Harcourt

Algebra 2

TIMOTHY D. KANOLD
EDWARD B. BURGER
JULI K. DIXON
MATTHEW R. LARSON
STEVEN J. LEINWAND

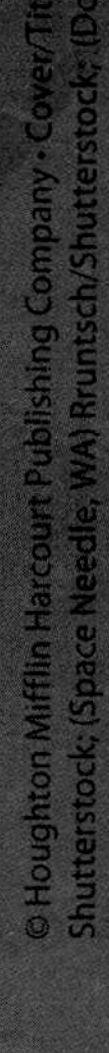

Printed in the U.S.A.

ISBN 978-0-544-38592-4

1 2 3 4 5 6 7 8 9 10 0868 22 21 20 19 18 17 16 15 14

4500484518 A B C D E F G

Authors

Timothy D. Kanold, Ph.D., is an award-winning international educator, author, and consultant. He is a former superintendent and director of mathematics and science at Adlai E. Stevenson High School District 125 in Lincolnshire, Illinois. He is a past president of the National Council of Supervisors of Mathematics (NCSM) and the Council for the Presidential Awardees of Mathematics (CPAM). He has served on several writing and leadership commissions for NCTM during the past decade. He presents motivational professional development seminars with a focus on developing professional learning communities (PLC's) to improve the teaching, assessing, and learning of students. He has recently authored nationally recognized articles, books, and textbooks for mathematics education and school leadership, including *What Every Principal Needs to Know about the Teaching and Learning of Mathematics*.

Edward B. Burger, Ph.D., is the President of Southwestern University, a former Francis Christopher Oakley Third Century Professor of Mathematics at Williams College, and a former vice provost at Baylor University. He has authored or coauthored more than sixty-five articles, books, and video series; delivered over five hundred addresses and workshops throughout the world; and made more than fifty radio and television appearances. He is a Fellow of the American Mathematical Society as well as having earned many national honors, including the Robert Foster Cherry Award for Great Teaching in 2010. In 2012, Microsoft Education named him a "Global Hero in Education."

Juli K. Dixon, Ph.D., is a Professor of Mathematics Education at the University of Central Florida. She has taught mathematics in urban schools at the elementary, middle, secondary, and post-secondary levels. She is an active researcher and speaker with numerous publications and conference presentations. Key areas of focus are deepening teachers' content knowledge and communicating and justifying mathematical ideas. She is a past chair of the NCTM Student Explorations in Mathematics Editorial Panel and member of the Board of Directors for the Association of Mathematics Teacher Educators.

Matthew R. Larson, Ph.D., is the K-12 mathematics curriculum specialist for the Lincoln Public Schools and served on the Board of Directors for the National Council of Teachers of Mathematics from 2010 to 2013. He is a past chair of NCTM's Research Committee and was a member of NCTM's Task Force on Linking Research and Practice. He is the author of several books on implementing the Common Core Standards for Mathematics. He has taught mathematics at the secondary and college levels and held an appointment as an honorary visiting associate professor at Teachers College, Columbia University.

Steven J. Leinwand is a Principal Research Analyst at the American Institutes for Research (AIR) in Washington, D.C., and has over 30 years in leadership positions in mathematics education. He is past president of the National Council of Supervisors of Mathematics and served on the NCTM Board of Directors. He is the author of numerous articles, books, and textbooks and has made countless presentations with topics including student achievement, reasoning, effective assessment, and successful implementation of standards.

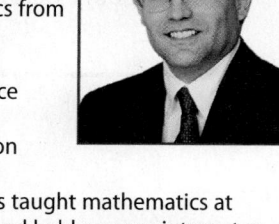

Performance Task Consultant

Robert Kaplinsky
Teacher Specialist, Mathematics
Downey Unified School District
Downey, California

STEM Consultants
Science, Technology, Engineering, and Mathematics

Michael A. DiSpezio
Global Educator
North Falmouth, Massachusetts

Michael R. Heithaus
Executive Director, School of Environment, Arts, and Society
Professor, Department of Biological Sciences
Florida International University
North Miami, Florida

Reviewers

Mindy Eden
Richwoods High School
Peoria School District
Peoria, IL

Dustin Johnson
Badger High School Math Teacher
Department Chair
Lake Geneva-Genoa City Union High School District
Lake Geneva, WI

Ashley D. McSwain
Murray High School
Murray City School District
Salt Lake City, UT

Rebecca Quinn
Doherty Memorial High School
Worcester Public Schools District
Worcester, MA

Ted Ryan
Madison LaFollette High School
Madison Metropolitan School District
Madison, WI

Tony Scoles
Fort Zumwalt School District
O'Fallon, MO

Cynthia L. Smith
Higley Unified School District
Gilbert, AZ

Phillip E. Spellane
Doherty Memorial High School
Worcester Public Schools District
Worcester, MA

Mona Toncheff
Math Content Specialist
Phoenix Union High School District
Phoenix, AZ

Functions

UNIT 1

COMMON CORE

Volume 1

MODULE 1 Analyzing Functions

COMMON CORE

MODULE 2 Absolute Value Functions, Equations, and Inequalities

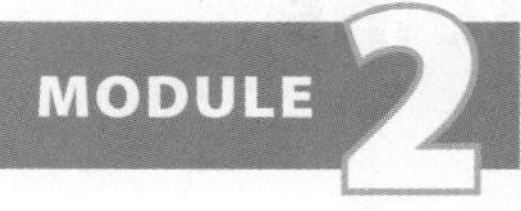

COMMON CORE

UNIT 2

Volume 1

Quadratic Functions, Equations, and Relations

MODULE 3 Quadratic Equations

COMMON CORE

MODULE 4 Quadratic Relations and Systems of Equations

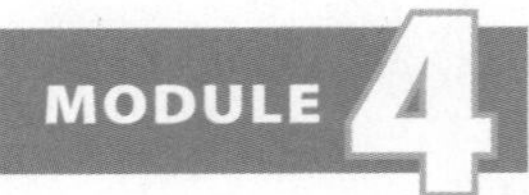

Polynomial Functions, Expressions, and Equations

UNIT 3

Volume 1

MODULE 5 Polynomial Functions

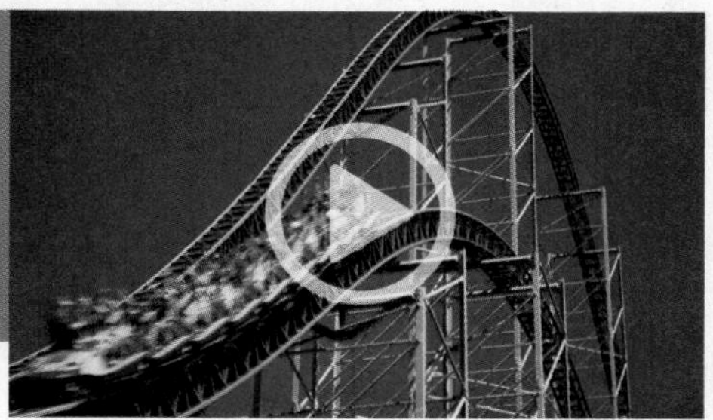

COMMON CORE

MODULE 6 Polynomials

COMMON CORE

Polynomial Equations

COMMON CORE

Rational Functions, Expressions, and Equations

Volume 1

Rational Functions

MODULE 9

Rational Expressions and Equations

COMMON CORE

UNIT 5

Rational Functions, Expressions, and Equations

Volume 1

MODULE 10 Radical Functions

COMMON CORE

MODULE 11 Radical Expressions and Equations

COMMON CORE

Exponential and Logarithmic Functions and Equations

UNIT 6

Volume 2

MODULE 12 Sequences and Series

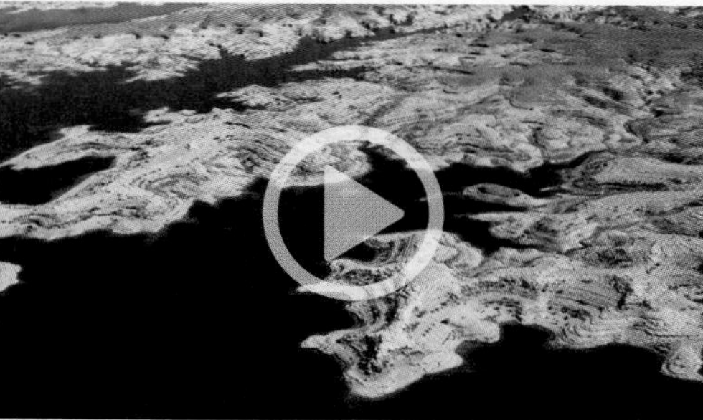

COMMON CORE

MODULE 13 Exponential Functions

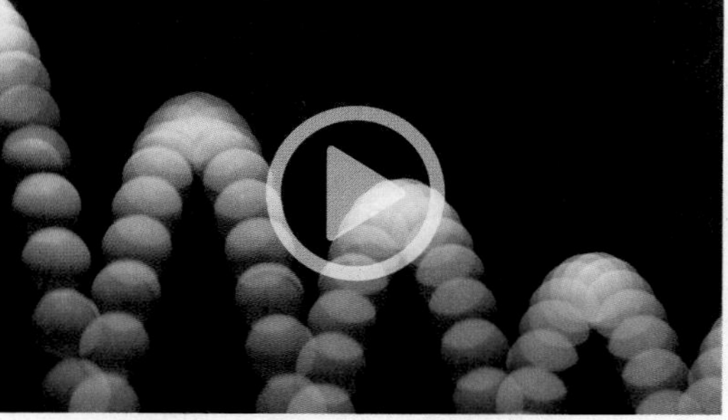

COMMON CORE

MODULE 14 Modeling with Exponential and Other Functions

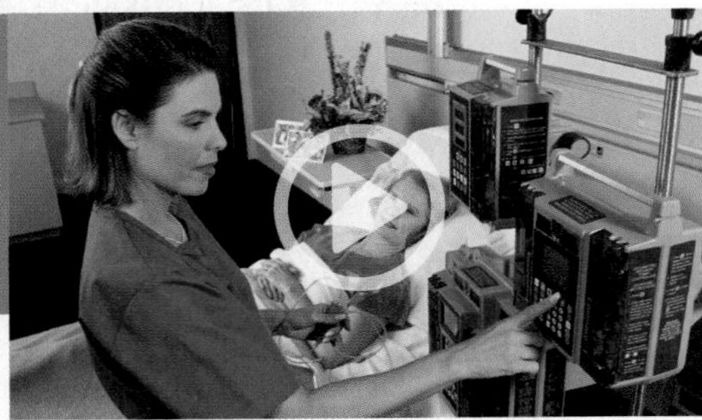

COMMON CORE

MODULE 15 Logarithmic Functions

COMMON CORE

MODULE 16 Logarithmic Properties and Exponential Equations

COMMON CORE

UNIT 7 Trigonometric Functions

Volume 2

MODULE 17 Unit-Circle Definition of Trigonometric Functions

MODULE 18 Graphing Trigonometric Functions

Probability

UNIT 8

COMMON CORE

Volume 2

MODULE 19 Introduction to Probability

COMMON CORE

MODULE 20 Conditional Probability and Independence of Events

COMMON CORE

MODULE 21 Probability and Decision Making

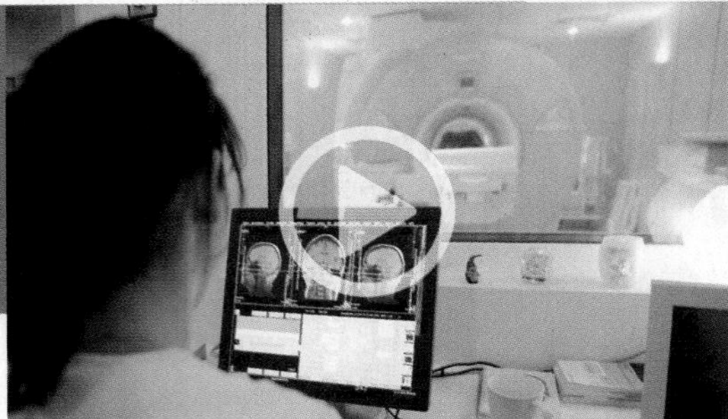

COMMON CORE

Statistics

MODULE 22 Gathering and Displaying Data

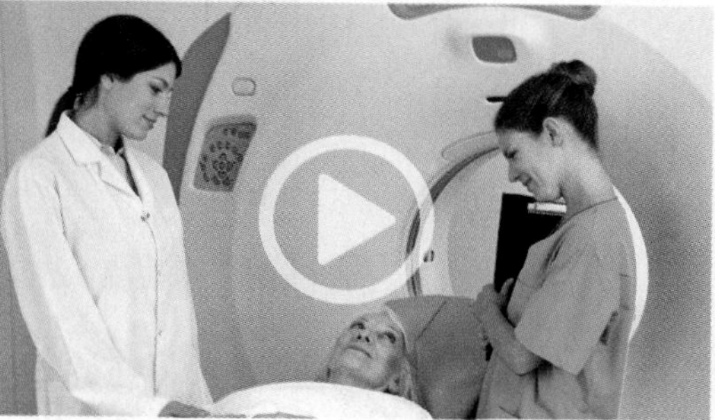

COMMON CORE

MODULE 23 Data Distributions

COMMON CORE

MODULE 24 Making Inferences from Data

COMMON CORE

HMH Algebra 2
Online State Resources

Scan the QR code or visit:
my.hrw.com/nsmedia/osp/2016/ma/hs/temp
for correlations and other state-specific resources.

Common Core State Standards

HMH ALGEBRA 2

Standard	Descriptor	Citations
Number and Quantity		
N-CN The Complex Number System		
Perform arithmetic operations with complex numbers.		
N-CN.A.1	Know there is a complex number i such that $i^2 = -1$, and every complex number has the form $a + bi$ with a and b real.	**SE:** 113–136, 127–138
N-CN.A.2	Use the relation $i^2 = -1$ and the commutative, associative, and distributive properties to add, subtract, and multiply complex numbers.	**SE:** 127–138, 139–152
Use complex numbers in polynomial identities and equations.		
N-CN.C.7	Solve quadratic equations with real coefficients that have complex solutions.	**SE:** 139–152
N-CN.C.8[1]	(+) Extend polynomial identities to the complex numbers.	**SE:** 309–320
N-CN.C.9[1]	(+) Know the Fundamental Theorem of Algebra; show that it is true for quadratic polynomials.	**SE:** 353–368
Algebra		
A-SSE Seeing Structure in Expressions		
Interpret the structure of expressions.		
A-SSE.A.1	Interpret expressions that represent a quantity in terms of its context. ★	**SE:** 249–264, 309–320, 401–418
A-SSE.A.1a[1]	Interpret parts of an expression, such as terms, factors, and coefficients. ★	**SE:** 249–264, 309–320
A-SSE.A.1b[1]	Interpret complicated expressions by viewing one or more of their parts as a single entity. ★	**SE:** 401–418
A-SSE.A.2	Use the structure of an expression to identify ways to rewrite it.	**SE:** 309–320, 425–438
CWrite expressions in equivalent forms to solve problems.		
A-SSE.B4	Derive the formula for the sum of a finite geometric series (when the common ratio is not 1), and use the formula to solve problems. ★	**SE:** 613–628

★ Indicates a modeling standard linking mathematics to everyday life, work, and decision-making.
(+) Indicates additional mathematics to prepare students for advanced courses.

Scan the QR code or visit my.hrw.com/nsmedia/osp/2016/ma/hs/te_1/temp for additional correlations and state specific resources.

Standard	Descriptor	Citations
A-APR Arithmetic with Polynomials and Rational Expressions		
Perform arithmetic operations on polynomials.		
A-APR.A.1 [1]	Understand that polynomials form a system analogous to the integers, namely, they are closed under the operations of addition, subtraction, and multiplication; add, subtract, and multiply polynomials.	**SE:** 271–282, 283–296, 297–308, 321–334
Understand the relationship between zeros and factors of polynomials.		
A-APR.B.2	Know and apply the Remainder Theorem: For a polynomial $p(x)$ and a number a, the remainder on division by $x - a$ is $p(a)$, so $p(a) = 0$ if and only if $(x - a)$ is a factor of $p(x)$.	**SE:** 341–352, 353–368
A-APR.B.3	Identify zeros of polynomials when suitable factorizations are available, and use the zeros to construct a rough graph of the function defined by the polynomial.	**SE:** 249–264, 309–320, 321–334, 341–352, 353–368
Use polynomial identities to solve problems.		
A-APR.C.4	Prove polynomial identities and use them to describe numerical relationships.	**SE:** 283–296
Rewrite rational expressions.		
A-APR.D.6	Rewrite simple rational expressions in different forms; write $\frac{a(x)}{b(x)}$ in the form $\frac{q(x) + r(x)}{b(x)}$, where $a(x)$, $b(x)$, $q(x)$, and $r(x)$ are polynomials with the degree of $r(x)$ less than the degree of $b(x)$, using inspection, long division, or, for the more complicated examples, a computer algebra system.	**SE:** 321–334, 381–400, 401–418
A-APR.D.7 [1]	(+) Understand that rational expressions form a system analogous to the rational numbers, closed under addition, subtraction, multiplication, and division by a nonzero rational expression; add, subtract, multiply, and divide rational expressions.	**SE:** 425–438, 439–452
A-CED Creating Equations		
Create equations that describe numbers or relationships.		
A-CED.A.1	Create equations and inequalities in one variable and use them to solve problems. ★	**SE:** 77–86, 87–100, 309–320, 453–466, 557–570

[1] These standards are not included in the PARCC Model Content Framework for Algebra 2.

Common Core State Standards (continued)

Standard	Descriptor	Citations
A-CED.A.2[1]	Create equations in two or more variables to represent relationships between quantities; graph equations on coordinate axes with labels and scales. ★	**SE:** 5–16, 17–30, 31–46, 65–76, 159–174, 175–188, 923–936
A-CED.A.3[1]	Represent constraints by equations or inequalities, and by systems of equations and/or inequalities, and interpret solutions as viable or non-viable options in a modeling context.	**SE:** 5–16, 159–174, 175–188, 203–222, 341–352, 453–466
A-CED.A.4[1]	Rearrange formulas to highlight a quantity of interest, using the same reasoning as in solving equations. ★	**SE:** 425–438, 439–452, 783–798
A-REI Reasoning with Equations and Inequalities		
Understand solving equations as a process of reasoning and explain the reasoning.		
A-REI.A.2	Solve simple rational and radical equations in one variable, and give examples showing how extraneous solutions may arise.	**SE:** 453–466, 557–570
Represent and solve equations and inequalities graphically.		
A-REI.D.11	Explain why the *x*-coordinates of the points where the graphs of the equations $y = f(x)$ and $y = g(x)$ intersect are the solutions of the equation $f(x) = g(x)$; find the solutions approximately, e.g., using technology to graph the functions, make tables of values, or find successive approximations. Include cases where $f(x)$ and/or $g(x)$ are linear, polynomial, rational, absolute value, exponential, and logarithmic functions. ★	**SE:** 77–86, 353–368, 923–936
Functions		
F-IF Interpreting Functions		
Interpret functions that arise in applications in terms of the context.		
F-IF.B.4	For a function that models a relationship between two quantities, interpret key features of graphs and tables in terms of the quantities, and sketch graphs showing key features given a verbal description of the relationship. ★	**SE:** 17–30, 65–76, 249–264, 495–512, 513–526, 871–888, 889–904, 905–922, 923–936
F-IF.B.5[1]	Relate the domain of a function to its graph and, where applicable, to the quantitative relationship it describes. ★	**SE:** 5–16

★ Indicates a modeling standard linking mathematics to everyday life, work, and decision-making.
(+) Indicates additional mathematics to prepare students for advanced courses.

Standard	Descriptor	Citations
F-IF.B.6	Calculate and interpret the average rate of change of a function (presented symbolically or as a table) over a specified interval. Estimate the rate of change from a graph. ★	**SE:** 17–30, 495–512, 513–526
Analyze functions using different representations.		
F-IF.C.7	Graph functions expressed symbolically and show key features of the graph, by hand in simple cases and using technology for more complicated cases. ★	**SE:** 31–46, 65–76, 87–100, 235–248, 249–264, 353–368, 495–512, 513–526, 543–556, 799–812, 871–888, 889–904, 905–922
F-IF.C.7b[1]	Graph square root, cube root, and piecewise-defined functions, including step functions and absolute value functions. ★	**SE:** 31–46, 65–76, 87–100, 495–512, 513–526, 543–556
F-IF.C.7c	Graph polynomial functions, identifying zeros when suitable factorizations are available, and showing end behavior. ★	**SE:** 235–248, 249–264, 353–368
F-IF.C.7e	Graph exponential and logarithmic functions, showing intercepts and end behavior, and trigonometric functions, showing period, midline, and amplitude. ★	**SE:** 799–812, 871–888, 889–904, 905–922
F-IF.C.8[1]	Write a function defined by an expression in different but equivalent forms to reveal and explain different properties of the function.	**SE:** 271–282, 381–400, 401–418, 439–452, 583–596, 597–612, 667–680, 681–696
F-IF.C.9	Compare properties of two functions each represented in a different way (algebraically, graphically, numerically in tables, or by verbal descriptions).	**SE:** 889–904, 905–922
F-BF Building Functions		
Build a function that models a relationship between two quantities.		
F-BF.A.1	Write a function that describes a relationship between two quantities. ★	**SE:** 271–282, 283–296, 381–400, 401–418, 439–452, 583–596, 597–612, 681–696
F-BF.A.1b	Combine standard function types using arithmetic operations. ★	**SE:** 271–282, 283–296, 381–400, 401–418, 439–452

Common Core State Standards (continued)

Standard	Descriptor	Citations
Build new functions from existing functions.		
F-BF.B.3	Identify the effect on the graph of replacing $f(x)$ by $f(x) + k$, $kf(x)$, $f(kx)$, and $f(x + k)$ for specific values of k (both positive and negative); find the value of k given the graphs. Experiment with cases and illustrate an explanation of the effects on the graph using technology.	**SE:** 31–46, 65–76, 235–248, 381–400, 495–512, 513–526, 871–888, 889–904, 905–922
F-BF.B.4	Find inverse functions.	**SE:** 47–58, 479–494
F-BF.B.4a	Solve an equation of the form $f(x) = c$ for a simple function f that has an inverse and write an expression for the inverse.	**SE:** 479–494
F-LE Linear, Quadratic, and Exponential Models		
Construct and compare linear, quadratic, and exponential models and solve problems.		
F-LE.A.4	For exponential models, express as a logarithm the solution to $ab^{ct} = d$ where a, c, and d are numbers and the base b is 2, 10, or e; evaluate the logarithm using technology. ★	**SE:** 799–812
F-TF Trigonometric Functions		
Extend the domain of trigonometric functions using the unit circle.		
F-TF.A.1	Understand radian measure of an angle as the length of the arc on the unit circle subtended by the angle.	**SE:** 825–838
F-TF.A.2	Explain how the unit circle in the coordinate plane enables the extension of trigonometric functions to all real numbers, interpreted as radian measures of angles traversed counterclockwise around the unit circle.	**SE:** 839–852
Model periodic phenomena with trigonometric functions.		
F-TF.B.5	Choose trigonometric functions to model periodic phenomena with specified amplitude, frequency, and midline. ★	**SE:** 923–936
Prove and apply trigonometric identities.		
F-TF.C.8	Prove the Pythagorean identity $\sin^2(\theta) + \cos^2(\theta) = 1$ and use it to find $\sin(\theta)$, $\cos(\theta)$, or $\tan(\theta)$ given $\sin(\theta)$, $\cos(\theta)$, or $\tan(\theta)$ and the quadrant of the angle.	**SE:** 853–864

★ Indicates a modeling standard linking mathematics to everyday life, work, and decision-making.
(+) Indicates additional mathematics to prepare students for advanced courses.

Standard	Descriptor	Citations
Statistics and Probability		
S-ID Interpreting Categorical and Quantitative Data		
Summarize, represent, and interpret data on a single count or measurement variable.		
S-ID.A.4	Use the mean and standard deviation of a data set to fit it to a normal distribution and to estimate population percentages. Recognize that there are data sets for which such a procedure is not appropriate. Use calculators, spreadsheets, and tables to estimate areas under the normal curve. ★	**SE:** 1095–1110, 1131–1140
S-IC Making Inferences and Justifying Conclusions		
Understand and evaluate random processes underlying statistical experiments.		
S-IC.A.1	Understand statistics as a process for making inferences to be made about population parameters based on a random sample from that population. ★	**SE:** 1083–1094
S-IC.A.2	Decide if a specified model is consistent with results from a given data-generating process, e.g., using simulation. ★	**SE:** 1117–1130
Make inferences and justify conclusions from sample surveys, experiments, and observational studies.		
S-IC.B.3	Recognize the purposes of and differences among sample surveys, experiments, and observational studies; explain how randomization relates to each. ★	**SE:** 1179–1192
S-IC.B.4	Use data from a sample survey to estimate a population mean or proportion; develop a margin of error through the use of simulation models for random sampling. ★	**SE:** 1141–1156, 1163–1178
S-IC.B.5	Use data from a randomized experiment to compare two treatments; use simulations to decide if differences between parameters are significant. ★	**SE:** 1193–1210
S-IC.B.6	Evaluate reports based on data. ★	**SE:** 1179–1192
S-MD Using Probability to Make Decisions		
Use probability to evaluate outcomes of decisions.		
S-MD.B.6[1]	(+) Use probabilities to make fair decisions (e.g., drawing by lots, using a random number generator). ★	**SE:** 1049–1058
S-MD.B.7[1]	(+) Analyze decisions and strategies using probability concepts (e.g., product testing, medical testing, pulling a hockey goalie at the end of a game). ★	**SE:** 1059–1070

Common Core Cluster Progressions

HMH Algebra 2 carefully develops the instructional progression of each cluster from the Common Core Standards. The table below shows where key topics from each cluster are taught in HMH Algebra 2.

HMH ALGEBRA 2

Common Core Clusters		Unit 1	Unit 2	Unit 3
N-CN.A	Perform arithmetic operations with complex numbers.		covered in full	
N-CN.C	Use complex numbers in polynomial identities and equations.		quadratics	other polynomials
A-SSE.A	Interpret the structure of expressions.			polynomials
A-SSE.B	Write expressions in equivalent forms to solve problems.			
A-APR.A	Perform arithmetic operations on polynomials.			polynomial
A-APR.B	Understand the relationship between zeros and factors of polynomials.			polynomials
A-APR.C	Use polynomial identities to solve problems.			covered in full
A-APR.D	Create equations that describe numbers or relationships.			polynomial long division
A-CED.A	Solve equations and inequalities in one variable.		quadratic with possibility of nonreal roots	polynomial
A-REI.A	Understand solving equations as a process of reasoning and explain the reasoning.			
A-REI.C	Solve systems of equations.		linear/ quadratic	
A-REI.D	Represent and solve equations and inequalities graphically.	absolute value	quadratic with possibility of nonreal roots	polynomial
F-IF.B	Interpret functions that arise in applications in terms of a context.	end behavior; interval and set notation	quadratic with possibility of nonreal roots	polynomial

	Unit 4	Unit 5	Unit 6	Unit 7	Unit 8	Unit 9
	rational					
			sums of geometric series			
	polynomials within rational expressions					
	rational expressions					
	rational	square- and cube-root functions	exponential and logarithmic	trigonometric		
	simple rational	simple radical				
	rational	radical	exponential and logarithmic	trigonometric		
	rational	radical	exponential and logarithmic	trigonometric		

Common Core Cluster Progressions (continued)

HMH ALGEBRA 2

Common Core Clusters		Unit 1	Unit 2	Unit 3
F-IF.C	Analyze functions using different representations.	piecewise	quadratic with possibility of nonreal roots	polynomial
F-BF.A	Build a function that models a relationship between two quantities.			polynomial
F-BF.B	Build new functions from existing functions.	generic functions		
F-LE.A	Construct and compare linear, quadratic, and exponential models and solve problems			
F-TF.A	Interpret expressions for functions in terms of the situation they model.			
F-TF.B	Model periodic phenomena with trigonometric functions.			
F-TF.C	Prove and apply trigonometric identities.			
G-GPE.A	Translate between the geometric description and the equation for a conic section.		covered in full	
S-ID.A	Summarize, represent, and interpret data on a single count or measurement variable.			
S-IC.A	Understand and evaluate random processes underlying statistical experiments.			
S-IC.B	Make inferences and justify conclusions from sample surveys, experiments and observational studies.			
S-CP.A	Understand independence and conditional probability and use them to interpret data.			
S-CP.B	Use the rules of probability to compute probabilities of compound events in a uniform probability model.			
S-MD.B	Use probability to evaluate outcomes of decisions.			

Unit 4	Unit 5	Unit 6	Unit 7	Unit 8	Unit 9
rational	radical	exponential and logarithmic	trigonometric		
rational	radical	exponential and logarithmic	trigonometric		
rational	radical	exponential	trigonometric		
		logarithms as solutions for exponentials			
			radian measure		
			sine and cosine functions		
			Pythagorean Identity and its derivatives		
					fit data to a normal distribution
					covered in full
					covered in full
				covered in full	
				covered in full	
				fair decisions, strategies, and testing	

Succeeding with HMH Algebra 2

HMH Algebra 2 is built on the 5E instructional model–Engage, Explore, Explain, Elaborate, Evaluate–to develop strong conceptual understanding and mastery of key mathematics standards.

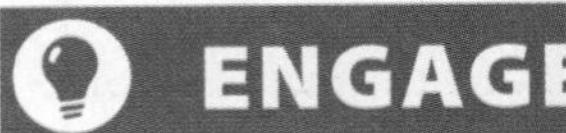

Preview the Lesson Performance Task in the Interactive Student Edition.

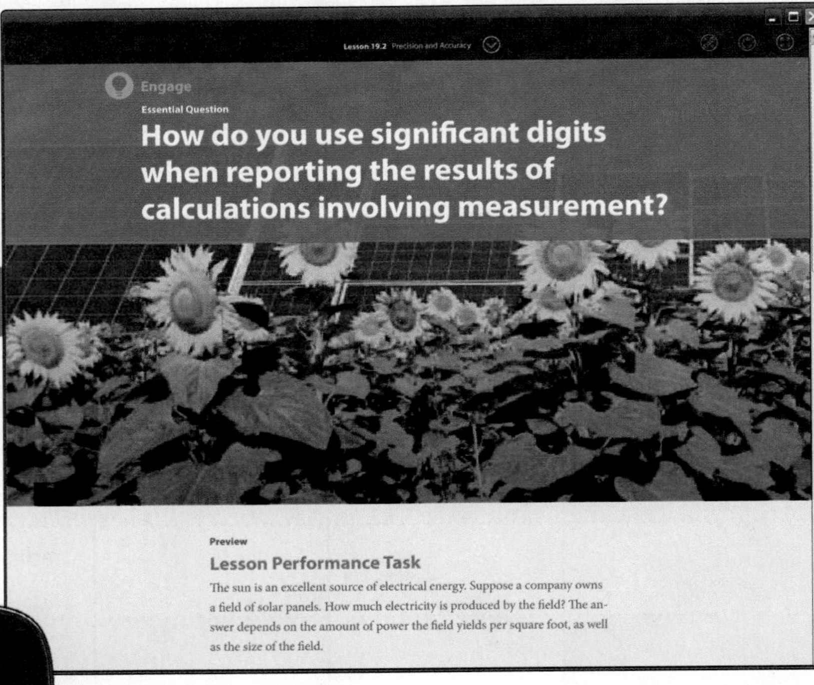

Lesson 19.2 Precision and Accuracy
Engage
Essential Question
How do you use significant digits when reporting the results of calculations involving measurement?
Preview
Lesson Performance Task
The sun is an excellent source of electrical energy. Suppose a company owns a field of solar panels. How much electricity is produced by the field? The answer depends on the amount of power the field yields per square foot, as well as the size of the field.

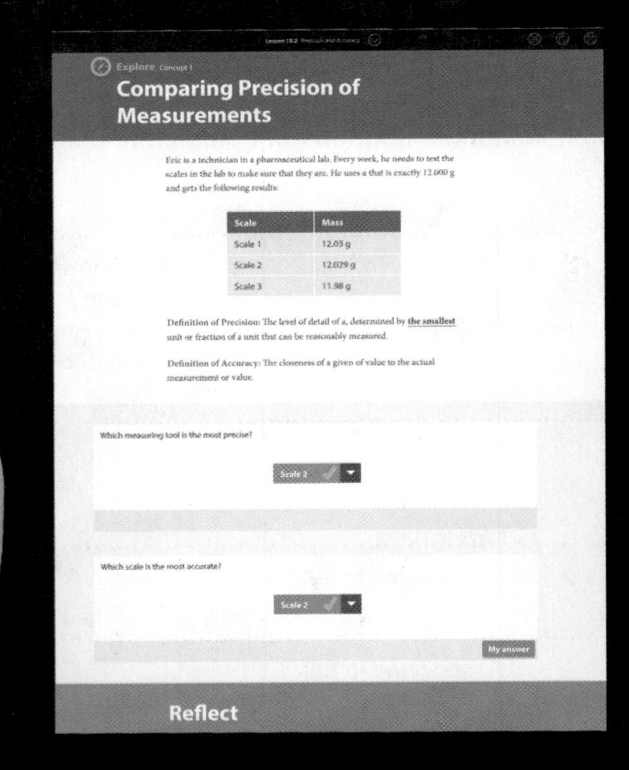

EXPLORE

Explore and interact with new concepts to develop a deeper understanding of mathematics in your book and the Interactive Student Edition.

Scan the QR code to access engaging videos, activities, and more in the Resource Locker for each lesson.

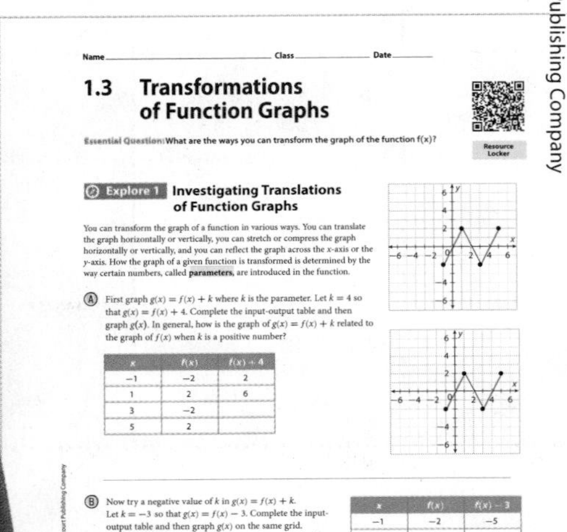

Name Class Date
1.3 Transformations of Function Graphs
Essential Question: What are the ways you can transform the graph of the function f(x)?
Resource Locker
Explore 1 Investigating Translations of Function Graphs

EXPLAIN

Learn concepts with step-by-step interactive examples. Every example is also supported by a Math On the Spot video tutorial.

reported value, 4.5 centimeters, up to, but not including, 0.5 units above it, 5.5 centimeters. The actual length, l, is within a range of possible values: centimeters. Similarly, a length given to the nearest tenth can actually range from 0.05 units below the reported value up to, but not including, 0.05 units above it. So a length reported as 4.5 cm could actually be as low as 4.45 cm or as high as nearly 4.55 cm.

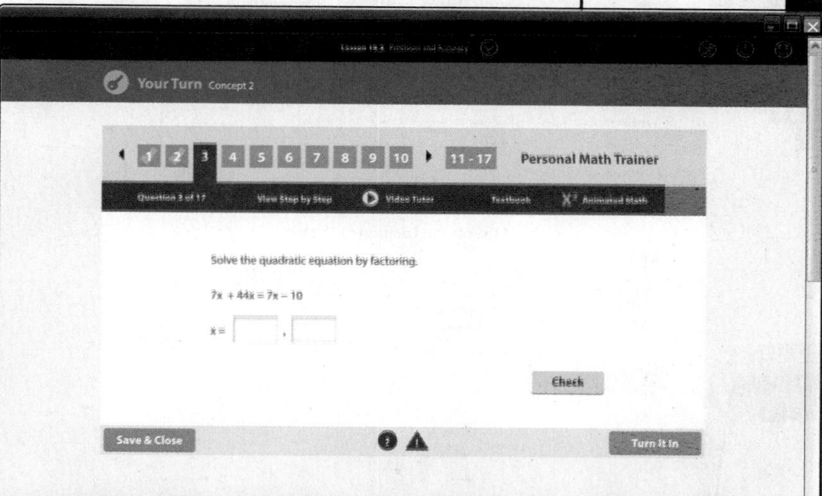

Explain 1 Completing the Square with Expressions

Finding the value of c needed to make an expression such as $x^2 + 6x + c$ into a perfect square trinomial is called **completing the square**.

Using algebra tiles, half of the x-tiles are placed along the right and bottom sides of the x^2-tile. The number of 1-tiles added is the square of the number of x-tiles on either side of the x^2-tile.

To complete the square for the expression $x^2 + bx + c$, replace c with $\left(\frac{b}{2}\right)^2$. The perfect square trinomial is $x^2 + bx + \left(\frac{b}{2}\right)^2$ and factors as $\left(x + \frac{b}{2}\right)^2$.

Example 1 Complete the square to form a perfect trinomial. Then factor the trinomial.

(A) $x^2 + 12x + c$

Identify b.	$b = 12$
Find c.	$c = \left(\frac{b}{2}\right)^2 = \left(\frac{12}{2}\right)^2 = 36$
Write the trinomial.	$x^2 + 12x + 36$
Factor the trinomial.	$x^2 + 12x + 36 = (x + 6)^2$

(B) $z^2 - 26z + c$

Identify b.	$b =$ ☐
Find c.	$c = \left(\frac{b}{2}\right)^2 = \left(\frac{☐}{2}\right)^2 =$ ☐
Write the trinomial.	$z^2 +$ ☐ $z +$ ☐
Factor the trinomial.	$z^2 +$ ☐ $z +$ ☐ $=$ ☐

Reflect

Complete the square to form a perfect square trinomial. Then factor the trinomial.

3. $a^2 + 18a +$ ☐

4. $p^2 - 5p +$ ☐

Your Turn

5. In Part A, b is positive and in Part B, b is negative. Does this affect the sign of c? Why or why not?

Module 8 460 Lesson 8

Check your understanding of new concepts and skills with Your Turn exercises in your book or online with Personal Math Trainer.

ELABORATE

Show your understanding and reasoning with Reflect and Elaborate questions.

Your Turn

10. The calculator screen shows the graph of $f(x) = 4x^2 - 8x - 5$. Explain how the graph supports the solution in Part B.

Elaborate

11. When solving a quadratic equation in the form $x^2 + bx + c = 0$ by completing the square, what is the purpose of moving the constant to the other side of the equation?

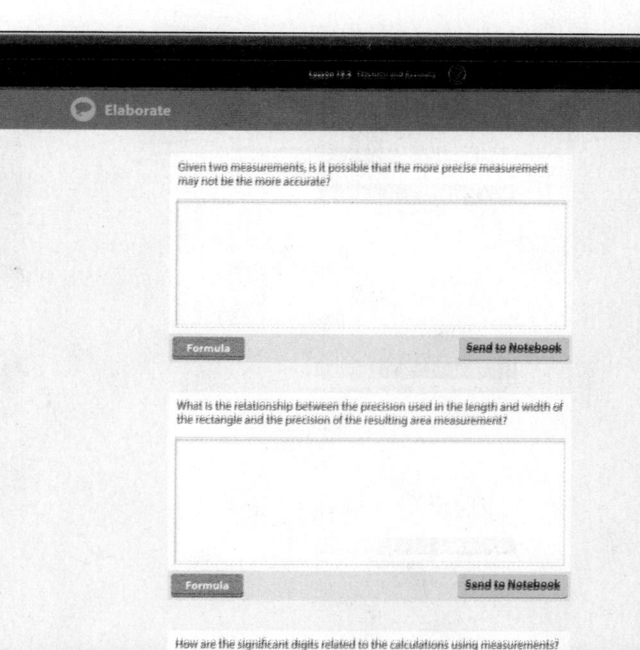

EVALUATE

Practice and apply skills and concepts with Evaluate exercises and a Lesson Performance Task in your book with plenty of workspace, or complete these exercises online with Personal Math Trainer.

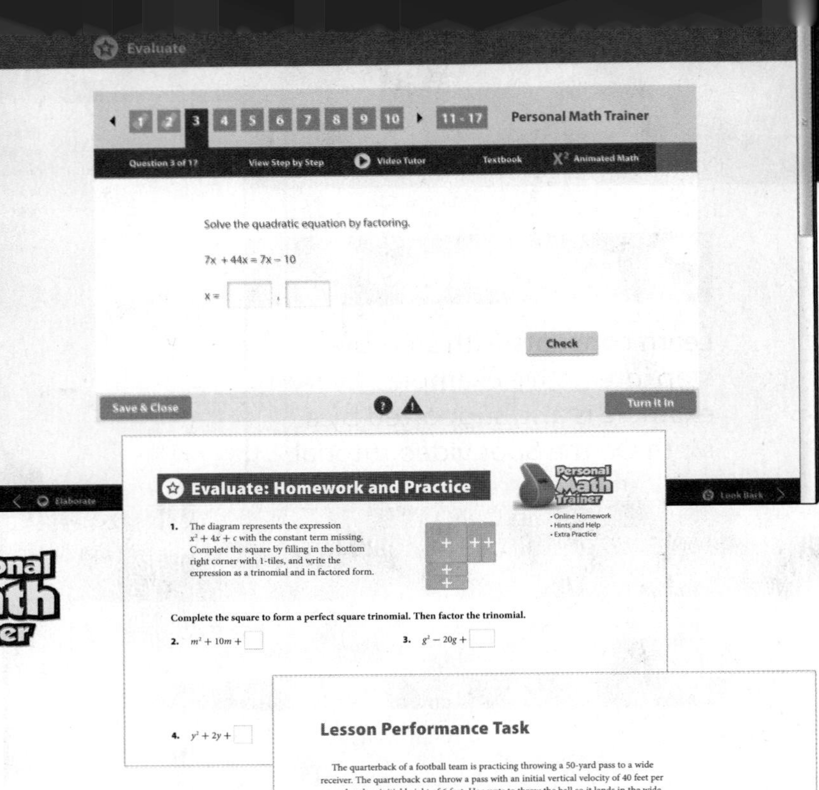

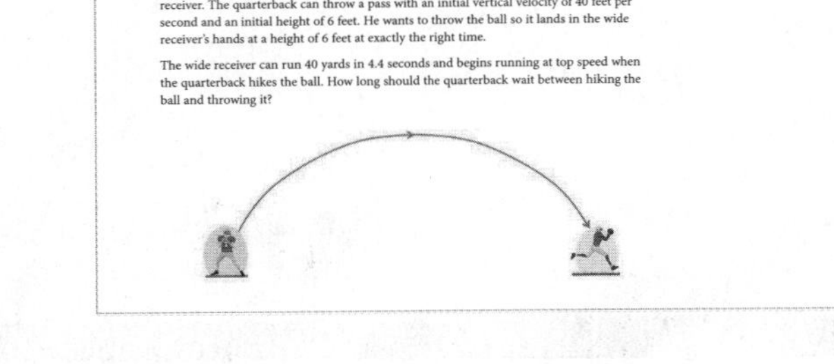

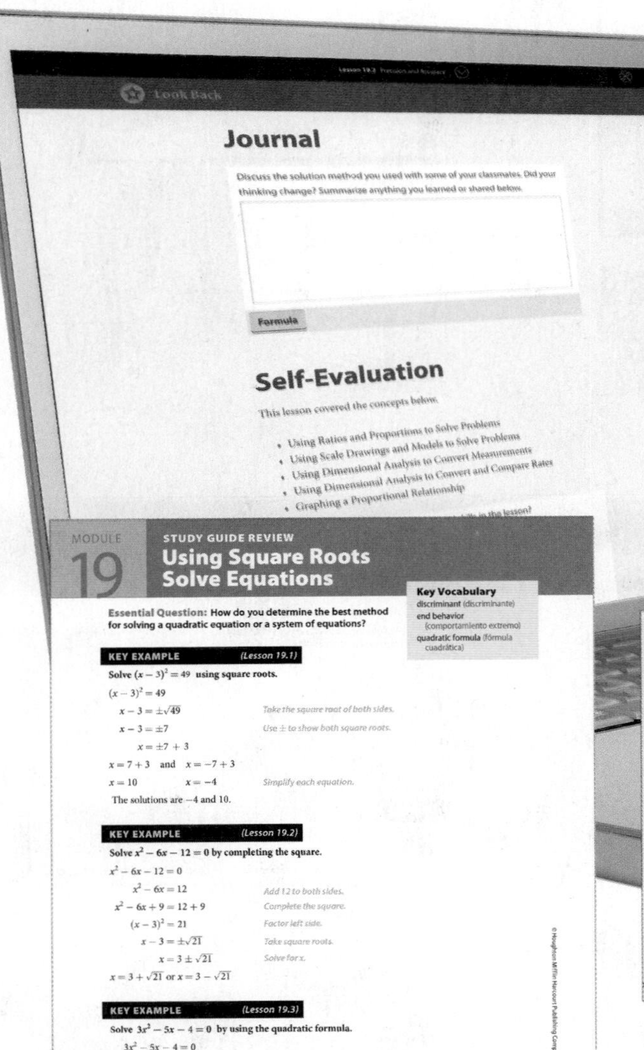

LOOK BACK

Review what you have learned and prepare for high-stakes tests with a variety of resources, including Study Guide Reviews, Performance Tasks, and Assessment Readiness test preparation.

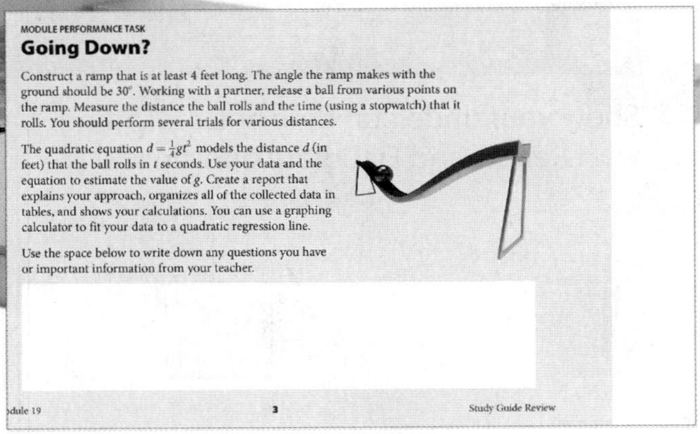

Professional Learning Communities

Synergy Through Collaboration

Tim Kanold
Program Author

Great teaching materials do not provide great education in and of themselves. Educators who collaborate in Professional Learning Communities can have a profound impact on their students. As a mathematics teacher, your grade-level or course-based collaborative team is the engine that can drive your professional learning and the professional learning community (PLC) process.

You and your colleagues hold a critical key to helping *all* students successfully learn the Common Core Mathematics Standards in your school. Through your hard work and the work of your collaborative team, effective instruction, assessment, and intervention practices become more coherent and focused.

The National Board for Professional Teaching Standards states the following:

> Seeing themselves as partners with other teachers, [faculty members] are dedicated to improving the profession. They care about the quality of teaching in their schools, and, to this end, their collaboration with colleagues is continuous and explicit. They recognize that collaborating in a professional learning community contributes to their own professional growth, as well as to the growth of their peers, for the benefit of student learning. Teachers promote the ideal that working collaboratively increases knowledge, reflection, and quality of practice and benefits the instructional program. (*Mathematics Standards for Teachers of Students Ages 11–18+*, ©2010, p. 75)

As a highly accomplished mathematics teacher you understand the value in the practice of effective collaboration with your colleagues. Teacher collaboration is not the icing on top of the proverbial cake of your work. Instead, it is the egg in the batter, holding the cake together.

As your school becomes a learning institution for the adults, it also becomes a learning institution dedicated to preparing all students for the future. The process of your collaboration in a PLC culture capitalizes on the fact that you and your colleagues come together with diverse experiences and knowledge to create a whole that is larger than the sum of the parts. Teacher collaboration is the solution to your sustained professional learning—the ongoing and never-ending process of growth necessary to meet the classroom demands of the CCSS expectations and the unit-by-unit mathematics content described in our series.

Functions

CONTENTS

Unit Pacing Guide

45-Minute Classes

Module 1

DAY 1	DAY 2	DAY 3	DAY 4	DAY 5
Lesson 1.1	Lesson 1.2	Lesson 1.2	Lesson 1.3	Lesson 1.3
DAY 6	**DAY 7**	**DAY 8**		
Lesson 1.4	Lesson 1.4	Module Review and Assessment Readiness		

Module 2

DAY 1	DAY 2	DAY 3	DAY 4	DAY 5
Lesson 2.1	Lesson 2.1	Lesson 2.2	Lesson 2.2	Lesson 2.3
DAY 6	**DAY 7**	**DAY 8**		
Lesson 2.3	Module Review and Assessment Readiness	Unit Review and Assessment Readiness		

90-Minute Classes

Module 1

DAY 1	DAY 2	DAY 3	DAY 4
Lesson 1.1 Lesson 1.2	Lesson 1.2 Lesson 1.3	Lesson 1.3 Lesson 1.4	Lesson 1.4 Module Review and Assessment Readiness

Module 2

DAY 1	DAY 2	DAY 3	DAY 4
Lesson 2.1	Lesson 2.2	Lesson 2.3	Module Review and Assessment Readiness Unit Review and Assessment Readiness

Program Resources

PLAN

HMH Teacher App

Access a full suite of teacher resources online and offline on a variety of devices. Plan present, and manage classes, assignments, and activities.

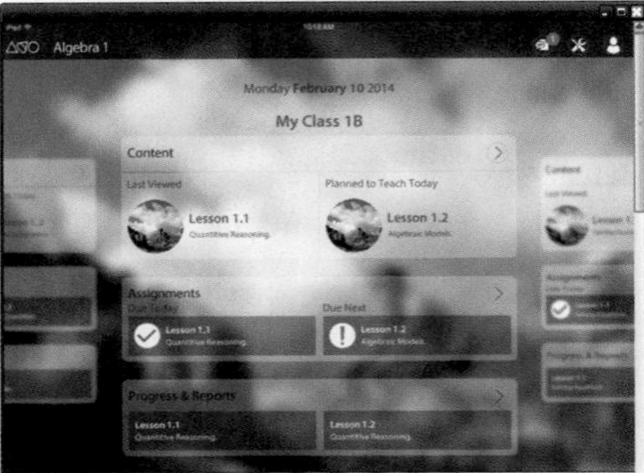

ePlanner **Easily plan your classes, create and view assignments, and access all program resources with your online, customizable planning tool.**

Professional Development Videos

Authors Juli Dixon and Matt Larson model successful teaching practices and strategies in actual classroom settings.

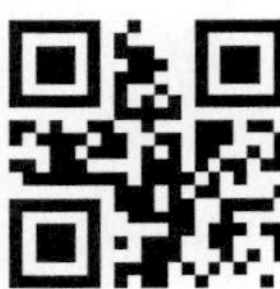

QR Codes **Scan with your smart phone to jump directly from your print book to online videos and other resources.**

Teacher's Edition

Support students with point-of-use Questioning Strategies, teaching tips, resources for differentiated instruction, additional activities, and more.

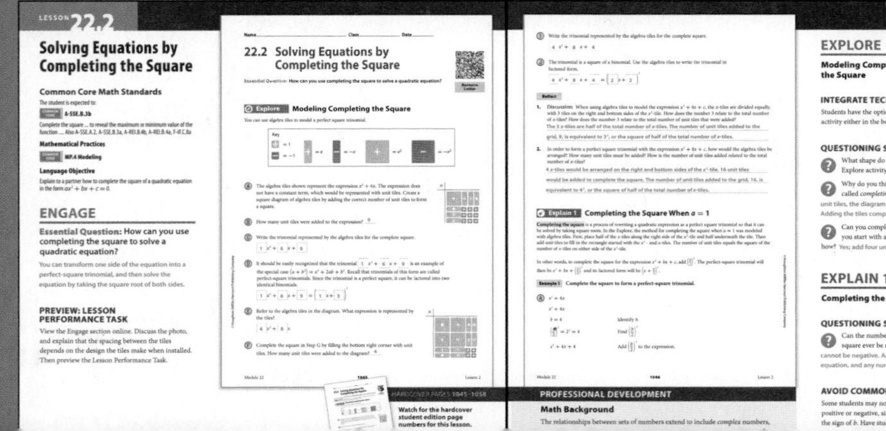

LESSON 22.2

Solving Equations by Completing the Square

EXPLORE

EXPLAIN 1

PROFESSIONAL DEVELOPMENT

ENGAGE AND EXPLORE

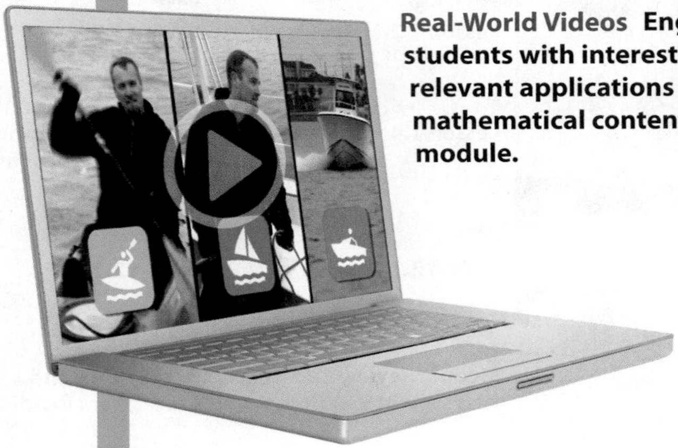

Real-World Videos **Engage students with interesting and relevant applications of the mathematical content of each module.**

Explore Activities

Students interactively explore new concepts using a variety of tools and approaches.

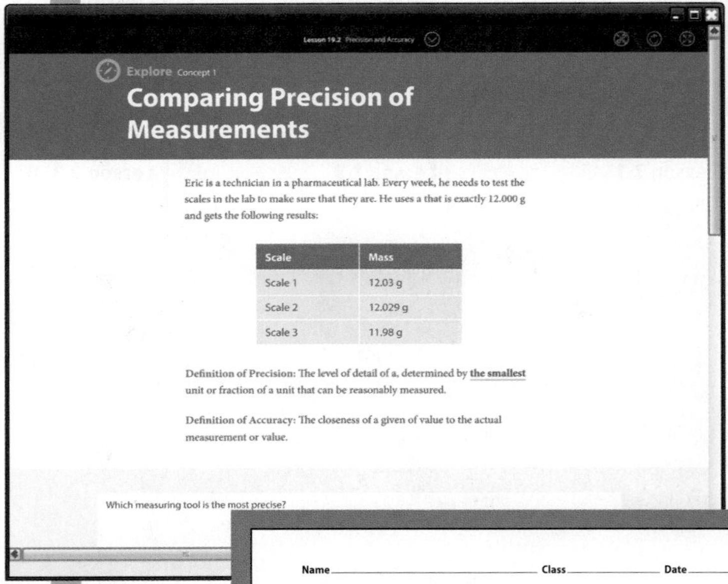

Explore Concept 1

Comparing Precision of Measurements

Eric is a technician in a pharmaceutical lab. Every week, he needs to test the scales in the lab to make sure that they are. He uses a that is exactly 12.000 g and gets the following results:

Scale	Mass
Scale 1	12.03 g
Scale 2	12.029 g
Scale 3	11.98 g

Definition of Precision: The level of detail of a, determined by the smallest unit or fraction of a unit that can be reasonably measured.

Definition of Accuracy: The closeness of a given of value to the actual measurement or value.

Which measuring tool is the most precise?

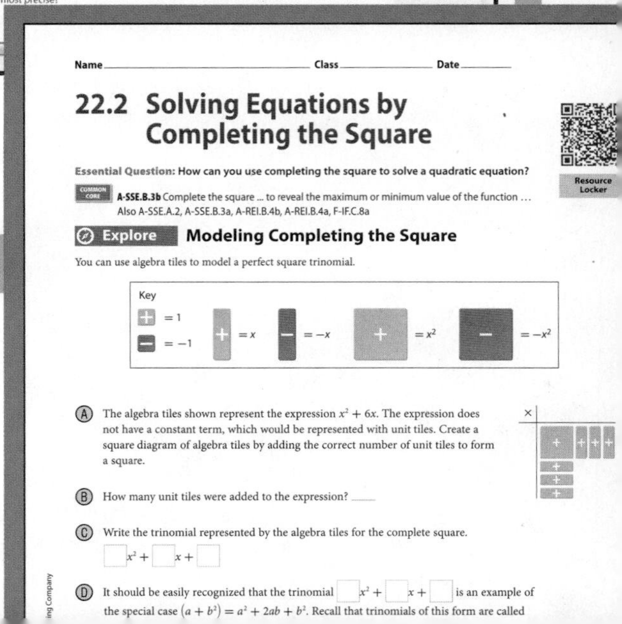

Name ______ Class ______ Date ______

22.2 Solving Equations by Completing the Square

Resource Locker

Essential Question: How can you use completing the square to solve a quadratic equation?

A-SSE.B.3b Complete the square ... to reveal the maximum or minimum value of the function ... Also A-SSE.A.2, A-SSE.B.3a, A-REI.B.4b, A-REI.B.4a, F-IF.C.8a

Explore **Modeling Completing the Square**

You can use algebra tiles to model a perfect square trinomial.

Key: $= 1$, $= -1$, $= x$, $= -x$, $= x^2$, $= -x^2$

(A) The algebra tiles shown represent the expression $x^2 + 6x$. The expression does not have a constant term, which would be represented with unit tiles. Create a square diagram of algebra tiles by adding the correct number of unit tiles to form a square.

(B) How many unit tiles were added to the expression? ____

(C) Write the trinomial represented by the algebra tiles for the complete square.

$\square x^2 + \square x + \square$

(D) It should be easily recognized that the trinomial $\square x^2 + \square x + \square$ is an example of the special case $(a + b^2) = a^2 + 2ab + b^2$. Recall that trinomials of this form are called

TEACH

Math On the Spot video tutorials, featuring program authors Dr. Edward Burger and Martha Sandoval-Martinez, accompany every example in the textbook and give students step-by-step instructions and explanations of key math concepts.

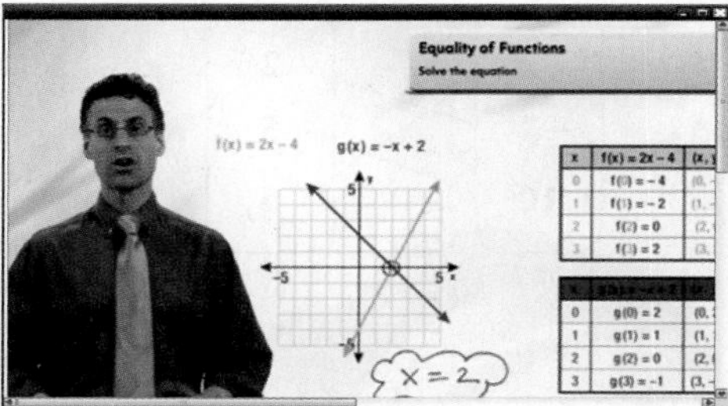

Interactive Teacher Edition

Customize and present course materials with collaborative activities and integrated formative assessment.

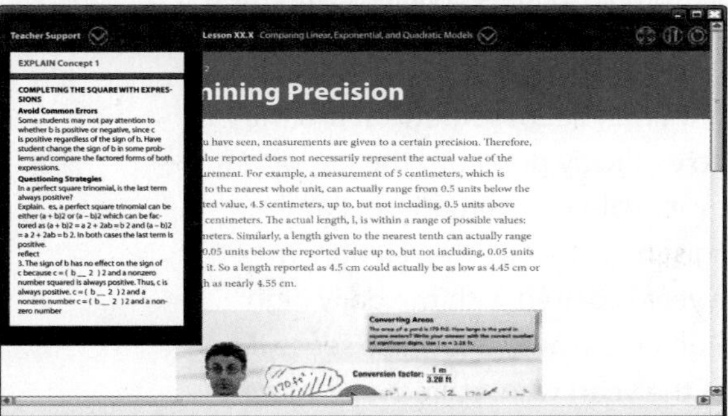

Differentiated Instruction Resources

Support all learners with Differentiated Instruction Resources, including

- **Leveled Practice and Problem Solving**
- **Reading Strategies**
- **Success for English Learners**
- **Challenge**

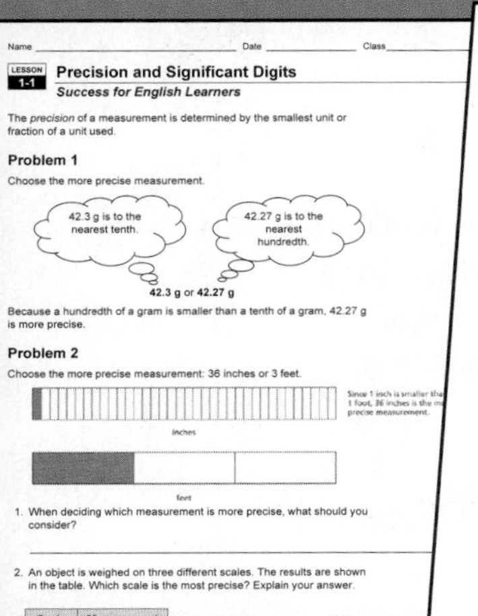

Name ______ Date ______ Class ______

LESSON 1-1 **Precision and Significant Digits**

Success for English Learners

The *precision* of a measurement is determined by the smallest unit or fraction of a unit used.

Problem 1

Choose the more precise measurement.

42.3 g is to the nearest tenth.

42.27 g is to the nearest hundredth.

42.3 g or **42.27 g**

Because a hundredth of a gram is smaller than a tenth of a gram, 42.27 g is more precise.

Problem 2

Choose the more precise measurement: 36 inches or 3 feet.

inches

feet

1. When deciding which measurement is more precise, what should you consider?

2. An object is weighed on three different scales. The results are shown in the table. Which scale is the most precise? Explain your answer.

Scale	Measurement

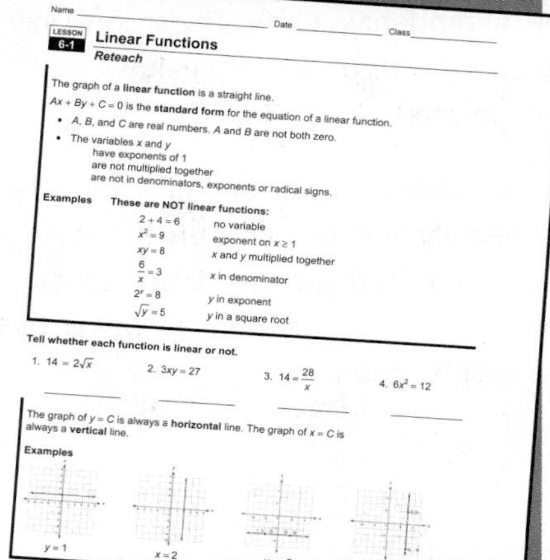

Name ______ Date ______ Class ______

LESSON 6-1 **Linear Functions**

Reteach

The graph of a **linear function** is a straight line.

$Ax + By + C = 0$ is the **standard form** for the equation of a linear function.

- A, B, and C are real numbers. A and B are not both zero.
- The variables x and y
  have exponents of 1
  are not multiplied together
  are not in denominators, exponents or radical signs.

Examples **These are NOT linear functions:**

$2 + 4 = 6$	no variable
$x^2 = 9$	exponent on $x \geq 1$
$xy = 8$	x and y multiplied together
$\frac{6}{x} = 3$	x in denominator
$2^y = 8$	y in exponent
$\sqrt{y} = 5$	y in a square root

Tell whether each function is linear or not.

1. $14 = 2\sqrt{x}$
2. $3xy = 27$
3. $14 = \frac{28}{x}$
4. $6x^2 = 12$

The graph of $y = C$ is always a **horizontal** line. The graph of $x = C$ is always a **vertical** line.

Examples

$y = 1$ $x = 2$ $y = -3$ $x = 3$

ASSESSMENT AND INTERVENTION

The Personal Math Trainer provides online practice, homework, assessments, and intervention. Monitor student progress through reports and alerts. Create and customize assignments aligned to specific lessons or Common Core standards.

- **Practice** – With dynamic items and assignments, students get unlimited practice on key concepts supported by guided examples, step-by-step solutions, and video tutorials.
- **Assessments** – Choose from course assignments or customize your own based on course content, Common Core standards, difficulty levels, and more.
- **Homework** – Students can complete online homework with a wide variety of problem types, including the ability to enter expressions, equations, and graphs. Let the system automatically grade homework, so you can focus where your students need help the most!
- **Intervention** – Let the Personal Math Trainer automatically prescribe a targeted, personalized intervention path for your students.

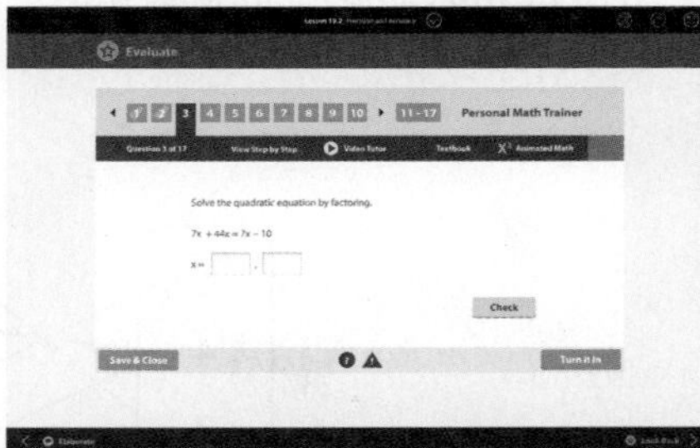

Focus on Higher Order Thinking

Raise the bar with homework and practice that incorporates higher-order thinking and mathematical practices in every lesson.

Assessment Readiness

Prepare students for success on high stakes tests for Algebra 2 with practice at every module and unit

Assessment Resources

Tailor assessments and response to intervention to meet the needs of all your classes and students, including

- Leveled Module Quizzes
- Leveled Unit Tests
- Unit Performance Tasks
- Placement, Diagnostic, and Quarterly Benchmark Tests
- Tier 1, Tier 2, and Tier 3 Resources

Math Background

Functions COMMON CORE F-IF.A.1

LESSONS 1.1 to 1.4

Many students have the mistaken belief that relations and functions must be described by equations. Presenting relations and functions as sets of ordered pairs right from the start helps avoid this misconception.

A *relation* is simply a set of ordered pairs. For a given relation, the set of all first values (or x-values) is the domain. The set of all second values (or y-values) is the range.

The ordered pairs in a relation may be given as a set. For example, the relation described by the set $\{(-1, 2), (4, 0), (4, 3), (7, -5)\}$ consists of four ordered pairs. The ordered pairs may also be presented in a table, graph, or a mapping diagram. This mapping diagram below describes the same relation as the set of ordered pairs.

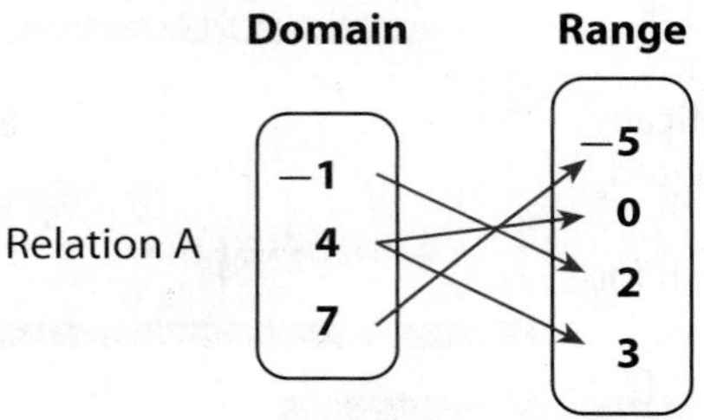

A relation can be described by the way it matches domain and range values. Relation A is one-to-many. This means there is at least one domain value (in this case, 4) that is paired with more than one range value (0 and 3).

A relation is many-to-one if more than one domain value is paired with a single range value. Relation B, shown below, is many-to-one because the domain values 0 and 9 are both paired with the range value 8.

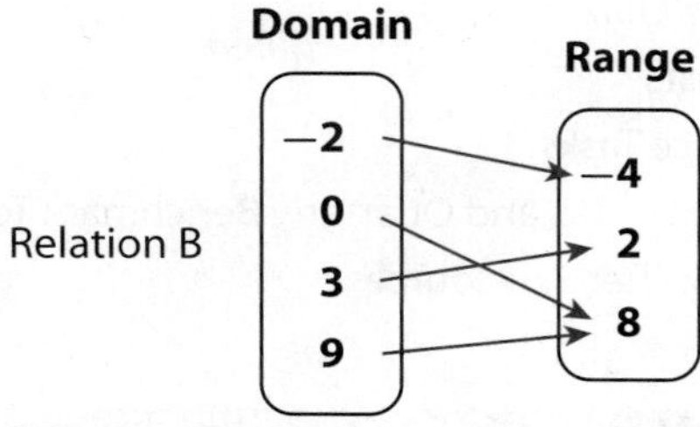

A relation is one-to-one if each domain value is paired with a unique range value and each range value is paired with a unique domain value. Relation C is one-to-one.

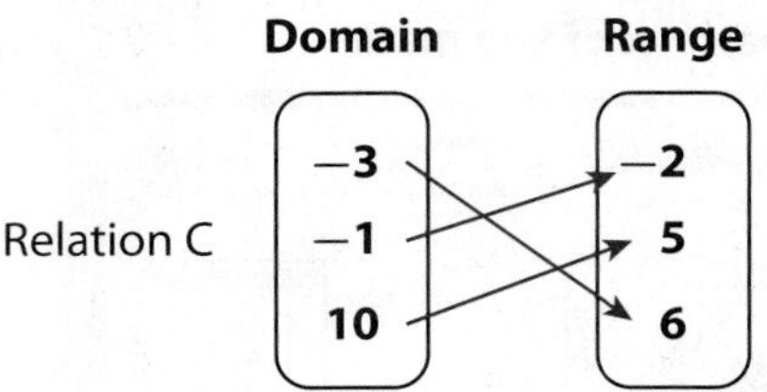

A *function* is a relation in which each domain value is paired with exactly one range value. Thus, every function is a relation, but not every relation is a function. In the above examples, relations B and C are functions. Relation A is not a function because the domain value 4 is paired with more than one range value.

The definition of function may seem somewhat arbitrary to students. It is helpful to explicitly point out the important role that functions play in real-world situations. For example, a meteorologist might study the relation in which each day of the year is paired with the daily high temperature in Los Angeles. It would not make sense if one domain value (a day of the year) were paired with more than one range value (a high temperature). This relation is a function, as are most relations that describe real-world situations.

This example illustrates that a function does not have to be defined with an equation or formula; the function above is not described by any formula that we understand. The real-world example also illustrates why the first value of a function is the independent variable and the second value is the dependent variable. The second value (e.g., temperature) depends on the first value (e.g., day of the year).

Functions may be one-to-one or many-to-one. The function that gives the daily high temperature in Los Angeles is likely to be many-to-one, as there may be several days that are paired with the same temperature. However, by definition a function cannot be one-to-many.

In general, it is fairly intuitive to see that functions may be many-to-one or one-to-one, but not one-to-many. Graphically, a single domain value with multiple range values will fail the "vertical line test" because there will be several points that are vertically aligned with one point on the horizontal axis.

Given the graph of a function, you can use the "horizontal line test" to determine whether the function is many-to-one or one-to-one. If there is a horizontal line that intersects the function's graph in more than one point, then the function is many-to-one. For example, the graph of $y = x^2$ fails the horizontal line test since, for example, the horizontal line $y = 4$ passes through $(-2, 4)$ and $(2, 4)$, both of which are on the function's graph. Therefore, this function is many-to-one. If a function passes the horizontal line test, the function is one-to-one. One-to-one functions are important because these are precisely the functions for which an inverse function exists. Students will learn about inverse functions in this unit.

When a function can be described by an equation, the function can be written in function notation. This notation offers a compact way to describe how the function maps input values to output values. For example, the notation $f(x) = 2x + 5$ means that the function f takes an input value x, multiplies it by 2, and then adds 5. The variable or expression on which a function operates is called the *argument* of the function. In this example, the argument is x.

One advantage of function notation is that it gives the option of changing the argument of the function. Using 2 as the argument of the function in the above example results in $f(2)$, which is a shorthand way of writing "the value of f at $x = 2$." The argument of a function can also be an expression. Thus, $f\left(x^2 + 1\right)$ means $2\left(x^2 + 1\right) + 5$. It is also possible to use another function as the argument of a function. For example, consider the function g given by $g(x) = x - 3$. Then $f\big(g(x)\big) = 2g(x) + 5$ or $2\,(x - 3) + 5$. Fluency in working with functions and function notation is an essential prerequisite for students' success in future mathematics classes.

Absolute Value

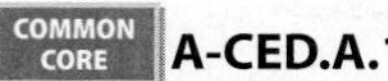

LESSONS 2.1 to 2.3

The absolute value of a number is the number's distance from 0 on a number line. More generally, $|x - a|$ represents the distance between x and a. Thus, the equation $|x - 1| = 3$ asks, "Which values of x are 3 units away from 1?" As the figure shows, there are two values of x that are 3 units away from 1, –2 and 4. So, this absolute-value equation has two solutions.

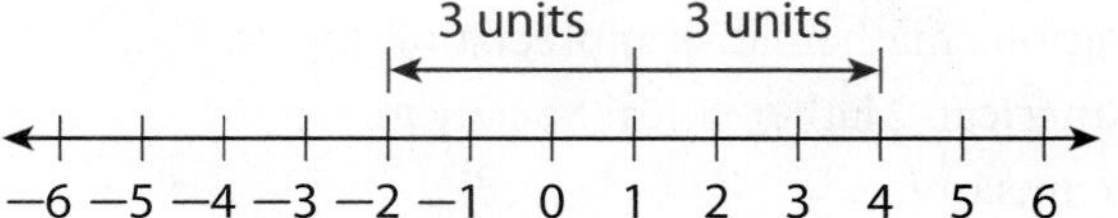

It is also possible for an absolute-value equation to have one solution, no solutions, or infinitely many solutions.

Absolute-value inequalities may be written using compound inequalities. Since the absolute value of x gives the distance of x from 0 on a number line, an inequality such as $|x| < 3$ represents all points less than 3 units from 0; that is, $x > -3$ AND $x < 3$, or $-3 < x < 3$. Similarly, $|x| > 3$ is the set of all points more than 3 units from 0, which is the compound inequality $x < -3$ OR $x > 3$.

Absolute value inequalities may be used to express a range of values. The absolute value of $x - a$ gives the distance between x and a on a number line. Therefore, the absolute-value inequality $|x - a| < k$ states that the distance between x and a is less than k. In other words, the inequality represents the set of all values of x that are less than k units from a.

This idea is useful in a variety of real-world applications. For example, suppose that a machine is set to cut pieces of fabric that are 2 meters long. For quality-assurance purposes, the pieces of fabric may differ from this length by at most 3 millimeters or 0.003 meter. The range of acceptable lengths is expressed by the inequality $|x - 2| \leq 0.003$. That is, the distance on a number line from x to 2 is at most 0.003. Equivalently, the relationship can be expressed with the compound inequality $-0.003 \leq x - 2 \leq 0.003$. By the Addition Property of Inequality, it is permissible to add 2 to each part of the inequality, which gives the range of acceptable lengths as $1.997 \leq x \leq 2.003$.

Functions

MATH IN CAREERS

Unit Activity Preview

After completing this unit, students will complete a Math in Careers task by creating and graphing an algebraic model for the revenue of a community theater at different ticket prices. Critical skills include representing real-world situations algebraically, determining domain and range, and interpreting graphs.

For more information about careers in mathematics as well as various mathematics appreciation topics, visit The American Mathematical Society at http://www.ams.org.

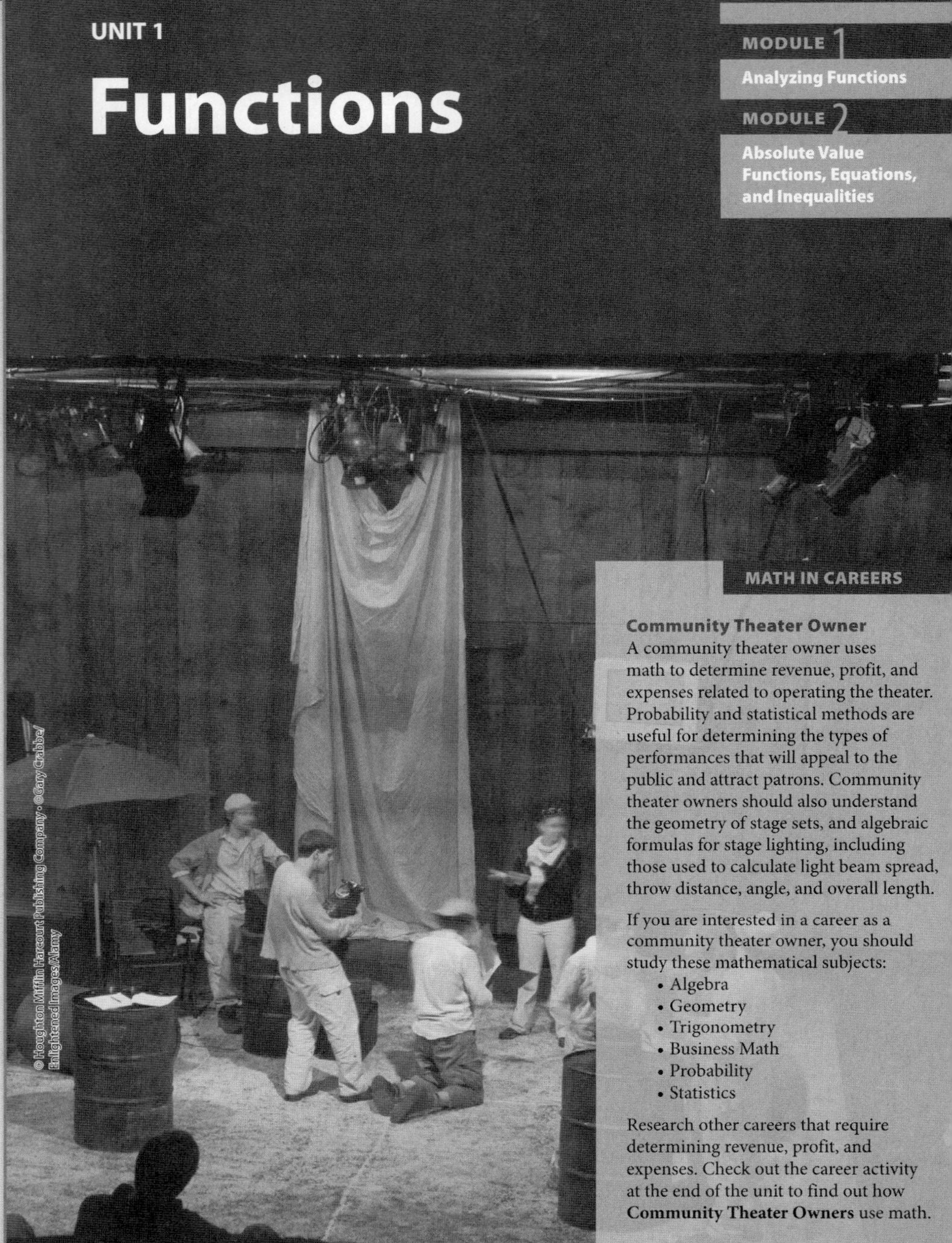

UNIT 1
Functions
MODULE 1
Analyzing Functions
MODULE 2
Absolute Value Functions, Equations, and Inequalities
MATH IN CAREERS
Community Theater Owner
A community theater owner uses math to determine revenue, profit, and expenses related to operating the theater. Probability and statistical methods are useful for determining the types of performances that will appeal to the public and attract patrons. Community theater owners should also understand the geometry of stage sets, and algebraic formulas for stage lighting, including those used to calculate light beam spread, throw distance, angle, and overall length.
If you are interested in a career as a community theater owner, you should study these mathematical subjects:
• Algebra
• Geometry
• Trigonometry
• Business Math
• Probability
• Statistics
Research other careers that require determining revenue, profit, and expenses. Check out the career activity at the end of the unit to find out how Community Theater Owners use math.
© Houghton Mifflin Harcourt Publishing Company • ©Gary Crabbe/ Enlightened Images/Alamy
1

TRACKING YOUR LEARNING PROGRESSION

Before	In this Unit	After
Students understand: • using variables and expressions to represent situations • locating points in a coordinate plane • solving equations • finding and interpreting *x*- and *y*-intercepts	Students will learn about: • analyzing functions, including domain, range and end behavior • transforming function graphs and inverses of functions • graphing, writing, and solving functions including absolute value functions, equations and inequalities	Students will study: • quadratic equations and their graphs • systems of linear and quadratic equations • parabolas • systems of linear inequalities

Reading Start-Up

Visualize Vocabulary

Use the ✔ words to complete the graphic. You can put more than one word on each spoke of the information wheel.

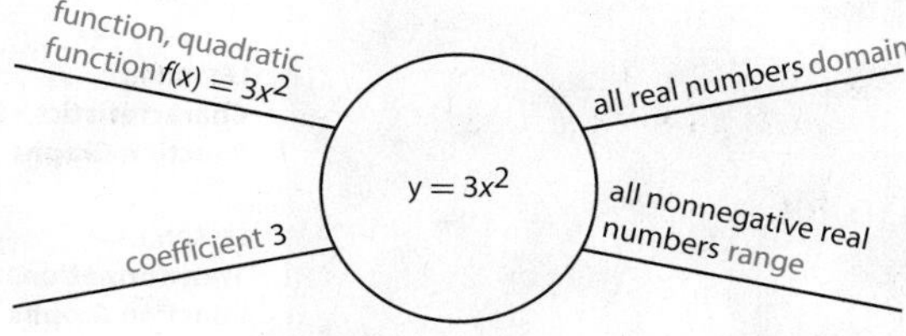

Vocabulary

Review Words

- ✔ coefficient *(coeficiente)*
- ✔ domain *(dominio)*
- ✔ function *(función)*
- ✔ inequality *(desigualdad)*
- ✔ interval *(intervalo)*
- ✔ quadratic function *(función cuadrática)*
- ✔ range *(rango)*
- ✔ transformation *(transformación)*

Preview Words

- conjunction *(conjunción)*
- disjunction *(disyunción)*
- even function *(función par)*
- inverse function *(función inversa)*
- odd function *(función impar)*
- parameter *(parámetro)*

Understand Vocabulary

To become familiar with some of the vocabulary terms in the module, consider the following. You may refer to the module, the glossary, or a dictionary.

1. A ___parameter___ is a constant in the equation of a curve that yields a family of similar curves as it changes.
2. A function $f(x)$ such that $f(x) = f(-x)$ is an ___even function___.
3. A compound statement that uses the word *or* is a ___disjunction___.

Active Reading

Three-Panel Flip Chart Before beginning each lesson, create a three-panel flip chart to help you summarize important aspects of the lesson. As you study each lesson, record algebraic examples of functions on the first flap, their graphs on the second flap, and analyses of the functions on the third flap. Add to flip charts from previous lessons by extending the analyses of the functions when possible. For equations and inequalities, record an example on the first flap, a worked out solution on the second flap, and a graph on the third flap.

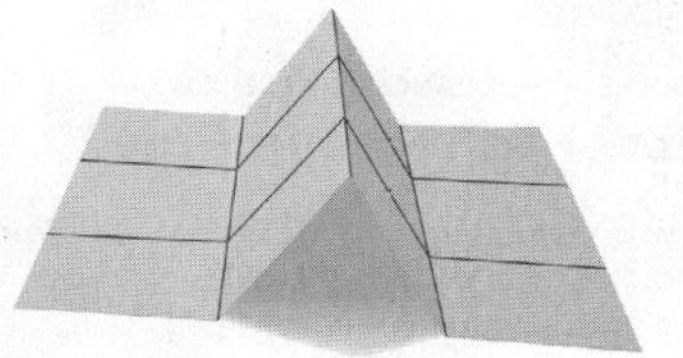

Reading Start Up

Have students complete the activities on this page by working alone or with others.

VISUALIZE VOCABULARY

The information wheel graphic helps students review vocabulary associated with quadratic functions. If time allows, discuss any other mathematical relationships among the vocabulary words.

UNDERSTAND VOCABULARY

Use the following explanations to help students learn the preview words.

The **end behavior** of a function is the behavior of the graph as x gets very large and as x gets very small. An **even function** has symmetric end behavior. To find the **inverse function** of an even function, the domain of the even function must be restricted.

ACTIVE READING

Students can use these reading and note-taking strategies to help them organize and understand the new concepts and vocabulary. Encourage them to ask for help as they review basic vocabulary, and for additional clarification, if needed, as they learn new academic vocabulary throughout the unit. They will encounter much of the vocabulary frequently in the remaining units.

ADDITIONAL RESOURCES

Differentiated Instruction

- Reading Strategies EL

Analyzing Functions

ESSENTIAL QUESTION:

Answer: Understanding how functions behave can help you choose the correct function to use when solving real-world problems.

PROFESSIONAL DEVELOPMENT VIDEO

Professional Development Video

Author Matt Larson models successful teaching practices in an actual high-school classroom.

Professional Development my.hrw.com

MODULE 1

Analyzing Functions

Essential Question: How can you analyze functions to solve real-world problems?

REAL WORLD VIDEO

Pole vaulting is just one of many track-and-field events that feature a person or object flying through the air. The path of a pole vaulter or of a shot put can be modeled using a quadratic function.

MODULE PERFORMANCE TASK PREVIEW

How High Does a Pole Vaulter Go?

In pole vaulting, a person jumps over a horizontal bar with the assistance of a long fiberglass or carbon-fiber pole. The flexible pole makes it possible for vaulters to achieve much greater heights than jumping without a pole. The goal is to clear the bar without knocking it down. How can mathematics be used to compare the heights of a pole vaulter for two different vaults? Let's jump in and find out!

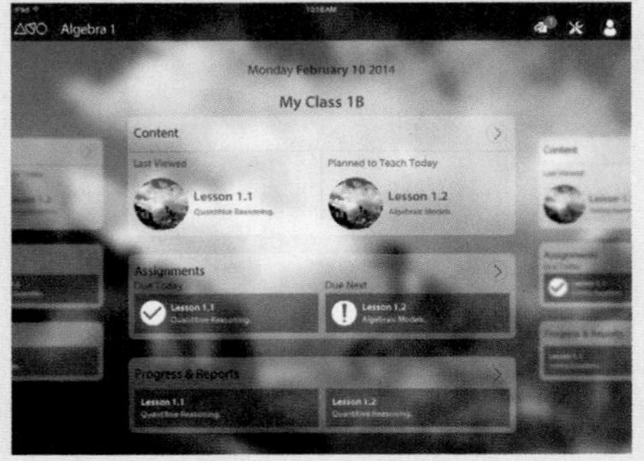

DIGITAL TEACHER EDITION

Access a full suite of teaching resources when and where you need them:

- Access content online or offline
- Customize lessons to share with your class
- Communicate with your students in real-time
- View student grades and data instantly to target your instruction where it is needed most

PERSONAL MATH TRAINER

Assessment and Intervention

Assign automatically graded homework, quizzes, tests, and intervention activities. Prepare your students with updated, Common Core-aligned practice tests.

Are YOU Ready?

Complete these exercises to review skills you will need for this chapter.

- Online Homework
- Hints and Help
- Extra Practice

Algebraic Representations of Transformations

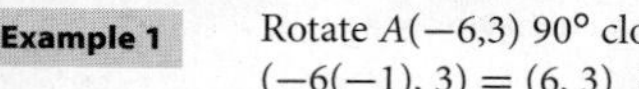

Example 1 Rotate $A(-6,3)$ 90° clockwise.
$(-6(-1), 3) = (6, 3)$ Multiply.
$A(-6, 3) \rightarrow A'(3, 6)$ Switch.

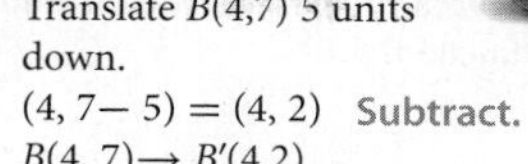

Translate $B(4,7)$ 5 units down.
$(4, 7-5) = (4, 2)$ Subtract.
$B(4, 7) \rightarrow B'(4,2)$

Find the location of A' given that A is $(1, 5)$.

1. Rotate 90° clockwise. $(5, -1)$

2. Translate 1 unit left. $(0, 5)$

3. Reflect across the x-axis. $(1, -5)$

Linear Functions

Example 2 Name the x- and y-intercepts for $y = -2x + 1$.
x-intercept: $0 = -2x + 1$, so $x = 0.5$. y-intercept: $y = -2(0) + 1 = 1$

Find the x- and y-intercepts for each equation.

4. $y = 8x - 4$
x-intercept: 0.5
y-intercept: -4

5. $y = -x + 12$
x-intercept: 12
y-intercept: 12

6. $y = 1.2x + 4.8$
x-intercept: -4
y-intercept: 4.8

Properties of Translations, Reflections, and Rotations

Example 3 The point $P(1, -8)$ is reflected across the y-axis. Name the quadrant that the image, P', is in.
$P(1, -8) \rightarrow P'(-1, -8)$, so P' is in Quadrant III.

Name the quadrant that $R(7,3)$ is in after the transformation.

7. reflection across the x-axis IV

8. translation 8 units down IV

9. rotation 270° clockwise II

Rate of Change and Slope

Example 4 Two points on a line are $(-3, 3)$ and $(4, 1)$. Find the slope.
$\frac{y_1 - y_2}{x_1 - x_2} = \frac{3 - 1}{-3 - 4} = -\frac{2}{7}$ The slope is $-\frac{2}{7}$.

Find the slope represented by the two points.

10. $(0, 5)$ and $(-9, -4)$ 1

11. $(6, -2)$ and $(1, -1)$ -0.2

12. $(-7, 3)$ and $(-4, -12)$ -5

Are You Ready?

ASSESS READINESS

Use the assessment on this page to determine if students need strategic or intensive intervention for the module's prerequisite skills.

ASSESSMENT AND INTERVENTION

RtI Response to Intervention TIER 1, TIER 2, TIER 3 SKILLS

Personal Math Trainer will automatically create a standards-based, personalized intervention assignment for your students, targeting each student's individual needs!

ADDITIONAL RESOURCES

See the table below for a full list of intervention resources available for this module.

Response to Intervention Resources also includes:

- Tier 2 Skill Pre-Tests for each Module
- Tier 2 Skill Post-Tests for each skill

Response to Intervention			Differentiated Instruction
Tier 1 Lesson Intervention Worksheets	**Tier 2** Strategic Intervention Skills Intervention Worksheets	**Tier 3** Intensive Intervention Worksheets available online	
Reteach 1.1 Reteach 1.2 Reteach 1.3 Reteach 1.4	4 Algebraic Representations... 18 Linear Functions 25 Properties of Translations... 27 Rate of Change and Slope	Building Block Skills 1, 22, 23, 27, 41, 42, 43, 44, 90, 103	Challenge worksheets Extend the Math Lesson Activities in TE

LESSON 1.1

Domain, Range, and End Behavior

Common Core Math Standards

The student is expected to:

F-IF.B.5

Relate the domain of a function to its graph and, where applicable, to the quantitative relationship it describes. Also A-CED.A.2, A-CED.A.3

Mathematical Practices

MP.6 Precision

Language Objective

With a partner, fill in a graphic organizer showing the domain, range, and end behavior of a function.

ENGAGE

Essential Question: How can you determine the domain, range, and end behavior of a function?

Possible answer: The domain consists of x values for which the function is defined or on which the real-world situation is based. The range consists of the corresponding $f(x)$ values. The end behavior describes what happens to the $f(x)$ values as the x values increase without bound or decrease without bound.

PREVIEW: LESSON PERFORMANCE TASK

View the online Engage. Discuss how the distance a car can travel is a function of the amount of gas in the car's gas tank. Have students identify the independent and dependent variables of the functional relationship. Then preview the Lesson Performance Task.

Name ______________ Class ______________ Date ______________

1.1 Domain, Range, and End Behavior

Resource Locker

Essential Question: How can you determine the domain, range, and end behavior of a function?

Explore Representing an Interval on a Number Line

An **interval** is a part of a number line without any breaks. A *finite interval* has two endpoints, which may or may not be included in the interval. An *infinite interval* is unbounded at one or both ends.

Suppose an interval consists of all real numbers greater than or equal to 1. You can use the inequality $x \geq 1$ to represent the interval. You can also use *set notation* and *interval notation*, as shown in the table.

Description of Interval	Type of Interval	Inequality	Set Notation	Interval notation
All real numbers from a to b, including a and b	Finite	$a \leq x \leq b$	$\{x \mid a \leq x \leq b\}$	$[a, b]$
All real numbers greater than a	Infinite	$x > a$	$\{x \mid x > a\}$	$(a, +\infty)$
All real numbers less than or equal to a	Infinite	$x \leq a$	$\{x \mid x \leq a\}$	$(-\infty, a]$

For set notation, the vertical bar means "such that," so you read $\{x \mid x \geq 1\}$ as "the set of real numbers x such that x is greater than or equal to 1."

For interval notation, do the following:

- Use a square bracket to indicate that an interval includes an endpoint and a parenthesis to indicate that an interval doesn't include an endpoint.
- For an interval that is unbounded at its positive end, use the symbol for positive infinity, $+\infty$. For an interval that unbounded at its negative end, use the symbol for negative infinity, $-\infty$. Always use a parenthesis with positive or negative infinity.

So, you can write the interval $x \geq 1$ as $[1, +\infty)$.

(A) Complete the table by writing the finite interval shown on each number line as an inequality, using set notation, and using interval notation.

Finite Interval	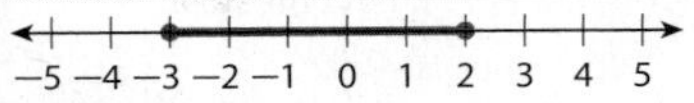 (number line −5 to 5: closed dot at −3, closed dot at 2)	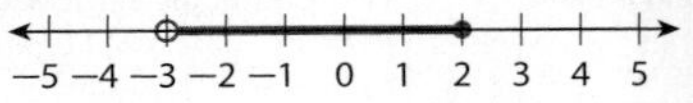 (number line −5 to 5: open dot at −3, closed dot at 2)
Inequality	$-3 \leq x \leq 2$	$-3 < x \leq 2$
Set Notation	$\{x \mid -3 \leq x \leq 2\}$	$\{x \mid -3 < x \leq 2\}$
Interval Notation	$[-3, 2]$	$(-3, 2]$

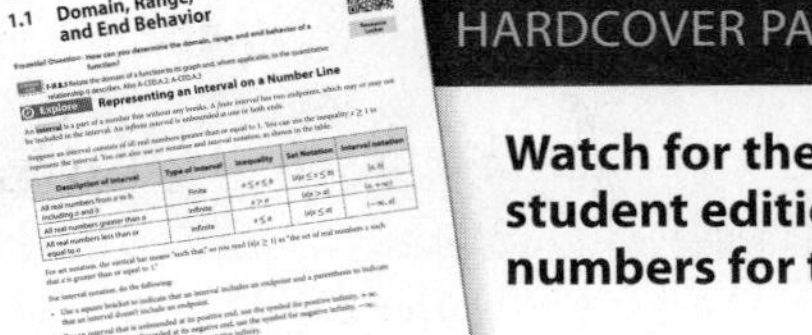

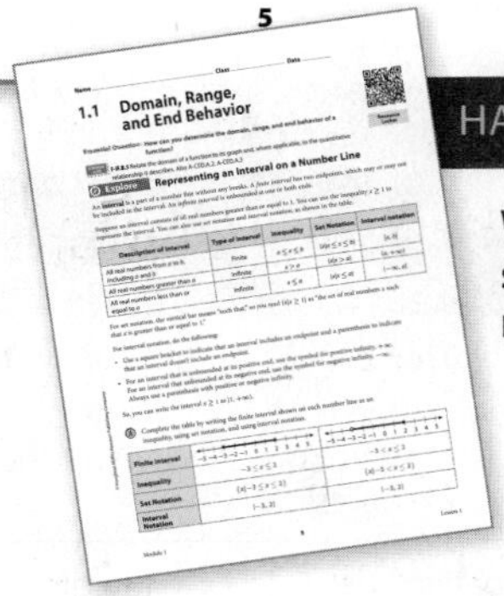

HARDCOVER PAGES 5–16

Watch for the hardcover student edition page numbers for this lesson.

Ⓑ Complete the table by writing the infinite interval shown on each number line as an inequality, using set notation, and using interval notation.

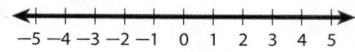

Infinite Interval	−5 −4 −3 −2 −1 0 1 2 3 4 5	−5 −4 −3 −2 −1 0 1 2 3 4 5
Inequality	$x \leq 2$	$x > 2$
Set Notation	$\{x \mid x \leq 2\}$	$\{x \mid x > 2\}$
Interval Notation	$(-\infty, 2]$	$(2, +\infty)$

Reflect

1. Consider the interval shown on the number line.

−5 −4 −3 −2 −1 0 1 2 3 4 5

a. Represent the interval using interval notation. $(-\infty, +\infty)$

b. What numbers are in this interval? **All real numbers**

2. What do the intervals [0, 5], [0, 5), and (0, 5) have in common? What makes them different?
All three intervals contain all the numbers between 0 and 5. The interval [0, 5] also includes the endpoints 0 and 5, the interval [0, 5) includes only the endpoint 0, and the interval (0, 5) does not contain either endpoint.

3. **Discussion** The symbol ∪ represents the *union* of two sets. What do you think the notation $(-\infty, 0) \cup (0, +\infty)$ represents?
All real numbers except 0

Explain 1 Identifying a Function's Domain, Range and End Behavior from its Graph

Recall that the *domain* of a function f is the set of input values x, and the *range* is the set of output values $f(x)$. The **end behavior** of a function describes what happens to the $f(x)$-values as the x-values either increase without bound (approach positive infinity) or decrease without bound (approach negative infinity). For instance, consider the graph of a linear function shown. From the graph, you can make the following observations.

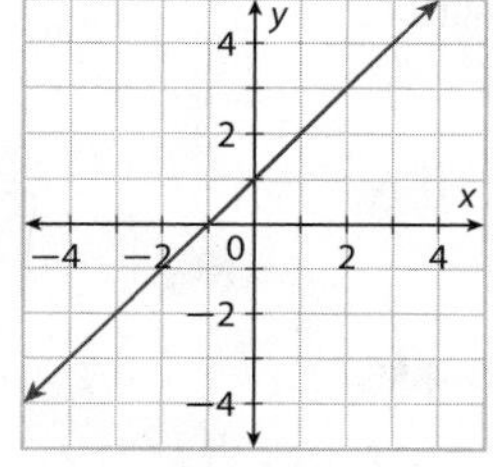

PROFESSIONAL DEVELOPMENT

Integrate Mathematical Practices

This lesson provides an opportunity to address Mathematical Practice **MP.6**, which calls for students to use the language of mathematics to communicate precisely and to "attend to precision." Students learn to describe intervals using inequalities, set notation, and interval notation. They also learn how to use mathematical notation to describe end behavior of a function.

EXPLORE

Representing an Interval on a Number Line

INTEGRATE TECHNOLOGY

Students have the option of completing the activity either in the book or online.

INTEGRATE MATHEMATICAL PRACTICES

Focus on Modeling

MP.4 Draw students' attention to the use of braces, parentheses, and brackets in the various representations. Make sure students can use the symbols correctly, and can explain the significance of the symbols in each type of notation.

EXPLAIN 1

Identifying a Function's Domain, Range, and End Behavior from its Graph

AVOID COMMON ERRORS

Some students may incorrectly identify the end behavior of a function that increases over the interval $(-\infty, 0)$ as "As $x \to -\infty, f(x) \to \infty$." Help students to see that for this part of the description, they must consider the behavior of the function as the values of x *decrease* (the behavior of the graph as observed from right to left), and not whether the function itself is an increasing or decreasing function.

QUESTIONING STRATEGIES

? Is it possible that a linear function with the domain {all real numbers} could have a range that is *not* {all real numbers}? Explain. **Yes; the function could be a constant function, such as $f(x) = 2$. The domain is {all real numbers}, but the range is {2}.**

Statement of End Behavior	Symbolic Form of Statement
As the x-values increase without bound, the $f(x)$-values also increase without bound.	As $x \to +\infty$, $f(x) \to +\infty$.
As the x-values decrease without bound, the $f(x)$-values also decrease without bound.	As $x \to -\infty$, $f(x) \to -\infty$.

Example 1 **Write the domain and the range of the function as an inequality, using set notation, and using interval notation. Also describe the end behavior of the function.**

Ⓐ The graph of the quadratic function $f(x) = x^2$ is shown.

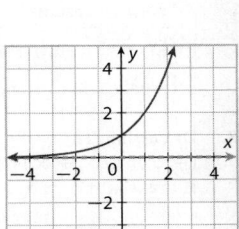

Domain:

Inequality: $-\infty < x < +\infty$

Set notation: $\{x \mid -\infty < x < +\infty\}$

Interval notation: $(-\infty, +\infty)$

Range:

Inequality: $y \geq 0$

Set notation: $\{y \mid y \geq 0\}$

Interval notation: $[0, +\infty)$

End behavior:

As $x \to +\infty$, $f(x) \to +\infty$.

As $x \to -\infty$, $f(x) \to +\infty$.

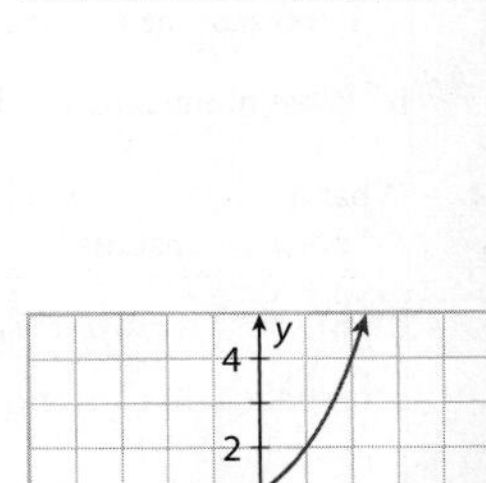

Ⓑ The graph of the exponential function $f(x) = 2^x$ is shown.

Domain:

Inequality: $-\infty < x < +\infty$

Set notation: $\{x \mid -\infty < x < +\infty\}$

Interval notation: $(-\infty, +\infty)$

Range:

Inequality: $y > 0$

Set notation: $\{y \mid y > 0\}$

Interval notation: $(0, +\infty)$

End behavior:

As $x \to +\infty$, $f(x) \to +\infty$.

As $x \to +\infty$, $f(x) \to 0$.

COLLABORATIVE LEARNING

Peer-to-Peer Activity

Have students work in pairs to draw the graph of a linear function with a restricted domain and keep the graph hidden from their partner. Have students describe the function's domain and range using one of the notation forms from the lesson, then exchange descriptions and try to draw each other's graph. Have students compare their graphs (which may differ) and discuss the results.

Reflect

4. Why is the end behavior of a quadratic function different from the end behavior of a linear function?
Unlike the graph of a linear function, the graph of a quadratic function has a turning point (the vertex), which changes the direction of the graph.

5. In Part B, the $f(x)$-values decrease as the x-values decrease. So, why can't you say that $f(x) \to -\infty$ as $x \to -\infty$?
The $f(x)$-values do not decrease without bound. They instead approach 0.

Your Turn

Write the domain and the range of the function as an inequality, using set notation, and using interval notation. Also describe the end behavior of the function.

6. The graph of the quadratic function $f(x) = -x^2$ is shown.

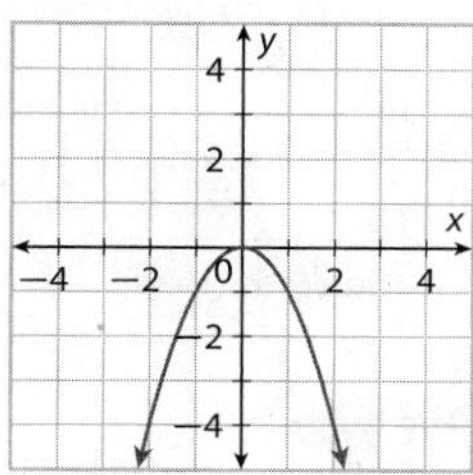

Domain: $-\infty < x < +\infty$, $\{x \mid -\infty < x < +\infty\}$, $(-\infty, +\infty)$
Range: $-\infty < y \leq 0$, $\{y \mid -\infty < y \leq 0\}$, $(-\infty, 0]$
End behavior: As $x \to +\infty$, $f(x) \to -\infty$; As $x \to -\infty$, $f(x) \to +\infty$.

Explain 2 Graphing a Linear Function on a Restricted Domain

Unless otherwise stated, a function is assumed to have a domain consisting of all real numbers for which the function is defined. Many functions—such as linear, quadratic, and exponential functions—are defined for all real numbers, so their domain, when written in interval notation, is $(-\infty, +\infty)$. Another way to write the set of real numbers is $\mathbb{R}$.

Sometimes a function may have a restricted domain. If the rule for a function and its restricted domain are given, you can draw its graph and then identify its range.

Example 2 **For the given function and domain, draw the graph and identify the range using the same notation as the domain.**

(A) $f(x) = \frac{3}{4}x + 2$ with domain $[-4, 4]$

Since $f(x) = \frac{3}{4}x + 2$ is a linear function, the graph is a line segment with endpoints at $(-4, f(-4))$, or $(-4, -1)$, and $(4, f(4))$, or $(4, 5)$. The endpoints are included in the graph.

The range is $[-1, 5]$.

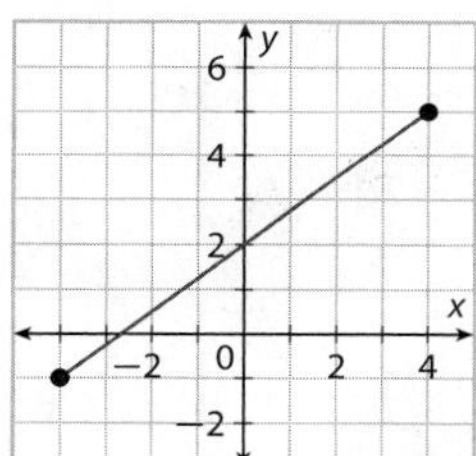

DIFFERENTIATE INSTRUCTION

Cognitive Strategies

If students have a difficult time consistently identifying the domain and range of functions, encourage them to use the phrase *depends on* instead of *is a function of*. For example, "The distance traveled by a car depends on the amount of gas in the tank." Help them to see that the elements of the range "depend on" the elements of the domain.

EXPLAIN 2

Graphing a Linear Function on a Restricted Domain

INTEGRATE MATHEMATICAL PRACTICES

Focus on Math Connections

MP.1 Remind students that the graph of a function represents the set of ordered pairs produced by the function. Help them to see that when they are using a graph to identify the range of a function, they are to identify the y values of those ordered pairs.

QUESTIONING STRATEGIES

? If a linear function has a restricted domain, must the range consist of a finite number of elements? Explain. **No. If the domain is restricted to an interval (or intervals), as opposed to a finite number of elements, the range could consist of infinitely many values. For example, the range of the function $f(x) = 3x$ with domain $[0, 5]$ is $[0, 15]$, an interval containing infinitely many numbers.**

? If the domain of a linear function consists of n elements, how many elements would there be in the range? Explain. **One, if the function is a constant function, or n if it is not. In a non-constant linear function, each element of the domain is paired with a different element of the range.**

(B) $f(x) = -x - 2$ with domain $\{x|x > -3\}$

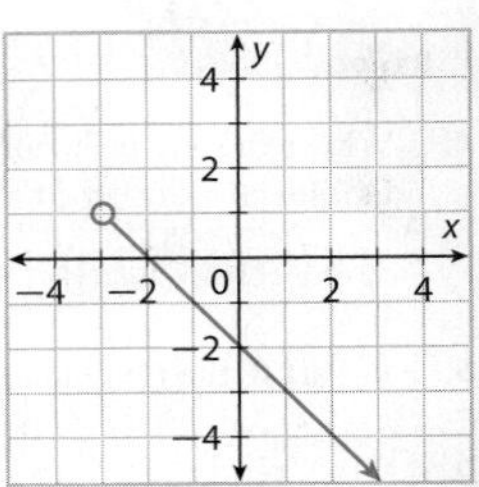

Since $f(x) = -x - 2$ is a linear function, the graph is a ray with its endpoint at $(-3, f(-3))$,

or **(−3, 1)**. The endpoint **is not** included in the graph.

The range is **$\{y|y < 1\}$**.

Reflect

7. In Part A, how does the graph change if the domain is $(-4, 4)$ instead of $[-4, 4]$?
The graph no longer includes the endpoints of the segment.

8. In Part B, what is the end behavior as x increases without bound? Why can't you talk about the end behavior as x decreases without bound?
As $x \to +\infty$, $f(x) \to -\infty$. Because the domain does not include values of x that are less than or equal to −3, the values of x cannot decrease without bound.

Your Turn

For the given function and domain, draw the graph and identify the range using the same notation as the domain.

9. $f(x) = -\frac{1}{2}x + 2$ with domain $-6 \le x < 2$

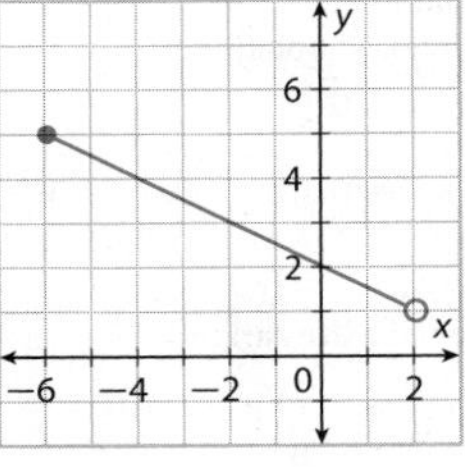

The range is $1 < y \le 5$.

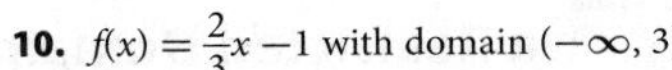

10. $f(x) = \frac{2}{3}x - 1$ with domain $(-\infty, 3]$

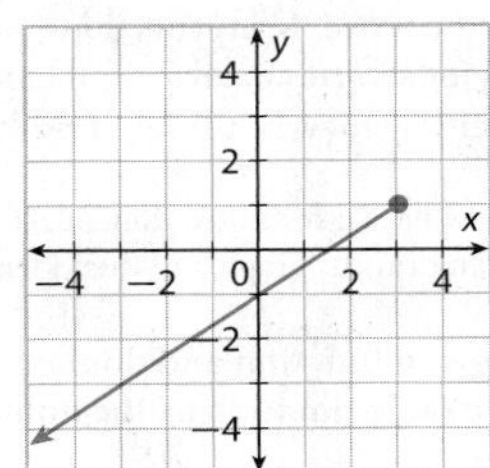

The range is $(-\infty, 1]$.

LANGUAGE SUPPORT EL

Connect Vocabulary

Have students work in pairs. Instruct one student to verbally describe the domain, range, and end behavior of a function without using those three terms. Have the other student fill in a graphic organizer with boxes titled *Domain, Range,* and *End behavior,* and write in the appropriate values under each box. Have students switch roles and repeat the exercise using a different function.

Explain 3 Modeling with a Linear Function

Recall that when a real-world situation involves a constant rate of change, a linear function is a reasonable model for the situation. The situation may require restricting the function's domain.

Example 3 **Write a function that models the given situation. Determine a domain from the situation, graph the function using that domain, and identify the range.**

(A) Joyce jogs at a rate of 1 mile every 10 minutes for a total of 40 minutes. (Use inequalities for the domain and range of the function that models this situation.)

Joyce's jogging rate is 0.1 mi/min. Her jogging distance d (in miles) at any time t (in minutes) is modeled by $d(t) = 0.1t$. Since she jogs for 40 minutes, the domain is restricted to the interval $0 \leq t \leq 40$.

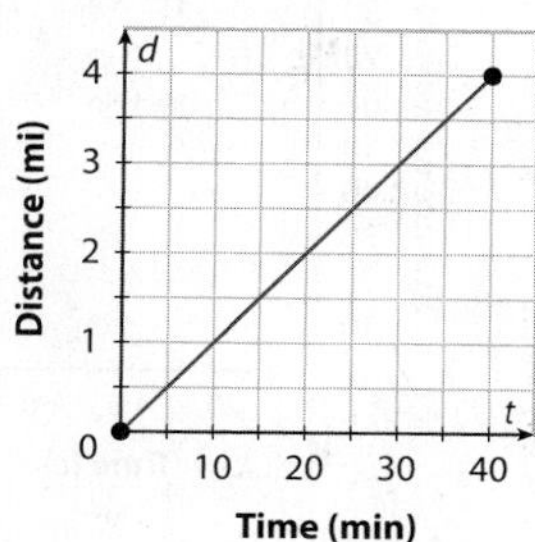

The range is $0 \leq d \leq 4$.

(B) A candle 6 inches high burns at a rate of 1 inch every 2 hours for 5 hours. (Use interval notation for the domain and range of the function that models this situation.)

The candle's burning rate is **−0.5** in./h. The candle's height h (in inches) at any time t (in hours) is modeled by $h(t) =$ **$6 - 0.5t$**. Since the candle burns for 5 hours, the domain is restricted to the interval [0, **5**].

The range is **[3.5, 6]**.

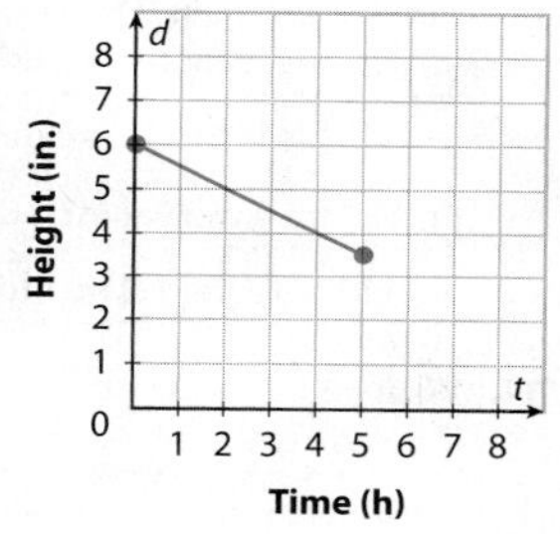

EXPLAIN 3

Modeling with a Linear Function

AVOID COMMON ERRORS

Some students may erroneously identify the domain of a function that represents a real-world situation as an interval, when in fact the domain consists only of specific numbers *within* the interval, such as integers or multiples of a particular rational number. Help students to avoid this error by encouraging them to ask themselves whether any number within the interval could be a realistic input value for the situation described by the function.

INTEGRATE MATHEMATICAL PRACTICES

Focus on Reasoning

MP.2 Encourage students to check their work by considering the reasonableness of the range of the function. Have them evaluate whether the values in the range seem realistic for the given situation.

ELABORATE

INTEGRATE MATHEMATICAL PRACTICES

Focus on Communication

MP.3 Discuss different strategies for determining the range of a function from a graph of the function. Have students describe methods they use, and illustrate their methods using graphs of different types of functions, including those with restricted domains.

QUESTIONING STRATEGIES

? Is it possible that a real-world situation can be modeled by a function whose domain consists of both positive and negative real numbers? If no, explain why not. If yes, give an example. Yes. Possible example: a function that describes the relationship between air temperature in degrees Fahrenheit and dew point, at a given level of humidity. The domain consists of all possible air temperatures in degrees Fahrenheit.

SUMMARIZE THE LESSON

? How do you identify and represent the domain, range, and end behavior of a function? To identify the domain, find the values of x for which the function is defined. To find the range, find the values of $f(x)$ for each value of x in the domain. There are different ways of representing the domain and range, including using inequalities, set notation, and interval notation. To find the end-behavior, consider what happens to the values of the range as the values of the domain increase or decrease without bound.

Reflect

11. In Part A, suppose Joyce jogs for only 30 minutes.

A. How does the domain change? **The domain is $0 \le t \le 30$ instead of $0 \le t \le 40$.**

B. How does the graph change? **The graph's right endpoint is (30, 3) instead of (40, 4).**

C. How does the range change? **The range is $0 \le d \le 3$ instead of $0 \le d \le 4$.**

Your Turn

12. While standing on a moving walkway at an airport, you are carried forward 25 feet every 15 seconds for 1 minute. Write a function that models this situation. Determine a domain from the situation, graph the function, and identify the range. Use set notation for the domain and range.

The walkway's rate of motion is $\frac{5}{3}$ ft/s. The distance d (in feet) you travel at any time t (in seconds) is modeled by $d(t) = \frac{5}{3}t$.

Domain: $\{t \mid 0 \le t \le 60\}$; range: $\{d \mid 0 \le d \le 100\}$.

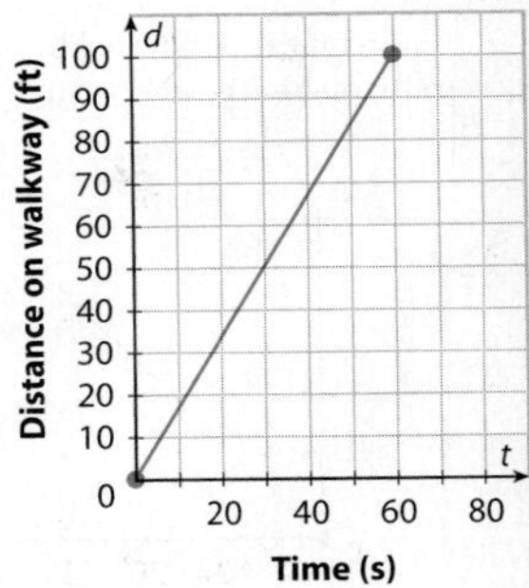

Elaborate

13. If a and b are real numbers such that $a < b$, use interval notation to write four different intervals having a and b as endpoints. Describe what numbers each interval includes.

$[a, b]$: This interval includes all real numbers between a and b, including both a and b.

$[a, b)$: This interval includes all real numbers between a and b, including a but not b.

$(a, b]$: This interval includes all real numbers between a and b, including b but not a.

(a, b): This interval includes all real numbers between a and b but does not include a or b.

14. What impact does restricting the domain of a linear function have on the graph of the function?

If the domain is bounded at both ends, the graph of the linear function is a line segment rather than a line. If the domain is bounded at only one end, the graph of the linear function is a ray rather than a line.

15. Essential Question Check-In How does slope determine the end behavior of a linear function with an unrestricted domain?

If slope is positive, the $f(x)$-values increase without bound as the x-values increase without bound, and the $f(x)$-values decrease without bound as the x-values decrease without bound. If the slope is negative, the end behavior reverses: The $f(x)$-values decrease without bound as the x-values increase without bound, and the $f(x)$-values increase without bound as the x-values decrease without bound.

Evaluate: Homework and Practice

- Online Homework
- Hints and Help
- Extra Practice

1. Write the interval shown on the number line as an inequality, using set notation, and using interval notation.

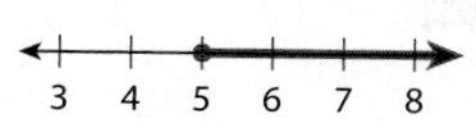

$x \geq 5$, $\{x|x \geq 5\}$, $[5, +\infty)$

2. Write the interval (5, 100] as an inequality and using set notation.

$5 < x \leq 100$; $\{x|5 < x \leq 100\}$

3. Write the interval $-25 \leq x < 30$ using set notation and interval notation.

$\{x| -25 \leq x < 30\}$, $[-25, 30)$

4. Write the interval $\{x| -3 < x < 5\}$ as an inequality and using interval notation.

$-3 < x < 5$, $(-3, 5)$

Write the domain and the range of the function as an inequality, using set notation, and using interval notation. Also describe the end behavior of the function or explain why there is no end behavior.

5. The graph of the quadratic function $f(x) = x^2 + 2$ is shown.

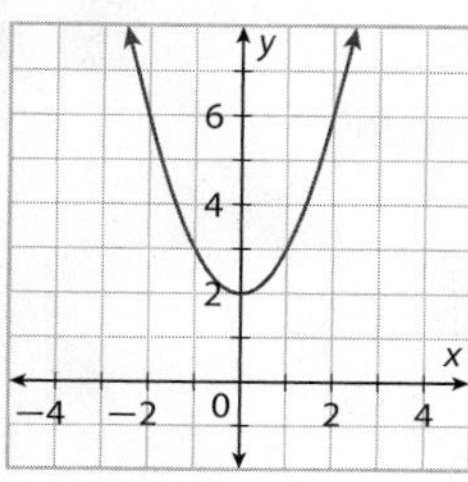

Domain: $-\infty < x < +\infty$, $\{x| -\infty < x < +\infty\}$, $(-\infty, +\infty)$
Range: $2 \leq y < +\infty$, $\{y|2 \leq y < +\infty\}$, $[2, +\infty)$
End behavior: As $x \to +\infty$, $f(x) \to +\infty$; As $x \to -\infty$, $f(x) \to +\infty$.

6. The graph of the exponential function $f(x) = 3^x$ is shown.

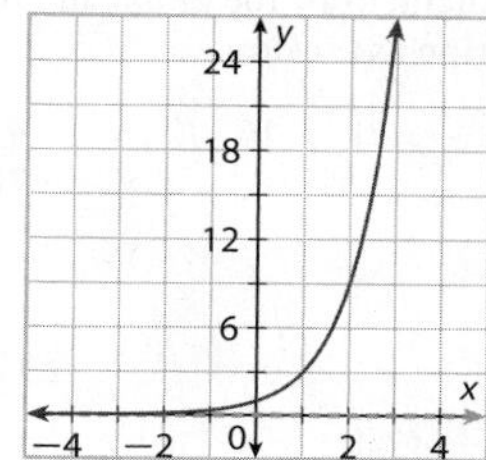

Domain: $-\infty < x < +\infty$, $\{x| -\infty < x < +\infty\}$, $(-\infty, +\infty)$
Range: $0 < y < +\infty$, $\{y|0 < y < +\infty\}$, $(0, +\infty)$
End behavior: As $x \to +\infty$, $f(x) \to +\infty$; As $x \to -\infty$, $f(x) \to 0$.

Exercise	Depth of Knowledge (D.O.K.)	COMMON CORE Mathematical Practices
1–8	**1** Recall of Information	**MP.2** Reasoning
9–10	**1** Recall of Information	**MP.4** Modeling
11	**1** Recall of Information	**MP.6** Precision
12	**2** Skills/Concepts	**MP.4** Modeling
13	**2** Skills/Concepts H.O.T.	**MP.3** Logic
14	**3** Strategic Thinking H.O.T.	**MP.6** Precision

EVALUATE

ASSIGNMENT GUIDE

Concepts and Skills	Practice
Explore Representing an Interval on a Number Line	Exercises 1–4
Example 1 Identifying a Function's Domain, Range, and End Behavior from its Graph	Exercises 5–8
Example 2 Graphing a Linear Function on a Restricted Domain	Exercises 9–10
Example 3 Modeling with a Linear Function	Exercises 11–12

VISUAL CUES

Some students may benefit from labeling the endpoints of an interval as *included* or *not included,* as indicated by the closed circle or open circle on the graph. They will then be sure to use the appropriate symbols when describing the interval using the different types of notation.

CONNECT VOCABULARY EL

Relate *end behavior* to the shape of the graph of different functions. Have students use words to describe the end behavior of each function by looking at the graph. For example, a function $f(x)$ appears to rise for positive x-values and fall for negative x-values.

MULTIPLE REPRESENTATIONS

When analyzing the graph of a function, students may find it easier to first describe the end behavior of the function in words. They then can translate their verbal descriptions into algebraic notation, making sure that the symbols accurately reflect their descriptions.

KINESTHETIC EXPERIENCE

To help students correctly identify end behavior, suggest that they use a finger to trace along the graph of a function, moving first from left to right, as $x \longrightarrow \infty$, and then from right to left, as $x \longrightarrow -\infty$. Help them to match their observations of the behavior of the graph to its correct description and notation.

7. The graph of the linear function $g(x) = 2x - 2$ is shown.

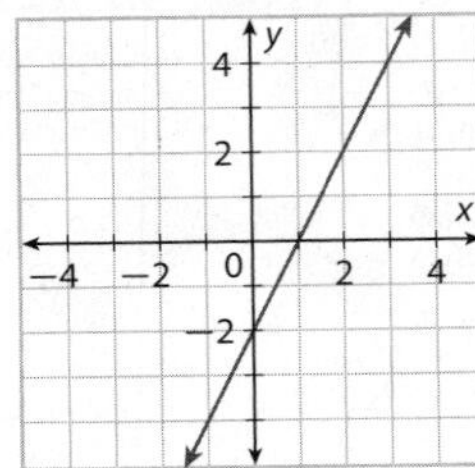

Domain: $-\infty < x < +\infty$, $\{x \mid -\infty < x < +\infty\}$, $(-\infty, +\infty)$

Range: $-\infty < y < +\infty$, $\{x \mid -\infty < y < +\infty\}$, $(-\infty, +\infty)$

End behavior: As $x \rightarrow +\infty$, $f(x) \rightarrow +\infty$; As $x \rightarrow -\infty$, $f(x) \rightarrow -\infty$.

8. The graph of a function is shown.

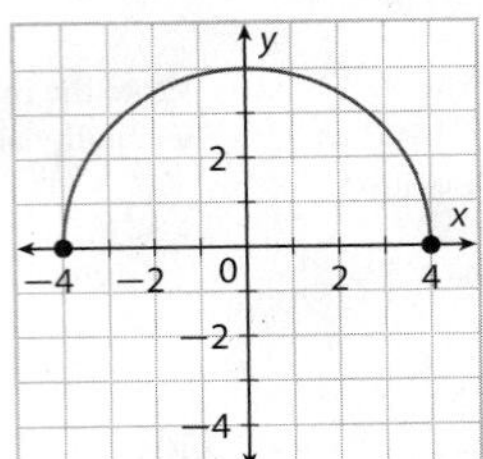

Domain: $-4 \leq x \leq 4$, $\{x \mid -4 \leq x \leq 4\}$, $[-4, 4]$

Range: $0 \leq y \leq 4$, $\{y \mid 0 \leq y \leq 4\}$, $[0, 4]$

There is no end behavior because the domain is bounded at both ends.

For the given function and domain, draw the graph and identify the range using the same notation as the domain.

9. $f(x) = -x + 5$ with domain $[-3, 2]$

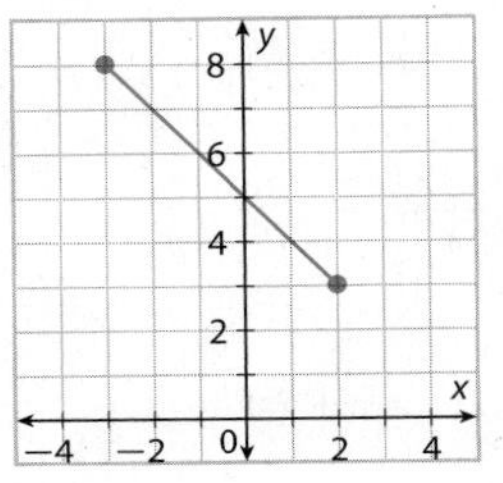

Since $f(x) = -x + 5$ is a linear function, the graph is a line segment with endpoints at $(-3, f(-3))$, or $(-3, 8)$, and $(2, f(2))$, or $(2, 3)$. The endpoints are included in the graph.

The range is $[3, 8]$.

10. $f(x) = \frac{3}{2}x + 1$ with domain $\{x \mid x > -2\}$

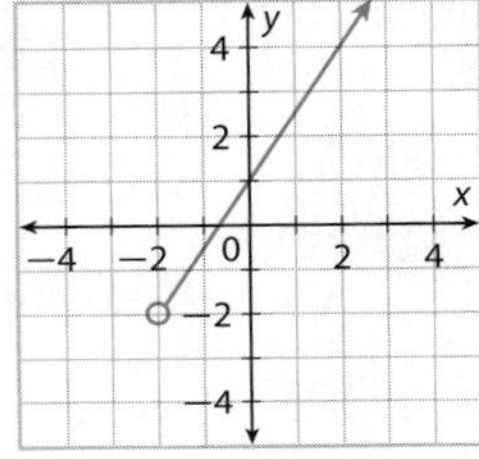

Since $f(x) = \frac{3}{2}x + 1$ is a linear function, the graph is a ray with its endpoint at $(-2, f(-2))$, or $(-2, -2)$. The endpoint is included in the graph.

The range is $\{y \mid y > -2\}$.

Exercise	Depth of Knowledge (D.O.K.)	COMMON CORE Mathematical Practices
15	2 Skills/Concepts H.O.T.	MP.4 Modeling

Write a function that models the given situation. Determine a domain from the situation, graph the function using that domain, and identify the range.

11. A bicyclist travels at a constant speed of 12 miles per hour for a total of 45 minutes. (Use set notation for the domain and range of the function that models this situation.)

The bicyclist's speed is 12 mi/h. The distance traveled d (in miles) at any time t (in hours) is modeled by $d(t) = 12t$. Since the bicyclist travels for 45 minutes, or 0.75 hour, the domain is restricted to the interval $\{t \mid 0 \leq t \leq 0.75\}$.

The range is $\{d \mid 0 \leq d \leq 9\}$.

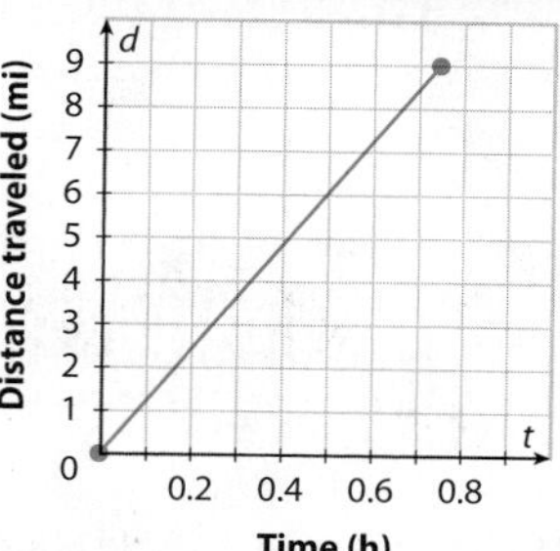

12. An elevator in a tall building starts at a floor of the building that is 90 meters above the ground. The elevator descends 2 meters every 0.5 second for 6 seconds. (Use an inequality for the domain and range of the function that models this situation.)

The elevator's rate of motion is −4 m/s. The elevator's height h (in meters) at any time t (in seconds) is modeled by $h(t) = 90 - 4t$. Since the elevator descends for 6 seconds, the domain is restricted to the interval $0 \leq t \leq 6$.

The range is $66 \leq h \leq 90$.

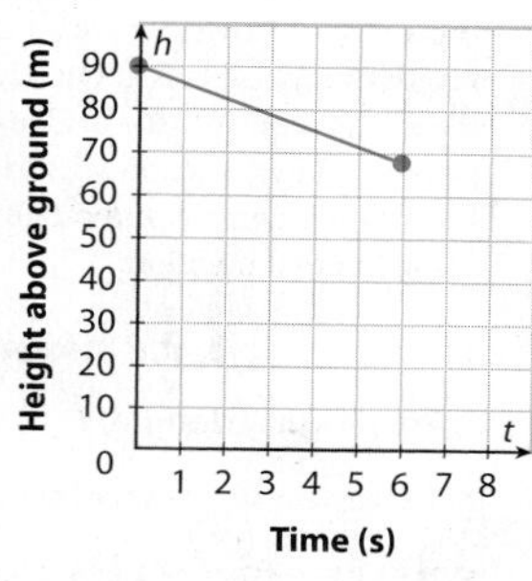

H.O.T. Focus on Higher Order Thinking

13. Explain the Error Cameron sells tickets at a movie theater. On Friday night, she worked from 4 p.m. to 10 p.m. and sold about 25 tickets every hour. Cameron says that the number of tickets, n, she has sold at any time t (in hours) can be modeled by the function $n(t) = 25t$, where the domain is $0 \leq t \leq 1$ and the range is $0 \leq n \leq 25$. Is Cameron's function, along with the domain and range, correct? Explain.

Cameron's function is correct, but the domain and range are incorrect. Cameron worked for a total of 6 hours, so the domain of the function should be $0 \leq t \leq 6$. After 6 hours, Cameron has sold $25 \times 6 = 150$ tickets. So, the range of the function should be $0 \leq n \leq 150$.

QUESTIONING STRATEGIES

When is the graph of a linear function with a restricted domain a line segment? When is it a ray? **It is a line segment when the domain is a closed interval. It is a ray when the domain is restricted to real numbers greater than or equal to a number, or less than or equal to a number.**

AVOID COMMON ERRORS

When attempting to model a real-world situation, students sometimes confuse the dependent and independent variables, thus reversing the domain and range. Help them to understand that the domain consists of the values represented by the independent variable, and that the range values are a function of the values of the domain.

PEER-TO-PEER DISCUSSION

Is it possible that a linear function with the domain {all real numbers} could have a range that is *not* {all real numbers}? Explain. Yes; the function could be a constant function, such as $f(x) = 2$. The domain is {all real numbers}, but the range is {2}.

You may want to have students work on the modeling questions in pairs, thus providing them with an opportunity to discuss each situation with a partner, and decide how to best model the situation using a function.

JOURNAL

Have students describe how to identify the domain and range of a function given its graph, or given the situation it models.

14. Multi-Step The graph of the cubic function $f(x) = x^3$ is shown.

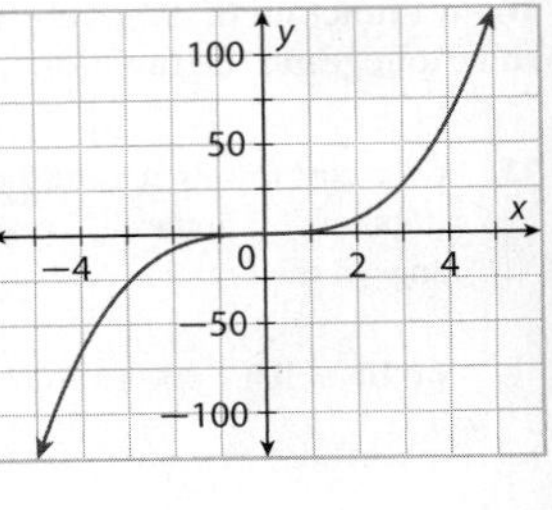

a. What are the domain, range, and end behavior of the function? (Write the domain and range as an inequality, using set notation, and using interval notation.)

b. How is the range of the function affected if the domain is restricted to [−4, 4]? (Write the range as an inequality, using set notation, and using interval notation.)

c. Graph the function with the restricted domain.

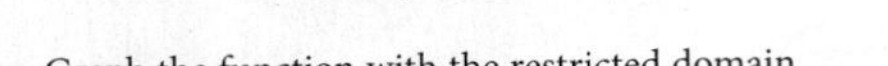

a. Domain: $-\infty < x < +\infty$, $\{x \mid -\infty < x < +\infty\}$, $(-\infty, +\infty)$

Range: $-\infty < x < +\infty$, $\{x \mid -\infty < x < +\infty\}$, $(-\infty, +\infty)$

End behavior: As $x \to +\infty$, $f(x) \to +\infty$; As $x \to -\infty$, $f(x) \to -\infty$.

b. Restricted range: $-64 \leq y \leq 64$, $\{y \mid -64 \leq y \leq +64\}$, $[-64, 64]$

c.

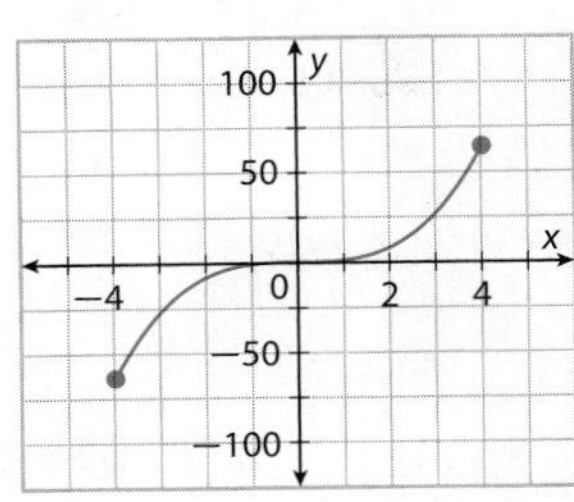

15. Represent Real-World Situations The John James Audubon Bridge is a cable-stayed bridge in Louisiana that opened in 2011. The height from the bridge deck to the top of the tower where a particular cable is anchored is about 500 feet, and the length of that cable is about 1200 feet. Draw the cable on a coordinate plane, letting the x-axis represent the bridge deck and the y-axis represent the tower. (Only use positive values of x and y.) Write a linear function whose graph models the cable. Identify the domain and range, writing each as an inequality, using set notation, and using interval notation.

Since the cable, the bridge deck, and the tower form a right triangle, find the length of the leg that lies on the x-axis by using the Length of bridge deck: Pythagorean Theorem.

$$a^2 + b^2 = c^2$$

$$500^2 + b^2 = 1200^2$$

$$b \approx 1091$$

slope: $m = \dfrac{500 - 0}{0 - 1091} = \dfrac{500}{-1091} \approx -0.46$

The y-intercept is 500.

So, the linear function is $y = -0.46x + 500$.

Domain:, $0 \leq x \leq 1091$, $\{x \mid 0 \leq x \leq 1091\}$, $[0, 1091]$

Range: $0 \leq y \leq 500$, $\{y \mid 0 \leq y \leq 500\}$, $[0, 500]$

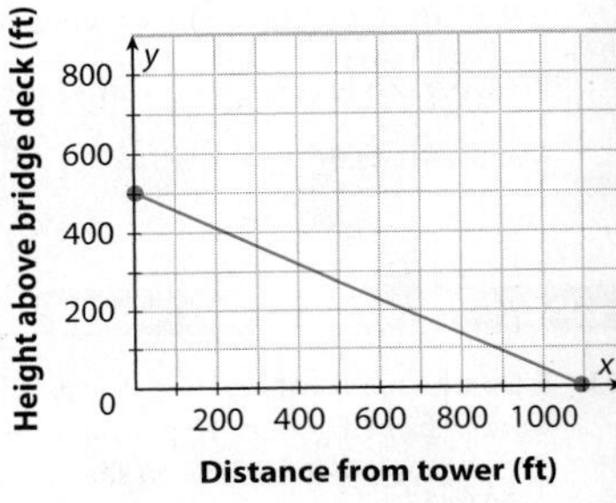

Lesson Performance Task

The fuel efficiency for a 2007 passenger car was 31.2 mi/gal. For the same model of car, the fuel efficiency increased to 35.6 mi/gal in 2012. The gas tank for this car holds 16 gallons of gas.

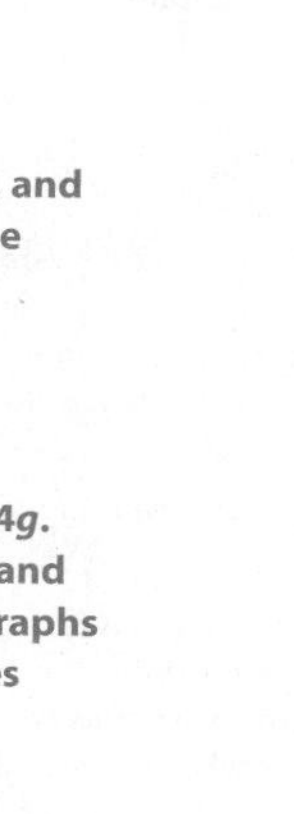

a. Write and graph a linear function that models the distance that each car can travel for a given amount of gas (up to one tankful).

b. Write the domain and range of each function using interval notation.

c. Write and simplify a function $f(g)$ that represents the *difference* in the distance that the 2012 car can travel and the distance that the 2007 car can travel on the same amount of gas. Interpret this function using the graphs of the functions from part a. Also find and interpret $f(16)$.

d. Write the domain and range of the difference function using set notation.

a. For both cars, let g be the amount of gas (in gallons) that each car uses, and let d be the distance (in miles) that each car travels. For the 2007 car, the linear model is $d_{2007}(g) = 31.2g$. For the 2012 car, the linear model is $d_{2012}(g) = 35.6g$.

b. The domain for the 2007 model is [0, 16], and the range is [0, 499.2]. The domain for the 2012 model is [0, 16], and the range is [0, 569.6].

c. The difference function is $f(g) = d_{2012}(g) - d_{2007}(g) = 35.6g - 31.2g = 4.4g$. This function gives the vertical distance between the graphs of $d_{2012}(g)$ and $d_{2007}(g)$. For instance, when $g = 16$, the vertical distance between the graphs is $f(16) = 4.4 \cdot 16 = 70.4$, which means the 2012 car can travel 70.4 miles farther on a tankful of gas than the 2007 car.

d. The domain is $\{g \mid 0 \leq g \leq 16\}$, and the range is $\{f(g) \mid 0 \leq f(g) \leq 70.4\}$.

EXTENSION ACTIVITY

Have students research the average fuel costs per gallon in 2007 and in 2012. Have students use the data to create a new graph representing the distance each car could travel for a given amount of money (up to the cost of a typical full tank). Ask students to describe the aspects of their graphs.

QUESTIONING STRATEGIES

? Why must restrictions be placed on the domain? **The tank only holds at most 16 gallons of gas and at least 0 gallons of gas. A graph with a negative number of gallons of gas or more than 16 gallons of gas would not make sense for this situation.**

? Why does the domain contain all of the points in the interval and not just the integer values? **The amount of gas used is continuous. There is a distance traveled for any value of g in the domain.**

INTEGRATE MATHEMATICAL PRACTICES

Focus on Communication

MP.3 Encourage students to relate the ranges that they wrote for the difference functions to their graphs. Have them determine whether the values in the range make sense in the real-world situation. Then have students explain whether it makes sense that as the number of gallons used increases, the difference in miles traveled by the two cars also increases.

Scoring Rubric

2 points: Student correctly solves the problem and explains his/her reasoning.

1 point: Student shows good understanding of the problem but does not fully solve or explain his/her reasoning.

0 points: Student does not demonstrate understanding of the problem.

LESSON 1.2

Characteristics of Function Graphs

Common Core Math Standards

The student is expected to:

F-IF.B.4

For a function that models a relationship between two quantities, interpret key features ... and sketch graphs showing key features.... Also A-CED.A.2, F-IF.B.6, S-ID.B.6

Mathematical Practices

MP.7 Using Structure

Language Objective

Explain to a partner where the local maximum and minimum values are on a graph of a function, and where the zero of a function is located on its graph.

ENGAGE

Essential Question: What are some of the attributes of a function, and how are they related to the function's graph?

Possible answer: A function may have positive or negative values, indicating whether the graph lies above or below the *x*-axis. It may increase or decrease on an interval, indicating where the graph rises or falls. It may have local maximum or minimum values, which are the *y* coordinates of the graph's turning points. It may have zeros, which are the *x* coordinates of the points where the graph crosses the *x*-axis.

PREVIEW: LESSON PERFORMANCE TASK

View the online Engage. Have students compare the historical variation in the area/extent of Arctic sea ice with current variation. Then preview the Lesson Performance Task.

Name ______________________ Class ______________ Date ________

1.2 Characteristics of Function Graphs

Resource Locker

Essential Question: What are some of the attributes of a function, and how are they related to the function's graph?

Explore Identifying Attributes of a Function from Its Graph

You can identify several attributes of a function by analyzing its graph. For instance, for the graph shown, you can see that the function's domain is $\{x|0 \le x \le 11\}$ and its range is $\{y| -1 \le y \le 1\}$. Use the graph to explore the function's other attributes.

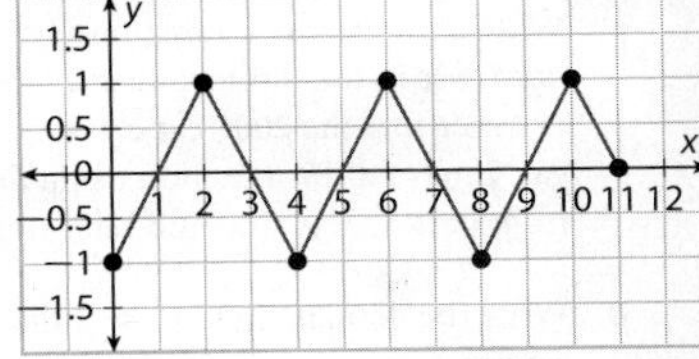

(A) The values of the function on the interval $\{x|1 < x < 3\}$ are positive/negative. (positive circled)

(B) The values of the function on the interval $\{x|8 < x < 9\}$ are positive/negative. (negative circled)

A function is **increasing** on an interval if $f(x_1) < f(x_2)$ when $x_1 < x_2$ for any *x*-values x_1 and x_2 from the interval. The graph of a function that is increasing on an interval rises from left to right on that interval. Similarly, a function is **decreasing** on an interval if $f(x_1) > f(x_2)$ when $x_1 < x_2$ for any *x*-values x_1 and x_2 from the interval. The graph of a function that is decreasing on an interval falls from left to right on that interval.

(C) The given function is increasing/decreasing on the interval $\{x|2 < x < 4\}$. (decreasing circled)

(D) The given function is increasing/decreasing on the interval $\{x|4 < x < 6\}$. (increasing circled)

For the two points $(x_1, f(x_1))$ and $(x_2, f(x_2))$ on the graph of a function, the **average rate of change** of a function is the ratio of the change in the function values, $f(x_2) - f(x_1)$, to the change in the *x*-values, $x_2 - x_1$. For a linear function, the rate of change is constant and represents the slope of the function's graph.

(E) What is the given function's average rate of change on the interval $\{x|0 \le x \le 2\}$?

$$\frac{f(2) - f(1)}{2 - 1} = \frac{1 - 0}{2 - 1} = \frac{1}{1} = 1$$

A function may change from increasing to decreasing or from decreasing to increasing at *turning points.* The value of $f(x)$ at a point where a function changes from increasing to decreasing is a **maximum value**. A maximum value occurs at a point that appears higher than all nearby points on the graph of the function. Similarly, the value of $f(x)$ at a point where a function changes from decreasing to increasing is a **minimum value**. A minimum value occurs at a point that appears lower than all nearby points on the graph of the function.

(F) At how many points does the given function change from increasing to decreasing? 3

HARDCOVER PAGES 17–30

Watch for the hardcover student edition page numbers for this lesson.

Ⓖ What is the function's maximum value at these points? 1

Ⓗ At how many points does the given function change from decreasing to increasing? 2

Ⓘ What is the function's minimum value at these points? −1

A **zero** of a function is a value of x for which $f(x) = 0$. On a graph of the function, the zeros are the x-intercepts.

Ⓙ How many x-intercepts does the given function's graph have? 6

Ⓚ Identify the zeros of the function. **1, 3, 5, 7, 9, 11**

Reflect

1. **Discussion** Identify three different intervals that have the same average rate of change, and state what the rate of change is.
Possible answers: The intervals $\{x|0 \leq x \leq 2\}$, $\{x|4 \leq x \leq 6\}$, and $\{x|8 \leq x \leq 10\}$ all have a rate of change of 1. The intervals $\{x|2 \leq x \leq 4\}$, $\{x|6 \leq x \leq 8\}$, and $\{x|10 \leq x \leq 11\}$ all have a rate of change of −1.

2. **Discussion** If a function is increasing on an interval $\{x|a \leq x \leq b\}$, what can you say about its average rate of change on the interval? Explain.
The average rate of change is positive, because the change in function values, $f(b) - f(a)$, must be positive. Since the change in x-values, $b - a$, is also positive, the ratio of $f(b) - f(a)$ to $b - a$ is positive.

Explain 1 Sketching a Function's Graph from a Verbal Description

By understanding the attributes of a function, you can sketch a graph from a verbal description.

Example 1 **Sketch a graph of the following verbal descriptions.**

Ⓐ Lyme disease is a bacterial infection transmitted to humans by ticks. When an infected tick bites a human, the probability of transmission is a function of the time since the tick attached itself to the skin. During the first 24 hours, the probability is 0%. During the next three 24-hour periods, the rate of change in the probability is always positive, but it is much greater for the middle period than the other two periods. After 96 hours, the probability is almost 100%. Sketch a graph of the function for the probability of transmission.

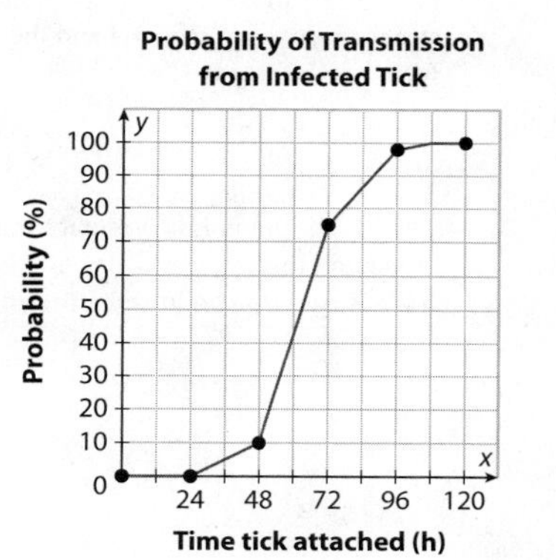

Identify the axes and scales.

The x-axis will be time (in hours) and will run from 0 to at least 96. The y-axis will be the probability of infection (as a percent) from 0 to 100.

PROFESSIONAL DEVELOPMENT

Integrate Mathematical Practices

This lesson provides an opportunity to address Mathematical Practice **MP.7**, which calls for students to find different ways of seeing situations by looking for patterns and making "use of structures." Students learn how the attributes of functions are represented graphically. They also learn how the graph of a set of data can be used to generate a function that approximates the data and can be used to make predictions about additional data points. Through these processes, students learn to make connections between functions and the situations they represent.

EXPLORE

Identifying Attributes of a Function from its Graph

INTEGRATE TECHNOLOGY

Students have the option of completing the Explore activity either in the book or online.

QUESTIONING STRATEGIES

What types of functions have no maximum or minimum values? **linear functions of the form $f(x) = mx + b$**

What types of functions have either a maximum value or a minimum value, but not both? **functions whose graphs are U-shaped (or ∩-shaped), such as quadratic functions**

EXPLAIN 1

Sketching a Function's Graph from a Verbal Description

QUESTIONING STRATEGIES

How does a graph depict an increase or decrease in the rate of change of a function? **If the rate of change increases, the graph becomes steeper. If it decreases, the graph becomes less steep.**

AVOID COMMON ERRORS

When sketching a graph from a verbal description, students may erroneously use the information provided about the rate of change to label the vertical axis of the graph. Help them to see that the rate of change is neither a value of x nor a value of $f(x)$, but is instead the ratio of the change in $f(x)$ values to the change in x-values over a given interval, which is reflected in the slope of the graph over that interval.

INTEGRATE MATHEMATICAL PRACTICES

Focus on Math Connections

MP.1 Help students to see the relationship between rate of change and slope of a line. Lead them to recognize that for linear functions, the rate of change and slope are identical, and that for non-linear functions, the rate of change is the slope of the line that approximates the given curve over a certain interval.

Identify key intervals.

The intervals are in increments of 24 hours: 0 to 24, 24 to 48, 48 to 96, and 96 to 120.

Sketch the graph of the function.

Draw a horizontal segment at $y = 0$ for the first 24-hour interval. The function increases over the next three 24-hour intervals with the middle one having the greatest increase (the steepest slope). After 96 hours, the graph is nearly horizontal at 100%.

(B) The incidence of a disease is the rate at which a disease occurs in a population. It is calculated by dividing the number of new cases of a disease in a given time period (typically a year) by the size of the population. **To avoid small decimal numbers, the rate is often expressed in terms of a large number of people rather than a single person.** For instance, the incidence of measles in the United States in 1974 was about 10 cases per 100,000 people.

From 1974 to 1980, there were drastic fluctuations in the incidence of measles in the United States. In 1975, there was a slight increase in incidence from 1974. The next two years saw a substantial increase in the incidence, which reached a maximum in 1977 of about 26 cases per 100,000 people. From 1977 to 1979, the incidence fell to about 5 cases per 100,000 people. The incidence fell much faster from 1977 to 1978 than from 1978 to 1979. Finally, from 1979 to 1980, the incidence stayed about the same. **Sketch a graph the function for the incidence of measles.**

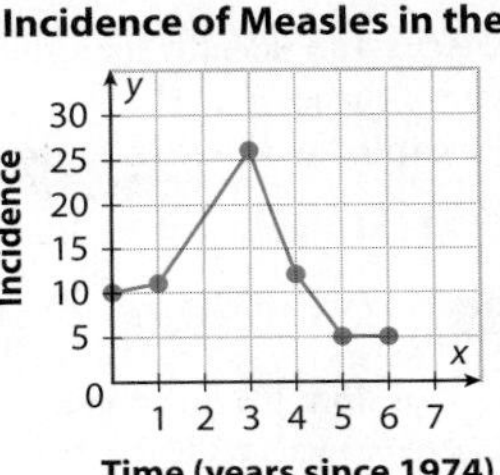

Identify the axes and scales.

The x-axis will represent time given by years and will run from 0 to ___6___. The y-axis will represent ___incidence of measles___, measured in cases per 100,000 people, and will run from 0 to 30.

Identify key intervals.

The intervals are one-year increments from ___0___ to ___6___.

Sketch the graph the function.

The first point on the graph is ___(0, 10)___. The graph slightly (rises)/falls from $x = 0$ to $x = 1$.

From $x = 1$ to $x = 3$, the graph (rises)/falls to a maximum y-value of ___26___. The graph rises/(falls) steeply from $x = 3$ to $x = 4$ and then rises/(falls) less steeply from $x = 4$ to $x = 5$. The graph is horizontal from $x = 5$ to $x = 6$.

Reflect

3. In Part B, the graph is horizontal from 1979 to 1980. What can you say about the rate of change for the function on this interval?

There is no change in the function's values, so the rate of change is 0.

COLLABORATIVE LEARNING

Peer-to-Peer Activity

Have students work in pairs. Instruct each student to graph a function similar to that shown in Example 1, keeping the graph hidden from the partner. Have students describe the graph's attributes to partners, and have the partners attempt to graph the function from the verbal description. Students should then compare graphs, and use the results to refine their descriptions (if necessary) to more accurately reflect the attributes of the functions.

Your Turn

4. A grocery store stocks shelves with 100 cartons of strawberries before the store opens. For the first 3 hours the store is open, the store sells 20 cartons per hour. Over the next 2 hours, no cartons of strawberries are sold. The store then restocks 10 cartons each hour for the next 2 hours. In the final hour that the store is open, 30 cartons are sold. Sketch a graph of the function.

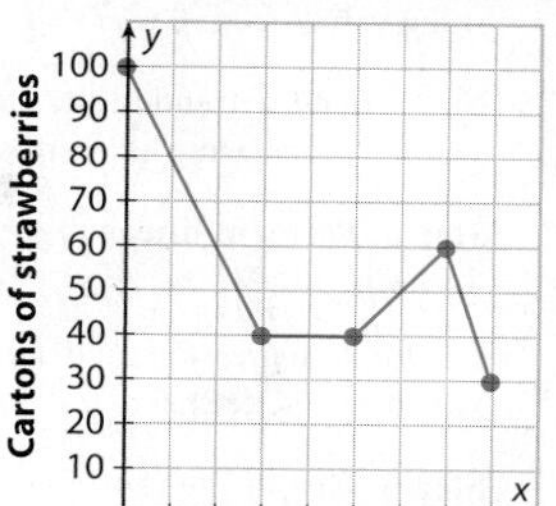

Explain 2 Modeling with a Linear Function

When given a set of paired data, you can use a scatter plot to see whether the data show a linear trend. If so, you can use a graphing calculator to perform linear regression and obtain a linear function that models the data. You should treat the least and greatest x-values of the data as the domain of the linear model.

When you perform linear regression, a graphing calculator will report the value of the *correlation coefficient* r. This variable can have a value from -1 to 1. It measures the direction and strength of the relationship between the variables x and y. If the value of r is negative, the y-values tend to decrease as the x-values increase. If the value of r is positive, the y-values tend to increase as the x-values increase. The more linear the relationship between x and y is, the closer that the value of r is to -1 or 1 (or the closer that the value of r^2 is to 1).

You can use the linear model to make predictions and decisions based on the data. Making a prediction within the domain of the linear model is called *interpolation*. Making a prediction outside the domain is called *extrapolation*.

Example 2 **Perform a linear regression for the given situation and make predictions.**

(A) A photographer hiked through the Grand Canyon. Each day she stored photos on a memory card for her digital camera. When she returned from the trip, she deleted some photos from each memory card, saving only the best. The table shows the number of photos she kept from all those stored on each memory card. Use a graphing calculator to create a scatter plot of the data, find a linear regression model, and graph the model. Then use the model to predict the number of photos the photographer will keep if she takes 150 photos.

Grand Canyon Photos

Photos Taken	Photos Kept
117	25
128	31
140	39
157	52
110	21
188	45
170	42

DIFFERENTIATE INSTRUCTION

Technology

Encourage students to try performing regression analysis using an online calculator. Finding online linear calculators is not difficult; a quick browser search will turn up several. Make sure that students adhere to the format in which ordered pairs are entered. Most online regression calculators require that data for points (a, b), (c, d), (e, f), (g, h) be entered as follows:

$a\ c\ e\ g$

$b\ d\ f\ h$

Programs typically plot the data points, show the line of best fit, and provide an equation for the line.

EXPLAIN 2

Modeling with a Linear Function

AVOID COMMON ERRORS

Students may think that they've made an error if their regression lines do not pass through many of the points on their graphs. Tell them that this does not indicate an error, and encourage them to think about the line of regression as a line about which the data clusters, not necessarily a line that connects the points.

CONNECT VOCABULARY EL

Relate the prefixes *inter* and *extra* in *interpolation* and *extrapolation* to their meanings in this context and in general English usage.

QUESTIONING STRATEGIES

When using interpolation to make a prediction from a linear regression model, the function may produce a value for a particular value of the domain that differs from the actual value given in the data set. How can this be justified? **The value produced by the model is a more likely value than the value in the actual data point, but other values are possible, as indicated by the points in the scatterplot.**

INTEGRATE TECHNOLOGY

Students can also use the table function on the graphing calculator to find additional values of the linear regression model.

Step 1: Create a scatter plot of the data.

Let x represent the number of photos taken, and let y represent the number of photos kept. Use a viewing window that shows x-values from 100 to 200 and y-values from 0 to 60.

Notice that the trend in the data appears to be roughly linear, with y-values generally increasing as x-values increase.

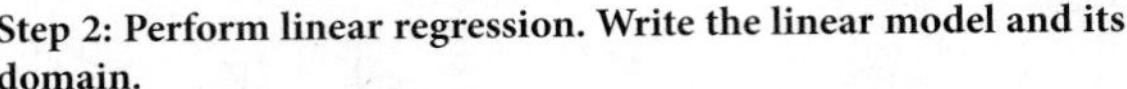

Step 2: Perform linear regression. Write the linear model and its domain.

```
LinReg
 y=ax+b
 a=.33097043
 b=-11.32573346
 r²=.7194927306
 r=.8482291734
```

The linear regression model is $y = 0.33x - 11.33$. Its domain is $\{x | 110 \leq x \leq 188\}$.

Step 3: Graph the model along with the data to obtain a visual check on the goodness of fit.

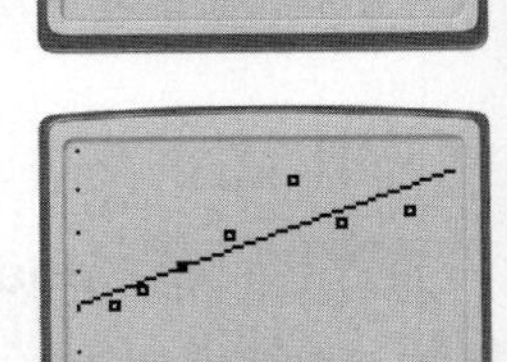

Notice that one of the data points is much farther from the line than the other data points are. The value of the correlation coefficient r would be closer to 1 without this data point.

Step 4: Predict the number of photos this photographer will keep if she takes 150 photos.

Evaluate the linear function when $x = 150$: $y = 0.33(150) - 11.33 \approx 38$. So, she will keep about 38 photos if she takes 150 photos.

(B) As a science project, Shelley is studying the relationship of car mileage (in miles per gallon) and speed (in miles per hour). The table shows the data Shelley gathered using her family's vehicle. Use a graphing calculator to create a scatter plot of the data, find a linear regression model, and graph the model. Then use the model to predict the gas mileage of the car at a speed of 20 miles per hour.

Speed (mi/h)	30	40	50	60	70
Mileage (mi/gal)	34.0	33.5	31.5	29.0	27.5

Step 1: Create a scatter plot of the data.

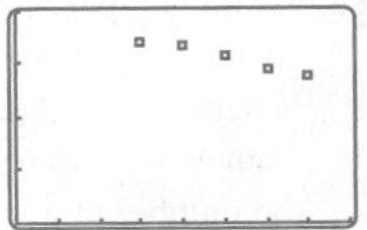

What do x and y represent?

Let x represent the car's speed, and let y represent the car's gas mileage.

What viewing window will you use?

Sample answer: Use a window that shows x-values from 0 to 80 and y-values from 0 to 40.

What trend do you observe?

Sample answer: The trend in the data appears to be quite linear, with y-values generally decreasing as x-values increase.

LANGUAGE SUPPORT EL

Connect Vocabulary

Have students work in pairs. Provide each pair with two or three graphs of a function. Have one student ask, "Where is the *local maximum value* of this function?" The other student should indicate the point on the graph where the function changes from increasing to decreasing. The first student asks, "How do you know?" The second student should explain why that point is the local maximum value. If both agree, they should label that point. They switch places, the second student asks about the local minimum value, and they repeat the procedure. By the end, each graph should be labeled with the local minimum and maximum values, and the zero of the function.

Step 2: Perform linear regression. Write the linear model and its domain.

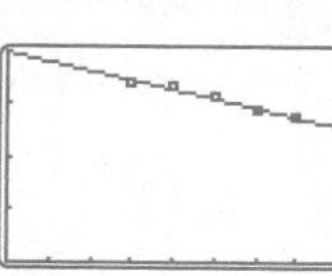

The linear regression model is $y = -0.175x + 39.85$. Its domain is $\{x|30 \le x \le 70\}$.

Step 3: Graph the model along with the data to obtain a visual check on the goodness of fit.

What can you say about the goodness of fit?

Sample answer: As expected from the fact that the value of *r* from Step 2 is very close to -1, the line passes through or comes close to passing through all the data points.

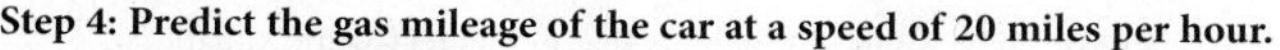

Step 4: Predict the gas mileage of the car at a speed of 20 miles per hour.

Evaluate the linear function when $x = 20$:

$y = -0.175(20) + 39.85 \approx 36.4$. So, the car's gas mileage should be about 36.4 mi/gal at a speed of 20 mi/h.

Reflect

5. Identify whether each prediction in Parts A and B is an interpolation or an extrapolation.
In Part A, the prediction is an interpolation. In Part B, the prediction is an extrapolation.

Your Turn

6. Vern created a website for his school's sports teams. He has a hit counter on his site that lets him know how many people have visited the site. The table shows the number of hits the site received each day for the first two weeks. Use a graphing calculator to find the linear regression model. Then predict how many hits there will be on day 15.

Day	1	2	3	4	5	6	7	8	9	10	11	12	13	14
Hits	5	10	21	24	28	36	33	21	27	40	46	50	31	38

The linear regression model is $y = 2.4x + 11$ where *x* represents the day and *y* represents the number of hits. The model predicts that on day 15 there will be $y = 2.4(15) + 11 = 47$ hits.

ELABORATE

INTEGRATE MATHEMATICAL PRACTICES

Focus on Critical Thinking

MP.3 Discuss with students the fact that not all data is suitable for representation by a linear regression model. Ask them to tell how they might go about determining the best type of regression model to use for a particular set of data.

QUESTIONING STRATEGIES

? When are values found through extrapolation most accurate? **when the values of *x* are close in value to the values of the given domain**

SUMMARIZE THE LESSON

? What are some of the attributes of a function that you can determine from its graph? **You can tell whether the function has a maximum value, a minimum value, and local maximum and minimum values. You can tell over which intervals the function increases or decreases. You can find the zeros of the function, and also determine the average rate of change.**

Elaborate

7. How are the attributes of increasing and decreasing related to average rate of change? How are the attributes of maximum and minimum values related to the attributes of increasing and decreasing?

If a function is increasing on an interval, then the average rate of change will be positive.

If a function is decreasing on an interval, then the average rate of change will be negative.

A maximum value occurs when the function changes from increasing to decreasing.

A minimum value occurs when the function changes from decreasing to increasing.

8. How can line segments be used to sketch graphs of functions that model real-world situations?

Line segments can be used to connect known data points. Connecting the points will provide a rough sketch of the function represented.

9. When making predictions based on a linear model, would you expect interpolated or extrapolated values to be more accurate? Justify your answer.

Interpolated values would be more accurate because they are within the domain of the model. Extrapolated values assume that the model still applies outside its domain, but that assumption may be incorrect.

10. Essential Question Check-In What are some of the attributes of a function?

A function may be positive or negative on specific intervals. It also may be increasing or decreasing on specific intervals. A function may have maximum or minimum values as well as zeros.

Evaluate: Homework and Practice

- Online Homework
- Hints and Help
- Extra Practice

The graph shows a function that models the value V (in millions of dollars of a stock portfolio as a function of time t (in months) over an 18-month period.

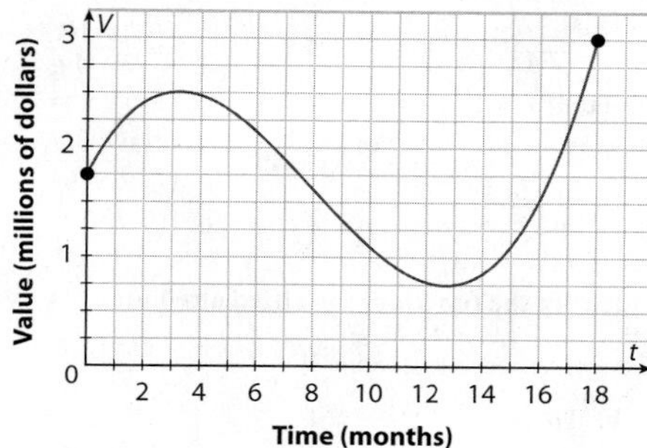

1. On what intervals is the function increasing? $\{t|3 \le t \le 13\}$

   On what intervals is the function decreasing? $\{t|0 \le t \le 13\}$ and $\{t|13 \le t \le 18\}$

2. Identify any maximum values and minimum values.
   A maximum value of 2.5 occurs at $x = 3$. A minimum value of 0.75 occurs at $x = 13$.

3. What are the function's domain and range?
   Domain: $\{t|0 \le t \le 18\}$; Range: The least $V(t)$-value is 0.75 (at $t = 3$) and the greatest $V(t)$-value is 3 (at $t = 18$), so the range is $\{V(t)|0.75 \le V(t) \le 3\}$.

The table of values gives the probability $P(n)$ for getting all 5's when rolling a number cube n times.

n	1	2	3	4	5
$P(n)$	$\frac{1}{6}$	$\frac{1}{36}$	$\frac{1}{216}$	$\frac{1}{1296}$	$\frac{1}{7776}$

4. Is $P(n)$ increasing or decreasing? Explain the significance of this.
   As the number of rolls increases, $P(n)$ is always decreasing. This implies that the more times a number cube is rolled, the less likely it is that every roll is a 5.

5. What is the end behavior of $P(n)$? Explain the significance of this.
   As n increases without bound, $P(n)$ approaches 0.

Exercise	Depth of Knowledge (D.O.K.)	COMMON CORE Mathematical Practices
1–5	1 Recall of Information	MP.4 Modeling
6	1 Recall of Information	MP.6 Precision
7–10	1 Recall of Information	MP.2 Reasoning
11–14	2 Skills/Concepts	MP.5 Using Tools
15–16	2 Skills/Concepts	MP.4 Modeling
17–18	2 Skills/Concepts H.O.T.	MP.5 Using Tools
19	3 Strategic Thinking H.O.T.	MP.4 Modeling
20	3 Strategic Thinking H.O.T.	MP.6 Precision

EVALUATE

ASSIGNMENT GUIDE

Concepts and Skills	Practice
Explore Identifying Attributes of a Function from its Graph	Exercise 1–10
Example 1 Sketching a Function's Graph from a Verbal Description	Exercises 11–13
Example 2 Modeling with a Linear Function	Exercises 14–18

INTEGRATE MATHEMATICAL PRACTICES

Focus on Math Connections

MP.1 Students should recognize that it is the nature of the algebraic expression used to define a function that determines the nature, and thus the attributes, of the related graph. Have students use their graphing calculators to explore how different types of functions produce graphs with differing attributes.

AVOID COMMON ERRORS

Some students may, in error, interpret the phrase *increasing rate of change* as meaning a positive rate of change, thus drawing a line (or line segment) with a positive slope. Help them to see that if the rate of change is increasing, the *slope* is increasing, (that is, not simply the values of $f(x)$), and the resulting graph is a curve.

CONNECT VOCABULARY EL

Have students "match" the graphs of different functions to descriptions of the highlighted vocabulary for this lesson, such as "This function is increasing/decreasing on an interval" or "The local minimum/maximum value of this function is at point (3, −2)" or "The average rate of change of this function is ____."

6. The table shows some values of a function. On which intervals is the function's average rate of change positive? Select all that apply.

x	0	1	2	3
f(x)	50	75	40	65

a. From $x = 0$ to $x = 1$

$\frac{f(1) - f(0)}{1 - 0} = \frac{75 - 50}{1 - 0} = 25$

b. From $x = 0$ to $x = 2$

$\frac{f(2) - f(0)}{2 - 0} = \frac{40 - 50}{2 - 0} = -5$

c. From $x = 0$ to $x = 3$

$\frac{f(3) - f(0)}{3 - 0} = \frac{65 - 50}{3 - 0} = 5$

d. From $x = 1$ to $x = 2$

$\frac{f(2) - f(1)}{2 - 1} = \frac{40 - 75}{2 - 1} = -35$

e. From $x = 1$ to $x = 3$

$\frac{f(3) - f(1)}{3 - 1} = \frac{65 - 75}{3 - 1} = -5$

f. From $x = 2$ to $x = 3$

$\frac{f(3) - f(2)}{3 - 2} = \frac{65 - 40}{3 - 2} = 25$

So, choices A, C, and F all have positive average rates of change.

Use the graph of the function $f(x)$ to identify the function's specified attributes.

7. Find the function's average rate of change over each interval.

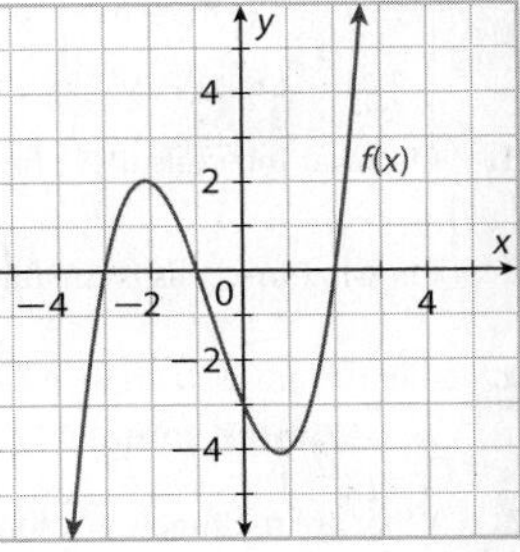

a. From $x = -3$ to $x = -2$

$\frac{f(-2) - f(-3)}{-2 - (-3)} = \frac{2 - 0}{-2 - (-3)} = 2$

b. From $x = -2$ to $x = 1$

$\frac{f(1) - f(-2)}{1 - (-2)} = \frac{-4 - 2}{1 - (-2)} = -2$

c. From $x = 0$ to $x = 1$

$\frac{f(1) - f(0)}{1 - 0} = \frac{-4 - (-3)}{1 - 0} = -1$

d. From $x = 1$ to $x = 2$

$\frac{f(2) - f(1)}{2 - 1} = \frac{0 - (-4)}{2 - 1} = 4$

e. From $x = -1$ to $x = 0$

$\frac{f(0) - f(-1)}{0 - (-1)} = \frac{-3 - 0}{0 - (-1)} = -3$

f. From $x = -1$ to $x = 2$

$\frac{f(2) - f(-1)}{2 - (-1)} = \frac{0 - 0}{2 - (-1)} = 0$

8. On what intervals are the function's values positive? **$\{x \mid -3 < x < -1\}$ and $\{x \mid x > 2\}$.**

9. On what intervals are the function's values negative? **$\{x \mid x < -3\}$ and $\{x \mid -1 < x < 2\}$.**

10. What zeros does the function have? **−3, −1, and 2.**

11. The following describes the United States nuclear stockpile from 1944 to 1974. From 1944 to 1958, there was a gradual increase in the number of warheads from 0 to about 5000. From 1958 to 1966, there was a rapid increase in the number of warheads to a maximum of about 32,000. From 1968 to 1970, there was a decrease in the number of warheads to about 26,000. Finally, from 1970 to 1974, there was a small increase to about 28,000 warheads. Sketch a graph of the function.

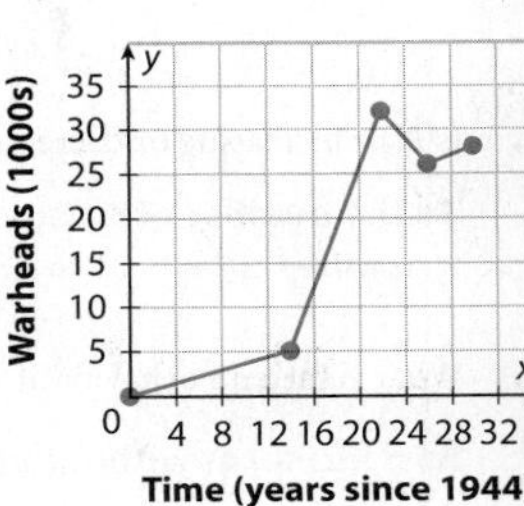

12. The following describes the unemployment rate in the United States from 2003 to 2013. In 2003, the unemployment rate was at 6.3%. The unemployment rate began to fall over the years and reached a minimum of about 4.4% in 2007. A recession that began in 2007 caused the unemployment rate to increase over a two-year period and reach a maximum of about 10% in 2009. The unemployment rate then decreased over the next four years to about 7.0% in 2013. Sketch a graph of the function.

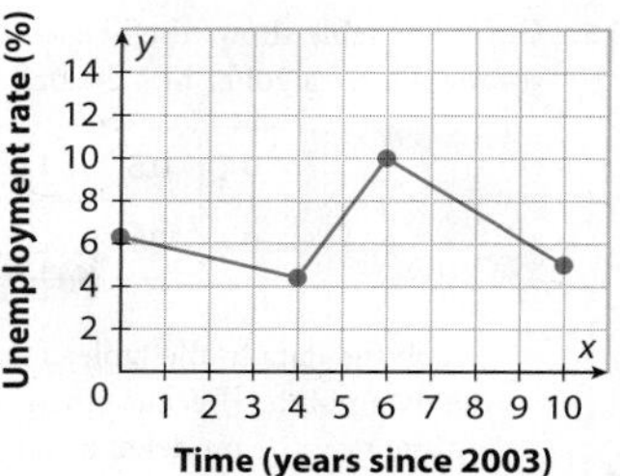

13. The following describes the incidence of mumps in the United States from 1984 to 2004. From 1984 to 1985, there was no change in the incidence of mumps, staying at about 1 case per 100,000 people. Then there was a spike in the incidence of mumps, which reached a peak of about 5.5 cases per 100,000 in 1987. Over the next year, there was a sharp decline in the incidence of mumps, to about 2 cases per 100,000 people in 1988. Then, from 1988 to 1989, there was a small increase to about 2.5 cases per 100,000 people. This was followed by a gradual decline, which reached a minimum of about 0.1 case per 100,000 in 1999. For the next five years, there was no change in the incidence of mumps. Sketch a graph of the function.

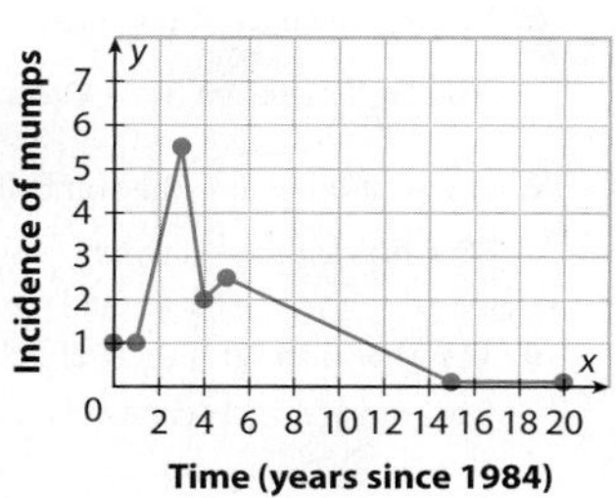

14. **Aviation** The table gives the lengths and wingspans of airplanes in an airline's fleet.

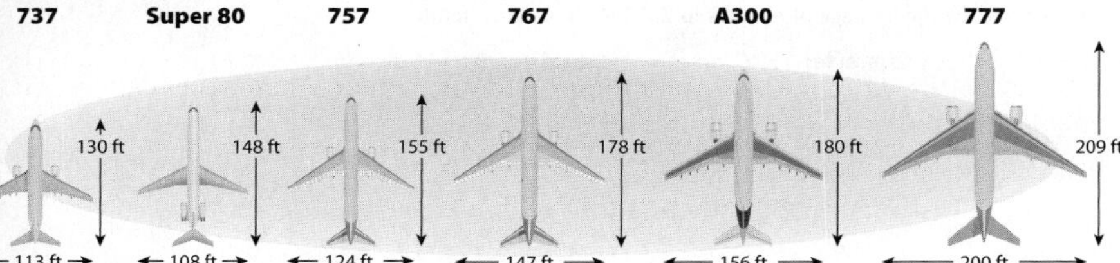

a. Make a scatter plot of the data with x representing length and y representing wingspan.

b. Sketch a line of fit.

c. Use the line of fit to predict the wingspan of an airplane with a length of 220 feet.

a and b.

c. about 200 feet

CURRICULUM INTEGRATION

Students with a particular interest in a topic in science, economics, or social science can be encouraged to find research papers in which data is collected and linear regression analysis is performed. For example, a medical drug trial might show data for the efficacy of a particular medicine and use linear regression to find a relationship between dosage and efficacy, or time and activity.

KINESTHETIC EXPERIENCE

Students may want to test their estimation skills by using a piece of uncooked spaghetti to approximate a line of best fit for a scatterplot of a set of data. They can then use a graphing calculator to find the regression line, and compare it to the estimate.

15. Golf The table shows the height (in feet) of a golf ball at various times (in seconds) after a golfer hits the ball into the air.

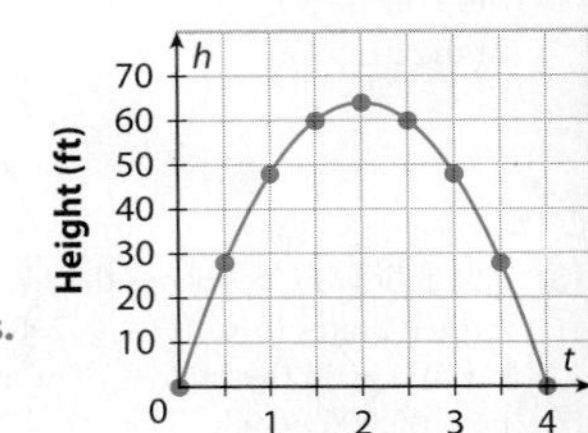

Time (s)	0	0.5	1	1.5	2	2.5	3	3.5	4
Height (ft)	0	28	48	60	64	60	48	28	0

a. Graph the data in the table. Then draw a smooth curve through the data points. (Because the golf ball is a projectile, its height h at time t can be modeled by a quadratic function whose graph is a parabola.)

b. What is the maximum height that the golf ball reaches?

The ball reaches a maximum height of 64 feet in 2 seconds.

c. On what interval is the golf ball's height increasing?

The height is increasing on the interval $\{x | 0 \leq x < 2\}$.

d. On what interval is the golf ball's height decreasing?

The height is decreasing on the interval $\{x | 2 < x \leq 4\}$.

16. The model $a = 0.25t + 29$ represents the median age a of females in the United States as a function of time t (in years since 1970).

a. Predict the median age of females in 1995.

1995 is 25 years after 1970, so $a = 0.25(25) + 29 \approx 35.3$.

b. Predict the median age of females in 2015 to the nearest tenth.

2015 is 45 years after 1970, so $a = 0.25(45) + 29 \approx 40.3$.

H.O.T. Focus on Higher Order Thinking

17. Make a Prediction Anthropologists who study skeletal remains can predict a woman's height just from length of her humerus, the bone between the elbow and the shoulder. The table gives data for humerus length and overall height for various women.

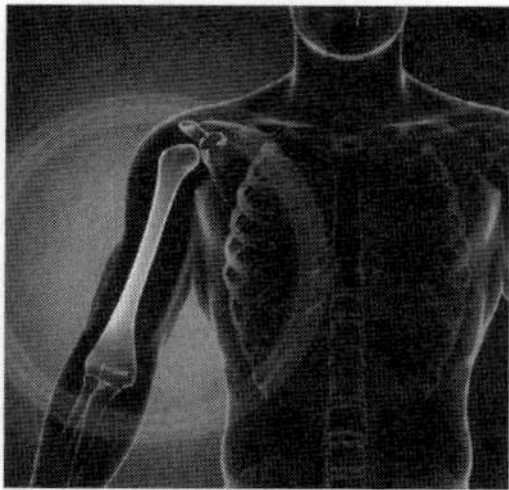

Humerus Length (cm)	35	27	30	33	25	39	27	31
Height (cm)	167	146	154	165	140	180	149	155

Using a graphing calculator, find the linear regression model and state its domain. Then predict a woman's height from a humerus that is 32 cm long, and tell whether the prediction is an interpolation or an extrapolation.

The linear regression model is $h = 2.75\ell + 71.97$ where ℓ is the length of a woman's humerus (in centimeters) and h is her overall height (in centimeters). The shortest length of a humerus given in the table is 27 centimeters, and the longest is 39 centimeters, so the domain of regression model is $\{\ell \mid 27 \le \ell \le 39\}$. When $\ell = 32$, $h = 2.75(32) + 71.97 \approx 160$, so the woman's height would be about 160 centimeters. Because 32 is in the domain of the regression model, the prediction is an interpolation.

18. Make a Prediction Hummingbird wing beat rates are much higher than those in other birds. The table gives data about the mass and the frequency of wing beats for various species of hummingbirds.

Mass (g)	3.1	2.0	3.2	4.0	3.7	1.9	4.5
Frequency of Wing Beats (beats per second)	60	85	50	45	55	90	40

a. Using a graphing calculator, find the linear regression model and state its domain.

The linear regression model is $b = -19.14m + 121.97$ where m is a hummingbird's mass (in grams) and f is the frequency of wing beats (in beats per second). The least mass given in the table is 1.9 grams, and the greatest mass is 4.5 grams, so the domain of the regression model is $\{m \mid 1.9 \le m \le 4.5\}$.

PEER-TO-PEER DISCUSSION

Ask students to discuss the real-world relevance and importance of knowing the attributes of a function that models a given situation. Have them use some of the situations provided in the exercises to illustrate their explanations.

JOURNAL

Have students describe how the attributes of increasing, decreasing, maximum values, and minimum values of a function are related, and how information about these attributes is helpful in drawing the graph of a function.

b. Predict the frequency of wing beats for a Giant Hummingbird with a mass of 19 grams.

When $m = 19$, $f = -19.14(19) + 121.97 \approx -242$, so the frequency of the wing beats is about -242 beats per second.

c. Comment on the reasonableness of the prediction and what, if anything, is wrong with the model.

A negative wing beat frequency makes no physical sense, so the prediction isn't reasonable. There is nothing wrong with the model. The prediction, which is an extrapolation, is based on a value of m that is far outside the domain of the model. The model simply doesn't account for a hummingbird with such an exteme mass.

19. Explain the Error A student calculates a function's average rate of change on an interval and finds that it is 0. The student concludes that the function is constant on the interval. Explain the student's error, and give an example to support your explanation.

The average rate of change on an interval uses only the endpoints of the interval in the calculation. If the endpoints happen to have the same y-coordinate, the average rate of change will be 0, but that doesn't mean the function remains constant throughout the interval. For instance, the average rate of change for $f(x) = x^2$ on the interval $\{x \mid -1 \le x \le 1\}$ is $\frac{f(1) - f(-1)}{1 - (-1)} = \frac{1 - 1}{1 - (-1)} = \frac{0}{1} = 0$, but the function is decreasing from $(-1, 1)$ to $(0, 0)$ and then increasing from $(0, 0)$ to $(1, 1)$, so the function is clearly not constant on the interval.

20. Communicate Mathematical Ideas Describe a way to obtain a linear model for a set of data without using a graphing calculator.

After making a scatter plot of the data, draw a line that appears to pass as close to the data points as possible. (It may pass through some of them, or it may not pass through any of them.) Choose two points on the line to calculate its slope m, and then substitute one of the points and the value of m into $y = mx + b$ to find the value of b, the line's y-intercept. Knowing the values m and b, write the model as $y = mx + b$.

Lesson Performance Task

Since 1980 scientists have used data from satellite sensors to calculate a daily measure of Arctic sea ice extent. Sea ice extent is calculated as the sum of the areas of sea ice covering the ocean where the ice concentration is greater than 15%. The graph here shows seasonal variations in sea ice extent for 2012, 2013, and the average values for the 1980s.

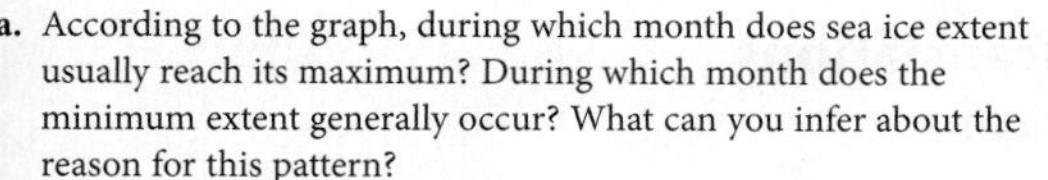

a. According to the graph, during which month does sea ice extent usually reach its maximum? During which month does the minimum extent generally occur? What can you infer about the reason for this pattern?

b. Sea ice extent reached its lowest level to date in 2012. About how much less was the minimum extent in 2012 compared with the average minimum for the 1980s? About what percentage of the 1980s average minimum was the 2012 minimum?

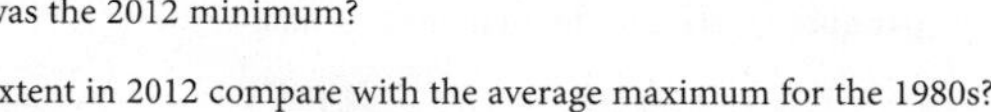

c. How does the maximum extent in 2012 compare with the average maximum for the 1980s? About what percentage of the 1980s average maximum was the 2012 maximum?

d. What do the patterns in the maximum and minimum values suggest about how climate change may be affecting sea ice extent?

e. How do the 2013 maximum and minimum values compare with those for 2012? What possible explanation can you suggest for the differences?

a. The maximum sea ice extent usually occurs in March and the minimum in September. We can infer that sea ice extent increases during the cold winter months, begins to decrease as ice melts in the spring, and reaches its minimum at the end of the summer.

b. The 2012 minimum was about 3.4 million km^2 compared with the 1980s average minimum of about 7.3 million km^2. Thus the 2012 minimum was about 3.9 million km^2 less, or about 47% of the 1980s average. Student answers should be within a reasonable range of these values given the scale of the graph.

c. The 2012 maximum is less than the average 1980s maximum, but the difference is less than with the minimum values. The 2012 maximum is about 92% of the 1980s average maximum.

d. The warmer temperatures associated with global climate change have drastically reduce the extent of sea ice during the summer but have had a much less significant effect on the extent during the winter.

e. The 2013 maximum was about the same as in 2012, but the 2013 minimum was actually about 1 million km^2 greater than in 2012. Students may suggest that while the overall trend is for decreasing minimum values, variations in specific climate conditions from year to year mean that minimum values may fluctuate.

EXTENSION ACTIVITY

Have students research the National Snow and Ice Data Center to learn more about the cryosphere, sea ice in general, the current condition of arctic sea ice, and changes that have occurred over the past year. Note that during 2013, summer weather patterns were very different from previous summers, as it was considerably cooler in 2013 than in prior years. Ask students to use the information they found to discuss any pattern of changes that are reflected in the maximum and minimum extent values.

AVOID COMMON ERRORS

Have students read the labels on the graph to ensure they understand that the values in the scale of the sea ice extent are to be multiplied by 10^6 (million) and that the units are kilometers squared, because the sea ice extent is calculated as an area of ice.

INTEGRATED MATHEMATICAL PRACTICES

Focus on Modeling

MP.4 Note that the graph of the Arctic Sea Ice Extent shows several sets of data that do not follow smooth curves. It may be helpful to begin analysis by placing a straightedge parallel to the x-axis (*Months*). The straightedge can be moved up slowly to determine the minimums and maximums for each set of data. A ruler can also be placed along the line that approximates the given curve of data between March and September for each year to help students compare their rates of change.

Scoring Rubric

2 points: Student correctly solves the problem and explains his/her reasoning.

1 point: Student shows good understanding of the problem but does not fully solve or explain his/her reasoning.

0 points: Student does not demonstrate understanding of the problem.

LESSON 1.3

Transformations of Function Graphs

Common Core Math Standards

The student is expected to:

F-BF.B.3

Identify the effect on the graph of replacing $f(x)$ by $f(x) + k$, $k\,f(x)$, $f(kx)$, and $f(x + k)$ for specific values of k ... find the value of k given the graphs. ... Also A-CED.A.2, F-IF.C.7b

Mathematical Practices

MP.2 Reasoning

Language Objective

Identify graphs of odd and even functions and justify reasoning with a partner.

ENGAGE

Essential Question: What are the ways you can transform the graph of the function $y = f(x)$?

Possible answer: The parameter h in $y = f(x - h)$ produces a horizontal translation of the graph of $y = f(x)$. The parameter k in $y = f(x) + k$ produces a vertical translation of the graph of $y = f(x)$. The parameter a in $y = af(x)$ produces a vertical stretch/compression of the graph of $y = f(x)$ and may also produce a reflection across the x-axis. The parameter b in $y = f\left(\frac{1}{b}x\right)$ produces a horizontal stretch/compression of the graph of $y = f(x)$ and may also produce a reflection across the y-axis.

PREVIEW: LESSON PERFORMANCE TASK

View the online Engage. Discuss the photo and the guidelines someone might need to follow when designing a chair. Then preview the Lesson Performance Task.

Name ______________________ Class ______________ Date ____________

1.3 Transformations of Function Graphs

Essential Question: What are the ways you can transform the graph of the function f(x)?

Resource Locker

Explore 1 Investigating Translations of Function Graphs

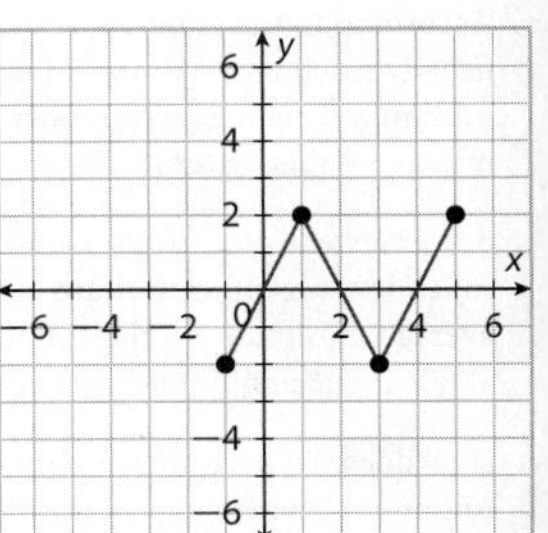

You can transform the graph of a function in various ways. You can translate the graph horizontally or vertically, you can stretch or compress the graph horizontally or vertically, and you can reflect the graph across the x-axis or the y-axis. How the graph of a given function is transformed is determined by the way certain numbers, called **parameters**, are introduced in the function.

(A) First graph $g(x) = f(x) + k$ where k is the parameter. Let $k = 4$ so that $g(x) = f(x) + 4$. Complete the input-output table and then graph $g(x)$. In general, how is the graph of $g(x) = f(x) + k$ related to the graph of $f(x)$ when k is a positive number?

x	f(x)	f(x) + 4
−1	−2	2
1	2	6
3	−2	2
5	2	6

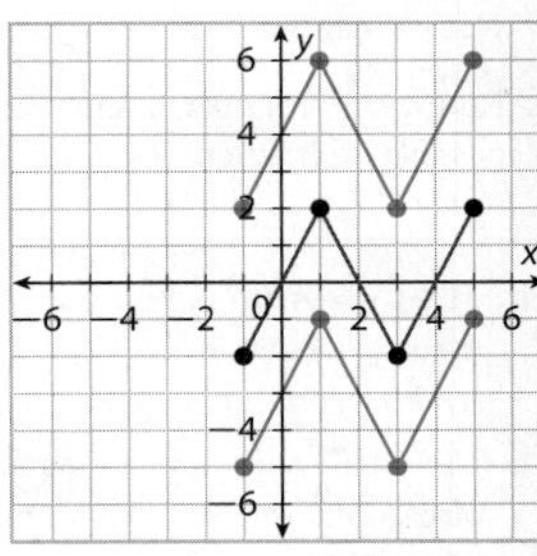

For $k > 0$, the graph of $g(x) = f(x) + k$ is the graph of $f(x)$ translated up k units.

(B) Now try a negative value of k in $g(x) = f(x) + k$. Let $k = -3$ so that $g(x) = f(x) - 3$. Complete the input-output table and then graph $g(x)$ on the same grid. In general, how is the graph of $g(x) = f(x) + k$ related to the graph of $f(x)$ when k is a negative number?

x	f(x)	f(x) − 3
−1	−2	−5
1	2	−1
1	−2	−5
5	2	−1

For $k < 0$, the graph of $g(x) = f(x) + k$ is the graph of $f(x)$ translated down $|k|$ units.

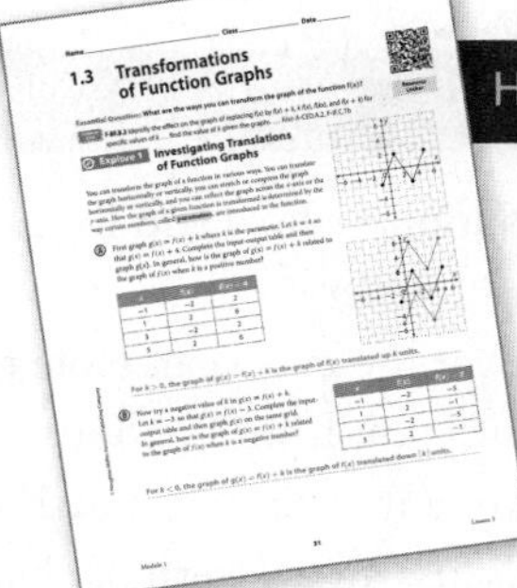

HARDCOVER PAGES 31–46

Watch for the hardcover student edition page numbers for this lesson.

Ⓒ Now graph $g(x) = f(x - h)$ where h is the parameter. Let $h = 2$ so that $g(x) = f(x - 2)$. Complete the mapping diagram and then graph $g(x)$. (To complete the mapping diagram, you need to find the inputs for g that produce the inputs for f after you subtract 2. Work backward from the inputs for f to the inputs for g by adding 2.) In general, how is the graph of $g(x) = f(x - h)$ related to the graph of $f(x)$ when h is a positive number?

Input for *g*	Input for *f*	Output for *f*	Output for *g*
1	−1	−2	−2
3	1	2	2
5	3	−2	−2
7	5	2	2

(Arrows from Input for *g* to Input for *f* labeled − 2.)

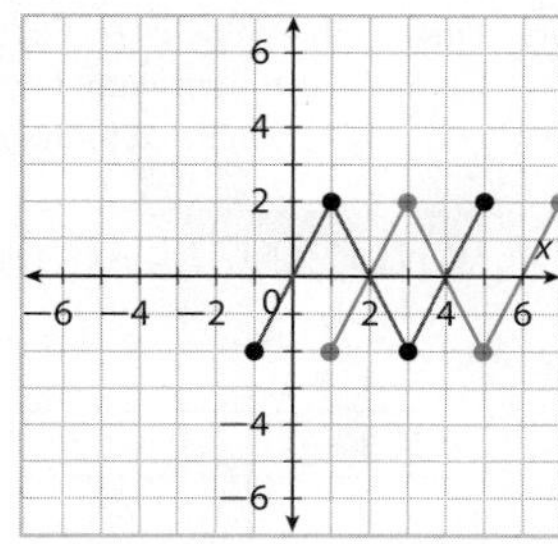

For $h > 0$, the graph of $g(x) = f(x - h)$ is the graph of $f(x)$ translated right h units.

Ⓓ **Make a Conjecture** How would you expect the graph of $g(x) = f(x - h)$ to be related to the graph of $f(x)$ when h is a negative number?

For $h < 0$, the graph of $g(x) = f(x - h)$ is the graph of $f(x)$ translated left $|h|$ units.

Reflect

1. Suppose a function $f(x)$ has a domain of $[x_1, x_2]$ and a range of $[y_1, y_2]$. When the graph of $f(x)$ is translated vertically k units where k is either positive or negative, how do the domain and range change?
The domain remains the same, and the range changes from $[y_1, y_2]$ to $[y_1 + k, y_2 + k]$.

2. Suppose a function $f(x)$ has a domain of $[x_1, x_2]$ and a range of $[y_1, y_2]$. When the graph of $f(x)$ is translated horizontally h units where h is either positive or negative, how do the domain and range change?
The domain changes from $[x_1, x_2]$ to $[x_1 - h, x_2 - h]$, and the range remains the same.

3. You can transform the graph of $f(x)$ to obtain the graph of $g(x) = f(x - h) + k$ by combining transformations. Predict what will happen by completing the table.

Sign of *h*	Sign of *k*	Transformations of the Graph of *f*(*x*)
+	+	Translate right *h* units and up *k* units.
+	−	**Translate right *h* units and down $\|k\|$ units.**
−	+	**Translate left $\|h\|$ units and up *k* units.**
−	−	**Translate left $\|h\|$ units and down $\|k\|$ units.**

PROFESSIONAL DEVELOPMENT

Math Background

Transformations change the graph of a function. When students understand the basic transformations (translation, reflection, stretch, and compression), they are better able to understand how to write the equation of a graph, and how to identify the graph of a function that has been transformed.

EXPLORE 1

Investigating Translations of Function Graphs

INTEGRATE TECHNOLOGY

Students have the option of completing the activity either in the book or online.

AVOID COMMON ERRORS

Students may confuse directions in horizontal translations. Emphasize that h is the number *subtracted* from x. For example, in $f(x - 3)$, the value of h is 3, a positive number, and therefore the translation is to the right.

QUESTIONING STRATEGIES

? Given the graph of a function $f(x)$, and the graph of the image of the function after a translation, how can you determine the rule for the function represented by the image? **You can select a particular point on the original graph (such as an endpoint of a segment, or a local maximum or minimum point), and see how its image was obtained. If the image is above or below the original point, the rule will involve adding or subtracting the number of units it was translated to $f(x)$. If the image is to the left or right of the original point, the rule will involve adding or subtracting the number of units it was translated to x in $f(x)$.**

EXPLORE 2

Investigating Stretches and Compressions of Function Graphs

QUESTIONING STRATEGIES

? On the coordinate plane, what is the difference between a stretch and a compression? **In a stretch, the points of the graph are pulled *away* from the x-axis. In a compression, they are pulled *toward* the x-axis.**

? On the coordinate plane, what is the difference between a horizontal stretch and a vertical stretch? **In a horizontal stretch, the points of the graph are pulled away from the y-axis. In a vertical stretch, the points of the graph are pulled away from the x-axis.**

Explore 2 Investigating Stretches and Compressions of Function Graphs

In this activity, you will consider what happens when you multiply by a positive parameter inside or outside a function. Throughout, you will use the same function $f(x)$ that you used in the previous activity.

(A) First graph $g(x) = a \cdot f(x)$ where a is the parameter. Let $a = 2$ so that $g(x) = 2f(x)$. Complete the input-output table and then graph $g(x)$. In general, how is the graph of $g(x) = a \cdot f(x)$ related to the graph of $f(x)$ when a is greater than 1?

x	f(x)	2f(x)
−1	−2	−4
1	2	4
3	−2	−4
5	2	4

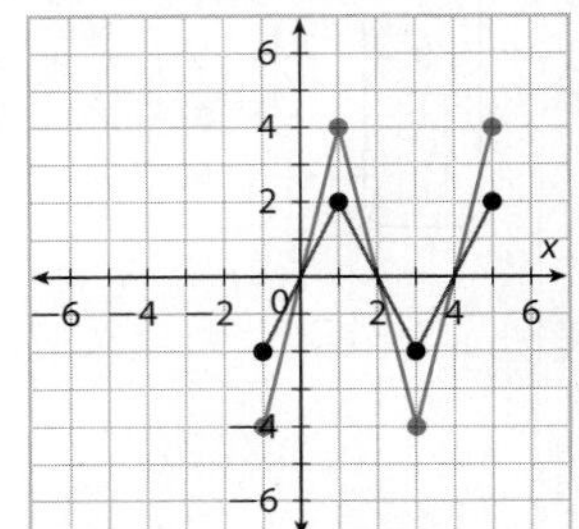

For $a > 1$, the graph of $g(x) = a \cdot f(x)$ is the graph of $f(x)$ stretched vertically (away from the x-axis) by a factor of a.

(B) Now try a value of a between 0 and 1 in $g(x) = a \cdot f(x)$. Let $a = \frac{1}{2}$ so that $g(x) = \frac{1}{2}f(x)$. Complete the input-output table and then graph $g(x)$. In general, how is the graph of $g(x) = a \cdot f(x)$ related to the graph of $f(x)$ when a is a number between 0 and 1?

x	f(x)	$\frac{1}{2}$f(x)
−1	−2	−1
1	2	1
3	−2	−1
5	2	1

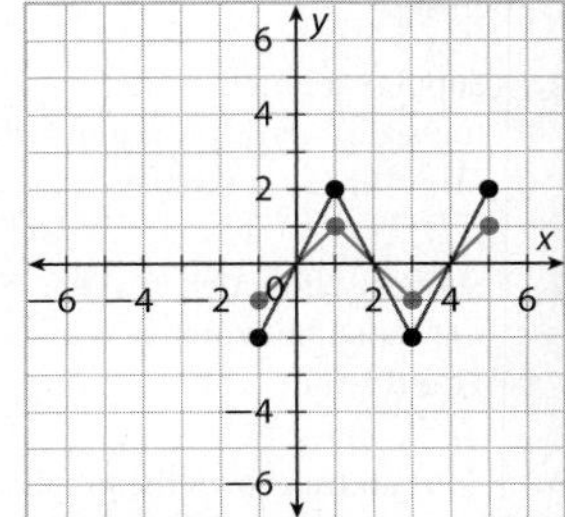

For $0 < a < 1$, the graph of $g(x) = a \cdot f(x)$ is the graph of $f(x)$ compressed vertically (toward the x-axis) by a factor of a.

COLLABORATIVE LEARNING

Peer-to-Peer Activity

Have students work in pairs. Provide students with three or four functions, and have them use a graphing calculator to explore how changes to the various parameters in each function affect the graph of the function. Once they start to make the connections, encourage them to try and predict each change before graphing the transformation.

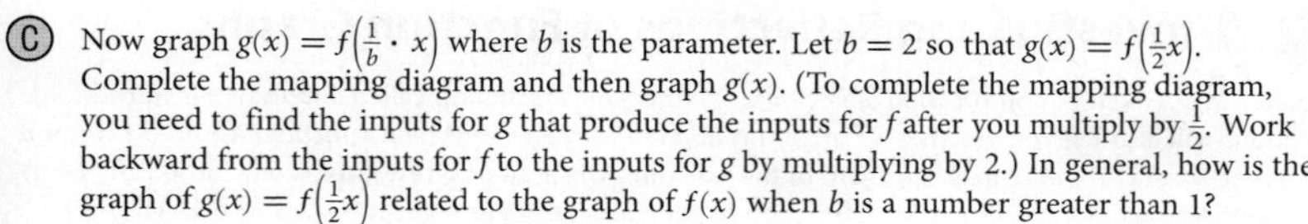

Ⓒ Now graph $g(x) = f\left(\frac{1}{b} \cdot x\right)$ where b is the parameter. Let $b = 2$ so that $g(x) = f\left(\frac{1}{2}x\right)$. Complete the mapping diagram and then graph $g(x)$. (To complete the mapping diagram, you need to find the inputs for g that produce the inputs for f after you multiply by $\frac{1}{2}$. Work backward from the inputs for f to the inputs for g by multiplying by 2.) In general, how is the graph of $g(x) = f\left(\frac{1}{2}x\right)$ related to the graph of $f(x)$ when b is a number greater than 1?

Input for g	Input for f	Output for f	Output for g
-2	-1	-2	-2
2	1	2	2
6	3	-2	-2
10	5	2	2

($\cdot \frac{1}{2}$)

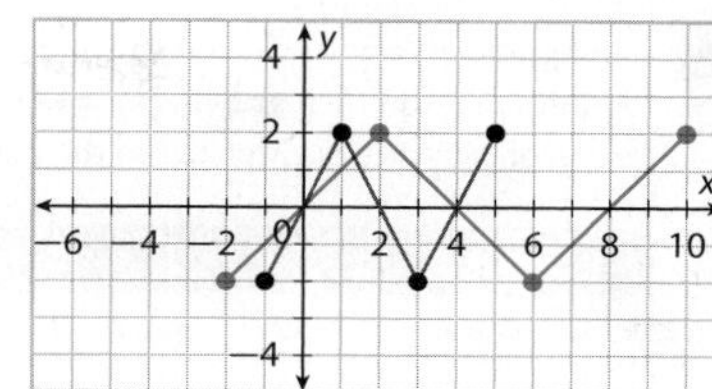

For $b > 1$, the graph of $g(x) = f\left(\frac{1}{b} \cdot x\right)$ is the graph of $f(x)$ stretched horizontally (away from the y-axis) by a factor of b.

Ⓓ **Make a Conjecture** How would you expect the graph of $g(x) = f\left(\frac{1}{b} \cdot x\right)$ to be related to the graph of $f(x)$ when b is a number between 0 and 1?

For $0 < b < 1$, the graph of $g(x) = f\left(\frac{1}{b} \cdot x\right)$ is the graph of $f(x)$ compressed horizontally (toward the y-axis) by a factor of b.

Reflect

4. Suppose a function $f(x)$ has a domain of $[x_1, x_2]$ and a range of $[y_1, y_2]$. When the graph of $f(x)$ is stretched or compressed vertically by a factor of a, how do the domain and range change?
The domain remains the same, and the range changes from $[y_1, y_2]$ to $[ay_1, ay_2]$.

5. You can transform the graph of $f(x)$ to obtain the graph of $g(x) = a \cdot f(x-h) + k$ by combining transformations. Predict what will happen by completing the table.

Value of a	Transformations of the Graph of $f(x)$
$a > 1$	Stretch vertically by a factor of a, and translate h units horizontally and k units vertically.
$0 < a < 1$	**Compress vertically by a factor of a, and translate h units horizontally and k units vertically.**

6. You can transform the graph of $f(x)$ to obtain the graph of $g(x) = f\left(\frac{1}{b}(x-h)\right) + k$ by combining transformations. Predict what will happen by completing the table.

Value of b	Transformations of the Graph of $f(x)$
$b > 1$	Stretch horizontally by a factor of b, and translate h units horizontally and k units vertically.
$0 < b < 1$	**Compress horizontally by a factor of b, and translate h units horizontally and k units vertically.**

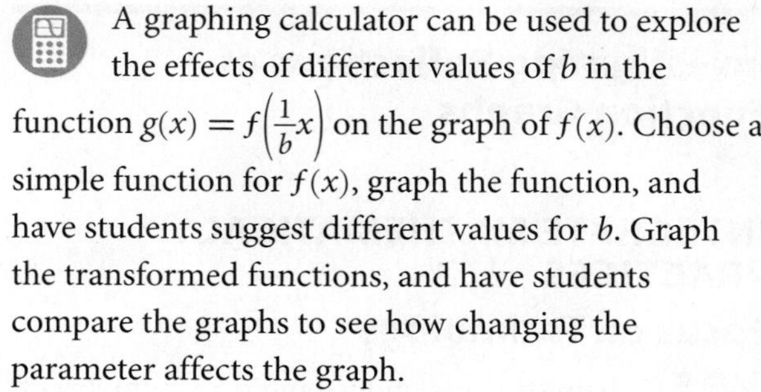

INTEGRATE TECHNOLOGY

A graphing calculator can be used to explore the effects of different values of b in the function $g(x) = f\left(\frac{1}{b}x\right)$ on the graph of $f(x)$. Choose a simple function for $f(x)$, graph the function, and have students suggest different values for b. Graph the transformed functions, and have students compare the graphs to see how changing the parameter affects the graph.

INTEGRATE MATHEMATICAL PRACTICES

Focus on Reasoning

MP.2 Prompt students to recognize that when the graph of a function passes through the origin, a transformation involving a stretch or a compression of the function will not affect the point at the origin. Ask students to justify how this is possible, when all points on either side of the origin *are* affected.

EXPLORE 3

Investigating Reflections of Function Graphs

INTEGRATE MATHEMATICAL PRACTICES

Focus on Technology

MP.5 To help students understand the symmetry of the graphs of even and odd functions, have students use a graphing calculator to graph $f(x) = x^2$ and $g(x) = f(-x) = (-x)^2$ to see that the two graphs coincide. This is a consequence of the fact that replacing x with $-x$ in a function rule causes the graph to be reflected across the y-axis. Since the graph of $f(x) = x^2$ is symmetric with respect to the y-axis, it is unaffected when x is replaced with $-x$.

Also have students graph $f(x) = x^3$, $g(x) = f(-x) = (-x)^3$, and $h(x) = -f(x) = -x^3$, and observe that the graphs of $g(x)$ and $h(x)$ coincide. The graph of $g(x)$ is a reflection of the graph of $f(x)$ across the y-axis, while the graph of $h(x)$ is a reflection of the graph of $f(x)$ across the x-axis. The graphs of $g(x)$ and $h(x)$ coincide because reflecting the graph of $f(x)$ across both axes does not change the graph, which is another way of saying that the graph of $f(x)$ has 180° rotational symmetry about the origin.

QUESTIONING STRATEGIES

? How do the domain and range of the function $g(x) = f(-x)$ compare to the domain and range of $f(x)$? **The domain of $g(x)$ consists of the opposites of the elements in the domain of $f(x)$. The range values are the same.**

Explore 3 Investigating Reflections of Function Graphs

When the parameter in a stretch or compression is negative, another transformation called a *reflection* is introduced. Examining reflections will also tell you whether a function is an *even function* or an *odd function*. An **even function** is one for which $f(-x) = f(x)$ for all x in the domain of the function, while an **odd function** is one for which $f(-x) = -f(x)$ for all x in the domain of the function. A function is not necessarily even or odd; it can be neither.

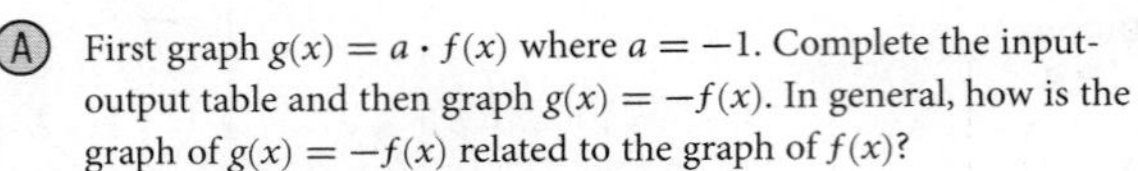

(A) First graph $g(x) = a \cdot f(x)$ where $a = -1$. Complete the input-output table and then graph $g(x) = -f(x)$. In general, how is the graph of $g(x) = -f(x)$ related to the graph of $f(x)$?

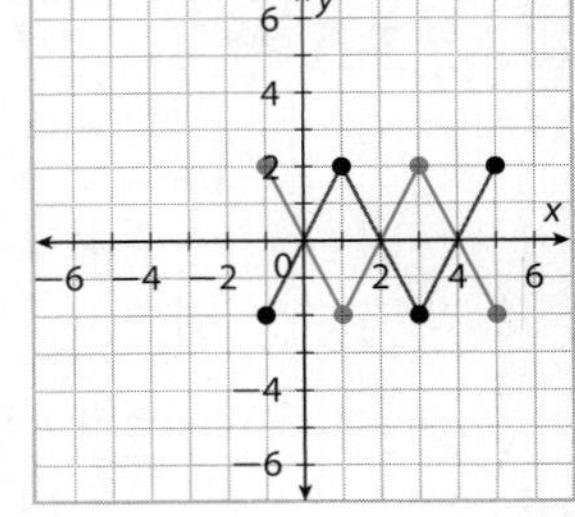

x	f(x)	−f(x)
−1	−2	2
1	2	−2
3	−2	2
5	2	−2

The graph of $g(x) = -f(x)$ is a reflection of the graph of $f(x)$ across the x-axis.

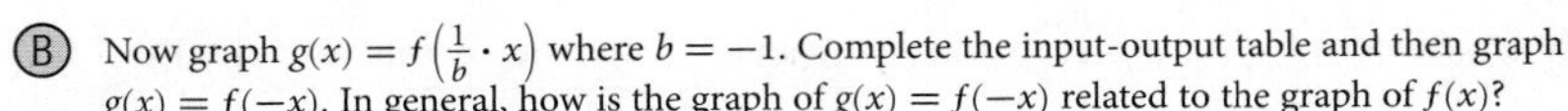

(B) Now graph $g(x) = f\left(\frac{1}{b} \cdot x\right)$ where $b = -1$. Complete the input-output table and then graph $g(x) = f(-x)$. In general, how is the graph of $g(x) = f(-x)$ related to the graph of $f(x)$?

Input for g	· (−1) → Input for f	Output for f	Output for g
1	−1	−2	−2
−1	1	2	2
−3	3	−2	−2
−5	5	2	2

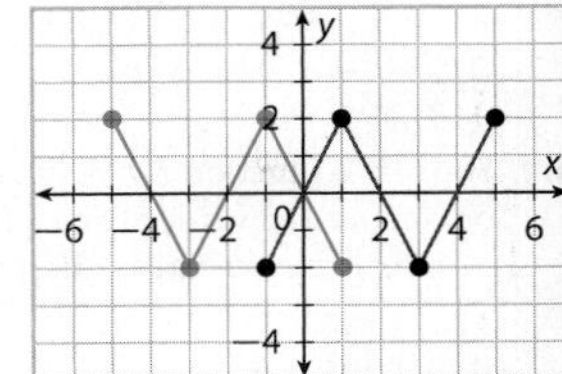

The graph of $g(x) = f(-x)$ is a reflection of the graph of $f(x)$ across the y-axis.

Reflect

7. **Discussion** Suppose a function $f(x)$ has a domain of $[x_1, x_2]$ and a range of $[x_1, x_2]$. When the graph of $f(x)$ is reflected across the x-axis, how do the domain and range change?
The domain remains the same, and the range changes from $[y_1, y_2]$ to $[-y_2, -y_1]$.

8. For a function $f(x)$, suppose the graph of $f(-x)$, which you know is a reflection of the graph of $f(x)$ across the y-axis, is identical to the graph of $f(x)$. What does this tell you about $f(x)$? Explain.
Because $f(x) = f(-x)$, $f(x)$ must be an even function.

9. Is the function whose graph you reflected across the axes in Steps A and B an even function, an odd function, or neither? Explain.
It is neither an even function nor an odd function, because the graph of $f(-x)$ in Step B is not identical to the graph of $f(x)$ nor is it identical to the graph of $-f(x)$ in Step A.

Explain 1 Transforming the Graph of the Parent Quadratic Function

You can use transformations of the graph of a basic function, called a *parent function*, to obtain the graph of a related function. To do so, focus on how the transformations affect reference points on the graph of the parent function.

For instance, the parent quadratic function is $f(x) = x^2$. The graph of this function is a U-shaped curve called a *parabola* with a turning point, called a *vertex*, at (0, 0). The vertex is a useful reference point, as are the points (−1, 1) and (1, 1).

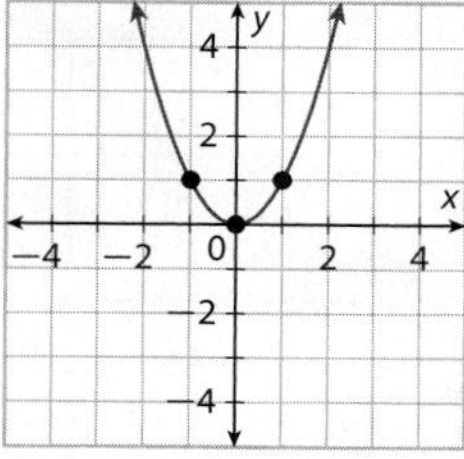

Example 1 **Describe how to transform the graph of $f(x) = x^2$ to obtain the graph of the related function $g(x)$. Then draw the graph of $g(x)$.**

Ⓐ $g(x) = -3f(x - 2) - 4$

Parameter and Its Value	Effect on the Parent Graph
$a = -3$	vertical stretch of the graph of $f(x)$ by a factor of 3 and a reflection across the x-axis
$b = 1$	Since $b = 1$, there is no horizontal stretch or compression.
$h = 2$	horizontal translation of the graph of $f(x)$ to the right 2 units
$k = -4$	vertical translation of the graph of $f(x)$ down 4 units

Applying these transformations to a point (x, y) on the parent graph results in the point $(x + 2, -3y - 4)$. The table shows what happens to the three reference points on the graph of $f(x)$.

Point on the Graph of $f(x)$	Corresponding Point on $g(x)$
(−1, 1)	$(-1 + 2, -3(1) - 4) = (1, -7)$
(0, 0)	$(0 + 2, -3(0) - 4) = (2, -4)$
(1, 1)	$(1 + 2, -3(1) - 4) = (3, -7)$

Use the transformed reference points to graph $g(x)$.

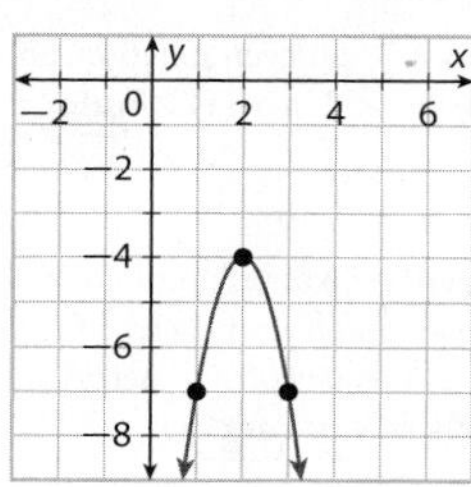

EXPLAIN 1

Transforming the Graph of the Parent Quadratic Function

QUESTIONING STRATEGIES

? When drawing the graph of a transformation of the function $f(x) = x^2$ that involves a reflection, a horizontal translation, and a vertical stretch, in which order should the transformations be applied to the graph of the parent function? Explain. The order does not matter. The graph of the new function will be the same no matter what the order.

? When drawing the graph of a transformation of the function $f(x) = x^2$ that involves a reflection, a vertical translation, and a horizontal compression, in which order should the transformations be applied to the graph of the parent function? Explain. The reflection and compression need to be applied before the vertical translation. The new function is a vertical translation of the graph of $f(x) = ax^2$.

DIFFERENTIATE INSTRUCTION

Visual Cues

Suggest that students write the general function $g(x) = af(x - h)^2 + k$, (or $f(x) = a(x - h)^2 + k$, depending on the context) above the specific function they are analyzing in order to correctly identify the parameters in the transformation.

Communicating Math

When analyzing transformed functions, have students list each parameter and its value, and then write a short phrase, such as "shift 5 units to the left" or "reflect over the x-axis" to indicate the meaning of each parameter. This may make it easier for the student to then construct the graph of the function.

INTEGRATE MATHEMATICAL PRACTICES

Focus on Math Connections

MP.1 Discuss with students how the attributes of a function (such as domain, range, maximum or minimum values, and intervals over which the function is increasing or decreasing) can be determined from the function written in the form $g(x) = af(x - h)^2 + k$, where $f(x)$ is the function $f(x) = x^2$.

(B) $g(x) = f\left(\frac{1}{2}(x + 5)\right) + 2$

Parameter and Its Value	Effect on the Parent Graph
$a =$ 1	The parent graph is unaffected.
$b =$ 2	The parent graph is (stretched)/compressed horizontally by a factor of 2. There is no reflection across the y-axis.
$h =$ −5	The parent graph is translated −5 units (horizontally)/vertically.
$k =$ 2	The parent graph is translated 2 units horizontally/(vertically).

Applying these transformations to a point on the parent graph results in the point $(2x - 5, y + 2)$. The table shows what happens to the three reference points on the graph of $f(x)$.

Point on the Graph of $f(x)$	Corresponding Point on the Graph of $g(x)$
(−1, 1)	$(2(-1) - 5, 1 + 2) = (-7, 3)$
(0, 0)	$(2(0) - 5, 0 + 2) = (-5, 2)$
(1, 1)	$(2(1) - 5, 1 + 2) = (-3, 3)$

Use the transformed reference points to graph $g(x)$.

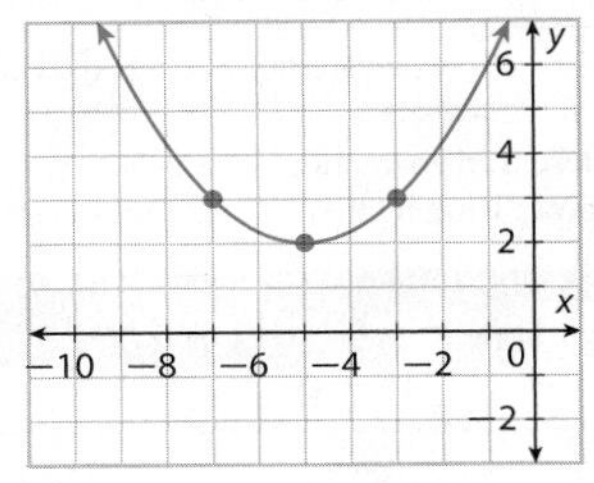

Reflect

10. Is the function $f(x) = x^2$ an even function, an odd function, or neither? Explain.
The function $f(x) = x^2$ is an even function because $f(-x) = f(x)$ for all values of x in its domain.

11. The graph of the parent quadratic function $f(x) = x^2$ has the vertical line $x = 0$ as its axis of symmetry. Identify the axis of symmetry for each of the graphs of $g(x)$ in Parts A and B. Which transformation(s) affect the location of the axis of symmetry?
In Part A, the axis of symmetry is $x = 2$. In Part B, the axis of symmetry is $x = -5$. Only a horizontal translation affects the location of the axis of symmetry.

LANGUAGE SUPPORT EL

Connect Vocabulary

Have students work individually and then with a partner on this activity. Give each student pictures on paper or graphing calculators showing images of the graphs of even and odd functions. Have each student identify whether the graph is an even or odd function. Once they decide, they should work with a partner. Each partner has to agree or disagree with the choices made by the other person, and explain why he/she agrees or disagrees. In their explanations, encourage the use of the terms *reflection, x-axis, y-axis, coincides with graph of f.*

Your Turn

12. Describe how to transform the graph of $f(x) = x^2$ to obtain the graph of the related function $g(x) = f\left(-4(x - 3)\right) + 1$. Then draw the graph of $g(x)$.

The graph of $g(x) = f\left(-4(x - 3)\right) + 1$ is a reflection of the graph of $f(x)$ across the y-axis, a horizontal compression by a factor of $\frac{1}{4}$, and a translation of 3 units to the right and 1 unit up.

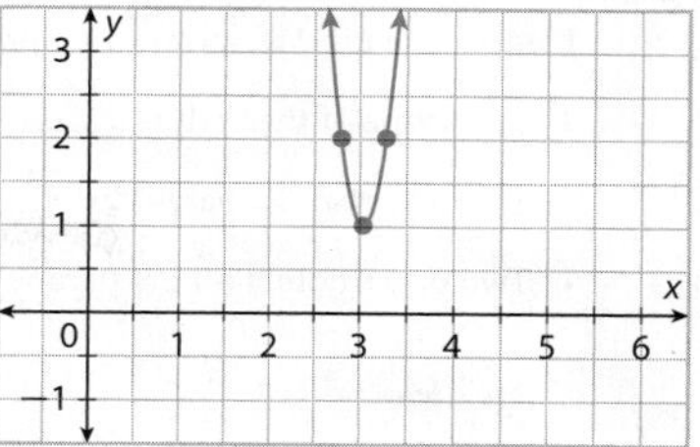

Graph of $f(x)$	Graph of $g(x)$
$(-1, 1)$	$\left(\frac{1}{4}(-1) + 3, 1 + 1\right) = \left(3\frac{1}{4}, 2\right)$
$(0, 0)$	$\left(\frac{1}{4}(0) + 3, 0 + 1\right) = (3, 1)$
$(1, 1)$	$\left(\frac{1}{4}(1) + 3, 1 + 1\right) = \left(2\frac{3}{4}, 2\right)$

Explain 2 Modeling with a Quadratic Function

You can model real-world objects that have a parabolic shape using a quadratic function. In order to fit the function's graph to the shape of the object, you will need to determine the values of the parameters in the function $g(x) = a \cdot f\left(\frac{1}{b}(x - h)\right) + k$ where $f(x) = x^2$. Note that because $f(x)$ is simply a squaring function, it's possible to pull the parameter b outside the function and combine it with the parameter a. Doing so allows you to model real-objects using $g(x) = a \cdot f(x - h) + k$, which has only three parameters.

When modeling real-world objects, remember to restrict the domain of $g(x) = a \cdot f(x - h) + k$ to values of x that are based on the object's dimensions.

Example 2

An old stone bridge over a river uses a parabolic arch for support. In the illustration shown, the unit of measurement for both axes is feet, and the vertex of the arch is point C. Find a quadratic function that models the arch, and state the function's domain.

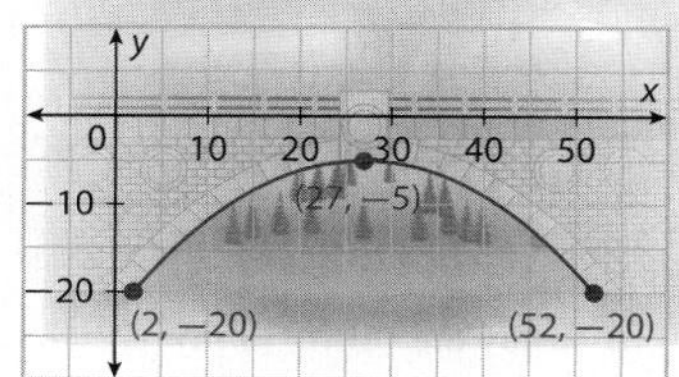

EXPLAIN 2

Modeling with a Quadratic Function

AVOID COMMON ERRORS

Students may use the wrong signs to indicate the horizontal and vertical translations. Reinforce that the number indicating the horizontal translation must be *subtracted* from x, whereas the number indicating the vertical translation must be *added* to the function.

QUESTIONING STRATEGIES

? When modeling a real-world object using a quadratic function, why do you need to restrict the domain of the function? **The graph of the function is part of a parabola. It has a left-most point and a right-most point. Thus, the domain consists only of values between, and including, those two points.**

INTEGRATE MATHEMATICAL PRACTICES

Focus on Modeling

MP.4 Have students brainstorm real-world objects that can be modeled using quadratic functions. Make a list of the objects mentioned, and have students discuss (in general terms) the value of the parameter a in $f(x) = a(x - h)^2 + k$, for each object.

Analyze Information

Identify the important information.

- The shape of the arch is a **parabola**.
- The vertex of the parabola is **$C(27, -5)$**.
- Two other points on the parabola are **$A(2, -20)$** and **$B(52, -20)$**.

Formulate a Plan

You want to find the values of the parameters a, h, and k in $g(x) = a \cdot f(x - h) + k$ where $f(x) = x^2$. You can use the coordinates of point **C** to find the values of h and k. Then you can use the coordinates of one of the other points to find the value of a.

Solve

The vertex of the graph of $g(x)$ is point C, and the vertex of the graph of $f(x)$ is the origin. Point C is the result of translating the origin 27 units to the right and 5 units down. This means that $h = 27$ and $k = -5$. Substituting these values into $g(x)$ gives $g(x) = a \cdot f(x - 27) - 5$. Now substitute the coordinates of point B into $g(x)$ and solve for a.

$g(x) = a \cdot f(x - 27) - 5$ Write the general function.

$g(\boxed{52}) = a \cdot f(52 - 27) - 5$ Substitute 52 for x.

$g(52) = a \cdot f(\boxed{25}) - 5$ Simplify.

$-20 = a \cdot f(\boxed{25}) - 5$ Replace $g(52)$ with -20, the y-value of B.

$-20 = a(625) - 5$ Evaluate $f(25)$.

$a = \boxed{-\frac{3}{125}}$ Simplify.

Substitute the value of a into $g(x)$.

$g(x) = -\frac{3}{125} f(x - 27) - 5$

The arch exists only between points A and B, so the domain of $g(x)$ is $\{x | 2 \leq x \leq 52\}$.

Justify and Evaluate

To justify the answer, verify that $g(2) = -20$.

$g(x) = -\frac{3}{125} f(x - 27) - 5$ Write the function.

$g(\boxed{2}) = -\frac{3}{125} f(\boxed{2} - 27) - 5$ Substitute 2 for x.

$= -\frac{3}{125} f(\boxed{-25}) - 5$ Subtract.

$= -\frac{3}{125} \cdot (\boxed{625}) - 5$ Evaluate $f(-25)$.

$= -20$ ✓ Simplify.

Your Turn

13. The netting of an empty hammock hangs between its supports along a curve that can be modeled by a parabola. In the illustration shown, the unit of measurement for both axes is feet, and the vertex of the curve is point C. Find a quadratic function that models the hammock's netting, and state the function's domain.

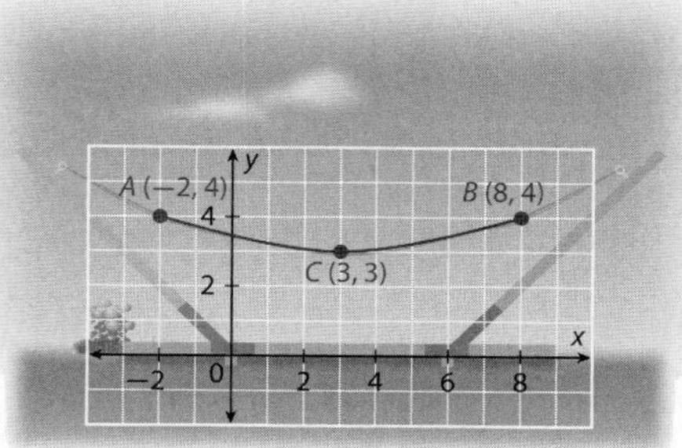

The vertex is (3, 3), so $h = 3$ and $k = 3$. Substitute the values of h and k into $g(x)$.
$g(x) = a \cdot f(x - 3) + 3$
Substitute (8, 4) into $g(x)$ and solve for a.
$4 = a \cdot f(8 - 3) + 3$
$4 = a \cdot f(5) + 3$
$4 = a \cdot 25 + 3$
$\frac{1}{25} = a$
So, $g(x) = \frac{1}{25} f(x - 3) + 3$. The netting exists only between points A and B, so the domain of $g(x)$ is $\{x \mid -2 \le x \le 8\}$.

Elaborate

14. What is the general procedure to follow when graphing a function of the form $g(x) = a \cdot f(x - h) + k$ given the graph of $f(x)$?
The general procedure for graphing $g(x)$ is to choose reference points on the graph of $f(x)$ and apply the transformations for $g(x)$ to them. In the case of $f(x) = x^2$, choose three points on the graph of $f(x)$: the vertex and one point on either side of the vertex. Each point (x, y) is transformed to the point $(x + h, ay + k)$. Use the new points to draw the graph of $g(x)$.

15. What are the general steps to follow when determining the values of the parameters a, h, and k in $f(x) = a(x - h)^2 + k$ when modeling a parabolic real-world object?
To model a parabolic real-world object, first define a coordinate system. Then identify three points on the object; ideally, one of the points should be the vertex. The coordinates of the vertex on the object, (x_v, y_v), are the values of h and k, respectively. Use a second point, (x_1, y_1), on the object to solve $y_1 = a(x_1 - x_v)^2 + y_v$ for a and get $a = \frac{y_1 - y_v}{(x_1 - x_v)^2}$. You can use the third point as a check on your results.

16. **Essential Question Check-In** How can the graph of a function $f(x)$ be transformed?
The graph can be stretched or compressed horizontally or vertically, it can be reflected across the x-axis or y-axis, and it can be translated horizontally or vertically.

ELABORATE

INTEGRATE MATHEMATICAL PRACTICES

Focus on Math Connections

MP.1 Remind students that the real zeros of a function are the x-intercepts of the graph of the function. Have them discuss how the number of real zeros of a function can be determined by knowing the values of a, h, and k in $f(x) = a(x - h)^2 + k$.

SUMMARIZE THE LESSON

How does each of the following transformations of $f(x) = x^2$ affect the values of a, h, and k in the function $g(x) = af(x - h)^2 + k$?

translation 3 units left $h = -3$

translation 3 units up $k = 3$

vertical stretch by a factor of 3 $a = 3$

reflection across the x-axis $a = -1$

EVALUATE

ASSIGNMENT GUIDE

Concepts and Skills	Practice
Explore 1 Investigating Translations of Function Graphs	Exercises 1–4
Explore 2 Investigating Stretches and Compressions of Function Graphs	Exercises 5–8
Explore 3 Investigating Reflections of Function Graphs	Exercises 9–14
Example 1 Transforming the Graph of the Parent Quadratic Function	Exercises 15–16
Example 2 Modeling with a Quadratic Function	Exercises 17–18

AVOID COMMON ERRORS

Students may confuse the concepts of *stretch* and *compression* (both vertical and horizontal). Tell them that they can evaluate the function for a specific value of x, and compare it to the value of $f(x)$. Plotting one or two of these points will provide a visual cue as to the nature of the translation.

Evaluate: Homework and Practice

- Online Homework
- Hints and Help
- Extra Practice

Write $g(x)$ in terms of $f(x)$ after performing the given transformation of the graph of $f(x)$.

1. Translate the graph of $f(x)$ to the left 3 units.

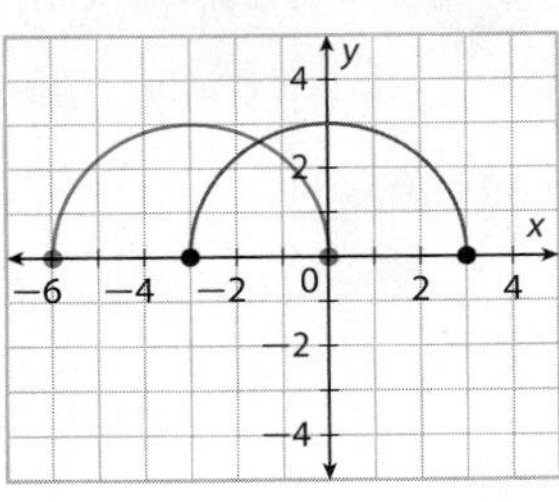

$g(x) = f(x + 3)$

2. Translate the graph of $f(x)$ up 2 units.

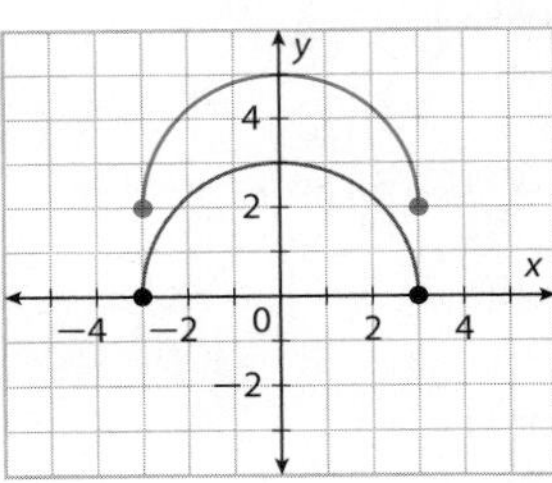

$g(x) = f(x) + 2$

3. Translate the graph of $f(x)$ to the right 4 units.

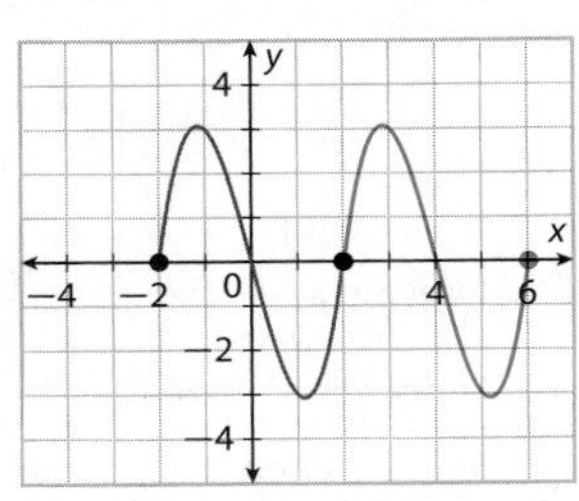

$g(x) = f(x - 4)$

4. Translate the graph of $f(x)$ down 3 units.

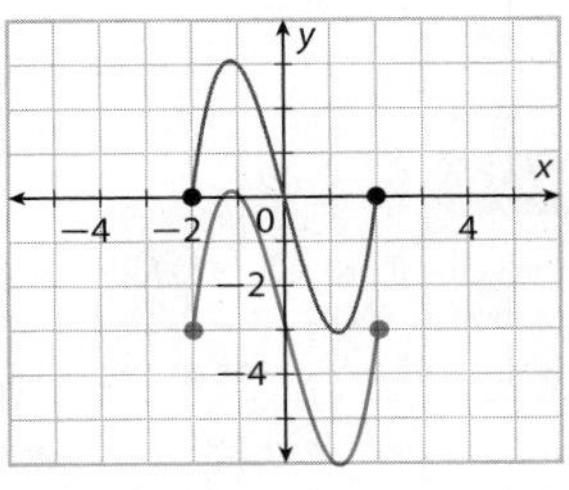

$g(x) = f(x) - 3$

5. Stretch the graph of $f(x)$ horizontally by a factor of 3.

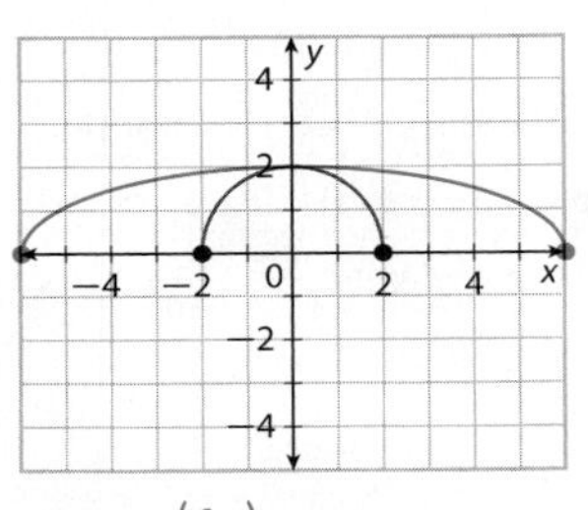

$g(x) = f\left(\frac{1}{3}x\right)$

6. Stretch the graph of $f(x)$ vertically by a factor of 2.

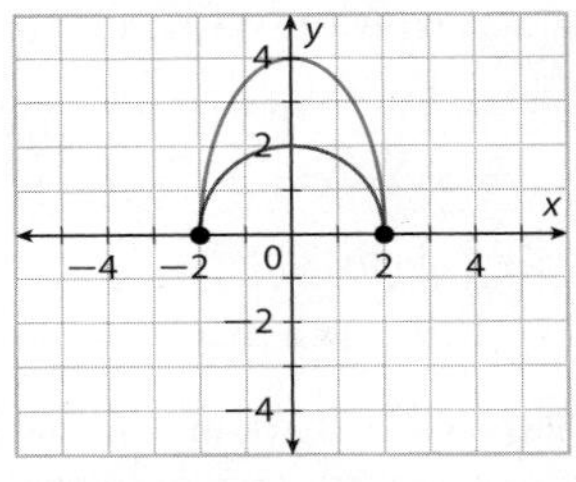

$g(x) = 2f(x)$

Exercise	Depth of Knowledge (D.O.K.)	COMMON CORE Mathematical Practices
1–4	1 Recall of Information	MP.4 Modeling
5–14	1 Recall of Information	MP.2 Reasoning
15–16	1 Recall of Information	MP.6 Precision
17–18	2 Skills/Concepts	MP.4 Modeling
19	3 Strategic Thinking H.O.T.	MP.2 Reasoning
20	3 Strategic Thinking H.O.T.	MP.6 Precision

7. Compress the graph of $f(x)$ horizontally by a factor of 3.

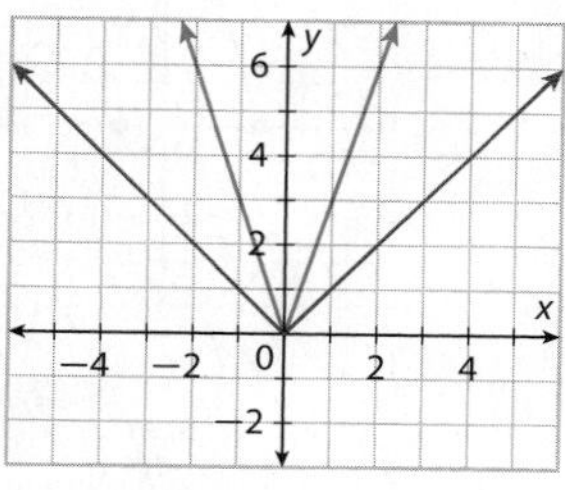

$g(x) = f(3x)$

8. Compress the graph of $f(x)$ vertically by a factor of 2.

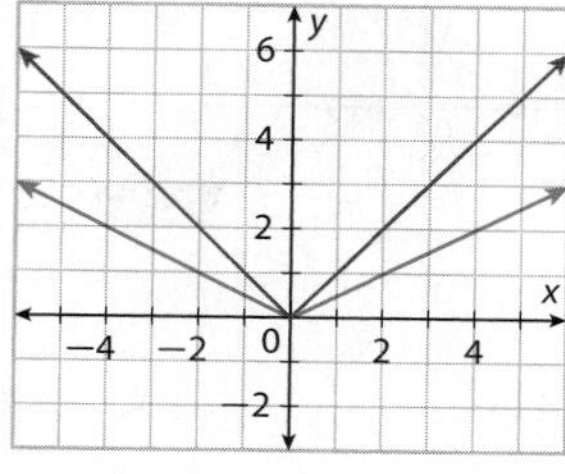

$g(x) = \frac{1}{2}f(x)$

9. Reflect the graph of $f(x)$ across the y-axis.

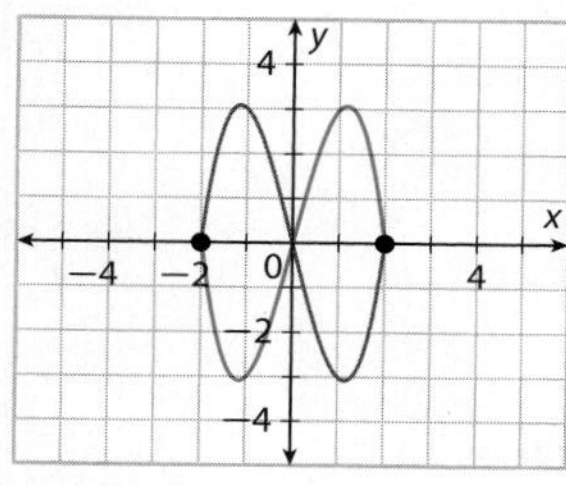

$g(x) = f(-x)$

10. Reflect the graph of $f(x)$ across the x-axis.

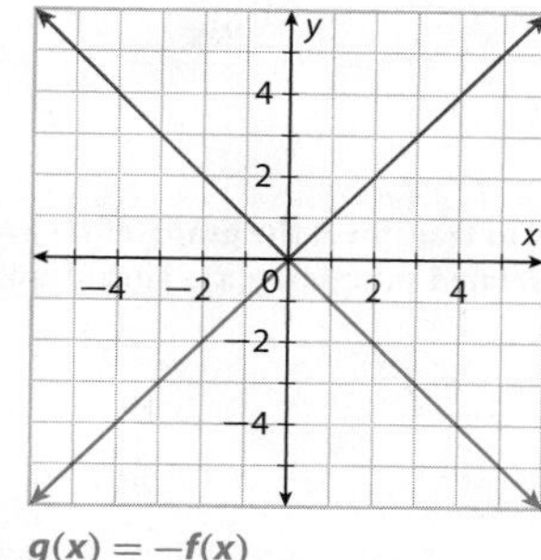

$g(x) = -f(x)$

11. Reflect the graph of $f(x)$ across the y-axis.

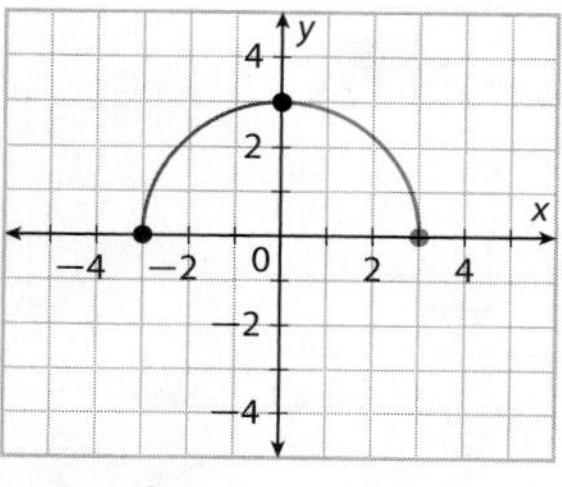

$g(x) = f(-x)$

12. Reflect the graph of $f(x)$ across the x-axis.

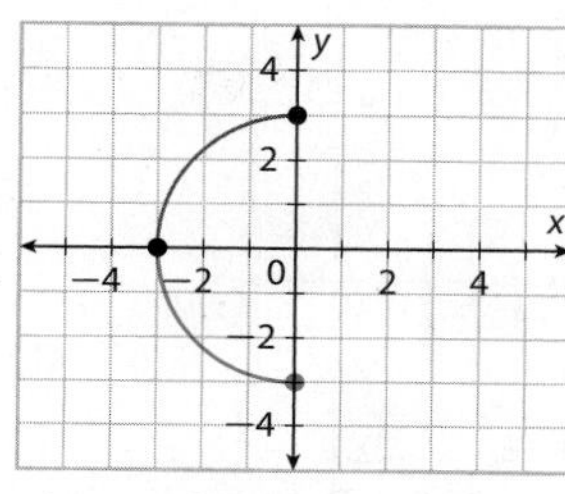

$g(x) = -f(x)$

CRITICAL THINKING

Given a function $f(x)$, how do the functions $g(x) = -f(x)$ and $h(x) = f(-x)$ differ in terms of their effects on the ordered pairs that belong to $f(x)$?

$g(x)$ is the function that negates the $f(x)$ values in each ordered pair; $h(x)$ negates the x-value in each ordered pair.

INTEGRATE MATHEMATICAL PRACTICES

Focus on Patterns

MP.8 Encourage students to use their graphing calculators to explore graphs of functions of higher degree and to see whether they can determine any patterns that would indicate when a function is even and when it is odd.

INTEGRATE TECHNOLOGY

Students can check their work by graphing their functions on a graphing calculator. This provides immediate feedback, as well as the opportunity to visually observe how corrections to the various parameters affect the graph of the function.

13. Determine if each function is an even function, an odd function, or neither.

a. 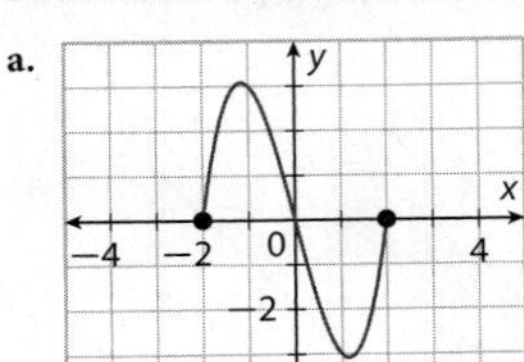

Odd function

b. 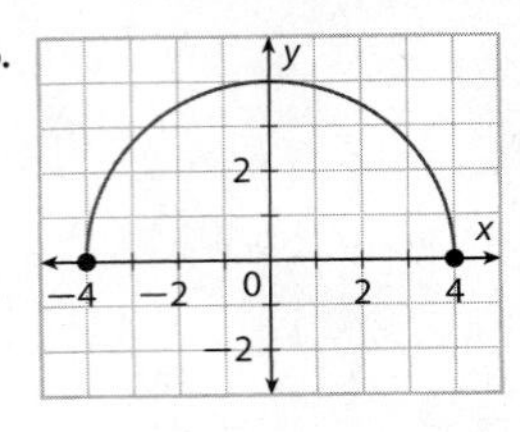

Even function

c. 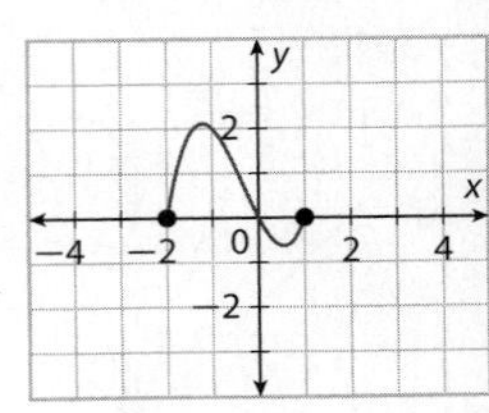

Neither

14. Determine whether each quadratic function is an even function. Answer *yes* or *no*.

a. $f(x) = 5x^2$ **Yes**

b. $f(x) = (x - 2)^2$ **No**

c. $f(x) = \left(\frac{x}{3}\right)^2$ **Yes**

d. $f(x) = x^2 + 6$ **Yes**

Describe how to transform the graph of $f(x) = x^2$ to obtain the graph of the related function $g(x)$. Then draw the graph of $g(x)$.

15. $g(x) = -\frac{f(x + 4)}{3}$

reflection of the graph of $f(x)$ across the x-axis, a vertical compression by a factor of $\frac{1}{3}$, and a translation of 4 units to the left

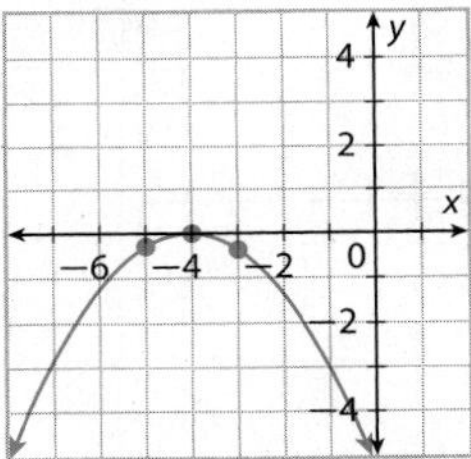

16. $g(x) = f(2x) + 2$

horizontal compression of the graph of $f(x)$ by a factor of $\frac{1}{2}$ and a translation of 2 units up

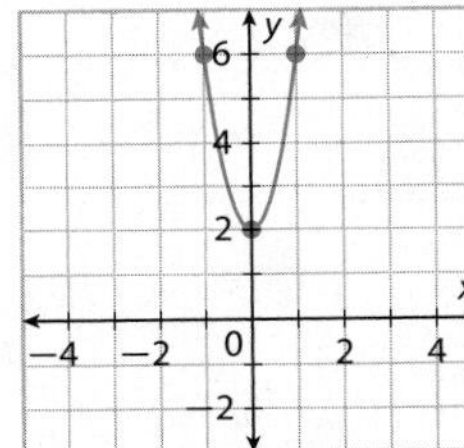

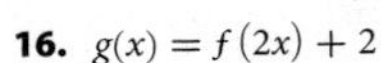

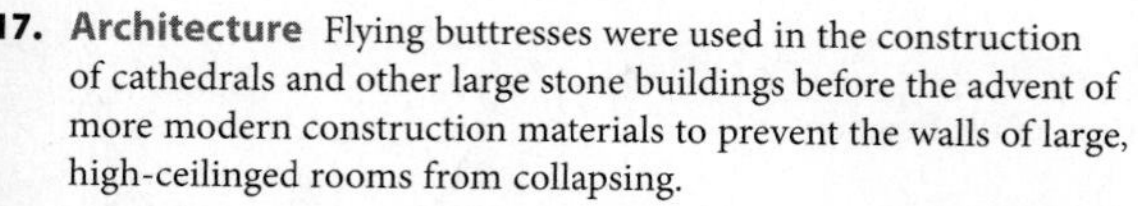

17. Architecture Flying buttresses were used in the construction of cathedrals and other large stone buildings before the advent of more modern construction materials to prevent the walls of large, high-ceilinged rooms from collapsing.

The design of a flying buttress includes an arch. In the illustration shown, the unit of measurement for both axes is feet, and the vertex of the arch is point *C*. Find a quadratic function that models the arch, and state the function's domain.

The vertex is $(2, 12)$, so $h = 2$ and $k = 12$. Substitute the values of h and k into $g(x)$. $g(x) = a \cdot f(x - 2) + 12$

Substitute $(8, 4)$ into $g(x)$ and solve for a.

$6 = a \cdot f(8 - 2) + 12$

$6 = a \cdot f(6) + 12$

$6 = a \cdot 36 + 12$

$-\frac{1}{6} = a$

So, $g(x) = -\frac{1}{6}f(x - 2) + 12$. The arch exists only between points C and B, so the domain of $g(x)$ is $\{x \mid 2 \leq x \leq 8\}$.

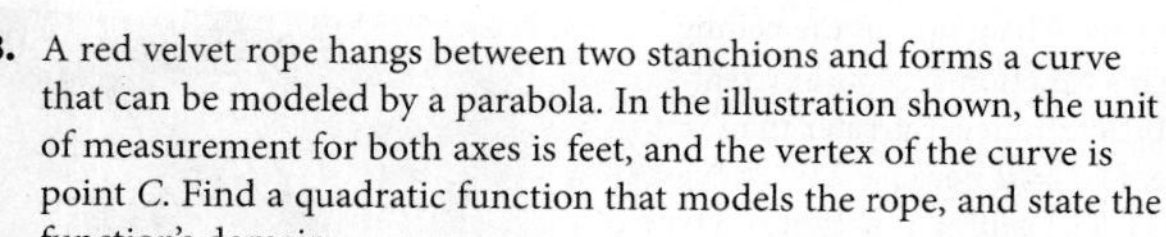

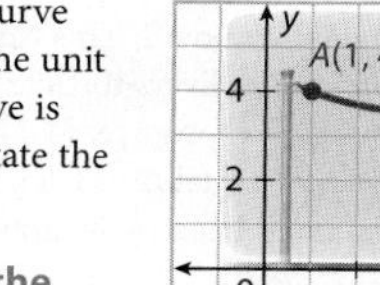

18. A red velvet rope hangs between two stanchions and forms a curve that can be modeled by a parabola. In the illustration shown, the unit of measurement for both axes is feet, and the vertex of the curve is point *C*. Find a quadratic function that models the rope, and state the function's domain.

The vertex is $(4, 3.5)$, so $h = 4$ and $k = 3.5$. Substitute the values of h and k into $g(x)$. $g(x) = a \cdot f(x - 4) + 3.5$

Substitute $(4, 3.5)$ into $g(x)$ and solve for a.

$4 = a \cdot f(7 - 4) + 3.5$

$4 = a \cdot f(3) + 3.5$

$4 = a \cdot 9 + 3.5$

$\frac{1}{18} = a$

So, $g(x) = \frac{1}{18}f(x - 4) + 3.5$. The rope exists only between points A and B, so the domain of $g(x)$ is $\{x \mid 1 \leq x \leq 7\}$.

INTEGRATE MATHEMATICAL PRACTICES

Focus on Reasoning

MP.2 Students can check their functions for correctness by substituting the coordinates of a point on the parabola into the rule to see whether the resulting equation is true.

CONNECT VOCABULARY EL

Review terms such as *horizontal translation, vertical translation, stretch/compression* by having students look at graphs with different parameters, and then show the kind of translation by using their hands. For example, holding a hand horizontally for a horizontal translation, and moving it up or down for a vertical one.

PEER-TO-PEER DISCUSSION

Ask students to discuss with a partner how a real-world situation that can be modeled by a vertical stretch of the parent quadratic function compares to a real-world situation that can be modeled by a vertical compression of the parent quadratic function. Have them share their conclusions with the class. **A situation that can be modeled by a vertical stretch of $f(x) = x^2$ will contain function values that will increase or decrease at a faster rate than the function values in a situation that can be modeled by a vertical compression of $f(x) = x^2$.**

JOURNAL

Have students explain how the parameters a, h, and k in the function $g(x) = af(x - h)^2 + k$ affect the graph of $f(x) = x^2$.

H.O.T. Focus on Higher Order Thinking

19. Multiple Representations The graph of the function $g(x) = \left(\frac{1}{2}x + 2\right)^2$ is shown.

Use the graph to identify the transformations of the graph of $f(x) = x^2$ needed to produce the graph of $g(x)$. (If a stretch or compression is involved, give it in terms of a horizontal stretch or compression rather than a vertical one.) Use your list of transformations to write $g(x)$ in the form $g(x) = f\left(\frac{1}{b}(x - h)\right) + k$. Then show why the new form of $g(x)$ is algebraically equivalent to the given form.

The graph of $g(x)$ shows that the graph of $f(x)$ has been stretched horizontally by a factor of 2 and translated to the left 4 units. So, $g(x) = f\left(\frac{1}{2}(x - (-4))\right)$. This equation is equivalent to the given form of $g(x)$ because $x - (-4)$ can be rewritten as $x + 4$, $\frac{1}{2}$ can be distributed to the terms of $x + 4$, and $f(x)$ can be replaced by the action (squaring) that it performs on its input values. So, $g(x) = f\left(\frac{1}{2}(x - (-4))\right) = f\left(\frac{1}{2}(x + 4)\right) = f\left(\frac{1}{2}x + 2\right) = \left(\frac{1}{2}x + 2\right)^2$.

20. Represent Real-World Situations The graph of the ceiling function, $f(x) = \lceil x \rceil$, is shown. This function accepts any real number x as input and delivers the least integer greater than or equal to x as output. For instance, $f1.3 = 2$ because 2 is the least integer greater than or equal to 1.3. The ceiling function is a type of *step function*, so named because its graph looks like a set of steps.

Write a function $g(x)$ whose graph is a transformation of the graph of $f(x)$ based on this situation: A parking garage charges \$4 for the first hour or less and \$2 for every additional hour or fraction of an hour. Then graph $g(x)$.

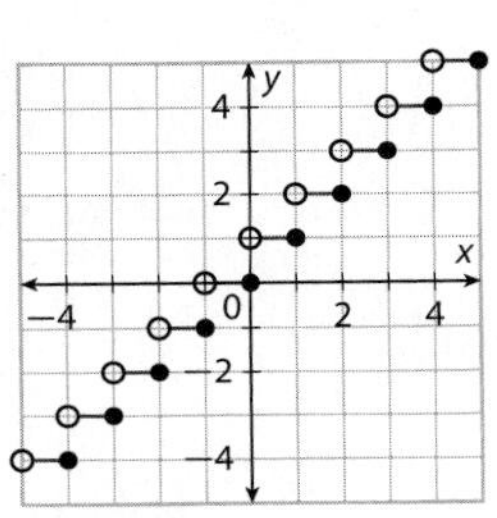

$g(x) = 2f(x) + 2$

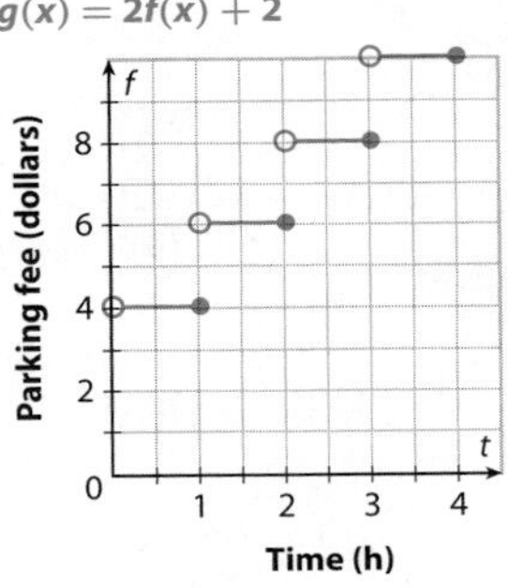

Lesson Performance Task

You are designing two versions of a chair, one without armrests and one with armrests. The diagrams show side views of the chair. Rather than use traditional straight legs for your chair, you decide to use parabolic legs. Given the function $f(x) = x^2$, write two functions, $g(x)$ and $h(x)$, whose graphs represent the legs of the two chairs and involve transformations of the graph of $f(x)$. For the chair without armrests, the graph of $g(x)$ must touch the bottom of the chair's seat. For the chair with armrests, the graph of $h(x)$ must touch the bottom of the armrest. After writing each function, graph it.

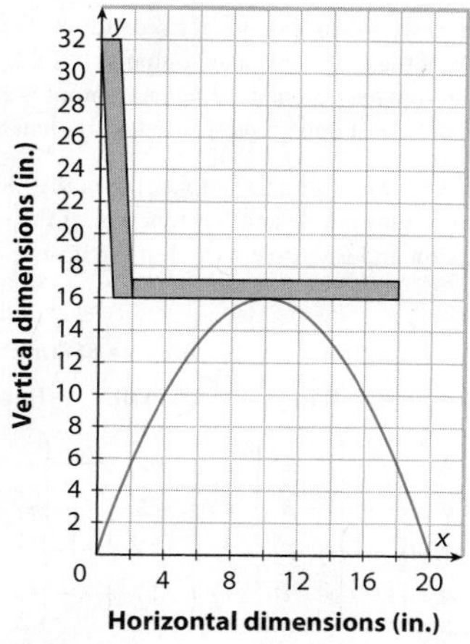

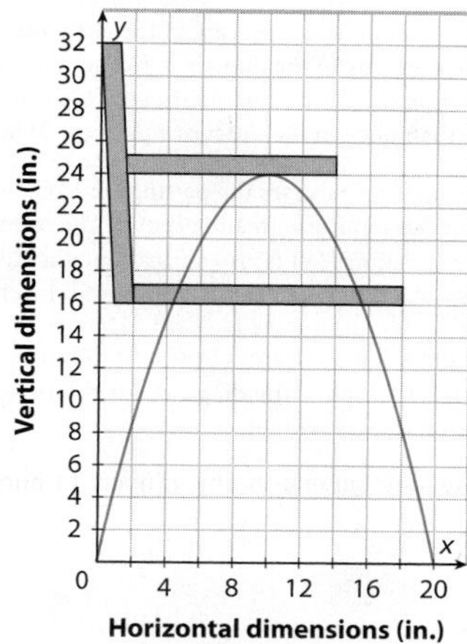

Sample answer: For the chair without armrests, let (10, 16) be the vertex of the parabola, and terminate the parabola at (0, 0) and (20, 0). The vertex is (10, 16), so $h = 10$ and $k = 16$. Substitute the values of h and k into $g(x)$. $g(x) = a \cdot f(x - 10) + 16$

Substitute (20, 0) into $g(x)$ and solve for a.

$0 = a \cdot f(20 - 10) + 16$

$0 = a \cdot f(10) + 16$

$0 = a \cdot 100 + 16$

$-0.16 = a$

So, $g(x) = -0.16f(x - 10) + 16$ with domain $\{x| 0 \leq x \leq 20\}$. The graph of $g(x)$ is shown.

For the chair with armrests, let (10, 24) be the vertex of the parabola, and again terminate the parabola at (0, 0) and (20, 0). Note that this parabola is a vertical stretch of the previous parabola by a factor of $\frac{24}{16} = 1.5$. So, $h(x) = 1.5\,g(x) = 1.5\left(-0.16f(x - 10) + 16\right)$ $= -0.24f(x - 10) + 24$, also with domain $\{x| 0 \leq x \leq 20\}$. The graph of $h(x)$ is shown.

EXTENSION ACTIVITY

Have students research the differences between a catenary curve and a parabolic curve and find examples of catenaries in real life (for example, a hanging cable, or the Gateway Arch in St. Louis). Students should find that the two types of curves look very similar in that they are both symmetrical and have similar shapes. A parabola in its simplest form is $f(x) = x^2$ while a catenary is of the form $f(x) = \cosh(x)$. Parabolas are often used to model catenaries when the differences between them are not consequential.

CONNECT VOCABULARY EL

Some students may not be familiar with the term *armrest*, a compound word made up of *arm* and *rest*. Show students an example of a chair with armrests and another without armrests. Discuss how the armrests in the given design need to have the support of the parabolic legs beneath them to provide the strength to hold up under the weight of a person leaning on the armrests.

QUESTIONING STRATEGIES

? Is a stretch or a compression used to form the legs of the chair with armrests? Is it vertical or horizontal? vertical stretch

? Why is it necessary for the values of a to be negative in the equations for the parabolas? The parabolas open downward.

? Which of the two chairs do you think is likely to be the more stable? Why? The chair with the armrests would be more stable because it is secured at two points on each pair of legs rather than just one point on each. The seat on the chair with the vertex centered on it could tip forward or backward depending on where the weight is shifted.

Scoring Rubric

2 points: Student correctly solves the problem and explains his/her reasoning.

1 point: Student shows good understanding of the problem but does not fully solve or explain his/her reasoning.

0 points: Student does not demonstrate understanding of the problem.

LESSON 1.4

Inverses of Functions

Common Core Math Standards

The student is expected to:

 **F-BF.B.4**

Find inverse functions. Also F-BF.B.4b(+)

Mathematical Practices

 **MP.4 Modeling**

Language Objective

Show or explain what the inverse of the graph of a function would look like and justify your reasoning to a partner.

ENGAGE

Essential Question: What is an inverse function, and how do you know it's an inverse function?

Possible answer: Given a function $f(x)$ that pairs domain values with range values, the inverse function $f^{-1}(x)$, if it exists, reverses those pairings. (The inverse function exists only when the original function is one-to-one or has had its domain restricted so that it becomes one-to-one.) The composition of $f(x)$ and $f^{-1}(x)$ is just x, and the graphs of $f(x)$ and $f^{-1}(x)$ are reflections across the line $y = x$.

PREVIEW: LESSON PERFORMANCE TASK

View the Engage section online. Discuss the photo, asking which would be more helpful and why: to obtain femur length as a function of height, or use the inverse function to find height as a function of femur length? Then preview the Lesson Performance Task.

Name ______________________ Class ______________ Date __________

1.4 Inverses of Functions

Resource Locker

Essential Question: What is an inverse function, and how do you know it's an inverse function?

Explore Understanding Inverses of Functions

Recall that a *relation* is any pairing of the elements of one set (the domain) with the elements of a second set (the range). The elements of the domain are called inputs, while the elements of the range are called outputs. A function is a special type of relation that pairs every input with exactly one output. In a *one-to-one function*, no output is ever used more than once in the function's pairings. In a *many-to-one function*, at least one output is used more than once.

An **inverse relation** reverses the pairings of a relation. If a relation pairs an input x with an output y, then the inverse relation pairs an input y with an output x. The inverse of a function may or may not be another function. If the inverse of a function $f(x)$ is also a function, it is called the **inverse function** and is written $f^{-1}(x)$. If the inverse of a function is not a function, then it is simply an inverse relation.

 The mapping diagrams show a function and its inverse. Complete the diagram for the inverse of the function.

Is the function one-to-one or many-to-one? Explain.

Function Domain	Function Range	Inverse Domain	Inverse Range
−4 →	−2	−2 →	−4
0 →	−3	−3 →	0
1 →	2	2 →	1
4 →	1	1 →	4

The function is one-to-one, because no output is ever used more than once in the function's pairings.

Is the inverse of the function also a function? Explain.

The inverse is a function, because for each input there is only one output.

 The mapping diagrams show a function and its inverse. Complete the diagram for the inverse of the function.

Is the function one-to-one or many-to-one? Explain.

Function Domain	Function Range
−4 →	−2
0 →	−3
1 →	2
4 →	2

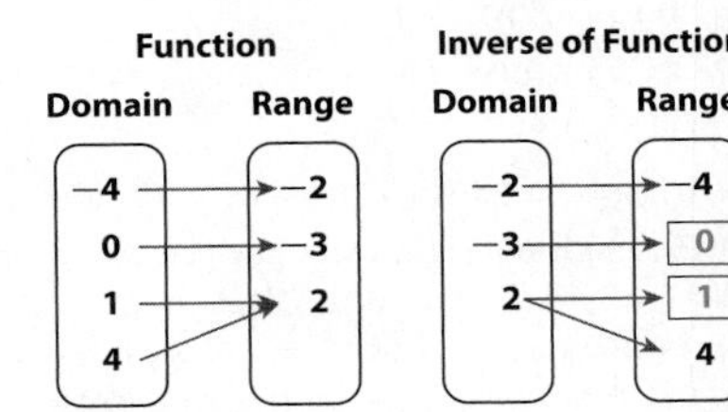

The function is many-to-one, because there are two inputs, 1 and 4, that have the same output.

Is the inverse of the function also a function? Explain.

The inverse is not a function, because the input 2 has two different outputs, 1 and 4.

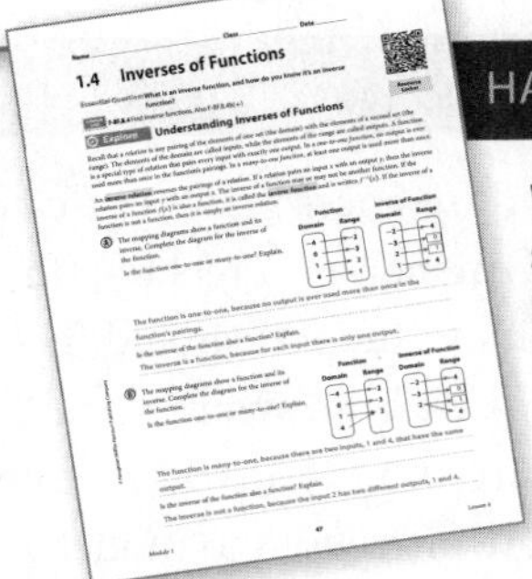

HARDCOVER PAGES 47–58

Watch for the hardcover student edition page numbers for this lesson.

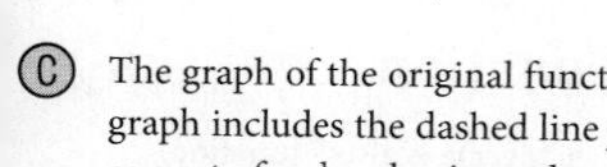

Ⓒ The graph of the original function in Step A is shown. Note that the graph includes the dashed line $y = x$. Write the inverse of the function as a set of ordered pairs and graph them.

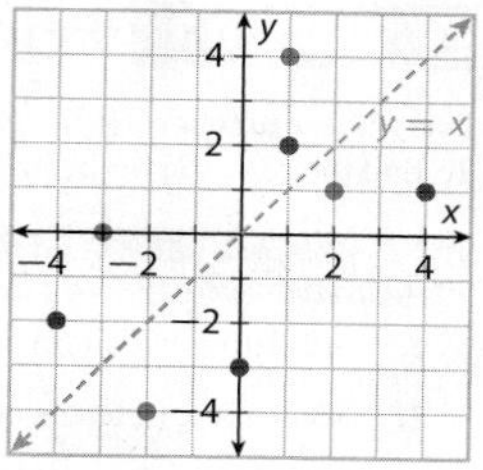

Function: $\{(-4, -2), (0, -3), (1, 2), (4, 1)\}$

Inverse of function:

$\{(-2, -4), (-3, 0), (2, 1), (1, 4)\}$

What do you observe about the graphs of the function and its inverse in relationship to the line $y = x$? Why does this make sense?

The graphs are reflections across the line $y = x$, which makes sense because the ordered pairs in a function and its inverse have their x- and y-coordinates reversed.

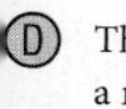

Ⓓ The **composition of two functions** $f(x)$ and $g(x)$, written $f(g(x))$ and read as "f of g of x," is a new function that uses the output of $g(x)$ as the input of $f(x)$. For example, consider the functions f and g with the following rules.

f: Add 1 to an input. g: Double an input.

Notice that $g(1) = 2(1) = 2$. So, $f(g(1)) = f(2) = 2 + 1 = 3$.

You can also find $g(f(x))$. Notice that $f(1) = 1 + 1 = 2$. So, $g(f(1)) = g(2) = 2(2) = 4$.

For these two functions, you can see that $f(g(1)) \neq g(f(1))$.

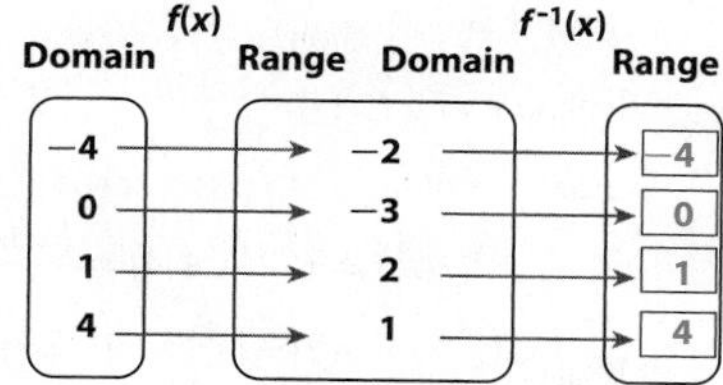

You can compose a function and its inverse. For instance, the mapping diagram shown illustrates $f^{-1}(f(x))$ where $f(x)$ is the original function from Step A and $f^{-1}(x)$ is its inverse. Notice that the range of $f(x)$ serves as the domain of $f^{-1}(x)$. Complete the diagram. What do you notice about the outputs of of $f^{-1}(f(x))$? Explain why this makes sense.

$f(x)$ Domain	Range / $f^{-1}(x)$ Domain	$f^{-1}(x)$ Range
−4	−2	−4
0	−3	0
1	2	1
4	1	4

The outputs of $f^{-1}(f(x))$ exactly match the inputs of $f^{-1}(f(x))$. That is, $f^{-1}(f(x)) = x$. The function takes each input and assigns it to an output. The inverse takes that output as an input, and assigns it back to the original function's input. So, the composition takes an input, assigns it to an output, and then assigns it back to the original input.

Reflect

- What is the relationship between the domain and range of a relation and its inverse?
The range of the original relation is the domain of the inverse relation, and the range of the inverse relation is the domain of the original relation.

- **Discussion** In Step D, you saw that for inverse functions, $f^{-1}(f(x)) = x$. What do you expect $f(f^{-1}(x))$ to equal? Explain.
It will also equal x. The function $f^{-1}(x)$ maps the output of $f(x)$ back to its input, so $f(f^{-1}(x))$ will then map that input back to the input of $f^{-1}(x)$.

PROFESSIONAL DEVELOPMENT

Math Background

A relation is a mapping of the elements of one set of numbers to the elements of another set, which produces a set of ordered pairs. A relation is a function if, for every input, there is exactly one output. The graph of a relation is a function if it passes the vertical line test, that is, if every possible vertical line drawn through the graph intersects it at no more than one point.

A function takes an input, applies a rule, and produces an output. The inverse of that function will use that output as its input and apply a rule to give the input of the original function as its output.

EXPLORE

Understanding Inverses of Functions

INTEGRATE TECHNOLOGY

Students have the option of completing the Explore activity either in the book or online.

AVOID COMMON ERRORS

Students often read $f^{-1}(x)$ as raising a function to the −1 power. Stress that in this notation −1 is not an exponent, even though it is written as a superscript.

QUESTIONING STRATEGIES

❓ What must be true about a function if its inverse is not a function? **The function must pair at least two inputs with the same output.**

EXPLAIN 1

Finding the Inverse of a Linear Function

QUESTIONING STRATEGIES

A linear function takes each real number, multiplies it by 2 and subtracts 4. What does the inverse of this function do to its input values? **The inverse function adds 4 to each input value, and divides the result by 2.**

INTEGRATE MATHEMATICAL PRACTICES

Focus on Reasoning

MP.2 Encourage students always to test an inverse function using the fact that if $f(a) = b$, then $f^{-1}(b) = a$.

QUESTIONING STRATEGIES

If the graph of a linear function and its inverse function are parallel, what must be true about the slopes of the graphs of the two functions? Explain. **The slope of each graph must be 1. These graphs will be parallel to the line $y = x$, whose slope is also 1.**

Explain 1 Finding the Inverse of a Linear Function

Every linear function $f(x) = mx + b$ where $m \neq 0$ is a one-to-one function. So, its inverse is also a function. To find the equation of the inverse function, use the fact that inverse functions undo each other's pairings.

To find the inverse of a function $f(x)$:	
1.	Substitute y for $f(x)$.
2.	Solve for x in terms of y.
3.	Switch x and y (since the inverse switches inputs and outputs).
4.	Replace y with $f^{-1}(x)$.

To check your work and verify that the functions are inverses, show that $f(f^{-1}(x)) = x$ and that $f^{-1}(f(x)) = x$.

Example 1 **Find the inverse function $f^{-1}(x)$ for the given function $f(x)$. Use composition to verify that the functions are inverses. Then graph the function and its inverse.**

Ⓐ $f(x) = 3x + 4$

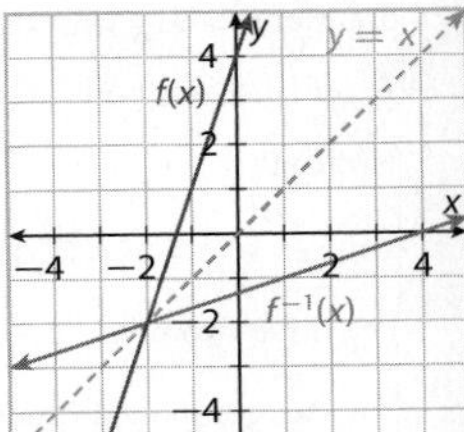

Replace $f(x)$ with y. $\quad y = 3x + 4$

Solve for x. $\quad y - 4 = 3x$

$$\frac{y-4}{3} = x$$

Switch x and y. $\quad y = \frac{x-4}{3}$

Replace y with $f^{-1}(x)$. $\quad f^{-1}(x) = \frac{x-4}{3}$

Check: Verify that $f^{-1}(f(x)) = x$ and $f(f^{-1}(x)) = x$.

$$f^{-1}(f(x)) = f^{-1}(3x + 4) = \frac{(3x+4)-4}{3} = \frac{3x}{3} = x$$

$$f(f^{-1}(x)) = f\left(\frac{x-4}{3}\right) = 3\left(\frac{x-4}{3}\right) + 4 = (x - 4) + 4 = x$$

Ⓑ $f(x) = 2x - 2$

Replace $f(x)$ with y. $\quad y = 2x - 2$

Solve for x. $\quad y + 2 = 2x$

$$\frac{y+2}{2} = x$$

Switch x and y. $\quad y = \frac{x+2}{2}$

Replace y with $f^{-1}(x)$. $\quad f^{-1}(x) = \frac{x+2}{2}$

Check: Verify that $f^{-1}(f(x)) = x$ and $f(f^{-1}(x)) = x$.

$$f^{-1}(f(x)) = f^{-1}(2x - 2) = \frac{(2x-2)+2}{2} = \frac{2x}{2} = x$$

$$f(f^{-1}(x)) = f\left(\frac{x+2}{2}\right) = 2\left(\frac{x+2}{2}\right) - 2 = (x + 2) - 2 = x$$

COLLABORATIVE LEARNING

Small Group Activity

Have students work in small groups. Have each group create a poster illustrating how inverse functions undo each other. Have them choose a function, and design an illustration that shows how the input and output values of the function and its inverse are related. Have groups share their posters with the class.

Reflect

3. What is the significance of the point where the graph of a linear function and its inverse intersect?
The lines intersect on the line $y = x$, which is where the value of the function and its inverse are the same.

4. The graph of a constant function $f(x) = c$ for any constant c is a horizontal line through the point $(0, c)$. Does a constant function have an inverse? Does it have an inverse function? Explain.
A constant function has an inverse, but not an inverse function. Its inverse is the vertical line through $(c, 0)$. But because a constant function assigns every input to the same output, it is a many-to-one function, and its inverse is not a function.

Your Turn

Find the inverse function $f^{-1}(x)$ for the given function $f(x)$. Use composition to verify that the functions are inverses. Then graph the function and its inverse.

5. $f(x) = -2x + 3$ **Replace f(x) with y, then solve for x.**

$$f(x) = -2x + 3$$

$$y = -2x + 3$$

$$\frac{-y+3}{2} = x$$

Switch x and y, then replace y with $f^{-1}(x)$.

$$\frac{-x+3}{2} = y \qquad f^{-1}(x) = \frac{-x+3}{2}$$

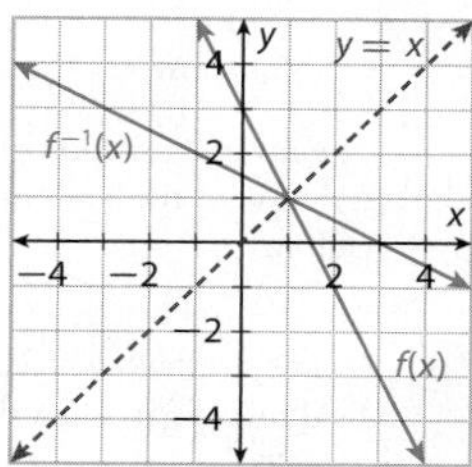

Explain 2 Modeling with the Inverse of a Linear Function

In a model for a real-world situation, the variables have specific real-world meanings. For example, the distance d (in miles) traveled in time t (in hours) at a constant speed of 60 miles per hour is $d = 60t$. Writing this in function notation as $d(t) = 60t$ emphasizes that this equation describes distance as a function of time.

You can find the inverse function for $d = 60t$ by solving for the independent variable t in terms of the dependent variable d. This gives the equation $t = \frac{d}{60}$. Writing this in function notation as $t(d) = \frac{d}{60}$ emphasizes that this equation describes time as a function of distance. Because the meanings of the variables can't be interchanged, you do not switch them at the end as you would switch x and y when working with purely mathematical functions. As you work with real-world models, you may have to restrict the domain and range.

EXPLAIN 2

Modeling with the Inverse of a Linear Function

INTEGRATE MATHEMATICAL PRACTICES

Focus on Math Connections

MP.1 Inverses may also be thought of as a pair of relations that switch the role of the dependent and independent variables. The dependent variable becomes the independent variable, and vice versa.

QUESTIONING STRATEGIES

How can you use the graph of a linear function that models a real-world situation to write the rule for the inverse of the function? **You can reflect the graph across the line $y = x$, identify the slope and the y-intercept of the image, and substitute into the equation $f(x) = mx + b$.**

INTEGRATE TECHNOLOGY

Students can use the table feature on a graphing calculator to observe that if (x, y) is a point on the graph of the original function, (y, x) is a point on the graph of the inverse function.

DIFFERENTIATE INSTRUCTION

Visual Cues

Visual learners may benefit from folding their papers over the line $y = x$. This will enable them to see that $f(x)$ and $f^{-1}(x)$ are reflections of each other over that line.

CONNECT VOCABULARY EL

Have students explain whether a function will have an inverse function or not from input/output tables and from graphs. Provide some terms and sentence stems that they can use to explain their reasoning, such as: "I know this function *(will/will not)* have an inverse because *(it is a one-to-one; it is a many to one; there is one x value for every y value*, etc.)." They should write their explanations using the terms and sentence stems, and then read their explanations aloud.

Example 2 **For the given function, state the domain of the inverse function using set notation. Then find an equation for the inverse function, and graph it. Interpret the meaning of the inverse function.**

(A) The equation $C = 3.5g$ gives the cost C (in dollars) as a function of the number of gallons of gasoline g when the price is $3.50 per gallon.

The domain of the function $C = 3.5g$ is restricted to nonnegative numbers to make real-world sense, so the range of the function also consists of non negative numbers. This means that the domain of the inverse function is $\{C \mid C \geq 0\}$

Solve the given equation for g to find the inverse function.

Write the equation. $C = 3.5g$

Divide both sides by 3.5. $\frac{C}{3.5} = g$

So, the inverse function is $g = \frac{C}{3.5}$.

Graph the inverse function.

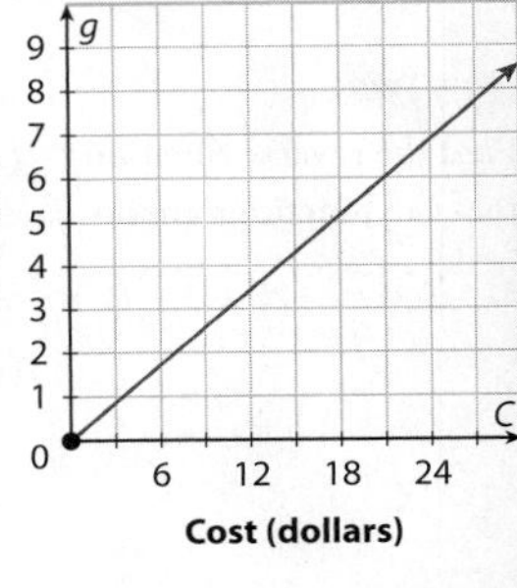

The inverse function gives the number of gallons of gasoline as a function of the cost (in dollars) when the price of gas is $3.50 per gallon.

(B) A car's gas tank, which can hold 14 gallons of gas, contains 4 gallons of gas when the driver stops at a gas station to fill the tank. The gas pump dispenses gas at a rate of 5 gallons per minute. The equation $g = 5t + 4$ gives the number of gallons of gasoline g in the tank as a function of the pumping time t(in minutes).

The range of the function $g = 5t + 4$ is the number of gallons of gas in the tank, which varies from 4 gallons to 4 gallons. So, the domain of the inverse function is $\{g \mid 4 \leq g \leq 14\}$.

Solve the given equation for g to find the inverse function.

Write the equation. $g = 5t + 4$

Simplify. $\frac{g - 4}{5} = t$

So, the inverse function is $t = \frac{g - 4}{5}$.

Graph the inverse function.

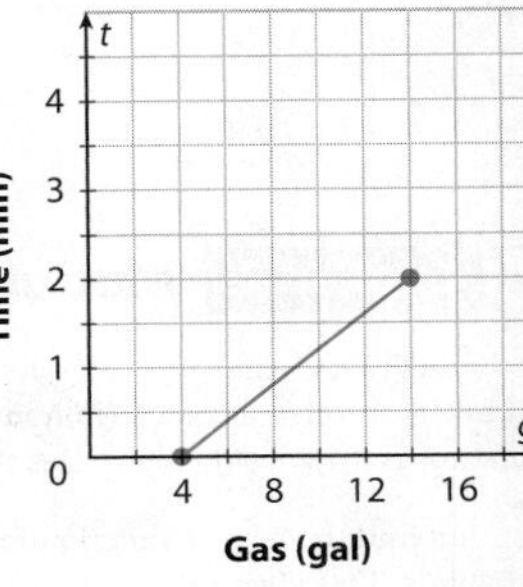

The inverse function gives the pumping time (in minutes) as a function of the amount of gas in the tank (in gallons).

LANGUAGE SUPPORT EL

Communicate Math

Have students work in pairs. Instruct one student to choose a graph of a function and ask the partner to sketch what the inverse of the graph would look like. Once the partner completes the sketch, the first student asks, "How do you know?" They then switch roles and repeat the process with a different graph. Encourage the pairs to use terms such as *reflection, inverse, function,* $y = x$.

Your Turn

For the given function, determine the domain of the inverse function. Then find an equation for the inverse function, and graph it. Interpret the meaning of the inverse function.

6. A municipal swimming pool containing 600,000 gallons of water is drained. The amount of water w (in thousands of gallons) remaining in the pool at time t (in hours) after the draining begins is $w = 600 - 2t$.

The range of $w = 600 - 20t$ is $\{w \mid 0 \le w \le 600\}$. This is the domain of the inverse function. Solve the given equation for t to find the inverse function.

$$w = 600 - 20t$$

$$\frac{w - 600}{-20} = t$$

$$-\frac{1}{20}w + 30 = t$$

The inverse function gives the time (in hours) the pool has been draining as a function of the amount of water (in thousands of gallons) remaining in the pool.

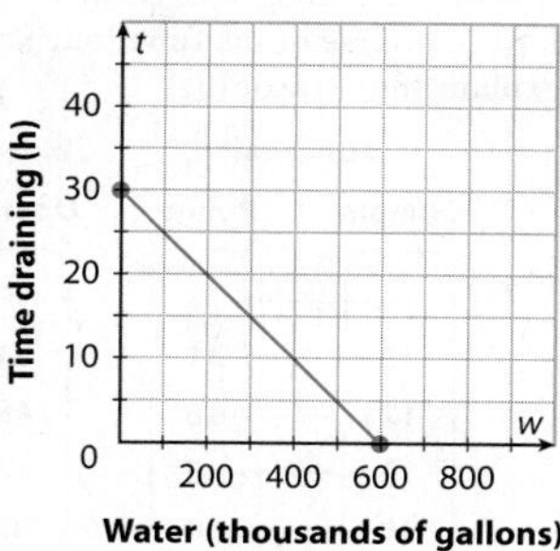

Elaborate

7. What must be true about a function for its inverse to be a function?

The function must be one-to-one.

8. A function rule indicates the operations to perform on an input to produce an output. What is the relationship between these operations and the operations indicated by the inverse function?

The inverse function undoes the operations of the original function. It performs the inverse operation of each original operation, and in the reverse order.

9. How can you use composition to verify that two functions $f(x)$ and $g(x)$ are inverse functions?

Find $f(g(x))$ and $g(f(x))$. If $f(g(x)) = x$ and $g(f(x)) = x$, then $f(x)$ and $g(x)$ are inverse functions.

10. Describe a real-world situation modeled by a linear function for which it makes sense to find an inverse function. Give an example of how the inverse function might also be useful.

Sample answer: Grapes are $1.80 per pound at the grocery store. The equation $C = 1.8w$ gives the cost C (in dollars) for grapes with a weight w (in pounds). The inverse function is $w = \frac{C}{1.8}$. It gives the weight of the grapes purchased as a function of their cost. You could use the inverse, for example, to find what weight of grapes you could buy for $5.

11. Essential Question Check-In What is an inverse relation?

It is a relation that reverses all the pairings of some other relation. If a relation pairs an input x with an output y, then the inverse relation pairs an input y with an output x.

ELABORATE

PEER-TO-PEER DISCUSSION

Ask students to discuss with a partner what must be true about the graph of a function in order for the inverse to be a function. The graph must pass a horizontal line test. That is, no two points of the graph can lie on the same horizontal line.

QUESTIONING STRATEGIES

If you find the inverse of the inverse of a function, will it necessarily be a function? Explain. Yes. The inverse of the inverse of a function is the original function.

SUMMARIZE THE LESSON

How do you find the inverse of a function, and how is the original function related to its inverse? To find the inverse of a function, replace $f(x)$ with y, solve for x, and then switch x and y. The output of a function is the input of the inverse function. The output of the inverse function is the input of the function. Because the coordinates of the ordered pairs are reversed, the graphs of the function and the inverse function are reflections across the line $y = x$.

EVALUATE

ASSIGNMENT GUIDE

Concepts and Skills	Practice
Explore Understanding Inverses of Functions	Exercises 1–4
Example 1 Finding the Inverse of a Linear Function	Exercises 5–10
Example 2 Modeling with the Inverse of a Linear Function	Exercises 11–12

AVOID COMMON ERRORS

Some students may have difficulty reflecting points in the line $y = x$. For these students, you may want to review the concept of reflection, and encourage them to use tracing paper, to fold paper, or to use a reflecting tool to correctly draw the reflection.

QUESTIONING STRATEGIES

? When finding the inverse of a function, why do you need to switch x and y after solving the equation for x? because the y-values of the original function become the x-values in the inverse, and vice-versa

Evaluate: Homework and Practice

• Online Homework
• Hints and Help
• Extra Practice

The mapping diagrams show a function and its inverse. Complete the diagram for the inverse of the function. Then tell whether the inverse is a function, and explain your reasoning.

1. 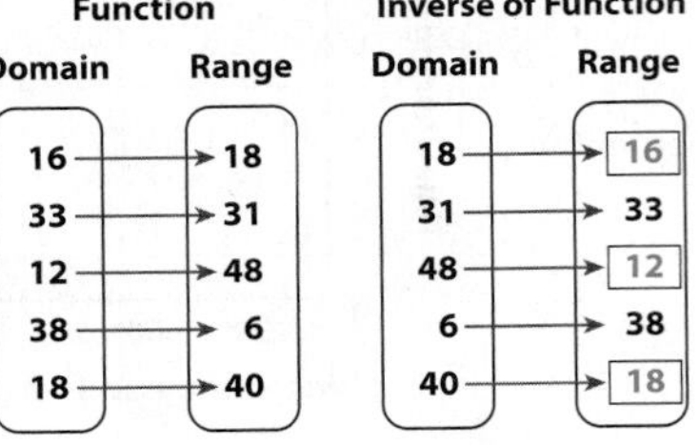

The inverse is a function, because for each input there is only one output.

2. 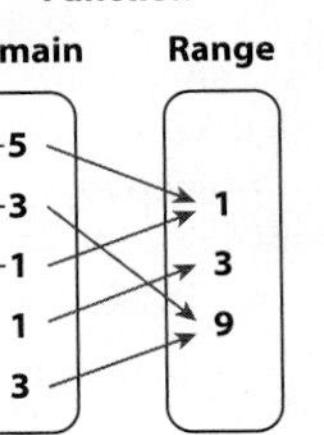

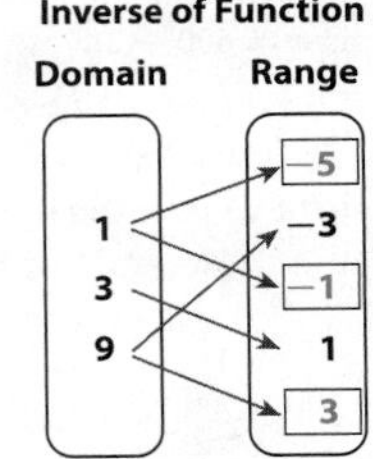

The inverse is not a function, because the inputs 1 and 9 each have two different outputs.

Write the inverse of the given function as a set of ordered pairs and then graph the inverse on the coordinate plane.

3. Function:
$\{(-4, -3), (-2, -4), (0, -2), (1, 0), (2, 3)\}$
Inverse of function:
$\{(-3, -4), (-4, -2), (-2, 0), (0, 1), (3, 2)\}$

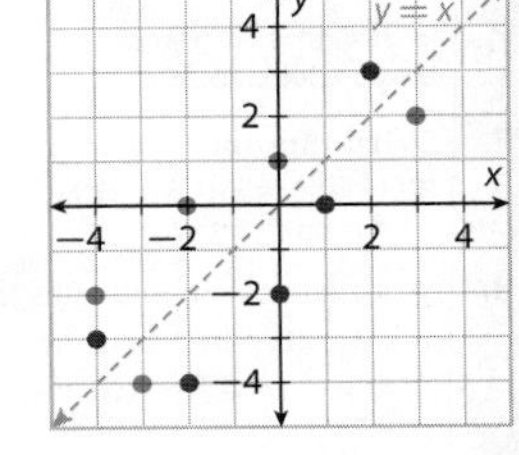

4. Function:
$\{(-3, -4), (-2, -3), (-1, 2), (1, 2), (2, 4), (3, 4)\}$
Inverse of function:
$\{(-4, -3), (-3, -2), (2, -1), (2, 1), (4, 2), (4, 3)\}$

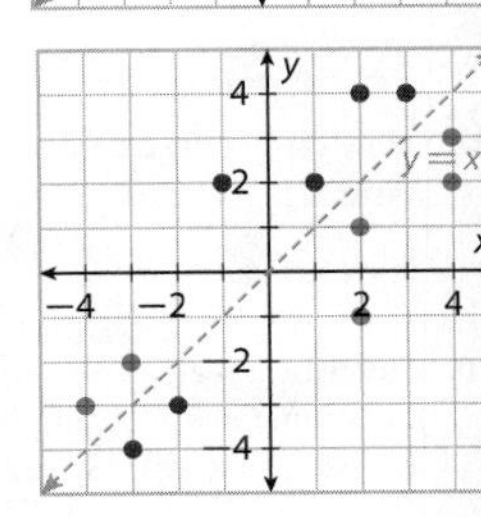

Find the inverse function $f^{-1}(x)$ for the given function $f(x)$.

5. $f(x) = 4x - 8$

Replace $f(x)$ with y, then solve for x.

$$y = 4x - 8$$
$$y + 8 = 4x$$
$$\frac{y + 8}{4} = x$$

Switch x and y, then replace y with $f^{-1}(x)$.

$$f^{-1}(x) = \frac{x + 8}{4}$$

6. $f(x) = \frac{x}{3}$

Replace $f(x)$ with y, then solve for x.

$$y = \frac{x}{3}$$
$$3y = x$$

Switch x and y, then replace y with $f^{-1}(x)$.

$$f^{-1}(x) = 3x$$

Exercise	Depth of Knowledge (D.O.K.)	COMMON CORE Mathematical Practices
1–4	**1** Recall of Information	**MP.2** Reasoning
5–8	**2** Skills/Concepts	**MP.5** Using Tools
9–10	**2** Skills/Concepts	**MP.4** Modeling
11–12	**2** Skills/Concepts	**MP.1** Problem Solving
13–15	**2** Skills/Concepts	**MP.2** Reasoning
16–17	**3** Strategic Thinking H.O.T.	**MP.6** Precision
18	**3** Strategic Thinking H.O.T.	**MP.4** Modeling

7. $f(x) = \frac{x+1}{6}$

Replace $f(x)$ with y, then solve for x.

$$y = \frac{x+1}{6}$$
$$6y = x + 1$$
$$6y - 1 = x$$

Switch x and y, then replace y with $f^{-1}(x)$.

$$f^{-1}(x) = 6x - 1$$

8. $f(x) = -0.75x$

Replace $f(x)$ with y, then solve for x.

$$y = -0.75x$$
$$y = -\frac{3}{4}x$$
$$-\frac{4}{3}y = x$$

Switch x and y, then replace y with $f^{-1}(x)$.

$$f^{-1}(x) = -\frac{4}{3}x$$

Find the inverse function $f^{-1}(x)$ for the given function $f(x)$. Use composition to verify that the functions are inverses. Then graph the function and its inverse.

9. $f(x) = -3x + 3$

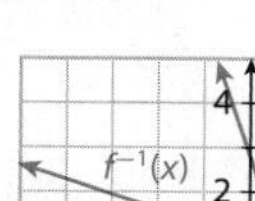
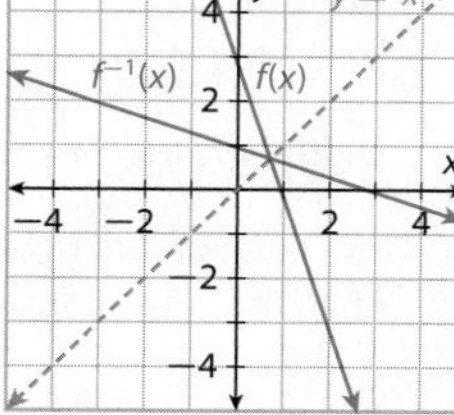

Replace $f(x)$ with y, then solve for x.

$$y = -3x + 3$$
$$y - 3 = -3x$$
$$\frac{y-3}{-3} = x$$
$$-\frac{1}{3}y + 1 = x$$

Switch x and y, then replace y with $f^{-1}(x)$.

$$f^{-1}(x) = -\frac{1}{3}x + 1$$

***Check:* Verify that $f^{-1}(f(x)) = x$ and $f(f^{-1}(x)) = x$.**

$$f^{-1}(f(x)) = f^{-1}(-3x + 3) = -\frac{1}{3}(-3x + 3) + 1 = (x - 1) + 1 = x$$

$$f(f^{-1}(x)) = f\left(-\frac{1}{3}x + 1\right) = -3\left(-\frac{1}{3}x + 1\right) + 3 = (x - 3) + 3 = x$$

10. $f(x) = \frac{2}{5}x - 2$

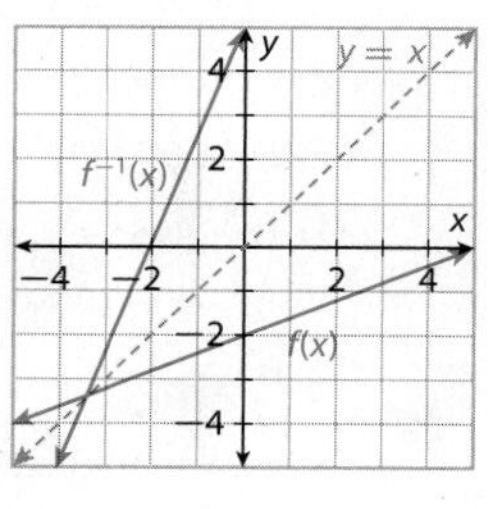

Replace $f(x)$ with y, then solve for x.

$$y = \frac{2}{5}x - 2$$
$$y + 2 = \frac{2}{5}x$$
$$\frac{5}{2}(y + 2) = x$$
$$\frac{5}{2}y + 5 = x$$

Switch x and y, then replace y with $f^{-1}(x)$.

$$f^{-1}(x) = \frac{5}{2}x + 5$$

***Check:* Verify that $f^{-1}(f(x)) = x$ and $f(f^{-1}(x)) = x$.**

$$f^{-1}(f(x)) = f^{-1}\left(\frac{2}{5}x - 2\right) = \frac{5}{2}\left(\frac{2}{5}x - 2\right) + 5 = (x - 5) + 5 = x$$

$$f(f^{-1}(x)) = f\left(\frac{5}{2}x + 5\right) = \frac{2}{5}\left(\frac{5}{2}x + 5\right) - 2 = (x + 2) - 2 = x$$

VISUAL CUES

It may be useful to note that when you are graphing an inverse, the y-intercepts of the original function become the x-intercepts of the inverse and vice-versa. So if you are graphing a line, it is easy to quickly establish the two points necessary to determine the inverse.

COMMUNICATING MATH

Ask students to discuss what is meant by the statement "Inverse functions undo each other." Have them use examples to illustrate their explanations.

For the given function, determine the domain of the inverse function. Then find an equation for the inverse function, and graph it. Interpret the meaning of the inverse function.

11. **Geometry** The equation $A = \frac{1}{2}(20)h$ gives the area A (in square inches) of a triangle with a base of 20 inches as a function of its height h (in inches).

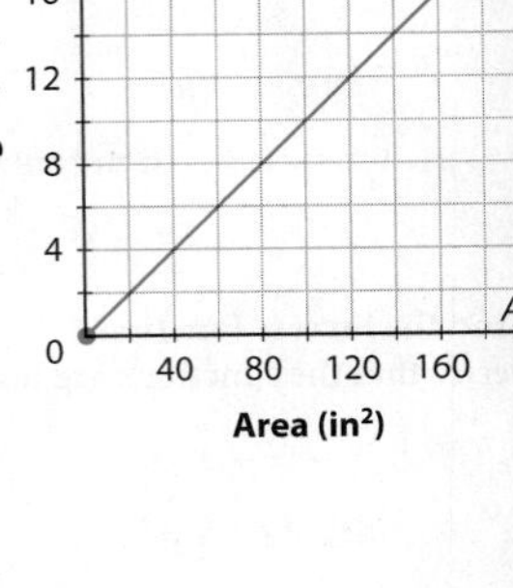

The domain of the function $A = \frac{1}{2}(20)h$ is restricted to nonnegative numbers to make real-world sense, so the range of the function also consists of nonnegative numbers. This means that the domain of the inverse function is $\{A | A \geq 0\}$.

$$A = \frac{1}{2}(20)h$$

$$A = 10h$$

$$\frac{A}{10} = h$$

So, the inverse function is $h = \frac{A}{10}$.

The inverse function gives the height (in inches) of a triangle with a base of 20 inches as a function of the area (in square inches) of the triangle.

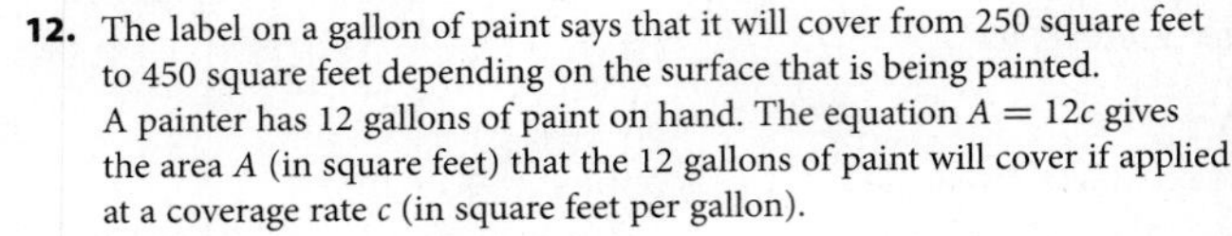

12. The label on a gallon of paint says that it will cover from 250 square feet to 450 square feet depending on the surface that is being painted. A painter has 12 gallons of paint on hand. The equation $A = 12c$ gives the area A (in square feet) that the 12 gallons of paint will cover if applied at a coverage rate c (in square feet per gallon).

The domain for the function $A = 12c$ is $\{c | 250 \leq c \leq 450\}$. The range for the function varies from a minimum area of $12(250) = 3000$ square feet to a maximum area of $12(450) = 5400$ square feet, so the domain of the inverse function is $\{A | 3000 \leq A \leq 5400\}$.

Solve the given equation for c to find the inverse function.

$$A = 12c$$

$$\frac{A}{12} = c$$

So, the inverse function is $c = \frac{A}{12}$.

The inverse function gives the coverage rate (in square feet per gallon) at which 12 gallons of paint must be applied as a function of the area covered (in square feet).

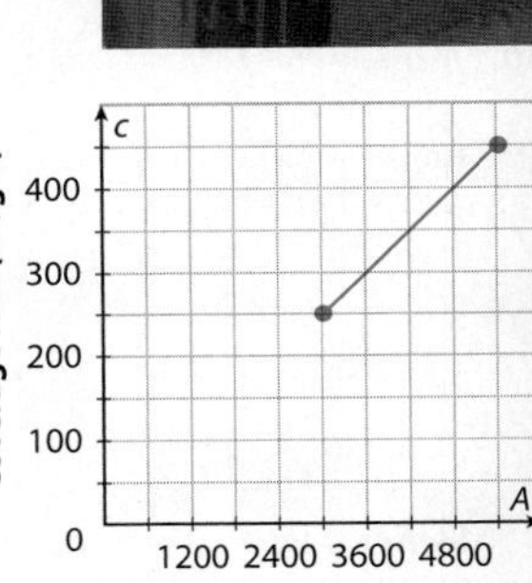

The graph of a function is given. Tell whether the function's inverse is a function, and explain your reasoning. If the inverse is not a function, tell how can you restrict the domain of the function so that its inverse is a function.

13.

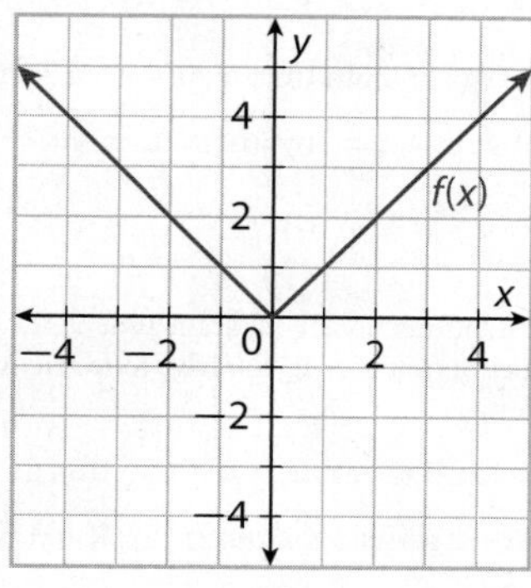

The function's inverse is not a function, because the function is many-to-one. If the domain is restricted to $\{x|x \leq 0\}$, $\{x|x \geq 0\}$, or some subset of these sets, the function becomes one-to-one, and the inverse is a function.

14.

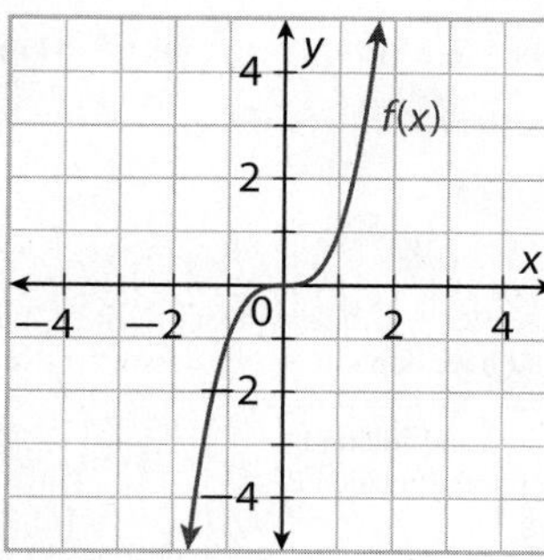

The function's inverse is a function, because the function is one-to-one.

15. Multiple Response Identify the domain intervals over which the inverse of the graphed function is also a function. Select all that apply.

A. $[4, +\infty)$ D. $(-\infty, +\infty)$ G. $(4, 8)$

B. $(0, +\infty)$ E. $(-\infty, 4]$ H. $(8, +\infty)$

C. $[-4, +\infty)$ F. $(-\infty, 4)$ I. $(0, 8]$

The solutions are any intervals in the domain of the function for which each range value is paired with only one domain value. So, the correct choices are A, B, F, and G.

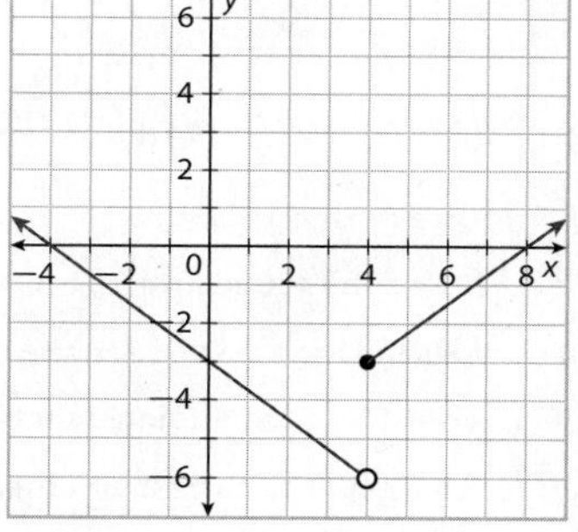

INTEGRATE MATHEMATICAL PRACTICES

Focus on Reasoning

MP.2 Students should compare the function and the inverse function that they write for each real-world situation, verifying that the two rules utilize inverse operations. Students should check to ensure that when the inverse function is evaluated for a particular value, the result is the input associated with that value from the original function.

JOURNAL

Have students describe a real-world situation in which it would be useful to find an inverse in order to answer a question.

H.O.T. Focus on Higher Order Thinking

16. **Draw Conclusions** Identify all linear functions that are their own inverse.

The line $y = x$ is its own inverse. Also, any line that is perpendicular to the line $y = x$ is its own inverse, since it will be its own reflection across that line. So, any linear function of the form $y = -x + b$ where b is a real number is its own inverse.

17. **Make a Conjecture** Among linear functions (excluding constant functions), quadratic functions, absolute value functions, and exponential functions, which types of function do you have to restrict the domain for the inverse to be a function? Explain.

You have to restrict the domains of quadratic functions and absolute value functions, because these functions are many-to-one functions. For instance, the quadratic function $f(x) = x^2$ pairs both -2 and 2 with 4, and the absolute value function $f(x) = |x|$ pairs both -2 and 2 with 2. On the other hand, linear functions (excluding constant functions) and exponential functions are one-to-one functions, so their domains do not need to be restricted.

18. **Find the Error** A student was asked to find the inverse of $f(x) = 2x + 1$. The student's work is shown. Explain why the student is incorrect and what the student should have done to get the correct answer.

> The function $f(x) = 2x + 1$ involves two operations: multiplying by 2 and adding 1. The inverse operations are dividing by 2 and subtracting 1. So, the inverse function is $f^{-1}(x) = \frac{x}{2} - 1$.

Composing the original function and what the student thinks is the inverse gives this result:

$$f^{-1}\left(f(x)\right) = \frac{2x+1}{2} - 1 = \left(x + \frac{1}{2}\right) - 1 = x - \frac{1}{2}$$

$$f\left(f^{-1}(x)\right) = 2\left(\frac{x}{2} - 1\right) + 1 = (x - 2) + 1 = x - 1$$

Since $f^{-1}\left(f(x)\right) \neq x$ and $f\left(f^{-1}(x)\right) \neq x$, the student's function is not the inverse function. To find the actual inverse function, the student should have recognized that not only does the inverse function use the inverse operations but also applies them in the reverse order. Since the original function multiplies by 2 first and then adds 1, the inverse function should subtract 1 first and then divide by 2. So, the inverse function is $f^{-1}(x) = \frac{x-1}{2}$, or $f^{-1}(x) = \frac{1}{2}x - \frac{1}{2}$.

Lesson Performance Task

In an anatomy class, a student measures the femur of an adult male and finds the length of the femur to be 50.0 cm. The student is then asked to estimate the height of the male that the femur came from.

The table shows the femur lengths and heights of some adult males and females. Using a graphing calculator, perform linear regression on the data to obtain femur length as a function of height (one function for adult males, one for adult females). Then find the inverse of each function. Use the appropriate inverse function to find the height of the adult male and explain how the inverse functions would be helpful to a forensic scientist.

Femur Length (cm)	30	38	46	54	62
Male Height (cm)	138	153	168	183	198
Female Height (cm)	132	147	163	179	194

A graphing calculator gives the regression equation for an adult male as $f = 0.533h_m - 43.6$ where h_m is male height (in centimeters) and f is femur length (in centimeters).

Find the inverse function.

$$f + 43.6 = 0.533h_m$$

$$\frac{f + 43.6}{0.533} = h_m$$

So, the inverse function is $h_m = \frac{f + 43.6}{0.533}$.

A graphing calculator gives the regression equation for an adult female as $f = 0.513h_f - 37.6$ where h_f is female height (in centimeters) and f is femur length (in centimeters).

Find the inverse function.

$$f + 37.6 = 0.513h_f$$

$$\frac{f + 37.6}{0.513} = h_f$$

So, the inverse function is $h_f = \frac{f + 37.6}{0.513}$.

Evaluate the inverse function for an adult male when $f = 50.0$.

$$h_m = \frac{50.0 + 43.6}{0.533} = \frac{93.6}{0.533} \approx 175.6$$

So, the male's height should be approximately 176 cm.

There are several ways this technique could be helpful to a forensic scientist. A forensic scientist could estimate the height of the individual and that would eliminate a portion of the missing persons files that need to be considered.

EXTENSION ACTIVITY

Have students measure the femur lengths (cm) and heights (cm) of 5 male students and record the data in a table. Then have students answer the questions in the Performance Task using their data instead of the data given. Have students explain how their results are similar or different from those found in the Performance Task, and also to note the reasons why the measurements cannot be as accurate. Discuss how technology such as an x-ray, CT scan, or MRI, could be used to improve accuracy.

CONNECT VOCABULARY EL

Some students may not be familiar with the term *femur* mentioned in this problem. Show students a diagram of a human skeleton. Explain that the femur is the only bone in the thigh and it is the longest, heaviest, and strongest bone in the human body.

INTEGRATE MATHEMATICAL PRACTICES

Focus on Critical Thinking

MP.3 Discuss with students whether or not this data set is suitable for representation by a linear regression model. Ask them to tell how they might go about determining the best type of regression model to use for this particular set of data.

AVOID COMMON ERRORS

Students may not divide the entire expression $f + 43.6$ by 0.533. Have students tell the order of the operations in the function (multiply, then subtract) and then tell the reverse of these operations (add, then divide). Since $f + 43.6$ cannot be simplified before dividing, have students put parentheses around the expression before dividing by 0.533: $h_m \frac{(f + 43.6)}{0.533}$.

Scoring Rubric

2 points: Student correctly solves the problem and explains his/her reasoning.

1 point: Student shows good understanding of the problem but does not fully solve or explain his/her reasoning.

0 points: Student does not demonstrate understanding of the problem.

Study Guide Review

ASSESSMENT AND INTERVENTION

Assign or customize module reviews.

MODULE PERFORMANCE TASK

COMMON CORE

Mathematical Practices: MP.1, MP.4, MP.6

SUPPORTING STUDENT REASONING

Students should begin this problem by graphing the two functions. Here are some issues they might bring up.

- **Does the graph represent the motion of the jumper in space?** Although the motion of a person vaulting over a pole can be modeled as projectile motion, which follows a parabolic path, in this case the parabola represents the height versus the time in the air, not the two-dimensional motion of the jumper.
- **Should all four quadrants be used for the graphs?** Ask students what each quadrant would mean in terms of the problem situation. Lead them to realize that only the first quadrant makes sense.

STUDY GUIDE REVIEW

Analyzing Functions

MODULE 1

Essential Question: How can you analyze functions to solve real-world problems?

Key Vocabulary
finite interval *(intervalo finito)*
infinite interval *(intervalo infinito)*
domain *(dominio)*
range *(rango)*
end behavior *(comportamiento final)*

KEY EXAMPLE *(Lesson 1.1)*

Write the domain and range of $f(x) = 3^x$ as an inequality, using set notation, and using interval notation. Then describe the end behavior of the function.

	Domain	Range
Inequality	$-\infty < x < +\infty$	$y > 0$
Set notation	$\{x \mid -\infty < x < +\infty\}$	$y \mid y > 0$
Interval notation	$(-\infty, +\infty)$	$(0, +\infty)$

End behavior: As $x \to +\infty$, $f(x) \to +\infty$, and as $x \to -\infty$, $f(x) \to 0$.

y
4
2
x
−4 −2 0 2 4
−2
−4

KEY EXAMPLE *(Lesson 1.3)*

Describe how to transform the graph of $f(x) = x^2$ to obtain the graph of the related function $g(x) = 2f(x - 1) + 3$.

Parameter	Effect on the Parent Graph
$a = 2$	vertical stretch of the graph of $f(x)$ by a factor of 2
$h = 1$	translation of the graph of $f(x)$ to the right 1 unit
$k = 3$	translation of the graph of $f(x)$ up 3 units

A point (x, y) on the graph of $f(x) = x^2$ becomes the point $(x + 1, 2y + 3)$.

KEY EXAMPLE *(Lesson 1.4)*

Find the inverse function $f^{-1}(x)$ for $f(x) = -2x + 3$.

$y = -2x + 3$ — Replace $f(x)$ with y.

$\frac{y-3}{-2} = x$ — Solve for x.

$y = \frac{x-3}{-2}$ — Switch x and y.

$f^{-1}(x) = \frac{x-3}{-2}$ — Replace y with $f^{-1}(x)$.

SCAFFOLDING SUPPORT

- Students should recognize that the horizontal axis is the time, so the non-zero x-intercept represents the time of flight.
- Students should understand that the maximum of the parabola corresponds to the maximum height of the jump.

EXERCISES

Write the domain and range of the function as an inequality, using set notation, and using interval notation. *(Lesson 1.1)*

1. 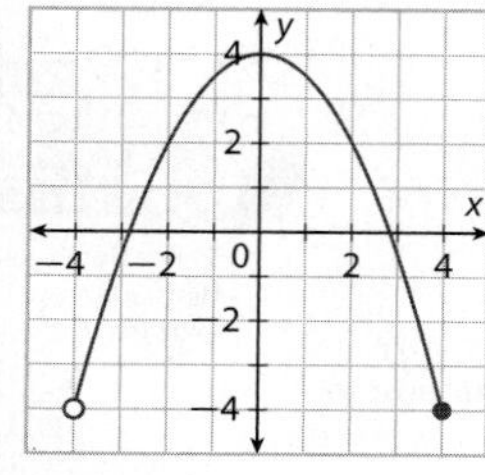

Domain:

Inequality: $-4 < x \leq 4$

Set notation: $\{x \mid -4 < x \leq 4\}$

Interval notation: $(-4, 4]$

Range:

Inequality: $-4 \leq y \leq 4$

Set Notation: $\{y \mid -4 \leq y \leq 4\}$

Interval Notation: $[-4, 4]$

2. 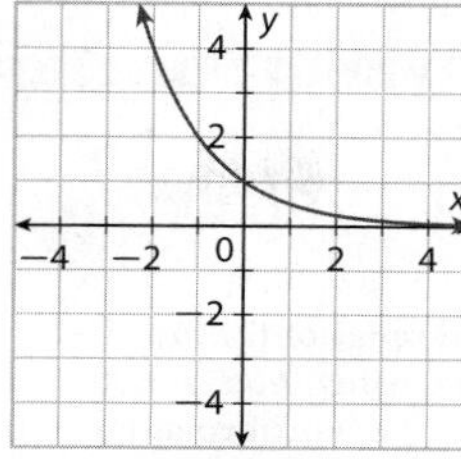

Domain:

Inequality: $-\infty < x < +\infty$

Set notation: $\{x \mid -\infty < x < +\infty\}$

Interval notation: $(-\infty, \infty)$

Range:

Inequality: $0 < y < \infty$

Set Notation: $\{y \mid 0 < y < \infty\}$

Interval Notation: $(0, \infty)$

Find the inverse function $f^{-1}(x)$ for the given function $f(x)$. *(Lesson 1.4)*

3. $f(x) = \frac{x+3}{5}$ $f^{-1}(x) = 5x - 3$

4. $f(x) = 2x + 6$ $f^{-1}(x) = \frac{x}{2} - 3$

5. Explain how to transform the graph of the function $f(x) = x^2$ to obtain the graph of the related function $g(x) = -2f(x + 1) - 3$. *(Lesson 1.3)*
Because the a value is -2, the graph is stretched by a factor of 2 and reflected across the x-axis. Because the h value is -1, the graph of $g(x)$ is translated 1 unit to the left of $f(x)$. Since the k value is -3, $g(x)$ is translated three units down from $f(x)$.

MODULE PERFORMANCE TASK

How High Does a Pole-Vaulter Go?

A pole-vaulter performs two vaults, which can be modeled using the functions $h_1(t) = 9.8t - 4.9t^2$ and $h_2(t) = 8.82t - 4.9t^2$ where h is the height in meters at time t in seconds. How do the two jumps compare graphically in terms of the vertexes and intercepts, and what do these represent? Which was the higher jump? How do you know?

Use your own paper to complete the task. Be sure to write down all your data and assumptions. Then use graphs, numbers, words, or algebra to explain how you reached your conclusions.

DISCUSSION OPPORTUNITIES

- How can you tell whose jump was higher by looking at the graph, table, or numbers?
- How can you tell whose jump went farther by looking at the graph, table, or numbers?

SAMPLE SOLUTION

Steps:

Graph both equations on the same coordinate grid, using the first quadrant only. Label the graphs to make them easier to recognize.

Compare the non-zero x-intercepts of the two graphs, which show the time the jumper was in the air. The longer the time of flight, the higher the jump.

Compare the vertices of the two graphs. These represent the maximum heights of the two jumps and the times at which they happened.

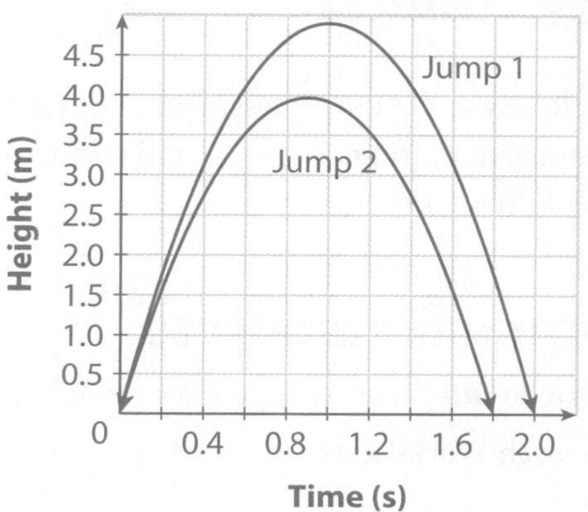

The first jump was the higher jump because the maximum height is greater; this can be seen from the graph.

Assessment Rubric

2 points: Student correctly solves the problem and explains his/her reasoning.

1 point: Student shows good understanding of the problem but does not fully solve or explain.

0 points: Student does not demonstrate understanding of the problem.

Ready to Go On?

ASSESS MASTERY

Use the assessment on this page to determine if students have mastered the concepts and standards covered in this module.

ASSESSMENT AND INTERVENTION

Access Ready to Go On? assessment online, and receive instant scoring, feedback, and customized intervention or enrichment.

ADDITIONAL RESOURCES

Response to Intervention Resources

- Reteach Worksheets

Differentiated Instruction Resources

- Reading Strategies EL
- Success for English Learners EL
- Challenge Worksheets

Assessment Resources

- Leveled Module Quizzes

1.1–1.4 Analyzing Functions

- Online Homework
- Hints and Help
- Extra Practice

Write the domain and range of the function $g(x) = 3x^2 - 4$ as an inequality, using set notation, and using interval notation. Then, compare the function to $f(x) = x^2$ and describe the transformations. *(Lessons 1.1, 1.3)*

1.	Domain	Range	Transformations
Inequality	$-\infty < x < +\infty$	$y \geq -4$	When compared to $f(x)$, $g(x)$ is stretched vertically by a factor of 3 and translated down 4 units.
Set notation	$\{x \mid -\infty < x < +\infty\}$	$\{y \mid y \geq -4\}$	
Interval notation	$(-\infty, +\infty)$	$[-4, +\infty)$	

Find the inverse for each linear function. *(Lesson 1.4)*

2. $f(x) = -2x + 4$

$f^{-1}(x) = \frac{x-4}{-2}$

3. $g(x) = \frac{x}{4} - 3$

$g^{-1}(x) = 4(x+3) = 4x + 12$

4. $h(x) = \frac{3}{4}x + 1$

$h^{-1}(x) = \frac{4}{3}(x-1) = \frac{4x-4}{3}$

5. $j(x) = 5x - 6$

$j^{-1}(x) = \frac{x+6}{5}$

ESSENTIAL QUESTION

6. What are two ways the graphed function could be used to solve real-world problems? *(Lesson 1.2)*

Possible Answers: The function could be used to show when the profit is rising or falling. The function could be used to find the profit at a certain year. The function could be used to find intervals of gain or loss in profit.

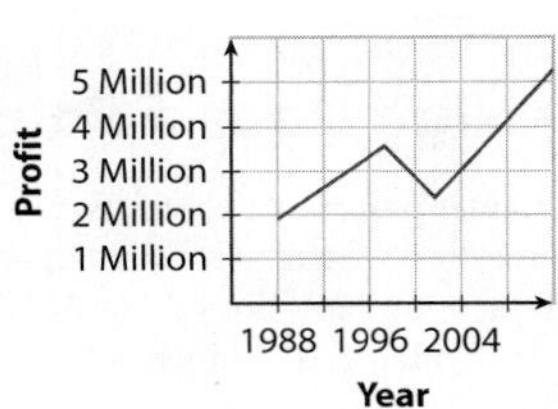

COMMON CORE Common Core Standards

Lesson	Items	Content Standards	Mathematical Practices
1.1, 1.3	1	**F-IF.B.5, A-CED.A.3**	**MP.6**
1.4	2	**F-IF.B.5, A-CED.A.2**	**MP.1**
1.4	3	**F-IF.B.5, A-CED.A.2**	**MP.1**
1.4	4	**F-IF.B.5, A-CED.A.2**	**MP.1**
1.4	5	**F-IF.B.5, A-CED.A.2**	**MP.1**

Assessment Readiness

1. Look at each equation. Does the graph of the equation have an end behavior that approaches infinity (∞) as $x \rightarrow -\infty$?
Select Yes or No for A–C.
   - **A.** $y = -2x - 5$ — ● Yes ○ No
   - **B.** $y = 5(x + 2)^2 - 3$ — ● Yes ○ No
   - **C.** $y = -3^x$ — ○ Yes ● No

2. Consider the linear equation $g(x) = -f(x + 3) - 2$. Choose True or False for each statement.
   - **A.** When compared to $f(x) = x^2$, $g(x)$ will have a vertical stretch of 3. — ○ True ● False
   - **B.** When compared to $f(x) = x^2$, $g(x)$ will be reflected over the x-axis. — ● True ○ False
   - **C.** When compared to $f(x) = x^2$, $g(x)$ will be translated left 3 units, and down 2 units. — ● True ○ False

3. A bike rider starts at a fast pace and rides 40 miles in 2 hours. He gets tired, and slows down, traveling only 20 miles in the next 3 hours. He takes a rest for an hour, then rides back to where he started at a steady pace without stopping for 4 hours. Draw a graph to match the real world situation. Explain your choices.

The slope from $x = 0$ to $x = 2$ is steeper than the slope from $x = 2$ to $x = 5$, because the bike rider was moving faster. He stopped for an hour, so the section from $x = 5$ to $x = 6$ is horizontal. For the ride home, the biker had no stops or changes in speed, so that line is straight.

4. The function to convert Fahrenheit to Celsius is $°C = f(°F) = \frac{5(°F - 32)}{9}$. The inverse function will convert Celsius to Fahrenheit. What is the inverse function? Explain how determining this inverse is different than determining the previous inverses.

$°F = f^{-1}(°C) = \frac{9(°C)}{5} + 32$; Possible Answer: The °F and °C do not need to be switched like the x and y did in the previous functions. They are both degree measures, and because of the real-world relationship, switching them wouldn't make sense.

Common Core Standards

Lesson	Items	Content Standards	Mathematical Practices
1.1	1	**F-IF.B.5**	**MP.7**
1.3	2	**F-IF.B.3**	**MP.7**
1.2	3	**F-IF.B.4**	**MP.4**
1.4	4	**F-BF.B.4**	**MP.2**

* Item integrates mixed review concepts from previous modules or a previous course.

MIXED REVIEW

Assessment Readiness

ASSESSMENT AND INTERVENTION

Assign ready-made or customized practice tests to prepare students for high-stakes tests.

ADDITIONAL RESOURCES

Assessment Resources

- Leveled Module Quizzes: Modified, B

AVOID COMMON ERRORS

Item 3 Some students will not consider each period of time as an addition to the previously mentioned time but will instead attempt to compact the graph into a total of four hours. Encourage students to read the question carefully, noting that each new time is for a new section and does not include the section already completed.

Absolute Value Functions, Equations, and Inequalities

ESSENTIAL QUESTION:

Answer: Understanding absolute value functions can help you solve real-world comparison and distance problems.

PROFESSIONAL DEVELOPMENT VIDEO

Professional Development Video
Author Matt Larson models successful teaching practices in an actual high-school classroom.
Professional Development
my.hrw.com

MODULE 2

Absolute Value Functions, Equations, and Inequalities

Essential Question: How can you use absolute value functions to solve real-world problems?

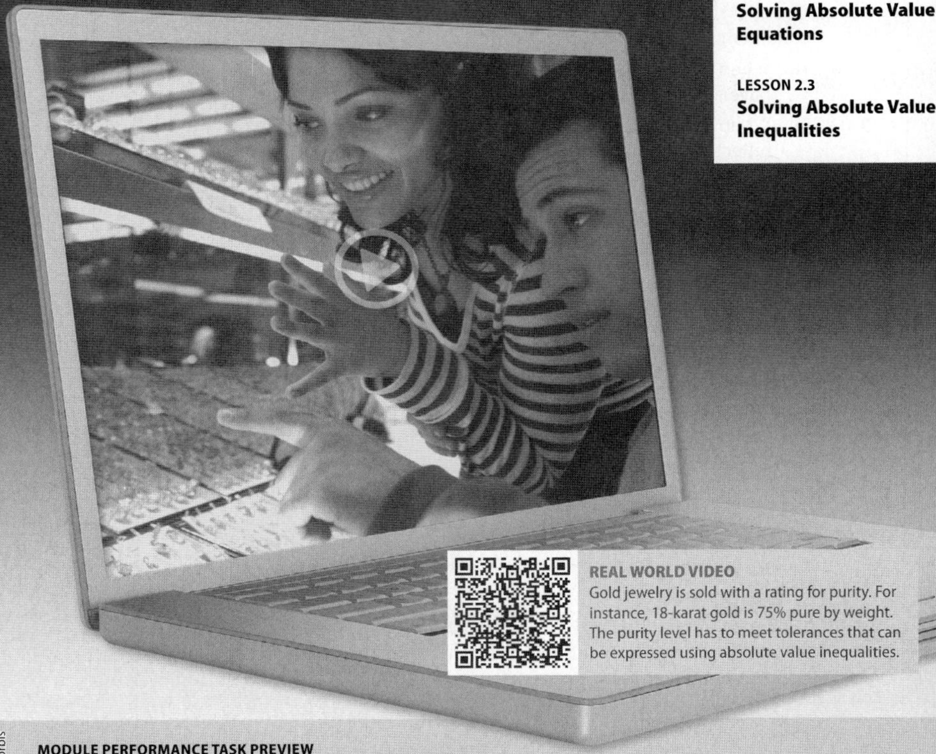

REAL WORLD VIDEO
Gold jewelry is sold with a rating for purity. For instance, 18-karat gold is 75% pure by weight. The purity level has to meet tolerances that can be expressed using absolute value inequalities.

MODULE PERFORMANCE TASK PREVIEW

What Is the Purity of Gold?

Because gold is such a soft metal, it is usually mixed with another metal such as copper or silver. Pure gold is 24 karat, and 18 karat indicates a mixture of 18 parts gold and 6 parts of another metal or metals. Imagine someone wants to sell you a ring and claims it is 18 karat. How can you use math to be sure the gold is indeed 18 karat? Let's find out!

Module 2 63

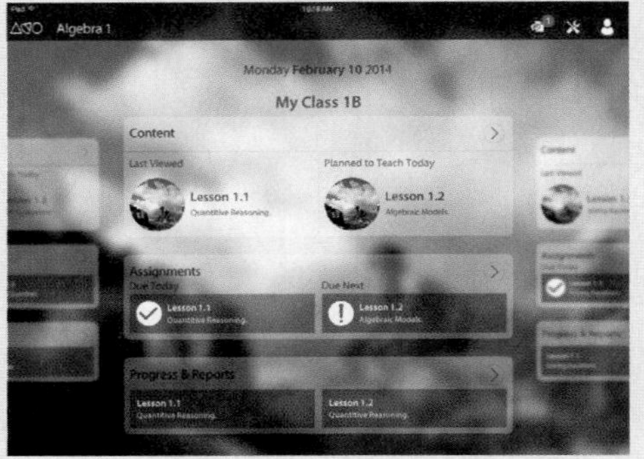

DIGITAL TEACHER EDITION

Access a full suite of teaching resources when and where you need them:

- Access content online or offline
- Customize lessons to share with your class
- Communicate with your students in real-time
- View student grades and data instantly to target your instruction where it is needed most

PERSONAL MATH TRAINER

Assessment and Intervention

Assign automatically graded homework, quizzes, tests, and intervention activities. Prepare your students with updated, Common Core-aligned practice tests.

Are YOU Ready?

Complete these exercises to review skills you will need for this chapter.

- Online Homework
- Hints and Help
- Extra Practice

One-Step Equations

Example 1 Solve $x - 6.8 = 2$ for x.

$x - 6.8 + 6.8 = 2 + 6.8$ Add.

$x = 8.8$ Combine like terms.

Solve each equation.

1. $r + 9 = 7$ **−2**

2. $\frac{w}{4} = -3$ **−12**

3. $10b = 14$ **1.4**

Slope and Slope-Intercept Form

Example 2 Find the slope and y-intercept of $3x - y = 24$.

$-3x + 3x - y = -3x + 6$ Write the equation in $y = mx + b$ form.

$-y(-1) = (-3x + 6)(-1)$

$y = 3x - 6$ The slope is 3 and the y-intercept is −6.

Find the slope and y-intercept for each equation.

4. $y - 8 = 2x + 9$ **slope: 2; y-intercept: 17**

5. $3y = 2(x - 3)$ **slope: $\frac{2}{3}$; y-intercept: −2**

6. $2y + 8x = 1$ **slope: −4; y-intercept: 0.5**

Linear Inequalities in Two Variables

Example 3 Graph $y < 2x - 3$.

Graph the y-intercept of $(0, -3)$.

Use the slope of 2 to plot a second point, and draw a line connecting the points.

Shade below the line.

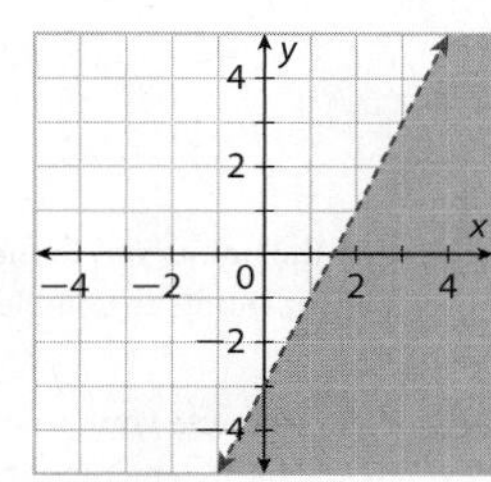

Graph and label each inequality on the coordinate plane.

7. $y \geq -x + 2$

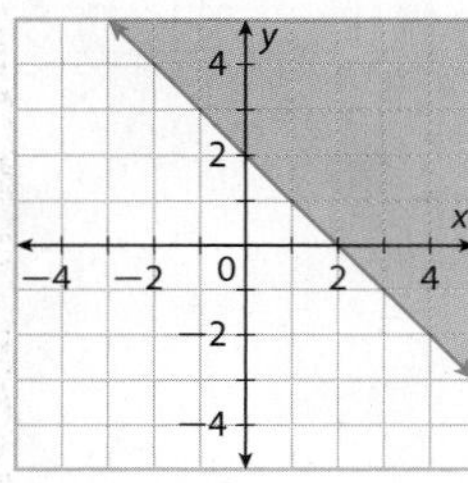

8. $y < x - 1$

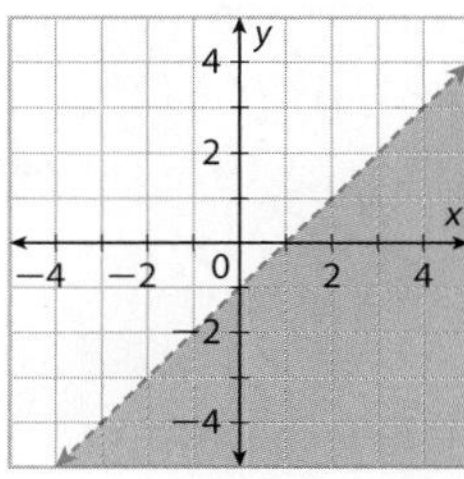

Response to Intervention			Differentiated Instruction
Tier 1 Lesson Intervention Worksheets	**Tier 2** Strategic Intervention Skills Intervention Worksheets	**Tier 3** Intensive Intervention Worksheets available online	
Reteach 2.1 Reteach 2.2 Reteach 2.3	18 Linear Functions 19 Linear Inequalities in Two Variables 23 One-Step Equations 24 One-Step Inequalities 31 Slope and Slope-Intercept Form	Building Block Skills 1, 22, 23, 27, 41, 42, 43, 44, 47, 89, 90, 94	Challenge worksheets Extend the Math Lesson Activities in TE

Are You Ready?

ASSESS READINESS

Use the assessment on this page to determine if students need strategic or intensive intervention for the module's prerequisite skills.

ASSESSMENT AND INTERVENTION

RtI Response to Intervention TIER 1, TIER 2, TIER 3 SKILLS

Personal Math Trainer will automatically create a standards-based, personalized intervention assignment for your students, targeting each student's individual needs!

ADDITIONAL RESOURCES

See the table below for a full list of intervention resources available for this module.

Response to Intervention Resources also includes:

- Tier 2 Skill Pre-Tests for each Module
- Tier 2 Skill Post-Tests for each skill

LESSON 2.1

Graphing Absolute Value Functions

Common Core Math Standards

The student is expected to:

F-IF.C.7b

Graph . . . piecewise-defined functions, including . . . absolute value functions. Also A-CED.A.2, F-IF.B.4, F-BF.B.3

Mathematical Practices

MP.4 Modeling

Language Objective

Identify the vertex, slope, and direction of the opening for a variety of absolute value functions by describing them to a partner.

ENGAGE

Essential Question: How can you identify the features of the graph of an absolute value function?

Possible answer: The domain consists of x values for which the function is defined or on which the real-world situation is based. The range consists of the corresponding $f(x)$ values. The end behavior describes what happens to the $f(x)$ values as the x values increase without bound or decrease without bound.

PREVIEW: LESSON PERFORMANCE TASK

View the Engage section online. Discuss the photo, how a musician might make an instrument play louder or softer, and how a graph might show an increase and then a decrease in loudness. Then preview the Lesson Performance Task.

Name ______ Class ______ Date ______

2.1 Graphing Absolute Value Functions

Resource Locker

Essential Question: How can you identify the features of the graph of an absolute value function?

Explore 1 Graphing and Analyzing the Parent Absolute Value Function

Absolute value, written as $|x|$, represents the distance between x and 0 on a number line. As a distance, absolute value is always positive. For every point on a number line, there is another point on the opposite side of 0 that is the same distance from 0. For example, both 5 and –5 are five units away from 0. Thus, $|-5| = 5$ and $|5| = 5$.

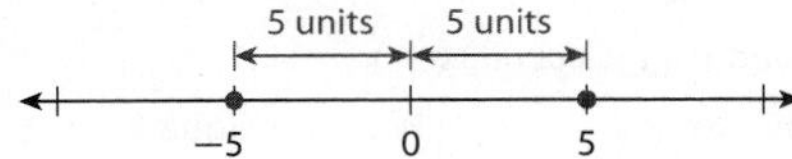

The absolute value function $|x|$, can be defined piecewise as $|x| = \begin{cases} x & x \geq 0 \\ -x & x < 0 \end{cases}$. When x is nonnegative, the function simply returns the number. When x is negative, the function returns the opposite of x.

(A) Complete the input-output table for $f(x)$.

$$f(x) = |x| = \begin{cases} x & x \geq 0 \\ -x & x < 0 \end{cases}$$

x	f(x)
–8	8
–4	4
0	0
4	4
8	8

(B) Plot the points you found on the coordinate grid. Use the points to complete the graph of the function.

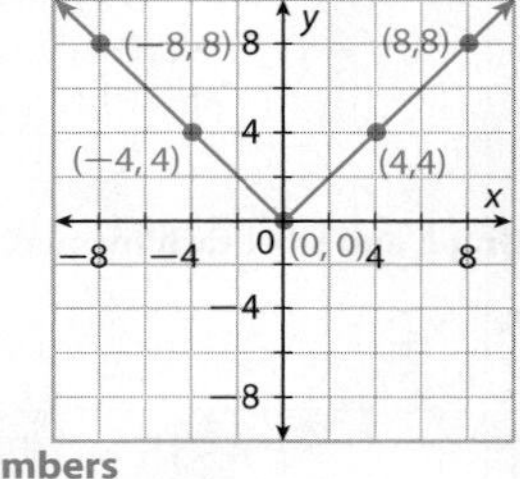

(C) Now, examine your graph of $f(x) = |x|$ and complete the following statements about the function.

$f(x) = |x|$ is symmetric about the **y-axis** and therefore is a(n) **even** function.

The domain of $f(x) = |x|$ is $(-\infty, \infty)$ **or the set of all real numbers**.

The range of $f(x) = |x|$ is $(0, \infty)$ **or the set of all nonnegative real numbers**.

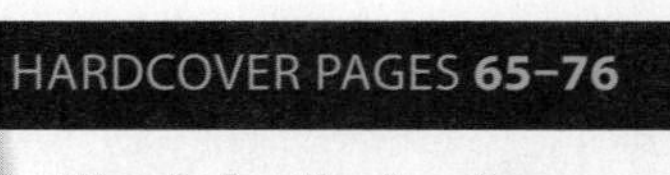

HARDCOVER PAGES 65–76

Watch for the hardcover student edition page numbers for this lesson.

Reflect

1. Use the definition of the absolute value function to show that $f(x) = |x|$ is an even function.

In an even function $f(x) = f(-x)$. $f(x) = |x|$ is defined piecewise, so there are two cases to examine: $x = 0$, $x \geq 0$, and $x < 0$. If $x \geq 0$ then $-x \leq 0$. You know $f(x) = x$ when $x \geq 0$. To find $f(-x)$, recall that $f(x) = -x$ when $x \leq 0$. In this case, $-x \leq 0$, so $f((-x)) = -(-x)$ or $f(-x) = x$. This shows that $f(x) = f(-x)$ when $x > 0$. If $x < 0$ then $-x > 0$. You know $f(x) = -x$ when $x < 0$. To find $f(-x)$, recall that $f(x) = x$ when $x > 0$. In this case, $-x > 0$, so $f(-x) = -x$. This shows that $f(x) = f(-x)$ when $x < 0$.

Explain 1 Graphing Absolute Value Functions

You can apply general transformations to absolute value functions by changing parameters in the equation $g(x) = a\left|\frac{1}{b}(x - h)\right| + k$.

Example 1 **Given the function $g(x) = a\left|\frac{1}{b}(x - h)\right| + k$, find the vertex of the function. Use the vertex and two other points to help you graph $g(x)$.**

(A) $g(x) = 4|x - 5| - 2$

The vertex of the parent absolute value function is at (0, 0).

The vertex of $g(x)$ will be the point to which (0, 0) is mapped to by $g(x)$.

$g(x)$ involves a translation of $f(x)$ 5 units to the right and 2 units down.

The vertex of $g(x)$ will therefore be at (5, –2).

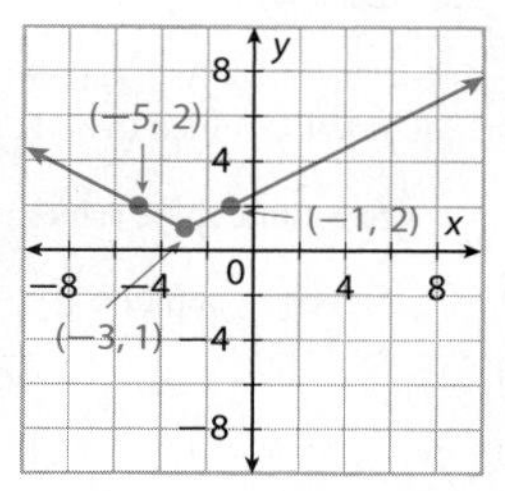

Next, determine the location to which each of the points (1, 1) and (–1, 1) on $f(x)$ will be mapped.

Since $a > 1$ then $g(x)$, in addition to a translation, is also a vertical stretch of $f(x)$ by a factor of 4. The x-coordinate of each point will be shifted 5 units to the right while the y-coordinate will be stretched by a factor of 4 and then moved down 2 units. So, (1, 1) moves to $(1 + 5, 4 \cdot |1| - 2) = (6, 2)$, and (–1, 1) moves to $(-1 + 5, 4 \cdot |1| - 2) = (4, 2)$. Now plot the three points and graph $g(x)$.

(B) $g(x) = \left|-\frac{1}{2}(x + 3)\right| + 1$

The vertex of the parent absolute value function is at (0, 0).

$g(x)$ is a translation of $f(x)$ **3** units to the **left** and **1** unit **up**.

The vertex of $g(x)$ will therefore be at (**–3**, **1**).

Next, determine to where the points (2, 2) and (–2, 2) on $f(x)$ will be mapped.

y
8
(–5, 2)
4
(–1, 2) x
–8 –4 0 4 8
(–3, 1) –4
–8

PROFESSIONAL DEVELOPMENT

Integrate Mathematical Practices

This lesson provides an opportunity to address Mathematical Practice **MP.4**, which calls for students to "model with mathematics." Students learn the meaning of the parameters a, b, h, and k in an absolute value function, and use those parameters to graph and draw conclusions about absolute value functions.

EXPLORE 1

Graphing and Analyzing the Parent Absolute Value Function

INTEGRATE TECHNOLOGY

Using calculators to graph the parent absolute value function can illustrate that other absolute value functions are transformations of the parent function.

CONNECT VOCABULARY EL

Students should recognize that the graph of the parent function relates to the definition of *absolute value*. For each coordinate point, the y–value tells how far each x–value is from 0.

EXPLAIN 1

Graphing Absolute Value Functions

AVOID COMMON ERRORS

Students who recognize that (0, 0) is the vertex for the parent absolute value function may try to find the vertex for a transformation function by substituting 0 for x. Remind students that the vertex cannot be determined by substitution.

QUESTIONING STRATEGIES

In a function in the form $g(x) = a\left|\frac{1}{b}(x - h)\right| + k$ which parameters can be used to find the vertex of the function? Explain. **h and k; the vertex of the function, will be at the coordinates (h, k).**

Why do some graphs of absolute value functions extend higher in one direction than in the other? **When one half of the function extends higher than the other half, that graph's vertex is not in the center of the portion of the coordinate plane shown.**

INTEGRATE TECHNOLOGY

Students can use a graphing calculator to check their graphs of absolute value functions by verifying that the points they found are correct.

CONNECT VOCABULARY EL

Relate *absolute value function* graphs to the graphs of other *linear functions* by showing that all of them can be stretched, compressed, and reflected. Encourage students to describe the shapes and slopes of absolute value functions in their own words: for example, *upside-down V-shaped, composed of two lines or linear pieces*, and so on.

EXPLAIN 2

Writing Absolute Value Functions from a Graph

INTEGRATE MATHEMATICAL PRACTICES

Focus on Communication

MP.3 In order to verify that expressions are equivalent, students can substitute values in equivalent forms of absolute value expressions. For example, students can show that $a\left|\frac{1}{b}(x-h)\right| = \frac{a}{b}\left|(x - h)\right|$ by substituting values for a, b, x, and h.

Since $|b| = 2$, $g(x)$ is also a **horizontal stretch** of $f(x)$ and since b is negative, a **reflection across the y-axis**.

The x-coordinate will move **3** units to the **left** and then **stretch** by a factor of **2**.

The y-coordinate will move **up 1** unit.

So, (2, 2) becomes $\left(2 - 3, \left|-\frac{1}{2} \cdot 2\right| + 1\right) = (-1, 2)$, and (−2, 2) becomes $(-5, 2)$. Now plot the three points and use them to sketch $g(x)$.

Your Turn

2. Given $g(x) = -\frac{1}{5}\left|(x + 6)\right| + 4$, find the vertex and two other points and use them to help you graph $g(x)$.

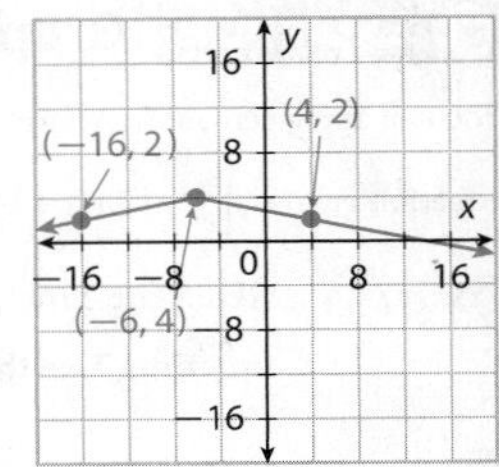

Vertex: $(h, k) = (-6, 4)$

$-1 < a < 0$ so $g(x)$ is a reflection; vertical compression by $\frac{1}{5}$.

$(10, 10) \rightarrow \left(10 - 6, -\frac{1}{5} \cdot |10| + 4\right) = (4, 2)$

$(-10, 10) \rightarrow (-16, 2)$ across the x-axis

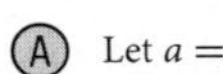 Explain 2 Writing Absolute Value Functions from a Graph

If an absolute value equation in the form $g(x) = a\left|\frac{1}{b}(x - h)\right| + k$ has values other than 1 for both a and b, you can rewrite that equation so that the value of at least one of a or b is 1.

When a and b are positive: $a\left|\frac{1}{b}(x - h)\right| = \left|\frac{a}{b}(x - h)\right| = \frac{a}{b}\left|(x - h)\right|$.

When a is negative and b is positive, you can move the opposite of a inside the absolute value expression. This leaves −1 outside the absolute value symbol: $-2\left|\frac{1}{b}\right| = -1(2)\left|\frac{1}{b}\right| = -1\left|\frac{2}{b}\right|$.

When b is negative, you can rewrite the equation without a negative sign, because of the properties of absolute value: $a\left|\frac{1}{b}(x - h)\right| = a\left|\frac{1}{-b}(x - h)\right|$. This case has now been reduced to one of the other two cases.

Example 2 **Given the graph of an absolute value function, write the function in the form $g(x) = a\left|\frac{1}{b}(x - h)\right| + k$.**

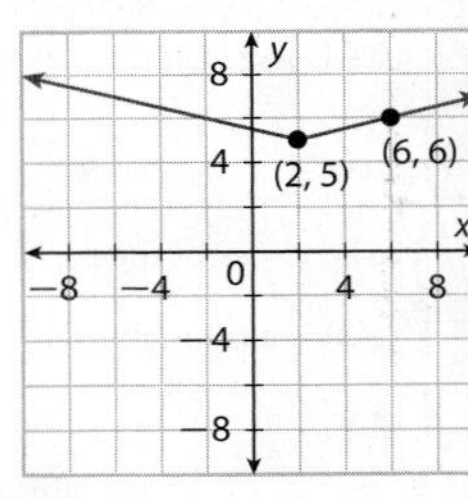

(A) Let $a = 1$.

The vertex of $g(x)$ is at (2, 5). This means that $h = 2$ and $k = 5$, and a was assumed to be 1.

Substitute these values into $g(x)$, giving $g(x) = \left|\frac{1}{b}(x - 2)\right| + 5$.

Choose a point on $g(x)$ like (6, 6), Substitute these values into $g(x)$, and solve for b.

COLLABORATIVE LEARNING

Peer-to-Peer Activity

Have students work in pairs to construct graphs with three parameters the same and one parameter different. Instruct one student to choose which parameter (a, b, h, or k) will be different. Both roll number cubes to determine the similar and different values. Have them create two graphs, then write a paragraph explaining how the different parameter affected the shape of each graph.

Substitute. $6 = \left|\frac{1}{b}(6-2)\right| + 5$

Simplify. $6 = \left|\frac{1}{b}(4)\right| + 5$

Subtract 5 from each side. $1 = \left|\frac{4}{b}\right|$

Rewrite the absolute value as two equations. $1 = \frac{4}{b}$ or $1 = -\frac{4}{b}$

Solve for b. $b = 4$ or $b = -4$

Based on the problem conditions, only consider $b = 4$. Substitute into $g(x)$ to find the equation for the graph.

$g(x) = \left|\frac{1}{4}(x-2)\right| + 5$

(B) Let $b = 1$.

The vertex of $g(x)$ is at **(1, 6)**. This means that $h =$ **1** and $k =$ **6**, and b was assumed to be 1.

Substitute these values into $g(x)$, giving $g(x) = a\left|x - \boxed{1}\right| = \boxed{6}$.

Now, choose a point on $g(x)$ with integer coordinates, $(0, \boxed{3})$.

Substitute these values into $g(x)$ and solve for a.

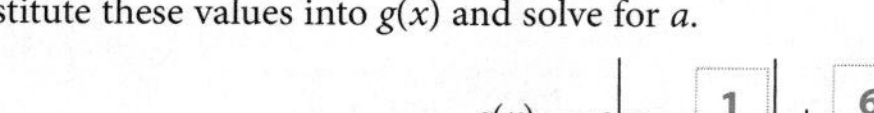

$g(x) = a\left|x - \boxed{1}\right| + \boxed{6}$

Substitute. $\boxed{3} = a|0-1| + 6$

Simplify. $\boxed{3} = a|-1| + 6$

Solve for a. $\boxed{-3} = a$

Therefore $g(x) = \boxed{-3|x-1|+6}$.

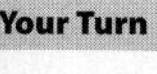

Your Turn

3. Given the graph of an absolute value function, write the function in the form $g(x) = a\left|\frac{1}{b}(x-h)\right| + k$.

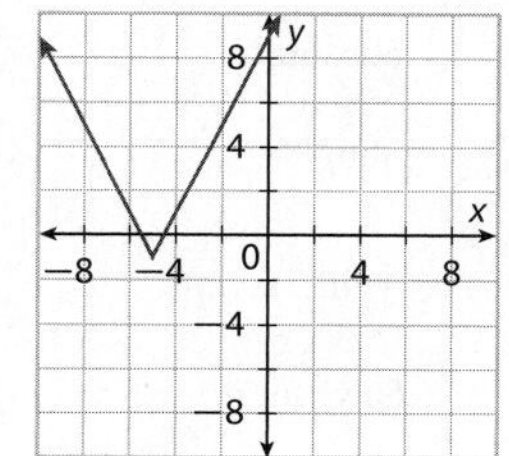

$a = 1$, vertex $= (-5, -1) = (h, k)$

$g(x) = \left|\frac{1}{b}(x-(-5))\right| - 1$

Choose (0, 9).

$9 = \left|\frac{1}{b}(0+5)\right| - 1$ **$b = \frac{1}{2}$ or $b = -\frac{1}{2}$**

$10 = \left|\frac{5}{b}\right|$ **$g(x) = \left|2(x+5)\right| - 1$**

QUESTIONING STRATEGIES

When writing an absolute function from a graph, how can you use the direction in which an absolute value function opens to check your work? **An absolute value function which opens upward will have a positive value for a, and an absolute value function which opens downward will have a negative value for a.**

DIFFERENTIATE INSTRUCTION

Critical Thinking

Discuss with students ways to determine if a graph of a function represents an absolute value function. Students should realize that an absolute value function has symmetry about a vertical line through the vertex, so the two pieces of the function will have equal but opposite slopes. Challenge students to show that the slopes of these two lines are opposites.

EXPLAIN 3

Modeling with Absolute Value Functions

INTEGRATE MATHEMATICAL PRACTICES

Focus on Critical Thinking

MP.3 When writing equations to solve real-world problems, discuss with students how to choose the part of the description that describes the origin. Students should understand that they can select an origin that will make the problem easy to solve.

Explain 3 Modeling with Absolute Value Functions

Light travels in a straight line and can be modeled by a linear function. When light is reflected off a mirror, it travels in a straight line in a different direction. From physics, the angle at which the light ray comes in is equal to the angle at which it is reflected away: the angle of incidence is equal to the angle of reflection. You can use an absolute value function to model this situation.

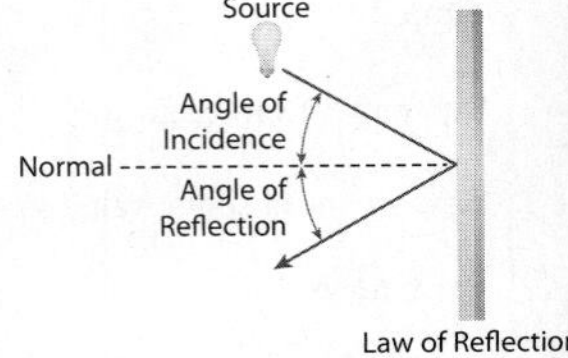

Law of Reflection

Example 3 **Solve the problem by modeling the situation with an absolute value function.**

At a science museum exhibit, a beam of light originates at a point 10 feet off the floor. It is reflected off a mirror on the floor that is 15 feet from the wall the light originates from. How high off the floor on the opposite wall does the light hit if the other wall is 8.5 feet from the mirror?

Analyze Information

Identify the important information.

- The model will be of the form $g(x) = $ $a\left|\frac{1}{b}(x-h)\right|+k$.
- The vertex of $g(x)$ is $(15, 0)$.
- Another point on $g(x)$ is $(0, 10)$.
- The opposite wall is 23.5 feet from the first wall.

Formulate a Plan

Let the base of the first wall be the origin. You want to find the value of $g(x)$ at $x = $ 23.5, which will give the height of the beam on the opposite wall. To do so, find the value of the parameters in the transformation of the parent function. In this situation, let $b = 1$. The vertex of $g(x)$ will give you the values of *h* and *k*. Use a second point to solve for a. Evaluate $g(23.5)$.

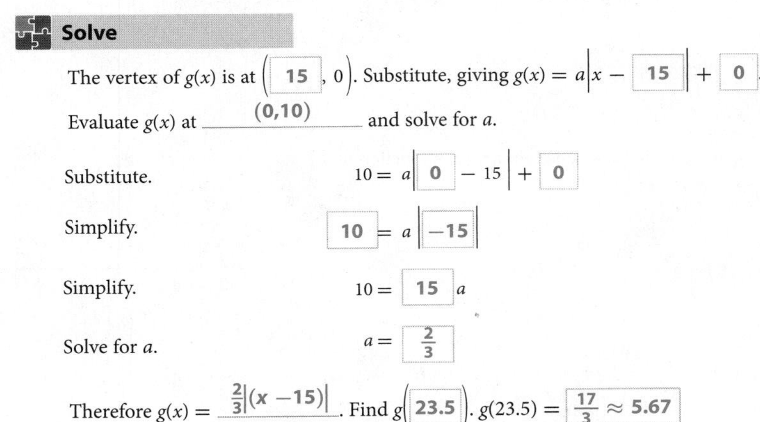

Solve

The vertex of $g(x)$ is at $(15, 0)$. Substitute, giving $g(x) = a|x - 15| + 0$.

Evaluate $g(x)$ at (0,10) and solve for a.

Substitute. $10 = a|0 - 15| + 0$

Simplify. $10 = a|-15|$

Simplify. $10 = 15a$

Solve for a. $a = \frac{2}{3}$

Therefore $g(x) = \frac{2}{3}|(x - 15)|$. Find $g(23.5)$. $g(23.5) = \frac{17}{3} \approx 5.67$

LANGUAGE SUPPORT EL

Connect Context

Discuss how the term *parent function* relates to the common use of the word *parent*. Students should understand that transformations of the parent absolute value function will always have certain characteristics in common with the parent function.

Justify and Evaluate

The answer of 5.67 makes sense because function is symmetric with respect to the line $x = 15$. This represents a distance that is a little more than twice as far from the beam's origin as it is from the spot where the beam hits the second wall. Since the beam originates at a height of 10 feet, it should hit the second wall at a height of a little over 5 feet.

Your Turn

4. Two students are passing a ball back and forth, allowing it to bounce once between them. If one student bounce-passes the ball from a height of 1.4 m and it bounces 3 m away from the student, where should the second student stand to catch the ball at a height of 1.2 m? Assume the path of the ball is linear over this short distance.

Let $a = 1$. vertex $= (3,0) = (h,k)$

Use the point $(0, 1.4)$ or $\left(0, \frac{7}{5}\right)$.

$$g(x) = \left|\frac{1}{b}(x-3)\right|$$
$$\frac{7}{5} = \left|\frac{1}{b}(0-3)\right|$$
$$\frac{7}{5} = \left|\frac{3}{b}\right|$$
$$\frac{7}{5} = \frac{3}{b} \text{ or } \frac{7}{5} = -\frac{3}{b}$$
$$b = \frac{15}{7} \text{ or } b = -\frac{15}{7}$$
$$g(x) = \left|\frac{7}{15}(x-3)\right|$$

Now, replace $g(x)$ with 1.2 or $\frac{6}{5}$ and solve for x. $\frac{6}{5} = \left|\frac{7}{15}(x-3)\right|$

$$\frac{6}{5} = \frac{7}{15}(x-3) \text{ or } -\frac{6}{5} = \frac{7}{15}(x-3)$$
$$x = \frac{39}{7} \approx 5.57 \text{ or } x = \frac{3}{7} \approx 0.43$$

Only $x = \frac{39}{7}$ makes sense (the second student has to be on the other side of the vertex from the first student). Therefore, the second student should stand 5.57 meters away from the first student.

Elaborate

5. In the general form of the absolute value function, what does each parameter represent?
h is horizontal translation, k is vertical translation, a is vertical stretch/compression and b is horizontal stretch/compression.

6. **Discussion** Explain why the vertex of $f(x) = |x|$ remains the same when $f(x)$ is stretched or compressed but not when it is translated.
The vertex of $f(x) = |x|$ is at $(0, 0)$. When $f(x)$ is stretched or compressed, one of these values is multiplied by a or b. In either case, the product is 0 so the coordinates remain $(0, 0)$. But when $f(x)$ is translated, h k is added to a coordinate, which changes the vertex.

7. **Essential Question Check-In** What are the features of the graph of an absolute value function?
The features are the vertex, the direction of opening, and the slope of each ray.

QUESTIONING STRATEGIES

The points A and B are both on the same absolute value function. If the x-value for Point A is greater than the x-value for Point B, can you determine which point has the greater y-value? Explain. No; depending on the values for a, b, h, and k, either point could have a greater y-value.

ELABORATE

INTEGRATE MATHEMATICAL PRACTICES

Focus on Math Connections

MP.1 The general form of the absolute value function is similar to the quadratic function in vertex form. Students can use the similarities between the forms to remember what each variable represents.

QUESTIONING STRATEGIES

What are the values for h, k, a, and b in the parent absolute value function? In the parent absolute value function, $h = 0$, $k = 0$, $a = 1$, and $b = 1$.

SUMMARIZE THE LESSON

How can you use the parameters of an absolute value function in general form to predict the shape of the function? The parameters h and k will tell you the coordinates for the vertex, (h, k). The signs of a and b will tell you whether the function opens upward or downward. The values used for a and b will tell you how much the function is stretched or compressed.

EVALUATE

ASSIGNMENT GUIDE

Concepts and Skills	Practice
Explain 1 Graphing Absolute Value Functions	Exercises 6–11
Explain 2 Writing Absolute Value Functions from a Graph	Exercises 12–13
Explain 3 Modeling with Absolute Value Functions	Exercises 14–17

INTEGRATE MATHEMATICAL PRACTICES

Focus on Critical Thinking

MP.3 When interpreting graphs of real-world absolute value functions, discuss with students what data is represented on the x–axis and what data is represented by the y–axis.

Evaluate: Homework and Practice

- Online Homework
- Hints and Help
- Extra Practice

Predict what the graph of each given function will look like. Verify your prediction using a graphing calculator. Then sketch the graph of the function.

1. 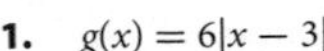 $g(x) = 6|x - 3|$

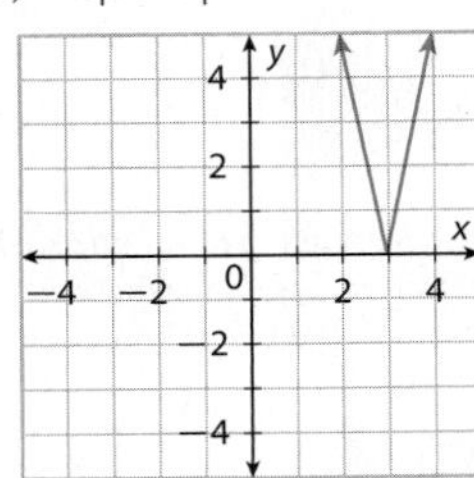

$g(x)$ is the graph of $f(x) = |x|$ vertically stretched by a factor of 6 and shifted 3 units to the right.

2. 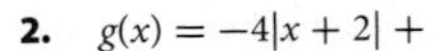 $g(x) = -4|x + 2| + 5$

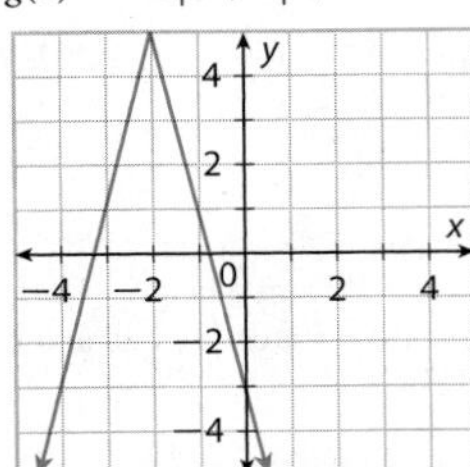

$g(x)$ is the graph of $f(x) = |x|$ vertically stretched by a factor of 4, shifted 2 units to the left, 5 units up and reflected across the x-axis.

3. $g(x) = \left|\frac{7}{5}(x - 6)\right| + 4$

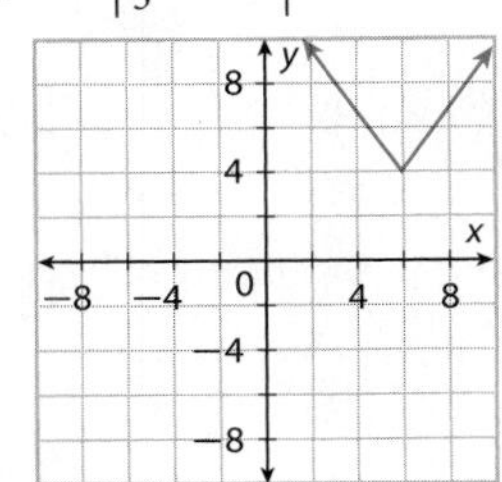

$g(x)$ is the graph of $f(x) = |x|$ horizontally compressed by a factor of $\frac{5}{7}$, shifted 6 units to the right and 4 units up.

4. $g(x) = \left|\frac{3}{7}(x - 4)\right| + 2$

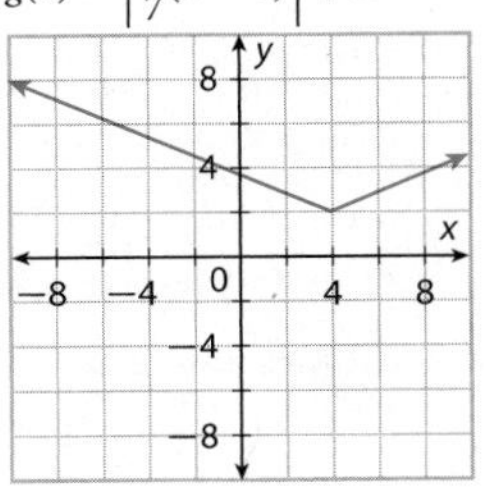

$g(x)$ is the graph of $f(x) = |x|$ horizontally stretched by a factor of $\frac{7}{3}$, shifted 4 units to the right, and 2 units up.

5. $g(x) = \frac{7}{4}|(x - 2)| - 3$

$g(x)$ is the graph of $f(x) = |x|$ vertically stretched by a factor of $\frac{7}{4}$, shifted 2 units to the right, and 3 units down.

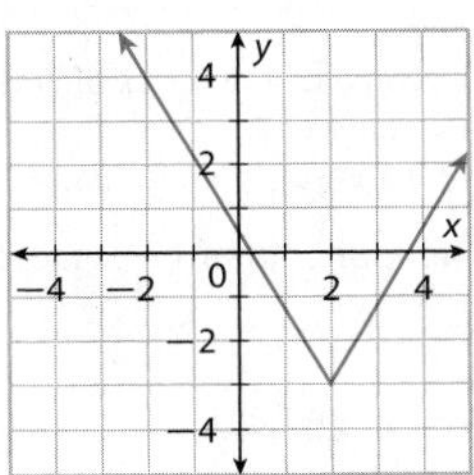

Exercise	Depth of Knowledge (D.O.K.)	COMMON CORE Mathematical Practices
1–5	**1** Recall of Information	**MP.2** Reasoning
6–11	**1** Recall of Information	**MP.5** Using Tools
12–13	**1** Recall of Information	**MP.2** Reasoning
14–17	**2** Skills/Concepts	**MP.4** Modeling
18	**2** Skills/Concepts H.O.T.	**MP.5** Using Tools

Graph the given function and identify the domain and range.

6. $g(x) = |x|$

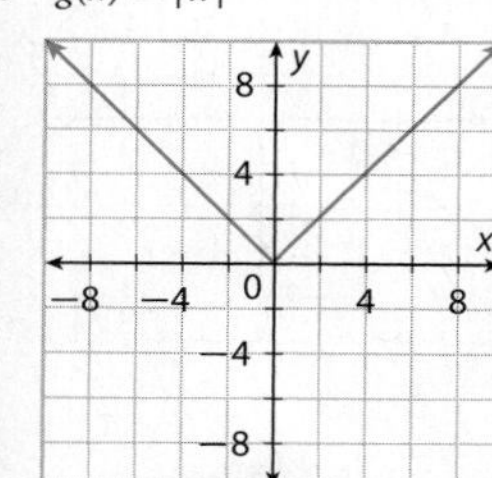

D: all real numbers; R: $y \geq 0$

7. $g(x) = \frac{4}{3}|(x-5)| + 7$

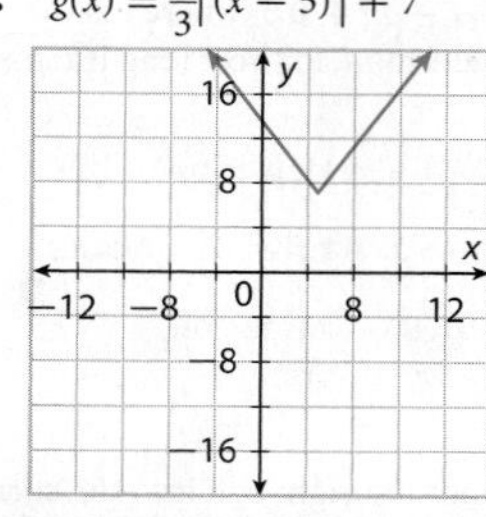

D: all real numbers; R: $y \geq 7$

8. $g(x) = -\frac{7}{6}|(x-2)|$

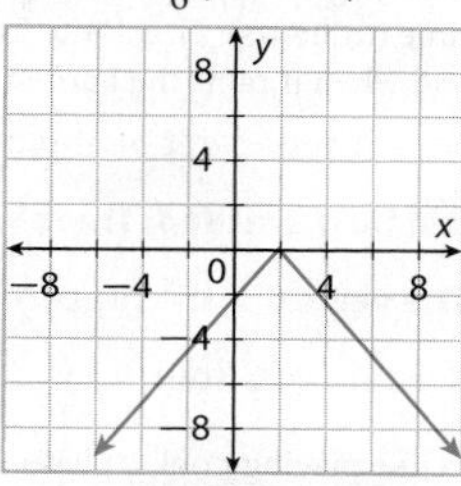

D: all real numbers; R: $y \leq 0$

9. $g(x) = \left|\frac{3}{4}(x-2)\right| - 7$

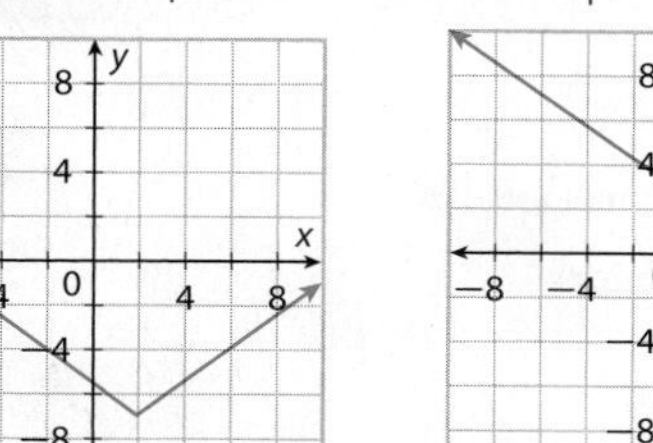

D: all real numbers; R: $y \geq -7$

10. $g(x) = \left|\frac{5}{7}(x-4)\right|$

D: all real numbers; R: $y \geq 0$

11. $g(x) = \left|-\frac{7}{3}(x+5)\right| - 4$

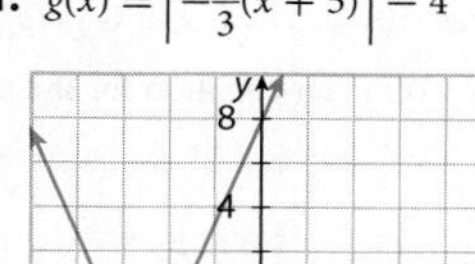

D: all real numbers; R: $y \geq -4$

Write the absolute value function in standard form for the given graph. Use *a* or *b* as directed, $b > 0$.

12. Let $a = 1$.

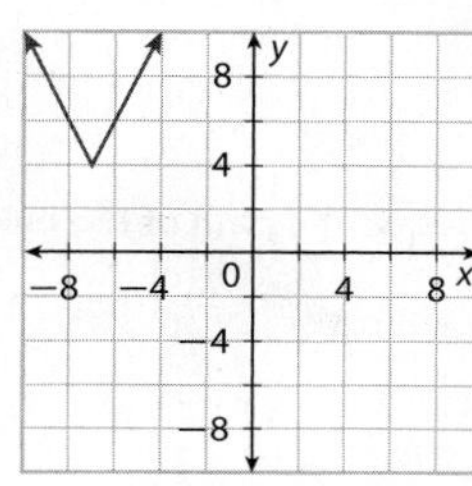

Vertex: $(-7, 4)$; equation $g(x) = \left|\frac{1}{b}(x+7)\right| + 4$

Use the point $(-6, 6)$: $6 = \left|\frac{1}{b}(-6+7)\right| + 4$

$$6 = \left|\frac{1}{b}(1)\right| + 4$$

$$2 = \left|\frac{1}{b}\right|$$

$$\frac{1}{b} = 2 \text{ or } \frac{1}{b} = -2$$

$$b = \frac{1}{2} \text{ or } b = -\frac{1}{2}$$

So the equation is $g(x) = |2(x+7)| + 4$.

13. Let $b = 1$.

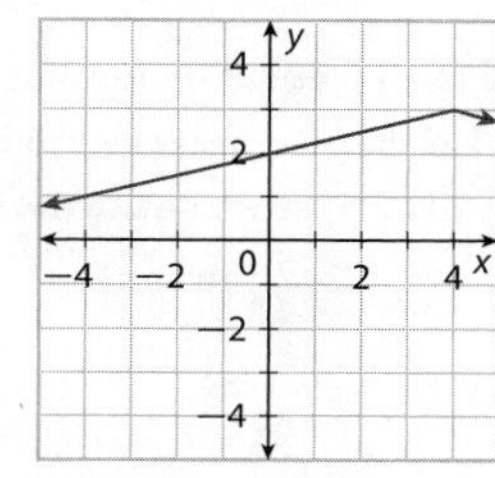

Vertex: $(4, 3)$; equation $g(x) = a|(x-4)| + 3$

Use the point $(0, 2)$: $2 = a|(0-4)| + 3$

$$2 = a|-4| + 3$$

$$2 = 4a + 3$$

$$-\frac{1}{4} = a$$

So the equation is $g(x) = -\frac{1}{4}|(x-4)| + 3$.

Exercise	Depth of Knowledge (D.O.K.)	COMMON CORE Mathematical Practices
19	**2** Skills/Concepts H.O.T.	**MP.1** Problem Solving
20	**3** Strategic Thinking H.O.T.	**MP.2** Reasoning

AVOID COMMON ERRORS

Students should know that the sign in front of the parameter h does not indicate whether to translate the function in a negative or positive direction along the x-axis. Remind students that a negative sign in front of h refers to a translation to the right, and a positive sign refers to a translation to the left.

MULTIPLE REPRESENTATIONS

Challenge students to check their answers to real-world absolute value problems by using different methods. Since absolute value functions have symmetry about the vertical line that contains the vertex, many real-world problems can be solved by drawing similar or congruent right triangles that use the lines of the absolute value function.

14. A rainstorm begins as a drizzle, builds up to a heavy rain, and then drops back to a drizzle. The rate r (in inches per hour) at which it rains is given by the function $r = -0.5|t - 1| + 0.5$, where t is the time (in hours). Graph the function. Determine for how long it rains and when it rains the hardest.

Since there can't be negative rainfall, the negative values can be discarded. Therefore, it rains for a total of 2 hours. The vertex of the graph is at (1, 0.5), so it rains the hardest at 1 hour.

15. While playing pool, a player tries to shoot the eight ball into the corner pocket as shown. Imagine that a coordinate plane is placed over the pool table. The eight ball is at $\left(5, \frac{5}{4}\right)$ and the pocket they are aiming for is at (10, 5). The player is going to bank the ball off the side at (6, 0).

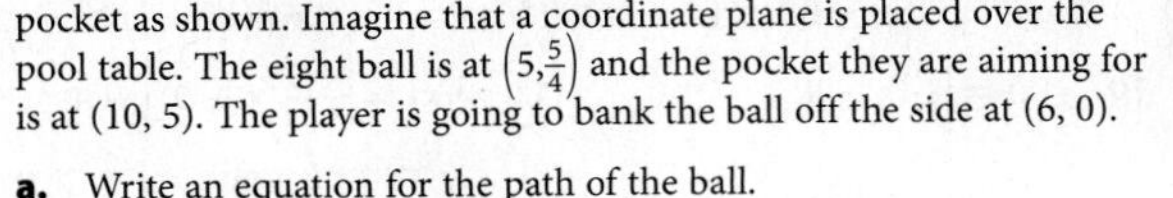

a. Write an equation for the path of the ball.

The vertex of the path of the ball is (6, 0), so the equation has the form $y = a|x - 6|$. Substitute the coordinates of the point $\left(5, \frac{5}{4}\right)$ into the equation and solve for a.

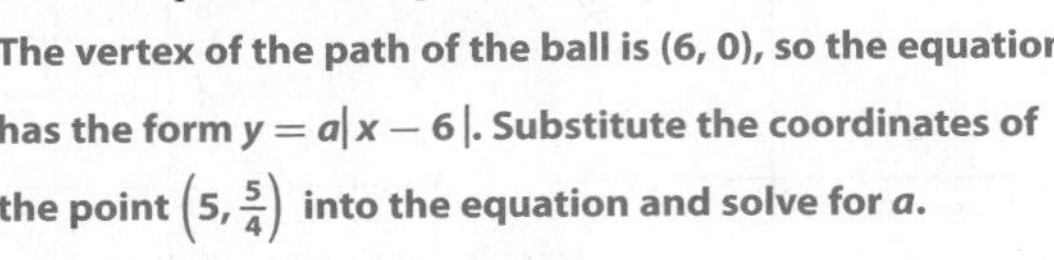

$$y = a|x - 6|$$

$$\frac{5}{4} = a|5 - 6|$$

$$\frac{5}{4} = a|-1|$$

$$\frac{5}{4} = a$$

An equation for the path of the ball is $y = \frac{5}{4}|x - 6|$.

b. Did the player make the shot? How do you know?

The player will make the shot if the point (10, 5) lies on the path of the ball.

$$5 \stackrel{?}{=} \frac{5}{4}|10 - 6|$$

$$5 \stackrel{?}{=} \frac{5}{4}|4|$$

$$5 = 5$$

The point (10, 5) satisfies the equation, so the player does make the shot.

16. Sam is sitting in a boat on a lake. She can get sunburnt from the sunlight that hits her directly and from sunlight that reflects off the water. Sunlight reflects off the water at the point (2, 0) and hits Sam at the point (3.5, 3). Write and graph the function that shows the path of the sunlight.

The vertex is (2, 0), so the equation has the form $y = a|x - 2|$.

Substitute (3.5, 3) into the equation and solve for a.

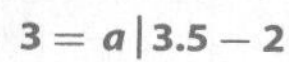

$3 = a|3.5 - 2|$

$3 = a|1.5|$

$2 = a$; An equation for the path of the sunlight is $y = 2|x - 2|$.

17. The Transamerica Pyramid is an office building in San Francisco. It stands 853 feet tall and is 145 feet wide at its base. Imagine that a coordinate plane is placed over a side of the building. In the coordinate plane, each unit represents one foot. Write an absolute value function whose graph is the V-shaped outline of the sides of the building, ignoring the "shoulders" of the building.

The vertex of the building is going to be the top, which will be at the point (72.5, 853), so the equation has the form $y = a|x - 72.5| + 853$. Substitute the coordinates of the point (145, 0) into the equation and solve for a.

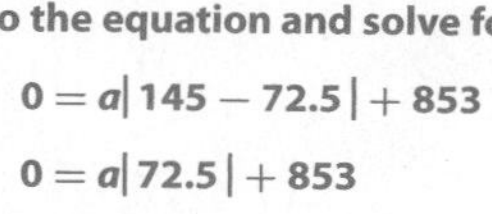

$$0 = a|145 - 72.5| + 853$$

$$0 = a|72.5| + 853$$

$$-\frac{1706}{145} = a$$

So, the equation has the form $y = -\frac{1706}{145}|x - 72.5| + 853$.

18. Match each graph with its function.

C $y = |x + 6| - 4$ **A** $y = |x - 6| - 4$ **B** $y = |x - 6| + 4$

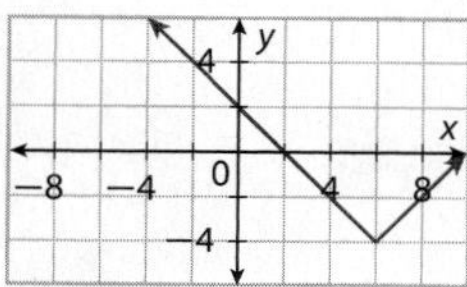

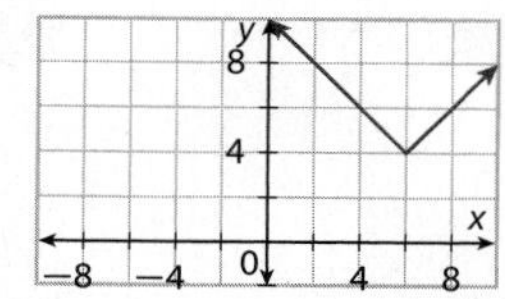

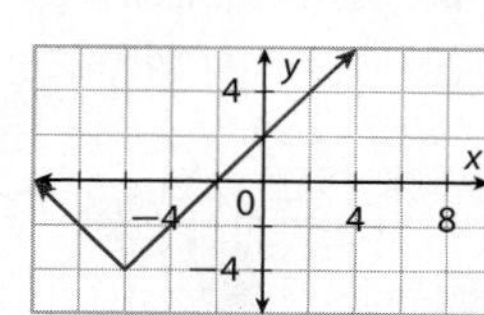

CRITICAL THINKING

Have students consider the significance of h in determining values of the domain for which an absolute value function is increasing and for which it is decreasing, and how the value of a is useful for refining this information.

JOURNAL

Have students describe what can be determined about the shape of an absolute value function by examining the values of a, b, h, and k.

H.O.T. Focus on Higher Order Thinking

19. Explain the Error Explain why the graph shown is not the graph of $y = |x + 3| + 2$. What is the correct equation shown in the graph?

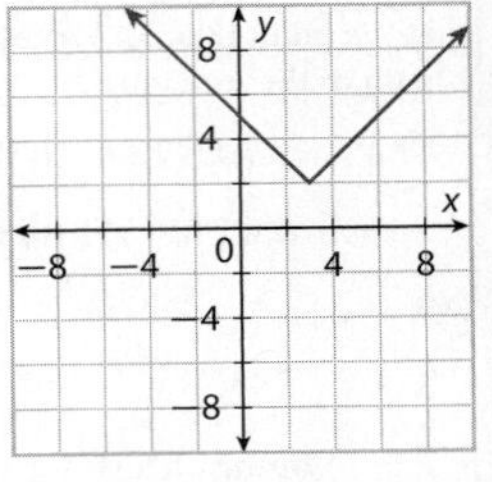

The graph shown cannot be the graph of $y = |x + 3| + 2$ because the $+3$ inside of the absolute value symbols means the graph should be shifted to the left 3 units. The graph shown is shifted to the right 3 units, so it represents $y = |x - 3| + 2$.

20. Multi-Step A golf player is trying to make a hole-in-one on the miniature golf green shown. Imagine that a coordinate plane is placed over the golf green. The golf ball is at (2.5, 2) and the hole is at (9.5, 2). The player is going to bank the ball off the side wall of the green at (6, 8).

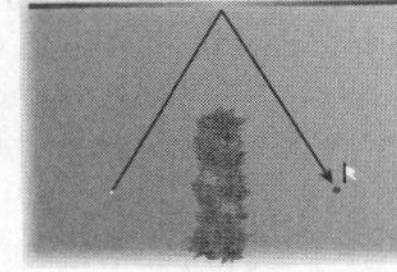

a. Write an equation for the path of the ball.

The vertex of the path of the ball is (6, 8), so the equation has the form $y = a|x - 6| + 8$. Substitute the coordinates of the point (2.5, 2) into the equation and solve for a.

$$y = a|x - 6| + 8$$
$$2 = a|2.5 - 6| + 8$$
$$2 = a|-3.5| + 8$$
$$2 = 3.5a + 8$$
$$-6 = 3.5a$$
$$-\frac{12}{7} = a$$

An equation for the path of the ball is $y = -\frac{12}{7}|x - 6| + 8$.

b. Use the equation in part a to determine if the player makes the shot.

The player will make the shot if the point (9.5, 2) lies on the path of the ball.

$$2 \stackrel{?}{=} -\frac{12}{7}|9.5 - 6| + 8$$
$$2 \stackrel{?}{=} -\frac{12}{7}|3.5| + 8$$
$$2 \stackrel{?}{=} -6 + 8$$
$$2 = 2$$

The point (9.5, 2) satisfies the equation, so the player does make the shot.

Lesson Performance Task

Suppose a musical piece calls for an orchestra to start at *fortissimo* (about 90 decibels), decrease steadily in loudness to *pianissimo* (about 50 decibels) in four measures, and then increase steadily back to *fortissimo* in another four measures.

a. Write a function to represent the sound level s in decibels

b. After how many measures should the orchestra be at the loudness of *mezzo forte* (about 70 decibels)?

c. Describe what the graph of this function would look like.

a. $s = a|m - 4| + 50$

$90 = a|0 - 4| + 50$

$90 = a|-4| + 50$

$90 = 4a + 50$

$40 = 4a$

$10 = a$

So, the equation is $s = 10|m - 4| + 50$.

b. Substitute 70 for s.

$70 = 10|m - 4| + 50$

$20 = 10|m - 4|$

$2 = |m - 4|$

$2 = m - 4$ OR $-2 = m - 4$

$6 = m$ $\quad$ $2 = m$

So, at both measures 2 and 4, the orchestra will be at the loudness of *mezzo forte*.

The graph will be of $f(x) = |x|$ shifted 4 units to the right, 50 units up, and vertically stretched by a factor of 10.

EXTENSION ACTIVITY

Have students consider these two situations:

- A note is played on an instrument, and then the instrument becomes silent.
- An empty room is noisier than a room furnished with rugs, drapes, and furniture.

Have students research where sound energy goes, and how sound vibrations dissipate, resulting in silence. Students should discover that sound energy is transmitted through the air and absorbed by many materials, especially those that are soft.

LANGUAGE SUPPORT EL

A *measure* or *bar* (*bar* is more common in British English, while *measure* is more common in American English) in musical notation is a segment of time defined by a given number of beats. Dividing music into measures helps a musician keep place in the written music and also keep time, or, stay in the proper rhythm.

CONNECT VOCABULARY EL

A *decibel*, dB, is a unit of how loud a sound is. On the decibel scale, 0 dB is used for a barely heard sound; normal conversation is about 60 dB; and 130 dB sound may cause pain. The word *decibel* is made up of two parts, *deci*, meaning one-tenth, and *bel*, named after Alexander Graham Bell.

INTEGRATE MATHEMATICAL PRACTICES

Focus on Modeling

MP.4 In this lesson, students have studied absolute value denoted by two vertical bars. In technology, the term *abs()* is often used. So, abs $(-2) = 2$ is the same as $|-2| = 2$.

INTEGRATE MATHEMATICAL PRACTICES

Focus on Critical Thinking

MP.3 Discuss with students which values of s have no associated value of m $(s < 50)$, one associated value of m $(s = 50)$, and more than one associated value of m $(s > 50.)$

Scoring Rubric

2 points: Student correctly solves the problem and explains his/her reasoning.

1 point: Student shows good understanding of the problem but does not fully solve or explain his/her reasoning.

0 points: Student does not demonstrate understanding of the problem.

LESSON 2.2

Solving Absolute Value Equations

Common Core Math Standards

The student is expected to:

 **A-CED.A.1**

Create equations and inequalities in one variable and use them to solve problems. Also A-REI.B.3, A-REI.D.11

Mathematical Practices

 **MP.6 Precision**

Language Objective

Explain to a partner why solutions to a variety of absolute value equations make sense and contain more than one solution, one solution, or no solution.

ENGAGE

Essential Question: How can you solve an absolute value equation?

Possible answer: Isolate the absolute value expression, then write two related equations with a disjunction, also known as an "or" statement.

PREVIEW: LESSON PERFORMANCE TASK

View the Engage section online. Discuss the photo and why this situation can be represented by a V-shaped path and an absolute value equation. Then preview the Lesson Performance Task.

Name ______ Class ______ Date ______

2.2 Solving Absolute Value Equations

Resource Locker

Essential Question: How can you solve an absolute value equation?

Explore Solving Absolute Value Equations Graphically

Absolute value equations differ from linear equations in that they may have two solutions. This is indicated with a **disjunction**, a mathematical statement created by a connecting two other statements with the word "or." To see why there can be two solutions, you can solve an absolute value equation using graphs.

(A) Solve the equation $2|x - 5| - 4 = 2$.

Plot the function $f(x) = 2|x - 5| - 4$ on the grid. Then plot the function $g(x) = 2$ as a horizontal line on the same grid, and mark the points where the plots intersect.

The points are (2, 2) and (8, 2).

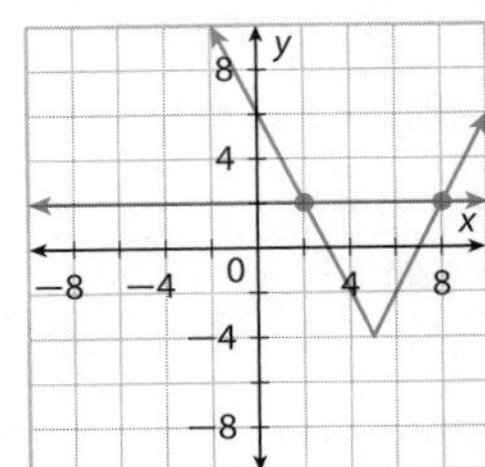

(B) Write the solution to this equation as a disjunction:

$x =$ **2** or $x =$ **8**

Reflect

1. Why might you expect most absolute value equations to have two solutions? Why not three or four?

If the absolute value expression is not equal to zero, the expression inside an absolute value can be either positive or negative. So, there can be at most two solutions. Looking at this graphically, an absolute value graph can intersect a horizontal line at most two times.

2. Is it possible for an absolute value equation to have no solutions? one solution? If so, what would each look like graphically?

Yes; yes; A graph with the horizontal line entirely below an upward-opening absolute value function, or above a downward-opening absolute value function, will not have points of intersection and the equation will have no solutions. A graph with the horizontal line passing through the vertex will have exactly 1 solution.

HARDCOVER PAGES 77–86

Watch for the hardcover student edition page numbers for this lesson.

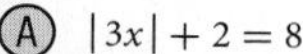

Explain 1 Solving Absolute Value Equations Algebraically

To solve absolute value equations algebraically, first isolate the absolute value on one side of the equation the same way you would isolate a variable. Then use the rule:

If $|x| = a$ (where a is a positive number), then $x = a$ OR $x = -a$.

Notice the use of a **disjunction** here in the rule for values of x. You cannot know from the original equation whether the expression inside the absolute value is positive or negative, so you must work through both possibilities to finish isolating x.

Example 1 **Solve each absolute value equation algebraically. Graph the solutions on a number line.**

(A) $|3x| + 2 = 8$

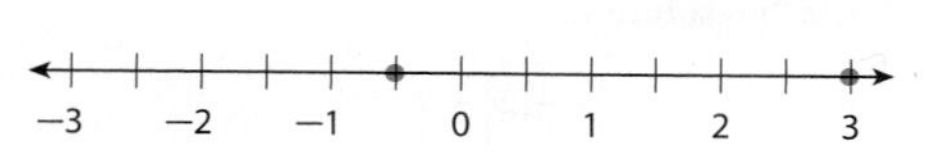

Subtract 2 from both sides. $|3x| = 6$

Rewrite as two equations. $3x = 6$ or $3x = -6$

Solve for x. $x = 2$ or $x = -2$

(B) $3|4x - 5| - 2 = 19$

Add 2 to both sides. $3|4x - 5| = 21$

Divide both sides by 3. $|4x - 5| = 7$

Rewrite as two equations. $4x - 5 = 7$ or $4x - 5 = -7$

Add 5 to all four sides. $4x = 12$ or $4x = -2$

Solve for x. $x = 3$ or $x = -\frac{1}{2}$

Your Turn

Solve each absolute value equation algebraically. Graph the solutions on a number line.

3. $\frac{1}{2}|x + 2| = 10$

$|x + 2| = 20$

$x + 2 = 20$ or $x + 2 = -20$

$x = 18$ or $x = -22$

4. $-2|3x - 6| + 5 = 1$

$-2|3x - 6| = -4$

$|3x - 6| = 2$

$3x - 6 = 2$ or $3x - 6 = -2$

$x = \frac{8}{3}$ or $x = \frac{4}{3}$

PROFESSIONAL DEVELOPMENT

Integrate Mathematical Practices

This lesson provides an opportunity to address Mathematical Practice **MP.6**, which calls for students to "attend to precision" and communicate precisely. Students find the solutions to absolute value equations both by graphing them, with and without technology, and through algebra. Students learn that *disjunction* is often used to express the solutions to absolute value equations, and they use the properties of algebra to accurately and efficiently find the solutions to various types of absolute value equations.

EXPLORE

Solving Absolute Value Equations Graphically

INTEGRATE TECHNOLOGY

Students have the option of completing the graphing activity either in the book or online.

QUESTIONING STRATEGIES

How do you solve an absolute value equation graphically? **Plot each side as if it were a separate function of x, and find the x-coordinates of the intersection points.**

Why do you write the solutions to the absolute value equation as a disjunction? **If two values of the variable both satisfy an equation, then one *or* the other can be correct.**

EXPLAIN 1

Solving Absolute Value Equations Algebraically

AVOID COMMON ERRORS

Some students may not isolate the absolute value expression on one side of the equation as a first step when solving the equation. Stress the importance of this step so that the equation is in the form $|x| = a$, which has the solution $x = a$ or $x = -a$.

QUESTIONING STRATEGIES

How do you interpret the solutions to an absolute value equation like $|x| = a$ on a number line? **Sample answer: The solutions are the same distance from 0 on either side of the number line.**

Why is it important to isolate the absolute value expression when solving an absolute value equation? **So you can remove the absolute value bars and rewrite the expression as a disjunction.**

EXPLAIN 2

Absolute Value Equations with Fewer than Two Solutions

QUESTIONING STRATEGIES

When does an absolute value equation have fewer than two solutions? when the absolute value is equal to zero or equal to a negative number

In the absolute value expression $d|ax+b|-c=-c$ for nonzero variables, how does d affect the solution? It does not affect it. The first step is to add c to both sides to get $d|ax+b|=0$. Because the product of a number and 0 is 0, you can divide both sides by d to get $|ax+b|=0$.

INTEGRATE TECHNOLOGY

A graphing calculator can be used to check the number of solutions to an absolute value equation. Graph each side of the equation as a function and then count the number of intersection points.

AVOID COMMON ERRORS

Some students may think that if an absolute value equation does not have two solutions, then there must be no solution. Explain to students that when the absolute value equals zero, there may be one solution. For example, $|3x+6|=0$ has one solution, −2, because 0 is neither positive nor negative.

Explain 2 Absolute Value Equations with Fewer than Two Solutions

You have seen that absolute value equations have two solutions when the isolated absolute value is equal to a positive number. When the absolute value is equal to zero, there is a single solution because zero is its own opposite. When the absolute value is equal to a negative number, there is no solution because absolute value is never negative.

Example 2 **Isolate the absolute value in each equation to determine if the equation can be solved. If so, finish the solution. If not, write "no solution."**

Ⓐ $-5|x+1|+2=12$

Subtract 2 from both sides.	$-5|x+1|=10$
Divide both sides by −5.	$|x+1|=-2$
Absolute values are never negative.	No Solution

Ⓑ $\frac{3}{5}|2x-4|-3=-3$

Add 3 to both sides.	$\frac{3}{5}|2x-4|=$ 0
Multiply both sides by $\frac{5}{3}$.	$|2x-4|=$ 0
Rewrite as one equation.	$2x-4=$ 0
Add 4 to both sides.	$2x=$ 4
Divide both sides by 2.	$x=$ 2

Your Turn

Isolate the absolute value in each equation to determine if the equation can be solved. If so, finish the solution. If not, write "no solution."

5. $3\left|\frac{1}{2}x+5\right|+7=5$

$3\left|\frac{1}{2}x+5\right|=-2$

$\left|\frac{1}{2}x+5\right|=-\frac{2}{3}$

No solution

6. $9\left|\frac{4}{3}x-2\right|+7=7$

$9\left|\frac{4}{3}x-2\right|=0$

$\left|\frac{4}{3}x-2\right|=0$

$x=\frac{3}{2}$

COLLABORATIVE LEARNING

Peer-to-Peer Activity

Have students work in pairs to brainstorm types of absolute value equations that have two solutions, one solution, or no solution. For example, instruct one student to write a conjecture about what type of absolute value equation has no solutions, and give an example. Then have the other student solve the example and write an explanation about whether the conjecture is correct or incorrect. Have students switch roles and repeat the exercise using an equation that has a different number of solutions.

Elaborate

7. Why is important to solve both equations in the disjunction arising from an absolute value equation? Why not just pick one and solve it, knowing the solution for the variable will work when plugged backed into the equation?
The solution to a mathematical equation is not simply any value of the variable that makes the equation work. Supplying only one value that works in the equation implies that it is the only value that works, which is incorrect.

8. **Discussion** Discuss how the range of the absolute value function differs from the range of a linear function. Graphically, how does this explain why a linear equation always has exactly one solution while an absolute value equation can have one, two, or no solutions?
The range of a non-constant linear function is all real numbers. The range of an absolute value function is $y \geq k$ if the function opens upward and $y \leq k$ if the function opens downward. Because the graph of a linear function is a line, a horizontal line will intersect it only once. Because the graph of an absolute value function is a V, a horizontal line can intersect it once, twice, or not at all.

9. **Essential Question Check-In** Describe, in your own words, the basic steps to solving absolute value equations and how many solutions to expect.
Isolate the absolute value expression. If the absolute value expression is equal to a positive number, solve for both the positive and negative case. If the absolute value expression is equal to zero, then remove the absolute value and solve the equation. There is one solution. If the absolute value expression is equal to a negative number, then there is no solution.

DIFFERENTIATE INSTRUCTION

Critical Thinking

Some students may need help in deciding whether absolute value equations have no solutions, one solution, or two solutions. You may want to suggest that they *always* follow this solving plan: (1) Write the original equation; then (2) isolate the absolute value expression on one side of the equal sign. It will have the form $|ax + b| = c$. (3) Rewrite the equation as two equations of the form $ax + b = c$ and $ax + b = -c$; and (4) solve each equation for x. There may be 0, 1, or 2 solutions. (5) If there are two solutions, write the answer using "or." (6) Check the solution(s) in the original problem.

ELABORATE

INTEGRATE MATHEMATICAL PRACTICES

Focus on Patterns

MP.8 Discuss with students how to solve an absolute value equation of the form $|ax + b| = c$. Students should routinely rewrite the next step as a disjunction, or a compound equation of the form $ax + b = c$ or $ax + b = -c$ and then solve each part of the equation.

QUESTIONING STRATEGIES

? How is the process of solving a linear absolute value equation like the process of solving a regular linear equation? **Both processes are similar initially, except that you isolate the absolute value in one case, but isolate the variable in the case of the linear equation. From there, the process is the same for each part of the disjunction of the two linear equations for the absolute value equation.**

PEER-TO-PEER ACTIVITY

Have students work in pairs. Have one student write an absolute value equation and have the partner solve it. The partner then explains why the solution(s) makes sense. Students switch roles and repeat the process. Encourage students to use the phrase "distance from zero" and the statement "This negative/positive integer makes the equation true."

SUMMARIZE THE LESSON

? How do you solve a linear absolute value equation? **Isolate the absolute value; write the absolute value as the disjunction of two linear equations; and solve each equation.**

EVALUATE

ASSIGNMENT GUIDE

Concepts and Skills	Practice
Explore Solving Absolute Value Equations Graphically	Exercise 1–4
Example 1 Solving Absolute Value Equations Algebraically	Exercises 5–8
Example 2 Absolute Value Equations with Fewer than Two Solutions	Exercises 9–16

INTEGRATE MATHEMATICAL PRACTICES

Focus on Reasoning

MP.2 Remind students to check their solutions by substituting the values into the original equation and verifying that both solutions make the equation true. When solving equations graphically, remind students that the x-value of an intersection point is a solution to the original equation.

Evaluate: Homework and Practice

- Online Homework
- Hints and Help
- Extra Practice

Solve the following absolute value equations by graphing.

1. $|x - 3| + 2 = 5$

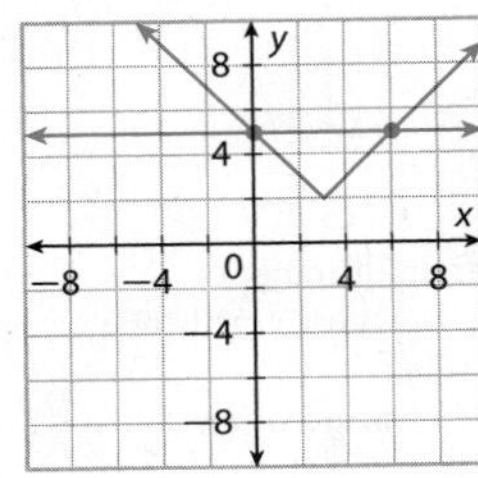

$x = 0$ or $x = 6$

2. $2|x + 1| + 5 = 9$

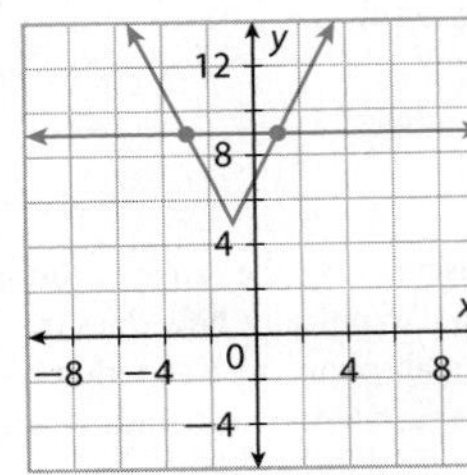

$x = -3$ or $x = 1$

3. $-2|x + 5| + 4 = 1$

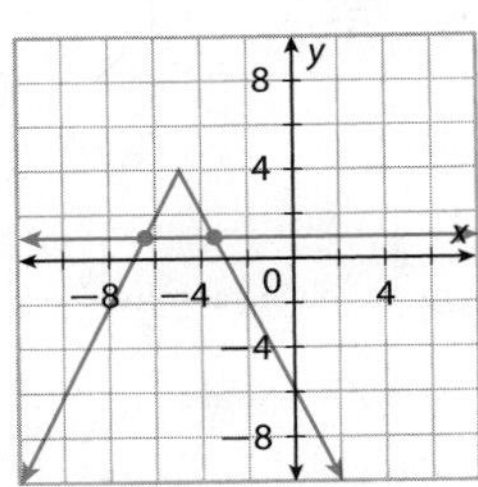

$x = -3\frac{1}{2}$ or $x = -6\frac{1}{2}$

4. $\left|\frac{3}{2}(x - 2)\right| + 3 = 2$

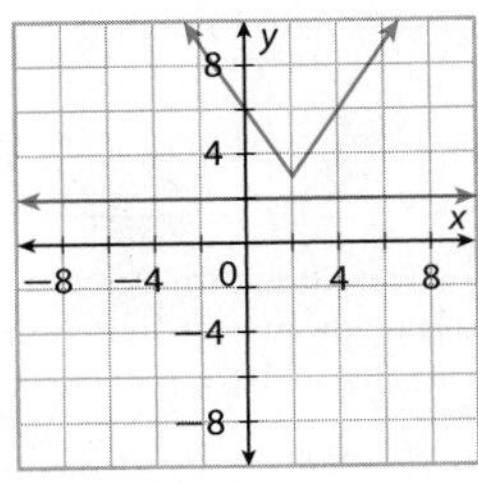

No solution

Solve each absolute value equation algebraically. Graph the solutions on a number line.

5. $|2x| = 3$

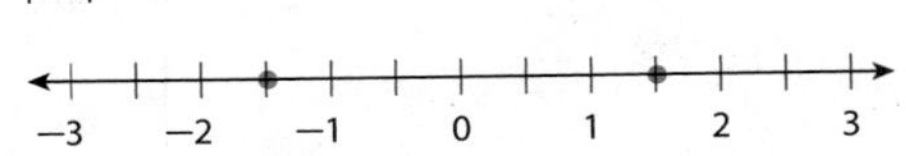

$2x = 3$ or $2x = -3$

$x = \frac{3}{2}$ or $x = -\frac{3}{2}$

6. $\left|\frac{1}{3}x + 4\right| = 3$

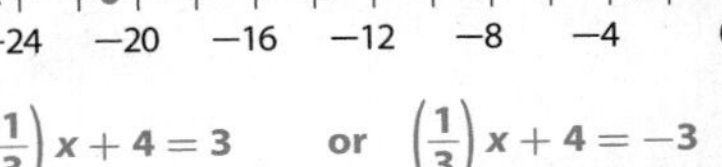

$\left(\frac{1}{3}\right)x + 4 = 3$ or $\left(\frac{1}{3}\right)x + 4 = -3$

$\left(\frac{1}{3}\right)x = -1$ or $\left(\frac{1}{3}\right)x = -7$

$x = -3$ or $x = -21$

Exercise	Depth of Knowledge (D.O.K.)	COMMON CORE Mathematical Practices
1–4	**2** Skills/Concepts	**MP.5** Using Tools
5–16	**2** Skills/Concepts	**MP.6** Precision
17	**3** Strategic Thinking	**MP.4** Modeling
18, 21	**3** Strategic Thinking	**MP.4** Modeling
19	**3** Strategic Thinking	**MP.6** Precision
20	**2** Skills/Concepts	**MP.6** Precision
22	**3** Strategic Thinking H.O.T.	**MP.3** Logic
23–25	**3** Strategic Thinking H.O.T.	**MP.6** Precision

7. $3|2x - 3| + 2 = 3$

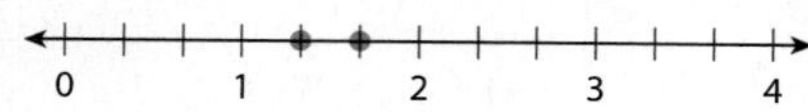

$$2x - 3 = \frac{1}{3}$$

$$2x - 3 = \frac{1}{3} \quad \text{or} \quad 2x - 3 = \frac{-1}{3}$$

$$2x = \frac{10}{3} \quad \text{or} \quad 2x = \frac{8}{3}$$

$$x = \frac{5}{3} \quad \text{or} \quad x = \frac{4}{3}$$

8. $-8|-x - 6| + 10 = 2$

$$-8|-x - 6| = -8$$

$$|-x - 6| = 1$$

$$-x - 6 = 1 \quad \text{or} \quad -x - 6 = -1$$

$$x = -7 \quad \text{or} \quad x = -5$$

Isolate the absolute values in the following equations to determine if they can be solved. If so, find and graph the solution(s). If not, write "no solution".

9. $\frac{1}{4}|x + 2| + 7 = 5$

$$\frac{1}{4}|x + 2| = -2$$

No solution

10. $-3|x - 3| + 3 = 6$

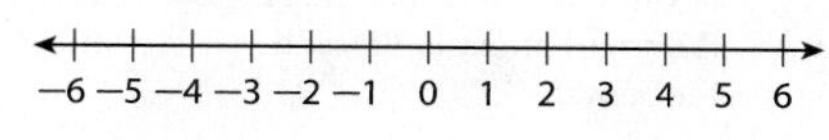

$$-3|x - 3| = 3$$

$$|x - 3| = -1$$

No solution

11. $2(|x + 4| + 3) = 6$

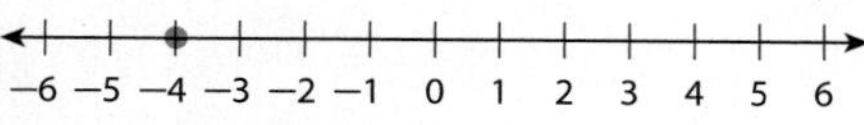

$$2|x + 4| + 6 = 6$$

$$2|x + 4| = 0$$

$$|x + 4| = 0$$

$$x = -4$$

12. $5|2x + 4| - 3 = -3$

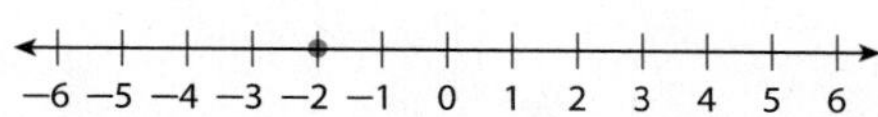

$$5|2x + 4| = 0$$

$$|2x + 4| = 0$$

$$2x + 4 = 0$$

$$x = -2$$

Solve the absolute value equations.

13. $|3x - 4| + 2 = 1$

$$|3x - 4| = -1$$

No solution

14. $7\left|\frac{1}{2}x + 3\frac{1}{2}\right| - 2 = 5$

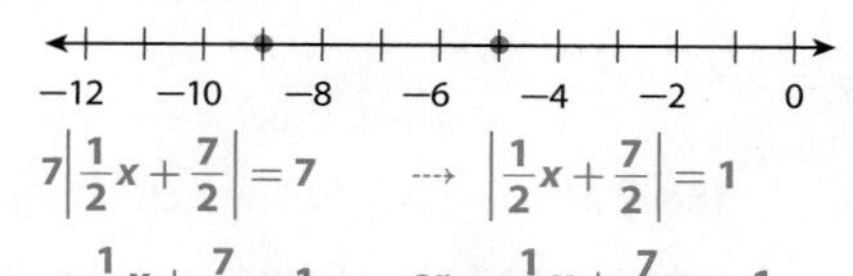

$$7\left|\frac{1}{2}x + \frac{7}{2}\right| = 7 \quad \longrightarrow \quad \left|\frac{1}{2}x + \frac{7}{2}\right| = 1$$

$$\frac{1}{2}x + \frac{7}{2} = 1 \quad \text{or} \quad \frac{1}{2}x + \frac{7}{2} = -1$$

$$\frac{1}{2}x = -\frac{5}{2} \quad \text{or} \quad \frac{1}{2}x = -\frac{9}{2}$$

$$x = -5 \quad \text{or} \quad x = -9$$

AVOID COMMON ERRORS

Students may erroneously include points on the graph *between* the solution points when they graph solutions. Remind students that the solution process gives 0, 1, or 2 solutions to an absolute value equation, not infinitely many solutions.

INTEGRATE MATHEMATICAL PRACTICES

Focus on Critical Thinking

MP.3 Ask students give examples of absolute value equations that have no solutions. Suggest that they think about how a graph of an equation with no solution will look. This graph should not show any points, so it is an empty graph.

INTEGRATE MATHEMATICAL PRACTICES

Focus on Modeling

MP.4 When modeling a problem in which an absolute value equation applies, have students start with a V-shaped diagram. This will help them remember that this type of function may have 0, 1, or 2 solutions to the associated equation, depending on the original real-world problem.

AVOID COMMON ERRORS

When solving absolute equations algebraically, watch for students who do not solve these equations by first rewriting them in the form $|ax + b| = c$. Remind them that the absolute value expression should be nonnegative before they proceed with the solution steps.

15. $|2(x + 5) - 3| + 2 = 6$

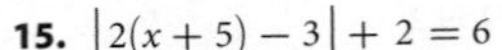

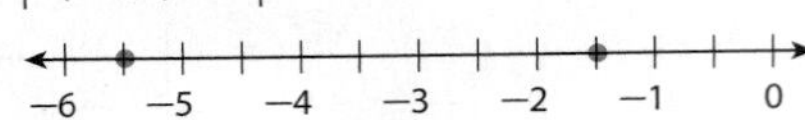

$|2x + 7| = 4$

$2x + 7 = 4$ or $2x + 7 = -4$

$2x = -3$ or $2x = -11$

$x = -\frac{3}{2}$ or $x = -\frac{11}{2}$

16. $-5|-3x + 2| - 2 = -2$

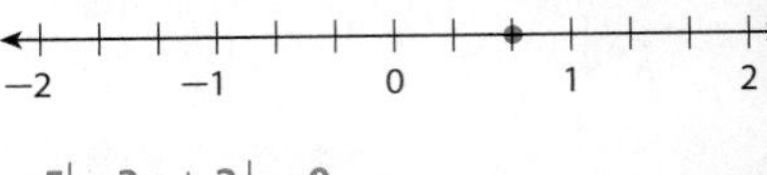

$-5|-3x + 2| = 0$

$|-3x + 2| = 0$

$-3x + 2 = 0$

$-3x = -2$

$x = \frac{2}{3}$

17. The bottom of a river makes a V-shape that can be modeled with the absolute value function, $d(h) = \frac{1}{5}|h - 240| - 48$, where d is the depth of the river bottom (in feet) and h is the horizontal distance to the left-hand shore (in feet).

A ship risks running aground if the bottom of its keel (its lowest point under the water) reaches down to the river bottom. Suppose you are the harbormaster and you want to place buoys where the river bottom is 30 feet below the surface. How far from the left-hand shore should you place the buoys?

$d(h) = -30$

$\frac{1}{5}|h - 240| - 48 = -30$

$h = 330$ or $h = 150$

The buoys should be placed at either 150 ft or 330 ft from the left-hand shore.

18. A flock of geese is flying past a photographer in a V-formation that can be described using the absolute value function $b(d) = \frac{3}{2}|d - 50|$, where $b(d)$ is the distance (in feet) of a goose behind the leader, and d is the distance from the photographer. If the flock reaches 27 feet behind the leader on both sides, find the distance of the nearest goose to the photographer.

$\frac{3}{2}|d - 50| = 27$

$d = 68$ feet or $d = 32$ feet

There are two geese 27 feet behind the leader, but only the one 32 feet from the photographer is the closest.

$d = 32$ feet

19. Geometry Find the points on the x-axis where a circle centered at (3, 0) with a radius of 5 crosses the x-axis. Use an absolute value equation and the fact that all points on a circle are the same distance (the radius) from the center.

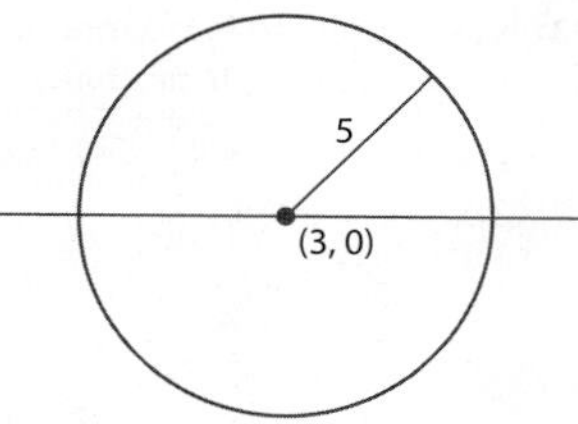

The points that are a distance of 5 from the center of the circle at $x = 3$ are given by $|x - 3| = 5$.

Solving $|x - 3| = 5$ gives $x = 8$ or $x = -2$.

The points are (−2, 0) and (8, 0).

20. Select the value or values of x that satisfy the equation $-\frac{1}{2}|3x - 3| + 2 = 1$.

Ⓐ $x = \frac{5}{3}$

B. $x = -\frac{5}{3}$

Ⓒ $x = \frac{1}{3}$

D. $x = -\frac{1}{3}$

E. $x = 3$

F. $x = -3$

G. $x = 1$

H. $x = -1$

$-\frac{1}{2}|3x - 3| = -1$

$|3x - 3| = 2$

$3x - 3 = 2$ **or** $3x - 3 = -2$

$3x = 5$ **or** $3x = 1$

$x = \frac{5}{3}$ **or** $x = \frac{1}{3}$

21. Terry is trying to place a satellite dish on the roof of his house at the recommended height of 30 feet. His house is 32 feet wide, and the height of the roof can be described by the function $h(x) = -\frac{3}{2}|x - 16| + 24$, where x is the distance along the width of the house. Where should Terry place the dish?

Use the model function to solve for x when $h(x) = 30$ feet.

$-\frac{3}{2}|x - 16| + 24 = 30$

$|x - 16| = -4$

No Solution. Terry does not have a spot on his roof that is 30 feet high.

H.O.T. Focus on Higher Order Thinking

22. Explain the Error While attempting to solve the equation $-3|x - 4| - 4 = 3$ a student came up with the following results. Explain the error and find the correct solution:

$-3|x - 4| - 4 = 3$

$-3|x - 4| = 7$

$|x - 4| = -\frac{7}{3}$

$x - 4 = -\frac{7}{3}$ or $x - 4 = \frac{7}{3}$

$x = \frac{5}{3}$ or $x = -\frac{19}{3}$

The student tried to replace the absolute value with two equations using the positive and negative values of the number on the other side of the equal sign. However, this number was negative and cannot be treated like a positive number. The isolated absolute value is equal to a negative number and therefore this equation has no solution.

SMALL GROUP ACTIVITY

Have students work in small groups to make a poster showing how to apply the steps for solving an absolute value equation. Give each group a different equation to solve. Then have each group present its poster to the rest of the class, and ask for a volunteer from the group to explain each step.

INTEGRATE MATHEMATICAL PRACTICES

Focus on Reasoning

MP.2 When solving absolute equations of the form $-|ax + b| = c$, where $c > 0$, students should recognize that the equation states that a negative absolute value is equal to a positive number. This is not possible because of the definition of absolute value, so while "solving the equation" gives numerical answers, these answers are not solutions to the original equation. You may want students to verify this by graphing. There will be no intersection points.

AVOID COMMON ERRORS

Watch for students who are confused by nested absolute value equations. Remind students to carefully write disjunctions for each part of the solution, as appropriate, using the same solution process they use for a single absolute equation.

PEER-TO-PEER DISCUSSION

Ask students to discuss with a partner what the solution to $|ax + b| = c$ means in terms of the graph of the related functions $f(x) = |ax + b|$ and $g(x) = c$. Then ask students to make conjectures about the solutions to $|ax + b| = c$ and the graphs of their related functions. Conjectures should include the possible number of intersection points and how the graph of the function looks. **The solutions to $|ax + b| = c$ are the x-coordinates of the intersection points of the related functions. Based on this, conjectures should include that the graphs of $f(x) = |ax + b|$ and $g(x) = c$ can have two, one, or no intersection points, and that the graph of $f(x)$ is V-shaped because this graph can intersect a line in two or fewer places.**

JOURNAL

Have students compare and contrast the methods they have learned for solving absolute value equations.

23. Communicate Mathematical Ideas Solve this absolute value equation and explain what algebraic properties make it possible to do so.

$3|x - 2| = 5|x - 2| - 7$

$3|x - 2| - 5|x - 2| = -7$			**Subtraction Property of Equality**
$(3 - 5)|x - 2| = -7$			**Distributive Property**
$|x - 2| = \frac{7}{2}$			**Division Property of Equality**
$x - 2 = \frac{7}{2}$	or	$x - 2 = -\frac{7}{2}$	**Definition of absolute value**
$x = \frac{11}{2}$	or	$x = -\frac{3}{2}$	**Addition Property of Equality**

24. Justify Your Reasoning This absolute value equation has nested absolute values. Use your knowledge of solving absolute value equations to solve this equation. Justify the number of possible solutions.

$||2x + 5| - 3| = 10$

Follow each possible solution path and use more disjunctions if needed.

$||2x + 5| - 3| = 10$

$|2x + 5| - 3 = 10$	or	$|2x + 5| - 3 = -10$
$|2x + 5| = 13$	or	$|2x + 5| = -7$
$|2x + 5| = 13$	or	No solution
$|2x + 5| = 13$		
$2x + 5 = 13$	or	$2x + 5 = -13$
$2x = 8$	or	$2x = -18$
$x = 4$	or	$x = -9$

There are two possible solutions because only one path produced solutions.

25. Check for Reasonableness For what type of real-world quantities would the negative answer for an absolute value equation not make sense?

Answers will vary. Sample answer: time, distance, height, length, speed

Lesson Performance Task

A snowball comes apart as a child throws it north, resulting in two halves traveling away from the child. The child is standing 12 feet south and 6 feet east of the school door, along an east-west wall. One fragment flies off to the northeast, moving 2 feet east for every 5 feet north of travel, and the other moves 2 feet west for every 5 feet north of travel. Write an absolute value function that describes the northward position, $n(e)$, of both fragments as a function of how far east of the school door they are. How far apart are the fragments when they strike the wall?

The fragments can be described as two lines originating at the child's coordinates, and then be replaced by a single absolute value function.

$$n(e) = \frac{5}{2}(e-6) \quad \text{or} \quad n(e) = -\frac{5}{2}(e-6)$$

$$n(e) = \frac{5}{2}|e-6|$$

To find where the fragments strike the school wall, solve for the eastward position when the fragments are 12 feet north of the child.

$$n(e) = \frac{5}{2}|e-6| = 12$$

$$|e-6| = \frac{24}{5}$$

$$e-6 = \frac{24}{5} \quad \text{or} \quad e-6 = -\frac{24}{5}$$

$$e = \frac{54}{5} \quad \text{or} \quad e = \frac{6}{5}$$

The fragments are $\left|\frac{54}{5} - \frac{6}{5}\right| = \left|\frac{48}{5}\right| = 9\frac{3}{5}$ **feet apart.**

EXTENSION ACTIVITY

Have students try to find an alternate solution method using the formula for the slope of a line. Student should find the coordinates for the snowball on the right to be $\left(10\frac{4}{5}, 12\right)$. Subtracting 6 from the value of x gives the distance from $(6, 12)$ to $(x, 12)$. That distance is $4\frac{4}{5}$ ft. The distance from the y-axis to the snowball on the left is $6 - 4\frac{4}{5} = 1\frac{1}{5}$ ft.

AVOID COMMON ERRORS

Some students may use the ratio $\frac{2}{5}$ in their equation instead of $\frac{5}{2}$. Explain that the snowball *rises* 5 feet north for every 2 feet west it *runs*. Thus, the ratio is $\frac{5}{2}$.

INTEGRATE MATHEMATICAL PRACTICES

Focus on Communication

MP.3 Discuss with students how solving for the eastward position solves for the distance of the snowball on the right, $e - 6 = \frac{24}{5}$, and the snowball on the left, $e - 6 = -\frac{24}{5}$. Then discuss how solving for e does not answer the problem. The difference between the two distances is equal to the distance the two are apart.

Scoring Rubric

2 points: Student correctly solves the problem and explains his/her reasoning.

1 point: Student shows good understanding of the problem but does not fully solve or explain his/her reasoning.

0 points: Student does not demonstrate understanding of the problem.

LESSON 2.3

Solving Absolute Value Inequalities

Common Core Math Standards

The student is expected to:

 **A-CED.A.1**

Create equations and inequalities in one variable and use them to solve problems. Also A-REI.B.3, F-IF.C.7b

Mathematical Practices

 **MP.4 Modeling**

Language Objective

Match absolute value equations and inequalities with their graphs, explaining and justifying reasoning.

ENGAGE

Essential Question: What are two ways to solve an absolute value inequality?

Possible answer: You can solve an absolute value inequality graphically or algebraically. For a graphical solution, treat each side of the inequality as a function and graph the two functions. Use the inequality symbol to determine the intervals on the x-axis where one graph lies above or below the other. For an algebraic solution, isolate the absolute value expression and rewrite the inequality as a compound inequality that doesn't involve absolute value so that you can finish solving the inequality.

PREVIEW: LESSON PERFORMANCE TASK

View the Engage section online. Discuss the names of the planets, the elliptical path the planets follow, and why the distance a planet is from the sun might relate to absolute value inequalities. Then preview the Lesson Performance Task.

Name ______ Class ______ Date ______

2.3 Solving Absolute Value Inequalities

Resource Locker

Essential Question: What are two ways to solve an absolute value inequality?

Explore Visualizing the Solution Set of an Absolute Value Inequality

You know that when solving an absolute value equation, it's possible to get two solutions. Here, you will explore what happens when you solve absolute value inequalities.

(A) Determine whether each of the integers from −5 to 5 is a solution of the inequality $|x| + 2 < 5$. Write *yes* or *no* for each number in the table. If a number is a solution, plot it on the number line.

−5 −4 −3 −2 −1 0 1 2 3 4 5

Number	Solution?
$x = -5$	no
$x = -4$	no
$x = -3$	no
$x = -2$	yes
$x = -1$	yes
$x = 0$	yes
$x = 1$	yes
$x = 2$	yes
$x = 3$	no
$x = 4$	no
$x = 5$	no

(B) Determine whether each of the integers from −5 to 5 is a solution of the inequality $|x| + 2 > 5$. Write *yes* or *no* for each number in the table. If a number is a solution, plot it on the number line.

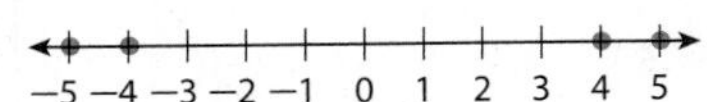

Number	Solution?
$x = -5$	yes
$x = -4$	yes
$x = -3$	no
$x = -2$	no
$x = -1$	no
$x = 0$	no
$x = 1$	no
$x = 2$	no
$x = 3$	no
$x = 4$	yes
$x = 5$	yes

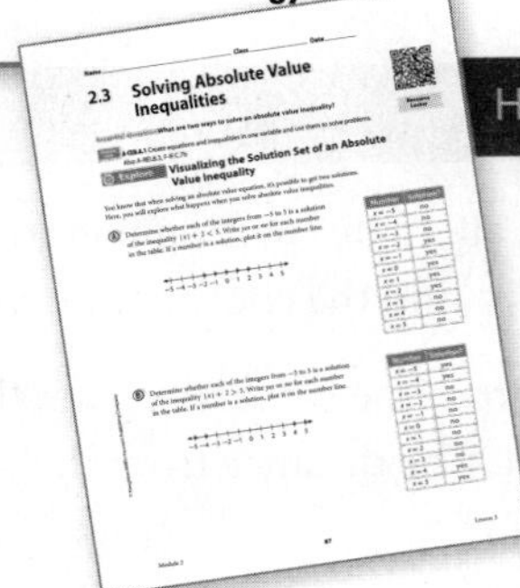

HARDCOVER PAGES 87–100

Watch for the hardcover student edition page numbers for this lesson.

(C) State the solutions of the equation $|x| + 2 = 5$ and relate them to the solutions you found for the inequalities in Steps A and B.

The solutions are -3 and 3. These are the only numbers that are not solutions of the inequalities $|x| + 2 < 5$ and $|x| + 2 > 5$.

(D) If x is any real number and not just an integer, graph the solutions of $|x| + 2 < 5$ and $|x| + 2 > 5$.

Graph of all real solutions of $|x| + 2 < 5$:

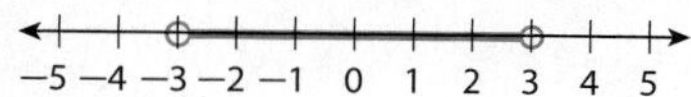

Graph of all real solutions of $|x| + 2 > 5$:

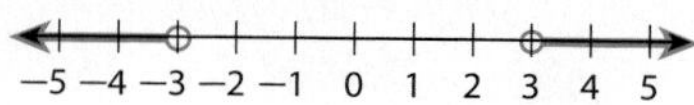

Reflect

1. It's possible to describe the solutions of $|x| + 2 < 5$ and $|x| + 2 > 5$ using inequalities that don't involve absolute value. For instance, you can write the solutions of $|x| + 2 < 5$ as $x > -3$ and $x < 3$. Notice that the word *and* is used because x must be both greater than -3 and less than 3. How would you write the solutions of $|x| + 2 > 5$? Explain.
   Write the solutions of $|x| + 2 > 5$ as $x < -3$ or $x > 3$. Use the word *or* because x must be either less than -3 or greater than 3; it can't be both.

2. Describe the solutions of $|x| + 2 \leq 5$ and $|x| + 2 \geq 5$ using inequalities that don't involve absolute value.
   The solutions of $|x| + 2 \leq 5$ are the values of x for which $x \geq -3$ and $x \leq 3$. The solutions of $|x| + 2 \geq 5$ are the values of x for which $x \leq 3$ or $x \geq 3$.

Explain 1 Solving Absolute Value Inequalities Graphically

You can use a graph to solve an absolute value inequality of the form $f(x) > g(x)$ or $f(x) < g(x)$, where $f(x)$ is an absolute value function and $g(x)$ is a constant function. Graph each function separately on the same coordinate plane and determine the intervals on the x-axis where one graph lies above or below the other. For $f(x) > g(x)$, you want to find the x-values for which the graph $f(x)$ is above the graph of $g(x)$. For $f(x) < g(x)$, you want to find the x-values for which the graph of $f(x)$ is below the graph of $g(x)$.

Example 1 **Solve the inequality graphically.**

(A) $|x + 3| + 1 > 4$

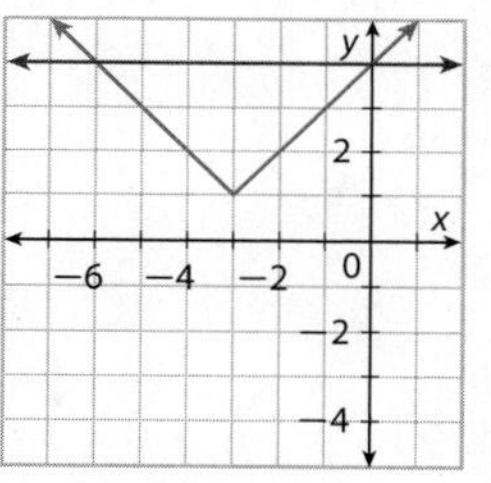

The inequality is of the form $f(x) > g(x)$, so determine the intervals on the x-axis where the graph of $f(x) = |x + 3| + 1$ lies above the graph of $g(x) = 4$.

The graph of $f(x) = |x + 3| + 1$ lies above the graph of $g(x) = 4$ to the left of $x = -6$ and to the right of $x = 0$, so the solution of $|x + 3| + 1 > 4$ is $x < -6$ or $x > 0$.

PROFESSIONAL DEVELOPMENT

Math Background

An absolute value inequality is often in the form $|ax + b| < c$ or $|ax + b| > c$. If the inequality is in the form $|ax + b| < c$, then it can be rewritten as the compound inequality $-c < ax + b < c$, and solved for x. The solution will be of the form $\frac{-c-b}{a} < x$ and $x < \frac{c-b}{a}$. If the inequality is in the form $|ax + b| > c$, it can be rewritten as the compound inequality $c < ax + b$ or $ax + b < -c$, and solved for x. The solution will be of the form $\frac{c-b}{a} < x$ or $x \frac{-c-b}{a}$. The solutions are easily adjusted for the "or equal" symbols.

EXPLORE

Visualizing the Solution Set of an Absolute Value Inequality

QUESTIONING STRATEGIES

How would you characterize the solutions to an absolute value inequality? **Sample answer: They lie either between two values or everywhere else except between the two values, depending on the inequality.**

Why do you write the solutions to the absolute value inequality as a compound inequality statement? **Sample answer: because the graphs of a compound inequality statement will include all of the solutions of the inequality**

EXPLAIN 1

Solving Absolute Value Inequalities Graphically

QUESTIONING STRATEGIES

How do you interpret which points are solutions of the graphs? **Sample answer: If $f(x) > g(x)$, the graph of $f(x)$ must be "above" the graph of $g(x)$. The solutions are the x-values in the interval along the x-axis where $f(x)$ has y-values greater than $g(x)$.**

How do you know when the endpoints of the solution interval on the x-axis are not included in the solution? **The original inequality is "$<$," not "$\leq$."**

Ⓑ $|x-2|-3<1$

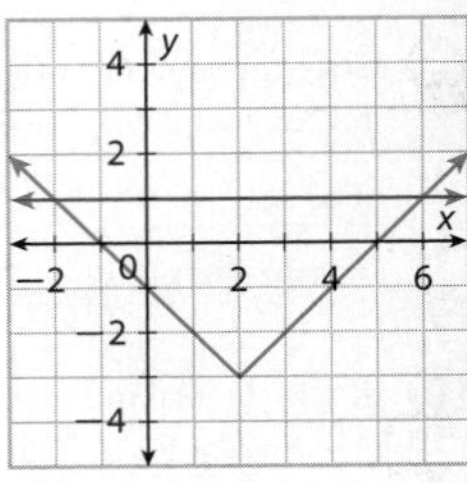

The inequality is of the form $f(x) < g(x)$, so determine the intervals on the x-axis where the graph of $f(x) = |x-2|-3$ lies **below** the graph of $g(x) = 1$.

The graph of $f(x) = |x-2|-3$ lies **below** the graph of $g(x) = 1$ between $x =$ **−2** and $x =$ **6**, so the solution of $|x-2|-3<1$ is $x >$ **−2** *and* $x <$ **6**.

Reflect

3. Suppose the inequality in Part A is $|x+3|+1 \geq 4$ instead of $|x+3|+1>4$. How does the solution change?

The solution now includes the endpoints of the interval: $x \leq -6$ *or* $x \geq 0$.

4. In Part B, what is another way to write the solution $x > -2$ and $x < 6$?

$-2 < x < 6$

5. **Discussion** Suppose the graph of an absolute value function $f(x)$ lies entirely above the graph of the constant function $g(x)$. What is the solution of the inequality $f(x) > g(x)$? What is the solution of the inequality $f(x) < g(x)$?

The solution of $f(x) > g(x)$ is all real numbers, because every point on the graph of $f(x)$ is above the corresponding point on the graph of $g(x)$. The solution of $f(x) < g(x)$ is no real number, because no point on the graph of $f(x)$ is below the corresponding point on the graph of $g(x)$.

Your Turn

6. Solve $|x+1|-4 \leq -2$ graphically.

The inequality is of the form $f(x) \leq g(x)$, so determine the intervals on the x-axis where the graph of $f(x) = |x+1|-4$ intersects or lies below the graph of $g(x) = -2$. The graph of $f(x) = |x+1|-4$ intersects the graph of $g(x) = -2$ at $x = -3$ and $x = 1$ and lies below the graph of $g(x) = -2$ between those x-values, so the solution of $|x+1|-4 \leq -2$ is $x \geq -3$ *and* $x \leq 1$.

COLLABORATIVE LEARNING

Small Group Activity

Have students work in groups to make a flowchart that explains how to solve each of the four types of an absolute value inequality of the form $|ax+b| \square c$ or $|ax-b| \square c$, where the box represents the inequality symbol. For example:

$|2x+3| \leq 6$ $|2x+3| < 6$ $|2x+3| < 6$ $|2x+3| \geq 6$

Ask each student in a group to finish one branch of the flowchart. Then have the group collate the branches to make the entire flowchart.

Explain 2 Solving Absolute Value Inequalities Algebraically

To solve an absolute value inequality algebraically, start by isolating the absolute value expression. When the absolute value expression is by itself on one side of the inequality, apply one of the following rules to finish solving the inequality for the variable.

Solving Absolute Value Inequalities Algebraically
1. If $|x| > a$ where a is a positive number, then $x < -a$ or $x > a$.
2. If $|x| < a$ where a is a positive number, then $-a < x < a$.

Example 2 **Solve the inequality algebraically. Graph the solution on a number line.**

Ⓐ $|4 - x| + 15 > 21$

$|4 - x| > 6$

$4 - x < -6$ or $4 - x > 6$

$-x < -10$ or $-x > 2$

$x > 10$ or $x < -2$

The solution is $x > 10$ or $x < -2$.

−6 −4 −2 0 2 4 6 8 10 12 14

Ⓑ $|x + 4| - 10 \leq -2$

$|x + 4| \leq$ **8**

$x + 4 \geq$ **−8** and $x + 4 \leq$ **8**

$x \geq$ **−12** and $x \leq$ **4**

The solution is $x \geq$ **−12** and $x \leq$ **4**,

or **−12** $\leq x \leq$ **4**.

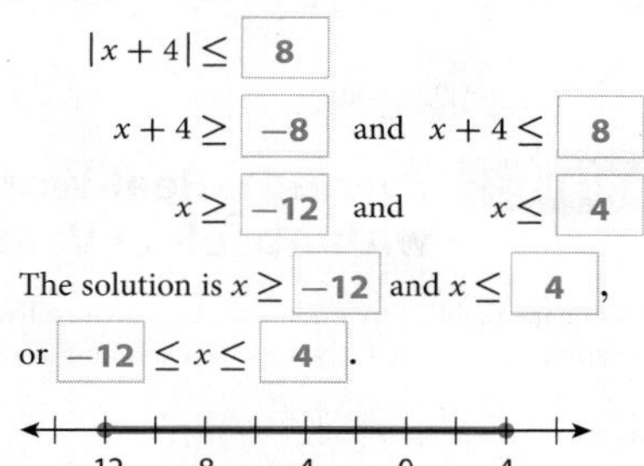

−12 −8 −4 0 4

Reflect

7. In Part A, suppose the inequality were $|4 - x| + 15 > 14$ instead of $|4 - x| + 15 > 21$. How would the solution change? Explain.
The first step in solving would be to subtract 15 from both sides and get $|4 - x| > -1$. At this point, the solving process can stop, because the absolute value of every number is greater than −1. So, the solution is all real numbers.

8. In Part B, suppose the inequality were $|x + 4| - 10 \leq -11$ instead of $|x + 4| - 10 \leq -2$. How would the solution change? Explain.
The first step in solving would be to add 10 to both sides and get $|x + 4| \leq -1$. At this point, the solving process can stop, because there are no real numbers whose absolute value is less than or equal to −1. So, the solution is no real number.

DIFFERENTIATE INSTRUCTION

Visual Cues

You may want students to use visual models to help them understand some simple inequalities as well as some real-world inequalities. For simple inequalities of the form $|x| < a$ or $|x| > a$, constructing a graph of possible solutions on a number line as a first step may be helpful. For a real-world problem, drawing a number line with all points graphed between the starting value and the tolerance amounts may be most helpful. This should help students visualize how to construct an inequality based on the graph.

EXPLAIN 2

Solving Absolute Value Inequalities Algebraically

QUESTIONING STRATEGIES

When does the graph of the solution to an inequality include the endpoints? **when the original inequality is $\leq$ or $\geq$**

When does the graph of the solution include the points between the endpoints found in the solution? **When the original inequality is $\leq$, the compound inequality is an "and" statement, so its graph includes the intersection of two graphs. These graphs intersect between the endpoints.**

INTEGRATE TECHNOLOGY

A graphing calculator can be used to check the solution graph for an inequality. For example, you would graph $y = |4 - x| + 15 > 21$ to check the solution for $|4 - x| + 15 > 21$. The graph will be a broken horizontal line above the x-axis with endpoints at −2 and 10. You must interpret the graph to be open at the endpoints. So, the solution graph is $x < -2$ or $x > 10$.

AVOID COMMON ERRORS

Some students confuse when to use *or* and *and* when rewriting an absolute value inequality. Remind students that when the inequality is $|ax + b| < c$ or $|ax + b| \leq c$, they should rewrite the inequality using *and*. When the inequality is $|ax + b| > c$ or $|ax + b| \geq c$, they should rewrite the inequality using *or*. Emphasize the importance of checking some of the solutions in the original inequality to help avoid this error.

EXPLAIN 3

Solving a Real-World Problem with Absolute Value Inequalities

QUESTIONING STRATEGIES

? When does an absolute value inequality apply to a real-world situation? Sample answer: When a model for the real-world situation includes a range of values where the sign of the difference between the values doesn't matter, you can write an absolute value model that will apply. For example, if the model is $|\ell - 3.25| \leq 0.02$, expanding the inequality gives $3.25 \leq \ell \leq 3.27$, which gives possible values on either side of ℓ.

INTEGRATE MATHEMATICAL PRACTICES

Focus on Reasoning

MP.2 Encourage students to solve the absolute value inequality for a real-world problem in the standard way: (1) Write a compound inequality using and or *or*, depending on the original problem; (2) solve each inequality; (3) rewrite the solution as a compound inequality using *and* or *or*; (4) graph the compound inequality if needed; and (5) check some solution points in the original problem to see if they make sense.

Your Turn

Solve the inequality algebraically. Graph the solution on a number line.

9. $3|x - 7| \geq 9$

$3|x - 7| \geq 9$

$|x - 7| \geq 3$

$x - 7 \leq -3$ or $x - 7 \geq 3$

$x \leq 4$ or $x \geq 10$

The solution is $x \leq 4$ or $x \geq 10$.

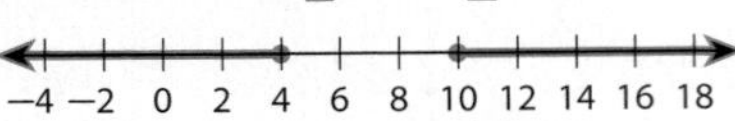

10. $|2x + 3| < 5$

$|2x + 3| < 5$

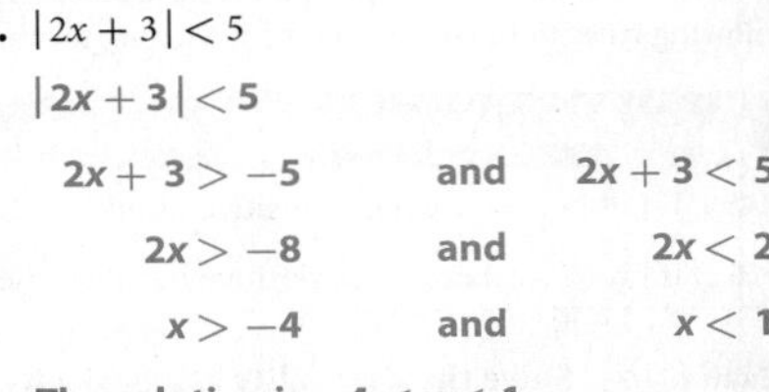

$2x + 3 > -5$ and $2x + 3 < 5$

$2x > -8$ and $2x < 2$

$x > -4$ and $x < 1$

The solution is $-4 < x < 1$.

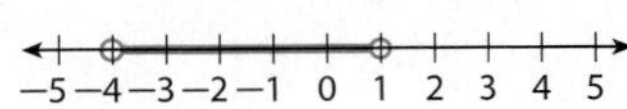

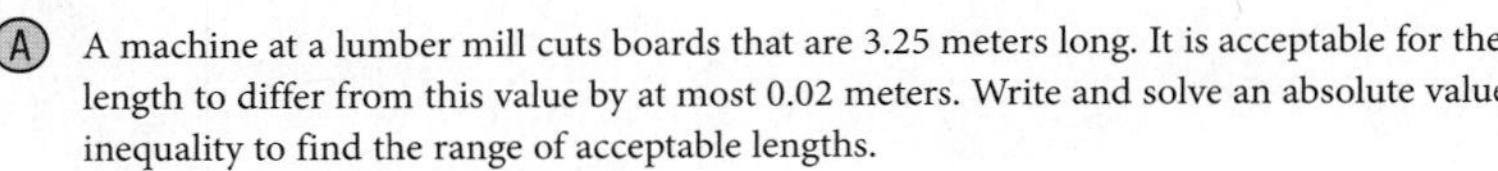

Explain 3 Solving a Real-World Problem with Absolute Value Inequalities

Absolute value inequalities are often used to model real-world situations involving a margin of error or *tolerance*. Tolerance is the allowable amount of variation in a quantity.

Example 3

Ⓐ A machine at a lumber mill cuts boards that are 3.25 meters long. It is acceptable for the length to differ from this value by at most 0.02 meters. Write and solve an absolute value inequality to find the range of acceptable lengths.

Analyze Information

Identify the important information.

- The boards being cut are 3.25 meters long.
- The length can differ by at most 0.02 meters.

Formulate a Plan

Let the length of a board be ℓ. Since the sign of the difference between ℓ and 3.25 doesn't matter, take the absolute value of the difference. Since the absolute value of the difference can be at most 0.02, the inequality that models the situation is

$|\ell - 3.25| \leq 0.02$.

Solve

$|\ell - 3.25| \leq 0.02$

$\ell - 3.25 \geq -0.02$ and $\ell - 3.25 \leq 0.02$

$\ell \geq 3.23$ and $\ell \leq 3.27$

So, the range of acceptable lengths is $3.23 \leq \ell \leq 3.27$

LANGUAGE SUPPORT EL

Connect Vocabulary

Help students understand the term *compound inequality* as it is used to solve an absolute value inequality. Have them recall that a disjunction is a compound statement joined by the word *or*. A disjunction applies to all inequalities of the form $|x| > a$ or $|x| \geq a$. Since inequalities can also be of the form $|x| < a$ or $|x| \leq a$, students also need to learn a compound statement joined by the word *and*. Have students use note cards to write examples of all four types of inequalities they may see in the lesson, and ask them to write the associated compound inequality with a graph of the solution set for each example.

 **Justify and Evaluate**

The bounds of the range are positive and close to **3.25**, so this is a reasonable answer.

The answer is correct since **3.23** $+ 0.02 = 3.25$ and **3.27** $- 0.02 = 3.25$.

Your Turn

11. A box of cereal is supposed to weigh 13.8 oz, but it's acceptable for the weight to vary as much as 0.1 oz. Write and solve an absolute value inequality to find the range of acceptable weights.

Let the weight of the cereal be w. The sign of the difference between w and 13.8 doesn't matter, so take the absolute value of the difference. Since the absolute value of the difference can be as much as 0.1, the inequality that models the situation is $|w - 13.8| \leq 0.1$.

Solve:

$|w - 13.8| \leq 0.1$

$w - 13.8 \geq 0.1$ **and** $w - 13.8 \leq 0.1$

$w \geq 13.7$ **and** $w \leq 13.9$

So, the range of acceptable weights of the cereal (in ounces) is $13.7 \leq w \leq 13.9$.

Elaborate

12. Describe the values of x that satisfy the inequalities $|x| < a$ and $|x| > a$ where a is a positive constant.

For $|x| < a$, the solutions are values of x between $-a$ and a. For $|x| > a$, the solutions are the values of x beyond $-a$ and a (that is, the values of x less than $-a$ or the values of x greater than a).

13. How do you algebraically solve an absolute value inequality?

Isolate the absolute value expression. Then rewrite the inequality as a compound inequality that uses either *and* or *or* and that doesn't involve absolute value. Finish solving for the variable.

14. Explain why the solution of $|x| > a$ is all real numbers if a is a negative number.

Since the absolute value of any number is always nonnegative, it is always greater than any negative number. So, all real numbers satisfy the inequality.

15. Essential Question Check-In How do you solve an absolute value inequality graphically?

Treat each side of the inequality as a function and graph the two functions. Use the inequality symbol to determine the intervals on the x-axis where one graph lies above or below the other.

ELABORATE

INTEGRATE MATHEMATICAL PRACTICES

Focus on Patterns

MP.8 Discuss with students how to solve an absolute value inequality of the form $|ax + b| < c$ and $|ax + b| > c$. Students should routinely rewrite the next step as a compound inequality using *and* or *or*, and then solve each part of the inequality.

QUESTIONING STRATEGIES

? How is solving an absolute value inequality like and different from solving an absolute value equation? **They are alike in that some of the solution steps are the same once a compound statement is written for the absolute value expression. They are different in that an absolute value inequality may be an *and* statement with infinitely many solutions as well as an *or* statement with infinitely many solutions, but an absolute value equation is only an *or* statement with two, one, or zero solutions.**

CONNECT VOCABULARY EL

Relate the word *conjunction* to its opposite, *disjunction* (discussed in the previous lesson). Explain that the prefix *con* means *to join.* For a conjunction to be true, all of its parts *(joined)* must be true.

SUMMARIZE THE LESSON

? How do you solve a linear absolute value inequality? **Isolate the absolute value expression; write the absolute value expression as a compound statement of two linear inequalities; solve each inequality; and rewrite the solution as a compound statement.**

EVALUATE

ASSIGNMENT GUIDE

Concepts and Skills	Practice
Explore Visualizing the Solution Set of an Absolute Value Inequality	Exercises 1–2
Example 1 Solving Absolute Value Inequalities Graphically	Exercises 3–10
Example 2 Solving Absolute Value Inequalities Algebraically	Exercises 11–16
Example 3 Solving a Real-World Problem with Absolute Value Inequalities	Exercises 17–22

INTEGRATE MATHEMATICAL PRACTICES

Focus on Reasoning

MP.2 Remind students to check their solutions by substituting some values into the original inequality and verifying that they make the inequality true. When solving inequalities graphically, remind students that the interval on the x-axis where $f(x) > g(x)$ or $f(x) < g(x)$ is makes up the solution set.

Evaluate: Homework and Practice

- Online Homework
- Hints and Help
- Extra Practice

1. Determine whether each of the integers from −5 to 5 is a solution of the inequality $|x - 1| + 3 \geq 5$. If a number is a solution, plot it on the number line.

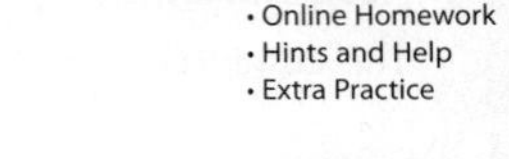

The integers from −5 to 5 that satisfy the inequality are −5, −4, −3, −2, −1, 3, 4, and 5.

2. Determine whether each of the integers from −5 to 5 is a solution of the inequality $|x + 1| - 2 \leq 1$. If a number is a solution, plot it on the number line.

The integers from −5 to 5 that satisfy the inequality are −4, −3, −2, −1, 0, 1, and 2.

Solve each inequality graphically.

3. $2|x| \leq 6$

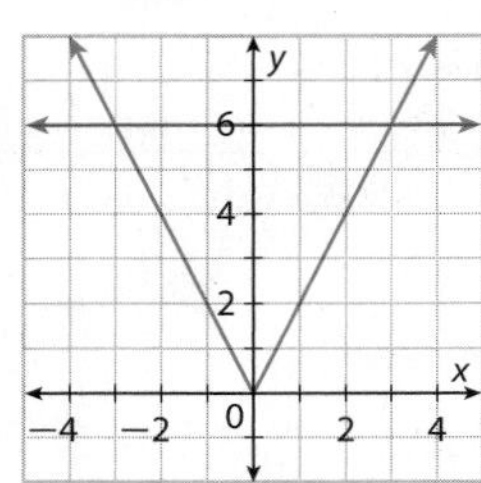

The solution is $-3 \leq x \leq 3$.

4. $|x - 3| - 2 > -1$

The solution is $x < 2$ or $x > 4$.

5. 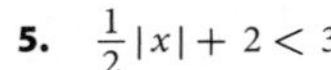 $\frac{1}{2}|x| + 2 < 3$

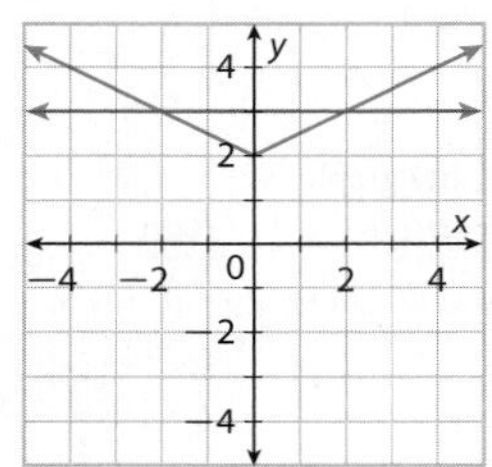

The solution is $-2 < x < 2$.

6. $|x + 2| - 4 \geq -2$

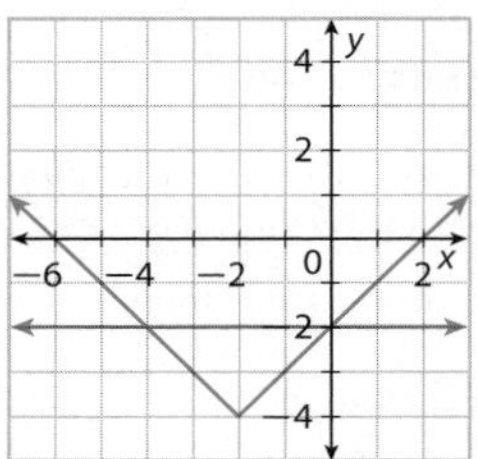

The solution is $x \leq -4$ or $x \geq 0$.

Exercise	Depth of Knowledge (D.O.K.)	COMMON CORE Mathematical Practices
1–2	**1** Recall of Information	**MP.6** Precision
3–6	**1** Recall of Information	**MP.4** Modeling
7–16	**2** Skills/Concepts	**MP.2** Reasoning
17–21	**2** Skills/Concepts	**MP.1** Problem Solving
22	**2** Skills/Concepts H.O.T.	**MP.4** Modeling
23	**3** Strategic Thinking H.O.T.	**MP.**6 Precision
24	**3** Strategic Thinking H.O.T.	**MP.**2 Reasoning

Match each graph with the corresponding absolute value inequality. Then give the solution of the inequality.

A. $2|x| + 1 > 3$ B. $2|x + 1| < 3$ C. $2|x| - 1 > 3$ D. $2|x - 1| < 3$

7. 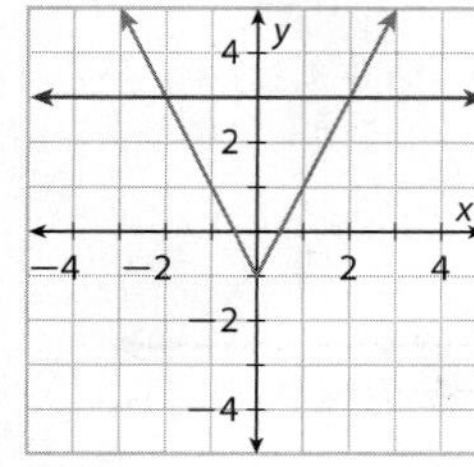

C. The solution is $x < -2$ or $x > 2$.

8. 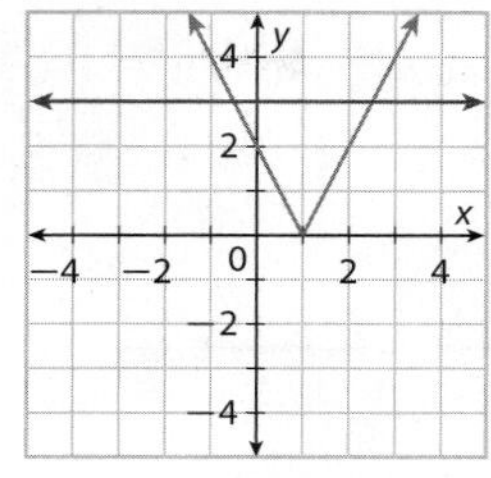

D. The solution is $-\frac{1}{2} < x < \frac{5}{2}$.

9. 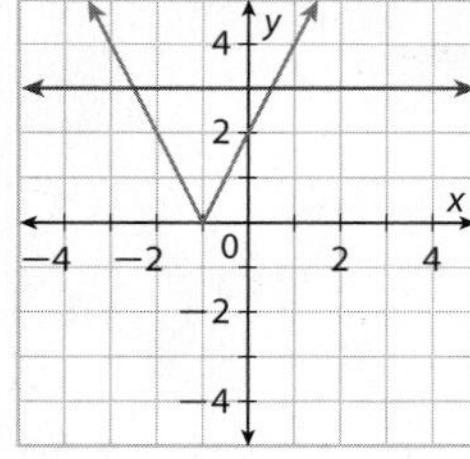

B. The solution is $-\frac{5}{2} < x < \frac{1}{2}$.

10. 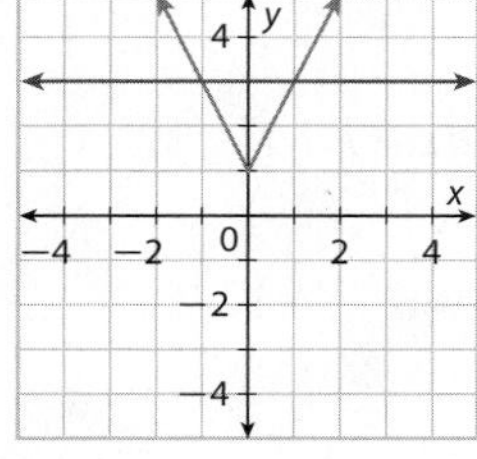

A. The solution is $x < -1$ or $x > 1$.

Solve each absolute value inequality algebraically. Graph the solution on a number line.

11. $2\left|x - \frac{7}{2}\right| + 3 > 4$

$$2\left|x - \frac{7}{2}\right| + 3 > 4$$

$$2\left|x - \frac{7}{2}\right| > 1$$

$$\left|x - \frac{7}{2}\right| > \frac{1}{2}$$

$$x - \frac{7}{2} < -\frac{1}{2} \text{ or } x - \frac{7}{2} > \frac{1}{2}$$

$$x < 3 \qquad x > 4$$

The solution is $x < 3$ or $x > 4$.

−2 −1 0 1 2 3 4 5 6 7 8 9

SMALL GROUP ACTIVITY

Have students work in small groups to make a poster showing how to apply the steps for solving an absolute value inequality. Give each group a different inequality to solve. Then have each group present its poster to the rest of the class, and ask for a volunteer from the group to explain each step.

INTEGRATE MATHEMATICAL PRACTICES

Focus on Math Connections

MP.1 Point out that the concept *margin of error* is used in surveys to describe how many percentage points higher or lower a poll result can be and still be considered a "true" figure, meaning a result that is representative of the population.

12. $|2x + 1| - 4 < 5$

$|2x + 1| - 4 < 5$

$|2x + 1| < 9$

$2x + 1 > -9$ and $2x + 1 < 9$

$2x > -10$ $\quad 2x < 8$

$x > -5$ $\quad x < 4$

The solution is $-5 < x < 4$.

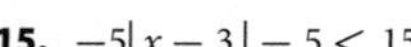

13. $3|x + 4| + 2 \geq 5$

$3|x + 4| + 2 \geq 5$

$3|x + 4| \geq 3$

$|x + 4| \geq 1$

$x + 4 \leq -1$ or $x + 4 \geq 1$

$x \leq -5$ $\quad x \geq -3$

The solution is $x \leq -5$ or $x \geq -3$.

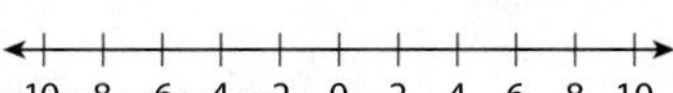

14. $|x + 11| - 8 \leq -3$

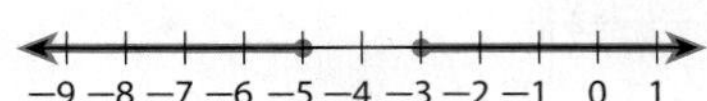

$|x + 11| - 8 \leq -3$

$|x + 11| \leq 5$

$x + 11 \geq -5$ and $x + 11 \leq 5$

$x \geq -16$ $\quad x \leq -6$

The solution is $-16 \leq x \leq -6$.

15. $-5|x - 3| - 5 < 15$

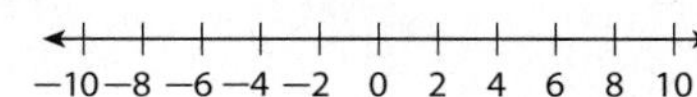

$-5|x - 3| < 20$

$|x - 3| > -4$

no real number

16. $8|x + 4| + 10 < 2$

$8|x + 4| < -8$

$|x + 4| < -1$

no real number

Solve each problem using an absolute value inequality.

17. The thermostat for a house is set to 68 °F, but the actual temperature may vary by as much as 2 °F. What is the range of possible temperatures?

Let the temperature in the house be T. The sign of the difference between T and 68 doesn't matter, so take the absolute value of the difference. Since the absolute value of the difference can be as much as 2, the inequality that models the situation is $|T - 68| \leq 2$.

$|T - 68| \leq 2$

$|T - 68| \geq -2$ and $|T - 68| \leq 2$

$T \geq 66$ $\quad T \leq 70$

The range of house temperatures (in degrees Fahrenheit) is $66 \leq T \leq 70$.

18. The balance of Jason's checking account is \$320. The balance varies by as much as \$80 each week. What are the possible balances of Jason's account?

Let the balance of Jason's account be B. The sign of the difference between B and 320 doesn't matter, so take the absolute value of the difference. Since the absolute value of the difference can be as much as 80, the inequality that models the situation is $|B - 320| \leq 80$.

$|B - 320| \leq 80$

$B - 320 \geq -80$ and $B - 320 \leq 80$

$B \geq 240$ $\quad B \leq 400$

The range of possible balances (in dollars) is $240 \leq B \leq 400$.

19. On average, a squirrel lives to be 6.5 years old. The lifespan of a squirrel may vary by as much as 1.5 years. What is the range of ages that a squirrel lives?

Let the age of a squirrel be a. The sign of the difference between a and 6.5 doesn't matter, so take the absolute value of the difference. Since the absolute value of the difference can be as much as 1.5, the inequality that models the situation is $|x - 6.5| \leq 1.5$.

$|x - 6.5| \leq 1.5$

$x - 6.5 \geq -1.5$ and $x - 6.5 \leq 1.5$

$x \geq 5$ $\quad x \leq 8$

The range of ages (in years) that a squirrel lives is $5 \leq a \leq 8$.

PEER-TO-PEER DISCUSSION

Ask students to discuss with a partner what the solution to an inequality of the form $|ax + b| < c$ means in terms of the graph of the related functions $f(x) = |ax + b|$ and $g(x) = c$. Then ask students to make conjectures about the solutions to $|ax + b| < c$ based on the graphs of their related functions. Conjectures should include the interval along the x-axis that represents the solutions and how the graphs of these functions look. **The solutions to $|ax + b| < c$ are points in the interval along the x-axis for which $f(x) < g(x)$. Based on this, conjectures should include that the graphs of $f(x) = |ax + b|$ and $g(x) = c$ show the interval of points that satisfy the compound statement $-c < ax + b < c$.**

AVOID COMMON ERRORS

Watch for students who confuse which type of compound statement to use, *and* or *or*. Remind students that the solution process gives infinitely many solutions to the inequality, and that the type of compound statement determines whether the solution points are between the endpoints or everywhere but between the endpoints.

20. You are playing a history quiz game where you must give the years of historical events. In order to score any points at all for a question about the year in which a man first stepped on the moon, your answer must be no more than 3 years away from the correct answer, 1969. What is the range of answers that allow you to score points?

Let your answer be a. The sign of the difference between a and 1969 doesn't matter, so take the absolute value of the difference. Since the absolute value of the difference can be no more than 3, the inequality that models the situation is $|a - 1969| \leq 3$.

$|a - 1969| \leq 3$

$a - 1969 \geq -3$ **and** $a - 1969 \leq 3$

$a \geq 1966 \qquad a \leq 1972$

The range of answers that allows you to score points is $1966 \leq a \leq 1972$.

21. The speed limit on a road is 30 miles per hour. Drivers on this road typically vary their speed around the limit by as much as 5 miles per hour. What is the range of typical speeds on this road?

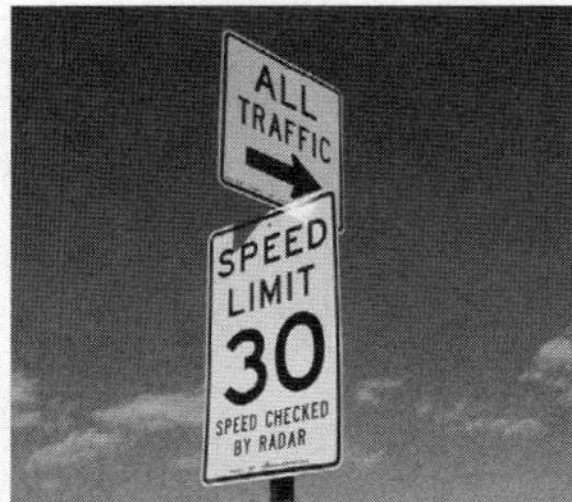

Let the speed of a car be s. The sign of the difference between s and 30 doesn't matter, so take the absolute value of the difference. Since the absolute value of the difference can be as much as 5, the inequality that models the situation is $|s - 30| \leq 5$.

$|s - 30| \leq 5$

$s - 30 \geq -5$ **and** $s - 30 \leq 5$

$s \geq 25 \qquad s \leq 35$

The range of typical speeds (in miles per hour) is $25 \leq s \leq 35$.

H.O.T. Focus on Higher Order Thinking

22. Represent Real-World Problems A poll of likely voters shows that the incumbent will get 51% of the vote in an upcoming election. Based on the number of voters polled, the results of the poll could be off by as much as 3 percentage points. What does this mean for the incumbent?

Let the incumbent's percentage of votes among all likely voters (not just those polled) be v. The sign of the difference between v and 51 doesn't matter, so take the absolute value of the difference. Since the absolute value of the difference can be as much as 3, the inequality that models the situation is $|v - 51| \leq 3$.

$|v - 51| \leq 3$

$v - 51 \geq -3$ **and** $v - 51 \leq 3$

$v \geq 48$ **and** $v \leq 54$

The range for the incumbent's percentage of votes among all likely voters is $48 \leq v \leq 54$, which means that the incumbent could still lose the election if the incumbent's percentage of votes among all likely voters (not just those polled) is less than 50%.

23. Explain the Error A student solved the inequality $|x - 1| - 3 > 1$ graphically. Identify and correct the student's error.

I graphed the functions $f(x) = |x - 1| - 3$ and $g(x) = 1$. Because the graph of $g(x)$ lies above the graph of $f(x)$ between $x = -3$ and $x = 5$, the solution of the inequality is $-3 < x < 5$.

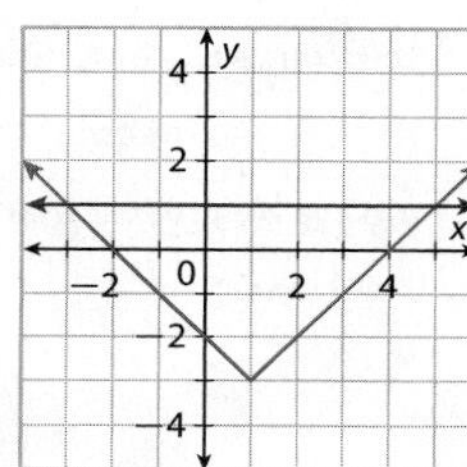

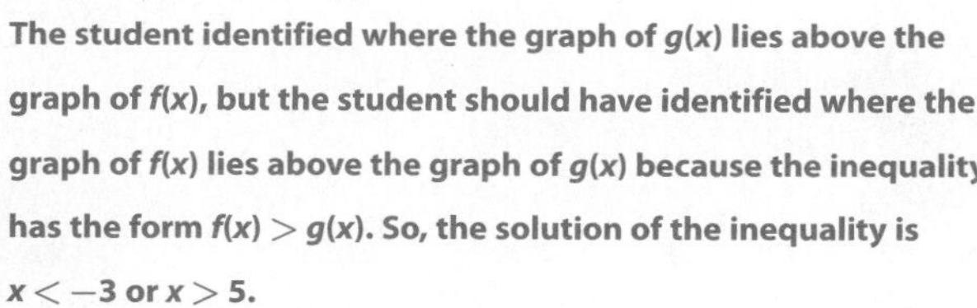

The student identified where the graph of $g(x)$ lies above the graph of $f(x)$, but the student should have identified where the graph of $f(x)$ lies above the graph of $g(x)$ because the inequality has the form $f(x) > g(x)$. So, the solution of the inequality is $x < -3$ or $x > 5$.

INTEGRATE MATHEMATICAL PRACTICES

Focus on Modeling

MP.4 When modeling a problem in which an absolute value inequality involving tolerance applies, have students start with a number line diagram. Have them plot the starting value and then all points within the tolerance range greater than and less than the starting value. This will provide a visual connection to the inequality that applies, depending on the original real-world problem.

JOURNAL

Have students compare and contrast the methods they have learned for solving absolute value inequalities.

24. Multi-Step Recall that a literal equation or inequality is one in which the constants have been replaced by letters.

a. Solve $|ax + b| > c$ for x. Write the solution in terms of a, b, and c. Assume that $a > 0$ and $c > 0$.

$|ax + b| > c$

$ax + b < -c$ **or** $ax + b > c$

$ax < -c - b$ $\quad$ $ax > c - b$

$x < \frac{-c-b}{a}$ $\quad$ $x > \frac{c-b}{a}$

The solution is $x < \frac{-c-b}{a}$ **or** $x > \frac{c-b}{a}$.

b. Use the solution of the literal inequality to find the solution of $|10x + 21| > 14$.

Substitute 10 for *a*, 21 for *b*, and 14 for *c* in the solution of the literal inequality and simplify.

The solution is $x < \frac{-14-21}{10}$ **or** $x > \frac{-14-21}{10}$**, which simplifies to** $x < -3.5$ **or** $x > -0.7$.

c. Explain why you must assume that $a > 0$ and $c > 0$ before you begin solving the literal inequality.

If $a = 0$, you would not be able to divide by a. If $a < 0$, you would need to reverse the direction of the inequality and get a different solution. If $c < 0$, the inequality would have no solution because $|ax + b|$ will always be greater than c. If $c = 0$, the inequality has an infinite number of solutions.

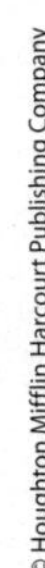

Lesson Performance Task

The distance between the Sun and each planet in our solar system varies because the planets travel in elliptical orbits around the Sun. Here is a table of the average distance and the variation in the distance for the five innermost planets in our solar system.

	Average Distance	Variation
Mercury	36 million miles	7.5 million miles
Venus	67.2 million miles	0.5 million miles
Earth	92.75 million miles	1.75 million miles
Mars	141 million miles	13 million miles
Jupiter	484 million miles	24 million miles

a. Write and solve an inequality to represent the range of distances that can occur between the Sun and each planet.

b. Calculate the percentage variation (variation divided by average distance) in the orbit of each of the planets. Based on these percentages, which planet has the most elliptical orbit?

Mercury $|x - 36| \leq 7.5$

$x - 36 \leq 7.5$ AND $x - 36 \geq -7.5$

$x \leq 43.5$ $\quad$ $x \geq 28.5$

ge for Mercury is $28.5 \leq x \leq 43.5$.

Venus $|x - 67.2| \leq 0.5$

$x - 67.2 \leq 0.5$ AND $x - 67.2 \geq -0.5$

$x \leq 67.7$ $\quad$ $x \geq 66.7$

ge for Venus is $66.7 \leq x \leq 67.7$.

Earth $|x - 92.75| \leq 1.75$

$x - 92.75 \leq 1.75$ AND $x - 92.75 \geq -1.75$

$x \leq 94.5$ $\quad$ $x \geq 91$

ge for Earth is $91 \leq x \leq 94.5$.

Mars $|x - 141| \leq 13$

$x - 141 \leq 13$ AND $x - 141 \geq -13$

$x \leq 154$ $\quad$ $x \geq 128$

Range for Mars is $128 \leq x \leq 154$.

Jupiter $|x - 484| \leq 24$

$x - 484 \leq 24$ AND $x - 484 \geq -24$

$x \leq 508$ $\quad$ $x \geq 460$

Range for Jupiter is $460 \leq x \leq 508$.

b. Mercury 21%, Venus 1%, Earth 2%, Mars 9%, Jupiter 5%; Mercury has the most elliptical orbit.

EXTENSION ACTIVITY

Have students research the dwarf planet Pluto to find its average distance and its range of distance from the sun. Students will find that Pluto is approximately 39.5 AU (astronomical units) from the sun. Pluto's closest point to the sun is 29.7 AU. Pluto's farthest point away from the sun is 49.7 AU. 1 AU is equal to Earth's distance from the sun, or 1 AU is about 93 million miles.

CONNECT CONTEXT EL

Some students may not be familiar with the meanings of *average distance* and *variation*. Draw a horizontal line segment on the board. To the left of the line segment, some distance away, draw the sun. At the middle point of the line segment write "average distance". To the right and left of the middle point write "variation". Explain that the planet's location is at some point on the line segment. Its exact location varies, but the average of all of its possible locations is the middle point.

AVOID COMMON ERRORS

Some students may subtract x (the range) from the average distance. For example, for Mercury they may write $|36 - x| \leq 7.5$ instead of $|x - 36| \leq 7.5$. Because they are finding the absolute value of the expression they will still get the correct range for Mercury.

Scoring Rubric

2 points: Student correctly solves the problem and explains his/her reasoning.

1 point: Student shows good understanding of the problem but does not fully solve or explain his/her reasoning.

0 points: Student does not demonstrate understanding of the problem.

Study Guide Review

ASSESSMENT AND INTERVENTION

Assign or customize module reviews.

MODULE PERFORMANCE TASK

Mathematical Practices: MP.1, MP.2, MP.4, MP.6, MP.7
A-REI.B.3

SUPPORTING STUDENT REASONING

Students should begin this problem by focusing on how they will go about determining the range of acceptable karat values for each ring.

SCAFFOLDING SUPPORT

- Help students to understand that because 1 karat is 1/24 of the whole, they can find the expected percent of gold in each ring by multiplying the karat value by 1/24 and then by 100% to find the percent.
- Students may not intuitively use an absolute value inequality but may instead find the percentage and see if it is within a range. Use this context to revisit the idea of absolute value inequalities. Specifically:
  low % < (ideal % − actual %) < high %
  corresponds to
  $$\frac{\text{high \%} - \text{low \%}}{2} < |\text{ideal \%} - \text{actual \%}|$$

STUDY GUIDE REVIEW

Absolute Value Functions, Equations, and Inequalities

MODULE 2

Essential Question: How can you use absolute value functions to solve real-world problems?

Key Vocabulary
absolute value *(valor absoluto)*
absolute-value equation *(ecuación de valor absoluto)*
coefficient *(coeficiente)*
disjunction *(disyunción)*
domain *(dominio)*
function *(función)*
inequality *(desigualdad)*
parameter *(parámetro)*
range *(rango)*
symmetry *(simetría)*
vertex *(vértice)*

KEY EXAMPLE *(Lesson 2.1)*

Given the function $g(x) = \left|\frac{1}{3}(x+6)\right| - 1$, predict what the graph will look like compared to the parent function, $f(x) = |x|$.

The graph of $g(x)$ will be the graph of $f(x)$ translated down 1 unit and left 6 units. There will also be a horizontal stretch of $f(x)$ by a factor of 3.

KEY EXAMPLE *(Lesson 2.2)*

Solve $6|2x+3| + 1 = 25$ algebraically.

$6\|2x+3\| = 24$	Subtract 1 from both sides.
$\|2x+3\| = 4$	Divide both sides by 6.
$2x+3 = 4$ or $2x+3 = -4$	Rewrite as two equations.
$2x = 1$ or $2x = -7$	Subtract 3 from all four sides.
$x = \frac{1}{2}$ or $x = -\frac{7}{2}$	Solve for x.
So, $x = \frac{1}{2}$ or $-\frac{7}{2}$.	

KEY EXAMPLE *(Lesson 2.3)*

Solve $|x+2| - 4 < 4$ algebraically, then graph the solution on a number line.

$$|x+2| - 4 < 4$$

$\|x+2\| < 8$	Add 4 to both sides.
$x+2 < 8$ or $x+2 > -8$	Rewrite as two inequalities.
$x < 6$ or $x > -10$	Subtract 2 from all four sides.

The solution is $x < 6$ or $x > -10$.

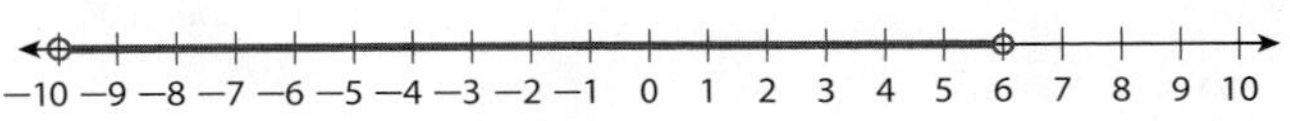

SCAFFOLDING SUPPORT (CONTINUED)

- Students should recognize that the range can be expressed as an absolute value inequality, for example, $t \geq |\text{ideal \%} - \text{actual \%}|$, where t is the tolerance.
- The tolerance is half a karat, so students will need to figure out the percentage for half a karat, which is $\frac{1}{2} \times \frac{1}{24} \times 100\% \approx 2.08\%$.

EXERCISES

Solve. *(Lessons 2.2, 2.3)*

1. $-10|x+2| = -70$

   $x = 5$ or $x = -9$

2. $|3x+7| = 27$

   $x = \frac{20}{3}$ or $x = -\frac{34}{3}$

3. $\frac{1}{7}|8+x| \leq 5$

   $-43 \leq x \leq 27$

4. $|x-2| - 5 > 10$

   $x > 17$ or $x < -13$

5. Explain how the graph of $g(x) = \left|\frac{3}{7}(x-4)\right| + 2$ compares to the graph of $h(x) = \frac{3}{7}(x-4) + 2$. *(Lesson 2.1)*

   Possible Answer: The graphs are the same at and to the right of $x = 4$. However, the graph of $g(x)$ is a reflection of $h(x)$ across $y = 2$ to the left of $x = 4$.

6. Leroy wants to place a chimney on his roof. It is recommended that the chimney be set at a height of at least 25 feet. The height of the roof is described by the function $r(x) = -\frac{4}{3}|x-10| + 35$, where x is the width of the roof. Where should Leroy place the chimney if the house is 40 feet wide? *(Lesson 2.3)*

   Leroy can place the chimney at or between 2.5 feet and 17.5 feet along the width of the roof.

MODULE PERFORMANCE TASK

What Is the Purity of Gold?

You have three gold rings labeled 10 karat, 14 karat, and 18 karat, and would like to know if the rings are correctly labeled. The table shows the results of an analysis of the rings.

Ring Label	Actual Percentage of Gold
10-karat	40.6%
14-karat	59.5%
18-karat	71.2%

In the United States, jewelry manufacturers are legally allowed a half karat tolerance. Determine which of the rings, if any, have an actual percentage of gold that falls outside this tolerance.

Use your own paper to list any additional information you will need and then complete the task. Be sure to write down all your data and assumptions. Then use graphs, numbers, words, or algebra to explain how you reached your conclusion.

DISCUSSION OPPORTUNITIES

- Why is it important to have tolerances on purity of gold?
- Some countries do not allow for negative tolerances on gold. What does this mean?

SAMPLE SOLUTION

First, calculate the expected percent of gold for each ring using $k \times \frac{1}{24} \times 100\%$.

Next, write an inequality for each karat value using the legal tolerance, $t \geq |\text{ideal \%} - \text{actual \%}|$, where $t = \frac{1}{2} \times \frac{1}{24} \times 100 \approx 2.08\%$.

Finally, use the inequality and the actual percentage values for each ring to determine if the rings are correctly labeled.

Karat	ideal percent	actual percent
10	$10 \times \frac{1}{24} \times 100\% \approx 41.7\%$	40.6%
14	$14 \times \frac{1}{24} \times 100\% \approx 58.3\%$	59.5%
18	$18 \times \frac{1}{24} \times 100\% \approx 75\%$	71.2%

Karat	$|\text{ideal \%} - \text{actual \%}|$	Correct label?
10	$|41.7\% - 40.6\%| = 1.1\% \leq 2.08\%$	Yes
14	$|58.3\% - 59.5\%| = 1.2\% \leq 2.08\%$	Yes
18	$|75\% - 71.2\%| = 3.8\% > 2.08\%$	No

Assessment Rubric

2 points: Student correctly solves the problem and explains his/her reasoning.

1 point: Student shows good understanding of the problem but does not fully solve or explain.

0 points: Student does not demonstrate understanding of the problem.

Ready to Go On?

ASSESS MASTERY

Use the assessment on this page to determine if students have mastered the concepts and standards covered in this module.

ASSESSMENT AND INTERVENTION

Access Ready to Go On? assessment online, and receive instant scoring, feedback, and customized intervention or enrichment.

ADDITIONAL RESOURCES

Response to Intervention Resources

- Reteach Worksheets

Differentiated Instruction Resources

- Reading Strategies EL
- Success for English Learners EL
- Challenge Worksheets

Assessment Resources

- Leveled Module Quizzes

Ready to Go On?

2.1–2.3 Absolute Value Functions, Equations, and Inequalities

- Online Homework
- Hints and Help
- Extra Practice

Solve. *(Lesson 2.1)*

1. $|-2x - 3| = 6$

$x = -\frac{9}{2}$ or $x = \frac{3}{2}$

2. $\frac{1}{4}|-4 - 3x| = 2$

$x = -4$ or $x = \frac{4}{3}$

3. $|3x + 8| = 2$

$x = -2$ or $x = -\frac{10}{3}$

4. $4|x + 7| + 3 = 59$

$x = -21$ or $x = 7$

Solve each inequality using the method indicated. *(Lesson 2.2)*

5. $|5x + 2| \leq 13$ (algebraically)

$-3 \leq x$ or $\leq \frac{11}{5}$

6. $|x - 2| + 1 \leq 5$ (graphically)

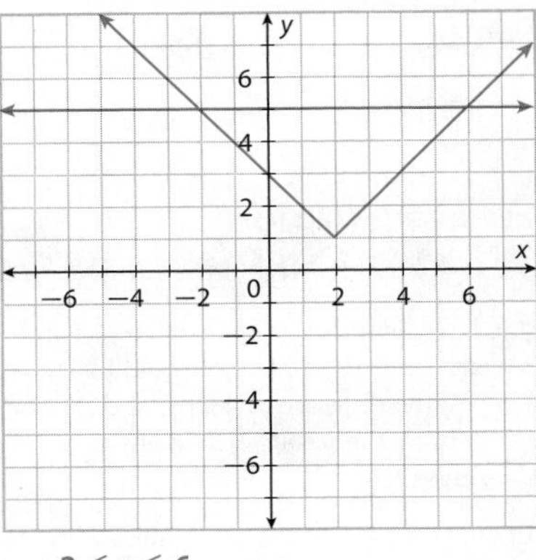

$-2 \leq x \leq 6$

ESSENTIAL QUESTION

7. Write a real world situation that could be modeled by $|x - 14| = 3$. *(Lesson 2.1)*

Possible Answer: There are supposed to be 14 biscuits in a frozen package, but there could be as many as 3 extra or 3 fewer in each bag, depending on the weight of the biscuits. Solving the equality will give the highest and lowest amounts of biscuits in the bag.

COMMON CORE Common Core Standards

Lesson	Items	Content Standards	Mathematical Practices
2.2	1	**A-CED.A.1, A-REI.B.3**	**MP.2**
2.2	2	**A-CED.A.1, A-REI.B.3**	**MP.2**
2.3	3	**A-CED.A.1, A-REI.B.3**	**MP.1**
2.3	4	**A-CED.A.1, A-REI.B.3**	**MP.1**
2.1	5	**F-IF.C.7b**	**MP.6**
2.3	6	**A-CED.A.1, A-REI.B.3**	**MP.6**

Assessment Readiness

1. Look at each inequality. Will the graph of the inequality be reflected over the x-axis when compared to $f(x) = |x|$? Select Yes or No for A–C.
   - **A.** $g(x) = 3|x - 4|$ ○ Yes ● No
   - **B.** $h(x) = -\frac{1}{2}|x|$ ● Yes ○ No
   - **C.** $j(x) = |x + 3| - 2$ ○ Yes ● No

2. Consider the absolute value equation $\frac{2}{3}|x - 4| + 2 = 5$ Choose True or False for each statement.
   - **A.** Solving $\frac{2}{3}|x - 4| + 2 = 5$ gives the same x-values as solving $\left|\frac{2}{3}(x - 4)\right| + 2 = 5.$ ● True ○ False
   - **B.** To solve the equation for x, the first step is to add 4 to both sides. ○ True ● False
   - **C.** Before the step to rewrite as two equations, the equation looks like: $|x - 4| = 3.$ ● True ○ False

3. Describe the domain, range, and vertex of the function $f(x) = 3|x - 4| + 2$. Explain your answers.

   The domain is $\{x \mid -\infty \leq x \leq \infty\}$ because the function continues in both positive and negative x directions without end. The range is $\{y \mid y \geq 2\}$ because the function starts at the y-value of 2, and opens upward. The vertex is (4, 2), because that is where the function changes direction.

4. Laurie wants to put a portable cellular phone mini-tower on her roof. The tower cannot be placed higher than 30 feet. The slant of her roof can be represented by the equation $r(x) = -\frac{1}{4}|x| + 60$. If her house is 40 feet wide, where could she place the tower? Explain.

   Since the tower cannot be more than 30 feet high, we solve the inequality $30 \geq -\frac{1}{4}|x| + 60$, which tells us that she cannot place the tower on the roof. The entire roof is more than 30 feet high.

MIXED REVIEW
Assessment Readiness

ASSESSMENT AND INTERVENTION

Assign ready-made or customized practice tests to prepare students for high-stakes tests.

ADDITIONAL RESOURCES

Assessment Resources

- Leveled Module Quizzes: Modified, B

AVOID COMMON ERRORS

Item 2 Some students will not realize that there is more than one way to solve a problem and that some steps can be completed in different ways, yet still be equivalent. Remind students of the different ways to solve problems, and that the way presented to them may not be the way they prefer to use.

COMMON CORE Common Core Standards

Lesson	Exercise	Content Standards	Mathematical Practices
1.3, 2.1	1*	F-IF.B.4, F-IF.C.7b	MP.5
2.2	2	A-REI.B.3	MP.1
1.1, 2.1	3*	F-IF.B.5, F-IF.C.7b	MP.5
2.3	4	A-REI.B.3	MP.1

* Item integrates mixed review concepts from previous modules or a previous course.

MIXED REVIEW

Assessment Readiness

ASSESSMENT AND INTERVENTION

Assign ready-made or customized practice tests to prepare students for high-stakes tests.

ADDITIONAL RESOURCES

Assessment Resources

- Leveled Unit Tests: Modified, A, B, C
- Performance Assessment

AVOID COMMON ERRORS

Item 8 Some students will automatically find the behavior of the functions as they approach positive infinity rather than negative infinity. Remind students to look to the left side of the graph when finding the end behavior as the graph approaches negative infinity.

UNIT 1 MIXED REVIEW

Assessment Readiness

- Online Homework
- Hints and Help
- Extra Practice

1. Consider the function $f(x) = 2(x - 1)^2 + 5$. Choose True or False for each statement.
   - **A.** The range is $y \geq 5$. ● True ○ False
   - **B.** The range is $y \geq 7$. ○ True ● False
   - **C.** The domain is $-\infty < x < \infty$. ● True ○ False

2. Consider the function $g(x) = -3f(x + 1) - 1$. Choose True or False for each statement.
   - **A.** When compared to $f(x) = 2x$, $g(x)$ will be reflected over the x-axis. ● True ○ False
   - **B.** When compared to $f(x) = 2x$, $g(x)$ will have a vertical stretch of 3. ● True ○ False
   - **C.** When compared to $f(x) = 2x$, $g(x)$ will be translated right 1 unit and up 1 unit. ○ True ● False

3. Consider the equation $f(x) = \frac{1}{2}x - 5$. Is the given equation the inverse of $f(x)$? Select Yes or No for A–C.
   - **A.** $f^{-1}(x) = 2x - 10$ ○ Yes ● No
   - **B.** $f^{-1}(x) = -\frac{1}{2}x + 5$ ○ Yes ● No
   - **C.** $f^{-1}(x) = 2x + 10$ ● Yes ○ No

4. Consider the equation $3|x - 2| + 6 = 12$. Choose True or False for each statement.
   - **A.** The equation can be solved using the Pythagorean Theorem. ○ True ● False
   - **B.** The solutions of the equation are $x = 4$ and $x = 0$. ● True ○ False
   - **C.** The first step to solving the equation could be subtracting 6 from both sides of the equation. ● True ○ False

5. Look at each function. Will the graph of the function be stretched or compressed in the horizontal direction when compared to $f(x) = |x|$? Select Yes or No for A–C.
   - **A.** $g(x) = 2|x + 1| - 4$ ● Yes ○ No
   - **B.** $h(x) = |x - 2| - 1$ ○ Yes ● No
   - **C.** $j(x) = \left|\frac{1}{2}x - 7\right| + 2$ ● Yes ○ No

COMMON CORE **Common Core Standards**

Items	Content Standards	Mathematical Practices
1	F-IF.B.5	MP.2
2	F-BF.B.3	MP.7
3	F-BF.B.4	MP.7
4	A-REI.B.3	MP.5
5	F-IF.C.7b	MP.2
6	F-IF.B.4	MP.4

* Item integrates mixed review concepts from previous modules or a previous course.

6. A triathlete is training for her next race and starts by swimming 2 miles in 1 hour. She rests for 1 hour and then rides her bike 100 miles in 5 hours. She rests another hour and runs 20 miles in 5 hours. Draw a graph showing the distance she travels over time. Explain your choice.

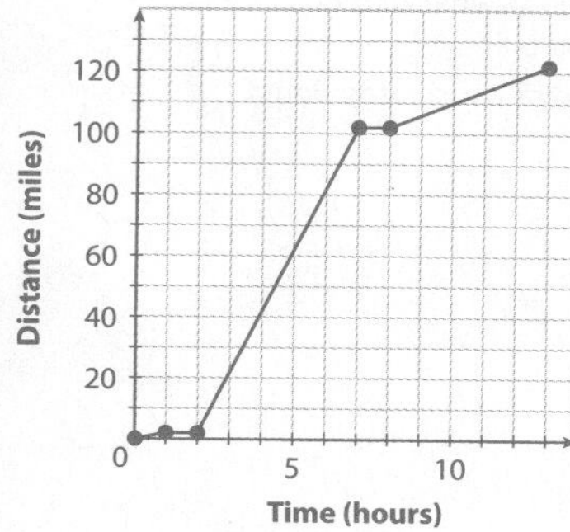

The slope between the x-values 2 and 7 is steeper than at other times because she was moving faster. When she stops to rest, the sections from 1 to 2 and 7 to 8 are horizontal. The slope from 0 to 1 is the most gradual because she was going slowest here.

7. The maximum number of oranges in a box of volume one cubic foot can be modeled by the inequality $|x - 17| \leq 5$, depending on the size of the oranges. Solve the inequality to find the minimum and maximum numbers of oranges in a box. Explain your answer.

The box can contain a minimum of 12 oranges and a maximum of 22 oranges. Possible answer: The inequality needs to be split into $x - 17 \leq 5$ and $x - 17 \geq -5$ before solving, so that will give $x \leq 22$ and $x \geq 12$, which can be combined to make $12 \leq x \leq 22$.

8. How does the end behavior of $f(x) = (x - 2)^2 + 3$ differ from that of $g(x) = -(3x + 7)^2 - 8$ as $x \rightarrow -\infty$? Explain your answer.

For $f(x)$, the end behavior approaches infinity as $x \rightarrow -\infty$. For $g(x)$, the end behavior approaches negative infinity as $x \rightarrow -\infty$. This is true because $f(x)$ opens upward, and $g(x)$ opens downward.

Performance Tasks

★ **9.** The revenue from an amusement park ride is given by the admission price of $3 times the number of riders. As part of a promotion, the first 10 riders ride for free.

A. What kind of transformation describes the change in the revenue based on the promotion?

B. Write a function rule for this transformation.

A. a horizontal shift 10 units right or a vertical shift 30 units down

B. possible answer: $f(x) = 3(x - 10)$

COMMON CORE Common Core Standards

Items	Content Standards	Mathematical Practices
7	A-REI.B.3	MP.6
8	F-IF.B.5	MP.6

* Item integrates mixed review concepts from previous modules or a previous course.

PERFORMANCE TASKS

There are three different levels of performance tasks:

* **Novice:** These are short word problems that require students to apply the math they have learned in straightforward, real-world situations.

** **Apprentice:** These are more involved problems that guide students step-by-step through more complex tasks. These exercises include more complicated reasoning, writing, and open ended elements.

*****Expert:** These are open-ended, nonroutine problems that, instead of stepping the students through, ask them to choose their own methods for solving and justify their answers and reasoning.

SCORING GUIDES

Item 9 (2 points)

a. 1 point for correct transformation

b. 1 point for correct function

SCORING GUIDES

Item 10 (6 points)

a. 2 points for correct transformation

b. 2 points for correct transformation

c. 2 points for correct choice

Item 11 (6 points)

a. 1 point for correct function
   1 point for correct range
   1 point for correct domain

b. 1 point for correct inverse function
   1 point for explanation

c. 1 point for correct interpretation

★★10. An automotive mechanic charges \$50 to diagnose the problem in a vehicle and \$65 per hour for labor to fix it.

A. If the mechanic increases his diagnostic fee to \$60, what kind of transformation is the graph of the total repair bill?

B. If the mechanic increases his labor rate to \$75 per hour, what kind of transformation is this to the graph of the total repair bill?

C. If it took 3 hours to repair your car, which of the two rate increases would have a greater effect on your total bill?

A. vertical translation

B. horizontal compression

C. the increase in the per-hour labor rate

★★★11. **Diving** Scuba divers must know that the deeper the dive, the greater the water pressure in pounds per square inch (psi) for fresh water diving, as shown in the table.

Depth (feet)	Pressure (psi)
34	29.4
68	44.1
102	58.8

A. Write the pressure as a function of depth, and identify a reasonable domain and range for this function.

B. Find the inverse of the function from part **A**. What does the inverse function represent?

C. The point (25.9, 25.9) is an approximate solution to both the function from part **A** and its inverse. What does this point mean in the context of the problem?

A. $P(d) = \frac{147}{340}d + 14.7$

D: $\{d \mid d \geq 0\}$; **R:** $\{P \mid P \geq 14.7\}$

B. $d(P) = \frac{340}{147}P - 34$

It represents depth as a function of pressure.

C. At 25.9 ft, the pressure is 25.9 psi.

MATH IN CAREERS

Community Theater Owner A community theater currently sells 200 season tickets at \$50 each. In order to increase its season-ticket revenue, the theater surveys its season-ticket holders to see if they would be willing to pay more. The survey finds that for every \$5 increase in the price of a season ticket, the theater would lose 10 season-ticket holders. What action, if any, should the theater owner take to increase revenue?

a. Let n be the number of \$5 price increases in the cost of a season ticket. Write an expression for the cost of a season ticket after n price increases, and an expression for the number of season-ticket holders after n price increases.

b. Use the expressions from part **a** to create a revenue function, $R(n)$, from the survey information.

c. Determine a constraint on the value of n. That is, write and solve an inequality that represents an upper bound on the value of n, then state a reasonable domain for the revenue function.

d. Graph the revenue function. Be sure to label the axes with the quantities they represent and indicate the axis scales by showing numbers for some grid lines.

e. Write a brief paragraph describing what actions the theater owner should take to maximize revenue. Include what happens to the number of season-ticket holders as well as the season-ticket prices.

a. cost of a season ticket: $50 + 5n$ number of season-ticket holders: $200 - 10n$

b. revenue = (number of season-ticket holders) · (cost of a season ticket)

$$R(n) = (200 - 10n)(50 + 5n)$$

c. $200 - 10n \geq 0$; $n \leq 20$;

domain: $\{0, 1, 2, ..., 20\}$

d.

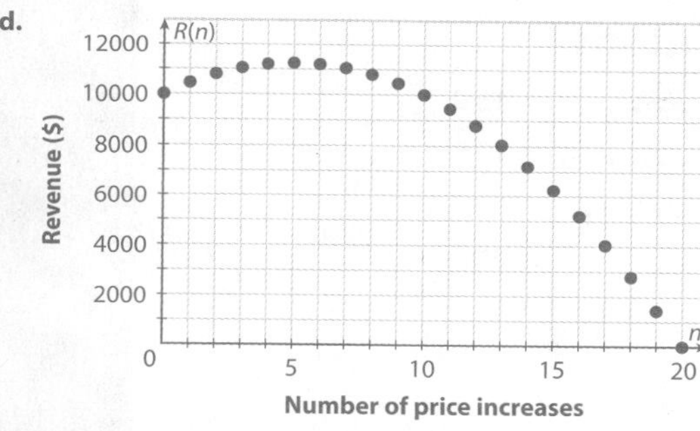

e. Maximize revenue by increasing the price of a season ticket to \$75. The number of ticket holders drops to 150, but revenue increases to \$11,250.

MATH IN CAREERS

Community Theater Owner In this Unit Performance Task, students can see how a community theater owner uses mathematics on the job.

For more information about careers in mathematics as well as various mathematics appreciation topics, visit the American Mathematical Society http://www.ams.org

SCORING GUIDES

Task (6 points)

a. 1 point for correct expressions

b. 1 point for correct function

c. 1 point for correct inequality and domain

d. 1 point for correct graph

e. 1 point for recommended actions
1 point for effects

UNIT 2

Quadratic Functions, Equations, and Relations

CONTENTS

Unit Pacing Guide

45-Minute Classes

Module 3

DAY 1	DAY 2	DAY 3	DAY 4	DAY 5
Lesson 3.1	Lesson 3.1	Lesson 3.2	Lesson 3.3	Lesson 3.3
DAY 6				
Module Review and Assessment Readiness				

Module 4

DAY 1	DAY 2	DAY 3	DAY 4	DAY 5
Lesson 4.1	Lesson 4.1	Lesson 4.2	Lesson 4.2	Lesson 4.3
DAY 6	DAY 7	DAY 8	DAY 9	DAY 10
Lesson 4.3	Lesson 4.4	Lesson 4.4	Module Review and Assessment Readiness	Unit Review and Assessment Readiness

90-Minute Classes

Module 3

DAY 1	DAY 2	DAY 2
Lesson 3.1	Lesson 3.2 Lesson 3.3	Lesson 3.3 Module Review and Assessment Readiness

Module 4

DAY 1	DAY 2	DAY 3	DAY 4	DAY 5
Lesson 4.1	Lesson 4.2	Lesson 4.3	Lesson 4.2	Module Review and Assessment Readiness Unit Review and Assessment Readiness

Program Resources

PLAN

HMH Teacher App

Access a full suite of teacher resources online and offline on a variety of devices. Plan present, and manage classes, assignments, and activities.

ePlanner **Easily plan your classes, create and view assignments, and access all program resources with your online, customizable planning tool.**

Professional Development Videos

Authors Juli Dixon and Matt Larson model successful teaching practices and strategies in actual classroom settings.

QR Codes **Scan with your smart phone to jump directly from your print book to online videos and other resources.**

Teacher's Edition

Support students with point-of-use Questioning Strategies, teaching tips, resources for differentiated instruction, additional activities, and more.

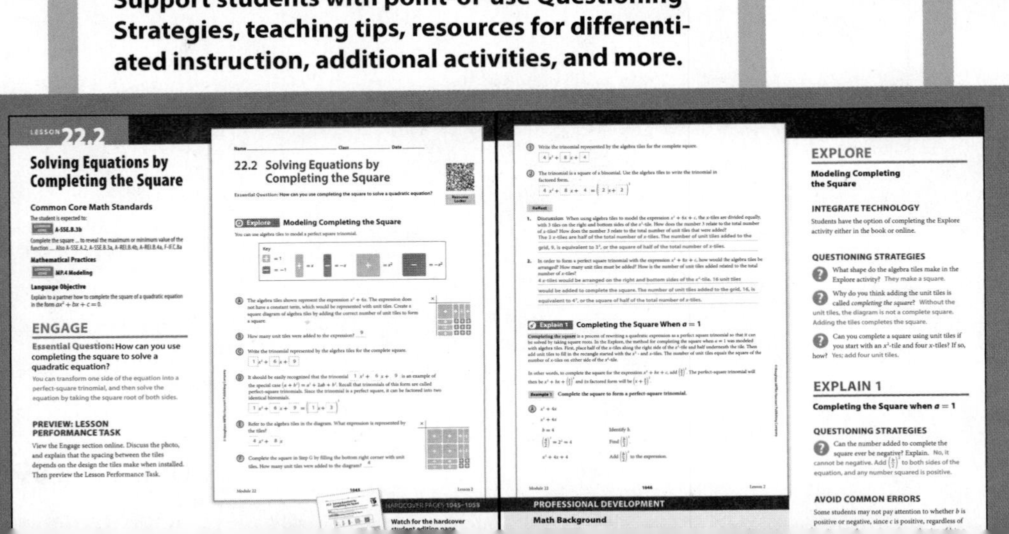

ENGAGE AND EXPLORE

Real-World Videos **Engage students with interesting and relevant applications of the mathematical content of each module.**

Explore Activities

Students interactively explore new concepts using a variety of tools and approaches.

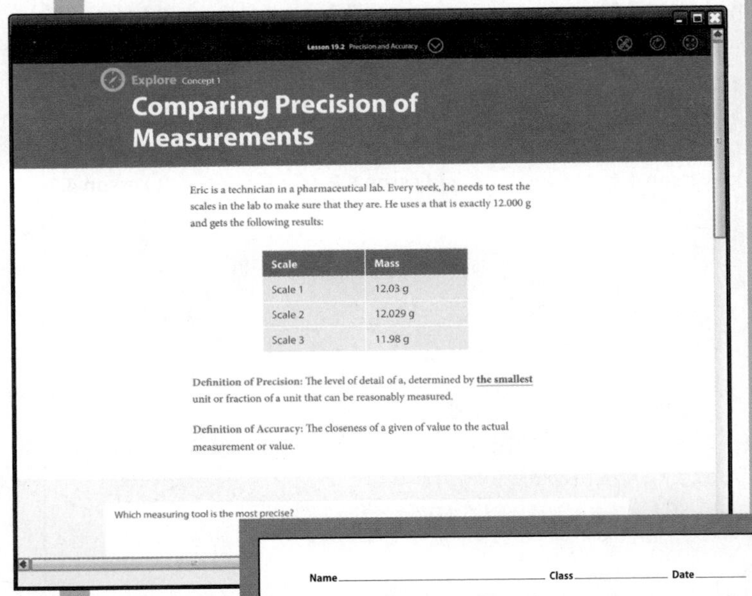
Lesson 19.2 Precision and Accuracy
Explore Concept 1
Comparing Precision of Measurements
Eric is a technician in a pharmaceutical lab. Every week, he needs to test the scales in the lab to make sure that they are. He uses a that is exactly 12.000 g and gets the following results:
Scale | Mass
Scale 1 | 12.03 g
Scale 2 | 12.029 g
Scale 3 | 11.98 g
Definition of Precision: The level of detail of a, determined by the smallest unit or fraction of a unit that can be reasonably measured.
Definition of Accuracy: The closeness of a given of value to the actual measurement or value.
Which measuring tool is the most precise?

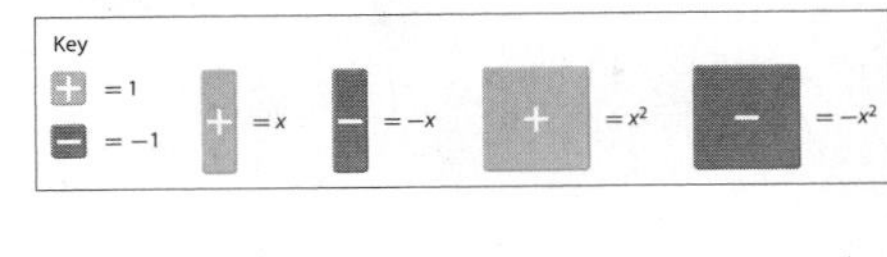
Name Class Date
22.2 Solving Equations by Completing the Square
Essential Question: How can you use completing the square to solve a quadratic equation?
A-SSE.B.3b Complete the square ... to reveal the maximum or minimum value of the function ...
Also A-SSE.A.2, A-SSE.B.3a, A-REI.B.4b, A-REI.B.4a, F-IF.C.8a
Explore Modeling Completing the Square
You can use algebra tiles to model a perfect square trinomial.

Ⓐ The algebra tiles shown represent the expression $x^2 + 6x$. The expression does not have a constant term, which would be represented with unit tiles. Create a square diagram of algebra tiles by adding the correct number of unit tiles to form a square.

Ⓑ How many unit tiles were added to the expression? ____

Ⓒ Write the trinomial represented by the algebra tiles for the complete square.

$\square x^2 + \square x + \square$

Ⓓ It should be easily recognized that the trinomial $\square x^2 + \square x + \square$ is an example of the special case $(a + b^2) = a^2 + 2ab + b^2$. Recall that trinomials of this form are called

TEACH

Math On the Spot video tutorials, featuring program authors Dr. Edward Burger and Martha Sandoval-Martinez, accompany every example in the textbook and give students step-by-step instructions and explanations of key math concepts.

Interactive Teacher Edition

Customize and present course materials with collaborative activities and integrated formative assessment.

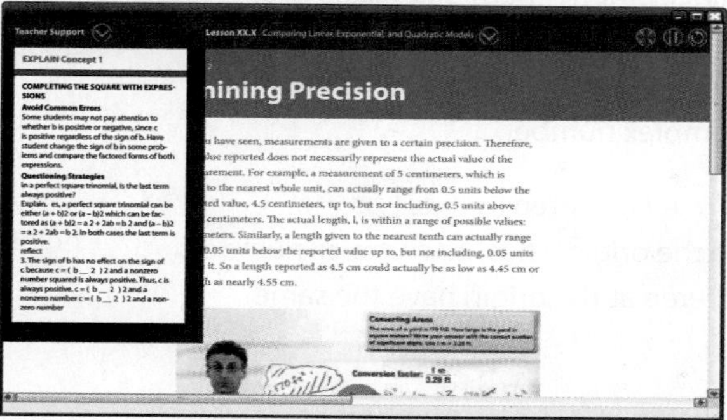

Differentiated Instruction Resources

Support all learners with Differentiated Instruction Resources, including

- **Leveled Practice and Problem Solving**
- **Reading Strategies**
- **Success for English Learners**
- **Challenge**

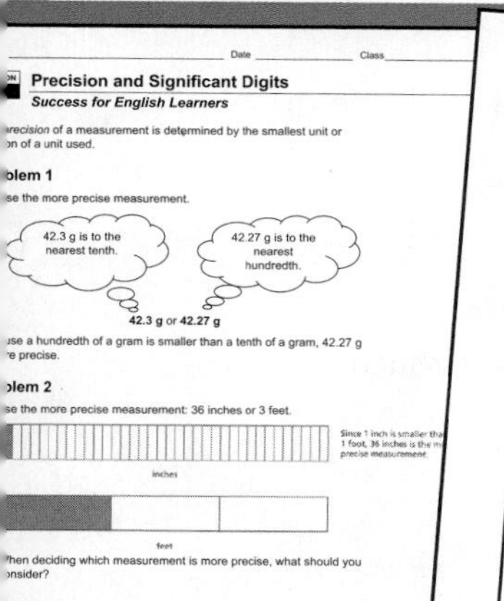

Date Class

Precision and Significant Digits

Success for English Learners

...recision of a measurement is determined by the smallest unit or ...on of a unit used.

...blem 1

...se the more precise measurement.

42.3 g is to the nearest tenth.

42.27 g is to the nearest hundredth.

42.3 g or 42.27 g

...use a hundredth of a gram is smaller than a tenth of a gram, 42.27 g ...e precise.

...blem 2

...se the more precise measurement: 36 inches or 3 feet.

Since 1 inch is smaller than 1 foot, 36 inches is the m... precise measurement.

inches

feet

...hen deciding which measurement is more precise, what should you ...nsider?

...n object is weighed on three different scales. The results are shown ... the table. Which scale is the most precise? Explain your answer.

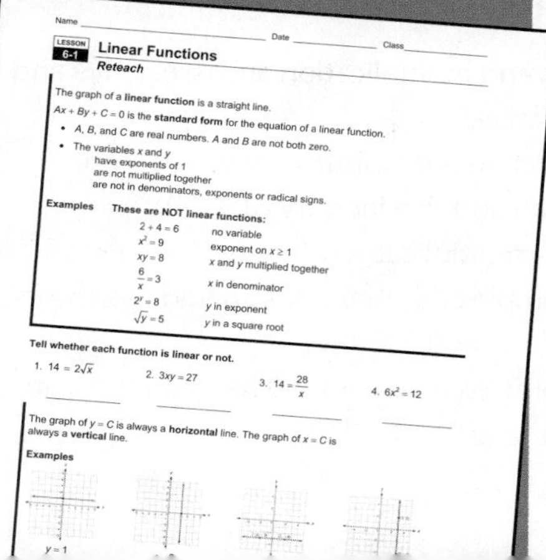

Name Date Class

LESSON 6-1 Linear Functions

Reteach

The graph of a **linear function** is a straight line.

$Ax + By + C = 0$ is the **standard form** for the equation of a linear function.

- A, B, and C are real numbers. A and B are not both zero.
- The variables x and y have exponents of 1, are not multiplied together, are not in denominators, exponents or radical signs.

Examples These are NOT linear functions:

$2 + 4 = 6$	no variable
$x^2 = 9$	exponent on $x \geq 1$
$xy = 8$	x and y multiplied together
$\frac{6}{x} = 3$	x in denominator
$2^x = 8$	y in exponent
$\sqrt{y} = 5$	y in a square root

Tell whether each function is linear or not.

1. $14 = 2\sqrt{x}$ 2. $3xy = 27$ 3. $14 = \frac{28}{x}$ 4. $6x^2 = 12$

The graph of $y = C$ is always a **horizontal** line. The graph of $x = C$ is always a **vertical** line.

Examples

$y = 1$

ASSESSMENT AND INTERVENTION

The Personal Math Trainer provides online practice, homework, assessments, and intervention. Monitor student progress through reports and alerts.

Create and customize assignments aligned to specific lessons or Common Core standards.

- **Practice** – With dynamic items and assignments, students get unlimited practice on key concepts supported by guided examples, step-by-step solutions, and video tutorials.
- **Assessments** – Choose from course assignments or customize your own based on course content, Common Core standards, difficulty levels, and more.
- **Homework** – Students can complete online homework with a wide variety of problem types, including the ability to enter expressions, equations, and graphs. Let the system automatically grade homework, so you can focus where your students need help the most!
- **Intervention** – Let the Personal Math Trainer automatically prescribe a targeted, personalized intervention path for your students.

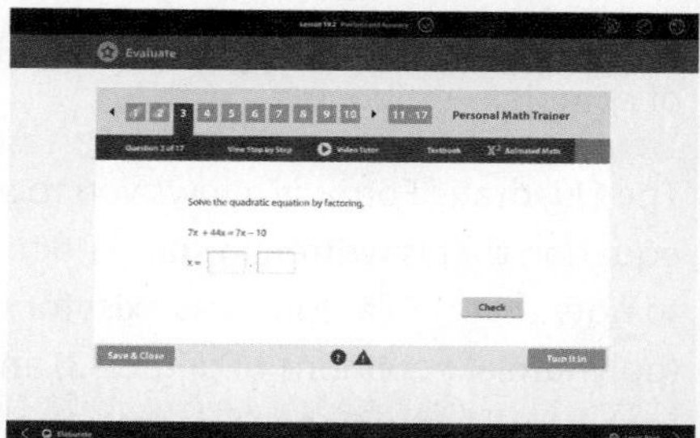

Focus on Higher Order Thinking

Raise the bar with homework and practice that incorporates higher-order thinking and mathematical practices in every lesson.

Assessment Readiness

Prepare students for success on high stakes tests for Algebra 2 with practice at every module and unit

Assessment Resources

Tailor assessments and response to intervention to meet the needs of all your classes and students, including

- Leveled Module Quizzes
- Leveled Unit Tests
- Unit Performance Tasks
- Placement, Diagnostic, and Quarterly Benchmark Tests
- Tier 1, Tier 2, and Tier 3 Resources

Math Background

Solving Quadratic Equations  A-REI.B.4

LESSONS 3.1 to 3.3

Every quadratic equation has two roots. Given a quadratic equation $ax^2 + bx + c = 0$ with real coefficients, the discriminant, $b^2 - 4ac$, may be used to characterize the roots over the complex numbers.

When the discriminant is positive, the roots are two distinct real numbers.

When the discriminant is zero, the two real roots are identical and the function may be written in factored form as $f(x) = a(x - r)^2$. In this case, we say the root has multiplicity 2.

When the discriminant is negative, the two roots are a pair of complex conjugates.

The Quadratic Formula allows you to solve any quadratic equation that is written in standard form. It is interesting to note that similar formulas exist for cubic equations (polynomial equations of degree 3) and quartic equations (polynomial equations of degree 4), although these formulas are much more complex than the Quadratic Formula. For polynomial equations of degree 5 and higher, there are no general formulas for the roots of the equation.

The Quadratic Formula is the algebraic result of completing the square with general coefficients. The derivation of the formula does not depend on the values *a*, *b*, and *c* being real numbers. This means that the Quadratic Formula may be used to solve quadratic equations in standard form even when the coefficients of the equation are complex numbers.

For example, consider the equation $y = x^2 - ix + 1$. In this case, $a = c = 1$ and $b = -i$. Substituting these values into the Quadratic Formula and simplifying gives the solutions $x = \frac{i \pm i\sqrt{5}}{2} = \frac{1 \pm \sqrt{5}}{2}i$. Note that when the coefficients of the quadratic equation are not real numbers, the complex roots are not conjugates.

Complex Numbers  N-CN.B.5

LESSONS 3.2 to 3.3

The complex numbers, C, are numbers of the form $a + bi$, where a and b are real numbers and $i = \sqrt{-1}$. Setting $b = 0$ shows that the real numbers are a subset of the complex numbers.

However, there are differences between the set of real numbers and the set of complex numbers. The real numbers have a natural linear order, reflecting the number-line model used to represent them. This means that given any two distinct real numbers, p and q, either $p < q$ or $p > q$. The complex numbers, in contrast, have no natural order.

The complex numbers may be represented using a coordinate system called the *complex plane*. This representation played a key role in helping complex numbers gain acceptance among mathematicians as a natural extension of the real numbers. The complex plane also gives visual meaning to the idea of the absolute value (or magnitude) of a complex number.

The absolute value of $a + bi$, written $|a + bi|$, is the distance from (a, b) to the origin. Thus, all complex numbers that lie on a circle centered at the origin have the same absolute value.

Addition and multiplication of complex numbers are defined as follows.

$$(a + bi) + (c + di) = (a + c) + (b + d)i$$
$$(a + bi)(c + di) = (ac - bd) + (ad + bc)i$$

Using these definitions, the complex numbers form a field. This means that the set of complex numbers, with addition and multiplication defined as above, has the following properties:

- Addition and multiplication are associative and commutative.
- Multiplication is distributive over addition.
- There is an additive identity $(0 + 0i)$.
- There is a multiplicative identity $(1 + 0i)$.
- Every complex number z has an additive inverse $-z$ such that $z + (-z) = 0$.
- Every complex number $z \neq 0$ has a multiplicative inverse z^{-1} such that $z \cdot z^{-1} = 1$.

These same properties hold for the real numbers, which also form a field. The only property that may be surprising for the complex numbers is the last one.

Given a nonzero complex number $a + bi$, its multiplicative inverse is $\frac{a - bi}{a^2 + b^2}$.

As described previously, complex numbers may be represented on the complex plane. For the purpose of understanding addition, complex numbers may also be represented by vectors; $a + bi$ is represented by the vector $\langle a, b\rangle$. From this perspective, addition of complex numbers can be understood as the sum of vectors. For example, to add $7 + 2i$ and $1 + 6i$, use the vectors $\langle 7, 2\rangle$ and $\langle 1, 6\rangle$. Vectors may be added by forming a parallelogram and drawing the diagonal. The figure shows that the sum of the vectors is $\langle 8, 8\rangle$ or $8 + 8i$. This matches the sum obtained by using the definition of addition of complex numbers.

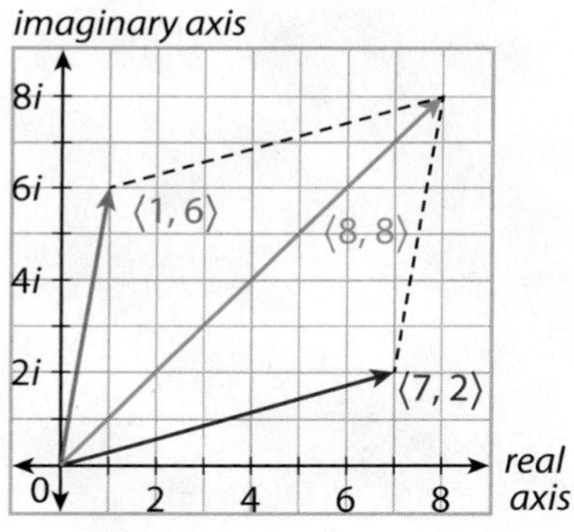

Complex-number multiplication can also be represented by vectors. The product of vectors *v* and *w*, *vw*, is the vector whose length is $|vw| = |v||w|$ and whose angle with respect to the positive real axis has the same measure as the sum of the measures of the angles formed by *v* and *w* with the positive real axis.

Amazingly, this is the same result obtained by using the definition of multiplication of complex numbers!

Forms of Quadratic Functions  A-SSE.A.2

LESSON 4.1

A *quadratic function* is a polynomial function of degree 2. The graph of every quadratic function is a parabola.

Quadratic functions may be written in three different forms, each having its advantages and disadvantages. The following summary of these forms highlights some of the information about the graph of the function that can immediately be gleaned from its form.

- **Vertex form**: $f(x) = a(x - h)^2 + k, a \neq 0$
The graph of the function is a parabola with vertex (h, k). The axis of symmetry of the parabola is $x = h$.
- **Standard form**: $f(x) = ax^2 + bx + c, a \neq 0$
The axis of symmetry of the parabola is $x = -\frac{b}{2a}$.
The vertex is $\left(-\frac{b}{2a}, f\left(\frac{-b}{2a}\right)\right)$.
- **Factored form**: $f(x) = a(x - r_1)(x - r_2), a \neq 0$
The values r_1 and r_2 are the zeros of the quadratic function. When r_1 and r_2 are real numbers, the parabola intersects the *x*-axis at $x = r_1$ and $x = r_2$.

Note that regardless of the form that is used, the value of *a* determines whether the parabola opens upward or downward. In particular, the parabola opens upward when $a > 0$ and downward when $a < 0$.

Thus, for $a > 0$, the *y*-value of the vertex is the minimum value of the function and for $a < 0$, the *y*-value of the vertex is the maximum value of the function. An important characteristic of quadratic functions is they always attain either a maximum value or a minimum value, but not both.

As students progress through this unit, they should become adept at working back and forth among the three forms of a quadratic equation. For example, they can complete the square to go from standard form to vertex form. By finding roots with the Quadratic Formula, students can transform any quadratic function in standard form to an equivalent function in factored form.

UNIT 2

Quadratic Functions, Equations, and Relations

MATH IN CAREERS

Unit Activity Preview

After completing this unit, students will complete a Math in Careers task by graphing and interpreting a quadratic function that models the profitability of a toy. Critical skills include completing the square, graphing quadratic functions, and interpreting graphs.

For more information about careers in mathematics as well as various mathematics appreciation topics, visit The American Mathematical Society at http://www.ams.org.

UNIT 2

Quadratic Functions, Equations, and Relations

MATH IN CAREERS

Toy Manufacturer A toy manufacturer uses math to calculate the cost of manufacturing, including labor and materials, as well as to predict sales, determine profits, and keep track of orders and inventory. Toy manufacturers study market trends and use statistics to understand the economics of supply and demand for their products. They may also apply three-dimensional modeling to determine the amount of materials needed for toy construction.

If you are interested in a career as a toy manufacturer, you should study these mathematical subjects:

- Algebra
- Geometry
- Trigonometry
- Business Math
- Technical Math

Research other careers that require understanding how to predict sales of goods. Check out the career activity at the end of the unit to find out how **Toy Manufacturers** use math.

TRACKING YOUR LEARNING PROGRESSION

Before	In this Unit	After
Students understand: • domain, range, and end behavior of function graphs • transformations and inverses of functions • graphing and solving quadratic functions • solving absolute value functions and quadratic equations and inequalities	Students will learn about: • quadratic equations • complex numbers • ways of solving quadratic equations • circles and parabolas • solving linear-quadratic systems of equations, linear systems in three variables	Students will study: • polynomial functions • adding, subtracting, multiplying, and dividing polynomials • solving polynomial equations • the Binomial Theorem

Reading Start-Up

Vocabulary

Review Words

- ✔ axis of symmetry *(eje de simetría)*
- ✔ discriminant *(discriminante)*
- ✔ elimination *(eliminación)*
- ✔ parabola *(parábola)*
- ✔ quadratic formula *(fórmula cuadrática)*
- ✔ quadratic formula *(fórmula cuadrática)*
- ✔ quadratic function *(función cuadrática)*
- ✔ substitution *(sustitución)*
- ✔ vertex *(vértice)*

Preview Words

- complex number *(número complejo)*
- directrix *(directriz)*
- focus *(foco)*
- imaginary number *(número imaginario)*
- matrix *(matriz)*

Visualize Vocabulary

Use the ✔ words to complete the graphic. Place one word in each of the four sections of the frame.

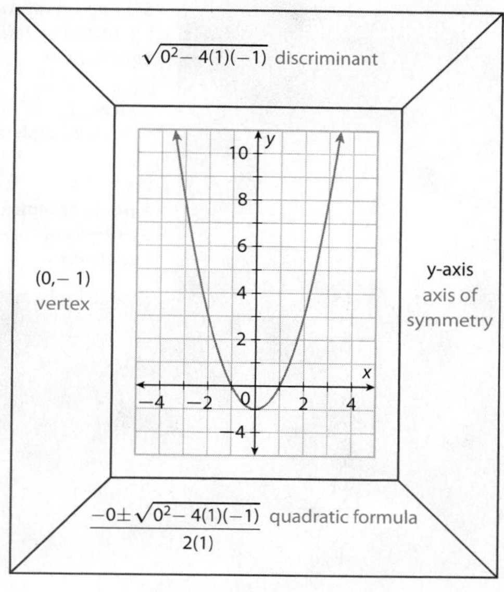

Understand Vocabulary

To become familiar with some of the vocabulary terms in the module, consider the following. You may refer to the module, the glossary, or a dictionary.

1. Every point on a parabola is equidistant from a fixed line, called the **directrix**, and a fixed point, called the **focus**.
2. A **complex number** is any number that can be written as $a + bi$, where a and b are real numbers and $i = \sqrt{-1}$.
3. A **matrix** is a rectangular array of numbers.

Active Reading

Four-Corner Fold Before beginning each lesson, create a four-corner fold to help you organize the characteristics of key concepts. As you study each lesson, define new terms, including an example and a graph or diagram where applicable.

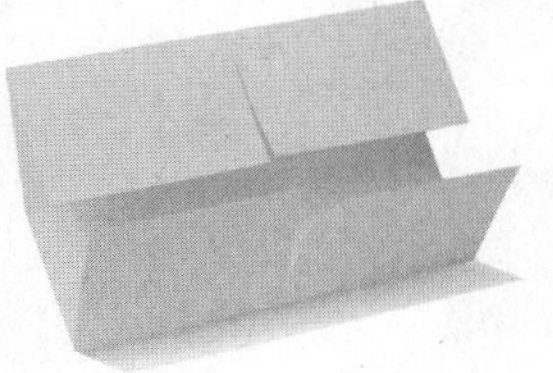

Reading Start Up

Have students complete the activities on this page by working alone or with others.

VISUALIZE VOCABULARY

The information frame graphic helps students review vocabulary associated with the graphs of quadratic functions. If time allows, discuss any other mathematical relationships among the vocabulary words.

UNDERSTAND VOCABULARY

Use the following explanations to help students learn the preview words.

> A parabola is defined by its relationship to its **focus**, a point on the axis of symmetry of the parabola, and its **directrix**, a given line on the other side of the parabola as the focus. The graph of a parabola that does not intersect the x-axis has roots that are **complex numbers**. A complex number has a real number part and an **imaginary number** part.

ACTIVE READING

Students can use these reading and note-taking strategies to help them organize and understand the new concepts and vocabulary. Encourage students to ask for help if they do not recognize a word or the reasoning behind an application. Discuss how students can apply prior knowledge and experiences to aid their understanding of quadratic functions, equations, and relations.

ADDITIONAL RESOURCES

Differentiated Instruction

- Reading Strategies EL

MODULE 3

Quadratic Equations and Inequalities

ESSENTIAL QUESTION:

Answer: Quadratic functions can help you solve problems involving business, science, and structural design.

PROFESSIONAL DEVELOPMENT VIDEO

Professional Development Video

Author Matt Larson models successful teaching practices in an actual high-school classroom.

Professional Development my.hrw.com

Quadratic Equations

MODULE 3

Essential Question: How can you use quadratic equations and inequalities to solve real-world problems?

REAL WORLD VIDEO
Safe drivers are aware of stopping distances and carefully judge how fast they can travel based on road conditions. Stopping distance is one of many everyday functions that can be modeled with quadratic equations.

MODULE PERFORMANCE TASK PREVIEW

Can You Stop in Time?

When a driver applies the brakes, the car continues to travel for a certain distance until coming to a stop. The stopping distance for a vehicle depends on many factors, including the initial speed of the car and road conditions. How far will a car travel after the brakes are applied? Let's hit the road and find out!

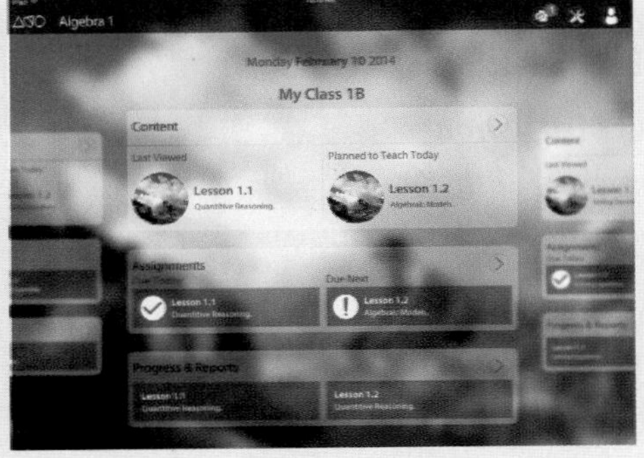

DIGITAL TEACHER EDITION

Access a full suite of teaching resources when and where you need them:

- Access content online or offline
- Customize lessons to share with your class
- Communicate with your students in real-time
- View student grades and data instantly to target your instruction where it is needed most

PERSONAL MATH TRAINER

Assessment and Intervention

Assign automatically graded homework, quizzes, tests, and intervention activities. Prepare your students with updated, Common Core-aligned practice tests.

Are YOU Ready?

Complete these exercises to review skills you will need for this chapter.

- Online Homework
- Hints and Help
- Extra Practice

One-Step Inequalities

Example 1 Solve $-2x \leq 9$ for x.
$x \geq -4.5$

Divide both sides by −2. Because you are dividing by a negative number, flip the inequality symbol.

Solve each inequality.

1. $n - 12 > 9$ — $n > 21$
2. $-3p < -27$ — $p > 9$
3. $\frac{k}{4} \geq -1$ — $k \geq -4$

Exponents

Example 2 Simplify $\frac{3a^5b^2}{9a^2b}$.

$$\frac{3a^5b^2}{9a^2b} = \frac{3^1a^5b^2}{3^2a^2b^1} = \frac{a^{5-2}b^{2-1}}{3^{2-1}} = \frac{a^3b}{3}$$

Subtract exponents when dividing.

Simplify each expression.

4. $\frac{16p^2}{2p^4}$ — $\frac{8}{p^2}$
5. $5vw^5 \cdot 2v^4$ — $10v^5w^5$
6. $\frac{3x^7y}{6x^4y^2}$ — $\frac{x^3}{2y}$

Solving Quadratic Equations by Factoring

Example 3 Factor to solve $x^2 + 2x - 15 = 0$ for x.

Pairs of factors of −15 are:
1 and −15
3 and −5
5 and −3
15 and −1

The pair with the sum of the middle term, 2, is 5 and −3.

$(x + 5)(x - 3) = 0$

Either $x + 5 = 0$ or $x - 3 = 0$, so x-values are −5 and 3.

Factor to solve each equation.

7. $x^2 - 7x + 6 = 0$ — 1, 6
8. $x^2 - 18x + 81 = 0$ — 9
9. $x^2 - 16 = 0$ — 4, −4

Are You Ready?

ASSESS READINESS

Use the assessment on this page to determine if students need strategic or intensive intervention for the module's prerequisite skills.

ASSESSMENT AND INTERVENTION

RtI Response to Intervention TIER 1, TIER 2, TIER 3 SKILLS

Personal Math Trainer will automatically create a standards-based, personalized intervention assignment for your students, targeting each student's individual needs!

ADDITIONAL RESOURCES

See the table below for a full list of intervention resources available for this module.

Response to Intervention Resources also includes:

- Tier 2 Skill Pre-Tests for each Module
- Tier 2 Skill Post-Tests for each skill

Response to Intervention			Differentiated Instruction
Tier 1 Lesson Intervention Worksheets	**Tier 2** Strategic Intervention Skills Intervention Worksheets	**Tier 3** Intensive Intervention Worksheets available online	
Reteach 3.1 Reteach 3.2 Reteach 3.3	9 Exponents 24 One-Step Inequalities 29 Rational Number... 30 Real Numbers 32 Solving Quadratic... 33 Solving Quadratic...	Building Block Skills 1, 4, 18, 20, 21, 34, 47, 61, 76, 94, 97, 100, 109	Challenge worksheets Extend the Math Lesson Activities in TE

LESSON 3.1

Solving Quadratic Equations by Taking Square Roots

Common Core Math Standards

The student is expected to:

 **N-CN.A.1**

Know there is a complex number i such that $i^2 = -1$, and every complex number has the form $a + bi$ with a and b real. Also A-REI.B.4b

Mathematical Practices

COMMON CORE **MP.4 Modeling**

Language Objective

Have students decide whether a given square root is an imaginary number (square root of a negative number) or a real number and explain their reasoning to a partner.

ENGAGE

Essential Question: What is an imaginary number, and how is it useful in solving quadratic equations?

Possible answer: An imaginary number has the form bi; b is a nonzero real number and i is the imaginary unit, which is defined to be equal to $\sqrt{-1}$. Imaginary numbers allow you to solve quadratic equations of the form $x^2 = a$ when a is a negative number.

PREVIEW: LESSON PERFORMANCE TASK

View the Engage section online. Discuss the photo and how a quadratic function can be used to model a suspension bridge. Then preview the Lesson Performance Task.

Name ________ Class ________ Date ________

3.1 Solving Quadratic Equations by Taking Square Roots

Resource Locker

Essential Question: What is an imaginary number, and how is it useful in solving quadratic equations?

Explore Investigating Ways of Solving Simple Quadratic Equations

There are many ways to solve a quadratic equation. Here, you will use three methods to solve the equation $x^2 = 16$: by graphing, by factoring, and by taking square roots.

(A) Solve $x^2 = 16$ by graphing.

First treat each side of the equation as a function, and graph the two functions, which in this case are $f(x) = x^2$ and $g(x) = 16$, on the same coordinate plane.

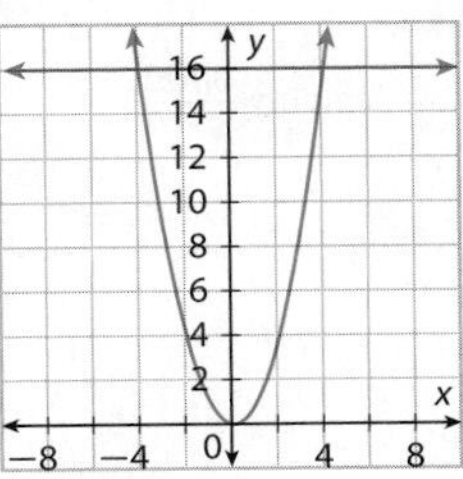

Then identify the x-coordinates of the points where two graphs intersect.

$x =$ [−4] or $x =$ [4]

(B) Solve $x^2 = 16$ by factoring.

This method involves rewriting the equation so that 0 is on one side in order to use the *zero-product property*, which says that the product of two numbers is 0 if and only if at least one of the numbers is 0.

Write the equation.	$x^2 = 16$
Subtract 16 from both sides.	$x^2 -$ [16] $= 0$
Factor the difference of two squares.	$(x +$ [4] $)(x - 4) = 0$
Apply the zero-product property.	$x +$ [4] $= 0$ or $x - 4 = 0$
Solve for x.	$x =$ [−4] or $x = 4$

(C) Solve $x^2 = 16$ by taking square roots.

A real number x is a *square root* of a nonnegative real number a provided $x^2 = a$. A square root is written using the radical symbol $\sqrt{}$. Every positive real number a has both a positive square root, written $\sqrt{a}$, and a negative square root, written $-\sqrt{a}$. For instance, the square roots of 9 are $\pm\sqrt{9}$ (read "plus or minus the square root of 9"), or ± 3. The number 0 has only itself as its square root: $\pm\sqrt{0} = 0$.

Write the equation.	$x^2 = 16$
Use the definition of square root.	$x = \pm\sqrt{16}$
Simplify the square roots.	$x =$ [±4]

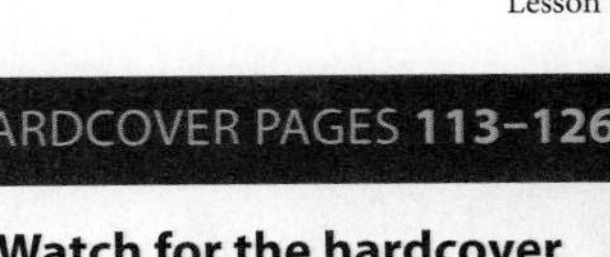

HARDCOVER PAGES 113–126

Watch for the hardcover student edition page numbers for this lesson.

Reflect

1. Which of the three methods would you use to solve $x^2 = 5$? Explain, and then use the method to find the solutions.
   The graphing method would give only approximate solutions, while the factoring method can't be used because $x^2 - 5$ isn't a difference of two squares. However, taking square roots gives $x = \pm\sqrt{5}$.

2. Can the equation $x^2 = -9$ be solved by any of the three methods? Explain.
   None of the three methods can be used. Attempting to use the graphing method results in a parabola and a line that don't intersect. Attempting to use the factoring method results in the expression $x^2 + 9$, which isn't factorable. Attempting to use square roots doesn't make sense because square roots of negative numbers aren't defined.

Explain 1 Finding Real Solutions of Simple Quadratic Equations

When solving a quadratic equation of the form $ax^2 + c = 0$ by taking square roots, you may need to use the following properties of square roots to simplify the solutions. (In a later lesson, these properties are stated in a more general form and then proved.)

Property Name	Words	Symbols	Numbers
Product property of square roots	The square root of a product equals the product of the square roots of the factors.	$\sqrt{ab} = \sqrt{a} \cdot \sqrt{b}$ where $a \geq 0$ and $b \geq 0$	$\sqrt{12} = \sqrt{4 \cdot 3} = \sqrt{4} \cdot \sqrt{3} = 2\sqrt{3}$
Quotient property of square roots	The square root of a fraction equals the quotient of the square roots of the numerator and the denominator.	$\sqrt{\frac{a}{b}} = \frac{\sqrt{a}}{\sqrt{b}}$ where $a \geq 0$ and $b > 0$	$\sqrt{\frac{5}{9}} = \frac{\sqrt{5}}{\sqrt{9}} = \frac{\sqrt{5}}{3}$

Using the quotient property of square roots may require an additional step of *rationalizing the denominator* if the denominator is not a rational number. For instance, the quotient property allows you to write $\sqrt{\frac{2}{7}}$ as $\frac{\sqrt{2}}{\sqrt{7}}$, but $\sqrt{7}$ is not a rational number. To rationalize the denominator, multiply $\frac{\sqrt{2}}{\sqrt{7}}$ by $\frac{\sqrt{7}}{\sqrt{7}}$ (a form of 1) and get this result: $\frac{\sqrt{2}}{\sqrt{7}} \cdot \frac{\sqrt{7}}{\sqrt{7}} = \frac{\sqrt{14}}{\sqrt{49}} = \frac{\sqrt{14}}{7}$.

PROFESSIONAL DEVELOPMENT

Math Background

Students encounter many functions in their study of mathematics. The simplest are the parent functions, including the parent linear function $f(x) = x$, the parent quadratic function $f(x) = x^2$, the parent cubic function $f(x) = x^2$, and the parent square root function $f(x) = \sqrt{x}$. Each parent function is the building block for the functions in its family. Understanding the parent functions is a first step in understanding equations and graphs of functions in general. For advanced functions, there may be no true parent function. There is no one parent exponential function, although $f(x) = b^x$ may be considered the parent for any base b, $b > 0$, and $b \neq 1$.

EXPLORE

Investigating Ways of Solving Simple Quadratic Equations

INTEGRATE MATHEMATICAL PRACTICES

Focus on Critical Thinking

MP.3 Discuss whether 1 can be used instead of 0 in the Zero Product Property to make a "One" Product Property. Have students show that if $ab = 1$, neither a nor b must equal 1. Have them consider −1 and other numbers and lead them to conclude that the property holds only for 0.

QUESTIONING STRATEGIES

How can you use the factored form of a quadratic equation to find the zeros of the related quadratic function? **Factor the equation, apply the Zero Product Property, and then solve the equation.**

What are the roots of an equation? **the values of the variable that make the equation true**

EXPLAIN 1

Finding Real Solutions of Simple Quadratic Equations

INTEGRATE TECHNOLOGY

When zeros occur at non-integer x-values, using a table to find them can be difficult. Show students that they can use a graphing calculator to find zeros by graphing the function and selecting **2:zero** from the **CALCULATE** menu.

AVOID COMMON ERRORS

When solving an equation of the form $x^2 = s$ where $s > 0$, students may look only for positive solutions. Be sure that students also look for negative solutions.

QUESTIONING STRATEGIES

? What is rationalizing the denominator? **eliminating the radical from a denominator by multiplying by a form of 1**

EXPLAIN 2

Solving a Real-World Problem Using a Simple Quadratic Equation

INTEGRATE MATHEMATICAL PRACTICES

Focus on Communication

MP.3 A variable followed by a subscript zero, as in V_0 or h_0, usually indicates an initial value of the variable. The zero indicates the value of the variable when the time t is 0.

Example 1 Solve the quadratic equation by taking square roots.

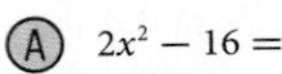

(A) $2x^2 - 16 = 0$

Add 16 to both sides. $2x^2 = 16$

Divide both sides by 2. $x^2 = 8$

Use the definition of square root. $x = \pm\sqrt{8}$

Use the product property. $x = \pm\sqrt{4} \cdot \sqrt{2}$

Simplify. $x = \pm 2\sqrt{2}$

(B) $-5x^2 + 9 = 0$

Subtract 9 from both sides. $-5x^2 = \mathbf{-9}$

Divide both sides by $\mathbf{-5}$. $x^2 = \mathbf{\frac{9}{5}}$

Use the definition of square root. $x = \pm\sqrt{\mathbf{\frac{9}{5}}}$

Use the quotient property. $x = \pm\mathbf{\frac{\sqrt{9}}{\sqrt{5}}}$

Simplify the numerator. $x = \pm\mathbf{\frac{3}{\sqrt{5}}}$

Rationalize the denominator. $x = \pm\mathbf{\frac{3\sqrt{5}}{5}}$

Your Turn

Solve the quadratic equation by taking square roots.

3. $x^2 - 24 = 0$

$\mathbf{x^2 = 24}$

$\mathbf{x = \pm\sqrt{24}}$

$\mathbf{x = \pm 2\sqrt{6}}$

4. $-4x^2 + 13 = 0$

$\mathbf{-4x^2 = -13}$

$\mathbf{x^2 = \frac{13}{4}}$

$\mathbf{x = \pm\frac{\sqrt{13}}{\sqrt{4}}}$

$\mathbf{x = \pm\frac{\sqrt{13}}{2}}$

Explain 2 Solving a Real-World Problem Using a Simple Quadratic Equation

Two commonly used quadratic models for falling objects near Earth's surface are the following:

- Distance fallen (in feet) at time t (in seconds): $d(t) = 16t^2$
- Height (in feet) at time t (in seconds): $h(t) = h_0 - 16t^2$ where h_0 is the object's initial height (in feet)

For both models, time is measured from the instant that the object begins to fall. A negative value of t would represent a time before the object began falling, so negative values of t are excluded from the domains of these functions. This means that for any equation of the form $d(t) = c$ or $h(t) = c$ where c is a constant, a negative solution should be rejected.

COLLABORATIVE LEARNING

Peer-to-Peer Activity

Have pairs of students work together to make note cards for each method they have learned to find the zeros of quadratic functions. Suggest that they describe the steps of the method as well as any advantages or disadvantages that they observed. Students can continue to add notes to the cards as they learn additional methods.

Example 2 **Write and solve an equation to answer the question. Give the exact answer and, if it's irrational, a decimal approximation (to the nearest tenth of a second).**

Ⓐ If you drop a water balloon, how long does it take to fall 4 feet?

Using the model $d(t) = 16t^2$, solve the equation $d(t) = 4$.

Write the equation. $16t^2 = 4$

Divide both sides by 16. $t^2 = \frac{1}{4}$

Use the definition of square root. $t = \pm\sqrt{\frac{1}{4}}$

Use the quotient property. $t = \pm\frac{1}{2}$

Reject the negative value of t. The water balloon falls 4 feet in $\frac{1}{2}$ second.

Ⓑ The rooftop of a 5-story building is 50 feet above the ground. How long does it take the water balloon dropped from the rooftop to pass by a third-story window at 24 feet?

50 ft

24 ft

Using the model $h(t) = h_0 - 16t^2$, solve the equation $h(t) = 24$. (When you reach the step at which you divide both sides by −16, leave 16 in the denominator rather than simplifying the fraction because you'll get a rational denominator when you later use the quotient property.)

Write the equation. $\boxed{50} - 16t^2 = \boxed{24}$

Subtract 50 from both sides. $-16t^2 = \boxed{-26}$

Divide both sides by −16. $t^2 = \boxed{\frac{26}{16}}$

Use the definition of square root. $t = \pm\sqrt{\boxed{\frac{26}{16}}}$

Use the quotient property to simplify. $t = \pm\boxed{\frac{\sqrt{26}}{4}}$

Reject the negative value of t. The water balloon passes by the third-story window in $\boxed{\frac{\sqrt{26}}{4}} \approx \boxed{1.3}$ seconds.

Reflect

5. **Discussion** Explain how the model $h(t) = h_0 - 16t^2$ is built from the model $d(t) = 16t^2$.
Think of $h(t)$, a falling object's height h at time t, as the distance that the object has *left* to fall. Since the total distance to fall is h_0, $h(t)$ is the distance left after subtracting the distance already fallen, $d(t)$, from h_0.

AVOID COMMON ERRORS

Because the word *maximum* is often associated with positive amounts, students may incorrectly assume that a quadratic function with a positive leading coefficient should have a maximum. Stress that, in fact, the "positive" parabola has a minimum and the "negative" parabola is the one with the maximum.

DIFFERENTIATE INSTRUCTION

Manipulatives

Students may benefit from using algebra tiles to practice factoring quadratic expressions. For example, show students how to model $x^2 + 6x + 8$ with algebra tiles. Then demonstrate that arranging the tiles in a rectangle models the product $(x + 2)(x + 4)$.

QUESTIONING STRATEGIES

What is the zero of a function? How does this translate when you use quadratic functions to model the height of a soccer ball after it is kicked? **The zero of a function is a value of the input x that makes the output $f(x)$ equal zero. In the case of a soccer ball, the zero of the function is the time it takes for the soccer ball to hit the ground after it is kicked.**

CONNECT VOCABULARY EL

Relate *imaginary unit* to real number or whole number units. Ask students to state what the square root of positive 1 is. Likewise, if the square root of −1 is the imaginary unit i, then its square is the original negative number (−1 in this case). Explain why imaginary units and imaginary numbers were invented—to define the square root of negative numbers.

EXPLAIN 3

Defining Imaginary Numbers

AVOID COMMON ERRORS

Some students may try to simplify a complex number by combining the real part and the imaginary part. For example, they may try to write $5 + 6i$ as $11i$. Emphasize that just as unlike terms in an algebraic expression cannot be combined, the real and imaginary parts of a complex number cannot be combined. Therefore, $5i + 6i = 11i$, but $5 + 6i \neq 5i + 6i$.

Your Turn

Write and solve an equation to answer the question. Give the exact answer and, if it's irrational, a decimal approximation (to the nearest tenth of a second).

6. How long does it take the water balloon described in Part B to hit the ground?

Using the model $h(t) = h_0 - 16t^2$, solve the equation $h(t) = 0$.

$$50 - 16t^2 = 0$$
$$-16t^2 = -50$$
$$t^2 = \frac{50}{16}$$
$$t = \pm\sqrt{\frac{50}{16}} = \frac{5\sqrt{2}}{4}$$

Reject the negative value of t. The water balloon hits the ground in $\frac{5\sqrt{2}}{4} \approx 1.8$ seconds.

7. On the moon, the distance d (in feet) that an object falls in time t (in seconds) is modeled by the function $d(t) = \frac{8}{3}t^2$. Suppose an astronaut on the moon drops a tool. How long does it take the tool to fall 4 feet?

Using the model $d(t) = \frac{8}{3}t^2$, solve the equation $d(t) = 4$.

$$\frac{8}{3}t^2 = 4$$
$$t^2 = \frac{3}{2}$$
$$t = \pm\sqrt{\frac{3}{2}} = \pm\frac{\sqrt{6}}{2}$$

Reject the negative value of t. The tool falls 4 feet in $\frac{\sqrt{6}}{2} \approx 1.2$ seconds.

Explain 3 Defining Imaginary Numbers

You know that the quadratic equation $x^2 = 1$ has two real solutions, the equation $x^2 = 0$ has one real solution, and the equation $x^2 = -1$ has no real solutions. By creating a new type of number called *imaginary numbers*, mathematicians allowed for solutions of equations like $x^2 = -1$.

Imaginary numbers are the square roots of negative numbers. These numbers can all be written in the form bi where b is a nonzero real number and i, called the **imaginary unit**, represents $\sqrt{-1}$. Some examples of imaginary numbers are the following:

- $2i$
- $-5i$
- $-\frac{i}{3}$ or $-\frac{1}{3}i$
- $i\sqrt{2}$ (Write the i in front of the radical symbol for clarity.)
- $\frac{i\sqrt{3}}{2}$ or $\frac{\sqrt{3}}{2}i$

Given that $i = \sqrt{-1}$, you can conclude that $i^2 = -1$. This means that the square of any imaginary number is a negative real number. When squaring an imaginary number, use the power of a product property of exponents: $(ab)^m = a^m \cdot b^m$.

LANGUAGE SUPPORT EL

Connect Vocabulary

Provide students with 4 to 6 "square root cards"—index cards displaying the square roots of several negative and positive integers. Working in pairs, one student shows a card and the other student decides the kind of number it represents. If both agree, the first student then finds the *square* of that square root. Students switch roles and repeat the process until all the cards have been used.

Example 3 Find the square of the imaginary number.

Ⓐ $5i$

$(5i)^2 = 5^2 \cdot i^2$
$= 25(-1)$
$= -25$

Ⓑ $-i\sqrt{2}$

$(-i\sqrt{2})^2 = \left(\boxed{-\sqrt{2}}\right)^2 \cdot i^2$
$= \boxed{2}(-1)$
$= \boxed{-2}$

Reflect

8. By definition, i is a square root of -1. Does -1 have another square root? Explain.
Yes, $-i$ is also a square root of -1 because squaring $-i$ also gives -1.

Your Turn

Find the square of the imaginary number.

9. $-2i$

$(-2i)^2 = (-2)^2 \cdot i^2$
$= 4(-1)$
$= -4$

10. $\frac{\sqrt{3}}{3}i$

$\left(\frac{\sqrt{3}}{3}i\right)^2 = \left(\frac{\sqrt{3}}{3}\right)^2 \cdot i^2$
$= \frac{3}{9}(-1)$
$= -\frac{1}{3}$

Explain 4 Finding Imaginary Solutions of Simple Quadratic Equations

Using imaginary numbers, you can solve simple quadratic equations that do not have real solutions.

Example 4 Solve the quadratic equation by taking square roots. Allow for imaginary solutions.

Ⓐ $x^2 + 12 = 0$

Write the equation.	$x^2 + 12 = 0$
Subtract 12 from both sides.	$x^2 = -12$
Use the definition of square root.	$x = \pm\sqrt{-12}$
Use the product property.	$x = \pm\sqrt{(4)(-1)(3)} = \pm 2i\sqrt{3}$

QUESTIONING STRATEGIES

What is an imaginary number? An imaginary unit i is defined as $\sqrt{-1}$. You can use the imaginary unit to write the square root of any negative number. Imaginary numbers can be written in the form bi, where b is a nonzero real number and i is the imaginary unit. $\sqrt{-1}$

EXPLAIN 4

Finding Imaginary Solutions of Simple Quadratic Equations

QUESTIONING STRATEGIES

What do you look for during the solving process to indicate that a quadratic equation might have imaginary solutions? The value x^2 is equal to a negative number or x is equal to the positive or negative square root of a negative number.

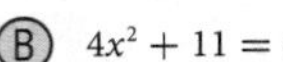

INTEGRATE MATHEMATICAL PRACTICES

Focus on Critical Thinking

MP.3 Ask how the imaginary solutions of a quadratic equation of the form $ax^2 = c$ are related, and what their sum might be. Students should see that the solutions are opposites and should surmise that their sum is 0.

ELABORATE

CONNECT VOCABULARY EL

A *family of functions* is a set of functions whose graphs have basic characteristics in common. Functions that are in the same family are transformations of their parent function.

QUESTIONING STRATEGIES

? How do you multiply powers with the same base when the exponents are rational? **Use the Product of Powers or Quotient of Powers and simplify.**

? Explain why recognizing parent functions is useful for graphing. **Recognizing the parent function can help you predict what the graph will look like and help you fill in the missing parts.**

SUMMARIZE THE LESSON

How can you solve equations involving square roots and cube roots? **Isolate the radical expression. If it is a square root, square both sides of the equation. If it is a cube root, cube both sides of the equation. Continue to solve by isolating the variable. For square root equations, check for extraneous solutions by substituting the solution(s) back into the original equation.**

(B) $4x^2 + 11 = 6$

Write the equation.	$4x^2 + 11 = 6$
Subtract 11 from both sides.	$\boxed{4}\,x^2 = \boxed{-5}$
Divide both sides by $\boxed{4}$.	$x^2 = \boxed{-\frac{5}{4}}$
Use the definition of square root.	$x = \pm\sqrt{\boxed{-\frac{5}{4}}}$
Use the qoutient property.	$x = \pm \boxed{\frac{\sqrt{5}}{2}i}$

Your Turn

Solve the quadratic equation by taking square roots. Allow for imaginary solutions.

11. $\frac{1}{4}x^2 + 9 = 0$

$\frac{1}{4}x^2 = -9$

$x^2 = -36$

$x = \pm\sqrt{-36}$

$x = \pm 6i$

12. $-5x^2 + 3 = 10$

$-5x^2 = 7$

$x^2 = -\frac{7}{5}$

$x = \pm\sqrt{-\frac{7}{5}}$

$x = \pm\frac{\sqrt{35}}{5}i$

Elaborate

13. The quadratic equations $4x^2 + 32 = 0$ and $4x^2 - 32 = 0$ differ only by the sign of the constant term. Without actually solving the equations, what can you say about the relationship between their solutions?
The first equation has imaginary solutions, while the second has real solutions, but the solutions will only differ by the factor of the imaginary unit *i*.

14. What kind of a number is the square of an imaginary number?
It is a negative real number.

15. Why do you reject negative values of t when solving equations based on the models for a falling object near Earth's surface, $d(t) = 16t^2$ for distance fallen and $h(t) = h_0 - 16t^2$ for height during a fall?
A negative value of *t* represents time before the fall, but both models deal only with time after the instant that the fall begins.

16. Essential Question Check-In Describe how to find the square roots of a negative number.
The square roots of a negative number, $-a$, are given by the imaginary unit *i* times the square roots of the corresponding positive number, *a*.

Evaluate: Homework and Practice

- Online Homework
- Hints and Help
- Extra Practice

1. Solve the equation $x^2 - 2 = 7$ using the indicated method.

   a. Solve by graphing.

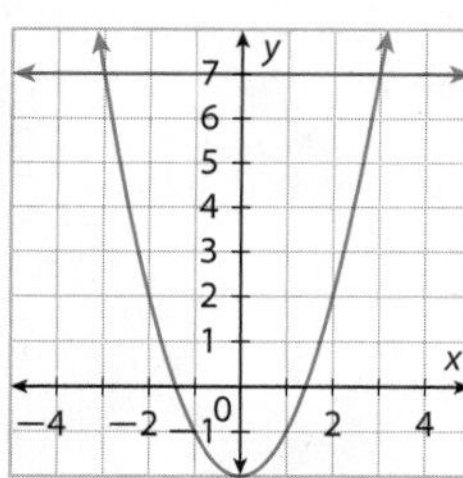

Treat each side of the equation as a function, and graph the two functions, which in this case are $f(x) = x^2 - 2$ and $g(x) = 7$, on the same coordinate plane. The x-coordinates of the two points where the graphs intersect are $x = -3$ and $x = 3$.

   b. Solve by factoring.

$$x^2 - 9 = 0$$
$$(x+3)(x-3) = 0$$
$$x + 3 = 0 \quad \text{or} \quad x - 3 = 0$$
$$x = -3 \quad \text{or} \quad x = 3$$

   c. Solve by taking square roots.

$$x^2 = 9$$
$$x = \pm\sqrt{9}$$
$$x = \pm 3$$

2. Solve the equation $2x^2 + 3 = 5$ using the indicated method.

   a. Solve by graphing.

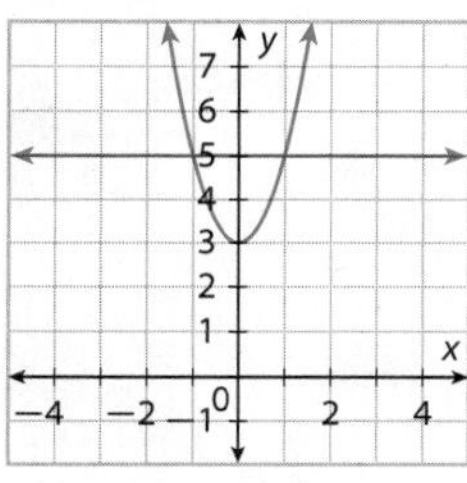

Treat each side of the equation as a function, and graph the two functions, which in this case are $f(x) = 2x^2 + 3$ and $g(x) = 5$, on the same coordinate plane. The x-coordinates of the two points where the graphs intersect are $x = -1$ and $x = 1$.

   b. Solve by factoring.

$$2x^2 - 2 = 0$$
$$2(x+1)(x-1) = 0$$
$$x + 1 = 0 \quad \text{or} \quad x - 1 = 0$$
$$x = -1 \quad \text{or} \quad x = 1$$

   c. Solve by taking square roots.

$$2x^2 = 2$$
$$x^2 = 1$$
$$x = \pm\sqrt{1}$$
$$x = \pm 1$$

Exercise	Depth of Knowledge (D.O.K.)	COMMON CORE Mathematical Practices
1–6	**1** Recall of Information	**MP.4** Modeling
7–10	**2** Skills/Concepts	**MP.4** Modeling
11–16	**2** Skills/Concepts	**MP.2** Reasoning
17–20	**2** Skills/Concepts	**MP.4** Modeling
21–22	**2** Skills/Concepts	**MP.5** Using Tools

EVALUATE

Personal Math Trainer

ASSIGNMENT GUIDE

Concepts and Skills	Practice
Explore Investigating Ways of Solving Simple Quadratic Equations	Exercises 1–2
Example 1 Finding Real Solutions of Simple Quadratic Equations	Exercises 2–6
Example 2 Solving a Real-World Problem Using a Simple Quadratic Equation	Exercises 7–10
Example 3 Defining Imaginary Numbers	Exercises 11–13
Example 4 Finding Imaginary Solutions of Simple Quadratic Equations	Exercises 15–18

AVOID COMMON ERRORS

When students draw the graph of a model of a quadratic function $F(x)$, they may draw a smooth curve through the points they plotted. Remind them that a reasonable domain of $F(x)$ consists of whole-number (or decimal) values. Therefore, the graph of the function is actually a set of discrete points rather than a smooth curve.

Solve the quadratic equation by taking square roots.

3. $4x^2 = 24$

$x^2 = 6$

$x = \pm\sqrt{6}$

4. $-\frac{x^2}{5} + 15 = 0$

$-\frac{x^2}{5} = -15$

$x^2 = 75$

$x = \pm\sqrt{75}$

$x = \pm 5\sqrt{3}$

5. $2(5 - 5x^2) = 5$

$10 - 10x^2 = 5$

$-10x^2 = -5$

$x^2 = \frac{1}{2}$

$x = \pm\sqrt{\frac{1}{2}}$

$x = \pm\frac{\sqrt{2}}{2}$

6. $3x^2 - 8 = 12$

$3x^2 = 20$

$x^2 = \frac{20}{3}$

$x = \pm\sqrt{\frac{20}{3}}$

$x = \pm\frac{\sqrt{20}}{\sqrt{3}} = \pm\frac{\sqrt{60}}{3} = \pm\frac{2\sqrt{15}}{3}$

Write and solve an equation to answer the question. Give the exact answer and, if it's irrational, a decimal approximation (to the nearest tenth of a second).

7. A squirrel in a tree drops an acorn. How long does it take the acorn to fall 20 feet?

Using the model $d(t) = 16t^2$, solve the equation $d(t) = 20$.

$16t^2 = 20$

$t^2 = \frac{5}{4}$

$t = \pm\sqrt{\frac{5}{4}}$

$t = \pm\frac{\sqrt{5}}{2}$

Reject the negative value of t. The acorn falls 20 feet in $\frac{\sqrt{5}}{2} \approx 1.1$ seconds.

8. A person washing the windows of an office building drops a squeegee from a height of 60 feet. How long does it take the squeegee to pass by another window washer working at a height of 20 feet?

Using the model $h(t) = h_0 - 16t^2$, solve the equation $h(t) = 20$.

$60 - 16t^2 = 20$

$-16t^2 = -40$

$t^2 = \frac{10}{4}$

$t = \pm\sqrt{\frac{10}{4}}$

$t = \pm\frac{\sqrt{10}}{2}$

Reject the negative value of t. The squeegee passes by the other window washer in $\frac{\sqrt{10}}{2} \approx 1.6$ seconds.

Exercise	Depth of Knowledge (D.O.K.)	COMMON CORE Mathematical Practices
23	**1** Recall of Information	**MP.2** Reasoning
24–25	**3** Strategic Thinking H.O.T.	**MP.4** Modeling
26	**3** Strategic Thinking H.O.T.	**MP.3** Logic

Geometry Determine the lengths of the sides of the rectangle using the given area. Give answers both exactly and approximately (to the nearest tenth).

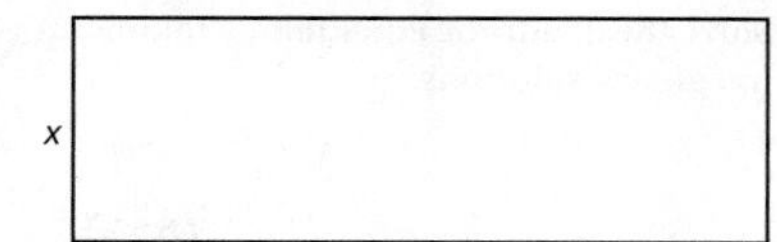

9. The area of the rectangle is 45 cm².

$$\begin{aligned}(\text{length})(\text{width}) &= \text{area}\\ (3x)(x) &= 45\\ 3x^2 &= 45\\ x^2 &= 15\\ x &= \pm\sqrt{15}\end{aligned}$$

Reject the negative value of x because length cannot be negative. So, the width of the rectangle is $\sqrt{15} \approx 3.9$ cm, and the length is $3\sqrt{15} \approx 11.6$ cm.

10. The area of the rectangle is 54 cm².

$$\begin{aligned}(\text{length})(\text{width}) &= \text{area}\\ (3x)(x) &= 54\\ 3x^2 &= 54\\ x^2 &= 18\\ x &= \pm\sqrt{18}\\ x &= \pm 3\sqrt{2}\end{aligned}$$

Reject the negative value of x because length cannot be negative. So, the width of the rectangle is $3\sqrt{2} \approx 4.2$ cm, and the length is $9\sqrt{2} \approx 12.7$ cm.

Find the square of the imaginary number.

11. $3i$

$$\begin{aligned}(3i)^2 &= 3^2 \cdot i^2\\ &= 9(-1)\\ &= -9\end{aligned}$$

12. $i\sqrt{5}$

$$\begin{aligned}(i\sqrt{5})^2 &= (\sqrt{5})^2 \cdot i^2\\ &= 5(-1)\\ &= -5\end{aligned}$$

13. $-i\frac{\sqrt{2}}{2}$

$$\begin{aligned}\left(-\frac{i\sqrt{2}}{2}\right)^2 &= \left(-\frac{\sqrt{2}}{2}\right)^2 \cdot i^2\\ &= \frac{1}{2}(-1)\\ &= -\frac{1}{2}\end{aligned}$$

Determine whether the quadratic equation has real solutions or imaginary solutions by solving the equation.

14. $15x^2 - 10 = 0$

$$\begin{aligned}15x^2 &= 10\\ x^2 &= \frac{2}{3}\\ x &= \pm\sqrt{\frac{2}{3}}\\ x &= \pm\frac{\sqrt{6}}{3}\end{aligned}$$

The solutions are real.

15. $\frac{1}{2}x^2 + 12 = 4$

$$\begin{aligned}\frac{1}{2}x^2 &= -8\\ x^2 &= -16\\ x &= \pm\sqrt{-16}\\ x &= \pm 4i\end{aligned}$$

The solutions are imaginary.

16. $5(2x^2 - 3) = 4(x^2 - 10)$

$$\begin{aligned}10x^2 - 15 &= 4x^2 - 40\\ 6x^2 &= -25\\ x^2 &= -\frac{25}{6}\\ x &= \pm\sqrt{-\frac{25}{6}}\\ x &= \pm\frac{5\sqrt{6}}{6}i\end{aligned}$$

The solutions are imaginary.

QUESTIONING STRATEGIES

? What is meant by reasonable domain? **A reasonable domain consists of the values of the independent variables that make sense in the context of the real-world situation.**

? What is the domain of a function? Why might it differ from the reasonable domain? **The domain of a function is all the values of the independent variable for which the function is defined. It may include values that represent physically impossible situations, such as a nearly infinite number of minutes.**

Solve the quadratic equation by taking square roots. Allow for imaginary solutions.

17. $x^2 = -81$

$x = \pm\sqrt{-81}$

$x = \pm 9i$

18. $x^2 + 64 = 0$

$x^2 = -64$

$x = \pm\sqrt{-64}$

$x = \pm 8i$

19. $5x^2 - 4 = -8$

$5x^2 = -4$

$x^2 = -\frac{4}{5}$

$x = \pm\sqrt{-\frac{4}{5}}$

$x = \pm\frac{2\sqrt{5}}{5}i$

20. $7x^2 + 10 = 0$

$7x^2 = -10$

$x^2 = -\frac{10}{7}$

$x = \pm\sqrt{-\frac{10}{7}}$

$x = \pm\frac{\sqrt{70}}{7}i$

Geometry Determine the length of the sides of each square using the given information. Give answers both exactly and approximately (to the nearest tenth).

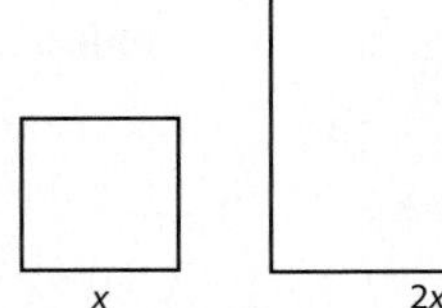

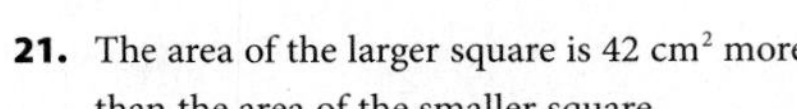

21. The area of the larger square is 42 cm^2 more than the area of the smaller square.

Use the formula for the area A of a square with side length s: $A = s^2$.

$(2x)^2 = x^2 + 42$

$4x^2 = x^2 + 42$

$3x^2 = 42$

$x^2 = 14$

$x = \pm\sqrt{14}$

Reject the negative value of x. The smaller square has a side length of $\sqrt{14} \approx 3.7$ cm, and the larger square has a side length of $2\sqrt{14} \approx 7.5$ cm.

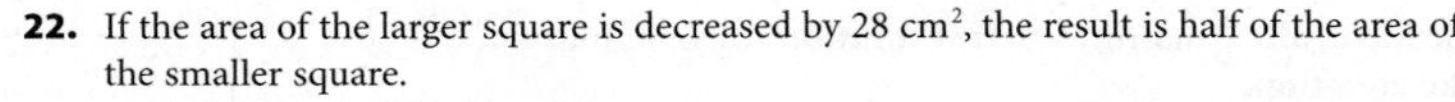

22. If the area of the larger square is decreased by 28 cm^2, the result is half of the area of the smaller square.

Use the formula for the area A of a square with side length s: $A = s^2$.

$(2x)^2 - 28 = \frac{1}{2}x^2$

$4x^2 - 28 = \frac{1}{2}x^2$

$\frac{7}{2}x^2 = 28$

$x^2 = 8$

$x = \pm\sqrt{8} = \pm 2\sqrt{2}$

Reject the negative value of x. The smaller square has a side length of $2\sqrt{2} \approx 2.8$ cm, and the larger square has a side length of $4\sqrt{2} \approx 5.7$ cm.

23. Determine whether each of the following numbers is real or imaginary.

a. i	☐ Real	X Imaginary
b. A square root of 5	X Real	☐ Imaginary
c. $(2i)^2$	X Real	☐ Imaginary
d. $(-5)^2$	X Real	☐ Imaginary
e. $\sqrt{-3}$	☐ Real	X Imaginary
f. $-\sqrt{10}$	X Real	☐ Imaginary

H.O.T. Focus on Higher Order Thinking

24. Critical Thinking When a batter hits a baseball, you can model the ball's height using a quadratic function that accounts for the ball's initial vertical velocity. However, once the ball reaches its maximum height, its vertical velocity is momentarily 0 feet per second, and you can use the model $h(t) = h_0 - 16t^2$ to find the ball's height h (in feet) at time t (in seconds) as it falls to the ground.

a. Suppose a fly ball reaches a maximum height of 67 feet and an outfielder catches the ball 3 feet above the ground. How long after the ball begins to descend does the outfielder catch the ball?

Using the model $h(t) = h_0 - 16t^2$, solve the equation $h(t) = 3$.

$$67 - 16t^2 = 3$$
$$-16t^2 = -64$$
$$t^2 = 4$$
$$t = \pm\sqrt{4}$$
$$t = \pm 2$$

Reject the negative value of t. The outfielder caught the ball 2 seconds after it reached its maximum height.

b. Can you determine (without writing or solving any equations) the total time the ball was in the air? Explain your reasoning and state any assumptions you make.

The other solution to the quadratic equation $h(t) = 3$, -2 seconds, is another time when the ball would have been 3 feet above the ground. This would have happened 2 seconds *before* the ball reached its maximum height. If you assume that the batter hit the ball at a height of 3 feet, then you can conclude that the ball was in the air for a total of 4 seconds.

PEER-TO-PEER DISCUSSION

Ask students to discuss with a partner a topic they would like to research to find a data set with time as the independent variable.

Students may find examples such as the length or weight of an animal as it grows; the populations of an endangered species in a city; the cost of a particular item; or a team's winning percentage. Have pairs of students then find information on the appropriate model for the data set.

JOURNAL

Have students write a journal entry that describes how they could apply their knowledge of graphs of quadratic functions to solve real-world problems.

25. Represent Real-World Situations The aspect ratio of an image on a screen is the ratio of image width to image height. An HDTV screen shows images with an aspect ratio of 16:9. If the area of an HDTV screen is 864 in^2, what are the dimensions of the screen?

The width of the screen must be some multiple of 16, and the height of screen must be the same multiple of 9. Let m be the common (positive) multiplier, so that the width is $16m$, the height is $9m$, and the ratio of width to height is $\frac{16m}{9m} = \frac{16}{9}$.

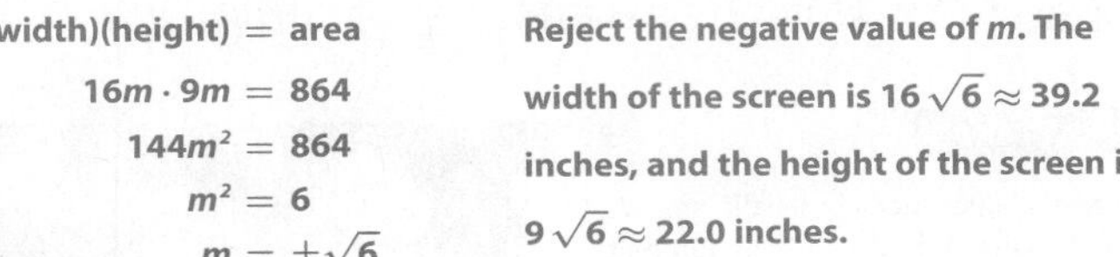

$$\begin{aligned} (\text{width})(\text{height}) &= \text{area} \\ 16m \cdot 9m &= 864 \\ 144m^2 &= 864 \\ m^2 &= 6 \\ m &= \pm\sqrt{6} \end{aligned}$$

Reject the negative value of m. The width of the screen is $16\sqrt{6} \approx 39.2$ inches, and the height of the screen is $9\sqrt{6} \approx 22.0$ inches.

26. Explain the Error Russell wants to calculate the amount of time it takes for a load of dirt to fall from a crane's clamshell bucket at a height of 16 feet to the bottom of a hole that is 32 feet deep. He sets up the following equation and tries to solve it.

$$\begin{aligned} 16 - 16t^2 &= 32 \\ -16t^2 &= 16 \\ t^2 &= -1 \\ t &= \pm\sqrt{-1} \\ t &= \pm i \end{aligned}$$

Does Russell's answer make sense? If not, find and correct Russell's error.

No, the time should not be an imaginary number of seconds. His error was using a positive number to represent the "height" of the bottom of the hole. If the hole is 32 feet deep, the bottom is at −32 feet relative to ground level.

$$\begin{aligned} 16 - 16t^2 &= -32 \\ -16t^2 &= -48 \\ t^2 &= 3 \\ t &= \pm\sqrt{3} \end{aligned}$$

Reject the negative value of t. The dirt took $\sqrt{3} \approx 1.7$ seconds to reach the bottom of the hole.

Lesson Performance Task

A suspension bridge uses two thick cables, one on each side of the road, to hold up the road. The cables are suspended between two towers and have a parabolic shape. Smaller vertical cables connect the parabolic cables to the road. The table gives the lengths of the first few vertical cables starting with the shortest one.

Displacement from the Shortest Vertical Cable (m)	Height of Vertical Cable (m)
0	3
1	3.05
2	3.2
3	3.45

Find a quadratic function that describes the height (in meters) of a parabolic cable above the road as a function of the horizontal displacement (in meters) from the cable's lowest point. Use the function to predict the distance between the towers if the parabolic cable reaches a maximum height of 48 m above the road at each tower.

Use a coordinate plane where the x-axis is located at the level of the road, and the y-axis is located at the shortest vertical cable. In this coordinate system, the general form of the height function is $h(x) = ax^2 + k$. Since the height of the shortest vertical cable is 3 m, $k = 3$ and $h(x) = ax^2 + 3$.

To find the value of a, use one the data for one of the vertical cables (other than the shortest one). For instance, substitute 1 for x and 3.05 for $h(x)$ and solve $h(x) = ax^2 + 3$ for a.

$h(x) = ax^2 + 3$

$h(1) = a \cdot 1^2 + 3$

$3.05 = a + 3$

$0.05 = a$

So, $h(x) = 0.05x^2 + 3$. Confirm that $h(2) = 3.2$ and $h(3) = 3.45$.

Set the height function equal to 48 and solve for x.

$$\begin{aligned} h(x) &= 48 \\ 0.05x^2 + 3 &= 48 \\ 0.05x^2 &= 45 \\ x^2 &= 900 \\ x &= \pm\sqrt{900} \\ x &= \pm 30 \end{aligned}$$

The two towers are at 30 m in opposite directions from the shortest vertical cable, so the distance between towers is $30 - (-30) = 60$ m.

QUESTIONING STRATEGIES

How can you tell without calculating whether a quadratic equation has imaginary roots? **Graph the equation, and if the graph does not intersect the x-axis, the solutions are imaginary.**

INTEGRATE MATHEMATICAL PRACTICES

Focus on Technology

MP.5 A graphing calculator or spreadsheet can also be used to quickly evaluate expressions for many values of the variable. Use the table feature of a graphing calculator to evaluate an expression for different unknown values.

EXTENSION ACTIVITY

The supporting cable on a suspension bridge is in the shape of a parabola, but a cable suspended from both ends takes the shape of a *catenary*. Have students research online to compare the shapes of a parabola and catenary. Some students might be interested in the equation for a catenary, $y = \frac{a}{2}\left(e^{x/a} + e^{-x/a}\right) = a \cosh\left(\frac{x}{a}\right)$, where a is the vertical distance from the x-axis to the vertex. Another topic of interest related to suspension bridges is the Tacoma Narrows Bridge collapse. Have students do an Internet search to find footage of this dramatic event.

Scoring Rubric

2 points: Student correctly solves the problem and explains his/her reasoning.

1 point: Student shows good understanding of the problem but does not fully solve or explain his/her reasoning.

0 points: Student does not demonstrate understanding of the problem.

LESSON 3.2

Complex Numbers

Common Core Math Standards

The student is expected to:

N-CN.A.2

Use the relation $i^2 = -1$ and the commutative, associative, and distributive properties to add, subtract, and multiply complex numbers. Also N-CN.A.1

Mathematical Practices

MP.2 Reasoning

Language Objective

Work with a partner to classify and justify the classification of real, complex, and imaginary numbers.

ENGAGE

Essential Question: What is a complex number and how do you add, subtract, and mutiply complex numbers?

Possible answer: A complex number has the form $a + bi$ where a and b are real numbers and i is the imaginary unit. You add and subtract complex numbers by combining like terms. You multiply complex numbers by using the distributive property, substituting -1 for i^2, and combining like terms.

PREVIEW: LESSON PERFORMANCE TASK

View the Engage section online. Discuss the photo and how complex numbers can be used to generate fractal patterns. Then preview the Lesson Performance Task.

Name ________ Class ________ Date ________

3.2 Complex Numbers

Essential Question: What is a complex number, and how can you add, subtract, and multiply complex numbers?

Resource Locker

Explore Exploring Operations Involving Complex Numbers

In this lesson, you'll learn to perform operations with *complex numbers,* which have a form similar to linear binomials such as $3 + 4x$ and $2 - x$.

(A) Add the binomials $3 + 4x$ and $2 - x$.

Group like terms. $(3 + 4x) + (2 - x) = (3 + \boxed{2}) + (4x + \boxed{-x})$

Combine like terms. $= (\boxed{5} + \boxed{3x})$

(B) Subtract $2 - x$ from $3 + 4x$.

Rewrite as addition. $(3 + 4x) - (2 - x) = (3 + 4x) + (-2 + \boxed{x})$

Group like terms. $= (3 + \boxed{-2}) + (4x + \boxed{x})$

Combine like terms. $= (\boxed{1} + \boxed{5x})$

(C) Multiply the binomials $3 + 4x$ and $2 - x$.

Use FOIL. $(3 + 4x)(2 - x) = 6 + (-3x) + \boxed{8x} + \boxed{-4x^2}$

Combine like terms. $= 6 + \boxed{5x} + \boxed{-4x^2}$

Reflect

1. In Step A, you found that $(3 + 4x) + (2 - x) = 5 + 3x$. Suppose $x = i$ (the imaginary unit). What equation do you get? $(3 + 4i) + (2 - i) = 5 + 3i$
2. In Step B, you found that $(3 + 4x) + (2 - x) = 1 + 5x$. Suppose $x = i$ (the imaginary unit). What equation do you get? $(3 + 4i) - (2 - i) = 1 + 5i$
3. In Step C, you found that $(3 + 4x)(2 - x) = 6 + 5x - 4x^2$. Suppose $x = i$ (the imaginary unit). What equation do you get? How you can further simplify the right side of this equation?
   $(3 + 4i)(2 - i) = 6 + 5i - 4i^2$; because $i^2 = -1$, the right side of this equation can be simplified to $6 + 5i - 4(-1)$, or $10 + 5i$.

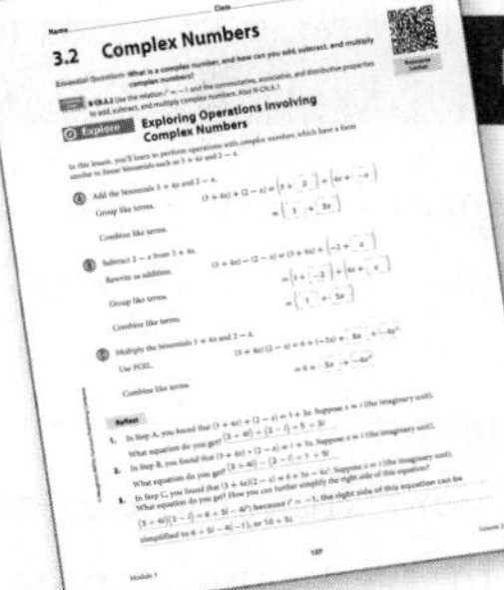

HARDCOVER PAGES 127–138

Watch for the hardcover student edition page numbers for this lesson.

Explain 1 Defining Complex Numbers

A **complex number** is any number that can be written in the form $a + bi$, where a and b are real numbers and $i = \sqrt{-1}$. For a complex number $a + bi$ a is called the *real part* of the number, and b is called the *imaginary part*. (Note that "imaginary part" refers to the real multiplier of i; it does not refer to the imaginary number bi.) The Venn diagram shows some examples of complex numbers.

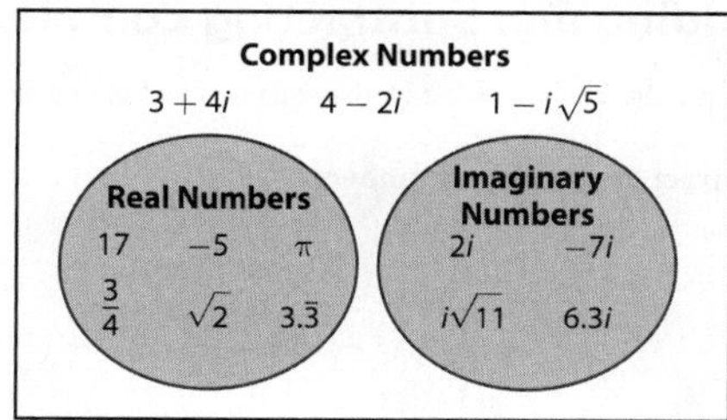

Notice that the set of real numbers is a subset of the set of complex numbers. That's because a real number a can be written in the form $a + 0i$ (whose imaginary part is 0). Likewise, the set of imaginary numbers is also a subset of the set of complex numbers, because an imaginary number bi(where $b \neq 0$) can be written in the form $0 + bi$(whose real part is 0).

Example 1 **Identify the real and imaginary parts of the given number. Then tell whether the number belongs to each of the following sets: real numbers, imaginary numbers, and complex numbers.**

(A) $9 + 5i$

The real part of $9 + 5i$ is 9, and the imaginary part is 5. Because both the real and imaginary parts of $9 + 5i$ are nonzero, the number belongs only to the set of complex numbers.

(B) $-7i$

The real part of $-7i$ is __0__, and the imaginary part is __−7__. Because the (real)/imaginary part is 0, the number belongs to these sets: imaginary numbers and complex numbers.

Your Turn

Identify the real and imaginary parts of the given number. Then tell whether the number belongs to each of the following sets: real numbers, imaginary numbers, and complex numbers.

4. 11

The real part of 11 is 11, and the imaginary part is 0. Because the imaginary part is 0, the number belongs to these sets: real numbers and complex numbers.

PROFESSIONAL DEVELOPMENT

Integrate Mathematical Practices

This lesson provides an opportunity to address Mathematical Practice **MP.2**, which calls for students to translate between multiple representations and to "reason abstractly and quantitatively." Students explore the relationship between operations with complex numbers and operations with binomials. They also describe how complex-number arithmetic operations follow from operations with rational numbers and square roots.

EXPLORE

Exploring Operations Involving Imaginary Numbers

INTEGRATE TECHNOLOGY

Students have the option of completing the activity either in the book or online.

QUESTIONING STRATEGIES

Do all complex numbers include an imaginary part? Explain. **No, a complex number does not always include an imaginary part. All real numbers are also complex numbers. The imaginary unit i is defined as $\sqrt{-1}$. You can use the imaginary unit to write the square root of any negative number.**

How can you tell which part of a complex number is the real part and which is the imaginary part? **In a number of the form $a + bi$, the real part is a, which does not have i as a factor. The imaginary part is bi, where b is a nonzero real number and i is the imaginary unit.**

EXPLAIN 1

Defining Complex Numbers

AVOID COMMON ERRORS

Students may write the conjugate of $a + bi$ as $-a-bi$. Caution them to change the sign only of bi, and not of a, when they write the complex conjugate.

QUESTIONING STRATEGIES

What are the components of a complex number? **A complex number has the form $a + bi$, where a and b are real numbers. Each term of $a + bi$ is given a name: a is called the *real part* and bi is called the *imaginary part*.**

EXPLAIN 2

Adding and Subtracting Complex Numbers

QUESTIONING STRATEGIES

Can the sum of two imaginary numbers be 0? yes, if both the real parts and the imaginary parts are opposites of each other

A *pure* imaginary number has no real part. When is the sum of two imaginary numbers a pure imaginary number? when the real parts are opposites, for example, $(6 + 4i) + (-6 - 8i) = -4i$

INTEGRATE MATHEMATICAL PRACTICES

Focus on Math Connections

MP.1 Quadratic equations are equations of degree 2, and therefore have a maximum of two real solutions. Sometimes the two real solutions are a double root, but many quadratic equations have zero real solutions. It is only by introducing complex numbers that we are able to find two solutions for all quadratic equations.

AVOID COMMON ERRORS

Some students may try to simplify a complex number by combining the real part and the imaginary part. Emphasize that just as unlike terms in an algebraic expression cannot be combined, neither can the real and imaginary parts of a complex number.

5. $-1 + i$

The real part of $-1 + i$ is -1, and the imaginary part is 1. Because both the real and imaginary parts of $-1 + i$ are nonzero, the number belongs only to the set of complex numbers.

Explain 2 Adding and Subtracting Complex Numbers

To add or subtract complex numbers, add or subtract the real parts and the imaginary parts separately.

Example 2 **Add or subtract the complex numbers.**

(A) $(-7 + 2i) + (5 - 11i)$

Group like terms. $(-7 + 2i) + (5 - 11i) = (-7 + 5) + (2i + (-11i))$

Combine like terms. $= -2 + (-9i)$

Write addition as subtraction. $= -2 - 9i$

(B) $(18 + 27i) - (2 + 3i)$

Group like terms. $(18 + 27i) - (2 + 3i) = \left(18 - \boxed{2}\right) + \left(\boxed{27i} - 3i\right)$

Combine like terms. $= \boxed{16} + \boxed{24}\,i$

Reflect

6. Is the sum $(a + bi) + (a - bi)$ where a and b are real numbers, a real number or an imaginary number? Explain.

$(a + bi) + (a - bi) = (a + a) + (bi + (-bi)) = 2a$

Since a is a real number, $2a$ is a real number. So, the sum $(a + bi) + (a - bi)$ is a real number.

Your Turn

Add or subtract the complex numbers.

7. $(17 - 16i) - (9 + 10i)$

$(17 - 6i) - (9 + 10i) = (17 - 9) + (-6i - 10i)$

$= 8 + (-16i)$

$= 8 - 16i$

8. $(16 + 17i) + (-8 - 12i)$

$(16 + 17i) + (-8 - 12i) = (16 + (-8)) + (17i + (-12i))$

$= 8 + 5i$

COLLABORATIVE LEARNING

Peer-to-Peer Activity

Have students work in pairs. Each student writes an addition and subtraction problem for an imaginary number $(a + bi)$, a pure imaginary number (bi), and a real number (a). The partners exchange papers and solve all six problems, then exchange papers again to check their answers.

Explain 3 Multiplying Complex Numbers

To multiply two complex numbers, use the distributive property to multiply each part of one number with each part of the other. Use the fact that $i^2 = -1$ to simplify the result.

Example 3 Multiply the complex numbers.

Ⓐ $(4 + 9i)(6 - 2i)$

Use the distributive property. $(4 + 9i)(6 - 2i) = 24 - 8i + 54i - 18i^2$

Substitute -1 for i^2. $= 24 - 8i + 54i - 18(-1)$

Combine like terms. $= 42 + 46i$

Ⓑ $(-3 + 12i)(7 + 4i)$

Use the distributive property. $(-3 + 12i)(7 + 4i) = \boxed{-21} - 12i + \boxed{84i} + 48i^2$

Substitute -1 for i^2. $= \boxed{-21} - 12i + \boxed{84i} + 48(-1)$

Combine like terms. $= \boxed{-69} + \boxed{72}\, i$

Reflect

9. Is the product of $(a + bi)(a - bi)$, where a and b are real numbers, a real number or an imaginary number? Explain.

$$(a + bi)(a - bi) = a^2 - abi + abi - b^2i^2$$
$$= a^2 - b^2(-1)$$
$$= a^2 + b^2$$

Since a and b are real numbers, $a^2 + b^2$ is a real number. So the product $(a + bi)(a - bi)$ is a real number.

Your Turn

Multiply the complex numbers.

10. $(6 - 5i)(3 - 10i)$

$$(6 - 15i)(3 - 10i) = 18 - 60i - 15i + 50i^2$$
$$= 18 - 60i - 15i + 50(-1)$$
$$= -32 - 75i$$

11. $(8 + 15i)(11 + i)$

$$(8 + 15i)(11 + i) = 88 + 8i + 165i + 15i^2$$
$$= 88 + 8i + 165i + 15(-1)$$
$$= 73 + 173i$$

DIFFERENTIATE INSTRUCTION

Visual Learners

To help visual learners see the relationships among the various types of numbers, show them the following diagram. Ask them to give examples of each type of number.

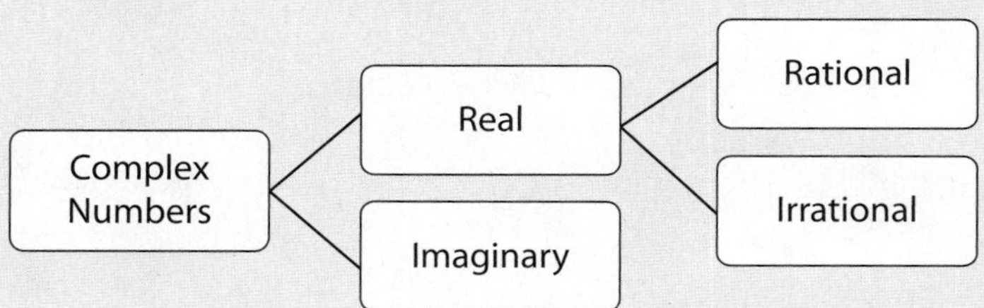

EXPLAIN 3

Multiplying Complex Numbers

QUESTIONING STRATEGIES

How is multiplying two imaginary numbers similar to the FOIL method? The same steps are used to multiply two imaginary numbers as are used to multiply two binomials.

If you use the FOIL method to multiply two imaginary numbers, which of the products, F, O, I, or L, are real? Which are pure imaginary? F and L are real; O and I are pure imaginary.

AVOID COMMON ERRORS

Some students may try to simplify a complex number by combining the real part and the imaginary part. Emphasize that just as unlike terms in an algebraic expression cannot be combined, neither can the real and imaginary parts of a complex number.

INTEGRATE MATHEMATICAL PRACTICES

Focus on Math Connections

MP.1 Reinforce how FOIL is used to multiply two binomials, such as the product of $2 + 3x$ and $1 - 4x$, before asking students to use FOIL to multiply two imaginary numbers, such as the product of $2 + 3i$ and $1 - 4i$. Show the work for the binomials side by side with the work for the imaginary numbers. Ask students to point out the similarities and differences in the work steps.

EXPLAIN 4

Solving a Real-World Problem Using Complex Numbers

QUESTIONING STRATEGIES

If two real-world quantities have values of $12 - 15i$ and $16 - 20i$, do you know which quantity is larger? Explain. **No; you can compare the real part only to the real part, and the imaginary part only to the imaginary part.**

INTEGRATE MATHEMATICAL PRACTICES

Focus on Critical Thinking

MP.3 Ask students to compare the product of $2 + 3i$ and $2 - 3i$ to the product of $3 + 2i$ and $3 - 2i$. Have them explain the relationship between the products. **Both have a value of 13. The first product is $(2 + 3i)(2 - 3i) = 2^2 - 6i + 6i - 9i^2 = 4 + 9 = 13$. The second has the same middle terms and has a value of $9 + 4 = 13$.**

Explain 4 Solving a Real-World Problem Using Complex Numbers

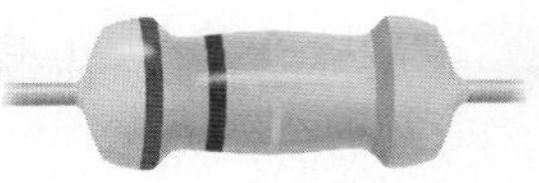

Electrical engineers use complex numbers when analyzing electric circuits. An electric circuit can contain three types of components: resistors, inductors, and capacitors. As shown in the table, each type of component has a different symbol in a circuit diagram, and each is represented by a different type of complex number based on the phase angle of the current passing through it.

Circuit Component	Symbol in Circuit Diagram	Phase Angle	Representation as a Complex Number
Resistor	(resistor symbol)	0°	A real number a
Inductor	(inductor symbol)	90°	An imaginary number bi where $b > 0$
Capacitor	(capacitor symbol)	−90°	An imaginary number bi where $b < 0$

A diagram of an alternating current (AC) electric circuit is shown along with the *impedance* (measured in ohms, Ω) of each component in the circuit. An AC power source, which is shown on the left in the diagram and labeled 120 V (for volts), causes electrons to flow through the circuit. Impedance is a measure of each component's opposition to the electron flow.

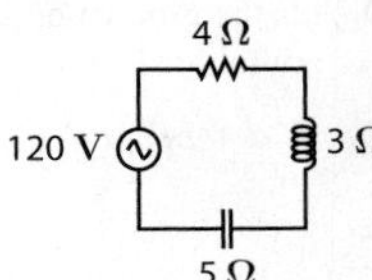

Example 4 **Use the diagram of the electric circuit to answer the following questions.**

(A) The total impedance in the circuit is the sum of the impedances for the individual components. What is the total impedance for the given circuit?

Write the impedance for each component as a complex number.

- Impedance for the resistor: 4
- Impedance for the inductor: $3i$
- Impedance for the capacitor: $-5i$

Then find the sum of the impedances.

Total impedance $= 4 + 3i + (-5i) = 4 - 2i$

(B) Ohm's law for AC electric circuits says that the voltage V (measured in volts) is the product of the current I (measured in amps) and the impedance Z (measured in ohms): $V = I \cdot Z$. For the given circuit, the current I is $24 + 12i$ amps. What is the voltage V for each component in the circuit?

Use Ohm's law, $V = I \cdot Z$, to find the voltage for each component. Remember that Z is the impedance from Part A.

Voltage for the resistor $= I \cdot Z = (24 + 12i)(\boxed{4}) = 96 + \boxed{48}\, i$

Voltage for the inductor $= I \cdot Z = (24 + 12i)(\boxed{3i}) = -36 + \boxed{72}\, i$

Voltage for the capacitor $= I \cdot Z = (24 + 12i)(\boxed{-5i}) = \boxed{60} - 120i$

Reflect

12. Find the sum of the voltages for the three components in Part B. What do you notice?

Sum of voltages $= (96 + 48i) + (-36 + 72i) + (60 - 120i)$

$= [96 + (-36) + 60] + [48i + 72i + (-120i)]$

$= 120i + 0i = 120$

The sum of the voltages equals the voltage supplied by the power source.

Your Turn

13. Suppose the circuit analyzed in Example 4 has a second resistor with an impedance of 2 Ω added to it. Find the total impedance. Given that the circuit now has a current of $18 + 6i$ amps, also find the voltage for each component in the circuit.

Total impedance $= 2 + 4 + 3i + (-5i) = 6 - 2i$

Voltage for the first resistor $= I \cdot Z = (18 + 6i)(4) = 72 + 24i$

Voltage for the second resistor $= I \cdot Z = (18 + 6i)(2) = 36 + 12i$

Voltage for the inductor $= I \cdot Z = (18 + 6i)(3i) = -18 + 54i$

Voltage for the capacitor $= I \cdot Z = (18 + 6i)(-5i) = 30 - 90i$

Elaborate

14. What kind of number is the sum, difference, or product of two complex numbers?

The sum, difference, or product of two complex numbers is always a complex number.

15. When is the sum of two complex numbers a real number? When is the sum of two complex numbers an imaginary number?

The sum of two complex numbers is a real number when the imaginary parts of the numbers are additive inverses or both 0. The sum of two complex numbers is an imaginary number when the real parts of the numbers are additive inverses or both 0.

LANGUAGE SUPPORT EL

Connect Vocabulary

Provide pairs of students with 6 to 8 "number cards" or index cards on which are different complex numbers, imaginary numbers, and real numbers. Ask them to sort the cards into those categories. Pairs must agree on the classifications and justify their decisions by writing a short explanation on each card. Students then identify the real and imaginary parts of the complex numbers by labeling.

CONNECT VOCABULARY EL

Have students complete a Venn diagram in which one circle contains real numbers and the other circle imaginary numbers. Emphasize that the overlap shows complex numbers. Have students write three examples of each kind of number in their diagrams.

ELABORATE

INTEGRATE MATHEMATICAL PRACTICES

Focus on Math Connections

MP.1 Relate the real and imaginary parts of a complex number to the real (horizontal) and imaginary (vertical) axes. Students should realize that points on the horizontal axis represent real numbers, points on the vertical axis represent pure imaginary numbers, and points in the quadrants represent complex numbers.

QUESTIONING STRATEGIES

? If you multiply a nonzero real number and an imaginary number, is the product real or imaginary? Why? **Imaginary; $c(bi) = cbi$, which is imaginary since cb is real and neither b nor c equals 0.**

SUMMARIZE THE LESSON

? How do you perform the various operations on complex numbers? **To add or subtract complex numbers, add or subtract their real parts and their imaginary parts separately. To multiply complex numbers, use the distributive property or the FOIL method. To divide complex numbers, multiply the numerator and denominator by the complex conjugate of the denominator.**

EVALUATE

ASSIGNMENT GUIDE

Concepts and Skills	Practice
Explore Exploring Operations Involving Imaginary Numbers	Exercise 1
Example 1 Defining Complex Numbers	Exercises 2–5
Example 2 Adding and Subtracting Complex Numbers	Exercises 6–9
Example 3 Multiplying Complex Numbers	Exercises 10–20

16. Discussion What are the similarities and differences between multiplying two complex numbers and multiplying two binomial linear expressions in the same variable?

The distributive property is used to multiply both complex numbers and binomial linear expressions. When two binomial linear expressions in the same variable are multiplied, the result is a trinomial quadratic expression. When two complex numbers are multiplied, the result is another complex number.

17. Essential Question Check-In How do you add and subtract complex numbers?

To add or subtract complex numbers, combine like terms.

Evaluate: Homework and Practice

- Online Homework
- Hints and Help
- Extra Practice

1. Find the sum of the binomials $3 + 2x$ and $4 - 5x$. Explain how you can use the result to find the sum of the complex numbers $3 + 2i$ and $4 - 5i$.

   $(3 + 2x) + (4 - 5x) = (3 + 4) + (2x - 5x) = 7 - 3x$

   Replacing x with the imaginary unit i gives this result: $(3 + 2i) + (4 - 5i) = 7 - 3i$.

2. Find the product of the binomials $1 - 3x$ and $2 + x$. Explain how you can use the result to find the product of the complex numbers $1 - 3i$ and $2 + i$.

   $(1 - 3x)(2 + x) = 2 - 6x + x - 3x^2 = 2 - 5x - 3x^2$

   Replacing x with the imaginary unit i gives this result: $(1 - 3i)(2 + i) = 1 - 5i - 3i^2$. Because $i^2 = -1$, the result can be further simplified as follows:

   $(1 - 3i)(2 + i) = 2 - 5i - 3i^2 = 2 - 5i - 3(-1) = 5 - 5i$

Identify the real and imaginary parts of the given number. Then tell whether the number belongs to each of the following sets: real numbers, imaginary numbers, and complex numbers.

3. $5 + i$

   The real part is 5, and the imaginary part is 1. Because both the real and imaginary parts are nonzero, the number belongs only to the set of complex numbers.

4. $7 - 6i$

   The real part is 7, and the imaginary part is −6. Because both the real and imaginary parts are nonzero, the number belongs only to the set of complex numbers.

Exercise	Depth of Knowledge (D.O.K.)	COMMON CORE Mathematical Practices
1–14	1 Recall of Information	MP.2 Reasoning
15–18	2 Skills/Concepts	MP.2 Reasoning
19–22	2 Skills/Concepts	MP.4 Modeling
23	2 Skills/Concepts	MP.2 Reasoning
24–25	3 Strategic Thinking H.O.T.	MP.2 Reasoning
26	2 Skills/Concepts H.O.T.	MP.3 Logic

5. 25

The real part is 25, and the imaginary part is 0. Because the imaginary part is 0, the number belongs to these sets: real numbers and complex numbers.

6. $i\sqrt{21}$

The real part is 0, and the imaginary part is $\sqrt{21}$. Because the real part is 0, the number belongs to these sets: imaginary numbers and complex numbers.

Add.

7. $(3 + 4i) + (7 + 11i)$

$$(3 + 4i) + (7 + 11i) = (3 + 7) + (4i + 11i) = 10 + 15i$$

8. $(2 + 3i) + (6 - 5i)$

$$(2 + 3i) + (6 - 5i) = (2 + 6) + (3i + 5i) = 8 - 2i$$

9. $(-1 - i) + (-10 + 3i)$

$$(-1 - i) + (-10 + 3i) = (-1 - 10) + (-i + 3i) = -11 + 2i$$

10. $(-9 - 7i) + (6 + 5i)$

$$(-9 - 7i) + (6 + 5i) = (-9 + 6) + (-7i + 5i) = -3 - 2i$$

Subtract.

11. $(2 + 3i) - (7 + 6i)$

$$(2 + 3i) - (7 + 6i) = (2 - 7) + (3i - 6i) = -5 - 3i$$

12. $(4 + 5i) - (14 - i)$

$$(4 + 5i) - (14 - i) = (4 - 14) + (5i - i) = -10 + 6i$$

13. $(-8 - 3i) - (-9 - 5i)$

$$(-8 - 3i) - (-9 - 5i) = (-8 + 9) + (-3i + 5i) = 1 + 2i$$

14. $(5 + 2i) - (5 - 2i)$

$$(5 + 2i) - (5 - 2i) = (5 - 5) + (2i - 2i) = 4i$$

Multiply.

15. $(2 + 3i)(3 + 5i)$

$$\begin{aligned}(2 + 3i)(3 + 5i) &= 6 + 10i + 9i + 15i^2\\ &= 6 + 10i + 9i + 15(-1)\\ &= -9 + 19i\end{aligned}$$

16. $(7 + i)(6 - 9i)$

$$\begin{aligned}(7 + i)(6 - 9i) &= 42 - 63i + 6i - 9i^2\\ &= 42 - 63i + 6i - 9(-1)\\ &= 51 - 57i\end{aligned}$$

17. $(-4 + 11i)(-5 - 8i)$

$$\begin{aligned}(-4 + 11i)(-5 - 8i) &= 20 + 32i - 55i - 88i^2\\ &= 20 + 32i - 55i - 88(-1)\\ &= 108 - 23i\end{aligned}$$

18. $(4 - i)(4 + i)$

$$\begin{aligned}(4 - i)(4 + i) &= 16 + 4i - 4i - i^2\\ &= 16 + 4i - 4i - (-1)\\ &= 17\end{aligned}$$

QUESTIONING STRATEGIES

What is a complex conjugate? Two complex numbers of the form $a + bi$ and $a - bi$ are complex conjugates. The product of complex conjugates is always a real number.

CRITICAL THINKING

Just as every real number corresponds to a point on the real number line, every complex number corresponds to a point in the *complex plane.* The complex plane has a horizontal axis called the *real axis* and a vertical axis called the *imaginary axis.* Ask students whether they can graph the line $y = 3x + 4$ on the complex plane.

AVOID COMMON ERRORS

Watch for students who simplify a complex number by combining the real part and the imaginary part. Clarify that just as unlike terms in an algebraic expression cannot be combined, real and imaginary parts of a complex number cannot be combined.

Use the diagram of the electric circuit and the given current to find the total impedance for the circuit and the voltage for each component.

19.

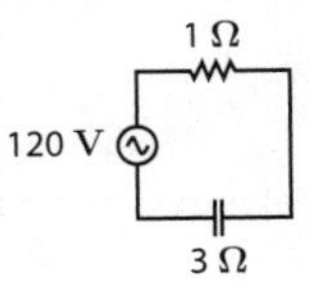

The circuit has a current of $12 + 36i$ amps.

Total impedance $= 1 - 3i$

Voltage for the resistor $= I \cdot Z$

$= (12 + 36i)(1)$

$= 12 + 36i$

Voltage for the capacitor $= I \cdot Z$

$= (12 + 36i)(-3i)$

$= 108 - 36i$

20.

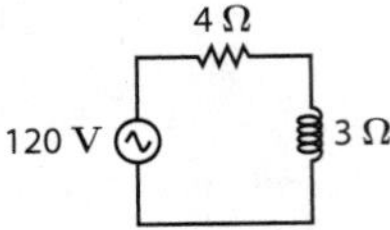

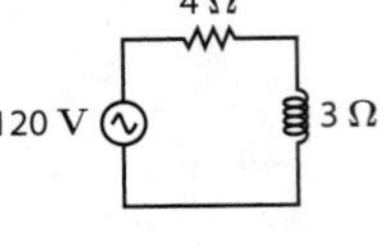

The circuit has a current of $19.2 - 14.4i$.

Total impedance $= 4 + 3i$

Voltage for the resistor $= I \cdot Z$

$= (19.2 - 14.4i)(4)$

$= 76.8 - 57.6i$

Voltage for the inductor $= I \cdot Z$

$= (19.2 - 14.4i)(-3$

$= 43.2 + 57.6i$

21.

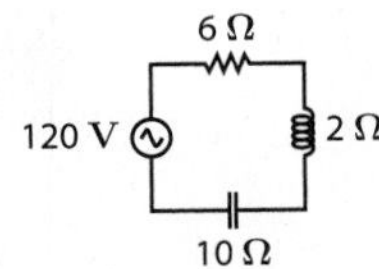

The circuit has a current of $7.2 + 9.6i$ amps.

Total impedance $= 6 + 2i + (-10i) = 6 - 8i$

Voltage for the resistor $= I \cdot Z$

$= (7.2 + 9.6i)(6)$

$= 43.2 + 57.6i$

Voltage for the inductor $= I \cdot Z$

$= (7.2 + 9.6i)(2i)$

$= -19.2 + 14.4i$

Voltage for the capacitor $= I \cdot Z$

$= (7.2 + 9.6i)(-10i)$

$= 96 - 72i$

22.

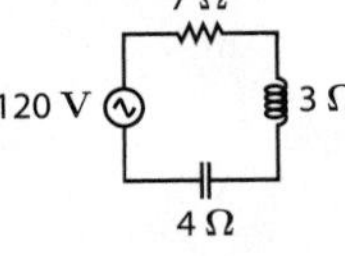

The circuit has a current of $16.8 + 2.4i$ amps.

Total impedance $= 7 + 3i + (-4i) = 7$

Voltage for the resistor $= I \cdot Z$

$= (16.8 + 2.4i)(7)$

$= 117.6 + 16.8i$

Voltage for the inductor $= I \cdot Z$

$= (16.8 + 2.4i)(3i)$

$= -7.2 + 50.4i$

Voltage for the capacitor $= I \cdot Z$

$= (16.8 + 2.4i)(-4i)$

$= 9.6 - 67.2i$

23. Match each product on the right with the corresponding expression on the left.

A. $(3 - 5i)(3 + 5i)$ ____B____ $-16 + 30i$

B. $(3 + 5i)(3 + 5i)$ ____D____ -34

C. $(-3 - 5i)(3 + 5i)$ ____A____ 34

D. $(3 - 5i)(-3 - 5i)$ ____C____ $16 - 30i$

A. $(3 - 5i)(3 + 5i) = 9 + 15i - 15i - 25i^2$
$= 9 + 15i - 15i - 25(-1)$
$= 34$

B. $(3 + 5i)(3 + 5i) = 9 + 15i + 15i + 25i^2$
$= 9 + 15i + 15i + 25(-1)$
$= -16 + 30i$

C. $(-3 - 5i)(3 + 5i) = -9 - 15i - 15i - 25i^2$
$= -9 - 15i - 15i - 25(-1)$
$= 16 - 30i$

D. $(3 - 5i)(-3 - 5i) = -9 - 15i + 15i + 25i^2$
$= -9 - 15i + 15i + 25(-1)$
$= -34$

H.O.T. Focus on Higher Order Thinking

24. Explain the Error While attempting to multiply the expression $(2 - 3i)(3 + 2i)$ a student made a mistake. Explain and correct the error.

$(2 - 3i)(3 + 2i) = 6 - 9i + 4i - 6i^2$
$= 6 - 9(-1) + 4(-1) - 6(1)$
$= 6 + 9 - 4 - 6$
$= 5$

The student incorrectly defined i as being equal to -1 instead of $\sqrt{-1}$. The student should have written the product as $6 - 9i + 4i - 6(-1) = 12 - 5i$.

INTEGRATE MATHEMATICAL PRACTICES

Focus on Math Connections

MP.1 Have students look for a pattern in powers of the imaginary unit i, going beyond i^2, the highest power used in the lesson. Students will need to deduce that all the higher powers can be simplified by repeatedly dividing out i^2.

PEER-TO-PEER DISCUSSION

Ask students to work with a partner to find examples of each of the following terms: a *complex number*, a *real number*, and an *imaginary number*. **complex: $a + bi$; real: a; imaginary: bi**

JOURNAL

Have students to write about how complex numbers can be applied to the real world. How might complex numbers help describe how electric circuits operate?

25. Critical Thinking Show that $\sqrt{3} + i\sqrt{3}$ and $-\sqrt{3} - i\sqrt{3}$ are the square roots of $6i$.

Show that the square of each number is $6i$.

$$\begin{aligned}(\sqrt{3} + i\sqrt{3})(\sqrt{3} + i\sqrt{3}) &= 3 + 3i + 3i + 3i^2 \\ &= 3 + 3i + 3i + 3(-1) \\ &= 6i\end{aligned}$$

$$\begin{aligned}(-\sqrt{3} - i\sqrt{3})(-\sqrt{3} - i\sqrt{3}) &= 3 + 3i + 3i + 3i^2 \\ &= 3 + 3i + 3i + 3(-1) \\ &= 6i\end{aligned}$$

26. Justify Reasoning What type of number is the product of two complex numbers that differ only in the sign of their imaginary parts? Prove your conjecture.

The product of two complex numbers that differ only in the sign of their imaginary parts is a real number. Proof: Let the complex numbers be $a + bi$ and $a - bi$ where a and b are real and $b \neq 0$. Multiplying the numbers gives the following result:

$$\begin{aligned}(a + bi)(a - bi) &= a^2 + abi - abi - b^2i^2 \\ &= a^2 - b^2(-1) \\ &= a^2 + b^2\end{aligned}$$

Since the set of real numbers is closed under all operations, $a^2 + b^2$ is a real number.

Lesson Performance Task

Just as real numbers can be graphed on a real number line, complex numbers can be graphed on a complex *plane*, which has a horizontal real axis and a vertical imaginary axis. When a Julia set that involves complex numbers is graphed on a complex plane, the result can be an elaborate self-similar figure called a *fractal*.

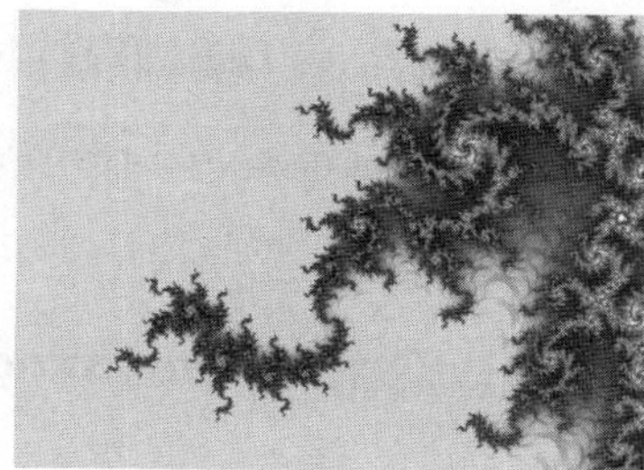

Consider Julia sets having the quadratic recursive rule $f(n+1) = (f(n))^2 + c$ for some complex number $f(0)$ and some complex constant c. For a given value of c, a complex number $f(0)$ either belongs or doesn't belong to the "filled-in" Julia set corresponding to c depending on what happens with the sequence of numbers generated by the recursive rule.

a. Letting $c = i$, generate the first few numbers in the sequence defined by $f(0) = 1$ and $f(n+1) = (f(n))^2 + i$. Record your results in the table.

n	$f(n)$	$f(n+1) = (f(n))^2 + i$
0	$f(0) = 1$	$f(1) = (f(0))^2 + i = (1)^2 + i = 1 + i$
1	$f(1) = 1 + i$	$f(2) = (f(1))^2 + i = (1+i)^2 + i =$ $3i$
2	$f(2) =$ $3i$	$f(3) = (f(2))^2 + i = (3i)^2 + i =$ $-9 + i$
3	$f(3) =$ $-9 + i$	$f(4) = (f(3))^2 + i = (-9 + i)^2 + i =$ $80i - 17i$

b. The *magnitude* of a complex number $a + bi$ is the real number $\sqrt{a^2 + b^2}$. In the complex plane, the magnitude of a complex number is the number's distance from the origin. If the magnitudes of the numbers in the sequence generated by a Julia set's recursive rule where $f(0)$ is the starting value remain bounded, then $f(0)$ belongs to the "filled-in" Julia set. If the magnitudes increase without bound, then $f(0)$ doesn't belong to the "filled-in" Julia set. Based on your completed table for $f(0) = 1$, would you say that the number belongs to the "filled-in" Julia set corresponding to $c = i$? Explain.

c. Would you say that $f(0) = i$ belongs to the "filled-in" Julia set corresponding to $c = i$? Explain.

b. The magnitude of $f(0) = 1$ is $\sqrt{1^2 + 0^2} = \sqrt{1} = 1$. The magnitude of $f(1) = 1 + i$ is $\sqrt{1^2 + 1^2} = \sqrt{2}$. The magnitude of $f(2) = 3i$ is $\sqrt{0^2 + 3^2} = \sqrt{9} = 3$. The magnitude of $f(3) = -9 + i$ is $\sqrt{(-9^2) + 1^2} = \sqrt{82}$. The magnitude of $f(4) = 80 - 17i$ is $\sqrt{80^2 + (-17)^2} = \sqrt{6689}$. The magnitudes appear to be increasing without bound, so $f(0) = 1$ does not belong to the "filled-in" Julia set.

c. For $f(0) = i$, the sequence of numbers generated by the recursive rule is $f(0) = i$, $f(1) = -1 + i$, $f(2) = -i$, $f(3) = -1 + i$, $f(3) = -1 + i$, $f(4) = -i$ and so on. Since the magnitudes of the numbers never exceed $\sqrt{2}$, $f(0) = i$ belongs to the "filled-in" Julia set.

EXTENSION ACTIVITY

Students can use the Julia set to generate a visual pattern. Each set of ordered pairs (a, b) in the grid represents a complex number $a + bi$. Use these complex numbers to calculate up to three iterations for the Julia set, using $c = 0$. Then find the absolute value of the result, which is $\sqrt{a^2 + b^2}$.

If $|Z_1|>2$, stop, and color that square red.

If $|Z_2|>2$, stop, and color that square green.

If $|Z_3|>2$, stop, and color that square blue.

Have students experiment with larger grids and with $c \neq 0$.

INTEGRATE MATHEMATICAL PRACTICES

Focus on Patterns

MP.8 Students should be able to recognize when iterations for the Julia set result in a constant or two distinct values which switch back and forth. Students can try different values of Z_0 and c to explore this phenomenon, such as $Z_0 = i - 1$, and $c = i + 1$, which returns a constant value $Z_n = -i + 1$.

AVOID COMMON ERRORS

Students may have difficulty with the notation $f(n + 1) = (f(n))^2 + c$. Have students read this aloud as: "$f(n + 1)$ equals the quantity $f(n)$ squared plus c." Note that the nested parentheses indicate that the entire quantity $f(n)$ is squared.

Scoring Rubric

2 points: Student correctly solves the problem and explains his/her reasoning.

1 point: Student shows good understanding of the problem but does not fully solve or explain his/her reasoning.

0 points: Student does not demonstrate understanding of the problem.

LESSON 3.3

Finding Complex Solutions of Quadratic Equations

Common Core Math Standards

The student is expected to:

COMMON CORE **N-CN.C.7**

Solve quadratic equations with real coefficients that have complex solutions. Also N-CN.C.2, A-REI.B.4b

Mathematical Practices

MP.2 Reasoning

Language Objective

Work with a partner or small group to determine whether solutions to quadratic equations are real or not real and justify reasoning.

ENGAGE

Essential Question: How can you find the complex solutions of any quadratic equation?

Possible answer: You can factor, if possible, to find real solutions; approximate from a graph; find a square root (which may be part of completing the square); or complete the square/quadratic formula. For the general equation $ax^2 + bx + c = 0$, you must either complete the square or use the quadratic formula to find the complex solutions of the equation.

PREVIEW: LESSON PERFORMANCE TASK

View the Engage section online. Discuss the photo and how to solve a quadratic equation to determine how high a baseball will go after it is hit. Then preview the Lesson Performance Task.

Name ________ Class ________ Date ________

3.3 Finding Complex Solutions of Quadratic Equations

Essential Question: How can you find the complex solutions of any quadratic equation?

Resource Locker

Explore Investigating Real Solutions of Quadratic Equations

(A) Complete the table.

$ax^2 + bx + c = 0$	$ax^2 + bx = -c$	$f(x) = ax^2 + bx$	$g(x) = -c$
$2x^2 + 4x + 1 = 0$	$2x^2 + 4x = -1$	$f(x) = 2x^2 + 4x$	$g(x) = -1$
$2x^2 + 4x + 2 = 0$	$2x^2 + 4x = -2$	$f(x) = 2x^2 + 4x$	$g(x) = -2$
$2x^2 + 4x + 3 = 0$	$2x^2 + 4x = -3$	$f(x) = 2x^2 + 4x$	$g(x) = -3$

(B) The graph of $f(x) = 2x^2 + 4x$ is shown. Graph each $g(x)$. Complete the table.

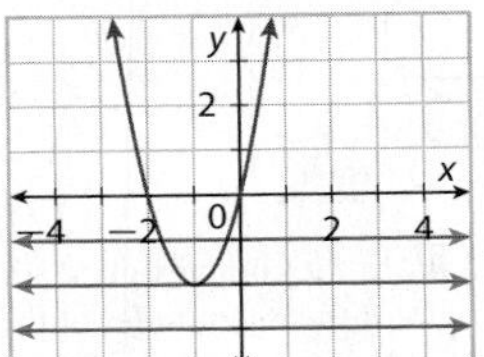

Equation	Number of Real Solutions
$2x^2 + 4x + 1 = 0$	2
$2x^2 + 4x + 2 = 0$	1
$2x^2 + 4x + 3 = 0$	0

(C) Repeat Steps A and B when $f(x) = -2x^2 + 4x$.

$ax^2 + bx + c = 0$	$ax^2 + bx = -c$	$f(x) = ax^2 + bx$	$g(x) = -c$
$-2x^2 + 4x - 1 = 0$	$-2x^2 + 4x = 1$	$f(x) = -2x^2 + 4x$	$g(x) = 1$
$-2x^2 + 4x - 2 = 0$	$-2x^2 + 4x = 2$	$f(x) = -2x^2 + 4x$	$g(x) = 2$
$-2x^2 + 4x - 3 = 0$	$-2x^2 + 4x = 3$	$f(x) = -2x^2 + 4x$	$g(x) = 3$

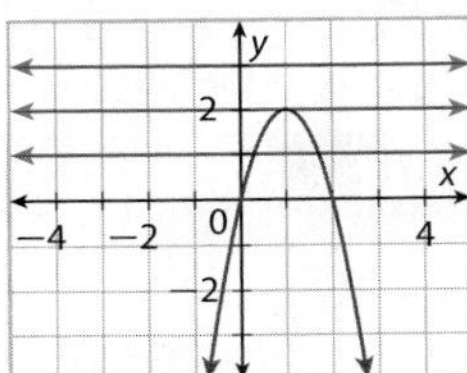

Equation	Number of Real Solutions
$-2x^2 + 4x - 1 = 0$	2
$-2x^2 + 4x - 2 = 0$	1
$-2x^2 + 4x - 3 = 0$	0

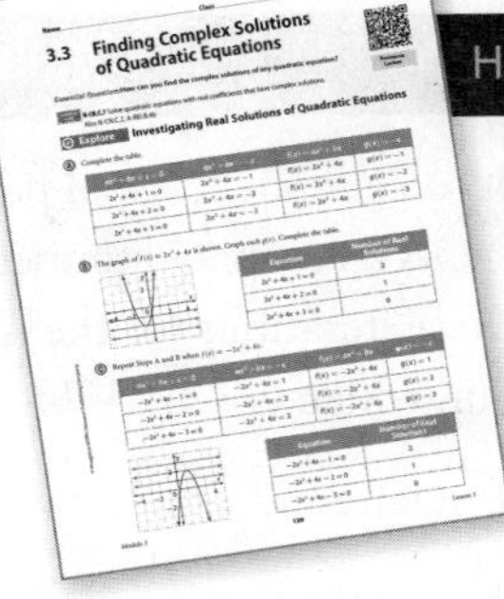

HARDCOVER PAGES 139–152

Watch for the hardcover student edition page numbers for this lesson.

Reflect

1. Look back at Steps A and B. Notice that the minimum value of $f(x)$ in Steps A and B is -2. Complete the table by identifying how many real solutions the equation $f(x) = g(x)$ has for the given values of $g(x)$.

Value of $g(x)$	Number of Real Solutions of $f(x) = g(x)$
$g(x) = -2$	1
$g(x) > -2$	2
$g(x) < -2$	0

2. Look back at Step C. Notice that the maximum value of $f(x)$ in Step C is 2. Complete the table by identifying how many real solutions the equation $f(x) = g(x)$ has for the given values of $g(x)$.

Value of $g(x)$	Number of Real Solutions of $f(x) = g(x)$
$g(x) = 2$	1
$g(x) > 2$	0
$g(x) < 2$	2

3. You can generalize Reflect 1: For $f(x) = ax^2 + bx$ where $a > 0$, $f(x) = g(x)$ where $g(x) = -c$ has real solutions when $g(x)$ is greater than or equal to the minimum value of $f(x)$. The minimum value of $f(x)$ is

$$f\left(-\frac{b}{2a}\right) = a\left(-\frac{b}{2a}\right)^2 + b\left(-\frac{b}{2a}\right) = a\left(\frac{b^2}{4a^2}\right) - \frac{b^2}{2a} = \frac{b^2}{4a} - \frac{b^2}{2a} = \frac{b^2}{4a} - \frac{2b^2}{4a} = -\frac{b^2}{4a}.$$

So, $f(x) = g(x)$ has real solutions when $g(x) \geq -\frac{b^2}{4a}$. Since $g(x) = -c$, you obtain:

Write the inequality. $g(x) \geq -\frac{b^2}{4a}$ Add $\frac{b^2}{4a}$ to both sides. $\frac{b^2}{4a} - c \geq 0$

Substitute $-c$ for $g(x)$. $-c \geq -\frac{b^2}{4a}$ Multiply both sides by $4a$, which is positive. $b^2 - 4ac \geq 0$

In other words, the equation $ax^2 + bx + c = 0$ where $a > 0$ has real solutions when $b^2 - 4ac \geq 0$.

Generalize the results of Reflect 2 in a similar way. What do you notice?

For $f(x) = ax^2 + bx$ where $a < 0$, $f(x) = g(x)$ where $g(x) = -c$ has real solutions when $g(x)$ is less than or equal to the maximum value of $f(x)$. The maximum value of $f(x)$ is $f\left(-\frac{b}{2a}\right) = -\frac{b^2}{4a}$.

So, $f(x) = g(x)$ has real solutions when $g(x) \leq -\frac{b^2}{4a}$. Since $g(x) = -c$, you obtain:

Write the inequality. $g(x) \leq -\frac{b^2}{4a}$ Add $\frac{b^2}{4a}$ to both sides. $\frac{b^2}{4a} - c \leq 0$

Substitute $-c$ for $g(x)$. $-c \leq -\frac{b^2}{4a}$ Multiply both sides by $4a$, which is negative. $b^2 - 4ac \geq 0$

Whether $a > 0$ or $a < 0$, $b^2 - 4ac \geq 0$ tells when $ax^2 + bx + c = 0$ has real solutions.

EXPLORE

Investigating Real Solutions of Quadratic Equations

INTEGRATE TECHNOLOGY

Students can use a graphing calculator to graph $f(x)$ and each function $g(x)$ to verify the number of real solutions to each equation.

QUESTIONING STRATEGIES

? If an equation is written in vertex form, what information can you use to find out if it has real solutions? **The sign of a determines the direction of the opening and the maximum or minimum value tells you whether there are real solutions.**

? How do you determine where the graph of a quadratic function crosses the x-axis? **You can find the x-intercepts of the graph of a quadratic function in standard form by factoring the function to get its intercept form. If the function is not factorable, the x-intercepts can be found by using the quadratic formula to find the zeros of the function.**

PROFESSIONAL DEVELOPMENT

Math Background

In Algebra 1, students used the quadratic formula to find real solutions to a quadratic equation. Students now revisit the formula to extend its use to complex solutions.

The sign of the expression $b^2 - 4ac$ determines whether the quadratic equation has two real solutions, one real solution, or two nonreal solutions. For cubic equations of the form $ax^3 + bx^2 + cx + d = 0$, the sign of the discriminant $b^2c^2 - 4ac^3 - 4b^3d - 27a^2d^2$ determines whether the equation has three real solutions, two real solutions, or one real solution.

EXPLAIN 1

Finding Complex Solutions by Completing the Square

QUESTIONING STRATEGIES

? How do you convert quadratic functions to vertex form? Explain. You can convert quadratic functions from standard form to vertex form $f(x) = a(x - h)^2 + k$ by completing the square on $ax^2 + bx$. You have to add and subtract the same constant to keep the function value the same.

INTEGRATE MATHEMATICAL PRACTICES

Focus on Technology

MP.5 Discuss with students how to use the graphing calculator to find a maximum or minimum value of a quadratic function. Students can solve problems algebraically and then use their graphing calculators to check their solutions.

Explain 1 Finding Complex Solutions by Completing the Square

Recall that completing the square for the expression $x^2 + bx$ requires adding $\left(\frac{b}{2}\right)^2$ to it, resulting in the perfect square trinomial $x^2 + bx + \left(\frac{b}{2}\right)^2$, which you can factor as $\left(x + \frac{b}{2}\right)^2$. Don't forget that when $x^2 + bx$ appears on one side of an equation, adding $\left(\frac{b}{2}\right)^2$ to it requires adding $\left(\frac{b}{2}\right)^2$ to the other side as well.

Example 1 **Solve the equation by completing the square. State whether the solutions are real or non-real.**

Ⓐ $3x^2 + 9x - 6 = 0$

1. Write the equation in the form $x^2 + bx = c$.

$$3x^2 + 9x - 6 = 0$$
$$3x^2 + 9x = 6$$
$$x^2 + 3x = 2$$

2. Identify b and $\left(\frac{b}{2}\right)^2$.

$$b = 3$$
$$\left(\frac{b}{2}\right)^2 = \left(\frac{3}{2}\right)^2 = \frac{9}{4}$$

3. Add $\left(\frac{b}{2}\right)^2$ to both sides of the equation.

$$x^2 + 3x + \frac{9}{4} = 2 + \frac{9}{4}$$

4. Solve for x.

$$\left(x + \frac{3}{2}\right)^2 = 2 + \frac{9}{4}$$
$$\left(x + \frac{3}{2}\right)^2 = \frac{17}{4}$$
$$x + \frac{3}{2} = \pm\sqrt{\frac{17}{4}}$$
$$x + \frac{3}{2} = \pm\frac{\sqrt{17}}{2}$$
$$x = -\frac{3}{2} \pm \frac{\sqrt{17}}{2}$$
$$x = \frac{-3 \pm \sqrt{17}}{2}$$

There are two real solutions: $\frac{-3 + \sqrt{17}}{2}$ and $\frac{-3 - \sqrt{17}}{2}$.

Ⓑ $x^2 - 2x + 7 = 0$

1. Write the equation in the form $x^2 + bx = c$.

$x^2 - 2x = -7$

2. Identify b and $\left(\frac{b}{2}\right)^2$.

$$b = \boxed{-2}$$
$$\left(\frac{b}{2}\right)^2 = \left(\frac{\boxed{-2}}{2}\right)^2 = \boxed{1}$$

3. Add $\left(\frac{b}{2}\right)^2$ to both sides.

$$x^2 - 2x + \boxed{1} = -7 + \boxed{1}$$

4. Solve for x.

$$x^2 + 2x\ \boxed{1} = -7 + \boxed{1}$$
$$\left(x - \boxed{1}\right)^2 = \boxed{-6}$$
$$x - \boxed{1} = \pm\sqrt{\boxed{-6}}$$
$$x = 1 \pm \sqrt{\boxed{-6}}$$

There are two real/non-real solutions: $1 + i\sqrt{6}$ and $1 - i\sqrt{6}$.

COLLABORATIVE LEARNING

Peer-to-Peer Activity

Have students work in pairs. Provide each pair with several quadratic equations written in various forms. Have one student verbally instruct the partner in how to find the nonreal solutions to the equation. Then have partners switch roles, repeating the activity for a different quadratic equation. Have students discuss how their steps for solving the equation were similar or different.

Reflect

4. How many complex solutions do the equations in Parts A and B have? Explain.
Each equation has two complex solutions, because the set of complex numbers includes all real numbers as well as all non-real numbers.

Your Turn

Solve the equation by completing the square. State whether the solutions are real or non-real.

5. $x^2 + 8x + 17 = 0$

$x^2 + 8x = -17$

$x^2 + 8x + 16 = -7 + 16$

$(x + 4)^2 = -1$

$x + 4 = \pm\sqrt{-1}$

$x = -4 \pm i$

There are two non-real solutions: $-4 + i$ and $-4 - i$.

6. $x^2 + 10x - 7 = 0$

$x^2 + 10x = 7$

$x^2 + 10x + 25 = 7 + 25$

$(x + 5)^2 = 32$

$x + 5 = \pm\sqrt{32}$

$x = -5 \pm 4\sqrt{2}$

There are two non-real solutions: $-5 + 4\sqrt{2}$ and $-5 - 4\sqrt{2}$.

Explain 2 Identifying Whether Solutions Are Real or Non-real

By completing the square for the general quadratic equation $ax^2 + bx + c = 0$, you can obtain the *quadratic formula*, $x = \frac{-b \pm \sqrt{b^2 - 4ac}}{2a}$, which gives the solutions of the general quadratic equation. In the quadratic formula, the expression under the radical sign, $b^2 - 4ac$, is called the *discriminant*, and its value determines whether the solutions of the quadratic equation are real or non-real.

Value of Discriminant	Number and Type of Solutions
$b^2 - 4ac > 0$	Two real solutions
$b^2 - 4ac = 0$	One real solution
$b^2 - 4ac < 0$	Two non-real solutions

Example 2 **Answer the question by writing an equation and determining whether the solutions of the equation are real or non-real.**

(A) A ball is thrown in the air with an initial vertical velocity of 14 m/s from an initial height of 2 m. The ball's height h (in meters) at time t (in seconds) can be modeled by the quadratic function $h(t) = -4.9t^2 + 14t + 2$. Does the ball reach a height of 12 m?

Set $h(t)$ equal to 12. $-4.9t^2 + 14t + 2 = 12$

Subtract 12 from both sides. $-4.9t^2 + 14t + 10 = 0$

Find the value of the discriminant. $14^2 - 4(-4.9)(-10) = 196 - 196 = 0$

Because the discriminant is zero, the equation as one real solution, so the ball does reach a height of 12 m.

EXPLAIN 2

Identifying Whether Solutions are Real or Non-real

QUESTIONING STRATEGIES

Does the discriminant give the solution of a quadratic equation? Explain. No, it gives the number and type of solution, but it does not give the actual solution.

AVOID COMMON ERRORS

Remind students that they must write the quadratic equation in standard form before applying the quadratic formula.

CONNECT VOCABULARY EL

Review vocabulary related to quadratic functions, such as *discriminant* and *real numbers,* by having students label the parts of a quadratic function written in various forms.

DIFFERENTIATE INSTRUCTION

Cognitive Strategies

Some students have trouble completing the square because there are so many steps. Show them how to break the process into three parts:

(1) Get the equation into the form needed for completing the square.

(2) Complete the square.

(3) Finish the solution by taking square roots of both sides and simplifying the results.

When students make errors, analyze their work carefully to see what part of the process is giving them trouble, and give them extra practice on that part of the process.

INTEGRATE MATHEMATICAL PRACTICES

Focus on Reasoning

MP.2 The discriminant can be used to distinguish between rational and irrational solutions. Give students several quadratic equations for which $b^2 - 4ac$ is positive, some with rational solutions, and some with irrational solutions. Ask them to make a conjecture about how the value of the discriminant is related to whether the solutions are rational or irrational. Students should be able to explain why the solutions will be rational when the value of the discriminant is a perfect square.

EXPLAIN 3

Finding Complex Solutions Using the Quadratic Formula

QUESTIONING STRATEGIES

? Why are there always two solutions to a quadratic equation that has nonreal solutions? How are they related? **Since $\sqrt{b^2 - 4ac}$ is not zero, its value will be both added to and subtracted from $-b$ in the numerator, resulting in two solutions; they are complex conjugates.**

? What is the general solution of a quadratic equation with only one solution? $x = -\dfrac{b}{2a}$

(B) A person wants to create a vegetable garden and keep the rabbits out by enclosing it with 100 feet of fencing. The area of the garden is given by the function $A(w) = w(50 - w)$ where w is the width (in feet) of the garden. Can the garden have an area of 700 ft²?

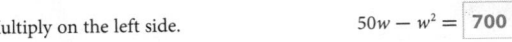

Set $A(w)$ equal to 700. $\qquad w(50 - w) = \boxed{700}$

Multiply on the left side. $\qquad 50w - w^2 = \boxed{700}$

Subtract 700 from both sides. $\qquad -w^2 + 50w - \boxed{700} = 0$

Find the value of the discriminant. $\qquad 50^2 - 4(-1)(-700) = 2500 - 2800 = -300$

Because the discriminant is [positive/zero/**negative**], the equation has [two real/one real/**two non-real**] solutions, so the garden [can/**cannot**] have an area of 700 ft².

Your Turn

Answer the question by writing an equation and determining if the solutions are real or non-real.

7. A hobbyist is making a toy sailboat. For the triangular sail, she wants the height h (in inches) to be twice the length of the base b (in inches). Can the area of the sail be 10 in²?

Write the area A of the sail as a function of b. $\qquad A = \frac{1}{2}b(2b) = b^2$

Substitute 10 for A. $\qquad 10 = b^2$

Subtract 10 from both sides. $\qquad 0 = b^2 - 10$

Find the discriminant. $\qquad 0^2 - 4(1)(-10) = 0 + 40 = 40$

Because the discriminant is positive, the equation has two real solutions, so the area of the sail can be 10 in².

Explain 3 Finding Complex Solutions Using the Quadratic Formula

When using the quadratic formula to solve a quadratic equation, be sure the equation is in the form $ax^2 + bx + c = 0$.

Example 3 **Solve the equation using the quadratic formula. Check a solution by substitution.**

(A) $-5x^2 - 2x - 8 = 0$

Write the quadratic formula. $\qquad x = \dfrac{-b \pm \sqrt{b^2 - 4ac}}{2a}$

Substitute values. $\qquad = \dfrac{-(-2) \pm \sqrt{-2^2 - 4(-5)(-8)}}{2(-5)}$

Simplify. $\qquad = \dfrac{2 \pm \sqrt{-156}}{-10} = \dfrac{1 \pm i\sqrt{39}}{-5}$

LANGUAGE SUPPORT EL

Communicate Math

Students play "How do you know?" Give students several cards containing quadratic equations; some have real number solutions, others nonreal or complex solutions. In small groups, students draw a card and state whether the solution is real or not real. They then answer the question "How do you know?" Players take turns and sort cards into piles according to the kind of solution. By the end of the game, all players in a group must agree on card placement.

So, the two solutions are $-\frac{1}{5} - \frac{i\sqrt{39}}{5}$ and $-\frac{1}{5} + \frac{i\sqrt{39}}{5}$.

Check by substituting one of the values.

Substitute. $-5\left(-\frac{1}{5} - \frac{i\sqrt{39}}{5}\right)^2 - 2\left(-\frac{1}{5} - \frac{i\sqrt{39}}{5}\right) - 8 \stackrel{?}{=} 0$

Square. $-5\left(\frac{1}{25} + \frac{2i\sqrt{39}}{25} - \frac{39}{25}\right) - 2\left(-\frac{1}{5} - \frac{i\sqrt{39}}{5}\right) - 8 \stackrel{?}{=} 0$

Distribute. $-\frac{1}{5} - \frac{2i\sqrt{39}}{5} + \frac{39}{5} + \frac{2}{5} + \frac{2i\sqrt{39}}{5} - 8 \stackrel{?}{=} 0$

Simplify. $\frac{40}{5} - 8 \stackrel{?}{=} 0$

$0 = 0$

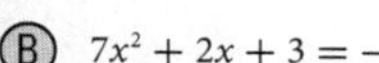 $7x^2 + 2x + 3 = -1$

Write the equation with 0 on one side. $7x^2 + 2x + \boxed{4} = 0$

Write the quadratic formula. $x = \frac{-b \pm \sqrt{b^2 - 4ac}}{2a}$

Substitute values. $= \frac{-\boxed{2} \pm \sqrt{\left(\boxed{2}\right)^2 - 4\left(\boxed{7}\right)\left(\boxed{4}\right)}}{2\left(\boxed{7}\right)}$

Simplify. $= \frac{-\boxed{2} \pm \sqrt{-\boxed{108}}}{14}$

$= \frac{-\boxed{2} \pm \boxed{6}\,i\sqrt{\boxed{3}}}{14} = \frac{-\boxed{1} \pm \boxed{3}\,i\sqrt{\boxed{3}}}{7}$

So, the two solutions are $-\frac{1}{7} + \frac{3i\sqrt{3}}{7}$ and $-\frac{1}{7} - \frac{3i\sqrt{3}}{7}$.

Check by substituting one of the values.

Substitute. $7\left(-\frac{1}{7} + \frac{3i\sqrt{3}}{7}\right)^2 + 2\left(-\frac{1}{7} + \frac{3i\sqrt{3}}{7}\right)^2 + 4 \stackrel{?}{=} 0$

Square. $7\left(\frac{1}{49} - \frac{6i\sqrt{3}}{49} - \frac{27}{49}\right)^2 + 2\left(-\frac{1}{7} + \frac{3i\sqrt{3}}{7}\right)^2 + 4 \stackrel{?}{=} 0$

Distribute. $\frac{1}{7} - \frac{6i\sqrt{3}}{7} - \frac{27}{7} - \frac{2}{7} + \frac{6i\sqrt{3}}{7} + 4 \stackrel{?}{=} 0$

$-\frac{28}{7} + 4 \stackrel{?}{=} 0$

Simplify. $0 = 0$

AVOID COMMON ERRORS

Students may have difficulty remembering the quadratic formula. Encourage students to copy the formula and have it on hand when they are working. Caution them to write the equation in standard form before identifying the values of *a*, *b*, and *c* to be used in the formula.

INTEGRATE MATHEMATICAL PRACTICES

Focus on Communication

MP.3 You may wish to point out that quadratic equations always have two roots. However, when the value of the discriminant is 0, the two roots happen to be the same. In this case, the quadratic is said to have a *double root.*

ELABORATE

INTEGRATE MATHEMATICAL PRACTICES

Focus on Critical Thinking

MP.3 Emphasize that choosing which method to use to solve a quadratic equation is as important as being able to use each method. Have students discuss when each method might be preferred.

AVOID COMMON ERRORS

Students may sometimes make a mistake in sign when calculating the discriminant, particularly when the quantity $4ac$ is less than 0. Remind them that subtracting a negative number is the same as adding the opposite, or positive, number. If a and c are opposite signs, the discriminant will always be positive.

SUMMARIZE THE LESSON

When does a quadratic equation have nonreal solutions, and how do you find them? When the value of the discriminant is negative, the quadratic equation will have two nonreal solutions. You find the solutions by using the quadratic formula to solve the equation, and then writing the solutions as a pair of complex conjugates of the form $a \pm bi$.

Your Turn

Solve the equation using the quadratic formula. Check a solution by substitution.

8. $6x^2 - 5x - 4 = 0$

$$x = \frac{-b \pm \sqrt{b^2 - 4ac}}{2a}$$
$$= \frac{-(-5) \pm \sqrt{(-5)^2 - 4(6)(-4)}}{2(6)}$$
$$= \frac{5 \pm \sqrt{121}}{12}$$
$$= \frac{5 \pm 11}{12}$$

So, the solutions are $\frac{5+11}{12} = \frac{4}{3}$ and $\frac{5-11}{12} = -\frac{1}{2}$.

Check

$$6\left(\frac{4}{3}\right)^2 - 5\left(\frac{4}{3}\right) - 4 \stackrel{?}{=} 0$$
$$\frac{32}{3} - \frac{20}{3} - 4 \stackrel{?}{=} 0$$
$$0 = 0$$

9. $x^2 + 8x + 12 = 2x$

$$x^2 + 6x + 12 = 0$$
$$x = \frac{-b \pm \sqrt{b^2 - 4ac}}{2a}$$
$$= \frac{-(-6) \pm \sqrt{(6)^2 - 4(1)(12)}}{2(1)}$$
$$= \frac{-6 \pm \sqrt{-12}}{2}$$
$$= \frac{-6 \pm 2i\sqrt{3}}{2}$$
$$= -3 \pm i\sqrt{3}$$

So, the solutions are $= -3 + i\sqrt{3}$ and $= -3 - i\sqrt{3}$.

Check

$$\left(-3 + i\sqrt{3}\right)^2 + 6\left(-3 + i\sqrt{3}\right) + 12 \stackrel{?}{=} 0$$
$$6 - 6i\sqrt{3} - 18 - 6i\sqrt{3} + 12 \stackrel{?}{=} 0$$
$$0 = 0$$

Elaborate

10. Discussion Suppose that the quadratic equation $ax^2 + bx + c = 0$ has $p + qi$ where $q \neq 0$ as one of its solutions. What must the other solution be? How do you know?

The other solution must be $p - qi$. The radical $\sqrt{b^2 - 4ac}$ in the quadratic formula produces imaginary numbers when $b^2 - 4ac < 0$. Since $\sqrt{b^2 - 4ac}$ is both added to and subtracted from $-b$ in the numerator of the quadratic formula, one solution will have the form $p + qi$, and the other will have the form $p - qi$.

11. Discussion You know that the graph of the quadratic function $f(x) = ax^2 + bx + c$ has the vertical line $x = -\frac{b}{2a}$ as its axis of symmetry. If the graph of $f(x)$ crosses the x-axis, where do the x-intercepts occur relative to the axis of symmetry? Explain.

The x-intercepts are the solutions of $f(x) = 0$, which are $x = \frac{-b \pm \sqrt{b^2 - 4ac}}{2a}$ by the quadratic formula. Writing the x-intercepts as $x = -\frac{b}{2a} \pm \frac{\sqrt{b^2 - 4ac}}{2a}$ shows that the x-intercepts are the same distance, $\frac{\sqrt{b^2 - 4ac}}{2a}$, away from the axis of symmetry, with one x-intercept on each side of the line: $x = -\frac{b}{2a} - \frac{\sqrt{b^2 - 4ac}}{2a}$ on the left and $x = -\frac{b}{2a} + \frac{\sqrt{b^2 - 4ac}}{2a}$ on the right.

12. Essential Question Check-In Why is using the quadratic formula to solve a quadratic equation easier than completing the square?

The quadratic formula is the result of completing the square on the general quadratic equation $ax^2 + bx + c = 0$. As long as any particular equation is in the form $ax^2 + bx + c = 0$, you can simply substitute the values of a, b, and c into the quadratic formula and obtain the solutions of the equation.

Evaluate: Homework and Practice

- Online Homework
- Hints and Help
- Extra Practice

1. The graph of $f(x) = x^2 + 6x$ is shown. Use the graph to determine how many real solutions the following equations have: $x^2 + 6x + 6 = 0$, $x^2 + 6x + 9 = 0$, and $x^2 + 6x + 12 = 0$. Explain.

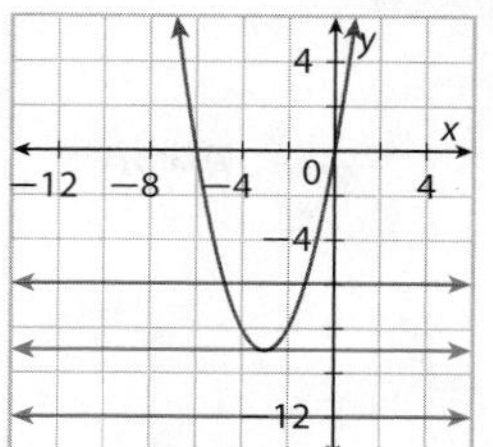

For each equation, subtract the constant from both sides to obtain these equations: $x^2 + 6x = -6$, $x^2 + 6x = -9$, and $x^2 + 6x = -12$. The graph of $g(x) = -6$ intersects the graph of $f(x)$ twice, so the equation $x^2 + 6x + 6 = 0$ has two real solutions. The graph of $g(x) = -9$ intersects the graph of $f(x)$ once, so the equation $x^2 + 6x + 9 = 0$ has one real solution. The graph of $g(x) = -12$ doesn't intersect the graph of $f(x)$, so the equation $x^2 + 6x + 12 = 0$ has no real solutions.

2. The graph of $f(x) = -\frac{1}{2}x^2 + 3x$ is shown. Use the graph to determine how many real solutions the following equations have: $-\frac{1}{2}x^2 + 3x - 3 = 0$, $-\frac{1}{2}x^2 + 3x - \frac{9}{2} = 0$, and $-\frac{1}{2}x^2 + 3x - 6 = 0$. Explain.

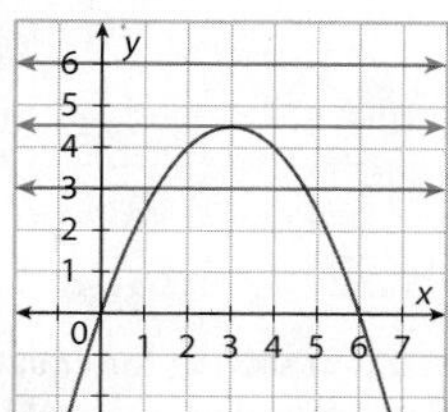

For each equation, subtract the constant from both sides to obtain these equations: $-\frac{1}{2}x^2 + 3x = 3$, $-\frac{1}{2}x^2 + 3x = \frac{9}{2}$, and $-\frac{1}{2}x^2 + 3x = 6$. The graph of $g(x) = 3$ intersects the graph of $f(x)$ twice, so the equation $-\frac{1}{2}x^2 + 3x - 3 = 0$ has two real solutions. The graph of $g(x) = \frac{9}{2}$ intersects the graph of $f(x)$ once, so the equation $-\frac{1}{2}x^2 + 3x - \frac{9}{2} = 0$ has one real solution. The graph of $g(x) = 6$ doesn't intersect the graph of $f(x)$, so the equation $-\frac{1}{2}x^2 + 3x - 6 = 0$ has no real solutions.

Solve the equation by completing the square. State whether the solutions are real or non-real.

3. $x^2 + 4x + 1 = 0$

$$x^2 + 4x = -1$$
$$x^2 + 4x + 4 = -1 + 4$$
$$(x + 2)^2 = 3$$
$$x + 2 = \pm\sqrt{3}$$
$$x = -2 \pm \sqrt{3}$$

two real solutions: $-2 + \sqrt{3}$ and $-2 - \sqrt{3}$.

4. $x^2 + 2x + 8 = 0$

$$x^2 + 2x = -8$$
$$x^2 + 2x + 1 = -8 + 1$$
$$(x + 1)^2 = -7$$
$$x + 1 = \pm\sqrt{-7}$$
$$x + 1 = \pm i\sqrt{7}$$
$$x = -1 \pm i\sqrt{7}$$

two non-real solutions: $-1 + i\sqrt{7}$ and $-1 - i\sqrt{7}$.

Exercise	Depth of Knowledge (D.O.K.)	COMMON CORE Mathematical Practices
1–8	1 Recall of Information	MP.2 Reasoning
9–16	1 Recall of Information	MP.3 Logic
17–20	2 Skills/Concepts	MP.2 Reasoning
21	1 Recall of Information	MP.3 Logic
22	3 Strategic Thinking H.O.T.	MP.3 Logic
23–24	3 Strategic Thinking H.O.T.	MP.4 Modeling

EVALUATE

ASSIGNMENT GUIDE

Concepts and Skills	Practice
Explore Investigating Real Solutions of Quadratic Equations	Exercises 1–2
Example 1 Finding Complex Solutions by Completing the Square	Exercises 3–8
Example 2 Identifying Whether Solutions are Real or Non-real	Exercises 9–16
Example 3 Finding Complex Solutions Using the Quadratic Formula	Exercises 17–20

CONNECT VOCABULARY EL

What information does the value of the discriminant give about a quadratic equation? **The value of the discriminant indicates the number and types of roots.**

VISUAL CUES

If students have difficulty evaluating the discriminant, have them organize the variables in a table. Ask students to create a table for each of the variables $(a, b, c, b^2, 4ac, b^2 - 4ac)$ and have them predict the number and type of solutions based on the variables they list in the table.

5. $x^2 - 5x = -20$

$$x^2 - 5x + \frac{25}{4} = -20 + \frac{25}{4}$$
$$\left(x - \frac{5}{2}\right)^2 = -\frac{55}{4}$$
$$x - \frac{5}{2} = \pm\sqrt{-\frac{55}{4}}$$
$$x - \frac{5}{2} = \pm\frac{i\sqrt{55}}{2}$$
$$x = \frac{5}{2} \pm \frac{i\sqrt{55}}{2}$$

two non-real solutions:
$\frac{5}{2} + \frac{i\sqrt{55}}{2}$ **and** $\frac{5}{2} - \frac{i\sqrt{55}}{2}$.

6. $5x^2 - 6x = 8$

$$x^2 - 1.2x = 1.6$$
$$x^2 - 1.2x + 0.36 = 1.6 + 0.36$$
$$(x - 0.6)^2 = 1.96$$
$$x - 0.6 = \pm\sqrt{1.96}$$
$$x - 0.6 = \pm 1.4$$
$$x = 0.6 \pm 1.4$$

two real solutions:
2 and −0.8.

7. $7x^2 + 13x = 5$

$$x^2 + \frac{13}{7}x = \frac{5}{7}$$
$$x^2 + \frac{13}{7}x + \frac{169}{196} = \frac{5}{7} + \frac{169}{196}$$
$$\left(x + \frac{13}{14}\right)^2 = \frac{309}{196}$$
$$x + \frac{13}{14} = \pm\sqrt{\frac{309}{196}}$$
$$x + \frac{13}{14} = \pm\frac{\sqrt{309}}{14}$$
$$x = -\frac{13}{14} \pm \frac{\sqrt{309}}{14}$$

two real solutions:
$\frac{-13 + \sqrt{309}}{14}$ **and** $\frac{-13 - \sqrt{309}}{14}$.

8. $-x^2 - 6x - 11 = 0$

$$x^2 + 6x + 11 = 0$$
$$x^2 + 6x + 9 = -11 + 9$$
$$(x + 3)^2 = -2$$
$$x + 3 = \pm\sqrt{-2}$$
$$x + 3 = \pm i\sqrt{2}$$
$$x = -3 \pm i\sqrt{2}$$

two non-real solutions:
$-3 + i\sqrt{2}$ **and** $-3 - i\sqrt{2}$.

Without solving the equation, state the number of solutions and whether they are real or non-real.

9. $-16x^2 + 4x + 13 = 0$

Find the discriminant.

$4^2 - 4(-16)(13) = 16 + 832 = 848$

Because the discriminant is positive, the equation has two real solutions.

10. $7x^2 - 11x + 10 = 0$

Find the discriminant.

$(-11)^2 - 4(7)(10) = 121 - 280 = -159$

Because the discriminant is negative, the equation has two non-real solutions.

11. $-x^2 - \frac{2}{5}x = 1$

$$-x^2 - \frac{2}{5}x - 1 = 0$$

Find the discriminant.

$\left(-\frac{2}{5}\right)^2 - 4(-1)(-1) = \frac{4}{25} - 4 = -\frac{96}{25}$

Because the discriminant is negative, the equation has two non-real solutions.

12. $4x^2 + 9 = 12x$

$$4x^2 - 12x + 9 = 0$$

Find the discriminant.

$(-12)^2 - 4(4)(9) = 144 - 144 = 0$

Because the discriminant is zero, the equation has one real solution.

Answer the question by writing an equation and determining whether the solutions of the equation are real or non-real.

13. A gardener has 140 feet of fencing to put around a rectangular vegetable garden. The function $A(w) = 70w - w^2$ gives the garden's area A (in square feet) for any width w (in feet). Does the gardener have enough fencing for the area of the garden to be 1300 ft^2?

Write an equation by setting $A(w)$ equal to 1300. Then rewrite the equation with 0 on one side. $70w - w^2 = 1300$

$$-w^2 + 70w - 1300 = 0$$

Find the discriminant. $70^2 - 4(-1)(-1300) = 4900 - 5200 = -300$

Because the discriminant is negative, the equation has two non-real solutions, so the gardener does not have enough fencing.

14. A golf ball is hit with an initial vertical velocity of 64 ft/s. The function $h(t) = -16t^2 + 64t$ models the height h (in feet) of the golf ball at time t (in seconds). Does the golf ball reach a height of 60 ft?

Write an equation by setting $h(t)$ equal to 60. Then rewrite the equation with 0 on one side. $-16t^2 + 64t = 60$

$$-16t^2 + 64t - 60 = 0$$

$$4t^2 - 16t + 15 = 0$$

Find the discriminant. $(-16)^2 - 4(4)(15) = 256 - 240 = 16$

Because the discriminant is positive, the equation has two real solutions, so the golf ball does reach a height of 60 ft.

15. As a decoration for a school dance, the student council creates a parabolic arch with balloons attached to it for students to walk through as they enter the dance. The arch is given by equation $y = x(5 - x)$, where x and y are measured in feet and where the origin is at one end of the arch. Can a student who is 6 feet 6 inches tall walk through the arch without ducking?

Write an equation by setting y equal to 6.5. Then rewrite the equation with 0 on one side. $x(5 - x) = 6.5$

$$5x - x^2 = 6.5$$

$$-x^2 + 5x - 6.5 = 0$$

Find the discriminant. $5^2 - 4(-1)(-6.5) = 25 - 26 = -1$

Because the discriminant is negative, the equation has two non-real solutions, so a student who is 6 feet 6 inches tall cannot walk through the arch without ducking.

PEER-TO-PEER DISCUSSION

Ask students to discuss with a partner how the graphs of the following three parabolas would look: a parabola with two real solutions, a parabola with one real solution, and a parabola with two nonreal solutions. Students should say that a parabola with two solutions will have two x-intercepts, and the parabola will open from the vertex toward the x-axis; that a parabola with one solution will have one x-intercept with the vertex on the x-axis; and that a parabola with two nonreal solutions will open from the vertex away from the axis and have no x-intercept.

16. A small theater company currently has 200 subscribers who each pay $120 for a season ticket. The revenue from season-ticket subscriptions is $24,000. Market research indicates that for each $10 increase in the cost of a season ticket, the theater company will lose 10 subscribers. A model for the projected revenue R (in dollars) from season-ticket subscriptions is $R(p) = (120 + 10p)(200 - 10p)$, where p is the number of $10 price increases. According to this model, is it possible for the theater company to generate $25,600 in revenue by increasing the price of a season ticket?

Write an equation by setting $R(p)$ equal to 25,600. Then rewrite the equation with 0 on one side. $(120 + 10p)(200 - 10p) = 25{,}600$

$$-100p^2 + 800p + 24{,}000 = 25{,}600$$
$$-100p^2 + 800p - 1600 = 0$$
$$p^2 - 8p + 16 = 0$$

Find the discriminant. $(-8)^2 - 4(1)(16) = 64 - 64 = 0$

Because the discriminant is zero, the equation has one real solution, so it is possible to generate $25,600 in revenue by increasing the price of a season ticket.

Solve the equation using the quadratic formula. Check a solution by substitution.

17. $x^2 - 8x + 27 = 0$

$$x = \frac{-b \pm \sqrt{b^2 - 4ac}}{2a}$$
$$= \frac{-(-8) \pm \sqrt{(-8)^2 - 4(1)(27)}}{2(1)}$$
$$= \frac{8 \pm \sqrt{-44}}{2}$$
$$= \frac{8 \pm 2i\sqrt{11}}{2}$$
$$= 4 \pm i\sqrt{11}$$

So, the solutions are

$4 + i\sqrt{11}$ and $4 - i\sqrt{11}$.

Check

$$(4 + i\sqrt{11})^2 - 8(4 + i\sqrt{11}) + 27 \stackrel{?}{=} 0$$
$$5 + 8i\sqrt{11} - 84 + i\sqrt{11} + 27 \stackrel{?}{=} 0$$
$$5 + 8i\sqrt{11} - 32 - 8i\sqrt{11} + 27 \stackrel{?}{=} 0$$
$$5 - 32 + 27 \stackrel{?}{=} 0$$
$$0 = 0$$

18. $x^2 - 30x + 50 = 0$

$$x = \frac{-b \pm \sqrt{b^2 - 4ac}}{2a}$$
$$= \frac{-(-30) \pm \sqrt{(-30)^2 - 4(1)(50)}}{2(1)}$$
$$= \frac{30 \pm \sqrt{700}}{2}$$
$$= \frac{30 \pm 10\sqrt{7}}{2}$$
$$= 15 \pm 5\sqrt{7}$$

So, the solutions are

$15 + 5\sqrt{7}$ and $15 - 5\sqrt{7}$.

Check

$$(15 + 5\sqrt{7})^2 - 30(15 + 5\sqrt{7}) + 50 \stackrel{?}{=} 0$$
$$400 + 150\sqrt{7} - 30(15 + 5\sqrt{7}) + 50 \stackrel{?}{=} 0$$
$$400 + 150\sqrt{7} - 450 - 150\sqrt{7} + 50 \stackrel{?}{=} 0$$
$$400 - 150 + 50 \stackrel{?}{=} 0$$
$$0 = 0$$

19. $x + 3 = x^2$

Rewrite the equation with 0 on one side.

$x^2 - x - 3 = 0$ **Use the quadratic formula.**

$$x = \frac{-b \pm \sqrt{b^2 - 4ac}}{2a}$$
$$= \frac{-(-1) \pm \sqrt{(-1)^2 - 4(1)(-3)}}{2(1)}$$
$$= \frac{1 \pm \sqrt{13}}{2}$$

So, the two solutions are $\frac{1+\sqrt{13}}{2}$ **and** $\frac{1-\sqrt{13}}{2}$.

Check

$$\left(\frac{1+\sqrt{13}}{2}\right)^2 - \left(\frac{1+\sqrt{13}}{2}\right) - 3 \stackrel{?}{=} 0$$
$$\frac{14+2\sqrt{13}}{4} - \left(\frac{1+\sqrt{13}}{2}\right) - 3 \stackrel{?}{=} 0$$
$$\frac{14+2\sqrt{13}}{4} - \left(\frac{2+2\sqrt{13}}{4}\right) - 3 \stackrel{?}{=} 0$$
$$\frac{12}{4} - 3 \stackrel{?}{=} 0$$
$$0 = 0$$

20. $2x^2 + 7 = 4x$

$2x^2 - 4x + 7 = 0$

$$x = \frac{-b \pm \sqrt{b^2 - 4ac}}{2a}$$
$$= \frac{-(-4) \pm \sqrt{(-4)^2 - 4(2)(7)}}{2(2)}$$
$$= \frac{4 \pm \sqrt{-40}}{4}$$
$$= \frac{4 \pm 2i\sqrt{10}}{4} = \frac{2 \pm i\sqrt{10}}{2}$$

So, the two solutions are $1 + \frac{i\sqrt{10}}{2}$ **and** $1 - \frac{i\sqrt{10}}{2}$.

Check.

$$2\left(1+\frac{i\sqrt{10}}{2}\right)^2 - 4\left(1+\frac{i\sqrt{10}}{2}\right) + 7 \stackrel{?}{=} 0$$
$$2\left(-\frac{3}{2} + i\sqrt{10}\right) - 4\left(1+\frac{i\sqrt{10}}{2}\right) + 7 \stackrel{?}{=} 0$$
$$-3 + 2i\sqrt{10} - 4 - 2i\sqrt{10} + 7 \stackrel{?}{=} 0$$
$$-3 - 4 + 7 \stackrel{?}{=} 0$$
$$0 = 0$$

21. Place an X in the appropriate column of the table to classify each equation by the number and type of its solutions.

Equation	Two Real Solutions	One Real Solution	Two Non-Real Solutions
$x^2 - 3x + 1 = 0$	X		
$x^2 - 2x + 1 = 0$		X	
$x^2 - x + 1 = 0$			X
$x^2 + 1 = 0$			X
$x^2 + x + 1 = 0$			X
$x^2 + 2x + 1 = 0$		X	
$x^2 + 3x + 1 = 0$	X		

AVOID COMMON ERRORS

Students need to be careful to avoid making sign errors when completing the square. Point out that when the rule representing vertex form is simplified, the result should be the original rule written in standard form. Students can use this fact to perform a quick check of the reasonableness of their results, and in order to catch any sign errors they may have made.

JOURNAL

Have students summarize how to use the discriminant to help solve any quadratic equation. Have them include examples of quadratic equations with one or two real solutions and with two nonreal solutions.

H.O.T. Focus on Higher Order Thinking

22. **Explain the Error** A student used the method of completing the square to solve the equation $-x^2 + 2x - 3 = 0$. Describe and correct the error.

$$-x^2 + 2x - 3 = 0$$
$$-x^2 + 2x = 3$$
$$-x^2 + 2x + 1 = 3 + 1$$
$$(x + 1)^2 = 4$$
$$x + 1 = \pm\sqrt{4}$$
$$x + 1 = \pm 2$$
$$x = -1 \pm 2$$

So, the two solutions are $-1 + 2 = 1$ and $-1 - 2 = -3$.

The student did not divide both sides by -1 first to make the coefficient of the x^2-term be 1. The correct solution is as follows.

$$x^2 - 2x + 3 = 0$$
$$x^2 - 2x = -3$$
$$x^2 - 2x + 1 = -3 + 1$$
$$(x - 1)^2 = -2$$
$$x - 1 = \pm\sqrt{-2}$$
$$x - 1 = \pm i\sqrt{2}$$
$$x = 1 \pm i\sqrt{2}$$

So, the two solutions are $1 + i\sqrt{2}$ and $1 - i\sqrt{2}$.

23. **Make a Conjecture** Describe the values of c for which the equation $x^2 + 8x + c = 0$ has two real solutions, one real solution, and two non-real solutions.

Find the value of the discriminant.

$b^2 - 4ac = 8^2 - 4(1)c = 64 - 4c$

The equation has two real solutions when the discriminant is positive, so solving $64 - 4c > 0$ for c gives $c < 16$. The equation has one real solution when the discriminant is zero, so solving $64 - 4c = 0$ for c gives $c = 16$. The equation has two non-real solutions when the discriminant is negative, so solving $64 - 4c < 0$ for c gives $c > 16$.

24. **Analyze Relationships** When you rewrite $y = ax^2 + bx + c$ in vertex form by completing the square, you obtain these coordinates for the vertex: $\left(-\frac{b}{2a}, c - \frac{b^2}{4a}\right)$. Suppose the vertex of the graph of $y = ax^2 + bx + c$ is located on the x-axis. Explain how the coordinates of the vertex and the quadratic formula are in agreement in this situation.

When the vertex is on the x-axis, the y-coordinate of the vertex must be 0, so $c - \frac{b^2}{4a} = 0$, which can be rewritten as $b^2 - 4ac = 0$. When you set y equal to 0 in $y = ax^2 + bx + c$ and solve for x, you get one real solution, namely, $x = -\frac{b}{2a}$, which is the x-coordinate of the vertex.

Lesson Performance Task

Matt and his friends are enjoying an afternoon at a baseball game. A batter hits a towering home run, and Matt shouts, "Wow, that must have been 110 feet high!" The ball was 4 feet off the ground when the batter hit it, and the ball came off the bat traveling vertically at 80 feet per second.

a. Model the ball's height h (in feet) at time t (in seconds) using the projectile motion model $h(t) = -16t^2 + v_0t + h$ where v_0 is the projectile's initial vertical velocity (in feet per second) and h_0 is the projectile's initial height (in feet). Use the model to write an equation based on Matt's claim, and then determine whether Matt's claim is correct.

b. Did the ball reach of a height of 100 feet? Explain.

c. Let h_{max} be the ball's maximum height. By setting the projectile motion model equal to h_{max}, show how you can find h_{max} using the discriminant of the quadratic formula.

d. Find the time at which the ball reached its maximum height.

a. The ball's height h at time t is given by $h(t) = -16t^2 + 80t + 4$. Matt's claim is that $h(t)$ at some time t. Applying the discriminant of the quadratic formula to the equation $-16t^2 + 80t + 4 = 110$, or $-16t^2 + 80t - 106 = 0$, gives $b^2 - 4ac = 80^2 - 4(-16)(-106) = 6400 - 6784 = -384$. Since the discriminant is negative, there are no real values of t that solve the equation, so Matt's claim is incorrect.

b. For the ball to reach of height of 100 feet, $h(t)$ must equal 100. Applying the discriminant of the quadratic formula to the equation $-16t^2 + 80t + 4 = 100$, or $-16t^2 + 80t - 96 = 0$, gives $b^2 - 4ac = 80^2 - 4(-16)(-96) = 6400 - 6144 = 256$. Since the discriminant is positive, there are two real values of t that solve the equation, so the ball did reach a height of 100 feet at two different times (once before reaching its maximum height and once after).

c. Setting $h(t)$ equal to h_{max} gives $-16t^2 + 80t + 4 = h_{max} = 0$, or $-16t^2 + 80t + 4 - h_{max} = 0$. Since the maximum height occurs for a single real value of t, the discriminant of the quadratic equation must equal 0.

$$\begin{aligned} b^2 - 4ac &= 0 \\ 80^2 - 4(-16)(4 - h_{max}) &= 0 \\ 6400 + 644 - h_{max} &= 0 \\ 64(4 - h_{max}) &= -6400 \\ 4 - h_{max} &= -100 \\ -h_{max} &= -104 \\ h_{max} &= 104 \end{aligned}$$

So, the ball reached a maximum height of 104 feet.

d. Solve the equation $-16t^2 + 80t + 4 = 104$, or $-16t^2 + 80t - 100 = 0$, using the quadratic formula. You already know that the discriminant is 0 when the ball reached its maximum height, so $t = \frac{-80 \pm \sqrt{0}}{2(-16)} = \frac{-80}{-32} = 2.5$. So, the ball reached its maximum height 2.5 seconds after it was hit.

EXTENSION ACTIVITY

On the moon, the force of gravity is $\frac{1}{6}$ Earth's gravity, so the equation for simple projectile motion for a ball hit at a height of 4 feet above the ground is $y = -\frac{16}{6}t^2 + vt + 4$. Have students determine if a baseball hit upward at a 45° angle and traveling at $v = 80$ ft/s on the moon reaches a height of 200 feet. They should find the real solutions. $t \approx 2.7$ and 27.3 s, so the ball does reach a height of 200 feet.

AVOID COMMON ERRORS

Students may sometimes make a mistake in sign when calculating the discriminant, particularly when the quantity $4ac$ is less than 0. Remind them that subtracting a negative number is the same as adding the opposite, or positive, number. If a and c have opposite signs, the discriminant will always be positive.

INTEGRATE TECHNOLOGY

Students can use a graphing utility to graph a parabola and find the maximum value.

QUESTIONING STRATEGIES

? How can the symmetry of a parabola help you to find the maximum or minimum if you know two different points on the graph with the same y-coordinate? The x-coordinate of the maximum or minimum will be halfway between the x-coordinates of the two points on the graph.

Scoring Rubric

2 points: Student correctly solves the problem and explains his/her reasoning.

1 point: Student shows good understanding of the problem but does not fully solve or explain his/her reasoning.

0 points: Student does not demonstrate understanding of the problem.

MODULE 3

Study Guide Review

ASSESSMENT AND INTERVENTION

Assign or customize module reviews.

MODULE PERFORMANCE TASK

COMMON CORE

Mathematical Practices: MP.1, MP.2, MP.4, MP.6
A-SSE.A.1, A-CED.A.1, A-CED.A.3, A-REI.B.4b

SUPPORTING STUDENT REASONING

Students should begin this problem by focusing on what information they will need. They can then do research, or you can provide them with specific information. They may not understand what the variables represent or why they would need to know them. Facilitate a conversation to discuss the factors that affect a car's stopping distance. Those factors include:

- Driver's reaction time: the driver won't brake instantly, so a number of seconds must be accounted for.
- Road slickness (called the *coefficient of friction*): depending on the type of road surface and its condition (wet, oily, dry) the car will slide farther.
- Speed: the faster the car goes, the longer it takes to stop.

Here is some of the information may ask for.

- **Typical driver reaction time:** The average reaction time is 1.5 seconds.
- **Coefficient of friction:** For a dry road, the coefficient of friction is about 0.7.

STUDY GUIDE REVIEW

Quadratic Equations

MODULE 3

Essential Question: How can you use quadratic equations to solve real-world problems?

Key Vocabulary
complex number *(número complejo)*
imaginary number *(número imaginario)*
imaginary unit *(unidad imaginaria)*
pure imaginary number *(número imaginario puro)*

KEY EXAMPLE *(Lessons 3.1, 3.2)*

Take square roots to solve the quadratic equations.

$3x^2 - 27 = 9$	
$3x^2 = 36$	Add 27 to both sides.
$x^2 = 12$	Divide both sides by 3.
$x = \pm\sqrt{12}$	Square root
$x = \pm\sqrt{4} \cdot \sqrt{3}$	Product Property
$x = \pm 2\sqrt{3}$	Simplify.

$x^2 + 20 = 0$	
$x^2 = -20$	Subtract 20 on both sides.
$x = \pm\sqrt{-20}$	Square root
$x = \pm\sqrt{(-1)(5)(4)}$	Product Property
$x = \pm 2i\sqrt{5}$	Simplify.

KEY EXAMPLE *(Lesson 3.3)*

Solve $2x^2 + 4x - 8 = 0$ by completing the square.

$2x^2 + 4x = 8$	Write the equation in the form $x^2 + bx = c$.
$x^2 + 2x = 4$	Divide both sides by 2.
$x^2 + 2x + 1 = 4 + 1$	Add $\left(\frac{b}{2}\right)^2$ to both sides of the equation.
$(x + 1)^2 = 5$	Solve for x.
$x + 1 = \pm\sqrt{5}$	
$x = -1 \pm \sqrt{5}$	

SCAFFOLDING SUPPORT

- Students should understand that the driver will not immediately brake after seeing the felled tree. The time between seeing the tree and hitting the brakes is the reaction time.
- Encourage students to use a quadratic inequality to solve this problem, for example $\frac{v^2}{2\mu g} + 1.5v \leq 125$.

EXERCISES

Solve using the method stated. *(Lessons 3.1, 3.3)*

1. $x^2 - 16 = 0$ (square root)

$x = \pm 4$

2. $2x^2 - 10 = 0$ (square root)

$x = \pm\sqrt{5}$

3. $3x^2 - 6x - 12 = 0$ (completing the square)

$x = 1 \pm \sqrt{7}$

4. $x^2 + 6x + 10 = 0$ (completing the square)

$x = -3 \pm i$

5. $x^2 - 4x + 4 = 0$ (factoring)

$x = 2$

6. $x^2 - x - 30 = 0$ (factoring)

$x = 6$ or $x = -5$

7. Explain if a quadratic equation can be solved using factoring. *(Lessons 3.1, 3.3)*

Possible Answer: If there is a common number where the factors multiply to make *c*, and the factors add to make *b*, then the quadratic equation can be solved by factoring. If a is something other than 1, a different approach is taken.

8. Can completing the square solve any quadratic equation? Explain. *(Lessons 3.1, 3.3)*

No. If the equation has a *b* value of 0, then completing the square will not solve the equation.

MODULE PERFORMANCE TASK

Can You Stop in Time?

A driver sees a tree fall across the road 125 feet in front of the car. The driver is barely able to stop the car before hitting the tree. What was the maximum speed in miles per hour that the car could have been traveling when the driver saw the tree fall?

The equation for braking distance is $d = \frac{s^2}{2\mu g}$, where d is braking distance, s is speed of the car, μ is the coefficient of friction between the tires and the road, and g is the acceleration due to gravity, 32.2 ft/s^2.

Start by listing on your own paper the information you will need and the steps you will take to solve the problem. Then complete the task, using numbers, words, or algebra to explain how you reached your conclusion.

SAMPLE SOLUTION

Assumptions

The driver has a typical reaction time of 1.5 s.

The coefficient of friction is 0.7.

Find an inequality to determine the stopping distance, including the distance traveled during the reaction time, which is 1.5*v*:

$$\frac{v^2}{2\mu g} + 1.5v \leq 125$$

Solve the quadratic inequality for *v* to find the maximum speed the driver could have been traveling.

$$\frac{v^2}{2(0.7)(32.2\text{ ft/s}^2)} + (1.5\text{ s})v \leq 125\text{ ft}$$

$$0.0222v^2 + 1.5v \leq 125$$

$$v^2 + \frac{1.5}{0.0222}v \leq \frac{125}{0.0222}$$

$$v^2 + 67.57v - 5630.63 \leq 0$$

Use the quadratic formula:

$$v^2 + 67.57v - 5630.63 = 0$$

$$v = \frac{-67.57 \pm \sqrt{(67.57)^2 - 4(-5630.63)}}{2}$$

$$v = -116.08, 48.51$$

Disregarding the negative solution, and converting to miles per hour:

$$48.51\text{ ft/s} \times \frac{0.682\text{ mi/hr}}{1\text{ ft/s}} \approx 33\text{ mph}$$

The driver's maximum speed was 33 miles per hour.

DISCUSSION OPPORTUNITIES

- What happens if the coefficient of friction is smaller, for example when the roads are wet? A wet road has a coefficient of friction of about 0.4.
- What does the negative solution mean in this context? Why can we disregard it?
- Students may have heard of the "3-second rule" of driving. Discuss how speed, reaction time, and stopping distance are related to this rule, and why it is important to follow it.

Assessment Rubric

2 points: Student correctly solves the problem and explains his/her reasoning.

1 point: Student shows good understanding of the problem but does not fully solve or explain.

0 points: Student does not demonstrate understanding of the problem.

Ready to Go On?

ASSESS MASTERY

Use the assessment on this page to determine if students have mastered the concepts and standards covered in this module.

ASSESSMENT AND INTERVENTION

Access Ready to Go On? assessment online, and receive instant scoring, feedback, and customized intervention or enrichment.

ADDITIONAL RESOURCES

Response to Intervention Resources

- Reteach Worksheets

Differentiated Instruction Resources

- Reading Strategies EL
- Success for English Learners EL
- Challenge Worksheets

Assessment Resources

- Leveled Module Quizzes

Ready to Go On?

3.1–3.3 Quadratic Equations

- Online Homework
- Hints and Help
- Extra Practice

Solve the equations by taking square roots, completing the square, factoring, or the quadratic formula. *(Lessons 3.1, 3.2, 3.3)*

1. $2x^2 - 16 = 0$

$x = \pm 2\sqrt{2}$

2. $2x^2 - 6x - 20 = 0$

$x = -2$ and $x = 5$

3. $2x^2 + 2x - 2 = 0$

$x = \frac{-1 \pm \sqrt{5}}{2}$

4. $x^2 + x = 30$

$x = -6$ and $x = 5$

5. $x^2 - 5x = 24$

$x = -3$ and $x = 8$

6. $-4x^2 + 8 = 24$

$x = \pm 2i$

7. $x^2 + 30 = 24$

$x = \pm i\sqrt{6}$

8. $x^2 + 4x + 3 = 0$

$x = -1$ or $x = -3$

ESSENTIAL QUESTION

9. Write a real world situation that could be modeled by the equation $7m \cdot 5m = 875$. *(Lesson 3.1)*

Possible Answer: The ratio of peanuts to raisins in a snack mix is 7 to 5. if there are 875 peanuts and raisins in the mix, how many raisins and how many peanuts are there?

COMMON CORE Common Core Standards

Lesson	Items	Content Standards	Mathematical Practices
3.1	1	**A-REI.B.4**	**MP.2**
3.1	2	**A-REI.B.4**	**MP.2**
3.1	3	**A-REI.B.4**	**MP.2**
3.1	4	**A-REI.B.4**	**MP.2**
3.1	5	**A-REI.B.4**	**MP.2**
3.2, 3.3	6–8	**A-REI.B.4, N-CN.A.1, N-CN.C.7**	**MP.2**

MODULE 3
MIXED REVIEW

Assessment Readiness

1. Which of the following equations, when graphed, has two x-intercepts?
   - **A.** $x^2 + 16 = 0$ ○ Yes ● No
   - **B.** $2x^2 - 20 = 10$ ● Yes ○ No
   - **C.** $-3x^2 - 6 = 0$ ○ Yes ● No

2. Consider the equation $4x^2 + 4x - 16 = 0$. Choose True or False for each statement.
   - **A.** To solve this equation using complete the square, $\left(\frac{b}{2}\right)^2 = \left(\frac{4}{2}\right)^2 = 4$. ○ True ● False
   - **B.** If solving this equation using factoring, then $(x + 4)(x - 4) = 0$ ○ True ● False
   - **C.** After completing the square, $x = -\frac{1}{2} \pm \frac{\sqrt{17}}{2}$. ● True ○ False

3. Consider the equation $ax^2 + bx = 25$. For what values of a and b would you solve this equation by taking a square root? For what values of a would the square root result in an imaginary number? Explain your answers.

   The variable b must be equal to 0. The variable a could be any number. For negative values of a, the square root would result in an imaginary number. For positive values of a, the square root would result in a real number.

4. Consider the equation $f(x) = ax^2 + bx + c$. For what values of a would the quadratic function open upward? For what values of a would the quadratic function open downward? What would happen to the function if the value of a were 0? Explain.

   For the quadratic function to open upward, a would need to be greater than 0. For the quadratic function to open downward, a would need to be less than 0. If the value of a is 0, then it would be a linear function, because the x^2 term would not be present.

MIXED REVIEW
Assessment Readiness

ASSESSMENT AND INTERVENTION

Assign ready-made or customized practice tests to prepare students for high-stakes tests.

ADDITIONAL RESOURCES

Assessment Resources

- Leveled Module Quizzes: Modified, B

AVOID COMMON ERRORS

Item 4 Some students will be distracted by the fact that there are no numbers in the problem, and they will try to assess a, b, and c. Remind the students to focus on the questions asked. In this case, they should focus only on a.

COMMON CORE Common Core Standards

Lesson	Items	Content Standards	Mathematical Practices
1.3, 3.1, 3.2	1*	**N-CN.A.1**	**MP.2**
3.3	2	**A-REI.B.4b**	**MP.1**
3.1, 3.3	3*	**N-CN.A.1, N-CN.C.7**	**MP.6**
3.1, 3.2, 3.3	4	**F-IF.B.4, S-ID.B.6a**	**MP.6**

* Item integrates mixed review concepts from previous modules or a previous course.

Quadratic Relations and Systems of Equations

ESSENTIAL QUESTION:

Answer: Systems of equations and inequalities help us maximize profits in business.

PROFESSIONAL DEVELOPMENT VIDEO

Professional Development Video

Author Matt Larson models successful teaching practices in an actual high-school classroom.

Professional Development
my.hrw.com

MODULE 4

Quadratic Relations and Systems of Equations

Essential Question: How can you use systems of equations to solve real-world problems?

REAL WORLD VIDEO
Video game designers need a solid understanding of algebra, including systems of quadratic equations, in order to program realistic interactions within the game environment.

MODULE PERFORMANCE TASK PREVIEW

How Can You Hit a Moving Target with a Laser Beam?

Video games can be a lot of fun. They can also help players to develop and hone skills such as following instructions, using logic in problem solving, hand-eye coordination, and fine motor and spatial abilities. Video game designers often use mathematics to program realistic interactions in the video world. How can math be used to aim a laser beam to hit a virtual clay disk flying through the air? Set your sights on the target and let's get started!

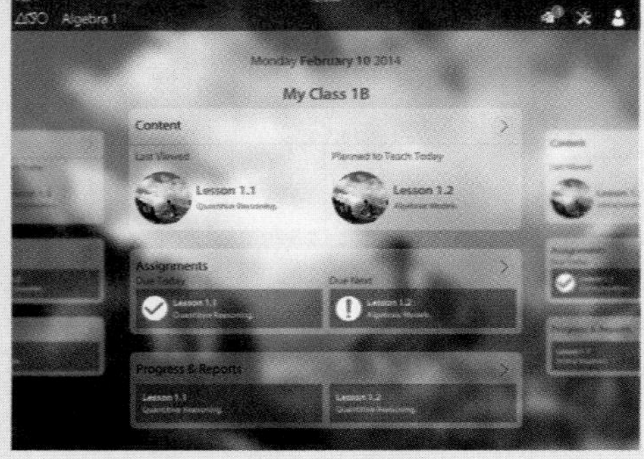

DIGITAL TEACHER EDITION

Access a full suite of teaching resources when and where you need them:

- Access content online or offline
- Customize lessons to share with your class
- Communicate with your students in real-time
- View student grades and data instantly to target your instruction where it is needed most

PERSONAL MATH TRAINER

Assessment and Intervention

Assign automatically graded homework, quizzes, tests, and intervention activities. Prepare your students with updated, Common Core-aligned practice tests.

Are YOU Ready?

Complete these exercises to review skills you will need for this chapter.

- Online Homework
- Hints and Help
- Extra Practice

Graphing Linear Nonproportional Relationships

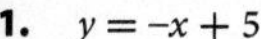
Example 1 Graph $y = -2x - 3$.

x	0	−2	−3
y	−3	1	3

Make a table of values. Plot the points and draw a line through them.

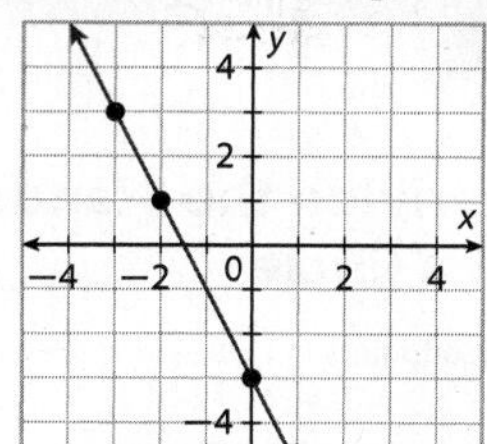

Graph each equation.

1. $y = -x + 5$

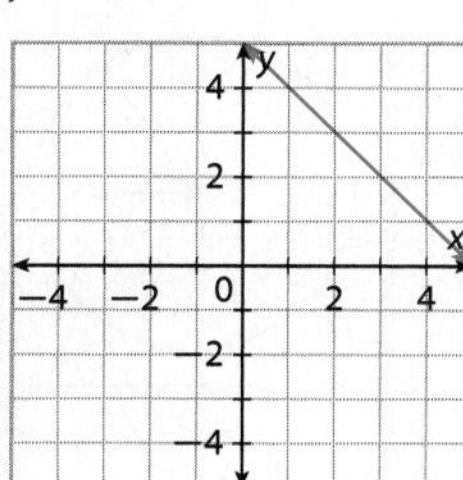

2. $y = 3x - 2$

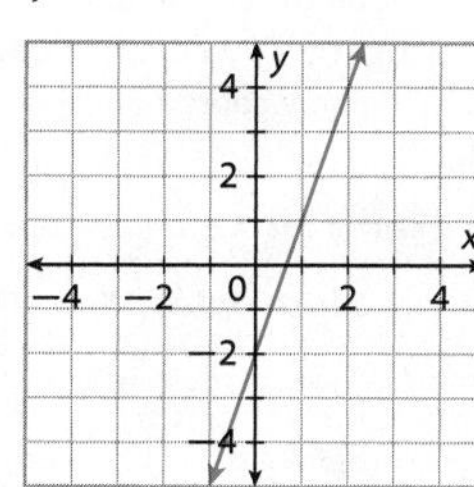

Multi-Step Equations

Example 2 Solve $4(x - 2) = 12$ for x.

$4x - 8 = 12$ Distribute.

$4x = 20$ Add 8 to both sides.

$x = 5$ Divide by 4.

Solve each equation.

3. $5 - 3x = 7(x - 1)$ 1.2 **4.** $3x + 2(x - 1) = 28$ 6 **5.** $2(6 - 5x) = 5x + 9$ 0.2

Solving Systems of Two Linear Equations

Example 3 Solve the system $\begin{cases} y = 2x + 8 \\ 3x + 2y = 2 \end{cases}$.

$3x + 2(2x + 8) = 2$ Substitute.

$x = -2$ Solve for x.

$y = 2(-2) + 8 = 4$ Solve for y.

The solution is $(-2, 4)$.

Solve each system.

6. $\begin{cases} y = 10 - 3x \\ 5x - y = 6 \end{cases}$ (2, 4) **7.** $\begin{cases} 2x - 3y = 4 \\ -x + 2y = 3 \end{cases}$ (17, 10) **8.** $\begin{cases} 5x - 2y = 4 \\ 3x + 2y = -12 \end{cases}$ (−1, −4.5)

Response to Intervention			Differentiated Instruction
Tier 1 Lesson Intervention Worksheets	**Tier 2** Strategic Intervention Skills Intervention Worksheets	**Tier 3** Intensive Intervention Worksheets available online	
Reteach 4.1 Reteach 4.2 Reteach 4.3 Reteach 4.4	14 Graphing Linear... 20 Multi-Step Equations 32 Solving Quadratic... 34 Solving Systems of... 35 Systems of... 36 The Quadratic...	Building Block Skills 21, 43, 44, 46, 91, 94, 97, 100	Challenge worksheets Extend the Math Lesson Activities in TE

Are You Ready?

ASSESS READINESS

Use the assessment on this page to determine if students need strategic or intensive intervention for the module's prerequisite skills.

ASSESSMENT AND INTERVENTION

RtI Response to Intervention TIER 1, TIER 2, TIER 3 SKILLS

Personal Math Trainer will automatically create a standards-based, personalized intervention assignment for your students, targeting each student's individual needs!

ADDITIONAL RESOURCES

See the table below for a full list of intervention resources available for this module.

Response to Intervention Resources also includes:

- Tier 2 Skill Pre-Tests for each Module
- Tier 2 Skill Post-Tests for each skill

LESSON 4.1

Circles

Common Core Math Standards

The student is expected to:

A-CED.A.3

Represent constraints by equations or inequalities, ... and interpret solutions as viable or nonviable options in a modeling context. Also A-CED.A.2, G-GPE.A.1, G-GPE.B.4

Mathematical Practices

COMMON CORE **MP.7 Using Structure**

Language Objective

Work with a partner to match graphs of circles to their equations in standard form.

ENGAGE

Essential Question: What is the standard form for the equation of a circle, and what does the standard form tell you about the circle?

Possible answer: The standard form for the equation of a circle is $(x-h)^2+(y-k)^2=r^2$, which tells you that the center is (h, k) and the radius is r.

PREVIEW: LESSON PERFORMANCE TASK

View the online Engage. Discuss the photo and the generally circular nature of radio-signal reception strength. Then preview the Lesson Performance Task.

Name __________ Class __________ Date __________

4.1 Circles

Essential Question: What is the standard form for the equation of a circle, and what does the standard form tell you about the circle?

Resource Locker

Explore Deriving the Standard-Form Equation of a Circle

Recall that a circle is the set of points in a plane that are a fixed distance, called the radius, from a given point, called the center.

Ⓐ The coordinate plane shows a circle with center $C(h, k)$ and radius r. $P(x, y)$ is an arbitrary point on the circle but is not directly above or below or to the left or right of C. $A(x, k)$ is a point with the same x-coordinate as P and the same y-coordinate as C. Explain why $\triangle CAP$ is a right triangle.

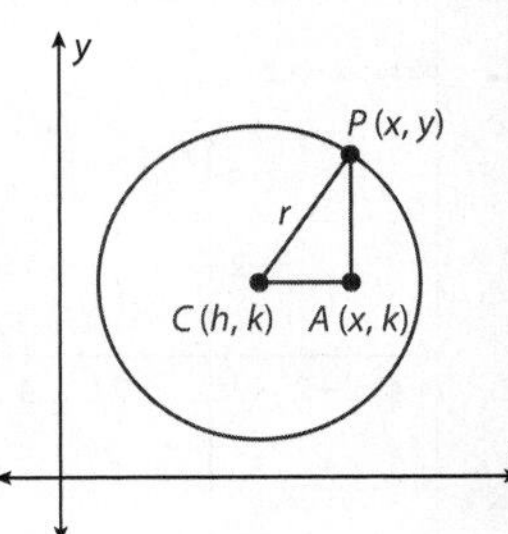

Since point A has the same x-coordinate as point P, segment PA is a vertical segment. Since point A has the same y-coordinate as point C, segment CA is a horizontal segment. This means that segments PA and CA are perpendicular, which means that $\angle CAP$ is a right angle and $\triangle CAP$ is a right triangle.

Ⓑ Identify the lengths of the sides of $\triangle CAP$. Remember that point P is arbitrary, so you cannot rely upon the diagram to know whether the x-coordinate of P is greater than or less than h or whether the y-coordinate of P is greater than or less than k, so you must use absolute value for the lengths of the legs of $\triangle CAP$. Also, remember that the length of the hypotenuse of $\triangle CAP$ is just the radius of the circle.

The length of segment AC is $|x-h|$.

The length of segment AP is $|y-k|$.

The length of segment CP is r.

Ⓒ Apply the Pythagorean Theorem to $\triangle CAP$ to obtain an equation of the circle.

$$(x-h)^2+(y-k)^2=r^2$$

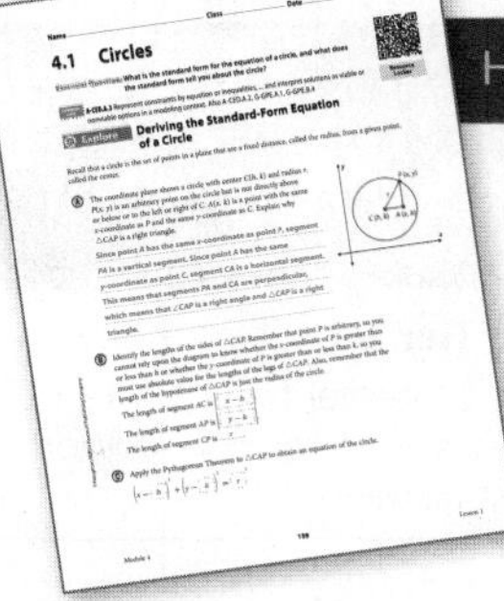

HARDCOVER PAGES 159–174

Watch for the hardcover student edition page numbers for this lesson.

Reflect

1. **Discussion** Why isn't absolute value used in the equation of the circle?
Since squaring removes any negative signs just as absolute value does, there's no need to take absolute value before squaring.

2. **Discussion** Why does the equation of the circle also apply to the cases in which P has the same x-coordinate as C or the same y-coordinate as C so that $\triangle CAP$ doesn't exist?
If P has the same x-coordinate as C, then P's y-coordinate must be either $k + r$ or $k - r$. So, $(x-h)^2 + (y-k)^2 = (h-h)^2 + ((k \pm r) - k)^2 = 0^2 + (\pm r)^2 = r^2$, and the equation of the circle is still satisfied. Similarly, if P has the same y-coordinate as C, then P's x-coordinate must be either $k + r$ or $k - r$. So, $(x-h)^2 + (y-k)^2 = ((h \pm r) - h)^2 + (k-k)^2 = (\pm r)^2 + 0^2 = r^2$, and the equation of the circle is still satisfied.

Explain 1 Writing the Equation of a Circle

The standard-form equation of a circle with center $C(h, k)$ and radius r is $(x-h)^2 + (y-k)^2 = r^2$. If you solve this equation for r, you obtain the equation $r = \sqrt{(x-h)^2 + (y-k)^2}$, which gives you a means for finding the radius of a circle when the center and a point $P(x, y)$ on the circle are known.

Example 1 Write the equation of the circle.

(A) The circle with center $C(-3, 2)$ and radius $r = 4$

Substitute -3 for h, 2 for k, and 4 for r into the general equation and simplify.

$$(x-(-3))^2 + (y-2)^2 = 4^2$$
$$(x+3)^2 + (y-2)^2 = 16$$

(B) The circle with center $C(-4, -3)$ and containing the point $P(2, 5)$

Step 1 Find the radius.

$$r = CP$$
$$= \sqrt{(\boxed{2} - (-4))^2 + (\boxed{5} - (-3))^2}$$
$$= \sqrt{(\boxed{6})^2 + (\boxed{8})^2}$$
$$= \sqrt{\boxed{36} + \boxed{64}}$$
$$= \sqrt{\boxed{100}} = \boxed{10}$$

Step 2 Write the equation of the circle.

$$(x-(-4))^2 + (y-(-3))^2 = \boxed{10}^2$$
$$(x+4)^2 + (y+3)^2 = \boxed{100}$$

PROFESSIONAL DEVELOPMENT

Math Background

The equation of a circle is based on the fact that all of the points on the circle are a fixed distance from a given point. This distance can be found using the Pythagorean Theorem. In the derivation, the fixed distance, the radius, is represented by the hypotenuse of a right triangle that has one vertex at the center of the circle, and one on the circle itself. Applying the Pythagorean Theorem produces the equation of the circle, $(x-h)^2 + (y-k)^2 = r^2$. Note that taking the square root of each side of this equation produces the equation $\sqrt{(x-h)^2 + (y-k)^2} = r$. This equation shows that the radius is the distance between the two points.

EXPLORE

Deriving the Standard-Form Equation of a Circle

INTEGRATE TECHNOLOGY

Students have the option of completing the Explore activity either in the book or online.

QUESTIONING STRATEGIES

Why does point A have coordinates (x, k)? It is below $P(x, y)$, which has x-coordinate x, and on the same horizontal line as $C(h, k)$, which has y-coordinate k.

Why is it necessary to use absolute value signs when representing the length of the legs of the right triangle? Since P could be any point on the circle, absolute value signs are used to make sure the length of each leg is a positive number.

EXPLAIN 1

Writing the Equation of a Circle

AVOID COMMON ERRORS

Some students may forget to square the radius when writing the equation. Others may take its square root. Help students to avoid making these errors by having them write r^2 above the place in the equation where they need to write the square of the radius.

QUESTIONING STRATEGIES

Do you need to be given the coordinates of the center to write an equation of a circle? If not, what other information could you use to find the center? Explain. No. If you know the endpoints of a diameter of the circle, you can find the coordinates of the center using the midpoint formula.

INTEGRATE MATHEMATICAL PRACTICES

Focus on Math Connections

MP.1 Discuss with students how the graph of the equation $(x-h)^2 + (y-k)^2 = r^2$ is a transformation of the graph of $x^2 + y^2 = r^2$. Have students describe the transformation and compare the two graphs.

EXPLAIN 2

Rewriting an Equation of a Circle to Graph the Circle

QUESTIONING STRATEGIES

How do you know what number to add to make perfect square trinomials when converting to standard form? Take half of the coefficient of the x term, and square it. Then do the same with the coefficient of the y term.

Once the equation is in standard form, how do you find the diameter of the circle? The diameter is 2 times the square root of the number that represents r^2.

Your Turn

Write the equation of the circle.

3. The circle with center $C(1, -4)$ and radius $r = 2$

$$(x-1)^2 + (y-(-4))^2 = 2^2$$
$$(x-1)^2 + (y+4)^2 = 4$$

4. The circle with center $C(-2, 5)$ and containing the point $P(-2, -1)$

Because points C and P have the same x-coordinate, the radius of the circle is just the absolute value of the difference of their y-coordinates, so $r = |5-(-1)| = |6| = 6$.

$$(x-(-2))^2 + (y-5)^2 = 6^2$$
$$(x+2)^2 + (y-5)^2 = 36$$

Explain 2 Rewriting an Equation of a Circle to Graph the Circle

Expanding the standard-form equation $(x-h)^2 + (y-k)^2 = r^2$ results in a general second-degree equation in two variables having the form $x^2 + y^2 + cx + dy + e = 0$. In order to graph such an equation or an even more general equation of the form $ax^2 + ay^2 + cx + dy + e = 0$. you must complete the square on both x and y to put the equation in standard form and identify the circle's center and radius.

Example 2 **Graph the circle after writing the equation in standard form.**

(A) $x^2 + y^2 - 10x + 6y + 30 = 0$

Write the equation. $x^2 + y^2 - 10x + 6y + 30 = 0$

Prepare to complete the square on x and y. $(x^2 - 10x + \blacksquare) + (y^2 + 6y + \blacksquare) = -30 + \blacksquare + \blacksquare$

Complete both squares. $(x^2 - 10x + 25) + (y^2 + 6y + 9) = -30 + 25 + 9$

Factor and simplify. $(x-5)^2 + (y+3)^2 = 4$

The center of the circle is $C(5, -3)$, and the radius is $r = \sqrt{4} = 2$.

Graph the circle.

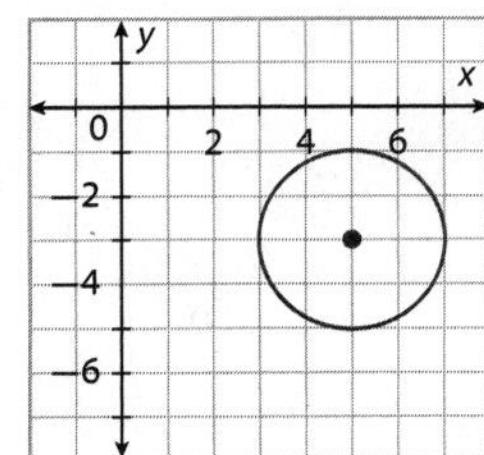

COLLABORATIVE LEARNING

Peer-to-Peer Activity

Have students work in pairs. Instruct each student in each pair to write an equation of a circle in standard form. Have them graph the circles, keeping their graphs hidden from their partners. Have them also convert their equations to the general form $ax^2 + by^2 + cx + dy + e = 0$ by expanding and combining like terms. Instruct students to exchange the general forms of their equations, write each other's equations in standard form, and draw the graph. Have students compare their work.

Ⓑ $4x^2 + 4y^2 + 8x - 16y + 11 = 0$

Write the equation.	$4x^2 + 4y^2 + 8x - 16y + 11 = 0$
Factor 4 from the x terms and the y terms.	$4(x^2 + 2x) + 4(y^2 - 4y) + 11 = 0$
Prepare to complete the square on x and y.	$4(x^2 + 2x + \blacksquare) + 4(y^2 - 4y + \blacksquare) = -11 + 4(\blacksquare) + 4(\blacksquare)$
Complete both squares.	$4(x^2 + 2x + \boxed{1}) + 4(y^2 - 4y + \boxed{4}) = -11 + 4(\boxed{1}) + 4(\boxed{4})$
Factor and simplify.	$4(x + \boxed{1})^2 + 4(y - \boxed{2})^2 = \boxed{9}$
Divide both sides by 4.	$(x + \boxed{1})^2 + (y - \boxed{2})^2 = \boxed{\frac{9}{4}}$

The center is $C(\boxed{-1}, \boxed{2})$, and the radius is $r = \sqrt{\boxed{\frac{9}{4}}} = \boxed{\frac{3}{2}}$.

Graph the circle.

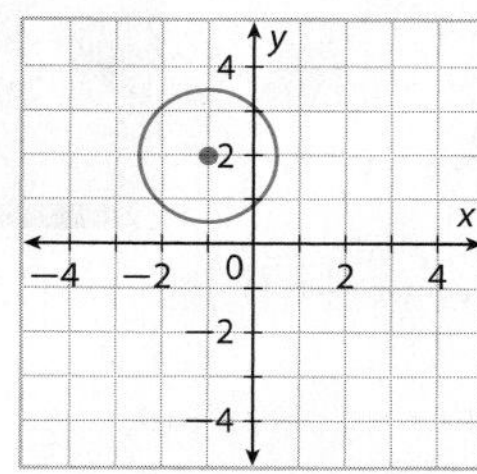

Your Turn

Graph the circle after writing the equation in standard form.

5. $x^2 + y^2 + 4x + 6y + 4 = 0$

$$x^2 + y^2 + 4x + 6y + 4 = 0$$
$$(x^2 + 4x) + (y^2 + 6y) = -4$$
$$(x^2 + 4x + 4) + (y^2 + 6y + 9) = -4 + 4 + 9$$
$$(x + 2)^2 + (y + 3)^2 = 9$$

The center is $C(-2, -3)$, and the radius is $r = \sqrt{9} = 3$.

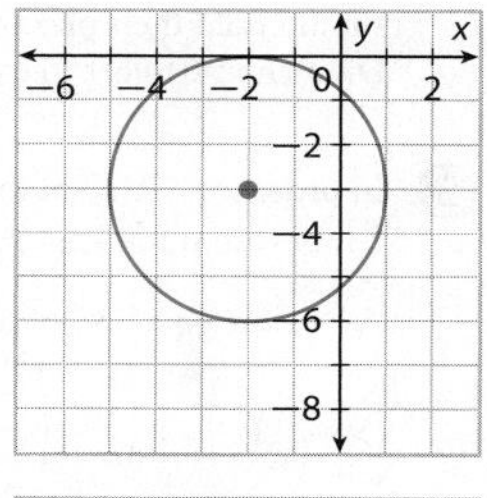

6. $9x^2 + 9y^2 - 54x - 72y + 209 = 0$

$$9x^2 + 9y^2 - 54x - 72y + 209 = 0$$
$$9(x^2 - 6x) + 9(y^2 - 8y) = -209$$
$$9(x^2 - 6x + 9) + 9(y^2 - 8y + 16) = -209 + 9(9) + 9(16)$$
$$9(x - 3)^2 + 9(y - 4)^2 = 16$$
$$(x - 3)^2 + (y - 4)^2 = \frac{16}{9}$$

The center is $C(3, 4)$, and the radius is $r = \sqrt{\frac{16}{9}} = \frac{4}{3}$.

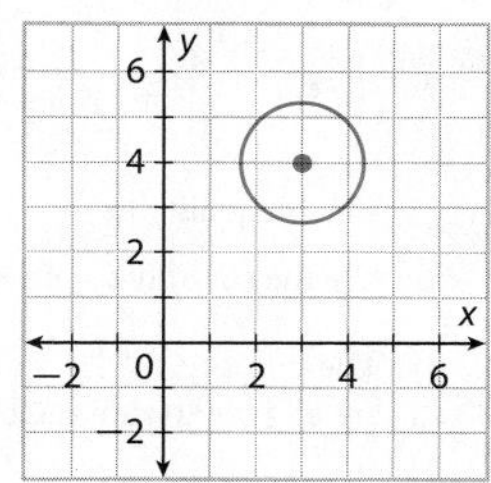

AVOID COMMON ERRORS

When adding the numbers to the constant term to maintain the equality, students may forget to multiply the number added to complete each square by the leading coefficient that was factored from the variable terms. Help them to avoid this error by encouraging them to circle the leading coefficients that have been factored out in the process of completing the square.

INTEGRATE MATHEMATICAL PRACTICES

Focus on Critical Thinking

MP.3 Have students compare how the completing-the-square process is used to write quadratic functions in vertex form with how it is used to write a circle in standard form. Have them describe both the similarities and the differences.

DIFFERENTIATE INSTRUCTION

Kinesthetic Experience

Prepare a length of string with a marker attached at one end. Display a coordinate plane. With a tack, tape, or some other means, attach the non-marker end of the string to an arbitrary point on the plane and draw a circle. Ask students to explain how they could use a point on the circle and the center to find the length of the string. Help them to see that they can construct a right triangle whose hypotenuse is the length of the string, and apply the Pythagorean Theorem to determine the length of the string.

EXPLAIN 3

Solving a Real-World Problem Involving a Circle

QUESTIONING STRATEGIES

? If you know the equation of a circle, how can you determine whether a given point lies inside, outside, or on the circle? **You can substitute the coordinates of the point for *x* and *y* in the equation of the circle, and see whether the value of $(x-h)^2+(y-k)^2$ is less than, greater than, or equal to the value of r^2. If it is less than r^2, the point lies inside the circle; if greater than, the point lies outside the circle; and if equal to, the point lies on the circle.**

INTEGRATE MATHEMATICAL PRACTICES

Focus on Reasoning

MP.2 Ask students to explain why points that are inside the circle satisfy the inequality $(x-h)^2+(y-k)^2<r^2$. Students should recognize that a point inside the circle would lie on a circle whose radius would be shorter than *r*, and whose equation would be $(x-h)^2+(y-k)^2={r_1}^2$, with $r_1<r$. Thus, ${r_1}^2<r^2$ and $(x-h)^2+(y-k)^2<r^2$.

Explain 3 Solving a Real-World Problem Involving a Circle

A circle in a coordinate plane divides the plane into two regions: points inside the circle and points outside the circle. Points inside the circle satisfy the inequality $(x-h)^2+(y-k)^2<r^2$, while points outside the circle satisfy the inequality $(x-h)^2+(y-k)^2>r^2$.

Example 3 **Write an inequality representing the given situation, and draw a circle to solve the problem.**

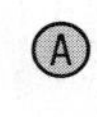

The table lists the locations of the homes of five friends along with the locations of their favorite pizza restaurant and the school they attend. The friends are deciding where to have a pizza party based on the fact that the restaurant offers free delivery to locations within a 3-mile radius of the restaurant. At which homes should the friends hold their pizza party to get free delivery?

Place	Location
Alonzo's home	A(3, 2)
Barbara's home	B(2, 4)
Constance's home	C(−2, 3)
Dion's home	D(0, −1)
Eli's home	E(1, −4)
Pizza restaurant	(−1, 1)
School	(1, −2)

Write the equation of the circle with center (−1, 1) and radius 3.

$(x-(-1))^2+(y-1)^2=3^2$, or $(x+1)^2+(y-1)^2=9$

The inequality $(x+1)^2+(y-1)^2<9$ represents the situation.
Plot the points from the table and graph the circle.

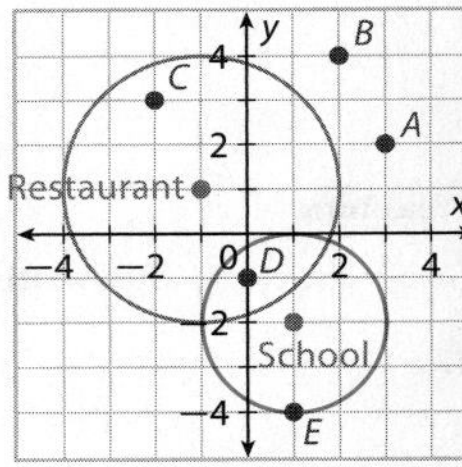

The points inside the circle satisfy the inequality. So, the friends should hold their pizza party at either Constance's home or Dion's home to get free delivery.

In order for a student to ride the bus to school, the student must live more than 2 miles from the school. Which of the five friends are eligible to ride the bus?

Write the equation of the circle with center (1, −2) and radius 2.

$(x-1)^2+(y-(-2))^2=2^2$

$(x-1)^2+(y+2)^2=4$

The inequality $(x-1)^2+(y+2)^2>4$ represents the situation.
Use the coordinate grid in Part A to graph the circle.

The points **outside** the circle satisfy the inequality. So, **Alonzo, Barbara, and Constance** are eligible to ride the bus.

LANGUAGE SUPPORT EL

Communicate Math

Have students work in pairs. Provide each pair of students with different graphs of circles and, on separate note cards or sheets of paper, the equations for those graphs. The first student chooses a graph and decides which equation goes with it, then explains why they are a match. The second student repeats the procedure using another graph and equation.

Reflect

7. For Part B, how do you know that point E isn't outside the circle?
The coordinates of point E are $(1, -4)$. Substituting 1 for x and -4 for y in $(x-1)^2+(y+2)^2$ gives $(1-1)^2+(-4+2)^2=0^2+(-2)^2=4$, so the coordinates of E satisfy the equation of the circle, which means that E is on the circle and not outside it.

Your Turn

Write an inequality representing the given situation, and draw a circle to solve the problem.

8. Sasha delivers newspapers to subscribers that live within a 4-block radius of her house. Sasha's house is located at point $(0, -1)$. Points A, B, C, D, and E represent the houses of some of the subscribers to the newspaper. To which houses does Sasha deliver newspapers?

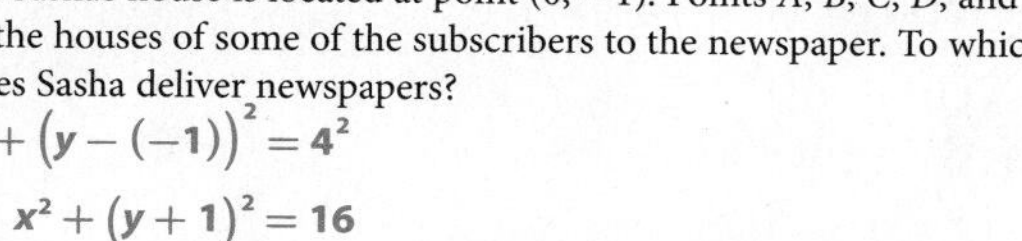

$$(x-0)^2+(y-(-1))^2=4^2$$
$$x^2+(y+1)^2=16$$

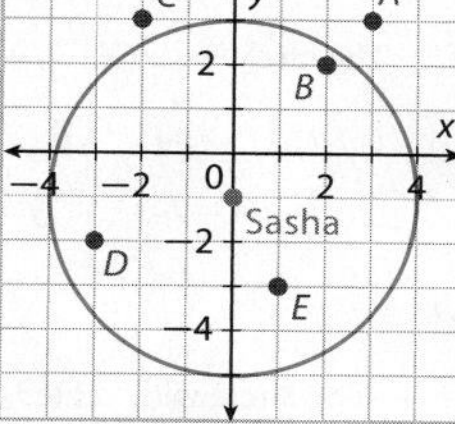

The inequality $x^2+(y+1)^2<16$ represents the situation.
The points inside the circle satisfy the inequality $x^2+(y+1)^2<16$.
So, Sasha delivers to the houses located at points B, D, and E.

Elaborate

9. Describe the process for deriving the equation of a circle given the coordinates of its center and its radius.
First, choose an arbitrary point P on the circle. Next, find a third point A that forms a right triangle with points C and P. Then, use the coordinates of the three points to find the lengths of segments CA and PA. (The length of segment CP is the circle's radius.) Finally, use the Pythagorean Theorem to write an equation of the circle.

10. What must you do with the equation $ax^2+ay^2+cx+dy+e=0$ in order to graph it?
Complete the square on x and y to write the equation in standard form. From the standard-form equation you can then identify the circle's center and radius, which you can then use to graph the circle.

11. What do the inequalities $(x-h)^2+(y-k)^2<r^2$ and $(x-h)^2+(y-k)^2>r^2$ represent?
The inequality $(x-h)^2+(y-k)^2<r^2$ represents points inside the circle with equation $(x-h)^2+(y-k)^2=r^2$, and the inequality $(x-h)^2+(y-k)^2>r^2$ represents points outside the circle.

12. **Essential Question Check-In** What information must you know or determine in order to write an equation of a circle in standard form?
You must know the center of the circle and its radius to write an equation of the circle in standard form. If only the center and a point on the circle are known, you can determine the radius from those two points.

ELABORATE

QUESTIONING STRATEGIES

How is the equation of a circle related to the equation $a^2+b^2=c^2$ from the Pythagorean Theorem? **The radius is c, and the lengths of the legs of the right triangle that has the radius as its hypotenuse are a and b.**

INTEGRATE MATHEMATICAL PRACTICES

Focus on Reasoning

MP.2 Discuss with students why, in the equation $ax^2+by^2+cx+dy+e=0$, a and b must be equal for the equation to be that of a circle. Focus their attention on the steps involved in converting the equation to the standard form of a circle, and on the roles of a and b in the conversion.

SUMMARIZE THE LESSON

How can you write the equation of a circle? **You can use the coordinates of the center for h and k, and the radius for r, in the equation $(x-h)^2+(y-k)^2=r^2$.**

EVALUATE

ASSIGNMENT GUIDE

Concepts and Skills	Practice
Explore Deriving the Standard-Form Equation of a Circle	
Example 1 Writing the Equation of a Circle	Exercises 1–4, 21, 24, 25
Example 2 Rewriting an Equation of a Circle to Graph the Circle	Exercises 5–12
Example 3 Solving a Real-World Problem Involving a Circle	Exercises 13–20, 22–23

QUESTIONING STRATEGIES

? How can you find the radius of a circle if you know the endpoints of a diameter of the circle? You can use the distance formula to find the length of the diameter and take half of that distance.

Evaluate: Homework and Practice

- Online Homework
- Hints and Help
- Extra Practice

Write the equation of the circle.

1. The circle with $C(4, -11)$ and radius $r = 16$

$$(x-h)^2 + (y-k)^2 = r^2$$
$$(x-4)^2 + (y-(-11))^2 = 16^2$$
$$(x-4)^2 + (y+11)^2 = 256$$

2. The circle with $C(-7, -1)$ and radius $r = 13$

$$(x-h)^2 + (y-k)^2 = r^2$$
$$(x-(-7))^2 + (y-(-1))^2 = 13^2$$
$$(x+7)^2 + (y+1)^2 = 169$$

3. The circle with center $C(-8, 2)$ and containing the point $P(-1, 6)$

$$\begin{aligned} r &= CP \\ &= \sqrt{(-1-(-8))^2 + (6-2)^2} \\ &= \sqrt{7^2 + 4^2} \\ &= \sqrt{49 + 16} \\ &= \sqrt{65} \end{aligned}$$
$$(x-h)^2 + (y-k)^2 = r^2$$
$$(x-(-8))^2 + (y-2)^2 = (\sqrt{65})^2$$
$$(x+8)^2 + (y-2)^2 = 65$$

4. The circle with center $C(5, 9)$ and containing the point $P(4, 8)$

$$\begin{aligned} r &= CP \\ &= \sqrt{(4-5)^2 + (8-9)^2} \\ &= \sqrt{(-1)^2 + (-1)^2} \\ &= \sqrt{1+1} \\ &= \sqrt{2} \end{aligned}$$
$$(x-h)^2 + (y-k)^2 = r^2$$
$$(x-5)^2 + (y-9)^2 = (\sqrt{2})^2$$
$$(x-5)^2 + (y-9)^2 = 2$$

In Exercises 5–12, graph the circle after writing the equation in standard form.

5. $x^2 + y^2 - 2x - 8y + 13 = 0$

$$x^2 + y^2 - 2x - 8y + 13 = 0$$
$$(x^2 - 2x) + (y^2 - 8y) = -13$$
$$(x^2 - 2x + 1) + (y^2 - 8y + 16) = -13 + 1 + 16$$
$$(x-1)^2 + (y-4)^2 = 4$$

The center of the circle is $C(1, 4)$, and the radius is $r = \sqrt{4} = 2$.

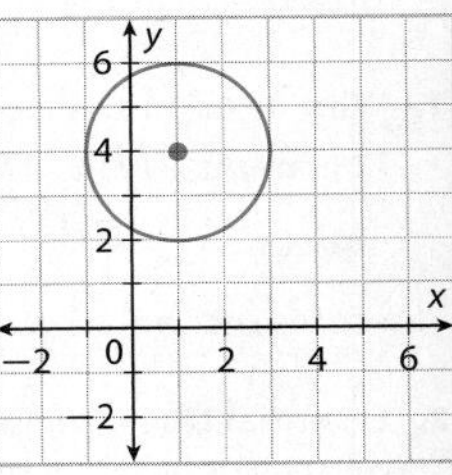

Exercise	Depth of Knowledge (D.O.K.)	COMMON CORE Mathematical Practices
1–12	**1** Recall of Information	**MP.7** Using Structure
13–20	**2** Skills/Concepts	**MP.4** Modeling
21	**2** Skills/Concepts	**MP.7** Using Structure
22–23	**3** Strategic Thinking H.O.T.	**MP.4** Modeling
24–25	**3** Strategic Thinking H.O.T.	**MP.2** Reasoning

Graph the circle after writing the equation in standard form.

6. $x^2 + y^2 + 6x - 10y + 25 = 0$

$$x^2 + y^2 + 6x - 10y + 25 = 0$$
$$(x^2 + 6x) + (y^2 - 10y) = -25$$
$$(x^2 + 6x + 9) + (y^2 - 10y + 25) = -25 + 9 + 25$$
$$(x + 3)^2 + (y - 5)^2 = 9$$

The center of the circle is $C(-3, 5)$, and the radius is $r = \sqrt{9} = 3$.

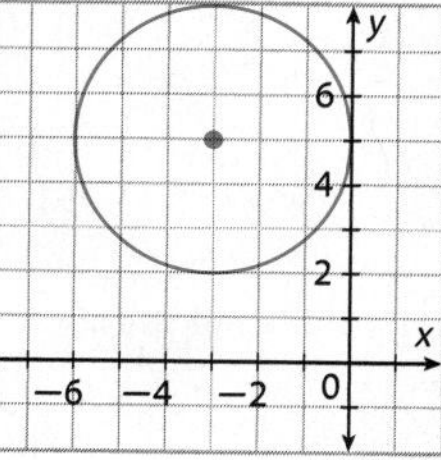

7. $x^2 + y^2 + 4x + 12y + 39 = 0$

$$x^2 + y^2 + 4x + 12y + 39 = 0$$
$$(x^2 + 4x) + (y^2 + 12y) = -39$$
$$(x^2 + 4x + 4) + (y^2 + 12y + 36) = -39 + 4 + 36$$
$$(x + 2)^2 + (y + 6)^2 = 1$$

The center of the circle is $C(-2, -6)$, and the radius is $r = \sqrt{1} = 1$.

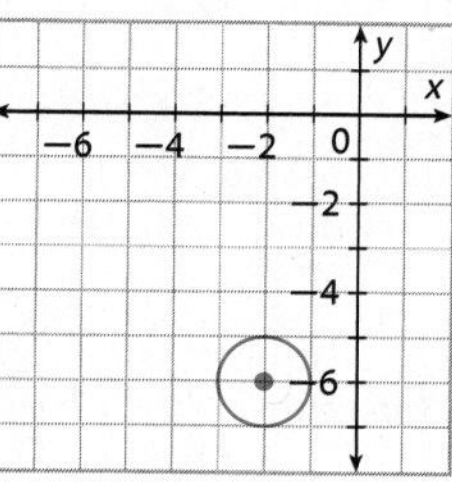

8. $x^2 + y^2 - 8x + 4y + 16 = 0$

$$x^2 + y^2 - 8x + 4y + 16 = 0$$
$$(x^2 - 8x) + (y^2 + 4y) = -16$$
$$(x^2 - 8x + 16) + (y^2 + 4y + 4) = -16 + 16 + 4$$
$$(x - 4)^2 + (y + 2)^2 = 4$$

The center of the circle is $C(4, -2)$, and the radius is $r = \sqrt{4} = 2$.

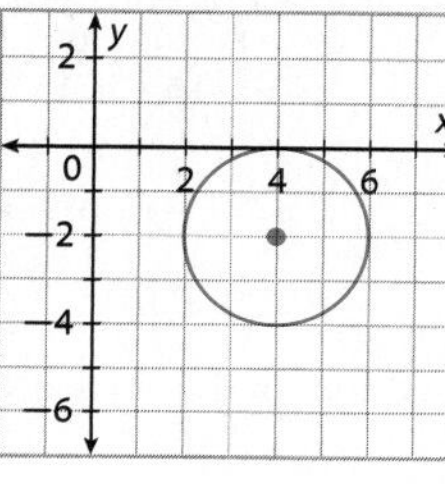

9. $8x^2 + 8y^2 - 16x - 32y - 88 = 0$

$$8x^2 + 8y^2 - 16x - 32y - 88 = 0$$
$$x^2 + y^2 - 2x - 4y - 11 = 0$$
$$(x^2 - 2x) + (y^2 - 4y) = 11$$
$$(x^2 - 2x + 1) + (y^2 - 4y + 4) = 11 + 1 + 4$$
$$(x - 1)^2 + (y - 2)^2 = 16$$

The center of the circle is $C(1, 2)$, and the radius is $r = \sqrt{16} = 4$.

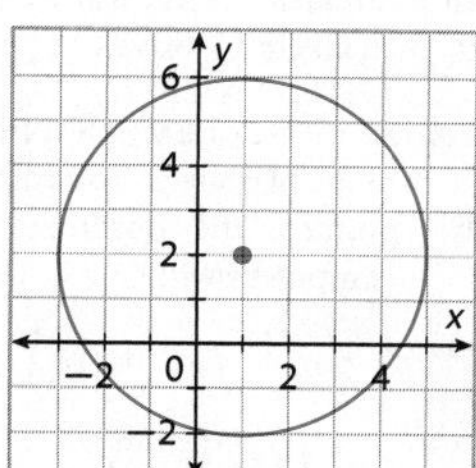

AVOID COMMON ERRORS

Students may forget to factor out the leading coefficients of x^2 and y^2 before completing the square. Reinforce that the coefficient of each squared term must be 1 when completing each square.

VISUAL CUES

Suggest that students circle the numbers being added to or subtracted from x and y, and circle the preceding addition or subtraction signs, to remind them to take the opposites of these numbers when identifying the coordinates of the center of the circle.

INTEGRATE MATHEMATICAL PRACTICES

Focus on Technology

MP.5 Students may ask how to graph a circle on a graphing calculator. Lead them to observe that a circle is not a function, so it cannot be entered on the **Y** = screen as one rule. Use an equation such as $(x+2)^2 + (y-3)^2 = 4$ to show how the equation can be solved for y and entered as two functions: the top half of the circle, $\left(y = 3 + \sqrt{4 - (x+2)^2}\right)$, and the bottom half of the circle, $\left(y = 3 - \sqrt{4 - (x+2)^2}\right)$.

10. $2x^2 + 2y^2 + 20x + 12y + 50 = 0$

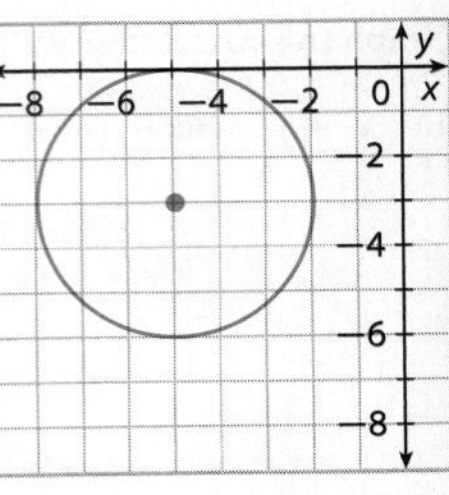

$$2x^2 + 2y^2 + 20x + 12y + 50 = 0$$
$$x^2 + y^2 + 10x + 6y + 25 = 0$$
$$(x^2 + 10x) + (y^2 + 6y) = -25$$
$$(x^2 + 10x + 25) + (y^2 + 6y + 9) = -25 + 25 + 9$$
$$(x+5)^2 + (y+3)^2 = 9$$

The center of the circle is $C(-5, -3)$, and the radius is $r = \sqrt{9} = 3$.

11. $12x^2 + 12y^2 - 96x - 24y + 201 = 0$

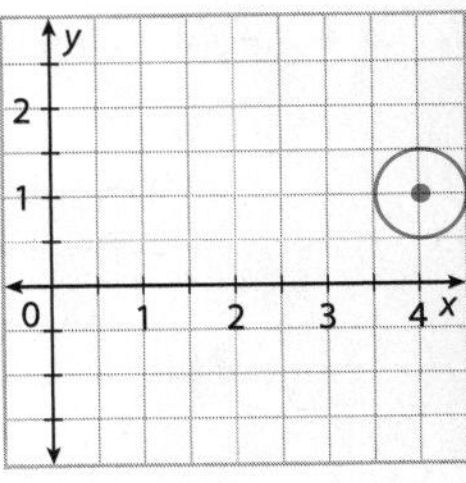

$$12x^2 + 12y^2 - 96x - 24y + 201 = 0$$
$$12(x^2 - 8x) + 12(y^2 - 2y) = -201$$
$$12(x^2 - 8x + 16) + 12(y^2 - 2y + 1) = -201 + 12(16) + 12(1)$$
$$12(x-4)^2 + 12(y-1)^2 = 3$$
$$(x-4)^2 + (y-1)^2 = \frac{1}{4}$$

The center of the circle is $C(4, 1)$, and the radius is $r = \sqrt{\frac{1}{4}} = \frac{1}{2}$.

12. $16x^2 + 16y^2 + 64x - 96y + 199 = 0$

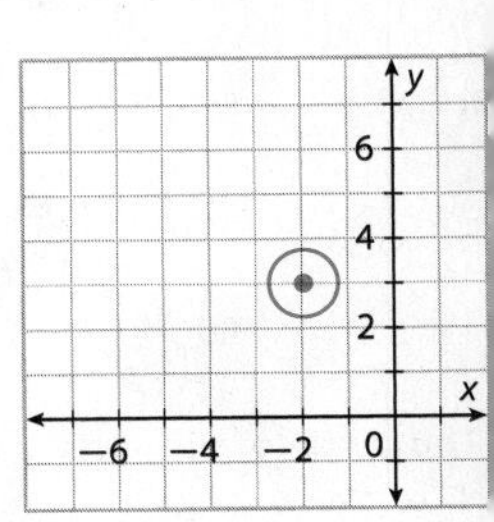

$$16x^2 + 16y^2 + 64x - 96y + 199 = 0$$
$$16(x^2 + 4x) + 16(y^2 - 6y) = -199$$
$$16(x^2 + 4x + 4) + 16(y^2 - 6y + 9) = -199 + 16(4) + 16(9)$$
$$16(x+2)^2 + 16(y-3)^2 = 9$$
$$(x+2)^2 + (y-3)^2 = \frac{9}{16}$$

The center of the circle is $C(-2, 3)$, and the radius is $r = \sqrt{\frac{9}{16}} = \frac{3}{4}$.

In Exercises 13–20, write an inequality representing the problem, and draw a circle to solve the problem.

13. A router for a wireless network on a floor of an office building has a range of 35 feet. The router is located at the point (30, 30). The lettered points in the coordinate diagram represent computers in the office. Which computers will be able to connect to the network through the router?

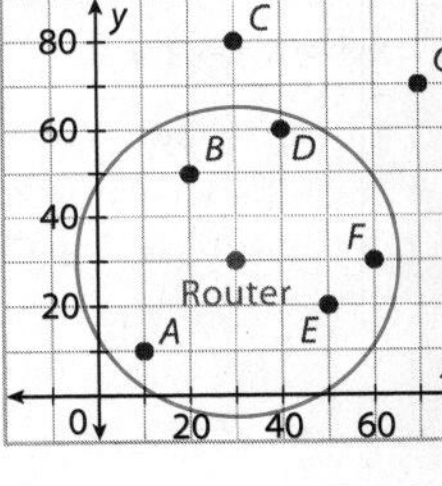

$$(x-30)^2 + (y-30)^2 = 35^2$$
$$(x-30)^2 + (y-30)^2 = 1225$$

The inequality $(x-30)^2 + (y-30)^2 \leq 1225$ represents the situation.

The points on or inside the circle satisfy the inequality. So, the computers located at points *A, B, D, E,* and *F* will be able to connect to the network.

Write an inequality representing the problem, and draw a circle to solve the problem.

14. The epicenter of an earthquake is located at the point $(20, -30)$. The earthquake is felt up to 40 miles away. The labeled points in the coordinate diagram represent towns near the epicenter. In which towns is the earthquake felt?

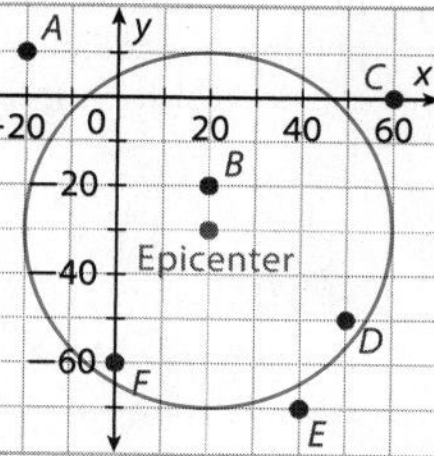

$$(x-20)^2+(y-(-30))^2=40^2$$
$$(x-20)^2+(y+30)^2=1600$$

The inequality $(x-20)^2+(y-30)^2<1600$ represents the situation.

The points inside the circle satisfy the inequality. So, the earthquake is felt in the towns located at points *B*, *D*, and *F*.

15. Aida's cat has disappeared somewhere in her apartment. The last time she saw the cat, it was located at the point $(30, 40)$. Aida knows all of the cat's hiding places, which are indicated by the lettered points in the coordinate diagram. If she searches for the cat within 25 feet of where she last saw it, which hiding places will she check?

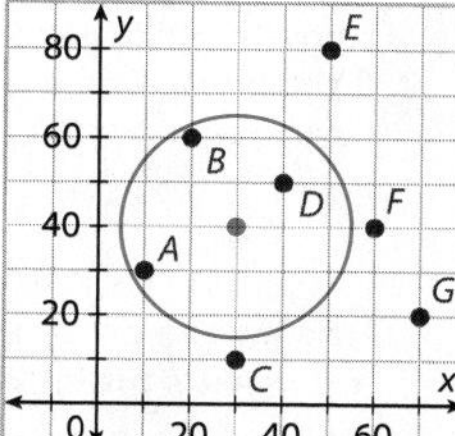

$$(x-30)^2+(y-40)^2=25^2$$
$$(x-30)^2+(y-40)^2=625$$

The inequality $(x-30)^2+(y-40)^2\le 625$ represents the situation.

The points on or inside the circle satisfy the inequality. So, Aida will search for the cat in its hiding places at points *A*, *B*, and *D*.

16. A rock concert is held in a large state park. The concert stage is located at the point $(-2, 2)$, and the music can be heard as far as 4 miles away. The lettered points in the coordinate diagram represent campsites within the park. At which campsites can the music be heard?

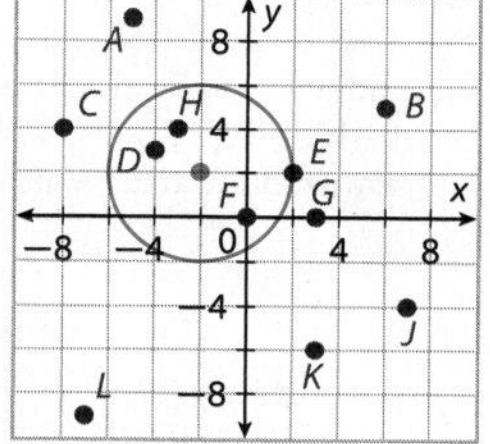

$$(x-(-2))^2+(y-2)^2=4^2$$
$$(x+2)^2+(y-2)^2=16$$

The inequality $(x+2)^2+(y-2)^2\le 16$ represents the situation.

The points on or inside the circle satisfy the inequality. So, the music can be heard at the campsites located at points *D*, *E*, *F* and *H*.

CONNECT VOCABULARY EL

Have students label the parts for the equation of a circle in standard form, identifying the parts that indicate the coordinates of the center and the radius.

17. **Business** When Claire started her in-home computer service and support business, she decided not to accept clients located more than 10 miles from her home. Claire's home is located at the point (5, 0), and the lettered points in the coordinate diagram represent the homes of her prospective clients. Which prospective clients will Claire not accept?

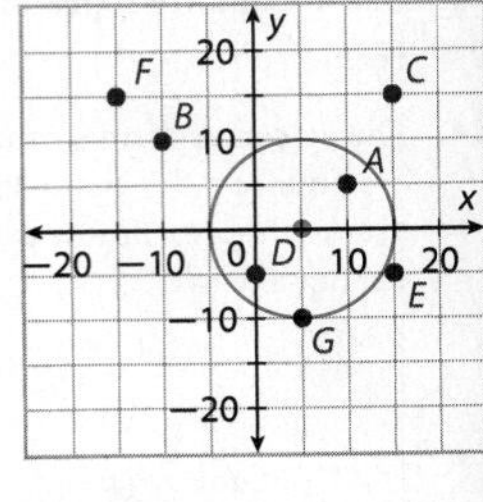

$$(x-5)^2+(y-0)^2=10^2$$
$$(x-5)^2+y^2=100$$

The inequality $(x-5)^2+y^2>100$ represents the situation. The points outside the circle satisfy the inequality. So, Claire should not accept the prospective clients located at points *B*, *C*, *E*, and *F*.

18. **Aviation** An airport's radar system detects airplanes that are in flight within a 60-mile radius of the airport. The airport is located at $(-20, 40)$. The lettered points in the coordinate diagram represent the locations of airplanes currently in flight. Which airplanes does the airport's radar system detect?

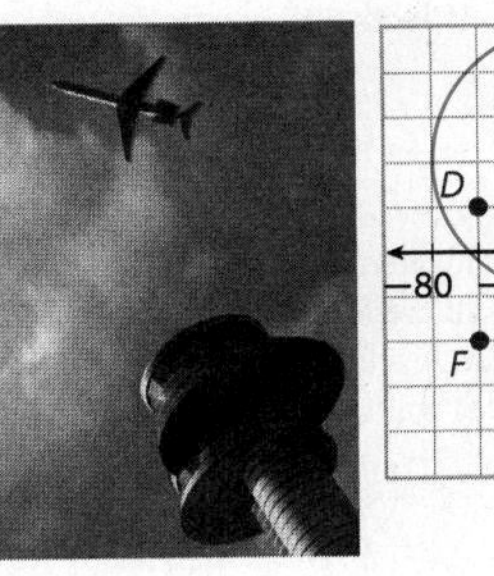

$$(x-(-20))^2+(y-40)^2=60^2$$
$$(x+20)^2+(y-40)^2=3600$$

The inequality $(x+20)^2+(y-40)^2\le 3600$ represents the situation.

The points on or inside the circle satisfy the inequality. So, the airport's radar system detects the airplanes at points *A*, *D*, *G*, and *J*.

19. Due to a radiation leak at a nuclear power plant, the towns within a 30-mile radius are to be evacuated. The nuclear power plant is located at the point $(-10, -10)$. The lettered points in the coordinate diagram represent the towns in the area. Which towns are in the evacuation zone?

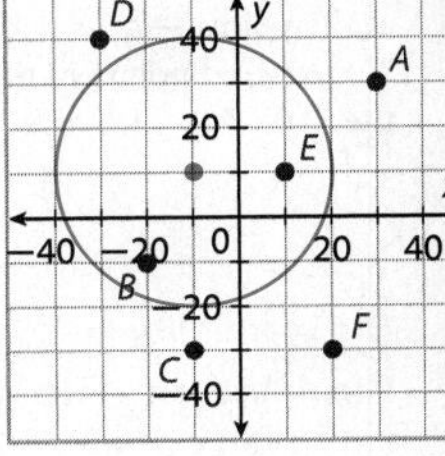

$$(x-(-10))^2+(y-(-10))^2=30^2$$
$$(x+10)^2+(y+10)^2=900$$

The inequality $(x+10)^2+(y+10)^2\le 900$ represents the situation.

The points on or inside the circle satisfy the inequality. So, the towns located at points *B*, *C*, and *E* are in the evacuation zone.

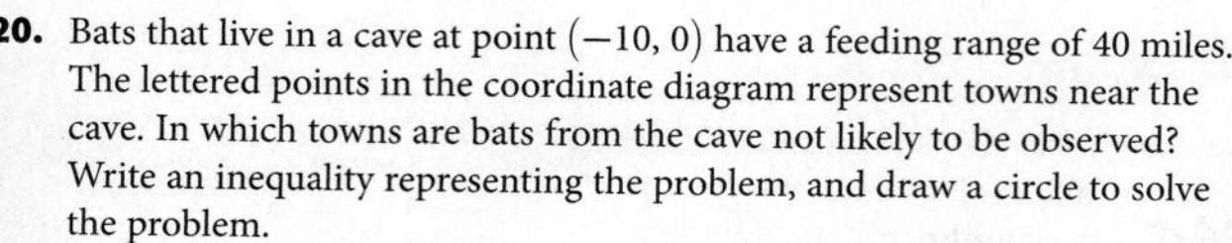

20. Bats that live in a cave at point $(-10, 0)$ have a feeding range of 40 miles. The lettered points in the coordinate diagram represent towns near the cave. In which towns are bats from the cave not likely to be observed? Write an inequality representing the problem, and draw a circle to solve the problem.

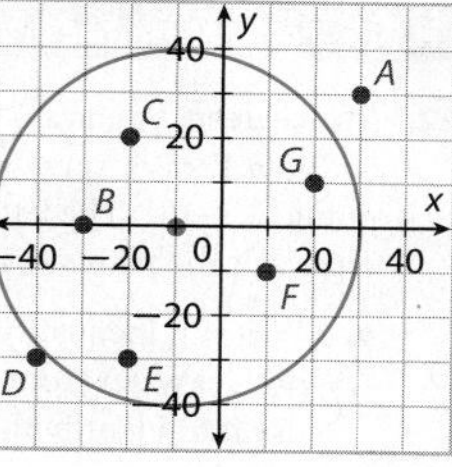

$$(x-(-10))^2+(y-0)^2=40^2$$
$$(x+10)^2+y^2=1600$$

The inequality $(x+10)^2+y^2>1600$ represents the situation.

The points outside the circle satisfy the inequality. So, bats from the cave are not likely to be observed in the towns located at points *A* and *D*.

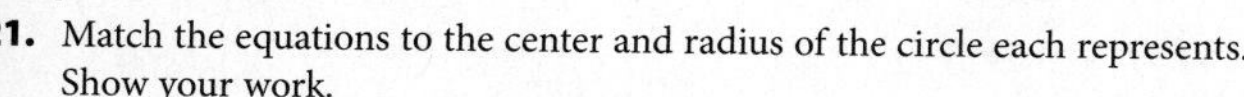

21. Match the equations to the center and radius of the circle each represents. Show your work.

A. $x^2+y^2+18x+22y-23=0$ ______ $C(9,-11);\ r=13$

B. $x^2+y^2-18x+22y+33=0$ ______ $C(9, 11);\ r=15$

C. $25x^2+25y^2-450x-550y-575=0$ ______ $C(-9,-11);\ r=15$

D. $25x^2+25y^2+450x-550y+825=0$ ______ $C(-9, 11);\ r=13$

A

$$x^2+y^2+18x+22y-23=0$$
$$(x^2+18x)+(y^2-22y)=23$$
$$(x^2+18x+81)+(y^2+22y+121)=23+81+121$$
$$(x+9)^2+(y+11)^2=225$$

The center of the circle is $C(-9,-11)$, and the radius is $r=\sqrt{225}=15$.

B

$$x^2+y^2-18x+22y+33=0$$
$$(x^2-18x)+(y^2+22y)=-33$$
$$(x^2-18x+81)+(y^2+22y+121)=-33+81+121$$
$$(x-9)^2+(y+11)^2=169$$

The center of the circle is $C(9,-11)$, and the radius is $r=\sqrt{169}=13$.

C

$$25x^2+25y^2-450x-550y-575=0$$
$$x^2+y^2-18x-22y-23=0$$
$$(x^2-18x)+(y^2-22y)=23$$
$$(x^2-18x+81)+(y^2-22y+121)=23+81+121$$
$$(x-9)^2+(y-11)^2=225$$

The center of the circle is $C(9, 11)$, and the radius is $r=\sqrt{225}=15$.

D

$$25x^2+25y^2+450x-550y+825=0$$
$$x^2+y^2+18x-22y=-33$$
$$(x^2+18x)+(y^2-22y)=-33$$
$$(x^2+18x+81)+(y^2-22y+121)=-33+81+121$$
$$(x+9)^2+(y-11)^2=169$$

The center of the circle is $(-9, 11)$, and the radius is $r=\sqrt{169}=13$.

Answers: B, C, A, D

H.O.T. Focus on Higher Order Thinking

22. Multi-Step A garden sprinkler waters the plants in a garden within a 12-foot spray radius. The sprinkler is located at the point $(5, -10)$. The lettered points in the coordinate diagram represent the plants. Use the diagram for parts a–c.

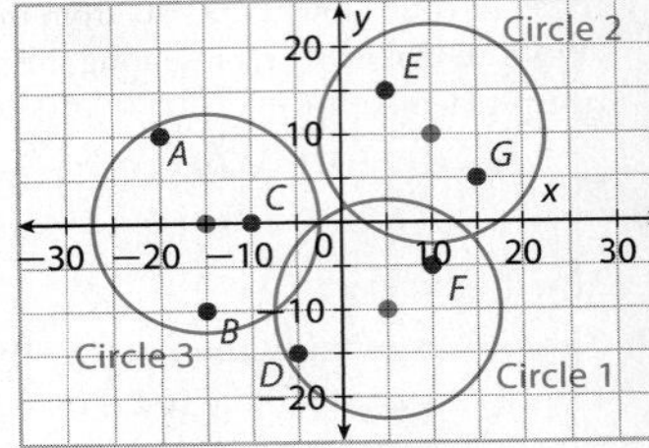

a. Write an inequality that represents the region that does not get water from the sprinkler. Then draw a circle and use it to identify the plants that do not get water from the sprinkler.

$$(x - 5)^2 + (y - (-10))^2 = 12^2$$
$$(x - 5)^2 + (y + 10)^2 = 144$$

The inequality $(x - 5)^2 + (y + 10)^2 > 144$ represents the situation. The points outside the circle satisfy the inequality. So, the plants located at points *A, B, C, E,* and *G* do not get water from the sprinkler.

b. Suppose a second sprinkler with the same spray radius is placed at the point $(10, 10)$. Write a system of inequalities that represents the region that does not get water from either sprinkler. Then draw a second circle and use it to identify the plants that do not get water from either sprinkler.

$$(x - 10)^2 + (y - 10)^2 = 12^2$$
$$(x - 10)^2 + (y - 10)^2 = 144$$

The system of inequalities $(x - 5)^2 + (y + 10)^2 > 144$ and $(x - 10)^2 + (y - 10)^2 > 144$ represents the situation. The points outside both circles satisfy the system of inequalities. So, the plants located at points *A, B,* and *C* would not get water from either sprinkler.

c. Where would you place a third sprinkler with the same spray radius so all the plants get water from a sprinkler? Write a system of inequalities that represents the region that does not get water from any of the sprinklers. Then draw a third circle to show that every plant receives water from a sprinkler.

Locate the sprinkler at the point $(-10, 0)$.

$$(x - (-10))^2 + (y - 0)^2 = 12^2$$
$$(x + 10)^2 + y^2 = 144$$

The system of inequalities $(x - 5)^2 + (y + 10)^2 > 144$ and $(x - 10)^2 + (y - 10)^2 > 144$ and $(x + 10)^2 + y^2 > 144$ represents the situation. The points outside all three circles satisfy the system of inequalities. So, there are no plants that would not get watered by any sprinkler.

23. Represent Real-World Situations The orbit of the planet Venus is nearly circular. An astronomer develops a model for the orbit in which the sun has coordinates $S(0, 0)$, the circular orbit of Venus passes through $V(41, 53)$, and each unit of the coordinate plane represents 1 million miles. Write an equation for the orbit of Venus. How far is Venus from the sun?

Since the center of the orbit is the sun, the radius of the orbit is *SV*.

$$\begin{aligned} r &= SV \\ &= \sqrt{(41-0)^2 + (53-0)^2} \\ &= \sqrt{41^2 + 53^2} \\ &= \sqrt{1681 + 2809} \\ &= \sqrt{4490} \\ &\approx 67 \end{aligned}$$

So, the equation of the orbit is $x^2 + y^2 = 67^2$, or $x^2 + y^2 = 4489$, and Venus is approximately 67 million miles from the sun.

24. Draw Conclusions The *unit circle* is defined as the circle with radius 1 centered at the origin. A *Pythagorean triple* is an ordered triple of three positive integers, (a, b, c), that satisfy the relationship $a^2 + b^2 = c^2$. An example of a Pythagorean triple is (3, 4, 5). In parts a–d, you will draw conclusions about Pythagorean triples.

a. Write the equation of the unit circle.

$$(x-h)^2 + (y-k)^2 = r^2$$
$$(x-0)^2 + (y-0)^2 = 1^2$$
$$x^2 + y^2 = 1$$

b. Use the Pythagorean triple (3, 4, 5) and the symmetry of a circle to identify the coordinates of two points on the part of the unit circle that lies in Quadrant I. Explain your reasoning.

Dividing both sides of $3^2 + 4^2 = 5^2$ by 5^2 gives $\frac{3^2}{5^2} + \frac{4^2}{5^2} = \frac{5^2}{5^2}$, or $\left(\frac{3}{5}\right)^2 + \left(\frac{4}{5}\right)^2 = 1$, so the points $\left(\frac{3}{5}, \frac{4}{5}\right)$ and $\left(\frac{4}{5}, \frac{3}{5}\right)$ are on the unit circle in Quadrant I.

PEER-TO-PEER DISCUSSION

Ask students to discuss with a partner how they can tell by inspecting a circle in the form $ax^2 + by^2 + cx + dy + e = 0$ whether the center of the circle lies on either the x- or y-axis. **The circle lies on the x-axis if $d = 0$. It lies on the y-axis if $c = 0$. It lies on both axes (at the origin) if both $c = 0$ and $d = 0$.**

JOURNAL

Have students describe how they can determine whether a point P lies on a circle if they know the radius of the circle and the coordinates of the center of the circle.

c. Use your answer from part b and the symmetry of a circle to identify the coordinates of six other points on the unit circle. This time, the points should be in Quadrants II, III, and IV.

Reflecting the points $\left(\frac{3}{5}, \frac{4}{5}\right)$ and $\left(\frac{4}{5}, \frac{3}{5}\right)$ across the y-axis gives the points $\left(-\frac{3}{5}, \frac{4}{5}\right)$ and $\left(-\frac{4}{5}, \frac{3}{5}\right)$.

Reflecting the points $\left(\frac{3}{5}, \frac{4}{5}\right)$ and $\left(\frac{4}{5}, \frac{3}{5}\right)$ across the x-axis gives the points $\left(\frac{3}{5}, -\frac{4}{5}\right)$ and $\left(\frac{4}{5}, -\frac{3}{5}\right)$.

Reflecting the points $\left(\frac{3}{5}, \frac{4}{5}\right)$ and $\left(\frac{4}{5}, \frac{3}{5}\right)$ across both axes gives the points $\left(-\frac{3}{5}, -\frac{4}{5}\right)$ and $\left(-\frac{4}{5}, -\frac{3}{5}\right)$.

d. Find a different Pythagorean triple and use it to identify the coordinates of eight points on the unit circle.

Answers will vary. Sample answer: The Pythagorean triple $(5, 12, 13)$ generates these eight points: $\left(\frac{5}{13}, \frac{12}{13}\right)$, $\left(\frac{12}{13}, \frac{5}{13}\right)$, $\left(-\frac{5}{13}, \frac{12}{13}\right)$, $\left(-\frac{12}{13}, \frac{5}{13}\right)$, $\left(\frac{5}{13}, -\frac{12}{13}\right)$, $\left(\frac{12}{13}, -\frac{5}{13}\right)$, $\left(-\frac{5}{13}, -\frac{12}{13}\right)$, and $\left(-\frac{12}{13}, -\frac{5}{13}\right)$.

25. Make a Conjecture In a two-dimensional plane, coordinates are given by ordered pairs of the form (x, y). You can generalize coordinates to three-dimensional space by using ordered pairs of the form (x, y, z) where the coordinate z is used to indicate displacement above or below the xy-plane. Generalize the standard-form equation of a circle to find the general equation of a sphere. Explain your reasoning.

Let the center of the sphere be $C(h, k, j)$, the radius be r, and an arbitrary point on the sphere be $P(x, y, z)$. The plane $z = j$ contains a circular cross section of the sphere and includes the points $C(h, k, j)$ and $P(x, y, j)$, which is the perpendicular projection of $P(x, y, z)$ onto the plane. The radius of the circular cross section is $CP' = \sqrt{(x-h)^2 + (y-k)^2}$. Applying the Pythagorean Theorem to $\triangle CP'P$, which is a right triangle, gives the following:

$$(CP')^2 + (P'P)^2 = (CP)^2$$

$$\left(\sqrt{(x-h)^2 + (y-k)^2}\right)^2 + (z-j)^2 = r^2$$

$$(x-h)^2 + (y-k)^2 + (z-j)^2 = r^2$$

Lesson Performance Task

A highway that runs straight east and west passes 6 miles south of a radio tower. The broadcast range of the station is 10 miles.

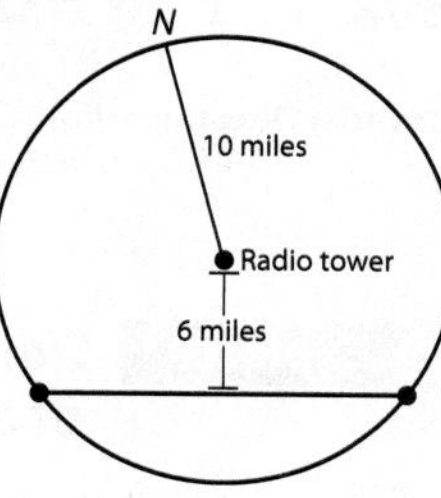

a. Determine the distance along the highway that a car will be within range of the radio station's signal.

b. Given that the car is traveling at a constant speed of 60 miles per hour, determine the amount of time the car is within range of the signal.

a. **The radius of the circle representing the broadcasting range is 10. Let the position of the radio tower be $(0, 0)$. Then the highway passes through $(0, -6)$ and so is represented by the line $y = -6$.**

Write the equation of the circle representing the range of the radio station's signal.

$$(x - 0)^2 + (y - 0)^2 = 10^2$$
$$x^2 + y^2 = 100$$

The highway intersects the circle at points where $y = -6$.

$$x^2 + (-6)^2 = 100$$
$$x^2 + 36 = 100$$
$$x^2 = 64$$
$$x = \pm\sqrt{64}$$
$$x = \pm 8$$

So, the highway intersects the circle at $(8, -6)$ and $(-8, -6)$.

The distance between the intersection points $(8, -6)$ and $(-8, -6)$ is $8 - (-8) = 16$ miles. So, the car will be within range of the radio station's signal for 16 miles.

b. $d = rt$

$$t = \frac{d}{r}$$
$$= \frac{16}{60}$$
$$= \frac{4}{15}$$

So, the car is within range of the signal for $\frac{4}{15}$ hour, or 16 minutes.

EXTENSION ACTIVITY

Have students consider a second highway that runs parallel to the first, 2 miles south of (below) the original highway. Ask how fast a car would need to go along this highway to be in range of the radio signal for the same amount of time as the first car? **The second car would be in range for $2\left(\sqrt{10^2 - 8^2}\right) = 12$ miles. The second car would need to travel $\frac{12}{16}(60) = 45$ miles per hour.**

Students could also research radio signals and ask whether they do have a circular range, and what conditions affect both AM and FM signals, either decreasing signal range (terrain, for example) or allowing a signal to be received a long distance from its source.

QUESTIONING STRATEGIES

? How do you know whether the beginning and ending points for the car are within broadcasting range? **Each point is 6 units vertically below the center point and at the end of a radius 10 units from the center. There are only two such points.**

AVOID COMMON ERRORS

Students who don't write the distance-rate-time formula may not take care in determining the amount of time that the car is within range of the signal, and thus using the reciprocal value, dividing 60 by 16 instead of the reverse. Remind them to structure their calculations and use formulas instead of just operating on numbers.

Scoring Rubric

2 points: Student correctly solves the problem and explains his/her reasoning.

1 point: Student shows good understanding of the problem but does not fully solve or explain his/her reasoning.

0 points: Student does not demonstrate understanding of the problem.

LESSON 4.2

Parabolas

Common Core Math Standards

The student is expected to:

 A-CED.A.2

Create equations in two or more variables to represent relationships between quantities; graph equations on coordinate axes with labels and scales. Also A-CED.A.3, G-GPE.A.2

Mathematical Practices

 MP.7 Using Structure

Language Objective

Explain to a partner what the focus and directrix of a parabola are.

Fill in and label a graphic organizer describing different types of parabolas.

ENGAGE

Essential Question: How is the distance formula connected with deriving equations for both vertical and horizontal parabolas?

Possible answer: When you use the distance formula to describe all the points that are equidistant from a given point and a horizontal line you get the equation of a vertical parabola. Similarly, when you use the distance formula to describe all the points that are equidistant from a given point and a vertical line, you get the equation of a horizontal parabola.

PREVIEW: LESSON PERFORMANCE TASK

View the Engage section online. Discuss the photo and how the shape of a parabola can be used to build a microphone. Then preview the Lesson Performance Task.

Name ______________ Class ______________ Date ______________

4.2 Parabolas

Essential Question: How is the distance formula connected with deriving equations for both vertical and horizontal parabolas?

Resource Locker

Explore Deriving the Standard-Form Equation of a Parabola

A **parabola** is defined as a set of points equidistant from a line (called the **directrix**) and a point (called the **focus**). The focus will always lie on the axis of symmetry, and the directrix will always be perpendicular to the axis of symmetry. This definition can be used to derive the equation for a horizontal parabola opening to the right with its vertex at the origin using the distance formula. (The derivations of parabolas opening in other directions will be covered later.)

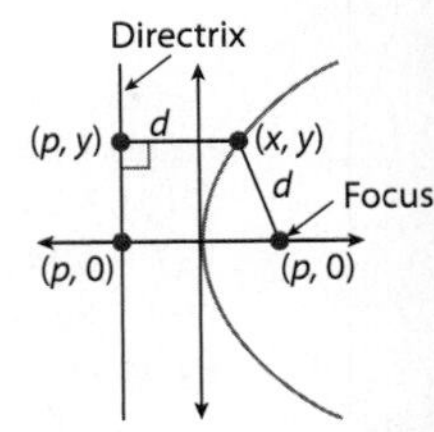

(A) The coordinates for the focus are given by $(p, 0)$.

(B) Write down the expression for the distance from a point (x, y) to the coordinates of the focus:

$$d = \sqrt{(x - p)^2 + (y - 0)^2}$$

(C) The distance from a point to a line is measured by drawing a perpendicular line segment from the point to the line. Find the point where a horizontal line from (x, y) intersects the directrix (defined by the line $x = -p$ for a parabola with its vertex on the origin).

$(-p, y)$

(D) Write down the expression for the distance from a point, (x, y) to the point from Step C:

$$d = \sqrt{(x - -p)^2 + (y - y)^2}$$

(E) Setting the two distances the same and simplifying gives.

$$\sqrt{(x-p)^2 + y^2} = \sqrt{(x+p)^2}$$

To continue solving the problem, square both sides of the equation and evaluate the squared binomials.

$$1\,x^2 + -2\,xp + 1\,p^2 + y^2 = 1\,x^2 + 2\,xp + 1\,p^2$$

(F) Collect terms.

$$0\,x^2 + -4\,px + 0\,p^2 + y^2 = 0$$

(G) Finally, simplify and arrange the equation into the **standard form for a horizontal parabola** (with vertex at (0, 0)):

$$y^2 = 4px$$

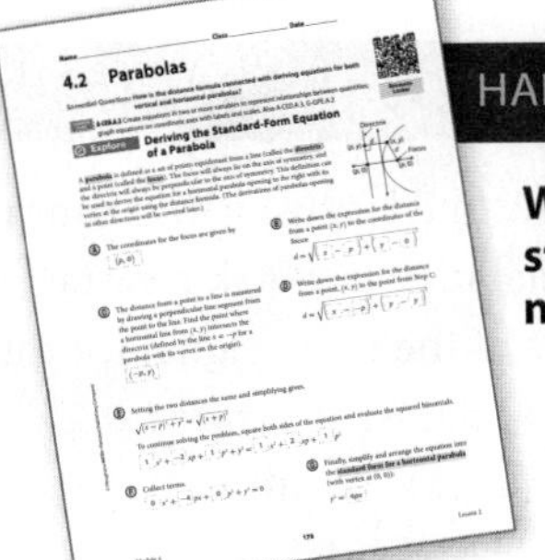

HARDCOVER PAGES 175–188

Watch for the hardcover student edition page numbers for this lesson.

Reflect

1. Why was the directrix placed on the line $x = -p$?
The directrix had to be as far from the vertex (at the origin) as the focus, but on the opposite side. So if the focus is at $(p, 0)$, the directrix has to intersect the x-axis at $(-p, 0)$. The line $x = -p$ is perpendicular to the axis of symmetry (the line connecting the focus and the origin) and contains the point $(-p, 0)$.

2. **Discussion** How can the result be generalized to arrive at the standard form for a horizontal parabola with a vertex at (h, k):
$(y - k)^2 = 4p(x - h)$?
A parabola with a vertex at (h, k) can be described by a horizontal shift of h to the right and a vertical shift of k upward, which can be achieved for any graph by substituting $(y - k)$ for y and $(x - h)$ for x.

Explain 1 Writing the Equation of a Parabola with Vertex at (0, 0)

The equation for a horizontal parabola with vertex at $(0, 0)$ is written in the standard form as $y^2 = 4px$. It has a vertical directrix along the line $x = -p$, a horizontal axis of symmetry along the line $y = 0$, and a focus at the point $(p, 0)$. The parabola opens toward the focus, whether it is on the right or left of the origin $(p > 0$ or $p < 0)$. Vertical parabolas are similar, but with horizontal directrices and vertical axes of symmetry:

Parabolas with Vertices at the Origin		
	Vertical	Horizontal
Equation in standard form	$x^2 = 4py$	$y^2 = 4px$
$p > 0$	Opens upward	Opens rightward
$p < 0$	Opens downward	Opens leftward
Focus	$(0, p)$	$(p, 0)$
Directrix	$y = -p$	$x = -p$
Axis of Symmetry	$x = 0$	$y = 0$

PROFESSIONAL DEVELOPMENT

Integrate Mathematical Practices

This lesson provides an opportunity to address Mathematical Practice **MP.7**, which calls for students to "look for and make use of structure." Students learn the relationships between quadratic equations and their graphs. Students learn that equations in the forms $(y - k)^2 = 4p(x - h)$ and $(x - h)^2 = 4p(y - k)$ have vertices (h, k), focus at either $(h + p, k)$ or $(h, k + p)$, and have the directrix $y = k - p$ or $x = h - p$.

EXPLORE

Deriving the Standard Form Equation of a Parabola

INTEGRATE MATHEMATICAL PRACTICES

Focus on Patterns

MP.8 Explain that if the equation of a parabola contains an x^2 term the parabola opens either up or down, while an equation that contains a y^2 term opens either right or left.

EXPLAIN 1

Writing the Equation of a Parabola with Vertex at (0, 0)

INTEGRATE MATHEMATICAL PRACTICES

Focus on Math Connections

MP.1 Explain that for an equation in the form $y = \frac{1}{4p}x^2$, the graph opens upward if $\frac{1}{4p}$ is positive and downward if $\frac{1}{4p}$ is negative. For an equation in the form $x = \frac{1}{4p}y^2$, the graph opens to the right if $\frac{1}{4p}$ is positive and to the left if $\frac{1}{4p}$ is negative.

QUESTIONING STRATEGIES

How can you find the directrix of a parabola with an equation in the form $y = \frac{1}{4p}x^2$ or $x = \frac{1}{4p}y^2$? **The directrix is p units from vertex. Remember that the parabola opens away from the directrix.**

Example 1 **Find the equation of the parabola from the description of the focus and directrix. Then make a sketch showing the parabola, the focus, and the directrix.**

Ⓐ Focus $(-8, 0)$, directrix $x = 8$

A vertical directrix means a horizontal parabola.

Confirm that the vertex is at $(0, 0)$:

a. The y-coordinate of the vertex is the same as the focus: 0.

b. The x-coordinate is halfway between the focus (-8) and the directrix $(+8)$: 0.

c. The vertex is at $(0, 0)$.

Use the expression for a horizontal parabola, $y^2 = 4px$, and replace p with the x coordinate of the focus: $y^2 = 4(-8)x$

Simplify: $y^2 = -32x$

Plot the focus and directrix and sketch the parabola.

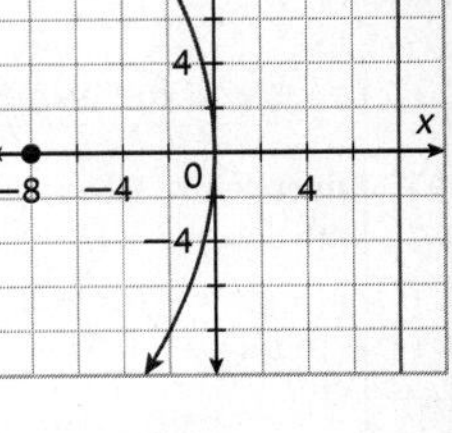

Ⓑ Focus $(0, -2)$, directrix $y = 2$

A vertical | horizontal directrix means a vertical | horizontal parabola.

Confirm that the vertex is at $(0, 0)$:

a. The x-coordinate of the vertex is the same as the focus: 0.

b. The y-coordinate is halfway between the focus, -2 and the directrix, 2 : 0

c. The vertex is at $(0, 0)$.

Use the expression for a vertical parabola, $x^2 = 4py$, and replace p with the x coordinate of the focus: $x^2 = 4 \cdot -2 \cdot y$

Simplify: $x^2 = -8y$

Plot the focus, the directrix, and the parabola.

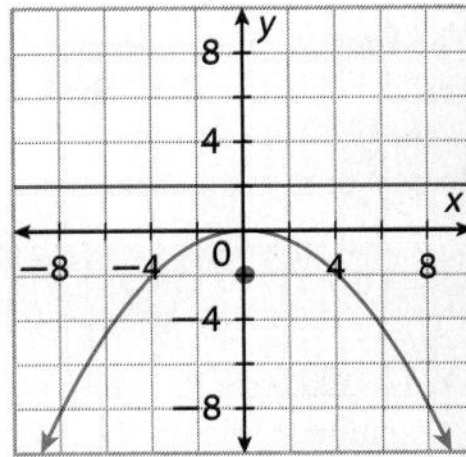

Your Turn

Find the equation of the parabola from the description of the focus and directrix. Then make a sketch showing the parabola, the focus, and the directrix.

3. Focus $(2, 0)$, directrix $x = -2$

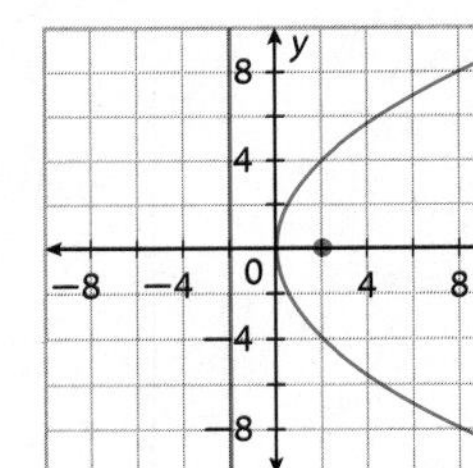

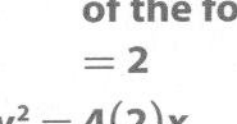

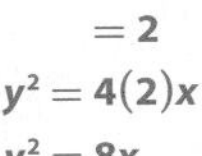

$p =$ **x-coordinate of the focus** $= 2$

$y^2 = 4(2)x$

$y^2 = 8x$

4. Focus $\left(0, -\frac{1}{2}\right)$, directrix $y = \frac{1}{2}$

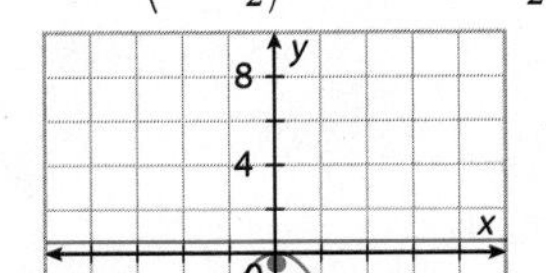

$p =$ **y-coordinate of the focus** $= \left(-\frac{1}{2}\right)$

$x^2 = 4\left(-\frac{1}{2}\right)y$

$x^2 = -2y$

COLLABORATIVE LEARNING

Peer-to-Peer Activity

Have students work in pairs. Instruct each student to create a design using graphs of parabolas. Students exchange designs and write the equations for the parabolas in the partner's design, including the domain and range of each curve.

Explain 2 Writing the Equation of a Parabola with Vertex at (h, k)

The standard equation for a parabola with a vertex (h, k) can be found by translating from $(0, 0)$ to (h, k): substitute $(x - h)$ for x and $(y - k)$ for y. This also translates the focus and directrix each by the same amount.

Parabolas with Vertex (h, k)		
	Vertical	Horizontal
Equation in standard form	$(x-h)^2 = 4p(y-k)$	$(y-k)^2 = 4p(x-h)$
$p > 0$	Opens upward	Opens rightward
$p < 0$	Opens downward	Opens leftward
Focus	$(h, k+p)$	$(h+p, k)$
Directrix	$y = k - p$	$x = h - p$
Axis of Symmetry	$x = h$	$y = k$

p is found halfway from the directrix to the focus:

- For vertical parabolas: $p = \dfrac{(y \text{ value of focus}) - (y \text{ value of directrix})}{2}$
- For horizontal parabolas: $p = \dfrac{(x \text{ value of focus}) - (x \text{ value of directrix})}{2}$

The vertex can be found from the focus by relating the coordinates of the focus to h, k, and p.

Example 2 **Find the equation of the parabola from the description of the focus and directrix. Then make a sketch showing the parabola, the focus, and the directrix.**

(A) Focus $(3, 2)$, directrix $y = 0$

A horizontal directrix means a vertical parabola.

$p = \dfrac{(y \text{ value of focus}) - (y \text{ value of directrix})}{2} = \dfrac{2-0}{2} = 1$

$h =$ the x-coordinate of the focus $= 3$

Solve for k: The y-value of the focus is $k + p$, so

$k + p = 2$

$k + 1 = 2$

$k = 1$

Write the equation: $(x - 3)^2 = 4(y - 1)$

Plot the focus, the directrix, and the parabola.

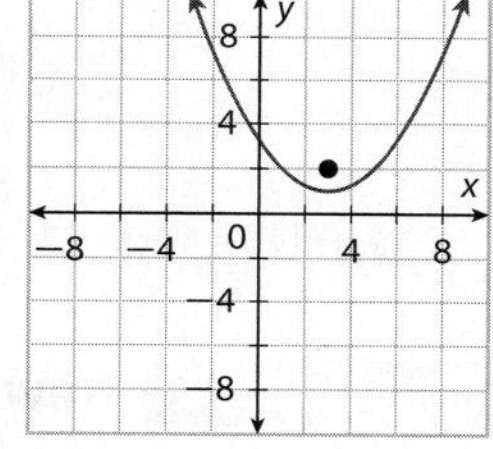

DIFFERENTIATE INSTRUCTION

Modeling

Students can write equations which model parabolic shapes that exist in the real world. These include bridges, arcs, and the paths traced in projectile motion.

Critical Thinking

Have students explain how to tell if the graph of a quadratic equation in standard form is a circle or parabola.

EXPLAIN 2

Writing the Equation of a Parabola with Vertex at *(h, k)*

INTEGRATE MATHEMATICAL PRACTICES

Focus on Critical Thinking

MP.3 The focus of a parabola can be found by using the formulas $(h + p, k)$ and $(h, k + p)$. Alternatively, students can graph the vertex, find the focus by determining the opening direction of the parabola, then count p units in the appropriate direction.

QUESTIONING STRATEGIES

Given values of h, k, and p, describe the similarities and differences between the graph of a parabola with an equation in the form $(y - k)^2 = 4p(x - h)$ and an equation in the form $(x - h)^2 = 4p(y - k)$. Similarities: Both graphs have a vertex at (h, k) and the distance to the focus is the same. Differences: The graph of the equation in the form $(y - k)^2 = 4p(x - h)$ opens to either the left or the right, while the graph of the equation in the form $(x - h)^2 = 4p(y - k)$ opens either upward or downward.

CONNECT VOCABULARY EL

Help students to understand the meanings of *focus*, *directrix*, and *axis of symmetry* by labeling these on the graph of a parabola.

EXPLAIN 3

Rewriting the Equation of a Parabola to Graph the Parabola

INTEGRATE TECHNOLOGY

Students can solve equations of parabolas for y and graph the corresponding function(s) on their graphing calculators. If the equation is for a parabola that opens left or right, the parabola needs to be graphed using two functions.

AVOID COMMON ERRORS

Some students may include both positive and negative values of $4p(x - h)$ when taking the square root of both sides of an equation in the form $(y - k)^2 = 4p(x - h)$. Remind them that when equations of this form are solved for y, the resulting equation should be in the form $y = \pm\sqrt{4p(x - h)} + k$.

Ⓑ Focus $(-1, -1)$, directrix $x = 5$

A vertical directrix means a **horizontal** parabola.

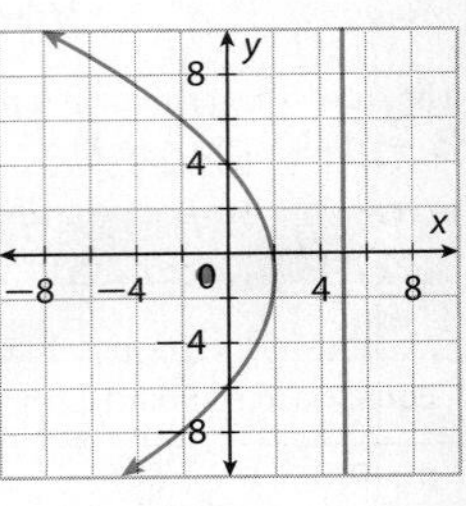

$p = \frac{(x \text{ value of focus}) - (x \text{ value of directrix})}{2} = \frac{-1 - 5}{2} = -3$

$k =$ the y-coordinate of the focus $= -1$

Solve for h: The x-value of the focus is $h + p$, so

$h + p = -1$

$h + (-3) = -1$

$h = 2$

Write the equation: $(y + 1)^2 = -12(x - 2)$

Your Turn

Find the equation of the parabola from the description of the focus and directrix. Then make a sketch showing the parabola, the focus, and the directrix.

5. Focus $(5, -1)$, directrix $x = -3$

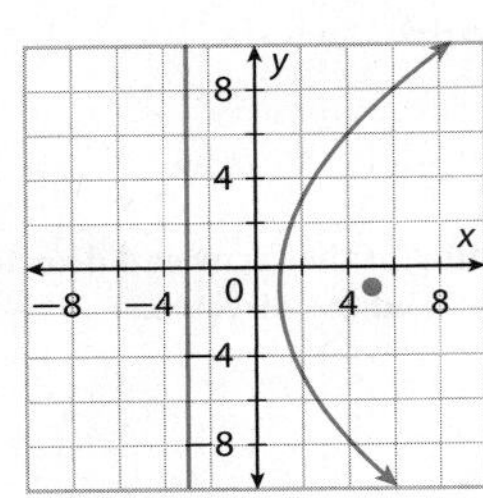

$p = \frac{5 - (-3)}{2} = 4$

$k = -1$

$h + p = h + (4) = 5 \rightarrow h = 1$

$(y + 1)^2 = 16(x - 1)$

6. Focus $(-2, 0)$, directrix $y = 4$

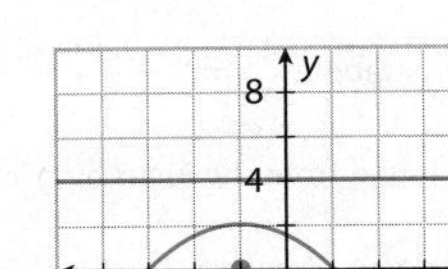

$p = \frac{0 - 4}{2} = -2$

$h = -2$

$k + p = k + (-2) = 0 \rightarrow k = 2$

$(x + 2)^2 = -8(y - 2)$

Explain 3 Rewriting the Equation of a Parabola to Graph the Parabola

A **second-degree equation in two variables** is an equation constructed by adding terms in two variables with powers no higher than 2. The general form looks like this:

$ax^2 + by^2 + cx + dy + e = 0$

Expanding the standard form of a parabola and grouping like terms results in a second-degree equation with either $a = 0$ or $b = 0$, depending on whether the parabola is vertical or horizontal. To graph an equation in this form requires the opposite conversion, accomplished by completing the square of the squared variable.

LANGUAGE SUPPORT EL

Connect Vocabulary

Have students work in pairs to fill in a graphic organizer. Write the word *parabola* in a circle in the middle of a sheet of paper. Fold the paper in fourths. Write *opens upward* in one corner of the paper, *opens downward* in another corner, *opens to the right* and *opens to the left* in the remaining corners. Have the students work together to sketch a parabola and write an equation for each kind of graph.

Example 3 **Convert the equation to the standard form of a parabola and graph the parabola, the focus, and the directrix.**

A $x^2 - 4x - 4y + 12 = 0$

Isolate the x terms and complete the square on x.

Isolate the x terms.	$x^2 - 4x = 4y - 12$
Add $\left(\frac{-4}{2}\right)^2$ to both sides.	$x^2 - 4x + 4 = 4y - 8$
Factor the perfect square trinomial on the left side.	$(x - 2)^2 = 4y - 8$
Factor out 4 from the right side.	$(x - 2)^2 = 4(y - 2)$

This is the standard form for a vertical parabola. Now find p, h, and k from the standard form in order to graph the parabola, focus, and directrix.

$4p = 4$	Vertex $= (2, 2)$
$p = 1$	Focus $= (2, k + p) = (2, 3)$
$h = 2$	Directrix:
$k = 2$	$y = k - p$
	$y = 1$

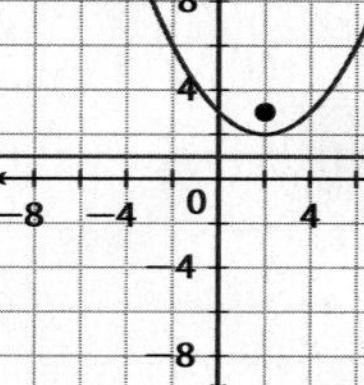

B $y^2 + 2x + 8y + 18 = 0$

Isolate the y terms.	$y^2 + 8y = -2x - 18$
Add $\left(\frac{8}{2}\right)^2$ to both sides.	$y^2 + 8y + 16 = -2x - 2$
Factor the perfect square trinomial.	$(y + 4)^2 = -2x - 2$
Factor out -2 on the right.	$(y + 4)^2 = -2(x + 1)$

Identify features to graph:

$p = -\frac{1}{2}$, $h = -1$, $k = -4$

Vertex $= (-1, -4)$

Focus $= \left(-\frac{3}{2}, -4\right)$

Directrix: $x = -\frac{1}{2}$

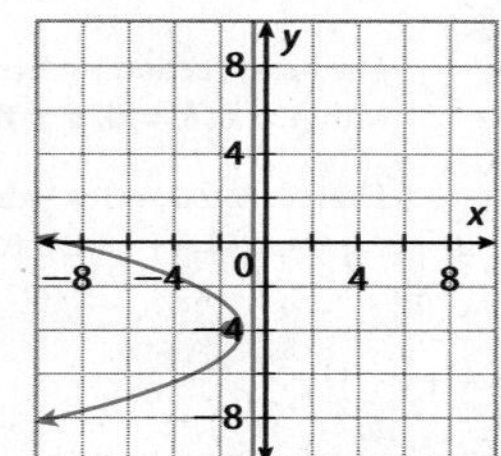

QUESTIONING STRATEGIES

? How would you solve an equation in the form $(x - h)^2 = 4p(y - k)$ for y in order to graph the equation on your graphing calculator? **Divide both sides of the equation by $4p$ and then add k to both sides of the equation.**

EXPLAIN 4

Solving a Real-World Problem

CONNECT VOCABULARY EL

Remind students that placing constraints on the values of x is equivalent to restricting the domain. Similarly, placing constraints on the values of y is equivalent to restricting the range.

Your Turn

Convert the equation to the standard form of a parabola and graph the parabola, the focus, and the directrix.

7. $y^2 - 12x - 4y + 64 = 0$

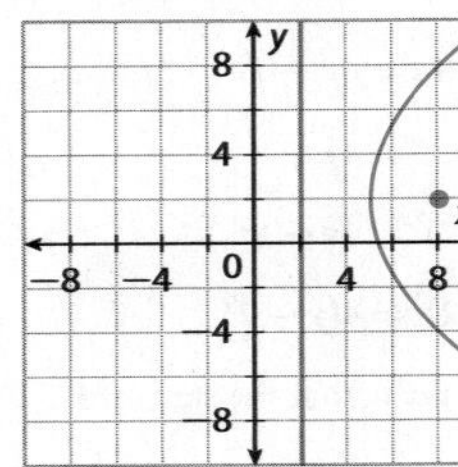

$$y^2 - 4y = 12x - 64$$
$$y^2 - 4y + 4 = 12x - 64 + 4$$
$$(y - 2)^2 = 12x - 60$$
$$(y - 2)^2 = 12(x - 5)$$

Vertex $= (5, 2)$, Focus $= (8, 2)$, Directrix: $x = 2$

8. $x^2 + 8x - 16y - 48 = 0$

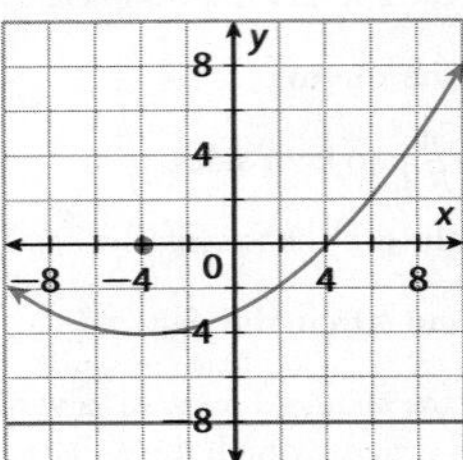

$$x^2 + 8x = 16y + 48$$
$$x^2 + 8x + 16 = 16y + 48 + 16$$
$$(x + 4)^2 = 16y + 64$$
$$(x + 4)^2 = 16(y + 4)$$

Vertex $= (-4, -4)$, Focus $= (-4, 0)$, Directrix: $y = -8$

 Explain 4 Solving a Real-World Problem

Parabolic shapes occur in a variety of applications in science and engineering that take advantage of the concentrating property of reflections from the parabolic surface at the focus.

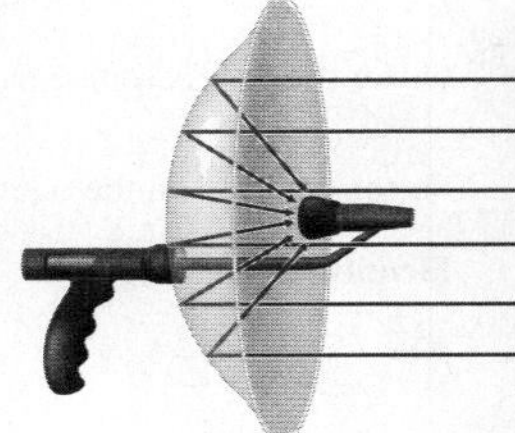

(A) Parabolic microphones are so-named because they use a parabolic dish to bounce sound waves toward a microphone placed at the focus of the parabola in order to increase sensitivity. The dish below has a cross section dictated by the equation $x = 32y^2$ where x and y are in inches. How far from the center of the dish should the microphone be placed?

The cross section matches the standard form of a horizontal parabola with $h = 0, k = 0, p = 8$.

Therefore the vertex, which is the center of the dish, is at $(0, 0)$ and the focus is at $(8, 0)$, 8 inches away.

Ⓑ A reflective telescope uses a parabolic mirror to focus light rays before creating an image with the eyepiece. If the focal length (the distance from the bottom of the mirror's bowl to the focus) is 140 mm and the mirror has a 70 mm diameter (width), what is the depth of the bowl of the mirror?

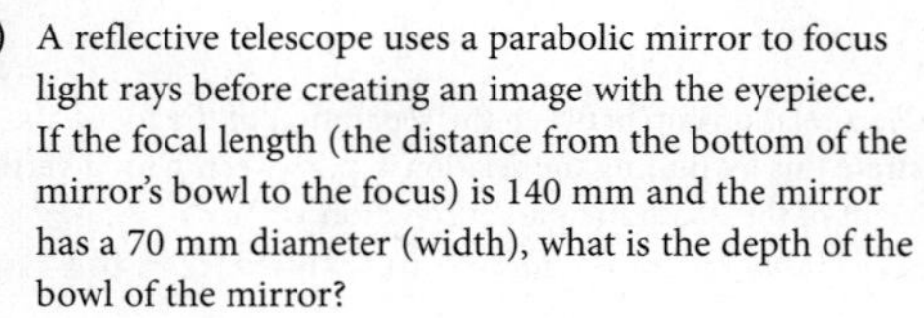

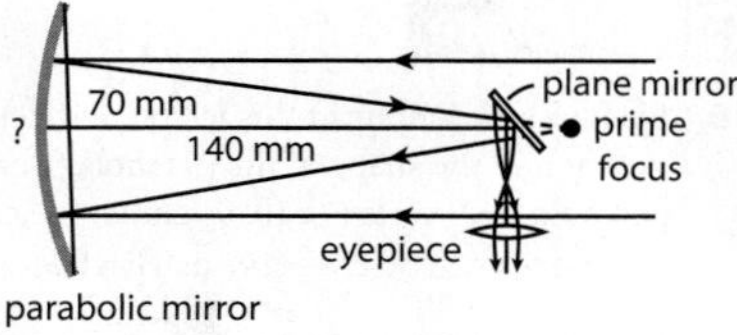

The distance from the bottom of the mirror's bowl to the focus is p. The vertex location is not specified (or needed), so use $(0, 0)$ for simplicity. The equation for the mirror is a horizontal parabola (with x the distance along the telescope and y the position out from the center).

$$\left(y - \boxed{0}\right)^2 = 4p\left(x - \boxed{0}\right)$$

$$y^2 = \boxed{560}\,x$$

Since the diameter of the bowl of the mirror is 70 mm, the points at the rim of the mirror have y-values of 35 mm and −35 mm. The x-value of either point will be the same as the x-value of the point directly above the bottom of the bowl, which equals the depth of the bowl. Since the points on the rim lie on the parabola, use the equation of the parabola to solve for the x-value of either edge of the mirror.

$$\boxed{35}^2 = \boxed{560}\,x$$

$$x \approx \boxed{2.19}\text{ mm}$$

The bowl is approximately 2.19 mm deep.

Your Turn

9. A football team needs one more field goal to win the game. The goalpost that the ball must clear is 10 feet (~3.3 yd) off the ground. The path of the football after it is kicked for a 35-yard field goal is given by the equation $y - 11 = -0.0125\,(x - 20)^2$, in yards. Does the team win?

$y - 11 = -0.0125(35 - 20)^2$

$y = 8.1875$

Since 8.1875 is greater than 3.3, the ball goes over the goalpost and the team wins the game.

ELABORATE

INTEGRATE MATHEMATICAL PRACTICES

Focus on Math Connections

MP.1 Explain that there are alternate forms for the equations of parabolas. Parabolas with vertices at the origin may be written in the forms $y = ax^2$ (for vertical parabolas) and $x = ay^2$ (for horizontal parabolas). Parabolas with vertices at points other than the origin may be written in the forms $(y-k)^2 = 4p(x-h)$ (vertical parabolas) and $(x-h)^2 = 4p(y-k)$ (horizontal parabolas). In these forms, $a = \frac{1}{4p}$.

SUMMARIZE THE LESSON

Explain how a parabola can be graphed given its equation. **Use the equation to graph the vertex of the parabola. Then find the value of p and determine the direction in which the parabola opens. Graph the focus and directrix accordingly. Substitute an x-value to find a point on the parabola. Graph the reflection of the point over the axis of symmetry. Then complete the graph.**

Elaborate

10. Examine the graphs in this lesson and determine a relationship between the separation of the focus and the vertex, and the shape of the parabola. Demonstrate this by finding the relationship between p for a vertical parabola with vertex of $(0, 0)$ and a, the coefficient of the quadratic parent function $y = ax^2$.

The parabola gets wider as the focus moves away from the vertex. To convert from the standard form of a parabola to the standard form of a quadratic, isolate y:

$x^2 = 4py$

$y = \frac{1}{4p}x^2 = ax^2$

$\Rightarrow a = \frac{1}{4p}$

11. Essential Question Check-In How is the distance formula used to go from the definition of a parabola based on focus and directrix to an equation that relates x and y?

Write the expressions for the distance from a point on the parabola to each of the focus and the directrix. Then equate the two distances per the definition of a parabola.

Evaluate: Homework and Practice

- Online Homework
- Hints and Help
- Extra Practice

Find the equation of the parabola with vertex at $(0, 0)$ from the description of the focus and directrix and plot the parabola, the focus, and the directrix.

1. Focus at $(3, 0)$, directrix: $x = -3$

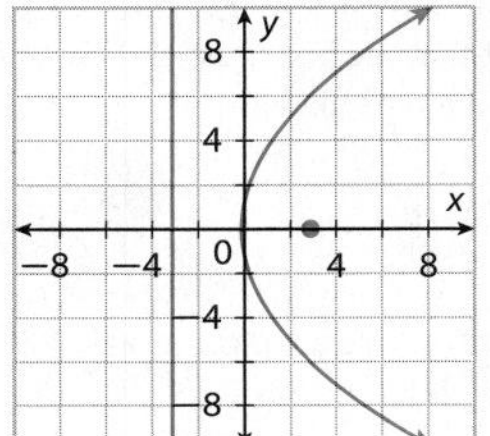

$y^2 = 4px$
$y^2 = 4(3)x$
$y^2 = 12x$

2. Focus at $(0, -5)$, directrix: $y = 5$

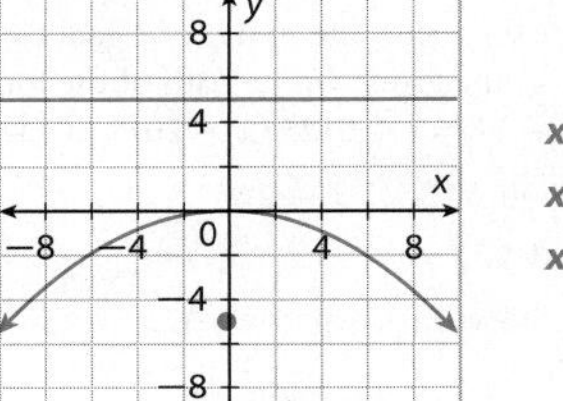

$x^2 = 4py$
$x^2 = 4(5)y$
$x^2 = 20y$

3. Focus at $(-1, 0)$, directrix: $x = 1$

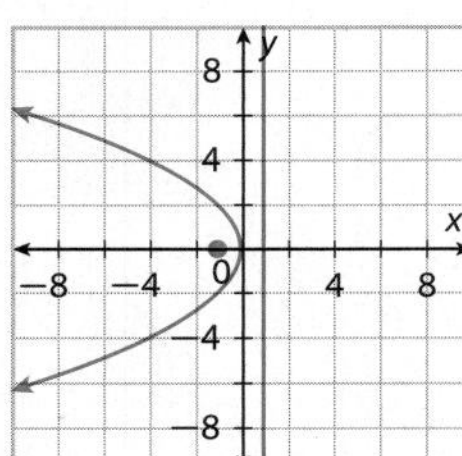

$y^2 = 4px$
$y^2 = 4(-1)x$
$y^2 = -4x$

4. Focus at $(0, 2)$, directrix: $y = -2$

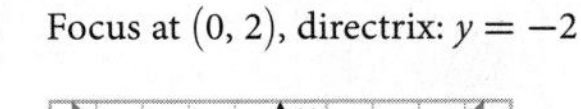

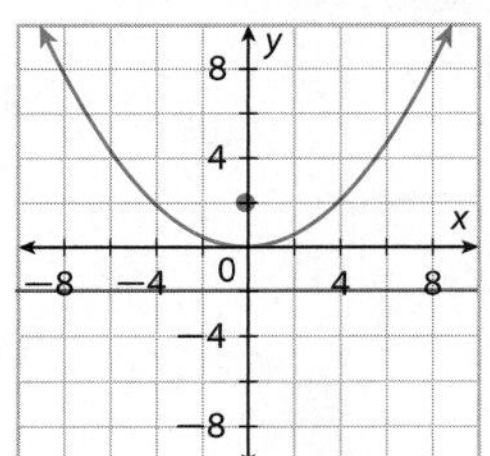

$x^2 = 4py$
$x^2 = 4(2)y$
$x^2 = 8y$

Find the equation of the parabola with the given information.

5. Vertex: $(-3, 6)$; Directrix: $x = -2.25$

$(y-k)^2 = 4p(x-h)$
$(y-6)^2 = 4(-1.25)(x+3)$
$(y-6)^2 = -5(x+3)$

6. Vertex: $(6, 20)$; Focus: $(6, -11)$

$(x-h)^2 = 4p(y-k)$
$(x-6)^2 = 4(-9)(y-20)$
$(x-6)^2 = -36(y-20)$

Find the equation of the parabola with vertex at (h, k) from the description of the focus and directrix and plot the parabola, the focus, and the directrix.

7. Focus at $(5, 3)$, directrix: $y = 7$

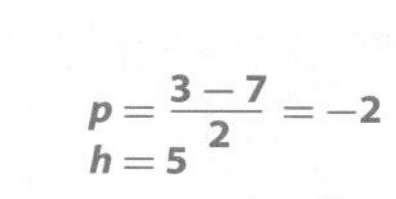

$p = \frac{3-7}{2} = -2$
$h = 5$
$k + p = k + (-2) = 3$
$k = 5$
$(x-5)^2 = -8(y-5)$

8. Focus at $(-3, 3)$, directrix: $x = 3$

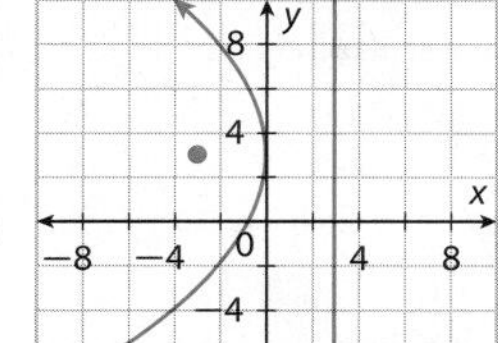

$p = \frac{-3-3}{2} = -3$
$k = 3$
$h + p = h + (-3) = -3$
$h = 0$
$(y-3)^2 = -12x$

Convert the equation to the standard form of a parabola and graph the parabola, the focus, and the directrix.

9. $y^2 - 20x - 6y - 51 = 0$

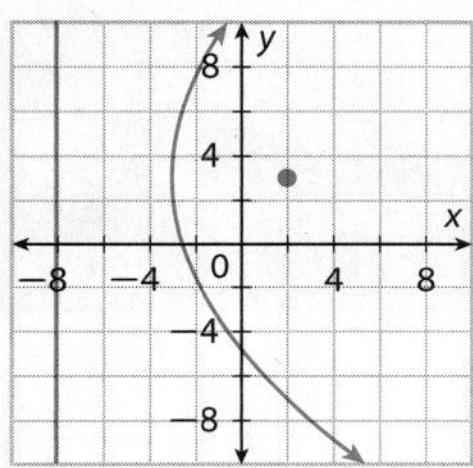

$y^2 - 6y = 20x + 51$
$y^2 - 6y + 9 = 20x + 51 + 9$
$(y-3)^2 = 20x + 60$
$(y-3)^2 = 20(x+3)$
Vertex $= (-3, 3)$, Focus $= (2, 3)$,
Directrix : $x = -8$

10. $x^2 - 14x - 12y + 73 = 0$

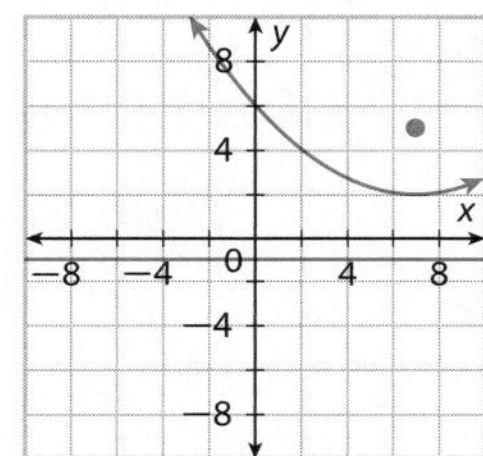

$x^2 - 14x = 12y - 73$
$x^2 - 14x + 49 = 12y - 73 + 49$
$(x-7)^2 = 12y - 24$
$(x-7)^2 = 12(y-2)$
Vertex $= (7, 2)$, Focus $= (7, 5)$,
Directrix : $x = -1$

11. Communications The equation for the cross section of a parabolic satellite television dish is $y = \frac{1}{50}x^2$, measured in inches. How far is the focus from the vertex of the cross section?

$y = \frac{1}{50}x^2 = \frac{1}{4 \cdot 12.5}x^2$
The focus is 12.5 in. from the vertex of the cross section.

Exercise	Depth of Knowledge (D.O.K.)	COMMON CORE Mathematical Practices
1–4	**1** Recall of Information	**MP.6** Precision
5–6	**1** Recall of Information	**MP.2** Reasoning
7–8	**1** Recall of Information	**MP.6** Precision
9–10	**2** Skills/Concepts	**MP.6** Precision
11–14	**2** Skills/Concepts	**MP.4** Modeling
15	**2** Skills/Concepts	**MP.6** Precision

EVALUATE

ASSIGNMENT GUIDE

Concepts and Skills	Practice
Explore Deriving the Standard Form Equation of a Parabola	Exercises 16–17
Example 1 Writing the Equation of a Parabola with Vertex at (0, 0)	Exercises 1–4
Example 2 Writing the Equation of a Parabola with Vertex at (h, k)	Exercises 5–8, 15
Example 3 Rewriting the Equation of a Parabola to Graph the Parabola	Exercises 9–10
Example 4 Solving a Real-World Problem	Exercises 11–14

INTEGRATE MATHEMATICAL PRACTICES

Focus on Reasoning

MP.2 Students can check that their parabolas have the correct widths by verifying that the distance across the parabola at the focus equals $4p$.

AVOID COMMON ERRORS

Some students may confuse the equations of horizontal and vertical parabolas. It may help them to make a chart listing the general equations for both horizontal and vertical parabolas.

12. Engineering The equation for the cross section of a spotlight is $y + 5 = \frac{1}{12}x^2$, measured in inches. Where is the bulb located with respect to the vertex of the cross section?

$y + 5 = \frac{1}{12}x^2$

$y + 5 = \frac{1}{4 \cdot 3}x^2$

The bulb is 3 in. from the vertex of the cross section.

13. When a ball is thrown into the air, the path that the ball travels is modeled by the parabola $y - 7 = -0.0175(x - 20)^2$, measured in feet. What is the maximum height the ball reaches? How far does the ball travel before it hits the ground?

The vertex of the parabola is (20, 7), so the maximum height of the ball is 7 feet.

$0 - 7 = -0.0175\,(x - 20)^2$

$\pm 20 = x - 20$

$x = 0, 40$

The ball travels 40 feet before it hits the ground.

14. A cable for a suspension bridge is modeled by the equation $y - 55 = 0.0025x^2$, where x is the horizontal distance, in feet, from the support tower and y is the height, in feet, above the water. How far is the lowest point of the cable above the water?

The vertex of the parabola is (0, 55), so the lowest point of the cables is 55 feet above the bridge.

15. Match each equation to its graph.

B $y + 1 = \frac{1}{16}(x - 2)^2$

C $y - 1 = \frac{1}{16}(x + 2)^2$

A $x + 1 = -\frac{1}{16}(y - 2)^2$

A.
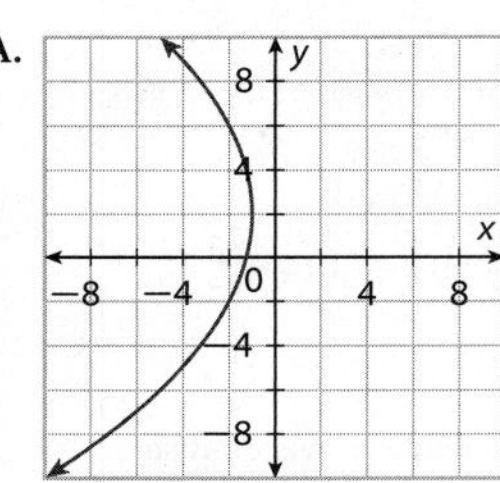

B.
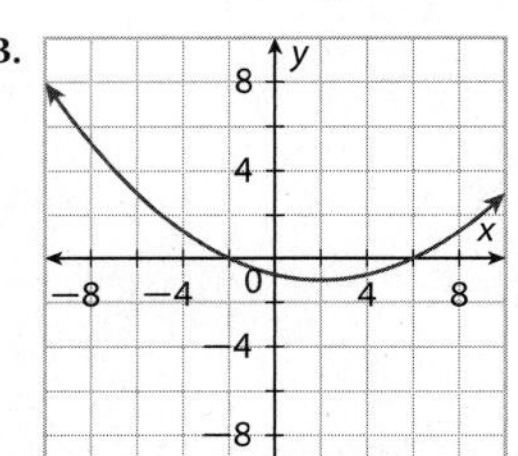

C.
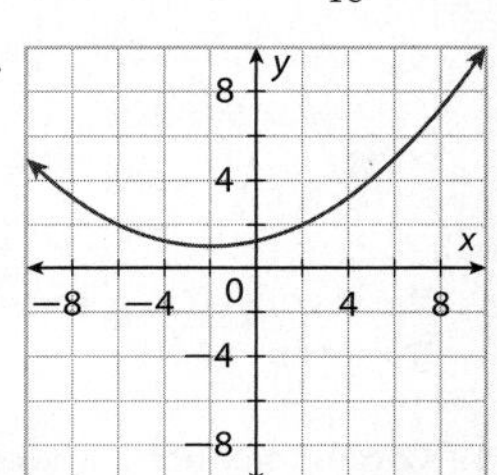

Exercise	Depth of Knowledge (D.O.K.)	COMMON CORE Mathematical Practices
16–17	3 Strategic Thinking	MP.2 Reasoning
18	2 Skills/Concepts H.O.T.	MP.4 Modeling
19	3 Strategic Thinking H.O.T.	MP.2 Reasoning
20	2 Skills/Concepts H.O.T.	MP.3 Logic

Derive the equation of the parabolas with the given information.

16. An upward pointing parabola with a focus at $(0, p)$ and a directrix at $(y = -p)$

distance from (x, y) to focus = distance from (x, y) to directrix

$$\sqrt{(x-0)^2 + (y-p)^2} = \sqrt{(x-x)^2 + (y+p)^2}$$
$$\sqrt{x^2 + (y-p)^2} = \sqrt{(y+p)^2}$$
$$x^2 + (y-p)^2 = (y+p)^2$$
$$x^2 + y^2 - 2py + p^2 = y^2 + 2py + p^2$$
$$x^2 = 4py$$

17. A rightward pointing parabola with a focus at $(-p, 0)$ and a directrix at $(y = -p)$

distance from (x, y) to focus = distance from (x, y) to directrix

$$\sqrt{(x+p)^2 + (y-0)^2} = \sqrt{(x-p)^2 + (y-y)^2}$$
$$(x+p)^2 + y^2 = (x-p)^2$$
$$x^2 + 2px + p^2 + y^2 = x^2 - 2px + p^2$$
$$y^2 = -4px$$

H.O.T. Focus on Higher Order Thinking

18. Multi-Step A tennis player hits a tennis ball while standing just behind the back end of the court. The path of the ball is modeled by the equation $y - 4 = -\frac{4}{1521}(x - 39)^2$. The tennis net is 3 feet high, and the total length of the court is 78 feet.

a. Explain why the ball will go over the net.

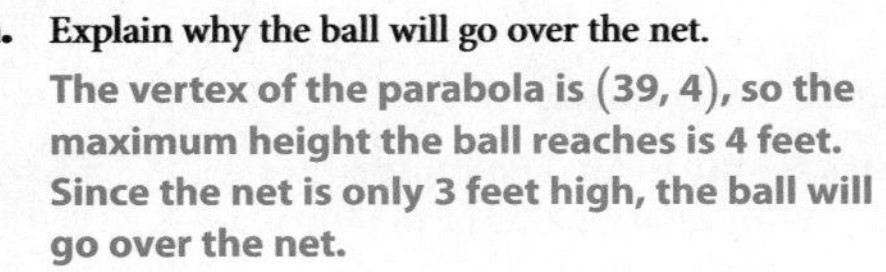

The vertex of the parabola is $(39, 4)$, so the maximum height the ball reaches is 4 feet. Since the net is only 3 feet high, the ball will go over the net.

b. How far is the net located from the player?

The ball will have traveled 39 feet from the player when it reaches the net, so the net is 39 feet from the player.

c. Will the ball land inside the court?

$$0 - 4 = -\frac{4}{1521}(x - 39)^2$$
$$-4 = -\frac{4}{1521}(x - 39)^2$$
$$1521 = (x - 39)^2$$
$$\pm 39 = x - 39$$
$$x = 0, 78$$

The ball will travel 78 feet before it hits the ground. Since the ball's path and the court are 78 feet long, but the ball started from behind the court, the ball will land inside the court.

CONNECT VOCABULARY EL

Have students find and label the *focus* and *directrix* of different parabolas and describe their locations in relation to the axis of symmetry and the vertex of each parabola.

JOURNAL

Have students compare and contrast the methods they have learned for graphing parabolas and writing equations for parabolas.

19. Critical Thinking The latus rectum of a parabola is the line segment perpendicular to the axis of symmetry through the focus, with endpoints on the parabola. Find the length of the latus rectum of the parabola. Justify your answer. Hint: Set the coordinate system such that the vertex is at the origin and it open rightward with the focus at $(p, 0)$.

The parabola that results has the equation: $y^2 = 4px$

The axis of symmetry of this parabola is the x-axis. The line containing the latus rectum is perpendicular to the x-axis and goes through the focus so it has an equation of $x = p$. Setting $x = p$ in the equation above and solving for y we obtain the coordinates of the endpoints of the latus rectum. Their coordinates are $(p, 2p)$ and $(p, -2p)$. The length of this segment is $2p - (-2p) = 4p$ as expected for a vertical segment with those endpoints.

$$y^2 = 4px$$
$$y^2 = 4p \cdot p$$
$$y^2 = 4p^2$$
$$y = \pm\sqrt{4p^2}$$
$$y = \pm 2p$$

20. Explain the Error Lois uses the parabola $y - 8 = -\frac{1}{18}(x + 2)^2$ and the distance formula to find the distance from the vertex of the parabola to the focus to be 12.7 units. Her work is shown.

$$d = \sqrt{(x-h)^2 + (y-k)^2}$$
$$= \sqrt{(-2-0)^2 + (8+4.5)^2}$$
$$= \sqrt{(-2)^2 + 12.5^2}$$
$$= \sqrt{4 + 156.25}$$
$$\approx 12.7$$

a. Explain what Lois did wrong, and then find the correct answer.

Lois did not use the correct coordinates for the focus. The coordinates of the vertex of the parabola are $(-2, 8)$, so the coordinates of the focus are $(-2, 8 + (-4.5)) = (-2, 3.5)$.

$$d = \sqrt{(x-h)^2 + (y-k)^2}$$
$$= \sqrt{(-2+2)^2 + (8-3.5)^2}$$
$$= \sqrt{4.5^2}$$
$$= 4.5$$

So, the focus is 4.5 units from the vertex of the parabola.

b. Is it necessary to use the distance formula to solve for the distance? Explain.

No. The distance is given by $|p|$. In this case, the distance is $|-4.5| = 4.5$.

Lesson Performance Task

Parabolic microphones are used for field audio during sports events. The microphones are manufactured such that the equation of their cross section is $x = \frac{1}{34}y^2$, in inches. The feedhorn part of the microphone is located at the focus.

a. How far is the feedhorn from the edge of the parabolic surface of the microphone?

b. What is the diameter of the microphone? Explain your reasoning.

c. If the diameter is increased by 5 inches, what is the new equation of the cross section of the microphone?

a. $x = \frac{1}{34}y^2 = \frac{1}{4 \cdot 8.5}y^2$

b. The point directly above the focus is at (p, y). Since $p = 8.5$, we can plug $(8.5, y)$ into the equation of the parabola and find $y = 17$. The radius is 17 inches, so the diameter is 34 inches.

c. The new diameter is 39 inches, so the new radius is 19.5 inches. So the point $(p, 19.5)$ directly above the focus is on the parabola.

$$x = \frac{1}{4p}y^2 \longrightarrow (p) = \frac{1}{4p}(19.5)^2 \longrightarrow p = 9.75$$

$$x = \frac{1}{4(9.75)}y^2 \longrightarrow x = \frac{1}{39}y^2$$

The new equation is $x = \frac{1}{39}y^2$.

EXTENSION ACTIVITY

Sound rays parallel to the axis of a parabolic microphone are reflected off its inner surface and pass through the focal point. To explore this phenomenon, have students graph the parabola $y = x^2$. The slope of any line tangent to a point on this parabola is $m = 2x$. Have students pick different points on the parabola (except the origin), draw tangent lines through these points, then draw a line parallel to the y-axis that ends at the point, forming an acute angle a, which students can measure using a protractor. Then have students draw a second line from the point, forming an angle with the tangent line congruent to a. Encourage the students to draw many lines, to observe that the lines intersect at the focus.

INTEGRATE TECHNOLOGY

Students can plot parabolas which open to the left or right using a calculator or a graphing program on a computer by first solving the equation $x^2 = 4py$ for y, and plotting two functions, $y = \pm\sqrt{4px}$.

QUESTIONING STRATEGIES

Ask students to derive $x^2 = 4py$ by assuming that the distance from the focus to a point on a parabola is equal to the shortest distance from that point to the directrix, and using the distance formula. $P(x, y)$ is on the parabola. The focal point is at $(0, p)$, the distance from P to $(0, p)$ is $\sqrt{(x-0)^2 + (y-p)^2}$, the distance from P to the directrix is $y - p$. Setting the two equal:

$$\sqrt{x^2 + (y-p)^2} = y + p$$

$$x^2 + (y-p)^2 = (y+p)^2$$

$$x^2 = 4py$$

Scoring Rubric

2 points: Student correctly solves the problem and explains his/her reasoning.

1 point: Student shows good understanding of the problem but does not fully solve or explain his/her reasoning.

0 points: Student does not demonstrate understanding of the problem.

LESSON 4.3

Solving Linear-Quadratic Equations

Common Core Math Standards

The student is expected to:

A-REI.C.7

Solve a simple system consisting of a linear equation and a quadratic equation in two variables algebraically and graphically.

Mathematical Practices

MP.1 Problem Solving

Language Objective

Work with a partner to explain, orally and in writing, how to solve a simple linear-quadratic system.

ENGAGE

Essential Question: How can you solve a system composed of a linear equation in two variables and a quadratic equation in two variables?

Possible answer: graphing; solving the linear equation for a variable and substituting it in the quadratic equation to solve for the other variable

PREVIEW: LESSON PERFORMANCE TASK

View the Engage section online. Discuss the photo and how to determine the distance a skier travels after leaving a ramp by solving a system of equations. Then preview the Lesson Performance Task.

Name__________ Class__________ Date__________

4.3 Solving Linear-Quadratic Systems

Resource Locker

Essential Question: How can you solve a system composed of a linear equation in two variables and a quadratic equation in two variables?

Explore Investigating Intersections of Lines and Graphs of Quadratic Equations

There are many real-world situations that can be modeled by linear or quadratic functions. What happens when the two situations overlap? Examine graphs of linear functions and quadratic functions and determine the ways they can intersect.

(A) Examine the two graphs below and determine the ways a line could intersect the parabola.

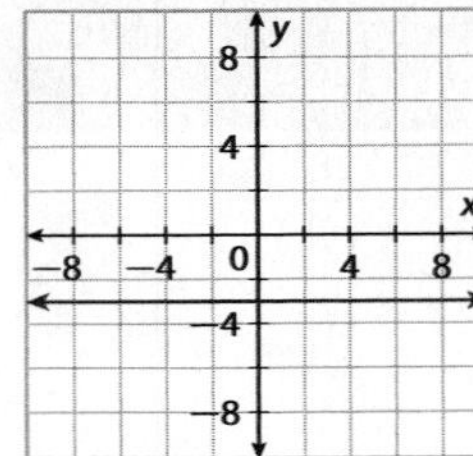
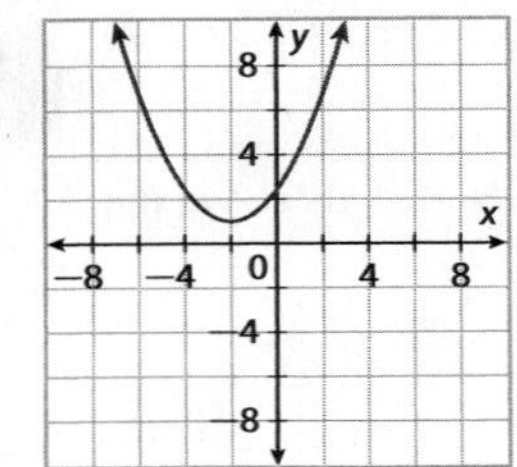

(B) Sketch three graphs of a line and a parabola: one that intersects in one point, one that intersects in two points, and one that does not intersect.

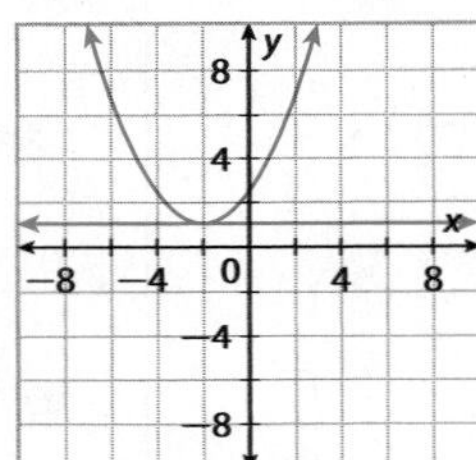
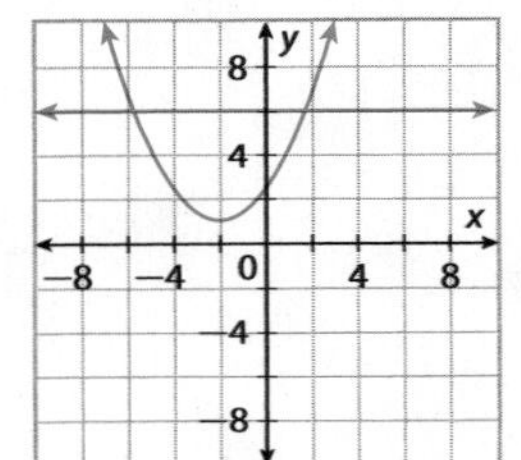
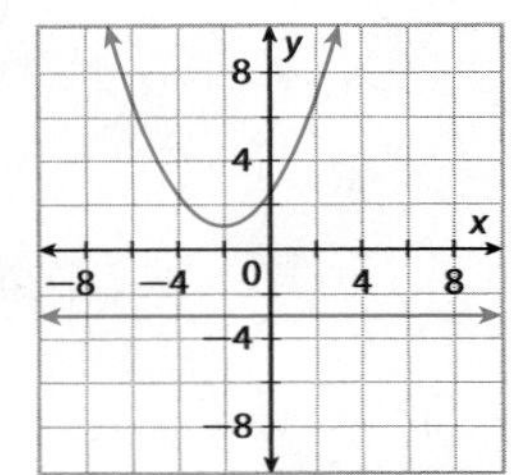

(C) So a linear function and a quadratic function can intersect at 0, 1, or 2 points.

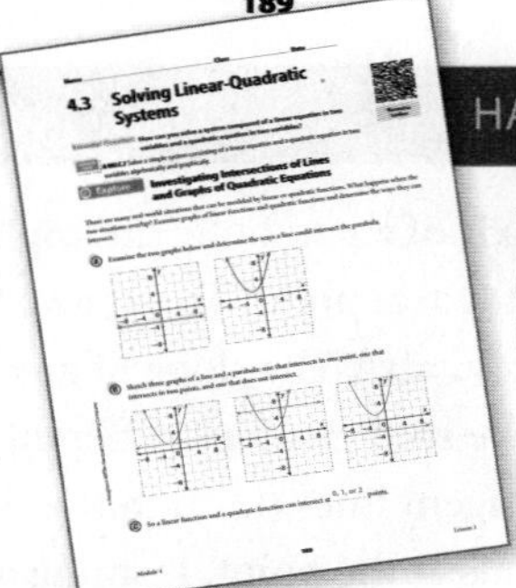

HARDCOVER PAGES **189–202**

Watch for the hardcover student edition page numbers for this lesson.

Reflect

1. If a line intersects a circle at one point, what is the relationship between the line and the radius of the circle at that point?
The line and the radius are perpendicular.

2. **Discussion** Does a line have to be horizontal to intersect a parabola at exactly one point?
No, it just has to be perpendicular to the axis of symmetry.

Explain 1 Solving Linear-Quadratic Systems Graphically

Graph each equation by hand and find the set of points where the two graphs intersect.

Example 1 **Solve the given linear-quadratic system graphically.**

(A) 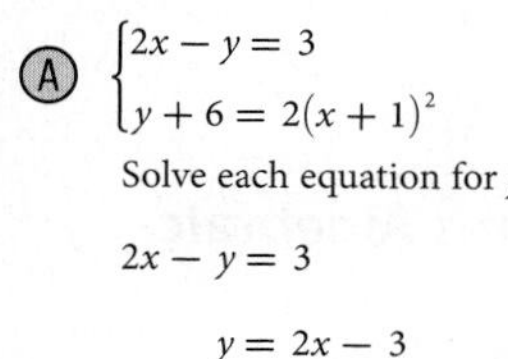

$\begin{cases} 2x - y = 3 \\ y + 6 = 2(x+1)^2 \end{cases}$

Solve each equation for y.

$2x - y = 3$

$y = 2x - 3$

$y + 6 = 2(x+1)^2$

$y = 2(x+1)^2 - 6$

Plot the line and the parabola.

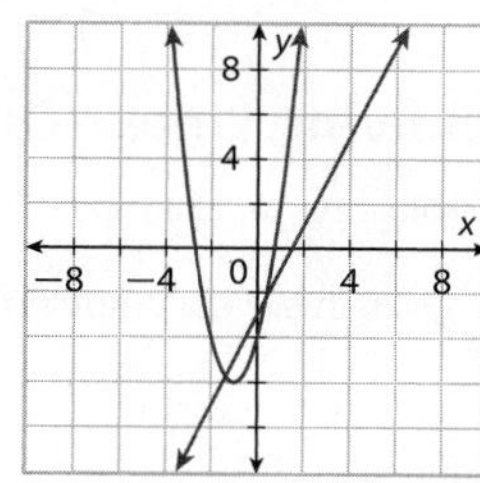

Find the approximate points of intersection: $(-1.4, -5.7)$ and $(0.4, -2.3)$.

Exact solutions are $\left(\frac{-1-\sqrt{3}}{2}, -\sqrt{3} - 4\right)$ and $\left(\frac{-1+\sqrt{3}}{2}, \sqrt{3} - 4\right)$.

(B) 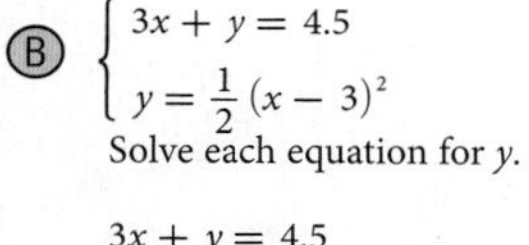

$\begin{cases} 3x + y = 4.5 \\ y = \frac{1}{2}(x-3)^2 \end{cases}$

Solve each equation for y.

$3x + y = 4.5$

$y =$ **$-3x + 4.5$**

$y =$ **$\frac{1}{2}(x-3)^2$**

Plot the line and the parabola on the axes provided.

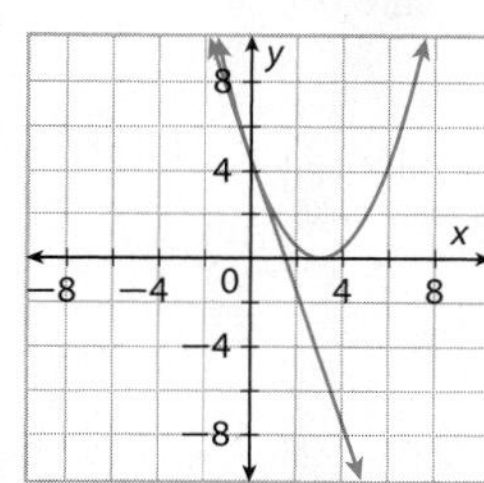

Find the approximate point(s) of intersection: **(0, 4.5)**.

PROFESSIONAL DEVELOPMENT

Learning Progressions

Students have already learned to graph lines, circles, and parabolas. In this lesson they are introduced to combining these graphs to solve linear-quadratic equations. In future lessons, students will learn to graph other systems of equations and inequalities, including linear systems in three variables and systems of linear inequalities.

EXPLORE

Investigating Intersections of Lines and Graphs of Quadratic Equations

INTEGRATE TECHNOLOGY

After solving both equations for y, students may graph the equations on their graphing calculators and find the solutions of the system by finding the intersections of the graphs.

QUESTIONING STRATEGIES

If a linear-quadratic system with no solution contains a quadratic equation that opens downward with a vertex at (3, 7), what is a possible equation for the linear equation? Why? **Equation $y = 8$; the maximum value of the quadratic equation is 7.**

EXPLAIN 1

Solving Linear-Quadratic Systems Graphically

INTEGRATE MATHEMATICAL PRACTICES

Focus on Reasoning

MP.2 The numbers of solutions of a linear-quadratic system varies. There may be 0, 1, or 2 solutions, because a line and a circle or parabola may intersect at 0,1, or 2 points.

QUESTIONING STRATEGIES

How do you know if the graph of a quadratic equation is a circle or parabola? **The equation of a circle contains both an x^2 and a y^2. The equation of a parabola contains only an x^2 or a y^2.**

EXPLAIN 2

Solving Quadratic Systems Algebraically

AVOID COMMON ERRORS

Students may forget to solve for both the positive and negative square roots when solving a quadratic equation containing y^2 for y. Encourage students to consider the number of possible solutions before solving.

Your Turn

Solve the given linear-quadratic system graphically.

3. $\begin{cases} y + 3x = 0 \\ y - 6 = -3x^2 \end{cases}$

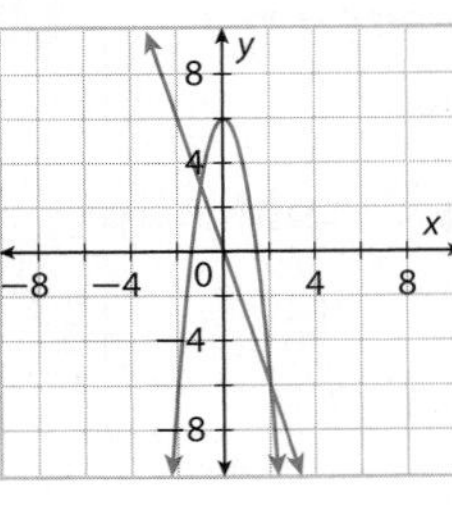

$(-1, 3)$ and $(2, -6)$

4. 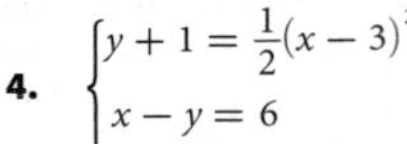

$\begin{cases} y + 1 = \frac{1}{2}(x - 3)^2 \\ x - y = 6 \end{cases}$

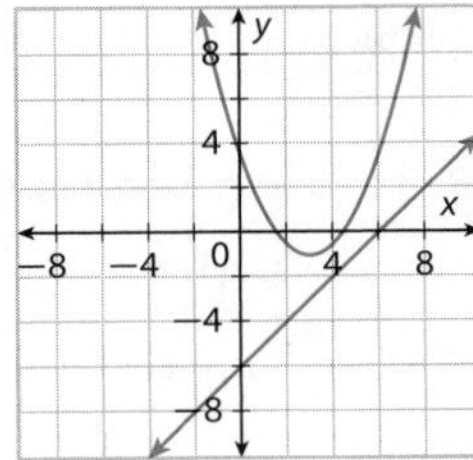

No solution

Explain 2 Solving Linear-Quadratic Systems Algebraically

Use algebra to find the solution. Use substitution or elimination.

Example 2 **Solve the given linear-quadratic system algebraically.**

(A) $\begin{cases} 3x - y = 7 \\ y + 4 = 2(x + 5)^2 \end{cases}$

Solve this system using elimination. First line up the terms.

$$7 + y = 3x$$
$$4 + y = 2(x + 5)^2$$

Subtract the second equation from the first to eliminate the y variable.

$$7 + y = 3x$$
$$-\left(4 + y = 2(x + 5^2)\right)$$
$$3 = 3x - 2(x + 5)^2$$

Solve the resulting equation for x using the quadratic formula.

$$3 = 3x - 2(x + 5)^2$$
$$3 = 3x - 2(x^2 + 10x + 25)$$
$$3 = 3x - 2x^2 - 20x - 50$$
$$0 = -2x^2 - 17x - 53$$
$$2x^2 + 17x + 53 = 0$$
$$x = \frac{-17 \pm \sqrt{17^2 - 4 \cdot 2 \cdot}}{2 \cdot 2}$$
$$= \frac{-17 \pm \sqrt{289 - 424}}{4}$$
$$= \frac{-17 \pm \sqrt{-135}}{4}$$

There is no real number equivalent to $\sqrt{-135}$, so the system has no solution.

COLLABORATIVE LEARNING

Peer-to-Peer Activity

Have students work in pairs. Have one student write a linear equation, and the other write a quadratic equation. Students trade equations and graph both equations on the same coordinate plane. Students find the solutions of the system of equations by identifying the points of intersection, then compare answers.

Ⓑ $\begin{cases} y = \frac{1}{4}(x-3)^2 \\ 3x - 2y = 13 \end{cases}$

Solve the system by substitution. The first equation is already solved for y. Substitute the expression $\frac{1}{4}(x-3)^2$ for y in the second equation.

$3x - 2\left(\frac{1}{4}(x-3)^2\right) = 13$

$$13 = 3x - 2\left(\frac{1}{4}(x-3)^2\right)$$

$$13 = 3x - \boxed{\frac{1}{2}}(x-3)^2$$

$$13 = 3x - \frac{1}{2}\left(\boxed{x^2 - 6x + 9}\right)$$

$$13 = 3x - \frac{1}{2}x^2 + 3x - \frac{9}{2}$$

$$13 = -\frac{1}{2}x^2 + \boxed{6x} - \frac{9}{2}$$

$$0 = -\frac{1}{2}x^2 + 6x - \frac{35}{2}$$

$$0 = x^2 \boxed{-12x + 35}$$

$$0 = \left(x \boxed{-5}\right)\left(x \boxed{-7}\right)$$

$$x = \left(\boxed{-5}\right) \text{ or } x = \left(\boxed{-7}\right)$$

Now, solve for x.

So the line and the parabola intersect at two points. Use the x-coordinates of the intersections to find the points.

Solve $3x - 2y = 13$ for y.

$$3x - 2y = 13$$

$$-2y = 13 - 3x$$

$$y = \boxed{-\left(\frac{13 - 3x}{2}\right)}$$

Find y when $x = 5$ and when $x = 7$.

$$y = -\frac{13 - 3 \cdot 5}{2} \qquad y = -\frac{13 - 3 \cdot 7}{2}$$

$$= -\frac{13 - 15}{2} \qquad = -\frac{13 - 21}{2}$$

$$= -\frac{-2}{2} \qquad = -\frac{-8}{2}$$

$$= 1 \qquad = 4$$

So the solutions to the system are **(5, 1) and (7, 4)**.

Reflect

5. How can you check algebraic solutions for reasonableness?
Graph the system and compare the algebraic solutions to the approximated solutions from the graph.

QUESTIONING STRATEGIES

Is it necessary to always solve the linear equation first and then substitute into the quadratic equation? Explain. **No. It is possible to solve the quadratic equation for one of the variables and then use substitution to solve the linear equation.**

DIFFERENTIATE INSTRUCTION

Cognitive Strategies

Emphasize the importance of considering whether there may be another way to solve the problem. Students may try elimination in a linear-quadratic system and then decide that they can easily solve the quadratic for a variable and use substitution instead.

EXPLAIN 3

Solving a Real-World Problem

INTEGRATE MATHEMATICAL PRACTICES

Focus on Communication

MP.3 You may ask students to work in pairs or small groups to identify other real-world situations that can be modeled by the intersection of a line and a circle or parabola.

Your Turn

Solve the given linear-quadratic system algebraically.

6. $\begin{cases} x - 6 = -\frac{1}{6}y^2 \\ 2x + y = 6 \end{cases}$

$2x + y = 6 \rightarrow y = 6 - 2x$

$x - 6 = -\frac{1}{6}y^2 \rightarrow x - 6 = -\frac{1}{6}(6 - 2x)^2$

Simplifies to $x\left(\frac{2}{3}x - 3\right) = 0.$

$x = 0$ or $x = \frac{9}{2}$

$y = 6 - 2(0)$ or $y = 6 - 2\left(\frac{9}{2}\right)$

$y = 6$ or $y = -3$

The solutions are $(0, 6)$ and $\left(\frac{9}{2}, -3\right)$.

7. $\begin{cases} x - y = 7 \\ x^2 - y = 7 \end{cases}$

$x - y = 7 \rightarrow y = x - 7$

$x^2 - y = 7 \rightarrow x^2 - (x - 7) = 7$

Simplifies to $x(x - 1) = 0.$

$x = 0$ or $x = 1$

$y = 0 - 7$ or $y = 1 - 7$

$y = -7$ or $y = -6$

The solutions are $(0, -7)$ and $(1, -6)$.

Explain 3 Solving Real-World Problems

You can use the techniques from the previous examples to solve real-world problems.

Example 3 Solve each problem.

(A) A tour boat travels around an island in a pattern that can be modeled by the equation $36x^2 + 25y^2 = 900$. A fishing boat approaches the island on a path that can be modeled by the equation $3x - 2y = -8$. Is there a danger of collision? If so, where?

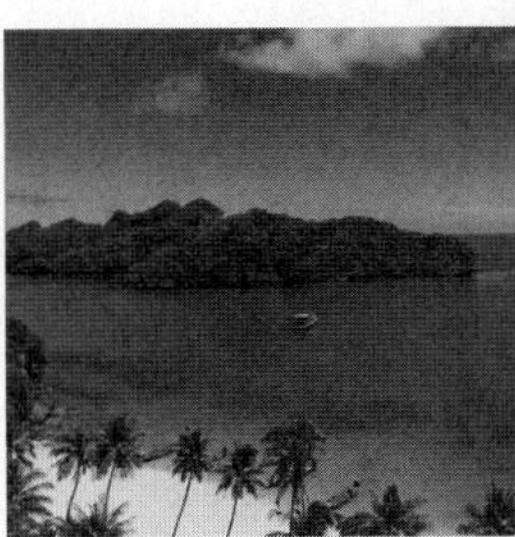

Write the system of equations.

$\begin{cases} 36x^2 + 25y^2 = 900 \\ 3x - 2y = -8 \end{cases}$

Solve the second equation for x.

$3x - 2y = -8$

$3x = 2y - 8$

$x = \frac{2y - 8}{3}$

LANGUAGE SUPPORT EL

Connect Vocabulary

Have students work in pairs. Have one student write and solve a simple system with a linear and quadratic equation algebraically and explain to the partner every step of the process. The partner must then solve the same system graphically, explaining every step of that process. The partners then write down the steps they used both algebraically and graphically to solve the system.

Substitute for x in the first equation.

$$36x^2 + 25y^2 = 900$$

$$36\left(\frac{2y-8}{3}\right)^2 + 25y^2 = 900$$

$$36\left(\frac{4y^2 - 32y + 64}{9}\right) + 25y^2 = 900$$

$$4(4y^2 - 32y + 64) + 25y^2 = 900$$

$$16y^2 - 128y + 256 + 25y^2 = 900$$

$$41y^2 - 128y - 644 = 0$$

Solve using the quadratic equation.

$$y = \frac{128 \pm \sqrt{128^2 - 4(41)(-664)}}{2(41)}$$

$$= \frac{128 \pm \sqrt{122{,}000}}{82}$$

$$= -2.70 \text{ or } 5.82$$

Collisions can occur when $y \approx -2.70$ or $y \approx 5.82$.

To find the x-values, substitute the y-values into $x = \frac{2y-8}{3}$.

$$x = \frac{2(-2.70) - 8}{3} \qquad x = \frac{2(5.82) - 8}{3}$$

$$= \frac{-5.40 - 8}{3} \qquad = \frac{11.64 - 8}{3}$$

$$= \frac{-13.40}{3} \qquad = \frac{3.64}{3}$$

$$= -4.47 \qquad = 1.21$$

So the boats could collide at either $(-4.47, -2.70)$ or $(1.21, 5.82)$.

QUESTIONING STRATEGIES

? How do you decide which variable to solve for first in a linear quadratic system when using the substitution method? Determine which solved-for variable will result in the simpler solving process when substituted in the quadratic equation.

? How can you check the reasonableness of your answer if one equation is that of a circle? Graph the system of equations using a graphing calculator, being sure to graph the two arcs of the circle as separate functions. Trace to see whether the solutions are points of intersection.

(B) The range of the signal from a radio station is bounded by a circle described by the equation $x^2 + y^2 = 2025$. A stretch of highway near the station is modeled by the equation $y - 15 = \frac{1}{20}x$. At which points, if any, does a car on the highway enter and exit the broadcast range of the station?

Write the system of equations.

$$\begin{cases} x^2 + y^2 = -2025 \\ y - 15 = \frac{1}{20}x \end{cases}$$

Solve the second equation for y.

$$y - 15 = \frac{1}{20}x$$

$$y = \boxed{\frac{1}{20}x + 15}$$

Substitute for x in the first equation.

$$x^2 + y^2 = 2025$$

$$x^2 + \left(\boxed{\frac{1}{20}x + 15}\right)^2 = 2025$$

$$x^2 + \boxed{\frac{1}{400}x^2 + \frac{3}{2}x + 225} = 2025$$

$$\boxed{\frac{401}{400}}x^2 + \frac{3}{2}x + 225 = 2025$$

$$\frac{401}{400}x^2 + \frac{3}{2}x - \boxed{1800} = 0$$

$$401x^2 + 600x - 720000 = 0$$

Solve using the quadratic formula.

$$y = \frac{-600 \pm \sqrt{600^2 - 4(401)(-720000)}}{2(401)}$$

$$= \frac{600 \pm \sqrt{1{,}155{,}240{,}000}}{802}$$

$$\approx \boxed{-41.63} \text{ or } \boxed{43.13} \text{ (rounded to the nearest hundredth)}$$

To find the y-values, substitute the x-values into $y = \frac{1}{20}x + 15$.

$$y = \frac{1}{20}(-41.63) + 15 \qquad y = \frac{1}{20}(43.13) + 15$$

$$= -\frac{41.63}{20} + 15 \qquad = \frac{43.13}{20} + 15$$

$$= -2.08 + 15 \qquad = 2.16 + 15$$

$$= 12.92 \qquad = 17.16$$

The car will be within the radio station's broadcast area between (−41.63, 12.92) and (43.13, 17.16

Your Turn

8. An asteroid is traveling toward Earth on a path that can be modeled by the equation $y = \frac{1}{28}x - 7$. It approaches a satellite in orbit on a path that can be modeled by the equation $\frac{x^2}{49} + \frac{y^2}{51} = 1$. What are the approximate coordinates of the points where the satellite and asteroid might collide?

Substitute $\frac{1}{28}x - 7$ into the second equation.

$$\frac{x^2}{49} + \frac{\left(\frac{1}{28}x - 7\right)^2}{51} = 1$$

$$\frac{x^2}{49} + \frac{1}{39984}x^2 - \frac{1}{102}x + \frac{49}{51} = 1$$

$$x = \frac{-(-392) \pm \sqrt{(-392)^2 - 4(817)(-1568)}}{2(817)}$$

$x = 1.65$ or $x = -1.17$

$y = \frac{1}{28}(1.65) - 7$ or $y = \frac{1}{28}(-1.17) - 7$

$y = -6.94$ or $y = -7.04$

The solutions are $(-1.17, -7.04)$ and $(1.65, -6.94)$.

9. The owners of a circus are planning a new act. They want to have a trapeze artist catch another acrobat in mid-air as the second performer comes into the main tent on a zip-line. If the path of the trapeze can be modeled by the parabola $y = \frac{1}{4}x^2 + 16$ and the path of the zip-line can be modeled by $y = 2x + 12$, at what point can the trapeze artist grab the second acrobat?

$(2x + 12) = \frac{1}{4}x^2 + 16$

Simplifies to $0 = (x - 4)(x - 4)$.

$x = 4$

$y = 2(4) + 12$

$y = 20$

The solution is $(4, 20)$.

Elaborate

10. A parabola opens to the left. Identify an infinite set of parallel lines that will intersect the parabola only once.

$\{y = a \mid a \in R\}$, the set of all lines parallel to the x-axis.

11. If a parabola can intersect the set of lines $\{x = a \mid a \in R\}$ in 0, 1, or 2 points, what do you know about the parabola?

The parabola cannot be expressed as a function; it fails the vertical line test.

12. Essential Question Check-In How can you solve a system composed of a linear equation in two variables and a quadratic equation in two variables?

Graphically or algebraically using substitution. Systems in which the quadratic equation only has one second-order term can be solved algebraically using elimination.

ELABORATE

INTEGRATE MATHEMATICAL PRACTICES

Focus on Reasoning

MP.2 Ask students how the squares of the variables in the quadratic equation affect the graph of the system and the solutions. Students should indicate that the graph of the linear equation is a line. If y is squared in the quadratic equation, the graph is a parabola opening up or down, if x is squared it opens left or right, and if both are squared, it is a circle. The number of solutions is 2, 1, or 0, regardless.

SUMMARIZE THE LESSON

What are the principal ways to solve a linear-quadratic system, and how do you determine the number of solutions? Algebraically and by graphing the system; solving the system will result two solutions, one solution, or no solution. When the system is solved by graphing, the number of solutions is determined by the number of intersection points.

EVALUATE

ASSIGNMENT GUIDE

Concepts and Skills	Practice
Explore Investigating Intersections of Lines and Graphs of Quadratic Equations	Exercises 1–2
Example 1 Solving Linear-Quadratic Systems Graphically	Exercises 3–8
Example 2 Solving Linear-Quadratic Systems Algebraically	Exercises 9–14
Example 3 Solving a Real-World Problem	Exercises 15–18

INTEGRATE MATHEMATICAL PRACTICES

Focus on Communication

MP.3 Group students in pairs. In turns, students tell partners what their preferred method of solving linear-quadratic systems is and why.

CONNECT VOCABULARY EL

Relate the term *linear system* to the idea that this kind of system has only linear equations, while a *linear-quadratic system* has one linear and one quadratic equation. Have students look at graphs on graphing calculators or in pictures to verify this.

Evaluate: Homework and Practice

1. How many points of intersection are on the graph? 1

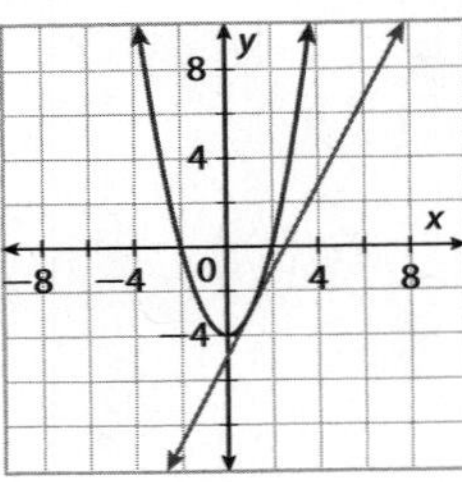

2. How many points of intersection are there on the graph of $\begin{cases} y = x^2 + 3x - 2 \\ y - x = 4 \end{cases}$?

2

Solve each given linear-quadratic system graphically.

3. $\begin{cases} y = -(x-2)^2 + 4 \\ y = -5 \end{cases}$

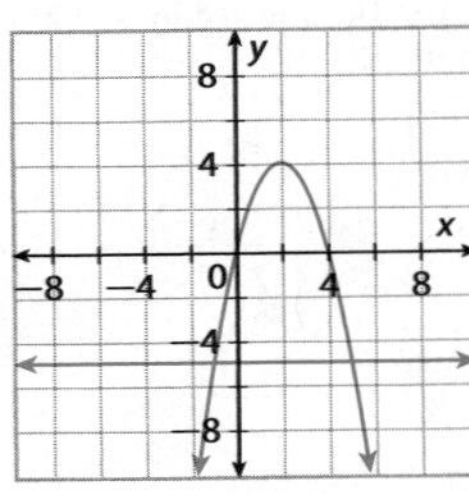

(−1, −5) and (5, −5)

4. $\begin{cases} y - 3 = (x-1)^2 \\ 2x + y = 5 \end{cases}$

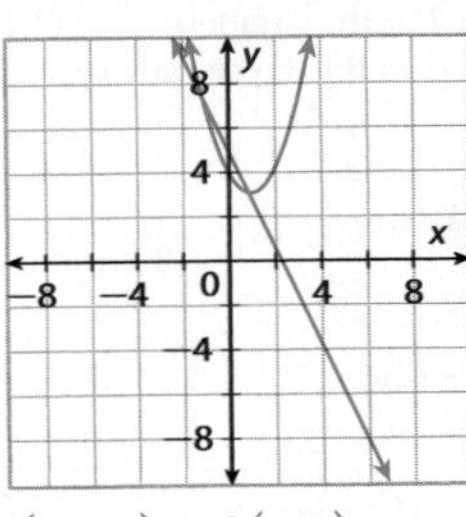

(−1, 7) and (1, 3)

5. $\begin{cases} x = y^2 - 5 \\ -x + 2y = 12 \end{cases}$

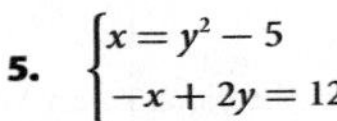

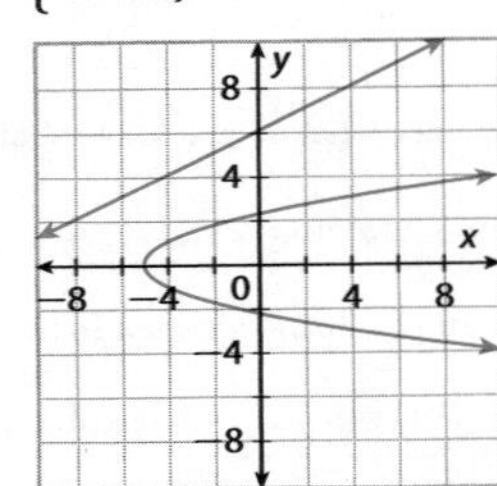

No solution

6. $\begin{cases} x - 4 = (y+1)^2 \\ 3x - y = 17 \end{cases}$

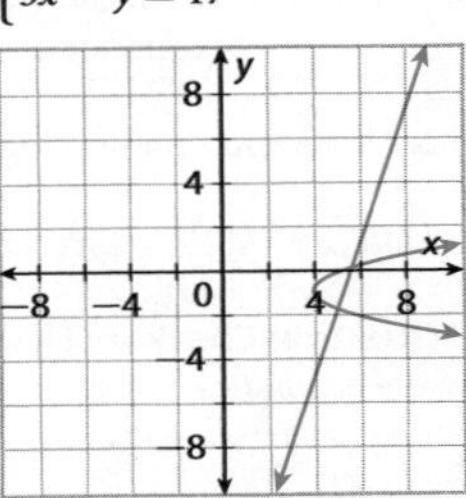

(5, −2) and approximately (5.78, 0.34

Exercise	Depth of Knowledge (D.O.K.)	COMMON CORE Mathematical Practices
1–2	**1** Recall of Information	**MP.6** Precision
3–8	**1** Recall of Information	**MP.5** Using Tools
9–14	**1** Recall of Information	**MP.3** Logic
15–18	**2** Skills/Concepts	**MP.4** Modeling
19–20	**2** Skills/Concepts	**MP.5** Using Tools
21	**2** Skills/Concepts	**MP.2** Reasoning

7. 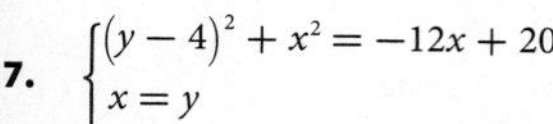
$\begin{cases}(y-4)^2 + x^2 = -12x + 20 \\ x = y\end{cases}$

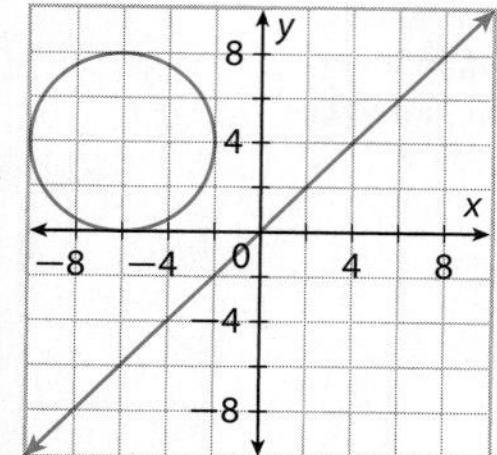

No solution

8. $\begin{cases}5 - y = x^2 + x \\ y + 1 = \frac{3}{4}x\end{cases}$

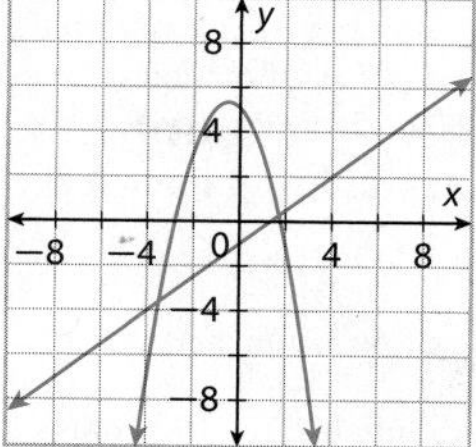

approximately $(-3.48, -3.61)$ and $(1.73, 0.29)$

Solve each linear-quadratic system algebraically.

9. $\begin{cases}6x + y = -16 \\ y + 7 = x^2\end{cases}$

$y + 7 = x^2 \quad \rightarrow \quad y = x^2 - 7$

$6x + y = -16 \rightarrow \quad = 6x + (x^2 - 7) = -16$

Simplifies to $(x + 3)(x + 3) = 0$

$x = (-3)$

$y + 7 = -3^2$

$y = 2$

The solution is $(-3, 2)$.

10. $\begin{cases}y - 5 = (x - 2)^2 \\ x + 2y = 6\end{cases}$

$x + 2y = 6 \quad \rightarrow \quad x = 6 - 2y$

$y - 5 = (x - 2)^2 \rightarrow \quad y - 5 = \left((6 - 2y) - 2\right)^2$

Simplifies to $0 = 4y^2 - 17y + 21$.

$y = \dfrac{-(-17) \pm \sqrt{(-17)^2 - 4(4)(21)}}{2(4)}$

$y = \dfrac{17 \pm \sqrt{-47}}{8}$

Since this is not a real number, this system has no solution.

11. $\begin{cases}y^2 - 26 = -x^2 \\ x - y = 6\end{cases}$

$x - y = 6 \quad \rightarrow \quad x - 6 = y$

$y^2 - 26 = -x^2 \rightarrow (x - 6)^2 - 26 = -x^2$

Simplifies to $(x - 1)(x - 5) = 0$.

$x = 1$ or $x = 5$

$1 - y = 6$ or $5 - y = 6$

$y = -5$ or $y = -1$

The solutions are $(1, -5)$ and $(5, -1)$.

12. $\begin{cases}y - 3 = x^2 - 2x \\ 2x + y = 1\end{cases}$

$2x + y = 1 \quad \rightarrow \quad y = 1 - 2x$

$y - 3 = x^2 - 2x \rightarrow (1 - 2x) - 3 = x^2 - 2x$

$(1 - 2x) - 3 = x^2 - 2x$

$-2 = x^2$

Since this is not a real number, this system has no solution.

13. $\begin{cases}y = x^2 + 1 \\ y - 1 = x\end{cases}$

$y - 1 = x \quad \rightarrow \quad y = x + 1$

$y = x^2 + 1 \rightarrow x + 1 = x^2 + 1$

Simplifies to $0 = x(x - 1)$.

$x = 0$ or $x = 1$

$y = x + 1$ or $y = x + 1$

$y = 0 + 1$ or $y = 1 + 1$

$y = 1$ or $y = 2$

The solutions $(0, 1)$ and $(1, 2)$.

14. $\begin{cases}y = x^2 + 2x + 7 \\ y - 7 = x\end{cases}$

$y - 7 = x \quad \rightarrow \quad y = x + 7$

$y = x^2 + 2x + 7 \rightarrow x + 7 = x^2 + 2x + 7$

Simplifies to $0 = x(x + 1)$.

$x = 0$ or $x = -1$

$y = x + 7$ or $y = x + 7$

$y = 0 + 7$ or $y = -1 + 7$

$y = 7$ or $y = 6$

The solutions are $(0, 7)$ and $(-1, 6)$.

INTEGRATE MATHEMATICAL PRACTICES

Focus on Math Connections

MP.1 Solving a linear-quadratic system by substitution will result in a quadratic equation. If the discriminant ($b^2 - 4ac$) is negative, there are no solutions. If the discriminant is 0, there is one solution, and if the discriminant is positive, there are two solutions.

Exercise	Depth of Knowledge (D.O.K.)	COMMON CORE Mathematical Practices
22	**3** Strategic Thinking H.O.T.	**MP.3** Logic
23	**3** Strategic Thinking H.O.T.	**MP.2** Reasoning
24	**3** Strategic Thinking H.O.T.	**MP.3** Logic

AVOID COMMON ERRORS

Students may try to find a solution when there is none. Remind students that a linear-quadratic system may not have a solution. This is the case when the graphs of the equations do not intersect.

INTEGRATE MATHEMATICAL PRACTICES

Focus on Technology

MP.5 When graphing a linear-quadratic system on a graphing calculator, students may need to use features such as *zoom* and *intersect* when a system appears to have one solution. It is possible that, upon further inspection, that there may be two solutions or no solution.

Write and solve a system of equations to find the solutions.

15. Jason is driving his car on a highway at a constant rate of 60 miles per hour when he passes his friend Alan whose car is parked on the side of the road. Alan has been waiting for Jason to pass so that he can follow him to a nearby campground. To catch up to Jason's passing car, Alan accelerates at a constant rate. The distance d, in miles, that Alan's car travels as a function of time t, in hours, since Jason's car has passed is given by $d = 3600t^2$. How long does it takes Alan's car to catch up with Jason's car?

Set the speeds equal and solve for t.

$60t = 3600t^2 \quad \rightarrow \quad t = 60t^2 \quad \rightarrow \quad t = \frac{1}{60}$

So it takes $\frac{1}{60}$ of an hour, or 1 minute, to catch up.

16. The flight of a cannonball toward a hill is described by the parabola $y = 2 + 0.12x - 0.002x^2$.

The hill slopes upward along a path given by $y = 0.15x$.

Where on the hill does the cannonball land?

Set the flight of the cannonball and the hill slope equal.

$0.15x = 2 + 0.12x - 0.002x^2 \rightarrow 0 = 2 - 0.03x - 0.002x^2$

$$x = \frac{-(-0.03) \pm \sqrt{(-0.03)^2 - 4(-0.002)(2)}}{2(-0.002)}$$

$x = -40$ or $x = 25$

The negative answer can be ignored.

$y = 0.15(25)$

$y = 3.75$

The cannonball lands on the hill at $(25, 3.75)$.

17. Amy throws a quarter from the top of a building at the same time that a balloon is released from the ground. The equation describing the height y above ground of the quarter in feet is $y = 64 - 2x^2$, where x is the time in seconds. The equation describing the elevation of the balloon in feet is $y = 6x + 8$, where x is the time in seconds. After how many seconds will the balloon and quarter pass each other? Check your solution for reasonableness.

Set the quarter's height above ground and the elevation of the balloon equal.

$6x + 8 = 64 - 2x^2$

$2x^2 + 6x - 56 = 0$

$2(x + 7)(x - 4) = 0$

$x = -7$ or $x = 4$

The negative result is meaningless in context. The quarter and the balloon will pass after 4 seconds.

18. The range of an ambulance service is a circular region bounded by the equation $x^2 + y^2 = 400$. A straight road within the service area is represented by $y = 3x + 20$. Find the length of the road that lies within the range of the ambulance service (round your answer to the nearest hundredth).

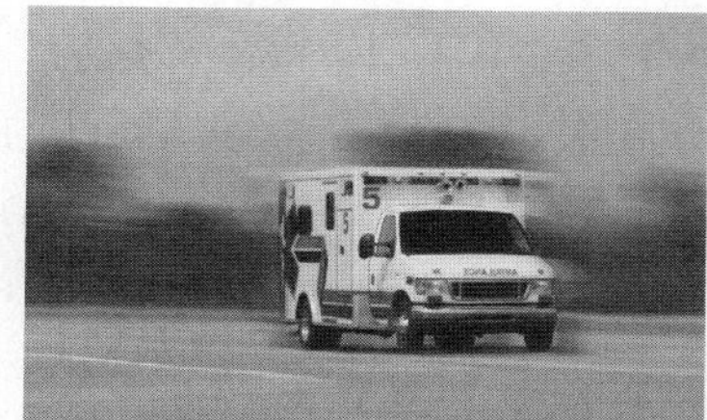

Recall that the distance formula is $d = \sqrt{(x_2 - x_1)^2 + (y_2 - y_1)^2}$.

$$\begin{cases} x^2 + y^2 = 400 \\ y = 3x + 20 \end{cases}$$

Substitute and solve for x.

$x^2 + (3x + 20)^2 = 400 \rightarrow x(x + 12) = 0$

$x = 0$ or $x = -12$

$y = 3x + 20$ or $y = 3x + 20$

$y = 3(0) + 20$ or $y = 3(-12) + 20$

$y = 20$ or $y = -16$

So, the endpoints are $(0, 20)$ and $(-12, -16)$. Use the distance formula.

$d = \sqrt{(-12 - 0)^2 + (-16 - 20)^2} = 12\sqrt{10} \approx 37.95$

The length of the road is approximately 37.95.

19. Match the equations with their solutions.

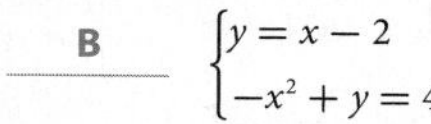

B $\begin{cases} y = x - 2 \\ -x^2 + y = 4x - 2 \end{cases}$ **A.** $(4, 3)\ (-4, -3)$

D $\begin{cases} y = (x - 2)^2 \\ y = -5x - 8 \end{cases}$ **B.** $(0, -2)\ (5, 3)$

A $\begin{cases} 4y = 3x \\ x^2 + y^2 = 25 \end{cases}$ **C.** $(2, 0)$

C $\begin{cases} y = (x - 2)^2 \\ y = 0 \end{cases}$ **D.** No solution

20. A student solved the system $\begin{cases} y - 7 = x^2 - 5x \\ y - 2x = 1 \end{cases}$ graphically and determined the only solution to be (1, 3). Was this a reasonable answer? How do you know?

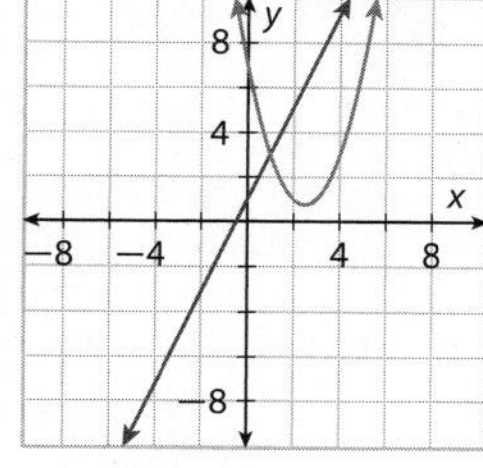

It was not reasonable. The linear function is not tangent to the quadratic function, so there will be a second solution, which occurs outside the boundary of the part of the coordinate plane shown on the grid.

AVOID COMMON ERRORS

When elimination requires subtracting equations, students may subtract only the terms they want to eliminate. Encourage them to multiply all of the terms by −1 and then add.

JOURNAL

Have students describe the ways they learned to solve linear-quadratic equations. Encourage students to include a solved example for each method.

H.O.T. Focus on Higher Order Thinking

21. Explain the Error A student was asked to come up with a system of equations, one linear and one quadratic, that has two solutions. The student gave $\begin{cases} y^2 = -(x+1)^2 + 9 \\ y = x^2 - 4x + 3 \end{cases}$ as the answer. What did the student do wrong?

The student did not give a linear equation. The first equation is a circle, and the second equation is a parabola.

22. Analyze Relationships The graph shows a quadratic function and a linear function $y = d$. If the linear function were changed to $y = d + 3$, how many solutions would the new system have? If the linear function were changed to $y = d - 5$, how many solutions would the new system have? Give reasons for your answers.

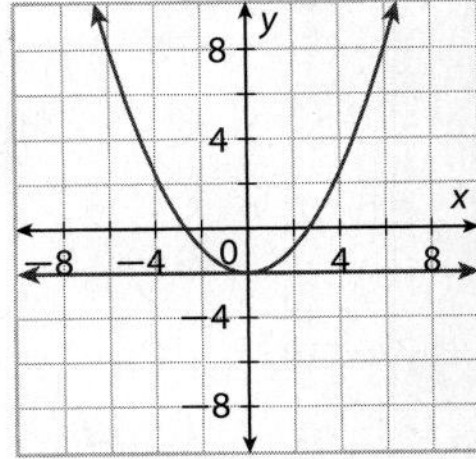

$y = d + 3$: two solutions; the line and the parabola currently intersect in one point. Translating the line up 3 units will result in the line intersecting the parabola in two points.

$y = d - 5$: no solution; the line and the parabola currently intersect in one point. Translating the line down 5 units will result in the line being entirely below the parabola, so there would be no points of intersection.

23. Make a Conjecture Given $y = 100x^2$ and $y = 0.0001x^2$, what can you say about any line that goes through the vertex of each but is not horizontal or vertical?

Any line that goes through the vertex but is not horizontal or vertical will go through some other point on each parabola.

24. Communicate Mathematical Ideas Explain why a system of a linear equation and a quadratic equation cannot have an infinite number of solutions.

Only if both equations described have the same curve would the system have an infinite number of solutions. A linear equation will always be a straight line, and a quadratic equation will never be a straight line.

Lesson Performance Task

uppose an aerial freestyle skier goes off a ramp with her path represented by the equation $= -0.024(x - 25)^2 + 40$. If the surface of the mountain is represented by the linear equation $= -0.5x + 25$, find the distance in feet the skier lands from the beginning of the ramp.

$0.5x + 25 = -0.024(x - 25)^2 + 40$

$0.5x + 25 = -0.024(x^2 - 50x + 625) + 40$

$0.5x + 25 = -0.024x^2 + 1.2x - 15 + 40$

$0.5x + 25 = -0.024x^2 + 1.2x + 25$

$0 = -0.024x^2 + 1.7x$

$0 = x(-0.024x + 1.7)$

$0 = -0.024x + 1.7 \qquad x = 0$

$-0.024x = -1.7$

$x = \frac{425}{6}$

$x \approx 70.83$

nce the value of 0 is where the skier meets the ramp, the skier lands out 71 feet from the ramp.

udents may also choose to solve the problem using a graphing lculator.

EXTENSION ACTIVITY

A thrown ball follows the equation $y = x - \frac{10}{v^2}x^2$, where v is the initial velocity of the ball in meters per second and distances are in meters. Have students graph the ball's trajectory for $v = 10, 20, 30$, and 40, and determine for what value of v the vertical height of the ball reaches $y = 10$ meters. Students should find that increasing v increases the vertical height of the ball as well as the horizontal distance it travels. For $v = 20$, the graphs $y = x - \frac{10}{v^2}x^2$ and $y = 10$ intersect at one point, (20, 10). For values of v greater than 20, the two graphs intersect at two points, which means the ball reaches a height of 10 meters twice in its trajectory, once when it is going up and once when it is going down.

QUESTIONING STRATEGIES

What is accomplished by setting the equations equal to each other? The solution is the x-value for which both equations are equal, so setting the equations equal to each other and solving for x gives you this value.

What is the vertex of the quadratic equation? How can you use this to determine whether the solution is reasonable? (25, 40); this indicates that the skier reaches her highest point at a horizontal distance of 25 feet from the takeoff point. Because the ramp slopes downward, the skier should land at least another 25 feet farther, or at least 50 feet from the takeoff point.

Scoring Rubric

2 points: Student correctly solves the problem and explains his/her reasoning.

1 point: Student shows good understanding of the problem but does not fully solve or explain his/her reasoning.

0 points: Student does not demonstrate understanding of the problem.

LESSON 4.4

Solving Linear Systems in Three Variables

Common Core Math Standards

The student is expected to:

A-REI.C.6

Solve systems of linear equations exactly .... Also A-CED.A.3

Mathematical Practices

MP.1 Problem Solving

Language Objective

Label the kind of solution methods shown to solve systems of three linear equations in three variables. Explain to a partner which method is easiest to use in a particular context and why.

ENGAGE

Essential Question: How can you find the solution(s) of a system of three linear equations in three variables?

Possible answer: Solve using substitution, elimination, or matrices.

PREVIEW: LESSON PERFORMANCE TASK

View the Engage section online. Discuss the photo and how you can use a system of linear equations to determine the number of different components of inline skates a company can afford to purchase. Then preview the Lesson Performance Task.

Name ______ Class ______ Date ______

4.4 Solving Linear Systems in Three Variables

Resource Locker

Essential Question: How can you find the solution(s) of a system of three linear equations in three variables?

Explore Recognizing Ways that Planes Can Intersect

Recall that a linear equation in two variables defines a line. Consider a *linear equation in three variables*. An example is shown.

$$5 = 3x + 2y + 6z$$

A **linear equation in three variables** has three distinct variables, each of which is either first degree or has a coefficient of zero.

Just as the two numbers that satisfy a linear equation in two variables are called an ordered pair, the three numbers that satisfy a linear equation in three variables are called an **ordered triple** and are written (x, y, z).

The set of all ordered pairs satisfying a linear equation in two variables forms a line. Likewise the set of all ordered triples satisfying a linear equation in three variables forms a plane.

Three linear equations in three variables, considered together, form **a system of three linear equations in three variables**. The solutions of a system like this depend on the ways three planes can intersect.

(A) The diagrams show some ways three planes can intersect. How many points lie on all 3 planes? 0

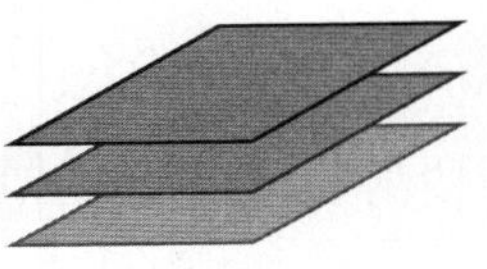

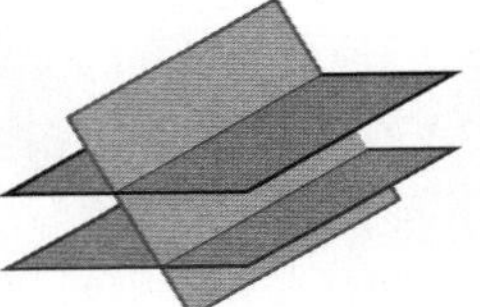

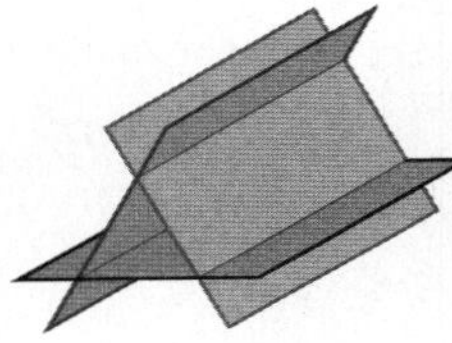

(B) The diagram shows three intersecting planes.

How many points lie on all 3 planes? 1

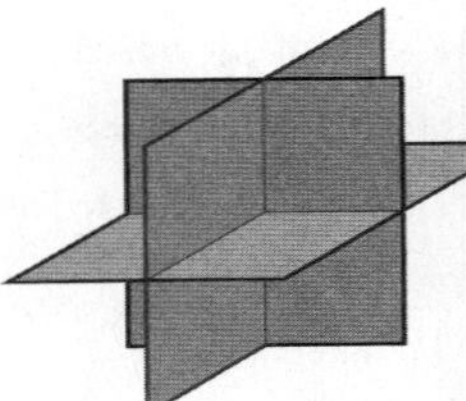

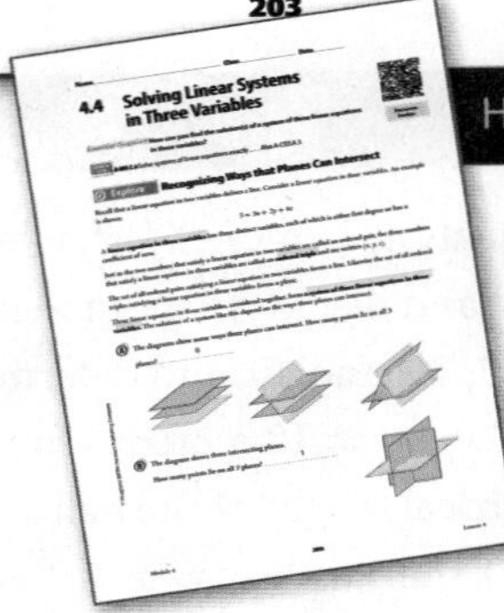

HARDCOVER PAGES 203–2

Watch for the hardcover student edition page numbers for this lesson.

Ⓒ The diagram shows planes intersecting in a different way.

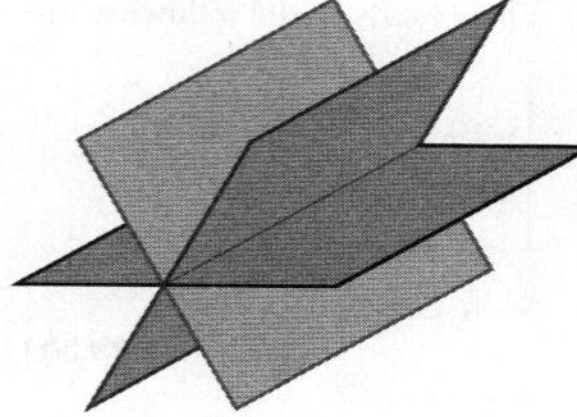

Describe the intersection. The intersection is a line.

How many points lie in all 3 planes? an infinite number

Reflect

. **Discussion** Give an example of three planes that intersect at exactly one point.
Sample answers: The three dimensional coordinate axes; three faces of a cube that share a common corner.

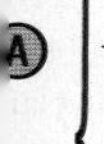

Explain 1 Solving a System of Three Linear Equations Using Substitution

system of three linear equations is solved in the same manner as a system of two linear equations. It just has more teps.

Example 1 **Solve the system using substitution.**

Ⓐ
$$\begin{cases} -2x + y + 3z = 20 & \boxed{1} \\ -3x + 2y + z = 21 & \boxed{2} \\ 3x - 2y + 3z = -9 & \boxed{3} \end{cases}$$

Choose an equation and variable to start with. The easiest equations to solve are those that have a variable with a coefficient of 1. Solve for y.

$-2x + y + 3z = 20$

$y = 2x - 3z + 20$

Now substitute for y in equations $\boxed{2}$ and $\boxed{3}$ and simplify.

$21 = -3x + 2(2x - 3z + 20) + z$	$-9 = 3x - 2(2x - 3z + 20) + 3z$
$21 = -3x + 4x - 6z + 40 + z$	$-9 = 3x - 4x + 6z - 40 + 3z$
$21 = x - 5z + 40$	$-9 = -x + 9z - 40$
$-19 = x - 5z \quad \boxed{4}$	$31 = -x + 9z \quad \boxed{5}$

EXPLORE

Recognizing Ways that Planes Can Intersect

INTEGRATE TECHNOLOGY

Have students draw three intersecting planes using an art application on their iPads.

INTEGRATE MATHEMATICAL PRACTICES

Focus on Modeling

MP.4 Sharing their diagrams of three intersecting planes with the class, students will see the possible ways three planes can intersect. Their intersection may be a line or a point. In some cases, three planes will not intersect.

EXPLAIN 1

Solving a System of Three Linear Equations Using Substitution

INTEGRATE MATHEMATICAL PRACTICES

Focus on Communication

MP.3 Have students explain to a partner the process of solving a system of three linear equations in three variables by substitution.

PROFESSIONAL DEVELOPMENT

Integrate Mathematical Practices

This lesson provides an opportunity to address Mathematical Practice **MP.1**, which calls for students to "makes sense of problems and persevere in solving them." Students solve systems of linear equations in three variables using three different methods: substitution, elimination, and matrices. Students are asked to choose among these methods to solve real-world problems, and verify that the solution is indeed reasonable.

QUESTIONING STRATEGIES

After solving one equation for a single variable, what is the next step when solving a system of three linear equations in three variables by substitution? Substitute into the two other original equations to get a system of two linear equations in two variables.

This results in the following linear system in two variables:

$$\begin{cases} -19 = x - 5z & \boxed{4} \\ 31 = -x + 9z & \boxed{5} \end{cases}$$

Solve equation [4] for x.

$x = 5z - 19$

Substitute into equation [5] and solve for z. Then use the value for z to find the values of x.

$31 = -(5z - 19) + 9z$ $31 = -x + 9(3)$

$31 = 4z + 19$ $31 = -x + 27$

$3 = z$ $-4 = x$

Finally, solve the equation for y when $x = -4$ and $z = 3$.

$y = 2x - 3z + 20$

$y = 2(-4) - 3(3) + 20$

$y = 3$

Therefore, the solution to the system of three linear equations is the ordered triple $(-4, 3, 3)$.

(B) There is a unique parabolic function passing through any three noncollinear points in the coordinate pla provided that no two of the points have the same x-coordinate. Find the parabola that passes through the points $(2, 1)$, $(-1, 4)$, and $(-2, 3)$.

The general form of a parabola is the quadratic equation $y = ax^2 + bx + c$. In order to find the equation of the parabola, we must identify the values of a, b, and c. Since each point lies on the parabola, substituting the coordinates of each point into the general equation produces a different equation.

$$\begin{cases} 1 = a(2)^2 + b(2) + c \\ 4 = a(-1)^2 + b(-1) + c \\ \boxed{3} = a\left(\boxed{-2}\right)^2 + b\left(\boxed{-2}\right) + c \end{cases} \Rightarrow \begin{cases} 1 = 4a + 2b + c & \boxed{1} \\ 4 = a - b + c & \boxed{2} \\ 3 = 4a - 2b + c & \boxed{3} \end{cases}$$

Choose an equation in which it is easier to isolate a variable. Solve equation [2] for c.

$c = 4 - a + \boxed{b}$ [2]

Now substitute for $c =$ in equations [1] and [3].

$1 = 4a + 2b + \left(\boxed{4 - a + b}\right)$ $3 = 4a - 2b + \left(\boxed{4 - a + b}\right)$

$1 = \boxed{3a} + 3b + 4$ $3 = 3a - \boxed{b} + 4$

$\boxed{-3} = 3a + 3b$ [4] $\boxed{-1} = 3a - b$ [5]

COLLABORATIVE LEARNING

Peer-to-Peer Activity

Have students work in groups of three. Give each group a system of three linear equations in three variables to solve. Explain that each student in a group should solve the system with a different method. Then, have students compare their solutions.

This results in the following linear system in two variables:

$$\begin{cases} 3a + 3b = -3 & [4] \\ 3a - b = -1 & [5] \end{cases}$$

Solve equation [5] for b.

$b = 3a + \boxed{1}$

Substitute into equation [4] and solve for a. Then use the value for a to find the values of b.

$3a + 3 + \left(\boxed{3a + 1}\right) = -3$

$3a + 9a + \boxed{3} = -3$

$12a = \boxed{-6}$

$a = \boxed{-\frac{1}{2}}$

$3\left(-\frac{1}{2}\right) + 3b = -3$

$\boxed{-\frac{3}{2}} + 3b = -3$

$3b = \boxed{-\frac{3}{2}}$

$b = \boxed{-\frac{1}{2}}$

Then use the values a and b to solve for c.

$c = 4 - a + b = 4 - \left(-\frac{1}{2}\right) + \left(-\frac{1}{2}\right) = 4$

So the equation of the parabola connecting (2, 1), (−1, 4), and (−2, 3) is

$y = \boxed{-\frac{1}{2}}x^2 - \boxed{\frac{1}{2}}x + \boxed{4}$.

Your Turn

3. $\begin{cases} x + 2y + z = 8 \\ 2x + y - z = 4 \\ x + y - 3z = 7 \end{cases}$

$x + 2y + z = 8 \rightarrow z = 8 - x - 2y$

Substitute for z in the other equations.

$2x + y - (8 - x - 2y) = 4 \quad x + y + 3(8 - x - 2y) = 7$

$\downarrow \quad \downarrow$

$x + y = 4 \quad -2x - 5y = -17$

Solving this system yields $x = 1$ and $y = 3$

$z = 8 - x - 2y \rightarrow z = 8 - 1 - 2(3) = 1$

So the ordered triple is (1, 3, 1).

4. $\begin{cases} 2x - y - 3z = 1 \\ 4x + 3y + 2z = -4 \\ -3x + 2y + 5z = -3 \end{cases}$

$2x - y - 3z = 1 \rightarrow 2x - 3z - 1 = y$

Substitute for y in the other equations.

$4x + 3(2x - 3z - 1) + 2z = -4 \quad -3x + 2(2x - 3z - 1) + 5z = -3$

$\downarrow \quad \downarrow$

$10x - 7z = -1 \quad x - z = -1$

Solving this system yields $x = 2$ and $z = 3$.

$2x - 3z - 1 = y \rightarrow 2(2) - 3(3) - 1 = y = -6$

So the ordered triple is (2, −6, 3).

DIFFERENTIATE INSTRUCTION

Visual Cues

Show students a graph of all of the possible ways three planes can intersect and have them identify the number and nature of the solutions in each case.

EXPLAIN 2

Solving a System of Three Linear Equations Using Elimination

AVOID COMMON ERRORS

When solving a system of three linear equations by elimination, students may choose two equations, eliminate one of the variables, and then choose another pair of the original equations and eliminate a different variable instead of the same variable. Tell them that although they now have an equivalent system, it does not help them solve if they do not eliminate the same variable.

Explain 2 Solving a System of Three Linear Equations Using Elimination

You can also solve systems of three linear equations using elimination.

Example 2

A
$$\begin{cases} -2x + y + 3z = 20 & \boxed{1} \\ -3x + 2y + z = 21 & \boxed{2} \\ 3x - 2y + 3z = -9 & \boxed{3} \end{cases}$$

Begin by looking for variables with coefficients that are either the same or additive inverses of each other. When subtracted or added, these pairs will eliminate that variable. Subtract equation $\boxed{3}$ from equation $\boxed{1}$ to eliminate the z variable.

$$\begin{array}{ll} \boxed{1} & -2x + y + 3z = 20 \\ \boxed{3} & \underline{3x - 2y + 3z = -9} \\ & -5x + 3y + 0 = 29 \quad \boxed{4} \end{array}$$

Next multiply $\boxed{2}$ by -3 and add it to $\boxed{1}$ to eliminate the same variable.

$$\begin{array}{llcl} \boxed{1} & -2x + y + 3z = 20 & & -2x + y + 3z = 20 \\ \boxed{2} & \underline{-3(-3x + 2y + z = 21)} & \Rightarrow & \underline{9x - 6y - 3z = -63} \\ & & & 7x - 5y + 0 = -43 \quad \boxed{5} \end{array}$$

This results in the system of two linear equations below.

$$\begin{cases} -5x + 3y = 29 & \boxed{4} \\ 7x - 5y = -43 & \boxed{5} \end{cases}$$

To solve this system, multiply $\boxed{4}$ by 5 and add the result to the product of $\boxed{5}$ and 3.

$$\begin{array}{llcl} \boxed{4} & 5(-5x + 3y = 29) & & -25 + 15y = 145 \\ \boxed{5} & \underline{3(7x - 5y = -43)} & \Rightarrow & \underline{21x - 15y = -129} \\ & & & -4x + 0 = 16 \\ & & & -4x = 16 \\ & & & x = -4 \end{array}$$

Substitute to solve for y and z.

$$\begin{array}{ll} -5x + 3y = 29 \quad [4] & -3x + 2y + z = 21 \quad [2] \\ -5(-4) + 3y = 29 & -3(-4) + 2(3) + z = 21 \\ y = 3 & z = 3 \end{array}$$

The solution to the system is the ordered triple $(-4, 3, 3)$.

LANGUAGE SUPPORT EL

Communicate Math

Give each pair of students a sheet with three linear equations and the beginnings of the three different solution methods for the system. Have them label the kind of solution method shown (elimination, substitution, matrices). The partners must agree that the labels are accurate and then describe which method is easiest for each of them and why.

Students then solve the systems using the chosen method, and compare solutions. Suggest students discuss any disagreements about a method's ease of use.

(B) $\begin{cases} x + 2y + 3z = 9 & \boxed{1} \\ x + 3y + 2z = 5 & \boxed{2} \\ x - 4y - z = -5 & \boxed{3} \end{cases}$

Begin by subtracting equation $\boxed{2}$ from equation $\boxed{1}$ to eliminate x.

$\boxed{1}$ $x + 2y + 3z = 9$

$\boxed{2}$ $x + 3y + 2z = 5$

$0x - y + z = 4$ $\boxed{4}$

Now subtract equation $\boxed{3}$ from equation $\boxed{1}$ to eliminate x.

$\boxed{1}$ $x + 2y + 3z = 9$

$\boxed{3}$ $x + 4y - z = 5$

$0x - 2y + 4z = 14$ $\boxed{5}$

This results in a system of two linear equations:

$\begin{cases} -y + z = 4 & \boxed{4} \\ -2y + 4z = 14 & \boxed{5} \end{cases}$

To solve this system, multiply equation $\boxed{5}$ by $-\frac{1}{2}$ and add it to equation $\boxed{4}$.

$\boxed{4}$ $-y + z = 4$ $\quad -y + z = 4$

$\boxed{5}$ $-\frac{1}{2}(-2y + 4z = 14) \Rightarrow y - 2z = -7$

$0y - z = -3$

$z = 3$

Substitute to solve for y and x.

$-y + z = 4$ [4] $\quad x + 2y + 3z = 4$ [1]

$-y + 3 = 4$ $\quad x + 2(-1) + 3(3) = 9$

$y = -1$ $\quad x = 2$

The solution to the system is the ordered triple $(2, -1, 3)$.

QUESTIONING STRATEGIES

? What will happen if you choose two of the three linear equations in the system, eliminate one of the three variables, then choose another pair of the original equations and eliminate a different variable? **You will then have a system of two equations in three variables that is impossible to solve.**

EXPLAIN 3

Solving a System of Three Linear Equations Using Matrices

AVOID COMMON ERRORS

Remember to write each equation in the form $ax + by + cz = d$ before writing the matrix so that the elements of the matrix are in the correct order.

Your Turn

5. $\begin{cases} x + 2y + z = 8 & \boxed{1} \\ 2x + y - z = 4 & \boxed{2} \\ x + y + 3z = 7 & \boxed{3} \end{cases}$

$$\begin{array}{r} x + 2y + z = 8 \\ + \; 2x + y - z = 4 \\ \hline 3x + 3y = 12 \end{array} \quad \Rightarrow \; x + y = 4$$

$$3(2x + y - z = 4) \;\Rightarrow\; 6x + 3y - 3z = 12$$

$$\begin{array}{r} + \; x + y + 3z = 7 \end{array} \qquad \begin{array}{r} + \; x + y + 3z = 7 \\ \hline 7x + 4y = 19 \end{array}$$

$$\begin{array}{r} -7(x + y = 4) \\ + \;\; 7x + 4y = 19 \\ \hline \end{array} \quad \Rightarrow \quad \begin{array}{r} -7x - 7y = -28 \\ + \;\; 7x + 4y = 19 \\ \hline 3y = 9 \\ y = 3 \end{array}$$

$x + (3) = 4 \rightarrow x = 1$

$x + 2y + z = 8 \rightarrow 1 + 2(3) + z = 8 \rightarrow z = 1$

So the ordered triple is $(1, 3, 1)$.

6. $\begin{cases} 2x - y - 3z = 1 & \boxed{1} \\ 4x + 3y + 2z = -4 & \boxed{2} \\ -3x + 2y + 5z = -3 & \boxed{3} \end{cases}$

$$\begin{array}{r} 3(2x - y - 3z = 1) \\ 4x + 3y + 2z = -4 \\ \hline 10x - 7z = -1 \end{array} \quad \Rightarrow \quad \begin{array}{r} 6x - 3y - 9z = 3 \\ 4x + 3y + 2z = - \\ \hline \end{array}$$

$$\begin{array}{r} 2(4x + 3y + 2z = -4) \\ -3(-3x + 2y + 5z = -3) \\ \hline \end{array} \quad \Rightarrow \quad \begin{array}{r} 8x + 6y + 4z = - \\ 9x - 6y - 15z = 9 \\ \hline 17x - 11z = 1 \end{array}$$

$$\begin{array}{r} 11(10x - 7z = -1) \\ -7(17x - 11z = 1) \\ \hline \end{array} \quad \Rightarrow \quad \begin{array}{r} 110x - 77z = -1 \\ -119x + 77z = -7 \\ \hline -9x = -1 \\ x = 2 \end{array}$$

$10x + 7z = -\,1 \rightarrow 10(2) - 7z = -1 \rightarrow z = 3$

$2x - y - 3z = 1 \rightarrow 2(2) - y - 3(3) = 1 \rightarrow y = -$

So the ordered triple is $(2, -6, 3)$.

Explain 3 Solving a System of Three Linear Equations Using Matrices

You can represent systems of three linear equations in a *matrix*. A **matrix** is a rectangular array of numbers enclosed in brackets. Matrices are referred to by size: an *m*-by-*n* matrix has *m* rows and *n* columns.

A system of three linear equations can be written in a 3-by-4 matrix as follows. First rearrange the equations so all of the variables are to the left of the equals sign and the constant term is to the right. Then, each row corresponds to an equation and each of the first three columns represents a variable. Each entry represents the coefficient of the variable represented by the column in the equation related to the row. The fourth column is the constants that were to the right of the equals sign.

The system $\begin{cases} 2x + y + 3z = 20 \\ 5x + 2y + z = 21 \\ 3x - 2y + 7z = 9 \end{cases}$ is expressed as $\begin{bmatrix} 2 & 1 & 3 & 20 \\ 5 & 2 & 1 & 21 \\ 3 & -2 & 7 & -9 \end{bmatrix}$ in matrix form.

Gaussian Elimination is a formalized process of using matrices to eliminate two of the variables in each equation in the system. This results in an easy way to view the solution set. The process involves using *elementary row operations* to generate equivalent matrices that lead to a solution.

The **elementary row operations** are

(1) Multiplying a row by a constant – When performing row multiplication, the product of the original value and the constant replaces each value in the row.

(2) Adding two rows – In row addition, each value in the second row mentioned in the addition is replaced by the sum of the values in the equivalent column of the two rows being summed. These operations can also be performed together.

The elimination can be continued past this point to a matrix in which the solutions can be simply read directly out of the matrix. You can use a graphing calculator to perform these operations. The commands are shown in the table.

Command	Meaning	Syntax
*row(	replace each value in the row indicated with the product of the current value and the given number	*row(value,matrix,row)
row+(	replace rowB with the sum of rowA and the current rowB	row+(matrix,rowA,rowB)
*row+(	replace rowB with the product of the given value and rowA added to the current value of rowB	*row+(value,matrix,rowA,rowB)

Example 3 **Solve the system of three linear equations using matrices.**

$$\begin{cases} -2x + y + 3z = 20 \\ -3x + 2y + z = 21 \\ 3x - 2y + 3z = -9 \end{cases}$$

Input the system as a 3-by-4 matrix. Multiply the first row by –0.5. Enter the command into your calculator. Press enter to view the result.

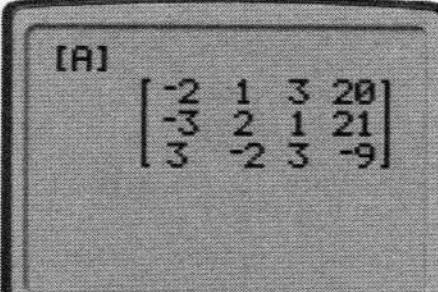

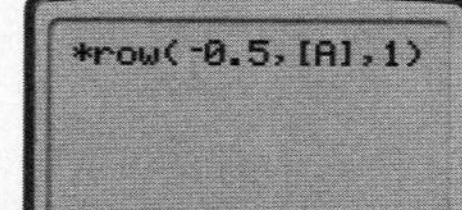

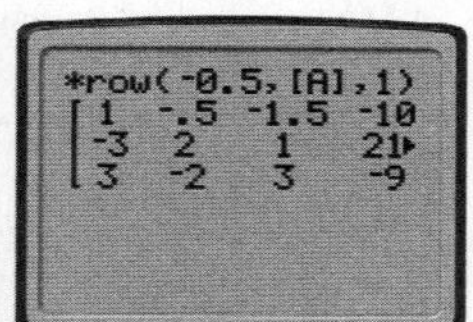

QUESTIONING STRATEGIES

What operations will produce a matrix that is row-equivalent to the original? Interchange two rows; multiply a row by a nonzero constant; then add a multiple of one row to another.

To reuse the resulting matrix, store it into Matrix B. Add 3 times row 1 to row 2. Press enter to view the result. Remember to store the result into a new matrix.

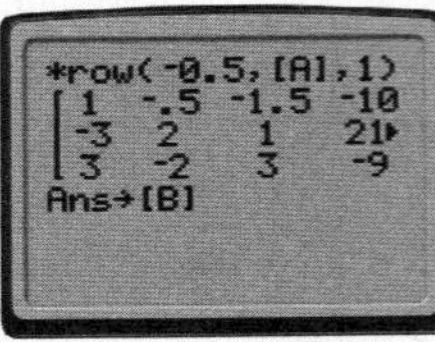

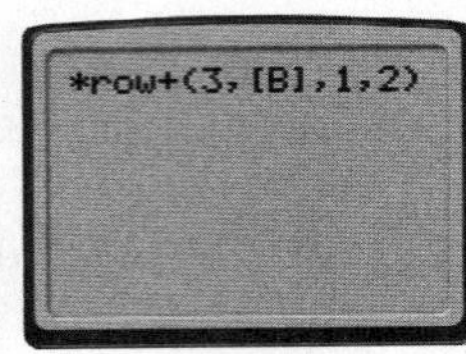

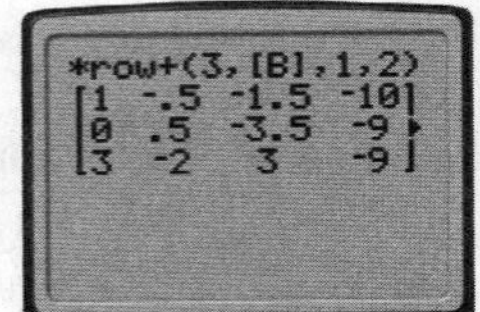

Multiply row 2 by 2. Add −3 times row 1 to row 3. Add 0.5 times row 2 to row 3.

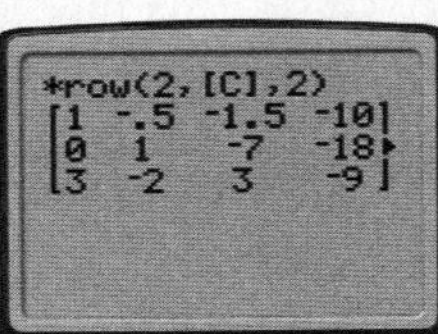

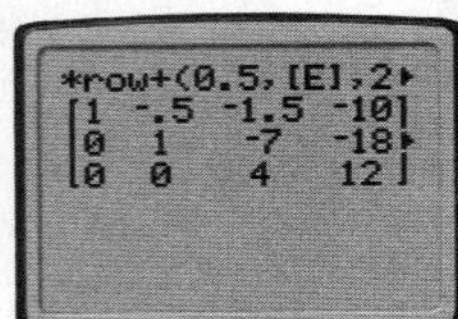

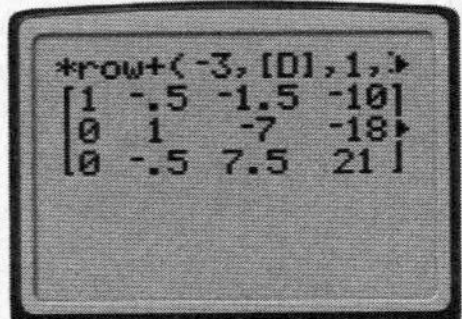

Multiply row 3 by 0.25. Add 7 times row 3 to row 2. Add 1.5 times row 3 to row 1.

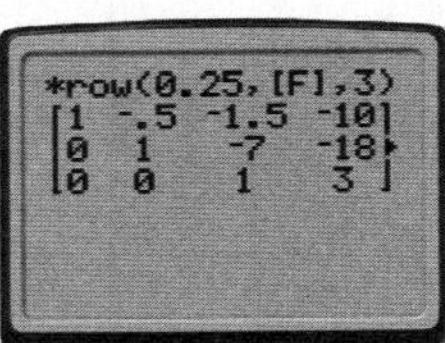

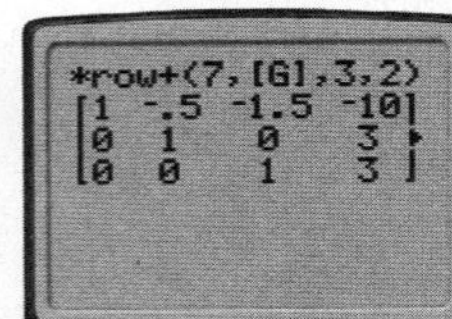

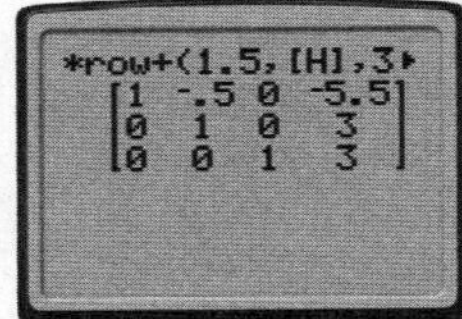

Add 0.5 times row 2 to row 1.

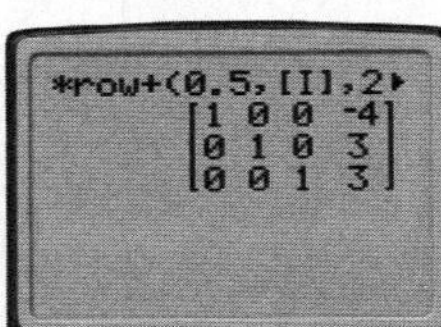

The first row tells us that $x = -4$, the second row tells us that $y = 3$, and the third row tells us that $z = 3$. So the solution is the ordered triple $(-4, 3, 3)$.

(B) $\begin{cases} x + 2y + 3z = 9 \\ x + 3y + 2z = 5 \\ x + 4y - z = -5 \end{cases}$

Write as a matrix.

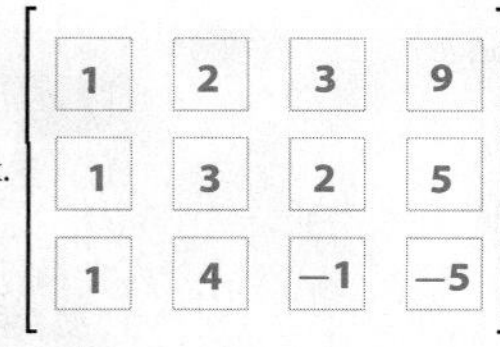

$$\begin{bmatrix} 1 & 2 & 3 & 9 \\ 1 & 3 & 2 & 5 \\ 1 & 4 & -1 & -5 \end{bmatrix}$$

Perform row operations.

$-r1 + r2$ $\begin{bmatrix} 1 & 2 & 3 & 9 \\ 0 & 1 & -1 & -4 \\ 1 & 4 & -1 & -5 \end{bmatrix}$

$-r1 + r3$ $\begin{bmatrix} 1 & 2 & 3 & 9 \\ 0 & 1 & -1 & -4 \\ 0 & 2 & -4 & -14 \end{bmatrix}$

$-2r2 + r3$ $\begin{bmatrix} 1 & 2 & 3 & 9 \\ 0 & 1 & -1 & -4 \\ 0 & 0 & -2 & -6 \end{bmatrix}$

$-0.5r3$ $\begin{bmatrix} 1 & 2 & 3 & 9 \\ 0 & 1 & -1 & -4 \\ 0 & 0 & 1 & 3 \end{bmatrix}$

$r3 + r2$ $\begin{bmatrix} 1 & 2 & 3 & 9 \\ 0 & 1 & 0 & -1 \\ 0 & 0 & 1 & 3 \end{bmatrix}$

$-3r3 + r1$ $\begin{bmatrix} 1 & 2 & 0 & 0 \\ 0 & 1 & 0 & -1 \\ 0 & 0 & 1 & 3 \end{bmatrix}$

$2r2 + r1$ $\begin{bmatrix} 1 & 0 & 0 & 2 \\ 0 & 1 & 0 & -1 \\ 0 & 0 & 1 & 3 \end{bmatrix}$

The solution is the ordered triple (2, −1, 3).

Your Turn

7. $\begin{cases} x + 2y + z = 8 \\ 2x + y - z = 4 \\ x + y + 3z = 7 \end{cases}$

Input the system as a 3-by-4 matrix. $\begin{bmatrix} 1 & 2 & 1 & 8 \\ 2 & 1 & -1 & 4 \\ 1 & 1 & 3 & 7 \end{bmatrix}$

Multiply row 1 by −2 and add it to row 2. Multiply row 1 by −1 and add it to row 3. Multiply row 2 by $-\frac{1}{3}$. Add row 2 to row 3. Multiply row 3 by $\frac{1}{3}$. Multiply row 3 by −1 and add it to row 1. Multiply row 3 by −1 and add it to row 2. Multiply row 2 by −1 and add it to row 1.

$\begin{bmatrix} 1 & 0 & 0 & 1 \\ 0 & 1 & 0 & 3 \\ 0 & 0 & 1 & 1 \end{bmatrix}$ **So, the solution of the system is (1, 3, 1).**

EXPLAIN 4

Solving a Real-World Problem

INTEGRATE MATHEMATICAL PRACTICES

Focus on Communication

MP.3 Have students work in pairs or small groups to write and solve another real-world problem that can be modeled with a system of three linear equations in three variables.

QUESTIONING STRATEGIES

? Will there always be a solution to a system of three linear equations in three variables written to model a real-world problem? **No. There will not always be a solution. There will not be a solution if all of the given parameters cannot be met.**

Explain 4 Solving a Real-World Problem

Example 4

(A) A child has \$6.17 in change in her piggy bank. The change consists of 113 coins in a mix of pennies, nickels, and quarters. If there are 8 times as many nickels as pennies, how many of each coin does the child have? Solve using substitution.

Begin by setting up a system of equations, and use p for the number of pennies, n for the number of nickels, and q for the number of quarters. Use the relationships in the problem statement to write the equations.

The total number of coins is the sum of the number of each coin. So, the first equation is $p + n + q = 113$.

The total value of the coins is \$6.17 or 617 cents (converting the value to cents will allow all coefficients to be integers). The second equation will be $p + 5n + 25q = 617$.

The third relationship given is that there are eight times as many nickels as pennies or, $n = 8p$. This gives the following system of equations:

$$\begin{cases} p + n + q = 113 & \boxed{1} \\ p + 5n + 25q = 617 & \boxed{2} \\ n = 8p & \boxed{3} \end{cases}$$

Equation $\boxed{3}$ is already solved for n. Substitute for n in equations $\boxed{1}$ and $\boxed{2}$ simplify.

$$p + (8p) + q = 113$$
$$9p + q = 113 \quad \boxed{4}$$

$$p + 5(8p) + 25q = 617$$
$$p + 40p + 25q = 617$$
$$41p + 25q = 617 \quad \boxed{5}$$

This results in the following linear system in two variables:

$$\begin{cases} 9p + q = 113 & \boxed{4} \\ 41p + 25q = 617 & \boxed{5} \end{cases}$$

Solve equation $\boxed{4}$ for q.

$$9p + q = 113$$
$$q = 113 - 9p$$

Substitute for q in equation $\boxed{5}$ and solve for p.

$$41p + 25(113 - 9p) = 617$$
$$41p + 2825 - 225p = 617$$
$$12 = p$$

Evaluate at $p = 12$ to find q and n.

$$q = 113 - 9p \qquad n = 8p$$
$$q = 113 - 9(12) \qquad n = 8(12)$$
$$q = 5 \qquad n = 96$$

The child's piggy bank contains 12 pennies, 96 nickels, and 5 quarters.

Ⓑ A student is shopping for clothes. The student needs to buy an equal number of shirts and ties. He also needs to buy four times as many shirts as pants. Shirts cost \$35, ties cost \$25, and pants cost \$40. If the student spends \$560, how many shirts, pants, and ties did he get?

Begin by setting up a system of equations, using s for the number of shirts, t for the number of ties, and p for the number pairs of pants. Use the relationships in the problem statement to write the equations.

The number of shirts is equal to the number of ties. So, the first equation is $s = t$.

The number of shirts is equal to 4 times the number of pairs of pants, so a second equation is $s =$ **4p**.

The total the student spent is the sum of the cost of the shirts, the ties, and the pairs of pants.

$35s + 25t + 40p =$ **560**

The system of equations is below.

$$\begin{cases} s = t & \boxed{1} \\ s = 4p & \boxed{2} \\ 35s + 25t + 40p = 560 & \boxed{3} \end{cases}$$

Equation 1 is already solved for t. Solve equation 2 for p.

$4p = s$

$p = \boxed{\frac{1}{4}s}$

Substitute for p and t in equation 3 and solve for s.

$$35s + 25(s) + 40\left(\frac{1}{4}s\right) = 560$$

$$35s + 25s + 10s = 560$$

$$\boxed{70}\,s = 560$$

$$s = \boxed{8}$$

Evaluate the equation solved for p above at $s = 8$ to find p.

$p = \frac{1}{4}s$

$p = \frac{1}{4}(8) = 2$

Recall that $s = t$, so $t = 8$.

The student bought **8** shirts, **8** ties, and **2** pairs of pants.

CONNECT VOCABULARY EL

Compare and contrast a system of three linear equations in three variables to the linear-quadratic systems discussed in the previous lesson. Have students complete a chart showing the similarities and differences between these two kinds of systems.

ELABORATE

AVOID COMMON ERRORS

Students may assume that systems have a single solution, namely, that the equations are unique and their graphs intersect at a point. Remind them that a system of three linear equations may be dependent; that is, all three equations may describe the same plane, or the system may be inconsistent, meaning there is no point or line in which all three planes intersect.

SUMMARIZE THE LESSON

? What are the principal methods of solving a real-world problem that can be modeled by a system of three linear equations in three variables? **Translate to a system, then use substitution, elimination, or matrices to solve it and apply the solution to the problem.**

Your Turn

8. Louie Dampier is the leading scorer in the history of the American Basketball Association (ABA). His 13,726 points were scored on two-point baskets, three-point baskets, and one-point free throws. In his ABA career, Dampier made 2144 more two-point baskets than free throws and 1558 more free throws than three-point baskets. How many three-point baskets, two-point baskets, and free throws did Dampier make?

$r = f + 2144 \Rightarrow r = (t + 1588) + 2144 \Rightarrow r = t + 3732$

$r = t + 1588$

$$2r + 3t + f = 13726$$
$$2(t + 3732) + 3t + (t + 1588) = 13726$$
$$t = 779$$

$f = 779 + 1588 = 2367$

↓

$r = (2367) + 2144 = 4511$

So, $t = 779$, $f = 2367$ and $r = 4511$.

Elaborate

9. If you are given a system of linear equations in three variables, but the system only has two equations, what happens when you try to solve it?

The solution will be a line because it will be in terms of two variables.

10. Discussion Why does a system need to have at least as many equations as unknowns to have a unique solution?

If there is not an equation for each variable, the solution processes outlined above cannot progress to the end, and you will be left with one variable defined only in terms of another.

11. Essential Question Check-In How can you find the solution to a system of three linear equations in three variables?

The system can be solved by substitution, elimination, or by using matrices.

Evaluate: Homework and Practice

- Online Homework
- Hints and Help
- Extra Practice

Solve the system using substitution.

1. $\begin{cases} 4x + y - 2z = -6 & 1 \\ 2x - 3y + 3z = 9 & 2 \\ x - 2y = 0 & 3 \end{cases}$

$x - 2y = 0 \rightarrow x = 2y$

Now substitute for x in the first and second equations and simplify.

$4(2y) + y - 2z = -6$

$\downarrow$

$9y - 2z = -6$

$2(2y) - 3y + 3z = 9$

$\downarrow$

$y + 3z = 9$

Solving this system yields $y = 0$ and $z = 3$

$x = 2(0) = 0$

So the ordered triple is $(0, 0, 3)$.

2. $\begin{cases} x + 5y + 3z = 4 & 1 \\ 4y - z = 3 & 2 \\ 6x - 2y + 4z = 0 & 3 \end{cases}$

$4y - z = 3 \rightarrow 4y - 3 = z$

$x + 5y + 3(4y - 3) = 4$

$\downarrow$

$x + 17y = 13$

$6x - 2y + 4(4y - 3) = 0$

$\downarrow$

$3x + 7y = 6$

Solving this system yields $x = 0.25$ and $y = 0.75$.

$z = 4y - 3 = 4(0.75) - 3 = 0$

So the ordered triple is $(0.25, 0.75, 0)$.

Solve the system using elimination.

3. $\begin{cases} 4x + y - 2z = -6 & 1 \\ 2x - 3y + 3z = 9 & 2 \\ x - 2y = 0 & 3 \end{cases}$

$3(4x + y - 2z = -6) \Rightarrow 12x + 3y - 6z = -18$

$\underline{2x - 3y + 3z = 9} \qquad \underline{2x - 3y + 3z = 9}$

$14x - 3z = -9$

$2(2x - 3y + 3z = 9) \Rightarrow 4x - 6y + 6z = 18$

$\underline{-3(x - 2y = 0)} \qquad \underline{-3x + 6y = 0}$

$x + 6z = 18$

$2(14x - 3z = -9) \Rightarrow 28x - 6z = -18$

$\underline{x + 6z = 18} \qquad \underline{x + 6z = 18}$

$29x = 0$

$x = 0$

$14x - 3z = -9 \rightarrow 14(0) - 3z = -9 \rightarrow z = 3$

$4x + y - 2z = -6 \rightarrow 4(0) + y - 2(3) = -6 \rightarrow y = 0$

So the ordered triple is $(0, 0, 3)$.

EVALUATE

ASSIGNMENT GUIDE

Concepts and Skills	Practice
Explore Recognizing Ways that Planes Can Intersect	Exercise 14
Example 1 Solving a System of Three Linear Equations Using Substitution	Exercises 1–2
Example 2 Solving a System of Three Linear Equations Using Elimination	Exercises 3–5
Example 3 Solving a System of Three Linear Equations Using Matrices	Exercises 6–7
Example 4 Solving a Real-World Problem	Exercises 11–13

INTEGRATE MATHEMATICAL PRACTICES

Focus on Modeling

MP.4 Have students work in small groups. Have each group use pieces of paper to model systems of three equations in three variables. Have each group model a consistent system with a single point as a solution, a consistent system with a line as a solution, an inconsistent system, and a dependent system.

Exercise	Depth of Knowledge (D.O.K.)	COMMON CORE Mathematical Practices
1–5	**1** Recall of Information	**MP.2** Reasoning
6–7	**1** Recall of Information	**MP.5** Using Tools
8–9	**1** Recall of Information	**MP.2** Reasoning
10	**2** Skills/Concepts	**MP.6** Precision
11–13	**2** Skills/Concepts	**MP.4** Modeling

AVOID COMMON ERRORS

Remind students that a system of three linear equations may have no solution (when all three planes do not intersect), a single solution (when the planes intersect at a single point), or an infinite number of solutions (when the planes intersect in a line and when the system is dependent).

4. $\begin{cases} x + 5y + 3z = 4 & 1 \\ 4y - z = 3 & 2 \\ 6x - 2y + 4z = 0 & 3 \end{cases}$

$$3(4y - z = 3) \Rightarrow 12y - 3z = 9$$
$$\underline{x + 5y + 3z = 4} \qquad \underline{x + 5y + 3z = 4}$$
$$x + 17y = 13$$

$$4(4y - z = 3) \Rightarrow 16y - 4z = 12$$
$$\underline{6x - 2y + 4z = 0} \qquad \underline{6x - 2y + 4z = 0}$$
$$6x + 14y = 12$$
$$\downarrow$$
$$3x + 7y = 6$$

$$-3(x + 17y = 13) \Rightarrow -3x - 51y = -39$$
$$\underline{3x + 7y = 6} \qquad \underline{3x + 7y = 6}$$
$$-44y = -33$$
$$y = 0.75$$

$x + 17y = 13 \rightarrow x + 17(0.75) = 13 \rightarrow x = 0.25$

$x + 5y + 3z = 4 \rightarrow 0.25 + 5(0.75) + 3z = 4 \rightarrow z = 0$

So the ordered triple is $(0.25, 0.75, 0)$.

5. $\begin{cases} 2x - y + 3z = -12 & 1 \\ -x + 2y - 3z = 15 & 2 \\ y + 5z = -6 & 3 \end{cases}$

$$2x - y + 3z = -12$$
$$\underline{-x + 2y - 3z = 15}$$
$$x + y = 3$$

$$5(-x + 2y - 3z = 15) \Rightarrow -5x + 10y - 15z = 75$$
$$\underline{3(y + 5z = -6)} \qquad \underline{3y + 15z = -18}$$
$$-5x + 13y = 57$$

$$5(x + y = 3) \Rightarrow 5x + 5y = 15z$$
$$\underline{-5x + 13y = 57} \qquad 5x + 13y = 57$$
$$18y = 72$$
$$y = 4$$

$x + y = 3 \rightarrow x + (4) = 3 \rightarrow x = -1$

$2x - y + 3z = -12 \rightarrow 2(-1) - 4 + 3z = -12$

$3z = -6 \rightarrow z = -2$

So the ordered triple is $(-1, 4, -2)$.

Exercise	Depth of Knowledge (D.O.K.)	COMMON CORE Mathematical Practices
14–15	**3** Strategic Thinking H.O.T.	**MP.3** Logic
16	**3** Strategic Thinking H.O.T.	**MP.6** Precision

Solve the system of three linear equations using matrices.

6. $\begin{cases} 4x + y - 2z = -6 & 1 \\ 2x - 3y + 3z = 9 & 2 \\ x - 2y = 0 & 3 \end{cases}$

Input the system as a 3-by-4 matrix.

[A] $\begin{bmatrix} 4 & 1 & -2 & -6 \\ 2 & -3 & 3 & 9 \\ 1 & -2 & 0 & 0 \end{bmatrix}$

Switch row 3 with row 1 to make the matrix easier to solve.

Multiply row 1 by −4 and add it to row 3.

Multiply row 1 by −2 and add it to row 2.

Multiply row 2 by −9 and add it to row 3.

Multiply row 3 by $-\frac{1}{29}$**.**

Multiply row 3 by −3 and add it to row 2.

Multiply row 2 by 2 and add it to row 1.

$\begin{bmatrix} 1 & 0 & 0 & 0 \\ 0 & 1 & 0 & 0 \\ 0 & 0 & 1 & 3 \end{bmatrix}$

So, the solution is (0, 0, 3).

7. $\begin{cases} x + 5y + 3z = 4 & 1 \\ 4y - z = 3 & 2 \\ 6x - 2y + 4z = 0 & 3 \end{cases}$

Input the system as a 3-by-4 matrix.

[A] $\begin{bmatrix} 1 & 5 & 3 & 4 \\ 0 & 4 & -1 & 3 \\ 6 & -2 & 4 & 0 \end{bmatrix}$

Multiply row 1 by −6 and add it to row 3.

Multiply row 2 by 8 and add it to row 3.

Multiply row 3 by $-\frac{1}{22}$**.**

Add row 3 to row 2.

Multiply row 2 by 0.25.

Multiply row 2 by −5 and add it to row 1.

Multiply row 3 by −3 and add it to row 1.

$\begin{bmatrix} 1 & 0 & 0 & .25 \\ 0 & 1 & 0 & .75 \\ 0 & 0 & 1 & 0 \end{bmatrix}$

So, the solution is (0.25, 0.75, 0).

QUESTIONING STRATEGIES

Can a system of three linear equations in three variables be solved by graphing on the coordinate plane? Why or why not? **No; graphing in three variables requires a dimension for each of the variables, so a third variable would require a third axis, and thus a three-dimensional coordinate system.**

MULTIPLE REPRESENTATIONS

Show students that there are other ways to solve systems that involve determinants or augmented matrices with row reduction. Show students how a two-by-two system can be solved by using these methods, then explain how the methods can be applied to three-by-three systems.

Solve the system of linear equations using your method of choice.

8. $\begin{cases} 2x - y + 3z = 5 & 1 \\ -6x + 3y - 9z = -15 & 2 \\ 4x - 2y + 6z = 10 & 3 \end{cases}$

$$\begin{array}{rcr} 2x - y + 3z = 5 & \rightarrow & 2x + 3z - 5 = y \\ -6x + 3(2x + 3z - 5) - 9z = -15 & & 4x - 2(2x + 3z - 5) + 6z = 10 \\ -6x + 6x + 9z - 15 - 9z = -15 & & 4x - 4x - 6z + 10 + 6z = 10 \\ -15 = -15 & & 10 = 10 \end{array}$$

Both equations are true, so the system has infinitely many solutions.

9. $\begin{cases} 3x + 4y - z = -7 & 1 \\ x - 5y + 2z = 19 & 2 \\ 5x + y - 2z = 5 & 3 \end{cases}$

$$\begin{array}{rcr} 3x + 4y - z = -7 & \rightarrow & 3x + 4y + 7 = z \\ x - 5y + 2(3x + 4y + 7) = 19 & \Rightarrow & 5x + y - 2(3x + 4y + 7) = 5 \\ x - 5y + 6x + 8y + 14 = 19 & & 5x + y - 6x - 8y - 14 = 5 \\ 7x + 3y = 5 & & -x - 7y = 19 \end{array}$$

Solving this system yields $x = 2$ and $y = -3$

$3x + 4y + 7 = z \rightarrow 3(2) + 4(-3) + 7 = z \rightarrow 1 = z$

So the ordered triple is $(2, -3, 1)$

10. Find the equation of the parabola passing through the points $(3, 7)$, $(30, -11)$, and $(0, -1)$.

Identify the values of *a*, *b*, and *c* for the general form of a parabola

$$\begin{array}{rcrcr} (7) = a(3)^2 + b(3) + c & & 7 = 9a + 3b + c & & 7 = 9a + 3b - 1 \\ (-11) = a(30)^2 + b(30) + c & \Rightarrow & -11 = 900a + 30b + c & \Rightarrow & -11 = 900a + 30b - 1 \\ (-1) = a(0)^2 + b(0) + c & & -1 = c & & \end{array}$$

$\Rightarrow \begin{cases} 8 = 9a + 3b \\ -1 = 90a + 3b \end{cases}$ **Solving this systems yields $b = 3$ and $a = -\frac{1}{9}$**

So, the equation of the parabola connecting $(3, 7)$, $(30, -11)$, and $(0, -1)$ is $y = -\frac{1}{9}x^2 + 3x -$

11. Geometry In triangle ABC, the measure of angle X is eight times the sum of the measures of angles Y and Z. The measure of angle Y is three times the measure of angle Z. What are the measures of the angles?

$Y = 3Z \qquad X = 8(Y + Z) = 8(3Z) + 8Z = 32Z$

Substitute the equations for X and Y in terms of Z into the first equation.

$X + Y + Z = 180 \rightarrow (32Z) + (3Z) + Z = 180 \rightarrow Z = 5$

$Y = 3(5) \qquad X = 8(15) + 8(5)$

$Y = 15 \qquad X = 160$

So, angle X is 160°, angle Y is 15°, and angle Z is 5°.

12. The combined age of three relatives is 120 years. James is three times the age of Dan, and Paul is two times the sum of the ages of James and Dan. How old is each person?

Choose an equation and variable to start with. The third equation is already solved for J. $J = 3D$

Now substitute for J in the second equation and simplify.

$P = 2J + 2D = 2(3D) + 2D = 8D$

$J + D + P = 120 \rightarrow (3D) + D + (8D) = 120 \rightarrow D = 10$

$J = 3D = 3(10) = 30$

$P = 2J + 2D = 2(30) + 2(10) = 80$

So, Dan is 10 years old, James is 30 years old, and Paul is 80 years old.

13. Economics At a stock exchange there were a total of 10,000 shares sold in one day. Stock A had four times as many shares sold as Stock B. The number of shares sold for Stock C was equal to the sum of Stock A and Stock B. How many shares of each stock were sold?

$A = 4B$

$C = A + B = (4B) + B = 5B$

$A + B + C = 10{,}000 \rightarrow (4B) + B + (5B) = 10{,}000 \rightarrow B = 1000$

$A = 4B = 4(1000) = 4000$

$C = A + B = (4000) + (1000) = 5000$

Stock A sold 4000 shares, stock B sold 1000 shares, and stock C sold 5000 shares.

JOURNAL

Have students list the methods they have learned for solving systems of three linear equations in three variables, and include an example problem for each method.

H.O.T. Focus on Higher Order Thinking

14. Communicate Mathematical Ideas Explain how you know when a system has infinitely many solutions or when it has no solutions.

If when solving the system you get a true statement (such as $0 = 0$), then that system has infinitely many solutions. If when solving the system you get a false statement (such as $1 = 3$), then that system will have no solution.

15. Explain the Error When given this system of equations, a student was asked to solve using matrices. Find and correct the student's error.

$$\begin{cases} 5x + 7y + 9x = 0 \\ x - y + z = -3 \\ 8x + y = 12 \end{cases}$$

$$\begin{bmatrix} 5 & 7 & 9 \\ 1 & -1 & 1 \\ 8 & 1 & 0 \end{bmatrix}$$

The student did not add the last column of numbers representing the values to the right of the equals sign. The correct matrix set up should be as follows.

$$\begin{bmatrix} 5 & 7 & 9 & 0 \\ 1 & -1 & 1 & -3 \\ 8 & 1 & 0 & 12 \end{bmatrix}$$

16. Critical Thinking Explain why the following system of equations cannot be solved.

$$\begin{cases} 7x + y + 6z = 1 \\ -x - 4y + 8z = 9 \end{cases}$$

When solving a system of equations, there must be at least as many equations as there are variables.

Lesson Performance Task

A company that manufactures inline skates needs to order three parts—part *A*, part *B*, and part *C*. For one shipping order the company needs to buy a total of 6000 parts. There are four times as many *B* parts as *C* parts. The total number of *A* parts is one-fifth the sum of the *B* and *C* parts. On previous orders, the costs had been $0.25 for part *A*, $0.50 for part *B*, and $0.75 for part *C*, resulting in a cost of $3000 for all the parts in one order. When filling out an order for new parts, the company sees that it now costs $0.60 for part *A*, $0.40 for part *B*, and $0.60 for part *C*. Will the company be able to buy the same quantity of parts at the same price as before with the new prices?

$$\begin{cases} A+B+C=6000 \\ A=\frac{1}{5}(B+C) \\ B=C \end{cases} \Rightarrow \begin{cases} A+(4C)+C=6000 \\ A=\frac{1}{5}((4C)+C) \\ B=4C \end{cases} \Rightarrow \begin{cases} A+5C=6000 \\ A=C \\ B=4C \end{cases}$$

$$\Rightarrow \begin{cases} (C)+5C=6000 \\ A=C \\ B=4C \end{cases} \Rightarrow \begin{cases} C=1000 \\ A=C \\ B=4C \end{cases} \Rightarrow \begin{cases} C=1000 \\ A=C \\ B=4C \end{cases} \Rightarrow \begin{cases} C=1000 \\ A=1000 \\ B=4(1000)=4000 \end{cases}$$

Determine the new costs of each part with the price change.

Part $A = 1000 \cdot 0.60 = 600$

Part $B = 4000 \cdot 0.40 = 1600$

Part $C = 1000 \cdot 0.60 = 600$

The total cost will now be $2800, so the company will be able to afford the parts it needs and can actually buy more.

EXTENSION ACTIVITY

The techniques for solving three equations in three unknowns can be extended to solve systems with four or more equations. Ask students to explore solution methods for solving systems of four or more equations, and to examine their graphing calculators' matrix-solving capabilities as well. Have students report on the methods used, as well as on the differences they found. They should note that graphing is not an option, because a fourth dimension, or greater, would be required.

INTEGRATE MATHEMATICAL PRACTICES

Focus on Modeling

MP.4 Because the information is listed in a long paragraph, students may have difficulty setting up the system. First have them read the statement of the problem and ask what the variables are. Have them consider each sentence of the paragraph separately and write it in simplified form, if necessary. Lightly crossing off each segment as it is turned into an equation will make it easier to see what remains to be modeled.

QUESTIONING STRATEGIES

? What quantities do each of the equations represent? **One equation represents the total number of parts, one represents the relationship between the numbers of units of A to the units of B and C, and one represents the relationship between the numbers of units of B to the units of C.**

Scoring Rubric

2 points: Student correctly solves the problem and explains his/her reasoning.

1 point: Student shows good understanding of the problem but does not fully solve or explain his/her reasoning.

0 points: Student does not demonstrate understanding of the problem.

Study Guide Review

ASSESSMENT AND INTERVENTION

Assign or customize module reviews.

MODULE PERFORMANCE TASK

COMMON CORE

Mathematical Practices: MP.1, MP.2, MP.4
A-REI.C.7, A-CED.A.2, F-BF.A.1

SUPPORTING STUDENT REASONING

Students should begin by focusing on how to represent the situation using algebra. They may choose to write functions to represent both the laser and the disk, or just use a coordinate point for the disk's maximum.

- **What two quantities are related in the functions?** The description of the disk relates horizontal distance to vertical height, so both functions should relate those quantities.
- **What type of function can I use to represent the disk and the laser?** The disk follows a parabolic path, but the laser is straight.
- **How do I represent where the designer points the laser?** You can find an equation that represents the path of the laser when it's fired correctly.

STUDY GUIDE REVIEW

Quadratic Relations and Systems of Equations

MODULE 4

Essential Question: How can you use systems of equations to solve real-world problems?

Key Vocabulary
directrix *(directriz)*
focus of a parabola *(foco de una parábola)*
linear equation in three variables *(ecuación lineal en tres variables)*
matrix *(matriz)*
ordered triple *(tripleta ordenada)*

KEY EXAMPLE *(Lesson 4.1)*

Write the equation of a circle that has a center at (−3, 5) and a radius of 9.

$(x-h)^2 + (y-k)^2 = r^2$	The standard form of the equation of a circle
$h = -3$	x-coordinate of center
$k = 5$	y-coordinate of center
$r = 9$	radius
$(x-(-3))^2 + (y-5)^2 = 9^2$	Substitute.
$(x+3)^2 + (y-5)^2 = 81$	Simplify.

KEY EXAMPLE *(Lesson 4.3)*

Solve the system using elimination.

$$\begin{cases} 5x + y = 10 \\ y + 2 = 3(x+4)^2 \end{cases}$$

$y - 10 = -5x$ First, line up the terms.

$y + 2 = 3(x+4)^2$

$y - 10 = -5x$ Subtract the second equation from the first.

$\cancel{-y} + (-2) = -3(x+4)^2$

$-12 = 5x - 3(x+4)^2$

$-12 = 5x - 3(x+4)^2$

$-12 = 5x - 3x^2 - 24x - 48$

$0 = -3x^2 - 19x - 36$ Solve the resulting equation for x.

$$x = \frac{19 \pm \sqrt{(-19)^2 - 4(-3)(-36)}}{2(-3)}$$

$$x = \frac{19 \pm i\sqrt{71}}{-6}$$

There is no real number equivalent, so the system has no solution.

SCAFFOLDING SUPPORT

- Encourage students to start by making a rough sketch of the scenario on graph paper. Be sure they take into account the fact that the laser is shot at an initial height of 5 feet.
- Students might also want to attempt to describe the angle of the laser using degrees. Encourage them to try, and point out that they will likely need to use trigonometry to figure out the angle. Provide assistance if needed. (The angle of inclination is $\tan^{-1}(5/6)$, or 39.8°.)

EXERCISES

Find the equation of the circle with the given characteristics. *(Lessons 4.1)*

1. Center: (3, 4)

Radius: 6

$(x-3)^2+(y-4)^2=36$

2. Center: (−7.5, 15)

Radius: 1.5

$(x+7.5)^2=(y-15)^2=2.25$

Find the center and radius of the given circle. *(Lessons 4.1)*

3. $(x-5)^2+(y-8)^2=144$

center: (5, 8)

radius: 12

4. $x^2+(y+6)^2=50$

center: (0, −6)

radius: $5\sqrt{2}$

Find the solution to the system of equations using graphing or elimination. *(Lessons 4.2, 4.3, 4.4)*

5. $\begin{cases}4x+3y=1\\ y=x^2-x-1\end{cases}$

$(1,-1)$ and $\left(-\frac{4}{3},\frac{19}{9}\right)$

6. $\begin{cases}x-3y=2\\ y=x^2+2x-34\end{cases}$

$(5,1)$ and $\left(-\frac{20}{3},-\frac{26}{9}\right)$

7. $\begin{cases}3x+5y-2z=-7\\ -2x+7y+6z=-3\\ 8x+3y-10z=-11\end{cases}$

infinitely many solutions

8. $\begin{cases}3x+24y+9z=9\\ x-8y-3z=37\\ 2x-16y-6z=75\end{cases}$

no solution

MODULE PERFORMANCE TASK

How Can You Hit a Moving Target with a Laser Beam?

A video game designer is creating a game similar to skeet shooting, where a player will use a laser beam to hit a virtual clay disk launched into the air. The disk is launched from the ground and, if nothing blows it up, it reaches a maximum height of 30 meters and returns to the ground 60 meters away. The laser is fired from a height of 5 meters above the ground. Where should the designer point the laser to hit the disk at its maximum height?

Use your own paper to complete the task. Be sure to write down all your data and assumptions. Then use graphs, numbers, words, or algebra to explain how you reached your conclusion.

SAMPLE SOLUTION

Assumptions:

The path of the clay disk can be described by a quadratic function, and it is not affected by air resistance.

The laser beam travels in a straight line.

If the clay disk is shot from (0, 0), reaches a maximum height of 30, and reaches the ground again at (60, 0), the vertex of the parabola describing the disk's path must be at (30, 30), halfway between the two *x*-intercepts.

The laser is shot from a height of 5 meters, so find the equation that goes through (0, 5) and (30, 30):

$$m=\frac{y_2-y_1}{x_2-x_1}=\frac{30-5}{30-0}=\frac{5}{6}$$

$$y-y_1=\frac{5}{6}(x-x_1)$$

$$y-5=\frac{5}{6}(x-0)$$

$$y=\frac{5}{6}x+5$$

The equation of the line describing the laser is $y=\frac{5}{6}x+5$.

DISCUSSION OPPORTUNITIES

- Students might realize that the laser beam could miss if it is fired at the wrong time. What additional information would they need to figure out when the laser should be fired to score a hit?
- Students may be unfamiliar with the context of skeet shooting. Have a class conversation about the trajectories for objects that are launched upward into the air before falling back to the ground.

Assessment Rubric

2 points: Student correctly solves the problem and explains his/her reasoning.

1 point: Student shows good understanding of the problem but does not fully solve or explain.

0 points: Student does not demonstrate understanding of the problem.

Ready to Go On?

ASSESS MASTERY

Use the assessment on this page to determine if students have mastered the concepts and standards covered in this module.

ASSESSMENT AND INTERVENTION

Access Ready to Go On? assessment online, and receive instant scoring, feedback, and customized intervention or enrichment.

ADDITIONAL RESOURCES

Response to Intervention Resources

- Reteach Worksheets

Differentiated Instruction Resources

- Reading Strategies EL
- Success for English Learners EL
- Challenge Worksheets

Assessment Resources

- Leveled Module Quizzes

Ready to Go On?

4.1–4.4 Quadratic Relations and Systems of Equations

- Online Homework
- Hints and Help
- Extra Practice

Find the equation of the circle with the given characteristics. *(Lessons 4.1)*

1. Center: (0, –2)
Radius: 1

$x^2 + (y + 2)^2 = 1$

2. Center: (–4, 4.5)
Radius: 16

$(x + 4)^2 + (y - 4.5)^2 = 256$

Find the center and radius of the given circle. *(Lesson 4.1)*

3. $x^2 + y^2 = 25$

center: (0, 0)

radius: 5

4. $(x - 18)^2 + (y + 18)^2 = 70$

center: (18, −18)

radius: $\sqrt{70}$

Solve the system of equations using any method. *(Lessons 4.2, 4.3, 4.4)*

5. $\begin{cases} y + 12 = 4x \\ y - 20 = x^2 - 8x \end{cases}$

(4, 4) and (8, 20)

6. $\begin{cases} y = x + 2 \\ 2y - 12 = 2x^2 - 8x \end{cases}$

(4, 6) and (1, 3)

7. $\begin{cases} x + y + z = 9 \\ x - 8y - z = -27 \\ 2x - y + z = 6 \end{cases}$

(5, 4, 0)

8. $\begin{cases} -3x - 12y - 3z = 0 \\ x + 4y + z = 10 \\ -2x - 8y - 2z = -34 \end{cases}$

no solution

ESSENTIAL QUESTION

9. Describe a real world situation that might involve three linear equations in three variables. *(Lesson 5.4)*

Possible Answer: You are trying to find the ages of three people. You know the sum of all three ages, the sum of the first two ages and twice the third, and the sum of the first and third ages and twice the second.

COMMON CORE Common Core Standards

Lesson	Items	Content Standards	Mathematical Practices
4.1	1–2	A-CED.A.2, G-GPE.A.1	MP.7
4.1	3–4	A-CED.A.2, G-GPE.A.1	MP.2
4.2, 4.3	5	A-REI.C.7	MP.1
4.2, 4.3	6	A-REI.C.7	MP.1
4.4	7	A-REI.C.6	MP.1
4.4	8	A-REI.C.6	MP.1

MODULE 4
MIXED REVIEW

Assessment Readiness

1. Look at each focus and directrix. Is the resulting parabola horizontal? Select Yes or No for A–C.
   - **A.** Focus $(-5, 0)$, Directrix $x = 5$ — ● Yes ○ No
   - **B.** Focus $(4, 0)$, Directrix $x = -4$ — ● Yes ○ No
   - **C.** Focus $(0, -3)$, Directrix $y = 3$ — ○ Yes ● No

2. Consider the system of equations $\begin{cases} y = x^2 + 6x + 10 \\ y + 6 = 2x \end{cases}$. Choose Yes or No for each statement.
   - **A.** Another way to write this system is $\begin{cases} y = x^2 + 6x + 10 \\ y = 2x - 6 \end{cases}$ — ● Yes ○ No
   - **B.** The only way to solve this system is by graphing. — ○ Yes ● No
   - **C.** There is only one solution to the system, $(-4, 2)$. — ○ Yes ● No

3. Explain how a system of three equations in three variables can have infinitely many solutions.

   To have infinitely many solutions, all three equations must be the same. So, all three equations should simplify to make the same coefficients for all of the variables and the same constant.

4. Robin solved a quadratic equation using the process shown. Describe and correct her mistake.

$$0 = \frac{x^2}{4} - 2x + 7$$

$$x = \frac{-(-2) \pm \sqrt{(-2)^2 - 4\left(\frac{1}{4}\right)(7)}}{2(1/4)}$$

$$= \frac{2 \pm \sqrt{-4 - 7}}{\frac{1}{2}}$$

$$= 4 \pm 2\sqrt{-11}$$

$$= 4 \pm 2i\sqrt{11}$$

When Robin squared the value of b, she said that $(-2)^2 = -4$. It should be positive 4, because $-2 \cdot -2 = 4$. The correct answer should be $4 \pm 2i\sqrt{3}$.

COMMON CORE

Common Core Standards

Lesson	Exercise	Content Standards	Mathematical Practices
4.2	1	**G-GPE.A.3**	**MP.7**
4.3	2	**A-REI.C.7**	**MP.2**
1.2, 4.4	3*	**A-REI.C.6, F-IF.B.4**	**MP.6**
3.3	4*	**N-CN.C.7**	**MP.3**

* Item integrates mixed review concepts from previous modules or a previous course.

MIXED REVIEW

Assessment Readiness

ASSESSMENT AND INTERVENTION

Assign ready-made or customized practice tests to prepare students for high-stakes tests.

ADDITIONAL RESOURCES

Assessment Resources

- Leveled Module Quizzes: Modified, B

AVOID COMMON ERRORS

Item 3 Many students will believe that systems of equations in three variables cannot have infinitely many solutions because they represent planes. Remind students that three planes can intersect in a line or overlap in the same plane. Each situation has infinitely many solutions.

MIXED REVIEW

Assessment Readiness

ASSESSMENT AND INTERVENTION

Assign ready-made or customized practice tests to prepare students for high-stakes tests.

ADDITIONAL RESOURCES

Assessment Resources

- Leveled Unit Tests: Modified, A, B, C
- Performance Assessment

AVOID COMMON ERRORS

Item 3 Many students will forget to divide by a before completing the square, therefore getting an incorrect answer for the $\left(\frac{b}{2}\right)^2$ term. Remind students that they can enter two equations from their solution steps into the calculator and use the table to confirm that the equations are equivalent.

UNIT 2 MIXED REVIEW

Assessment Readiness

- Online Homework
- Hints and Help
- Extra Practice

1. Consider the function $f(x) = 3(x-7)^2 + 2$. Choose True or False for each statement.

A. The axis of symmetry for $f(x)$ is $x = 7$. ● True ○ False

B. The range is $\{ y \mid y \in \Re \}$. ○ True ● False

C. The vertex of $f(x)$ is $(7, -2)$. ○ True ● False

2. Look at each quadratic equation. Does the equation have real roots? Select Yes or No for A–C.

A. $x^2 - 25 = 0$ ● Yes ○ No

B. $-\frac{1}{2}x^2 - 3 = 0$ ○ Yes ● No

C. $3x^2 - 4 = 2$ ● Yes ○ No

3. Consider the equation $3x^2 - 12x + 15 = 0$. Choose True or False for each statement.

A. If solving this equation using factoring, then $(x-5)(x+1) = 0$. ○ True ● False

B. After completing the square, $x = -2 \pm \sqrt{11}$. ○ True ● False

C. To solve this equation using complete the square, $\left(\frac{b}{2}\right)^2 = \left(\frac{-4}{2}\right)^2 = 4$. ● True ○ False

4. Consider the system of equations $\begin{cases} y = 2x^2 - 3x + 5 \\ y - 3 = x \end{cases}$. Choose True or False for each statement.

A. The only way to solve this equation is by elimination. ○ True ● False

B. Another way to write this system is $\begin{cases} y = 2x^2 - 3x + 5 \\ y = x + 3 \end{cases}$ ● True ○ False

C. There are three possible solutions to the system. ○ True ● False

5. Look at each focus and directrix. Is the resulting parabola vertical? Select Yes or No for A–C.

A. Focus $(6, -3)$, Directrix $x = 2$ ○ Yes ● No

B. Focus $(-4, -2)$, Directrix $y = -3$ ● Yes ○ No

C. Focus $(0, 1)$, Directrix $y = 2$ ● Yes ○ No

COMMON CORE

Common Core Standards

Items	Content Standards	Mathematical Practices
1*	F-IF.B.4, F-IF.B.5	MP.1
2	N-CN.A.2, N-CN.C.7	MP.2
3	A-SSE.3	MP.5
4	A-REI.C.7	MP.2
5	G-GPE.A.2	MP.2
6	F-IF.B.4	MP.4

* Item integrates mixed review concepts from previous modules or a previous course.

6. Marcia shoots an arrow that hits a bull's–eye 80 feet away. Before hitting the bull's–eye, the arrow reaches a maximum height of 16 feet at the midway point, 40 feet. If the bull's–eye is considered to be at (80, 0), what function (in intercept form) could represent the path of the arrow if x is the horizontal distance from Marcia and $h(x)$ represents the height of the arrow in relation to the horizontal distance? How high is the arrow above the ground after traveling 20 feet? Explain.

$h(x) = -\frac{1}{100}x(x - 80)$; At 20 feet from where the arrow is shot, the arrow is 12 feet above the horizontal distance.; Possible answer: Substitute 20 for x, then solve to find the height of the arrow.

7. Consider the equation $-4x^2 + x = 3$. What method should be used to most easily solve the equation if you have a choice between taking the square root, completing the square, using the quadratic formula, or factoring? Explain your reasoning, and then solve the equation.

Sample answer: Use the quadratic formula. Because the variable b is not zero, taking the square root is not possible, and the equation cannot be factored easily. To use completing the square, the coefficient on x^2 should be 1, which gives fractions for the coefficient on x and the constant. The best choice is to use the quadratic formula: $x = \frac{1}{8} \pm i\frac{\sqrt{47}}{8}$.

8. Ronald says $f(x) = 0.5x + 1.5$ is the inverse of $g(x) = -1.5x + 4$. Is Ronald's answer correct? Explain why or why not.

No; the inverse of $g(x) = -1.5x + 4$ can be found by subtracting 4 from both sides, then dividing by -1.5. So, the inverse is $g^{-1}(x) = -\frac{2}{3}x + \frac{8}{3}$.

Performance Tasks

9. Keille is building a rectangular pen for a pet rabbit. She can buy wire fencing in a roll of 40 ft or a roll of 80 ft. The graph shows the area of pens she can build with each type of roll.

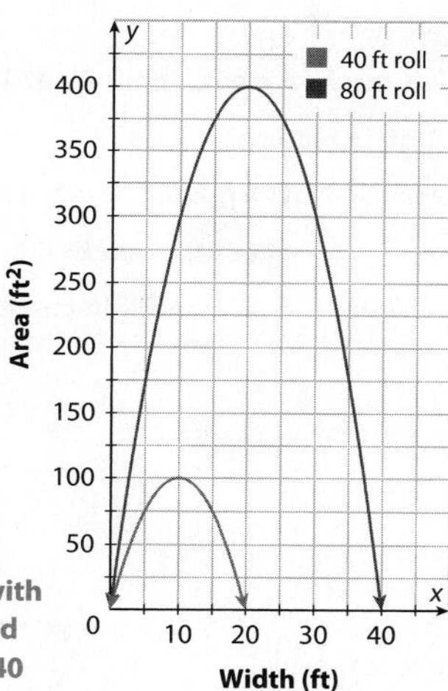

A. Describe the function for an 80 ft roll of fencing as a transformation of the function for a 40 ft roll of fencing.

B. Is the largest pen Keille can build with an 80 ft roll of fencing twice as large as the largest pen she can build with a 40 ft roll of fencing? Explain.

A. translation 10 units right and 300 units up

B. No; the largest pen Keille can build with an 80 ft roll has an area of 400 ft², and the largest pen she can build with a 40 ft roll has an area of 100 ft². Therefore, a roll that is twice as long allows her to build a pen with 4 times the area.

PERFORMANCE TASKS

There are three different levels of performance tasks:

***Novice:** These are short word problems that require students to apply the math they have learned in straightforward, real-world situations.

****Apprentice:** These are more involved problems that guide students step-by-step through more complex tasks. These exercises include more complicated reasoning, writing, and open ended elements.

*****Expert:** These are open-ended, nonroutine problems that, instead of stepping the students through, ask them to choose their own methods for solving and justify their answers and reasoning.

SCORING GUIDES

Item 9 (2 points)

a. 1 point for correct transformation

b. 1 point for correct answer and explanation

COMMON CORE

Common Core Standards

Items	Content Standards	Mathematical Practices
7	N-CN.C.7	MP.6
8*	F-BF.B.4	MP.3

* Item integrates mixed review concepts from previous modules or a previous course.

SCORING GUIDES

Item 10 (2 points)

a. 1 point for correct maximum

b. 1 point for correct answer and comparison

Item 11 (6 points)

a. 1 point for correct function

b. 1 point for correct function

c. 1 point for correct quadratic output
1 point for correct linear output

d. 1 point for correct model
1 point for explanation

★★10. The spittlebug is the world's highest-jumping animal relative to its body length of about 6 millimeters. The height h of a spittlebug's jump in millimeters can be model by the function $h(t) = -4000t^2 + 3000t$, where t is the time in seconds.

A. What is the maximum height that the spittlebug will reach?

B. What is the ratio of a spittlebug's maximum jumping height to its body length? In the best human jumpers, this ratio is about 1.38 to 1. Compare the ratio for spittlebugs with the ratio for the best human jumpers.

A. 562.5 mm

B. 93.75 to 1; Possible answer: the ratio for spittlebugs is more than 67 times as great as the ratio for humans.

★★★11. The light produced by high-pressure sodium vapor streetlamps for different energy usages is shown in the table.

High-Pressure Sodium Vapor Streetlamps					
Energy Use (watts)	35	50	70	100	150
Light Output (lumens)	2250	4000	5800	9500	16,000

A. Find a quadratic model for the light output with respect to energy use.

B. Find a linear model for the light output with respect to energy use.

C. Apply each model to estimate the light output in lumens of a 200-watt bulb.

D. Which model gives the better estimate? Explain.

A. $y = 0.187x^2 + 84.3x - 863.6$

B. $y = 119x - 2159$

C. quadratic model output, about 23,476 lumens; linear model output, about 21,641 lumens

D. Possible answer: The quadratic model would probably give a better estimate of the light output for higher values of energy usage because the data points lie along a slight curve.

MATH IN CAREERS

Toy Manufacturer A company is marketing a new toy. The function $s(p) = -50p^2 + 3000p$ models how the total sales s of the toy, in dollars, depends on the price p of the toy, in dollars.

a. Complete the square to write the function in vertex form.

b. Graph the function. Be sure to label the axes with the quantities they represent and indicate the axis scales by showing numbers for some grid lines.

c. What is the vertex of the graph? What does the vertex represent in this situation?

d. The model predicts that total sales will be $40,000 when the toy price is $20. At what other price does the model predict that the total sales will be $40,000? Use the symmetry of the graph to support your answer.

e. According to the model, at what nonzero price should the manufacturer expect to sell no toys? How can you determine this price using the graph?

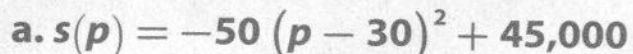

a. $s(p) = -50\,(p - 30)^2 + 45{,}000$

b.

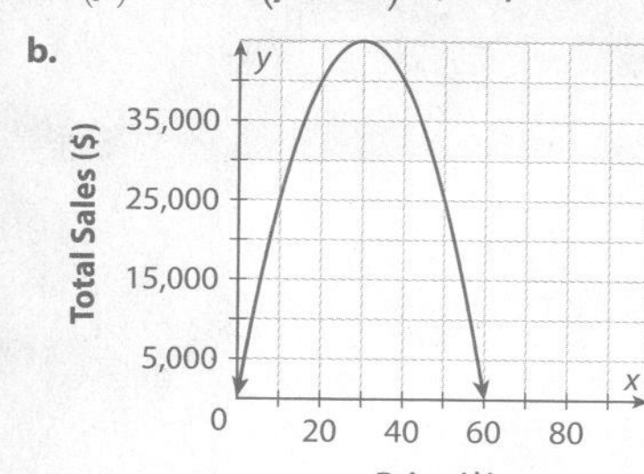

c. (30, 45,000); the toy price ($30) that is predicted to result in the greatest total sales ($45,000).

d. $40; The point (20, 40,000) is 10 units to the left of the vertex. Based on the symmetry of the graph, there will also be a point 10 units to the right of the vertex with a *y*-coordinate of 40,000. This point is (40, 40,000).

e. $60; This corresponds to the point (60, 0), which means that the total sales is zero when the price is $60.

MATH IN CAREERS

Toy Manufacturer In this Unit Performance Task, students can see how a toy manufacturer uses mathematics on the job.

For more information about careers in mathematics as well as various mathematics appreciation topics, visit the American Mathematical Society http://www.ams.org

SCORING GUIDES

Task (6 points)

a. 1 point for correct function

b. 1 point for correct graph

c. 1 point for correct vertex and interpretation

d. 1 point for correct price and explanation

e. 1 point for correct price
   1 point for explanation

UNIT 3

Polynomial Functions, Expressions, and Equations

CONTENTS

Unit Pacing Guide

45-Minute Classes

Module 5

DAY 1	DAY 2	DAY 3	DAY 4	
Lesson 5.1	Lesson 5.1	Lesson 5.2	Module Review and Assessment Readiness	

Module 6

DAY 1	DAY 2	DAY 3	DAY 4	DAY 5
Lesson 6.1	Lesson 6.2	Lesson 6.2	Lesson 6.3	Lesson 6.4
DAY 6	**DAY 7**	**DAY 8**		
Lesson 6.5	Lesson 6.5	Module Review and Assessment Readiness		

Module 7

DAY 1	DAY 2	DAY 3	DAY 4	DAY 5
Lesson 7.1	Lesson 7.1	Lesson 7.2	Lesson 7.2	Module Review and Assessment Readiness
DAY 6				
Unit Review and Assessment Readiness				

90-Minute Classes

Module 1

DAY 1	DAY 2
Lesson 5.1	Lesson 6.2 Module Review and Assessment Readiness

Module 6

DAY 1	DAY 2	DAY 3	DAY 4
Lesson 6.1 Lesson 6.2	Lesson 6.2 Lesson 6.3	Lesson 6.4 Lesson 6.5	Lesson 6.5 Module Review and Assessment Readiness

Module 7

DAY 1	DAY 2	DAY 3
Lesson 7.1	Lesson 7.2	Module Review and Assessment Readiness Unit Review and Assessment Readiness

Program Resources

PLAN

HMH Teacher App

Access a full suite of teacher resources online and offline on a variety of devices. Plan present, and manage classes, assignments, and activities.

ePlanner **Easily plan your classes, create and view assignments, and access all program resources with your online, customizable planning tool.**

Professional Development Videos

Authors Juli Dixon and Matt Larson model successful teaching practices and strategies in actual classroom settings.

QR Codes **Scan with your smart phone to jump directly from your print book to online videos and other resources.**

Teacher's Edition

Support students with point-of-use Questioning Strategies, teaching tips, resources for differentiated instruction, additional activities, and more.

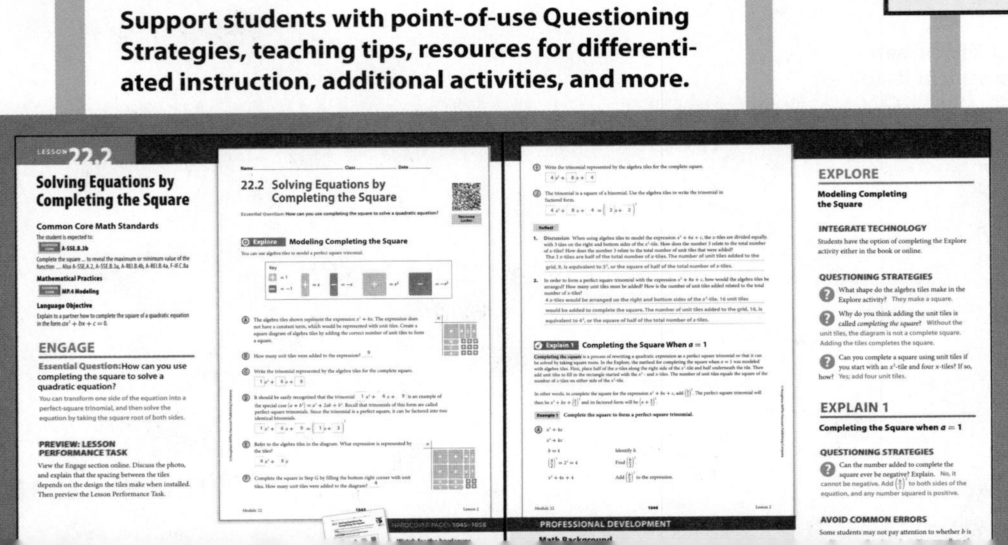

ENGAGE AND EXPLORE

Real-World Videos **Engage students with interesting and relevant applications of the mathematical content of each module.**

Explore Activities

Students interactively explore new concepts using a variety of tools and approaches.

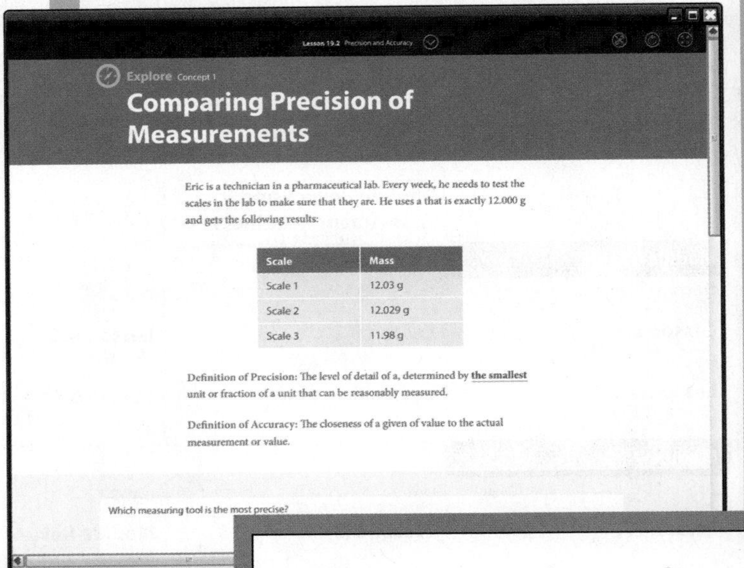

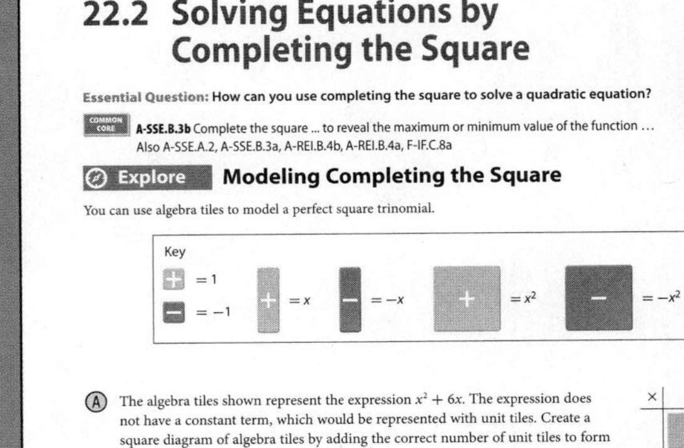

22.2 Solving Equations by Completing the Square
Essential Question: How can you use completing the square to solve a quadratic equation?
Explore Modeling Completing the Square
You can use algebra tiles to model a perfect square trinomial.

TEACH

Math On the Spot video tutorials, featuring program authors Dr. Edward Burger and Martha Sandoval-Martinez, accompany every example in the textbook and give students step-by-step instructions and explanations of key math concepts.

Interactive Teacher Edition

Customize and present course materials with collaborative activities and integrated formative assessment.

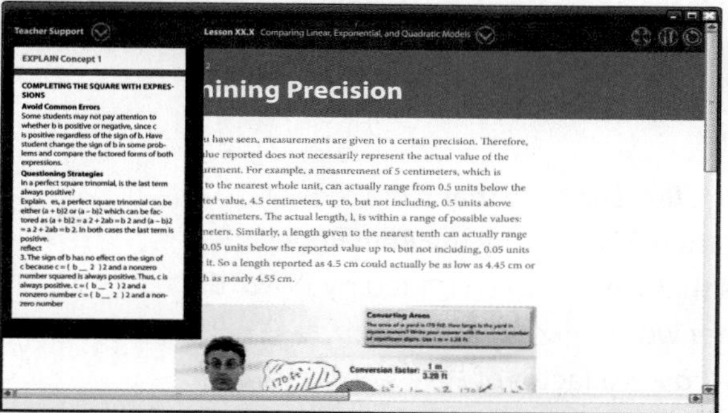

Differentiated Instruction Resources

Support all learners with Differentiated Instruction Resources, including

- **Leveled Practice and Problem Solving**
- **Reading Strategies**
- **Success for English Learners**
- **Challenge**

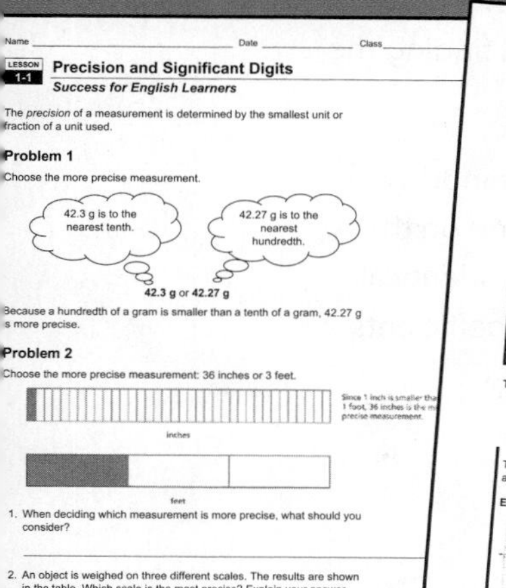

Name ______ Date ______ Class ______

LESSON 1-1 **Precision and Significant Digits**

Success for English Learners

The *precision* of a measurement is determined by the smallest unit or fraction of a unit used.

Problem 1

Choose the more precise measurement.

42.3 g is to the nearest tenth.

42.27 g is to the nearest hundredth.

42.3 g or 42.27 g

Because a hundredth of a gram is smaller than a tenth of a gram, 42.27 g is more precise.

Problem 2

Choose the more precise measurement: 36 inches or 3 feet.

inches

feet

1. When deciding which measurement is more precise, what should you consider?

2. An object is weighed on three different scales. The results are shown in the table. Which scale is the most precise? Explain your answer.

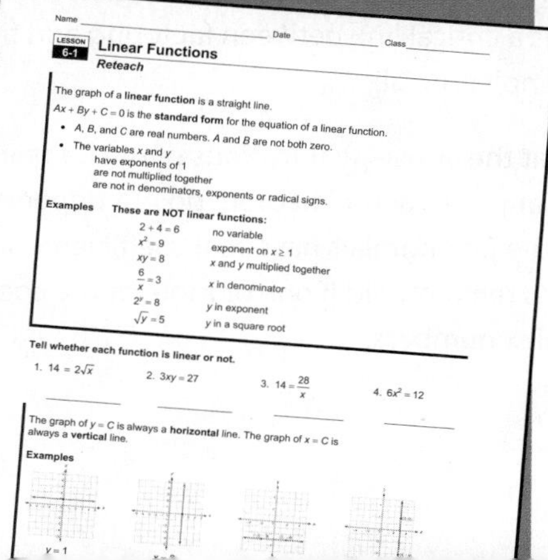

Name ______ Date ______ Class ______

LESSON 6-1 **Linear Functions**

Reteach

The graph of a **linear function** is a straight line.

$Ax + By + C = 0$ is the **standard form** for the equation of a linear function.

- A, B, and C are real numbers. A and B are not both zero.
- The variables x and y
  have exponents of 1
  are not multiplied together
  are not in denominators, exponents or radical signs.

Examples These are NOT linear functions:

$2 + 4 = 6$	no variable
$x^2 = 9$	exponent on $x \geq 1$
$xy = 8$	x and y multiplied together
$\frac{6}{x} = 3$	x in denominator
$2^x = 8$	x in exponent
$\sqrt{y} = 5$	y in a square root

Tell whether each function is linear or not.

1. $14 = 2\sqrt{x}$
2. $3xy = 27$
3. $14 = \frac{28}{x}$
4. $6x^2 = 12$

The graph of $y = C$ is always a **horizontal** line. The graph of $x = C$ is always a **vertical** line.

Examples

$y = 1$

ASSESSMENT AND INTERVENTION

The Personal Math Trainer provides online practice, homework, assessments, and intervention. Monitor student progress through reports and alerts. Create and customize assignments aligned to specific lessons or Common Core standards.

- **Practice** – With dynamic items and assignments, students get unlimited practice on key concepts supported by guided examples, step-by-step solutions, and video tutorials.
- **Assessments** – Choose from course assignments or customize your own based on course content, Common Core standards, difficulty levels, and more.
- **Homework** – Students can complete online homework with a wide variety of problem types, including the ability to enter expressions, equations, and graphs. Let the system automatically grade homework, so you can focus where your students need help the most!
- **Intervention** – Let the Personal Math Trainer automatically prescribe a targeted, personalized intervention path for your students.

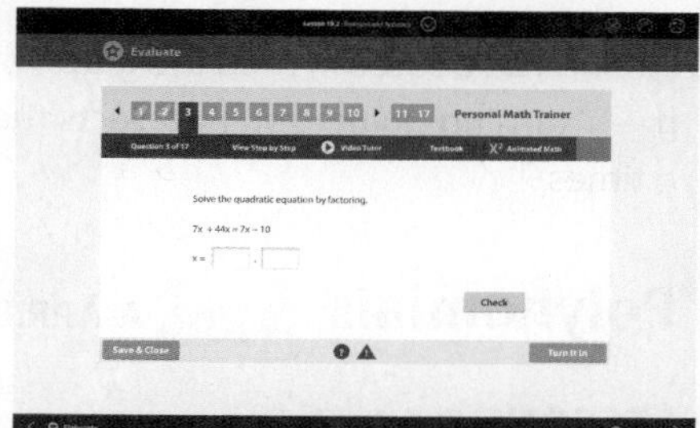

Focus on Higher Order Thinking

Raise the bar with homework and practice that incorporates higher-order thinking and mathematical practices in every lesson.

Assessment Readiness

Prepare students for success on high stakes tests for Algebra 2 with practice at every module and unit

Assessment Resources

Tailor assessments and response to intervention to meet the needs of all your classes and students, including

- Leveled Module Quizzes
- Leveled Unit Tests
- Unit Performance Tasks
- Placement, Diagnostic, and Quarterly Benchmark Tests
- Tier 1, Tier 2, and Tier 3 Resources

Math Background

Graphing Polynomial Functions COMMON CORE F-IF.C.7c

LESSONS 5.1 and 5.2

There are some basic characteristics exhibited by the graphs of all polynomial functions. Students can use these characteristics to help determine whether they have correctly graphed a polynomial function. For all polynomial functions $y = P(x)$,

- The graph of $y = P(x)$ is a smooth, continuous curve. If $P(x)$ has degree 2 or greater, then the curve is nonlinear.

- As x approaches $+\infty$, $P(x)$ approaches $+\infty$ or $-\infty$. Similarly, as x approaches $-\infty$, $P(x)$ approaches $+\infty$ or $-\infty$. In other words, the graph of a polynomial function never "levels off" or approaches an asymptote.

- If $P(x)$ has degree n, then the graph of $y = P(x)$ has at most $n - 1$ turning points and intersects the x-axis no more than n times.

Polynomials  A-APR.B.2

LESSONS 6.1 to 6.5

Polynomials have a central role in high school algebra, so it is essential that students be able to identify, describe, and classify them. A polynomial is an expression involving a sum of whole-number powers of one or more variables that are multiplied by coefficients.

Any polynomial in one variable may be written in the form $a_n x^n + \ldots + a_2 x^2 + a_1 x + a_0$. Unless otherwise specified, the coefficients a_i are generally restricted to real numbers, although many of the key results of this chapter also hold for polynomials with complex coefficients.

It is instructive to compare division of polynomials with division of whole numbers. Consider two whole numbers, p and d, with $d \neq 0$. When we divide p by d, we say that the quotient is a whole number q and the remainder is a whole number r such that $p = dq + r$ and $0 \leq r < d$. (Note that if $r \geq d$, we would be able to continue dividing.)

Equivalently, $\frac{p}{d} = q + \frac{r}{d}$.

Division of polynomials is much the same. Given polynomials $P(x)$ and $D(x)$, where $D(x) \neq 0$, we can write $\frac{P(x)}{D(x)} = Q(x) + \frac{R(x)}{D(x)}$, where the remainder $R(x)$ is a polynomial whose degree is less than that of $D(x)$. (If the degree of $R(x)$ were not less than the degree of $D(x)$ we would be able to continue dividing.)

Equivalently, $P(x) = Q(x)D(x) + R(x)$

This last expression can be used to justify the Remainder Theorem.

Notice that when $D(x)$ is a linear divisor of the form $x - a$, the expression becomes $P(x) = Q(x)(x - a) + r$, where the remainder r is a real number. (This is because $x - a$ has degree 1, so the remainder polynomial $R(x)$ must have degree 0. That is, the remainder is a constant.) Letting $x = a$ shows that $P(a) = r$.

The Remainder Theorem has an important corollary called the Factor Theorem.

To derive this theorem, first suppose that a is a root of the polynomial $P(x)$. Then $P(a) = 0$. By the Remainder Theorem, this means that when $P(x)$ is divided by $x - a$, the remainder is 0. In other words, $P(x) = Q(x)(x - a) + 0$, which means that $x - a$ a is a factor of $P(x)$. Conversely, if $x - a$ is a factor of $P(x)$, then $P(x) = Q(x)(x - a)$ and it is easy to see that $P(a) = Q(a)(a - a) = 0$.

The Factor Theorem neatly summarizes these results as follows:

For any polynomial $P(x)$, $x - a$ is a factor of $P(x)$ if and only if $P(a) = 0$.

This theorem has important practical applications because it provides a critical link between factoring and finding the roots of a polynomial.

Notice that the above justifications of the Remainder Theorem and the Factor Theorem do not depend on the fact that the polynomials have real coefficients. Identical arguments remain valid if one or more of the coefficients are complex numbers.

This is an example of how algebra can be viewed as a discipline of ever expanding generalizations. In this case, division of whole numbers serves as a model that can be generalized to division of polynomials with complex coefficients. In fact, the model can be generalized to division of polynomials whose coefficients are in any field.

Solutions of Polynomial Equations

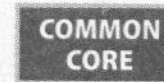

F-IF.C.7d

LESSONS 7.1 and 7.2

This unit provides an array of tools that can be used, sometimes in combination with each other, to find the roots of a polynomial.

The first of these tools is the Factor Theorem, which states that $x - a$ is a factor of the polynomial $P(x)$ if and only if a is a root of $P(x)$; in other words, $P(a) = 0$. This establishes a crucial link between factoring and finding roots.

A second tool is the Rational Root Theorem. Given a polynomial $P(x)$ with integer coefficients, this theorem states that every rational root of $P(x)$ has the form $\frac{p}{q}$ where p is a factor of the constant term of $P(x)$ and q is a factor of the leading coefficient.

The main steps in the proof of this theorem are outlined below.

Write $P(x)$ as $a_nx^n + a_{n-1}x^{n-1} + \ldots a_1x + a_0$. Suppose that $\frac{p}{q}$ is a root of $P(x)$, where p and q are integers and $\frac{p}{q}$ is written in lowest terms so that p and q have no common factors. Since $P\left(\frac{p}{q}\right) = 0$, we have

$$a_n\left(\frac{p}{q}\right)^n + a_{n-1}\left(\frac{p}{q}\right)^{n-1} + \ldots a_1\left(\frac{p}{q}\right) + a_0 = 0.$$

Multiply both sides of the equation by q^{n-1}:

$$a_n\left(\frac{p^n}{q}\right) + a_{n-1}p^{n-1} + \ldots + a_1pq^{n-2} + a_0q^{n-1} = 0 \text{ or}$$

$$a_n\left(\frac{p^n}{q}\right) = -a_{n-1}p^{n-1} - \ldots - a_1pq^{n-2} = a_0q^{n-1}$$

The expression on the right side of this equation is an integer. Therefore $a_n\left(\frac{p^n}{q}\right)$ is an integer and q must be a factor of a_np^n. Since p and q have no factors in common, q must be a factor of a_n. To show that p is a factor of a_0, multiply both sides of the original equation by $\left(\frac{q^n}{p}\right)$ and use a similar argument.

A third tool in the search for roots is the Irrational Root theorem: If a polynomial $P(x)$ with rational coefficients has a root of the form $a + b\sqrt{c}$, where a and b are rational and $\sqrt{c}$ is irrational, then $a - b\sqrt{c}$ is also a root of $P(x)$. This theorem comes with an important caveat. Note that the theorem does not say that all irrational roots are of the form $a + b\sqrt{c}$ nor that all irrational roots come in conjugate pairs. It only states that irrational roots of the form $a + b\sqrt{c}$ come in conjugate pairs. Consider the polynomial $x^3 - 2$. One of the roots is obviously $\sqrt[3]{2}$. This is the one and only irrational root; the other two roots are complex conjugates.

The Fundamental Theorem of Algebra ties everything together. It states that every polynomial function of degree $n \geq 1$ has n zeros (counting multiplicities) in the field of complex numbers. Note that this theorem applies even in the case where the polynomial function has complex coefficients.

In other words, the field of complex numbers is algebraically closed. In contrast, the field of real numbers is not algebraically closed, as demonstrated by the example $x^3 - 2$ above.

The first complete proof of the Fundamental Theorem of Algebra is generally credited to Carl Friedrich Gauss. He published one proof in his Ph.D. thesis of 1799, but he considered the result so important that he gave several different proofs over the course of his lifetime.

UNIT 3

Polynomial Functions, Expressions, and Equations

MATH IN CAREERS

Unit Activity Preview

After completing this unit, students will complete a Math in Careers task by evaluating and subtracting quadratic functions representing the labor force of the United States. Critical skills include evaluating polynomial functions and operations with polynomials.

For more information about careers in mathematics as well as various mathematics appreciation topics, visit The American Mathematical Society at http://www.ams.org.

UNIT 3

Polynomial Functions, Expressions, and Equations

27%
22%
8%
43%

MATH IN CAREERS

Statistician Statisticians use math to describe patterns and relationships. Statisticians design surveys and collect data, and rely on mathematical modeling and computational methods to analyze their findings. They use these findings and analyses to help solve problems in various fields, such as business, engineering, the sciences, and government.

If you are interested in a career as a statistician, you should study these mathematical subjects:

- Algebra
- Geometry
- Calculus
- Differential Equations
- Probability
- Statistics

Research other careers that require understanding and analyzing data. Check out the career activity at the end of the unit to find out how **Statisticians** use math.

TRACKING YOUR LEARNING PROGRESSION

Before	In this Unit	After
Students understand: • complex numbers • solving quadratic equations • parabolas • solving systems of equations	Students will learn about: • polynomial functions • operations with polynomials • finding rational solutions of polynomial equations • finding complex solutions of polynomial equations	Students will study: • graphing rational functions • operations with rational expressions • solving rational equations

Reading Start-Up

Visualize Vocabulary

Use the review words to complete the chart.

factor	a number or expression that divides a product exactly.
real number	a rational or irrational number
term	a number, variable, product, or quotient in an expression
parameter	one of the constants in a function or equation that may be changed
transformation	a change in the size, position, or shape of a figure or graph
coefficient	a numerical factor in a term of an algebraic expression

Vocabulary

Review Words

✔ coefficient *(coeficiente)*
✔ factor *(factor)*
✔ parameter *(parámetro)*
✔ real number *(número real)*
✔ term *(término)*
✔ transformation *(transformación)*

Preview Words

binomial *(binomio)*
cubic function *(función cúbica)*
monomial *(monomio)*
polynomial *(polinomio)*
root *(raíz)*
trinomial *(trinomio)*

Understand Vocabulary

To become familiar with some of the vocabulary terms in the module, consider the following. You may refer to the module, the glossary, or a dictionary.

1. A polynomial with two terms is a binomial.
2. A polynomial function of degree 3 is a cubic function.
3. A root of a polynomial is a zero of the function associated with that polynomial.

Active Reading

Key-Term Fold Before beginning the unit, create a key-term fold to help you organize what you learn. Write a vocabulary term on each tab of the key-term fold. Under each tab, write the definition of the term and an example.

Reading Start Up

Have students complete the activities on this page by working alone or with others.

VISUALIZE VOCABULARY

The chart helps students review vocabulary associated with functions, expressions, equations, and graphs of functions. If time allows, discuss mathematical relationships among the vocabulary words, especially between parameters and transformations.

UNDERSTAND VOCABULARY

Use the following explanations to help students learn the preview words.

A **monomial** is a product of a variable or variables and a coefficient. A **polynomial** is a monomial or sum of monomials. A **binomial** is a polynomial with two terms. A **trinomial** is a polynomial with three terms. A **cubic function** is a third degree polynomial function.

ACTIVE READING

Students can use these reading and note-taking strategies to help them organize and understand the new concepts and vocabulary. Encourage students to ask for help if they do not understand the definition of a new term. Suggest that students include multiple examples in their key-term folds.

ADDITIONAL RESOURCES

Differentiated Instruction

- Reading Strategies EL

MODULE 5

Polynomial Functions

ESSENTIAL QUESTION:

Answer: You can use polynomial functions to analyze and predict weather patterns, or track complicated financial trends.

PROFESSIONAL DEVELOPMENT VIDEO

Professional Development Video

Author Matt Larson models successful teaching practices in an actual high-school classroom.

Professional Development my.hrw.com

MODULE 5

Polynomial Functions

Essential Question: How can polynomial functions help to solve real-world problems?

REAL WORLD VIDEO
Engineers who design roller coasters use mathematics, including polynomial functions, to model the shape of the track.

MODULE PERFORMANCE TASK PREVIEW

What's the Function of a Roller Coaster?

Nothing compares with riding a roller coaster. The thrill of a steep drop, the breathtaking speed, and the wind in your face make the ride unforgettable. How can a polynomial function model the path of a roller coaster? Hang on to your seat and let's find out!

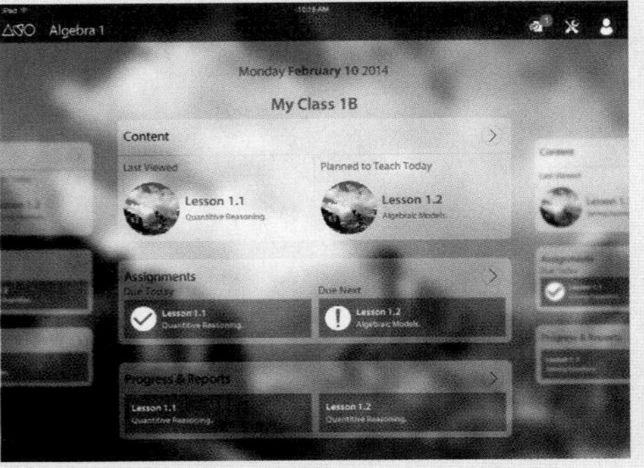

DIGITAL TEACHER EDITION

Access a full suite of teaching resources when and where you need them:

- Access content online or offline
- Customize lessons to share with your class
- Communicate with your students in real-time
- View student grades and data instantly to target your instruction where it is needed most

PERSONAL MATH TRAINER

Assessment and Intervention

Assign automatically graded homework, quizzes, tests, and intervention activities. Prepare your students with updated, Common Core-aligned practice tests.

Are YOU Ready?

Complete these exercises to review skills you will need for this chapter.

- Online Homework
- Hints and Help
- Extra Practice

Classifying Polynomials

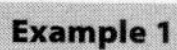

Example 1 Classify the polynomial $2x^4 + x^3 - 1$ by its degree and number of terms.

Because the greatest exponent is 4, this is a quartic polynomial.

Because the polynomial has three terms, it is a trinomial.

The polynomial $2x^4 + x^3 - 1$ is a quartic trinomial.

Classify the polynomial by its degree and number of terms.

1. $3x^3$

cubic monomial

2. $9x - 3y + 7$

linear trinomial

3. $x^2 - 4$

quadratic binomial

4. $x^5 + x^4$

degree 5 binomial

5. $5x^3 - 7y^2 + 2$

cubic trinomial

6. x

linear monomial

Transforming Cubic Functions

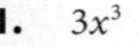

Example 2 The graph of $f(x) = 0.5(x - 3)^3 + 2$ is transformed 4 units right and 5 units down. Write the new function.

The inflection point is $(3, 2)$. Its location after the transformation is $(3 + 4, 2 - 5)$, or $(7, -3)$.

After the transformation, the function is $f'(x) = 0.5(x - 7)^3 - 3$.

Write the new function after the given transformation.

7. $g(x) = 0.25(x - 6)^3 - 1$
10 units left, 7 units down

$g'(x) = 0.25(x + 4)^3 - 8$

8. $h(x) = (x + 9)^3 - 5$
6 units right, 4 units up

$h'(x) = (x + 3)^3 - 1$

9. $f(x) = -0.5(x + 8)^3 + 12$
1 unit left, 3 units up

$f'(x) = -0.5(x + 9)^3 + 15$

10. $f(x) = x^3$
3 units right, 2 units up

$f'(x) = (x - 3)^3 + 2$

11. $g(x) = 5(x + 1)^3 - 4$
1 unit right, 4 units up

$g'(x) = 5x^3$

12. $h(x) = (x - 5)^3 + 5$
0.5 unit right, 1.5 units down

$h'(x) = (x - 5.5)^3 + 3.5$

Response to Intervention			Differentiated Instruction
Tier 1 Lesson Intervention Worksheets	**Tier 2** Strategic Intervention Skills Intervention Worksheets	**Tier 3** Intensive Intervention Worksheets available online	
Reteach 5.1 Reteach 5.2	5 Classifying Polynomials 37 Transforming Cubic Functions	Building Block Skills 29, 41, 43, 76	Challenge worksheets Extend the Math Lesson Activities in TE

Are You Ready?

ASSESS READINESS

Use the assessment on this page to determine if students need strategic or intensive intervention for the module's prerequisite skills.

ASSESSMENT AND INTERVENTION

Personal Math Trainer

RtI Response to Intervention TIER 1, TIER 2, TIER 3 SKILLS

Personal Math Trainer will automatically create a standards-based, personalized intervention assignment for your students, targeting each student's individual needs!

ADDITIONAL RESOURCES

See the table below for a full list of intervention resources available for this module.

Response to Intervention Resources also includes:

- Tier 2 Skill Pre-Tests for each Module
- Tier 2 Skill Post-Tests for each skill

LESSON 5.1

Graphing Cubic Functions

Common Core Math Standards

The student is expected to:

COMMON CORE **F-BF.B.3**

Identify the effect on the graph of replacing *f*(*x*) by *f*(*x*) + *k*, *k f*(*x*), *f*(*kx*), and *f*(*x* + *k*) for specific values of *k* ... find the value of *k* given the graphs. ... Also F-IF.C.7c, F.BF.A.1

Mathematical Practices

COMMON CORE **MP.6 Precision**

Language Objective

Explain to a partner how to predict transformations of a basic cubic function.

ENGAGE

Essential Question: How are the graphs of $f(x) = a(x-h)^3 + k$ and $f(x) = \left(\frac{1}{b}(x-h)\right)^3 + k$ related to the graph of $f(x) = x^3$?

Possible answer: Both graphs involve transformations of the graph of $f(x) = x^3$. The first involves vertically stretching or compressing the graph of $f(x) = x^3$, reflecting it across the *x*-axis if $a < 0$, and translating it horizontally and vertically. The second involves horizontally stretching or compressing the graph of $f(x) = x^3$, reflecting it across the *y*-axis if $b < 0$, and translating it horizontally and vertically.

PREVIEW: LESSON PERFORMANCE TASK

View the Engage section online. Discuss the photo and how the volume of a spherical aquarium can be described by a cubic function. Then preview the Lesson Performance Task.

Name ______ Class ______ Date ______

5.1 Graphing Cubic Functions

Resource Locker

Essential Question: How are the graphs of $f(x) = a(x-h)^3 + k$ and $f(x) = \left(\frac{1}{b}(x-h)\right)^3 + k$ related to the graph of $f(x) = x^3$?

Explore 1 Graphing and Analyzing $f(x) = x^3$

You know that a quadratic function has the standard form $f(x) = ax^2 + bx + c$ where *a*, *b*, and *c* are real numbers and $a \neq 0$. Similarly, a **cubic function** has the standard form $f(x) = ax^3 + bx^2 + cx + d$ where *a*, *b*, *c* and *d* are all real numbers and $a \neq 0$. You can use the basic cubic function, $f(x) = x^3$, as the parent function for a family of cubic functions related through transformations of the graph of $f(x) = x^3$.

(A) Complete the table, graph the ordered pairs, and then pass a smooth curve through the plotted points to obtain the graph of $f(x) = x^3$.

x	$y = x^3$
−2	−8
−1	−1
0	0
1	1
2	8

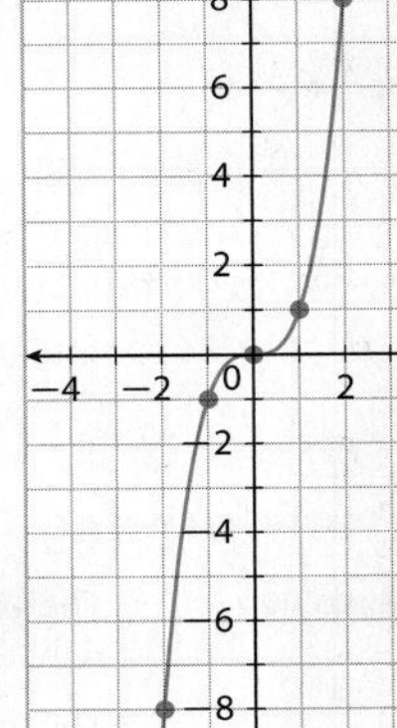

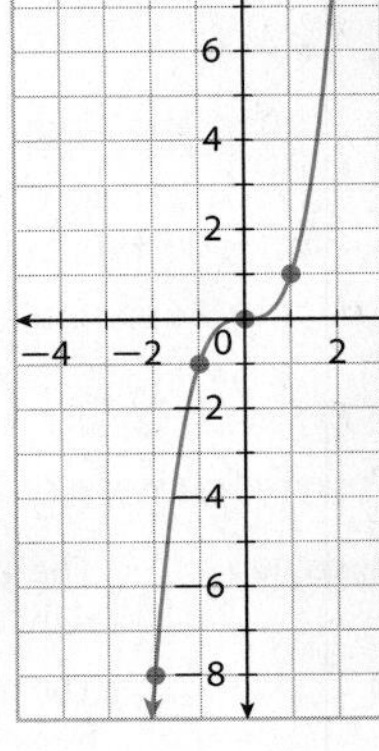

(B) Use the graph to analyze the function and complete the table.

Attributes of $f(x) = x^3$	
Domain	$\mathbb{R}$
Range	$\mathbb{R}$
End behavior	As $x \to +\infty$, $f(x) \to$ $+\infty$. As $x \to -\infty$, $f(x) \to$ $-\infty$.
Zeros of the function	$x = 0$
Where the function has positive values	$x > 0$
Where the function has negative values	$x < 0$
Where the function is increasing	The function increases throughout its domain.
Where the function is decreasing	The function never decreases.
Is the function even $(f(-x) = f(x))$, odd $(f(-x) = -f(x))$, or neither?	Odd, because $(x)^3 =$ $-x^3$.

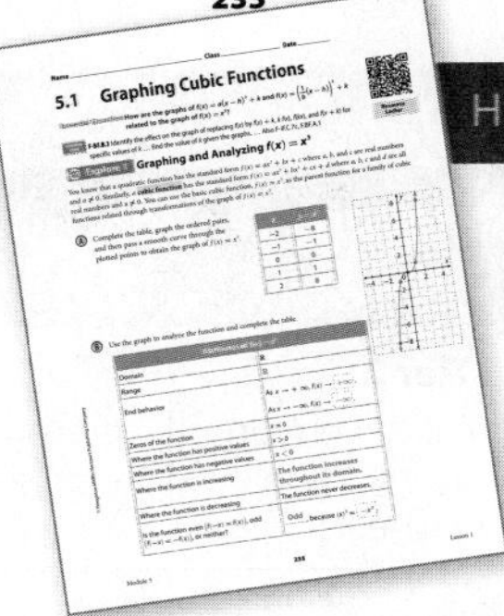

HARDCOVER PAGES 235–248

Watch for the hardcover student edition page numbers for this lesson.

Reflect

1. How would you characterize the rate of change of the function on the intervals $[-1, 0]$ and $[0, 1]$ compared with the rate of change on the intervals $[-2, -1]$ and $[1, 2]$? Explain.
The rate of change on all four intervals is positive because the function is increasing. However, the rate of change on the intervals $[-1, 0]$ and $[0, 1]$ is much less than the rate of change on the intervals $[-2, -1]$ and $[1, 2]$, because the graph rises more slowly on the intervals $[-1, 0]$ and $[0, 1]$ than it does on the intervals $[-2, -1]$ and $[1, 2]$.

2. A graph is said to be *symmetric about the origin* (and the origin is called the graph's *point of symmetry*) if for every point (x, y) on the graph, the point $(-x, -y)$ is also on the graph. Is the graph of $f(x) = x^3$ symmetric about the origin? Explain.
Yes, because for every point $(x, y) = (x, x^3)$ on the graph of the function, the point $(-x, (-x)^3) = (-x, -x^3) = (-x, -y)$ is also on the graph.

3. The graph of $g(x) = (-x)^3$ is a reflection of the graph of $f(x) = x^3$ across the y-axis, while the graph of $h(x) = -x^3$ is a reflection of the graph of $f(x) = x^3$ across the x-axis. If you graph $g(x)$ and $h(x)$ on a graphing calculator, what do you notice? Explain why this happens.
The graphs of $g(x)$ and $h(x)$ are the same because $f(x)$ is an odd function (that is, $f(-x) = -f(x)$). Given that $g(x) = f(-x)$ and $h(x) = -f(x)$, you have $g(x) = h(x)$.

Explain 1 Graphing Combined Transformations of $f(x) = x^3$

When graphing transformations of $f(x) = x^3$, it helps to consider the effect of the transformations on the three reference points on the graph of $f(x)$: $(-1, -1)$, $(0, 0)$, and $(1,1)$. The table lists the three points and the corresponding points on the graph of $g(x) = a\left(\frac{1}{b}(x - h)\right)^3 + k$. Notice that the point $(0, 0)$, which is the point of symmetry for the graph of $f(x)$, is affected only by the parameters h and k. The other two reference points are affected by all four parameters.

$f(x) = x^3$		$g(x) = a\left(\frac{1}{b}(x-h)\right)^3 + k$	
x	y	x	y
-1	-1	$-b + h$	$-a + k$
0	0	h	k
1	1	$b + h$	$a + k$

PROFESSIONAL DEVELOPMENT

Math Background

A cubic function is a polynomial function of degree 3. The standard form of a cubic function is $f(x) = ax^3 + bx^2 + cx + d$ where a, b, c, and d are real numbers and $a \neq 0$. Each function of the family of cubic functions is increasing or decreasing over its entire domain, depending on the sign of the leading coefficient of x^3. There also may be *turning points* and *relative maximum* and *relative minimum* points, depending on the transformations of the graph of $f(x) = x^3$. The domain and range of cubic functions are the set of all real numbers. The inverse of a cubic function may or may not be a function. If the graph has turning points, its inverse is not a function.

EXPLORE

Graphing and Analyzing $f(x) = x^3$

INTEGRATE TECHNOLOGY

Students can use a graphing calculator to graph and generate table values for the function $y = x^3$.

QUESTIONING STRATEGIES

How do you verify that the graph of $f(x) = x^3$ has symmetry about the origin? Show that if (x, y) is a point on the graph, then $(-x, -y)$ is also a point on the graph.

How is the graph of $f(x) = x^3$ similar to the graph of $f(x) = x$? The domain and range for both functions $(-\infty, \infty)$ are ; the end behavior for both functions is $f(x) \to -\infty$ as $x \to -\infty$, and $f(x) \to \infty$ as $x \to +\infty$.

EXPLAIN 1

Graphing Combined Transformations of $f(x) = x^3$

INTEGRATE MATHEMATICAL PRACTICES

Focus on Patterns

MP.8 Point out that to graph the function $f(x) = a(x - h)^3 + k$, you identify the point of symmetry (h, k) and use the value of a to draw the graph through two additional points $(-1 + h, -a + k)$ and $(1 + h, a + k)$. So, to graph $f(x) = 2(x - 3)^3 + 1$, first identify the point of symmetry, $(3, 1)$. Then identify points $(-1 + 3, -2 + 1) = (2, -1)$, and $(1 + 3, 2 + 1) = (4, 3)$ as additional reference points. A smooth curve through these three points is a good beginning for the graph.

QUESTIONING STRATEGIES

? What is the point of symmetry for a graph of the form $f(x) = \left(\frac{1}{b}(x-h)\right)^3 + k$? **(h, k)**

? How does a negative value for b affect the graph of $f(x) = \left(\frac{1}{b}(x-h)\right)^3 + k$? **The graph is reflected across the y-axis.**

Example 1 **Identify the transformations of the graph of $f(x) = x^3$ that produce the graph of the given function $g(x)$. Then graph $g(x)$ on the same coordinate plane as the graph of $f(x)$ by applying the transformations to the reference points $(-1, -1)$, $(0, 0)$, and $(1, 1)$.**

 $g(x) = 2(x-1)^3 - 1$

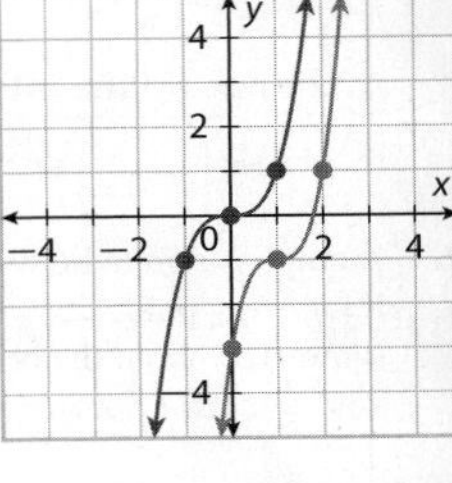

The transformations of the graph of $f(x)$ that produce the graph of $g(x)$ are:

- a vertical stretch by a factor of 2
- a translation of 1 unit to the right and 1 unit down

Note that the translation of 1 unit to the right affects only the x-coordinates of points on the graph of $f(x)$, while the vertical stretch by a factor of 2 and the translation of 1 unit down affect only the y-coordinates.

$f(x) = x^3$		$g(x) = 2(x-1)^3 - 1$	
x	y	x	y
−1	−1	$-1 + 1 = 0$	$2(-1) - 1 = -3$
0	0	$0 + 1 = 1$	$2(0) - 1 = -1$
1	1	$1 + 1 = 2$	$2(1) - 1 = 1$

 $g(x) = \left(2(x+3)\right)^3 + 4$

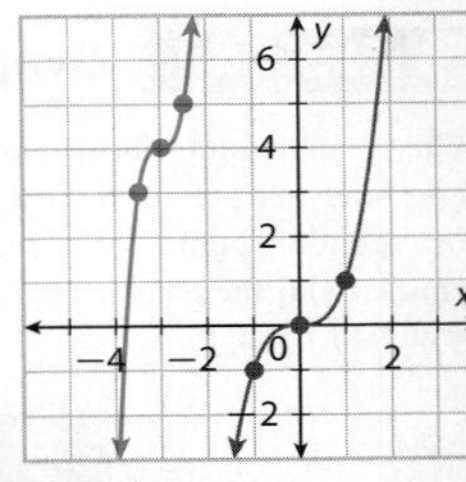

The transformations of the graph of $f(x)$ that produce the graph of $g(x)$ are:

- a horizontal compression by a factor of $\frac{1}{2}$
- a translation of 3 units to the left and 4 units up

Note that the horizontal compression by a factor of $\frac{1}{2}$ and the translation of 3 units to the left affect only the x-coordinates of points on the graph of $f(x)$, while the translation of 4 units up affects only the y-coordinates.

$f(x) = x^3$		$g(x) = \left(2(x+3)\right)^3 + 4$	
x	y	x	y
−1	−1	$\frac{1}{2}(-1) + -3 = -3\frac{1}{2}$	$-1 + 4 = 3$
0	0	$\frac{1}{2}(0) + -3 = -3$	$0 + 4 = 4$
1	1	$\frac{1}{2}(1) + -3 = -2\frac{1}{2}$	$1 + 4 = 5$

COLLABORATIVE LEARNING

Whole Class Activity

Have groups of students create posters to describe the transformations to the graph of $f(x) = x^3$ when graphing $f(x) = a(x-h)^3 + k$. Have them write an example function in the top cell of a graphic organizer. Then, in each cell below the example function, have them list the variable and describe the nature of the transformation.

Your Turn

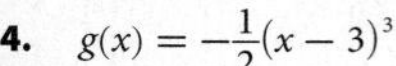

Identify the transformations of the graph of $f(x) = x^3$ that produce the graph of the given function $g(x)$. Then graph $g(x)$ on the same coordinate plane as the graph of $f(x)$ by applying the transformations to the reference points $(-1, -1)$, $(0, 0)$, and $(1, 1)$.

4. $g(x) = -\frac{1}{2}(x - 3)^3$

The transformations of the graph of $f(x)$ that produce the graph of $g(x)$ are:

- a vertical compression by a factor of $\frac{1}{2}$
- a reflection across the x-axis
- a translation of 3 units to the right

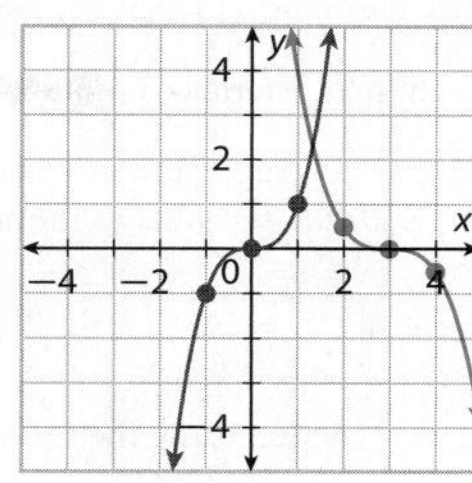

Note that the translation of 3 units to the right affects only the x-coordinates of points on the graph of $f(x)$, while the vertical compression by a factor of $\frac{1}{2}$ and the reflection across the x-axis affect only the y-coordinates. Points: $\left(2, \frac{1}{2}\right)$, $(3, 0)$, and $\left(4, -\frac{1}{2}\right)$

Explain 2 Writing Equations for Combined Transformations of $f(x) = x^3$

Given the graph of the transformed function $g(x) = a\left(\frac{1}{b}(x - h)\right)^3 + k$, you can determine the values of the parameters by using the same reference points that you used to graph $g(x)$ in the previous example.

Example 2 **A general equation for a cubic function $g(x)$ is given along with the function's graph. Write a specific equation by identifying the values of the parameters from the reference points shown on the graph.**

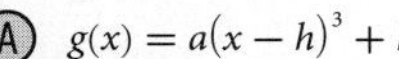

Ⓐ $g(x) = a(x - h)^3 + k$

Identify the values of h and k from the point of symmetry.

$(h, k) = (2, 1)$, so $h = 2$ and $k = 1$.

Identify the value of a from either of the other two reference points.

The rightmost reference point has general coordinates $(h + 1, a + k)$. Substituting 2 for h and 1 for k and setting the general coordinates equal to the actual coordinates gives this result:

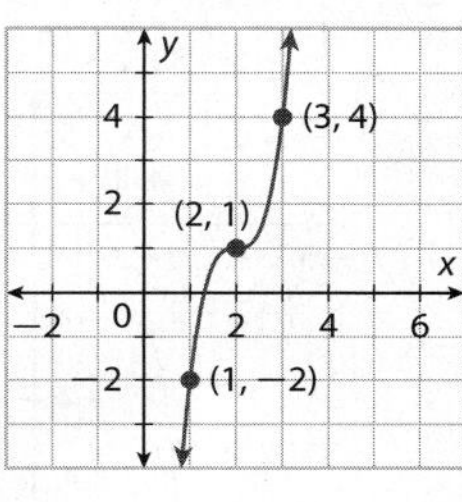

$(h + 1, a + k) = (3, a + 1) = (3, 4)$, so $a = 3$.

Write the function using the values of the parameters: $g(x) = 3(x - 2)^3 + 1$

EXPLAIN 2

Writing Equations for Combined Transformations of $f(x) = x^3$

AVOID COMMON ERRORS

For students having difficulty identifying the parameters in the graph of $g(x) = a\left(\frac{1}{b}(x - h)\right)^3 + k$, have them start with identifying the images of the reference points $(-1, -1)$, $(0, 0)$, $(1, 1)$ from the graph of $f(x) = x^3$. Then have them solve for the parameters a, b, h, and k using the image points and $(-b + h, -a + k)$, (h, k), or $(b + h, a + k)$, respectively.

DIFFERENTIATE INSTRUCTION

Critical Thinking

Have students form pairs. Give each pair of students a cubic function in general form and a graphing calculator. Have them graph the parent function $f(x) = x^3$ and then discuss how their given cubic function will be transformed based the graph of the parent function. Include choices such as reflection across the x-axis, reflection across the y-axis, horizontal and vertical shifts, and horizontal and vertical stretches. Have them graph their given functions to verify their predictions.

QUESTIONING STRATEGIES

Why does the general form $f(x) = a(x - h)^3 + k$ or $f(x) = \left(\frac{1}{b}(x - h)\right)^3 + k$ need to be specified before finding the equation of the transformed function? **The general form must be specified so that a unique equation can be found.**

(B) $g(x) = \left(\frac{1}{b}x - h\right)^3 + k$

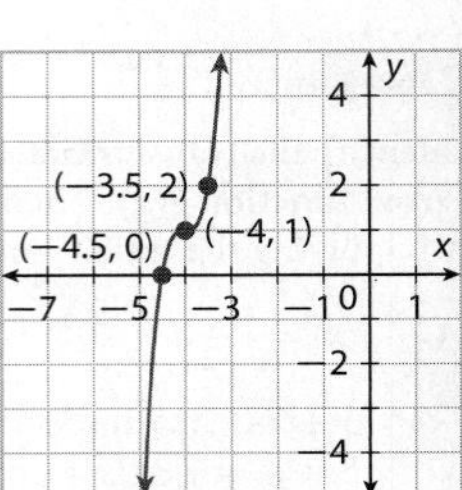

Identify the values of h and k from the point of symmetry.

$(h, k) = (-4, \boxed{1})$, so $h = -4$ and $k = \boxed{1}$.

Identify the value of b from either of the other two reference points.

The rightmost reference point has general coordinates $(b + h, 1 + k)$. Substituting -4 for h and $\underline{1}$ for k and setting the general coordinates equal to the actual coordinates gives this result:

$(b + h, 1 + \boxed{1}) = (b - 4, \boxed{2}) = (-3.5, 2)$, so $b = \boxed{0.5}$.

Write the function using the values of the parameters, and then simplify.

$$g(x) = \left(\frac{1}{\boxed{0.5}}\left(x - \boxed{-4}\right)\right)^3 + \boxed{1}$$

or

$$g(x) = \left(\boxed{2}\left(x + \boxed{4}\right)\right)^3 + \boxed{1}$$

Your Turn

A general equation for a cubic function $g(x)$ is given along with the function's graph. Write a specific equation by identifying the values of the parameters from the reference points shown on the graph.

5. $g(x) = a(x - h)^3 + k$

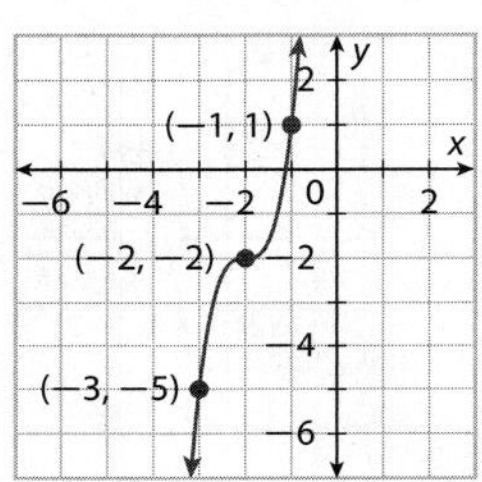

$(h, k) = (-2, -2)$, so $h = -2$ and $k = -2$.

$(h + 1, a + k) = (-2 + 1, a - 2) = (-1, 1)$, so $a = 3$.

$g(x) = 3(x + 2)^3 - 2$

6. $g(x) = \left(\frac{1}{b}(x - h)\right)^3 + k$

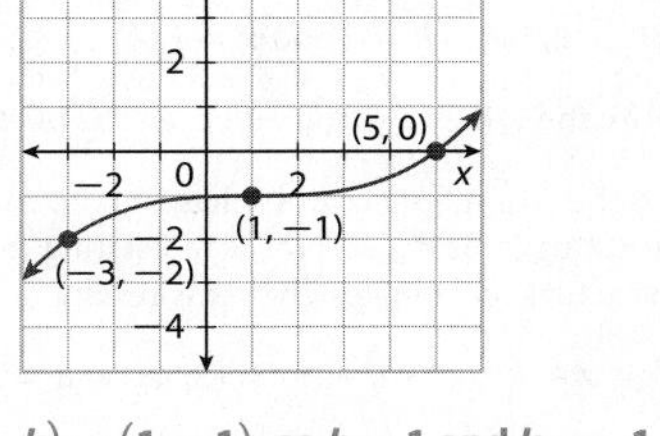

$(h, k) = (1, -1)$, so $h = 1$ and $k = -1$.

$(b + h, 1 + k) = (b + 1, 1 - 1) = (5, 0)$, so $b = 4$

$g(x) = \left(\frac{1}{4}(x - 1)\right)^3 - 1$

LANGUAGE SUPPORT EL

Connect Vocabulary

Have students work in pairs. Instruct one student to explain the effect of any transformation of the parent function $f(x) = x^3$. While the first student explains, the second student writes down the steps in the explanation. They switch roles and repeat the procedure for another change, such as the effect of b on the graph of $g(x) = \frac{1}{b}x^3$. The goal is to support students as they learn to articulate their understanding—at first, using their own words, then moving towards more mathematically precise explanations.

Explain 3 Modeling with a Transformation of $f(x) = x^3$

You may be able to model a real-world situation that involves volume with a cubic function. Sometimes mass may also be involved in the problem. Mass and volume are related through *density*, which is defined as an object's mass per unit volume. If an object has mass m and volume V, then its density d is $d = \frac{m}{V}$. You can rewrite the formula as $m = dV$ to express mass in terms of density and volume.

Example 3 **Use a cubic function to model the situation, and graph the function using calculated values of the function. Then use the graph to obtain the indicated estimate.**

(A) Estimate the length of an edge of a child's alphabet block (a cube) that has a mass of 23 g and is made from oak with a density of 0.72 g/cm³.

Let ℓ represent the length (in centimeters) of an edge of the block. Since the block is a cube, the volume V (in cubic centimeters) is $V(\ell) = \ell^3$. The mass m (in grams) of the block is $m(\ell) = 0.72 \cdot V(\ell) = 0.72\ell^3$. Make a table of values for this function.

Length (cm)	Mass (g)
0	0
1	0.72
2	5.76
3	19.44
4	46.08

Draw the graph of the mass function, recognizing that the graph is a vertical compression of the graph of the parent cubic function by a factor of 0.72. Then draw the horizontal line $m = 23$ and estimate the value of ℓ where the graphs intersect.

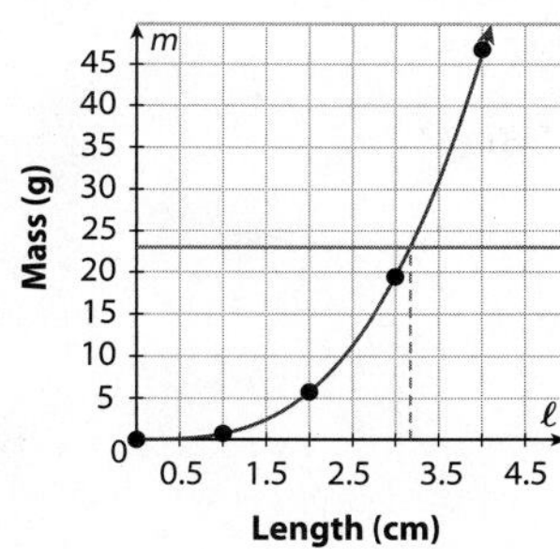

The graphs intersect where $\ell \approx 3.2$, so the edge length of the child's block is about 3.2 cm.

EXPLAIN 3

Modeling with a Transformation of $f(x) = x^3$

QUESTIONING STRATEGIES

? How is the density formula for a sphere of radius r, $m(r) = DV(r)$ with mass m, density D, and volume V related to the volume of a sphere, $V(r) = \frac{4}{3}\pi r^3$, with radius r? The mass of the sphere is the product of the density and the volume, so $m(r) = \frac{4}{3}\pi Dr^3$.

? What kind of transformation does the equation $m(r) = \frac{4}{3}\pi Dr^3$ show? a vertical stretch of the function $m(r) = r^3$ by a factor of $\frac{4}{3}\pi D$

(B) Estimate the radius of a steel ball bearing with a mass of 75 grams and a density of 7.82 g/cm³.

Let r represent the radius (in centimeters) of the ball bearing. The volume V (in cubic centimeters) of the ball bearing is $V(r) = \boxed{\frac{4}{3}\pi}\ r^3$. The mass m (in grams) of the ball bearing is $m(r) = 7.82 \cdot V(r) = \boxed{32.76}\ r^3$.

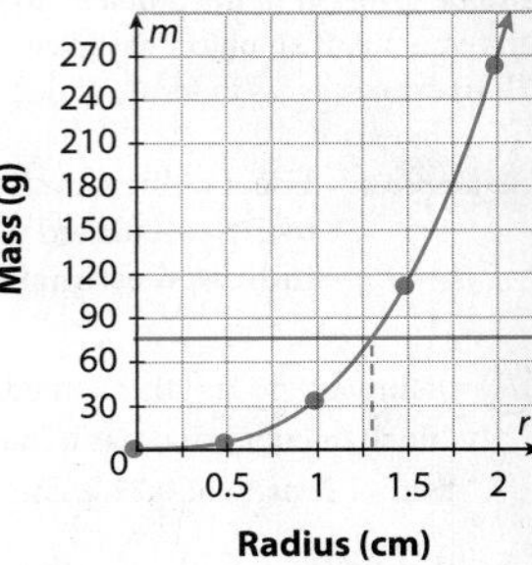

Radius (cm)	Mass (g)
0	0
0.5	4.10
1	32.76
1.5	110.57
2	262.08

Draw the graph of the mass function, recognizing that the graph is a vertical **stretch** of the graph of the parent cubic function by a factor of **7.82**. Then draw the horizontal line $m = \boxed{75}$ and estimate the value of r where the graphs intersect.

The graphs intersect where $r \approx \boxed{1.3}$, so the radius of the steel ball bearing is about **1.3** cm.

Reflect

7. **Discussion** Why is it important to plot multiple points on the graph of the volume function.
Because you are using the graph to estimate the value of the independent variable from a given value of the dependent variable, the graph should be as accurate as possible.

Your Turn

Use a cubic function to model the situation, and graph the function using calculated values of the function. Then use the graph to obtain the indicated estimate.

8. Polystyrene beads fill a cube-shaped box with an effective density of 0.00076 kg/cm³ (which accounts for the space between the beads). The filled box weighs 6 kilograms while the empty box had weighed 1.5 kilograms. Estimate the inner edge length of the box.

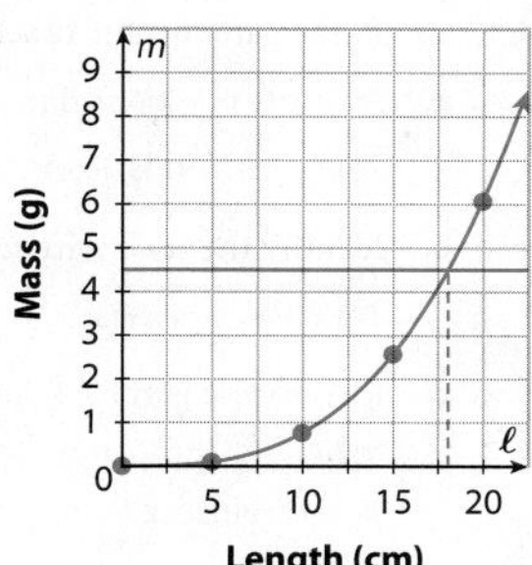

Let ℓ represent the length (in centimeters) of an inner edge of the box. Since the box is a cube, the volume V (in cubic centimeters) is $V(\ell) = \ell^3$. The mass m (in kilograms) of the polystyrene beads in the box is $m(\ell) = 0.00076 \cdot V(\ell) = 0.00076\ell^3$. Make a table of values for this function.

Length (cm)	Mass (kg)
0	0
5	0.095
10	0.76
15	2.565
20	6.08

Draw the graph of the mass function, recognizing that the graph is a vertical compression of the graph of the parent cubic function by a factor of 0.00076. Then draw the horizontal line $m = 6 - 1.5 = 4.5$ and estimate the value of ℓ where the graphs intersect.

The graphs intersect where $\ell \approx 18$, so the inner edge length of the box is about 18 cm.

Elaborate

9. Identify which transformations (stretches or compressions, reflections, and translations) of $f(x) = x^3$ change the following attributes of the function.

a. End behavior

Reflections across the x-axis $(a < 0)$ and reflections across the y-axis $(b < 0)$ change the end behavior.

b. Location of the point of symmetry

Vertical translations $(k \neq 0)$ and horizontal translations $(h \neq 0)$ change the location of the point of symmetry.

c. Symmetry about a point

No transformations change the function's symmetry about a point.

10. Essential Question Check-In Describe the transformations you must perform on the graph of $f(x) = x^3$ to obtain the graph of $f(x) = a(x - h)^3 + k$.

If $a < 0$, reflect the parent graph across the x-axis. Then either stretch the graph vertically by a factor of a if $|a| > 1$ or compress the graph vertically by a factor of a if $|a| < 1$. Finally, translate the graph h units horizontally and k units vertically.

ELABORATE

INTEGRATE MATHEMATICAL PRACTICES

Focus on Critical Thinking

MP.3 Before students graph any cubic function, encourage them to predict how the graph will look based on the leading coefficient of x when the function is written in general form $g(x) = a\left(\frac{1}{b}(x - h)\right)^3 + k$, and on the values of h and k.

SUMMARIZE THE LESSON

? If $a = 1$, $b = 1$, $h = 0$ and $k = 0$, which values would you change in $f(x) = a\left(\frac{1}{b}(x - h)\right)^3 + k$ to perform each of the type of transformations of $f(x) = x^3$? **Translate: change the value of h or k; stretch or compress vertically: change the value of a; reflect across the x-axis: change the sign of a; stretch or compress horizontally: change the value of b; reflect across the y-axis: change the sign of b.**

EVALUATE

ASSIGNMENT GUIDE

Concepts and Skills	Practice
Explore Graphing and Analyzing $f(x) = x^3$	Exercise 1
Example 1 Graphing Combined Transformations of $f(x) = x^3$	Exercises 10–17
Example 2 Writing Equations for Combined Transformations of $f(x) = x^3$	Exercises 18–21
Example 3 Modeling with a Transformation of $f(x) = x^3$	Exercises 22–23

INTEGRATE TECHNOLOGY

When graphing a cubic function or any other function on a graphing calculator, students should choose a good viewing window: one that displays the important characteristics of the graph. As a class, have students brainstorm what should show on the graphing screen. Sample answer: the end behavior; the turning point, or point of symmetry of the graph; the x-axis of the graph

Evaluate: Homework and Practice

• Online Homework
• Hints and Help
• Extra Practice

1. Graph the parent cubic function $f(x) = x^3$ and use the graph to answer each question.

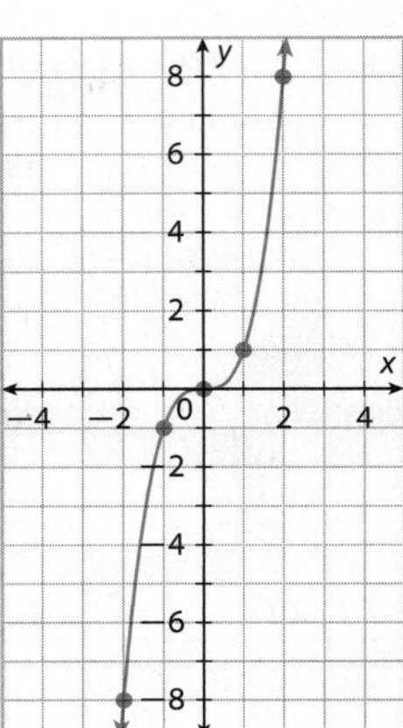

a. State the function's domain and range.

The domain is $\mathbb{R}$, and the range is $\mathbb{R}$.

b. Identify the function's end behavior.

As $x \to +\infty, f(x) \to +\infty$. As $x \to -\infty, f(x) \to -\infty$.

c. Identify the graph's x- and y-intercepts.

The graph's only x-intercept is 0. The graph's only y-intercept is 0.

d. Identify the intervals where the function has positive values and where it has negative values.

The function has positive values on the interval $(0, +\infty)$ and negative values on the interval $(-\infty, 0)$.

e. Identify the intervals where the function is increasing and where it is decreasing.

The function is increasing throughout its domain. The function never decreases.

f. Tell whether the function is even, odd, or neither. Explain.

The function is odd because $f(-x) = (-x)^3 = -x^3 = -f(x)$.

g. Describe the graph's symmetry.

The graph is symmetric about the origin.

Describe how the graph of $g(x)$ is related to the graph of $f(x) = x^3$.

2. $g(x) = (x - 4)^3$

translation of the graph of $f(x)$ right 4 units.

3. $g(x) = -5x^3$

vertical stretch of the graph of $f(x)$ by a factor of 5 and a reflection across the x-axis.

4. $g(x) = x^3 + 2$

translation of the graph of $f(x)$ up 2 units.

5. $g(x) = (3x)^3$

horizontal compression of the graph of $f(x)$ by a factor of $\frac{1}{3}$.

Exercise	Depth of Knowledge (D.O.K.)	COMMON CORE Mathematical Practices
1–10	1 Recall of Information	MP.2 Reasoning
11–17	2 Skills/Concepts	MP.2 Reasoning
18–20	3 Strategic Thinking	MP.4 Modeling
21	2 Skills/Concepts	MP.2 Reasoning
22	3 Strategic Thinking H.O.T.	MP.3 Logic

6. $g(x) = (x + 1)^3$

translation of the graph of $f(x)$ left 1 unit.

7. $g(x) = \frac{1}{4}x^3$

vertical compression of the graph of $f(x)$ by a factor of $\frac{1}{4}$.

8. $g(x) = x^3 - 3$

translation of the graph of $f(x)$ down 3 units.

9. $g(x) = \left(-\frac{2}{3}x\right)^3$

horizontal stretch of the graph of $f(x)$ by a factor of $\frac{3}{2}$ as well as a reflection across the y-axis.

Identify the transformations of the graph of $f(x) = x^3$ that produce the graph of the given function $g(x)$. Then graph $g(x)$ on the same coordinate plane as the graph of $f(x)$ by applying the transformations to the reference points $(-1, -1)$, $(0, 0)$, and $(1, 1)$.

10. $g(x) = \left(\frac{1}{3}x\right)^3$

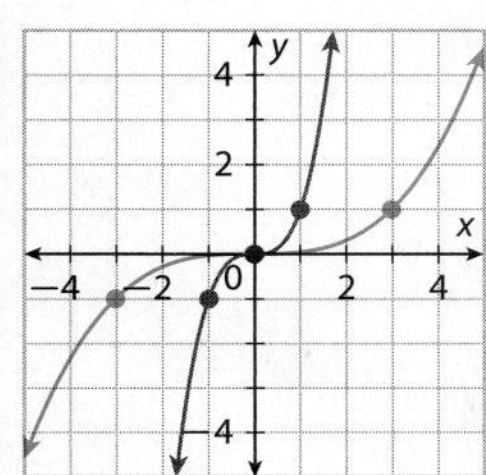

a horizontal stretch by a factor of 3. Reference points on the graph of $g(x)$ are $(-3, -1)$, $(0, 0)$, and $(3, 1)$.

11. $g(x) = \frac{1}{3}x^3$

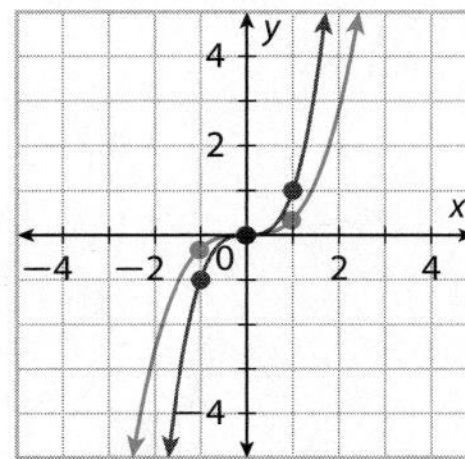

a vertical compression by a factor of $\frac{1}{3}$. Reference points on the graph of $g(x)$ are $\left(-1, -\frac{1}{3}\right)$, $(0, 0)$ and $\left(1, \frac{1}{3}\right)$.

12. $g(x) = (x - 4)^3 - 3$

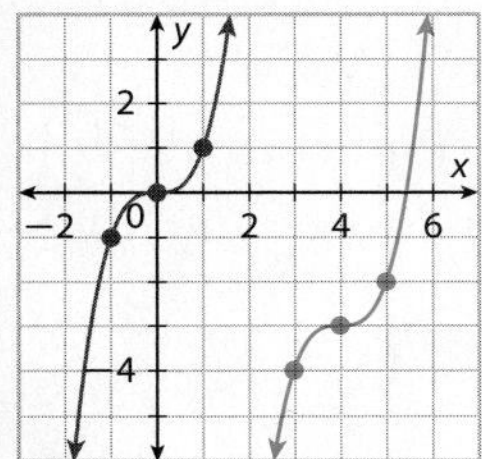

translation of 4 units to the right and 3 units down. Reference points on the graph of $g(x)$ are $(3, -4)$, $(4, -3)$, and $(5, -2)$.

13. $g(x) = (x + 1)^3 + 2$

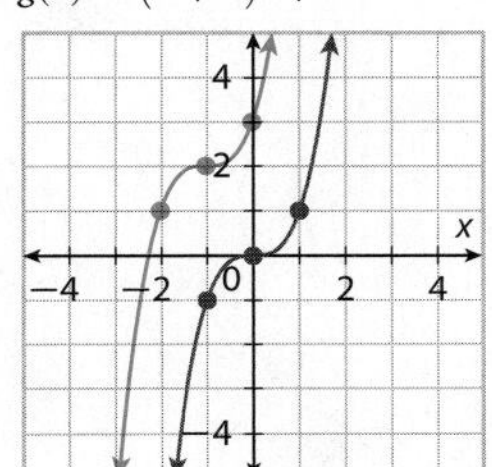

a translation of 1 unit to the left and 2 units up. Reference points on the graph of $g(x)$ are $(-1, 1)$, $(-1, 2)$, and $(0, 3)$.

AVOID COMMON ERRORS

Students may be confused about where to start when finding the equation for a combined transformation of the graph of $f(x) = x^3$. Explain that they should compare the corresponding points of the graph to the reference points of the graph of $f(x) = x^3$. If the graph is stretched or compressed horizontally, then they may use the form $f(x) = \left(\frac{1}{b}(x - h)\right)^3 + k$. If the graph is stretched or compressed vertically, then they may use the form $f(x) = a(x - h)^3 + k$.

INTEGRATE MATHEMATICAL PRACTICES

Focus on Modeling

MP.4 Suggest that students make a graphic organizer similar to the one below to help them remember the differences in the types of transformations of $f(x) = x^3$. Suggest students choose one or more cubic functions from this exercise set and give an example of each type of transformation.

Transformation	Example
Vertical shift	
Horizontal shift	
Vertical stretch	
Horizontal compression	

INTEGRATE MATHEMATICAL PRACTICES

Focus on Math Connections

MP.1 Point out that another name for the point of symmetry of a cubic function in this lesson is *the inflection point.* This is the point for which the "curvature" of the graph changes. For a cubic equation with a positive leading coefficient, the rate of change in the y-values of the graph decreases as x approaches this point from below and then begins to increase again as x increases past the point. In later mathematics classes, students will find that the slope of the curve at this point is 0.

A general equation for a cubic function $g(x)$ is given along with the function's graph. Write a specific equation by identifying the values of the parameters from the reference points shown on the graph.

14. $g(x) = \left(\frac{1}{b}(x - h)\right)^3 + k$

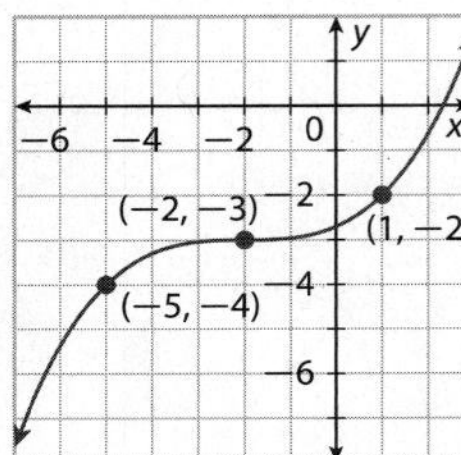

$(h, k) = (-2, -3)$, so $h = -2$ and $k = -3$.

$(b + h, 1 + k) = (b - 2, 1 - 3) = (1, -2)$, so $b = 3$.

$g(x) = \left(\frac{1}{3}(x + 2)\right)^3 - 3$

15. $g(x) = a(x - h)^3 + k$

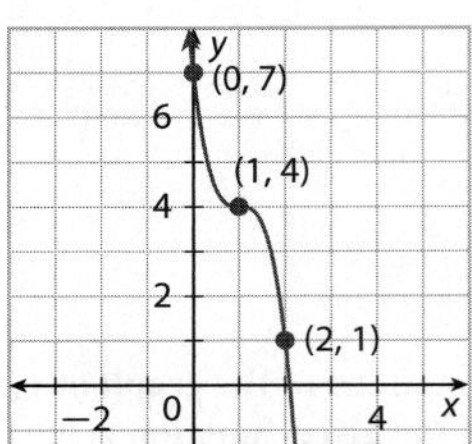

$(h, k) = (1, 4)$, so $h = 1$ and $k = 4$.

$(h + 1, a + k) = (1 + 1, a + 4) = (1, 2)$, so $a =$

$g(x) = -3(x - 1)^3 + 4$

16. 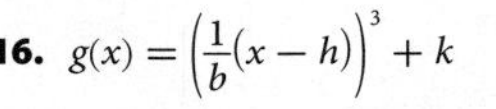 $g(x) = \left(\frac{1}{b}(x - h)\right)^3 + k$

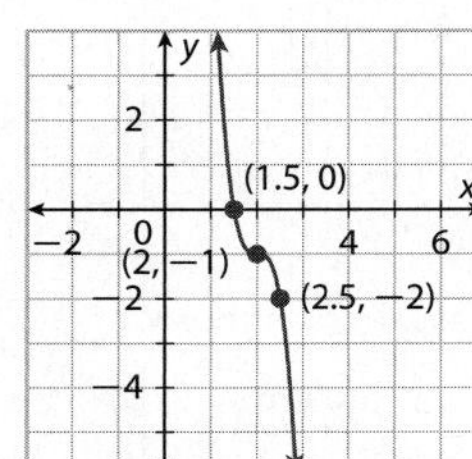

$(h, k) = (2, -1)$, so $h = 2$ and $k = -1$.

$(b + h, 1 + k) = (b + 2, 1 - 1) = (1.5, 0)$,

so $b = -0.5$.

$g(x) = \left(\frac{1}{-0.5}(x - 2)\right)^3 - 1 = \left(-2(x - 2)\right)^3 - 1$

17. $g(x) = a(x - h)^3 + k$

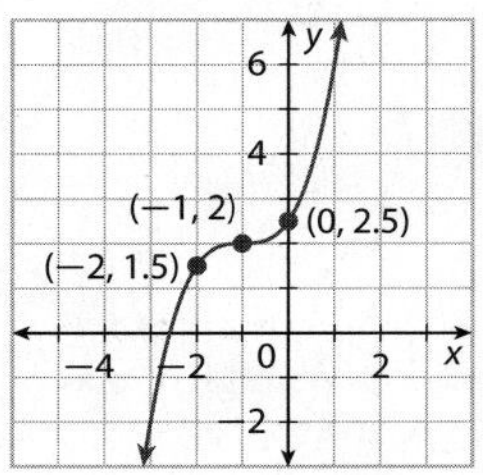

$(h, k) = (-1, 2)$, so $h = -1$ and $k = 2$.

$(h + 1, a + k) = (-1 + 1, a + 2) = (0, 2.5)$,

so $a = 0.5$.

$g(x) = 0.5(x + 1)^3 + 2$

Use a cubic function to model the situation, and graph the function using calculated values of the function. Then use the graph to obtain the indicated estimate.

18. Estimate the edge length of a cube of gold with a mass of 1 kg. The density of gold is 0.019 kg/cm³.

The volume V (in cubic centimeters) of the cube is $V(\ell) = \ell^3$. The mass m (in kilograms) of the cube is $m(\ell) = 0.019 \cdot V(\ell) = 0.019\ell^3$.

Length (cm)	Mass (g)
0	0
1	0.019
2	0.152
3	0.513
4	1.216

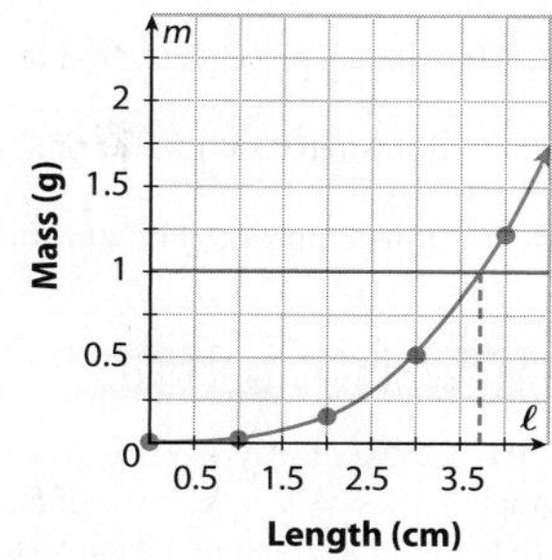

The graphs intersect where $\ell \approx 3.75$, so the edge length of the cube of gold is about 3.75 centimeters.

19. A proposed design for a habitable Mars colony is a semispherical biodome used to maintain a breathable atmosphere for the colonists. Estimate the radius of the biodome if it is required to contain 5.5 billion cubic feet of air.

Since the biodome is a hemisphere, the volume V (in billions of cubic feet) of the biodome is $V(r) = \frac{1}{2}\left(\frac{4}{3}\pi r^3\right) \approx 2.09r^3$.

Radius (thousands of feet)	Volume (billions of cubic feet)
0	0
0.5	0.26
1	2.09
1.5	7.05
2	16.72

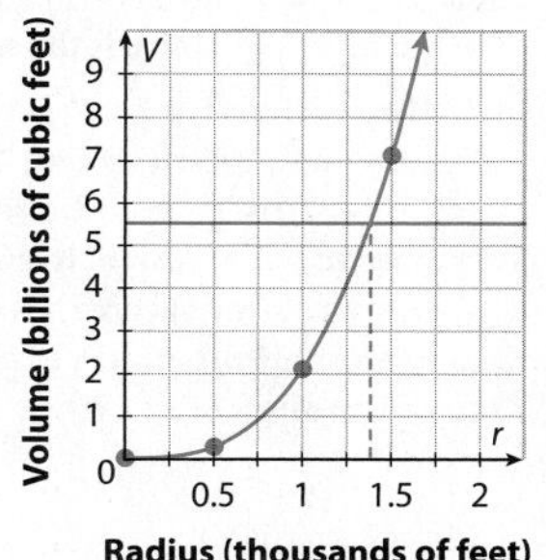

The graphs intersect where $r \approx 1.4$, so the radius of the biodome is about 1.4 thousand (1400) ft.

INTEGRATE MATHEMATICAL PRACTICES

Focus on Modeling

MP.4 For modeling problems involving geometry, review the formulas for the volumes of a sphere and rectangular prism. Students should recall that the volume V of a sphere can be found with the formula $V = \frac{4}{3}\pi r^3$, where r is the radius, and the volume of a rectangular prism is $V = lwh$, where l is the length of the rectangular base, w is the width of the base, and h is the height of the prism.

CONNECT VOCABULARY EL

To help students remember how the words *shift, stretch,* and *compression* are used in the context of this lesson, remind students that a *shift* is a translation, a transformation that does not change the shape or size of the original figure as the figure moves on the coordinate plane. A *stretch* (or *compression*), on the other hand, represents what happens to the graph of the parent figure if the leading coefficient of x is not equal to one. Reference points from the transformed graph will have more space between the corresponding y-values ("stretched") than the parent graph, or less space between the y-values ("compressed") than points on the parent graph. You can see these changes on the graph for small values of x.

PEER-TO-PEER DISCUSSION

Have students work in pairs. Instruct one student in each pair to sketch the graph of a cubic function of the form $f(x) = a(x - h)^3 + k$, while the other gives verbal instructions for each step. Then have the student who sketched the graph write the steps that were followed. Have students switch roles and repeat the exercise using a cubic function of the form $f(x) = [(\frac{1}{b})(x - h)]^3 + k$.

JOURNAL

Have students compare and contrast algebraic representations of vertical and horizontal transformations of cubic functions.

20. Multiple Response Select the transformations of the graph of the parent cubic function that result in the graph of $g(x) = (3(x - 2))^3 + 1$.

A. Horizontal stretch by a factor of 3

(B.) Horizontal compression by a factor of $\frac{1}{3}$

C. Vertical stretch by a factor of 3

D. Vertical compression by a factor of $\frac{1}{3}$

(E.) Translation 1 unit up

F. Translation 1 unit down

G. Translation 2 units left

(H.) Translation 2 units right

H.O.T. Focus on Higher Order Thinking

21. Justify Reasoning Explain how horizontally stretching (or compressing) the graph of $f(x) = x^3$ by a factor of b can be equivalent to vertically compressing (or stretching) the graph of $f(x) = x^3$ by a factor of a.

Horizontally stretching or compressing the graph of the parent cubic function by a factor of b results in the graph of the function $g(x) = \left(\frac{1}{b}x\right)^3$. You can rewrite $g(x)$ as follows:

$$g(x) = \left(\frac{1}{b}x\right)^3 = \left(\frac{1}{b}\right)^3 \cdot x^3 = \frac{1}{b^3} \cdot x^3$$

The function is now in the form $g(x) = ax^3$ where $a = \frac{1}{b^3}$. Notice that when $|b| > 1$, $|a| < 1$, which means that a horizontal stretch is equivalent to a vertical compression. Similarly, when $|b| < 1$, $|a| > 1$, which means that a horizontal compression is equivalent to a vertical stretch.

22. Critique Reasoning A student reasoned that $g(x) = (x - h)^3$ can be rewritten as $g(x) = x^3 - h^3$, so a horizontal translation of h units is equivalent to a vertical translation of $-h^3$ units. Is the student correct? Explain.

No, the student isn't correct. There is no property of exponents that allows you to distribute an exponent to a sum or difference, so $g(x) = (x - h)^3$ cannot be rewritten in the form $g(x) = x^3 + k$. From a geometric perspective, it doesn't make sense to think that there can be a vertical translation of a graph that is equivalent to a horizontal translation of the graph except in the trivial case where the graph is not moved at all $(h = k = 0)$.

Lesson Performance Task

Julio wants to purchase a spherical aquarium and fill it with salt water, which has an average density of 1.027 g/cm^3. He has found a company that sells four sizes of spherical aquariums.

Aquarium Size	Diameter (cm)
Small	15
Medium	30
Large	45
Extra large	60

a. If the stand for Julio's aquarium will support a maximum of 50 kg, what is the largest size tank that he should buy? Explain your reasoning.

b. Julio's friend suggests that he could buy a larger tank if he uses fresh water, which has a density of 1.0 g/cm^3. Do you agree with the friend? Why or why not?

a. **The volume V (in cubic centimeters) of a sphere with diameter d (in centimeters) is $V(d) = \frac{3}{4}\pi\left(\frac{d}{2}\right)^3 = \frac{\pi}{6}d^3$. If the sphere is filled with salt water having a density of 1.027 g/cm3, then the mass m (in kilograms) of the salt water is $m(V) = \frac{1.027}{1000}V = 0.001027V$. The table summarizes the volume and mass of salt water for each size of tank.**

Aquarium Size	Volume (cm^3)	Mass of Water (kg)
Small	1,760	1.81
Medium	14,100	14.5
Large	47,700	49.0
Extra large	113,000	116

Some students may say that Julio should buy the large tank, because the mass of the water, 49.0 kg, is less than 50 kg. Other students may say that he should buy the medium tank, because he has to consider the mass of the empty tank, which will likely make the total mass greater than 50 kg.

b. **Students' answers will depend on how they answered Part a. If they answered that Julio should buy the large tank, then the minor difference in density will have no effect on his choice. If they said he should buy the medium tank, some students may decide that the lesser density of fresh water might reduce the mass of the water just enough to allow him to buy the large tank.**

EXTENSION ACTIVITY

Julio decides he wants to fill one-third of his aquarium with sand that has a density of 1.6 g/cm^3. The remaining two-thirds of the aquarium will be filled with water. Have students answer the questions in the Performance Task using this new information. Then have them graph the mass in the aquarium compared with the aquarium size, both with and without the sand. Ask them how the addition of the sand affects the total mass in the aquarium and if this information will help Julio decide between a Medium and a Large tank.

AVOID COMMON ERRORS

Make sure students are multiplying the volume by the density instead of dividing by the density. Have students write the units next to the values as they do the calculation. If the units cancel properly, the final units should be mass. Ask students what the real-life consequence of dividing by the density would be.

QUESTIONING STRATEGIES

? Why would using fresh water allow Julio to buy a larger tank? **Fresh water has a lower density and therefore has a lower mass for the same volume.**

? If the diameter of the Medium tank is twice the diameter of the Small tank, why isn't the volume of the Medium tank twice that of the Small tank? **The volume is described by a cubic function. The ratio of the volumes is the ratio of their diameters cubed.**

? Why is it important to know the density of the water? **The density is the mass per volume. If the volume is known, then the density will give the mass that the volume will hold.**

Scoring Rubric

2 points: The student's answer is an accurate and complete execution of the task or tasks.

1 point: The student's answer contains attributes of an appropriate response but is flawed.

0 points: The student's answer contains no attributes of an appropriate response.

LESSON 5.2

Graphing Polynomial Functions

Common Core Math Standards

The student is expected to:

 **F-IF.C.7c**

Graph polynomial functions, identifying zeros when suitable factorizations are available, and showing end behavior. Also A-SSE.A.1a, A-APR.B.3, F-IF.B.4

Mathematical Practices

 **MP.7 Using Structure**

Language Objective

Work with a partner or small group to match function types to their equations or definitions.

ENGAGE

Essential Question: How do you sketch the graph of a polynomial function in intercept form?

Determine the end behavior based on the degree and whether or not the function includes a negative constant factor. Identify and plot the x-intercepts. Use the factors to determine the sign of the function's values on the intervals determined by the x-intercepts. Sketch the graph by showing where it crosses the x-axis, where it is tangent to the x-axis, and roughly where turning points occur.

PREVIEW: LESSON PERFORMANCE TASK

View the Engage section online. Discuss the photo, asking the students to list the known quantities for the sheet of cardboard and the unknown variables for the box. Then preview the Lesson Performance Task.

Name ______________ Class ______________ Date ______________

5.2 Graphing Polynomial Functions

Resource Locker

Essential Question: How do you sketch the graph of a polynomial function in intercept form?

Explore 1 Investigating the End Behavior of the Graphs of Simple Polynomial Functions

Linear, quadratic, and cubic functions belong to a more general class of functions called *polynomial functions*, which are categorized by their degree. Linear functions are polynomial functions of degree 1, quadratic functions are polynomial functions of degree 2, and cubic functions are polynomial functions of degree 3. In general, a **polynomial function of degree n** has the standard form $p(x) = a_nx^n + a_{n-1}x^{n-1} + \ldots + a_2x^2 + a_1x + a_0$, where $a_n, a_{n-1}, \ldots, a_2, a_1$, and a_0 are real numbers called the *coefficients* of the expressions $a_nx^n, a_{n-1}x^{n-1}, \ldots, a_2x^2, a_1x$, and a_0, which are the *terms* of the polynomial function. (Note that the constant term, a_0, appears to have no power of x associated with it, but since $x^0 = 1$, you can write a_0 as a_0x^0 and treat a_0 as the coefficient of the term.)

A polynomial function of degree 4 is called a *quartic* function, while a polynomial function of degree 5 is called a *quintic* function. After degree 5, polynomial functions are generally referred to by their degree, as in "a sixth-degree polynomial function."

(A) Use a graphing calculator to graph the polynomial functions $f(x) = x$, $f(x) = x^2$, $f(x) = x^3$, $f(x) = x^4$, $f(x) = x^5$, and $f(x) = x^6$. Then use the graph of each function to determine the function's domain, range, and end behavior. (Use interval notation for the domain and range.)

Function	Domain	Range	End Behavior
$f(x) = x$	$(-\infty, +\infty)$	$(-\infty, +\infty)$	As $x \to +\infty$, $f(x) \to$ $+\infty$. As $x \to -\infty$, $f(x) \to$ $-\infty$.
$f(x) = x^2$	$(-\infty, +\infty)$	$[0, +\infty)$	As $x \to +\infty$, $f(x) \to$ $+\infty$. As $x \to -\infty$, $f(x) \to$ $+\infty$.
$f(x) = x^3$	$(-\infty, +\infty)$	$(-\infty, +\infty)$	As $x \to +\infty$, $f(x) \to$ $+\infty$. As $x \to -\infty$, $f(x) \to$ $-\infty$.
$f(x) = x^4$	$(-\infty, +\infty)$	$[0, +\infty)$	As $x \to +\infty$, $f(x) \to$ $+\infty$. As $x \to -\infty$, $f(x) \to$ $+\infty$.
$f(x) = x^5$	$(-\infty, +\infty)$	$(-\infty, +\infty)$	As $x \to +\infty$, $f(x) \to$ $+\infty$. As $x \to -\infty$, $f(x) \to$ $-\infty$.
$f(x) = x^6$	$(-\infty, +\infty)$	$[0, +\infty)$	As $x \to +\infty$, $f(x) \to$ $+\infty$. As $x \to -\infty$, $f(x) \to$ $+\infty$.

HARDCOVER PAGES 249–264

Watch for the hardcover student edition page numbers for this lesson.

 Use a graphing calculator to graph the polynomial functions $f(x) = -x$, $f(x) = -x^2$, $f(x) = -x^3$, $f(x) = -x^4$, $f(x) = -x^5$, and $f(x) = -x^6$. Then use the graph of each function to determine the function's domain, range, and end behavior. (Use interval notation for the domain and range.)

Function	Domain	Range	End Behavior
$f(x) = -x$	$(-\infty, +\infty)$	$(-\infty, +\infty)$	As $x \to +\infty$, $f(x) \to -\infty$. As $x \to -\infty$, $f(x) \to +\infty$.
$f(x) = -x^2$	$(-\infty, +\infty)$	$(-\infty, 0]$	As $x \to +\infty$, $f(x) \to -\infty$. As $x \to -\infty$, $f(x) \to -\infty$.
$f(x) = -x^3$	$(-\infty, +\infty)$	$(-\infty, +\infty)$	As $x \to +\infty$, $f(x) \to -\infty$. As $x \to -\infty$, $f(x) \to +\infty$.
$f(x) = -x^4$	$(-\infty, +\infty)$	$(-\infty, 0]$	As $x \to +\infty$, $f(x) \to -\infty$. As $x \to -\infty$, $f(x) \to -\infty$.
$f(x) = -x^5$	$(-\infty, +\infty)$	$(-\infty, +\infty)$	As $x \to +\infty$, $f(x) \to -\infty$. As $x \to -\infty$, $f(x) \to +\infty$.
$f(x) = -x^6$	$(-\infty, +\infty)$	$(-\infty, 0]$	As $x \to +\infty$, $f(x) \to -\infty$. As $x \to -\infty$, $f(x) \to -\infty$.

Reflect

 How can you generalize the results of this Explore for $f(x) = x^n$ and $f(x) = -x^n$ where n is positive whole number?

The domains of the functions $f(x) = x^n$ and $f(x) = -x^n$ are both $(-\infty, +\infty)$. The ranges depend on whether n is even or odd. If n is odd, the ranges of $f(x) = x^n$ and $f(x) = -x^n$ are both $(-\infty, +\infty)$. If n is even, the range of $f(x) = x^n$ is $[0, +\infty)$ while the range of $f(x) = -x^n$ is $(-\infty, 0]$. The end behavior of $f(x) = -x^n$ is always the opposite of the end behavior of $f(x) = x^n$.

EXPLORE 1

Investigating the End Behavior of the Graphs of Simple Polynomial Functions

INTEGRATE TECHNOLOGY

Students have the option of completing the graphing calculator activity either in the book or online.

QUESTIONING STRATEGIES

Suppose $f(x) \to +\infty$ as $x \to -\infty$. What does this statement tell you about the graph of $f(x) = x^n$ and the direction in which you are moving on the x-axis? What can you say about the value of n? **The statement says that as you move to the left along the negative x-axis so x decreases without bound, the graph of $f(x) = x^n$ rises without bound. This is true of the graph of $f(x) = x^n$ when n is even.**

Does any function of the form $f(x) = x^n$ have end behavior where $f(x) \to -\infty$ as $x \to +\infty$? Explain. **No; this would mean that as you move right along the positive x-axis, the graph of $f(x) = x^n$ falls without bound, which is not true of the graph of $f(x) = x^n$ for all values of n.**

PROFESSIONAL DEVELOPMENT

Integrate Mathematical Practices

This lesson provides an opportunity to address Mathematical Practice **MP.7**, which calls for students to "look for and make use of structure." Students analyze some of the attributes of polynomial functions. Specifically, they examine domain, range, intercepts, turning points, and end behavior. They also investigate the x-intercepts of graphs of polynomial functions, and how they relate to the factored form of the related polynomial expression. Students also analyze polynomial functions in real-world contexts.

EXPLORE 2

Investigating the x-intercepts and Turning Points of the Graphs of Polynomial Functions

CONNECT VOCABULARY EL

Relate *turning point* to driving a car north and then turning the car to drive south. Explain that the *turning point* is the point at which the car reverses direction.

Explore 2 Investigating the x-intercepts and Turning Points of the Graphs of Polynomial Functions

The cubic function $f(x) = x^3$ has three factors, all of which happen to be x. One or more of the x's can be replaced with other linear factors in x, such as $x - 2$, without changing the fact that the function is cubic. In general, a polynomial function of the form $p(x) = a(x - x_1)(x - x_2)...(x - x_n)$ where $a, x_1, x_2,...,$ and x_n are real numbers (that are not necessarily distinct) has degree n where n is the number of variable factors.

The graph of $p(x) = a(x - x_1)(x - x_2)...(x - x_n)$ has $x_1, x_2,...,$ and x_n as its x-intercepts, which is why the polynomial is said to be in *intercept form*. Since the graph of $p(x)$ intersects the x-axis only at its x-intercepts, the graph must move away from and then move back toward the x-axis between each pair of successive x-intercepts, which means that the graph has a *turning point* between those x-intercepts. Also, instead of crossing the x-axis at an x-intercept, the graph can be *tangent* to the x-axis, and the point of tangency becomes a turning point because the graph must move toward the x-axis and then away from it near the point of tangency.

The y-coordinate of each turning point is a maximum or minimum value of the function. A maximum or minimum value is called *global* or *absolute* if the function never takes on a value that is greater than the maximum or less than the minimum. On the other hand, a maximum or minimum value is called *local* or *relative* if the function does take on values that are greater than the maximum or less than the minimum somewhere outside an interval where the maximum or minimum value occurs.

(A) Use a graphing calculator to graph the cubic functions $f(x) = x^3$, $f(x) = x^2(x - 2)$, and $f(x) = x(x - 2)(x + 2)$. Then use the graph of each function to answer the questions in the table.

Function	$f(x) = x^3$	$f(x) = x^2(x - 2)$	$f(x) = x(x - 2)(x + 2)$
How many distinct factors does $f(x)$ have?	1	2	3
What are the graph's x-intercepts?	0	0, 2	0, 2, −2
Is the graph tangent to the x-axis or does it cross the x-axis at each x-intercept?	Crosses at $x = 0$	Tangent at $x = 0$; crosses at $x = 2$	Crosses at all three x-intercepts
How many turning points does the graph have?	0	2	2
How many global maximum values? How many local?	No maximum values	No global maximum values, but one local maximum value	No global maximum values, but one local maximum value
How many global minimum values? How many local?	No minimum values	No global minimum values, but one local minimum value	No global minimum values, but one local minimum value

COLLABORATIVE LEARNING

Peer-to-Peer Activity

Have students work in pairs. Instruct one student in each pair to sketch the graph of a polynomial function in intercept form while the other gives verbal instructions for each step. Then have the student who sketched the graph write the steps that were followed. Have students switch roles and repeat the exercise using a different polynomial function in intercept form. Encourage students to display and use a sign table for their graphs.

Ⓑ Use a graphing calculator to graph the quartic functions $f(x) = x^4$, $f(x) = x^3(x-2)$, $f(x) = x^2(x-2)(x+2)$, and $f(x) = x(x-2)(x+2)(x+3)$. Then use the graph of each function to answer the questions in the table.

Function	$f(x) = x^4$	$f(x) = x^3(x-2)$	$f(x) = x^2(x-2)(x+2)$	$f(x) = x(x-2)(x+2)(x+3)$
How many distinct factors?	1	2	3	4
What are the x-intercepts?	0	0, 2	0, 2, −2	0, 2, −2, −3
Tangent to or cross the x-axis at x-intercepts?	Tangent at $x = 0$	Crosses at both x-intercepts	Tangent at $x = 0$; crosses at $x = 2$ and $x = -2$	Crosses at all four x-intercepts
How many turning points?	1	2	3	3
How many global maximum values? How many local?	No maximum values	No maximum values	No global maximum values, but one local maximum value	No global maximum values, but one local maximum value
How many global minimum values? How many local?	One global minimum value and no local minimum values	One global minimum value and no local minimum values	One global minimum value (which occurs twice) and no local minimum values	One global minimum value and one local minimum value

Reflect

2. What determines how many x-intercepts the graph of a polynomial function in intercept form has?
Each distinct factor produces one x-intercept.

3. What determines whether the graph of a polynomial function in intercept form crosses the x-axis or is tangent to it at an x-intercept?
If the factor that produces the x-intercept is raised to an odd power, the graph will cross the x-axis. If the factor is raised to an even power, the graph will be tangent to the x-axis.

4. Suppose you introduced a factor of −1 into each of the quartic functions in Step B. (For instance, $f(x) = x^4$ becomes $f(x) = -x^4$.) How would your answers to the questions about the functions and their graphs change?
Since each function's graph would be reflected across the x-axis, a maximum value would become a minimum value and vice versa. This would change the answers to the questions about global and local maximum and minimum values. For instance, $f(x) = x^4$ has no maximum values, one global minimum value, and no local minimum values, whereas $f(x) = -x^4$ would have one global maximum value, no local maximum values, and no minimum values.

QUESTIONING STRATEGIES

How is the number of variable factors of a polynomial function related to the degree of the polynomial? **They are equal.**

Where are the turning points of a polynomial function located? How are the local maxima and minima related to the turning points? **Between consecutive pairs of x-intercepts; the local maxima and minima occur at the turning points.**

DIFFERENTIATE INSTRUCTION

Visual Clues

When discussing local maxima and minima, have students cover irrelevant parts of the graph with a sheet of paper to help them focus on the local extreme value of interest.

Cognitive Strategies

Suggest that all students create reference cards that show the general shapes of polynomial functions of degrees 2 through 5. Students can think of the cards as a "vocabulary of graphs" and use them when graphing polynomial functions.

EXPLAIN 1

Sketching the Graph of Polynomial Functions in Intercept Form

AVOID COMMON ERRORS

To determine end behavior, students can multiply all factors, but they may make errors in the complex calculation. Point out that end behavior is determined by the term with the greatest degree. If a function is written in factored from, then the highest-degree term is the product of all the first terms of the factors, as long as any repeated factors are considered individually. So, if $f(x) = (3x + 1)^2(x - 1) = (3x + 1)(3x + 1)(x - 1)$, then the leading term is $(3x)(3x)(x) = 9x^3$, and the polynomial has the same end behavior as $f(x) = x^3$.

 **Explain 1** Sketching the Graph of Polynomial Functions in Intercept Form

Given a polynomial function in intercept form, you can sketch the function's graph by using the end behavior, the x-intercepts, and the sign of the function values on intervals determined by the x-intercepts. The sign of the function values tells you whether the graph is above or below the x-axis on a particular interval. You can find the sign of the function values by determining the sign of each factor and recognizing what the sign of the product of those factors is.

Example 1 Sketch the graph of the polynomial function.

Ⓐ $f(x) = x(x + 2)(x - 3)$

Identify the end behavior. For the function $p(x) = a(x - x_1)(x - x_2)\ldots(x - x_n)$, the end behavior is determined by whether the degree n is even or odd and whether the constant factor a is positive or negative. For the given function $f(x)$, the degree is 3 and the constant factor a, which is 1, is positive, so $f(x)$ has the following end behavior:

As $x \to +\infty, f(x) \to +\infty$.

As $x \to -\infty, f(x) \to -\infty$.

Identify the graph's x-intercepts, and then use the sign of $f(x)$ on intervals determined by the x-intercepts to find where the graph is above the x-axis and where it's below the x-axis.

The x-intercepts are $x = 0$, $x = -2$, and $x = 3$. These three x-intercepts divide the x-axis into four intervals: $x < -2$, $-2 < x < 0$, $0 < x < 3$, and $x > 3$.

Interval	Sign of the Constant Factor	Sign of x	Sign of $x + 2$	Sign of $x - 3$	Sign of $f(x) = x(x+2)(x-3)$
$x < -2$	+	−	−	−	−
$-2 < x < 0$	+	−	+	−	+
$0 < x < 3$	+	+	+	−	−
$x > 3$	+	+	+	+	+

So, the graph of $f(x)$ is above the x-axis on the intervals $-2 < x < 0$ and $x > 3$, and it's below the x-axis on the intervals $x < -2$ and $0 < x < 3$.

Sketch the graph.

While you should be precise about where the graph crosses the x-axis, you do not need to be precise about the y-coordinates of points on the graph that aren't on the x-axis. Your sketch should simply show where the graph lies above the x-axis and where it lies below the x-axis.

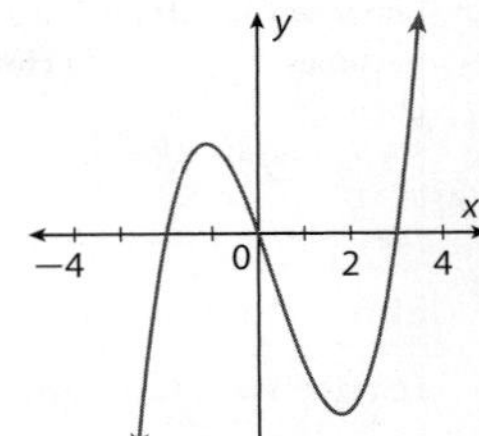

LANGUAGE SUPPORT EL

Connect Vocabulary

Distribute note cards to students. Have half the students write the names of the types of functions addressed in this lesson, such as *cubic, quartic, quadratic,* and *linear,* writing one name per card. Have the other half of the students write a definition (*a function with a degree of* 3, for example, or *an equation*) on each card. Place the name cards in one pile and the definition cards in another. Students shuffle the cards, place them face down, and take turns turning over one card from each pile. If they have a match, they must explain to the rest of the group why it is a match.

(B) $f(x) = -(x - 4)(x - 1)(x + 1)(x + 2)$

Identify the end behavior.

As $x \to +\infty$, $f(x) \to$ $-\infty$.

As $x \to -\infty$, $f(x) \to$ $-\infty$.

Identify the graph's x-intercepts, and then use the sign of $f(x)$ on intervals determined by the x-intercepts to find where the graph is above the x-axis and where it's below the x-axis.

The x-intercepts are $x =$ -2, $x =$ -1, $x =$ 1, $x =$ 4.

Interval	Sign of the Constant Factor	Sign of $x - 4$	Sign of $x - 1$	Sign of $x + 1$	Sign of $x + 2$	Sign of $f(x) = -(x - 4)(x - 1)(x + 1)(x + 2)$
$x < -2$	−	−	−	−	−	−
$-2 < x < -1$	−	−	−	−	+	+
$-1 < x < 1$	−	−	+	+	+	−
$1 < x < 4$	−	−	+	+	+	+
$x > 4$	−	+	+	+	+	−

So, the graph of $f(x)$ is above the x-axis on the intervals

$-2 < x < -1$ and $1 < x < 4$, and

it's below the x-axis on the intervals $x < -2$, $-1 < x < 1$,

and $x > 4$.

Sketch the graph.

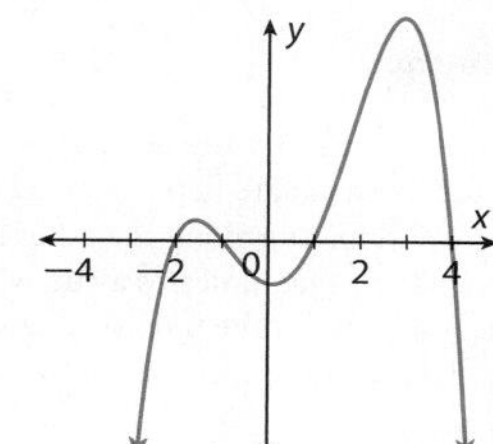

QUESTIONING STRATEGIES

? When sketching the graph of a polynomial function in intercept form, how do you know when the graph is tangent to the x-axis? **When the same zero values occur an even number of times in the factorization of the polynomial, the graph of the function is tangent to the x-axis at that value.**

? What are you finding when you find $f(0)$? **the graph's y-intercept**

EXPLAIN 2

Modeling with a Polynomial Function

INTEGRATE TECHNOLOGY

On a graphing calculator, students can enter a polynomial function in standard or modified intercept form. For example, a cubic function can be entered using the general form $f(x) = (a_1x + b_1)(a_2x + b_2)(a_3x + b_3)$, which is not quite intercept form.

Your Turn

Sketch the graph of the polynomial function.

5. $f(x) = -x^2(x - 4)$

As $x \to +\infty$, $f(x) \to -\infty$.

As $x \to -\infty$, $f(x) \to +\infty$.

The x-intercepts are $x = 0$ and $x = 4$.

Interval	Sign of the Constant Factor	Sign of x^2	Sign of $x - 4$	Sign of $f(x) = x^2(x - 4)$
$x < 0$	−	+	−	+
$0 < x < 4$	−	+	−	+
$x > 4$	−	+	+	−

So, the graph of $f(x)$ is above the x-axis on the intervals $x < 0$ and $0 < x < 4$, and it's below the x-axis on the interval $x > 4$.

Explain 2 Modeling with a Polynomial Function

You can use cubic functions to model real-world situations. For example, you find the volume of a box (a rectangular prism) by multiplying the length, width, and height. If each dimension of the box is given in terms of x, then the volume is a cubic function of x.

Example 2

To create an open-top box out of a sheet of cardboard that is 9 inches long and 5 inches wide, you make a square flap of side length x inches in each corner by cutting along one of the flap's sides and folding along the other side. (In the first diagram, a solid line segment in the interior of the rectangle indicates a cut, while a dashed line segment indicates a fold.) After you fold up the four sides of the box (see the second diagram), you glue each flap to the side it overlaps. To the nearest tenth, find the value of x that maximizes the volume of the box.

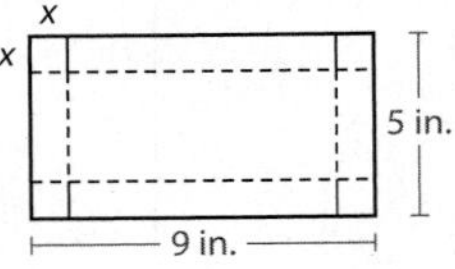

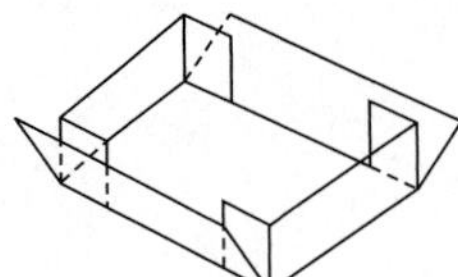

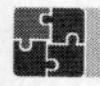

Analyze Information

Identify the important information.

A square flap of side length x inches is made in each corner of a rectangular sheet of cardboard.

The sheet of cardboard measures 9 inches by 5 inches.

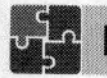

Formulate a Plan

Find the dimensions of the box once the flaps have been made and the sides have been folded up. Create a volume function for the box, graph the function on a graphing calculator, and use the graph to find the value of x that maximizes the volume.

Solve

1. Write expressions for the dimensions of the box.

   Length of box: $9 - \boxed{2x}$

   Width of box: $5 - \boxed{2x}$

   Height of box: $\boxed{x}$

2. Write the volume function and determine its domain.

   $V(x) = \left(9 - \boxed{2x}\right)\left(5 - \boxed{2x}\right)\boxed{x}$

   Because the length, width, and height of the box must all be positive, the volume function's domain is determined by the following three constraints:

   $9 - 2x > 0$, or $x < \boxed{4.5}$

   $5 - 2x > 0$, or $x < \boxed{2.5}$

   $x > 0$

   Taken together, these constraints give a domain of $0 < x < \boxed{2.5}$.

3. Use a graphing calculator to graph the volume function on its domain.

   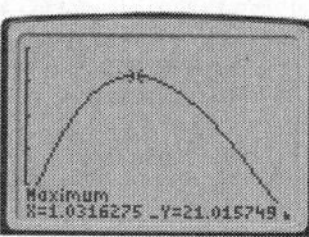

   Adjust the viewing window so you can see the maximum. From the graphing calculator's **CALC** menu, select **4: maximum** to locate the point where the maximum value occurs.

   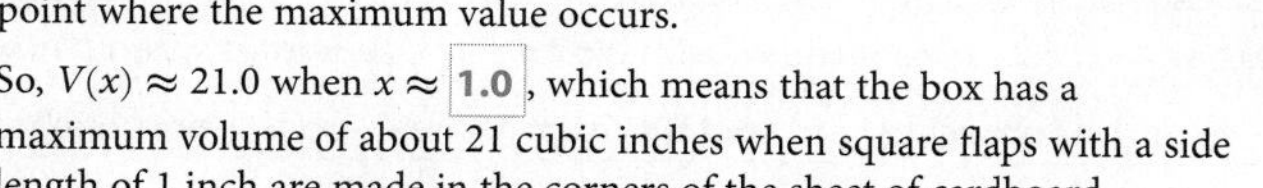

   So, $V(x) \approx 21.0$ when $x \approx \boxed{1.0}$, which means that the box has a maximum volume of about 21 cubic inches when square flaps with a side length of 1 inch are made in the corners of the sheet of cardboard.

QUESTIONING STRATEGIES

? Why do the constraints on x for length and width not simply require that x be nonnegative? **The constraints on x describe those values of x that make expressions for length and width nonnegative values.**

? How can you generalize from this situation to finding the domain for any volume function? **Since length, height, and width will always be nonnegative, the domain of a volume function will always require that the independent variable take on only those values that make each dimension nonnegative.**

ELABORATE

INTEGRATE MATHEMATICAL PRACTICES

Focus on Critical Thinking

MP.3 Before students graph any polynomial functions, encourage them to predict how the graph should look based on the degree and end behavior of the function. If the function is in intercept form, encourage students to predict the number and location of the turning points.

QUESTIONING STRATEGIES

What is the degree of any volume function? Explain. **Three; geometrically, volume is related to a figure with three dimensions, so it will be represented by a function of degree 3.**

SUMMARIZE THE LESSON

What are some of the key attributes of a polynomial function of degree n that you can determine from the graph of the function? **You can determine the x-intercepts and therefore the real zeros of the function, and the approximate location of the turning points. You can also determine the maximum and minimum values, the end behavior, and whether the degree of the leading coefficient is even or odd, and positive or negative.**

Justify and Evaluate

Making square flaps with a side length of 1 inch means that the box will be 7 inches long, 3 inches wide, and 1 inch high, so the volume is 21 cubic inches. As a check on this result, consider making square flaps with a side length of 0.9 inch and 1.1 inches:

$V(0.9) = (9 - 1.8)(5 - 1.8)(0.9) =$ **20.736**

$V(1.1) = (9 - 2.2)(5 - 2.2)(1.1) =$ **20.944**

Both volumes are slightly less than 21 cubic inches, which suggests that 21 cubic inches is the maximum volume.

Reflect

6. **Discussion** Although the volume function has three constraints on its domain, the domain involves only two of them. Why?
All three inequalities must be satisfied simultaneously. Any x-value that satisfies $x < 2.5$ also satisfies $x < 4.5$, so the constraint $x \leq 4.5$ has no impact on the domain.

Your Turn

7. To create an open-top box out of a sheet of cardboard that is 25 inches long and 13 inches wide, you make a square flap of side length x inches in each corner by cutting along one of the flap's sides and folding along the other. (In the diagram, a solid line segment in the interior of the rectangle indicates a cut, while a dashed line segment indicates a fold.) Once you fold up the four sides of the box, you glue each flap to the side it overlaps. To the nearest tenth, find the value of x that maximizes the volume of the box.

x
x
13
25 in.

The length of the box is $25 - 2x$, the width is $13 - 2x$, and the height is x. So, the volume func is $V(x) = (25 - 2x)(13 - 2x)x$ with a domain of $0 < x < 6.5$ determined by the constraints tha three dimensions of the box must be nonnegative. Maximum volume is about 402 cubic inche when square flaps with a side length of 2.7 inches are made in the corners.

Elaborate

8. Compare and contrast the domain, range, and end behavior of $f(x) = x^n$ when n is even and when n is odd.
The domains are always the same, but when n is even, the range contains only numbers greater than or equal to 0, whereas when n is odd, the range is all real numbers. When n is even, $f(x)$ approaches $+\infty$ as x approaches both $-\infty$ and $+\infty$, whereas when n is odd, $f(x)$ approaches $-\infty$ as x approaches $-\infty$ and $f(x)$ approaches $+\infty$ as x approaches $+\infty$.

9. **Essential Question Check-In** For a polynomial function in intercept form, why is the constant factor important when graphing the function?
The sign of the constant factor has an impact on the end behavior of the function. It also has an impact on whether the y-coordinates of turning points represent maximum or minimum values.

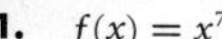

Evaluate: Homework and Practice

- Online Homework
- Hints and Help
- Extra Practice

Use a graphing calculator to graph the polynomial function. Then use the graph to determine the function's domain, range, and end behavior. (Use interval notation for the domain and range.)

1. $f(x) = x^7$

Domain: $(-\infty, +\infty)$

Range: $(-\infty, +\infty)$

End behavior: As $x \to +\infty$, $f(x) \to + \infty$.

As $x \to -\infty$, $f(x) \to -\infty$.

2. $f(x) = -x^9$

Domain: $(-\infty, +\infty)$

Range: $(-\infty, +\infty)$

End behavior: As $x \to +\infty$, $f(x) \to -\infty$.

As $x \to -\infty$, $f(x) \to +\infty$.

3. $f(x) = x^{10}$

Domain: $(-\infty, +\infty)$

Range: $[0, +\infty)$

End behavior: As $x \to +\infty$, $f(x) \to +\infty$.

As $x \to -\infty$, $f(x) \to +\infty$.

4. $f(x) = -x^8$

Domain: $(- \infty, +\infty)$

Range: $(-\infty, 0]$

End behavior: As $x \to +\infty$, $f(x) \to -\infty$.

As $x \to -\infty$, $f(x) \to -\infty$.

Use a graphing calculator to graph the function. Then use the graph to determine the number of turning points and the number and type (global or local) of any maximum or minimum values.

5. $f(x) = x(x + 1)(x + 3)$

The graph has two turning points. The function has one local maximum value and one local minimum value.

6. $f(x) = (x + 1)^2(x - 1)(x - 2)$

The graph has three turning points. The function has one local maximum value, one global minimum value, and one local minimum value.

7. $f(x) = -x(x - 2)^2$

The graph has two turning points. The function has one local maximum value and one local minimum value.

8. $f(x) = -(x - 1)(x + 2)^3$

The graph has one turning point. The function has one global maximum value.

Exercise	Depth of Knowledge (D.O.K.)	COMMON CORE Mathematical Practices
1-8	**2** Skills/Concepts	**MP.2** Reasoning
9–11	**2** Skills/Concepts	**MP.4** Modeling
12–13	**3** Strategic Thinking	**MP.5** Using Tools
14–17	**3** Strategic Thinking	**MP.4** Modeling
18	**2** Skills/Concepts	**MP.2** Reasoning
19	**3** Strategic Thinking H.O.T.	**MP.3** Logic

EVALUATE

ASSIGNMENT GUIDE

Concepts and Skills	Practice
Explore 1 Investigating the End Behavior of the Graphs of Simple Polynomial Functions	Exercises 1–4
Explore 2 Investigating the x-intercepts and Turning Points of the Graphs of Polynomial Functions	Exercises 5–8
Example 1 Sketching the Graph of Polynomial Functions in Intercept Form	Exercises 9–11
Example 2 Modeling with a Polynomial Function	Exercises 12–13

INTEGRATE MATHEMATICAL PRACTICES

Focus on Reasoning

MP.2 Students should recognize that the characteristics of the expression that defines a polynomial function determine the nature, and thus the attributes, of the graph of the function. Have students use grid paper and/or their graphing calculators to explore how different types of polynomial functions produce graphs with similar and differing attributes.

AVOID COMMON ERRORS

Students may have difficulty identifying the leading coefficient and therefore the expected end behavior of a polynomial function. Emphasize that students must either write the polynomial in standard form with the highest power first, or multiply the variable terms of the factors of the polynomial, if the polynomial is expressed in intercept form.

INTEGRATE MATHEMATICAL PRACTICES

Focus on Modeling

MP.4 Suggest that students make a flow chart illustrating the process of graphing a factorable polynomial function. They can choose one polynomial function from this lesson and describe how each step would be applied.

Sketch the graph the polynomial function.

9. $f(x) = x^2(x - 2)$

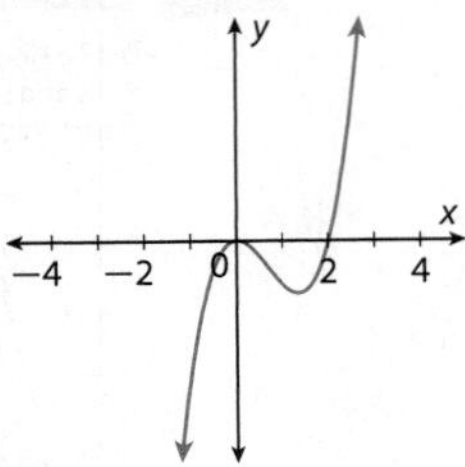

As $x \to +\infty$, $f(x) \to +\infty$. As $x \to -\infty$, $f(x) \to -\infty$.

The x-intercepts are $x = 0$ and $x = 2$.

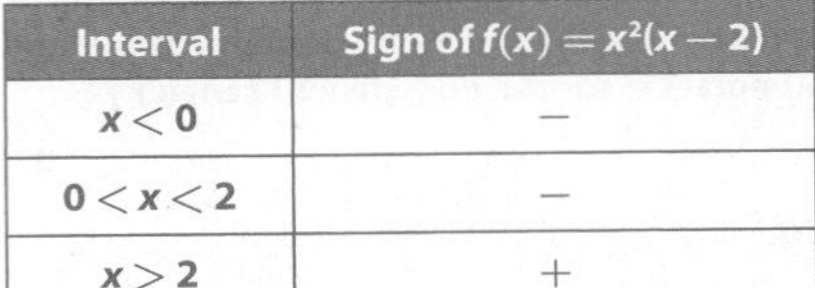

Interval	Sign of $f(x) = x^2(x - 2)$
$x < 0$	−
$0 < x < 2$	−
$x > 2$	+

So, the graph of $f(x)$ is above the x-axis on the interval $x > 2$, and it's below the x-axis on the intervals $x < 0$ and $0 < x < 2$.

10. $f(x) = -(x + 1)(x - 2)(x - 3)$

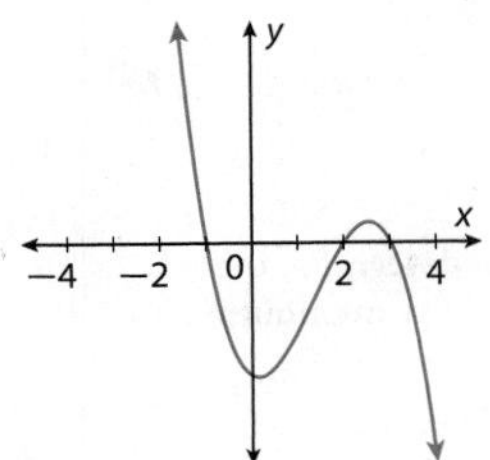

As $x \to +\infty$, $f(x) \to -\infty$. As $x \to -\infty$, $f(x) \to +\infty$.

The x-intercepts are $x = -1$, $x = 2$ and $x = 3$.

Interval	Sign of $f(x) = -(x + 1)(x - 2)(x - 3)$
$x < -1$	+
$-1 < x < 2$	−
$2 < x < 3$	+
$x > 3$	−

So, the graph of $f(x)$ is above the x-axis on the intervals $x < -1$ and $2 < x < 3$, and it's below the x-axis on the intervals $-1 < x < 2$ and $x > 3$.

11. $f(x) = x(x + 2)^2(x - 1)$

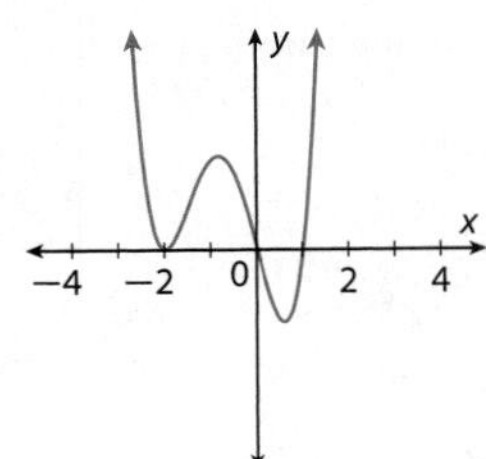

As $x \to +\infty$, $f(x) \to +\infty$.

As $x \to -\infty$, $f(x) \to +\infty$.

The x-intercepts are $x = -2$, $x = 0$, and $x = 1$.

Interval	Sign of $f(x) = x(x + 2)^2(x - 1)$
$x < -2$	+
$-2 < x < 0$	+
$0 < x < 1$	−
$x > 1$	+

So, the graph of $f(x)$ is above the x-axis on the intervals $x < -2$, $-2 < x < 0$, and $x > 1$, it's below the x-axis on the intervals $0 < x < 1$.

Exercise	Depth of Knowledge (D.O.K.)	COMMON CORE Mathematical Practices
20	**3** Strategic Thinking H.O.T.	**MP.2** Reasoning
21	**3** Strategic Thinking H.O.T.	**MP.4** Modeling

12. To create an open-top box out of a sheet of cardboard that is 6 inches long and 3 inches wide, you make a square flap of side length x inches in each corner by cutting along one of the flap's sides and folding along the other. Once you fold up the four sides of the box, you glue each flap to the side it overlaps. To the nearest tenth, find the value of x that maximizes the volume of the box.

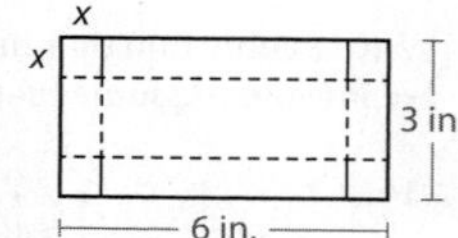

The length of the box is $6 - 2x$, the width is $3 - 2x$, and the height is x. So, the volume function is $V(x) = (6 - 2x)(3 - 2x)x$ with a domain of $0 < x < 1.5$. Maximum volume is 5.2 cubic inches when square flaps with a side length of 0.6 inch are made in the corners.

13. The template shows how to create a box from a square sheet of cardboard that has a side length of 36 inches. In the template, solid line segments indicate cuts, dashed line segments indicate folds, and grayed rectangles indicate pieces removed. The vertical strip that is 2 inches wide on the left side of the template is a flap that will be glued to the side of the box that it overlaps when the box is folded up. The horizontal strips that are $\frac{x}{2}$ inches wide at the top and bottom of the template are also flaps that will overlap to form the top and bottom of the box when the box is folded up. Write a volume function for the box in terms of x only. (You will need to determine a relationship between x and y first.) Then, to the nearest tenth, find the dimensions of the box with maximum volume.

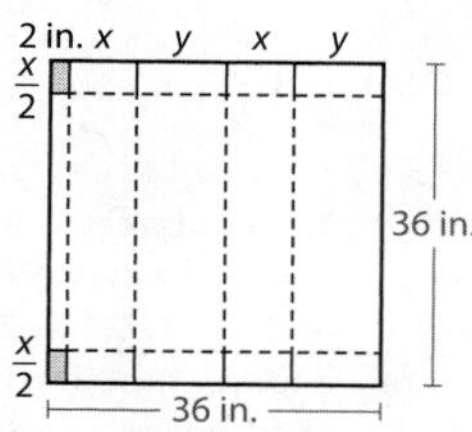

To find the relationship between x and y, use that fact that $2 + x + y + x + y = 36$, so $x + y = 17$, or $y = 17 - x$. Then the dimensions of the box are x, $17 - x$, and $36 - 2\left(\frac{x}{2}\right)$, or $36 - x$. The volume function is $V(x) = x(17 - x)(36 - x)$. The domain of the function is determine by the constraints $x > 0$; $17 - x > 0$, or $x < 17$; and $36 - x > 0$, or $x < 36$. So, the domain of the function is $0 < x < 17$. Using the graphing calculator to locate the graph's highest point on the interval $(0, 17)$, you find that the box has a maximum volume of about 2032 cubic inches when the dimensions of the box are 7.3 inches, 9.7 inches, and 28.7 inches.

INTEGRATE MATHEMATICAL PRACTICES

Focus on Math Connections

MP.1 Suggest that students work in small groups to discuss why the sign of the leading coefficient affects the end behavior of a polynomial function, and how the degree of the polynomial is related to the end behavior.

INTEGRATE MATHEMATICAL PRACTICES

Focus on Math Connections

MP.1 Students may have difficulty when asked to graph a polynomial function. This may be because they do not have an overall sense of how the graph should look, or because they do not graph enough points between the zeros to accurately represent the function. Suggest that they determine the end behavior before starting a graph, and then choose at least two points between each zero to sketch the graph.

Write a cubic function in intercept form for the given graph, whose x-intercepts are integers. Assume that the constant factor a is either 1 or −1.

14.

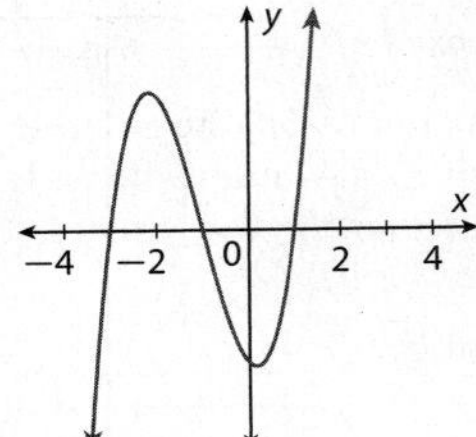

The x-intercepts are $x = -3$, $x = -1$, and $x = 1$. The related factors are $x + 3$, $x + 1$, and $x - 1$. Since there are three factors and the function is cubic, each factor must be raised to the first power. So, the general function is $f(x) = a(x + 3)(x + 1)(x - 1)$ for some constant factor a. Given the function's end behavior, a must be positive. So, the specific function with $a = 1$ is $f(x) = (x + 3)(x + 1)(x - 1)$.

15.

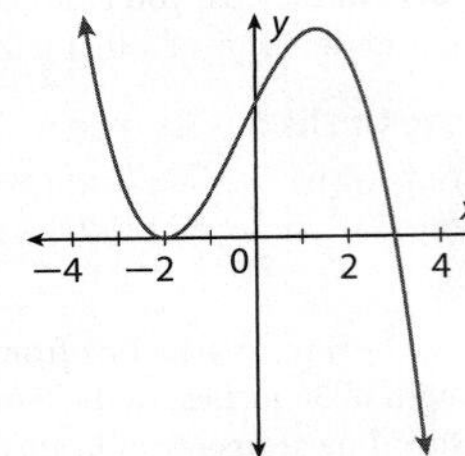

The x-intercepts are $x = -2$ and $x = 3$. The related factors are $x + 2$ and $x - 3$. Since there are only two factors and the function is cubic, one of the factors must be squared. Given that the graph is tangent to the x-axis at $x = -2$, the factor $x + 2$ must be squared. So, the general function is $f(x) = a(x + 2)^2(x - 3)$ for some constant factor a. Given the function's end behavior, a must be negative. So, the specific function with $a = -1$ is $f(x) = -(x + 2)^2(x - 3)$.

Write a quartic function in intercept form for the given graph, whose x-intercepts are integers. Assume that the constant factor a is either 1 or −1.

16.

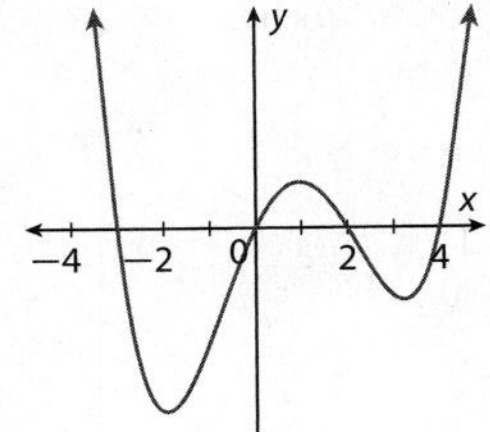

The x-intercepts are $x = -3$, $x = 0$, $x = 2$, and $x = 4$. The related factors are $x + 3$, x, $x - 2$, and $x - 4$. Since there are four factors and the function is quartic, each factor must be raised to the first power. So, the general function is $f(x) = ax(x + 3)(x - 2)(x - 4)$ for some constant factor a. Given the function's end behavior, a must be positive. So, the specific function with $a = 1$ is $f(x) = x(x + 3)(x - 2)(x - 4)$.

17.

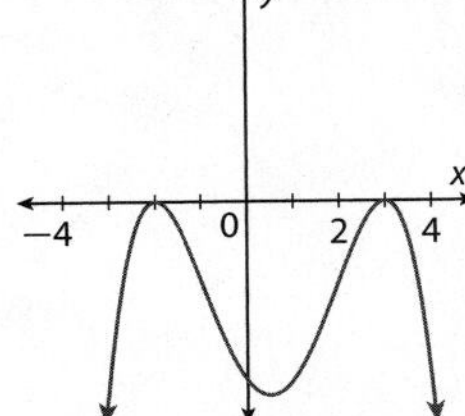

The x-intercepts are $x = -2$ and $x = 3$. The related factors are $x + 2$ and $x - 3$. Since there are only two factors and the function is quartic, one or both factors must be raised to a power other than 1. Given that the graph is tangent to the x-axis at both $x = -2$ and $x = 3$, both the factor $x + 2$ and the factor $x - 3$ must be squared. So, the general function is $f(x) = a(x + 2)^2(x - 3)^2$ for some constant factor a. Given the function's end behavio[r], a must be negative. So, the specific functio[n] with $a = -1$ is $f(x) = -(x + 2)^2(x - 3)^2$.

18. Multiple Response Select all statements that apply to the graph of $f(x) = (x - 1)^2(x + 2)$.

(A.) The x-intercepts are $x = 1$ and $x = -2$.

B. The x-intercepts are $x = -1$ and $x = 2$.

C. The graph crosses the x-axis at $x = 1$ and is tangent to the x-axis at $x = -2$.

D. The graph crosses the x-axis at $x = -1$ and is tangent to the x-axis at $x = 2$.

(E.) The graph is tangent to the x-axis at $x = 1$ and crosses the x-axis at $x = -2$.

F. The graph is tangent to the x-axis at $x = -1$ and crosses the x-axis at $x = 2$.

G. A local minimum occurs on the interval $-2 < x < 1$, and a local maximum occurs at $x = 1$.

(H.) A local maximum occurs on the interval $-2 < x < 1$, and a local minimum occurs at $x = 1$.

I. A local minimum occurs on the interval $-1 < x < 2$, and a local maximum occurs at $x = 2$.

J. A local maximum occurs on the interval $-1 < x < 2$, and a local minimum occurs at $x = 2$.

H.O.T. Focus on Higher Order Thinking

19. Explain the Error A student was asked to sketch the graph of the function $f(x) = x^2(x - 3)$. Describe what the student did wrong. Then sketch the correct graph.

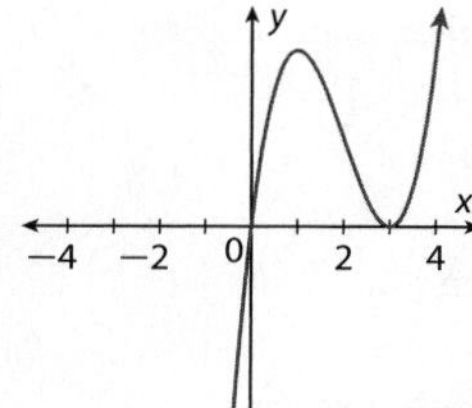

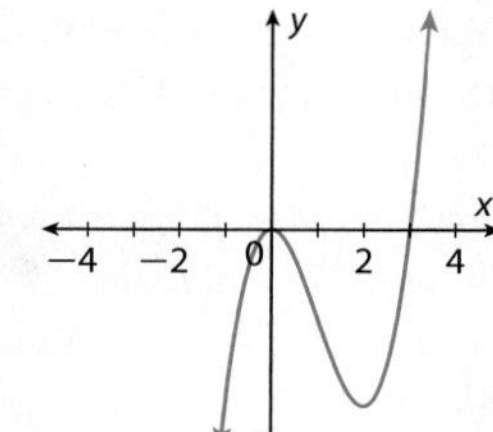

The student sketched the graph so that it crosses the x-axis at $x = 0$ and is tangent to the x-axis at $x = 3$. Instead, the graph should be tangent to the x-axis at $x = 0$ and cross the x-axis at $x = 3$.

AVOID COMMON ERRORS

Students may write the wrong power for a factor of a polynomial function. Explain that if they know the multiplicity of a zero, they automatically know the power of the corresponding factor. If they are told the function is cubic or quartic, then they know that the power is 3 or 4.

CONNECT VOCABULARY EL

To help students remember the words associated with the attributes of a polynomial function, have them make note cards for each attribute, including cards for *domain, range, x-intercepts, turning points, maxima and minima,* and *end behavior.* Ask them to write a description of the attribute, show an example polynomial function and its graph, and list any other attribute that this particular graph may also have. Make sure they use the proper notation for end behavior in their descriptions. Then have students make a poster showing the graph of a polynomial of degree three or higher with all of the applicable attributes included as labels on the graph.

PEER-TO-PEER DISCUSSION

Have students work in pairs. Instruct one student in each pair to sketch the graph of a cubic function of the form $f(x) = (x + b_1)(x + b_2)(x + b_3)$, while the other gives verbal instructions for each step. Then have the student who sketched the graph write the steps that were followed and determine the attributes of the graph. Have students switch roles and repeat the exercise using a quartic function of the form $f(x) = (x + b_1)(x + b_2)(x + b_3)(x + b_4)$.

JOURNAL

Have students describe how the attributes of a polynomial function are determined from the function written in intercept form, and how information about these attributes is helpful in drawing the graph of the function.

20. Make a Prediction Knowing the characteristics of the graphs of cubic and quartic functions in intercept form, sketch the graph of the quintic function $f(x) = x^2(x + 2)(x - 2)^2$.

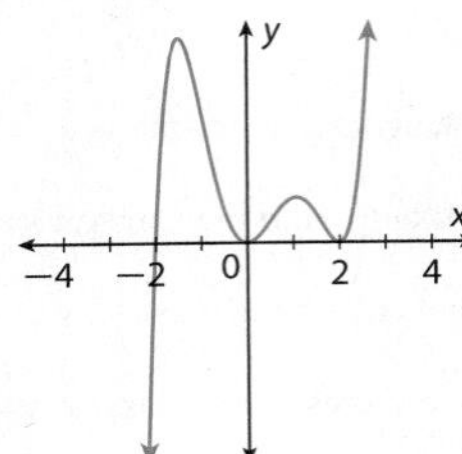

21. Represent Real-World Situations A rectangular piece of sheet metal is rolled and riveted to form a circular tube that is open at both ends, as shown. The sheet metal has a perimeter of 36 inches. Each of the two sides of the rectangle that form the two ends of the tube has a length of x inches, and the tube has a circumference of $x - 1$ inches because an overlap of 1 inch is needed for the rivets. Write a volume function for the tube in terms of x. Then, to the nearest tenth, find the value of x that maximizes the volume of the tube.

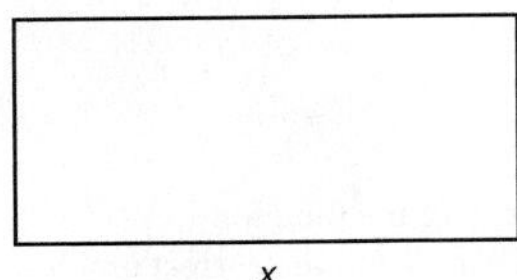

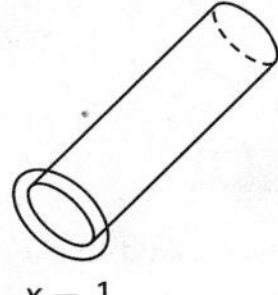

Given that x represents one dimension of the rectangle, let y represent the other dimension. Since the perimeter of the rectangle is 36 inches, you know that $2x + 2y = 36$, so $x + y = 18$, and $y = 18 - x$. Since $x - 1$ represents the circumference of the tube, you know that $2\pi r = x - 1$ where r is the radius of the tube, so $r = \frac{x-1}{2\pi}$. Since the tube is a cylinder with radius r and height y, the volume function is $V(x) = \pi r^2 y = \pi\left(\frac{(x-1)^2}{4\pi^2}\right)(18 - x) = \frac{\pi}{4}(x - 1)^2(18 - x)$. The domain of the function is determined by the constraints $x > 0$; $x - 1 > 0$, or $x > 1$; and $18 - x > 0$, or $x < 18$. So, the domain of the function is $1 < x < 18$. Using the graphing calculator to locate the graph's highest point, you find that the tube has a maximum volume of about 572 cubic inches when the length of the sides of the rectangle that form the ends of the tube is 12.3 inches.

Lesson Performance Task

The template shows how to create a box with a lid from a sheet of card stock that is 10 inches wide and 24 inches long. In the template, solid line segments indicate cuts, and dashed line segments indicate folds. The square flaps, each with a side length of x inches, are glued to the sides they overlap when the box is folded up. The box has a bottom and four upright sides. The lid, which is attached to one of the upright sides, has three upright sides of its own. Assume that the three sides of the lid can be tucked inside the box when the lid is closed.

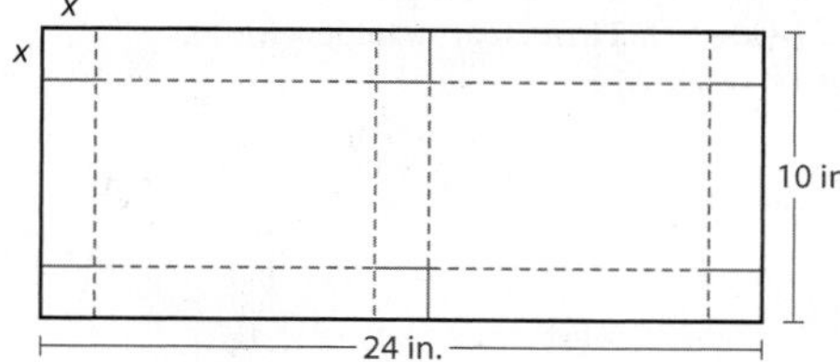

a. Write a polynomial function that represents the volume of the box, and state its domain.

b. Use a graphing calculator to find the value of x that will produce the box with maximum volume. What are the dimensions of that box?

a. **The volume function is $V(x) = x(10 - 2x)\left(\frac{1}{2}(24 - 3x)\right)$, or $V(x) = x(10 - 2x)\left(12 - \frac{3}{2}x\right)$. The domain of the function is determined by the constraints $x > 0$; $10 - 2x > 0$, or $x < 5$; and $12 - \frac{3}{2}x > 0$, or $x < 8$. So, the domain of the function is $0 < x < 5$.**

b. **Using a graphing calculator to graph the function and locate the graph's highest point on the interval $(0, 5)$, you find that the box has a maximum volume of 108 cubic inches when $x = 2$ so that the dimensions of the box are 2 inches, 6 inches, and 9 inches.**

EXTENSION ACTIVITY

The box in this Performance Task was an open box, that is, it had no top. Ask students to research ways to create a *closed* box from a sheet of cardstock. Have them find boxes in their daily lives that they can disassemble to two-dimensional form. Ask students how, based on the resulting two-dimensional geometry, they would set up an equation for the volume of the box, and whether they would be able to determine a maximum volume based on that equation.

CONNECT VOCABULARY EL

Some students may not be familiar with the term *card stock*. Have a student volunteer describe *card stock* (a sturdy paper used to make cards) and compare it to other materials such as *cardboard* or *paper*.

INTEGRATE MATHEMATICAL PRACTICES

Focus on Modeling

MP.4 Ask students how they can determine the length, width, and height of the box from the two-dimensional diagram. Have them draw a 3D picture of the final box, labeling the appropriate edge x and writing formulas for the other two sides. Ask students what x represents on the final box. **the length of one side of the box, or the height of a short, flat box**

QUESTIONING STRATEGIES

? Why do we use the interval (0, 4.25) to find the function maximum? **Those are the realistic values of the distance x.**

? Why can't x-values between 4.25 and 5.5 be used to find a function maximum? **$V(x)$ is negative between these values, and a volume cannot be negative.**

? What would a box look like if x were very close to 0? **It would appear to be a piece of cardboard with no height.**

? What happens to the box when x is very close to 4.25? **The narrow end of the box shrinks to 0, and there is no flap to fold up.**

Scoring Rubric

2 points: Student correctly solves the problem and explains his/her reasoning.

1 point: Student shows good understanding of the problem but does not fully solve or explain his/her reasoning.

0 points: Student does not demonstrate understanding of the problem.

Study Guide Review

ASSESSMENT AND INTERVENTION

Assign or customize module reviews.

MODULE PERFORMANCE TASK

COMMON CORE

Mathematical Practices: MP.1, MP.2, MP.3, MP.4, MP.5
F-IF.B.4, F-IF.C.7c, A-APR.B.3

SUPPORTING STUDENT REASONING

Students should begin by asking what information is contained in the polynomial function. Here is some of the information they may ask for.

- **Is the graph of the polynomial the spatial model of the track?** Yes, the polynomial is the two-dimensional representation of the actual roller coaster track.
- **What does it mean when the polynomial function goes below the x-axis?** Students might be baffled by this, because the x-axis in this model is ground level. When the function is negative, this means the roller coaster is below ground, going through a tunnel.

Polynomial Functions

Essential Question: How can polynomial functions help to solve real-world problems?

Key Vocabulary
cubic function *(función cúbica)*
polynomial function *(función polinomial)*

KEY EXAMPLE *(Lesson 5.1)*

Identify the transformations of the graph $f(x) = x^3$ that produce the graph of the function $g(x) = \frac{1}{3}(x + 2)^3$. Then create a table with the corresponding input and output values.

- a vertical compression by a factor of $\frac{1}{3}$
- a translation of 2 units to the left

x	$f(x) = x^3$	$g(x) = \frac{1}{3}(x + 2)^3$
−2	−8	$\frac{1}{3}(-2 + 2)^3 = 0$
−1	−1	$\frac{1}{3}(-1 + 2)^3 = \frac{1}{3}$
0	0	$\frac{1}{3}(0 + 2)^3 = \frac{8}{3}$
1	1	$\frac{1}{3}(1 + 2)^3 = 9$
2	8	$\frac{1}{3}(2 + 2)^3 = \frac{64}{3}$

KEY EXAMPLE *(Lesson 5.2)*

Use a graphing calculator to graph $g(x) = x(x - 2)^2 (x + 3)$. Then use the graph to determine the number of turning points and minimums or maximums.

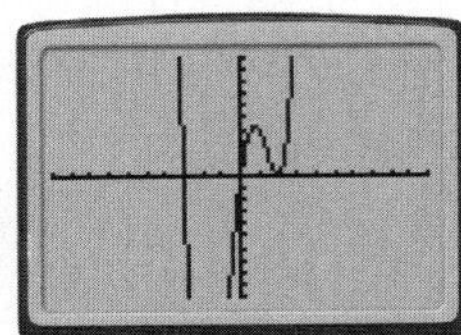

According to the graph, there are three turning points, one local maximum, one local minimum, and one global minimum.

SCAFFOLDING SUPPORT

- Students should recognize that the zeroes of the polynomial are $x = 50$, $x = 200$, and $x = 250$, and these occur when the function intersects the x-axis.
- Encourage students to graph the polynomial, and use the graph to interpret the behavior of the roller coaster.
- Students can describe the ride in terms of the intervals where the graph is increasing and decreasing, with explanations of what these mean in the context.
- Students do not need exact values for the intervals and the maxima and minima; instead they should focus on interpreting the *meaning* of the graph; rough estimates are acceptable.

EXERCISES

Identify the transformations of the graph $f(x) = x^3$ that produce the graph of the function. *(Lesson 5.1)*

1. $g(x) = \left(-\frac{1}{4}(x+2)\right)^3 + 3$

a horizontal stretch by a factor of 4
a reflection across the y-axis
a translation of 2 units left and 3 units up

2. $h(x) = \frac{1}{3}(x-4)^3$

a vertical compression by a factor of $\frac{3}{3}$
a translation of 4 units right

Use the graphing calculator to graph each function, then use the graph to determine the number of turning points, maximums, and minimums. *(Lesson 5.2)*

3. $s(x) = x(x+2)(x+1)^2$

3 turning points
1 local maximum
2 global minimums

4. $h(x) = x^2(x-3)(x+2)(x-2)$

4 turning points
2 local maximums
2 local minimums

5. Write a real world situation that could be modeled by the equation $V(w) = w(5w)(3w)$. *(Lesson 5.2)*

Possible Answer: Let w represent the width of a box. Then the length is five times the width, and the height is three times the width. If the width is between 8 and 10 inches, find the highest and lowest possible volume.

MODULE PERFORMANCE TASK

What's the Function of a Roller Coaster?

An engineer is designing part of a roller coaster track that can be modeled by the polynomial function

$$f(x) = 2.0 \times 10^{-6} x^4 - 0.0011x^3 + 0.195x^2 - 12.25x + 250$$

where $f(x)$ is the height in feet of a roller coaster car above ground level, and x is the horizontal distance in feet. For this section of track, the domain is $0 \leq x \leq 250$.

The factored form of this function is

$$f(x) = 2.0 \times 10^{-6}(x-200)(x-250)(x-50)^2.$$

Describe the experience of a rider who is riding a roller coaster on this track.

Use your own paper to complete the task. Be sure to write down all your data and assumptions. Then use graphs, numbers, words, or algebra to explain how you reached your conclusion.

DISCUSSION OPPORTUNITIES

- What other key factor would be important in assessing how exciting this roller coaster would be to ride? Discuss how speed is important for a roller coaster, and what reasonable speeds might be. Students can also research the different parameters of existing roller coasters.

SAMPLE SOLUTION

Assumptions

The x-axis is at ground level.

Method

Graph the function on a coordinate grid. Explore the portions of the graph that are decreasing and increasing, the zeroes, and the maxima and minima. When the graph is decreasing, the roller coaster is descending, when the graph is increasing, the roller coaster is ascending. When the graph is below the x-axis, the roller coaster is underground.

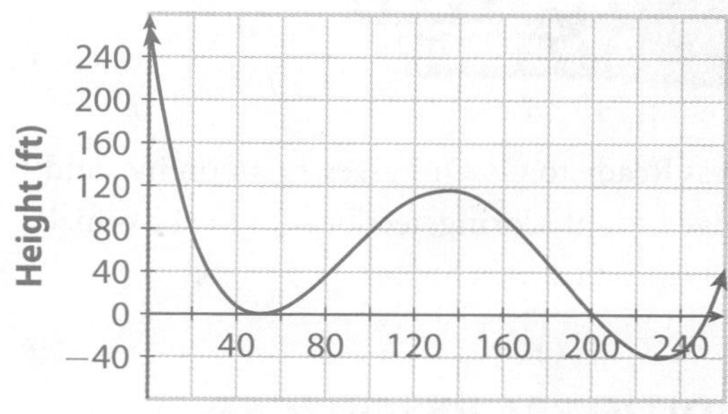

Analysis

The total horizontal distance for this portion of the track is 260 feet. The roller coaster starts 250 feet above the ground, and while traveling a horizontal distance of 50 feet descends to ground level, a vertical drop of 250 feet. The roller coaster then ascends to a height of about 108 feet, while traveling a horizontal distance of about 84 feet, then descends, going underground to a depth of about 39 feet while traveling about 94 feet horizontally, then finally ascends again, rising above the ground to a total vertical distance of 250 feet.

Assessment Rubric

2 points: Student correctly solves the problem and explains his/her reasoning.

1 point: Student shows good understanding of the problem but does not fully solve or explain.

0 points: Student does not demonstrate understanding of the problem.

Ready to Go On?

ASSESS MASTERY

Use the assessment on this page to determine if students have mastered the concepts and standards covered in this module.

ASSESSMENT AND INTERVENTION

Access Ready to Go On? assessment online, and receive instant scoring, feedback, and customized intervention or enrichment.

ADDITIONAL RESOURCES

Response to Intervention Resources

- Reteach Worksheets

Differentiated Instruction Resources

- Reading Strategies EL
- Success for English Learners EL
- Challenge Worksheets

Assessment Resources

- Leveled Module Quizzes

Ready to Go On?

5.1–5.2 Polynomial Functions

- Online Homework
- Hints and Help
- Extra Practice

Identify the transformations of the graph of $f(x) = x^3$ that produce the graph of $g(x) = -\frac{1}{4}(x+4)^3$. Apply the transformations to the reference points (–1, –1), (0, 0), and (1, 1) *(Lesson 5.1)*

1. Changes to x.

A translation of 4 units to the left.

2. Changes to y.

A vertical compression by a factor of $\frac{4}{4}$, and a reflection across the x-axis.

3. Apply the transformations using the changes to x and y.

$f(x) = x^3$		$g(x) = -\frac{1}{4}(x+4)^3$	
x	y	x	y
−1	−1	−5	$\frac{1}{4}$
0	0	−4	0
1	1	−3	$-\frac{1}{4}$

Graph the given function on your graphing calculator. Use the graph to state the number of turning points in the graph and the x-intercepts. *(Lesson 5.2)*

4. $g(x) = x^2(x-3)$

2 turning points; $x = 0$ and $x = 3$

5. $h(x) = (x-4)(x-3)(x+2)^2$

3 turning points; $x = -2$, $x = 3$, and $x = 4$

ESSENTIAL QUESTION

6. Give a real world example of a cubic function. *(Lesson 5.1)*
Possible Answer: Finding the side length of a sandbox in the shape of a rectangular prism when given the volume and the side lengths in terms of x.

COMMON CORE Common Core Standards

Lesson	Items	Content Standards	Mathematical Practices
5.1	1	**F-BF.B.3**	**MP.7**
5.1	2	**F-BF.B.3**	**MP.7**
5.1	3	**F-BF.B.3**	**MP.2**
5.2	4	**F-IF.C.7c, A-APR.B.3, F-IF.B.4**	**MP.5**
5.2	5	**F-IF.C.7c, A-APR.B.3, F-IF.B.4**	**MP.5**

MODULE 5
MIXED REVIEW

Assessment Readiness

1. Look at each equation. Is the vertex of the graph translated to the right and up when compared to $f(x) = x^3$?
Select Yes or No for A–C.
   - **A.** $y = (x + 6)^3 + 2$ ○ Yes ● No
   - **B.** $y = 5x^3 + 7$ ○ Yes ● No
   - **C.** $y = (x - 4)^3 + 2$ ● Yes ○ No

2. Consider the equation $h(x) = x(x - 1)(x + 3)^2$. Choose True or False for each statement.
   - **A.** There are four turning points in the graph. ○ True ● False
   - **B.** The graph crosses the x-axis at −3, −1, 0, and 1. ○ True ● False
   - **C.** The graph has a global maximum. ○ True ● False

3. Write a quartic function in intercept form for the given graph. Assume that the constant factor a is either 1 or −1. Explain your answer.

$f(x) = x(x + 2)(x - 3)(x - 5)$; the x-intercepts are $x = -2$, $x = 0$, $x = 3$, and $x = 5$. The related factors are $x + 2$, x, $x - 3$, and $x - 5$. There are four intercepts, and it is a quartic function, so each factor will be raised to the power of 1. Since the constant factor a is 1, the general function is $f(x) = (x + 2)x(x - 3)(x - 5)$ or $f(x) = x(x + 2)(x - 3)(x - 5)$.

4. An ottoman shaped like a rectangular prism has a length of x, a width two inches shorter than the length, and a height two inches taller than the length. Write the function that represents the volume; then find the length, width, and height of the ottoman if the volume is 5760 in^3.

$V(x) = x(x - 2)(x + 2) = x^3 - 4x$; $\ell = 18$ inches, $w = 16$ inches, and $h = 20$ inches

MIXED REVIEW
Assessment Readiness

ASSESSMENT AND INTERVENTION

Assign ready-made or customized practice tests to prepare students for high-stakes tests.

ADDITIONAL RESOURCES

Assessment Resources

- Leveled Module Quizzes: Modified, B

AVOID COMMON ERRORS

Item 4 Some students will have a hard time creating the equation for volume when the sides are given to them in terms of polynomials. Encourage the students to draw and label a picture to help them see what should be substituted into the equation.

Common Core Standards

Lesson	Items	Content Standards	Mathematical Practices
1.3, 5.1	1*	F-BF.B.3	MP.6
5.2	2	F-IF.C.7c	MP.1
1.2, 5.2	3*	F-IF.B.4, F-IF.C.7c	MP.6
5.1	4	G-GMD.A.3	MP.2

* Item integrates mixed review concepts from previous modules or a previous course.

MODULE 6

Polynomials

ESSENTIAL QUESTION:

Answer: Polynomials can be used to model surface area or volume of three-dimensional objects, such as packaging.

PROFESSIONAL DEVELOPMENT VIDEO

Professional Development Video

Author Matt Larson models successful teaching practices in an actual high-school classroom.

Professional Development my.hrw.com

MODULE 6

Polynomials

Essential Question: How can you use polynomials to solve real-world problems?

REAL WORLD VIDEO
Meteorologists use mathematics and computer models to analyze climate patterns and forecast weather. For example, polynomial functions can be used to model temperature patterns.

MODULE PERFORMANCE TASK PREVIEW

What's the Temperature?

The weather is always a topic for conversation. Is it hot or cold outside? Is it T-shirt and shorts weather, or should you bundle up? What were the high and low temperatures for a particular day? You might suspect that the outdoor temperature follows a pattern. How can you use a polynomial to model the temperature? Let's find out!

Module 6 269

DIGITAL TEACHER EDITION

Access a full suite of teaching resources when and where you need them:

- Access content online or offline
- Customize lessons to share with your class
- Communicate with your students in real-time
- View student grades and data instantly to target your instruction where it is needed most

PERSONAL MATH TRAINER

Assessment and Intervention

Assign automatically graded homework, quizzes, tests, and intervention activities. Prepare your students with updated, Common Core-aligned practice tests.

Are YOU Ready?

Complete these exercises to review skills you will need for this chapter.

Adding and Subtracting Polynomials

Example 1 Subtract.

$(7a^3 - 4a^2 + 11) - (3a^2 - 2a + 5)$

$7a^3 - 4a^2 + 11 - 3a^2 + 2a - 5$ Multiply by -1.

$7a^3 - 7a^2 + 2a + 6$ Combine like terms.

- Online Homework
- Hints and Help
- Extra Practice

Add or subtract the polynomials.

1. $(m^5 + 4m^2 + 6) - (3m^5 - 8m^2)$ **$-2m^5 + 12m^2 + 6$**
2. $(k^2 + 3k + 1) + (k^2 - 8)$ **$2k^2 + 3k - 7$**

Algebraic Expressions

Example 2 Simplify the expression $5x^3 - 10x^2 + x^3 + 10$.

$6x^3 - 10x^2 + 10$ Combine like terms.

Simplify each expression.

3. $6x - 2x^2 - 2x$ **$-2x^2 + 4x$**
4. $(5x)(2x^2) - x^2$ **$10x^3 - x^2$**
5. $4(2x - 3y) + 2(x + y)$ **$10x - 10y$**
6. $4(a + b) - 7(a + 2b)$ **$-3a - 10b$**

Multiplying Polynomials

Example 3 Multiply. $(2a - b)(a + ab + b)$

$(2a - b)(a + ab + b) = 2a(a + ab + b) - b(a + ab + b)$

$= 2a \cdot a + 2a \cdot ab + 2a \cdot b - b \cdot a - b \cdot ab - b \cdot b$

$= 2a^2 + 2a^2b + 2ab - ab - ab^2 - b^2$

$= 2a^2 + 2a^2b + ab - ab^2 - b^2$

Multiply the polynomials.

7. $(x^2 - 4)(x + y)$ **$x^3 + x^2y - 4x - 4y$**
8. $(3m + 2)(3m^2 - 2m + 1)$ **$9m^3 - m + 2$**

Response to Intervention			Differentiated Instruction
Tier 1 Lesson Intervention Worksheets	**Tier 2** Strategic Intervention Skills Intervention Worksheets	**Tier 3** Intensive Intervention Worksheets available online	
Reteach 6.1 Reteach 6.2 Reteach 6.3 Reteach 6.4 Reteach 6.5	2 Adding... 3 Algebraic Expressions 10 Factoring Polynomials 11 Factoring Special... 12 Factoring Trinomials 22 Multiplying...	Building Block Skills 24, 25, 27, 33, 34, 62, 64, 84	Challenge worksheets Extend the Math Lesson Activities in TE

Are You Ready?

ASSESS READINESS

Use the assessment on this page to determine if students need strategic or intensive intervention for the module's prerequisite skills.

ASSESSMENT AND INTERVENTION

RtI Response to Intervention TIER 1, TIER 2, TIER 3 SKILLS

Personal Math Trainer will automatically create a standards-based, personalized intervention assignment for your students, targeting each student's individual needs!

ADDITIONAL RESOURCES

See the table below for a full list of intervention resources available for this module.

Response to Intervention Resources also includes:

- Tier 2 Skill Pre-Tests for each Module
- Tier 2 Skill Post-Tests for each skill

LESSON 6.1

Adding and Subtracting Polynomials

Common Core Math Standards

The student is expected to:

COMMON CORE **A-APR.A.1**

Understand that polynomials form a system . . . closed under the operations of addition, subtraction, ...; add, subtract, . . . polynomials. Also F-BF.A.1b

Mathematical Practices

 **MP.2 Reasoning**

Language Objective

Students work in pairs to create a "parts of a polynomial" chart.

ENGAGE

Essential Question: How do you add or subtract two polynomials, and what type of expression is the result?

First, add or subtract like terms. The sum or difference is another polynomial.

PREVIEW: LESSON PERFORMANCE TASK

View the Engage section online. Discuss the photo and how the records of maximum and minimum temperatures provide data for two functions. Have the students identify the independent and dependent variables of the two functions. Then preview the Lesson Performance Task.

Name ____________ Class ________ Date ________

6.1 Adding and Subtracting Polynomials

Resource Locker

Essential Question: How do you add or subtract two polynomials, and what type of expression is the result?

Explore Identifying and Analyzing Monomials and Polynomials

A polynomial function of degree n has the *standard form* $p(x) = a_nx^n + a_{n-1}x^{n-1} + \ldots + a_2x^2 + a_1x + a_0$, where $a_n, a_{n-1}, \ldots, a_2, a_1$, and a_0 are real numbers. The expression $a_nx^n + a_{n-1}x^{n-1} + \ldots a_2x^2 + a_1x + a_0$ is called a **polynomial**, and each term of a polynomial is called a **monomial**. A monomial is the product of a number and one or more variables with whole-number exponents. A polynomial is a monomial or a sum of monomials. The *degree of a monomial* is the sum of the exponents of the variables, and the *degree of a polynomial* is the degree of the monomial term with the greatest degree. The *leading coefficient* of a polynomial is the coefficient of the term with the greatest degree.

(A) Identify the monomials: x^3, $y + 3y^2 - 5y^3 + 10$, a^2bc^{12}, 76

Monomials: $x^3, a^2bc^{12}, 76$

Not monomials: $y + 3y^2 - 5y^3 + 10$

(B) Identify the degree of each monomial.

Monomial	x^3	a^2bc^{12}	76
Degree	3	15	0

(C) Identify the terms of the polynomial $y + 3y^2 - 5y^3 + 10$. $y, 3y^2, -5y^3, 10$

(D) Identify the coefficient of each term.

Term	y	$3y^2$	$-5y^3$	10
Coefficient	1	3	−5	10

(E) Identify the degree of each term.

Term	y	$3y^2$	$-5y^3$	10
Degree	1	2	3	0

(F) Write the polynomial in standard form. $-5y^3 + 3y^2 + y + 10$

(G) What is the leading coefficient of the polynomial? −5

HARDCOVER PAGES 271–282

Watch for the hardcover student edition page numbers for this lesson.

Reflect

1. **Discussion** How can you find the degree of a polynomial with multiple variables in each term?
Find the degree of each term by adding the exponents of each variable. The degree of the polynomial is the degree of the term with the highest degree.

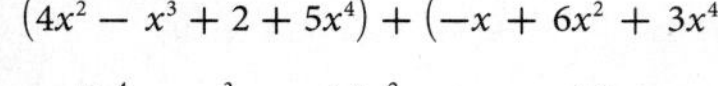 **Adding Polynomials**

To add polynomials, combine like terms.

Example 1 **Add the polynomials.**

(A) $(4x^2 - x^3 + 2 + 5x^4) + (-x + 6x^2 + 3x^4)$

$$\begin{array}{rrrrr} 5x^4 & -x^3 & +4x^2 & & +2 \\ +3x^4 & & +6x^2 & -x & \\ \hline 8x^4 & -x^3 & +10x^2 & -x & +2 \end{array}$$

Write in standard form.
Align like terms.
Add.

(B) $(10x - 18x^3 + 6x^4 - 2) + (-7x^4 + 5 + x + 2x^3)$

$(6x^4 - 18x^3 + 10x - 2) + (-7x^4 + 2x^3 + x + 5)$ Write in standard form.

$= \left(6x^4 - \boxed{7x^4}\right) + \left(\boxed{-18x^3} + 2x^3\right) + \left(\boxed{10x} + x\right) + \left(-2 + \boxed{5}\right)$ Group like terms.

$= \boxed{-x^4} - 16x^3 + \boxed{11x} + 3$ Add.

Reflect

2. Is the sum of two polynomials always a polynomial? Explain.
Yes. Because the two addends are the sums of monomials, adding them also results in a sum of monomials, which is by definition a polynomial.

Your Turn

Add the polynomials.

3. $(17x^4 + 8x^2 - 9x^7 + 4 - 2x^3) + (11x^3 - 8x^2 + 12)$
$(-9x^7 + 17x^4 - 2x^3 + 8x^2 + 4) + (11x^3 - 8x^2 + 12)$
$= (-9x^7) + (17x^4) + (-2x^3 + 11x^3) + (-8x^2 - 8x^2) + (4 + 12)$
$= -9x^7 + 17x^4 + 9x^3 + 16$

4. $(-8x + 3x^{11} + x^6) + (4x^4 - x + 17)$
$(3x^{11} + x^6 - 8x) + (4x^4 - x + 17)$
$= (3x^{11}) + (x^6) + (4x^4) + (-8x - x) + (17)$
$= 3x^{11} + x^6 + 4x^4 - 9x + 17$

EXPLORE

Identifying and Analyzing Monomials and Polynomials

INTEGRATE TECHNOLOGY

Students have the option of completing the polynomial activity either in the book or online.

QUESTIONING STRATEGIES

How do you find the degree of a term containing one variable with no exponent on the variable? Why? **The degree is 1; a variable such as x is equivalent to x^1.**

How do you recognize the leading coefficient? **Write the polynomial in standard form. It is the coefficient of the term with the highest degree.**

EXPLAIN 1

Adding Polynomials

AVOID COMMON ERRORS

Students often add polynomials using the same method each time, either horizontally or vertically. Point out that if the polynomials have many terms, adding them vertically may prevent errors because students can line up like terms and leave gaps if terms of some degrees are missing. If the polynomials have only a few terms, adding them horizontally may be more convenient, especially when using mental math.

PROFESSIONAL DEVELOPMENT

Learning Progressions

In this lesson, students extend their earlier work with quadratic and cubic polynomial functions to explore the arithmetic of polynomials of degree n. A polynomial is an expression involving a sum of whole-number powers of one or more variables that are multiplied by coefficients. It has the form $p(x) = a_nx^n + a_{n-1}x^{n-1} + \ldots + a_2x^2 + a_1x + a_0$ where $a_n, a_{n-1}, \ldots, a_2, a_1$, and a_0 are real numbers, and each term of the expression is called a *monomial*. Unless otherwise specified, the coefficients a_i are generally restricted to real numbers, although many of the key results of this module also hold for polynomials with complex coefficients, which students will learn in future courses.

QUESTIONING STRATEGIES

? Is it possible to add three or more polynomials? Explain how. **Yes, you can add three or more polynomials, either by writing the polynomials vertically, aligning like terms, and adding their coefficients, or by writing the polynomials horizontally, grouping like terms, and adding their coefficients.**

? Are the commutative and associative properties of addition true for the addition of polynomials? Explain. **Yes, the sum is the same regardless of the order in which polynomials are added. If three or more polynomials are added, the sum is the same regardless of how the polynomials are grouped.**

EXPLAIN 2

Subtracting Polynomials

INTEGRATE MATHEMATICAL PRACTICES

Focus on Math Connections

MP.1 Point out that subtracting like terms in polynomials is just like subtracting numbers. For a term with the same variables and exponents like x^2y^5, which we'll call *something*, it is: 8 something minus 5 something is 3 something, 6 something minus −4 something is 10 something, and so on. Have students think up more of these analogous patterns.

QUESTIONING STRATEGIES

? Is it necessary to write polynomials in standard form before subtracting them? Explain. **No, as long as you group like terms before subtracting and keep track of signs correctly, the results will be the same. However, it is good practice to write the difference as a polynomial in standard form.**

Explain 2 Subtracting Polynomials

To subtract polynomials, combine like terms.

Example 2 Subtract the polynomials.

(A) $(12x^3 + 5x - 8x^2 + 19) - (6x^2 - 9x + 3 - 18x^3)$

Write in standard form.	$12x^3$	$-8x^2$	$+5x$	$+19$
Align like terms and add the opposite.	$+18x^3$	$-6x^2$	$+9x$	-3
Add.	$30x^3$	$-14x^2$	$+14x$	$+16$

(B) $(-4x^2 + 8x^3 + 19 - 5x^5) - (9 + 2x^2 + 10x^5)$

Write in standard form and add the opposite. $(-5x^5 + 8x^3 - 4x^2 + 19) + (-10x^5 - 2x^2 - 9)$

Group like terms $= \left(-5x^5 - \boxed{10x^5}\right) + \left(\boxed{8x^3}\right) + \left(\boxed{-4x^2} - 2x^2\right) + \left(\boxed{19} - \right.$

Add $= \boxed{-15x^5} + 8x^3 - \boxed{6x^2} + 10$

Reflect

5. Is the difference of two polynomials always a polynomial? Explain.
Yes. Finding the difference of two polynomials is the same as finding the sum of the first polynomial and the opposite of the second. The sum of two polynomials is always a polynomial, so the difference of two polynomials is also always a polynomial.

Your Turn

Subtract the polynomials.

6. $(23x^7 - 9x^4 + 1) - (-9x^4 + 6x^2 - 31)$
$= (23x^7 - 9x^4 + 1) + (9x^4 - 6x^2 - 31)$
$= (23x^7) + (-9x^4 + 9x^4) + (-6x^2) + (1 - 31)$
$= 23x^7 - 6x^2 - 30$

7. $(7x^3 + 13x - 8x^5 + 20x^2) - (-2x^5 + 9x^2)$
$(-8x^5 + 7x^3 + 20x^2 + 13x) + (2x^5 - 9x^2)$
$= (-8x^5 + 2x^5) + (7x^3) + (20x^2 - 9x^2) + (13x)$
$= -6x^5 + 7x^3 + 11x^2 + 13x$

COLLABORATIVE LEARNING

Whole Class Activity

Have groups of students create posters to describe how to add or subtract polynomials. Have them write an example addition (or subtraction) problem in the top cell of a graphic organizer. Then have them write each of the steps below it in one box, with an explanation in words alongside it in another box. Have students use arrows to connect the steps.

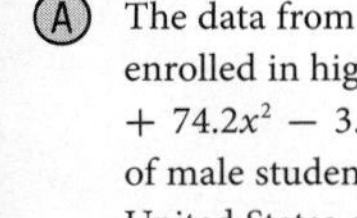

Explain 3 Modeling with Polynomial Addition and Subtraction

Polynomial functions can be used to model real-world quantities. If two polynomial functions model quantities that are two parts of a whole, the functions can be added to find a function that models the quantity as a whole. If the polynomial function for the whole and a polynomial function for a part are given, subtraction can be used to find the polynomial function that models the other part of the whole.

Example 3 **Find the polynomial that models the problem and use it to estimate the quantity.**

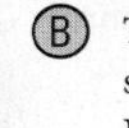

(A) The data from the U.S. Census Bureau for 2005–2009 shows that the number of male students enrolled in high school in the United States can be modeled by the function $M(x) = -10.4x^3 + 74.2x^2 - 3.4x + 8320.2$, where x is the number of years after 2005 and $M(x)$ is the number of male students in thousands. The number of female students enrolled in high school in the United States can be modeled by the function $F(x) = -13.8x^3 + 55.3x^2 + 141x + 7880$, where x is the number of years after 2005 and $F(x)$ is the number of female students in thousands. Estimate the total number of students enrolled in high school in the United States in 2009.

In the equation $T(x) = M(x) + F(x)$, $T(x)$ is the total number of students in thousands.

Add the polynomials.

$$(-10.4x^3 + 74.2x^2 - 3.4x + 8320.2) + (-13.8x^3 + 55.3x^3 + 141x + 7880)$$

$$= (-10.4x^3 - 13.8x^3) + (74.2x^2 + 55.3x^2) + (-3.4x + 141x) + (8320.2 + 7880)$$

$$= -24.2x^3 + 129.5x^2 + 137.6x + 16{,}200.2$$

The year 2009 is 4 years after 2005, so substitute 4 for x.

$$-24.2(4)^3 + 129.5(4)^2 + 137.6(4) + 16{,}200.2 \approx 17{,}274$$

About 17,274 thousand students were enrolled in high school in the United States in 2009.

(B) The data from the U.S. Census Bureau for 2000–2010 shows that the total number of overseas travelers visiting New York and Florida can be modeled by the function $T(x) = 41.5x^3 - 689.1x^2 + 4323.3x + 2796.6$, where x is the number of years after 2000 and $T(x)$ is the total number of travelers in thousands. The number of overseas travelers visiting New York can be modeled by the function $N(x) = -41.6x^3 + 560.9x^2 - 1632.7x + 6837.4$, where x is the number of years after 2000 and $N(x)$ is the number of travelers in thousands. Estimate the total number of overseas travelers to Florida in 2008.

In the equation $F(x) = T(x) \boxed{-} N(x)$, $F(x)$ is the number of travelers to Florida in thousands.

Subtract the polynomials.

$$(41.5x^3 - 689.1x^2 + 4323.3x + 2796.6) \boxed{-} (-41.6x^3 + 560.9x^2 - 1632.7x + 6837.4)$$

$$= (41.5x^3 - 689.1x^2 + 4323.3x + 2796.6) + (41.6x^3 - 560.9x^2 + 1632.7x - 6837.4)$$

DIFFERENTIATE INSTRUCTION

Visual Cues

Have students use color coding to circle and identify the like terms when adding or subtracting polynomials. They can also include arrows to help them identify like terms when adding polynomials in horizontal form.

Multiple Representations

Have students make a poster showing the methods for adding and subtracting polynomials horizontally and vertically. For each method, students should provide an example.

AVOID COMMON ERRORS

Regardless of the method they use to subtract polynomials, students may not remember to distriubute the subtraction operation to all terms in the second polynomial. The result is that the first term is subtracted while the others are added. Remind students to always watch for this potential mistake. Encourage students to check their answers; just as a numerical difference can be checked by addition, students can check a polynomial difference by addition.

EXPLAIN 3

Modeling with Polynomial Addition and Subtraction

INTEGRATE MATHEMATICAL PRACTICES

Focus on Modeling

MP.4 Many real-world situations in fields ranging from education and business to engineering and physics can be modeled by polynomial functions over a restricted domain. Students are provided polynomials that model real-world situations. Polynomial functions can also be fit to data for analysis. By adding and subtracting polynomials, students extend the model to determine relationships in the data.

QUESTIONING STRATEGIES

? How can adding or subtracting polynomials help you model a real-world quantity? **Sample answer: Since the sum or difference of two or more polynomials is a polynomial, then the sums or differences of polynomials that model quantities can also can model a quantity.**

ELABORATE

QUESTIONING STRATEGIES

How do the degrees of the monomial terms of two polynomials affect how they are added or subtracted? **Sample answer: Since only like terms can be added or subtracted, the degrees of the monomial terms are important. To be like terms, they must have the same degree, and they also must have the same variable with the same exponent.**

CONNECT VOCABULARY EL

To help students remember words and concepts related to polynomials, have them make a table similar to the one below showing names, degrees, and examples of polynomials in standard form up to degree 5.

Classifying Polynomials By Degree		
Name	**Degree**	**Example**
Constant	0	-9
Linear	1	$x+4$
Quadratic	2	x^2+3x-1
⋮	⋮	⋮

SUMMARIZE THE LESSON

What points should you remember when adding or subtracting polynomials? **Sample answer: combine like terms, write in standard form, align like terms**

$= \left(41.5x^3 + \boxed{41.6x^3}\right) + \left(\boxed{-689.1x^2} - 560.9x^2\right) + \left(\boxed{4323.3x} + 1632.7x\right) + \left(2796.6 - \boxed{6837.4}\right)$

$= \boxed{83.1}x^3 - \boxed{1250}x^2 + \boxed{5956}x - \boxed{4040.8}$

The year 2008 is 8 years after 2000, so substitute $\boxed{8}$ for x.

$83.1(8)^3 - 1250(8)^2 + 5956(8) - 4040.8 \approx \boxed{6154}$

About $\boxed{6154}$ thousand overseas travelers visited Florida in 2008.

Your Turn

8. According to the data from the U.S. Census Bureau for 1990–2009, the number of commercially owned automobiles in the United States can be modeled by the function $A(x) = 1.4x^3 - 130.6x^2 + 1831.3x + 128{,}141$, where x is the number of years after 1990 and $A(x)$ is the number of automobiles in thousands. The number of privately-owned automobiles in the United States can be modeled by the function $P(x) = -x^3 + 24.9x^2 - 177.9x + 1709.5$, where x is the number of years after 1990 and $P(x)$ is the number of automobiles in thousands. Estimate the total number of automobiles owned in 2005.

In the equation $T(x) = A(x) + P(x)$, $T(x)$is the total number of automobiles in thousands. Add the polynomials.

$\left(1.4x^3 - 130.6x^2 + 1831.3x + 128141\right) + \left(-x^3 + 24.9x^2 - 177.9x + 1709.5\right)$

$= \left(1.4x^3 - x^3\right) + \left(-130.6x^2 + 24.9x^2\right) + \left(1831.3x - 177.9x\right) + \left(128{,}141 + 1709.5\right)$

$= 0.4x^3 - 105.7x^2 + 1653.4x + 129{,}850.5$

The year 2005 is 15 years after 1990, so substitute 15 for x.

$0.4(15)^3 - 105.7(15)^2 + 1653.4(15) + 129{,}850.5 = 132{,}219$

So, 132,219 thousand automobiles were owned the United States in 2005.

Elaborate

9. How is the degree of a polynomial related to the degrees of the monomials that comprise the polynomial?
The degree of a polynomial is the degree of the monomial term with the highest degree. The degree of a monomial is the sum of the exponents of the variables.

10. How is polynomial subtraction based on polynomial addition?
Subtracting two polynomials is the same as adding the first polynomial to the opposite of the second.

11. How would you find the model for a whole if you have polynomial functions that are models for the two distinct parts that make up that whole?
To find the function that models the whole, add the two polynomial functions that model the two distinct parts.

12. Essential Question Check-In What is the result of adding or subtracting polynomials?
The result is always a polynomial.

LANGUAGE SUPPORT EL

Connect Vocabulary

Have students work in pairs. Instruct one student in each pair to write a polynomial of degree 4 in standard form on a large sheet of construction paper. Both students then write terms from this lesson on separate sticky notes, including terms such as *leading coefficient, monomial, degree, term, first term, coefficient.* Students then decide where to correctly place the sticky notes on the polynomial expression.

Evaluate: Homework and Practice

- Online Homework
- Hints and Help
- Extra Practice

1. Write the polynomial $-23x^7 + x^9 - 6x^3 + 10 + 2x^2$ in standard form, and then identify the degree and leading coefficient.

Standard Form: $x^9 - 23x^7 - 6x^3 + 2x^2 + 10$

Degree: 9

Leading Coefficient: 1

Add the polynomials.

2. $(82x^8 + 21x^2 - 6) + (18x + 7x^8 - 42x^2 + 3)$
$= (82x^8 + 21x^2 - 6) + (7x^8 - 42x^2 + 18x + 3)$
$= (82x^8 + 7x^8) + (21x^2 - 42x^2) + (18x) + (-6 + 3)$
$= 89x^8 - 21x^2 + 18x - 3$

3. $(15x - 121x^{12} + x^9 - x^7 + 3x^2) + (x^7 - 68x^2 - x^9)$
$= (-121x^{12} + x^9 - x^7 + 3x^2 + 15x) + (-x^9 + x^7 - 68x^2)$
$= (-121x^{12}) + (x^9 - x^9) + (-x^7 + x^7) + (3x^2 - 68x^2) + (15x)$
$= -121x^{12} - 65x^2 + 15x$

4. $(16 - x^2) + (-18x^2 + 7x^5 - 10x^4 + 5)$
$= (-x^2 + 16) + (7x^5 - 10x^4 - 18x^2 + 5)$
$= (7x^5) + (-10x^4) + (-x^2 - 18x^2) + (16 + 5)$
$= 7x^5 - 10x^4 - 19x^2 + 21$

5. $(x + 1 - 3x^2) + (8x - 21x^2 + 1)$
$= (-3x^2 + x + 1) + (21x^2 + 8x - 1)$
$= (-3x^2 + 21x^2) + (x + 8x) + (1 - 1)$
$= 18x^2 + 9x$

6. $(64 + x^3 - 8x^2) + (7x + 3 - x^2) + (19x^2 - 7x - 2)$
$= (x^3 - 8x^2 + 64) + (-x^2 + 7x + 3) + (19x^2 - 7x - 2)$
$= (x^3) + (-8x^2 - x^2 + 19x^2) + (7x - 7x) + (64 + 3 - 2)$
$= x^3 + 10x^2 + 65$

7. $(x^4 - 7x^3 + 2 - x) + (2x^3 - 3) + (1 - 5x^3 - x^4 + x)$
$= (x^4 - 7x^3 - x + 2) + (2x^3 - 3) + (-x^4 - 5x^3 + x + 1)$
$= (x^4 - x^4) + (-7x^3 + 2x^3 - 5x^3) + (-x + x) + (2 - 3 + 1)$
$= -10x^2$

Subtract the polynomials.

8. $(-2x + 23x^5 + 11) - (5 - 9x^3 + x)$
$= (23x^5 - 2x + 11) + (9x^3 - x - 5)$
$= (23x^5) + (9x^3) + (-2x - x) + (11 - 5)$
$= 23x^5 + 9x^3 - 3x + 6$

Exercise	Depth of Knowledge (D.O.K.)	COMMON CORE Mathematical Practices
1–12	1 Recall of Information	MP.2 Reasoning
13–20	2 Skills/Concepts	MP.4 Modeling
21	2 Skills/Concepts	MP.2 Reasoning
22, 25	3 Strategic Thinking H.O.T.	MP.2 Reasoning
23	3 Strategic Thinking H.O.T.	MP.1 Problem Solving
24	3 Strategic Thinking H.O.T.	MP.4 Modeling

EVALUATE

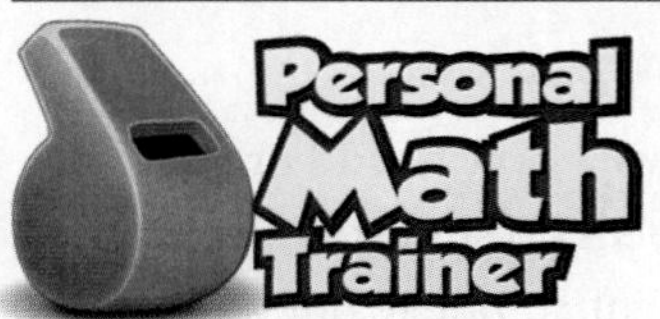

ASSIGNMENT GUIDE

Concepts and Skills	Practice
Explore Identifying and Analyzing Monomials and Polynomials	Exercise 1
Example 1 Adding Polynomials	Exercises 2–6
Example 2 Subtracting Polynomials	Exercises 7–13
Example 3 Modeling with Polynomial Addition and Subtraction	Exercises 14–20

INTEGRATE TECHNOLOGY

When adding or subtracting two polynomials in one variable, students can graph the expressions before they are added (or subtracted), and after. The graphs should be coincident. The *trace* feature in graphing calculators can also be used to find the certain values for real-world polynomial functions that are graphed.

INTEGRATE MATHEMATICAL PRACTICES

Focus on Communication

MP.3 Help students clarify how to add or subtract polynomials by having them do some of the exercises in groups. Have one student complete one step of the addition (or subtraction) process, including an explanation of the process, then pass the problem to another student, who completes the second step, including an explanation. Continue passing the problem until it is complete.

9. $(7x^3 + 68x^4 - 14x + 1) - (-10x^3 + 8x + 23)$
$= (68x^4 + 7x^3 - 14x + 1) + (10x^3 - 8x - 23)$
$= (68x^4) + (7x^3 + 10x^3) + (-14x - 8x) + (1 - 23)$
$= 68x^4 + 17x^3 - 22x - 22$

10. $(57x^{18} - x^2) - (6x - 71x^3 + 5x^2 + 2)$
$= (57x^{18} - x^2) + (71x^3 + 5x^2 - 6x - 2)$
$= (57x^{18}) + (71x^3) + (-x^2 - 5x^2) + (-6x) + (-2)$
$= 57x^{18} + 71x^3 - 6x^2 - 6x - 2$

11. $(9x - 12x^3) - (5x^3 + 7x - 2)$
$= (-12x^3 + 9x) + (-5x^3 - 7x + 2)$
$= (-12x^3 - 5x^3) + (9x - 7x) + (2)$
$= -17x^3 + 2x + 2$

12. $(3x^5 - 9) - (11 + 13x^2 - x^4) - (10x^2 + x^4)$
$= (3x^5 - 9) + (x^4 - 13x^2 - 11) + (-x^4 - 10x^2)$
$= (3x^5) + (x^4 - x^4) + (-13x^2 - 10x^2) + (-9 - 11)$
$= 3x^5 - 23x^2 - 20$

13. $(10x^2 - x + 4) - (5x + 7) + (6x - 11)$
$= (10x^2 - x + 4) + (-5x - 7) + (6x - 11)$
$= (10x^2) + (-x - 5x + 6x) + (4 - 7 - 11)$
$= 10x^2 - 14$

Find the polynomial that models the problem and use it to estimate the quantity.

14. A rectangle has a length of x and a width of $5x^3 + 4 - x^2$. Find the perimeter of the rectangle when the length is 5 feet.

$P(x) = \ell(x) + \ell(x) + w(x) + w(x)$
$= x + x + (5x^3 + 4 - x^2) + (5x^3 + 4 - x^2)$
$= (5x^3 + 5x^3) + (-x^2 - x^2) + (x + x) + (4 + 4)$
$= 10x^3 - 2x^2 + 2x + 8$
$P(5) = 10(5)^3 - 2(5)^2 + 2(5) + 8 = 1218$
The perimeter is 1218 feet.

15. A rectangle has a perimeter of $6x^3 + 9x^2 - 10x + 5$ and a length of x. Find the width of the rectangle when the length is 21 inches.

$$\begin{aligned} w(x) + w(x) &= P(x) - \ell(x) - \ell(x) \\ &= (6x^3 + 9x^2 - 10x + 5) - x - x \\ &= 6x^3 + 9x^2 + (-10x - x - x) + 5 \\ &= 6x^3 + 9x^2 - 12x + 5 \end{aligned}$$

$2w(21) = 6(21)^3 + 9(21)^2 - 12(21) + 5 = 59{,}288$

Since 59,288 is twice the width, the width of the rectangle is half of this, or 29,644.

The width is 29,644 inches when the length is 21 inches.

16. Cho is making a garden, where the length is x feet and the width is $4x - 1$ feet. He wants to add garden stones around the perimeter of the garden once he is done. If the garden is 4 feet long, how many feet will Cho need to cover with garden stones?

$$\begin{aligned} P(x) &= \ell(x) + \ell(x) + w(x) + w(x) \\ &= x + x + (4x - 1) + (4x - 1) \\ &= (x + x + 4x + 4x) + (-1 - 1) \\ &= 10x - 2 \end{aligned}$$

$P(4) = 10(4) - 2 = 38$

The perimeter is 38 feet when the length is 4 feet long, so Cho will need to cover 38 feet with garden stones.

17. Employment The data from the U.S. Census Bureau for 1980–2010 shows that the median weekly earnings of full-time male employees who have at least a bachelor's degree can be modeled by the function $M(x) = 0.009x^3 - 0.29x^2 + 30.7x + 439.6$, where x is the number of years after 1980 and $M(x)$ is the median weekly earnings in dollars. The median weekly earnings of all full-time employees who have at least a bachelor's degree can be modeled by the function $T(x) = 0.012x^3 - 0.46x^2 + 56.1x + 732.3$, where x is the number of years after 1980 and $T(x)$ is the median weekly earnings in dollars. Estimate the median weekly earnings of a full-time female employee with at least a bachelor's degree in 2010.

In the equation $F(x) = T(x) - M(x)$, $F(x)$ is the median weekly earnings in dollars.

$$\begin{aligned} &(0.012x^3 - 0.46x^2 + 56.1x + 732.3) - (0.009x^3 - 0.29x^2 + 30.7x + 439.6) \\ &= (0.012x^3 - 0.46x^2 + 56.1x + 732.3) + (-0.009x^3 + 0.29x^2 - 30.7x - 439.6) \\ &= (0.012x^3 - 0.009x^3) + (-0.46x^2 - 0.29x^2) + (56.1x - 30.7x) + (732.3 - 439.6) \\ &= 0.003x^3 - 0.17x^2 + 25.4x + 292.7 \end{aligned}$$

The year 2010 is 30 years after 1980, so substitute 30 for x.

$0.003(30)^3 - 0.17(30)^2 + 25.4(30) + 292.7 \approx 983$

INTEGRATE MATHEMATICAL PRACTICES

Focus on Math Connections

MP.1 Remind students that they have previously worked with polynomial functions and they should build on that knowledge. Have students write a quartic polynomial function f in standard form and identify the leading coefficient and the number of terms. Then have them graph f, describe the graph, and give other attributes of the polynomial, including the expected end behavior.

AVOID COMMON ERRORS

Students may identify the wrong term as the leading coefficient or find the wrong degree of a polynomial. They may benefit from rewriting polynomials in standard form before identifying the degree and leading coefficient.

18. Business From data gathered in the period 2008–2012, the yearly amount of U.S. exports can be modeled by the function $E(x) = -228x^3 + 2552.8x^2 - 6098.5x + 11{,}425.8$, where x is the number of years after 2008 and $E(x)$ is the amount of exports in billions of dollars. The yearly amount of U.S. imports can be modeled by the function $I(x) = -400.4x^3 + 3954.4x^2 - 11{,}128.8x + 17{,}749.6$, where x is the number of years after 2008 and $I(x)$ is the amount of imports in billions of dollars. Estimate the total amount the United States imported and exported in 2012.

In the equation $T(x) = E(x) + I(x)$, $T(x)$ is the total number of imports and exports in billions.

$$\left(-228x^3 + 2252.8x^2 - 6098.5x + 11{,}425.8\right) + \left(-400.4x^3 + 3954.4x^2 - 11{,}128.8x + 17{,}749.6\right)$$

$$= \left(-228x^3 - 400.4x^3\right) + \left(2252.8x^2 + 3954.4x^2\right) + \left(-6098.5x - 11{,}128.8x\right) + \left(11{,}425.8 + 17{,}7\right.$$

$$= -628.4x^3 + 6207.2x^2 - 17{,}227.3x + 29{,}175.4$$

The year 2008 is 4 years after 2012, so substitute 4 for x.

$$-628.4(4)^3 + 6207.2(4)^2 - 17{,}227.3(4) + 29{,}175.4 \approx 19{,}364$$

19. Education From data gathered in the period 1970–2010, the number of full-time students enrolled in a degree-granting institution can be modeled by the function $F(x) = 8.7x^3 - 213.3x^2 + 2015.5x + 3874.9$, where x is the number of years after 1970 and $F(x)$ is the number of students in thousands. The number of part-time students enrolled in a degree-granting institution can be modeled by the function $P(x) = 12x^3 - 285.3x^2 + 2217x + 1230$, where x is the number of years after 1970 and $P(x)$ is the number of students in thousands. Estimate the total number of students enrolled in a degree-granting institution in 2000.

In the equation $T(x) = F(x) + P(x)$, $T(x)$ is the total number of students in thousands.

$$\left(8.7x^3 - 213.3x^2 + 2015.5 + 3874.9\right) + \left(12x^3 - 285.3x^2 + 2217x + 1230\right)$$

$$= \left(8.7x^3 + 12x^3\right) + \left(-213.3x^2 - 285.3x^2\right) + \left(2015.5x + 2217x\right) + \left(3874.9 + 1230\right)$$

$$= 20.7x^3 - 498.6x^2 + 4232.5x + 5104.9$$

The year 2000 is 30 years after 1970, so substitute 30 for x.

$$20.7(30)^3 - 498.6(30)^2 + 4232.5(30) + 5104.9 \approx 242{,}240$$

About 242,240 thousand students were enrolled in 2000.

20. Geography The data from the U.S. Census Bureau for 1982–2003 shows that the surface area of the United States that is covered by rural land can be modeled by the function $R(x) = 0.003x^3 - 0.086x^2 - 1.2x + 1417.4$, where x is the number of years after 1982 and $R(x)$ is the surface area in millions of acres. The total surface area of the United States can be modeled by the function $T(x) = 0.0023x^3 + 0.034x^2 - 5.9x + 1839.4$, where x is the number of years after 1982 and is the surface area in millions of acres. Estimate the surface area of the United States that is not covered by rural land in 2001.

In the equation $N(x) = T(x) - R(x)$, $N(x)$ is the surface area in millions of acres that is not covered by rural land.

$(0.0023x^3 + 0.034x^2 - 5.9x + 1839.4) - (0.003x^3 - 0.086x^2 - 1.2x + 1417.4)$
$= (0.0023x^3 + 0.034x^2 - 5.9x + 1839.4) + (-0.003x^3 + 0.086x^2 + 1.2x - 1417.4)$
$= (0.0023x^3 + 0.003x^3) + (0.034x^2 + 0.086x^2) + (-5.9x + 1.2x) + (1839.4 - 1417.4)$
$= -0.0007x^3 + 0.12x^2 - 4.7x + 422$
$N(19) = -0.0007(19)^3 + 0.12(19)^2 - 4.7(19) + 422 \approx 371$

About 371 millions of acres were not covered by rural land in 2001.

21. Determine which polynomials are monomials. Choose all that apply.

a. (circled) $4x^3y$
b. $12 - x^2 + 5x$
c. $152 + x$
d. (circled) 783
e. (circled) x
f. $19x^{-2}$
g. (circled) $4x^4x^2$

H.O.T. Focus on Higher Order Thinking

22. Explain the Error Colin simplified $(16x + 8x^2y - 7xy^2 + 9y - 2xy) - (-9xy + 8xy^2 + 10x^2y + x - 7y)$. His work is shown below. Find and correct Colin's mistake.

$(16x + 8x^2y - 7xy^2 + 9y - 2xy) - (-9xy + 8xy^2 + 10x^2y + x - 7y)$
$= (16x + 8x^2y - 7xy^2 + 9y - 2xy) + (9xy - 8xy^2 - 10x^2y - x + 7y)$
$= (16x - x) + (8x^2y - 7xy^2 - 8xy^2 - 10x^2y) + (9y + 7y) + (-2xy + 9xy)$
$= 15x - 17x^2y^2 + 16y + 7xy$

Colin incorrectly combined the terms $8x^2y$, $-7xy^2$, $8xy^2$ and $10x^2y$. The like terms are $8x^2y$ and $10x^2y$, and $-7xy^2$ and $8xy^2$.

$(16x + 8x^2y - 7xy^2 + 9y - 2xy) - (-9xy + 8xy^2 + 10x^2y + x - 7y)$
$= (16x + 8x^2y - 7xy^2 + 9y - 2xy) + (9xy - 8xy^2 - 10x^2y - x + 7y)$
$= (16x - x) + (8x^2y - 10x^2y) + (-7xy^2 - 8xy^2) + (9y + 7y) + (-2xy + 9xy)$
$= 15x - 2x^2y - 15xy^2 + 16y + 7xy$

INTEGRATE MATHEMATICAL PRACTICES

Focus on Communication

MP.3 When students work with polynomials and their exponents, they might confuse coefficients and exponents. Have students read problems aloud, stating the terms clearly and carefully–for example, either "four x" or "x to the fourth"—as appropriate.

AVOID COMMON ERRORS

Students may make sign errors when subtracting polynomials. Point out that rewriting the subtraction of polynomials as an addition of the opposite may prevent errors.

PEER-TO-PEER DISCUSSION

Instruct one student in each pair to write two polynomials in standard form while the other student gives verbal instructions for adding the polynomials. Then have students switch roles and repeat the exercise, giving instructions for subtracting the polynomials.

JOURNAL

Have students write about how polynomials are related to monomials, and how the degrees of monomials are important when adding or subtracting polynomials.

23. Critical Reasoning Janice is building a fence around a portion of her rectangular yard. The length of yard she will enclose is x, and the width is $2x^2 - 98x + 5$, where the measurements are in feet. If the length of the enclosed yard is 50 feet and the cost of fencing is \$13 per foot, how much will Janice need to spend on fencing?

In the equation $P(x) = l(x) + l(x) + w(x) + w(x)$, $P(x)$ is the perimeter of the enclosed yard in feet.

$x + x + (2x^2 - 98x + 5) + (2x^2 - 98x + 5)$

$= (2x^2 + 2x^2) + (x + x - 98x - 98x) + (5 + 5)$

$= 4x^2 - 194x + 10$

$P(50) = 4(50)^2 - 194(50) + 10 = 310$

The perimeter of the yard is 310 feet.

$\$13 \cdot 310 = \$4030$

Janice will need to spend \$4030 on fencing.

24. Multi-Step Find a polynomial expression for the perimeter of a trapezoid with legs of length x and bases of lengths $7x^3 + 2x$ and $x^2 + 3x - 10$ where each is measured in inches.

a. Find the perimeter of the trapezoid if the length of one leg is 6 inches.

b. If the length is increased by 5 inches, will the perimeter also increase? By how much?

$P(x) = x + x + (7x^3 + 2x) + (x^2 + 3x - 10)$

$= (7x^3) + (x^2) + (x + x + 2x + 3x) + (-10)$

$= 7x^3 + x^2 - 7x - 10$

a. $7(6)^3 + (6)^2 + 7(6) - 10 = 1580$

The perimeter is 1580 inches.

b. $7(11)^3 + (11)^2 + 7(11) - 10 = 9505$

$9505 - 1580 = 7925$

The perimeter will increase by 7925 inches.

25. Communicate Mathematical Ideas Present a formal argument for why the set of polynomials is closed under addition and subtraction. Use the polynomials $ax^m + bx^m$ and $ax^m - bx^m$, for real numbers a and b and whole number m, to justify your reasoning.

$ax^m + bx^m = (a + b)x^m$

The sum of two monomials, ax^m and bx^m, is another monomial, $(a + b)x^m$.

$ax^m - bx^m = (a - b)x^m$

The difference of two monomials, ax^m and bx^m, is another monomial, $(a - b)x^m$

So, the sum or difference of two polynomials is a sum of monomials, which is another polynomial.

esson Performance Task

he table shows the average monthly maximum and minimum temperatures for Death Valley roughout one year.

Month	Maximum Temperature	Minimum Temperature
January	67	40
February	73	46
March	82	55
April	91	62
May	101	73
June	110	81
July	116	88
August	115	86
September	107	76
October	93	62
November	77	48
December	65	38

se a graphing calculator to find a good fourth-degree polynomial regression model for both e maximum and minimum temperatures. Then find a function that models the range in onthly temperatures and use the model to estimate the range during September. How does e range predicted by your model compare with the range shown in the table?

aximum temperature model:

$_{max}(t) = 0.0319t^4 - 0.962t^3 + 8.12t^2 - 15.2t + 76.2$

inimum temperature model:

$_{min}(t) = 0.0372t^4 - 1.08t^3 + 8.97t^2 - 17.8t + 51.4$

here t is time (1 = Jan., 2 = Feb., etc.) and T is temperature (degrees Fahrenheit).

e range of monthly temperatures is the difference of the maximum and minimum mperatures.

$(t) = T_{max}(t) - T_{min}(t)$

$(t) = (0.0319t^4 - 0.962t^3 + 8.12t^2 - 15.2t + 76.2) - (0.0372t^4 - 1.08t^3 + 8.97t^2 - 17.8t + 51.4)$

$(t) = (0.0319t^4 - 0.0372t^4) + (-0.962t^3 + 1.08t^3) + (8.12t^2 - 8.97t^2) + (-15.2t + 17.8t) + (76.2 - 51.4)$

$(t) = -0.0053t^4 + 0.118t^3 - 0.85t^2 + 2.6t + 24.8$

$9) = -0.0053(9)^4 + 0.118(9)^3 - 0.85(9)^2 + 2.6(9) + 24.8$

$9) = -0.0053(6561) + 0.118(729) - 0.85(81) + 2.6(9) + 24.8$

$9) = -34.8 + 86.0 - 68.9 + 23.4 + 24.8 = 30.5$

e predicted range in temperatures in September is about 30.5 degrees, which is in agreement ith the September temperatures shown in the data table.

EXTENSION ACTIVITY

Have the students use their maximum and minimum temperature models to alculate the *average* temperature for the month of September. Then have students esearch the actual average temperature in Death Valley for September. Ask students whether their models accurately predicted the average temperature and, f not, what might account for the difference. **For example, the data might be based on different time periods, and so a September model would not be accurate.**

CONNECT CONTEXT EL

Some students may not be familiar with the name and location of *Death Valley*. Point out the location on a map, and explain how the high temperatures relate to the name *Death Valley*.

AVOID COMMON ERRORS

Some students may introduce sign errors when doing subtraction. When two functions are subtracted, all terms in the second set of parentheses should change sign: $(a + b) - (-c + d) = a + b + c - d$.

INTEGRATE MATHEMATICAL PRACTICES

Focus on Critical Thinking

MP.3 Ask students how they might improve the accuracy of their models. Have them discuss the advantages of adding more data points versus using a higher-order polynomial.

Scoring Rubric

2 points: Student correctly solves the problem and explains his/her reasoning.

1 point: Student shows good understanding of the problem but does not fully solve or explain his/her reasoning.

0 points: Student does not demonstrate understanding of the problem.

Multiplying Polynomials

Common Core Math Standards

The student is expected to:

A-APR.A.1

Understand that polynomials form a system ... closed under ... multiplication; ... multiply polynomials. Also A-APR.C.4, F-BF.A.1b

Mathematical Practices

MP.4 Modeling

Language Objective

Work in pairs to complete a compare and contrast chart for adding/subtracting and multiplying polynomials.

ENGAGE

Essential Question: How do you multiply polynomials, and what type of expression is the result?

Possible answer: You multiply two polynomials by multiplying each term of one polynomial with each term of the other polynomial. The product is another polynomial.

PREVIEW: LESSON PERFORMANCE TASK

View the Engage section online. Discuss the photo and how the total amount of oil produced is a function of both the number of wells and the amount produced by each well. Then preview the Lesson Performance Task.

Name ____________ Class ________ Date ________

6.2 Multiplying Polynomials

Essential Question: How do you multiply polynomials, and what type of expression is the result?

Resource Locker

Explore Analyzing a Visual Model for Polynomial Multiplication

The volume of a rectangular prism is the product of the length, width, and height of that prism. If the dimensions are all known, then the volume is a simple calculation. What if some of the dimensions are given as *binomials*? A **binomial** is a polynomial with two terms. How would you find the volume of a rectangular prism that is $x + 3$ units long, $x + 2$ units wide, and x units high? The images below show two methods for finding the solution.

$V = \text{length} \times \text{width} \times \text{height}$
$= (x + 3)(x + 2)x$

$v = v_1 + v_2 + v_3 + v_4$

v_2 = volume of this piece
v_1 = volume of this piece
v_4 = volume of this piece
v_3 = volume of this piece

(A) The first model shows the rectangular prism, and its volume is calculated directly as the product of two binomials and a monomial.

(B) The second image divides the rectangular prism into **four** smaller prisms, the dimensions of which are each **monomials**.

(C) The volume of a cube (V_1) where all sides have a length of x, is $x \cdot x \cdot x = x^3$.

(D) The volume of a rectangular prism (V_2) with dimensions x by x by 2 is $x \cdot x \cdot 2 = 2x^2$.

(E) The volume of a rectangular prism (V_3) with dimensions x by x by 3 is $x \cdot x \cdot 3 = 3x^2$.

(F) The volume of a rectangular prism (V_4) with dimensions x by 3 by 2 is $x \cdot 3 \cdot 2 = 6x$.

(G) So the volume of the rectangular prism is the sum of the volumes of the four smaller regions.

$$V_1 + V_2 + V_3 + V_4 = x^3 + 2x^2 + 3x^2 + 6x$$
$$= x^3 + 5x^2 + 6x$$

HARDCOVER PAGES 283–296

Watch for the hardcover student edition page numbers for this lesson.

Reflect

1. If all three dimensions were binomials, how many regions would the rectangular prism be divided into?
8

2. **Discussion** Can this method be applied to finding the volume of other simple solids? Are there solids that this process would be difficult to apply to? Are there any solids that this method cannot be applied to?
Yes. It would be difficult to find the volume of any shape, such as a pyramid or sphere, that did not subdivide into smaller iterations of that shape and did not stack together well.

Explain 1 Multiplying Polynomials

Multiplying polynomials involves using the product rule for exponents and the distributive property. The product of two monomials is the product of the coefficients and the sum of the exponents of each variable.

$$5x \cdot 6x^3 = 30x^{1+3} \qquad -2x^2y^4z \cdot 5y^2z = -10x^2y^{4+2}z^{1+1}$$
$$= 30x^4 \qquad = -10x^2y^6z^2$$

When multiplying two binomials, the distributive property is used. Each term of one polynomial must be multiplied by each term of the other.

$$\begin{aligned}(2+3x)(1+x) &= 2(1+x) + 3x(x+1)\\ &= 2(1) + 2(x) + 3x(x) + 3x(1)\\ &= 2 + 2x + 3x^{1+1} + 3x\\ &= 2 + 5x + 3x^2\end{aligned}$$

The polynomial $2 + 5x + 3x^2$ is called a **trinomial** because it has three terms.

Example 1 **Perform the following polynomial multiplications.**

(A) $(x+2)(1-4x+2x^2)$

Find the product by multiplying horizontally.

$(x+2)(2x^2-4x+1)$	Write the polynomials in standard form.
$x(2x^2) + x(-4x) + x(1) + 2(2x^2) + 2(-4x) + 2(1)$	Distribute the x and the 2.
$2x^3 - 4x^2 + x + 4x^2 - 8x + 2$	Simplify.
$2x^3 - 7x + 2$	Combine like terms.

Therefore, $(x+2)(2x^2-4x+1) = 2x^3 - 7x + 2$.

PROFESSIONAL DEVELOPMENT

Math Background

In the previous lesson, students discovered that polynomials are closed under addition and subtraction. In this lesson, students learn that polynomials are also closed under multiplication; the product of two polynomials is a polynomial. When we multiply two nonzero integers p by q, we say that the *product* is an integer pq such that each digit of q is multiplied by each digit of p, and then the partial products are added. Multiplication of polynomials is much the same. Given polynomials $P(x)$ and $Q(x)$, where both $P(x)$ and $Q(x) \neq 0$, we can write $P(x) \cdot Q(x) = R(x)$. $R(x)$ will be a simplified polynomial with like terms combined.

EXPLORE

Analyzing a Visual Model for Polynomial Multiplication

INTEGRATE TECHNOLOGY

Students have the option of completing the polynomial multiplication activity either in the book or online.

QUESTIONING STRATEGIES

How does a polynomial model the volume of a real-world figure like a rectangular prism with variable dimensions? **The volume of a figure like a rectangular prism can be written as a cubic polynomial because the polynomial represents three dimensions. For the rectangular prism, the cubic may be a product of the dimensions.**

EXPLAIN 1

Multiplying Polynomials

AVOID COMMON ERRORS

Students often are unsure whether to multiply polynomials horizontally or vertically. Point out that if the polynomials have many terms, multiplying them vertically may prevent errors because vertical multiplication is familiar, and the locations of the product terms are similar to place value in a numerical product. If the polynomials have few terms, multiplying horizontally may be more convenient, as long as the student remembers to use the distributive property to multiply each term of one polynomial by all other terms of the other polynomial.

QUESTIONING STRATEGIES

Is the commutative property of multiplication true for the multiplication of polynomials? Explain. **Yes, the product will be the same regardless of the order in which polynomials are multiplied.**

After you have multiplied two polynomials, how can you make sure you have not missed any terms in the process? **Before simplifying, the product of a polynomial with *m* terms and a polynomial with *n* terms has *mn* terms, so count the number of terms in the product.**

EXPLAIN 2

Modeling with Polynomial Multiplication

INTEGRATE MATHEMATICAL PRACTICES

Focus on Patterns

MP.8 Point out that using a table with color to organize the products may be helpful when finding the product of real-world polynomials. For example, to find $(x^2 + 3x - 5)(x^2 - x + 1)$, the table below might be used, with the terms of each trinomial either above the columns, or alongside the rows.

	x^2	$-x$	$+1$
x^2	x^4	$-x^3$	$+x^2$
$+3x$	$+3x^3$	$-3x^2$	$+3x$
-5	$-5x^2$	$+5x$	-5

Like terms, shown with the same color, are combined to complete the product.

(B) $(3x - 4)(2 + x - 7x^2)$

Find the product by multiplying vertically.

$$\begin{array}{r} -7x^2 + \boxed{x} + 2 \\ 3x - 4 \\ \hline \boxed{28x^2} - 4x - 8 \\ \boxed{-21x^3} + 3x^2 + 6x \quad \\ \hline -21x^3 + \boxed{31x^2} + 2x - 8 \end{array}$$

Write each polynomial in standard form.

Multipy -4 and $(-7x^2 + x + 2)$.

Multipy $\boxed{3x}$ and $(-7x^2 + x + 2)$.

Combine like terms.

Therefore, $(3x - 4)(2 + x - 7x^2) = \underline{-21x^3 + 31x^2 + 2x - 8}$.

Your Turn

3. $(3 + 2x)(4 - 7x + 5x^2)$

$2x(5x^2) + 2x(-7x) + 2x(4) + 3(5x^2) + 3(-7x) + 3(4)$ — **Distribute the 2x and the 3.**

$10x^3 - 14x^2 + 8x + 15x^2 - 21x + 12$ — **Simplify.**

$10x^3 + x^2 - 13x + 12$ — **Combine like terms.**

4. $(x - 6)(3 - 8x - 4x^2)$

$x(-4x^2) + x(-8x) + x(3) - 6(-4x^2) - 6(-8x) - 6(3)$ — **Distribute the x and the −6.**

$-14x^3 - 8x^2 + 3x + 24x^2 + 48x - 18$ — **Simplify.**

$-14x^3 + 16x^2 + 51x - 18$ — **Combine like terms.**

Explain 2 Modeling with Polynomial Multiplication

Many real-world situations can be modeled with polynomial functions. Sometimes, a situation will arise in which a model is needed that combines two quantities modeled by polynomial functions. In this case, the desired model would be the product of the two known models.

Example 2 **Find the polynomial function modeling the desired relationship.**

(A) Mr. Silva manages a manufacturing plant. From 1990 through 2005, the number of units produced (in thousands) can be modeled by $N(x) = 0.02x^2 + 0.2x + 3$. The average cost per unit (in dollars) can be modeled by $C(x) = -0.002x^2 - 0.1x + 2$, where x is the number of years since 1990. Write a polynomial $T(x)$ that can be used to model Mr. Silva's total manufacturing cost for those years.

The total manufacturing cost is the product of the number of units made and the cost per unit.

$T(x) = N(x) \cdot C(x)$

COLLABORATIVE LEARNING

Small Group Activity

Have groups of students describe how to multiply polynomials. Ask them to write an example multiplication problem in a graphic organizer similar to the one shown. Students then pass the organizer to another student, who writes in the next step and describes it. They continue to pass the organizers until each problem is solved and all steps are explained. A Sample organizer is shown.

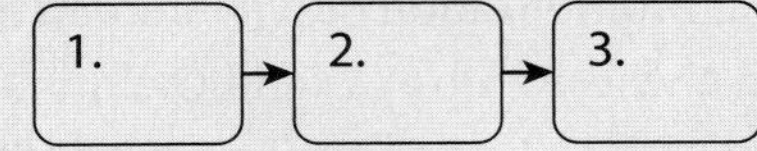

Multiply the two polynomials.

$$
\begin{array}{rrrrr}
 & & 0.02x^2 & +\ 0.2x & +\ 3 \\
 & \times & -\ 0.002x^2 & -\ 0.1x & +\ 2 \\
\hline
 & & 0.04x^2 & +\ 0.4x & +\ 6 \\
 & -0.002x^3 & -\ 0.02x^2 & -\ 0.3x & \\
-0.00004x^4 & -\ 0.0004x^3 & -\ 0.006x^2 & & \\
\hline
-0.00004x^4 & -\ 0.0024x^3 & +\ 0.014x^2 & +\ 0.1x & +\ 6
\end{array}
$$

Therefore, the total manufacturing cost can be modeled by the following polynomial, where x is the number of years since 1990.

$T(x) = -0.00004x^4 - 0.0024x^3 + 0.014x^2 + 0.1x + 6$

(B) Ms. Liao runs a small dress company. From 1995 through 2005, the number of dresses she made can be modeled by $N(x) = 0.3x^2 - 1.6x + 14$, and the average cost to make each dress can be modeled by $C(x) = -0.001x^2 - 0.06x + 8.3$, where x is the number of years since 1995. Write a polynomial that can be used to model Ms. Liao's total dressmaking costs, $T(x)$, for those years.

The total dressmaking cost is the product of the number of dresses made and the cost per dress.

$T(x) = N(x) \cdot C(x)$

Multiply the two polynomials.

$$
\begin{array}{rrrrr}
 & & 0.3x^2 & -\ 1.6x & +\ 14 \\
 & \times & -\ 0.001x^2 & \boxed{-0.06x} & +\ 8.3 \\
\hline
 & & 2.49x^2 & -\ 13.28x & \boxed{+116.2} \\
 & -0.018x^3 & \boxed{+0.096x^2} & -\ 0.84x & \\
-0.0003x^{\boxed{4}} & +\ 0.0016x^3 & -\ 0.014x^2 & & \\
\hline
-0.0003x^{\boxed{4}} & -\ 0.0164x^3 & +\ 2.572x^2 & \boxed{-14.12x} & +\ 116.2
\end{array}
$$

Therefore, the total dressmaking cost can be modeled by the following polynomial, where x is the number of years since 1995.

$T(x) = \underline{-0.0003x^4 - 0.0164x^3 + 2.572x^2 - 14.12x + 116.2}$

QUESTIONING STRATEGIES

? What property of exponents is used to find the partial products? **When you multiply two powers with the same base, you add their exponents.**

DIFFERENTIATE INSTRUCTION

Multiple Representations

Have students work in small groups to multiply two polynomials, such as $(x^2 + 3x - 5)(x^2 - x + 1)$. Each student in the group should choose a different method, such as multiplying horizontally, multiplying vertically, or using a table. Have students discuss the ways in which the methods are alike and the ways in which they differ.

EXPLAIN 3

Verifying Polynomial Identities

AVOID COMMON ERRORS

Students may think that they need to analyze each side of a polynomial equation in order to verify that the equation expresses a polynomial identity. Point out that if one side of the equation is a monomial, then that side is complete. There may be more than one way to proceed, but the arithmetic operations must be performed on both sides, if necessary, until the two sides match.

QUESTIONING STRATEGIES

? How do you verify a polynomial identity? **You perform the operations indicated on each side of the identity until the two sides match.**

Your Turn

5. Brent runs a small toy store specializing in wooden toys. From 2000 through 2012, the number of toys Brent made can be modeled by $N(x) = 0.7x^2 - 2x + 23$, and the average cost to make each toy can be modeled by $C(x) = -0.004x^2 - 0.08x + 25$, where x is the number of years since 2000. Write a polynomial that can be used to model Brent's total cost for making the toys, $T(x)$, for those years.

The total cost is the product of the number of toys made and the cost per toy.

Multiply the two polynomials.

$$\begin{array}{rrrrr}
 & & 0.7x^2 & -2x & +23 \\
 & \times & -0.004x^2 & -0.08x & +25 \\
\hline
 & & 17.5x^2 & -50x & +575 \\
 & -0.056x^3 & 0.16x^2 & -1.84x & \\
-0.0028x^4 & 0.008x^3 & -0.092x^2 & & \\
\hline
-0.0028x^4 & -0.048x^3 & +17.568x^2 & -51.84x & +575
\end{array}$$

Therefore, the total cost of making the toys can be modeled by the following polynomial, where x is the number of years since 2000.

$T(x) = -0.0028x^4 - 0.064x^3 + 17.248x^2 - 51.84x + 575$

Explain 3 Verifying Polynomial Identities

You have already seen certain special polynomial relationships. For example, a difference of two squares can be easily factored: $x^2 - a^2 = (x + a)(x - a)$. This equation is an example of a **polynomial identity**, a mathematical relationship equating one polynomial quantity to another. Another example of a polynomial identity is

$$(x + a)^2 - (x - a)^2 = 4ax.$$

The identity can be verified by simplifying one side of the equation to match the other.

Example 3 **Verify the given polynomial identity.**

(A) $(x + a)^2 - (x - a)^2 = 4ax$

The right side of the identity is already fully simplified. Simplify the left-hand side.

$$(x + a)^2 - (x - a)^2 = 4ax$$

$$x^2 + 2ax + a^2 - (x^2 - 2ax + a^2) = 4ax \qquad \text{Use the sum of the two squares and the difference of two squares identities.}$$

$$x^2 + 2ax + a^2 - x^2 + 2ax - a^2 = 4ax \qquad \text{Rearrange terms.}$$

$$\cancel{x^2} - \cancel{x^2} + 2ax + 2ax + \cancel{a^2} - \cancel{a^2} = 4ax \qquad \text{Simplify.}$$

$$4ax = 4ax$$

Therefore, $(x + a)^2 - (x - a)^2 = 4ax$ is a true statement.

LANGUAGE SUPPORT EL

Communicate Math

Have students complete a chart like the following showing similarities and differences:

Operation	Add and Subtract Polynomials	Multiply Polynomials
Alike	The result is another polynomial.	The result is another polynomial.
Different	You can only add and subtract like terms.	You don't need to multiply like terms.

Ⓑ $(a + b)(a^2 - ab + b^2) = a^3 + b^3$

The right side of the identity is already fully simplified. Simplify the left-hand side.

$$(a + b)(a^2 - ab + b^2) = a^3 + b^3$$

$a(a^2) + a(\boxed{-ab}) + a(b^2) + b(a^2) + \boxed{b}(-ab) + b(b^2) = a^3 + b^3$ Distribute a and b.

$a^3 - a^2b + ab^2 + \boxed{a^2b} - ab^2 + \boxed{b^3} = a^3 + b^3$ **Simplify.**

$a^3 - \boxed{a^2b} + a^2b^2 - \boxed{ab^2} + b^3 = a^3 + b^3$ Rearrange terms.

$a^3 \boxed{+} b^3 = a^3 + b^3$ Combine like terms.

Therefore, $(a + b)(a^2 - ab + b^2) = a^3 + b^3$ is a **true** statement.

Your Turn

6. Show that $a^5 - b^5 = (a - b)(a^4 + a^3b + a^2b^2 + ab^3 + b^4)$.

The left side of the identity is already fully simplified. Simplify the right-hand side.

$a^5 - b^5 = a(a^4) + a(a^3b) + a(a^2b^2) + a(ab^3) + a(b^4) - b(a^4) - b(a^3b) - b(a^2b^2) - b(ab^3) - b(b^4)$

$a^5 - b^5 = a^5 + a^4b + a^3b^2 + a^2b^3 + ab^4 - a^4b - a^3b^2 - a^2b^3 - ab^4 - b^5$

$a^5 - b^5 = a^5 - b^5$

7. Show that $(a - b)(a^2 + ab + b^2) = a^3 - b^3$.

The right side of the identity is already fully simplified. Simplify the left-hand side.

$a(a^2) + a(ab) + a(b^2) - b(a^2) - b(ab) - b(b^2) = a^3 - b^3$ **Distribute a and b.**

$a^3 + a^2b + ab^2 - a^2b - ab^2 - b^3 = a^3 - b^3$ **Simplify.**

$a^3 - b^3 = a^3 - b^3$ **Combine like terms.**

Explain 4 Using Polynomial Identities

The most obvious use for polynomial identities is simplifying algebraic expressions, but polynomial identities often turn out to have nonintuitive uses as well.

Example 4 **For each situation, find the solution using the given polynomial identity.**

Ⓐ The polynomial identity $(x^2 + y^2)^2 = (x^2 - y^2)^2 + (2xy)^2$ can be used to identify Pythagorean triples. Generate a Pythagorean triple using $x = 4$ and $y = 3$.

Substitute the given values into the identity.

$$(4^2 + 3^2)^2 = (4^2 - 3^2)^2 + (2 \cdot 4 \cdot 3)^2$$
$$(16 + 9)^2 = (16 - 9)^2 + (24)^2$$
$$(25)^2 = (7)^2 + (24)^2$$
$$625 = 49 + 576$$
$$625 = 625$$

Therefore, 7, 24, 25 is a Pythagorean triple.

EXPLAIN 4

Using Polynomial Identities

CONNECT VOCABULARY EL

Students may not understand *identity* in the context of using polynomials' identities. Tell them that once an identity is established, they should then apply the identity to numbers, much as they would apply a known formula to a geometric figure. In the process of using the identity, they do *not* re-verify the identity.

QUESTIONING STRATEGIES

How are polynomial identities used? **They may be used to simplify algebraic expressions or to find shortcuts for polynomial-based formulas or mental math calculations.**

AVOID COMMON ERRORS

Regardless of the method students use to multiply polynomials, a common error is to use the properties of exponents incorrectly, multiplying exponents that should be added. Remind students that the product of two powers with the same base is the base raised to the sum of the powers, or $b^m \bullet b^n = b^{m+n}$.

(B) The identity $(x + y)^2 = x^2 + 2xy + y^2$ can be used for mental-math calculations to quickly square numbers.

Find the square of 27.

Find two numbers whose sum is equal to 27.

Let $x =$ **20** and $y = 7$

Evaluate

$$\left(20 + \boxed{7}\right)^2 = 20^2 + \boxed{2 \cdot 20 \cdot 7} + 7^2$$

$$27^2 = 400 + \boxed{280} + 49$$

$$27^2 = \boxed{729}$$

Verify by using a calculator to find 27^2.

$27^2 =$ **729**

Your Turn

8. The identity $(x + y)(x - y) = x^2 - y^2$ can be used for mental-math calculations to quickly multiply two numbers in specific situations.

Find the product of 37 and 43. (Hint: What values should you choose for x and y so the equation calculates the product of 37 and 43?)

Substitute $x = 40$ and $y = 3$ into the identity and evaluate.

$$(40 + 3)(40 - 3) = 40^2 - 3^2$$

$$43 \cdot 37 = 1600 - 9$$

$$43 \cdot 37 = 1591$$

9. The identity $(x - y)^2 = x^2 - 2xy + y^2$ can also be used for mental-math calculations to quickly square numbers.

Find the square of 18. (Hint: What values should you choose for x and y so the equation calculates the square of 18?)

$25 - 7 = 18$

Substitute $x = 25$ and $y = 7$ into the identity and evaluate.

$$(25 - 7)^2 = 25^2 - 2 \cdot 25 \cdot 7 + 7^2$$

$$18^2 = 625 - 350 + 49 = 625 - 301 = 324$$

Elaborate

0. What property is employed in the process of polynomial multiplication?
The distributive property.

1. How can you use unit analysis to justify multiplying two polynomial models of real-world quantities?
The units of the polynomials need to combine in such a way that their product is the desired unit.

2. Give an example of a polynomial identity and how it's useful.
See student work; answers will vary.

3. **Essential Question Check-In** When multiplying polynomials, what type of expression is the product?
A polynomial

Evaluate: Homework and Practice

- Online Homework
- Hints and Help
- Extra Practice

The dimensions for a rectangular prism are $x + 5$ for the length, $x + 1$ for the width, and x for the height. What is the volume of the prism?
$(x + 5)(x + 1)x = x^3 + 6x^2 + 5x$

rform the following polynomial multiplications.

$(3x - 2)(2x^2 + 3x - 1)$

$3x(2x^2) + 3x(3x) + 3x(-1) - 2(2x^2) - 2(3x) - 2(-1)$	**Distribute the $3x$ and the -2.**
$6x^3 + 9x^2 - 3x - 4x^2 - 6x + 2$	**Simplify.**
$6x^3 + 5x^2 - 9x + 2$	**Combine like terms.**

$(x^3 + 3x^2 + 1)(3x^2 + 6x - 2)$

		x^3	$+3x^2$		$+1$		
		$\times$	$3x^2$	$+6x$	-2		
		$-2x^3$	$-6x^2$		-2		Multiply -2 and $(x^3 + 3x^2 + 1)$.
	$6x^4$	$+18x^3$		$+6x$			Multiply $6x$ and $(x^3 + 3x^2 + 1)$.
$3x^5$	$+ 9x^4$		$+3x^2$				Multiply $3x^2$ and $(x^3 + 3x^2 + 1)$.
$3x^5$	$+15x^4$	$+16x^3$	$-3x^2$	$+6x$	-2		Combine like terms.

Exercise	Depth of Knowledge (D.O.K.)	COMMON CORE Mathematical Practices
1	**1** Recall of Information	**MP.6** Precision
2–7	**1** Recall of Information	**MP.6** Precision
8–11	**2** Skills/Concepts	**MP.4** Modeling
12–21	**2** Skills/Concepts	**MP.2** Reasoning
22	**3** Strategic Thinking	**MP.2** Reasoning
23	**3** Strategic Thinking	**MP.5** Using Tools

ELABORATE

QUESTIONING STRATEGIES

? How is the distributive property used to multiply two polynomials? **Each monomial term of one polynomial must be multiplied by the entire other polynomial, so the distributive property applies.**

CONNECT VOCABULARY EL

Relate the prefixes *bi-* and *tri-* to the meaning of *binomial* (two terms) and *trinomial* (three terms).

SUMMARIZE THE LESSON

? What points should you remember when multiplying polynomials? **Use the distributive property to multiply every term of one polynomial by every term of the other polynomial, combine like terms, and align like terms.**

EVALUATE

ASSIGNMENT GUIDE

Concepts and Skills	Practice
Explore Analyzing a Visual Model for Polynomial Multiplication	Exercise 1
Example 1 Multiplying Polynomials	Exercises 2–7
Example 2 Modeling with Polynomial Multiplication	Exercises 8–11
Example 3 Verifying Polynomial Identities	Exercises 12–15
Example 4 Using Polynomial Identities	Exercises 16–21

INTEGRATE TECHNOLOGY

Point out that when multiplying two polynomials in one variable, students can graph the expressions before they are multiplied and, again, after they are multiplied. The graphs should be coincident.

4. $(x^2 + 9x + 7)(3x^2 + 9x + 5)$

$$\begin{array}{rrrrrl} & & x^2 & +9x & +7 & \\ & \times & 3x^2 & +9x & +5 & \\ \hline & & 5x^2 & +45x & +35 & \text{Multiply 5 and } (x^2+9x+7). \\ & 9x^3 & +81x^2 & +63x & & \text{Multiply } 9x \text{ and } (x^2+9x+7). \\ 3x^4 & +27x^3 & +21x^2 & & & \text{Multiply } 3x^2 \text{ and } (x^2+9x+7). \\ \hline 3x^4 & +36x^3 & +107x^2 & +108x & +35 & \text{Combine like terms.} \end{array}$$

5. $(2x + 5y)(3x^2 - 4xy + 2y^2)$

$2x(3x^2) + 2x(-4xy) + 2x(2y^2) + 5y(3x^2) + 5y(-4xy) + 5y(2y^2)$ **Distribute the $2x$ and the**

$6x^3 - 8x^2y + 4xy^2 + 15x^2y - 20xy^2 + 20y^3$ **Simplify.**

$6x^3 + 7x^2y - 16xy^2 + 10y^3$ **Combine like terms.**

6. $(x^3 + x^2 + 1)(x^2 - x - 5)$

$$\begin{array}{rrrrrrl} & & x^3 & +x^2 & & +1 & \\ & \times & & x^2 & -x & -5 & \\ \hline & & -5x^3 & -5x^2 & & -5 & \text{Multiply } -5 \text{ and } (x^3+x^2+1). \\ & -x^4 & -x^3 & & -x & & \text{Multiply } -x \text{ and } (x^3+x^2+1). \\ x^5 & +x^4 & & x^2 & & & \text{Multiply } x^2 \text{ and } (x^3+x^2+1). \\ \hline x^5 & & -6x^3 & -4x^2 & -x & -5 & \text{Combine like terms.} \end{array}$$

7. $(4x^2 + 3x + 2)(3x^2 + 2x - 1)$

$$\begin{array}{rrrrrl} & & 4x^2 & +3x & +2 & \\ \hline & \times & 3x^2 & +2x & -1 & \\ & & -4x^2 & -3x & -2 & \text{Multiply } -1 \text{ and } (4x^2+3x+2). \\ & 8x^3 & +6x^2 & +4x & & \text{Multiply } 2x \text{ and } (4x^2+3x+2). \\ 12x^4 & +9x^3 & +6x^2 & & & \text{Multiply } 3x^2 \text{ and } (4x^2+3x+2). \\ \hline 12x^4 & +17x^3 & +8x^2 & +x & -2 & \text{Combine like terms.} \end{array}$$

Exercise	Depth of Knowledge (D.O.K.)	COMMON CORE Mathematical Practices
24	3 Strategic Thinking H.O.T.	MP.2 Reasoning
25	3 Strategic Thinking H.O.T.	MP.3 Logic
26	3 Strategic Thinking H.O.T.	MP.2 Reasoning

Write a polynomial function to represent the new value.

8. The volume of a stock or number of shares traded on a given day is $S(x) = x^5 - 3x^4 + 10x^2 - 6x + 30$. The average cost of a share of a stock on a given day is $C(x) = 0.004x^4 - 0.02x^2 + 0.3x + 4$.

The value is equal to the number of shares traded times the cost per share.

$V(x) = (x^5 - 3x^4 + 10x^2 - 6x + 30)(0.004x^4 - 0.02x^2 + 0.3x + 4)$

$$
\begin{array}{rrrrrrrrrr}
 & & & & x^5 & -3x^4 & & +10x^2 & -6x & +30 \\
 & & & \times & & 0.004x^4 & & -0.02x^2 & +0.3x & +4 \\
\hline
 & & & & 4x^5 & -12x^4 & & +40x^2 & -24x & +120 \\
 & & & 0.3x^6 & -0.9x^5 & & +3x^3 & -1.8x^2 & +9x & \\
 & & -0.002x^7 & +0.06x^6 & & -0.2x^4 & +0.12x^3 & -0.6x^2 & & \\
0.004x^9 & -0.012x^8 & & +0.04x^6 & -0.024x^5 & +0.12x^4 & & & & \\
\hline
0.004x^9 & -0.012x^8 & -0.02x^7 & +0.4x^6 & +3.076x^5 & -12.08x^4 & +3.12x^3 & +37.6x^2 & -15x & +120
\end{array}
$$

$V(x) = 0.004x^4 - 0.012x^8 - 0.02x^7 + 0.4x^6 + 3.076x^5 - 12.08x^4 = 3.12x^3 + 37.6x^2 - 15x + 120$

9. A businessman models the number of items (in thousands) that his company sold from 1998 through 2004 as $N(x) = -0.1x^3 + x^2 - 3x + 4$ and the average price per item (in dollars) as $P(x) = 0.2x + 5$, where x represents the number of years since 1998. Write a polynomial $R(x)$ that can be used to model the total revenue for this company.

The total revenue will be the product of the number of items sold and the price each item is sold at.

Multiply the two polynomials.

$R(x) = (0.2x + 5)(-0.1x^3 + x^2 - 3x + 4)$

$= 0.2x(-0.1x^3) + 0.2x(x^2) + 0.2x(-3x) + 0.2x(4) + 5(-0.1x^3) + 5(x^2) + 5(-3x) + 5(4)$

$= -0.02x^4 + 0.2x^3 - 0.6x^2 + 0.8x - 0.5x^3 + 5x^2 - 15x + 20$

$= -0.02x^4 - 0.3x^3 + 4.4x^2 - 14.2x + 20$

10. Biology A biologist has found that the number of branches on a certain rare tree in its first few years of life can be modeled by the polynomial $b(y) = 4y^2 + y$. The number of leaves on each branch can be modeled by the polynomial $l(y) = 2y^3 + 3y^2 + y$, where y is the number of years after the tree reaches a height of 6 feet. Write a polynomial describing the total number of leaves on the tree.

$T(y) = (4y^2 + y)(2y^3 + 3y^2 + y)$

$= 8y^5 + 12y^4 + 4y^3 + 2y^4 + 3y^3 + y^2$

$= 8y^5 + 16y^4 + 7y^3 + y^2$

INTEGRATE MATHEMATICAL PRACTICES

Focus on Communication

MP.3 Help students clarify how to multiply polynomials by having them work in groups. Have one student complete one step of the multiplication process, including an explanation of the process, then pass the problem to another student, who completes the second step, including an explanation. Continue passing the problem until it is complete.

MULTIPLE REPRESENTATIONS

To help students structure how to multiply polynomials, have them use tables similar to the one shown below for $(x^2 + 2x + 1)(x^3 + 3x - 2)$. These diagrams provide more visual support than the more standard vertical method. Have students share their tables with a partner, describing the patterns they see and telling how they got their product polynomials.

	x^3	$3x$	-2
x^2			
$2x$			
1			

11. Physics An object thrown in the air has a velocity after t seconds that can be described by $v(t) = -9.8t + 24$ (in meters/second) and a height $h(t) = -4.9t^2 + 24t + 60$ (in meters). The object has mass $m = 2$ kilograms. The kinetic energy of the object is given by $K = \frac{1}{2}mv^2$, and the potential energy is given by $U = 9.8mh$. Find an expression for the total kinetic and potential energy $K + U$ as a function of time. What does this expression tell you about the energy of the falling object?

$K = \frac{1}{2}(2)(-9.8t + 24)^2$

$K = (-9.8t + 24)^2$

$K = 96.04t^2 - 470.4t + 576$

$U = 9.8(2)(-4.9t^2 + 24t + 60)$

$U = -96.04t^2 + 470.4t + 1176$

$K + U = (96.04t^2 - 470.4t + 576) + (-96.04t^2 + 470.4t + 1176)$

$= 1752$

Since the sum is a constant, this means that the energy of the object is constant and that as it gains kinetic energy by falling, it loses the same amount of potential energy.

Verify the given polynomial identity.

12. $(x + y + z)^2 = x^2 + y^2 + z^2 + 2xy + 2xz + 2yz$

The right side of the identity is already fully simplified. Simplify the left-hand side.

$(x + y + z)^2 = x(x) + x(y) + x(z) + y(x) + y(y) + y(z) + z(x) + z(y) + z(z)$

$= x^2 + xy + xz + yx + y^2 + yz + zx + zy + z^2$

$= x^2 + y^2 + z^2 + xy + yx + xz + zx + yz + zy$

$= x^2 + y^2 + z^2 + 2xy + 2xz + 2yz$

13. $a^5 + b^5 = (a + b)(a^4 - a^3b + a^2b^2 - ab^3 + b^4)$

The left side of the identity is already fully simplified. Simplify the right-hand side.

$$\begin{array}{r} a^4 - a^3b + a^2b^2 - ab^3 + b^4 \\ \times \qquad a + b \\ \hline a^4b - a^3b^2 + a^2b^3 - ab^4 + b^5 \\ a^5 - a^4b + a^3b^2 - a^2b^3 + ab^4 \qquad \\ \hline a^5 \qquad\qquad\qquad + b^5 \end{array}$$

14. $x^4 - y^4 = (x - y)(x + y)(x^2 + y^2)$

The left side of the identity is already fully simplified. Simplify the right-hand side. Examine $(x - y)(x + y)(x^2 + y^2)$. Recall that $(x + y)(x - y) = x^2 - y^2$. Substitute on the right side of the equation.

$x^4 - y^4 = (x^2 - y^2)(x^2 + y^2)$

$x^4 - y^4 = x^2(x^2) + x^2(y^2) - y^2(x^2) - y^2(y^2)$

$x^4 - y^4 = x^4 - y^4$

15. $(a^2+b^2)(x^2+y^2)=(ax-by)^2+(bx+ay)^2$

$$a^2(x^2)+a^2(y^2)+b^2(x^2)+b^2(y^2)=(ax)^2-2(ax)(by)+(by)^2+(bx)^2+2(bx)(ay)+(ay)^2$$
$$a^2x^2+a^2y^2+b^2x^2+b^2y^2=a^2x^2-2axby+b^2y^2+b^2x^2+2axby+a^2y^2$$
$$a^2x^2+a^2y^2+b^2x^2+b^2y^2=a^2x^2+a^2y^2+b^2x^2+b^2y^2$$

Evaluate the following polynomials using one or more of these identities.
$(x+y)^2=x^2+2xy+y^2$, $(x+y)(x-y)=x^2-y^2$, or $(x-y)^2=x^2-2xy+y^2$.

16. 43^2

$$43^2=(40+3)^2 = 1600+240+9 = 1849$$

17. 32^2

$$32^2=(30+2)^2 = 900+120+4 = 1024$$

18. 89^2

$$89^2=(90-1)^2 = 8100-180+1 = 7921$$

19. 47^2

$$47^2=(50-3)^2 = 2500-300+9 = 2209$$

20. $54 \cdot 38$

$$\begin{aligned}54\cdot 38&=(46+8)(46-8)\\&=46^2-8^2\\&=(50-4)^2-64\\&=50^2-2\cdot 50\cdot 4+4^2-64\\&=2500-400+16-64\\&=1052\end{aligned}$$

21. $58 \cdot 68$

$$\begin{aligned}58\cdot 68&=(63+5)(63-5)\\&=63^2-5^2\\&=(60+3)^2-25\\&=60^2+2\cdot 60\cdot 3+3^2-25\\&=3600+360+9-25\\&=3944\end{aligned}$$

22. Explain the Error Two students used binomial expansion to expand $(a+b)^2$. Which answer is incorrect? Identify the error.

A	*B*
$(a+b)^2$	$(a+b)^2$
$1a^2b^0+2a^2b^1+1a^0b^2$	$1a^2b^2+2a^1b^1+1a^0b^0$
$a^2+2ab+b^2$	$a^2b^2+2ab+1$

Answer B is incorrect because the powers of *b* should begin at 0 and increase, not decrease.

INTEGRATE MATHEMATICAL PRACTICES

Focus on Modeling

MP.4 When students multiply polynomials, they may leave out some of the partial products. Tell students to write down all of the partial products and circle the monomial in each one. Then ask them to draw arrows from the monomial in the first polynomial to the matching monomial in the second polynomial.

AVOID COMMON ERRORS

When using the rules for some special products of polynomials, students often forget to apply the power of a power property of exponents to the coefficients of terms in the polynomial. Suggest that students first write the coefficient and variable within parentheses, with the exponent applied to both, and then simplify.

PEER-TO-PEER DISCUSSION

Instruct one student in each pair to write two polynomials in standard form while the other student gives verbal instructions for multiplying the polynomials. Then have students switch roles, repeat the exercise, and give instructions for multiplying two new polynomials.

JOURNAL

Have students make a table describing the methods for multiplying polynomials. Give examples for multiplying monomials, binomials, and trinomials, as well as for verifying polynomial identities.

23. Determine how many terms there will be after performing the polynomial multiplication.

a. $(5x)(3x)$	X 1	2	3	4
b. $(3x)(2x+1)$	1	X 2	3	4
c. $(x+1)(x-1)$	1	X 2	3	4
d. $(x+2)(3x^2-2x+1)$	1	2	3	X 4

a. $(5x)(3x) = 15x^2$ **1 term**

b. $(3x)(2x+1) = 6x^2 + 3x$ **2 terms**

c. $(x+1)(x-1) = x^2 - 1$ **2 terms**

d. $(x+2)(3x^2-2x+1) = 3x^3 + 4x^2 - 3x + 2$ **4 terms**

H.O.T. Focus on Higher Order Thinking

24. Multi-Step Given the polynomial identity: $x^6 + y^6 = (x^2 + y^2)(x^4 - x^2y^2 + y^4)$

a. Verify directly by expanding the right hand side.

$x^6 + y^6 = (x^2+y^2)(x^4 - x^2y^2 + y^4)$

$x^6 + y^6 = x^2(x^4) + x^2(-x^2y^2) + x^2(y^4) + y^2(x^4) + y^2(-x^2y^2) + y^2(y^4)$

$x^6 + y^6 = x^6 - x^4y^2 + x^2y^4 + x^4y^2 - x^2y^4 + y^6$

$x^6 + y^6 = x^6 + x^4y^2 - x^4y^2 + x^2y^4 - x^2y^4 + y^6$

$x^6 + y^6 = x^6 + y^6$

b. Use another polynomial identity to verify this identity. (Note that $a^6 = (a^2)^3 = (a^3)^2$)

Use $a^6 = (a^2)^3$ to replace $x^6 + y^6$ with $(x^2)^3 + (y^2)^3$.

Now use the identity for the sum of two cubes, $(a+b)(a^2 - ab + b^2) = a^3 + b^3$ to simplify $(x^2)^3 + (y^2)^3$.

$(x^2)^3 + (y^2)^3 = (x^2+y^2)((x^2)^2 - (2x^2)(y^2) + (y^2)^2)$

$= (x^2+y^2)(x^4 - 2x^2y^2 + y^4)$

25. Communicate Mathematical Ideas Explain why the set of polynomials is closed under multiplication.

Since $ax^m \cdot bx^n = abx^{m+n}$ for real numbers a and b and whole numbers m and n, the product of two monomials is another monomial. Therefore, the product of two polynomials, which are sums of monomials, is again a sum of monomials, which is another polynomial.

26. Critical Thinking Explain why every other term of the expansion of $(x-y)^5$ is negative when $(x-y)$ is raised to the fifth.

When the power is odd the term is negative, and when the power is even the term is positive.

Lesson Performance Task

The table presents data about oil wells in the state of Oklahoma from 1992 through 2008.

Year	Number of Wells	Average Daily Oil Production per Well (Barrels)
2008	83,443	2.178
2007	82,832	2.053
2006	82,284	2.108
2005	82,551	2.006
2004	83,222	2.10
2003	83,415	2.12
2002	83,730	2.16
2001	84,160	2.24
2000	84,432	2.24
1999	85,043	2.29
1998	85,691	2.49
1997	86,765	2.62
1996	88,144	2.66
1995	90,557	2.65
1994	91,289	2.73
1993	92,377	2.87
1992	93,192	2.99

a. Given the data in this table, use polynomial regression to find models for the number of producing wells and average daily well output in terms of t years since 1992.

b. Find a function modeling the total daily oil output for the state of Oklahoma.

a. Producing oil wells: $W(t) = 0.884t^3 + 39.6t^2 - 1510t + 93700$.
Average daily output (in barrels per well): $O(t) = 0.00418t^2 - 0.125t + 3.01$
where t equals time ($1992 = 1$, $1993 = 2$, etc.)

b.

$$\begin{array}{rrrrrr}
 & & 0.884t^3 & +39.6t^2 & -1510t & +93700 \\
\times & & & 0.00418t^2 & -0.125t & +3.01 \\
\hline
 & & 2.66084t^3 & +119.196t^2 & -4545.1t & +282037 \\
 & -0.1105t^4 & -4.95t^3 & +188.75t^2 & -11712.5t & \\
0.00369512t^5 & +0.165528t^4 & -6.3118t^3 & +391.666t^2 & & \\
\hline
0.00369512t^5 & +0.055028t^4 & -8.60096t^3 & +699.612t^2 & -16257.6t & +282037
\end{array}$$

To the correct number of significant figures,
$D(t) = 0.00370t^5 + 0.0550t^4 - 8.60t^3 + 700t^2 - 16300t + 28200$

EXTENSION ACTIVITY

Have students research the price of oil per barrel for each year from 1992 to 2008 and use polynomial regression to find a model $P(t)$ for the price of oil. Then have students use the model and the daily output model $O(t)$ they determined in the Performance Task to find a function modeling the total value of oil produced each day by the state of Oklahoma. Ask students to calculate the daily oil income in 1992 and compare it to 2008.

INTEGRATE MATHEMATICAL PRACTICES

Focus on Reasoning

MP.2 Ask students to look at the data table and describe any trends they see in number of wells and daily output over time. **Both decrease with time.** Based on these trends, have students predict the behavior of the total daily oil output over time. **It will decrease.** Have students graph the total daily output function $D(t)$ for the time period from 1992 to 2008 to test their predictions.

AVOID COMMON ERRORS

Some students may multiply exponents instead of adding them. Polynomials have two types of numerical values: exponents and coefficients. In the term $0.884t^3$, the coefficient is 0.884 and the exponent is 3. Have students explain what to do with each value when multiplying two polynomials. **Multiply the coefficients and add the exponents.**

Scoring Rubric

2 points: Student correctly solves the problem and explains his/her reasoning.
1 point: Student shows good understanding of the problem but does not fully solve or explain his/her reasoning.
0 points: Student does not demonstrate understanding of the problem.

The Binomial Theorem

Common Core Math Standards

The student is expected to:

A-APR.C.5(+)

Know and apply the Binomial Theorem for the expansion of $(x + y)^n$ in powers of x and y for a positive integer n, where x and y are any numbers, with coefficients determined for example by Pascal's Triangle. Also A-APR.A.1, S-CP.A.1, S-CP.B.7

Mathematical Practices

MP.7 Using Structure

Language Objective

Work with a partner to create a poster of terms used in this lesson, such as Binomial Theorem, binomial probability, binomial experiment and Pascal's Triangle.

ENGAGE

Essential Question: How is the Binomial Theorem useful?

Possible answer: You can use the Binomial Theorem to expand a whole-number power of a binomial. The theorem gives the terms of the expansion as a product of a binomial coefficient (based on Pascal's Triangle), a power of one of the terms of the binomial, and a power of the other term in the binomial. The Binomial Theorem is also useful in calculating probabilities for a binomial experiment.

PREVIEW: LESSON PERFORMANCE TASK

View the online Engage. Discuss the photo and what it means for a player to be an 85% free-throw shooter. Then preview the Lesson Performance Task.

Name________________________ Class____________ Date__________

6.3 The Binomial Theorem

Resource Locker

Essential Question: How is the Binomial Theorem useful?

Explore 1 Generating Pascal's Triangle

Pascal's Triangle is a famous number pattern named after the French mathematician Blaise Pascal (1623–1662). You can use Pascal's Triangle to help you expand a power of a binomial of the form $(a + b)^n$.

Use the tree diagram shown to generate Pascal's Triangle. Notice that from each node in the diagram to the nodes immediately below it there are two paths, a left path (L) and a right path (R). You can describe a path from the single node in row 0 to any other node in the diagram using a string of Ls and Rs.

First, notice that there is only one possible path to each node in row 1, which is why a 1 appears in those nodes. In row 2, there is only one possible path, LL, to the first node and only one possible path, RR, to the last node, but there are two possible paths, LR and RL, to the center node.

(A) Complete only rows 3 and 4 of Pascal's Triangle. (You will complete rows 5 and 6 in Step C.) In each node, write the number of possible paths from the top down to that node.

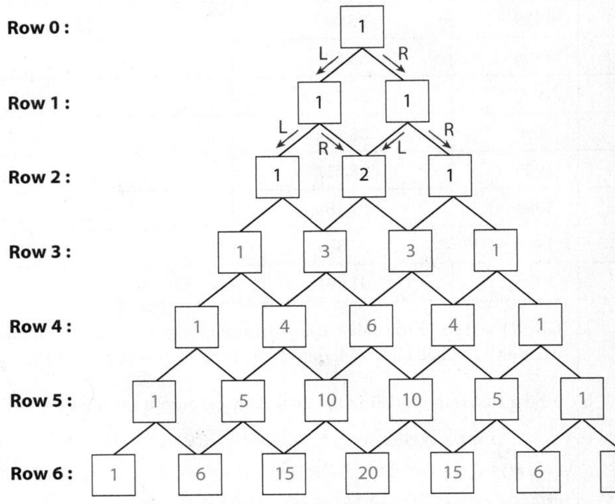

(B) Look for patterns in the tree diagram.

What is the value in the first and last node in each row? 1

For every other node, the value in the node is the sum of the two values above it.

(C) Using the patterns in Step B, go back to Pascal's Triangle in Step A and complete rows 5 and 6.

Answers for this step are shown in Step A.

HARDCOVER PAGES 297–30

Watch for the hardcover student edition page numbers for this lesson.

Reflect

1. Using strings of Ls and Rs, write the paths that lead to the second node in row 3 of Pascal's Triangle. How are the paths alike, and how are they different?
The paths that lead to the second node in row 3 are LLR, LRL, and RLL. These paths contain the same elements, but in different orders.

2. The path LLRLR leads to which node in which row of Pascal's Triangle? What is the value of that node?
The path LLRLR leads to the third node in row 5. This node has a value of 10.

Explore 2 Relating Pascal's Triangle to Powers of Binomials

As shown, the value in position r of row n of Pascal's Triangle is written as ${}_nC_r$, where the position numbers in each row start with 0. In this Explore, you will see how the values in Pascal's Triangle are related to powers of a binomial.

Row 0 : → ${}_0C_0$

Row 1 : → ${}_1C_0$ ${}_1C_1$

Row 2 : → ${}_2C_0$ ${}_2C_1$ ${}_2C_2$

Row 3 : → ${}_3C_0$ ${}_3C_1$ ${}_3C_2$ ${}_3C_3$

(A) Expand each power.

$(a+b)^0 =$ **1**

$(a+b)^1 =$ **$a+b$**

$(a+b)^2 =$ **$a^2+2ab+b^2$** Square of a binomial

$(a+b)^3 =$ **$a^3+3a^2b+3ab^2+b^3$** Multiply $(a+b)^2$ by $(a+b)$.

$(a+b)^4 =$ **$a^4+4a^3b+6a^2b^2+4ab^3+b^4$** Multiply $(a+b)^3$ by $(a+b)$.

(B) Identify the patterns in the expanded form of $(a+b)^n$.

- The exponents of a start at **n** and [increase/decrease] by **1** each term. (decrease circled)
- The exponents of b start at **0** and [increase/decrease] by **1** each term. (increase circled)
- The sum of the exponents in each term is **n**.
- The coefficients of the terms in the expanded form of $(a+b)^n$ are the values in row **n** of Pascal's Triangle.

Reflect

3. How many terms are in the expanded form of $(a+b)^n$?
There are $n+1$ terms in the expanded form of $(a+b)^n$.

4. Without expanding the power, determine the middle term of $(a+b)^6$. Explain how you found your answer.
Since the coefficient is ${}_6C_3 = 20$, the exponents of a and b have a sum of 6, and the exponents of the middle term are the same when n is even, the middle term must be $20a^3b^3$.

5. Without expanding the power, determine the first term of $(a+b)^{15}$. Explain how you found your answer.
The first term of $(a+b)^{15}$ is a^{15} since the first term of $(a+b)^n$ is always a^n.

PROFESSIONAL DEVELOPMENT

Learning Progressions

In the previous lesson, students learned how to multiply polynomials. They also learned the rules for finding squares and cubes of binomials. In this lesson, students continue their work with multiplication of polynomials, examining the patterns formed when binomials are raised to even higher powers. They explore the patterns found in Pascal's Triangle, and learn how to use the Binomial Theorem to expand powers of binomials. Students also apply the Binomial Theorem to a situation involving binomial probabilities.

EXPLORE 1

Generating Pascal's Triangle

INTEGRATE TECHNOLOGY

Students have the option of completing the Explore activity either in the book or online.

QUESTIONING STRATEGIES

Which row of Pascal's Triangle has 12 values? **row 11**

What do you notice if you read any row of Pascal's Triangle from right to left? **The values are the same as when read from left to right. Each row is symmetric about a vertical line through the number at the top of the triangle.**

EXPLORE 2

Relating Pascal's Triangle to Powers of Binomials

QUESTIONING STRATEGIES

What position in Pascal's Triangle is represented as ${}_5C_2$? Explain. **Position 2 of row 5; ${}_nC_r$ represents position r of row n.**

What number in row 15 of Pascal's Triangle is the same number as ${}_{15}C_4$? Explain how you know. **${}_{15}C_{11}$; Because the pattern is symmetric, the number in the fourth position in the row will be the same as that in the fourth position from the end of the row.**

EXPLAIN 1

Expanding Powers of Binomials Using the Binomial Theorem

QUESTIONING STRATEGIES

What must be true about the degree of each term in the expansion? **It must be equal to the exponent to which the binomial is raised.**

Will the coefficient of the second term of every binomial raised to the fourth power always be 4? Explain. **No. If the coefficient of one or both of the terms in the binomial is not 1, the coefficient in the expansion will be 4 times the coefficient of the first term raised to the third power times the coefficient of the second term.**

AVOID COMMON ERRORS

When expanding a power of a binomial like $(2x + 3)^4$, students may raise the x in $2x$ to appropriate powers but not the coefficient 2. For instance, they may think that the first term in the expansion of $(2x + 3)^4$ is $2x^4$ instead of $(2x)^4 = 16x^4$. Similarly, students may forget to use the numbers from Pascal's Triangle in an expansion. For example, they may think that the second term in the expansion of $(2x + 3)^4$ is $(2x)^3(3)^1 = 24x^3$ instead of $4(2x)^3(3)^1 = 96x^3$.

INTEGRATE TECHNOLOGY

If the binomial contains only one variable, students can use a graphing calculator to check the accuracy of the expansion. Students can enter the original expression and the expanded form as two separate functions and check to see that the graphs are identical.

Explain 1 Expanding Powers of Binomials Using the Binomial Theorem

The **Binomial Theorem** states the connection between the terms of the expanded form of $(a + b)^n$ and Pascal's Triangle.

Binomial Theorem

For any whole number n, the binomial expansion of $(a + b)^n$ is given by
$(a + b)^n = {}_nC_0a^nb^0 + {}_nC_1a^{n-1}b^1 + {}_nC_2a^{n-2}b^2 + \ldots + {}_nC_{n-1}a^1b^{n-1} + {}_nC_na^0b^n$
where ${}_nC_r$ is the value in position r (where r starts at 0) of the nth row of Pascal's Triangle.

Since it can be cumbersome to look up numbers from Pascal's Triangle each time you want to expand a power of a binomial, you can use a calculator instead. To do so, enter the value of n, press, go to the **PRB** menu, select **3:nCr**, and then enter the value of r. The calculator screen shows the values for ${}_6C_1$, ${}_6C_2$, and ${}_6C_3$.

```
6 nCr 1
            6
6 nCr 2
           15
6 nCr 3
           20
```

Example 1 Use the Binomial Theorem to expand each power of a binomial.

 $(x - 2)^3$

Step 1 Identify the values in row 3 of Pascal's Triangle.

1, 3, 3, and 1

Step 2 Expand the power as described by the Binomial Theorem, using the values from Pascal's Triangle as coefficients.

$(x - 2)^3 = 1x^3(-2)^0 + 3x^2(-2)^1 + 3x^1(-2)^2 + 1x^0(-2)^3$

Step 3 Simplify.

$(x - 2)^3 = x^3 - 6x^2 + 12x - 8$

 $(x + y)^7$

Step 1 Use a calculator to determine the values of ${}_7C_0$, ${}_7C_1$, ${}_7C_2$, ${}_7C_3$, ${}_7C_4$, ${}_7C_5$, ${}_7C_6$, and ${}_7C_7$.

1, 7, 21, 35, 35, 21, 7, and 1

Step 2 Expand the power as described by the Binomial Theorem, using the values of ${}_7C_0$, ${}_7C_1$, ${}_7C_2$, ${}_7C_3$, ${}_7C_4$, ${}_7C_5$, ${}_7C_6$, and ${}_7C_7$ as coefficients.

$(x + y)^7 = \boxed{1}x^{\boxed{7}}y^{\boxed{0}} + \boxed{7}x^{\boxed{6}}y^{\boxed{1}} + \boxed{21}x^{\boxed{5}}y^{\boxed{2}} + \boxed{35}x^{\boxed{4}}y^{\boxed{3}}$
$+ \boxed{35}x^{\boxed{3}}y^{\boxed{4}} + \boxed{21}x^{\boxed{2}}y^{\boxed{5}} + \boxed{7}x^{\boxed{1}}y^{\boxed{6}} + \boxed{1}x^{\boxed{0}}y^{\boxed{7}}$

Step 3 Simplify.

$(x + y)^7 = x^{\boxed{7}} + \boxed{7}x^{\boxed{6}}y + \boxed{21}x^{\boxed{5}}y^{\boxed{2}} + \boxed{35}x^{\boxed{4}}y^{\boxed{3}} + \boxed{35}x^{\boxed{3}}y^{\boxed{4}}$
$+ \boxed{21}x^{\boxed{2}}y^{\boxed{5}} + \boxed{7}xy^{\boxed{6}} + y^{\boxed{7}}$

COLLABORATIVE LEARNING

Small Group Activity

Have students work in groups of 3 or 4. Instruct each group to design an experiment that models the situation in Example 2. Have them perform their experiment 50 times, recording the result of each trial. Have them use their results to verify the probabilities calculated using the Binomial Theorem. Have each group present their model and their results to the class.

Reflect

6. What happens to the signs of the terms in the expanded form of $(x - 2)^3$? Why does this happen?
The signs alternate between positive and negative because -2 to an even power is positive while -2 to an odd power is negative.

7. If the number 11 is written as the binomial $(10 + 1)$, how can you use the Binomial Theorem to find 11^2, 11^3, and 11^4? What is the pattern in the digits?
$11^2 = 10^2 + 2(10)(1) + 1^2 = 121$
$11^3 = 10^3 + 4(10)^2(1) + 4(10)(1)^2 + 1^3 = 1331$
$11^4 = 10^4 + 4(10)^3(1) + 6(10)^2(1)^2 + 4(10)(1)^3 + 1^4 = 14{,}641$
The digits are the values in the rows of Pascal's Triangle.

Your Turn

8. Use the Binomial Theorem to expand $(x - y)^4$.
The values in row 4 of Pascal's Triangle are 1, 4, 6, 4, and 1.

$$(x - y)^4 = 1x^4(-y)^0 + 4x^3(-y)^1 + 6x^2(-y)^2 + 4x^1(-y)^3 + 1x^0(-y)^4$$
$$= x^4 - 4x^3y + 6x^2y^2 - 4xy^3 + y^4$$

Explain 2 Solving a Real-World Problem Using Binomial Probabilities

Recall that the probability of an event A is written as $P(A)$ and is expressed as a number between 0 and 1, where 0 represents impossibility and 1 represents certainty.

When dealing with probabilities, you will find these two rules helpful.

1. **Addition Rule for Mutually Exclusive Events:** If events A and B are *mutually exclusive* (that is, they cannot occur together), then $P(A \text{ or } B) = P(A) + P(B)$. For example, when rolling a die, getting a 1 and getting a 2 are mutually exclusive events, so $P(1 \text{ or } 2) = P(1) + P(2) = \frac{1}{6} + \frac{1}{6} = \frac{1}{3}$.
2. **Complement Rule:** The *complement* of event A consists of all of the possible outcomes that are not part of A, and the probability that A does not occur is $P(\text{not } A) = 1 - P(A)$. For example, when rolling a die, the probability of not getting a 2 is $P(\text{not } 2) = 1 - P(2) = 1 - \frac{1}{6} = \frac{5}{6}$.

A **binomial experiment** involves many trials where each trial has only two possible outcomes: success or failure. If the probability of success in each trial is p and the probability of failure in each trial is $q = 1 - p$, the **binomial probability** of exactly r success in n trials is given by $P(r) = {}_nC_r p^r q^{n-r}$. Since ${}_nC_r = {}_nC_n - r$, you can rewrite $P(r)$ as $P(r) = {}_nC_{n-r} p^r q^{n-r}$, which represents the $(n - r)$th term in the expanded form of $(p + q)^n$.

DIFFERENTIATE INSTRUCTION

Kinesthetic Experience

Kinesthetic learners may benefit from moving a physical object, such as a coin or other marker, along the paths in Pascal's Triangle. For instance, you could give each of 16 students a unique pathway to follow using a four-letter sequence of Ls and Rs, such as RRLR. Those 16 students would then move their markers along the paths to determine at what node in row 4 of the triangle they land. By surveying the 16 students, you would find how many students landed at each of the five nodes in row 4, thereby generating the numbers in that row of Pascal's Triangle.

EXPLAIN 2

Solving a Real-World Problem Using Binomial Probabilities

CONNECT VOCABULARY EL

Have students relate the prefix *bi-* to the number two. A binomial expression has two terms. A binomial experiment has two outcomes. This connection should help students understand some of the essential terms in this lesson. Relate the prefix to binomial probability and the Binomial Theorem as well.

QUESTIONING STRATEGIES

Why are the probabilities multiplied by ${}_nC_r$? because that is the number of different ways the outcome could occur

INTEGRATE MATHEMATICAL PRACTICES

Focus on Math Connections

MP.1 Students have experience calculating probabilities for various types of experiments. Reinforce that in *binomial* experiments, each trial has only two possible outcomes. Compare this to the rolling of a number cube for which there are six possible outcomes. However, if the experiment is such that only rolling a 6 is considered a success, then the experiment is a binomial experiment.

AVOID COMMON ERRORS

Students may sometimes confuse p and q. Remind them that p is the probability of success and that q is the probability of failure, $1 - p$. Have them note that the sum of the probabilities they enter in the formula must be 1. Prompt them to consider and discuss why this is so.

For visually challenged students, have them consider that the loop in p faces forward, the loop in q faces backward.

Example 2 **One in 5 boats traveling down a river bypass a harbor at the mouth of the river and head out to sea. Currently, 4 boats are traveling down the river and approaching the mouth of the river.**

(A) What is the probability that exactly 2 of the 4 boats head out to sea?

The probability that a boat will head out to sea is $\frac{1}{5}$, or 0.2.

Substitute 4 for n, 2 for r, 0.2 for p, and 0.8 for q.

$$P(2) = {}_4C_2(0.2)^2(0.8)^{4-2}$$
$$= 6(0.2)^2(0.8)^2$$
$$= 6(0.04)(0.64)$$
$$= 0.1536$$

So, the probability that exactly 2 of the 4 boats will head out to sea is 0.1536, or 15.36%.

(B) What is the probability that at least 2 of the 4 boats will head out to sea?

To find the probability that at least 2 of the 4 boats will head out to sea, find the probability that 2, **3**, or **4** boats will head out to sea and add the probabilities.

From Part A, you know that $P(2) = 0.1536$.

$$P(3) = {}_4C_{\boxed{3}}(0.2)^{\boxed{3}}(0.8)^{\boxed{1}}$$
$$= 4\left(\boxed{0.008}\right)\left(\boxed{0.8}\right)$$
$$= \boxed{0.0256}$$

$$P(4) = {}_4C_{\boxed{4}}(0.2)^{\boxed{4}}(0.8)^{\boxed{0}}$$
$$= 1\left(\boxed{0.0016}\right)\left(\boxed{1}\right)$$
$$= \boxed{0.0016}$$

$$P(\text{at least } 2) = P(2 \text{ or } 3 \text{ or } 4)$$
$$= P(2) + P(3) + P(4)$$
$$= 0.1536 + \boxed{0.0256} + \boxed{0.0016}$$
$$= \boxed{0.1808}$$

So, the probability that at least 2 of the 4 boats will head out to sea is 0.1808, or 18.08%.

LANGUAGE SUPPORT EL

Communicate Math

Have students work in pairs to create and complete a poster with a large table showing the information below.

Term	Picture or Equation	Explanation
Binomial Theorem		
Binomial probability		
Binomial experiment		
Pascal's Triangle		

Reflect

9. In words, state the complement of the event that at least 2 of the 4 boats will head out to sea. Then find the probability of the complement.
The complement of the event that at least 2 of the 4 boats will head out to sea is the event that fewer than 2 boats will head out to sea. To find the probability of the complement, subtract the probability found in Part B from 1.
$P(\text{fewer than } 2) = 1 - 0.1808 = 0.9192$
So, the probability that fewer than 2 boats will head out to sea is 0.9192, or 91.92%.

Your Turn

10. Students are assigned randomly to 1 of 3 guidance counselors at a school. What is the probability that Ms. Banks, one of the school's guidance counselors, will get exactly 2 of the next 3 students assigned?
The probability that a student will be assigned to Ms. Banks is $\frac{1}{3}$.

$$P(2) = {}_3C_2\left(\frac{1}{3}\right)^2\left(\frac{2}{3}\right)^1$$
$$= 3\left(\frac{1}{9}\right)\left(\frac{2}{3}\right)$$
$$= \frac{2}{9} \approx 0.222$$

The probability that Ms. Banks will get exactly 2 of the next 3 students is $\frac{2}{9}$, or about 22.2%.

Elaborate

11. How do the numbers in one row of Pascal's Triangle relate to the numbers in the previous row?
The first and last numbers in a row of Pascal's Triangle are both 1. Every other number is the sum of the two numbers immediately above it in the previous row.

12. How does Pascal's Triangle relate to the power of a binomial?
For a binomial raised to the *n*th power, each term in the expanded form of the power includes a number in row *n* of Pascal's Triangle as a factor.

13. The expanded form of $(p + q)^3$ is $p^3 + 3p^2q + 3pq^2 + q^3$. In terms of a binomial experiment with a probability p of success and a probability q of failure on each trial, what do each of the terms p^3, $3p^2q$, $3pq^2$, and q^3 represent?
The terms p^3, $3p^2q$, $3pq^2$, and q^3 represent the probabilities of exactly 0, 1, 2, and 3 successes, respectively, in 3 trials of a binomial experiment.

14. **Essential Question Check-In** The Binomial Theorem says that the expanded form of $(a + b)^n$ is a sum of terms of the form ${}_nC_r a^{n-r} b^r$ for what values of r?
The values of *r* are 0, 1, 2, ..., *n*.

ELABORATE

INTEGRATE MATHEMATICAL PRACTICES

Focus on Critical Thinking

MP.3 Have students discuss why the number ${}_nC_r$ for particular values of n and r in Pascal's Triangle is the same number used for the coefficient of a binomial probability of exactly r successes in n trials. Prompt them to consider how they found the numbers in the triangle initially in the Explore, and the relationship to the meaning of the coefficient in the binomial probability.

CONNECT VOCABULARY EL

Ask students to use their own words to explain what *mutually exclusive events* are and to provide an example.

SUMMARIZE THE LESSON

How do you use the Binomial Theorem to expand powers of binomials? **To expand a binomial raised to the *n*th power, identify the values in row *n* of Pascal's Triangle. Expand the power as described in the Binomial Theorem, using the values from Pascal's Triangle as multipliers of the terms. Then simplify each term.**

EVALUATE

ASSIGNMENT GUIDE

Concepts and Skills	Practice
Explore 1 Generating Pascal's Triangle	Exercises 1, 24
Explore 2 Relating Pascal's Triangle to Powers of Binomials	Exercise 25
Example 1 Expanding Powers of Binomials Using the Binomial Theorem	Exercises 2–18, 23
Example 2 Solving a Real-World Problem Using Binomial Probabilities	Exercises 19–22, 26

COOPERATIVE LEARNING

Have students work in pairs to practice constructing Pascal's Triangle. Encourage them to look for patterns in the resulting triangle that can help them readily obtain the coefficients they need for any given binomial expansion or probability.

Evaluate: Homework and Practice

• Online Homework
• Hints and Help
• Extra Practice

1. The path LLRRLLR leads to which node in which row of Pascal's Triangle? What is the value of that node?

The path LLRLR leads to the fourth node in row 7. This node has a value of $15 + 20 = 35$ when Pascal's Triangle in Explore 1 is extended to row 7.

2. Without expanding the power, determine the middle term of $(a + b)^8$. Explain how you found your answer.

Since the coefficient is ${}_8C_4 = 70$, the exponents of a and b have a sum of 8, and the exponents of the middle term are the same when n is even, the middle term must be $70a^4b^4$.

Use the Binomial Theorem to expand each power of a binomial.

3. $(x + 6)^3$

$(x + 6)^3 = 1x^3(6)^0 + 3x^2(6)^1 + 3x^1(6)^2 + 1x^0(6)^3$

$= x^3 + 18x^2 + 108x + 216$

4. $(x - 5)^4$

$(x - 5)^4 = 1x^4(-5)^0 + 4x^3(-5)^1 + 6x^2(-5)^2 + 4x^1(-5)^3 + 1x^0(-5)^4$

$= x^4 - 20x^3 + 150x^2 - 500x + 625$

5. $(x + 3)^6$

$(x + 3)^6 = 1x^6(3)^0 + 6x^5(3)^1 + 15x^4(3)^2 + 20x^3(3)^3 + 15x^2(3)^4 + 6x^1(3)^5 + 1x^0(3)^6$

$= x^6 + 18x^5 + 135x^4 + 540x^3 + 1215x^2 + 1458x + 729$

6. $(2x - 1)^3$

$(2x - 1)^3 = 1(2x)^3(-1)^0 + 3(2x)^2(-1)^1 + 3(2x)^1(-1)^2 + 1(2x)^0(-1)^3$

$= 8x^3 - 12x^2 + 6x - 1$

7. $(3x + 4)^5$

$(3x + 4)^5 = 1(3x)^5(4)^0 + 5(3x)^4(4)^1 + 10(3x)^3(4)^2 + 10(3x)^2(4)^3 + 5(3x)^1(4)^4 + 1(3x)^0($

$= 243x^5 + 1620x^4 + 4320x^3 + 5760x^2 + 3840x + 1024$

8. $(2x - 3)^7$

$(2x - 3)^7 = 1(2x)^7(-3)^0 + 7(2x)^6(-3)^1 + 21(2x)^5(-3)^2 + 35(2x)^4(-3)^3 + 35(2x)^3(-3)^4$

$+ 21(2x)^2(-3)^5 + 7(2x)^1(-3)^6 + 1(2x)^0(-3)^7$

$= 128x^7 - 1344x^6 + 6048x^5 - 15{,}120x^4 + 22{,}680x^3 - 20{,}412x^2 + 10{,}206x - 2187$

Exercise	Depth of Knowledge (D.O.K.)	COMMON CORE Mathematical Practices
1–12	**1** Recall of Information	**MP.7** Using Structure
13–16	**1** Recall of Information	**MP.5** Using Tools
17–19	**1** Recall of Information	**MP.2** Reasoning
20	**2** Skills/Concepts	**MP.2** Reasoning
21	**1** Recall of Information	**MP.7** Using Structure
22–23	**1** Recall of Information	**MP.5** Using Tools

. $(x + 2y)^5$

$(x + 2y)^5 = 1x^5(2y)^0 + 5x^4(2y)^1 + 10x^3(2y)^2 + 10x^2(2y)^3 + 5x^1(2y)^4 + 1x^0(2y)^5$

$= x^5 + 10x^4y + 40x^3y^2 + 80x^2y^3 + 80xy^4 + 32y^5$

0. $(3x - y)^4$

$(3x - y)^4 = 1(3x)^4(-y)^0 + 4(3x)^3(-y)^1 + 6(3x)^2(-y)^2 + 4(3x)^1(-y)^3 + 1(3x)^0(-y)^4$

$= 81x^4 - 108x^3y + 54x^2y^2 - 12xy^3 + y^4$

1. $(5x + y)^4$

$(5x - y)^4 = 1(5x)^4y^0 + 4(5x)^3y^1 + 6(5x)^2y^2 + 4(5x)^1y^3 + 1(5x)^0y^4$

$= 625x^4 + 500x^3y + 150x^2y^2 + 20xy^3 + y^4$

2. $(x - 6y)^5$

$(x + 6y)^5 = 1x^5(-6y)^0 + 5x^4(-6y)^1 + 10x^3(-6y)^2 + 10x^2(-6y)^3 + 5x^1(-6y)^4 + 1x^0(-6y)^5$

$= x^5 - 30x^4y + 360x^3y^2 - 2160x^2y^3 + 6480xy^4 - 7776y^5$

3. $(5x - 4y)^3$

$(5x - 4y)^3 = 1(5x)^3(-4y)^0 + 3(5x)^2(-4y)^1 + 3(5x)^1(-4y)^2 + 1(5x)^0(-4y)^3$

$= 125x^3 - 300x^2y + 240xy^2 - 64y^3$

4. $(4x + 3y)^6$

$(4x + 3y)^6 = 1(4x)^6(3y)^0 + 6(4x)^5(3y)^1 + 15(4x)^4(3y)^2 + 20(4x)^3(3y)^3 + 15(4x)^2(3y)^4$

$+ 6(4x)^1(3y)^5 + 1(4x)^0(3y)^6$

$= 4096x^6 + 18{,}432x^5y + 34{,}560x^4y^2 + 34{,}560x^3y^3 + 19{,}440x^2y^4 + 5832xy^5 + 729y^6$

Use the Binomial Theorem to find the specified term of the given power of a binomial. (Remember that r starts at 0 in the Binomial Theorem, so finding, say, the second term means that $r = 1$.)

5. Find the fourth term in the expanded form of $(x - 1)^6$.

Let $n = 6$, $r = 3$, $a = x$, and $b = -1$ in ${}_nC_ra^{n-r}b^r$.

${}_6C_3x^{6-3}(-1)^3 = 20x^3(-1)^3 = -20x^3$

6. Find the second term in the expanded form of $(2x + 1)^4$.

Let $n = 4$, $r = 1$, $a = 2x$, and $b = 1$ in ${}_nC_ra^{n-r}b^r$.

${}_4C_1(2x)^{4-1}(1)^1 = 4(2x)^3(1)^1 = 32x^3$

7. Find the third term in the expanded form of $(3x - 2y)^5$.

Let $n = 5$, $r = 2$, $a = 3x$, and $b = 2y$ in ${}_nC_ra^{n-r}b^r$.

${}_5C_2(3x)^{5-2}(-2y)^2 = 10(3x)^3(-2y)^2 = 1080x^3y^2$

8. Find the fifth term in the expanded form of $(6x + 8y)^7$.

Let $n = 7$, $r = 4$, $a = 6x$, and $b = 8y$ in ${}_nC_ra^{n-r}b^r$.

${}_7C_4(6x)^{7-4}(8y)^4 = 35(6x)^3(8y)^4 = 30{,}965{,}760x^3y^4$

Exercise	Depth of Knowledge (D.O.K.)	COMMON CORE Mathematical Practices
24, 26	2 Skills/Concepts H.O.T.	MP.3 Logic
25	3 Strategic Thinking H.O.T.	MP.3 Logic

QUESTIONING STRATEGIES

If a term in a binomial being raised to a power has a coefficient other than 1, what happens to that coefficient when the power is expanded using the Binomial Theorem? **The coefficient is raised to the same power as the variable for each term and then multiplied by the corresponding value from Pascal's Triangle.**

AVOID COMMON ERRORS

Students may use the coefficients from the wrong row of Pascal's Triangle when expanding powers of binomials. Remind them that the coefficients needed for the expansion of $(a + b)^n$ will be found in the row of Pascal's Triangle that contains $n + 1$ numbers.

VISUAL CUES

Before they begin the expansion of a binomial raised to a power, some students may find it helpful to write out a fill-in-the-blank framework, such as

$(\_ + \_)^4 =$

$(\_)^4 + 4(\_)^3(\_) + 6(\_)^2(\_)^2 + 4(\_)(\_)^3 + (\_)^4.$

First, have them find the appropriate numbers from Pascal's Triangle. Then, they can fill in the exponents for the powers of the first term of the binomial in descending order: 4, 3, 2, 1, 0, and the exponents for the powers of the second term of the binomial in ascending order: 0, 1, 2, 3, 4. If the binomial has the form $(a - b)^n$, remind students to alternate the signs of the terms in the expansion, starting with a positive first term. They can then enter the values of a and b and simplify, being sure to apply each exponent to both the variable and its coefficient for variable terms.

INTEGRATE MATHEMATICAL PRACTICES

Focus on Critical Thinking

MP.3 To ensure that students understand the parameters that constitute a binomial experiment, have them brainstorm real-world situations that lend themselves to binomial probability contexts. Then ask them to discuss events for which it might be easier to find the probability of the *complement* of the event in order to determine the probability of the event itself, than to determine the probability of the event directly.

Ellen takes a multiple-choice quiz that has 5 questions, with 4 answer choices for each question.

19. What is the probability that she will get exactly 2 answers correct by guessing?

The probability that Ellen will get any one answer correct is $\frac{1}{4}$.

$P(2) = {}_5C_2\left(\frac{1}{4}\right)^2\left(\frac{3}{4}\right)^3 = 10\left(\frac{1}{26}\right)\left(\frac{27}{64}\right) = \frac{135}{512} \approx 0.264$

So, the probability that Ellen will get exactly 2 answers correct by guessing is $\frac{135}{512}$, or about 26.4%.

20. What is the probability that Ellen will get at least 3 answers correct by guessing?

$$P(3) = {}_5C_3\left(\frac{1}{4}\right)^3\left(\frac{3}{4}\right)^2 = 10\left(\frac{1}{64}\right)\left(\frac{9}{16}\right) = \frac{45}{512}$$

$$P(4) = {}_5C_4\left(\frac{1}{4}\right)^4\left(\frac{3}{4}\right)^1 = 5\left(\frac{1}{256}\right)\left(\frac{3}{4}\right) = \frac{15}{1024}$$

$$P(5) = {}_5C_5\left(\frac{1}{4}\right)^5\left(\frac{3}{4}\right)^0 = 1\left(\frac{1}{1024}\right)(1) = \frac{1}{1024}$$

$$\begin{aligned} P(\text{at least } 3) &= P(3 \text{ or } 4 \text{ or } 5) \\ &= P(3) + P(4) + P(5) \\ &= \frac{45}{512} + \frac{15}{1024} + \frac{1}{1024} = \frac{53}{512} \approx 0.104 \end{aligned}$$

So, the probability that Ellen will get at least 3 answers correct by guessing is $\frac{53}{512}$ or about 10.4%.

Manufacturing A machine that makes a part used in cars has a 98% probability of producing the part within acceptable tolerance levels. The machine makes 25 parts per hour.

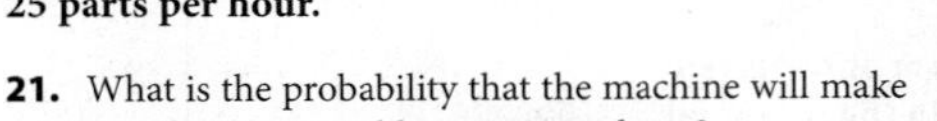

21. What is the probability that the machine will make exactly 20 acceptable parts in an hour?

The probability that the machine will make an acceptable part is 0.98.

$P(20) = {}_{25}C_{20}\,(0.98)^{20}\,(0.02)^5 \approx 0.000114$

The probability that the machine will produce exactly 20 acceptable parts is about 0.000114, or about 0.0114%.

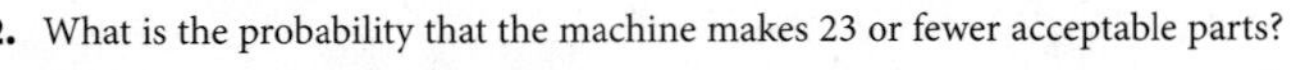

22. What is the probability that the machine makes 23 or fewer acceptable parts?

$$\begin{aligned} P(23 \text{ or fewer}) &= 1 - P(24 \text{ or } 25) = 1 - [P(24) + P(25)] \\ &= 1 - [{}_{25}C_{24}\,(0.98)^{24}\,(0.02)^1 + {}_{25}C_{25}\,(0.98)^{25}\,(0.02)^0] \\ &\approx 1 - [0.3079 + 0.6035] = 0.0886 \end{aligned}$$

So, the probability that the machine will produce 23 or fewer acceptable parts is about 0.0886, or about 8.86%.

23. Match each term of an expanded power of a binomial on the right with the corresponding description of the term on the left. (Remember that r starts at 0 in the Binomial Theorem, so finding, say, the second term means that $r = 1$.)

A. Fifth term in the expanded form of $(x + 2)^6$	B	$640x^2$
B. Fourth term in the expanded form of $(x + 4)^5$	D	$48x^2$
C. Third term in the expanded form of $(x + 8)^4$	A	$240x^2$
D. Second term in the expanded form of $(x + 16)^3$	C	$384x^2$

A. Fifth term: $_6C_4x^{6-4}(2)^4 = 15x^2(16) = 240x^2$
B. Fourth term: $_5C_3x^{5-3}(4)^3 = 10x^2(64) = 640x^2$
C. Third term: $_4C_2x^{4-2}(8)^2 = 6x^2(64) = 384x^2$
D. Third term: $_3C_1x^{3-1}(16)^1 = 3x^2(16) = 48x^2$

H.O.T. Focus on Higher Order Thinking

24. Construct Arguments Identify the symmetry in the rows of Pascal's Triangle and give an argument based on strings of Ls and Rs to explain why the symmetry exists.

When presented in a tree diagram as in Explore 1, Pascal's Triangle has reflection symmetry in the vertical line that passes through the node at the top of the tree. This means that in any row n, $_nC_r = {}_nC_{n-r}$. The symmetry exists because for each string of Ls and Rs that takes you to a node on the left side of the line of symmetry, you can replace each L with an R and each R with an L to obtain a string that takes you to the corresponding node (in the same row) on the right side of the line of symmetry. For instance, in row 4, the string LLRL takes you to the node in position 1, while the "mirror-image" string RRLR takes you to the node in position 3. This means that there will be the same number of pathways to get to position 1 as there are to get to position 3, so $_4C_1 = {}_4C_{4-1}$.

25. Communicate Mathematical Ideas Explain why the numbers from Pascal's Triangle show up in the Binomial Theorem.

If you think of a tree diagram like the one for Pascal's Triangle but with *a* and *b* substituted for L and R, you can see that a pathway from the top of the tree down to the node in, say, position 2 (counting from 0) of row 5, generates a string such as *aabab*, which is one way to produce the term with the variable part a^3b^2 in the expanded form of $(a + b)^5$. (In essence, the string *aabab* tells you to use the *a*-terms from the first, second, and fourth factors in the product $(a + b)(a + b)(a + b)(a + b)(a + b)$ and to use the *b*-terms from the third and fifth factors.) There are 9 other pathways that lead to position 2 of row 5: *bbaaa, abbaa, aabba, aaabb, baaab, abaab, baaba, ababa,* and *babaa*. So, there is a total of 10, or $_5C_2$, ways to produce the term with the variable part a^3b^2, which means that a^3b^2 has a coefficient of $_5C_2$. In general, the term in the expanded form of $(a + b)^n$ with the variable part $a^{n-r}b^r$ has the coefficient $_nC_r$, which is what the Binomial Theorem tells you.

WORLD HISTORY

Students may be interested to learn more about Blaise Pascal and Pascal's Triangle. Born in 1623, Pascal was a child prodigy who was building calculating machines by the time he was a teenager. The computer programming language Pascal is named for him. Encourage students to look for other patterns in Pascal's Triangle, such as horizontal sums (the rows add to powers of 2) and patterns that form the Fibonacci sequence.

MULTIPLE REPRESENTATIONS

In higher mathematics, the notation $\binom{n}{r}$ is used instead of $_nC_r$. Students might create a version of Pascal's Triangle using this notation.

JOURNAL

Have students describe the steps they would take to expand $(3c + 2d)^4$ using the Binomial Theorem.

26. Represent Real-World Situations A small airline overbooks flights on the assumption that some passengers will not show up. The probability that a passenger shows up is 0.8. What number of tickets can the airline sell for a 20-seat flight and still have a probability of seating everyone that is at least 90%? Explain your reasoning.

For the probability that everyone is seated to be at least 90%, the probability that too many passengers show up must be no more than 10%. First, consider the case where 21 tickets are sold and 21 passengers show up:

$$P(\text{21 passengers show up}) = {}_{21}C_{21}(0.8)^{21}(0.2)^0 \approx 1(0.0092)(1) = 0.0092 = 0.92\%$$

Next, consider the case where 22 tickets are sold and either 21 or 22 passengers show up:

$$\begin{aligned} P(\text{21 or 22 passengers show up}) &= P(21) + P(22) \\ &= {}_{22}C_{21}(0.8)^{21}(0.2)^1 + {}_{22}C_{22}(0.8)^{22}(0.2)^0 \\ &\approx 22(0.0092)(0.2) + 1(0.0074)(1) \\ &\approx 0.0405 + 0.0074 \\ &= 0.0479 = 4.79\% \end{aligned}$$

Next, consider the case where 23 tickets are sold and 21, 22, or 23 passengers show up:

$$\begin{aligned} P(\text{21, 22, or 23 passengers show up}) &= P(21) + P(22) + P(23) \\ &= {}_{23}C_{21}(0.8)^{21}(0.2)^2 + {}_{23}C_{22}(0.8)^{22}(0.2)^1 \\ &\quad + {}_{23}C_{23}(0.8)^{23}(0.2)^0 \\ &\approx 0.0931 + 0.0340 + 0.0059 \\ &= 0.1330 = 13.3\% \end{aligned}$$

So, the airline can sell 22 tickets for a 20-seat flight and still have a probability of seating everyone that is at least 90%.

Lesson Performance Task

Suppose that a basketball player has just been fouled while attempting a 3-point shot and is awarded three free throws. Given that the player is 85% successful at making free throws, calculate the probability that the player successfully makes zero, one, two, or all three of the free throws. Which situation is most likely to occur?

The number of trials, or free throws, the player gets is 3, so let $n = 3$. The player's probability of success is 0.85, so $p = 0.85$. This means the player's probability of failure is $1 - 0.85 = 0.15$. So, $q = 0.15$. Find the binomial probabilities of making the possible numbers of free throws.

Player makes zero free throws:

The number of successes is 0, so $r = 0$.

$$P(0) = {}_3C_0(0.85)^0(0.15)^{3-0} = 1(1)(0.003375) = 0.003375$$

The probability that the player makes zero free throws is 0.3375%.

Player makes one free throw:

The number of successes is 1, so $r = 1$.

$$P(1) = {}_3C_1(0.85)^1(0.15)^{3-1} = 3(0.85)(0.0225) = 0.057375$$

The probability that the player makes one free throw is 5.7375%.

Player makes two free throws:

The number of successes is 2, so $r = 2$.

$$P(2) = {}_3C_2(0.85)^2(0.15)^{3-2} = 3(0.7225)(0.15) = 0.325125$$

The probability that the player makes two free throws is 32.5125%.

Player makes three free throws:

The number of successes is 3, so $r = 3$.

$$P(3) = {}_3C_3(0.85)^3(0.15)^{3-3} = 1(0.614125)(1) = 0.614125$$

The probability that the player makes all three free throws is 61.4125%.

Because 61.4125% is the highest probability, the player is most likely to make all three free throws.

EXTENSION ACTIVITY

Have students consider what free-throw shooting percentage gives a player better than a 50% chance of making all or none of any number of free throws. For example, have them find what free-throw shooting percentage gives a player a better than 50% chance of making both of two free throws, and what percentage gives a player better than a 50% chance of making all three of three free throws. Then have students consider a better than 50% chance of missing both or of missing all three. Students can generalize these results. **When $P > \sqrt{0.5}$, the chance of making 2 of 2 free throws is greater than 50%, so $P > 70.7\%$. When $P > \sqrt[3]{0.5}$, the chance of making 3 of 3 free throws is greater than 50%, so $P > 79.4\%$. The chances of missing both or of missing all three are these numbers subtracted from 100%: 29.3% and 20.6%.**

AVOID COMMON ERRORS

Students may neglect to include the binomial coefficients in their calculations. This will not cause incorrect probabilities when $r = n$ or when $r = 0$, because ${}_nC_r = 1$ in these cases, but it will cause incorrect probabilities in all other cases. Remind students that there is more than one way to make or miss 2 of 3 free throws, so the binomial coefficient must be used as a multiplier to account for these ways. It will help them remember to always write the binomial coefficient, even when they know the value is 1.

INTEGRATE MATHEMATICAL PRACTICES

Focus on Technology

MP.5 Graphing calculators can evaluate binomial coefficients. To evaluate ${}_7C_3$ using the appropriate keys and menus, use the sequence 7, ***nCr***, 3 **ENTER**.

Scoring Rubric

2 points: Student correctly solves the problem and explains his/her reasoning.

1 point: Student shows good understanding of the problem but does not fully solve or explain his/her reasoning.

0 points: Student does not demonstrate understanding of the problem.

LESSON 6.4

Factoring Polynomials

Common Core Math Standards

The student is expected to:

 **A-SSE.A.2**

Use the structure of an expression to identify ways to rewrite it. Also N-CN.C.8(+), A-SSE.A.1a, A-APR.B.3, A-CED.A.1

Mathematical Practices

 **MP.8 Patterns**

Language Objective

Work with a partner to complete a chart detailing how factoring can be used.

ENGAGE

Essential Question: What are some ways to factor a polynomial, and how is factoring useful?

Possible answer: Methods include factoring out the greatest common monomial factor, recognizing special factoring patterns, and factoring by grouping. Factoring is useful when solving polynomial equations because the zero-product property can be applied to the factored polynomial on one side of the equation as long as the other side is 0.

PREVIEW: LESSON PERFORMANCE TASK

View the Engage section online. Discuss the photo and how the volume of the flower bed is related to its outer and inner dimensions. Then preview the Lesson Performance Task.

Name ______________ Class ______________ Date ______________

6.4 Factoring Polynomials

Essential Question: What are some ways to factor a polynomial, and how is factoring useful?

Resource Locker

Explore Analyzing a Visual Model for Polynomial Factorization

Factoring a polynomial of degree n involves finding factors of lesser a degree that can be multiplied together to produce the polynomial. When a polynomial has degree 3, for example, you can think of it as a rectangular prism whose dimensions you need to determine.

(A) The volumes of the parts of the rectangular prism are as follows:

Red: $V = x^3$

Green: $V = 2x^2$

Yellow: $V = 8x$

Blue: $V = 4x^2$

Total volume: $V = x^3 + 6x^2 + 8x$

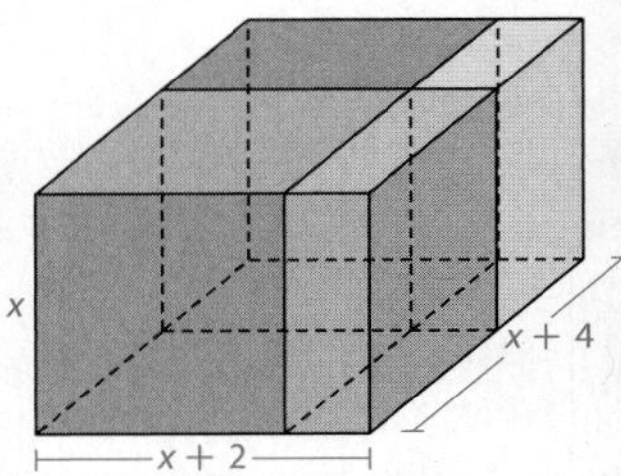

Volume $= x^3 + 6x^2 + 8x$

(B) The volume of the red piece is found by cubing the length of one side. What is the height of this piece?

x

(C) The volume of a rectangular prism is $V = lwh$, where l is the length, w is the width, and h is the height of the prism. Notice that the green prism shares two sides with the cube. What are the lengths of these two sides?

x and x

(D) What is the length of the third side of the green prism?

Divide by both of the known dimensions to find the missing side length. $\frac{2x^2}{x \cdot x} = 2$

The length of the last side is 2.

(E) You showed that the width of the cube is $\underline{x}$ and the width of the green prism is $\underline{2}$. What is the width of the entire prism?

$x + 2$

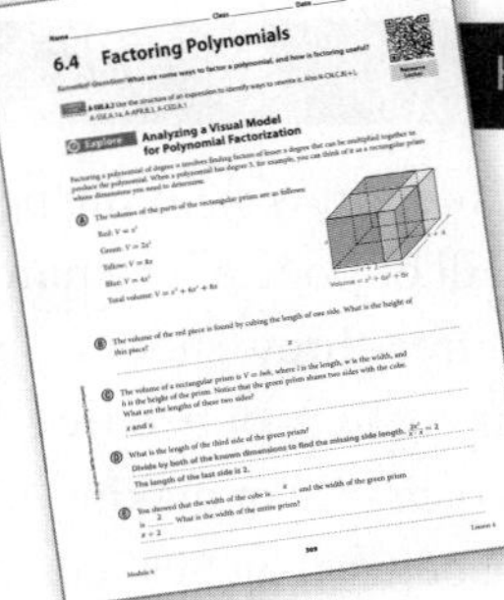

HARDCOVER PAGES 309–320

Watch for the hardcover student edition page numbers for this lesson.

Ⓕ You determined that the length of the green piece is x. Use the volume of the yellow piece and the information you have derived to find the length of the prism.

Since the volume of the yellow piece is 8x, the height of the yellow piece is x, and the width of the yellow piece is 2, simply divide out to find that the last remaining side length is 4.

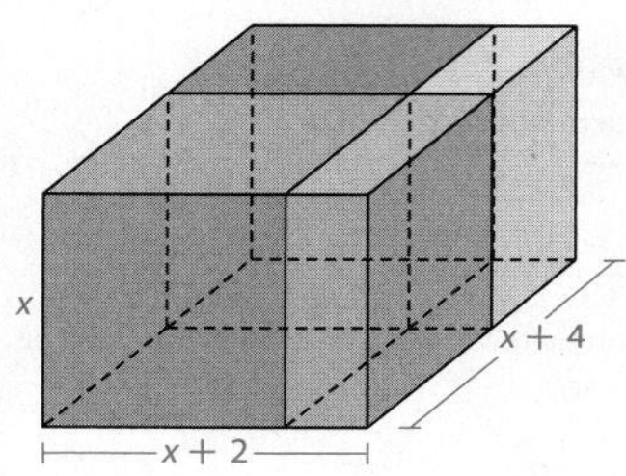

Volume $= x^3 + 6x^2 + 8x$

Ⓖ Since the dimensions of the overall prism are x, $x + 2$, and $x + 4$, the volume of the overall prism can be rewritten in factored form as $V = (x)(x + 2)(x + 4)$. Multiply these polynomials together to verify that this is equal to the original given expression for the volume of the overall figure.

$V = x^3 + 6x^2 + 8x$

Reflect

1. **Discussion** What is one way to double the volume of the prism?
Sample Answer: One way to double the volume of the prism is to double the height of the prism.

Explain 1 Factoring Out the Greatest Common Monomial First

Most polynomials cannot be *factored over the integers*, which means to find factors that use only integer coefficients. But when a polynomial can be factored, each factor has a degree less than the polynomial's degree. While the goal is to write the polynomial as a product of linear factors, this is not always possible. When a factor of degree 2 or greater cannot be factored further, it is called an **irreducible factor**.

Example 1 Factor each polynomial over the integers.

Ⓐ $6x^3 + 15x^2 + 6x$

$6x^3 + 15x^2 + 6x$	Write out the polynomial.
$x(6x^2 + 15x + 6)$	Factor out a common monomial, an x.
$3x(2x^2 + 5x + 2)$	Factor out a common monomial, a 3.
$x(2x + 1)(x + 2)$	Factor into simplest terms.

Note: The second and third steps can be combined into one step by factoring out the greatest common monomial.

PROFESSIONAL DEVELOPMENT

Integrate Mathematical Practices

This lesson provides an opportunity to address Mathematical Practice **MP.8**, which calls for students to "look for and express regularity in repeated reasoning." Students are already familiar with multiplying polynomials but, in this lesson, they must analyze the conditions that help them factor a polynomial, or rewrite it as the product of individual factors of lesser degree. These factors, when multiplied, give the original polynomial. Many methods of factoring, including special factoring patterns, are presented so that students can analyze the polynomial and explain which method gives the factorization more easily. Factoring polynomials is a useful tool for solving polynomial equations by using the zero-product property.

EXPLORE

Analyzing a Visual Model for Polynomial Factorization

INTEGRATE TECHNOLOGY

Students have the option of completing the polynomial factorization activity either in the book or online.

QUESTIONING STRATEGIES

How is factoring useful when determining the variable dimensions of a polynomial model like a rectangular prism? **Factoring is useful when the volumes of parts of a three-dimensional model are known and can be added to get the variable dimensions of the figure. Since factoring is the opposite of multiplying, the polynomial can then be written in factored form and multiplied to give the volume of the whole figure.**

EXPLAIN 1

Factoring Out the Greatest Common Monomial First

AVOID COMMON ERRORS

Students often forget to factor out the greatest common monomial as the first step in factoring. Point out that if the terms of a polynomial have a greatest common factor, it almost always should be factored first, before analyzing the remainder of the terms for factoring. Emphasize that sometimes finding the greatest common factor is the only way to factor some polynomials.

QUESTIONING STRATEGIES

How can you tell if the terms of a polynomial have a greatest common factor? **Each of the terms has a number that divides all of the terms and/or a power of a variable that divides each term. The common monomial factor is a product of this number and the power of one or more of the variables.**

What does it mean for a polynomial to be "factored completely"? **The greatest monomial factor is factored out and the remaining polynomial is factored into factors that cannot be factored further: they are *irreducible*.**

EXPLAIN 2

Recognizing Special Factoring Patterns

INTEGRATE MATHEMATICAL PRACTICES

Focus on Patterns

MP.8 Students should review the factoring patterns they learned in Algebra 1, including: difference of two squares: $a^2 - b^2 = (a + b)(a - b)$; and perfect square trinomials: $a^2 + 2ab + b^2 = (a + b)^2$ and $a^2 - 2ab + b^2 = (a - b)^2$. Emphasize that there are two more useful factoring patterns in this lesson: sum of two cubes: $a^3 + b^3 = (a + b)(a^2 - ab + b^2)$ and difference of two cubes: $a^3 - b^3 = (a - b)(a^2 + ab + b^2)$. Students should see that each of the factors is irreducible.

(B) $2x^3 - 20x$

$\underline{2x}^{\,3} - \underline{20}\,x$ — Write out the polynomial.

$\underline{2x}\,(x^2 - 10)$ — Factor out the greatest common monomial.

Reflect

2. Why wasn't the factor $x^2 - 10$ further factored?
Since 10 does not have any two factors that sum to 0, $(x^2 - 10)$ is irreducible over the integers.

3. Consider what happens when you factor $x^2 - 10$ over the real numbers and not merely the integers. Find a such that $x^2 - 10 = (x - a)(x + a)$.
$a = \sqrt{10}$

Your Turn

4. $3x^3 + 7x^2 + 4x$

$x(3x^2 + 7x + 4)$ — **Factor out a common monomial, an x.**

$x(3x + 4)(x + 1)$ — **Factor into simplest terms.**

Explain 2 Recognizing Special Factoring Patterns

Remember the factoring patterns you already know:

Difference of two squares: $a^2 - b^2 = (a + b)(a - b)$

Perfect square trinomials: $a^2 + 2ab + b^2 = (a + b)^2$ and $a^2 - 2ab + b^2 = (a - b)^2$

There are two other factoring patterns that will prove useful:

Sum of two cubes: $a^3 + b^3 = (a + b)(a^2 - ab + b^2)$

Difference of two cubes: $a^3 - b^3 = (a - b)(a^2 + ab + b^2)$

Notice that in each of the new factoring patterns, the quadratic factor is irreducible over the integers.

Example 2 **Factor the polynomial using a factoring pattern.**

(A) $27x^3 + 64$

$27x^3 + 64$ — Write out the polynomial.

$27x^3 = (3x)^3$ — Check if $27x^3$ is a perfect cube.

$64 = (4)^3$ — Check if 64 is a perfect cube.

$a^3 + b^3 = (a + b)(a^2 - ab + b^2)$ — Use the sum of two cubes formula to factor.

$(3x)^3 + 4^3 = (3x + 4)((3x)^2 - (3x)(4) + 4^2)$

$27x^3 + 64 = (3x + 4)(9x^2 - 12x + 16)$

COLLABORATIVE LEARNING

Small Group Activity

Help groups of students review the factoring patterns they learned in previous courses along with how to factor the sum or difference of two cubes. Provide each student with an example of one type of factoring, and ask them to show and explain the first step in factoring their problem. Then they pass the problem to another student, who writes the next step and explains it. They continue to pass the problem until each problem is completely factored and all steps are explained. Encourage them to use these as examples of the types of factoring when they write about factoring in their journals.

(B) $8x^3 - 27$

$8\underline{x}^3 - 27$	Write out the polynomial.
$8x^3 = (\underline{2}x)^3$	Check if $8x^3$ is a perfect cube.
$27 = (\underline{3})^3$	Check if 27 is a perfect cube.
$a^3 - b^3 = (a-b)(a^2 + ab + b^2)$	Use the difference of two cubes formula to factor.
$8x^3 - 27 = (\underline{2}x - \underline{3})(\underline{4}x^2 + \underline{6}x + \underline{9})$	

Reflect

5. The equation $8x^3 - 27 = 0$ has three roots. How many of them are real, what are they, and how many are nonreal?

To find the roots of the given expression, notice that the expression is the difference of cubes. Use the difference of cubes formula to factor $8x^3 - 23$

$8x^3 - 27 = (2x-3)(4x^2 + 6x + 9)$

To find the first root, set $2x - 3$ equal to 0 and solve for x.

$2x - 3 = 0$

$2x = 3$

$x = \frac{3}{2}$

Therefore $\frac{3}{2}$ is a real root. Next, look at $4x^2 + 6x + 9$ Notice that because the polynomial is irreducible over the integers, the quadratic formula must be used to solve for the roots.

$$x = \frac{-6 \pm \sqrt{6^2 - 4(4)(9)}}{2(4)}$$

$$= \frac{-6 \pm \sqrt{36 - 144}}{8}$$

$$= \frac{-6 \pm \sqrt{-108}}{8}$$

As the number under the square root symbol is negative, both of the values of x will be nonreal numbers. Therefore, the one real root is $\frac{3}{2}$ and two roots are nonreal.

Your Turn

6. $40x^4 + 5x$

$40x^4 + 5x$	**Write out the polynomial.**
$5x(8x^3 + 1)$	**Factor out $5x$.**
$8x^3 = (2x)^3$	**Check if $8x^3$ is a perfect cube.**
$1 = (1)^3$	**Check if 1 is a perfect cube.**
$a^3 + b^3 = (a+b)(a^2 - ab + b^2)$	**Use the formula to factor.**
$8x^3 + 1 = (2x+1)(4x^2 - 2x + 1)$	
$5x(8x^3 + 1) = 5x(2x+1)(4x^2 - 2x + 1)$	
$40x^4 + 5x = 5x(2x+1)(4x^2 - 2x + 1)$	

QUESTIONING STRATEGIES

What are the steps for using the sum or difference of cubes formulas to factor? **Factor out the greatest monomial factor, rewrite as the sum or difference of perfect cubes, and then apply the sum or difference of cubes formula.**

DIFFERENTIATE INSTRUCTION

Communicating Math

Give groups of students several different polynomials to factor. Have all students explain their reasoning or describe the procedures they used to factor the polynomial completely. Encourage them to make visual aids or graphic organizers to help them with their explanations. Ask for a volunteer from each group to summarize to the class how to factor a polynomial.

EXPLAIN 3

Factoring by Grouping

AVOID COMMON ERRORS

Students may not have a systematic approach to factoring. They will find it easier to factor by grouping if they use a strategy of looking for a common monomial factor, checking the factoring patterns, checking if factoring by grouping applies to their problem, and so on.

QUESTIONING STRATEGIES

? How do you factor a polynomial by grouping? **Rearrange the terms so that when they are grouped they will have common factors; group the terms; factor each group, using factoring patterns if necessary; then rearrange and assemble the factors using the distributive property.**

EXPLAIN 4

Solving a Real-World Problem by Factoring a Polynomial

INTEGRATE MATHEMATICAL PRACTICES

Focus on Math Connections

MP.1 Discuss with students how to use the zero-product property in the context of factoring and solving a real-world polynomial equation. Tell them that once a polynomial equation is established that models the real-world situation, then they apply the known information to the polynomial and rewrite it in a form (with zero on one side) that makes it possible to factor and solve the polynomial using the zero-product property.

Explain 3 Factoring by Grouping

Another technique for factoring a polynomial is grouping. If the polynomial has pairs of terms with common factors, factor by grouping terms with common factors and then factoring out the common factor from each group. Then look for a common factor of the groups in order to complete the factorization of the polynomial.

Example 3 **Factor the polynomial by grouping.**

(A) $x^3 + x^2 + x + 1$

Write out the polynomial.	$x^3 - x^2 + x - 1$
Group by common factor.	$(x^3 - x^2) + (x - 1)$
Factor.	$x^2(x - 1) + 1(x - 1)$
Regroup.	$(x^2 + 1)(x - 1)$

(B) $x^4 + x^3 + x + 1$

Write out the polynomial.	$x^4 + x^3 + x + 1$
Group by common factor.	$(\underline{x^4} + \underline{x^3}) + (x + 1)$
Factor.	$\underline{x^3}(x + 1) + \underline{1}(x + 1)$
Regroup.	$(\underline{x^3} + \underline{1})(x + 1)$
Apply sum of two cubes to the first term.	$(\underline{x^2} - \underline{x} + 1)(x + 1)(x + 1)$
Substitute this into the expression and simplify.	$(\underline{x + 1})^2(\underline{x^2} - \underline{x} + 1)$

Your Turn

7. $x^3 + 3x^2 + 3x + 2$

$x^3 + 3x^2 + 3x + 2$	**Write out the polynomial.**
$(x^3 + 2x^2) + (x^3 + 3x + 3)$	**Group by common factor.**
$x^2(x + 2) + (x + 1)(x + 2)$	**Factor.**
$(x^2 + x + 1)(x + 2)$	**Regroup.**

Explain 4 Solving a Real-World Problem by Factoring a Polynomial

Remember that the zero-product property is used in solving factorable quadratic equations. It can also be used in solving factorable polynomial equations.

Example 4 **Write and solve a polynomial equation for the situation described.**

A water park is designing a new pool in the shape of a rectangular prism. The sides and bottom of the pool are made of material 5 feet thick. The length must be twice the height (depth), and the interior width must be three times the interior height. The volume of the box must be 6000 cubic feet. What are the exterior dimensions of the pool?

The dimensions of the interior of the pool, as described by the problem, are the following:

$h = x - 5$

$w = 3x - 15$

$l = 2x - 10$

The formula for volume of a rectangular prism is $V = lwh$. Plug the values into the volume equation.

$V = (x - 5)(3x - 15)(2x - 10)$

$V = (x - 5)(6x^2 - 60x + 150)$

$V = 6x^3 - 90x^2 + 450x - 750$

Now solve for $V = 6000$.

$6000 = 6x^3 - 90x^2 + 450x - 750$

$0 = 6x^3 - 90x^2 + 450x - 6750$

Factor the resulting new polynomial.

$6x^3 - 90x^2 + 450x - 6750$

$= 6x^2(x - 15) + 450(x - 15)$

$= (6x^2 + 450)(x - 15)$

The only real root is $x = 15$.

The interior height of the pool will be 10 feet, the interior width 30 feet, and the interior length 20 feet. Therefore, the exterior height is 15 feet, the exterior length is 30 feet, and the exterior width is 40 feet.

Engineering To build a hefty wooden feeding trough for a zoo, its sides and bottom should be 2 feet thick, and its outer length should be twice its outer width and height.

What should the outer dimensions of the trough be if it is to hold 288 cubic feet of water?

Volume = Interior Length(feet) · Interior Width(feet) · Interior Height(feet)

$288 = (\underline{2x} - 4)(\underline{x} - 4)(\underline{x} - 2)$

$288 = \underline{2}x^3 - \underline{16}x^2 + \underline{40}x - \underline{32}$

$0 = \underline{2}x^3 - \underline{16}x^2 + \underline{40}x - \underline{320}$

$0 = \underline{2x^2}(x - \underline{8}) + \underline{40}(x - \underline{8})$

$0 = \underline{2}(x^2 + \underline{20})(x - \underline{8})$

The only real solution is $x = \underline{8}$. The trough is $\underline{16}$ feet long, $\underline{8}$ feet wide, and $\underline{8}$ feet high.

QUESTIONING STRATEGIES

? How is the zero-product property used to solve a polynomial equation? **The polynomial equation is rewritten so that 0 is on one side, and then the equation is factored. The zero-product property states that if each factor is set equal to zero and solved, then the values obtained are solutions to the original polynomial equation.**

ELABORATE

QUESTIONING STRATEGIES

How do you determine whether a polynomial is not factorable? **First determine that the terms do not have a common factor, that no factoring pattern applies to the terms of the polynomial, and that there is no other way to rewrite the polynomial as the product of irreducible factors.**

COGNITIVE STRATEGIES

To help students remember the formulas for the sum and difference of cubes, you may wish to use the mnemonic device SOPPS for the order of the terms in the second factor:

Square Opposite-sign Product Plus Square.

SUMMARIZE THE LESSON

Have students make a graphic organizer that lists their own methods of factoring a polynomial completely. The lists should include factoring out the greatest monomial factor, applying rules for factoring the sum and difference of two cubes, and previously learned rules such as factoring the difference of two squares.

Your Turn

8. **Engineering** A new shed is being designed in the shape of a rectangular prism. The shed's side and bottom should be 3 feet thick. Its outer length should be twice its outer width and height.
What should the outer dimensions of the shed be if it is to have 972 cubic feet of space?

Volume = Interior Length(feet) · Interior Width(feet) · Interior Height(feet)

$972 = (2x - 6)(x - 6)(x - 3)$

$972 = 2x^3 - 24x^2 + 90x - 108$

$0 = 2x^3 - 24x^2 + 90x - 1080$

$0 = 2x^2(x - 12) + 90(x - 12)$

$0 = 2(x^2 + 45)(x - 12)$

The only real solution is $x = 12$. The shed is 24 feet long, 12 feet wide, and 12 feet high.

Elaborate

9. Describe how the method of grouping incorporates the method of factoring out the greatest common monomial.
By grouping, you are treating a binomial common to both groups as a monomial to be factored out.

10. How do you decide if an equation fits in the sum of two cubes pattern?
If there are two terms in the equation being summed together and these terms are perfect cubes, then it fits the sum of two cubes pattern.

11. How can factoring be used to solve a polynomial equation of the form $p(x) = a$, where a is a nonzero constant?
Subtract a to get $p(x) - a = 0$. Factor out common monomials or use grouping to factor the polynomial.

12. **Essential Question Check-In** What are two ways to factor a polynomial?
Recognizing special factoring patterns and factoring by grouping

LANGUAGE SUPPORT EL

Connect Vocabulary

Have students work together to complete a table like the one shown.

Useful Ways to Factor Polynomials	
Perfect square trinomials:	$a^2 + 2ab + b^2 = (a + b)^2$ and $a^2 - 2ab + b^2 = (a - b)^2$
Sum of two cubes:	$a^3 + b^3 = (a + b)(a^2 - ab + b^2)$
Difference of two cubes:	$a^3 - b^3 = (a - b)(a^2 + ab + b^2)$

Evaluate: Homework and Practice

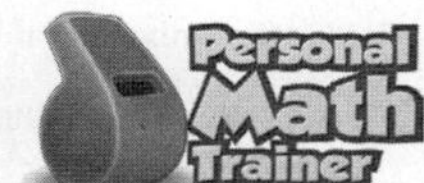

- Online Homework
- Hints and Help
- Extra Practice

Factor the polynomial, or identify it as irreducible.

1. $x^3 + x^2 - 12x$

$x(x^2 + x - 12)$

$x(x + 4)(x - 3)$

2. $x^3 + 5$

Irreducible.

3. $x^3 - 125$

$x^3 = (1x)^3$

$125 = (5)^3$

$a^3 - b^3 = (a - b)(a^2 + ab + b^2)$

$x^3 - 125 = (x - 5)(x^2 + 5x + 25)$

4. $x^3 + 5x^2 + 6x$

$x(x^2 + 5x + 6)$

$x((x^2 + 2x) + (3x + 6))$

$x(x(x + 2) + 3(x + 2))$

$x(x + 2)(x + 3)$

5. $8x^3 + 125$

$8x^3 = (2x)^3 \quad 125 = (5)^3$

$a^3 + b^3 = (a + b)(a^2 - ab + b^2)$

$8x^3 + 125 = (2x + 5)(4x^2 - 10x + 25)$

6. $2x^3 + 6x$

$2x^3 + 6x$

$2x(x^2 + 3)$

7. $216x^3 + 64$

$8(27x^3 + 8)$

$27x^3 = (3x)^3 \quad 8 = (2)^3$

$a^3 + b^3 = (a + b)(a^2 - ab + b^2)$

$216x^3 + 64 = 8(3x + 2)(9x^2 - 6x + 4)$

8. $8x^3 - 64$

$8(x^3 - 8)$

$8(x - 2)(x^2 - 2x + 4)$

9. $10x^3 - 80$

$10(x^3 - 8)$

$x^3 = (1x)^3 \quad 8 = (2)^3$

$a^3 - b^3 = (a - b)(a^2 + ab + b^2)$

$10x^3 - 80 = 10(x - 2)(x^2 + 2x + 4)$

10. $2x^4 + 7x^3 + 5x^2$

$x^2(2x^2 + 7x + 5)$

$x^2((2x^2 + 5x) + (2x + 5))$

$x^2(x(2x + 5) + 1(2x + 5))$

$x^2(x + 1)(2x + 5)$

11. $x^3 + 10x^2 + 16x$

$x(x^2 + 10x + 16)$

$x((x^2 + 2x) + (8x + 16))$

$x(x(x + 2) + 8(x + 2))$

$x(x + 2)(x + 8)$

12. $x^3 + 9769$

Irreducible.

Exercise	Depth of Knowledge (D.O.K.)	COMMON CORE Mathematical Practices
1–18	**1** Recall of Information	**MP.5** Using Tools
19–22	**2** Skills/Concepts	**MP.4** Modeling
23	**1** Recall of Information	**MP.2** Reasoning
24	**1** Recall of Information	**MP.3** Logic
25–26	**2** Skills/Concepts	**MP.3** Logic
27–29	**3** Strategic Thinking H.O.T.	**MP.2** Reasoning

EVALUATE

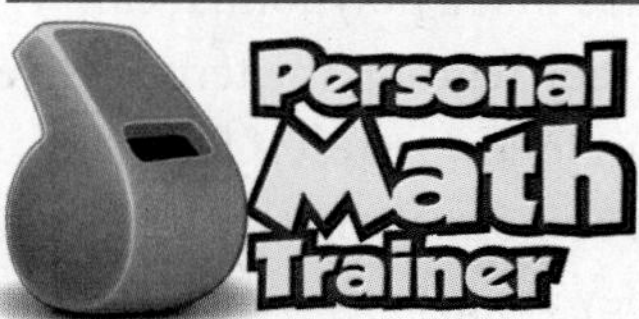

ASSIGNMENT GUIDE

Concepts and Skills	Practice
Explore Analyzing a Visual Model for Polynomial Factorization	
Example 1 Factoring Out the Greatest Common Monomial Factor First	Exercises 1–2, 4, 6, 10–12
Example 2 Recognizing Special Factoring Patterns	Exercises 3, 5, 7–9
Example 3 Factoring by Grouping	Exercises 13–18
Example 4 Solving a Real-World Problem by Factoring a Polynomial	Exercises 19–22

INTEGRATE TECHNOLOGY

Emphasize that students should use caution when checking answers on a graphing calculator. The calculator provides support that the answer is correct, but it cannot be used to *prove* correctness.

AVOID COMMON ERRORS

Students may not recognize that a polynomial can sometimes be factored if they regroup the terms. Give students a pattern they can follow to test if factoring by grouping applies to a polynomial: first, rearrange the terms so that when they are grouped, they will have common factors; group the terms; factor each group, using factoring patterns if necessary; then, rearrange and assemble the factors using the distributive property

INTEGRATE MATHEMATICAL PRACTICES

Focus on Math Connections

MP.1 After students have solved a polynomial equation using the zero-product property, help them understand and recall that the zeros of the polynomial function $f(x)$ associated with the polynomial equation are the values of x where the graph of the polynomial function crosses the x-axis. The zeros of a function $f(x)$ are also equivalent to the solutions of the equation $f(x) = 0$ and are related to the factors of the polynomial.

Factor the polynomial by grouping.

13. $x^3 + 8x^2 + 6x + 48$

$x^2(x + 8) + 6(x + 8)$

$(x^2 + 6)(x + 8)$

14. $x^3 + 4x^2 - x - 4$

$x^2(x + 4) - 1(x + 4)$

$(x^2 - 1)(x + 4)$

$(x - 1)(x + 1)(x + 4)$

15. $8x^4 + 8x^3 + 27x + 27$

$8x^3(x + 1) + 27(x + 1)$

$(8x^3 + 27)(x + 1)$

$(2x + 3)(4x^2 - 6x + 9)(x + 1)$

16. $27x^4 + 54x^3 - 64x - 128$

$27x^3(x + 2) - 64(x + 2)$

$(27x^3 - 64)(x + 2)$

$(3x - 4)(9x^2 + 12x + 16)(x + 2)$

17. $x^3 + 2x^2 + 3x + 6$

$x^2(x + 2) + 3(x + 2)$

$(x^2 + 3)(x + 2)$

18. $4x^4 - 4x^3 - x + 1$

$4x^4 - 4x^3 - x + 1$

$4x^3(x - 1) - 1(x - 1)$

$(4x^3 - 1)(x - 1)$

Write and solve a polynomial equation for the situation described.

19. Engineering A new rectangular outbuilding for a farm is being designed. The outbuilding's side and bottom should be 4 feet thick. Its outer length should be twice its outer width and height. What should the outer dimensions of the outbuilding be if it is to hold 2304 cubic feet?

$2304 = (2x - 8)(x - 8)(x - 4)$

$2304 = 2x^3 - 32x^2 + 160x - 256$

$0 = 2x^3 - 32x^2 + 160x - 2560$

$0 = 2x^2(x - 16) + 160(x - 16)$

$0 = 2(x^2 + 80)(x - 16)$

The only real solution is $x = 16$. The outbuilding is 32 feet long, 24 feet wide, and 24 feet hig

20. Arts A piece of rectangular crafting supply is being cut for a new sculpture. You want its length to be 4 times its height and its width to be 2 times its height. If you want the wood to be 64 cubic centimeters, what will its length, width, and height be?

$V = (4x)(2x)(x)$

$V = 8x^3$

$64 = 8x^3$

$8 = x^3$

$2 = x$

The length of the piece of crafting supply will be 8 cm, the width 4 cm, and the height 2 cm.

21. **Engineering** A new rectangular holding tank is being built. The tank's side and bottom should be 1 foot thick. Its outer length should be twice its outer width and height.

What should the outer dimensions of the tank be if it is to hold 36 cubic feet?

$$36 = (2x - 2)(x - 2)(x - 1)$$
$$36 = 2x^3 - 8x^2 + 10x - 4$$
$$0 = 2x^3 - 8x^2 + 10x - 40$$
$$0 = 2x^2(x - 4) + 10(x - 4)$$
$$0 = 2(x^2 + 5)(x - 4)$$

The only real solution is $x = 4$. The tank is 8 feet long, 4 feet wide, and 4 feet high.

22. **Construction** A piece of granite is being cut for a building foundation. You want its length to be 8 times its height and its width to be 3 times its height. If you want the granite to be 648 cubic yards, what will its length, width, and height be?

$$V = (8x)(3x)(x)$$
$$V = 24x^3$$
$$648 = 24x^3$$
$$27 = x^3$$
$$3 = x$$

The length of the slab will be 24 yards, the width 9 yards, and the height 3 yards.

23. State which, if any, special factoring pattern each of the following polynomial functions follows:

a. $x^2 - 4$ **difference of two squares**

b. $3x^3 + 5$ **none**

c. $4x^2 + 25$ **none**

d. $16x^3 + 375$ **sum of two cubes**

e. $64x^3 - x^2 + 1$ **none**

H.O.T. Focus on Higher Order Thinking

24. **Communicate Mathematical Ideas** What is the relationship between the degree of a polynomial and the degree of its factors?

The degree of a polynomial is always at least 1 larger than the degree of any of its factors.

25. **Critical Thinking** Why is there no sum-of-two-squares factoring pattern?

There is no sum-of-two-squares factoring pattern because any sum of two squares will only have complex roots as an answer.

INTEGRATE MATHEMATICAL PRACTICES

Focus on Patterns

MP.8 Point out that students should review the factoring patterns they learned in Algebra 1 as well as the two useful factoring patterns in this lesson:

Sum of two cubes:

$a^3 + b^3 = (a + b)(a^2 - ab + b^2)$;

Difference of two cubes:

$a^3 - b^3 = (a - b)(a^2 + ab + b^2)$

Emphasize that the exercises may go beyond factoring over the integers and may include factoring over the real numbers or complex numbers.

AVOID COMMON ERRORS

Some students may not be sure of the point at which a polynomial has been factored completely. Discuss ways to determine whether the factoring is complete, checking that the greatest monomial factor has been factored out, and making sure that each factor is itself irreducible.

PEER-TO-PEER DISCUSSION

Instruct one student in each pair to write a polynomial while the other student gives verbal instructions for factoring the polynomial. Then have students switch roles, and repeat the exercise, giving instructions for factoring a different polynomial.

JOURNAL

Have students make a table describing the methods and patterns for factoring polynomials. Give examples of using the sum and difference of two cubes and of factoring polynomials by grouping.

26. Explain the Error Jim was trying to factor a polynomial function and produced the following result:

$3x^3 + x^2 + 3x + 1$	Write out the polynomial.
$3x^2(x + 1) + 3(x + 1)$	Group by common factor.
$3(x^2 + 1)(x + 1)$	Regroup.

Explain Jim's error.

Jim misgrouped the polynomial function. He should have grouped the function like this:

$3x^3 + x^2 + 3x + 1$	**Write out the polynomial.**
$3x(x^2 + 1) + 1(x^2 + 1)$	**Group by common factor.**
$(x^2 + 1)(3x + 1)$	**Regroup.**

27. Factoring can also be done over the complex numbers. This allows you to find all the roots of an equation, not just the real ones.

Complete the steps showing how to use a special factor identity to factor $x^2 + 4$ over the complex numbers.

$x^2 + 4$	Write out the polynomial.
$x^2 - (-4)$	**Rewrite as a difference of two squares.**
$(x + \sqrt{-4})\ (x - \sqrt{-4})$	Factor.
$(x + 2i)\ (x - 2i)$	Simplify.

28. Find all the complex roots of the equation $x^4 - 16 = 0$.

$(x^2 + 4)(x^2 - 4) = 0$

$(x^2 + 4)(x - 2)(x + 2) = 0$

Factors $(x - 2)$ and $(x + 2)$ will yield real roots. factor $(x^2 + 4)$ will yield comples roots.

$x^2 + 4$

$x^2 - (-4)$

$(x + \sqrt{-4})(x - \sqrt{-4})$

$(x + 2i)(x - 2i)$

$x + 2i = 0$ **or** $x - 2i = 0$

$x = -2i$ $\quad x = 2i$

The complex roots of the equation $x^4 - 16 = 0$ are $x = -2i$ and $x = 2i$.

29. Factor $x^3 + x^2 + x + 1$ over the complex numbers.

$x^3 + x^2 + x + 1$

$x^2(x + 1) + 1(x + 1)$

$(x + 1)(x^2 + 1)$

$(x + 1)[x^2 - (-1)]$

$(x + 1)(x + \sqrt{-1})(x - \sqrt{-1})$

$(x + 1)(x + i)(x - i)$

Therefore, $x^3 + x^2 + x + 1 = (x + 1)(x + i)(x - i)$

Lesson Performance Task

Sabrina is building a rectangular raised flower bed. The boards on the two shorter sides are 6 inches thick, and the boards on the two longer sides are 4 inches thick. Sabrina wants the outer length of her bed to be 4 times its height and the outer width to be 2 times its height. She also wants the boards to rise 4 inches above the level of the soil in the bed. What should the outer dimensions of the bed be if she wants it to hold 3136 cubic inches of soil?

Let x = the external height

Volume = Interior Lenght(inches) · Interior Width(inches) · Interior Height (inches)

$$3136 = (4x - 12)(2x - 8)(x - 4)$$

$$3136 = 8x^3 - 88x^2 + 320x - 384$$

$$0 = 8x^3 - 88x^2 + 320x - 3520$$

$$0 = 8x^2(x - 11) + 320(x - 11)$$

$$0 = (8x^2 + 320)(x - 11)$$

$x = 11$ is the only real solution

Thus the external dimensions must be 44 inches long by 22 inches wide by 11 inches high.

EXTENSION ACTIVITY

Have students design a circular flower bed using a tire or other doughnut-shaped object. Have them discuss the constraints they would put on the dimensions of the bed and on the volume of the soil. Then ask them to set up a polynomial equation for the interior volume of the bed and solve for the unknown dimension. Have students discuss what shape would be best for a garden bed and why. **A rectangular bed that is long and narrow allows the gardener to easily reach all plants without stepping on the soil.**

LANGUAGE SUPPORT EL

Some students may not be familiar with the term *flower bed*. Explain that a *bed* can refer to an area for a garden. It may be enclosed by fencing, boards, or logs, and is sometimes built from the ground to a height of several inches to make it easier for the gardener to work in the soil. Have them look at the photo of the flower bed and describe any similarities they see between it and a bed that a person might sleep on. **Both are rectangular, flat, and low to the ground.**

QUESTIONING STRATEGIES

? Why is it important to move all the terms of the equation to one side? **The other side will then be zero, and you can use the zero-product property to solve for the solution.**

? If the final factoring gives more than one solution, how can you determine the correct one? **The answer must make sense for the problem. If the question is asking for a length of a board, then a negative answer would not be realistic. The answer must be positive.**

Scoring Rubric

2 points: Student correctly solves the problem and explains his/her reasoning.

1 point: Student shows good understanding of the problem but does not fully solve or explain his/her reasoning.

0 points: Student does not demonstrate understanding of the problem.

LESSON 6.5

Dividing Polynomials

Common Core Math Standards

The student is expected to:

 **A-APR.D.6**

Rewrite simple rational expressions in different forms; write $a(x)/b(x)$ in the form $q(x) + r(x)/b(x)$, ... using inspection, long division, ... Also A-APR.A.1, A-APR.B.3

Mathematical Practices

 **MP.2 Reasoning**

Language Objective

Work in small groups to complete a compare and contrast chart for dividing polynomials.

ENGAGE

Essential Question: What are some ways to divide polynomials, and how do you know when the divisor is a factor of the dividend?

Possible answer: You can divide polynomials using long division or, for a divisor of the form $x - a$, synthetic division. The divisor is a factor of the dividend when the remainder is 0.

PREVIEW: LESSON PERFORMANCE TASK

View the Engage section online. Discuss the photo and how the number of teams and the attendance are both functions of time. Then preview the Lesson Performance Task.

Name______________________ Class______________ Date__________

6.5 Dividing Polynomials

Resource Locker

Essential Question: What are some ways to divide polynomials, and how do you know when the divisor is a factor of the dividend?

 Explore Evaluating a Polynomial Function Using Synthetic Substitution

Polynomials can be written in something called nested form. A polynomial in nested form is written in such a way that evaluating it involves an alternating sequence of additions and multiplications. For instance, the nested form of $p(x) = 4x^3 + 3x^2 + 2x + 1$ is $p(x) = x(x(4x + 3) + 2) + 1$, which you evaluate by starting with 4, multiplying by the value of x, adding 3, multiplying by x, adding 2, multiplying by x, and adding 1.

Ⓐ Given $p(x) = 4x^3 + 3x^2 + 2x + 1$, find $p(-2)$.

Rewrite $p(x)$ as $p(x) = x(x(4x + 3) + 2) + 1$.

Multiply. $-2 \cdot 4 = -8$

Add. $-8 + 3 = -5$

Multiply. $-5 \cdot -2 = 10$

Add. $10 + 2 = 12$

Multiply. $12 \cdot 2 = -24$

Add. $-24 + 1 = -23$

You can set up an array of numbers that captures the sequence of multiplications and additions needed to find $p(a)$. Using this array to find $p(a)$ is called **synthetic substitution**.

Given $p(x) = 4x^3 + 3x^2 + 2x + 1$, find $p(-2)$ by using synthetic substitution. The dashed arrow indicates bringing down, the diagonal arrows represent multiplication by -2, and the solid down arrows indicate adding.

The first two steps are to bring down the leading number, 4, then multiply by the value you are evaluating at, -2.

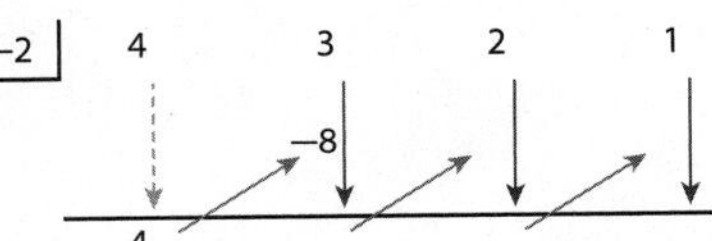

 Add 3 and -8.

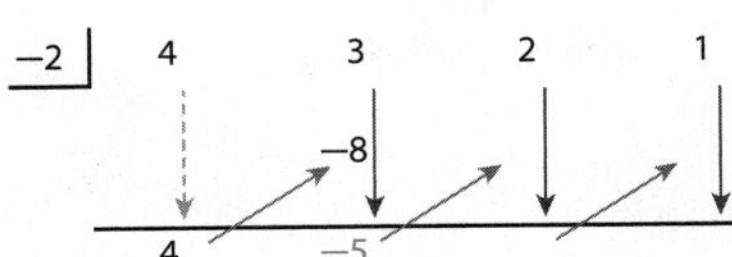

HARDCOVER PAGES 321–334

Watch for the hardcover student edition page numbers for this lesson.

Ⓒ Multiply the previous answer by −2.

$$\begin{array}{r|rrrr} -2 & 4 & 3 & 2 & 1 \\ & & -8 & 10 & \\ \hline & 4 & -5 & & \end{array}$$

Ⓓ Continue this sequence of steps until you reach the last addition.

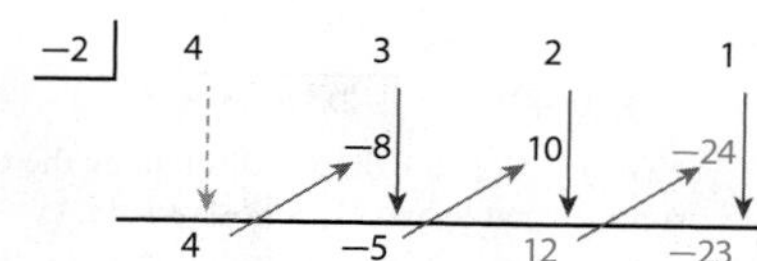

Ⓔ 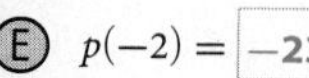

$p(-2) = -23$

Reflect

1. **Discussion** After the final addition, what does this sum correspond to?
The final sum represents the value of $p(x)$ where $x = -2$.

Explain 1 Dividing Polynomials Using Long Division

Recall that arithmetic long division proceeds as follows.

```
Divisor      23 ← Quotient
         12) 277 ← Dividend
             24
             ---
              37
              36
             ---
               1 ← Remainder
```

Notice that the long division leads to the result $\frac{dividend}{divisor} = quotient + \frac{remainder}{divisor}$. Using the numbers from above, the arithmetic long division leads to $\frac{277}{12} = 23 + \frac{1}{12}$. Multiplying through by the divisor yields the result $dividend = (divisor)(qoutient) + remainder$. (This can be used as a means of checking your work.)

Example 1 **Given a polynomial divisor and dividend, use long division to find the quotient and remainder. Write the result in the form *dividend = (divisor)(quotient) + remainder* and then carry out the multiplication and addition as a check.**

Ⓐ $(4x^3 + 2x^2 + 3x + 5) \div (x^2 + 3x + 1)$

Begin by writing the dividend in standard form, including terms with a coefficient of 0 (if any).

$4x^3 + 2x^2 + 3x + 5$

Write division in the same way as you would when dividing numbers.

$x^2 + 3x + 1 \overline{) 4x^3 + 2x^2 + 3x + 5}$

EXPLORE

Evaluating a Polynomial Function Using Synthetic Substitution

INTEGRATE TECHNOLOGY

Students have the option of completing the polynomial division activity either in the book or online.

QUESTIONING STRATEGIES

What operation are you doing and what are you finding when you use synthetic substitution on the polynomial function $p(x)$ to find $p(a)$? You are dividing the polynomial function $p(x)$ by the quantity $(x - a)$, and you are finding the value of $p(a)$.

EXPLAIN 1

Dividing Polynomials Using Long Division

AVOID COMMON ERRORS

Students may have difficulty relating the familiar long-division process for whole numbers to identifying the process for polynomials using the algorithm for finding $dividend = (divisor)(quotient) + remainder$. Point out that polynomial long division leads to this result: $\frac{dividend}{divisor} = quotient + \frac{remainder}{divisor}$, which is equivalent to $dividend = (divisor)(quotient) + remainder$ if you multiply each term by the divisor. Showing an example of arithmetic long division alongside an example of polynomial division may help students make the connection.

PROFESSIONAL DEVELOPMENT

Math Background

Division of polynomials is related to division of whole numbers. Given polynomials $P(x)$ and $D(x)$, where $D(x) \neq 0$, we can write $\frac{P(x)}{D(x)} = Q(x) + \frac{R(x)}{D(x)}$, where the remainder $R(x)$ is a polynomial whose degree is less than that of $D(x)$. (If the degree of $R(x)$ were not less than the degree of $D(x)$, we would be able to continue dividing.) Equivalently, $P(x) = Q(x) \cdot D(x) + R(x)$. This last expression can be used to justify the Remainder Theorem. Notice that when $D(x)$ is a linear divisor of the form $x - a$, the expression becomes $P(x) = Q(x)(x - a) + r$, where the remainder r is a real number.

QUESTIONING STRATEGIES

? How can you tell if you are finished solving a polynomial division problem? **The remainder has a degree less than the degree of the divisor, or has degree 0.**

? What do you write as the final answer for a polynomial division problem? **The answer should be written as the product of factors plus the remainder, where one factor is the divisor and the other factor is the quotient.**

Find the value you need to multiply the divisor by so that the first term matches with the first term of the dividend. In this case, in order to get $4x^2$, we must multiply x^2 by $4x$. This will be the first term of the quotient.

$$\begin{array}{r} 4x \\ x^2+3x+1\overline{)\,4x^3+2x^2+3x+5} \end{array}$$

Next, multiply the divisor through by the term of the quotient you just found and subtract that value from the dividend. $(x^2+3x+1)(4x) = 4x^3+12x^2+4x$, so subtract $4x^3+12x^2+4x$ from $4x^3+2x^2+3x+5$.

$$\begin{array}{r} 4x \\ x^2+3x+1\overline{)\,4x^3+2x^2+3x+5} \\ \underline{-(4x^3+12x^2+4x)} \\ -10x^2-x+5 \end{array}$$

Taking this difference as the new dividend, continue in this fashion until the largest term of the remaining dividend is of lower degree than the divisor.

$$\begin{array}{r} 4x-10 \\ x^2+3x+1\overline{)\,4x^3+2x^2+3x+5} \\ \underline{-(4x^3+12x^2+4x)} \\ -10x^2-x+5 \\ \underline{-(-10x^2-30x-10)} \\ 29x+15 \end{array}$$

Since $29x+5$ is of lower degree than x^2+3x+1, stop. $29x+15$ is the remainder.

Write the final answer.

$4x^3+2x^2+3x+5 = (x^2+3x+1)(4x-10)+29x+15$

Check.

$$\begin{aligned} 4x^3+2x^2+3x+5 &= (x^2+3x+1)(4x-10)+29x+15 \\ &= 4x^3+12x^2+4x-10x^2-30x-10+29x+15 \\ &= 4x^3+2x^2+3x+5 \end{aligned}$$

 $(6x^4+5x^3+2x+8) \div (x^2+2x-5)$

Write the dividend in standard form, including terms with a coefficient of 0.

$6x^4+5x^3+0x^2+2x+8$

Write the division in the same way as you would when dividing numbers.

$$x^2+2x-5\overline{)\,6x^4+5x^3+0x^2+2x+8}$$

COLLABORATIVE LEARNING

Small Group Activity

Help groups of students practice dividing polynomials using synthetic division. Provide each student with a different example of polynomial division, and ask them to show and explain the first step in dividing with synthetic division. Then have them pass the problem to another student, who writes the next step and explains it. They continue to pass the problem until each problem is completely solved and all steps are explained. The last student summarizes by giving the quotient and remainder in polynomial form. Encourage students to use these as examples of dividing polynomials when they write in their journals.

Divide.

$$\begin{array}{r} 6x^2 - \boxed{7x} + \boxed{44} \\ x^2 + 2x - 5 \overline{\big) 6x^4 + 5x^3 + 0x^2 + 2x + 8} \\ -(6x^4 + 12x^3 - 30x^2) \\ \hline -7x^3 + 30x^2 + 2x \\ -\left(-7x^3 \boxed{-14x^2 + 35x}\right) \\ \hline \boxed{44x^2 - 33x} + 8 \\ -\left(\boxed{44x^2 + 88x - 220}\right) \\ \hline \boxed{-121x + 228} \end{array}$$

Write the final answer.

$6x^4 + 5x^3 + 2x + 8 = \boxed{(x^2 + 2x - 5)(6x^2 - 7x + 44) - 121x + 228}$

Check.

$$\begin{aligned} 6x^4 + 5x^3 + 2x + 8 &= (x^2 + 2x - 5)(6x^2 - 7x + 44) - 121x + 228 \\ &= 6x^4 - 7x^3 + 44x^2 + 12x^3 - 14x^2 + 88x - 30x^2 + 35x - 220 - 121x + 228 \\ &= 6x^4 + 5x^3 + 2x + 8 \end{aligned}$$

Reflect

2. How do you include the terms with 0 coefficients?
You represent the term with 0 as the coefficient, e.g, 0x.

Your Turn

Use long division to find the quotient and remainder. Write the result in the form *dividend* = (*divisor*)(*qoutient*) + *remainder* and then carry out a check.

3. $(15x^3 + 8x - 12) \div (3x^2 + 6x + 1)$

$$\begin{array}{r} 5x - 10 \\ 3x^2 + 6x + 1 \overline{\big) 15x^3 + 0x^2 + 8x - 12} \\ -(15x^3 + 30x^2 + 5x) \\ \hline -30x^2 + 3x - 12 \\ -(-30x^2 - 60x - 10) \\ \hline 63x - 2 \end{array}$$

$(3x^2 + 6x + 1)(5x - 10) + 63x - 2$

$= 15x^3 - 30x^2 + 30x^2 - 60x + 5x - 10 +$

$63x - 2$

$= 15x^3 + 8x - 12$

DIFFERENTIATE INSTRUCTION

Graphic Organizers

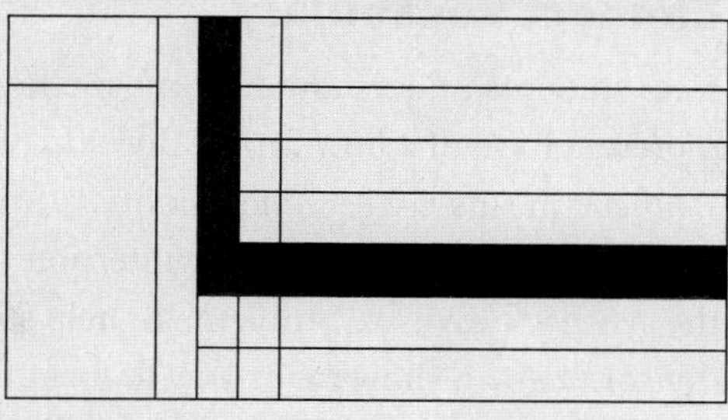

Have groups of students create graphic organizers to help them divide polynomials using synthetic division. Have them show how to organize a problem into a form similar to the one shown. Then have them use organizers to write each of the steps, explain what goes into each of the cells, and then interpret the results.

EXPLAIN 2

Dividing $p(x)$ by $x - a$ Using Synthetic Division

INTEGRATE MATHEMATICAL PRACTICES

Focus on Patterns

MP.8 Students should quickly see that there are patterns in synthetic division. Have students use arrows and expressions, if necessary, to help them understand the patterns. For example, $(2x^2 + 7x + 9) \div (x + 2)$ may be shown as:

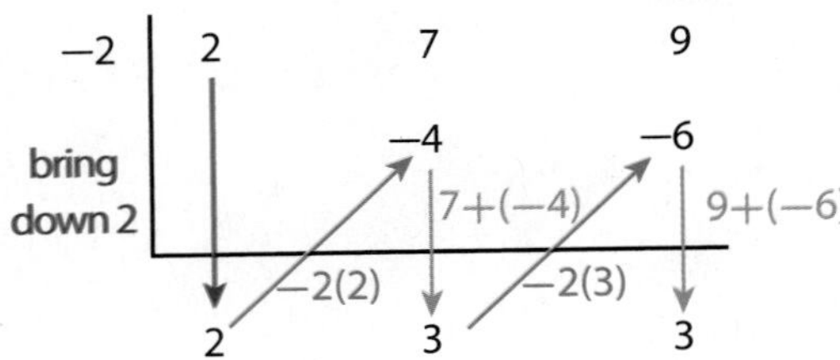

Students should notice that the divisor is −2 because the form of the divisor is $(x - a)$, or $(x - (-2))$; the rows are added; the remainder is the last digit in the last row, 3; and the last row includes the coefficients of the quotient, starting with the power of the variable decreased by 1.

$$(2x^2 + 7x + 9) \div (x + 2) = 2x + 3 + \frac{3}{x+2}$$

4. $(9x^4 + x^3 + 11x^2 - 4) \div (x^2 + 16)$

$$\begin{array}{r} 9x^2 + x - 133 \\ x^2 + 16 \overline{) 9x^4 + x^3 + 11x^2 + 0x - 4} \\ -(9x^4 + 0x^3 + 144x^2) \\ \hline x^3 - 133x^2 + 0x \\ -(x^3 + 0x^2 + 16x) \\ \hline -133x^2 - 16x - 4 \\ -(-133x^2 + 0x - 2128) \\ \hline -16x + 2124 \end{array}$$

$(x^2 + 16)(9x^2 + x - 133) - 16x + 2124$

$= 9x^4 + x^3 - 133x^2 + 144x^2 + 16x - 2128 - 16x + 2124$

$= 9x^4 + x^3 + 11x^2 - 4$

Explain 2 Dividing $p(x)$ by $x - a$ Using Synthetic Division

Compare long division with synthetic substitution. There are two important things to notice. The first is that $p(a)$ is equal to the remainder when $p(x)$ is divided by $x - a$. The second is that the numbers to the left of $p(a)$ in the bottom row of the synthetic substitution array give the coefficients of the quotient. For this reason, synthetic substitution is also called **synthetic division**.

Long Division	Synthetic Substitution
$\begin{array}{r} 3x^2 + 10x + 20 \\ x - 2 \overline{) 3x^3 + 4x^2 + 0x + 10} \\ -(3x^3 - 6x^2) \\ \hline 10x^2 + 0x \\ -(10x^2 - 20x) \\ \hline 20x + 10 \\ -20x - 40 \\ \hline 50 \end{array}$	$\begin{array}{r\|rrrr} 2 & 3 & 4 & 0 & 10 \\ & & 6 & 20 & 40 \\ \hline & 3 & 10 & 20 & 50 \end{array}$

Example 2 **Given a polynomial $p(x)$, use synthetic division to divide by $x - a$ and obtain the quotient and the (nonzero) remainder. Write the result in the form $p(x) = (x - a)$ (quotient) $+ p(a)$ then carry out the multiplication and addition as a check.**

Ⓐ $(7x^3 - 6x + 9) \div (x + 5)$

By inspection, $a = -5$. Write the coefficients and a in the synthetic division format.

$$\begin{array}{r\|rrrr} -5 & 7 & 0 & -6 & 9 \\ \hline & & & & \end{array}$$

Bring down the first coefficient. Then multiply and add for each column.

$$\begin{array}{r\|rrrr} -5 & 7 & 0 & -6 & 9 \\ & & -35 & 175 & -845 \\ \hline & 7 & -35 & 169 & -839 \end{array}$$

Write the result, using the non-remainder entries of the bottom row as the coefficients.

$(7x^2 - 6x + 9) = (x + 5)(7x^2 - 35x + 169) - 836$

Check.

$(7x^3 - 6x + 9) = (x + 5)(7x^2 - 35x + 169) - 836$

$= 7x^3 - 35x^2 - 35x^2 - 175x + 169x + 845 - 836$

$= 7x^3 - 6x + 9$

LANGUAGE SUPPORT EL

Connect Vocabulary

Help students understand how the method *synthetic division* is used as a symbolic representation of a polynomial division problem. Point out that the English word *synthetic* means *not genuine, unnatural, artificial, or contrived*. That implies they will have to understand how to interpret the numerical results in the last row of the synthetic division problem. To help students remember the value of a for the divisor $(x - a)$, show them how to form the equation $x - a = 0$, and then solve that equation for a. This procedure will remind students to use the correct sign for the divisor.

(B) $(4x^4 - 3x^2 + 7x + 2) \div \left(x - \frac{1}{2}\right)$

Find a. Then write the coefficients and a in the synthetic division format.

Find $a = \boxed{\frac{1}{2}}$

$$\frac{1}{2} \,\big|\; 4 \quad 0 \quad -3 \quad 7 \quad 2$$

Bring down the first coefficient. Then multiply and add for each column.

$$\begin{array}{r|rrrrr} \frac{1}{2} & 4 & 0 & -3 & 7 & 2 \\ & & 2 & 1 & -1 & 3 \\ \hline & 4 & 2 & -2 & 6 & \boxed{5} \end{array}$$

Write the result.

$(4x^4 - 3x^2 + 7x + 2) = \boxed{\left(x - \frac{1}{2}\right)(4x^3 + 2x^2 - 2x + 6) + 5}$

Check.

$$(4x^4 - 3x^2 + 7x + 2) = \left(x - \frac{1}{2}\right)(4x^3 + 2x^2 - 2x + 6) + 5$$
$$= 4x^4 + 2x^3 - 2x^2 + 6x - 2x^3 - x^2 + x - 3 + 5$$
$$= 4x^4 + 3x^2 + 7x + 2$$

Reflect

5. Can you use synthetic division to divide a polynomial by $x^2 + 3$? Explain.
No, the divisor must be a linear binomial in the form $x - a$; $x^2 + 3$ is a quadratic binomial.

Your Turn

Given a polynomial $p(x)$, use synthetic division to divide by $x - a$ and obtain the quotient and the (nonzero) remainder. Write the result in the form $p(x) = (x - a)(quotient) + p(a)$. You may wish to perform a check.

6. $(2x^3 + 5x^2 - x + 7) \div (x - 2)$

$$\begin{array}{r|rrrr} 2 & 2 & 5 & -1 & 7 \\ & & 4 & 18 & 34 \\ \hline & 2 & 9 & 17 & \boxed{41} \end{array}$$

$$(x - 2)(2x^2 + 9x + 17) + 41$$
$$= 2x^3 - 4x^2 + 9x^2 - 18x + 17x - 34 + 41$$
$$= 2x^3 + 5x^2 - x + 7$$

7. $(6x^4 + 25x^3 - 3x + 5) \div \left(x + \frac{1}{3}\right)$

$$\begin{array}{r|rrrrr} -\frac{1}{3} & 6 & -25 & 0 & -3 & 5 \\ & & -2 & 9 & -3 & 2 \\ \hline & 6 & -27 & 9 & -6 & \boxed{7} \end{array}$$

$$\left(x + \frac{1}{3}\right)(6x^3 - 27x^2 + 9x - 6) + 7$$
$$= 6x^4 + 2x^3 - 27x^3 - 9x^2 + 9x^2 + 3x - 6x$$
$$- 2 + 7$$
$$= 6x^4 - 25x^3 - 3x + 5$$

QUESTIONING STRATEGIES

How can you recognize the quotient and remainder when using the synthetic division method? **The bottom row of the synthetic division problem gives the coefficients of the quotient along with the remainder of the division problem.**

EXPLAIN 3

Using the Remainder Theorem and Factor Theorem

QUESTIONING STRATEGIES

How are the Remainder Theorem and the Factor Theorem related? The Remainder Theorem implies that if a polynomial $p(x)$ is divided by $x - a$, and the remainder $p(a) = 0$, then $(x - a)$ is a factor of the polynomial. The Factor Theorem says that if $(x - a)$ is a factor of $p(x)$, you can rewrite the polynomial as the quotient $q(x)$ times this factor, or $p(x) = (x - a)q(x)$.

Explain 3 Using the Remainder Theorem and Factor Theorem

When $p(x)$ is divided by $x - a$, the result can be written in the form $p(x) = (x - a)q(x) + r$ where $q(x)$ is the quotient and r is a number. Substituting a for x in this equation gives $p(a) = (a - a)q(a) + r$. Since $a - a = 0$, this simplifies to $p(a) = r$. This is known as the **Remainder Theorem**.

If the remainder $p(a)$ in $p(x) = (x - a)q(x) + p(a)$ is 0, then $p(x) = (x - a)q(x)$, which tells you that $x - a$ is a factor of $p(x)$. Conversely, if $x - a$ is a factor of $p(x)$, then you can write $p(x)$ as $p(x) = (x - a)q(x)$, and when you divide $p(x)$ by $x - a$, you get the quotient $q(x)$ with a remainder of 0. These facts are known as the **Factor Theorem**.

Example 3 **Determine whether the given binomial is a factor of the polynomial $p(x)$. If so, find the remaining factors of $p(x)$.**

Ⓐ $p(x) = x^3 + 3x^2 - 4x - 12$; $(x + 3)$

Use synthetic division.

$$\begin{array}{r|rrrr} -3 & 1 & 3 & -4 & -12 \\ & & -3 & 0 & 12 \\ \hline & 1 & 0 & -4 & \boxed{0} \end{array}$$

Since the remainder is 0, $x + 3$ is a factor.

Write $q(x)$ and then factor it.

$q(x) = x^2 - 4 = (x + 2)(x - 2)$

So, $p(x) = x^3 + 3x^2 - 4x - 12 = (x + 2)(x - 2)(x + 3)$.

Ⓑ $p(x) = x^4 - 4x^3 - 6x^2 + 4x + 5$; $(x + 1)$

Use synthetic division.

$$\begin{array}{r|rrrrr} -1 & 1 & -4 & -6 & 4 & 5 \\ & & -1 & 5 & 1 & -5 \\ \hline & 1 & -5 & -1 & 5 & \boxed{0} \end{array}$$

Since the remainder is 0, $(x + 1)$ is a factor. Write $q(x)$.

$q(x) = x^3 - 5x^2 - x + 5$

Now factor $q(x)$ by grouping.

$q(x) = x^3 - 5x^2 - x + 5$

$= x^2(x - 5) - (x - 5)$

$= (x^2 - 1)(x - 5)$

$= (x + 1)(x - 1)(x - 5)$

So, $p(x) = x^4 - 4x^3 - 6x^2 + 4x + 5 = (x + 1)(x + 1)(x - 1)(x - 5)$.

Your Turn

Determine whether the given binomial is a factor of the polynomial $p(x)$. If it is, find the remaining factors of $p(x)$.

8. $p(x) = 2x^4 + 8x^3 + 2x + 8; (x + 4)$

$$\begin{array}{r|rrrrr} -4 & 2 & 8 & 0 & 2 & 8 \\ & & -8 & 0 & 0 & -8 \\ \hline & 2 & 0 & 0 & 2 & 0 \end{array}$$

Since the remainder is 0, $(x + 4)$ is a factor.

$q(x) = 2x^3 + 2 = 2(x^3 + 1) = (x + 1)(x^2 - x + 1)$

So, $p(x) = 2x^4 + 8x^3 + 2x + 8$

$= 2(x + 1)(x^2 - x + 1)(x + 4)$

9. $p(x) = 3x^3 - 2x + 5; (x - 1)$

$$\begin{array}{r|rrrr} 1 & 3 & 0 & -2 & 5 \\ & & 3 & 3 & 1 \\ \hline & 3 & 3 & 1 & 6 \end{array}$$

Since the remainder is 6, $x - 1$ is not a factor.

Elaborate

10. Compare long division and synthetic division of polynomials.
The numbers generated by synthetic division are equal to the coefficients of the terms of the polynomial quotient, including the remainder. They are essentially the same process.

11. How does knowing one linear factor of a polynomial help find the other factors?
If one linear factor of the polynomial is known, synthetic division can be used to find the product of the other factors, which may be easily factorable.

12. What conditions must be met in order to use synthetic division?
The divisor must be a linear binomial with a leading coefficient of 1. The dividend must be written in standard form with 0 representing any missing terms.

13. **Essential Question Check-In** How do you know when the divisor is a factor of the dividend?
The divisor is a factor of the dividend when the remainder is 0.

ELABORATE

QUESTIONING STRATEGIES

When do you use synthetic substitution, and when do you synthetic division? You use synthetic substitution when you want to find the function value of a polynomial for a certain number. You use synthetic division when you want to find the quotient of polynomial division.

INTEGRATE MATHEMATICAL PRACTICES

Focus on Communication

MP.3 Have students work in pairs to complete a chart like the following, showing similarities and differences:

	Alike	Different
Long Division		
Synthetic Substitution or Division		

SUMMARIZE THE LESSON

How do you explain the process of synthetic division, and when and why it is useful? What are possible sources of error in the process? Synthetic division is a division process that uses only the coefficients of a polynomial. If the last sum is 0, then the binomial is a factor of the polynomial; possible errors are not bringing down the first coefficient, forgetting to add instead of subtract, and forgetting to include coefficients that are 0.

EVALUATE

ASSIGNMENT GUIDE

Concepts and Skills	Practice
Explore Evaluating a Polynomial Function Using Synthetic Substitution	Exercises 1–4
Example 1 Dividing Polynomials Using Long Division	Exercises 5–8
Example 2 Dividing $p(x)$ by $x - a$ Using Synthetic Division	Exercises 9–11
Example 3 Using the Remainder Theorem and Factor Theorem	Exercises 12–15

AVOID COMMON ERRORS

Students might make errors in signs when doing synthetic division and synthetic substitution because values are added rather than subtracted as in long division. Remind them that terms are always added for synthetic substitution and synthetic division.

AVOID COMMON ERRORS

Students may be confused about when to use synthetic division and when to use long division. Point out that for a divisor other than a linear binomial with leading coefficient 1, long division is the best method. It may, however, be possible to divide the dividend and divisor by a constant to make the leading coefficient 1.

Evaluate: Homework and Practice

- Online Homework
- Hints and Help
- Extra Practice

Given $p(x)$, find $p(-3)$ by using synthetic substitution.

1. $p(x) = 8x^3 + 7x^2 + 2x + 4$

$$\begin{array}{r|rrrr} -3 & 8 & 7 & 2 & 4 \\ & & -24 & 51 & -159 \\ \hline & 8 & -17 & 53 & -155 \end{array}$$

$p(-3) = -155$

2. $p(x) = x^3 + 6x^2 + 7x - 25$

$$\begin{array}{r|rrrr} -3 & 1 & 6 & 7 & -25 \\ & & -3 & -9 & 6 \\ \hline & 1 & 3 & -2 & -19 \end{array}$$

$p(-3) = -19$

3. $p(x) = 2x^3 + 5x^2 - 3x$

$$\begin{array}{r|rrrr} -3 & 2 & 5 & -3 & 0 \\ & & -6 & 3 & 0 \\ \hline & 2 & -1 & 0 & 0 \end{array}$$

$p(-3) = 0$

4. $p(x) = -x^4 + 5x^3 - 8x + 45$

$$\begin{array}{r|rrrrr} -3 & -1 & 5 & 0 & -8 & 45 \\ & & 3 & -24 & 72 & -192 \\ \hline & -1 & 8 & -24 & 64 & -147 \end{array}$$

$p(-3) = -147$

Given a polynomial divisor and dividend, use long division to find the quotient and remainder. Write the result in the form *dividend* = (*divisor*)(*quotient*) + *remainder*. You may wish to carry out a check.

5. $(18x^3 - 3x^2 + x - 1) \div (x^2 - 4)$

$$\begin{array}{r} 18x - 3 \\ x^2 - 4 \overline{)\, 18x^3 - 3x^2 + x - 1} \\ -(18x^3 + 0x^2 - 72x) \\ \hline -3x^2 + 73x - 1 \\ -(-3x^2 + 0x + 12) \\ \hline 73x - 13 \end{array}$$

Check.

$(x^2 - 4)(18x - 3) + 73x - 13$

$= 18x^3 - 72x - 3x^2 + 12 + 73x - 13$

$= 18x^3 - 3x^2 + x - 1$

6. $(6x^4 + x^3 - 9x + 13) \div (x^2 + 8)$

$$\begin{array}{r} 6x^2 + x - 48 \\ x^2 + 8 \overline{)\, 6x^4 + x^3 + 0x^2 - 9x + 13} \\ -(6x^4 + 0x^3 + 48x^2) \\ \hline x^3 - 48x^2 - 9x \\ -(x^3 + 0x^2 + 8x) \\ \hline -48x^2 - 17x + 13 \\ -(-48x^2 + 0x - 384) \\ \hline -17x + 397 \end{array}$$

Check.

$(x^2 + 8)(6x^2 + x - 48) - 17x + 397$

$= 6x^4 + x^3 - 48x^2 + 48x^2 + 8x - 384 - 17x + 397$

$= 6x^4 + x^3 - 9x + 13$

Exercise	Depth of Knowledge (D.O.K.)	COMMON CORE Mathematical Practices
1–15	**1** Recall of Information	**MP.2** Reasoning
16–19	**2** Skills/Concepts	**MP.4** Modeling
20	**2** Skills/Concepts	**MP.2** Reasoning
21	**3** Strategic Thinking H.O.T.	**MP.2** Reasoning
22	**3** Strategic Thinking H.O.T.	**MP.6** Precision
23	**3** Strategic Thinking H.O.T.	**MP.2** Reasoning

7. $(x^4 + 6x - 2.5) \div (x^2 + 3x + 0.5)$

$$\begin{array}{r} x^2 - 3x + 8.5 \\ x^2 + 3x + 0.5 \overline{)\, x^4 + 0x^3 + 0x^2 + 6x - 2.5} \\ \underline{-(x^4 + 3x^3 + 0.5x^2)} \\ -3x^3 - 0.5x^2 + 6x \\ \underline{-(-3x^3 - 9x^2 - 1.5x)} \\ 8.5x^2 + 7.5x - 2.5 \\ \underline{-(8.5x^2 + 25.5x + 4.25)} \\ -18x - 6.75 \end{array}$$

Check.

$(x^2 + 3x + 0.5)(x^2 - 3x + 8.5) - 18x - 6.75$

$= x^4 - 3x^3 + 8.5x^2 + 3x^3 - 9x^2 + 25.5x + 0.5x^2$

$- 1.5x + 4.25 - 18x - 6.75$

$= x^4 + 6x - 2.5$

8. $(x^3 + 250x^2 + 100x) \div \left(\frac{1}{2}x^2 + 25x + 9\right)$

$$\begin{array}{r} 2x + 400 \\ \frac{1}{2}x^2 + 25x + 9 \overline{)\, x^3 + 250x^2 + 100x + 0} \\ \underline{-(x^3 + 50x^2 + x)} \\ 200x^2 + 82x + 0 \\ \underline{-(200x^2 + 10,000x + 3600)} \\ -9918x - 3600 \end{array}$$

Check.

$\left(\frac{1}{2}x^2 + 25 + 9\right)(2x + 400) - 9918x - 3600$

$= x^3 + 200x^2 + 50x^2 + 10,000x + 18x + 3600$

$- 9918x - 3600$

$= x^3 + 250x^2 + 100x$

Given a polynomial $p(x)$, use synthetic division to divide by $x - a$ and obtain the quotient and the (nonzero) remainder. Write the result in the form $p(x) = (x - a)(\text{quotient}) + p(a)$. You may wish to carry out a check.

9. $(7x^3 - 4x^2 - 400x - 100) \div (x - 8)$

8	7	−4	−400	−100
		56	416	−128
	7	52	16	28

$(x - 8)(7x^2 + 52x + 16) + 28$

$= 7x^3 - 56x^2 + 52x^2 - 416x + 16x - 128 + 28$

$= 7x^3 - 4x^2 - 400x - 100$

10. $(8x^4 - 28.5x^2 - 9x + 10) \div (x + 0.25)$

−0.25	8	0	−28.5	−9	10
		−2	0.5	7	−0.5
	8	−2	−28	−2	9.5

$(x + 0.25)(8x^3 - 2x^2 - 28x - 2) + 9.5$

$= 8x^4 + 2x^3 - 2x^3 - 0.5x^2 - 28x^2 - 7x - 2x$

$- 0.5 + 9.5$

$= 8x^4 - 28.5x^2 - 9x + 10$

11. $(2.5x^3 + 6x^2 - 5.5x - 10) \div (x + 1)$

−1	2.5	6	−5.5	−10
		−2.5	−3.5	9
	2.5	3.5	−9	−1

$(x + 1)(2.5x^2 + 3.5x - 9) - 1$

$= 2.5x^3 + 2.5x^2 + 3.5x^2 + 3.5x - 9x - 9 - 1$

$= 2.5x^3 + 6x^2 - 5.5x - 10$

AVOID COMMON ERRORS

A common error when doing synthetic division is to subtract the second row rather than adding it. Show students a long division problem alongside its solution, using synthetic division to emphasize that the results will be different if they make this error.

Determine whether the given binomial is a factor of the polynomial $p(x)$. If so, find the remaining factors of $p(x)$.

12. $p(x) = x^3 + 2x^2 - x - 2;\ (x + 2)$

−2	1	2	−1	−2
		−2	0	2
	1	0	−1	0

$x + 2$ is a factor.

$x^2 - 1 = (x + 1)(x - 1)$

So, $p(x) = x^3 + 2x^2 - x - 2$

$= (x + 1)(x - 1)(x + 2)$.

13. $p(x) = 2x^4 + 6x^3 - 5x - 10;\ (x + 2)$

−2	2	6	0	−5	−10
		−4	−4	8	−6
	2	2	−4	3	−16

$x + 2$ is not a factor.

14. $p(x) = x^3 - 22x^2 + 157x - 360;\ (x - 8)$

8	1	−22	157	−360
		8	−112	360
	1	−14	45	0

$x - 8$ is a factor.

$x^2 - 14x + 45 = (x - 5)(x - 9)$

So, $p(x) = x^3 - 22x^2 + 157x - 360 = (x - 5)(x - 9)(x - 8)$.

15. $p(x) = 4x^3 - 12x^2 + 2x - 5;\ (x - 3)$

3	4	−12	2	−5
		12	0	6
	4	0	2	1

$x - 3$ is not a factor.

16. The volume of a rectangular prism is modeled by the function $V(x) = x^3 - 8x^2 + 19x - 12$. Given $V(1) = 0$ and $V(3) = 0$, identify the other value of x for which $V(x) = 0$, which will give the missing dimension of the prism.

1	1	−8	19	−12
		1	−7	12
	1	−7	12	0

This gives the expression $x^2 - 7x + 12$.

3	1	−7	12
		3	−12
	1	−4	0

This gives the expression $x - 4$, which is the missing dimension. $V(4) = 0$

17. Given that the height of a rectangular prism is $x + 2$ and the volume is $x^3 - x^2 - 6x$, write an expression that represents the area of the top face of the prism.

$$\begin{array}{r|rrrr} -2 & 1 & -1 & -6 & 0 \\ & & -2 & 6 & 6 \\ \hline & 1 & -3 & 0 & \boxed{0} \end{array}$$

So, the area can be represented by $x^2 - 3x$.

18. Physics A Van de Graaff generator is a machine that produces very high voltages by using small, safe levels of electric current. One machine has a current that can be modeled by $I(t) = t + 2$, where $t > 0$ represents time in seconds. The power of the system can be modeled by $P(t) = 0.5t^3 + 6t^2 + 10t$. Write an expression that represents the voltage of the system. Recall that $V = \frac{P}{I}$.

$$\begin{array}{r|rrrr} -2 & 0.5 & 6 & 10 & 0 \\ & & -1 & -10 & 0 \\ \hline & 0.5 & 5 & 0 & \boxed{0} \end{array}$$

The voltage can be represented by $0.5t^2 + 5t$.

19. Geometry The volume of a hexagonal pyramid is modeled by the function $V(x) = \frac{1}{3}x^3 + \frac{4}{3}x^2 + \frac{2}{3}x - \frac{1}{3}$. Given the height $x + 1$, use polynomial division to find an expression for the area of the base.

(Hint: For a pyramid, $V = \frac{1}{3}Bh$.)

$V(x) = \frac{1}{3}(x^3 + 4x^2 + 2x - 1)$.

$$\begin{array}{r|rrrr} -1 & 1 & 4 & 2 & -1 \\ & & -1 & -3 & 1 \\ \hline & 1 & 3 & -1 & \boxed{0} \end{array}$$

So, the area of the base can be represented by $x^2 + 3x - 1$.

20. Explain the Error Two students used synthetic division to divide $3x^3 - 2x - 8$ by $x - 2$. Determine which solution is correct. Find the error in the other solution.

A.	B.
$\begin{array}{r\|rrrr} 2 & 3 & 0 & -2 & -8 \\ & & 6 & 12 & 20 \\ \hline & 3 & 6 & 10 & 12 \end{array}$	$\begin{array}{r\|rrrr} 2 & 3 & 0 & -2 & -8 \\ & & -6 & 12 & -20 \\ \hline & 3 & -6 & 10 & -28 \end{array}$

Student A is correct. Student B used the incorrect sign of *a*.

INTEGRATE MATHEMATICAL PRACTICES

Focus on Math Connections

MP.1 Emphasize the conditions that must be met to use synthetic division: The divisor must be a linear binomial with a leading coefficient of 1. The dividend must be written in standard form with 0 representing any missing terms.

Discuss the characteristics of synthetic division that make it synthetic: there are no variables, only coefficients; and addition is used instead of subtraction.

INTEGRATE MATHEMATICAL PRACTICES

Focus on Reasoning

MP.2 Point out that students should review how to do synthetic division and long division when the dividend is missing terms for some powers of the variable. Emphasize that they must include the missing terms written as zero times the power of the variable to complete the division.

PEER-TO-PEER DISCUSSION

Instruct one student in each pair to solve a polynomial division problem using long division, while the other student solves it by using synthetic division. Then have students switch roles and repeat the exercise for a new division problem with a polynomial that does not have a linear factor. Then have them discuss their results and any preferences they have for one method or the other.

JOURNAL

Have students describe a mnemonic device that can help them remember the steps in synthetic division.

H.O.T. Focus on Higher Order Thinking

21. Multi-Step Use synthetic division to divide $p(x) = 3x^3 - 11x^2 - 56x - 50$ by $(3x + 4)$. Then check the solution.

Rewrite $3x + 4$ as $\left(x + \frac{4}{3}\right)$.

$-\frac{4}{3}$	3	−11	−56	−50
		−4	20	48
	3	−15	−36	−2

The quotient needs to be divided by 3.

$$\frac{3x^2 - 15x - 36}{3} = x^2 - 5x - 12$$

Check.

$$(3x + 4)\left(\frac{3x^2 - 15x - 36}{3}\right) - 2$$

$$(3x + 4)(x^2 - 5x - 12) - 2$$

$$= 3x^3 + 4x^2 - 15x^2 - 20x - 36x - 48 - 2$$

$$= 3x^3 - 11x^2 - 56x - 50$$

22. Critical Thinking The polynomial $ax^3 + bx^2 + cx + d$ is factored as $3(x - 2)(x + 3)(x - 4)$. What are the values of a and d? Explain.

$a = 3$; $d = 72$; The value of a is the leading coefficient, 3; the value of d is the product of the constant terms of each factor and the leading coefficient 3.

23. Analyze Relationships Investigate whether the set of whole numbers, the set of integers, and the set of rational numbers are closed under each of the four basic operations. Then consider whether the set of polynomials in one variable is closed under the four basic operations, and determine whether polynomials are like whole numbers, integers, or rational numbers with respect to closure. Use the table to organize.

	Whole Numbers	Integers	Rational Numbers	Polynomials
Addition	Yes	Yes	Yes	Yes
Subtraction	No	Yes	Yes	Yes
Multiplication	Yes	Yes	Yes	Yes
Division (by nonzero)	No	No	Yes (nonzero)	Yes (nonzero)

Polynomials are similar to rational numbers with respect to closure. They are closed under each operation if division is nonzero.

Lesson Performance Task

The table gives the attendance data for all divisions of NCAA Women's Basketball.

NCAA Women's Basketball Attendance			
Season	**Years since 2006–2007**	**Number of teams in all 3 divisions**	**Attendance (in thousands) for all 3 divisions**
2006–2007	0	1003	10,878.3
2007–2008	1	1013	11,120.8
2008–2009	2	1032	11,160.3
2009–2010	3	1037	11,134.7
2010–2011	4	1048	11,160.0
2011–2012	5	1055	11,201.8

Enter the data from the second, third, and fourth columns of the table and perform polynomial regression on the data pairs (t, T) and (t, A) where $t =$ years since the 2006–2007 season, $T =$ number of teams, and $A =$ attendance (in thousands). For each set of data pairs, choose the regression model having the least degree that best fits the data.

Then create a model for the average attendance per team: $A_{avg}(t) = \frac{A(t)}{T(t)}$. Carry out the division to write $A_{avg}(t)$ in the form *quadratic quotient* + $\frac{remainder}{T(t)}$.

Use an online computer algebra system to carry out the division of $A(t)$ by $T(t)$.

Models:

$T(t) = 10.57t + 1005$

$A(t) = 13.80t^3 - 121.6t^2 + 329.8t + 10{,}880$

Online computer algebra system result:

$$A_{avg}(t) = 1.30558t^2 - 135.64t + 12{,}927.9 - \frac{12{,}981{,}600}{10.57t + 1005}$$

EXTENSION ACTIVITY

Have students research the attendance for a specific NCAA women's basketball team for a single season. Have them compare that number to the value calculated from the model $A_{avg}(t)$ for the same year. Ask the students how accurate the model is in predicting the attendance for that team and what some of the sources of error might be

AVOID COMMON ERRORS

Students may try to include the "3 divisions" in their calculation, perhaps by dividing the number of teams or attendance by 3. Explain to students that a *division* is a group of schools that compete against each other and there 3 such groups, or divisions, for college basketball. Explain that this number is irrelevant for this calculation. What is important is that the numbers in the table represent the total number of teams and the total attendance for all of women's collegiate basketball.

INTEGRATE MATHEMATICAL PRACTICES

Focus on Reasoning

MP.2 Have students highlight the *remainder* in the final function $A_{avg}(t)$. Ask them if the remainder is zero or nonzero and what a nonzero remainder means. Have students discuss the significance of a remainder for a function that describes attendance per team. If the attendance is 315.8 fans per team, ask students if the 0.8 represents an actual person or if it results from a limitation of the model.

Scoring Rubric

2 points: Student correctly solves the problem and explains his/her reasoning.

1 point: Student shows good understanding of the problem but does not fully solve or explain his/her reasoning.

0 points: Student does not demonstrate understanding of the problem.

Study Guide Review

ASSESSMENT AND INTERVENTION

Assign or customize module reviews.

MODULE PERFORMANCE TASK

COMMON CORE

Mathematical Practices: MP.1, MP.2, MP.4, MP.6, MP.7
A-APR.A.1, A-CED.A.2, F-BF.A.1

SUPPORTING STUDENT REASONING

Students should be able to find the maximum temperature, and then focus on thinking about how to compress the given polynomial to find the minimum function.

- **How do I find the minimum function?** Note that the meteorologist thinks a vertical compression will create a reasonable minimum function. Begin by finding a scale factor.

STUDY GUIDE REVIEW

Polynomials

MODULE 6

Essential Question: How can you use polynomials to solve real-world problems?

Key Vocabulary
binomial *(binomio)*
monomial *(monomio)*
polynomial *(polinomio)*
synthetic division *(división sintética)*
trinomial *(trinomio)*

KEY EXAMPLE *(Lesson 6.1)*

Subtract: $(5x^4 - x^3 + 2x + 1) - (2x^3 + 3x^2 - 4x - 7)$

$$\begin{array}{rrrrr} 5x^4 & -x^3 & 0x^2 & 2x & 1 \\ + & -2x^3 & -3x^2 & 4x & 7 \\ \hline 5x^4 & -3x^3 & -3x^2 & +6x & +8 \end{array}$$

Write in standard form.
Align like terms and add the opposite.
Add.

Therefore, $(5x^4 - x^3 + 2x + 1) - (2x^3 + 3x^2 - 4x - 7) = 5x^4 - 3x^3 - 3x^2 + 6x + 8$.

KEY EXAMPLE *(Lesson 6.2)*

Multiply: $(3x - 2)(2x^2 - 5x + 1)$

$(3x - 2)(2x^2 - 5x + 1)$ — Write in standard form.

$3x(2x^2) + 3x(-5x) + 3x(1) + (-2)(2x^2) + (-2)(-5x) + (-2)(1)$ — Distribute the $3x$ and the -2.

$6x^3 - 15x^2 + 3x - 4x^2 + 10x - 2$ — Simplify.

$6x^3 - 19x^2 + 13x - 2$ — Combine like terms.

Therefore, $(3x - 2)(2x^2 - 5x + 1) = 6x^3 - 19x^2 + 13x - 2$.

KEY EXAMPLE *(Lesson 6.5)*

Divide: $(x^3 + 10x^2 + 13x + 36) \div (x + 9)$

$$\begin{array}{r} x^2 + x + 4 \\ x+9 \overline{) \, x^3 + 10x^2 + 13x + 36} \\ -(x^3 + 9x^2) \quad\quad\quad\quad \\ \hline x^2 + 13x \quad\quad \\ -(x^2 + 9x) \quad\quad \\ \hline 4x + 36 \\ -(4x + 36) \\ \hline 0 \end{array}$$

In order to get x^3, multiply by x^2.
Multiply the divisor through by x^2, then subtract.
In order to get x^2, multiply by x.
Multiply the divisor through by x, then subtract.
In order to get $4x$, multiply by 4.
Multiply the divisor through by 4, then subtract.

Therefore, $(x^3 + 10x^2 + 13x + 36) \div (x + 9) = x^2 + x + 4$.

SCAFFOLDING SUPPORT

- To find the polynomial for $T_{\min}(x)$, students should recognize that they will need to determine a scale factor to apply to $T_{\max}(x)$. They can find this by calculating the ratio of the minimum to the maximum monthly temperatures, and taking the average of these. They should find the scale factor is approximately 0.66.
- Note that polynomials will vary depending on rounding. Encourage students to use four decimal places.

EXERCISES

Solve. *(Lessons 6.1, 6.2, 6.5)*

1. $(9x^2 + 2x + 12) + (7x^2 + 10x - 13)$

$16x^2 + 12x - 1$

2. $(6x^6 - 4x^5) - (10x^5 - 15x^4 + 8)$

$6x^6 - 14x^5 + 15x^4 - 8$

3. $(x - 3)(4x^2 - 2x + 3)$

$4x^3 - 14x^2 + 9x - 9$

4. $(9x^4 + 27x^3 + 23x^2 + 10x) \div (x^2 + 2x)$

$9x^2 + 9x + 5$

5. Mr. Alonzo runs a car repair garage. The average income from repairing a car can be modeled by $C(x) = 45x + 150$. If, for one year, the number of cars repaired can be modeled by $N(x) = 9x^2 + 7x + 6$, write a polynomial that can be used to model Mr. Alonzo's business income for that year. Explain. *(Lesson 6.2)*

$C(x) \cdot N(x) = (45x + 150) \cdot (9x^2 + 7x + 6) = 405x^3 + 1665x^2 + 1320x + 900$; To get the total for the entire year, you would multiply the average income by the number of cars.

MODULE PERFORMANCE TASK

What's the Temperature?

A meteorologist studying the temperature patterns for Redding, California, found the average of the daily minimum and maximum temperatures for each month, but the August temperatures are missing.

Month	Jan	Feb	Mar	Apr	May	June	July	Aug	Sep	Oct	Nov	Dec
Average Max Temperature (°F)	55.3	61.3	62.5	69.6	80.5	90.4	98.3	?	89.3	77.6	62.1	54.7
Average Min Temperature (°F)	35.7	40	41.7	46	52.3	61.8	64.7	?	58.8	49.2	41.4	35.2

How can she find the averages for August? She began by fitting the polynomial function shown below to the data for the average maximum temperature, where x is the month, with $x = 1$ corresponding to January, and the temperature is in degrees Fahrenheit.

$$T_{max}(x) = 0.0095x^5 - 0.2719x^4 + 2.5477x^3 - 9.1882x^2 + 17.272x + 45.468$$

She also thinks that a vertical compression of this function will create a function that fits the average minimum temperature data for Redding.

Use this information to find the average high and low temperature for August. Use graphs, numbers, words, or algebra to explain how you reached your conclusion.

SAMPLE SOLUTION

Assumptions

- The given model fits the data.

First, evaluate the given polynomial at $x = 8$ to find the average maximum temperature for August. The estimated average maximum temperature is 97.6°F.

Then, find a reasonable scale factor to apply to the maximum function to create the minimum function. One way is to find the ratio of the minimum temperature to the maximum temperature for each month, and then average them. The ratios vary from 0.634 to 0.683, and have an average of 0.656.

Multiply the maximum function by this scale factor to produce the minimum function:

$$T_{min}(x) = 0.00623x^5 - 0.1784x^4 + 1.6713x^3 - 6.0275x^2 + 11.3304x + 29.827$$

Evaluate this function at $x = 8$ to find the estimated average minimum temperature for August, which is 63.8°F.

DISCUSSION OPPORTUNITIES

- What would the shape of the polynomial be for different cities? For example, how would the polynomial change for a city near the equator?
- How would the results change if a polynomial with lesser degree is used instead? How does the degree of the polynomial affect the fit?

Assessment Rubric

2 points: Student correctly solves the problem and explains his/her reasoning.

1 point: Student shows good understanding of the problem but does not fully solve or explain.

0 points: Student does not demonstrate understanding of the problem.

Ready to Go On?

ASSESS MASTERY

Use the assessment on this page to determine if students have mastered the concepts and standards covered in this module.

ASSESSMENT AND INTERVENTION

Access Ready to Go On? assessment online, and receive instant scoring, feedback, and customized intervention or enrichment.

ADDITIONAL RESOURCES

Response to Intervention Resources

- Reteach Worksheets

Differentiated Instruction Resources

- Reading Strategies EL
- Success for English Learners EL
- Challenge Worksheets

Assessment Resources

- Leveled Module Quizzes

6.1–6.5 Polynomials

- Online Homework
- Hints and Help
- Extra Practice

Factor the polynomial. *(Lesson 6.4)*

1. $3x^2 + 4x - 4$

$(3x - 2)(x + 2)$

2. $2x^3 + 4x^2 - 30x$

$2x(x + 5)(x - 3)$

3. $9x^2 - 25$

$(3x + 5)(3x - 5)$

4. $4x^2 - 16x + 16$

$4(x - 2)^2$

Complete the polynomial operation. *(Lesson 6.1, 6.2, 6.3, 6.5)*

5. $(8x^3 - 2x^2 - 4x + 8) + (5x^2 + 6x - 4)$

$8x^3 + 3x^2 + 2x + 4$

6. $(-4x^2 - 2x + 8) - (x^2 + 8x - 5)$

$-5x^2 - 10x + 13$

7. $5x(x + 2)(3x - 7)$

$15x^3 - 5x^2 - 70x$

8. $(3x^3 + 12x^2 + 11x - 2) \div (x + 2)$

$3x^2 + 6x - 1$

9. $(x + y)^6$

$x^6 + 6x^5y + 15x^4y^2 + 20x^3y^3 + 15x^2y^4 + 6xy^5 + y^6$

ESSENTIAL QUESTION

10. Write a real-world situation that would require adding polynomials. *(Lesson 6.1)*

Possible Answer: A farmer is fencing in a triangular piece of land. One side can be represented by $x + 4$, another by $3x + 7$, and the last by $8x - 5$. What polynomial represents the amount of fencing he will need to surround the land?

COMMON CORE Common Core Standards

Lesson	Items	Content Standards	Mathematical Practices
6.4	1–4	**A-SSE.A.2**	**MP.2**
6.1	5	**A-APR.A.1**	**MP.2**
6.1	6	**A-APR.A.1**	**MP.2**
6.2	7	**A-APR.A.1**	**MP.2**
6.5	8	**A-APR.A.1, A-APR.D.6**	**MP.2**
6.3	9	**A-APR.A.1, A-APR.C.5**	**MP.2**

MODULE 6
MIXED REVIEW

Assessment Readiness

1. Look at each polynomial division problem. Can the polynomials be divided without a remainder?
Select Yes or No for A–C.
   - **A.** $(3x^3 - 5x^2 + 10x + 4) \div (3x + 1)$ ● Yes ○ No
   - **B.** $(2x^2 - 5x - 1) \div (x - 3)$ ○ Yes ● No
   - **C.** $(x^3 - 4x^2 + 2x - 3) \div (x + 2)$ ○ Yes ● No

2. Consider the polynomial $x^3 - x^2 - 6x$.
Select True or False for each statement.
   - **A.** $6x$ can be factored out of every term. ○ True ● False
   - **B.** The completely factored polynomial is $x(x + 2)(x - 3)$. ● True ○ False
   - **C.** $f(x) = x^3 - x^2 - 6x$ has a global minimum. ○ True ● False

3. Alana completed a problem where she had to find the sum of the polynomials $(3x^2 + 8x - 4)$ and $(-8x^3 - 3x + 4)$. Her answer is 0. Describe and correct her mistake. When graphed, how many times does the sum change directions?

   The only way to get 0 is to combine all of the x terms, instead of considering the x terms with their exponents. Since x terms with different exponents cannot be combined, that is the mistake she made. The correct answer is $-8x^3 + 3x^2 + 5x$; The sum changes direction 2 times.

4. A rectangular plot of land has a length of $(2x^2 + 5x - 20)$ and a width of $(3x + 4)$. What polynomial represents the area of the plot of land? Explain how you got your answer.

   $6x^3 + 23x^2 - 40x - 80$; Possible answer: I multiplied the polynomials. First, I multiplied every term in the first polynomial by $3x$, then I multiplied every term in the first polynomial by 4. After that, I combined like terms.

Common Core Standards

Lesson	Items	Content Standards	Mathematical Practices
6.5	1	A-APR.D.6	MP.1
5.2, 6.4	2*	A-APR.A.1, A-SSE.A.2	MP.2
5.2, 6.1	3*	A-APR.A.1, F-IF.C.7c	MP.3
6.2	4	F-IF.C.7c	MP.6

* Item integrates mixed review concepts from previous modules or a previous course.

MIXED REVIEW
Assessment Readiness

ASSESSMENT AND INTERVENTION

Assign ready-made or customized practice tests to prepare students for high-stakes tests.

ADDITIONAL RESOURCES

Assessment Resources

- Leveled Module Quizzes: Modified, B

AVOID COMMON ERRORS

Item 2 Some students may not understand the difference between "global minimum" and "local minimum." Ask them to think of the words *local* and *global* outside of their mathematical meanings. *Local* means nearby, while *global* refers to the entire world (or function).

MODULE 7

Polynomial Equations

ESSENTIAL QUESTION:

Answer: Polynomial equations can be used to model roller coasters and firework displays.

PROFESSIONAL DEVELOPMENT VIDEO

Professional Development Video
Author Matt Larson models successful teaching practices in an actual high-school classroom.
Professional Development
my.hrw.com

Polynomial Equations

MODULE 7

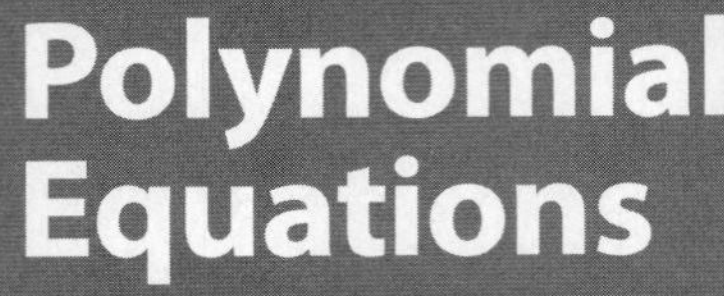

Essential Question: How can you use polynomial equations to solve real-world problems?

LESSON 7.1
Finding Rational Solutions of Polynomial Equations

LESSON 7.2
Finding Complex Solutions of Polynomial Equations

REAL WORLD VIDEO
The population of the Texas horned lizard has decreased rapidly, and the species is now considered threatened. Biologists use polynomials and other mathematical models to study threatened and endangered species.

MODULE PERFORMANCE TASK PREVIEW

What Do Polynomials Have to Do with Endangered Species?

A species is considered to be endangered when the population is so low that the species is at risk of becoming extinct. Biologists use mathematics to model the population of species, and they use their models to help them predict the future population and to determine whether or not a species is at risk of extinction. How can a polynomial be used to model a species population? Let's find out!

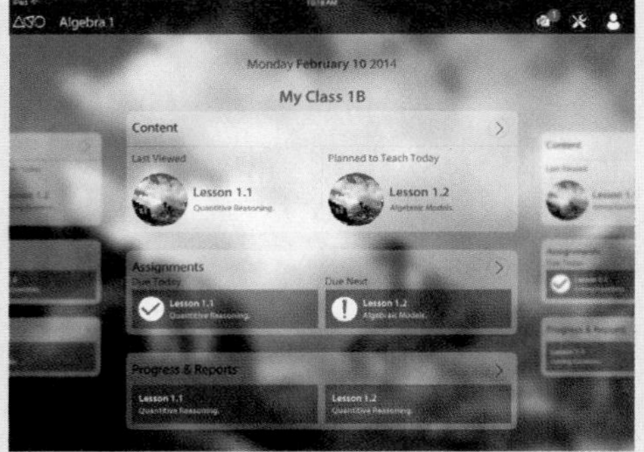

DIGITAL TEACHER EDITION

Access a full suite of teaching resources when and where you need them:

- Access content online or offline
- Customize lessons to share with your class
- Communicate with your students in real-time
- View student grades and data instantly to target your instruction where it is needed most

PERSONAL MATH TRAINER

Assessment and Intervention

Assign automatically graded homework, quizzes, tests, and intervention activities. Prepare your students with updated, Common Core-aligned practice tests.

Are YOU Ready?

Complete these exercises to review skills you will need for this chapter.

- Online Homework
- Hints and Help
- Extra Practice

Real Numbers

Example 1 Compare $2\sqrt{64}$ and $\sqrt{225}$.

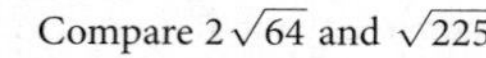

$2\sqrt{64} = 2 \cdot 8$ and $\sqrt{225} = 15$ — Evaluate the radicals.

$16 > 15$ — Multiply and compare.

Since $16 > 15$, $2\sqrt{64} > \sqrt{225}$.

Compare. Use > or <.

1. $4\sqrt{25}$ __<__ $25\sqrt{4}$
2. $0.75\sqrt{144}$ __<__ $8\sqrt{16}$
3. $2.2\sqrt{100}$ __>__ $3\sqrt{36}$

Add and Subtract Rational Numbers

Example 2 Add $\frac{3}{4} + \frac{5}{6}$.

$\left(\frac{3}{3}\right) \cdot \frac{3}{4} + \left(\frac{2}{2}\right) \cdot \frac{5}{6}$ — The LCM is 12. Multiply by 1.

$\frac{9}{12} + \frac{10}{12}$ — Add.

$\frac{19}{12}$

Add or subtract.

4. $\frac{1}{3} + \frac{5}{8}$ __$\frac{23}{24}$__
5. $\frac{7}{12} - \frac{4}{9}$ __$\frac{5}{36}$__
6. $\frac{9}{8} - \frac{5}{6}$ __$\frac{7}{24}$__

Equations Involving Exponents

Example 3 Solve $x^2 + 3x - 10 = 0$ for x.

$(x - 2)(x + 5) = 0$ — Factor.

Either $(x - 2) = 0$ or $(x + 5) = 0$

$x = 2$ or $x = -5$ — Solve.

The solutions for x are 2 and –5.

Solve for x.

7. $x^2 - 5x + 4 = 0$ __1, 4__
8. $x^2 + 11x + 30 = 0$ __−6, −5__
9. $x^2 + 6x = 16$ __−8, 2__

Response to Intervention			Differentiated Instruction
Tier 1 Lesson Intervention Worksheets	**Tier 2** Strategic Intervention Skills Intervention Worksheets	**Tier 3** Intensive Intervention Worksheets available online	
Reteach 7.1 Reteach 7.2	1 Add and Subtract Rational Numbers 7 Equations Involving Exponents 30 Real Numbers	Building Block Skills 2, 3, 4, 18, 20, 29, 75, 76, 100, 109	Challenge worksheets Extend the Math Lesson Activities in TE

Are You Ready?

ASSESS READINESS

Use the assessment on this page to determine if students need strategic or intensive intervention for the module's prerequisite skills.

ASSESSMENT AND INTERVENTION

RtI Response to Intervention TIER 1, TIER 2, TIER 3 SKILLS

Personal Math Trainer will automatically create a standards-based, personalized intervention assignment for your students, targeting each student's individual needs!

ADDITIONAL RESOURCES

See the table below for a full list of intervention resources available for this module.

Response to Intervention Resources also includes:

- Tier 2 Skill Pre-Tests for each Module
- Tier 2 Skill Post-Tests for each skill

Finding Rational Solutions of Polynomial Equations

Common Core Math Standards

The student is expected to:

A-APR.B.2

Know and apply the Remainder Theorem: For a polynomial $p(x)$ and a number a, the remainder on division by $x - a$ is $p(a)$, so $p(a) = 0$ if and only if $(x - a)$ is a factor of $p(x)$. Also A-APR.B.3, A-CED.A.3

Mathematical Practices

MP.2 Reasoning

Language Objective

Explain to a partner how to identify the factors of a polynomial function.

ENGAGE

Essential Question: How do you find the rational roots of a polynomial equation?

Use the Rational Root Theorem to identify possible rational roots. Check each by using synthetic substitution. If a rational root is found, repeat the process on the quotient obtained from the bottom row of the synthetic substitution. Continue to find rational roots in this way until the quotient is quadratic, at which point you can try factoring to identify the last two rational roots.

PREVIEW: LESSON PERFORMANCE TASK

View the Engage section online. Discuss the photo and how the number of tourists in any given year can vary depending on many factors. Then preview the Lesson Performance Task.

Name ______________ Class ______________ Date ______________

7.1 Finding Rational Solutions of Polynomial Equations

Resource Locker

Essential Question: How do you find the rational roots of a polynomial equation?

Explore Relating Zeros and Coefficients of Polynomial Functions

The zeros of a polynomial function and the coefficients of the function are related. Consider the polynomial function $f(x) = (x + 2)(x - 1)(x + 3)$.

(A) Identify the zeros of the polynomial function. **The zeros are $x = -2$, $x = 1$, and $x = -3$.**

(B) Multiply the factors to write the function in standard form.

$$f(x) = (x + 2)(x - 1)(x + 3)$$
$$= (x^2 + 2x - x - 2)(x + 3)$$
$$= (x^2 + x - 2)(x + 3)$$
$$= x^3 + 3x^2 + x^2 + 3x - 2x - 6$$
$$= x^3 + 4x^2 + x - 6$$

(C) How are the zeros of $f(x)$ related to the standard form of the function? **Each of the zeros of the polynomial function is a factor of the constant term in the standard form.**

(D) Now consider the polynomial function $g(x) = (2x + 3)(4x - 5)(6x - 1)$. Identify the zeros of this function.

The zeros are $x = -\frac{3}{2}$, $x = \frac{5}{4}$, and $x = \frac{1}{6}$.

(E) Multiply the factors to write the function in standard form.

$$g(x) = (2x + 3)(4x - 5)(6x - 1)$$
$$= (8x^2 - 10x + 12x - 15)(6x - 1)$$
$$= (8x^2 + 2x - 15)(6x - 1)$$
$$= 48x^3 - 8x^2 + 12x^2 - 2x - 90x + 15$$
$$= 48x^3 + 4x^2 - 92x + 15$$

(F) How are the zeros of $g(x)$ related to the standard form of the function?

Each of the numerators of the zeros is a factor of the constant term, 15, and each of the denominators is a factor of the leading coefficient, 48.

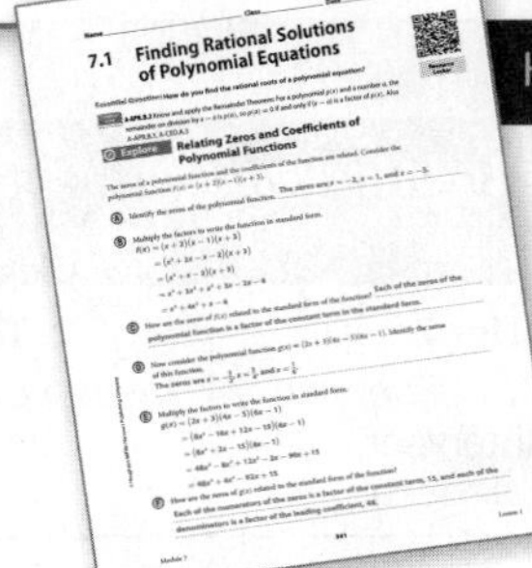

HARDCOVER PAGES 341–352

Watch for the hardcover student edition page numbers for this lesson.

Reflect

In general, how are the zeros of a polynomial function related to the function written in standard form?
Each of the numerators of the zeros is a factor of the constant term. Each of the denominators of the zeros is a factor of the leading coefficient.

Discussion Does the relationship from the first Reflect question hold if the zeros are all integers? Explain.
Yes; If the zeros are all integers, each of them can be written with a denominator of 1. Each of the numerators is still a factor of the constant term.

If you use the zeros, you can write the factored form of $g(x)$ as $g(x) = \left(x + \frac{3}{2}\right)\left(x - \frac{5}{4}\right)\left(x - \frac{1}{6}\right)$, rather than as $g(x) = (2x + 3)(4x - 5)(6x - 1)$. What is the relationship of the factors between the two forms? Give this relationship in a general form.
In each factor, the denominator of the fraction becomes the coefficient of the variable. In general, if the zero is $-\frac{b}{a}$, the factor can be written as $(ax + b)$.

Explain 1 Finding Zeros Using the Rational Zero Theorem

a polynomial function $p(x)$ is equal to $(a_1x + b_1)(a_2x + b_2)(a_3x + b_3)$, where a_1, a_2, a_3, b_1, b_2, and b_3 e integers, the leading coefficient of $p(x)$ will be the product $a_1a_2a_3$ and the constant term will be e product $b_1b_2b_3$. The zeros of $p(x)$ will be the rational numbers $-\frac{b_1}{a_1}$, $-\frac{b_2}{a_2}$, $-\frac{b_3}{a_3}$.

omparing the zeros of $p(x)$ to its coefficient and constant term shows that the numerators of the olynomial's zeros are factors of the constant term and the denominators of the zeros are factors of e leading coefficient. This result can be generalized as the Rational Zero Theorem.

Rational Zero Theorem

If $p(x)$ is a polynomial function with integer coefficients, and if $\frac{m}{n}$ is a zero of $p(x)$ $\left(p\left(\frac{m}{n}\right) = 0\right)$, then m is a factor of the constant term of $p(x)$ and n is a factor of the leading coefficient of $p(x)$.

Example 1 **Find the rational zeros of the polynomial function; then write the function as a product of factors. Make sure to test the possible zeros to find the actual zeros of the function.**

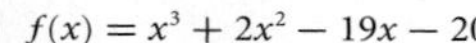

A) $f(x) = x^3 + 2x^2 - 19x - 20$

a. Use the Rational Zero Theorem to find all possible rational zeros.
Factors of -20: $\pm1, \pm2, \pm4, \pm5, \pm10, \pm20$

b. Test the possible zeros. Use a synthetic division table to organize the work. In this table, the first row represents the coefficients of the polynomial, the first column represents the divisors, and the last column represents the remainders.

$\frac{m}{n}$	1	2	−19	−20
1	1	3	−16	−36
2	1	4	−11	−42
4	1	6	5	0
5	1	7	16	60

PROFESSIONAL DEVELOPMENT

Integrate Mathematical Practices

This lesson provides an opportunity to address Mathematical Practice **MP.2**, which calls for students to translate between multiple representations and to "reason abstractly and quantitatively." Students explore the relationship between the factors of a polynomial function and its zeros. They learn how to identify the zeros given the factors, and the factors given the zeros. They then explore the relationships between the rational zeros of a function and its leading coefficient and constant term, establishing the Rational Zero Theorem.

EXPLORE

Relating Zeros and Coefficients of Polynomial Functions

INTEGRATE TECHNOLOGY

Students have the option of completing the Explore activity either in the book or online.

QUESTIONING STRATEGIES

? What is the relationship between the factors of a polynomial function and the zeros of the function? **The zeros are the values of x found by setting each factor equal to 0 and solving for x.**

? If a zero of a polynomial function is $\frac{7}{13}$, what do you know about the coefficients when the polynomial is written in standard form? **7 is a factor of the constant term and 13 is a factor of the leading coefficient.**

EXPLAIN 1

Finding Zeros Using the Rational Zero Theorem

QUESTIONING STRATEGIES

? Is every zero of a polynomial function represented in the set of numbers given by the Rational Zero Theorem? **No. The Rational Zero Theorem gives only those zeros that are rational numbers. A polynomial function can also have zeros that are irrational numbers or imaginary numbers.**

AVOID COMMON ERRORS

Some students may forget to include 1 and −1 in their list of possible rational zeros. You may want to suggest that they write these first so that they are not inadvertently left off the list.

QUESTIONING STRATEGIES

? If the leading coefficient of a polynomial function with integer coefficients is 1, what can you conclude about the function's rational zeros? Explain your reasoning. **They must be integers, because when you apply the Rational Zero Theorem, q can equal only 1 or −1 in $\frac{p}{q}$.**

c. Factor the polynomial. The synthetic division by 4 results in a remainder of 0, so 4 is a zero and the polynomial in factored form is given as follows:

$(x-4)(x^2+6x+5)=0$

$(x-4)(x+5)(x+1)=0$

$x=4, x=-5, \text{ or } x=-1$

The zeros are $x=4$, $x=-5$, or $x=-1$.

(B) $f(x)=x^4-4x^3-7x^2+22x+24$

a. Use the Rational Zero Theorem to find all possible rational zeros.

Factors of −24: ± 1, ± 2, ± 3, ± 4, ± 6, ± 8, ± 12, ± 24

b. Test the possible zeros. Use a synthetic division table.

$\frac{m}{n}$	1	−4	−7	22	24
1	1	−3	−10	12	36
2	1	−2	−11	0	24
3	1	−1	−10	−8	0

c. Factor the polynomial. The synthetic division by 3 results in a remainder of 0, so 3 is a zero and the polynomial in factored form is given as follows:

$(x-3)(x^3-x^2-10x-8)=0$

d. Use the Rational Zero Theorem again to find all possible rational zeros of $g(x)=x^3-x^2-10x-8$.

Factors of −8: ± 1, ± 2, ± 4, ± 8

e. Test the possible zeros. Use a synthetic division table.

$\frac{m}{n}$	1	−1	−10	−8
1	1	0	−10	−18
2	1	1	−8	−24
3	1	2	−4	−20
4	1	3	2	0

f. Factor the polynomial. The synthetic division by 4 results in a remainder of 0, so 4 is a zero and the polynomial in factored form is:

$(x-3)(x-4)(1x^2+3x+2)=0$

$(x-3)(x-4)(x+2)(x+1)=0$

$x=3, x=4, x=-2, \text{ or } x=-1$

The zeros are $x=3, x=4, x=-2, \text{ or } x=-1$.

COLLABORATIVE LEARNING

Small Group Activity

Have students work in groups of 3–4 students. Instruct each group to create a fifth-degree polynomial function with rational zeros, not all of which are integers. Ask them to write their functions in standard from. Have groups exchange functions, and have each group create a poster showing how to apply the Rational Zero Theorem to find the zeros of the function. Students' posters should also show verification that each number is indeed a zero of the function.

Reflect

4. How is using synthetic division on a 4th degree polynomial to find its zeros different than using synthetic division on a 3rd degree polynomial to find its zeros?

To find the zeros of a 4th degree polynomial using synthetic division, you need to use synthetic division to reduce that polynomial to a 3rd degree polynomial and then use synthetic division again to reduce that polynomial to a quadratic polynomial that can be factored, if possible.

5. Suppose you are trying to find the zeros the function $f(x) = x^2 + 1$. Would it be possible to use synthetic division on this polynomial? Why or why not?

It would not be possible to find the zeros of this polynomial using synthetic substitution because the function has no rational roots, only complex roots.

6. Using synthetic division, you find that $\frac{1}{2}$ is a zero of $f(x) = 2x^3 + x^2 - 13x + 6$. The quotient from the synthetic division array for $f\left(\frac{1}{2}\right)$ is $2x^2 + 2x - 12$. Show how to write the factored form of $f(x) = 2x^3 + x^2 - 13x + 6$ using integer coefficients.

Using $\frac{1}{2}$ as a zero and the quotient $2x^2 + 2x - 12$ you can write $f(x) = 2x^3 + x^2 - 13x + 6$ as $f(x) = \left(x - \frac{1}{2}\right)(2x^2 + 2x - 12)$.

$$f(x) = \left(x - \frac{1}{2}\right)(2x^2 + 2x - 12) = \left(x - \frac{1}{2}\right)(2)(x^2 + x - 6)$$
$$= (2x - 1)(x^2 + x - 6) = (2x - 1)(x + 3)(x - 2)$$

Your Turn

7. Find the zeros of $f(x) = x^3 - 2x^2 - 8x$.

a. Use the Rational Zero Theorem. Factors of 8: $\pm1, \pm2, \pm4, \pm8$

b. Test the possible zeros to find one that is actually a zero.

$\frac{m}{n}$	1	−2	−8	0
1	1	−1	−9	−9
2	1	0	−8	−16
4	1	2	0	0

c. Factor the polynomial using 4 as a zero.

$(x - 4)(x^2 + 2x) = 0$

$(x - 4)(x)(x + 2) = 0$

$x = 4, x = 0$, or $x = -2$ **The zeros are $x = 4, x = 0$, or $x = -2$.**

INTEGRATE MATHEMATICAL PRACTICES

Focus on Math Connections

MP.1 Remind students that a zero of a function is a number from the domain that the function pairs with 0. Discuss that, for this reason, a graph of the function will have an x-intercept at each zero. Students can then make a concrete connection between the rational zeros they identify for a function, and the role the zeros play in the graph of the function.

DIFFERENTIATE INSTRUCTION

Visual Cues

Encourage students to circle the leading coefficient in the function and to write "q is a factor of" above it, and to circle the constant term in the function and to write "p is a factor of" above it. This will be helpful when applying the Rational Zero Theorem, and will keep students from erroneously writing the reciprocals of the possible rational zeros, especially since the usages of p and q appear in reverse alphabetical order with respect to the function.

EXPLAIN 2

Solving a Real-World Problem Using the Rational Root Theorem

CONNECT VOCABULARY EL

Explain how the words *zeros* and *roots* (or solutions) have similar meanings but are used in different contexts. The *zeros* of a function are the *roots* (or solutions) of the related equation.

QUESTIONING STRATEGIES

? Why is it necessary to rewrite the equation so that it is equal to 0? **In order to find the roots of an equation using the Rational Root Theorem, the equation must be in the form $p(x) = 0$.**

? What information is obtained by applying the Rational Zero Theorem to a polynomial function? **A list of all possible rational zeros of the function**

Explain 2 Solving a Real-World Problem Using the Rational Root Theorem

Since a zero of a function $f(x)$ is a value of x for which $f(x) = 0$, finding the zeros of a polynomial function $p(x)$ is the same thing as find the solutions of the polynomial equation $p(x) = 0$. Because a solution of a polynomial equation is known as a **root**, the Rational Zero Theorem can be also expressed as the Rational Root Theorem.

Rational Root Theorem

If the polynomial $p(x)$ has integer coefficients, then every rational root of the polynomial equation $p(x) = 0$ can be written in the form $\frac{m}{n}$, where m is a factor of the constant term of $p(x)$ and n is a factor of the leading coefficient of $p(x)$.

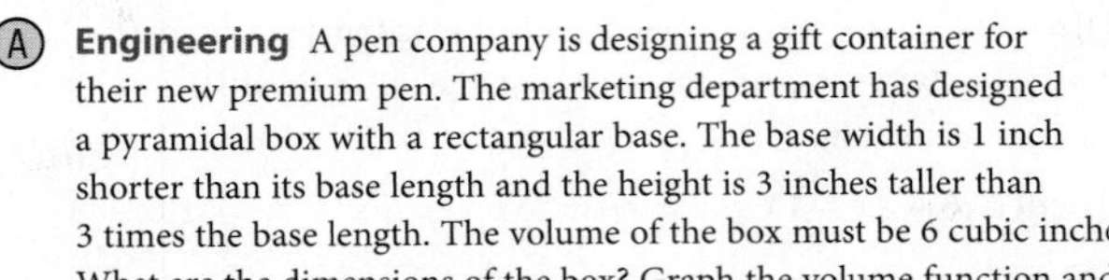

(A) **Engineering** A pen company is designing a gift container for their new premium pen. The marketing department has designed a pyramidal box with a rectangular base. The base width is 1 inch shorter than its base length and the height is 3 inches taller than 3 times the base length. The volume of the box must be 6 cubic inches. What are the dimensions of the box? Graph the volume function and the line $y = 6$ on a graphing calculator to check your solution.

A. Analyze Information

The important information is that the base width must be **1** inch shorter than

the base length, the height must be **3** inches taller than 3 times the base length,

and the box must have a volume of **6** cubic inches.

B. Formulate a Plan

Write an equation to model the volume of the box.

Let x represent the base length in inches. The base width is **$x - 1$** and the height is **$3x + 3$**, or **$3(x + 1)$**.

$$\frac{1}{3}\ell w h = V$$

$$\frac{1}{3}(\underline{x})(x - \underline{1})(3)(x + \underline{1}) = \underline{6}$$

$$\underline{1}\,x^3 - \underline{1}\,x - \underline{6} = 0$$

C. Solve

Use the Rational Root Theorem to find all possible rational roots.

Factors of −6: ± 1, ± 2, ± 3, ± 6

Test the possible roots. Use a synthetic division table.

$\frac{m}{n}$	1	0	−1	−6
1	1	1	0	−6
2	1	2	3	0
3	1	3	8	18

Factor the polynomial. The synthetic division by 2 results in a remainder of 0, so 2 is a root and the polynomial in factored form is as follows:

$(1x - 2)(1x^2 + 3x + 8) = 0$

The quadratic polynomial produces only complex roots, so the only possible answer for the base length is 2 inches. The base width is 1 inch and the height is 9 inches.

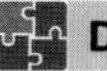

D. Justify and Evaluate

The x-coordinates of the points where the graphs of two functions, f and g, intersect is the solution of the equation $f(x) = g(x)$. Using a graphing calculator to graph the volume function and $y = 6$ results in the graphs intersecting at the point (2, 6).

Since the x-coordinate is 2, the answer is correct.

Your Turn

8. **Engineering** A box company is designing a new rectangular gift container. The marketing department has designed a box with a width 2 inches shorter than its length and a height 3 inches taller than its length. The volume of the box must be 56 cubic inches. What are the dimensions of the box?

A. **The box width must be 2 inches shorter than the length, the height must be 3 inches taller than the width, and the box must have a volume of 56 cubic inches.**

B. **Let x represent the length in inches. The width is $x - 2$ and the height is $x + 3$.**

$$\ell wh = V$$

$$(x)(x-2)(x+3) = 56$$

$$x^3 + x^2 - 6x = 56$$

$$x^3 + x^2 - 6x - 56 = 0$$

INTEGRATE MATHEMATICAL PRACTICES

Focus on Critical Thinking

MP.3 Prompt students to recognize that any rational roots found by factoring the resulting quadratic polynomial must be numbers that were identified as possible rational roots initially. This may help them to catch errors in factoring, or in performing the synthetic division.

ELABORATE

INTEGRATE MATHEMATICAL PRACTICES

Focus on Technology

MP.5 Have students discuss how they could use a graphing utility to help determine which numbers from their list of possible rational zeros are more likely than others to be zeros. Students should recognize that they can use the x-intercepts of the graph to help them focus in on which numbers on their lists are good candidates to test as possible zeros.

QUESTIONING STRATEGIES

? If a cubic function has only one rational root, what will be true about the quadratic polynomial quotient that results from synthetic division by the rational root? It will not be factorable over the set of integers.

SUMMARIZE THE LESSON

? How can you use the Rational Root Theorem to find the rational solutions of a polynomial equation? You can write the equation in the form $p(x) = 0$, and then use the theorem to identify possible roots of the equation. These roots will be of the form $\frac{p}{q}$. You can then test the possible roots using synthetic substitution. If you can reduce the polynomial to a quadratic, you can try factoring the quadratic to find any other rational roots.

C. Use the Rational Root Theorem. Factors of -56: $\pm1, \pm2, \pm4, \pm7, \pm8, \pm14, \pm28, \pm56$
Test the possible roots to find one that is actually a root. Use a synthetic division table.

$\frac{p}{q}$	1	1	−6	−56
1	1	2	−4	−60
2	1	3	0	−56
4	1	5	14	0

Factor the polynomial. using 4 as a root.
$(x - 4)(x^2 + 5x + 14)$
The quadratic polynomial produces only complex roots. The only possible answer for the length is 4 inches. The width is 2 inches and the height is 7 inches.

D. Using a graphing calculator, the graphs intersect at $(4, 56)$, which validates the answer.

Elaborate

9. For a polynomial function with integer coefficients, how are the function's coefficients and rational zeros related?
The rational zeros of a polynomial function with integer coefficients are in the form $\frac{m}{n}$, where m is a factor of the constant term and n is a factor of the leading coefficient.

10. Describe the process for finding the rational zeros of a polynomial function with integer coefficients.
Using the Rational Zero Theorem to find all possible rational zeros, test the possible zeros to find one that is actually a zero by using a synthetic division table to organize the work and factor the polynomial.

11. How is the Rational Root Theorem useful when solving a real-world problem about the volume of an object when the volume function is a polynomial and a specific value of the function is given?
The theorem is useful in this case because it allows you to find the rational roots of the polynomial equation created when you set the volume function equal to the given value. By rewriting the equation so that one side is 0, you can use the Rational Root Theorem to find the dimension given by the variable and then find the other dimensions.

12. Essential Question Check-In What does the Rational Root Theorem find?
The Rational Root Theorem finds the possible rational roots of a polynomial equation.

LANGUAGE SUPPORT EL

Communicating Math

Have students work in pairs. Instruct one student to write a polynomial function in factor form. Have the second student identify the zeros of the function and explain why they are the zeros. The students switch roles and repeat the process. Repeat the example from the lesson to provide a format.

Evaluate: Homework and Practice

- Online Homework
- Hints and Help
- Extra Practice

Find the rational zeros of each polynomial function then write each function in factored form.

1. $f(x) = x^3 - x^2 - 10x - 8$

   Factors of −8: ±1, ±2, ±4, ±8

   4 is a zero.

   $(x-4)(x^2+3x+2)=0$
   $(x-4)(x+2)(x+1)=0$
   $x=4, x=-2, \text{ or } x=-1$
   $f(x)=(x-4)(x+2)(x+1)$

2. $f(x) = x^3 + 2x^2 - 23x - 60$

   Factors of −60: ±1, ±2, ±3, ±4, ±5, ±6, ±10, ±12, ±15, ±20, ±30, ±60

   5 is a zero.

   $(x-5)(x^2+7x+12)=0$
   $(x-5)(x+3)(x+4)=0$
   $x=5, x=-3, \text{ or } x=-4$
   $f(x)=(x-5)(x+3)(x+4)$

3. $j(x) = 2x^3 - x^2 - 13x - 6$

   Factors of −6: ±1, ±2, ±3, ±6

   3 is a zero.

   $(x-3)(2x^2+5x+2)=0$
   $(x-3)(2x+1)(x+2)=0$
   $x=3, x=-\frac{1}{2}, \text{ or } x=-2$
   $j(x)=(x-3)(2x+1)(x+2)$

4. $g(x) = x^3 - 9x^2 + 23x - 15$

   Factors of −15: ±1, ±3, ±5, ±15

   1 is a zero.

   $(x-1)(x^2-8x+15)=0$
   $(x-4)(x-5)(x-3)=0$
   $x=4, x=5, \text{ or } x=3$
   $g(x)=(x-4)(x-5)(x-3)$

5. $h(x) = x^3 - 5x^2 + 2x + 8$

   Factors of 8: ±1, ±2, ±4, ±8

   2 is a zero.

   $(x-2)(x^2-3x-4)=0$
   $(x-2)(x-4)(x+1)=0$
   $x=2, x=4, \text{ or } x=-1$
   $m(x)=(x-2)(x-4)(x+1)$

6. $h(x) = 6x^3 - 7x^2 - 9x - 2$

   Factors of −2: ±1, ±2

   2 is a zero.

   $(x-2)(6x^2+5x+1)=0$
   $(x-2)(2x+1)(3x+1)=0$
   $x=2, x=-\frac{1}{2}, \text{ or } x=-\frac{1}{3}$
   $h(x)=(x-2)(2x+1)(3x+1)$

7. $s(x) = x^3 - x^2 - x + 1$

   Factors of 1: ±1

   1 is a zero.

   $(x-1)(x^2-1)=0$
   $(x-1)(x+1)(x-1)=0$
   $x=1 \text{ or } x=-1$
   $s(x)=(x-1)(x+1)(x-1)$

8. $t(x) = x^3 + x^2 - 8x - 12$

   Factors of −12: ±1, ±2, ±3, ±4, ±6, ±12

   3 is a zero.

   $(x-3)(x^2+4x+4)=0$
   $(x-3)(x+2)(x+2)=0$
   $x=3 \text{ or } x=-2$
   $t(x)=(x-3)(x+2)(x+2)$

Exercise	Depth of Knowledge (D.O.K.)	COMMON CORE Mathematical Practices
1–12	**1** Recall of Information	**MP.5** Using Tools
13–17	**2** Skills/Concepts	**MP.4** Modeling
18–19	**2** Skills/Concepts H.O.T.	**MP.3** Logic
20	**3** Strategic Thinking H.O.T.	**MP.2** Reasoning
21	**3** Strategic Thinking H.O.T.	**MP.3** Logic

EVALUATE

ASSIGNMENT GUIDE

Concepts and Skills	Practice
Explore Relating Zeros and Coefficients of Polynomial Functions	Exercise 17
Example 1 Finding Zeros Using the Rational Zero Theorem	Exercises 2–12
Example 2 Solving a Real-World Problem Using the Rational Root Theorem	Exercises 13–16

INTEGRATE MATHEMATICAL PRACTICES

Focus on Patterns

MP.8 Students can use patterns in the signs of the terms in the polynomial function to help them decide which of the possible rational zeros to test. For example, if the signs of the terms in the polynomial function (or in the quotient after dividing synthetically) are all positive, students need not check any positive numbers on their lists.

AVOID COMMON ERRORS

Students may incorrectly conclude that a polynomial function that has n rational zeros has only n real zeros. Explain that the function may have irrational zeros as well, and irrational zeros are real zeros.

CONNECT VOCABULARY EL

Have students, in their own words, explain how the Rational Zero Theorem and the Rational Root Theorem are related (for example, a solution of a polynomial equation is often called a root).

9. $k(x) = x^4 + 5x^3 - x^2 - 17x + 12$

Factors of 12: $\pm1, \pm2, \pm3, \pm4, \pm6, \pm12$

1 is a zero.

Factor the polynomial.

$(x-1)(x^3+6x^2+5x-12)$

Factors of 12: $\pm1, \pm2, \pm3, \pm4, \pm6, \pm12$

1 is a zero.

$(x-1)(x-1)(x^2+7x+12) = 0$

$(x-1)(x-1)(x+3)(x+4) = 0$

$x = 1, x = -3,$ **or** $x = -4$

$k(x) = (x-1)(x-1)(x+3)(x+4)$

10. $g(x) = x^4 - 6x^3 + 11x^2 - 6x$

$g(x) = x(x^3 - 6x^2 + 11x - 6)$

Factors of 6: $\pm1, \pm2, \pm3, \pm6$

1 is a zero.

$(x)(x-1)(x^2-5x+6) = 0$

$(x)(x-1)(x-3)(x-2) = 0$

$x = 1, x = 0, x = 3,$ **or** $x = 2$

$g(x) = (x)(x-1)(x-3)(x-2)$

11. $h(x) = x^4 - 2x^3 - 3x^2 + 4x + 4$

Factors of 4: $\pm1, \pm2, \pm4$

2 is a zero.

$(x-2)(x^3-3x-2)$

Factors of 2: $\pm1, \pm2$

2 is a zero.

$(x-2)(x-2)(x^2+2x+1) = 0$

$(x-2)(x-2)(x+1)(x+1) = 0$

$x = -1$ **or** $x = 2$

$h(x) = (x-2)(x-2)(x+1)(x+1)$

12. $f(x) = x^4 - 5x^2 + 4$

Factors of 4: $\pm1, \pm2, \pm4$

1 is a zero.

$f(x) = (x-1)(x^3+x^2-4x-4)$

Factors of -4: $\pm1, \pm2, \pm4$

2 is a zero.

$(x-1)(x-2)(x^2+3x+2) = 0$

$(x-1)(x-2)(x+2)(x+1) = 0$

$x = 1, x = 2, x = -2,$ **or** $x = -1$

$f(x) = (x-1)(x-2)(x+2)(x+1)$

13. Manufacturing A laboratory supply company is designing a new rectangular box in which to ship glass pipes. The company has created a box with a width 2 inches shorter than its length and a height 9 inches taller than twice its length. The volume of each box must be 45 cubic inches. What are the dimensions?

Let x represent the length in inches. Then the width is $x - 2$ and the height is $2x + 9$.

$$\ell wh = V$$

$$(x)(x-2)(2x+9) = 0$$

$$2x^3 + 5x^2 - 18x = 45$$

$$2x^3 + 5x^2 - 18x - 45 = 0$$

Factors of -45: $\pm1, \pm3, \pm5, \pm9, \pm15, \pm45$

3 is a root.

$(x-3)(2x^2+11x+15) = 0$

The quadratic factor produces only complex roots. The only possible answer for the length is 3 inches. The width is 1 inch and the height is 15 inches.

4. **Engineering** A natural history museum is building a pyramidal glass structure for its tree snake exhibit. Its research team has designed a pyramid with a square base and with a height that is 2 yards more than a side of its base. The volume of the pyramid must be 147 cubic yards. What are the dimensions?

Let x represent the side of the square base in yards. The height is $x + 2$.

$$\frac{1}{3}\ell wh = V$$
$$\frac{1}{3}(x)(x)(x+2) = 147$$
$$\frac{1}{3}(x^3 + 2x^2) = 147$$
$$x^3 + 2x^2 = 441$$

$x^3 + 2x^2 - 441 = 0$ **Factors of -441: $\pm1, \pm3, \pm7, \pm9, \pm21, \pm49, \pm63, \pm147, \pm441$**

7 is a root.

$$(x-7)(x^2 + 9x + 63) = 0$$

The quadratic factor produces only complex roots. So, each side of the base is 7 yards and the height is 9 yards.

5. **Engineering** A paper company is designing a new, pyramid-shaped paperweight. Its development team has decided that to make the length of the paperweight 4 inches less than the height and the width of the paperweight 3 inches less than the height. The paperweight must have a volume of 12 cubic inches. What are the dimensions of the paperweight?

Let x represent the height in inches. The length is $x - 4$ and the width is $x - 3$.

$$\frac{1}{3}\ell wh = V$$
$$\frac{1}{3}(x-4)(x-3)(x) = 12$$
$$\frac{1}{3}(x^3 - 7x^2 + 12x) = 12$$
$$x^3 - 7x^2 + 12x = 36$$
$$x^3 - 7x^2 + 12x - 36 = 0$$

Factors of -36: $\pm1, \pm2, \pm3, \pm4, \pm6, \pm9, \pm12, \pm18, \pm36$

6 is a root.

$$(x-6)(x^2 - x + 6) = 0$$

The quadratic factor produces only complex roots. So, the height is 6 inches, the length is 2 inches, and the width is 3 inches.

CRITICAL THINKING

Discuss with students *why* the Rational Root Theorem works, by applying it to a quadratic equation, such as $2x^2 + x - 15 = 0$, and showing how the process of solving the equation by factoring focuses on the factors of p and q in a way that is similar to the process of the Rational Root Theorem. Focus students' attention on how p is the product of the first coefficients of the factors, and q is the product of the constant terms of the factors.

PEER-TO-PEER DISCUSSION

Ask students to discuss with a partner how the Rational Root Theorem, in conjunction with the Zero Product Property, enables them to solve real-world problems that can be modeled by polynomial equations. **The Rational Root Theorem can be used to identify possible solutions. Identifying one or more of the solutions from the list of possible solutions can help you to write the equation in factored form. You can then use the Zero Product Property to set each factor equal to zero and solve for other possible solutions.**

JOURNAL

Have students describe how they could use the Rational Zero Theorem to write a polynomial function in intercept form.

16. Match each set of roots with its polynomial function.

A. $x = 2, x = 3, x = 4$ **B** $f(x) = (x + 2)(x - 4)\left(x - \frac{3}{2}\right)$

B. $x = -2, x = -4, x = \frac{3}{2}$ **C** $f(x) = \left(x - \frac{1}{2}\right)\left(x - \frac{5}{4}\right)\left(x + \frac{7}{3}\right)$

C. $x = \frac{1}{2}, x = \frac{5}{4}, x = \frac{-7}{3}$ **A** $f(x) = (x - 2)(x - 2)(x - 2)$

D. $x = \frac{-4}{5}, x = \frac{6}{7}, x = 4$ **D** $f(x) = \left(x + \frac{4}{5}\right)\left(x - \frac{6}{7}\right)(x - 4)$

17. Identify the zeroes of $f(x) = (x + 3)(x - 4)(x - 3)$, write the function in standard form, and state how the zeros are related to the standard form.

The zeroes of $f(x)$ are $x = -3$, $x = 4$, and $x = 3$.

$f(x) = (x + 3)(x - 4)(x - 3) = (x^2 + 3x - 4x - 12)(x - 3)$

$= (x^2 - x - 12)(x - 3) = x^3 - 3x^2 - x^2 + 3x - 12x + 36$

$= x^3 - 4x^2 - 9x + 36$

The zeros of $f(x)$ are all factors of the constant term in the polynomial function.

H.O.T. Focus on Higher Order Thinking

18. Critical Thinking Consider the polynomial function $g(x) = 2x^3 - 6x^2 + \pi x + 5$. Is it possible to use the Rational Zero Theorem and synthetic division to factor this polynomial? Explain.

No; it is not possible because the function contains a term, πx, whose coefficient is irrational and, therefore, not an integer.

19. Explain the Error Sabrina was told to find the zeros of the polynomial function $h(x) = x(x - 4)(x + 2)$. She stated that the zeros of this polynomial are $x = 0$, $x = -4$, and $x = 2$. Explain her error.

For any factor $(ax + b)$, a zero occurs at $-\frac{b}{a}$. Sabrina forgot to include the negative sign when converting from her factors to the zeros.

20. Justify Reasoning If $\frac{c}{b}$ is a rational zero of a polynomial function $p(x)$, explain why $bx - c$ must be a factor of the polynomial.

Since $p\left(\frac{c}{b}\right) = 0$, $x - \frac{c}{b}$ is a factor of $p(x)$ by the Factor Theorem. So, $p(x) = \left(x - \frac{c}{b}\right)q(x)$ and $p(x) = \frac{b}{b}\left(x - \frac{c}{b}\right)q(x) = \frac{1}{b}(bx - c)q(x)$, which shows that $bx - c$ is a factor of $p(x)$.

21. Justify Reasoning A polynomial function $p(x)$ has degree 3, and its zeros are -3, 4, and 6. What do you think is the equation of $p(x)$? Do you think there could be more than one possibility? Explain.

$p(x) = (x + 3)(x - 4)(x - 6)$; any constant multiple of $p(x)$ will also have degree 3 and the same zeros, so the equation can be any function of the form $p(x) = a(x + 3)(x - 4)(x - 6)$ where $a \neq 0$.

Lesson Performance Task

For the years from 2001–2010, the number of Americans traveling to other countries by plane can be represented by the polynomial function $A(t) = 20t^4 - 428t^3 + 2760t^2 - 4320t + 33,600$, where A is the number of thousands of Americans traveling abroad by airplane and t is the number of years since 2001. In which year were there 40,000,000 Americans traveling abroad? Use the Rational Root Theorem to find your answer.
[Hint: consider the function's domain and range before finding all possible rational roots.]

$$A(t) = 20t^4 - 428t^3 + 2760t^2 - 4320t + 33,600$$
$$40,000 = 20t^4 - 428t^3 + 2760t^2 - 4320t + 33,600$$
$$0 = 20t^4 - 428t^3 + 2760t^2 - 4320t - 6400$$

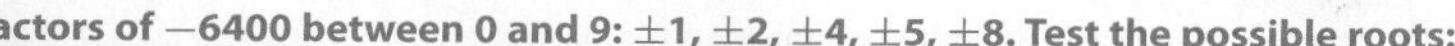

Factors of −6400 between 0 and 9: ±1, ±2, ±4, ±5, ±8. Test the possible roots:

$\frac{p}{q}$	20	−428	2760	−4320	−6400
1	20	−408	2352	−1968	−8368
2	20	−388	1984	−352	−7104
4	20	−348	1368	1152	−1792
5	20	−328	1120	1280	0
8	20	−268	616	608	1536

$(x - 5)(20x^3 - 328x^2 + 1120x + 1280)$

Factors of 1280 between 0 and 9: ±1, ±2, ±4, ±5, ±8. Test the possible roots to find one that is actually a root.

$\frac{p}{q}$	20	−328	1120	1280
1	20	−308	812	2092
2	20	−288	544	2368
4	20	−248	128	1792
5	20	−228	20	1380
8	20	−168	−224	512

Because the cubic polynomial factor has only irrational roots, $x = 5$ years returns the only solution. In other words, there were 40,000,000 Americans traveling overseas by air in 2006.

AVOID COMMON ERRORS

Some students may set $A(t)$ equal to 40,000,000, which is the number given in the problem. Ask students to check to units of A. thousands of Americans. Have students divide 40,000,000 by 1,000 to get the correct value for A, 40,000. More precisely, A is 40,000 thousands of Americans.

QUESTIONING STRATEGIES

Why is it useful to know a function's domain when solving for the roots? **If the domain consists only of rational numbers, then the roots must be rational. For example, if the domain consists of the integers from 0 to 9, then the roots must be rational because integers are rational numbers.**

Why does the domain consist only of integers? **The domain is the number of years since 2001. The function only makes sense for integer values.**

EXTENSION ACTIVITY

Have students research the factors that affect tourist numbers, such as changes in economic status, or the safety of a destination. Have students discuss who might use a model of tourist numbers like $A(t)$ and how it might be used. Ask students to describe situations in which it would be useful to input a value of t to calculate the number of tourists, and in what situations it would be useful to do the inverse—use a given number of tourists and solve for the roots.

Scoring Rubric

2 points: Student correctly solves the problem and explains his/her reasoning.

1 point: Student shows good understanding of the problem but does not fully solve or explain his/her reasoning.

0 points: Student does not demonstrate understanding of the problem.

LESSON 7.2

Finding Complex Solutions of Polynomial Equations

Common Core Math Standards

The student is expected to:

 **A-APR.B.2**

Know and apply the Remainder Theorem: .... Also N-CN.C.9(+), A-REI.D.11, A-APR.B.3, F-IF.C.7c

Mathematical Practices

 **MP.7 Using Structure**

Language Objective

Complete a "Solving Polynomial Equations" chart with a partner.

ENGAGE

Essential Question: What do the Fundamental Theorem of Algebra and its corollary tell you about the roots of the polynomial equation $p(x) = 0$ where $p(x)$ has degree n?

The equation has exactly n complex roots provided that you count the multiplicities of the roots.

PREVIEW: LESSON PERFORMANCE TASK

View the Engage section online. Discuss the photo and what variables you might use to describe the amount of violence in a movie. Then preview the Lesson Performance Task.

Name ______ Class ______ Date ______

7.2 Finding Complex Solutions of Polynomial Equations

Resource Locker

Essential Question: What do the Fundamental Theorem of Algebra and its corollary tell you about the roots of the polynomial equation p(x) = 0 where p(x) has degree n?

Explore Investigating the Number of Complex Zeros of a Polynomial Function

You have used various algebraic and graphical methods to find the roots of a polynomial equation $p(x) = 0$ or the zeros of a polynomial function $p(x)$. Because a polynomial can have a factor that repeats, a zero or a root can occur multiple times.

The polynomial $p(x) = x^3 + 8x^2 + 21x + 18 = (x + 2)(x + 3)^2$ has -2 as a zero once and -3 as a zero twice, or *with multiplicity 2*. The **multiplicity** of a zero of $p(x)$ or a root of $p(x) = 0$ is the number of times that the related factor occurs in the factorization.

In this Explore, you will use algebraic methods to investigate the relationship between the degree of a polynomial function and the number of zeros that it has.

(A) Find all zeros of $p(x) = x^3 + 7x^2$. Include any multiplicities greater than 1.

$p(x) = x^3 + 7x^2$

Factor out the GCF. $p(x) = \boxed{x^2}(x + 7)$

What are all the zeros of $p(x)$? 0 (mult. 2), −7

(B) Find all zeros of $p(x) = x^3 - 64$. Include any multiplicities greater than 1.

$p(x) = x^3 - 64$

Factor the difference of two cubes. $p(x) = \left(x \boxed{-} 4\right)\left(x^2 + \boxed{4x} + \boxed{16}\right)$

What are the real zeros of $p(x)$? 4

Solve $x^2 + 4x + 16 = 0$ using the quadratic formula.

$$x = \frac{-b \pm \sqrt{b^2 - 4ac}}{2a}$$

$$x = \frac{\boxed{-4} \pm \sqrt{4^2 - 4 \cdot 1 \cdot \boxed{16}}}{2 \cdot \boxed{1}} \quad x = \frac{-4 \pm \sqrt{\boxed{-48}}}{2} \quad x = \frac{-4 \pm \boxed{4i}\sqrt{3}}{2}$$

$x = -2 \pm 2i\sqrt{3}$

What are the non-real zeros of $p(x)$? $-2 + 2i\sqrt{3}, -2 - 2i\sqrt{3}$

HARDCOVER PAGES 353–368

Watch for the hardcover student edition page numbers for this lesson.

Ⓒ Find all zeros of $p(x) = x^4 + 3x^3 - 4x^2 - 12x$. Include any multiplicities greater than 1.

$$p(x) = x^4 + 3x^3 - 4x^2 - 12x$$

Factor out the GCF. $p(x) = x\left(\boxed{x^3 + 3x^2 - 4x - 12}\right)$

Group terms to begin factoring by grouping. $p(x) = x\left((x^3 + 3x^2) - \left(\boxed{4x + 12}\right)\right)$

Factor out common monomials. $p(x) = x\left(\boxed{x^2}(x + 3) - \boxed{4}(x + 3)\right)$

Factor out the common binomial. $p(x) = x(x + 3)(x^2 - 4)$

Factor the difference of squares. $p(x) = x(x + 3)\left(\boxed{x + 2}\right)\left(\boxed{x - 2}\right)$

What are all the zeros of $p(x)$? **0, −3, −2, 2**

Ⓓ Find all zeros of $p(x) = x^4 - 16$. Include any multiplicities greater than 1.

$$p(x) = x^4 - 16$$

Factor the difference of squares. $p(x) = \left(\boxed{x^2 - 4}\right)(x^2 + 4)$

Factor the difference of squares. $p(x) = \left(\boxed{x + 2}\right)\left(\boxed{x - 2}\right)(x^2 + 4)$

What are the real zeros of $p(x)$? **−2, 2**

Solve $x^2 + 4 = 0$ by taking square roots.

$x^2 + 4 = 0$

$x^2 = -4$

$x = \pm\sqrt{-4}$

$x = \pm\ \boxed{2i}$

What are the non-real zeros of $p(x)$? **−2i, 2i**

PROFESSIONAL DEVELOPMENT

Learning Progressions

Students have learned factoring techniques in earlier lessons, and a more general technique for finding zeros of polynomial functions and solutions of polynomial equations based on the Rational Zero/Root Theorem in the previous lesson. They have also learned how to use the quadratic formula to solve quadratic equations. In this lesson, students pull all these techniques together in order to understand and use the Fundamental Theorem of Algebra.

EXPLORE

Investigating the Number of Complex Zeros of a Polynomial Function

INTEGRATE TECHNOLOGY

Students have the option of completing the Explore activity either in the book or online.

QUESTIONING STRATEGIES

? When would you need to use the quadratic formula to find a zero? **When one of the factors of the polynomial is a non-factorable quadratic polynomial.**

INTEGRATE MATHEMATICAL PRACTICES

Focus on Patterns

MP.8 Encourage students to look for patterns in their results. They can make connections between the degree of each polynomial and the number of zeros, and between a function's characteristics and their effects on the nature of its zeros. Students can also be prompted to make conjectures about the number of each type of zero (real and non-real) that could exist for polynomials of varying degrees.

(E) Find all zeros of $p(x) = x^4 + 5x^3 + 6x^2 - 4x - 8$. Include multiplicities greater than 1.

By the Rational Zero Theorem, possible rational zeros are ± 1, ± 2, ± 4, and ± 8. Use a synthetic division table to test possible zeros.

$\frac{m}{n}$	1	5	6	−4	−8
1	1	6	12	8	0

The remainder is 0, so 1 is/is not a zero.

$p(x)$ factors as $(x - 1)\left(x^3 + 6x^2 + 12x + 8\right)$.

Test for zeros in the cubic polynomial.

$\frac{m}{n}$	1	6	12	8
1	1	7	19	27
−1	1	5	7	1
2	1	8	28	64
−2	1	4	4	0

−2 a zero.

$p(x)$ factors as $(x - 1)(x + 2)\left(x^2 + 4x + 4\right)$. The quadratic is a perfect square trinomial.

So, $p(x)$ factors completely as $p(x) = (x - 1)\,(x + 2)^3$.

What are all the zeros of $p(x)$? 1, −2 (mult. 3)

Complete the table to summarize your results from Steps A–E.

Polynomial Function in Standard Form	Polynomial Function Factored over the Integers	Real Zeros and Their Multiplicities	Non-real Zeros and Their Multiplicities
$p(x) = x^3 + 7x^2$	$p(x) = x^2(x + 7)$	0 (mult. 2); −7	None
$p(x) = x^3 - 64$	$p(x) = (x - 4)(x^2 + 4x + 16)$	4	$-2 + 2i\sqrt{3}$; $-2 - 2i\sqrt{3}$
$p(x) = x^4 + 3x^3 - 4x^2 - 12x$	$p(x) = x(x + 3)(x + 2)(x - 2)$	0; −3; −2; 2	None
$p(x) = x^4 - 16$	$p(x) = (x - 2)(x + 2)(x^2 + 4)$	−2; 2	$-2i$; $2i$
$p(x) = x^4 + 5x^3 + 6x^2 - 4x - 8$	$p(x) = (x - 1)(x + 2)^3$	1, −2 (mult. 3)	None

COLLABORATIVE LEARNING

Peer-to-Peer Activity

Provide pairs of students with a fourth degree polynomial equation and a fifth degree polynomial equation. Have them work together to determine the number of possible combinations of types of roots for each equation. Then have them graph their equations, and use the graphs to help predict which combination of roots will be the correct combination for each function. Challenge them to solve the equations to verify their predictions.

Reflect

1. Examine the table. For each function, count the number of unique zeros, both real and non-real. How does the number of unique zeros compare with the degree?
The number of unique zeros is less than or equal to the degree.

2. Examine the table again. This time, count the total number of zeros for each function, where a zero of multiplicity m is counted as m zeros. How does the total number of zeros compare with the degree?
The total number of zeros is the same as the degree of the function.

3. **Discussion** Describe the apparent relationship between the degree of a polynomial function and the number of zeros it has.
The number of zeros of a polynomial function is the same as the degree of the function when you include complex zeros and count the multiplicities of the zeros in the total.

 Explain 1 Applying the Fundamental Theorem of Algebra to Solving Polynomial Equations

The Fundamental Theorem of Algebra and its corollary summarize what you have observed earlier while finding rational zeros of polynomial functions and in completing the Explore.

The Fundamental Theorem of Algebra

Every polynomial function of degree $n \geq 1$ has at least one zero, where a zero may be a complex number.

Corollary: Every polynomial function of degree $n \geq 1$ has exactly n zeros, including multiplicities.

Because the zeros of a polynomial function $p(x)$ give the roots of the equation $p(x) = 0$, the theorem and its corollary also extend to finding all roots of a polynomial equation.

Example 1 **Solve the polynomial equation by finding all roots.**

(A) $2x^3 - 12x^2 - 34x + 204 = 0$

The polynomial has degree 3, so the equation has exactly 3 roots.

$$2x^3 - 12x^2 - 34x + 204 = 0$$

Divide both sides by 2. $\quad x^3 - 6x^2 - 17x + 102 = 0$

Group terms. $\quad (x^3 - 6x^2) - (17x - 102) = 0$

Factor out common monomials. $\quad x^2(x - 6) - 17(x - 6) = 0$

Factor out the common binomial. $\quad (x^2 - 17)(x - 6) = 0$

One root is $x = 6$. Solving $x^2 - 17 = 0$ gives $x^2 = 17$, or $x = \pm\sqrt{17}$.

The roots are $-\sqrt{17}$, $\sqrt{17}$, and 6.

EXPLAIN 1

Applying the Fundamental Theorem of Algebra to Solving Polynomial Equations

INTEGRATE MATHEMATICAL PRACTICES

Focus on Math Connections

MP.1 Substantiate The Fundamental Theorem of Algebra and its corollary by applying them to solutions of linear equations and easily factorable quadratic equations, with which students are familiar. Include examples of quadratic equations that have roots with multiplicity of 2.

DIFFERENTIATE INSTRUCTION

Communicating Math

Understanding the concept of the degree of a polynomial is important in applying the Fundamental Theorem of Algebra and its corollary. Students (especially English language learners) may benefit from a rigorous review of finding degrees of polynomials written in standard form, factored form, and with terms in varying orders of degree. Focus on polynomials that contain only single-variable monomials. Check that students can explain how to find the degree of the polynomial for each of the different forms.

QUESTIONING STRATEGIES

? If, after using synthetic substitution to test all possible rational roots of a cubic equation, you find only one root of the equation, can you conclude that the remaining roots are imaginary? Explain. **No. The remaining roots may be imaginary or they may be irrational.**

(B) $x^4 - 6x^2 - 27 = 0$

The polynomial has degree 4, so the equation has exactly 4 roots.

Notice that $x^4 - 6x^2 - 27$ has the form $u^2 - 6u - 27$, where $u = x^2$. So, you can factor it like a quadratic trinomial.

$$x^4 - 6x^2 - 27 = 0$$

Factor the trinomial. $\left(x^2 - \boxed{9}\right)\left(x^2 + \boxed{3}\right) = 0$

Factor the difference of squares. $\left(x + \boxed{3}\right)\left(x - \boxed{3}\right)(x^2 + 3) = 0$

The real roots are -3 and 3. Solving $x^2 + 3 = 0$ gives $x^2 = -3$, or

$x = \pm\sqrt{-3} = \pm \boxed{i}\sqrt{\boxed{3}}$.

The roots are $-3, 3, -i\sqrt{3}, i\sqrt{3}$.

Reflect

4. Restate the Fundamental Theorem of Algebra and its corollary in terms of the roots of equations.

Theorem: For every polynomial of degree $n \geq 1$, the equation $p(x) = 0$ has at least one root, where a root may be a complex number. Corollary: For every polynomial of degree $n \geq 1$, the equation $p(x) = 0$ has exactly n roots, when you include multiplicity.

Your Turn

Solve the polynomial equation by finding all roots.

5. $8x^3 - 27 = 0$

$(2x - 3)(4x^2 + 6x + 9) = 0$

$2x - 3 = 0$

$x = \frac{3}{2}$

$4x^2 + 6x + 9 = 0$

$x = \frac{-(6) \pm \sqrt{(6)^2 - 4(4)(9)}}{2(4)}$

$x = \frac{-6 \pm \sqrt{-108}}{8} = \frac{-6 \pm 6i\sqrt{3}}{8}$

$x = \frac{-3 \pm 3i\sqrt{3}}{4}$, or $-\frac{3}{4} \pm \frac{3}{4}i\sqrt{3}$

The roots are $\frac{3}{2}$, $\frac{-3 + 3i\sqrt{3}}{4}$, and $\frac{-3 - 3i\sqrt{3}}{4}$.

6. $p(x) = x^4 - 13x^3 + 55x^2 - 91x$

$x(x^3 - 13x^2 + 55x - 91) = 0$

One root is $x = 0$.

Possible rational roots: $\pm1, \pm7, \pm13, \pm91$.

Use synthetic division to test for roots.

A second root is $x = 7$.

Solve $x^2 - 6x + 13 = 0$.

$x = \frac{-(-6) \pm \sqrt{(-6)^2 - 4(1)(13)}}{2 \cdot 1}$

$x = \frac{6 \pm \sqrt{-16}}{2} = \frac{6 \pm 4i}{2}$

$x = 3 \pm 2i$

The roots are 0, 7, $3 + 2i$, and $3 - 2i$.

LANGUAGE SUPPORT EL

Communicate Math

Have students work in pairs. Have them write the theorems in this module for solving polynomial equations, the Rational Zero Theorem, Rational Roots Theorem, and the Fundamental Theorem of Algebra, and then work together to explain the theorems in their own words. Then have students write the explanations and give an example for each theorem.

Explain 2 Writing a Polynomial Function From Its Zeros

You may have noticed in finding roots of quadratic and polynomial equations that any irrational or complex roots come in pairs. These pairs reflect the "±" in the quadratic formula. For example, for any of the following number pairs, you will never have a polynomial equation for which only one number in the pair is a root.

$$\sqrt{5} \text{ and } -\sqrt{5};\ 1 + \sqrt{7} \text{ and } 1 - \sqrt{7};\ i \text{ and } -i;\ 2 + 14i \text{ and } 2 - 14i;\ \frac{11}{6} + \frac{1}{6}i\sqrt{3} \text{ and } \frac{11}{6} - \frac{1}{6}i\sqrt{3}$$

The irrational root pairs $a + b\sqrt{c}$ and $a - b\sqrt{c}$ are called *irrational conjugates*. The complex root pairs $a + bi$ and $a - bi$ are called *complex conjugates*.

Irrational Root Theorem

If a polynomial $p(x)$ has rational coefficients and $a + b\sqrt{c}$ is a root of the equation $p(x) = 0$, where a and b are rational and $\sqrt{c}$ is irrational, then $a - b\sqrt{c}$ is also a root of $p(x) = 0$.

Complex Conjugate Root Theorem

If $a + bi$ is an imaginary root of a polynomial equation with real-number coefficients, then $a - bi$ is also a root.

Because the roots of the equation $p(x) = 0$ give the zeros of a polynomial function, corresponding theorems apply to the zeros of a polynomial function. You can use this fact to write a polynomial function from its zeros. Because irrational and complex conjugate pairs are a sum and difference of terms, the product of irrational conjugates is always a rational number and the product of complex conjugates is always a real number.

$$(2 - \sqrt{10})(2 + \sqrt{10}) = 2^2 - (\sqrt{10})^2 = 4 - 10 = -6 \qquad (1 - i\sqrt{2})(1 + i\sqrt{2}) = 1^2 - (i\sqrt{2})^2 = 1 - (-1)(2) = 3$$

Example 2 **Write the polynomial function with least degree and a leading coefficient of 1 that has the given zeros.**

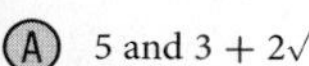

(A) 5 and $3 + 2\sqrt{7}$

Because irrational zeros come in conjugate pairs, $3 - 2\sqrt{7}$ must also be a zero of the function.

Use the 3 zeros to write a function in factored form, then multiply to write it in standard form.

	$p(x) = \left[x - (3 + 2\sqrt{7})\right]\left[x - (3 - 2\sqrt{7})\right](x - 5)$
Multiply the first two factors using FOIL.	$= \left[x^2 - (3 - 2\sqrt{7})x - (3 + 2\sqrt{7})x + (3 + 2\sqrt{7})(3 - 2\sqrt{7})\right](x - 5)$
Multipy the conjugates.	$= \left[x^2 - (3 - 2\sqrt{7})x - (3 + 2\sqrt{7})x + (9 - 4 \cdot 7)\right](x - 5)$
Combine like terms.	$= \left[x^2 + (-3 + 2\sqrt{7} - 3 - 2\sqrt{7})x + (-19)\right](x - 5)$
Simplify.	$= \left[x^2 - 6x - 19\right](x - 5)$
Distributive property	$= x(x^2 - 6x - 19) - 5(x^2 - 6x - 19)$
Multiply.	$= x^3 - 6x^2 - 19x - 5x^2 + 30x + 95$
Combine like terms.	$= x^3 - 11x^2 + 11x + 95$

The polynomial function is $p(x) = x^3 - 11x^2 + 11x + 95$.

EXPLAIN 2

Writing a Polynomial Function From its Zeros

QUESTIONING STRATEGIES

? If one zero of a fourth degree polynomial function is rational, what must be true about the other three zeros? **One of the three must also be rational. The other two could be either irrational conjugates or imaginary conjugates.**

? Is it possible for a fifth degree polynomial equation to have no real zeros? Explain. **No. Since imaginary zeros occur in conjugate pairs, there could be at most 4 imaginary zeros. Therefore, at least one zero must be real.**

AVOID COMMON ERRORS

Students may make errors when multiplying factors of the form $(x - a)$, where a is an irrational number such as $3 + \sqrt{2}$ or an imaginary number such as $1 - 4i$. Encourage them to multiply each of these types of factors with the factor that contains the conjugate of the irrational or imaginary number first, and show them how to use grouping to make the multiplication easier.

INTEGRATE MATHEMATICAL PRACTICES

Focus on Critical Thinking

MP.3 Have students discuss how they could write the rule for a third degree polynomial function whose graph passes through $(1+\sqrt{2}, 0)$ and the origin. Then have them find the function, and use a graphing calculator to check their work.

 2, 3 and $1-i$

Because complex zeros come in conjugate pairs, $\underline{1+i}$ must also be a zero of the function.

Use the 4 zeros to write a function in factored form, then multiply to write it in standard form.

$$p(x) = \left[x-(1+i)\right]\left[x-\left(\boxed{1-i}\right)\right](x-2)(x-3)$$

Multiply the first two factors using FOIL. $= \left[x^2-(1-i)x-\left(\boxed{1+i}\right)x+(1+i)(1-i)\right](x-2)(x-3)$

Multipy the conjugates. $= \left[x^2-(1-i)x-(1+i)x+\left(1-\left(\boxed{-1}\right)\right)\right](x-2)(x-3)$

Combine like terms. $= \left[x^2+(-1+i-1+i)x+2\right](x-2)(x-3)$

Simplify. $= \left(\boxed{x^2-2x+2}\right)(x-2)(x-3)$

Multipy the binomials. $= (x^2-2x+2)\boxed{(x^2-5x+6)}$

Distributive property $= x^2(x^2-5x+6)\boxed{-2x}(x^2-5x+6)+2(x^2-5x+6)$

Multipy. $= (x^4-5x^3-6x^2)+(-2x^3+10x^2-12x)+(2x^2-10x+12)$

Combine like terms. $= \boxed{x^4-7x^3+18x^2-22x+12}$

The polynomial function is $p(x) = \underline{x^4-7x^3+18x^2-22x+12}$.

Reflect

7. Restate the Irrational Root Theorem in terms of the zeros of polynomial functions.

If a polynomial function $p(x)$ has rational coefficients and $a+b\sqrt{c}$ is a zero of the function, where a and b are rational and $\sqrt{c}$ is irrational, then $a-b\sqrt{c}$ is also a zero of $p(x)$.

8. Restate the Complex Conjugates Zero Theorem in terms of the roots of equations.

If $a+bi$ is an imaginary zero of a polynomial function $p(x)$ with real-number coefficients, then $a-bi$ is also a zero of $p(x)$.

Your Turn

Write the polynomial function with the least degree and a leading coefficient of 1 that has the given zeros.

9. $2 + 3i$ and $4 - 7\sqrt{2}$

The polynomial function must also have $2 - 3i$ and $4 + 7\sqrt{2}$ as zeros.

$$p(x) = \left[x - (2 + 3i)\right]\left[x - (2 - 3i)\right]\left[x - \left(4 + 7\sqrt{2}\right)\right]\left[x - \left(4 - 7\sqrt{2}\right)\right]$$

$$= \left[x^2 - (2 - 3i)x - (2 + 3i)x + (2 + 3i)(2 - 3i)\right]\left[x^2 - \left(4 - 7\sqrt{2}\right)x - \left(4 + 7\sqrt{2}\right)x + \left(4 + 7\sqrt{2}\right)\left(4 - 7\sqrt{2}\right)\right]$$

$$= \left[x^2 - (2 - 3i)x - (2 + 3i)x + (4 - 9(-1))\right]\left[x^2 - \left(4 - 7\sqrt{2}\right)x - \left(4 + 7\sqrt{2}\right)x + (16 - 49 \cdot 2)\right]$$

$$= \left[x^2 + (-2 + 3i - 2 - 3i)x + 13\right]\left[x^2 + \left(-4 + 7\sqrt{2} - 4 - 7\sqrt{2}\right)x - 82\right]$$

$$= (x^2 - 4x + 13)(x^2 - 8x - 82)$$

$$= x^2(x^2 - 8x - 82) - 4x(x^2 - 8x - 82) + 13(x^2 - 8x - 82)$$

$$= (x^4 - 8x^3 - 82x^2) + (-4x^3 + 32x^2 + 328x) + (13x^2 - 104x - 1066)$$

$$= x^4 - 12x^3 - 37x^2 + 224x - 1066$$

The polynomial function is $p(x) = x^4 - 12x^3 - 37x^2 + 224x - 1066$.

Explain 3 Solving a Real-World Problem by Graphing Polynomial Functions

You can use graphing to help you locate or approximate any real zeros of a polynomial function. Though a graph will not help you find non-real zeros, it can indicate that the function has non-real zeros. For example, look at the graph of $p(x) = x^4 - 2x^2 - 3$.

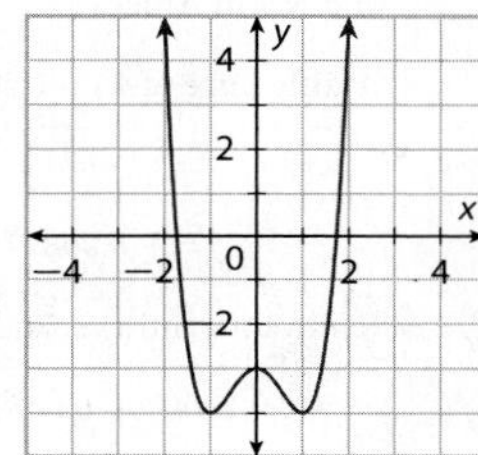

The graph intersects the x-axis twice, which shows that the function has two real zeros. By the corollary to the Fundamental Theorem of Algebra, however, a fourth degree polynomial has four zeros. So, the other two zeros of $p(x)$ must be non-real. The zeros are $-\sqrt{3}$, $\sqrt{3}$, i, and $-i$. (A polynomial whose graph has a turning point on the x-axis has a real zero of even multiplicity at that point. If the graph "bends" at the x-axis, there is a real zero of odd multiplicity greater than 1 at that point.)

EXPLAIN 3

Solving a Real-World Problem by Graphing Polynomial Functions

INTEGRATE MATHEMATICAL PRACTICES

Focus on Modeling

MP.4 Lead students to recognize that the solution of the problem is *not* a zero of either $p(x)$ or $q(x)$; however, it *is* a zero of the difference function $p(x) - q(x)$. This can be confirmed from the graphs of the three functions.

QUESTIONING STRATEGIES

? Why do the methods shown in Parts A and B produce the same solution? **When you solve the equation $p(x) = q(x)$, you are finding the value of x for which the two functions are equal. Since $p(x)$ is equal to $q(x)$ at this value of x, this is the value that would make their difference, $p(x) - q(x)$, equal to 0.**

(A) The following polynomial models approximate the total oil consumption C (in millions of barrels per day) for North America (NA) and the Asia Pacific region (AP) over the period from 2001 to 2011, where t is in years and $t = 0$ represents 2001.

$$C_{NA}(t) = 0.00494t^4 - 0.0915t^3 + 0.442t^2 - 0.239t + 23.6$$

$$C_{AP}(t) = 0.00877t^3 - 0.139t^2 + 1.23t - 21.1$$

Use a graphing calculator to plot the functions and approximate the x-coordinate of the intersection in the region of interest. What does this represent in the context of this situation? Determine when oil consumption in the Asia Pacific region overtook oil consumption in North America using the requested method.

Graph $Y1 = 0.00494x^4 - 0.0915x^3 + 0.442x^2 - 0.239x + 23.6$ and $Y2 = 0.00877x^3 - 0.139x^2 + 1.23x + 21.1$. Use the "Calc" menu to find the point of intersection. Here are the results for Xmin = 0, Xmax = 10, Ymin = 20, Ymax = 30. (The graph for the Asia Pacific is the one that rises upward on all segments.)

Intersection X=5.305603 Y=25.022918

The functions intersect at about $x = 5$, which represents the year 2006. This means that the models show oil consumption in the Asia Pacific equaling and then overtaking oil consumption in North America about 2006.

(B) Find a single polynomial model for the situation in Example 3A whose zero represents the time that oil consumption for the Asia Pacific region overtakes consumption for North America. Plot the function on a graphing calculator and use it to find the x-intercept.

Let the function $C_D(t)$ represent the difference in oil consumption in the Asia Pacific and North America.

A difference of 0 indicates **the time that consumption is equal**.

$$\boxed{C_D(t)} = \boxed{C_{AP}(t)} - C_{NA}(t)$$

$$= -0.00877t^3 - 0.139t^2 + 1.23t + 21.1 - (0.00494t^4 - 0.0915t^3 + 0.442t^2 - 0.239t + 23.6)$$

Remove parentheses and rearrange terms.

$$= -0.00494t^4 + 0.00877t^3 + 0.0915t^3 - 0.139t^2 - 0.442t^2 + 1.23t + 0.239t + 21.1 - 23.6$$

Combine like terms. Round to three significant digits.

$$= \mathbf{-0.00494t^4 + 0.100t^3 - 0.581t^2 + 1.47t - 2.50}$$

Graph $C_D(t)$ and find the x-intercept. (The graph with Ymin = −4, Ymax = 6 is shown.)

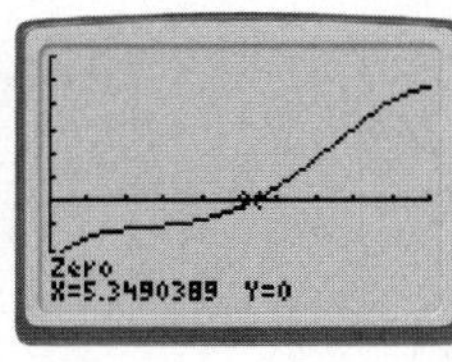

Within the rounding error, the results for the x-coordinate of the intersection of $C_{NA}(t)$ and $C_{AP}(t)$ and the x-intercept of $C_D(t)$ are the same.

Your Turn

10. An engineering class is designing model rockets for a competition. The body of the rocket must be cylindrical with a cone-shaped top. The cylinder part must be 60 cm tall, and the height of the cone must be twice the radius, as shown. The volume of the payload region must be 558π cm³ in order to hold the cargo. Use a graphing calculator to graph the rocket's payload volume as a function of the radius x. On the same screen, graph the constant function for the desired payload. Find the intersection to find x.

Let V represent the volume of the payload region.

$V = V_{cone} + V_{cylinder}$

$$V(x) = \frac{1}{3}\pi x^2(2x) + \pi x^2(60) = \frac{2}{3}\pi x^3 + 60\pi x^2$$

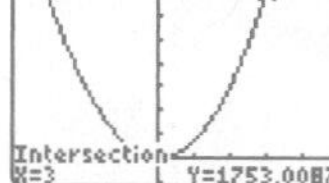

To find x when the volume is 558π, graph

$y = \frac{2}{3}\pi x^3 + 60\pi x^2$ and $y = 558\pi$ and

find the points of intersection.

Because the radius must be positive, the radius of the rocket is 3 cm.

Elaborate

11. What does the degree of a polynomial function $p(x)$ tell you about the zeros of the function or the roots of the equation $p(x) = 0$?
The degree tells you how many zeros or roots there are when you include complex zeros or roots and count the multiplicities of repeated zeros or roots.

12. A polynomial equation of degree 5 has the roots 0.3, 2, 8, and 10.6 (each of multiplicity 1). What can you conclude about the remaining root? Explain your reasoning.
The remaining root must be rational. This is because any irrational roots or imaginary roots always occur in conjugate pairs. So, if there were an irrational or imaginary root, there would have to be two of them.

13. **Discussion** Describe two ways you can use graphing to determine when two polynomial functions that model a real-world situation have the same value.
You can graph both functions on the same coordinate grid and find the x-value of any point where the two graphs intersect. Also, you can form a new function that is the difference of the two original functions. The zeros of this function will also be the x-values where the original functions have the same value.

14. **Essential Question Check-In** What are possible ways to find all the roots of a polynomial equation?
By the corollary to the Fundamental Theorem of Algebra, you know that the number of roots equals the degree of the equation. You can factor when possible, and use the Rational Root theorem along with the Zero Product Property to find rational roots. You can use the quadratic formula to find irrational or complex roots.

ELABORATE

INTEGRATE MATHEMATICAL PRACTICES

Focus on Patterns

MP.8 Lead students to the generalization that a polynomial function of odd degree must have an odd number (counting repeated zeros) of real zeros and, in particular, must have at least one real zero.

QUESTIONING STRATEGIES

? A fourth degree polynomial function has only the zeros −2, 3, and 4. How can this be true given the requirement of the Corollary of the Fundamental Theorem of Algebra, which states that a polynomial of degree n has exactly n zeros? **One of the zeros must occur twice. The corollary requires that repeated zeros be counted multiple times.**

INTEGRATE MATHEMATICAL PRACTICES

Focus on Critical Thinking

MP.3 Ask students to discuss the possibility of two polynomial functions that model a real-world situation having more than one value for which they are equal. Have them discuss the implications of this situation on the graphs of the functions and on the graph of the difference function.

SUMMARIZE THE LESSON

? How can you use the Fundamental Theorem of Algebra, its corollary, and the Irrational Conjugates and Complex Conjugates Theorems to determine the possible combinations of types of zeros of a polynomial function? **You can use the Fundamental Theorem of Algebra and its corollary to find the total number of zeros of the function. Then you can use the fact that irrational and imaginary zeros occur in conjugate pairs to determine the possible combinations.**

EVALUATE

ASSIGNMENT GUIDE

Concepts and Skills	Practice
Explore Investigating the Number of Complex Zeros of a Polynomial Function	Exercises 1–2
Example 1 Applying the Fundamental Theorem of Algebra to Solving Polynomial Equations	Exercises 3–4
Example 2 Writing a Polynomial Function From its Zeros	Exercises 5–8
Example 3 Solving a Real-World Problem by Graphing Polynomial Functions	Exercises 9–11

QUESTIONING STRATEGIES

? How does the Rational Zero Theorem help you find zeros that are not rational? **The Rational Zero Theorem can be used to identify rational zeros and the corresponding factors. Then, other methods, such as the quadratic formula, may be used to find other zeros that are irrational or imaginary.**

Evaluate: Homework and Practice

• Online Homework
• Hints and Help
• Extra Practice

Find all zeros of $p(x)$. Include any multiplicities greater than 1.

1. $p(x) = 3x^3 - 10x^2 + 10x - 4$

Possible rational zeros are $\pm1, \pm2, \pm4, \pm\frac{1}{3}, \pm\frac{2}{3}, \pm\frac{4}{3}$.

2 is a zero. $p(x) = (x-2)(3x^2 - 4x + 2)$

Solve $3x^2 - 4x + 2 = 0$.

$$x = \frac{-(-4) \pm \sqrt{(-4)^2 - 4(3)(2)}}{2(3)}$$

$$x = \frac{4 \pm \sqrt{-8}}{6} = \frac{4 \pm 2i\sqrt{2}}{6} = \frac{2 \pm i\sqrt{2}}{3}$$

The zeros of $p(x)$ are 2, $\frac{2+i\sqrt{2}}{3}$, and $\frac{2-i\sqrt{2}}{3}$.

2. $p(x) = x^3 - 3x^2 + 4x - 12$

$$\begin{aligned} p(x) &= x^3 - 3x^2 + 4x - 12 \\ &= (x^3 - 3x^2) + (4x - 12) \\ &= x^2(x-3) + 4(x-3) \\ &= (x^2+4)(x-3) \end{aligned}$$

3 is a zero.

Solve $x^2 + 4 = 0$.

$x^2 = -4$

$x = \pm\sqrt{-4} = \pm 2i$

The zeros of $p(x)$ are 3, $-2i$, and $2i$.

Solve the polynomial equation by finding all roots.

3. $2x^3 - 3x^2 + 8x - 12 = 0$

$$(2x^3 - 3x^2) + (8x - 12) = 0$$
$$x^2(2x-3) + 4(2x-3) = 0$$
$$(x^2+4)(2x-3) = 0$$
$$2x - 3 = 0$$
$$x = \frac{3}{2}$$
$$x^2 + 4 = 0$$
$$x^2 = -4$$
$$x = \pm\sqrt{-4} = \pm 2i$$

The roots are $\frac{3}{2}$, $-2i$, and $2i$.

4. $x^4 - 5x^3 + 3x^2 + x = 0$

$x(x^3 - 5x^2 + 3x + 1) = 0$

0 is a root.

Possible rational roots are 1 and -1.

1 is a root.

$x(x-1)(x^2 - 4x - 1) = 0$

Solve $x^2 - 4x - 1 = 0$.

$$x = \frac{-(-4) \pm \sqrt{(-4)^2 - 4(1)(-1)}}{2(1)}$$

$$x = \frac{4 \pm \sqrt{20}}{2} = \frac{4 \pm 2\sqrt{5}}{2} = 2 \pm \sqrt{5}$$

The roots are 0, 1, $2+\sqrt{5}$, and $2-\sqrt{5}$.

Exercise	Depth of Knowledge (D.O.K.)	COMMON CORE Mathematical Practices
1–8	**2** Skills/Concepts	**MP.2** Reasoning
9–10	**2** Skills/Concepts	**MP.6** Precision
11	**2** Skills/Concepts	**MP.4** Modeling
12	**3** Strategic Thinking	**MP.2** Reasoning
13–14	**3** Strategic Thinking H.O.T.	**MP.2** Reasoning
15	**3** Strategic Thinking H.O.T.	**MP.2** Reasoning

Write the polynomial function with least degree and a leading coefficient of 1 that has the given zeros.

5. 0, $\sqrt{5}$, and 2

Because irrational zeros come in conjugate pairs, $-\sqrt{5}$ must also be a zero.

$$\begin{aligned} p(x) &= x(x-\sqrt{5})(x+\sqrt{5})(x-2) \\ &= x(x^2-5)(x-2) \\ &= x(x^3-2x^2-5x+10) \\ &= x^4-2x^3-5x^2+10x \end{aligned}$$

6. $4i$, 2, and -2

Because complex zeros come in conjugate pairs, $-4i$ must also be a zero.

$$\begin{aligned} p(x) &= (x-2)(x+2)(x-4i)(x+4i) \\ &= (x^2-4)(x^2+16) \\ &= x^4+12x^2-64 \end{aligned}$$

7. 1, -1 (multiplicity 3), and $3i$

Because complex zeros come in conjugate pairs, $-3i$ must also be a zero.

$$\begin{aligned} p(x) &= (x-1)(x+1)^3(x-3i)(x+3i) \\ &= \left[(x-1)(x+1)\right](x+1)^2(x-3i)(x+3i) \\ &= (x^2-1)(x^2+2x+1)(x^2+9) \\ &= (x^4+8x^2-9)(x^2+2x+1) \\ &= x^4(x^2+2x+1)+8x^2(x^2+2x+1)-9(x^2+2x+1) \\ &= x^6+2x^5+x^4+8x^4+16x^3+8x^2-9x^2-18x-9 \\ &= x^6+2x^5+9x^4+16x^3-x^2-18x-9 \end{aligned}$$

8. 3(multiplicity of 2) and $3i$

Because complex zeros come in conjugate pairs, $-3i$ must also be a zero.

$$\begin{aligned} p(x) &= (x-3)^2(x-3i)(x+3i) \\ &= (x^2-6x+9)(x^2+9) \\ &= x^2(x^2-6x+9)+9(x^2-6x+9) \\ &= x^4-6x^3+9x^2+9x^2-54x+81 \\ &= x^4-6x^3+18x^2-54x+81 \end{aligned}$$

AVOID COMMON ERRORS

Students often make sign errors when writing factors for zeros or roots that are irrational, such as $2-\sqrt{5}$, or imaginary, such as $2+i$. Encourage them to use parentheses within parentheses when writing the factors, and to be careful to apply the distributive property when removing the parentheses or regrouping the terms.

INTEGRATE MATHEMATICAL PRACTICES

Focus on Reasoning

MP.2 Have students discuss *why* irrational roots of a polynomial equation with rational coefficients must occur in conjugate pairs. Have them consider the resulting polynomial if, for example, only one of three factors of a cubic polynomial equation contained an irrational number.

VISUAL CUES

Have students graph several of the functions using a graphing calculator to provide a visual connection between each type of zero (rational, irrational, and imaginary), and its representation on the graph of the function. Help students to see how irrational zeros can be approximated from x-intercepts. Lead them to observe that a function that has only imaginary zeros has no x-intercepts.

CRITICAL THINKING

Students may be interested to find that they can test irrational and imaginary zeros of a polynomial function using synthetic substitution. Encourage them to use this process to check their work.

9. Forestry Height and trunk volume measurements from 10 giant sequoias between the heights of 220 and 275 feet in California give the following model, where h is the height in feet and V is the volume in cubic feet.

$$V(h) = 0.131h^3 - 90.9h^2 + 21{,}200h - 1{,}627{,}400$$

The "President" tree in the Giant Forest Grove in Sequoia National Park has a volume of about 45,100 cubic feet. Use a graphing calculator to plot the function $V(h)$ and the constant function representing the height of the President tree together. (Use a window of 220 to 275 for X and 30,000 to 55,000 for Y.) Find the x-coordinate of the intersection of the graphs. What does this represent in the context of this situation?

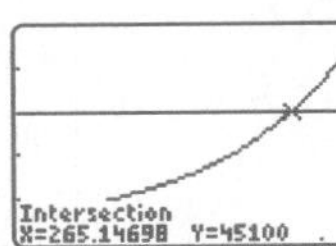

The x-coordinate of the intersection gives the model's predicted height for a tree with the volume of the President tree. This predicted height is about 265 feet.

10. Business Two competing stores, store A and store B, opened the same year in the same neighborhood. The annual revenue R (in millions of dollars) for each store t years after opening can be approximated by the polynomial models shown.

$$R_A(t) = 0.0001\left(-t^4 + 12t^3 - 77t^2 + 600t + 13{,}650\right)$$

$$R_B(t) = 0.0001\left(-t^4 + 36t^3 - 509t^2 + 3684t + 3390\right)$$

Using a graphing calculator, graph the models from $t = 0$ to $t = 10$, with a range of 0 to 2 for R. Find the x-coordinate of the intersection of the graphs, and interpret the graphs.

Graph Y1 $= 0.0001\left(-x^4 + 12x^3 - 77x^2 + 600x + 13{,}650\right)$ for R_A.
Graph Y2 $= 0.0001\left(-x^4 + 36x^3 - 509x^2 + 3684x + 3390\right)$ for R_B.
Then find the point of intersection.
The functions intersect at $x = 9$, which corresponds to having the same annual revenue 9 years after the stores opened.

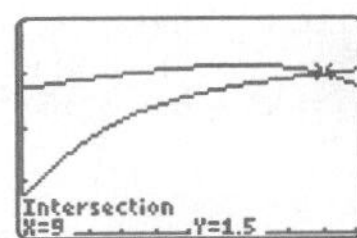

11. Personal Finance A retirement account contains cash and stock in a company. The cash amount is added to each week by the same amount until week 32, then that same amount is withdrawn each week. The functions shown model the balance B (in thousands of dollars) over the course of the past year, with the time t in weeks.

$B_C(t) = -0.12|t - 32| + 13$

$B_S(t) = 0.00005t^4 - 0.00485t^3 + 0.1395t^2 - 1.135t + 15.75$

Use a graphing calculator to graph both models (Use 0 to 20 for range.). Find the x-coordinate of any points of intersection. Then interpret your results in the context of this situation.

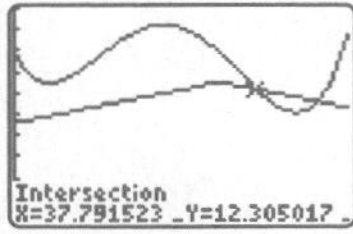

The graphs intersect at x-values of about 38 and 47. This means that at those weeks of the year, the cash balance and stock balance in the account were the same.

12. Match the roots with their equation.

A. 1   **A, B, E, F** $x^4 + x^3 + 2x^2 + 4x - 8 = 0$

B. −2   **A, B, C, D** $x^4 - 5x^2 + 4 = 0$

C. 2

D. −1

E. $2i$

F. $-2i$

$x^4 + x^3 + 2x^2 + 4x - 8 = 0$ in factored form is $(x - 1)(x + 2)(x^2 + 4) = 0$. Roots are 1, −2, $2i$, and $-2i$.

$x^4 - 5x^2 + 4 = 0$ in factored form is $(x + 1)(x - 1)(x + 2)(x - 2) = 0$. Roots are −1, 1, −2, and 2.

LANGUAGE SUPPORT EL

Connect Vocabulary

Remind students that they learned complex numbers have a real and an imaginary part. The complex conjugate of $a + bi$ is $a - bi$, and similarly the complex conjugate of $a - bi$ is $a + bi$. This consists of changing the sign of the imaginary part of a complex number. The real part is left unchanged.

PEER-TO-PEER DISCUSSION

Ask students to discuss with a partner why, although the Rational Root Theorem can always be used to help find the roots of a cubic equation, it may not be useful for finding the roots of a fourth degree polynomial equation. **Since a cubic equation has three roots, at least one of them will be rational (since irrational and imaginary roots occur in conjugate pairs). The other two roots, no matter what type, can be found by factoring or by using the quadratic formula. A fourth degree equation will have four roots, none of which may be rational, so the Rational Root Theorem will not be of help.**

JOURNAL

Have students describe how they would go about finding the roots of a fifth degree polynomial equation if they know that at least two of the roots are rational.

H.O.T. Focus on Higher Order Thinking

13. **Draw Conclusions** Find all of the roots of $x^6 - 5x^4 - 125x^2 + 15{,}625 = 0$. (Hint: Rearrange the terms with a sum of cubes followed by the two other terms.)

$$(x^6 + 15{,}625) - 25x^4 - 625x^2 = 0$$
$$\left[(x^2)^3 + 25^3\right] - 25x^4 - 625x^2 = 0$$
$$(x^2 + 25)(x^4 - 25x^2 + 625) - 25x^2(x^2 + 25) = 0$$
$$(x^2 + 25)(x^4 - 25x^2 + 625 - 25x^2) = 0$$
$$(x^2 + 25)(x^4 - 50x^2 + 625) = 0$$
$$(x^2 + 25)(x^2 - 25)^2 = 0$$
$$(x^2 + 25)\left[(x + 5)(x - 5)\right]^2 = 0$$

The roots are -5 and 5, each with multiplicity 2, and $-5i$ and $5i$.

14. **Explain the Error** A student is asked to write the polynomial function with least degree and a leading coefficient of 1 that has the zeros $1 + i$, $1 - i$, $\sqrt{2}$, and -3. The student writes the product of factors shown, and multiplies them together to obtain $p(x) = x^4 + (1 - \sqrt{2})x^3 - (4 + \sqrt{2})x^2 + (6 + 4\sqrt{2})x - 6\sqrt{2}$. What error did the student make? What is the correct function?

The function must have 5 zeros. The zero $\sqrt{2}$ must be paired with its conjugate, $-\sqrt{2}$.

$$\begin{aligned} p(x) &= \left[x - (1 + i)\right]\left[x - (1 - i)\right](x - \sqrt{2})(x + \sqrt{2})(x + 3) \\ &= \left[x^2 - (1 - i)x - (1 + i)x + (1 + i)(1 - i)\right](x^2 - 2)(x + 3) \\ &= \left[x^2 + (-1 + i - 1 - i)x + (1 - (-1))\right](x^3 + 3x^2 - 2x - 6) \\ &= (x^2 - 2x + 2)(x^3 + 3x^2 - 2x - 6) \\ &= (x^5 + 3x^4 - 2x^3 - 6x^2) + (-2x^4 - 6x^3 + 4x^2 + 12x) + (2x^3 + 6x^2 - 4x - 12) \\ &= x^5 + x^4 - 6x^3 + 4x^2 + 8x - 12 \end{aligned}$$

15. **Critical Thinking** What is the least degree of a polynomial equation that has $3i$ as a root with a multiplicity of 3, and $2 - \sqrt{3}$ as a root with multiplicity 2? Explain.

The least degree is 10. Since $3i$ is a root 3 times, then $-3i$ must also be a root 3 times. Since $2 - \sqrt{3}$ is a root 2 times, then $2 + \sqrt{3}$ must also be a root 2 times, and $3 + 3 + 2 + 2 = 10$.

Lesson Performance Task

In 1984 the MPAA introduced the PG-13 rating to their movie rating system. Recently, scientists measured the incidences of a specific type of violence depicted in movies. The researchers used specially trained coders to identify the specific type of violence in one half of the top grossing movies for each year since 1985. The trend in the average rate per hour of 5-minute segments of this type of violence in movies rated G/PG, PG-13, and R can be modeled as a function of time by the following equations:

$$V_{G/PG}(t) = -0.015t + 1.45$$

$$V_{PG\text{-}13}(t) = 0.000577t^3 - 0.0225t^2 + 0.26t + 0.8$$

$$V_R(t) = 2.15$$

V is the average rate per hour of 5-minute segments containing the specific type of violence in movies, and t is the number of years since 1985.

a. Interestingly, in 1985 or $t = 0$, $V_{G/PG}(0) > V_{PG\text{-}13}(0)$. Can you think of any reasons why this would be true?

b. What do the equations indicate about the relationship between $V_{G/PG}(t)$ and $V_{PG\text{-}13}(t)$ as t increases?

Graph the models for $V_{G/PG}(t)$ and $V_{PG\text{-}13}(t)$ and find the year in which $V_{PG\text{-}13}(t)$ will be greater than $V_{G/PG}(t)$.

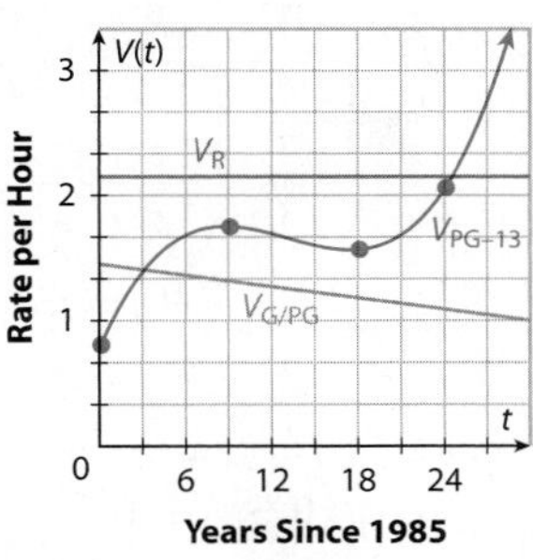

a. Possible answers include but are not limited to

- **The rating of PG-13 was poorly understood by the people responsible for rating the films.**
- **Films released in the years immediately following 1985 had been scripted, filmed, and/or edited before the rating was fully understood by the film studios, so they hadn't separated the specific type of violence out of the G/PG movies.**

b. The equations indicate that as t increases, $V_{PG\text{-}13}(t)$ will eventually be greater than $V_{G/PG}(t)$. $V_{G/PG}(t)$ is a linear function with a negative first term so its end behavior on the right is decreasing to negative infinity while the leading term of $V_{PG\text{-}13}(t)$ is positive, so its end behavior on the right is increasing to infinity.

c. The functions intersect at a value of $t \approx 3$, which indicates that the average rate per hour of 5-minute segments of violence in movies rated PG-13 first surpassed the average hourly rate in movies rated G/PG in 1988.

EXTENSION ACTIVITY

Have students research the top-grossing movie for each year since 1985 and whether it was rated *G*, *PG*, *PG*-13, or *R*. Have students discuss whether the success of a movie is related to its rating. Ask them if they think the amount of violence in a movie makes it more or less popular.

CONNECT VOCABULARY EL

Students may not be familiar with the abbreviations of the movie rating system. Explain that the abbreviations indicate how appropriate the movie is for difference audiences. A *G* rating means the movie is for *General* audiences. A *PG* rating means *Parental Guidance* is suggested. A *PG-13* rating means *Parental Guidance* is suggested and the movie may not be appropriate for children under age *13*. An *R* rating means entrance is *Restricted;* an adult must accompany children under 17.

AVOID COMMON ERRORS

Students may think that the models $V(t)$ give the total amount of violence in a movie. Ask students what the units of $V(t)$ are. **number of 5-minute segments per hour** Ask students how to calculate the total minutes of violence in a movie. **Multiply $V(t)$ by 5 and then multiply by the length of the movie in minutes.**

INTEGRATE MATHEMATICAL PRACTICES

Focus on Communication

MP.3 Discuss with students why $V_{PG\text{-}13}$ increases to infinity as t increases. Ask them if it makes sense that $V_{PG\text{-}13}$ becomes greater than V_R and whether they think this will actually happen. Have students explain how they could create a model that would more accurately predict $V_{PG\text{-}13}$ for future years..

Scoring Rubric

2 points: Student correctly solves the problem and explains his/her reasoning.

1 point: Student shows good understanding of the problem but does not fully solve or explain his/her reasoning.

0 points: Student does not demonstrate understanding of the problem.

Study Guide Review

ASSESSMENT AND INTERVENTION

Assign or customize module reviews.

MODULE PERFORMANCE TASK

Mathematical Practices: MP.1, MP.3, MP.4, MP.5
F-IF.B.4, F-IF.B.5, F-IF.C.7c, A-REI.D.10

SUPPORTING STUDENT REASONING

Students should begin by thinking about what information is contained in the given polynomial function, and what the best method is for understanding the change in population over time.

- **How should I find out how the polynomial behaves?** Point out that a graph may allow students to see the overall behavior of the polynomial better than a table of values or set of points.

STUDY GUIDE REVIEW

Polynomial Equations

MODULE 7

Essential Question: How can you use polynomial equations to solve real-world problems?

Key Vocabulary
root *(raíz)*
multiplicity *(multiplicidad)*

KEY EXAMPLE *(Lesson 7.1)*

Find the rational zeros of $f(x) = x^3 + 6x^2 + 11x + 6$; then write the function as a product of factors.

Factors of 6: $\pm1, \pm2, \pm3, \pm6$ — Use the Rational Zero Theorem.

Test the roots in a synthetic division table.

$\frac{m}{n}$	1	6	11	6
1	1	7	18	24
2	1	8	27	60
3	1	9	38	120
6	1	12	83	504
−1	1	5	6	0

$(x+1)(x^2+5x+6)$ — Factor the trinomial.

$(x+1)(x+2)(x+3)$

$x=-1, x=-2, x=-3$

KEY EXAMPLE *(Lesson 7.2)*

Find all the zeros of $m(x) = 2x^4 - 4x^3 + 8x^2 - 16x$.

$2x^4 - 4x^3 - 8x^2 - 16x$

$2x(x^3 - 2x^2 - 4x + 8)$ — Factor out the GCF.

$2x((x^3 - 2x^2) - (4x - 8))$ — Group the terms.

$2x(x^2(x-2) - 4(x-2))$ — Factor out common monomials.

$2x(x^2-4)(x-2)$ — Factor out the common binomial.

$2x(x+2)(x-2)(x-2)$ — Difference of two squares

So, the zeros of $m(x)$ are 0, −2, 2 (mult. 2).

SCAFFOLDING SUPPORT

- Students should realize that their first step should be to graph the polynomial.
- Encourage students to consider the meaning of their graphs, especially the end behavior of the polynomial.
- Ask students to determine a reasonable domain, which in this case is $0 \le x \le 17$, because for $x > 17$, $f(x) < 0$, and it is not possible to have a negative population.

EXERCISES

Rewrite the function as a product of factors, and state all of the zeros. *(Lessons 7.1, 7.2)*

1. $r(x) = x^3 + 13x^2 + 48x + 36$

$r(x) = (x + 6)^2(x + 1)$

roots: −6 (mult. 2), −1

2. $m(x) = 3x^4 - 3x^2$

$m(x) = 3x^2(x + 1)(x - 1)$

roots: 0 (mult. 2), −1, 1

3. $n(x) = x^3 + 5x^2 - 8x - 12$

$n(x) = (x + 6)(x - 2)(x + 1)$

roots: −6, 2, −1

4. $p(x) = x^3 - 8$

$p(x) = (x - 2)(x^2 + 2x + 4)$

roots: $2, -1 + i\sqrt{3}, -1 - i\sqrt{3}$

5. $b(x) = x^4 - 81$

$b(x) = (x - 3)(x + 3)(x^2 + 9)$

roots: $3, -3, 3i, -3i$

6. $t(x) = 15x^3 + 27x^2 - 6x$

$t(x) = 3x(x + 2)(5x - 1)$

roots: $0, -2, \frac{1}{5}$

7. Give an example of a fourth-degree polynomial function with all real zeros. Explain how you got your function. *(Lesson 7.1)*

$f(x) = x^3 + 7x^2 + 4x - 12$; I created some binomials $(x + 6)$, $(x + 2)$, and $(x - 1)$, then multiplied them all together to create the equation. Since it started with binomials with real number roots, all of the roots of the resulting product will have all real number roots as well.

MODULE PERFORMANCE TASK

What Do Polynomials Have to Do With Endangered Species?

A biologist has been studying a particular species of frog in an area for many years and has compiled population data. She used the data to create a model of the population, given here, where x is the years since 2000.

$$P(x) = -x^4 + 27x^3 - 198x^2 + 372x + 1768$$

Describe the trends for the population, and explain what the model predicts for the future population of this species of frog.

Use your own paper to complete the task. Be sure to write down all your data and assumptions. Then use graphs, numbers, words, or algebra to explain how you reached your conclusions.

DISCUSSION OPPORTUNITIES

- Imagine that the frog population in 2015 is found to be 4000. How does this affect the model, and your prediction about the future frog population?
- Is it possible to bring a species on the brink of extinction back to a level at which the species is no longer in danger? What are some examples of this happening?

SAMPLE SOLUTION

Assumptions

- The given model fits the population over time.

First, graph the polynomial, using the first quadrant.

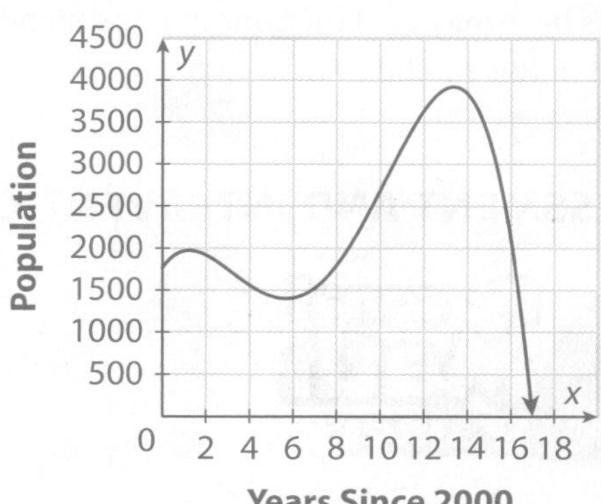

The graph of the polynomial appears to have a zero at $x = 17$. Evaluating the polynomial at $x = 17$ confirms that it is a zero.

Analysis

In 2000, the frog population was 1768, and there was an increase in the population until early 2001, when the population began to decrease. In about the middle of 2005, the population again began to increase, reaching a peak population of almost 4000 around the middle of 2013. The future of this population does not look promising, and if the trend continues to fit the model, the species will be extinct by 2017.

Assessment Rubric

2 points: Student correctly solves the problem and explains his/her reasoning.

1 point: Student shows good understanding of the problem but does not fully solve or explain.

0 points: Student does not demonstrate understanding of the problem.

Ready to Go On?

ASSESS MASTERY

Use the assessment on this page to determine if students have mastered the concepts and standards covered in this module.

ASSESSMENT AND INTERVENTION

Access Ready to Go On? assessment online, and receive instant scoring, feedback, and customized intervention or enrichment.

ADDITIONAL RESOURCES

Response to Intervention Resources

- Reteach Worksheets

Differentiated Instruction Resources

- Reading Strategies EL
- Success for English Learners EL
- Challenge Worksheets

Assessment Resources

- Leveled Module Quizzes

Ready to Go On?

7.1–7.2 Polynomial Functions

- Online Homework
- Hints and Help
- Extra Practice

Write the function as a product of factors. *(Lesson 7.1)*

1. $f(x) = 7x^3 - 14x^2 - x + 2$

$f(x) = (x - 2)(7x^2 - 1)$

2. $g(x) = 3x^2 + 2x - 8$

$g(x) = (x + 2)(3x - 4)$

3. $h(x) = 4x^2 - 25$

$h(x) = (2x + 5)(2x - 5)$

4. $t(x) = 8x^3 - 512$

$t(x) = 8(x - 4)(x^2 + 4x + 16)$

List the roots. *(Lessons 7.1, 7.2)*

5. $m(x) = x^4 + 3x^2 - 18$

$\sqrt{3}, -\sqrt{3}, i\sqrt{6}, -i\sqrt{6}$

6. $r(x) = x^3 + 3x^2 - x - 3$

$-3, 1, -1$

7. $q(x) = x^3 - 1$

$1, \frac{-1 + i\sqrt{3}}{2}, \frac{-1 - i\sqrt{3}}{2}$

8. $p(x) = 9x^2 - 100$

$-\frac{10}{3}, \frac{10}{3}$

ESSENTIAL QUESTION

9. Give an example of how factoring polynomials might be used in geometry. *(Lesson 7.1)*

Possible Answer: If given the area of a rectangle as a polynomial, the polynomial could be factored to find the possible side lengths of the rectangle in terms of the variable.

COMMON CORE Common Core Standards

Lesson	Items	Content Standards	Mathematical Practices
7.1	1–4	**A-APR.B.2, A-APR.B.3**	**MP.7**
7.1, 7.2	5	**A-APR.B.2, A-APR.B.3, N-CN.C.9**	**MP.2**
7.1	6	**A-APR.B.2, A-APR.B.3**	**MP.2**
7.1, 7.2	7	**A-APR.B.2, A-APR.B.3, N-CN.C.9**	**MP.2**
7.1	8	**A-APR.B.2, A-APR.B.3**	**MP.2**

MODULE 7
MIXED REVIEW

Assessment Readiness

1. Look at each equation. Does the polynomial have all real roots? Select Yes or No for A–C?

		Yes	No
A.	$f(x) = x^4 - 2x^2 - 5$	○ Yes	● No
B.	$g(x) = x^2 - 9$	● Yes	○ No
C.	$h(x) = x^4 - 256$	○ Yes	● No

2. Consider the polynomial equation $m(x) = x^4 - 16x^2$. Choose True or False for each statement.

		True	False
A.	There will be both real and imaginary roots to this polynomial.	○ True	● False
B.	Factoring the polynomial involves the difference of two squares.	● True	○ False
C.	The roots of the polynomial are 0 (mult.2), 4, −4.	● True	○ False

3. Explain why some polynomial functions with real coefficients have non-real zeros.

If a polynomial function has degree n and m real zeros (where m includes multiplicities and where $m < n$), then it must have $n - m$ non-real zeros by the Fundamental Theorem of Algebra. If the polynomial function has real coefficients, then $n - m$ must be an even number, and the non-real zeros are pairs of complex conjugates by the Complex Conjugates Theorem.

4. By analyzing a quickly growing oil town, an analyst states that the predicted population P of the town t years from now can be modeled by the function $P(t) = 5x^3 - 2x^2 + 15{,}000$. If we assume the function is true, in approximately how many years will the town have a population of 225,000? How did you get your answer?

Approximately 35 years; Sample answer: I put the equation into the $y =$ portion of my calculator and then looked at the table to see where y is closest to 225,000.

Common Core Standards

Lesson	Items	Content Standards	Mathematical Practices
7.1, 7.2	1	**A-APR.B.2**	**MP.1**
6.4, 7.1	2*	**A-SSE.A.2, A-APR.B.2**	**MP.2**
7.2	3	**A-APR.B.2**	**MP.6**
5.2, 7.2	4*	**A-APR.B.2, F-IF.C.7c**	**MP.4**

* Item integrates mixed review concepts from previous modules or a previous course.

MIXED REVIEW

Assessment Readiness

ASSESSMENT AND INTERVENTION

Assign ready-made or customized practice tests to prepare students for high-stakes tests.

ADDITIONAL RESOURCES

Assessment Resources

- Leveled Module Quizzes: Modified, B

AVOID COMMON ERRORS

Item 3 Some students will have trouble with the concept of imaginary roots. Because they are called imaginary, students may not think that the roots will cause a change in direction. Explain that the word *imaginary* does not mean that the roots do not have any effect.

MIXED REVIEW
Assessment Readiness

ASSESSMENT AND INTERVENTION

Assign ready-made or customized practice tests to prepare students for high-stakes tests.

ADDITIONAL RESOURCES

Assessment Resources

- Leveled Unit Tests: Modified, A, B, C
- Performance Assessment

AVOID COMMON ERRORS

Item 3 Some students will forget that polynomials can be factored more than one way. Encourage students to fully multiply the original polynomial so they can compare it to the answer choices and find equivalent expressions.

UNIT 3 MIXED REVIEW

Assessment Readiness

Personal Math Trainer

- Online Homework
- Hints and Help
- Extra Practice

1. Identify the transformations of the graph of $f(x) = x^3$ that produce the graph of the function $g(x) = -2(x - 5)^3$. Select True or False for each statement.

A. When compared with $f(x)$, the graph of $g(x)$ is vertically compressed by a factor of $\frac{1}{2}$. ○ True ● False

B. When compared with $f(x)$, the graph of $g(x)$ is translated 5 units to the right. ● True ○ False

C. When compared with $f(x)$, the graph of $g(x)$ is reflected across the x-axis. ● True ○ False

2. Consider the polynomial $3x^3 + 9x^2 - 12x$. Select True or False for each statement.

A. $3x$ can be factored out of every term. ● True ○ False

B. The polynomial cannot be factored as it is written. ○ True ● False

C. The completely factored polynomial is $3x(x - 1)(x + 4)$. ● True ○ False

3. Consider the polynomial operation $3x(x - 2)(5x + 2)$. Is the expression equivalent? Select Yes or No for A–D

A. $(3x^2 - 6x)(5x + 2)$ ● Yes ○ No

B. $3x(5x^2 - 8x - 4)$ ● Yes ○ No

C. $15x^3 - 24x^2 - 12x$ ● Yes ○ No

D. $3x(5x^2 - 5x - 2)$ ○ Yes ● No

4. Consider the polynomial function $g(x) = 3x^3 + 6x^2 - 9x$. Select True or False for each statement.

A. The polynomial has only real roots. ● True ○ False

B. Factoring the polynomial involves a common monomial. ● True ○ False

C. The roots of the polynomial are 0, –3, 1, 3. ○ True ● False

5. Consider the function $m(x) = x^4 - 16$. Are these roots to the equation? Select Yes or No for A–C.

A. $-2i, 2i$ ● Yes ○ No

B. $2 \pm 2i$ ○ Yes ● No

C. $-2, 2$ ● Yes ○ No

COMMON CORE

Common Core Standards

Items	Content Standards	Mathematical Practices
1*	**F-BF.B.3**	**MP.7**
2	**A-SSE.A.2**	**MP.2**
3	**A-APR.A.1**	**MP.5**
4	**A-APR.B.2**	**MP.1**
5	**A-APR.B.2**	**MP.1**
6	**F-IF.C.7**	**MP.5**

* Item integrates mixed review concepts from previous modules or a previous course.

6. Use a graphing calculator to graph the function $f(x) = -x(x+1)(x-4)^2$, and then use the graph to determine the number of turning points and minimums or maximums.

According to the graph, there are three turning points, one local maximum, one local minimum, and one global maximum.

7. Ms. Flores grows tomatoes on her farm. The price per pound of tomatoes can be modeled by $P(x) = 20x + 4$. If the total income that she wants to earn from tomatoes for one year can be modeled by $I(x) = 60x^3 - 8x^2 + 136x + 28$, write a polynomial that can be used to model the pounds of tomatoes Ms. Flores needs to grow in one year. Explain your answer.

$I(x) \div P(x) = (60x^3 - 8x^2 + 136x + 28) \div (20x + 4) = 3x^2 - x + 7$; To get the total pounds of tomatoes, divide the total income for the year by the price per pound.

8. During a discussion in class, Hannah stated that she liked the quadratic formula more than completing the square and factoring, because it works on every quadratic equation. The teacher then proposed the equation $-3x(x+7) = 14$. Explain how Hannah can adjust this equation so she can use the quadratic formula to solve it.

Possible answer: To use the quadratic formula, the equation will need to be in the form $ax^2 + bx + c = 0$, so Hannah would need to distribute the $-3x$ through the parentheses, then subtract 14 from both sides to get it in the correct form. The equation would be $-3x^2 - 21x - 14 = 0$.

Performance Tasks

9. A bottom for a box can be made by cutting congruent squares from each of the four corners of a piece of cardboard. The volume of a box made from an 8.5-by-11-inch piece of cardboard would be represented by $V(x) = x(11 - 2x)(8.5 - 2x)$, where x is the side length of one square.

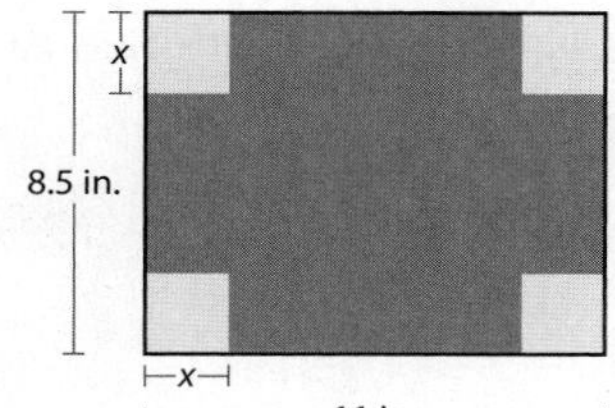

A. Express the volume as a sum of monomials.

B. Find the volume when $x = 1$ inch.

A. $4x^3 - 39x^2 + 93.5x$

B. 58.5 in^3

PERFORMANCE TASKS

There are three different levels of performance tasks:

* **Novice:** These are short word problems that require students to apply the math they have learned in straightforward, real-world situations.

** **Apprentice:** These are more involved problems that guide students step-by-step through more complex tasks. These exercises include more complicated reasoning, writing, and open ended elements.

*****Expert:** These are open-ended, nonroutine problems that, instead of stepping the students through, ask them to choose their own methods for solving and justify their answers and reasoning.

SCORING GUIDES

Item 9 (2 points)

a. 1 point for correct polynomial

b. 1 point for correct volume

Common Core Standards

Items	Content Standards	Mathematical Practices
7	A-APR.D.6	MP.4
8*	A-REI.B.4b	MP.3

* Item integrates mixed review concepts from previous modules or a previous course.

SCORING GUIDES

Item 10 (2 points)

a. 1 point for correct model

b. 1 point for reasonable estimate

Item 11 (6 points)

a. 1 point for correct factoring

b. 1 point for correct value

c. 1 point for correct value
1 point for correct interpretation

d. 2 points for explanation

★★**10.** The volume of several planets in cubic kilometers can be modeled by $v(d) = \frac{1}{6}\pi d^3$, where d is the diameter of the planet in kilometers. The mass of each planet in kilograms in terms of diameter d can be modeled by $M(d) = (3.96 \times 10^{12})d^3 - (6.50 \times 10^{17})d^2 + (2.56 \times 10^{22})d - 5.56 \times 10^{25}$.

A. The density of a planet in kilograms per cubic kilometer can be found by dividing the planet's mass by its volume. Use polynomial division to find a model for the density of a planet in terms of its diameter.

B. Use the model to estimate the density of Jupiter, with diameter $d = 142{,}984$ km.

A. $D(d) = \frac{2.376 \times 10^{13}}{\pi} + \frac{(-3.9 \times 10^{18})d^2 + (1.536 \times 10^{23})d - 3.336 \times 10^{26}}{\pi d^3}$

B. 1.236×10^{12} **kg/km**^{3}

★★★**11.** The profit of a small business (in thousands of dollars) since it was founded can be modeled by the polynomial $f(t) = -t^4 + 44t^3 - 612t^2 + 2592t$, where t represents the number of years since 1980.

A. Factor $f(t)$ completely.

B. What was the company's profit in 1985?

C. Find and interpret $f(15)$.

D. What can you say about the company's long-term prospects?

A. $f(t) = -t(t - 8)(t - 18)(t - 18)$

B. $2,535,000

C. $f(15) = -945$, **the company lost $945,000 in 1995.**

D. Possible answer: The company will continue to lose money after breaking even in 1998.

MATH IN CAREERS

Statistician According to data from the U.S. Census Bureau, the total number of people in the United States labor force can be approximated by the function $T(x) = -0.011x^2 + 2x + 107$, where x is the number of years since 1980 and $T(x)$ is the number of workers in millions. The number of women in the United States labor force can be approximated by the function $W(x) = -0.012x^2 + 1.26x + 45.5$.

a. Use the function $T(x)$ to estimate the number of workers in millions in 2010.

b. Write a polynomial function $M(x)$ that models the number of men in the labor force, and explain how you found your function.

c. Use the function found in part *b* to estimate the number of male workers in millions in 2010.

d. Explain how you could have found the answer to part *c* without using the function $M(x)$.

a. 157.1

b. $M(x) = 0.001x^2 + 74x + 61.5$, $M(x) = T(x) - W(x)$

c. 84.6

d. You can use the function $W(x)$ to find the number of female workers in 2010 and subtract this value from the total number of workers found in part a.

MATH IN CAREERS

Statistician In this Unit Performance Task, students can see how a statistician uses mathematics on the job.

For more information about careers in mathematics as well as various mathematics appreciation topics, visit the American Mathematical Society http://www.ams.org

SCORING GUIDES

Task (6 points)

a. 1 point for correct value

b. 1 point for correct function
1 point for explanation

c. 1 point for correct value

d. 2 points for correct explanation

UNIT 4

Rational Functions, Expressions, and Equations

CONTENTS

Unit Pacing Guide

45-Minute Classes

Module 8

DAY 1	DAY 2	DAY 3	DAY 4
Lesson 8.1	Lesson 8.2	Lesson 8.2	Module Review and Assessment Readiness

Module 9

DAY 1	DAY 2	DAY 3	DAY 4	DAY 5
Lesson 9.1	Lesson 9.1	Lesson 9.2	Lesson 9.2	Lesson 9.3

DAY 6	DAY 7	DAY 8
Lesson 9.3	Module Review and Assessment Readiness	Unit Review and Assessment Readiness

90-Minute Classes

Module 8

DAY 1	DAY 2
Lesson 8.1 Lesson 8.2	Lesson 8.2 Module Review and Assessment Readiness

Module 9

DAY 1	DAY 2	DAY 3	DAY 4
Lesson 9.1	Lesson 9.2	Lesson 9.3	Module Review and Assessment Readiness Unit Review and Assessment Readiness

Program Resources

PLAN

HMH Teacher App

Access a full suite of teacher resources online and offline on a variety of devices. Plan present, and manage classes, assignments, and activities.

Algebra 1
Monday February 10 2014
My Class 1B
Content
Lesson 1.1
Lesson 1.2
Assignments
Progress & Reports

ePlanner **Easily plan your classes, create and view assignments, and access all program resources with your online, customizable planning tool.**

Professional Development Videos

Authors Juli Dixon and Matt Larson model successful teaching practices and strategies in actual classroom settings.

QR Codes **Scan with your smart phone to jump directly from your print book to online videos and other resources.**

Teacher's Edition

Support students with point-of-use Questioning Strategies, teaching tips, resources for differentiated instruction, additional activities, and more.

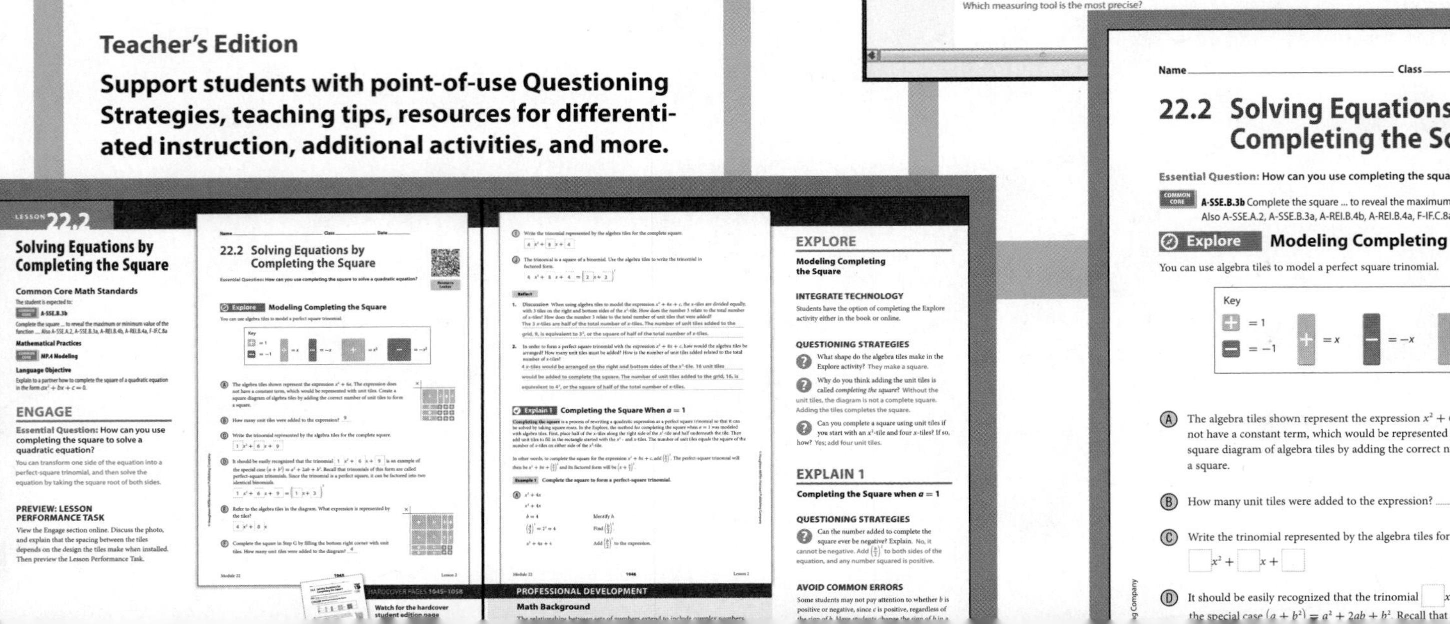
Solving Equations by Completing the Square
ENGAGE
22.2 Solving Equations by Completing the Square
EXPLORE
Modeling Completing the Square
EXPLAIN 1
Completing the Square when $a = 1$
PROFESSIONAL DEVELOPMENT

ENGAGE AND EXPLORE

Real-World Videos **Engage students with interesting and relevant applications of the mathematical content of each module.**

Explore Activities

Students interactively explore new concepts using a variety of tools and approaches.

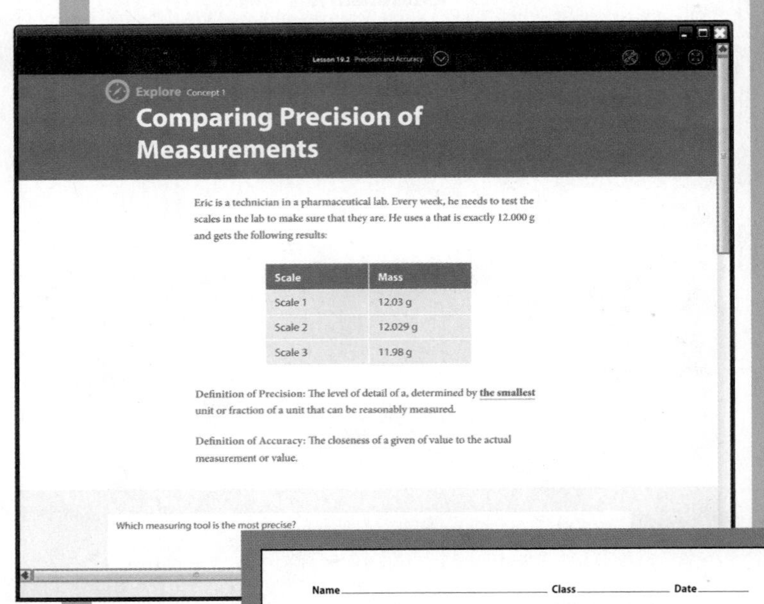
Explore Concept 1
Comparing Precision of Measurements
Eric is a technician in a pharmaceutical lab. Every week, he needs to test the scales in the lab to make sure that they are. He uses a that is exactly 12.000 g and gets the following results:
Scale | Mass
Scale 1 | 12.03 g
Scale 2 | 12.029 g
Scale 3 | 11.98 g
Definition of Precision: The level of detail of a, determined by the smallest unit or fraction of a unit that can be reasonably measured.
Definition of Accuracy: The closeness of a given of value to the actual measurement or value.
Which measuring tool is the most precise?

Name ____ Class ____ Date ____

22.2 Solving Equations by Completing the Square

Essential Question: How can you use completing the square to solve a quadratic equation?

A-SSE.B.3b Complete the square ... to reveal the maximum or minimum value of the function ... Also A-SSE.A.2, A-SSE.B.3a, A-REI.B.4b, A-REI.B.4a, F-IF.C.8a

Explore **Modeling Completing the Square**

You can use algebra tiles to model a perfect square trinomial.

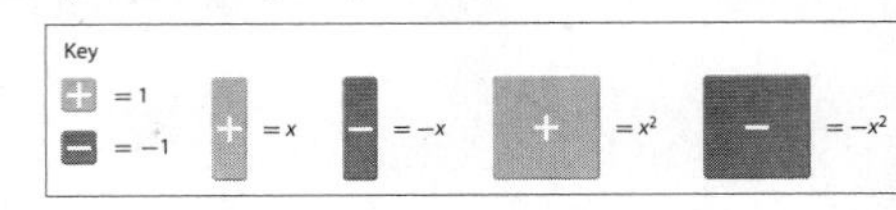

Ⓐ The algebra tiles shown represent the expression $x^2 + 6x$. The expression does not have a constant term, which would be represented with unit tiles. Create a square diagram of algebra tiles by adding the correct number of unit tiles to form a square.

Ⓑ How many unit tiles were added to the expression? ____

Ⓒ Write the trinomial represented by the algebra tiles for the complete square.
☐x^2 + ☐x + ☐

Ⓓ It should be easily recognized that the trinomial ☐x^2 + ☐x + ☐ is an example of the special case $(a + b^2) = a^2 + 2ab + b^2$. Recall that trinomials of this form are called

TEACH

Math On the Spot video tutorials, featuring program authors Dr. Edward Burger and Martha Sandoval-Martinez, accompany every example in the textbook and give students step-by-step instructions and explanations of key math concepts.

Interactive Teacher Edition

Customize and present course materials with collaborative activities and integrated formative assessment.

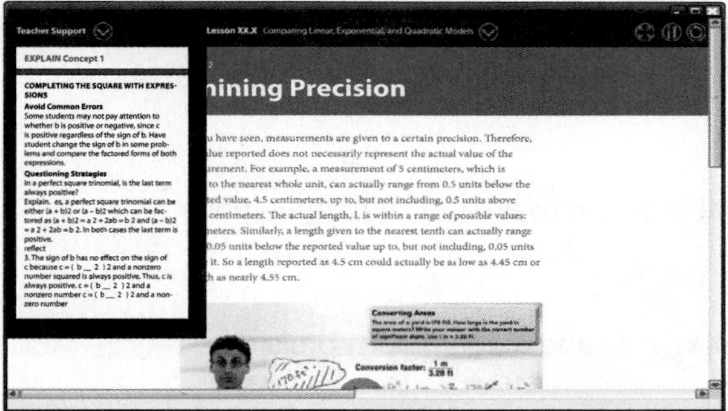

Differentiated Instruction Resources

Support all learners with Differentiated Instruction Resources, including

- **Leveled Practice and Problem Solving**
- **Reading Strategies**
- **Success for English Learners**
- **Challenge**

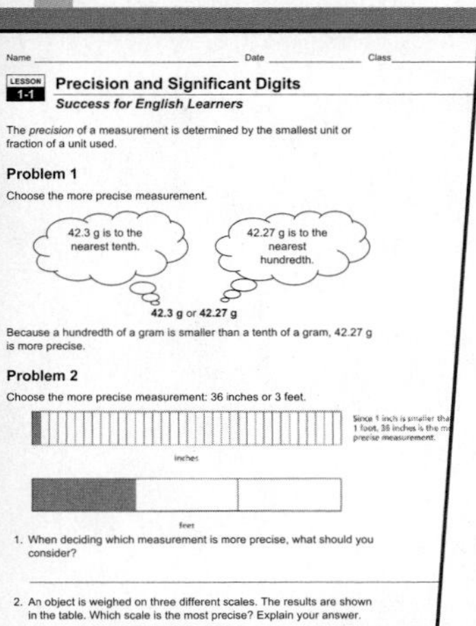

Name ______ Date ______ Class ______

LESSON 1-1 **Precision and Significant Digits**
Success for English Learners

The *precision* of a measurement is determined by the smallest unit or fraction of a unit used.

Problem 1

Choose the more precise measurement.

42.3 g is to the nearest tenth.

42.27 g is to the nearest hundredth.

42.3 g or 42.27 g

Because a hundredth of a gram is smaller than a tenth of a gram, 42.27 g is more precise.

Problem 2

Choose the more precise measurement: 36 inches or 3 feet.

Since 1 inch is smaller than 1 foot, 36 inches is the more precise measurement.

inches

feet

1. When deciding which measurement is more precise, what should you consider?

2. An object is weighed on three different scales. The results are shown in the table. Which scale is the most precise? Explain your answer.

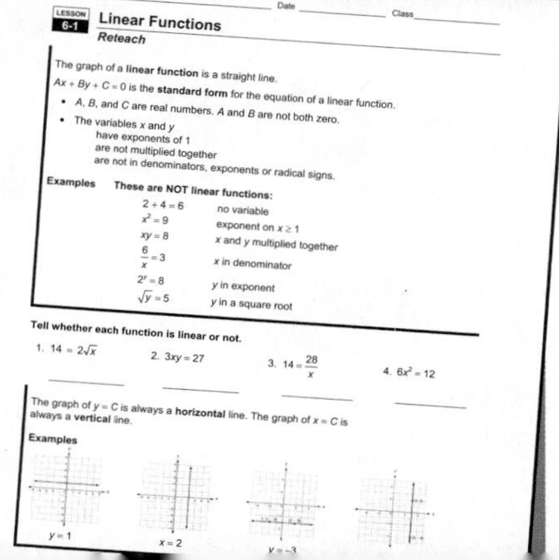

Name ______ Date ______ Class ______

LESSON 6-1 **Linear Functions**
Reteach

The graph of a **linear function** is a straight line.

$Ax + By + C = 0$ is the **standard form** for the equation of a linear function.

- A, B, and C are real numbers. A and B are not both zero.
- The variables x and y
  have exponents of 1
  are not multiplied together
  are not in denominators, exponents or radical signs.

Examples **These are NOT linear functions:**

$2 + 4 = 6$	no variable
$x^2 = 9$	exponent on $x \geq 1$
$xy = 8$	x and y multiplied together
$\frac{6}{x} = 3$	x in denominator
$2^y = 8$	y in exponent
$\sqrt{y} = 5$	y in a square root

Tell whether each function is linear or not.

1. $14 = 2\sqrt{x}$ 2. $3xy = 27$ 3. $14 = \frac{28}{x}$ 4. $6x^2 = 12$

The graph of $y = C$ is always a **horizontal** line. The graph of $x = C$ is always a **vertical** line.

Examples

$y = 1$ $x = 2$ $y = -3$

ASSESSMENT AND INTERVENTION

The Personal Math Trainer provides online practice, homework, assessments, and intervention. Monitor student progress through reports and alerts. Create and customize assignments aligned to specific lessons or Common Core standards.

- **Practice** – With dynamic items and assignments, students get unlimited practice on key concepts supported by guided examples, step-by-step solutions, and video tutorials.
- **Assessments** – Choose from course assignments or customize your own based on course content, Common Core standards, difficulty levels, and more.
- **Homework** – Students can complete online homework with a wide variety of problem types, including the ability to enter expressions, equations, and graphs. Let the system automatically grade homework, so you can focus where your students need help the most!
- **Intervention** – Let the Personal Math Trainer automatically prescribe a targeted, personalized intervention path for your students.

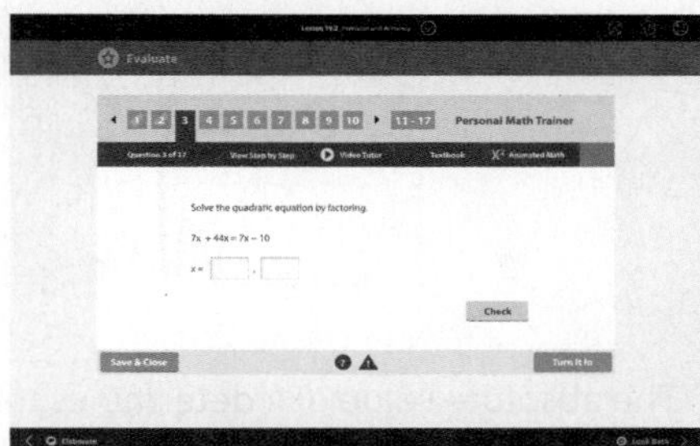

Focus on Higher Order Thinking

Raise the bar with homework and practice that incorporates higher-order thinking and mathematical practices in every lesson.

Assessment Readiness

Prepare students for success on high stakes tests for Algebra 2 with practice at every module and unit

Assessment Resources

Tailor assessments and response to intervention to meet the needs of all your classes and students, including

- Leveled Module Quizzes
- Leveled Unit Tests
- Unit Performance Tasks
- Placement, Diagnostic, and Quarterly Benchmark Tests
- Tier 1, Tier 2, and Tier 3 Resources

Math Background

Rational Functions  F-IF.C.7d

LESSON 8.1

This unit deals with rational expressions and rational functions.

The simplest rational functions are given by *inverse variations*. Specifically, an inverse variation is a function of the form $y = \frac{k}{x}$, where k is a nonzero constant.

The graph of an inverse variation is a *hyperbola*. The x- and y-axes are asymptotes.

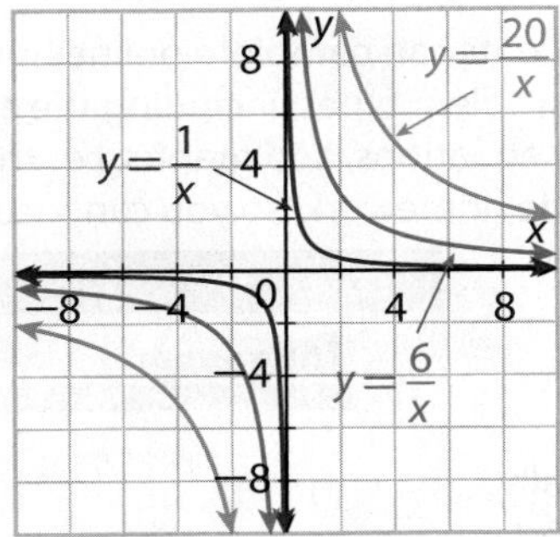

The absolute value of k determines the shape of the hyperbola. The smaller the absolute value of k, the closer the curve is to the origin. This is illustrated in the graphs of $y = \frac{k}{x}$, for $k = 1$, $k = 6$, and $k = 20$.

Rational Expressions A-APR.A.1

LESSONS 9.1 to 9.3

A *rational expression* is a quotient of two polynomials.

Students should realize, however, that a rational expression may be written in a form in which it is not immediately obvious that the expression is a quotient of polynomials.

Consider the following expression.

$$\frac{(x-1)^2}{x(x+2)^{-2}}$$

Using the Negative Exponent Property, the expression may be rewritten as

$$\frac{(x-1)^2(x+2)^2}{x}$$

Squaring both binomials in the numerator and then multiplying shows that the expression is indeed a rational expression.

Operations on rational expressions are similar to operations on fractions.

For example, if $a(x)$, $b(x)$, $c(x)$, and $d(x)$ are polynomials, then

$$\frac{a(x)}{b(x)} + \frac{c(x)}{d(x)} = \frac{a(x)d(x) + b(x)c(x)}{b(x)d(x)}$$

except where $b(x) = 0$ and $d(x) = 0$.

As with fractions, it is generally best to simplify rational expressions before adding, subtracting, multiplying, or dividing.

A set of numbers is *closed*, or has *closure*, under a given operation if the result of the operation on any two numbers in the set is also in the set.

For example, the set of real numbers is closed under addition, because adding any two real numbers results in another real number. Likewise, the real numbers are closed under subtraction, multiplication and division (by a nonzero real number), because performing these operations on two real numbers always yields another real number.

Polynomials are closed under the same operations as integers. Rational expressions are closed under addition, subtraction, multiplication, and division by a nonzero rational expression.

A *rational function* has the form

$$f(x) = \frac{p(x)}{q(x)},$$

where $p(x)$ and $q(x)$ are polynomials.

Note that $q(x)$ may be a constant, in which case the rational function simplifies to a polynomial. However, $q(x)$ is generally taken to be a polynomial of degree greater than or equal to 1 in order to restrict the discussion to rational functions that are not polynomials.

The graph of a rational function has a vertical asymptote at each real value of x for which $q(x) = 0$ and $p(x) = 0$.

However, not every rational function has vertical asymptotes. For example, the rational function

$$f(x) = \frac{1}{x^2 + 1}$$

has a denominator that is never 0, and the graph of this function is a continuous curve.

It is also interesting to note that rational functions may have asymptotes that are neither horizontal nor vertical.

The following figure shows the graph of

$$f(x) = \frac{x^2 - 2x - 3}{x - 2}.$$

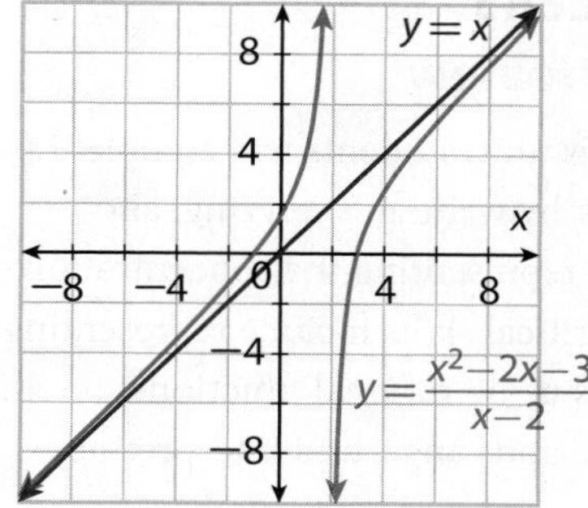

Using long division, this function may be written as

$$f(x) = x - \frac{3}{x - 2}$$

For very large values of $|x|$, $\frac{3}{x-2}$ is close to 0, so the value of $f(x)$ is close to that of the function $g(x) = x$.

Thus, the line $y = x$ is an asymptote.

Rational Functions, Expressions, and Equations

MATH IN CAREERS

Unit Activity Preview

After completing this unit, students will complete a Math in Careers task by writing, analyzing, and graphing a function representing the concentration of acid in a mixture. Critical skills include representing real-world situations using rational functions, determining domain and range, and interpreting asymptotes.

For more information about careers in mathematics as well as various mathematics appreciation topics, visit The American Mathematical Society at http://www.ams.org.

UNIT 4

Rational Functions, Expressions, and Equations

MODULE 8
Rational Functions

MODULE 9
Rational Expressions and Equations

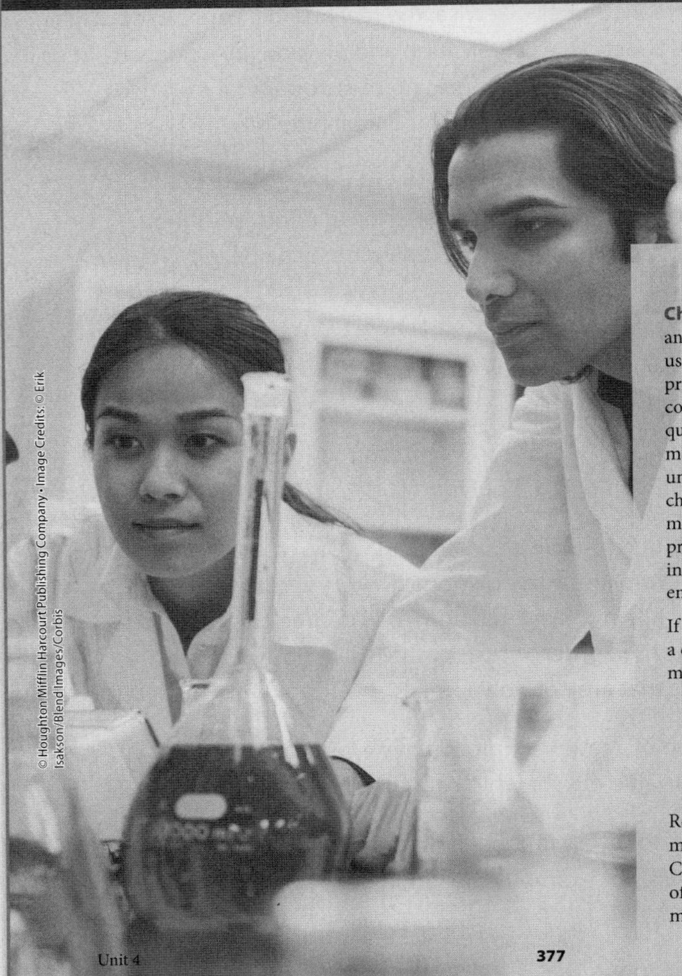

MATH IN CAREERS

Chemist Chemists study the properties and composition of substances. They use the mathematics of ratios and proportions to determine the atomic composition of materials and the quantities of atoms needed to synthesize materials. They use geometry to understand the physical structures of chemical compounds. Chemists also use mathematical models to understand and predict behavior of chemical interaction including reaction rates and activation energies.

If you are interested in a career as a chemist, you should study these mathematical subjects:

- Geometry
- Algebra
- Calculus
- Differential Equations
- Statistics

Research other careers that require using mathematical models to predict behavic Check out the career activity at the end of the unit to find out how **Chemists** us math.

TRACKING YOUR LEARNING PROGRESSION

Before	In this Unit	After
Students understand: • adding, subtracting, multiplying, factoring, and dividing polynomial functions • combining rational expressions by various operations • finding rational and complex solutions of polynomial equations	Students will learn about: • graphing rational functions • adding and subtracting rational expressions • multiplying and dividing rational expressions • graphing and solving rational equations	Students will study: • inverses of quadratic and cubic functions • graphing square root functions • graphing cube root functions • simplifying radical expressions and solving radical equations

Reading Start-Up

Visualize Vocabulary

Use the ✓ words to complete the chart.

range	the set of output values of a function or relation
direct variation	a linear relationship between two variables, x and y, that can be written in the form $y = kx$, where k is a nonzero constant
reciprocal	the multiplicative inverse of a number
parent function	the simplest function with the defining characteristics of the function family
domain	the set of all possible input values of a relation or function
rational expression	an algebraic expression whose numerator and denominator are polynomials

Vocabulary

Review Words

- ✓ direct variation (*variación directa*)
- ✓ domain (*dominio*)
- ✓ parent function (*función madre*)
- ✓ range (*rango*)
- ✓ rational expression (*expresión racional*)
- ✓ reciprocal (*recíproco*)

Preview Words

- asymptote (asíntota)
- closure (cerradura)
- inverse variation (variación inversa)
- rational function (función racional)

Understand Vocabulary

To become familiar with some of the vocabulary terms in the module, consider the following. You may refer to the module, the glossary, or a dictionary.

1. **Inverse variation** is a relationship between two variables, x and y, that can be written in the form $y = \frac{k}{x}$, where k is a nonzero constant and $x \neq 0$.
2. A line that a graph approaches as the value of the variable becomes extremely large or small is a/an **asymptote**.
3. A function whose rule can be written as a rational expression is a/an **rational function**.

Active Reading

Double-Door Fold Before beginning each lesson, create a double-door fold to compare the characteristics of two expressions, functions, or variations. This can help you identify the similarities and differences between the topics.

Reading Start Up

Have students complete the activities on this page by working alone or with others.

VISUALIZE VOCABULARY

The chart helps students review important vocabulary associated with rational expressions and parent functions. If time allows, brainstorm aspects of rational expressions that may need special consideration when they are defined as functions.

UNDERSTAND VOCABULARY

Use the following explanations to help students learn the preview words.

> A **rational function** is a ratio of two polynomial functions. A rational function has a **discontinuity** at any value that makes the denominator equal to zero. A line that the graph of a rational function gets closer and closer to but never reaches is an **asymptote**. **Inverse variation** is an example of a rational function.

ACTIVE READING

Students can use these reading and note-taking strategies to help them organize and understand the new concepts and vocabulary. Encourage students to use mathematical vocabulary often and precisely as they refer to their double-door folds. Remind them to ask about any terms that seem unclear.

ADDITIONAL RESOURCES

Differentiated Instruction

- Reading Strategies EL

MODULE 8

Rational Functions

ESSENTIAL QUESTION:

Answer: Many real-world situations that involve dividing one quantity by another can be represented by rational functions. For example, any per-capita measure will likely be best represented by a rational function.

PROFESSIONAL DEVELOPMENT VIDEO

Professional Development Video
Author Matt Larson models successful teaching practices in an actual high-school classroom.
Professional Development
my.hrw.com

MODULE 8

Rational Functions

Essential Question: How can you use rational functions to solve real-world problems?

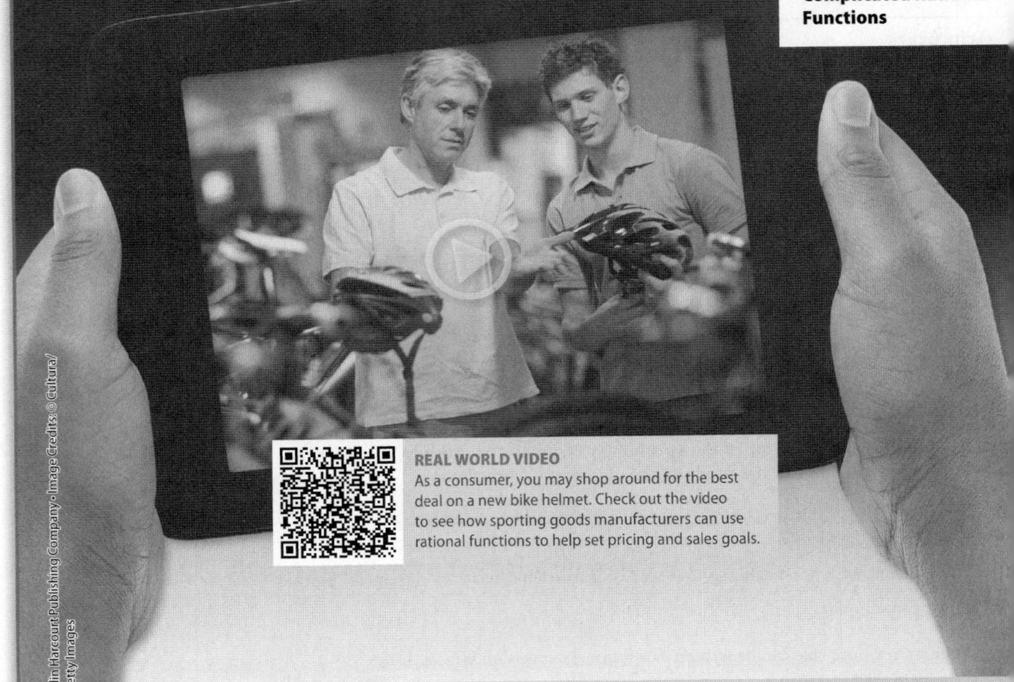

REAL WORLD VIDEO
As a consumer, you may shop around for the best deal on a new bike helmet. Check out the video to see how sporting goods manufacturers can use rational functions to help set pricing and sales goals.

MODULE PERFORMANCE TASK PREVIEW

What Is the Profit?

Like any business, a manufacturer of bike helmets must pay attention to ways to minimize costs and maximize profit. Businesses use mathematical functions to calculate and predict various quantities, including profits, costs, and revenue. What are some of the ways a business can use a profit function? Let's find out!

DIGITAL TEACHER EDITION

Access a full suite of teaching resources when and where you need them:

- Access content online or offline
- Customize lessons to share with your class
- Communicate with your students in real-time
- View student grades and data instantly to target your instruction where it is needed most

PERSONAL MATH TRAINER

Assessment and Intervention

Assign automatically graded homework, quizzes, tests, and intervention activities. Prepare your students with updated, Common Core-aligned practice tests.

Are YOU Ready?

Complete these exercises to review skills you will need for this chapter.

- Online Homework
- Hints and Help
- Extra Practice

Graphing Linear Nonproportional Relationships

Example 1 Graph $y = -\frac{1}{2}x - 3$

Plot the y-intercept $(0, -3)$

The slope is $-\frac{1}{2}$, so from $(0, -3)$, plot the next point up 1 and left 2.

Draw a line through the two points.

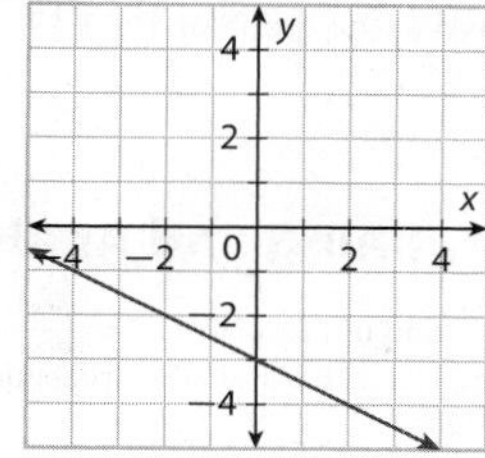

Graph each relationship.

1. $y = 3x - 4$

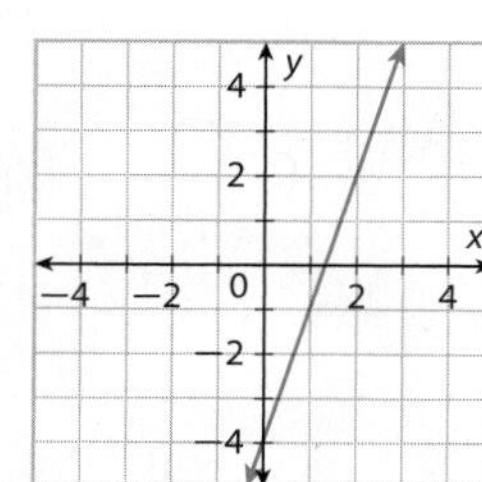

2. $y = -\frac{3}{4}x + 1$

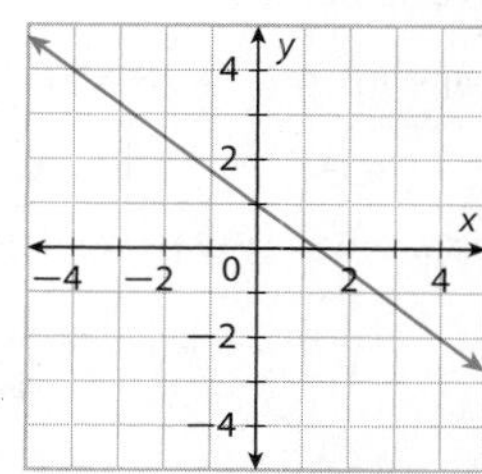

Direct and Inverse Variation

Example 2 The graph of a direct variation function passes through $(1, 10)$. Write the equation for the function.

$k = \frac{y}{x} = \frac{10}{1} = 10$, so the equation is $y = 10x$.

Example 3 The graph of an inverse variation function passes through $(4, 3)$. Write the equation for the function.

$k = xy = 4 \cdot 3 = 12$, so the equation is $y = \frac{12}{x}$.

Write a direct variation equation for the graph that passes through the point.

3. $(2, 5)$ $y = \frac{5}{2}x$
4. $(3, 6)$ $y = 2x$
5. $(4, 1)$ $y = \frac{1}{4}x$

Write an inverse variation equation for the graph that passes through the point.

6. $(8, 1)$ $y = \frac{8}{x}$
7. $(5, 10)$ $y = \frac{50}{x}$
8. $(2, 6)$ $y = \frac{12}{x}$

Response to Intervention			Differentiated Instruction
Tier 1 Lesson Intervention Worksheets	**Tier 2** Strategic Intervention Skills Intervention Worksheets	**Tier 3** Intensive Intervention Worksheets available online	
Reteach 8.1 Reteach 8.2	6 Direct Variation 14 Graphing Linear Nonproportional Relationships 15 Graphing Linear Proportional Relationships 17 Inverse Variation	Building Block Skills 41, 43, 44, 46, 94, 96	Challenge worksheets Extend the Math Lesson Activities in TE

Are You Ready?

ASSESS READINESS

Use the assessment on this page to determine if students need strategic or intensive intervention for the module's prerequisite skills.

ASSESSMENT AND INTERVENTION

RtI Response to Intervention TIER 1, TIER 2, TIER 3 SKILLS

Personal Math Trainer will automatically create a standards-based, personalized intervention assignment for your students, targeting each student's individual needs!

ADDITIONAL RESOURCES

See the table below for a full list of intervention resources available for this module.

Response to Intervention Resources also includes:

- Tier 2 Skill Pre-Tests for each Module
- Tier 2 Skill Post-Tests for each skill

Graphing Simple Rational Functions

Common Core Math Standards

The student is expected to:

 F-IF.C.7d(+)

Graph rational functions, identifying ... asymptotes ..., and showing end behavior. Also A-APR.D.6, F-BF.B.3

Mathematical Practices

 MP.4 Modeling

Language Objective

Explain to a partner the characteristics of the graphs of rational functions.

ENGAGE

Essential Question: How are the graphs of $f(x) = a\left(\frac{1}{x-h}\right) + k$ and $f(x) = \frac{1}{b(x-h)} + k$ related to the graph of $f(x) = \frac{1}{x}$?

Possible answer: Both graphs involve transformations of the graph of $f(x) = \frac{1}{x}$. The first equation involves vertically stretching or compressing the graph of $f(x) = \frac{1}{x}$ by a factor of a, reflecting it across the x-axis if $a < 0$, and translating it h units horizontally and k units vertically. The second equation involves horizontally stretching or compressing the graph of $f(x) = \frac{1}{x}$ by a factor of b, reflecting it across the y-axis if $b < 0$, and translating it h units horizontally and k units vertically.

PREVIEW: LESSON PERFORMANCE TASK

View the Engage section online. Discuss the photo and how a one-time fee can be converted to a monthly fee. Then preview the Lesson Performance Task

Name ______ Class ______ Date ______

8.1 Graphing Simple Rational Functions

Resource Locker

Essential Question: How are the graphs of $f(x) = a\left(\frac{1}{x-h}\right) + k$ and $f(x) = \frac{1}{\frac{1}{b}(x-h)} + k$ related to the graph of $f(x) = \frac{1}{x}$?

Explore 1 Graphing and Analyzing $f(x) = \frac{1}{x}$

A **rational function** is a function of the form $f(x) = \frac{p(x)}{q(x)}$ where $p(x)$ and $q(x)$ are polynomials. The most basic rational function with a variable expression in the denominator is $f(x) = \frac{1}{x}$.

(A) State the domain of $f(x) = \frac{1}{x}$.

The function accepts all real numbers except 0, because division by 0 is undefined. So, the function's domain is as follows:

- As an inequality: $x <$ 0 or $x >$ 0
- In set notation: $\{x \mid x \neq 0\}$
- In interval notation (where the symbol $\cup$ means *union*): $(-\infty, 0) \cup (0, +\infty)$

(B) Determine the end behavior of $f(x) = \frac{1}{x}$.

First, complete the tables.

x Increases without Bound	
x	$f(x) = \frac{1}{x}$
100	0.01
1000	0.001
10,000	0.0001

x Decreases without Bound	
x	$f(x) = \frac{1}{x}$
−100	−0.01
−1000	−0.001
−10,000	−0.0001

Next, summarize the results.

- As $x \to +\infty$, $f(x) \to$ 0.
- As $x \to -\infty$, $f(x) \to$ 0.

HARDCOVER PAGES 381–400

Watch for the hardcover student edition page numbers for this lesson.

(C) Be more precise about the end behavior of $f(x) = \frac{1}{x}$, and determine what this means for the graph of the function.

You can be more precise about the end behavior by using the notation $f(x) \to 0^+$, which means that the value of $f(x)$ approaches 0 from the positive direction (that is, the value of $f(x)$ is positive as it approaches 0), and the notation $f(x) \to 0^-$, which means that the value of $f(x)$ approaches 0 from the negative direction. So, the end behavior of the function is more precisely summarized as follows:

- As $x \to +\infty$, $f(x) \to$ 0^+.
- As $x \to -\infty$, $f(x) \to$ 0^-.

The end behavior indicates that the graph of $f(x)$ approaches, but does not cross, the [x-axis/y-axis], so that axis is an asymptote for the graph.

(D) Examine the behavior of $f(x) = \frac{1}{x}$ near $x = 0$, and determine what this means for the graph of the function.

First, complete the tables.

x Approaches 0 from the Positive Direction	
x	$f(x) = \frac{1}{x}$
0.01	100
0.001	1000
0.0001	10,000

x Approaches 0 from the Negative Direction	
x	$f(x) = \frac{1}{x}$
−0.01	−100
−0.001	−1000
−0.0001	−10,000

Next, summarize the results.

- As $x \to 0^+$, $f(x) \to$ $+\infty$.
- As $x \to 0^-$, $f(x) \to$ $-\infty$.

The behavior of $f(x) = \frac{1}{x}$ near $x = 0$ indicates that the graph of $f(x)$ approaches, but does not cross, the [x-axis/y-axis], so that axis is also an asymptote for the graph.

(E) Graph $f(x) = \frac{1}{x}$.

First, determine the sign of $f(x)$ on the two parts of its domain.

- When x is a negative number, $f(x)$ is a [positive/negative] number.
- When x is a positive number, $f(x)$ is a [positive/negative] number.

Next, complete the tables.

Negative Values of *x*	
x	$f(x) = \frac{1}{x}$
−2	−0.5
−1	−1
−0.5	−2

Positive Values of *x*	
x	$f(x) = \frac{1}{x}$
0.5	2
1	1
2	0.5

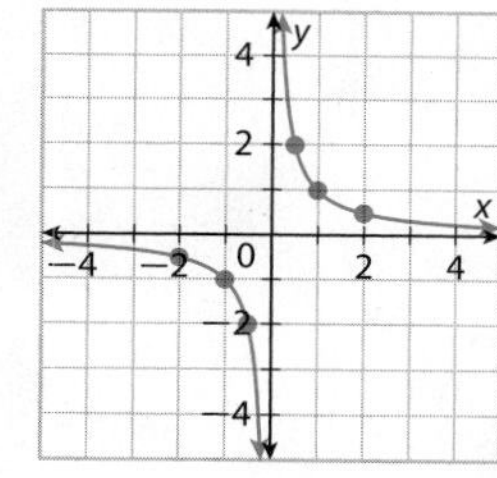

Finally, use the information from this step and all previous steps to draw the graph. Draw asymptotes as dashed lines.

PROFESSIONAL DEVELOPMENT

Learning Progressions

Previously, students looked at polynomial functions and their transformations, inverse variation applications, and the graphs of rational functions of the form $f(x) = \frac{a}{x}$ in the first quadrant. Students now extend that knowledge by graphing and transforming the graph of the parent function $f(x) = \frac{1}{x}$. They learn how the values of h and k are related to the graph of $f(x) = \frac{a}{x-h} + k$ and graph rational functions in the general form $\frac{ax+b}{cx+d}$, where $bx + c$ and $dx + e$ are both linear functions. In the next lesson, students examine the quotients of linear and quadratic polynomials, and discontinuities.

EXPLORE

Graphing and Analyzing $f(x) = \frac{1}{x}$

INTEGRATE TECHNOLOGY

Students may complete the Explore activity either in the book or online.

QUESTIONING STRATEGIES

? Why are there two parts to the graph of the rational function? **There are positive values and negative values for *x*, but no value when *x* is 0.**

? Why isn't the graph symmetric across the *y*-axis? **Positive values of *x* result in positive values of *y*, but negative values of *x* result in negative values of *y*.**

(F) State the range of $f(x) = \frac{1}{x}$.

The function takes on all real numbers except **0**, so the function's range is as follows:

- As an inequality: $y <$ **0** or $y >$ **0**
- In set notation: $\{y | y \neq$ **0**$\}$
- In interval notation (where the symbol $\cup$ means *union*): $(-\infty,$ **0**$) \cup ($**0**$, +\infty)$

(G) Identify the intervals where the function is increasing and where it is decreasing.

The function is never increasing.

The function is decreasing on the intervals $(-\infty, 0)$ and $(0, +\infty)$.

(H) Determine whether $f(x) = \frac{1}{x}$ is an even function, an odd function, or neither.

$f(-x) = \frac{1}{-x} = -\frac{1}{x} = -f(x)$ so $f(x) = \frac{1}{x}$ is an odd function.

Reflect

1. How does the graph of $f(x) = \frac{1}{x}$ show that the function has no zeros?

The graph of the function never crosses the *x*-axis.

2. **Discussion** A graph is said to be *symmetric about the origin* (and the origin is called the graph's *point of symmetry*) if for every point (x, y) on the graph, the point $(-x, -y)$ is also on the graph. Is the graph of $f(x) = \frac{1}{x}$ symmetric about the origin? Explain.

Yes, because for every point $(x, y) = \left(x, \frac{1}{x}\right)$ on the graph of the function, the point $\left(-x, \frac{1}{-x}\right) = \left(-x, -\frac{1}{x}\right) = (-x, -y)$ is also on the graph.

3. What line is a line of symmetry for the graph of $f(x) = \frac{1}{x}$?

The line $y = x$.

COLLABORATIVE LEARNING

Peer-to-Peer Activity

Have students work in pairs. Give each pair graphs of eight transformed rational functions labeled A through H, and cards with the eight functions on them. Set aside one additional graph and function that do not match. Have each pair match the correct functions and graphs and then decide why the remaining graph and function do not match.

Explain 1 Graphing Simple Rational Functions

When graphing transformations of $f(x) = \frac{1}{x}$, it helps to consider the effect of the transformations on the following features of the graph of $f(x)$: the vertical asymptote, $x = 0$; the horizontal asymptote, $y = 0$; and two reference points, $(-1, -1)$ and $(1, 1)$. The table lists these features of the graph of $f(x)$ and the corresponding features of the graph of $g(x) = a\left(\frac{1}{\frac{1}{b}(x-h)}\right) + k$. Note that the asymptotes are affected only by the parameters h and k, while the reference points are affected by all four parameters

Feature	$f(x) = \frac{1}{x}$	$g(x) = a\left(\frac{1}{\frac{1}{b}(x-h)}\right) + k$
Vertical asymptote	$x = 0$	$x = h$
Horizontal asymptote	$y = 0$	$y = k$
Reference point	$(-1, -1)$	$(-b + h, -a + k)$
Reference point	$(1, 1)$	$(b + h, a + k)$

Example 1 **Identify the transformations of the graph of $f(x) = \frac{1}{x}$ that produce the graph of the given function $g(x)$. Then graph $g(x)$ on the same coordinate plane as the graph of $f(x)$ by applying the transformations to the asymptotes $x = 0$ and $y = 0$ to the reference points $(-1, -1)$ and $(1, 1)$. Also state the domain and range of $g(x)$ using inequalities, set notation, and interval notation.**

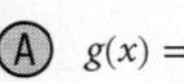 $g(x) = 3\left(\frac{1}{x-1}\right) + 2$

The transformations of the graph of $f(x)$ that produce the graph of $g(x)$ are:

- a vertical stretch by a factor of 3
- a translation of 1 unit to the right and 2 units up

Note that the translation of 1 unit to the right affects only the x-coordinates, while the vertical stretch by a factor of 3 and the translation of 2 units up affect only the y-coordinates.

Feature	$f(x) = \frac{1}{x}$	$g(x) = 3\left(\frac{1}{x-h}\right) + 2$
Vertical asymptote	$x = 0$	$x = 1$
Horizontal asymptote	$y = 0$	$y = 2$
Reference point	$(-1, -1)$	$(-1 + 1, 3(-1) + 2) = (0, -1)$
Reference point	$(1, 1)$	$(1 + 1, 3(1) + 2) = (2, 5)$

Domain of $g(x)$:

Inequality: $x < 1$ or $x > 1$

Set notation: $\{x \mid x \neq 1\}$

Interval notation: $(-\infty, 1) \cup (1, +\infty)$

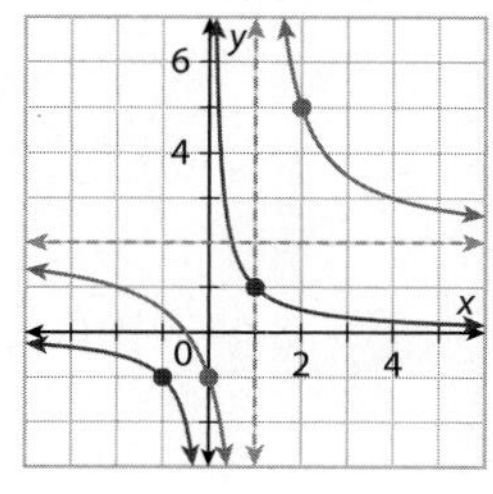

Range of $g(x)$:

Inequality: $y < 2$ or $y > 2$

Set notation: $\{y \mid y \neq 2\}$

Interval notation: $(-\infty, 2) \cup (2, +\infty)$

DIFFERENTIATE INSTRUCTION

Multiple Representations

Interpersonal learners may benefit from working in pairs, with one student graphing a quotient of linear functions by rewriting the function in graphing form and the other graphing the function by making a table of values and plotting points. Students should compare the strategies by identifying at least one advantage and one disadvantage for each method.

EXPLAIN 1

Graphing Simple Rational Functions

QUESTIONING STRATEGIES

What is the midpoint of the x-coordinates of the two reference points? (h, k)

because $\frac{(-b+h)+(b+h)}{2} = \frac{2h}{2} = h$

and $\frac{(-a+k)+(a+k)}{2} = \frac{2k}{2} = k$

AVOID COMMON ERRORS

Students may make errors when finding a reference point. Have students check them with respect to each other by finding whether they are centered at (h, k), as above.

CONNECT VOCABULARY EL

Connect the term *rational function* to *rational numbers*, including fractions. Remind students that a simple rational function has polynomials in the numerator and denominator.

(B) $g(x) = \frac{1}{2(x+3)} - 1$

The transformations of the graph of $f(x)$ that produce the graph of $g(x)$ are:

- a horizontal compression by a factor of $\frac{1}{2}$
- a translation of 3 units to the left and 1 unit down

Note that the horizontal compression by a factor of $\frac{1}{2}$ and the translation of 3 units to the left affect only the x-coordinates of points on the graph of $f(x)$, while the translation of 1 unit down affects only the y-coordinates.

Feature	$f(x) = \frac{1}{x}$	$g(x) = \frac{1}{2(x+3)} - 1$
Vertical asymptote	$x = 0$	$x = -3$
Horizontal asymptote	$y = 0$	$y = -1$
Reference point	$(-1, -1)$	$\left(\frac{1}{2}(-1) - 3, -1 - 1\right) = \left(-3\frac{1}{2}, -2\right)$
Reference point	$(1, 1)$	$\left(\frac{1}{2}(1) - 3, 1 - 1\right) = \left(-2\frac{1}{2}, 0\right)$

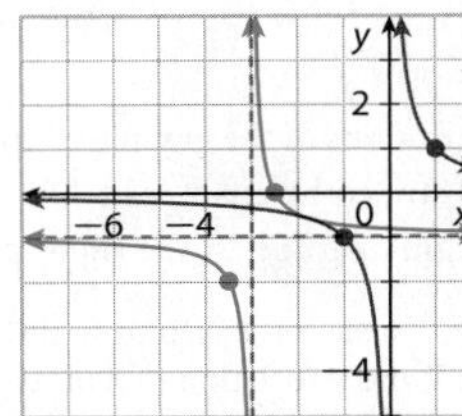

Domain of $g(x)$:

Inequality: $x < -3$ or $x > -3$

Set notation: $\{x \mid x \neq -3\}$

Interval notation: $(-\infty, -3) \cup (-3, +\infty)$

Range of $g(x)$:

Inequality: $y < -1$ or $y > -1$

Set notation: $\{y \mid y \neq -1\}$

Interval notation: $(-\infty, -1) \cup (-1, +\infty)$

Your Turn

Identify the transformations of the graph of $f(x) = \frac{1}{x}$ that produce the graph of the given function $g(x)$. Then graph $g(x)$ on the same coordinate plane as the graph of $f(x)$ by applying the transformations to the asymptotes $x = 0$ and $y = 0$ to the reference points $(-1, -1)$ and $(1, 1)$. Also state the domain and range of $g(x)$ using inequalities, set notation, and interval notation.

4. $g(x) = -0.5\left(\frac{1}{x+1}\right) - 3$

The transformations of the graph of $f(x)$ that produce the graph of $g(x)$ are:

- a vertical compression by a factor of $\frac{1}{2}$
- a reflection across the x-axis
- a translation of 1 units to the left and 3 units down

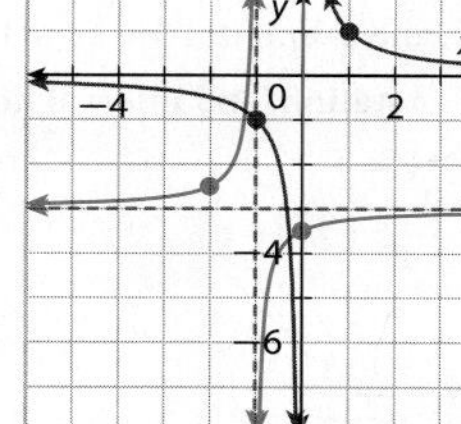

Vert. Asymp: $x = 0$ becomes $x = -1$

Horiz. Asymp: $y = 0$ becomes $y = -3$

$(-1, -1)$ becomes $\left(-2, -\frac{5}{2}\right)$

$(1, 1)$ becomes $\left(0, -\frac{7}{2}\right)$

Domain of $g(x)$:

Inequality: $x < -1$ or $x > -1$

Set notation: $\{x \mid x \neq -1\}$

Interval notation: $(-\infty, -1) \cup (-1, +\infty)$

Range of $g(x)$:

Inequality: $y < -3$ or $y > -3$

Set notation: $\{y \mid y \neq -3\}$

Interval notation: $(-\infty, -3) \cup (-3, +\infty)$

5. $g(x) = \frac{1}{-0.5(x-2)} + 1$

The transformations of the graph of $f(x)$ that produce the graph of $g(x)$ are:

- a horizontal stretch by a factor of 2
- a reflection across the y-axis
- a translation of 2 units to the right and 1 unit up

Vert. Asymp: $x = 0$ becomes $x = 2$

Horiz. Asymp: $y = 0$ becomes $y = 1$

$(-1, -1)$ becomes $(4, -0)$

$(1, 1)$ becomes $(0, 2)$

Domain of $g(x)$:

Inequality: $x < 2$ or $x > 2$

Set notation: $\{x \mid x \neq 2\}$

Interval notation: $(-\infty, 2) \cup (2, +\infty)$

Range of $g(x)$:

Inequality: $y < 1$ or $y > 1$

Set notation: $\{y \mid y \neq 1\}$

Interval notation: $(-\infty, 1) \cup (1, +\infty)$

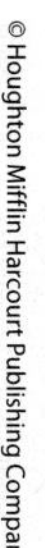

EXPLAIN 2

Rewriting Simple Rational Functions in Order to Graph Them

INTEGRATE MATHEMATICAL PRACTICES

Focus on Math Connections

MP.1 Remind students that division by a linear factor in the form $x - h$ can be done by synthetic division. However, for simple quotients, it is quicker to use long division.

AVOID COMMON ERRORS

Students may not get the correct sign of the remainder when performing long division. Remind them to consider the operation signs. For example, when subtracting $3x - 3$ from $3x - 4$, the result is -1.

Explain 2 Rewriting Simple Rational Functions in Order to Graph Them

When given a rational function of the form $g(x) = \frac{mx + n}{px + q}$, where $m \neq 0$ and $p \neq 0$, you can carry out the division of the numerator by the denominator to write the function in the form $g(x) = a\left(\frac{1}{x - h}\right) + k$ or $g(x) = \frac{1}{\frac{1}{b}(x - h)} + k$ in order to graph it.

Example 2 **Rewrite the function in the form $g(x) = a\left(\frac{1}{x - h}\right) + k$ or $g(x) = \frac{1}{\frac{1}{b}(x - h)} + k$ and graph it. Also state the domain and range using inequalities, set notation, and interval notation.**

(A) $g(x) = \dfrac{3x - 4}{x - 1}$

Use long division.

$$\begin{array}{r} 3 \\ x - 1 \overline{)\ 3x - 4} \\ \underline{3x - 3} \\ -1 \end{array}$$

So, the quotient is 3, and the remainder is -1. Using the fact that $dividend = quotient + \frac{remainder}{divisor}$, you have $g(x) = 3 + \frac{-1}{x - 1}$, or $g(x) = -\frac{1}{x - 1} + 3$.

The graph of $g(x)$ has vertical asymptote $x = 1$, horizontal asymptote $y = 3$, and reference points $\left(-1 + 1, -(-1) + 3\right) = (0, 4)$ and $(1 + 1, -(1) + 3) = (2, 2)$.

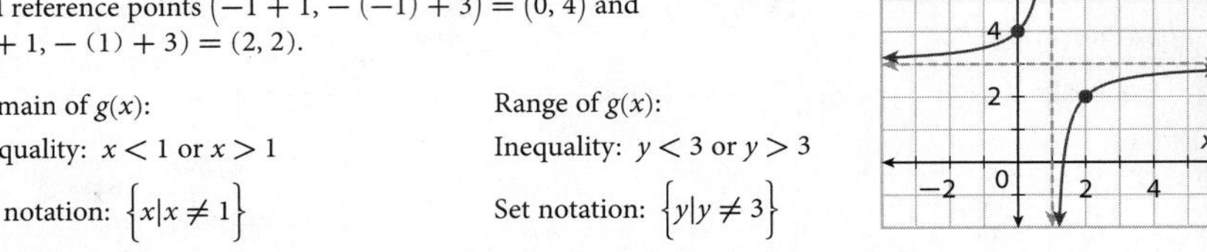

Domain of $g(x)$:

Inequality: $x < 1$ or $x > 1$

Set notation: $\{x | x \neq 1\}$

Interval notation: $(-\infty, 1) \cup (1, +\infty)$

Range of $g(x)$:

Inequality: $y < 3$ or $y > 3$

Set notation: $\{y | y \neq 3\}$

Interval notation: $(-\infty, 3) \cup (3, +\infty)$

 $g(x) = \dfrac{4x - 7}{-2x + 4}$

Use long division.

$$\begin{array}{r} -2 \\ -2x + 4 \overline{)\ 4x - 7} \\ \underline{4x - 8} \\ \boxed{1} \end{array}$$

So, the quotient is -2, and the remainder is $\underline{1}$. Using the fact that $dividend = quotient + \frac{remainder}{divisor}$, you have

$$g(x) = -2 + \frac{\boxed{1}}{-2x + 4}, \text{ or } g(x) = \frac{\boxed{1}}{-2\left(x - \boxed{2}\right)} - 2.$$

The graph of $g(x)$ has vertical asymptote $x = \boxed{2}$, horizontal asymptote $y = -2$, and reference points $\left(-\frac{1}{2}(-1) + \boxed{2}, -1 - 2\right) = \left(\boxed{2\frac{1}{2}}, -3\right)$ and $\left(-\frac{1}{2}(1) + \boxed{2}, 1 - 2\right) = \left(\boxed{1\frac{1}{2}}, -1\right)$.

Domain of $g(x)$:

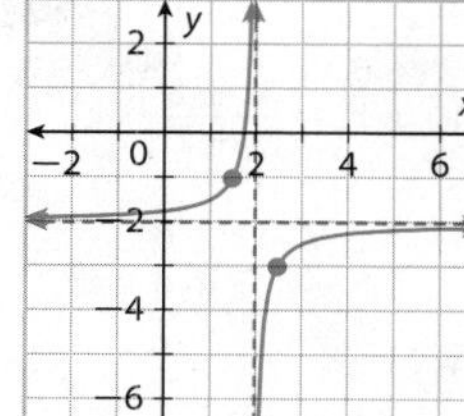

Inequality: $x < \boxed{2}$ or $x > \boxed{2}$

Set notation: $\left\{x \mid x \neq \boxed{2}\right\}$

Interval notation: $\left(-\infty, \boxed{2}\right) \cup \left(\boxed{2}, +\infty\right)$

Range of $g(x)$:

Inequality: $y < \boxed{-2}$ or $y > \boxed{-2}$

Set notation: $\left\{y \mid y \neq \boxed{-2}\right\}$

Interval notation: $\left(-\infty, \boxed{-2}\right) \cup \left(\boxed{-2}, +\infty\right)$

6. In Part A, the graph of $g(x)$ is the result of what transformations of the graph of $f(x) = \frac{1}{x}$?

The graph of $g(x)$ is a reflection of the graph of $f(x)$ across the x-axis and a translation 1 unit to the right and 3 units up.

7. In Part B, the graph of $g(x)$ is the result of what transformations of the graph of $f(x) = \frac{1}{x}$?

The graph of $g(x)$ is a horizontal compression of the graph of $f(x)$ by a factor of $\frac{1}{2}$ and a translation 2 units to the right and 2 units down.

QUESTIONING STRATEGIES

? Why are the domain and range of the graphs of rational functions disjunctions *or* inequalities, and not conjunctions? **The domain does not include the x-asymptote , but it does contain the values of x on each side of the asymptote. This is also true of the range and the y-asymptote.**

EXPLAIN 3

Writing Simple Rational Functions

QUESTIONING STRATEGIES

? How do you know that the graph can be modeled by a rational function? There is a vertical asymptote; a horizontal asymptote; as x decreases without bound, $f(x)$ approaches the y-asymptote; as x increases without bound, $f(x)$ approaches the y-asymptote; as x approaches the x-asymptote from the left, $f(x) \to -\infty$; as x approaches the x-asymptote from the right, $f(x) \to \infty$.

Your Turn

Rewrite the function in the form $g(x) = a\left(\frac{1}{x-h}\right) + k$ or $g(x) = \frac{1}{\frac{1}{b}(x-h)} + k$ and graph it. Also state the domain and range using inequalities, set notation, and interval notation.

8. $g(x) = \dfrac{3x+8}{x+2}$

$$\begin{array}{r} 3 \\ x+2\,\overline{)\,3x+8} \\ 3x+6 \\ \hline 2 \end{array}$$

So, $g(x) = 3 + \dfrac{2}{x+2}$, or $g(x) = 2\left(\dfrac{1}{x+2}\right) + 3$.

The graph of $g(x)$ has vertical asymptote $x = -2$, horizontal asymptote $y = -3$, and reference points $(-1-2, 2(-1)+3) = (-3, 1)$ and $(1-2, 2(1)+3) = (-1, 5)$.

Domain of $g(x)$:

Inequality: $x < -2$ or $x > -2$

Set notation: $\{x \mid x \neq -2\}$

Interval notation: $(-\infty, -2) \cup (-2, +\infty)$

Range of $g(x)$:

Inequality: $y < 3$ or $y > 3$

Set notation: $\{y \mid y \neq 3\}$

Interval notation: $(-\infty, 3) \cup (3, +\infty)$

Explain 3 Writing Simple Rational Functions

When given the graph of a simple rational function, you can write its equation using one of the general forms $g(x) = a\left(\frac{1}{x-h}\right) + k$ and $g(x) = \frac{1}{\frac{1}{b}(x-h)} + k$ after identifying the values of the parameters using information obtained from the graph.

Example 3

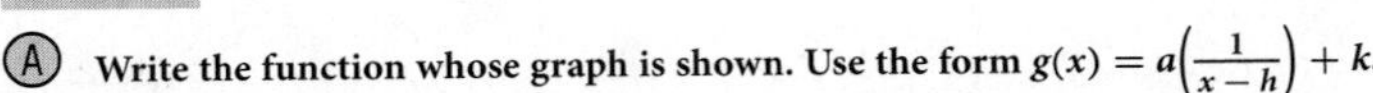

(A) **Write the function whose graph is shown. Use the form $g(x) = a\left(\frac{1}{x-h}\right) + k$.**

Since the graph's vertical asymptote is $x = 3$, the value of the parameter h is 3. Since the graph's horizontal asymptote is $y = 4$, the value of the parameter k is 4.

Substitute these values into the general form of the function.

$$g(x) = a\left(\frac{1}{x-3}\right) + 4$$

Now use one of the points, such as $(4, 6)$, to find the value of the parameter a.

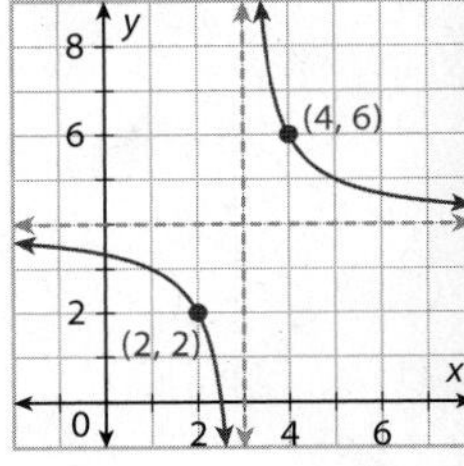

$$g(x) = a\left(\frac{1}{x-3}\right) + 4$$
$$6 = a\left(\frac{1}{4-3}\right) + 4$$
$$6 = a + 4$$
$$2 = a$$

So, $g(x) = 2\left(\frac{1}{x-3}\right) + 4$.

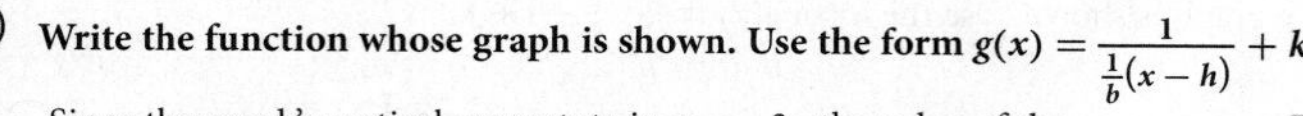

Ⓑ **Write the function whose graph is shown. Use the form $g(x) = \dfrac{1}{\frac{1}{b}(x-h)} + k$.**

Since the graph's vertical asymptote is $x = -3$, the value of the parameter h is -3. Since the graph's horizontal asymptote is $y = \boxed{-1}$, the value of the parameter k is $\underline{-1}$.

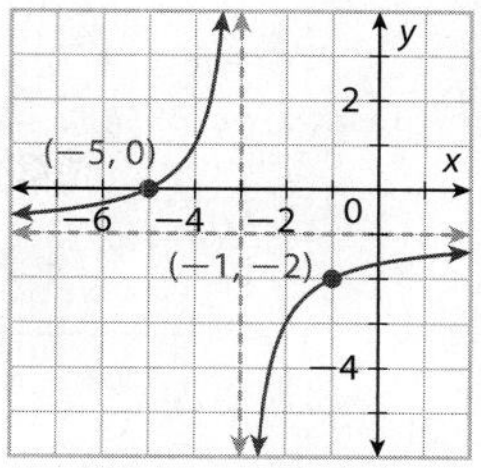

Substitute these values into the general form of the function.

$$g(x) = \frac{1}{\frac{1}{b}(x+3)} + \boxed{-1}$$

Now use one of the points, such as $(-5, 0)$, to find the value of the parameter a.

$$g(x) = \frac{1}{\frac{1}{b}(x+3)} + \boxed{-1}$$

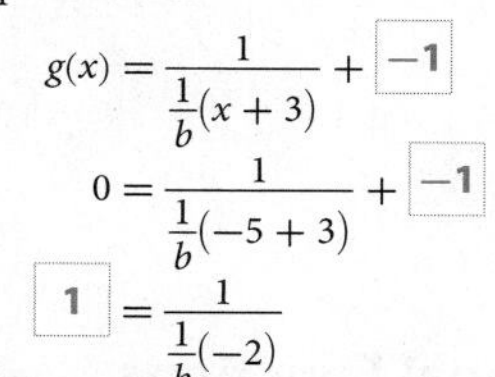

$$0 = \frac{1}{\frac{1}{b}(-5+3)} + \boxed{-1}$$

$$\boxed{1} = \frac{1}{\frac{1}{b}(-2)}$$

$$\frac{1}{b}(-2) \cdot \boxed{1} = 1$$

$$\frac{1}{b} = \boxed{\frac{-1}{2}}$$

$$b = \boxed{-2}$$

So, $g(x) = \dfrac{1}{\frac{1}{\boxed{-2}}(x+3)} + \boxed{-1}$, or $g(x) = \dfrac{1}{-0.5(x+3)} - 1$.

Reflect

9. Discussion In Parts A and B, the coordinates of a second point on the graph of $g(x)$ are given. In what way can those coordinates be useful?

You can use those coordinates as a check on the correctness of the equation by substituting the coordinates into the equation and seeing if you get a true statement.

Your Turn

10. Write the function whose graph is shown. Use the form $g(x) = a\left(\frac{1}{x-h}\right) + k$.

$h = -2$

$k = 1$

Use the point $(-3, 5)$:

$$g(x) = a\left(\frac{1}{x+2}\right) + 1$$

$$5 = a\left(\frac{1}{-3+2}\right) + 1$$

$$5 = -a + 1$$

$$4 = -a$$

$$-4 = a$$

So, $g(x) = -4\left(\frac{1}{x+2}\right) + 1$.

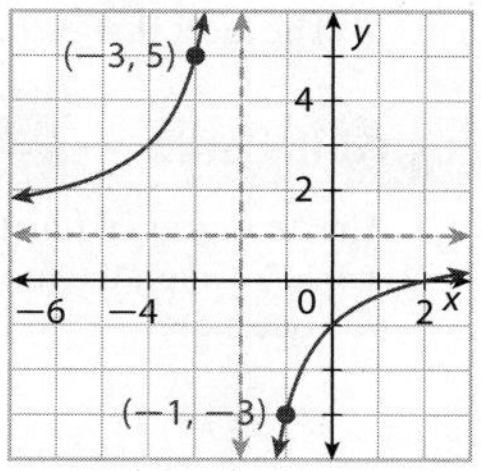

EXPLAIN 4

Modeling with Simple Rational Functions

QUESTIONING STRATEGIES

? What indicates that a rational function is a good model for a situation? **A constant quantity divided among varying numbers of another quantity is one possibility.**

11. Write the function whose graph is shown. Use the form $g(x) = \frac{1}{\frac{1}{b}(x-h)} + k$.

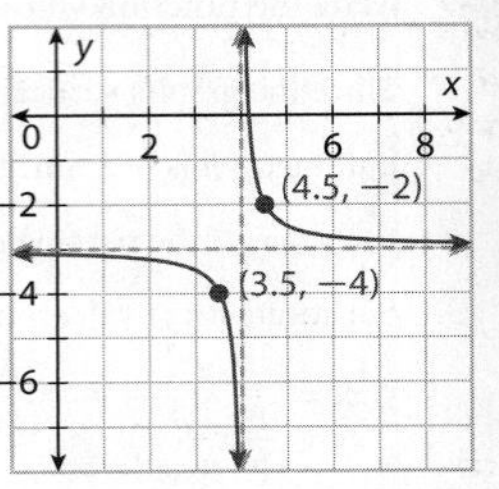

$h = 4$

$k = -3$

Use the point $(4.5, -2)$:

$g(x) = \frac{1}{\frac{1}{b}(x-4)} + -3$

$-2 = \frac{1}{\frac{1}{b}(4.5-4)} - 3$

$-2 = \frac{1}{\frac{1}{b}(0.5)} - 3$

$1 = \frac{1}{\frac{1}{b}(0.5)}$

$\frac{1}{b}(0.5) = 1$

$\frac{1}{b} = 2$

$b = \frac{1}{2}$

So, $g(x) = \frac{1}{2(x-4)} - 3$.

Explain 4 Modeling with Simple Rational Functions

In a real-world situation where there is a shared cost and a per-person or per-item cost, you can model the situation using a rational function that has the general form $f(x) = \frac{a}{x-h} + k$ where $f(x)$ is the total cost for each person or item.

Example 4

(A) **Mary and some of her friends are thinking about renting a car while staying at a beach resort for a vacation. The cost per person for staying at the beach resort is \$300, and the cost of the car rental is \$220. If the friends agree to share the cost of the car rental, what is the minimum number of people who must go on the trip so that the total cost for each person is no more than \$350?**

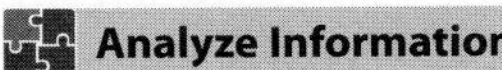

Analyze Information

Identify the important information.

- The cost per person for the resort is \$300.
- The cost of the car rental is \$220.
- The most that each person will spend is \$350.

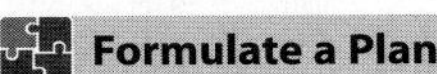

Formulate a Plan

Create a rational function that gives the total cost for each person. Graph the function, and use the graph to answer the question.

Solve

Let p be the people who agree to go on the trip. Let $C(p)$ be the cost (in dollars) for each person.

$C(p) = \frac{220}{p} + 300$

Graph the function, recognizing that the graph involves two transformations of the graph of the parent rational function:

- a vertical stretch by a factor of 220
- a vertical translation of 300 units up

Also draw the line $C(p) = 350$.

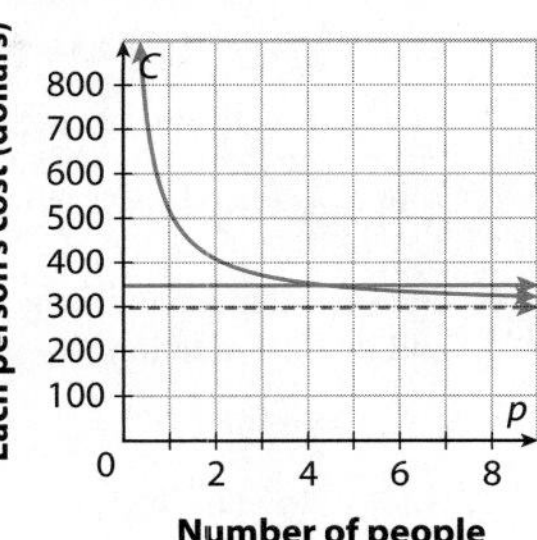

The graphs intersect between $p = 4$ and $p = 5$, so the minimum number of people who must go on the trip in order for the total cost for each person to be no more than $350 is 5.

Justify and Evaluate

Check the solution by evaluating the function $C(p)$. Since $C(4) = 355 > 350$ and $C(5) = 344 < 350$, the minimum number of people who must go on the trip is 5.

Your Turn

12. Justin has purchased a basic silk screening kit for applying designs to fabric. The kit costs $200. He plans to buy T-shirts for $10 each, apply a design that he creates to them, and then sell them. Model this situation with a rational function that gives the average cost of a silk-screened T-shirt when the cost of the kit is included in the calculation. Use the graph of the function to determine the minimum number of T-shirts that brings the average cost below $17.50.

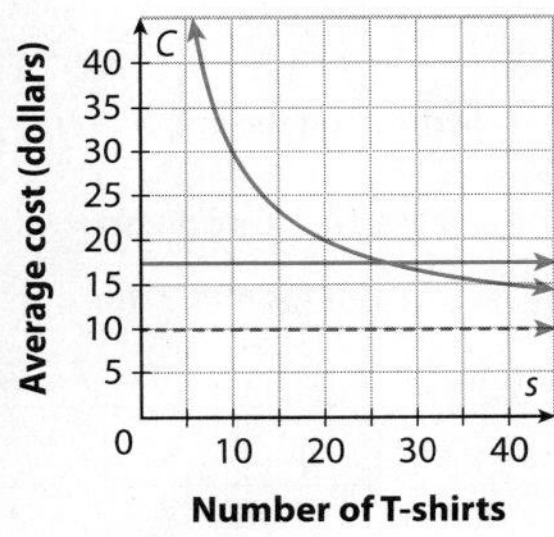

Let s be the number of T-shirts. Let $C(s)$ be the average cost (in dollars) of the silk-screened T-shirts when the cost of the kit is included. $C(s) = \frac{200}{s} + 10$

The graphs appear to intersect between $s = 26$ and $s = 27$. Since $C(26) = \frac{200}{26} + 10 \approx 17.69$ and $C(27) = \frac{200}{27} + 10 \approx 17.41$, the minimum number of T-shirts that brings the average cost below $17.50 is 27.

INTEGRATE MATHEMATICAL PRACTICES

Focus on Technology

MP.5 Students can graph a rational function using a graphing calculator, and use the TRACE function to explore the relationship between the quantities. After TRACE is pressed, the left and right arrow keys move the cursor along the graph. As the cursor moves, its x- and y-coordinates are updated at the bottom of the viewing window.

ELABORATE

INTEGRATE MATHEMATICAL PRACTICES

Focus on Critical Thinking

MP.3 Ask how could you graph $C(a) = \frac{a+5}{a+20}$ in the first quadrant without using a graphing calculator. Elicit that you know that the graph begins at (0, 0.25) and that you can determine that the graph has $C(a) = 1$ as its horizontal asymptote (which is the function's end behavior as a increases without bound). You can then make a table of values for several positive values of a, plot the points, and draw a smooth curve that approaches the line $C(a) = 1$ for greater values of a.

QUESTIONING STRATEGIES

? For the function $f(x) = \frac{2x-5}{x-4}$, what attributes of the graph can be directly read from the coefficients? **$y = 2$ is the horizontal asymptote, $x = 4$ is the vertical asymptote.**

SUMMARIZE THE LESSON

? How do you transform the graph of $f(x) = \frac{1}{x}$? **$f(x) = a\left(\frac{1}{\frac{1}{b}x - h}\right) + k$ vertically stretches or compresses the graph of $f(x) = \frac{1}{x}$ by a factor of a and reflects it across the x-axis if $a < 0$, horizontally stretches or compresses the graph by a factor of b and reflects it across the y-axis if $b < 0$, and translates it h units horizontally and k units vertically.**

Elaborate

13. Compare and contrast the attributes of $f(x) = \frac{1}{x}$ and the attributes of $g(x) = -\frac{1}{x}$.

Both functions have a domain that excludes 0 and a range that excludes 0. The graphs of both functions have the x-axis and the y-axis as asymptotes. However, the graphs approach the asymptotes from different directions. (For instance, while the graph of $f(x)$ approaches the x-axis from the positive direction as x increases without bound, the graph of $g(x)$ approaches the x-axis from the negative direction as x increases without bound.) The graph of $f(x)$ lies in Quadrants I and III, whereas the graph of $g(x)$ lies in Quadrants II and IV. While $f(x)$ decreases on both parts of its domain, $g(x)$ increases on both parts of its domain.

14. State the domain and range of $f(x) = a\left(\frac{1}{x-h}\right) + k$ using inequalities, set notation, and interval notation.

Domain:

Inequality: $x < h$ or $x > h$

Set notation: $\{x | x \neq h\}$

Interval notation: $(-\infty, h) \cup (h, +\infty)$

Range:

Inequality: $y < k$ or $y > k$

Set notation: $\{y | y \neq k\}$

Interval notation: $(-\infty, k) \cup (k, +\infty)$

15. Given that the model $C(p) = \frac{100}{p} + 50$ represents the total cost C (in dollars) for each person in a group of p people when there is a shared expense and an individual expense, describe what the expressions $\frac{100}{p}$ and 50 represent.

The expression $\frac{100}{p}$ represents each person's share of a \$100 expense for the group. The expression 50 represents an individual expense of \$50.

16. Essential Question Check-In Describe the transformations you must perform on the graph of $f(x) = \frac{1}{x}$ to obtain the graph of $f(x) = a\left(\frac{1}{x-h}\right) + k$.

If $a < 0$, reflect the parent graph across the x-axis. Then either stretch the graph vertically by a factor of $|a|$ if $|a| > 1$ or compress the graph vertically by a factor of $|a|$ if $0 < |a| < 1$. Finally, translate the graph h units right if $h > 0$, $|h|$ units left if $h < 0$, k units up if $k > 0$, and $|k|$ units down if $k < 0$.

LANGUAGE SUPPORT EL

Communicate Math

Have students work in pairs to look at graphs of rational functions and their equations. The first student describes the graph to the second student, identifying the asymptotes and the domain, range, and end behavior of the function. Students switch roles and repeat the process with a different rational function and its graph.

Evaluate: Homework and Practice

- Online Homework
- Hints and Help
- Extra Practice

Describe how the graph of $g(x)$ is related to the graph of $f(x) = \frac{1}{x}$.

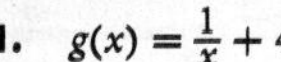

1. $g(x) = \frac{1}{x} + 4$

The graph of $g(x)$ is a translation of the graph of $f(x)$ up 4 units.

2. $g(x) = 5\left(\frac{1}{x}\right)$

The graph of $g(x)$ is a vertical stretch of the graph of $f(x)$ by a factor of 5.

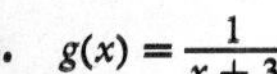

3. $g(x) = \frac{1}{x+3}$

The graph of $g(x)$ is a translation of the graph of $f(x)$ left 3 units.

4. $g(x) = \frac{1}{0.1x}$

The graph of $g(x)$ is a horizontal stretch of the graph of $f(x)$ by a factor of 10.

5. $g(x) = \frac{1}{x} - 7$

The graph of $g(x)$ is a translation of the graph of $f(x)$ down 7 units.

6. $g(x) = \frac{1}{x-8}$

The graph of $g(x)$ is a translation of the graph of $f(x)$ right 8 units.

7. $g(x) = -0.1\left(\frac{1}{x}\right)$

The graph of $g(x)$ is a vertical compression of the graph of $f(x)$ by a factor of 0.1 as well as a reflection of the graph of $f(x)$ across the x-axis.

8. $g(x) = \frac{1}{-3x}$

The graph of $g(x)$ is a horizontal compression of the graph of $f(x)$ by a factor of $\frac{1}{3}$ as well as a reflection of the graph of $f(x)$ across the y-axis.

Identify the transformations of the graph of $f(x)$ that produce the graph of the given function $g(x)$. Then graph $g(x)$ on the same coordinate plane as the graph of $f(x)$ by applying the transformations to the asymptotes $x = 0$ and $y = 0$ and to the reference points $(-1, -1)$ and $(1, 1)$. Also state the domain and range of $g(x)$ using inequalities, set notation, and interval notation.

9. $g(x) = 3\left(\frac{1}{x+1}\right) - 2$

The transformations are:

- a vertical stretch by a factor of 3
- a translation of 1 unit to the left and 2 units down

Domain of $g(x)$:

Inequality: $x < -1$ or $x > -1$

Set notation: $\{x \mid x \neq -1\}$

Interval notation: $(-\infty, -1) \cup (-1, +\infty)$

Range of $g(x)$:

Inequality: $y < -2$ or $y > -2$

Set notation: $\{y \mid y \neq -2\}$

Interval notation: $(-\infty, -2) \cup (-2, +\infty)$

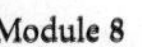

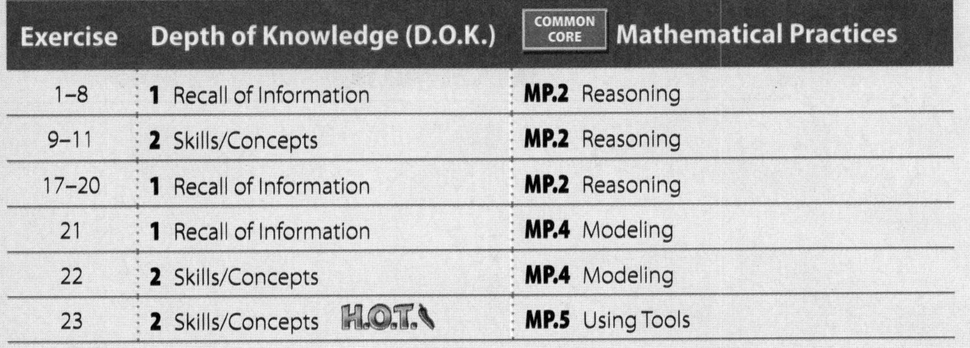

Exercise	Depth of Knowledge (D.O.K.)	COMMON CORE Mathematical Practices
1–8	1 Recall of Information	MP.2 Reasoning
9–11	2 Skills/Concepts	MP.2 Reasoning
17–20	1 Recall of Information	MP.2 Reasoning
21	1 Recall of Information	MP.4 Modeling
22	2 Skills/Concepts	MP.4 Modeling
23	2 Skills/Concepts H.O.T.	MP.5 Using Tools

EVALUATE

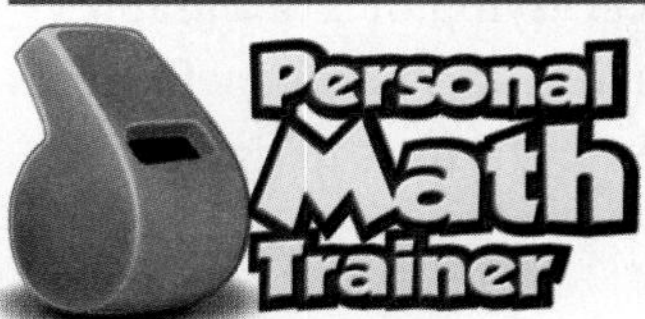

ASSIGNMENT GUIDE

Concepts and Skills	Practice
Explore Graphing and Analyzing $f(x) = \frac{1}{x}$	
Example 1 Graphing Simple Rational Functions	Exercises 9–12
Example 2 Rewriting Simple Rational Functions in Order to Graph Them	Exercises 13–16
Example 3 Writing Simple Rational Functions	Exercises 17–20
Example 4 Modeling with Simple Rational Functions	Exercises 21–22

QUESTIONING STRATEGIES

If the coordinates of (h, k) are $(-6, 15)$ and a and b are each equal to 2, what are the coordinates of the reference points? $(-2 + (-6), (-2 + 15) = (-8, 13)$ and $(2 + (-6), (2 + 15) = (-4, 17)$

VISUAL CUES

After horizontal and vertical asymptotes of a graph have been identified, visual learners may benefit from drawing horizontal and vertical arrows to find the reference points.

10. $g(x) = \dfrac{1}{-0.5(x-3)} + 1$

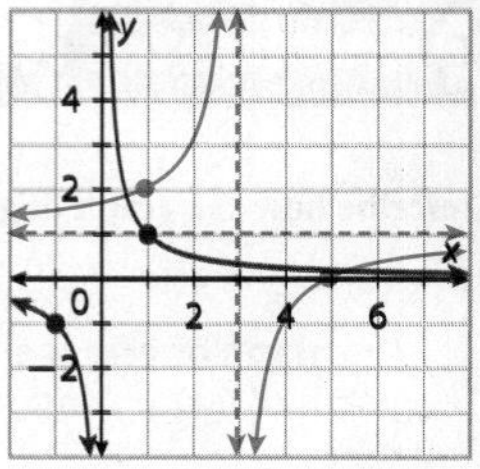

The transformations are:

- **a horizontal stretch by a factor of 2**
- **a reflection across the y-axis**
- **a translation of 3 units to the right and 1 unit up**

Domain of $g(x)$:

Inequality: $x < 3$ **or** $x > 3$

Set notation: $\{x \mid x \neq 3\}$

Interval notation: $(-\infty, 3) \cup (3, +\infty)$

Range of $g(x)$:

Inequality: $y < 1$ **or** $y > 1$

Set notation: $\{y \mid y \neq 1\}$

Interval notation: $(-\infty, 1) \cup (1, +\infty)$

11. $g(x) = -0.5\left(\dfrac{1}{x-1}\right) - 2$

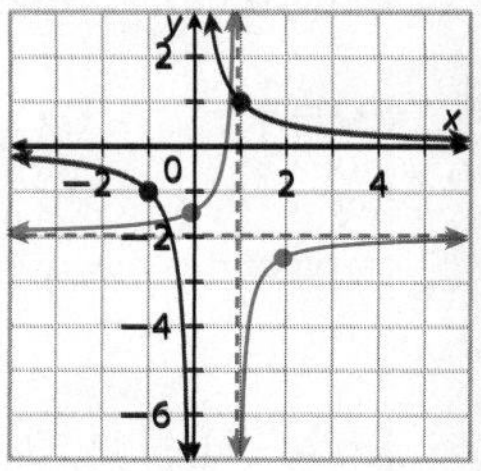

The transformations are:

- **a vertical compression by a factor of $\frac{1}{2}$**
- **a reflection across the x-axis**
- **a translation of 1 unit to the right and 2 units down**

Domain of $g(x)$:

Inequality: $x < 1$ **or** $x > 1$

Set notation: $\{x \mid x \neq 1\}$

Interval notation: $(-\infty, 1) \cup (1, +\infty)$

Range of $g(x)$:

Inequality: $y < -2$ **or** $y > -2$

Set notation: $\{y \mid y \neq -2\}$

Interval notation: $(-\infty, -2) \cup (-2, +\infty)$

12. $g(x) = \dfrac{1}{2(x+2)} + 3$

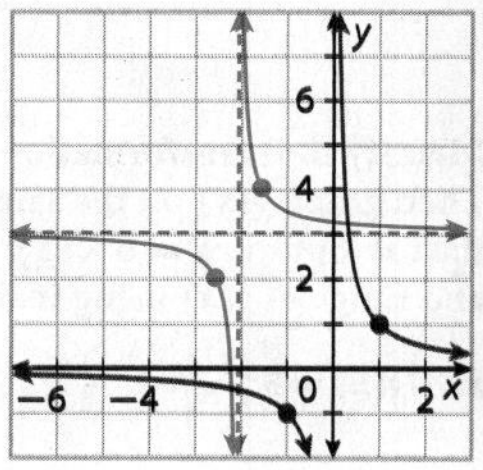

The transformations are:

- **a horizontal compression by a factor of $\frac{1}{2}$**
- **a translation of 2 units to the left and 3 units up**

Domain of $g(x)$:

Inequality: $x < -2$ **or** $x > -2$

Set notation: $\{x \mid x \neq -2\}$

Interval notation: $(-\infty, -2) \cup (-2, +\infty)$

Range of $g(x)$:

Inequality: $y < 3$ **or** $y > 3$

Set notation: $\{y \mid y \neq 3\}$

Interval notation: $(-\infty, 3) \cup (3, +\infty)$

Exercise	Depth of Knowledge (D.O.K.)	COMMON CORE Mathematical Practices
24–25	3 Strategic Thinking H.O.T.	MP.3 Logic

Rewrite the function in the form $g(x) = a\frac{1}{(x-h)} + k$ or $g(x) = \frac{1}{\frac{1}{b}(x-h)} + k$ and graph it. Also state the domain and range using inequalities, set notation, and interval notation.

13. $g(x) = \frac{3x-5}{x-1}$

$$\begin{array}{r} 3 \\ x-1\,\overline{)\,3x-5} \\ \underline{3x-3} \\ -2 \end{array}$$

$g(x) = -2\left(\frac{1}{x-1}\right) + 3$

Vert. Asymp: $x = 1$

Horiz. Asymp: $y = 3$

$(-1, -1)$ becomes $(0, 5)$

$(1, 1)$ becomes $(2, 1)$

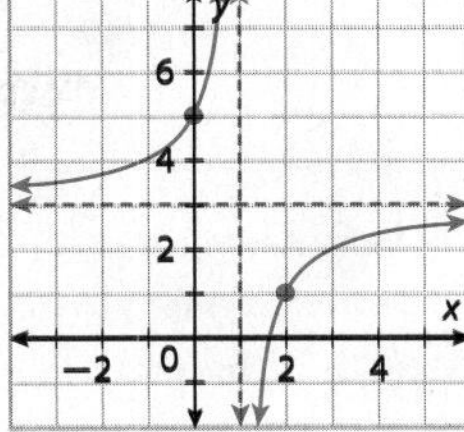

Domain of $g(x)$:

Inequality: $x < 1$ or $x > 1$

Set notation: $\{x \mid x \neq 1\}$

Interval notation: $(-\infty, 1) \cup (1, +\infty)$

Range of $g(x)$:

Inequality: $y < 3$ or $y > 3$

Set notation: $\{y \mid y \neq 3\}$

Interval notation: $(-\infty, 3) \cup (3, +\infty)$

14. $g(x) = \frac{x+5}{0.5x+2}$

$$\begin{array}{r} 2 \\ 0.5x+2\,\overline{)\,x+5} \\ \underline{x+4} \\ 1 \end{array}$$

$g(x) = \frac{1}{0.5(x+4)} + 2.$

Vert. Asymp: $x = -4$

Horiz. Asymp: $y = 2$

$(-1, -1)$ becomes $(-6, 1)$

$(1, 1)$ becomes $(-2, 3)$

Domain of $g(x)$:

Inequality: $x < -4$ or $x > -4$

Set notation: $\{x \mid x \neq -4\}$

Interval notation: $(-\infty, -4) \cup (-4, +\infty)$

Range of $g(x)$:

Inequality: $y < 2$ or $y > 2$

Set notation: $\{y \mid y \neq 2\}$

Interval notation: $(-\infty, 2) \cup (2, +\infty)$

15. $g(x) = \frac{-4x+11}{x-2}$

$$\begin{array}{r} -4 \\ x-2\,\overline{)\,-4x+11} \\ \underline{-4x+8} \\ 3 \end{array}$$

$g(x) = 3\left(\frac{1}{x-2}\right) - 4$

Vert. Asymp: $x = 2$

Horiz. Asymp: $y = -4$

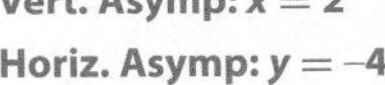

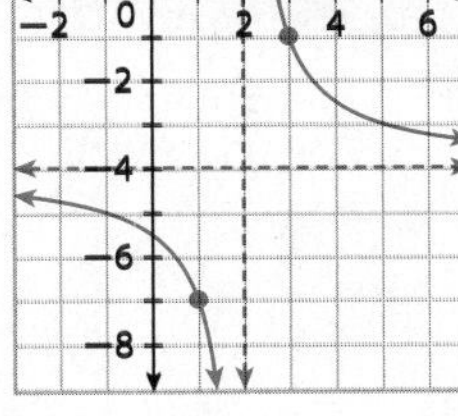

$(-1, -1)$ becomes $(1, -7)$

$(1, 1)$ becomes $(3, -1)$

Domain of $g(x)$:

Inequality: $x < 2$ or $x > 2$

Set notation: $\{x \mid x \neq 2\}$

Interval notation: $(-\infty, 2) \cup (2, +\infty)$

Range of $g(x)$:

Inequality: $y < -4$ or $y > -4$

Set notation: $\{y \mid y \neq -4\}$

Interval notation: $(-\infty, -4) \cup (-4, +\infty)$

CONNECT VOCABULARY EL

Relate the term *reference point* to the noun *reference,* meaning *a source of information.* A *reference* on a job application is person who serves as a source for information about the applicant.

AVOID COMMON ERRORS

For real-world problems, students may not check to see whether the domain is continuous or discrete, and if it is discrete, how a solution should be rounded. Stress the importance of checking whether solutions are defined or whether it is appropriate to round up or down.

16. $g(x) = \dfrac{4x + 13}{-2x - 6}$

$$\begin{array}{r} -2 \\ -2x - 6\,\overline{)\,4x + 13} \\ \underline{4x + 12} \\ 1 \end{array}$$

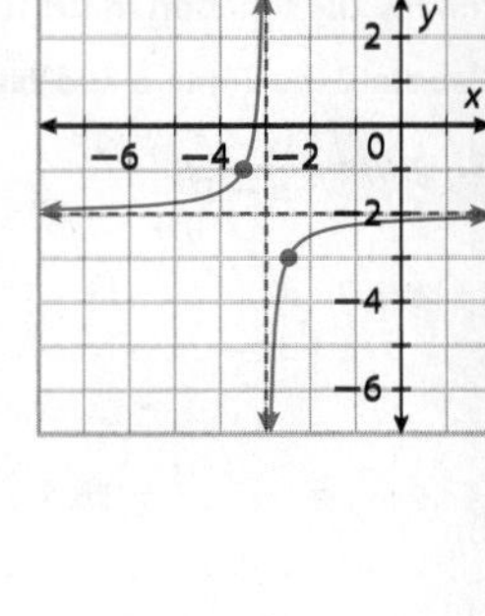

$g(x) = \dfrac{1}{-2(x+3)} - 2$

Vert. Asymp: $x = -3$

Horiz. Asymp: $y = -2$

$(-1, -1)$ becomes $\left(\frac{-5}{2}, -3\right)$

$(1, 1)$ becomes $\left(\frac{-7}{2}, -1\right)$

Domain of $g(x)$:

Inequality: $x < -3$ or $x > -3$

Set notation: $\{x | x \neq -3\}$

Interval notation: $(-\infty, -3) \cup (-3, +\infty)$

Range of $g(x)$:

Inequality: $y < -2$ or $y > -2$

Set notation: $\{y | y \neq -2\}$

Interval notation: $(-\infty, -2) \cup (-2, +w\infty)$

17. Write the function whose graph is shown. Use the form $g(x) = a\left(\frac{1}{x-h}\right) + k$.

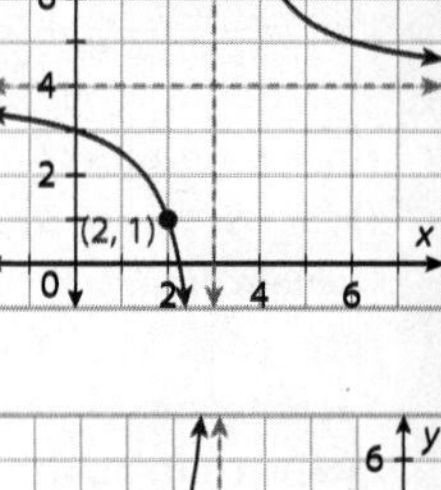

$h = 3$

$k = 4$

Use the point $(4, 7)$:

$7 = a\left(\dfrac{1}{4-3}\right) + 4$

$3 = a$

$g(x) = 3\left(\dfrac{1}{x-3}\right) + 4$

18. Write the function whose graph is shown. Use the form $g(x) = \dfrac{1}{\frac{1}{b}(x-h)} + k$

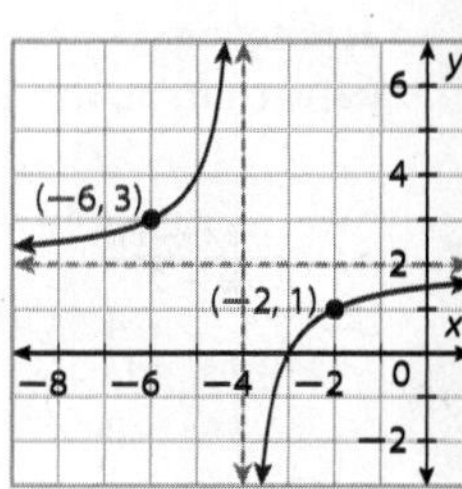

$h = -4$

$k = 2$

Use the point $(-2, 1)$:

$1 = \dfrac{1}{\frac{1}{b}(-2+4)} + 2$

$b = -2$

$g(x) = \dfrac{1}{-\frac{1}{2}(x+4)} + 2$

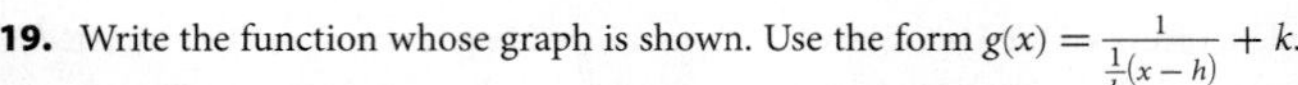

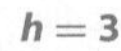

19. Write the function whose graph is shown. Use the form $g(x) = \frac{1}{\frac{1}{b}(x-h)} + k$.

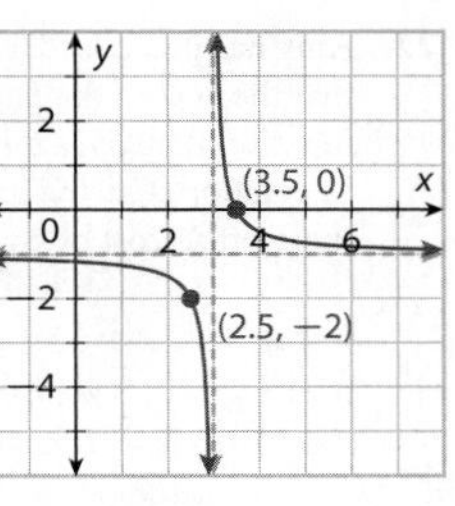

$h = 3$

$k = -1$

Use the point (3.5, 0):

$$0 = \frac{1}{\frac{1}{b}(3.5 - 3)} - 1$$

$$b = \frac{1}{2}$$

$$g(x) = \frac{1}{2(x-3)} - 1$$

20. Write the function whose graph is shown. Use the form $g(x) = a\left(\frac{1}{x-h}\right) + k$

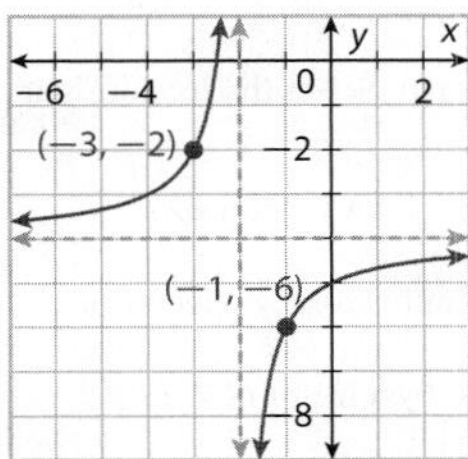

$h = -2$

$k = -4$

Use the point (−1, −6):

$$-6 = a\left(\frac{1}{-1+2}\right) - 4$$

$$-2 = a$$

$$g(x) = -2\left(\frac{1}{x+2}\right) - 4$$

21. Maria has purchased a basic stained glass kit for $100. She plans to make stained glass suncatchers and sell them. She estimates that the materials for making each suncatcher will cost $15. Model this situation with a rational function that gives the average cost of a stained glass suncatcher when the cost of the kit is included in the calculation. Use the graph of the function to determine the minimum number of suncatchers that brings the average cost below $22.50.

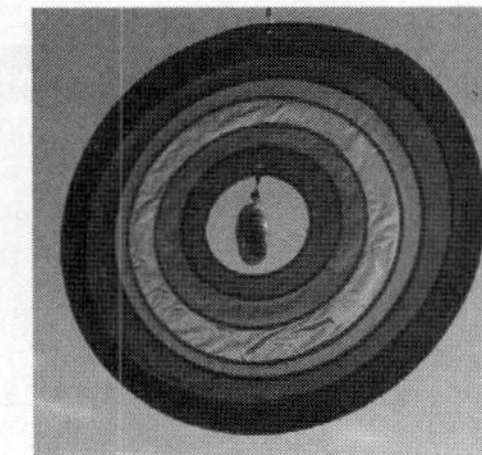

Let s be the number of suncatchers that Maria makes. Let $C(s)$ be the average cost (in dollars) of a suncatcher when the cost of the kit is included.

$$C(s) = \frac{100}{s} + 15$$

The graphs appear to intersect between $s = 13$ and $s = 14$. Since $C(13) = \frac{100}{13} + 15 \approx 22.69$ and $C(14) = \frac{100}{14} + 15 \approx 22.14$, the minimum number of suncatchers that brings the average cost below $22.50 is 14.

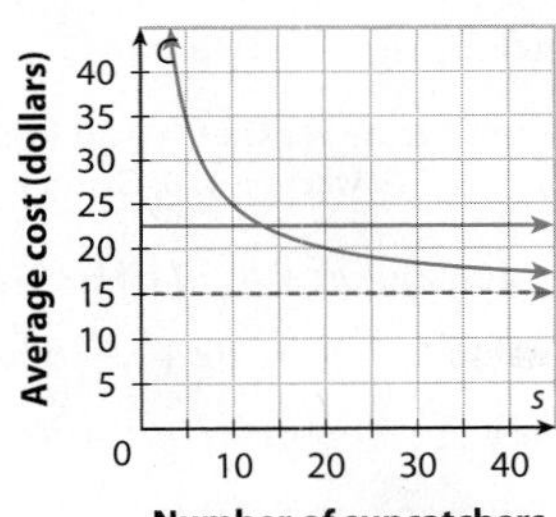

INTEGRATE MATHEMATICAL PRACTICES

Focus on Math Connections

MP.1 Students may lightly connect the reference points to see that they are symmetric about (h, k).

JOURNAL

Have students make a table that shows the steps for graphing a function of the form $\frac{bx+c}{dx+e}$ by two methods: (1) writing the function in graphing form before graphing and (2) graphing the function without writing the function in graphing form first.

22. Amy has purchased a basic letterpress kit for \$140. She plans to make wedding invitations. She estimates that the cost of the paper and envelope for each invitation is \$2. Model this situation with a rational function that gives the average cost of a wedding invitation when the cost of the kit is included in the calculation. Use the graph of the function to determine the minimum number of invitations that brings the average cost below \$5.

Let w be the number of wedding invitations that Maria makes. Let $C(w)$ be the average cost (in dollars) of a wedding invitation when the cost of the kit is included.

$C(w) = \frac{140}{w} + 2$

The graphs appear to intersect between $w = 46$ and $w = 47$. Since $C(46) = \frac{140}{46} + 2 \approx 5.04$ and $C(47) = \frac{140}{47} + 2 \approx 4.98$, the minimum number of invitations that brings the average below \$5 is 47.

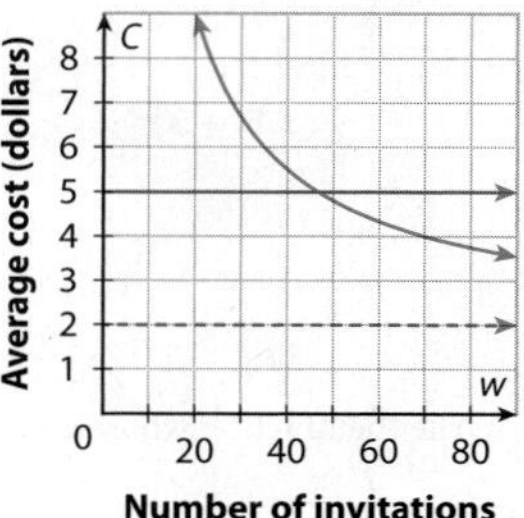

23. Multiple Response Select the transformations of the graph of the parent rational function that result in the graph of $g(x) = \frac{1}{2(x-3)} + 1$

A. Horizontal stretch by a factor of 2

(B.) Horizontal compression by a factor of $\frac{1}{2}$

C. Vertical stretch by a factor of 2

D. Vertical compression by a factor of $\frac{1}{2}$

(E.) Translation 1 unit up

F. Translation 1 unit down

(G.) Translation 3 units right

H. Translation 3 units left

H.O.T. Focus on Higher Order Thinking

24. Justify Reasoning Explain why, for positive numbers a and b, a vertical stretch or compression of the graph of $f(x) = \frac{1}{x}$ by a factor of a and, separately, a horizontal stretch or compression of the graph of $f(x)$ by a factor of b result in the same graph when a and b are equal.

A horizontal stretch or compression of the graph of $f(x)$ by a factor of b is given by $f\left(\frac{1}{b}x\right)$, which you can rewrite as follows: $f\left(\frac{1}{b}x\right) = \frac{1}{\frac{1}{b}x} = \frac{1}{\frac{1}{b}} \cdot \frac{1}{x} = b \cdot \frac{1}{x} = b \cdot f(x)$. Since a vertical stretch or compression of the graph of $f(x)$ by a factor of a is given by $a \cdot f(x)$, you can conclude that the two transformations are identical provided $a = b$.

25. Communicate Mathematical Ideas Determine the domain and range of the rational function $g(x) = \frac{mx+n}{px+q}$ where $p \neq 0$. Give your answer in set notation, and explain your reasoning.

The domain consists of all real numbers except for the value of x that makes the denominator equal to 0. Solving $px + q = 0$ for x gives $x = -\frac{q}{p}$. So, the domain is $\left\{x \middle| x \neq -\frac{p}{q}\right\}$. When you divide the numerator by the denominator, the quotient determines the horizontal asymptote of the graph, and this y-value is the only real number that isn't in the range of the function. Dividing $mx + n$ by $px + q$ gives a quotient of $\frac{m}{p}$, so the range is $\left\{y \middle| y \neq \frac{m}{p}\right\}$.

Lesson Performance Task

Graham wants to take snowboarding lessons at a nearby ski resort that charges $40 per week for a class that meets once during the week for 1 hour and gives him a lift ticket valid for 4 hours. The resort also charges a one-time equipment-rental fee of $99 for uninterrupted enrollment in classes. The resort requires that learners pay for three weeks of classes at a time.

a. Write a model that gives Graham's average weekly enrollment cost (in dollars) as a function of the time (in weeks) that Graham takes classes.

b. How much would Graham's average weekly enrollment cost be if he took classes only for the minimum of three weeks?

c. For how many weeks would Graham need to take classes for his average weekly enrollment cost to be at most $60? Describe how you can use a graphing calculator to graph the function from part a in order to answer this question, and then state the answer.

a. Let t be the time (in weeks) that Graham takes classes. Let $C(t)$ be Graham's average weekly enrollment cost (in dollars) when the rental fee is included. The model is $C(t) = \frac{99}{t} + 40$.

b. If Graham takes classes for 3 weeks, his average weekly enrollment cost is $C(3) = \frac{99}{3} + 40 = \$73$.

c. To find when Graham's average weekly enrollment cost will be at most $60, graph $y = \frac{99}{x} + 40$ and $y = 60$ on a graphing calculator and find the x-coordinate of the point where the graphs intersect. The graphing calculator gives 4.95 as that x-coordinate. So, since Graham must pay for three weeks of classes at a time, he will need to take classes for 6 weeks in order to have an average weekly enrollment cost of at most $60.

EXTENSION ACTIVITY

Ask students to graph the cumulative amount Graham has spent on his membership at the ski resort after x months. Ask them to describe the parent function and tell what translation they need to make. Then have them discuss when Graham might want to use this function and when he would want to use the function in the Performance Task.

INTEGRATE MATHEMATICAL PRACTICES

Focus on Communication

MP.3 Ask students to describe the domain and range of the continuous function $f(x)$ in the Performance Task. Then ask them how the domain and range are different for the real-world situation. Have them discuss how the constraints in the real-world situation affect the domain and range.

QUESTIONING STRATEGIES

? What effect does the monthly fee have on $f(x)$? **It translates $f(x)$ up or down the y-axis.**

? As x increases, why does $f(x)$ approach the monthly fee? **The initial fee of $240 is spread out over more months, so its monthly contribution becomes smaller and smaller.**

Scoring Rubric

2 points: Student correctly solves the problem and explains his/her reasoning.

1 point: Student shows good understanding of the problem but does not fully solve or explain his/her reasoning.

0 points: Student does not demonstrate understanding of the problem.

LESSON 8.2

Graphing More Complicated Rational Functions

Common Core Math Standards

The student is expected to:

 **F-IF.C.7d(+)**

Graph rational functions, identifying zeros and asymptotes when suitable factorizations are available, and showing end behavior. Also A-SSE.A.1b, A-APR.D.6

Mathematical Practices

COMMON CORE **MP.8 Patterns**

Language Objective

Students describe and explain the key features of the graph of a complicated rational function.

ENGAGE

Essential Question: What features of the graph of a rational function should you identify in order to sketch the graph? How do you identify those features?

Possible answer: Identify vertical asymptotes and "holes," based on the factors of the function's denominator, horizontal asymptotes, and slant asymptotes, based on an analysis of the function's end behavior; x-intercepts based on the factors of the function's numerator, where the graph lies above or below the x-axis, based on an analysis of the signs of the factors in both the numerator and denominator.

PREVIEW: LESSON PERFORMANCE TASK

View the Engage section online. Discuss the photo and how the radius of a baseball is a function of its volume. Then preview the Lesson Performance Task.

Name ________________ Class ________ Date ________

8.2 Graphing More Complicated Rational Functions

Resource Locker

Essential Question: What features of the graph of a rational function should you identify in order to sketch the graph? How do you identify those features?

Explore 1 Investigating Domains and Vertical Asymptotes of More Complicated Rational Functions

You know that the rational function $f(x) = \frac{1}{x-2} + 3$ has the domain $\{x | x \neq 2\}$ because the function is undefined at $x = 2$. Its graph has the vertical asymptote $x = 2$ because as $x \to 2^+$ (x approaches 2 from the right), $f(x) \to +\infty$, and as $x \to 2^-$ (x approaches 2 from the left), $f(x) \to -\infty$. In this Explore, you will investigate the domains and vertical asymptotes of other rational functions.

(A) Complete the table by identifying each function's domain based on the x-values for which the function is undefined. Write the domain using an inequality, set notation, and interval notation. Then state the equations of what you think the vertical asymptotes of the function's graph are.

Function	Domain	Possible Vertical Asymptotes
$f(x) = \frac{x+3}{x-1}$	Inequality: $x < 1$ or $x > 1$ Set notation: $\{x \mid x \neq 1\}$ Interval notation: $(-\infty, 1) \cup (1, +\infty)$	$x = 1$
$f(x) = \frac{(x+5)(x-1)}{x+1}$	Inequality: $x < 1$ or $x > -1$ Set notation: $\{x \mid x \neq -1\}$ Interval notation: $(-\infty, -1) \cup (-1, +\infty)$	$x = -1$
$f(x) = \frac{x-4}{(x+1)(x-1)}$	Inequality: $x < -1$ or $-1 < x < 1$ or $x > 1$ Set notation: $\{x \mid x \neq -1 \text{ and } x \neq 1\}$ Interval notation: $(-\infty, -1) \cup (-1, 1) \cup (1, +\infty)$	$x = -1, x = 1$
$f(x) = \frac{2x^2 - 3x + 9}{x^2 - x - 6}$	Inequality: $x < -2$ or $-2 < x < 3$ or $x > 3$ Set notation: $\{x \mid x \neq -2 \text{ and } x \neq 3\}$ Interval notation: $(-\infty, -2) \cup (-2, 3) \cup (3, +\infty)$	$x = -2, x = 3$

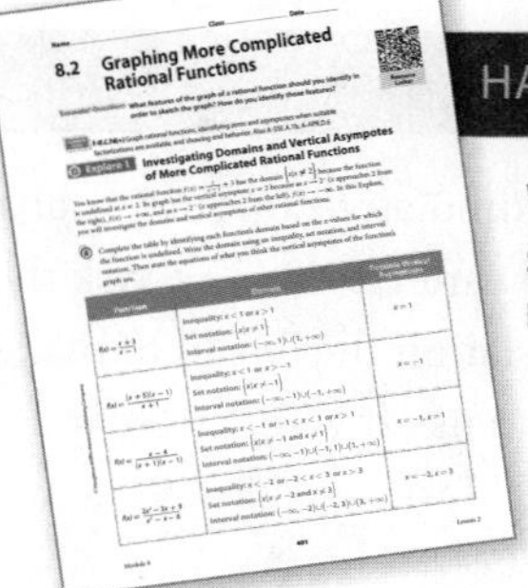

HARDCOVER PAGES 401–418

Watch for the hardcover student edition page numbers for this lesson.

Ⓑ Using a graphing calculator, graph each of the functions from Step A, and check to see if vertical asymptotes occur where you expect. Are there any unexpected results?

The graphs of the first three functions have the expected vertical asymptotes. The graph of the fourth function, however, has a vertical asymptote at $x = -2$ but not at $x = 3$.

Ⓒ Examine the behavior of $f(x) = \frac{x+3}{x-1}$ near $x = 1$.

First, complete the tables.

x approaches 1 from the right	
x	$f(x) = \frac{x+3}{x-1}$
1.1	41
1.01	401
1.001	4001

x approaches 1 from the left	
x	$f(x) = \frac{x+3}{x-1}$
0.9	−39
0.99	−399
0.999	−3999

Next, summarize the results.

- As $x \to 1^+$, $f(x) \to$ $+\infty$.
- As $x \to 1^-$, $f(x) \to$ $-\infty$.

The behaviour of $f(x) = \frac{x+3}{x-1}$ near $x = 1$ shows that the graph of $f(x)$ (has)/does not have a vertical asymptote at $x = 1$.

Ⓓ Examine the behavior of $f(x) = \frac{(x+5)(x-1)}{(x+1)}$ near $x = -1$.

First, complete the tables.

x approaches −1 from the right	
x	$f(x) = \frac{(x+5)(x-1)}{x+1}$
−0.9	−77.9
−0.99	−797.99
−0.999	−7997.999

x approaches −1 from the left	
x	$f(x) = \frac{(x+5)(x-1)}{x+1}$
−1.1	81.9
−1.01	801.99
−1.001	8001.999

Next, summarize the results.

- As $x \to -1^+$, $f(x) \to$ $-\infty$.
- As $x \to -1^-$, $f(x) \to$ $+\infty$.

The behavior of $f(x) = \frac{(x+5)(x-1)}{(x+1)}$ near $x = -1$ shows that the graph of $f(x)$ (has)/does not have a vertical asymptote at $x = -1$.

PROFESSIONAL DEVELOPMENT

Learning Progressions

Previously, students learned to graph, find asymptotes, and describe domain, range, and end behavior of rational functions of the form $f(x) = \frac{ax+b}{cx+d}$. They used long division to write linear divided by linear functions as a quotient plus a remainder, learned the basics about domain, range, and end behavior, and transformed the parent function $f(x) = \frac{1}{x}$ to graph rational functions. Students apply these skills to more complex rational functions such a quadratic divided by linear functions.

EXPLORE

Investigating Domains and Vertical Asymptotes of More Complicated Rational Functions

AVOID COMMON ERRORS

Remind students if the numerator and denominator have the same zero, the result is a point discontinuity, which will not be visible on a graphing calculator. The x-value at which the point discontinuity exists must be excluded from the domain, and the corresponding y-value must be excluded from the range.

(E) Examine the behavior of $f(x) = \dfrac{x - 4}{(x + 1)(x - 1)}$ near $x = -1$ and $x = 1$.

First, complete the tables. Round results to the nearest tenth.

x approaches −1 from the right	
x	$f(x) = \dfrac{x-4}{(x+1)(x-1)}$
−0.9	25.8
−0.99	250.8
−0.999	2500.8

x approaches −1 from the left	
x	$f(x) = \dfrac{x-4}{(x+1)(x-1)}$
−1.1	−24.3
−1.01	−249.3
−1.001	−2499.3

x approaches 1 from the right	
x	$f(x) = \dfrac{x-4}{(x+1)(x-1)}$
1.1	−13.8
1.01	−148.8
1.001	−1498.8

x approaches 1 from the left	
x	$f(x) = \dfrac{x-4}{(x+1)(x-1)}$
0.9	16.3
0.99	151.3
0.999	1501.3

Next, summarize the results.

- As $x \to -1^+$, $f(x) \to$ $+\infty$.
- As $x \to -1^-$, $f(x) \to$ $-\infty$.
- As $x \to 1^+$, $f(x) \to$ $-\infty$.
- As $x \to 1^-$, $f(x) \to$ $+\infty$.

The behavior of $f(x) = \frac{x-4}{(x+1)(x-1)}$ near $x = -1$ shows that the graph of $f(x)$ has/does not have a vertical asymptote at $x = -1$. The behavior of $f(x) = \frac{x-4}{(x+1)(x-1)}$ near $x = 1$ shows that the graph of $f(x)$ has/does not have a vertical asymptote at $x = 1$.

(F) Examine the behavior of $f(x) = \dfrac{2x^2 - 3x - 9}{x^2 - x - 6}$ near $x = -2$ and $x = 3$.

First, complete the tables. Round results to the nearest ten thousandth if necessary.

x approaches −2 from the right	
x	$f(x) = \dfrac{2x^2-3x-9}{x^2-x-6}$
−1.9	−8
−1.99	−98
−1.999	−998

x approaches −2 from the left	
x	$f(x) = \dfrac{2x^2-3x-9}{x^2-x-6}$
−2.1	12
−2.01	102
−2.001	1002

COLLABORATIVE LEARNING

Peer-to-Peer Activity

Have students work in pairs. Give one student in each pair a rational function of the form $f(x) = \dfrac{(x+a)(x+b)}{(x+c)(x+d)}$, where a, b, c, and d are integers. Have that student describe the function solely in terms of its zeros, asymptotes, and holes, if any. The partner should attempt to write a rational function that fits this description. Pairs can then discuss their results. Point out that more than one rational function can have the same zeros, asymptotes, and holes.

x approaches 3 from the right	
x	$f(x) = \frac{2x^2 - 3x - 9}{x^2 - x - 6}$
3.1	1.803922
3.01	1.800399
3.001	1.800040

x approaches 3 from the left	
x	$f(x) = \frac{2x^2 - 3x - 9}{x^2 - x - 6}$
2.9	1.795918
2.99	1.799599
2.999	1.799960

Next, summarize the results.

- As $x \to -2^+$, $f(x) \to$ $-\infty$.
- As $x \to -2^-$, $f(x) \to$ $+\infty$.
- As $x \to 3^+$, $f(x) \to$ 1.8.
- As $x \to 3^-$, $f(x) \to$ 1.8.

The behavior of $f(x) = \frac{2x^2 - 3x - 9}{x^2 - x - 6}$ near $x = -2$ shows that the graph of $f(x)$ (has)/does not have a vertical asymptote at $x = -2$. The behavior of $f(x) = \frac{2x^2 - 3x - 9}{x^2 - x - 6}$ near $x = 3$ shows that the graph of $f(x)$ has/(does not have) a vertical asymptote at $x = 3$.

Reflect

1. Rewrite $f(x) = \frac{2x^2 - 3x - 9}{x^2 - x - 6}$ so that its numerator and denominator are factored. How does this form of the function explain the behavior of the function near $x = 3$?

With the function written in the form $f(x) = \frac{(2x+3)(x-3)}{(x+2)(x-3)}$, you can see that the numerator and denominator have a common factor of $x - 3$. In effect, the function behaves just like the function $g(x) = \frac{2x+3}{x+2}$ except that $f(x)$ is not defined at $x = 3$. However, $f(x)$ approaches $g(3) = 1.8$ as x approaches 3.

2. **Discussion** When you graph $f(x) = \frac{2x^2 - 3x - 9}{x^2 - x - 6}$ on a graphing calculator, you can't tell that the function is undefined for $x = 3$. How does using the calculator's table feature help? What do you think the graph should look like to make it clear that the function is undefined at $x = 3$?

The table feature will display an error message for the function's value at $x = 3$. Because the graph has a "hole" at $x = 3$, there should be an open circle at the point $(3, 1.8)$.

DIFFERENTIATE INSTRUCTION

Critical Thinking

Show how to find the oblique asymptote for a quadratic/linear function by synthetic division rather than long division.

EXPLAIN 1

Sketching the Graphs of More Complicated Rational Functions

AVOID COMMON ERRORS

Students may try to graph without factoring and will miss holes and discontinuities. Remind students to factor quadratic expressions when possible. If they determine that the numerator and denominator share a common linear factor, it should be crossed out and the function simplified. There is a hole in the graph at the x-value where the shared linear factor equals zero.

Explain 1 Sketching the Graphs of More Complicated Rational Functions

As you have seen, there can be breaks in the graph of a rational function. These breaks are called *discontinuities*, and there are two kinds:

1. When a rational function has a factor in the denominator that is not also in the numerator, an *infinite discontinuity* occurs at the value of x for which the factor equals 0. On the graph of the function, an infinite discontinuity appears as a vertical asymptote.

2. When a rational function has a factor in the denominator that is also in the numerator, a *point discontinuity* occurs at the value of x for which the factor equals 0. On the graph of the function, a point discontinuity appears as a "hole."

The graph of a rational function can also have a horizontal asymptote. It is determined by the degrees and leading coefficients of the function's numerator and denominator. If the numerator is a polynomial $p(x)$ in standard form with leading coefficient a and the denominator is a polynomial $q(x)$ in standard form with leading coefficient b, then an examination of the function's end behavior gives the following results.

Relationship between Degree of $p(x)$ and Degree of $q(x)$	Equation of Horizontal Asymptote (if one exists)
Degree of $p(x) < $ degree of $q(x)$	$y = 0$
Degree of $p(x) = $ degree of $q(x)$	$y = \frac{a}{b}$
Degree of $p(x) > $ degree of $q(x)$	There is no horizontal asymptote. The function instead increases or decreases without bound as x increases or decreases without bound. In particular, when the degree of the numerator is 1 more than the degree of the denominator, the function's graph approaches a slanted line, called a *slant asymptote*, as x increases or decreases without bound.

You can sketch the graph of a rational function by identifying where vertical asymptotes, "holes," and horizontal asymptotes occur. Using the factors of the numerator and denominator, you can also establish intervals on the x-axis where either an x-intercept or a discontinuity occurs and then check the signs of the factors on those intervals to determine whether the graph lies above or below the x-axis.

LANGUAGE SUPPORT EL

Vocabulary Development

Have students work in pairs. They should complete a chart like the following, using the different types of rational functions identified in this lesson and the previous lesson.

Rational Function	Example	Vertical Asymptotes	Graph
f(*x*) = *constant/linear*			
f(*x*) = *linear/linear*			
f(*x*) =*quadratic/linear*			
f(*x*) = *quadratic/quadratic*			

Example 1 **Sketch the graph of the given rational function. (If the degree of the numerator is 1 more than the degree of the denominator, find the graph's slant asymptote by dividing the numerator by the denominator.) Also state the function's domain and range using inequalities, set notation, and interval notation. (If your sketch indicates that the function has maximum or minimum values, use a graphing calculator to find those values to the nearest hundredth when determining the range.)**

Ⓐ $f(x) = \frac{x+1}{x-2}$

Identify vertical asymptotes and "holes."

The function is undefined when $x - 2 = 0$, or $x = 2$. Since $x - 2$ does not appear in the numerator, there is a vertical asymptote rather than a "hole" at $x = 2$.

Identify horizontal asymptotes and slant asymptotes.

The numerator and denominator have the same degree and the leading coefficient of each is 1, so there is a horizontal asymptote at $y = \frac{1}{1} = 1$.

Identify x-intercepts.

An x-intercept occurs when $x + 1 = 0$, or $x = -1$.

Check the sign of the function on the intervals $x < -1$, $-1 < x < 2$, and $x > 2$.

Interval	Sign of $x+1$	Sign of $x-2$	Sign of $f(x) = \frac{x+1}{x-2}$
$x < -1$	−	−	+
$-1 < x < 2$	+	−	−
$x > 2$	+	+	+

Sketch the graph using all this information. Then state the domain and range.

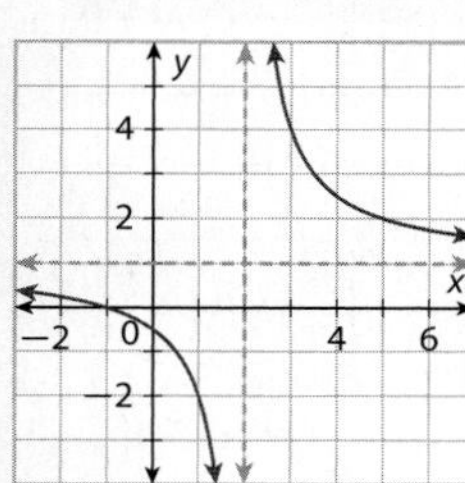

Domain:

Inequality: $x < 2$ or $x > 2$

Set notation: $\{x \mid x \neq 2\}$

Interval notation: $(-\infty, 2) \cup (2, +\infty)$

Range:

Inequality: $y < 1$ or $y > 1$

Set notation: $\{y \mid y \neq 1\}$

Interval notation: $(-\infty, 1) \cup (1, +\infty)$

QUESTIONING STRATEGIES

? How do you find the vertical asymptotes of a rational equation? **Simplify the equation by eliminating any factors that are in both the numerator and denominator. There is a linear asymptote at x-values for which the denominator equals zero in the simplified equation.**

(B) $f(x) = \dfrac{x^2 + x - 2}{x + 3}$

Factor the function's numerator.

$$f(x) = \frac{x^2 + x - 2}{x + 3} = \frac{(x - 1)(x + 2)}{x + 3}$$

Identify vertical asymptotes and "holes."

The function is undefined when $x + 3 = 0$, or $x = \boxed{-3}$. Since $x + 3$ does not appear in the numerator, there is a vertical asymptote rather than a "hole" at $x = \boxed{-3}$.

Identify horizontal asymptotes and slant asymptotes.

Because the degree of the numerator is 1 more than the degree of the denominator, there is no horizontal asymptote, but there is a slant asymptote. Divide the numerator by the denominator to identify the slant asymptote.

$$\begin{array}{r} x - \boxed{2} \\ x + 3 \overline{\smash{)}\, x^2 + x - 2} \\ \underline{x^2 + 3x} \\ -2x - 2 \\ \underline{-2x - 6} \\ 4 \end{array}$$

So, the line $y = x - \boxed{2}$ is the slant asymptote.

Identify x-intercepts.

There are two x-intercepts: when $x - 1 = 0$, or $x = \boxed{1}$, and when $x + 2 = 0$, or $x = \boxed{-2}$.

Check the sign of the function on the intervals $x < -3$, $-3 < x < -2$, $-2 < x < 1$, and $x > 1$.

Interval	Sign of $x + 3$	Sign of $x + 2$	Sign of $x - 1$	Sign of $f(x) = \frac{(x-1)(x+2)}{x+3}$
$x < -3$	−	−	−	−
$-3 < x < -2$	+	−	−	+
$-2 < x < 1$	+	+	−	−
$x > 1$	+	+	+	+

Sketch the graph using all this information. Then state the domain and range.

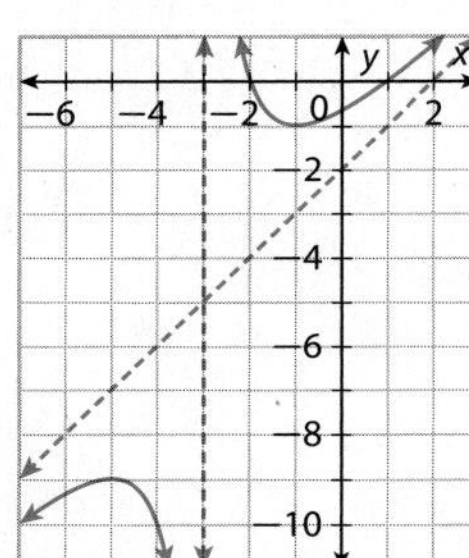

Domain:

Inequality: $x < \boxed{-3}$ or $x > \boxed{-3}$

Set notation: $\{x \mid x \neq \boxed{-3}\}$

Interval notation: $(-\infty, \boxed{-3}) \cup (\boxed{-3}, +\infty)$

The sketch indicates that the function has a maximum value and a minimum value. Using **3:minimum** from the **CALC** menu on a graphing calculator gives -1 as the minimum value. Using **4:maximum** from the **CALC** menu on a graphing calculator gives -5 as the maximum value.

Range: Inequality: $y < \boxed{-5}$ or $y > \boxed{-1}$

Set notation: $\left\{y \mid y < \boxed{-5} \text{ or } y > \boxed{-1}\right\}$ Interval notation: $\left(-\infty, \boxed{-5}\right) \cup \left(\boxed{-1}, +\infty\right)$

Your Turn

Sketch the graph of the given rational function. (If the degree of the numerator is 1 more than the degree of the denominator, find the graph's slant asymptote by dividing the numerator by the denominator.) Also state the function's domain and range using inequalities, set notation, and interval notation. (If your sketch indicates that the function has maximum or minimum values, use a graphing calculator to find those values to the nearest hundredth when determining the range.)

3. $f(x) = \dfrac{x+1}{x^2 + 3x - 4}$

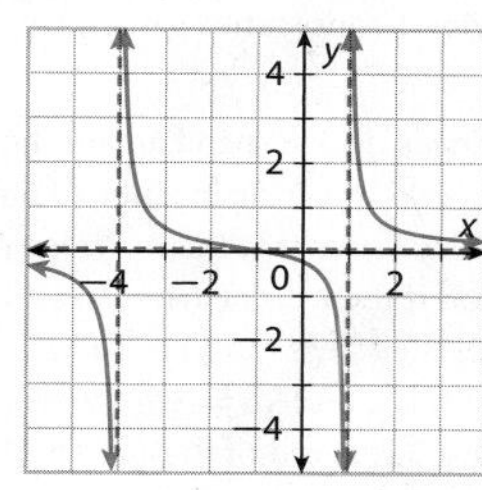

$f(x) = \dfrac{x+1}{x^2 + 3x - 4} = \dfrac{x+1}{(x-1)(x+4)}$

There are vertical asymptotes at $x = -4$ and $x = 1$.

There is a horizontal asymptote at $y = 0$.

There is an x-intercept at $x = -1$.

Check the sign of the function on the intervals $x < -4$, $-4 < x < -1$, $-1 < x < 1$, and $x > 1$.

Domain:

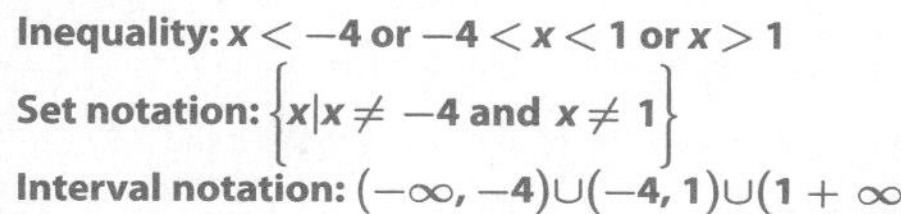

Inequality: $x < -4$ or $-4 < x < 1$ or $x > 1$

Set notation: $\left\{x \mid x \neq -4 \text{ and } x \neq 1\right\}$

Interval notation: $(-\infty, -4) \cup (-4, 1) \cup (1 + \infty)$

Range:

Inequality: $-\infty < y < +\infty$

Set notation: $\left\{y \mid -\infty < y < +\infty\right\}$

Interval notation: $(-\infty, +\infty)$

Explain 2 Modeling with More Complicated Rational Functions

When two real-world variable quantities are compared using a ratio or rate, the comparison is a rational function. You can solve problems about the ratio or rate by graphing the rational function.

Example 2 **Write a rational function to model the situation, or use the given rational function. State a reasonable domain and range for the function using set notation. Then use a graphing calculator to graph the function and answer the question.**

Ⓐ A baseball team has won 32 games out of 56 games played, for a winning percentage of $\frac{32}{56} \approx 0.571$. How many consecutive games must the team win to raise its winning percentage to 0.600?

Let w be the number of consecutive games to be won. Then the total number of games won is the function $T_{\text{won}}(W) = 32 + w$, and the total number of games played is the function $T_{\text{played}}(W) = 56 + w$.

EXPLAIN 2

Modeling with More Complicated Rational Functions

AVOID COMMON ERRORS

Students may not realize when to look for a slant asymptote. Remind students to find the slant asymptote of quadratic/linear rational functions.

QUESTIONING STRATEGIES

? What are three ways to write the domain and range of a function? set notation, with inequalities, interval notation

The rational function that gives the team's winning percentage p (as a decimal) is $p(w) = \frac{T_{won}(W)}{T_{played}(W)} = \frac{32 + w}{56 + w}$.

The domain of the rational function is $\{w \mid w \geq 0$ and w is a whole number$\}$. Note that you do not need to exclude -56 from the domain, because only nonnegative whole-number values of w make sense in this situation.

Since the function models what happens to the team's winning percentage from consecutive wins (no losses), the values of $p(w)$ start at 0.571 and approach 1 as w increases without bound. So, the range is $\{p \mid 0.571 \leq p < 1\}$.

Graph $y = \frac{32 + x}{56 + x}$ on a graphing calculator using a viewing window that shows 0 to 10 on the x-axis and 0.5 to 0.7 on the y-axis. Also graph the line $y = 0.6$. To find where the graphs intersect, select **5: intersect** from the **CALC** menu.

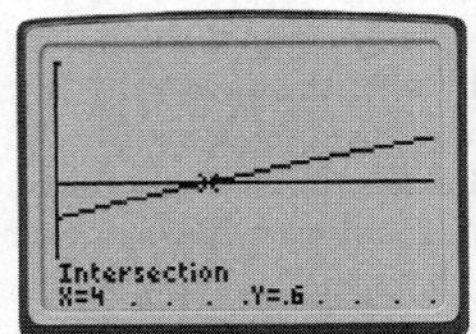

So, the team's winning percentage (as a decimal) will be 0.600 if the team wins 4 consecutive games.

(B) Two friends decide spend an afternoon canoeing on a river. They travel 4 miles upstream and 6 miles downstream. In still water, they know that their average paddling speed is 5 miles per hour. If their canoe trip takes 4 hours, what is the average speed of the river's current? To answer the question, use the rational function $t(c) = \frac{4}{5 - c} + \frac{6}{5 + c} = \frac{50 - 2c}{(5 - c)(5 + c)}$ where c is the average speed of the current (in miles per hour) and t is the time (in hours) spent canoeing 4 miles against the current at a rate of $5 - c$ miles per hour and 6 miles with the current at a rate of $5 + c$ miles per hour.

In order for the friends to travel upstream, the speed of the current must be less than their average paddling speed, so the domain of the function is $\{c \mid 0 \leq c <$ 5 $\}$. If the friends canoed in still water ($c = 0$), the trip would take a total of $\frac{4}{5} + \frac{6}{5} =$ 2 hours.

As c approaches 5 from the left, the value of $\frac{6}{5 + c}$ approaches $\frac{6}{10} = 0.6$ hour, but the value of $\frac{4}{5 - c}$ increases without bound. So, the range of the function is $\{t \mid t \geq$ 2 $\}$.

Graph $y = \frac{50 - 2x}{(5 - x)(5 + x)}$ on a graphing calculator using a viewing window that shows 0 to 5 on the x-axis and 2 to 5 on the y-axis. Also graph the line $y =$ 4. To find where the graphs intersect, select **5:intersect** from the **CALC** menu. The calculator shows that the average speed of the current is about 3.8 miles per hour.

Your Turn

Write a rational function to model the situation, or use the given rational function. State a reasonable domain and range for the function using set notation. Then use a graphing calculator to graph the function and answer the question.

4. A saline solution is a mixture of salt and water. A $p\%$ saline solution contains $p\%$ salt and $(100 - p)\%$ water by mass. A chemist has 300 grams of a 4% saline solution that needs to be strengthened to a 6% solution by adding salt. How much salt should the chemist add?

Let s be the amount (in grams) of salt added to the saline solution. The mass of the salt in the solution before any more salt is added is $0.04(300) = 12$ grams, so the mass m(in grams) of the salt in the solution after more salt is added is $m_{salt}(s) = 12 + s$. The mass m(in grams) of the solution after more salt is added is $m_{solution}(s) = 300 + s$. So, after more salt is added, the percent p (as a decimal) of the mass of solution that is salt is the rational function $p(s) = \frac{M_{salt}(s)}{M_{solution}(s)} = \frac{12+s}{300+s}$.

The domain of the rational function is $\{s \mid s \geq 0\}$. The percent of salt in the solution starts at 0.04 and approaches 1 as s increases without bound, so the range is $\{p \mid 0.04 \leq p < 1\}$.

Graphing $y = \frac{12+x}{300+x}$ and $y = 0.06$ on a graphing calculator with a window that shows 0.04 to 0.07 on the x-axis and 0 to 10 on the y-axis and then locating the point where the graphs intersect, you find that the amount of salt that the chemist should add is about 6.4 grams.

Elaborate

5. How can you show that the vertical line $x = c$, where c is a constant, is an asymptote for the graph of a rational function?

Examine the behavior of the function as x approaches c from both the left and the right. If the values of the function increase or decrease without bound, the line is an asymptote.

6. How can you determine the end behavior of a rational function?

Divide the function's numerator by the denominator. The quotient gives the function's end behavior. For instance, if the quotient is a constant c, then the values of the function approach c as x increases or decreases without bound (that is, the horizontal line $y = c$ is an asymptote for the graph).

7. Essential Question Check-In How do you identify any vertical asymptotes and "holes" that the graph of a rational function has?

Factor the function's numerator and denominator. If a factor of the denominator is not also a factor of the numerator, then a vertical asymptote occurs at the x-value for which the factor equals 0. If a factor of the denominator is also a factor of the numerator, then a "hole" occurs at the x-value for which the factor equals 0.

ELABORATE

INTEGRATE MATHEMATICAL PRACTICES

Focus on Patterns

MP.8 The rules for finding horizontal asymptotes covered in this lesson can be extended to rational functions other than linear/linear, linear/quadratic, quadratic/linear, and quadratic/quadratic functions. When the degree of the numerator is smaller than the degree of the denominator, the horizontal asymptote is $y = 0$. When the degree of the numerator is larger than the degree of the denominator, there is no horizontal asymptote. When the degrees of the numerator and denominator are equal, the horizontal asymptote is $y = \frac{a_1}{a_2}$.

SUMMARIZE THE LESSON

How do you graph rational functions? Factor if possible, cancel factors common to numerator and denominator, find horizontal, oblique, and vertical asymptotes, plug in x-values to find points, and remember to graph a hole (or point discontinuity) where a cancelled factor equals zero.

EVALUATE

ASSIGNMENT GUIDE

Concepts and Skills	Practice
Explore Investigating Domains and Vertical Asymptotes of More Complicated Rational Functions	Exercises 1–2
Explain 1 Sketching the Graphs of More Complicated Rational Functions	Exercises 7–12
Explain 2 Modeling With More Complicated Rational Functions	Exercises 13–16

INTEGRATE MATHEMATICAL PRACTICES

Focus on Math Connections

MP.1 A function in the form $f(x) = \frac{a}{x-h} + k$ can be graphed by transforming the parent function $f(x) = \frac{1}{x}$. It can also be rewritten as a linear/linear rational function by finding a common denominator and rewriting the function as a single fraction.

Evaluate: Homework and Practice

- Online Homework
- Hints and Help
- Extra Practice

State the domain using an inequality, set notation, and interval notation. For any x-value excluded from the domain, state whether the graph has a vertical asymptote or a "hole" at that x-value. Use a graphing calculator to check your answer.

1. $f(x) = \frac{x+5}{x+1}$

Domain:

Inequality: $x < -1$ or $x > -1$

Set notation: $\{x \mid x \neq -1\}$

Interval notation: $(-\infty, -1) \cup (-1, +\infty)$

vertical asymptote at $x = 3$

2. $f(x) = \frac{x^2 + 2x - 3}{x^2 - 4x + 3}$

Domain:

Inequality: $x < 1$ or $1 < x < 3$ or $x > 3$

Set notation: $\{x \mid x \neq 1 \text{ and } x \neq 3\}$

Interval notation: $(-\infty, 1) \cup (1, 3) \cup (3,$

a "hole" at $x = 1$; a vertical asymptote at x

Divide the numerator by the denominator to write the function in the form $f(x) = \text{quotient} + \frac{\text{remainder}}{\text{divisor}}$ and determine the function's end behavior. Then, using a graphing calculator to examine the function's graph, state the range using an inequality, set notation, and interval notation.

3. $f(x) = \frac{3x+1}{x-2}$

So, $f(x) = 3 + \frac{7}{x-2}$. As x increases or decreases without bound, $f(x)$ approaches 3.

Range:

Inequality: $y < 3$ or $y > 3$

Set notation: $\{y \mid y \neq 3\}$

Interval notation: $(-\infty, 3) \cup (3, +\infty)$

4. $f(x) = \frac{x}{(x-2)(x+3)}$

So, $f(x) = 0 + \frac{x}{(x-2)(x+3)}$. As x increases or decreases without bound, $f(x)$ approaches 0.

Range:

Inequality: $-\infty < y < -\infty$

Set notation: $\{y \mid -\infty < y < -\infty\}$

Interval notation: $(-\infty, +\infty)$

5. $f(x) = \frac{x^2 - 5x + 6}{x - 1}$

So, $f(x) = x - 4 + \frac{2}{x-1}$. As x increases without bound, $f(x)$ increases without bound, and as x decreases without bound, $f(x)$ decreases without bound.

Range (approximate):

Inequality: $y < -5.83$ or $y > -0.17$

Set notation: $\{y \mid y < -5.83 \text{ or } y > -0.17\}$

Interval notation: $(-\infty, -5.83) \cup (-0.17, +\infty)$

6. $f(x) = \frac{4x^2 - 1}{x^2 + x - 2}$

So, $f(x) = 4 + \frac{-4x+7}{x^2+x-2}$. As x increases or decreases without bound, $f(x)$ approaches 4.

Range (approximate):

Inequality: $y < 0.51$ or $y > 3.49$

Set notation: $\{y \mid y < 0.51 \text{ or } y > 3.49\}$

Interval notation: $(-\infty, 0.51) \cup (3.49,$

Exercise	Depth of Knowledge (D.O.K.)	COMMON CORE Mathematical Practices
1–6	2 Skills/Concepts	MP.4 Modeling
7–12	2 Skills/Concepts	MP.5 Using Tools
13–16	2 Skills/Concepts	MP.4 Modeling
17	2 Skills/Concepts	MP.2 Reasoning
18	3 Strategic Thinking H.O.T.	MP.6 Precision
19	3 Strategic Thinking H.O.T.	MP.3 Logic

Sketch the graph of the given rational function. (If the degree of the numerator is 1 more than the degree of the denominator, find the graph's slant asymptote by dividing the numerator by the denominator.) Also state the function's domain and range using inequalities, set notation, and interval notation. (If your sketch indicates that the function has maximum or minimum values, use a graphing calculator to find those values to the nearest hundredth when determining the range.)

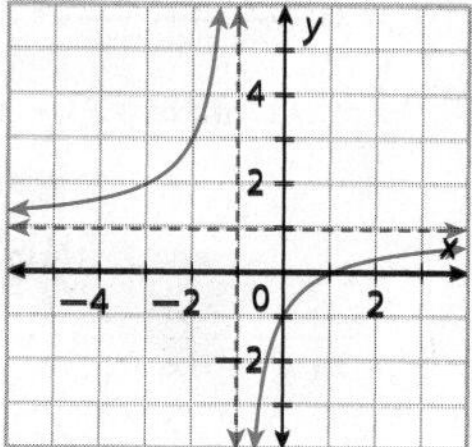

7. $f(x) = \frac{x-1}{x+1}$

There is a vertical asymptote at $x = -1$.

There is a horizontal asymptote at $y = 1$.

There is an x-intercept at $x = 1$.

Check the sign of the function on the intervals $x < -1$, $-1 < x < 1$, and $x > 1$.

Domain:

Inequality: $x < -1$ or $x > -1$

Set notation: $\{x \mid x \neq -1\}$

Interval notation: $(-\infty, -1) \cup (-1, +\infty)$

Range:

Inequality: $y < 1$ or $y > 1$

Set notation: $\{y \mid y \neq 1\}$

Interval notation: $(-\infty, 1) \cup (1, +\infty)$

8. $f(x) = \frac{x-1}{(x-2)(x+3)}$

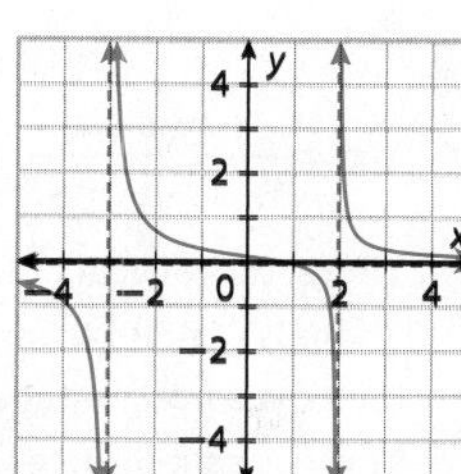

There is a vertical asymptote at $x = -3$ and $x = 2$.

There is a horizontal asymptote at $y = 0$.

There is an x-intercept at $x = 1$.

Check the sign of the function on the intervals $x < -3$, $-3 < x < 1$, $1 < x < 2$, and $x > 2$.

Domain:

Inequality: $x < -3$ or $-3 < x < 2$ or $x > 2$

Set notation: $\{x \mid x \neq -3 \text{ and } x \neq 2\}$

Interval notation: $(-\infty, -3) \cup (-3, 2) \cup (2, +\infty)$

Range:

Inequality: $-\infty < y < +\infty$

Set notation: $\{y \mid -\infty < y < +\infty\}$

Interval notation: $(-\infty, +\infty)$

AVOID COMMON ERRORS

Students may assume that when quadratic/linear functions cannot be simplified by cancelling a factor common to the numerator and denominator, that no asymptote exists. Remind students to find the oblique asymptote by dividing the numerator by the denominator. The quotient is the oblique asymptote.

9. $f(x) = \dfrac{(x+1)(x-1)}{x+2}$

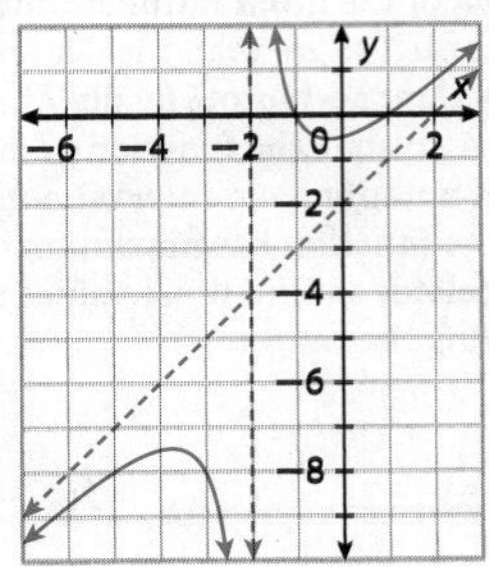

There is a vertical asymptote at $x = -2$.

$$f(x) = \frac{(x+1)(x-1)}{x+2} = \frac{x^2 - 1}{x+2}$$

$$\begin{array}{r}
x - 2 \\
x + 2\,\overline{)\,x^2 + 0x - 1} \\
\underline{x^2 + 2x} \\
-2x - 1 \\
\underline{-2x - 4} \\
3
\end{array}$$

The line $y = x - 2$ is a slant asymptote.

There are x-intercepts at $x = -1$ and $x = 1$.

Check the sign of the function on the intervals $x < -2$, $-2 < x < -1$, $-1 < x < 1$, and $x > 1$.

Domain:

Inequality: $x < -2$ or $x > -2$

Set notation: $\{x \mid x \neq -2\}$

Interval notation: $(-\infty, -2) \cup (-2, +\infty)$

Range (approximate):

Inequality: $y < -0.54$ or $y > -7.46$

Set notation: $\{y \mid y < -0.54 \text{ or } y > -7.46\}$

Interval notation: $(-\infty, -0.54) \cup (-7.46, +\infty$

10. $f(x) = \dfrac{-3x(x-2)}{(x-2)(x+2)}$

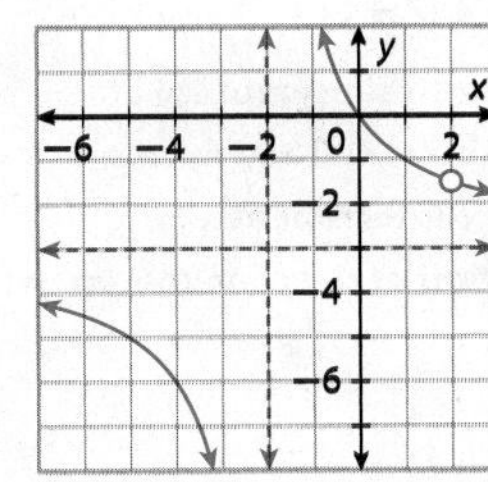

There is a vertical asymptote at $x = -2$

There is a "hole" at $x = 2$.

There is a horizontal asymptote at $y = -3$.

There is an x-intercept at $x = 0$.

Check the sign of the function on the intervals $x < -2$, $-2 < x < 0$, $0 < x < 2$, and $x > 2$.

Domain:

Inequality: $x < -2$ or $-2 < x < 2$ or $x > 2$

Set notation: $\{x \mid x \neq -2 \text{ and } x \neq 2\}$

Interval notation: $(-\infty, -2) \cup (-2, 2) \cup (2, +\infty)$

Range:

Inequality: $y < -3$ or $y > -3$

Set notation: $\{y \mid y \neq -3\}$

Interval notation: $(-\infty, -3) \cup (-3, +$

1. $f(x) = \frac{x^2 + 2x - 4}{x - 1}$

$(x) = \frac{x^2 + 2x - 4}{x - 1} = \frac{(x + 4)(x - 2)}{x - 1}$

here is a vertical asymptote at $x = 1$.

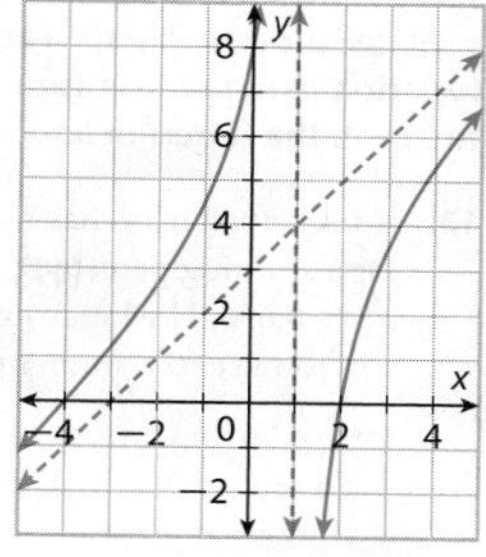

$$\begin{array}{r} x + 3 \\ - 1 \overline{) x^2 + 2x - 4} \\ \underline{x^2 - x} \\ 3x - 4 \\ \underline{3x - 3} \\ -1 \end{array}$$

The line $y = x + 3$ is a slant asymptote.

There are x-intercepts at $x = 2$ and $x = -4$.

Check the sign of the function on the intervals $x < -4$, $-4 < x < 1$, $1 < x < 2$, and $x > 2$.

omain:

Inequality: $x < 1$ or $x > 1$

Set notation: $\{x | x \neq 1\}$

Interval notation: $(-\infty, 1) \cup (1, +\infty)$

Range:

Inequality: $-\infty < y < +\infty$

Set notation: $\{y | -\infty < y < +\infty\}$

Interval notation: $(-\infty, +\infty)$

2. $f(x) = \frac{2x^2 - 4x}{x^2 + 4x + 4}$

$f(x) = \frac{2x^2 - 4x}{x^2 + 4x + 4} = \frac{2x(x - 2)}{(x + 2)^2}$

There is a vertical asymptote at $x = -2$.

$$\begin{array}{r} 2 \\ x^2 + 4x + 4 \overline{) 2x^2 - 4x + 0} \\ \underline{2x^2 + 8x + 8} \\ -12x - 8 \end{array}$$

There is a horizontal asymptote at $y = 2$. There are x-intercepts at $x = 0$ and $x = 2$.

Check the sign of the function on the intervals

$x < -2$, $-2 < x < 0$, $0 < x < 2$, and $x > 2$.

Domain:

Inequality: $x < -2$ or $x > -2$

Set notation: $\{x | x \neq -2\}$

Interval notation: $(-\infty, -2) \cup (-2, +\infty)$

Range (approximate):

Inequality: $y > -0.67$

Set notation: $\{y | y > -0.67\}$

Interval notation: $(-0.67, +\infty)$

AVOID COMMON ERRORS

Students may try to graph first and find asymptotes afterward. Remind students to always start by identifying vertical and horizontal asymptotes, before graphing a rational function. The asymptotes are guidelines, or a framework, for the graph.

Write a rational function to model the situation, or use the given rational function. State a reasonable domain and range for the function using set notation. Then use a graphing calculator to graph the function and answer the question.

13. A basketball team has won 16 games out of 23 games played, for a winning percentage (expressed as a decimal) of $\frac{16}{23} \approx 0.696$. How many consecutive games must the team win to raise its winning percentage to 0.750?

Let w be the number of consecutive games to be won. Then the total number of games won is the function $T_{won}(w) = 16 + w$, and the total number of games played is the function $T_{played}(w) = 23 + w$.

The rational function that gives the team's winning percentage p (as a decimal) is $p(w) = \frac{T_{won}(w)}{T_{played}(w)} = \frac{16 + w}{23 + w}$. The domain of the rational function is $\{w \mid w \geq 0 \text{ and } w \text{ is a whole number}\}$. Since the values of $p(w)$ start at 0.696 and approach 1 as w increases without bound, the range is $\{p \mid 0.696 \leq p < 1\}$.

Graphing $y = \frac{16 + x}{23 + x}$ and $y = 0.75$ on a graphing calculator with a window that shows 0 to 10 on the x-axis and 0.6 to 0.8 on the y-axis and then locating the point where the graphs intersect, you find that the number of consecutive wins needed to bring the team's winning percentage to 0.750 is 5.

14. So far this season, a baseball player has had 84 hits in 294 times at bat, for a batting average of $\frac{84}{294} \approx 0.286$. How many consecutive hits must the player get to raise his batting average to 0.300?

Let h be the number of consecutive hits. Then the total number of hits is the function $T_{hits}(h) = 84 + h$, and the total number of times at bat is the function $T_{at\ bats}(h) = 294 + h$. The rational function that gives the player's batting average a (as a decimal) is $a(h) = \frac{T_{hits}(h)}{T_{at\ bats}(h)} = \frac{84 + h}{294 + h}$.

The domain of the rational function is $\{h \mid h \geq 0 \text{ and } h \text{ is a whole number}\}$. Since the values of $a(h)$ start at 0.286 and approach 1 as h increases without bound, the range is $\{a \mid 0.286 \leq a < 1\}$.

Graphing $y = \frac{84 + x}{294 + x}$ and $y = 0.3$ on a graphing calculator with a window that shows 0 to 10 on the x-axis and 0.2 to 0.4 on the y-axis and then locating the point where the graphs intersect, you find that the number of consecutive hits needed to bring the player's batting average to 0.300 is 6.

15. A kayaker traveled 5 miles upstream and then 8 miles downstream on a river. The average speed of the current was 3 miles per hour. If the kayaker was paddling for 5 hours, what was the kayaker's average paddling speed? To answer the question, use the rational function $t(s) = \frac{5}{s-3} + \frac{8}{s+3} = \frac{13s-9}{(s-3)(s+3)}$ where s is the kayaker's average paddling speed (in miles per hour) and t is the time (in hours) spent kayaking 5 miles against the current at a rate of $s - 3$ miles per hour and 8 miles with the current at a rate of $s + 3$ miles per hour.

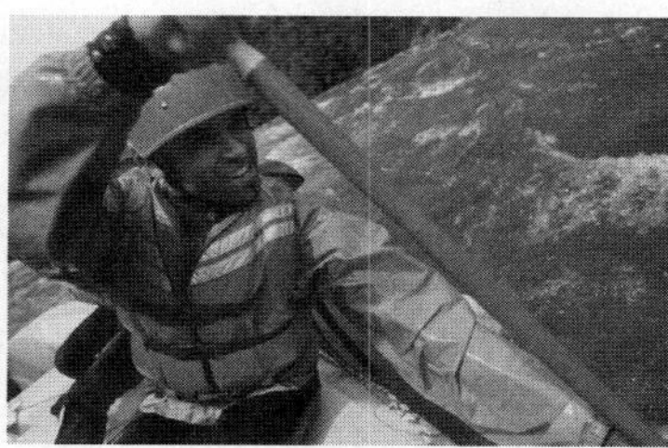

In order for the kayaker to travel upstream, the paddling speed must exceed the speed of the current, so the domain of the function is $\left\{s \mid s > 3\right\}$. As s approaches 3 from the right, $t(s)$ increases without bound, and as s increases without bound, $t(s)$ approaches 0. So, the range of the function is $\left\{t \mid t > 0\right\}$.

Graphing $y = \frac{13x - 9}{(x-3)(x+3)}$ and $y = 5$ on a graphing calculator with a window that shows 3 to 10 on the x-axis and 0 to 6 on the y-axis and then locating the point where the graphs intersect, you find that the kayaker's paddling speed was about 4.3 miles per hour.

16. In aviation, *air speed* refers to a plane's speed in still air. A small plane maintains a certain air speed when flying to and from a city that is 400 miles away. On the trip out, the plane flies against a wind, which has an average speed of 40 miles per hour. On the return trip, the plane flies with the wind. If the total flight time for the round trip is 3.5 hours, what is the plane's average air speed? To answer this question, use the rational function $t(s) = \frac{400}{s-40} + \frac{400}{s+40} = \frac{800s}{(s-40)(s+40)}$ air speed (in miles per hour) and t is the total flight time (in hours) for the round trip.

In order for the plane to make progress when flying against the wind, the plane's air speed must be greater than the speed of the wind, so the domain of the function is $\left\{s \mid s > 40\right\}$. As s approaches 40 from the right, $t(s)$ increases without bound, and as s increases without bound, $t(s)$ approaches 0. So, the range of the function is $\left\{t \mid t > 0\right\}$.

Graphing $y = \frac{800x}{(x-40)(x+40)}$ and $y = 3.5$ on a graphing calculator with a window that shows 0 to 500 on the x-axis and 0 to 5 on the y-axis and then locating the point where the graphs intersect, you find that the plane's average air speed is about 235 miles per hour.

JOURNAL

Have students outline the process of graphing more complex rational functions in their journals. Suggest that they incorporate several examples.

17. Multiple Response Select the statements that apply to the rational function $f(x) = \frac{x-2}{x^2 - x + 6}$.

(A.) The function's domain is $\left\{x \mid x \neq -2 \text{ and } x \neq 3\right\}$.

B. The function's domain is $\left\{x \mid x \neq -2 \text{ and } x \neq -3\right\}$.

C. The function's range is $\left\{y \mid y \neq 0\right\}$.

(D.) The function's range is $\left\{y \mid -\infty < y < +\infty\right\}$.

(E.) The function's graph has vertical asymptotes at $x = -2$ and $x = 3$.

F. The function's graph has a vertical asymptote at $x = -3$ and a "hole" at $x = 2$.

(G.) The function's graph has a horizontal asymptote at $y = 0$.

H. The function's graph has a horizontal asymptote at $y = 1$.

H.O.T. Focus on Higher Order Thinking

18. Draw Conclusions For what value(s) of a does the graph of $f(x) = \frac{x+a}{x^2 + 4x + 3}$ have a "hole"? Explain. Then, for each value of a, state the domain and the range of $f(x)$ using interval notation.

The graph of f(x) has a "hole" if the numerator is a factor of the denominator. Since $x^2 + 4x + 3 = (x+1)(x+3)$, there are two values of a for which the graph of f(x) has a "hole": $a = 1$ and $a = 3$. The domain of the function $f(x) = \frac{x+1}{x^2+4x+3}$ is $(-\infty, -3) \cup (-3, -1) \cup (-1, +\infty)$ and the range is $(-\infty, 0) \cup \left(0, \frac{1}{2}\right) \cup \left(\frac{1}{2}, +\infty\right)$. The domain of the function $f(x) = \frac{x+3}{x^2+4x+3}$ is $(-\infty, -3) \cup (-3, -1) \cup (-1, +\infty)$, and the range is $\left(-\infty, -\frac{1}{2}\right) \cup \left(-\frac{1}{2}, 0\right) \cup (0, +\infty)$.

19. Critique Reasoning A student claims that the functions $f(x) = \frac{4x^2 - 1}{4x + 2}$ and $g(x) = \frac{4x + 2}{4x^2 - 1}$ have different domains but identical ranges. Which part of the student's claim is correct, and which is false? Explain.

The domain of f(x) is $\left\{x \mid x \neq -\frac{1}{2}\right\}$, while the domain of g(x) is $\left\{x \mid x \neq -\frac{1}{2} \text{ and } x \neq \frac{1}{2}\right\}$, so the student's claim is correct with respect to the domains. The range of f(x) is $\left\{y \mid y \neq -1\right\}$, while the range of g(x) is $\left\{y \mid y \neq -1 \text{ and } y \neq 0\right\}$, so the student's claim is incorrect with respect to the ranges.

Lesson Performance Task

In professional baseball, the smallest allowable volume of a baseball is 92.06% of the largest allowable volume, and the range of allowable radii is 0.04 inch.

a. Let r be the largest allowable radius (in inches) of a baseball. Write expressions, both in terms of r, for the largest allowable volume of the baseball and the smallest allowable volume of the baseball. (Use the formula for the volume of a sphere, $V = \frac{4}{3}\pi r^3$.)

b. Write and simplify a function that gives the ratio R of the smallest allowable volume of a baseball to the largest allowable volume.

c. Use a graphing calculator to graph the function from part b, and use the graph to find the smallest allowable radius and the largest allowable radius of a baseball. Round your answers to the nearest hundredth.

a. Largest allowable volume: $\frac{4}{3}\pi r^3$

Smallest allowable volume: $\frac{4}{3}\pi(r - 0.04)^3$

b. $R(r) = \dfrac{\frac{4}{3}\pi(r - 0.04)^3}{\frac{4}{3}\pi r^3} = \dfrac{(r - 0.04)^3}{r^3}$

c. Graph $y = \dfrac{(x - 0.04)^3}{x^3}$ and $y = 0.9206$ on a graphing calculator, and find the x-coordinate of the point where the graphs intersect. The graphs intersect at $x = 1.47$ to the nearest hundredth, so the largest allowable radius is 1.47 inches. The smallest allowable radius is $1.47 - 0.04 = 1.43$ inches.

EXTENSION ACTIVITY

Have students discuss whether the solution graphs would be different if the baseball were a cube with a side of length x. Have students determine the largest and smallest allowable lengths for the side of the cube when the smallest allowable volume is 92.06% of the largest allowable volume, and the range of allowable lengths is 0.04 inches. Have students compare the function for this situation to the one they derived in the Performance Task.

AVOID COMMON ERRORS

Students may set the ratio of volumes to 92.06 instead of 0.9206. Have students explain what a percentage is, and ask them what 92.06% means in this situation. Have students graph $y = 92.06$ and $y = 0.9206$, and ask them which one gives a solution for this problem.

INTEGRATE MATHEMATICAL PRACTICES

Focus on Critical Thinking

MP.3 Have students discuss the significance of the percentage 92.06% when solving this problem by graphing. Ask them to describe the behavior of the solution as the percentage varies. Ask them what will happen to the graph as the range of allowable radii gets smaller or larger.

Scoring Rubric

2 points: Student correctly solves the problem and explains his/her reasoning.

1 point: Student shows good understanding of the problem but does not fully solve or explain his/her reasoning.

0 points: Student does not demonstrate understanding of the problem.

Study Guide Review

ASSESSMENT AND INTERVENTION

Assign or customize module reviews.

MODULE PERFORMANCE TASK

Mathematical Practices: MP.1, MP.2, MP.4, MP.6
F-BF.A.1b, F-IF.B.4

SUPPORTING STUDENT REASONING

Students should begin by filling in the table with the missing information. Here are questions students may ask.

- **How do I find the revenue?** Multiply the retail price given for the style of helmet by the number of helmets. This is the amount of money the store takes in for that size order.
- **What is the relationship among profit, revenue, and cost?** $P = R - C$
- **Where can I record the profit per helmet in the table?** Suggest that they use the Profit row for this and use scratch paper for the total profit per batch, or vice versa.

STUDY GUIDE REVIEW

Rational Functions

MODULE 8

Essential Question: How can you use rational functions to solve real-world problems?

Key Vocabulary
asymptote *(asíntota)*
constant of variation *(constante de variación)*
parent function *(función madre)*
rational function *(función racional)*

KEY EXAMPLE *(Lesson 8.1)*

Graph $y = -\frac{1}{x-2}$. State the domain, range, y-intercept, and identify any asymptotes.

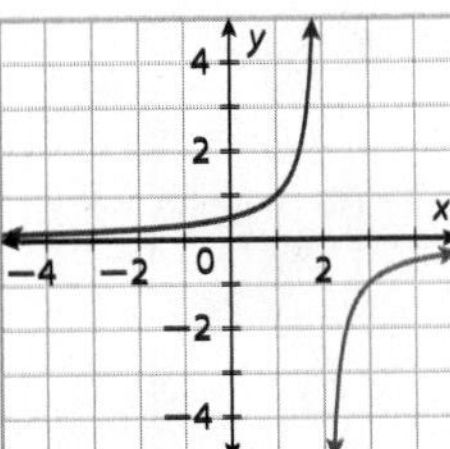

Domain: $x < 2$ or $x > 2$
Range: $y < 0$ or $y > 0$
y-intercept: $\left(0, \frac{1}{2}\right)$
The graph has a vertical asymptote at $x = 2$ and a horizontal asymptote at $y = 0$.

KEY EXAMPLE *(Lesson 8.2)*

Graph $y = \frac{2x^2}{x+2}$. State the domain, range, x-intercept, and identify any asymptotes.

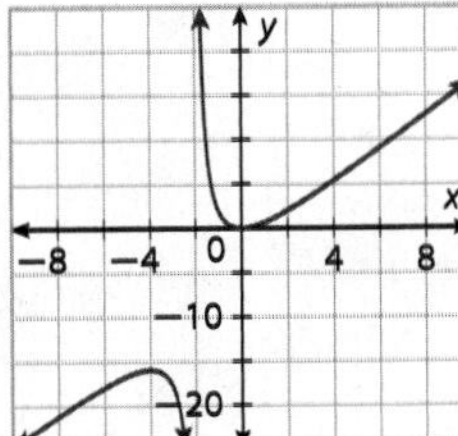

Domain: $x < -2$ or $x > -2$
Range: $y \leq -16$ or $y \geq 0$
The numerator has 0 as its only zero, so the x-intercept is $(0, 0)$.
The denominator has -2 as its only zero, so the graph has a vertical asymptote at $x = -2$.

SCAFFOLDING SUPPORT

- Students might make a scatterplot that shows profit trends for each type of helmet, or they could look at the data in the table and notice trends.
- Watch for students who misuse the Cost formula given in the table.
- You may want to suggest that students find a formula for determining the profit per helmet based on the number of helmets.

EXERCISES

Describe how the graph of $g(x)$ is related to the graph of $f(x) = \frac{1}{x}$. *(Lesson 8.1)*

1. $g(x) = \frac{1}{x+4}$

   g is f translated 4 units left

2. $g(x) = \frac{1}{x-2} + 3$

   g is f translated 2 units right and 3 units up

3. $g(x) = \frac{-1}{x+3}$

   g is f reflected across the x-axis and translated 3 units left

Graph the function using a graphing calculator. State the domain, x-intercept(s), and identify asymptotes. *(Lesson 8.2)*

4. $f(x) = \frac{x^2 - 3x}{x+4}$

   Domain: $x < -4$ or $x > -4$

   x-intercepts: $x = 0, 3$

   asymptotes: $x = -4$

5. $f(x) = \frac{x-3}{x^2 + 6x + 5}$

   Domain: $x < -5$ or $-5 < x < -1$ or $x > -1$

   x-intercept: $x = 3$

   asymptotes: $x = -5, x = -1, y = 0$

6. $f(x) = -\frac{(x^2 - 4)}{(x+1)}$

   Domain: $x < -1$ or $x > -1$

   x-intercepts: $x = -2, 2$

   asymptotes: $x = -1$

MODULE PERFORMANCE TASK

What Is the Profit?

A sporting goods store sells two styles of bike helmets: Style A for $30 each and Style B for $40 each. The store is trying to calculate its average profit on each style of helmet, using the rational function $A(x) = \frac{P(x)}{x}$, where $P(x)$ is the profit on the sale of x helmets. The helmet supplier offers a of volume discount for orders up to 500 helmets, using the cost formulas shown in the table. For each style, how does per-helmet profit change as the number of helmets increases? What is the maximum per-helmet profit?

Number of Helmets (x)	100	200	300	400	500
Style A					
Revenue					
Cost: $100 + (20 - 0.01x)x$					
Profit					
Style B					
Revenue					
Cost: $250 + (30 - 0.03x)x$					
Profit					

Start by organizing your data in the table. Then use your own paper to complete the task. Use graphs, numbers, words, or algebra to explain how you reached your conclusion.

SAMPLE SOLUTION

Compute a formula for finding the profit per helmet based on the number of helmets. If x represents the number of helmets for Style A,

$$A(x) = \frac{P(x)}{x} = \frac{R - C}{x}$$

$$A(x) = \frac{30x - [100 + (20 - 0.01x)x]}{x}$$

$$A(x) = \frac{0.01x^2 + 10x - 100}{x}$$

So for Style A, (number of helmets, profit per helmet) $= \left(x, \frac{0.01x^2 + 10x - 100}{x}\right)$.

Similarly, for Style B, (number of helmets, profit per helmet) $= \left(x, \frac{0.03x^2 + 10x - 250}{x}\right)$.

Now, use these formulas to find some per-helmet profit figures and list them in a table:

Style A	Style B
(100, $10.00)	(100, $10.50)
(200, $11.50)	(200, $14.75)
(300, $12.67)	(300, $18.17)
(400, $13.75)	(400, $21.38)
(500, $14.80)	(500, $24.50)

Style A profits increase from $10 per helmet to a maximum of $14.80 per helmet. Style B profits increase from $10.50 per helmet to a maximum of $24.50 per helmet. Style B profits increase more quickly than Style A profits.

DISCUSSION OPPORTUNITIES

- Ask students to speculate whether the profit functions are linear. Ask them to explain their reasoning.
- Ask students to discuss which constants in the expressions for Style B brought about the more rapid increase in profits. Invite students to justify their opinions.

Assessment Rubric

2 points: Student correctly solves the problem and explains his/her reasoning.

1 point: Student shows good understanding of the problem but does not fully solve or explain.

0 points: Student does not demonstrate understanding of the problem.

Ready to Go On?

ASSESS MASTERY

Use the assessment on this page to determine if students have mastered the concepts and standards covered in this module.

ASSESSMENT AND INTERVENTION

Access Ready to Go On? assessment online, and receive instant scoring, feedback, and customized intervention or enrichment.

ADDITIONAL RESOURCES

Response to Intervention Resources

- Reteach Worksheets

Differentiated Instruction Resources

- Reading Strategies EL
- Success for English Learners EL
- Challenge Worksheets

Assessment Resources

- Leveled Module Quizzes

Ready to Go On?

8.1–8.2 Rational Functions

Personal Math Trainer

- Online Homework
- Hints and Help
- Extra Practice

Describe how the graph of $g(x)$ is related to the graph of $f(x) = \frac{1}{x}$. *(Lesson 8.2)*

1. $g(x) = \frac{5}{x} - 3$

   g is *f* vertically stretched by a factor of 5 and translated 3 units down

2. $g(x) = \frac{1}{-0.5(x-2)} + 4$

   g is *f* horizontally stretched by a factor of 2, reflected across the *y*-axis, and translated 2 units right and 4 units up

3. $g(x) = \frac{-1}{x} + 5$

   g is *f* reflected across the x-axis and translated 5 units up

Graph the function using a graphing calculator. State the domain, *x*-intercept(s), and identify asymptotes. *(Lessons 8.2, 8.3)*

4. $f(x) = \frac{2x-4}{x+3}$

   Domain: $x < -3$ or $x > -3$

   x-intercept: $x = 2$

   asymptotes: $x = -3, y = 2$

5. $f(x) = \frac{x^2-9}{x-2}$

   Domain: $x < 2, x > 2$

   x-intercepts: $x = -3, 3$

   asymptotes: $x = 2$

6. $f(x) = -\frac{(x+2)}{(x^2+3x)}$

   Domain: $x < -3, -3 < x < 0, x > 0$

   x-intercept: $x = -2$

   asymptotes: $x = -3, x = 0$

ESSENTIAL QUESTION

7. How do you identify the asymptotes of a rational function?

   Possible Answer: The graph has vertical asymptotes for every value of the variable that makes the denominator 0. It has a horizontal asymptote if the degree of the denominator is less than or equal to the degree of the numerator.

COMMON CORE Common Core Standards

Lesson	*Items*	Content Standards	Mathematical Practices
8.1	1–3	**F-IF.C.7d, A-APR.D.6, F-BF.B.3**	**MP.6**
8.2	4–6	**F-IF.C.7d, A-SSE.A.1b**	**MP.5**

MODULE 8
MIXED REVIEW

Assessment Readiness

1. Consider the equation $x^2 - 64 < 0$. Is the given inequality a solution set of the equation?
Select Yes or No for A–C.
   - **A.** $x < -8$ or $x > -8$ ○ Yes ● No
   - **B.** $-8 < x < -8$ ● Yes ○ No
   - **C.** $-64 < x < -64$ ○ Yes ● No

2. Consider the equation $y = \frac{2x+5}{x-1}$. Select True or False for each statement.
   - **A.** The line $x = 1$ is an asymptote. ● True ○ False
   - **B.** The point (0, –5) lies on the graph. ● True ○ False
   - **C.** The function is undefined for $x = -1$. ○ True ● False

3. Consider the equation $\frac{(x^2+5x+4)}{(x^2-9)}$. State the domain, range, and x- and y-intercepts, and identify any asymptotes.

   Domain: $x < -3, -3 < x < 3, x > 3$

   Range: $\{y \mid y$ is a real number$\}$

   x-intercepts: $x = -4, -1$

   y-intercept: $y = \frac{4}{9}$

   asymptotes: $x = -3, x = 3$

4. You have subscribed to a cable television service. The cable company charges a one-time installation fee of \$30 and a monthly fee of \$50. Write a model that gives the average cost per month as a function of months subscribed to the service. After how many months will the average cost be \$56? Explain your thinking and identify any asymptotes on the graph of the function.

   $C = \frac{30 + 50m}{m}$, where C represents average cost and m represents number of months; 5 months; $m = 0$ is a vertical asymptote and $C = 50$ is a horizontal asymptote

MODULE 8

MIXED REVIEW

Assessment Readiness

ASSESSMENT AND INTERVENTION

Assign ready-made or customized practice tests to prepare students for high-stakes tests.

ADDITIONAL RESOURCES

Assessment Resources

- Leveled Module Quizzes: Modified, B

AVOID COMMON ERRORS

Item 4 Students may be reluctant to place a variable in both the numerator and the denominator of the function. Explain that if they have translated carefully and correctly, their functions will be correct.

Common Core Standards

Lesson	Items	Content Standards	Mathematical Practices
3.1	1*	**A-REI.B.4b**	**MP.2**
8.2, 8.3	2	**F-IF.C.7d**	**MP.7**
8.1	3	**A-CED.A.2, N-Q.A.1**	**MP.1**
1.2, 8.2, 8.3	4*	**F-IF.B.4, F-IF.C.7d, N-Q.A.1**	**MP.4**

* Item integrates mixed review concepts from previous modules or a previous course.

Rational Expressions and Equations

ESSENTIAL QUESTION:

Answer: Rational expressions and equations can be used to model comparisons between per-capita expenditures or rates of speed.

PROFESSIONAL DEVELOPMENT VIDEO

Professional Development Video

Author Matt Larson models successful teaching practices in an actual high-school classroom.

Professional Development

my.hrw.com

MODULE 9

Rational Expressions and Equations

Essential Question: How can you use rational expressions and equations to solve real-world problems?

REAL WORLD VIDEO
Robotic arms and other prosthetic devices are among the wonders of robotics. Check out some of the other cutting-edge applications of modern robotics.

MODULE PERFORMANCE TASK PREVIEW

Robots and Resistors

Robotics engineers design robots and develop applications for them, such as executing high-precision tasks in factories, cleaning toxic waste, and locating and defusing bombs. People who work in robotics are skilled in areas such as electronics and computer programming. How can a rational expression be used to help design the circuitry for a robot? Let's find out!

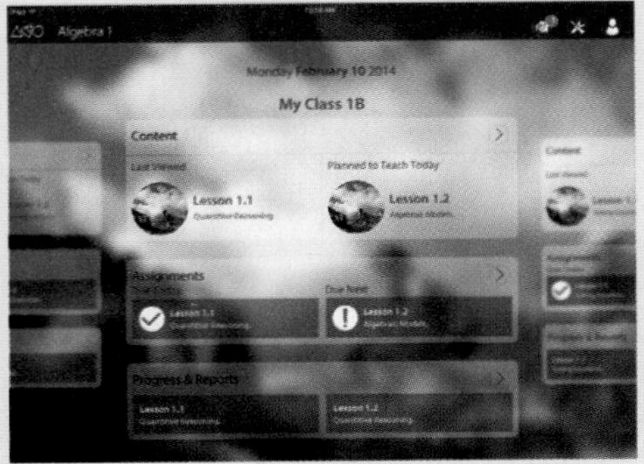

DIGITAL TEACHER EDITION

Access a full suite of teaching resources when and where you need them:

- Access content online or offline
- Customize lessons to share with your class
- Communicate with your students in real-time
- View student grades and data instantly to target your instruction where it is needed most

PERSONAL MATH TRAINER

Assessment and Intervention

Assign automatically graded homework, quizzes, tests, and intervention activities. Prepare your students with updated, Common Core-aligned practice tests.

Complete these exercises to review skills you will need for this chapter.

- Online Homework
- Hints and Help
- Extra Practice

Graphing Linear Proportional Relationships

Example 1 Graph $y = \frac{1}{2}x$.

When $x = 0$, $y = 0$, so plot $(0, 0)$ on the graph.

The slope is $\frac{1}{2}$, so from $(0, 0)$, plot the next point up 1 and over 2.

Draw a line through the two points.

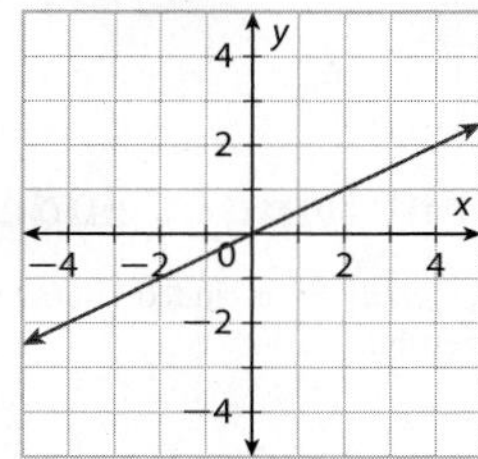

Graph each proportional relationship.

1. $y = 2x$

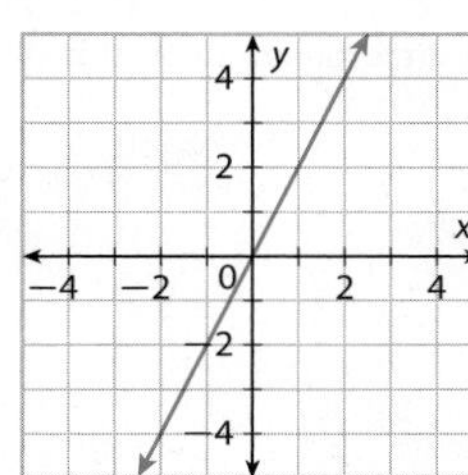

2. $y = \frac{2}{3}x$

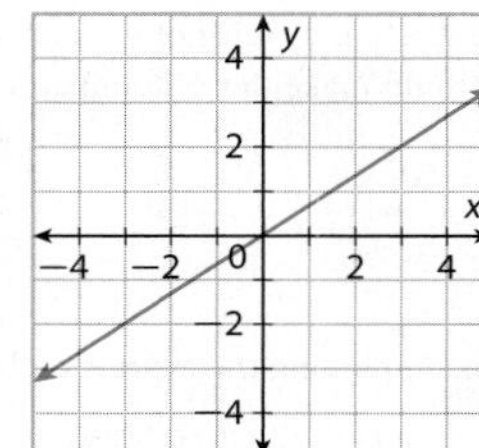

Direct and Inverse Variation

Example 2 In a direct variation the constant is 4 and its graph passes through $(x, 10)$. Find x.

$y = kx \rightarrow 10 = 4x \rightarrow x = 2.5$

Example 3 In an inverse variation the constant is 2.4 and its graph passes through $(6, y)$. Find y.

$k = xy \rightarrow 2.4 = 6y \rightarrow y = 0.4$

Find the missing variable for each direct variation.

3. $k = -1$; $(x, -5)$ 5

4. $k = 3$; $(9, y)$ 27

5. $k = \frac{1}{3}$; $(x, -2)$ −6

Find the missing variable for each inverse variation.

6. $k = 8$; $(x, -10)$ −0.8

7. $k = -2$; $(5, y)$ −0.4

8. $k = 6$; $(x, 1.5)$ 4

Response to Intervention			Differentiated Instruction
Tier 1 Lesson Intervention Worksheets	**Tier 2** Strategic Intervention Skills Intervention Worksheets	**Tier 3** Intensive Intervention Worksheets available online	
Reteach 9.1 Reteach 9.2 Reteach 9.3	6 Direct Variation 14 Graphing Linear Nonproportional Relationships 15 Graphing Linear Proportional Relationships 17 Inverse Variation	Building Block Skills 41, 46, 43, 44, 46, 94, 96	Challenge worksheets Extend the Math Lesson Activities in TE

Are You Ready?

ASSESS READINESS

Use the assessment on this page to determine if students need strategic or intensive intervention for the module's prerequisite skills.

ASSESSMENT AND INTERVENTION

RtI Response to Intervention TIER 1, TIER 2, TIER 3 SKILLS

Personal Math Trainer will automatically create a standards-based, personalized intervention assignment for your students, targeting each student's individual needs!

ADDITIONAL RESOURCES

See the table below for a full list of intervention resources available for this module.

Response to Intervention Resources also includes:

- Tier 2 Skill Pre-Tests for each Module
- Tier 2 Skill Post-Tests for each skill

LESSON 9.1

Adding and Subtracting Rational Expressions

Common Core Standards

The student is expected to:

 **A-APR.D.7(+)**

Understand that rational expressions form a system analogous to the rational numbers, ...; add, subtract, . . . rational expressions. Also A-SSE.A.2

Mathematical Practices

COMMON CORE **MP.7 Using Structure**

Language Objective

Explain to a partner how to simplify a rational expression and how to add and subtract rational expressions.

ENGAGE

Essential Question: How can you add and subtract rational expressions?

Possible answer: Convert them to like denominators, then add the numerators, all the while keeping track of the combined excluded values.

PREVIEW: LESSON PERFORMANCE TASK

View the Engage section online. Discuss the photo and how the river's current can either help the kayaker go faster or slow the kayaker down. Then preview the Lesson Performance Task.

Name ______ Class ______ Date ______

9.1 Adding and Subtracting Rational Expressions

Essential Question: How can you add and subtract rational expressions?

Explore Identifying Excluded Values

Given a rational expression, identify the excluded values by finding the zeroes of the denominator. If possible, simplify the expression.

(A) $\frac{(1 - x^2)}{x - 1}$

The denominator of the expression is $x - 1$.

(B) Since division by 0 is not defined, the excluded values for this expression are all the values that would make the denominator equal to 0.

$x - 1 = 0$

$x = 1$

(C) Begin simplifying the expression by factoring the numerator.

$$\frac{(1 - x^2)}{x - 1} = \frac{(1 - x)(1 + x)}{x - 1}$$

(D) Divide out terms common to both the numerator and the denominator.

$$\frac{(1 - x^2)}{x - 1} = \frac{\cancel{(1 - x)}(1 + x)}{-\cancel{(1 - x)}} = -(1 + x) = -1 - x$$

(E) The simplified expression is

$$\frac{(1 - x^2)}{x - 1} = -1 - x, \text{ whenever } x \neq 1$$

(F) What is the domain for this function? What is its range?

Its domain is all real numbers except $x = 1$. Its range is all real numbers except $y = -2$.

Reflect

1. What factors can be divided out of the numerator and denominator?
Common factors

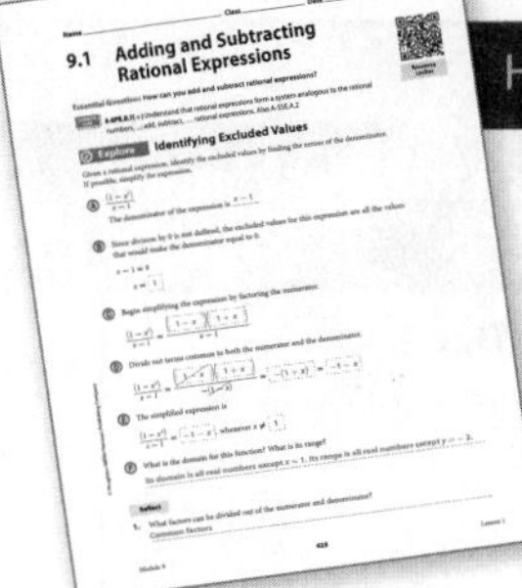

HARDCOVER PAGES **425–438**

Watch for the hardcover student edition page numbers for this lesson.

Explain 1 Writing Equivalent Rational Expressions

Given a rational expression, there are different ways to write an equivalent rational expression. When common terms are divided out, the result is an equivalent but simplified expression.

Example 1 Rewrite the expression as indicated.

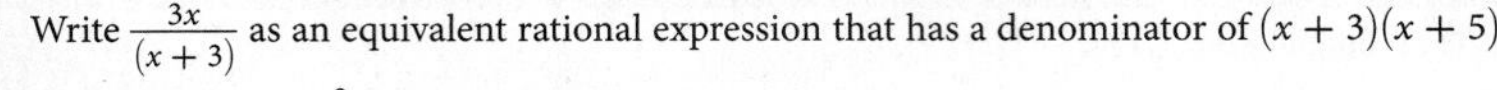

(A) Write $\frac{3x}{(x+3)}$ as an equivalent rational expression that has a denominator of $(x+3)(x+5)$.

The expression $\frac{3x}{(x+3)}$ has a denominator of $(x+3)$.

The factor missing from the denominator is $(x+5)$.

Introduce a common factor, $(x+5)$.

$$\frac{3x}{(x+3)} = \frac{3x(x+5)}{(x+3)(x+5)}$$

$\frac{3x}{(x+3)}$ is equivalent to $\frac{3x(x+5)}{(x+3)(x+5)}$.

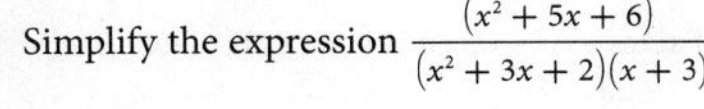

(B) Simplify the expression $\frac{(x^2+5x+6)}{(x^2+3x+2)(x+3)}$.

Write the expression. $\frac{(x^2+5x+6)}{(x^2+3x+2)(x+3)}$

Factor the numerator and denominator. $\frac{(x+2)(x+3)}{(x+1)(x+2)(x+3)}$

Divide out like terms. $\frac{1}{x+1}$

Your Turn

2. Write $\frac{5}{5x-25}$ as an equivalent expression with a denominator of $(x-5)(x+1)$.

$$\frac{5}{5x-25} = \frac{5}{5(x-5)} = \frac{1}{x-5} = \frac{1(x+1)}{(x-5)(x+1)} = \frac{x+1}{(x-5)(x+1)}$$

3. Simplify the expression $\frac{(x+x^3)(1-x^2)}{(x^2-x^6)}$.

$$\frac{(x+x^3)(1-x^2)}{(x^2-x^6)} = \frac{x(1+x^2)(1-x^2)}{x^2(1-x^4)} = \frac{x(1+x^2)(1-x^2)}{x^2(1+x^2)(1-x^2)} = \frac{\cancel{x}\cancel{(1+x^2)}\cancel{(1-x^2)}}{x^{\cancel{2}}\cancel{(1+x^2)}\cancel{(1-x^2)}} = \frac{1}{x}$$

PROFESSIONAL DEVELOPMENT

Integrate Mathematical Practices

Operations on rational expressions are similar to operations on fractions. For example,

$$\frac{a(x)}{b(x)} + \frac{c(x)}{d(x)} = \frac{a(x)d(x) + b(x)c(x)}{b(x)d(x)}$$

except where $b(x) = 0$ and/or $d(x) = 0$. As with fractions, it is generally best to simplify rational expressions before adding, subtracting, multiplying, or dividing. Note that in the above equation, the denominator $b(x)d(x)$ may not be the *least* common denominator of the two rational expressions.

EXPLORE

Identifying Excluded Values

INTEGRATE TECHNOLOGY

Students have the option of completing the Explore activity either in the book or online.

QUESTIONING STRATEGIES

? When identifying excluded values, why is it not necessary to consider values of the variable that make the numerator equal to 0? **If the numerator is 0 and the denominator is nonzero, the fraction is defined and is equal to 0, so values that make the numerator 0 do not need to be excluded (as long as they don't also make the denominator 0).**

? Why are there no excluded values for the rational expression $\frac{x}{x^2+4}$? **There are no real numbers for which $x^2 + 4$ equals 0.**

EXPLAIN 1

Writing Equivalent Rational Expressions

AVOID COMMON ERRORS

Students sometimes make errors writing the simplified form of a rational expression in which all factors of the numerator divide out with common factors from the denominator. These students may write the simplified denominator as the final answer, forgetting that there is a factor of 1 that remains in the numerator. To help students avoid this error, encourage them to write a 1 above or below any factor that divides out, and to multiply the 1's with any remaining factors when writing the final rational expression.

QUESTIONING STRATEGIES

When simplifying a rational expression, when might it be helpful to factor −1 from either the numerator or the denominator? **when the expressions in the numerator and the denominator are not both written in descending form, or when the leading coefficient of one or both expressions is negative**

INTEGRATE MATHEMATICAL PRACTICES

Focus on Math Connections

MP.1 To help students understand why rational expressions such as $\frac{x+2}{2}$ cannot be simplified, have them substitute a number, such as 6, for x and compare the value of $\frac{6+2}{2}$ to $\frac{6+\cancel{2}^{1}}{\cancel{2}_{1}}$. Point out that the two expressions are not equivalent. Tell students they can use this substitute-and-check strategy in other situations when they are not sure whether their action produces an equivalent expression.

Explain 2 Identifying the LCD of Two Rational Expressions

Given two or more rational expressions, the least common denominator (LCD) is found by factoring each denominator and finding the least common multiple (LCM) of the factors. This technique is useful for the addition and subtraction of expressions with unlike denominators.

Least Common Denominator (LCD) of Rational Expressions

To find the LCD of rational expressions:

1. Factor each denominator completely. Write any repeated factors as powers.
2. List the different factors. If the denominators have common factors, use the highest power of each common factor.

Example 2 Find the LCD for each set of rational expressions.

A $\frac{-2}{3x-15}$ and $\frac{6x}{4x+28}$

Factor each denominator completely.

$3x - 15 = 3(x - 5)$

$4x + 28 = 4(x + 7)$

List the different factors.

$3, 4, x - 5, x + 7$

The LCD is $3 \cdot 4(x - 5)(x + 7)$,

or $12(x - 5)(x + 7)$.

B $\frac{-14}{x^2 - 11x + 24}$ and $\frac{9}{x^2 - 6x + 9}$

Factor each denominator completely.

$x^2 - 11x + 24 =$ **$(x-3)(x-8)$**

$x^2 - 6x + 9 =$ **$(x-3)(x-3)$**

List the different factors.

$x - 3$ and **$x - 8$**

Taking the highest power of $(x - 3)$,

the LCD is **$(x-3)^2(x-8)$**.

Reflect

4. **Discussion** When is the LCD of two rational expressions not equal to the product of their denominators?
When a factor appears one or more times in each denominator

Your Turn

Find the LCD for each set of rational expressions.

5. $\frac{x+6}{8x-24}$ and $\frac{14x}{10x-30}$

$8x - 24 = 8(x - 3)$
$= 2^3(x - 3)$
$10x - 30 = 10(x - 3)$
$= 2 \cdot 5(x - 3)$
factors: 2, 5, $x - 3$
Taking the highest power of 2, the LCD is $2^3 \cdot 5(x - 3) = 40(x - 3)$.

6. $\frac{12x}{15x+60} = \frac{5}{x^2+9x+20}$

$15x + 60 = 15(x + 4)$
$= 3 \cdot 5(x + 4)$
$x^2 + 9x + 20 = (x + 4)(x + 5)$
factors: 3, 5, $x + 4$, $x + 5$
The LCD is $3 \cdot 5(x + 4)(x+5) = 15(x + 4)(x+5)$.

COLLABORATIVE LEARNING

Peer-to-Peer Activity

Pair advanced students with classmates who are struggling with adding and subtracting rational expressions with unlike denominators. Encourage the advanced students to start by trying to diagnose which part of the process is causing the most trouble and to focus on helping with the appropriate skills. By explaining the process, advanced students will develop a deeper understanding of the concepts and struggling students will benefit from peer instruction.

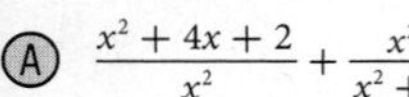 Adding and Subtracting Rational Expressions

Adding and subtracting rational expressions is similar to adding and subtracting fractions.

Example 3 **Add or subtract. Identify any excluded values and simplify your answer.**

(A) $\frac{x^2 + 4x + 2}{x^2} + \frac{x^2}{x^2 + x}$

Factor the denominators. $\frac{x^2 + 4x + 2}{x^2} + \frac{x^2}{x(x + 1)}$

Identify where the expression is not defined. The first expression is undefined when $x = 0$. The second expression is undefined when $x = 0$ and when $x = -1$.

Find a common denominator. The LCM for x^2 and $x(x + 1)$ is $x^2(x + 1)$.

Write the expressions with a common denominator by multiplying both by the appropriate form of 1. $\frac{(x + 1)}{(x + 1)} \cdot \frac{x^2 + 4x + 2}{x^2} + \frac{x^2}{x(x + 1)} \cdot \frac{x}{x}$

Simplify each numerator. $= \frac{x^3 + 5x^2 + 6x + 2}{x^2(x + 1)} + \frac{x^3}{x^2(x + 1)}$

Add. $= \frac{2x^3 + 5x^2 + 6x + 2}{x^2 x + 1}$

Since none of the factors of the denominator are factors of the numerator, the expression cannot be further simplified.

 $\frac{2x^2}{x^2 - 5x} - \frac{x^2 + 3x - 4}{x^2}$

Factor the denominators. $\frac{2x^2}{\boxed{x(x - 5)}} - \frac{x^2 + 3x - 4}{x^2}$

Identify where the expression is not defined. The first expression is undefined when $x = 0$ and when $x = 5$. The second expression is undefined when $x = 0$.

Find a common denominator. The LCM for $x(x - 5)$ and x^2 is $x^2(x - 5)$.

Write the expressions with a common denominator by multiplying both by the appropriate form of 1. $\boxed{\frac{x}{x}} \cdot \frac{2x^2}{x(x - 5)} - \frac{x^2 + 3x - 4}{x^2} \cdot \frac{x - 5}{x - 5}$

Simplify each numerator. $= \frac{2x^3}{x^2(x - 5)} - \frac{x^3 - 2x^2 - 19x + 20}{x^2(x - 5)}$

Subtract. $= \frac{\boxed{x^3} + 2x^2 + 19x - 20}{x^2(x - 5)}$

Since none of the factors of the denominator are factors of the numerator, the expression cannot be further simplified.

DIFFERENTIATE INSTRUCTION

Communicating Math

It may be beneficial to have students verbally describe the steps involved in adding and subtracting rational expressions. Ensure that students' descriptions are accurate, but allow them to use their own words to describe the steps. Pay careful attention, in students' explanations, to how they find the common denominator, and how they convert the numerators of the fractions to obtain equivalent expressions. Students may also benefit from hearing how other students describe these steps.

EXPLAIN 3

Adding and Subtracting Rational Expressions

AVOID COMMON ERRORS

Students may make sign errors when combining the numerators in a problem involving the subtraction of two rational expressions. To avoid this, reinforce the importance of writing the numerator being subtracted in parentheses and carefully applying the distributive property before combining like terms.

QUESTIONING STRATEGIES

? How do you find the LCD of rational expressions? **First, factor each denominator. Then write the product of the factors of the denominators. If the denominators have common factors, use the highest power of that factor found in any of the denominators.**

? What steps do you use to rewrite the expressions with like denominators? **Multiply each numerator by any factors of the LCD that were not factors of its original denominator. Use the LCD for the denominator.**

PEER-TO-PEER DISCUSSION

Ask students to consider whether the product of the denominators can always be used as the common denominator when adding or subtracting fractions with unlike denominators. Have them experiment to see what happens in situations in which the product is not the *least* common denominator. **The product can be used, but the result will need to be simplified.**

Your Turn

Add each pair of expressions, simplifying the result and noting the combined excluded values. Then subtract the second expression from the first, again simplifying the result and noting the combined excluded values.

7. $-x^2$ and $\frac{1}{(1-x^2)}$

Addition:

$$-x^2 + \frac{1}{(1-x^2)} = \frac{(-x^2)(1-x^2)}{(1-x^2)} + \frac{1}{(1-x^2)}$$
$$= \frac{x^4 - x^2 + 1}{(1-x^2)}$$
$$= \frac{x^4 - x^2 + 1}{(1+x)(1-x)}, x \neq \pm 1$$

Subtraction:

$$-x^2 - \frac{1}{(1-x^2)} = \frac{(-x^2)(1-x^2)}{(1-x^2)} - \frac{1}{(1-x^2)}$$
$$= \frac{x^4 - x^2 - 1}{(1+x)(1-x)}, x \neq \pm 1$$

8. $\frac{x^2}{(4-x^2)}$ and $\frac{1}{(2-x)}$

Addition:

$$\frac{x^2}{(4-x^2)} + \frac{1}{(2+x)} = \frac{x^2}{(2+x)(2-x)} + \frac{1}{(2+x)}$$
$$= \frac{x^2}{(2+x)(2-x)} + \frac{(2-x)}{(2+x)(2-x)}$$
$$= \frac{x^2 + (2-x)}{(2+x)(2-x)}$$
$$= \frac{x^2 - x + 2}{(2+x)(2-x)}, x \neq \pm 2$$

Subtraction:

$$\frac{x^2}{(4-x^2)} - \frac{1}{(2+x)} = \frac{x^2}{(2+x)(2-x)} - \frac{(2-x)}{(2+x)(2-}$$
$$= \frac{x^2 - (2-x)}{(2+x)(2-x)}$$
$$= \frac{x^2 + x - 2}{(2+x)(2-x)}$$
$$= \frac{(x+2)(x-1)}{(2+x)(2-x)}$$
$$= \frac{(x-1)}{(2-x)}, x \neq \pm 2$$

Explain 4 Adding and Subtracting with Rational Models

Rational expressions can model real-world phenomena, and can be used to calculate measurements of those phenomena.

Example 4 **Find the sum or difference of the models to solve the problem.**

(A) Two groups have agreed that each will contribute \$2000 for an upcoming trip. Group A has 6 more people than group B. Let x represent the number of people in group A. Write and simplify an expression in terms of x that represents the difference between the number of dollars each person in group A must contribute and the number each person in group B must contribute.

$$\frac{2000}{x} - \frac{2000}{x-6} = \frac{2000(x-6)}{x(x-6)} - \frac{2000x}{(x-6)x}$$
$$= \frac{2000x + 12{,}000 - 2000x}{x(x-6)}$$
$$= \frac{12{,}000}{x(x-6)}$$

(B) A freight train averages 30 miles per hour traveling to its destination with full cars and 40 miles per hour on the return trip with empty cars. Find the total time in terms of d. Use the formula $t = \frac{d}{r}$.

Let d represent the one-way distance.

Total time: $\frac{d}{30} + \frac{d}{40} = \frac{d \cdot \boxed{40}}{30 \cdot \boxed{40}} + \frac{d \cdot \boxed{30}}{40 \cdot \boxed{30}}$

$$= \frac{d \cdot \boxed{40} + d \cdot \boxed{30}}{\boxed{1200}}$$

$$= \frac{\boxed{7}}{\boxed{120}} d$$

Your Turn

9. A hiker averages 1.4 miles per hour when walking downhill on a mountain trail and 0.8 miles per hour on the return trip when walking uphill. Find the total time in terms of d. Use the formula $t = \frac{d}{r}$.

Let d represent the one-way distance.

Total time: $\frac{d}{1.4} + \frac{d}{0.8} = \frac{d \cdot 0.8}{1.4 \cdot 0.8} + \frac{d \cdot 1.4}{0.8 \cdot 1.4}$

$$= \frac{d \cdot 0.8 + d \cdot 1.4}{1.12}$$
$$= \frac{2.2}{1.12}d$$
$$= \frac{55}{28}d$$

LANGUAGE SUPPORT EL

Communicate Math

Have students work in pairs. Provide each pair of students with some rational expressions written on sticky notes or index cards and with some addition and subtraction problems. Have the first student explain the steps to simplify a rational expression while the second student writes notes. Students switch roles and repeat the process with an addition problem, then again with a subtraction problem.

EXPLAIN 4

Adding and Subtracting with Rational Models

QUESTIONING STRATEGIES

? What is the significance of the excluded values of a rational expression that models a real-world situation? The excluded values are numbers that are not possible values of the independent variable in the given situation.

INTEGRATE MATHEMATICAL PRACTICES

Focus on Technology

MP.5 Students can use a graphing calculator to compare the graph of the function defined by the original sum or difference with the graph of the function defined by the final simplified expression. The graphs should be identical.

ELABORATE

INTEGRATE MATHEMATICAL PRACTICES

Focus on Critical Thinking

MP.3 Ask students to discuss why values that are excluded from an addend in a sum of rational expressions must be excluded from the final simplified form of the sum, even if that value does not make the simplified expression undefined.

QUESTIONING STRATEGIES

? Why does the rational expression $\frac{x^2+1}{x^2-1}$ have two excluded values, but the expression $\frac{x^2-1}{x^2+1}$ have none? **The denominator of the first rational expression is equal to 0 when $x = 1$ and when $x = -1$. There is no real number that makes the denominator of the second expression equal to 0.**

SUMMARIZE THE LESSON

? How do you subtract two rational expressions? **If the denominators are like, subtract the numerators and write the result as the numerator over the common denominator. If the denominators are not alike, find the LCD, convert each rational expression to an equivalent expression having the LCD, and then follow the steps described above. If the second numerator contains more than one term, be careful to apply the distributive property when subtracting.**

10. Yvette ran at an average speed of 6.20 feet per second during the first two laps of a race and an average speed of 7.75 feet per second during the second two laps of a race. Find her total time in terms of d, the distance around the racecourse.

Total time: $\frac{2d}{6.2} + \frac{2d}{7.75}$

$$\frac{2d}{6.2} + \frac{2d}{7.75} = \frac{2(7.75 + 6.2)d}{7.75 \cdot 6.2}$$

$$= \frac{(2)(13.95)d}{48.05}$$

$$\cong 0.58d$$

Elaborate

11. Why do rational expressions have excluded values?

Excluded values would make the expression undefined.

12. How can you tell if your answer is written in simplest form?

When none of the factors of the denominator are factors of the numerator, the answer is written in simplest form.

13. Essential Question Check-In Why must the excluded values of each expression in a sum or difference of rational expressions also be excluded values for the simplified expression?

You cannot add or subtract undefined expressions so any value that makes one expression in a sum or difference undefined has to be an excluded value for the simplified expression.

Evaluate: Homework and Practice

- Online Homework
- Hints and Help
- Extra Practice

Given a rational expression, identify the excluded values by finding the zeroes of the denominator.

1. $\dfrac{x-1}{x^2+3x-4}$

$\dfrac{x-1}{x^2+3x-4} = \dfrac{x-1}{(x+4)(x-1)}$

$x \neq 1, x \neq -4$

2. $\dfrac{4}{x(x+17)}$

$\dfrac{4}{x(x+17)}$

$x \neq 0, x \neq -17$

Write the given expression as an equivalent rational expression that has the given denominator.

3. Expression: $\frac{x-7}{x+8}$

Denominator: $x^3 + 8x^2$

$x^3 + 8x^2 = x^2(x+8)$

$\dfrac{x-7}{x+8} = \dfrac{(x-7)x^2}{(x+8)x^2} = \dfrac{x^2(x-7)}{x^3+8x^2}$ or $\dfrac{x^3-7x^2}{x^3+8x^2}$

4. Expression: $\frac{3x^3}{3x-6}$

Denominator: $(2-x)(x^2+9)$

$\dfrac{3x^3}{3x-6} = \dfrac{x^3}{x-2} = \dfrac{-x^3}{2-x} = \dfrac{-x^3(x^2+9)}{(2-x)(x^2+9)}$

Simplify the given expression.

5. $\dfrac{(-4-4x)}{(x^2-x-2)}$

$\dfrac{(-4-4x)}{(x^2-x-2)} = \dfrac{-4(1+x)}{(x-2)(x+1)}$

$= \dfrac{-4\cancel{(1+x)}}{(x-2)\cancel{(1+x)}}$

$= \dfrac{-4}{(x-2)}$

$= \dfrac{4}{(2-x)}$

6. $\dfrac{-x-8}{x^2+9x+8}$

$\dfrac{-x-8}{x^2+9x+8} = \dfrac{-1\cancel{(x+8)}}{\cancel{(x+8)}(x+1)} = \dfrac{-1}{(x+1)}$

7. $\dfrac{6x^2+5x+1}{3x^2+4x+1}$

$\dfrac{6x^2+5x+1}{3x^2+4x+1} = \dfrac{\cancel{(3x+1)}(2x+1)}{\cancel{(3x+1)}(x+1)} = \dfrac{(2x+1)}{(x+1)}$

8. $\dfrac{x^4-1}{x^2+1}$

$\dfrac{x^4-1}{x^2+1} = \dfrac{\cancel{(x^2+1)}(x^2-1)}{\cancel{(x^2+1)}} = (x^2-1)$

Find the LCD for each set of rational expressions.

9. $\dfrac{x}{2x+16}$ and $\dfrac{-4x}{3x-27}$

$2x + 16 = 2(x+8)$

$3x - 27 = 3(x-9)$

List the different factors.

$2, 3, x+8, x-9$

LCD: $2 \cdot 3(x+8)(x-9) = 6(x+8)(x-9)$

10. $\dfrac{x^2-4}{5x-30}$ and $\dfrac{5x+13}{7x-42}$

Denominator factors: $5, 7, x-6$

$5 \cdot 7 \cdot (x-6) = 35(x-6)$

Exercise	Depth of Knowledge (D.O.K.)	COMMON CORE Mathematical Practices
1–2	**1** Recall of Information	**MP.5** Using Tools
3–24	**2** Skills/Concepts	**MP.2** Reasoning
25–27	**2** Skills/Concepts	**MP.4** Modeling
28	**3** Strategic Thinking H.O.T.	**MP.4** Modeling
29–30	**2** Skills/Concepts	**MP.4** Modeling
31–32	**3** Strategic Thinking H.O.T.	**MP.3** Logic

EVALUATE

ASSIGNMENT GUIDE

Concepts and Skills	Practice
Explore Identifying Excluded Values	Exercises 1–2
Example 1 Writing Equivalent Rational Expressions	Exercises 3–8
Example 2 Identifying the LCD of Two Rational Expressions	Exercises 9–14
Example 3 Adding and Subtracting Rational Expressions	Exercises 15–24
Example 4 Adding and Subtracting with Rational Models	Exercises 25–28

QUESTIONING STRATEGIES

? Why do some rational expressions have excluded values while others do not? **The denominators of some rational expressions contain factors that are equal to 0 for one or more values of *x*. Those rational expressions will have excluded values, since the rational expression is undefined for those values of *x*. In other rational expressions, no value of *x* makes the denominator equal to 0, so there are no excluded values.**

AVOID COMMON ERRORS

Students often list only the values that make the simplest form of a rational expression undefined. Stress the importance of recording all of the values for which the original expression is undefined.

INTEGRATE MATHEMATICAL PRACTICES

Focus on Math Connections

MP.1 Remind students that they can check their answers to a subtraction problem by adding the answer to the subtrahend to see if the result is the minuend. (If $a - b = c$, then $c + b = a$.) This is especially useful for checking that no sign errors were made when subtracting.

11. $\dfrac{4x + 12}{x^2 + 5x + 6}$ and $\dfrac{5x + 15}{10x + 20}$

$x^2 + 5x + 6 = (x + 2)(x + 3)$

$10x + 20 = 10(x + 2)$

$= 2 \cdot 5(x + 2)$

List the different factors.

$2, 5, x + 2, x + 3$

LCD: $2 \cdot 5(x + 2)(x + 3) = 10(x + 2)(x + 3)$

12. $\dfrac{-11}{x^2 - 3x - 28}$ and $\dfrac{2}{x^2 - 2x - 24}$

$x^2 - 3x - 28 = (x - 7)(x + 4)$

$x^2 - 2x - 24 = (x + 4)(x - 6)$

List the different factors.

$x - 7, x - 6, x + 4$

LCD: $(x - 7)(x - 6)(x + 4)$

13. $\dfrac{12}{3x^2 - 21x - 54}$ and $\dfrac{-1}{21x^2 - 84}$

$3x^2 - 21x - 54 = 3(x - 9)(x + 2)$

$21x^2 - 84x = 21(x + 2)(x - 2)$

$= 3 \cdot 7\,(x + 2)(x - 2)$

List the different factors.

$3, 7, x - 9, x + 2, x - 2$

LCD: $3 \cdot 7(x - 9)(x + 2)(x - 2)$

$= 21(x - 9)(x + 2)(x - 2)$

14. $\dfrac{3x}{5x^2 - 40x + 60}$ and $\dfrac{17}{-7x^2 + 56x + 84}$

$5x^2 - 40x + 60 = 5(x - 6)(x - 2)$

$-7x^2 + 56x + 84 = -7(x - 6)(x - 2)$

List the different factors.

$5, -7, x - 6, x - 2$

LCD: $5(-7)(x - 6)(x - 2)$

$= -35(x - 6)(x - 2)$

Add or subtract the given expressions, simplifying each result and noting the combined excluded values.

15. $\dfrac{1}{1 + x} + \dfrac{1 - x}{x}$

$$\frac{1}{1+x} + \frac{1-x}{x} = \frac{1x}{(1+x)x} + \frac{(1-x)(1+x)}{x(1+x)}$$

$$= \frac{x + 1 - x^2}{x(1+x)}$$

$$= \frac{-x^2 + x + 1}{x(1+x)},\ x \neq 0, -1$$

16. $\dfrac{x + 4}{x^2 - 4} + \dfrac{-2x - 2}{x^2 - 4}$

$$\frac{x+4}{x^2-4} + \frac{-2x-2}{x^2-4} = \frac{x+4-2x-2}{x^2-4}$$

$$= \frac{(-x+2)}{(x+2)(x-2)}$$

$$= \frac{-(x-2)}{(x+2)(x-2)}$$

$$= \frac{-1}{(x+2)},\ x \neq \pm 2$$

17. $\dfrac{1}{2+x} - \dfrac{2-x}{x}$

$$\frac{1}{2+x} - \frac{2-x}{x} = \frac{1x}{(2+x)x} - \frac{(2-x)(2+x)}{x(2+x)}$$
$$= \frac{x-(-x^2+4)}{x(x+2)}$$
$$= \frac{x+(x^2-4)}{x(x+2)}$$
$$= \frac{x^2+x-4}{x(x+2)},\ x \neq 0, -2$$

18. $\dfrac{4x^4+4}{x^2+1} - \dfrac{8}{x^2+1}$

$$\frac{4x^4+4}{x^2+1} - \frac{8}{x^2+1} = \frac{4x^4+4-8}{x^2+1}$$
$$= \frac{4x^4-4}{x^2+1}$$
$$= \frac{4(x^4-1)}{(x^2+1)}$$
$$= \frac{4\cancel{(x^2+1)}(x^2-1)}{\cancel{(x^2+1)}}$$
$$= 4(x^2-1)$$

$(x^2+1) = 0$ has no real solutions so no values are excluded.

19. $\dfrac{x^4-2}{x^2-2} + \dfrac{2}{-x^2+2}$

$$\frac{x^4-2}{x^2-2} + \frac{2}{-x^2+2} = \frac{x^4-2}{x^2-2} + \frac{-2}{x^2-2}$$
$$= \frac{x^4-4}{x^2-2}$$
$$= \frac{\cancel{(x^2-2)}(x^2+2)}{\cancel{(x^2-2)}}$$
$$= x^2+2,\ x \neq \pm\sqrt{2}$$

20. $\dfrac{1}{x^2+3x-4} - \dfrac{1}{x^2-3x+2}$

$$\frac{1}{x^2+3x-4} - \frac{1}{x^2-3x+2} = \frac{1}{(x-1)(x+4)} - \frac{1}{(x-1)(x-2)}$$
$$= \frac{(x-2)}{(x-1)(x+4)(x-2)} - \frac{x+4}{(x-1)(x-2)(x+4)}$$
$$= \frac{(x-2)-(x+4)}{(x-1)(x+4)(x-2)}$$
$$= \frac{-6}{(x-1)(x+4)(x-2)},\ x \neq -4, 1, 2$$

21. $\dfrac{3}{x^2-4} - \dfrac{x+5}{x+2}$

$$\frac{3}{x^2-4} - \frac{x+5}{x+2} = \frac{3}{(x+2)(x-2)} - \frac{x+5}{x+2}$$
$$= \frac{3}{(x+2)(x-2)} - \frac{(x+5)(x-2)}{(x+2)(x-2)}$$
$$= \frac{3-(x+5)(x-2)}{(x+2)(x-2)}$$
$$= \frac{3-(x^2+3x-10)}{(x+2)(x-2)}$$
$$= \frac{3-x^2-3x+10}{(x+2)(x-2)}$$
$$= \frac{-x^2-3x+13}{(x+2)(x-2)},\ x \neq \pm 2$$

22. $\dfrac{-3}{9x^2-4} + \dfrac{1}{3x^2+2x}$

$$\frac{-3}{9x^2-4} + \frac{1}{3x^2+2x} = \frac{-3}{(3x+2)(3x-2)} + \frac{1}{x(3x+2)}$$
$$= \frac{-3x}{x(3x+2)(3x-2)} + \frac{(3x-2)}{x(3x+2)(3x-2)}$$
$$= \frac{-2}{x(3x+2)(3x-2)},\ x \neq 0, \pm\frac{2}{3}$$

MODELING

When working with rational expressions that represent real-world situations, students should recognize that not only must they consider excluded values that are based on the algebraic nature of the denominators of the expressions, but they also need to consider values that must be excluded due to the limitations on the domain in the given situation.

VISUAL CUES

When students simplify rational expressions, suggest that they highlight each different factor in the numerator and denominator with a different color by using highlighters or colored pencils. This process can help them keep track of common factors, as shown below.

$$\frac{x^2(x+1)(x-2)^2}{x(x+3)(x+1)} = \frac{x(x-2)^2}{x+3}$$

23. $\frac{x-2}{x+2} + \frac{1}{x^2-4} - \frac{x+2}{2-x}$

$$\frac{x-2}{x+2} + \frac{1}{x^2-4} - \frac{x+2}{2-x} = \frac{x-2}{x+2} + \frac{1}{(x+2)(x-2)} + \frac{x+2}{x-2}$$

$$= \frac{(x-2)(x-2)}{(x+2)(x-2)} + \frac{1}{(x+2)(x-2)} + \frac{(x+2)(x+2)}{(x-2)(x+2)}$$

$$= \frac{x^2-4x+4+1+x^2+4x+4}{(x+2)(x-2)}$$

$$= \frac{2x^2+9}{(x+2)(x-2)}, x \neq \pm 2$$

24. $\frac{x-3}{x+3} - \frac{1}{x-3} + \frac{x+2}{3-x}$

$$\frac{x-3}{x+3} - \frac{1}{x-3} + \frac{x+2}{3-x} = \frac{x-3}{x+3} + \frac{-1}{x-3} + \frac{-x-2}{x-3}$$

$$= \frac{x-3}{x+3} + \frac{-x-3}{x-3}$$

$$= \frac{(x-3)(x-3)}{(x+3)(x-3)} + \frac{(-x-3)(x+3)}{(x-3)(x+3)}$$

$$= \frac{x^2-6x+9-x^2-6x-9}{(x-3)(x+3)}$$

$$= \frac{-12x}{(x-3)(x+3)}, x \neq \pm 3$$

25. The owner of store A and store B wants to know the average cost of both stores. Store A has an average cost of $\frac{100+2q}{q}$, and store B has an average cost of $\frac{200+q}{2q}$, where both stores have the same output, q. Find an expression to represent the cost of both stores.

$$\frac{100+2q}{q} + \frac{200+q}{2q} = \frac{(2)(100+2q)}{(2)q} + \frac{200+q}{2q}$$

$$= \frac{200+4q+200+q}{2q}$$

$$= \frac{400+5q}{2q}$$

The cost can be represented by $= \frac{400+5q}{2q}$.

26. An auto race consists of 8 laps. A driver completes the first 3 laps at an average speed of 185 miles per hour and the remaining laps at an average speed of 200 miles per hour. Let d represent the length of one lap. Find the time in terms of d that it takes the driver to complete the race.

$$\frac{3d}{185} + \frac{5d}{200} = \frac{3d(200)}{185(200)} + \frac{5d(185)}{200(185)}$$

$$= \frac{600d+925d}{37{,}000}$$

$$= \frac{61d}{1480} \text{ hours}$$

27. The junior and senior classes of a high school are cleaning up a beach. Each class has pledged to clean 1600 meters of shoreline. The junior class has 12 more students than the senior class. Let s represent the number of students in the senior class. Write and simplify an expression in terms of s that represents the difference between the number of meters of shoreline each senior must clean and the meters each junior must clean.

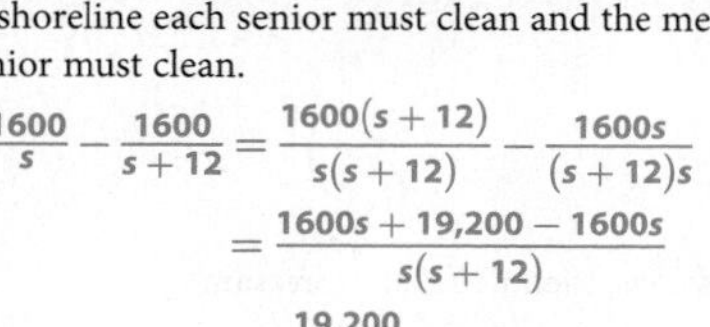

$$\frac{1600}{s} - \frac{1600}{s+12} = \frac{1600(s+12)}{s(s+12)} - \frac{1600s}{(s+12)s}$$
$$= \frac{1600s + 19{,}200 - 1600s}{s(s+12)}$$
$$= \frac{19{,}200}{s(s+12)} \text{ meters}$$

28. Architecture The Renaissance architect Andrea Palladio believed that the height of a room with vaulted ceilings should be the harmonic mean of the length and width. The harmonic mean of two positive numbers a and b is equal to $\frac{2}{\frac{1}{a}+\frac{1}{b}}$. Simplify this expression. What are the excluded values? What do they mean in this problem?

$\frac{2}{\frac{1}{a}+\frac{1}{b}} = \frac{2}{\frac{1b}{ab}+\frac{1a}{ba}} = \frac{2}{\left(\frac{b+a}{ab}\right)} = \frac{2ab}{a+b}$, **excluding** $a = 0, b = 0, a = -b$.

These values do not occur because geometric lengths are positive.

29. Match each expression with the correct excluded value(s).

a. $\frac{3x+5}{x+2}$ C — no excluded values

b. $\frac{1+x}{x^2-1}$ D — $x \neq 0, -2$

c. $\frac{3x^4-12}{x^2+4}$ B — $x \neq 1, -1$

d. $\frac{3x+6}{x^2(x+2)}$ A — $x \neq -2$

A. $\frac{3x+5}{x+2}, x \neq -2$

B. $\frac{1+x}{x^2-1}, x \neq 1, -1$

C. $\frac{3x^4-12}{x^2+4}$, **no excluded values**

D. $\frac{3x+6}{x^2(x+2)}, x \neq 0, -2$

CONNECT VOCABULARY EL

Have students explain why a rational expression has excluded values for a denominator of zero, using what they know about fractions or ratios to explain. Help them by re-voicing or clarifying their explanations, as needed.

JOURNAL

Have students compare the method used to add two rational numbers to the method used to add two rational expressions. Have them use specific examples to illustrate their explanations.

H.O.T. Focus on Higher Order Thinking

30. Explain the Error George was asked to write the expression $2x - 3$ with excluded values placed one at a time at $x = 1$, $x = 2$, and $x = -3$. He wrote the following expressions:

a. $\frac{2x - 3}{x - 1}$

b. $\frac{2x - 3}{x - 2}$

c. $\frac{2x - 3}{x + 3}$

What error did George make? Write the correct expressions, then write an expression that has all three excluded values.

George wrote expressions that had the correct excluded values, but his expressions are not equivalent to $2x - 3$. The correct expressions should be the following:

a. $\frac{(2x-3)(x-1)}{x-1}$

b. $\frac{(2x-3)(x-2)}{x-2}$

c. $\frac{(2x-3)(x+3)}{x+3}$

$2x - 3 = \frac{(2x-3)(x-1)(x-2)(x+3)}{(x-1)(x-2)(x+3)}, x \neq 1, 2, -3$

31. Communicate Mathematical Ideas Write a rational expression with excluded values at $x = 0$ and $x = 17$.

Answers may vary. Sample answer:

$\frac{a}{x(x-17)}$

32. Critical Thinking Sketch the graph of the rational equation $y = \frac{x^2 + 3x + 2}{x + 1}$. Think about how to graphically show that a graph exists over a domain except at one point.

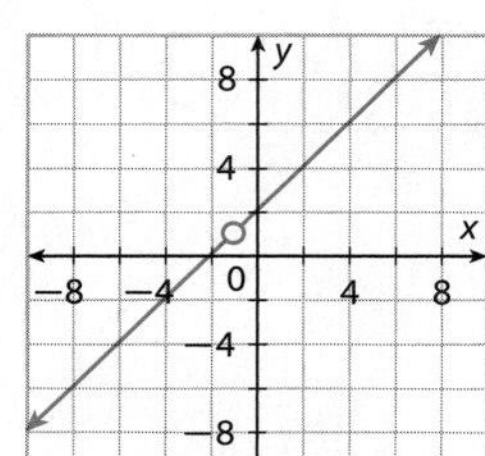

This expression has an excluded value at $x = -1$. This can be shown on the graph with a hole at that one point.

Lesson Performance Task

A kayaker spends an afternoon paddling on a river. She travels 3 miles upstream and 3 miles downstream in a total of 4 hours. In still water, the kayaker can travel at an average speed of 2 miles per hour. Based on this information, can you estimate the average speed of the river's current? Is your answer reasonable?

Next, assume the average speed of the kayaker is an unknown, k, and not necessarily 2 miles per hour. What is the range of possible average kayaker speeds under the rest of the constraints?

Total time is equal to time upstream plus time downstream.

$$T = \frac{D}{r_1} + \frac{D}{r_2} = D\left(\frac{1}{r_1} + \frac{1}{r_2}\right) = D\left(\frac{r_1 + r_2}{r_1 r_2}\right)$$

$$\frac{T}{D}(r_1 r_2) = r_1 + r_2$$

Substitute for r_1 and r_2:

$$\frac{T}{D}(2 - c)(2 + c) = (2 - \cancel{c}) + (2 + \cancel{c}) = 4$$

$$(4 - c^2) = 4\frac{D}{T}$$

$$c^2 - 4 = -4\frac{D}{T}$$

Plug in specific constants:

$$c^2 = -4\frac{D}{T} + 4 = -\cancel{4}\left(\frac{3}{\cancel{4}}\right) + 4 = -3 + 4 = 1$$

$$c = \pm\sqrt{1} = \pm 1$$

The answer is 1 mile per hour only because the speed in this context cannot be negative.

To figure out the range of speeds of the kayaker in the river, we replace k for 2 above.

$$\frac{T}{D}(k - c)(k + c) = (k - \cancel{c}) + (k + \cancel{c}) = 2k$$

$$(k^2 - c^2) = 2k\frac{D}{T}$$

$$c^2 - k^2 = -2k\frac{D}{T}$$

$$c^2 = -2k\frac{D}{T} + k^2$$

$$c = \pm\sqrt{-2k\frac{D}{T} + k^2} \rightarrow -2k\frac{D}{T} + k^2 \geq 0$$

$$k^2 \geq 2k\frac{D}{T}$$

$$k \geq 2\frac{D}{T} = 2 \cdot \frac{3}{4} = 1.5 \text{ miles per hour}$$

The kayaker has to go at least 1.5 miles per hour regardless of the speed of the current.

EXTENSION ACTIVITY

Have students explain how the presence of a strong wind might affect the time it takes the kayaker to travel up and down the river. Ask the students how they would account for the wind in their calculations. **Add or subtract a wind factor when calculating the rates. For example, for an upstream wind the speed of the kayaker upstream would be $r_1 = 2 - c - w$ and the speed of the kayaker downstream would be $r_1 = 2 - c + w$, where w is the corrective factor for the wind.**

CONNECT VOCABULARY EL

Some students may not be familiar with the term *kayak*. Have a student volunteer describe a kayak. Explain that *kayak* is used both as a noun and as a verb, and that the person paddling a kayak is called a *kayaker*.

AVOID COMMON ERRORS

Students may divide the total distance (6 miles) by the total time (4 hours) to get an average speed of 1.5 miles per hour, but this is incorrect. Ask students why the upstream and downstream travel times need to be calculated separately. **The kayaker is traveling at a different speed in each direction due to the river current.** Ask students what quantity is the same in both directions. **distance** Ask students what quantities are different in each direction. **the travel time and speed of the kayaker**

Scoring Rubric

2 points: Student correctly solves the problem and explains his/her reasoning.

1 point: Student shows good understanding of the problem but does not fully solve or explain his/her reasoning.

0 points: Student does not demonstrate understanding of the problem.

Multiplying and Dividing Rational Expressions

Common Core Math Standards

The student is expected to:

A-APR.D.7(+)

Understand that rational expressions form a system ... closed under addition, subtraction, multiplication, and division by a nonzero rational expression; ... multiply, and divide rational expressions. Also F-BF.A.1b

Mathematical Practices

COMMON CORE **MP.8 Patterns**

Language Objective

Explain to a partner the steps for multiplying and dividing rational expressions.

ENGAGE

Essential Question: How can you multiply and divide rational expressions?

To find the product of rational expressions, factor each numerator and denominator, multiply the numerators and denominators, and simplify the resulting rational expression that is the product. To find the quotient of rational expressions, multiply by the reciprocal of the divisor and then follow the steps for multiplying rational expressions.

PREVIEW: LESSON PERFORMANCE TASK

View the Engage section online. Discuss the photo and how the heat generated by a runner's body could depend on height. Then preview the Lesson Performance Task.

Name ____________ Class ________ Date ________

9.2 Multiplying and Dividing Rational Expressions

Resource Locker

Essential Question: How can you multiply and divide rational expressions?

Explore Relating Multiplication Concepts

Use the facts you know about multiplying rational numbers to determine how to multiply rational expressions.

(A) How do you multiply $\frac{4}{5} \cdot \frac{5}{6}$?

Multiply 4 by **5** to find the **numerator** of the product, and multiply 5 by **6** to find the **denominator**.

(B) $\frac{4}{5} \cdot \frac{5}{6} = \frac{20}{30}$

(C) To simplify, factor the numerator and denominator.

$20 = 2 \cdot 2 \cdot 5$

$30 = 2 \cdot 3 \cdot 5$

(D) Cancel common factors in the numerator and denominator to simplify the product.

$\frac{4}{5} \cdot \frac{5}{6} = \frac{20}{30} = \frac{2 \cdot 2 \cdot 5}{2 \cdot 3 \cdot 5} = \frac{2}{3}$

(E) Based on the steps used for multiplying rational numbers, how can you multiply the rational expression $\frac{x+1}{x-1} \cdot \frac{3}{2(x+1)}$?

Multiply $x + 1$ by 3 to find the numerator of the product, and multiply $x - 1$ by $2(x + 1)$ to find the denominator. Then cancel common factors to simplify the product.

Reflect

1. **Discussion** Multiplying rational expressions is similar to multiplying rational numbers. Likewise, dividing rational expressions is similar to dividing rational numbers. How could you use the steps for dividing rational numbers to divide rational expressions?

When dividing rational numbers, multiply by the reciprocal of the divisor and follow the steps for multiplying rational numbers. So, when dividing rational expressions, multiply by the reciprocal of the divisor and follow the steps for multiplying rational expressions.

HARDCOVER PAGES 439–452

Watch for the hardcover student edition page numbers for this lesson.

Explain 1 Multiplying Rational Expressions

To multiply rational expressions, multiply the numerators to find the numerator of the product, and multiply the denominators to find the denominator. Then, simplify the product by cancelling common factors.

Note the excluded values of the product, which are any values of the variable for which the expression is undefined.

Example 1 **Find the products and any excluded values.**

(A) $\dfrac{3x^2}{x^2-2x-8} \cdot \dfrac{2x^2-6x-20}{x^2-3x-10}$

$\dfrac{3x^2}{x^2-2x-8} \cdot \dfrac{2x^2-6x-20}{x^2-3x-10} = \dfrac{3x^2}{(x+2)(x-4)} \cdot \dfrac{2(x+2)(x-5)}{(x+2)(x-5)}$ Factor the numerators and denominators.

$= \dfrac{6x^2(x+2)(x-5)}{(x+2)(x-4)(x+2)(x-5)}$ Multiply the numerators and multiply the denominators.

$= \dfrac{6x^2\cancel{(x+2)}\cancel{(x-5)}}{\cancel{(x+2)}(x-4)(x+2)\cancel{(x-5)}}$ Cancel the common factors in the numerator and denominator.

$= \dfrac{6x^2}{(x+2)(x-4)}$

Determine what values of x make each expression undefined.

$\dfrac{3x^2}{x^2-2x-8}$: The denominator is 0 when $x = -2$ and $x = 4$.

$\dfrac{2x^2-6x-20}{x^2-3x-10}$: The denominator is 0 when $x = -2$ and $x = 5$.

Excluded values: $x = -2$, $x = 4$, and $x = 5$

(B) $\dfrac{x^2-8x}{14(x^2+8x+15)} \cdot \dfrac{7x+35}{x+8}$

$\dfrac{x^2-8x}{14(x^2+8x+15)} \cdot \dfrac{7x+35}{x+8} = \dfrac{x(x-8)}{14(x+3)(x+5)} \cdot \dfrac{7(x+5)}{x+8}$ Factor the numerators and denominators.

$= \dfrac{7x(x-8)(x+5)}{14(x+3)(x+5)(x+8)}$ Multiply the numerators and multiply the denominators.

$= \dfrac{x(x-8)}{2(x+3)(x+8)}$ Cancel the common factors in the numerator and denominator.

Determine what values of x make each expression undefined.

$\dfrac{x^2-8x}{14(x^2+8x+15)}$: The denominator is 0 when $x = -3$ and $x = -5$.

$\dfrac{7x+35}{x+8}$: The denominator is 0 when $x = -8$.

Excluded values: $x = -3$, $x = -5$, and $x = -8$

PROFESSIONAL DEVELOPMENT

Learning Progressions

Students learned how to simplify rational expressions in the previous lesson. They also know how to multiply and divide numerical fractions. Here, they combine those skills to multiply and divide rational expressions. Students apply their knowledge of factoring, as well as of multiplying polynomials, to simplify expressions involving multiplication and division of rational expressions. The concept of excluded values will carry over into later studies, for example, in excluding extraneous values in the simplification of logarithms.

EXPLORE

Relating Multiplication Concepts

INTEGRATE TECHNOLOGY

Students have the option of completing the Explore activity either in the book or online.

QUESTIONING STRATEGIES

What are two different ways of multiplying $\dfrac{2x^2y}{6xy} \cdot \dfrac{3y}{4x}$? **Multiply across and then simplify the result, or divide out common factors of the numerators and denominators and then multiply across. In either case, the result will be $\dfrac{y}{4}$.**

EXPLAIN 1

Multiplying Rational Expressions

AVOID COMMON ERRORS

Students sometimes confuse multiplying rational expressions with cross-multiplying. Point out that cross-multiplying takes place across an equal sign when solving equations of the form $\frac{a}{b} = \frac{c}{d}$. Tell students to use the equal sign as the cue to cross multiply. When multiplying rational expressions, multiply straight across.

QUESTIONING STRATEGIES

Why should you factor the numerators and the denominators before you multiply? **It makes it easier to multiply because you can divide out common factors from a numerator and a denominator before multiplying.**

INTEGRATE MATHEMATICAL PRACTICES

Focus on Reasoning

MP.2 Students should recognize that multiplying two rational expressions does not introduce excluded values. The excluded values of the product are the combined excluded values of the original rational expressions. Students can use this fact to help detect errors in their work.

EXPLAIN 2

Dividing Rational Expressions

QUESTIONING STRATEGIES

? How is the procedure for dividing rational expressions related to multiplying rational expressions? **Dividing by an expression is equivalent to multiplying by its reciprocal. Once division is converted to multiplication, you can carry out the steps for multiplying rational expressions.**

? Why must you exclude values of the variable that make the numerator of the divisor 0? **If the numerator of a fraction is 0, then the fraction equals 0. Since division by 0 is undefined, the divisor cannot be equal to 0.**

Your Turn

Find the products and any excluded values.

2. $\frac{x^2-9}{x^2-5x-24} \cdot \frac{x-8}{2x^2-18x}$

$= \frac{(x+3)(x-3)}{(x+3)(x-8)} \cdot \frac{x-8}{2x(x-9)}$

$= \frac{(x+3)(x-3)(x-8)}{2x(x+3)(x-8)(x-9)}$

$= \frac{(x-3)}{2x(x-9)}$

Excluded values: $x = -3$, $x = 8$, $x = 0$, and $x = 9$

3. $\frac{x}{x-9} \cdot \frac{3x-27}{x+1}$

$= \frac{x}{(x-9)} \cdot \frac{3(x-9)}{x+1}$

$= \frac{3x(x-9)}{(x-9)(x+1)}$

$= \frac{3x}{x+1}$

Excluded values: $x = -1$ and $x = 9$

Explain 2 Dividing Rational Expressions

To divide rational expressions, change the division problem to a multiplication problem by multiplying by the reciprocal. Then, follow the steps for multiplying rational expressions.

Example 2 **Find the quotients and any excluded values.**

(A) $\frac{(x+7)^2}{x^2} \div \frac{x^2+9x+14}{x^2+x-2}$

$\frac{(x+7)^2}{x^2} \div \frac{x^2+9x+14}{x^2+x-2} = \frac{(x+7)^2}{x^2} \cdot \frac{x^2+x-2}{x^2+9x+14}$ — Multiply by the reciprocal.

$= \frac{(x+7)(x+7)}{x^2} \cdot \frac{(x+2)(x-1)}{(x+7)(x+2)}$ — Factor the numerators and denominators.

$= \frac{(x+7)(x+7)(x+2)(x-1)}{x^2(x+7)(x+2)}$ — Multiply the numerators and multiply the denominators.

$= \frac{(x\cancel{+7})(x+7)(x\cancel{+2})(x-1)}{x^2(x\cancel{+7})(x\cancel{+2})}$ — Cancel the common factors in the numerator and denominator.

$= \frac{x+7(x-1)}{x^2}$

Determine what values of x make each expression undefined.

$\frac{(x+7)^2}{x}$: The denominator is 0 when $x = 0$.

$\frac{x^2+9x+14}{x^2+x-2}$: The denominator is 0 when $x = -2$ and $x = 1$.

$\frac{x^2+x-2}{x^2+9x+14}$: The denominator is 0 when $x = -7$ and $x = -2$.

Excluded values: $x = 0$, $x = -7$, $x = 1$, and $x = -2$

COLLABORATIVE LEARNING

Peer-to-Peer Activity

Have students work in pairs. Instruct each pair to create a problem involving the division of two rational expressions by working backward from the factored form of the numerators and denominators. Have them rewrite the problem, multiplying the factors in each numerator and denominator. Then have them exchange problems with another pair, and find the quotient. Have each pair compare their answer to the answer determined by the students who created the problem.

(B) $\dfrac{6x}{3x-30} \div \dfrac{9x^2-27x-36}{x^2-10x}$

$\dfrac{6x}{3x-30} \div \dfrac{9x^2-27x-36}{x^2-10x} = \dfrac{6x}{3x-30} \cdot \dfrac{\boxed{x^2-10x}}{\boxed{9x^2-27x-36}}$ Multiply by the reciprocal.

$= \dfrac{6x}{3\left(\boxed{x-10}\right)} \cdot \dfrac{x\left(\boxed{x-10}\right)}{9(x+1)\left(\boxed{x-4}\right)}$ Factor the numerators and denominators.

$= \dfrac{6x^2\left(\boxed{x-10}\right)}{27\left(\boxed{x-10}\right)(x+1)\left(\boxed{x-4}\right)}$ Multiply the numerators and multiply the denominators.

$= \dfrac{\boxed{2x^2}}{\boxed{9(x+1)(x-4)}}$ Cancel the common factors in the numerator and denominator.

Determine what values of x make each expression undefined.

$\dfrac{6x}{3x-30}$: The denominator is 0 when $\boxed{x=10}$.

$\dfrac{9x^2-27x-36}{x^2-10x}$: The denominator is 0 when $\boxed{x=10 \text{ and } x=0}$.

$\dfrac{x^2-10x}{9x^2-27x-36}$: The denominator is 0 when $\boxed{x=-1 \text{ and } x=4}$.

Excluded values: $\boxed{x=0, x=10, x=-1, \text{ and } x=4}$

Your Turn

Find the quotients and any excluded values.

4. $\dfrac{x+11}{4x} \div \dfrac{2x+6}{x^2+2x-3}$

$= \dfrac{x+11}{4x} \cdot \dfrac{x^2+2x-3}{2x+6}$

$= \dfrac{(x+11)}{4x} \cdot \dfrac{(x-1)(x+3)}{2(x+3)}$

$= \dfrac{(x+11)(x-1)(x+3)}{8x(x+3)}$

$= \dfrac{(x+11)(x-1)}{8x}$

Excluded values: $x=0$, $x=1$, and $x=-3$

5. $\dfrac{20}{x^2-7x} \div \dfrac{5x^2-40x}{x^2-15x+56}$

$= \dfrac{20}{x^2-7x} \cdot \dfrac{x^2-15x+56}{5x^2-40x}$

$= \dfrac{20}{x(x-7)} \cdot \dfrac{(x-8)(x-7)}{5x(x-8)}$

$= \dfrac{20(x-8)(x-7)}{5x^2(x-7)(x-8)}$

$= \dfrac{4}{x^2}$

Excluded values: $x=0$, $x=7$, and $x=8$

INTEGRATE MATHEMATICAL PRACTICES

Focus on Critical Thinking

MP.3 Prompt students to recognize that they can check their solutions to division problems by multiplying the quotient by the divisor and checking to see that the result is the dividend.

DIFFERENTIATE INSTRUCTION

Graphic Organizers

Have students copy and complete the graphic organizer shown below, writing a worked-out example in each box.

	Numerical Fractions	Rational Expressions
Adding		
Subtracting		
Multiplying		
Dividing		

EXPLAIN 3

Activity: Investigating Closure

AVOID COMMON ERRORS

Students may think that a single example is sufficient to prove that a set is closed. While a single counterexample is enough to prove that a set is not closed, the general result must be proven to show closure. For example, the integer division $8 \div 2 = 4$ is an integer, but the integers are not closed under division.

QUESTIONING STRATEGIES

? How do you determine whether a set of polynomials or rational expressions is closed under a given operation? **Define the members of the described set. Then investigate the set to determine whether the given operation always results in a member of the set.**

INTEGRATE MATHEMATICAL PRACTICES

Focus on Communication

MP.3 For most students, it will be easier to give a counter example to show that a set is *not* closed than to explain why a set *is* closed. Encourage students to use variables such as a and b to represent elements of the set, and try to determine the general result of the operation on a and b.

Explain 3 Activity: Investigating Closure

A set of numbers is said to be closed, or to have **closure**, under a given operation if the result of the operation on any two numbers in the set is also in the set.

(A) Recall whether the set of whole numbers, the set of integers, and the set of rational numbers are closed under each of the four basic operations.

	Addition	Subtraction	Multiplication	Division
Whole Numbers	Closed	Not Closed	Closed	Not Closed
Integers	Closed	Closed	Closed	Not Closed
Rational Numbers	Closed	Closed	Closed	Closed

(B) Look at the set of rational expressions. Use the rational expressions $\frac{p(x)}{q(x)}$ and $\frac{r(x)}{s(x)}$ where $p(x)$, $q(x)$, $r(x)$ and $s(x)$ are nonzero. Add the rational expressions.

$$\frac{p(x)}{q(x)} + \frac{r(x)}{s(x)} = \frac{p(x)s(x) + q(x)r(x)}{q(x)s(x)}$$

(C) Is the set of rational expressions closed under addition? Explain.
Yes; since $q(x)$ and $s(x)$ are nonzero, $q(x)s(x)$ is nonzero. So, $\frac{p(x)s(x) + q(x)r(x)}{q(x)s(x)}$ is again a rational expression.

(D) Subtract the rational expressions.

$$\frac{p(x)}{q(x)} - \frac{r(x)}{s(x)} = \frac{p(x)s(x) - q(x)r(x)}{q(x)s(x)}$$

(E) Is the set of rational expressions closed under subtraction? Explain.
Yes; since $q(x)$ and $s(x)$ are nonzero, $q(x)s(x)$ is nonzero. So, $\frac{p(x)s(x) - q(x)r(x)}{q(x)s(x)}$ is again a rational expression.

(F) Multiply the rational expressions.

$$\frac{p(x)}{q(x)} \cdot \frac{r(x)}{s(x)} = \frac{p(x)r(x)}{q(x)s(x)}$$

(G) Is the set of rational expressions closed under multiplication? Explain.
Yes; since $q(x)$ and $s(x)$ are nonzero, $q(x)s(x)$ is nonzero. So, $\frac{p(x)r(x)}{q(x)s(x)}$ is again a rational expression.

(H) Divide the rational expressions.

$$\frac{p(x)}{q(x)} \div \frac{r(x)}{s(x)} = \frac{p(x)s(x)}{q(x)r(x)}$$

(I) Is the set of rational expressions closed under division? Explain.
Yes; since $q(x)$ and $r(x)$ are nonzero, $q(x)r(x)$ is nonzero. So, $\frac{p(x)s(x)}{q(x)r(x)}$ is again a rational expression.

Reflect

6. Are rational expressions most like whole numbers, integers, or rational numbers? Explain.
Rational expressions are like rational numbers because both the set of rational expressions and the set of rational numbers are closed under all four basic operations.

Explain 4 Multiplying and Dividing with Rational Models

Models involving rational expressions can be solved using the same steps to multiply or divide rational expressions.

Example 3 **Solve the problems using rational expressions.**

(A) Leonard drives 40 miles to work every day. One-fifth of his drive is on city roads, where he averages 30 miles per hour. The other part of his drive is on a highway, where he averages 55 miles per hour. The expression $\frac{d_c r_h + d_h r_c}{r_c r_h}$ represents the total time spent driving, in hours. In the expression, d_c represents the distance traveled on city roads, d_h represents the distance traveled on the highway, r_c is the average speed on city roads, and r_h is the average speed on the highway. Use the expression to find the average speed of Leonard's drive.

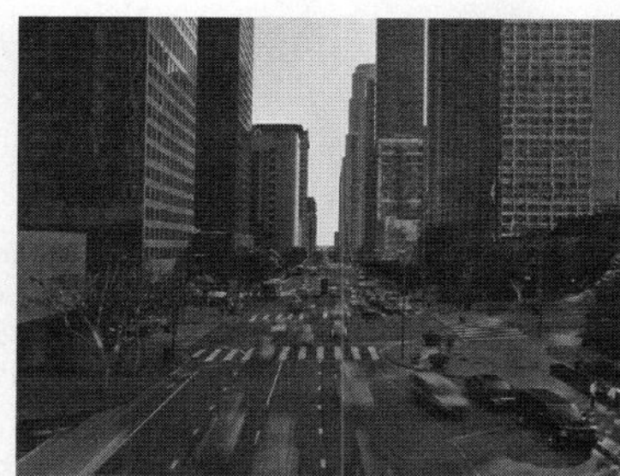

The total distance traveled is 40 miles. Find an expression for the average speed, r, of Leonard's drive.

$$r = \text{Total distance traveled} \div \text{Total time}$$
$$= 40 \div \frac{d_c r_h + d_h r_c}{r_c r_h}$$
$$= 40 \cdot \frac{r_c r_h}{d_c r_h + d_h r_c}$$
$$= \frac{40 r_c r_h}{d_c r_h + d_h r_c}$$

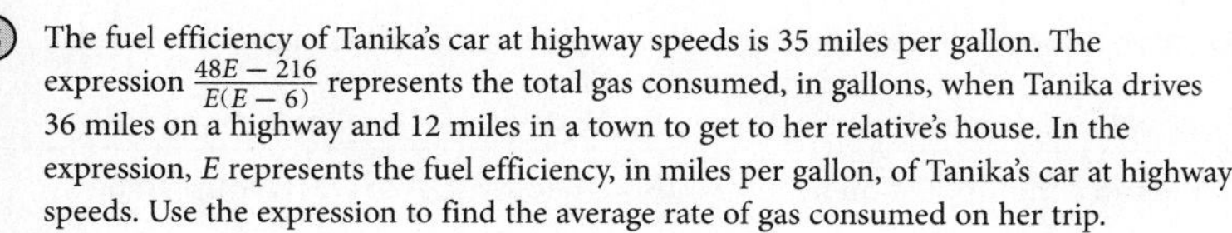

Find the values of d_c and d_h.

$d_c = \frac{1}{5}(40) = 8$ miles

$d_h = 40 - 8 = 32$ miles

Solve for r by substituting in the given values from the problem.

$$r = \frac{d r_c r_h}{d_c r_h + d_h r_c}$$
$$= \frac{40 \cdot 55 \cdot 30}{8 \cdot 55 + 32 \cdot 30}$$
$$\approx 47 \text{ miles per hour}$$

The average speed of Leonard's drive is about 47 miles per hour.

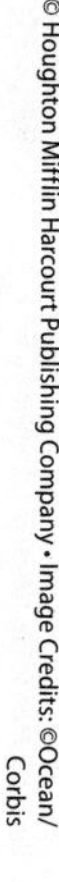

(B) The fuel efficiency of Tanika's car at highway speeds is 35 miles per gallon. The expression $\frac{48E - 216}{E(E-6)}$ represents the total gas consumed, in gallons, when Tanika drives 36 miles on a highway and 12 miles in a town to get to her relative's house. In the expression, E represents the fuel efficiency, in miles per gallon, of Tanika's car at highway speeds. Use the expression to find the average rate of gas consumed on her trip.

EXPLAIN 4

Multiplying and Dividing with Rational Models

QUESTIONING STRATEGIES

? How do you determine the excluded values in a real-world problem that involves dividing two rational expressions? **Find the values that make each denominator 0 and that make the numerator of the divisor 0. Also, determine numbers that are not reasonable values for the independent variable in the situation.**

INTEGRATE MATHEMATICAL PRACTICES

Focus on Modeling

MP.4 Discuss with students how the rational expressions used in the example model the situation. Discuss what each numerator and denominator represents, and why a quotient of these quantities is an appropriate model.

ELABORATE

INTEGRATE MATHEMATICAL PRACTICES

Focus on Communication

MP.3 Call upon students to describe each step involved in the solution to a problem involving division of two rational expressions. Make sure they use accurate mathematical language in describing not only the division process, but also how to identify excluded values of the variable.

SUMMARIZE THE LESSON

? How do you divide two rational expressions? **Multiply the first rational expression by the reciprocal of the second. Factor each numerator and denominator, and then multiply numerators and multiply denominators. Divide out common factors of the numerators and denominators.**

The total distance traveled is 48 miles. Find an expression for the average rate of gas consumed, g, on Tanika's trip.

$g =$ Total gas consumed $\div$ Total distance traveled

$$= \frac{48E - 216}{E(E-6)} \div 48$$

$$= \frac{48E - 216}{48E(E-6)}$$

The value of E is 35.

Solve for g by substituting in the value of E.

$$g = \frac{48(35) - 216}{48(35)(35 - 6)}$$

$$= \frac{1464}{48{,}720}$$

$$\approx 0.03$$

The average rate of gas consumed on Tanika's trip is about 0.03 gallon per mile.

Your Turn

7. The distance traveled by a car undergoing constant acceleration, a, for a time, t, is given by $d = v_0t + \frac{1}{2}at^2$ where v_0 is the initial velocity of the car. Two cars are side by side with the same initial velocity. One car accelerates and the other car does not. Write an expression for the ratio of the distance traveled by the accelerating car to the distance traveled by the nonaccelerating car as a function of time.

Let A be the acceleration of the accelerating car.

Accelerating car: $d = v_0t + \frac{1}{2}At^2$

Nonaccelerating car: $d = v_0t + \frac{1}{2}(0)t^2 = v_0t$

$$\frac{\text{Distance of accelerating car}}{\text{Distance of nonaccelerating car}} = \frac{v_0t + \frac{1}{2}At^2}{v_0t}$$

$$= \frac{v_0t}{v_0t} + \frac{\frac{1}{2}At^2}{v_0t}$$

$$= 1 + \frac{At}{2v_0}$$

The ratio as a function of time is $1 + \frac{At}{2v_0}$.

Elaborate

8. Explain how finding excluded values when dividing one rational expression by another is different from multiplying two rational expressions.
When finding excluded values of a product of two rational expressions, find the values of x for which the denominator of the one of the expressions is 0. When finding excluded values when dividing one rational expression by another, find the values of x for which the denominator of the first expression or the numerator of the second expression is 0.

9. Essential Question Check-In How is dividing rational expressions related to multiplying rational expressions?
When dividing rational expressions, find the reciprocal of the divisor and change the division problem to a multiplication problem. Then follow the steps for multiplying rational expressions.

LANGUAGE SUPPORT EL

Communicate Math

Have students work in pairs. Provide each pair of students with some rational expressions to multiply or divide, written on sticky notes or index cards. Have the first student explain the steps to multiply rational expressions while the second student writes notes. Students switch roles and repeat the process for a division problem, highlighting the additional step of using the reciprocal.

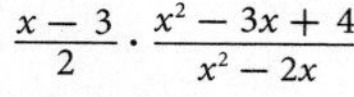

Evaluate: Homework and Practice

• Online Homework
• Hints and Help
• Extra Practice

1. Explain how to multiply the rational expressions.

$\frac{x-3}{2} \cdot \frac{x^2-3x+4}{x^2-2x}$

Multiply $x - 13$ by $x^2 - 3x + 4$ to get the numerator of the product. Multiply 2 by $x^2 - 2x$ to get the denominator of the product. Then, simplify by cancelling common factors in the numerator and the denominator.

Find the products and any excluded values.

2. $\frac{x}{3x-6} \cdot \frac{x-2}{x+9}$

$= \frac{x}{3(x-2)} \cdot \frac{x-2}{x+9}$

$= \frac{x(x-2)}{3(x-2)(x+9)}$

$= \frac{x}{3(x+9)}$

Excluded values: $x = 2$ and $x = -9$

3. $\frac{5x^2+25x}{2} \cdot \frac{4x}{x+5}$

$= \frac{5x(x+5)}{2} \cdot \frac{4x}{x+5}$

$= \frac{20x^2(x+5)}{2(x+5)}$

$= 10x^2$

Excluded values: $x = -5$

4. $\frac{x^2-2x-15}{10x+30} \cdot \frac{3}{x^2-3x-10}$

$= \frac{(x-5)(x+3)}{10(x+3)} \cdot \frac{3}{(x+2)(x-5)}$

$= \frac{3(x-5)(x+3)}{10(x+3)(x+2)(x-5)}$

$= \frac{3}{10(x+2)}$

Excluded values: $x = -3$, $x = -2$, and $x = 5$

5. $\frac{x^2-1}{x^2+5x+4} \cdot \frac{x^2}{x^2-x}$

$= \frac{(x-1)(x+1)}{(x+4)(x+1)} \cdot \frac{x^2}{x(x-1)}$

$= \frac{(x-1)(x+1)x^2}{x(x+4)(x+1)(x-1)}$

$= \frac{x}{x+4}$

Excluded values: $x = -4$, $x = -1$, and $x = 0$, and $x = 1$

Exercise	Depth of Knowledge (D.O.K.)	COMMON CORE Mathematical Practices
1	**1** Recall of Information	**MP.6** Precision
2–13	**1** Recall of Information	**MP.2** Reasoning
14–17	**2** Skills/Concepts	**MP.6** Precision
18–20	**2** Skills/Concepts	**MP.4** Modeling
21–22	**3** Strategic Thinking H.O.T.	**MP.2** Reasoning
23	**2** Skills/Concepts H.O.T.	**MP.4** Modeling

EVALUATE

ASSIGNMENT GUIDE

Concepts and Skills	Practice
Explore Relating Multiplication Concepts	Exercise 1
Example 1 Multiplying Rational Expressions	Exercises 2–7
Example 2 Dividing Rational Expressions	Exercises 8–13
Example 3 Activity: Investigating Closure	Exercises 14–17
Example 4 Multiplying and Dividing with Rational Models	Exercises 18–20

AVOID COMMON ERRORS

When multiplying rational expressions, students may divide out by common factors and then, erroneously, cross-multiply instead of multiplying straight across. Remind them that cross-multiplying is used to solve equations, and that when multiplying two rational expressions, they must multiply straight across.

AVOID COMMON ERRORS

When identifying excluded values for quotients of rational expressions, students may consider values that cause the denominators to be zero, but they may forget to consider values that cause the divisor itself to be 0. For example, the divisor $\frac{x^2 - 36}{x^2 - 4x}$ will have a value of 0 when $x = 6$ or $x = -6$, so these values must also be excluded values.

6. $\frac{x^2 + 14x + 33}{4x} \cdot \frac{x^2 - 3x}{x + 3} \cdot \frac{8x - 56}{x^2 + 4x - 77}$

$= \frac{(x + 11)(x + 3)}{4x} \cdot \frac{x(x - 3)}{x + 3} \cdot \frac{8(x - 7)}{(x + 11)(x - 7)}$

$= \frac{8x(x + 11)(x + 3)(x - 3)(x - 7)}{4x(x + 3)(x + 11)(x - 7)}$

$= 2(x - 3)$

Excluded values: $x = 0, x = -3, x = -11$, and $x = 7$

7. $\frac{9x^2}{x - 6} \cdot \frac{x^2 - 36}{3x - 6} \cdot \frac{3}{4x^2 + 24x}$

$= \frac{9x^2}{x - 6} \cdot \frac{(x + 6)(x - 6)}{3(x - 2)} \cdot \frac{3}{4x(x + 6)}$

$= \frac{27x^2(x + 6)(x - 6)}{12x(x - 6)(x - 2)(x + 6)}$

$= \frac{9x}{4(x - 2)}$

Excluded values: $x = 6, x = 2, x = 0$ and $x = -6$

Find the quotients and any excluded values.

8. $\frac{5x^2 + 10x}{x^2 + 2x + 1} \div \frac{20x + 40}{x^2 - 1}$

$= \frac{5x^2 + 10x}{x^2 + 2x + 1} \cdot \frac{x^2 - 1}{20x + 40}$

$= \frac{5x(x + 2)}{(x + 1)(x + 1)} \cdot \frac{(x + 1)(x - 1)}{20(x + 2)}$

$= \frac{5x(x + 2)(x + 1)(x - 1)}{20(x + 1)(x + 1)(x + 2)}$

$= \frac{x(x - 1)}{4(x + 1)}$

Excluded values: $x = 1, x = -1$, and $x = -2$

9. $\frac{x^2 - 9x + 18}{x^2 + 9x + 18} \div \frac{x^2 - 36}{x^2 - 9}$

$= \frac{x^2 - 9x + 18}{x^2 + 9x + 18} \cdot \frac{x^2 - 9}{x^2 - 36}$

$= \frac{(x - 6)(x - 3)}{(x + 6)(x + 3)} \cdot \frac{(x + 3)(x - 3)}{(x + 6)(x - 6)}$

$= \frac{(x - 6)(x - 3)(x + 3)(x - 3)}{(x + 6)(x + 3)(x + 6)(x - 6)}$

$= \frac{(x - 3)^2}{(x + 6)^2}$

Excluded values: $x = \pm 6, x = \pm 3$

10. $\frac{-x^2 + x + 20}{5x^2 - 25x} \div \frac{x + 4}{2x - 14}$

$= \frac{-x^2 + x + 20}{5x^2 - 25x} \cdot \frac{2x^2 - 14}{x + 4}$

$= \frac{-(x + 4)(x - 5)}{5x(x - 5)} \cdot \frac{2(x - 7)}{x + 4}$

$= \frac{-2(x + 4)(x - 5)(x - 7)}{5x(x - 5)(x + 4)}$

$= \frac{-2(x - 7)}{5x}$

Excluded values: $x = 0, x = 5, x = 7$ and $x = -4$

11. $\frac{x + 3}{x^2 + 8x + 15} \div \frac{x^2 - 25}{x - 5}$

$= \frac{x + 3}{x^2 + 8x + 15} \cdot \frac{x - 5}{x^2 - 25}$

$= \frac{x + 3}{(x + 5)(x + 3)} \cdot \frac{x - 5}{(x + 5)(x - 5)}$

$= \frac{(x + 3)(x - 5)}{(x + 5)(x + 3)(x + 5)(x - 5)}$

$= \frac{1}{(x + 5)^2}$

Excluded values: $x = -5, x = -3$, an[d] $x = 5$

12. $\dfrac{x^2-10x+9}{3x} \div \dfrac{x^2-7x-18}{x^2+2x}$

$= \dfrac{x^2-10x+9}{3x} \cdot \dfrac{x^2+2x}{x^2-7x-18}$

$= \dfrac{(x-1)(x-9)}{3x} \cdot \dfrac{x(x+2)}{(x+2)(x-9)}$

$= \dfrac{x(x-1)(x-9)(x+2)}{3x(x+2)(x-9)}$

$= \dfrac{x-1}{3}$

Excluded values: $x = 0$, $x = -2$, and $x = 9$

13. $\dfrac{8x+32}{x^2+8x+16} \div \dfrac{x^2-6x}{x^2-2x-24}$

$= \dfrac{8x+32}{x^2+8x+16} \cdot \dfrac{x^2-2x-24}{x^2-6x}$

$= \dfrac{8(x+4)}{(x+4)(x+4)} \cdot \dfrac{(x+4)(x-6)}{x(x-6)}$

$= \dfrac{8(x+4)(x+4)(x-6)}{x(x+4)(x+4)(x-6)}$

$= \dfrac{8}{x}$

Excluded values: $x = 0$, $x = -4$, and $x = 6$

Let $p(x) = \frac{1}{x+1}$ and $q(x) = \frac{1}{x-1}$. Find the result and determine whether the result of performing each operation is another rational expression.

14. $p(x) + q(x)$

$\frac{2x}{(x+1)(x-1)}$; yes, $p(x) + q(x)$ is a rational expression because the set of rational expressions is closed under addition.

15. $p(x) - q(x)$

$\frac{-2}{(x+1)(x-1)}$; yes, $p(x) - q(x)$ is a rational expression because the set of rational expressions is closed under subtraction.

16. $p(x) \cdot q(x)$

$\frac{1}{(x+1)(x-1)}$; yes, $p(x) \cdot q(x)$ is a rational expression because the set of rational expressions is closed under multiplication.

17. $p(x) \div q(x)$

$\frac{x-1}{x+1}$; yes, $p(x) \div q(x)$ is a rational expression because the set of rational expressions is closed under division.

SMALL GROUP ACTIVITY

Have students work in small groups to make a poster showing how to divide two rational expressions. Give each group a different problem, each consisting of polynomials that require several different factoring strategies. Then have each group present its poster to the rest of the class, explaining each step.

INTEGRATE MATHEMATICAL PRACTICES

Focus on Technology

MP.5 Students can use a graphing calculator to compare the graph of the function defined by the original product or quotient with the graph of the function defined by the final simplified expression. If the expressions are equivalent, the graphs should be identical.

18. The distance a race car travels is given by the equation $d = v_0t + \frac{1}{2}at^2$ where v_0 is the initial speed of the race car, a is the acceleration, and t is the time travelled. Near the beginning of a race, the driver accelerates for 9 seconds at a rate of 4 m/s². The driver's average speed was 75 m/s. Find the driver's average speed during the acceleration.

The average speed is equal to the distance traveled divided by the time.

$$r = \frac{d}{t} = \frac{t\left(v_0 + \frac{1}{2}at\right)}{t} = v_0 + \frac{1}{2}at$$

Substitute the known values into the equation to find r.

$$r = v_0 + \frac{1}{2}at = 75 + \frac{1}{2}(4)(9) = 93$$

The average speed during the acceleration is 93 meters per second.

19. Julianna is designing a circular track that will consist of three concentric rings, each one set 6 meters apart. Find an expression for the ratio of the length of the outer ring to the length of the middle ring and another for the ratio of the length of the outer ring to length of the inner ring. If the radius of the inner ring is set at 90 meters, how many times longer is the outer ring than the middle ring and the inner ring?

Length of inner ring: $2\pi r$

Length of middle track: $2\pi(r + 6)$

Length of outer ring: $2\pi(r + 12)$

$$\frac{\text{Length of outer ring}}{\text{Length of middle ring}} = \frac{2\pi(r + 12)}{2\pi(r + 6)} = \frac{r + 12}{r + 6}$$

$$\frac{\text{Length of outer ring}}{\text{Length of inner ring}} = \frac{2\pi(r + 12)}{2\pi r} = \frac{r + 12}{r}$$

Substitute 90 for r.

$$\frac{90 + 12}{90 + 6} = \frac{102}{96} = 1.0625$$

$$\frac{90 + 12}{90} = \frac{102}{90} \approx 1.13$$

The outer ring is 1.0625 times longer than the middle ring and about 1.13 times longer than the inner ring.

20. Geometry Find a rational expression for the ratio of the surface area of a cylinder to the volume of a cylinder. Then find the ratio when the radius is 3 inches and the height is 10 inches.

Surface Area $= 2\pi r^2 + 2\pi rh$

Volume $= \pi r^2 h$

$$\frac{\text{Surface Area}}{\text{Volume}} = \frac{2\pi r^2 + 2\pi rh}{\pi r^2 h} = \frac{2\pi r(r+h)}{\pi r^2 h} = \frac{2(r+h)}{rh}$$

Substitute 3 for r and 10 for h.

$$\frac{2(3+10)}{(3)(10)} = \frac{26}{30} = \frac{13}{15}$$

The ratio of the cylinder's surface area to its volume 13:15.

H.O.T. Focus on Higher Order Thinking

21. Explain the Error Maria finds an equivalent expression to $\frac{x^2-4x-45}{3x-15} \div \frac{6x^2-150}{x^2-5x}$. Her work is shown. Find and correct Maria's mistake.

$$\frac{x^2-4x-45}{3x-15} \div \frac{6x^2-150}{x^2-5x} = \frac{(x-9)(x+5)}{3(x-5)} \div \frac{6(x+5)(x-5)}{x(x-5)}$$
$$= \frac{6(x-9)(x+5)(x+5)(x-5)}{3x(x-5)(x-5)}$$
$$= \frac{2(x-9)(x-5)^2}{x(x-5)}$$

Maria did not multiply by the reciprocal.

$$\frac{x^2-4x-45}{3x-15} \div \frac{6x^2-150}{x^2-5x} = \frac{x^2-4x-45}{3x-15} \cdot \frac{x^2-5x}{6x^2-150}$$
$$= \frac{(x-9)(x+5)}{3(x-5)} \cdot \frac{x(x-5)}{6(x+5)(x-5)}$$
$$= \frac{x(x-9)(x+5)(x-5)}{18x(x-5)(x+5)(x-5)}$$
$$= \frac{x(x-9)}{18(x-5)}$$

22. Critical Thinking Multiply the rational expression. What do you notice about the expression?

$$\left(\frac{3}{x-4} + \frac{x^3-4x}{8x^2-32}\right)\left(\frac{3x+18}{x^2+2x-24} - \frac{x}{8}\right) = \left(\frac{3}{x-4} + \frac{x(x+2)(x-2)}{8(x+2)(x-2)}\right)\left(\frac{3x+6}{x-4x+6} - \frac{x}{8}\right)$$
$$= \left(\frac{3}{x-4} + \frac{x}{8}\right)\left(\frac{3}{x-4} - \frac{x}{8}\right)$$
$$= \left(\frac{3}{x-4}\right)^2 - \left(\frac{x}{8}\right)^2$$
$$= \frac{3}{x-4} \cdot \frac{3}{x-4} - \frac{x}{8} \cdot \frac{x}{8}$$
$$= \frac{9}{(x-4)^2} - \frac{x^2}{64}$$

The expression is the difference of two squares.

MODELING

When working with rational expressions that represent real-world situations, students should recognize that not only must they consider excluded values that are based on the algebraic nature of the rational expressions, but they also need to consider values that must be excluded due to the limitations on the domain in the given situation.

CONNECT VOCABULARY EL

Have students complete a vocabulary chart using rational numbers and rational expressions, with examples of both fractions and rational expressions. Include the terms used in this lesson: *numerator, denominator, factor, reciprocal.*

JOURNAL

Have students compare and contrast the method they have learned for multiplying rational expressions with the method they have learned for adding rational expressions.

23. Multi-Step Jordan is making a garden with an area of $x^2 + 13x + 30$ square feet and a length of $x + 3$ feet.

a. Find an expression for the width of Jordan's garden.

$$x^2 + 13x + 30 \div x + 3 = \frac{x^2 + 13x + 30}{1} \cdot \frac{1}{x+3}$$

$$= \frac{(x+10)(x+3)}{1} \cdot \frac{1}{x+3}$$

$$= \frac{(x+10)(x+3)}{x+3}$$

$$= x + 10$$

Jordan's garden is $x + 10$ feet wide.

b. If Karl makes a garden with an area of $3x^2 + 48x + 180$ square feet and a length of $x + 6$, how many times larger is the width of Jon's garden than Jordan's?

$$3x^2 + 48x + 180 \div x + 6 = \frac{3x^2 + 48x + 180}{1} \cdot \frac{1}{x+6}$$

$$= \frac{3(x+10)(x+6)}{1} \cdot \frac{1}{x+6}$$

$$= \frac{3(x+10)(x+6)}{x+6}$$

$$= 3(x + 10)$$

Karl's garden is 3 times wider than Jordan's garden.

c. If x is equal to 4, what are the dimensions of both Jordan's and Karl's gardens?

Jordan's garden:

Length: $4 + 3 = 7$ feet

Width: $4 + 10 = 14$ feet

Karl's garden:

Length: $4 + 6 = 10$ feet

Width: $3(4 + 10) = 42$ feet

Lesson Performance Task

Who has the advantage, taller or shorter runners? Almost all of the energy generated by a long-distance runner is released in the form of heat. For a runner with height H and speed V, the rate hg of heat generated and the rate h_r of heat released can be modeled by $h_g = k_1H^3V^2$ and $h_r = k_2H^2$, k_1 and k_2 being constants. So, how does a runner's height affect the amount of heat she releases as she increases her speed?

First, set up the ratio for the amount of heat generated by the runner to the amount of heat released by dividing the value h_g by h_r.

$$\frac{h_g}{h_r} = \frac{k_1H^3V^2}{k_2H^2}$$

Next, simplify the ratio by combining terms.

$$\frac{h_g}{h_r} = \frac{k_1HV^2}{k_2}$$

When $\frac{h_g}{h_r}$ is equal to 1, the amount of heat released is the same as the amount of heat generated. You can use this condition as a way to determine the relationship of height to speed. Setting the ratio equal to 1, you isolate speed on one side of the equation.

$$\frac{k_2}{k_1H} = V^2$$

Since k_1 and k_2 are constants, you see that as a runner's height increases, the speed required to maintain the balance of heat generated to heat released gets smaller. Therefore, a shorter runner can run at a higher speed and not lose as much heat as taller runner does.

EXTENSION ACTIVITY

Ask students to rework the problem, this time with the heat generated modeled by $h_g = k_1H^3V$. Ask them to describe the relation between speed and height, and to tell how that relation differs from the answer they calculated in the Performance Task. Ask them whether this model gives shorter runners a greater or lesser advantage, compared to the model in the Performance Task. **Shorter runners still have an advantage over taller runners, but it is not as great.**

AVOID COMMON ERRORS

Students may think that the amount of heat released by the runner is independent of speed because $h_r = k_2H^2$, which is independent of V. Ask students where the heat comes from before it is released. **generated by runner** Then ask what the expression is for the heat generated, and ask whether it depends on V. **$h_g = k_1H^3V^2$; yes** Then have students write the equation for the situation that occurs when the amount of heat released is equal to the amount of heat generated.

INTEGRATE MATHEMATICAL PRACTICES

Focus on Math Connections

MP.1 Have students draw a graph for the relation they obtained between height and speed. Ask them what information they need to draw the exact graph for the relation. **the constants k_1 and k_2** Then, have students discuss whether this graph helps them determine an ideal height for a runner.

Scoring Rubric

2 points: Student correctly solves the problem and explains his/her reasoning.

1 point: Student shows good understanding of the problem but does not fully solve or explain his/her reasoning.

0 points: Student does not demonstrate understanding of the problem.

LESSON 9.3

Solving Rational Equations

Common Core Math Standards

The student is expected to:

COMMON CORE **A-REI.A.2**

Solve simple rational and radical equations in one variable, and give examples showing how extraneous solutions may arise. Also A-CED.A.1, A-CED.A.3, A-REI.A.1

Mathematical Practices

COMMON CORE **MP.3 Logic**

Language Objective

Describe to a partner how to solve rational equations.

ENGAGE

Essential Question: What methods are there for solving rational equations?

Rational equations can be solved algebraically by finding the LCM of the denominators of the rational expressions and multiplying each side of the equation by that LCM. When the equation is simplified, the result is a polynomial equation that can be solved by factoring, graphing, and other methods. Rational equations also can be solved by graphing. For example, each side of a rational equation may be entered as a function. The solution is the *x*-coordinate(s) of the point(s) at which the graphs intersect.

PREVIEW: LESSON PERFORMANCE TASK

View the Engage section online. Discuss the photo and ask students to list the information they would need to calculate the profit per item. Then preview the Lesson Performance Task.

Name ______ Class ______ Date ______

9.3 Solving Rational Equations

Essential Question: What methods are there for solving rational equations?

Resource Locker

Explore Solving Rational Equations Graphically

A rational equation is an equation that contains one or more rational expressions. The time t in hours it takes to travel d miles can be determined by using the equation $t = \frac{d}{r}$, where r is the average rate of speed. This equation is an example of a rational equation. One method to solving rational equations is by graphing.

Solve the rational equation $\frac{x}{x-3} = 2$ by graphing.

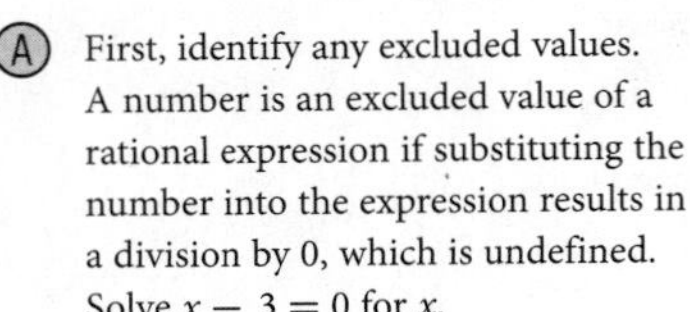

(A) First, identify any excluded values. A number is an excluded value of a rational expression if substituting the number into the expression results in a division by 0, which is undefined. Solve $x - 3 = 0$ for x.

$x - 3 = 0$

$x = $ 3

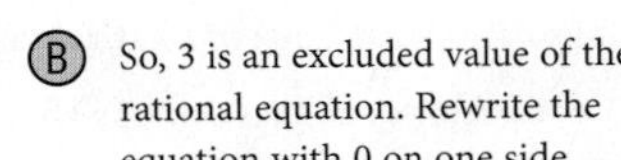

(B) So, 3 is an excluded value of the rational equation. Rewrite the equation with 0 on one side.

$\frac{x}{x-3} = 2$

$\frac{x}{x-3} - 2 = 0$

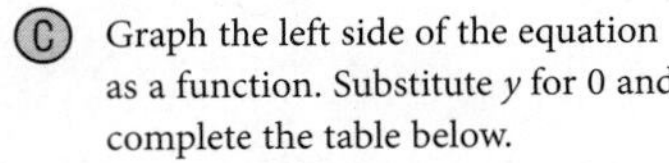

(C) Graph the left side of the equation as a function. Substitute y for 0 and complete the table below.

x	y	(x, y)
0	−2	(0, −2)
1	−2.5	(1, −2.5)
2	−4	(2, −4)
4	2	(4, 2)
5	0.5	(5, 0.5)
9	−0.5	(9, −0.5)

(D) Use the table to graph the function.

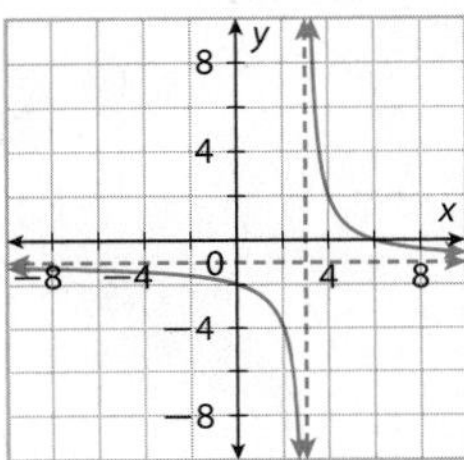

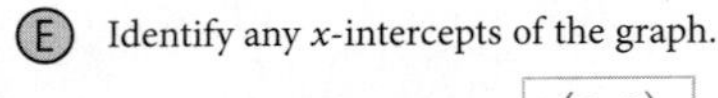

(E) Identify any x-intercepts of the graph.

There is an x-intercept at (6, 0).

(F) Is the value of x an excluded value? What is the solution of $\frac{x}{x-3} = 2$?

No, $x = 6$ is not an excluded value.

The solution of $\frac{x}{x-3} = 2$ is $x = 6$.

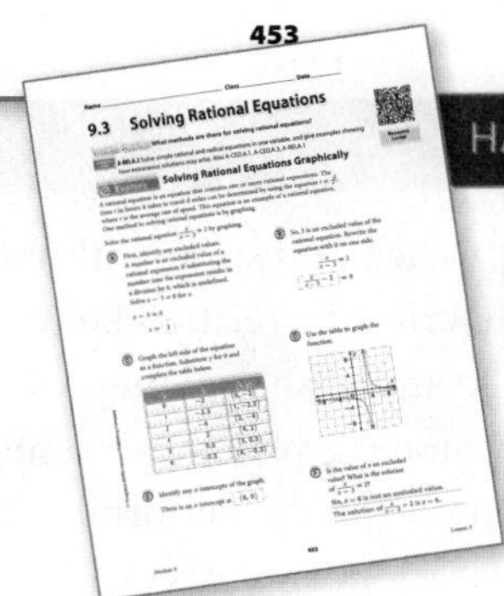

HARDCOVER PAGES 453–466

Watch for the hardcover student edition page numbers for this lesson.

Reflect

1. **Discussion** Why does rewriting a rational equation with 0 on one side help with solving the equation?
Rewriting the equation with 0 on one side helps because the expression on the other side can be graphed and the solution is the x-intercept.

Explain 1 Solving Rational Equations Algebraically

Rational equations can be solved algebraically by multiplying through by the LCD and solving the resulting polynomial equation. However, this eliminates the information about the excluded values of the original equation. Sometimes an excluded value of the original equation is a solution of the polynomial equation, and in this case the excluded value will be an **extraneous solution** of the polynomial equation. Extraneous solutions are not solutions of an equation.

Example 1 Solve each rational equation algebraically.

(A) $\frac{3x+7}{x-5} = \frac{5x+17}{2x-10}$

Identify any excluded values.

$x - 5 = 0 \qquad 2x - 10 = 0$
$x = 5 \qquad x = 5$

The excluded value is 5.
Identify the LCD by finding all factors of the denominators.

$2x - 10 = 2(x - 5)$

The different factors are 2 and $x - 5$.

The LCD is $2(x - 5)$.

Multiply each term by the LCD. $\frac{3x+7}{x-5} \cdot 2(x-5) = \frac{5x+17}{2(x-5)} \cdot 2(x-5)$

Divide out common factors. $\frac{3x+7}{\cancel{x-5}} \cdot 2\cancel{(x-5)} = \frac{5x+17}{\cancel{2}\cancel{(x-5)}} \cdot \cancel{2}\cancel{(x-5)}$

Simplify. $(3x+7)2 = 5x + 17$

Use the Distributive Property. $6x + 14 = 5x + 17$

Solve for x. $x + 14 = 17$

$x = 3$

The solution $x = 3$ is not an excluded value. So, $x = 3$ is the solution of the equation.

PROFESSIONAL DEVELOPMENT

Integrate Mathematical Practices

This lesson provides an opportunity to address Mathematical Practice **MP.3**, which calls for students to "construct viable arguments." Students learn that they can solve rational equations graphically, by writing a related function and finding the zeros of the function. They also learn to solve rational equations algebraically, multiplying the equation by the LCD and converting it into an equivalent polynomial equation. Students draw connections between the excluded values of the expressions and the extraneous solutions of the equation.

EXPLORE

Solving Rational Equations Graphically

INTEGRATE TECHNOLOGY

Students have the option of completing the Explore activity either in the book or online.

INTEGRATE MATHEMATICAL PRACTICES

Focus on Math Connections

MP.1 Students should recognize that the x-intercepts represent the solutions of the equation because they are the zeros of the related function. Help them to make this connection, emphasizing that a point with coordinates $(x, 0)$ represents a value of x for which the function is equal to 0.

QUESTIONING STRATEGIES

? If the two sides of the equation are graphed as separate functions, will the graphs intersect, and if so, where? **Yes; the graphs will intersect at the point or points whose x-values are the solutions of the equation.**

EXPLAIN 1

Solving Rational Equations Algebraically

QUESTIONING STRATEGIES

? How does finding the LCD of the rational expressions and multiplying each side of the equation by the LCD turn the rational equation into a polynomial equation? **After the multiplication of both sides by the LCD has been carried out, common factors in the numerators and denominators can be divided out. The resulting denominators on each side are 1, and since the numerators are polynomials, the equation becomes a polynomial equation.**

CONNECT VOCABULARY EL

Have students look up the definition of *extraneous* and relate its use in this context to its use in non-mathematical contexts.

QUESTIONING STRATEGIES

How can you tell whether a solution of a rational equation is extraneous? **It is extraneous if it is an excluded value for one of the rational expressions in the equation.**

INTEGRATE TECHNOLOGY

Students can use the graphing method presented in the Explore to check their solutions. Have them graph the corresponding function and compare its zeros to the solutions found algebraically.

(B) $\frac{2x-9}{x-7} + \frac{x}{2} = \frac{5}{x-7}$

Identify any excluded values.

$x - 7 = 0$

$x = \boxed{7}$

The excluded value is **7**.

Identify the LCD.

The different factors are **2 and $x - 7$**.

The LCD is **$2(x-7)$**.

Multiply each term by the LCD. $\frac{2x-9}{x-7} \cdot \boxed{2(x-7)} + \frac{x}{2} \cdot \boxed{2(x-7)} = \frac{5}{x-7} \cdot \boxed{2(x-7)}$

Divide out common factors. $\frac{2x-9}{\cancel{x-7}} \cdot \boxed{2\cancel{(x-7)}} + \frac{x}{\cancel{2}} \cdot \boxed{\cancel{2}(x-7)} = \frac{5}{\cancel{x-7}} \cdot \boxed{2\cancel{(x-7)}}$

Simplify. $\boxed{2}(2x-9) + x\left(\boxed{x-7}\right) = 5\left(\boxed{2}\right)$

Use the Distributive Property. $\boxed{4x-18} + x^2 - 7x = \boxed{10}$

Write in standard form. $\boxed{x^2 - 3x - 28} = 0$

Factor. $\left(\boxed{x-7}\right)\left(\boxed{x+4}\right) = 0$

Use the Zero Product Property. $x - 7 = 0$ or $\boxed{x+4} = 0$

Solve for x. $x = 7$ or $x = \boxed{-4}$

The solution $x = \boxed{7}$ is extraneous because it is an excluded value. The only solution is $x = \boxed{-4}$.

Your Turn

Solve each rational equation algebraically.

2. $\frac{8}{x+3} = \frac{x+1}{x+6}$

Excluded values: -3 and -6

LCD: $(x+3)(x+6)$

$$\frac{8}{x+3} \cdot (x+3)(x+6) = \frac{x+1}{x+6} \cdot (x+3)(x+6)$$

$$\frac{8}{\cancel{x+3}} \cdot \cancel{(x+3)}(x+6) = \frac{x+1}{\cancel{x+6}} \cdot (x+3)\cancel{(x+6)}$$

$$8(x+6) = (x+1)(x+3)$$

$$8x + 48 = x^2 + 4x + 3$$

$$0 = x^2 - 4x - 45$$

$$0 = (x+9)(x+5)$$

$$x = 9 \text{ or } x = 5$$

The solutions are $x = 9$ or $x = -5$.

COLLABORATIVE LEARNING

Small Group Activity

Have students work in groups of 3–4 students. Provide each group with a different rational equation to solve. Instruct students to create a poster showing the equation solved using three different methods: graphically using one function, graphically using two functions, and algebraically. Remind students to look for and to indicate extraneous solutions. Have students share their posters with the class.

Explain 2 Solving a Real-world Problem with a Rational Equation

Rational equations are used to model real-world situations. These equations can be solved algebraically.

Example 2 **Use a rational equation to solve the problem.**

(A) Kelsey is kayaking on a river. She travels 5 miles upstream and 5 miles downstream in a total of 6 hours. In still water, Kelsey can travel at an average speed of 3 miles per hour. What is the average speed of the river's current?

Analyze Information

Identify the important information:

- The answer will be the average speed of **the current**.
- Kelsey spends **6 hours** kayaking.
- She travels **5 miles** upstream and **5 miles** downstream.
- Her average speed in still water is **3 miles per hour**.

Formulate a Plan

Let c represent the speed of the current in miles per hour. When Kelsey is going upstream, her speed is equal to her speed in still water **minus** c. When Kelsey is going downstream, her speed is equal to her speed in still water **plus** c.

The variable c is restricted to **positive real numbers**.

Complete the table.

	Distance (mi)	Average speed (mi/h)	Time (h)
Upstream	5	$3 - c$	$\frac{5}{3 - c}$
Downstream	5	$3 + c$	$\frac{5}{3 + c}$

Use the results from the table to write an equation.
total time = time upstream + time downstream

$$6 = \boxed{\frac{5}{3 - c}} + \boxed{\frac{5}{3 + c}}$$

DIFFERENTIATE INSTRUCTION

Multiple Representations

Point out to students that they can use the table feature of a graphing calculator to check their solutions to rational equations. They can enter the left side of the equation as Y1 and the right side as Y2. Then, by using the table feature, they can verify that Y1 and Y2 have the same values of x that they determined by using algebra.

EXPLAIN 2

Solving a Real-World Problem with a Rational Equation

AVOID COMMON ERRORS

Students may need to be reminded to check to see whether the solutions of their equations are extraneous solutions. Remind them to also consider restrictions that are imposed on the variable due to the context of the application.

QUESTIONING STRATEGIES

? How could you solve the problem graphically? **Graph each side of the equation as a function and find the points of intersection of the two graphs. The x-values of the points of intersection will be the solutions of the equation.**

INTEGRATE MATHEMATICAL PRACTICES

Focus on Modeling

MP.4 Discuss with students how the rational expressions used in the example model the situation. Have students describe what each numerator and denominator represents, and why the equation models the real-world relationship described in the problem.

Solve

$3 - c = 0 \qquad 3 + c = 0$

$\boxed{3} = c \qquad c = \boxed{-3}$

Excluded values: **3 and −3**

LCD: **$(3 - c)(3 + c)$**

Multiply by the LCD. $\quad 6 \cdot \boxed{(3 - c)(3 + c)} = \frac{5}{3 - c} \cdot \boxed{(3 - c)(3 + c)} + \frac{5}{3 + c} \cdot \boxed{(3 - c)(3 + c)}$

Divide out common factors. $\quad 6 \cdot \boxed{(3 - c)(3 + c)} = \frac{5}{\cancel{3 - c}} \cdot \boxed{(\cancel{3 - c})(3 + c)} + \frac{5}{\cancel{3 + c}} \cdot \boxed{(3 - c)(\cancel{3 + c})}$

Simplify. $\quad 6 \cdot \boxed{(3 - c)(3 + c)} = 5 \cdot \boxed{3 + c} + 5 \cdot \boxed{3 - c}$

Use the Distributive Property. $\quad \boxed{54 - 6c^2} = 15 + 5c + \boxed{15 - 5c}$

Write in standard form. $\quad 0 = \boxed{6c^2 - 24}$

Factor. $\quad 0 = 6(c + 2)\left(\boxed{c - 2}\right)$

Use the Zero Product Property. $\quad c + 2 = 0$ or $\boxed{c - 2} = 0$

Solve for c. $\quad c = \boxed{-2}$ or $c = \boxed{2}$

There **are no** extraneous solutions. The solutions are **$c = -2$ or $c = 2$**.

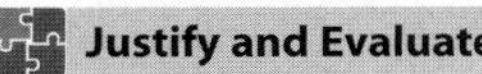

Justify and Evaluate

The solution $c = \boxed{-2}$ is unreasonable because the speed of the current cannot be **negative,** but the solution $c = \boxed{2}$ is reasonable because the speed of the current can be **positive**. If the speed of the current is **2 miles per hour**, it would take Kelsey **5** hour(s) to go upstream and **1** hour(s) to go downstream, which is a total of **6** hours.

Reflect

3. Why does the domain of the variable have to be restricted in real-world problems that can be modeled with a rational equation?

The variable must make sense in a real-world context. The speed of the current cannot be negative or 0, so the domain of *c* had to be restricted to positive real numbers.

Your Turn

4. Kevin can clean a large aquarium tank in about 7 hours. When Kevin and Lara work together, they can clean the tank in 4 hours. Write and solve a rational equation to determine how long, to the nearest tenth of an hour, it would take Lara to clean the tank if she works by herself. Explain whether the answer is reasonable.

Kevin's rate: $\frac{1}{7}$ of the tank per hour

Lara's rate: $\frac{1}{t}$ of the tank per hour, where t is the time in hours needed to clean the tank alone.

The domain of t must be positive real numbers.

Kevin's rate · hours worked + Lara's rate · hours worked = 1 complete job

$\frac{1}{7}(4) + \frac{1}{t}(4) = 1$

Excluded value: 0; LCD: $7t$

$$\frac{1}{7}(4) + \frac{1}{t}(4) = 1$$
$$\frac{1}{7}(4) \cdot 7 \cdot t + \frac{1}{t}(4) \cdot 7 \cdot t = 1 \cdot 7 \cdot t$$
$$4t + 1 \cdot 4 \cdot 7 = 1 \cdot 7 \cdot t$$
$$4t + 28 = 7t$$
$$28 = 3t$$
$$9\frac{1}{3} = t$$

It would take Lara about 9 hours and 20 minutes to clean the tank by herself. The answer is reasonable because $9\frac{1}{3}$ is positive and $\frac{1}{7}(4) + \frac{1}{9\frac{1}{3}}(4) = 1$.

Elaborate

5. Why is it important to check solutions to rational equations?
To make sure that there are no extraneous solutions.

6. Why can extraneous solutions to rational equations exist?
Because the process of multiplying through by the LCD loses the information about excluded values.

7. **Essential Question Check In** How can you solve a rational equation without graphing?
Rational equations can be solved algebraically by finding the LCM of the denominators of the rational expressions and multiplying each side of the equation by that LCM. When the equation is simplified, the result is a polynomial equation that can be solved.

ELABORATE

INTEGRATE MATHEMATICAL PRACTICES

Focus on Critical Thinking

MP.3 Discuss with students how the algebraic process of converting a rational equation into a polynomial equation can introduce extraneous solutions. Lead them to recognize that polynomial expressions themselves do not have excluded values and, therefore, the solutions to a polynomial equation will all satisfy the polynomial equation. However, if the polynomial equation is derived from a rational equation, any excluded values of the rational equation that are solutions of the polynomial equation will be extraneous.

SUMMARIZE THE LESSON

How can you use the LCD of the rational expressions in an equation to solve the equation? **You can multiply each term in the equation by the LCD. This will change the rational equation into a polynomial equation. You can then solve the polynomial equation, being careful to check whether any of the solutions are extraneous.**

LANGUAGE SUPPORT EL

Communicate Math

Have students work in pairs to complete a chart shown on solving rational equations.

Type of Equation	Type of Solution	Notes Explaining Steps
Rational: Write an equation	Graphical	For example, rewrite with 0 on one side and graph the function on the other side.
Rational: Write an equation	Algebraic	For example, find the LCD by factoring, etc.

EVALUATE

ASSIGNMENT GUIDE

Concept and Skills	Practice
Explore Solving Rational Equations Graphically	Exercises 1–2
Example 1 Solving Rational Equations Algebraically	Exercises 3–8
Example 2 Solving a Real-World Problem with a Rational Equation	Exercises 9–16

AVOID COMMON ERRORS

If students do not obtain an appropriate graph, they may have made errors either in entering the function (or functions) or in choosing an appropriate viewing window. The most common error in entering a rational function is to omit the parentheses around the complete numerator and the complete denominator. Check students' calculators to catch errors and guide them in correcting any errors.

Evaluate: Homework and Practice

- Online Homework
- Hints and Help
- Extra Practice

Solve each rational equation by graphing using a table of values.

1. $\frac{x}{x+4} = -3$

Excluded value: $x = -4$

$\frac{x}{x+4} = -3$

$\frac{x}{x+4} + 3 = 0$

x	y	(x, y)
−8	5	(−8, 5)
−6	6	(−6, 6)
−5	8	(−5, 8)
−3.5	−4	(−3.5, −4)
−2	2	(−2, 2)
0	3	(0, 3)

The x-intercept is at $(-3, 0)$. The solution is $x = -3$.

2. $\frac{x}{2x - 10} = 3$

Excluded value: $x = 5$

$\frac{x}{2x-10} = 3$

$\frac{x}{2x-10} - 3 = 0$

x	y	(x, y)
0	−3	(0, −3)
3	−3.75	(3, −3.75)
4	−5	(4, −5)
5.5	2.5	(5.5, 2.5)
7	−1.25	(7, −1.25)
10	−2	(10, −2)

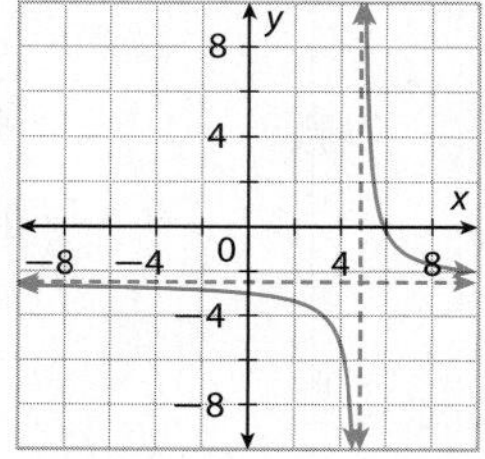

The x-intercept is at $(6, 0)$. The solution is $x = 6$.

Solve each rational equation algebraically.

3. $\frac{9}{4x} - \frac{5}{6} = -\frac{13}{12x}$

Excluded value: $x = 0$

LCD: $2 \cdot 2 \cdot 3 \cdot x = 12x$

$\frac{9}{4x} \cdot 12x - \frac{5}{6} \cdot 12x = -\frac{13}{12x} \cdot 12x$

$9 \cdot 3 - 5 \cdot 2x = -13$

$27 - 10x = -13$

$-10x = -40$

$x = 4$

The solution is $x = 4$.

4. $\frac{3}{x+1} + \frac{2}{7} = 2$

Excluded value: $x = -1$

LCD: $7(x + 1)$

$\frac{3}{x+1} \cdot 7(x+1) + \frac{2}{7} \cdot 7(x+1) = 2 \cdot 7(x+1)$

$3 \cdot 7 + 2(x+1) = 2 \cdot 7(x+1)$

$21 + 2x + 2 = 14x + 14$

$-12x + 9 = 0$

$-12x = -9$

$x = \frac{3}{4}$

Exercise	Depth of Knowledge (D.O.K.)	COMMON CORE Mathematical Practices
1–2	**2** Skills/Concepts	**MP.6** Precision
3–8	**1** Recall of Information	**MP.2** Reasoning
9–16	**2** Skills/Concepts	**MP.4** Modeling
17	**1** Recall of Information	**MP.2** Reasoning
18	**3** Strategic Thinking H.O.T.	**MP.2** Reasoning
19	**3** Strategic Thinking H.O.T.	**MP.6** Precision

5. $\frac{56}{x^2 - 2x - 15} - \frac{6}{x+3} = \frac{7}{x-5}$

$x = 5$ or $x = -3$

Excluded values: 5 and -3

LCD: $(x-5)(x+3)$

$$\frac{56}{(x-5)(x+3)} \cdot (x-5)(x+3) - \frac{6}{x+3} \cdot (x-5)(x+3) = \frac{7}{x-5} \cdot (x-5)(x+3)$$

$$56 - 6(x-5) = 7(x+3)$$

$$56 - 6x + 30 = 7x + 21$$

$$65 = 13x$$

$$5 = x$$

The solution is $x = 5$ is extraneous. There is no solution.

6. $\frac{x^2 - 29}{x^2 - 10x + 21} = \frac{6}{x-7} + \frac{5}{x-3}$

$x^2 - 10x + 21 = 0$

$(x-7)(x-3) = 0$

$x - 7 = 0$ or $x - 3 = 0$

$x = 7$ or $x = 3$

Excluded values: 7 and 3

LCD: $(x-7)(x-3)$

$$\frac{x^2 - 29}{(x-7)(x-3)} \cdot (x-7)(x-3) = \frac{6}{x-7} \cdot (x-7)(x-3) + \frac{5}{x-3} \cdot (x-7)(x-3)$$

$$\frac{x^2 - 29}{\cancel{(x-7)}\cancel{(x-3)}} \cdot \cancel{(x-7)}\cancel{(x-3)} = \frac{6}{\cancel{x-7}} \cdot \cancel{(x-7)}(x-3) + \frac{5}{\cancel{x-3}} \cdot (x-7)\cancel{(x-3)}$$

$$x^2 - 29 = 6(x-3) + 5(x-7)$$

$$x^2 - 29 = 6x - 18 + 5x - 35$$

$$x^2 - 29 = 11x - 53$$

$$x^2 - 11x + 24 = 0$$

$$(x-3)(x-8) = 0$$

$$x - 3 = 0 \text{ or } x - 8 = 0$$

$$x = 3 \text{ or } x = 8$$

The solution $x = 3$ is extraneous. The solution is $x = 8$.

CRITICAL THINKING

Ask students to consider whether it is possible to solve a rational equation by multiplying each of its terms by a common denominator that is not the *least* common denominator of the rational expressions. Have them predict how the result of doing this would compare to using the LCD, and test their predictions using one or more of the exercises.

INTEGRATE MATHEMATICAL PRACTICES

Focus on Reasoning

MP.2 Students can check their solutions by substituting the values into the original equations and verifying that they make the equation true. Students should observe that any extraneous solutions would make one or more of the rational expressions undefined.

Exercise	Depth of Knowledge (D.O.K.)	COMMON CORE Mathematical Practices
20	**3** Strategic Thinking H.O.T.	**MP.3** Logic
21	**3** Strategic Thinking H.O.T.	**MP.5** Using Tools

QUESTIONING STRATEGIES

How is the LCD of two rational expressions related to each denominator? **It is a multiple of each of the denominators.**

When is the LCD of two rational expressions the product of the denominators? **When the denominators have no common factors.**

7. $\frac{5}{2x+6} - \frac{1}{6} = \frac{2}{x+4}$

Excluded values: −3 and −4

LCD: $2 \cdot 3 \cdot (x+3)(x+4)$

$$\frac{5}{2(x+3)} \cdot 2 \cdot 3 \cdot (x+3)(x+4) - \frac{1}{2 \cdot 3} \cdot 2 \cdot 3 \cdot (x+3)(x+4) = \frac{2}{x+4} \cdot 2 \cdot 3 \cdot (x+3)(x+4)$$

$$\frac{5}{\cancel{2}\cancel{(x+3)}} \cdot \cancel{2} \cdot 3 \cdot \cancel{(x+3)}(x+4) - \frac{1}{\cancel{2 \cdot 3}} \cdot \cancel{2 \cdot 3} \cdot (x+3)(x+4) = \frac{2}{\cancel{x+4}} \cdot 2 \cdot 3 \cdot (x+3)\cancel{(x+4)}$$

$$5 \cdot 3 \cdot (x+4) - 1 \cdot (x+3)(x+4) = 2 \cdot 2 \cdot 3 \cdot (x+3)$$

$$15x + 60 - x^2 - 7x - 12 = 12x + 36$$

$$-x^2 + 8x + 48 = 12x + 36$$

$$0 = x^2 - 4x + 12$$

$$0 = (x-2)(x+6)$$

$$x = 2 \text{ or } x = -6$$

The solution is $x = 2$ or $x = -6$.

8. $\frac{5}{x^2 - 3x + 2} - \frac{1}{x-2} = \frac{x+6}{3x-3}$

Excluded values: 1 and 2

$3x - 3 = 3(x-1)$

LCD: $3(x-1)(x-2)$

$$\frac{5}{(x-1)(x-2)} \cdot 3(x-1)(x-2) - \frac{1}{x-2} \cdot 3(x-1)(x-2) = \frac{x+6}{3(x-1)} \cdot 3(x-1)(x-2)$$

$$\frac{5}{\cancel{(x-1)}\cancel{(x-2)}} \cdot 3\cancel{(x-1)}\cancel{(x-2)} - \frac{1}{\cancel{x-2}} \cdot 3(x-1)\cancel{(x-2)} = \frac{x+6}{\cancel{3(x-1)}} \cdot \cancel{3(x-1)}(x-2)$$

$$5 \cdot 3 - 1 \cdot 3(x-1) = (x+6)(x-2)$$

$$15 - 3x + 3 = x^2 + 4x - 12$$

$$0 = x^2 + 7x - 30$$

$$0 = (x+10)(x-3)$$

$$x = -10 \text{ or } x = 3$$

The solution is $x = -10$ or $x = 3$.

For 15 and 16, write a rational equation for each real-world application. Do not solve.

9. A save percentage in lacrosse is found by dividing the number of saves by the number of shots faced. A lacrosse goalie saved 9 of 12 shots. How many additional consecutive saves s must the goalie make to raise his save percentage to 0.850?

Number of saves: $9 + s$

Number of shots: $12 + s$

$$\frac{9 + s}{12 + s} = 0.850$$

10. Jake can mulch a garden in 30 minutes. Together, Jake and Ross can mulch the same garden in 16 minutes. How much time t, in minutes, will it take Ross to mulch the garden when working alone?

Jake's rate · minutes worked $= \frac{1}{30}(16)$

Ross' rate · minutes worked $= \frac{1}{t}(16)$

$$\frac{1}{30}(16) + \frac{1}{t}(16) = 1$$

11. Geometry A new ice skating rink will be approximately rectangular in shape and will have an area of 18,000 square feet. Using an equation for the perimeter P, of the skating rink in terms of its width W, what are the dimensions of the skating rink if the perimeter is 580 feet?

$$L \cdot W = 18{,}000$$

$$L = \frac{18{,}000}{W}$$

$$P = 2(L + W)$$

$$580 = 2\left(\frac{18{,}000}{W} + W\right)$$

$$580W = 2(18{,}000 + W^2)$$

$$290W = 18{,}000 + W^2$$

$$0 = W^2 - 290W + 18{,}000$$

$$W = 200 \text{ or } W = 90$$

The dimensions are 200 feet by 90 feet.

12. Water flowing through both a small pipe and a large pipe can fill a water tank in 9 hours. Water flowing through the large pipe alone can fill the tank in 17 hours. Write an equation that can be used to find the amount of time t, in hours, it would take to fill the tank using only the small pipe.

large pipe's rate · hours worked $= \frac{1}{17}(9)$

Small pipe's rate · hours worked $= \frac{1}{t}(9)$

$$\frac{1}{17}(9) + \frac{1}{t}(9) = 1$$

COMMUNICATING MATH

Call upon students to present their solutions to the class. Ask them to describe how they determined the LCD and how they transformed the rational equation into a polynomial equation. Have them describe the steps of the solution process, and tell how they identified any extraneous solutions.

AVOID COMMON ERRORS

When solving a rational equation that models a real-world situation, students may erroneously believe that any negative solution must be an extraneous solution. Help them to see that this is not necessarily the case, and remind them to reflect upon the rational expressions contained in the original equation and their excluded values.

13. A riverboat travels at an average of 14 km per hour in still water. The riverboat travels 110 km east up the Ohio River and 110 km west down the same river in a total of 17.5 hours. To the nearest tenth of a kilometer per hour, what was the speed of the current of the river?

The variable c is the speed of the current in km per hour.

Time upstream: $\frac{110}{14 - c}$

Time downstream: $\frac{110}{14 + c}$

$$\frac{110}{14 - c} + \frac{110}{14 + c} = 17.5$$

Excluded values: $-14, 14$

LCD: $(14 - c)(14 + c)$

$$\frac{110}{14 - c}(14 - c)(14 + c) + \frac{110}{14 + c}(14 - c)(14 + c) = 17.5(14 - c)(14 + c)$$
$$110(14 + c) + 110(14 - c) = 17.5(14 - c)(14 + c)$$
$$3080 = 3430 - 17.5c^2$$
$$-350 = -17.5c^2$$
$$20 = c^2$$
$$\pm 4.5 \approx c$$

The solution $c = -4.5$ does not make sense in context because the speed cannot be negative. So, the speed of the current is about 4.5 km/h.

14. A baseball player's batting average is equal to the number of hits divided by the number of at bats. A professional player had 139 hits in 515 at bats in 2012 and 167 hits in 584 at bats in 2013. Write and solve an equation to find how many additional consecutive hits h the batter would have needed to raise his batting average in 2012 to be at least equal to his average in 2013.

2012: $\frac{139 + h}{515 + h}$

2013: $\frac{167}{587}$

$$\frac{139 + h}{515 + h} = \frac{167}{584}$$

Excluded value: -515

LCD: $584(515 + h)$

$$\frac{139 + h}{515 + h} \cdot 584(515 + h) = \frac{167}{584} \cdot 584(515 + h)$$
$$\frac{139 + h}{\cancel{515 + h}} \cdot 584(\cancel{515 + h}) = \frac{167}{\cancel{584}} \cdot \cancel{584}(515 + h)$$
$$(139 + h)584 = 167(515 + h)$$
$$81{,}176 + 584h = 86{,}005 + 167h$$
$$417h = 4829$$
$$h \approx 11.58$$

The number of hits must be a whole number. The player would need 12 consecutive hits to raise his batting average in 2012 to be at least equal to his average in 2013.

15. The time required to deliver and install a computer network at a customer's location is $t = 5 + \frac{2d}{r}$, where t is time in hours, d is the distance (in miles), from the warehouse to the customer's location, and r is the average speed of the delivery truck. If it takes 8.2 hours for an employee to deliver and install a network for a customer located 80 miles from the warehouse, what is the average speed of the delivery truck?

Excluded value: $r \neq 0$

LCD: r

$$t = 5 + \frac{2d}{r}$$
$$8.2 = 5 + \frac{2(80)}{r}$$
$$8.2 \cdot r = 5 \cdot r + \frac{2(80)}{r} \cdot r$$
$$8.2r = 5r + 160$$
$$3.2r = 160$$
$$r = 50$$

The average speed of the truck is 50 mph.

16. Art A glassblower can produce several sets of simple glasses in about 3 hours. When the glassblower works with an apprentice, the job takes about 2 hours. How long would it take the apprentice to make the same number of sets of glasses when working alone?

The variable t is time in hours it would take for the apprentice.

$\frac{1}{3}(2) + \frac{1}{t}(2) = 1$

Excluded value: 0

LCD: $3t$

$$\frac{1}{3}(2) + \frac{1}{t}(2) = 1$$
$$\frac{1}{3}(2) \cdot 3t + \frac{1}{t}(2) \cdot 3t = 1 \cdot 3t$$
$$2t + 2 \cdot 3 = 2t$$
$$6 = t$$

It would take the apprentice about 6 hours.

17. Which of the following equations have at least two excluded values? Select all that apply.

A. $\frac{3}{x} + \frac{1}{5x} = 1$ — **excluded value: 0**

(B.) $\frac{x-4}{x-2} + \frac{3}{x} = \frac{5}{6}$ — **excluded values: 0 and 2**

C. $\frac{x}{x-6} + 1 = \frac{5}{2x-12}$ — **excluded value: 6**

D. $\frac{2x-3}{x^2 - 10x + 25} + \frac{3}{7} = \frac{1}{x-5}$ — **excluded value: 5**

(E.) $\frac{7}{x+2} + \frac{3x-4}{x^2 + 5x + 6} = 9$ — **excluded values: −2 and −3**

PEER-TO-PEER DISCUSSION

Ask students to discuss with a partner how solving a proportion by cross-multiplying is similar to solving a rational equation by multiplying through by the LCD. **Students should recognize that cross-multiplying produces the same result as if they had multiplied both sides of the equation by the product of the denominators. The product of the denominators may not be the *least* common denominator, but it will transform the rational equation into a polynomial equation.**

JOURNAL

Have students make a list of the steps involved in solving a rational equation algebraically.

H.O.T. Focus on Higher Order Thinking

18. **Critical Thinking** An equation has the form $\frac{a}{x} + \frac{x}{b} = c$, where a, b, and c are constants and $b \neq 0$. How many solutions could this equation have? Explain.

0, 1, or 2; the equation becomes $x^2 - bcx + ab = 0$ after multiplying by the LCD and putting the equation in standard form. The number of solutions of x depends on the values of a, b, and c.

19. **Multiple Representations** Write an equation whose graph is a straight line, but with an open circle at $x = 4$.

The graph of $y = \frac{(x-4)(x-3)}{x-4} = \frac{x^2 - 7x + 12}{x-4}$ has the same graph as $y = x - 3$ but has an open circle at $x = 4$.

20. **Justify Reasoning** Explain why the excluded values do not change when multiplying by the LCD to add or subtract rational expressions.

The function was defined not to exist at those points, so if an alternate form of the equation is to be equivalent, the new form must not exist at those points either.

21. **Critical Thinking** Describe how you would find the inverse of the rational function $f(x) = \frac{x-1}{x-2}$, $x \neq 2$. Then find the inverse.

Substitute y for x in the expression, and substitute x for $f(x)$. Then solve for y.

$y = \frac{x-1}{x-2} \longrightarrow x = \frac{y-1}{y-2}$

$x(y-2) = (y-1)$	**Multiply.**
$yx - 2x = y - 1$	**Distribute.**
$yx - y = 2x - 1$	**Collect y terms.**
$y(x-1) = 2x - 1$	**Factor.**
$y = \frac{2x-1}{x-1}$	**Divide.**

The inverse function $f^{-1}(x)$ is $f^{-1}(x) = \frac{2x-1}{x-1}$, $x \neq 1$.

Lesson Performance Task

Kasey creates comedy sketch videos and posts them on a popular video website and is selling an exclusive series of sketches on DVD. The total cost to make the series of sketches is $989. The materials cost $1.40 per DVD and the shipping costs $2.00 per DVD. Kasey plans to sell the DVDs for $12 each.

a. Let d be the number of DVDs Kasey sells. Create a profit-per-item model from the given information by writing a rule for $C(d)$, the total costs in dollars, $S(d)$, the total sales income in dollars, $P(d)$, the profit in dollars, and $P_{PI}(d)$, the profit per item sold in dollars.

b. What is the profit per DVD if Kasey sells 80 DVDs? Does this value make sense in the context of the problem?

c. Then use the function $P_{PI}(d)$ from part a to find how many DVDs Kasey would have to sell to break even. Identify all excluded values.

a. $C(d) = 989 + 1.4d + 2d = 989 + 3.4d$

$S(d) = 12d$

$P(d) = 12d - (989 + 3.4d) = 8.6d - 989$

$P_{PI}(d) = \frac{8.6d - 989}{d}$

b. $P_{PI}(80) = \frac{8.6(80) - 989}{(80)}$

$= \frac{-301}{80}$

≈ -3.76

Kasey would have a profit of −$3.76 per DVD sold. This value makes sense because the costs are greater than the amount of sales.

c. The excluded value is $d = 0$.

$0 = \frac{8.6d - 989}{d}$

$0 \cdot d = \frac{8.6d - 989}{d} \cdot d$

$0 = 8.6d - 989$

$989 = 8.6d$

$115 = d$

Kasey would have to sell 115 DVDs to break even.

EXTENSION ACTIVITY

Have students consider starting a bakery business to sell bread at a farmer's market. Have students choose a price per loaf and estimate the number of loaves they would have to sell in order to make a profit, assuming they start by buying a 50-pound bag of flour. Then have students create a model for the profit per loaf of bread, taking into account all relevant costs. After inputting all known values, have students discuss whether they would adjust the price or the sales goal in order to make a profit.

CONNECT VOCABULARY EL

Students may not understand the concept of *profit.* Explain that the money you receive when selling an item is called the *sales income,* but this is not the same thing as profit. To calculate the profit, first find how much it *costs* to produce the item. The *profit* is the money left over after subtracting the costs from the income.

INTEGRATE MATHEMATICAL PRACTICES

Focus on Reasoning

MP.2 Have students graph the profit per item $P_{PI}(d)$ for the number of necklaces sold, d. Have them discuss the maximum profit Bailey can make and what limits the profit. Have students explain how the profit per item changes as the number of items sold increases. **The profit will approach $8.60 per item, but it will never reach it because the cost of materials per necklace must be subtracted.**

Scoring Rubric

2 points: Student correctly solves the problem and explains his/her reasoning.

1 point: Student shows good understanding of the problem but does not fully solve or explain his/her reasoning.

0 points: Student does not demonstrate understanding of the problem.

Study Guide Review

ASSESSMENT AND INTERVENTION

Assign or customize module reviews.

MODULE PERFORMANCE TASK

COMMON CORE

Mathematical Practices: MP.1, MP.2, MP.3, MP.4, MP.6, MP.7
A-APR.D.7

SUPPORTING STUDENT REASONING

Students should begin by focusing on how to set up the problem. They can then do research, or you can provide them with specific information. Here is some of the information they may ask for.

- **What is the relationship for total resistance for resistors in parallel?**
  $\frac{1}{R_T} = \frac{1}{R_1} + \frac{1}{R_2} + \frac{1}{R_3} + \ldots + \frac{1}{R_n}$, for n resistors.

STUDY GUIDE REVIEW

Rational Expressions and Equations

MODULE 9

Essential Question: How can you use rational expressions and equations to solve real-world problems?

Key Vocabulary
closure *(cerradura)*
extraneous solution *(solución extraña)*
rational expression *(expresión racional)*
reciprocal *(recíproco)*

KEY EXAMPLE *(Lesson 9.1)*

Add the expression $\frac{1}{3+x} + \frac{3-x}{x}$, simplify the result, and note the excluded values.

$\frac{1}{3+x} + \frac{3-x}{x} = \frac{1x}{(3+x)x} + \frac{(3-x)(3+x)}{x(3+x)}$ Write with like denominators.

$= \frac{x + (9 - x^2)}{x(x+3)}$ Add.

$= \frac{-x^2 + x + 9}{x(x+3)}, x \neq -3, 0$ Simplify.

KEY EXAMPLE *(Lesson 9.2)*

Find the quotient of $\frac{x+3}{x+2} \div \frac{x^2-9}{2x-4}$ and note any excluded values.

$\frac{x+3}{x+2} \div \frac{x^2-9}{2x-4} = \frac{x+3}{x+2} \cdot \frac{2x-4}{x^2-9}$ Multiply by the reciprocal.

$= \frac{x+3}{x+2} \cdot \frac{2(x-2)}{(x+3)(x-3)}$ Factor the numerators and denominators.

$= \frac{2\cancel{(x+3)}(x-2)}{(x+2)\cancel{(x+3)}(x-3)}$ Multiply and cancel the common factors.

$= \frac{2(x-2)}{(x+2)(x-3)}; x \neq \pm 2, \pm 3$

KEY EXAMPLE *(Lesson 9.3)*

Solve the rational equation algebraically.

$$\frac{x}{x-3} + \frac{x}{2} = \frac{6x}{2x-6}$$

$2\cancel{(x-3)}\frac{x}{\cancel{x-3}} + \cancel{2}(x-3)\frac{x}{\cancel{2}} = 2\cancel{(x-3)}\frac{6x}{\cancel{2x-6}}$ Multiply each term by the LCD and divide out common factors.

$2x + x(x-3) = 6x$ Simplify.

$x^2 - 7x = 0$ Write in standard form.

$x(x-7) = 0$ Factor.

$x = 0$ or $x = 7$ Solve for x.

SCAFFOLDING SUPPORT

- If students are having difficulty adding long series of fractions, you may wish to suggest that they try using decimals instead.

EXERCISES

Add or subtract the given expressions, simplify the result, and note the excluded values. *(Lesson 9.1)*

1. $\frac{6x+6}{x^2-9} + \frac{-3x+3}{x^2-9}$

   $\frac{3}{x-3}$

   Excluded values: $x \neq \pm 3$

2. $\frac{4}{x^2-1} - \frac{x+2}{x-1}$

   $\frac{-x^2-3x+2}{(x-1)(x+1)}$

   Excluded values: $x \neq \pm 1$

Multiply or divide the given expressions, simplify the result, and note the excluded values. *(Lesson 9.2)*

3. $\frac{x^2-4x-5}{3x-15} \cdot \frac{4}{x^2-2x-3}$

   $\frac{4}{3x-9}$

   Excluded values: $x \neq -1, 3, 5$

4. $\frac{x+2}{x-4} \div \frac{x}{3x-12}$

   $\frac{3(x+2)}{x}$

   Excluded values: $x \neq 0, 4$

Solve each rational equation algebraically. *(Lesson 9.3)*

5. $x - \frac{10}{x} = 3$

   $x = -2$ or $x = 5$

6. $\frac{5}{x+1} = \frac{2}{x+4}$

   $x = -6$

MODULE PERFORMANCE TASK

Robots and Resistors

An engineer is designing part of a circuit that will control a robot. The circuit must have a certain total resistance to function properly. The engineer plans to use several resistors in *parallel*, which means each resistor is on its own branch of the circuit. The resistors available for this project are 20, 50, 80, and 200-ohm.

How can the engineer design a parallel circuit with a total resistance of 10 ohms using a maximum of 5 resistors, at least two of which must be different values? Find at least two possible circuit configurations that meet these criteria.

For another part of the circuit, the engineer wants to use resistors in parallel to create a total resistance of 6 ohms. Can she do it using the available resistor values? If so, how? If not, explain why not.

Begin by listing in the space below all of the information you will need to solve the problem. Then use your own paper to complete the task. Be sure to write down all your data and assumptions. Then use graphs, numbers, words, or algebra to explain how you reached your conclusion.

SAMPLE SOLUTION

The available resistance values are 20, 50, 80, and 200 ohms. Use the equation for the total resistance of parallel resistors, $\frac{1}{R_T} = \frac{1}{R_1} + \frac{1}{R_2} + \frac{1}{R_3} + \ldots + \frac{1}{R_n}$, to find a combination of resistors that results in $R_T = 10$ ohms. One way to do this is to find the reciprocal of each resistor value, and use these to find the combinations which, when added, result in the reciprocal of the total resistance:

$\frac{1}{R_T} = \frac{1}{10} = 0.1$, $\frac{1}{20\text{ ohm}} = 0.05$,

$\frac{1}{50\text{ ohm}} = 0.02$, $\frac{1}{80\text{ ohm}} = 0.0125$, and

$\frac{1}{200\text{ ohm}} = 0.005$.

One possible configuration is one 20-ohm, one 50-ohm, two 80-ohm, and one 200-ohm resistor:

$$\frac{1}{R_T} = 0.1 = 0.05 + 0.02 + 2(0.025) + 0.005$$

Another possible configuration is four 80-ohm and one 20-ohm resistor:

$$\frac{1}{R_T} = 0.1 = 4(0.0125) + 0.05$$

A third possible configuration is one 20-ohm, two 50-ohm, and two 200-ohm resistors:

$$\frac{1}{R_T} = 0.1 = 0.05 + 2(0.02) + 2(0.005)$$

However, it is not possible to use these resistors in parallel to create 6 ohms of total resistance. One way to see this is to examine the reciprocal of 6: $\frac{1}{6} = 0.1\overline{6}$, a repeating decimal. No sum of non-repeating decimals will create a repeating decimal.

DISCUSSION OPPORTUNITIES

- Lead students in discussing the meaning of *electrical resistance*. What do they think happens when total resistance increases?
- Will adding more resistors in parallel ever cause total resistance to increase?

Assessment Rubric

2 points: Student correctly solves the problem and explains his/her reasoning.

1 point: Student shows good understanding of the problem but does not fully solve or explain.

0 points: Student does not demonstrate understanding of the problem.

Ready to Go On?

ASSESS MASTERY

Use the assessment on this page to determine if students have mastered the concepts and standards covered in this module.

ASSESSMENT AND INTERVENTION

Access Ready to Go On? assessment online, and receive instant scoring, feedback, and customized intervention or enrichment.

ADDITIONAL RESOURCES

Response to Intervention Resources

- Reteach Worksheets

Differentiated Instruction Resources

- Reading Strategies EL
- Success for English Learners EL
- Challenge Worksheets

Assessment Resources

- Leveled Module Quizzes

9.1–9.3 Rational Expressions and Equations

- Online Homework
- Hints and Help
- Extra Practice

Perform the indicated operations, simplify the result, and note any excluded values. *(Lessons 9.1, 9.2)*

1. $\frac{4}{x+5} + \frac{2x}{x^2-25}$

$\frac{2(3x-10)}{(x+5)(x-5)}; x \neq \pm 5$

2. $\frac{3x+2}{x-2} - \frac{x+5}{x-2}$

$\frac{2x-3}{x-2}; x \neq 2$

3. $\frac{x+3}{x+2} \cdot \frac{2x-4}{x^2-9}$

$\frac{2(x-2)}{(x+2)(x-3)}; x \neq -2, \pm 3$

4. $\frac{x-3}{x-4} \div \frac{x-2}{x^2-16}$

$\frac{(x-3)(x+4)}{(x-2)}; x \neq 2, \pm 4$

Solve each rational equation. *(Lesson 9.3)*

5. $\frac{3}{x+2} + \frac{3}{2x+4} = \frac{x}{2x+4}$

$x = 9$

6. $\frac{x}{x-8} = \frac{24-2x}{x-8}$

no solution

7. $\frac{8x}{x^2-4} - \frac{4}{x+2} = \frac{8}{x^2-4}$

$x = 0$

8. $\frac{3x}{x+1} + \frac{6}{2x} = \frac{7}{x}$

$x = -\frac{2}{3}, 2$

ESSENTIAL QUESTION

9. How do you add or subtract rational expressions and identify any excluded values?

Possible Answer: To add or subtract rational expressions, find and apply the LCD and then simplify. For each situation, the excluded values are the values that make the denominator 0 in the original form or in the simplified form.

COMMON CORE Common Core Standards

Lesson	*Items*	Content Standards	Mathematical Practices
9.1	1	**A-APR.D.7, A-SSE.A.2**	**MP.2**
9.1	2	**A-APR.D.7, A-SSE.A.2**	**MP.2**
9.2	3	**A-APR.D.7**	**MP.2**
9.2	4	**A-APR.D.7**	**MP.2**
9.3	5–8	**A-REI.A.2**	**MP.1**

MODULE 9
MIXED REVIEW

Assessment Readiness

1. Look at each expression. Is it equivalent to $x - 3$? Select Yes or No for A–C.

   A. $\frac{(x-3)(x+5)}{x+3} + \frac{x+3}{x+5}$ ○ Yes ● No

   B. $\frac{x+3}{x+5} + \frac{x-3}{x+5}$ ○ Yes ● No

   C. $\frac{(x+3)(x+5)}{x-5} \div \frac{x+5}{x-5}$ ○ Yes ● No

2. Consider finding how many roots a quadratic equation has. Choose True or False for each statement.

   A. The quadratic equation $x^2 - 12 = 0$ has real roots. ● True ○ False

   B. The quadratic equation $x^2 + 25 = 0$ has imaginary roots. ● True ○ False

   C. The quadratic equation $-8x^2 + 20 = 0$ has one real root, and one imaginary root. ○ True ● False

3. A hiker averages 0.6 mile per hour walking up a mountain trail and 1.3 miles per hour walking down the trail. Find the total time in terms of d. Explain your answer.

   Total time is approximately 2.44*d*. The time to go up or down is found using $t = \frac{d}{r}$. The total time is given by adding the time up to the time down: $\frac{d}{0.6} + \frac{d}{1.3} = \frac{1.9d}{0.78} = 2.44d$

4. A restaurant has two pastry ovens. When both ovens are used, it takes about 3 hours to bake the bread needed for one day. When only the large oven is used, it takes about 4 hours to bake the bread for one day. About how long would it take to bake the bread for one day if only the small oven were used? Explain how you got your answer.

   12 hours; (rate of large oven · hours worked) + (rate of small oven · hours worked) = 1 complete job: $\frac{1}{4}(3) + \frac{1}{h}(3) = 1$; $3h + 12 = 4h$, $h = 12$

MIXED REVIEW

Assessment Readiness

ASSESSMENT AND INTERVENTION

Assign ready-made or customized practice tests to prepare students for high-stakes tests.

ADDITIONAL RESOURCES

Assessment Resources

- Leveled Module Quizzes: Modified, B

AVOID COMMON ERRORS

Item 3 Some students may have difficulty with this problem because the substituted value is in the denominator. Remind students to divide 1 by the denominator to get the non-fractional coefficient of d.

Common Core Standards

Lesson	Items	Content Standards	Mathematical Practices
9.1, 9.2	1	A-APR.D.6, A-APR.D.7	MP.1
3.1, 3.2	2*	N-CN.A.1, N.CN.A.2	MP.2
1.2, 9.1	3*	A-CED.A.2, A-APR.D.7, N-Q.A.1	MP.6
9.3	4	A-REI.A.2, N-Q.A.1	MP.4

* Item integrates mixed review concepts from previous modules or a previous course.

MIXED REVIEW

Assessment Readiness

ASSESSMENT AND INTERVENTION

Assign ready-made or customized practice tests to prepare students for high-stakes tests.

ADDITIONAL RESOURCES

Assessment Resources

- Leveled Unit Tests: Modified, A, B, C
- Performance Assessment

AVOID COMMON ERRORS

Item 5 Some students will miss that the relationship is inversely proportional, and instead they will interpret the relationship as direct variation. Remind students to read carefully, and highlight, circle, or underline key words to solve the problem.

UNIT 4 MIXED REVIEW

Assessment Readiness

- Online Homework
- Hints and Help
- Extra Practice

1. Consider the equations. Does the equation have an asymptote at 5? Choose Yes or No for A–C.

A. $y = \frac{3x^3}{x-5}$ ● Yes ○ No

B. $y = \frac{x^2(x-4)}{x-4}$ ○ Yes ● No

C. $y = \frac{3x^2-6}{(x-2)(x-5)}$ ● Yes ○ No

2. Consider the equations $f(x) = \frac{1}{x}$ and $g(x) = 1 + \frac{1}{x+5}$. Select True or False for each statement.

A. $g(x)$ is translated 1 unit up and 5 units left from $f(x)$. ● True ○ False

B. $g(x)$ is translated 1 unit up and 5 units right from $f(x)$. ○ True ● False

C. $g(x)$ is reflected over the x-axis in comparison to $f(x)$. ○ True ● False

3. Consider each equation. Does the equation have the solutions $x = -6, 4$? Choose Yes or No for A–C.

A. $x + 2 = \frac{24}{x+6}$ ○ Yes ● No

B. $\frac{x+2}{x} = 24$ ○ Yes ● No

C. $x + 2 = \frac{24}{x}$ ● Yes ○ No

4. Consider each expression. Are the values $x = 0$ and $x = 2$ excluded? Choose Yes or No for A–C.

A. $\frac{1}{x+2} + \frac{4+x}{x}$ ○ Yes ● No

B. $\frac{1}{x-2} + \frac{4+x}{x}$ ● Yes ○ No

C. $\frac{1}{x^2-2} + \frac{4+x}{x^2+2}$ ○ Yes ● No

COMMON CORE

Common Core Standards

Items	Content Standards	Mathematical Practices
1	**F-BF.B.3, F-IF-C.7**	**MP.7**
2*	**F-BF.B.3**	**MP.7**
3	**A-REI.A.2**	**MP.1**
4	**A-APR.D.7**	**MP.2**
5	**F-BF.B.A.1**	**MP.6**
6	**A-REI.A.2**	**MP.4**
7*	**A-APR.A.1**	**MP.4**

* Item integrates mixed review concepts from previous modules or a previous course.

5. The time t it takes Sam to drive to his grandmother's house is inversely proportional to the speed v at which he drives. Write an equation for the one-way travel time. If it takes Sam 5 hours driving 50 miles per hour, how long would it take him if he drove at 65 miles per hour? Explain your answer.

$t = \frac{k}{v}$, where $k = 250$ miles. If $v = 65$ miles per hour, then , after substituting into the equation, we find $t \approx 3.8$ hours.

6. A town has two trucks to collect garbage. When both trucks are in use, they take 6 hours to collect all the garbage. When only the small truck is in use, it takes 24 hours to collect the garbage. How long would it take to collect the garbage if only the large truck is in service? Explain your answer.

8 hours; (rate of large truck · hours) + (rate of small truck · hours) = 1 complete collection:

$\frac{1}{x}(6) + \frac{1}{24}(6) = 1$; $144 + 6x = 24x$; $x = 8$

7. A farmer needs $3x^2 - 4x + 10$ seeds for each of $x^3 + 5x - 20$ fields. What expression would represent the seeds the farmer needs to plant all of the fields? Is $x = 1$ a reasonable value for this representation? Explain your answers.

(fields) · (seeds per field) = seeds for all fields;

$3x^5 - 4x^4 + 25x^3 - 80x^2 + 130x - 200$ $x = 1$ is not a reasonable value for x because the solution for the expression is negative, and there is no way the farmer needs a negative number of seeds for his fields.;

Performance Tasks

* 8. For a car moving with initial speed v_0 and acceleration a, the distance d that the car travels in time t is given by $d = v_0 t + \frac{1}{2}at^2$.

A. Write a rational expression in terms of t for the average speed of the car during a period of acceleration. Simplify the expression.

B. During a race, a driver accelerates for 3 s at a rate of 10 ft/s² in order to pass another car. The driver's initial speed was 264 ft/s. What was the driver's average speed during the acceleration?

A. $\frac{v_0 t + \frac{1}{2}at^2}{t} = v_0 + \frac{1}{2}at$

B. 279 ft/s

PERFORMANCE TASKS

There are three different levels of performance tasks:

* **Novice:** These are short word problems that require students to apply the math they have learned in straightforward, real-world situations.

** **Apprentice:** These are more involved problems that guide students step-by-step through more complex tasks. These exercises include more complicated reasoning, writing, and open ended elements.

*****Expert:** These are open-ended, nonroutine problems that, instead of stepping the students through, ask them to choose their own methods for solving and justify their answers and reasoning.

SCORING GUIDES

Item 8 (2 points)

a. 1 point for correct, simplified rational expression

b. 1 point for correct average speed

SCORING GUIDES

Item 9 (6 points)

a. 1 point for expression for 2001 winner
1 point for expression for 2002 winner

b. 2 points for correct equation
2 points for correct answer

Item 10 (6 points)

a. 2 points for correct simplified expression

b. 2 points for correct table

c. 2 points for correct answer

★★ **9.** The average speed for the winner of the 2002 Indy 500 was 25 mi/h greater than the average speed for the 2001 winner. In addition, the 2002 winner completed the 500 mi race 32 min faster than the 2001 winner.

A. Let *s* represent the average speed of the 2001 winner in miles per hour. Write expressions in terms of *s* for the time in hours that it took the 2001 and 2002 winners to complete the race.

B. Write a rational equation that can be used to determine *s*. Solve your equation to find the average speed of the 2001 winner to the nearest mile per hour.

A. 2001 winner: $\frac{500}{s}$; 2002 winner: $\frac{500}{s+25}$

B. Possible answer: $\frac{500}{s} = \frac{500}{s+25} + \frac{32}{60}$; 141 mi/h

★★★**10.** The Renaissance architect Andrea Palladio preferred that the length and width of rectangular rooms be limited to certain ratios. These ratios are listed in the table. Palladio also believed that the height of a room with vaulted ceilings should be the harmonic mean of the length.

Rooms with a Width of 30 ft		
Length-to-Width Ratio	**Length (ft)**	**Height (ft)**
2:1	**60**	**40**
3:2	**45**	**36**
4:3	**40**	**34.3**
5:3	**50**	**37.5**
$\sqrt{2}$:1	**42.4**	**35.1**

A. The harmonic mean of two positive numbers *a* and *b* is equal to $\frac{2}{\frac{1}{a}+\frac{1}{b}}$. Simplify this expression.

B. Complete the table for a rectangular room with a width of 30 feet that meets Palladio's requirements for its length and height. If necessary, round to the nearest tenth.

C. A Palladian room has a length-to-width ratio of 4:3. If the length of this room is doubled, what effect should this change have on the room's width and height, according to Palladio's principles?

A. $\frac{2ab}{a+b}$

B. See table.

C. Both the width and the height will double.

MATH IN CAREERS

Chemist A chemist mixes 5 mL of an acid with 15 mL of water. The concentration of acid in the acid-and-water mix is $\frac{5}{5+15} = \frac{5}{20} = 25\%$. If the chemist adds more acid to the mix, then the concentration C becomes a function of the additional amount a of acid added to the mix.

a. Write a rule for the function $C(a)$.

b. What is a reasonable domain for this function? Explain.

c. What concentration of acid does pure water have? What concentration of acid does pure acid have? So, what are the possible values of $C(a)$?

d. Graph the function. Be sure to label the axes with the quantities they represent and indicate the axis scales by showing numbers for some grid lines.

e. Analyze the function's rule to determine the vertical asymptote of the function's graph. Why is the asymptote irrelevant in this situation?

f. Analyze the function's rule to determine the horizontal asymptote of the function's graph. What is the relevance of the asymptote in this situation?

a. $C(a) = \frac{5+a}{20+a}$

b. $a \geq 0$**; The amount of acid added must be nonnegative.**

c. Pure water is 0% acid; pure acid is 100% acid; $0\% \leq C(a) \leq 100\%$ **or** $0 \leq C(a) \leq 1$

d.

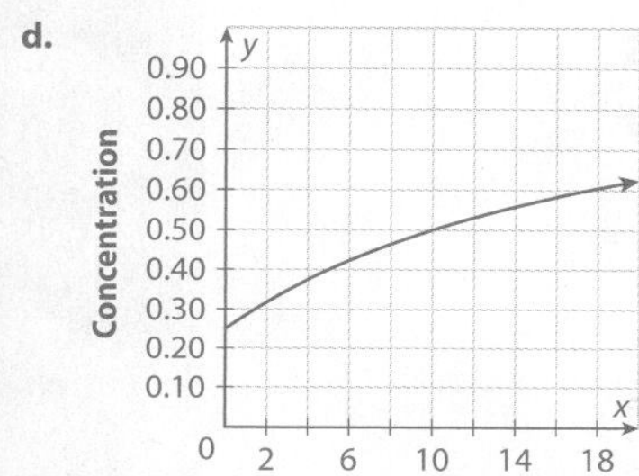

e. vertical asymptote: $x = -20$**; Only nonnegative values of** x **are being considered.**

f. horizontal asymptote: $y = 1$**; When the chemist adds lots of acid to the mix, the concentration of acid in the mix approaches that of pure acid (concentration = 1).**

MATH IN CAREERS

Chemist In this Unit Performance Task, students can see how a chemist uses mathematics on the job.

For more information about careers in mathematics as well as various mathematics appreciation topics, visit the American Mathematical Society http://www.ams.org

SCORING GUIDES

Task (6 points)

a. 1 point for correct function

b. 1 point for correct domain and explanation

c. 1 point for correct answers

d. 1 point for correct graph

e. 1 point for correct asymptote and explanation

f. 1 point for correct asymptote and explanation

Rational Functions, Expressions, and Equations

CONTENTS

Unit Pacing Guide

45-Minute Classes

Module 10

DAY 1	DAY 2	DAY 3	DAY 4	DAY 5
Lesson 10.1	Lesson 10.1	Lesson 10.2	Lesson 10.2	Lesson 10.3
DAY 6				
Module Review and Assessment Readiness				

Module 11

DAY 1	DAY 2	DAY 3	DAY 4	DAY 5
Lesson 11.1	Lesson 11.1	Lesson 11.2	Lesson 11.2	Lesson 11.3
DAY 6	DAY 7	DAY 8		
Lesson 11.3	Module Review and Assessment Readiness	Unit Review and Assessment Readiness		

90-Minute Classes

Module 10

DAY 1	DAY 2	DAY 3
Lesson 10.1	Lesson 10.2	Lesson 10.3 Module Review and Assessment Readiness

Module 11

DAY 1	DAY 2	DAY 3	DAY 4
Lesson 11.1	Lesson 11.2	Lesson 11.3	Module Review and Assessment Readiness Unit Review and Assessment Readiness

Program Resources

PLAN

HMH Teacher App

Access a full suite of teacher resources online and offline on a variety of devices. Plan present, and manage classes, assignments, and activities.

ePlanner **Easily plan your classes, create and view assignments, and access all program resources with your online, customizable planning tool.**

Professional Development Videos

Authors Juli Dixon and Matt Larson model successful teaching practices and strategies in actual classroom settings.

QR Codes **Scan with your smart phone to jump directly from your print book to online videos and other resources.**

Teacher's Edition

Support students with point-of-use Questioning Strategies, teaching tips, resources for differentiated instruction, additional activities, and more.

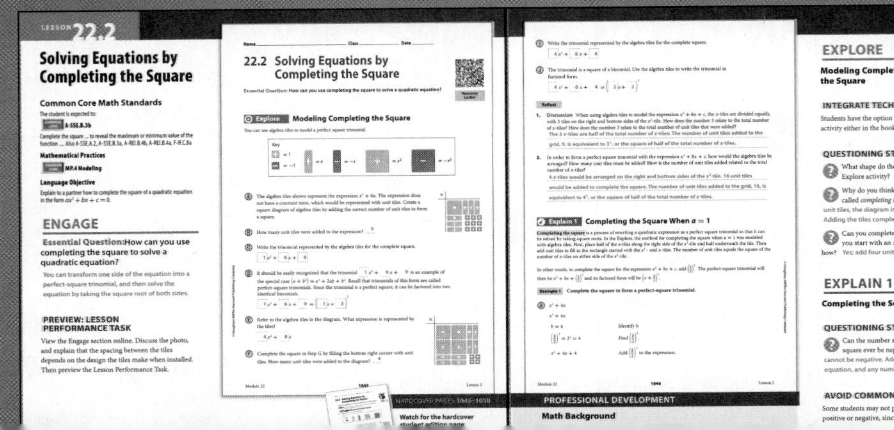

ENGAGE AND EXPLORE

Real-World Videos **Engage students with interesting and relevant applications of the mathematical content of each module.**

Explore Activities

Students interactively explore new concepts using a variety of tools and approaches.

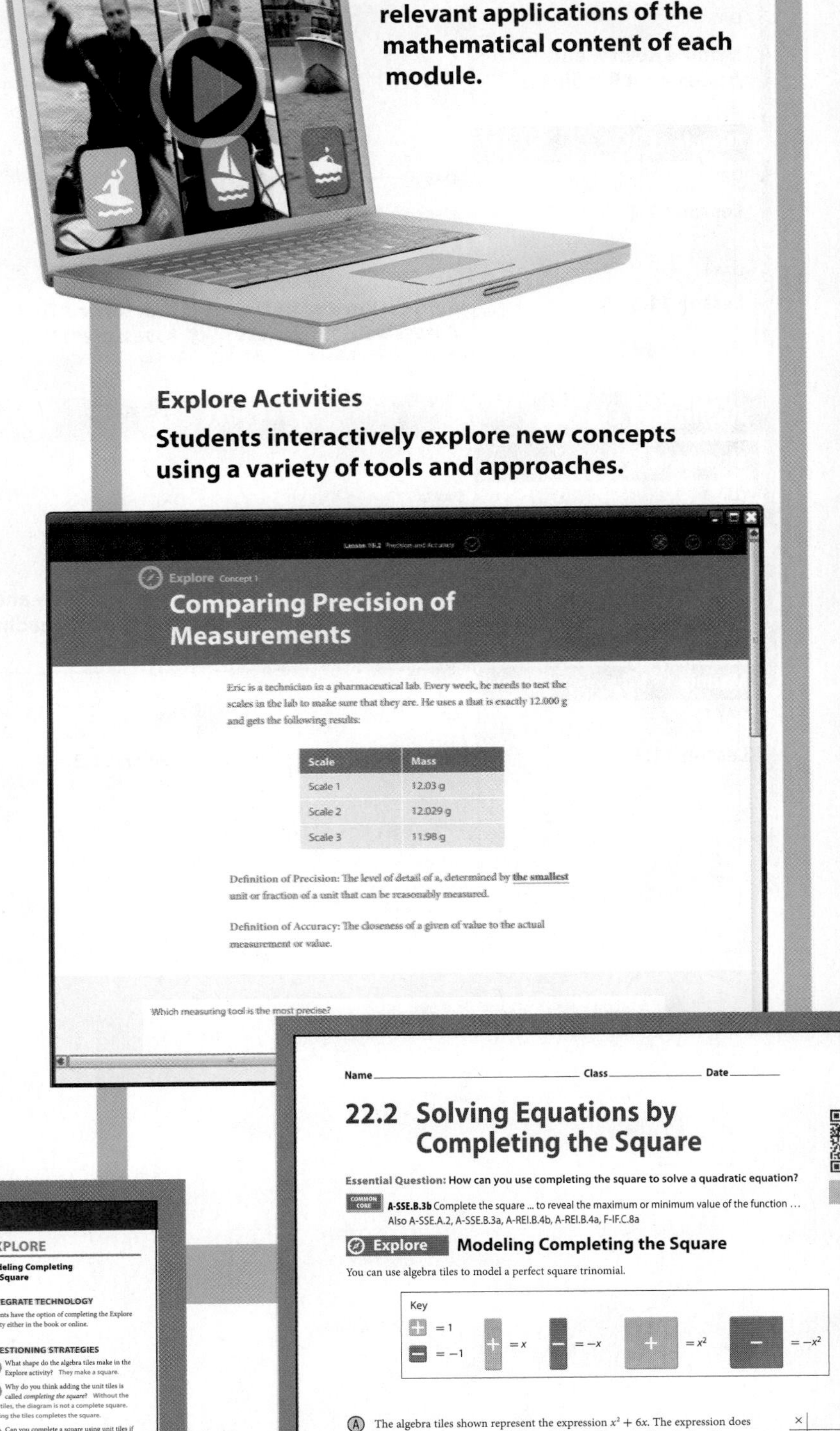

Explore Concept 1
Comparing Precision of Measurements
Eric is a technician in a pharmaceutical lab. Every week, he needs to test the scales in the lab to make sure that they are. He uses a that is exactly 12.000 g and gets the following results:
Scale | Mass
Scale 1 | 12.03 g
Scale 2 | 12.029 g
Scale 3 | 11.98 g
Definition of Precision: The level of detail of a, determined by the smallest unit or fraction of a unit that can be reasonably measured.
Definition of Accuracy: The closeness of a given of value to the actual measurement or value.
Which measuring tool is the most precise?
22.2 Solving Equations by Completing the Square
Essential Question: How can you use completing the square to solve a quadratic equation?
Explore Modeling Completing the Square
You can use algebra tiles to model a perfect square trinomial.

TEACH

Math On the Spot video tutorials, featuring program authors Dr. Edward Burger and Martha Sandoval-Martinez, accompany every example in the textbook and give students step-by-step instructions and explanations of key math concepts.

Interactive Teacher Edition

Customize and present course materials with collaborative activities and integrated formative assessment.

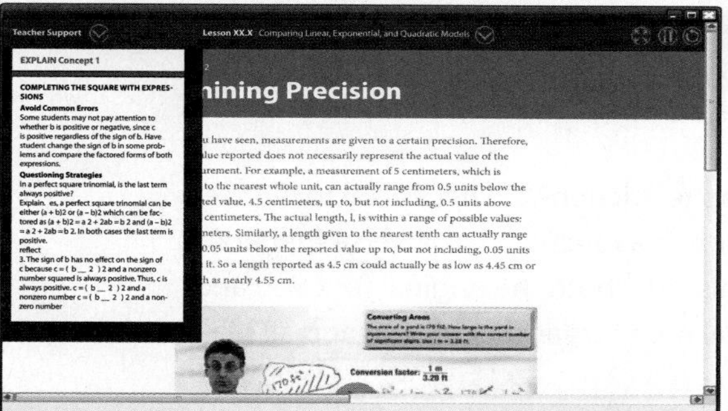

Differentiated Instruction Resources

Support all learners with Differentiated Instruction Resources, including

- **Leveled Practice and Problem Solving**
- **Reading Strategies**
- **Success for English Learners**
- **Challenge**

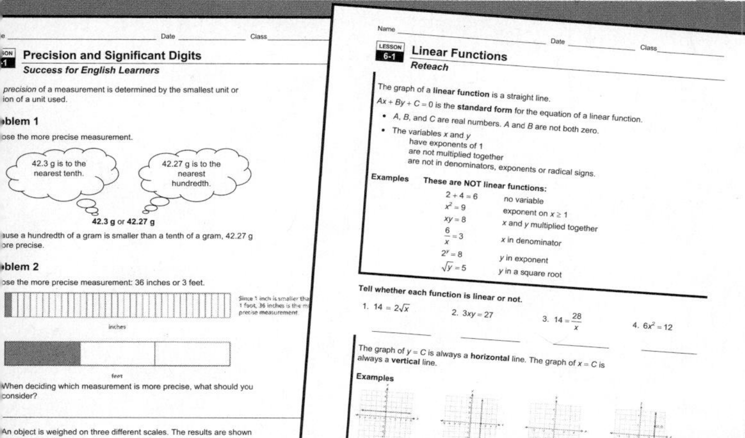

Precision and Significant Digits
Success for English Learners

precision of a measurement is determined by the smallest unit or ...ion of a unit used.

Problem 1
...ose the more precise measurement.

42.3 g is to the nearest tenth. 42.27 g is to the nearest hundredth.

42.3 g or 42.27 g

...ause a hundredth of a gram is smaller than a tenth of a gram, 42.27 g ...ore precise.

Problem 2
...ose the more precise measurement: 36 inches or 3 feet.

When deciding which measurement is more precise, what should you consider?

An object is weighed on three different scales. The results are shown in the table. Which scale is the most precise? Explain your answer.

Name ______ Date ______ Class ______

LESSON 6-1 Linear Functions
Reteach

The graph of a **linear function** is a straight line.
$Ax + By + C = 0$ is the **standard form** for the equation of a linear function.
- A, B, and C are real numbers. A and B are not both zero.
- The variables x and y
  have exponents of 1
  are not multiplied together
  are not in denominators, exponents or radical signs.

Examples — These are NOT linear functions:

$2 + 4 = 6$	no variable
$x^2 = 9$	exponent on $x \geq 1$
$xy = 8$	x and y multiplied together
$\frac{6}{x} = 3$	x in denominator
$2^x = 8$	y in exponent
$\sqrt{y} = 5$	y in a square root

Tell whether each function is linear or not.

1. $14 = 2\sqrt{x}$ 2. $3xy = 27$ 3. $14 = \frac{28}{x}$ 4. $6x^2 = 12$

The graph of $y = C$ is always a **horizontal** line. The graph of $x = C$ is always a **vertical** line.

Examples

ASSESSMENT AND INTERVENTION

The Personal Math Trainer provides online practice, homework, assessments, and intervention. Monitor student progress through reports and alerts. Create and customize assignments aligned to specific lessons or Common Core standards.

- **Practice** – With dynamic items and assignments, students get unlimited practice on key concepts supported by guided examples, step-by-step solutions, and video tutorials.
- **Assessments** – Choose from course assignments or customize your own based on course content, Common Core standards, difficulty levels, and more.
- **Homework** – Students can complete online homework with a wide variety of problem types, including the ability to enter expressions, equations, and graphs. Let the system automatically grade homework, so you can focus where your students need help the most!
- **Intervention** – Let the Personal Math Trainer automatically prescribe a targeted, personalized intervention path for your students.

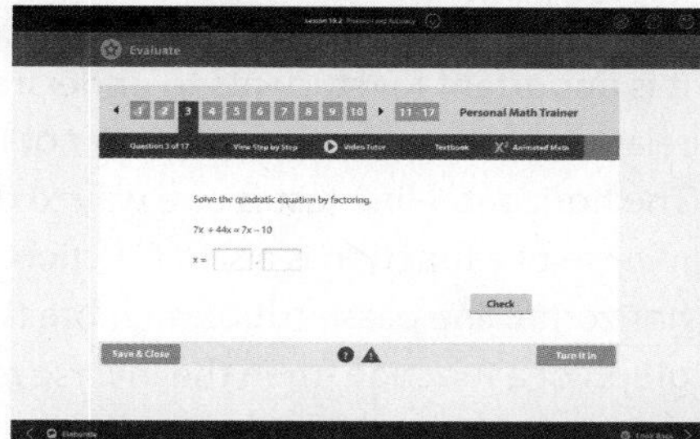

Focus on Higher Order Thinking

Raise the bar with homework and practice that incorporates higher-order thinking and mathematical practices in every lesson.

Assessment Readiness

Prepare students for success on high stakes tests for Algebra 2 with practice at every module and unit

Assessment Resources

Tailor assessments and response to intervention to meet the needs of all your classes and students, including

- Leveled Module Quizzes
- Leveled Unit Tests
- Unit Performance Tasks
- Placement, Diagnostic, and Quarterly Benchmark Tests
- Tier 1, Tier 2, and Tier 3 Resources

Math Background

Radical Functions  F-BF.B.4

LESSONS 10.1 to 10.3

When two nonzero real numbers are multiplicative inverses of each other, their product is the multiplicative identity, 1.

In other words, for $a \neq 0$, $a \cdot \frac{1}{a} = 1$. Analogously, when two functions f and g are inverses, their composition is the identity function.

This may be expressed symbolically as $f(g(x)) = x$ and $g(f(x)) = x$. In less formal terms, these equations show that f and g "undo" each other. That is, the composition of f and g, in either order, takes the input value x and returns the output value x.

In this case, $g(x)$ is called the inverse of $f(x)$ and it may be named $f^1(x)$.

It is important for students to understand that the inverse relation of a function may or may not itself be a function. The horizontal-line test is one way to decide whether the inverse of a function is also a function. Specifically, if no horizontal line passes through more than one point on the graph of a function, then the inverse relation is a function.

This is because the graph of the inverse relation, which can be found by reflecting the graph of the original function across the line $y = x$, will pass the vertical-line test.

The horizontal-line test is a way of checking to see if a function is one-to-one. In a one-to-one function, each y-value is paired with exactly one x-value. Thus, f is one-to-one if for every a and b in its domain, $f(a) = f(b)$ implies $a = b$.

The conditions under which the inverse relation of a function is itself a function may now be restated as follows: A function is one-to-one if and only if its inverse relation is a function.

Given a relation defined by a set of ordered pairs (x, y), the inverse relation is the set of ordered pairs (y, x). Thus, the graph of an inverse relation is the reflection of the graph of the original relation across the line $y = x$. The following graph shows that $y = \pm\sqrt{x}$ is the inverse relation of $y = x^2$.

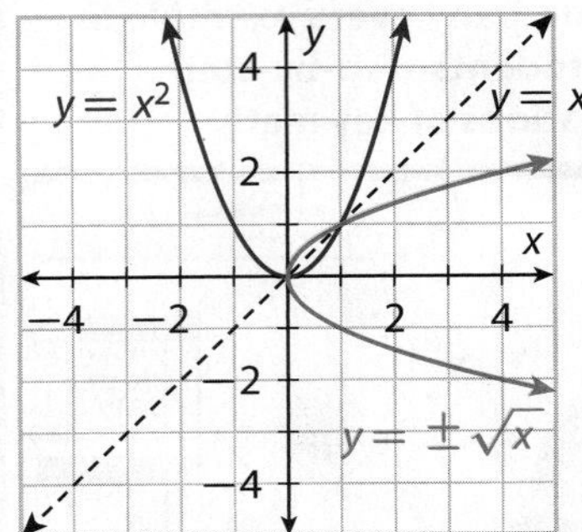

While $y = x^2$ is a function, we can see immediately from the graph that $y = \pm\sqrt{x}$ is not. The relation becomes a function when the domain of $y = x^2$ is restricted to nonnegative values of x. In this case, the inverse function is the principal square root of x; that is, $y = \sqrt{x}$. This corresponds to the portion of the graph of $y = \pm\sqrt{x}$ that lies on or above the x-axis.

Note that for $y = x^3$ no restrictions are necessary to ensure that the inverse relation is a function. The inverse function is simply $y = \sqrt[3]{x}$. In this case, both the original function and its inverse have all real numbers as the domain and all real numbers as the range.

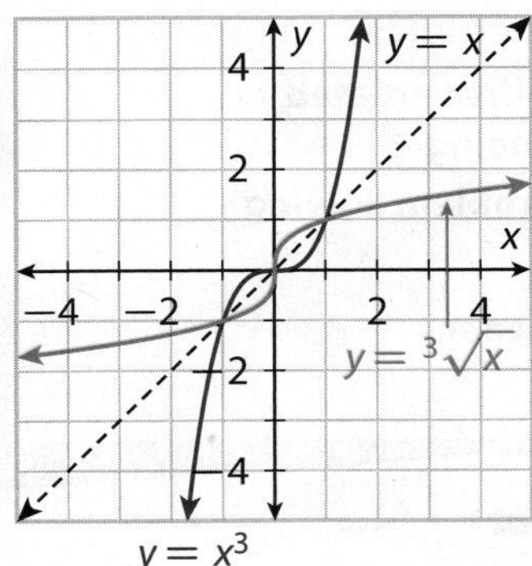

Rational Exponents  N-RN.A.2

LESSON 11.1

Rational exponents are defined to be consistent with definitions and properties for integer exponents.

For example, given a real number a, we want to define $a^{\frac{1}{2}}$ so that it is consistent with the Power of a Power Property; it must be true that

$$\left(a^{\frac{1}{3}}\right)^3 = a^{\frac{1}{3}\cdot 3} = a^1 = a.$$

This shows that $a^{\frac{1}{3}}$ must be the cube root of a:

$$a^{\frac{1}{3}} = \sqrt[3]{a}$$

In general, for any natural number n, $a^{\frac{1}{n}} = \sqrt[n]{a}$.

Similarly, in defining $a^{\frac{m}{n}}$, where m is an integer and n is a natural number, the Power of a Power Property should be true:

$$a^{\frac{m}{n}} = \left(a^{\frac{1}{n}}\right)^m = (a^m)^{\frac{1}{n}}$$

Using $a^{\frac{1}{n}} = \sqrt[n]{a}$ shows that the required definition is

$$a^{\frac{m}{n}} = \left(\sqrt[n]{a}\right)^m = \sqrt[n]{a^m}$$

Exponents can be extended to irrational numbers. For example, to find the value of 2^{π}, first consider the following sequence:

3.1, 3.14, 3.142, 3.1416, 3.14159, …

This sequence gets closer and closer to π, so it is reasonable to expect that the sequence below gets closer and closer to 2^{π}.

$2^{\frac{31}{10}}, 2^{\frac{314}{100}}, 2^{\frac{3142}{1000}}, 2^{\frac{31416}{10000}}, 2^{\frac{314159}{100000}}, \ldots$

A rigorous treatment of irrational exponents requires concepts from calculus, but this informal explanation may help students understand why the domain of functions such as $f(x) = 2^{\pi}$ is all real numbers.

UNIT 5

Radical Functions, Expressions, and Equations

MATH IN CAREERS

Unit Activity Preview

After completing this unit, students will complete a Math in Careers task by finding a quadratic function that models BMI data. Critical skills include fitting a function to data, finding appropriate domain and range, and finding the inverse of a function.

For more information about careers in mathematics as well as various mathematics appreciation topics, visit The American Mathematical Society at http://www.ams.org.

UNIT 5

Radical Functions, Expressions, and Equations

MODULE 10
Radical Functions

MODULE 11
Radical Expressions and Equations

MATH IN CAREERS

Nutritionist Nutritionists provide services to individuals and institutions, such as schools and hospitals. Nutritionists must be able to calculate the amounts of different substances in a person's diet, including calories, fat, vitamins, and minerals. They must also calculate measures of fitness, such as body mass index. Nutritionists must use statistics when reviewing nutritional studies in scientific journals.

If you are interested in a career as a nutritionist, you should study these mathematical subjects:

- Algebra
- Statistics
- Business Math

Research other careers that require proficiency in understanding statistics in scientific articles. Check out the career activity at the end of the unit to find out how **Nutritionists** use math.

TRACKING YOUR LEARNING PROGRESSION

Before	In this Unit	After
Students understand: • graphing simple and more complicated rational functions • combining rational expressions by various operations • graphing and solving rational equations	Students will learn about: • inverses of quadratic and cubic functions • graphing square root functions • graphing cube root functions • simplifying radical expressions • solving radical equations	Students will study: • arithmetic and geometric sequences • exponential growth and decay functions • exponential functions with *e*

Reading Start-Up

Visualize Vocabulary

Use the ✓ words to complete the graphic. Put just one word in each section of the square.

Invese function The function that results from exchanging the input and output values of a function.	**Many-to-one function** A function where each element of the range may correspond to more than one element of the domain.
One-to-one function A function where each element of the range corresponds to only one element of the domain.	**Composition of functions** A situation with two functions in which the output of one function is used as the input for the other.

Function Types

Vocabulary

Review Words

✓ composition of functions (*composición de funciones*)
extraneous solution (*solución extraña*)
✓ inverse function (*función inversa*)
✓ many-to-one function (*función muchos a uno*)
✓ one-to-one function (*función uno a uno*)
radical expression (*expresión radical*)

Preview Words

cube root function (función de raíz cúbica)
index (índice)
square root function (función de raíz cuadrada)

Understand Vocabulary

To become familiar with some of the vocabulary terms in the module, consider the following. You may refer to the module, the glossary, or a dictionary.

1. A function whose rule contains a variable under a square-root sign is a **square root function**.
2. A function whose rule contains a variable under a cube-root sign is a **cube root function**.
3. In the radical expression $\sqrt[n]{x}$, n is the **index**.

Active Reading

Pyramid Fold Before beginning a module, create a pyramid fold to help you take notes from each lesson in the module. The three sides of the pyramid can summarize information about function families, their graphs, and their characteristics.

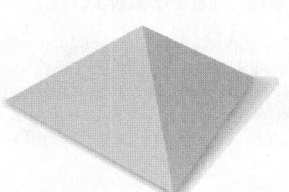

Reading Start Up

Have students complete the activities on this page by working alone or with others.

VISUALIZE VOCABULARY

The chart helps students review important vocabulary associated with functions and radical expressions. If time allows, ask students to supply examples for each, or several, of the review terms.

UNDERSTAND VOCABULARY

Use the following explanations to help students learn the preview words.

The inverse of a quadratic function with a restricted domain is a **square root function**. The inverse of a cubic function is a **cube root function**. The **index** of a square root expression is 2, while the index of a cube root expression is 3.

ACTIVE READING

Students can use these reading and note-taking strategies to help them organize and understand the new concepts and vocabulary. Encourage students to apply familiar vocabulary they have learned in earlier units to help find patterns in the structure of new terms. Emphasize the importance of seeking clarification of confusing or unfamiliar terms.

ADDITIONAL RESOURCES

Differentiated Instruction

- Reading Strategies EL

MODULE 10

Radical Functions

ESSENTIAL QUESTION:

Answer: Radical functions can often be used to describe relationships found in the natural world; for example, the relationship between the age and weight of an animal is often a radical function.

PROFESSIONAL DEVELOPMENT VIDEO

Professional Development Video

Author Matt Larson models successful teaching practices in an actual high-school classroom.

Professional Development
my.hrw.com

MODULE 10

Radical Functions

Essential Question: How can you use radical functions to solve real-world problems?

REAL WORLD VIDEO
A rocket must generate enough thrust to achieve escape velocity from Earth's gravitational field. Check out some of the calculations and preparations that go into a successful launch.

MODULE PERFORMANCE TASK PREVIEW

We Have Liftoff!

If you throw a ball straight up, it will eventually come back down. But if you could throw it with enough initial velocity, it would escape Earth's surface and go into orbit. If you could throw it even faster, it might even escape the solar system. What is the escape velocity for Earth, the minimum velocity for an object to leave Earth's surface and not return? What about the velocity necessary to escape other planets? Let's take off and find out!

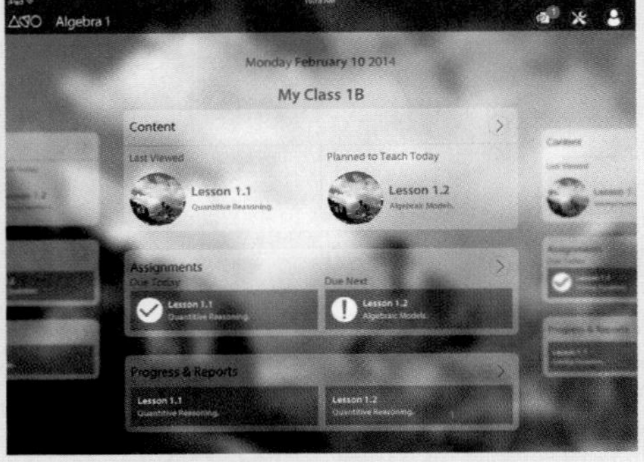

DIGITAL TEACHER EDITION

Access a full suite of teaching resources when and where you need them:

- Access content online or offline
- Customize lessons to share with your class
- Communicate with your students in real-time
- View student grades and data instantly to target your instruction where it is needed most

PERSONAL MATH TRAINER

Assessment and Intervention

Assign automatically graded homework, quizzes, tests, and intervention activities. Prepare your students with updated, Common Core-aligned practice tests.

Are YOU Ready?

Complete these exercises to review skills you will need for this chapter.

- Online Homework
- Hints and Help
- Extra Practice

Exponents

Example 1 Simplify .

$$x^2 \cdot x^3 - 2x^4 \cdot x = x^{2+3} - 2x^{4+1}$$
$$= x^5 - 2x^5$$
$$= -x^5$$

Simplify each expression.

1. $5x^3 \cdot 2x$ — $10x^4$
2. $-x^4 \cdot x^3$ — $-x^7$
3. $4x^2(2xy - x^2)$ — $8x^3y - 4x^4$

Inverse Linear Functions

Example 2 Write the inverse function of $y = x + 9$.

$y - 9 = x + 9 - 9$ Subtract.

$y - 9 = x$ Simplify.

The inverse function of $y = x + 9$ is $x = y - 9$.

Example 3 Write the inverse function of $y = \frac{x}{-22}$.

$(-22)y = -\frac{x}{22}(-22)$ Multiply.

$-22y = x$ Simplify.

The inverse function of $y = \frac{x}{-22}$ is $x = -22y$.

Write the inverse of each function.

4. $y = x - 6$ — $x = y + 6$
5. $y = 7x$ — $x = \frac{y}{7}$
6. $y = \frac{1}{2}x$ — $x = 2y$
7. $y = x + 11$ — $x = y - 11$
8. $y = -18x$ — $x = -\frac{y}{18}$
9. $y = 21 + x$ — $x = y - 21$

Response to Intervention			Differentiated Instruction
Tier 1 Lesson Intervention Worksheets	**Tier 2** Strategic Intervention Skills Intervention Worksheets	**Tier 3** Intensive Intervention Worksheets available online	
Reteach 10.1 Reteach 10.2 Reteach 10.3	9 Exponents 16 Inverse Linear Functions	Building Block Skills 76, 85, 100	Challenge worksheets Extend the Math Lesson Activities in TE

Are You Ready?

ASSESS READINESS

Use the assessment on this page to determine if students need strategic or intensive intervention for the module's prerequisite skills.

ASSESSMENT AND INTERVENTION

RtI Response to Intervention TIER 1, TIER 2, TIER 3 SKILLS

Personal Math Trainer will automatically create a standards-based, personalized intervention assignment for your students, targeting each student's individual needs!

ADDITIONAL RESOURCES

See the table below for a full list of intervention resources available for this module.

Response to Intervention Resources also includes:

- Tier 2 Skill Pre-Tests for each Module
- Tier 2 Skill Post-Tests for each skill

LESSON 10.1

Inverses of Simple Quadratic and Cubic Functions

Common Core Math Standards

The student is expected to:

 **F-BF.B.4a**

Solve an equation of the form $f(x) = c$ for a simple function f that has an inverse and write an expression for the inverse. Also F-BF.B.4b(+), F-BF.B.4c(+), F-BF.B.4d(+)

Mathematical Practices

COMMON CORE **MP.2 Reasoning**

Language Objective

Fill in an organizer of quadratic and cubic functions and their inverses.

ENGAGE

Essential Question: What functions are the inverses of quadratic and cubic functions, and how can you find them?

Possible answer: Square root functions are the inverses of quadratic functions, with the included restricted domain. Cube root functions are the inverses of cubic functions. You can find the inverse functions by using inverse operations and switching the variables, but must restrict the domain of a quadratic function.

PREVIEW: LESSON PERFORMANCE TASK

View the Engage section online. Discuss the photo and how the irrigation area can be described by a quadratic function. Ask students to list the variables involved in the function. Then preview the Lesson Performance Task.

Name ______________ Class ______________ Date ______________

10.1 Inverses of Simple Quadratic and Cubic Functions

Resource Locker

Essential Question: What functions are the inverses of quadratic functions and cubic functions, and how can you find them?

Explore Finding the Inverse of a Many-to-One Function

The function $f(x)$ is defined by the following ordered pairs: $(-2, 4)$, $(-1, 2)$, $(0, 0)$, $(1, 2)$, and $(2, 4)$.

(A) Find the inverse function of $f(x)$, $f^{-1}(x)$, by reversing the coordinates in the ordered pairs.

$(4, -2)$, $(2, -1)$, $(0, 0)$, $(2, 1)$, $(4, 2)$

(B) Is the inverse also a function? Explain.

No; the x-values 2 and 4 are both paired with more than one y-value.

(C) If necessary, restrict the domain of $f(x)$ such that the inverse, $f^{-1}(x)$, is a function.

The domain of $f(x)$ should be restricted to $\{x \mid x \geq 0\}$

(D) With the restricted domain of $f(x)$, what ordered pairs define the inverse function $f^{-1}(x)$?

$(0, 0)$, $(2, 1)$, $(4, 2)$

Reflect

1. **Discussion** Look again at the ordered pairs that define $f(x)$. Without switching the order of the coordinates, how could you have known that the inverse of $f(x)$ would not be a function?
When two or more coordinates have the same y-value but unique x-values, the inverse of that function will have coordinates in which the same x-value maps to more than one y-value, and thus will not be a function. That is, if a function is many-to-one, its inverse will not be a function.

2. How will restricting the domain of $f(x)$ affect the range of its inverse?
Since the domain of a function is the same as the range of its inverse, the restriction will apply to both.

HARDCOVER PAGES 479–494

Watch for the hardcover student edition page numbers for this lesson.

 Explain 1 Finding and Graphing the Inverse of a Simple Quadratic Function

The function $f(x) = x^2$ is a many-to-one function, so its domain must be restricted in order to find its inverse function. If the domain is restricted to $x \geq 0$, then the inverse function is $f^{-1}(x) = \sqrt{x}$; if the domain is restricted to $x \leq 0$, then the inverse function is $f^{-1}(x) = -\sqrt{x}$.

The inverse of a quadratic function is a **square root function**, which is a function whose rule involves $\sqrt{x}$. **The parent square root function** is $g(x) = \sqrt{x}$. A square root function is defined only for values of x that make the expression under the radical sign nonnegative.

Example 1 **Restrict the domain of each quadratic function and find its inverse. Confirm the inverse relationship using composition. Graph the function and its inverse.**

(A) $f(x) = 0.5x^2$

Restrict the domain. $\{x|x \geq 0\}$

Find the inverse.

Replace $f(x)$ with y.	$y = 0.5x^2$
Multiply both sides by 2.	$2y = x^2$
Use the definition of positive square root.	$\sqrt{2y} = x$
Switch x and y to write the inverse.	$\sqrt{2x} = y$
Replace y with $f^{-1}(x)$.	$f^{-1}(x) = \sqrt{2x}$

Confirm the inverse relationship using composition.

$$f^{-1}(f(x)) = f^{-1}(0.5x^2)$$
$$= \sqrt{2(0.5x^2)}$$
$$= \sqrt{x^2}$$
$$= x \text{ for } x \geq 0$$

Since $f^{-1}(f(x)) = x$ for $x \geq 0$, it has been confirmed that $f^{-1}(x) = \sqrt{2x}$ for $x \geq 0$ is the inverse function of $f(x) = 0.5x^2$ for $x \geq 0$.

Graph $f^{-1}(x)$ by graphing $f(x)$ and reflecting $f(x)$ over the line $y = x$.

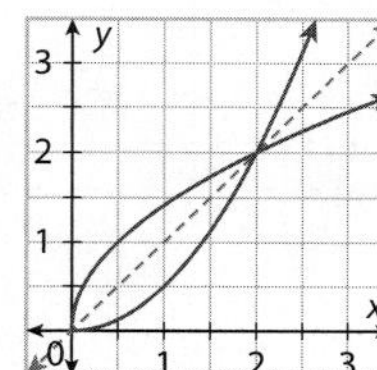

PROFESSIONAL DEVELOPMENT

Math Background

The domain of any even function $f(x) = x^n$ where $n = 2, 4, 6, \ldots$ needs to be restricted for the inverse to also be a function. This is because these functions are not one-to-one. If the domain is not restricted, then reflecting its graph across the line $y = x$ yields a graph that fails the vertical line test. This is because every non-zero real number has two nth roots when n is even, one positive and one negative. In contrast, the domain of any odd function $f(x) = x^n$ where $n = 1, 3, 5, \ldots$ need not be restricted for the inverse to also be a function. This is because every real number has a single nth root when n is odd, either positive, negative, or zero at the origin.

EXPLORE

Finding the Inverse of a Many-to-One Function

INTEGRATE TECHNOLOGY

Encourage students to investigate the DrawInv function of their graphing calculators. Have them graph $Y1 = X^2$, then use DrawInv Y1 to add the graph of the inverse to the screen.

QUESTIONING STRATEGIES

? How can you tell if a set of ordered pairs that represents a function has an inverse that is a function? **Check to see whether each ordered pair has a unique *y*-value.**

EXPLAIN 1

Finding and Graphing the Inverse of a Simple Quadratic Function

QUESTIONING STRATEGIES

? What characteristic of the graph of a quadratic function tells you that the domain needs to be restricted for the inverse to be a function? **The U-shape tells you that the function is not one-to-one, and that its inverse will not be a function unless the domain is restricted.**

? How do you find the domain and range of the inverse of a quadratic function? **The domain will be the range of the original quadratic function. The range will be the domain of the original quadratic function, restricted to values either greater than or equal to, or less than or equal to, the value of *x* that produces the minimum or maximum value of the original function.**

INTEGRATE MATHEMATICAL PRACTICES

Focus on Math Connections

MP.1 Remind students how the vertical line test can be used to determine whether the graph of a relation represents a function. Help them see that the horizontal line test can be used to see whether a function has an inverse that is a function. Lead them to recognize how applying the horizontal line test to the graph of the original function is related to applying the vertical line test to the graph of the inverse of the function.

(B) $f(x) = x^2 - 7$

Find the inverse.

Restrict the domain. $\{x \mid x \geq 0\}$

Replace $f(x)$ with y. $y = x^2 - 7$

Add 7 to both sides. $y + 7 = x^2$

Use the definition of positive square root. $\sqrt{y+7} = x$

Switch x and y to write the inverse. $\sqrt{x+7} = y$

Replace y with $f^{-1}(x)$. $\sqrt{x+7} = f^{-1}(x)$

Confirm the inverse relationship using composition.

$$f^{-1}(f(x)) = f^{-1}\left(x^2 - 7\right)$$
$$= \sqrt{(x^2 - 7) + 7}$$
$$= \sqrt{x^2}$$
$$= x \text{ for } x \geq 0$$

Since $f^{-1}(f(x)) = x$ for $x \geq 0$ it has been confirmed that $f^{-1}(x) = \sqrt{x+7}$ for $x \geq -7$ is the inverse function of $f(x) = x^2 - 7$ for $x \geq 0$.

Graph $f^{-1}(x)$ by graphing $f(x)$ and reflecting $f(x)$ over the line $y = x$.

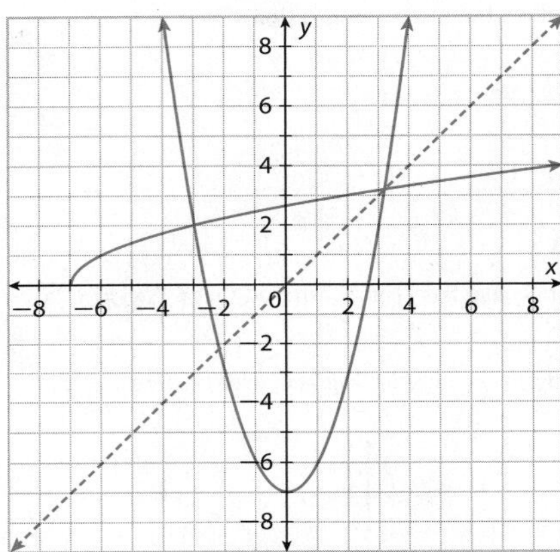

COLLABORATIVE LEARNING

Peer-to-Peer Activity

Have students work in pairs. Provide each pair with a function of the form $f(x) = ax^3 + c$. Have students find $f^{-1}(x)$, the inverse of the function. Then have them graph both $f(x)$ and $f^{-1}(x)$ on the same coordinate grid. Have them check their work by verifying that if (x, y) belongs to $f(x)$, then (y, x) belongs to $f^{-1}(x)$.

Your Turn

Restrict the domain of each quadratic function and find its inverse. Confirm the inverse relationship using composition. Graph the function and its inverse.

3. $f(x) = 3x^2$

Restrict the domain. $\{x \mid x \geq 0\}$.

Find the inverse.

Replace $f(x)$ with y.	$y = 3x^2$
Divide both sides by 3.	$\frac{y}{3} = x^2$
Use the definition of positive square root.	$\sqrt{\frac{y}{3}} = x$
Switch x and y to write the inverse.	$\sqrt{\frac{x}{3}} = y$
Replace y with $f^{-1}(x)$.	$\sqrt{\frac{x}{3}} = f^{-1}(x)$

Confirm the inverse relationship using composition.

$$f^{-1}(f(x)) = f^{-1}(3x^2) = \sqrt{\frac{3x^2}{3}} = \sqrt{x^2} = x \text{ for } x \geq 0$$

Since $f^{-1}(f(x)) = x$ for $x \geq 0$, it has been confirmed that $f^{-1}(x) = \sqrt{\frac{x}{3}}$ for $x \geq 0$ is the inverse function of $f(x) = 3x^2$ for $x \geq 0$.

Graph $f^{-1}(x)$ by graphing $f(x)$ and reflecting $f(x)$ over the line $y = x$.

Explain 2 Finding the Inverse of a Quadratic Model

In many instances, quadratic functions are used to model real-world applications. It is often useful to find and interpret the inverse of a quadratic model. Note that when working with real-world applications, it is more useful to use the notation $x(y)$ for the inverse of $y(x)$ instead of the notation $y^{-1}(x)$.

Example 2 **Find the inverse of each of the quadratic functions. Use the inverse to solve the application.**

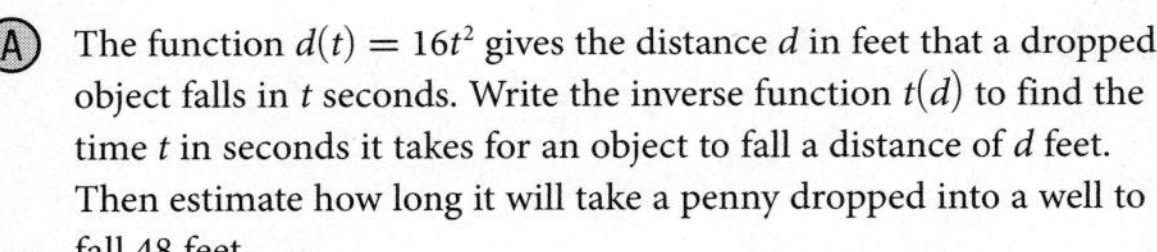

Ⓐ The function $d(t) = 16t^2$ gives the distance d in feet that a dropped object falls in t seconds. Write the inverse function $t(d)$ to find the time t in seconds it takes for an object to fall a distance of d feet. Then estimate how long it will take a penny dropped into a well to fall 48 feet.

The original function $d(t) = 16t^2$ is a quadratic function with a domain restricted to $t \geq 0$.

Find the inverse function.

Write $d(t)$ as d.	$d = 16t^2$
Divide both sides by 16.	$\frac{d}{16} = t^2$
Use the definition of positive square root.	$\sqrt{\frac{d}{16}} = t$

AVOID COMMON ERRORS

Students may make algebraic errors when finding the inverse of a function such as $f(x) = 5x^2$. Reinforce that students should isolate x^2 before taking the square root of each side, and that when taking the square root, they must take the square root of the entire expression on the other side of the equation, not just of the variable.

EXPLAIN 2

Finding the Inverse of a Quadratic Model

QUESTIONING STRATEGIES

How does the inverse of a function relate to the original function in a real-world application? It tells you how to find the value of what was the independent variable in the original function, given the value of what was the dependent variable.

DIFFERENTIATE INSTRUCTION

Graphic Organizers

Students may benefit from summarizing what they've learned in a graphic organizer like the one shown below. Encourage students to add graphs.

	Linear	Quadratic	Cubic
Functions	$f(x) = ax$ $f^{-1}(x) = \frac{x}{a}$	$f(x) = ax^2$ $f^{-1}(x) = \sqrt{\frac{x}{a}}$	$f(x) = ax^3$ $f^{-1}x = \sqrt[3]{\frac{x}{a}}$
Restrictions	$f(x)$ must have nonzero slope	Domain of $f(x)$: nonnegative values	No restrictions

Write t as $t(d)$. $\sqrt{\frac{d}{16}} = t(d)$

The inverse function is $t(d) = \sqrt{\frac{d}{16}}$ for $d \geq 0$.

Use the inverse function to estimate how long it will take a penny dropped into a well to fall 48 feet. Substitute $d = 48$ into the inverse function.

Write the function. $t(d) = \sqrt{\frac{d}{16}}$

Substitute 48 for d. $t(48) = \sqrt{\frac{48}{16}}$

Simplify. $t(48) = \sqrt{3}$

Use a calculator to estimate. $t(48) \approx 1.7$

So, it will take about 1.7 seconds for a penny to fall 48 feet into the well.

(B) The function $E(v) = 4v^2$ gives the kinetic energy E in Joules of an 8-kg object that is traveling at a velocity of v meters per second. Write and graph the inverse function $v(E)$ to find the velocity v in meters per second required for an 8-kg object to have a kinetic energy of E Joules. Then estimate the velocity required for an 8-kg object to have a kinetic energy of 60 Joules.

The original function $E(v) = 4v^2$ is a **quadratic** function with a domain restricted to v **≥ 0**.

Find the inverse function.

Write $E(v)$ as E. $\boxed{E} = 4v^2$

Divide both sides by 4. $\boxed{\frac{E}{4}} = v^2$

Use the definition of positive square root. $\boxed{\sqrt{\frac{E}{4}}} = v$

Write v as $v(E)$. $v(E) = \sqrt{\frac{E}{4}}$

The inverse function is $v(E) =$ $\sqrt{\frac{E}{4}}$ for E ≥ 0.

Use the inverse function to estimate the velocity required for an 8-kg object to have a kinetic energy of 60 Joules.

Substitute $E = 60$ into the inverse function.

Write the function. $v(E) = \boxed{\sqrt{\frac{E}{4}}}$

Substitute 60 for E. $v\left(\boxed{60}\right) = \boxed{\sqrt{\frac{60}{4}}}$

Simplify. $v(60) = \sqrt{15}$

Use a calculator to estimate. $v(60) \approx 3.9$

So, an 8-kg object with kinetic energy of 60 Joules is traveling at a velocity of **3.9** meters per second.

Your Turn

Find the inverse of the quadratic function. Use the inverse to solve the application.

4. The function $A(r) = \pi r^2$ gives the area of a circular object with respect to its radius r. Write the inverse function $r(A)$ to find the radius r required for area of A. Then estimate the radius of an circular object that has an area of 40 cm^2.

The original function has a domain restricted to $r \geq 0$.

$$A = \pi r^2$$
$$\frac{A}{\pi} = r^2$$
$$\sqrt{\frac{A}{\pi}} = r$$
$$\sqrt{\frac{A}{\pi}} = r(A)$$
$$r(A) = \sqrt{\frac{A}{\pi}}$$
$$r(40) = \sqrt{\frac{40}{\pi}}$$
$$r(40) \approx 3.6$$

So, a circular object with an area of 40 cm^2 will have a radius of about 3.6 cm.

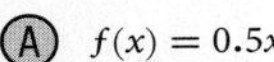

Explain 3 Finding and Graphing the Inverse of a Simple Cubic Function

Note that the function $f(x) = x^3$ is a one-to-one function, so its domain does not need to be restricted in order to find its inverse function. The inverse of $f(x) = x^3$ is $f^{-1}(x) = \sqrt[3]{x}$.

The inverse of a cubic function is a **cube root function**, which is a function whose rule involves $\sqrt[3]{x}$. The **parent cube root function** is $g(x) = \sqrt[3]{x}$.

Example 3 **Find the inverse of each cubic function. Confirm the inverse relationship using composition. Graph the function and its inverse.**

(A) $f(x) = 0.5x^3$

Find each inverse. Graph the function and its inverse.

Replace $f(x)$ with y.	$y = 0.5x^3$
Multiply both sides by 2.	$2y = x^3$
Use the definition of cube root.	$\sqrt[3]{2y} = x$
Switch x and y to write the inverse.	$\sqrt[3]{2x} = y$
Replace y with $f^{-1}(x)$.	$\sqrt[3]{2x} = f^{-1}(x)$

Confirm the inverse relationship using composition.

$$f^{-1}(f(x)) = f^{-1}(0.5x^3)$$
$$= \sqrt[3]{2(0.5x^3)}$$
$$= \sqrt[3]{x^3}$$
$$= x$$

INTEGRATE TECHNOLOGY

A graphing calculator can be used to verify that functions are inverses of each other. Students can graph the two functions and the function $f(x) = x$, and check that the graphs of their functions are reflections of each other across the graph of $f(x) = x$.

EXPLAIN 3

Finding and Graphing the Inverse of a Simple Cubic Function

QUESTIONING STRATEGIES

Why is there no need to restrict the domain of a simple cubic function before finding its inverse? Because it is a one-to-one function, its inverse is also a function.

How does the domain of a cube root function compare with the domain of a square root function? Why? The domain of a cube root function is all real numbers. The domain of a cube root function is the values of x that make the expression inside the square root greater than or equal to zero. The square root of a negative number is not a real number, but the cube root of a negative number is a real number.

Since $f^{-1}(f(x)) = x$, it has been confirmed that $f^{-1}(x) = \sqrt[3]{2x}$ is the inverse function of $f(x) = 0.5x^3$.

Graph $f^{-1}(x)$ by graphing $f(x)$ and reflecting $f(x)$ over the line $y = x$.

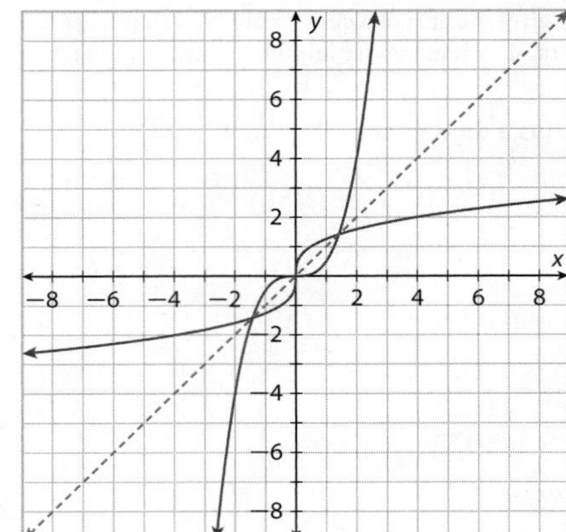

(B) $f(x) = x^3 - 9$

Find the inverse.

Replace $f(x)$ with y. $\boxed{y} = x^3 - 9$

Add 9 to both sides. $\boxed{y + 9} = x^3$

Use the definition of cube root. $\boxed{\sqrt[3]{y + 9}} = x$

Switch x and y to write the inverse. $\underline{\sqrt[3]{x + 9} = y}$

Replace y with $f^{-1}(x)$. $\underline{\sqrt[3]{x + 9} = f^{-1}(x)}$

Confirm the inverse relationship using composition.

$$f^{-1}(f(x)) = f^{-1}\left(\boxed{x^3 - 9}\right)$$

$$= \boxed{\sqrt[3]{(x^3 - 9) + 9}}$$

$$= \boxed{\sqrt[3]{x^3}}$$

$$= \boxed{x}$$

Since $f^{-1}(f(x)) = \boxed{x}$, it has been confirmed that $f^{-1}(x) = \boxed{\sqrt[3]{x + 9}}$ is the inverse function of $f(x) = x^3 - 9$.

Graph $f^{-1}(x)$ by graphing $f(x)$ and reflecting $f(x)$ over the line $y = x$.

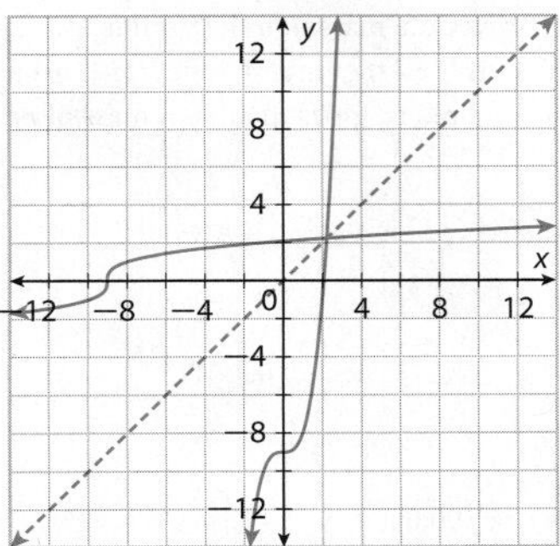

Your Turn

Find each inverse. Graph the function and its inverse.

5. $f(x) = 2x^3$

Find the inverse.

Replace $f(x)$ with y. $y = 2x^3$

Divide both sides by 2. $\frac{y}{2} = x^3$

Use the definition of cube root. $\sqrt[3]{\frac{y}{2}} = x$

Switch x and y to write the inverse. $\sqrt[3]{\frac{x}{2}} = y$

Replace y with $f^{-1}(x)$. $\sqrt[3]{\frac{x}{2}} = f^{-1}(x)$

Confirm the inverse relationship using composition.

$$f^{-1}(f(x)) = f^{-1}(2x^3)$$
$$= \sqrt[3]{\frac{2x^3}{2}}$$
$$= \sqrt[3]{x^3}$$
$$= x$$

Since $f^{-1}(f(x)) = x$, it has been confirmed that $f^{-1}(x) = \sqrt[3]{\frac{x}{2}}$ is the inverse function of $f(x) = 2x^3$.
Graph $f^{-1}(x)$ by graphing $f(x)$ and reflecting $f(x)$ over the line $y = x$.

Explain 4 Finding the Inverse of a Cubic Model

In many instances, cubic functions are used to model real-world applications. It is often useful to find and interpret the inverse of cubic models. As with quadratic real-world applications, it is more useful to use the notation $x(y)$ for the inverse of $y(x)$ instead of the notation $y^{-1}(x)$.

INTEGRATE MATHEMATICAL PRACTICES

Focus on Technology

MP.5 The table feature on a graphing calculator can be used to verify that two functions are inverses of each other. Students can enter both functions, and use the table to verify that if (x, y) belongs to Y1, then (y, x) belongs to Y2.

EXPLAIN 4

Finding the Inverse of a Cubic Model

QUESTIONING STRATEGIES

? How do you determine the domain and range of the inverse of the function in a real-world application? **The domain is the range of the original function, and the range is the domain of the original function. Domains may need to be restricted to values that are reasonable values of the independent variable in the given context.**

INTEGRATE MATHEMATICAL PRACTICES

Focus on Communication

MP.3 To ensure that students understand the relationship between the function and its inverse in this context, ask them to describe real-world questions that could more easily be answered using the original function, and those that could more easily be answered using the inverse function.

Example 4 **Find the inverse of each of the following cubic functions.**

(A) The function $m(L) = 0.00001L^3$ gives the mass m in kilograms of a red snapper of length L centimeters. Find the inverse function $L(m)$ to find the length L in centimeters of a red snapper that has a mass of m kilograms.

The original function $m(L) = 0.00001L^3$ is a cubic function.

Find the inverse function.

Write $m(L)$ as m. $\quad m = 0.00001L^3$

Multiply both sides by 100,000. $\quad 100{,}000m = L^3$

Use the definition of cube root. $\quad \sqrt[3]{100{,}000m} = L$

Write L as $L(m)$. $\quad \sqrt[3]{100{,}000m} = L(m)$

The inverse function is $L(m) = \sqrt[3]{100{,}000m}$.

(B) The function $A(r) = \frac{4}{3}\pi r^3$ gives the surface area A of a sphere with radius r. Find the inverse function $r(A)$ to find the radius r of a sphere with surface area A.

The original function $A(r) = \frac{4}{3}\pi r^3$ is a **cubic** function.

Find the inverse function.

Write $A(r)$ as A. $\quad A = \frac{4}{3}\pi r^3$

Divide both sides by $\frac{4}{3}\pi$. $\quad \frac{3}{4\pi}A = r^3$

Use the definition of cube root. $\quad \sqrt[3]{\frac{3}{4\pi}A} = r$

Write r as $r(A)$. $\quad \sqrt[3]{\frac{3}{4\pi}A} = r(A)$

The inverse function is $r(A) = \sqrt[3]{\frac{3}{4\pi}A}$.

Your Turn

6. The function $m(r) = \frac{44}{3}\pi r^3$ gives the mass in grams of a spherical lead ball with a radius of r centimeters. Find the inverse function $r(m)$ to find the radius r of a lead sphere with mass m.

$$m = \frac{44}{3}\pi r^3$$

$$\frac{3}{44\pi}m = r^3$$

$$\sqrt[3]{\frac{3}{44\pi}m} = r$$

$$\sqrt[3]{\frac{3}{44\pi}m} = r(m)$$

Elaborate

7. What is the general form of the inverse function for the function $f(x) = ax^2$? State any restrictions on the domains.
The inverse of $f(x) = ax^2$ is $f^{-1}(x) = \sqrt{\frac{x}{a}}$, where the domain of both functions must be restricted to $\{x \mid x \geq 0\}$.

8. What is the general form of the inverse function for the function $f(x) = ax^3$? State any restrictions on the domains.
The inverse of $f(x) = ax^3$ is $f^{-1}(x) = \sqrt[3]{\frac{x}{a}}$. There are no restrictions on the domains.

9. **Essential Question Check-In** Why must the domain be restricted when finding the inverse of a quadratic function, but not when finding the inverse of a cubic function?
The inverse function of a quadratic function is a square root function, which is not defined for nonnegative values of x, whereas the inverse function of a cubic function is a cube root function, which is defined for all real number values of x.

Evaluate: Homework and Practice

- Online Homework
- Hints and Help
- Extra Practice

Restrict the domain of the quadratic function and find its inverse. Confirm the inverse relationship using composition. Graph the function and its inverse.

1. $f(x) = 0.2x^2$

Restrict the domain to $\{x \mid x \geq 0\}$.

$$y = 0.2x^2$$
$$5y = x^2$$
$$\sqrt{5y} = x$$
$$\sqrt{5x} = y$$
$$\sqrt{5x} = f^{-1}(x)$$

$$f^{-1}(f(x)) = f^{-1}(0.2x^2)$$
$$= \sqrt{5(0.2x^2)}$$
$$= \sqrt{x^2}$$
$$= x \text{ for } x \geq 0$$

Since $f^{-1}(f(x)) = x$ for $x \geq 0$, it has been confirmed that $f^{-1}(x) = \sqrt{5x}$ for $x \geq 0$ is the inverse function of $f(x) = 0.2x^2$ for $x \geq 0$.

ELABORATE

INTEGRATE MATHEMATICAL PRACTICES

Focus on Critical Thinking

MP.3 Ask students to consider whether the end behavior of the graph of a function can be used to determine the need to restrict the domain in order for the inverse to be a function. Lead them to recognize that when the end behavior is the same as x approaches either ∞ or $-\infty$ (as is the case with a quadratic function), it *is* an indicator. However, when this is not the case, it is not possible to tell whether the function is one-to-one. Have students consider, for example, the graph of a cubic function that has a local maximum and a local minimum. This function is not one-to-one, but other cubic functions, such as $f(x) = x^3$, are.

SUMMARIZE THE LESSON

How do you find the function that is the inverse of a quadratic function? What type of function is the inverse? **Substitute y for $f(x)$, solve for x, and then switch x and y. The result is a square root function. You must restrict the domain of the original function so that the inverse will be a function.**

LANGUAGE SUPPORT EL

Communicate Math

Have students work in pairs. Ask them to discuss how to fill in a chart like the one below and, when they reach agreement about an entry, to take turns adding it to the chart.

Type of Function	Example equation	Graph of function
Quadratic function		
Inverse:		
Cubic function		
Inverse:		

EVALUATE

ASSIGNMENT GUIDE

Concepts and Skills	Practice
Explore Finding the Inverse of a Many-to-One Function	
Example 1 Finding and Graphing the Inverse of a Simple Quadratic Function	Exercises 1–6
Example 2 Finding the Inverse of a Quadratic Model	Exercises 7–8
Example 3 Finding and Graphing the Inverse of a Simple Cubic Function	Exercises 9–12
Example 4 Finding the Inverse of a Cubic Model	Exercises 13–15

QUESTIONING STRATEGIES

? Why is it important to know whether a function is one-to-one when finding its inverse? **Because if it is not one-to-one, you need to restrict the domain for the inverse to be a function.**

2. $f(x) = 8x^2$

Restrict the domain to $\{x \mid x \geq 0\}$.

$y = 8x^2$

$\frac{y}{8} = x^2$

$\sqrt{\frac{y}{8}} = x$

$\sqrt{\frac{x}{8}} = y$

$\sqrt{\frac{x}{8}} = f^{-1}(x)$

$f^{-1}(f(x)) = f^{-1}(8x^2)$

$= \sqrt{\frac{8x^2}{8}}$

$= \sqrt{x^2}$

$= x$ for $x \geq 0$

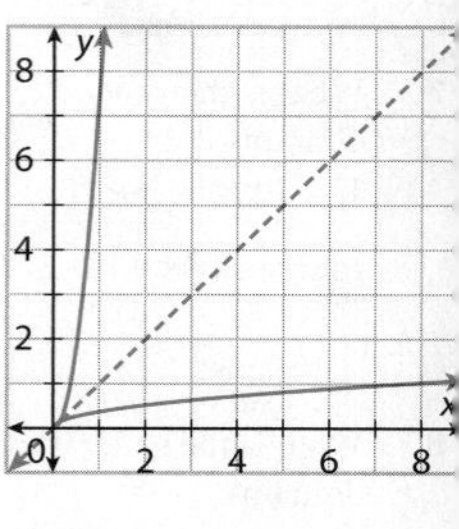

Since $f^{-1}(f(x)) = x$ for $x \geq 0$, it has been confirmed that $f^{-1}(x) = \sqrt{\frac{x}{8}}$ for $x \geq 0$ is the inverse function of $f(x) = 8x^2$ for $x \geq 0$.

3. $f(x) = x^2 + 10$

Restrict the domain to $\{x \mid x \geq 10\}$.

$y = x^2 + 10$

$y - 10 = x^2$

$\sqrt{y - 10} = x$

$\sqrt{x - 10} = y$

$\sqrt{x - 10} = f^{-1}(x)$

$f^{-1}(f(x)) = f^{-1}(x^2 + 10)$

$= \sqrt{(x^2 + 10) - 10}$

$= \sqrt{x^2}$

$= x$ for $x \geq 0$

Since $f^{-1}(f(x)) = x$ for $x \geq 10$, it has been confirmed that $f^{-1}(x) = \sqrt{x - 10}$ for $x \geq 10$ is the inverse function of $f(x) = x^2 + 10$ for $x \geq 0$.

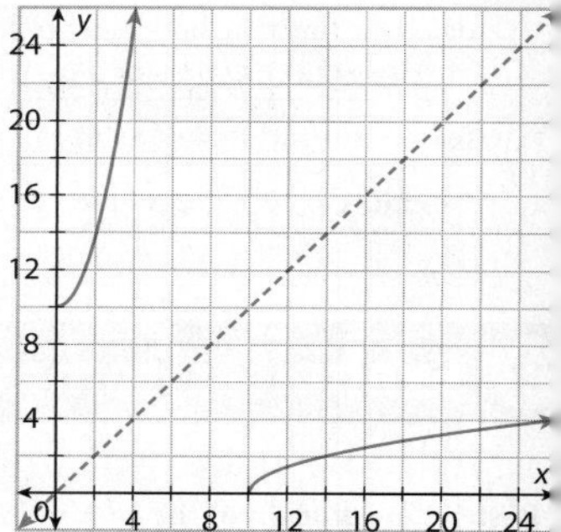

Restrict the domain of the quadratic function and find its inverse. Confirm the inverse relationship using composition.

4. $f(x) = 15x^2$

Restrict the domain to $\{x \mid x \geq 0\}$.

$y = 15x^2$

$\frac{y}{15} = x^2$

$\sqrt{\frac{y}{15}} = x$

$\sqrt{\frac{x}{15}} = y$

$\sqrt{\frac{x}{15}} = f^{-1}(x)$

$f^{-1}(f(x)) = f^{-1}(15x^2)$

$= \sqrt{\frac{15x^2}{15}}$

$= \sqrt{x^2}$

$= x$ for $x \geq 0$

Since $f^{-1}(f(x)) = x$ for $x \geq 0$, it has been confirmed that $f^{-1}(x) = \sqrt{\frac{x}{15}}$ for $x \geq 0$ is the inverse function of $f(x) = 15x^2$ for $x \geq 0$.

Exercise	Depth of Knowledge (D.O.K.)	COMMON CORE Mathematical Practices
1–6	**2** Skills/Concepts	**MP.3** Logic
7–8	**3** Strategic Thinking	**MP.4** Modeling
9–10	**2** Skills/Concepts	**MP.6** Precision
11–12	**2** Skills/Concepts	**MP.2** Reasoning
13–15	**3** Strategic Thinking	**MP.4** Modeling
16,18	**3** Strategic Thinking H.O.T.	**MP.2** Reasoning
17	**3** Strategic Thinking H.O.T.	**MP.4** Modeling

$f(x) = x^2 - \frac{3}{4}$

Restrict the domain to $\left\{x \middle| \ x \geq -\frac{3}{4}\right\}$.

$$y = x^2 - \frac{3}{4}$$
$$y + \frac{3}{4} = x^2$$
$$\sqrt{y + \frac{3}{4}} = x$$
$$\sqrt{x + \frac{3}{4}} = y$$
$$\sqrt{x + \frac{3}{4}} = f^{-1}(x)$$

$$f^{-1}(f(x)) = f^{-1}\left(x^2 - \frac{3}{4}\right)$$
$$= \sqrt{\left(x^2 - \frac{3}{4}\right) + \frac{3}{4}}$$
$$= \sqrt{x^2}$$
$$= x \text{ for } x \geq 0$$

Since $f^{-1}(f(x)) = x$ for $x \geq -\frac{3}{4}$, it has been confirmed that $f^{-1}(x) = \sqrt{x + \frac{3}{4}}$ for $x \geq -\frac{3}{4}$ is the inverse function of $f(x) = x^2 - \frac{3}{4}$ for $x \geq 0$.

$f(x) = 0.7x^2$

Restrict the domain to $\{x| \ x \geq 0\}$.

$$y = 0.7x^2$$
$$\frac{10}{7}y = x^2$$
$$\sqrt{\frac{10}{7}y} = x$$
$$\sqrt{\frac{10}{7}x} = y$$
$$\sqrt{\frac{10}{7}x} = f^{-1}(x)$$

$$f^{-1}(f(x)) = f^{-1}\left(\frac{7}{10}x^2\right)$$
$$= \sqrt{\frac{10}{7}\left(\frac{7}{10}x^2\right)}$$
$$= \sqrt{x^2}$$
$$= x \text{ for } x \geq 0$$

Since $f^{-1}(f(x)) = x$ for $x \geq 0$, it has been confirmed that $f^{-1}(x) = \sqrt{\frac{10}{7}x}$ for $x \geq 0$ is the inverse function of $f(x) = 0.7x^2$ for $x \geq 0$.

The function $d(s) = \frac{1}{14.9}s^2$ models the average depth d in feet of the water over which a tsunami travels, where s is the speed in miles per hour. Write the inverse function $s(d)$ to find the speed required for a depth of d feet. Then estimate the speed of a tsunami over water with an average depth of 1500 feet.

$$d(s) = \frac{1}{14.9}s^2$$
$$d = \frac{1}{14.9}s^2$$
$$14.9d = s^2$$
$$\sqrt{14.9d} = s$$
$$\sqrt{14.9d} = s(d)$$
$$s(d) = \sqrt{14.9d}$$
$$s(1500) = \sqrt{14.9(1500)}$$
$$s(1500) \approx 150$$

So, the speed of a tsunami over water with an average depth of 1500 feet is about 150 mi/h.

AVOID COMMON ERRORS

Students may, in error, believe that if the graph of a relation passes the horizontal line test, then the relation is one-to-one. Help them to see that the horizontal line test can be used only to test whether a *function* is one-to-one. In other words, the graph must first pass the vertical line test.

INTEGRATE MATHEMATICAL PRACTICES

Focus on Modeling

MP.4 Discuss with students how a function and its inverse can both model a given real-world situation, even if one is a power function and the other is a radical function.

8. The function $x(T) = 9.8\left(\frac{T}{2\pi}\right)^2$ gives the length x in meters for a pendulum to swing for a period of T seconds. Write the inverse function to find the period of a pendulum in seconds. The period of a pendulum is the time it takes the pendulum to complete one back-and-forth swing. Find the period of a pendulum with length of 5 meters.

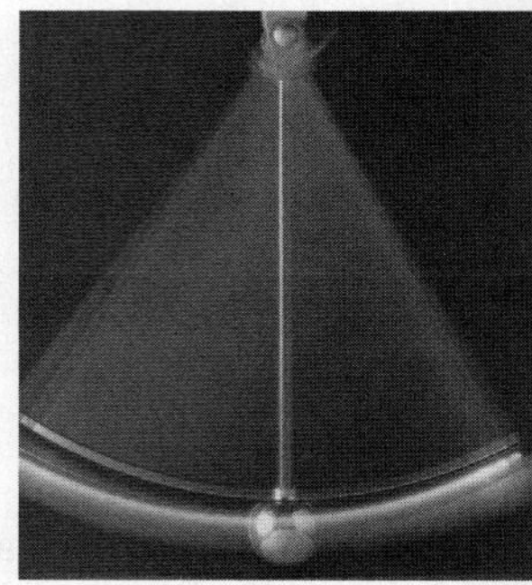

$$x(T) = 9.8\left(\frac{T}{2\pi}\right)^2$$

$$x = 9.8\left(\frac{T}{2\pi}\right)^2$$

$$\frac{x}{9.8} = \left(\frac{T}{2\pi}\right)^2$$

$$\sqrt{\frac{x}{9.8}} = \frac{T}{2\pi}$$

$$2\pi\sqrt{\frac{x}{9.8}} = T$$

$$2\pi\sqrt{\frac{x}{9.8}} = T(x)$$

$$T(x) = 2\pi\sqrt{\frac{x}{9.8}}$$

$$T(5) = 2\pi\sqrt{\frac{5}{9.8}}$$

$$T(45) \approx 4.5$$

The period of a pendulum with a length of 5 meters is about 4.5 seconds.

Find the inverse of each cubic function. Confirm the inverse relationship using composition. Graph the function and its inverse.

9. $f(x) = 0.25x^3$

$$y = 0.25x^3$$

$$4y = x^3$$

$$\sqrt[3]{4y} = x$$

$$\sqrt[3]{4x} = y$$

$$\sqrt[3]{4x} = f^{-1}(x)$$

$$f^{-1}(f(x)) = f^{-1}(0.25x^3)$$

$$= \sqrt[3]{4(0.25x^3)}$$

$$= \sqrt[3]{x^3}$$

$$= x$$

Since $f^{-1}(f(x)) = x$, it has been confirmed that $f^{-1}(x) = \sqrt[3]{4x}$ is the inverse function of $f(x) = 0.25x^3$.

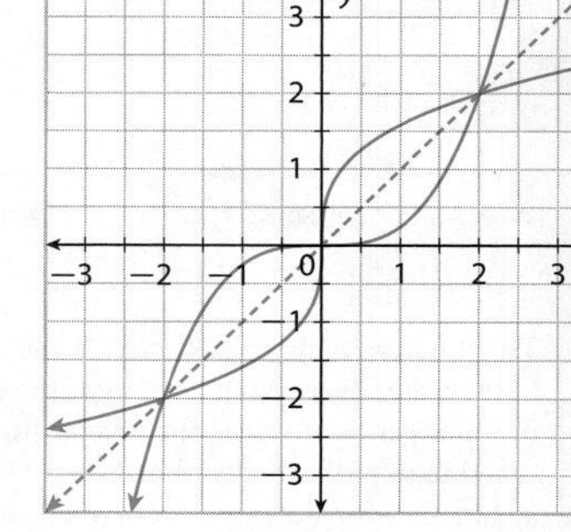

10. $f(x) = -12x^3$

$$y = -12x^3$$

$$\frac{y}{-12} = x^3$$

$$\sqrt[3]{-\frac{y}{12}} = x$$

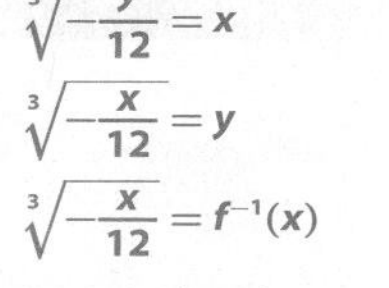

$$\sqrt[3]{-\frac{x}{12}} = y$$

$$\sqrt[3]{-\frac{x}{12}} = f^{-1}(x)$$

$$f^{-1}(f(x)) = f^{-1}(-12x^3)$$

$$= \sqrt[3]{\frac{-12x^3}{-12}}$$

$$= \sqrt[3]{x^3}$$

$$= x$$

Since $f^{-1}(f(x)) = x$, it has been confirmed that $f^{-1}(x) = \sqrt[3]{-\frac{x}{12}}$ is the inverse function of $f(x) = -12x^3$.

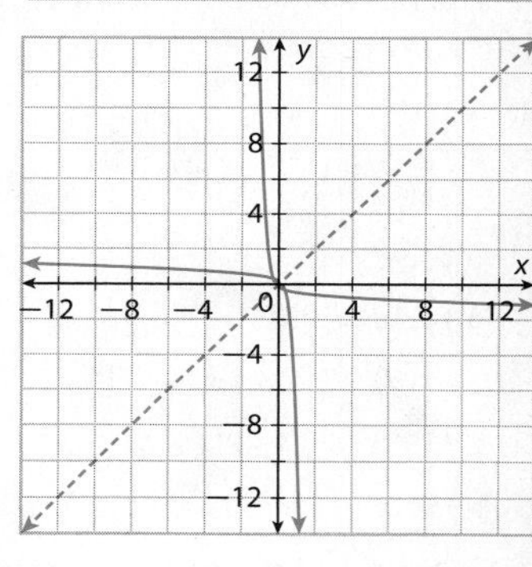

Find the inverse of the cubic function. Confirm the inverse relationship using composition.

1. $f(x) = x^3 - \frac{5}{6}$

$$y = x^3 - \frac{5}{6}$$
$$y + \frac{5}{6} = x^3$$
$$\sqrt[3]{y + \frac{5}{6}} = x$$
$$\sqrt[3]{x + \frac{5}{6}} = y$$
$$\sqrt[3]{x + \frac{5}{6}} = f^{-1}(x)$$

$$f^{-1}(f(x)) = f^{-1}\left(x^3 - \frac{5}{6}\right)$$
$$= \sqrt[3]{\left(x^3 - \frac{5}{6}\right) + \frac{5}{6}}$$
$$= \sqrt[3]{x^3}$$
$$= x$$

Since $f^{-1}(f(x)) = x$, it has been confirmed that $f^{-1}(x) = \sqrt[3]{x + \frac{5}{6}}$ is the inverse function of $f(x) = x^3 - \frac{5}{6}$.

2. $f(x) = x^3 + 9$

$$y = x^3 + 9$$
$$y - 9 = x^3$$
$$\sqrt[3]{y - 9} = x$$
$$\sqrt[3]{x - 9} = y$$
$$\sqrt[3]{x - 9} = f^{-1}(x)$$

$$f^{-1}(f(x)) = f^{-1}(x^3 + 9)$$
$$= \sqrt[3]{(x^3 + 9) - 9}$$
$$= \sqrt[3]{x^3}$$
$$= x$$

Since $f^{-1}(f(x)) = x$, $f^{-1}(x) = \sqrt[3]{x - 9}$ is the inverse function of $f(x) = x^3 + 9$.

3. The function $m(r) = 31r^3$ models the mass in grams of a spherical zinc ball as a function of the ball's radius in centimeters. Write the inverse model to represent the radius r in cm of a spherical zinc ball as a function of the ball's mass m in g.

$$m(r) = 31r^3$$
$$m = 31r^3$$
$$\frac{m}{31} = r^3$$
$$\sqrt[3]{\frac{m}{31}} = r$$
$$\sqrt[3]{\frac{m}{31}} = r(m)$$

4. The function $m(r) = 21r^3$ models the mass in grams of a spherical titanium ball as a function of the ball's radius in centimeters. Write the inverse model to represent the radius r in centimeters of a spherical titanium ball as a function of the ball's mass m in grams.

$$m(r) = 21r^3$$
$$m = 21r^3$$
$$\frac{m}{21} = r^3$$
$$\sqrt[3]{\frac{m}{21}} = r$$
$$\sqrt[3]{\frac{m}{21}} = r(m)$$

MULTIPLE REPRESENTATIONS

Discuss with students how symbolic representations, graphs, and tables of values can all be used to analyze the relationship between a quadratic or cubic function and its inverse. Help students to make connections among the various representations. Different learners may find that one type of representation is more useful than others in aiding their understanding.

INTEGRATE TECHNOLOGY

Encourage students to use both the graphing feature and the table feature on a graphing calculator to help solve problems and to check their work.

PEER-TO-PEER DISCUSSION

Ask students to discuss with a partner how restricting the domain of $f(x) = x^2$ to $x \leq 0$, instead of to $x \geq 0$, affects the domain and range of the inverse of the function. **The domain of the inverse function will be the same as if the restriction were $x \geq 0$, but the range will be $f(x) \leq 0$, instead of $f(x) \geq 0$. The inverse function would be $f^{-1}(x) = -\sqrt{x}$.**

JOURNAL

Have students describe the functions that are inverses of quadratic functions and cubic functions. Have them explain why it is sometimes necessary to restrict the domain of a function when finding its inverse.

15. The weight w in pounds that a shelf can support can be modeled by $w(d) = 82.9d^3$ where d is the distance, in inches, between the supports for the shelf. Write the inverse model to represent the distance d in inches between the supports of a shelf as a function of the weight w in pounds that the shelf can support.

$$w(d) = 82.9d^3$$
$$w = 82.9d^3$$
$$\frac{w}{82.9} = d^3$$
$$\sqrt[3]{\frac{w}{82.9}} = d$$
$$\sqrt[3]{\frac{w}{82.9}} = d(w)$$

H.O.T. Focus on Higher Order Thinking

16. Explain the Error A student was asked to find the inverse of the function $f(x) = \left(\frac{x}{2}\right)^3 + 9$. What did the student do wrong? Find the correct inverse.

$$f(x) = \left(\frac{x}{2}\right)^3 + 9$$
$$y = \left(\frac{x}{2}\right)^3 + 9$$
$$y - 9 = \left(\frac{x}{2}\right)^3$$
$$2y - 18 = x^3$$
$$\sqrt[3]{2y - 18} = x$$
$$y = \sqrt[3]{2y - 18}$$
$$f^{-1}(x) = \sqrt[3]{2y - 18}$$

The student multiplied both sides by 2 before taking the cube root of both sides. The student should have taken the cube root of both sides first, and then multiplied by 2.

$$f(x) = \left(\frac{x}{2}\right)^3 + 9$$
$$y = \left(\frac{x}{2}\right)^3 + 9$$
$$y - 9 = \left(\frac{x}{2}\right)^3$$
$$\sqrt[3]{y - 9} = \frac{x}{2}$$
$$2\sqrt[3]{y - 9} = x$$
$$y = 2\sqrt[3]{x - 9}$$
$$f^{-1}(x) = 2\sqrt[3]{x - 9}$$

17. Multi-Step A framing store uses the function $\left(\frac{c - 0.2}{0.5}\right)^2 = a$ to determine the total area of a piece of glass with respect to the cost before installation of the glass. Write the inverse function for the cost c in dollars of glass for a picture with an area of a in square centimeters. Then write a new function to represent the total cost C the store charges if it costs $6.00 for installation. Use the total cost function to estimate the cost if the area of the glass is 192 cm^2.

$$\left(\frac{c - 0.2}{0.5}\right)^2 = a$$
$$\frac{c - 0.2}{0.5} = \sqrt{a}$$
$$c - 0.2 = 0.5\sqrt{a}$$
$$c = 0.5\sqrt{a} + 0.2$$

$$C = c + 6$$
$$C = 0.5\sqrt{a} + 6.2$$
$$C = 0.5\sqrt{192} + 6.2$$
$$C = 13.13$$

The total cost with installation would be $13.13.

18. Make a Conjecture The function $f(x) = x^2$ must have its domain restricted to have its inverse be a function. The function $f(x) = x^3$ does not need to have its domain restricted to have its inverse be a function. Make a conjecture about which power functions need to have their domains restricted to have their inverses be functions and which do not.

A power function whose power is even will have to have its domain restricted. A power function whose power is odd does not have to have its domain restricted.

Lesson Performance Task

One method used to irrigate crops is the center-pivot irrigation system. In this method, sprinklers rotate in a circle to water crops. The challenge for the farmer is to determine where to place the pivot in order to water the desired number of acres. The farmer knows the area but needs to find the radius of the circle necessary to define that area. How can the farmer determine this from the formula for the area of a circle $A = \pi r^2$? Find the formula the farmer could use to determine the radius necessary to irrigate a given number of acres, A. (Hint: One acre is 43,560 square feet.) What would be the radius necessary for the sprinklers to irrigate an area of 133 acres?

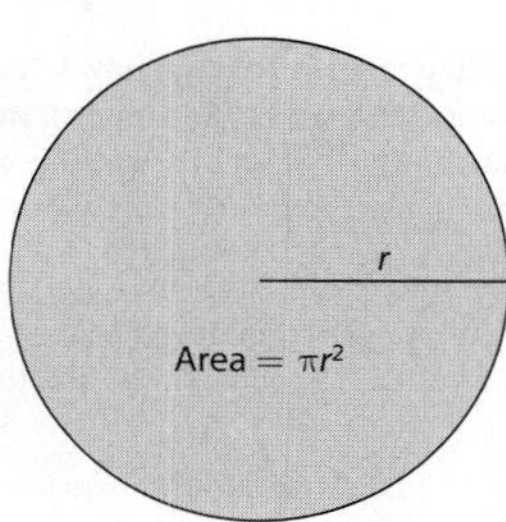

Use the area of a circle.

$$A = \pi r^2$$

$$43{,}560A = \pi r^2$$

$$\frac{43{,}560A}{\pi} = \frac{\pi r^2}{\pi}$$

$$\frac{43{,}560A}{\pi} = r^2$$

$$\sqrt{\frac{43{,}560A}{\pi}} = r$$

$$118\sqrt{A} \approx r$$

By substituting in the number of acres for A, you get the radius necessary to define a circle with the same area as that number of acres.

The radius necessary to irrigate an area of 133 acres would be:

$r \approx 118\sqrt{A}$

$r \approx 118\sqrt{133}$

$r \approx 1361$ ft

This would be a little over $\frac{1}{4}$ of a mile.

EXTENSION ACTIVITY

Explain to students that the farmer is trying to conserve water and is limited to 3 million gallons of water for each irrigation. If the crops need 2 inches of water per irrigation to be productive, have students calculate the maximum radius of the circular area the farmer can irrigate. (Hint: 1 gallon is approximately 0.13 cubic feet.) **The volume of water is given by $V = \pi r^2 d$, where d is the depth of water. Solving for the inverse function gives $r = \sqrt{\frac{V}{\pi d}} = 863$ feet.**

CONNECT VOCABULARY EL

Some students may not be familiar with the term *pivot*. Explain to students that a *pivot* is *a point from which something rotates.* Draw a circle, and mark the center of the circle. Explain to students that a rotating sprinkler defines a circle, and the pivot point, where the sprinkler is located, is at the center of the circle.

QUESTIONING STRATEGIES

? Why is a quadratic function used in this problem? **Area is a two-dimensional quantity, and when both dimensions are the same, the area is proportional to the square of the dimension. For example, the area of a circle is proportional to the radius squared.**

? What are the domain and range of the inverse function $r = 118\sqrt{A}$, and how are they restricted by the real-world situation? **The domain is $A \geq 0$, and the range is $r \geq 0$. Both quantities must be greater than or equal to zero because length and area cannot be negative.**

Scoring Rubric

2 points: Student correctly solves the problem and explains his/her reasoning.

1 point: Student shows good understanding of the problem but does not fully solve or explain his/her reasoning.

0 points: Student does not demonstrate understanding of the problem.

LESSON 10.2

Graphing Square Root Functions

Common Core Math Standards

The student is expected to:

F-IF.C.7b

Graph square root ... functions. Also F-IF.B.4, F-IF.B.6, F-BF.B.3

Mathematical Practices

COMMON CORE **MP.4 Modeling**

Language Objective

Discus with a partner how the graphs of square root functions compare with quadratic functions.

ENGAGE

Essential Question: How can you use transformations of a parent square root function to graph functions of the form $f(x) = a\sqrt{x-h} + k$ or $g(x) = \sqrt{\frac{1}{b}(x-h)} + k$?

Possible answer: You can use the parameters *a*, *b*, *h*, and *k* to transform points on the parent function and use those transformed points to draw the graph of $f(x)$ or $g(x)$.

PREVIEW: LESSON PERFORMANCE TASK

View the Engage section online. Discuss the photo and how a representative sample can give information about the entire batch. Then preview the Lesson Performance Task.

Name ______ Class ______ Date ______

10.2 Graphing Square Root Functions

Essential Question: How can you use transformations of a parent square root function to graph functions of the form $g(x) = a\sqrt{(x-h)} + k$ or $g(x) = \sqrt{\frac{1}{b}(x-h)} + k$?

Resource Locker

Explore Graphing and Analyzing the Parent Square Root Function

Although you have seen how to use imaginary numbers to evaluate square roots of negative numbers, graphing complex numbers and complex valued functions is beyond the scope of this course. For purposes of graphing functions based on the square roots (and in most cases where a square root function is used in a real-world example), the domain and range should both be limited to real numbers.

The square root function is the inverse of a quadratic function with a domain limited to positive real numbers. The quadratic function must be a one-to-one function in order to have an inverse, so the domain is limited to one side of the vertex. The square root function is also a one-to-one function as all inverse functions are.

(A) The domain of the square root function (limited to real numbers) is given by $\{x \mid x \geq 0\}$

(B) Fill in the table.

x	$f(x) = \sqrt{x}$
0	0
1	1
4	2
9	3

(C) Plot the points on the graph, and connect them with a smooth curve.

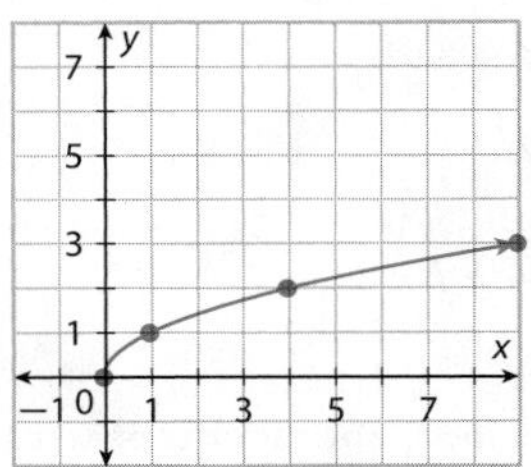

(D) Recall that the range of this function is the inverse of the parent quadratic $(f(x) = x^2)$ with a domain limited to the nonnegative real numbers. Write the range of this square root function:

$\{y \mid y \geq 0\}$.

(E) The graph appears to be getting flatter as x increases, indicating that the rate of change decreases as x increases.

(F) Describe the end behavior of the square root function, $f(x) = \sqrt{x}$. $f(x) \rightarrow \infty$ as $x \rightarrow \infty$

HARDCOVER PAGES 495–512

Watch for the hardcover student edition page numbers for this lesson.

Reflect

1. **Discussion** Why does the end behavior of the square root function only need to be described at one end?
The function is not defined for negative values of x, and so its behavior as x approaches negative infinity is also not defined. The discrete point $(0, 0)$ does not describe end behavior even though the function "ends" there.

2. The solution to the equation $x^2 = 4$ is sometimes written as $x = \pm 2$. Explain why the inverse of $f(x) = x^2$ cannot similarly be written as $g(x) = \pm\sqrt{x}$ in order to use all reals as the domain of $f(x)$.
Functions, including functions that are inverses of other functions, must have a single range value for each domain value. The $\pm$ symbol is shorthand for "positive or negative" and indicates two different range values for a single domain value. This is counter to the definition of function.

Explore 2 Predicting the Effects of Parameters on the Graphs of Square Root Functions

You have learned how to transform the graph of a function using reflections across the x- and y-axes, vertical and horizontal stretches and compressions, and translations. Here, you will apply those transformations to the graph of the square root function $f(x) = \sqrt{x}$.

When transforming the parent function $f(x) = \sqrt{x}$, you can get functions of the form

$g(x) = a\sqrt{(x - h)} + k$ or $g(x) = \sqrt{\frac{1}{b}(x - h)} + k$.

For each parameter, predict the effect on the graph of the parent function, and then confirm your prediction with a graphing calculator.

(A) Predict the effect of the parameter, h, on the graph of $g(x) = \sqrt{x - h}$ for each function.

a. $g(x) = \sqrt{x - 2}$: The graph is a **translation** of the graph of $f(x)$ [(right)/left/up/down] 2 units.

b. $g(x) = \sqrt{x + 2}$: The graph is a **translation** of the graph of $f(x)$ [right/(left)/up/down] 2 units.

Check your answers using a graphing calculator.

(B) Predict the effect of the parameter k on the graph of $g(x) = \sqrt{x} + k$ for each function.

a. $g(x) = \sqrt{x} + 2$: The graph is a **translation** of the graph of $f(x)$ [right/(up)/left/down] 2 units.

b. $g(x) = \sqrt{x} - 2$: The graph is a **translation** of the graph of $f(x)$ [right/up/left/(down)] 2 units.

Check your answers using a graphing calculator.

PROFESSIONAL DEVELOPMENT

Learning Progressions

Students have learned how parameters affect the graphs of quadratic functions, absolute value functions, and rational functions. In this lesson, these concepts are extended to the graphs of square root functions. Students analyze how the parameters a, b, h, and k, in functions of the form $f(x) = a\sqrt{x - h} + k$ and $f(x) = \sqrt{\frac{1}{b}(x - h)} + k$ affect the graph of the parent square root function, $f(x) = \sqrt{x}$. They then use this knowledge to graph square root functions, and to analyze graphs to determine the functions they represent.

EXPLORE 1

Graphing and Analyzing the Parent Square Root Function

INTEGRATE TECHNOLOGY

Students have the option of completing the Explore activity either in the book or online.

QUESTIONING STRATEGIES

How do you know that the graph of $f(x) = \sqrt{x}$ does not have a horizontal asymptote? **As the value of x increases, the square root of x increases without bound, so there is no horizontal asymptote. (As $x \to \infty$, $f(x) \to \infty$.) The function is an increasing function, and the range is all non-negative real numbers.**

EXPLORE 2

Predicting the Effects of Parameters on the Graphs of Square Root Functions

QUESTIONING STRATEGIES

For functions of the form $f(x) = a\sqrt{x}$, why does a value of a that is between 0 and 1 create a vertical compression of the graph of the parent function? **The function value for each x-value is multiplied by a number less than 1, making it less than the corresponding value for the parent function; this pulls the graph closer to the x-axis.**

INTEGRATE MATHEMATICAL PRACTICES

Focus on Math Connections

MP.1 Discuss with students how they can use what they know about how the various parameters affect the graphs of quadratic functions to make predictions about how the parameters will affect the graphs of square root functions.

(C) Predict the effect of the parameter a on the graph of $g(x) = a\sqrt{x}$ for each function.

a. $g(x) = 2\sqrt{x}$: The graph is a **vertical** stretch of the graph of $f(x)$ by a factor of **2**.

b. $g(x) = \frac{1}{2}\sqrt{x}$: The graph is a **vertical** compression of the graph of $f(x)$ by a factor of $\frac{1}{2}$.

c. $g(x) = -\frac{1}{2}\sqrt{x}$: The graph is a **vertical** compression of the graph of $f(x)$ by a factor of $\frac{1}{2}$ as well as a **reflection** across the ***x*-axis**.

d. $g(x) = -2\sqrt{x}$: The graph is a **vertical** stretch of the graph of $f(x)$ by a factor of **2** as well as a **reflection** across the ***x*-axis**.

Check your answers using a graphing calculator.

(D) Predict the effect of the parameter, b, on the graph of $g(x) = \sqrt{\frac{1}{b}x}$ for each function.

a. $g(x) = \sqrt{\frac{1}{2}x}$: The graph is a **horizontal** stretch of the graph of $f(x)$ by a factor of **2**.

b. $g(x) = \sqrt{2x}$: The graph is a **horizontal** compression of the graph of $f(x)$ by a factor of $\frac{1}{2}$.

c. $g(x) = \sqrt{-\frac{1}{2}x}$: The graph is a **horizontal** stretch of the graph of $f(x)$ by a factor of **2** as well as a **reflection** across the ***y*-axis**.

d. $g(x) = \sqrt{-2x}$: The graph is a **horizontal** compression of the graph of $f(x)$ by a factor of $\frac{1}{2}$ as well as a **reflection** across the ***y*-axis**.

Check your answers using a graphing calculator.

Reflect

3. **Discussion** Describe what the effect of each of the transformation parameters is on the domain and range of the transformed function.

Each value in the domain shifts left by $|h|$ if h is positive and right by $|h|$ if h is negative. h has no effect on the range. If a is negative, it changes the sign of each value in the range, but a has no effect on the domain. Each value in the range shifts up by $|k|$ if k is positive and down by $|k|$ if k is negative. k has no effect on the domain. If b is negative, it changes the sign of each value in the domain, but b has no effect on the range.

COLLABORATIVE LEARNING

Peer-to-Peer Activity

Have students work in pairs. Have each student write a function of the form $f(x) = a\sqrt{x-h} + k$ but keep it hidden from the partner. Have students graph their functions on graph paper, exchange them with partners, and try to determine the function represented by the partner's graph. Have partners check each other's work. Then have the students repeat the activity using functions of the form $f(x) = \sqrt{\frac{1}{b}(x-h)} + k$.

Explain 1 Graphing Square Root Functions

Vhen graphing transformations of the square root function, it is useful to consider the effect of the transformation n two reference points, $(0, 0)$ and $(1, 1)$, that lie on the parent function, and where they map to on the transformed unction, $g(x)$.

$f(x) = \sqrt{x}$		$g(x) = a\sqrt{x - h} + k$		$g(x) = \sqrt{\frac{1}{b}(x - h)} + k$	
x	y	x	y	x	y
0	0	h	k	h	k
1	1	$h + 1$	$k + a$	$h + b$	$k + 1$

he reference points can be found by recognizing that the initial point of the graph is translated from $(0, 0)$ to $h, k)$. From the initial point, find the next reference point by going up or down by $|a|$ or left or right by $|b|$, epending on the parameter used and its sign.

ransformations of the square root function also affect the domain and range. In order to work with real valued nputs and outputs, the domain of the square root function cannot include values of x that result in a negative-valued xpression. Negative values of x can be in the domain, as long as they result in nonnegative values of the expression hat is inside the square root. Similarly, the value of the square root function is positive by definition, but multiplying he square root function by a negative number, or adding a constant to it changes the range and can result in negative alues of the transformed function.

Example 1 **For each of the transformed square root functions, find the transformed reference points and use them to plot the transformed function on the same graph with the parent function. Describe the domain and range using set notation.**

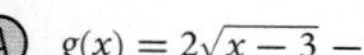

A) $g(x) = 2\sqrt{x - 3} - 2$

To find the domain:

Square root input must be nonnegative. $x - 3 \geq 0$

Solve the inequality for x. $x \geq 3$

The domain is $\{x \mid x \geq 3\}$.

To find the range:

The square root function is nonnegative. $\sqrt{x - 3} \geq 0$

Multiply by 2 $2\sqrt{x - 3} \geq 0$

Subtract 2. $2\sqrt{x - 3} - 2 \geq -2$

Subraction in $g(x)$. $g(x) \geq -2$

Since $g(x)$ is greater than or equal to -2 for all x in the domain, the range is $\{y \mid y \geq -2\}$.

$(0, 0) \rightarrow (3, -2)$

$(1, 1) \rightarrow (4, 0)$

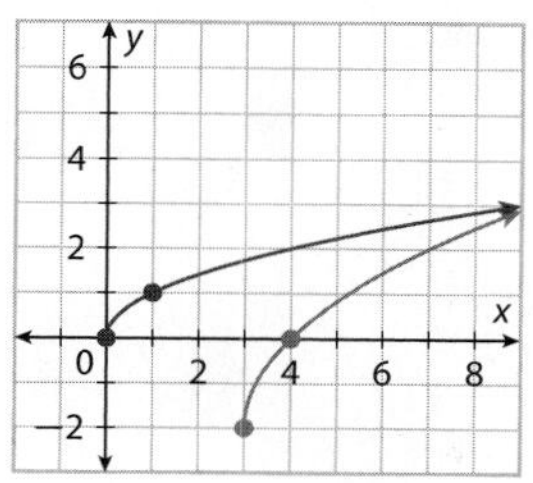

DIFFERENTIATE INSTRUCTION

Kinesthetic Experience

Have students work in pairs. Have each pair place a transparency sheet over a heet of graph paper with the axes labeled. Have them graph the radical function $(x) = a\sqrt{x - h} + k$ on the transparency for $h = 0$ and $k = 0$. Then have them nove the transparency to represent changes in h and k, and write the function that epresents the transformation. Students can use a graphing calculator to check heir answers.

EXPLAIN 1

Graphing Square Root Functions

QUESTIONING STRATEGIES

? What is an example of a negative value of x that is in the domain of a square root function? Why is it part of the domain? **In the function $g(x) = \sqrt{x + 10}$, x can be -6 because it results in a nonnegative square root, $g(x) = \sqrt{-6 + 10} = \sqrt{4}$.**

? What effect do h and k have on the domain and range of a square root function? **The domain is all real numbers greater than or equal to h. The range is all real numbers greater than or equal to k if $a > 0$, and less than or equal to k if $a < 0$.**

INTEGRATE MATHEMATICAL PRACTICES

Focus on Technology

MP.5 Students can use a graphing calculator to help them better understand the effects of a stretch or a compression. Have them graph both the parent function and the given function on the calculator so they can see how the rate of change of the function is reflected in the graph.

PEER-TO-PEER DISCUSSION

Ask students to discuss with a partner the difference between a vertical stretch and a horizontal stretch. Have them use graphs exhibiting each of these attributes to describe the comparison in their own words. Then ask them to do the same for vertical and horizontal compressions. Have them share their descriptions with the class.

(B) $g(x) = \sqrt{-\frac{1}{2}(x-2)} + 1$

To find the domain:

Square root input must be nonnegative. $-\frac{1}{2}(x-2) \geq$ **0**

Multiply both sides by −2. $x - 2$ **$\leq$** 0

Add 2 to both sides. **x** ≤ 2

Expressed in set notation, the domain is $\{x \mid$ **$x \leq 2$** $\}$.

To find the range:

The square root function is nonnegative. $\sqrt{-\frac{1}{2}(x-2)}$ **$\geq$** 0

Add 1 both sides $\sqrt{-\frac{1}{2}(x-2)} + 1 \geq$ **1**

Substitute in **$g(x)$**. $g(x) \geq 1$

Since $g(x)$ is greater than 1 for all x in the domain,

the range (in set notation) is $\{y \mid$ **$y \geq 1$** $\}$.

$(0, 0) \rightarrow$ **(2, 1)**

$(1, 1) \rightarrow$ **(0, 2)**

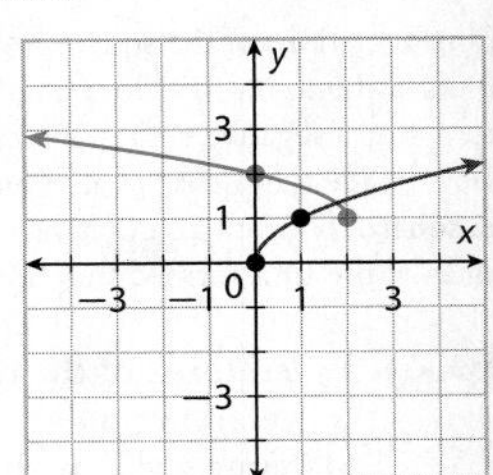

Your Turn

For each of the transformed square root functions, find the transformed reference points and use them to plot the transformed function on the same graph with the parent function. Describe the domain and range using set notation.

4. $g(x) = -3\sqrt{x-2} + 3$

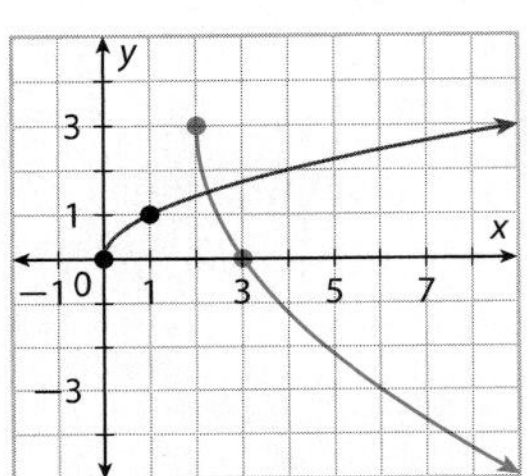

To find the domain: $x - 2 \geq 0$

$x \geq 2$

The domain is $\{x \mid x \geq 2\}$.

To find the range: $\sqrt{x-2} \geq 0$

$-3\sqrt{x-2} \leq 0$

$-3\sqrt{x-3} + 3 \leq 3$

$g(x) \leq 3$

The range is $\{y \mid y \leq 3\}$.

LANGUAGE SUPPORT EL

Communicate Math

Have students work in pairs to complete a chart similar to the following, comparing and contrasting quadratic and square root functions.

Type of Function	Example	Description	Similarities	Differences

5. $g(x) = \sqrt{\frac{1}{3}(x+2)} + 1$

To find the domain: $\frac{1}{3}(x+2) \geq 0$

$x + 2 \geq 0$

$x \geq -2$

The domain is $\{x \mid x \geq -2\}$.

To find the range: $\sqrt{\frac{1}{3}(x+2)} \geq 0$

$\sqrt{\frac{1}{3}(x+2)} + 1 \geq 1$

$g(x) \geq 1$

The range is $\{y \mid y \geq 1\}$.

Explain 2 Writing Square Root Functions

Given the graph of a square root function and the form of the transformed function, either $g(x) = a\sqrt{x-h} + k$ or $g(x) = \sqrt{\frac{1}{b}(x-h)} = k$, the transformation parameters can be determined from the transformed reference points. In either case, the initial point will be at (h, k) and readily apparent. The parameter a can be determined by how far up or down the second point (found at $x = h + 1$) is from the initial point, or the parameter b can be determined by how far to the left or right the second point (found at $y = k + 1$) is from the initial point.

Example 2 **Write the function that matches the graph using the indicated transformation format.**

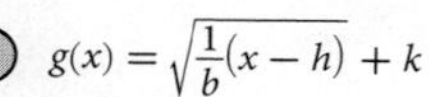

Ⓐ $g(x) = \sqrt{\frac{1}{b}(x-h)} + k$

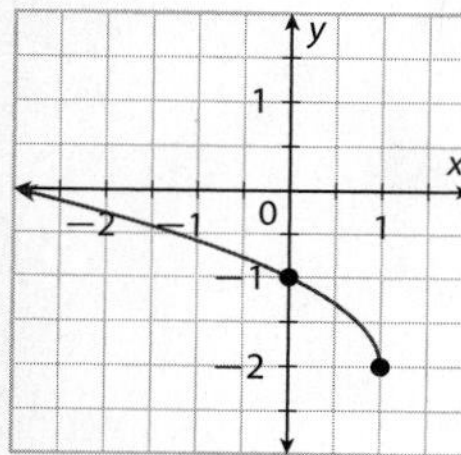

Initial point: $(h, k) = (1, -2)$

Second point:

$(h + b, k + 1) = (0, -1)$

$1 + b = 0$

$b = -1$

The function is $g(x) = \sqrt{-1(x-1)} - 2$.

EXPLAIN 2

Writing Square Root Functions

QUESTIONING STRATEGIES

How can you tell the signs of h and k by looking at the graph? **You can see which way the graph of the parent function has been translated. If it has been translated to the right, h is positive. If it has been translated to the left, h is negative. If it has been translated up, k is positive. If it has been translated down, k is negative.**

AVOID COMMON ERRORS

Students may forget that when indicating a horizontal stretch or compression of the parent graph, the reciprocal of the stretch or compression factor, and not the factor itself, is placed under the radical sign. Present a side-by-side comparison of a stretch and a compression to remind students of the proper procedure.

INTEGRATE TECHNOLOGY

Students can use a graphing calculator to check their work. They can enter their functions and use the graphing feature to check that the graphs of their functions match the given graph.

(B) $g(x) = a\sqrt{x - h} + k$

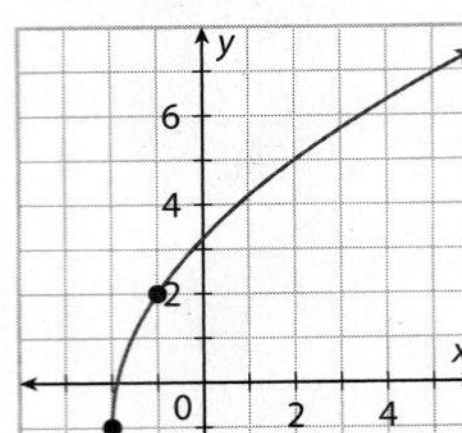

Initial point: $(h, k) = (-2, -1)$

Second point:

$(h + 1, k + a) = (-1, 2)$

$-1 + a = 2$

$a = 3$

The function is $g(x) = 3\sqrt{x + 2} - 1$.

Your Turn

Write the function that matches the graph using the indicated transformation format.

6. $g(x) = \sqrt{\frac{1}{b}(x - h)} + k$

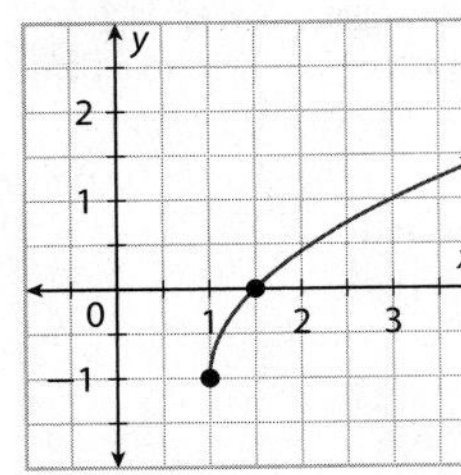

$(h, k) = (1, -1)$

$(h + b, k + 1) = \left(\frac{3}{2}, 0\right)$

$1 + b = \frac{3}{2}$

$b = \frac{1}{2}$

$g(x) = \sqrt{2(x - 1)} - 1$

7. $g(x) = a\sqrt{(x - h)} + k$

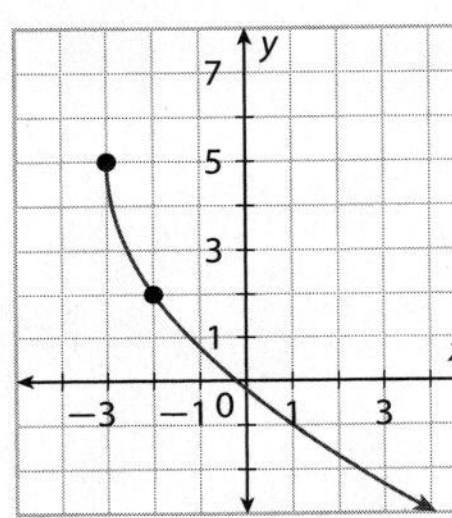

$(h, k) = (-3, 5)$

$(h + 1, k + a) = (-2, 2)$

$5 + a = 2$

$a = -3$

$g(x) = -3\sqrt{x + 3} + 5$

Explain 3 Modeling with Square Root Functions

Square root functions that model real-world situations can be used to investigate average rates of change.

Recall that the average rate of change of the function $f(x)$ over an interval from x_1 to x_2 is given by

$$\frac{f(x_2) - f(x_1)}{x_2 - x_1}.$$

Example 3 **Use a calculator to evaluate the model at the indicated points, and connect the points with a curve to complete the graph of the model. Calculate the average rates of change over the first and last intervals and explain what the rate of change represents.**

(A) The approximate period T of a pendulum (the time it takes a pendulum to complete one swing) is given in seconds by the formula $T = 0.32\sqrt{\ell}$, where ℓ is the length of the pendulum in inches. Use lengths of 2, 4, 6, 8, and 10 inches.

First find the points for the given x-values.

Length (inches)	Period (seconds)
2	0.45
4	0.64
6	0.78
8	0.91
10	1.01

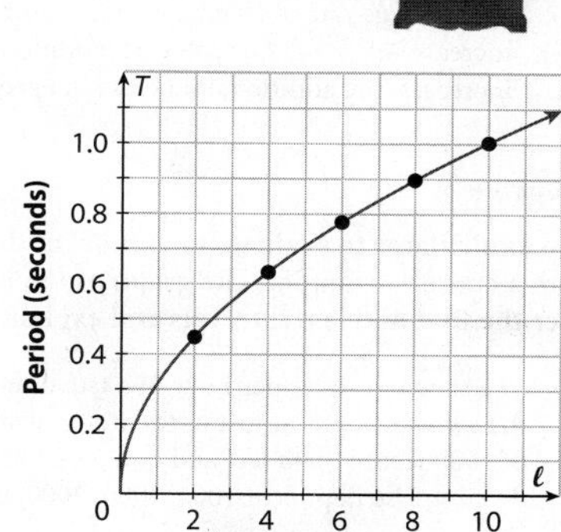

Plot the points and draw a smooth curve through them.

Find the average increase in period per inch increase in the pendulum length for the first interval and the last interval.

First interval:

$$\text{rate of change} = \frac{0.64 - 0.45}{4 - 2} = 0.095$$

Last Interval:

$$\text{rate of change} = \frac{1.01 - 0.91}{10 - 8} = 0.05$$

The average rate of change is less for the last interval. The average rate of change represents the increase in pendulum period with each additional inch of length. As the length of the pendulum increases, the increase in period time per inch of length becomes less.

EXPLAIN 3

Modeling with Square Root Functions

QUESTIONING STRATEGIES

How can you summarize the rate of change of a square root function of the form $f(x) = a\sqrt{x}$ when a is a positive number? How is this reflected in the graph of the function? **As values of x increase, the rate of change decreases. The graph shows a rising curve that gets less and less steep (i.e., flatter) as x approaches infinity.**

Ⓑ A car with good tires is on a dry road. The speed, in miles per hour, from which the car can stop in a given distance d, in feet, is given by $s(d) = \sqrt{96d}$. Use distances of 20, 40, 60, 80, and 100 feet.

First, find the points for the given x-values.

Distance	20	40	60	80	100
Speed	43.8	62.0	75.9	87.6	98.0

Plot the points and draw a smooth curve through them.

First interval:

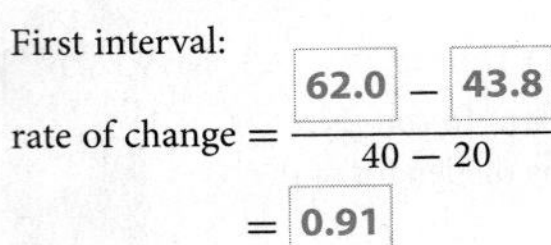

rate of change $= \dfrac{\boxed{62.0} - \boxed{43.8}}{40 - 20}$

$= \boxed{0.91}$

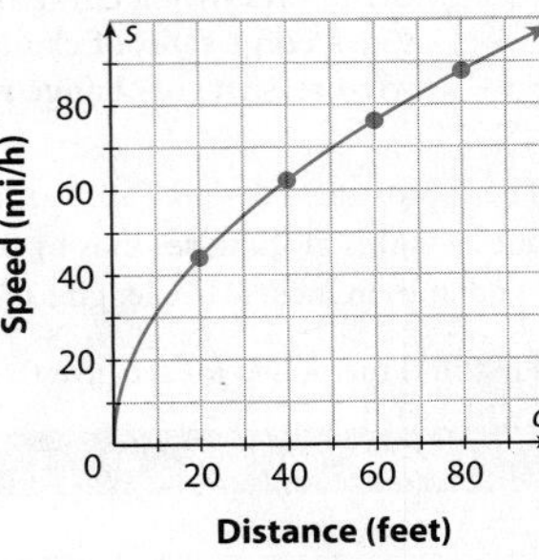

Last Interval:

rate of change $= \dfrac{\boxed{98.0} - \boxed{87.6}}{100 - 80}$

$= \boxed{0.52}$

The average rate of change is **less** for the last interval. The average rate of change represents the increase in **speed** with each additional **foot of distance**. As the available stopping distance increases, the additional increase in speed per foot of stopping distance **decreases**.

Your Turn

Use a calculator to evaluate the model at the indicated points, and connect the points with a curve to complete the graph of the model. Calculate the average rates of change over the first and last intervals and explain what the rate of change represents.

8. The speed in miles per hour of a tsunami can be modeled by the function $s(d) = 3.86\sqrt{d}$, where d is the average depth in feet of the water over which the tsunami travels. Graph this function from depths of 1000 feet to 5000 feet and compare the change in speed with depth from the shallowest interval to the deepest. Use depths of 1000, 2000, 3000, 4000, and 5000 feet for the x-values.

Points: (1000, 122.1), (2000, 172.6), (3000, 211.4), (4000, 244.1), (5000, 272.9)

First interval: $= \dfrac{172.6 - 122.1}{2000 - 1000}$

$= 0.0505$

Last Interval: $= \dfrac{272.9 - 244.1}{5000 - 4000}$

$= 0.0288$

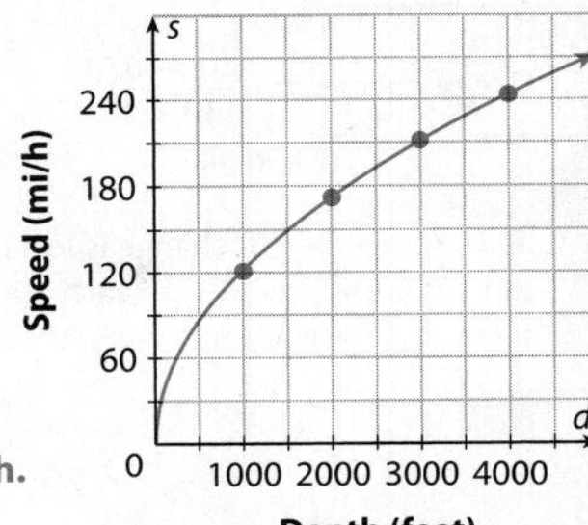

The average rate of change is less for the last interval. The average rate of change represents the increase in tsunami speed with each additional foot of depth. The speed increases less with each additional foot of depth.

Elaborate

9. What is the difference between the parameters inside the radical (b and h) and the parameters outside the radical (a and k)?
The inside parameters are horizontal transformations and the outside parameters are vertical transformations.

10. Which transformations change the square root function's end behavior?
vertical reflections ($a < 0$) and horizontal reflections ($b < 0$)

11. Which transformations change the square root function's initial point location?
horizontal translations ($h \neq 0$) and vertical translations ($k \neq 0$)

12. Which transformations change the square root function's domain?
horizontal translations ($h \neq 0$) and horizontal reflections ($a < 0$)

13. Which transformations change the square root function's range?
vertical translations ($k \neq 0$) and vertical reflections ($b < 0$)

14. **Essential Question Check-In** Describe in your own words the steps you would take to graph a function of the form $g(x) = a\sqrt{x - h} + k$ or $g(x) = \sqrt{\frac{1}{b}(x - h)} + k$ if you were given the values of h and k and using either a or b.
Start with the point (h, k), which is the endpoint of the function. If $g(x) = a\sqrt{x - h} + k$ is used, a second reference point will be located over by 1 to the right and up by a (or down by $|a|$ if $a < 0$). If $g(x) = \sqrt{\frac{1}{b}(x - h)} + k$ is used, the second reference point is found by moving up by 1 and to the right by b (or left by $|b|$ if $b < 0$). Draw a half parabola that goes through both reference points and continues past the second point.

ELABORATE

INTEGRATE MATHEMATICAL PRACTICES

Focus on Math Connections

MP.1 Enhance students' understanding of the different effects produced by a and b by having them complete a table of values for $x = 0, 1, 4, 16$, and 64 and the functions $f(x) = \sqrt{x}$, $g(x) = 4\sqrt{x}$, $h(x) = \sqrt{4x}$, and $j(x) = \sqrt{\frac{1}{4}x}$, and compare the values across the functions. Students can then plot the points and graph the different functions to see how the effects of the parameters are reflected in the graphs.

QUESTIONING STRATEGIES

? How can you use the rule for a square root function to determine the x-intercept of its graph? **Find the value of x that makes the function equal to 0. This can be found by inspection, or by setting the rule equal to 0 and solving for x.**

SUMMARIZE THE LESSON

? How is the graph of $f(x) = a\sqrt{x - h} + k$ related to the graph of $f(x) = \sqrt{x}$? **Its starting point is at (h, k), instead of (0, 0). It is stretched vertically by a factor of a if $|a| > 1$, or compressed vertically by a factor of a if $0 < |a| < 1$. If $a < 0$, then the graph is decreasing instead of increasing.**

EVALUATE

ASSIGNMENT GUIDE

Concepts and Skills	Practice
Explore 1 Graphing and Analyzing the Parent Square Root Function	Exercises 1
Explore 2 Predicting the Effects of Parameters on the Graphs of Square Root Functions	Exercises 2–5
Example 1 Graphing Square Root Functions	Exercises 6–13
Example 2 Writing Square Root Functions	Exercises 14–17
Example 3 Modeling with Square Root Functions	Exercises 18–21

INTEGRATE MATHEMATICAL PRACTICES

Focus on Critical Thinking

MP.3 Mario says that the domain of the square root function is the set of all positive real numbers. Is he correct? Explain. **He is not correct, because the domain also includes 0. The domain is the set of all non-negative real numbers.**

Evaluate: Homework and Practice

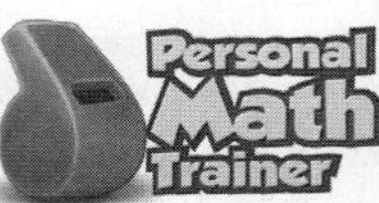

- Online Homework
- Hints and Help
- Extra Practice

1. Graph the functions $f(x) = \sqrt{x}$ and $g(x) = -\sqrt{x}$ on the same grid. Describe the domain, range and end behavior of each function. How are the functions related?

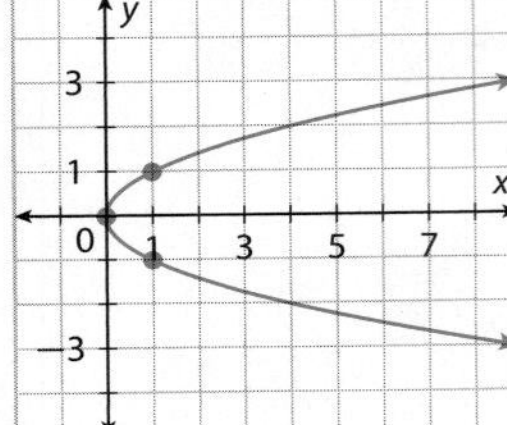

	$f(x) = \sqrt{x}$	$g(x) = -\sqrt{x}$
Domain	$\{x \mid x \geq 0\}$	$\{x \mid x \geq 0\}$
Range	$\{y \mid y \geq 0\}$	$\{y \mid y \geq 0\}$
End Behavior	$f(x) \to \infty$ as $x \to \infty$	$g(x) \to -\infty$ as $x \to \infty$

The functions are reflections of each other over the x-axis.

Describe the transformations of $g(x)$ from the parent function $f(x) = \sqrt{x}$.

2. $g(x) = \sqrt{\frac{1}{2}x} + 1$

Stretch horizontally by a factor of 2 and translate up by 1.

3. $g(x) = -5\sqrt{x+1} - 3$

Stretch vertically by a factor of 5, reflect across x-axis, and translate down by 1 and left by 3.

4. $g(x) = \frac{1}{4}\sqrt{x-5} - 2$

Compress vertically by 4, and translate right by 5 and down by 2.

5. $g(x) = \sqrt{-7(x-7)}$

Compress horizontally by a factor of 7, reflect across y-axis, and translate right by 7.

Describe the domain and range of each function using set notation.

6. $g(x) = \sqrt{\frac{1}{3}(x-1)}$

$\frac{1}{3}(x-1) \geq 0$

$x - 1 \geq 0$

$x \geq 1$

Domain: $\{x \mid x \geq 1\}$

$\sqrt{\frac{1}{3}(x-1)} \geq 0$

$g(x) \geq 0$

Range: $\{y \mid y \geq 0\}$

7. $g(x) = 3\sqrt{x+4} + 3$

$x + 4 \geq 0$

$x \geq -4$

Domain: $\{x \mid x \geq -4\}$

$\sqrt{x+4} \geq$

$3\sqrt{x+4} \geq$

$3\sqrt{x+4} + 3 \geq$

$g(x) \geq$

Range: $\{y \mid y \geq 3\}$

8. $g(x) = \sqrt{-5(x+1)} + 2$

$-5(x+1) \geq 0$

$x + 1 \leq 0$

$x \leq -1$

Domain: $\{x \mid x \leq -1\}$

$\sqrt{-5(x+1)} \geq 0$

$\sqrt{-5(x+1)} + 2 \geq 2$

$g(x) \geq 2$

Range: $\{y \mid y \geq 2\}$

9. $g(x) = -7\sqrt{x-3} - 5$

$x - 3 \geq 0$

$x \geq 3$

Domain: $\{x \mid x \geq 3\}$

$\sqrt{x-3} \geq 0$

$-7\sqrt{x-3} \leq 0$

$-7\sqrt{x-3} - 5 \leq -$

$g(x) \leq -$

Range: $\{y \mid y \leq -5\}$

Exercise	Depth of Knowledge (D.O.K.)	COMMON CORE Mathematical Practices
1	**1** Recall of Information	**MP.6** Precision
2–5	**2** Skills/Concepts	**MP.2** Reasoning
6–13	**2** Skills/Concepts	**MP.4** Modeling
14–17	**2** Skills/Concepts	**MP.2** Reasoning
18–21	**2** Skills/Concepts	**MP.4** Modeling
22	**2** Skills/Concepts	**MP.2** Reasoning

Plot the transformed function $g(x)$ on the grid with the parent function, $f(x) = \sqrt{x}$.

10. $g(x) = -\sqrt{x} + 3$

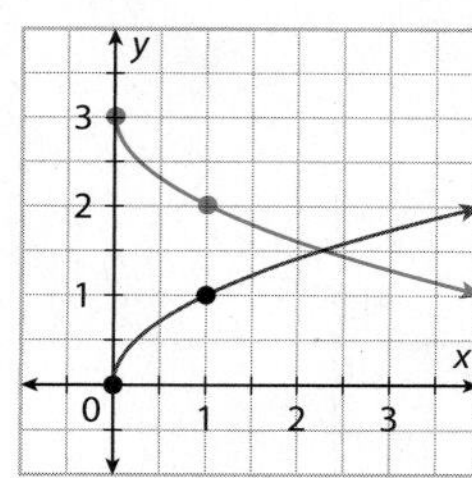

$x \geq 0$

domain: $\{x \mid x \geq 0\}$.

$\sqrt{x} \geq 0$

$-\sqrt{x} \leq 0$

$-\sqrt{x} + 3 \leq 3$

$g(x) \leq 3$

range: $\{y \mid y \leq 3\}$.

11. $g(x) = \sqrt{\frac{1}{3}(x + 4)} - 1$

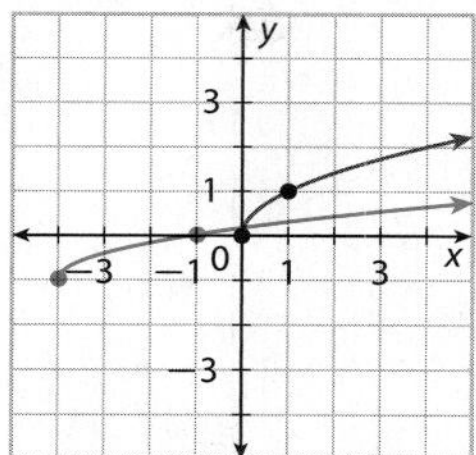

$\frac{1}{3}(x + 4) \geq 0$

$x + 4 \geq 0$

$x \geq -4$

domain: $\{x \mid x \geq -4\}$.

$\sqrt{\frac{1}{3}(x + 4)} \geq 0$

$\sqrt{\frac{1}{3}(x + 4)} - 1 \geq -1$

$g(x) \geq -1$

range: $\{y \mid y \geq -1\}$.

12. $g(x) = \sqrt{-\frac{2}{3}\left(x - \frac{1}{2}\right)} - 2$

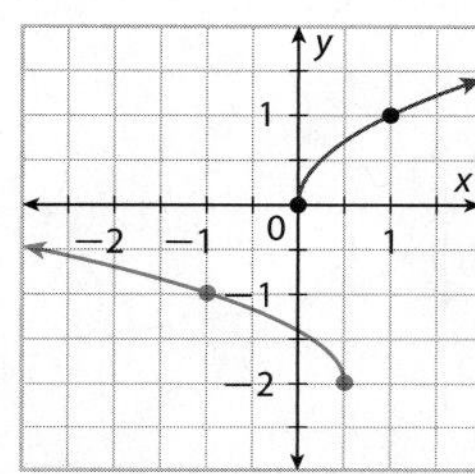

$-\frac{2}{3}\left(x - \frac{1}{2}\right) \geq 0$

$x - \frac{1}{2} \leq 0$

$x \leq \frac{1}{2}$

domain $\left\{x \mid x \leq \frac{1}{2}\right\}$.

To find the range:

$\sqrt{-\frac{2}{3}\left(x - \frac{1}{2}\right)} \geq 0$

$\sqrt{-\frac{2}{3}\left(x - \frac{1}{2}\right)} - 2 \geq -2$

$g(x) \geq -2$

range $\left\{y \mid y \geq -2\right\}$.

13. $g(x) = 4\sqrt{x + 3} - 4$

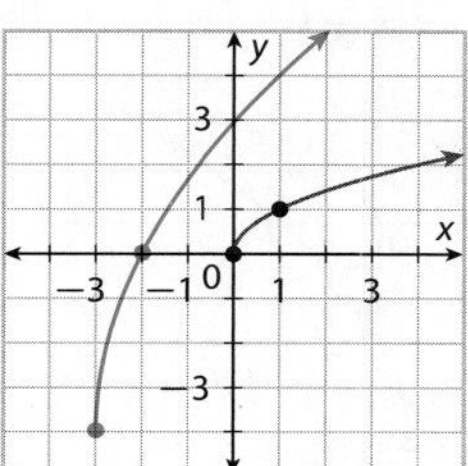

$x + 3 \geq 0$

$x \geq -3$

domain: $\{x \mid x \geq -3\}$.

$\sqrt{x + 3} \geq 0$

$4\sqrt{x + 3} \geq 0$

$4\sqrt{x + 3} - 4 \geq -4$

$g(x) \geq -4$

range: $\{y \mid y \leq -4\}$.

Exercise	Depth of Knowledge (D.O.K.)	COMMON CORE Mathematical Practices
23–24	**3** Strategic Thinking H.O.T.	**MP.2** Reasoning
25	**3** Strategic Thinking H.O.T.	**MP.4** Modeling

QUESTIONING STRATEGIES

? What do the coordinates of the starting point tell you about how the graph of the parent function was transformed? **The x-coordinate tells you how far the graph was translated in the horizontal direction. The y-coordinate tells you how far the graph was translated in the vertical direction.**

VISUAL CUES

Suggest that students draw the graph of the parent square root function on the same coordinate grid as the given graph so that they can see whether the given graph represents a stretch or compression of the graph of the parent function.

Write the function that matches the graph using the indicated transformation format.

14. $g(x) = \sqrt{\frac{1}{b}(x - h)} + k$

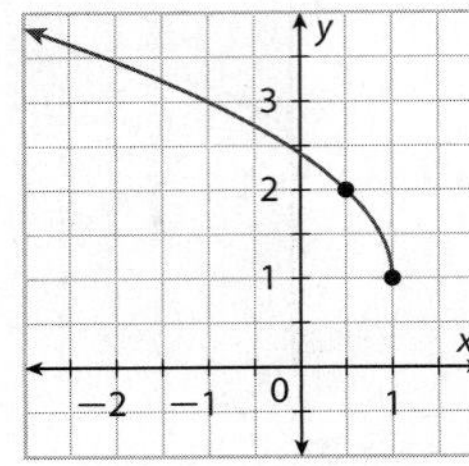

$(h, k) = (1, 1)$

$(h + b, k + 1) = \left(\frac{1}{2}, 2\right)$

$1 + b = \frac{1}{2}$

$b = -\frac{1}{2}$

$g(x) = \sqrt{-2(x - 1)} + 1$

15. $g(x) = \sqrt{\frac{1}{b}(x - h)} + k$

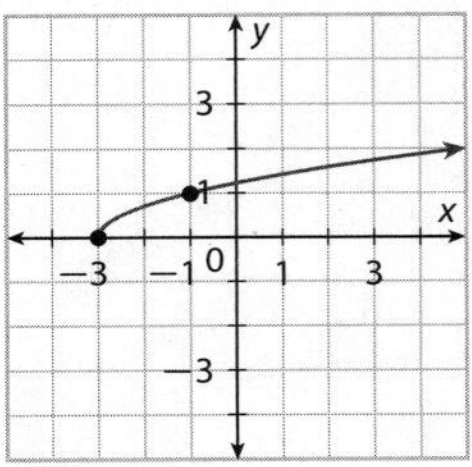

$(h, k) = (-3, 0)$

$(h + b, k + 1) = (-1, 1)$

$-3 + b = -1$

$b = 2$

$g(x) = \sqrt{\frac{1}{2}(x + 3)}$

16. $g(x) = a\sqrt{x - h} + k$

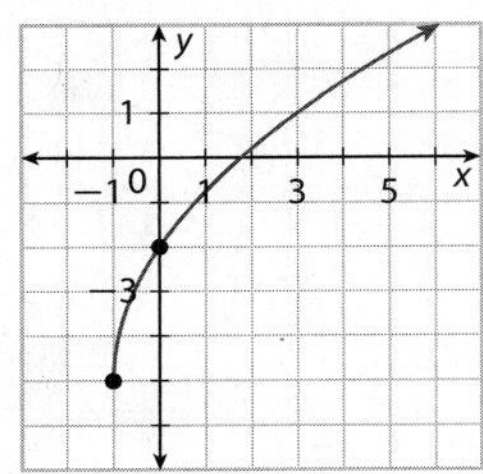

$(h, k) = (-1, -5)$

$(h + 1, k + a) = (0, -2)$

$-5 + a = -2$

$a = 3$

$g(x) = 3\sqrt{x + 1} - 5$

17. $g(x) = a\sqrt{x - h} + k$

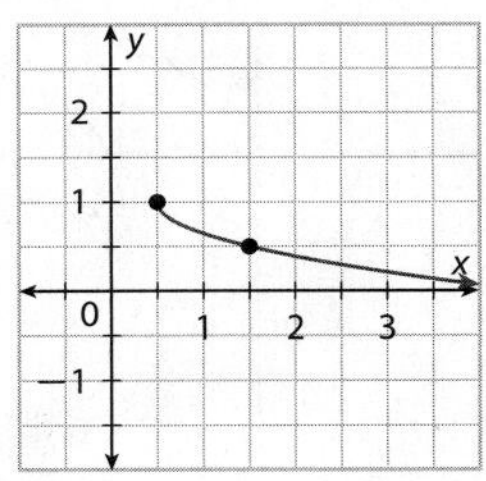

$(h, k) = \left(\frac{1}{2}, 1\right)$

$(h + 1, k + a) = \left(\frac{3}{2}, \frac{1}{2}\right)$

$1 + a = \frac{1}{2}$

$a = -\frac{1}{2}$

$g(x) = -\frac{1}{2}\sqrt{x - \frac{1}{2}} + 1$

Use a calculator to evaluate the model at the indicated points, and connect the points with a curve to complete the graph of the model. Calculate the average rates of change over the first and last intervals and explain what the rate of change represents.

18. A farmer is trying to determine how much fencing to buy to make a square holding pen with a 6-foot gap for a gate. The length of fencing, f, in feet, required as a function of area, A, in square feet, is given by $f(A) = 4\sqrt{A} - 6$. Evaluate the function from 20 ft² to 100 ft² by calculating points every 20 ft².

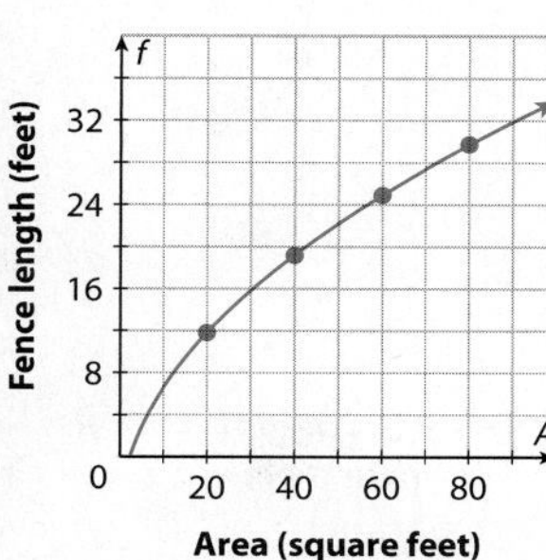

points: (20, 11.9), (40, 19.3), (60, 25.0), (80, 29.8), (100, 34.0)

First Interval: $= \dfrac{19.3 - 11.9}{40 - 20}$ $= 0.37$

Last Interval: $= \dfrac{34.0 - 29.8}{100 - 80}$ $= 0.21$

The rate of change represents the extra fence length required for each additional square foot of pen area. The rate of change decreases with increasing area. So, the extra fence length needed decreases as the area increases.

19. The speed, s, in feet per second, of an object dropped from a height, h, in feet, is given by the formula $s(h) = \sqrt{64h}$. Evaluate the function for heights of 0 feet to 25 feet by calculating points every 5 feet.

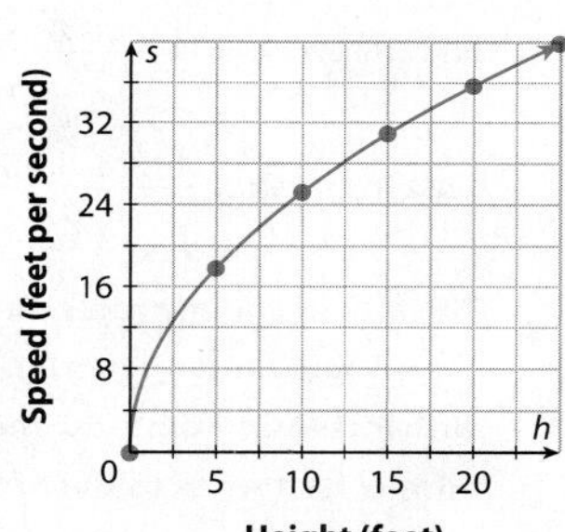

points: (0, 0), (5, 17.9), (10, 25.3), (15, 31.0), (20, 35.8), (25, 40.0)

First Interval: $= \dfrac{17.9 - 0}{5 - 0}$ $= 3.58$

Last Interval: $= \dfrac{40.0 - 35.9}{25 - 20}$ $= 0.84$

The rate of change represents additional speed in feet per second for each additional foot of height. The rate of change decreases with increasing height. So, the additional speed decreases as the height increases.

MULTIPLE REPRESENTATIONS

Encourage students to make a table of values for the function in order to find additional points on the graph. This will help them to draw a more accurate curve.

AVOID COMMON ERRORS

When graphing a function of the form $f(x) = a\sqrt{x - h} + k$ with $a < 0$, some students may perform the translation first and then perform the reflection. Help them to see that the function indicates a vertical translation of the graph of $f(x) = a\sqrt{x - h}$ by k units, so the graph needs to be reflected before it is translated vertically.

20. Water is draining from a tank at an average speed, s, in feet per second, characterized by the function $s(d) = 8\sqrt{d - 2}$, where d is the depth of the water in the tank in feet. Evaluate the function for depths of 2, 3, 4, and 5 feet.

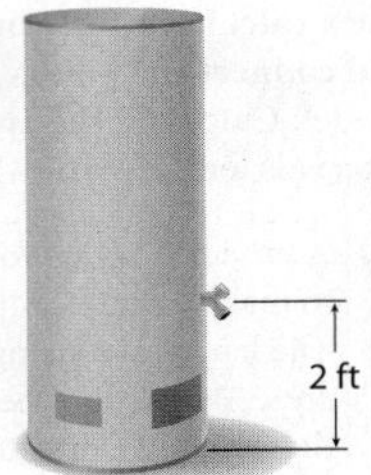

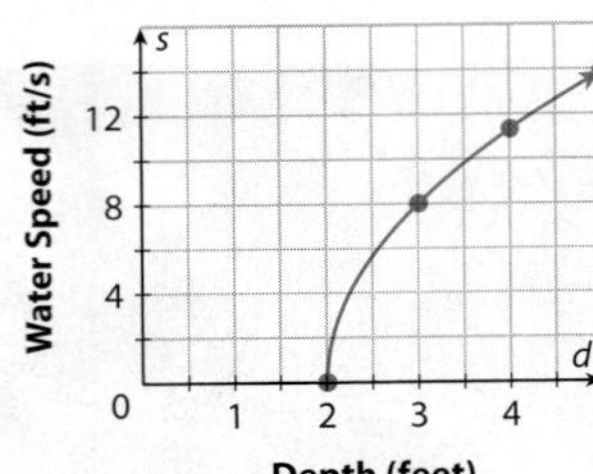

points: (2, 0.00), (3, 8.00), (4, 11.31), (5, 13.86)

First Interval: $= \frac{8.00 - 0}{3 - 2} = 8.00$

Last Interval: $= \frac{13.86 - 11.31}{5 - 4} = 2.55$

The rate of change represents the increase in water velocity for every additional foot of depth. The rate of change decreases with increasing depth. So, the increase in water velocity decreases as the depth increases.

21. A research team studies the effects from an oil spill to develop new methods in oil clean-up. In the spill they are studying, the damaged oil tanker spilled oil into the ocean, forming a roughly circular spill pattern. The spill expanded out from the tanker, increasing the area at a rate of 100 square meters per hour. The radius of the circle is given by the function $r = \sqrt{\frac{100}{\pi}t}$, where t is the time (in hours) after the spill begins. Evaluate the function at hours 0, 1, 2, 3, and 4.

Points: (0, 0), (1, 5.64), (2, 7.98), (3, 9.77), (4, 11.28)

First Interval: $= \frac{5.64 - 0}{1 - 0} = 5.64$

Last Interval: $= \frac{11.28 - 9.77}{4 - 3} = 1.51$

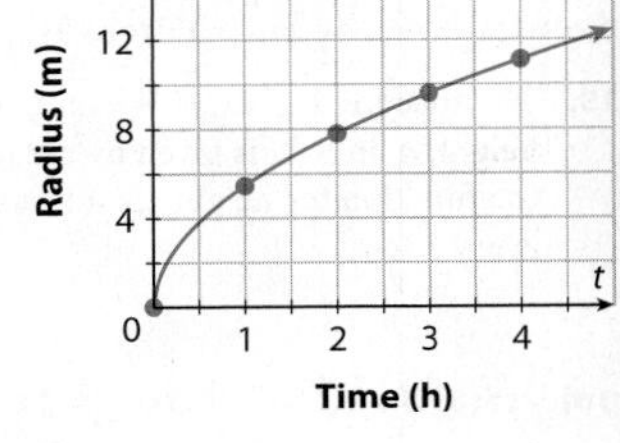

The rate of change represents the increase in meters of the oil spill radius per hour. The rate of change decreases with increasing time. So, the increase in the radius of the oil spill decreases as the time increases.

22. Give all of the transformations of the parent function $f(x) = \sqrt{x}$ that result in the function $g(x) = \sqrt{-2(x-3)} + 2$.

A. Horizontal stretch
(B.) Horizontal compression
(C.) Horizontal reflection
(D.) Horizontal translation
E. Vertical stretch
F. Vertical compression
G. Vertical reflection
(H.) Vertical translation

H.O.T. Focus on Higher Order Thinking

23. **Draw Conclusions** Describe the transformations to $f(x) = \sqrt{x}$ that result in the function $g(x) = \sqrt{-8x + 16} + 3$.

$$\begin{aligned} g(x) &= \sqrt{-8x + 16} + 3 \\ &= \sqrt{-8(x-2)} + 3 \\ &= 2\sqrt{-2(x-2)} + 3 \end{aligned}$$

Horizontal compression by 2, a horizontal reflection, a vertical stretch by 2, a translation of 2 to the right, and a translation of 3 up.

24. **Analyze Relationships** Show how a horizontally stretched square root function can sometimes be replaced by a vertical compression by equating the two forms of the transformed square root function.

$$g(x) = a\sqrt{x} = \sqrt{\frac{1}{b}x}$$

What must you assume about a and b for this replacement to result in the same function?

$$\begin{aligned} a\sqrt{x} &= \sqrt{\frac{1}{b}x} \\ a\sqrt{x} &= \sqrt{\frac{1}{b}} \cdot \sqrt{x} \\ a &= \sqrt{\frac{1}{b}} \end{aligned}$$

a and b must be positive numbers.

CONNECT VOCABULARY EL

Students should check their understanding of the terms *domain, range, end behavior,* and *parent function* as they revisit these terms from previous lessons. Ask them to state what the terms mean for the functions they are graphing.

JOURNAL

Have students explain how to find the equation of a transformed square root function given the starting point and another point on the graph.

25. Multi-Step On a clear day, the view across the ocean is limited by the curvature of Earth. Objects appear to disappear below the horizon as they get farther from an observer. For an observer at height h above the water looking at an object with a height of H (both in feet), the approximate distance (d) in miles at which the object drops below the horizon is given by $d(h) = 1.21\sqrt{h + H}$.

a. What is the effect of the object height, H, on the graph of $d(h)$?

The graph is translated left by *H* feet.

b. What is the domain of the function $d(h)$? Explain your answer.

The domain is given by $\{h : h \geq 0\}$. Although values of *h* between $-H$ and 0 might seem reasonable because the expression under the square root symbol is still not negative, a negative value of *h* corresponds to being underwater, where the visibility over the horizon is not modeled by the function.

c. Plot two functions of distance required to see an object over the horizon versus observer height: one for seeing a 2-foot-tall buoy and one for seeing a 20-foot-tall sailboat. Calculate points every 10 feet from 0 to 40 feet.

Observer Height (ft)	Buoy Distance (mi)
0	1.7
10	4.2
20	5.7
30	6.8
40	7.8

Observer Height (ft)	Sailboat Distance (mi)
0	5.4
10	6.6
20	7.7
30	8.6
40	9.4

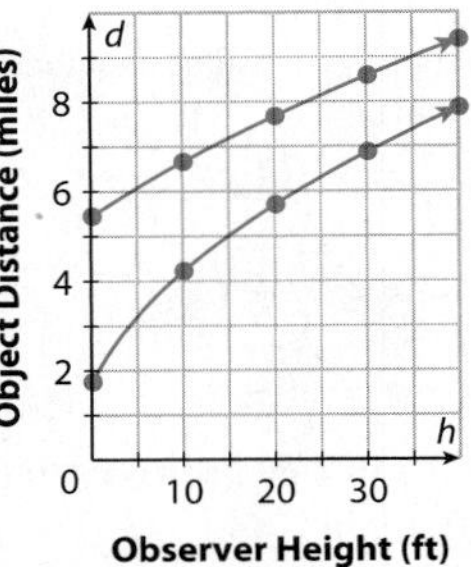

d. Where is the greatest increase in viewing distance with observer height?

From 0 to 10 feet observing the 2-foot tall buoy.

Lesson Performance Task

With all the coffee beans that come in for processing, a coffee manufacturer cannot sample all of them. Suppose one manufacturer uses the function $s(x) = \sqrt{x} + 1$ to determine how many beans that it must take from x containers in order to obtain a good representative sample. How does this function relate to the function $f(x) = \sqrt{x}$? Graph both functions. How many samples should be taken from a shipment of 45 containers of beans? Explain why this can only be a whole number answer.

The function $s(x)$ is function $f(x)$ shifted 1 unit up.

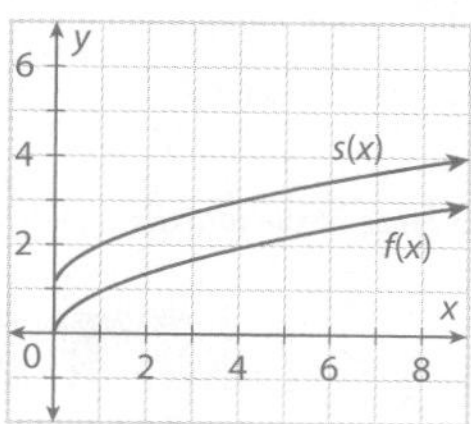

If 45 containers of beans come in, then:

$s(x) = \sqrt{x} + 1$

$s(45) = \sqrt{45} + 1$

$s(45) \approx 8$

About 8 samples should be taken from them. The answer must be a whole number, because whatever amount of beans is taken, it still represents 1 sample.

EXTENSION ACTIVITY

If the manufacturer wants to increase the sample size to get a more accurate picture of the quality of the shipment, how can the model $s(x) = \sqrt{x} + 1$ be adjusted to increase the sample size? **Apply a vertical stretching to get $s(x) = \sqrt{x} + 1$, where $a > 1$, or increase the shift in the y direction to get $s(x) = \sqrt{x} + k$, where $k > 1$.**

Ask students what might be a disadvantage of increasing the sample size. **If the beans are destroyed during the sampling process, then the manufacturer has lost more of its inventory.**

AVOID COMMON ERRORS

Some students may think that the function $s(x) = \sqrt{x} + 1$ translates the function $f(x) = \sqrt{x}$ in the x direction because the $+1$ is on the same side of the equation as the variable x. Explain to students that $s(x) = \sqrt{x} + 1 = f(x) + 1$, which means that $s(x)$ is $f(x)$ increased by 1. Ask students to write the function $t(x)$ that translates $f(x)$ in the x direction one unit. **$t(x) = \sqrt{x + 1}$**

QUESTIONING STRATEGIES

? What are the domain and range of the mathematical function $s(x) = \sqrt{x} + 1$? **The domain is $x \geq 0$, and the range is $y > 1$. Both include continuous values.**

? What are the domain and range of $s(x)$ for the problem situation? Why does this differ from the domain and range of the function? **The domain is integers $x \geq 1$, and the range is integers $y \geq 2$. A domain value of 0 would mean that 1 bean was taken from zero containers, which does not make sense.**

Scoring Rubric

2 points: Student correctly solves the problem and explains his/her reasoning.

1 point: Student shows good understanding of the problem but does not fully solve or explain his/her reasoning.

0 points: Student does not demonstrate understanding of the problem.

LESSON 10.3

Graphing Cube Root Functions

Common Core Math Standards

The student is expected to:

F-IF.C.7b

Graph . . . cube root ... functions. Also F-IF.B.4, F-IF.B.6, F-BF.B.3

Mathematical Practices

MP.4 Modeling

Language Objective

Describe how the graph of a cube root functions differs from the graph of a square root function.

ENGAGE

Essential Question: How can you use transformations of a parent cube root function to graph functions of the form $f(x) = a\sqrt[3]{x - h} + k$ or $g(x) = \sqrt[3]{\frac{1}{b}(x - h)} + k$?

Possible answer: For , $f(x)$, the graph is a vertical stretch or compression of the parent graph by a factor of a. When $|a| > 1$, the graph is a vertical stretch; when $0 < |a| < 1$, the graph is a vertical compression. For $g(x)$ the graph is a horizontal stretch or compression of the parent graph by a factor of b. When $|b| > 1$, the graph is a horizontal stretch, and when $0 < |b| < 1$, the graph is a horizontal compression.

PREVIEW: LESSON PERFORMANCE TASK

View the Engage section online. Discuss the photo and how an object's density can affect its size. Have students list variables that might be useful when calculating an object's size. Then preview the Lesson Performance Task.

Name ______________ Class ______________ Date ______________

10.3 Graphing Cube Root Functions

Resource Locker

Essential Question: How can you use transformations of parent cube root functions to graph functions of the form $f(x) = a\sqrt[3]{(x - h)} + k$ or $g(x) = \sqrt[3]{\frac{1}{b}(x - h)} + k$?

Explore 1 Graphing and Analyzing the Parent Cube Root Function

The cube root parent function is $f(x) = \sqrt[3]{x}$. To graph $f(x)$, choose values of x and find corresponding values of y. Choose both negative and positive values of x.

Graph the function $f(x) = \sqrt[3]{x}$. Identify the domain and range of the function.

(A) Make the table of values.

x	y	x, y
−8	−2	(−8, −2)
−1	−1	(−1, −1)
0	0	(0, 0)
1	1	(1, 1)
8	2	(8, 2)

(B) Use the table to graph the function.

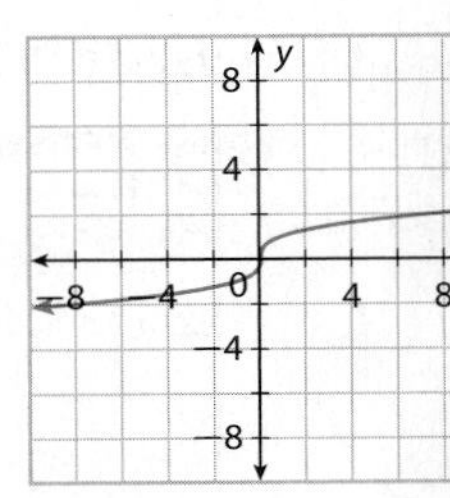

(C) Identify the domain and range of the function.

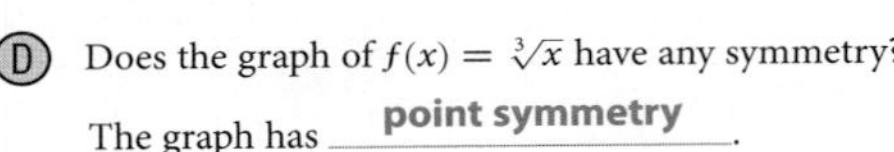

The domain is the **set of all real numbers**.

The range is **set of all real numbers**.

(D) Does the graph of $f(x) = \sqrt[3]{x}$ have any symmetry?

The graph has **point symmetry**.

Reflect

1. Can the radicand in a cube root function be negative?
Yes, because the cube of a negative number is negative.

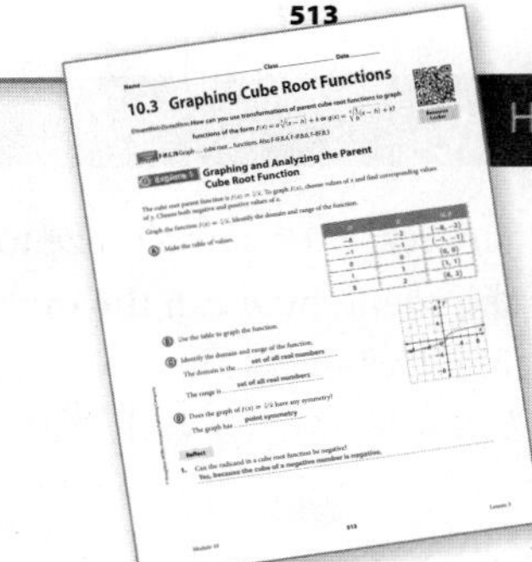

HARDCOVER PAGES 513–52

Watch for the hardcover student edition page numbers for this lesson.

Explain 1 Graphing Cube Root Functions

Transformations of the Cube Root Parent Function $f(x) = \sqrt[3]{x}$

Transformation	$f(x)$ Notation	Examples
Vertical translation	$f(x) + k$	$y = \sqrt[3]{x} + 3$ 3 units up $y = \sqrt[3]{x} - 4$ 4 units down
Horizontal translation	$f(x - h)$	$y = \sqrt[3]{x - 2}$ 2 units right $y = \sqrt[3]{x + 1}$ 1 units left
Vertical stretch/compression	$af(x)$	$y = 6\sqrt[3]{x}$ vertical stretch by 6 $y = \frac{1}{2}\sqrt[3]{x}$ vertical compression by $\frac{1}{2}$
Horizontal stretch/ compression	$f\left(\frac{1}{b}x\right)$	$y = \sqrt[3]{\frac{1}{5}x}$ horizontal stretch by 5 $y = \sqrt[3]{3x}$ horizontal compression by $\frac{1}{3}$
Reflection	$-f(x)$ $f(-x)$	$y = -\sqrt[3]{x}$ across x-axis $y = \sqrt[3]{-x}$ across y-axis

For the function $f(x) = a\sqrt[3]{x - h} + k$, (h, k) is the graph's point of symmetry. Use the values of a, h, and k to draw each graph. For example, the point $(1, 1)$ on the graph of the parent function becomes the point $(1 + h, a + k)$ on the graph of the given function.

Example 1 **Graph the cube root functions.**

(A) Graph $g(x) = 2\sqrt[3]{x - 3} + 5$.

The transformations of the graph of $f(x) = \sqrt[3]{x}$ that produce the graph of $g(x)$ are:

- a vertical stretch by a factor of 2
- a translation of 3 units to the right and 5 units up

Choose points on $f(x) = \sqrt[3]{x}$ and find the transformed corresponding points on $g(x) = 2\sqrt[3]{x - 3} + 5$.

Graph $g(x) = 2\sqrt[3]{x - 3} + 5$ using the transformed points.

$f(x) = \sqrt[3]{x}$	$g(x) = 2\sqrt[3]{x - 3} + 5$
$(-8, -2)$	$(-5, 1)$
$(-1, -1)$	$(2, 3)$
$(0, 0)$	$(3, 5)$
$(1, 1)$	$(4, 7)$
$(8, 2)$	$(11, 9)$

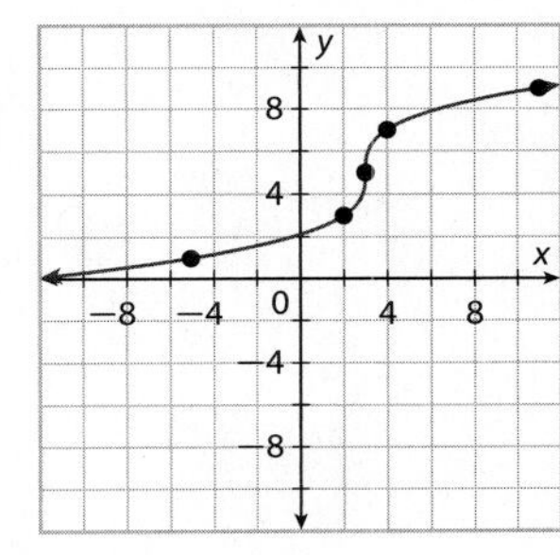

PROFESSIONAL DEVELOPMENT

Learning Progressions

Previously, students learned how parameters affect the graphs of square root functions. In this lesson, students analyze how the parameters a, b, h, and k, in functions of the form $f(x) = a\sqrt[3]{x - h} + k$ and $f(x) = \sqrt[3]{\frac{1}{b}(x - h)} + k$, affect the graph of the parent cube root function, $f(x) = \sqrt[3]{x}$. They then use this knowledge to graph cube root functions, and to analyze graphs to determine the functions they represent. This will help students when they work with radical functions with indices greater than 3. They will be able to distinguish between the attributes of functions with even indices and those with odd indices, and apply transformations to the graphs of those functions.

EXPLORE

Graphing and Analyzing the Parent Cube Root Function

INTEGRATE TECHNOLOGY

Students have the option of completing the Explore activity either in the book or online.

QUESTIONING STRATEGIES

How do you know that the graph of $f(x) = \sqrt[3]{x}$ does not have any horizontal asymptotes? As the value of x increases, the cube root of x increases without bound, and as the value of x decreases, the cube root of x decreases without bound, so there are no horizontal asymptotes. (As $x \to \infty$, $f(x) \to \infty$, and as $x \to -\infty$, $f(x) \to -\infty$.) The function is an increasing function, and the range is all real numbers.

EXPLAIN 1

Graphing Cube Root Functions

INTEGRATE MATHEMATICAL PRACTICES

Focus on Critical Thinking

MP.3 When graphing a cube-root function, students can create a table of values, and use the points from the table to help them to draw a more accurate curve. Discuss with students how to choose values of x that will make this work easier. Lead them to recognize that they need to choose values of x that make the *radicand* a perfect cube (positive or negative), not necessarily values of x that are themselves perfect cubes.

AVOID COMMON ERRORS

Students may sometimes restrict the domain of cube root functions to values of the variable that make the radicand non-negative. Remind students that radicals with odd indices have real roots even when the radicand is negative. Therefore, they should graph cube root functions over the set of all real numbers.

QUESTIONING STRATEGIES

? What effect do h and k have on the domain and range of a cube root function? **None; the domain and range are both the set of all real numbers, regardless of the values of h and k.**

Graph $g(x) = \sqrt[3]{\frac{1}{2}(x - 10)} + 4$.

The transformations of the graph of $f(x) = \sqrt[3]{x}$ that produce the graph of $g(x)$ are:

- a horizontal stretch by a factor of 2
- a translation of 10 units to the right and 4 units up

Choose points on $f(x) = \sqrt[3]{x}$ and find the transformed corresponding points on $g(x) = \sqrt[3]{\frac{1}{2}(x - 10)} + 4$.

Graph $g(x) = \sqrt[3]{\frac{1}{2}(x - 10)} + 4$ using the transformed points.

$f(x) = \sqrt[3]{x}$	$g(x) = \sqrt[3]{\frac{1}{2}(x - 10)} + 4$
(−8, −2)	**(−6, 2)**
(−1, −1)	**(8, 3)**
(0, 0)	**(10, 4)**
(1, 1)	**(12, 5)**
(8, 2)	**(26, 6)**

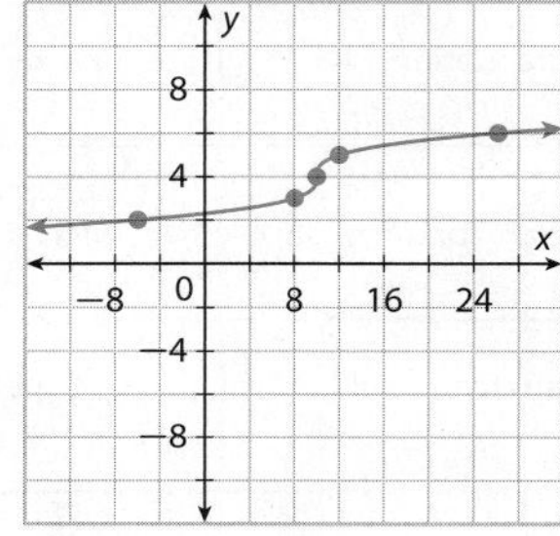

Your Turn

Graph the cube root function.

2. Graph $g(x) = \sqrt[3]{x - 3} + 6$.

transformations:
- **a translation of 3 units to the right and 6 units up**

$f(x) = \sqrt[3]{x}$	$g(x) = \sqrt[3]{x - 3} + 6$
(−8, −2)	**(−5, 4)**
(−1, −1)	**(2, 5)**
(0, 0)	**(3, 6)**
(1, 1)	**(4, 7)**
(8, 2)	**(11, 8)**

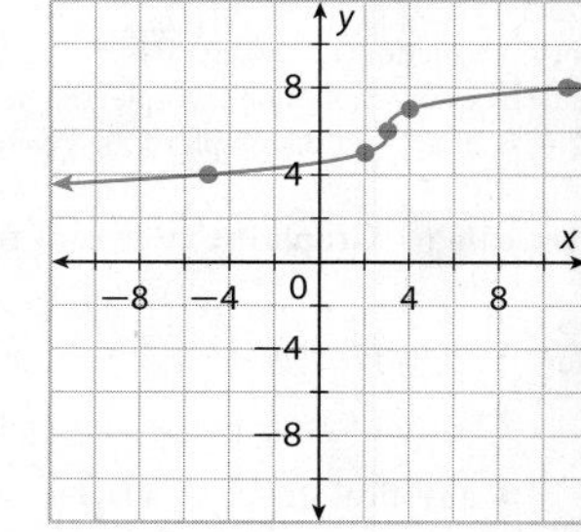

COLLABORATIVE LEARNING

Whole Class Activity

Project a large coordinate grid on the board. Have a student draw the graph of $f(x) = \sqrt[3]{x}$ on the grid. Select five students, and place each student's first initial on one of the following points on the graph: (−8, −2), (−1, −1), (0, 0), (1, 1), (8, 2). Have the students point to "their" points on the projected graph. Then present a cube root function, such as $f(x) = -3\sqrt[3]{x + 1} + 4$ or $f(x) = \sqrt[3]{\frac{1}{2}(x - 3)} - 2$, and have each of the five students move his or her finger (or a pointer) to its new location on the graph of the given function. Have the other students in the class check for correctness. Then repeat the activity for other students using different functions.

Explain 2 Writing Cube Root Functions

Given the graph of the transformed function $g(x) = a\sqrt[3]{\frac{1}{b}(x-h)} + k$, you can determine the values of the parameters by using the reference points $(-1, 1)$, $(0, 0)$, and $(1, 1)$ that you used to graph $g(x)$ in the previous example.

Example 2 **For the given graphs, write a cube root function.**

(A) Write the function in the form $g(x) = a\sqrt[3]{x-h} + k$.

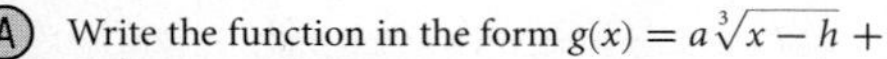

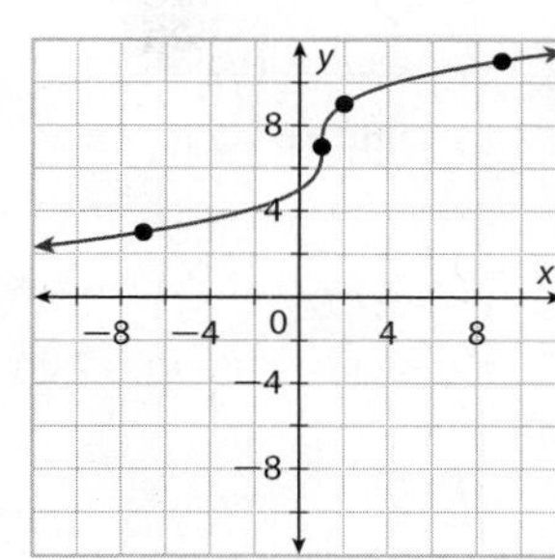

Identify the values of a, h, and k.

Identify the values of h and k from the point of symmetry.

$(h, k) = (1, 7)$, so $h = 1$ and $k = 7$.

Identify the value of a from either of the other two reference points $(-1, 1)$ or $(1, 1)$.

The reference point $(1, 1)$ has general coordinates $(h + 1, a + k)$. Substituting 1 for h and 7 for k and setting the general coordinates equal to the actual coordinates gives this result:

$(h + 1, a + k) = (2, a + 7) = (2, 9)$, so $a = 2$.

$a = 2$ $\quad h = 1$ $\quad k = 7$

The function is $g(x) = 2\sqrt[3]{x-1} + 7$.

(B) Write the function in the form $g(x) = \sqrt[3]{\frac{1}{b}(x-h)} + k$.

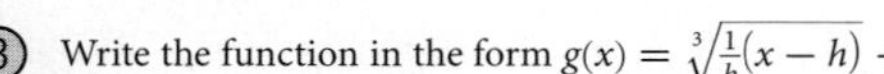

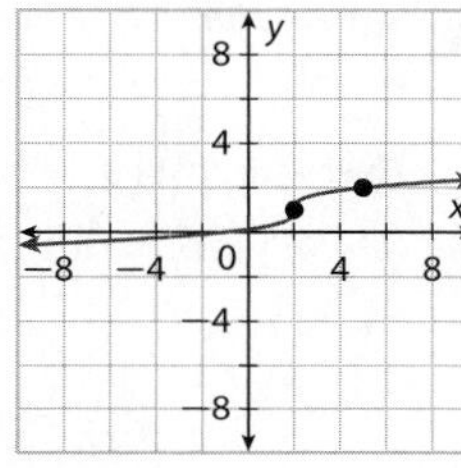

Identify the values of b, h, and k.

Identify the values of h and k from the point of symmetry.

$(h, k) = (2, \boxed{1})$ so $h = 2$ and $k = \boxed{1}$.

Identify the value of b from either of the other two reference points.

The rightmost reference point has general coordinates $(b + h, 1 + k)$. Substituting 2 for h and 1 for k and setting the general coordinates equal to the actual coordinates gives this result:

$(b + h, 1 + \boxed{1}) = (b + 2, \boxed{2}) = (5, 2)$, so $b = \boxed{3}$.

$b = \boxed{3}$ $\quad h = \boxed{2}$ $\quad k = \boxed{1}$

The function is $g(x) = \sqrt[3]{\frac{1}{3}(x-2)} + 1$.

EXPLAIN 2

Writing Cube Root Functions

QUESTIONING STRATEGIES

How can you identify the point to which (0, 0) from the graph of the parent function was translated in the graph of a cube root function? **The point (0, 0) is translated to the point at which the curvature of the graph changes.**

DIFFERENTIATE INSTRUCTION

Multiple Representations

Have students complete the table to examine the effects produced by a and b. Students can graph the functions to see the effects.

x	$f(x) = \sqrt[3]{x}$	$g(x) = 8\sqrt[3]{x}$	$g(x) = \sqrt[3]{8x}$	$g(x) = \sqrt[3]{\frac{1}{8}x}$
−64	−4	−32	−8	−2
−8	−2	−16	−4	−1
−1	−1	−8	−2	−0.5
0	0	0	0	0
1	1	8	2	0.5
8	2	16	4	1
64	4	32	8	2

AVOID COMMON ERRORS

It is easy for students to forget that when indicating a horizontal stretch or compression of the parent graph, the reciprocal of the stretch or compression factor, and not the factor itself, is placed under the radical sign. Present a side-by-side comparison of a stretch and a compression to remind students of the proper procedure.

INTEGRATE TECHNOLOGY

Students can use a graphing calculator to check their work. They can enter their functions, and use the graphing feature to check that the graphs of their functions match the given graph.

Your Turn

For the given graphs, write a cube root function.

3. Write the function in the form $g(x) = a\sqrt[3]{x-h} + k$.

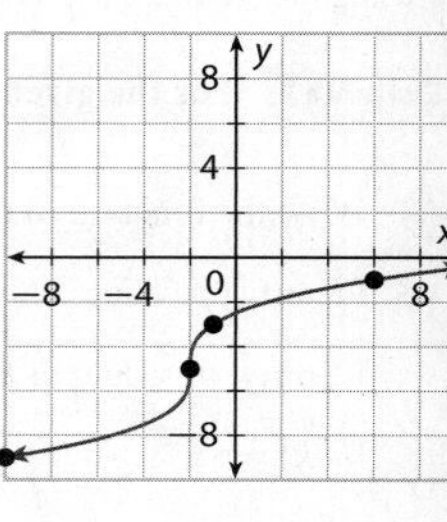

$(h, k) = (-2, -5)$, so $h = -2$ and $k = -5$.

The reference point $(1, 1)$ has general coordinates $(h+1, a+k)$.

Substituting -2 for h and -5 for k and setting the general coordinates equal to the actual coordinates gives this result:

$(h+1, a+k) = (-1, a-5) = (-1, -3)$, so $a = 2$.

The function is $g(x) = 2\sqrt[3]{(x+2)} - 5$.

4. Write the function in the form $g(x) = \sqrt[3]{\frac{1}{b}(x-h)} + k$.

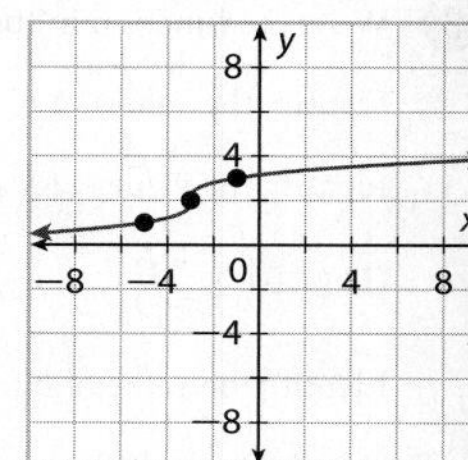

$(h, k) = (-3, 2)$, so $h = -3$ and $k = 2$.

The rightmost reference point has general coordinates $(b+h, 1+k)$.

$(b+h, 1+2) = (b-3, 3) = (-1, 3)$, so $b = 2$.

The function is $g(x) = \sqrt[3]{\frac{1}{2}(x+3)} + 2$

LANGUAGE SUPPORT EL

Communicate Math

Have students work in pairs to complete a chart similar to the following, comparing and contrasting square root and cube root functions.

Type of Function	Example	Description	Similarities	Differences

 **Explain 3**

Modeling with Cube Root Functions

You can use cube root functions to model real-world situations.

Example 3

Ⓐ The shoulder height h (in centimeters) of a particular elephant is modeled by the function $h(t) = 62.1\sqrt[3]{t} + 76$, where t is the age (in years) of the elephant. Graph the function and examine its average rate of change over the equal t-intervals $(0, 20)$, $(20, 40)$, and $(40, 60)$. What is happening to the average rate of change as the t-values of the intervals increase? Use the graph to find the height when $t = 35$.

Graph $h(t) = 62.1\sqrt[3]{t} + 76$.

The graph is the graph of $f(x) = \sqrt[3]{x}$ translated up 76 and stretched vertically by a factor of 62.1. Graph the transformed points $(0, 76)$, $(8, 200.2)$, $(27, 262.3)$, and $(64, 324.4)$. Connect the points with a smooth curve.

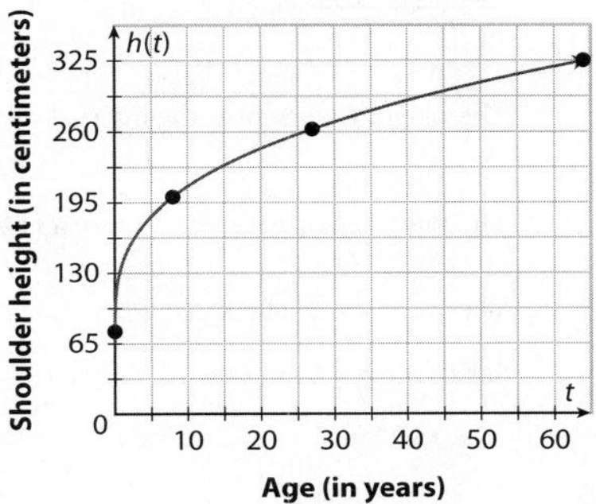

First interval:

$$\text{Average Rate of change} \approx \frac{244.6 - 76}{20 - 0} = 8.43$$

Second interval:

$$\text{Average Rate of change} \approx \frac{288.4 - 244.6}{40 - 20} = 2.19$$

Third interval:

$$\text{Average Rate of change} \approx \frac{319.1 - 288.4}{60 - 40} = 1.54$$

The average rate of change is becoming less.

Drawing a vertical line up from 35 gives a value of about 280 cm.

EXPLAIN 3

Modeling with Cube Root Functions

QUESTIONING STRATEGIES

? What information about the situation is better illustrated by the graph than by the function rule? **The graph makes it easier to see the behavior of the function as the values of x increase.**

INTEGRATE MATHEMATICAL PRACTICES

Focus on Math Connections

MP.1 Instruct students to find the inverse of the function in the example. Have them compare the two functions. Then have them discuss the types of questions that could be answered better by the inverse function than by the original function.

(B) The velocity of a 1400-kilogram car at the end of a 400-meter run is modeled by the function $v = 15.2\sqrt[3]{p}$, where v is the velocity in kilometers per hour and p is the power of its engine in horsepower. Graph the function and examine its average rate of change over the equal p-intervals $(0, 60)$, $(60, 120)$, and $(120, 180)$. What is happening to the average rate of change as the p-values of the intervals increase? Use the function to find the velocity when p is 100 horsepower.

Graph $V = 15.2\sqrt[3]{p}$.

The graph is the graph of $f(x) = \sqrt[3]{x}$ stretched **vertically** by a factor of 15.2. Graph the transformed points $(0, 0)$, $(8,$ **30.4**$)$, $(27,$ **45.6**$)$, $(64,$ **60.8**$)$, $(125,$ **76**$)$, and $(216,$ **91.2**$)$.

Connect the points with a smooth curve.

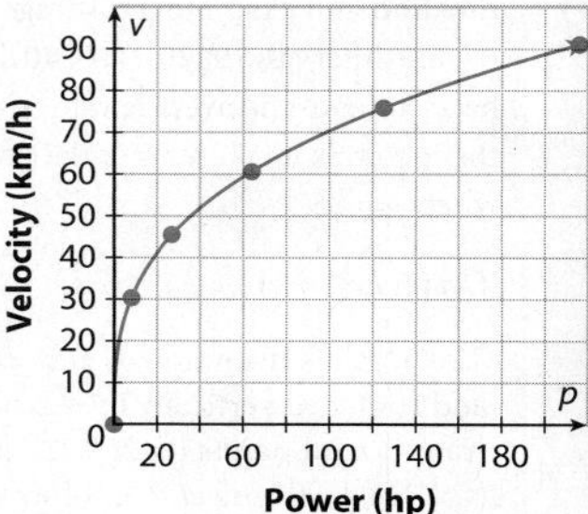

The rate of change over the interval $(0, 60)$ is $\frac{59.5 - 0}{60 - 0}$ which is about **0.99**.

The rate of change over the interval $(60, 120)$ is $\frac{75.0 - 59.5}{120 - 60}$ whichis about **0.26**.

The rate of change over the interval $(120, 180)$ is $\frac{85.8 - 75.0}{180 - 120}$ which is about **0.18**.

The average rate of change is becoming **less**.

Substitute $p = 100$ in the function.

$v = 15.2\sqrt[3]{p}$

$v = 15.2\sqrt[3]{100}$

$v \approx 15.2(4.64)$

$v = 70.5$

The velocity is about **70.5** km/h.

Your Turn

5. The fetch is the length of water over a wind that is blowing in the same direction. The function $s(f) = 7.1\sqrt[3]{f}$, relates the speed of the wind s in kilometers per hour to the fetch f in kilometers. Graph the function and examine its average rate of change over the intervals $(20, 80)$, $(80, 140)$, and $(140, 200)$. What is happening to the average rate of change as the f-values of the intervals increase? Use the function to find the speed of the wind when $f = 64$.

first interval: $\frac{30.6 - 19.3}{80 - 20} \approx 0.19.$

second interval: $\frac{36.9 - 30.6}{140 - 80} \approx 0.11.$

third interval: $\frac{41.5 - 36.9}{200 - 140} \approx 0.08.$

The average rate of change is becoming less.

The speed of the wind is about 28.4 km/h.

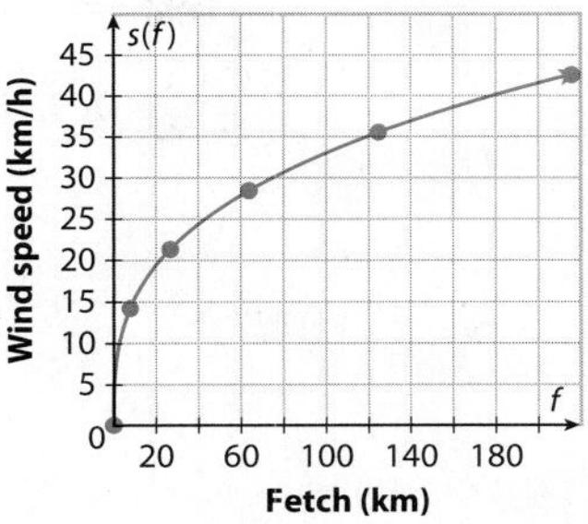

Elaborate

6. **Discussion** Why is the domain of $f(x) = \sqrt[3]{x}$ all real numbers?
Answers may vary. Sample answer: You can take the cube root of negative numbers, zero, and positive numbers, so the value of the radicand in $\sqrt[3]{x}$ can be positive, negative, or zero, which makes the domain all real numbers.

7. Identify which transformations (stretches or compressions, reflections, and translations) of $f(x) = x^3$ change the following attributes of the function.

   a. Location of the point of symmetry

   b. Symmetry about a point

   a. Vertical translations $(k \neq 0)$ and horizontal translations $(h \neq 0)$ change the location of the point of symmetry.

   b. No transformations change the function's symmetry about a point.

8. **Essential Question Check-In** How do parameters a, b, h, and k effect the graphs of $f(x) = a\sqrt[3]{(x - h)} + k$ and $g(x) = \sqrt[3]{\frac{1}{b}(x - h)} + k$?
The graph of $f(x)$ is a vertical stretch or compression of the graph of the parent function by a factor of a. When $|a| > 1$, the graph of $f(x)$ is a vertical stretch, and when $0 < |a| < 1$, the graph of $f(x)$ is a vertical compression. The graph of $g(x)$ is a horizontal stretch or compression of the graph of the parent function by a factor of b. When $|b| > 1$ the graph of $g(x)$ is a horizontal stretch, and when $0 < |b| < 1$ the graph of $g(x)$ is a horizontal compression. In both cases, the graphs are translated left or right by h and up or down by k.

ELABORATE

INTEGRATE MATHEMATICAL PRACTICES

Focus on Critical Thinking

MP.3 Have students consider *why*, when a factor of $\frac{1}{b}$ is introduced in the radicand, a horizontal stretch or compression of the graph of the parent function occurs. Have students work in small groups to discuss how this parameter affects the pairing of values by the function. Encourage them to use both the graphing and table features of the graphing calculator to investigate why this occurs.

SUMMARIZE THE LESSON

How is the graph of $f(x) = a\sqrt[3]{x - h} + k$ related to the graph of $f(x) = \sqrt[3]{x}$? **The point at which the curvature of the graph changes is at (h, k) instead of $(0, 0)$. It is stretched vertically by a factor of a if $|a| > 1$, or compressed vertically by a factor of a if $0 < |a| < 1$. If $a < 0$, then the graph is decreasing instead of increasing.**

EVALUATE

ASSIGNMENT GUIDE

Concepts and Skills	Practice
Explore Graphing and Analyzing the Parent Cube Root Function	Exercises 1–2
Example 1 Graphing Cube Root Functions	Exercises 9–11
Example 2 Writing Cube Root Functions	Exercises 12–14
Example 3 Modeling with Cube Root Functions	Exercises 15–16

INTEGRATE MATHEMATICAL PRACTICES

Focus on Communication

MP.3 Students can check that they've used accurate language to describe the transformations by graphing the given function and checking to see if the graph matches the description. If students are having difficulty, you may want to suggest that they work on these problems with a partner, verbalizing and then refining their descriptions with the partner.

MULTIPLE REPRESENTATIONS

Encourage students to make a table of values for the function in order to find additional points on the graph. This will help them to draw a more accurate curve.

Evaluate: Homework and Practice

- Online Homework
- Hints and Help
- Extra Practice

1. Graph the function $g(x) = \sqrt[3]{x} + 3$. Identify the domain and range of the function.

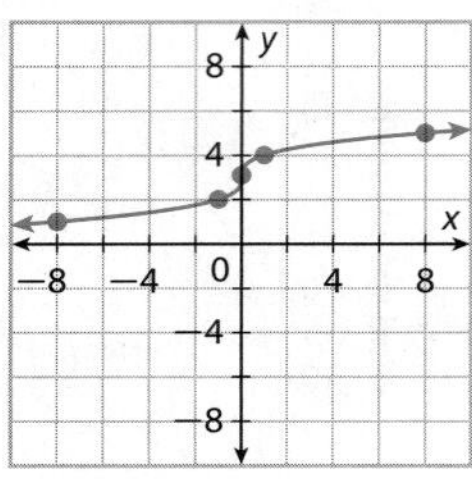

Make a table of values.

x	y	(x, y)
−8	1	(−8, 1)
−1	2	(−1, 2)
0	3	(0, 3)
1	4	(1, 4)
8	5	(8, 5)

Use the table to graph the function.

The domain is all real numbers.

The range is all real numbers.

2. Graph the function $g(x) = \sqrt[3]{x} - 5$. Identify the domain and range of the function.

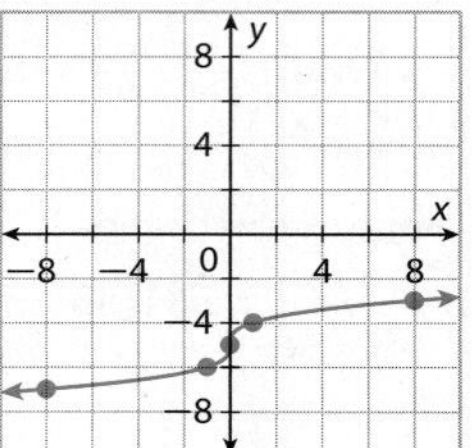

Make a table of values.

x	y	(x, y)
−8	−7	(−8, −7)
−1	−6	(−1, −6)
0	−5	(0, −5)
1	−4	(1, −4)
8	−3	(8, −3)

Use the table to graph the function.

The domain is all real numbers.

The range is all real numbers.

Predict the effect of parameters on the graphs of cube root functions.

3. $g(x) = \sqrt[3]{x} + 6$

The graph of $g(x) = \sqrt[3]{x} + 6$ is the graph of $f(x) = \sqrt[3]{x}$ translated 6 units up.

4. $g(x) = \sqrt[3]{x - 5}$

The graph of $g(x) = \sqrt[3]{x - 5}$ is the graph of $f(x) = \sqrt[3]{x}$ translated 5 units right.

5. $g(x) = \frac{1}{3}\sqrt[3]{-x}$

The graph of $g(x) = \frac{1}{3}\sqrt[3]{-x}$ is the graph of $f(x) = \sqrt[3]{x}$ compressed vertically by a factor of $\frac{1}{3}$ and reflected across the y-axis.

6. $g(x) = \sqrt[3]{5x}$

The graph of $g(x) = \sqrt[3]{5x}$ is the graph of $f(x) = \sqrt[3]{x}$ compressed horizontally by a factor of $\frac{1}{5}$.

7. $g(x) = -2\sqrt[3]{x} + 3$

The graph of $g(x) = -2\sqrt[3]{x} + 3$ is the graph of $f(x) = \sqrt[3]{x}$ translated 3 units up , reflected across the x-axis, and vertically stretched by a factor of 2.

8. $g(x) = \sqrt[3]{x + 4} - 3$

The graph of $g(x) = \sqrt[3]{x + 4} - 3$ is the graph of $f(x) = \sqrt[3]{x}$ translated 4 units left and 3 units down.

Exercise	Depth of Knowledge (D.O.K.)	COMMON CORE Mathematical Practices
1–2	**1** Recall of Information	**MP.4** Modeling
3–8	**2** Skills/Concepts	**MP.2** Reasoning
9–14	**2** Skills/Concepts	**MP.6** Precision
15–16	**2** Skills/Concepts	**MP.4** Modeling
17	**2** Skills/Concepts	**MP.6** Precision
18	**2** Skills/Concepts	**MP.4** Modeling

Graph the cube root functions.

9. $g(x) = 3\sqrt[3]{x+4}$

transformations:

- a vertical stretch by a factor of 3
- a translation of 4 units to the left

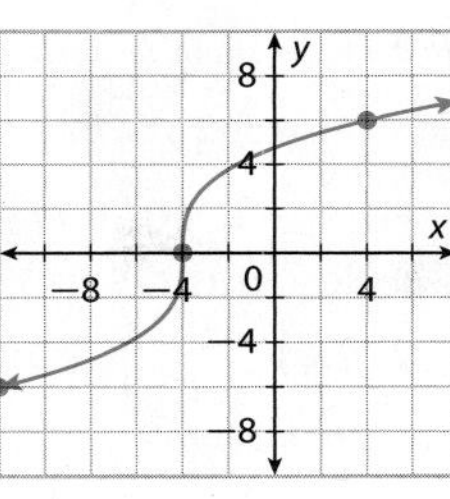

$f(x) = \sqrt[3]{x}$	$g(x) = 3\sqrt[3]{x+4}$
(−8, −2)	(−12, −6)
(−1, −1)	(−5, −3)
(0, 0)	(−4, 0)
(1, 1)	(−3, 3)
(8, 2)	(4, 6)

10. $g(x) = 2\sqrt[3]{x} + 3$

transformations:

- a vertical stretch by a factor of 2
- a translation of 3 units up

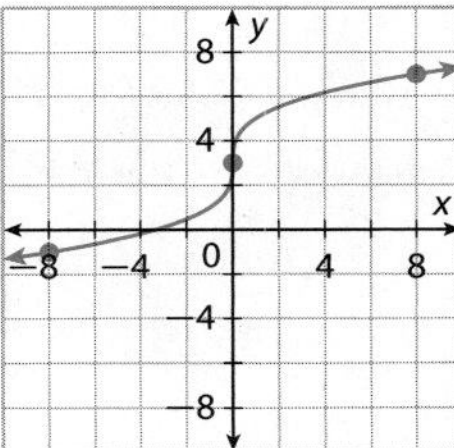

$f(x) = \sqrt[3]{x}$	$g(x) = 2\sqrt[3]{x} + 3$
(−8, −2)	(−8, −1)
(−1, −1)	(−1, 1)
(0, 0)	(0, 3)
(1, 1)	(1, 5)
(8, 2)	(8, 7)

11. $g(x) = \sqrt[3]{x-3} + 2$

transformations:

- a translation of 3 units to the right and 2 units up

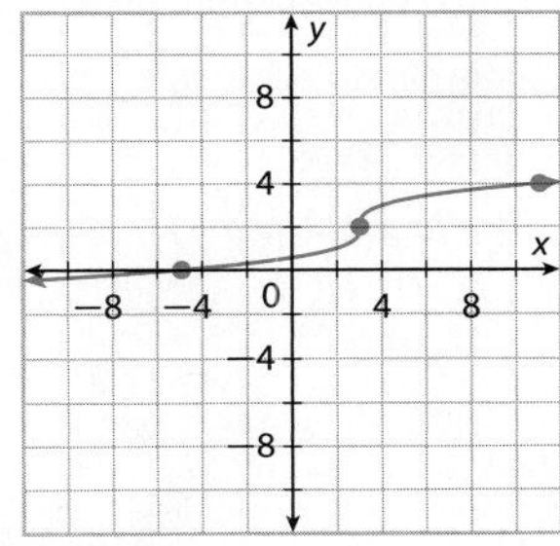

$f(x) = \sqrt[3]{x}$	$g(x) = \sqrt[3]{x-3} + 2$
(−8, −2)	(−5, 0)
(−1, −1)	(2, 1)
(0, 0)	(3, 2)
(1, 1)	(4, 3)
(8, 2)	(11, 4)

Exercise	Depth of Knowledge (D.O.K.)	COMMON CORE Mathematical Practices
19–21	**2** Skills/Concepts	**MP.2** Reasoning
22	**3** Strategic Thinking H.O.T.	**MP.2** Reasoning
23–24	**3** Strategic Thinking H.O.T.	**MP.3** Logic

COOPERATIVE LEARNING

Have students work in small groups. Have each group make a poster showing how to graph a function of the form $f(x) = a\sqrt[3]{x-h} + k$ and a function of the form $f(x) = \sqrt[3]{\frac{1}{b}(x-h)} + k$. Give each group different functions to graph. Then have each group present its poster to the rest of the class, explaining each step.

VISUAL CUES

Suggest that students draw the graph of the parent cube root function on the same coordinate grid as the given graph so that they can see whether the given graph represents a stretch or compression of the graph of the parent function.

AVOID COMMON ERRORS

When graphing a function of the form $f(x) = a\sqrt[3]{x - h} + k$ with $a < 0$, some students may perform the translation first and then perform the reflection. Help them to see that the function indicates a vertical translation of the graph of $f(x) = a\sqrt[3]{x - h}$ by k units, so the graph needs to be reflected before it is translated vertically.

PEER-TO-PEER DISCUSSION

Ask students to discuss with a partner how they can use the rule for a cube root function to determine the x- and y-intercepts of its graph. **To find the x-intercept, set the rule equal to 0 and solve for x. To find the y-intercept, substitute 0 for x and solve for y.**

For the given graphs, write a cube root function.

12. Write the function in the form $g(x) = a\sqrt[3]{x - h} + k$.

$(h, k) = (-2, -2)$, so $h = -2$ and $k = -2$.

The reference point $(1, 1)$ has general coordinates $(h + 1, a + k)$.

$(h + 1, a + k) = (-1, a - 2) = (-1, 1)$ so $a = 3$.

The function is $g(x) = 3\sqrt[3]{x + 2} - 2$.

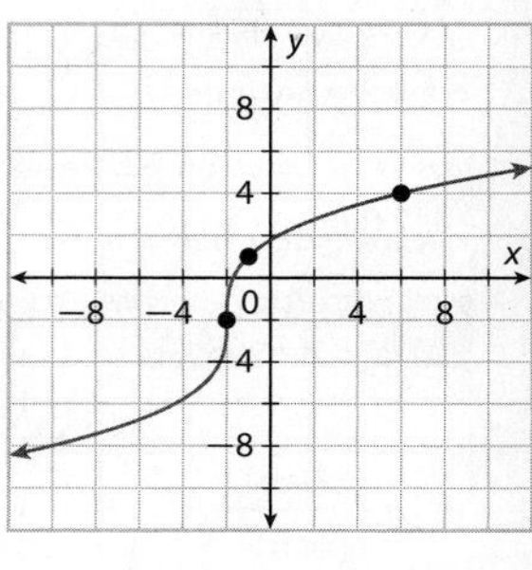

13. Write the function in the form $g(x) = a\sqrt[3]{x - h} + k$.

$(h, k) = (2, -6)$, so $h = 2$ and $k = -6$.

The reference point $(1, 1)$ has general coordinates $(h + 1, a + k)$.

$(h + 1, a + k) = (3, a - 6) = (3, -8)$ so $a = -2$.

The function is $g(x) = -2\sqrt[3]{x - 2} - 6$.

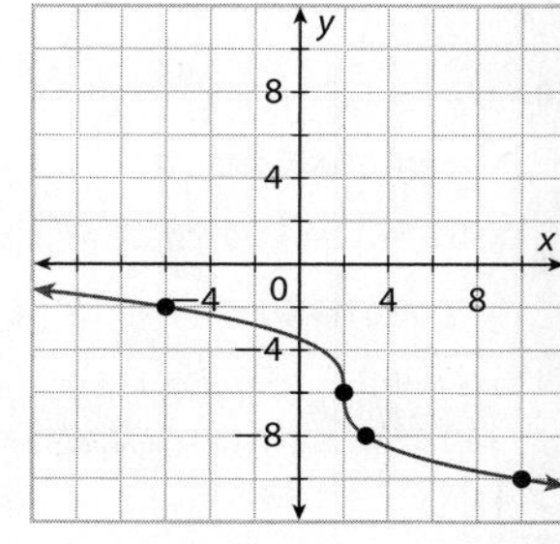

14. Write the function in the form $g(x) = \sqrt[3]{\frac{1}{b}(x - h)} + k$.

$(h, k) = (-4, -3)$, so $h = -4$ and $k = -3$.

The reference point $(1, 1)$ has general coordinates $(b + h, 1 + k)$.

$(b + h, 1 - 3) = (b - 4, -2) = (-2, -2)$, so $b = 2$.

The function is $g(x) = \sqrt[3]{\frac{1}{2}(x + 4)} - 3$.

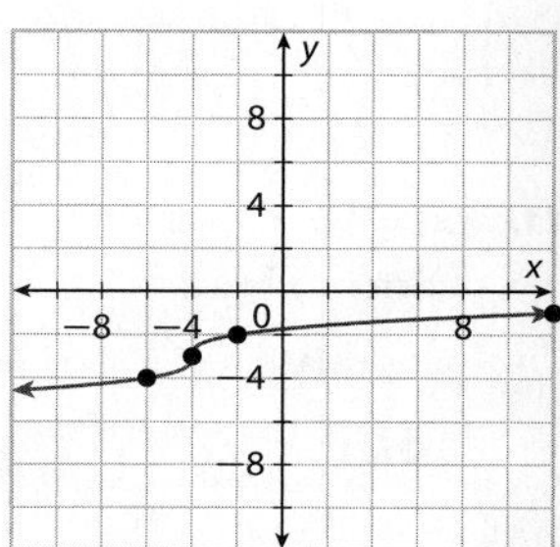

15. The length of the side of a cube is modeled by $s = \sqrt[3]{V}$. Graph the function. Use the graph to find s when $V = 48$.

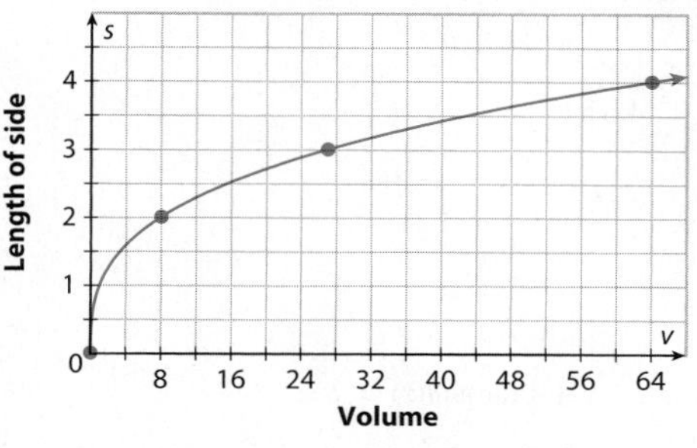

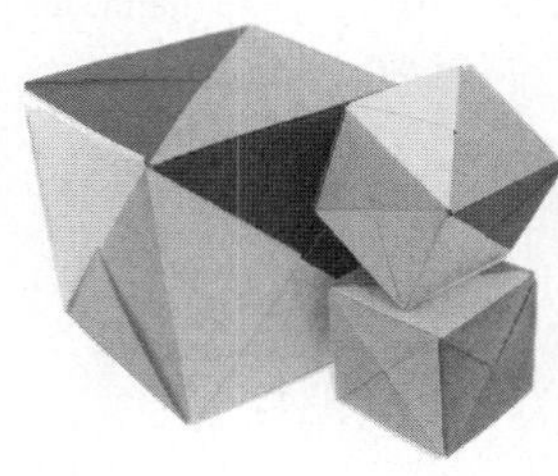

Drawing a vertical line up from $V = 48$ up to the graph gives a value of about 3.6 for s. When $V = 48$, $s \approx 3.6$.

16. The radius of a stainless steel ball, in centimeters, can be modeled by $r(m) = 0.31\sqrt[3]{m}$, where m is the mass of the ball in grams. Use the function to find r when $m = 125$.

$\mathbf{r(125) = 0.31\sqrt[3]{125}}$

$\mathbf{r(125) = 0.31(5)}$

$\mathbf{r(125) = 1.55}$

A stainless steel ball bearing with a mass of 125 grams has a radius of 1.55 centimeters.

17. Describe the steps for graphing $g(x) = \sqrt[3]{x + 8} - 11$.

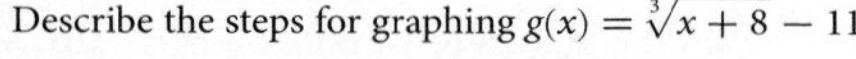

1. Graph the parent function $f(x) = \sqrt[3]{x}$.

2. Translate the graph of $f(x) = \sqrt[3]{x}$ 8 units to the left.

3. Translate the graph of $f(x) = \sqrt[3]{x}$ 11 units down.

18. Modeling Write a situation that can be modeled by a cube root function. Give the function.

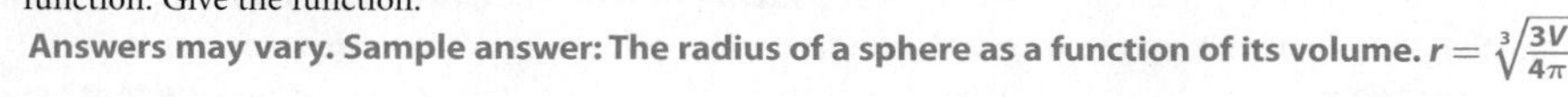

Answers may vary. Sample answer: The radius of a sphere as a function of its volume. $r = \sqrt[3]{\frac{3V}{4\pi}}$

19. Find the y-intercept for the function $y = a\sqrt[3]{x - h} + k$.

To find the y-intercept, let $x = 0$ in the equation.

$\mathbf{y = a\sqrt[3]{x - h} + k}$

$\mathbf{y = a\sqrt[3]{0 - h} + k}$

$\mathbf{y = a\sqrt[3]{-h} + k}$ **or** $\mathbf{y = -ah^{1/3} + k}$

CONNECT VOCABULARY EL

Ask students to articulate what a square root function is and how it is related to a quadratic function. Then have them explain what a cube root function is and how it is related to a cubic function.

JOURNAL

Have students compare and contrast the process of graphing a cube root function with that of graphing a square root function.

20. Find the x-intercept for the function $y = a\sqrt[3]{x - h} + k$.

To find the x-intercept, let $y = 0$ in the equation.

$$y = a\sqrt[3]{x-h} + k$$
$$0 = a\sqrt[3]{x-h} + k$$
$$-k = a\sqrt[3]{x-h}$$
$$\frac{-k}{a} = \sqrt[3]{x-h}$$
$$\frac{(-k)^3}{a^3} = x - h$$
$$\frac{(-k)^3}{a^3} + h = x$$

21. Describe the translation(s) used to get $g(x) = \sqrt[3]{x - 9} + 12$ from $f(x) = \sqrt[3]{x}$. Select all that apply.

- (**A.**) translated 9 units right
- **B.** translated 9 units left
- **C.** translated 9 units up
- **D.** translated 9 units down
- **E.** translated 12 units right
- **F.** translated 12 units left
- (**G.**) translated 12 units up
- **H.** translated 12 units down

H.O.T. Focus on Higher Order Thinking

22. Explain the Error Tim says that to graph $g(x) = \sqrt[3]{x - 6} + 3$, you need to translate the graph of $f(x) = \sqrt[3]{x}$ 6 units to the left and then 3 units up. What mistake did he make?

Tim thought the general form for the translated graph was $f(x) = a\sqrt[3]{(x + h)} + k$ instead of $f(x) = a\sqrt[3]{(x - h)} + k$. The graph of $f(x) = \sqrt[3]{x}$ should be translated 6 units to the right.

23. Communicate Mathematical Ideas Why does the square root function have a restricted domain but the cube root function does not?

Answers may vary. Sample answer: If you square a negative number you always get a positive number. Thus, you cannot take a square root of a negative number and this restricts the domain of the square root function to nonnegative numbers. However, if you cube a negative number, you get another negative number. Thus, you can take the cube root of a negative number, a positive number, and zero. Therefore, the domain of the cube root function is all real numbers.

24. Justify Reasoning Does a horizontal translation and a vertical translation of the function $f(x) = \sqrt[3]{x}$ affect the function's domain or range? Explain.

No, the domain and the range of $f(x) = \sqrt[3]{x}$ is all real numbers. After a horizontal or vertical translation, the domain or range will still be all real numbers.

Lesson Performance Task

The side length of a 243-gram copper cube is 3 centimeters. Use this information to write a model for the radius of a copper sphere as a function of its mass. Then, find the radius of a copper sphere with a mass of 50 grams. How would changing the material affect the function?

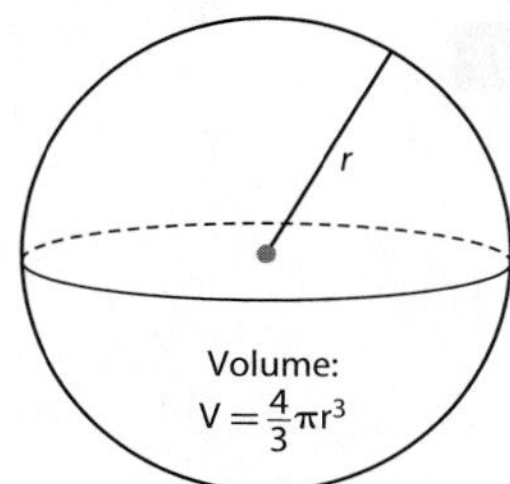

The mass of an object is equal to the object's volume times its density. Find the density of the copper using the information given for the cube. Density is mass divided by volume.

$$\frac{243 \text{ g}}{(3 \text{ cm})^3} = \frac{243 \text{ g}}{27 \text{ cm}^3} = 9 \text{ g/cm}^3$$

The density of the copper is 9 g/cm³.

The volume of a sphere is given by the formula $V = \frac{4}{3}\pi r^3$.

$$m(r) = \left(\frac{4}{3}\pi r^3\right)(9)$$
$$= 12\pi r^3$$

So, the mass of the copper sphere written as a function of its radius is $m(r) = 12\pi r^3$.

Now, rewrite the function so the radius is a function of the mass.

$$m(r) = 12\pi r^3$$
$$m = 12\pi r^3$$
$$\frac{1}{12\pi} m = r^3$$
$$\sqrt[3]{\frac{1}{12\pi} m} = r$$
$$\sqrt[3]{\frac{1}{12\pi} m} = r(m)$$
$$0.3\sqrt[3]{m} \approx r(m)$$

Substitute 50 for m in the function and solve for the radius.

$$r(50) = 0.3\sqrt[3]{50}$$
$$\approx 1.1$$

So, the radius of a 50-gram copper sphere is about 1.1 centimeters.

Changing the material of the sphere changes the function, because when density changes, the function $m(r)$ changes.

EXTENSION ACTIVITY

Have students write a general equation for the radius r with the density D as a variable. $r(m) = \sqrt[3]{\frac{3}{4\pi D}m}$ Then have them explain how the density D affects the graph of the function $r(m)$. **If $0 < D < 1$, then D causes a horizontal compression of the graph. If $D > 1$, then D causes a horizontal stretch of the graph.**

AVOID COMMON ERRORS

Some students may not take the cube root of the constant factor when solving for r. The cube root must be applied to coefficients on both sides of the equation. When solving for r in $r^3 = \frac{1}{12\pi}m$, the cube root must be applied to both $\frac{1}{12\pi}$ and m: $r = \sqrt[3]{\frac{1}{12\pi}}\sqrt[3]{m}$.

INTEGRATE MATHEMATICAL PRACTICES

Focus on Communication

MP.3 Have students discuss whether the size of an object always varies as the cube root of its mass. Have students consider different shapes and determine the size of the object in terms of its mass. Ask students to explain when the size might be the cube root of its mass and when it might be a different function.

Scoring Rubric

2 points: Student correctly solves the problem and explains his/her reasoning.

1 point: Student shows good understanding of the problem but does not fully solve or explain his/her reasoning.

0 points: Student does not demonstrate understanding of the problem.

Study Guide Review

ASSESSMENT AND INTERVENTION

Assign or customize module reviews.

MODULE PERFORMANCE TASK

Mathematical Practices: MP.1, MP.2, MP.4, MP.6
A-REI.A.2

SUPPORTING STUDENT REASONING

Students should begin by focusing on how to set up the problem. They can then do research, or you can provide them with specific information. Here is some of the information they may ask for.

- **What is the radius of Earth?** Earth's radius is approximately 6.37×10^6 m.
- **What is g on Earth's surface?** The standard value for g is 9.8 m/s^2. Point out that they've already used this value in the context of projectile motion.

STUDY GUIDE REVIEW

Radical Functions

Essential Question: How can you use radical functions to solve real-world problems?

Key Vocabulary
cube root function (*función de raíz cúbica*)
index (*índice*)
inverse function (*función inversa*)
square root function (*función de raíz cuadrada*)

KEY EXAMPLE (*Lesson 10.1*)

Find the inverse function $f^{-1}(x)$ for $f(x) = 2x^3 + 10$.

Replace $f(x)$ with y.	$y = 2x^3 + 10$
Solve for x^3.	$\frac{y-10}{2} = x^3$
Take the cube root.	$\sqrt[3]{\frac{y-10}{2}} = x$
Switch x and y.	$y = \sqrt[3]{\frac{x-10}{2}}$
Replace y with $f^{-1}(x)$.	$f^{-1}(x) = \sqrt[3]{\frac{x-10}{2}}$

KEY EXAMPLE (*Lesson 10.2*)

Graph $y = -\sqrt{x-3} + 2$. Describe the domain and range.

Sketch the graph of $y = -\sqrt{x}$.
It begins at the origin and passes through $(1, -1)$.
For $y = -\sqrt{x-3} + 2$, $h = 3$ and $k = 2$.
Shift the graph of $y = -\sqrt{x}$ right 3 units and up 2 units. The graph begins at $(3, 2)$ and passes through $(4, 1)$.
Domain: $\{x : x \geq 3\}$ Range: $\{y : y \leq 2\}$

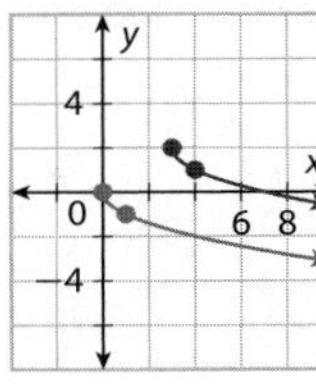

KEY EXAMPLE (*Lesson 10.3*)

Graph $y = \sqrt[3]{x+2} - 4$.

Sketch the graph of $y = \sqrt[3]{x}$.
It passes through $(-1, -1)$, $(0, 0)$, and $(1, 1)$.
For $y = \sqrt[3]{x+2} - 4$, $h = -2$ and $k = -4$.
Shift the graph of $y = \sqrt[3]{x}$ left 2 units and down 4 units. The graph passes through $(-3, -5)$, $(-2, -4)$, and $(-1, -3)$.

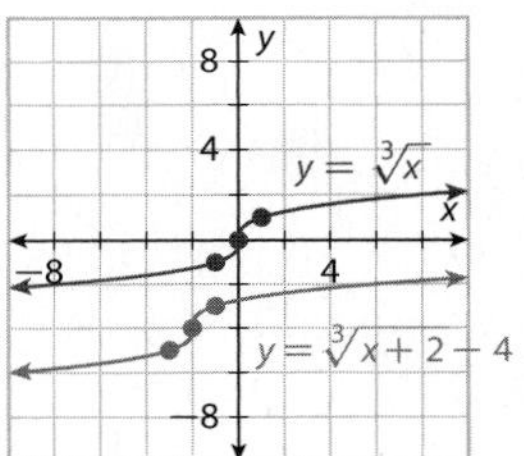

SCAFFOLDING SUPPORT

- Students may be confused by the inclusion of mass information in the table. Explain that mass isn't included in the escape velocity formula—it is extraneous information.
- Students may notice that the values they calculate for v_{escape} can vary due to differences in rounding.

EXERCISES

Find the inverse of each function. Restrict the domain where necessary. *(Lesson 10.1)*

1. $f(x) = 16x^2$

   $f^{-1}(x) = \frac{\sqrt{x}}{4}$; D: $\{x \mid x \geq 0\}$

2. $f(x) = x^3 - 20$

   $f^{-1}(x) = \sqrt[3]{x + 20}$

Identify the transformations of the graph $f(x) = \sqrt{x}$ that produce the graph of the function. *(Lesson 10.2)*

3. $g(x) = -\sqrt{4x}$

   a horizontal compression by a factor of $\frac{1}{4}$

   a reflection across the *x*-axis

4. $h(x) = \frac{1}{2}\sqrt{x} + 1$

   a vertical compression by a factor of $\frac{1}{2}$

   a translation 1 unit up

Identify the transformations of the graph $f(x) = \sqrt[3]{x}$ that produce the graph of the function. *(Lesson 10.3)*

5. $g(x) = 4\sqrt[3]{x}$

   a vertical stretch by a factor of 4

6. $h(x) = \sqrt[3]{x - 5} + 3$

   a translation 5 units right and 3 units up

MODULE PERFORMANCE TASK

We Have Liftoff!

A rocket scientist is designing a rocket to visit the planets in the solar system. The velocity that is needed to escape a planet's gravitational pull is called the escape velocity. The escape velocity depends on the planet's radius and its mass, according to the equation $V_{escape} = \sqrt{2gR}$, where R is the radius and g is the gravitational constant for the particular planet. The rocket's maximum velocity is exactly double Earth's escape velocity. For which planets will the rocket have enough velocity to escape the planet's gravity?

Planet	Radius (m)	Mass (kg)	g (m/s^2)
Mercury	2.43×10^6	3.20×10^{23}	3.61
Venus	6.07×10^6	4.88×10^{24}	8.83
Mars	3.38×10^6	6.42×10^{23}	3.75
Jupiter	6.98×10^7	1.90×10^{27}	26.0
Saturn	5.82×10^7	5.68×10^{26}	11.2
Uranus	2.35×10^7	8.68×10^{25}	10.5
Neptune	2.27×10^7	1.03×10^{26}	13.3

Begin by listing in the space below any additional information you will need to solve the problem. Then use your own paper to complete the task. Be sure to write down all your data and assumptions. Then use graphs, numbers, words, or algebra to explain how you reached your conclusions.

DISCUSSION OPPORTUNITIES

- Would the escape velocity for an asteroid be larger than or smaller than the escape velocity for a large planet?
- You may wish to discuss the relationship between radius, mass, and g: $g = k\frac{M}{R^2}$, where k is a constant. Challenge students to find the value of the constant.

SAMPLE SOLUTION

Method

Research Earth's radius and value of g, then calculate the escape velocity.

$$v_{escape} = \sqrt{2gR}$$
$$= \sqrt{2(9.8)(6.37 \times 10^6)}$$
$$= \sqrt{124,852,000}$$
$$\approx 11,173.72 \text{ m/s}$$

The rocket is able to go double that speed, or about 22,348 m/s.

Calculate escape velocities for each of the other planets and compare them:

Planet	Radius (m)	g	v_{escape} (m/s)
Mercury	2.43×10^6	3.6	4183
Venus	6.07×10^6	8.9	10,395
Mars	3.38×10^6	3.8	5068
Jupiter	6.98×10^7	26.1	60,362
Saturn	5.82×10^7	11.2	36,107
Uranus	2.35×10^7	10.5	22,215
Neptune	2.27×10^7	13.4	24,665

The rocket can visit Mercury, Venus, Mars, and Uranus, but not Jupiter, Saturn, or Neptune.

Assessment Rubric

2 points: Student correctly solves the problem and explains his/her reasoning.

1 point: Student shows good understanding of the problem but does not fully solve or explain.

0 points: Student does not demonstrate understanding of the problem.

Ready to Go On?

ASSESS MASTERY

Use the assessment on this page to determine if students have mastered the concepts and standards covered in this module.

ASSESSMENT AND INTERVENTION

Access Ready to Go On? assessment online, and receive instant scoring, feedback, and customized intervention or enrichment.

ADDITIONAL RESOURCES

Response to Intervention Resources

- Reteach Worksheets

Differentiated Instruction Resources

- Reading Strategies EL
- Success for English Learners EL
- Challenge Worksheets

Assessment Resources

- Leveled Module Quizzes

Ready to Go On?

10.1–10.3 Radical Functions

- Online Homework
- Hints and Help
- Extra Practice

Find the inverse of each function. State any restrictions on the domain. *(Lesson 10.1)*

1. $f(x) = x^2 + 9$

$f^{-1}(x) = \sqrt{x-9}$; D: $\{x \mid x \geq 9\}$

2. $f(x) = -7x^3$

$f^{-1}(x) = \sqrt[3]{-\frac{x}{7}}$

3. $f(x) = -2x^3 + 1$

$f^{-1}(x) = \sqrt[3]{\frac{1-x}{2}}$

4. $f(x) = 5x^2 + 3$

$f^{-1}(x) = \sqrt{\frac{x-3}{5}}$; D: $\{x \mid x \geq 3\}$

Identify the transformations of the graph $f(x) = \sqrt{x}$ or $h(x) = \sqrt[3]{x}$ that produce the graph of the function. *(Lessons 10.2, 10.3)*

5. $g(x) = \frac{1}{3}\sqrt{x-5} - 4$

g is f vertically compressed by $\frac{1}{3}$ and translated right 5 and down 2

6. $g(x) = \sqrt[3]{4x} + 3$

g is h horizontally compressed by 4 and translated 3 units up

7. $g(x) = \sqrt{x-4} - 1$

g is f translated right 4 and down 1

8. $g(x) = \sqrt[3]{7x+10}$

g is h horizontally compressed by a factor of 7 and translated $\frac{10}{7}$ units left

ESSENTIAL QUESTION

9. How do you use a parent square root or cube root function to graph a transformation of the function? *(Lessons 10.2, 10.3)*

Possible Answer: Use the parameters *a*, *b*, *h*, and *k* to transform points from the parent function. Use the transformed points to draw the graph.

COMMON CORE Common Core Standards

Lesson	*Items*	Content Standards	Mathematical Practices
10.1	1–4	**F-BF.B.4a, F-BF.B.4d**	**MP.2**
10.2	5	**F-IF.C.7b, F-IF.B.4, F-BF.B.3**	**MP.7**
10.3	6	**F-IF.C.7b, F-IF.B.4, F-BF.B.3**	**MP.7**
10.2	7	**F-IF.C.7b, F-IF.B.4, F-BF.B.3**	**MP.7**
10.3	8	**F-IF.C.7b, F-IF.B.4, F-BF.B.3**	**MP.7**

MODULE 10
MIXED REVIEW

Assessment Readiness

1. Look at each equation. Is it the inverse of $f(x) = x^3 - 16$? Select Yes or No for A–C.

A. $f^{-1}(x) = \sqrt[3]{x - 16}$ ○ Yes ● No

B. $f^{-1}(x) = \sqrt[3]{x + 16}$ ● Yes ○ No

C. $f^{-1}(x) = \sqrt[3]{x} + 16$ ○ Yes ● No

2. Consider the graphed function. Choose True or False for each statement.

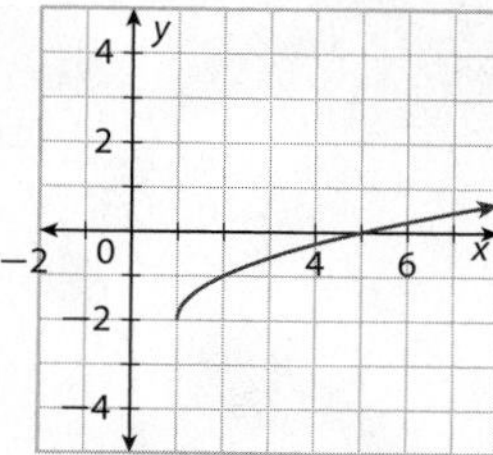

A. The equation for the function is $y = \sqrt{x - 1} - 2$. ● Yes ○ No

B. The function has exactly one y-intercept. ○ Yes ● No

C. The range of the function is $y \leq -2$. ○ Yes ● No

3. A plane's average speed when flying from one city to another is 550 mi/h and is 430 mi/h on the return flight. To the nearest mile per hour, what is the plane's average speed for the entire trip? Explain your answer.

483 mph; since the distance to and from the city is the same, the equation for finding the average speed is $\frac{2}{\frac{1}{550\text{ mi/h}} + \frac{1}{430\text{mi/h}}}$, which is equal to approximately 483 mi/h.

4. The kinetic energy E (in joules) of a 1250-kilogram compact car is given by the equation $E = 625s^2$, where s is the speed of the car (in meters per second). Write an inverse model that gives the speed of the car as a function of its kinetic energy. If the kinetic energy doubles, will the speed double? Explain why or why not.

$s = \frac{\sqrt{E}}{25}$; no. Possible answer: since E is under a square root symbol, when it doubles s only increases by a factor of $\sqrt{2}$.

Common Core Standards

Lesson	Items	Content Standards	Mathematical Practices
10.1	1	**F-BF.4.a**	**MP.2**
10.2	2	**F-IF.C.7b**	**MP.6**
9.3	3*	**A-REI.A.2, N-Q.A.1**	**MP.4**
1.4, 3.1, 10.1	4*	**F-BF.B.4a**	**MP.4**

* Item integrates mixed review concepts from previous modules or a previous course.

MIXED REVIEW

Assessment Readiness

ASSESSMENT AND INTERVENTION

Assign ready-made or customized practice tests to prepare students for high-stakes tests.

ADDITIONAL RESOURCES

Assessment Resources

- Leveled Module Quizzes: Modified, B

AVOID COMMON ERRORS

Item 3 Many students will fall back on their usual definition of "average" and add the speeds together, and then divide by 2. Remind students to double-check the formula for average speed before completing the problem.

MODULE 11

Radical Expressions and Equations

ESSENTIAL QUESTION:

Answer: Solving radical equations can allow you to evaluate claims or make predictions in situations that involve radical relationships, such as the stopping distance of a car.

PROFESSIONAL DEVELOPMENT VIDEO

Professional Development Video
Author Matt Larson models successful teaching practices in an actual high-school classroom.
Professional Development
my.hrw.com

MODULE 11

Radical Expressions and Equations

Essential Question: How can you use radical expressions and equations to solve real-world problems?

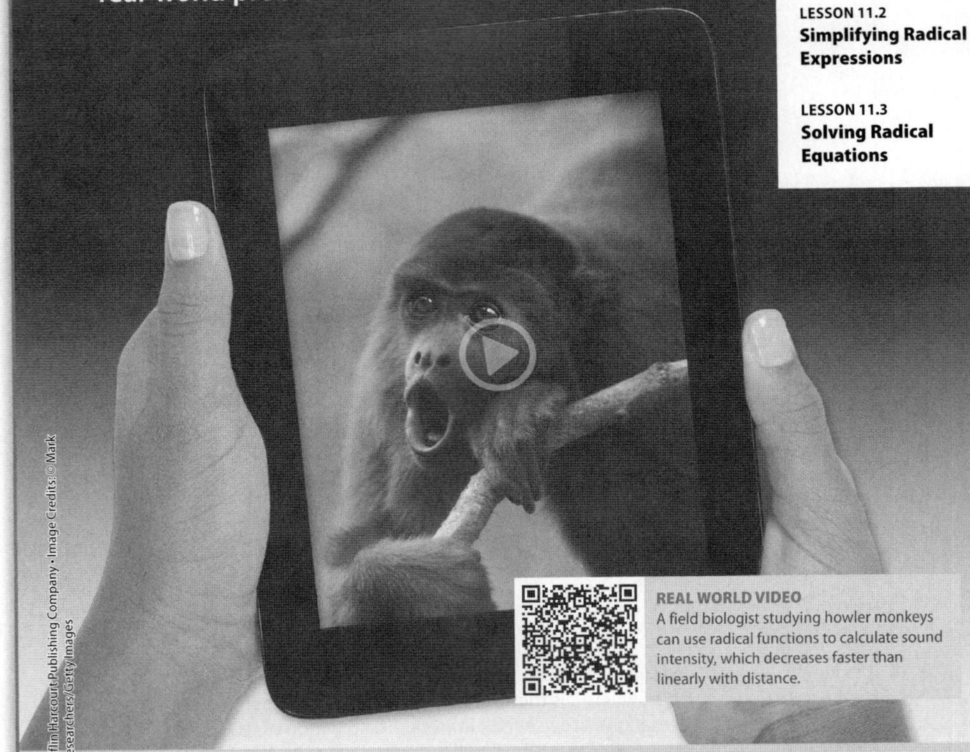

REAL WORLD VIDEO
A field biologist studying howler monkeys can use radical functions to calculate sound intensity, which decreases faster than linearly with distance.

MODULE PERFORMANCE TASK PREVIEW

Don't Disturb the Neighbors!

The loudness of a sound is subjective and depends on the listener's sensitivity to the frequencies of the sound waves. An objective measure, sound intensity, can be used to measure sounds. Sound intensity decreases the farther you get from the source of a sound. How far away do your neighbors have to be so that a loud band does not bother them? Let's find out!

Module 11 531

DIGITAL TEACHER EDITION

Access a full suite of teaching resources when and where you need them:

- Access content online or offline
- Customize lessons to share with your class
- Communicate with your students in real-time
- View student grades and data instantly to target your instruction where it is needed most

PERSONAL MATH TRAINER

Assessment and Intervention

Assign automatically graded homework, quizzes, tests, and intervention activities. Prepare your students with updated, Common Core-aligned practice tests.

Are YOU Ready?

Complete these exercises to review skills you will need for this chapter.

Personal Math Trainer
- Online Homework
- Hints and Help
- Extra Practice

Exponents

Example 1 Simplify $(x^3)^2 + x \cdot x^3 + 3x^4$.

$(x^3)^2 + x \cdot x^3 + 3x^4 = (x^3)(x^3) + x \cdot x^3 + 3x^4$ Start with the raised power.

$= x^{3+3} + x^{1+3} + 3x^4$ Add exponents.

$= x^6 + x^4 + 3x^4$ Simplify.

$= x^6 + 4x^4$ Add like terms.

Simplify each expression.

1. $(-x^5)^2$ $-x^{10}$

2. $(3x^2)^3 - x^4 \cdot x^2$ $26x^6$

3. $3x(2x)^2$ $12x^3$

Inverse Linear Functions

Example 2 Write the inverse function of $y = 10x - 4$.

$y + 4 = 10x$ Isolate the x-term.

$\frac{y+4}{10} = \frac{10x}{10}$ Divide.

The inverse function of $y = 10x - 4$ is $x = \frac{y+4}{10}$.

Write the inverse function.

4. $y = 3x + 1$ $x = \frac{y-1}{3}$

5. $y = 2(x - 9)$ $x = \frac{y+18}{2}$

6. $y = \frac{1}{4}(3x + 4)$ $x = \frac{4y-4}{3}$

Rational and Radical Exponents

Example 3 Write $\sqrt[9]{a^3}$ using a rational exponent.

$\sqrt[9]{a^3} = a^{\frac{3}{9}} = a^{\frac{1}{3}}$

Write each radical expression using a rational exponent.

7. $\sqrt[2]{x^5}$ $x^{\frac{5}{2}}$

8. $\sqrt[4]{a^2 b}$ $a^{\frac{1}{2}} b^{\frac{1}{4}}$

9. $\sqrt[4]{p^8 q^2}$ $p^2 q^{\frac{1}{2}}$

Are You Ready?

ASSESS READINESS

Use the assessment on this page to determine if students need strategic or intensive intervention for the module's prerequisite skills.

ASSESSMENT AND INTERVENTION

RtI Response to Intervention TIER 1, TIER 2, TIER 3 SKILLS

Personal Math Trainer will automatically create a standards-based, personalized intervention assignment for your students, targeting each student's individual needs!

ADDITIONAL RESOURCES

See the table below for a full list of intervention resources available for this module.

Response to Intervention Resources also includes:

- Tier 2 Skill Pre-Tests for each Module
- Tier 2 Skill Post-Tests for each skill

Response to Intervention			Differentiated Instruction
Tier 1 Lesson Intervention Worksheets	**Tier 2** Strategic Intervention Skills Intervention Worksheets	**Tier 3** Intensive Intervention Worksheets available online	
Reteach 11.1 Reteach 11.2 Reteach 11.3	9 Exponents 16 Inverse Linear Functions 28 Rational and Radical Exponents	Building Block Skills 29, 75, 76, 85, 100	Challenge worksheets Extend the Math Lesson Activities in TE

LESSON 11.1

Radical Expressions and Rational Exponents

Common Core Math Standards

The student is expected to:

N-RN.A.1

Explain how the definition . . . of rational exponents follows from ... properties of integer exponents ..., allowing for a notation for radicals in terms of rational exponents.

Mathematical Practices

MP.6 Precision

Language Objective

Identify, with a partner, matching radical expressions and rational equations.

ENGAGE

Essential Question: How are rational exponents related to radicals and roots?

Possible answer: Rational exponents and radicals are both ways to represent roots of quantities. The denominator of a rational exponent and the index of a radical represent the root. The rational exponent $\frac{m}{n}$ on a quantity represents the mth power of the nth root of the quantity or the nth root of the mth power of the quantity, where n is the index of the radical.

PREVIEW: LESSON PERFORMANCE TASK

View the Engage section online. Discuss the photo and how both the air temperature and the wind speed can contribute to the wind chill. Then preview the Lesson Performance Task.

Name ______________________ Class ____________ Date ________

11.1 Radical Expressions and Rational Exponents

Resource Locker

Essential Question: How are rational exponents related to radicals and roots?

Explore Defining Rational Exponents in Terms of Roots

Remember that a number a is an nth root of a number b if $a^n = b$. As you know, a square root is indicated by $\sqrt{\ }$ and a cube root by $\sqrt[3]{\ }$. In general, the nth root of a real number a is indicated by $\sqrt[n]{a}$, where n is the **index** of the radical and a is the radicand. (Note that when a number has more than one real root, the radical sign indicates only the principal, or positive, root.)

A *rational exponent* is an exponent that can be expressed as $\frac{m}{n}$, where m is an integer and n is a natural number. You can use the definition of a root and properties of equality and exponents to explore how to express roots using rational exponents.

(A) How can you express a square root using an exponent? That is, if $\sqrt{a} = a^m$, what is m?

Given	$\sqrt{a} = a^m$
Square both sides.	$(\sqrt{a})^2 = (a^m)^2$
Definition of square root	$a = (a^m)^2$
Power of a power property	$a = a^{2m}$
Definition of first power	$a^{1} = a^{2m}$
The bases are the same, so equate exponents.	$1 = 2m$
Solve.	$m = \frac{1}{2}$
So,	$\sqrt{a} = a^{\frac{1}{2}}$.

(B) How can you express a cube root using an exponent? That is, if $\sqrt[3]{a} = a^m$, what is m?

Given	$\sqrt[3]{a} = a^m$
Cube both sides.	$(\sqrt[3]{a})^3 = (a^m)^3$
Definition of cube root	$a = (a^m)^3$
Power of a power property	$a = a^{3m}$

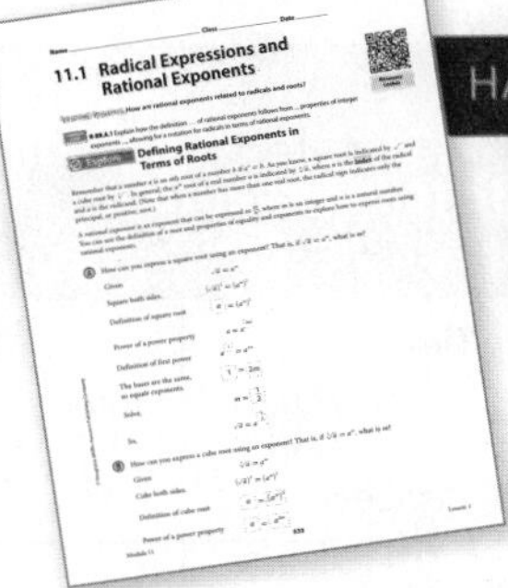

HARDCOVER PAGES 533–542

Watch for the hardcover student edition page numbers for this lesson.

Definition of first power $a^1 = a^{3m}$

The bases are the same, so equate exponents. $1 = 3m$

Solve. $m = \frac{1}{3}$

So, $\sqrt[3]{a} = a^{\frac{1}{3}}$.

Reflect

Discussion Examine the reasoning in Steps A and B. Can you apply the same reasoning for any *n*th root, $\sqrt[n]{a}$, where *n* is a natural number? Explain. What can you conclude?

Yes; the only difference is that instead of squaring or cubing both sides and using the definition of square root or cube root, you raise both sides to the *n*th power and use the definition of *n*th root. The other reasoning is exactly the same. You can conclude that finding the $\frac{1}{n}$ power is the same as finding the *n*th root, or that $\sqrt[n]{a} = a^{\frac{1}{n}}$.

For a positive number *a*, under what condition on *n* will there be only one real *n*th root? two real *n*th roots? Explain.

When *n* is odd; when *n* is even; for an odd power like x^3 or x^5, every distinct value of *x* gives a unique result, so there is only one number that raised to the power will give the result, or one *n*th root. For example, there is one fifth root of 32 because 2 is the only number whose fifth power is 32. For an even power like x^2 or x^4, there are two values of *x* (opposites of each other) that raised to the power will give the result. For example, there are two fourth roots of 81 because 3^4 and $(-3)^4$ both equal 81.

For a negative number *a*, under what condition on *n* will there be no real *n*th roots? one real *n*th root? Explain.

When *n* is even; when *n* is odd; no even power of any number is negative, but every number—positive or negative—has exactly one *n*th root when *n* is odd.

EXPLORE

Defining Rational Exponents in Terms of Roots

INTEGRATE TECHNOLOGY

Students have the option of completing the Explore activity either in the book or online.

QUESTIONING STRATEGIES

? When rewriting a radical expression by using a rational exponent, where do you place the index of the radical? **in the denominator of the rational exponent**

? How does knowing that $a^{\frac{1}{n}} = \sqrt[n]{a}$ help you to simplify the expression $16^{0.25}$? **You can rewrite the fraction as $\frac{1}{4}$. So $16^{0.25} = 16^{\frac{1}{4}} = \sqrt[4]{16} = 2$.**

AVOID COMMON ERRORS

Students may need to be reminded that although, for example, both 3 and –3 are fourth roots of 81, the expression $\sqrt[4]{81}$ indicates the *positive* (principal) fourth root of 81, or 3. Thus, the expression $81^{\frac{1}{4}}$ simplifies to 3, not to both 3 and –3.

CONNECT VOCABULARY EL

In order to use accurate language in their explanations and questions, students need to understand the difference between the terms *radical* and *radicand*. Some students may not be familiar with the term *radicand*. Explain that it is *the number or expression under the radical sign*. When converting a radical expression to a power, the radicand becomes the base of the power.

PROFESSIONAL DEVELOPMENT

Learning Progressions

In this lesson, students learn about rational exponents, and how to translate between radical expressions and expressions containing rational exponents. Students will use these skills in the next lesson, where they will learn how to apply the properties of rational exponents to simplify expressions containing radicals or rational exponents. They will also apply these skills to the solving of real-world problems that can be modeled by radical functions.

EXPLAIN 1

Translating Between Radical Expressions and Rational Exponents

QUESTIONING STRATEGIES

? What does the numerator of a rational exponent indicate? the power of the expression What does the denominator indicate? the index of the radical

INTEGRATE MATHEMATICAL PRACTICES

Focus on Critical Thinking

MP.3 Discuss with students that when finding the value of a number raised to a rational exponent, they can evaluate either the root or the power first. Lead them to see that it is often easier to evaluate the root first, since doing so enables students to work with smaller numbers.

Explain 1 Translating Between Radical Expressions and Rational Exponents

In the Explore, you found that a rational exponent $\frac{m}{n}$ with $m = 1$ represents an nth root, or that $a^{\frac{1}{n}} = \sqrt[n]{a}$ for positive values of a. This is also true for negative values of a when the index is odd. When $m \neq 1$, you can think of the numerator m as the power and the denominator n as the root. The following ways of expressing the exponent $\frac{m}{n}$ are equivalent.

Rational Exponents

For any natural number n, integer m, and real number a when the nth root of a is real:

Words	Numbers	Algebra
The exponent $\frac{m}{n}$ indicates the mth power of the nth root of a quantity.	$27^{\frac{2}{3}} = (\sqrt[3]{27})^2 = 3^2 = 9$	$a^{\frac{m}{n}} = (\sqrt[n]{a})^m$
The exponent $\frac{m}{n}$ indicates the nth root of the mth power of a quantity.	$4^{\frac{3}{2}} = \sqrt{4^3} = \sqrt{64} = 8$	$a^{\frac{m}{n}} = \sqrt[n]{a^m}$

Notice that you can evaluate each example in the "Numbers" column using the equivalent definition.

$$27^{\frac{2}{3}} = \sqrt[3]{27^2} = \sqrt[3]{729} = 9 \qquad 4^{\frac{3}{2}} = (\sqrt{4})^3 = 2^3 = 8$$

Example 1 **Translate radical expressions into expressions with rational exponents, and vice versa. Simplify numerical expressions when possible. Assume all variables are positive.**

(A) a. $(-125)^{\frac{4}{3}}$ b. $x^{\frac{11}{8}}$ c. $\sqrt[5]{6^4}$ d. $\sqrt[4]{x^3}$

a. $(-125)^{\frac{4}{3}} = (\sqrt[3]{-125})^4 = (-5)^4 = 625$

b. $x^{11/8} = \sqrt[8]{x^{11}}$ or $(\sqrt[8]{x})^{11}$

c. $\sqrt[5]{6^4} = 6^{\frac{4}{5}}$

d. $\sqrt[4]{x^3} = x^{\frac{3}{4}}$

(B) a. $\left(\frac{81}{16}\right)^{\frac{3}{4}}$ b. $(xy)^{\frac{5}{3}}$ c. $\sqrt[3]{11^6}$ d. $\sqrt[3]{\left(\frac{2x}{y}\right)^5}$

a. $\left(\frac{81}{16}\right)^{\frac{3}{4}} = \left(\sqrt[4]{\frac{81}{16}}\right)^3 = \left(\frac{3}{2}\right)^3 = \frac{27}{8}$

b. $(xy)^{\frac{5}{3}} = \sqrt[3]{(xy)^5}$ or $\left(\sqrt[3]{xy}\right)^5$

c. $\sqrt[3]{11^6} = 11^{\frac{6}{3}} = 11^2 = 121$

d. $\sqrt[3]{\left(\frac{2x}{y}\right)^5} = \left(\frac{2x}{y}\right)^{\frac{5}{3}}$

COLLABORATIVE LEARNING

Peer-to-Peer Activity

Have students work in pairs. Instruct each pair to create a quiz for another pair to take. Have them create five questions that involve simplifying a power that contair a rational exponent, and that contain expressions which can be simplified without the use of a calculator. Have pairs exchange quizzes with other pairs, work on the quiz with their partners, and check their answers with the pair that created the quiz.

Reflect

4. How can you use a calculator to show that evaluating $0.001728^{\frac{4}{3}}$ as a power of a root and as a root of a power are equivalent methods?

As a power of a root: Enter $\sqrt[3]{0.001728}$ to obtain 0.12. Then enter 0.12^4 to obtain 0.00020736.

As a root of a power: Enter 0.001728^4. Then find $\sqrt[3]{(\text{Ans.})}$. The result is again 0.00020736.

Your Turn

5. Translate radical expressions into expressions with rational exponents, and vice versa. Simplify numerical expressions when possible. Assume all variables are positive.

a. $\left(-\frac{32}{243}\right)^{\frac{2}{5}}$

$\left(-\frac{32}{243}\right)^{\frac{2}{5}} = \left(\sqrt[5]{-\frac{32}{243}}\right)^2 = \left(-\frac{2}{3}\right)^2 = \frac{4}{9}$

b. $(3y)^{\frac{b}{c}}$

$(3y)^{\frac{b}{c}} = \left(\sqrt[c]{3y}\right)^b$ or $\sqrt[c]{(3y)^b}$

c. $\sqrt[3]{0.5^9}$

$\sqrt[3]{0.5^9} = 0.5^{\frac{9}{3}} = 0.5^3 = 0.125$

d. $\left(\sqrt[u]{st}\right)^v$

$\left(\sqrt[u]{st}\right)^v = (st)^{\frac{v}{u}}$

Explain 2 Modeling with Power Functions

The following functions all involve a given power of a variable.

$A = \pi r^2$ (area of a circle)

$V = \frac{4}{3}\pi r^3$ (volume of a sphere)

$T = 1.11 \cdot L^{\frac{1}{2}}$ (the time T in seconds for a pendulum of length L feet to complete one back-and-forth swing)

These are all examples of *power functions*. A power function has the form $y = ax^b$ where a is a real number and b is a rational number.

Example 2 **Solve each problem by modeling with power functions.**

(A) **Biology** The function $R = 73.3\sqrt[4]{M^3}$, known as Kleiber's law, relates the basal metabolic rate R in Calories per day burned and the body mass M of a mammal in kilograms. The table shows typical body masses for some members of the cat family.

Typical Body Mass	
Animal	**Mass (kg)**
House cat	4.5
Cheetah	55
Lion	170

EXPLAIN 2

Modeling with Power Functions

QUESTIONING STRATEGIES

How is a power function related to a radical function? **It is the same as the related radical function, just a way of expressing the function with a rational exponent instead of a radical.**

How do you identify the restrictions on the domain of a power function that represents a real-world situation? **The domain must be restricted to numbers that make x^b a real number, and further restricted to numbers that make sense in the context of the situation.**

DIFFERENTIATE INSTRUCTION

Cognitive Strategies

Students who continue to confuse the conversion of the numerator and denominator of the rational exponent to the exponent and index of the related radical expression may benefit from writing $\frac{e}{i}$ (e for exponent, i for index) next to the rational exponent before converting to the radical expression.

INTEGRATE TECHNOLOGY

A graphing calculator can be used to explore the graph of the power function in the example. Students can also use the **TABLE** feature to identify the value of the function for different values of the domain.

a. Rewrite the formula with a rational exponent.

b. What is the value of R for a cheetah to the nearest 50 Calories?

c. From the table, the mass of the lion is about 38 times that of the house cat. Is the lion's metabolic rate more or less than 38 times the cat's rate? Explain.

```
73.3*55^(3/4)
      1480.389485
```

a. Because $\sqrt[n]{a^m} = a^{\frac{m}{n}}$, $\sqrt[4]{M^3} = M^{\frac{3}{4}}$, so the formula is $R = 73.3M^{\frac{3}{4}}$.

b. Substitute 55 for M in the formula and use a calculator.

The cheetah's metabolic rate is about 1500 Calories.

c. Less; find the ratio of R for the lion to R for the house cat.

$$\frac{73.3(170)^{\frac{3}{4}}}{73.3(4.5)^{\frac{3}{4}}} = \frac{170^{\frac{3}{4}}}{4.5^{\frac{3}{4}}} \approx \frac{47.1}{3.1} \approx 15$$

The metabolic rate for the lion is only about 15 times that of the house cat.

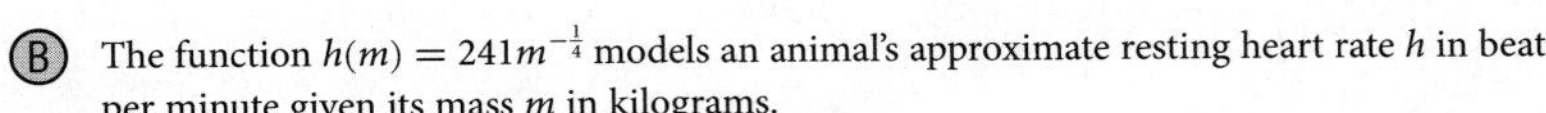

B The function $h(m) = 241m^{-\frac{1}{4}}$ models an animal's approximate resting heart rate h in beats per minute given its mass m in kilograms.

a. A common shrew has a mass of only about 0.01 kg. To the nearest 10, what is the model's estimate for this shrew's resting heart rate?

b. What is the model's estimate for the resting heart rate of an American elk with a mass of 300 kg?

c. Two animal species differ in mass by a multiple of 10. According to the model, about what percent of the smaller animal's resting heart rate would you expect the larger animal's resting heart rate to be?

a. Substitute 0.01 for m in the formula and use a calculator.

$$h(m) = 241\left(0.01\right)^{-\frac{1}{4}} \approx 760$$

The model estimates the shrew's resting heart rate to be about 760 beats per minute.

b. Substitute 300 for m in the formula and use a calculator.

$$h(m) = 241\left(300\right)^{-\frac{1}{4}} \approx 60$$

The model estimates the elk's resting heart rate to be about 60 beats per minute.

c. Find the ratio of $h(m)$ for the larger animal to the smaller animal. Let 1 represent the mass of the smaller animal.

$$\frac{241 \cdot 10^{-\frac{1}{4}}}{241 \cdot 1^{-\frac{1}{4}}} = 10^{-\frac{1}{4}} = \frac{1}{10^{\frac{1}{4}}} \approx 0.56$$

You would expect the larger animal's resting heart rate to be about 56% of the smaller animal's resting heart rate.

Reflect

6. What is the difference between a power function and an exponential function?
A power function involves a given power of a variable, while an exponential function involves a variable power of a given number (the base).

7. In Part B, the exponent is negative. Are the results consistent with the meaning of a negative exponent that you learned for integers? Explain.
Yes; a power with a negative integer exponent is the reciprocal of the corresponding positive power. So, for example, for the elk, this would mean that $300^{-\frac{1}{4}} = \frac{1}{300^{\frac{1}{4}}}$. Using the calculator again, $h(m) = 241\left(\frac{1}{300^{\frac{1}{4}}}\right) \approx 60$, which is consistent.

Your Turn

8. Use Kleiber's law from Part A.
   a. Find the basal metabolic rate for a 170 kilogram lion to the nearest 50 Calories. Then find the formula's prediction for a 70 kilogram human.
   Kleiber's law for lion: $73.3(170)^{\frac{3}{4}} \approx 3450$ Calories
   Kleiber's law for human: $73.3(70)^{\frac{3}{4}} \approx 1750$ Calories
   b. Use your metabolic rate result for the lion to find what the basal metabolic rate for a 70 kilogram human *would* be *if* metabolic rate and mass were directly proportional. Compare the result to the result from Part a.
   If metabolic rate and mass were directly proportional then $\frac{3450 \text{ Cal}}{170 \text{ kg}} = \frac{x \text{ Cal}}{70 \text{ kg}}$, so $170x = (3450)(70)$, or $x = \left(\frac{241{,}500}{170}\right) \approx 1400$ Cal. so, the rate for a human would be significantly lower than the actual prediction from Kleiber's law. Kleiber's law indicates that smaller organisms have a higher metabolic rate per kilogram of mass than do larger organisms.

Elaborate

9. Explain how can you use a radical to write and evaluate the power $4^{2.5}$.
You can first rewrite the decimal as the fraction $\frac{25}{10} = \frac{5}{2}$. Then $4^{2.5} = 4^{\frac{5}{2}} = \left(\sqrt{4}\right)^5 = 2^5 = 32$.

10. When $y = kx$ for some constant k, y varies directly as x. When $y = kx^2$, y varies directly as the square of x; and when $y = k\sqrt{x}$, y varies directly as the square root of x. How could you express the relationship $y = kx^{\frac{3}{5}}$ for a constant k?
***y* varies directly as the three-fifths power of *x*.**

11. **Essential Question Check-In** Which of the following are true? Explain.
   - To evaluate an expression of the form $a^{\frac{m}{n}}$, first find the nth root of a. Then raise the result to the mth power.
   - To evaluate an expression of the form $a^{\frac{m}{n}}$, first find the mth power of a. Then find the nth root of the result.

They are both true. For a real number *a* and integers *m* and *n* with $n \neq 0$, $a^{\frac{m}{n}} = \left(\sqrt[n]{a}\right)^m = \sqrt[n]{a^m}$, so the order in which you find the root or power does not matter.

CONNECT VOCABULARY EL

For English language learners, differentiating between the words *rational* and *radical* can be difficult, both in print and in speech. Continue to make explicit connections between the terms' meanings and symbols each time they are used.

ELABORATE

INTEGRATE MATHEMATICAL PRACTICES

Focus on Reasoning

MP.2 Ask students to consider how they can use the fact that $a^{\frac{m}{n}} = \sqrt[n]{a^m}$ to prove that $\sqrt[k]{5^k} = 5$, given that k is any positive integer. Then ask them to create some examples using other bases and different values of k to verify this identity.

SUMMARIZE THE LESSON

How can you rewrite a radical expression as an exponential expression and vice versa? **You can write a radical expression as the radicand raised to a fraction in which the numerator is the power of the radicand and the denominator is the index of the radical. You can write an exponential expression with the base of the exponent as the radicand, the denominator of the exponent as the index, and the numerator of the exponent as the power.**

LANGUAGE SUPPORT EL

Visual Cues

Have students work in pairs. Provide each pair with index cards on which are written either rational expressions or matching radical expressions. Include some radical expressions with square roots, rational expressions with rational exponents with a numerator of 1, and so on. Have students match cards and use colors or shapes to circle matching powers and indices. Suggest they write a 2 as an index of a square root, and a 1 as a power, to show an appropriate match for the special cases mentioned above.

EVALUATE

ASSIGNMENT GUIDE

Concepts and Skills	Practice
Explore Defining Rational Exponents in Terms of Roots	
Example 1 Translating Between Radical Expressions and Rational Exponents	Exercises 1–16
Example 2 Modeling with Power Functions	Exercises 17–20

QUESTIONING STRATEGIES

If the radicand is a negative number, what must be true about the index? Explain. **The index must be odd. This is because even roots of negative numbers are not real numbers. (You can't raise a real number to an even power and get a negative number.)**

VISUAL CUES

Suggest that students circle the denominator in the rational exponent, and draw a curved arrow from the denominator, passing beneath the base, to a point in front of the expression, indicating that it becomes the index of the radical in the converted expression.

Evaluate: Homework and Practice

- Online Homework
- Hints and Help
- Extra Practice

Translate expressions with rational exponents into radical expressions. Simplify numerical expressions when possible. Assume all variables are positive.

1. $64^{\frac{5}{3}}$

   $64^{\frac{5}{3}} = \left(\sqrt[3]{64}\right)^5 = 4^5 = 1024$

2. $x^{\frac{p}{q}}$

   $x^{\frac{p}{q}} = \sqrt[q]{x^p}$ or $\left(\sqrt[q]{x}\right)^p$

3. $(-512)^{\frac{2}{3}}$

   $(-512)^{\frac{2}{3}} = \left(\sqrt[3]{-512}\right)^2 = (-8)^2 = 64$

4. $3^{\frac{2}{7}}$

   $3^{\frac{2}{7}} = \sqrt[7]{3^2} = \sqrt[7]{9}$

5. $-\left(\frac{729}{64}\right)^{\frac{5}{6}}$

   $-\left(\frac{729}{64}\right)^{\frac{5}{6}} = -\left(\sqrt[6]{\frac{729}{64}}\right)^5 = -\left(\frac{3}{2}\right)^5 = -\frac{243}{32}$

6. $0.125^{\frac{4}{3}}$

   $0.125^{\frac{4}{3}} = \left(\sqrt[3]{0.125}\right)^4 = 0.5^4 = 0.0625$

7. $vw^{\frac{2}{3}}$

   $vw^{\frac{2}{3}} = v\sqrt[3]{w^2}$ or $v\left(\sqrt[3]{w}\right)^2$

8. $(-32)^{0.6}$

   $(-32)^{0.6} = (-32)^{\frac{3}{5}} = \left(\sqrt[5]{-32}\right)^3 = (-2)^3 = -8$

Translate radical expressions into expressions with rational exponents. Simplify numerical expressions when possible. Assume all variables are positive.

9. $\sqrt[7]{y^5}$

   $\sqrt[7]{y^5} = y^{\frac{5}{7}}$

10. $\sqrt[7]{-6^6}$

    $\sqrt[7]{-6^6} = (-6)^{\frac{6}{7}}$

11. $\sqrt[3]{3^{15}}$

    $\sqrt[3]{3^{15}} = 3^{\frac{15}{3}} = 3^5 = 243$

12. $\sqrt[4]{(\pi z)^3}$

    $\sqrt[4]{(\pi z)^3} = (\pi z)^{\frac{3}{4}}$

13. $\sqrt[6]{(bcd)^4}$

    $\sqrt[6]{(bcd)^4} = (bcd)^{\frac{4}{6}} = (bcd)^{\frac{2}{3}}$

14. $\sqrt{6^6}$

    $\sqrt{6^6} = 6^{\frac{6}{2}} = 6^3 = 216$

15. $\sqrt[5]{32^2}$

    $\sqrt[5]{32^2} = 32^{\frac{2}{5}} = 2^2 = 4$

16. $\sqrt[3]{\left(\frac{4}{x}\right)^9}$

    $\sqrt[3]{\left(\frac{4}{x}\right)^9} = \left(\frac{4}{x}\right)^{\frac{9}{3}} = \left(\frac{4}{x}\right)^3 = \frac{4^3}{x^3} = \frac{64}{x^3}$

Exercise	Depth of Knowledge (D.O.K.)	COMMON CORE Mathematical Practices
1–16	**1** Recall of Information	**MP.5** Using Tools
17	**2** Skills/Concepts	**MP.2** Reasoning
18–20	**2** Skills/Concepts	**MP.4** Modeling
21	**1** Recall of Information	**MP.5** Using Tools
22	**3** Strategic Thinking H.O.T.	**MP.2** Reasoning
23–24	**3** Strategic Thinking H.O.T.	**MP.3** Logic

17. **Music** Frets are small metal bars positioned across the neck of a guitar so that the guitar can produce the notes of a specific scale. To find the distance a fret should be placed from the bridge, multiply the length of the string by $2^{-\frac{n}{12}}$, where n is the number of notes higher than the string's root note. Where should a fret be placed to produce a F note on a B string (6 notes higher) given that the length of the string is 64 cm?

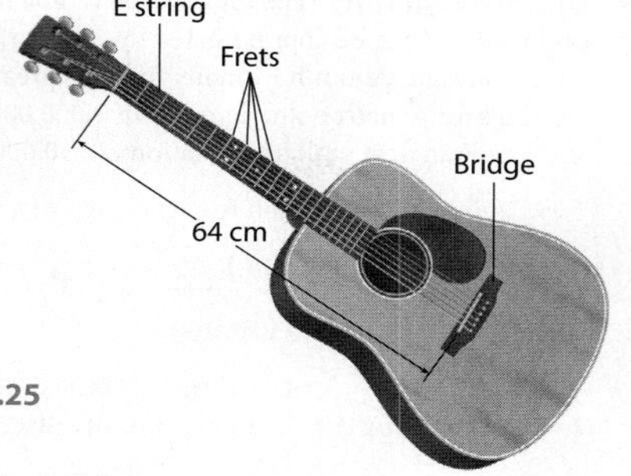

$$64\left(2^{-\frac{n}{12}}\right) = 64\left(2^{-\frac{6}{12}}\right) = 64\left(2^{-\frac{1}{2}}\right) = 64\left(\frac{1}{2^{\frac{1}{2}}}\right) \approx 45.25$$

The fret should be placed about 45.25 cm from the bridge.

18. **Meteorology** The function $W = 35.74 + 0.6215T - 35.75V^{\frac{4}{25}} + 0.4275TV^{\frac{4}{25}}$ relates the windchill temperature W to the air temperature T in degrees Fahrenheit and the wind speed V in miles per hour. Use a calculator to find the wind chill temperature to the nearest degree when the air temperature is 28 °F and the wind speed is 35 miles per hour.

$$\begin{aligned} W &= 35.74 + 0.6215T - 35.75V^{\frac{4}{25}} + 0.4275TV^{\frac{4}{25}} \\ &= 35.74 + 0.6215(28) - 35.75(35)^{\frac{4}{25}} + 0.4275(28)\left(35^{\frac{4}{25}}\right) \\ &\approx 11.14 \end{aligned}$$

The windchill temperature is about 11°F.

19. **Astronomy** New stars can form inside a cloud of interstellar gas when a cloud fragment, or *clump*, has a mass M greater than the *Jean's mass* M_J. The Jean's mass is $M_J = 100n^{-\frac{1}{2}}(T + 273)^{\frac{3}{2}}$ where n is the number of gas molecules per cubic centimeter and T is the gas temperature in degrees Celsius. A gas clump has $M = 137$, $n = 1000$, and $T = -263$. Will the clump form a star? Justify your answer.

Yes; for this n and T, the Jean's mass is $M_J = 100(1000)^{-\frac{1}{2}}(-263 + 273)^{\frac{3}{2}} = \frac{100}{1000^{\frac{1}{2}}}(10)^{\frac{3}{2}} = 100$. The mass of the clump, 137, is greater than the Jean's mass, 100, so the clump will form a star.

AVOID COMMON ERRORS

When using a calculator to evaluate an expression that contains a rational exponent, students often forget to put parentheses around the exponent. Use an example, such as $8^{\frac{1}{3}}$, which students can simplify mentally, to show that the value of the expression when entered without parentheses is not the same as the value of the expression when entered correctly.

INTEGRATE TECHNOLOGY

Students can use a graphing calculator to check their work. The **MATH** submenu, in the **MATH** menu, contains a cube root function as well as a function that can be used for radicals with other indices.

INTEGRATE MATHEMATICAL PRACTICES

Focus on Communication

MP.3 To help solidify students' understanding, have them verbalize their solutions to the exercises using accurate language. For a problem involving the simplification of , $32^{\frac{3}{5}}$ for example, a student might describe the solution in this way: "Thirty-two raised to the three-fifths power is equal to the fifth root of thirty-two raised to the third power, which is equal to two raised to the third power, which is equal to eight."

PEER-TO-PEER DISCUSSION

Ask students to work with a partner to determine two expressions of the form , $a^{\frac{m}{n}}$ where $\frac{m}{n}$ is not an integer, that are equal in value. Have students share their examples with the class and look for commonalities. **Possible answers: $4^{\frac{5}{2}}$ and $8^{\frac{5}{3}}$, $27^{\frac{2}{3}}$ and $81^{\frac{1}{2}}$**

JOURNAL

Have students write two different representations, one as a radical and the other as a power, of the principal fourth root of the cube of 81. Then have them describe how they would find this value.

20. Urban geography The total wages W in a metropolitan area compared to its total population p can be approximated by a power function of the form $W = a \cdot p^{\frac{9}{8}}$ where a is a constant. About how many times as great does the model predict the total earnings for a metropolitan area with 3,000,000 people will be as compared to a metropolitan area with a population of 750,000?

Find the ratio of wages for the larger metropolitan area to the smaller one.

$$\frac{a \cdot 3{,}000{,}000^{\frac{9}{8}}}{a \cdot 750{,}000^{\frac{9}{8}}} = \frac{3{,}000{,}000^{\frac{9}{8}}}{750{,}000^{\frac{9}{8}}} \approx 4.8$$

The total wages for the larger metropolitan area will be about 4.8 times as great as the total wages for the smaller metropolitan area.

21. Which statement is true?

A. In the expression $8x^{\frac{3}{4}}$, $8x$ is the radicand.

B. In the expression $(-16)x^{\frac{4}{5}}$, 4 is the index.

(C.) The expression $1024^{\frac{n}{m}}$ represents the mth root of the nth power of 1024.

D. $50^{-\frac{2}{5}} = -50^{\frac{2}{5}}$

E. $\sqrt{(xy)^3} = xy^{\frac{3}{2}}$

H.O.T. Focus on Higher Order Thinking

22. Explain the Error A teacher asked students to evaluate $10^{-\frac{3}{5}}$ using their graphing calculators. The calculator entries of several students are shown below. Which entry will give the incorrect result? Explain.

```
10^(-3/5)    5√(10^-3)    10^-.6    1/10^(5/3)    (1/10^(1/5))^3
```

$\frac{1}{10^{\frac{5}{3}}}$; the negative exponent means to take the reciprocal of the corresponding positive power. The corresponding positive power is $\frac{3}{5}$, so the correct entry is $\frac{1}{10^{\frac{3}{5}}}$.

23. Critical Thinking The graphs of three functions of the form $y = ax^{\frac{m}{n}}$ are shown for a specific value of a, where m and n are natural numbers. What can you conclude about the relationship of m and n for each graph? Explain.

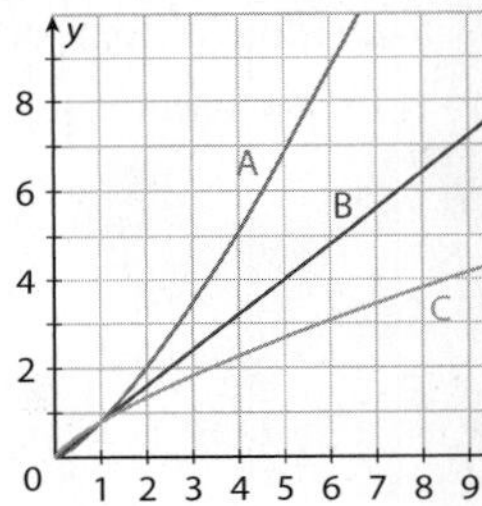

For graph B, $m = n$, that is, $y = ax$. This is because the graph is that of a line, for which the exponent on x is 1 and the graph has a constant rate of change (slope). For graph A, $m > n$. This is because for a power greater than 1, the average rate of change of the graph increases as x increases, that is, the graph gets steeper. For graph C, $m < n$. This is because for a power less than 1, the average rate of change of the graph decreases as x increases, that is, the graph gets less steep.

24. Critical Thinking For a negative real number a, under what condition(s) on m and n $(n \neq 0)$ is $a^{\frac{m}{n}}$ a real number? Explain. (Assume $\frac{m}{n}$ is written in simplest form.)

If n is odd you can find a real number odd root for every real number, positive or negative. But if n is even (so m is odd since the fraction is in lowest terms), then you are trying to find an even root of a negative number (in $\sqrt[n]{a^m}$, a^m is negative), which is not possible.

Lesson Performance Task

The formula $W = 35.74 + 0.6215T - 35.75V^{\frac{4}{25}} + 0.4275TV^{\frac{4}{25}}$ relates the wind chill temperature W to the air temperature T in degrees Fahrenheit and the wind speed V in miles per hour. Find the wind chill to the nearest degree when the air temperature is 40 °F and the wind speed is 35 miles per hour. If the wind chill is about 23 °F to the nearest degree when the air temperature is 40 °F, what is the wind speed to the nearest mile per hour?

a. Start by substituting the values for air temperature and wind speed.

$$W = 35.74 + 0.6215T - 35.75V^{\frac{4}{25}} + 0.4275TV^{\frac{4}{25}}$$

$$W = 35.74 + 0.6215(40) - 35.75(35)^{\frac{4}{25}} + 0.4275(40)(35)^{\frac{4}{25}}$$

Rewrite the formula in terms of roots and powers.

$$W = 35.74 + 0.6215(40) - 35.75\left(\sqrt[25]{35}\right)^4 + 0.4275(40)\left(\sqrt[25]{35}\right)^4$$

Evaluating the formula gives 27.659, which can be rounded to give a wind chill of about 28 °F.

b. Begin by substituting in the values you know.

$$W = 35.74 + 0.6215T - 35.75V^{\frac{4}{25}} + 0.4275TV^{\frac{4}{25}}$$

$$23 = 35.74 + 0.6215(40) - 35.75(V)^{\frac{4}{25}} + 0.4275(40)(V)^{\frac{4}{25}}$$

Then evaluate what you can and then rewrite the formula to solve for V.

$$23 = 35.74 + 24.86 - 35.75(V)^{\frac{4}{25}} + 17.1(V)^{\frac{4}{25}} = 60.6 - 18.65(V)^{\frac{4}{25}}$$

$$-37.6 = -18.65(V)^{\frac{4}{25}}$$

$$\left(\frac{37.6}{18.65}\right)^{\frac{25}{4}} = V$$

$$\left(\sqrt[4]{\frac{37.6}{18.65}}\right)^{25} = V$$

$$\left(\sqrt[4]{2.016}\right)^{25} = V$$

$$80 \approx V$$

A wind speed of 80 miles per hour makes an air temperature of 40 °F feel like 23 °F.

EXTENSION ACTIVITY

Have students derive an equation for the wind chill when the temperature is in degrees Celsius and the wind speed is in kilometers per hour. Have students explain how the two equations are different. Ask students how the unit conversion affects the exponents to which the variables are raised. **The exponents remain the same. The unit conversion affects only the coefficients of the terms.**

AVOID COMMON ERRORS

When solving the equation for V, some students may raise each *term* in the equation to the power $\frac{25}{4}$. Ask students what they need to do first. **Isolate the variable V on one side of the equation.**

Mention that after the equation is in the form $V^{\frac{4}{25}} = \frac{37.6}{18.65}$, each *side* of the equation can be raised to the power $\frac{25}{4}$.

INTEGRATE MATHEMATICAL PRACTICES

Focus on Critical Thinking

MP.3 Have students discuss whether the wind chill is influenced more by the air temperature or by the wind speed. Have students explain how the fractional exponents affect the influence of the wind speed. Ask students if the wind speed would have a larger or smaller effect if the exponents were integers.

Scoring Rubric

2 points: Student correctly solves the problem and explains his/her reasoning.

1 point: Student shows good understanding of the problem but does not fully solve or explain his/her reasoning.

0 points: Student does not demonstrate understanding of the problem.

LESSON 11.2

Simplifying Radical Expressions

Common Core Math Standards

The student is expected to:

 **N-RN.A.2**

Rewrite expressions involving radicals and rational exponents using the properties of exponents. Also F-IF.C.7b

Mathematical Practices

 **MP.8 Patterns**

Language Objective

Explain to a partner the steps for simplifying rational exponents and radical expressions.

ENGAGE

Essential Question: How can you simplify expressions containing rational exponents or radicals involving nth roots?

Possible answer: You can use the same properties of exponents for rational exponents as for integer exponents, apply the properties of square roots to radicals involving *n*th roots, and translate between radical form and rational exponent form whenever it is helpful.

PREVIEW: LESSON PERFORMANCE TASK

View the Engage section online. Discuss the photo and how the volume and surface area of a sphere have a common variable. Then preview the Lesson Performance Task.

Name ________________ Class ________ Date ________

11.2 Simplifying Radical Expressions

Resource Locker

Essential Question: How can you simplify expressions containing rational exponents or radicals involving *n*th roots?

Explore Establishing the Properties of Rational Exponents

In previous courses, you have used properties of integer exponents to simplify and evaluate expressions, as shown here for a few simple examples:

$4^2 \cdot 4^3 = 4^{2+3} = 4^5 = 1024$ $\qquad$ $(4 \cdot x)^2 = 4^2 \cdot x^2 = 16x^2$

$(4^2)^3 = 4^{2 \cdot 3} = 4^6 = 4096$ $\qquad$ $\frac{4^2}{4^3} = 4^{2-3} = 4^{-1} = \frac{1}{4}$

$\left(\frac{4}{x}\right)^3 = \frac{4^3}{x^3} = \frac{64}{x^3}$

Now that you have been introduced to expressions involving rational exponents, you can explore the properties that apply to simplifying them.

(A) Let $a = 64$, $b = 4$, $m = \frac{1}{3}$, and $n = \frac{3}{2}$. Evaluate each expression by substituting and applying exponents individually, as shown.

Expression	Substitute	Simplify	Result
$a^m \cdot a^n$	$64^{\frac{1}{3}} \cdot 64^{\frac{3}{2}}$	$4 \cdot 512$	2048
$(a \cdot b)^n$	$(64 \cdot 4)^{\frac{3}{2}}$	$256^{\frac{3}{2}}$	**4096**
$(a^m)^n$	$\left(64^{\frac{1}{3}}\right)^{\frac{3}{2}}$	$4^{\frac{3}{2}}$	**8**
$\frac{a^n}{a^m}$	$\frac{64^{\frac{3}{2}}}{64^{\frac{1}{3}}}$	$\frac{512}{4}$	**128**
$\left(\frac{a}{b}\right)^n$	$\left(\frac{64}{4}\right)^{\frac{3}{2}}$	$16^{\frac{3}{2}}$	**64**

HARDCOVER PAGES 543–556

Watch for the hardcover student edition page numbers for this lesson.

Ⓑ Complete the table again. This time, however, apply the rule of exponents that you would use for integer exponents.

Expression	Apply Rule and Substitute	Simplify	Result
$a^m \cdot a^n$	$64^{\frac{1}{3}+\frac{3}{2}}$	$64^{\frac{11}{6}}$	2048
$(a \cdot b)^n$	$64^{\frac{3}{2}} \cdot 4^{\frac{3}{2}}$	$512 \cdot 8$	4096
$(a^m)^n$	$64^{\frac{1}{3} \cdot \frac{3}{2}}$	$64^{\frac{1}{2}}$	8
$\frac{a^n}{a^m}$	$64^{\frac{3}{2}-\frac{1}{3}}$	$64^{\frac{7}{6}}$	128
$\left(\frac{a}{b}\right)^n$	$\frac{64^{\frac{3}{2}}}{4^{\frac{3}{2}}}$	$\frac{512}{8}$	64

Reflect

1. Compare your results in Steps A and B. What can you conclude?
Applying the same rules as for integer exponents gives the same results as applying the exponents individually. The properties of rational exponents are the same as the corresponding properties of integer exponents.

2. In Steps A and B, you evaluated $\frac{a^n}{a^m}$ two ways. Now evaluate $\frac{a^m}{a^n}$ two ways, using the definition of negative exponents. Are your results consistent with your previous conclusions about integer and rational exponents?

$\frac{a^m}{a^n} = \frac{64^{\frac{1}{3}}}{64^{\frac{3}{2}}} = \frac{4}{512} = \frac{1}{128}$;

$\frac{a^m}{a^n} = 64^{\frac{1}{3}-\frac{3}{2}} = 64^{-\frac{7}{6}} = \frac{1}{64^{\frac{7}{6}}} = \frac{1}{128}$;

Yes, working with negative rational exponents is consistent with working with negative integer exponents.

EXPLORE

Establishing the Properties of Rational Exponents

INTEGRATE TECHNOLOGY

Students have the option of completing the Explore activity either in the book or online.

QUESTIONING STRATEGIES

? If an expression consists of a variable raised to a negative exponent, how can you rewrite the expression with a positive exponent? **Rewrite the expression as the reciprocal of the variable raised to the opposite of the exponent.**

? How does that help you write the simplified form of $\frac{x^{\frac{1}{4}}}{x^{\frac{3}{4}}}$ with a positive exponent? **You can subtract the exponents, and then apply the rule to the answer.** $\frac{x^{\frac{1}{4}}}{x^{\frac{3}{4}}} = x^{\frac{1}{4}-\frac{3}{4}} = x^{-\frac{1}{2}} = \left(\frac{1}{x}\right)^{\frac{1}{2}}$

PROFESSIONAL DEVELOPMENT

Learning Progressions

This lesson extends concepts and properties that students have learned in previous courses and lessons. Students are familiar with the properties of exponents, and have used them to simplify expressions containing integer exponents. They also were introduced to the *n*th roots and the meaning of rational exponents in the previous lesson. In this lesson, students combine these concepts, extending the properties to expressions containing rational exponents. They also learn about the properties of *n*th roots. Students will apply these skills in the following lesson, where they will use them to solve radical equations.

EXPLAIN 1

Simplifying Rational-Exponent Expressions

AVOID COMMON ERRORS

Students may, in error, multiply or divide the common bases in a product or quotient of powers. Help them to see that the simplified product (or quotient) represents factors of the common base. Use a numerical example with integer exponents, such as $2^3 \cdot 2^4$, to help students see why this is so.

QUESTIONING STRATEGIES

How do you multiply powers with the same base when the exponents are rational? **Add the exponents, and write the result as a power of the common base.**

How do you divide powers with the same base when the exponents are rational? **Subtract the exponents, and write the result as a power of the common base.**

INTEGRATE TECHNOLOGY

Students can use a graphing calculator to check their work. Review the correct use of parentheses when entering expressions containing rational exponents. Also, encourage them to use parentheses around the numerator and the denominator of a quotient of expressions.

Explain 1 Simplifying Rational-Exponent Expressions

Rational exponents have the same properties as integer exponents.

Properties of Rational Exponents

For all nonzero real numbers *a* and *b* and rational numbers *m* and *n*

Words	Numbers	Algebra
Product of Powers Property To multiply powers with the same base, add the exponents.	$12^{\frac{1}{2}} \cdot 12^{\frac{3}{2}} = 12^{\frac{1}{2}+\frac{3}{2}} = 12^2 = 144$	$a^m \cdot a^n = a^m + n$
Quotient of Powers Property To divide powers with the same base, subtract the exponents.	$\frac{125^{\frac{2}{3}}}{125^{\frac{1}{3}}} = 125^{\frac{2}{3}-\frac{1}{3}} = 125^{\frac{1}{3}} = 5$	$\frac{a^m}{a^n} = a^{m-n}$
Power of a Power Property To raise one power to another, multiply the exponents.	$\left(8^{\frac{2}{3}}\right)^3 = 8^{\frac{2}{3}\cdot 3} = 8^2 = 64$	$(a^m)^n = a^{m \cdot n}$
Power of a Product Property To find a power of a product, distribute the exponent.	$(16 \cdot 25)^{\frac{1}{2}} = 16^{\frac{1}{2}} \cdot 25^{\frac{1}{2}} = 4 \cdot 5 = 20$	$(ab)^m = a^m b^m$
Power of a Quotient Property To find the power of a qoutient, distribute the exponent.	$\left(\frac{16}{81}\right)^{\frac{1}{4}} = \frac{16^{\frac{1}{4}}}{81^{\frac{1}{4}}} = \frac{2}{3}$	$\left(\frac{a}{b}\right)^m = \frac{a^m}{b^m}$

Example 1 **Simplify the expression. Assume that all variables are positive. Exponents in simplified form should all be positive.**

(A) **a.** $25^{\frac{3}{5}} \cdot 25^{\frac{7}{5}}$

Product of Powers Prop. $= 25^{\frac{3}{5}+\frac{7}{5}}$

Simplify. $= 25^2$

$= 625$

b. $\frac{8^{\frac{1}{3}}}{8^{\frac{2}{3}}}$

Quotient of Powes Prop. $= 8^{\frac{1}{3}-\frac{2}{3}}$

Simplify. $= 8^{-\frac{1}{3}}$

Definition of neg. power $= \frac{1}{8^{\frac{1}{3}}}$

Simplify. $= \frac{1}{2}$

COLLABORATIVE LEARNING

Peer-to-Peer Activity

Have students work in pairs. Provide each pair with several fairly complex expressions to simplify. Instruct one student in each pair to simplify one of the expressions while the other gives verbal instructions for each step. Then have the student who simplified the expression write an explanation next to each step, describing what was done. Have students switch roles and repeat the exercise using a different expression.

(B) a. $\left(\frac{y^{\frac{4}{3}}}{16y^{\frac{2}{3}}}\right)^{\frac{3}{2}}$

Quotient of Powers Prop. $= \left(\frac{y^{\frac{4}{3}-\frac{2}{3}}}{16}\right)^{\frac{3}{2}}$

Simplify. $= \left(\frac{y^{\frac{2}{3}}}{16}\right)^{\frac{3}{2}}$

Power of a Quotient Prop. $= \frac{\left(y^{\frac{2}{3}}\right)^{\frac{3}{2}}}{16^{\frac{3}{2}}}$

Power of a power Prop. $= \frac{y^{\frac{2}{3}\cdot\frac{3}{2}}}{16^{\frac{3}{2}}}$

Simplify. $= \frac{y}{64}$

b. $\left(27x^{\frac{3}{4}}\right)^{\frac{2}{3}}$

Power of a Product Prop. $= 27^{\frac{2}{3}}\left(x^{\frac{3}{4}}\right)^{\frac{2}{3}}$

Power of a Power Prop. $= 27^{\frac{2}{3}}\left(x^{\frac{3}{4}\cdot\frac{2}{3}}\right)$

Simplify. $= 9x^{\frac{1}{2}}$

Your Turn

Simplify the expression. Assume that all variables are positive. Exponents in simplified form should all be positive.

3. $\left(12^{\frac{2}{3}}\cdot 12^{\frac{4}{3}}\right)^{\frac{3}{2}}$

$\left(12^{\frac{2}{3}}\cdot 12^{\frac{4}{3}}\right)^{\frac{3}{2}} = \left(12^{\frac{2}{3}+\frac{4}{3}}\right)^{\frac{3}{2}} = \left(12^{2}\right)^{\frac{3}{2}}$

$= 12^{2\cdot\frac{3}{2}} = 12^{3} = 1728$

4. $\frac{\left(6x^{\frac{1}{3}}\right)^{2}}{x^{\frac{5}{3}}y}$

$\frac{\left(6x^{\frac{1}{3}}\right)^{2}}{x^{\frac{5}{3}}y} = \frac{6^{2}x^{\frac{1}{3}\cdot 2}}{x^{\frac{5}{3}}y} = \frac{36x^{\frac{2}{3}}}{x^{\frac{5}{3}}y} = \frac{36x^{\frac{2}{3}-\frac{5}{3}}}{y}$

$= \frac{36x^{-1}}{y} = \frac{36}{xy}$

Explain 2 Simplifying Radical Expressions Using the Properties of Exponents

When you are working with radical expressions involving *n*th roots, you can rewrite the expressions using rational exponents and then simplify them using the properties of exponents.

Example 2 **Simplify the expression by writing it using rational exponents and then using the properties of rational exponents. Assume that all variables are positive. Exponents in simplified form should all be positive.**

(A) $x\left(\sqrt[3]{2y}\right)\left(\sqrt[3]{4x^2y^2}\right)$

Write using rational exponents. $= x(2y)^{\frac{1}{3}}\left(4x^2y^2\right)^{\frac{1}{3}}$

Power of a Product Property $= x\left(2y\cdot 4x^2y^2\right)^{\frac{1}{3}}$

Power of a Powers Property $= x\left(8x^2y^3\right)^{\frac{1}{3}}$

Power of a Product Property $= x\left(2x^{\frac{2}{3}}y\right)$

Power of Powers Property $= 2x^{\frac{5}{3}}y$

DIFFERENTIATE INSTRUCTION

Communicating Math

For many students, the descriptive sentences in the first column of each table of properties will be the most helpful when applying the various properties. Have students read these out loud, and use the examples in the second column to check for understanding. Encourage students to memorize the sentences, rewording them in their own words, as necessary, to clarify the instruction. Then show them how repeating the sentence that applies, at each step of the simplification process, can provide the guidance they need to correctly apply each property.

EXPLAIN 2

Simplifying Radical Expressions Using the Properties of Exponents

QUESTIONING STRATEGIES

How does knowing the relationship between roots and expressions containing rational exponents help you to simplify expressions containing radicals? **Convert each radical to an expression containing a rational exponent, and then apply the rules for exponents.**

How do the properties of exponents help you to multiply two radicals that have the same radicands but different indices? **Convert each radical to an expression containing a rational exponent, add the exponents, and then write the result as a power of the common radicand.**

INTEGRATE MATHEMATICAL PRACTICES

Focus on Communication

MP.3 Enhance students' understanding of the properties and relationships used to simplify these expressions by having them explain each step, identifying the properties being applied. You may want to provide students with additional examples, then have them explain the steps of their own, and possibly each other's, work.

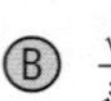

EXPLAIN 3

Simplifying Radical Expressions Using the Properties of *n*th Roots

QUESTIONING STRATEGIES

How do you rationalize a denominator that contains an *n*th root? **Multiply the numerator and denominator of the fraction by the *n*th root of enough factors of the radicand to create a perfect *n*th root.**

AVOID COMMON ERRORS

After learning the product and quotient properties for *n*th roots, students may assume there are similar properties for sums and differences. Show students, by numerical example, that $\sqrt[n]{a+b} \neq \sqrt[n]{a} + \sqrt[n]{b}$ and $\sqrt[n]{a+b} \neq \sqrt[n]{a} - \sqrt[n]{b}$ for $a, b > 0$.

(B) $\dfrac{\sqrt{64y}}{\sqrt[3]{64y}}$

White using rational exponents.	$= \dfrac{(64y)^{\frac{1}{2}}}{(64y)^{\frac{1}{3}}}$
Quotient of Powers Property	$= (64y)^{\boxed{\frac{1}{2}-\frac{1}{3}}}$
Simplify.	$= (64y)^{\boxed{\frac{1}{6}}}$
Power of a Product Property	$= \boxed{64^{\frac{1}{6}}y^{\frac{1}{6}}}$
Simplify.	$= \boxed{2y^{\frac{1}{6}}}$

Your Turn

5. $\dfrac{\sqrt{x^3}}{\sqrt[3]{x^2}}$

$\dfrac{\sqrt{x^3}}{\sqrt[3]{x^2}} = \dfrac{(x^3)^{\frac{1}{2}}}{(x^2)^{\frac{1}{3}}} = \dfrac{x^{\frac{3}{2}}}{x^{\frac{2}{3}}} = x^{\frac{3}{2}-\frac{2}{3}} = x^{\frac{5}{6}}$

6. $\sqrt[5]{16^3} \cdot \sqrt[4]{4^5} \cdot \sqrt[3]{4^2}$

$\sqrt[6]{16^3} \cdot \sqrt[4]{4^6} \cdot \sqrt[3]{8^2}$

$= 16^{\frac{1}{2}} \cdot 4^{\frac{3}{2}} \cdot 8^{\frac{2}{3}}$

$= (2^4)^{\frac{1}{2}} \cdot (2^2)^{\frac{3}{2}} \cdot (2^3)^{\frac{2}{3}}$

$= 2^2 \cdot 2^3 \cdot 2^2$

$= 2^7$

$= 128$

Explain 3 Simplifying Radical Expressions Using the Properties of nth Roots

From working with square roots, you know, for example, that $\sqrt{8} \cdot \sqrt{2} = \sqrt{8 \cdot 2} = \sqrt{16} = 4$ and $\dfrac{\sqrt{8}}{\sqrt{2}} \cdot = \sqrt{\dfrac{8}{2}} = \sqrt{4} = 2$. The corresponding properties also apply to *n*th roots.

Properties of *n*th Roots

For a > 0 and b > 0

Words	Numbers	Algebra
Product of Property of Roots The *n*th root of a product is equal to the product of the *n*th roots.	$\sqrt[3]{16} = \sqrt[3]{8} \cdot \sqrt[3]{2} = 2\sqrt[3]{2}$	$\sqrt[n]{ab} = \sqrt[n]{a} \cdot \sqrt[n]{b}$
Quotient of Property of Roots The *n*th root of a Quotient is equal to the Quotient of the *n*th roots.	$\sqrt{\dfrac{25}{16}} = \dfrac{\sqrt{25}}{\sqrt{16}} = \dfrac{5}{4}$	$\sqrt[n]{\dfrac{a}{b}} = \dfrac{\sqrt[n]{a}}{\sqrt[n]{b}}$

Example 3 **Simplify the expression using the properties of nth roots. Assume that all variables are positive. Rationalize any irrational denominators.**

Ⓐ $\sqrt[3]{256x^3y^7}$

	$\sqrt[3]{256x^3y^7}$
Write 256 as a power.	$= \sqrt[3]{2^8 \cdot x^3y^7}$
Product Property of Roots	$= \sqrt[3]{2^6 \cdot x^3y^6} \cdot \sqrt[3]{2^2 \cdot y}$
Factor out perfect cubes.	$= \sqrt[3]{2^6} \cdot \sqrt[3]{x^3} \cdot \sqrt[3]{y^6} \cdot \sqrt[3]{4y}$
Simplify.	$= 4xy^2\sqrt[3]{4y}$

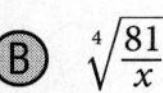 $\sqrt[4]{\frac{81}{x}}$

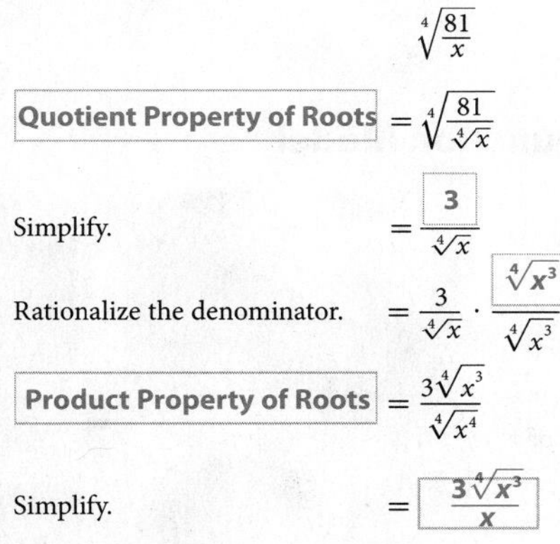

	$\sqrt[4]{\frac{81}{x}}$
Quotient Property of Roots	$= \frac{\sqrt[4]{81}}{\sqrt[4]{x}}$
Simplify.	$= \frac{3}{\sqrt[4]{x}}$
Rationalize the denominator.	$= \frac{3}{\sqrt[4]{x}} \cdot \frac{\sqrt[4]{x^3}}{\sqrt[4]{x^3}}$
Product Property of Roots	$= \frac{3\sqrt[4]{x^3}}{\sqrt[4]{x^4}}$
Simplify.	$= \frac{3\sqrt[4]{x^3}}{x}$

Reflect

7. In Part B, why was $\sqrt[4]{x^3}$ used when rationalizing the denominator? What factor would you use to rationalize a denominator of $\sqrt[5]{4y^3}$?

It was chosen to make the product of the radicands be a perfect fourth power so that the fourth root could be taken; $\sqrt[5]{8y^2}$.

INTEGRATE MATHEMATICAL PRACTICES

Focus on Reasoning

MP.2 Have each student work with a partner to use the relationship between radicals and rational exponents to derive the quotient property of roots, $\sqrt[n]{\frac{a}{b}} = \frac{\sqrt[n]{a}}{\sqrt[n]{b}}$. Have students justify each step of their derivations.

EXPLAIN 4

Rewriting a Radical-Function Model

QUESTIONING STRATEGIES

? How can you check that the simplified form of the expression is equivalent to the original expression? You could graph both expressions as functions on a graphing calculator and make sure their graphs are the same. You could also evaluate both expressions for several values and make sure the resulting values are the same.

Your Turn

Simplify the expression using the properties of *n*th roots. Assume that all variables are positive.

8. $\sqrt[3]{216x^{12}y^{15}}$

$\sqrt[3]{216x^{12}y^{15}} = \sqrt[3]{6^3} \cdot \sqrt[3]{x^{12}} \cdot \sqrt[3]{y^{15}} = 6x^4y^5$

9. $\sqrt[4]{\frac{16}{x^{14}}}$

$= \frac{\sqrt[4]{16}}{\sqrt[4]{x^{14}}}$

$= \frac{2}{\sqrt[4]{x^{12}} \cdot \sqrt[4]{x^2}}$

$= \frac{2}{\sqrt[4]{x^{12}}} \cdot \frac{1}{\sqrt[4]{x^2}}$

$= \frac{2}{x^3} \cdot \frac{1}{\sqrt[4]{x^2}} \cdot \frac{\sqrt[4]{x^2}}{\sqrt[4]{x^2}}$

$= 2\frac{\sqrt[4]{x^2}}{x^4}$

Explain 4 Rewriting a Radical-Function Model

When you find or apply a function model involving rational powers or radicals, you can use the properties in this lesson to help you first find a simpler expression for the model.

(A) **Manufacturing** A can that is twice as tall as its radius has the minimum surface area for the volume it contains. The formula $S = 6\pi\left(\frac{V}{2\pi}\right)^{\frac{2}{3}}$ expresses the surface area of a can with this shape in terms of its volume.

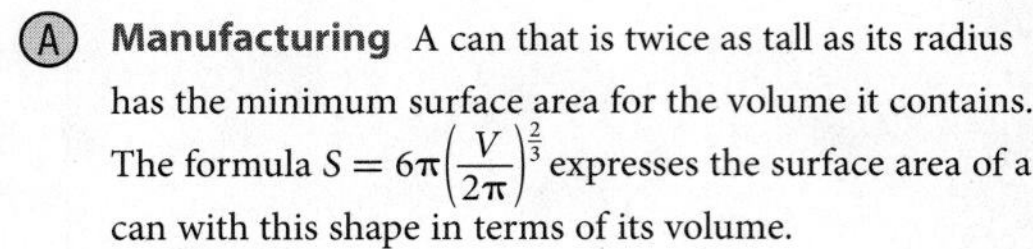

a. Use the properties of rational exponents to simplify the expression for the surface area. Then write the approximate model with the coefficient rounded to the nearest hundredth.

b. Graph the model using a graphing calculator. What is the surface area in square centimeters for a can with a volume of 440 cm³?

a.	$S = 6\pi\left(\frac{V}{2\pi}\right)^{\frac{2}{3}}$
Power of a Quotient Property	$= 6\pi \cdot \frac{V^{\frac{2}{3}}}{(2\pi)^{\frac{2}{3}}}$
Group Powers of 2π.	$= \frac{3(2\pi)}{(2\pi)^{\frac{2}{3}}} \cdot V^{\frac{2}{3}}$
Quotient of Powers Property	$= 3(2\pi)^{1-\frac{2}{3}} \cdot V^{\frac{2}{3}}$
Simplify.	$= 3(2\pi)^{\frac{1}{3}} \cdot V^{\frac{2}{3}}$
Use a calculator.	$\approx 5.54V^{\frac{2}{3}}$

A simplified model is $S = 3(2\pi)^{\frac{1}{3}} \cdot V^{\frac{2}{3}}$, which gives $S \approx 5.54V^{\frac{2}{3}}$.

b.

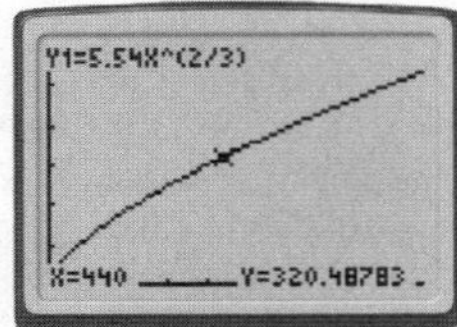

The surface area is about 320 cm^2.

B **Commercial fishing** The buoyancy of a fishing float in water depends on the volume of air it contains. The radius of a spherical float as a function of its volume is given by $r = \sqrt[3]{\frac{3V}{4\pi}}$.

a. Use the properties of roots to rewrite the expression for the radius as the product of a coefficient term and a variable term. Then write the approximate formula with the coefficient rounded to the nearest hundredth.

b. What should the radius be for a float that needs to contain 4.4 ft^3 of air to have the proper buoyancy?

a. $r = \sqrt[3]{\frac{3V}{4\pi}}$

Rewrite radicand. $= \sqrt[3]{\frac{3}{4\pi} \cdot \boxed{V}}$

Product Property of Roots $= \sqrt[3]{\frac{3}{4\pi}} \cdot \boxed{\sqrt[3]{V}}$

Use a calculator $\approx \boxed{0.62\sqrt[3]{V}}$

The rewritten formula is $r = \boxed{\sqrt[3]{\frac{3}{4\pi}} \cdot \sqrt[3]{V}}$, which gives $r \approx \boxed{0.62\sqrt[3]{V}}$.

b. Substitute 4.4 for V.

$r = 0.62\sqrt[3]{4.4} \approx \boxed{1.02}$

The radius is about 1.0 feet.

Reflect

10. Discussion What are some reasons you might want to rewrite an expression involving radicals into an expression involving rational exponents?

By rewriting radical expressions, especially complicated ones and those involving *n*th roots and powers in the radicand, rewriting using rational exponents lets you use the properties of rational exponents to make simplification easier. Also, rational exponents make it easier to enter an expression into a calculator for evaluation or graphing.

ELABORATE

QUESTIONING STRATEGIES

? Can you use the properties of rational exponents to simplify $\sqrt{a} \cdot \sqrt[3]{b}$? Explain. **No; in rational exponent form, the expression is $a^{\frac{1}{2}} \cdot b^{\frac{1}{3}}$. Because the bases are different, the product of powers property does not apply, and the expression cannot be simplified.**

SUMMARIZE THE LESSON

? How can the properties of exponents be applied to the simplification of expressions containing rational exponents and to those containing radicals? **For expressions containing rational exponents, the properties of exponents can be applied directly. For radical expressions, convert the radical expressions to exponent form using the fact that $\sqrt[n]{a^m} = a^{\frac{m}{n}}$, and then apply the properties.**

Your Turn

11. The surface area as a function of volume for a box with a square base and a height that is twice the side length of the base is $S = 10\left(\frac{V}{2}\right)^{\frac{2}{3}}$. Use the properties of rational exponents to simplify the expression for the surface area so that no fractions are involved. Then write the approximate model with the coefficient rounded to the nearest hundredth.

$S = 10\left(\frac{V}{2}\right)^{\frac{2}{3}} = 10 \cdot \frac{V^{\frac{2}{3}}}{2^{\frac{2}{3}}} = \frac{5 \cdot 2}{2^{\frac{2}{3}}} \cdot V^{\frac{2}{3}} = 5\left(2^{1-\frac{2}{3}}\right)V^{\frac{2}{3}} = 5 \cdot 2^{\frac{1}{3}}V^{\frac{2}{3}} \approx 6.30V^{\frac{2}{3}}$

The expression is $S = 5 \cdot 2^{\frac{1}{3}}V^{\frac{2}{3}}$, which gives $S = 6.30V^{\frac{2}{3}}$.

Elaborate

12. In problems with a radical in the denominator, you rationalized the denominator to remove the radical. What can you do to remove a rational exponent from the denominator? Explain by giving an example.

You can multiply the expression by a form of 1 so that the denominator of the resulting expression has an exponent that is an integer. For example, for $\frac{6}{x^{\frac{2}{5}}}$, multiply the numerator and denominator by $x^{\frac{3}{5}}$: $\frac{6}{x^{\frac{2}{5}}} \cdot \frac{x^{\frac{3}{5}}}{x^{\frac{3}{5}}} = \frac{6x^{\frac{3}{5}}}{x^{\frac{2}{5}+\frac{3}{5}}} = 6x^{\frac{3}{5}}x$.

13. Show why $\sqrt[n]{a^n}$ is equal to a for all natural numbers a and n using the definition of nth roots and using rational exponents.

By definition, the nth root of a number b is the number whose nth power is b. So the nth root of a^n is the number whose nth power is a^n, or a. Using rational exponents, the nth root is indicated by the exponent $\frac{1}{n}$, so $\sqrt[n]{a^n} = (a^n)^{\frac{1}{n}} = a^{n \cdot \frac{1}{n}} = a^{\frac{n}{n}} = a^1 = a$.

14. Show that the Product Property of Roots is true using rational exponents.

The nth root is indicated by the exponent $\frac{1}{n}$, so $\sqrt[n]{ab} = (ab)^{\frac{1}{n}} = a^{\frac{1}{n}} \cdot b^{\frac{1}{n}} = \sqrt[n]{a} \cdot \sqrt[n]{b}$.

15. Essential Question Check-In Describe the difference between applying the Power of a Power Property and applying the Power of a Product Property for rational exponents using an example that involves both properties.

Possible answer: Consider the expression $\left(4^{\frac{2}{3}}x^{\frac{4}{3}}\right)^{\frac{3}{4}}$. This is the $\frac{3}{4}$ power of the product of $4^{\frac{2}{3}}$ and $x^{\frac{4}{3}}$. The result is the product of the $\frac{3}{4}$ power of each factor: $\left(4^{\frac{2}{3}}\right)^{\frac{3}{4}}\left(x^{\frac{4}{3}}\right)^{\frac{3}{4}}$. This expression contains the $\frac{3}{4}$ power of the power $4^{\frac{2}{3}}$ and the $\frac{3}{4}$ power of the power $x^{\frac{4}{3}}$. Simplifying then gives $\left(4^{\frac{2}{3}}\right)^{\frac{3}{4}}\left(x^{\frac{4}{3}}\right)^{\frac{3}{4}} = 4^{\frac{1}{2}} \cdot x^1 = 2x$

LANGUAGE SUPPORT EL

Communicate Math

Have students work in pairs. The first student explains the steps for simplifying rational exponents to the second student, including the properties involved. The second student takes notes and writes down the steps, and repeats them back using his or her own words. Students switch roles and repeat the procedure for radical expressions involving nth roots.

Evaluate: Homework and Practice

- Online Homework
- Hints and Help
- Extra Practice

Simplify the expression. Assume that all variables are positive. Exponents in simplified form should all be positive.

1. $\left(\left(\frac{1}{16}\right)^{-\frac{2}{3}}\right)^{\frac{3}{4}}$

$\left(\left(\frac{1}{16}\right)^{-\frac{2}{3}}\right)^{\frac{3}{4}} = \left(\frac{1}{16}\right)^{-\frac{2}{3}\cdot\frac{3}{4}} = \left(\frac{1}{16}\right)^{-\frac{1}{2}} = 16 = 4$

2. $\frac{x^{\frac{1}{3}} \cdot x^{\frac{5}{6}}}{x^{\frac{1}{6}}}$

$\frac{x^{\frac{1}{3}} \cdot x^{\frac{5}{6}}}{x^{\frac{1}{6}}} = \frac{x^{\frac{1}{3}+\frac{5}{6}}}{x^{\frac{1}{6}}} = x^{\frac{1}{3}+\frac{5}{6}-\frac{1}{6}} = x$

3. $\frac{9^{\frac{3}{2}} \cdot 9^{\frac{1}{2}}}{9^{-2}}$

$\frac{9^{\frac{3}{2}} \cdot 9^{\frac{1}{2}}}{9^{-2}} = \frac{9^{\frac{3}{2}+\frac{1}{2}}}{9^{-2}} = \frac{9^2}{9^{-2}} = 9^{2-(-2)} = 9^4 = 6561$

4. $\left(\frac{16^{\frac{5}{3}}}{16^{\frac{5}{6}}}\right)^{\frac{9}{5}}$

$\left(\frac{16^{\frac{5}{3}}}{16^{\frac{5}{6}}}\right)^{\frac{9}{5}} = \left(16^{\frac{5}{3}-\frac{5}{6}}\right)^{\frac{9}{5}} = \left(16^{\frac{5}{6}}\right)^{\frac{9}{5}} = 16^{\frac{3}{2}} = 4^3 = 64$

5. $\frac{2xy}{\left(x^{\frac{1}{3}}y^{\frac{2}{3}}\right)^{\frac{3}{2}}}$

$\frac{2xy}{\left(x^{\frac{1}{3}}y^{\frac{2}{3}}\right)^{\frac{3}{2}}} = \frac{2xy}{x^{\frac{1}{3}\cdot\frac{3}{2}}y^{\frac{2}{3}\cdot\frac{3}{2}}} = \frac{2xy}{x^{\frac{1}{2}}y} = 2x^{1-\frac{1}{2}} = 2x^{\frac{1}{2}}$

6. $\frac{3y^{\frac{3}{4}}}{2xy^{\frac{3}{2}}}$

$\frac{3y^{\frac{3}{4}}}{2xy^{\frac{3}{2}}} = \frac{3y^{\frac{3}{4}-\frac{3}{2}}}{2x} = \frac{3y^{-\frac{3}{4}}}{2x} = \frac{3}{2xy^{\frac{3}{4}}}\left(\frac{y^{\frac{1}{4}}}{y^{\frac{1}{4}}}\right) = \frac{3y^{\frac{1}{4}}}{2xy}$

Simplify the expression by writing it using rational exponents and then using the properties of rational exponents. Assume that all variables are positive. Exponents in simplified form should all be positive.

7. $\sqrt[4]{25} \cdot \sqrt[3]{5}$

$\sqrt[4]{25} \cdot \sqrt[3]{5} = 25^{\frac{1}{4}} \cdot 5^{\frac{1}{3}} = (5^2)^{\frac{1}{4}} \cdot 5^{\frac{1}{3}}$
$= 5^{\frac{1}{2}} \cdot 5^{\frac{1}{3}} = 5^{\frac{1}{2}+\frac{1}{3}} = 5^{\frac{5}{6}}$

8. $\frac{\sqrt[4]{2^{-2}}}{\sqrt[9]{2^{-9}}}$

$\frac{\sqrt[4]{2^{-2}}}{\sqrt[6]{2^{-9}}} = \frac{2^{-\frac{1}{2}}}{2^{-\frac{3}{2}}} = 2^{-\frac{1}{2}-\left(-\frac{3}{2}\right)} = 2^1 = 2$

9. $\frac{\sqrt[4]{3^3} \cdot \sqrt[3]{x^2}}{\sqrt{3x}}$

$\frac{\sqrt[4]{3^3} \cdot \sqrt[3]{x^2}}{\sqrt{3x}} = \frac{(3^3)^{\frac{1}{4}} \cdot x^{\frac{2}{3}}}{(3x)^{\frac{1}{2}}} = \frac{\frac{3}{4} \cdot x^{\frac{2}{3}}}{3^{\frac{1}{2}} \cdot x^{\frac{1}{2}}}$
$= 3^{\frac{3}{4}-\frac{1}{2}} \cdot x^{\frac{2}{3}-\frac{1}{2}} = 3^{\frac{1}{4}} \cdot x^{\frac{1}{6}}$

10. $\frac{\sqrt[4]{x^4y^6} \cdot \sqrt{x^6}}{y}$

$\frac{\sqrt[4]{x^4y^6} \cdot \sqrt{x^6}}{y} = \frac{(x^4y^6)^{\frac{1}{4}} \cdot (x^6)^{\frac{1}{2}}}{y}$
$= \frac{x \cdot y^{\frac{3}{2}} \cdot x^3}{y} = x^{1+3} \cdot y^{\frac{3}{2}-1} = x^4y^{\frac{1}{2}}$

Exercise	Depth of Knowledge (D.O.K.)	COMMON CORE Mathematical Practices
1	**1** Recall of Information	**MP.3** Logic
2–16	**1** Recall of Information	**MP.5** Using Tools
17–20	**2** Skills/Concepts	**MP.4** Modeling
21	**2** Skills/Concepts H.O.T.	**MP.3** Logic
22–23	**3** Strategic Thinking H.O.T.	**MP.3** Logic

EVALUATE

ASSIGNMENT GUIDE

Concepts and Skills	Practice
Explore Establishing the Properties of Rational Exponents	
Example 1 Simplifying Rational-Exponent Expressions	Exercises 1–6
Example 2 Simplifying Radical Expressions Using the Properties of Exponents	Exercises 7–12
Example 3 Simplifying Radical Expressions Using the Properties of *n*th Roots	Exercises 13–16
Example 4 Rewriting a Radical-Function Model	Exercises 17–18

QUESTIONING STRATEGIES

? When do you add the exponents on two expressions? **when the expressions have the same base and they are being multiplied**

? When do you apply the power of a power property? **when an expression containing an exponent is being raised to another exponent**

INTEGRATE MATHEMATICAL PRACTICES

Focus on Reasoning

MP.2 Discuss with students that there is often more than one way to go about simplifying these types of expressions. Encourage students to be aware of this, and to use one method to check their results found using a different method.

VISUAL CUES

For expressions that involve applying the power of a product property or the power of a quotient property, suggest that students use arrows to show the exponent being applied to each factor in the product or to each factor in the numerator and denominator in the quotient. In this way, students may avoid errors such as forgetting to apply the exponent to a numerical coefficient or to a variable that does not contain an exponent.

AVOID COMMON ERRORS

Students may make errors in rationalizing denominators when the index is greater than 2. For example, when trying to rationalize an expression such as $\frac{\sqrt[5]{2}}{\sqrt[5]{x}}$, they may multiply by $\frac{\sqrt[5]{x}}{\sqrt[5]{x}}$, instead of $\frac{\sqrt[5]{x^4}}{\sqrt[5]{x^4}}$, as if the index were 2 instead of 5. Help them to see that this choice does not make the radicand a perfect fifth, which is the goal of rationalizing this denominator. Reinforce that the resulting exponent must be a multiple of the index.

11. $\dfrac{\sqrt[6]{s^4t^9}}{\sqrt[3]{st}}$

$$\frac{\sqrt[6]{s^4t^9}}{\sqrt[3]{st}} = \frac{(s^4t^9)^{\frac{1}{6}}}{(st)^{\frac{1}{3}}} = \frac{s^{\frac{2}{3}}t^{\frac{3}{2}}}{s^{\frac{1}{3}}t^{\frac{1}{3}}}$$
$$= s^{\frac{2}{3}-\frac{1}{3}}t^{\frac{3}{2}-\frac{1}{3}} = s^{\frac{1}{3}}t^{\frac{7}{6}}$$

12. $\sqrt[4]{27} \cdot \sqrt{3} \cdot \sqrt[6]{81^3}$

$$\sqrt[4]{27} \cdot \sqrt{3} \cdot \sqrt[6]{81^3} = 27^{\frac{1}{4}} \cdot 3^{\frac{1}{2}} \cdot 81^{\frac{1}{2}}$$
$$= (3^3)^{\frac{1}{4}} \cdot 3^{\frac{1}{2}} \cdot 9 = 3^{\frac{3}{4}} \cdot 3^{\frac{1}{2}} \cdot 3^2 = 3^{\frac{3}{4}+\frac{1}{2}+2}$$
$$= 3^{\frac{13}{4}} = 3^3 \cdot 3^{\frac{1}{4}} = 27 \cdot 3^{\frac{1}{4}}$$

Simplify the expression using the properties of *n*th roots. Assume that all variables are positive. Rationalize any irrational denominators.

13. $\dfrac{\sqrt{36} \cdot \sqrt[4]{216}}{\sqrt[4]{6}}$

$$= \frac{\sqrt[4]{36 \cdot 216}}{\sqrt[4]{6}} = \frac{\sqrt[4]{36 \cdot 216}}{6} = \sqrt[4]{36 \cdot 36}$$
$$= \sqrt[4]{6^2 \cdot 6^2} = \sqrt[4]{6^4} = 6$$

14. $\sqrt[4]{4096x^6y^8}$

$$= \sqrt[4]{8^4x^6y^8} = \sqrt[4]{8^4} \cdot \sqrt[4]{x^4} \cdot \sqrt[4]{y^8} \cdot \sqrt[4]{x^2}$$
$$= 8xy^2\sqrt[4]{x^2} = 8xy^2\sqrt{x}$$

15. $\dfrac{\sqrt[3]{x^8y^4}}{\sqrt[3]{x^2y}}$

$$= \sqrt[3]{\frac{x^8y^4}{x^2y}} = \sqrt[3]{x^{8-2}y^{4-1}} = \sqrt[3]{x^6} \cdot \sqrt[3]{y^3} = x^2y$$

16. $\sqrt[5]{\dfrac{125}{w^6}} \cdot \sqrt[5]{25v}$

$$= \sqrt[5]{\frac{125 \cdot 25v}{w^6}} = \sqrt[5]{\frac{5^3 \cdot 5^2 \cdot v}{w^5 \cdot w}} = \sqrt[5]{\frac{5^5}{w^5}} \cdot \sqrt[5]{\frac{v}{w}}$$
$$= \sqrt[5]{\left(\frac{5}{w}\right)^5} \cdot \sqrt[5]{\frac{v}{w}} = \frac{5}{w} \cdot \frac{\sqrt[5]{v}}{\sqrt[5]{w}} \cdot \frac{\sqrt[5]{w^4}}{\sqrt[5]{w^4}}$$
$$= \frac{5}{w} \cdot \frac{\sqrt[5]{vw^4}}{\sqrt[5]{w^5}} = \frac{5\sqrt[5]{vw^4}}{w^2}$$

17. Weather The volume of a sphere as a function of its surface area is given by $V = \frac{4\pi}{3}\left(\frac{S}{4\pi}\right)^{\frac{3}{2}}$.

a. Use the properties of roots to rewrite the expression for the radius as the product of a simplified coefficient term (with positive exponents) and a variable term. Then write the approximate formula with the coefficient rounded to the nearest thousandth.

b. A spherical weather balloon has a surface area of 500 ft². What is the approximate volume of the balloon?

a. $$V = \frac{4\pi}{3} \cdot \left(\frac{S}{4\pi}\right)^{\frac{3}{2}} = \frac{4\pi}{3} \cdot \frac{S^{\frac{3}{2}}}{(4\pi)^{\frac{3}{2}}} = \frac{1}{3} \cdot (4\pi)^{1-\frac{3}{2}} \cdot S^{\frac{3}{2}}$$
$$= \frac{1}{3} \cdot (4\pi)^{-\frac{1}{2}} \cdot S^{\frac{3}{2}} = \frac{1}{3} \cdot \frac{1}{(4\pi)^{\frac{1}{2}}} \cdot S^{\frac{3}{2}} = \frac{1}{6\pi^{\frac{1}{2}}} \cdot S^{\frac{3}{2}}$$
$$\approx 0.094S^{\frac{3}{2}}$$

b. $V \approx 0.094(500)^{\frac{3}{2}} \approx 1050 \text{ ft}^3$

18. Amusement parks An amusement park has a ride with a free fall of 128 feet. The formula $t = \sqrt{\frac{2d}{g}}$ gives the time t in seconds it takes the ride to fall a distance of d feet. The formula $v = \sqrt{2gd}$ gives the velocity v in feet per second after the ride has fallen d feet. The letter g represents the gravitational constant.

a. Rewrite each formula so that the variable d is isolated. Then simplify each formula using the fact that $g \approx 32$ ft/s^2.

a. $t = \sqrt{\frac{2d}{g}} = \sqrt{\frac{2}{g}} \cdot \sqrt{d} \approx \sqrt{\frac{2}{32}} \cdot \sqrt{d} = \sqrt{\frac{1}{16}} \cdot \sqrt{d}$
$= \frac{1}{4}\sqrt{d}$;

$v = \sqrt{2gd} = \sqrt{2g} \cdot \sqrt{d} \approx \sqrt{2(32)} \cdot \sqrt{d} = \sqrt{64} \cdot \sqrt{d}$
$= 8\sqrt{d}$

The formulas are $t = \sqrt{\frac{2}{g}} \cdot \sqrt{d}$, **or** $t \approx \frac{1}{4}\sqrt{d}$, **and** v
$= \sqrt{2g} \cdot \sqrt{d}$, **or** $v \approx 8\sqrt{d}$.

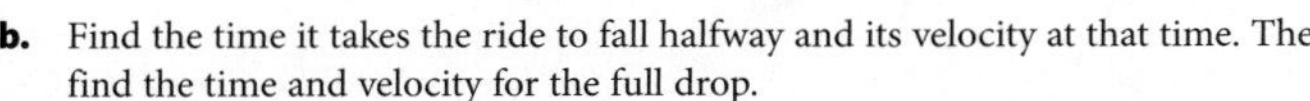

b. Find the time it takes the ride to fall halfway and its velocity at that time. Then find the time and velocity for the full drop.

b. halfway: $d = 64$ **ft, so** $t = \frac{1}{4}\sqrt{64} = 2$ **s and** $v = 8\sqrt{64} = 64$ **ft/s;**

full drop: $d = 128$ **ft, so** $t = \frac{1}{4}\sqrt{128} = \frac{1}{4}\sqrt{64(2)} = 2\sqrt{2}$ **s, or about 2.8 s, and**

$v = 8\sqrt{128} = 8\sqrt{64(2)} = 64\sqrt{2}$ **ft/s, or about 87 ft/s**

c. What is the ratio of the time it takes for the whole drop to the time it takes for the first half? What is the ratio of the velocity after the second half of the drop to the velocity after the first half? What do you notice?

c. $\frac{\text{whole time}}{\text{1st half time}} = \frac{\sqrt{2}}{2} = \sqrt{2} \approx 1.41$;

$\frac{\text{velocity at end}}{\text{velocity halfway}} = \frac{64\sqrt{2}}{64} = \sqrt{2} \approx 1.41$; **the ratios are the same**

19. Which choice(s) is/are equivalent to $\sqrt{2}$?

(A.) $\left(\sqrt[8]{2}\right)^4$

B. $\frac{2^3}{2^{-\frac{5}{2}}}$

(C.) $\left(4^{\frac{2}{3}} \cdot 2^{\frac{2}{3}}\right)^{\frac{1}{4}}$

(D.) $\frac{\sqrt[3]{2^2}}{\sqrt[6]{2}}$

(E.) $\frac{\sqrt{2^{-\frac{3}{4}}}}{\sqrt{2^{-\frac{7}{4}}}}$

TECHNOLOGY

Encourage students to use a graphing calculator to check their work. To check problems involving the simplification of variable expressions, suggest that students assign values to the variables and use the calculator to check that the value of the original expression and the value of the simplified expression are the same when evaluated for the same values of the variables.

JOURNAL

Have students describe how the properties of *n*th roots are similar to the corresponding properties of rational exponents.

20. Home Heating A propane storage tank for a home is shaped like a cylinder with hemispherical ends, and a cylindrical portion length that is 4 times the radius.

The formula $S = 12\pi\left(\frac{3V}{16\pi}\right)^{\frac{2}{3}}$ expresses the surface area of a tank with this shape in terms of its volume.

a. Use the properties of rational exponents to rewrite the expression for the surface area so that the variable V is isolated. Then write the approximate model with the coefficient rounded to the nearest hundredth.

a. $S = 12\pi\left(\frac{3V}{16\pi}\right)^{\frac{2}{3}} = 12\pi\left(\frac{3}{16\pi}\right)^{\frac{2}{3}} \cdot V^{\frac{2}{3}} \approx 5.76V^{\frac{2}{3}}$

b. Graph the model using a graphing calculator. What is the surface area in square feet for a tank with a volume of 150 ft³ ?

b.

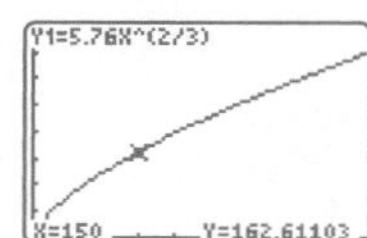

The surface area is about 162 ft².

H.O.T. Focus on Higher Order Thinking

21. Critique Reasoning Aaron's work in simplifying an expression is shown. What mistake(s) did Aaron make? Show the correct simplification.

$625^{-\frac{1}{3}} \div 625^{-\frac{4}{3}}$
$= 625^{-\frac{1}{3}-\left(-\frac{4}{3}\right)}$
$= 625^{-\frac{1}{3}\left(-\frac{3}{4}\right)}$
$= 625^{\frac{1}{4}}$
$= 5$

Aaron incorrectly applied the Quotient of Powers Property. He should have subtracted the exponents.

$625^{-\frac{1}{3}} \div 625^{-\frac{4}{3}}$
$= 625^{-\frac{1}{3}-\left(-\frac{4}{3}\right)} = 625^{-\frac{1}{3}+\frac{4}{3}} = 625^1 = 625$

22. Critical Thinking Use the definition of *n*th root to show that the Product Property of Roots is true, that is, that $\sqrt[n]{ab} = \sqrt[n]{a} \cdot \sqrt[n]{b}$. (Hint: Begin by letting x be the *n*th root of a and letting y be the *n*th root of b.)

Let x be the nth root of a and let y be the *n*th root of b. Then by the definition of *n*th root, $a = x^n$ and $b = y^n$. So, $ab = x^n y^n = (xy)^n$. This means by definition that xy is the *n*th root of ab, or $\sqrt[n]{ab} = xy$. But $xy = \sqrt[n]{a} \cdot \sqrt[n]{b}$, so $\sqrt[n]{ab} = \sqrt[n]{a} \cdot \sqrt[n]{b}$.

23. Critical Thinking For what real values of a is $\sqrt[4]{a}$ greater than a? For what real values of a is $\sqrt[5]{a}$ greater than a?

for $0 < a < 1$; for $a < -1$ or $0 < a < 1$

Lesson Performance Task

You've been asked to help decorate for a school dance, and the theme chosen is "The Solar System." The plan is to have a bunch of papier-mâché spheres serve as models of the planets, and your job is to paint them. All you're told are the volumes of the individual spheres, but you need to know their surface areas so you can get be sure to get enough paint. How can you write a simplified equation using rational exponents for the surface area of a sphere in terms of its volume?

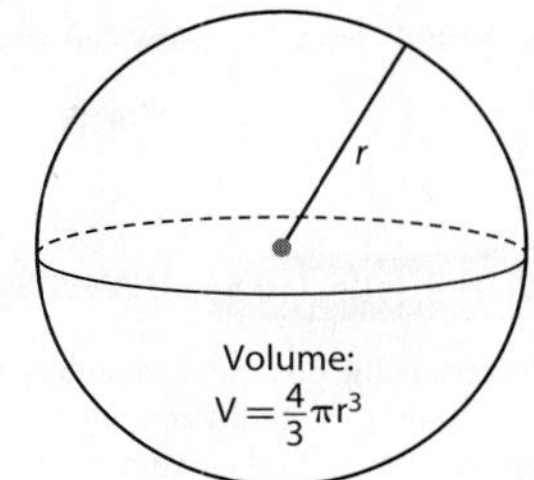

(The formula for the volume of a sphere is $V = \frac{4}{3}\pi r^3$ and the formula for the surface area of a sphere is $A = 4\pi r^2$.)

Solve the volume formula for *r*.

$$V = \frac{4}{3}\pi r^3$$

$$\frac{3V}{4\pi} = r^3$$

$$\sqrt[3]{\frac{3V}{4\pi}} = r$$

$$\left(\frac{3V}{4\pi}\right)^{\frac{1}{3}} = r$$

Substitute the value for *r* into the formula for surface area and simplify.

$$A = 4\pi r^2$$

$$= 4\pi\left[\left(\frac{3V}{4\pi}\right)^{\frac{1}{3}}\right]^2 \quad \textbf{Substitute.}$$

$$= 4\pi\left[\frac{3V}{4\pi}\right]^{\frac{2}{3}} \quad \textbf{Multiply exponents.}$$

$$= 4\pi\frac{(3V)^{\frac{2}{3}}}{(4\pi)^{\frac{2}{3}}} \quad \textbf{Distribute the exponent.}$$

$$= (4\pi)^{\frac{1}{3}}(3V)^{\frac{2}{3}} \quad \textbf{Subtract exponents.}$$

The surface area in terms of the volume is equal to $A = (4\pi)^{\frac{1}{3}}(3V)^{\frac{2}{3}}$.

EXTENSION ACTIVITY

Have students research the equations for the surface area and volume for a truncated *icosidodecahedron*, a 32-face solid similar to a soccer ball. Have students derive an equation for the surface area in terms of the volume, and then have them discuss whether they will need more or less paint to cover this shape, compared to painting a sphere.

AVOID COMMON ERRORS

When dividing one term by another, some students may divide the exponents instead of subtracting. Explain that to simplify $\frac{4\pi}{(4\pi)^{\frac{2}{3}}}$, you subtract the exponents: $1 - \frac{2}{3} = \frac{1}{3}$. The simplified term would then be $(4\pi)^{\frac{1}{3}}$.

INTEGRATE MATHEMATICAL PRACTICES

Focus on Modeling

MP.4 Have students discuss why the final exponent of V turns out to be $\frac{2}{3}$. Have them relate the numbers in the rational exponent to the geometry of the situation. Have them discuss whether the exponent would be $\frac{2}{3}$ if the shape were something other than a sphere.

Scoring Rubric

2 points: Student correctly solves the problem and explains his/her reasoning.

1 point: Student shows good understanding of the problem but does not fully solve or explain his/her reasoning.

0 points: Student does not demonstrate understanding of the problem.

LESSON 11.3

Solving Radical Equations

Common Core Math Standards

The student is expected to:

A-REI.A.2

Solve simple rational and radical equations in one variable, and give examples showing how extraneous solutions may arise. Also A-CED.A.1, A-REI.A.1

Mathematical Practices

MP.7 Using Structure

Language Objective

Work with a partner to complete a table to solve rational and radical equations.

ENGAGE

Essential Question: How can you solve equations involving square roots and cube roots?

First, combine terms to simplify, if possible. If there is one radical expression, isolate it on one side of the equation. Then, to solve the equation, square both sides when a square root is involved, and cube both sides when a cube root is involved. Finally, solve the resulting equation for the variable, remembering to check for extraneous solutions

PREVIEW: LESSON PERFORMANCE TASK

View the Engage section online. Discuss the photo and how the strength of a tornado depends on its wind speed. Then preview the Lesson Performance Task.

Name ______ Class ______ Date ______

11.3 Solving Radical Equations

Essential Question: How can you solve equations involving square roots and cube roots?

Resource Locker

Explore Investigating Solutions of Square Root Equations

When solving quadratic equations, you have learned that the number of real solutions depends upon the values in the equation, with different equations having 0, 1, or 2 real solutions. How many real solutions does a square root equation have? In the Explore, you will investigate graphically the numbers of real solutions for different square root equations.

(A) Remember that you can graph the two sides of an equation as separate functions to find solutions of the equation: a solution is any x-value where the two graphs intersect.

The graph of $y = \sqrt{x-3}$ is shown on a calculator window of $-4 \leq x \leq 16$ and $-2 \leq y \leq 8$. Reproduce the graph on your calculator. Then add the graph of $y = 2$.

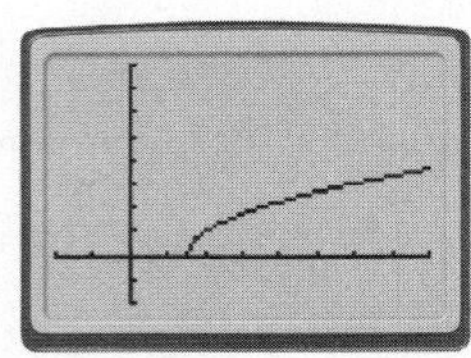

How many solutions does the equation $\sqrt{x-3} = 2$ have? __one__ How do you know?

The graphs intersect at one point.

On your calculator, replace the graph of $y = 2$ with the graph of $y = -1$.

How many solutions does the equation $\sqrt{x-3} = -1$ have? __zero__ How do you know?

The graphs never intersect.

(B) Graph $y = \sqrt{x-3} + 2$ on your calculator (you can use the same viewing window as in Step A).

Add the graph of $y = 3$ to the graph of $y = \sqrt{x-3} + 2$.

How many solutions does $\sqrt{x-3} + 2 = 3$ have? __one__

Replace the graph of $y = 3$ with the graph of $y = 1$.

How many solutions does $\sqrt{x-3} + 2 = 1$ have? __zero__

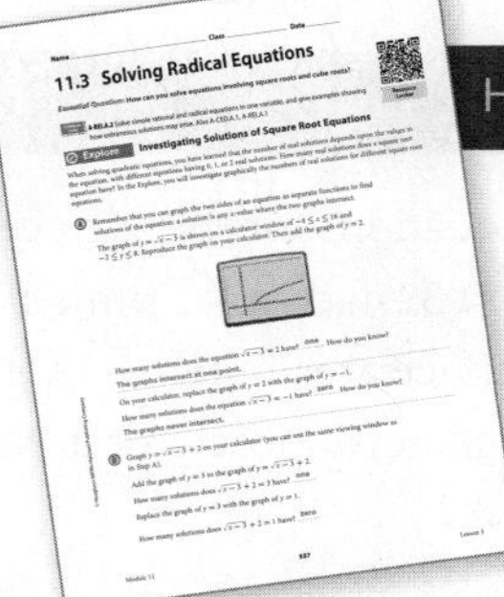

HARDCOVER PAGES 557–570

Watch for the hardcover student edition page numbers for this lesson.

Ⓒ Graph both sides of $\sqrt{4x-4} = x+1$ as separate functions on your calculator.

How many solutions does $\sqrt{4x-4} = x+1$ have? zero

Replace the graph of $y = x+1$ with the graph of $y = \frac{1}{2}x$.

How many solutions does $\sqrt{4x-4} = \frac{1}{2}x$ have? two

Replace the graph of $y = \frac{1}{2}x$ with the graph of $y = 2x-5$.

How many solutions does $\sqrt{4x-4} = 2x-5$ have? one

Ⓓ Graph both sides of $\sqrt{2x-3} = \sqrt{x}$ as separate functions on your calculator.

How many solutions does $\sqrt{2x-3} = \sqrt{x}$ have? one

Replace the graph of $y = \sqrt{x}$ with the graph of $y = \sqrt{2x+3}$.

How many solutions does $\sqrt{2x-3} = \sqrt{2x+3}$ have? zero

Reflect

1. For a square root equation of the form $\sqrt{bx-h} = c$, what can you conclude about the number of solutions based on the sign of c?
When c is nonnegative, there is one solution. When c is negative, there are no solutions.

2. For a square root equation of the form $\sqrt{bx-h} + k = c$, what can you conclude about the number of solutions based on the values of k and c?
When $k \le c$, there is one solution. When $k > c$, there are no solutions.

3. For a cube root equation of the form $\sqrt[3]{bx-h} = c$, will the number of solutions depend on the sign of c? Explain.
No, a cubic expression can have negative roots.

4. The graphs in the second part of Step D appear to be get closer and closer as x increases. How can you be sure that they never meet, that is, that $\sqrt{2x-3} = \sqrt{2x+3}$ really has no solutions?
The graphs have the same shape. They are just different horizontal translations of $y = \sqrt{2x}$, one to the right and one to the left.

Explain 1 Solving Square Root and $\frac{1}{2}$-Power Equations

A *radical equation* contains a variable within a radical or a variable raised to a (non-integer) rational power. To solve a square root equation, or, equivalently, an equation involving the power $\frac{1}{2}$, you can square both sides of the equation and solve the resulting equation.

Because opposite numbers have the same square, squaring both sides of an equation may introduce an apparent solution that is not an actual solution (an extraneous solution). For example, while the only solution of $x = 2$ is 2, the equation that is the square of each side, $x^2 = 4$, has two solutions, -2 and 2. But -2 is not a solution of the original equation.

PROFESSIONAL DEVELOPMENT

Math Background

In this lesson, students use inverse operations to solve radical equations, which are equations in which the variable is in the radicand. For example, since the inverse of taking a cube root is raising to the third power, equations containing a cube root of a variable expression can be solved by cubing both sides of the equation. Squaring both sides of an equation may produce an extraneous solution; that is, a solution that is not a solution of the original equation.

EXPLORE

Investigating Solutions of Square Root Equations

INTEGRATE TECHNOLOGY

Students have the option of completing the Explore activity either in the book or online.

QUESTIONING STRATEGIES

? How can the **INTERSECT** feature on your calculator help you solve a radical equation by graphing? **You can graph the function represented by each side of the equation and find the x-value of the point of intersection, or determine that one does not exist.**

EXPLAIN 1

Solving Square Root and $\frac{1}{2}$-Power Equations

QUESTIONING STRATEGIES

? Why do you need to square both sides of the equation? **Squaring is the inverse of taking a square root, so squaring the side that contains the radical gets rid of the radical sign. You have to square the other side, too, in order to maintain the equality.**

? Why don't all of the apparent solutions check? **When you square both sides of an equation, you can introduce an extraneous, or false, solution.**

AVOID COMMON ERRORS

When solving equations containing square roots, students may forget to square the entire quantity on each side. Caution students not to square terms individually when solving an equation such as $\sqrt{x+4} = x-2$. Point out that when both sides of this equation are squared, the result is $x+4 = (x-2)^2$, not $x+4 = x^2 - 2^2$.

INTEGRATE MATHEMATICAL PRACTICES

Focus on Math Connections

MP.1 Ask students to describe the relationship between the algebraic method used to solve a quadratic equation of the form $x^2 = a$ and the algebraic method used to solve a radical equation of the form $\sqrt{x} = b$. Lead them to see that the operations used to solve each equation are inverses of each other.

INTEGRATE TECHNOLOGY

Students can use a spreadsheet to check their solutions. They can enter a possible solution in cell A1. In cell A2, they can enter the left side of the equation, using A1 as the variable. In cell B2, they can enter the right side of the equation, also using A1 as the variable. If the values in cells A2 and B2 are equal, the value in cell A1 is a solution.

CONNECT VOCABULARY EL

Continue to make explicit the relationship between square roots, squaring, and raising something to the power of 2; and cube roots and cubing to the power of 3. It is easy to overlook that what is familiar to native English speakers (the connection of *cube*, a 6-sided object, with the number 3, for example) may not be to English language learners.

Example 1 **Solve the equation. Check for extraneous solutions.**

(A) $2 + \sqrt{x + 10} = x$

	$2 + \sqrt{x + 10} = x$
Isolate the radical.	$\sqrt{x + 10} = x - 2$
Square both sides.	$\left(\sqrt{x + 10}\right)^2 = (x - 2)^2$
Simplify.	$x + 10 = x^2 - 4x + 4$
Simplify.	$0 = x^2 - 5x - 6$
Factor.	$0 = (x - 6)(x + 1)$
Zero Product Property	$x = 6$ or $x = -1$

Check:

$2 + \sqrt{x + 10} = x$	$2 + \sqrt{x + 10} = x$
$2 + \sqrt{6 + 10} \stackrel{?}{=} x$	$2 + \sqrt{-1 + 10} \stackrel{?}{=} -1$
$2 + \sqrt{16} \stackrel{?}{=} 6$	$2 + \sqrt{9} \stackrel{?}{=} -1$
$6 = 6$ ✓	$5 \neq -1$ ✓
$x = 6$ is a solution.	$x = -1$ is not a solution.

The solution is $x = 6$.

(B) $(x + 6)^{\frac{1}{2}} - (2x - 4)^{\frac{1}{2}} = 0$

Rewrite with radicals.	$\sqrt{x + 6} - \sqrt{2x - 4} = 0$
Isolate radicals on each side.	$\sqrt{x + 6} = \boxed{\sqrt{2x - 4}}$
Square both sides.	$\left(\sqrt{x + 6}\right)^2 = \left(\boxed{\sqrt{2x - 4}}\right)^2$
Simplify.	$\boxed{x + 6} = \boxed{2x - 4}$
Solve.	$\boxed{10} = x$

Check:

$\sqrt{x + 6} - \sqrt{2x - 4} = 0$

$\sqrt{10 + 6} - \sqrt{2\left(\boxed{10}\right) - 4} \stackrel{?}{=} 0$

$\boxed{\sqrt{16}} - \boxed{\sqrt{16}} \stackrel{?}{=} 0$

$\boxed{0} = 0$

The solution is $\underline{x = 10}$.

COLLABORATIVE LEARNING

Peer-to-Peer Activity

Have students work in pairs. Challenge each pair to write a radical equation that meets the following conditions.

- The solution of the equation is 6.
- The equation contains $2x$ on one side and $3x$ on the other.
- The radicand is the sum of a variable expression and a constant.

Have students then solve their equations, and identify any extraneous solutions. Have each pair share their work. **Example:** $\sqrt{2x + 4} = 3x - 14, \frac{32}{9}$

Reflect

5. Graph the solution from Part A on a graphing calculator. How can you tell from the graph that there is an extraneous solution?

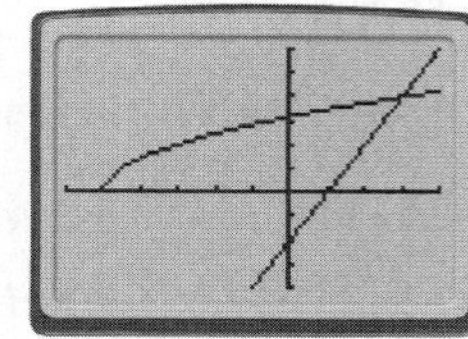

The graphs intersect at only 1 point, at the solution $x = 6$, so there is only one solution.

The graphs do not intersect at the apparent solution $x = -1$.

Your Turn

6. Solve $(x + 5)^{\frac{1}{2}} - 2 = 1$.

$$(x + 5)^{\frac{1}{2}} - 2 = 1$$
$$(x + 5)^{\frac{1}{2}} = 3$$
$$\left((x + 5)^{\frac{1}{2}}\right)^2 = 3^2$$
$$x + 5 = 9$$
$$x = 4$$

Check:

$$(4 + 5)^{\frac{1}{2}} - 2 \stackrel{?}{=} 1$$
$$3 - 2 \stackrel{?}{=} 1$$
$$1 = 1 \checkmark$$

The solution is $x = 4$.

Explain 2 Solving Cube Root and $\frac{1}{3}$-Power Equations

You can solve radical equations that involve roots other than square roots by raising both sides to the index of the radical. So, to solve a cube root equation, or, equivalently, an equation involving the power $\frac{1}{3}$, you can cube both sides of the equation and solve the resulting equation.

Example 2 **Solve the equation.**

(A) $\sqrt[3]{x + 2} + 7 = 5$

	$\sqrt[3]{x + 2} + 7 = 5$
Isolate the radical.	$\sqrt[3]{x + 2} = -2$
Cube both sides.	$\left(\sqrt[3]{x + 2}\right)^3 = (-2)^3$
Simplify.	$x + 2 = -8$
Solve for x	$x = -10$

The solution is $x = -10$.

DIFFERENTIATE INSTRUCTION

Cognitive Strategies

Students have already solved many equations by performing the same operation on both sides to isolate the variable. They also have observed how inverse operations "undo" each other. Help them to see that they will be using this same idea to solve radical equations. The only difference is that they will be adding a new operation—raising both sides of an equation to a power—and that this operation may introduce extraneous solutions.

EXPLAIN 2

Solving Cube Root and $\frac{1}{3}$-Power Equations

INTEGRATE MATHEMATICAL PRACTICES

Focus on Critical Thinking

MP.3 Discuss with students why raising both sides of an equation to an even power may produce extraneous solutions, but raising to an odd power does not. Provide an opportunity for them to better understand *why* this is so by having them square and cube both sides of the equation $x = 5$, and consider solutions of the resulting equations.

QUESTIONING STRATEGIES

If an equation contains a variable expression raised to the one-third power, can the solution process produce extraneous solutions? How do you know? **No; to solve the equation, you would need to cube both sides, and cubing both sides of an equation does not introduce the possibility of extraneous solutions.**

(B) $\sqrt[3]{x-5} = x + 1$

$$\sqrt[3]{x-5} = x + 1$$

Cube both sides. $\left(\sqrt[3]{x-5}\right)^3 = (x+1)^3$

Simplify $x - 5 = x^3 + 3x^2 + 3x + 1$

Simplify. $0 = x^3 + 3x^2 + 2x + 6$

Begin to factor by grouping. $0 = x^2\left(x + 3\right) + 2\left(x + 3\right)$

Complete factoring $0 = (x^2 + 2)\left(x + 3\right)$

By the Zero Product Property, $x^2 + 2 = 0$ or $x + 3 = 0$.

Because there are no values of x for which $x^2 = -2$, the only solution is $x = -3$.

Reflect

7. **Discussion** Part A shows checking for extraneous solutions, while Part B does not. While it is always wise to check your answers, can a cubic equation have an extraneous solution? Explain your answer.
No; while every positive number has two square roots, every number—positive or negative—has exactly one cube root. That is, the cube of every number is unique. So, when you cube both sides of an equation, you do not introduce the possibility of another number having the same cube as an actual solution.

Your Turn

8. Solve $2(x - 50)^{\frac{1}{3}} = -10.$

$$2(x-50)^{\frac{1}{3}} = -10$$
$$(x-50)^{\frac{1}{3}} = -5$$
$$\left((x-50)^{\frac{1}{3}}\right)^3 = (-5)^3$$
$$x - 50 = -125$$
$$x = -75$$

Explain 3 Solving a Real-World Problem

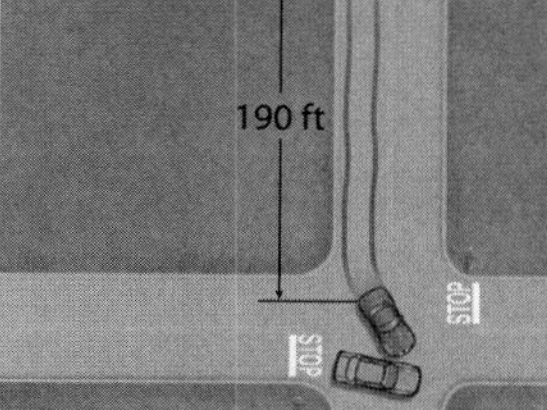

Ⓐ **Driving** The speed s in miles per hour that a car is traveling when it goes into a skid can be estimated by using the formula $s = \sqrt{30fd}$, where f is the coefficient of friction and d is the length of the skid marks in feet.

After an accident, a driver claims to have been traveling the speed limit of 55 mi/h. The coefficient of friction under the conditions at the time of the accident was 0.6, and the length of the skid marks is 190 feet. Is the driver telling the truth about the car's speed? Explain.

Use the formula to find the length of a skid at a speed of 55 mi/h. Compare this distance to the actual skid length of 190 feet.

$$s = \sqrt{30fd}$$

Substitute 55 for s and 0.6 for f $\quad 55 = \sqrt{30(0.6)d}$

Simplify. $\quad 55 = \sqrt{18d}$

Square both sides. $\quad 55^2 = \left(\sqrt{18d}\right)^2$

Simplify. $\quad 3025 = 18d$

Solve for d. $\quad 168 \approx d$

If the driver had been traveling at 55 mi/h, the skid marks would measure about 168 feet. Because the skid marks actually measure 190 feet, the driver must have been driving faster than 55 mi/h.

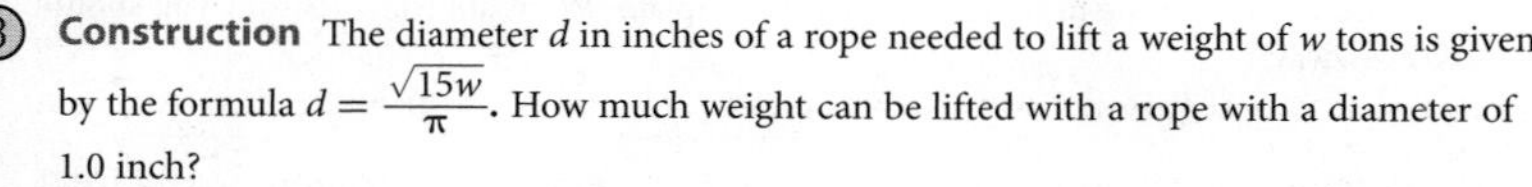

Ⓑ **Construction** The diameter d in inches of a rope needed to lift a weight of w tons is given by the formula $d = \frac{\sqrt{15w}}{\pi}$. How much weight can be lifted with a rope with a diameter of 1.0 inch?

Use the formula for the diameter as a function of weight, and solve for the weight given the diameter.

$$d = \frac{\sqrt{15w}}{\pi}$$

Substitute. $\quad \boxed{1.0} = \frac{\sqrt{15w}}{\pi}$

Square both sides. $\quad \boxed{\pi} = \boxed{\sqrt{15w}}$

Isolate the radical. $\quad \left(\boxed{\pi}\right)^2 = \left(\sqrt{15w}\right)^2$

Simplify. $\quad \boxed{\pi^2} = 15w$

Solve for w. $\quad \boxed{0.66} \approx w$

A rope with a diameter of 1.0 can hold about 0.66 ton, or about 1300 pounds.

EXPLAIN 3

Solving a Real-World Problem

QUESTIONING STRATEGIES

What are the restrictions on the variables in a square root function that models a real-world situation? **The variables in the radicand are restricted to values that make the radicand non-negative. Also, the values of the variables are restricted to values that make sense in the given context.**

INTEGRATE MATHEMATICAL PRACTICES

Focus on Modeling

MP.4 Discuss with students how each function models the given situation, explaining the relationship between the indicated variables. Help students to recognize that a model involving a square root relationship is the inverse of a model that involves a quadratic relationship.

ELABORATE

QUESTIONING STRATEGIES

If the only apparent solution of a radical equation is an extraneous solution, what will be true about the graphs of the functions represented by the expressions on each side of the equation? Explain. **The graphs will not intersect. The introduction of extraneous solutions is a consequence of algebraic manipulation. The solving of a radical equation by graphing produces only true solutions, represented by the *x*-coordinate of the point or points of intersection. If an equation has no true solution, the graphs will not intersect.**

SUMMARIZE THE LESSON

How do you solve an equation that contains a radical? **First, isolate the radical. Then raise both sides of the equation to the power equal to the index of the radical. Finally, solve the resulting equation for the variable, and check for extraneous solutions.**

Your Turn

9. **Biology** The trunk length (in inches) of a male elephant can be modeled by $l = 23\sqrt[3]{t} + 17$, where t is the age of the elephant in years. If a male elephant has a trunk length of 100 inches, about what is his age?

$$l = 23\sqrt[3]{t} + 17$$
$$100 = 23\sqrt[3]{t} + 17$$
$$83 = 23\sqrt[3]{t}$$
$$3.61 = \sqrt[3]{t}$$
$$(3.61)^3 = \left(\sqrt[3]{t}\right)^3$$
$$47 \approx t$$

The elephant is about 47 years old.

Elaborate

10. A student asked to solve the equation $\sqrt{4x+8} + 9 = 1$ isolated the radical, squared both sides, and solved for x to obtain $x = 14$, only to find out that the apparent solution was extraneous. Why could the student have stopped trying to solve the equation after isolating the radical?
Isolating the radical gives $\sqrt{4x+8} = -8$. Because the principal square root of a quantity cannot be negative, it is clear that there will be no real solution.

11. When you see a cube root equation with the radical expression isolated on one side and a constant on the other, what should you expect for the number of solutions? Explain. What are some reasons you should check your answer anyway?
There will always be one solution since there is a unique cube root for every real number. You should check your answer anyway, even though there won't be extraneous solutions, to make sure you haven't made any computational mistakes. Also, in a real-world context, you need to make sure the answer makes sense in the situation.

12. **Essential Question Check-In** Solving a quadratic equation of the form $x^2 = a$ involves taking the square root of both sides. Solving a square root equation of the form $\sqrt{x} = b$ involves squaring both sides of the equation. Which of these operations can create an equation that is not equivalent to the original equation? Explain how this affects the solution process.
Squaring both sides; squaring both sides can create an apparent solution that is not a solution of the original equation, that is, an extraneous solution. This means that you must be sure to check for extraneous solutions.

LANGUAGE SUPPORT EL

Communicate Math

Have students work in pairs to complete a table similar to the following, showing how to solve radical equations and equations with $\frac{1}{2}$ and $\frac{1}{3}$ power exponents. Have students write notes outlining the process next to each solution.

Type of equation	Solution	Notes explaining steps
Radical: square root		
Radical with $\frac{1}{2}$ power exponent		
Radical: cube root		
Radical with $\frac{1}{3}$ power exponent		

✩ Evaluate: Homework and Practice

Personal Math Trainer
- Online Homework
- Hints and Help
- Extra Practice

Solve the equation.

1. $\sqrt{x-9}=5$

$\left(\sqrt{x-9}\right)^2=5^2$

$x-9=25$

$x=34$

Check:

$\sqrt{34-9}\stackrel{?}{=}5$

$\sqrt{25}=5\checkmark$

The solution is $x=34$.

2. $\sqrt{3x}=6$

$\left(\sqrt{3x}\right)^2=6^2$

$3x=36$

$x=12$

Check:

$\sqrt{3(12)}\stackrel{?}{=}6$

$\sqrt{36}=6\checkmark$

The solution is $x=12$.

3. $\sqrt{x+3}=x+1$

$\left(\sqrt{x+3}\right)^2=(x+1)^2$

$x+3=x^2+2x+1$

$0=x^2+x-2$

$0=(x+2)(x-1)$

$x=-2$ or $x=1$

Check:

$\sqrt{-2+3}\stackrel{?}{=}-2+1$

$\sqrt{1}\neq-1\checkmark$

$\sqrt{1+3}\stackrel{?}{=}1+1$

$\sqrt{4}=2\checkmark$

The solution is $x=1$.

4. $\sqrt{(15x+10)}=2x+3$

$\left(\sqrt{15x-10}\right)^2=(2x+3)^2$

$15x+10=4x^2+12x+9$

$0=4x^2-3x-1$

$0=(4x+1)(x-1)$

$x=-\frac{1}{4}$ or $x=1$

Check:

$\sqrt{15\left(-\frac{1}{4}\right)+10}\stackrel{?}{=}2\left(-\frac{1}{4}\right)+3$

$\sqrt{\frac{25}{4}}=\frac{5}{2}\checkmark$

$\sqrt{15(1)+10}\stackrel{?}{=}2(1)+3$

$\sqrt{25}=5\checkmark$

The solution are $x=-\frac{1}{4}$ and $x=1$.

Exercise	Depth of Knowledge (D.O.K.)	COMMON CORE Mathematical Practices
1–16	1 Recall of Information	**MP.5** Using Tools
17–20	2 Skills/Concepts	**MP.4** Modeling
21	1 Recall of Information	**MP.5** Using Tools
22–24	2 Skills/Concepts H.O.T.	**MP.3** Logic
25	3 Strategic Thinking H.O.T.	**MP.3** Logic

EVALUATE

ASSIGNMENT GUIDE

Concepts and Skills	Practice
Explore Investigating Solutions of Square Root Equations	Exercises 21–22
Example 1 Solving Square-Root and $\frac{1}{2}$-Power Equations	Exercises 1–8
Example 2 Solving Cube-Root and $\frac{1}{3}$-Power Equations	Exercises 9–16
Example 3 Solving a Real-World Problem	Exercises 17–20

QUESTIONING STRATEGIES

? How do you know by which power you should raise both sides of the equation? **If it's a radical equation, raise both sides to the same power as the index. If the equation has a rational exponent, rewrite it as a radical equation, then follow the rule above.**

? How can you tell whether a solution to a radical equation is extraneous? **If the solution doesn't satisfy the original radical equation, it is extraneous.**

VISUAL CUES

Suggest that students circle or highlight the index of a radical equation so that they know to which power to raise each side of the equation when solving it. For square-root equations, have them write in the index of 2.

COMMUNICATING MATH

Have students describe how it is possible for a solution found using valid algebraic steps to not be a solution of the original equation.

5. $(x + 4)^{\frac{1}{2}} = 6$

$\left((x+4)^{\frac{1}{2}}\right)^2 = 6^2$

$x + 4 = 36$

$x = 32$

Check:

$(32 + 4)^{\frac{1}{2}} \stackrel{?}{=} 6$

$36^{\frac{1}{2}} = 6$ ✓

The solution is $x = 12$.

6. $(45 - 9x)^{\frac{1}{2}} = x - 5$

$\left((45 - 9x)^{\frac{1}{2}}\right)^2 = (x-5)^2$

$45 - 9x = x^2 - 10x + 25$

$0 = x^2 - x - 20$

$0 = (x+4)(x-5)$

$x = -4$ or $x = 5$

Check:

$(45 - 9(-4))^{\frac{1}{2}} \stackrel{?}{=} -4 - 5$

$81^{\frac{1}{2}} \neq -9$

$(45 - 9(5))^{\frac{1}{2}} \stackrel{?}{=} 5 - 5$

$0^{\frac{1}{2}} = 0$ ✓

The solution is $x = 5$.

7. $(x - 6)^{\frac{1}{2}} = x - 2$

$\left((x-6)^{\frac{1}{2}}\right)^2 = (x-2)^2$

$x - 6 = x^2 - 4x + 4$

$0 = x^2 - 5x + 10$

$x = \dfrac{-b \pm \sqrt{b^2 - 4ac}}{2a}$

$= \dfrac{5 \pm \sqrt{(-5)^2 - 4(1)(10)}}{2(1)}$

$= \dfrac{5 \pm \sqrt{-15}}{2}$

The discriminant is negative. There are no real solutions.

8. $4(x - 2)^{\frac{1}{2}} = (x + 13)^{\frac{1}{2}}$

$\left(4(x-2)^{\frac{1}{2}}\right)^2 = \left((x+13)^{\frac{1}{2}}\right)^2$

$4^2 \cdot (x - 2) = x + 13$

$16x - 32 = x + 13$

$15x = 45$

$x = 3$

Check:

$4(3 - 2)^{\frac{1}{2}} \stackrel{?}{=} (3 + 13)^{\frac{1}{2}}$

$4 \cdot 1^{\frac{1}{2}} \stackrel{?}{=} 16^{\frac{1}{2}}$

$4 = 4$

The solution is $x = 3$.

9. $5 - \sqrt[3]{x-4} = 2$

$5 - \sqrt[3]{x-4} = 2$

$-\sqrt[3]{x-4} = -3$

$\sqrt[3]{x-4} = 3$

$\left(\sqrt[3]{x-4}\right)^3 = 3^3$

$x - 4 = 27$

$x = 31$

10. $2\sqrt[3]{3x+2} = \sqrt[3]{4x-9}$

$2\sqrt[3]{3x+2} = \sqrt[3]{4x-9}$

$\left(2\sqrt[3]{3x+2}\right)^3 = \left(\sqrt[3]{4x-9}\right)^3$

$2^3(3x+2) = 4x - 9$

$24x + 16 = 4x - 9$

$20x = -25$

$x = -\dfrac{5}{4}$

11. $\sqrt[3]{69x + 35} = x + 5$

$$\left(\sqrt[3]{69x+35}\right)^3 = (x+5)^3$$
$$69x + 35 = (x^2 + 10x + 25)(x + 5)$$
$$69x + 35 = x^3 + 15x^2 + 75x + 125$$
$$0 = x^3 + 15x^2 + 6x + 90$$
$$0 = x^2(x + 15) + 6(x + 15)$$
$$0 = (x^2 + 6)(x + 15)$$

Because there are no values of x for which $x^2 = -6$, the only solution $x = -15$.

12. $\sqrt[3]{x + 5} = x - 1$

$$\left(\sqrt[3]{x+5}\right)^3 = (x-1)^3$$
$$x + 5 = (x^2 - 2x + 1)(x - 1)$$
$$x + 5 = x^3 - x^2 - 2x^2 + 2x + x - 1$$
$$x + 5 = x^3 - 3x^2 + 3x - 1$$
$$0 = x^3 - 3x^2 + 2x - 6$$
$$0 = x^2(x - 3) + 2(x - 3)$$
$$0 = (x^2 + 2)(x - 3)$$

Because there are no values of x for which $x^2 = -2$, the only solution is $x = 3$.

13. $(x + 7)^{\frac{1}{3}} = (4x)^{\frac{1}{3}}$

$$\left((x+7)^{\frac{1}{3}}\right)^3 = \left((4x)^{\frac{1}{3}}\right)^3$$
$$x + 7 = 4x$$
$$7 = 3x$$
$$\frac{7}{3} = x$$

14. $(5x + 1)^{\frac{1}{4}} = 4$

$$\left((5x+1)^{\frac{1}{4}}\right)^4 = 4^4$$
$$5x + 1 = 256$$
$$5x = 255$$
$$x = 51$$

Check:

$$\left(5(51) + 1\right)^{\frac{1}{4}} \stackrel{?}{=} 4$$
$$256^{\frac{1}{4}} = 4 \checkmark$$

The solution is $x = 51$.

15. $(-9x - 54)^{\frac{1}{3}} = -2x + 3$

$$\left((-9x-54)^{\frac{1}{3}}\right)^3 = (-2x+3)^3$$
$$-9x - 54 = (4x^2 - 6x + 9)(-2x + 3)$$
$$-9x - 54 = -8x^3 + 24x^2 - 36x + 27$$
$$0 = -8x^3 + 24x^2 - 27x + 81$$
$$0 = -8x^2(x - 3) - 27(x - 3)$$
$$0 = (-8x^2 - 27)(x - 3)$$
$$0 = (8x^2 + 27)(x - 3)$$

Because there are no values of x for which $8x^2 = -27$, the only solution is $x = 3$.

16. $2(x - 1)^{\frac{1}{5}} = (2x - 17)^{\frac{1}{5}}$

$$\left(2(x-1)^{\frac{1}{5}}\right)^5 = \left((2x-17)^{\frac{1}{5}}\right)^5$$
$$2^5(x - 1) = 2x - 17$$
$$32x - 32 = 2x - 17$$
$$30x = 15$$
$$x = \frac{1}{2}$$

QUESTIONING STRATEGIES

How could you use a graphing calculator to solve an equation such as $\sqrt{3 - 2x} = 5 - \sqrt{1 - x}$? **You could enter the left side of the equation as Y1 and the right side as Y2, graph the two functions, and find the x-coordinate of the point of intersection. You could also use the TABLE feature to find the x-value that produces the same y-value for the two functions.**

AVOID COMMON ERRORS

Some students believe that if a radical equation has two apparent solutions, one of them must be extraneous. To reinforce that this is not the case, have them solve the equation $\sqrt{5x - 14} = x - 2$ by graphing the functions defined by each side of the equation, and observing that their graphs intersect in two points. The solutions of the equation are the x-coordinates of these points, $x = 3$ and $x = 6$.

INTEGRATE MATHEMATICAL PRACTICES

Focus on Reasoning

MP.2 Ask students to consider the equation $\sqrt{3x - 5} = -2$, and how it is possible to know, without solving the equation, that it has no solution. Lead them to recognize that this is because the principal square root of a number is never negative; therefore, no value of x will satisfy the equation. Then have students solve the equation, both algebraically and graphically, and discuss their results.

17. **Driving** The formula for the speed versus skid length in Example 3A assumes that all 4 wheel brakes are working at top efficiency. If this is not true, another parameter is included in the equation so that the equation becomes $s = \sqrt{30fdn}$ where n is the percent braking efficiency as a decimal. Accident investigators know that the rear brakes failed on a car, reducing its braking efficiency to 60%. On a dry road with a coefficient of friction of 0.7, the car skidded 250 feet. Was the car going above the speed limit of 60 mi/h when the skid began?

Find the skid length at 60 mi/h.

$$s = \sqrt{30fdn}$$
$$60 = \sqrt{30(0.7)d(0.6)}$$
$$60 = \sqrt{12.6d}$$
$$60^2 = \left(\sqrt{12.6d}\right)^2$$
$$3600 = 12.6d$$
$$286 \approx d$$

Because expected skid length under the conditions is 286 feet, and the actual skid distance was 250 feet, the car was not exceeding the speed limit when the skid began.

18. **Anatomy** The surface area S of a human body in square meters can be approximated by $S = \sqrt{\frac{hm}{36}}$ where h is height in meters and m is mass in kilograms. A basketball player with a height of 2.1 meters has a surface area of about 2.7 m^2. What is the player's mass?

$$s = \sqrt{\frac{hm}{36}}$$
$$2.7 = \sqrt{\frac{2.1m}{36}}$$
$$2.7^2 = \left(\sqrt{\frac{2.1m}{36}}\right)^2$$
$$7.29 = \frac{2.1m}{36}$$
$$7.29\left(\frac{36}{2.1}\right) = m$$
$$125 \approx m$$

The player has a mass of about 125 kg.

19. **Biology** The approximate antler length L (in inches) of a deer buck can be modeled by $L = 9\sqrt[3]{t} + 15$ where t is the age in years of the buck. If a buck has an antler length of 36 inches, what is its age?

$L = 9\sqrt[3]{t} + 15$

$36 = 9\sqrt[3]{t} + 15$

$21 = 9\sqrt[3]{t}$

$\frac{7}{3} = \sqrt[3]{t}$

$\left(\frac{7}{3}\right)^3 = \left(\sqrt[3]{t}\right)^3$

$12.7 \approx t$

The buck is about 13 years old.

20. **Amusement Parks** For a spinning amusement park ride, the velocity v in meters per second of a car moving around a curve with radius r meters is given by $v = \sqrt{ar}$ where a is the car's acceleration in m/s^2. If the ride has a maximum acceleration of 30 m/s^2 and the cars on the ride have a maximum velocity of 12 m/s, what is the smallest radius that any curve on the ride may have?

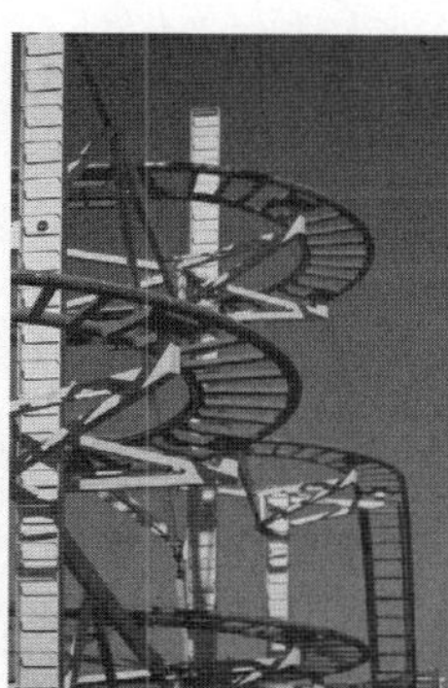

$v = \sqrt{ar}$

$12 = \sqrt{30r}$

$12^2 = \left(\sqrt{30r}\right)^2$

$144 = 30r$

$4.8 = r$

The smallest radius that any curve on the ride may have is about 4.8 meters.

21. For each radical equation, state the number of solutions that exist.

A. $\sqrt{x - 4} = -5$ **No solutions**

B. $\sqrt{x - 4} + 6 = 11$ **One solution**

C. $4 = -2\sqrt[3]{x + 2}$ **One solution**

D. $\sqrt{x + 40} = 0$ **One solution**

E. $\sqrt[3]{2x + 5} = -18$ **One solution**

INTEGRATE MATHEMATICAL PRACTICES

Focus on Reasoning

MP.2 Ask students to generalize what they've learned about the solving of equations containing square roots and cube roots to the solving of equations containing roots with other indices. Then ask them to consider how they might apply these ideas to the solving of equations containing variable expressions raised to rational exponents. For both types of equations, have students discuss when the possibility of extraneous solutions would exist.

CRITICAL THINKING

Challenge students to solve the equation $\sqrt[3]{2x} - \sqrt{3x} = 0$ algebraically. The equation can be solved by adding $\sqrt{3x}$ to both sides of the equation, cubing both sides of the resulting equation, and then squaring both sides of that resulting equation. The solutions are $x = 0$ and $x = \frac{4}{27}$.

JOURNAL

Have students describe how inverse operations are used to solve radical equations.

H.O.T. Focus on Higher Order Thinking

22. Critical Thinking For an equation of the form $\sqrt{x + a} = b$ where b is a constant, does the sign of a affect whether or not there is a solution for a given value of b? If so, how? If not, why not?

No; if you think of the graph of each side of the equation, the value of a just indicates a horizontal shift of the graph of the square root function and does not affect its range. So, it will not affect whether or not its graph and the graph of $y = b$ intersect.

23. Explain the Error Below is a student's work in solving the equation $2\sqrt{3x + 3} = 12$. What mistake did the student make? What is the correct solution?

$$2\sqrt{3x + 3} = 12$$
$$2\left(\sqrt{3x + 3}\right)^2 = 12^2$$
$$2(3x + 3) = 144$$
$$6x + 6 = 144$$
$$x = 23$$

When the student squared both sides, the coefficient 2 should also have been squared:

$$2\sqrt{3x + 3} = 12$$
$$\left(2\sqrt{3x + 3}\right)^2 = 12^2$$
$$4(3x + 3) = 144$$
$$12x + 12 = 144$$
$$12x = 132$$
$$x = 11$$

24. Communicate Mathematical Ideas Describe the key difference between solving radical equations for which you solve by raising both sides to an even power and those you solve by raising both sides to an odd power.

Odd roots can be found for all values of the radicand, positive or negative, but even roots can only be found when the radicand is nonnegative. This means that raising both sides to an odd power will not introduce any extraneous solutions, since every cube is unique. But raising both sides to an even power may introduce extraneous solutions, since even powers of opposites are the same.

25. Critical Thinking How could you solve an equation for which one side is a rational power radical expression and the other side is a constant? Give an example. Under what condition would you have to be especially careful to check your solutions?

Possible answer: One way is to raise both sides to the reciprocal power. For example, to solve $(2x - 3)^{\frac{3}{5}} = 8$, raise both sides to the $\frac{5}{3}$ power to obtain $2x - 3 = 32$, which has the solution $x = 17.5$. You would need to be especially careful when the denominator of the power is even, indicating an even root.

Lesson Performance Task

For many years scientists have used a scale known as the Fujita Scale to categorize different types of tornados in relation to the velocity of the winds produced. The formula used to generate the scale is given by $V = k(F + 2)^{\frac{3}{2}}$. The scale employs a constant, k, and the tornado's category number to determine wind speed. If you wanted to determine the different category numbers, how could you solve the radical equation for the variable F? (The value for k is about 14.1.) Solve the equation for F then verify the different categories using the minimum wind velocity. Do the values seem reasonable given the value for k?

Fujita Tornado Scale

Damage Level	Category	Minimum Wind Velocity (mi/h)	Calculations
Moderate	F1	73	$F = \sqrt[3]{\frac{73^2}{14.1^2}} - 2 \approx .9927$
Significant	F2	113	$F = \sqrt[3]{\frac{113^2}{14.1^2}} - 2 \approx 2.0047$
Severe	F3	158	$F = \sqrt[3]{\frac{158^2}{14.1^2}} - 2 \approx 3.0076$
Devastating	F4	207	$F = \sqrt[3]{\frac{207^2}{14.1^2}} - 2 \approx 3.9956$
Incredible	F5	261	$F = \sqrt[3]{\frac{261^2}{14.1^2}} - 2 \approx 4.9976$

$$V = k(F + 2)^{\frac{3}{2}}$$
$$V = 14.1(F + 2)^{\frac{3}{2}}$$
$$\frac{V}{14.1} = \frac{14.1(F + 2)^{\frac{3}{2}}}{14.1}$$
$$\frac{V}{14.1} = (F + 2)^{\frac{3}{2}}$$
$$\left(\frac{V}{14.1}\right)^2 = (F + 2)^{\left(\frac{3}{2}\right)2}$$
$$\frac{V^2}{14.1^2} = (F + 2)^3$$
$$\sqrt[3]{\frac{V^2}{14.1^2}} = \sqrt[3]{(F + 2)^3}$$
$$\sqrt[3]{\frac{V^2}{14.1^2}} = F + 2$$
$$\sqrt{\frac{V^2}{14.1^2}} - 2 = F$$

The values seem reasonable for the given value of *k*.

EXTENSION ACTIVITY

Have students research the equation relating wind velocity to the Beaufort scale number, a measure of wind speed covering a broad range of phenomena, including tornadoes. Have students solve the equation for the Beaufort number, and then calculate the Beaufort number for the minimum wind velocities of each category of the Fujita scale. Have students discuss the relation between the Beaufort and Fujita scales.

AVOID COMMON ERRORS

Some students may distribute the exponent to all terms in a set of parentheses. For example, students may want to write $V = k(F + 2)^{\frac{3}{2}}$ as $V = k\left(F^{\frac{3}{2}} + 2^{\frac{3}{2}}\right)$ in order to isolate F. Instead, explain to students that they need to raise both sides of the equation to the reciprocal of the exponent:
$$V^{\frac{2}{3}} = \left(k(F + 2)^{\frac{3}{2}}\right)^{\frac{2}{3}} = k^{\frac{2}{3}}(F + 2)$$

INTEGRATE MATHEMATICAL PRACTICES

Focus on Reasoning

MP.2 Have students discuss whether a linear wind scale would be more useful than a nonlinear one. Have students explain how they would compare tornadoes based on their Fujita numbers. Have students discuss the challenges of designing a scale for tornado strength.

Scoring Rubric

2 points: Student correctly solves the problem and explains his/her reasoning.

1 point: Student shows good understanding of the problem but does not fully solve or explain his/her reasoning.

0 points: Student does not demonstrate understanding of the problem.

Study Guide Review

ASSESSMENT AND INTERVENTION

Assign or customize module reviews.

MODULE PERFORMANCE TASK

Mathematical Practices: MP.1, MP.2, MP.4, MP.6
A-REI.A.2, A-CED.A.4

SUPPORTING STUDENT REASONING

Students should begin by finding the formula that relates sound intensity, power wattage, and distance. They can research this, or you can provide them with specific information. Here is some of the information they may ask for:

- **What is the formula for the sound intensity with regard to distance from the sound source?** $I = \frac{P}{4\pi d^2}$, where I represents the intensity, P represents the power in watts, and d represents the distance from the power source.
- **Is the power the same as the intensity?** The power is the constant wattage at the source of the sound, and the intensity is what the ear can hear at a certain distance from the source.

Radical Expressions and Equations

Essential Question: How can you use radical expressions and equations to solve real-world problems?

Key Vocabulary
extraneous solution (*solución extraña*)
radical expression (*expresión radical*)
rational exponent (*exponente racional*)

KEY EXAMPLE *(Lesson 11.1)*

Evaluate the expression.

$\left(\sqrt[4]{16}\right)^5 = 2^5 = 32$

$27^{\frac{4}{3}} = \left(\sqrt[3]{27}\right)^4 = 3^4 = 81$

KEY EXAMPLE *(Lesson 11.2)*

Write the expression in simplest form. Assume all variables are positive.

$\sqrt[3]{48} = \sqrt[3]{8 \cdot 6}$	Factor out a perfect cube.
$= \sqrt[3]{8} \cdot \sqrt[3]{6}$	Apply the Product Property of Radicals.
$= 2\sqrt[3]{6}$	Evaluate.
$\left(\frac{x^4}{y^8}\right)^{\frac{1}{2}} = \frac{(x^4)^{\frac{1}{2}}}{(y^8)^{\frac{1}{2}}}$	Apply the Power of a Quotient Property.
$= \frac{x^{4 \cdot \frac{1}{2}}}{y^{8 \cdot \frac{1}{2}}}$	Apply the Power of a Power Property.
$= \frac{x^2}{y^4}$	Simplify.

KEY EXAMPLE *(Lesson 11.3)*

Solve the equation. $\sqrt{x+15} = x - 5$

$\left(\sqrt{x+15}\right)^2 = (x-5)^2$	Square both sides.
$x + 15 = x^2 - 10x + 25$	
$x^2 - 11x + 10 = 0$	Write in standard form.
$(x-10)(x-1) = 0$	Factor.
$x = 10$ or $x = 1$	Solve for x.
$\sqrt{10+15} \stackrel{?}{=} 10 - 5$ $\sqrt{1+15} \stackrel{?}{=} 1 - 5$	Check.
$5 = 5$ $4 \neq -4$	

The solution $x = 1$ is extraneous. The only solution is $x = 10$.

SCAFFOLDING SUPPORT

- Challenge interested students to find the “elegant” solution, the one that requires the least amount of effort.
- For students needing more support, you may want to provide the formula along with the problem.
- Watch for students who substitute the intensity for P and the watts for I.

EXERCISES

Evaluate the expression. *(Lesson 11.1)*

1. $\sqrt[3]{-64}$

   -4

2. $81^{\frac{1}{4}}$

   3

3. $256^{\frac{3}{4}}$

   64

Write the expression in simplest form. Assume that all variables are positive. *(Lesson 11.2)*

4. $\sqrt[3]{80}$

   $2\sqrt[3]{10}$

5. $(3^4 \cdot 5^4)^{-\frac{1}{4}}$

   $\frac{1}{15}$

6. $(25a^{10}b^{16})^{\frac{1}{2}}$

   $5a^5b^8$

7. $\sqrt[5]{\frac{c}{d^8}}$

   $\frac{\sqrt[5]{cd^2}}{d^2}$

Solve each equation. *(Lesson 11.3)*

8. $\sqrt[3]{5x - 4} = 2$

   $\frac{12}{5}$

9. $\sqrt{x + 6} - 7 = -2$

   19

MODULE PERFORMANCE TASK

Don't Disturb the Neighbors!

The faintest sound an average person can detect has an intensity of 1×10^{-12} watts per square meter, where watts are a unit of power. The intensity of a sound is given by $I = \frac{P}{4\pi d^2}$, where P is the power of the sound and d is the distance from the source. Yolanda wants to throw a party at her house and plans to invite a band to perform. The power of the sound from the band's speakers is typically 3.0 watts. Yolanda's neighborhood has a rule that between 7 p.m. and 11 p.m., a sound intensity up to $I = 5.0 \times 10^{-5}$ W/m² is acceptable; after 11 p.m., the acceptable intensity is $I = 5.0 \times 10^{-7}$ W/m². How far away would Yolanda's closest neighbors need to be for the band to play till 11 p.m.? How far would they need to be for the band to play all night?

Start by listing in the space below the information you will need to solve the problem. Then use your own paper to complete the task. Be sure to write down all your data and assumptions. Then use graphs, numbers, words, or algebra to explain how you reached your conclusion.

DISCUSSION OPPORTUNITIES

- Ask students about the benefits and disadvantages of having noise restrictions within a community. Consider the standpoints of party-givers, neighbors, and law enforcement.
- Ask students about the reasonableness of this neighborhood's noise restriction. Under what circumstances might it be too strict or too lenient?

SAMPLE SOLUTION

Solve $I = \frac{P}{4\pi d^2}$ for d.

$$d^2 = \frac{P}{4\pi I}$$

$$d = \sqrt{\frac{P}{4\pi I}}$$

For 7 to 11 p.m., $I = 5.0 \times 10^{-5}$ and $P = 3$.

$$\text{So, } d = \sqrt{\frac{3}{4\pi \cdot 5 \times 10^{-5}}} = \sqrt{\frac{3 \times 10^5}{20\pi}}$$

$$\approx 69.1 \text{ m}$$

For after 11 p.m., $I = 5.0 \times 10^{-7}$ and $P = 3$.

$$d = \sqrt{\frac{3}{4\pi \cdot 5 \times 10^{-7}}} = \sqrt{\frac{3 \times 10^7}{20\pi}}$$

$$\approx 691.8 \text{ m}$$

Before 11 p.m., the nearest neighbor should be no closer than 69.1 m. After 11 p.m., the nearest neighbor should be no closer than 691.8 m.

Assessment Rubric

2 points: Student correctly solves the problem and explains his/her reasoning.

1 point: Student shows good understanding of the problem but does not fully solve or explain.

0 points: Student does not demonstrate understanding of the problem.

Ready to Go On?

ASSESS MASTERY

Use the assessment on this page to determine if students have mastered the concepts and standards covered in this module.

ASSESSMENT AND INTERVENTION

Access Ready to Go On? assessment online, and receive instant scoring, feedback, and customized intervention or enrichment.

ADDITIONAL RESOURCES

Response to Intervention Resources

- Reteach Worksheets

Differentiated Instruction Resources

- Reading Strategies EL
- Success for English Learners EL
- Challenge Worksheets

Assessment Resources

- Leveled Module Quizzes

11.1–11.3 Radical Expressions and Equations

- Online Homework
- Hints and Help
- Extra Practice

Simplify each expression. Assume that all variables are positive. *(Lessons 11.1, 11.2)*

1. $32^{\frac{1}{5}}$

2

2. $\left(\sqrt[3]{64}\right)^4$

256

3. $\sqrt[3]{27x^6}$

$\mathbf{3x^2}$

4. $\sqrt[4]{2x^6y^8}$

$\mathbf{xy^2\sqrt[4]{2x^2}}$

Solve each equation. *(Lesson 11.3)*

5. $\sqrt{10x} = 3\sqrt{x+1}$

9

6. $\sqrt[3]{2x-2} = 6$

109

7. $(4x+7)^{\frac{1}{2}} = 3$

0.5

8. $(x+3)^{\frac{1}{3}} = -6$

−219

ESSENTIAL QUESTION

9. How do you solve a radical equation and identify any extraneous roots?

Possible Answer: Raise both sides of the equation to the power that will make the variable have a whole number exponent. Then solve the polynomial equation. Use substitution to check for extraneous roots.

COMMON CORE Common Core Standards

Lesson	Items	Content Standards	Mathematical Practices
11.1, 11.2	1	**N-RN.A.1, N-RN.A.2**	**MP.2**
11.1, 11.2	2	**N-RN.A.1, N-RN.A.2**	**MP.2**
11.1, 11.2	3	**N-RN.A.1, N-RN.A.2**	**MP.2**
11.1, 11.2	4	**N-RN.A.1, N-RN.A.2**	**MP.2**
11.3	5–8	**A-REI.A.2**	**MP.2**

MODULE 11
MIXED REVIEW

Assessment Readiness

1. Look at each expression. Can the expression be simplified to a rational number? Select Yes or No for A–C.
   - **A.** $\sqrt{2} + \sqrt{2}$ ○ Yes ● No
   - **B.** $\sqrt{4} \cdot \sqrt{20}$ ○ Yes ● No
   - **C.** $(\sqrt{12})^2$ ● Yes ○ No

2. Consider the function $f(x) = \frac{2x^2 - 5x - 3}{x - 3}$. Choose True or False for each statement.
   - **A.** This function looks like a straight line when graphed. ● True ○ False
   - **B.** There is a hole in this function at $(3, 7)$. ● True ○ False
   - **C.** There is a hole in this function at $(-0.5, 0)$. ○ True ● False

3. Explain how to find the product of $(4 - 3i)(2 - i)$, then state the product.

   Possible answer: Using the FOIL method, every term can be multiplied, which gives $8 - 4i - 6i + 3i^2$ after combining like terms, and considering that $i^2 = -1$, the final answer is $5 - 10i$.

   $8 - 4i - 6i + 3i^2$

   $8 - 10i + 3(-1)$

   $8 - 10i - 3$

   $5 - 10i$

4. The formula $s = \sqrt{\frac{A}{4.828}}$ can be used to approximate the side length s of a regular octagon with area A. A stop sign is shaped like a regular octagon with a side length of 12.4 in. To the nearest square inch, what is the area of the stop sign? Explain how you got your answer.

   742 in²: Substitute $s = 12.4$ in the formula and solve:

   $$12.4 = \sqrt{\frac{A}{4.828}}$$

   $$153.76 = \frac{A}{4.828}$$

   $$A \approx 742$$

COMMON CORE Common Core Standards

Lesson	Items	Content Standards	Mathematical Practices
11.1	1	N-RN.A.1	MP.1
8.1, 8.2	2*	F-BF.B.3, F-IF.C.7d	MP.2
3.2	3*	N-CN.A.1, N-CN.A.2	MP.6
11.3	4	A-REI.A.2	MP.4

* Item integrates mixed review concepts from previous modules or a previous course.

MIXED REVIEW

Assessment Readiness

ASSESSMENT AND INTERVENTION

Assign ready-made or customized practice tests to prepare students for high-stakes tests.

ADDITIONAL RESOURCES

Assessment Resources

- Leveled Module Quizzes: Modified, B

AVOID COMMON ERRORS

Item 3 Some students will forget that $i^2 = -1$, and they will instead treat i like a variable. Remind students that i is not a variable but the imaginary unit.

UNIT 5

MIXED REVIEW

Assessment Readiness

ASSESSMENT AND INTERVENTION

Assign ready-made or customized practice tests to prepare students for high-stakes tests.

ADDITIONAL RESOURCES

Assessment Resources

- Leveled Unit Tests: Modified, A, B, C
- Performance Assessment

AVOID COMMON ERRORS

Item 4 Some students will have trouble solving these by hand, as they will find cube roots difficult to work with. Remind students that, as long as parentheses are used properly, these can be evaluated using a graphing calculator.

UNIT 5 MIXED REVIEW

Assessment Readiness

Personal Math Trainer

- Online Homework
- Hints and Help
- Extra Practice

1. Consider the graph of $g(x) = \frac{1}{3}\sqrt{x-1}$ as related to the graph of $f(x) = \sqrt{x}$. Select True or False for each statement.

A. $g(x)$ is a vertical stretching by a factor of $\frac{1}{3}$ and a translation of 1 unit up from $f(x)$. ○ True ● False

B. $g(x)$ is a vertical compression by a factor of $\frac{1}{3}$ and a translation 1 unit right from $f(x)$. ● True ○ False

C. $g(x)$ is a vertical compression by a factor of $\frac{1}{3}$ and a translation 1 unit left from $f(x)$. ○ True ● False

2. Consider each transformation in relation to $f(x) = \sqrt[3]{x}$. Select True or False for each statement.

A. $g(x) = 5\sqrt[3]{x+1} - 2$ is a transformation of $f(x)$ by a vertical stretch by a factor of 5 and a translation 1 unit left and 2 units down. ● True ○ False

B. $g(x) = 5\sqrt[3]{x-1} + 2$ is a transformation of $f(x)$ by a horizontal stretch by a factor of 5 and a translation of 1 unit left and 2 units down. ○ True ● False

C. $g(x) = \frac{1}{5}\sqrt[3]{x+1} - 2$ is a transformation of $f(x)$ by a horizontal stretch by a factor of $\frac{1}{5}$ and a translation of 1 unit left and 2 units down. ● True ○ False

3. Consider each equation. Is the equation the inverse of $f(x) = \frac{1}{2}x^3 + 5$? Choose Yes or No for A–C.

A. $f^{-1}(x) = \sqrt[3]{2(x-5)}$ ● Yes ○ No

B. $f^{-1}(x) = \sqrt[3]{2(x+5)}$ ○ Yes ● No

C. $f^{-1}(x) = \sqrt[3]{\frac{1}{2}(x-5)}$ ○ Yes ● No

4. Consider each expression. Can the expression be simplified to 25? Choose Yes or No for A–C.

A. $\left(\sqrt[2]{125}\right)^3$ ○ Yes ● No

B. $\left(\sqrt[3]{125}\right)^2$ ● Yes ○ No

C. $\left(\sqrt{125}\right)^{\frac{1}{3}}$ ○ Yes ● No

COMMON CORE Common Core Standards

Items	Content Standards	Mathematical Practices
1	**F-IF.C.7**	**MP.7**
2	**F-IF.C.7**	**MP.6**
3*	**F-BF.B.4**	**MP.1**
4	**N-RN.A.1**	**MP.1**
5*	**A-REI.A.2, F-BF.A.4**	**MP.4**
6	**A-REI.A.2**	**MP.6**
7	**N-RN.A.2**	**MP.3**

* Item integrates mixed review concepts from previous modules or a previous course.

5. A company produces canned tomatoes. They want the height h of each can to be twice the diameter d. Write an equation for the surface area A of the can in terms of the radius r. If the company wants to use no more than 90 square inches of metal for each can, what is the maximum radius of the can they will produce?

$A = 10\pi r^2$; Solve for the inverse function: $r = \sqrt{\frac{A}{10\pi}}$. The maximum radius is $r = \sqrt{\frac{90}{10\pi}} \approx 1.7$ inches.

6. The period T of a pendulum in seconds is given by $T = 2\pi\sqrt{\frac{L}{9.81}}$, where L is the length of the pendulum in meters. If you want to use a pendulum as a clock, with a period of 2 seconds, how long should the pendulum be?

Approximately 1 meter.

Solve for L in terms of T: $L = 9.81\left(\frac{T}{2\pi}\right)^2$. Then substitute for T:

$L = 9.81\left(\frac{2}{2\pi}\right)^2 \approx 1$ meter

7. Tandra says that $\sqrt[3]{\frac{8x^6}{y}}$ can be simplified to $\frac{2x^2}{\sqrt[3]{y}}$. Elizabeth says that $\sqrt[3]{\frac{6x^6}{y}}$ can be simplified to $\frac{2x^2}{\sqrt[3]{y}}$. Who is correct, or are they both correct? Explain.

Tandra is correct, and Elizabeth is incorrect; $\sqrt[3]{6} \approx 1.82$, not 2. The rest of the expression is fine.

Performance Tasks

★ 8. The formula $P = 73.3\sqrt[4]{m^3}$, known as Kleiber's law, relates the metabolism rate P of an organism in Calories per day and the body mass m of the organism in kilograms. The table shows the typical body mass of several members of the cat family.

Typical Body Mass	
Animal	**Mass(kg)**
House cat	4.5
Cheetah	55.0
Lion	170.0

A. What is the metabolism rate of a cheetah to the nearest Calorie per day?

B. Approximately how many more Calories of food does a lion need to consume each day than a house cat does?

A. 1480 Cal/day

B. 3224 Cal

PERFORMANCE TASKS

There are three different levels of performance tasks:

* **Novice:** These are short word problems that require students to apply the math they have learned in straightforward, real-world situations.

** **Apprentice:** These are more involved problems that guide students step-by-step through more complex tasks. These exercises include more complicated reasoning, writing, and open ended elements.

*****Expert:** These are open-ended, nonroutine problems that, instead of stepping the students through, ask them to choose their own methods for solving and justify their answers and reasoning.

SCORING GUIDES

Item 8 (2 points)

a. 1 point for correct metabolism rate

b. 1 point for correct difference

SCORING GUIDES

Item 9 (6 points)

a. 2 points for correct answer

b. 2 points for correct difference

c. 2 points for correct time

Item 10 (6 points)

a. 2 points for correct graph
1 point for correct parent function

b. 2 points for correct description

c. 1 point for correct answer

★★ **9.** On a clear day, the approximate distance d in miles that a person can see is given by $d = 1.2116\sqrt{h}$, where h is the person's height in feet above the ocean.

A. To the nearest tenth of a mile, how far can the captain on a clipper ship 15 feet above the ocean see?

B. How much farther, to the nearest tenth of a mile, will a sailor at the top of a mast 120 feet above the ocean be able to see than will the captain?

C. A pirate ship is approaching the clipper ship at a relative speed of 10 miles per hour. Approximately how many minutes sooner will the sailor be able to see the pirate ship than will the captain?

A. 4.7 mi

B. 8.6 mi farther

C. about 52 min sooner

★★★**10.** The time it takes a pendulum to make one complete swing back and forth depends on its string length, as shown in the table.

String Length (m)	2	4	6	8	10
Time (s)	2.8	4.0	4.9	5.7	6.3

A. Graph the relationship between string length and time, and identify the parent function which best describes the data.

B. The function $T(x) = 2\pi\sqrt{\frac{x}{9.8}}$ gives the period in seconds of a pendulum of length x. The period of a pendulum is the time it takes the pendulum to complete one back-and-forth swing. Describe the graph of T as a transformation of $f(x) = \sqrt{x}$.

C. By what factor must the length of a pendulum be increased to double its period?

A.

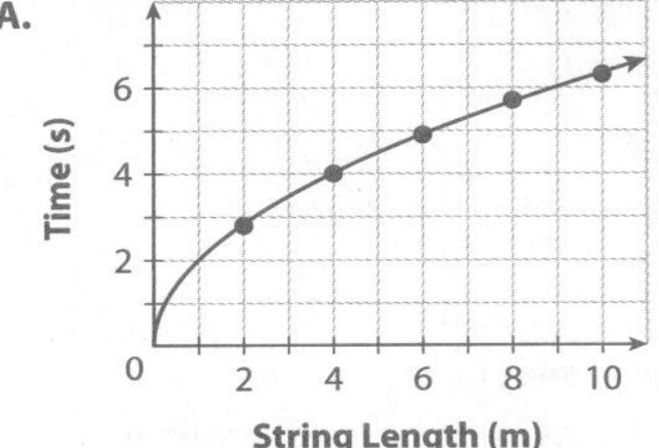

square root function

B. Possible answer: The graph of *T* is a vertical stretch of the graph of *f* by a factor of 2π and a horizontal stretch of the graph of *f* by a factor of 9.8.

C. by a factor of 4

MATH IN CAREERS

Nutritionist Body mass index (BMI) is a measure used to determine healthy body mass based on a person's height. BMI is calculated by dividing a person's mass in kilograms by the square of his or her height in meters. The median BMI measures for a group of boys, ages 2 to 10 years are given in the chart below.

Age of Boys	2	3	4	5	6	7	8	9	10
Median BMI	16.6	16.0	15.6	15.4	15.4	15.5	15.8	16.2	16.6

a. Create a scatter plot for the data in the table, treating age as the independent variable x and median BMI as the dependent variable y.

b. Use a calculator to find a quadratic regression model for the data. What is your model?

c. Give the domain of $f(x)$ based on the data set. Because $f(x)$ is quadratic, it is not one-to-one and its inverse is not a function. Restrict the domain of $f(x)$ to values of x for which $f(x)$ is increasing so that its inverse will be a function. What is the restricted domain of $f(x)$?

d. Find and graph the inverse of $f(x)$. What does $f^{-1}(x)$ model?

a.

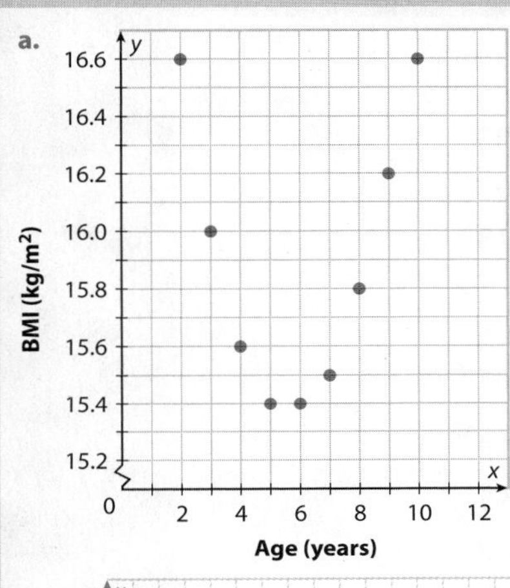

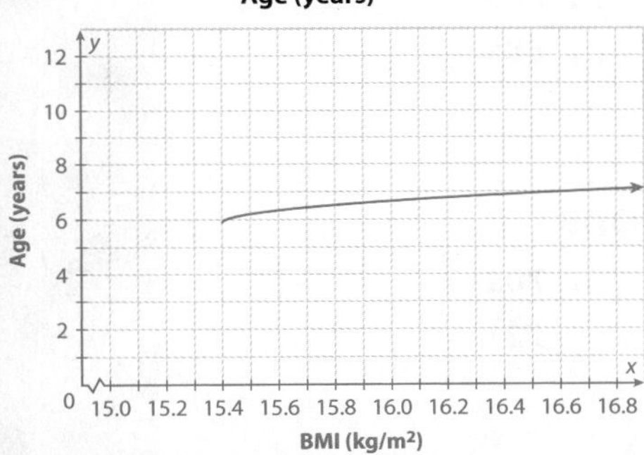

b. $f(x) = 0.0763x^2 - 0.897x + 18.0$

c. domain: $\{x \mid 2 \le x \le 10\}$

restricted domain: $\{x \mid 5.88 \le x \le 10\}$

d. $f^{-1}(x) = \sqrt{x - 15.4} + 5.88$

The inverse function models a boy's age as a function of median BMI.

MATH IN CAREERS

Nutritionist In this Unit Performance Task, students can see how a nutritionist uses mathematics on the job.

For more information about careers in mathematics as well as various mathematics appreciation topics, visit the American Mathematical Society http://www.ams.org

SCORING GUIDES

Task (6 points)

a. 1 point for correct scatter plot

b. 1 point for correct model

c. 1 point for correct original domain
1 point for correct restricted domain

d. 1 point for correct inverse and graph
1 point for correct description

Exponential and Logarithmic Functions and Equations

CONTENTS

Unit Pacing Guide

45-Minute Classes

Module 12

DAY 1	DAY 2	DAY 3	DAY 4	DAY 5
Lesson 12.1	Lesson 12.1	Lesson 12.2	Lesson 12.2	Lesson 12.3
DAY 6				
Module Review and Assessment Readiness				

Module 13

DAY 1	DAY 2	DAY 3	DAY 4	DAY 5
Lesson 13.1	Lesson 13.1	Lesson 13.2	Lesson 13.2	Lesson 13.3
DAY 6	**DAY 7**	**DAY 8**		
Lesson 13.4	Lesson 13.4	Module Review and Assessment Readiness		

Module 14

DAY 1	DAY 2	DAY 3	DAY 4
Lesson 14.1	Lesson 14.1	Lesson 14.2	Module Review and Assessment Readiness

Module 15

DAY 1	DAY 2	DAY 3	DAY 4
Lesson 15.1	Lesson 15.2	Lesson 15.2	Module Review and Assessment Readiness

Module 16

DAY 1	DAY 2	DAY 3	DAY 4	DAY 5
Lesson 16.1	Lesson 16.1 Lesson 16.2	Lesson 16.2	Module Review and Assessment Readiness	Unit Review and Assessment Readiness

90-Minute Classes

Module 12

DAY 1	DAY 2	DAY 3
Lesson 12.1	Lesson 12.2	Lesson 12.3 Module Review and Assessment Readiness

Module 13

DAY 1	DAY 2	DAY 3	DAY 4
Lesson 13.1 Lesson 13.2	Lesson 13.2	Lesson 13.3 Lesson 13.4	Lesson 13.4 Module Review and Assessment Readiness

Module 14

DAY 1	DAY 2
Lesson 14.1	Lesson 14.2 Module Review and Assessment Readiness

Module 15

DAY 1	DAY 2
Lesson 15.1 Lesson 15.2	Lesson 15.2 Module Review and Assessment Readiness

Module 16

DAY 1	DAY 2	DAY 3
Lesson 16.1	Lesson 16.2	Module and Unit Review and Assessment Readiness

Program Resources

PLAN

HMH Teacher App

Access a full suite of teacher resources online and offline on a variety of devices. Plan present, and manage classes, assignments, and activities.

Algebra 1
Monday February 10 2014
My Class 1B
Content
Lesson 1.1
Lesson 1.2
Assignments
Progress & Reports

ePlanner **Easily plan your classes, create and view assignments, and access all program resources with your online, customizable planning tool.**

Professional Development Videos

Authors Juli Dixon and Matt Larson model successful teaching practices and strategies in actual classroom settings.

QR Codes **Scan with your smart phone to jump directly from your print book to online videos and other resources.**

Teacher's Edition

Support students with point-of-use Questioning Strategies, teaching tips, resources for differentiated instruction, additional activities, and more.

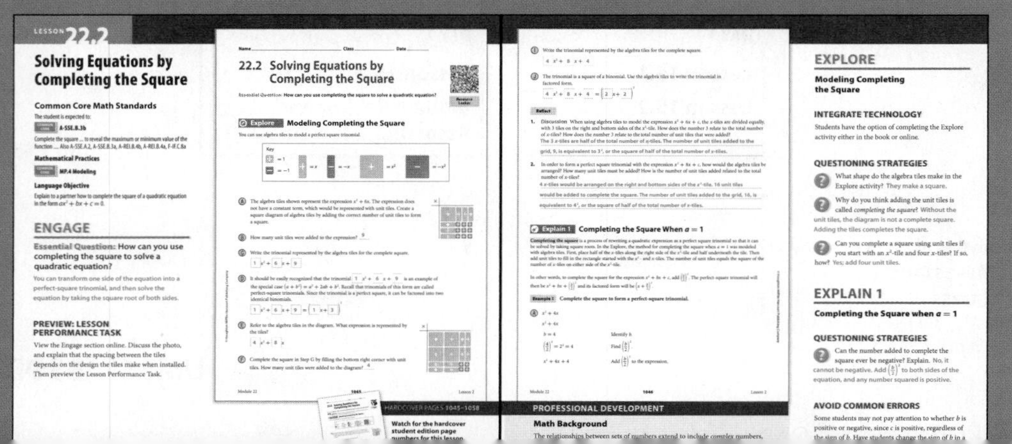

LESSON 22.2
Solving Equations by Completing the Square
ENGAGE
EXPLORE
EXPLAIN 1
PROFESSIONAL DEVELOPMENT

ENGAGE AND EXPLORE

Real-World Videos **Engage students with interesting and relevant applications of the mathematical content of each module.**

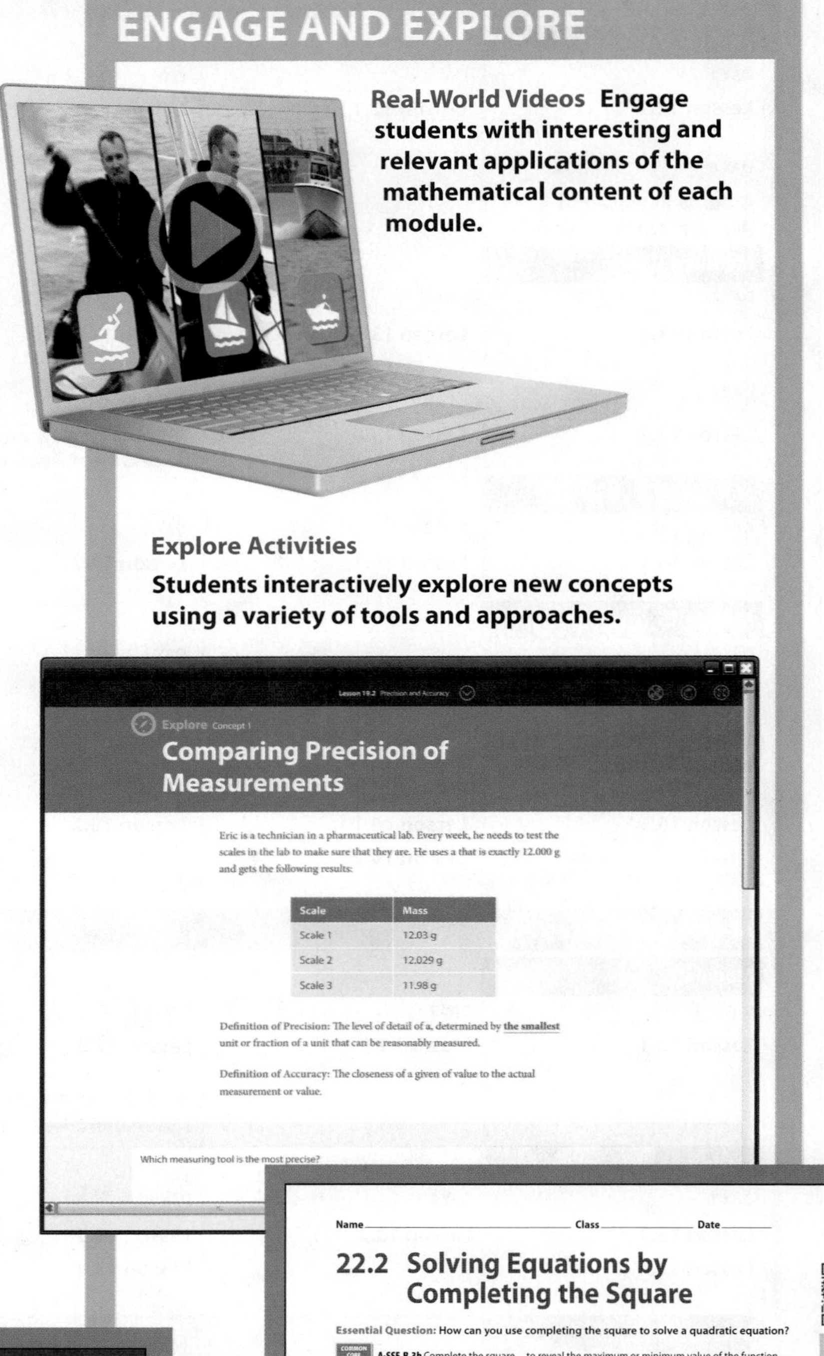

Explore Concept 1
Comparing Precision of Measurements
Eric is a technician in a pharmaceutical lab. Every week, he needs to test the scales in the lab to make sure that they are. He uses a that is exactly 12.000 g and gets the following results:
Scale | Mass
Scale 1 | 12.03 g
Scale 2 | 12.029 g
Scale 3 | 11.98 g
Definition of Precision: The level of detail of a, determined by the smallest unit or fraction of a unit that can be reasonably measured.
Definition of Accuracy: The closeness of a given of value to the actual measurement or value.
Which measuring tool is the most precise?

Explore Activities

Students interactively explore new concepts using a variety of tools and approaches.

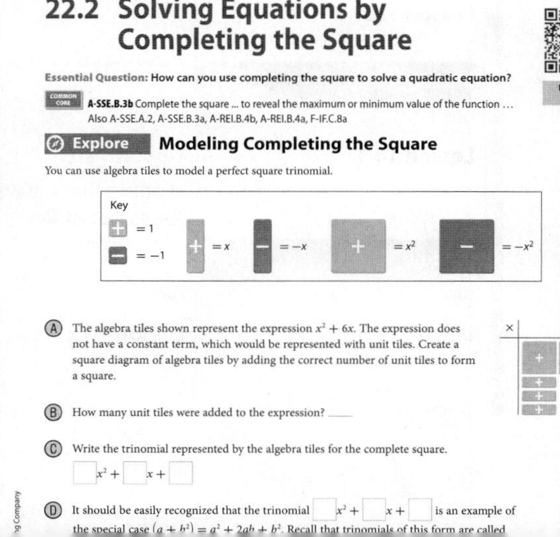

Name_______ Class_______ Date_______

22.2 Solving Equations by Completing the Square

Essential Question: How can you use completing the square to solve a quadratic equation?

A-SSE.B.3b Complete the square ... to reveal the maximum or minimum value of the function ... Also A-SSE.A.2, A-SSE.B.3a, A-REI.B.4b, A-REI.B.4a, F-IF.C.8a

Explore Modeling Completing the Square

You can use algebra tiles to model a perfect square trinomial.

Key: + = 1; − = −1; = x; = $-x$; = x^2; = $-x^2$

(A) The algebra tiles shown represent the expression $x^2 + 6x$. The expression does not have a constant term, which would be represented with unit tiles. Create a square diagram of algebra tiles by adding the correct number of unit tiles to form a square.

(B) How many unit tiles were added to the expression? ____

(C) Write the trinomial represented by the algebra tiles for the complete square.
$\square x^2 + \square x + \square$

(D) It should be easily recognized that the trinomial $\square x^2 + \square x + \square$ is an example of the special case $(a + b^2) = a^2 + 2ab + b^2$. Recall that trinomials of this form are called

TEACH

Math On the Spot video tutorials, featuring program authors Dr. Edward Burger and Martha Sandoval-Martinez, accompany every example in the textbook and give students step-by-step instructions and explanations of key math concepts.

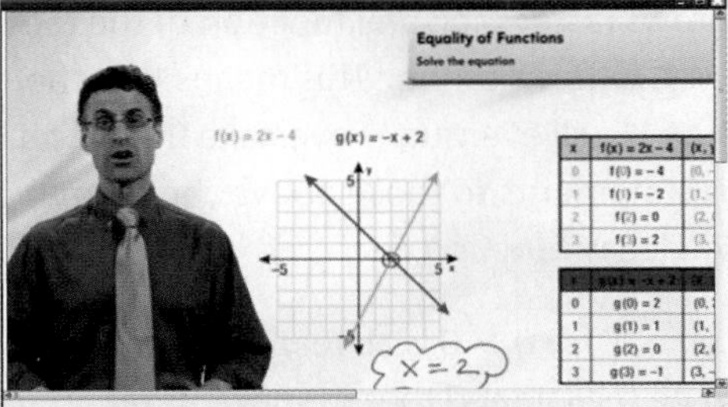

Interactive Teacher Edition

Customize and present course materials with collaborative activities and integrated formative assessment.

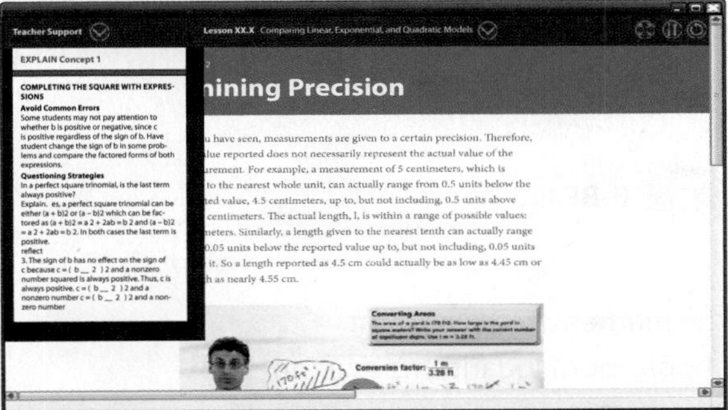

Differentiated Instruction Resources

Support all learners with Differentiated Instruction Resources, including

- **Leveled Practice and Problem Solving**
- **Reading Strategies**
- **Success for English Learners**
- **Challenge**

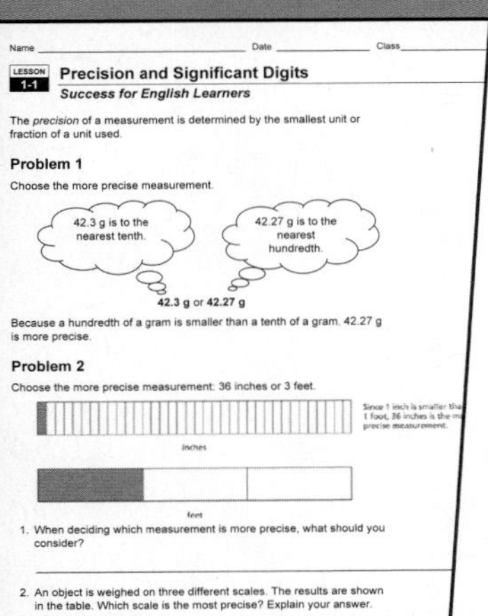

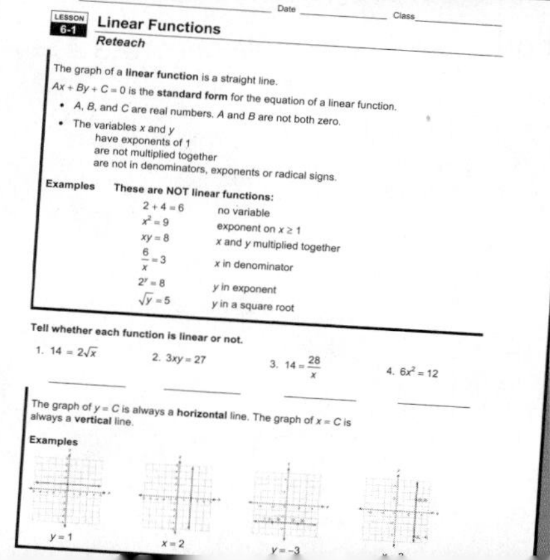

ASSESSMENT AND INTERVENTION

The Personal Math Trainer provides online practice, homework, assessments, and intervention. Monitor student progress through reports and alerts. Create and customize assignments aligned to specific lessons or Common Core standards.

- **Practice** – With dynamic items and assignments, students get unlimited practice on key concepts supported by guided examples, step-by-step solutions, and video tutorials.
- **Assessments** – Choose from course assignments or customize your own based on course content, Common Core standards, difficulty levels, and more.
- **Homework** – Students can complete online homework with a wide variety of problem types, including the ability to enter expressions, equations, and graphs. Let the system automatically grade homework, so you can focus where your students need help the most!
- **Intervention** – Let the Personal Math Trainer automatically prescribe a targeted, personalized intervention path for your students.

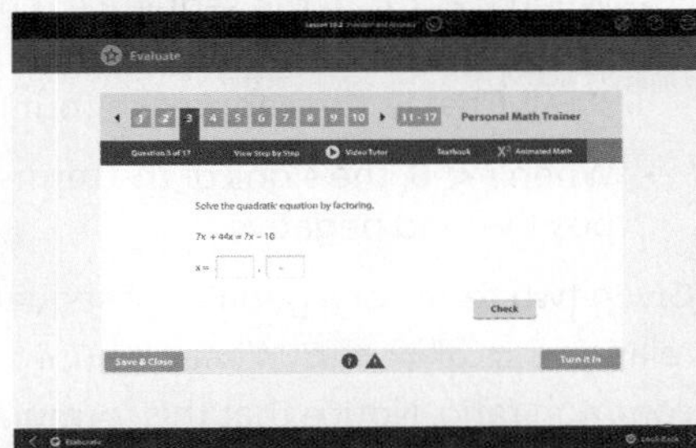

Focus on Higher Order Thinking

Raise the bar with homework and practice that incorporates higher-order thinking and mathematical practices in every lesson.

Assessment Readiness

Prepare students for success on high stakes tests for Algebra 2 with practice at every module and unit

Assessment Resources

Tailor assessments and response to intervention to meet the needs of all your classes and students, including

- Leveled Module Quizzes
- Leveled Unit Tests
- Unit Performance Tasks
- Placement, Diagnostic, and Quarterly Benchmark Tests
- Tier 1, Tier 2, and Tier 3 Resources

Math Background

Geometric Sequences COMMON CORE F-LE.A.2

LESSON 12.2

In a geometric sequence, the ratio of successive terms is a constant called the common ratio r $(r \neq 1)$. The nth term of a geometric sequence can be found by multiplying the first term by r $(n - 1)$ times; equivalently, $a_n = a_1 \cdot r^{n-1}$.

This general rule is analogous to the equation of an exponential function, $y = ab^x$, and a geometric sequence may be viewed as an exponential function whose domain is restricted to the natural numbers. For $a_1 > 0$, the value of r determines the nature of the geometric sequence.

- When $r > 1$, the sequence represents exponential growth. The terms of the sequence become arbitrarily large.
- When $0 < r < 1$, the sequence represents exponential decay. The terms of the sequence become arbitrarily small. That is, they approach (but never equal) 0.
- When $r < 0$, the signs of the terms alternate between positive and negative.

Given two terms of a geometric sequence, a_m and a_n, the relationship $a^n = a_m r^{n-m}$ may be used to calculate the common ratio. Notice that this formula holds whether $m < n$ or $m > n$, and that the formula reduces to the general rule for the nth term when $m = 1$.

Exponential Functions COMMON CORE F-IF.C.8b

LESSONS 13.1 and 13.2

An exponential function is a function of the form $f(x) = ab^x$, where $a \neq 0$, $b > 0$, and $b \neq 1$. If $a = 1$, this becomes $f(x) = b^x$. The figure below shows the shape of the graph of $y = b^x$, for $0 < b < 1$ and $b > 1$. Note that in both cases, the graph passes through $(0, 1)$ because any value raised to the 0 power is equal to 1.

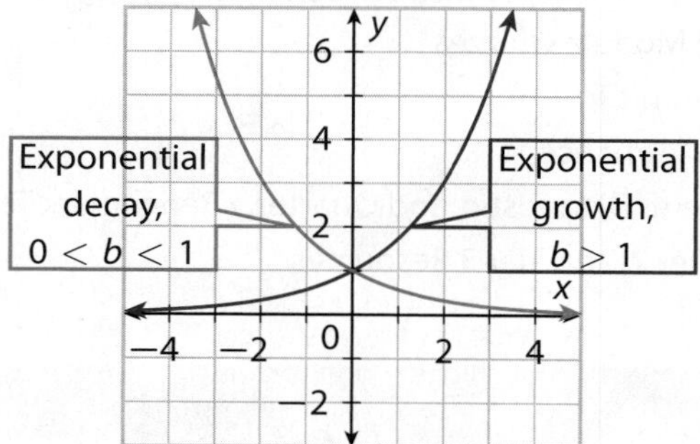

Look more closely at the graph of the exponential growth function, $y = b^x$ for $b > 1$. The curve is nearly flat for $x < 0$. More precisely, as $x \to -\infty$, the curve gets arbitrarily close to the x-axis without ever touching it. This is because $b^x > 0$ for all x. For positive values of x, the graph makes it clear that $f(x) = b^x$ increases rapidly. In fact, the exponential growth function grows faster than any function of the form $f(x) = x^n$ where n is a whole number. This means that the graph of $y = b^x$ $(b > 1)$ will eventually overtake the graph of $y = x^n$. (Analogous statements to those above can be made for the exponential decay function.)

The domain of $f(x) = b^x$ for $b > 0$ is all real numbers. However, it should be mentioned that we have so far defined powers only for certain values of exponents. In other words, students can evaluate the function $y = 2^x$ at $x = 7$, $x = 12$, and $x = -12$, but how should the function be evaluated for $x = 0.743$? And how should the function be evaluated for irrational values of x, such as $x = \sqrt{2}$? Students will learn more about rational exponents later.

The Base *e*  F-BF.B.5

LESSONS 13.3

The first reference to the mathematical constant e appeared in 1618 in a book about logarithms by John Napier. Although the constant is essential in the study of exponential and logarithmic functions, it may be most easily understood by algebra students when it is first presented in the context of compound interest.

The compound interest formula $A = P\left(1 + \frac{r}{n}\right)^{nt}$ gives the total amount of money A at the end of t years for an initial investment P with an interest rate r that is compounded n times per year. When \$1 is invested at 100% interest for one year, the formula becomes $A = P\left(1 + \frac{1}{n}\right)^n$.

The table gives the value of A for various values of n.

n	A
2	2.25
5	$\approx$ 2.4883
10	$\approx$ 2.5927
100	$\approx$ 2.7048
1000	$\approx$ 2.7169

The table suggests that as n grows arbitrarily large, the value of A does not grow arbitrarily large, but approaches a limiting value. This value, which is defined to be the constant e, is approximately 2.718281828459045. Written using the limit notation of calculus,

$$e = \lim_{n \to \infty}\left(1 + \frac{1}{n}\right)^n$$

The constant e is an irrational number that may seem far from "natural." However, the constant does arise naturally in many different areas of mathematics. For example, the value of e may also be defined in terms of an infinite series:

$$e = \frac{1}{0!} + \frac{1}{1!} + \frac{1}{2!} + \frac{1}{3!} + \cdots$$

The natural logarithm is the logarithm with base e. This logarithm is generally written as ln, rather than $\log_e$. The natural logarithm has an important role in calculus, where it can be shown that for any positive number a, ln a is the area under the curve $y = \frac{1}{x}$ from $x = 1$ to $x = a$.

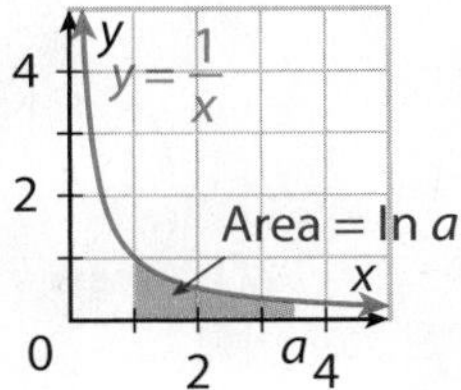

For an algebra course, it is important to impress upon students the fact that the natural logarithm has all of the usual properties of logarithms, and hence all of the usual properties of exponents. For example, $\ln(mn) = \ln m + \ln n$.

It is also important for students to understand and remember the inverse relationship $f(x) = e^x$ and $f(x) = \ln x$. In particular,

- $e^{\ln x} = x$ for all $x > 0$; and
- $\ln e^x = x$ for all real values of x.

Logarithms  F-BF.B.5

LESSONS 15.1 to 16.2

A logarithm is an exponent.
Given $b^x = a$ for $b > 0$ and $b \neq 1$, you can write the equivalent equation $\log_b a = x$. In other words, $\log_b a$ is the power to which b must be raised in order to obtain a. This can be expressed as $b^{\log_b a} = a$. In other words, $f(x) = \log_b x$ and $g(x) = b^x$ are inverse functions.

Because logarithms are exponents, any property of logarithms may be proved by citing the corresponding property of exponents. For example, given positive numbers m, n, and b $(b \neq 1)$, $\log_b mn = \log_b m + \log_b n$. This property is related to the Product of Powers Property of exponents. Specifically, let $\log_b m = x$ and let $\log_b n = y$. Then $b^x = m$, $b^y = n$, and $b^x b^y = mn$. By the Product of Powers Property, $b^{x+y} = mn$, and by the definition of a logarithm, $\log_b mn = x + y$. Thus, $\log_b mn = \log_b m + \log_b n$.

Logarithms were first proposed as a labor-saving device in the early 17th century by the Scottish nobleman John Napier. At the time, astronomers spent long hours on arithmetical calculations used to predict planetary motion. Napier realized that the properties of logarithms could be used to turn problems that required multiplication and division of very large numbers into problems that required only addition and subtraction. The first tables of common logarithms $(b = 10)$ were published in 1617. Until the advent of computers and calculators, such tables were essential for many mathematical calculations. For example, to find $\sqrt[5]{67}$, you would first rewrite the expression as $y = 67^{\frac{1}{5}}$. Taking the common logarithm of both sides of the equation gives $\log y = \log 67^{\frac{1}{5}}$ or $\log y = \frac{1}{5}\log 67$. (Note that common logarithms are typically written without a base.) You would then use a table to find log 67 and divide this value by 5. Finally, you would again use the table to find the value of y that has this logarithm. This calculation method later became the basis for calculating with slide rules.

Exponential and Logarithmic Functions and Equations

MATH IN CAREERS

Unit Activity Preview

After completing this unit, students will complete a Math in Careers task by writing and using a function that describes the decay of a radioactive substance. Critical skills include representing exponential decay, interpreting exponential functions, and finding the inverses of functions.

For more information about careers in mathematics as well as various mathematics appreciation topics, visit The American Mathematical Society at http://www.ams.org.

UNIT 6

Exponential and Logarithmic Functions and Equations

MATH IN CAREERS

Nuclear Medicine Technologist
Nuclear medicine technologists use technology to create images, or *scans*, of parts of a patient's body. They must understand the mathematics of exponential decay of radioactive materials. Nuclear medicine technologists analyze data from the scan, which are presented to a specialist for diagnosis.

If you are interested in a career as a nuclear medicine technologist, you should study these mathematical subjects:

- Algebra
- Statistics
- Calculus

Check out the career activity at the end of the unit to find out how **Nuclear Medicine Technologists** use math.

TRACKING YOUR LEARNING PROGRESSION

Before	In this Unit	After
Students understand: • inverses of functions • square root functions • radical expressions and equations	Students will learn about: • exponential and logarithmic functions • arithmetic and geometric sequences • exponential growth and decay • the base *e*	• the unit circle • radian measure • graphing and transforming trigonometric functions

Reading Start-Up

Visualize Vocabulary

Use the ✓ words to complete the graphic.

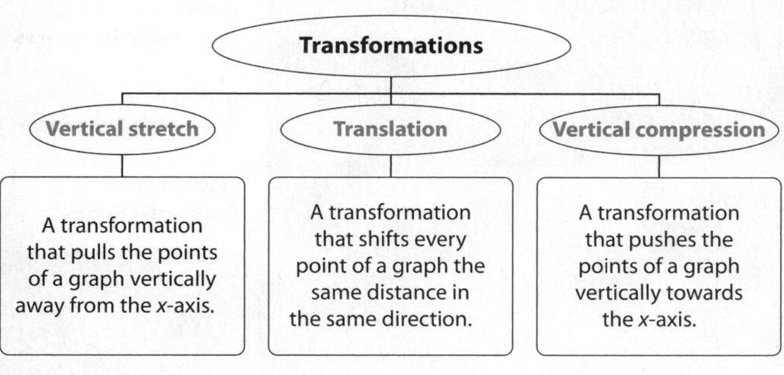

Transformations
Vertical stretch
Translation
Vertical compression
A transformation that pulls the points of a graph vertically away from the x-axis.
A transformation that shifts every point of a graph the same distance in the same direction.
A transformation that pushes the points of a graph vertically towards the x-axis.

Vocabulary

Review Words

- asymptote (*asíntota*)
- inverse function (*función inversa*)
- ✔ translation (*traslación*)
- ✔ vertical compression (*compresión vertical*)
- ✔ vertical stretch (*estiramiento vertical*)

Preview Words

- explicit formula (*fórmula explícita*)
- geometric sequence (*sucesión geométrica*)
- logarithmic function (*función logarítmica*)
- recursive formula (*fórmula recurrente*)

Understand Vocabulary

To become familiar with some of the vocabulary terms in the module, consider the following. You may refer to the module, the glossary, or a dictionary.

1. A sequence in which the ratio of successive terms is a constant r, where $r \neq 0$ or 1 , is a **geometric sequence**.
2. A **recursive formula** is a rule for a sequence in which one or more previous terms are used to generate the next term.
3. A **logarithmic function** is the inverse of an exponential function.

Active Reading

Booklet Before beginning the unit, create a booklet to help you organize what you learn. Each page of the booklet should correspond to a lesson in the unit and summarize the most important information from the lesson. Include definitions, examples, and graphs to help you recall the main elements of the lesson. Highlight the main idea and use colored pencils to help you illustrate any important concepts or differences.

Reading Start Up

Have students complete the activities on this page by working alone or with others.

VISUALIZE VOCABULARY

The case diagram helps students review important vocabulary associated with functions and transformations related to their graphs. If time allows, discuss how to recognize examples of the terms related to graphing.

UNDERSTAND VOCABULARY

Use the following explanations to help students learn the preview words.

An **exponential function** is a function in which the independent variable is an exponent. The inverse of an exponential function is a **logarithmic function**. In a **geometric sequence**, each term is related by a common ratio. The **explicit formula** for a geometric sequence is an exponential function.

ACTIVE READING

Students can use these reading and note-taking strategies to help them organize and understand the new concepts and vocabulary. Encourage students to ask for additional help in understanding the vocabulary used to denote a specific type of exponential or logarithmic equation.

ADDITIONAL RESOURCES

Differentiated Instruction

- Reading Strategies EL

Sequences and Series

ESSENTIAL QUESTION:

Answer: Sequences and series help us to make predictions based on previous patterns in data.

PROFESSIONAL DEVELOPMENT VIDEO

Professional Development Video

Author Matt Larson models successful teaching practices in an actual high-school classroom.

Professional Development my.hrw.com

MODULE 12

Sequences and Series

Essential Question: How do sequences and series help to solve real-world problems?

REAL WORLD VIDEO
Fractal geography is the study of fractal patterns that occur in geographic features such as coastlines and watersheds. Check out how geometric series are involved in determining the area and perimeter of fractals.

MODULE PERFORMANCE TASK PREVIEW

How Big Is That Snowflake?

Did you ever make cutout snowflakes in school? If you did, you folded the paper a few times and snipped little triangles from the edges. The more you snipped, the more you decreased the overall area. In this module, you'll explore a fractal pattern called a Koch snowflake that starts with a triangle and adds smaller and smaller triangles to the edges. So, what is the total area of a Koch snowflake? The answer to this will crystalize later in the module.

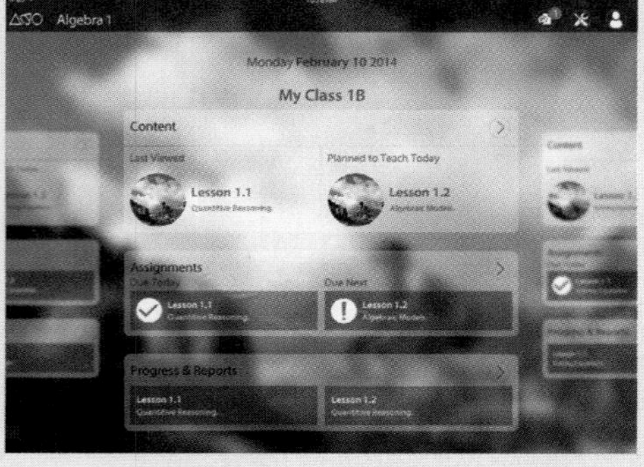

DIGITAL TEACHER EDITION

Access a full suite of teaching resources when and where you need them:

- Access content online or offline
- Customize lessons to share with your class
- Communicate with your students in real-time
- View student grades and data instantly to target your instruction where it is needed most

PERSONAL MATH TRAINER

Assessment and Intervention

Assign automatically graded homework, quizzes, tests, and intervention activities. Prepare your students with updated, Common Core-aligned practice tests.

Are YOU Ready?

Complete these exercises to review skills you will need for this chapter.

Personal Math Trainer

- Online Homework
- Hints and Help
- Extra Practice

Real Numbers

Example 1 Add: $\frac{5}{6}+\frac{5}{7}+\frac{5}{8}$

$\frac{5}{2\cdot 3}+\frac{5}{7}+\frac{5}{2^3}$ Use prime factors in denominators.

$\frac{5(2^2\cdot 7)}{2\cdot 3(2^2\cdot 7)}+\frac{5(2^3\cdot 3)}{7(2^3\cdot 3)}+\frac{5(3\cdot 7)}{2^3(3\cdot 7)}$ Use the LCD to rewrite fractions.

$\frac{365}{168}$ Simplify and add numerators.

Add.

1. $\frac{1}{2}+\frac{2}{3}+\frac{3}{4}$ $\frac{23}{12}$
2. $\frac{2}{3}+\frac{1}{2}+\frac{2}{5}$ $\frac{47}{30}$
3. $\frac{1}{8}+\frac{3}{10}+\frac{5}{12}$ $\frac{101}{120}$

Exponential Functions

Example 2 Write the values for $f(x)$ for $x = \{3, 4, 5\}$, if

$f(x)=\frac{1}{8}(4)^x$

$f(3)=\frac{1}{8}(4)^3=\frac{1}{8}(64)=8$

$f(4)=\frac{1}{8}(4)^4=\frac{1}{8}(256)=32$

$f(5)=\frac{1}{8}(4)^5=\frac{1}{8}(1024)=128$

The solution set is {8, 32, 128}.

Write the solution set for $f(x)$ for $x = \{3, 4, 5\}$.

4. $f(x) = 0.2(5)^x$ {25, 125, 625}
5. $f(x)=\frac{2}{3}(3)^x$ {18, 54, 162}
6. $f(x) = 0.75(2)^x$ {6, 12, 24}

Response to Intervention			*Differentiated Instruction*
Tier 1 Lesson Intervention Worksheets	**Tier 2** Strategic Intervention Skills Intervention Worksheets	**Tier 3** Intensive Intervention Worksheets available online	
Reteach 12.1 Reteach 12.2 Reteach 12.3	3 Algebraic Expressions 13 Geometric Sequences 20 Multi-Step Equations	Building Block Skills 27, 29, 75, 76, 91, 109	Challenge worksheets Extend the Math Lesson Activities in TE

Are You Ready?

ASSESS READINESS

Use the assessment on this page to determine if students need strategic or intensive intervention for the module's prerequisite skills.

ASSESSMENT AND INTERVENTION

RtI Response to Intervention TIER 1, TIER 2, TIER 3 SKILLS

Personal Math Trainer will automatically create a standards-based, personalized intervention assignment for your students, targeting each student's individual needs!

ADDITIONAL RESOURCES

See the table below for a full list of intervention resources available for this module.

Response to Intervention Resources also includes:

- Tier 2 Skill Pre-Tests for each Module
- Tier 2 Skill Post-Tests for each skill

LESSON 12.1

Arithmetic Sequences

Common Core Math Standards

The student is expected to:

F-BF.A.2

Write arithmetic and geometric sequences both recursively and with an explicit formula, use them to model situations, and translate between the two forms. Also A-CED.A.2, F-IF.A.3, F-BF.A.1a, F-LE.A.2

Mathematical Practices

MP.7 Using Structure

Language Objective

Work with a partner to match the graph of an arithmetic sequence to its explicit and recursive rule.

ENGAGE

Essential Question: What are algebraic ways to define an arithmetic sequence?

Possible answer: An arithmetic sequence can be defined explicitly by the rule $f(n) = a + dn$ for integer values of n greater than or equal to 0, or by the rule $f(n) = a + d(n - 1)$ for integer values of n greater than or equal to 1, depending on whether you want the initial value of the sequence to correspond to 0 or 1. An arithmetic sequence can also be defined recursively by the rule $f(0) = a$ and $f(n) = f(n - 1) + d$ for $n \geq 1$, or by the rule $f(1) = a$ and $f(n) = f(n - 1) + d$ for $n \geq 2$.

PREVIEW: LESSON PERFORMANCE TASK

View the online Engage. Discuss the photo and the fact that many group rental prices are a function of the number of people in the group. Then preview the Lesson Performance Task.

Name ______ Class ______ Date ______

12.1 Arithmetic Sequences

Essential Question: What are algebraic ways to define an arithmetic sequence?

Resource Locker

Explore Investigating Arithmetic Sequences

Consider a staircase where the vertical distance between steps is 7.5 inches and you must walk up 14 steps to get from the first floor to the second floor, a total vertical distance of 105 inches. Define two functions: $B(s)$, which models the distance from the bottom of the staircase (the first floor) to the bottom of your foot, and $T(s)$, which models the distance from the bottom of your foot to the top of the staircase (the second floor). For both functions, the independent variable s represents the number of steps that you have walked up.

(A) Complete the table. Show your calculations.

s	$B(s)$	$T(s)$
0	0	105
1	$0 + 7.5 = 7.5$	$105 - 7.5 = 97.5$
2	$0 + 2(7.5) = 15$	$105 - 2(7.5) = 90$
3	$0 + 3(7.5) = 22.5$	$105 - 3(7.5) = 82.5$
4	$0 + 4(7.5) = 30$	$105 - 4(7.5) = 75$

(B) Based on the patterns in the table, write rules for the two functions in terms of s.

$B(s) = 0 + 7.5s$

$T(s) = 105 - 7.5s$

(C) Identify the domain and range of $B(s)$.

- The domain of $B(s)$ is $\{0, 1, 2, 3, 4, 5, 6, 7, 8, 9, 10, 11, 12, 13, 14\}$.
- The range of $B(s)$ is $\{0, 7.5, 15, 22.5, 30, 37.5, 45, 52.5, 60, 67.5, 75, 82.5, 90, 97.5, 105\}$.

HARDCOVER PAGES 583–596

Watch for the hardcover student edition page numbers for this lesson.

Ⓓ Graph $B(s)$.

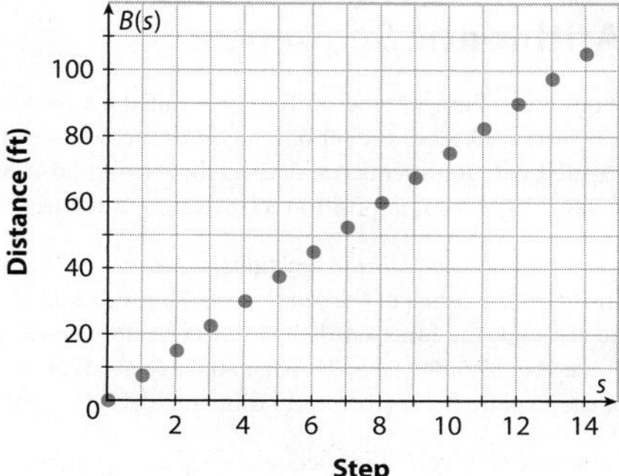

Ⓔ Identify the domain and range of $T(s)$.

- The domain of $T(s)$ is

{0, 1, 2, 3, 4, 5, 6, 7, 8, 9, 10, 11, 12, 13, 14}.

- The range of $T(s)$ is

{105, 97.5, 90, 82.5, 75, 67.5, 60, 52.5, 45, 37.5, 30, 22.5, 15, 7.5, 0}.

Ⓕ Graph $T(s)$.

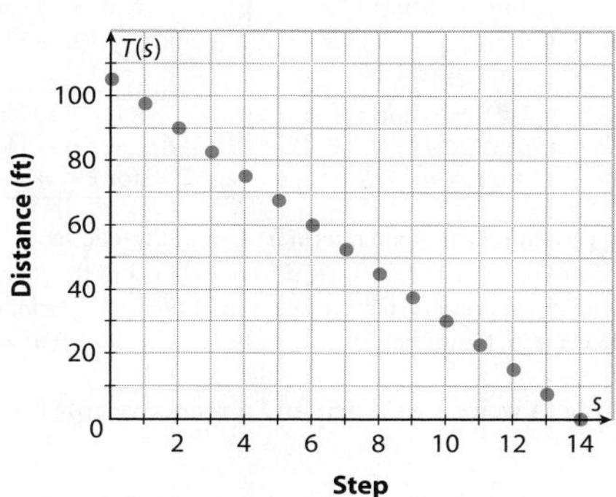

Reflect

1. Both $B(s)$ and $T(s)$ are linear functions, but their graphs consist of discrete points. Why?
The independent variable *s* has only whole-number values from 0 to 14, so only points whose *s*-coordinates are whole numbers from 0 to 14 are graphed.

2. How are $B(s)$ and $T(s)$ different? Why?
$B(s)$ is an increasing function because the distance from the bottom of the staircase increases with each step. $T(s)$ is a decreasing function because the distance from the top of the staircase decreases with each step.

EXPLORE

Investigating Arithmetic Sequences

INTEGRATE TECHNOLOGY

Students have the option of completing the Explore activity either in the book or online.

QUESTIONING STRATEGIES

? How do you know that the ranges of the two functions must be the same? **The ranges of both functions consist of the same set of measurements, but are paired with different values from the domain.**

INTEGRATE MATHEMATICAL PRACTICES

Focus on Reasoning

MP.2 Have students discuss how it is possible that the two functions can have the same domain and range, yet one is an increasing function and the other is a decreasing function. Ask them to explain how the function rules indicate that one function is increasing and the other decreasing.

PROFESSIONAL DEVELOPMENT

Learning Progressions

Students are familiar with the concept of functions and know that a function assigns exactly one output to each input. Students understand that a function has a domain and a range, and how to evaluate functions for inputs in their domains. They now extend these concepts and skills to sequences, observing that a sequence can be thought of as a function that maps consecutive integers (the elements of the domain) to the terms of the sequence (the elements of the range). They analyze both explicit rules and recursive rules for these functions, and learn to identify the types of functions that produce arithmetic sequences. Students also explore graphs of arithmetic sequences, and model real-world situations using arithmetic sequences.

EXPLAIN 1

Writing Explicit and Recursive Rules for Arithmetic Sequences

QUESTIONING STRATEGIES

What information do you need to know in order to find the 8th term of an arithmetic sequence by using its recursive rule? the 7th term and the common difference

If you know the second term and the common difference of an arithmetic sequence, can you write an explicit rule for the sequence? If so, explain how. Yes; you can subtract the common difference from the second term to get the first term. Then, you can substitute the first term and the common difference into the general explicit rule to get the explicit rule for the sequence.

AVOID COMMON ERRORS

Some students may confuse n and the nth term. Explain that n is the position number in the sequence, and the nth term is the term in that position.

INTEGRATE MATHEMATICAL PRACTICES

Focus on Patterns

MP.8 Have students compare the explicit form of the function when the domain is $n \geq 0$ with the form when the domain is $n \geq 1$. Lead them to recognize how the multiplier of the common difference needs to be $n - 1$ when the first term of the sequence is associated with 1 instead of 0.

CONNECT VOCABULARY EL

Have students look up the definition of *recursive* and relate its use in non-mathematical situations to its use here.

Explain 1 Writing Explicit and Recursive Rules for Arithmetic Sequences

A **sequence** is an ordered list of numbers. Each number in the list is called a *term* of the sequence. You can think of a sequence as a function with a subset of the set of integers as the domain and the set of terms of the sequence as the range. An **explicit rule** for a sequence defines the term in position n as a function of n. A **recursive rule** for a sequence defines the term in position n by relating it to one or more previous terms.

An **arithmetic sequence**, also known as a *discrete linear function*, is a sequence for which consecutive terms have a *common difference*. For instance, the terms of the sequence 0, 7.5, 15, 22.5, 30, 37.5, 45, 52.5, 60, 67.5, 75, 82.5, 90, 97.5, 105, which are the values of the function $B(s)$ from the Explore, have a common difference of 7.5. Likewise, the terms of the sequence 105, 97.5, 90, 82.5, 75, 67.5, 60, 52.5, 45, 37.5, 30, 22.5, 15, 7.5, 0, which are the values of the function $T(s)$ from the Explore, have a common difference of −7.5. Both sequences are arithmetic.

You can write different explicit and recursive rules for a sequence depending on what integer you use as the position number for the initial term of the sequence. The most commonly used starting position numbers are 0 and 1. The table shows rules for the sequences that you examined in the Explore.

	Sequence	
	0, 7.5, 15, 22.5, 30, 37.5, 45, 52.5, 60, 67.5, 75, 82.5, 90, 97.5, 105	105, 97.5, 90, 82.5, 75, 67.5, 60, 52.5, 45, 37.5, 30, 22.5, 15, 7.5, 0
Explicit rule when starting position is 0	$f(n) = 0 + 7.5n$ for $0 \leq n \leq 14$	$f(n) = 105 - 7.5n$ for $0 \leq n \leq 14$
Explicit rule when starting position is 1	$f(n) = 0 + 7.5(n - 1)$ for $1 \leq n \leq 15$	$f(n) = 105 - 7.5(n - 1)$ for $1 \leq n \leq 15$
Recursive rule when starting position is 0	$f(0) = 0$ and $f(n) = f(n - 1) + 7.5$ for $1 \leq n \leq 14$	$f(0) = 105$ and $f(n) = f(n - 1) - 7.5$ for $1 \leq n \leq 14$
Recursive rule when starting position is 1	$f(1) = 0$ and $f(n) = f(n - 1) + 7.5$ for $2 \leq n \leq 15$	$f(1) = 105$ and $f(n) = f(n - 1) - 7.5$ for $2 \leq n \leq 15$

In general, when 0 is the starting position for the initial term a of an arithmetic sequence with common difference d, the sequence has the explicit rule $f(n) = a + dn$ for $n \geq 0$ and the recursive rule $f(0) = a$ and $f(n) = f(n-1) + d$ for $n \geq 1$. When 1 is the starting position of the initial term, the sequence has the explicit rule $f(n) = a + d(n - 1)$ for $n \geq 1$ and the recursive rule $f(1) = a$ and $f(n) = f(n-1) + d$ for $n \geq 2$.

Example 1 **Use the given table to write an explicit and a recursive rule for the sequence.**

n	0	1	2	3	4	5
$f(n)$	2	5	8	11	14	17

First, check the differences of consecutive values of $f(n)$:

$5 - 2 = 3$, $8 - 5 = 3$, $11 - 8 = 3$, $14 - 11 = 3$, and $17 - 14 = 3$

The differences are the same, so the sequence is arithmetic.

The initial term a of the sequence is 2, and its position number is 0. As already observed, the common difference d is 3.

So, the explicit rule for the sequence is $f(n) = 2 + 3n$ for $0 \leq n \leq 5$. The recursive rule is $f(0) = 2$ and $f(n) = f(n - 1) + 3$ for $1 \leq n \leq 5$.

COLLABORATIVE LEARNING

Peer-to-Peer Activity

Have students work in pairs. Instruct each student in each pair to create an arithmetic sequence, and to write a recursive rule for the sequence. Have partners exchange recursive rules, use the rule to generate the first 10 terms of the sequence, and write an explicit rule for the sequence. Have partners check each other's work.

n	1	2	3	4	5	6
$f(n)$	29	25	21	17	13	9

First, check the differences of consecutive values of $f(n)$:

$25 - 29 =$ **−4**, $21 - 25 =$ **−4**, $17 - 21 =$ **−4**, $13 - 17 =$ **−4**, and $9 - 13 =$ **−4**

The differences are the same, so the sequence [(is)/is not] arithmetic.

The initial term a of the sequence is **29**, and its position number is **1**. As already observed, the common difference d is **−4**.

So, the explicit rule for the sequence is $f(n) =$ **29 − 4n** for **1** $\leq n \leq$ **6**. The recursive rule is $f($**1**$) =$ **29** and $f(n) = f(n-1) +$ **−4** for **2** $\leq n \leq$ **6**.

Your Turn

Use the given table to write an explicit and a recursive rule for the sequence.

3.

n	0	1	2	3	4	5
$f(n)$	−7	−2	3	8	13	18

The sequence is arithmetic because consecutive terms have a common difference of 5. Since the initial term −7 corresponds to $n = 0$, the explicit rule is $f(n) = -7 + 5n$ for $0 \leq n \leq 5$. The recursive rule is $f(0) = -7$ and $f(n) = f(n-1) + 5$ for $1 \leq n \leq 5$.

4.

n	1	2	3	4	5	6
$f(n)$	11	5	−1	−7	−13	−19

The sequence is arithmetic because consecutive terms have a common difference of −6. Since the initial term 11 corresponds to $n = 1$, the explicit rule is $f(n) = 11 - 6(n-1)$ for $1 \leq n \leq 6$. The recursive rule is $f(1) = 11$ and $f(n) = f(n-1) - 6$ for $2 \leq n \leq 6$.

DIFFERENTIATE INSTRUCTION

Multiple Representations

Present students with a context that can be modeled by an arithmetic sequence. Have them construct a table of values showing n and $f(n)$ for the sequence. Then have them graph the sequence, and write both an explicit and a recursive rule to generate the terms of the sequence. Finally, have them explain how the multiple representations are related.

EXPLAIN 2

Graphing Arithmetic Sequences

QUESTIONING STRATEGIES

? How can you use the graph of a sequence to determine whether the sequence is arithmetic? **See if the graph consists of points that lie in a straight line. If so, the sequence is arithmetic. If not, it is not.**

? How can you use the graph of a sequence to determine whether the common difference is a positive number or a negative number? **If the graph is increasing, the common difference is a positive number. If it is decreasing, the common difference is a negative number.**

Explain 2 Graphing Arithmetic Sequences

As you saw in the Explore, the graph of an arithmetic sequence consists of points that lie on a line. The arithmetic sequence 3, 7, 11, 15, 19 has a final term, so it is called a *finite* sequence and its graph has a countable number of points. The arithmetic sequence 3, 7, 11, 15, 19, ... does not have a final term (indicated by the three dots), so it is called an *infinite* sequence and its graph has infinitely many points. Since you cannot show the complete graph of an infinite sequence, you should simply show as many points as the grid allows.

Example 2 **Write the terms of the given arithmetic sequence and then graph the sequence.**

Ⓐ 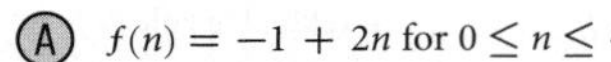
$f(n) = -1 + 2n$ for $0 \leq n \leq 4$

Make a table of values.

n	$f(n)$
0	$-1 + 2(0) = -1$
1	$-1 + 2(1) = 1$
2	$-1 + 2(2) = 3$
3	$-1 + 2(3) = 5$
4	$-1 + 2(4) = 7$

So, the sequence is $-1, 1, 3, 5, 7$.

Graph the sequence.

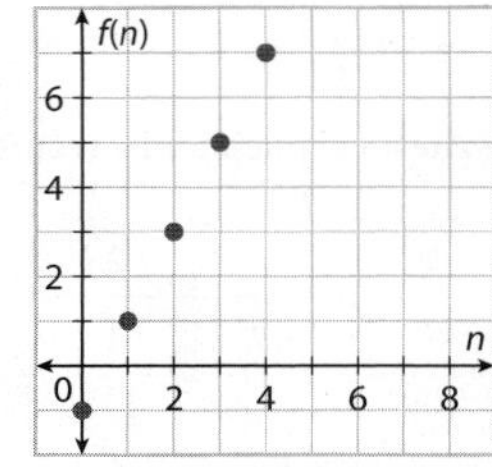

Ⓑ $f(1) = 4$ and $f(n) = f(n - 1) - 0.25$ for $n \geq 2$

Make a table of values, bearing in mind that the table could be extended because the sequence is infinite.

n	$f(n)$
1	4
2	$f(2) = f(1) - 0.25 = 4 - 0.25 =$ **3.75**
3	$f(3) = f(2) - 0.25 =$ **3.75** $- 0.25 =$ **3.5**
4	$f(4) = f(3) - 0.25 =$ **3.5** $- 0.25 =$ **3.25**
5	$f(5) = f(4) - 0.25 =$ **3.25** $- 0.25 =$ **3**

So, the sequence is **4, 3.75, 3.5, 3.25, 3, ...**.

Graph the sequence.

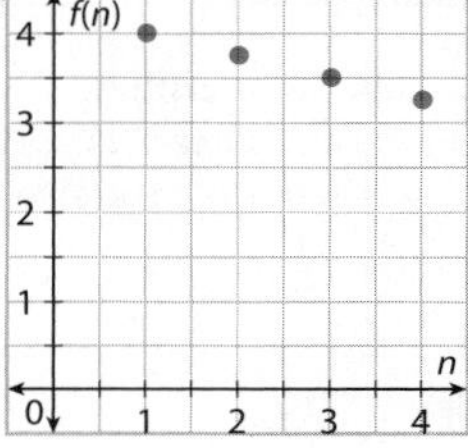

LANGUAGE SUPPORT EL

Communicate Math

Have students work in pairs, and provide them with explicit and recursive rules for sequences. On separate sheets, provide the graphs for those rules. Have the first student choose a graph to match a rule, and explain to the partner why it is a match. Students then switch roles and repeat for a recursive rule.

Help students articulate why the graphs for these sequences are points and not smooth lines. Compare graphs with smooth curves to graphs with points to help students evaluate the two kinds of graphs.

Your Turn

Write the terms of the given arithmetic sequence and then graph the sequence.

5. $f(n) = 8 - \frac{2}{3}(n - 1)$ for $1 \leq n \leq 7$

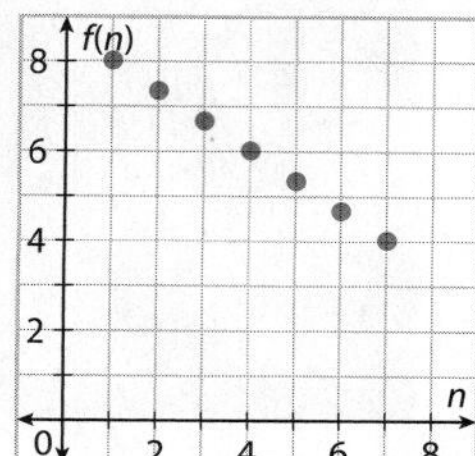

$8, 7\frac{1}{3}, 6\frac{2}{3}, 6, 5\frac{1}{3}, 4\frac{2}{3}, 4$

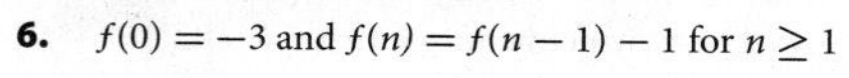

6. $f(0) = -3$ and $f(n) = f(n - 1) - 1$ for $n \geq 1$

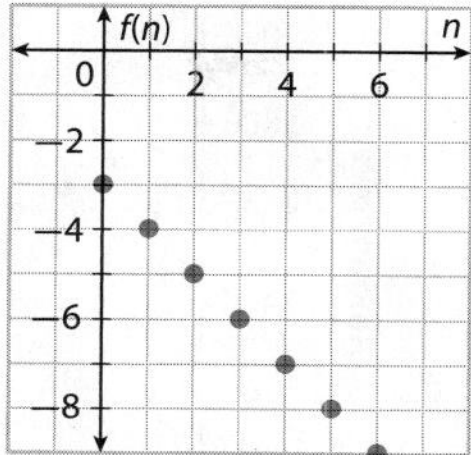

$-3, -4, -5, -6, \ldots$

Explain 3 Modeling with Arithmetic Sequences

Some real-world situations, like the situation in the Explore, can be modeled with an arithmetic sequence. You can then use a rule for the sequence to solve problems related to the situation.

Example 3 **Write a recursive rule and an explicit rule for an arithmetic sequence that models the situation. Then use the rule to answer the question.**

(A) There are 19 seats in the row nearest the stage of a theater. Each row after the first one has 2 more seats than the row before it. How many seats are in the 13th row?

Let n represent the row number, starting with 1 for the first row. The verbal description gives you a recursive rule: $f(1) = 19$ and $f(n) = f(n - 1) + 2$ for $n \geq 2$. Since the initial term is 19 and the common difference is 2, an explicit rule is $f(n) = 19 + 2(n - 1)$ for $n \geq 1$.

To find the number of seats in the 13th row, find using the explicit rule.

$f(13) = 19 + 2(13) = 45$

So, there are 45 seats in the 13th row.

INTEGRATE MATHEMATICAL PRACTICES

Focus on Communication

MP.3 Have students describe the difference between a function that represents an arithmetic sequence, and the function that represents the line that passes through the points of the graph of the sequence.

EXPLAIN 3

Modeling with Arithmetic Sequences

QUESTIONING STRATEGIES

Which rule in Part A does it make sense to find first? **Find the recursive rule. Then use the recursive rule to find the explicit rule and solve the problem.**

Which rule in Part B does it make sense to find first? **Find the explicit rule. Then use the explicit rule to find the recursive rule and solve the problem.**

INTEGRATE MATHEMATICAL PRACTICES

Focus on Modeling

MP.4 Discuss with students why it is possible to model the situation in the example using a function for an arithmetic sequence. Discuss not only the nature of the context, but also the domain and range.

INTEGRATE TECHNOLOGY

Students can use the table feature on a graphing calculator to check their work. If the table is set to display values of x beginning with 1 and increasing by 1, the table will show all of the terms in the sequence.

 A student with a part-time job borrowed money from her parents to purchase a bicycle. The graph shows the amount the student owes her parents as she makes equal weekly payments. The amount owed is shown only for the first 5 weeks.

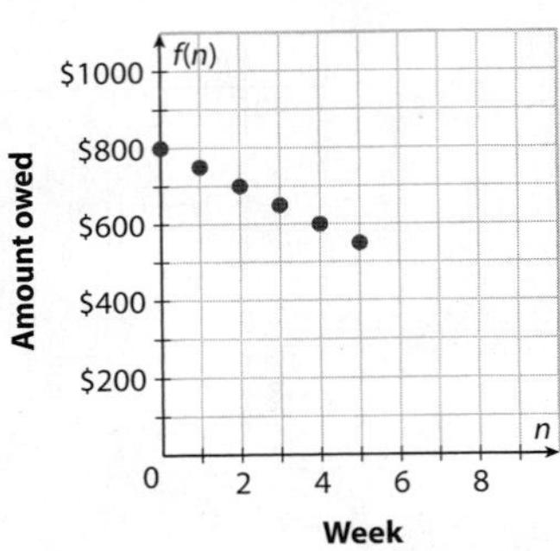

In how many weeks after purchasing the bicycle will the loan be paid off?

Let n represent the number of weeks since the loan was made, starting with **0** for the time at which the loan was made. The sequence of amounts owed is arithmetic because the weekly payments are **equal**. To determine the amount of the weekly payment, let $f(n)$ represent the amount owed at week n, and observe from the graph that $f(0) =$ **800** and $f(2) =$ **700**. The general explicit rule for the sequence is $f(n) = a + dn$. Substituting 2 for n, the value of $f(0)$ for a, and the value of $f(2)$ for $f(n)$ in $f(n) = a + dn$, you can solve for the common difference d:

$$f(2) = f(0) + 2d$$

$$700 = 800 + 2d$$

$$-100 = 2d$$

$$-50 = d$$

So, the amount of the weekly payment is **$50**, and an explicit rule for the sequence is $f(n) = 800 + (-50)n$. A recursive rule for the sequence is $f(0) = 800$ and $f(n) = f(n-1) + -50$.

To determine when the loan will be paid off, you want to find the value of n for which $f(n) = 0$. Use the explicit rule.

$$f(n) = 0$$

$$800 + (-50)n = 0$$

$$-50n = -800$$

$$n = 16$$

So, the loan will be paid off in **16** weeks.

Your Turn

Write a recursive rule and an explicit rule for an arithmetic sequence that models the situation. Then use the rule to answer the question.

7. The starting salary for a summer camp counselor is $395 per week. In each of the subsequent weeks, the salary increases by $45 to encourage experienced counselors to work for the entire summer. If the salary is $710 for the last week of the camp, for how many weeks does the camp run?

Let n represent the week number, starting with 1 for the first week. The verbal description gives you a recursive rule: $f(1) = 395$ and $f(n) = f(n-1) + 45$ for $n \geq 2$. Since the initial term is 395 and the common difference is 45, an explicit rule is $f(n) = 395 + 45(n-1)$ for $n \geq 1$. To determine how long the camp runs, find the value of n for which $f(n) = 710$. Use the explicit rule;

$395 + 45(n-1) = 710$; $n = 8$; so, the summer camp runs for 8 weeks.

8. The graph shows the length, in inches, of a row of grocery carts when various numbers of carts are nested together. What is the length of a row of 25 nested carts?

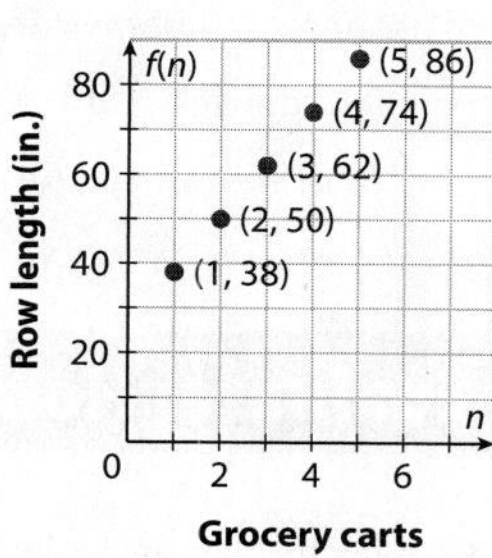

The point (1, 38) tells you that the initial term of the sequence is 38. Check the differences of consecutive values of $f(n)$:

$50 - 38 = 12$, $62 - 50 = 12$, $74 - 62 = 12$, and $86 - 74 = 12$;

The differences are the same, so the sequence is arithmetic.

An explicit rule for the sequence is $f(n) = 38 + 12(n-1)$ for $n \geq 1$. A recursive rule is $f(1) = 38$ and $f(n) = f(n-1) + 12$ for $n \geq 2$.

Use the explicit rule to find $f(25)$.

$f(25) = 38 + 12(25 - 1) = 326$;

so, a row of 25 nested shopping carts is 326 inches, or 27 feet 2 inches, long.

Elaborate

9. Discussion Is it easier to use an explicit rule or a recursive rule to find the 10th term in an arithmetic sequence? Explain.

It is easier to use an explicit rule to find the 10th term of the sequence. When using an explicit rule, you need to evaluate a function only once. To use the recursive rule, you need to evaluate a function nine times: First find the second term using the known value of the first term. Then find the third term using the value of the second term. Continue the process of obtaining the next term from the previous term until you get to the 10th term.

ELABORATE

QUESTIONING STRATEGIES

? Why is the slope of a linear function that defines an arithmetic sequence equal to the common difference of the arithmetic sequence? **The slope of a linear function describes the vertical change for 1 unit of horizontal change in the graph of the function. If 1 unit of horizontal change corresponds to a change of 1 in the position number for the sequence, then the vertical change corresponds to the common difference between two terms.**

INTEGRATE MATHEMATICAL PRACTICES

Focus on Critical Thinking

MP.3 Ask students to describe how to find the first term of an arithmetic sequence when they know the 20th term and the common difference. Have them find a solution using both explicit and recursive methods.

SUMMARIZE THE LESSON

? How can you use a function rule to define an arithmetic sequence? **You can write an explicit rule that generates each term of the sequence from the term number, or a recursive rule that generates each term from the term that comes before it.**

EVALUATE

ASSIGNMENT GUIDE

Concepts and Skills	Practice
Explore Investigating Arithmetic Sequences	Exercises 1, 16
Example 1 Writing Explicit and Recursive Rules for Arithmetic Sequences	Exercises 2–7, 19
Example 2 Graphing Arithmetic Sequences	Exercises 8–11, 17–18
Example 3 Modeling with Arithmetic Sequences	Exercises 12–15

10. What do you know about the terms in an arithmetic sequence with a common difference of 0?

If the common difference in a sequence is 0, then the terms of the sequence are all the same number. Explicit rule (using $n = 0$): $f(n) = a + 0n = a$; Recursive rule: $f(0) = a$ and $f(n) = f(n-1) + 0$, so $f(n) = f(n-1) = \ldots = f(1) = f(0) = a$

11. Describe the difference between the graph of an arithmetic sequence with a positive common difference and the graph of an arithmetic sequence with a negative common difference.

The graph of a sequence with a positive common difference follows a line with a positive slope (the line rises from left to right). The graph of a sequence with a positive common difference follows a line with a negative slope (the line falls from left to right).

12. Essential Question Check-In Does the rule $f(n) = -2 + 5n$ for $n \geq 0$ define an arithmetic sequence, and is the rule explicit or recursive? How do you know?

The rule $f(n) = -2 + 5n$ for $n \geq 0$ defines an arithmetic sequence with an initial term of -2 and a common difference of 5. The rule is explicit because it allows you to calculate the value of the term in position n directly. (A recursive rule would relate the term in position n to one or more previous terms.)

Evaluate: Homework and Practice

- Online Homework
- Hints and Help
- Extra Practice

1. Consider the staircase in the Explore. How would the functions $B(s)$ and $T(s)$ change if the staircase were a spiral staircase going from the first floor to the third floor, with the same step height and distance between floors?

The rule for $B(s)$ would remain unchanged while the rule for $T(s)$ would become $T(s) = 210 - 7.5s$.

The domain of each function would change from $\{0, 1, 2, \ldots, 14\}$ to $\{0, 1, 2, \ldots, 28\}$.

The range of each function would likewise change from $\{0, 7.5, 15, \ldots, 105\}$ to $\{0, 7.5, 15, \ldots, 210\}$.

These changes for the functions are all based on the fact that the staircase spans an additional floor. The fact that it is now a spiral staircase doesn't affect the functions.

Exercise	Depth of Knowledge (D.O.K.)	COMMON CORE Mathematical Practices
1	**1** Recall of Information	**MP.2** Reasoning
2–11	**2** Skills/Concepts	**MP.7** Using Structure
12–15	**2** Skills/Concepts	**MP.4** Modeling
16	**2** Skills/Concepts	**MP.7** Using Structure
17–18	**3** Strategic Thinking H.O.T.	**MP.3** Logic
19	**3** Strategic Thinking H.O.T.	**MP.6** Precision

Use the given table to write an explicit and a recursive rule for the sequence.

2.

n	0	1	2	3	4
$f(n)$	−6	1	8	15	22

The sequence is arithmetic because consecutive terms have a common difference of 7. Since the initial term −6 corresponds to $n = 0$, the explicit rule is $f(n) = -6 + 7n$ for $0 \leq n \leq 4$. The recursive rule is $f(0) = -6$ and $f(n) = f(n - 1) + 7$ for $1 \leq n \leq 4$.

3.

n	0	1	2	3	4
$f(n)$	8	5	2	−1	−4

The sequence is arithmetic because consecutive terms have a common difference of −3. Since the initial term 8 corresponds to $n = 0$, the explicit rule is $f(n) = 8 - 3n$ for $0 \leq n \leq 4$. The recursive rule is $f(0) = 8$ and $f(n) = f(n - 1) - 3$ for $1 \leq n \leq 4$.

Given the recursive rule for an arithmetic sequence, write the explicit rule.

4. $f(0) = 6$ and $f(n) = f(n - 1) + 5$ for $n \geq 1$

The initial term 6 corresponds to $n = 0$. The common difference is 5. So, the explicit rule is $f(n) = 6 + 5n$ for $n \geq 0$.

5. $f(1) = 19$ and $f(n) = f(n - 1) - 10$ for $n \geq 2$

The initial term 19 corresponds to $n = 1$. The common difference is −10. So, the explicit rule is $f(n) = 19 - 10(n - 1)$ for $n \geq 1$.

Given the explicit rule for an arithmetic sequence, write the recursive rule.

6. $f(n) = 9.6 - 0.2(n - 1)$ for $n \geq 1$

The initial term 9.6 corresponds to $n = 1$. The common difference is −0.2. So, the recursive rule is $f(1) = 9.6$ and $f(n) = f(n - 1) - 0.2$ for $n \geq 2$.

7. $f(n) = 14 + 8n$ for $n \geq 0$

The initial term 14 corresponds to $n = 0$. The common difference is 8. So, the recursive rule is $f(0) = 14$ and $f(n) = f(n - 1) + 8$ for $n \geq 1$.

Write the terms of the given arithmetic sequence and then graph the sequence.

8. $f(n) = 7 - \frac{1}{2}n$ for $n \geq 0$

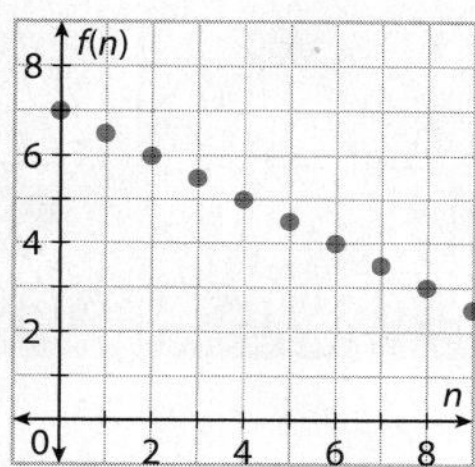

$7, 6\frac{1}{2}, 6, 5\frac{1}{2}, \ldots$

9. $f(n) = 3 + 2(n - 1)$ for $1 \leq n \leq 5$

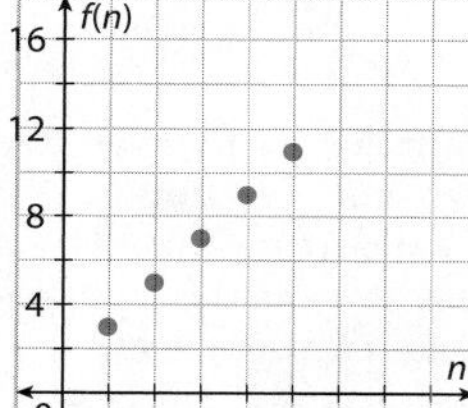

3, 5, 7, 9, 11

QUESTIONING STRATEGIES

? How is the domain of a linear function restricted if the function defines an arithmetic sequence? **The domain is restricted to either the whole numbers or the natural numbers or, if the sequence is finite, a subset of the whole numbers.**

VISUAL CUES

Students may find it easier to make the connection between $f(n)$ and n if they write a framework showing the term number beneath a blank for the term itself, as in the example below.

$$\frac{2}{(1)}, \frac{5}{(2)}, \frac{8}{(3)}, \frac{11}{(4)}, \ldots, \frac{2 + 3(n - 1)}{(n)}$$

COMMUNICATE MATH EL

The words *explicit* and *recursive* can be difficult to pronounce and use. As students work in small groups, model how to use these terms in context and how to pronounce them, without correcting students' pronunciation.

AVOID COMMON ERRORS

Some students may think that they should draw a line through the points on the graph of an arithmetic sequence. Remind them that the domain of a sequence consists only of integers, and point out that a line would contain points whose x-coordinates are not integers.

INTEGRATE MATHEMATICAL PRACTICES

Focus on Reasoning

MP.2 Ask students to tell what conclusions they can draw about an arithmetic sequence with a graph containing the point (6, 0). Students should conclude that either the first term of the sequence is a negative number and the common difference is a positive number, or that the first term of the sequence is a positive number and the common difference is a negative number.

10. $f(1) = -0.5$ and $f(n) = f(n-1) - 0.5$ for $n \geq 1$

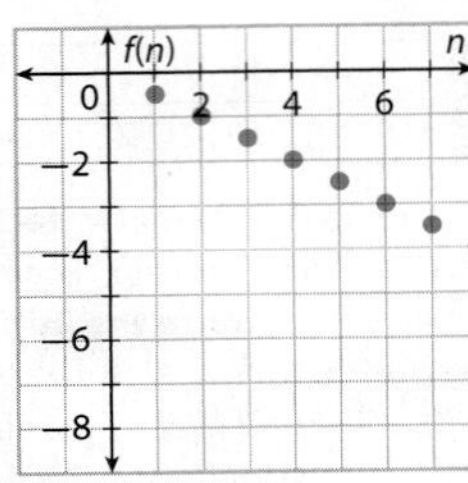

$-0.5, -1, -1.5, -2, \ldots$

11. $f(0) = -5$ and $f(n) = f(n-1) + 3$ for $0 \leq n \leq 4$

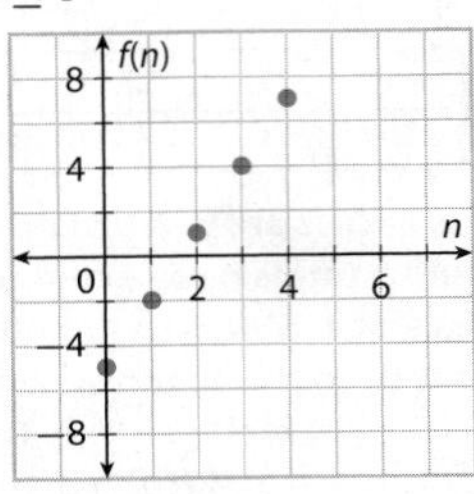

$-5, -2, 1, 4, 7$

Write a recursive rule and an explicit rule for an arithmetic sequence that models the situation. Then use the rule to answer the question.

12. Thomas begins an exercise routine for 20 minutes each day. Each week he plans to add 5 minutes per day to the length of his exercise routine. For how many minutes will he exercise each day of the 6th week?

Let n represent the week number, starting with 1 for the first week. The verbal description gives you a recursive rule: $f(1) = 20$ and $f(n) = f(n-1) + 5$ for $n \geq 2$. Since the initial term is 20 and the common difference is 5, an explicit rule is $f(n) = 20 + 5(n-1)$ for $n \geq 1$.

To find the number of minutes spent exercising each day of the 6th week, find $f(6)$ using the explicit rule.

$f(6) = 20 + 5(6-1) = 20 + 25 = 45$

So, Thomas will exercise 45 minutes each day during the 6th week.

13. The Louvre pyramid in Paris, France, is built of glass panes. There are 4 panes in the top row, and each additional row has 4 more panes than the previous row. How many panes are in the 17th row?

Let n represent the row number, starting with 1 for the first row. The verbal description gives you a recursive rule: $f(1) = 4$ and $f(n) = f(n-1) + 4$ for $n \geq 2$. Since the initial term is 4 and the common difference is 4, an explicit rule is $f(n) = 4 + 4(n-1)$ for $n \geq 1$.

To find the number of panes of glass in the 17th row, find $f(17)$ using the explicit rule.

$f(17) = 4 + 4(17-1) = 4 + 64 = 68$

So, there are 68 panes in the 17th row.

14. Clarissa is buying a prom dress on layaway. The dress costs $185. She makes a down payment of $20 to put the dress on layaway and then makes weekly payments of $15. In how many weeks is the dress paid off?

Let n represent the number of weeks, starting with 0 for the time at which she makes the down payment but not a weekly payment. Since she makes a down payment of $20, the remaining balance owed on the dress is $165. An explicit rule for the sequence of weekly balances is $f(n) = 165 - 15n$ for $n \geq 0$. Since the initial term is 165 and the common difference is -15, a recursive rule is $f(0) = 165$ and $f(n) = f(n-1) - 15$ for $n \geq 1$.

To find when the dress is paid off, solve $f(n) = 0$ using the explicit rule.

$$165 - 15n = 0$$
$$-15n = -165$$
$$n = 11$$

So, the dress will be paid off in 11 weeks.

15. The graph shows the height, in inches, of a stack of various numbers of identical plastic cups. The stack of cups will be placed on a shelf with 12 inches of vertical clearance with the shelf above. What number of cups can be in the stack without having a tight fit?

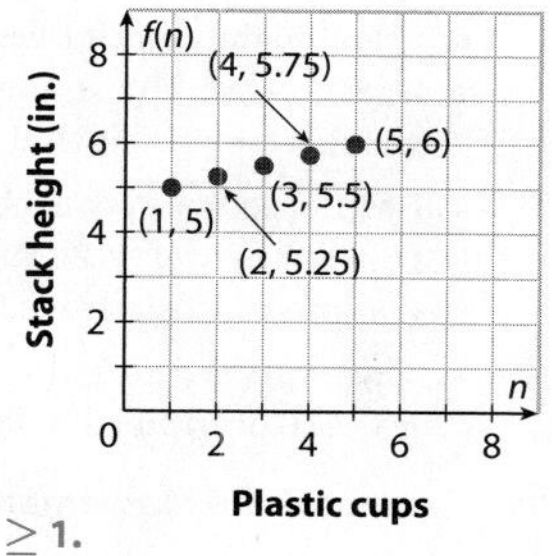

The point $(1, 5)$ tells you that the initial term of the sequence is 5. Check the differences of consecutive values of $f(n)$:

$5.25 - 5 = 0.25$, $5.5 - 5.25 = 0.25$, $5.75 - 5.5 = 0.25$, and $6 - 5.75 = 0.25$

The differences are the same, so the sequence is arithmetic.

An explicit rule for the sequence is $f(n) = 5 + 0.25(n-1)$ for $n \geq 1$.
A recursive rule is $f(1) = 5$ and $f(n) = f(n-1) + 0.25$ for $n \geq 2$.

To avoid a tight fit, there must be a gap between the top of the stack and the shelf above, so the maximum height of the stack is 11.75 inches. Using the explicit rule, solve $f(n) = 11.75$.

$$5 + 0.25(n-1) = 11.75$$
$$0.25(n-1) = 6.75$$
$$n - 1 = 27$$
$$n = 28$$

So, a stack of 28 plastic cups will fit on the shelf without having a tight fit.

16. Determine whether or not each of the following sequences is arithmetic. Select the correct response for each lettered part.

Sequence	Arithmetic	Not arithmetic
A. 1, 1, 2, 3, 5, 8, 13, 21, 34	☐	☒
B. 1, 4, 7, 10, 13, 16, 19	☒	☐
C. 1, 2, 4, 9, 16, 25	☐	☒
D. −4, 3, 10, 17, 24, 31	☒	☐
E. $\frac{1}{2}, \frac{2}{3}, \frac{3}{4}, \frac{4}{5}, \frac{5}{6}, \frac{6}{7}, \frac{7}{8}, \frac{8}{9}$	☐	☒
F. 18.5, 13, 7.5, 2, −3.5, −9	☒	☐

PEER-TO-PEER DISCUSSION

Ask students to discuss with a partner how they could write an explicit rule for an arithmetic sequence if they are given a recursive rule for the sequence. **You could use the recursive rule to identify a and d. If a is $f(0)$, you could substitute a and d into $f(n) = a + dn$. If a is $f(1)$, you could substitute a and d into $f(n) = a + d(n - 1)$.**

JOURNAL

Have students describe how an arithmetic sequence is related to a linear function.

H.O.T. Focus on Higher Order Thinking

17. Multiple Representations The graphs of two arithmetic sequences are shown.

Graph of sequence A

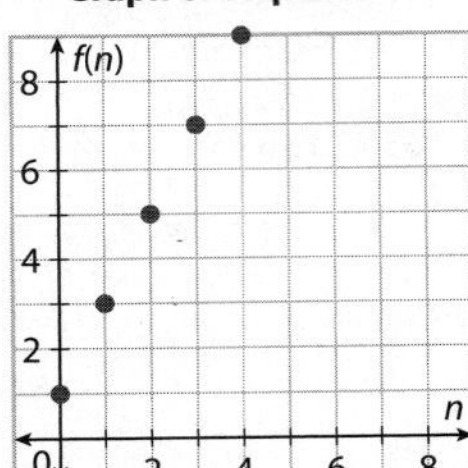

Graph of sequence B

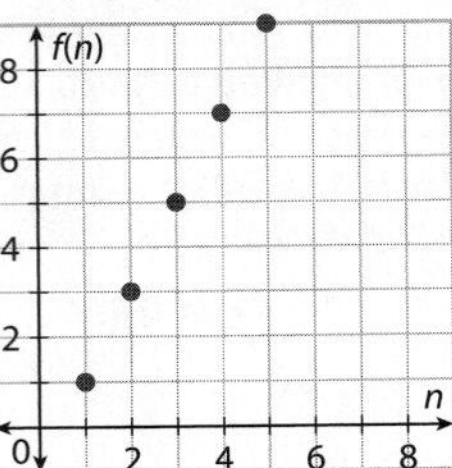

a. Are the sequences the same or different? Explain.

b. Write an explicit rule for each sequence.

c. How do the explicit rules indicate the geometric relationship between the two graphs?

a. In each case, the sequence is 1, 3, 5, 7, 9, . . . because the points on each graph have those numbers as their second coordinates.

b. For sequence A, the initial term is $f(0) = 1$ and the common difference is 2, so an explicit rule is $f(n) = 1 + 2n$ for $n \geq 0$. For sequence B, the initial term is $f(1) = 1$ and the common difference is 2, so an explicit rule is $f(n) = 1 + 2(n - 1)$ for $n \geq 1$.

c. The explicit rule for sequence B is the result of replacing n in the rule for sequence A with $n - 1$. Doing so translates the graph of sequence A to the right 1 unit.

18. Communicate Mathematical Ideas You know that if $(x_1, f(x_1))$ and $(x_2, f(x_2))$ are two points on the graph of a linear function, the slope of the function's graph is $m = \frac{f(x_2) - f(x_1)}{x_2 - x_1}$. Suppose $(n_1, f(n_1))$ and $(n_2, f(n_2))$ are two points on the graph of an arithmetic sequence with the explicit rule $f(n) = a + dn$. What does the expression $\frac{f(n_2) - f(n_1)}{n_2 - n_1}$ tell you about the arithmetic sequence? Justify your answer.

The expression $\frac{f(n_2) - f(n_1)}{n_2 - n_1}$ gives the sequence's common difference, as follows:

$$\frac{f(n_2) - f(n_1)}{n_2 - n_1} = \frac{(a + dn_2) - (a + dn_1)}{n_2 - n_1}$$
$$= \frac{a + dn_2 - a - dn_1}{n_2 - n_1}$$
$$= \frac{a - a + dn_2 - dn_1}{n_2 - n_1}$$
$$= \frac{d(n_2 - n_1)}{n_2 - n_1}$$
$$= d$$

19. Construct Arguments Show how the recursive rule $f(0) = a$ and $f(n) = f(n - 1) + d$ for $n \geq 0$ generates the explicit rule $f(n) = a + dn$ for $n \geq 0$.

$f(0) = a$

$f(1) = f(0) + d = a + d$

$f(2) = f(1) + d = (a + d) + d = a + 2d$

$f(3) = f(2) + d = (a + 2d) + d = a + 3d$

$f(4) = f(3) + d = (a + 3d) + d = a + 4d$

Generalizing these results gives $f(n) = a + dn$.

Lesson Performance Task

The graph shows how the cost of a personal transporter tour depends on the number of participants. Write explicit and recursive rules for the cost of the tour. Then calculate the cost of the tour for 12 participants.

Examine the points:

n	1	2	3	4	5
$f(n)$	75	100	125	150	175

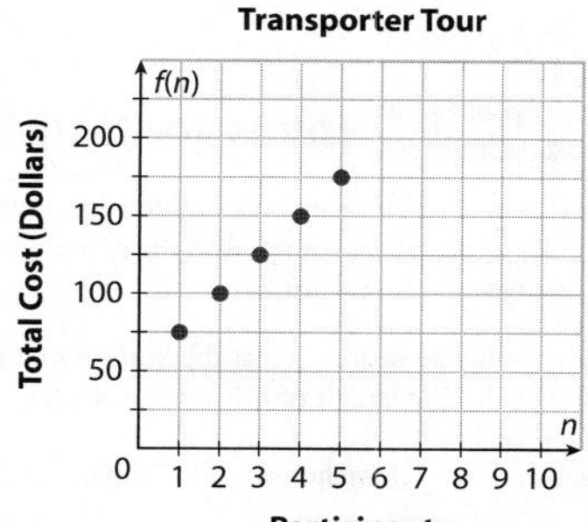

Notice that the difference between consecutive terms is constant, so the graph can be modeled by an arithmetic sequence. The common difference is $d = 25$.

Explicit rule:

$f(n) = a + d(n - 1)$

$= 75 + 25(n - 1)$

Recursive rule:

$f(1) = a$, and $f(n) = f(n - 1) + d$

$f(1) = 75$, and $d = 25$

So, a recursive rule is $f(1) = 75$, and $f(n) = f(n - 1) + 25$ for $n \geq 2$.

When there are 12 participants, $n = 12$.

$f(n) = 75 + 25(12 - 1) = 75 + 25(11) = 350$

The total cost of the tour for 12 participants is $350.

EXTENSION ACTIVITY

Have students solve the following problem.

The first three terms of an arithmetic sequence are $3x - 1$, $4x + 3$, and $7x - 1$. What are the values of the next two terms?

Then have them consider how they could create problems like this one. Have students work in pairs to show how they developed their problems and to test whether they work. **$a_2 - a_1 = a_3 - a_2$; $d = (4x + 3) - (3x - 1) = x + 4$ and $d = (7x - 1) - (4x + 3) = 3x - 4$.**

So, $x + 4 = 3x - 4$, and $x = 4$. The terms are $3(4) - 1 = 11$, $4(4) + 3 = 19$, and $7(4) - 1 = 27$, $d = 8$, so the next two terms are 35 and 43.

CONNECT VOCABULARY EL

Students may or may not have heard the word *segue*, which means transition, or they may assume, from its pronunciation, that it is spelled "segway." They may encounter *segue* in print and pronounce it "seeg" or be unsure of its meaning.

Have students write and pronounce the word correctly. Note that the Segway™ vehicle was named to indicate that riding it would be a smooth transition.

INTEGRATE MATHEMATICAL PRACTICES

Focus on Communication

MP.3 Have students describe the situation and resulting data to be modeled if someone reversed *a* and *d* in the recursive rule. **Reversing *a* and *d* would result in $25 + 75(n - 1)$ and would thus fit the data below.**

n	1	2	3	4
$f(n)$	25	100	175	250

This would indicate a cost of $25 for the first passenger and $75 for each additional passenger.

QUESTIONING STRATEGIES

How would the data differ if the recursive rule had reversed *a* and *d*? **The domain is restricted to either the whole numbers or the natural numbers or, if the sequence is finite, a subset of the whole numbers.**

Scoring Rubric

2 points: Student correctly solves the problem and explains his/her reasoning.

1 point: Student shows good understanding of the problem but does not fully solve or explain his/her reasoning.

0 points: Student does not demonstrate understanding of the problem.

LESSON 12.2

Geometric Sequences

Common Core Math Standards

The student is expected to:

F.BF.A.2

Write ... geometric sequences both recursively and with an explicit formula, use them to model situations, and translate between the two forms. Also F.IF.A.3, F.IF.C.7e, F.BF.A.1a, F.LE.A.2

Mathematical Practices

COMMON CORE **MP.2 Reasoning**

Language Objective

Complete a geometric sequences chart using words, symbols, and graphs.

ENGAGE

Essential Question: How can you define a geometric sequence algebraically?

Possible answer: A geometric sequence can be defined explicitly by the rule $f(n) = ar^n$ for integer values of n greater than or equal to 0, or by the rule $f(n) = ar^{n-1}$ for integer values of n greater than or equal to 1, depending on whether you want the initial value of the sequence to correspond to 0 or to 1. A geometric sequence can also be defined recursively by the rules $f(0) = a$ and $f(n) = f(n-1) \cdot r$ for $n \geq 1$, or by the rules $f(1) = a$ and $f(n) = f(n-1) \cdot r$ for $n \geq 2$.

PREVIEW: LESSON PERFORMANCE TASK

View the Engage section online. Discuss the photo and how the sounds from a musical instrument might be a function of frequency. Then preview the Lesson Performance Task.

Name ______ Class ______ Date ______

12.2 Geometric Sequences

Essential Question: How can you define a geometric sequence algebraically?

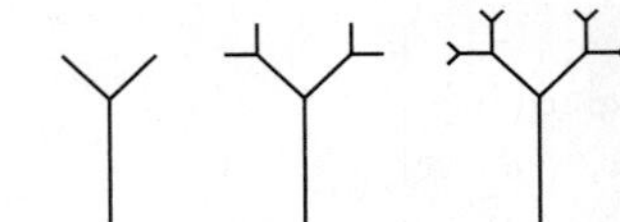

Explore Investigating Geometric Sequences

As a tree grows, limbs branch off of the trunk, then smaller limbs branch off these limbs and each branch splits off into smaller and smaller copies of itself the same way throughout the entire tree. A mathematical object called a *fractal tree* resembles this growth.

Start by drawing a vertical line at the bottom of a piece of paper. This is Stage 0 of the fractal tree and is considered to be one 'branch'. The length of this branch defines 1 unit.

For Stage 1, draw 2 branches off of the top of the first branch. For this fractal tree, each smaller branch is $\frac{1}{2}$ the length of the previous branch and is at a 45-degree angle from the direction of the parent branch. The first four iterations, Stages 0-3, are shown.

(A) In Stage 2, there are 2 branches drawn on the end of each of the 2 branches drawn in Stage 1. There are [4] new branches in Stage 2. Each one of these branches will be $\frac{1}{2}$ the length of its predecessors or [$\frac{1}{4}$] unit in length.

(B) For Stage 3, there are 8 new branches in total. To draw Stage 4, a total of [16] branches must be drawn and to draw Stage 5, a total of [32] branches must be drawn. Thus, each stage adds [2] times as many branches as the previous stage did.

(C) Complete the table.

Stage	New Branches	Pattern	New Branches as a Power
Stage 0	1	1	2^0
Stage 1	2	$2 \cdot 1$	2^1
Stage 2	4	$2 \cdot 2$	2^2
Stage 3	8	$2 \cdot 4$	2^3
Stage 4	16	$2 \cdot 8$	2^4
Stage 5	32	$2 \cdot 16$	2^5
Stage 6	64	$2 \cdot 32$	2^6

HARDCOVER PAGES 597–612

Watch for the hardcover student edition page numbers for this lesson.

Ⓓ The procedure for each stage after Stage 0 is to draw **2** branches on **each** branch added in the previous step.

Ⓔ Using the description above, write an equation for the number of new branches in a stage given the previous stage. Represent stage s as N_s; Stage 3 will be N_3.

$N_4 = \boxed{2} \cdot \boxed{N_3}$ $\quad$ $N_6 = \boxed{2} \cdot \boxed{N_5}$

$N_5 = \boxed{2} \cdot \boxed{N_4}$ $\quad$ $N_s = \boxed{2} \cdot \boxed{N_{s-1}}$

Ⓕ Rewrite the rule for Stage s as a function $N(s)$ that has a stage number as an input and the number of new branches in the stage as an output.

$N(s) = \boxed{2^s}$

Ⓖ Recall that the domain of a function is the set of all numbers for which the function is defined. $N(s)$ is a function of s and s is the stage number. Since the stage number refers to the **number of times** the tree has branched, it has to be **a whole number**.

Write the domain of $N(s)$ in set notation.

$\{s \mid s$ is a **whole** number$\}$

Ⓗ Similarly, the range of a function is the set of all possible values that the function can output over the domain. Let $N(s) = b$, the **number of new branches**.

The range of $N(s)$ is $\{1, 2, 4, \boxed{8}, \boxed{16}, \boxed{32}, \ldots\}$.

The range of $N(s)$ is $\{N \mid N = 2^n$, where n is **a whole number**$\}$.

Ⓘ Graph the first five values of $N(s)$ on the axes provided.

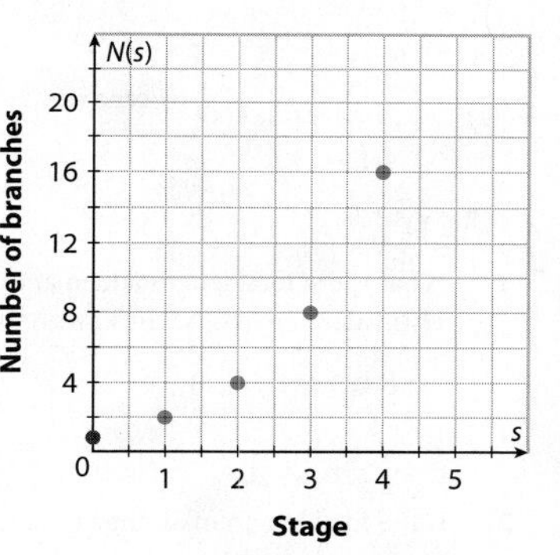

Ⓙ As s increases, $N(s)$ **increases**.

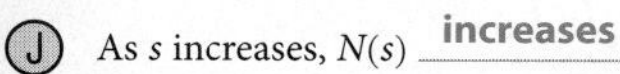

$N(s)$ is **an increasing** function.

EXPLORE

Investigating Geometric Sequences

AVOID COMMON ERRORS

Be sure students pay attention to the domain of the function that defines a sequence. For example, if the domain of $f(n) = n^2 + 1$ is $\{0, 1, 2, 3, \ldots\}$ rather than $\{1, 2, 3, 4, \ldots\}$, then the function generates the sequence 1, 2, 5, 10, … rather than the sequence 2, 5, 10, 17, ….

PROFESSIONAL DEVELOPMENT

Learning Progressions

Previously, students studied arithmetic sequences and wrote general recursive and explicit rules for them. In this lesson, students will study the same aspects of geometric sequences as they learn to recognize a geometric sequence by seeing that each term is related to the previous term by a common ratio.

Students will use the general rules for geometric sequences to write both recursive and explicit rules for specific sequences. Students will also learn about geometric series, which are formed by adding the terms of a geometric sequence. This will prepare them to expand their knowledge of common ratios into continuous situations in their study of exponential functions.

QUESTIONING STRATEGIES

? Can a sequence with repeating terms, such as 1, 1, 2, 2, 3, 3,..., be a function? **Yes, the domain of the function is the set of counting numbers and the set of terms is the range. Values can be repeated in the range of a function.**

? Predict the next term in the sequence $\frac{1}{8}, \frac{1}{4}, \frac{3}{8}, \frac{1}{2}, \frac{5}{8}, \ldots$ Explain your reasoning. **$\frac{3}{4}$; Each term is $\frac{1}{8}$ more than the previous term, so the next term $\frac{1}{8}$ more than $\frac{5}{8}$.**

? What is the tenth term of the sequence $f(n) = 3n$ when the domain is the set of consecutive integers starting with 1? Explain how to find it. **30; evaluate $3n$ for $n = 10$.**

Ⓚ Complete the table for branch length.

Stage Number	Number of Branches	Branch Length
0	1	1
1	2	$\frac{1}{2}$
2	4	$\frac{1}{4}$
3	8	$\frac{1}{8}$
4	16	$\frac{1}{16}$
5	32	$\frac{1}{32}$
⋮	⋮	⋮
n	2^n	$\frac{1}{2^n}$

Ⓛ Write $L(s)$ expressing the branch length as a function of the Stage.

$L(s) = \left(\frac{1}{2}\right)^{s}$

Ⓜ Write the domain and range of $L(s)$ in set notation.

The domain of $L(s)$ is $\{s \mid s$ is a **whole** number$\}$.

The range of $L(s)$ is $\left\{1, \frac{1}{2}, \frac{1}{4}, \frac{1}{8}, \frac{1}{16}, \frac{1}{32}, \ldots\right\}$.

The range of $L(s)$ is $\left\{L \mid L = \left(\frac{1}{2}\right)^n\right.$, where n is **a whole number**$\}$.

Ⓝ Graph the first five values of $N(s)$ on the axes provided. The fifth point has been graphed for you.

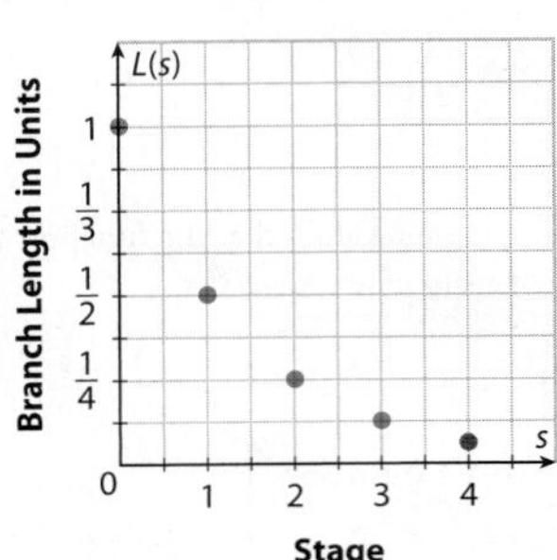

Ⓞ As s increases, $L(s)$ **decreases**. $L(s)$ is **a decreasing** function.

Reflect

1. What is the total length added at each stage?
The total length added at each stage is the number of new branches times the length of each branch. $N(s) \cdot L(s) = 2^s\left(\frac{1}{2}\right)^s = 2^s 2^{-s} = 2^0 = 1$

2. Is the total length of all the branches a sequence? If so, identify the sequence.
The total length is a sequence: 1, 2, 3, . . . s, . . .

COLLABORATIVE LEARNING

Peer-to-Peer Activity

Have pairs of students work together to create a graphic organizer outlining the process for writing explicit and recursive rules for geometric sequences. Include details about how the first term of the sequence and the common ratio are incorporated into each rule.

 Explain 1

Writing Explicit and Recursive Rules for Geometric Sequences

A sequence is a set of numbers related by a common rule. All sequences start with an initial term. In a **geometric sequence**, the ratio of any term to the previous term is constant. This constant ratio is called the **common ratio** and is denoted by r $(r \neq 1)$. In the **explicit form** of the sequence, each term is found by evaluating the function $f(n) = ar^n$ or $f(n) = ar^{n-1}$ where a is the initial value and r is the common ratio, for some whole number n. Note that there are two forms of the explicit rule because it is permissible to call the initial value the first term or to call ar the first term.

A geometric sequence can also be defined recursively $f(n) = r \cdot f(n-1)$ where either $f(0) = a$ or $f(1)$, again depending on the way the terms of the sequence are numbered. $f(n) = r \cdot f(n-1)$ is called the **recursive rule** for the sequence.

Example 1 **Write the explicit and recursive rules for a geometric sequence given a table of values.**

 A

n	0	1	2	3	4	...	$j-1$	j	...
$f(n)$	3	6	12	24	48	...	$ar^{(j-1)}$	ar^j	...

Determine a and r, then write the explicit and recursive rules.

Find the common ratio: $\frac{f(n)}{f(n-1)} = r$. $\qquad \frac{f(1)}{f(0)} = \frac{6}{3} = 2 = r$

Find the initial value, $a = f(0)$, from the table. $\qquad f(0) = 3 = a$

Find the explicit rule: $f(n) = ar^n$. $\qquad f(n) = 3 \cdot (2)^n$

Write the recursive rule. $\qquad f(n) = 2 \cdot f(n-1), n \geq 1$ and $f(0) = 3$

The explicit rule is $f(n) = 3 \cdot (2)^n$ and the recursive rule is $f(n) = 2 \cdot f(n-1), n \geq 1$ and $f(0) = 3$.

 B

n	1	2	3	4	5	...	$j-1$	j	...
$f(n)$	$\frac{1}{25}$	$\frac{1}{5}$	1	5	25	...	$ar^{(j-1)}$	ar^j	...

Determine a and r, then write the explicit and recursive rules.

Find the common ratio: $\frac{f(n)}{f(n-1)} = r$. $\qquad \frac{f(4)}{f(3)} = \frac{5}{1} = 5 = r$

Find the initial value, $a = f(1)$, from the table. $\qquad f(1) = \frac{1}{25} = a$

Find the explicit rule: $f(n) = ar^{n-1}$. $\qquad f(n) = \frac{1}{25} \cdot (5)^{n-1}$

Write the recursive rule. $\qquad f(n) = 5 \cdot f(n-1), n \geq 2$ and $f(1) = 5$

The explicit rule is $f(n) = \frac{1}{25} \cdot (5)^{n-1}$ and the recursive rule is $f(n) = 5 \cdot f(n-1), n \geq 2$ where $f(1) = 5$.

EXPLAIN 1

Writing Explicit and Recursive Rules for Geometric Sequences

AVOID COMMON ERRORS

When applying the sum formula for geometric series, students may subtract the values in the numerator before applying the exponent. Remind them that exponents are evaluated before addition and subtraction in the order of operations.

DIFFERENTIATE INSTRUCTION

Visual Cues

Visual learners may benefit by drawing diagrams that illustrate how the nth term of a sequence with a recursive rule is generated by the terms that come before it. Suggest that students use arrows to show how previous terms become the inputs to generate the terms that follow.

INTEGRATE MATHEMATICAL PRACTICES

Focus on Math Connections

MP.1 After students have written general algebraic formulas for recursive and explicit rules for geometric sequences, compare the process for substituting values for the variables in the formulas for geometric sequences with the process for arithmetic sequences. Point out the similarities, such as the use of a common difference in arithmetic sequences, and the use of a common ratio in geometric sequences. Also, point out the differences, such as how the common difference is added in a recursive rule for an arithmetic sequence, while the common ratio is multiplied in a recursive rule for a geometric sequence.

QUESTIONING STRATEGIES

What is a recursive rule for a geometric sequence with a first term of 3 and a common ratio of −2? $f(1) = 3$ and $f(n) = f(n) = f(n-1) \cdot (-2)$ for $n \geq 2$.

What is an explicit rule for a geometric sequence with a first term of $\frac{5}{6}$ and a common ratio of $\frac{1}{3}$? $f(n) = \frac{-5}{6} \cdot \left(\frac{1}{3}\right)^{n-1}$

If you know the second term and the common ratio of a geometric sequence, can you write an explicit rule for the sequence? Explain. **Yes; you can divide the second term by the common ratio to get the first term. Then, you can substitute the first term and the common ratio into the general explicit rule to get the explicit rule for the sequence.**

Reflect

3. **Discussion** If you were told that a geometric sequence had an initial value of $f(5) = 5$, could you write an explicit and a recursive rule for the function? What would the explicit rule be?

Yes. The form of the rules would change depending on r, but because the sequence is geometric, it would have both forms of the rules. The explicit rule would be $f(n) = 5r^{n-1}$ for some r.

Your Turn

Write the explicit and recursive rules for a geometric sequence given a table of values.

4.

n	0	1	2	3	4	5	6	...
$f(n)$	$\frac{1}{27}$	$\frac{1}{9}$	$\frac{1}{3}$	1	3	9	27	...

Common ratio: $\frac{f(4)}{f(3)} = \frac{3}{1} = 3 = r$

Initial value: $f(0) = \frac{1}{27} = a$

Explicit Form: $f(n) = \frac{1}{27} \cdot (3)^n$

Recursive Form: $f(n) = 3 \cdot f(n-1), n \geq 1$ and $f(0) = \frac{1}{27}$

5.

n	1	2	3	4	5	6	7	...
$f(n)$	0.001	0.01	0.1	1	10	100	1000	...

Common ratio: $\frac{f(5)}{f(4)} = \frac{10}{1} = 10 = r$

Initial value: $f(1) = 0.001 = a$

Explicit Form: $f(n) = 0.001 \cdot (10)^{n-1}$

Recursive Form: $f(n) = 0.001 \cdot f(n-1), n \geq 2$ and $f(1) = 0.001$

LANGUAGE SUPPORT EL

Communicate Math

Have students work in pairs. Ask students to complete a chart like the one below, to show and explain the relationship between a recursive rule and an explicit rule for a geometric sequence, and describe its graph.

Type of sequence	Explicit Rule	Recursive Rule	Graph
Geometric	*(write and describe)*	*(write equation and describe)*	

Explain 2 Graphing Geometric Sequences

To graph a geometric sequence given an explicit or a recursive rule you can use the rule to generate a table of values and then graph those points on a coordinate plane. Since the domain of a geometric sequence consists only of whole numbers, its graph consists of individual points, not a smooth curve.

Example 2 **Given either an explicit or recursive rule for a geometric sequence, use a table to generate values and draw the graph of the sequence.**

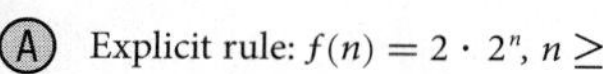

(A) Explicit rule: $f(n) = 2 \cdot 2^n, n \geq 0$

Use a table to generate points.

n	0	1	2	3	4	5	...
$f(n)$	2	4	8	16	32	64	...

Plot the first three points on the graph.

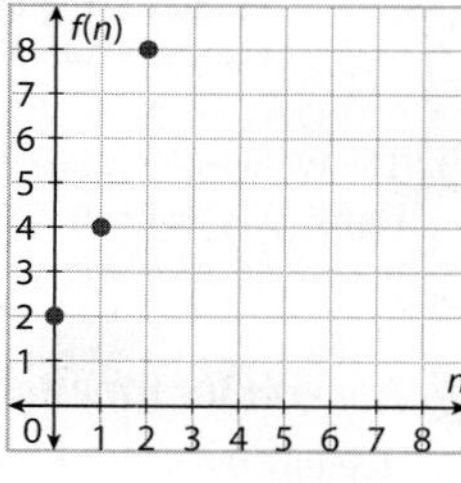

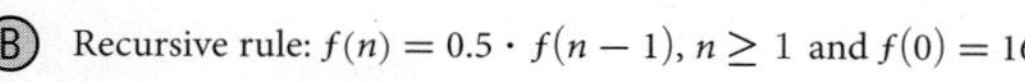

(B) Recursive rule: $f(n) = 0.5 \cdot f(n - 1), n \geq 1$ and $f(0) = 16$

Use a table to generate points.

n	0	1	2	3	4	5	6	...
$f(n)$	16	8	4	2	1	0.5	0.25	...

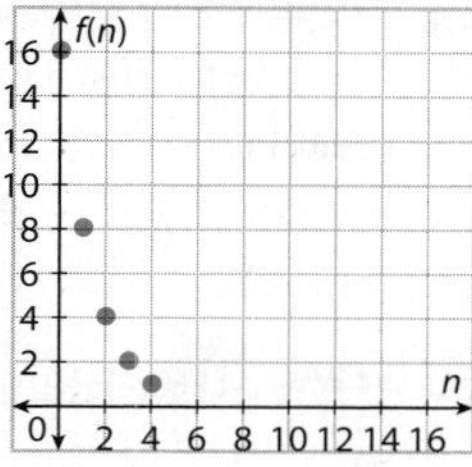

Your Turn

Given either an explicit or recursive rule for a geometric sequence, use a table to generate values and draw the graph of the sequence.

6. $f(n) = 3 \cdot 2^{n-1}, n \geq 1$

n	1	2	3	4	5	...
$f(n)$	3	6	12	24	48	...

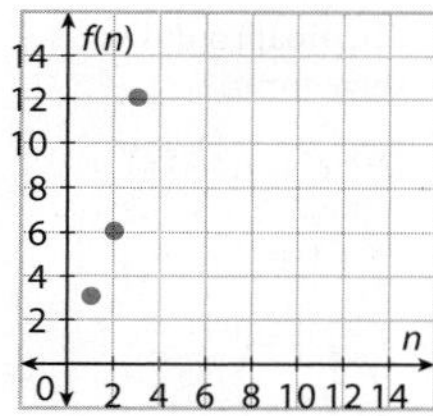

7. $f(n) = 3 \cdot f(n - 1), n \geq 2$ and $f(1) = 2$

n	1	2	3	4	5	...
$f(n)$	2	6	18	54	162	...

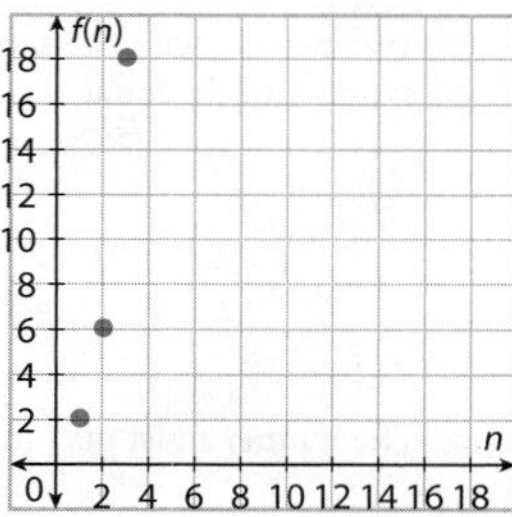

EXPLAIN 2

Graphing Geometric Sequences

AVOID COMMON ERRORS

When looking at a graph with points plotted for only a few values of n, students may incorrectly determine that a geometric sequence is linear and is thus an arithmetic sequence. To avoid this misunderstanding, have students use more values of n and extend both the table and the graph.

QUESTIONING STRATEGIES

How is the domain restricted in the graph of a geometric sequence? **The domain is restricted to a subset of the set of whole numbers.**

How does the graph of a geometric sequence for which the common ratio r is greater than 1 compare with the graph of a geometric sequence for which $0 < r < 1$? **The graph for the geometric sequence with $r > 1$ rises from left to right as x increases, at first slowly and then at an increasingly fast rate. The graph for $0 < r < 1$ falls from left to right as x increases, at first quickly, and then at an increasingly slower rate.**

EXPLAIN 3

Modeling With a Geometric Sequence

QUESTIONING STRATEGIES

? Suppose you began with $f(0)$ as the starting value instead of $f(1)$. Could you still solve the problem? **Yes; you would need to add 1 to the final value of *n*.**

Explain 3 Modeling With a Geometric Sequence

Given a real-world situation that can be modeled with a geometric sequence, you can use an explicit or a recursive rule to answer a question about the situation.

Example 3 **Write both an explicit and recursive rule for the geometric sequence that models the situation. Use the sequence to answer the question asked about the situation.**

(A) The Wimbledon Ladies' Singles Championship begins with 128 players. Each match, two players play and only one moves to the next round. The players compete until there is one winner. How many rounds must the winner play?

Analyze Information

Identify the important information:

- The first round requires 64 matches, so $a =$ 64.
- The next round requires half as many matches, so $r = \frac{1}{2}$.

Formulate a Plan

Using the fact that the domain starts at 1 and the first round has 128 players, create the explicit rule and the recursive rule for the tournament. The final round will have 1 match(es), so substitute this value into the explicit rule and solve for n.

Solve

The explicit rule is $f(n)$ $64 \cdot \left(\frac{1}{2}\right)^{n-1}$, $n = \geq 1$.

The recursive rule is $f(n) = \frac{1}{2} \cdot f(n-1)$, $n \geq 2$ and $f(1) = 64$.

The final round will have 1 match, so substitute 1 for $f(n)$ into the explicit rule and solve for n.

$$f(n) = 64 \cdot \left(\frac{1}{2}\right)^{n-1}$$

$$1 = 64 \cdot \left(\frac{1}{2}\right)^{n-1}$$

$$\frac{1}{64} = \left(\frac{1}{2}\right)^{n-1}$$

$$\left(\frac{1}{2}\right)^{6} = \left(\frac{1}{2}\right)^{n-1}$$

Two powers with the same positive base other than 1 are equal if and only if the exponents are equal.

$$\left(\frac{1}{2}\right)^{6} = \left(\frac{1}{2}\right)^{n-1}$$

$$6 = n - 1$$

$$7 = n$$

The winner must play in 7 rounds.

Justify and Evaluate

The answer of 7 rounds makes sense because using the explicit rule gives $f(7) =$ 1 and the final round will have 1 match(es). This result can be checked using the recursive rule, which again results in $f(7) =$ 1.

Your Turn

Write both an explicit and recursive rule for the geometric sequence that models the situation. Use the sequence to answer the question asked about the situation.

8. A particular type of bacteria divides into two new bacteria every 20 minutes. A scientist growing the bacteria in a laboratory begins with 200 bacteria. How many bacteria are present 4 hours later?

$n = \{0, 1, 2, \ldots\}$ $n =$ number of 20 minute time increments

$r = 2$ The bacteria doubles every 20 minutes.

$f(0) = 200$ Initial value of 200 bacteria at the beginning

Explicit rule: $f(n) = 200 \cdot 2^n$

Recursive rule: $f(n) = 2 \cdot f(n-1), n \geq 0$ and $f(0) = 200$

When 4 hours elapse in this model, $n = 12$, the number of 20-minute increments in 4 hours. Using $n = 12$, there are $f(12) = 200 \cdot 2^{12} = 819,200$ bacteria present after 4 hours.

Elaborate

9. Describe the difference between an explicit rule for a geometric sequence and a recursive rule.

An explicit rule allows you to compute any value in the sequence directly and a recursive rule requires you to compute a value from the previous value.

10. How would you decide to use $n = 0$ or $n = 1$ as the starting value of n for a geometric sequence modeling a real-world situation?

A time-based sequence, such as bacterial growth, typically starts with $n = 0$, which corresponds to a time of 0, meaning that no time has elapsed. For a single-elimination tournament, $n = 1$ typically corresponds to the first round.

11. Essential Question Check-In How can you define a geometric sequence in an algebraic way? What information do you need to write these rules?

You can define a geometric sequence explicitly by the rule $f(n) = ar^n$ for whole number values of n or by the rule $f(n) = ar^{n-1}$ for integer values of n greater than or equal to 1. A geometric sequence can also be defined recursively by the rule $f(0) = a$ and $f(n) = f(n-1) \cdot r$ for $n \geq 1$ or by the rule $f(1) = a$ and $f(n) = f(n-1) \cdot r$ for $n \geq 2$. In both types of rules, you will need to determine the common ratio and an initial value.

ELABORATE

INTEGRATE MATHEMATICAL PRACTICES

Focus on Math Connections

MP.1 Have students consider whether the *Fibonacci sequence*, where $f(1) = 1, f(2) = 1$, and $f(n-1) + f(n-2)$ for $n \geq 3$, is a geometric sequence after the first two terms, an arithmetic sequence, or neither. Students should generate the first few terms and decide that it is neither. Let them know that as n gets very large, the terms approach a geometric sequence with a common ratio approaching the golden ratio, $\frac{1+\sqrt{2}}{2} = 1.618$.

QUESTIONING STRATEGIES

How can you write a rule of a geometric sequence?

To write a recursive rule, assume $f(1)$ is given and use the general rule $f(n) - 1 \cdot r$ for $n \geq 2$, where r is the common ratio. To write an explicit rule, use the general rule $f(n) = f(1) \cdot r^{n-1}$, where $f(1)$ is the first term in the sequence and r is the common ratio.

SUMMARIZE THE LESSON

What is the difference between arithmetic and geometric sequences? What is the difference between a geometric sequence and a geometric series? Arithmetic sequences have a common difference, while geometric sequences have a common ratio. A geometric series is the indicated sum of the terms of a geometric sequence.

EVALUATE

ASSIGNMENT GUIDE

Concepts and Skills	Practice
Explore Investigating Geometric Sequences	Exercises 1–3
Example 1 Writing Explicit and Recursive Rules for Geometric Sequences	Exercises 4–7
Example 2 Graphing Geometric Sequences	Exercises 8–11
Example 3 Modeling with a Geometric Sequence	Exercises 12–17

Connect Vocabulary EL

Connect the terms *arithmetic sequence* and *geometric sequence* to the idea of patterns. Encourage students to discuss the similarities and differences between these two types of sequences. Help students talk about linear variation versus exponential variation as you listen to their explanations.

Evaluate: Homework and Practice

- Online Homework
- Hints and Help
- Extra Practice

You are creating self-similar fractal trees. You start with a trunk of length 1 unit (at Stage 0). Then the trunk splits into two branches each one-third the length of the trunk. Then each one of these branches splits into two new branches, with each branch one-third the length of the previous one.

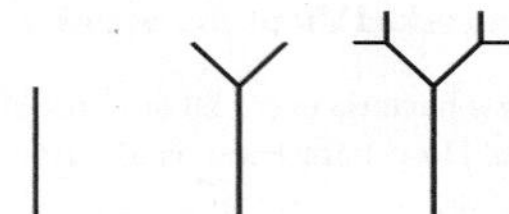

1. Can the length of the new branches at each stage be described with a geometric sequence? Explain. If so, find the explicit form for the length of each branch.

Yes. The sequence of lengths of the new branches per stage has a common ratio relating them and an initial value. Since the new branches are one-third as long as the branches of the previous stage, the common ratio r is $\frac{1}{3}$. The initial condition is $f(0) = a = 1$. Here, the domain is all whole numbers since the first stage is Stage 0. The explicit form is: $f(n) = \left(\frac{1}{3}\right)^n, n \geq 0$.

2. Can the number of new branches at each stage be described with a geometric sequence? Explain. If so, find the recursive rule for the number of new branches.

Yes. The common ratio is $r = 2$ because the number of new branches created at each stage is double the number of branches from the previous stage. The initial condition is $f(0) = a = 1$ because there is one branch, the trunk, at Stage 0. Consequently, the recursive form is $f(n) = 2 \cdot f(n-1), n \geq 1$ and $f(0) = a = 1$. The explicit form is: $f(n) = 2^n, n \geq 0$.

3. Can the total length of the new branches at each stage be modeled with a geometric sequence? Explain. (The total length of the new branches is the sum of the lengths of all the new branches.)

Yes. The total length is the product of the explicit forms of both functions, the number of new branches per stage times their individual length: $f(n) = \left(\frac{1}{3}\right)^n 2^n = \left(\frac{2}{3}\right)^n, n \geq 0$. This is a geometric sequence.

Exercise	Depth of Knowledge (D.O.K.)	COMMON CORE Mathematical Practices
1–3	2 Skills/Concepts	MP.3 Logic
4–6	1 Recall of Information	MP.2 Reasoning
7–11	2 Skills/Concepts	MP.2 Reasoning
12–14	2 Skills/Concepts	MP.4 Modeling
15	3 Strategic Thinking	MP.4 Modeling
16	2 Skills/Concepts	MP.4 Modeling
17–18	3 Strategic Thinking H.O.T.	MP.3 Logic

Write the explicit and recursive rules for a geometric sequence given a table of values.

4.

n	0	1	2	3	4	...
$f(n)$	0.1	0.3	0.9	2.7	8.1	...

Common Ratio: $\frac{f(1)}{f(0)} = \frac{0.3}{0.1} = 3 = r$

Initial Value: $f(0) = 0.1 = a$

Explicit Form: $f(n) = 0.1 \cdot (3)^n$

Recursive Form: $f(n) = 3 \cdot f(n-1), n \geq 1$ and $f(0) = 0.1$

5.

n	0	1	2	3	4	...
$f(n)$	100	10	1	0.1	0.01	...

Common Ratio: $\frac{f(2)}{f(1)} = \frac{1}{10} = 0.1 = r$

Initial Value: $f(0) = 100 = a$

Explicit Form: $f(n) = 100 \cdot (0.1)^n$

Recursive Form: $f(n) = 0.1 \cdot f(n-1), n \geq 1$ and $f(0) = 100$

6.

n	1	2	3	4	5	...
$f(n)$	1000	100	10	1	0.1	...

Common Ratio: $\frac{f(4)}{f(3)} = \frac{1}{10} = 0.1 = r$

Initial Value: $f(1) = 1000 = a$

Explicit Form: $f(n) = 1000 \cdot (0.1)^{n-1}$

Recursive Form: $f(n) = 0.1 \cdot f(n-1), n \geq 2$ and $f(1) = 1000$

7.

n	1	2	3	4	5	...
$f(n)$	10^{50}	10^{47}	10^{44}	10^{41}	10^{38}	...

Common Ratio: $\frac{f(2)}{f(1)} = \frac{10^{47}}{10^{50}} = 10^{-3} = r$

Initial Value: $f(1) = 10^{50} = a$

Explicit Form: $f(n) = 10^{50} \cdot (10^{-3})^{n-1}$

Recursive Form: $f(n) = 10^{-3} \cdot f(n-1), n \geq 2$ and $f(1) = 10^{50}$

INTEGRATE MATHEMATICAL PRACTICES

Focus on Math Connections

MP.1 Ask students to consider the following situation: a collectible purchased for $100 increases in value by either $15 per year or by 10% per year. Have students discuss which increase they would prefer and why. Possible answers may include: "the 10% increase would be better after 10 years or more." Explain that this situation can be used to compare an arithmetic sequence with a geometric sequence.

AVOID COMMON ERRORS

A graph for a geometric sequence may look like an arithmetic sequence when only a few points are plotted. Encourage students to use more values of n by extending their table and graph.

Given either an explicit or recursive rule for a geometric sequence, use a table to generate values and draw the graph of the sequence.

8. $f(n) = \left(\frac{1}{2}\right) \cdot 4^n,\ n \geq 0$

n	0	1	2	3	4	...
$f(n)$	0.5	2	8	32	128	...

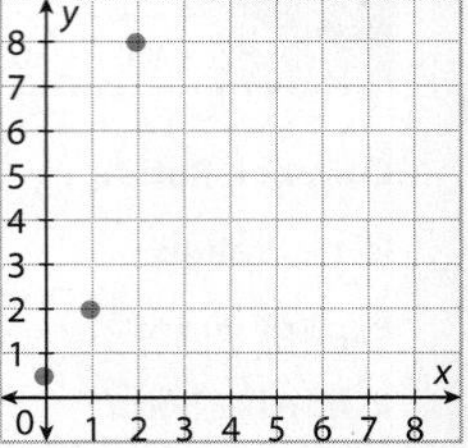

9. $f(n) = 2 \cdot f(n-1),\ n \geq 1$ and $f(0) = 0.5$

n	0	1	2	3	4	...
$f(n)$	0.5	1	2	4	8	...

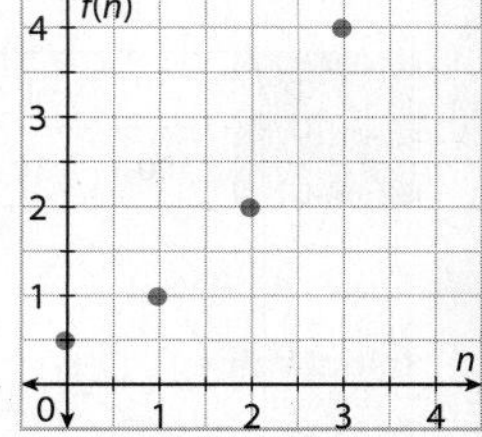

10. $f(n) = 0.5 \cdot f(n-1),\ n \geq 2$ and $f(1) = 8$

n	1	2	3	4	5	...
$f(n)$	8	4	2	1	0.5	...

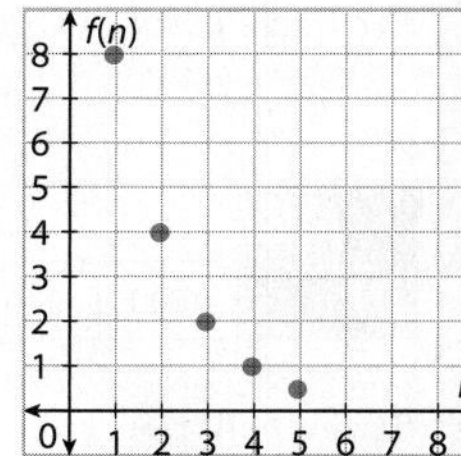

11. $f(n) = \frac{2}{3} \cdot f(n-1),\ n \geq 2$ and $f(1) = 1$

n	1	2	3	4	5	...
$f(n)$	1	0.666...	0.444...	0.296...	0.197...	...

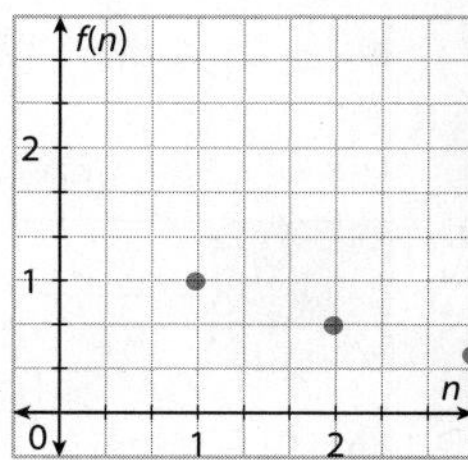

Write both an explicit and recursive rule for the geometric sequence that models the situation. Use the sequence to answer the question asked about the situation.

12. The Alphaville Youth Basketball committee is planning a single-elimination tournament. The committee wants the winner to play 4 games. How many teams should the committee invite?

Explicit rule: $f(n) = 2^n, n \geq 1$

Recursive rule: $f(n) = 2 \cdot f(n-1), n \geq 2$ and $f(1) = 2$

$f(4) = 2^4 = 16$

16 teams

13. An online video game tournament begins with 1024 players. Four players play in each game. In each game there is only one winner, and only the winner advances to the next round. How many games will the winner play?

$a = 256 \quad r = \frac{1}{4}$

Explicit rule: $f(n) = 256\left(\frac{1}{4}\right)^{n-1}, n \geq 1$

Recursive rule: $f(n) = \left(\frac{1}{4}\right) \cdot f(n-1),\ n \geq 2.$

and $f(1) = 256$

$f(n) = 256\left(\frac{1}{4}\right)^{n-1}$

$1 = 256\left(\frac{1}{4}\right)^{n-1}$

$\frac{1}{256} = \left(\frac{1}{4}\right)^{n-1}$

$\left(\frac{1}{4}\right)^4 = \left(\frac{1}{4}\right)^{n-1}$

$4 = n - 1$

$5 = n$

The winner plays 5 games.

14. Genealogy You have 2 biological parents, 4 biological grandparents, and 8 biological great-grandparents.

a. How many direct ancestors do you have if you trace your ancestry back 6 generations? How many direct ancestors do you have if you go back 12 generations?

Explicit rule: $a = 1, r = 2,$ and $f(n) = 2^n, n \geq 0$

Recursive rule: $f(n) = 2 \cdot f(n-1), n > 1$ and $f(0) = 1$

$f(6) = 2^6 = 64$ and $f(12) = 2^{12} = 4096.$

You have 64 ancestors back 6 generations and 4096 ancestors back 12 generations.

b. What if...? How does the explicit rule change if you are considered the first generation?

$a = 1, r = 2, f(n) = ar^{n-1} = 2^{n-1}, n \geq 1$

PEER-TO-PEER DISCUSSION

Pair students. Have one student write the first five terms of a geometric sequence and have the other student describe how to give its rule in both recursive and explicit forms. Then have students switch roles.

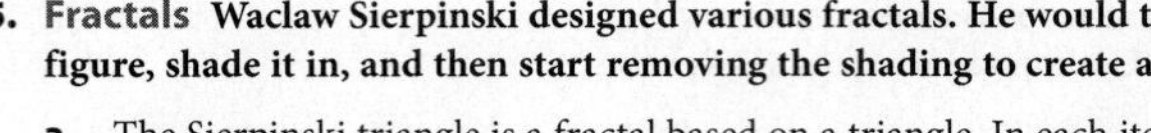

15. Fractals Waclaw Sierpinski designed various fractals. He would take a geometric figure, shade it in, and then start removing the shading to create a fractal pattern.

a. The Sierpinski triangle is a fractal based on a triangle. In each iteration, the center of each shaded triangle is removed.

Given that the area of the original triangle is 1 square unit, write a sequence for the area of the nth iteration of the Sierpinski triangle. (The first iteration is the original triangle.)

$r = \frac{3}{4}$

$a = 1$

Explicit rule: $f(n) = \left(\frac{3}{4}\right)^{n-1}, n \geq 1$

Recursive rule: $f(n) = \left(\frac{3}{4}\right) \cdot f(n-1), n \geq 2$ **and** $f(1) = 1$

b. The Sierpinski carpet is a fractal based on a square. In each iteration, the center of each shaded square is removed.

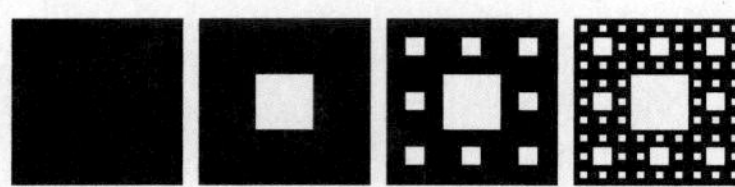

Given that the area of the original square is 1 square unit, write a sequence for the area of the nth iteration of the Sierpinski carpet. (The first iteration is the original square.)

$r = \frac{8}{9}$

$a = 1$

Explicit rule: $f(n) = \left(\frac{8}{9}\right)^{n-1}, n \geq 1$

Recursive rule: $f(n) = \left(\frac{8}{9}\right) \cdot f(n-1), n \geq 2$ **and** $f(1) = 1$

c. Find the shaded area of the fourth iteration of the Sierpinski carpet.

$f(4) = \left(\frac{8}{9}\right)^{4-1}$

$= \frac{512}{729}$

$\approx$ **0.702 square unit**

16. A piece of paper is 0.1 millimeter thick. When folded, the paper is twice as thick.

a. Find both the explicit and recursive rule for this geometric sequence.

Let n, the domain, be the number of folds, starting with 0 folds. Since the domain is the whole numbers, use $f(n) = ar^n$ for the explicit rule. At 0 folds, the paper is 0.1 millimeter thick.

$f(0) = 0.1 = a$

$r = 2$

Explicit rule: $f(n) = 0.1(2)^n$

Recursive rule: $f(n) = 2 \cdot f(n - 1)$, $n \geq 1$ and $f(0) = 0.1$

b. Studies have shown that you can fold a piece of paper a maximum of 7 times. How thick will the paper be if it is folded on top of itself 7 times?

$f(7) = 0.1(2)^7 = 0.1 \cdot 128 = 12.8$

The paper would be 12.8 millimeters thick after 7 folds.

c. Assume that you could fold the paper as many times as you want. How many folds would be required for the paper to be taller than Mount Everest at 8850 meters? (*Hint:* Use a calculator to generate two large powers of 2 and check if the required number of millimeters is between those two powers. Continue to refine your guesses.)

First, convert 8850 meters into millimeters: 8850 meters = 8,850,000 millimeters. Set $f(n) = 8{,}850{,}000$. Find the value of n corresponding to $f(n) = 8{,}850{,}000$.

$f(n) = 8{,}850{,}000 = 0.1(2)^n$

$88{,}500{,}000 = 2^n$

$2^{26} < 88{,}500{,}000 < 2^{27}$

It will take 27 folds to surpass Mount Everest in height.

JOURNAL

Have students write a journal entry that describes any initial confusion or difficulty they may have encountered in working with geometric sequences and series. Have students describe strategies for correcting or preventing these difficulties.

H.O.T. Focus on Higher Order Thinking

17. Justify Reasoning Suppose you have the following table of points of a geometric sequence. The table is incomplete so you do not know the initial value. Explain why each of the following can or cannot be the rules for the function in the table.

n	...	4	5	6	7	...
$f(n)$	...	6	12	24	48	...

a. $f(n) = 2^n$

b. $f(n) = \frac{3}{8} \cdot (2)^n$

c. $f(n) = 2 \cdot f(n-1), n \geq 1$ and $f(0) = 6$

d. $f(n) = \frac{3}{4} \cdot (2)^{n-1}$

e. $f(n) = 2 \cdot f(n-1), n \geq 1$ and $f(0) = \frac{3}{8}$

f. $f(n) = 2 \cdot f(n-1), n \geq 1$ and $f(1) = \frac{3}{4}$

g. $f(n) = (1.5) \cdot (2)^{n-2}$

h. $f(n) = 3 \cdot (2)^{n-3}$

A is incorrect because $f(4) = 6$, and if A were correct, then $f(4) = 16$.

C is incorrect because $f(4) = 6$ and so $f(0) \neq 6$. If $n = 0$ is in the domain, then $f(0) = \frac{3}{8} = 0.375$.

B, D, E, F, G, and H are all possible correct rules for different initial whole number values for n ranging from 0 to 3.

18. Communicate Mathematical Ideas Show that the rules $f(n) = ar^n$ for $n \geq 0$ and $f(n) = ar^{n-1}$ for $n \geq 1$ for a geometric sequence are equivalent.

To show these rules are equivalent, let $j = n - 1$ and rewrite the second rule.

$f(n) = ar^{n-1}$ for $n \geq 1$	Second rule
$f(j+1) = ar^j$ for $(j+1) \geq 1$	Let $j = n-1$ (or $n = j+1$) and substitute.
$f(j) = ar^j$ for $j \geq 0$	Simplify and get first rule.

Thus, you have the first rule for a geometric sequence with the variable name for the variable changed to j instead of n: $f(j) = ar^j$ for $j \geq 0$. Therefore, the rules are equivalent.

Lesson Performance Task

Have you ever heard of musical octaves? Octaves are defined as the interval between the same musical note in a higher or lower pitch. Octaves are geometric sequences. For example, the table shows the frequencies produced by playing the note D in ascending octaves, D_0 being the lowest D note audible to the human ear.

Scale of D's	
Note	**Frequency (Hz)**
D_0	18.35
D_1	35.71
D_2	73.42
D_3	146.83

a. Explain how to write an explicit rule and a recursive rule for the frequency of D notes in hertz, where $n = 1$ represents D_1.

Find the common ratio. $r = \frac{D_2}{D_1} = \frac{73.42}{35.71} \approx 2$ $\quad r = \frac{D_3}{D_2} = \frac{146.83}{73.42} \approx 2$

The common ratio is about 2.

Identify the first term a_1. $a_1 = D_1 = 35.71$

explicit rule $f(n) = 35.71(2)^{n-1}$

recursive rule: $f(1) = 35.71$ and $f(n) = f(n-1) \cdot 2$ for $n \geq 2$

b. The note commonly called "middle D" is D_4. Use the explicit rule or the recursive rule from part **a** to predict the frequency for middle D.

Using the explicit rule: $f(4) = 35.71(2)^{(4)-1}$

$= 285.68$

The frequency of middle D is about 285.68 Hz.

c. Humans generally cannot hear sounds with frequencies greater than 20,000 Hz. What is the first D note that humans cannot hear? Explain.

Use a graphing calculator to solve. $20{,}000 = 35.71(2)^{n-1}$

$n \approx 10.13$.

The first D note that humans cannot hear is D_{11} because n can only be an integer and $f(10) = 35.71(2)^{(10)-1} \approx 18{,}283.5$, which is less than 20,000.

EXTENSION ACTIVITY

Have students research the relationship between frequency and wavelength. Then have students write the geometric sequence for the sound *wavelength* of the octaves D_n. Have students compare this sequence to the one for sound frequencies. $f = \frac{v}{\lambda}$, where v is the speed of sound and λ is the wavelength. $\lambda_n = \frac{v}{a_1}\left(\frac{1}{2}\right)^{n-1}$ is a *decreasing* geometric sequence.

AVOID COMMON ERRORS

Students may calculate r as $\frac{D_1}{D_2} = \frac{1}{2}$ rather than $\frac{D_2}{D_1} = 2$. Explain that $r = \frac{D_1}{D_2}$ will give a decreasing sequence, but the Performance Task describes an increasing sequence. Therefore, r must be greater than 1.

INTEGRATE MATHEMATICAL PRACTICES

Focus on Math Connections

MP.1 Have students explain why a geometric sequence is appropriate for modeling the frequencies of octaves. Have students describe the behavior of linear and quadratic functions and discuss how octave frequencies would behave if they were modeled by these functions.

Scoring Rubric

2 points: Student correctly solves the problem and explains his/her reasoning.

1 point: Student shows good understanding of the problem but does not fully solve or explain his/her reasoning.

0 points: Student does not demonstrate understanding of the problem.

LESSON 12.3

Geometric Series

Common Core Math Standards

The student is expected to:

A-SSE.B.4

Derive the formula for the sum of a finite geometric series (when the common ratio is not 1), and use the formula to solve problems.
Also A-SSE.A.2

Mathematical Practices

MP.7 Using Structure

Language Objective

Explain to a partner how to find the sum of a finite geometric series.

ENGAGE

Essential Question: How do you find the sum of a finite geometric series?

Possible answer: Identify the first term *a*, the common ratio *r*, and the number of terms, *n*. Then apply the formula $S(n) = a\left(\frac{1-r^n}{1-r}\right)$ to find the sum of the geometric series.

PREVIEW: LESSON PERFORMANCE TASK

View the online Engage. Discuss how loan balances are reduced by payments but also grow, at the same time. Then preview the Lesson Performance Task.

Name _______________ Class _______________ Date _______________

12.3 Geometric Series

Essential Question: How do you find the sum of a finite geometric series?

Resource Locker

Explore 1 Investigating a Geometric Series

A **series** is the expression formed by adding the terms of a sequence. If the sequence is geometric and has a finite number of terms, it is called a **finite geometric series**. In this Explore, you will generate several related finite geometric series and find a formula for calculating the sum of each series.

(A) Start with a rectangular sheet of paper and assume the sheet has an area of 1 square unit. Cut the sheet in half and lay down one of the half-pieces. Then cut the remaining piece in half, and lay down one of the quarter-pieces as if rebuilding the original sheet of paper. Continue the process: At each stage, cut the remaining piece in half, and lay down one of the two pieces as if rebuilding the original sheet of paper.

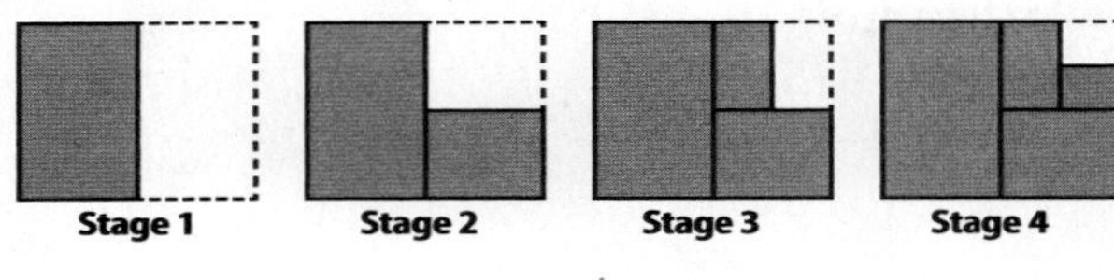

n/a

(B) Complete the table by expressing the total area of the paper that has been laid down in two ways:

- as the sum of the areas of the pieces that have been laid down, and
- as the difference between 1 and the area of the remaining piece.

Stage	Sum of the areas of the pieces that have been laid down	Difference of 1 and the area of the remaining piece
1	$\frac{1}{2}$	$1 - \frac{1}{2} = \boxed{\frac{1}{2}}$
2	$\frac{1}{2} + \boxed{\frac{1}{4}} = \boxed{\frac{3}{4}}$	$1 - \boxed{\frac{1}{4}} = \boxed{\frac{3}{4}}$
3	$\frac{1}{2} + \boxed{\frac{1}{4}} + \boxed{\frac{1}{8}} = \boxed{\frac{7}{8}}$	$1 - \boxed{\frac{1}{8}} = \boxed{\frac{7}{8}}$
4	$\frac{1}{2} + \boxed{\frac{1}{4}} + \boxed{\frac{1}{8}} + \boxed{\frac{1}{16}} = \boxed{\frac{15}{16}}$	$1 - \boxed{\frac{1}{16}} = \boxed{\frac{15}{16}}$

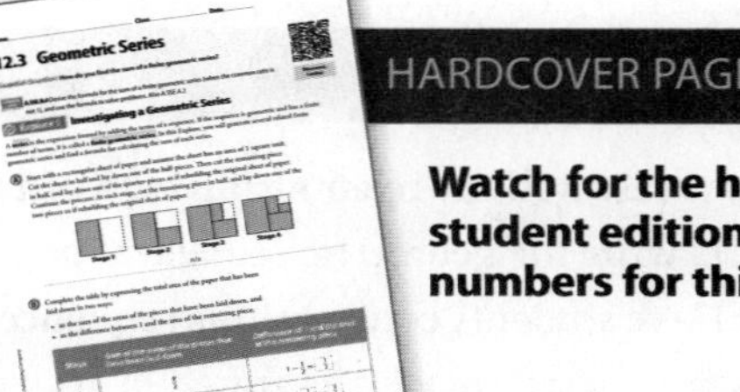

HARDCOVER PAGES 613–628

Watch for the hardcover student edition page numbers for this lesson.

Reflect

1. Write the sequence formed by the areas of the individual pieces that are laid down. What type of sequence is it?
The sequence formed by the areas of the individual pieces laid down is $\frac{1}{2}, \frac{1}{4}, \frac{1}{8}, \frac{1}{16}, \ldots$. It is a geometric sequence with a common ratio of $\frac{1}{2}$.

2. In the table from Step B, you wrote four related finite geometric series: $\frac{1}{2}, \frac{1}{2} + \frac{1}{4}, \frac{1}{2} + \frac{1}{4} + \frac{1}{8}$, and $\frac{1}{2} + \frac{1}{4} + \frac{1}{8} + \frac{1}{16}$. One way you found the sum of each series was simply to add up the terms. Describe another way you found the sum of each series.
Subtract the last term in the series from 1.

3. If the process of cutting the remaining piece of paper and laying down one of the two pieces is continued, you obtain the finite geometric series $\frac{1}{2} + \frac{1}{4} + \ldots + \left(\frac{1}{2}\right)^n$ at the nth stage. Use your answer to the previous question to find the sum of this series.
$1 - \left(\frac{1}{2}\right)^n$

Explore 2 Deriving a Formula for the Sum of a Finite Geometric Series

To find a general formula for the sum of a finite geometric series with n terms, begin by writing the series as $S(n) = a + ar + ar^2 + \ldots + ar^{n-1}$.

(A) Find an expression for $rS(n)$.

$$rS(n) = ar + ar^2 + ar^{\boxed{3}} \ldots + ar^{\boxed{n}}$$

(B) Find an expression for $S(n) - rS(n)$ by aligning like terms and subtracting.

$$S(n) = a + ar + ar^2 + \ldots + ar^{n-1}$$
$$-rS(n) = ar + ar^2 + \ldots + ar^{n-1} + ar^n$$
$$S(n) - rS(n) = a + \boxed{0} + \boxed{0} + \ldots + \boxed{0} - ar^n$$

(C) Simplify the expression for $S(n) - rS(n)$.

$$S(n) - rS(n) = \boxed{a - ar^n}$$

(D) Factor the left and right sides of the equation in Step C.

$$S(n)\boxed{1 - r} = \boxed{a}(1 - r^{\boxed{n}})$$

(E) Divide both sides of the equation in Step D by $1 - r$.

$$S(n) = a\left(\frac{\boxed{1} - \boxed{r^n}}{1 - r}\right)$$

PROFESSIONAL DEVELOPMENT

Learning Progressions

In the previous lesson, students learned to recognize a geometric sequence by observing that each term was related to the previous term by a common ratio. Students used the general rules for geometric sequences to write both recursive and explicit rules for specific sequences. Students will now learn about geometric series, which are formed by adding the terms of a geometric sequence. They will derive a formula that can be used to find the sum of a geometric series given the first term of the series, the common ratio, and the number of terms in the series. They will then use the formula to find the sum of a geometric series and to solve real-world problems that can be modeled by a geometric series.

EXPLORE 1

Investigating a Geometric Series

INTEGRATE TECHNOLOGY

Students have the option of completing the Explore activity either in the book or online.

QUESTIONING STRATEGIES

? What happens to the total area of the pieces laid down as the number of stages, n, increases? **As n increases, the total area of the pieces laid down gets closer to 1, the area of the paper.**

EXPLORE 2

Deriving a Formula for the Sum of a Finite Geometric Series

QUESTIONING STRATEGIES

? Why does subtracting $rS(n)$ from $S(n)$ result in the difference between the last term of $rS(n)$ and the first term of $S(n)$? **because the other terms are common to both expansions and subtract out to 0**

? What restrictions are there on the values of r that can be used in the formula for the sum of a geometric series? **The value of r cannot be 1, because $1 - r$ is in a denominator in the formula for the sum, and division by zero is undefined.**

INTEGRATE MATHEMATICAL PRACTICES

Focus on Modeling

MP.4 Discuss with students the meaning of the variables in the formula, and ask them to tell how their values can be identified for any given geometric series. Also, check to ensure that students understand what the resulting value of $S(n)$ represents.

EXPLAIN 1

Finding the Sum of a Finite Geometric Series

AVOID COMMON ERRORS

When applying the formula for the sum of a finite geometric series, students may subtract the values in the numerator before applying the exponent. Remind them that exponents are evaluated before addition and subtraction in the order of operations.

QUESTIONING STRATEGIES

How do you find n for a geometric series when only the first few terms and the last term are given? **Set the last term equal to $a(r)^{n-1}$, substitute for a and r, and solve for n.**

How can you tell if you need to substitute a negative number for r? **If the signs of the terms of the series alternate, then r is a negative number.**

INTEGRATE TECHNOLOGY

Students can use the **Seq** mode of a graphing calculator to check their work by using the appropriate **LIST** options for the sum of a sequence.

Reflect

4. Check to see if the formula in Step E gives the same result as the answer you wrote for Reflect 3.
   The finite geometric series in Reflect 3 has an initial term a equal to $\frac{1}{2}$, a common ratio r equal to $\frac{1}{2}$, and n terms. The formula above gives this sum: $S(n) = \frac{1}{2}\left(\frac{1-\left(\frac{1}{2}\right)^n}{1-\frac{1}{2}}\right) = \frac{1}{2}\left(\frac{1-\left(\frac{1}{2}\right)^n}{\frac{1}{2}}\right) = 1 - \left(\frac{1}{2}\right)^n$. This agrees with the sum from Reflect 3.

5. What restrictions are there on the values of r that can be used in the formula for the sum of a finite geometric series? Explain.
   $r \neq 1$, because $r = 1$ would result in division by 0 in the formula.

Explain 1 Finding the Sum of a Finite Geometric Series

The formula $S(n) = a\left(\frac{1-r^n}{1-r}\right)$ for the sum of a geometric series requires knowing the values of a, r, and n.

Recall that you learned how to find a and r for a geometric sequence, and the technique is no different for a series: a is the value of the first term, and r is the ratio of any two successive terms. To find n, you can simply count the terms if they are all listed. For instance, for the finite geometric series $3 + 6 + 12 + 24 + 48$, you can see that $a = 3$, $r = 2$, and $n = 5$.

If some of the terms of a finite geometric series have been replaced by an ellipsis, as in $2 + 6 + 18 + \ldots + 1458$, you obviously can't count the terms. One way to deal with this situation is to generate the missing terms by using the common ratio, which in this case is 3. The next term after 18 is $3(18) = 54$, and repeated multiplications by 3 to generate successive terms gives $2 + 6 + 18 + 54 + 162 + 486 + 1458$, so the series has 7 terms.

Another way to find the number of terms in $2 + 6 + 18 + \ldots + 1458$ is to recognize that the nth term in a geometric series is ar^{n-1}. For the series $2 + 6 + 18 + \ldots + 1458$ whose nth term is $2(3)^{n-1}$, find n as follows:

$2(3)^{n-1} = 1458$	Set the nth term equal to the last term.
$(3)^{n-1} = 729$	Divide both as power of 3
$(3)^{n-1} = 3^6$	Write 729 as a power of 3
$n - 1 = 6$	When the bases are the same, you can equate the exponents.
$n = 7$	Add 1 to both sides

Find the sum of the finite geometric series.

(A) $5 + 15 + 45 + 135 + 405 + 1215$

Step 1 Find the values of a, r, and n.

The first term in the series is a.	$a = 5$
Find the common ratio r by dividing two successive terms.	$r = \frac{15}{5} = 3$
Count the terms to find n.	$n = 6$

COLLABORATIVE LEARNING

Peer-to-Peer Activity

Have students work in pairs. Instruct each student to create a finite geometric series consisting of 10 to 15 terms. Have them find the sum of each series. Then have them exchange series with their partners, giving them only the series' first three terms and the last term. Students should not tell the partner the number of terms in the series. Have students find the sums of the series they are given, and compare their results with their partners.

Step 2 Use the formula $S(n) = a\left(\frac{1-r^n}{1-r}\right)$.

Substitute the values of a, r, and n. $S(6) = 5\left(\frac{1-3^6}{1-3}\right)$

Evaluate the power in the numerator. $= 5\left(\frac{1-729}{1-3}\right)$

Simplify the numerator and denominator. $= 5\left(\frac{-728}{-2}\right)$

Simplify the fraction. $= 5(364)$

Multiply. $= 1820$

(B) $\frac{1}{4} + \frac{1}{8} + \frac{1}{16} + \dots + \frac{1}{512}$

Step 1 Find the values of a, r, and n.

The first term in the series is a. $a = \boxed{\frac{1}{4}}$

Find the common ratio by dividing two successive terms. $r = \frac{\frac{1}{8}}{\boxed{\frac{1}{4}}} = \boxed{\frac{1}{2}}$

Set the nth term, $\frac{1}{4}\left(\frac{1}{2}\right)^{n-1}$, equal to the last term to find n. $\frac{1}{4}\left(\frac{1}{2}\right)^{n-1} = \boxed{\frac{1}{512}}$

Multiply both sides by $\boxed{}$. $\left(\frac{1}{2}\right)^{n-1} = \frac{1}{128}$

Write $\frac{1}{128}$ as a power of $\frac{1}{2}$. $\left(\frac{1}{2}\right)^{n-1} = \left(\frac{1}{2}\right)^{\boxed{7}}$

Equate the exponents. $n - 1 = \boxed{7}$

Add 1 to both sides. $n = \boxed{8}$

Step 2 Use the formula $S(n) = a\left(\frac{1-r^n}{1-r}\right)$.

Substitute the values of a, r, and n. $S(8) = \boxed{\frac{1}{4}}\left(\frac{1-\left(\boxed{\frac{1}{2}}\right)^{\boxed{8}}}{1-\boxed{\frac{1}{2}}}\right)$

Evaluate the power in the numerator. $= \frac{1}{4}\left(\frac{1-\boxed{\frac{1}{256}}}{1-\frac{1}{2}}\right)$

Simplify the numerator and denominator. $= \frac{1}{4}\left(\frac{\boxed{\frac{255}{256}}}{\frac{1}{2}}\right)$

Simplify the fraction. $= \frac{1}{4}\left(\boxed{\frac{255}{128}}\right)$

Multiply. $= \boxed{\frac{255}{521}}$

DIFFERENTIATE INSTRUCTION

Modeling

Learners who have trouble visualizing area may benefit from using a strip of paper in the Explore activity instead of a sheet of paper. Starting with a strip of paper whose length is taken to be 1 unit, students can fold it in half, cut at the crease, and lay down one of the halves. By repeating the process and laying down the successive halves end to end, students will still be able to complete the table, but they will be focused on length rather than area.

Your Turn

Find the sum of the finite geometric series.

6. $1 - 2 + 4 - 8 + 16 - 32$

$a = 1$

$r = \frac{-2}{1} = -2$

$n = 6$

$S(6) = 1\left(\frac{1-(-2)^6}{1-(-2)}\right)$

$= \frac{1-64}{3}$

$= \frac{-63}{3}$

$= -21$

7. $\frac{1}{2} - \frac{1}{4} + \frac{1}{8} \ldots - \frac{1}{256}$

$a = \frac{1}{2}$

$r = \frac{-\frac{1}{4}}{\frac{1}{2}} = -\frac{1}{2}$

$\frac{1}{2}\left(-\frac{1}{2}\right)^{n-1} = -\frac{1}{256}$

$\left(-\frac{1}{2}\right)^{n-1} = -\frac{1}{128}$

$\left(-\frac{1}{2}\right)^{n-1} = \left(-\frac{1}{2}\right)^7$

$n - 1 = 7$

$n = 8$

$S(8) = \frac{1}{2}\left(\frac{1-\left(-\frac{1}{2}\right)^8}{1-\left(-\frac{1}{2}\right)}\right)$

$= \frac{1}{2}\left(\frac{1-\frac{1}{256}}{1+\frac{1}{2}}\right)$

$= \frac{1}{2}\left(\frac{\frac{255}{256}}{\frac{3}{2}}\right)$

$= \frac{1}{2}\left(\frac{85}{128}\right)$

$= \frac{85}{256}$

LANGUAGE SUPPORT EL

Communicate Math

Have students work in pairs. Ask the first student to choose a finite geometric series and explain to the second student how to find the sum. The second student writes down the steps, and reads them back to the first student. Have both students edit the steps that have been written down until they are satisfied with the result.

Listen as students talk to ensure that they are not confusing the terms *sequence* and *series.* If you notice confusion, step in and point out the mathematical difference between the two terms.

 Explain 2 Solving a Real-World Problem Involving a Finite Geometric Series

Some financial problems can be modeled by geometric series. For instance, an *annuity* involves equal payments made at regular intervals for a fixed amount of time. Because money can be invested and earn interest, comparing the value of money today to the value of money in the future requires accounting for the effect of interest. The *future value* of an annuity is how much the annuity payments will be worth at some point in the future. The *present value* of an annuity is how much the annuity payments are worth in the present.

Although an interest rate is typically expressed as an annual rate, it can be converted to a rate for other periods of time. For instance, an annual interest rate of $r\%$ results in a monthly interest rate of $\frac{r}{12}\%$. In general, if interest is earned n times per year, an annual interest rate of $r\%$ is divided by n.

Example 2

(A) Niobe is saving for a down payment on a new car, which she intends to buy a year from now. At the end of each month, she deposits \$200 from her paycheck into a dedicated savings account, which earns 3% annual interest that is applied to the account balance each month. After making 12 deposits, how much money will Niobe have in her savings account?

Niobe is interested in the future value of her annuity (savings plan). A 3% annual interest rate corresponds to a $\frac{3}{12}\% = 0.25\%$ monthly interest rate.

First, calculate the sequence of end-of-month account balances. Recognize the recursive nature of the calculations:

- The end-of-month balance for month 1 is \$200 because the first deposit of \$200 is made at the end of the month, but the deposit doesn't earn any interest that month.
- The end-of-month balance for any other month is the sum of the previous month's end-of-month balance, the interest earned on the previous month's end-of-month balance, and the next deposit.

So, if $B(m)$ represents the account balance for month m, then a recursive rule for the account balances is $B(1) = 200$ and $B(m) = B(m-1) + B(m-1) \cdot 0.0025 + 200$. Notice that you can rewrite the equation $B(m) = B(m-1) + B(m-1) \cdot 0.0025 + 200$ as $B(m) = B(m-1) \cdot 1.0025 + 200$ by using the Distributive Property.

EXPLAIN 2

Solving a Problem Involving a Finite Geometric Series

QUESTIONING STRATEGIES

? Why is r equal to the sum of 1 and the interest rate? Multiplying by the sum of 1 and the interest rate produces 100% of the amount of money that is in the account plus the interest on that money. This is the multiplier from year to year.

INTEGRATE MATHEMATICAL PRACTICES

Focus on Communication

MP.3 Ask students to explain *why* this problem can be modeled using a geometric series. Have them brainstorm other, related real-world situations that would also lend themselves to this type of model and solution.

COMMUNICATE MATH EL

Help students understand the difference between the word *finite* and the word *infinite*. They may not be as familiar with *finite* as they are with *infinite*, which is more commonly used in ordinary speech.

Month	End-of-month balance of account
1	200
2	$200 \cdot 1.0025 + 200$
3	$[200(1.0025) + 200] \cdot 1.0025 + 200 = 200(1.0025)^2 + 200(1.0025) + 200$
4	$[200(1.0025)^2 + 200(1.0025) + 200] \cdot 1.0025 + 200 = 200(1.0025)^3 + 200(1.0025)^2 + 200(1.0025) + 200$
⋮	⋮
12	$[200(1.0025)^{10} + \cdots + 200] \cdot 1.0025 + 200 = 200(1.0025)^{11} + \cdots + 200(1.0025) + 200$

Next, find the sum of the finite geometric series that represents the end-of-month balance after 12 deposits. You may find it helpful to use the commutative property to rewrite $200(1.0025)^{11} + \cdots + 200(1.0025) + 200$ as $200 + 200(1.0025) + \cdots + 200(1.0025)^{11}$ so that it's easier to see that the initial term a is 200 and the common ratio r is 1.0025. Also, you know from the recursive process that this series has 12 terms. Apply the formula for the sum of a finite geometric series in order to obtain the final balance of the account.

$$S(12) = 200\left(\frac{1 - 1.0025^{12}}{1 - 1.0025}\right)$$

To evaluate the expression for the sum, use a calculator. You may find it helpful to enter the expression in parts and rely upon the calculator's Answer feature to accumulate the results. (You should avoid rounding intermediate calculations, because the round-off errors will compound and give an inaccurate answer.)

So, Niobe will have $2433.28 in her account after she makes 12 deposits.

(B) Niobe decides to postpone buying a new car because she wants to get a new smart
phone instead. She can pay the phone's full price of $580 up front, or she can agree to pay an extra $25 per month on her phone bill over the course of a two-year contract for phone service.

What is the present cost to Niobe if she agrees to pay $25 per month for two years, assuming that she could put the money for the payments in a savings account that earns 3% annual interest and make $25 monthly withdrawals for two years?

As in Part A, a 3% annual interest rate becomes a 0.25% monthly interest rate. If Niobe puts some money M_1 in the savings account and lets it earn interest for 1 month, then she will have $M_1 + 0.0025M_1$, or $1.0025M_1$, available to make her first phone payment. Since she wants $1.0025M_1$ to equal $25, M_1 must equal $\frac{\$25}{1.0025} \approx \$24.94$. This means that the present cost of her first phone payment is $24.94, because that amount of money will be worth $25 in 1 month after earning $0.06 in interest.

Similarly, if Niobe puts some additional money M_2 in the savings account and lets it earn interest for 2 months, then she will have $1.0025M_2$ after 1 month and $1.0025(1.0025M_2)$, or $(1.0025)^{2}M_2$, after 2 months. Since she wants $(1.0025)^{2}M_2$ to equal \$25, M_2 must equal $\frac{\$25}{(1.0025)^{2}} \approx \$24.88$.

This means that the present cost of her second phone payment is \$ 24.88. It also means that she must deposit a total of $M_1 + M_2 = \$24.94 + \$24.88 = \$49.82$ in the savings account in order to have enough money for her first two phone payments.

Generalize these results to complete the following table.

Number of Payments	Present of Payments
1	$\frac{25}{1.0025}$
2	$\frac{25}{1.0025} + \frac{25}{(1.0025)^2}$
3	$\frac{25}{1.0025} + \frac{25}{(1.0025)^2} + \frac{25}{(1.0025)^{3}}$
⋮	⋮
24	$\frac{25}{1.0025} + \frac{25}{(1.0025)^2} + \cdots + \frac{25}{(1.0025)^{24}}$

Find the sum of the finite geometric series that represents the present cost of 24 payments.

$a = \frac{25}{0.0025}$

$r = \frac{1}{1.0025}$

$n = 24$

$$S(24) = \frac{25}{1.0025}\left(\frac{1 - \left(\frac{1}{1.0025}\right)^{24}}{1 - \frac{1}{1.0025}}\right)$$

≈ 581.65

Although Niobe will end up making total payments of $\$25 \cdot 24 = \$600$, the present cost of the payments is \$581.65, which is only slightly more than the up-front price of the phone.

ELABORATE

INTEGRATE MATHEMATICAL PRACTICES

Focus on Critical Thinking

MP.3 Ask students to explain how the formula $S(n) = \frac{a - r \cdot ar^n - 1}{1 - r}$ is equivalent to $S(n) = a\left(\frac{1 - r^n}{1 - r}\right)$. Have them describe the conditions that would make one form easier to use than the other.

SUMMARIZE THE LESSON

? What is a geometric series? What is the difference between an arithmetic series and a geometric series? A geometric series is the indicated sum of the terms of a geometric sequence. Arithmetic series are the sums of arithmetic sequences, which have a common difference, while geometric series are sums of geometric sequences, which have a common ratio.

Your Turn

8. A lottery winner is given the choice of collecting \$1,000,000 immediately or collecting payments of \$6000 per month for the next 20 years. Assuming the lottery money can be invested in an account with an annual interest rate of 6% that is applied monthly, find the present value of the lottery's delayed-payout plan in order to compare it with the lump-sum plan and decide which plan is better.

The monthly interest rate is $\frac{6}{12} = 0.5\%$. This means that the present value of the first payment is $\frac{\$6000}{1.005} \approx \$5970.15$. The present value of the first two payments is $\frac{\$6000}{1.005} + \frac{\$6000}{(1.005)^2} \approx \$11,910.60$. Since there are 240 payments, the present value of all the payments is $\frac{\$6000}{1.005} + \frac{\$6000}{(1.005)^2} + \cdots + \frac{\$6000}{(1.005)^{240}}$. Since $a = \frac{6000}{1.005}$, $r = \frac{1}{1.005}$, and $n = 240$, the sum of the finite geometric series is: $S(240) = \frac{6000}{1.005}\left(\frac{1 - \left(\frac{1}{1.005}\right)^{240}}{1 - \frac{1}{1.005}}\right) \approx 837,484.63$

The present value of the delayed-payout plan, \$837,484.63, is less than the lump-sum plan, so it makes sense to go with the lump-sum plan.

Elaborate

9. An alternative way of writing the formula for the sum of a finite geometric series is $S(n) = \frac{a - r \cdot ar^{n-1}}{1 - r}$. Describe in words how to find the sum of a finite geometric series using this formula.

Find the difference of the first term and the product of the common ratio and the last term. Divide that difference by the difference of 1 and the common ratio.

10. Describe how to find the number of terms in a finite geometric series when some of the terms have been replaced by an ellipsis.

One way is to identify the common ratio and generate the missing terms by repeatedly multiplying by the common ratio. Another way is to use the fact that the nth term of a geometric series is ar^{n-1}, set this expression equal to the last term of the given geometric series, and solve for n.

11. Discussion When analyzing an annuity, why is it important to determine the annuity's present value or future value?

Because the payments of an annuity occur over time, the value of each of those payments changes when the interest earned is taken into account. In order to make a decision about an annuity, you need to consider the value of the payments all at the same time, either now (present value) or at some point in the future (future value).

12. Essential Question Check-In What is the formula for the sum of the finite geometric series $a + ar + ar^2 + \cdots + ar^{n-1}$?

$S(n) = a\left(\frac{1 - r^n}{1 - r}\right)$

Evaluate: Homework and Practice

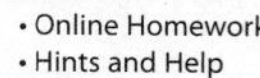

1. Suppose you start with a square piece of paper that you divide into four quarters, cutting out an L-shaped piece using three of the quarters and laying it down to create the first term of a geometric series. You then use the remaining quarter to repeat the process three more times, as shown.

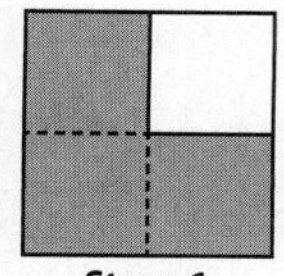
Stage 1

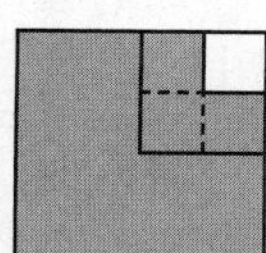
Stage 2

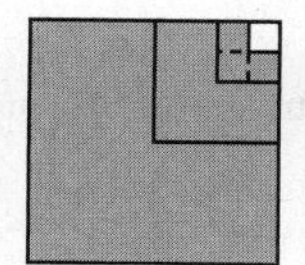
Stage 3

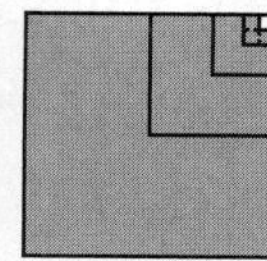
Stage 4

a. Complete the table.

Stage	Sum of the areas of the pieces that have been laid down	Difference of 1 and the area of the remaining piece
1	$\frac{3}{4}$	$1 - \frac{1}{4} = \frac{3}{4}$
2	$\frac{3}{4} + \frac{3}{16} = \frac{15}{16}$	$1 - \frac{1}{16} = \frac{15}{16}$
3	$\frac{3}{4} + \frac{3}{16} + \frac{3}{64} = \frac{63}{64}$	$1 - \frac{1}{64} = \frac{63}{64}$
4	$\frac{3}{4} + \frac{3}{16} + \frac{3}{64} + \frac{3}{256} = \frac{255}{256}$	$1 - \frac{1}{256} = \frac{255}{256}$

b. Generalize the results in the table: At stage n, the second column gives you the finite geometric series $\frac{3}{4} + \frac{3}{16} + \cdots + 3\left(\frac{1}{4}\right)^n$. The third column gives you a way to find the sum of this series. What formula does the third column give you?

$\frac{3}{4} + \frac{3}{16} + \cdots + 3\left(\frac{1}{4}\right)^n = 1 - \left(\frac{1}{4}\right)^n$

c. Show that the general formula for the sum of a finite geometric series agrees with the specific formula from part b.

In the general formula $S(n) = a\left(\frac{1 - r^n}{1 - r}\right)$, let $a = \frac{3}{4}$ and $r = \frac{1}{4}$.

$$S(n) = a\left(\frac{1-r^n}{1-r}\right) = \frac{3}{4}\left(\frac{1-\left(\frac{1}{4}\right)^n}{1-\frac{1}{4}}\right) = \frac{3}{4}\left(\frac{1-\left(\frac{1}{4}\right)^n}{\frac{3}{4}}\right) = 1 - \left(\frac{1}{4}\right)^n$$

2. In a later lesson you will learn how to use polynomial division to show that $\frac{x^n - 1}{x - 1} = x^{n-1} + x^{n-2} + \cdots + x^2 + x + 1$ for any integer n greater 0. Use this identity as an alternative method of deriving the formula for the sum of a finite geometric series with n terms. That is, given the series $a + ar + ar^2 + \cdots + ar^{n-1}$, show that its sum is $a\left(\frac{1 - r^n}{1 - r}\right)$.

Factor out a from all terms. $\quad a + ar + ar^2 + \cdots + ar^{n-1} = a\left(1 + r + r^2 + \cdots + r^{n-1}\right)$

Replace the series using the supplied identity. $\quad = a\left(\frac{r^n - 1}{r - 1}\right)$

Multiply the numerator and denominator by −1. $\quad = a\left(\frac{1 - r^n}{1 - r}\right)$

Exercise	Depth of Knowledge (D.O.K.)	COMMON CORE Mathematical Practices
1	**2** Skills/Concepts	**MP.5** Using Tools
2	**3** Strategic Thinking	**MP.3** Logic
3–12	**2** Skills/Concepts	**MP.2** Reasoning
13–18	**2** Skills/Concepts	**MP.4** Modeling
19	**2** Skills/Concepts H.O.T.	**MP.2** Reasoning
20–21	**3** Strategic Thinking H.O.T.	**MP.3** Logic

EVALUATE

ASSIGNMENT GUIDE

Concepts and Skills	Practice
Explore 1 Investigating a Geometric Series	Exercise 1
Explore 2 Deriving a Formula for the Sum of a Finite Geometric Series	Exercise 2
Example 1 Finding the Sum of a Finite Geometric Series	Exercises 3–12, 21
Example 2 Solving a Problem Involving a Finite Geometric Series	Exercises 13–20

QUESTIONING STRATEGIES

? If you know the sum of the first 10 terms of a geometric series, and you know the 10th term and the common ratio, how can you find the sum of the first 11 terms of the series? **You can multiply the 10th term by the common ratio to find the 11th term, and add it to the sum of the first 10 terms.**

COMMUNICATING MATH

Students may benefit from writing out a list of the steps involved in finding the sum of a geometric series. They can write down how to identify the value of each variable in the formula, how to substitute into the formula, and how to simplify the resulting expression correctly.

Find the sum of the finite geometric series.

3. $-3 + 6 - 12 + 24 - 48 + 96 - 192 + 384$

$a = -3, r = -2, n = 8$

$S(8) = -3\left(\frac{1-(-2)^8}{1-(-2)}\right)$

$= -3\left(\frac{1-256}{1-(-2)}\right) = 255$

4. $6 - 4 + \frac{8}{3} - \frac{16}{9} + \frac{32}{17}$

$a = 6, r = -\frac{2}{3}, n = 5$

$S(5) = 6\left(\frac{1-\left(-\frac{2}{3}\right)^5}{1-\left(-\frac{2}{3}\right)}\right)$

$= \frac{110}{27} \approx 4.07$

Determine how many terms the geometric series has, and then find the sum of the series.

5. $-12 - 4 - \frac{4}{3} - \cdots - \frac{4}{243}$

$a = -12$

$r = \frac{-4}{-12} = \frac{1}{3}$

$-12\left(\frac{1}{3}\right)^{n-1} = -\frac{4}{243}$

$\left(\frac{1}{3}\right)^{n-1} = \frac{1}{729} = \left(\frac{1}{3}\right)^6$

$n = 7$

$S(7) = -12\left(\frac{1-\left(\frac{1}{3}\right)^7}{1-\frac{1}{3}}\right)$

$= -\frac{4372}{243} \approx -17.99$

6. $0.3 + 0.03 + 0.003 + \cdots + 0.000003$

$a = 0.3, r = 0.1, n = 6$

$S(6) = 0.3\left(\frac{(1-(0.1)^6)}{1-0.1}\right) = 0.333333$

7. $6 + 30 + 150 + \cdots + 468{,}750$

$a = 6$

$r = \frac{30}{6} = 5$

$6 \cdot 5^{n-1} = 468{,}750$

$5^{n-1} = 78{,}125 = 5^7$

$n = 8$

$S(8) = 6\left(\frac{1-5^8}{1-5}\right) = 585{,}936$

8. $-3 + 9 - 27 + \cdots - 177{,}147$

$a = -3$

$r = \frac{9}{-3} = -3$

$-3(-3)^{n-1} = -177{,}147$

$(-3)^{n-1} = 59{,}049 = (-3)^{10}$

$n = 11$

$S(11) = -3\left(\frac{1-(-3)^{11}}{1-(-3)}\right) = -132{,}86$

Write the finite geometric series from its given description, and then find its sum.

9. A geometric series that starts with 2, ends with −6250, and has a common ratio of −5

$2 - 10 + 50 - 250 + 1250 - 6250$

$a = 2, r = -5, n = 6$

$S(6) = 2\left(\frac{1-(-5)^6}{1-(-5)}\right) = -5208$

10. A geometric series with 5 terms that begins with 1 and has a common ratio of $\frac{1}{3}$.

$1 + \frac{1}{3} + \frac{1}{9} + \frac{1}{27} + \frac{1}{81}$

$a = 1, r = \frac{1}{3}, n = 5$

$S(5) = 1\left(\frac{1-\left(\frac{1}{3}\right)^5}{1-\frac{1}{3}}\right) = \frac{121}{81} \approx 1.49$

11. A geometric series with 7 terms that begins with 1000 and successively decreases by 20%

1000 + 800 + 640 + 512 + 409.6 + 327.68 + 262.144

$a = 1000$

$r = 1 - 0.2 = 0.8$

$n = 7$

$S(7) = 1000\left(\frac{1 - (0.8)^7}{1 - 0.8}\right) = 3951.424$

12. A geometric series where the first term is −12, the last term is −972, and each term after the first is triple the previous term

−12 − 36 − 108 − 324 − 972

$a = -12, r = 3, n = 5$

$S(5) = -12\left(\frac{1 - 3^5}{1 - 3}\right) = -1452$

13. **Chess** The first international chess tournament was held in London in 1851. This single-elimination tournament (in which paired competitors played matches and only the winner of a match continued to the next round) began with 16 competitors. How many matches were played?

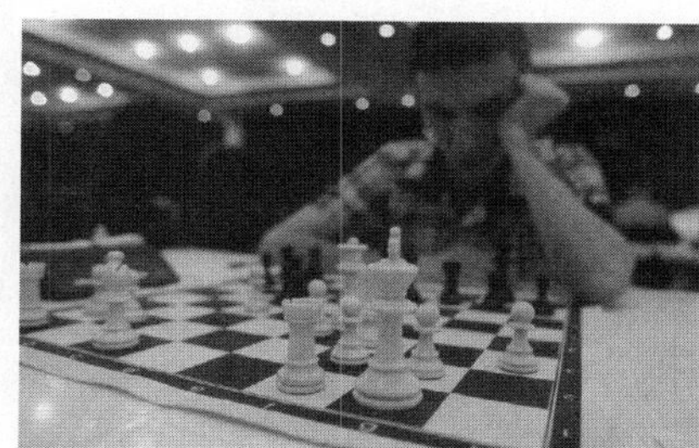

Each round had half the number of competitors remaining, so $r = \frac{1}{2}$. The tournament started with 16 competitors and 8 matches in the first round, so $a = 8$. The last round had a single match. The number of rounds was n.

$8\left(\frac{1}{2}\right)^{n-1} = 1$

$\frac{1}{2}^{n-1} = \frac{1}{8}$

$n - 1 = 3$

$n = 4$

$S(4) = 8\left(\frac{1 - \left(\frac{1}{2}\right)^4}{1 - \frac{1}{2}}\right) = 8\left(\frac{1 - \frac{1}{16}}{1 - \frac{1}{2}}\right) = 15$

So, a total of 15 matches were played.

14. A ball is dropped from an initial height and allowed to bounce repeatedly. On the first bounce (one up-and-down motion), the ball reaches a height of 32 inches. On each successive bounce, the ball reaches 75% of its previous height. What is the total vertical distance that the ball travels in 10 bounces? (Do not include the initial height from which the ball is dropped.)

After the first bounce, the ball travels 32 inches up and 32 inches down. On every bounce, the ball travels twice the bounce height.

$64 + 64(0.75) + 64(0.75)^2 + \cdots + 64(0.75)^9$

$a = 64, r = 0.75, n = 10$

$S(10) = 64\left(\frac{1 - (0.75)^{10}}{1 - 0.75}\right) \approx 241.6$

So, the ball travels a vertical distance of about 241.6 inches (about 20.1 feet) in 10 bounces.

INTEGRATE MATHEMATICAL PRACTICES

Focus on Critical Thinking

MP.3 Encourage students to check their answers for reasonableness. A sum that seems too great or too small may be an indication that they made an error when simplifying the expression for the sum.

AVOID COMMON ERRORS

Students may think that when the terms of a series are negative, they should substitute a negative number for r. Show them that this is incorrect reasoning, using an example to illustrate that when the common ratio is a negative number, the signs of the terms in the series alternate.

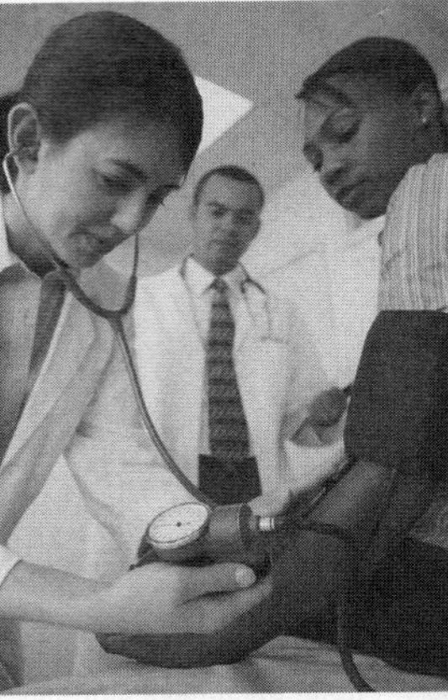

15. Medicine During a flu outbreak, health officials record 16 cases the first week, 56 new cases the second week, and 196 new cases the third week.

a. Assuming the pattern of new cases continues to follow a geometric sequence, what total number of new cases will have been recorded by the fifth week?

$a = 16, r = \frac{56}{16} = \frac{7}{2}, n = 5$

$$S(5) = 16\left(\frac{1 - \left(\frac{7}{2}\right)^5}{1 - \frac{7}{2}}\right)$$

$$= 16\left(\frac{1 - \frac{16{,}807}{32}}{1 - \frac{7}{2}}\right) = 3355$$

So, a total of 3355 new cases will have been recorded by the fifth week.

b. How many weeks will it take for the total number of recorded cases to exceed 40,000?

$$16\left(\frac{1 - \left(\frac{7}{2}\right)^n}{1 - \frac{7}{2}}\right) > 40{,}000$$

$$16\left(\frac{(3.5)^n - 1}{2.5}\right) > 40{,}000$$

$$6.4\left((3.5)^n - 1\right) > 40{,}000$$

$$(3.5)^n - 1 > 6250$$

$$(3.5)^n > 6251$$

Checking values of n shows that $(3.5)^6 \approx 1838 < 6251$ and $(3.5)^7 \approx 6434 > 6251$.

So, the number of cases will exceed 40,000 in the seventh week.

16. Finance A person deposits \$5000 into an investment account at the end of each year for 10 years. The account earns 4% interest annually. What is the future value of the annuity after the 10th deposit?

The account balance after the 10th deposit is given by the series $5000 + 5000(1.07) + 5000(1.07)^2 + \ldots + 5000(1.07)^9$.

$a = 5000$

$r = 1.04$

$n = 10$

$$S(10) = 5000\left(\frac{1 - (1.04)^{10}}{1 - 1.04}\right)$$

$$\approx 60{,}030.54$$

So, the future value of the annuity after the 10th deposit is \$60,030.54.

17. Business A business wants to buy a parcel of land in order to expand its operations. The owner of the land offers two purchase options: Buy the land today for $100,000, or buy the land in five equal payments of $22,000 where the payments are due a year apart and the first payment is due immediately. The chief financial officer for the business determines that money set aside for the purchase of the land can be invested and earn 5.4% interest annually. Which purchase option is the better deal for the business? Explain.

The present value of the delayed-payment option is

$$22{,}000 + \frac{22{,}000}{1.054} + \frac{22{,}000}{(1.054)^2} + \frac{22{,}000}{(1.054)^3} + \frac{22{,}000}{(1.054)^4}.$$

(The first payment is not discounted because it is made immediately.)

The sum of this finite geometric series is $S(5) = 22{,}000\left(\frac{1-\left(\frac{1}{1.056}\right)^5}{1-\frac{1}{1.056}}\right) \approx 98{,}935.79.$

Since the delayed-payment option saves the business about $1000, it is the better deal.

18. Match each finite geometric series on the left with its sum on the right.

A. $2 + 6 + 18 + \cdots + 1458$ B   1094

B. $2 - 6 + 18 - \cdots + 1458$ D   −2186

C. $-2 + 6 - 18 + \cdots - 1458$ A   2186

D. $-2 -6 -8 - \cdots - 1458$ C   −1094

A. $a = 2, r = 3$, and $n = 7$, so $S(7) = 2\left(\frac{1-3^7}{1-3}\right) = 2186.$

B. $a = 2, r = -3$, and $n = 7$, so $S(7) = 2\left(\frac{1-(-3)^7}{1-(-3)}\right) = 1094.$

C. $a = -2, r = -3$, and $n = 7$, so $S(7) = -2\left(\frac{1-(-3)^7}{1-(-3)}\right) = -1094.$

D. $a = -2, r = 3$ and $n = 7$, so $S(7) = -2\left(\frac{1-3^7}{1-3}\right) = -2186.$

H.O.T. Focus on Higher Order Thinking

19. Represent Real-World Problems The formula for the future value FV of an annuity consisting of n regular payments of p dollars at an interest rate of i (expressed as a decimal) is $FV = p\left(\frac{(1+i)^n - 1}{i}\right)$, which is valid for any payment rate (such as monthly or annually) as long as the interest rate has the same time unit. The formula assumes that the future value is calculated when the last payment is made. Show how to derive this formula.

The future value of the annuity is given by the finite geometric series $p + p(1+i) + p(1+i)^2 + \cdots + p(1+i)^{n-1}$. Use the formula for the sum of a finite geometric series with $a = p$ and $r = 1 + i$.

$$FV = p\left(\frac{1-(1+i)^n}{1-(1+i)}\right) = p\left(\frac{1-(1+i)^n}{1-1-i}\right) = p\left(\frac{1-(1+i)^n}{-i}\right) = p\left(\frac{(1+i)^n - 1}{i}\right)$$

PEER-TO-PEER DISCUSSION

Ask students to discuss with a partner whether the sum of the first 5 terms of a geometric series can be equal to 0. Call upon pairs to present their conclusions to the class, and have them justify their reasoning. If the sum of the first 5 terms of a geometric series is 0, then $a\left(\frac{1-r^5}{1-r}\right) = 0$, which means that either $a = 0$ or $1 - r^5 = 0$. If $1 - r^5 = 0$, then $r = 1$. Since, in a geometric series, a cannot be 0 and r cannot be 1, it is not possible for the sum to be 0. (Note that if $r = 1$, the fraction in the formula is undefined.)

JOURNAL

Have students explain the difference between a geometric sequence and a geometric series, and describe how to use the formula to find the sum of a geometric series.

20. Represent Real-World Problems The formula for the present value PV of an annuity consisting of n regular payments of p dollars at an interest rate of i (expressed as a decimal) is $PV = p\left(\frac{1-(1+i)^{-n}}{i}\right)$, which is valid for any payment rate (such as monthly or annually) as long as the interest rate has the same time unit. The formula assumes that the present value is calculated one time unit before the first payment is made. Show how to derive this formula.

The present value of the annuity is given by the finite geometric series $\frac{p}{1+i} + \frac{p}{(1+i)^2} + \cdots + \frac{p}{(1+i)^n}$. Use the formula for the sum of a finite geometric series with $a = \frac{p}{1+i}$ and $r \frac{1}{1+i}$.

$$PV = \frac{p}{1+i}\left(\frac{1-\left(\frac{1}{1+i}\right)^n}{1-\frac{1}{1+i}}\right) = \frac{p}{1+i}\left(\frac{1-(1+i)^{-n}}{1-\frac{1}{1+i}}\right)$$

$$= \frac{p}{1+i}\left(\frac{1-(1+i)^{-n}}{\frac{1+i-1}{1+i}}\right) = \frac{p}{1+i}\left(\frac{1-(1+i)^{-n}}{\frac{i}{i+1}}\right)$$

$$= p\left(\frac{1-(1+i)^{-n}}{i}\right)$$

21. Draw Conclusions Consider whether it's possible for the infinite geometric series $a + ar + ar^2 + \cdots$ to have a finite sum. Since the formula $S(n) = a\left(\frac{1-r^n}{1-r}\right)$ gives the sum of the first n terms of the series, a reasonable approach to finding the sum of all terms in the series is to determine what happens to $S(n)$ as n increases without bound. Use this approach on each of the following series and draw a conclusion.

a. $1 + 2 + 4 + 8 + \cdots$

a. For the series $1 + 2 + 4 + 8 + \cdots$, $a = 1$ and $r = 2$.

$S(n) = 1\left(\frac{1-2^n}{1-2}\right) = \frac{1-2^n}{-1} = 2^{n-1}$

As $n \to +\infty$ $S(n) \to +\infty$, so a reasonable conclusion is that this series does not have a finite sum.

b. $1 + \frac{1}{2} + \frac{1}{4} + \frac{1}{8} + \cdots$

b. For the series $1 + \frac{1}{2} + \frac{1}{4} + \frac{1}{8} + \cdots$, $a = 1$ and $r = \frac{1}{2}$.

$$S(n) = 1\left(\frac{1-\frac{1^n}{2}}{1-\frac{1}{2}}\right) = \frac{1-\left(\frac{1}{2}\right)^n}{\frac{1}{2}} = 2 - 2\left(\frac{1}{2}\right)^n$$

As $n \to +\infty$ $S(n) \to 2$, so a reasonable conclusion is that this series has a sum of 2.

Lesson Performance Task

You've finally purchased your dream home after saving for a long time. You've made a nice down payment, and your mortgage loan is $150,000. It is a 30-year loan with an annual interest rate of 4.5%, which is calculated monthly. Find a formula for calculating monthly mortgage payments. Then find the monthly payment needed to pay off your mortgage loan.

Let P be the principal, r be the monthly interest rate expressed as a decimal, and m be the monthly payment.

The balance at the end of each month is equal to the balance at the end of the prior month, plus the new interest, minus the monthly payment:

First month: $P(1+r)-m$

Second month: $[P(1+r)-m](1+r)=P(1+r)^2-m(1+r)-m$

Third month: $[P(1+r)^2-m(1+r)-m](1+r)=P(1+r)^3-m(1+r)^2-m(1+r)-m$

Notice the pattern in the loan balance:

$$P(1+r)^n-m(1+r)^{n-1}-m(1+r)^{n-2}-\cdots-m(1+r)-m$$
$$=P(1+r)^n-m\left[(1+r)^{n-1}+(1+r)^{n-2}+\cdots+(1+r)+1\right]$$

The expression in brackets above, $(1+r)^{n-1}+(1+r)^{n-2}+\cdots+(1+r)+1$, is a geometric series with n terms and a common ratio of $1+r$. Use the formula to find the sum of the geometric series.

$$(1+r)^{n-1}+(1+r)^{n-2}+\cdots+(1+r)+1=1\left[\frac{1-(1+r)^n}{1-(1+r)}\right]=\frac{1-(1+r)^n}{-r}=\frac{(1+r)^n-1}{r}$$

Now substitute the expression for the sum into the expression for the loan balance.

$$P(1+r)^n-m\left[\frac{(1+r)^n-1}{r}\right]$$

To pay off the loan, you need to get to a loan balance of $0. Find an expression for the monthly payment that allows you to do this.

$$P(1+r)^n-m\left[\frac{(1+r)^n-1}{r}\right]=0\rightarrow m\left[\frac{(1+r)^n-1}{r}\right]=P(1+r)^n$$

$$m=\frac{P(1+r)^n}{\frac{(1+r)^n-1}{r}}=P\left[\frac{r(1+r)^n}{(1+r)^n-1}\right]$$

Since the interest is compounded monthly, r is equal to the annual interest rate, 4.5%, divided by 12, or $\frac{0.045}{12}=0.00375$. The term of the loan is for 30 years, so the number of months is $n=12\cdot30=360$. P is the amount of the loan, or $150,000. Substitute for P, r, and n to find the monthly payment m.

$$m=150{,}000\left[\frac{(0.00375)(1+0.00375)^{360}}{(1+0.00375)^{360}-1}\right]\approx 760.03$$

A monthly payment of $760.03 is needed to pay off the mortgage loan in 30 years.

EXTENSION ACTIVITY

Have students research minimum payments on loans and credit cards. Suggest that they find a minimum monthly payment for an outstanding balance and a given interest rate that would result in a constant loan balance each month. For example, a minimum monthly payment of $50 on a $3000 loan at 20% annual interest would result in a constant balance because the monthly payment equals the interest incurred during the first month. Any payment of less than $50 would result in the balance *increasing* each month.

QUESTIONING STRATEGIES

? What is the loan balance in month n? $p(1+r)^n-m(1+r)^{n-1}-m(1+r)^{n-2}-\ldots-m(1+r)-m$

? What value can be factored from all but the first term in the expansion of the monthly loan balance? $-m$, the monthly payment

INTEGRATE MATHEMATICAL PRACTICES

Focus on Technology

MP.5 Recursive formulas lend themselves well to spreadsheets. Copying a formula to an array of cells applies the formula recursively. Note that one or more cell references may need to be absolute, however, if, for example, the interest rate is entered as a reference.

A spreadsheet can be used to check whether the monthly payment will pay off the loan amount after 360 payments.

Scoring Rubric

2 points: Student correctly solves the problem and explains his/her reasoning.

1 point: Student shows good understanding of the problem but does not fully solve or explain his/her reasoning.

0 points: Student does not demonstrate understanding of the problem.

MODULE 12

Study Guide Review

ASSESSMENT AND INTERVENTION

Assign or customize module reviews.

MODULE PERFORMANCE TASK

Mathematical Practices: MP.1, MP.2, MP.4, MP.7, MP.8
F-BF.A.2, A-SSE.B.4

SUPPORTING STUDENT REASONING

Students should begin this problem by finding the total area of the Koch triangle after each of the first three iterations. Here is some of the information they may ask for.

- **Can we substitute a real value for each side of the triangle?** Students can start with a side length of 2, which results in an area of $\sqrt{3}$ for the original triangle.

SCAFFOLDING SUPPORT

- Suggest that students use a table to organize their work. Headings might include: Iteration number, Area of Original Triangle, Area of each New Triangle, Number of New Triangles, and Total Area.

STUDY GUIDE REVIEW

Sequences and Series

MODULE 12

Essential Question: How can you use exponential functions to solve real-world problems?

Key Vocabulary
arithmetic sequence *(sucesión arithmética)*
explicit rule *(regla explícita)*
finite geometric series *(serie geométrica finito)*
geometric sequence *(sucesión geométrica)*
recursive rule *(regla recurrente)*
sequence *(sucesión)*
series *(regla recurrente)*

KEY EXAMPLE *(Lesson 12.2)*

Write the explicit rule for the sequence described by the points $(0, 4), (1, -2), (2, -8), (3, -14), \ldots$

$f(0) = 4 \rightarrow a = 4$ — Use the fact that $f(0) = a$ to find a.
$f(1) = a + d$ — Use $f(1) = a + d$ to find d.
$f(1) = 4 + d$
$-2 = 4 + d$
$d = -6$
$f(n) = 4 - 6n$ — Substitute a and d into $f(n) = a + dn$

The explicit rule for the sequence is $f(n) = 4 - 6n$.

KEY EXAMPLE *(Lesson 12.2)*

Find the 12th term of the geometric sequence 5, 15, 45,...

$r = \frac{15}{5} = 3$ — Find the common ratio of the sequence.
$a_n = a_1 r^{n-1}$ — Write the formula for a geometric sequence
$a_{12} = 5(3)^{12-1}$ — Substitute in a, r, and n.
$a_{12} = 5(177{,}147)$ — Use a calculator to solve for a_{12}.
$a_{12} = 885{,}735$ — Simplify.

The 12th term of the geometric sequence is 885,735.

KEY EXAMPLE *(Lesson 12.3)*

Find the sum of the geometric series $2 - 4 + 8 - 16 + 32 - 64$.

$a = 2, r = \frac{-4}{2} = -2, n = 6$ — Find the values of a, r, and n.

$S(n) = 2\left(\frac{1 - r^n}{1 - r}\right)$

$S(6) = 2\left(\frac{1 - (-2)^6}{1 - (-2)}\right)$ — Use the sum formula

$S(6) = -42$

The sum for the geometric series is -42.

SCAFFOLDING SUPPORT (CONTINUED)

- You may wish to challenge students to find a general formula for the area of the snowflake after n iterations. One form of this formula is $A_n = \frac{a_0}{5}\left(8 - 3\left(\frac{4}{9}\right)^n\right)$, where a_0 is the area of the original triangle.

EXERCISES

1. If the first three terms of a geometric sequence are 3, 12, and 48, what is the seventh term? *(Lesson 12.2)*

   12,288

Write the explicit rule for the algebraic sequence. In every sequence, the first term is the $f(0)$ term. *(Lesson 12.1)*

2. 5, 7, 9, 11, 13 ...

   $f(n) = 5 + 2n$

3.

x	0	1	2	3	4
y	−3	1	5	9	13

   $f(n) = -3 + 4n$

Find the sum of the geometric series. *(Lesson 12.1)*

4. 4 + 16 + 64 + 256 + ... + 16,384

   21,844

5. 3 − 6 + 12 − 24 + ... − 1536

   −1023

6. −2 − 6 − 18 − 54 − 162

   −242

7. −2 + 8 − 32 + ... +2048

   1638

MODULE PERFORMANCE TASK

How Big Is That Snowflake?

The Koch snowflake is special kind of shape called a fractal. It begins with an equilateral triangle. In the first iteration, each side of the triangle is divided into thirds. The middle third of each side becomes the base of a new equilateral triangle. In the second iteration, each of the sides is divided into thirds, forming the base of a new equilateral triangle. To make the full snowflake, this process continues infinitely. The first two iterations and the original triangle are shown.

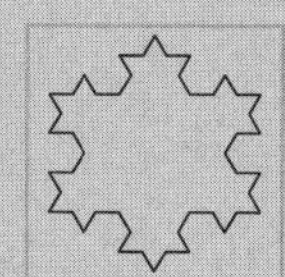

What is the area of the Koch triangle after three iterations? By what factor is the area of the original triangle increased? Start on your own paper by listing the information you will need to solve the problem. Be sure to write down all your data and assumptions. Then use graphs, numbers, tables, words, or algebra to explain how you reached your conclusion.

DISCUSSION OPPORTUNITIES

- Discuss with students how they might create a similar figure from a square, and how their solutions would change.
- Students may wonder about the area of the completed Koch snowflake. Lead them in a discussion of what they think and why. You may wish to reveal that if the iterations were to continue indefinitely, the total area would be 1.6 times the area of the original triangle.

SAMPLE SOLUTION

The area of the original triangle is, $\frac{1}{2} \cdot 2 \cdot \sqrt{3}$, or $\sqrt{3}$.

In the first iteration, each side of the 3 original sides has a triangle added. The figure now has 12 sides, each with a length of $\frac{2}{3}$. The added areas are $3\left(0.5 \cdot \frac{2}{3} \cdot \frac{1}{3} \cdot \sqrt{3}\right) = \frac{1}{3}\sqrt{3}$, and the total area is $\sqrt{3} + \frac{1}{3}\sqrt{3}$, or $\frac{4}{3}\sqrt{3}$.

In the second iteration, each of the 12 sides has a triangle added. The figure now has 48 sides, each with a length of $\frac{2}{9}$. The added areas are $12\left(0.5 \cdot \frac{2}{9} \cdot \frac{1}{9} \cdot \sqrt{3}\right) = \frac{4}{27}\sqrt{3}$, and the total area is $\frac{4}{3}\sqrt{3} + \frac{4}{27}\sqrt{3}$, or $\frac{40}{27}\sqrt{3}$.

In the third iteration, each of the 48 sides has a triangle added. The figure now has 144 sides, each of length $\frac{2}{27}$. The added areas are $48\left(0.5 \cdot \frac{2}{27} \cdot \frac{1}{27} \cdot \sqrt{3}\right)$, or $\frac{16}{243}\sqrt{3}$, and the total area is $\frac{40}{27}\sqrt{3} + \frac{16}{243}\sqrt{3}$, or $\frac{376}{243}\sqrt{3}$.

After 3 iterations, the total area of the snowflake is about $\frac{376}{243} = 1.55$ times the area of the original triangle.

Assessment Rubric

2 points: Student correctly solves the problem and explains his/her reasoning.

1 point: Student shows good understanding of the problem but does not fully solve or explain his/her reasoning.

0 points: Student does not demonstrate understanding of the problem.

Ready to Go On?

ASSESS MASTERY

Use the assessment on this page to determine if students have mastered the concepts and standards covered in this module.

ASSESSMENT AND INTERVENTION

Access Ready to Go On? assessment online, and receive instant scoring, feedback, and customized intervention or enrichment.

ADDITIONAL RESOURCES

Response to Intervention Resources

- Reteach Worksheets

Differentiated Instruction Resources

- Reading Strategies EL
- Success for English Learners EL
- Challenge Worksheets

Assessment Resources

- Leveled Module Quizzes

12.1–12.3 Sequences and Series

- Online Homework
- Hints and Help
- Extra Practice

Write a recursive rule and an explicit rule for each sequence. *(Lessons 12.1, 12.2)*

1. 9, 27, 81, 243,…

$f(1) = 9$ and $f(n) = f(n-1) \cdot 3$, $f(n) = 9(3)^{n-1}$

2. 4, −3, −10, −17, ...

$f(0) = 4$ and $f(n) = f(n-1) - 7$, $f(n) = 4 - 7n$

Find the stated term of the geometric sequence. *(Lesson 12.2)*

3. −3, −6, −12, −24, ...; 9th term

−768

4. 4, −12, 36, −108, ...; 11th term

236,196

Find the sum of the geometric series. *(Lesson 12.3)*

5. 10 − 20 + 40 − 80 + 160 − ... + 2560

1710

6. −1 + 3 − 9 + 27 − ... − 6561

−4921

7. 2 + 12 + 72 + 432 + 2592 + 15,552

18,662

8. 7 − 7 + 7 − 7 + 7 − ... + 7

7

ESSENTIAL QUESTION

9. How can you tell whether a sequence is geometric or algebraic?

Possible Answer: An algebraic sequence has a common number that is added or subtracted from the previous term every time. A geometric sequence has a number that is multiplied by the previous term every time.

COMMON CORE Common Core Standards

Lesson	Items	Content Standards	Mathematical Practices
12.1	1	**F-BF.A.2**	**MP.2**
12.1	2	**F-BF.A.2**	**MP.2**
12.2	3	**F-BF.A.2**	**MP.2**
12.2	4	**F-BF.A.2**	**MP.2**
12.3	5–8	**A-SSE.B.4**	**MP.2**

MODULE 12
MIXED REVIEW

Assessment Readiness

1. Consider each sequence. Is the sequence geometric? Select Yes or No for A–D.
   - **A.** 10, 15, 20, 25,... ○ Yes ● No
   - **B.** 5, 15, 45, 135,... ● Yes ○ No
   - **C.** 1, 3, 5, 7,... ○ Yes ● No
   - **D.** 2, 4, 8, 16,... ● Yes ○ No

2. Consider the series 1, 5, 9, 13, 17, ... Choose True or False for each statement.
   - **A.** If n represents the position in the sequence the algebraic expression for the sequence, is $4n - 3$. ● True ○ False
   - **B.** If n represents the position in the sequence, the algebraic expression for the sequence is $n + 4$. ○ True ● False
   - **C.** There is no algebraic expression for the sequence, because it is a geometric sequence. ○ True ● False

3. Give the first five terms of the sequence $2n + 1$, and then create an example of a real world situation that could match the arithmetic sequence. If the sequence were plotted on a coordinate plane, what kind of function would it be?

   3, 5, 7, 9, 11; Possible answer: A baker makes tiered cakes. The top tier is always 3 inches in radius. Each additional layer has a radius 2 inches larger than the previous layer.; linear

4. Solve $\frac{3}{4}|x + 3| - 8 = 4$ for x. Explain your method.

   $x = 13$ or -19; Possible answer: To solve an absolute value equation, first isolate the absolute value expression. In this case, we get $|x + 3| = 16$. Then, write two equations, one where the right side is positive and one where it is negative: $x + 3 = 16$ and $x + 3 = -16$. Solve each as usual.

5. Explain the difference between a geometric sequence and a geometric series.

   A geometric sequence is a list of terms. Each term is related to the previous term by a common ratio. A geometric series is the sum of the terms in a geometric sequence.

COMMON CORE Common Core Standards

Lesson	Items	Content Standards	Mathematical Practices
12.2	1	**F-BF.A.2**	**MP.1**
12.1	2	**F-BF.A.2**	**MP.7**
1.2, 12.1	3*	**F-BF.A.2, F-IF.B.4**	**MP.4**
2.2	4*	**A-REI.B.3**	**MP.6**
12.1, 12.3	5	**A-SSE.B.4, F-BF.A.2**	**MP.6**

* Item integrates mixed review concepts from previous modules or a previous course.

MIXED REVIEW

Assessment Readiness

ASSESSMENT AND INTERVENTION

Assign ready-made or customized practice tests to prepare students for high-stakes tests.

ADDITIONAL RESOURCES

Assessment Resources

- Leveled Module Quizzes: Modified, B

AVOID COMMON ERRORS

Item 4 Some students will solve an absolute value equation as if the absolute value symbols were parentheses. Remind students that most absolute value equations have two solutions: a solution that gives a positive value inside the absolute value symbol and a solution that gives a negative value inside the absolute value symbol.

MODULE 13

Exponential Functions

ESSENTIAL QUESTION:

Answer: Exponential functions can be used to compute the age of a relic based on the half-lives of a carbon isotope. They are also used to predict the size of a population at some future time.

PROFESSIONAL DEVELOPMENT VIDEO

Professional Development Video

Author Matt Larson models successful teaching practices in an actual high-school classroom.

Professional Development
my.hrw.com

MODULE 13

Exponential Functions

Essential Question: How can you use exponential functions to solve real-world problems?

REAL WORLD VIDEO
Check out how exponential functions can be used to model the path of a bouncing ball and other real-world patterns.

MODULE PERFORMANCE TASK PREVIEW

That's the Way the Ball Bounces

The height that a ball reaches after bouncing off a hard surface depends on several factors, including the height from which the ball was dropped and the material the ball is made of. The height of each successive bounce will be less than the previous bounce. How can mathematical modeling be used to represent a bouncing ball? Let's find out!

DIGITAL TEACHER EDITION

Access a full suite of teaching resources when and where you need them:

- Access content online or offline
- Customize lessons to share with your class
- Communicate with your students in real-time
- View student grades and data instantly to target your instruction where it is needed most

PERSONAL MATH TRAINER

Assessment and Intervention

Assign automatically graded homework, quizzes, tests, and intervention activities. Prepare your students with updated, Common Core-aligned practice tests.

Are YOU Ready?

Complete these exercises to review skills you will need for this chapter.

Personal Math Trainer
- Online Homework
- Hints and Help
- Extra Practice

Real Numbers

Example 1 Write the multiplicative inverse of 0.3125.

$0.3125 = \frac{3125}{10{,}000}$ Write the decimal as a fraction.

$= \frac{5}{16} \rightarrow \frac{16}{5}$ Simplify, then take the reciprocal.

The multiplicative inverse of 0.3125 is $\frac{16}{5}$.

Write the multiplicative inverse.

1. 1.125 $\frac{8}{9}$

2. −0.6875 $-\frac{16}{11}$

3. 0.444 $\frac{250}{111}$

Exponential Functions

Example 2 Evaluate $12(1.5)^{x-5}$ for $x = 8$.

$12(1.5)^{8-5}$ Substitute.

$12(1.5)^{3}$ Simplify.

$12(3.375) = 40.5$ Evaluate the exponent. Multiply.

Evaluate each expression.

4. $30(1.1)^{5x}; x = 0.4$ 36.3

5. $8(2.5)^{\frac{x}{3}}; x = 12$ 312.5

6. $2(x)^{2x+9}; x = -3$ −54

Geometric Sequences

Example 3 List the first four terms of the sequence if $t_1 = 2$ and $t_n = -3t_{n-1}$.

$t_2 = -3t_{2-1} = -3t_1 = -3 \cdot 2 = -6$ Find the second term.

$t_3 = -3t_{3-1} = -3t_2 = -3 \cdot (-6) = 18$ Find the third term.

$t_4 = -3t_{4-1} = -3t_3 = -3 \cdot 18 = -54$ Find the fourth term.

The first four terms are 2, −6, 18, and −54.

List the first four terms of the sequence.

7. $t_1 = 0.02$
$t_n = 5t_{n-1}$
0.02, 0.1, 0.5, 2.5

8. $t_1 = 3$
$t_n = 0.5t_{n-1}$
3, 1.5, 0.75, 0.375

Are You Ready?

ASSESS READINESS

Use the assessment on this page to determine if students need strategic or intensive intervention for the module's prerequisite skills.

ASSESSMENT AND INTERVENTION

RtI Response to Intervention TIER 1, TIER 2, TIER 3 SKILLS

Personal Math Trainer will automatically create a standards-based, personalized intervention assignment for your students, targeting each student's individual needs!

ADDITIONAL RESOURCES

See the table below for a full list of intervention resources available for this module.

Response to Intervention Resources also includes:

- Tier 2 Skill Pre-Tests for each Module
- Tier 2 Skill Post-Tests for each skill

Response to Intervention			Differentiated Instruction
Tier 1 Lesson Intervention Worksheets	**Tier 2** Strategic Intervention Skills Intervention Worksheets	**Tier 3** Intensive Intervention Worksheets available online	
Reteach 13.1 Reteach 13.2 Reteach 13.3 Reteach 13.4	8 Exponential Functions 13 Geometric Sequences 30 Real Numbers	Building Block Skills 18, 20, 29, 75, 76, 100, 109	Challenge worksheets Extend the Math Lesson Activities in TE

Exponential Growth Functions

Common Core Math Standards

The student is expected to:

COMMON CORE **F.BF.B.3**

Identify the effect on the graph of replacing $f(x)$ by $f(x) + k$, $k\,f(x)$, $f(kx)$, and $f(x + k)$ for specific values of k (both positive and negative); ... Also F.IF.C.7e, F.LE.A.2, A.REI.D.11

Mathematical Practices

COMMON CORE **MP.4 Modeling**

Language Objective

In a small group, match graphs to their corresponding exponential growth functions.

ENGAGE

Essential Question: How is the graph of $g(x) = ab^{x-h} + k$ where $b > 1$ related to the graph of $f(x) = b^x$?

The graph of $g(x) = ab^{x-h} + k$ involves transformations of the graph of $f(x) = b^x$. In particular, the graph of $g(x)$ is a vertical stretch or compression of the graph of $f(x)$ by a factor of $|a|$, a reflection of the graph across the x-axis if $a < 0$, and a translation of the graph h units horizontally and k units vertically.

PREVIEW: LESSON PERFORMANCE TASK

View the Engage section online. Discuss the photo and the possible ways to model the growth of an investment over time. Then preview the Lesson Performance Task.

Name________________ Class________________ Date________________

13.1 Exponential Growth Functions

Essential Question: How is the graph of $g(x) = ab^{x-h} + k$ where $b > 1$ related to the graph of $f(x) = b^x$?

Resource Locker

Explore 1 Graphing and Analyzing $f(x) = 2^x$ and $f(x) = 10^x$

An **exponential function** is a function of the form $f(x) = b^x$, where the base b is a positive constant other than 1 and the exponent x is a variable. Notice that there is no single parent exponential function because each choice of the base b determines a different function.

(A) Complete the input-output table for each of the parent exponential functions below.

x	$f(x) = 2^x$
−3	$\frac{1}{8}$
−2	$\frac{1}{4}$
−1	$\frac{1}{2}$
0	1
1	2
2	4
3	8

x	$p(x) = 10^x$
−3	$\frac{1}{1000}$
−2	$\frac{1}{100}$
−1	$\frac{1}{10}$
0	1
1	10
2	100
3	1000

(B) Graph the parent functions $f(x) = 2^x$ and $p(x) = 10^x$ by plotting points.

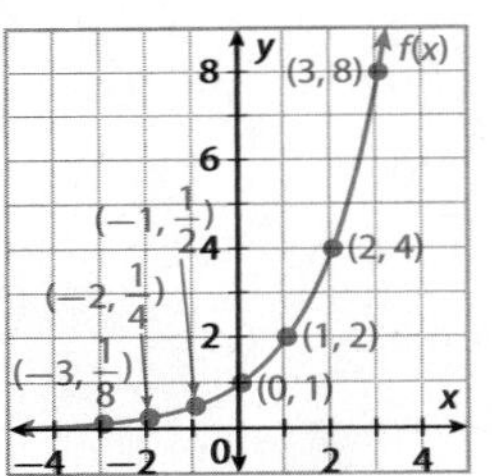

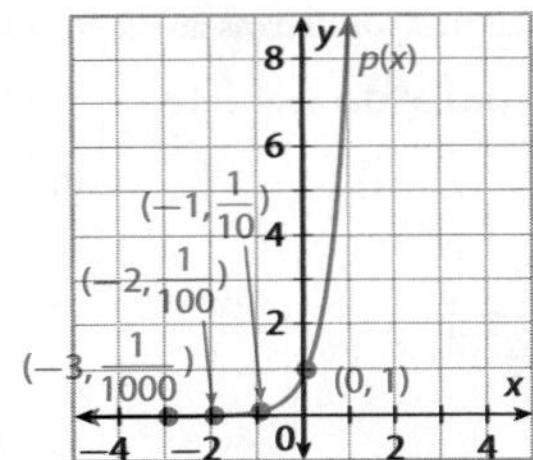

HARDCOVER PAGES 635–650

Watch for the hardcover student edition page numbers for this lesson.

Ⓒ What is the domain of each function?

Domain of $f(x) = 2^x$: $\{x \mid -\infty < x < \infty\}$

Domain of $p(x) = 10^x$: $\{x \mid -\infty < x < \infty\}$

Ⓓ What is the range of each function?

Range of $f(x) = 2^x$: $\{y \mid 0 < x < \infty\}$

Range of $p(x) = 10^x$: $\{y \mid 0 < x < \infty\}$

Ⓔ What is the y-intercept of each function?

y-intercept of $f(x) = 2^x$: 1

y-intercept of $p(x) = 10^x$: 1

Ⓕ What is the trend of each function?

In both $f(x) = 2^x$ and $p(x) = 10^x$, as the value of x increases, the value of y (increases)/ decreases.

Reflect

1. Will the domain be the same for every exponential function? Why or why not?
Yes, because the value of the exponent x can be any real number.

2. Will the range be the same for every exponential function in the form $f(x) = b^x$, where b is a positive constant? Why or why not?
Yes, because the value of b^x where b is a positive number greater than 1 will always be a positive number.

3. Will the value of the y-intercept be the same for every exponential function? Why or why not?
Yes, because a non-zero base raised to the power of 0 is always equal to 1.

Explain 1 Graphing Combined Transformations of $f(x) = b^x$ Where $b > 1$

A given exponential function $g(x) = a(b^{x-h}) + k$ with base b can be graphed by recognizing the difference between the given function and its parent function, $f(x) = b^x$. These differences define the parameters of the transformation, where k represents the vertical translation, h is the horizontal translation, and a represents either the vertical stretch or compression of the exponential function and whether it is reflected across the x-axis. You can use these parameters to see what happens to two reference points during the transformation. Two points that are easily visualized on the parent exponential function are $(0, 1)$ and $(1, b)$. The parent exponential function also has an asymptote at $y = 0$.

The given function is the parent function translated horizontally h units to the right, stretched or compressed by a factor of a, and translated up k units. Also, if $a < 0$, then the parent function is reflected across the x-axis before it is translated vertically. The point $(0, 1)$ becomes $(h, a + k)$ and $(1, b)$ becomes $(1 + h, ab + k)$. The asymptote becomes $y = k$.

PROFESSIONAL DEVELOPMENT

Learning Progressions

In this lesson, students see that an exponential function is not just a function with an exponent, but a function whose independent variable is in the exponent. Therefore, $f(x) = 2^x$ is an exponential function, but $g(x) = x^2$ is not. Students will graph most of the exponential functions in this lesson by hand and will see that the graphs of exponential growth functions approach a horizontal asymptote as x decreases without bound. In the next lesson, they will examine exponential decay functions, which approach the horizontal asymptote as x increases without bound.

EXPLORE

Graphing and Analyzing $f(x) = 2^x$ and $f(x) = 10^x$

QUESTIONING STRATEGIES

❓ Does the graph of $f(x) = bx^2$ have a vertical asymptote? Why or why not? **No; the function is defined for all real values of x.**

❓ Why can't the value of b be 1? **When $b = 1$, the function is the constant function $f(x) = 1$.**

EXPLAIN 1

Graphing Combined Transformations of $f(x) = b^x$ Where $b > 1$

INTEGRATE MATHEMATICAL PRACTICES

Focus on Modeling

MP.4 Visual learners can use colored pencils to sketch each of the intermediate steps in obtaining a graph of $g(x)$, a combined transformation from the graph of $f(x)$. For example, students might first draw the horizontal translation, then a reflection across the x-axis, and finally the vertical translation.

AVOID COMMON ERRORS

When translating to obtain the graph of $f(x) = b^{x-h}$, students often interpret the sign of h incorrectly and translate the parent graph in the wrong direction. A major cause of this error is the presence of the subtraction sign in the expression $x - h$. Remind students that this subtraction sign is not the sign of h.

The graphs of $f(x) = 2^x$ and $p(x) = 10^x$ are shown below with the reference points and asymptotes labeled.

$f(x) = 2^x$	$p(x) = 10^x$
(graph)	(graph)

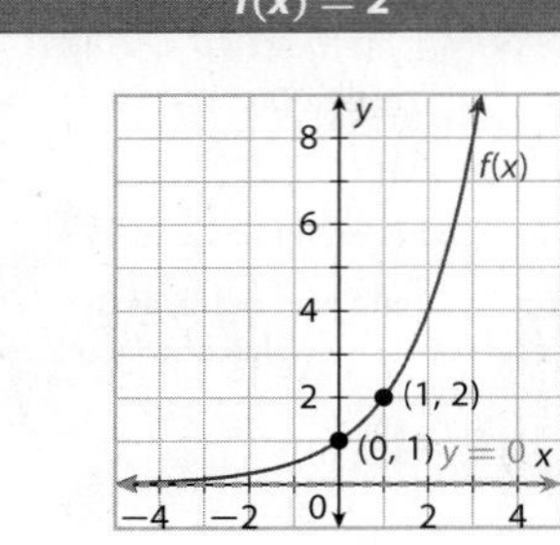

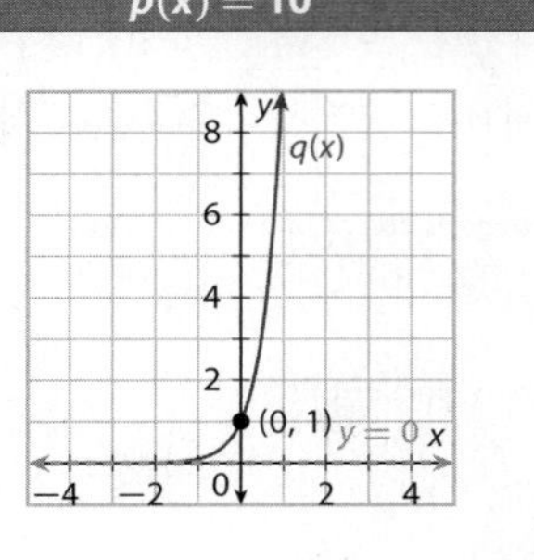

Example 1 **State the domain and range of the given function. Then identify the new values of the reference points and the asymptote. Use these values to graph the function.**

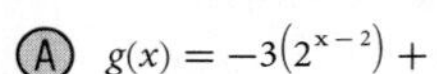

(A) $g(x) = -3(2^{x-2}) + 1$

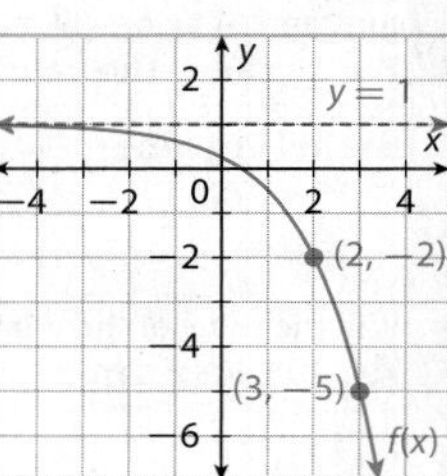

The domain of $g(x) = -3(2^{x-2}) + 1$ is $\{x \mid -\infty < x < \infty\}$.

The range of $g(x) = -3(2^{x-2}) + 1$ is $\{y \mid y < 1\}$.

Examine $g(x)$ and identify the parameters.

$a = -3$, which means that the function is reflected across the x-axis and vertically stretched by a factor of 3.

$h = 2$, so the function is translated 2 units to the right.

$k = 1$, so the function is translated 1 unit up.

The point $(0, 1)$ becomes $(h, a + k)$.

$$(h, a + k) = (2, -3 + 1)$$
$$= (2, -2)$$

$(1, b)$ becomes $(1 + h, ab + k)$.

$$(1 + h, ab + k) = (1 + 2, -3(2) + 1)$$
$$= (3, -6 + 1)$$
$$= (3, -5)$$

The asymptote becomes $y = k$.

$y = k \quad \rightarrow \quad y = 1$

Plot the transformed points and asymptote and draw the curve.

COLLABORATIVE LEARNING

Peer-to-Peer Activity

Have pairs of students work together to make a table showing the effects of the constant a on the graphs of $g(x) = ab^{x-h} + k$ if $a > 1$ and if $a < -1$. In the table, have students include a sketch of each graph, as well as information about how changing the value of a affects function characteristics such as asymptotes and end behavior.

Ⓑ $q(x) = 1.5(10^{x-3}) - 5$

The domain of $q(x) = 1.5(10^{x-3}) - 5$ is $\{x| -\infty < x < \infty\}$.

The range of $q(x) = 1.5(10^{x-3}) - 5$ is $\{y| y > -5\}$.

Examine $q(x)$ and identify the parameters.

$a = $ 1.5 so the function is stretched vertically by a factor of 1.5.

$h = $ 3 so the function is translated 3 units to the right.

$k = $ −5 so the function is translated 5 units down.

The point $(0,1)$ becomes $(h, a + k)$.

$(h, a + k) = (3, 1.5 - 5) = (3, -3.5)$

$(1, b)$ becomes $(1 + h, ab + k)$.

$(1 + h, ab + k) = (1 + 3, 1.5(10) - 5) = (4, 10)$

The asymptote becomes $y = k$.

$y = k \quad \rightarrow \quad y = -5$

Plot the transformed points and asymptote and draw the curve.

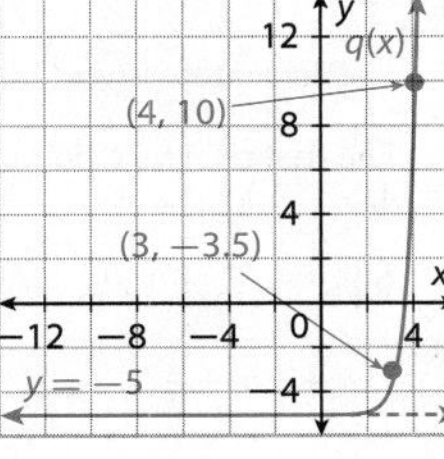

Your Turn

4. $g(x) = 4(2^{x+2}) - 6$

The domain of $g(x) = 4(2^{x+2}) - 6$ is $\{x| -\infty < x < \infty\}$.

The range of $g(x) = 4(2^{x+2}) - 6$ is $\{y| y > -6\}$.

$a = 4$ $\quad h = -2$ $\quad k = -6$

The asymptote becomes $y = -6$.

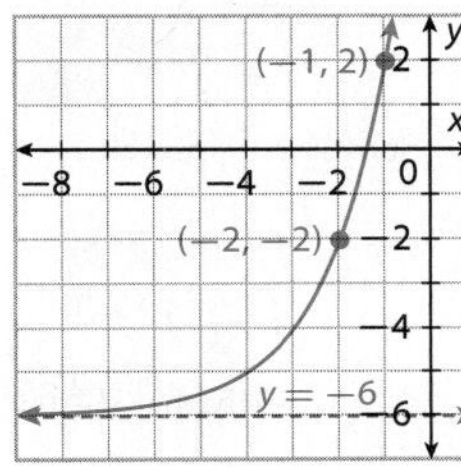

5. $q(x) = -\frac{3}{5}(10^{x+2}) + 3$

The domain of $q(x) = -\frac{3}{5}(10^{x+2}) + 3$ is $\{x| -\infty < x < \infty\}$.

The range of $q(x) = -\frac{3}{5}(10^{x+2}) + 3$ is $\{y| y < 3\}$.

$a = -\frac{3}{5}$ $\quad h = -2$ $\quad k = 3$

The asymptote becomes $y = 3$.

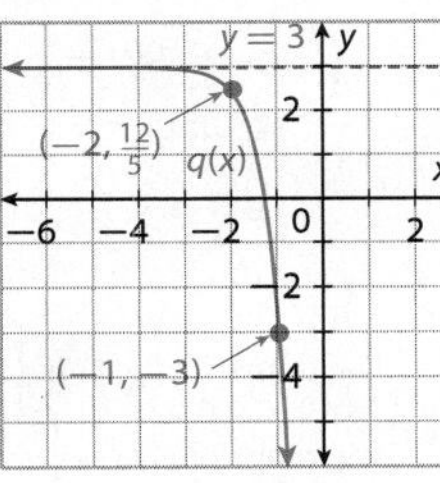

QUESTIONING STRATEGIES

? Can you transform the graph of $f(x) = b^x$ so that it has a turning point? **No; the graph will be ever increasing from the horizontal asymptote or ever decreasing to the horizontal asymptote, no matter which transformation is used.**

DIFFERENTIATE INSTRUCTION

Kinesthetic Experience

For kinesthetic learners, draw a coordinate plane on the board so that the origin is close to a given student's shoulder height. Have the student stand in front of the plane, aligned with the y-axis, and then arrange his or her arms to roughly model the graph of an exponential function $f(x) = ab^x$ for different values of b for $a = 1$ and for $a = -1$.

EXPLAIN 2

Writing Equations for Combined Transformations of $f(x) = b^x$ Where $b > 1$

INTEGRATE TECHNOLOGY

Students can check the equations they write by graphing the transformed functions on their graphing calculators. Have them use the **TRACE** or **TABLE** feature to identify coordinates of points in the resulting graph.

Explain 2 Writing Equations for Combined Transformations of $f(x) = b^x$ Where $b > 1$

Given the graph of an exponential function, you can use your knowledge of the transformation parameters to write the function rule for the graph. Recall that the asymptote will give the value of k and the x-coordinate of the first reference point is h. Then let y_1 be the y-coordinate of the first point and solve the equation $y_1 = a + k$ for a.

Finally, use a, h, and k to write the function in the form $g(x) = a\left(b^{x-h}\right) + k$.

Example 2 **Write the exponential function that will produce the given graph, using the specified value of b. Verify that the second reference point is on the graph of the function. Then state the domain and range of the function in set notation.**

Ⓐ Let $b = 2$.

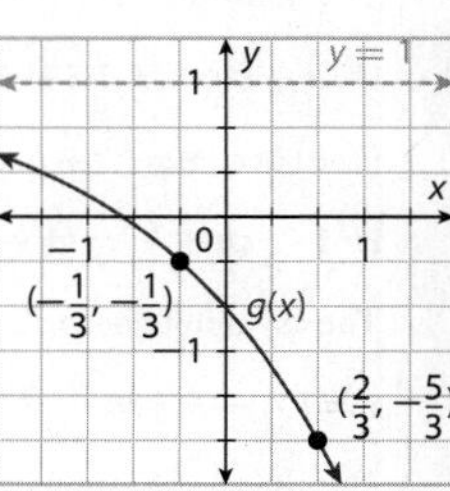

The asymptote is $y = 1$, showing that $k = 1$.

The first reference point is $\left(-\frac{1}{3}, -\frac{1}{3}\right)$. This shows that $h = -\frac{1}{3}$ and that $a + k = -\frac{1}{3}$.

Substitute $k = 1$ and solve for a.

$$a + k = -\frac{1}{3}$$
$$a + 1 = -\frac{1}{3}$$
$$a = -\frac{4}{3}$$
$$h = -\frac{1}{3}$$
$$k = 1$$

Substitute these values into $g(x) = a\left(b^{x-h}\right) + k$ to find $g(x)$.

$$g(x) = a\left(b^{x-h}\right) + k$$
$$= -\frac{4}{3}\left(2^{x+\frac{1}{3}}\right) + 1$$

Verify that $g\left(\frac{2}{3}\right) = -\frac{5}{3}$.

$$g\left(\frac{2}{3}\right) = -\frac{4}{3}\left(2^{\frac{2}{3}+\frac{1}{3}}\right) + 1$$
$$= -\frac{4}{3}\left(2^1\right) + 1$$
$$= -\frac{4}{3}(2) + 1$$
$$= \frac{3}{3} - \frac{8}{3}$$
$$= -\frac{5}{3}$$

The domain of $g(x)$ is $\left\{x \mid -\infty < x < +\infty\right\}$.

The range of $g(x)$ is $\left\{y \mid y < 1\right\}$.

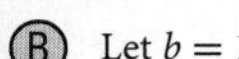

(B) Let $b = 10$.

The asymptote is $y = 6$, showing that $k = 6$.

The first reference point is $(-4, 4.4)$. This shows that $h = -4$ and that $a + k = 4.4$. Substitute for k and solve for a.

$a + k = 4.4$

$a + 6 = 4.4$

$a = -1.6$ $h = -4$ $k = 6$

Substitute these values into $q(x) = a(b^{x-h}) + k$ to find $q(x)$.

$q(x) = a(b^{x-h}) + k = -1.6\left(10^{x--4}\right) + 6$

Verify that $q(-3) = -10$.

$q(-3) = -1.6\left(10^{-3--4}\right) + 6$

$= -1.6\left(10^{1}\right) + 6$

$= -16 + 6$

$= -10$

The domain of $q(x)$ is $\{x \mid -\infty < x < +\infty\}$. The range of $q(x)$ is $\{y \mid y < 6\}$.

Your Turn

Write the exponential function that will produce the given graph, using the specified value of *b*. Verify that the second reference point is on the graph of the function. Then state the domain and range of the function in set notation.

6. $b = 2$

The asymptote is $y = -\frac{5}{2} \rightarrow k = -\frac{5}{2}$, showing that $k = -\frac{5}{2}$.

The first reference point is $(3, -1) \rightarrow h = 3$ and $a + k = -1$. Substitute k and solve for a.

$a + k = -1$

$a - \frac{5}{2} = -1$

$a = \frac{3}{2}$

$a = \frac{3}{2}; h = 3; k = -\frac{5}{2}$

$g(x) = \frac{3}{2}(2^{x-3}) - \frac{5}{2}$

Verify that $g(4) = \frac{1}{2}$.

$g(4) = \frac{3}{2}(2^{4-3}) - \frac{5}{2} = \frac{1}{2}$

The domain of $g(x)$ is $\{x \mid -\infty < x < +\infty\}$.

The range of $g(x)$ is $\left\{y \mid y > -\frac{5}{2}\right\}$.

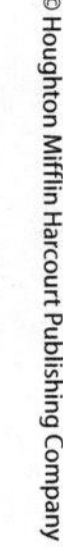

QUESTIONING STRATEGIES

? How do you find h and k from the first reference point? **The x-coordinate of the first reference point is h. Substitute the value of k in the equation $y = a + k$ to find a.**

? How do you use the second reference point? **After you substitute a, h, and k and find the function, substitute the coordinates of the second reference point to check that the function includes this point.**

EXPLAIN 3

Modeling With Exponential Growth Functions

AVOID COMMON ERRORS

Students may multiply the initial amount by the growth factor and then raise that product to the exponent. Remind students to apply the order of operations. The exponent applies only to the growth factor.

QUESTIONING STRATEGIES

What is the exponential growth function $f(t) = a(1 + r)^t$ if the growth rate is 0.05%? Why? $f(t) = a(1.0005)^t$, because 0.05 written as a decimal is 0.0005

When should you round exponential growth calculations? Round during the last step only. Rounding earlier will compound errors.

Explain 3 Modeling with Exponential Growth Functions

An **exponential growth function** has the form $f(t) = a(1 + r)^t$ where $a > 0$ and r is a constant percent increase (expressed as a decimal) for each unit increase in time t. That is, since $f(t + 1) = (1 + r) \cdot f(t) = f(t) + r \cdot f(t)$, the value of the function increases by $r \cdot f(t)$ on the interval $[t, t + 1]$. The base $1 + r$ of an exponential growth function is called the **growth factor**, and the constant percent increase r, in decimal form, is called the **growth rate**.

Example 3 **Find the function that corresponds with the given situation. Then use the graph of the function to make a prediction.**

(A) Tony purchased a rare guitar in 2000 for \$12,000. Experts estimate that its value will increase by 14% per year. Use a graph to find the number of years it will take for the value of the guitar to be \$60,000.

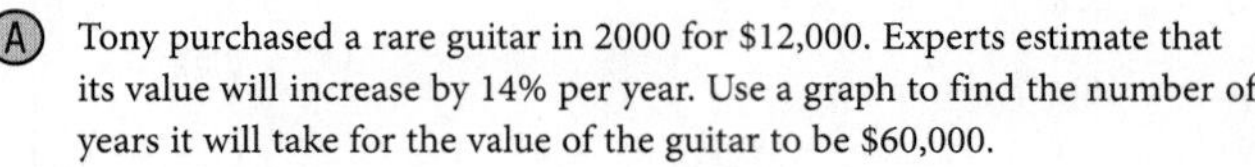

Write a function to model the growth in value for the guitar.

$f(t) = a(1 + r)^t$

$= 12,000(1 + 0.14)^t$

$= 12,000(1.14)^t$

Use a graphing calculator to graph the function.

Use the graph to predict when the guitar will be worth \$60,000.

Use the TRACE feature to find the t-value where $f(t) \approx 60,000$.

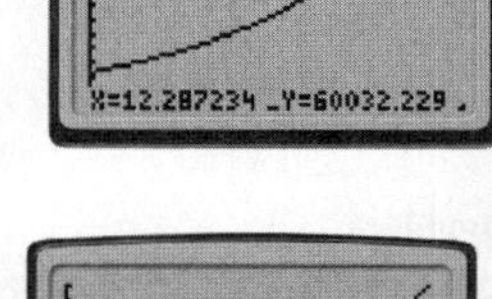

So, the guitar will be worth \$60,000 approximately 12.29 years after it was purchased.

(B) At the same time that Tony bought the \$12,000 guitar, he also considered buying another rare guitar for \$15,000. Experts estimated that this guitar would increase in value by 9% per year. Determine after how many years the two guitars will be worth the same amount.

Write a function to model the growth in value for the second guitar.

$g(t) = a(1 + r)^t$

$= \boxed{15,000}\left(1 + \boxed{0.09}\right)^t$

$= \boxed{15,000}\left(\boxed{1.09}\right)^t$

Use a graphing calculator to graph the two functions.

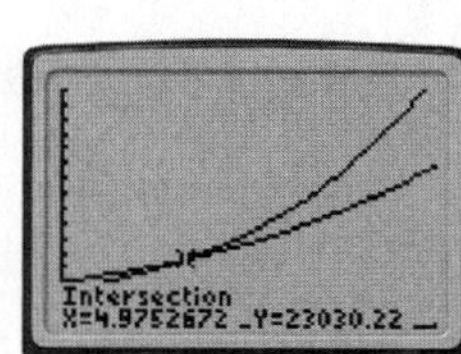

Use the graph to predict when the two guitars will be worth the same amount.

Use the intersection feature to find the t-value where $g(t) = \boxed{f(t)}$.

So, the two guitars will be worth the same amount 4.98 years after 2000.

Reflect

7. In part A, find the average rates of change over the intervals $(0, 4)$, $(4, 8)$, and $(8, 12)$. Do the rates increase, decrease, or stay the same?

The average rate of change from 0 to 4 is $\frac{20,267.52 - 12,000}{4 - 0} = 2066.88$, the average rate of change from 4 to 8 is $\frac{34,231.04 - 20,267.52}{8 - 4} = 3490.88$, and the average rate of change from 8 to 12 is $\frac{57,814.86 - 34,231.04}{12 - 8} = 5895.96$. Between each interval, the average rate of change gets larger, so the rates are increasing for increasing values of x.

Your Turn

Find the function that corresponds with the given situation. Then graph the function on a calculator and use the graph to make a prediction.

8. John researches a baseball card and finds that it is currently worth \$3.25. However, it is supposed to increase in value 11% per year. In how many years will the card be worth \$26?

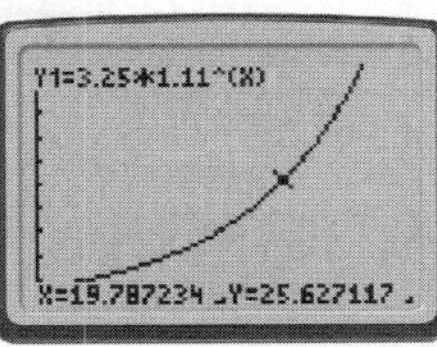

Write a function to model the growth in value for the baseball card.
$g(t) = a(1 + r)^t = 3.25(1 + 0.11)^t = 3.25(1.11)^t$.
Graphing the function and using the trace function to determine when $g(x) \approx 26$ result in $x \approx 20$.
So, the card will be worth \$26 approximately 20 years after John purchased it.

Elaborate

9. How are reference points helpful when graphing transformations of $f(x) = b^x$ or when writing equations for transformed graphs?

Reference points help when graphing transformations because all of the points of the parent graph are affected in the same manner. So by shifting each reference point by the same value or ratio, the transformed graph can be drawn. Similarly, the points of a transformed graph can be compared to the reference points on the parent graph to determine the values of a, h, and k in order to find the equation of the transformed graph.

10. Give the general form of an exponential growth function and describe its parameters.

A function $f(x) = ab^x$ is an exponential growth function, where $a > 0$ and $b > 1$.

11. **Essential Question Check-In** Which transformations of $f(x) = b^x$ change the function's end behavior? Which transformations change the function's y-intercept?

Reflections across the x-axis change the function's end behavior by making the reflected function increase toward the asymptote as x tends to negative infinity and decrease toward negative infinity as x tends to infinity. Vertical translations also change the function's end behavior since they affect the graph's asymptote. Vertical translations, horizontal translations, vertical stretches and compressions, and reflections across the x-axis all affect the location of the graph's y-intercept.

LANGUAGE SUPPORT EL

Communicate Math

Have students work in pairs. Each student writes an exponential growth function in the form $f(x) = b^x$ on an index card, and sketches its graph on another card. Students shuffle the index cards and lay them face down in an array. They take turns turning two cards over, trying to match the graph of the function to its equation. Students must justify why they think they do or don't have a match.

ELABORATE

CONNECT VOCABULARY EL

Have students begin to create a list of words associated with exponential functions, and later their inverses, beginning with *growth* and *interest*, then later adding vocabulary such as *decay*, *e*, and *logarithms*.

INTEGRATE MATHEMATICAL PRACTICES

Focus on Critical Thinking

MP.3 When students have the option of several points to use as a reference point and the y-intercept is one such point, students should find that it is easier to use the y-intercept than the other points for calculations.

SUMMARIZE THE LESSON

What are the effects of the constant a on the graph of $g(x) = ab^{x-h} + k$? **If $a > 1$, the graph of the parent function $f(x) = b^x$ is stretched vertically by a factor of a. If $0 < a < 1$, the graph is shrunk vertically by a factor of a. If $a < -1$, the graph of $f(x) = b^x$ is stretched vertically by a factor of $|a|$ and reflected across the x-axis. If $-1 < a < 0$, the graph of $f(x) = b^x$ is shrunk vertically by a factor of $|a|$ and reflected across the x-axis.**

EVALUATE

ASSIGNMENT GUIDE

Concepts and Skills	Practice
Explore Graphing and Analyzing $f(x) = 2^x$ and $f(x) = 10^x$	
Example 1 Graphing Combined Transformations of $f(x) = b^x$ where $b > 1$	Exercises 9–14
Example 2 Writing Equations for Combined Transformations of $f(x) = b^x$ where $b > 1$	Exercises 15–17
Example 3 Modeling With Exponential Growth Functions	Exercises 18–22

AVOID COMMON ERRORS

When translating the graph of $g(x) = ab^{x-h} + k$, students commonly interpret the sign of h incorrectly and translate the parent graph in the wrong direction. A major cause of this error is the presence of the subtraction sign in the expression $x - h$. Remind students that this subtraction sign is not the sign of h. In the expression $x - 2$, for instance, $h = 2$ (a positive number), so the translation is to the right. To identify the value of h in the expression $x + 2$, students should rewrite it as $x - (-2)$, which means that $h = -2$, so the translation is to the left.

Evaluate: Homework and Practice

- Online Homework
- Hints and Help
- Extra Practice

Describe the effect of each transformation on the parent function. Graph the parent function and its transformation. Then determine the domain, range, and y-intercept of each function.

1. $f(x) = 2^x$ and $g(x) = 2(2^x)$

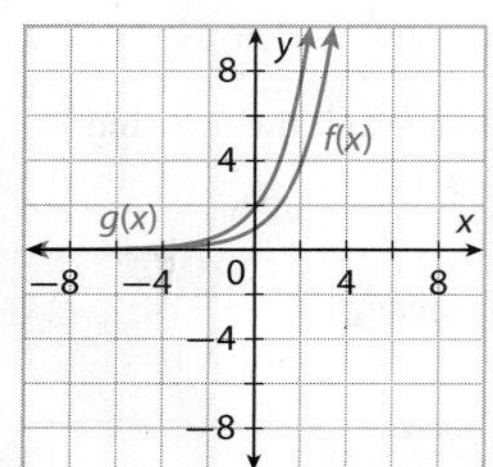

$g(x)$ is a vertical stretch (or horizontal compression) of $f(x)$. The domain of $f(x)$ is $\{x|-\infty < x < \infty\}$ and the range is $\{y|y > 0\}$. The domain of $g(x)$ is $\{x|-\infty < x < \infty\}$ and the range is $\{y|y > 0\}$. The y-intercept of $f(x)$ is 1 and the y-intercept of $g(x)$ is 2.

2. $f(x) = 2^x$ and $g(x) = -5(2^x)$

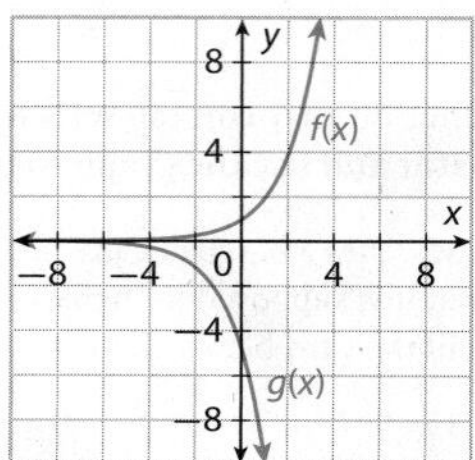

$g(x)$ is a vertical stretch (or horizontal compression) of $f(x)$ combined with a reflection about the x-axis. The domain of $f(x)$ is $\{x|-\infty < x < \infty\}$ and the range is $\{y|y > 0\}$. The domain of $g(x)$ is $\{x|-\infty < x < \infty\}$ and the range is $\{y|y < 0\}$. The y-intercept of $f(x)$ is 1 and the y-intercept of $g(x)$ is −5.

3. $f(x) = 2^x$ and $g(x) = 2^{x+2}$

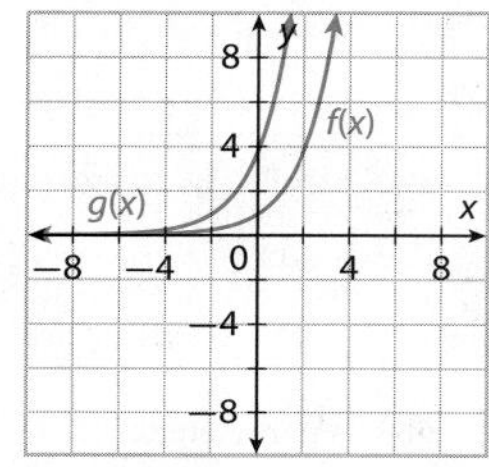

$g(x)$ is a shift to the left by 2 of $f(x)$. The domain of $f(x)$ is $\{x|-\infty < x < \infty\}$ and the range is $\{y|y > 0\}$. The domain of $g(x)$ is $\{x|-\infty < x < \infty\}$ and the range is $\{y|y > 0\}$. The y-intercept of $f(x)$ is 1 and the y-intercept of $g(x)$ is 4.

4. $f(x) = 2^x$ and $g(x) = 2^x + 5$

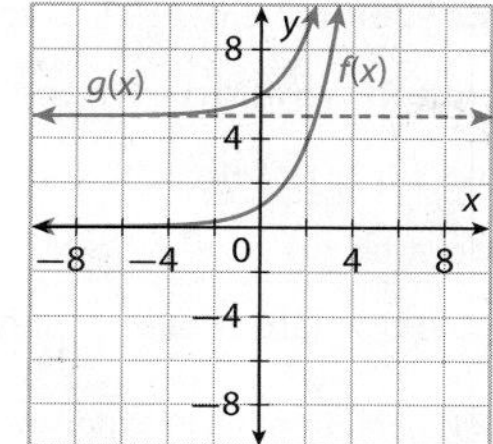

$g(x)$ is a shift upward by 5 of $f(x)$. The domain of $f(x)$ is $\{x|-\infty < x < \infty\}$ and the range is $\{y|y > 0\}$. The domain of $g(x)$ is $\{x|-\infty < x < \infty\}$ and the range is $\{y|y > 5\}$. The y-intercept of $f(x)$ is 1 and the y-intercept of $g(x)$ is 6.

Exercise	Depth of Knowledge (D.O.K.)	COMMON CORE Mathematical Practices
1–8	**1** Recall of Information	**MP.6** Precision
9–14	**2** Skills/Concepts	**MP.2** Reasoning
15–17	**2** Skills/Concepts	**MP.2** Reasoning
18–22	**2** Skills/Concepts	**MP.4** Modeling
23	**3** Strategic Thinking H.O.T.	**MP.2** Reasoning
24	**3** Strategic Thinking H.O.T.	**MP.3** Logic

5. $f(x) = 10^x$ and $g(x) = 2(10^x)$

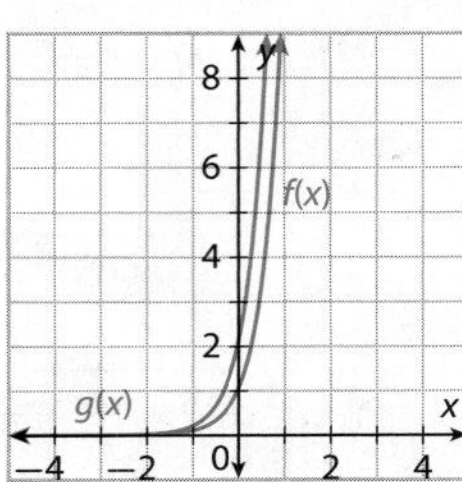

$g(x)$ is a vertical stretch (or horizontal compression) of $f(x)$. The domain of $f(x)$ is $\{x \mid -\infty < x < \infty\}$ and the range is $\{y \mid y > 0\}$. The domain of $g(x)$ is $\{x \mid -\infty < x < \infty\}$ and the range is $\{y \mid y > 0\}$. The y-intercept of $f(x)$ is 1 and the y-intercept of $g(x)$ is 2.

6. $f(x) = 10^x$ and $g(x) = -4(10^x)$

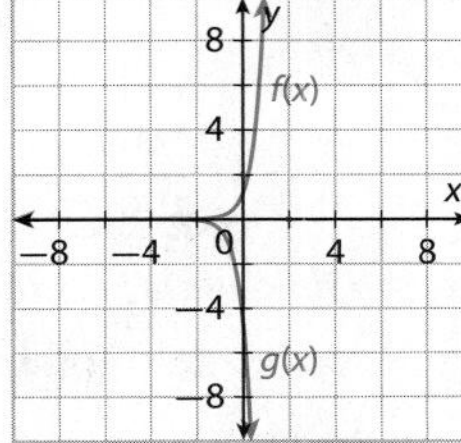

$g(x)$ is a vertical stretch (or horizontal compression) of $f(x)$ combined with a reflection about the x-axis. The domain of $f(x)$ is $\{x \mid -\infty < x < \infty\}$ and the range is $\{y \mid y > 0\}$. The domain of $g(x)$ is $\{x \mid -\infty < x < \infty\}$ and the range is $\{y \mid y < 0\}$. The y-intercept of $f(x)$ is 1 and the y-intercept of $g(x)$ is -4.

7. $f(x) = 10^x$ and $g(x) = 10^{x-2}$

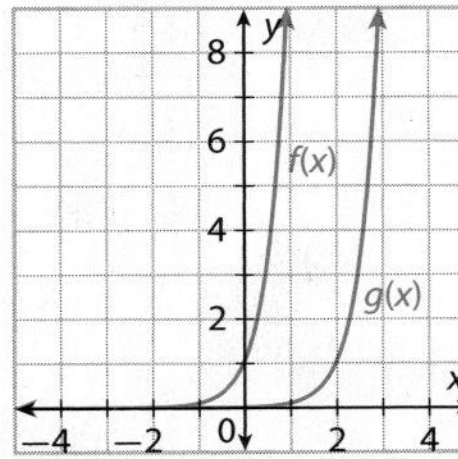

$g(x)$ is a shift to the right by 2 of $f(x)$. The domain of $f(x)$ is $\{x \mid -\infty < x < \infty\}$ and the range is $\{y \mid y > 0\}$. The domain of $g(x)$ is $\{x \mid -\infty < x < \infty\}$ and the range is $\{y \mid y > 0\}$. The y-intercept of $f(x)$ is 1 and the y-intercept of $g(x)$ is $\frac{1}{100}$.

8. $f(x) = 10^x$ and $g(x) = 10^x - 6$

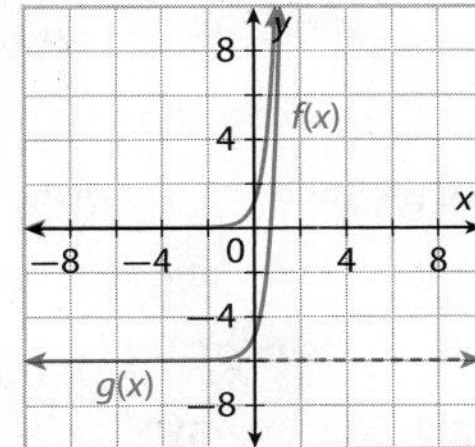

$g(x)$ is a shift downward by 6 of $f(x)$. The domain of $f(x)$ is $\{x \mid -\infty < x < \infty\}$ and the range is $\{y \mid y > 0\}$. The domain of $g(x)$ is $\{x \mid -\infty < x < \infty\}$ and the range is $\{y \mid y > -6\}$. The y-intercept of $f(x)$ is 1 and the y-intercept of $g(x)$ is -5.

9. Describe the graph of $g(x) = 2^{(x-3)} - 4$ in terms of $f(x) = 2^x$.

The graph is shifted down by 4 and right by 3.

10. Describe the graph of $g(x) = 10^{(x+7)} + 6$ in terms of $f(x) = 10^x$.

The graph is shifted up by 6 and left by 7.

PEER-TO-PEER DISCUSSION

Ask students to discuss with a partner how they would transform $f(x) = 1.1^x$ and $g(x) = -1.1^x$. Have them choose a translation and a stretch, write the rule, and sketch the graphs. If desired, have students choose an axis to reflect the function across and repeat.

State the domain and range of the given function. Then identify the new values of the reference points and the asymptote. Use these values to graph the function.

11. $h(x) = 2(3^{x+2}) - 1$

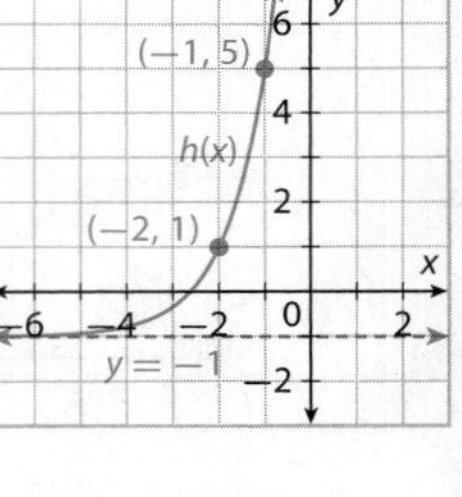

The domain of $h(x) = 2(3^{x+2}) - 1$ is $\{x \mid -\infty < x < \infty\}$.

The range of $h(x) = 2(3^{x+2}) - 1$ is $\{y \mid y > -1\}$.

$a = 2$ so the function is vertically stretched by a factor of 2.

$h = -2$ so the function is translated 2 units to the left.

$k = -1$ so the function is translated 1 unit down.

The point $(0, 1)$ becomes $(-2, 1)$.

The point $(1, 3)$ becomes $(-1, 5)$.

The asymptote becomes $y = -1$.

12.  $k(x) = -0.5(4^{x-1}) + 2$

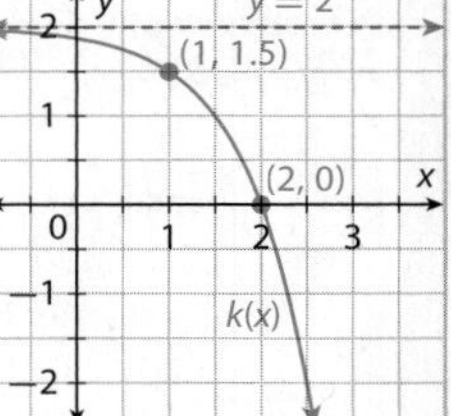

The domain of $k(x) = -0.5(4^{x-1}) + 2$ is $\{x \mid -\infty < x < \infty\}$.

The range of $k(x) = -0.5(4^{x-1}) + 2$ is $\{y \mid y < 2\}$.

a is negative so function is reflected across x–axis

$a = 0.5$ so the function is vertically compressed by a factor of $\frac{1}{2}$.

$h = 1$ so the function is translated 1 unit to the right.

$k = 2$ so the function is translated 2 units up.

The point $(0, 1)$ becomes $(1, 1.5)$.

The point $(1, 4)$ becomes $(2, 0)$.

The asymptote becomes $y = 2$.

13. 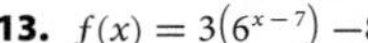 $f(x) = 3(6^{x-7}) - 8$

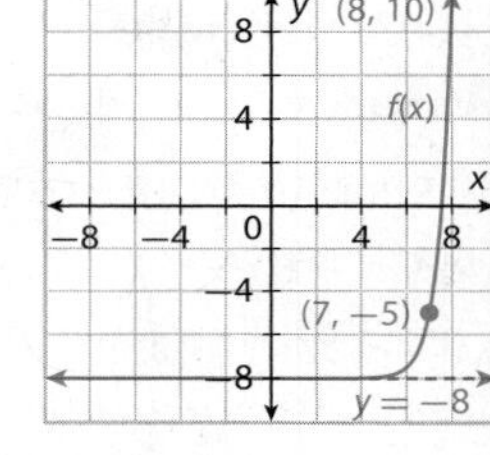

The domain of $f(x) = 3(6^{x-7}) - 8$ is $\{x \mid -\infty < x < \infty\}$.

The range of $f(x) = 3(6^{x-7}) - 8$ is $\{y \mid y > -8\}$.

$a = 3$ so the function is vertically stretched by a factor of 3.

$h = 7$ so the function is translated 7 units to the right.

$k = -8$ so the function is translated 8 units down.

The point $(0, 1)$ becomes $(7, -8)$.

The point $(1, 6)$ becomes $(8, 10)$.

The asymptote becomes $y = -8$.

14. $f(x) = -3(2^{x+1}) + 3$

The domain of $f(x) = -3(2^{x+1}) + 3$ is $\{x \mid -\infty < x < \infty\}$.

The range of $f(x) = -3(2^{x+1}) + 3$ is $\{y \mid y < 3\}$.

a is negative so function is reflected across x-axis

$a = -3$ so the function is vertically stretched by a factor of 3.

$h = -1$ so the function is translated 1 unit to the left.

$k = 3$ so the function is translated 3 units up.

The point $(0, 1)$ becomes $(-1, 0)$.

The point $(1, 2)$ becomes $(0, -3)$.

The asymptote becomes $y = 3$.

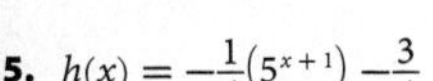

15. $h(x) = -\frac{1}{4}(5^{x+1}) - \frac{3}{4}$

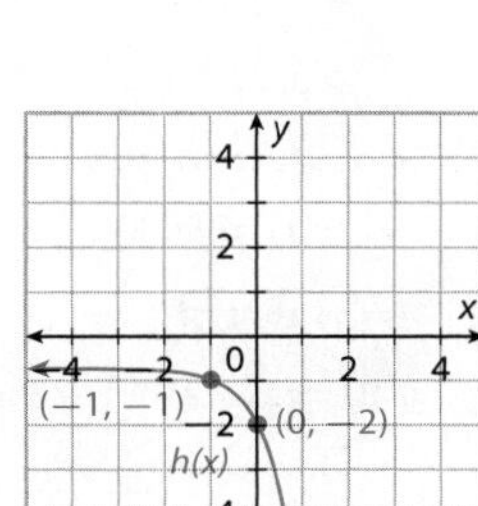

The domain of $h(x) = -\frac{1}{4}(5^{x+1}) - \frac{3}{4}$ is $\{x \mid -\infty < x < \infty\}$.

The range of $h(x) = \frac{-1}{4}(5^{x+1}) - \frac{3}{4}$ is $\left\{y \mid y < -\frac{3}{4}\right\}$.

a is negative so function is reflected across x-axis

$a = -\frac{1}{4}$ so the function is vertically compressed by a factor of $\frac{1}{4}$.

$h = -1$ so the function is translated 1 unit to the left.

$k = -\frac{3}{4}$ so the function is translated $\frac{3}{4}$ unit down.

The point $(0, 1)$ becomes $(-1, -1)$.

The point $(1, 5)$ becomes $(0, -2)$.

The asymptote becomes $y = -\frac{3}{4}$.

16. $p(x) = 2(4^{x-3}) - 5$

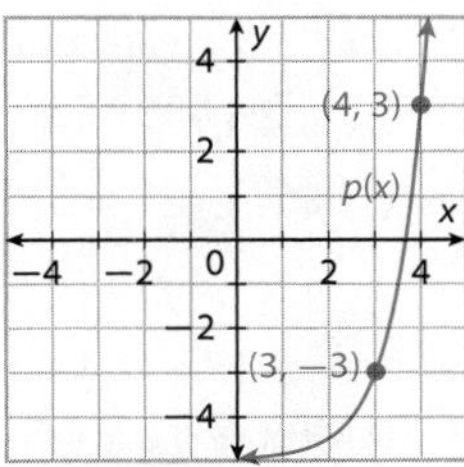

The domain of $p(x) = 2(4^{x-3}) - 5$ is $\{x \mid -\infty < x < \infty\}$.

The range of $p(x) = 2(4^{x-3}) - 5$ is $\{y \mid y > -5\}$

$a = 2$ so the function is vertically stretched by a factor of 2.

$h = 3$ so the function is translated 3 unit to the right.

$k = -5$ so the function is translated 5 unit down.

The point $(0, 1)$ becomes $(3, -3)$.

The point $(1, 4)$ becomes $(4, 3)$.

The asymptote becomes $y = -5$.

INTEGRATE TECHNOLOGY

Students may find it useful to use a spreadsheet to calculate values they use repeatedly. For example, after they enter the values of a, b, h, and k in separate cells, they can calculate coordinates of two reference points as formulas using these values.

Write the exponential function that will produce the given graph, using the specified value of b. Verify that the second reference point is on the graph of the function. Then state the domain and range of the function in set notation.

17. $b = 2$

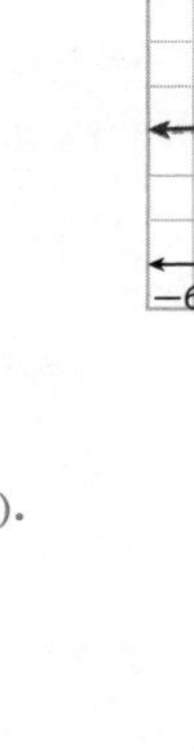

The asymptote is $y = 3 \rightarrow k = 3$.

The first reference point is $(-1, 5.2) \rightarrow h = -1$

and $a + k = 5.2$. Substitute for k and solve for a.

$a + k = 5.2$

$a + 3 = 5.2$

$a = 2.2$

$a = 2.2; h = -1; k = 3$

Substitute these values into $g(x) = a(b^{x-h}) + k$ to find $g(x)$.

$g(x) = 2.2(2^{x+1}) + 3$

Verify that $g(0) = 7.4$.

$g(0) = 2.2(2^{0+1}) + 3 = 7.4$

The domain of $g(x)$ is $\{x | -\infty < x < +\infty\}$.

The range of $g(x)$ is $\{y | y > 3\}$.

18. $b = 10$

The asymptote is $y = 4 \rightarrow k = 4$. 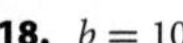

The first reference point is $(-2, 3.7) \rightarrow h = -2$ and

$a + k = 3.7$. Substitute for k and solve for a.

$a + k = 3.7$

$a + 4 = 3.7$

$a = -0.3$

$a = -0.3; h = -2; k = 4$

Substitute these values into $q(x) = a(b^{x-h}) + k$ to find $q(x)$.

$q(x) = -0.3(10^{x+2}) + 4$

Verify that $q(-1) = 1$.

$q(-1) = -0.3(10^{-1+2}) + 4 = 1$

The domain of $q(x)$ is $\{x | -\infty < x < +\infty\}$.

The range of $q(x)$ is $\{y | y < 4\}$.

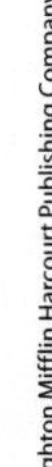

Find the function that corresponds with the given situation. Then graph the function on a calculator and use the graph to make a prediction.

19. A certain stock opens with a price of \$0.59. Over the first three days, the value of the stock increases on average by 50% per day. If this trend continues, how many days will it take for the stock to be worth \$6?

$f(t) = a(1 + r)^t$

$= 0.59\ (1 + 0.5)^t$

$= 0.59(1.5)^t$

Graphing the function and using the trace function to determine when $f(x) = 6$ result in $x \approx 5.74$.

So, it will take approximately 5.74 days for the stock to be worth \$6.

20. Sue has a lamp from her great-grandmother. She has it appraised and finds it is worth \$1000. She wants to sell it, but the appraiser tells her that the value is appreciating by 8% per year. In how many years will the value of the lamp be \$2000?

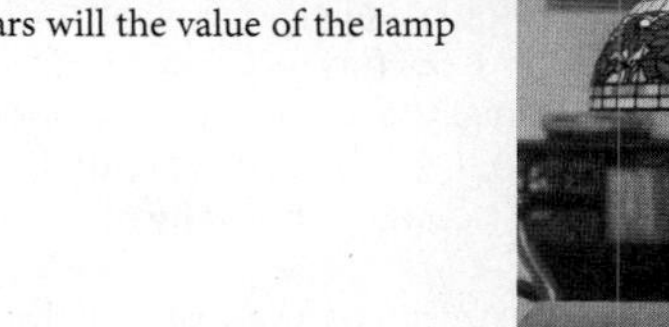

$f(t) = a(1 + r)^t$

$= 1000(1 + 0.08)^t$

$= 1000(1.08)^t$

Graphing the function and using the trace function to determine when $f(x) = 2000$ result in $x \approx 9.04$.

So, it will take approximately 9.04 years for the value of the lamp to be worth \$2000.

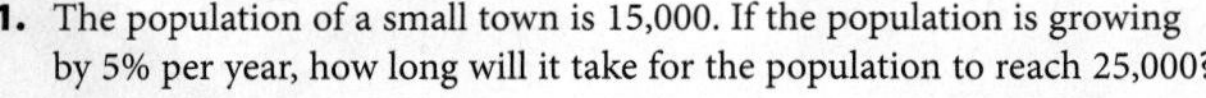

21. The population of a small town is 15,000. If the population is growing by 5% per year, how long will it take for the population to reach 25,000?

$f(t) = a(1 + r)^t$

$= 15{,}000(1 + 0.05)^t$

$= 15{,}000(1.05)^t$

Graphing the function and using the trace function to determine when $f(x) = 25{,}000$ result in $x \approx 10.47$.

So, it will take approximately 10.47 years for the population to reach 25,000.

JOURNAL

Have students describe the steps they would take to graph $f(x) = 2^{x+1} - 1$ and describe and explain the transformations from the parent function.

22. Bill invests \$3000 in a bond fund with an interest rate of 9% per year. If Bill does not withdraw any of the money, in how many years will his bond fund be worth \$5000?

$$f(t) = a(1 + r)^t$$
$$= 3000(1 + 0.09)^t$$
$$= 3000(1.09)^t$$

Graphing the function and using the trace function to determine when $f(x) = 5000$ result in $x \approx 5.96$.

So, it will take approximately 5.96 years for Bill's bond fund to reach \$5000.

H.O.T. Focus on Higher Order Thinking

23. Analyze Relationships Compare the end behavior of $g(x) = 2^x$ and $f(x) = x^2$. How are the graphs of the functions similar? How are they different?

For $g(x) = 2^x$, as $x \to +\infty$, $g(x) \to +\infty$ and as $x \to -\infty$, $g(x) \to 0$.
For $f(x) = x^2$, as $x \to +\infty$, $f(x) \to +\infty$ and as $x \to -\infty$, $f(x) \to +\infty$.
The two functions have the same end behavior as $x \to +\infty$, however as $x \to -\infty$, $f(x) = x^2$ is unbounded, whereas $g(x) = 2^x$ is bounded below by 0.

24. Explain the Error A student has a baseball card that is worth \$6.35. He looks up the appreciation rate and finds it to be 2.5% per year. He wants to find how much it will be worth after 3 years. He writes the function $f(t) = 6.35(2.5)^t$ and uses the graph of that function to find the value of the card in 3 years.

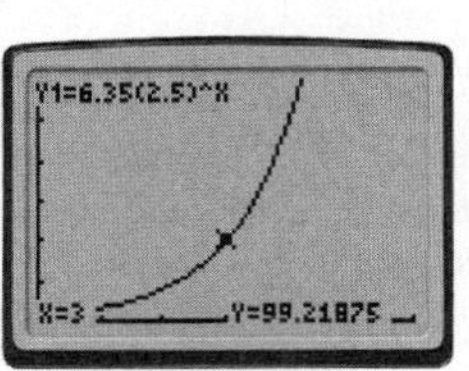

According to his graph, his card will be worth about \$99.22 in 3 years. What did the student do wrong? What is the correct answer?

The student forgot to convert the growth rate to a decimal. The function should be $f(t) = 6.35(1.025)^t$. Using the correct function and graph gives $f(3) = 6.8382555$. So, in three years, the card will be worth about \$6.84.

Lesson Performance Task

Like all collectables, the price of an item is determined by what the buyer is willing to pay and the seller is willing to accept. The estimated value of a 1948 Tucker 48 in excellent condition has risen at an approximately exponential rate from about \$500,000 in December 2006 to about \$1,400,000 in December 2013.

a. Find an equation in the form $V(t) = V_0(1 + r)^t$, where V_0 is the value of the car in dollars in December 2006, r is the average annual growth rate, t is the time in years since December 2006, and $V(t)$ is the value of the car in dollars at time t. (Hint: Substitute the known values and solve for r.)

b. What is the interpretation for the value of r?

c. If this trend continues, what would be the value of the car in December 2017?

a. December 2013 is 7 years from December 2006. Substitute 500,000 for V_0, 7 for t, and 1,400,000 for $V(t)$.

$1{,}400{,}000 = 500{,}000(1 + r)^7$

Solve for r.

$\frac{1{,}400{,}000}{500{,}000} = \frac{500{,}000(1 + r)^7}{500{,}000}$

$2.8 = (1 + r)^7$

$\sqrt[7]{2.8} = \sqrt[7]{(1 + r)^7}$

$1.158 \approx 1 + r$

$0.158 \approx r$

$V(t) = 500{,}000(1.158)^t$

b. The average annual growth rate for the value of a 1948 Tucker 48 is about 15.8%.

c. In December 2017, $t = 11$.

$V(11) = 500{,}000(1.158)^{11}$

$\approx 2{,}510{,}522.73$

The car would have a value of about \$2,510,522.73.

EXTENSION ACTIVITY

Have students research the average growth rate of the stock market from 2006 to 2013. Then have students write an exponential growth function $V(t) = V_0(1 + r)^t$ for the average growth of an initial investment $V_0 = \$500,000$. Have students compare the value of the car to the value of the stock investment in 2013.

CONNECT VOCABULARY EL

Some students may not be familiar with the terms used in this Lesson Performance Task. Have a student volunteer describe the words *appreciate, fold,* and *fetch.*

QUESTIONING STRATEGIES

? If the car value increased by a constant amount each year, how could the car's value be modeled? **with a linear equation**

? Does the function $V(t)$ have an upper limit? **Mathematically, no. But in a real-world situation, circumstances might limit the value of the car.**

Scoring Rubric

2 points: Student correctly solves the problem and explains his/her reasoning.

1 point: Student shows good understanding of the problem but does not fully solve or explain his/her reasoning.

0 points: Student does not demonstrate understanding of the problem.

LESSON 13.2

Exponential Decay Functions

Common Core Math Standards

The student is expected to:

COMMON CORE **F.BF.B.3**

Identify the effect on the graph of replacing f(x) by f(x) + k, k f(x), f(kx), and f(x + k) for specific values of k (both positive and negative); ... Also F.IF.C.7e, F.LE.A.2, A.REI.D.11

Mathematical Practices

COMMON CORE **MP.4 Modeling**

Language Objective

Work with a partner to compare and contrast exponential decay and exponential growth functions.

ENGAGE

Essential Question: How is the graph of $g(x) = ab^{x-h} + k$ where $0 < b < 1$ related to the graph of $f(x) = b^x$?

Possible answer: The graph of $g(x) = ab^{x-h} + k$ involves transformations of the graph of $f(x) = b^x$. In particular, the graph of $g(x)$ is a vertical stretch or compression of the graph of $f(x)$ by a factor of $|a|$, a reflection of the graph across the x-axis if $a < 0$, and a translation of the graph h units horizontally and k units vertically.

PREVIEW: LESSON PERFORMANCE TASK

View the Engage section online. Discuss the photo and why it might be important to know the amount of a radioactive isotope remaining in the environment. Then preview the Lesson Performance Task.

Name ________ Class ________ Date ________

13.2 Exponential Decay Functions

Essential Question: How is the graph of $g(x) = ab^{x-h} + k$ where $0 < b < 1$ related to the graph of $f(x) = b^x$?

Resource Locker

Explore 1 Graphing and Analyzing $f(x) = \left(\frac{1}{2}\right)^x$ and $f(x) = \left(\frac{1}{10}\right)^x$

Exponential functions with bases between 0 and 1 can be transformed in a manner similar to exponential functions with bases greater than 1. Begin by plotting the parent functions of two of the more commonly used bases: $\frac{1}{2}$ and $\frac{1}{10}$.

(A) To begin, fill in the table in order to find points along the function $f(x) = \left(\frac{1}{2}\right)^x$. You may need to review the rules of the properties of exponents, including negative exponents.

x	$f(x) = \left(\frac{1}{2}\right)^x$
−3	8
−2	4
−1	2
0	1
1	$\frac{1}{2}$
2	$\frac{1}{4}$
3	$\frac{1}{8}$

(B) What does the end behavior of this function appear to be as x increases?

$f(x)$ approaches 0.

(C) Plot the points on the graph and draw a smooth curve through them.

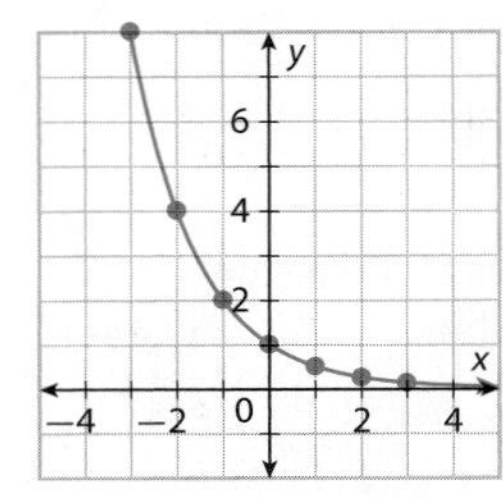

(D) Complete the table for $f(x) = \left(\frac{1}{10}\right)^x$.

x	$f(x) = \left(\frac{1}{10}\right)^x$
−3	1000
−2	100
−1	10
0	1
1	$\frac{1}{10}$
2	$\frac{1}{100}$
3	$\frac{1}{1000}$

(E) Plot the points on the graph and draw a smooth curve through them.

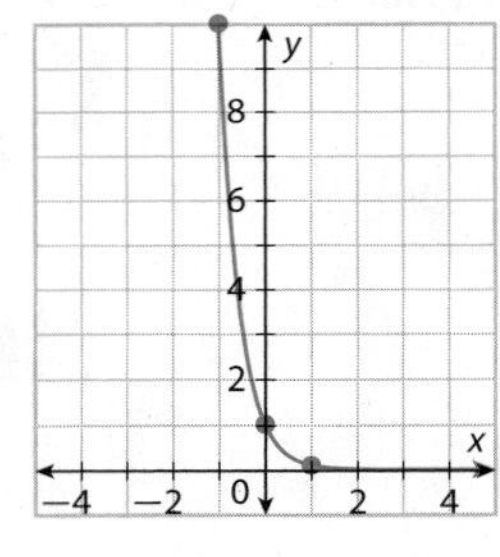

HARDCOVER PAGES 651–666

Watch for the hardcover student edition page numbers for this lesson.

Ⓕ Fill in the following table of properties:

	$f(x) = \left(\frac{1}{2}\right)^x$	$f(x) = \left(\frac{1}{10}\right)^x$
Domain	$\{x \mid -\infty < x < \infty\}$	$\{x \mid -\infty < x < \infty\}$
Range	$\{y \mid y > 0\}$	$\{y \mid y > 0\}$
End behavior as $x \to \infty$	$f(x) \to 0$	$f(x) \to 0$
End behavior as $x \to -\infty$	$f(x) \to \infty$	$f(x) \to \infty$
y-intercept	$(0, 1)$	$(0, 1)$

Ⓖ Both of these functions decrease/increase throughout the domain. (decrease circled)

Ⓗ Of the two functions, $f(x) = \left(\frac{1}{10}\right)^x$ decreases faster.

Reflect

1. **Make a Conjecture** Look at the table of properties for the functions. What do you notice? Make a conjecture about these properties for exponential functions of the form $f(x) = \left(\frac{1}{n}\right)^x$, where n is a constant.
The domain, range, end behavior, and y-intercept are the same for both functions. These same properties apply to all exponential functions of the form $f(x) = \left(\frac{1}{n}\right)^x$.

Explain 1 Graphing Combined Transformations of $f(x) = b^x$ Where $0 < b < 1$

When graphing transformations of $f(x) = b^x$ where $0 < b < 1$, it is helpful to consider the effect of the transformation on two reference points, $(0, 1)$ and $\left(-1, \frac{1}{b}\right)$, as well as the effect on the asymptote, $y = 0$. The table shows these reference points and the asymptote $y = 0$ for $f(x) = b^x$ and the corresponding points and asymptote for the transformed function, $g(x) = ab^{x-h} + k$.

PROFESSIONAL DEVELOPMENT

Math Background

Students will graph most of the exponential functions in this lesson by hand. They will see that the graphs of exponential decay functions approach the positive x-axis as x increases without bound, so the x-axis is an asymptote for the graph of any function of the form $f(x) = b^x$ where $b > 0$ and $b \neq 1$. Students will also transform the graphs of exponential functions and discover how the transformations affect the asymptote, y-intercept, and rate of increase or decrease, and write transformed functions for graphs based upon the asymptote and two points on the graph, the reference points.

EXPLORE

Graphing and Analyzing $f(x) = \left(\frac{1}{2}\right)^x$ and $f(x) = \left(\frac{1}{10}\right)^x$

INTEGRATE TECHNOLOGY

Make sure that students are comfortable using their calculators to graph exponential functions. They may need to practice putting in the appropriate domains and ranges.

QUESTIONING STRATEGIES

? What is the decay factor in an exponential decay function? **the base b of an exponential decay function $y = ab^x$ where $a > 0$**

? What is the parent function for exponential decay functions? **$f(x) = b^x$ where $0 < b < 1$ is the parent function for the family of exponential decay functions with base b.**

EXPLAIN 1

Graphing Combined Transformations of $f(x) = b^x$ Where $0 < b < 1$

INTEGRATE MATHEMATICAL PRACTICES

Focus on Modeling

MP.4 As a starting point for graphing combined transformations, students should be aware that the graph of $f(x) = ab^x$ always passes through the points $(0, a)$ and $(1, ab)$.

QUESTIONING STRATEGIES

? What is the horizontal asymptote of the graph $f(x) = a \cdot b^{x-h} + k$ where $b = \frac{1}{2}$? **The horizontal asymptote of the graph $f(x)$ is $y = k$.**

? For the graph of $f(x) = a \cdot b^{x-h} + k$ where $b = \frac{1}{2}$ and (h, k) is at the origin, what are the reference points? **$(0, a)$ and $(-1, 2a)$**

	$f(x) = b^x$	$g(x) = ab^{x-h} + k$
First reference point	$(0, 1)$	$(h, a + k)$
Second reference point	$\left(-1, \frac{1}{b}\right)$	$\left(h - 1, \frac{a}{b} + k\right)$
Asymptote	$y = 0$	$y = k$

Example 1 **For each of the transformed functions, use the reference points and the asymptote to draw the transformed function on the grid with the parent function. Then describe the domain and range of the transformed function using set notation.**

(A) $g(x) = 3\left(\frac{1}{2}\right)^{x-2} - 2$

Identify parameters: $a = 3$ $b = \frac{1}{2}$ $h = 2$ $k = -2$

Find reference points:

$(h, a + k) = (2, 3 - 2) = (2, 1)$

$\left(h - 1, \frac{a}{b} + k\right) = \left(2 - 1, \frac{3}{\frac{1}{2}} - 2\right) = (1, 4)$

Find the asymptote: $y = -2$

Plot the points and draw the asymptote. Then connect the points with a smooth curve that approaches the asymptote without crossing it.

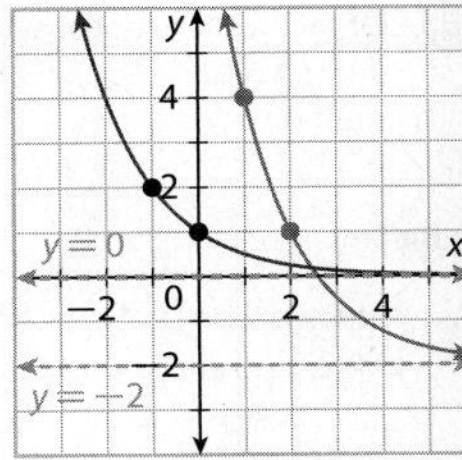

Domain: $\{x \mid -\infty < x < \infty\}$

Range: $\{y \mid y > -2\}$

(B) $g(x) = -\left(\frac{1}{10}\right)^{x+2} + 8$

Identify parameters:

$a =$ **−1** $b =$ **$\frac{1}{10}$** $h =$ **−2** $k =$ **8**

Find reference points:

$(h,$ **$a + k$**$) = (-2, -1 + 8)\ (-2, 7)$

$\left(h - 1, \frac{a}{b} + k\right) = \left(-2 - 1, \frac{-1}{\frac{1}{10}} + 8\right) = ($**−3**, **−2**$)$

COLLABORATIVE LEARNING

Peer-to-Peer Activity

Have pairs of students work together to create a graphic organizer to compare and contrast exponential growth functions and exponential decay functions.

Find the asymptote:

$y = \boxed{8}$

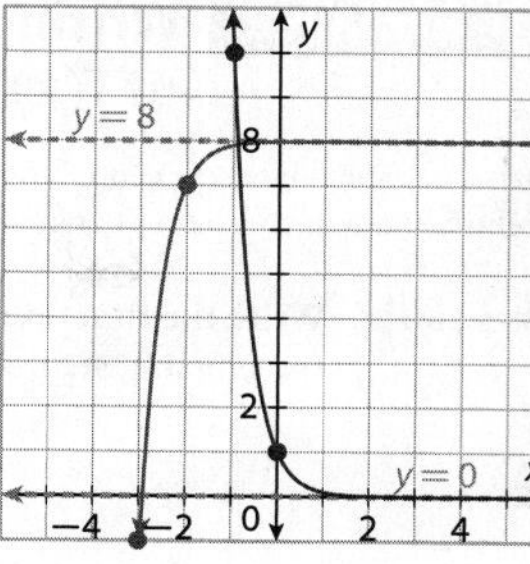

Plot the points and draw the asymptote. Then connect the points with a smooth curve that approaches the asymptote without crossing it.

Domain: $\{x \mid \boxed{-\infty < x < \infty}\}$

Range: $\{y \mid \boxed{y < 8}\}$

Reflect

2. Which parameters make the domain and range of $g(x)$ differ from those of the parent function? Write the transformed domain and range for $g(x)$ in set notation.

None of the parameters alter the domain, which is all real numbers for both the parent and transformed functions. The parameter a alters the range if it is less than 0, and the parameter k alters the finite end of the range. Domain: $\{x \mid -\infty < x < \infty\}$; Range ($a > 0$): $\{y \mid y > k\}$; Range ($a < 0$): $\{y \mid y < k\}$

Your Turn

For the transformed function, use the reference points and the asymptote to draw the transformed function on the grid with the parent function. Then describe the domain and range of the transformed function using set notation.

3. $g(x) = 3\left(\frac{1}{3}\right)^{x+2} - 4$

Identify parameters:

$a = 3$; $b = \frac{1}{3}$; $h = -2$; $k = -4$

Find reference points:

$(h, a + k) = (-2, 3 - 4) = (-2, -1)$

$\left(h - 1, \frac{a}{b} + k\right) = \left(-2 - 1, \frac{3}{\frac{1}{3}} - 4\right) = (-3, 5)$

Find the asymptote: $y = -4$

Domain: $\{x \mid -\infty < x < \infty\}$

Range: $\{y \mid y > -4\}$

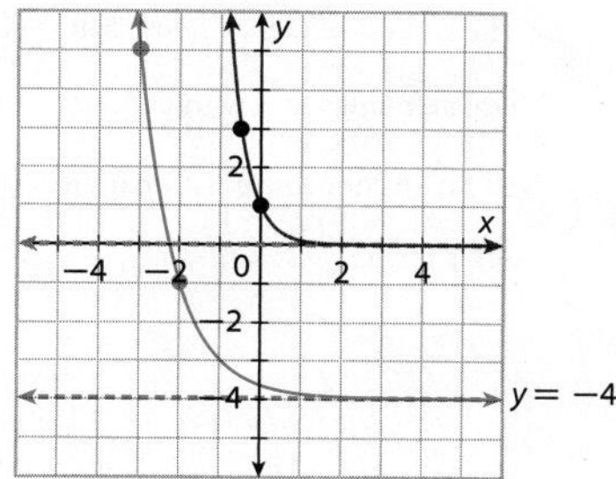

CONNECT VOCABULARY EL

Connect the terms *decay* and *growth* to life. When something alive grows, it tends to become taller and larger. When something alive decays, it tends to get smaller; it takes up less space.

DIFFERENTIATE INSTRUCTION

Communicating Math

Have students make up their own functions in the form $y = ab^{x-h} + k$ for different a, h, and k values, and then discuss the transformations with each other.

EXPLAIN 2

Writing Equations for Combined Transformations of $f(x) = b^x$ where $0 < b < 1$

INTEGRATE TECHNOLOGY

Students can check the equations they write by graphing the functions on their graphing calculators. Have them use the **TRACE** or **TABLE** feature to identify coordinates of points in the resulting graph.

 Explain 2 **Writing Equations for Combined Transformations of $f(x) = b^x$ where $0 < b < 1$**

Given a graph of an exponential function, $g(x) = ab^{x-h} + k$, the reference points and the asymptote can be used to identify the transformation parameters in order to write the function rule.

Example 2 **Write the function represented by this graph and state the domain and range using set notation.**

Ⓐ

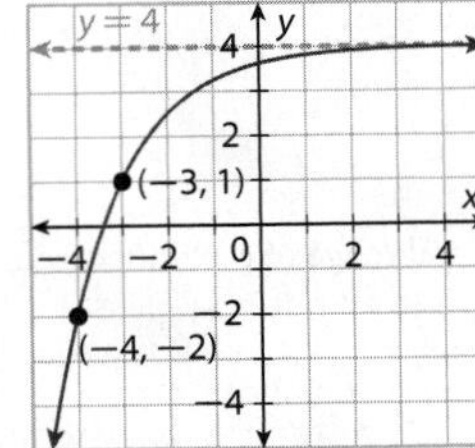

Find k from the asymptote: $k = 4$.

The first reference point is at $(-3, 1)$.

Equate point value with parameters-based expression. $(-3, 1) = (h, a + k)$

Use the x-coordinate to solve for h. $h = -3$

Use the y-coordinate to solve for a. $a = 1 - k$

$= -3$

The second reference point is at $(-4, -2)$.

Equate point value with parameters-based expression. $(-4, -2) = \left(h - 1, \frac{a}{b} + k\right)$

Equate y-coordinate with parameters. $\frac{-3}{b} + 4 = -2$

Solve for b. $\frac{-3}{b} = -6$

$b = \frac{-3}{-6}$

$= \frac{1}{2}$

$g(x) = -3\left(\frac{1}{2}\right)^{x+3} + 4$

Domain: $\{x \mid -\infty < x < \infty\}$

Range: $\{y \mid y < 4\}$

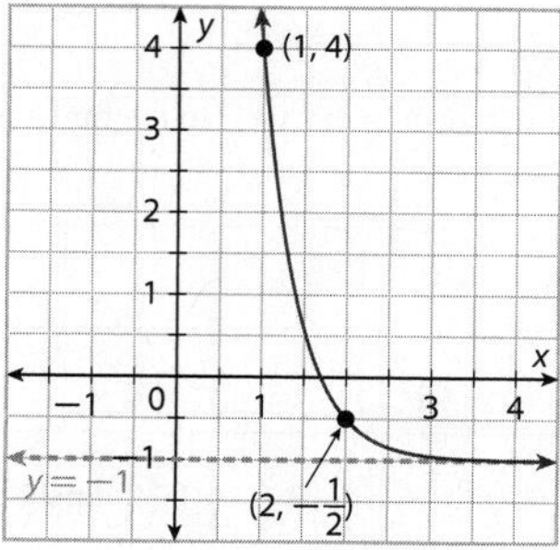

Find k from the asymptote: $k = \boxed{-1}$.

The first reference point is at $\left(\boxed{2}, \boxed{-\frac{1}{2}}\right)$, so $\left(\boxed{2}, -\frac{1}{2}\right) = \left(h, \boxed{a + k}\right)$

$h = \boxed{2}$ $\quad a = \boxed{-\frac{1}{2}} - k$

$= \boxed{\frac{1}{2}}$

The second reference point is at $\left(\boxed{1}, \boxed{4}\right)$, so $\left(\boxed{1}, 4\right) = \left(h - 1, \boxed{\frac{a}{b} + k}\right)$

$\dfrac{\boxed{\frac{1}{2}}}{b} - 1 = \boxed{4}$

$\dfrac{\frac{1}{2}}{b} = \boxed{5}$

$b = \dfrac{\frac{1}{2}}{5}$

$= \boxed{\frac{1}{10}}$

$g(x) = \boxed{\frac{1}{2}} \left(\frac{1}{10}\right)^{x - \boxed{2}} - \boxed{-1}$

Domain: $\{x \mid -\infty < x < \infty\}$

Range: $\{y \mid y \boxed{>} -1\}$

QUESTIONING STRATEGIES

? For a given value of k and a first reference point of (6, 8), how do you find the values of h and a? **The value of h is 6 and the value of a is $8 - k$.**

? For a given value of k and a and a second reference point of (4, 10), how do you find the values of b? **Set the value of $\frac{a}{b} + k$ to 10, substitute the values of a and k, and solve for b.**

Reflect

4. Compare the y-intercept and the asymptote of the function shown in this table to the function plotted in Example 2A.

x	−5	−4	−3	−2	−1	0	1	2
$g(x)$	−10	−4	−4	$\frac{1}{2}$	$1\frac{1}{4}$	$1\frac{5}{8}$	$1\frac{13}{16}$	$1\frac{29}{32}$

The y-intercept appears to have moved down by 2 units from $\left(3\frac{5}{8} \text{ to } 1\frac{5}{8}\right)$, and the asymptote appears to have moved down by 2 units as well (from 4 to 2).

5. Compare the y-intercept and the asymptote of the function shown in this table to the function plotted in Example 2B.

x	−3	−2	−1	0	1	2
$g(x)$	49	4	−0.5	−0.95	−0.995	−0.9995

The y-intercept is not apparent in the graph but must be larger than 10, while the table shows that the y- intercept is at −0.95. The asymptote of both functions appears to be −1.

Your Turn

Write the function represented by this graph and state the domain and range using set notation.

6.

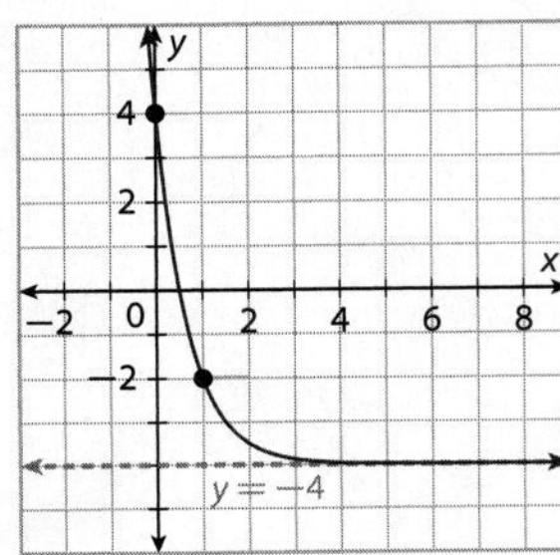

Asymptote: $y = -4$, so $k = -4$

First reference point: $(1, -2)$

$h = 1$

$a = -2 - (-4) = 2$

$(1, -2) = (h, a + k)$

Second reference point: $(0, 4)$

$(0, 4) = \left(h - 1, \frac{a}{b} + k\right)$

$\frac{2}{b} - 4 = 4$

$\frac{2}{b} = 8$

$b = \frac{1}{4}$

$g(x) = 2\left(\frac{1}{4}\right)^{x-1} - 4$

Domain: $\{x \mid -\infty < x < \infty\}$

Range: $\{y \mid y > -4\}$

Explain 3 Modeling with Exponential Decay Functions

An **exponential decay function** has the form $f(t) = a(1 - r)^t$ where $a > 0$ and r is a constant percent decrease (expressed as a decimal) for each unit increase in time t. That is, since $f(t + 1) = (1 - r) \cdot f(t) = f(t) - r \cdot f(t)$, the value of the function decreases by $r \cdot f(t)$ on the interval $[t, t + 1]$. The base $1 - r$ of an exponential decay function is called the **decay factor**, and the constant percent decrease r, in decimal form, is called the **decay rate**.

Example 3 **Given the description of the decay terms, write the exponential decay function in the form $f(t) = a(1 - r)^t$ and graph it with a graphing calculator.**

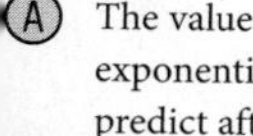

Ⓐ The value of a truck purchased new for \$28,000 decreases by 9.5% each year. Write an exponential function for this situation and graph it using a calculator. Use the graph to predict after how many years the value of the truck will be \$5000.

"Purchased new for \$28,000..." $a = 28{,}000$

"...decreases by 9.5% each year." $r = 0.095$

Substitute parameter values. $V_T(t) = 28{,}000(1 - 0.095)^t$

Simplify. $V_T(t) = 28{,}000(0.905)^t$

Graph the function with a graphing calculator. Use WINDOW to adjust the graph settings so that you can see the function and the function values that are important.

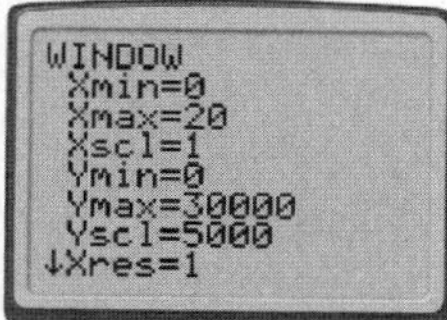

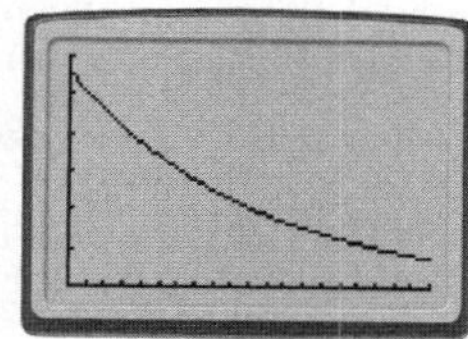

Find when the value reaches \$5000 by finding the intersection between $V_T(t) = 28{,}000(0.905)^t$ and $V_T(t) = 5000$ on the calculator.

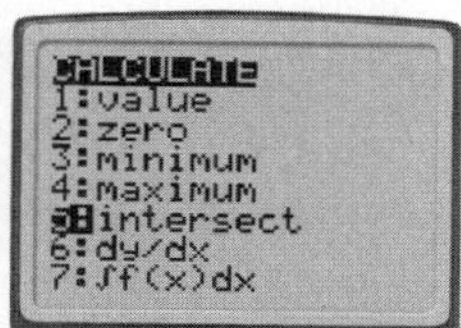

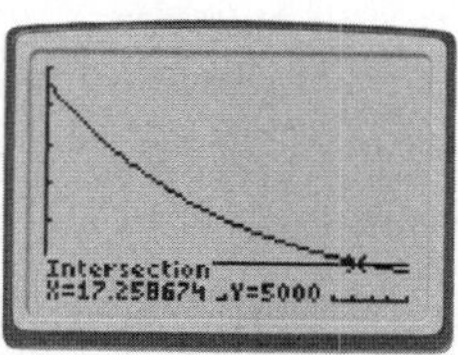

The intersection is at the point (17.26, 5000), which means after 17.26 years, the truck will have a value of \$5000.

LANGUAGE SUPPORT EL

Graphic Organizers

Have each pair of students complete a compare and contrast Venn diagram to show the similarities and differences between exponential decay and exponential growth functions. Encourage students to discuss and show the similarities and differences between their graphs, their equations, and so on.

EXPLAIN 3

Modeling With Exponential Decay Functions

QUESTIONING STRATEGIES

? How is the decay factor related to the percent of decrease in value? The sum of the decay factor and the percent of decrease is 1. For example, for a percent of decrease of 23%, the decay factor is 0.77.

INTEGRATE MATHEMATICAL PRACTICES

Focus on Critical Thinking

MP.3 Explain the concept of depreciation and how it is used in the business world. Discuss the difference between an item losing the same *dollar amount* of value each year, known as *straight-line depreciation,* and the item losing the same *percent* of its value each year, a type of depreciation which is based on an exponential decay model.

Ⓑ The value of a sports car purchased new for $45,000 decreases by 15% each year. Write an exponential function for the depreciation of the sports car, and plot it along with the previous example. After how many years will the two vehicles have the same value if they are purchased at the same time?

"Purchased new for $45,000..." $\boxed{a} = 45{,}000$

"...decreases by 15% each year." $r = \boxed{0.15}$

Substitute parameter values. $V_c(t) = \boxed{45{,}000}\left(1 - \boxed{0.15}\right)^t$

Simplify. $V_c(t) = 45{,}000\left(\boxed{0.85}\right)^t$

Add this plot to the graph for the truck value from Example A and find the intersection of the two functions to determine when the values are the same.

The intersection point is $\left(\boxed{7.567}, \boxed{13{,}155}\right)$.

After $\boxed{7.567}$ years, the values of both vehicles will be $\$\boxed{13{,}155}$.

Reflect

7. What reference points could you use if you plotted the value function for the sports car on graph paper? Confirm that the graph passes through them using the calculate feature on a graphing calculator.

The transformation parameters are $a = 45{,}000$, $h = 0$, and $k = 0$. The parent function is $b = 0.85$. The reference points are $(h, a + k) = (0, 45{,}000)$ and $\left(h - 1, \frac{a}{b} + k\right) = (-1, 52{,}941)$. Using the calculate feature confirms the graph passes through $(0, 45{,}000)$ and $(-1, 52{,}941)$.

8. Using the sports car from example B, calculate the average rate of value change over the course of the first year and the second year of ownership. What happens to the absolute value of the rate of change from the first interval to the second? What does this mean in this situation?

Average rate of change during the interval from t_0 to $t_1 = \frac{f(t_1) - f(t_0)}{t_1 - t_0}$

First year: rate of change $= \frac{45{,}000 \cdot 0.85 - 45{,}000}{1 - 0} = -\$6750$ per year

Second year: rate of change $= \frac{45{,}000 \cdot (0.85)^2 - 45{,}000 \cdot 0.85}{2 - 1} = -\$5737.50$ per year

The absolute value of the rate of change decreased during the second interval. This means that the car depreciates less each year than the year before.

Your Turn

9. On federal income tax returns, self-employed people can depreciate the value of business equipment. Suppose a computer valued at \$2765 depreciates at a rate of 30% per year. Use a graphing calculator to determine the number of years it will take for the computer's value to be \$350.

$v(t) = 2765(1 - 0.3)^t = 2765(0.7)^t$

Intersect with $v(t) = 350$

Using a graphing calculator, the intersection point is at $(5.79, 350)$.

It will take about 5.79 years for the value of the computer to drop to \$350.

Elaborate

10. Which transformations of $f(x) = \left(\frac{1}{2}\right)^x$ or $f(x) = \left(\frac{1}{10}\right)^x$ change the function's end behavior?

Vertical translations change the asymptote and thus the lower end behavior as x increases.

Reflections across the x-axis change the end behavior as x decreases, from approaching positive infinity to approaching negative infinity.

11. Which transformations change the location of the graph's y-intercept?

Vertical translations, horizontal translations, vertical stretches/compressions, and reflections across the x-axis all change the y-intercept.

12. Discussion How are reference points and asymptotes helpful when graphing transformations of $f(x) = \left(\frac{1}{2}\right)^x$ or $f(x) = \left(\frac{1}{10}\right)^x$ or when writing equations for transformed graphs?

Reference points and asymptotes are easy to transform and have a simple relationship to the function parameters $(a, h, \text{and } k)$ associated with the transformation. The point $(0, 1)$ becomes $(h, a + k)$, the point $\left(-1, \frac{1}{b}\right)$ becomes $\left(h - 1, \frac{a}{b} + k\right)$, and the asymptote $y = 0$ becomes $y = k$.

13. Give the general form of an exponential decay function based on a known decay rate and describe its parameters.

$f(t) = a(1 - r)^t$

a is the starting value, or the value at $t = 0$.

r is the decay rate, or what fraction of the value is lost per unit of time.

$(1 - r)$ is the decay factor, or what fraction of the previous value remains after the passage of a unit of time.

14. Essential Question Check-In How is the graph of $f(x) = b^x$ used to help graph the function $g(x) = ab^{x-h} + k$?

The graph of $g(x) = ab^{x-h} + k$ can be taken from the basic shape of the parent function, $f(x) = b^x$, with transformations applied based on the parameters a, h, and k.

ELABORATE

QUESTIONING STRATEGIES

How do you rewrite exponential decay functions to answer questions about the functions? Properties of exponents can be used to rewrite exponential functions to show specific growth or decay factors.

SUMMARIZE THE LESSON

What does the graph of an exponential decay function look like? An exponential decay function is a function of the form $y = ab^x$ $f(x) = b^x$ with $a > 0$ and $0 < b < 1$. Exponential decay models describe situations in which a quantity decreases by a fixed percent each time period. The graph of an exponential decay function is a curve that falls from left to right and gets less and less steep as x increases. The x-axis, or a line parallel to it, is a horizontal asymptote of the graph.

EVALUATE

ASSIGNMENT GUIDE

Concepts and Skills	Practice
Example 1 Graphing Combined Transformations of $f(x) = b^x$ where $0 < b < 1$.	Exercises 5–8
Example 2 Writing Equations for Combined Transformations of $f(x) = b^x$ where $0 < b < 1$	Exercises 12–13
Example 3 Modeling With Exponential Decay Functions	Exercises 14–16

Evaluate: Homework and Practice

- Online Homework
- Hints and Help
- Extra Practice

Describe the transformation(s) from each parent function and give the domain and range of each function.

1. $g(x) = \left(\frac{1}{2}\right)^x + 3$

Vertical translation up by 3.

Domain: $\{x \mid -\infty < x < \infty\}$

Range: $\{y \mid y > 3\}$

2. $g(x) = \left(\frac{1}{10}\right)^{x+4}$

Horizontal translation left by 4.

Domain: $\{x \mid -\infty < x < \infty\}$

Range: $\{y \mid y > 0\}$

3. $g(x) = -\left(\frac{1}{10}\right)^{x-1} + 2$

Reflection across the x-axis, translation right by 1 and up by 2.

Domain: $\{x \mid -\infty < x < \infty\}$

Range: $\{y \mid y < 2\}$

4. $g(x) = 3\left(\frac{1}{2}\right)^{x+3} - 6$

Vertical stretch by a factor of 3, translation left by 3 and down by 6.

Domain: $\{x \mid -\infty < x < \infty\}$

Range: $\{y \mid y > -6\}$

For each of the transformed functions, use the reference points and the asymptote to draw the transformed function on the grid with the parent function. Then describe the domain and range of the transformed function using set notation.

5. $g(x) = -2\left(\frac{1}{2}\right)^{x-1} + 2$

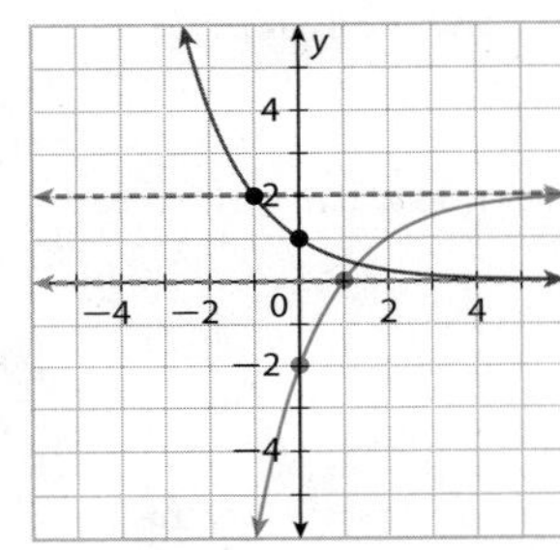

Identify parameters: $a = -2; b = \frac{1}{2}; h = 1; k = 2$

Find reference points:

$(h, a + k) = (1, -2 + 2) = (1, 0)$

$\left(h - 1, \frac{a}{b} + k\right) = 1 - 1, \frac{-2}{\frac{1}{2}} + 2 = (0, -2)$

Find the asymptote: $y = 2$

Domain: $\{x \mid -\infty < x < \infty\}$

Range: $\{y \mid y < 2\}$

Exercise	Depth of Knowledge (D.O.K.)	COMMON CORE Mathematical Practices
1–4	**2** Skills/Concepts	**MP.2** Reasoning
5–8	**2** Skills/Concepts	**MP.4** Modeling
9–10	**2** Skills/Concepts	**MP.2** Reasoning
11–13	**2** Skills/Concepts	**MP.4** Modeling
14	**3** Strategic Thinking H.O.T.	**MP.6** Precision
15–17	**3** Strategic Thinking H.O.T.	**MP.2** Reasoning

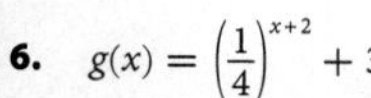

6. $g(x) = \left(\frac{1}{4}\right)^{x+2} + 3$

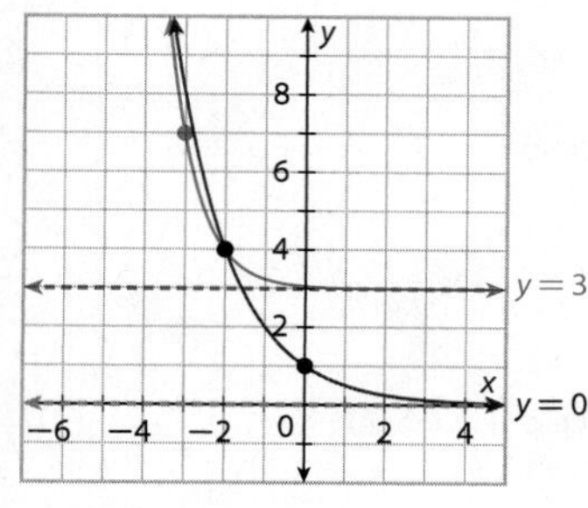

Identify parameters: $a = 1; b = \frac{1}{4}; h = -2; k = 3$

Find reference points:

$$(h, a + k) = (-2, 1 + 3) = (-2, 4)$$

$$\left(h - 1, \frac{a}{b} + k\right) = \left(-2 - 1, \frac{1}{\frac{1}{4}} + 3\right) = (-3, 7)$$

Find the asymptote: $y = 3$

Domain: $\left\{x \mid -\infty < x < \infty\right\}$

Range: $\left\{y \mid y > 3\right\}$

7. $g(x) = \frac{1}{2}\left(\frac{1}{3}\right)^{x-\frac{1}{2}} + 2$

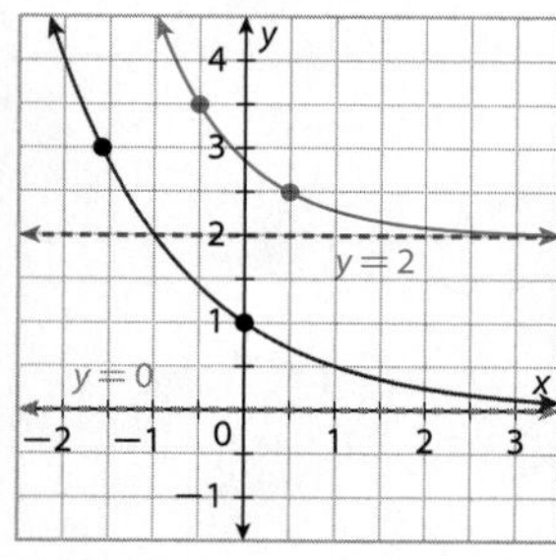

Identify parameters: $a = \frac{1}{2}; b = \frac{1}{3}; h = \frac{1}{2}; k = 2$

Find reference points:

$$(h, a + k) = \left(\frac{1}{2}, \frac{1}{2} + 2\right) = \left(\frac{1}{2}, \frac{5}{2}\right)$$

$$\left(h - 1, \frac{a}{b} + k\right) = \left(\frac{1}{2} - 1, \frac{\frac{1}{2}}{\frac{1}{3}} + 2\right) = \left(-\frac{1}{2}, \frac{7}{2}\right)$$

Find the asymptote: $y = 2$

Domain: $\left\{x \mid -\infty < x < \infty\right\}$

Range: $\left\{y \mid y > 2\right\}$

8. $g(x) = -3\left(\frac{1}{2}\right)^{x+2} + 7$

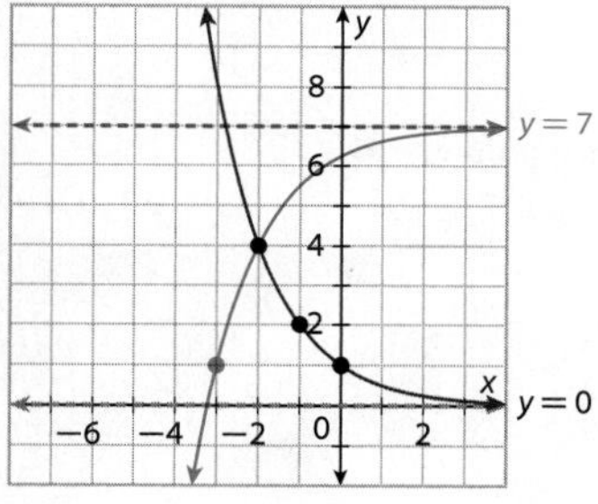

Identify parameters: $a = -3; b = \frac{1}{2}; h = -2; k = 7$

Find reference points:

$$(h, a + k) = (-2, -3 + 7) = (-2, 4)$$

$$\left(h - 1, \frac{a}{b} + k\right) = \left(-2 - 1, \frac{-3}{\frac{1}{2}} + 7\right) = (-3, 1)$$

Find the asymptote: $y = 7$

Domain: $\left\{x \mid -\infty < x < \infty\right\}$

Range: $\left\{y \mid y < 7\right\}$

AVOID COMMON ERRORS

Some students may think that a horizontal shift in the graph of an exponential function affects the domain. Demonstrate that the domain of all exponential functions and their translations is the set of all real numbers, just as with quadratic functions. Go back to the definition of domain and point out that the value of x can be any real number in any exponential growth or decay function or any translation of these functions. You might use a graphing calculator demonstration to reinforce this idea visually.

Write the function represented by each graph and state the domain and range using set notation.

9.

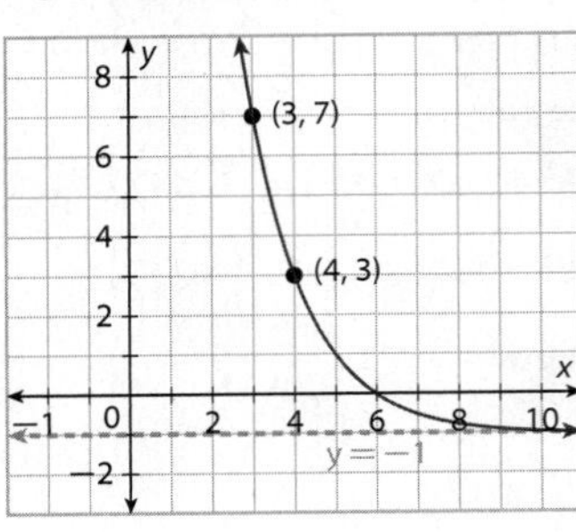

Asymptote:

$y = -1$

$k = -1$

First reference point: $(4, 3)$

$(4, 3) = (h, a + k)$

$h = 4$

$a = 3 - (-1)$

$a = 4$

Second reference point: $(3, 7)$

$(3, 7) = \left(h - 1, \frac{a}{b} + k\right)$

$\frac{4}{b} - 1 = 7$

$\frac{4}{b} = 8$

$b = \frac{4}{8}$

$b = \frac{1}{2}$

$g(x) = 4\left(\frac{1}{2}\right)^{x-4} - 1$

Domain: $\{x \mid -\infty < x < \infty\}$

Range: $\{y \mid y > -1\}$

10.

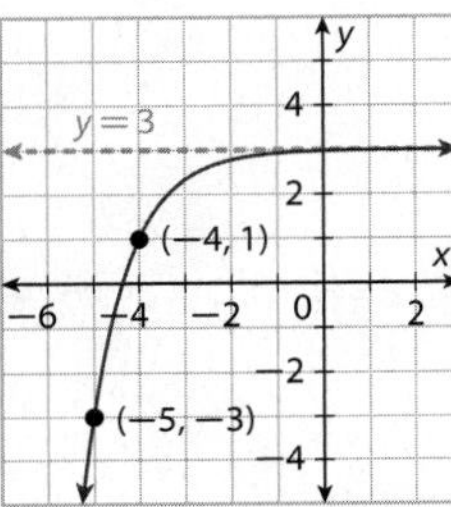

Asymptote:

$y = 3$

$k = 3$

First reference point: $(-4, 1)$

$(-4, 1) = (h, a + k)$

$h = -4$

$a = 1 - 3$

$a = -2$

Second reference point: $(-5, -3)$

$(-5, -3) = \left(h - 1, \frac{a}{b} + k\right)$

$\frac{-2}{b} + 3 = -3$

$\frac{-2}{b} = -6$

$b = \frac{-2}{-6}$

$b = \frac{1}{3}$

$g(x) = -2\left(\frac{1}{3}\right)^{x+4} + 3$

Domain: $\{x \mid -\infty < x < \infty\}$

Range: $\{y \mid y < 3\}$

Write the exponential decay function described in the situation and use a graphing calculator to answer each question asked.

11. Medicine A quantity of insulin used to regulate sugar in the bloodstream breaks down by about 5% each minute after the injection. A bodyweight-adjusted dose is generally 10 units. How long does it take for the remaining insulin to be half of the original injection?

$I(t) = 10(1 - 0.05)^t$

$= 10(0.95)^t$

Half of the original injection (10) is 5. Use a graph to find the intersection with $I(t) = 5$.

Intersection point is at $(13.5, 5)$.

It takes about 13.5 minutes.

12. Paleontology Carbon-14 is a radioactive isotope of carbon that is used to date fossils. There are about 1.5 atoms of carbon-14 for every trillion atoms of carbon in the atmosphere, which known as 1.5 ppt (parts per trillion). Carbon in a living organism has the same concentration as carbon-14. When an organism dies, the carbon-14 content decays at a rate of 11.4% per millennium (1000 years). Write the equation for carbon-14 concentration (in ppt) as a function of time (in millennia) and determine how old a fossil must be that has a measured concentration of 0.2 ppt.

$c(t) = 1.5(1 - 0.114)^t$

$= 1.5(0.886)^t$

Intersection point is at $(16.65, 0.2)$.

The fossil is about 16.65 millennia, or 16,650 years old.

13. Music Stringed instruments like guitars and pianos create a note when a string vibrates back and forth. The distance that the middle of the string moves from the center is called the amplitude (a), and for a guitar, it starts at 0.75 mm when a note is first struck. Amplitude decays at a rate that depends on the individual instrument and the note, but a decay rate of about 25% per second is typical. Calculate the time it takes for an amplitude of 0.75 mm to reach 0.1 mm.

$a(t) = 0.75(1 - 0.25)^t$

$= 0.75(0.75)^t$

Intersection point is at $(7.004, 0.1)$.

The amplitude will reach 0.1 mm in about 7 seconds.

PEER-TO-PEER DISCUSSION

Ask students to brainstorm and discuss two specific, real-world situations, one of exponential growth and one of exponential decay. For each situation, ask students to discuss how the graphs should look and tell how they would go about creating equations to help them model real-world data.

JOURNAL

Have students write about the two types of exponential models, and describe how they differ from polynomial models such as quadratic and cubic.

H.O.T. Focus on Higher Order Thinking

14. Analyze Relationships Compare the graphs of $f(x) = \left(\frac{1}{2}\right)^x$ and $g(x) = x^{\frac{1}{2}}$. Which of the following properties are the same? Explain.

a. Domain $\{x \mid -\infty < x < \infty\}$; $\{x \mid x \geq 0\}$

b. Range $\{y \mid y > 0\}$; $\{y \mid y \geq 0\}$

c. End behavior as x increases $f(x) \to 0$; $g(x) \to \infty$

d. End behavior as x decreases $f(x) \to \infty$; $g(x)$ is not defined for values less than 0.

None are the same.

15. Communicate Mathematical Ideas A quantity becomes half as much during each given time period. Another quantity becomes one-quarter as much during the same given time period. Determine each decay rate, state which is greater, and explain your results.

The decay rate of the first quantity is 50% because the decay factor is $1 - r = \frac{1}{2}$, so the decay rate equals $\frac{1}{2}$, or 50%. The decay rate of the second quantity is 75% because the decay factor is $1 - r = \frac{1}{4}$, so the decay rate is $\frac{3}{4}$, or 75%. The decay rate of the second quantity is greater.

16. Multiple Representations Exponential decay functions are written as transformations of the function $f(x) = b^x$, where $0 < b < 1$. However, it is also possible to use negative exponents as the basis of an exponential decay function. Use the properties of exponents to show why the function $f(x) = 2^{-x}$ is an exponential decay function.

Given	$f(x) = 2^{-x}$
Power of a power property	$= (2^{-1})^x$
Property of negative exponents	$= \left(\frac{1}{2}\right)^x$

The last result is in the form $f(x) = b^x$ where $0 < b < 1$ and is therefore an exponential decay function.

17. Represent Real-World Problems You buy a video game console for \$500 and sell it 5 years later for \$100. The resale value decays exponentially over time. Write a function that represents the resale value, R, in dollars over the time, t, in years. Explain how you determined your function.

$R(t) = 500(0.725)^t$; Sample answer: I used the general exponential decay function $f(x) = ab^x$ and substituted 100 for $f(x)$, 500 for a, and 5 for x, resulting in $100 = 500(b^5)$. I then solved for b by dividing 100 by 500 to get 0.2 and then took the fifth root of 0.2, resulting in 0.724779, which I rounded to 0.725.

Lesson Performance Task

Sodium-24 is a radioactive isotope of sodium used as a diagnostic aid in medicine. It undergoes radioactive decay to form the stable isotope magnesium-24 and has a half-life of about 15 hours. This means that, in this time, half the amount of a sample mass of sodium-24 decays to magnesium-24. Suppose we start with an initial mass of of 100 grams sodium-24.

a. Use the half-life of sodium-24 to write an exponential decay function of the form $m_{Na}(t) = m_0(1 - r)^t$, where m_0 is the initial mass of sodium-24, r is the decay rate, t is the time in hours, and $m_{Na}(t)$ is the mass of sodium-24 at time t. What is the meaning of r?

Substitute 50 for $m_{Na}(t)$, 100 for a_0, and 15 for t in the function.

$$50 = 100(1 - r)^{15}$$
$$0.5 = (1 - r)^{15}$$
$$\sqrt[15]{0.5} = \sqrt[15]{(1 - r)^{15}}$$
$$0.955 \approx 1 - r$$
$$0.045 \approx r$$
$$m_{Na}(t) = 100(0.955)^t$$

The value of r means that the mass of sodium-24 is reduced by 4.5% each hour.

b. The combined amounts of sodium-24 and magnesium-24 must equal m_0, or 100, for all possible values of t. Show how to write a function for $m_{Mg}(t)$, the mass of magnesium-24 as a function of t.

The sum of the mass of magnesium-24 and sodium-24 is equal to m_0, which is 100.

$$m_{Mg}(t) + m_{Na}(t) = m_0$$
$$m_{Mg}(t) + m_{Na}(t) = 100$$

Solve for $m_{Mg}(t)$.

$$m_{Mg}(t) = 100 - m_{Na}(t)$$

Substitute $100(0.955)^t$ for $m_{Na}(t)$

$$m_{Mg}(t) = 100 - 100(0.955)^t$$

c. Use a graphing calculator to graph $m_{Na}(t)$ and $m_{Mg}(t)$. Describe the graph of $m_{Mg}(t)$ as a series of transformations of $m_{Na}(t)$. What does the intersection of the graphs represent?

The graph of $m_{Mg}(t)$ is a reflection of the graph of $m_{Na}(t)$ across the t-axis and a translation of 100 units vertically. The intersection of the graphs represents the point where the mass of sodium-24 is equal to the mass of magnesium-24, which occurs at the first half-life of sodium-24.

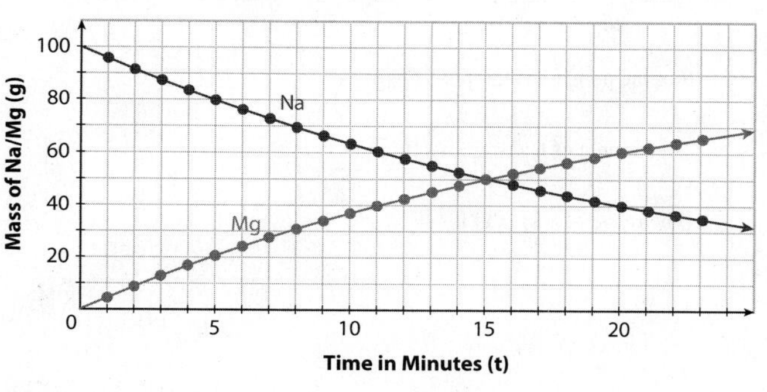

EXTENSION ACTIVITY

Have students research the half-life of technetium-99m, another radioactive isotope widely used in medicine. Have students write an exponential decay function for an initial mass of 100 grams. Then have students graph this function and compare it to the one for sodium-24. Have students discuss the difference in decay rates and how that might affect a real-world situation.

AVOID COMMON ERRORS

Students may set r equal to -0.045 because this is a decay situation. However, this would make the term $(1 - r)^t$ greater than one, and the function $m_{Na}(t)$ would become a growth function. Explain to students that the term $(1 - r)^t$ already contains the minus sign that turns $m_{Na}(t)$ into a decay function.

INTEGRATE MATHEMATICAL PRACTICES

Focus on Communication

MP.3 Have students consider the graphs for $m_{Na}(t)$ and $m_{Mg}(t)$, and have them explain which is exponential decay and which is exponential growth, based on the properties of the graphs. Have students discuss whether they can determine from the graphs the final values of the functions as t gets very large.

Scoring Rubric

2 points: Student correctly solves the problem and explains his/her reasoning.

1 point: Student shows good understanding of the problem but does not fully solve or explain his/her reasoning.

0 points: Student does not demonstrate understanding of the problem.

LESSON 13.3

The Base *e*

Common Core Math Standards

The student is expected to:

COMMON CORE **F.BF.B.3**

Identify the effect on the graph of replacing $f(x)$ by $f(x) + k$, $kf(x)$, $f(kx)$, and $f(x + k)$ for specific values of k (both positive and negative); ... Also F.IF.C.7e, A.REI.D.11

Mathematical Practices

MP.1 Problem Solving

Language Objective

Work with a partner to explain, in words, how the graph of a transformed exponential function with base *e* compares to the same transformation on graphs of other exponential functions.

ENGAGE

Essential Question: How is the graph of $g(x) = ae^{x-h} + k$ related to the graph of $f(x) = e^x$?

Possible answer: The graph of $g(x) = ae^{x-h} + k$ involves transformations of the graph of $f(x) = e^x$. In particular, the graph of $g(x)$ is a vertical stretch or compression of the graph of $f(x)$ by a factor of $|a|$, a reflection of the graph across the x-axis if $a < 0$, and a translation of the graph h units horizontally and k units vertically.

PREVIEW: LESSON PERFORMANCE TASK

View the Engage section online. Discuss the photo and why it would be useful to have a mathematical model for the amount of carbon dioxide in the atmosphere. Then preview the Lesson Performance Task.

Name ______________________ Class ______________ Date ________

13.3 The Base *e*

Essential Question: How is the graph of $g(x) = ae^{x-h} + k$ related to the graph of $f(x) = e^x$?

Resource Locker

Explore 1 Graphing and Analyzing $f(x) = e^x$

The following table represents the function $f(x) = \left(1 + \frac{1}{x}\right)^x$ for several values of x.

x	1	10	100	1000	...
$f(x)$	2	2.5937...	2.7048...	2.7169...	...

As the value of x increases without bound, the value of $f(x)$ approaches a number whose decimal value is 2.718... This number is irrational and is called e. You can write this in symbols as $f(x) \to e$ as $x \to +\infty$.

If you graph $f(x)$ and the horizontal line $y = e$, you can see that $y = e$ is the horizontal asymptote of $f(x)$.

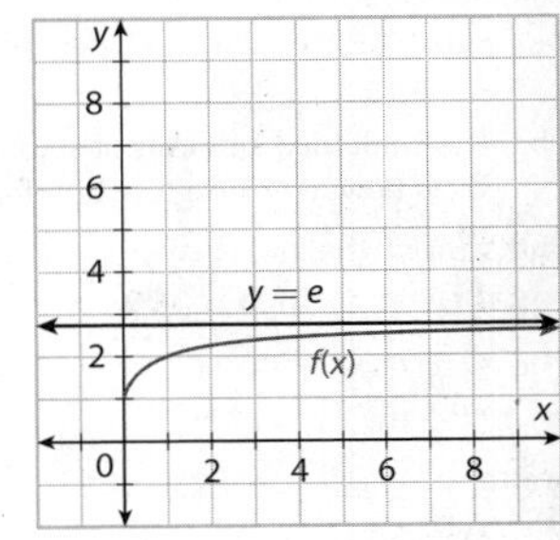

Even though e is an irrational number, it can be used as the base of an exponential function. The number e is sometimes called the natural base of an exponential function and is used extensively in scientific and other applications involving exponential growth and decay.

(A) Fill out the table of values below for the function $f(x) = e^x$. Use decimal approximations.

x	−10	−1	−0.5	0	0.5	1	1.5	2
$f(x) = e^x$	4.54×10^{-5}	$\frac{1}{e} = 0.367...$	0.606...	1	$\sqrt{e} =$ 1.648...	2.718...	4.481...	7.389

(B) Plot the points on a graph.

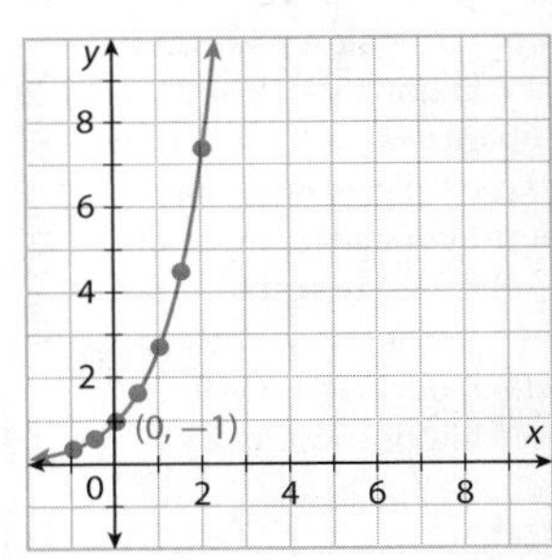

(C) The domain of $f(x) = e^x$ is $\{x \mid -\infty < x < \infty\}$.

The range of $f(x) = e^x$ is $\{y \mid y > 0\}$.

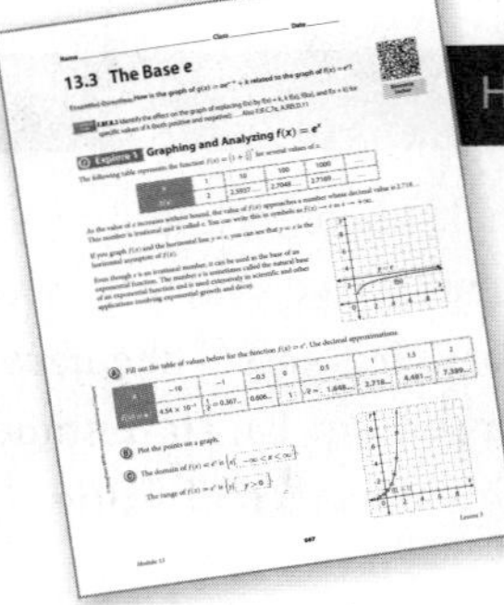

Watch for the hardcover student edition page numbers for this lesson.

(D) Is the function increasing or decreasing? For what values of x is it increasing/decreasing?

The function is increasing throughout its domain for all values of x.

(E) The function's y-intercept is $(0, \boxed{1})$ because $f(0) = e^0 = \boxed{1}$ and $x = 0$ is in the domain of the function.

(F) Another point on the graph that can be used as a reference point is $(1, \boxed{e})$.

(G) Identify the end behavior.

$f(x) \to \boxed{\infty}$ as $x \to \infty$

$f(x) \to \boxed{0}$ as $x \to -\infty$

There is a horizontal asymptote at $y = \boxed{0}$.

Reflect

1. What is the relationship between the graphs of $f(x) = e^x$, $g(x) = 2^x$, and $h(x) = 3^x$? (Hint: Sketch the graphs on your own paper.)

$2 < e < 3$, so $2^x < e^x < 3^x$. Thus $g(x) < f(x) < h(x)$ and the graph of $f(x)$ is between the graphs of $h(x)$ and $g(x)$.

Explain 1 Graphing Combined Transformations of $f(x) = e^x$

When graphing combined transformations of $f(x) = e^x$ that result in the function $g(x) = a \cdot e^{x-h} + k$, it helps to focus on two reference points on the graph of $f(x)$, $(0, 1)$ and $(1, e)$, as well as on the asymptote $y = 0$. The table shows these reference points and the asymptote $y = 0$ for $f(x) = e^x$ and the corresponding points and asymptote for the transformed function, $g(x) = a \cdot e^{x-h} + k$.

	$f(x) = e^x$	$g(x) = a \cdot e^{x-h} + k$
First reference point	$(0, 1)$	$(h, a + k)$
Second reference point	$(1, e)$	$(h + 1, ae + k)$
Asymptote	$y = 0$	$y = k$

PROFESSIONAL DEVELOPMENT

Integrate Mathematical Practices

This lesson provides an opportunity to address Mathematical Practice **MP.1**, which calls for students to "make sense of problems and persevere in solving them." The natural base, e, is used in many applications of continuous change, from compound interest to applications of probability, statistics, and trigonometry. Students are introduced to the base e, the graph of $f(x) = e^x$, and transformations of the graph. They write equations for combined transformations of $f(x) = e^x$, model exponential functions with base e, and solve related real-world problems.

EXPLORE

Graphing and Analyzing $f(x) = e^x$

INTEGRATE MATHEMATICAL PRACTICES

Focus on Math Connections

MP.1 Discuss with students their previous experience with the irrational number π, which is so important in geometric relationships. Explain that in this lesson they will learn about another irrational constant, e, which is also applicable to many situations.

QUESTIONING STRATEGIES

? What is $f(0)$? What does this tell you about the graph of $f(x) = e^x$? **1; the graph passes through the point $(0,1)$.**

? Does the graph of $f(x) = e^x$ ever intersect the x–axis? Why or why not? **No; there is no value for x for which $e^x = 0$. As x decreases without bound, e^x approaches but never reaches 0.**

INTEGRATE MATHEMATICAL PRACTICES

Focus on Patterns

MP.8 Have students find the values of $\frac{1}{x}$ for $x = 1$, 10, 100, and 100. Then, have them find the values of $1 + \frac{1}{x}$ for the same values. Ask them to describe what happens as x becomes greater.

EXPLAIN 1

Graphing Combined Transformations of $f(x) = e^x$

QUESTIONING STRATEGIES

? What are two reference points on the graph of $f(x) = e^x$ that will help when graphing combined transformations? **$(0, 1)$ and $(1, e)$, as well as the asymptote $y = 0$**

Example 1 **Given a function of the form $g(x) = a \cdot e^{x-h} + k$, identify the reference points and use them to draw the graph. State the transformations that compose the combined transformation, the asymptote, the domain, and range. Write the domain and range using set notation.**

 $g(x) = 3 \cdot e^{x+1} + 4$

Compare $g(x) = 3 \cdot e^{x+1} + 4$ to the general form $g(x) = a \cdot e^{x-h} + k$ to find that $h = -1$, $k = 4$, and $a = 3$.

Find the reference points of $f(x) = 3 \cdot e^{x+1} + 4$.

$(0, 1) \rightarrow (h, a + k) = (-1, 3 + 4) = (-1, 7)$

$(1, e) \rightarrow (h + 1, ae + k) = (-1 + 1, 3e + 4) = (0, 3e + 4)$

State the transformations that compose the combined transformation.

$h = -1$, so the graph is translated 1 unit to the left.

$k = 4$, so the graph is translated 4 units up.

$a = 3$, so the graph is vertically stretched by a factor of 3.

a is positive, so the graph is not reflected across the x-axis.

The asymptote is vertically shifted to $y = k$, so $y = 4$.

The domain is $\left\{x \middle| -\infty < x < \infty\right\}$.

The range is $\left\{y \middle| y > 4\right\}$.

Use the information to graph the function $g(x) = 3 \cdot e^{x+1} + 4$.

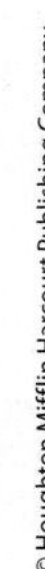

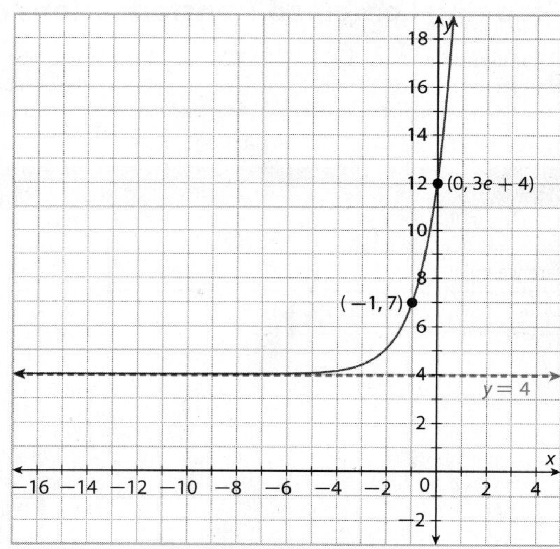

COLLABORATIVE LEARNING

Peer-to-Peer Activity

Have pairs of students work together to find real-world data that would fit an exponential growth model of the form $f(x) = ae^{cx}$ where c is a positive constant. Have students write a paragraph about how understanding the exponential growth model can help them predict trends in the data.

Ⓑ $g(x) = -0.5 \cdot e^{x-2} - 1$

Compare $g(x) = -0.5 \cdot e^{x-2} - 1$ to the general form $g(x) = a \cdot e^{x-h} + k$ to find that $h =$ 2, $k =$ −1, and $a =$ −0.5.

Find the reference points of $g(x) = -0.5 \cdot e^{x-2} - 1$.

$(0, 1) \rightarrow (h, a + k) = (2, -0.5 + -1) = (2, -1.5)$

$(1, e) \rightarrow (h + 1, ae + k) = (2 + 1, -0.5e + -1) = (3, -0.5e - 1)$

State the transformations that compose the combined transformation.

$h =$ 2, so the graph is translated 2 units to the right.

$k =$ −1, so the graph is translated 1 unit down.

$a =$ −0.5, so the graph is vertically compressed by a factor of 0.5.

a is negative, so the graph is reflected across the x-axis.

The asymptote is vertically shifted to $y = k$, so $y =$ −1.

The domain is $\{x \mid -\infty < x < \infty\}$.

The range is $\{y \mid y < -1\}$.

Use the information to graph the function $g(x) = -0.5 \cdot e^{x-2} - 1$.

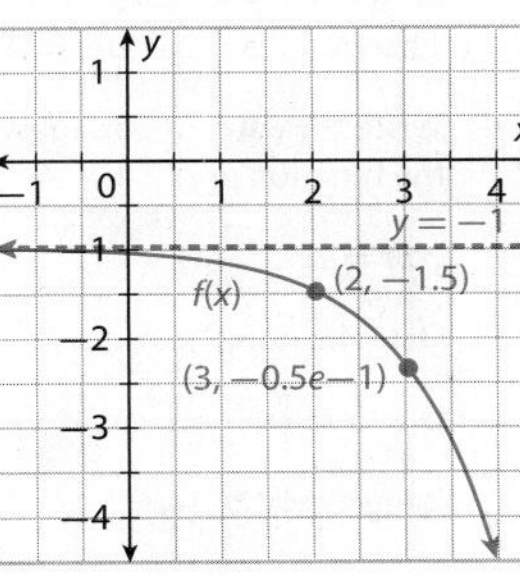

Your Turn

Given a function of the form $g(x) = a \cdot e^{x-h} + k$, identify the reference points and use them to draw the graph. State the asymptote, domain, and range. Write the domain and range using set notation.

2. $g(x) = (-1) \cdot e^{x+2} - 3$

$a = -1; h = -2; k = -3$

Reference points:

$(0, 1) \rightarrow (-2, -4)$

$(1, e) \rightarrow (-1, -e - 3)$

asymptote: $y = -3$

Domain: $\{x \mid -\infty < x < \infty\}$

Range: $\{y \mid y < -3\}$

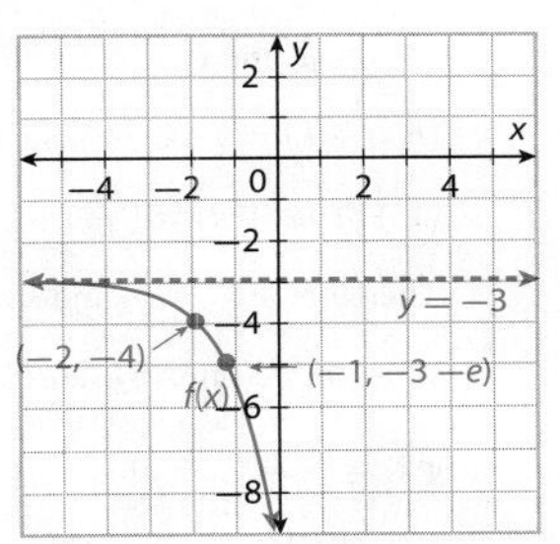

INTEGRATE TECHNOLOGY

Tell students that most calculators can calculate only logs with two bases, one of which is base 10. Ask students to study their calculators and find any keys that might be related to logs. If necessary, guide them to the similarity of the **LOG** key and the **LN** key.

DIFFERENTIATE INSTRUCTION

Curriculum Integration

Encourage students to research the history and significance of the number *e*, using the Internet and/or a library. Have students work either individually or in a small group to write reports on their findings or to present their findings orally to classmates. Both written reports and oral presentations should include graphics.

EXPLAIN 2

Writing Equations for Combined Transformations of $f(x) = e^x$

AVOID COMMON ERRORS

When students see the equation $y = ae^{rx}$, they may think that e is a variable because they are used to letters representing variables and because there are several other variables in the equation. Make sure that they understand that e is in fact a constant—a specific irrational number like π.

QUESTIONING STRATEGIES

? What are two reference points on the graph of $f(x) = e^x$ that will help when writing equations for combined transformations? $(0,1)$ and $(1,e)$

? How is the first reference point transformed from the point $(0, 1)$ in the graph of $f(x) = e^x$? The x-coordinate is moved to h, and the y-coordinate is moved to k and stretched away from it vertically by a factor of a.

Explain 2 Writing Equations for Combined Transformations of $f(x) = e^x$

If you are given the transformed graph $g(x) = a \cdot e^{x-h} + k$, it is possible to write the equation of the transformed graph by using the reference points $(h, a + k)$ and $(1 + h, ae + k)$.

Example 2 **Write the function whose graph is shown. State the domain and range in set notation.**

(A) First, look at the labeled points on the graph.

$(h, a + k) = (4, 6)$

$(1 + h, ae + k) = (5, 2e + 4)$

Find a, h, and k.

$(h, a + k) = (4, 6)$, so $h = 4$.

$(1 + h, ae + k) = (5, 2e + 4)$, so $ae + k = 2e + 4$.
Therefore, $a = 2$ and $k = 4$.

Write the equation by substituting the values of a, h, and k into the function $g(x) = a \cdot e^{x-h} + k$.

$g(x) = 2e^{x-4} + 4$

State the domain and range.

Domain: $\{x \mid -\infty < x < \infty\}$

Range: $\{y \mid y > 4\}$

(B) First, look at the labeled points on the graph.

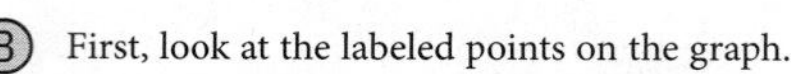

$(h, a + k) = (-4, -8)$

$(1 + h, ae + k) = (-3, -2e - 6)$

Find a, h, and k.

$(h, a + k) = (-4, -8)$, so $h = -4$.

$(1 + h, ae + k) = (-3, -2e - 6)$, so $ae + k = -2e - 6$.

Therefore, $a = -2$ and $k = -6$.

Write the equation by substituting the values of a, h, and k into the function $g(x) = a \cdot e^{x-h} + k$.

$g(x) = -2e^{x+4} - 6$

State the domain and range.

Domain: $\{x \mid -\infty < x < \infty\}$

Range: $\{y \mid y < -6\}$

LANGUAGE SUPPORT EL

Communicate Math

Have students work together to complete the table for a specific transformation applied to each of the functions.

Type of Function	Equation	Graph	Comparison to other graphs in this table
Exponential with base 2			
Exponential with base 10			
Exponential with base e			

Your Turn

Write the function whose graph is shown. State the domain and range in set notation.

3.

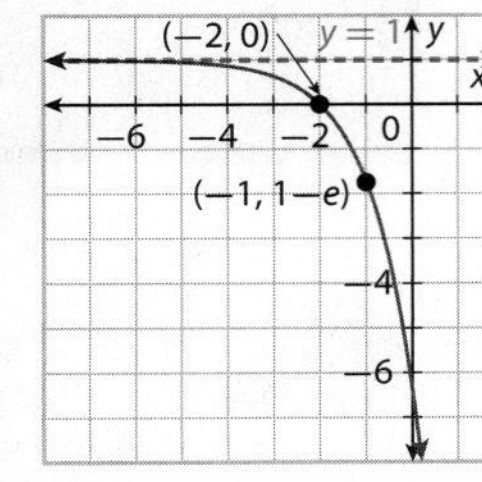

Find a, h, and k.

$(h, a + k) = (-2, 0)$, so $h = -2$.

$(1 + h, ae + k) = (-1, 1 - e)$, so

$ae + k = -e + 1$. Therefore, $a = -1$ and $k = 1$.

$g(x) = -e^{x+2} + 1$

Domain: $\{x \mid -\infty < x < \infty\}$

Range: $\{y \mid y < 1\}$

Explain 3 Modeling with Exponential Functions Having Base e

Although the function $f(x) = e^x$ has base $e \approx 2.718$, the function $g(x) = e^{cx}$ can have any positive base (other than 1) by choosing an appropriate positive or negative value of the constant c. This is because you can write $g(x)$ as $(e^c)^x$ by using the Power of a Power Property of Exponents.

Example 3 **Solve each problem using a graphing calculator. Then determine the growth rate or decay rate of the function.**

(A) The Dow Jones index is a stock market index for the New York Stock Exchange. The Dow Jones index for the period 1980-2000 can be modeled by $V_{DJ}(t) = 878e^{0.121t}$, where t is the number of years after 1980. Determine how many years after 1980 the Dow Jones index reached 3000.

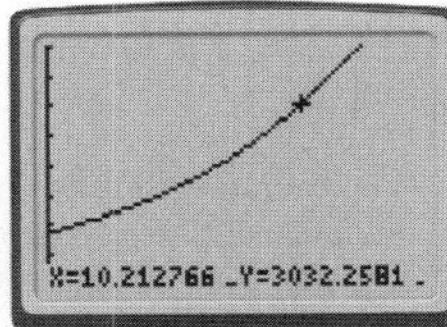

Use a graphing calculator to graph the function.

The value of the function is about 3000 when $x \approx 10.2$. So, the Dow Jones index reached 3000 after 10.2 years, or after the year 1990.

In an exponential growth model of the form $f(x) = ae^{cx}$, the growth factor $1 + r$ is equal to e^c.

To find r, first rewrite the function in the form $f(x) = a(e^c)^x$.

$V_{DJ}(t) = 878e^{0.121t}$

$= 878(e^{0.121})^t$

Find r by using $1 + r = e^c$.

$1 + r = e^c$

$1 + r = e^{0.121}$

$r = e^{0.121} - 1 \approx 0.13$

So, the growth rate is about 13%.

EXPLAIN 3

Modeling With Exponential Functions Having Base e

INTEGRATE MATHEMATICAL PRACTICES

Focus on Critical Thinking

MP.3 Have students consider how they would use natural decay functions to solve scientific half-life problems.

(B) The Nikkei 225 index is a stock market index for the Tokyo Stock Exchange. The Nikkei 225 index for the period 1990-2010 can be modeled by $V_{N225}(t) = 23{,}500e^{-0.0381t}$, where t is the number of years after 1990. Determine how many years after 1990 the Nikkei 225 index reached 15,000.

Use a graphing calculator to graph the function.

The value of the function is about 15,000 when $x \approx$ 12. So, the Nikkei 225 index reached 15,000 after 12 years, or after the year 2002.

In an exponential decay model of the form $f(x) = ae^{cx}$, the decay factor $1 - r$ is equal to e^c.

To find r, first rewrite the function in the form $f(x) = a(e^c)^x$.

$V_{N225}(t) = 23{,}500e^{-0.0381t}$

$= 23{,}500\left(e^{-0.0381}\right)^t$

Find r by using $1 - r = e^c$.

$1 - r = e^c$

$1 - r = e^{-0.0381}$

$r = 1 - e^{-0.0381} \approx 0.037$

So, the growth rate is 3.7 %.

Your Turn

4. A paleontologist uncovers a fossil of a saber-toothed cat in California. The paleontologist analyzes the fossil and concludes that the specimen contains 15% of its original carbon-14. The percent of original carbon-14 in a specimen after t years can be modeled by $N(t) = 100e^{-0.00012t}$, where t is the number of years after the specimen died. Use a graphing calculator to determine the age of the fossil. Then determine the decay rate of the function.

Using a graphing calculator gives a value for the function of about 15 when $x \approx 15{,}800$. So, the fossil is about 15,800 years old.

The decay factor $1 - r$ is equal to e^c in the function $f(x) = ae^{cx}$.

Rewrite the function in the form $f(x) = a(e^c)^x$.

$N(t) = 100e^{-0.00012t} = 100\left(e^{-0.00012}\right)^t$

$1 - r = e^{-0.00012}$

$r = 1 - e^{-0.00012}$

Elaborate

5. Which transformations of $f(x) = e^x$ change the function's end behavior?
Vertical translations change the function's end behavior because they affect the graph's asymptote.

6. Which transformations change the location of the graph's y-intercept?
Vertical translations, horizontal translations, vertical stretches/compressions, and reflections across the x-axis all change the location of the graph's y-intercept.

7. Why can the function $f(x) = ae^{cx}$ be used as an exponential growth model and as an exponential decay model? How can you tell if the function represents growth or decay?
If you rewrite the function in the form $f(x) = a(e^c)^x$, e^c can be equal to the growth factor, $1 + r$, or the decay factor, $1 - r$. If the constant c is positive, then the function models exponential growth, and if the constant c is negative, then the function models exponential decay.

8. **Essential Question Check-In** How are reference points helpful when graphing transformations of $f(x) = e^x$ or when writing equations for transformed graphs?
Reference points can be found from the equation and then used to graph transformations of $f(x) = e^x$. Reference points can also be used to write the equation for a transformed graph by giving the values of the constants in the equation.

Evaluate: Homework and Practice

• Online Homework
• Hints and Help
• Extra Practice

1. What is the greatest value of $f(x) = \left(1 + \frac{1}{x}\right)^x$ for any positive value of x?
The greatest value is e because as $x \to \infty$, $f(x) \to e$.

2. Identify the key attributes of $f(x) = e^x$, including the domain and range in set notation, the end behavior, and all intercepts.
The domain is $\{x \mid -\infty < x < \infty\}$ and the range is $\{y \mid y > 0\}$. As x approaches $-\infty$, $f(x)$ approaches 0 and as x approaches ∞, $f(x)$ approaches ∞. The function does not have any x-intercepts but has a y-intercept of 1.

ELABORATE

QUESTIONING STRATEGIES

How do you find the growth rate of a function of the form $f(x) = ae^{cx}$ where c is a positive constant? **Rewrite the function as $f(x) = a(e^c)^x$ and subtract 1 from the base e^c. If the growth factor $1 + r$ equals e^c, then the growth rate r is $e^c - 1$.**

How do you find the decay rate of a function of the form $f(x) = ae^{cx}$ where c is a negative constant? **Rewrite the function as $f(x) = a(e^c)^x$ and subtract the base e^c from 1. If the decay factor $1 - r$ equals e^c, then the decay rate equals $1 - e^c$.**

SUMMARIZE THE LESSON

How does the graph of $f(x) = e^x$ compare to graphs of exponential functions with other bases? **Because $e > 1$, $f(x)$ is an exponential growth function, so its graph rises from left to right. The graph rises more quickly than the graph of $f(x) = 2^x$ and less quickly than the graph of $f(x) = 3^x$.**

EVALUATE

ASSIGNMENT GUIDE

Concepts and Skills	Practice
Explore Graphing and Analyzing $f(x) = e^x$	Exercises 1–2
Example 1 Graphing Combined Transformations of $f(x) = e^x$	Exercises 7–11
Example 2 Writing Equations for Combined Transformations of $f(x) = e^x$	Exercises 12–13
Example 3 Modeling With Exponential Functions Having Base e	Exercises 14–15

AVOID COMMON ERRORS

Students are accustomed to letters representing variables and so may become confused when working with e. Remind them that, like π, e is a constant representing an irrational number.

Predict the effect of the parameters h, k, or a on the graph of the parent function $f(x) = e^x$. Identify any changes of domain, range, or end behavior.

3. $g(x) = f\left(x - \frac{1}{2}\right)$

The graph is translated $\frac{1}{2}$ unit to the right. There is no effect on the domain, range, or end behavior.

4. $g(x) = f(x) - \frac{5}{2}$

The graph is translated down $\frac{5}{2}$ units. There is no effect on the domain or end behavior but the range changes to $\left\{y \middle| -\frac{5}{2} < y < \infty\right\}$.

5. $g(x) = -\frac{1}{4} f(x)$

The graph is vertically compressed by a factor of $\frac{1}{4}$ and reflected across the x-axis. There is no effect on the domain, but the range changes to $\left\{y \middle| -\infty < y < 0\right\}$. The end behavior as $x \to -\infty$ does not change, but the end behavior as $x \to \infty$ changes from $g(x) \to \infty$ to $g(x) \to -\infty$.

6. $g(x) = \frac{27}{2} f(x)$

The graph is vertically stretched by a factor of $\frac{27}{2}$. There is no effect on the domain, range, or end behavior.

7. The graph of $f(x) = ce^x$ crosses the y-axis at $(0, c)$, where c is some constant. Where does the graph of $g(x) = f(x) - d$ cross the y-axis?

$(0, c - d)$

Given the function of the form $g(x) = a \cdot e^{x-h} + k$, identify the reference points and use them to draw the graph. State the domain and range in set notation.

8. $g(x) = e^{x-1} + 2$

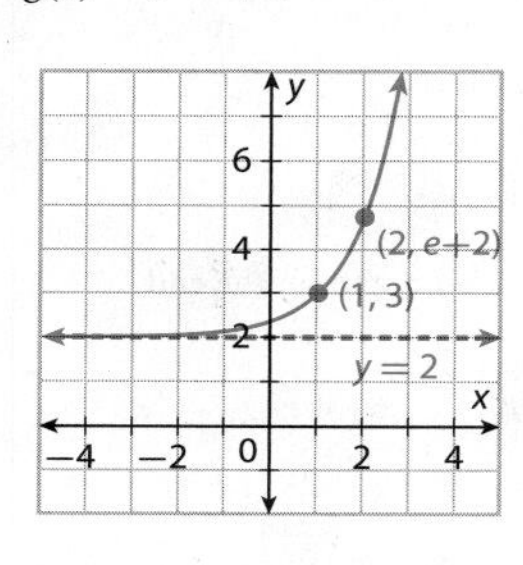

$a = 1; h = 1; k = 2$

$(0, 1) \to (1, 3); (1, e) \to (2, e + 2)$

Domain: $\{x | -\infty < x < \infty\}$

Range: $\{y | y > 2\}$

9. $g(x) = -e^{x+1} - 1$

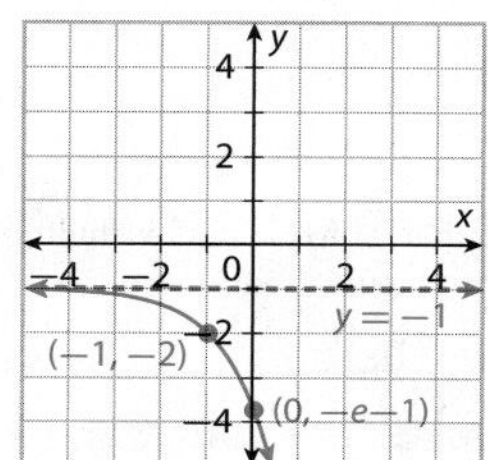

$a = -1; h = -1; k = -1$

$(0, 1) \to (-1, -2); (1, e) \to (0, -e - 1)$

Domain: $\{x | -\infty < x < \infty\}$

Range: $\{y | y < -1\}$

Exercise	Depth of Knowledge (D.O.K.)	COMMON CORE Mathematical Practices
1	**2** Skills/Concepts	**MP.2** Reasoning
2–6	**1** Recall of Information	**MP.2** Reasoning
7–11	**1** Recall of Information	**MP.4** Modeling
12–13	**1** Recall of Information	**MP.2** Reasoning
14–15	**2** Skills/Concepts	**MP.4** Modeling
16	**3** Strategic Thinking H.O.T.	**MP.3** Logic

10. $g(x) = \frac{3}{2}e^{x-1} - 3$

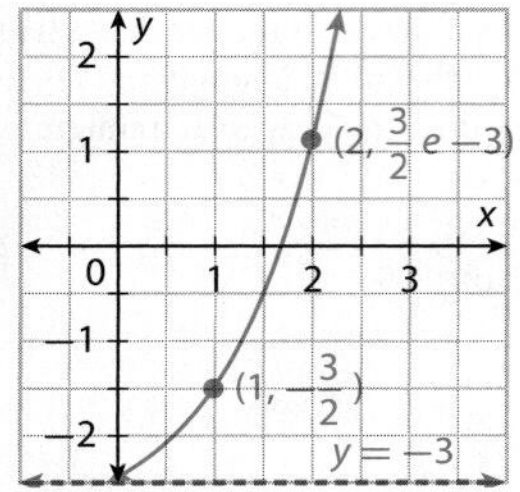

$a = \frac{3}{2}; h = 1; k = -3$

Reference points:

$(0, 1) \rightarrow \left(1, -\frac{3}{2}\right)$

$(1, e) \rightarrow \left(2, \frac{3}{2}e - 3\right)$

Domain: $\{x \mid -\infty < x < \infty\}$

Range: $\{y \mid y > -3\}$

11. $g(x) = -\frac{5}{3}e^{x-4} + 2$

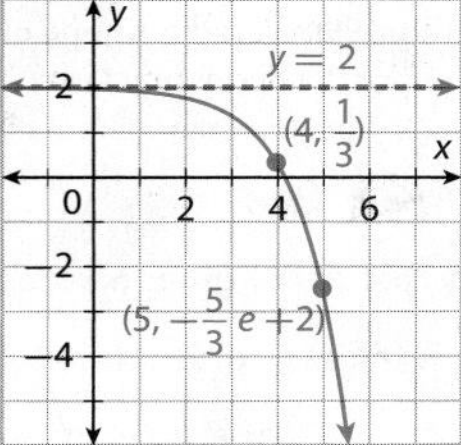

$a = -\frac{5}{3}; h = 4; k = 2$

Reference points:

$(0, 1) \rightarrow \left(4, \frac{1}{3}\right)$

$(1, e) \rightarrow \left(5, -\frac{5}{3}e + 2\right)$

Domain: $\{x \mid -\infty < x < \infty\}$

Range: $\{y \mid y < 2\}$

Write the function whose graph is shown. State the domain and range in set notation.

12.

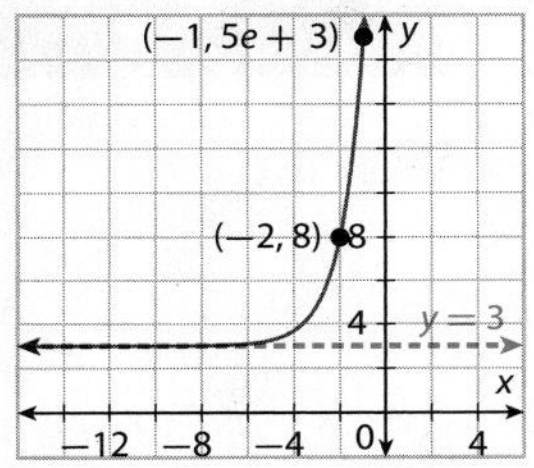

Find *a*, *h*, and *k*.

$(h, a + k) = (-2, 8)$, so $h = -2$.

$(1 + h, ae + k) = (-1, 5e + 3)$, so

$ae + k = 5e + 3$. Therefore,

$a = 5$ and $k = 3$.

$g(x) = 5e^{x+2} + 3$

Domain: $\{x \mid -\infty < x < \infty\}$

Range: $\{y \mid y > 3\}$

13.

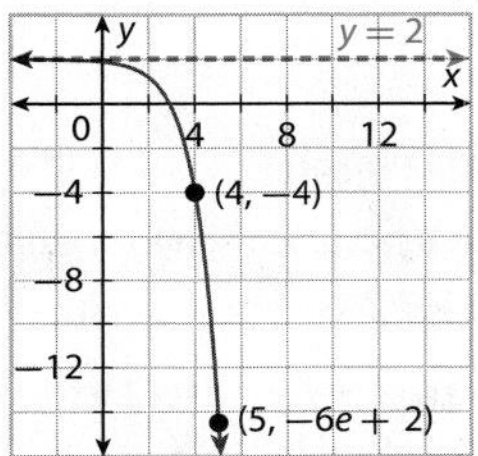

Find *a*, *h*, and *k*.

$(h, a + k) = (4, -4)$, so $h = 4$.

$(1 + h, ae + k) = (5, -6e + 2)$, so

$ae + k = -6e + 2$. Therefore,

$a = -6$ and $k = 2$.

$g(x) = -6e^{x-4} + 2$

Domain: $\{x \mid -\infty < x < \infty\}$

Range: $\{y \mid y < 2\}$

Exercise	Depth of Knowledge (D.O.K.)	COMMON CORE Mathematical Practices
17	**3** Strategic Thinking H.O.T.	**MP.4** Modeling
18	**3** Strategic Thinking H.O.T.	**MP.2** Reasoning

INTEGRATE MATHEMATICAL PRACTICES

Focus on Math Connections

MP.1 Like π, e is an irrational number, so its decimal form never repeats and never terminates. Its value is approximately 2.71828. The function $f(x) = e^x$ is special in mathematics because it is the only exponential function $f(x) = b^x$ whose derivative is equal to itself. For that reason, e is sometimes called *the natural base.*

Solve each problem using a graphing calculator. Then determine the growth rate or decay rate of the function.

14. Medicine Technetium-99m, a radioisotope used to image the skeleton and the heart muscle, has a half-life of about 6 hours. Use the decay function $N(t) = N_0e^{-0.1155t}$, where N_0 is the initial amount and t is the time on hours, to determine how many hours it takes for a 250 milligram dose to decay to 16 milligrams.

Let $N(t) = 16$ and $N_0 = 250$.

Using a graphing calculator gives a value for the function of about 16 when $x \approx 24$. So, it takes approximately 24 hours.

The decay factor $1 - r$ is equal to e^c in the function $f(x) = ae^{cx}$.

Rewrite the function in the form $f(x) = a(e^c)^x$.

$$N(t) = 250e^{-0.1155t} = 250\left(e^{-0.1155}\right)^t$$

$$1 - r = e^c$$

$$1 - r = e^{-0.1155}$$

$$1 - e^{-0.1155} = r$$

15. Ecology The George River herd of caribou in Canada was estimated to be about 4700 in 1954 and grew at an exponential rate to about 472,000 in 1984. Use the exponential growth function $P(t) = P_0e^{0.154t}$, where P_0 is the initial population, t is the time in years after 1954, and $P(t)$ is the population at time t, to determine how many years after 1984 the herd reached 25 million.

Let $P(t) = 25{,}000{,}000$ and $P_0 = 472{,}000$.

Using a graphing calculator gives a value for the function of about 25,000,000 when $x \approx 26$. So, the herd reached 25 million after approximately 26 years, or after 2010.

The growth factor $1 + r$ is equal to e^c.

Rewrite the function in the form $f(x) = a(e^c)^x$.

$$P(t) = 472{,}000e^{0.154t} = 472{,}000\left(e^{0.154}\right)^t$$

$$1 + r = e^c$$

$$1 + r = e^{0.154}$$

$$r = e^{0.154} - 1$$

H.O.T. Focus on Higher Order Thinking

16. Explain the Error A classmate claims that the function $g(x) = -4e^{x-5} + 6$ is the parent function $f(x) = e^x$ reflected across the y-axis, vertically compressed by a factor of 4, translated to the left 5 units, and translated up 6 units. Explain what the classmate described incorrectly and describe $g(x)$ as a series of transformations of $f(x)$.

The classmate incorrectly described a reflection across the y-axis, a vertical compression by a factor of 4, and a translation to the left 5 units. The function $g(x) = -4e^{x-5} + 6$ is the parent function $f(x) = e^x$ reflected across the x-axis, vertically stretched by a factor of 4, translated to the right 5 units, and translated up 6 units.

17. Multi-Step Newton's law of cooling states that the temperature of an object decreases exponentially as a function of time, according to $T = T_s + (T_0 - T_s)e^{-kt}$, where T_0 is the initial temperature of the liquid, T_s is the surrounding temperature, and k is a constant. For a time in minutes, the constant for coffee is approximately 0.283. The corner coffee shop has an air temperature of 70°F and serves coffee at 206°F. Coffee experts say coffee tastes best at 140°F.

a. How long does it take for the coffee to reach its best temperature?

Let $T = 140$, $T_s = 70$, $T_0 = 206$, and $k = 0.283$.

$T = 70 + (206 - 70)e^{-0.283t} = 70 + 136e^{-0.283t}$

Using a graphing calculator gives a value for the function of about 140 when $x \approx 2.3$. So, it takes approximately 2.3 minutes for the coffee to cool to 140 °F.

b. The air temperature on the patio outside the coffee shop is 86 °F. How long does it take for coffee to reach its best temperature there?

Let $T_s = 86$.

$T = 86 + (206 - 86)e^{-0.283t} = 86 + 120e^{-0.283t}$

Using a graphing calculator gives a value of about 140 for the function when $x \approx 2.8$. So, it takes approximately 2.8 minutes for the coffee to cool to 140 °F on the patio.

PEER-TO-PEER DISCUSSION

Ask students to discuss with a partner the similarities and differences between e and π, as well as their uses in the real world.

JOURNAL

Have students write a journal entry summarizing what they know about e and about the family of graphs of $f(x) = e^x$. Entries should include information that helps them identify transformations of the graph.

c. Find the time it takes for the coffee to cool to 71°F in both the coffee shop and the patio. Explain how you found your answer.

Coffee Shop:

Using a graphing calculator gives a value for the function of about 71 when $x \approx 17$. So, it takes approximately 17 minutes for the coffee to cool to 71 °F inside the coffee shop.

Patio:

The equation of the horizontal asymptote of the graph of the function for the patio is $y = 86$, the outside air temperature. Thus, the range of the function is $\{y \mid y > 86\}$. Since $71 < 86$, a temperature of 71°F is not possible for this function. So, the coffee will never cool to 71°F on the patio.

18. Analyze Relationships The graphing calculator screen shows the graphs of the functions $f(x) = 2^x$, $f(x) = 10^x$, and $f(x) = e^x$ on the same coordinate grid. Identify the common attributes and common point(s) of the three graphs. Explain why the point(s) is(are) common to all three graphs.

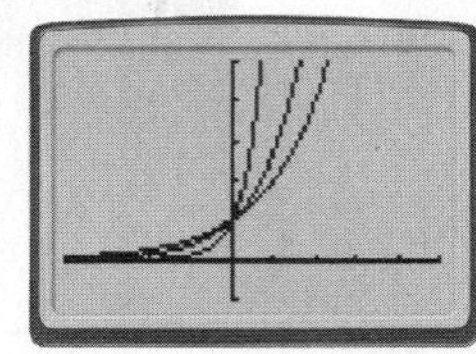

Common domain: $\{x \mid -\infty < x < \infty\}$

Common range: $\{y \mid y > 0\}$

Common *y*-intercept: 1

The point $(0, 1)$ is common to all three functions because the functions evaluated at 0 are all 1:

$f(0) = 2^0 = 1$

$f(0) = 10^0 = 1$

$f(0) = e^0 = 1$

Lesson Performance Task

The ever-increasing amount of carbon dioxide in Earth's atmosphere is an area of concern for many scientists. In order to more accurately predict what the future consequences of this could be, scientists make mathematic models to extrapolate past increases into the future. A model developed to predict the annual mean carbon dioxide level L in Earth's atmosphere in parts per million t years after 1960 is $L(t) = 36.9 \cdot e^{0.0223t} + 280$.

a. Use the function $L(t)$ to describe the graph of $L(t)$ as a series of transformations of $f(t) = e^t$.

b. Find and interpret $L(80)$, the carbon dioxide level predicted for the year 2040. How does it compare to the carbon dioxide level in 2015?

c. Can $L(t)$ be used as a model for all positive values of t? Explain.

Parts per million (ppm) of CO_2 in atmosphere: 600, 500, 400, 300, 200, 100, 0

20 40 60 80

Years (t) since 1960

a. The graph of $L(t)$ is a horizontal stretch of $f(t)$ by a factor of $\frac{1}{0.0223} \approx 44.843$, a vertical stretch of 36.9, and a translation of 280 units vertically.

b. $L(80) = 36.9 \cdot e^{0.0223(80)} + 280$

$\approx 36.9 \cdot 5.954 + 280$

≈ 499.703

The annual mean carbon dioxide level will be about 499.703 parts per million in 2040.

Next, find t for 2015.

$2015 - 1960 = 55$

$L(55) = 36.9 \cdot e^{0.0223(55)} + 280$

$\approx 36.9 \cdot 3.409 + 280$

≈ 405.792

$499.703 - 405.792 \approx 93.911$

The annual mean carbon dioxide level in 2040 will be about 93.911 parts per million greater than in 2015.

c. No, because the annual mean carbon dioxide level is in parts per million, so $L(t)$ cannot be greater than 1,000,000. Also, the annual mean carbon dioxide level will have to stop growing exponentially as it approaches 1,000,000 because there are other elements in the atmosphere, such as nitrogen, that cannot disappear.

EXTENSION ACTIVITY

Have students calculate the time t when the carbon dioxide level will have doubled from its 1960 level. Have them discuss whether this will happen within their lifetimes. **Set $L(t) = 2L(0)$ and solve for t. The carbon dioxide level will have doubled after about 101 years, or in 2061.**

LANGUAGE SUPPORT EL

Some students may not be familiar with the term *extrapolate*. Explain that it means *to use data from the past to predict values in the future.* Draw a graph and label the x-axis from 1960 to 2060. Explain that all values to the left of the current year have been measured in the past and they can be used to create a model for values to the right of the current year.

QUESTIONING STRATEGIES

? How is the variable t defined in the Lesson Performance Task? **t is the number of years after 1960.**

? What is the domain for the function $L(t)$? **For the mathematical function, the domain is $-\infty < t < \infty$. However, for this Performance Task, the domain is all integers t such that $t \geq 0$ and $L < 1{,}000{,}000$.**

? How can you write the equation so the variable t is the actual year itself, and how does this change the graph of $L(t)$? **$L(t) = 36.9e^{0.0223(t-1960)} + 280$. The graph is shifted to the right by 1960 units.**

Scoring Rubric

2 points: Student correctly solves the problem and explains his/her reasoning.

1 point: Student shows good understanding of the problem but does not fully solve or explain his/her reasoning.

0 points: Student does not demonstrate understanding of the problem.

LESSON 13.4

Compound Interest

Common Core Math Standards

The student is expected to:

 **F-LE.A.2**

Construct linear and exponential functions, including arithmetic and geometric sequences, given a graph, a description of a relationship, or two input-output pairs (include reading these from a table). Also F.IF.C.7e, F-IF.C.7, A-REI.D.11

Mathematical Practices

COMMON CORE **MP.4 Modeling**

Language Objective

Explain to a partner what simple interest is and what compound interest is.

ENGAGE

Essential Question: How do you model the value of an investment that earns compound interest?

Possible answer: You must know the principal (amount invested) P, the annual interest rate r, and the number of times per year, n, that the interest is compounded. Then, the value V of the investment at time t (in years) is $V(t) = P\left(1 + \frac{r}{n}\right)^{nt}$. This model becomes $V(t) = Pe^{rt}$ when the interest is compounded continuously.

PREVIEW: LESSON PERFORMANCE TASK

View the online Engage. Discuss the photo and the concept of investing to meet a changing goal amount. Then preview the Lesson Performance Task.

Name________ Class________ Date________

13.4 Compound Interest

Essential Question: How do you model the value of an investment that earns compound interest?

Resource Locker

Explore Comparing Simple and Compound Interest

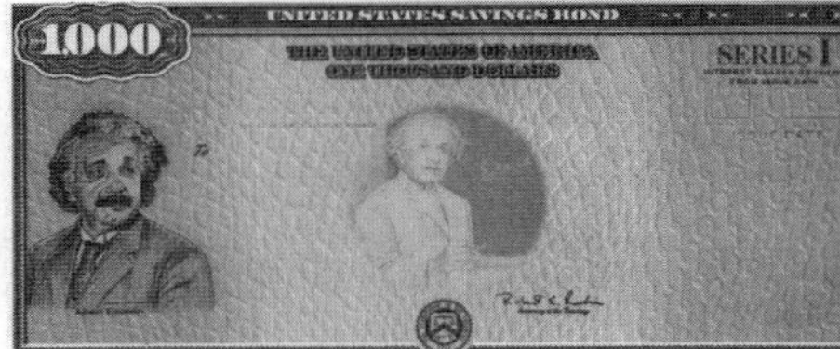

A *bond* is a type of investment that you buy with cash and for which you receive interest either as the bond matures or when it matures. A *conventional bond* generates an interest payment, sometimes called a *coupon payment*, on a regular basis, typically twice a year. The interest payments end when the bond matures and the amount you paid up-front is returned to you.

A *zero-coupon bond*, on the other hand, requires you to invest less money up-front and pays you its maturity value, which includes all accumulated interest, when the bond matures. Over the life of the bond, the interest that is earned each period itself earns interest until the bond matures.

The basic difference between a conventional bond and a zero-coupon bond is the type of interest earned. A conventional bond pays simple interest, whereas a zero-coupon bond pays **compound interest**, which is interest that earns interest.

(A) For \$1000, you can buy a conventional bond that has a maturity value of \$1000, has a maturity date of 4 years, and pays 5% annual interest. Calculate the interest that the investment earns annually by completing the table. (Bear in mind that interest earned is paid to you and not reinvested.)

Conventional Bond			
Year	Value of Investment at Beginning of Year	Interest Earned for Year (Paid to the Investor)	Value of Investment at End of Year
0			\$1000
1	\$1000	\$1000(0.05) = \$ 50	\$ 1000
2	\$1000	\$1000(0.05) = \$ 50	\$ 1000
3	\$1000	\$1000(0.05) = \$ 50	\$ 1000
4	\$1000	\$1000(0.05) = \$ 50	\$ 1000

HARDCOVER PAGES 681–696

Watch for the hardcover student edition page numbers for this lesson.

(B) For \$822.70, you can buy a zero-coupon bond that has a maturity value of \$1000, has a maturity date of 4 years, and pays 5% annual interest. Calculate the interest that the investment earns annually by completing the table. (Bear in mind that interest earned is reinvested and not paid to you until the bond matures.)

Zero-Coupon Bond			
Year	Value of Investment at Beginning of Year	Interest Earned for Year (Reinvested)	Value of Investment at End of Year
0			\$822.70
1	\$822.70	\$822.70(0.05) = \$ **41.14**	\$822.70 + \$ **41.14** = \$ **863.84**
2	\$ **863.84**	\$ **863.84** (0.05) = \$ **43.19**	\$ **863.84** + \$ **43.19** = \$ **907.03**
3	\$ **907.03**	\$ **907.03** (0.05) = \$ **45.35**	\$ **907.03** + \$ **45.35** = \$ **952.38**
4	\$ **952.38**	\$ **952.38** (0.05) = \$ **47.62**	\$ **952.38** + \$ **47.62** = \$1000

Reflect

1. Describe the difference between how simple interest is calculated and how compound interest is calculated.
Simple interest is paid back to the investor, and only calculated from the initial amount invested. So, the interest amount is a constant value. Compound interest is reinvested. It is first calculated from the initial amount invested. Then, the interest is added to the initial amount invested and calculated again from this new value. So, the interest amount grows exponentially over time.

2. If $V(t)$ represents the value of an investment at time t, in whole numbers of years starting with $t = 0$ and ending with $t = 4$, write a constant function for the last column in the first table and an exponential function for the last column in the second table.
In the last column of the first table, the value of the investment is a constant \$1000. So, $V(t) = 1000$. In the last column of the second table, the value of the investment grows exponentially with an initial investment of \$822.70 and an annual growth rate of 5%. So, $V(t) = 822.70(1.05)^t$.

EXPLORE

Comparing Simple and Compound Interest

INTEGRATE TECHNOLOGY

Students have the option of completing the Explore activity either in the book or online.

QUESTIONING STRATEGIES

? Which type of bond generates the most interest? How much more interest is generated by this type of bond? **The conventional bond generates more interest than the zero-coupon bond.**

? If you are an investor, what is the advantage of investing in the zero-coupon bond? **You may invest less money.**

PROFESSIONAL DEVELOPMENT

Math Background

The compound interest formula $V(t) = P\left(1 + \frac{r}{n}\right)^{nt}$ gives the total amount of money $V(t)$ at the end of t years for an initial investment P with an interest rate r that is compounded n times per year. When \$1 is invested at 100% interest for 1 year, the formula becomes $V(1) = \left(1 + \frac{1}{n}\right)^n$. The table gives the value of $V(1)$ for various values of n. The table suggests that as n grows larger, the value of $V(1)$ approaches a limiting value. This value, which is defined to be the constant e, is about 2.718281828459045. Written using the limit notation of calculus, $e = \lim_{n\to\infty}\left(1 + \frac{1}{n}\right)^n$.

n	$V(1)$
2	2.25
5	≈ 2.4883
10	≈ 2.5937
100	≈ 2.7048
1000	≈ 2.7169

EXPLAIN 1

Modeling Interest Compounded Annually

QUESTIONING STRATEGIES

What is the difference between simple interest and interest compounded annually? **Simple interest is interest earned on the principal. Interest compounded annually is interest earned on the principal and on the interest.**

When is the simple interest earned on an investment equal to interest that is compounded annually? **At the end of the first year, assuming the interest rates are the same.**

COMMUNICATE MATH EL

The term *compound* has many meanings. It means one thing in science, another in the everyday world (for example, an *army compound),* and still another in mathematics. Talk with students about the word's different meanings, specifying its particular meaning in math class.

INTEGRATE MATHEMATICAL PRACTICES

Focus on Math Connections

MP.1 Discuss with students how compound interest is an example of exponential growth. Help them to see that the formula for compound interest is an exponential function.

Explain 1 Modeling Interest Compounded Annually

Recall that the general exponential growth function is $f(t) = a(1 + r)^t$. When this function is applied to an investment where interest is compounded annually at a rate r, the function is written as $V(t) = P(1 + r)^t$ where $V(t)$ is the value V of the investment at time t and P is the *principal* (the amount invested).

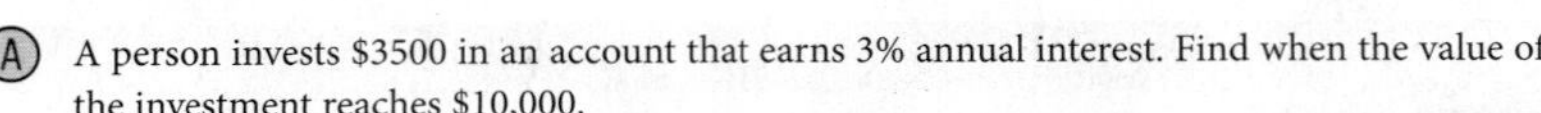

(A) A person invests $3500 in an account that earns 3% annual interest. Find when the value of the investment reaches $10,000.

Let $P = 3500$ and $r = 0.03$. Then $V(t) = P(1 + r)^t = 3500(1.03)^t$.

Graph $y = 3500(1.03)^x$ on a graphing calculator. Also graph the line $y = 10{,}000$ and find the point where the graphs intersect.

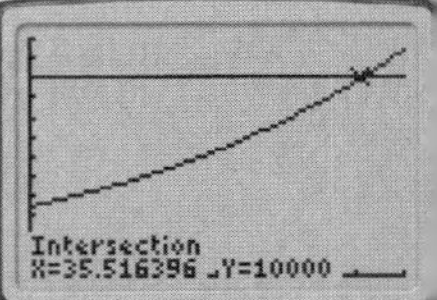

The value of the function is 10,000 at $x \approx 35.5$. So, the investment reaches a value of $10,000 in approximately 35.5 years.

(B) A person invests $200 in an account that earns 6.25% annual interest. Find when the value of the investment reaches $5000.

Let $P =$ **200** and $r =$ **0.0625**. Then $V(t) = P(1 + r)^t =$ **200** (**1.0625**)^t.

Graph the function on a graphing calculator. Also graph the line

$y =$ **5000** and find the point of intersection.

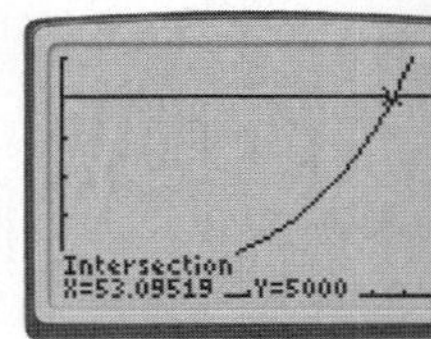

The value of the function is **5000** at $x \approx$ **53.1**. So, the investment reaches a value of $5000 in approximately **53.1** years.

Your Turn

3. A person invests $1000 in an account that earns 5.5% annual interest. Find when the value of the investment has doubled.

Let $P = 1000$ and $r = 0.055$. Then $V(t) = P(1 + r)^t = 1000(1.055)^t$. Graphing $y = 1000(1.055)^x$ along with the line $y = 2000$ shows that the value of the function is 2000 at $x \approx 12.9$. So, the investment reaches a value of $2000 in approximately 12.9 years.

COLLABORATIVE LEARNING

Small Group Activity

Have students work in groups of 3 to 4. Instruct students to use the Internet to research various types of investments and the interest programs they offer. Have them create a scenario for each type of investment they identify, and show how the investment grows over time. Have them create posters showing the results of their research and present the posters to the class.

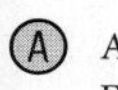 Explain 2

Modeling Interest Compounded More than Once a Year

Interest may be earned more frequently than once a year, such as semiannually (every 6 months), quarterly (every 3 months), monthly, and even daily. If the number of times that interest is compounded in a year is n, then the interest rate per compounding period is $\frac{r}{n}$ (where r is the annual interest rate), and the number of times that interest is compounded in t years is nt. So, the exponential growth function becomes $V(t) = P\left(1 + \frac{r}{n}\right)^{nt}$.

(A) A person invests \$1200 in an account that earns 2% annual interest compounded quarterly. Find when the value of the investment reaches \$1500.

Let $P = 1200$, $r = 0.02$, and $n = 4$. Then $V(t) = P\left(1 + \frac{r}{n}\right)^{nt} = 1200\left(1 + \frac{0.02}{4}\right)^{4t} = 1200(1.005)^{4t}$.

Graph the function $y = 1200(1.005)^{4x}$ on a graphing calculator. Also graph the line $y = 1500$ and find the point where the graphs intersect.

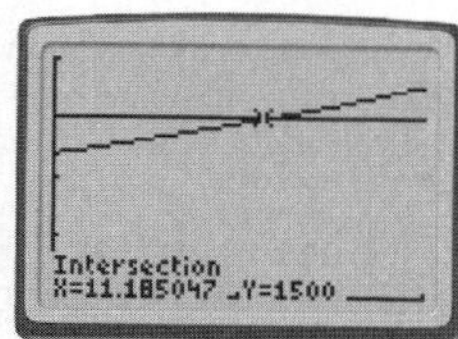

The value of the function is 1500 at $x \approx 11.2$. So, the investment reaches a value of \$1500 in approximately 11.2 years.

 (B) A person invests \$600 in an account that earns 6.25% annual interest compounded semiannually. Find when the value of the investment reaches \$1700.

Let $P = $ 600, $r = $ 0.0625, and $n = $ 2.

Then $V(t) = P\left(1 + \frac{r}{n}\right)^{nt} = 600\left(1 + \frac{0.0625}{2}\right)^{2t} = 600(1.03125)^{2t}$.

Graph the function on a graphing calculator. Also graph the line $y = $ 1700 and find the point where the graphs intersect.

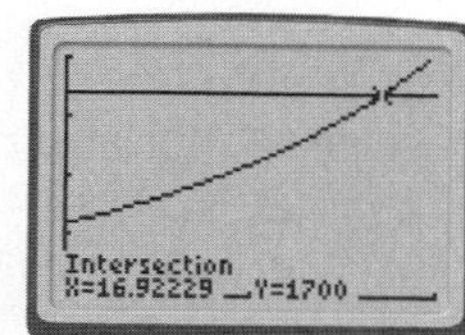

The value of the function is 1700 at $x \approx$ 16.9. So, the investment reaches a value of \$1700 in approximately 16.9 years.

DIFFERENTIATE INSTRUCTION

Communicating Math

Some students may feel overwhelmed by the complexity of the functions presented in the lesson. These students may benefit from rewriting the formulas using words in place of the various variables. Students can then use their "verbal formulas" to solve the problems. After achieving some success, students will likely feel less anxious about working with the formulas in their traditional forms.

EXPLAIN 2

Modeling Interest Compounded More Than Once a Year

AVOID COMMON ERRORS

Some students may mistake the number of months in a compounding period for the number of compounding periods per year. For example, for interest compounded quarterly, students may let $n = 3$, since quarterly means every 3 months. Clarify that n represents the number of *times* the interest is compounded each year.

QUESTIONING STRATEGIES

Why does the amount of interest earned increase as the frequency of compounding increases? **The more often the interest is compounded, the sooner the new interest is added to the balance on which the interest is earned.**

INTEGRATE MATHEMATICAL PRACTICES

Focus on Technology

MP.5 Use a graphing calculator to illustrate how increasing the number of compounding periods per year increases the rate of growth of an investment. Have students graph and compare several functions, each based on the same initial investment, interest rate, and time period, but for varying values of n.

EXPLAIN 3

Modeling Interest Compounded Continuously

QUESTIONING STRATEGIES

How is interest that is compounded continuously different from interest that is compounded daily? Interest that is compounded daily has 365 (or 366) compounding periods per year. Interest that is compounded continuously has, theoretically, infinitely many compounding periods per year.

AVOID COMMON ERRORS

Some students may, in error, raise the product of P and e to the exponent rt. Reinforce that the order of operations dictates that e be raised to the exponent, with the result multiplied by P.

Your Turn

4. A person invests $8000 in an account that earns 6.5% annual interest compounded daily. Find when the value of the investment reaches $20,000.

Let $P = 8000$, $r = 0.065$, and $n = 365$. Then $V(t) = P\left(1 + \frac{r}{n}\right)^{nt} = 8000\left(1 + \frac{0.065}{365}\right)^{365t}$ $\approx 8000(1.000178)^{365t}$. Graphing along $y = 8000(1.000178)^{365x}$ along with the $y = 20{,}000$ shows that the value of the function is 20,000 at $x = 14.1$. So, the investment reaches a value of $20,000 in approximately 14.1 years.

Explain 3 Modeling Interest Compounded Continuously

By letting $m = \frac{n}{r}$, you can rewrite the model $V(t) = P\left(1 + \frac{r}{n}\right)^{nt}$ as $V(t) = P\left(1 + \frac{1}{m}\right)^{mrt}$ because $\frac{r}{n} = \frac{1}{m}$ and $nt = mrt$. Then, rewriting as $V(t) = P\left(1 + \frac{1}{m}\right)^{mrt}$ as $V(t) = P\left[\left(1 + \frac{1}{m}\right)^{m}\right]^{rt}$ and letting n increase without bound, which causes m to increase without bound, you see that $\left(1 + \frac{1}{m}\right)^{m}$ approaches e, and the model simply becomes $V(t) = Pe^{rt}$. This model gives the value of an investment with principal P and annual interest rate r when interest is compounded *continuously*.

(A) A person invests $5000 in an account that earns 3.5% annual interest compounded continuously. Find when the value of the investment reaches $12,000.

Let $P = 5000$ and $r = 0.035$. Then $V(t) = 5000e^{0.035t}$.

Graph $y = 5000e^{0.035x}$. on a graphing calculator. Also graph the line $y = 12{,}000$ and find the point where the graphs intersect.

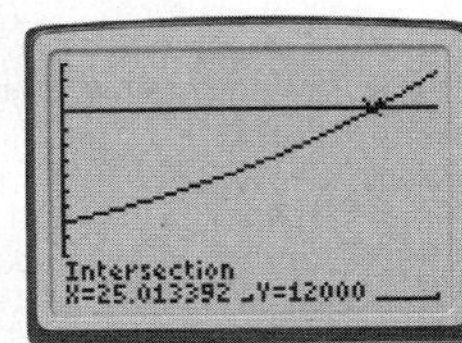

The value of the function is 12,000 at $x \approx 25$. So, the investment reaches a value of $12,000 in approximately 25 years.

LANGUAGE SUPPORT EL

Communicate Math

Have students work in pairs. Ask the first student to explain what simple interest is and how to find it, while the second student takes notes. The students switch roles; the second student explains what compound interest is and how to find it, while the first student takes notes. The first student should then do the same for constant compounding. Ask the pair to work together to read their notes and make any edits needed to complete their explanations.

(B) The principal amount, \$350, earns 6% annual interest compounded continuously. Find when the value reaches \$1800.

Let $P =$ **350** and $r =$ **0.06**. Then $V(t) =$ **350** $e^{\mathbf{0.06}t}$.

Graph the function on a graphing calculator. Also graph the line $y =$ **1800** and find the point where the graphs intersect.

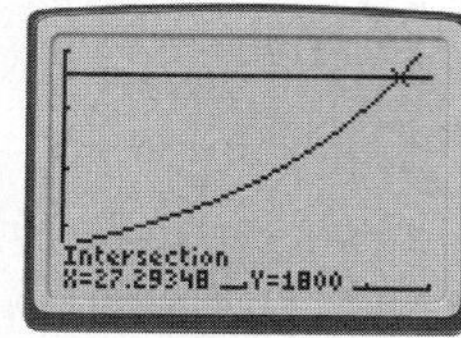

The value of the function is **1800** at $x \approx$ **27.3**. So, the investment reaches a value of \$1800 in approximately **27.3** years.

Your Turn

5. A person invests \$1550 in an account that earns 4% annual interest compounded continuously. Find when the value of the investment reaches \$2000.

Let $P = 1550$ and $r = 0.04$. Then $V(t) = 1550e^{0.04t}$. Graphing $y = 1550e^{0.04x}$ along with the line $y = 2000$ shows that the value of the function is 2000 at $x \approx 6.4$. So, the investment reaches a value of \$2000 in approximately 6.4 years.

Explain 4 Finding and Comparing Effective Annual Interest Rates

The value-of-an-investment function $V(t) = P\left(1 + \frac{r}{n}\right)^{nt} = P\left[\left(1 + \frac{r}{n}\right)^{n}\right]^{t}$, where interest is compounded n times per year, is an exponential function of the form $f(t) = ab^t$ where $a = P$ and $b = \left(1 + \frac{r}{n}\right)^{n}$. When the base of an exponential function is greater than 1, the function is an exponential growth function where the base is the growth factor and 1 less than the base is the growth rate. So, the growth rate for $V(t) = P\left(1 + \frac{r}{n}\right)^{nt}$ is $b - 1 = \left(1 + \frac{r}{n}\right)^{n} - 1$. This growth rate is called the investment's *effective annual interest rate R*, whereas r is called the investment's *nominal annual interest rate*.

Similarly, for the value-of-an-investment function $V(t) = Pe^{rt} = P\left[e^{r}\right]^{t}$, where interest is compounded continuously, the growth factor is e^r, and the growth rate is $e^r - 1$. So, in this case, the effective annual interest rate is $R = e^r - 1$.

For an account that earns interest compounded more than once a year, the effective annual interest rate is the rate that would produce the same amount of interest if interest were compounded annually instead. The effective rate allows you to compare two accounts that have different nominal rates and different compounding periods.

EXPLAIN 4

Finding and Comparing Effective Annual Interest Rates

QUESTIONING STRATEGIES

Which is greater, the nominal annual interest rate or its effective annual interest rate? Explain. **The effective annual interest rate is greater because it takes into account the interest that is generated on the interest.**

INTEGRATE MATHEMATICAL PRACTICES

Focus on Math Connections

MP.1 The concept of compound interest provides an opportunity to informally discuss the idea of a limiting process. As the frequency of compounding increases, the process gets closer and closer to continuous compounding. Tell students that the study of limiting processes is important in more advanced mathematics, especially calculus.

Ⓐ Arturo plans to make a deposit in one of the accounts shown in the table. To maximize the interest that the account earns, which account should he choose?

	Account X	Account Y
Nominal Annual Interest Rate	2.5%	2.48%
Compounding Period	Quarterly	Monthly

For Account X, interest is compounded quarterly, so $n = 4$. The nominal rate is 2.5%, so $r = 0.025$.

$R_X = \left(1 + \frac{r}{n}\right)^n - 1$ Use the formula for the effective rate.

$= \left(1 + \frac{0.025}{4}\right)^4 - 1$ Substitute.

≈ 0.02524 Simplify.

For Account Y, interest is compounded monthly, so $n = 12$. The nominal rate is 2.48%, so $r = 0.0248$.

$R_Y = \left(1 + \frac{r}{n}\right)^n - 1$ Use the formula for the effective rate.

$= \left(1 + \frac{0.0248}{12}\right)^{12} - 1$ Substitute.

≈ 0.02508 Simplify.

Account X has an effective rate of 2.524%, and Account Y has an effective rate of 2.508%, so Account X has a greater effective rate, and Arturo should choose Account X.

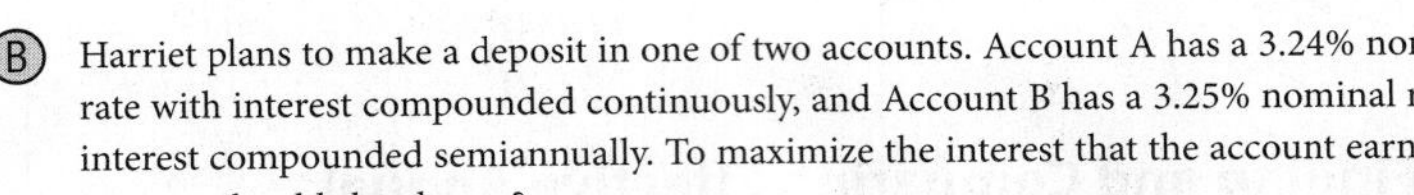

Ⓑ Harriet plans to make a deposit in one of two accounts. Account A has a 3.24% nominal rate with interest compounded continuously, and Account B has a 3.25% nominal rate with interest compounded semiannually. To maximize the interest that the account earns, which account should she choose?

For Account A, interest is compounded continuously. The nominal rate is 3.24%, so $r =$ 0.0324 .

$R_A = e^r - 1$ Use the formula for the effective rate.

$= e^{0.0324} - 1$ Substitute.

$\approx$ 0.03293 Simplify.

For Account B, interest is compounded semiannually, so so $n =$ 2. The nominal rate is 3.25%, so $r =$ 0.0325

$R_B = \left(1 + \frac{r}{n}\right)^n - 1$ Use the formula for the effective rate.

$= \left(1 + \frac{0.0325}{2}\right)^{2} - 1$ Substitute.

≈ 0.03276 Simplify.

Account A has an effective rate of 3.293%, and Account B has an effective rate of 3.276%, so Account A has a greater effective rate, and Harriet should choose Account A.

Your Turn

6. Jaclyn plans to make a deposit in one of the accounts shown in the table. To maximize the interest that the account earns, which account should she choose?

	Account X	Account Y
Nominal Annual Interest Rate	4.24%	4.18%
Compounding Period	Annually	Daily

For Account X, interest is compounded annually, so $n = 1$. The nominal rate is 4.24%, so $r = 0.0424$.

$R_X = \left(1 + \frac{r}{n}\right)^n - 1$

$= \left(1 + \frac{0.0424}{1}\right)^1 - 1$

$= 0.0424$

For Account Y, interest is compounded daily, so $n = 365$. The nominal rate is 4.18%, so $r = 0.0418$.

$R_Y = \left(1 + \frac{r}{n}\right)^n - 1$

$= \left(1 + \frac{0.0418}{365}\right)^{365} - 1$

≈ 0.04268

Account X has an effective rate of 4.24%, and Account Y has an effective rate of 4.268%, so Account Y has a greater effective rate, and Jaclyn should choose Account Y.

ELABORATE

INTEGRATE MATHEMATICAL PRACTICES

Focus on Communication

MP.3 Ask students to describe how the three functions used to model investments earning compound interest are related. Students should point out that the functions are all exponential growth functions, but that the growth factors differ in each case. Ensure that students use correct language in describing the mathematical relationships that exist among the functions.

SUMMARIZE THE LESSON

? What functions can you use to model investments that earn compound interest? **You can use $V(t) = P(1 + r)^t$ to model interest that is compounded annually. You can use $V(t) = P\left(1 + \frac{r}{n}\right)^{nt}$ to model interest that is compounded n times per year. You can use $V(t) = Pe^{rt}$ to model interest that is compounded continuously.**

Elaborate

7. Explain the difference between an investment's nominal annual interest rate and its effective annual interest rate.

An investment's nominal annual interest rate is the interest rate r that is used in the value function $V(t) = P\left(1 + \frac{r}{n}\right)^{nt}$ or $V(t) = Pe^{rt}$. The investment's effective annual interest rate is the interest rate R that would need to be used in the value function $V(t) = P(1 + R)^t$, where interest is compounded annually, to produce the same amount of annual interest as the investment actually earns.

8. **Essential Question Check-In** List the three functions used to model an investment that earns compound interest at an annual rate r. Identify when each function is used.

The three functions used to model an investment that earns compound interest at an annual rate r are $V(t) = P(1 + r)^t$, $V(t) = P\left(1 + \frac{r}{n}\right)^{nt}$, and $V(t) = Pe^{rt}$. The function $V(t) = P(1 + r)^t$ is used when interest is compounded annually. The function $V(t) = P\left(1 + \frac{r}{n}\right)^{nt}$ is used when interest is compounded more than once a year but not continuously. The function $V(t) = Pe^{rt}$ used when interest is compounded continuously.

Evaluate: Homework and Practice

- Online Homework
- Hints and Help
- Extra Practice

1. A person invests \$2560 in an account that earns 5.2% annual interest. Find when the value of the investment reaches \$6000.

Let $P = 2560$ and $r = 0.052$. Then $V(t) = P(1 + r)^t = 2560(1.052)^t$. Graphing $y = 2560(1.052)^x$ along with the line $y = 6000$ shows that the value of the function is 6000 at $x \approx 16.8$. So, the investment reaches a value of \$6000 in approximately 16.8 years.

2. A person invests \$1800 in an account that earns 2.46% annual interest. Find when the value of the investment reaches \$3500.

Let $P = 1800$ and $r = 0.0246$. Then $V(t) = P(1 + r)^t = 1800(1.0246)^t$. Graphing $y = 1800(1.0246)^x$ along with the line $y = 3500$ shows that the value of the function is 3500 at $x \approx 27.4$. So, the investment reaches a value of \$3500 in approximately 27.4 years.

3. Emmanuel invests \$3600 and Kelsey invests \$2400. Both investments earn 3.8% annual interest. How much longer will it take Kelsey's investment to reach \$10,000 than Emmanuel's investment?

Emmanuel's investment:

Let $P = 3600$ and $r = 0.038$. Then $V(t) = P(1 + r)^t = 3600(1.038)^t$. Graphing $y = 3600(1.038)^x$ along with the line $y = 10{,}000$ shows that the value of the function is 10,000 at $x \approx 27.4$. So, the investment reaches a value of \$10,000 in approximately 27.4 years.

Kelsey's investment:

Let $P = 2400$ and $r = 0.038$. Then $V(t) = P(1 + r)^t = 2400(1.038)^t$. Graphing $y = 2400(1.038)^x$ along with the line $y = 10{,}000$ shows that the value of the function is 10,000 at $x \approx 38.3$. So, the investment reaches a value of \$10,000 in approximately 38.3 years.

So, it takes Kelsey's investment approximately $38.3 - 27.4 = 10.9$ years longer to reach a value of \$10,000.

4. Jocelyn invests \$1200 in an account that earns 2.4% annual interest. Marcus invests \$400 in an account that earns 5.2% annual interest. Find when the value of Marcus's investment equals the value of Jocelyn's investment and find the common value of the investments at that time.

For Jocelyn's investment, let $P = 1200$ and $r = 0.024$. Then $V(t) = P(1 + r)^t = 1200(1.024)^t$.

For Marcus's investment, let $P = 400$ and $r = 0.052$. Then $V(t) = P(1 + r)^t = 400(1.052)^t$.

The graphs of $y = 1200(1.024)^x$ and $y = 400(1.052)^x$ intersect at approximately the point $(40.7, 3152.42)$.

So, the value of Marcus's investment equals the value of Jocelyn's investment after approximately 40.7 years. The common value of the investments is approximately \$3152.42.

5. A person invests \$350 in an account that earns 3.65% annual interest compounded semiannually. Find when the value of the investment reaches \$5675.

Let $P = 350$, $r = 0.0365$, and $n = 2$.

Then $V(t) = P\left(1 + \frac{r}{n}\right)^{nt} = 350\left(1 + \frac{0.0365}{2}\right)^{2t} = 350(1.01825)^{2t}$.

Graphing $y = 350(1.01825)^{2x}$ along with the line $y = 5675$, shows that the value of the function is 5675 at $x \approx 77$. So, the investment reaches a value of \$5675 in approximately 77 years.

Exercise	Depth of Knowledge (D.O.K.)	COMMON CORE Mathematical Practices
1–2	**1** Recall of Information	**MP.6** Precision
3–4	**2** Skills/Concepts	**MP.5** Using Tools
5–7	**1** Recall of Information	**MP.6** Precision
8	**2** Skills/Concepts	**MP.5** Using Tools
9–10	**1** Recall of Information	**MP.6** Precision
11	**2** Skills/Concepts	**MP.5** Using Tools
12–13	**1** Recall of Information	**MP.4** Modeling

EVALUATE

ASSIGNMENT GUIDE

Concepts and Skills	Practice
Explore Comparing Simple and Compound Interest	
Example 1 Modeling Interest Compounded Annually	Exercises 1–4, 18
Example 2 Modeling Interest Compounded More Than Once a Year	Exercises 5–8, 15–17
Example 3 Modeling Interest Compounded Continuously	Exercises 9–11
Example 4 Finding and Comparing Effective Annual Interest Rates	Exercises 12–14

VISUAL CUES

Suggest that students circle the numbers in the problem and, next to each number, write the variable for which the number will be substituted.

AVOID COMMON ERRORS

The formulas presented in this lesson each contain numerous variables. Because of this, students may mistake *e*, in the formula for investments that earn interest that is compounded continuously, as a variable, and look to make a substitution when applying this formula to a problem. To avoid this, suggest that students underline *e* when using this formula, to remind them that *e* is a number, not a variable, and that no number is substituted for *e*.

QUESTIONING STRATEGIES

If $I(t)$ is a function that represents the amount of interest earned on an account in which interest is compounded continuously, what rule can you write for $I(t)$? $I(t) = Pe^{rt} - P$

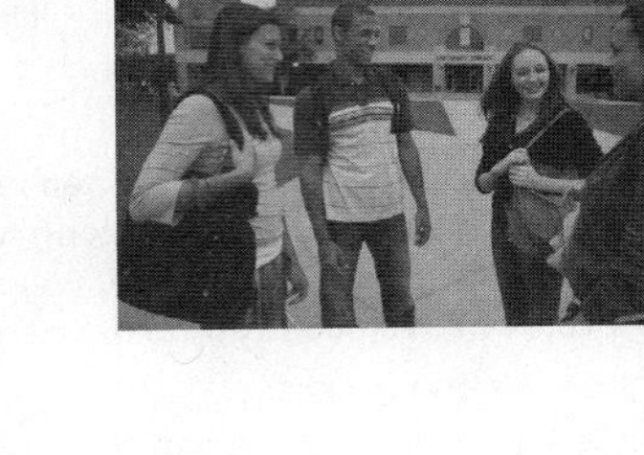

6. Molly invests $8700 into her son's college fund, which earns 2% annual interest compounded daily. Find when the value of the fund reaches $12,000.

Let $P = 8700$, $r = 0.02$, and $n = 365$.

Then $V(t) = P\left(1 + \frac{r}{n}\right)^{nt} = 8700\left(1 + \frac{0.02}{365}\right)^{365t}$

$\approx 8700(1.0000548)^{365t}$.

Graphing $y = 8700(1.0000548)^{365x}$ along with the line $y = 12{,}000$ shows that the value of the function is 12,000 at $x \approx 16.1$. So, the fund reaches a value of $12,000 in approximately 16.1 years.

7. A person invests $200 in an account that earns 1.98% annual interest compounded quarterly. Find when the value of the investment reaches $500.

Let $P = 200$, $r = 0.0198$, and $n = 4$.

Then $V(t) = P\left(1 + \frac{r}{n}\right)^{nt} = 200\left(1 + \frac{0.0198}{4}\right)^{4t} \approx 200(1.00495)^{4t}$.

Graphing $y = 200(1.00495)^{4x}$ along with the line $y = 500$, shows that the value of the function is 500 at $x \approx 46.4$. So, the investment reaches a value of $500 in approximately 46.4 years.

8. Hector invests $800 in an account that earns 6.98% annual interest compounded semiannually. Rebecca invests $1000 in an account that earns 5.43% annual interest compounded monthly. Find when the value of Hector's investment equals the value of Rebecca's investment and find the common value of the investments at that time.

For Hector's investment, let $P = 800$, $r = 0.0698$, and $n = 2$.

Then $V(t) = P\left(1 + \frac{r}{n}\right)^{nt} = 800\left(1 + \frac{0.0698}{2}\right)^{2t} \approx 800(1.0349)^{2t}$.

For Rebecca's investment, let $P = 1000$, $r = 0.0543$, and $n = 12$.

Then $V(t) = P\left(1 + \frac{r}{n}\right)^{nt} = 1000\left(1 + \frac{0.0543}{12}\right)^{12t} = 1000(1.004525)^{12t}$.

The graphs of $y = 800(1.0349)^{2x}$ and $y = 1000(1.004525)^{12x}$ intersect at approximately the point $(15.5, 2310.98)$.

So, the value of Hector's investment equals the value of Rebecca's investment after approximately 15.5 years. The common value of the investments is approximately $2310.98.

Exercise	Depth of Knowledge (D.O.K.)	COMMON CORE Mathematical Practices
14–15	2 Skills/Concepts	MP.5 Using Tools
16	3 Strategic Thinking H.O.T.	MP.5 Using Tools
17	3 Strategic Thinking H.O.T.	MP.3 Logic
18	3 Strategic Thinking H.O.T.	MP.2 Reasoning

9. A person invests \$6750 in an account that earns 6.23% annual interest compounded continuously. Find when the value of the investment reaches \$15,000.

Let $P = 6750$ and $r = 0.0623$. Then $V(t) = Pe^{rt} = 6570e^{0.0623t}$. Graphing $y = 6750e^{0.0623x}$ along with the line $y = 15{,}000$ shows that the value of the function is 15,000 at $x \approx 12.8$. So, the investment reaches a value of \$9500 in approximately 12.8 years.

10. A person invests \$465 in an account that earns 3.1% annual interest compounded continuously. Find when the value of the investment reaches \$2400.

Let $P = 465$ and $r = 0.031$. Then $V(t) = Pe^{rt} = 465e^{0.031t}$. Graphing $y = 465e^{0.031x}$ along with the line $y = 2400$ shows that the value of the function is 2400 at $x \approx 52.9$. So, the investment reaches a value of \$2400 in approximately 52.9 years.

11. Lucy invests \$800 in an account that earns 6.12% annual interest compounded continuously. Juan invests \$1600 in an account that earns 3.9% annual interest compounded continuously. Find when the value of Lucy's investment equals the value of Juan's investment and find the common value of the investments at that time.

For Lucy's investment, let $P = 800$ and $r = 0.0612$. Then $V(t) = Pe^{rt} = 800e^{0.0612t}$.

For Juan's investment, let $P = 1600$ and $r = 0.039$. Then $V(t) = Pe^{rt} = 1600e^{0.039t}$.

The graphs of $y = 800e^{0.0612x}$ and $y = 1600e^{0.039x}$ intersect at approximately the point (31.2, 5407.00).

So, the value of Lucy's investment equals the value of Juan's investment after approximately 31.2 years. The common value of the investments is approximately \$5407.00.

12. Paula plans to make a deposit in one of the accounts shown in the table. To maximize the interest that the account earns, which account should she choose?

	Account X	Account Y
Nominal Annual Interest rate	2.83%	2.86%
Compounding Period	Continuously	Annually

For Account X, interest is compounded continuously. The nominal rate is 2.83%, so $r = 0.0283$.

$$\begin{aligned} R_X &= e^r - 1 \\ &= e^{0.0283} - 1 \\ &\approx 0.0287 \end{aligned}$$

For Account Y, interest is compounded annually, so $n = 1$. The nominal rate is 2.86%, so $r = 0.0286$.

$$\begin{aligned} R_Y &= \left(1 + \frac{r}{n}\right)^n - 1 \\ &= \left(1 + \frac{0.0286}{1}\right)^1 - 1 \\ &\approx 0.0286 \end{aligned}$$

Account X has an effective rate of 2.87%, and Account Y has an effective rate of 2.86%, so Account X has a greater effective rate, and Paula should choose Account X.

COGNITIVE STRATEGIES

As a memory device, students may find it helpful to remember that the *effect*ive annual interest rate is a result of the *effect* that the compounding of the interest has on the nominal interest rate.

INTEGRATE MATHEMATICAL PRACTICES

Focus on Math Connections

MP.1 Students may be interested to learn that five of the most famous numbers in mathematics (e, i, π, 1, and 0) are related to each other by the seemingly simple equation $e^{i\pi} + 1 = 0$. Students will learn the derivation of this relationship in more advanced courses.

13. Tanika plans to make a deposit to one of two accounts. Account A has a 3.77% nominal rate with interest compounded daily, and Account B has a 3.8% nominal rate with interest compounded monthly. To maximize the interest that the account earns, which account should she choose?

For Account A, interest is compounded daily, so $n = 365$. The nominal rate is 3.78%, so $r = 0.0378$.

$$R_A = \left(1 + \frac{r}{n}\right)^n - 1$$
$$= \left(1 + \frac{0.0378}{365}\right)^{365} - 1$$
$$\approx 0.0385$$

For Account B, interest is compounded monthly, so $n = 12$. The nominal rate is 3.8%, so $r = 0.038$.

$$R_B = \left(1 + \frac{r}{n}\right)^n - 1$$
$$= \left(1 + \frac{0.038}{12}\right)^{12} - 1$$
$$\approx 0.0387$$

Account A has an effective rate of 3.85%, and Account B has an effective rate of 3.87%, so Account B has a greater effective rate, and Tanika should choose Account B.

14. Kylie plans to deposit $650 in one of the accounts shown in the table. She chooses the account with the greater effective rate. How much money will she have in her account after 10 years?

	Account X	Account Y
Nominal Annual Interest Rate	4.13%	4.12%
Compounding Period	Semiannually	Monthly

For Account X, interest is compounded semiannually, so $n = 2$. The nominal rate is 4.13%, so $r = 0.0413$.

$$R_X = \left(1 + \frac{r}{n}\right)^n - 1$$
$$= \left(1 + \frac{0.0413}{2}\right)^{2} - 1$$
$$\approx 0.0417$$

For Account Y, interest is compounded monthly, so $n = 4$. The nominal rate is 4.12%, so $r = 0.0412$.

$$R_Y = \left(1 + \frac{r}{n}\right)^n - 1$$
$$= \left(1 + \frac{0.0412}{4}\right)^{4} - 1$$
$$\approx 0.0418$$

Account Y has the greater effective rate, so Kylie chooses Account Y.

The value of Kylie's investment after 10 years is:

$$V(10) = 650\left(1 + \frac{0.0412}{4}\right)^{4(10)}$$
$$\approx 979.33$$

So, Kylie will have $979.33 in her account after 10 years.

15. A person invests $2860 for 15 years in an account that earns 4.6% annual interest. Match each description of a difference in interest earned on the left with the actual difference listed on the right.

A. Difference between compounding interest semiannually and annually ___C___ $14.89

B. Difference between compounding interest quarterly and semiannually ___B___ $21.98

C. Difference between compounding interest monthly and quarterly ___E___ $0.25

D. Difference between compounding interest daily and monthly ___A___ $42.75

E. Difference between compounding interest continuously and daily ___D___ $7.27

A. $V_S(15) - V_A(15) = 2860\left(1 + \frac{0.046}{2}\right)^{2(15)} - 2860(1 + 0.046)^{15}$

$\approx 5657.64 - 5614.89 = 42.75$

B. $V_Q(15) - V_S(15) = 2860\left(1 + \frac{0.046}{4}\right)^{4(15)} - 2860\left(1 + \frac{0.046}{2}\right)^{2(15)}$

$\approx 5679.62 - 5657.64 = 21.98$

C. $V_M(15) - V_Q(15) = 2860\left(1 + \frac{0.046}{12}\right)^{12(15)} - 2860\left(1 + \frac{0.046}{4}\right)^{4(15)}$

$\approx 5694.51 - 5679.62 = 14.89$

D. $V_D(15) - V_M(15) = 2860\left(1 + \frac{0.046}{365}\right)^{365(15)} - 2860\left(1 + \frac{0.046}{12}\right)^{12(15)}$

$\approx 5701.78 - 5694.51 = 7.27$

E. $V_D(15) - V_M(15) = 2860e^{0.046(15)} - 2860\left(1 + \frac{0.046}{365}\right)^{365(15)}$

$\approx 5702.03 - 5701.78 = 0.25$

H.O.T. Focus on Higher Order Thinking

16. **Multi-Step** Ingrid and Harry are saving to buy a house. Ingrid invests $5000 in an account that earns 3.6% interest compounded quarterly. Harry invests $7500 in an account that earns 2.8% interest compounded semiannually.

a. Find a model for each investment.

Ingrid's investment:

Let $P = 5000$, $r = 0.036$, and $n = 4$. Then $V(t) = P\left(1 + \frac{r}{n}\right)^{nt}$

$= 5000\left(1 + \frac{0.036}{4}\right)^{4t} = 5000(1.009)^{4t}$.

Harry's investment:

Let $P = 7500$, $r = 0.028$, and $n = 2$. Then $V(t) = P\left(1 + \frac{r}{n}\right)^{n}$

$= 7500\left(1 + \frac{0.028}{2}\right)^{2t} = 7500(1.014)^{2t}$.

PEER-TO-PEER DISCUSSION

Ask students to work with a partner to make a conjecture as to how much more money an investment of $10,000 would make at a rate of 4% compounded annually for 5 years versus 4% compounded monthly for 5 years. Then have them apply the formulas from this lesson to check their conjectures. **Students should find that when the interest is compounded monthly, the investment earns $43.44 more interest ($12,209.97 − $12,166.53).**

JOURNAL

Have students describe the concept of compound interest, citing the different types of compound interest, and explaining why the functions that model investments that earn compound interest are exponential growth functions.

b. Use a graphing calculator to find when the combined value of their investments reaches $15,000.

The combined value of the investments is $V(t) = 5000(1.009)^{4t} + 7500(1.014)^{2t}$. Graphing the function $y = 5000(1.009)^{4x} + 7500(1.014)^{2x}$ along with the line $y = 15{,}000$ shows that the value of the function is 15,000 at $x \approx 5.9$. So, the combined investment reaches a value of $15,000 after approximately 5.9 years.

17. Explain the Error A student is asked to find when the value of an investment of $5200 in an account that earns 4.2% annual interest compounded quarterly reaches $16,500. The student uses the model $V(t) = 5200(1.014)^{3t}$ and finds that the investment reaches a value of $16,500 after approximately 27.7 years. Find and correct the student's error.

The interest is compounded quarterly. This means that the interest is compounded every 3 months, or 4 times per year. The value of n in the function $V(t) = P\left(1 + \frac{r}{n}\right)^{nt}$ is the number of times the interest is compounded per year, so the student should have used 4 instead of 3.

Let $P = 5200$, $r = 0.042$, and $n = 4$. Then $V(t) = P\left(1 + \frac{r}{n}\right)^{nt} = 5200\left(1 + \frac{0.042}{4}\right)^{4t}$ $= 5200(1.0105)^{4t}$. Graphing $y = 5000(1.0105)^{4x}$ along with the line $y = 16{,}500$ shows that the value of the function is 16,500 at $x \approx 27.6$. So, the investment reaches a value of $16,500 after approximately 27.6 years.

18. Communicate Mathematical Ideas For a certain price, you can buy a zero-coupon bond that has a maturity value of $1000, has a maturity date of 4 years, and pays 5% annual interest. How can the present value (the amount you pay for the bond) be determined from the future value (the amount you get when the bond matures)?

The future value of the investment is $1000. The interest is compounded annually, so use the value function $V(t) = P(1 + r)^t$ to find the present value of the investment.

Let $r = 0.05$, $t = 4$, and $V(4) = 1000$. Solve for the present value P.

$$P(1 + 0.05)^4 = 1000$$

$$P(1.05)^4 = 1000$$

$$P = \frac{1000}{(1.05)^4}$$

$$P \approx 822.70$$

So, the present value of the investment is $822.70.

Lesson Performance Task

The grandparents of a newborn child decide to establish a college fund for her. They invest \$10,000 into a fund that pays 4.5% interest compounded continuously.

a. Write a model for the value of the investment over time and find the value of the investment when the child enters college at 18 years old.

b. In 2013, the average annual public in-state college tuition was \$8893, which was 2.9% above the 2012 cost. Use these figures to write a model to project the amount of money needed to pay for one year's college tuition 18 years into the future. What amount must be invested in the child's college fund to generate enough money in 18 years to pay for the first year's college tuition?

a. Use the formula for continuously compounded interest, with $P = 10{,}000$, $r = 0.045$, and $t = 18$.

$$V(t) = Pe^{rt}$$
$$= 10{,}000e^{(0.045)(18)}$$
$$= 10{,}000e^{0.81}$$
$$\approx 22{,}479.08$$

The value of the investment when the child enters college is \$22,479.08.

b. To estimate the cost in 18 years, use the formula for compound annual interest with $P = 8893$, $r = 0.029$, and $t = 18$.

$$V(t) = P(1 + r)^t$$
$$= 8893(1 + 0.029)^{18}$$
$$= 8893(1.029)^{18}$$
$$\approx 14{,}877.33$$

The model predicts that tuition will cost \$14,877.33 eighteen years into the future.

Now, use the continuously compounded interest formula to find what initial principal P yields a value in 18 years of \$14,877.33 when $r = 0.045$.

$$14{,}877.33 = Pe^{rt}$$
$$14{,}877.33 = Pe^{(0.045)(18)}$$
$$14{,}877.33 = Pe^{0.81}$$
$$\frac{14{,}877.33}{e^{0.81}} = P$$
$$\approx 6618.30$$

The amount that must be invested is \$6618.30.

EXTENSION ACTIVITY

Have students research the historical tuition costs of different four-year colleges and predict the savings needed to cover the projected tuitions for 4 years beginning 18–21 years from now. Have them consider different investment amounts and interest rates that would meet those costs, and present their findings to the class.

AVOID COMMON ERRORS

Students should compare the answers in Parts A and B of the Lesson Performance Task and re-read the original question in each part to determine whether the answers are reasonable.

INTEGRATE MATHEMATICAL PRACTICES

Focus on Modeling

MP.4 Students may consider alternative ways to approach the problem. For example, the growth during years 18–21 could also be considered, which would require a larger investment. Encourage students to pursue additional possibilities based on different constraints. Note that the growth rate will certainly change over time, so projections are unlikely to be very accurate.

Scoring Rubric

2 points: Student correctly solves the problem and explains his/her reasoning.

1 point: Student shows good understanding of the problem but does not fully solve or explain his/her reasoning.

0 points: Student does not demonstrate understanding of the problem.

Study Guide Review

ASSESSMENT AND INTERVENTION

Assign or customize module reviews.

MODULE PERFORMANCE TASK

Mathematical Practices: MP.1, MP.2, MP.4, MP.7
F-BF.B.3, F-LE.A.1c, F-LE.A.2

SUPPORTING STUDENT REASONING

Students should begin by thinking about how to fit an exponential function to the two data sets. They can then do research, or you can provide them with specific information. Here is some of the information they may ask for.

- **Why does the height of a bouncing ball decrease?** This is a consequence of conservation of energy. Each time the ball is compressed (when it hits the floor), some of its initial energy is transformed into the energy of deformation, reducing the available energy of motion (kinetic energy).
- **What form of exponential function works for the data?** Students should find that $h = h_0 r^n$ works for the two data sets.

Exponential Functions

Essential Question: How can you use exponential functions to solve real-world problems?

Key Vocabulary
exponential decay *(decremento exponencial)*
exponential function *(función exponencial)*
exponential growth *(crecimiento exponencial)*

KEY EXAMPLE *(Lesson 13.2)*

$g(x) = 3^{x+1}$ is a transformation of the function $f(x) = 3^x$. Sketch a graph of $g(x) = 3^{x+1}$.

$g(x) = 3^{x+1} = f(x+1)$

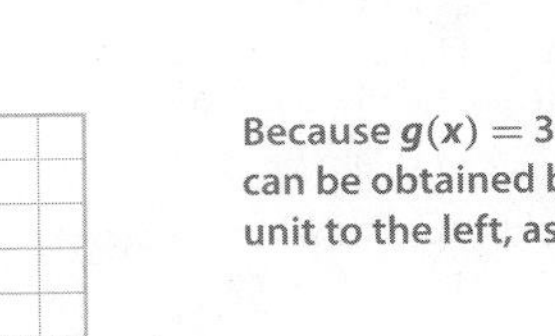

Because $g(x) = 3^{x+1} = f(x+1)$, the graph of g can be obtained by shifting the graph of f one unit to the left, as shown.

The solid line represents $f(x) = 3^x$.
The dashed line represents $g(x) = 3^{x+1}$.

KEY EXAMPLE *(Lesson 13.4)*

Which of the following accounts has a greater effective rate?

	Account X	Account Y
Nominal Interest Rate	3.5%	3.49%
Compounding Period	Quarterly	Weekly

$R_x = \left(1 + \frac{r}{n}\right)^n - 1$ — Use the formula for the effective rate.

$= \left(1 + \frac{0.035}{4}\right)^4 - 1$ — Substitute.

≈ 0.03546 — Simplify.

$R_y = \left(1 + \frac{r}{n}\right)^n - 1$ — Use the formula for the effective rate.

$= \left(1 + \frac{0.0349}{52}\right)^{52} - 1$ — Substitute.

≈ 0.0355 — Simplify.

Account Y has the higher effective rate.

SCAFFOLDING SUPPORT

- Remind students that to fit an exponential function to a data set, they should first calculate the ratio of consecutive outputs for evenly spaced inputs.
- Encourage students to use n, the number of bounces, as the independent variable, and h, the height, as the dependent variable.

EXERCISES

Sketch the graphs of the following transformations. *(Lessons 13.1, 13.2, 13.3)*

1. $g(x) = -2(0.5)^x$

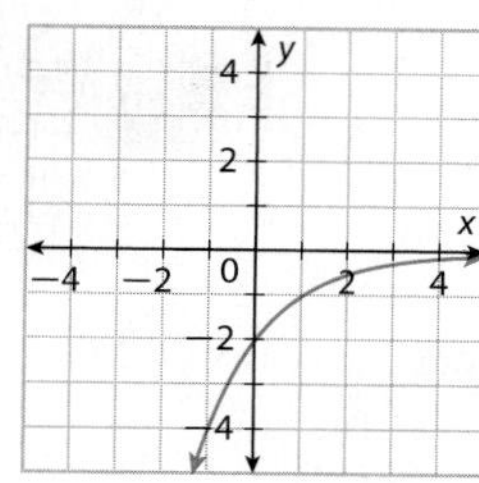

2. $f(x) = \left(\frac{1}{2}\right)^{-x}$

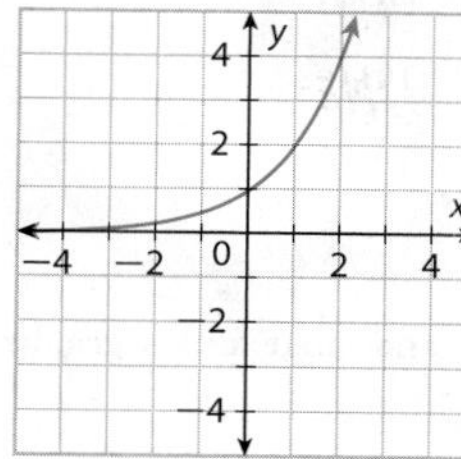

3. $f(x) = 2e^{x-2} + 1$

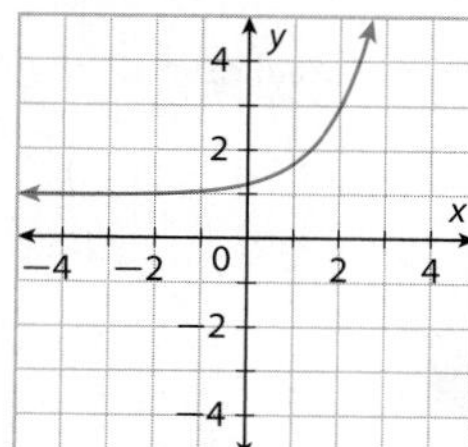

4. $g(x) = \left(\frac{3}{5}\right)^x$

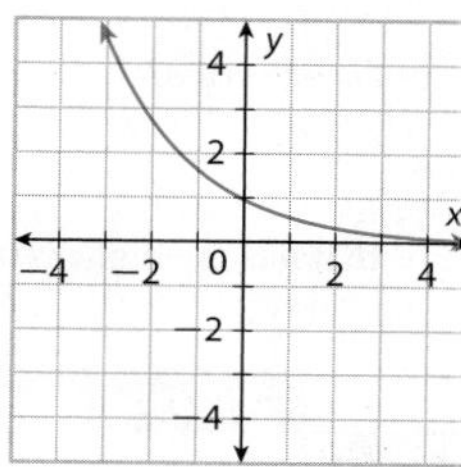

MODULE PERFORMANCE TASK

That's The Way the Ball Bounces

Kingston is a chemical engineer who is testing the "bounciness" of two novel materials. He formed each material into two equal-sized spheres. Kingston then dropped each sphere on a hard surface and measured the heights the spheres reached after each bounce. The results are shown in the table.

	Heights (cm)					
	h_0	h_1	h_2	h_3	h_4	h_5
Material A	90	63.0	44.1	30.9	21.6	15.1
Material B	90	49.5	27.2	15.0	8.2	4.5

Use the data to create mathematical models for the heights of the spheres. Compare the two materials. One of the two materials will be used for the tip of a pogo stick. Which material should Kingston recommend and why?

Use your own paper to complete the task. Be sure to write down all your data and assumptions. Then use graphs, numbers, words, or algebra to explain how you reached your conclusion.

SAMPLE SOLUTION

Method

First, find the ratio $\frac{h_n + 1}{h_n}$ and use this for r in the equation $h = h_0r^n$. h_0 is the starting height, which is 90 cm in both cases.

For material A, the average of the ratios is 0.70, so the equation is

$h_{\text{Material A}} = 90(0.7)^n$.

For Material B, the average of the ratios is 0.55, so the equation is

$h_{\text{Material A}} = 90(0.55)^n$.

You can plot the functions on the same coordinate grid.

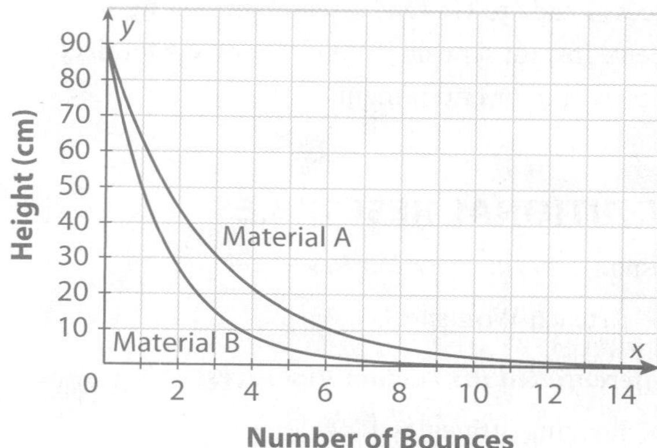

Material A has more "bounciness" because it bounces higher than does Material B, and also bounces more times before coming to rest.

Sample answer: Kingston should recommend Material A for the tip of the pogo stick, because a "bouncier" material will result in the potential for higher jumps.

DISCUSSION OPPORTUNITIES

- What are some other uses for very bouncy materials?
- Is the exponential model $h = h_0r^n$ realistic as n approaches infinity? Why or why not?

Assessment Rubric

2 points: Student correctly solves the problem and explains his/her reasoning.

1 point: Student shows good understanding of the problem but does not fully solve or explain.

0 points: Student does not demonstrate understanding of the problem.

Ready to Go On?

ASSESS MASTERY

Use the assessment on this page to determine if students have mastered the concepts and standards covered in this module.

ASSESSMENT AND INTERVENTION

Access Ready to Go On? assessment online, and receive instant scoring, feedback, and customized intervention or enrichment.

ADDITIONAL RESOURCES

Response to Intervention Resources

- Reteach Worksheets

Differentiated Instruction Resources

- Reading Strategies **EL**
- Success for English Learners **EL**
- Challenge Worksheets

Assessment Resources

- Leveled Module Quizzes

Ready to Go On?

13.1–13.4 Exponential Functions

- Online Homework
- Hints and Help
- Extra Practice

State the domain and range for the graphs of the following functions. *(Lessons 13.1, 13.2)*

1. $y = \left(\frac{1}{4}\right)^x$

The domain is all real numbers.

The range is $y \geq 0$.

2. $y = \left(\frac{1}{3}\right)^{(x-2)} + 2$

The domain is all real numbers.

The range is $y \geq 2$.

3. $y = -3 \cdot 2^{x+2}$

The domain is all real numbers.

The range is $y \leq 0$.

4. $y = 3^{x-2} - 1$

The domain is all real numbers.

The range is $y \geq -1$.

Identify the account that has the higher effective rate. *(Lessons 13.4)*

5.

	Account X	Account Y
Nominal Interest Rate	5%	5.2%
Compounding Period	Daily	Annually

Account Y

6.

	Account A	Account B
Nominal Interest Rate	2.65%	2.6%
Compounding Period	Quarterly	Continuously

Account A

ESSENTIAL QUESTION

7. How can you tell whether an exponential function models exponential growth or exponential decay?

Possible Answer: When the function is in the form $f(x) = ab^x$, if $b > 1$, the function models exponential growth, and if $0 < b < 1$, the function models exponential decay.

COMMON CORE Common Core Standards

Lesson	*Items*	Content Standards	Mathematical Practices
13.1	1	**F-BF.B.3**	**MP.6**
13.1	2	**F-BF.B.3**	**MP.6**
13.1	3	**F-BF.B.3**	**MP.6**
13.1	4	**F-BF.B.3**	**MP.6**
13.3	5	**F-LE.A.2**	**MP.6**
13.3	6	**F-LE.A.2**	**MP.6**

MODULE 13
MIXED REVIEW

Assessment Readiness

1. Consider the base of exponential functions. Will the given base cause exponential growth? Select Yes or No for A–C.
   - **A.** A base between 0 and 1 — ○ Yes ● No
   - **B.** A base greater than 1 — ● Yes ○ No
   - **C.** A base equal to 1 — ○ Yes ● No

2. Consider an investment of \$500 compounded annually with 3% interest. Choose True or False for each statement.
   - **A.** After 3 years, if no money is withdrawn, the account will have \$546.36 — ● Yes ○ No
   - **B.** The account will gain \$15.00 every year. — ○ Yes ● No
   - **C.** After 5 years, if no money is withdrawn, the account will have \$562.75. — ○ Yes ● No

3. Jordan said that the asymptote of $y = \left(\frac{1}{2}\right)^{x-2} + 3$ is $y = 2$. Describe and correct his mistake.

   Jordan looked in the wrong place to find the asymptote. The asymptote is the constant in the equation, not the constant in the exponent. The asymptote is $y = 3$.

4. Describe how $f(x) = |x|$ is changed to create $g(x) = \frac{3}{4}|x + 3| - 8$.

   The vertex is moved from $(0, 0)$ to $(-3, -8)$, and there is a horizontal stretch because of the value of a: $\frac{3}{4}$.

5. The graphs of $f(x) = 2^x$, $f(x) = 10^x$ and $f(x) = e^x$ all pass through a common point. Explain why the point $(0, 1)$ is common to all three functions.

   Any number except 0 raised to the 0 power is equal to 1. So, $2^0 = 10^0 = e^0 = 1$.

MIXED REVIEW
Assessment Readiness

ASSESSMENT AND INTERVENTION

Assign ready-made or customized practice tests to prepare students for high-stakes tests.

ADDITIONAL RESOURCES

Assessment Resources

- Leveled Module Quizzes: Modified, B

AVOID COMMON ERRORS

Item 2 Many students have trouble with compound interest and will revert to simple interest with any interest problem. Remind students to check their formulas and read the problem carefully to see which kind of interest they are looking for.

COMMON CORE **Common Core Standards**

Lesson	Items	Content Standards	Mathematical Practices
13.2	1	**F-BF.B.3**	**MP.6**
13.4	2	**F-LE.A.2**	**MP.1**
1.2, 13.2	3*	**F-BF.B.3**	**MP.3**
2.1	4*	**F-BF.B.3, F-IF.C.7b**	**MP.6**
13.1	5	**A-SSE.C.3c, F-IF.D.8b, F-BF.B.3**	**MP.8**

* Item integrates mixed review concepts from previous modules or a previous course.

Modeling with Exponential and Other Functions

ESSENTIAL QUESTION:

Answer: Being able to decide what type of function best fits a set of data allows you to make accurate predictions about a wide variety of different types of relationships.

PROFESSIONAL DEVELOPMENT VIDEO

Professional Development Video

Author Matt Larson models successful teaching practices in an actual high-school classroom.

Professional Development my.hrw.com

MODULE 14

Modeling with Exponential and Other Functions

Essential Question: How can modeling with exponential and other functions help you to solve real-world problems?

REAL WORLD VIDEO Most people have to save up money for a major purchase like a car or new home. Check out some of the factors to consider when investing for long-term goals.

MODULE PERFORMANCE TASK PREVIEW

Double Your Money!

If you had some money to invest, how would you pick the investment option that would let your money grow fastest? The return on an investment depends on factors such as the length of time of the investment and the return rate. How can you use an exponential model to find out when an investment will double in value? Let's find out!

DIGITAL TEACHER EDITION

Access a full suite of teaching resources when and where you need them:

- Access content online or offline
- Customize lessons to share with your class
- Communicate with your students in real-time
- View student grades and data instantly to target your instruction where it is needed most

PERSONAL MATH TRAINER

Assessment and Intervention

Assign automatically graded homework, quizzes, tests, and intervention activities. Prepare your students with updated, Common Core-aligned practice tests.

Are YOU Ready?

Complete these exercises to review skills you will need for this chapter.

- Online Homework
- Hints and Help
- Extra Practice

Writing Linear Equations

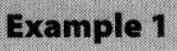

Write an equation for the line that passes through the points $(2, 3)$ and $(4, -1)$.

$\frac{-1-3}{4-2} = \frac{-4}{2} = -2$	Find the slope.
So $y = -2x + b$	Substitute slope for m in $y = mx + b$.
$(3) = -2(2) + b$	Substitute $(2, 3)$ for x- and y-values.
$b = 7$	Solve for b.

The equation is $y = -2x + 7$.

Write an equation for the line that passes through the given points.

1. $(2, -5), (6, -3)$ $y = 0.5x - 6$
2. $(4, -3), (-2, 15)$ $y = -3x + 9$
3. $(4, 7), (-2, -2)$ $y = 1.5x + 1$

Transforming Linear Functions

Example 2 Write the equation of $y = 9x - 2$ after a reflection across the x-axis followed by a reflection across the y-axis.

$y = -1(9x - 2) \rightarrow y = -9x + 2$	Reflection across the x-axis
$y = -9(-x) + 2 \rightarrow y = 9x + 2$	Reflection across the y-axis
So $y = 9x - 2$	Reflected across both axes is $y = 9x + 2$.

Write the equation of each function after a reflection across both axes.

4. $y = 2x + 1$ $y = 2x - 1$
5. $y = -3x - 4$ $y = -3x + 4$
6. $y = -0.2x + 6$ $y = -0.2x - 6$

Equations Involving Exponents

Example 3 Solve $x^{\frac{2}{3}} = 16$ for x.

$\left(x^{\frac{2}{3}}\right)^{\frac{3}{2}} = \pm (16)^{\frac{3}{2}}$	Raise both sides to the same power.
$x = \pm \left(16^{\frac{1}{2}}\right)^3 = \pm (4)^3 = \pm 64$	Evaluate the right side.
So, $x = \pm 64$.	

Solve for x.

7. $x^6 = 4096$ ± 4
8. $x^{\frac{3}{2}} = 27$ 9
9. $\frac{1}{3}x^{\frac{2}{5}} = 3$ ± 243

Response to Intervention			Differentiated Instruction
Tier 1 Lesson Intervention Worksheets	**Tier 2** Strategic Intervention Skills Intervention Worksheets	**Tier 3** Intensive Intervention Worksheets available online	
Reteach 14.1 Reteach 14.2	7 Equations Involving Exponents 9 Exponents 15 Graphing Linear... 31 Slope... 38 Transforming Linear... 40 Writing Linear...	Building Block Skills 29, 41, 43, 44, 46, 52, 75, 76, 96, 100, 103, 111	Challenge worksheets Extend the Math Lesson Activities in TE

Are You Ready?

ASSESS READINESS

Use the assessment on this page to determine if students need strategic or intensive intervention for the module's prerequisite skills.

ASSESSMENT AND INTERVENTION

RtI Response to Intervention TIER 1, TIER 2, TIER 3 SKILLS

Personal Math Trainer will automatically create a standards-based, personalized intervention assignment for your students, targeting each student's individual needs!

ADDITIONAL RESOURCES

See the table below for a full list of intervention resources available for this module.

Response to Intervention Resources also includes:

- Tier 2 Skill Pre-Tests for each Module
- Tier 2 Skill Post-Tests for each skill

LESSON 14.1

Fitting Exponential Functions to Data

Common Core Math Standards

The student is expected to:

 **S.ID.B.6a**

Fit a function to the data; use functions fitted to data to solve problems in the context of the data. Also A.CED.A.2, F.IF.B.4, F.IF.C.7e

Mathematical Practices

 **MP.5 Using Tools**

Language Objective

Explain to a partner how to find an exponential regression model.

ENGAGE

Essential Question: What are ways to model data using an exponential function of the form $f(x) = ab^x$?

One way is to roughly fit an exponential function to the data by identifying the initial value a and estimating the growth factor b. Another way is to perform exponential regression using a graphing calculator.

PREVIEW: LESSON PERFORMANCE TASK

View the Engage section online. Discuss the photo and ask students what data they would need to model the number and size of farms. Then preview the Lesson Performance Task.

Name________________ Class____________ Date________

14.1 Fitting Exponential Functions to Data

Resource Locker

Essential Question: What are ways to model data using an exponential function of the form $f(x) = ab^x$?

Explore — Identifying Exponential Functions from Tables of Values

Notice for an exponential function $f(x) = ab^x$ that $f(x+1) = ab^{x+1}$. By the product of powers property, $ab^{x+1} = a(b^x \cdot b^1) = ab^x \cdot b = f(x) \cdot b$. So, $f(x+1) = f(x) \cdot b$. This means that increasing the value of x by 1 multiplies the value of $f(x)$ by b. In other words, for successive integer values of x, each value of $f(x)$ is b times the value before it, or, equivalently, the ratio between successive values of $f(x)$ is b. This gives you a test to apply to a given set of data to see whether it represents exponential growth or decay.

Each table gives function values for successive integer values of x. Find the ratio of successive values of $f(x)$ to determine whether each set of data can be modeled by an exponential function.

 A

x	0	1	2	3	4
$f(x)$	1	4	16	64	256

$\frac{f(1)}{f(0)} = 4$; $\frac{f(2)}{f(1)} = 4$; $\frac{f(3)}{f(2)} = 4$; $\frac{f(4)}{f(3)} = 4$

The data (are)/are not exponential.

 B

x	0	1	2	3	4
$f(x)$	1	7	13	19	25

$\frac{f(1)}{f(0)} = 7$; $\frac{f(2)}{f(1)} = \frac{13}{7}$; $\frac{f(3)}{f(2)} = \frac{19}{13}$; $\frac{f(4)}{f(3)} = \frac{25}{19}$

The data are/are not exponential.

 C

x	0	1	2	3	4
$f(x)$	1	4	13	28	49

$\frac{f(1)}{f(0)} = 4$; $\frac{f(2)}{f(1)} = \frac{13}{4}$; $\frac{f(3)}{f(2)} = \frac{28}{13}$; $\frac{f(4)}{f(3)} = \frac{7}{4}$

The data are/(are not) exponential.

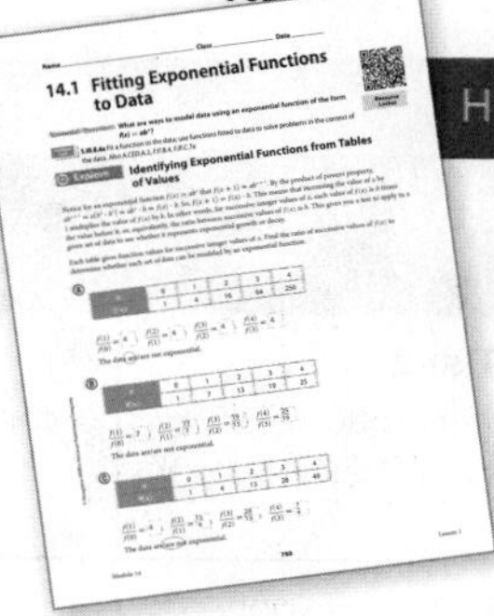

HARDCOVER PAGES 703–720

Watch for the hardcover student edition page numbers for this lesson.

x	0	1	2	3	4
$f(x)$	1	0.25	0.0625	0.015625	0.00390625

$\frac{f(1)}{f(0)} = \frac{1}{4}$; $\frac{f(2)}{f(1)} = \frac{1}{4}$; $\frac{f(3)}{f(2)} = \frac{1}{4}$; $\frac{f(4)}{f(3)} = \frac{1}{4}$

The data (are)/are not exponential.

Reflect

1. In which step(s) does the table show exponential growth? Which shows exponential decay? What is the base of the growth or decay?

Step A shows exponential growth with a base of 4; Step D shows exponential decay with a base of $\frac{1}{4}$.

2. In which step are the data modeled by the exponential function $f(x) = 4^{-x}$?

Step D

3. What type of function model would be appropriate in each step not modeled by an exponential function? Explain your reasoning.

In Step B, a linear model is appropriate because there is a constant change of 6 in the function value for every change of 1 in the value of x. In Step C, a quadratic model is appropriate because the second differences of the function values are constant: the first differences are 3, 9, 15, and 21, so the second differences are all 6.

4. **Discussion** In the introduction to this Explore, you saw that the ratio between successive terms of $f(x) = ab^x$ is b. Find and simplify an expression for $f(x + c)$ where c is a constant. Then explain how this gives you a more general test to determine whether a set of data can be modeled by an exponential function.

$f(x + c) = ab^{x+c} = a(b^x \cdot b^c) = ab^x \cdot b^c = f(x) \cdot b^c$; This means that increasing the value of x by c multiplies the value of $f(x)$ by b^c. The ratio $\frac{f(x+c)}{f(x)} = \frac{f(x) \cdot b^c}{f(x)} = b^c$. In other words, the ratio is constant. So, if x-values in a set of data differ by *any* constant amount and the ratio of function values at those x-values is constant, then an exponential model is appropriate.

Explain 1 Roughly Fitting an Exponential Function to Data

As the answer to the last Reflect question above indicates, if the ratios of successive values of the dependent variable in a data set for equally-spaced values of the independent variable are equal, an exponential function model fits. In the real world, sets of data rarely fit a model perfectly, but if the ratios are approximately equal, an exponential function can still be a good model.

PROFESSIONAL DEVELOPMENT

Learning Progressions

In this lesson, students continue their study of fitting models to data from algebra. They previously learned how to find linear and quadratic models for data, and now apply these techniques to exponential data sets. They find exponential regression equations both by examining tables of values and by using graphing calculators. They compare scatter plots of the data with graphs of functions associated with the regression equation, using technology. A comparison of these two graphs can help determine how well the regression model fits the data.

EXPLORE

Identifying Exponential Functions From Tables of Values

INTEGRATE TECHNOLOGY

Students have the option of completing the exponential function activity either in the book or online.

QUESTIONING STRATEGIES

? How do you tell from a table whether the function that fits the data is exponential? **Examine successive $f(x)$-values. The function is exponential if the ratio between values is constant when the values of the independent variable are equally spaced.**

? How can you tell whether a function that fits the data is an exponential growth function or an exponential decay function? **If the ratio between successive $f(x)$ values is greater than 1, then the function is exponential growth. If the ratio is between 0 and 1, then the function is exponential decay.**

EXPLAIN 1

Roughly Fitting an Exponential Function to Data

AVOID COMMON ERRORS

Some students may not interpret a table correctly when they look for exponential models. Caution them to clearly identify the parameters for the dependent variable and the independent variable when they describe the function. Tell them to look for a constant ratio between the dependent variable values as the independent variable increases in equally spaced increments.

QUESTIONING STRATEGIES

? How can you tell, just from analyzing a table, that a linear model would not be a good fit? The amount of increase in the values for the dependent variable is not close to being constant.

? How can you tell that a regression equation represents an exponential growth function? The value of b in an equation of the form $f(x) = ab^x$ is greater than 1.

Example 1

Ⓐ **Population Statistics** The table gives the official population of the United States for the years 1790 to 1890.

Year	Total Population
1790	3,929,214
1800	5,308,483
1810	7,239,881
1820	9,638,453
1830	12,860,702
1840	17,063,353
1850	23,191,876
1860	31,443,321
1870	38,558,371
1880	50,189,209
1890	62,979,766

Create an approximate exponential model for the data set. Then graph your function with a scatter plot of the data and assess its fit.

It appears that the ratio of the population in each decade to the population of the decade before it is pretty close to one and one third, so an exponential model should be reasonable.

For a model of the form $f(x) = ab^x$, $f(0) = a$. So, if x is the number of decades after 1790, the value when $x = 0$ is a, the initial population in 1790, or 3,929,214.

One way to estimate the growth factor, b, is to find the population ratios from decade to decade and average them:

$$\frac{1.35 + 1.36 + 1.33 + 1.33 + 1.33 + 1.36 + 1.36 + 1.23 + 1.30 + 1.26}{10} \approx 1.32$$

An approximate model is $f(x) = 3.93(1.32)^x$, where $f(x)$ is in millions.

The graph is shown.

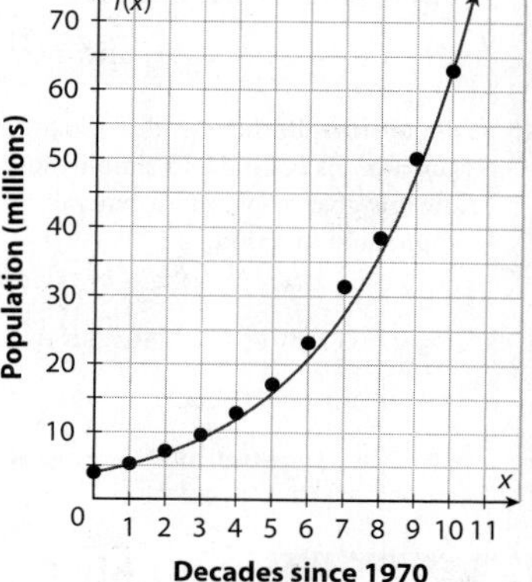

The graph looks like a good fit for the data. All of the points lie on, or close to, the curve.

Another way to estimate b is to choose a point other than $(0, a)$ from the scatter plot that appears would lie on, or very close to, the best-fitting exponential curve. Substitute the coordinates in the general formula and solve for b. For the plot shown, the point (8, 38.56) looks like a good choice.

$$38.56 = 3.93 \cdot b^8$$

$$(9.81)^{\frac{1}{8}} \approx (b^8)^{\frac{1}{8}}$$

$$1.33 \approx b$$

This value of b results in a model very similar to the previous model.

COLLABORATIVE LEARNING

Peer-to-Peer Activity

Have students work in pairs to find regression equations for data sets and to graph the data sets. Have one student enter the data into a graphing calculator and find the regression equation, and the other student graph the data as a scatter plot, then graph the function associated with the regression equation. Have students switch roles and repeat the exercise using another set of data.

Ⓑ **Movies** The table shows the decline in weekly box office revenue from its peak for one of 2013's top-grossing summer movies.

Week	Revenue (in Millions of Dollars)
0	95.3
1	55.9
2	23.7
3	16.4
4	8.8
5	4.8
6	3.3
7	1.9
8	1.1
9	0.6

Create an approximate exponential model for the data set. Then graph your function with a scatter plot of the data and assess its fit.

Find the value of a in $f(x) = ab^x$.

When $x = 0$, $f(x) =$ **95.3**. So, $a =$ **95.3**.

Find an estimate for b.

Approximate the revenue ratios from week to week and average them:

$$\frac{0.59 + 0.42 + 0.69 + 0.54 + \boxed{0.55 + 0.69 + 0.58 + 0.58} + 0.55}{\boxed{9}} \approx \boxed{0.58}$$

An approximate model is $f(x) = \boxed{95.3(0.58)^x}$.

The graph looks like a very good fit for the data. All of the points except one (2 weeks after peak revenue) lie on, or very close to, the curve.

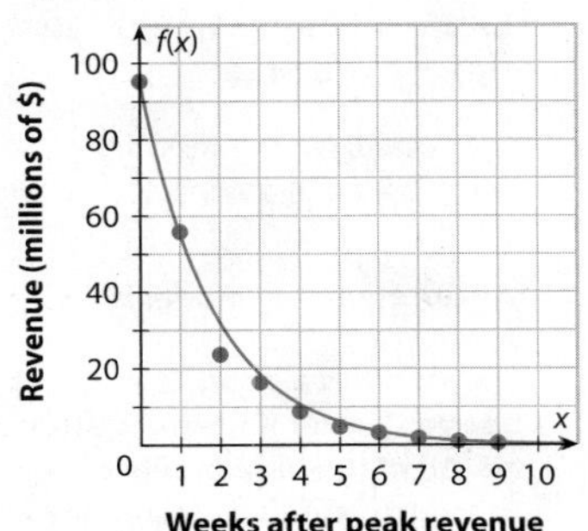

DIFFERENTIATE INSTRUCTION

Critical Thinking

Some students may need help understanding how to interpret the regression equations for real-world exponential models. Have them work in small groups to discuss how a regression equation is found and what the meaning of each parameter in the equation is. Ask one student to explain what the value of a represents in a real-world exponential model, and have another student explain what the value of b represents. Have a third student predict what a change in the value of a means in terms of the real-world data set, and then check the prediction by re-entering the data into the calculator and finding a new regression equation.

Your Turn

5. Fisheries The total catch in tons for Iceland's fisheries from 2002 to 2010 is shown in the table.

Year	Total Catch (Millions of Tons)
2002	2.145
2003	2.002
2004	1.750
2005	1.661
2006	1.345
2007	1.421
2008	1.307
2009	1.164
2010	1.063

Create an approximate exponential model for the data set. Then graph your function with a scatter plot of the data and assess its fit.

Let x represent years after 2002 and $f(x)$ represent the catch in millions of tons. Then $f(0) = a = 2.145$.

Estimate b by averaging the catch ratios from year to year:

$$\frac{0.93 + 0.87 + 0.95 + 0.81 + 1.06 + 0.92 + 0.89 + 0.91}{8} \approx 0.92$$

An approximate model is $f(x) = 2.15(0.92)^x$, where $f(x)$ is in million of tons.

The model is a good fit, but it appears that it would be even better if it were shifted down just a little bit. All of the data points except for 2006 are close to the curve, but the point for 2006 does not follow the general trend anyway.

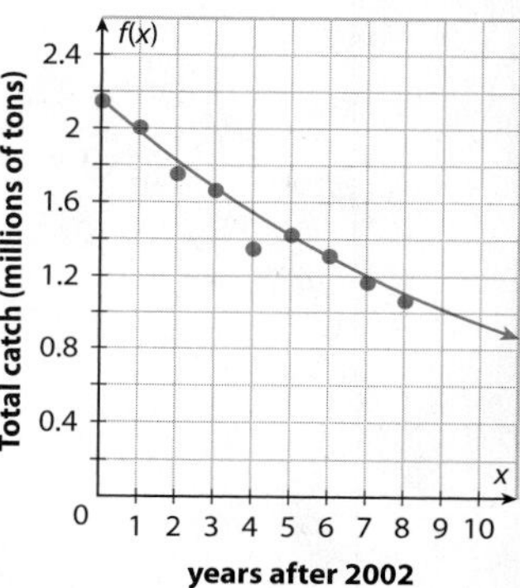

Explain 2 Fitting an Exponential Function to Data Using Technology

Previously you have used a graphing calculator to find a linear regression model of the form $y = ax + b$ to model data, and have also found quadratic regression models of the form $y = ax^2 + bx + c$. Similarly, you can use a graphing calculator to perform exponential regression to produce a model of the form $f(x) = ab^x$.

Example 2

 **Population Statistics** Use the data from Example 1 Part A and a graphing calculator to find the exponential regression model for the data, and show the graph of the model with the scatter plot.

Using the STAT menu, enter the number of decades since 1790 in List1 and the population to the nearest tenth of a million in List2.

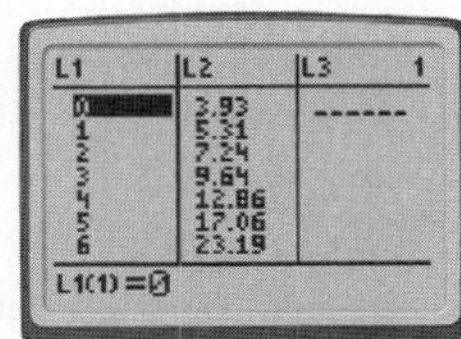

Using the STAT CALC menu, choose "ExpReg" and press ENTER until you see this screen:

An approximate model is $f(x) = 4.116(1.323)^x$.

Making sure that STATPLOT is turned "On," enter the model into the Y = menu either directly or using the VARS menu and choosing "Statistics," "EQ," and "RegEQ.") The graphs are shown using the ZoomStat window:

Plotted with the second graph from Example 1 (shown dotted), you can see that the graphs are nearly identical.

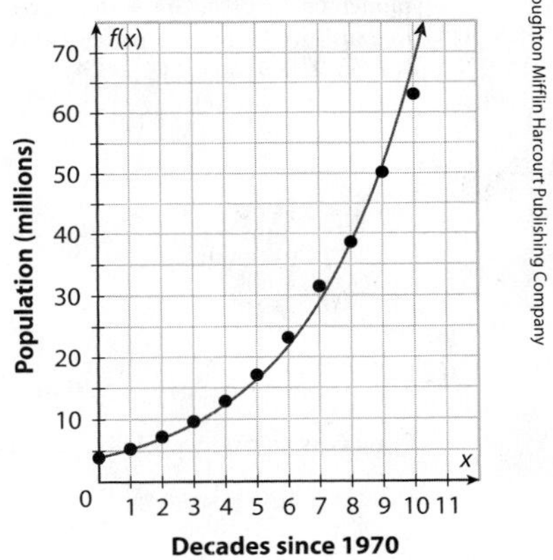

EXPLAIN 2

Fitting an Exponential Function to Data Using Technology

QUESTIONING STRATEGIES

? How can you compare the regression equation found with a graphing calculator to the model you derive from your own calculations? **View the graph of the data set together with the graph of the function for the regression model.**

? What does the value of r represent in the graphing calculator model? **the *correlation coefficient,* which roughly indicates how closely the model fits the data overall**

AVOID COMMON ERRORS

Students may graph regression equations on the graphing calculator using rounded values for a and b. Remind them that after performing the regression, the calculator stores very accurate estimations for these values. Students may need help accessing the exponential regression equation and ensuring that those values will be used in graphing the regression model.

(B) **Movies** Use the data from Example 1 Part B and a graphing calculator to find the exponential regression model for the data. Graph the regression model on the calculator, then graph the model from Example 1 on the same screen using a dashed curve. How do the graphs of the models compare? What can you say about the actual decline in revenue from one week after the peak to two weeks after the peak compared to what the regression model indicates?

Enter the data and perform exponential regression.

The model (using 3 digits of precision is $f(x) =$ **$86.2(0.576)^x$**.

The graphs of the models are very close, but the regression equation starts with a lower initial value, and comes closer to the data point that the first model misses by the most. The last several weeks the models appear to be very close together. From the data, the decline from one week after the peak to two weeks after the peak was significantly larger than accounted for by the regression model.

Reflect

6. **Discussion** The U.S. population in 2014 was close to 320 million people. What does the regression model in Part A predict for the population in 2014? What does this tell you about extrapolating far into the future using an exponential model? How does the graph of the scatter plot with the regression model support this conclusion? (Note: The decade-to-decade U.S. growth dropped below 30% to stay after 1880, and below 20% to stay after 1910. From 2000 to 2010, the rate was below 10%.)
About 2.2 billion people; you should be very cautious about predicting far into the future: the graph of an exponential growth model rises faster and faster, so it is hard to maintain this growth over a long period of time in the real world. In the graph, you can see that after about 1860, the growth already begins to fall below the model's prediction, and for 1890, the actual population is well below the model's prediction.

Your Turn

7. **Fisheries** Use the data from YourTurn5 and a graphing calculator to find the exponential regression model for the data. Graph the regression model on the calculator, then graph the model from your answer to YourTurn5 on the same screen. How do the graphs of the models compare?
$f(x) = 2.119(0.9174)^x$

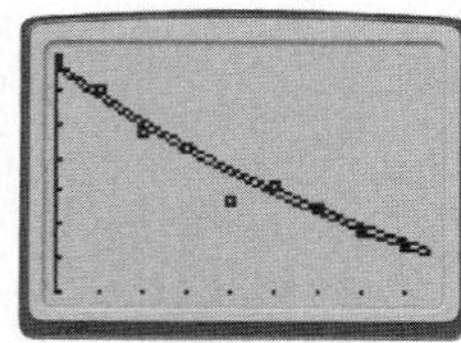

The graphs are close together with almost the exact same amount of curvature. The regression model lies just a little lower than the model from YourTurn3, and thus is a better model.

 Explain 3

Solving a Real-World Problem Using a Fitted Exponential Function

In the real world, the purpose of finding a mathematical model is to help identify trends or patterns, and to use them to make generalizations, predictions, or decisions based on the data.

Example 3

 The Texas population increased from 20.85 million to 25.15 million from 2000 to 2010.

a. Assuming exponential growth during the period, write a model where $x = 0$ represents the year 2000 and $x = 1$ represents the year 2010. What was the growth rate over the decade?

b. Use the power of a power property of exponents to rewrite the model so that b is the yearly growth factor instead of the growth factor for the decade. What is the yearly growth rate for this model? Verify that the model gives the correct population for 2010.

c. The Texas population was about 26.45 million in 2013. How does this compare with the prediction made by the model?

d. Find the model's prediction for the Texas population in 2035. Do you think it is reasonable to use this model to guide decisions about future needs for water, energy generation, and transportation needs. Explain your reasoning.

a. For a model of the form $f(x) = ab^x$, a $= f(0)$, so $a = 20.85$. To find an estimate for b, substitute $(x, f(x)) = (1, 25.5)$ and solve for b.

$$f(x) = a \cdot b^x$$

$$25.15 = 20.85 \cdot b^1$$

$$\frac{25.15}{20.85} = b$$

$$1.206 \approx b$$

An approximate model is $f(x) = 20.85(1.206)^x$. The growth rate was about 20.6%.

b. Because there are 10 years in a decade, the 10th power of the new b must give 1.206, the growth factor for the decade. So, $b^{10} = 1.206$, or $b = 1.206^{\frac{1}{10}}$. Use the power of a power property:

$$f(x) = 20.85(1.206)^x = 20.85\left(1.206^{\frac{1}{10}}\right)^{10x} \approx 20.85(1.019)^{10x}$$

Because x is decades after 2000, this is equivalent to $f(x) = 20.85(1.019)^x$ where x is years after 2000.

The model gives a 2010 population of $f(x) = 20.85(1.019)^{10} \approx 25.17$. This agrees with the actual population within a rounding error.

c. Substitute $x = 13$ into the model $f(x) = 20.85(1.019)^x$:

$$f(13) = 20.85(1.019)^{13} \approx 26.63$$

The prediction is just a little bit higher than the actual population.

d. For 2035, $x = 35$: $f(35) = 20.85(1.019)^{35} \approx 40.3$. The model predicts a Texas population of about 40 million in 2035. Possible answer: Because it is very difficult to maintain a high growth rate with an already very large population, and with overall population growth slowing, it seems unreasonable that the population would increase from 25 to 40 million so quickly. But because using the model to project even to 2020 gives a population of over 30 million, it seems reasonable to make plans for the population to grow by several million people over a relatively short period.

EXPLAIN 3

Solving a Real-World Problem Using a Fitted Exponential Function

QUESTIONING STRATEGIES

? For two sets of data, how might you decide whether one is better fit by an exponential regression equation than the other? **Compare the values of r or look at the graphs and data points together. The one with a better fit may be obvious visually, or you may find the one with the greater value of r may be a better fit.**

? How can you use an exponential model for a real-world situation to help you make decisions? **The trends shown by an exponential growth or decay model may be useful in making decisions based upon predictions, if those trends seem reliable.**

INTEGRATE MATHEMATICAL PRACTICES

Focus on Reasoning

MP.2 Encourage students to use the functionality of the graphing calculator to view the scatter plot of a data set along with the function associated with the regression equation. If the graph of the function shows that the scatter plot is not very well correlated with the function, then the model may not be a good representation of the data.

(B) The average revenue per theater for the movie in Part B of the previous Examples is shown in the graph. (Note that for this graph, Week 0 corresponds to Week 2 of the graphs from the previous Examples.) The regression model is $y = 5.65(0.896)^x$.

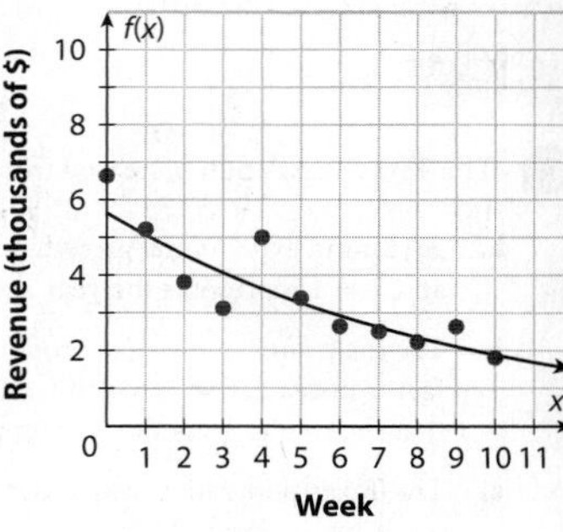

a. From Week 3 to Week 4, there is a jump of over 60% in the average weekly revenue per theater, but the total revenue for the movie for the corresponding week fell by over 30%. What must have occurred for this to be true?

There must have been a sharp reduction in the number of theaters showing the movie.

b. A new theater complex manager showing a similar summer movie in a single theater worries about quickly dropping revenue the first few weeks, and wants to stop showing the movie. Suppose you are advising the manager. Knowing that the model shown reflects the long-term trend well for such movies, what advice would you give the manager?

Possible answer: Be careful about removing the movie too quickly. Unless the amount of weekly revenue needed is very high, the model indicates that the longer-term trend may decline more slowly than the short-term trend.

Reflect

8. Discussion Consider the situation in Example 3B about deciding when to stop showing the movie. How does an understanding of what other theater managers might do affect your decision?

Possible answer: If too many managers keep showing the movie, the average revenue will drop more quickly, but if too many stop showing the movie, the average revenue per theater could rise sharply, so knowing what other managers might help you know when it is wise to do the opposite.

Your Turn

9. Graph the regression model for the catch in Icelandic fisheries, $f(x) = 2.119(0.9174^x)$, to find when the model predicts the total catches to drop below 0.5 million tons (remember that $x = 0$ corresponds to 2002). Should the model be used to project actual catch into the future? Why or why not? What are some considerations that the model raises about the fishery?

About 2018 or 2019; no, the model shows the fishery declining rapidly; possible elaboration: The model indicates that the reasons for the decline must be found and necessary changes made to ensure the productivity of the fishery. Some of these considerations are the total catch in the fisheries by other countries as well as by Iceland, whether and where overfishing is taking place, the health of the overall ocean environment in the areas, the health of the harvestable fish population as well as of species that it depends on, how quickly populations of different species can recover, and so on.

Elaborate

10. How can you tell whether a given set of data can reasonably be modeled using an exponential function?
If the ratios of successive values of the dependent variable in a data set for equally-spaced values of the independent variable are approximately equal, an exponential function model is reasonable.

11. What are some ways that an exponential growth or decay model can be used to guide decisions, preparations, or judgments about the future?
Possible answer: A city undergoing exponential growth with current trends projected to continue can use a growth model to help guide decisions to plan for increased water and electricity needs, transportation infrastructure needs, economic growth and opportunity needs, land use needs, and so on. For a species whose population is undergoing exponential decline, the model can help identify the need for understanding the causes of the decline and to institute land use or other strategies to help restore the population.

12. Essential Question Check-In What are some ways to find an approximate exponential model for a set of data without using a graphing calculator?
You can use the value when $x = 0$ to find the value of a. To find an estimate for b, you can average the (approximately constant) ratios of the successive terms, or choose a ratio between terms that looks representative. Another way to estimate b is to choose a point other than $(0, a)$ from the scatter plot that appears would lie on, or very close to, the best-fitting exponential curve. Then substitute the coordinates of this point into the general exponential model $f(x) = ab^x$ and solve for b.

ELABORATE

INTEGRATE MATHEMATICAL PRACTICES

Focus on Patterns

MP.8 Discuss with students how to determine whether an exponential model fits a data set. Give them several data sets and have them predict which data sets are exponential. Then have them enter the data sets into a graphing calculator to check their graphs.

QUESTIONING STRATEGIES

? What does a real-world exponential model $y = ab^x$ describe in terms of a set of data? The value of a represents a starting data point for $x = 0$. If x represents time passed, then a is the value before any time has passed. The value of b represents the growth or decay factor, or the rate of growth or decay between the data points. It may be close to the ratio of two y-values of a data set.

SUMMARIZE THE LESSON

? How do you find an exponential regression equation of the form $f(x) = ab^x$? You can substitute the values of several data points to find the value of a, and then find the overall ratio of successive values of $f(x)$ to find b. You can also use a graphing calculator to find the exponential regression equation.

LANGUAGE SUPPORT EL

Communicate Math

Help students to understand how the term *regression equation* is used to express an exponential model. Explain that a *regression* is *a statistical analysis of data*, and that a *regression equation* may be *the result of analyzing data*. Ask them to enter data values into a graphing calculator as lists, and then observe a scatter plot of the data. Explain how to activate the calculator's regression features and how to obtain the values of the variables in the regression equation of the form $f(x) = ab^x$ for the data.

EVALUATE

ASSIGNMENT GUIDE

Concepts and Skills	Practice
Explore Identifying Exponential Functions From Tables of Values	Exercises 1–8
Example 1 Roughly Fitting an Exponential Function to Data	Exercises 9, 10, 16
Example 2 Fitting an Exponential Function to Data Using Technology	Exercises 9, 11, 14
Example 3 Solving a Real-World Problem Using a Fitted Exponential Function	Exercises 9, 12, 13, 15

INTEGRATE MATHEMATICAL PRACTICES

Focus on Reasoning

MP.2 Remind students to check their exponential models by substituting the values from data points into the model and verifying that the model is a good fit. Remind students that a graph of the model may not pass through any of the actual data points in a scatter plot of the data.

Evaluate: Homework and Practice

- Online Homework
- Hints and Help
- Extra Practice

Determine whether each set of data can be modeled by an exponential function. If it can, tell whether it represents exponential growth or exponential decay. If it can't, tell whether a linear or quadratic model is instead appropriate.

1.

x	0	1	2	3	4
$f(x)$	2	6	18	54	162

Ratios of successive terms: $\frac{6}{2} = 3$, $\frac{18}{6} = 3$, $\frac{54}{18} = 3$, $\frac{162}{54} = 3$

The ratios are constant and greater than 1; exponential growth.

2.

x	1	2	3	4	5	6
$f(x)$	1	2	3	5	8	13

Ratios of successive terms: $\frac{2}{1}, \frac{3}{2}, \frac{5}{3}, \frac{8}{5}, \frac{13}{8}$

The ratios are not constant. Also, the first and second differences are not equal. Not exponential, linear, nor quadratic.

3.

x	0	1	2	3	4
$f(x)$	2	8	18	32	50

Ratios of successive terms: $\frac{8}{2} = 4$, $\frac{18}{8} = \frac{9}{4}$, $\frac{32}{18} = \frac{16}{9}$, $\frac{50}{32} = \frac{25}{16}$

The ratios are not constant. First differences: 6, 10, 14, 18. Second differences: 4, 4, 4. The second differences are constant, so a quadratic model is appropriate.

4.

x	5	10	15	20	25
$f(x)$	76.2	66.2	59.1	50.9	44.6

Ratios of successive terms: $\frac{66.2}{76.2} \approx 0.87$, $\frac{59.1}{66.2} \approx 0.89$, $\frac{50.9}{59.1} \approx 0.86$, $\frac{44.6}{50.9} \approx 0.88$

The ratios are approximately constant and less than 1; exponential decay.

Exercise	Depth of Knowledge (D.O.K.)	COMMON CORE Mathematical Practices
1–8	**1** Recall of Information	**MP.2** Reasoning
9–13	**1** Recall of Information	**MP.4** Modeling
14–16	**2** Skills/Concepts H.O.T.	**MP.3** Logic

Three students, Anja, Ben, and Celia, are asked to find an approximate exponential model for the data shown. Use the data and scatter plot for Exercises 5–7.

x	0	1	2	3	4	5	6	7	8	9	10
$f(x)$	10	6.0	5.4	3.9	3.7	2.3	1.4	1.0	0.9	0.8	0.5

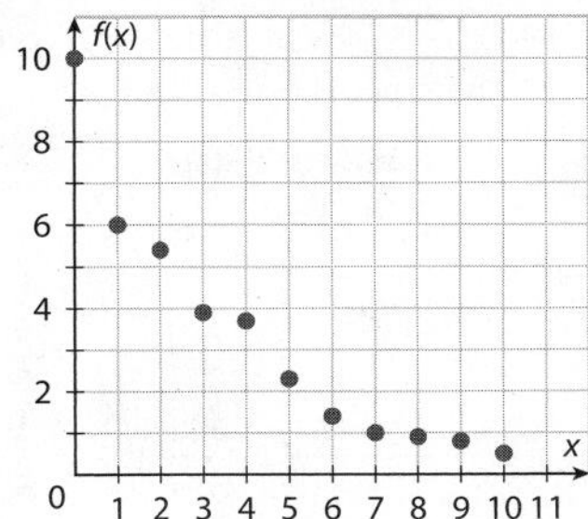

5. To find an approximate exponential model, Anja uses the first data point to find a, and then estimates b by finding the ratio of the first two function values. What is her model?

From $(0, 10)$, $f(0) = a \cdot b^0 = a$, so $a = 10$.

$b \approx \frac{6.0}{10} = 0.60$

Anja's model is $f(x) = 10(0.60)^x$.

6. To find his model, Ben uses the first and last data points. What is his model?

The points are $(0, 10)$ and $(10, 0.5)$. From $(0, 10)$, $f(0) = a \cdot b^0 = a$, so $a = 10$.

Substitute the coordinates of $(10, 0.5)$ into the model and solve for b.

$$f(x) = a \cdot b^x$$
$$0.5 = 10 \cdot b^{10}$$
$$0.05^{\frac{1}{10}} = b$$
$$0.74 \approx b$$

Ben's model is $f(x) = 10(0.74)^x$.

7. Celia thinks that because the drop between the first two points is so large, the best model might actually have a y-intercept a little below 10. She uses $(0, 9.5)$ to estimate a in her model. To estimate b, she finds the average of the ratios of successive data values. What is her model? (Use two digits of precision for all quantities.)

From $(0, 9.5)$, $f(0) = a \cdot b^0 = a$, so $a = 9.5$.

Estimate b: $\frac{0.60 + 0.90 + 0.72 + 0.95 + 0.62 + 0.61 + 0.71 + 0.90 + 0.89 + 0.63}{10} \approx 0.76$

Celia's model is $f(x) = 9.5(0.76)^x$.

COOPERATIVE LEARNING

Have students work in small groups to make a poster showing how to apply the steps for finding a regression equation using technology. Give each group a different data set and have them include a scatter plot of the data. Then have each group present its poster to the rest of the class, and ask for a volunteer from the group to explain each step.

INTEGRATE MATHEMATICAL PRACTICES

Focus on Modeling

MP.4 When modeling a problem in which an exponential regression equation applies, have students start with a scatter plot of the data. This will help them remember that the data points should be increasing (or decreasing) at a rapid rate, depending on the original real-world problem.

8. **Classic Cars** The data give the estimated value in dollars of a model of classic car over several years.

15,4300	16,2100	17,300	18,400	19,600	20,700	22,000

a. Find an approximate exponential model for the car's value by averaging the successive ratios of the value. Then make a scatter plot of the data, graph your model with the scatter plot, and assess its fit to the data.

Let $x = 0$ represent the year corresponding to the value \$15,300. Let $f(x)$ be in thousands of dollars.

From the point $(0, 15.3)$, $a = 15.3$.

Estimate b by averaging the value ratios from year to year:

$$\frac{1.052 + 1.068 + 1.064 + 1.065 + 1.056 + 1.063}{6}$$

≈ 1.061

An approximate model is $f(x) = 15.3(1.061)^x$.

The model fits the data very well.

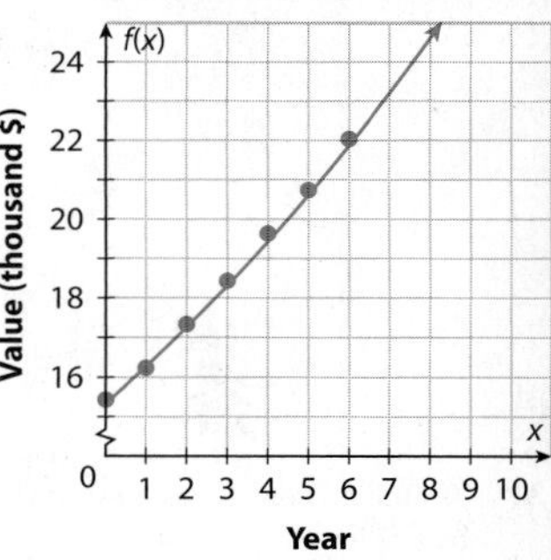

b. In the last year of the data, a car enthusiast spends \$15,100 on a car of the given model that is in need of some work. The owner then spends \$8300 restoring it. Use your model to create a table of values with a graphing calculator. How long does the function model predict the owner should keep the car before it can be sold for a profit of at least \$5000?

The owner spent a total of \$23,400 for the car. To make a profit of at least \$5000, the selling price must be at least \$28,400.

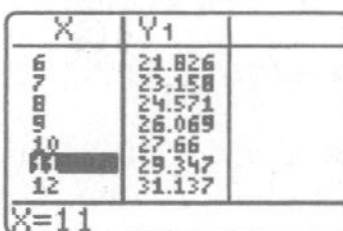

X	Y1
6	21.826
7	23.158
8	24.571
9	26.069
10	27.66
11	29.347
12	31.137

X=11

The table shows the value exceeding \$28,400 at year 11. Because the owner bought the car at year 6 of the model, this means that the model predicts that the owner needs to wait for about 5 years.

9. **Movies** The table shows the average price of a movie ticket in the United States from 2001 to 2010.

Year	2001	2002	2003	2004	2005	2006	2007	2008	2009	2010
Price ($)	5.66	5.81	6.03	6.21	6.41	6.55	6.88	7.18	7.50	7.89

a. Make a scatter plot of the data. Then use the first point and another point on the plot to find an approximate exponential model for the average ticket price. Then graph the model with your scatter plot and assess its fit to the data.

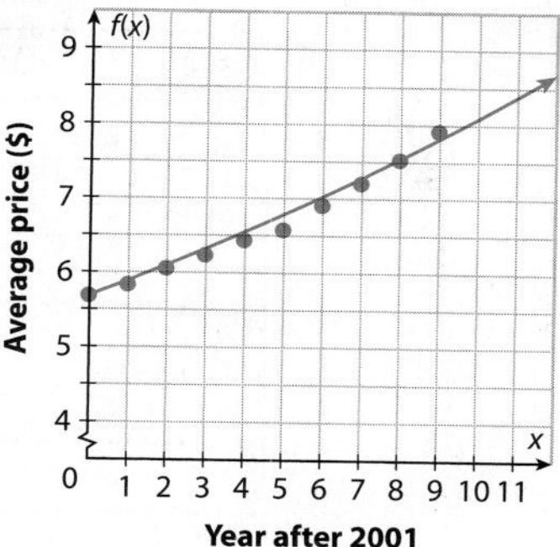

Possible answer: Let x represent years after 2001. From the point $(0, 5.66)$, $a = 5.66$. Choose the point for 2009, $(8, 7.50)$ and substitute the coordinates into the model.

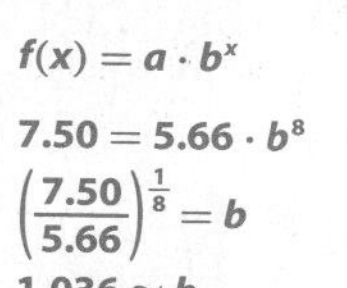

$f(x) = a \cdot b^x$

$7.50 = 5.66 \cdot b^8$

$\left(\frac{7.50}{5.66}\right)^{\frac{1}{8}} = b$

$1.036 \approx b$

An approximate model is $f(x) = 5.66(1.036)^x$. Overall, the model fits the trend fairly well, though it overestimates the price a little in the middle of the data, and passes below the last data point.

b. Use a graphing calculator to find a regression model for the data, and graph the model with the scatter plot. How does this model compare to your previous model?

Regression model: $f(x) = 5.59(1.037)^x$

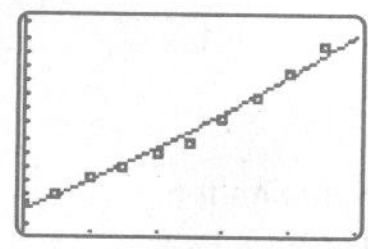

The regression model is very close to the model in Exercise 6. Its graph starts just a bit below the first model's graph, and it rises a tiny bit more steeply, but the models are very close together at the end of the period of the data.

c. What does the regression model predict for the average cost in 2014? How does this compare with the actual 2014 cost of about $8.35? A theater owner uses the model in 2010 to project income for 2014 assuming average sales of 490 tickets per day at the predicted price. If the actual price is instead $8.35, did the owner make a good business decision? Explain.

Prediction: $f(13) = 5.59(1.037)^{13} \approx$ $8.96; this is about $.616 more per ticket than the actual. No, for the year, the revenue shortfall would be about $490(365)(0.66) \approx$ $109,000, which is a large amount of money. $0.61 accounts for about 7% of the individual ticket price which is a large amount.

INTEGRATE MATHEMATICAL PRACTICES

Focus on Reasoning

MP.2 When analyzing a regression equation, ask students to make sure the equation makes sense with respect to the original data set. Have them check several data points in the model to see if the model fits the points fairly closely. Caution them that the actual values of a and b in an exponential model of the form $f(x) = ab^x$ may not appear anywhere in the actual data set.

CONNECT VOCABULARY EL

For students familiar with the term *line of best fit* as used in linear regression models, it is useful to connect this idea to a notion of "curve of best fit" for exponential (or quadratic) regression. Modeling these types of regression models may help them understand the idea of a "curve of best fit."

AVOID COMMON ERRORS

Students may have difficulty interpreting a real-world exponential model. Explain that the model may be limited by the constraints of the data, but it may still provide insights for decision-making. Emphasize that students may have to estimate the trend in the data if it is to be extrapolated.

10. Pharmaceuticals A new medication is being studied to see how quickly it is metabolized in the body. The table shows how much of an initial dose of 15 milligrams remains in the bloodstream after different intervals of time.

Hours Since Administration	Amount Remaining (mg)
0	15
1	14.3
2	13.1
3	12.4
4	11.4
5	10.7
6	10.2
7	9.8

a. Use a graphing calculator to find a regression model. Use the calculator to graph the model with the scatter plot. How much of the drug is eliminated each hour?

a. Model: $f(x) = 15.0(0.937)^x$

The decay factor is 0.937, so the hourly decay rate is $1 - 0.937 = 0.063$, or 6.3%.

(Answers might vary slightly due to rounding.)

b. The half-life of a drug is how long it takes for half of the drug to be broken down or eliminated from the bloodstream. Using the Table function, what is the half-life of the drug to the nearest hour?

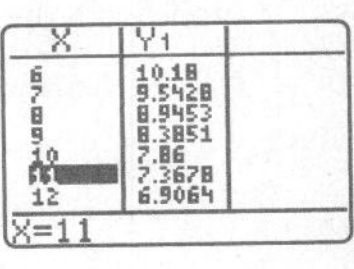

b. The half-life is the time to reduce the amount of medication to 7.5 mg.

The half-life is about 11 hours.

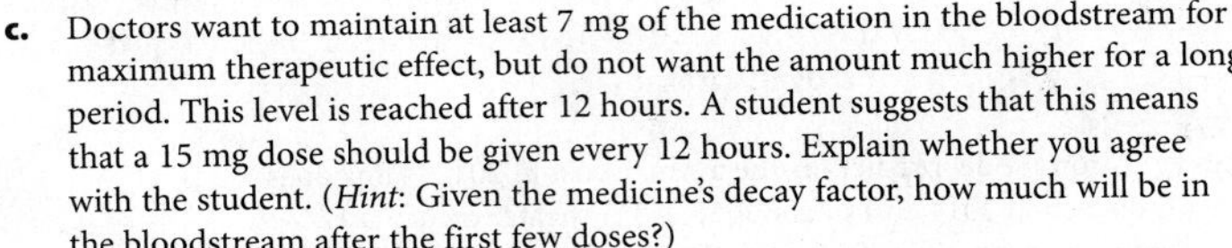

c. Doctors want to maintain at least 7 mg of the medication in the bloodstream for maximum therapeutic effect, but do not want the amount much higher for a long period. This level is reached after 12 hours. A student suggests that this means that a 15 mg dose should be given every 12 hours. Explain whether you agree with the student. (*Hint*: Given the medicine's decay factor, how much will be in the bloodstream after the first few doses?)

c. No; if a second 15 mg is given after 12 hours, it will be added to the remaining 7 mg to make a total of 22 mg. So, 12 hours after the second dose, $22(0.937)^{12} \approx 10$ mg will remain. If a third dose is given, then $25(0.937)^{12} \approx 11.5$ mg will remain after 12 hours. If a fourth dose is given, then $26.5(0.937)^{12} \approx 12.1$ mg will remain after 12 more hours. So, the minimum amount remaining is well above 7 mg, and is increasing, which could cause side effects.

11. Housing The average selling price of a unit in a high-rise condominium complex over 5 consecutive years was approximately \$184,300; \$195,600; \$204,500; \$215,300; \$228,200.

a. Find an exponential regression model where x represents years after the initial year and $f(x)$ is in thousands of dollars.

$f(x) \approx 184.6(1.054)^x$, where x is in years

b. A couple wants to buy a unit in the complex. First, they want to save 20% of the selling price for a down payment. What is the model that represents 20% of the average selling price for a condominium?

The 20% is a constant percent, so multiply the model by 0.2:

$f(x) \approx 0.2 \cdot 184.6(1.054)^x = 36.92(1.054)^x$.

c. At the time that the average selling price is \$228,200 (or when $x = 4$), the couple has \$20,000 saved toward a down payment. They are living with family, and saving \$1000 per month. Graph the model from Part *b* and a function that represents the couple's total savings on the same calculator screen. How much longer does the model predict it will take them to save enough money?

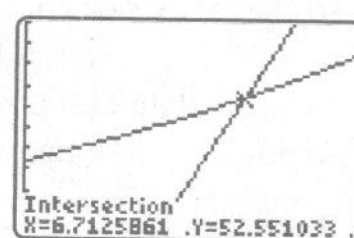

The price model is $f(x) = 36.92(1.054)^x$. The couple's saving is linear, and contains the point $(4, 20)$. They save \$12,000 per year, so the slope is 12.

Use point-slope form:

$$f(x) - 20 = 12(x - 4)$$
$$f(x) = 12(x - 4) + 20$$
$$f(x) = 12x - 28$$

The savings model is $f(x) = 12x - 28$.

Because $x = 4$ at the start of the monthly savings, it will take about 2.7 years to save enough for the down payment.

12. Business growth The growth in membership in thousands of a rapidly-growing Internet site over its first few years is modeled by $f(x) = 60(3.61)^x$ where x is in years and $x = 0$ represents the first anniversary of the site. Rewrite the model so that the growth factor represents weeks instead of years. What is the weekly growth factor? What does this model predict for the membership 20 weeks after the anniversary?

Use the power of a power property:

$f(x) = 60(3.61)^x = 60\left(3.61^{\frac{1}{52}}\right)^{52x} = 60(1.025)^{52x}$; the weekly growth factor is 1.025.

Because x is in years and x weeks is about $\frac{x}{52}$ of a year, the model for x in weeks is $f(x) = 60(1.025)^{52\left(\frac{x}{52}\right)} = 60(1.025)^x$. So $f(20) = 60(1.025)^x \approx 98$. The model predicts about 98,000 members 20 weeks after the anniversary.

AVOID COMMON ERRORS

When finding regression equations using a graphing calculator, students may not interpret the data properly before entering it into the calculator's data lists. Remind them, for example, that if the independent variable represents years since 2015, the first data point should include $x = 1$, not $x = 2016$.

PEER-TO-PEER DISCUSSION

Ask students to discuss with a partner what the regression equation of the form $f(x) = ab^x$ means in terms of the data set. Then ask students to make conjectures about the scatter plot of the data set, and about how the graph of the function associated with the regression equation might correlate with the scatter plot. Ask how the two graphs that are superimposed will look if the model closely represents the data or if the model is not a good fit for the data. **The regression equation for a data set is a representation of the overall exponential trend in the data. If the regression equation closely fits the data and gives a good model, then the graph of the function associated with the regression equation should fit the scatter plot closely. If the model is not a good fit for the data, few of the scatter plot points will be on or near the graph of the function for the regression equation.**

JOURNAL

Have students use words, graphs, and/or tables to describe a situation that would be modeled by an exponential function.

13. Which data set can be modeled by an exponential function $f(x) = ab^x$?

(a.) (0, 0.1), (1, 0.5), (2, 2.5), (3, 12.5)

b. (0, 0.1), (1, 0.2), (2, 0.3), (3, 0.4)

c. (0, 1), (1, 2), (2, 4), (4, 8)

d. (0, 0.8), (1, 0.4), (2, 0.10), (3, 0.0125)

H.O.T. Focus on Higher Order Thinking

14. Error analysis From the data (2, 72.2), (3, 18.0), (4, 4.4), (5, 1.1), (6, 0.27), a student sees that each change of 1 in x corresponds to a change in $f(x)$ of very close to 0.25, so that an exponential model is appropriate. From the first term, the student obtains $a = 72.2$, and writes the model $f(x) = 72.2(0.25)^x$. The student graphs the model with the data and observes that it does not fit the data well. What did the student do wrong? Correct the student's model.

Because the x-coordinate of the first data pair is not 0, the student should not have used the y-coordinate for a. When $x = 2$, $f(2) = 72.2(0.25)^2 \approx 4.5$, which is not correct. The x-value must be 0 for the corresponding $f(x)$ value to be a. To correct this, subtract 2 from the exponent in the model to obtain $f(x) = 72.2(0.25)^{x-2}$. Then $x = 2$ gives the value 72.2 for $f(2)$, while maintaining the correct ratio for b. (Note that the reasonable domain should be restricted to $x \geq 2$.)

15. Critical thinking For the data (0, 5), (1, 4), (2, 3.5), (3, 3.25), (4, 3.125), (5, 3.0625), the ratio of consecutive y-values is not constant, so you cannot write an exponential model $f(x) = ab^x$. But the difference in the values from term to term, 1, 0.5, 0.25, 0.125, 0.0625, shows exponential decay with a decay factor of 0.5. How can you use this fact to write a model of the data that contains an exponential expression of the form ab^x?

Notice that subtracting 3 from each y-value gives (0, 2), (1, 1), (2, 0.5), (3, 0.25), (4, 0.125), (5, 0.0625). This can be modeled by $f(x) = 2(0.5)^x$, so adding 3 to each function value will give the original data. So, you can use the model $f(x) = 2(0.5)^x + 3$.

16. Challenge Suppose that you have two data points (x_1, y_1) and (x_2, y_2) that you know are fitted by an exponential model $f(x) = ab^x$. Can you always find an equation for the model? Explain.

Yes; you have $y_1 = ab^{x_1}$ and $y_2 = b^{x_2}$. From the first, you know that $a = \frac{y_1}{b^{x_1}}$. You can substitute this into the second equation to obtain $y_2 = \frac{y_1}{b^{x_1}} b^{x_2}$. Because you know all the values except b, you can solve for b, and then use that value to then solve for a.

Lesson Performance Task

According to data from the U.S. Department of Agriculture, the number of farms in the United States has been decreasing over the past several decades. During this time, however, the average size of each farm has increased.

Farms in the United States	
Year	**Farms (Millions)**
1940	6.35
1950	5.65
1960	3.96
1970	2.95
1980	2.44
1990	2.15
2000	2.17

a. From 1940 to 1980, the average size of a U.S. farm can be modeled by the function $A(t) = 174e^{0.022t}$ where t is the number of years since 1940 and A is the average farm size in acres. What was the average farm size in 1940? In 1980?

Since 1940 is the base year, the average farm size was 174 acres. Since 1980 is 40 years past the base year $t = 40$.

$$A(t) = 174e^{0.022t}$$
$$A(40) = 174e^{0.022(40)}$$
$$\approx 419.5$$

The average farm size in 1980 is about 419.5 acres.

b. The table shows the number of farms in the United States from 1940 to 2000. Find an exponential model for the data using a calculator.

Possible Answer: $N(t) = 6.14(0.98)^t$

c. If you were to determine the exponential model without a calculator, would the value for a be the same as the value from the calculator? Explain your answer.

No, if you were to write this by hand, the value of a would be 6.35 because that is the initial value in 1940.

d. Based on the data in the table, predict what the number of farms in the United States in 2014.

$$N(t) = 6.14(0.98)^t$$
$$N(74) = 6.14(0.98)^{74}$$
$$\approx 1.38$$

The formula predicts that there will be about 1.38 million farms in 2014.

e. Using a graphing calculator, determine how many years it takes for the number of farms to decrease by 50%.

About 33 years.

f. Using a graphing calculator, determine when the number of farms in the United States will fall below 1 million.

Around 2030.

g. Does an exponential model seem appropriate for all of the data listed in the table? Why or why not?

For the most part it does, however the data rises from 1990 to 2000 which does not seem to fit perfectly with an exponential decay model.

EXTENSION ACTIVITY

Have students write a function $F(t)$ for the total acreage being farmed in the United States as a function of time, where t is the number of years since 1940. Have students graph $F(t)$, and then have them discuss whether the total amount of farmland is increasing or decreasing.

$F(t) = A(t)N(t) \approx 1068\, e^{0.022t}\, (0.98)^t$. The total farmland $F(t)$ is increasing.

AVOID COMMON ERRORS

Students may use the actual year as the variable t in the function $A(t)$. Explain that 1940 is the base year and t is the number of years since 1940. Ask students what number they should use for the variable t. **Subtract 1940 from the year in the question, and use the resulting value for t.**

INTEGRATE MATHEMATICAL PRACTICES

Focus on Critical Thinking

MP.3 Have students discuss the limitations of using an exponential model for the size of a farm or for the number of farms. Have students explain whether it makes sense for the average size of a farm to increase indefinitely.

Scoring Rubric

2 points: Student correctly solves the problem and explains his/her reasoning.

1 point: Student shows good understanding of the problem but does not fully solve or explain his/her reasoning.

0 points: Student does not demonstrate understanding of the problem.

LESSON 14.2

Choosing Among Linear, Quadratic, and Exponential Models

Common Core Math Standards

The student is expected to:

S.ID.B.6a

Fit a function to the data; use functions fitted to data to solve problems in the context of the data. Also A.CED.A.2, F.IF.B.4, F.IF.C.7e

Mathematical Practices

MP.5 Using Tools

Language Objective

With a partner, describe, in general, how to determine which kind of model is best represented by points on a coordinate plane.

ENGAGE

Essential Question: How do you choose among linear, quadratic, and exponential models for a given set of data?

Possible answer: Look at a scatter plot of the data to see the general trend and then choose a model that best represents the trend. In some cases, selecting a model is not a clear-cut process, and you may need to consider more than one model.

PREVIEW: LESSON PERFORMANCE TASK

View the Engage section online. Discuss the photo and have students describe what trends they would look for when choosing a model for a particular investment. Then preview the Lesson Performance Task.

Name ______________________ Class ____________ Date ____________

14.2 Choosing Among Linear, Quadratic, and Exponential Models

Resource Locker

Essential Question: How do you choose among, linear, quadratic, and exponential models for a given set of data?

Explore Developing Rules of Thumb for Visually Choosing a Model

When you work with data, you may not know whether a linear, quadratic, or exponential model will be a good fit. If the data lie along a curve that rises and then falls or falls and then rises, the data may be well-fitted by a quadratic model. But sometimes it may not be as clear. Consider the following scatter plots.

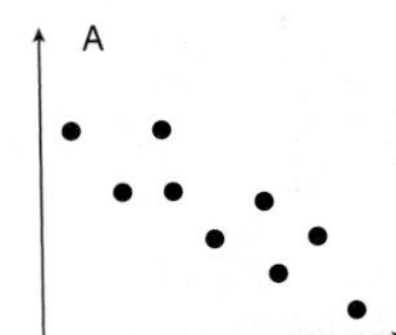

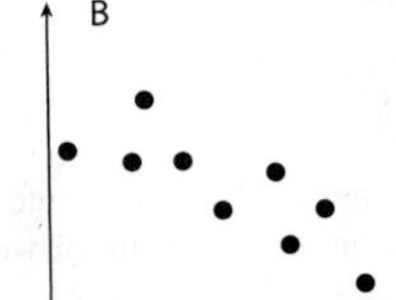

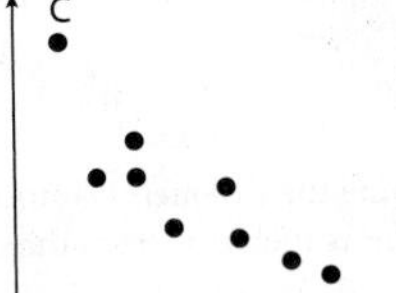

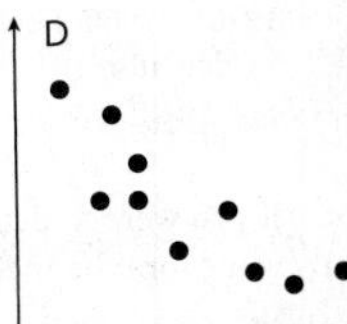

(A) Look at scatter plot A. Do you think a linear model will be appropriate? Explain your reasoning. If you think a linear model is appropriate, what do you know about the lead coefficient?

Yes; though the data do not lie closely along a single line, there is no apparent curvature to the data. The lead coefficient will be negative since it represents the slope.

(B) Look at scatter plot B. What is different now that indicates that another kind of model might be appropriate? What characteristics would this model have?

The lower position of the first point makes it look like the data might be showing some curvature, specifically, like one side of a parabola opening downward. This indicates that a quadratic model with a negative leading coefficient might be appropriate.

(C) Look at scatter plot C. What about this plot indicates that yet another kind of model might be appropriate? What characteristics would this model have?

Plot C might be showing some curvature in the opposite direction of plot B, that is, with an upward curve instead of a downward curve. The right side looks like it might be dropping so that the *x*-axis is an asymptote. So Plot C might be appropriately modeled by an exponential decay model, that is, an exponential model with a base that is less than 1.

HARDCOVER PAGES 721–73

Watch for the hardcover student edition page numbers for this lesson.

Ⓓ Look at scatter plot D. This plot is very similar to plot C, but what indicates that a different model would be appropriate? What characteristics would this model have?

The plot looks to be curving up a little less steeply at the left. Also, at its right it looks like it could be beginning to change direction to curve back upward. These facts indicate that a quadratic model with a positive leading coefficient might be appropriate.

Reflect

1. When can it be difficult to distinguish whether a quadratic or an exponential model is most appropriate?
If the data are all on one side of the vertex of a parabola, it can be hard to tell the curve from that of an exponential curve since there is no apparent change of direction.

2. Under what circumstances might it be difficult to tell exponential or quadratic data from linear data?
If the base *b* of an exponential model is very close to 1, it can be hard to see the curvature of the data, especially if they are not tightly aligned along the model. If the data lie along a very "wide" parabola the curve can be hard to see. In general, if you are "zoomed in" on a small part of an exponential or quadratic graph it can be hard to see the curvature.

3. For data that do not lie tightly along a curve or line, what is different about the last data point that can make it potentially more misleading than other points?
Since there are no data points following it, if it shows a change in steepness or direction, it can be harder to tell if this is actually true or if the change is more of a random variation.

Explain 1 Modeling with a Linear Function

As noted in the Explore, it is not always immediately clear what kind of model best represents a data set. With experience, your ability to recognize signs and reasons for choosing one model over another will increase.

Example 1 **Examine each scatter plot. Then complete the steps below.**

Step 1: Choose the data set that appears to be best modeled by a linear function. Explain your choice, whether you think a linear model will be a close fit, and whether any other model might possibly be appropriate. What characteristics do you expect the linear model will have?

Step 2: Enter the data for your choice into your graphing calculator in two lists, and perform linear regression. Then give the model, defining your variables. What are the initial value and the rate of change of the model?

Step 3: Graph the model along with the scatter plot using your calculator, then assess how well the model appears to fit the data.

PROFESSIONAL DEVELOPMENT

Math Background

In this lesson, students continue their study of fitting models by exploring how to choose among linear, quadratic, or exponential models. A linear model may be appropriate if a scatter plot of the data generally has a linear trend line. Points of the scatter plot may be roughly scattered equally above and below the trend line. A quadratic model may be appropriate if the scatter plot shows a roughly parabolic shape (symmetric about an axis of symmetry). An exponential model may be appropriate if the scatter plot is always increasing (or decreasing) rapidly.

EXPLORE

Developing Rules of Thumb for Visually Choosing a Model

INTEGRATE TECHNOLOGY

Students have the option of completing the choosing a model activity either in the book or online.

QUESTIONING STRATEGIES

? How do you use a scatter plot to tell whether the function it represents is linear, quadratic, or exponential? **If the points generally follow a line, choose linear. If the points rise and then fall, or fall and then rise, choose quadratic. If the points rise or fall rapidly, choose exponential.**

EXPLAIN 1

Modeling with a Linear Function

QUESTIONING STRATEGIES

? How is the coefficient of x in the linear regression model related to the slope of the fitted linear function? **In each case, the coefficient of *x* is the slope.**

? How can you use a linear regression model to make a decision from the data? **If the model proves to be a good fit, you can make a relevant prediction with some degree of confidence, and then use the prediction to make a decision.**

Ⓐ **Wildlife Conservation** Data sets and scatter plots for populations over time of four endangered, threatened, or scarce species are shown.

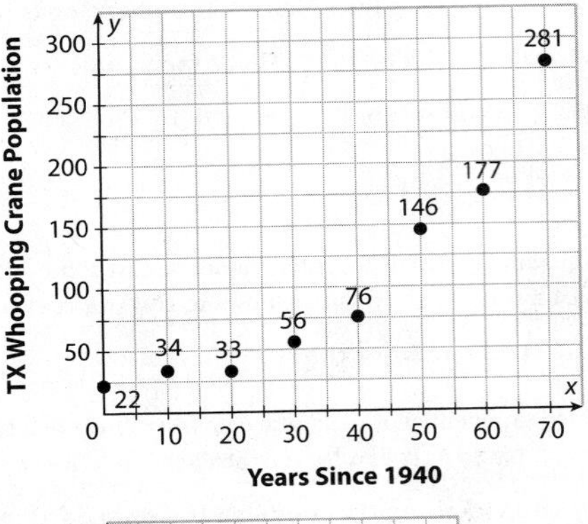

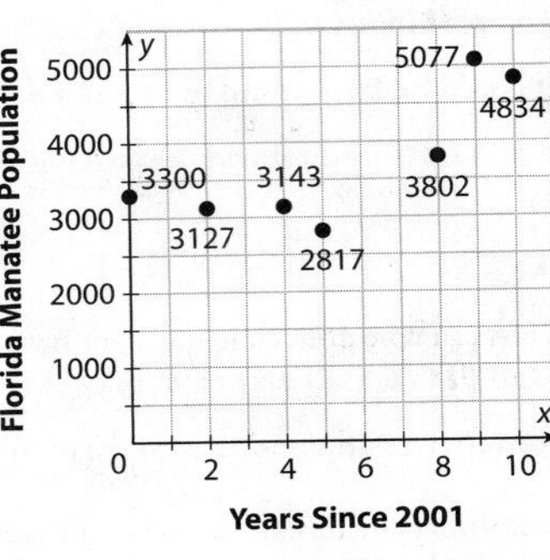

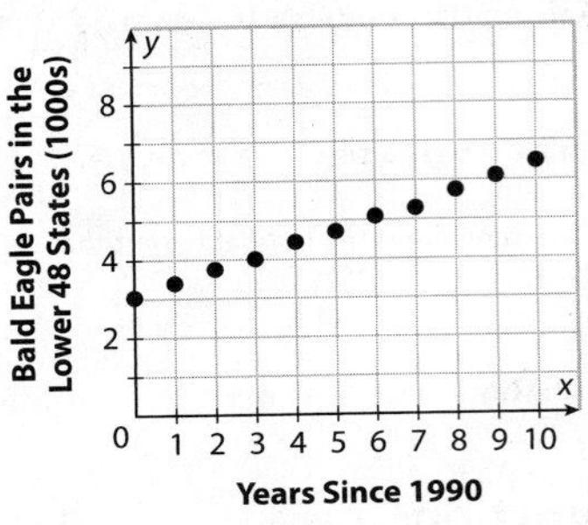

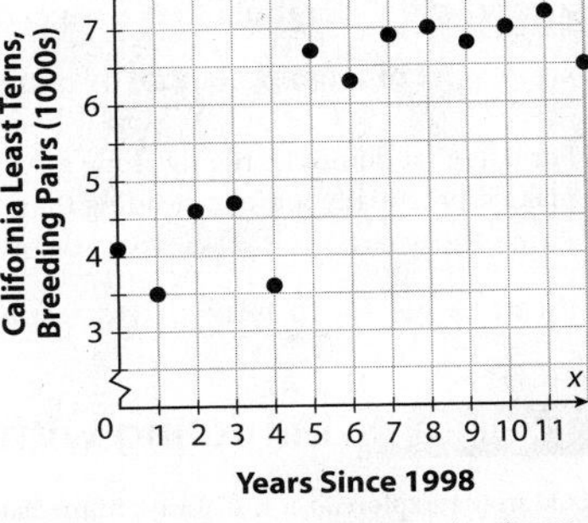

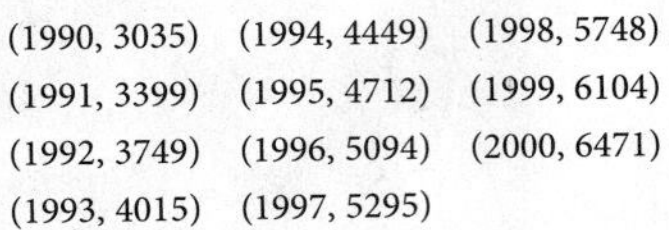

(1990, 3035) (1994, 4449) (1998, 5748)
(1991, 3399) (1995, 4712) (1999, 6104)
(1992, 3749) (1996, 5094) (2000, 6471)
(1993, 4015) (1997, 5295)

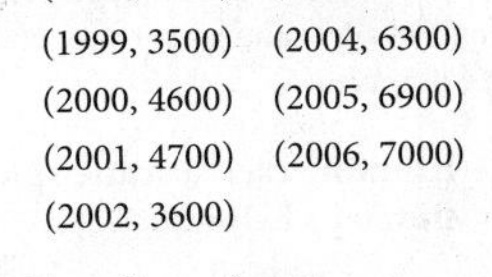

(1998, 4100) (2003, 6700) (2007, 680
(1999, 3500) (2004, 6300) (2008, 700
(2000, 4600) (2005, 6900) (2009, 720
(2001, 4700) (2006, 7000) (2010, 650
(2002, 3600)

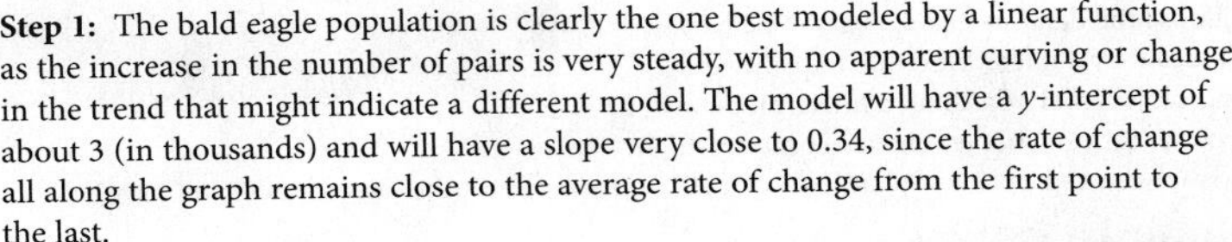

Step 1: The bald eagle population is clearly the one best modeled by a linear function, as the increase in the number of pairs is very steady, with no apparent curving or changes in the trend that might indicate a different model. The model will have a y-intercept of about 3 (in thousands) and will have a slope very close to 0.34, since the rate of change all along the graph remains close to the average rate of change from the first point to the last.

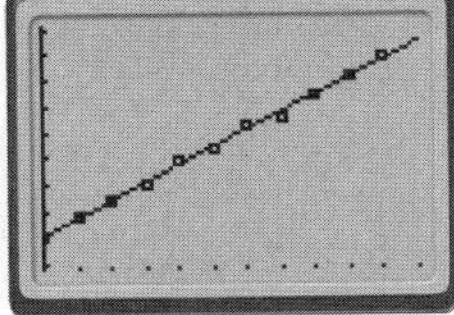

Step 2: A regression model is $y = 338.2x + 3042$ where x is the number of years after 1990 and y is the number of breeding pairs in thousands. The initial value is 3042, and the rate of change is about 338 pairs per year.

Step 3: The model is a very close fit to the data. It fits both the overall trend and the individual points very closely.

COLLABORATIVE LEARNING

Peer-to-Peer Activity

Have students work in pairs to find regression equations for data sets and their graphs. Have one student enter the data into a graphing calculator and find all three possible regression equations, linear, quadratic, and exponential. Have the student analyze the equations and make a suggestion about which model to choose. Have the other student graph the data as a scatter plot and then graph the chosen model over the scatter plot to verify or disprove that the chosen model is the best one. Then have students switch roles and repeat the exercise using another set of data.

(B) **Automobiles** Data sets and scatter plots for various statistics about changes in automobiles of different model years are shown.

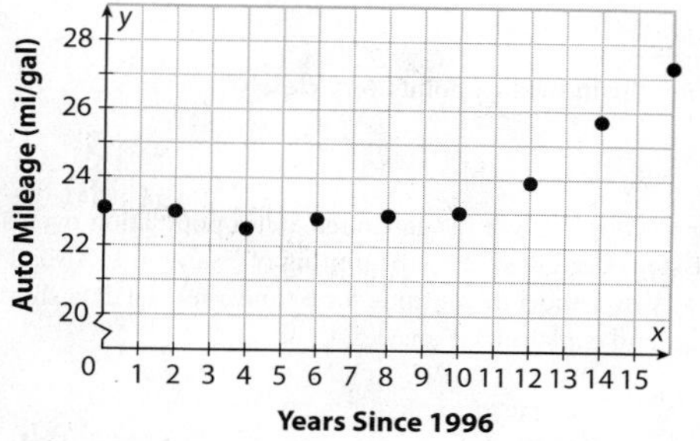

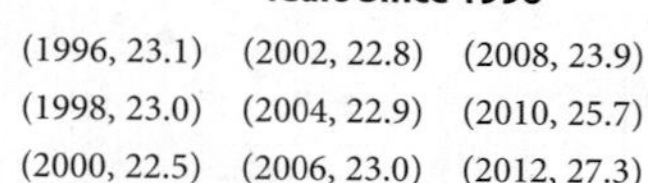

(1996, 23.1) (2002, 22.8) (2008, 23.9)
(1998, 23.0) (2004, 22.9) (2010, 25.7)
(2000, 22.5) (2006, 23.0) (2012, 27.3)

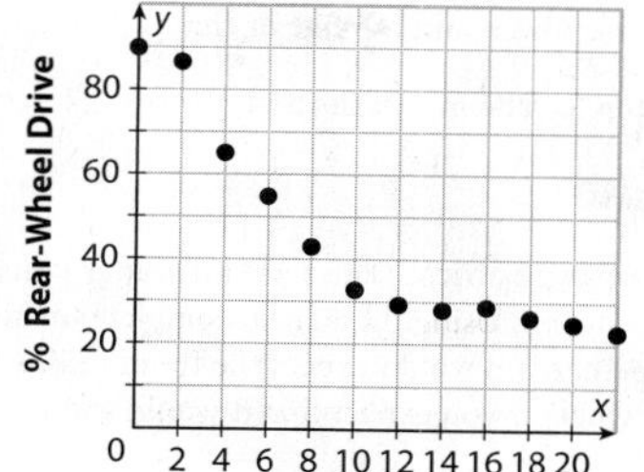

(1977, 89.8) (1985, 42.9) (1993, 28.8)
(1979, 86.5) (1987, 32.8) (1995, 26.3)
(1981, 65.0) (1989, 29.3) (1997, 24.9)
(1983, 54.8) (1991, 28.1) (1999, 22.9)

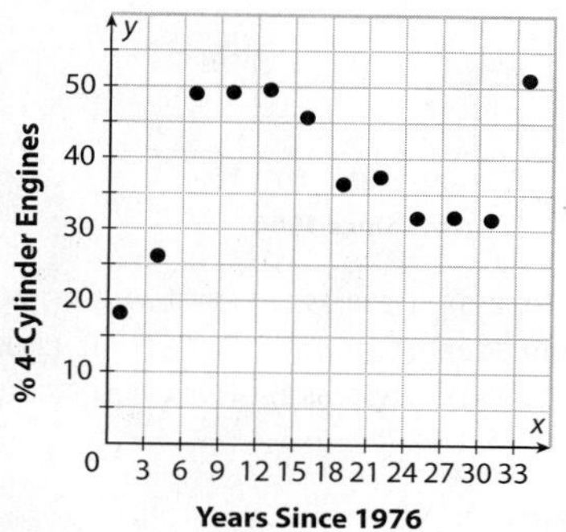

(1976, 18.2) (1988, 49.6) (2000, 31.7)
(1979, 26.2) (1991, 45.7) (2003, 31.8)
(1982, 49.0) (1994, 36.4) (2006, 31.5)
(1985, 49.2) (1997, 37.4) (2009, 51.1)

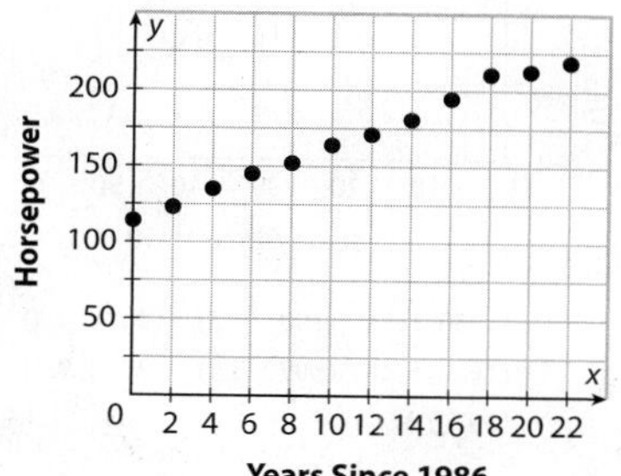

(1986, 114) (1994, 152) (2002, 195)
(1988, 123) (1996, 164) (2004, 211)
(1990, 135) (1998, 171) (2006, 213)
(1992, 145) (2000, 181) (2008, 219)

Step 1: The **horsepower data** are the data best modeled by a linear function, as the increase in **horsepower** over time is very steady, with the amount of increase never varying too much from the trend. All of the other data sets show clear variation in the rate of change. The model will have a y-intercept of about **114** and will have a positive slope that should be close to the overall average rate of change of **about 5**, since the rate of change all along the graph remains close to the average rate of change from the first point to the last.

DIFFERENTIATE INSTRUCTION

Critical Thinking

Some students may need help understanding how to choose among real-world linear, quadratic, or exponential models. Have them work in small groups to discuss how to choose a model after visually analyzing a scatter plot. Then have students use a graphing calculator to find a regression equation for all three types of models and compare them. Provide students with several data sets, and ask each student to choose a model, justify the choice, and then let the group critique it.

AVOID COMMON ERRORS

Some students may not recall the properties of linear models that can help them find a model for a data set. Remind students that the first differences in the $f(x)$ values are constant when a linear model is appropriate. For a real-world linear model, the first differences should be almost constant.

Step 2: A regression model is $y = 4.967x + 113.9$ where x is the number of years after 1986 and y is the **114 horsepower** for the model year. The initial value is about 114 horsepower, and the rate of change is about **5 horsepower per year**.

Step 3: The model fits both the overall trend and the individual points very closely.

Your Turn

4. Demographics Data sets and scatter plots for various changes in the United States population over time are shown. Using these data, complete the three steps described at the beginning of Example 1. Also, tell whether you would expect the trend indicated by your model to continue for a time after the data shown, or whether you expect that it would soon change, and explain your answer.

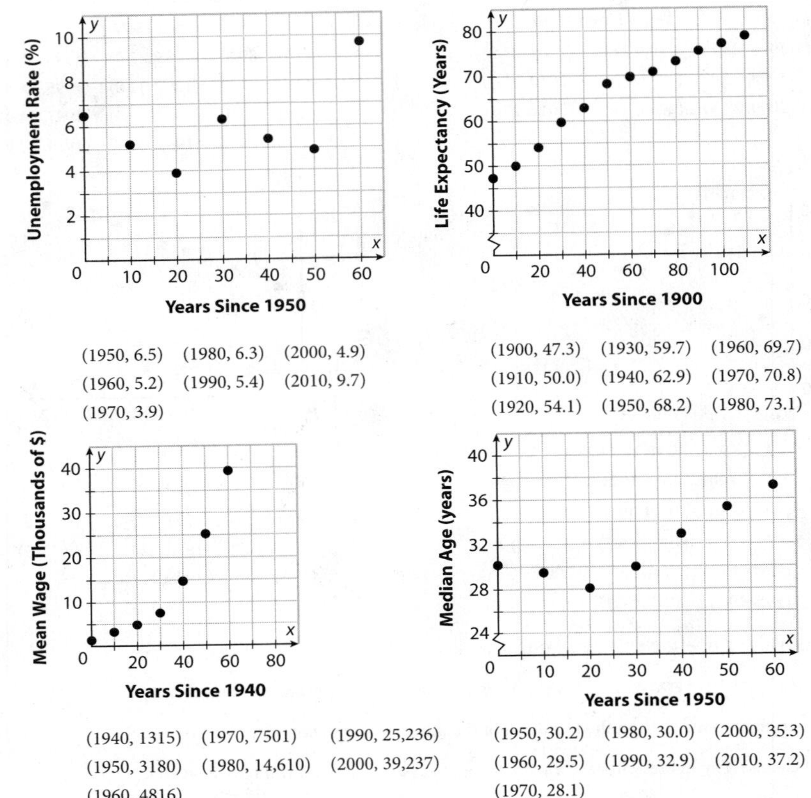

(1950, 6.5) (1980, 6.3) (2000, 4.9)
(1960, 5.2) (1990, 5.4) (2010, 9.7)
(1970, 3.9)

(1900, 47.3) (1930, 59.7) (1960, 69.7) (1990, 75
(1910, 50.0) (1940, 62.9) (1970, 70.8) (2000, 77
(1920, 54.1) (1950, 68.2) (1980, 73.1) (2010, 78

(1940, 1315) (1970, 7501) (1990, 25,236)
(1950, 3180) (1980, 14,610) (2000, 39,237)
(1960, 4816)

(1950, 30.2) (1980, 30.0) (2000, 35.3)
(1960, 29.5) (1990, 32.9) (2010, 37.2)
(1970, 28.1)

Step 1: The life expectancy data are the data best modeled by a linear function, as its plot is the only one that does not show a distinct curve or change of direction. Although the average rate of change over the first and second halves of the data are somewhat different, the trend appears linear over the last several data points. The regression line will be a reasonably good fit, but not be really close. It will have a positive slope fairly close to the data's overall average rate of change of about 0.28.

LANGUAGE SUPPORT EL

Communicate Math

Have students create a list of words that have been associated with linear, quadratic, and exponential models, such as *slope, first differences, second differences, growth, decay,* and so on. This list can be used to eliminate some models when attempting to fit a model to data. For example, a data set that records the growth of bacteria will probably demonstrate exponential growth. This may allow students to avoid the need to first look for common differences.

4. (continued)

Step 2: A regression model is y = 0.2901x + 49.62 where x is the number of years after 1900 and y is the life expectancy in years. The initial value is about 49.6 years, and the rate of change is about 0.29 years per year, or about 2.9 years increase in life expectancy per decade.

Step 3: The model is a good approximation of the overall trend, but it passes above, then below, then above the data points again, and is rising faster than the data at the end.

Possible answer: I think the model may overestimate the life expectancy going forward, since it is rising faster than the data toward the end of the period. It does seem reasonable to predict that the increase can continue at about the rate shown by the data beginning in 1950, although with any significant health or medical advances, it could increase more.

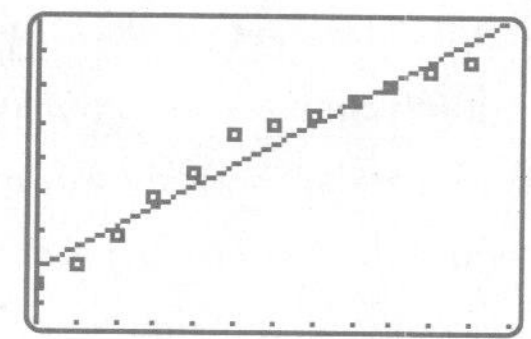

Explain 2 Modeling With a Quadratic Function

Example 2 Using the groups of data sets and their scatter plots from Example 1:

Step 1: Choose the data set that appears to be best modeled by a quadratic function. Explain your choice, whether you think a quadratic model will be a close fit, and whether any other model might possibly be appropriate. What characteristics do you expect the quadratic model will have?

Step 2: Enter the data for your choice into your graphing calculator in two lists, and perform quadratic regression. Then give the model, defining your variables.

Step 3: Graph the model along with the scatter plot using your calculator, then assess how well the model appears to fit the data.

(A) Use the data about animal populations in Example 1 Part A.

Step 1: The Florida manatee population appears to be the one best modeled by a quadratic function, as its scatter plot is the only one with a clear change in direction, and it clearly would not be well represented by a linear or exponential model. The whooping crane data might also be fit fairly well on one side of a quadratic model, but it might also be exponential. The quadratic model for the manatee population will have a positive leading coefficient since it opens upward, but it is hard to predict what the y-intercept or the vertex will be. Because graph is not very symmetrical, the fit may not be very close.

Step 2: A regression model is $y = 48.50x^2 - 317.3x + 3411$ where x is the number of years after 2001 and y is the number of manatees

Step 3: The model is not a close fit, but it does look like an appropriate model for the overall trend during the time of the data. It misses the horizontal position for the vertex by a fairly wide margin, but otherwise is not too far from the data.

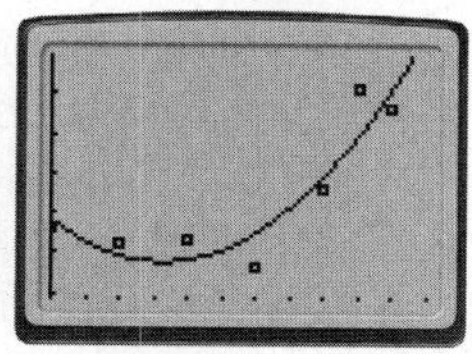

EXPLAIN 2

Modeling with a Quadratic Function

QUESTIONING STRATEGIES

? How can you use a scatter plot to tell whether a quadratic model will have a positive or negative leading coefficient? If the points of the scatter plot roughly form a parabola that opens downward, then the model will have a negative leading coefficient. If the points open upward, then the model will have a positive leading coefficient.

? If the graph of the data points is ever increasing for real-world data, does this mean that an exponential function is more appropriate than a quadratic model? No; for example, for the area of a square of side length s, the area is ever increasing, but a quadratic model is more appropriate. The domain does not include negative values.

AVOID COMMON ERRORS

Some students may not recall the properties of quadratic models that can help them find a model for a data set. Remind students that the second differences in the $f(x)$ values are constant when a quadratic model is appropriate. For a real-world quadratic model, the second differences should be almost constant. Suggest that students find the differences when there is only a small amount of data, so that they will not confuse the quadratic model with an exponential model.

 Use the data about automobiles in Example 1 Part B.

Step 1:

The miles per gallon data appear to be the data best modeled by a quadratic function, as its scatter plot seems to show a change of direction and a minimum point. The % Rear-Wheel Drive data looks approximately quadratic for a while, but the data continue to decline at the right, so a quadratic model would not be a good fit. Also, part of the percent 4-Cylinder data looks somewhat quadratic with a negative leading coefficient, but the graph changes direction again, indicating that a cubic model would be much more appropriate. The quadratic model for miles per gallon will have a positive leading coefficient since it opens upward. It appears that the vertex will not be too far from the minimum point on the plot, though it may be a little to the right.

Step 2:

Step 2: A regression model is $y = 0.0390x^2 - 0.3922x + 23.40$ where x is the number of years after 1996 and y is the average miles per gallon.

Step 3:

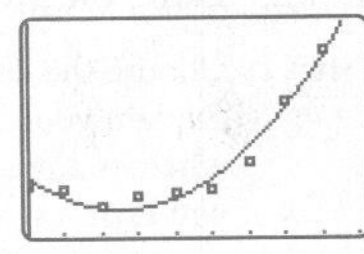

The model is a fairly close fit to the data. Its minimum reflects the actual minimum miles per gallon closely, and the model reflects the trend at the right side of the data well.

Reflect

5. **Discussion** The Florida manatee has been under consideration for being downgraded from endangered to threatened. Do you believe the graph and model of the manatee population in Part A of this Example support this concept or argue against it? Explain your reasoning.
Possible answer: Argue against it; first, the data span a time of only six years. It is true that the population the last three years is considerably above the previous years, but there is far too little data to show a clear long-term trend. Also, though the model is increasing sharply at its right edge, the last data point drops from the previous one. This emphasizes that you should be extremely cautious about making predictions into the future from the model.

6. How might the model for miles per gallon affect a decision on when to purchase a car?
Possible answer: The model is showing a rapid gain in miles per gallon going forward. This seems likely to continue for a while given the emphasis on fuel economy, so if you want to get the best choice of more efficient vehicles, you might want to wait a little longer.

Your Turn

7. Using the data in Your Turn Exercise 4, complete the three steps described at the beginning of Example 2. Also, tell whether you would expect the trend indicated by your model to continue for a time after the data shown, or whether you expect that it would soon change, and explain your answer.

Step 1: The median age data appear to be the data best modeled by a quadratic function, as its scatter plot seems to show a single change of direction and a minimum point. The quadratic model for median age will have a positive leading coefficient since it opens upward. It appears that the vertex will not be too far from the minimum point on the plot, but the model's fit will not be very close, as the data appear to lie closer to the graph of an absolute value function.

Step 2: A regression model is $y = 0.004048x^2 - 0.1093x + 29.90$ where x is the number of years after 1950 and y is the median age in years.

Step 3: The model approximates the data trend pretty well, except that it misses the minimum data point by a considerable amount. It is also rising more quickly than the data at its right side.

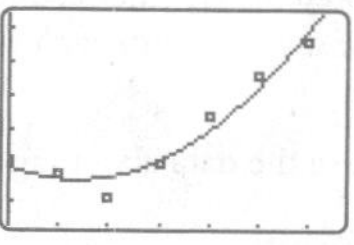

Possible answer: I think the model will not be accurate going forward because of the nature of the data set. The drop in median age around 1950 corresponds to the Baby Boom after World War II, when birth rates were very high.

Explain 3 Modeling with an Exponential Function

Example 3 **Using the groups of data sets and their scatter plots from Example 1:**

Step 1: Choose the data set that appears to be best modeled by an exponential function. Explain your choice, whether you think an exponential model will be a close fit, and whether any other model might possibly be appropriate. What characteristics do you expect the exponential model will have?

Step 2: Enter the data for your choice into your graphing calculator in two lists, and perform exponential regression. Then give the model, defining your variables. What are the initial value, growth or decay factor, and growth or decay rate of the model?

Step 3: Graph the model along with the scatter plot using your calculator, then assess how well the model appears to fit the data.

EXPLAIN 3

Modeling with an Exponential Function

QUESTIONING STRATEGIES

? What characteristics of a data set make you think that an exponential model is appropriate? **The ratio of successive $f(x)$ values is close to being constant.**

? If a data set has a y-intercept of 62 and contains the point (5, 100), what would you expect the exponential model to be, roughly? **about $y = 62(1.1)^x$**

INTEGRATE MATHEMATICAL PRACTICES

Focus on Reasoning

MP.2 Encourage students to use the functionality of a graphing calculator to make a scatter plot of a data set and then choose a model for the data. Then ask them to find linear, quadratic, and exponential regression equations for the data and graph each of the functions associated with the regression equations. Have them use the graphs to explain whether they chose the correct model from the initial scatter plot.

 Use the data about animal populations in Example 1 Part A.

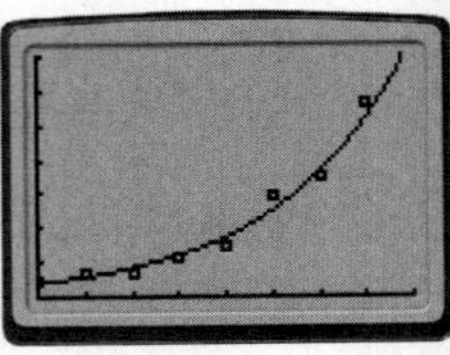

Step 1: The whooping crane population appears to be the one best modeled by an exponential function, as it rises increasingly quickly, but does not reflect a change in direction as a quadratic model can. Though the whooping crane plot is nearly linear in its midsection, the slow initial rise and fast later rise indicate that an exponential model is better. The California least tern data show a significant jump, but no clear pattern. An appropriate whooping crane model shows exponential growth, so the parameter b is greater than 1. Because the growth is not very large considering the time period of 70 years, however, the yearly growth factor will not be much above 1.

Step 2: A regression model is $y = 20.05(1.0374)^x$ where x is the number of years after 1940 and y is the population. The initial value for the model is 20 whooping cranes. The growth factor is 1.0374, and the growth rate is 0.0374, or about 3.74% per year.

Step 3: The model is very good fit for the data. Some data points are a little above the curve and some a little below, but the fit is close and reflects the trend very well.

 Use the data about automobiles in Example 1 Part B.

Step 1:

The percent of cars with rear-wheel drive data appears to be the data best modeled by an exponential function (exponential decay), as overall, the graph drops less and less steeply with time. None of the other plots has this characteristic. Because the data indicate exponential decay instead of growth, the parameter *b* is less than 1. The model will likely not be a really close fit, as is appears that the ratio of *y*-values from term to term varies a fair amount.

Step 2:

A regression model is $y = 80.45(0.9371)^x$ where x is the number of years after 1977 and y is the percent of cars with rear-wheel drive. The initial value for the model is 80.45%. The decay factor is 0.9371, and the decay rate is $1 - 0.9371 = 0.0629$, or about 6.3%.

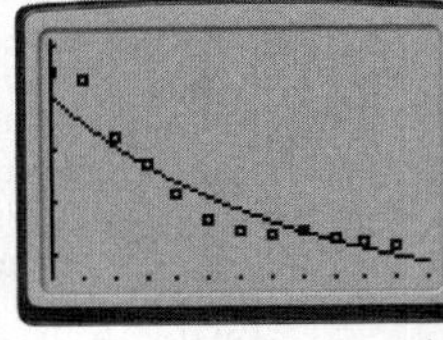

Step 3:

The model is a fairly good fit, but not a close fit. The model falls well below the first two data points, and does not represent the middle of the data well. It does match the trend better toward the end of the data, though the model's decay rate is a little too high for the actual data.

Reflect

8. **Discussion** What does the model for the whooping crane population predict for the population in 2040? Do you think it is possible that the whooping crane will be removed from the endangered species list any time in the next few decades? Explain.

$y = 20.05(1.0374)^{100} \approx 788$; Possible answer: no; even if the exponential growth in the model remains close to accurate over the next several decades, the growth rate is so slow and the total population of birds so small that the population will remain at risk for the foreseeable future.

Your Turn

9. Using the data in YourTurn Exercise 4, complete the three steps described at the beginning of Example 3. Also, tell whether you would expect the trend indicated by your model to continue for a time after the data shown, or whether you expect that it would soon change, and explain your answer.

Step 1: The mean full-time wage appears to be the one best modeled by an exponential function, as it rises increasingly quickly, but does not reflect a change in direction.

Step 2: A regression model is $y = 1.539(1.0567)^x$ where x is the number of years after 1940 and y is the mean full-time wage in thousands of dollars. The initial value for the model is 1.539, or about \$1540. The growth factor is 1.0567, and the growth rate is 0.0567, or about 5.67% per year. Because $1.0567^{10} \approx 1.74$, this is a growth rate of about 74% per decade.

Step 3: The model is a fairly good fit, but not a close fit. The model falls well below the first two data points, and does not represent the middle of the data well. It does match the trend better toward the end of the data.

Possible answer: I think the model will need to be modified so that the rate of increase will be somewhat less than the model indicates.

Elaborate

10. **Discussion** How does making a prediction from a model help make a decision or judgment based on a given set of data?

The model gives you the ability to predict a specific output for a given input, which a scatter plot will not do. Then you can use this prediction along with your knowledge of the context and trends to help you make a reasonable decision or judgment.

ELABORATE

INTEGRATE MATHEMATICAL PRACTICES

Focus on Patterns

MP.8 Discuss with students how to determine what type of model fits a data set. Give them several data sets and have them predict which data sets are linear, quadratic, or exponential. Then have them enter the data sets into a graphing calculator to check their predictions.

AVOID COMMON ERRORS

Students may find that they if they enter a value of 0 for y in a data set and do an exponential regression, the calculator signals an error. Remind students that the x-axis is an asymptote for the exponential function $f(x) = ab^x$ and that this function cannot have a value of 0. The best model for the data may still be exponential, but the data may need to be translated first and the model adjusted for the translation.

SUMMARIZE THE LESSON

? If the data does not appear to be rising or falling in a particular pattern from left to right when graphed, what can you determine about the best model for the data? **A quadratic or exponential model is not appropriate. A linear model is a good fit if the data are close to a trend line, which will be somewhat horizontal. If the data vary wildly from any trend line, none of these models may be appropriate.**

EVALUATE

ASSIGNMENT GUIDE

Concepts and Skills	Practice
Explore Developing Rules of Thumb for Visually Choosing a Model	Exercise 1
Example 1 Modeling with a Linear Function	Exercises 2, 6, 10
Example 2 Modeling with a Quadratic Function	Exercises 3, 5, 7, 11
Example 3 Modeling with an Exponential Function	Exercises 4, 9–10

INTEGRATE MATHEMATICAL PRACTICES

Focus on Reasoning

MP.2 Remind students to check their models by substituting the values from data points into the model and verifying that the model is a good fit. When making a scatter plot of the data, remind students that a graph of the model may not pass through many of the data points.

CONNECT VOCABULARY EL

Continue connecting the idea of exponential decay or growth to graphs showing a rapid increase or decrease in trend lines or curves. The more you can connect visual representations to words, the easier it is for English Language Learners to make connections with the terms' meanings.

11. Describe the process for obtaining a regression model using a graphing calculator.

To obtain a regression model using a graphing calculator, enter the data into two statistics lists, then go to the statistics calculation menu, where you can choose among the types of regression models the calculator can find. Then perform the regression after making sure that you choose data in the correct lists. To also see the model graphed with a scatter plot, make sure the statistics plot is tuned on and set to a scatter plot, and enter the model into the Y = menu either directly or by accessing the variables menu, choosing the statistics menu, and then selecting the regression equation. You can then enter an appropriate window or use the statistics zoom window.

12. Essential Question Check-In How can a scatter plot of a data set help you determine the best type of model to choose for the data?

A scatter plot can show patterns in the data that are not apparent from a list or table of the data, especially if the data show variability from term to term that may hide a clear trend. For example, the ratio of values from term to term may appear to vary more than you would expect for an exponential model to be a good choice, but a scatter plot might show that this variability hides a clear exponential trend overall.

Evaluate: Homework and Practice

- Online Homework
- Hints and Help
- Extra Practice

1. Match each scatter plot with the most appropriate model from the following. Do not use any choice more than once.

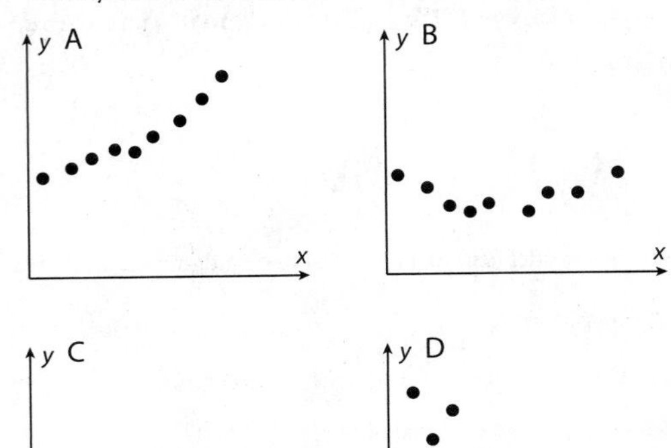

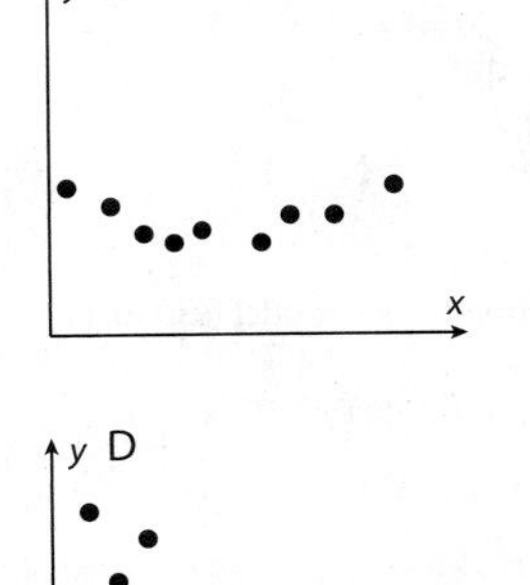

I. quadratic, $a > 0$
II. quadratic, $a < 0$
III. linear, $a < 0$
IV. exponential, $b > 1$
V. exponential, $b < 1$

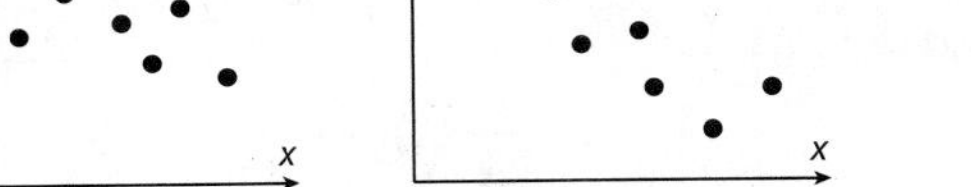

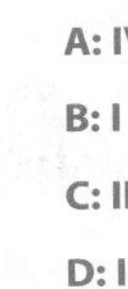

A: IV
B: I
C: II
D: III

Exercise	Depth of Knowledge (D.O.K.)	COMMON CORE Mathematical Practices
1–7	1 Recall of Information	MP.4 Modeling
8–10	1 Recall of Information	MP.2 Reasoning
2	2 Skills/Concepts	MP.3 Logic
9–11	3 Strategic Thinking H.O.T.	MP.3 Logic

In Exercises 2–5, for the data set given:

a. Create a scatter plot of the data. What kind of model do you think is most appropriate? Why? What characteristics do you expect that this model will have?

b. Use a graphing calculator to find an equation of the regression model. Then interpret the model, including the meaning of important parameters.

c. Graph the regression model with its scatter plot using a graphing calculator. How well does the model fit?

d. Answer the question following the data.

2. Population Demographics The data set shows the number of Americans living in multigenerational households.

Year	Number (in Millions)
1950	32
1960	27
1970	26
1980	28
1990	35
2000	42
2010	52

What does the model predict for the number in 2020? in 2040? Are these numbers reasonable? Explain.

a. Quadratic; the data show a clear quadratic-shaped curve opening upward. The model will have a positive value for the lead coefficient *a*. The fit should be close, with the *y*-intercept very near the 1950 number of 32 million Americans and the vertex near the minimum point in 1970.

b. The model is $y = 0.01488x^2 - 0.5393x + 31.40$ where *x* is the number of years since 1950 and *y* is the number in millions of Americans living in multigenerational households. The parameter $c = 31.40$ gives the model's prediction for the 1950 number.

y
56
48
40
32
24
0
10 20 30 40 50 60
x
# of Americans (Millions)
Years Since 1950

c. The model is a very close fit for the individual values and for the overall trend.

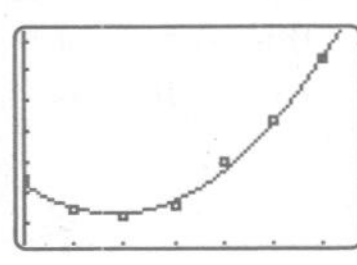

d. 2020: $y = 0.01488(70)^2 - 0.5393(70) + 31.40 \approx 67$ million;
2040: $y = 0.01488(90)^2 - 0.5393(90) + 31.40 \approx 103$ million;
Possible answer: The first number seems fairly reasonable, as it is not far in the future of the model and the model trend looks pretty strong. The second number is not reasonable, as it is far in the future and the overall population is growing much too slowly for this to happen without a large cultural change.

COOPERATIVE LEARNING

Have students work in small groups to make a poster showing how to choose a model for a data set. Give each group a different data set from among linear, quadratic, and exponential data. Then have each group present its poster to the rest of the class, and ask for a volunteer from the group to explain their model choice.

AVOID COMMON ERRORS

Some students may not choose the best model when they are exploring data sets. Suggest that they use the visual connection to a scatter plot to help them decide. Remind them that if the first differences in the $f(x)$ values are constant, then the model should be linear. If the second differences are constant, the model should be quadratic. If the ratios of the $f(x)$ values are constant, the model should be exponential.

3. **Cycling** The data set shows the inseam length for different frame sizes for road bicycles.

Frame Size (cm)	Inseam Length (cm)
46	69
48	71
49	74
51	76
53	79
54	81
58	86
60	89
61	91

Jarrell has an inseam of 84 cm, but the table does not give a frame size for him. He graphs the model on a graphing calculator and finds that a y-value of 84 is closest to an x-value of 56. He decides he needs a 56 cm frame. Do you think this is a reasonable conclusion. Explain.

a. Linear; the data show a clear linear pattern with no significant variation from it. The fit should be very close. The model will have a positive value for a since the graph is rising. Because the data are very far from the y-axis, the y-intercept of the model will not be meaningful in this context.

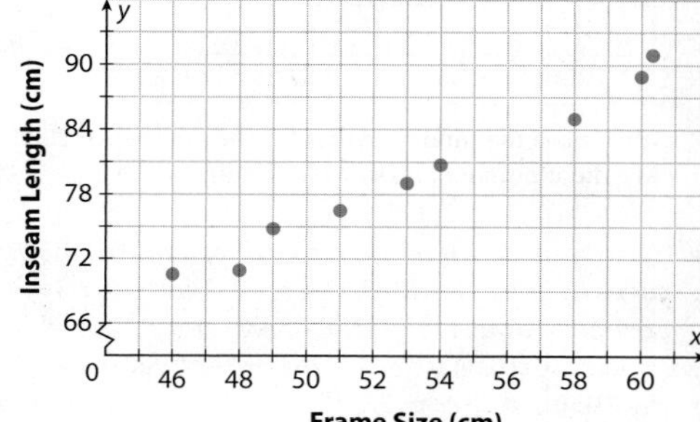

b. The model is $y = 1.454x + 2.008$ where x is the frame size in cm and y is the inseam length in cm. The rate of change indicated by the model is 1.454 additional cm of inseam length per cm increase in frame size.

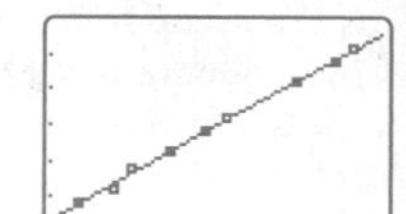

c. The model is an extremely close fit for the individual values and for the overall trend.

d. Possible answer: Yes; the model is a very close fit to the data. Also, this data point lies within the domain and range of the model data, so it should be safe to make the conclusion.

4. Population Geography The data set shows the percent of the U.S. population living in central cities.

What does your model predict for the percent of the population living in central cities in 2010? How much confidence would you have in this prediction? Explain. Given that the actual number for 2010 was about 36.9%, does this support your judgment?

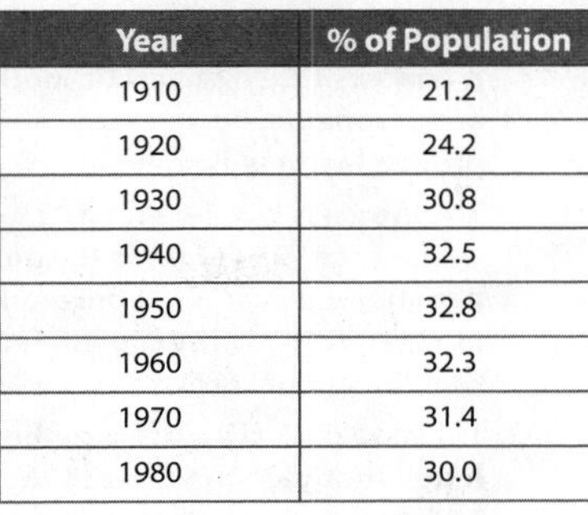

Year	% of Population
1910	21.2
1920	24.2
1930	30.8
1940	32.5
1950	32.8
1960	32.3
1970	31.4
1980	30.0

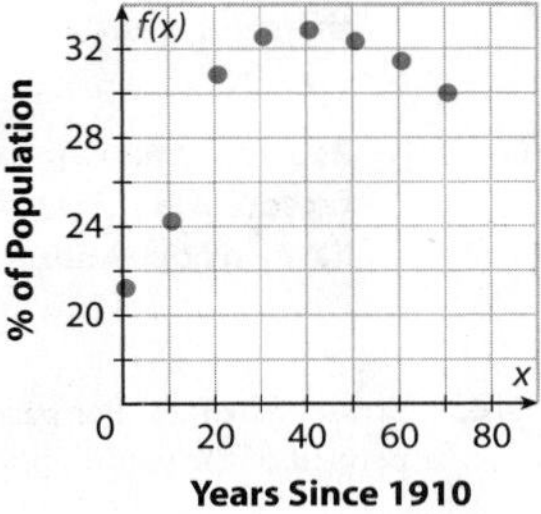

a. Quadratic; the data show what looks to be a downward-opening U-shape. Because it is opening downward, the model will have a negative value for the lead coefficient *a*. The model should fit fairly closely, but because the data to the right of the vertex are curving less slowly than the data to the left, the model may not show the trend too well to the right.

b. The model is $y = -0.006060x^2 + 0.5461x + 20.89$ where x is the number of years since 1910 and y is the percent of the population living in central cities. The parameter $c = 20.89$. gives the model's prediction for the 1910 number.

c. The model is a fairly close fit for the individual data values. It does, however, look to drop more quickly to the right than the data values indicate.

d. 2010: $y = -0.006060(100)^2 + 0.5461(100) + 20.89 \approx 15\%$;

Possible answer: Very little confidence; the model appears that it will underestimate the percent even for 1990, and 2010 is much farther out from the domain of the data. The actual value of 36.9% supports this conclusion. Not only did the decline in the percent living in central cities slow its decline, but it actually increased.

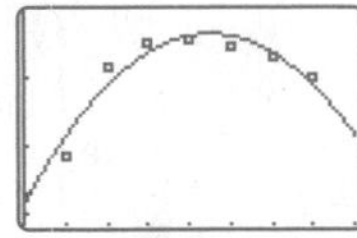

5. Animal Migration The data set shows the number of bald eagles counted passing a particular location on a migration route. Predict the number of bald eagles in 2033. How much confidence do you have in this prediction?

Year	Number of Eagles
1973	41
1978	79
1983	384
1988	261
1993	1725
1998	3289
2003	3356

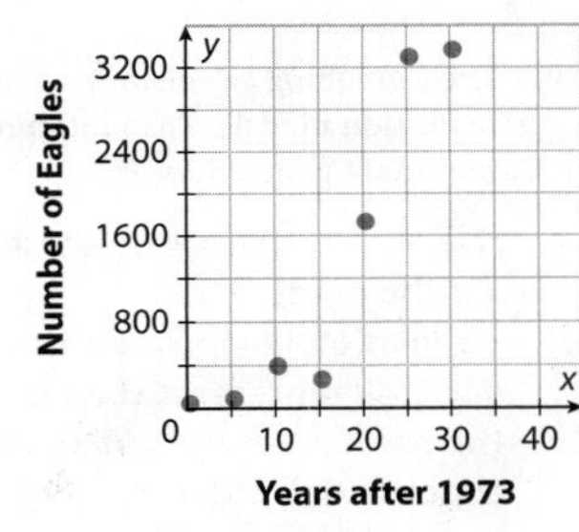

a. Exponential; the data are a clearly not linear, and appear to roughly approximate exponential growth, though

INTEGRATE MATHEMATICAL PRACTICES

Focus on Reasoning

MP.2 When analyzing a regression equation, ask students to make sure the equation makes sense with respect to the original data set. Have them check several data points in the model to see if the model fits the points fairly closely. If not, they can try a different regression model. Caution them that the values generated by the model may not appear anywhere in the actual data set.

AVOID COMMON ERRORS

Watch for students who do not know how to interpret a real-world model. Explain that the model may be limited by the constraints of the data and that for small amounts of data, more than one type of model may seem appropriate. Caution students that they may have to estimate the trend in the data if the data is to be extrapolated beyond the data points.

5. (continued)

it appears that a quadratic model could also be reasonable. Because the model shows growth, the growth factor will be greater than 1.

b. **The model is $y = 44.94(1.172)^x$ where x is the number of years since 1973 and y is the number of eagles counted. The parameter $a = 44.94$ is the model's estimate for the initial number in 1973. The growth factor is 1.172, which means that the annual growth rate is 17.2% annually.**

c. **The model is very closely to the first two data points, though it does not pass too close to the other points individually. Still, the model does look like a reasonable approximation of the data trend.**

d. **2033: $y = 44.94(1.172)^{60} \approx 614{,}171$**

Possible answer: very little confidence; there are many factors that affect eagle population, so the population would likely not continue to grow exponentially at the same rate.

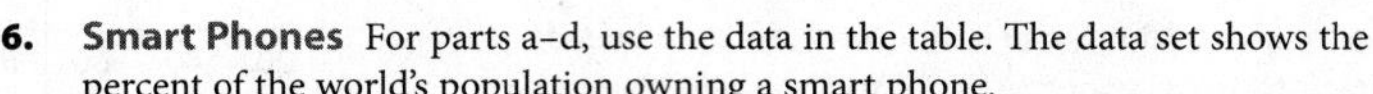

6. Smart Phones For parts a–d, use the data in the table. The data set shows the percent of the world's population owning a smart phone.

a. Create a scatter plot of the data.

Year	% of Population
2006	1
2007	3
2008	4
2009	5
2010	7
2011	11
2012	16
2013	22

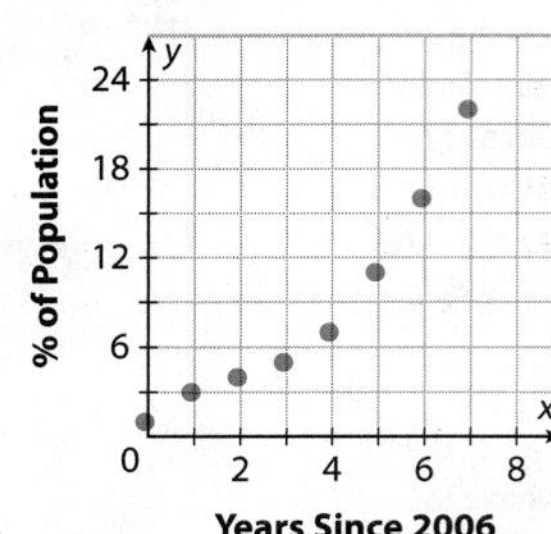

b. Use a graphing calculator to find equations for both exponential and quadratic regression models. Then interpret the models, including the meaning of important parameters.

The models are $y = 1.49(1.49)^x$ and $y = 0.446x^2 - 0.327x + 1.96$ where x is the number of years since 2006 and y is the percent of the world's population having a smart phone. In the exponential model the parameter $a = 1.49$ represents the initial percent in 2006. This is also represented by the parameter $c = 1.96$ in the quadratic model. The growth factor in the exponential model is 1.49, representing an annual growth rate of 49%.

c. Graph both regression models with the scatter plot using a graphing calculator. Do both models fit the data well? Does one seem significantly better than the other?

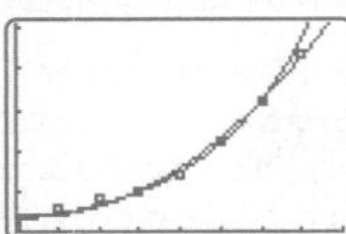

Both models fit the data well. The exponential model is a little closer to the initial value, but the quadratic model is better at the end of the data set, as the exponential model seems to be rising a little too quickly.

d. For how long after the data set do you think either model will be a good predictor? Explain your reasoning.

Possible answer: A couple of years at most; because the data give percent, exponential or even quadratic growth cannot continue long because a smaller and smaller percent of the world's population will be available for expansion—and the percent can never rise above 100. So the rate of increase must slow more and more as it gets closer to 100%. The exponential model predicts 80% only 3 years later, which is very unreasonable. Even the slower-rising quadratic model predicts 62% only 5 years later, which is also unreasonable.

7. Stock Market The data set gives the U.S. stock market's average annual return rates by for each of the last 11 decades.

Decade Ending	Annual Return Rate (%)
1910	9.96
1920	4.20
1930	14.95
1940	−0.63
1950	8.72
1960	19.28
1970	7.78
1980	5.82
1990	17.57
2000	18.17
2010	3.1

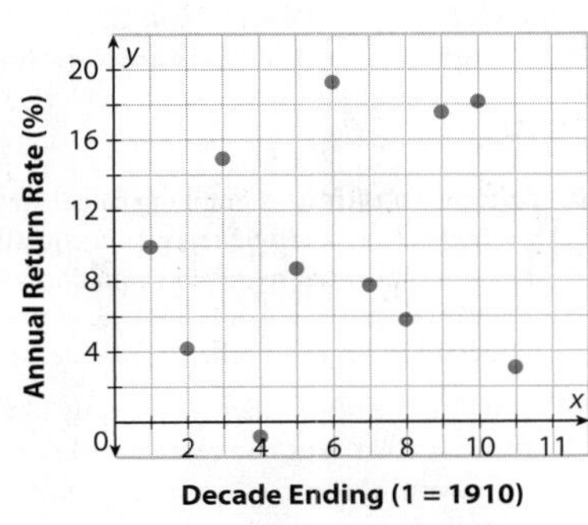

a. Make a scatter plot of the data.

b. What kind of model do you think is most appropriate for the data? Explain your reasoning.

Possible answer: No model; there is no apparent pattern to the data.

c. Do the data give any kind of prediction about investing in the stock market for the future? Explain.

Possible answer: The data give some prediction in the sense that they show that over the course of a decade, stocks have nearly always risen, and usually by at least several percent per year during the decade. So while the data give very little indication about any short period of time, they show that over a long enough time stocks generally rise several percent annually.

INTEGRATE MATHEMATICAL PRACTICES

Focus on Modeling

MP.4 Remind students that they can make a scatter plot of data in order to make a prediction about the type of model that will fit the data. Then, they can do linear, quadratic, and exponential regressions in the same way to verify their predictions.

WHOLE CLASS DISCUSSION

Lead a class discussion about how to distinguish linear, quadratic, and exponential regression equations for data sets. Ask students to make conjectures about the characteristics of the scatter plots for these models and to describe how the scatter plots should look when the model closely represents the data and when the model is not a good fit for the data.

JOURNAL

Have students use words, graphs, calculators, and/or tables to explain how to choose a model for a data set

H.O.T. Focus on Higher Order Thinking

8. **Explain the Error** Out of curiosity, Julia enters the stock market data from Exercise 7 into her calculator and performs linear and quadratic regression. As she expected, there is almost no fit to the data at all. She then tries exponential regression, and get the message "ERR: DOMAIN." Why does she get this message?

   The data contain a negative value, but exponential regression works only with positive data values.

9. **Critical Thinking** A student enters the road bicycle data from Exercise 3, accidentally performs quadratic regression instead of linear, and has the calculator graph the regression model with the scatter plot. The student sees this graph:

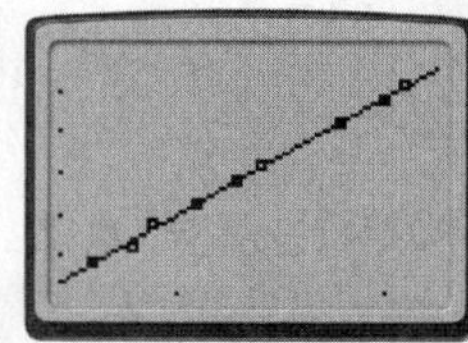

   The model graphed by the calculator is $y = -0.001241x^2 + 1.587x - 1.549$. It is obviously a very close fit to the data, and looks almost identical to the linear model. Explain how this can be true. (*Hint*: What happens when you zoom out?)

   Possible answer: When you keep zooming out, you see that the model is actually parabolic in shape (opening downward), but to find a quadratic model, the calculator has had to make the neighborhood of the data such a tiny, tiny part of the curve of the parabola that it appears basically straight where it passes through the data. Additionally, the parameter a in front of the *x* squared term in quadratic model is close to 0 and very small compared to *b*, and *c*.

10. **Critical Thinking** A graphing calculator returns a linear regression equation $y = ax + b$, a quadratic regression equation $y = ax^2 + bx + c$, and an exponential regression equation $y = a \cdot b^x$. For exponential regression, a is always positive, which is not true of the other models. How does an exponential model differ from the other two models regarding translations of a parent function?

    The linear and quadratic models have a term that indicates a vertical shift, but the exponential model does not. All of the exponential regression models will have the *x*-axis as an asymptote.

11. **Extension** In past work, you have used the correlation coefficient r, which indicates how well a line fits the data. The closer $|r|$ is to 1, the better the fit, and the closer to 0, the worse the fit. When you perform quadratic or exponential regression with a calculator, the *coefficient of determination* r^2 or R^2 serves a similar purpose. Return to the smart phone data in Exercise 6, and perform the quadratic and exponential regression again. (Make sure that "Diagnostics" is turned on in the Catalog menu of your calculator first.) Which model is the closer fit to the data, that is, for which model is R^2 closest to 1?

    quadratic model: $R^2 \approx 0.99$

    exponential model: $r^2 \approx 0.96$

    The quadratic model is a slightly closer fit.

Lesson Performance Task

A student is given $50 to invest. The student chooses the investment very well. The following data shows the amount that the investment is worth over several years.

x (Years)	y (Dollars)
0	50
1	147
2	462
3	1411
4	4220
5	4431
6	4642

a. Determine an appropriate model for the data. If it is reasonable to break up the data so that you can use different models over different parts of the time, then do so. Explain the reasoning for choosing your model(s).

From year 0 to year 4 the common ratio between the dollar values is always very close to 3. This suggests that an exponential model is most appropriate. Then from year 4 to year 6 there is a common difference of 211, which suggests that a linear model best fits this part of the data.

b. Write a situation that may reflect the given data.

Possible Explanation: The student invested the $50 in a small company that quickly became successful and grew into a large company. The student then sold all the stock and moved that amount into an account that earned 5% simple interest over the next two years.

EXTENSION ACTIVITY

Suppose the student in the Performance Task puts part of the money in the stock market and the rest in a savings account. Have students discuss how they could create a model that would describe the total return for the student's money.
The total return could be the sum of a linear model and an exponential model.

AVOID COMMON ERRORS

Students may answer that the years 0 to 4 are best modeled by the rising curve of a parabola because the numbers are increasing quickly. Have students calculate the ratio $\frac{y_x}{y_{x-1}}$ for years 0 to 4.
The ratio is 3. Explain that an exponential model is best for data values that have a common ratio.

INTEGRATE MATHEMATICAL PRACTICES

Focus on Reasoning

MP.2 Have students extrapolate the data in the table to the years beyond year 6. Have students discuss what assumptions they can and cannot make about the future returns. Have students discuss whether the exponential function of years 0 to 4 will have an effect on the extrapolation past year 6.

Scoring Rubric

2 points: Student correctly solves the problem and explains his/her reasoning.

1 point: Student shows good understanding of the problem but does not fully solve or explain his/her reasoning.

0 points: Student does not demonstrate understanding of the problem.

Study Guide Review

ASSESSMENT AND INTERVENTION

Assign or customize module reviews.

MODULE PERFORMANCE TASK

Mathematical Practices: MP.1, MP.2, MP.4, MP.5, MP.6
F-LE.A.1c, F-LE.A.2, F-BF.A.1

SUPPORTING STUDENT REASONING

Students should begin by thinking about how to find models for each plan. They can then do research, or you can provide them with specific information. Here is some of the information they may ask for.

- **What are the formulas for compound interest and continuously compounded interest?** $A = P\left(1 + \frac{r}{n}\right)^{nt}$ and $A = Pe^{rt}$
- **How can I find the value of t algebraically?** Students will not be able to find t algebraically, because they haven't been introduced to logarithms yet. Tell them that estimating the time to the nearest tenth of a year is accurate enough.

STUDY GUIDE REVIEW

Modeling with Exponential and Other Functions

MODULE 14

Essential Question: How can modeling with exponential and other functions help you to solve real-world problems?

Key Vocabulary
exponential regression
(regresión exponencial)

KEY EXAMPLE *(Lesson 14.1)*

What type of function is illustrated in the table?

x	-1	0	1	2	3
$f(x)$	9	3	1	$\frac{1}{3}$	$\frac{1}{9}$

Whenever x increases by 1, $f(x)$ is multiplied by the common ratio of $\frac{1}{3}$. Since this ratio is less than 1, the table represents an exponential decay function.

KEY EXAMPLE *(Lesson 14.2)*

Create a scatter plot for the data in the table. Treat age as the independent variable x and median BMI as the dependent variable y. Then, use a graphing calculator to find an appropriate regression model of the data. Explain why you chose that particular type of function.

Age	2	3	4	5	6	7	8	9	10
Median BMI	16.5	16.0	15.2	15.2	15.6	15.6	15.8	16.0	16.3

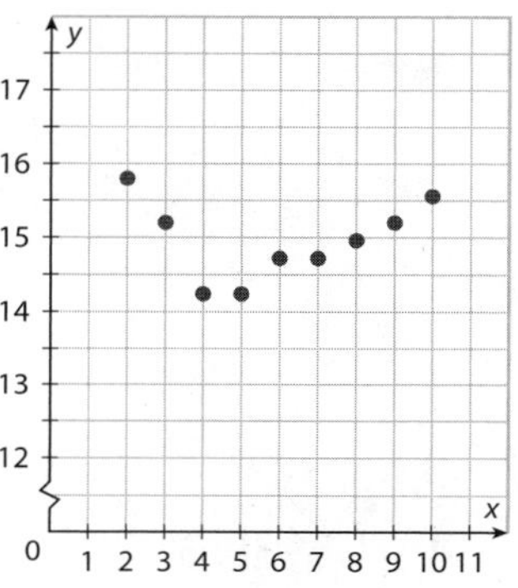

A quadratic regression of the data on a graphing calculator produces the equation $y = 0.0636x^2 - 0.7503x + 17.5867$. A quadratic function was chosen because the data points generally lie on a curve that approximates a parabola.

SCAFFOLDING SUPPORT

- Make sure students know how to use the compound interest formula: n is the number of compounding periods per year, r is the rate in decimal form, and t is the time in years.
- If they are reluctant to use guess and check, reassure them that it is necessary for this particular problem.

EXERCISES

Choose the type of function (linear, quadratic, or exponential) you would use to model the data. *(Lesson 14.2)*

1.

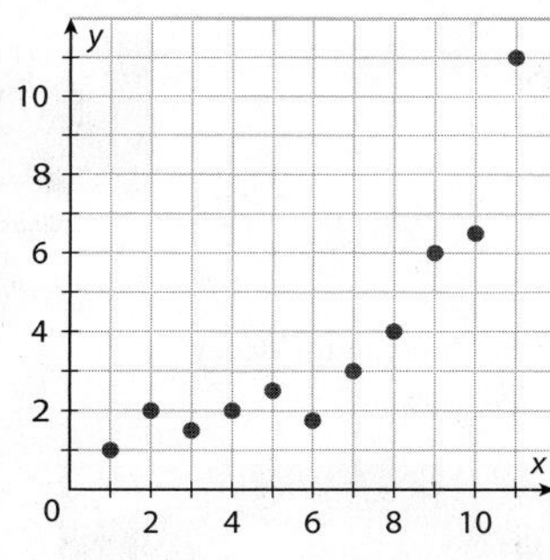

exponential function

2.

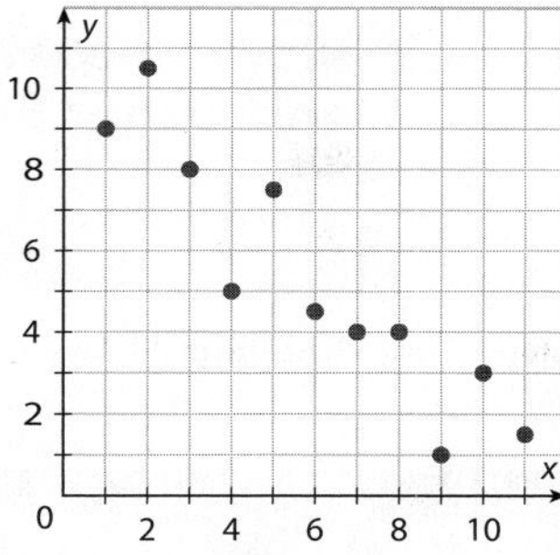

linear function

3. How does the Product of Powers Property of Exponents help you in deciding whether a given set of data is exponential? *(Lesson 14.1)*

For an exponential function $f(x) = ab^x$, you can use the Product of Powers Property of Exponents to get the following result: $f(x+1) = ab^{x+1} = ab^x \cdot b^1 = f(x) \cdot b$. You can conclude that when the value of x increases by 1, the value of $f(x)$ is multiplied by b. If you know this information, you can decide whether a given set of data is exponential.

MODULE PERFORMANCE TASK

Double Your Money

Jenna was a game show participant and won \$10,000! She eventually wants to use the money as a down payment on a home but is not quite ready for such a big commitment. She decides to invest the money and plans to use it once the amount reaches \$20,000. She researches various investment opportunities and would like to choose the one that will let her money double fastest.

Plan	Interest Rate	Compounding
Plan A	5.2%	Quarterly
Plan B	4.8%	Monthly
Plan C	4.25%	Continuously

To the nearest tenth of a year, how long will each plan take to double Jenna's money? Which should Jenna choose? Use your own paper to complete the task. Be sure to write down all your data and assumptions. Then use graphs, numbers, words, or algebra to explain how you reached your conclusion.

SAMPLE SOLUTION

Find models for each of the three investment plans, using $A = P\left(1 + \frac{r}{n}\right)^{nt}$ or $A = Pe^{rt}$.

Plan A: $n = 4$; $r = 0.05$; $P = 10,000$

$$20,000 = 10,000\left(1 + \frac{0.052}{4}\right)^{4 \cdot t}$$

Plan B: $n = 12$; $r = 0.048$; $P = 10,000$

$$20,000 = 10,000\left(1 + \frac{0.048}{12}\right)^{12 \cdot t}$$

Plan C: $r = 0.0425$; $P = 10,000$

$$20,000 = 10,000e^{0.0425t}$$

Now, graph each plan to get an estimate of when it will reach \$20,000:

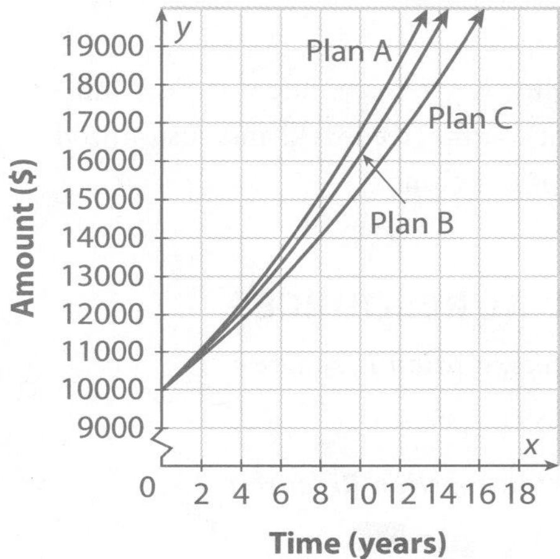

Finally, use a series of guesses to find a more precise value for each plan, to the nearest tenth of a year. This goes quickly using the table feature of a graphing calculator.

Plan A takes about 13.4 years to double, plan B takes about 14.5 years, and Plan C takes about 16.3 years. Jenna should choose plan A.

DISCUSSION OPPORTUNITIES

- What is e? Aside from continuously compounded interest, what is it used for?
- Does it appear that increasing the rate of compounding increases the value of an investment a lot, or just a little? Does moving from monthly compounding to continuous compounding make a big difference?

Assessment Rubric

2 points: Student correctly solves the problem and explains his/her reasoning.

1 point: Student shows good understanding of the problem but does not fully solve or explain.

0 points: Student does not demonstrate understanding of the problem.

Ready to Go On?

ASSESS MASTERY

Use the assessment on this page to determine if students have mastered the concepts and standards covered in this module.

ASSESSMENT AND INTERVENTION

Access Ready to Go On? assessment online, and receive instant scoring, feedback, and customized intervention or enrichment.

ADDITIONAL RESOURCES

Response to Intervention Resources

- Reteach Worksheets

Differentiated Instruction Resources

- Reading Strategies EL
- Success for English Learners EL
- Challenge Worksheets

Assessment Resources

- Leveled Module Quizzes

14.1–14.2 Modeling with Exponential and Other Functions

- Online Homework
- Hints and Help
- Extra Practice

The isotope X has a half-life of 10 days. Complete the table showing the decay of a sample of X. *(Lessons 14.1, 14.2)*

1.

Number of Half-Lives	Number of Days (t)	Percent of Isotope Remaining (p)
0	0	100
1	10	50
2	20	**25**
3	**30**	**12.5**
4	**40**	**6.25**

2. Write the decay rate per half-life, r, as a fraction.

$$r = \frac{1}{2}$$

3. Write an expression for the number of half-lives in t days.

$$\frac{t}{10}$$

4. Write a function that models this situation. The function $p(t)$ should give the percent of the isotope remaining after t days.

$$p(t) = 100\left(\frac{1}{2}\right)^{\frac{t}{10}}$$

ESSENTIAL QUESTION

5. What are two ways you can find an exponential function that models a given set of data?

Possible Answer: You can perform an exponential regression using a graphing calculator. Or, you can identify the initial value of a and estimate the growth or decay factor of b.

COMMON CORE Common Core Standards

Lesson	*Items*	Content Standards	Mathematical Practices
14.1	1	**S-ID.B.6a**	**MP.2**
14.1	2	**S-ID.B.6a**	**MP.2**
14.1	3	**S-ID.B.6a**	**MP.2**
14.1, 14.2	4	**S-ID.B.6a**	**MP.7**

MODULE 14
MIXED REVIEW

Assessment Readiness

1. Look at each exponential function. Does the function pass through (1, 2) and (3, 50)? Select Yes or No for A–C.

   A. $y = \frac{3}{5} \cdot 5^x$ ○ Yes ● No

   B. $y = \frac{2}{5} \cdot 5^x$ ● Yes ○ No

   C. $y = \frac{1}{2} \cdot 5^x$ ○ Yes ● No

2. Consider the function $y = -2\left(\frac{1}{4}\right)^{x+1} + 7$. Choose True or False for each statement.

   A. The asymptote of the function is $y = 7$. ● True ○ False

   B. The asymptote of the function is $x = 7$. ○ True ● False

   C. The function has no asymptote. ○ True ● False

3. Are there real solutions to the equation $x^3 - 5x^2 = 0$? Explain, then state the roots.

   There are two real-number solutions at 0 and 5. When the function is graphed, that is where it touches the *x*-axis.

4. Describe the type of function illustrated in the table. Explain.

x	4	5	6	7	8
y	−4	−3	−4	−7	−12

   Possible answer: When placed into the calculator in the STAT function, the quadratic regression equation fits the data better than any of the other regressions. Therefore, the function should be quadratic.

5. How can you use the pattern formed by the points on a scatterplot to determine whether to fit the data to a linear, quadratic, or exponential function?

   If the points on a scatterplot of the data generally follow a line, a linear function is the most appropriate model to choose. If the points follow a curve with both rises and falls, then a quadratic function is more appropriate. If the points follow a curve that rises or falls rapidly on one side and flattens on the other, an exponential is the best choice

COMMON CORE

Common Core Standards

Lesson	Items	Content Standards	Mathematical Practices
14.1	1	**S-ID.B.6**	**MP.1**
13.2	2*	**F-BF.B.3**	**MP.2**
7.1	3*	**A-APR.B.2**	**MP.6**
14.1	4	**S-ID.B.6**	**MP.7**
14.2	5	**S-ID.B.6**	**MP.6**

* Item integrates mixed review concepts from previous modules or a previous course.

MIXED REVIEW

Assessment Readiness

ASSESSMENT AND INTERVENTION

Assign ready-made or customized practice tests to prepare students for high-stakes tests.

ADDITIONAL RESOURCES

Assessment Resources

- Leveled Module Quizzes: Modified, B

AVOID COMMON ERRORS

Item 4 Students may find it difficult to find the shape of a function when given only a table or set of points. Encourage students to represent data visually to better see its shape.

MODULE 15

Logarithmic Functions

ESSENTIAL QUESTION:

Answer: Logarithmic functions are often found in relationships involving sensory data. For example, the relationship between the number of photons hitting a retina and the perceived brightness is logarithmic.

PROFESSIONAL DEVELOPMENT VIDEO

Professional Development Video

Author Matt Larson models successful teaching practices in an actual high-school classroom.

Professional Development
my.hrw.com

Logarithmic Functions

MODULE 15

Essential Question: How can you use logarithmic functions to solve real-world problems?

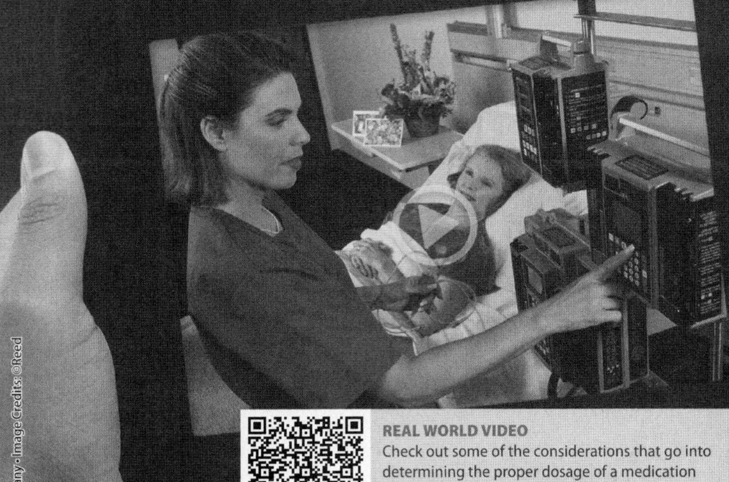

REAL WORLD VIDEO
Check out some of the considerations that go into determining the proper dosage of a medication and learn about the role of logarithmic functions in this process.

MODULE PERFORMANCE TASK PREVIEW

What's the Dosage?

Scientists working in the pharmaceutical industry discover, develop, and test drugs for everything from relieving a headache to controlling high blood pressure. One important question regarding a specific drug is how long the drug stays in a person's system. How can logarithmic functions be used to answer this question? Let's find out!

DIGITAL TEACHER EDITION

Access a full suite of teaching resources when and where you need them:

- Access content online or offline
- Customize lessons to share with your class
- Communicate with your students in real-time
- View student grades and data instantly to target your instruction where it is needed most

PERSONAL MATH TRAINER

Assessment and Intervention

Assign automatically graded homework, quizzes, tests, and intervention activities. Prepare your students with updated, Common Core-aligned practice tests.

Are YOU Ready?

Complete these exercises to review skills you will need for this chapter.

Personal Math Trainer
- Online Homework
- Hints and Help
- Extra Practice

Exponents

Example 1 Rewrite $x^{-3}y^2$ using only positive exponents.

$x^{-3}y^2 = \frac{y^2}{x^3}$

Rewrite each expression using only positive exponents.

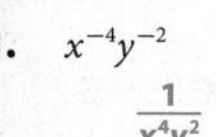

1. $x^{-4}y^{-2}$ $\frac{1}{x^4y^2}$
2. x^8y^{-5} $\frac{x^8}{y^5}$
3. $\frac{x^{-1}}{y^{-2}}$ $\frac{y^2}{x}$

Rational and Radical Exponents

Example 2 Write $\sqrt[4]{a^6b^4}$ using rational exponents.

$\sqrt[4]{a^6b^4} = (a^6b^4)^{\frac{1}{4}}$ Remove the radical symbol.

$= a^{\frac{3}{2}}b$ Simplify.

Write the expression using rational exponents.

4. $\sqrt[6]{a^3b^{12}}$ $a^{\frac{1}{2}}b^2$
5. $\sqrt[3]{ab^2}$ $a^{\frac{1}{3}}b^{\frac{2}{3}}$
6. $\sqrt[4]{81a^{12}b^8}$ $3a^3b^2$

Graphing Linear Nonproportional Relationships

Example 3 Graph $y = -3x + 1$.

Graph the y-intercept of $(0, 1)$.

Use the slope $\frac{-3}{1}$ to plot a second point.

Draw a line through the two points.

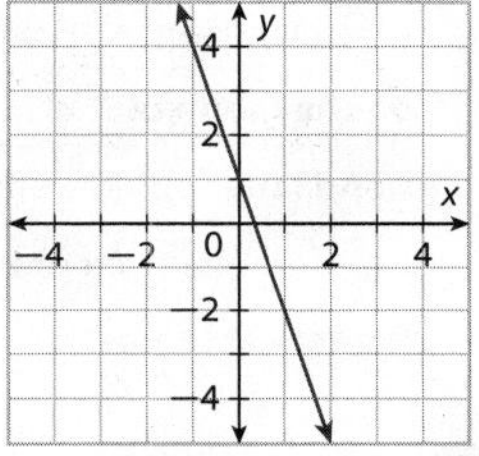

Graph each equation.

7. $y = \frac{2}{3}x - 4$

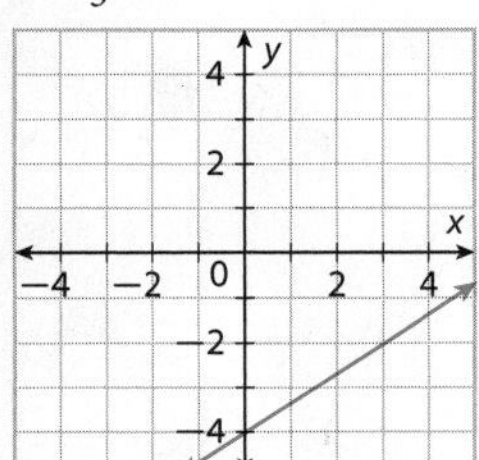

8. $y = 2x + 3$

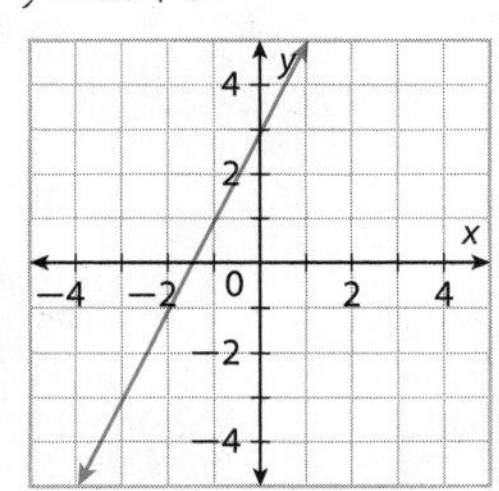

Response to Intervention			Differentiated Instruction
Tier 1 Lesson Intervention Worksheets	**Tier 2** Strategic Intervention Skills Intervention Worksheets	**Tier 3** Intensive Intervention Worksheets available online	
Reteach 15.1 Reteach 15.2	9 Exponents 14 Graphing Linear Nonproportional Relationships 28 Rational and Radical Exponents	Building Block Skills 29, 43, 44, 46, 75, 76, 94, 100	Challenge worksheets Extend the Math Lesson Activities in TE

Are You Ready?

ASSESS READINESS

Use the assessment on this page to determine if students need strategic or intensive intervention for the module's prerequisite skills.

ASSESSMENT AND INTERVENTION

RtI Response to Intervention TIER 1, TIER 2, TIER 3 SKILLS

Personal Math Trainer will automatically create a standards-based, personalized intervention assignment for your students, targeting each student's individual needs!

ADDITIONAL RESOURCES

See the table below for a full list of intervention resources available for this module.

Response to Intervention Resources also includes:

- Tier 2 Skill Pre-Tests for each Module
- Tier 2 Skill Post-Tests for each skill

LESSON 15.1

Defining and Evaluating a Logarithmic Function

Common Core Math Standards

The student is expected to:

F.BF.B.5(+)

Understand the inverse relationship between exponents and logarithms and use this relationship to solve problems involving logarithms and exponents. Also F.IF.C.7, F.IF.C.7e, F.IF.A.2

Mathematical Practices

COMMON CORE **MP.2 Reasoning**

Language Objective

Discuss with a partner the relationship between exponential and logarithmic functions.

ENGAGE

Essential Question: What is the inverse of the exponential function $f(x) = b^x$ where $b > 0$ and $b \neq 1$, and what is the value of $f^{-1}(b^m)$ for any real number m?

Possible answer: The inverse of $f(x) = b^x$ is $f^{-1}(x) = \log_b x$, the logarithm with base b of x. The value of $f^{-1}(b^m)$ is m because the inverse function accepts a power of b as an input and delivers the exponent as an output.

PREVIEW: LESSON PERFORMANCE TASK

View the Engage section online. Discuss the photo and how air pressure is a function of altitude. Then preview the Lesson Performance Task.

Name ______ Class ______ Date ______

15.1 Defining and Evaluating a Logarithmic Function

Resource Locker

Essential Question: What is the inverse of the exponential function $f(x) = b^x$ where $b > 0$ and $b \neq 1$, and what is the value of $f^{-1}(b^m)$ for any real number m?

Explore Understanding Logarithmic Functions as Inverses of Exponential Functions

An exponential function such as $f(x) = 2^x$ accepts values of the exponent as inputs and delivers the corresponding power of 2 as the outputs. The inverse of an exponential function is called a **logarithmic function**. For $f(x) = 2^x$, the inverse function is written $f^{-1}(x) = \log_2 x$, which is read either as "the logarithm with base 2 of x" or simply as "log base 2 of x." It accepts powers of 2 as inputs and delivers the corresponding exponents as outputs.

(A) Graph $f^{-1}(x) = \log_2 x$ using the graph of $f(x) = 2^x$ shown. Begin by reflecting the labeled points on the graph of $f(x) = 2^x$ across the line $y = x$ and labeling the reflected points with their coordinates. Then draw a smooth curve through the reflected points.

Graph $f^{-1}(x) = \log_2 x$ using the graph of $f(x) = 2^x$ shown. Begin by reflecting the labeled points on the graph of $f(x) = 2^x$ across the line $y = x$ and labeling the reflected points with their coordinates. Then draw a smooth curve through the reflected points.

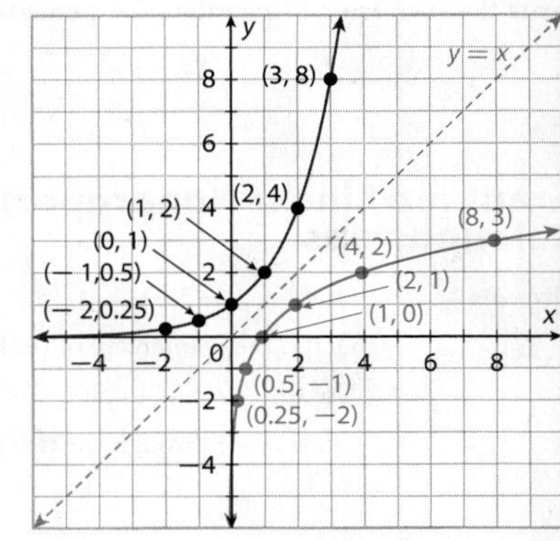

(B) Using the labeled points on the graph of $f^{-1}(x)$, complete the following statements.

$f^{-1}(0.25) = \log_2$ **0.25** $=$ **−2**

$f^{-1}(0.5) = \log_2$ **0.5** $=$ **−1**

$f^{-1}(1) = \log_2$ **1** $=$ **0**

$f^{-1}(2) = \log_2$ **2** $=$ **1**

$f^{-1}(4) = \log_2$ **4** $=$ **2**

$f^{-1}(8) = \log_2$ **8** $=$ **3**

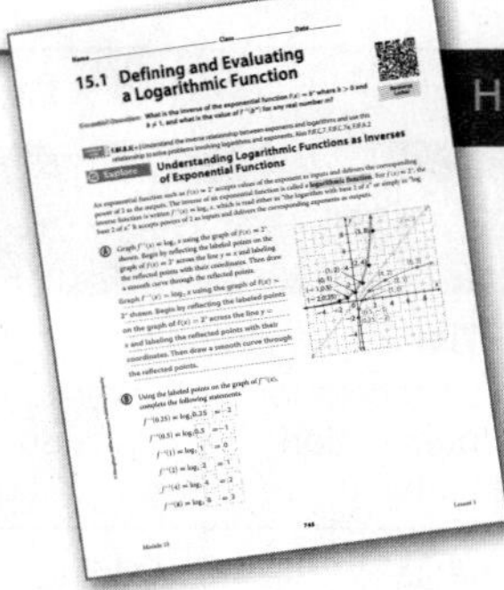

Watch for the hardcover student edition page numbers for this lesson.

Reflect

1. Explain why the domain of $f(x) = 2^x$ doesn't need to be restricted in order for its inverse to be a function.
The exponential function $f(x) = 2^x$ is a one-to-one function, so its inverse is a function.

2. State the domain and range of $f^{-1}(x) = \log_2 x$ using set notation.
The domain is $\{x | x > 0\}$, and the range is $\{y | -\infty < y < +\infty\}$.

3. Identify any intercepts and asymptotes for the graph of $f^{-1}(x) = \log_2 x$.
The graph has an x-intercept at $x = 1$ and no y-intercepts. The y-axis $(x = 0)$ is the graph's asymptote.

4. Is $f^{-1}(x) = \log_2 x$ an increasing function or a decreasing function?
The function is an increasing function.

5. How does $f^{-1}(x) = \log_2 x$ behave as x increases without bound? As x decreases toward 0?
As $x \to +\infty$, $f^{-1}(x) \to +\infty$. As $x \to 0^+$, $f^{-1}(x) \to -\infty$.

6. Based on the inverse relationship between $f(x) = 2^x$ and $f^{1}(x) = \log_2 x$, complete this statement:

$f^{-1}(16) = \log_2 \boxed{16} = \boxed{4}$ because $f\left(\boxed{4}\right) = \boxed{16}$.

Explain 1 Converting Between Exponential and Logarithmic Forms of Equations

In general, the exponential function $f(x) = b^x$, where $b > 0$ and $b \neq 1$, has the logarithmic function $f^{-1}(x) = \log_b x$ as its inverse. For instance, if $f(x) = 3^x$, then $f^{-1}(x) = \log_3 x$, and if $f(x) = \left(\frac{1}{4}\right)^x$, then $f^{-1}(x) = \log_{\frac{1}{4}} x$. The inverse relationship between exponential functions and logarithmic functions also means that you can write any exponential equation as a logarithmic equation and any logarithmic equation as an exponential equation.

Exponential Equation	Logarithmic Equation
$b^x = a$	$\log_b a = x$

$$b > 0, b \neq 1$$

PROFESSIONAL DEVELOPMENT

Learning Progressions

Students have learned about functions and their inverses in previous lessons. They have also learned about exponential functions. In this lesson, students learn that the inverse of an exponential function is called a *logarithmic function*. They learn how to evaluate logarithmic functions, and how to work with logarithmic functions that model real-world situations. In the following lesson, students will learn to how to graph logarithmic functions.

EXPLORE

Understanding Logarithmic Functions as Inverses of Exponential Functions

INTEGRATE TECHNOLOGY

Students have the option of completing the Explore activity either in the book or online.

QUESTIONING STRATEGIES

? Why does reflecting the graph of the exponential function across the line $y = x$ produce the graph of a logarithmic function? Because the graphs of inverse functions are reflections across the line $y = x$, and the inverse of an exponential function is a logarithmic function.

? How do you know that the graph of the logarithmic function has no horizontal asymptotes? The graph of the exponential function has no vertical asymptotes.

INTEGRATE MATHEMATICAL PRACTICES

Focus on Communication

MP.3 Have students discuss the attributes of the graph of the logarithmic function. Ask them to identify the domain and range of the function, and any intercepts. Also have them determine whether the function is increasing or decreasing, and describe its end behavior. Have them compare these attributes to those of the graph of the exponential function.

EXPLAIN 1

Converting Between Exponential and Logarithmic Forms of Equations

QUESTIONING STRATEGIES

? In the expression $\log_b y = x$, what does b represent? **b is the base in the power b^x.**

? In the expression $\log_b y = x$, what does x represent? **x is the exponent in the power b^x.**

? In the equation $\log_b y = x$, what does y represent? **y is the value of b^x in the equation $b^x = y$.**

Example 1 **Complete the table by writing each given equation in its alternate form.**

Exponential Equation	Logarithmic Equation
$4^3 = 64$	?
?	$\log_5 \frac{1}{25} = -2$
$\left(\frac{2}{3}\right)^p = q$	?
?	$\log_{\frac{1}{2}} m = n$

Think of each equation as involving an exponential function or a logarithmic function. Identify the function's base, input, and output. For the inverse function, use the same base but switch the input and output.

Think of the equation $4^3 = 64$ as involving an exponential function with base 4. The input is 3, and the output is 64. So, the inverse function (a logarithmic function) also has base 4, but its input is 64, and its output is 3.

Think of the equation $\log_5 \frac{1}{25} = -2$ as involving a logarithmic function with base 5. The input is $\frac{1}{25}$, and the output is -2. So, the inverse function (an exponential function) also has base 5, but its input is -2, and its output is $\frac{1}{25}$.

Think of the equation $\left(\frac{2}{3}\right)^p = q$ as involving an exponential function with base $\frac{2}{3}$. The input is p, and the output is q. So, the inverse function (a logarithmic function) also has base $\frac{2}{3}$, but its input is q, and its output is p.

Think of the equation $\log_{\frac{1}{2}} m = -n$ as involving a logarithmic function with base $\frac{1}{2}$. The input is m, and the output is n. So, the inverse function (an exponential function) also has base $\frac{1}{2}$, but its input is n, and its output is m.

Exponential Equation	Logarithmic Equation
$4^3 = 64$	$\log_4 64 = 3$
$5^{-2} = \frac{1}{25}$	$\log_5 \frac{1}{25} = -2$
$\left(\frac{2}{3}\right)^p = q$	$\log_{\frac{2}{3}} q = p$
$\left(\frac{1}{2}\right)^n = m$	$\log_{\frac{1}{2}} m = n$

COLLABORATIVE LEARNING

Peer-to-Peer Activity

Ask students, "What are some powers you know by heart?" Write some of these on one side of the board. Explain that for every power they know, they already know the logarithm. Write the logarithmic form alongside each of their exponential equations, with assistance from students. Review the meanings of positive and negative exponents. Be sure that students are comfortable moving back and forth between exponential and logarithmic forms.

Ⓑ

Exponential Equation	Logarithmic Equation
$3^5 = 243$	$\log_3 243 = 5$
$4^{-3} = \frac{1}{64}$	$\log_4 \frac{1}{64} = -3$
$\left(\frac{3}{4}\right)^r = s$	$\log_{\frac{3}{4}} s = r$
$\left(\frac{1}{5}\right)^w = v$	$\log_{\frac{1}{5}} v = w$

Think of the equation $3^5 = 243$ as involving an exponential function with base 3. The input is **5**, and the output is **243**. So, the inverse function (a logarithmic function) also has base 3, but its input is **243**, and its output is **5**.

Think of the equation $\log_4 \frac{1}{64} = -3$ as involving a logarithmic function with base **4**. The input is $\frac{1}{64}$, and the output is **−3**. So, the inverse function (an exponential function) also has base **4**, but its input is **−3**, and its output is $\frac{1}{64}$.

Think of the equation $\left(\frac{3}{4}\right)^r = s$ as involving an exponential function with base $\frac{3}{4}$. The input is **r**, and the output is *s*. So, the inverse function (a logarithmic function) also has base $\frac{3}{4}$, but its input is *s*, and its output is **r**.

Think of the equation $\log_{\frac{1}{5}} v = w$ as involving a logarithmic function with base $\frac{1}{5}$. The input is **v**, and the output is **w**. So, the inverse function (an exponential function) also has base $\frac{1}{5}$, but its input is **w**, and its output is **v**.

Reflect

7. A student wrote the logarithmic form of the exponential equation $5^0 = 1$ as $\log_5 0 = 1$. What did the student do wrong? What is the correct logarithmic equation?

The student forgot to switch the input and output when writing the logarithmic equation. The correct equation is $\log_5 1 = 0$.

Your Turn

8. Complete the table by writing each given equation in its alternate form.

Exponential Equation	Logarithmic Equation
$10^4 = 10{,}000$	$\log_{10} 10{,}000 = 4$
$2^{-4} = \frac{1}{16}$	$\log_2 \frac{1}{16} = -4$
$\left(\frac{2}{5}\right)^c = d$	$\log_{\frac{2}{5}} d = c$
$\left(\frac{1}{3}\right)^y = x$	$\log_{\frac{1}{3}} x = y$

CONNECT VOCABULARY EL

Help students to make a connection between the *base* of an exponent and the *base* of the related logarithm, and transfer their understanding of the base of an exponent to its use with logarithms. This will make it easier for them to convert between forms.

DIFFERENTIATE INSTRUCTION

Auditory Cues

The following rhyme may help students remember how to rewrite an exponential equation in logarithmic form.

To convert it to the log form,
Remember each component.
The base goes at the bottom,
And the log is the exponent!

EXPLAIN 2

Evaluating Logarithmic Functions by Thinking in Terms of Exponents

QUESTIONING STRATEGIES

? When evaluating a logarithm such as $\log_2 x$ for some specified value of x, what are you trying to find? **the exponent to which you raise 2 to get x**

Explain 2 Evaluating Logarithmic Functions by Thinking in Terms of Exponents

The logarithmic function $f(x) = \log_b x$ accepts a power of b as an input and delivers an exponent as an output. In cases where the input of a logarithmic function is a recognizable power of b, you should be able to determine the function's output. You may find it helpful first to write a logarithmic equation by letting the output equal x and then to rewrite the equation in exponential form. Once the bases on each side of the exponential equation are equal, you can equate their exponents to find x.

Example 2

Ⓐ If $f(x) = \log_{10} x$, find $f(1000)$, $f(0.01)$, and $f(\sqrt{10})$.

$f(1000) = x$	$f(0.01) = x$	$f(\sqrt{10}) = x$
$\log_{10} 1000 = x$	$\log_{10} 0.01 = x$	$\log_{10} \sqrt{10} = x$
$10^x = 1000$	$10^x = 0.01$	$10^x = \sqrt{10}$
$10^x = 10^3$	$10^x = 10^{-2}$	$10^x = 10^{\frac{1}{2}}$
$x = 3$	$x = -2$	$x = \frac{1}{2}$
So, $f(1000) = 3$.	So, $f(0.01) = -2$.	So, $f(\sqrt{10}) = \frac{1}{2}$.

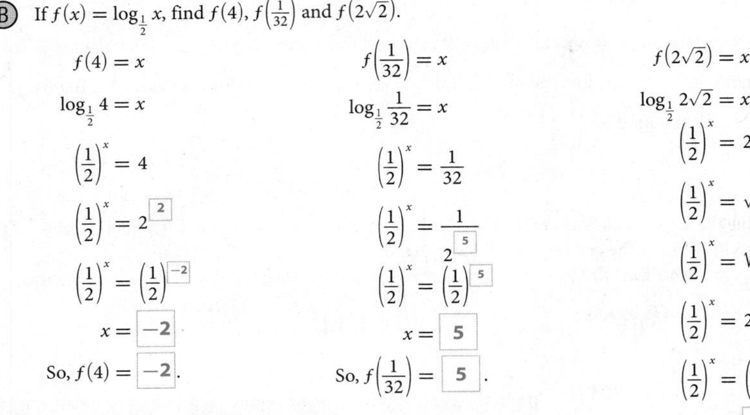

Ⓑ If $f(x) = \log_{\frac{1}{2}} x$, find $f(4)$, $f\left(\frac{1}{32}\right)$ and $f(2\sqrt{2})$.

$f(4) = x$	$f\left(\frac{1}{32}\right) = x$	$f(2\sqrt{2}) = x$
$\log_{\frac{1}{2}} 4 = x$	$\log_{\frac{1}{2}} \frac{1}{32} = x$	$\log_{\frac{1}{2}} 2\sqrt{2} = x$
$\left(\frac{1}{2}\right)^x = 4$	$\left(\frac{1}{2}\right)^x = \frac{1}{32}$	$\left(\frac{1}{2}\right)^x = 2\sqrt{2}$
$\left(\frac{1}{2}\right)^x = 2^{\boxed{2}}$	$\left(\frac{1}{2}\right)^x = \frac{1}{2^{\boxed{5}}}$	$\left(\frac{1}{2}\right)^x = \sqrt{2^2 \cdot 2}$
$\left(\frac{1}{2}\right)^x = \left(\frac{1}{2}\right)^{\boxed{-2}}$	$\left(\frac{1}{2}\right)^x = \left(\frac{1}{2}\right)^{\boxed{5}}$	$\left(\frac{1}{2}\right)^x = \sqrt{2^{\boxed{3}}}$
$x = \boxed{-2}$	$x = \boxed{5}$	$\left(\frac{1}{2}\right)^x = 2^{\boxed{\frac{3}{2}}}$
So, $f(4) = \boxed{-2}$.	So, $f\left(\frac{1}{32}\right) = \boxed{5}$.	$\left(\frac{1}{2}\right)^x = \left(\frac{1}{2}\right)^{\boxed{-\frac{3}{2}}}$
		$x = \boxed{-\frac{3}{2}}$
		So $f(2\sqrt{2}) = \boxed{-\frac{3}{2}}$.

LANGUAGE SUPPORT EL

Communicating Math

Give each pair of students an equation of an exponential function, and ask them to work together to graph it. Then ask them to decide on what the inverse, or logarithmic function, is, write the equation, and graph it.

Your Turn

9. If $f(x) = \log_7 x$, find $f(343)$, $f\left(\frac{1}{49}\right)$, and $f(\sqrt{7})$.

$f(343) = x$
$\log_7 343 = x$
$7^x = 343$
$7^x = 7^3$
$x = 3$
So, $f(343) = 3$.

$f\left(\frac{1}{49}\right) = x$
$\log_7 \frac{1}{49} = x$
$7^x = \frac{1}{49}$
$7^x = \frac{1}{7^2}$
$7^x = 7^{-2}$
$x = -2$
So, $f\left(\frac{1}{49}\right) = -2$.

$f(\sqrt{7}) = x$
$\log_7 \sqrt{7} = x$
$7^x = \sqrt{7}$
$7^x = 7^{\frac{1}{2}}$
$x = \frac{1}{2}$
So, $f(\sqrt{7}) = \frac{1}{2}$.

Explain 3 Evaluating Logarithmic Functions Using a Scientific Calculator

You can use a scientific calculator to find the logarithm of any positive number x when the logarithm's base is either 10 or e. When the base is 10, you are finding what is called the *common logarithm* of x, and you use the calculator's LOG key because $\log_{10} x$ is also written as $\log x$ (where the base is understood to be 10). When the base is e, you are finding what is called the *natural logarithm* of x, and you use the calculator's LN key because $\log_e x$ is also written as $\ln x$.

Example 3 **Use a scientific calculator to find the common logarithm and the natural logarithm of the given number. Verify each result by evaluating the appropriate exponential expression.**

 13

First, find the common logarithm of 13. Round the result to the thousandths place and raise 10 to that number to confirm that the power is close to 13.

log(13)
1.113943352
$10^{1.114}$
13.00169578

So, $\log 13 \approx 1.114$.

Next, find the natural logarithm of 13. Round the result to the thousandths place and raise e to that number to confirm that the power is close to 13.

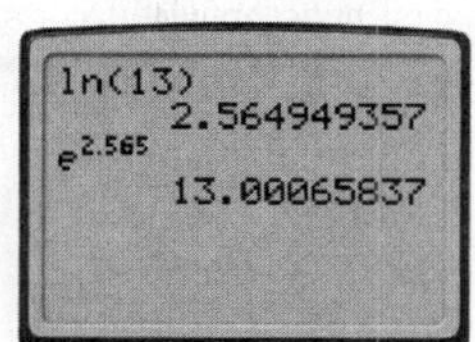

So, $\ln 13 \approx 2.565$.

INTEGRATE MATHEMATICAL PRACTICES

Focus on Communication

MP.3 As students work through these problems, have them verbalize their thought processes. This will enable you to check for understanding, and will also provide an opportunity for students who are struggling to hear how other students are thinking about these problems.

AVOID COMMON ERRORS

When evaluating logarithmic expressions, students sometimes confuse logs that are negative numbers with those that are fractions. For example, when asked to evaluate $\log_4 \frac{1}{16}$, students may think the value must be a fraction, since the argument is a fraction. Help them to see that the value must instead be a negative number, in this case −2, in order for 4^2 to be in the denominator of the fraction.

EXPLAIN 3

Evaluating Logarithmic Functions Using a Scientific Calculator

QUESTIONING STRATEGIES

? Why does the calculator return an error message when you enter log (−1)? You cannot take the log of a negative number. There is no number to which 10 can be raised to get −1.

INTEGRATE MATHEMATICAL PRACTICES

Focus on Technology

MP.5 Discuss with students how to check their answers for reasonableness. Reinforce that when they are finding a common log, they are finding the power of 10 that produces the number, and that when they are finding the natural log, they are finding the power of a base that is a bit less than 3.

INTEGRATE MATHEMATICAL PRACTICES

Focus on Reasoning

MP.2 Ask students to discuss how they can tell which is greater, ln 20 or log 20, without using a calculator. **Students should reason that since ln 20 has a base of *e* and log 20 has a base of 10, and because $e < 10$, the power of *e* that equals 20 must be greater than the power of 10 that equals 20. Therefore ln 20 > log 20.**

(B) 0.42

First, find the common logarithm of 0.42. Round the result to the thousandths place and raise 10 to that number to confirm that the power is close to 0.42.

$\log 0.42 \approx \boxed{-0.377}$

$10^{\boxed{-0.377}} \approx 0.42$

Next, find the natural logarithm of 0.42. Round the result to the thousandths place and raise *e* to that number to confirm that the power is close to 0.42.

$\ln 0.42 \approx \boxed{-0.868}$

$e^{\boxed{-0.868}} \approx 0.42$

Reflect

10. For any $x > 1$, why is $\log x < \ln x$?
Because the base of log *x* is 10, the base of ln *x* is *e*, and 10 > *e*, the number to which 10 is raised to obtain *x*, should be less than the number to which *e* is raised to obtain *x*.

Your Turn

Use a scientific calculator to find the common logarithm and the natural logarithm of the given number. Verify each result by evaluating the appropriate exponential expression.

11. 0.25

$\log 4 \approx -0.602$

$10^{-0.602} \approx 4$

$\ln 4 \approx -1.386$

$e^{-1.386} \approx 4$

12. 4

$\log 0.25 \approx 0.602$

$10^{0.602} \approx 0.25$

$\ln 0.25 \approx 1.386$

$e^{1.386} \approx 0.25$

Explain 4 Evaluating a Logarithmic Model

There are standard scientific formulas that involve logarithms, such as the formulas for the acidity level (pH) of a liquid and the intensity level of a sound. It's also possible to develop your own models involving logarithms by finding the inverses of exponential growth and decay models.

Example 4

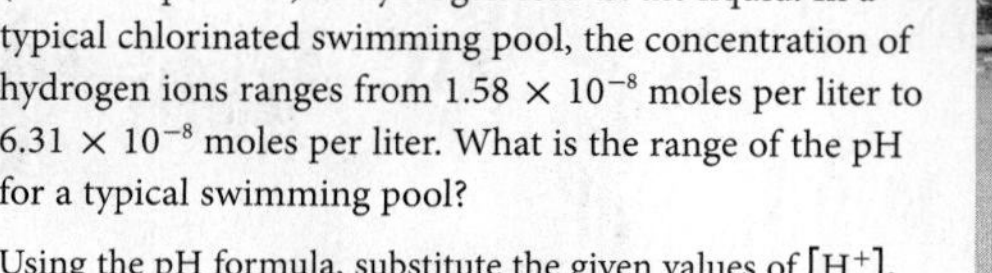

Ⓐ The acidity level, or pH, of a liquid is given by the formula $\text{pH} = \log \frac{1}{[H^+]}$ where $[H^+]$ is the concentration (in moles per liter) of hydrogen ions in the liquid. In a typical chlorinated swimming pool, the concentration of hydrogen ions ranges from 1.58×10^{-8} moles per liter to 6.31×10^{-8} moles per liter. What is the range of the pH for a typical swimming pool?

Using the pH formula, substitute the given values of $[H^+]$.

$$\text{pH} = \log\left(\frac{1}{6.31 \times 10^{-8}}\right)$$

$$\approx \log 15{,}800{,}000$$

$$\approx 7.2$$

$$\text{pH} = \log\left(\frac{1}{1.58 \times 10^{-8}}\right)$$

$$\approx \log 63{,}300{,}000$$

$$\approx 7.8$$

So, the pH of a swimming pool ranges from 7.2 to 7.8.

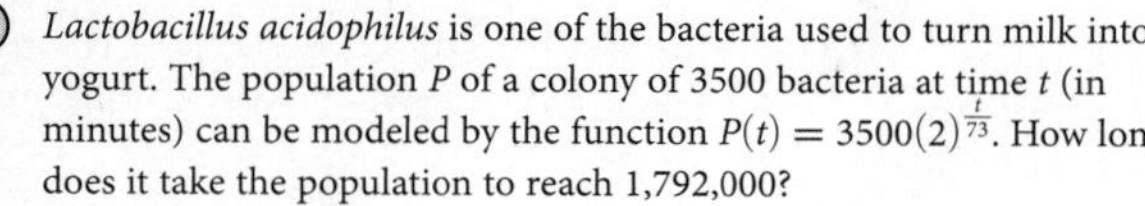

Ⓑ *Lactobacillus acidophilus* is one of the bacteria used to turn milk into yogurt. The population P of a colony of 3500 bacteria at time t (in minutes) can be modeled by the function $P(t) = 3500(2)^{\frac{t}{73}}$. How long does it take the population to reach 1,792,000?

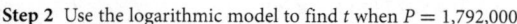

Step 1 Solve $P = 3500(2)^{\frac{t}{73}}$ for t.

Write the model. $P = 3500(2)^{\frac{t}{73}}$

Divide both sides by 3500. $\frac{P}{\boxed{3500}} = (2)^{\frac{t}{73}}$

Rewrite in logarithmic form. $\log_2 \frac{P}{\boxed{3500}} = \frac{t}{73}$

Multiply both sides by 73. $73 \log_2 \frac{P}{\boxed{3500}} = t$

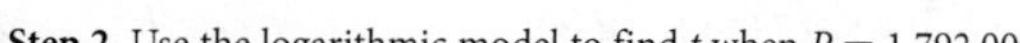

Step 2 Use the logarithmic model to find t when $P = 1{,}792{,}000$.

$$t = 73 \log_2 \frac{P}{\boxed{3500}} = 73 \log_2 \frac{1{,}792{,}000}{\boxed{3500}}$$

$$= 73 \log_2 \boxed{512} = 73\left(\boxed{9}\right) = \boxed{657}$$

So, the bacteria population will reach 1,792,000 in $\underline{657}$ minutes, or about $\underline{11}$ hours.

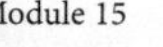

EXPLAIN 4

Evaluating a Logarithmic Model

QUESTIONING STRATEGIES

? When rewriting an exponential model in logarithmic form, how do you know what number to use for the base of the logarithmic expression? **The base will be the base from the power in the exponential expression.**

ELABORATE

QUESTIONING STRATEGIES

What is the inverse of the function $f(x) = \log x$? $f(x) = 10^x$

What is the inverse of the function $f(x) = \ln x$? $f(x) = e^x$

INTEGRATE MATHEMATICAL PRACTICES

Focus on Critical Thinking

MP.3 Ask students to give examples of logarithmic expressions that can be simplified using mental math, and those that would require a calculator. Then ask them to describe the differences between the two types of expressions.

SUMMARIZE THE LESSON

What is a logarithmic function? A logarithmic function is the inverse of an exponential function. It pairs inputs with the power of the given base that produces the input value.

Your Turn

13. The intensity level L (in decibels, dB) of a sound is given by the formula $L = 10 \log \frac{I}{I_0}$ where I is the intensity (in watts per square meter, W/m^2) of the sound and I_0 is the intensity of the softest audible sound, about 10^{-12} W/m^2. What is the intensity level of a rock concert if the sound has an intensity of 3.2 W/m^2?

$$L = 10 \log \frac{3.2}{10^{-12}}$$
$$= 10 \log(3.2 \times 10^{12})$$
$$\approx 10(12.5)$$
$$= 125$$

So, the sound of the rock concert has an intensity level of about 125 dB.

14. The mass (in milligrams) of beryllium-11, a radioactive isotope, in a 500-milligram sample at time t (in seconds) is given by the function $m(t) = 500e^{-0.05t}$. When will there be 90 milligrams of beryllium-11 remaining?

Solve $m = 500e^{-0.05t}$ for t.

$$m = 500e^{-0.05t}$$
$$\frac{m}{500} = e^{-0.05t}$$
$$\ln \frac{m}{500} = -0.05t$$
$$-20 \ln \frac{m}{500} = t$$

Use the model to find t when $m = 90$.

$$m = -20 \ln \frac{t}{500}$$
$$= -20 \ln \frac{90}{500}$$
$$= -20 \ln 0.18$$
$$\approx -20(-1.715)$$
$$\approx 34$$

So, there will be 90 milligrams of beryllium-11 left after about 34 seconds.

Elaborate

15. What is a logarithmic function? Give an example.

A logarithmic function is a function with a given base that accepts a power of the base as an input and outputs the exponent for the base. For example, $f(x) = \log_2 x$ is a logarithmic function with base 2, and $f(64) = \log_2 64 = 6$ because $64 = 2^6$.

16. How can you turn an exponential model that gives y as a function of x into a logarithmic model that gives x as a function of y?

Solve for x in terms of y in three basic steps:

1. Isolate the power of the base on one side of the equation.

2. Rewrite the equation in logarithmic form.

3. Isolate x.

17. Essential Question Check-In Write the inverse of the exponential function $f(x) = b^x$ where $b > 0$ and $b \neq 1$.

The inverse function is $f^{-1}(x) = \log_b x$.

Evaluate: Homework and Practice

- Online Homework
- Hints and Help
- Extra Practice

1. Complete the input-output table for $f(x) = \log_2 x$. Plot and label the ordered pairs from the table. Then draw the complete graph of $f(x)$.

x	$f(x)$
0.25	−2
0.5	−1
1	0
2	1
4	2
8	3

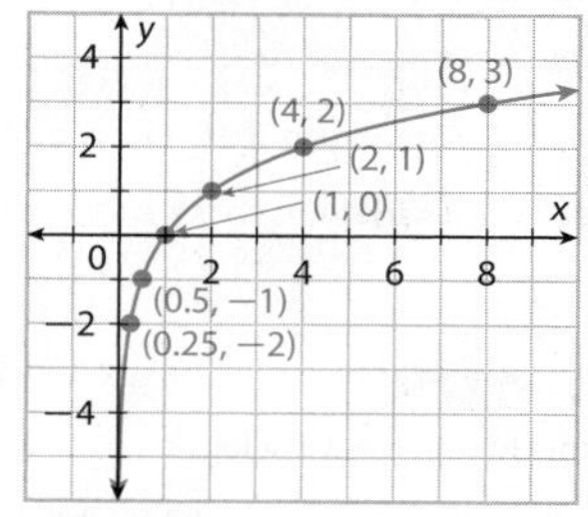

2. Use the graph of $f(x) = \log_2 x$ to do the following.
   - **a.** State the function's domain and range using set notation.
   - **b.** Identify the function's end behavior.
   - **c.** Identify the graph's x- and y-intercepts.
   - **d.** Identify the graph's asymptotes.
   - **e.** Identify the intervals where the function has positive values and where it has negative values.
   - **f.** Identify the intervals where the function is increasing and where it is decreasing

a. **The domain is $\{x \mid x > 0\}$, and the range is $\{y \mid -\infty < y < +\infty\}$.**

b. **As $x \to +\infty$, $f(x) \to +\infty$. As $x \to 0^+$, $f(x) \to -\infty$.**

c. **The graph's only x-intercept is 1. The graph has no y-intercepts.**

d. **The graph has the y-axis as an asymptote.**

e. **The function has negative values on the interval $(0, 1)$ and positive values on the interval $(1, +\infty)$.**

f. **The function is increasing throughout its domain. The function never decreases.**

Exercise	Depth of Knowledge (D.O.K.)	COMMON CORE Mathematical Practices
1–2	**1** Recall of Information	**MP.6** Precision
3–4	**2** Skills/Concepts	**MP.2** Reasoning
5–12	**1** Recall of Information	**MP.2** Reasoning
13–15	**2** Skills/Concepts	**MP.2** Reasoning
16–19	**1** Recall of Information	**MP.5** Using Tools
20–21	**2** Skills/Concepts	**MP.4** Modeling
22	**1** Recall of Information	**MP.4** Modeling

EVALUATE

Personal Math Trainer

ASSIGNMENT GUIDE

Concepts and Skills	Practice
Explore Understanding Logarithmic Functions as Inverses of Exponential Functions	Exercises 1–2
Example 1 Converting Between Exponential and Logarithmic Forms of Equations	Exercises 3–12
Example 2 Evaluating Logarithmic Functions by Thinking in Terms of Exponents	Exercises 13–15
Example 3 Evaluating Logarithmic Functions Using a Scientific Calculator	Exercises 16–19
Example 4 Evaluating a Logarithmic Model	Exercises 20–25

QUESTIONING STRATEGIES

? How do the domain and range of $f(x) = \log_b x$ differ from the domain and range of $f(x) = b^x$ when $b > 1$? **The domain of $f(x) = \log_b x$ is all real numbers, while the domain of $f(x) = b^x$ is non-negative numbers. The range of $f(x) = \log_b x$ is non-negative numbers, while the range of $f(x) = b^x$ is all real numbers.**

AVOID COMMON ERRORS

When evaluating logarithmic functions for radicals, students may think that they need to first simplify the radical. Explain that often it is easier to write the radical in exponential form and leave it in that form so that its base can be compared to the base of the logarithm.

3. Consider the exponential function $f(x) = 3^x$.

a. State the function's domain and range using set notation.

b. Describe any restriction you must place on the domain of the function so that its inverse is also a function.

c. Write the rule for the inverse function.

d. State the inverse function's domain and range using set notation.

a. The domain of $f(x)$ is $\{x \mid -\infty < x < +\infty\}$, and the range is $\{y \mid y > 0\}$.

b. The exponential function is one-to-one, so no restriction on its domain is needed in order for its inverse to be a function.

c. $f^{-1}(x) = \log_3 x$

d. The domain of $f^{-1}(x)$ is $\{x \mid x > 0\}$, and the range is $\{y \mid -\infty < y < +\infty\}$.

4. Consider the logarithmic function $f(x) = \log_4 x$.

a. State the function's domain and range using set notation.

b. Describe any restriction you must place on the domain of the function so that its inverse is also a function.

c. Write the rule for the inverse function.

d. State the inverse function's domain and range using set notation.

a. The domain of $f(x)$ is $\{x \mid x > 0\}$, and the range is $\{y \mid -\infty < y < +\infty\}$.

b. The logarithmic function is one-to-one, so no restriction on its domain is needed in order for its inverse to be a function.

c. $f^{-1}(x) = 4^x$

d. The domain of $f^{-1}(x)$ is $\{x \mid -\infty < x < +\infty\}$, and the range is $\{y \mid y > 0\}$.

Write the given exponential equation in logarithmic form.

5. $5^3 = 125$

$\log_5 125 = 3$

6. $\left(\frac{1}{10}\right)^{-2} = 100$

$\log_{\frac{1}{10}} 100 = -2$

7. $3^m = n$

$\log_3 n = m$

8. $\left(\frac{1}{2}\right)^p = q$

$\log_{\frac{1}{2}} q = p$

Write the given logarithmic equation in exponential form.

9. $\log_6 1296 = 4$

$6^4 = 1296$

10. $\log_{\frac{1}{4}} \frac{1}{64} = 3$

$\left(\frac{1}{4}\right)^3 = \frac{1}{64}$

11. $\log_8 x = y$

$8^y = x$

12. $\log_{\frac{2}{3}} c = d$

$\left(\frac{2}{3}\right)^d = c$

Exercise	Depth of Knowledge (D.O.K.)	COMMON CORE Mathematical Practices
23	2 Skills/Concepts H.O.T.	MP.3 Logic
24–25	3 Strategic Thinking H.O.T.	MP.3 Logic

13. If $f(x) = \log_3 x$, find $f(243)$, $f\left(\frac{1}{27}\right)$, and $f(\sqrt{27})$.

$f(243) = x$

$\log_3 243 = x$

$3^x = 243$

$3^x = 3^5$

$x = 5$

So, $f(243) = 5$.

$f\left(\frac{1}{27}\right) = x$

$\log_3 \frac{1}{27} = x$

$3^x = \frac{1}{27}$

$3^x = \frac{1}{3^3}$

$3^x = 3^{-3}$

$x = -3$

So, $f\left(\frac{1}{27}\right) = -3$.

$f(\sqrt{27}) = x$

$\log_3 \sqrt{27} = x$

$3^x = \sqrt{27}$

$3^x = \sqrt{3^3}$

$3^x = 3^{\frac{3}{2}}$

$x = \frac{3}{2}$

So, $f(\sqrt{27}) = \frac{3}{2}$.

14. If $f(x) = \log_6 x$, find $f(36)$, $f\left(\frac{1}{6}\right)$ and $f(6\sqrt[3]{6})$

$f(36) = x$

$\log_6 36 = x$

$6^x = 36$

$6^x = 6^2$

$x = 2$

So, $f(36) = 2$.

$f\left(\frac{1}{6}\right) = x$

$\log_6 \frac{1}{6} = x$

$6^x = \frac{1}{6}$

$6^x = 6^{-1}$

$x = -1$

So, $f\left(\frac{1}{6}\right) = -1$.

$f(6\sqrt[3]{6}) = x$

$\log_6(6\sqrt[3]{6}) = x$

$6^x = 6\sqrt[3]{6}$

$6^x = \sqrt[3]{6^3 \cdot 6}$

$6^x = \sqrt[3]{6^4}$

$6^x = 6^{\frac{4}{3}}$

$x = \frac{4}{3}$

So, $f(6\sqrt[3]{6}) = \frac{4}{3}$.

15. If $f(x) = \log_{\frac{1}{4}} x$, find $f\left(\frac{1}{64}\right)$, $f(256)$, and $f(\sqrt[3]{16})$

$f\left(\frac{1}{64}\right) = x$

$\log_{\frac{1}{4}} \frac{1}{64} = x$

$\left(\frac{1}{4}\right)^x = \frac{1}{64}$

$\left(\frac{1}{4}\right)^x = \frac{1}{4^3}$

$\left(\frac{1}{4}\right)^x = \left(\frac{1}{4}\right)^3$

$x = 3$

So, $f\left(\frac{1}{64}\right) = 3$.

$f(256) = x$

$\log_{\frac{1}{4}} 256 = x$

$\left(\frac{1}{4}\right)^x = 256$

$\left(\frac{1}{4}\right)^x = 4^4$

$\left(\frac{1}{4}\right)^x = \left(\frac{1}{4}\right)^{-4}$

$x = -4$

So, $f(256) = -4$.

$f(\sqrt[3]{16}) = x$

$\log_{\frac{1}{4}} \sqrt[3]{16} = x$

$\left(\frac{1}{4}\right)^x = \sqrt[3]{16}$

$\left(\frac{1}{4}\right)^x = \sqrt[3]{4^2}$

$\left(\frac{1}{4}\right)^x = 4^{\frac{2}{3}}$

$\left(\frac{1}{4}\right)^x = \left(\frac{1}{4}\right)^{-\frac{2}{3}}$

$x = -\frac{2}{3}$

So, $f\sqrt[3]{16} = -\frac{2}{3}$

TECHNOLOGY

To help students reinforce their understanding of common and natural logarithms, encourage them to try to approximate their answers before entering the expressions into a calculator.

KINESTHETIC EXPERIENCE

To help students remember how to convert from logarithmic form to exponential form, have them repeatedly trace a counterclockwise "circle" in the equation using their fingers. For example, in the equation $\log_b a = x$, they should trace the path from b to x to a, while saying "b to the x equals a." Encourage students to do this when rewriting numerical examples, as well.

Use a scientific calculator to find the common logarithm and the natural logarithm of the given number. Verify each result by evaluating the appropriate exponential expression.

16. 19

$\log 19 \approx 1.279$

$10^{1.279} \approx 19$

$\ln 19 \approx 2.944$

$e^{2.944} \approx 19$

17. 9

$\log 9 \approx 0.954$

$10^{0.954} \approx 9$

$\ln 9 \approx 2.197$

$e^{2.197} \approx 9$

18. 0.6

$\log 0.6 \approx -0.222$

$10^{-0.222} \approx 0.6$

$\ln 0.6 \approx -0.511$

$e^{-0.511} \approx 0.6$

19. 0.31

$\log 0.31 \approx -0.509$

$10^{-0.509} \approx 0.31$

$\ln 0.31 \approx -1.171$

$e^{-1.171} \approx 0.31$

20. The acidity level, or pH, of a liquid is given by the formula $pH = \log \frac{1}{[H^+]}$ where $[H^+]$ is the concentration (in moles per liter) of hydrogen ions in the liquid. What is the pH of iced tea with a hydrogen ion concentration of 0.000158 mole per liter?

$$pH = \log \frac{1}{0.000158}$$

$$\approx \log(6329)$$

$$\approx 3.8$$

The pH of the iced tea is about 3.8.

21. The intensity level L (in decibels, dB) of a sound is given by the formula $L = 10 \log \frac{I}{I_0}$ where I is the intensity (in watts per square meter, W/m^2) of the sound and I_0 is the intensity of the softest audible sound, about 10^{-12} W/m^2. What is the intensity level of a lawn mower if the sound has an intensity of 0.00063 W/m^2?

$$L = 10 \log \frac{0.00063}{10^{-12}}$$

$$= 10 \log(6.3 \times 10^8)$$

$$\approx 10(8.8)$$

$$\approx 88$$

So, the sound of the lawn mower has an intensity level of about 88 dB.

22. Match each liquid with its pH given the concentration of hydrogen ions in the liquid.

Liquid	Hydrogen Ion Concentration		pH
A. Cocoa	5.2×10^{-7}	G	3.5
B. Cider	7.9×10^{-4}	C	3.3
C. Ginger Ale	4.9×10^{-4}	F	2.4
D. Honey	1.3×10^{-4}	E	4.5
E. Buttermilk	3.2×10^{-5}	A	6.3
F. Cranberry juice	4.0×10^{-3}	I	6.4
G. Pinneapple juice	3.1×10^{-4}	B	3.1
H. Tomato juice	6.3×10^{-2}	H	1.2
I. Carrot juice	4.0×10^{-7}	D	3.9

H.O.T. Focus on Higher Order Thinking

23. **Explain the Error** Jade is taking a chemistry test and has to find the pH of a liquid given that its hydrogen ion concentration is 7.53×10^{-9} moles per liter. She writes the following.

$$\text{pH} = \ln \frac{1}{[\text{H}^+]}$$
$$= \ln \frac{1}{7.53 \times 10^9}$$
$$\approx 18.7$$

She knows that the pH scale ranges from 1 to 14, so her answer of 18.7 must be incorrect, but she runs out of time on the test. Explain her error and find the correct pH.

The formula for finding the pH uses the common logarithm, not the natural logarithm. She should have found

$$\log \frac{1}{[\text{H}^+]}$$

$$\text{pH} = \log \frac{1}{[\text{H}^+]}$$
$$= \log \frac{1}{7.53 \times 10^{-9}}$$
$$\approx 8.1$$

So, the pH of the liquid is about 8.1.

CONNECT VOCABULARY EL

To tap into prior knowledge, have students articulate how logarithmic functions are related to exponential functions (inverses) and how they can use the rules of exponents with logarithms.

PEER-TO-PEER DISCUSSION

Ask students to discuss with a partner how to find the value of $\ln\frac{1}{e}$ without using a calculator. Then have them discuss their reasoning with the class.

If $\ln\frac{1}{e} = x$, then $e^x = \frac{1}{e}$. Since $\frac{1}{e} = e^{-1}$, $x = -1$.

JOURNAL

Have students define a logarithmic function and describe how to transform an exponential function into a logarithmic function.

24. Multi-step Exponential functions have the general form $f(x) = ab^{x-h} + k$ where a, b, h, and k are constants, $a \neq 0$, $b > 0$, and $b \neq 1$.

a. State the domain and range of $f(x)$ using set notation.

b. Show how to find $f^{-1}(x)$. Give a description of each step you take.

c. State the domain and range of $f^{-1}(x)$ using set notation.

a. The domain of f(x) is $\{x \mid -\infty < x < +\infty\}$, and the range is $\{y \mid y > k\}$ if $a > 0$ or $\{y \mid y < k\}$ if $a < 0$.

b.

$f(x) = ab^{x-h} + k$	Write the function.
$y = ab^{x-h} + k$	Replace $f(x)$ with y.
$y - k = ab^{x-h}$	Subtract k from both sides.
$\frac{y-k}{a} = b^{x-h}$	Divide both sides by a.
$\log_b \frac{y-k}{a} = x - h$	Rewrite the equation in logarithmic form.
$h + \log_b \frac{y-k}{a} = x$	Add h to both sides.
$h + \log_b \frac{x-k}{a} = y$	Switch x and y.
$h + \log_b \frac{x-k}{a} = f^{-1}(x)$	Replace y with $f^{-1}(x)$

c. The domain of $f^{-1}(x)$ is $\{x \mid x > k\}$ if $a > 0$ or $\{x \mid x < k\}$ if $a < 0$, and the range is $\{y \mid -\infty < y < +\infty\}$.

25. Justify Reasoning Evaluate each expression without using a calculator. Explain your reasoning.

a. $\ln e^2$

b. $10^{\log 7}$

c. $4^{\log_2 5}$

a. Let $f(x) = \ln x$. Then $f^{-1}(x) = e^x$.

$\ln e^2 = f(e^2)$
$= f(f^{-1}(2))$
$= 2$

b. Let $f(x) = 10^x$. Then $f^{-1}(x) = \log x$.

$10^{\log 7} = f(\log 7)$
$= f(f^{-1}(7))$
$= 7$

c. $4^{\log_2 5} = (2^2)^{\log_2 5}$
$= 2^{2\log_2 5}$
$= 2^{\log_2 5 + \log_2 5}$
$= (2^{\log_2 5})(2^{\log_2 5})$

Let $g(x) = 2^x$. Then $g^{-1}(x) = \log_2 x$.

$2^{\log_2 5} = g^{(\log_2 5)}$
$= g(g^{-1}(5))$
$= 5$

Substitute 5 for $2^{\log_2 5}$ in $4^{\log_2 5} = (2^{\log_2 5})(2^{\log_2 5})$

$4^{\log_2 5} = (2^{\log_2 5})(2^{\log_2 5})$
$= (5)(5)$
$= 25$

Lesson Performance Task

Skydivers use an instrument called an altimeter to determine their height above Earth's surface. An altimeter measures atmospheric pressure and converts it to altitude based on the relationship between pressure and altitude. One model for atmospheric pressure P (in kilopascals, kPa) as a function of altitude a (in kilometers) is $P = 100e^{-a/8}$.

a. Since an altimeter measures pressure directly, pressure is the independent variable for an altimeter. Rewrite the model $P = 100e^{-a/8}$ so that it gives altitude as a function of pressure.

b. To check the function in part a, use the fact that atmospheric pressure at Earth's surface is about 100 kPa.

c. Suppose a skydiver deploys the parachute when the altimeter measures 87 kPa. Use the function in part a to determine the skydiver's altitude. Give your answer in both kilometers and feet. (1 kilometer ≈ 3281 feet)

a. Solve $P = 100e^{-a/8}$ for a.

$$P = 100e^{-a/8}$$
$$\frac{P}{100} = e^{-a/8}$$
$$\ln\frac{P}{100} = -\frac{a}{8}$$
$$-8\ln\frac{P}{100} = a$$

b. Substitution 100 for P in $a = -8\ln\frac{P}{100}$ gives $a = -8\ln\frac{100}{100} = -8\ln 1 = -8(0) = 0$.

Since an altitude of 0 km corresponds to being on Earth's surface, the function checks.

c. Substitution 87 for P in $a = -8\ln\frac{P}{100}$ gives $a = -8\ln\frac{87}{100} = -8\ln 0.87 \approx 1.1$.

So, the skydrive opens the parachute at an altitude of about 1.1 kilometers, or $1.1(3281) \approx 3600$ feet.

EXTENSION ACTIVITY

Have students research the height at which pilots are required to wear a pressure suit to protect them from low atmospheric pressure. about 15,000 meters Have students calculate the atmospheric pressure at this altitude, and then have them calculate the atmospheric pressure at the top of Mount Everest. 15 kPa and 33 kPa Have students discuss whether mountain climbers are in danger from the effects of low atmospheric pressure.

AVOID COMMON ERRORS

Students may solve for h by taking the base10 logarithm of both sides of the equation rather than the natural logarithm, ln. Explain that the natural log has base e, and because the equation has e raised to a power, they must take the natural log in order to isolate h.

INTEGRATE MATHEMATICAL PRACTICES

Focus on Math Connections

MP.1 Have students discuss the significance of the minus sign in the formula for P. Have students explain why the formula for h has a minus sign and yet the height must be a positive number.

Scoring Rubric

2 points: Student correctly solves the problem and explains his/her reasoning.

1 point: Student shows good understanding of the problem but does not fully solve or explain his/her reasoning.

0 points: Student does not demonstrate understanding of the problem.

LESSON 15.2

Graphing Logarithmic Functions

Common Core Math Standards

The student is expected to:

COMMON CORE **F.BF.B.3**

Identify the effect on the graph of replacing $f(x)$ by $f(x) + k$, $k\,f(x)$, $f(kx)$, and $f(x + k)$ for specific values of k (both positive and negative); ... Also F.IF.C.7e, A.CED.A.2, F.IF.B.4

Mathematical Practices

COMMON CORE **MP.7 Using Structure**

Language Objective

Work with a partner to compare and contrast the graphs of exponential and logarithmic functions.

ENGAGE

Essential Question: How is the graph of $g(x) = a\log_b(x - h) + k$ where $b > 0$ and $b \neq 1$ related to the graph of $f(x) = \log_b x$?

The graph of $g(x) = a\log_b(x - h) + k$ involves transformations of the graph of $f(x) = \log_b x$. In particular, the graph of $g(x)$ is a vertical stretch or compression of the graph of $f(x)$ by a factor of $|a|$, a reflection of the graph across the x-axis if $a < 0$, and a translation of the graph h units horizontally and k units vertically.

PREVIEW: LESSON PERFORMANCE TASK

View the Engage section online. Discuss the photo and have students suggest the first step they would take to find models for this data set. Then preview the Lesson Performance Task.

Name ____________ Class ____________ Date ____________

15.2 Graphing Logarithmic Functions

Resource Locker

Essential Question: How is the graph of $g(x) = a\log_b(x - h) + k$ where $b > 0$ and $b \neq 1$ related to the graph of $f(x) = \log_b x$?

Explore 1 Graphing and Analyzing Parent Logarithmic Functions

The graph of the logarithmic function $f(x) = \log_2 x$, which you analyzed in the previous lesson, is shown. In this Explore, you'll graph and analyze other basic logarithmic functions.

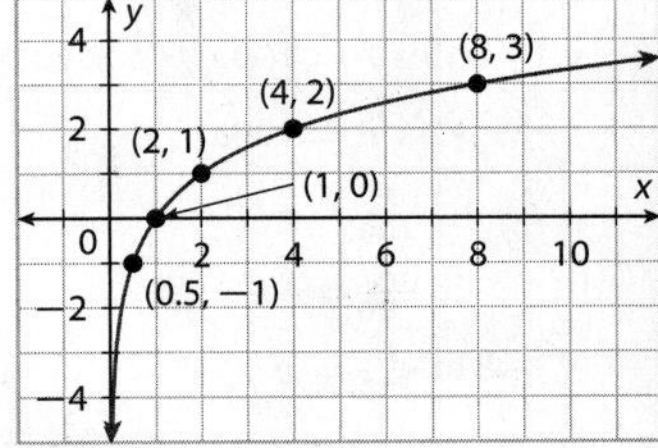

(A) Complete the table for the function $f(x) = \log x$. (Remember that when the base of a logarithmic function is not specified, it is understood to be 10.) Then plot and label the ordered pairs from the table and draw a smooth curve through the points to obtain the graph of the function.

x	$f(x) = \log x$
0.1	−1
1	0
10	1

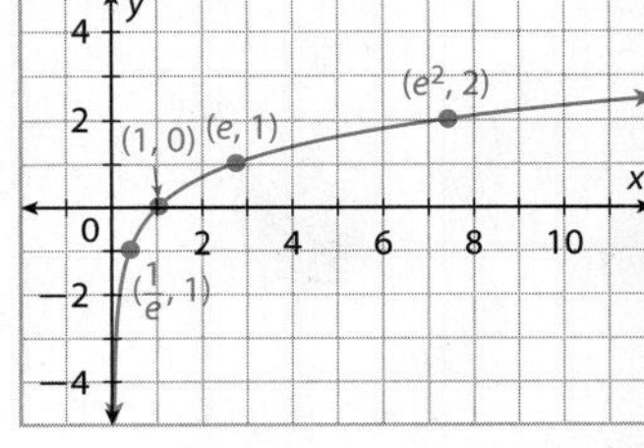

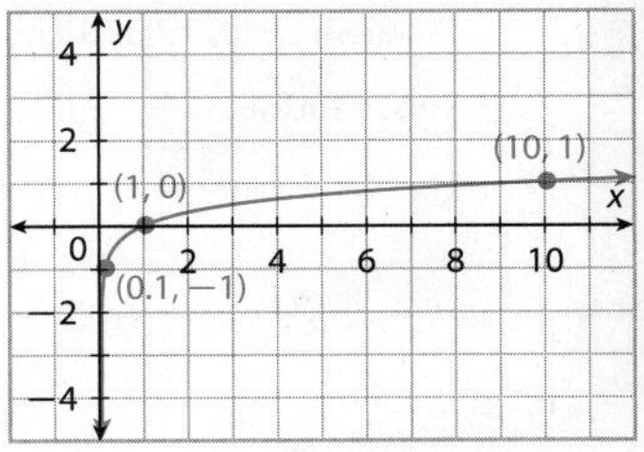

(B) Complete the table for the function $f(x) = \ln x$. (Remember that the base of this function is e). Then plot and label the ordered pairs from the table and draw a smooth curve through the points to obtain the graph of the function.

x	$f(x) = \ln x$
$\frac{1}{e} \approx 0.368$	−1
1	0
$e \approx 2.72$	1
$e^2 \approx 7.39$	2

(graph: points $(1, 0)$, $(e, 1)$, $(e^2, 2)$, $(\frac{1}{e}, -1)$)

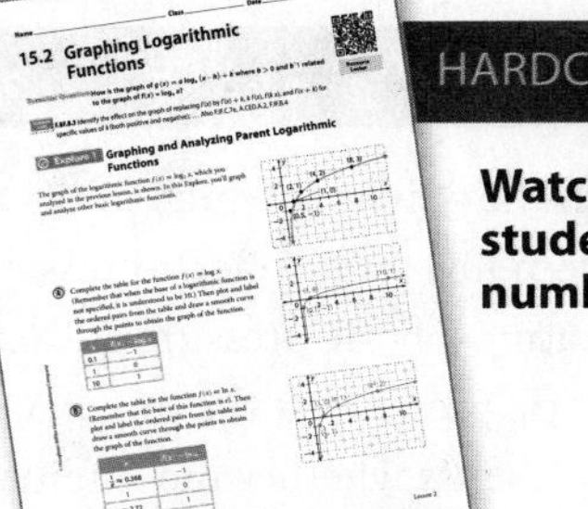

HARDCOVER PAGES 761–776

Watch for the hardcover student edition page numbers for this lesson.

Ⓒ Analyze the two graphs from Steps A and B, and then complete the table.

Function	$f(x) = \log_2(x)$	$f(x) = \log x$	$f(x) = \ln x$
Domain	$\{x \mid x > 0\}$	$\{x \mid x > 0\}$	$\{x \mid x > 0\}$
Range	$\{y \mid 0 < y < \infty\}$	$\{y \mid -\infty < y < +\infty\}$	$\{y \mid -\infty < y < +\infty\}$
End behavior	As $x \to +\infty, f(x) \to +\infty$. As $x \to 0^+, f(x) \to -\infty$.	**As $x \to +\infty, f(x) \to +\infty$. As $x \to 0^+, f(x) \to -\infty$.**	**As $x \to +\infty, f(x) \to +\infty$. As $x \to 0^+, f(x) \to -\infty$.**
Vertical and horizontal asymptotes	Vertical asymptote at $x = 0$; no horizontal asymptote	**Vertical asymptote at $x = 0$; no horizontal asymptote**	**Vertical asymptote at $x = 0$; no horizontal asymptote**
Intervals where increasing or decreasing	Increasing throughout its domain	**Increasing throughout its domain**	**Increasing throughout its domain**
Intercepts	x-intercept at (1, 0); no y-intercepts	**x-intercept at (1, 0); no y-intercepts**	**x-intercept at (1, 0); no y-intercepts**
Intervals where positive or negative	Positive on $(1, +\infty)$; negative on $(0, 1)$	**Positive on $(1, +\infty)$; negative on $(0, 1)$**	**Positive on $(1, +\infty)$; negative on $(0, 1)$**

Reflect

1. What similarities do you notice about all logarithmic functions of the form $f(x) = \log_b x$ where $b > 1$? What differences do you notice?

They all have a vertical asymptote at $x = 0$, an x-intercept at 1, are always increasing, and they have the same end behavior. The rates of change are different.

EXPLORE

Graphing and Analyzing Parent Logarithmic Functions

INTEGRATE TECHNOLOGY

Students have the option of completing the Explore activity either in the book or online.

QUESTIONING STRATEGIES

? What point or points do all of the graphs have in common? **(1, 0)**

? Why does each of the graphs contain this point? **Because $\log_b 1 = 0$ for all nonzero values of b.**

PROFESSIONAL DEVELOPMENT

Learning Progressions

In previous lessons, students learned how different parameters affect the graphs of various types of functions, including quadratic, radical, and exponential functions. In this lesson, they complete their study of transformations in Algebra 2 by applying what they've learned to the graphs of logarithmic functions. They predict how changing the parameters of a logarithmic function will transform the graph of the function, and how those changes affect the attributes of the function, including its domain and range, its asymptote, and its end behavior.

EXPLAIN 1

Graphing Combined Transformations of $f(x) = \log_b x$ Where $b > 1$

QUESTIONING STRATEGIES

? Why is the equation of the asymptote $x = h$? **Because the asymptote of $f(x) = \log_b x$ is the vertical line $x = 0$, and it is being translated h units in the horizontal direction.**

Explain 1 Graphing Combined Transformations of $f(x) = \log_b x$ Where $b > 1$

When graphing transformations of $f(x) = \log_b x$ where $b > 1$, it helps to consider the effect of the transformations on the following features of the graph of $f(x)$: the vertical asymptote, $x = 0$, and two reference points, $(1, 0)$ and $(b, 1)$. The table lists these features as well as the corresponding features of the graph of $g(x) = a \log_b (x - h) + k$.

Function	$f(x) = \log_b x$	$g(x) = a \log_b (x - h) + k$
Asymptote	$x = 0$	$x = h$
Reference point	$(1, 0)$	$(1 + h, k)$
Reference point	$(b, 1)$	$(b + h, a + k)$

Example 1 **Identify the transformations of the graph of $f(x) = \log_b x$ that produce the graph of the given function $g(x)$. Then graph $g(x)$ on the same coordinate plane as the graph of $f(x)$ by applying the transformations to the asymptote $x = 0$ and to the reference points $(1, 0)$ and $(b, 1)$. Also state the domain and range of $g(x)$ using set notation.**

 $g(x) = -2 \log_2 (x - 1) - 2$

The transformations of the graph of $f(x) = \log_2 x$ that produce the graph of $g(x)$ are as follows:

- a vertical stretch by a factor of 2
- a reflection across the x-axis
- a translation of 1 unit to the right and 2 units down

Note that the translation of 1 unit to the right affects only the x-coordinates of points on the graph of $f(x)$, while the vertical stretch by a factor of 2, the reflection across the x-axis, and the translation of 2 units down affect only the y-coordinates.

Function	$f(x) = \log_2 x$	$g(x) = -2 \log_2 (x - 1) - 2$
Asymptote	$x = 0$	$x = 1$
Reference point	$(1, 0)$	$(1 + 1, -2(0) - 2) = (2, -2)$
Reference point	$(2, 1)$	$(2 + 1, -2(1) - 2) = (3, -4)$

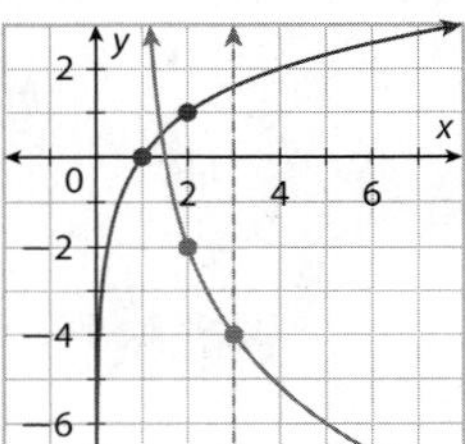

Domain: $\{x \mid x > 1\}$

Range: $\{y \mid \infty < y < +\infty\}$

COLLABORATIVE LEARNING

Peer-to-Peer Activity

Have students work in pairs. Provide each pair with an exponential function. Have them graph their function, and then use the points on the graph to graph the inverse of the function. Have them write an equation of the inverse function using what they've learned about inverse functions and transformations. Then have each pair present their work to the class.

(B) $g(x) = 2\log(x + 2) + 4$

The transformations of the graph of $f(x) = \log x$ that produce the graph of $g(x)$ are as follows:

- a vertical stretch by a factor of 2
- a translation of 2 units to the left and 4 units up

Note that the translation of 2 units to the left affects only the x-coordinates of points on the graph of $f(x)$, while the vertical stretch by a factor of 2 and the translation of 4 units up affect only the y-coordinates.

Function	$f(x) = \log x$	$g(x) = 2\log(x+2) + 4$
Asymptote	$x = 0$	$x = -2$
Reference point	$(1, 0)$	$(1 - 2, 2(0) + 4) = (-1, 4)$
Reference point	$(10, 1)$	$(10 - 2, 2(1) + 4) = (8, 6)$

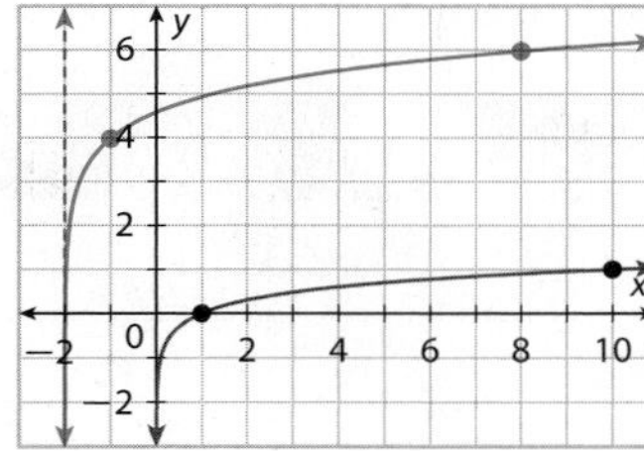

Domain: $\{x \mid x > -2\}$

Range: $\{y \mid -\infty < y < +\infty\}$

INTEGRATE MATHEMATICAL PRACTICES

Focus on Math Connections

MP.1 Discuss with students how a vertical compression affects the rate of change of the graph of a logarithmic function. Have them compare the "steepness" of the graphs of $f(x) = \log x$ and $g(x) = \frac{1}{2}\log x$ in the intervals $(0, 1)$ and $(1, +\infty)$. Students should observe that the graph of $g(x)$ is steeper than the graph of $f(x)$ in the first interval, and less steep in the second interval.

DIFFERENTIATE INSTRUCTION

Visual Cues

Visual learners can benefit from using colored pencils to graph the intermediate stages when transforming the graph of the parent function, $f(x) = \log_b x$, to the graph of $g(x) = a\log_b(x - h) + k$. For example, one color can be used to graph a reflection across the x-axis if $a < 0$, a different color can be used to graph any vertical stretch or compression of the reflected graph, and a third color can be used to graph the translation of the previous graph.

Your Turn

Identify the transformations of the graph of $f(x) = \log_b x$ that produce the graph of the given function $g(x)$. Then graph $g(x)$ on the same coordinate plane as the graph of $f(x)$ by applying the transformations to the asymptote $x = 0$ and to the reference points $(1, 0)$ and $(b, 1)$. Also state the domain and range of $g(x)$ using set notation.

2. $g(x) = \frac{1}{2}\log_2(x + 1) + 2$

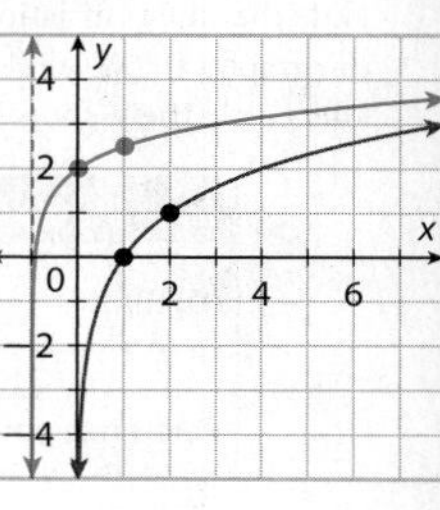

Domain: $\{x \mid x > -1\}$

Range: $\{y \mid -\infty < y < +\infty\}$

The transformations of the graph of $f(x) = \log_2 x$ that produce the graph of $g(x)$ are as follows:

- a vertical compression by a factor of $\frac{1}{2}$
- a translation of 1 unit to the left and 2 units up

Note that the translation of 1 unit to the left affects only the x-coordinates of points on the graph of $f(x)$, while the vertical compression by a factor of $\frac{1}{2}$ and the translation of 2 units up affect only the y-coordinates.

Function	$f(x) = \log_2 x$	$g(x) = \frac{1}{2}\log_2(x + 1) + 2$
Asymptote	$x = 0$	$x = -1$
Reference point	$(1, 0)$	$\left(1 - 1, \frac{1}{2}(0) + 2\right) = (0, 2)$
Reference point	$(2, 1)$	$\left(2 - 1, \frac{1}{2}(1) + 2\right) = \left(1, 2\frac{1}{2}\right)$

Explain 2 Writing, Graphing, and Analyzing a Logarithmic Model

You can obtain a logarithmic model for real-world data either by performing logarithmic regression on the data or by finding the inverse of an exponential model if one is available.

Example 2 **A biologist studied a population of foxes in a forest preserve over a period of time. The table gives the data that the biologist collected.**

Years Since Study Began	Fox Population
0	55
2	72
3	99
5	123
8	151
12	234
15	336
18	475

From the data, the biologist obtained the exponential model $P = 62(1.12)^t$ where P is the fox population at time t (in years since the study began). The biologist is interested in having a model that gives the time it takes the fox population to reach a certain level.

(A) One way to obtain the model that the biologist wants is to perform logarithmic regression on a graphing calculator using the data set but with the variables switched (that is, the fox population is the independent variable and time is the dependent variable). After obtaining the logarithmic regression model, graph it on a scatter plot of the data. Analyze the model in terms of whether it is increasing or decreasing as well as its average rate of change from $P = 100$ to $P = 200$, from $P = 200$ to $P = 300$, and from $P = 300$ to $P = 400$. Do the model's average rates of change increase, decrease, or stay the same? What does this mean for the fox population?

Using a graphing calculator, enter the population data into one list (L1) and the time data into another list (L2).

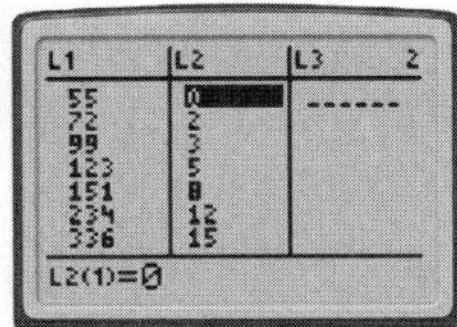

EXPLAIN 2

Writing, Graphing, and Analyzing a Logarithmic Model

QUESTIONING STRATEGIES

? How are the exponential model presented in the Example and the logarithmic model obtained using regression related? **They are inverses of each other.**

? Why do you reverse the coordinates of the data points when entering the data into the calculator? **because you are finding the equation of the inverse function**

INTEGRATE MATHEMATICAL PRACTICES

Focus on Technology

MP.5 Students can use the table feature of a graphing calculator to compare the values of the two functions for particular values of the independent variable. Students should find that the functions produce values that are roughly equivalent.

Perform logarithmic regression by pressing the STAT key, choosing the **CALC** menu, and selecting **9:LnReg**. Note that the calculator's regression model is a natural logarithmic function.

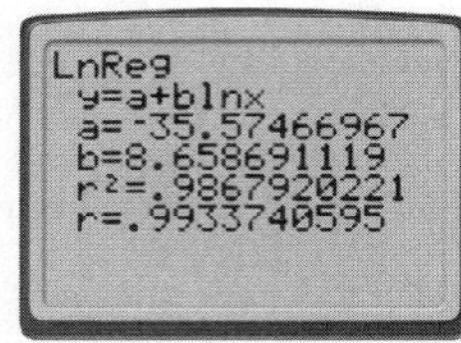

So, the model is $t = -35.6 + 8.66 \ln P$. Graphing this model on a scatter plot of the data visually confirms that the model is a good fit for the data.

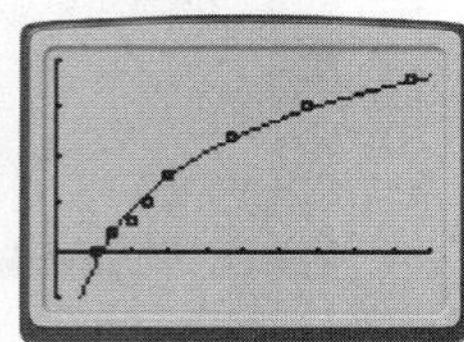

From the graph, you can see that the function is increasing. To find the model's average rates of change, divide the change in t (the dependent variable) by the change in P (the independent variable):

Average rate of change $= \frac{t_2 - t_1}{P_2 - P_1}$

Population	Number of Years to Reach That Population	Average Rate of Change
100	$t = -35.6 + 8.66 \ln 100 \approx 4.3$	
200	$t = -35.6 + 8.66 \ln 200 \approx 10.3$	$\frac{10.3 - 4.3}{200 - 100} = \frac{6.0}{100} = 0.060$
300	$t = -35.6 + 8.66 \ln 300 \approx 13.8$	$\frac{13.8 - 10.3}{300 - 200} = \frac{3.5}{100} = 0.035$
400	$t = -35.6 + 8.66 \ln 400 \approx 16.3$	$\frac{16.3 - 13.8}{400 - 300} = \frac{2.5}{100} = 0.025$

The model's average rates of change are decreasing. This means that as the fox population grows, it takes less time for the population to increase by another 100 foxes.

(B) Another way to obtain the model that the biologist wants is to find the inverse of the exponential model. Find the inverse model and compare it with the logarithmic regression model.

In order to compare the inverse of the biologist's model, $P = 62(1.12)^t$, with the logarithmic regression model, you must rewrite the biologist's model with base e so that the inverse will involve a natural logarithm. This means that you want to find a constant c such that $e^c = 1.12$. Writing the exponential equation $e^c = 1.12$ in logarithmic form gives $c = \ln 1.12$, so $c =$ **0.113** to the nearest thousandth.

Replacing 1.12 with $e^{0.113}$ in the biologist's model gives $P = 62\left(e^{0.113}\right)^t$, or $P = 62\,e^{0.113t}$. Now find the inverse of this function.

Write the equation. $P = 62e^{0.113t}$

Divide both sides by 62. $\frac{P}{62} = e^{0.113t}$

Write in logarithmic form. $\ln \frac{P}{62} = 0.113t$

Divide both sides by **0.113**. $8.85 \ln \frac{P}{62} = t$

So, the inverse of the exponential model is $t = 8.85 \ln \frac{P}{62}$. To compare this model with the logarithmic regression model, use a graphing calculator to graph both $y = 8.85 \ln \frac{x}{62}$ and $y = -35.6 + 8.66 \ln x$. You observe that the graphs (roughly coincide)/significantly diverge, so the models are (basically equivalent)/very different.

Reflect

3. **Discussion** In a later lesson, you will learn the quotient property of logarithms, which states that $\log_b \frac{m}{n} = \log_b m - \log_b n$ for any positive numbers m and n. Explain how you can use this property to compare the two models in Example 3.

You can use the quotient property of logarithms to rewrite $t = 8.85 \ln \frac{P}{62}$ as follows:

$t = 8.85 \ln \frac{P}{62} = 8.85(\ln P - \ln 62) \approx 8.85(\ln P - 4.13) \approx 8.85 \ln P - 36.6$

Comparing this result with the logarithmic regression model $t = -35.6 + 8.66 \ln P$ shows that the corresponding constants in the two equations are approximately equal.

Your Turn

4. Maria made a deposit in a bank account and left the money untouched for several years. The table lists her account balance at the end of each year.

Years Since the Deposit Was Made	Account Balance
0	$1000.00
1	$1020.00
2	$1040.40
3	$1061.21

ELABORATE

QUESTIONING STRATEGIES

? Which transformations of $f(x) = \log_b x$ change the function's domain? **horizontal translations**

? Which transformations of $f(x) = \log_b x$ change the function's range? **No transformations change the range. The range of logarithmic functions is all real numbers.**

SUMMARIZE THE LESSON

? How do the values of a, h, and k in the function $g(x) = a\log_b(x - h) + k$ tell you how to transform the graph of the function $f(x) = \log_b x$? **h tells you how far to translate the graph horizontally; k tells you how far to translate the graph vertically; a tells you if there is a vertical stretch or compression and, if $a < 0$, that there is a reflection across the x-axis.**

a. Write an exponential model for the account balance as a function of time (in years since the deposit was made).

b. Find the inverse of the exponential model after rewriting it with a base of e. Describe what information the inverse gives.

c. Perform logarithmic regression on the data (using the account balance as the independent variable and time as the dependent variable). Compare this model with the inverse model from part b.

a. The ratio of the account balances for consecutive years is 1.02, so an exponential model for the data is $B = 1000(1.02)^t$ where B is the account balance at time t (in years since the deposit was made).

b. First, find the constant c such that $e^c = 1.02$. Rewriting $e^c = 1.02$ in logarithmic form gives $c = \ln 1.02 \approx 0.02$. Then, find the inverse of $B = 1000(e^{0.02})^t = 1000e^{0.02t}$.

$$B = 1000e^{0.02t}$$

$$\frac{B}{1000} = e^{0.02t}$$

$$\ln \frac{B}{1000} = 0.02t$$

$$50 \ln \frac{B}{1000} = t$$

So, the inverse of the exponential model is $t = 50 \ln \frac{B}{1000}$, which gives the time it takes for the account balance to reach a certain level.

c. A graphing calculator gives the logarithmic regression model $t = -349 + 50.5 \ln B$. Graphing this model and the inverse model from part b shows that the models are basically equivalent.

Elaborate

5. Which transformations of $f(x) = \log_b(x)$ change the function's end behavior (both as x increases without bound and as x decreases toward 0 from the right)? Which transformations change the location of the graph's x-intercept?
Reflections across the x-axis change the end behavior. Horizontal and vertical translations affect the x-intercept.

6. How are reference points helpful when graphing transformations of $f(x) = \log_b(x)$?
Reference points provide a guide to the general shape of a transformed graph.

7. What are two ways to obtain a logarithmic model for a set of data?
Perform logarithmic regression on the data, or find the inverse of an exponential model if one is available.

8. **Essential Question Check-In** Describe the transformations you must perform on the graph of $f(x) = \log_b(x)$ to obtain the graph of $g(x) = a\log_b(x - h) + k$.
If $a < 0$, reflect the parent graph across the x-axis. Then either stretch the graph vertically by a factor of a if $|a| > 1$ or compress the graph vertically by a factor of a if $|a| < 1$. Finally, translate the graph h units horizontally and k units vertically.

LANGUAGE SUPPORT EL

Communicate Math

Have students work in pairs to complete a compare and contrast chart like the one below.

Type of function	Equation	Graph	Similarities and Differences
Exponential			
Logarithmic			

Evaluate: Homework and Practice

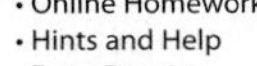

1. Graph the logarithmic functions $f(x) = \log_2 x$, $f(x) = \log x$, and $f(x) = \ln x$ on the same coordinate plane. To distinguish the curves, label the point on each curve where the y-coordinate is 1.

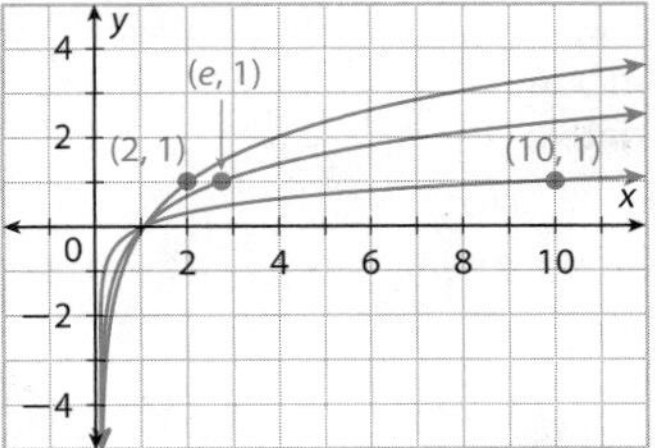

2. Describe the attributes that the logarithmic functions $f(x) = \log_2 x$, $f(x) = \log x$, and $f(x) = \ln x$ have in common and the attributes that make them different. Attributes should include domain, range, end behavior, asymptotes, intercepts, intervals where the functions are positive and where they are negative, intervals where the functions are increasing and where they are decreasing, and the average rate of change on an interval.

Attributes that the functions have in common:

- **The domain of all three functions is $\{x \mid x > 0\}$.**
- **The range of all three functions is $\{y \mid -\infty < y < +\infty\}$.**
- **All three functions have the same end behavior: As $x \to +\infty$, $f(x) \to +\infty$. As $x \to 0^+$, $f(x) \to -\infty$.**
- **The graphs of all three functions have the same vertical asymptote: $x = 0$ (the y-axis).**
- **The graphs of all three functions have the same x-intercept, at $x = 1$, and no y-intercept.**
- **All three functions are increasing throughout their domains.**
- **All three functions are negative on the interval $(0, 1)$ and positive on the interval $(1, +\infty)$.**

Attributes that make the functions different:

- **Each function has a different average rate of change on a given interval.**

For instance, on the interval $[0, 1]$, the average rate of change for $f(x) = \log_2 x$ is $\frac{\log_2 2 - \log_2}{2 - 1} = \frac{1 - 0}{1} = 1$, the average rate of change for $f(x) = \log x$ is $\frac{\log 2 - \log 1}{2 - 1} \approx \frac{0.301 - 0}{1} = 0.301$, and the average rate of change for $f(x) = \ln x$ is $\frac{\ln 2 - \ln 1}{2 - 1} \approx \frac{0.693 - 0}{1} = 0.693$.

Exercise	Depth of Knowledge (D.O.K.)	COMMON CORE Mathematical Practices
1	**1** Recall of Information	**MP.4** Modeling
2	**2** Skills/Concepts	**MP.4** Modeling
3–4	**2** Skills/Concepts	**MP.2** Reasoning
5–8	**2** Skills/Concepts	**MP.4** Modeling
9–10	**3** Strategic Thinking	**MP.4** Modeling
11–13	**3** Strategic Thinking H.O.T.	**MP.3** Logic

EVALUATE

ASSIGNMENT GUIDE

Concepts and Skills	Practice
Explore Graphing and Analyzing Parent Logarithmic Functions	Exercises 1–2
Example 1 Graphing Combined Transformations of $f(x) = \log_b x$ Where $b > 1$	Exercises 4–8
Example 2 Writing, Graphing, and Analyzing a Logarithmic Model	Exercises 9–10

QUESTIONING STRATEGIES

? Do translations of the graph of a logarithmic function affect the domain and/or the range of the function? Explain. **A horizontal translation affects the domain, but not the range. A vertical translation does not affect the domain or the range, because the range is always all real numbers.**

AVOID COMMON ERRORS

Students may find that functions grow so quickly (exponential) or slowly (logarithmic) that it will appear that the functions are asymptotic when they are not. Remind students that exponential graphs have only horizontal asymptotes, while logarithmic graphs have only vertical asymptotes.

3. For each of the six functions, describe how its graph is a transformation of the graph of $f(x) = \log_2 x$. Also identify what attributes of $f(x) = \log_2 x$ change as a result of the transformation. Attributes to consider are the domain, the range, the end behavior, the vertical asymptote, the x-intercept, the intervals where the function is positive and where it is negative, and whether the function increases or decreases throughout its domain.

a. $g(x) = \log_2 x - 5$

The graph of $g(x)$ is a vertical translation of the graph of $f(x)$ down 5 units. The attributes that change are the x-intercept and the intervals where the function is positive and where it is negative.

b. $g(x) = 4 \log_2 x$

The graph of $g(x)$ is a vertical stretch of the graph of $f(x)$ by a factor of 4. No attributes change.

c. $g(x) = \log_2 (x + 6)$

The graph of $g(x)$ is a horizontal translation of the graph of $f(x)$ left 6 units. The attributes that change are the domain, the end behavior, the vertical asymptote, the x-intercept, and the intervals where the function is positive and where it is negative.

d. $g(x) = -\frac{3}{4} \log_2 x$

The graph of $g(x)$ is a vertical compression of the graph of $f(x)$ by a factor of $\frac{3}{4}$ as well as a reflection across the x-axis. The attributes that change are the end behavior and whether the function increases or decreases throughout its domain.

e. $g(x) = \log_2 x + 7$

The graph of $g(x)$ is a vertical translation of the graph of $f(x)$ up 7 units. The attributes that change are the x-intercept and the intervals where the function is positive and where it is negative.

f. $g(x) = \log_2 (x - 8)$

The graph of $g(x)$ is a horizontal translation of the graph of $f(x)$ right 8 units. The attributes that change are the domain, the end behavior, the vertical asymptote, the x-intercept, and the intervals where the function is positive and where it is negative.

Identify the transformations of the graph of $f(x) = \log_b x$ that produce the graph of the given function $g(x)$. Then graph $g(x)$ on the same coordinate plane as the graph of $f(x)$ by applying the transformations to the asymptote $x = 0$ and to the reference points $(1, 0)$ and $(b, 1)$. Also state the domain and range of $g(x)$ using set notation.

4. $g(x) = -4 \log_2 (x + 2) + 1$

The transformations of the graph of $f(x) = \log_2 x$ that produce the graph of $g(x)$ are as follows:

- **a vertical stretch by a factor of 4**
- **a reflection across the x-axis**
- **a translation of 2 units to the left and 1 unit up**

Domain: $\{x \mid x > -2\}$ Range: $\{y \mid -\infty < y < +\infty\}$

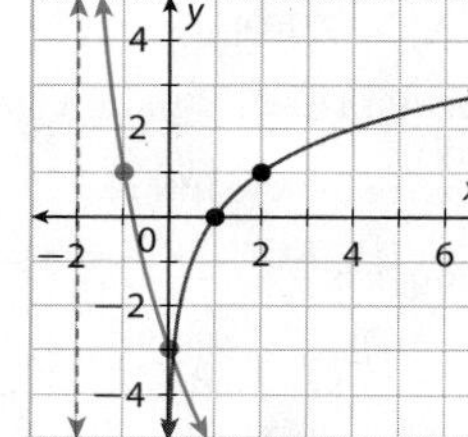

5. $g(x) = 3\log(x - 1) - 1$

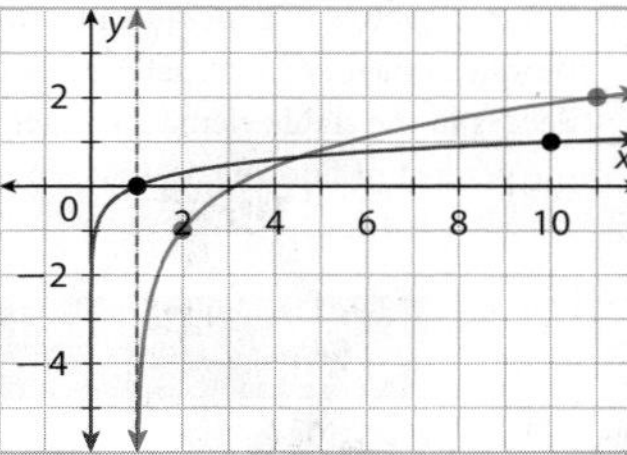

The transformations of the graph of $f(x) = \log x$ that produce the graph of $g(x)$ are as follows:

- **a vertical stretch by a factor of 3**
- **a translation of 1 unit to the right and 1 unit down**

Domain: $\{x \mid x > 1\}$ **Range:** $\{y \mid -\infty < y < +\infty\}$

6. $f(x) = \frac{1}{2}\log_2(x - 1) - 2$

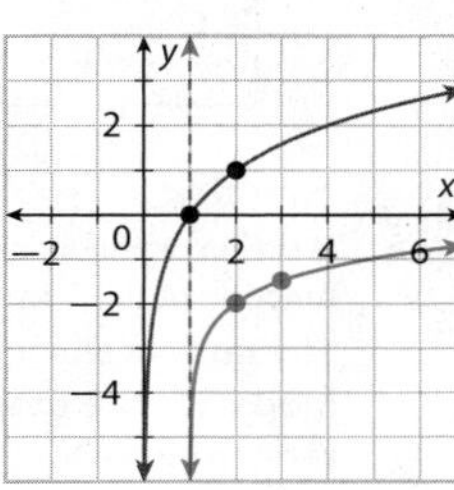

The transformations of the graph of $f(x) = \log_2 x$ that produce the graph of $g(x)$ are as follows:

- **a vertical compression by a factor of $\frac{1}{2}$**
- **a translation of 1 unit to the right and 2 units down**

Note that the translation of 1 unit to the right affects only the x-coordinates of points on the graph of $f(x)$, while the vertical compression by a factor of $\frac{1}{2}$ and the translation of 2 units down affect only the y-coordinates.

Domain: $\{x \mid x > 1\}$ **Range:** $\{y \mid -\infty < y < +\infty\}$

7. $g(x) = -4\ln(x - 4) + 3$

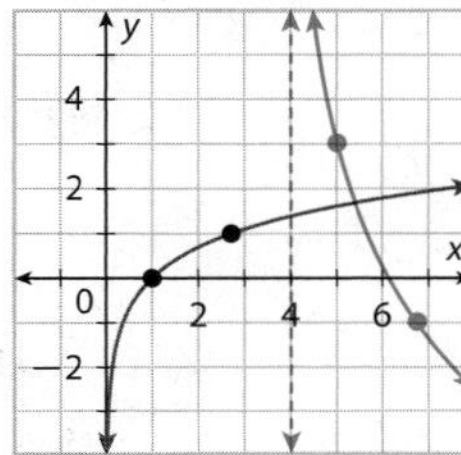

The transformations of the graph of $f(x) = \ln x$ that produce the graph of $g(x)$ are as follows:

- **a vertical compression by a factor of 4**
- **a reflection across the x-axis**
- **a translation of 4 units to the right and 3 units up**

Domain: $\{x \mid x > 4\}$ **Range:** $\{y \mid -\infty < y < +\infty\}$

8. $g(x) = -2\log(x + 2) + 5$

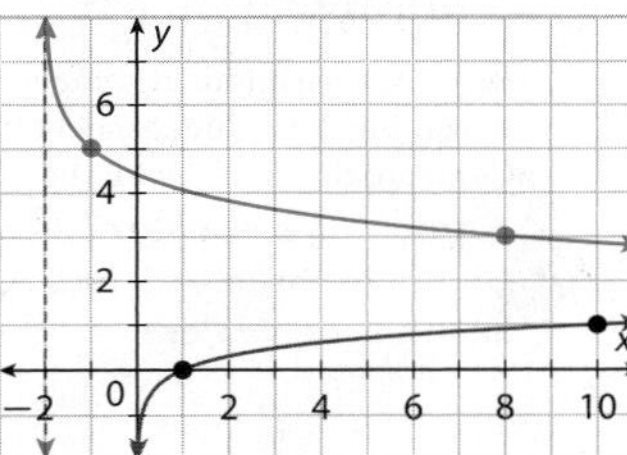

The transformations of the graph of $f(x) = \log x$ that produce the graph of $g(x)$ are as follows:

- **a vertical stretch by a factor of 2**
- **a reflection across the x-axis**
- **a translation of 2 units to the left and 5 units up**

Domain: $\{x \mid x > -2\}$ **Range:** $\{y \mid -\infty < y < +\infty\}$

MULTIPLE REPRESENTATIONS

Help students to recognize how, in each of the applications, the resulting equation represents the data. Use graphs and the table feature of the graphing calculator to ensure that students make connections among the various representations.

COMMUNICATING MATH

Students may find it helpful to write a verbal description of the transformations that are indicated by the function rule before attempting to draw the graph of the transformed function.

9. The radioactive isotope fluorine-18 is used in medicine to produce images of internal organs and detect cancer. It decays to the stable element oxygen-18. The table gives the percent of fluorine-18 that remains in a sample over a period of time.

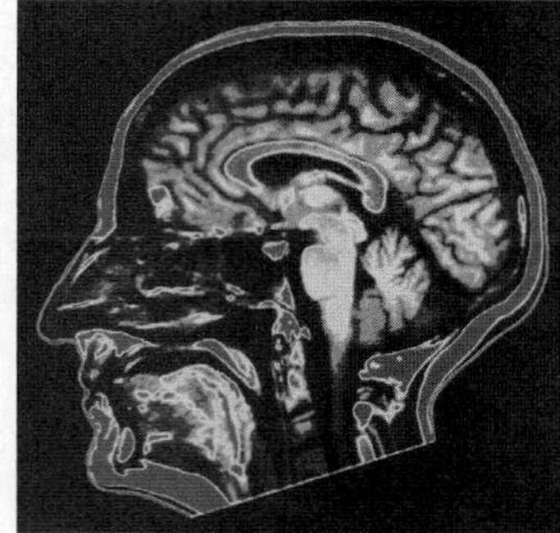

Time (hours)	Percent of Fluorine-18 Remaining
0	100
1	68.5
2	46.9
3	32.1

a. Write an exponential model for the percent of fluorine-18 remaining as a function of time (in hours).

The ratio of the percents for consecutive hours is about 68.5, so an exponential model for the data is $p = 100(0.685)^t$ where p is the percent of fluorine-18 remaining at time t (in hours).

b. Find the inverse of the exponential model after rewriting it with a base of e. Describe what information the inverse gives.

First, find the constant c such that $e^c = 0.685$. Rewriting $e^c = 0.685$ in logarithmic form gives $c = \ln 0.685 \approx -0.378$. Then, find the inverse of $p = 100(e^{-0.378})^t = 100\,e^{-0.378t}$.

$$p = 100e^{-0.378t}$$

$$\frac{p}{100} = e^{-0.378t}$$

$$\ln \frac{p}{100} = -0.378t$$

$$-2.65 \ln \frac{p}{100} = t$$

So, the inverse of the exponential model is $t = -2.65 \ln \frac{p}{100}$, which gives the time it takes for the percent of fluorine-18 remaining to reach a certain level.

c. Perform logarithmic regression on the data (using the percent of fluorine-18 remaining as the independent variable and time as the dependent variable). Compare this model with the inverse model from part b.

A graphing calculator gives the logarithmic regression model $t = 12.2 - 2.64 \ln p$. Graphing this model and the inverse model from part b shows that the models are basically equivalent.

10. During the period between 2001–2011, the average price of an ounce of gold doubled every 4 years. In 2001, the average price of gold was about $270 per ounce.

Year	Average Price of an Ounce of Gold
2001	$271.04
2002	$309.73
2003	$363.38
2004	$409.72
2005	$444.74
2006	$603.46
2007	$695.39
2008	$871.96
2009	$972.35
2010	$1224.53
2011	$1571.52

a. Write an exponential model for the average price of an ounce of gold as a function of time (in years since 2001).

An exponential model for the average price P of gold (in dollars per ounce) is $P = 270(2)^{\frac{t}{4}}$ where t is the time in years since 2001.

b. Find the inverse of the exponential model after rewriting it with a base of e. Describe what information the inverse gives.

First, rewrite $P = 270(2)^{\frac{t}{4}}$ as $P = 270\left(2^{\frac{1}{4}}\right)^t$. Next, find the constant c such that $e^c = 2^{\frac{1}{4}} \approx 1.19$. Rewriting $e^c \approx 1.19$ in logarithmic form gives $c \approx \ln 1.19 \approx 0.174$. Finally, find the inverse of $P = 270\left(e^{0.174}\right)^t = 270\,e^{0.174t}$.

$$P = 270\,e^{0.174t}$$

$$\frac{P}{270} = e^{0.174t}$$

$$\ln \frac{P}{270} = 0.174t$$

$$5.75 \ln \frac{P}{270} = t$$

So, the inverse of the exponential model is $t = 5.75 \ln \frac{P}{270}$, which gives the time it takes for the average price of gold to reach a certain level.

c. Perform logarithmic regression on the data in the table (using the average price of gold as the independent variable and time as the dependent variable). Compare this model with the inverse model from part b.

A graphing calculator gives the logarithmic regression model $t = -31.3 + 5.67 \ln P$. Graphing this model and the inverse model from part b shows that the models are basically equivalent.

PEER-TO-PEER DISCUSSION

Ask students to work with a partner to determine the domain and range of the function $f(x) = \log_b(-x)$. **The domain is all negative real numbers. The range is all real numbers.**

JOURNAL

Have students describe how to use transformations of the graph of the parent logarithmic function $f(x) = \log_2 x$ to graph the function $g(x) = a\log_2 (x - h) + k$.

H.O.T. Focus on Higher Order Thinking

11. Multiple Representations For the function $g(x) = \log (x - h)$, what value of the parameter h will cause the function to pass through the point $(7, 1)$? Answer the question in two different ways: once by using the function's rule, and once by thinking in terms of the function's graph.

Using the function's rule:

$gx = \log (x - h)$

$1 = \log (7 - h)$

$10^1 = 7 - h$

$3 = -h$

$-3 = h$

Thinking in terms of the function's graph:

The graph of $g(x) = \log (x - h)$ is the graph of $f(x) = \log x$ translated h units horizontally. Since the graph of $f(x)$ passes through the point $(10,1)$, shifting the graph left 3 units causes it to pass through the point $(7, 1)$. A shift of 3 units to the left means that $h = -3$.

12. Explain the Error A student drew the graph of $g(x) = 2 \log_{\frac{1}{2}}(x - 2)$ as shown. Explain the error that the student made, and draw the correct graph.

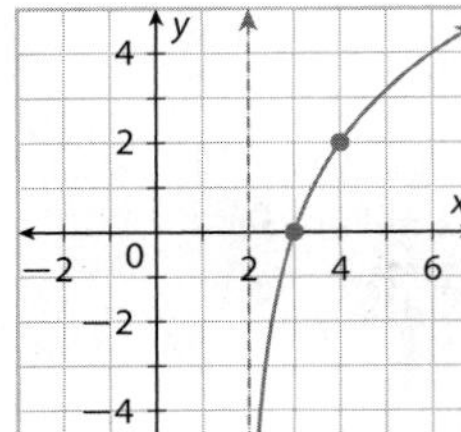

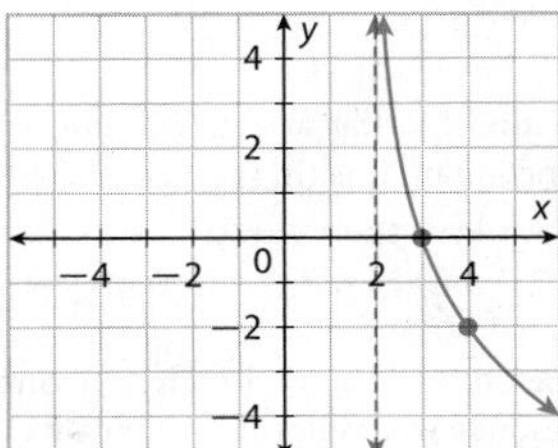

The student overlooked the fact that the base of the logarithmic function is $\frac{1}{2}$, not 2. When the function is rewritten with a base of 2, it becomes $g(x) = -2 \log_2(x - 2)$, which means that in addition to vertically stretching the graph of $f(x) = \log_2 x$ by a factor of 2 and translating the graph 2 units to the right, the student must reflect the graph across the x-axis.

13. Construct Arguments Prove that $\log_{\frac{1}{b}} x = -\log_b x$ for any positive value of b not equal to 1. Begin the proof by setting $\log_{\frac{1}{b}} x$ equal to m and rewriting the equation in exponential form.

Let $\log_{\frac{1}{b}} x = m$. In exponential form, the equation is $\left(\frac{1}{b}\right)^m = x$, so $\left(b^{-1}\right)^m = x$ and $b^{-m} = x$. In logarithmic form, the equation $b^{-m} = x$ is $\log_b x = -m$, or $-\log_b x = m$. By the transitive property of equality, $\log_{\frac{1}{b}} x = -\log_b x$.

Lesson Performance Task

Given the following data about the heights of chair seats and table tops for children, make separate scatterplots of the ordered pairs (age of child, chair seat height) and the ordered pairs (age of child, table top height). Explain why a logarithmic model would be appropriate for each data set. Perform a logarithmic regression on each data set, and describe the transformations needed to obtain the graph of the model from the graph of the parent function $f(x) = \ln x$.

Age of Child (years)	Chair Seat Height (inches)	Table Top Height (inches)
1	5	12
1.5	6.5	14
2	8	16
3	10	18
5	12	20
7.5	14	22
11	16	25

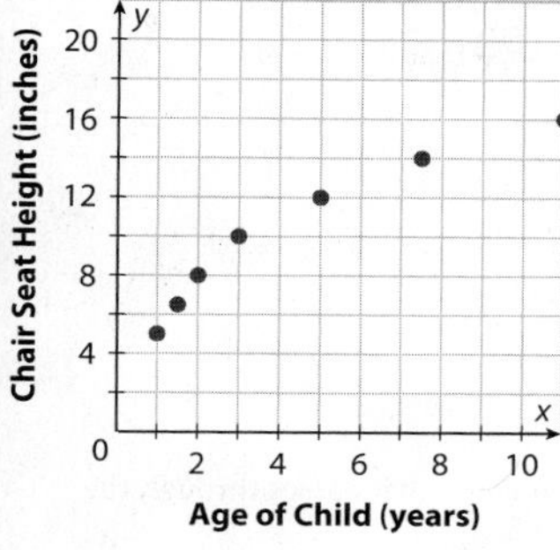

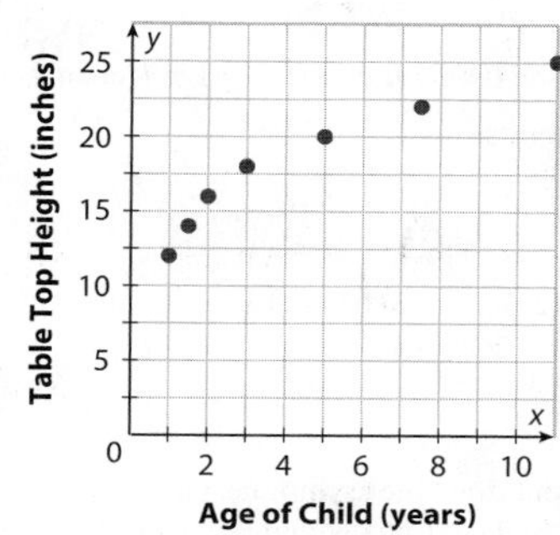

In both graphs, the average rate of change between consecutive points is always positive and decreases as the independent variable (age of a child) increases. So, a logarithmic model is appropriate for both data sets.

Logarithmic regression for (age of child, chair seat height) is $y = 4.83 + 4.59 \ln x$ where x is the age of a child and y is the chair seat height. The graph of $y = 4.83 + 4.59 \ln x$ is the graph of $f(x) = \ln x$ vertically stretched by a factor of 4.59 and translated up 4.83 units.

Logarithmic regression for (age of child, table top height) is $y = 12.05 + 5.19 \ln x$ where x is the age of a child and y is the chair seat height. The graph of $y = 12.05 + 5.19 \ln x$ is the graph of $f(x) = \ln x$ vertically stretched by a factor of 5.19 and translated up 12.05.

EXTENSION ACTIVITY

Have students measure the chair and table heights for five classmates. Have students ask the age of each classmate, and then have them plot this data on the graphs they drew in the Lesson Performance Task. Have students discuss whether the data they measured could be modeled by the same function they found for the younger children, and why or why not.

AVOID COMMON ERRORS

Students may graph the age on the y-axis and the other variables on the x-axis. Explain that the variable in common (in this case, the age) is usually graphed on the x-axis so the other variables can be more easily compared. Have students describe the resulting function if the age is graphed on the y-axis. **It is the inverse of the function being sought.**

INTEGRATE MATHEMATICAL PRACTICES

Focus on Communication

MP.3 Have students discuss the differences between the two graphs. Have students explain why the table height graph is not simply the chair height graph translated upward and how this could be related to the size of the child.

Scoring Rubric

2 points: Student correctly solves the problem and explains his/her reasoning.

1 point: Student shows good understanding of the problem but does not fully solve or explain his/her reasoning.

0 points: Student does not demonstrate understanding of the problem.

Study Guide Review

ASSESSMENT AND INTERVENTION

Assign or customize module reviews.

MODULE PERFORMANCE TASK

Mathematical Practices: MP.1, MP.2, MP.3, MP.4, MP.5
F-BF.B.5, S-ID.B.6a

SUPPORTING STUDENT REASONING

Students should begin by thinking about how to find a model for the amount of drug in the bloodstream. They can then do research, or you can provide them with specific information. Here is some of the information they may ask for.

- **How can technology be used to fit a logarithmic function to data?** Some students may use graphing calculators to fit data; others may prefer using a computer spreadsheet or an online graphing program. Students can research these methods and choose the one that best suits their needs.

STUDY GUIDE REVIEW

Logarithmic Functions

MODULE 15

Essential Question: How can you use logarithmic functions to solve real-world problems?

Key Vocabulary
asymptote (*asíntota*)
common logarithm (*logaritmo común*)
logarithm (*logaritmo*)
logarithmic function (*función logarítmica*)
natural logarithm (*logaritmo natural*)

KEY EXAMPLE *(Lesson 15.1)*

Evaluate $f(x) = \log_4 x$ when $x = 1024$.

$f(1024) = \log_4 1024$

$4^{f(1024)} = 1024$ by definition of logarithm

$4^{f(1024)} = 4^5$ because $4^5 = 1024$

$f(1024) = 5$

KEY EXAMPLE *(Lesson 15.2)*

Graph $f(x) = 3\log_2(x+1) - 4$.

The parameters for $f(x) = a\log_b(x-h) + k$ are $a = 3$, $b = 2$, $h = -1$, and $k = -4$.

Find reference points:

$(1+h, k) = (0, -4)$

$(b+h, a+k) = (2-1, 3-4) = (1, -1)$

The two reference points are $(0, -4)$ and $(1, -1)$.

Find the asymptote:

$x = h = -1$

Plot the points and draw the asymptote. Connect the points with a curve that passes through the reference points and continually draws nearer the asymptote.

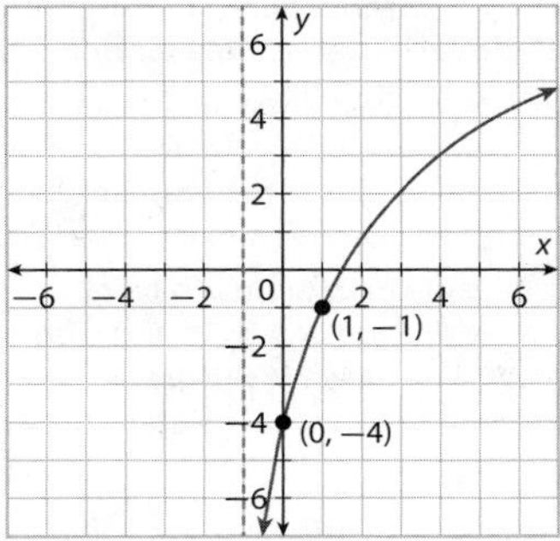

SCAFFOLDING SUPPORT

- Encourage students to calculate the amount of drug in the bloodstream after a single dose at different times, first putting the information in a table and then graphing it.
- Students might recognize that both the amount of drug in the bloodstream after one dose and the amount of drug in the bloodstream after periodic dosages can be modeled using recursive formulas.

EXERCISES

Evaluate each logarithmic function for the given value. *(Lesson 15.1)*

1. $f(x) = \log_2 x$, for $f(256)$

$f(256) = 8$

2. $f(x) = \log_9 x$, for $f(6561)$

$f(6561) = 4$

Graph each function. *(Lesson 15.2)*

3. $f(x) = 2\log_3 (x - 2) + 1$

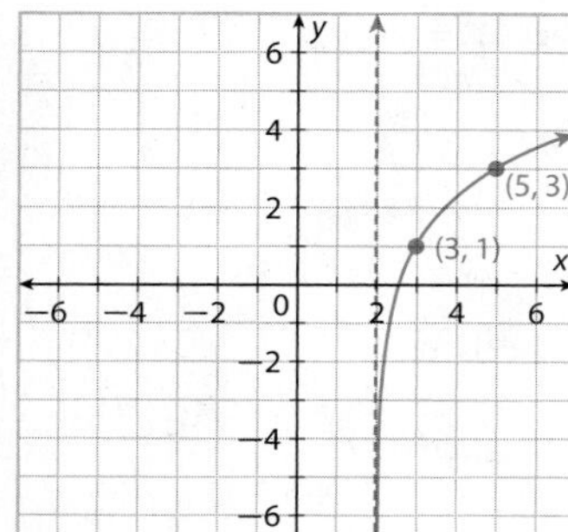

4. $f(x) = \log_5 (x + 1) - 1$

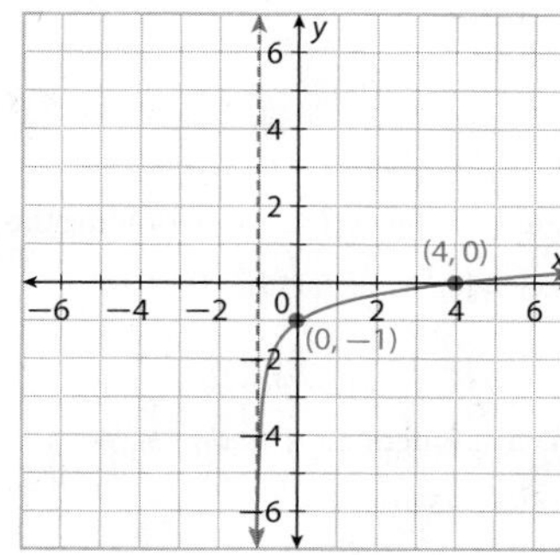

MODULE PERFORMANCE TASK

What's the Dosage?

Kira is a scientist working for a pharmaceutical lab and has developed a new drug. According to her research, 30% of the drug is eliminated from the bloodstream every 6 hours. Her initial dosage plan is to have the patient take a 1200 mg pill of the drug every 12 hours.

The patient needs to have at least 500 mg of the drug in the bloodstream at all times, but the total amount should never exceed 2500 mg. The drug should be taken for no more than 4 days. Does Kira's proposed dosage plan meet the medical requirements for the drug? Find a function that describes the amount of drug in the patient's bloodstream as a function of the number of doses.

Start by listing in the space below the information you will need to solve the problem. Then use your own paper to complete the task. Be sure to write down all your data and assumptions. Then use graphs, numbers, words, or algebra to explain how you reached your conclusion.

SAMPLE SOLUTION

First, find the amount of drug remaining in the bloodstream when the second dose is given. Every 6 hours, 70% of the drug remains, so after 12 hours, $1200 \times 0.7 \times 0.7 = 588$ mg is left. The dosage plan meets the minimum requirement.

Now, make a table of the amount of the drug in the patient's bloodstream after various numbers of doses. To do this, multiply the total amount at the last dose by $0.7 \times 0.7 = 0.49$, then add the amount of the new dose, 1200 mg. We should look at a total of 8 doses, since that is equivalent to the maximum time of taking the drug, 4 days.

Number of Doses	Amount of Medication in Bloodstream (mg)
1	1200
2	$(1200 \times 0.49) + 1200 = 1788$
3	$(1788 \times 0.49) + 1200 \approx 2076.1$
4	$(2076.1 \times 0.49) + 1200 \approx 2217.3$
5	$(2217.3 \times 0.49) + 1200 \approx 2286.5$
6	$(2286.5 \times 0.49) + 1200 \approx 2320.4$
7	$(2320.4 \times 0.49) + 1200 \approx 2337$
8	$(2337 \times 0.49) + 1200 \approx 2345.1$

So, the total dosage never exceeds the maximum. Both requirements are met. Now, graph the data in a scatterplot.

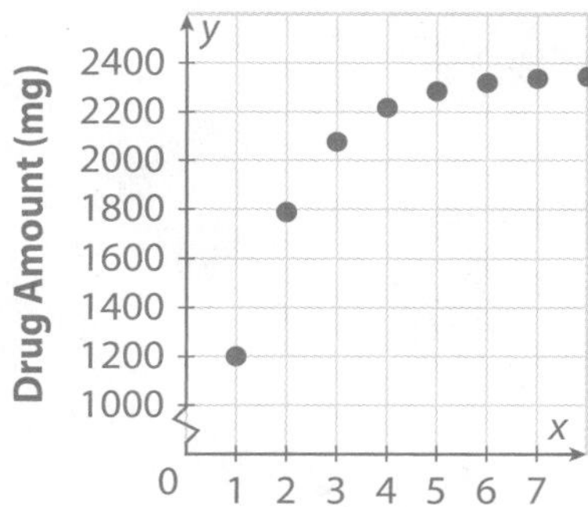

The data appear to form a logarithmic curve. Use regression to find a reasonable model:

$y = 545.82 \ln(x) + 1347.8$

The model is not perfect but has an R^2 value of more than 0.9.

Assessment Rubric

2 points: Student correctly solves the problem and explains his/her reasoning.

1 point: Student shows good understanding of the problem but does not fully solve or explain.

0 points: Student does not demonstrate understanding of the problem.

DISCUSSION OPPORTUNITIES

- Why can't a coordinate point with $x = 0$ be used to fit a logarithmic function?
- Why is it more important, with respect to the maximum allowable amount of drug in a patient's bloodstream, to focus on the amount after each dose, instead of looking more closely at what happens between doses?

Ready to Go On?

ASSESS MASTERY

Use the assessment on this page to determine if students have mastered the concepts and standards covered in this module.

ASSESSMENT AND INTERVENTION

Access Ready to Go On? assessment online, and receive instant scoring, feedback, and customized intervention or enrichment.

ADDITIONAL RESOURCES

Response to Intervention Resources

- Reteach Worksheets

Differentiated Instruction Resources

- Reading Strategies EL
- Success for English Learners EL
- Challenge Worksheets

Assessment Resources

- Leveled Module Quizzes

Ready to Go On?

15.1–15.2 Logarithmic Functions

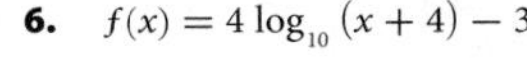

- Online Homework
- Hints and Help
- Extra Practice

Rewrite the given equation in exponential format. *(Lesson 15.1)*

1. $\log_6 x = r$

$6^r = x$

2. $\log_{\frac{3}{4}} 12x = 35y$

$\left(\frac{3}{4}\right)^{35y} = 12x$

Evaluate each logarithmic function for the given value. *(Lesson 15.1)*

3. $f(x) = \log_5 x$ for $f(125)$

$f(125) = 3$

4. $f(x) = \log_3 x$ for $f(729)$

$f(729) = 6$

Graph each function. *(Lesson 15.2)*

5. $f(x) = -3 \log_e (x + 1) + 2$

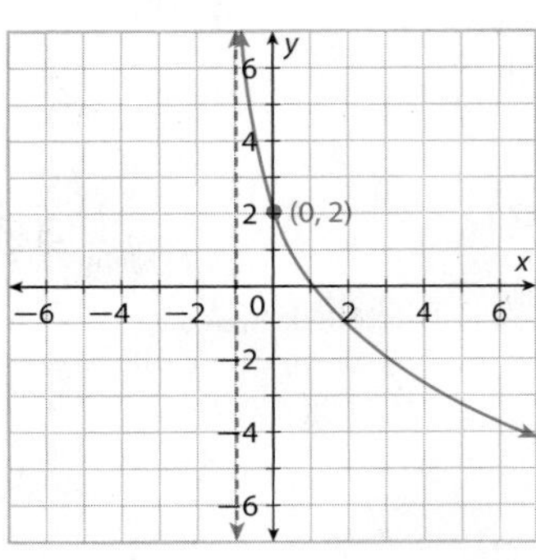

6. $f(x) = 4 \log_{10} (x + 4) - 3$

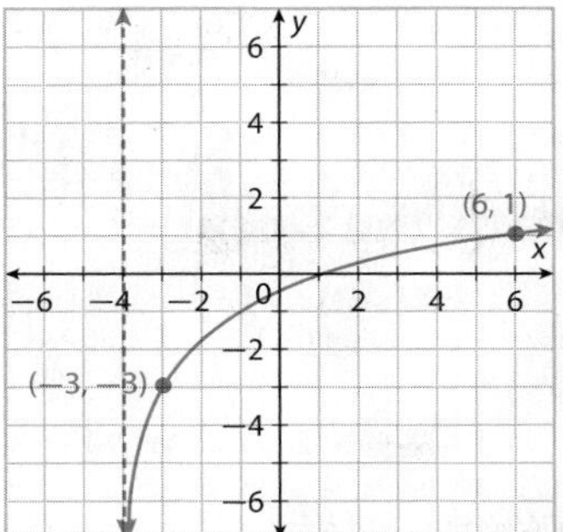

ESSENTIAL QUESTION

7. How is the graph of the logarithmic function $f(x) = \log_4 x$ related to the graph of the exponential function $g(x) = 4^x$?

They are inversely related, so the graph of $f(x)$ is the reflection of the graph of $g(x)$ over the line $y = x$.

COMMON CORE Common Core Standards

Lesson	Items	Content Standards	Mathematical Practices
15.1	1	**F-BF.B.5**	**MP.2**
15.1	2	**F-BF.B.5**	**MP.2**
15.1	3	**F-BF.B.5**	**MP.2**
15.1	4	**F-BF.B.5**	**MP.2**
15.2	5	**F-BF.B.3**	**MP.7**
15.2	6	**F-BF.B.3**	**MP.7**

MODULE 15
MIXED REVIEW

Assessment Readiness

1. Consider each function. Does the function show exponential decay? Select Yes or No for A–C.
   A. $f(x) = \left(\frac{1}{4}\right)^x$ ● Yes ○ No
   B. $f(x) = 1.6\left(\frac{3}{4}\right)^x$ ● Yes ○ No
   C. $f(x) = \frac{3}{5}(1.1)^x$ ○ Yes ● No

2. Consider the function $f(x) = \frac{1}{4}\log_5(x+3) - 2$. Choose True or False for each statement.
   A. The domain of this function is $\{x \mid x > -3\}$. ● True ○ False
   B. There is no range to this function. ○ True ● False
   C. The range of this function is $\{y \mid y > -2\}$ ○ True ● False

3. Shelby is canoeing in a river. She travels 4 miles upstream and 4 miles downstream in a total of 5 hours. In still water, Shelby can travel at an average speed of 2 miles per hour. To the nearest tenth, what is the average speed of the river's current? Explain.

   Upstream speed $= 2 - r$, Downstream speed $= 2 + r$, total time is the upstream time $\frac{4}{2-r}$ plus downstream time $\frac{4}{2+r}$ and is equal to 5 hours.

   $$\frac{4}{2-r} + \frac{4}{2+r} = 5$$
   $$4(2+r) + 4(2-r) = 5(2+r)(2-r)$$
   $$8 + 4r + 8 - 4r = 20 - 5r^2$$
   $$5r^2 = 4$$
   $$r = \pm\frac{2\sqrt{5}}{5} \approx 0.9$$

4. Researchers have found that after 25 years of age, the average size of the pupil in a person's eye decreases. The relationship between pupil diameter d (in millimeters) and age a (in years) can be modeled by $d = -2.1158 \log_e a + 13.669$. What is the average diameter of a pupil for a person 25 years old? 50 years old? Explain how you got your answer.

   about 6.86 mm; about 5.39 mm; use a calculator to evaluate the expression for $a = 25$ and $a = 50$

Common Core Standards

Lesson	Items	Content Standards	Mathematical Practices
13.2	1*	F-BF.B.3	MP.1
15.1	2	F-BF.B.5	MP.2
9.3	3*	A-REI.A.2,N-Q.A.1	MP.4
15.1	4	F-BF.B.5	MP.4

* Item integrates mixed review concepts from previous modules or a previous course.

MIXED REVIEW

Assessment Readiness

ASSESSMENT AND INTERVENTION

Assign ready-made or customized practice tests to prepare students for high-stakes tests.

ADDITIONAL RESOURCES

Assessment Resources

- Leveled Module Quizzes: Modified, B

AVOID COMMON ERRORS

Item 4 When using a calculator to solve a logarithmic function, some students will forget to consider the base of the logarithmic function. Remind students that the calculator's log button is in base 10, and they will need to use the change of base formula to evaluate logarithms in other bases.

MODULE 16

Logarithmic Properties and Exponential Equations

ESSENTIAL QUESTION:

Answer: Logarithms allow you to "undo" exponential operations. When you are given the output of an exponential function and wish to find the input, you use properties of logarithms to find the solution.

PROFESSIONAL DEVELOPMENT VIDEO

Professional Development Video

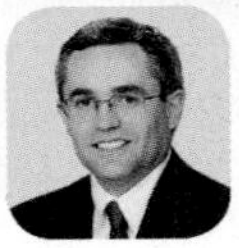

Author Matt Larson models successful teaching practices in an actual high-school classroom.

Professional Development

my.hrw.com

MODULE 16

Logarithmic Properties and Exponential Equations

Essential Question: How do the properties of logarithms allow you to solve real-world problems?

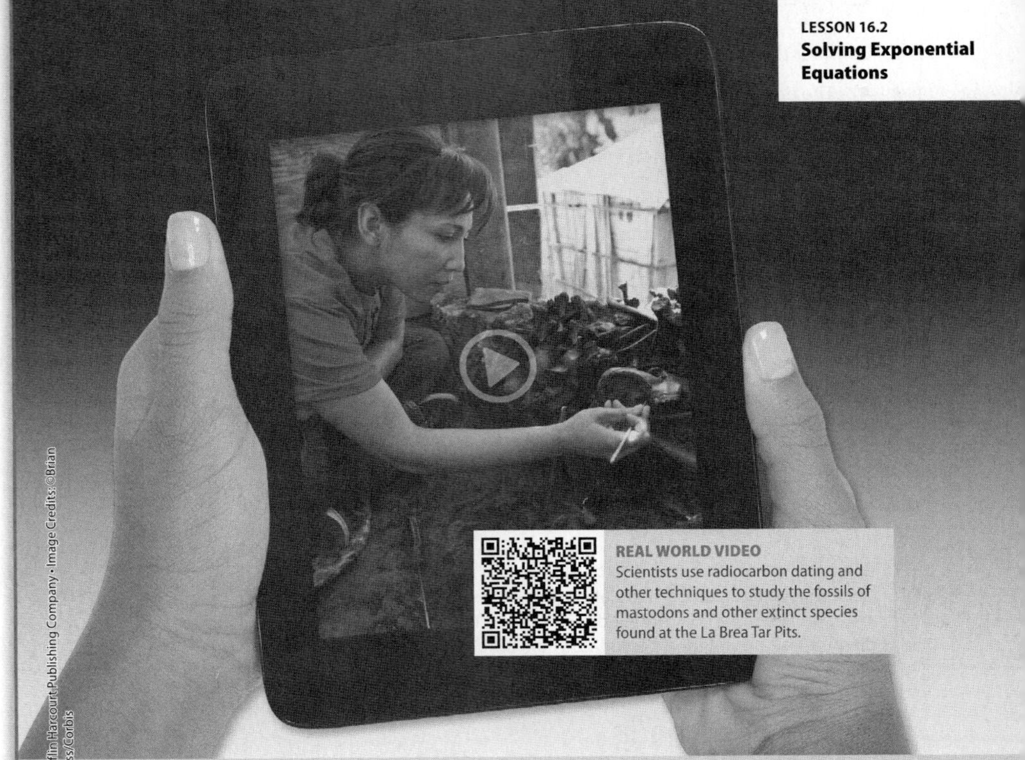

REAL WORLD VIDEO
Scientists use radiocarbon dating and other techniques to study the fossils of mastodons and other extinct species found at the La Brea Tar Pits.

MODULE PERFORMANCE TASK PREVIEW

How Old Is That Bone?

All living organisms contain carbon. Carbon has two main isotopes, carbon-12 and carbon-14. C-14 is radioactive and decays at a steady rate. Living organisms continually replenish their stores of carbon, and the ratio between C-12 and C-14 stays relatively constant. When the organism dies, this ratio changes at a known rate as C-14 decays. How can we use a logarithmic equation and carbon dating to determine the age of a mastodon bone? Let's find out!

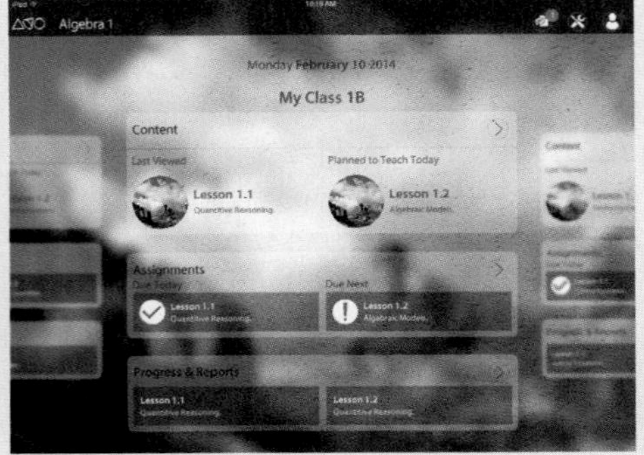

DIGITAL TEACHER EDITION

Access a full suite of teaching resources when and where you need them:

- Access content online or offline
- Customize lessons to share with your class
- Communicate with your students in real-time
- View student grades and data instantly to target your instruction where it is needed most

PERSONAL MATH TRAINER

Assessment and Intervention

Assign automatically graded homework, quizzes, tests, and intervention activities. Prepare your students with updated, Common Core-aligned practice tests.

Are YOU Ready?

Complete these exercises to review skills you will need for this chapter.

• Online Homework
• Hints and Help
• Extra Practice

Exponents

Example 1 Simplify $\frac{40 \cdot x^6 y}{5x^2 y^5}$.

$\frac{40 \cdot x^6 y}{5x^2 y^5} = \frac{40}{5} \cdot x^{6-2} y^{1-5}$ Subtract exponents.

$= \frac{8x^4}{y^4}$ Simplify.

Simplify each expression.

1. $\frac{xy^2}{x^3 y^2}$ $\frac{1}{x^2}$

2. $\frac{18x^3y^7}{2y^5}$ $9x^3y^2$

3. $\frac{12x^4}{8x^9y}$ $\frac{3}{2x^5y}$

Multi-Step Equations

Example 2 Solve $3(5 - 2x) = -x$ for x.

$15 - 6x = -x$ Distribute the 3.

$15 = 5x$ Add $6x$ to both sides.

$3 = x$ Divide both sides by 5.

The solution is $x = 3$.

Solve.

4. $5(4x + 9) = 2x$ -2.5

5. $3(x + 12) = 2(4 - 2x)$ -4

6. $(x - 2)^2 = 4(x + 1)$ 0, 8

Equations Involving Exponents

Example 3 Solve $2x^{\frac{1}{3}} - 1 = 3$ for x.

$2x^{\frac{1}{3}} = 4$ Add 1 to both sides.

$x^{\frac{1}{3}} = 2$ Divide both sides by 2.

$\left(x^{\frac{1}{3}}\right)^3 = (2)^3$ Raise both sides to the power of 3.

$x = 8$ Simplify.

Solve.

7. $3x^{\frac{1}{4}} + 2 = 11$ 81

8. $8x^{\frac{1}{2}} + 20 = 100$ 100

9. $4x^{\frac{1}{3}} + 15 = 35$ 125

Are You Ready?

ASSESS READINESS

Use the assessment on this page to determine if students need strategic or intensive intervention for the module's prerequisite skills.

ASSESSMENT AND INTERVENTION

Personal Math Trainer

RtI Response to Intervention TIER 1, TIER 2, TIER 3 SKILLS

Personal Math Trainer will automatically create a standards-based, personalized intervention assignment for your students, targeting each student's individual needs!

ADDITIONAL RESOURCES

See the table below for a full list of intervention resources available for this module.

Response to Intervention Resources also includes:

- Tier 2 Skill Pre-Tests for each Module
- Tier 2 Skill Post-Tests for each skill

Response to Intervention			Differentiated Instruction
Tier 1 Lesson Intervention Worksheets	**Tier 2** Strategic Intervention Skills Intervention Worksheets	**Tier 3** Intensive Intervention Worksheets available online	
Reteach 16.1 Reteach 16.2	7 Equations Involving Exponents 9 Exponents 20 Multi-Step Equations 28 Rational and Radical Exponents	Building Block Skills 29, 75, 76, 91, 100	Challenge worksheets Extend the Math Lesson Activities in TE

LESSON 16.1

Properties of Logarithms

Common Core Math Standards

The student is expected to:

F.BF.B.5(+)

Understand the inverse relationship between exponents and logarithms and use this relationship to solve problems involving logarithms and exponents.

Mathematical Practices

MP.6 Precision

Language Objective

Work with a small group to discuss and record the properties of logarithms and exponents.

ENGAGE

Essential Question: What are the properties of logarithms?

Logarithms have properties that are related to the properties of exponents. There is a Product Property of Logarithms, a Quotient Property of Logarithms, and a Power Property of Logarithms. There is also a Change of Base Property of Logarithms.

PREVIEW: LESSON PERFORMANCE TASK

View the Engage section online. Discuss the photo, asking which would be more useful: a model for the population as a function of time or a model for time as a function of the population. Then preview the Lesson Performance Task.

Name ______ Class ______ Date ______

16.1 Properties of Logarithms

Essential Question: What are the properties of logarithms?

Resource Locker

Explore 1 Investigating the Properties of Logarithms

You can use a scientific calculator to evaluate a logarithmic expression.

(A) Evaluate the expressions in each set using a scientific calculator.

Set A		Set B	
$\log \frac{10}{e} \approx$	0.566	$\frac{1}{\log e} \approx$	2.303
$\ln 10 \approx$	2.303	$1 + \log e \approx$	1.434
$\log e^{10} \approx$	4.343	$1 - \log e \approx$	0.566
$\log 10e \approx$	1.434	$10 \log e \approx$	4.343

(B) Match the expressions in Set A to the equivalent expressions in Set B.

$\log \frac{10}{e} =$ $1 - \log e$

$\ln 10 =$ $\frac{1}{\log e}$

$\log e^{10} =$ $10 \log e$

$\log 10e =$ $1 + \log e$

Reflect

1. How can you check the results of evaluating the logarithmic expressions in Set A? Use this method to check each.

Use the exponential form of the equations to check the results.

$\log \frac{10}{e} \approx 0.566$	$\ln 10 \approx 2.303$
$\frac{10}{e} \approx 10^{0.566}$	$10 \approx e^{2.303}$
$3.679 \approx 3.681$	$10 \approx 10.004$
$\log e^{10} \approx 4.343$	$\log 10e \approx 1.434$
$e^{10} \approx 10^{4.343}$	$10e \approx 10^{1.434}$
$22{,}026.47 \approx 22{,}029.265$	$27.183 \approx 27.164$

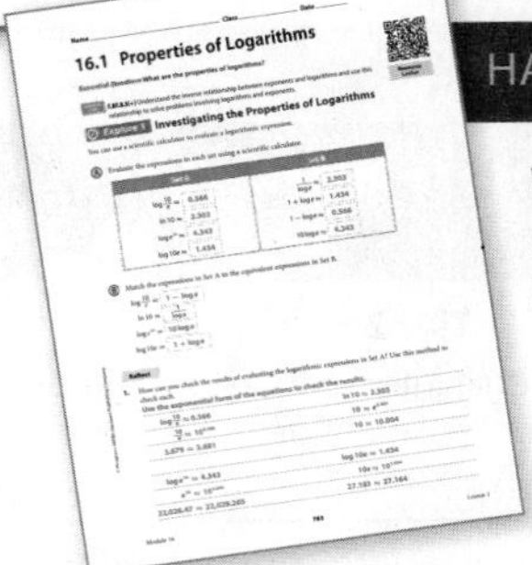

HARDCOVER PAGES 783–79

Watch for the hardcover student edition page numbers for this lesson.

2. **Discussion** How do you know that $\log e$ and $\ln 10$ are reciprocals? Given that the expressions are reciprocals, show another way to represent each expression.
$(\log e)(\ln 10) = 1$, so the expressions are reciprocals.

$\log e = \frac{1}{\ln 10}$ and $\ln 10 = \frac{1}{\log e}$.

Explore 2 Proving the Properties of Logarithms

A logarithm is the exponent to which a base must be raised in order to obtain a given number. So $\log_b b^m = m$. It follows that $\log_b b^0 = 0$, so $\log_b 1 = 0$. Also, $\log_b b^1 = 1$, so $\log_b b = 1$. Additional properties of logarithms are the Product Property of Logarithms, the Quotient Property of Logarithms, the Power Property of Logarithms, and the Change of Base Property of Logarithms. Given positive numb ers m, n, and b $(b \neq 1)$, prove the Product Property of Logarithms.

Properties of Logarithms			
For any positive numbers a, m, n, b $(b \neq 1)$, and c $(c \neq 1)$, the following properties hold.			
Definition-Based Properties	$\log_b b^m = m$	$\log_b 1 = 0$	$\log_b b = 1$
Product Property of Logarithms	$\log_b mn = \log_b m + \log_b n$		
Quotient Property of Logarithms	$\log_b \frac{m}{n} = \log_b m - \log_b n$		
Power Property of Logarithms	$\log_b m^n = n\log_b m$		
Change of Base Property of Logarithms	$\log_c a = \frac{\log_b a}{\log_b c}$		

(A) Let $x = \log_b m$ and $y = \log_b n$. Rewrite the expressions in exponential form.

$m =$ **b^x**

$n =$ **b^y**

(B) Substitute for m and n.

$\text{Log}_b\, mn = \log_b \left(\mathbf{b^x \cdot b^y} \right)$

(C) Use the Product of Powers Property of Exponents to simplify.

$\log_b (b^x \cdot b^y) = \log_b b^{\mathbf{x \cdot y}}$

(D) Use the definition of a logarithm $\log_b b^m = m$ to simplify further.

$\log_b b^{x+y} =$ **$x + y$**

(E) Substitute for x and y.

$x + y =$ **$\log_b m + \log_b n$**

PROFESSIONAL DEVELOPMENT

Integrate Mathematical Practices

This lesson provides an opportunity to address Mathematical Practice **MP.6**, which calls for students to "attend to precision." Students learn that, because of the inverse relationship between logarithms and exponents, the properties of logarithms are similar to the properties of exponents, and that exponents can be manipulated in logarithmic form using properties analogous to those in exponential form. They make explicit use of the properties of logarithms to evaluate expressions and to solve problems using logarithmic models.

EXPLORE 1

Investigating the Properties of Logarithms

INTEGRATE TECHNOLOGY

Students have the option of completing the Explore activity either in the book or online.

QUESTIONING STRATEGIES

? What is the base for logarithms written as log *x*? for logarithms written as ln *x*? **The base for log x is 10. The base for ln x is e.**

? How do you enter *e* on a graphing calculator? **Press 2nd e^x and enter 1 as the value of x.**

EXPLORE 2

Proving the Properties of Logarithms

QUESTIONING STRATEGIES

? Which property of exponents is similar to the Product Property of Logarithms? Why? **The Product of Powers Property; both use addition to rewrite an expression involving multiplication.**

? Which property of exponents is similar to the Quotient Property of Logarithms? Why? **The Quotient of Powers Property; both use subtraction to rewrite an expression involving division.**

INTEGRATE MATHEMATICAL PRACTICES

Focus on Technology

MP.5 A calculator has keys for common logs (that is, logs with base 10) and natural logs (logs with base *e*). Discuss with students how the Change of Base Property makes a generic logarithm key, one in which a base must be specified, unnecessary.

INTEGRATE MATHEMATICAL PRACTICES

Focus on Math Connections

MP.1 Explain to students that since logarithms are exponents, the properties of logarithms directly mirror the properties of exponents. Use numerical examples to show this relationship. For example, show how the Product Property of Logarithms, which can be illustrated by the equation

$$\begin{aligned}\log_2(4 \cdot 8) &= \log_2 4 + \log_2 8\\ &= 2 + 3\\ &= 5\end{aligned}$$

is related to the Product Property of Exponents, which can be illustrated by the related equation

$2^2 \cdot 2^3 = 2^{2+3} = 2^5$.

EXPLAIN 1

Using the Properties of Logarithms

AVOID COMMON ERRORS

Students sometimes employ the Product Property of Logarithms when there is no product. Show them that a logarithm is not "distributable" over the addends in a sum.

$$\log_2(8 + 32) \neq \log_2 8 + \log_2 32$$

$$\log_2 40 \neq 3 + 5$$

$$\log_2 40 \neq 8$$

QUESTIONING STRATEGIES

Can you extend the Product Property of Logarithms to more than two factors? If so, give a numerical example to justify your answer. **Yes; sample answer:**

$$\begin{aligned}\log_2 64 &= \log_2 (2)(4)(8)\\ &= \log_2 2 + \log_2 4 + \log_2 8\\ &= 1 + 2 + 3\\ &= 6\end{aligned}$$

and $2^6 = 64$

Reflect

3. Prove the Power Property of Logarithms. Justify each step of your proof.
Let $x = \log_b m$. Then $m = b^x$.

$\log_b m^n = \log_b(b^x)^n$	**Substitution**
$= \log_b b^{xn}$	**Power of a Power Property of Exponents**
$= xn$	**Definition of a logarithm**
$= (\log_b m)(n)$	**Substitution**
$= n \log_b m$	**Commutative Property**

Explain 1 Using the Properties of Logarithms

Logarithmic expressions can be rewritten using one or more of the properties of logarithms.

Example 1 **Express each expression as a single logarithm. Simplify if possible. Then check your results by converting to exponential form and evaluating.**

(A) $\log_3 27 - \log_3 81$

$\log_3 27 - \log_3 81 = \log_3\left(\frac{27}{81}\right)$	Quotient Property of Logarithms
$= \log_3\left(\frac{1}{3}\right)$	Simplify.
$= \frac{\log\left(\frac{1}{3}\right)}{\log 3}$	Change of Base Property of Logarithms
$\approx \frac{-0.477}{0.477}$	Evaluate the logarithms.
$= -1$	Simplify.

Check:

$\log_3\left(\frac{1}{3}\right) = -1$

$\frac{1}{3} = 3^{-1}$

$\frac{1}{3} = \frac{1}{3}$

COLLABORATIVE LEARNING

Peer-to-Peer Activity

Have students work in pairs. Ask them to write three numerical examples for each of the definition-based properties of logarithms. Then have them write a written description of what each property states, and the reason why each is true.

B $\log_5\left(\frac{1}{25}\right) + \log_5 625$

$\log_5\left(\frac{1}{25}\right) + \log_5 625 = \log_5\left(\frac{1}{25} \cdot 625\right)$ — Product Property of Logarithms

$= \log_5 25$ — Simplify.

$= \frac{\log 25}{\log 5}$ — Change of Base Property of Logarithms

$\approx \frac{1.398}{0.699}$ — Evaluate the logarithms.

$= 2$ — Simplify

Check:

$\log_5 25 = 2$

$25 = 5^2$

$25 = 25$

'our Turn

.press each expression as a single logarithm. Simplify if possible.

$\log_4 64^3$

$\log_4 64^3 = 3\log_4 64$

$= 3\left(\frac{\log 64}{\log 4}\right)$

$\approx 3\left(\frac{1.806}{0.602}\right)$

$= 9$

5. $\log_8 18 - \log_8 2$

$\log_8 18 - \log_8 2 = \log_8\left(\frac{18}{2}\right)$

$= \log_8 9$

$= \frac{\log(9)}{\log(8)}$

$\approx \frac{0.9542}{0.9031}$

≈ 1.057

Explain 2 Rewriting a Logarithmic Model

ere are standard formulas that involve logarithms, such as the formula for measuring the loudness of sounds. e loudness of a sound $L(I)$, in decibels, is given by the function $L(I) = 10\log\left(\frac{I}{I_0}\right)$, where I is the sound's intensity watts per square meter and I_0 is the intensity of a barely audible sound. It's also possible to develop logarithmic dels from exponential growth or decay models of the form $f(t) = a(1 + r)^t$ or $f(t) = a(1 - r)^t$ by finding the erse.

DIFFERENTIATE INSTRUCTION

Multiple Representations

tudents may benefit from adding a column to the table of Properties of ,ogarithms, and writing numerical examples to illustrate each property. This einforces students' understanding of the properties, and also provides them with nodels that they can use when applying the properties to other examples.

INTEGRATE TECHNOLOGY

Students can use a graphing calculator and the Change of Base Property to check their work. Show students how to enter the expressions on the calculator, being careful to use parentheses correctly to set off the argument in each expression.

EXPLAIN 2

Rewriting a Logarithmic Model

QUESTIONING STRATEGIES

How does knowing the Properties of Logarithms help you to solve a real-world problem that can be modeled by a logarithmic function? **You can use the properties to simplify the logarithmic expressions in the function rule.**

For the value of $t \log_b(1 + r)$ to equal t, what must be true? **b must equal $1 + r$.**

Example 2 Solve the problems using logarithmic models.

Ⓐ During a concert, an orchestra plays a piece of music in which its volume increases from one measure to the next, tripling the sound's intensity. Find how many decibels the loudness of the sound increases between the two measures.

Let I be the intensity in the first measure. So $3I$ is the intensity in the second measure.

Increase in loudness $= L(3I) - L(I)$	Write the expression.
$= 10\log\left(\frac{3I}{I_0}\right) - 10\log\left(\frac{I}{I_0}\right)$	Substitute.
$= 10\left(\log\left(\frac{3I}{I_0}\right) - \log\left(\frac{I}{I_0}\right)\right)$	Distributive Property
$= 10\left(\log 3 + \log\left(\frac{I}{I_0}\right) - \log\left(\frac{I}{I_0}\right)\right)$	Product Property of Logarithms
$= 10\log 3$	Simplify.
≈ 4.77	Evaluate the logarithm.

So the loudness of sound increases by about 4.77 decibels.

Ⓑ The population of the United States in 2012 was 313.9 million. If the population increases exponentially at an average rate of 1% each year, how long will it take for the population to double?

The exponential growth model is $P = P_0(1+r)^t$, where P is the population in millions after t years, P_0 is the population in 2012, and r is the average growth rate.

$P_0 = 313.9$

$P = 2P_0 =$ **627.8**

$r = 0.01$

Find the inverse model of $P = P_0(1 + r)^t$.

$P = P_0(1 + r)^t$	Exponential model
$\frac{P}{P_0} = (1 + r)^t$	Divide both sides by P_0.
$\log_{1+r}\left(\frac{P}{P_0}\right) = \log_{\boxed{1+r}}(1 + r)^t$	Take the log of both sides.

$$\log_{1+r}\left(\frac{P}{P_0}\right) = t$$

Definition of a logarithm

$$\frac{\log\left(\frac{P}{P_0}\right)}{\log\left((1+r)\right)} = t$$

Change of Base Property of Logarithms

Substitute and solve for t.

$$t = \frac{\log\left(\frac{627.8}{313.9}\right)}{\log\left(1 + 0.01\right)}$$

Substitute.

$$= \frac{\log 2}{\log 1.01}$$

Simplify.

$$= \frac{0.301}{0.004}$$

Evaluate the logarithms.

$$= 75.25$$

Simplify.

The population of the United States will double in **75.25** years from 2012, or in the year **2087**.

Your Turn

A bank account receives 0.06% annual interest compounded monthly. The balance B of the account after t months is given by the equation $B = B_0(1.06)^t$, where B_0 is the starting balance. If the account starts with a balance of \$250, how long will it take to triple the balance of the account?

$B_0 = 250$

$B = 3B_0 = 750$

Find the inverse model of $B = B_0(1.06)^t$.

$$B = B_0(1.06)^t$$

$$\log_{1.06} B = \log_{1.06}\left(B_0(1.06)^t\right)$$

$$\log_{1.06} B = \log_{1.06} B_0 + \log_{1.06}(1.06)^t$$

$$\log_{1.06} B - \log_{1.06} B_0 = \log_{1.06}(1.06)^t$$

$$\log_{1.06}\left(\frac{B}{B_0}\right) = t$$

$$\frac{\log_{1.06}\left(\frac{B}{B_0}\right)}{\log 1.06} = t$$

ELABORATE

INTEGRATE MATHEMATICAL PRACTICES

Focus on Critical Thinking

MP.3 Discuss with students the difference between the expressions $\log_b m^n$ and $(\log_b m)^n$. Help them to see that the Power Property of Logarithms applies only to the first of the two expressions. Have them evaluate each expression for a set of values, such as $b = 3$, $m = 81$, and $n = 2$, to prove that only $\log_b m^n$ is equal to $n\log_b m$.

SUMMARIZE THE LESSON

? How can you use the Properties of Logarithms to simplify a logarithmic expression? If the expression involves the log of a product, you can write it as the sum of the log of each factor. If it involves the log of a quotient, you can write it as the difference between the log of the dividend and the log of the divisor. If it involves the log of a power, you can write it as the product of the exponent and the log of the base.

Substitute and solve for t.

$$t = \frac{\log\left(\frac{750}{250}\right)}{\log 1.06} = \frac{\log 3}{\log 1.06} \approx \frac{0.477}{0.025} \approx 19.08$$

The balance of the account will triple after 19.08 months.

Elaborate

7. On what other properties do the proofs of the properties of logarithms rely?

The proofs of the properties of logarithms rely on related properties of exponents.

8. What properties of logarithms would you use to rewrite the expression $\log_7 x + \log_7 4x$ as a single logarithm?

Use the Product Property of Logarithms and the Power Property of Logarithms.

9. Explain how the properties of logarithms are useful in finding the inverse of an exponential growth or decay model.

After taking the logarithm of both sides of an exponential growth or decay model, use the Power Property of Logarithms and the other properties as needed to isolate the other variable.

10. **Essential Question Check-In** State the Product, Quotient, and Power Properties of Logarithms in a simple sentence.

The log of a product is equal to the sum of the logs of its factors.

The log of a quotient is equal to the log of the dividend minus the log of the divisor.

The log of a power is equal to the product of the exponent and the log of the base.

LANGUAGE SUPPORT EL

Communicate Math

Have small groups of students work together to complete a *Properties of Logarithms and Exponents* chart. Ask them to match related properties.

Properties of Logarithms	Properties of Exponents

Evaluate: Homework and Practice

- Online Homework
- Hints and Help
- Extra Practice

Express each expression as a single logarithm. Simplify if possible.

1. $\log_9 12 + \log_9 546.75$

$$\begin{aligned}\log_9 12 + \log_9 546.75 &= \log_9(12 \cdot 546.75)\\ &= \log_9 6561\\ &= \frac{\log 6561}{\log 9}\\ &= 4\end{aligned}$$

2. $\log_2 2.5 - \log_2 25.6$

$$\begin{aligned}\log_2 76.8 - \log_2 1.2 &= \log_2\left(\frac{76.8}{1.2}\right)\\ &= \log_2 64\\ &= \frac{\log 64}{\log 2}\\ &= 6\end{aligned}$$

3. $\log_{\frac{2}{5}} 0.0256^3$

$$\begin{aligned}\log_{\frac{2}{5}} 0.0256^3 &= 3\log_{\frac{2}{5}} 0.0256\\ &= 3\left(\frac{\log 0.0256}{\log\left(\frac{2}{5}\right)}\right)\\ &= 3(4) = 12\end{aligned}$$

4. $\log_{11} 11^{23}$

$$\begin{aligned}\log_{11} 11^{23} &= 23\log_{11} 11\\ &= 23\end{aligned}$$

5. $\log_5 5^{x+1} + \log_4 256^2$

$$\begin{aligned}\log_5 5^{x+1} + \log_4 256^2 &= (x+1) + 2\log_4 256\\ &= x + 1 + 2\left(\frac{\log 256}{\log 4}\right)\\ &= x + 1 + (24)\\ &= x + 9\end{aligned}$$

6. $\log(\log_7 98 - \log_7 2)^x$

$$\begin{aligned}\log(\log_7 98 - \log_7 2)^{10} &= \log\left(\log_7\left(\frac{98}{2}\right)\right)^x\\ &= \log(\log_7 49)^x\\ &= \log\left(\frac{\log 49}{\log 7}\right)^x\\ &= \log(2)^x\\ &= x\log 2 \approx 0.301x\end{aligned}$$

7. $\log_{x+1}(x^2 + 2x + 1)^3$

$$\begin{aligned}\log_{x+1}(x^2 + 2x + 1)^3 &= \log_{x+1}\left((x+1)^2\right)^3\\ &= \log_{x+1}(x+1)^6\\ &= 6\log_{x+1}(x+1)\\ &= 6(1) = 6\end{aligned}$$

8. $\log_4 5 + \log_4 12 - \log_4 3.75$

$$\begin{aligned}\log_4 5 + \log_4 12 - \log_4 3.75 &= \log_4(5 \cdot 12) - \log_4 3.75\\ &= \log_4 60 - \log 3.75\\ &= \log_4\left(\frac{60}{3.75}\right)\\ &= \log_4 16\\ &= 2\end{aligned}$$

Exercise	Depth of Knowledge (D.O.K.)	COMMON CORE Mathematical Practices
1–8	**1** Recall of Information	**MP.5** Using Tools
9–16	**2** Skills/Concepts	**MP.4** Modeling
17	**2** Skills/Concepts	**MP.2** Reasoning
18–19	**3** Strategic Thinking	**MP.2** Reasoning
20	**3** Strategic Thinking H.O.T.	**MP.4** Modeling
21	**2** Skills/Concepts H.O.T.	**MP.3** Logic
22	**2** Skills/Concepts H.O.T.	**MP.3** Logic

EVALUATE

ASSIGNMENT GUIDE

Concepts and Skills	Practice
Explore 1 Investigating the Properties of Logarithms	Exercise 17
Explore 2 Proving the Properties of Logarithms	Exercises 18–19
Example 1 Using the Properties of Logarithms	Exercises 1–8
Example 2 Rewriting a Logarithmic Model	Exercises 9–16

AVOID COMMON ERRORS

Students may be tempted to write a difference of logarithms as a quotient, which is an improper use of the Quotient Property of Logarithms. Demonstrate the following:

$$\log_2 32 - \log_2 8 \neq \frac{\log_2 32}{\log_2 8}$$
$$5 - 3 \neq \frac{5}{3}$$

QUESTIONING STRATEGIES

When simplifying the expression $\log xy^n$, which property do you apply first, the Product Property of Logarithms or the Power Property of Logarithms? Explain. **You apply the Product Property of Logarithms first, because the exponent applies only to y. Then apply the Power Property of Logarithms to the expression containing y.**

$$\log xy^n = \log x + \log y^n$$
$$= \log x + n\log y$$

Solve the problems using logarithmic models.

9. **Geology** Seismologists use the Richter scale to express the energy, or magnitude, of an earthquake. The Richter magnitude of an earthquake M is related to the energy released in ergs E shown by the formula $M = \frac{2}{3}\log\left(\frac{E}{10^{11.8}}\right)$. In 1964, an earthquake centered at Prince William Sound, Alaska registered a magnitude of 9.2 on the Richter scale. Find the energy released by the earthquake.

$$9.2 = \frac{2}{3}\log\left(\frac{E}{10^{11.8}}\right)$$
$$13.8 = \log\left(\frac{E}{10^{11.8}}\right)$$
$$13.8 = \log E - \log 10^{11.8}$$
$$13.8 = \log E - 11.8$$
$$25.6 = \log E$$
$$10^{25.6} = E$$
$$10^{25.6} = 10^{6} \cdot 10^{25} = 3.98 \times 10^{25}$$
$$3.98 \times 10^{25} = E$$

The energy released by an earthquake with a magnitude of 9.2 is 3.98×10^{25} ergs.

10. **Astronomy** The difference between the apparent magnitude (brightness) m of a star and its absolute magnitude M is given by the formula $m - M = 5\log\frac{d}{10}$, where d is the distance of the star from the Earth, measured in parsecs. Find the distance d of the star Rho Oph from Earth, where Rho Oph has an apparent magnitude of 5.0 and an absolute magnitude −0.4.

$$5.0 - (-0.4) = 5\log\frac{d}{10}$$
$$\frac{5.4}{5} = \log\frac{d}{10}$$
$$(1.08) = \log d - \log 10$$
$$1.08 = \log d - (1)$$
$$2.08 = \log d$$
$$10^{2.08} = d$$
$$120.2 \approx d$$

Rho Oph is about 120.2 parsecs from Earth.

Exercise	Depth of Knowledge (D.O.K.)	COMMON CORE Mathematical Practices
23	3 Strategic Thinking H.O.T.	MP.2 Reasoning

1. The intensity of the sound of a conversation ranges from 10^{-10} watts per square meter to 10^{-6} watts per square meter. What is the range in the loudness of the conversation? Use $I_0 = 10^{-12}$ watts per square meter.

$$L(10^{-10}) = 10\log\left(\frac{10^{-10}}{10^{-12}}\right)$$
$$= 10\log 10^{2}$$
$$= 10(2) = 20$$

Find the loudness of the conversation at 10^{-6} watts per square meter.

$$L(10^{-6}) = 10\log\left(\frac{10^{-6}}{10^{-12}}\right)$$
$$= 10\log 10^{6}$$
$$= 10(6) = 60$$

The loudness of the conversation ranges from 20 decibels to 60 decibels.

2. The intensity of sound from the stands of a football game is 25 times as great when the home team scores a touchdown as it is when the away team scores. Find the difference in the loudness of the sound when the two teams score.

Let I be the intensity when the away team scores.

So $25I$ is the intensity when the home team scores.

Difference in loudness $= L(25I) - L(I)$

$$= 10\log\left(\frac{25I}{I_0}\right) - 10\log\left(\frac{I}{I_0}\right)$$
$$= 10\left(\log\left(25\frac{I}{I_0}\right) - \log\left(\frac{I}{I_0}\right)\right)$$
$$= 10\left(\log 25 + \log\left(\frac{I}{I_0}\right) - \log\left(\frac{I}{I_0}\right)\right)$$
$$= 10\log 25 \approx 13.98$$

So the difference in the loudness of sound is about 13.98 decibels.

CRITICAL THINKING

Challenge students to find a way to use the Change of Base Property to find the value of $\log_8 16$ without the use of a calculator.

$$\log_8 16 = \frac{\log_2 16}{\log_2 8} = \frac{4}{3}$$

Then have them create other examples of this type, demonstrating the usefulness of this property.

COGNITIVE STRATEGIES

Students may have trouble remembering whether an expression such as $\log_3 5$ is equal to $\frac{\log 5}{\log 3}$ or $\frac{\log 3}{\log 5}$. These students may find it helpful to remember that the *base* in the logarithmic expression goes in the denominator, the bottom or "base" of the fraction. Alternatively, they might remember that the number written lower than the other number goes in the lower part of the fraction.

13. Finance A stock priced at $40 increases at a rate of 8% per year. Write and evaluate a logarithmic expression for the number of years that it will take for the value of the stock to reach $50.

$$P = P_0(1 + r)^t$$

$$\log_{1+r} P = \log_{1+r}\left(P_0 (1 + r)^t\right)$$

$$\log_{1+r} P = \log_{1+r} P_0 + \log_{1+r} (1 + r)^t$$

$$\log_{1+r} P - \log_{1+r} P_0 = \log_{1+r} (1 + r)^t$$

$$\log_{1+r}\left(\frac{P}{P_0}\right) = t(1)$$

$$\frac{\log\left(\frac{P}{P_0}\right)}{\log (1 + r)} = t$$

$P_0 = 40, P = 50, r = 0.08$

$$t = \frac{\log\left(\frac{50}{40}\right)}{\log(1 + 0.08)} = \frac{\log 1.25}{\log 1.08} \approx \frac{0.097}{0.033} \approx 2.94$$

It will take about 2.94 years to reach $50.

14. Suppose that the population of one endangered species decreases at a rate of 4% per year. In one habitat, the current population of the species is 143. After how long will the population drop below 30?

Find the inverse model of $P = P_0 (1 - r)^t$.

$$P = P_0(1 - r)^t$$

$$\log_{1-r} P = \log_{1-r}\left(P_0(1 - r)^t\right)$$

$$\log_{1-r} P = \log_{1-r} P_0 + \log_{1-r} (1 - r)^t$$

$$\log_{1-r} P - \log_{1-r} P_0 = \log_{1-r} (1 - r)^t$$

$$\log_{1-r}\left(\frac{P}{P_0}\right) = t(1)$$

$$\frac{\log\left(\frac{P}{P_0}\right)}{\log(1 - r)} = t$$

$P_0 = 143, P = 30, r = 0.04$

$$t = \frac{\log\left(\frac{30}{143}\right)}{\log(1 - 0.04)} \approx \frac{\log 0.21}{\log 0.96} \approx \frac{-0.678}{-0.018} \approx 37.7$$

The population will drop to below 30 after about 37.7 years.

15. The population P of bacteria in a culture after t minutes is given by the equation $P = P_0(1.12)^t$, where P_0 is the initial population. If the number of bacteria starts at 200, how long will it take for the population to increase to 1000?

$$P = P_0(1.12)^t$$

$$\log_{1.12} P = \log_{1.12}\left(P_0(1.12)^t\right)$$

$$\log_{1.12} P = \log_{1.12} P_0 + \log_{1.12}(1.12)^t$$

$$\log_{1.12} P - \log_{1.12} P_0 = \log_{1.12}(1.12)^t$$

$$\log_{1.12}\left(\frac{P}{P_0}\right) = t(1)$$

$$\frac{\log\left(\frac{P}{P_0}\right)}{\log(1.12)} = t$$

$P_0 = 200, P = 1000$

$$t = \frac{\log\left(\frac{1000}{200}\right)}{\log 1.12} = \frac{\log 5}{\log 1.12} \approx \frac{0.699}{0.049} \approx 14.3$$

It will take about 14.3 minutes for the population to increase to 1000.

16. **Chemistry** Most swimming pool experts recommend a pH of between 7.0 and 7.6 for water in a swimming pool. Use $\text{pH} = -\log\left[H^+\right]$ and write an expression for the difference in hydrogen ion concentration over this pH range.

Find the hydrogen ion concentration for a pH of 7.0.

$$7.0 = -\log\left[H^+\right]$$

$$-7.0 = \log\left[H^+\right]$$

$$10^{-7.0} = H^+$$

Find the hydrogen ion concentration for a pH of 7.6.

$$7.6 = -\log\left[H^+\right]$$

$$-7.6 = \log\left[H^+\right]$$

$$10^{-7.6} = H^+$$

The difference in hydrogen ion concentration over the pH range is $10^{-7.0} - 10^{-7.6}$.

INTEGRATE MATHEMATICAL PRACTICES

Focus on Reasoning

MP.2 Discuss with students how the Properties of Logarithms can be used to find values which otherwise cannot be easily found, using mental math. For example, show how the Quotient Property of Logarithms can be used to find the value of $\log_5 50 - \log_5 2$, an expression containing two logs, neither of which is an integer.

$$\begin{aligned}\log_5 50 - \log_5 2 &= \log_5\left(\frac{50}{2}\right)\\ &= \log_5 25\\ &= 2\end{aligned}$$

Ask students to create other examples in which applying the properties makes it possible to find the value using mental math.

VISUAL CUES

Suggest that students circle the exponents on the arguments in a logarithmic expression to help them remember to apply the Power Property of Logarithms when they arrive at the appropriate point of the simplification process.

17. Match the logarithmic expressions to equivalent expressions.

a. $\log_2 4x$ — **C** — $2x$

b. $\log_2 \frac{x}{4}$ — **A** — $2 + \log_2 x$

c. $\log_2 4^x$ — **E** — $\frac{\log x}{\log 2}$

d. $\log_2 x^4$ — **D** — $4\log_2 x$

e. $\log_2 x$ — **B** — $\log_2 x - 2$

$$\log_2 4x = \log_2 4 + \log_2 x$$
$$= 2 + \log_2 x$$
$$\log_2 \frac{x}{4} = \log_2 x - \log_2 4$$
$$= \log_2 x - 2$$
$$\log_2 4^x = x\log_2 4$$
$$= 2x$$
$$\log_2 x^4 = 4\log_2 x$$
$$\log_2 x = \frac{\log x}{\log_2}$$

18. Prove the Quotient Property of Logarithms. Justify each step of your proof.

Let $x = \log_b m$ and $y = \log_b n$. Then $m = b^x$ and $n = b^y$ by the definition of a logarithm.

$\log_b \frac{m}{n} = \log_b \frac{b^x}{b^y}$	**Substitution**
$= \log_b b^{x-y}$	**Quotient of Powers Property of Exponents**
$= x - y$	**Definition of a logarithm**
$= \log_b m - \log_b n$	**Substitution**

19. Prove the Change of Base Property of Logarithms. Justify each step of your proof.

Let $x = \log_c a$. Then $a = c^x$ by the definition of a logarithm.

$a = c^x$	**Definition of a logarithm**
$\log_b a = \log_b c^x$	**Take the logarithm of both sides.**
$\log_b a = x\log_b c$	**Power Property of Logarithms**
$\frac{\log_b a}{\log_b c} = x$	**Divide both sides by $\log_b c$.**
$\frac{\log_b a}{\log_b c} = \log_c a$	**Substitution**

H.O.T. Focus on Higher Order Thinking

20. Multi-Step The radioactive isotope Carbon-14 decays exponentially at a rate of 0.0121% each year.

a. How long will it take 250 g of Carbon-14 to decay to 100 g?

The exponential decay model is $A = A_0\,(1 - r)^t$, where A is the population after t years, A_0 is the initial population, and r is the decay rate.

$$P = P_0(1 - r)^t$$

$$\log_{1-r} P = \log_{1-r}\left(P_0(1 - r)^t\right)$$

$$\log_{1-r} P = \log_{1-r} P_0 + \log_{1-r}(1 - r)^t$$

$$\log_{1-r} P - \log_{1-r} P_0 = \log_{1-r}(1 - r)^t$$

$$\log_{1-r} \frac{P}{P_0} = t(1)$$

$$\frac{\log\left(\frac{P}{P_0}\right)}{\log(1 - r)} = t$$

$A_0 = 250, A = 100, r = 0.000121$

$$t = \frac{\log\left(\frac{100}{250}\right)}{\log(1 - 0.000121)} = \frac{\log(0.4)}{\log 0.999879} \approx 7573$$

It will take about 7573 years for 250 g of Carbon-14 to decay 100g.

b. The half-life for a radioactive isotope is the amount of time it takes for the isotope to reach half its initial value. What is the half-life of Carbon-14?

The initial value is 250 g, so half the initial value is 125 g.

$$t = \frac{\log\left(\frac{125}{250}\right)}{\log(1 - 0.000121)} = \frac{\log 0.5}{\log 0.999879} \approx 5730$$

The half-life of Carbon-14 is about 5730 years.

JOURNAL

Have students describe how to prove the properties of logarithms.

21. Explain the Error A student simplified the expression $\log_2 8 + \log_3 27$ as shown. Explain and correct the student's error.

$\log_2 8 + \log_3 27 = \log(8 \cdot 27)$

$= \log(216)$

≈ 2.33

Since the two terms have different bases, the Product Property of Logarithms cannot be used to simplify the expression.

$\log_2 8 + \log_3 27 = \frac{\log 8}{\log 2} + \frac{\log 27}{\log 3}$

$\approx \frac{0.903}{0.301} + \frac{1.431}{0.477}$

$= 3 + 3$

≈ 6

22. Communicate Mathematical Ideas Explain why it is not necessary for a scientific calculator to have both a key for common logs and a key for natural logs.

The natural logarithm is the common logarithm to the base *e*. So $\ln x = \log_e x$.

Using the Change of Base Property of Logarithms, this expression can be rewritten as $\frac{\log x}{\log e}$. This expression can then be evaluated for a given value of *x* using just the common log key on a scientific calculator.

23. Analyze Relationships Explain how to find the relationship between $\log_b a$ and $\log_{\frac{1}{b}} a$.

Rewrite both expressions using the same base.

$\log_b a = \frac{\log a}{\log b}$ **and** $\log_{\frac{1}{b}} a = \frac{\log a}{\log\left(\frac{1}{b}\right)}$

$\frac{\log a}{\log\left(\frac{1}{b}\right)} = \frac{\log}{\log b^{-1}} = \frac{\log a}{-\log b} = -\frac{\log a}{\log b}$

So $\log_{\frac{1}{b}} a$ is the opposite of $\log_b a$.

Lesson Performance Task

Given the population data for the state of Texas from 1920–2010, perform exponential regression to obtain an exponential growth model for population as a function of time (represent 1920 as 0).

Obtain a logarithmic model for time as a function of population two ways: (1) by finding the inverse of the exponential model, and (2) by performing logarithmic regression on the same set of data but using population as the independent variable and time as the dependent variable. Then confirm that the two expressions are equivalent by applying the properties of logarithms.

Year	U.S. Census Count
1920	4,663,228
1930	5,824,715
1940	6,414,824
1950	7,711,194
1960	9,579,677
1970	11,196,730
1980	14,229,191
1990	16,986,335
2000	20,851,820
2010	25,145,561

(1) The exponential model will be of the form $P(t) = P_0(1+r)^t$, where P_0 is the population in 1920, t is the number of years after 1920, r is the average annual growth rate, and $P(t)$ is the population t years after 1920. To calculate r, we will use the years 1920 and 1930.

$$P(t) = P_0(1+r)^t$$
$$5{,}824{,}715 = 4{,}663{,}228(1+r)^{10}$$
$$1.249 \approx (1+r)^{10}$$
$$\sqrt[10]{1.249} \approx \sqrt[10]{(1+r)^{10}}$$
$$1.022 \approx 1+r$$
$$0.022 \approx r$$

So the exponential model is $y = 4{,}663{,}228(1.022)^x$.

Use inverse operations to solve for x.

$$\frac{y}{4{,}663{,}228} = (1.022)^x$$
$$\log_{1.022}\left(\frac{y}{4{,}663{,}228}\right) = \log_{1.022}(1.022^x)$$
$$\log_{1.022}\left(\frac{y}{4{,}663{,}228}\right) = x$$

(2) Perform a logarithmic regression: $y = -814.74 + 53.14\ln x$

$$\log_{1.022}\left(\frac{x}{4{,}663{,}228}\right) = -814.74 + 53.14\ln(x)$$
$$\frac{\ln\left(\frac{x}{4{,}663{,}228}\right)}{\ln(1.022)} = -814.74 + 53.14\ln(x)$$

EXTENSION ACTIVITY

Have students research the world population for every decade starting in 1920. Then have students find or estimate an exponential model for the population as a function of time and consider how they would determine when the population would reach milestones such as 10 or 15 billion. Have students also discuss whether the population of Texas is growing at a larger or smaller rate than the world population, and what the reasons for the difference might be.

AVOID COMMON ERRORS

Students may forget that the growth rate is r, but the base of the exponent is $1 + r$. Remind them that a resulting value greater than 1 for r indicates a growth rate of over 100%. Remind them that the appropriate exponential model is $P(t) = P_0(1+r)^t$, not $P(t) = P_0 r^t$.

INTEGRATE MATHEMATICAL PRACTICES

Focus on Math Connections

MP.1 Have students discuss whether it is more useful to have a model of population as a function of time, $P(t)$, or a model of time as a function of population, $t(P)$. Have students describe real-world situations in which each of these models would be meaningful.

Scoring Rubric

2 points: Student correctly solves the problem and explains his/her reasoning.

1 point: Student shows good understanding of the problem but does not fully solve or explain his/her reasoning.

0 points: Student does not demonstrate understanding of the problem.

Solving Exponential Equations

Common Core Math Standards

The student is expected to:

F-LE.A.4

For exponential models, express as a logarithm the solution to $ab^{ct} = d$ where *a*, *c*, and *d* are numbers and the base *b* is 2, 10, or *e*; evaluate the logarithm using technology. Also F-IF.C.7e

Mathematical Practices

MP.5 Using Tools

Language Objective

Have students work with a partner to describe the steps for solving linear, exponential, and now logarithmic equations algebraically and graphically.

ENGAGE

Essential Question: What are some ways you can solve an equation of the form $ab^x = c$, where a and c are nonzero real numbers and b is greater than 0 and not equal to 1?

You can graph both sides of the equation and look for the point of intersection, or you can take the logarithm of both sides and solve algebraically.

PREVIEW: LESSON PERFORMANCE TASK

View the Engage section online. Discuss the photo and how the frequencies of piano notes are related by an exponential function rather than a linear function. Then preview the Lesson Performance Task.

Name ________ Class ________ Date ________

16.2 Solving Exponential Equations

Essential Question: What are some ways you can solve an equation of the form $ab^x = c$, where a and c are nonzero real numbers and b is greater than 0 and not equal to 1?

Resource Locker

Explore Solving Exponential Equations Graphically

One way to solve exponential equations is graphically. First, graph each side of the equation separately. The point(s) at which the two graphs intersect are the solutions of the equation.

(A) First, look at the equation $275e^{0.06x} = 1000$. To solve the equation graphically, split it into two separate equations.

$y_1 = $ **$275e^{0.06x}$**

$y_2 = $ **1000**

(B) What will the graphs of y_1 and y_2 look like?

The graph of y_1 will be increasing exponentially, and the graph of y_2 will be a horizontal line.

(C) Graph y_1 and y_2 using a graphing calculator.

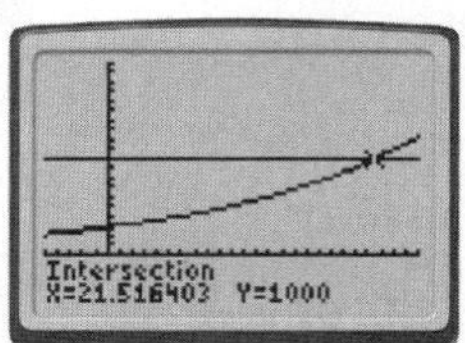

(D) The x-coordinate of the point of intersection is approximately **21.5**.

(E) So, the solution of the equation is $x \approx$ **21.5**.

(F) Now, look at the equation $10^{2x} = 10^4$. Split the equation into two separate equations.

$y_1 = $ **10^{2x}**

$y_2 = $ **10^4**

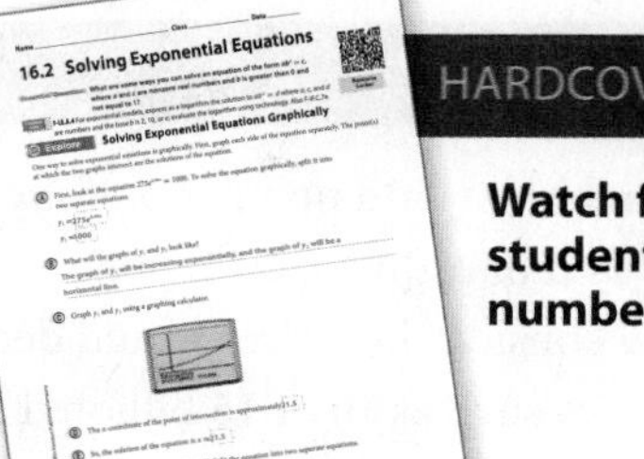

HARDCOVER PAGES 799–812

Watch for the hardcover student edition page numbers for this lesson.

Ⓖ What will the graphs of y_1 and y_2 look like?

The graph of y_1 will be increasing exponentially, and the graph of y_2 will be a horizontal line.

Ⓗ Graph y_1 and y_2 using a graphing calculator.

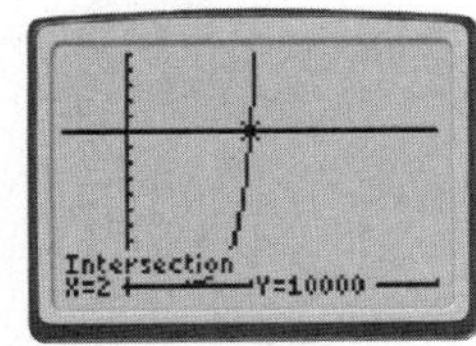

Ⓘ The x-coordinate of the point of intersection is **2**.

Ⓙ So, the solution of the equation is $x \approx$ **2**.

Reflect

1. How can you check the solution of an exponential equation after it is found graphically?
Substitute the solution in for the value of x in the equation and use a calculator to evaluate.

Explain 1 Solving Exponential Equations Algebraically

In addition to solving exponential equations graphically, exponential equations can be solved algebraically. One way to solve exponential equations is to rewrite them in logarithmic form. Another way is to use the Property of Equality for Logarithmic Equations which states that for any positive numbers x, y, and b $(b \neq 1)$, $\log_b x = \log_b y$ if and only if $x = y$.

Example 1 **Solve the equations. Give the exact solution and an approximate solution to three decimal places.**

Ⓐ $10 = 5e^{4x}$

$10 = 5e^{4x}$	Original equation
$2 = e^{4x}$	Divide both sides by 5.
$\ln 2 = 4x$	Rewrite in logarithmic form.
$\frac{\ln 2}{4} = \frac{4x}{4}$	Divide both sides by 4.
$\frac{\ln 2}{4} = x$	Simplify.
$0.173 \approx x$	Evaluate. Round to three decimal places.

PROFESSIONAL DEVELOPMENT

Learning Progressions

In previous lessons, students solved exponential equations in which both sides of the equation could be written as powers with the same base. Now that students have learned about logarithms, they can solve exponential equations in which the bases are not the same. Students will solve these exponential equations both graphically and algebraically by taking the logarithm of both sides. Students should notice the similarities between the Property of Equality for Logarithmic Equations and the Property of Equality for Exponential Equations.

EXPLORE

Solving Exponential Equations Graphically

INTEGRATE TECHNOLOGY

Students have the option of completing the Explore activity either in the book or online.

QUESTIONING STRATEGIES

? Why would there be no solution if the right side of the equation were a number less than or equal to 0? **The graph of the left side of the equation has a horizontal asymptote at the x-axis, so there would be no intersection point for the two functions and no value of the domain for which both functions are to have the same value.**

EXPLAIN 1

Solving Exponential Equations Algebraically

QUESTIONING STRATEGIES

? How do you use the Property of Equality for Exponential Equations to solve the equation $2^{6x} = 8^{x+1}$? **Write both sides of the equation as powers of 2, then set the exponents equal, and solve for x.**

$$2^{6x} = (2^3)^{x+1}$$
$$6x = 3x + 3$$
$$x = 1$$

? Why is it not possible to use the Property of Equality for Exponential Equations to solve the equation $2^{6x} = 10^{x+1}$? **because 2 and 10 cannot be written as powers of the same base**

? How does the Property of Equality for Logarithmic Equations enable you to solve the equation $2^{6x} = 10^{x+1}$? **The bases of the powers do not need to be the same. You can take the log of both sides.**

INTEGRATE MATHEMATICAL PRACTICES

Focus on Reasoning

MP.2 Discuss with students how the Property of Equality for Logarithmic Equations can be verified by applying the definition of a logarithm to the equation $\log_b x = \log_b y$, rewriting it in exponential form.

If $\log_b x = \log_b y$, then $b^{\log_b y} = x$.

By the Definition-Based Properties of Logarithms, $b^{\log_b y} = y$.

Therefore, $x = y$.

AVOID COMMON ERRORS

Some students may apply the Property of Equality for Logarithmic Equations incorrectly, taking the log of each term of an equation. Correct this error, instructing students to try to transform the equation so that there is only one term on each side of the equal sign. At that point, they can take the log of the expression on each side of the equation.

(B) $5^x - 4 = 7$

$5^x - 4 = 7$	Original equation
$5^x - 4 + \boxed{4} = 7 + \boxed{4}$	Add $\boxed{4}$ to both sides.
$5^x = \boxed{11}$	Simplify.
$\log 5^x = \log \boxed{11}$	Take the common logarithm of both sides.
$\boxed{x \log 5} = \log 11$	Power Property of Logarithms
$x = \dfrac{\log \boxed{11}}{\log \boxed{5}}$	Divide both sides by $\log 5$.
$x \approx \boxed{1.490}$	Evaluate. Round to three decimal palces.

Reflect

2. Consider the equation $2^{x-3} = 85$. How can you solve this equation using logarithm base 2?
Take the logarithm base 2 of both sides. Then rewrite $\log_2 85$ using the Change of Base Property of Logarithms so the exact solution can be found using a scientific calculator.

$$2^{x-3} = 85$$
$$\log_2 2^{x-3} = \log_2 85$$
$$(x-3)\log_2 2 = \log_2 85$$
$$x - 3 = \log_2 85$$
$$x = \log_2 85 + 3 \quad x = \frac{\log 85}{\log 2} + 3 \quad x \approx 9.409$$

3. **Discussion** When solving an exponential equation with base e, what is the benefit of taking the natural logarithm of both sides of the equation?
Taking the natural logarithm of both sides will result in on one side, which simplifies to 1.

Your Turn

Solve the equations. Give the exact solution and an approximate solution to three decimal places.

4. $2e^{x-1} + 5 = 80$

$$2e^{x-1} = 75$$
$$e^{x-1} = 37.5$$
$$\ln e^{x-1} = \ln 37.5$$
$$(x-1)(\ln e) = \ln 37.5$$
$$(x-1)(1) = \ln 37.5$$
$$x = \ln 37.5 + 1 \approx 4.624$$

5. $6^{3x} = 12$

$$\log 6^{3x} = \log 12$$
$$3x \log 6 = \log 12$$
$$x = \frac{\log 12}{3 \log 6} \approx 0.462$$

COLLABORATIVE LEARNING

Peer-to-Peer Activity

Have students work in pairs. Provide each pair with identical sets of several different exponential equations, and ask them to solve each equation two different ways. Have pairs share their solutions with the class, comparing their work with that of the other pairs of students. Discuss the results.

Explain 2 Solve a Real-World Problem by Solving an Exponential Equation

Suppose that $250 is deposited into an account that pays 4.5% compounded quarterly. The equation $A = P\left(1 + \frac{r}{4}\right)^n$ gives the amount A in the account after n quarters for an initial investment P that earns interest at a rate r. Solve for n to find how long it will take for the account to contain at least $500.

Analyze Information

Identify the important information.

- The initial investment P is $ 250.
- The interest rate is 4.5 %, so r is 0.045.
- The amount A in the account after n quarters is $ 500.

Formulate a Plan

Solve the equation for $A = P\left(1 + \frac{r}{4}\right)^n$ for n by substituting in the known information and using logarithms.

Solve

$500 = 250\left(1 + \frac{0.045}{4}\right)^n$ Substitute.

$2 = \left(1 + \frac{0.045}{4}\right)^n$ Divide both sides by 250.

$2 = 1.01125^n$ Evaluate the expression in parentheses.

$\log 2 = \log 1.01125^n$ Take the common logarithm of both sides.

$\log 2 = n \log 1.01125$ Power Property of Logarithms

$\frac{\log 2}{\log 1.01125} = n$ Divide both sides by log 1.01125.

$61.96 \approx n$ Evaluate.

EXPLAIN 2

Solving a Real-World Problem by Solving an Exponential Equation

QUESTIONING STRATEGIES

When working with a formula that models a real-world situation, how can you tell whether you will need to take the log of both sides of the equation? **You need to take the log of both sides of the equation if the variable for which you are solving is in the exponent.**

DIFFERENTIATE INSTRUCTION

Multiple Representations

Some students may suggest using the definition of a logarithm to solve an equation such as $5^{x+3} = 12$, rewriting the equation in logarithmic form, and using the Change of Base Property to solve for x.

$$x + 3 = \log_5 12$$
$$x = \frac{\log 12}{\log 5} - 3 \approx -1.46$$

Students should be encouraged to use this alternate method when possible, if they prefer. Show them how this leads to the same result as taking the log of both sides.

INTEGRATE MATHEMATICAL PRACTICES

Focus on Modeling

MP.4 Discuss with students how the formula for compound interest changes for different compounding periods. Help them to see that the value of A increases as the number of compounding periods per year increases. Show how this concept leads to the formula for situations in which the interest is compounded continuously.

ELABORATE

INTEGRATE MATHEMATICAL PRACTICES

Focus on Technology

MP.5 Discuss with students how to determine an appropriate viewing window when solving an exponential equation graphically. Discuss how the constants and coefficients in the equation can be used as a guide.

QUESTIONING STRATEGIES

? How does the Property of Equality for Logarithmic Equations make it possible to solve an exponential equation? **It moves the variable out of the exponent so it can be isolated.**

SUMMARIZE THE LESSON

? What are the steps for solving an exponential equation algebraically? **Transform the equation so that there is only one term on each side of the equal sign. Then take the log (or the ln) of both sides of the equation. This moves the variable out of the exponent(s). Then solve the resulting equation for the variable.**

Justify and Evaluate

It will take about **61.96** quarters, or about **15.5** years, for the account to contain at least $500.

Check by substituting this value for n in the equation and solving for A.

$A = 250\left(1 + \frac{0.045}{4}\right)^{61.96}$ Substitute.

$= 250\left(1.01125\right)^{61.96}$ Evaluate the expression in parentheses.

$\approx 250\left(2\right)$ Evaluate the exponent.

≈ 500 Multiply.

So, the answer is reasonable.

Your Turn

6. Suppose that $250 is deposited into an account that pays 4.5% compounded quarterly. The equation $A = P\left(1 + \frac{r}{4}\right)^n$ gives the amount A in the account after n quarters for an initial investment P that earns interest at a rate r. Solve for n to find how long it will take for the account to contain at least $500.

How long will it take to triple a $250 initial investment in an account that pays 4.5% compounded quarterly?

$P = 250;\ A = 3P = 750;\ r = 0.045$

$750 = 250\left(1 + \frac{0.045}{4}\right)^n$

$3 = (1.01125)^n$

$\log 3 = \log 1.01125^n$

$\log 3 = n \log 1.01125$

$n = \frac{\log 3}{\log 1.01125} \approx 98.2$

It will take about 98.2 quarters, or about 24.6 years, to triple.

Elaborate

7. Describe how to solve an exponential equation graphically.
An exponential equation can be solved graphically by graphing the two sides of the equation and determining where they intersect.

8. **Essential Question Check-In** Describe how to solve an exponential equation algebraically.
An exponential equation can be solved algebraically by taking the logarithm of both sides of the equation and using the properties of logarithms to evaluate.

LANGUAGE SUPPORT EL

Communicating Math

Have students work in pairs to first discuss and then fill in a chart like the one below. Tell students the blank row is to be completed once they have solved logarithmic equations, in the next lesson.

Equation	Algebraic solution	Graphical solution	Summary of similarities and differences
linear			
exponential			
logarithmic			

Evaluate: Homework and Practice

- Online Homework
- Hints and Help
- Extra Practice

Solve the equations graphically.

1. $4e^{0.1x} = 60$

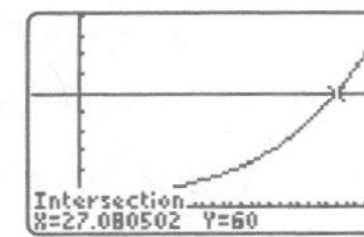

The x-coordinate of the point where the graphs intersect is ≈ 27.1. So, the solution is $x \approx 27.1$.

2. $120e^{2x} = 75e^{3x}$

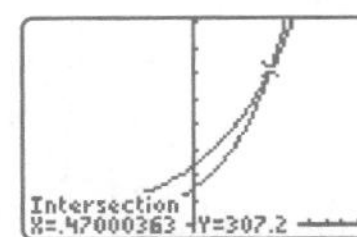

The x-coordinate of the point at which the graphs intersect is ≈ 0.47. So, the solution is ≈ 0.47.

3. $5 = 625e^{0.02x}$

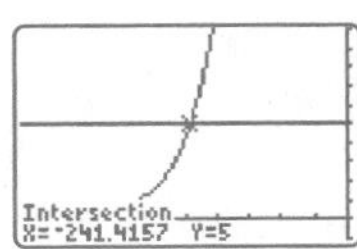

The x-coordinate of the point at which the graphs intersect is ≈ -241.4. So, the solution is $x \approx -241.4$.

Exercise	Depth of Knowledge (D.O.K.)	COMMON CORE Mathematical Practices
1–5	**1** Recall of Information	**MP.2** Reasoning
6–11	**1** Recall of Information	**MP.5** Using Tools
12–19	**2** Skills/Concepts	**MP.4** Modeling
20	**2** Skills/Concepts	**MP.2** Reasoning
21	**3** Strategic Thinking H.O.T.	**MP.3** Logic
22–23	**3** Strategic Thinking H.O.T.	**MP.4** Modeling

EVALUATE

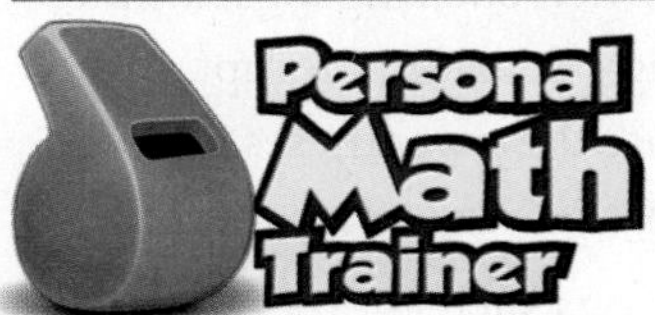

ASSIGNMENT GUIDE

Concepts and Skills	Practice
Explore Solving Exponential Equations Graphically	Exercises 1–5
Example 1 Solving Exponential Equations Algebraically	Exercises 6–11
Example 2 Solving a Real-World Problem by Solving an Exponential Equation	Exercises 12–19

TECHNOLOGY

Have students provide the window they used for graphing each equation. Have them share their strategies for determining the windows with their classmates, so that students who are struggling with this may gain some insight.

AVOID COMMON ERRORS

It is easy to make errors when entering logarithmic expressions on a graphing calculator. Prompt students to be sure to close the parentheses after entering the argument for each log. Have them practice entering expressions such as $\frac{\log 12}{2\log 5 + \log 3}$, and checking them for correctness.

Solve the equations graphically. Then check your solutions algebraically.

4. $10e^{6x} = 5e^{-3x}$

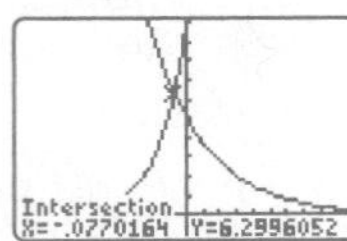

The x-coordinate of the point at which the graphs intersect is ≈ -0.08.

So, the solution is $x \approx -0.08$.

Check:

$$10e^{6(-0.08)} \approx 5e^{-3(-0.08)}$$
$$10e^{-0.48} \approx 5e^{0.24}$$
$$\frac{10}{5} \approx \frac{e^{0.24}}{e^{-0.48}}$$
$$2 \approx e^{0.72}$$
$$2 \approx 2.05$$

The answer is reasonable.

5. $450e^{0.4x} = 2000$

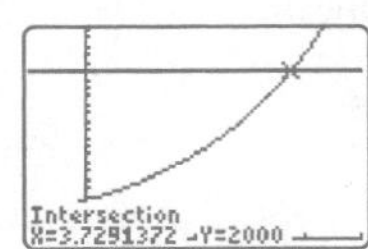

The x-coordinate of the point at which the graphs intersect is $x \approx 3.73$.

So, the solution is $x \approx 3.73$.

Check:

$$450e^{0.4(3.73)} \approx 2000$$
$$450e^{1.492} \approx 2000$$
$$2000.69 \approx 2000$$

The answer is reasonable.

Solve the equations. Give the exact solution and an approximate solution to three decimal places.

6. $6^{3x-9} - 10 = -3$

$$6^{3x-9} - 10 = -3$$
$$6^{3x-9} = 7$$
$$\log 6^{3x-9} = \log 7$$
$$(3x-9)\log 6 = \log 7$$
$$3x - 9 = \frac{\log 7}{\log 6}$$
$$x = \frac{1}{3}\left(\frac{\log 7}{\log 6} + 9\right) \approx 3.362$$

7. $7e^{3x} = 42$

$$7e^{3x} = 42$$
$$e^{3x} = 6$$
$$\ln e^{3x} = \ln 6$$
$$3x \ln e = \ln 6$$
$$3x(1) = \ln 6$$
$$x = \frac{\ln 6}{3} \approx 0.597$$

8. $11^{6x+2} = 12$

$$11^{6x+2} = 12$$
$$\log 11^{6x+2} = \log 12$$
$$(6x+2)\log 11 = \log 12$$
$$6x + 2 = \frac{\log 12}{\log 11}$$
$$6x = \frac{\log 12}{\log 11} - 2$$
$$x = \frac{1}{6}\left(\frac{\log 12}{\log 11} - 2\right) \approx -0.161$$

9. $e^{\frac{2x-1}{3}} = 250$

$$e^{\frac{2x-1}{3}} = 250$$
$$\ln e^{\frac{2x-1}{3}} = \ln 250$$
$$\left(\frac{2x-1}{3}\right)\ln e = \ln 250$$
$$\left(\frac{2x-1}{3}\right)(1) = \ln 250$$
$$2x - 1 = 3\ln 250$$
$$x = \frac{3\ln 250 + 1}{2} \approx 8.782$$

10. $(10^x)^2 + 90 = 105$

$$(10^x)^2 + 90 = 105$$
$$10^{2x} = 15$$
$$\log 10^{2x} = \log 15$$
$$2x \log 10 = \log 15$$
$$2x(1) = \log 15$$
$$x = \frac{\log 15}{2} \approx 0.588$$

11. $5^{\frac{x}{4}} = 30$

$$5^{\frac{x}{4}} = 30$$
$$\log 5^{\frac{x}{4}} = \log 30$$
$$\frac{x}{4} \log 5 = \log 30$$
$$x = \frac{4 \log 30}{\log 5} \approx 8.453$$

Solve.

12. The price P of a gallon of gas after t years is given by the equation $P = P_0(1 + r)^t$, where P_0 is the initial price of gas and r is the rate of inflation. If the price of a gallon of gas is currently \$3.25, how long will it take for the price to rise to \$4.00 if the rate of inflation is 10.5%?

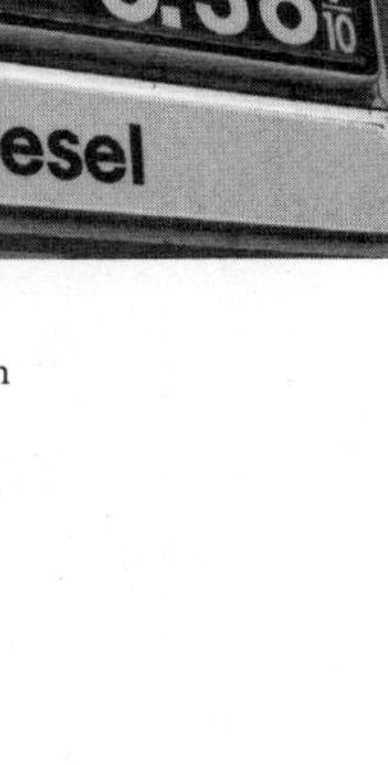

$$4 = 3.25(1.105)^t$$
$$1.231 \approx 1.105^t$$
$$\log 1.231 \approx \log 1.105^t$$
$$\log 1.231 \approx t \log 1.105$$
$$t \approx \frac{\log 1.231}{\log 1.105} \approx 2$$

It will take about 2 years for the price of gas to rise to \$4.00.

13. Finance The amount A in a bank account after t years is given by the equation $A = A_0\left(1 + \frac{r}{6}\right)^{6t}$, where A_0 is the initial amount and r is the interest rate. Suppose there is \$600 in the account. If the interest rate is 4%, after how many years will the amount triple?

$$1800 = 600\left(1 + \frac{0.04}{6}\right)^{6t}$$
$$3 = \left(1 + \frac{0.04}{6}\right)^{6t}$$
$$3 \approx 1.0067^{6t}$$
$$\log 3 \approx \log 1.0067^{6t}$$
$$\log 3 \approx 6t \log 1.0067$$
$$t \approx \frac{\log 3}{\log 1.0067} \approx 27.4$$

The amount in the account will triple after about 27.4 years.

INTEGRATE MATHEMATICAL PRACTICES

Focus on Reasoning

MP.2 Encourage students to check their solutions for correctness by substituting the value into the original equation and verifying that it makes the equation true. Point out that this will help them identify any errors, and encourage them to double check that they've entered the logarithmic expressions correctly in the graphing calculator. Impress upon students that errors working with these expressions are often a result of missing, or incorrect use of, parentheses.

QUESTIONING STRATEGIES

When is it preferable to take the natural log, as opposed to the common log, of both sides of an exponential equation that models a real-world situation? when the base of the power in the model is e

14. A baseball player has a 25% chance of hitting a home run during a game. For how many games will the probability of hitting a home run in every game drop to 5%?

Let n be the number of times at bat.

$$P(\text{home run in every game}) = 0.25^n$$
$$0.05 = 0.25^n$$
$$\log 0.05 = \log 0.25^n$$
$$\log 0.05 = n \log 0.25$$
$$n = \frac{\log 0.05}{\log 0.05} \approx 2$$

The probability of hitting all home runs drops to 5% for about 2 games.

15. Meteorology In one part of the atmosphere where the temperature is a constant −70 °F, pressure can be expressed as a function of altitude by the equation $P(h) = 128(10)^{-0.682h}$, where P is the atmospheric pressure in kilopascals (kPa) and h is the altitude in kilometers above sea level. The pressure ranges from 2.55 kPa to 22.9 kPa in this region. What is the range of altitudes?

Find the altitude for a pressure of 2.55 kPa.

$$2.55 = 128(10)^{-0.0682h}$$
$$0.0199 \approx 10^{-0.0682h}$$
$$\log 0.0199 \approx \log 10^{-0.0682h}$$
$$\log 0.0199 \approx -0.0682h \log 10$$
$$\log 0.0199 \approx -0.0682h(1)$$
$$h \approx \frac{\log 0.0199}{0.0682} \approx 24.94$$

Find the altitude for a pressure of 22.9 kPa.

$$22.9 = 128(10)^{-0.0682h}$$
$$0.1789 \approx 10^{-0.0682h}$$
$$\log 0.1789 \approx \log 10^{-0.0682h}$$
$$\log 0.1789 \approx -0.0682h \log 10$$
$$\log 0.1789 \approx -0.0682h(1)$$
$$h \approx -\frac{\log 0.1789}{0.0682} \approx 10.96$$

The altitude ranges from about 10.96 km to about 24.94 km above sea level.

16. You can choose a prize of either a \$20,000 car or one penny on the first day, double that (2 cents) on the second day, and so on for a month. On what day would you receive at least the value of the car?

\$20,000 is 2,000,000 cents. On day 1, you would receive 1 cent, or 2^0 cents. On day 2, you would receive 2 cents, or 2^1 cents, and so on. So, on day n you would receive 2^{n-1} cents.

$$2^{n-1} = 2{,}000{,}000$$
$$\log 2^{n-1} = \log 2{,}000{,}000$$
$$(n-1)\log 2 = \log 2{,}000{,}000$$
$$n - 1 = \frac{\log 2{,}000{,}000}{\log 2}$$
$$n = \frac{\log 2{,}000{,}000}{\log 2} + 1 \approx 21.93$$

You would receive at least the value of the car on day 22.

17. Population The population of a small coastal resort town, currently 3400, grows at a rate of 3% per year. This growth can be expressed by the exponential equation $P = 3400(1 + 0.03)^t$, where P is the population after t years. Find the number of years it will take for the population to reach 10,000.

$$10{,}000 = 34{,}00(1 + 0.03)^t$$
$$2.94 \approx (1.03)^t$$
$$\log 2.94 \approx \log 1.03^t$$
$$\log 2.94 \approx t \log 1.03$$
$$t \approx \frac{\log 2.94}{\log 1.03} \approx 36.5$$

It will take about 36.5 years for the population to reach 10,000.

18. A veterinarian has instructed Harrison to give his 75-lb dog one 325-mg aspirin tablet for arthritis. The amount of aspirin A remaining in the dog's body after t minutes can be expressed by $A = 325\left(\frac{1}{2}\right)^{\frac{t}{15}}$. How long will it take for the amount of aspirin to drop to 50 mg?

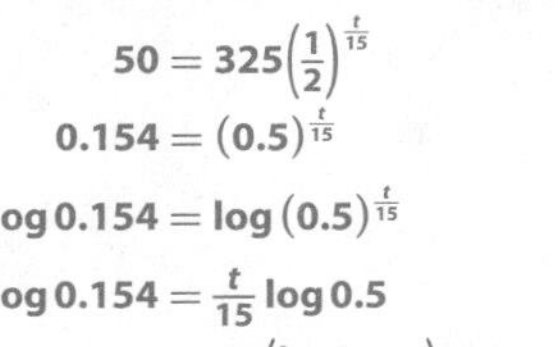

$$50 = 325\left(\frac{1}{2}\right)^{\frac{t}{15}}$$
$$0.154 = (0.5)^{\frac{t}{15}}$$
$$\log 0.154 = \log (0.5)^{\frac{t}{15}}$$
$$\log 0.154 = \frac{t}{15} \log 0.5$$
$$t = 15\left(\frac{\log 0.154}{\log 0.5}\right) \approx 40.5$$

It will take about 40.5 minutes for the amount of aspirin to drop to 50 mg.

19. Agriculture The number of farms in Iowa (in thousands) can be modeled by $N(t) = 119(0.987)^t$, where t is the number of years since 1980. According to the model, when will the number of farms in Iowa be about 80,000?

$$80 = 119(0.987)^t$$

$$0.672 \approx 0.987^t$$

$$\log 0.672 \approx \log 0.987^t$$

$$\log 0.672 \approx t \log 0.987$$

$$t \approx \frac{\log 0.672}{\log 0.987} \approx 30$$

The number of farms in Iowa will be about 80,000 after about 30 years, or around 2010.

20. Match the equations with the solutions.

a. $9e^{3x} = 27$ — **B** $x \approx 1.099$

b. $9e^{x} = 27$ — **D** $x \approx 1.022$

c. $9e^{3x-4} = 27$ — **A** $x \approx 0.366$

d. $9e^{3x} + 2 = 27$ — **C** $x \approx 1.700$

$$9e^{3x} = 27$$
$$e^{3x} = 3$$
$$\ln e^{3x} = \ln 3$$
$$3x \ln e = \ln 3$$
$$3x(1) = \ln 3$$
$$x = \frac{\ln 3}{3} \approx 0.366$$

$$9e^{3x} = 27$$
$$e^{x} = 3$$
$$\ln e^{x} = \ln 3$$
$$x \ln e = \ln 3$$
$$x(1) = \ln 3 \approx 1.099$$

$$9e^{3x-4} = 27$$
$$e^{3x-4} = 3$$
$$\ln e^{3x-4} = \ln 3$$
$$(3x-4)\ln e = \ln 3$$
$$(3x-4)(1) = \ln 3$$
$$3x = \ln 3 + 4$$
$$x = \frac{\ln 3 + 4}{3} \approx 1.700$$

$$9e^{x} + 2 = 27$$
$$9e^{x} = 25$$
$$e^{x} = \frac{25}{9}$$
$$\ln e^{x} = \ln \frac{25}{9}$$
$$x \ln e = \ln \frac{25}{9}$$
$$x(1) = \ln \frac{25}{9} \approx 1.022$$

H.O.T. Focus on Higher Order Thinking

21. Explain the Error A student solved the equation $e^{4x} - 6 = 10$ as shown. Find and correct the student's mistake. Is there an easier way to solve the problem? Verify that both methods result in the same answer.

$$e^{4x} - 6 = 10$$
$$e^{4x} = 16$$
$$\log e^{4x} = \log 16$$
$$4x \log e = \log 16$$
$$4x(1) = \log 16$$
$$x = \frac{\log 16}{4}$$
$$x \approx 0.301$$

The student evaluated log *e* incorrectly. log *e* is not equal to 1. The student should have evaluated the logarithm correctly or used the natural log.

$$e^{4x} - 6 = 10$$
$$e^{4x} = 16$$
$$\log e^{4x} = \log 16$$
$$4x \log e = \log 16$$
$$x = \frac{1}{4}\frac{\log 16}{\log e} \approx 0.693$$

$$e^{4x} - 6 = 10$$
$$e^{4x} = 16$$
$$\ln e^{4x} = \ln 16$$
$$4x \ln e = \ln 16$$
$$4x(1) = \ln 16$$
$$x = \frac{\ln 16}{4} \approx 0.693$$

22. Multi-Step The amount A in an account after t years is given by the equation $A = Pe\,rt$, where P is the initial amount and r is the interest rate.

a. Find an equation that models approximately how long it will take for the initial amount P in the account to double with the interest rate r. Write the equation in terms of the interest rate expressed as a percent.

$$2P = Pe^{rt}$$
$$2 = e^{rt}$$
$$\ln 2 = \ln e^{rt}$$
$$\ln 2 = rt \ln e$$
$$\ln 2 = rt(1)$$
$$t = \frac{\ln 2}{r} \approx \frac{0.69}{r}$$
$$t \approx \frac{69}{r\%}$$

The equation that models approximately how long it will take for the initial amount to double is $t \approx \frac{69}{r\%}$.

PEER-TO-PEER DISCUSSION

Have students work with a partner to find two different ways of solving the equation $16^x = 32^{x-2}$ algebraically, one solution without the use of logs, and the other using logs. Have students compare the methods, and discuss their similarities with the class. **To solve without using logs, rewrite each expression as a power of 2, set the resulting exponents equal, and solve for *x*, To solve using logs, take the log of both sides (ideally, using logs of base 2), apply the Power Property of Logarithms, and solve the resulting equation for *x*. Both methods should lead to the solution $x = 10$.**

JOURNAL

Have students describe the methods they have learned for solving exponential equations.

b. The Rule of 72 states that you can find the approximate time it will take to double your money by dividing 72 by the interest rate. The rule uses 72 instead of 69 because 72 has more divisors, making it easier to calculate mentally. Use the Rule of 72 to find the approximate time it takes to double an initial investment of $300 with an interest rate of 3.75%. Determine that this result is reasonable by solving the equation $A = P_0(1.0375)^t$, where A is the amount after t years and P_0 is the initial investment.

$$t \approx \frac{72}{3.75} = 19.2$$

By the Rule of 72, the amount will double in about 19.2 years.

Check:

$$600 = 300(1.0375)^t$$
$$2 = 1.0375^t$$
$$\log 2 = \log 1.0375^t$$
$$\log 2 = t \log 1.0375$$
$$t = \frac{\log 2}{\log 1.0375} \approx 18.8$$

The results are approximately equal, so 19.2 years is reasonable.

23. Represent Real-World Problems Suppose you have an initial mass M_0 of a radioactive substance with a half-life of h. Then the mass of the parent isotopes at time t is $P(t) = M_0\left(\frac{1}{2}\right)^{\frac{t}{h}}$. Since the substance is decaying from the original parent isotopes into the new daughter isotopes while the mass of all the isotopes remains constant, the mass of the daughter isotopes at time t is $D(t) = M_0 - P(t)$. Find when the masses of the parent isotopes and daughter isotopes are equal. Explain the meaning of your answer and why it makes sense.

To find when the masses of the parent isotopes and daughter isotopes are equal, solve $D(t) = P(t)$

$$D(t) = P(t)$$
$$M_0 - M_0\left(\frac{1}{2}\right)^{\frac{t}{h}} = M_0\left(\frac{1}{2}\right)^{\frac{t}{h}}$$
$$M_0 = 2M_0\left(\frac{1}{2}\right)^{\frac{t}{h}}$$
$$\frac{M_0}{2M_0} = (0.5)^{\frac{t}{h}}$$
$$0.5 = (0.5)^{\frac{t}{h}}$$
$$\log 0.5 = \log (0.5)^{\frac{t}{h}}$$
$$\log 0.5 = \frac{t}{h} \log 0.5$$
$$h = t$$

The masses of the parent isotopes and daughter isotopes are equal when $t = h$. So, the masses of the isotopes will be equal after 1 half-life. This makes sense because after one half-life, the mass of the parent isotopes will be $\frac{1}{2}$ of the initial mass. Since the parent isotopes decay into the daughter isotopes, the other half is now made of daughter isotopes. So, the two masses are equal.

Lesson Performance Task

The frequency of a note on the piano, in Hz, is related to its position on the keyboard by the function $f(n) = 440 \cdot 2^{\frac{n}{12}}$, where n is the number of keys above or below the note concert A, concert A being the A key above middle C on the piano. Using this function, find the position n of the key that has a frequency of 110 Hz. Why is this number a negative value?

$$110 = 440 \cdot 2^{\frac{n}{12}}$$

$$0.25 = 2^{\frac{n}{12}}$$

$$\log_2 0.25 = \log_2 2^{\frac{n}{12}}$$

$$-2 = \frac{n}{12}$$

$$-24 = n$$

24 keys to the left, or lower of, concert A.

A negative value for n means that the key is to the left of, or lower on the keyboard than, concert A.

EXTENSION ACTIVITY

Have students research the whole tone scale, a scale that has been used in Western classical music, jazz, and Indian classical music. Have students write the function $w(n)$ that gives the frequencies of the notes in the scale, and then have them compare it to the function for the frequencies of piano notes in the Performance Task. **A function that includes the note concert A is $w(n) = 440 \cdot 2^{\frac{n}{6}}$. The whole tone scale is a six-note scale corresponding to every other note on the piano keyboard.**

AVOID COMMON ERRORS

When solving for the exponent of $2^{\frac{n}{12}}$, students may take the square root instead of $\log_2$. Explain that you would take the square root if 2 were the exponent: n^2. But, in this problem, 2 is the base, so you need to take the log base 2: $\log_2 2^{\frac{n}{12}} = \frac{n}{12}$.

QUESTIONING STRATEGIES

? What is the rate of growth for the frequencies of the notes on the piano? **The rate of growth is 2 every 12 units.**

? How often does the frequency double? **every 12 keys (every 8 diatonic degrees)**

? How many keys are in an octave? **An octave is two notes whose frequencies are in a ratio of 1 to 2. An octave is divided into 12 notes, or keys, on the keyboard.**

Scoring Rubric

2 points: Student correctly solves the problem and explains his/her reasoning.

1 point: Student shows good understanding of the problem but does not fully solve or explain his/her reasoning.

0 points: Student does not demonstrate understanding of the problem.

MODULE 16

Study Guide Review

ASSESSMENT AND INTERVENTION

Assign or customize module reviews.

MODULE PERFORMANCE TASK

Mathematical Practices: MP.1, MP.2, MP.4, MP.6, MP.7
F-BF.5, F-LE.4

SUPPORTING STUDENT REASONING

Students should begin by thinking about how to find a model for the age of a carbon-containing material. They can then do research, or you can provide them with specific information. Here is some of the information they may ask for.

- **What is the formula for radiocarbon dating?** Encourage students to derive this formula by solving the half-life formula for t. The formula is $N = N_0(0.5)^{\frac{t}{t_{\frac{1}{2}}}}$, where N is the amount of C-14 currently in the sample, N_0 is the original amount of C-14, $t_{\frac{1}{2}}$ is the half-life of C-14, and t is the time in years.
- **What is the half–life of carbon-14?** 5,730 years

STUDY GUIDE REVIEW

Logarithmic Properties and Exponential Equations

MODULE 16

Essential Question: How do the properties of logarithms allow you to solve real-world problems?

Key Vocabulary
exponential equation
(ecuación exponencial)

KEY EXAMPLE *(Lesson 16.1)*

Simplify: $\log_5 5^{x+2} + \log_2 16^3$.

Apply properties of logarithms.

$$\begin{aligned}\log_5 5^{x+2} + \log_2 16^3 &= (x+2)\log_5 5 + 3\log_2 16\\ &= (x+2) + 3\log_2(2^4)\\ &= x + 2 + 3(4)\\ &= x + 14\end{aligned}$$

KEY EXAMPLE *(Lesson 16.2)*

Solve the equation: $4^{3x+1} = 6$.

$$4^{3x+1} = 6$$

$$\log 4^{3x+1} = \log 6 \quad \text{Take the log of both sides.}$$

$$(3x+1)\log 4 = \log 6 \quad \text{Bring down the exponent.}$$

$$3x + 1 = \frac{\log 6}{\log 4} \quad \text{Rearrange to isolate } x.$$

$$3x = \frac{\log 6}{\log 4} - 1$$

$$x = \frac{1}{3}\left(\frac{\log 6}{\log 4} - 1\right) \approx 0.0975$$

SCAFFOLDING SUPPORT

- Remind students of the properties of logarithms:
  $\log_a(u \cdot v) = \log_a(u) + \log_a(v)$
  $\log_a \frac{u}{v} = \log_a(u) - \log_a(v)$
  $\log_a(u^n) = n\log_a(u)$
  $\log_a(a^b) = b$
- If students have trouble deriving the formula for carbon dating, you may wish to provide it: $t = t_{\frac{1}{2}} \times \frac{\ln\left(\frac{N}{N_0}\right)}{\ln(0.5)}$. The meanings of the variables are given above.

EXERCISES

Use properties of logarithms to simplify. *(Lesson 16.1)*

1. $\log_{\frac{3}{5}} 0.216^4$

   12

2. $\log_4 4^{x-2} + \log_3 243^2$

   $x + 8$

3. $\log_8 0.015625^x$

   $-2x$

4. $\log 10^{2x+1} + \log_3 9$

   $2x + 3$

Solve each equation. *(Lesson 16.2)*

5. $5^x = 50$

   $\frac{\log 50}{\log 5} \approx 2.43$

6. $6^{x+2} = 45$

   $\frac{\log 45}{\log 6} - 2 \approx 0.125$

7. $20^{2x+3} = 15$

   $\frac{1}{2}\left(\frac{\log 15}{\log 20} - 3\right) \approx -1.048$

8. $3^{5x+1} = 150$

   $\frac{1}{5}\left(\frac{\log 150}{\log 3} - 1\right) \approx 0.712$

MODULE PERFORMANCE TASK

How Old Is That Bone?

The La Brea Tar Pits in Los Angeles contain one of the best preserved collections of Pleistocene vertebrates, including over 660 species of organisms. An archeologist working at La Brea Tar Pits wants to assess the age of a mastodon bone fragment she discovered. She measures that the fragment has 22% as much carbon-14 as typical living tissue. Given that the half-life of carbon-14 is 5370 years, what is the bone fragment's age?

Start by listing in the space below the information you will need to solve the problem. Then use your own paper to complete the task. Be sure to write down all your data and assumptions. Then use graphs, numbers, words, or algebra to explain how you reached your conclusion.

DISCUSSION OPPORTUNITIES

- Do you think C-14 dating would be useful for finding the age of a dinosaur fossil? Why or why not?
- Why can't carbon dating be used to date stone tools?

SAMPLE SOLUTION

Assumptions

- The ratio of carbon-12 to carbon-14 in the atmosphere has been constant since the organism from which the sample originated died.

Method

Starting from the half-life formula, derive the formula for carbon dating by solving for t. Use the properties of logarithms.

$$N = N_0 (0.5)^{t/t_{1/2}}$$

$$\frac{N}{N_0} = (0.5)^{t/t_{1/2}}$$

$$\ln \frac{N}{N_0} = \frac{t}{t_{\frac{1}{2}}} \cdot \ln(0.5)$$

$$t = t_{\frac{1}{2}} \cdot \frac{\ln \frac{N}{N_0}}{\ln(0.5)}$$

Use this formula, with $t_{\frac{1}{2}} = 5730$, $N_0 = 100$, and $N = 22$, to calculate the age of the fragment:

$$t = 5730 \cdot \frac{\ln \frac{22}{100}}{\ln(0.5)} \approx 12,500 \text{ years}$$

Assessment Rubric

2 points: Student correctly solves the problem and explains his/her reasoning.

1 point: Student shows good understanding of the problem but does not fully solve or explain.

0 points: Student does not demonstrate understanding of the problem.

Ready to Go On?

ASSESS MASTERY

Use the assessment on this page to determine if students have mastered the concepts and standards covered in this module.

ASSESSMENT AND INTERVENTION

Access Ready to Go On? assessment online, and receive instant scoring, feedback, and customized intervention or enrichment.

ADDITIONAL RESOURCES

Response to Intervention Resources

- Reteach Worksheets

Differentiated Instruction Resources

- Reading Strategies EL
- Success for English Learners EL
- Challenge Worksheets

Assessment Resources

- Leveled Module Quizzes

Ready to Go On?

16.1–16.2 Logarithmic Properties and Exponential Equations

- Online Homework
- Hints and Help
- Extra Practice

Use properties of logarithms to simplify. *(Lesson 16.1)*

1. $\log_{\frac{6}{5}} 2.0736^5$

   20

2. $\log_2 3.2 - \log_2 0.025$

   7

3. $\log_7 7^{2x-1} + \log_3 81^2$

   $2x + 7$

4. $\log_5 125 - \log 10^{5x}$

   $-5x + 3$

Solve each equation. Give the exact solution and an approximate solution to three decimal places. *(Lesson 16.2)*

5. $7^{2x} = 30$

   $\frac{\log 30}{2\log 7} \approx 0.874$

6. $5^{2x-1} = 20$

   $0.5\left(\frac{\log 20}{\log 5} + 1\right) \approx 1.431$

7. $2^{0.5x+7} = 215$

   $2\left(\frac{\log 215}{\log 2} - 7\right) \approx 1.496$

8. $10^{3x-3} = 15$

   $\frac{1}{3}\left(\frac{\log 15}{\log 10} + 3\right) \approx 1.392$

ESSENTIAL QUESTION

9. How do you solve an exponential equation algebraically?

   Possible answer: Begin by taking the logarithm of both sides. This allows you to use the Power Property of Logarithms to bring down the variable, putting it in front of the logarithm. Then, use arithmetic operations to isolate the variable in the normal way. At the end of the process, you will likely need to use a calculator to find the value of a logarithmic expression.

COMMON CORE Common Core Standards

Lesson	Items	Content Standards	Mathematical Practices
16.1	1	**F-BF.B.5**	**MP.7**
16.1	2	**F-BF.B.5**	**MP.7**
16.1	3	**F-BF.B.5**	**MP.7**
16.1	4	**F-BF.B.5**	**MP.7**
16.2	5–8	**F-LE.A.4**	**MP.2**

MODULE 16
MIXED REVIEW

Assessment Readiness

1. For each function below, determine if the function has an inverse defined for all real numbers. Select Yes or No for **A–C.**

   A. $f(x) = 4x^3 - 1$ ● Yes ○ No

   B. $f(x) = \sqrt{3x} + 2$ ● Yes ○ No

   C. $f(x) = 4x^2 + 2$ ○ Yes ● No

2. Consider the equation $8^{x+1} = 12$. Choose True or False for each statement.

   A. After bringing down the exponent, the equation is $(x + 1)\log 8 = \log 12$. ● True ○ False

   B. The equation cannot be solved because the bases are not the same. ○ True ● False

   C. The approximate value of x is 0.195. ● True ○ False

3. At a constant temperature, the pressure, P, of an enclosed gas is inversely proportional to the volume, V, of the gas. If $P = 50$ pounds per square inch when $V = 30$ cubic inches, how can you find the pressure when the volume is 125 cubic inches?

   Possible answer: The formula $y = \frac{k}{x}$ can be used. You can assume P is x, and V is y. That would make the first equation $30 = \frac{k}{50}$, so $k = 1500$. From there, $125 = \frac{1500}{x}$, so $x = 12$. The amount of pressure needed is 12 pounds per square inch.

4. $A = P(1 + r)^n$ gives amount A in an account after n years after an initial investment P that earns interest at an annual rate r. How long will it take for \$250 to increase to \$500 at 4% annual interest? Explain how you got your answer.

   About 17.67 years; Possible explanation: Substitute, then use logarithms to solve for n:

$$500 = 250(1.04)^n$$
$$2 = 1.04^n$$
$$\log 2 = n\log 1.04$$
$$\frac{\log 2}{\log 1.04} = n$$
$$17.67 \approx n$$

Common Core Standards

Lesson	Items	Content Standards	Mathematical Practices
10.1, 15.1	1*	F-BF.B.5, F-BF.4.A	MP.1
16.2	2	F-LE.A.4	MP.2
8.1	3*	N-Q.A.2	MP.6
16.2	4	F-LE.A.4	MP.6

* Item integrates mixed review concepts from previous modules or a previous course.

MIXED REVIEW

Assessment Readiness

ASSESSMENT AND INTERVENTION

Assign ready-made or customized practice tests to prepare students for high-stakes tests.

ADDITIONAL RESOURCES

Assessment Resources

- Leveled Module Quizzes: Modified, B

AVOID COMMON ERRORS

Item 1 Some students will miss that the item is asking about the inverse of each function. Remind students to read the entire question carefully, and highlight or underline key words.

MIXED REVIEW

Assessment Readiness

ASSESSMENT AND INTERVENTION

Assign ready-made or customized practice tests to prepare students for high-stakes tests.

ADDITIONAL RESOURCES

Assessment Resources

- Leveled Unit Tests: Modified, A, B, C
- Performance Assessment

AVOID COMMON ERRORS

Item 2 Students can easily miss or forget the word *not*. Encourage students to read carefully and to circle or highlight the word *not* anytime they see it in a question stem or solution.

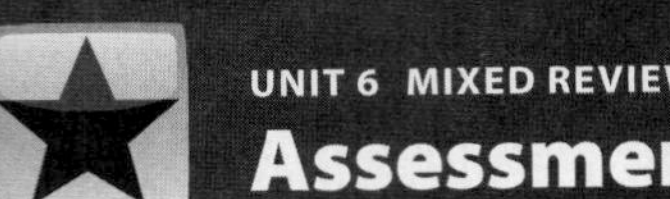

UNIT 6 MIXED REVIEW

Assessment Readiness

- Online Homework
- Hints and Help
- Extra Practice

1. Consider each sequence rule. Does the rule match the geometric sequence 5, 10, 20, 40, 80, ... ? Select Yes or No for A–C.

A. $a_n = 5(2)^n$ ○ Yes ● No

B. $a_n = 10(2n)$ ○ Yes ● No

C. $a_n = 5(2)^{n-1}$ ● Yes ○ No

2. Consider a situation where a population doubles every five years. Select True or False for each statement.

A. The situation could be modeled with an exponential equation. ● True ○ False

B. The situation could not be modeled with a quadratic equation. ● True ○ False

C. The situation could be modeled with a linear equation. ○ True ● False

3. Consider the function $f(x) = \log_6 x$. Select True or False for each statement. What is $f(216)$?

A. To evaluate $f(216)$, one way is to type it into the calculator as log 216 divided by log 6. ● True ○ False

B. There is no way to evaluate $\log_6$ in the calculator, because the log function in the calculator has a base of 10. ○ True ● False

C. When the function is evaluated for $x = 216$, $f(216) \approx 3$. ● True ○ False

4. Consider each equation. Is the equation the inverse function of $f(x) = 8x^3 + 2$?

A. $f^{-1}(x) = \frac{\sqrt[2]{x-2}}{2}$ ○ Yes ● No

B. $f^{-1}(x) = \frac{\sqrt[3]{x-2}}{2}$ ● Yes ○ No

C. $f^{-1}(x) = \frac{\sqrt[3]{x-2}}{8}$ ○ Yes ● No

D. $f^{-1}(x) = \frac{\sqrt[3]{x+2}}{2}$ ○ Yes ● No

COMMON CORE Common Core Standards

Items	Content Standards	Mathematical Practices
1	**F-BF.A.2**	**MP.1**
2	**S-ID.B.6**	**MP.6**
3	**F-BF.B.5**	**MP.5**
4*	**F-BF.B.4**	**MP.2**
5	**S-ID.B.6**	**MP.4**
6*	**A-APR.A.1**	**MP.2**
7	**F-LE.A.4**	**MP.6**

* Item integrates mixed review concepts from previous modules or a previous course.

5. In science class, Danny watched a video that talked about a type of spore that would have the following amount of spores in the petri dish each hour:

Hours	0	1	2	3	4
Spores	1	3	9	27	81

Danny wants to match the growth of the spores to a linear, quadratic, or exponential model. Using the information given, which model matches the spore growth? Explain.

An exponential model; Possible answer: The growth isn't constant, so it can't be a linear model. The spores increase too quickly to be a quadratic. The only model that fits well is an exponential model.

6. A circular plot of land has a radius $3x - 1$. What is the polynomial representing the area of the land? Explain your answer.

Area $= \pi r^2 = \pi(3x - 1)^2 = \pi(9x^2 - 6x + 1)$; Possible answer: Since the radius is a polynomial, the final answer will also be a polynomial. The FOIL method can be used to square the radius.

7. The number of bacteria growing in a petri dish after n hours can be modeled by $b(t) = b_0 r^n$, where b_0 is the initial number of bacteria and r is the rate at which the bacteria grow. If the number of bacteria quadruples after 1 hour, how many hours will it take to produce 51,200 bacteria if there are initially 50 bacteria? Explain your answer.

Substituting the rate $(r = 4)$, final amount of bacteria $(b = 51{,}200)$, and the initial bacteria $(b_0 = 50)$ into $\frac{b(t)}{b_0} = r^n$ gives $n = 5$ hours.

Performance Tasks

8. The amount of freight transported by rail in the United States was about 580 billion *ton-miles* in 1960 and has been increasing at a rate of 2.32% per year since then.

A. Write and graph a function representing the amount of freight, in billions of ton-miles, transported annually (1960 = year 0).

B. In what year would you predict that the number of ton-miles would have exceeded or would exceed 1 trillion (1000 billion)?

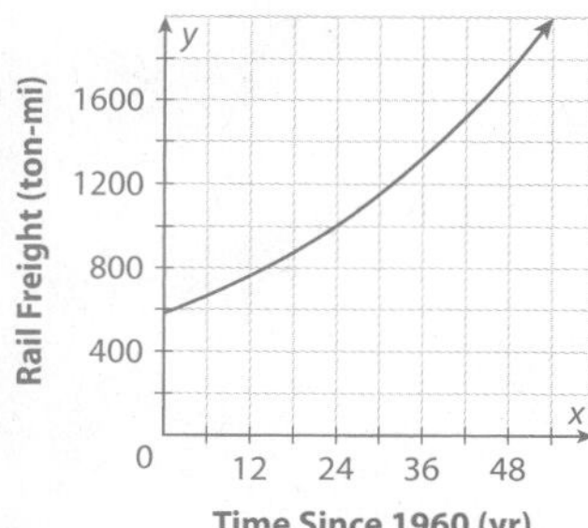

A. $f(t) = 580\,(1.0232)^t$

B. year 24, or 1984

PERFORMANCE TASKS

There are three different levels of performance tasks:

* **Novice:** These are short word problems that require students to apply the math they have learned in straightforward, real-world situations.

** **Apprentice:** These are more involved problems that guide students step-by-step through more complex tasks. These exercises include more complicated reasoning, writing, and open ended elements.

*****Expert:** These are open-ended, nonroutine problems that, instead of stepping the students through, ask them to choose their own methods for solving and justify their answers and reasoning.

SCORING GUIDES

Item 8 (2 points)

a. 1 point for correct function

b. 1 point for correct prediction

SCORING GUIDES

Item 9 (6 points)

a. 2 points for correct value

b. 2 points for correct answer
   2 points for explanation

Item 10 (6 points)

a. 2 points for correct values

b. 1 point for correct intensity
   1 point for correct placement

c. 1 point for correct answer
   1 point for explanation

★★★ **9.** In one part of the atmosphere where the temperature is a constant −70°F, from about 11 km to 25 km above sea level, pressure can be expressed as a function of altitude by the equation $P(h) = 128(10)^{-0.0682h}$, where P is the atmospheric pressure in kilopascals (kPa) and h is the altitude in kilometers above sea level.

A. What is the altitude, to the nearest tenth of a kilometer, where the pressure is 5.54 kPa?

B. A kilopascal is 0.145 psi. Would the model predict a sea-level pressure less than or greater than the actual sea-level pressure, 14.7 psi? Explain.

A. 20.0 km

B. greater; The model predicts sea-level to be 128 kPa, which converts to 18.6 psi.

★★★ **10.** The loudness of sound is measured on a logarithmic scale according to the formula $L = 10\log\left(\frac{I}{I_0}\right)$, where L is the loudness of sound in decibels (dB), I is the intensity of sound, and I 0 is the intensity of the softest audible sound.

Sound	Intensity
Jet takeoff	$10^{15}I_0$
Jackhammer	$10^{12}I_0$
Hair dryer	$10^{7}I_0$
Whisper	$10^{3}I_0$
Leaves rustling	$10^{2}I_0$
Softest audible sound	I_0

A. Find the loudness in decibels of each sound listed in the table.

B. The sound at a rock concert is found to have a loudness of 110 decibels. Find the intensity of this sound. Where should this sound be placed in the table in order to preserve the order from least to greatest intensity?

C. A decibel is $\frac{1}{10}$ of a bel. Is a jet plane louder than a sound that measures 20 bels? Explain.

A. jet: 150 dB; jackhammer: 120 dB; hair-dryer: 70 dB; whisper: 30 dB; leaves: 20 dB; softest audible: 0 dB

B. 10^{11} I_0, below jackhammer

C. No; 20 bels is 200 dB

MATH IN CAREERS

Nuclear Medicine Technologist The radioactive properties of the isotope technetium-99m can be used in combination with a tin compound to map circulatory system disorders. Technetium-99m has a half-life of 6 hours.

a. Write an exponential decay function that models this situation. The function $p(t)$ should give the percent of the isotope remaining after t hours.

b. Describe domain, range, and the end behavior of $p(t)$ as t increases without bound for the function found in part a.

c. Write the inverse of the decay function. Use a common logarithm for your final function.

d. How long does it take until 5% of the technetium-99m remains? Round to the nearest tenth of an hour.

a. $p(t) = 100\left(\frac{1}{2}\right)^{\frac{t}{6}}$

b. The domain is the number of hours that have passed: $t \geq 0$.

The range is the percent of technetium-99m remaining after t hours: $0 < p(t) \leq 100$. As t increases without bound, $p(t)$ approaches 0.

c. $t(p) = -19.93\log p + 39.86$

d. 25.9 hours

MATH IN CAREERS

Nuclear Medicine Technologist In this Unit Performance Task, students can see how a nuclear medicine technologist uses mathematics on the job.

For more information about careers in mathematics as well as various mathematics appreciation topics, visit the American Mathematical Society http://www.ams.org

SCORING GUIDES

Task (6 points)

a. 1 point for correct function

b. 1 point for correct domain and range
1 point for correct end behavior

c. 2 points for correct function

d. 1 point for correct value

UNIT 7

Trigonometric Functions

CONTENTS

Unit Pacing Guide

45-Minute Classes

Module 17

DAY 1	DAY 2	DAY 3	DAY 4	DAY 5
Lesson 17.1	Lesson 17.2	Lesson 17.2	Lesson 17.3	Lesson 17.3
DAY 6				
Module Review and Assessment Readiness				

Module 18

DAY 1	DAY 2	DAY 3	DAY 4	DAY 5
Lesson 18.1	Lesson 18.1	Lesson 18.2	Lesson 18.3	Lesson 18.4
DAY 6	DAY 7	DAY 8		
Lesson 18.4	Module Review and Assessment Readiness	Unit Review and Assessment Readiness		

90-Minute Classes

Module 17

DAY 1	DAY 2	DAY 3
Lesson 17.1 Lesson 17.2	Lesson 17.2 Lesson 17.3	Lesson 17.3 Module Review and Assessment Readiness

Module 18

DAY 1	DAY 2	DAY 3	DAY 4
Lesson 18.1	Lesson 18.2 Lesson 18.3	Lesson 18.4	Module Review and Assessment Readiness Unit Review and Assessment Readiness

Program Resources

PLAN

HMH Teacher App

Access a full suite of teacher resources online and offline on a variety of devices. Plan present, and manage classes, assignments, and activities.

ePlanner **Easily plan your classes, create and view assignments, and access all program resources with your online, customizable planning tool.**

Professional Development Videos

Authors Juli Dixon and Matt Larson model successful teaching practices and strategies in actual classroom settings.

QR Codes **Scan with your smart phone to jump directly from your print book to online videos and other resources.**

Teacher's Edition

Support students with point-of-use Questioning Strategies, teaching tips, resources for differentiated instruction, additional activities, and more.

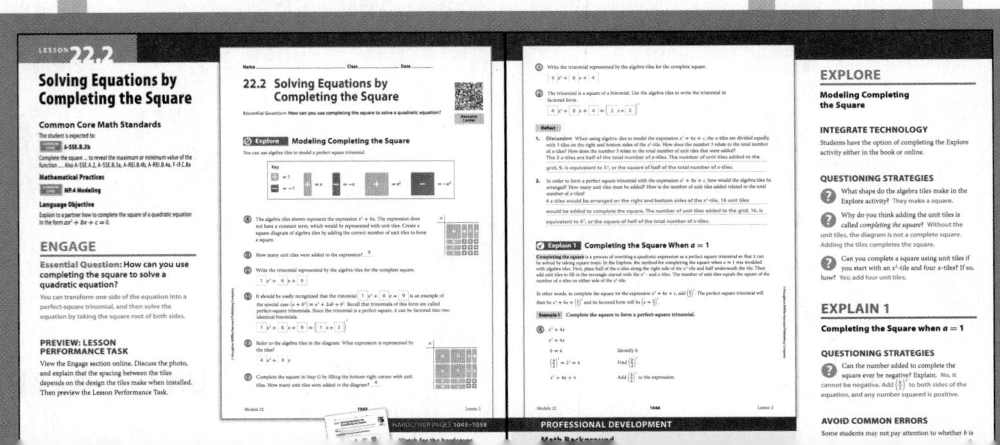

LESSON 22.2
Solving Equations by Completing the Square
ENGAGE
EXPLORE
Modeling Completing the Square
INTEGRATE TECHNOLOGY
QUESTIONING STRATEGIES
EXPLAIN 1
Completing the Square when a = 1
AVOID COMMON ERRORS
PROFESSIONAL DEVELOPMENT

ENGAGE AND EXPLORE

Real-World Videos **Engage students with interesting and relevant applications of the mathematical content of each module.**

Explore Activities

Students interactively explore new concepts using a variety of tools and approaches.

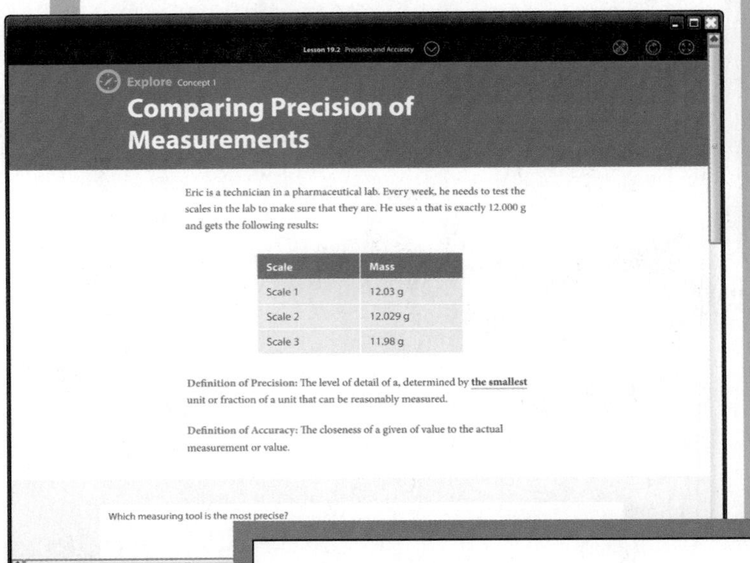

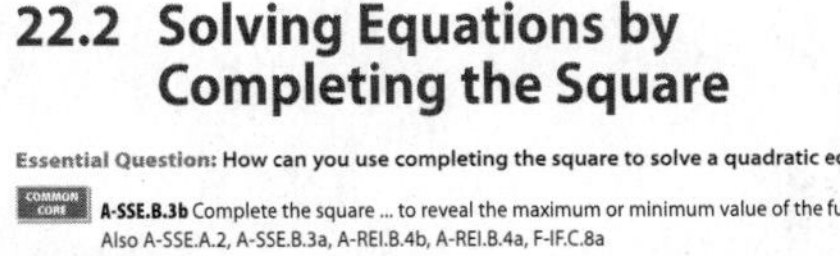

TEACH

Math On the Spot video tutorials, featuring program authors Dr. Edward Burger and Martha Sandoval-Martinez, accompany every example in the textbook and give students step-by-step instructions and explanations of key math concepts.

Interactive Teacher Edition

Customize and present course materials with collaborative activities and integrated formative assessment.

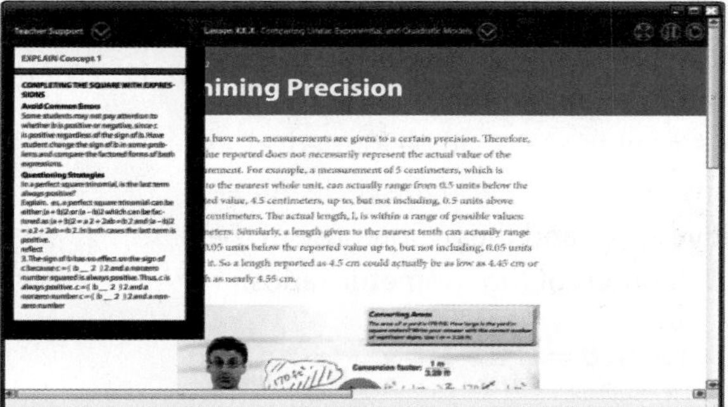

Differentiated Instruction Resources

Support all learners with Differentiated Instruction Resources, including

- **Leveled Practice and Problem Solving**
- **Reading Strategies**
- **Success for English Learners**
- **Challenge**

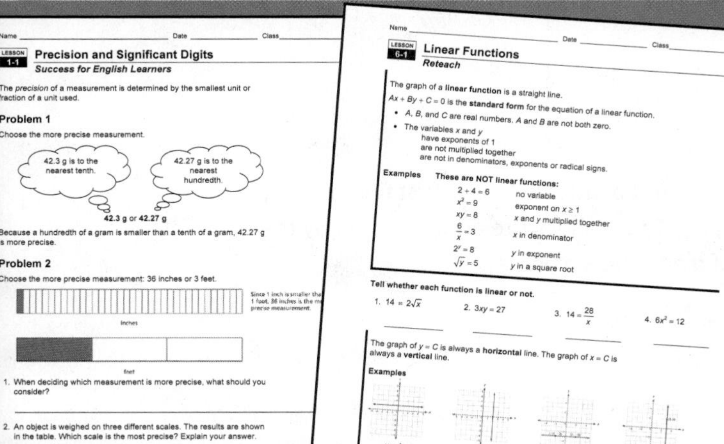

Name ______ Date ______ Class ______

LESSON 1-1 **Precision and Significant Digits**

Success for English Learners

The *precision* of a measurement is determined by the smallest unit or fraction of a unit used.

Problem 1

Choose the more precise measurement.

42.3 g is to the nearest tenth.

42.27 g is to the nearest hundredth.

42.3 g or 42.27 g

Because a hundredth of a gram is smaller than a tenth of a gram, 42.27 g is more precise.

Problem 2

Choose the more precise measurement: 36 inches or 3 feet.

Inches

feet

1. When deciding which measurement is more precise, what should you consider?

2. An object is weighed on three different scales. The results are shown in the table. Which scale is the most precise? Explain your answer.

Name ______ Date ______ Class ______

LESSON 6-1 **Linear Functions**

Reteach

The graph of a **linear function** is a straight line.

$Ax + By + C = 0$ is the **standard form** for the equation of a linear function.

- A, B, and C are real numbers. A and B are not both zero.
- The variables x and y
  - have exponents of 1
  - are not multiplied together
  - are not in denominators, exponents or radical signs.

Examples **These are NOT linear functions:**

$2 + 4 = 6$	no variable
$x^2 = 9$	exponent on $x \geq 1$
$xy = 8$	x and y multiplied together
$\frac{6}{x} = 3$	x in denominator
$2^y = 8$	y in exponent
$\sqrt{y} = 5$	y in a square root

Tell whether each function is linear or not.

1. $14 = 2\sqrt{x}$ ______
2. $3xy = 27$ ______
3. $14 = \frac{28}{x}$ ______
4. $6x^2 = 12$ ______

The graph of $y = C$ is always a **horizontal** line. The graph of $x = C$ is always a **vertical** line.

Examples

$y = 1$ $x = 2$

ASSESSMENT AND INTERVENTION

The Personal Math Trainer provides online practice, homework, assessments, and intervention. Monitor student progress through reports and alerts. Create and customize assignments aligned to specific lessons or Common Core standards.

- **Practice** – With dynamic items and assignments, students get unlimited practice on key concepts supported by guided examples, step-by-step solutions, and video tutorials.
- **Assessments** – Choose from course assignments or customize your own based on course content, Common Core standards, difficulty levels, and more.
- **Homework** – Students can complete online homework with a wide variety of problem types, including the ability to enter expressions, equations, and graphs. Let the system automatically grade homework, so you can focus where your students need help the most!
- **Intervention** – Let the Personal Math Trainer automatically prescribe a targeted, personalized intervention path for your students.

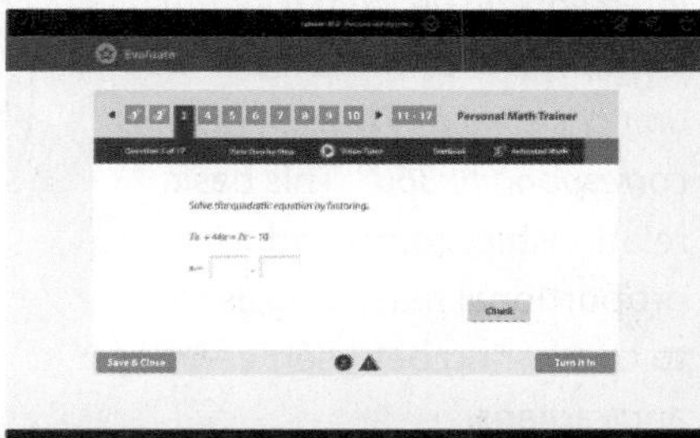

Focus on Higher Order Thinking

Raise the bar with homework and practice that incorporates higher-order thinking and mathematical practices in every lesson.

Assessment Readiness

Prepare students for success on high stakes tests for Algebra 2 with practice at every module and unit

Assessment Resources

Tailor assessments and response to intervention to meet the needs of all your classes and students, including

- Leveled Module Quizzes
- Leveled Unit Tests
- Unit Performance Tasks
- Placement, Diagnostic, and Quarterly Benchmark Tests
- Tier 1, Tier 2, and Tier 3 Resources

Math Background

Arc Length and Radian Measure

F-TF.A.1

LESSON 17.1

In the most general terms, an *arc* is *any smooth curve that joins two points.*In the context of circles, an *arc* is *a continuous portion of a circle*. An arc of a circle is closely related to the central angle that is defined by the endpoints of the arc and the center of the circle. Students should be aware that most of the theorems about arcs have proofs that depend on working back and forth between properties of arcs and properties of angles.

A *radian is a unit of angle measure* that may be defined as follows: *In a unit circle, a central angle that measures 1 radian intercepts an arc with a length of 1 unit. The circumference of the unit circle is 2π . Thus, 2π radians correspond to 360°*. This basic relationship, combined with proportional reasoning, is the key to converting between degrees and radians.

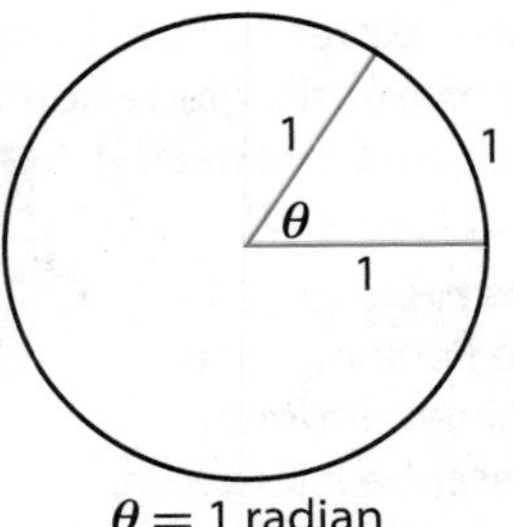

$\theta = 1$ radian

Students may wonder why radians are needed at all. They should be aware that radians give rise to more natural relationships than do degrees. For example, in a circle of radius *r*, the arc length s intercepted by a central angle θ is given by $s = r\theta$, but this simple formula holds only when θ is measured in radians. Students will see additional examples when they study calculus, in which all angles are measured in radians.

Trigonometric Functions

F-TF.A.2

LESSON 17.2

In geometry, students learned that two triangles are similar if two angles of one triangle are congruent to two angles of the other triangle. This postulate, known as *Angle-Angle (AA) Similarity*, provides the starting point for the study of trigonometry.

The right triangles that follow all contain a right angle and a 28° angle, so they are similar by AA Similarity. This means that

$\frac{A}{B} = \frac{JK}{JL} = \frac{PQ}{PR}$.

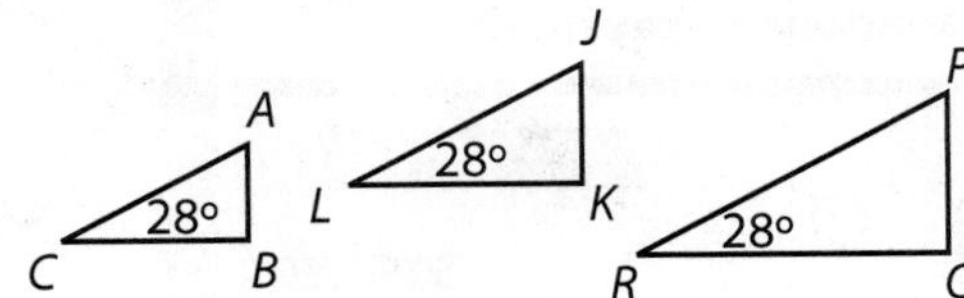

Thus, for any right triangles that contain a 28° angle, the ratio of the length of the leg opposite that angle to the length of the hypotenuse is the same. This ratio is defined to be the sine of 28°, written *sin 28°*. Other trigonometric ratios are defined by forming ratios of other combinations of side lengths.

Once the trigonometric functions have been defined for acute angles, it is easy to extend the definitions to other angle measures. To do this, we begin with a unit circle in the coordinate plane. A right triangle can be formed, as shown, by choosing any point $P(x_1, y_1)$ on the circle. Angle θ is formed by the positive *x*-axis and the hypotenuse of the right triangle. By the definitions of trigonometric ratios,

$\sin \theta = y_1$, $\cos \theta = x_1$, and $\tan \theta = \frac{y_1}{x_1}$.

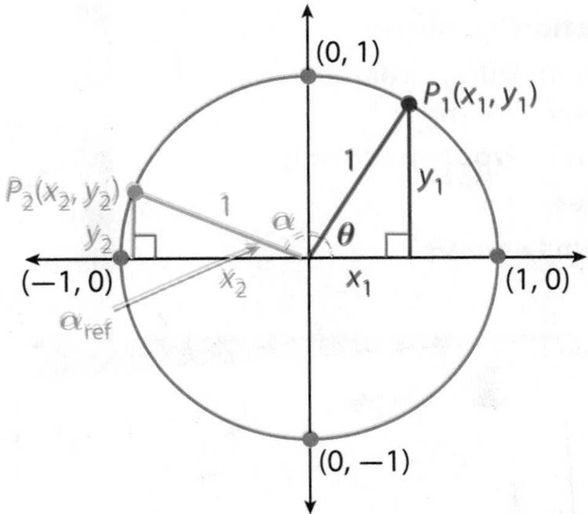

For an angle that is not acute, such as α, first find the *reference angle*, α_{ref}. This is the acute angle formed by the terminal side of *a* and the *x*-axis.

For α in the diagram, $\alpha_{ref} = 180 - \alpha$.
Construct a right triangle as shown and find the trigonometric ratios for α_{ref}; these are defined to be the trigonometric ratios for α. In other words,

$\sin \alpha = y_2$, $\cos \alpha = x_2$, and $\tan \alpha = \frac{y_2}{x_2}$.

However, the above is subject to one important caveat. Notice that y_2 is positive, while x_2 is negative; hence $\cos \alpha$ and $\tan \alpha$ are both negative. This will be true for any angle whose terminal side lies in Quadrant II.

The same process is used for angles greater than 180°: always find the reference angle between the terminal side and the *x*-axis. The diagram below shows which trigonometric ratios are positive for angles in each quadrant.

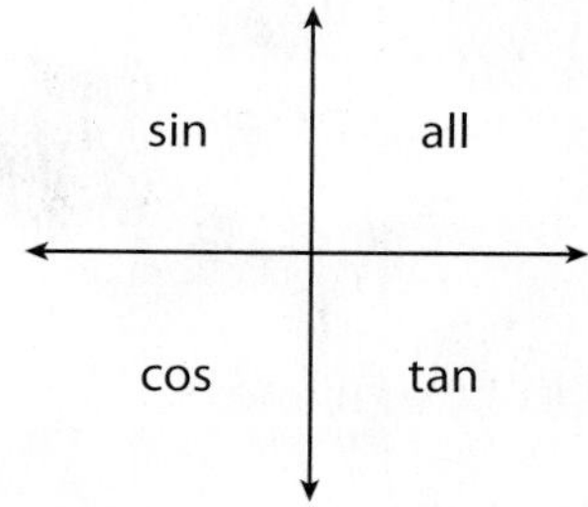

Sine and Cosine Graphs

F-IF.C.7e

LESSON 18.1

The sine and cosine functions are periodic functions with period 2π. As students work with the graphs of these functions, they should begin to recognize several important characteristics of the graphs.

Both the sine and cosine functions have graphs that are smooth, nonlinear curves.

- Both the sine and cosine functions have amplitude 1.
- The graph of $y = \sin x$ passes through the origin.
- The graphs of $y = \sin x$ and $y = \cos x$ have identical shapes. The graph of $y = \cos x$ is a translation $\frac{\pi}{2}$ units to the left of the graph of $y = \sin x$.

This last point is especially important. In algebraic terms, it states that $\cos x = \sin\left(x + \frac{\pi}{2}\right)$. This relationship can be verified by using the identity
$\sin (A + B) = \sin A \cos B + \cos A \sin B$.

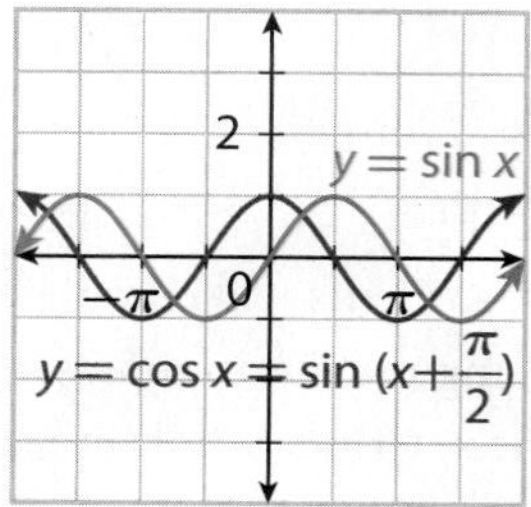

Students should be aware that knowing the basic shapes of the graphs of the sine and cosine functions can help them remember the values of these functions.

For example, students sometimes have difficulty remembering whether $\sin \frac{\pi}{2} = 0$ or $\cos \frac{\pi}{2} = 0$. A quick sketch of either graph should help them see that the latter equation is correct.

Tangent Graphs

F-IF.C.7e

LESSON 18.2

The tangent function has period π. This period is less than that of the sine or cosine function. Thus, the graph of the tangent function repeats more frequently on a given interval than the sine or cosine function does. The function $y = \tan x$ is undefined at $x = \frac{\pi}{2} + n\pi$, where *n* is an integer. Therefore, the graph of $y = \tan x$ has vertical asymptotes at these values of *x*.

The graph of $y = \tan x$ demonstrates an interesting feature of the function. As *x* approaches $\frac{\pi}{2}$ from the left (that is, $x < \frac{\pi}{2}$), tan x approaches infinity; as *x* approaches $\frac{\pi}{2}$ from the right (that is, $x > \frac{\pi}{2}$), tan *x* approaches negative infinity. The same is true at each vertical asymptote.

Once students are familiar with the graph of the tangent function, they can sketch the graph of the cotangent function by recalling the reciprocal relationship of the functions. In particular, where the graph of $y = \tan x$ has an *x*-intercept, the graph of $y = \cot x$ has an asymptote. Where the graph of $y = \tan x$ has an asymptote, the graph of
$y = \cot x$ has an *x*-intercept.

Trigonometric Functions

MATH IN CAREERS

Unit Activity Preview

After completing this unit, students will complete a Math in Careers task by using models to represent the motion of a paddle wheel. Critical skills include graphing a trigonometric function, describing what its parameters mean for the real-world situation, and using the function model to make a prediction.

For more information about careers in mathematics as well as various mathematics appreciation topics, visit The American Mathematical Society at http://www.ams.org.

UNIT 7

Trigonometric Functions

MODULE 17
Unit-Circle Definition of Trigonometric Functions

MODULE 18
Graphing Trigonometric Functions

MATH IN CAREERS

Boat Builder A boat builder builds and repairs all types of marine vessels, from sailboats to riverboats. Boat builders are responsible for drafting a boat's design; building the frame, hull, deck, and cabins; and fitting the engine. Boat builders often use computer technologies when designing a boat and must use geometry and trigonometry when interpreting blueprints and shaping and cutting materials to specified measurements. Boat builders need to be able to estimate and calculate costs of materials and labor and to understand mathematical models of different aspects of boats and boating.

If you are interested in a career as a boat builder, you should study these mathematical subjects:

- Geometry
- Algebra
- Trigonometry
- Business Math

Check out the career activity at the end of the unit to find out how **Boat Builders** use math.

TRACKING YOUR LEARNING PROGRESSION

Before	In this Unit	After
Students understand: • exponential functions • sequences • the base e • logarithmic functions	Students will learn about: • defining trigonometric functions with the unit circle • angles of rotation and radian measure • evaluating trigonometric functions • transformations of the graphs of trigonometric functions	Students will study: • probability • permutations and combinations • independent and dependent events • using probability to make fair decisions

Reading Start-Up

Visualize Vocabulary

Use the ✔ words to complete the graphic.

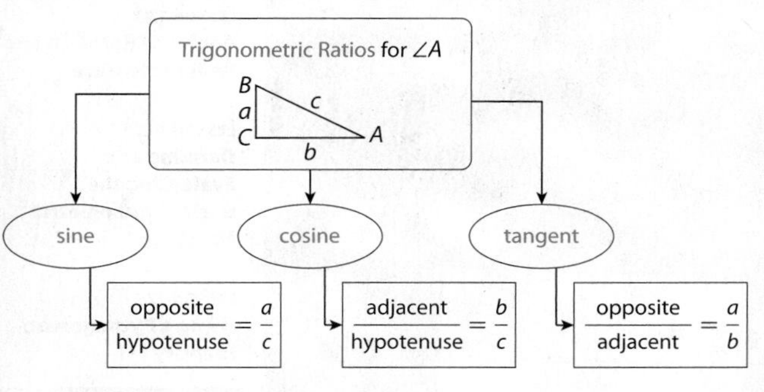

Vocabulary

Review Words

- ✔ cosine *(coseno)*
- ✔ sine *(seno)*
- ✔ tangent *(tangente)*
- ✔ trigonometric ratio *(razón trigonométrica)*

Preview Words

- amplitude *(amplitud)*
- angle of rotation *(ángulo de referencia)*
- cosecant function *(función cosecante)*
- cotangent function *(función cotangente)*
- period *(periodo)*
- periodic function *(function periódica)*
- radian *(radián)*
- reference angle *(ángulo de rotación)*
- secant function *(función secante)*

Understand Vocabulary

To become familiar with some of the vocabulary terms in the module, consider the following. You may refer to the module, the glossary, or a dictionary.

1. An **angle of rotation** is formed by a rotating ray, called the terminal side, and a stationary ray, called the initial side.
2. A **periodic function** repeats exactly in regular intervals.
3. The **amplitude** of a periodic function is half the difference of the maximum and minimum values and is always positive.

Active Reading

Layered Book Before beginning each module in this unit, create a layered book to help you summarize the information in each lesson. Each flap of the layered book can correspond to definitions and examples of the trigonometric functions, their graphs, and transformations. Write details of each function on the appropriate flap to create a summary of the module.

Reading Start Up

Have students complete the activities on this page by working alone or with others.

VISUALIZE VOCABULARY

The information graphic helps students review vocabulary associated with the three basic trigonometric functions. If time allows, discuss how each trigonometric ratio differs, including mnemonics that students might know.

UNDERSTAND VOCABULARY

Use the following explanations to help students learn the preview words.

The trigonometric functions sine, cosine, and tangent have reciprocal functions called the **cosecant**, **secant** and **cotangent**, respectively. Trigonometric functions are examples of **periodic functions** because they have a repeating pattern. The **period** of a trigonometric function is a measure of its repeating interval, and **amplitude** measures its variation in one period.

ACTIVE READING

Students can use these reading and note-taking strategies to help them organize and understand the new concepts and vocabulary. Encourage students to ask for help if they do not recognize a word or the reasoning behind an application.

ADDITIONAL RESOURCES

Differentiated Instruction

- Reading Strategies EL

MODULE 17

Unit-Circle Definition of Trigonometric Functions

ESSENTIAL QUESTION:

Answer: Visual arts programmers for video games and computer-generated drawings use unit circle definitions of trigonometric functions to rotate a figure on the screen.

PROFESSIONAL DEVELOPMENT VIDEO

Professional Development Video

Author Matt Larson models successful teaching practices in an actual high-school classroom.

Professional Development
my.hrw.com

MODULE 17

Unit-Circle Definition of Trigonometric Functions

Essential Question: How can the unit-circle definition of trigonometric functions help to solve real-world problems?

REAL WORLD VIDEO
How does a digital device like a smartphone display time on an analog clock? You may be surprised to learn that the answer involves trigonometry.

MODULE PERFORMANCE TASK PREVIEW

Telling Time with Trig

Imagine you are designing an analog clock widget that can be displayed on a variety of digital devices. You have to solve the problem of how to convert digital information about time into the corresponding positions of the hands of the clock. How can you use trigonometry to program your clock to display time accurately? It's time to find out!

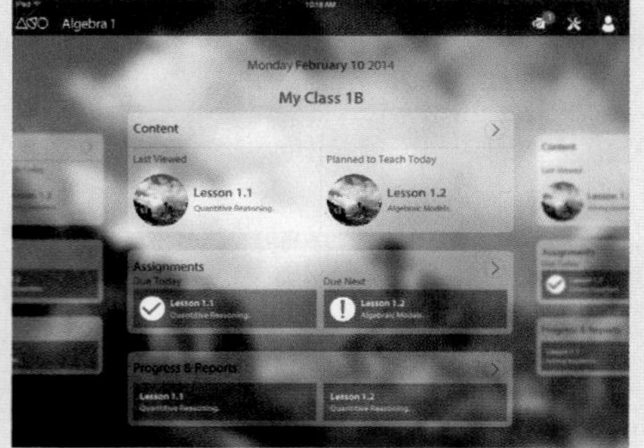

DIGITAL TEACHER EDITION

Access a full suite of teaching resources when and where you need them:

- Access content online or offline
- Customize lessons to share with your class
- Communicate with your students in real-time
- View student grades and data instantly to target your instruction where it is needed most

PERSONAL MATH TRAINER

Assessment and Intervention

Assign automatically graded homework, quizzes, tests, and intervention activities. Prepare your students with updated, Common Core-aligned practice tests.

Are YOU Ready?

Complete these exercises to review skills you will need for this chapter.

- Online Homework
- Hints and Help
- Extra Practice

Pythagorean Theorem

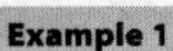
Example 1 Two sides of a right triangle measure 3 units and 1.5 units. Find the length of the third side. If possible, find the angle measures.

Use the Pythagorean Theorem $a^2 + b^2 = c^2$ to find the missing length.

The third side is either a leg or a hypotenuse.

If it's a hypotenuse, then it is c in the Pythagorean formula: $(1.5)^2 + 3^2 = c^2$, and $c = \sqrt{(1.5)^2 + 3^2} = \sqrt{2.25 + 9} = \sqrt{11.25} \approx 3.35$. The ratio of the side lengths is $1.5 : 3 : 3.35$, so this triangle is not a special right triangle.

If it's a leg, then it is a in the Pythagorean formula: $a^2 + 1.5^2 = 3^2$, and $a = \sqrt{3^2 - 1.5^2} = \sqrt{9 - 2.25} = 1.5\sqrt{3}$. Since the ratio of the sides $1.5 : 1.5\sqrt{3} : 3$ are in the form $a : a\sqrt{3} : 2a$, the triangle is a 30°-60°-90° special right triangle.

Two side lengths of a right triangle are given. Find the length of the missing side. If possible, find the angle measures of the triangle.

1. $4\sqrt{3}, 2\sqrt{3}$ — **6: 30°–60°–90°; $2\sqrt{15}$**

2. 8, 15 — **17; $\sqrt{161}$**

3. $3\sqrt{2}, 3$ — **3: 45°-45°-90°; $3\sqrt{3}$**

Distance Formula

Example 2 Find the distance between the points $(7, -1)$ and $(16, 11)$.

$$d = \sqrt{(x_1 - x_2)^2 + (y_1 - y_2)^2} = \sqrt{(7 - 16)^2 + (-1 - 11)^2}$$
$$= \sqrt{81 + 144} = \sqrt{225} = 15$$

The distance is 15.

Find the distance between the given points.

4. $(-4, 20)$ and $(3, -4)$ — **25**

5. $(8, 9)$ and $(0, -6)$ — **17**

6. $(2.5, -2)$ and $(-5, 2)$ — **8.5**

Are You Ready?

ASSESS READINESS

Use the assessment on this page to determine if students need strategic or intensive intervention for the module's prerequisite skills.

ASSESSMENT AND INTERVENTION

RtI Response to Intervention TIER 1, TIER 2, TIER 3 SKILLS

Personal Math Trainer will automatically create a standards-based, personalized intervention assignment for your students, targeting each student's individual needs!

ADDITIONAL RESOURCES

See the table below for a full list of intervention resources available for this module.

Response to Intervention Resources also includes:

- Tier 2 Skill Pre-Tests for each Module
- Tier 2 Skill Post-Tests for each skill

Response to Intervention			Differentiated Instruction
Tier 1 Lesson Intervention Worksheets	**Tier 2** Strategic Intervention Skills Intervention Worksheets	**Tier 3** Intensive Intervention Worksheets available online	
Reteach 17.1 Reteach 17.2 Reteach 17.3	44 Distance and Midpoint Formula 53 Pythagorean Theorem 55 Sine and Cosine Ratios 56 Special Right Triangles 58 Tangent Ratio	Building Block Skills 10, 11, 27, 38, 45, 46, 50, 69, 70, 79, 90, 91, 95, 98, 99, 100, 104	Challenge worksheets Extend the Math Lesson Activities in TE

LESSON 17.1

Angles of Rotation and Radian Measure

Common Core Math Standards

The student is expected to:

F-TF.A.1

Understand radian measure of an angle as the length of the arc on the unit circle subtended by the angle. Also G-C.C.5

Mathematical Practices

MP.8 Patterns

Language Objective

Work with a partner to complete a chart that shows an angle's initial and terminal sides, and the defining standard position of an angle.

ENGAGE

Essential Question: What is the relationship between the unit circle and radian measure?

Possible answer: The unit circle is a circle centered at the origin with a radius of 1 and a circumference of 2π. An angle of rotation that intercepts an arc on the unit circle whose length is 1 has a measure defined as 1 radian. So, there are 2π radians in an angle that makes one full revolution.

PREVIEW: LESSON PERFORMANCE TASK

View the online Engage. Discuss the photo and how a centrifuge simulates the forces that astronauts encounter. Then preview the Lesson Performance Task.

Name__________ Class__________ Date__________

17.1 Angles of Rotation and Radian Measure

Resource Locker

Essential Question: What is the relationship between the unit circle and radian measure?

Explore 1 Drawing Angles of Rotation and Finding Coterminal Angles

In trigonometry, an **angle of rotation** is an angle formed by the starting and ending positions of a ray that rotates about its endpoint. The angle is in *standard position* in a coordinate plane when the starting position of the ray, or *initial side* of the angle, is on the positive x-axis and has its endpoint at the origin. To show the amount and direction of rotation, a curved arrow is drawn to the ending position of the ray, or *terminal side* of the angle.

In geometry, you were accustomed to working with angles having measures between 0° and 180°. In trigonometry, angles can have measures greater than 180° and even less than 0°. To see why, think in terms of revolutions, or complete circular motions. Let θ be an angle of rotation in standard position.

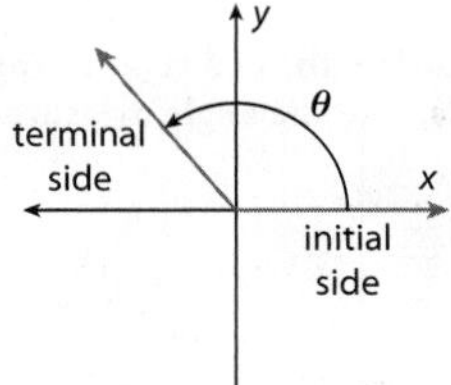

- If the rotation for an angle θ is less than 1 revolution in a counterclockwise direction, then the measure of θ is between 0° and 360°. An angle of rotation measured *clockwise* from standard position has a *negative* angle measure. **Coterminal angles** are angles that share the same terminal side. For example, the angles with measures of 257° and −103° are coterminal, as shown.

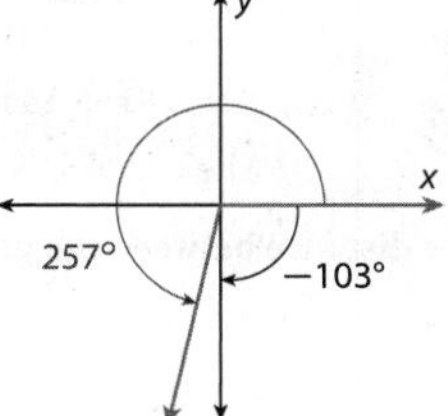

- If the rotation for θ is more than 1 revolution but less than 2 revolutions in a counterclockwise direction, then the measure of θ is between 360° and 720°, as shown. Because you can have any number of revolutions with an angle of rotation, there is a counterclockwise angle of rotation corresponding to any positive real number and a clockwise angle of rotation corresponding to any negative real number.

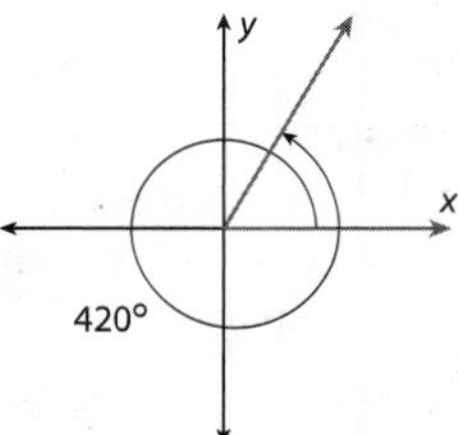

HARDCOVER PAGES 825–838

Watch for the hardcover student edition page numbers for this lesson.

Ⓐ Draw an angle of rotation of 310°. In what quadrant is the terminal side of the angle?

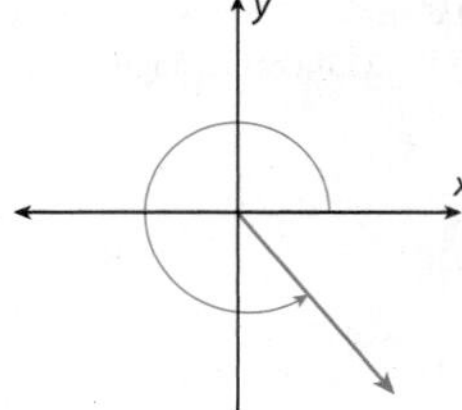

The terminal side is in Quadrant IV.

Ⓑ On the same graph from the previous step, draw a positive coterminal angle. What is the angle measure of your angle?

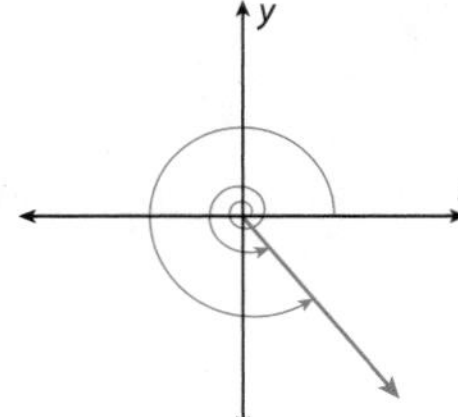

Possible angle shown, with measure of 670°.

Ⓒ On the same graph from the previous two steps, draw a negative coterminal angle. What is the angle measure of your angle?

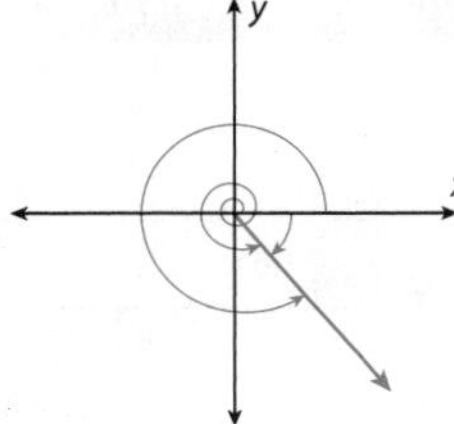

Possible angle shown, with measure of −50°.

Reflect

1. Is the measure of an angle of rotation in standard position completely determined by the position of its terminal side? Explain.
No; there are infinitely many angles of rotation, both positive and negative, that can be drawn in standard position with a given terminal side.

2. Find the measure between 720° and 1080° of an angle that is coterminal with an angle that has a measure of −30°. In addition, describe a general method for finding the measure of any angle that is coterminal with a given angle.
The measure will be 1050°, since 720 and 1080 are consecutive multiples of 360 and $-30 + 1080 = 1050$. In general, you can find the measure of any angle that is coterminal with a given angle by adding or subtracting a multiple of 360° from the given angle's measure.

PROFESSIONAL DEVELOPMENT

Integrate Mathematical Practices

This lesson includes opportunities to address Mathematical Practice Standard **MP.8**, "Look for and express regularity in repeated reasoning." Drawing angles helps students visualize the fact that the measures of coterminal angles differ by multiples of ±360°. Students apply this fact to calculate measures of angles coterminal with a given angle.

EXPLORE 1

Drawing Angles of Rotation and Finding Coterminal Angles

INTEGRATE TECHNOLOGY

Students have the option of completing the activity either in the book or online.

QUESTIONING STRATEGIES

? What is the difference between a 180° angle of rotation and a −180° angle of rotation? **They have the same terminal side, but the positive angle has a counterclockwise rotation, while the negative angle has a clockwise rotation.**

? What is the difference between a 90° angle of rotation and a −90° angle of rotation? **The positive angle has its terminal side along the positive *y*-axis. The negative angle has its terminal side along the negative *y*–axis.**

EXPLORE 2

Understanding Radian Measure

AVOID COMMON ERRORS

Students may seek to add a unit symbol or abbreviation to radian measures. Tell them that although they may see the abbreviation *rad* used to refer to radians, radian measures do not require a unit symbol or an abbreviation. Degree measures should always have a degree symbol; angle measures without a symbol or unit abbreviation should be assumed to be radians.

QUESTIONING STRATEGIES

What happens to the intercepted arc length s as the radius increases? Explain. It increases. As the radius increases, so does the circumference, which increases the length of the intercepted arc.

What will be the ratio of arc length to radius for a 60° central angle in a circle of radius 10 feet? For a 60° central angle in a circle of any radius? $\frac{\pi}{3}$; $\frac{\pi}{3}$

Explore 2 Understanding Radian Measure

The diagram shows three circles centered at the origin. The arcs that are on the circle between the initial and terminal sides of the 225° central angle are called *intercepted arcs.*

$\overset{\frown}{AB}$ is on a circle with radius 1 unit.

$\overset{\frown}{CD}$ is on a circle with radius 2 units.

$\overset{\frown}{EF}$ is on a circle with radius 3 units.

Notice that the intercepted arcs have different lengths, although they are intercepted by the same central angle of 225°. You will now explore how these arc lengths are related to the angle.

(A) The angle of rotation is 225 degrees counterclockwise.

There are 360 degrees in a circle.

225° represents $\frac{5}{8}$ of the total number of degrees in a circle.

So, the length of each intercepted arc is $\frac{5}{8}$ of the total circumference of the circle that it lies on.

(B) Complete the table. To find the length of the intercepted arc, use the fraction you found in the previous step. Give all answers in terms of π.

Radius, r	Circumference, C ($C = 2\pi r$)	Length of Intercepted Arc, s	Ratio of Arc Length to Radius, $\frac{s}{r}$
1	$2\pi(1) = 2\pi$	$\frac{5}{8} \cdot 2\pi = \frac{10\pi}{8} = \frac{5\pi}{4}$	$\frac{5\pi}{4} \div 1 = \frac{5\pi}{4}$
2	$2\pi(2) = 4\pi$	$\frac{5}{8} \cdot 4\pi = \frac{20\pi}{8} = \frac{5\pi}{2}$	$\frac{5\pi}{2} \div 2 = \frac{5\pi}{4}$
3	$2\pi(3) = 6\pi$	$\frac{5}{8} \cdot 6\pi = \frac{30\pi}{8} = \frac{15\pi}{4}$	$\frac{15\pi}{4} \div 3 = \frac{5\pi}{4}$

Reflect

3. What do you notice about the ratios $\frac{s}{r}$ in the fourth column of the table?
All of the ratios are equal to $\frac{5\pi}{4}$.

4. When the ratios of the values of a variable y to the corresponding values of another variable x all equal a constant k, y is said to be *proportional* to x, and the constant k is called the *constant of proportionality*. Because $\frac{y}{x} = k$, you can solve for y to get $y = kx$. In the case of the arcs that are intercepted by a 225° angle, is the arc length s proportional to the radius r? If so, what is the constant of proportionality, and what equation gives s in terms of r?
Yes; the constant of proportionality is $\frac{5\pi}{4}$, and the equation is $s = \frac{5\pi}{4}r$.

5. Suppose that the central angle is 270° instead of 225°. Would the arc length s still be proportional to the radius r? If so, would the constant of proportionality still be the same? Explain.
Yes; s is still proportional to r, but the constant of proportionality would become $\frac{3\pi}{2}$. This is because a 270° angle represents $\frac{3}{4}$ of a circle. For example, on a circle of radius 2: $r = 2$, $s = \frac{3}{4} \cdot 4\pi = 3\pi$, and $\frac{s}{r} = \frac{3\pi}{2}$.

COLLABORATIVE LEARNING

Whole Class Activity

Have students put masking tape around a few circular objects to mark the circumferences. Have them lay the masking tape pieces flat on the desk and measure the radius of each circular object. Then have them measure how many radii fit onto each tape piece by marking off each whole number of radii. Each should be a bit more than 6. Have students relate the number to the circumference formula. Students can then trace the circle onto paper, and put the masking tape back on the circle. Have them draw a central angle that is the width of one of these radius lengths. This is an angle that is one *radian angle,* or *radius,* wide.

Explain 1 Converting Between Degree Measure and Radian Measure

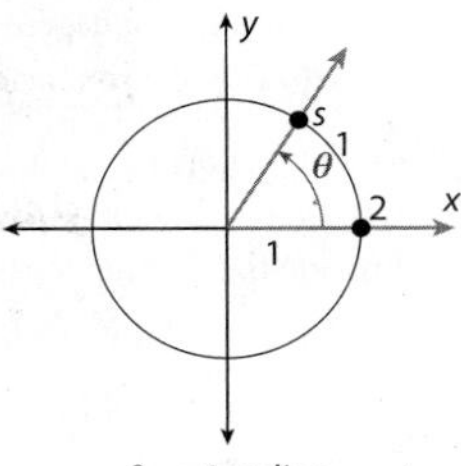

$\theta = 1$ radian

For a central angle θ that intercepts an arc of length s on a circle with radius r, the **radian measure** of the angle is the ratio $\theta = \frac{s}{r}$. In particular, on a *unit circle*, a circle centered at the origin with a radius of 1 unit, $\theta = s$. So, 1 *radian* is the angle that intercepts an arc of length 1 on a unit circle, as shown.

Recall that there are 360° in a full circle. Since the circumference of a circle of radius r is $s = 2\pi r$, the number of radians in a full circle is $\frac{2\pi r}{r} = 2\pi$. Therefore, $360° = 2\pi$ radians. So, $1° = \frac{2\pi}{360} = \frac{\pi}{180}$ radians and 1 radian $= \frac{360}{2\pi} = \frac{180}{\pi}$ degrees. This result is summed up in the following table.

CONVERTING DEGREES TO RADIANS	CONVERTING RADIANS TO DEGREES
Multiply the number of degrees by $\left(\frac{\pi \text{ radians}}{180°}\right)$.	Multiply the number of radians by $\left(\frac{180°}{\pi \text{ radians}}\right)$.

Example 1 Convert each measure from degrees to radians or from radians to degrees.

(A)

Degree measure	Radian measure
20°	$\frac{\pi}{180°} \cdot 20° = \frac{\pi}{9}$
315°	$\frac{\pi}{180°} \cdot 315° = \frac{7\pi}{4}$
600°	$\frac{\pi}{180°} \cdot 600° = \frac{10\pi}{3}$
−60°	$\frac{\pi}{180°} \cdot (-60°) = -\frac{\pi}{3}$
−540°	$\frac{\pi}{180°} \cdot (-540°) = -3\pi$

(B)

Radian measure	Degree measure
$\frac{\pi}{8}$	$\frac{180°}{\pi} \cdot \frac{\pi}{8} = $ 22.5°
$\frac{4\pi}{3}$	$\frac{180}{\pi} \cdot \frac{4\pi}{3} = $ 240°
$\frac{9\pi}{2}$	$\frac{180}{\pi} \cdot \frac{9\pi}{2} = 810°$
$-\frac{7\pi}{12}$	$\frac{180}{\pi} \cdot \left(-\frac{7\pi}{12}\right) = -105°$
$-\frac{13\pi}{6}$	$\frac{180}{\pi} \cdot \left(-\frac{13\pi}{6}\right) = -390°$

DIFFERENTIATE INSTRUCTION

Multiple Representations

Give students copies of blank unit circles to label. Suggest that students use colored pencils to help them organize the information. Over the course of the unit, have them add to the circle. For example, students might circle the measures of all angles with the same reference angle in the same color. Students can use their unit circles as references throughout this unit.

EXPLAIN 1

Converting Between Degree Measure and Radian Measure

CONNECT VOCABULARY EL

Help students differentiate between a *radian* and a *radius*. These two words can be easily confused when English learners are listening to explanations, especially because they associate the term *radius* with a circle.

INTEGRATE MATHEMATICAL PRACTICES

Focus on Math Connections

MP.1 Since the circumference of a circle C is equal to $2\pi r$, and a radian measure is $1r$, there are $2\pi \approx 6.283$ radians in a circle. Thus, a radian is between one seventh and one sixth of a circle.

QUESTIONING STRATEGIES

? What is the radian measure for a central angle of 180°? π

? If the radian measure is 1, what can you say about the arc length of the angle and the radius of the circle? They are equal.

? How can you check that you are using your conversion factor between degrees and radians correctly? When you convert an angle measure from degrees to radians, the ratio of the degree measure to the radian measure should be about 57.3°.

? As a quick check of your conversion, you can look at values. If $0° < d° < 180°$, between what values will the corresponding radians be? $0 < \theta < \pi$ If $180° < d° < 360°$, between what values will the corresponding radians be? $\pi < \theta < 2\pi$

Reflect

6. Which is larger, a degree or a radian? Explain.

A radian is larger, since it is equivalent to $\frac{180°}{\pi} \approx 57.3°$.

7. The unit circle below shows the measures of angles of rotation that are commonly used in trigonometry, with radian measures outside the circle and degree measures inside the circle. Provide the missing measures.

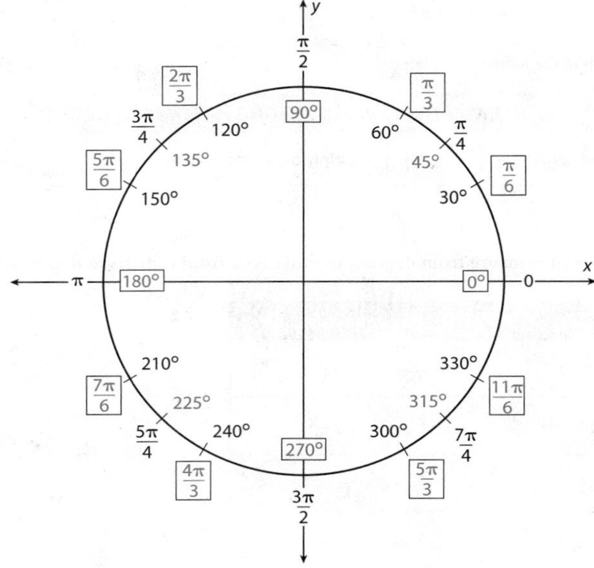

Your Turn

Convert each measure from degrees to radians or from radians to degrees.

8. −495°

$\frac{\pi}{180°} \cdot (-495°) = -\frac{11\pi}{4}$

9. $\frac{13\pi}{12}$

$\frac{180}{\pi} \cdot \left(\frac{13\pi}{12}\right) = 195°$

LANGUAGE SUPPORT EL

Communicate Math

Have students work in pairs to complete a table like the one below. Once students are familiar with radian measure, they can use this table as a reference throughout the lesson.

Term	Drawing or diagram	Explanation
1 radian angle in standard position		
Initial side		
Terminal side		
Coterminal angle		

Explain 2 Solving a Real-World Problem Involving Arc Length

As you saw in the first Explain, for a central angle θ in radian measure, $\theta = \frac{s}{r}$ where s is the intercepted arc length. Multiplying both sides of the equation by r gives the arc length formula for a circle:

Arc Length Formula
For a circle of radius r, the arc length s intercepted by a central angle θ (measured in radians) is given by the following formula. $$s = r\theta$$

Many problems involving arc length also involve *angular velocity*, which is the angle measure through which an object turns in a given time interval. For example, the second hand of a clock has an angular velocity of 360° per minute, or 6° per second. Angular velocity may also be expressed in radians per unit of time. This makes finding the arc length traversed in an amount of time especially easy by using the arc length formula.

 **The Sun** A point on the Sun's equator makes a full revolution once every 25.38 days. The Sun has a radius of about 432,200 miles at its equator. What is the angular velocity in radians per hour of a point on the Sun's equator? What distance around the sun's axis does the point travel in one hour? How does this compare with the distance of about 1038 miles traveled by a point on Earth's equator in an hour?

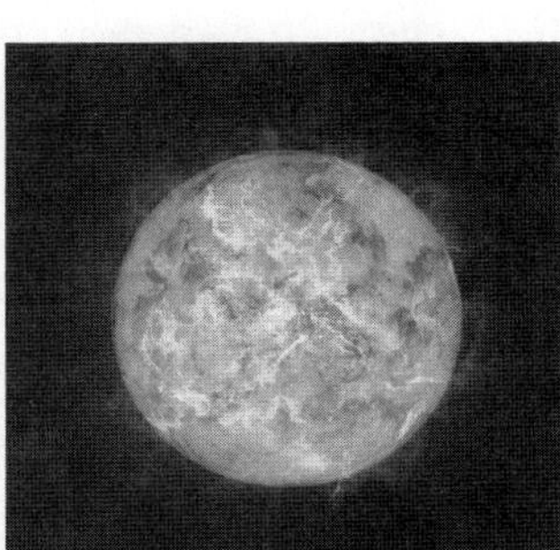

One revolution is 2π radians. The angular velocity in radians per day is $\frac{2\pi}{25.38}$. Convert this to radians per hour.

$$\frac{2\pi \text{ radians}}{25.38 \text{ days}} \cdot \frac{1 \text{ day}}{24 \text{ hours}} = \frac{2\pi \text{ radians}}{25.38(24) \text{ hours}}$$

$$\approx 0.01032 \text{ radians/h}$$

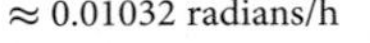

The distance the point travels in an hour is the arc length it traverses in an hour.

$$s = r\theta$$
$$= 432{,}200(0.01032)$$
$$\approx 4460$$

The point travels about 4460 miles around the Sun's axis in an hour. This is more than 4 times farther than a point on Earth's equator travels in the same time.

 **The Earth** Earth's equator is at a latitude of 0°. The Arctic circle is at a latitude of 66.52°N. The diameter of the equator is 7926 miles. The diameter of the Arctic circle is 3150 miles.

a. Find the angular velocity in degrees per minute of a point on the equator and of a point on the Arctic circle.

b. How far does a point on the Equator travel in 15 minutes?

c. How long will it take a point on the Arctic circle to travel this distance?

EXPLAIN 2

Solving a Real-World Problem Involving Arc Length

CONNECT VOCABULARY EL

The prefix *radi-* comes from the Latin word for *ray* and means *extending from a central location.* This meaning is seen in words such as *radius, radiate, radial,* and *radio.*

AVOID COMMON ERRORS

Some students may think that multiplying the diameter of a circle by some number n either multiplies both the arc length and radian measure by n or leaves both unchanged. Remind them that when $n \neq 1$, multiplying by n multiplies arc length by n but leaves the radian measure unchanged.

QUESTIONING STRATEGIES

? How could you find average angular speed? **Divide the total number of degrees in a rotation by the time in which the rotation occurred.**

INTEGRATE MATHEMATICAL PRACTICES

Focus on Math Connections

MP.1 The number of radians in a central angle of a circle is the measure of the intercepted arc in radian units.

a. Every point on Earth completes 1 revolution of **360** degrees each 24 hours, so the angular velocities of the points will be the same. Convert the angular velocity to degrees per minute.

$$\frac{\boxed{360}^\circ}{\boxed{24}\text{ h}} \cdot \frac{1\text{ h}}{60\text{ min}} = \frac{\boxed{360}^\circ}{24(60)\text{ min}} = \boxed{0.25}\,^\circ/\text{min}$$

The angular velocity is $\boxed{0.25}^\circ$/min.

b. Multiply the time by the angular velocity to find the angle through which a point rotates in 15 minutes.

$$\boxed{15}\text{ min} \cdot 0.25^\circ/\text{min} = \boxed{3.75}^\circ$$

Write a proportion to find the distance to the nearest tenth that this represents at the equator, where Earth's circumference is $\boxed{\pi} \cdot 7926$ miles.

$$\frac{3.75^\circ}{\boxed{360}^\circ} = \frac{x\text{ mi}}{\boxed{\pi} \cdot 7926\text{ mi}}$$

$$x = \frac{3.75\pi(7926)}{360}$$

$$x \approx \boxed{259.4}$$

A point at the equator travels about **259.4** miles in 15 minutes.

c. Write a proportion to find the angle of rotation to the nearest thousandth required to move a point 259.4 miles on the Arctic circle, where the circumference is $\boxed{\pi} \cdot 3150$ miles.

$$\frac{259.4\text{ mi}}{\boxed{\pi} \cdot 3150\text{ mi}} = \frac{x^\circ}{\boxed{360}^\circ}$$

$$x = \frac{259.4(360)}{3150\pi}$$

$$x \approx \boxed{9.437}$$

Use the angular velocity to find the time t to the nearest hundredth required for a point on the Arctic circle to move through an angle of rotation of 9.437°.

$$\left(\boxed{0.25}^\circ/\text{min}\right)(t\text{ min}) = 9.437^\circ$$

$$t \approx \boxed{37.75}$$

It takes about **37.75** minutes for a point on the Arctic circle to travel the same distance that a point on the equator travels in 15 minutes.

Reflect

10. How does using an angle of rotation to find the length of the arc on a circle intercepted by the angle differ when degrees are used from when radians are used?

When radians are used, you can find the arc length by simply multiplying the radius of the circle times the angle. When degrees are used, you must write a proportion equating the ratio of the measure of the angle to 360 degrees and the ratio of the unknown arc length to the circumference of the circle. Then you can solve for the arc length.

Your Turn

11. **Astronomy** A neutron star (an incredibly dense collapsed star) in the Sagittarius Galaxy has a radius of 10 miles and completes a full revolution every 0.0014 seconds. Find the angular velocity of the star in radians per second, then use this velocity to determine how far a point on the equator of the star travels each second. How does this compare to the speed of light (about 186,000 mi/sec)?

Find the angular velocity.

$\frac{2\pi \text{ radians}}{0.0014 \text{ second}} \approx 4490$ **radians/second**

The distance the point travels in a second is the arc length it traverses in a second.

$s = r\theta = 10(4490) \approx 45{,}000$

The point travels about 45,000 miles around the star's axis in one second. Because $\frac{45{,}000}{186{,}000} \approx 0.24$, **this is about one fourth the speed of light.**

12. **Geography** The northeastern corner of Maine is due north of the southern tip of South America in Chile. The difference in latitude between the locations is 103°. Using both degree measure and radian measure, and a north-south circumference of Earth of 24,860 miles, find the distance between the two locations.

Using degrees:

$\frac{103°}{360°} = \frac{x \text{ mi}}{24{,}860 \text{ mi}}$

$360x = 103(24{,}860)$

$x = \frac{103(24{,}860)}{360}$

$x \approx 7110$

The distance is about 7100 miles.

Using radians:

First convert to radians.

$\frac{\pi}{180°} \cdot 103° = \frac{103\pi}{180}$

Use the arc length formula.

$S = r\theta = \frac{24{,}860}{2\pi}\left(\frac{103\pi}{180}\right) \approx 7110$

The distance is about 7100 miles.

Elaborate

13. Given the measure of two angles of rotation, how can you determine whether they are coterminal without actually drawing the angles?

If the difference between the angles is an integer multiple of 360 degrees or 2π radians, then they are coterminal angles.

14. What is the conversion factor to go from degrees to radians? What is the conversion factor to go from radians to degrees? How are the conversion factors related?

The conversion factor to go from degrees to radians is $\frac{\pi \text{ radians}}{180°}$, while the conversion factor to go from radians to degrees is $\frac{180°}{\pi \text{ radians}}$. The two conversion factors are reciprocals of each other.

15. **Essential Question Check-In** What is the relationship between a circle with radius 1 centered at the origin and the measure of an angle of rotation with endpoint at the origin of 1 radian?

The angle of rotation that intercepts an arc whose length is 1 on this circle has a measure of 1 radian. So, there are 2π radians in a full rotation.

ELABORATE

INTEGRATE MATHEMATICAL PRACTICES

Focus on Math Connections

MP.1 Point out to students that they can convert between degrees and radians by using the proportion $\frac{r \text{ radians}}{\pi \text{ radians}} = \frac{d \text{ degrees}}{180 \text{ degrees}}$, where r is the measure of an angle θ in radians and d is its measure in degrees.

QUESTIONING STRATEGIES

? When determining angular velocity, is it better to have the angle measure in degrees or radians? **in radians, because you can directly convert to arc length**

SUMMARIZE THE LESSON

? How can the unit circle be used to determine arc length for a circle with radius r? Explain. **The unit circle has a radius of 1 and a circumference of 2π. An angle of rotation that intercepts an arc on the unit circle whose length is 1 has a measure defined as 1 radian, so for an arc on a circle with radius r, there are $2\pi r$ radians in an angle that makes one full revolution.**

EVALUATE

ASSIGNMENT GUIDE

Concepts and Skills	Practice
Explore 1 Drawing Angles of Rotation and Finding Coterminal Angles	Exercises 15–17
Explore 2 Understanding Radian Measure	Exercise 21
Example 1 Converting Between Degree Measure and Radian Measure	Exercises 1–8, 14
Example 2 Solving a Real-World Problem Involving Arc Length	Exercises 9–13

CONNECT VOCABULARY EL

Make sure students can articulate what makes a unit circle distinct from just any circle drawn on the coordinate plane. Help them make connections and increase their mathematical vocabularies by using the terms *origin, coordinate plane, x*- and *y-axes* and so on, as you help them explain.

Evaluate: Homework and Practice

- Online Homework
- Hints and Help
- Extra Practice

Draw the indicated angle of rotation in standard position.

1. A positive angle coterminal to 130°

Possible answer:

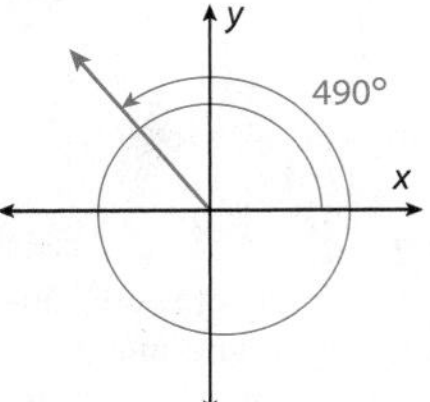

2. A negative angle coterminal to 130°

Possible answer:

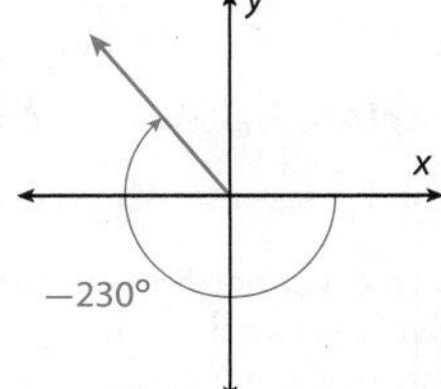

For each angle, find the nearest two positive coterminal angles and the nearest two negative coterminal angles.

3. 84°

$84° + 360° = 444°, 84° + 2(360°) = 804°,$
$84° - 360° = -276°, 84° - 2(360°) = -636°$

4. 420°

$420° - 360° = 60°, 420° + 360° = 780°,$
$420° - 2(360°) = -300°, 420° - 3(360°) = -$

5. $-\frac{\pi}{3}$

$-\frac{\pi}{3} + 2\pi = \frac{5\pi}{3}, -\frac{\pi}{3} + 2(2\pi) = \frac{11\pi}{3},$
$-\frac{\pi}{3} - 2\pi = -\frac{7\pi}{3}, -\frac{\pi}{3} - 2(2\pi) = -\frac{13\pi}{3}$

6. $\frac{5\pi}{2}$

$\frac{5\pi}{2} - 2\pi = \frac{\pi}{2}, \frac{5\pi}{2} + 2\pi = \frac{9\pi}{2},$
$\frac{5\pi}{2} - 2(2\pi) = -\frac{3\pi}{2}, \frac{5\pi}{2} - 3(2\pi) = -\frac{7\pi}{2}$

Convert each measure from degrees to radians or from radians to degrees.

7. 70°

$\frac{\pi}{180°} \cdot 70° = \frac{7\pi}{18}$

8. −270°

$\frac{\pi}{180°} \cdot (-270°) = -\frac{3\pi}{2}$

9. −945°

$\frac{\pi}{180°} \cdot (-945°) = -\frac{21\pi}{4}, \text{ or } -5\frac{1}{4}\pi$

10. 2160°

$\frac{\pi}{180°} \cdot 2160° = 12\pi$

11. $\frac{33\pi}{18}$

$\frac{180°}{\pi} \cdot \frac{33\pi}{18} = 330°$

12. $\frac{11\pi}{4}$

$\frac{180°}{\pi} \cdot \frac{11\pi}{4} = 495°$

13. $-\frac{5\pi}{3}$

$\frac{180°}{\pi} \cdot \left(-\frac{5\pi}{3}\right) = -300°$

14. $-\frac{7\pi}{2}$

$\frac{180°}{\pi} \cdot \left(-\frac{7\pi}{2}\right) = -630°$

Exercise	Depth of Knowledge (D.O.K.)	COMMON CORE Mathematical Practices
1–8	**1** Recall of Information	**MP.7** Using Structure
9–10	**1** Recall of Information	**MP.2** Reasoning
11–12	**2** Skills/Concepts	**MP.2** Reasoning
13	**3** Strategic Thinking	**MP.2** Reasoning
14	**1** Recall of Information	**MP.5** Using Tools
15–17	**1** Recall of Information	**MP.4** Modeling

15. Geography A student in the United States has an friend overseas with whom she corresponds by computer. The foreign student says, "If you write the latitude and longitude of my school in radians instead of degrees, you get the coordinates 0.6227 radians north latitude and 2.438 radians east longitude". Convert the coordinates back to degrees. Then use a globe, map, or app to identify the city.

$\frac{180°}{\pi \text{ radians}} \cdot 0.6227 \text{ radians} = 35.68°;$

$\frac{180°}{\pi \text{ radians}} \cdot 2.438 \text{ radians} = 139.69°$

The coordinates are 35.68° north latitude and 139.69° east longitude. The school is in Tokyo, Japan.

16. Geography If a ship sailed due south from Iceland to Antarctica, it would sail through an angle of rotation of about 140° around Earth's center. Find this measure in radians. Then, using 3960 miles for Earth's radius, find how far the ship would travel.

$\frac{\pi \text{ radians}}{180°} \cdot 140° = \frac{7\pi}{9} \text{ radians}; s = r\theta = 3960 \cdot \frac{7\pi}{9} \approx 9700;$

The ship would travel about 9700 miles.

17. Geography Acapulco, Mexico and Hyderabad, India both lie at 17° north latitude, and lie very nearly halfway around the world from each other in an east-west direction. The radius of Earth at a latitude of 17° is about 3790 miles. Suppose that you could fly from Acapulco directly west to Hyderabad or fly directly north to Hyderabad. Which way would be shorter, and by how much? Use 3960 miles for Earth's radius. (Hint: To fly directly north, you would go from 17° north latitude to 90° north latitude, and then back down to 17° north latitude.)

Flying west, the plane goes halfway around a circle with radius of 3790 miles:

$\frac{1}{2} \cdot 2\pi r = \pi r = \pi \cdot 3790 \approx 11{,}900 \text{ mi}$

Flying north, the plane travels over an angle of rotation of $2(90° - 17°) = 146°$.

$\frac{146°}{360°} = \frac{x \text{ mi}}{2\pi \cdot 3960 \text{ mi}} \rightarrow x \approx 10{,}100 \text{ mi}$

It would be about 11,900 − 10,100 = 1800 miles shorter to fly over the North Pole.

Exercise	Depth of Knowledge (D.O.K.)	COMMON CORE Mathematical Practices
18	**1** Recall of Information	**MP.5** Using Tools
19	**3** Strategic Thinking	**MP.3** Logic
20–23	**2** Skills/Concepts	**MP.3** Logic
24, 26–27	**3** Strategic Thinking H.O.T.	**MP.3** Logic
25	**2** Skills/Concepts H.O.T.	**MP.1** Problem Solving

KINESTHETIC EXPERIENCE

Have students sit in a circle around a clearly labeled set of x- and y-axes on the floor. Call out an angle and have the student closest to that angle measure stand up. Be sure to call both positive and negative angles.

AVOID COMMON ERRORS

Students who commonly make errors in calculations should always go back to the basic relationship $360° = 2\pi$ radians, or about 6.28 radians, to help them form a rough estimate of the size of the answer before they calculate.

INTEGRATE MATHEMATICAL PRACTICES

Focus on Critical Thinking

MP.3 Remind students to check that their answers are reasonable. When comparing the rotations of two spheres where one is much larger than the other but has a shorter rotational period, the second body should rotate through a much smaller angle than does the first, in the same period of time.

18. Planetary Exploration "Opportunity" and "Phoenix" are two of the robotic explorers on Mars. Opportunity landed at 2° south latitude, where Mars' radius is about 2110 miles. Phoenix landed at 68° north latitude, where Mars' radius is about 790 miles. Mars rotates on its axis once every 24.6 Earth-hours. How far does each explorer travel as Mars rotates by 1 radian? How many hours does it take Mars to rotate 1 radian? Using this answer, how fast is each explorer traveling around Mars' axis in miles per hour?

The distance s is given by the formula $s = r\theta$. Because $\theta = 1$, this is just $s = r$. So, Opportunity travels 2110 miles and Phoenix travels 790 miles.

Mars rotates 2π radians every 24.6 hours. So, its angular velocity is $\frac{2\pi \text{ radians}}{24.6 \text{ h}} \approx 0.2554$ radians/h. Find the time t to rotate 1 radian.

$$(t \text{ h})(0.2554 \text{ radians/h}) = 1 \text{ radian}$$
$$t = \frac{1}{0.2554}$$
$$t \approx 3.92$$

It takes about 3.92 hours to rotate one radian.

Opportunity: $\frac{2110 \text{ mi}}{3.92 \text{ h}} \approx 540$ **mi/h**

Phoenix: $\frac{790 \text{ mi}}{3.92 \text{ h}} \approx 200$ **mi/h**

19. Earth's Rotation The 40th parallel of north latitude runs across the United States through Philadelphia, Indianapolis, and Denver. At this latitude, Earth's radius is about 3030 miles. The earth rotates with an angular velocity of $\frac{\pi}{12}$ radians (or 15°) per hour toward the east. If a jet flies due west with the same angular velocity relative to the ground at the equinox, the sun as viewed from the jet will stop in the sky. How fast in miles per hour would the jet have to travel west at the 40th parallel for this to happen?

By the arc length formula, the number of miles represented by an angle of $\frac{\pi}{12}$ radians where Earth's radius is 3030 miles is $s = r\theta = 3030\left(\frac{\pi}{12}\right) \approx 793$. The jet would have to fly about 793 mi/h.

20. Our Galaxy It is about 30,000 light years from our solar system to the center of the Milky Way Galaxy. The solar system revolves around the center of the Milky Way with an angular velocity of about 2.6×10^{-8} radians per year.

a. What distance does the solar system travel in its orbit each year?

b. Given that a light year is about 5.88×10^{12} miles, how fast is the solar system circling the center of the galaxy in miles per hour?

a. $s = r\theta = 30{,}000(2.6 \times 10^{-8}) \approx 7.8 \times 10^{-4}$ **light years**

b. $\left(\frac{7.8 \times 10^{-4} \text{ light years}}{\text{year}}\right)\left(\frac{5.88 \times 10^{12} \text{ mi}}{\text{light year}}\right)\left(\frac{1 \text{ year}}{365 \text{ days}}\right)\left(\frac{1 \text{ day}}{24 \text{ h}}\right) \approx 520{,}000$ **mi/hr**

21. **Driving** A windshield wiper blade turns through an angle of 135°. The bottom of the blade traces an arc with a 9-inch radius. The top of the blade traces an arc with a 23-inch radius. To the nearest inch, how much longer is the top arc than the bottom arc?

Notice that is 135° is $\frac{\pi}{180} \cdot 135 = \frac{3\pi}{4}$ radians.

Top arc: $s = r\theta = 23\left(\frac{3\pi}{4}\right) \approx 54.2$

Bottom arc: $s = r\theta = 9\left(\frac{3\pi}{4}\right) \approx 21.2$

The difference is $54.2 - 21.2 = 33$ inches.

22. **Cycling** You are riding your bicycle, which has tires with a 30-inch diameter, at a steady 15 miles per hour. What is the angular velocity of a point on the outside of the tire in radians per second?

Convert miles per hour to inches per second.

$$\left(\frac{15\text{ mi}}{1\text{ hr}}\right)\left(\frac{5280\text{ ft}}{1\text{ mi}}\right)\left(\frac{12\text{ in.}}{1\text{ ft}}\right)\left(\frac{1\text{ hr}}{60\text{ min}}\right)\left(\frac{1\text{ min}}{60\text{ sec}}\right) = 264\text{ in./sec}$$

A point on the tire travels 264 inches in one second.

The circumference of the tire is $C = \pi d = 30\pi$ in.

Find the number of revolutions per second that the tire makes.

$$\frac{264\text{ in./sec}}{30\pi\text{ in./revolution}} \simeq 2.80\text{ revolutions/sec}$$

Convert revolutions per second to radians per second.

$$\frac{2.80\text{ revolutions}}{1\text{ sec}}\left(\frac{2\pi\text{ radians}}{1\text{ revolution}}\right) = 5.6\pi\text{ radians/sec}$$

23. Select all angles that are coterminal with an angle of rotation of 300°.

A. −420°

B. 2100°

C. −900°

D. $-\frac{\pi}{3}$ radians

E. $\frac{23\pi}{3}$ radians

F. $-\frac{7\pi}{3}$ radians

A, B, D, E, F

Note that $\frac{\pi}{180°} \cdot 300° = \frac{5\pi}{3}$ radians.

A. $-420° = 300° - 2(360°)$

B. $2100° = 300° + 5(360°)$

C. −900° falls between $300° - 3(360°) = -780°$ and $300° - 4(360°) = -1140°$.

D. $-\frac{\pi}{3} = \frac{5\pi}{3} - 2\pi$

E. $\frac{23\pi}{3} = \frac{5\pi}{3} + 6\pi$

F. $-\frac{7\pi}{3} = \frac{5\pi}{3} - 4\pi$

H.O.T. Focus on Higher Order Thinking

24. **Explain the Error** Lisa was told that a portion of the restaurant on the Space Needle in Seattle rotates at a rate of 8 radians per hour. When asked to find the distance through which she would travel if she sat at a table 40 feet from the center of rotation for a meal lasting 2 hours, she produced the following result:

$\theta = \frac{s}{r}$

$8 = \frac{s}{40}$

$320 = s$ The distance is 320 feet.

Lisa did the calculation correctly in finding the distance per hour, but because the meal lasted two hours, the total distance is the rate times the time, or 640 feet.

INTEGRATE MATHEMATICAL PRACTICES

Focus on Math Connections

MP.1 Emphasize that radian measures are often written with fractions. This notation has the advantage of giving exact values instead of decimal approximations. However, when measuring lengths or distances in an actual situation, the decimal value may be required.

JOURNAL

Have students write a journal entry describing what radian measure is, how it is used, and showing how to convert between radians and degrees. Students should explain the conversion formulas in words.

25. Represent Real-World Problems The minute hand on a clock has an angular velocity of 2π radians/hour, while the hour hand has an angular velocity of $\frac{\pi}{6}$ radians/hour. At 12:00, the hour and second hands both point straight up. The two hands will next come back together sometime after 1:00. At what exact time will this happen? (Hint: You want to find the next time when the angle of rotation made by the hour hand is coterminal with the angle made by the minute hand after it has first completed one full revolution.)

Let t represent the number of hours after 12:00. Then the minute hand rotates $2\pi t$ radians in t hours and the hour hand rotates $\frac{\pi}{6}t$ radians in the same time. The hands will come together after the hour hand has gone $\frac{\pi}{6}t$ radians and the minute hand has gone one full revolution of 2π radians plus the $\frac{\pi}{6}t$ radians that the hour hand has moved. This gives us a second expression for the angle of rotation of the minute hand from 12:00 until the hands next come together. Equate the expressions and solve for t.

$$2\pi t = 2\pi + \frac{\pi}{6}t$$
$$2t = 2 + \frac{1}{6}t$$
$$12t = 12 + t$$
$$11t = 12$$
$$t = \frac{12}{11}$$

The hands will come together after $1\frac{1}{11}$ hours. Because $\frac{1}{11}\text{ h} = \frac{60}{11} = 5\frac{5}{11}$ min, this is about halfway between 1:05 and 1:06.

26. Critical Thinking Write a single rational expression that can be used to represent all angles that are coterminal with an angle of $\frac{5\pi}{8}$ radians.

The angles will have the form $\frac{5\pi}{8} + n(2\pi)$ where n is an integer representing a number of revolutions, positive or negative, around the unit circle. Then: $\frac{5\pi}{8} + n(2\pi) = \frac{5\pi}{8} + \frac{8 \cdot n(2\pi)}{8} + \frac{5\pi + 16\pi n}{8}$, or $\frac{(5 + 16n)\pi}{8}$.

27. Extension You know that the length s of the arc intercepted on a circle of radius r by an angle of rotation of θ radians is $s = r\theta$. Find an expression for the area of the sector of the circle with radius r that has a central angle of θ radians. Explain your reasoning.

$\frac{1}{2}r^2\theta$; A full circle has an area of πr^2. A full circle is 2π radians, so an angle of θ radians is $\frac{\theta}{2\pi}$ of the circle. Find the portion of the area of a full circle that this represents: $\frac{\theta}{2\pi} \cdot \pi r^2 \frac{\theta}{2} \cdot r^2 = \frac{1}{2}r^2\theta$.

Lesson Performance Task

At a space exploration center, astronauts are training on a human centrifuge that has a diameter of 70 feet.

a. The centrifuge makes 72 complete revolutions in 2 minutes. What is the angular velocity of the centrifuge in radians per second? What distance does an astronaut travel around the center each second?

Find the number of revolutions per second.

$\frac{72 \text{ revolutions}}{2 \text{ min}} \cdot \frac{1 \text{ min}}{60 \text{ s}} = \frac{3}{5} \text{ revolution/s}$

Because 1 revolution is 2π radians, $\frac{3}{5}$ revolution is $\frac{3}{5} \cdot 2\pi = \frac{6\pi}{5}$ radians.

Find the length of the arc intercepted by an angle of $\frac{6\pi}{5}$ radians for a circle with a radius of $75 \div 2 = 35$ feet.

$s = r\theta = 35\left(\frac{6\pi}{5}\right) = 42\pi \approx 132$

The astronaut travels about 132 feet each second.

b. Acceleration is the rate of change of velocity with time. An object moving at a constant velocity v in circular motion with a radius of r has an acceleration a of $a = \frac{v^2}{r}$. What is the astronaut's acceleration? (Note that the acceleration will have units of feet per second *squared*.)

To find acceleration, first find the velocity. To do this, divide the number of feet traveled by the number of seconds elapsed.

$a = \frac{v^2}{r} = \frac{(42\pi \text{ ft/s})^2}{35 \text{ ft}} \approx 497 \text{ ft/s}^2$

The acceleration is about 497 ft/s².

c. One "g" is the acceleration caused on Earth's surface by gravity. This acceleration is what gives you your weight. Some roller coasters can produce an acceleration in a tight loop of 5 or even 6 g's. Earth's gravity produces an acceleration of 32 ft/s². How many g's is the astronaut experiencing in the centrifuge?

Convert 497 ft/s² to g's.

$497 \text{ ft/s}^2 \cdot \frac{1 \text{ g}}{32 \text{ ft/s}^2} \approx 15.5 \text{ g}$

The astronaut is experiencing about 15.5 g's.

EXTENSION ACTIVITY

Have students research the centrifugal forces created by spinning amusement park rides; how the rides are designed for safety; and why only healthy adults are allowed to ride them. Students may need to determine the relationship between *g* forces and the centrifugal forces of rotational acceleration. Have students present their findings to the class.

AVOID COMMON ERRORS

When converting, some students may be confused by the acceleration units ft/s² and m/s² due to the "per second squared" notation. Explain that, in converting, these units cancel, so this conversion is like, for example, converting feet to meters.

INTEGRATE MATHEMATICAL PRACTICES

Focus on Critical Thinking

MP.3 Students can solve for the number of revolutions in several ways. They may first see that 30 seconds is $\frac{1}{4}$ of 2 minutes, or convert both units to minutes. Encourage students to do this but to use a formal thinking process they can repeat for more complicated numbers. Have students share equivalent methods.

Scoring Rubric

2 points: Student correctly solves the problem and explains his/her reasoning.

1 point: Student shows good understanding of the problem but does not fully solve or explain his/her reasoning.

0 points: Student does not demonstrate understanding of the problem.

LESSON 17.2

Defining and Evaluating the Basic Trigonometric Functions

Common Core Math Standards

The student is expected to:

F-TF.A.2

Explain how the unit circle in the coordinate plane enables the extension of trigonometric functions to all real numbers, interpreted as radian measures of angles traversed counterclockwise around the unit circle. Also F-TF.A.3(+)

Mathematical Practices

MP.7 Using Structure

Language Objective

Label sine, cosine, and tangent in right triangles drawn within a unit circle.

ENGAGE

Essential Question: How does the unit circle allow the trigonometric functions to be defined for all real numbers instead of just for acute angles?

Possible answer: If a right triangle is formed in a unit circle with its base along the positive x-axis and its hypotenuse from the origin to the point (x, y) where the terminal side of an acute angle of rotation intersects the unit circle, the cosine of the angle is x and the sine of the angle is y. Defining the cosine and sine functions as the value of x and the value of y of this point on the unit circle for any real number angle of rotation in radians allows you to extend these functions to all real numbers. The tangent function is then defined as the ratio of y to x, and so is defined for all real numbers whose cosine is nonzero.

Name ________ Class ________ Date ________

17.2 Defining and Evaluating the Basic Trigonometric Functions

Resource Locker

Essential Question: How does the unit circle allow the trigonometric functions to be defined for all real numbers instead of just for acute angles?

Explore Using Special Right Triangles in a Unit Circle

In geometry, you learned that sine, cosine, and tangent are ratios of the lengths of the sides of a right triangle. In particular, if θ is an acute angle in a right triangle, then:

$$\sin\theta = \frac{\text{length of the opposite leg}}{\text{length of the hypotenuse}}$$

$$\cos\theta = \frac{\text{length of the adjacent leg}}{\text{length of the hypotenuse}}$$

$$\tan\theta = \frac{\text{length of the opposite leg}}{\text{length of the adjacent leg}}$$

You also studied two sets of special right triangles: those with angles of 45°—45°—90° and those with angles 30° —60° —90°, and found a general relationship for the lengths of the three sides in each type of triangle:

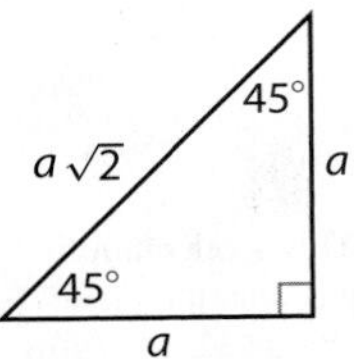

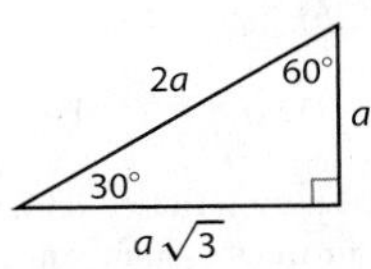

The variable, a, can take any positive value. To see how these triangles and the values of sine, cosine, and tangent for their angles relate to the unit circle, the hypotenuse must have a length of 1. This corresponds to leg lengths of $\frac{\sqrt{2}}{2}$ for the 45° —45° —90° triangle, and leg lengths of $\frac{\sqrt{3}}{2}$ and $\frac{1}{2}$ for the 30° —60° —90° triangle.

(A) A 45° —45° —90° triangle has been inscribed inside a unit circle.

- Sketch the result of reflecting the triangle across the y-axis.
- Sketch the result of reflecting the triangle across the x-axis.
- Sketch the result of reflecting the triangle across both axes.

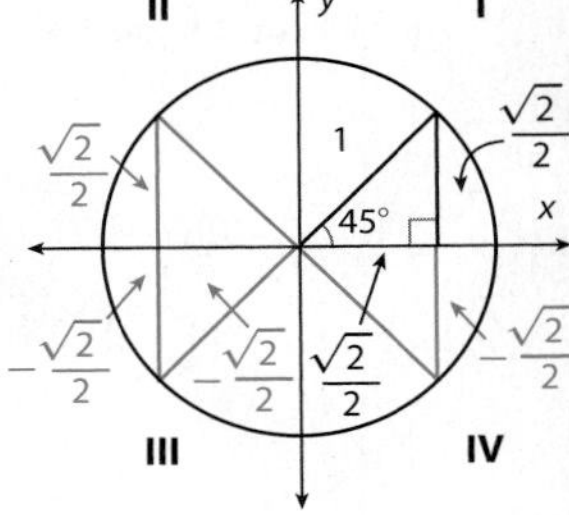

HARDCOVER PAGES 839–852

Watch for the hardcover student edition page numbers for this lesson.

You should have a triangle in each of the four quadrants.

- For each triangle you drew, indicate the *signed* length of each leg. For example, a leg pointing left or down from the x- or y-axis should have a negative value.

Use the signed lengths of the legs and the ratios associated with the trigonometric functions to fill in the table.

	Quadrant I $0° < \theta < 90°$	Quadrant II $90° < \theta < 180°$	Quadrant III $180° < \theta < 270°$	Quadrant IV $270° < \theta < 360°$
Angle of rotation, θ	45°	135°	225°	315°
$\sin\theta$	$\frac{\sqrt{2}}{2}$	$\frac{\sqrt{2}}{2}$	$-\frac{\sqrt{2}}{2}$	$-\frac{\sqrt{2}}{2}$
$\cos\theta$	$\frac{\sqrt{2}}{2}$	$-\frac{\sqrt{2}}{2}$	$-\frac{\sqrt{2}}{2}$	$\frac{\sqrt{2}}{2}$
$\tan\theta$	1	-1	1	-1

(B) Repeat the process from Step A for the 30° —60° —90° triangle that has been inscribed in the unit circle.

- Sketch the three reflected triangles and label the signed lengths of the legs.
- Use the signed lengths of the legs and the ratios associated with the trigonometric functions to fill in the table.

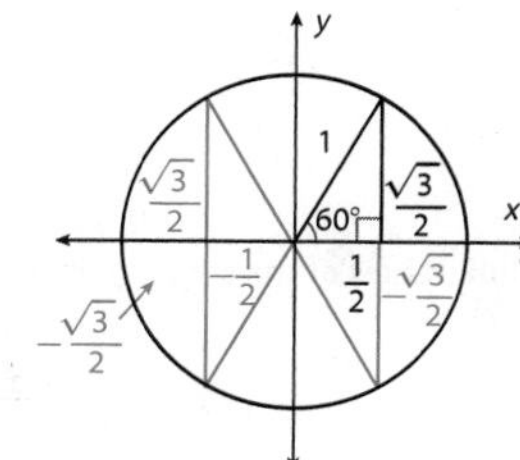

	Quadrant I $0° < \theta < 90°$	Quadrant II $90° < \theta < 180°$	Quadrant III $180° < \theta < 270°$	Quadrant IV $270° < \theta < 360°$
Angle of rotation, θ	60°	120°	240°	300°
$\sin\theta$	$\frac{\sqrt{3}}{2}$	$\frac{\sqrt{3}}{2}$	$-\frac{\sqrt{3}}{2}$	$-\frac{\sqrt{3}}{2}$
$\cos\theta$	$\frac{1}{2}$	$-\frac{1}{2}$	$-\frac{1}{2}$	$\frac{1}{2}$
$\tan\theta$	$\sqrt{3}$	$-\sqrt{3}$	$\sqrt{3}$	$-\sqrt{3}$

PROFESSIONAL DEVELOPMENT

Math Background

The sine, cosine, and tangent functions—sometimes called *circular functions*—are used when modeling periodic motion. Periodic motion has a pattern that is repeated at regular intervals. Examples include the swinging of a pendulum and the progress of a wave (light, sound, or ocean wave).

This lesson connects students' past experience with triangle trigonometry to the study of circular trigonometry. Later in the unit, students will investigate real-world applications of trigonometry involving periodic phenomena.

PREVIEW: LESSON PERFORMANCE TASK

View the online Engage. Discuss the photo of the racetrack and the fact that you can find relative positions along the track by overlaying a coordinate system on top of it. Then preview the Lesson Performance Task.

EXPLORE

Using Special Right Triangles in a Unit Circle

INTEGRATE TECHNOLOGY

Students have the option of completing the Explore activity either in the book or online.

QUESTIONING STRATEGIES

? How does reflecting the triangle across the y-axis affect the signed leg lengths? The length of the horizontal leg becomes the opposite of the original value; the length of the vertical leg remains the same.

? How does reflecting the triangle across the x-axis affect the signed leg lengths? The length of the vertical leg becomes the opposite of the original value; the length of the horizontal leg remains the same.

INTEGRATE MATHEMATICAL PRACTICES

Focus on Patterns

MP.8 Have students look for patterns in the tables that they create for the 30° and 60° angles. Have students use what they know about special right triangles to explain the patterns in the values. Students can also use what they've learned about angles of rotation to make generalizations about the patterns in the signs.

Ⓒ Repeat the process for this 30° —60° —90° triangle that has been inscribed in the unit circle.

- Sketch the three reflected triangles and label the signed lengths of the legs.
- Use the signed lengths of the legs and the ratios associated with the trigonometric functions to fill in the table.

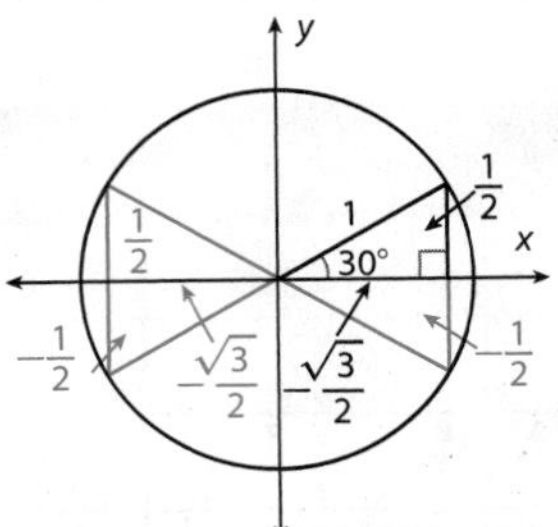

	Quadrant I $0° < \theta < 90°$	Quadrant II $90° < \theta < 180°$	Quadrant III $180° < \theta < 270°$	Quadrant IV $270° < \theta < 360°$
Angle of rotation, θ	30°	150°	210°	330°
$\sin\theta$	$\frac{1}{2}$	$\frac{1}{2}$	$-\frac{1}{2}$	$-\frac{1}{2}$
$\cos\theta$	$\frac{\sqrt{3}}{2}$	$-\frac{\sqrt{3}}{2}$	$-\frac{\sqrt{3}}{2}$	$\frac{\sqrt{3}}{2}$
$\tan\theta$	$\frac{\sqrt{3}}{3}$	$-\frac{\sqrt{3}}{3}$	$\frac{\sqrt{3}}{3}$	$-\frac{\sqrt{3}}{3}$

Reflect

1. What do you observe about the absolute values of the trigonometric functions in any row of each table?
   They are the same.

2. Identify which quadrants have positive values for $\sin\theta$ and which quadrants have negative values. Do the same for $\cos\theta$ and $\tan\theta$.
   $\sin\theta$: Quadrants I and II have positive values and Quadrants III and IV have negative values.
   $\cos\theta$: Quadrants I and IV have positive values and Quadrants II and III have negative values.
   $\tan\theta$: Quadrants I and III have positive values and Quadrants II and IV have negative values.

3. How do the signed lengths of the triangles' legs relate to the point where the triangle intersects the unit circle? Use this to relate the coordinates of the intersection points to the trigonometric functions of the angle, θ.
   The signed horizontal lengths are the x-coordinates of the points and the signed vertical lengths are the y-coordinates of the points. Because all four triangles have a hypotenuse length of 1, the x-coordinates also represent $\cos\theta$ and the y-coordinates also represent $\sin\theta$ at the points where the rotation angle intersects the unit circle.

COLLABORATIVE LEARNING

Peer-to-Peer Activity

Have students work in pairs. Instruct each pair to identify four angles whose terminal sides lie in different quadrants, each of which has a special angle for a reference angle. Insist that not all of the angles have the same reference angle. Then have each pair create a poster illustrating how to find the values of the sine, cosine, and tangent of each angle (without the use of a calculator). Have pairs share their work with the class.

Explain 1 Evaluating the Basic Trigonometric Functions for Special Angles

In the Explore, each of the reflected triangles has an inner angle with a vertex on the center of the circle whose measure is equal to the measure of the corresponding angle of the original triangle. These four angles serve as *reference angles* for the rotation angles listed in the table. This concept can be extended to any rotation angle.

The **reference angle** of a rotation angle is the acute angle from the terminal side of the rotation angle to the x-axis.

For rotation angles that represent less than one full revolution $\left(0° \leq \theta < 360° \text{ or } 0 \leq \theta < 2\pi\right)$ the measure of the reference angle can be found using a quadrant dependent formula. The quadrant also determines the signs of the trigonometric function. The formulas and signs are summarized in the table.

	Reference angle (θ')		Sign		
Quadrant	**Degrees**	**Radians**	**Sin**	**Cos**	**Tan**
I	$\theta' = \theta$	$\theta' = \theta$	+	+	+
II	$\theta' = 180° - \theta$	$\theta' = \pi - \theta$	+	−	−
III	$\theta' = \theta - 180°$	$\theta' = \theta - \pi$	−	−	+
IV	$\theta' = 360° - \theta$	$\theta' = 2\pi - \theta$	−	+	−

To find the values of the trigonometric functions of an angle θ you can use the ratios from the reference angle to find the absolute values of the functions, and then you can use the quadrant to determine the sign of the functions.

What about rotation angles larger than a full rotation? You have already observed that the values of $\cos\theta$ and $\sin\theta$ match the x- and y-coordinates where the terminal side of the angle intersects the circle.

Using this as the definition for sine and cosine, and including the definition of tangent as $\frac{y}{x}$, the trigonometric functions can be extended to any angle. Angles representing multiple revolutions, and negative angles give the same result for any trigonometric function as the coterminal angle between 0° and 360°.

Example 1 **Evaluate the trigonometric function by using the quadrant and the reference angle to determine the sign and absolute value of the function value.**

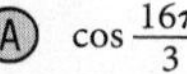 $\cos\frac{16\pi}{3}$

Identify the coterminal angle between 0 and 2π. $\frac{16}{3}\pi = 4\pi + \frac{4}{3}\pi$

Find the reference angle for Quadrant III. $\theta' = \frac{4}{3}\pi - \pi$

$\theta' = \frac{\pi}{3}$

Identify the special right triangle angle. $\theta' = \frac{\pi}{3} \times \frac{180°}{\pi} = 60°$

Use the sides of a 30° −60° −90° triangle. $\cos\theta' = \frac{1}{2}$

Apply the sign of cosine in Quadrant III. $\cos\frac{16}{3}\pi = -\cos\frac{\pi}{3}$

$= -\frac{1}{2}$

EXPLAIN 1

Evaluating the Basic Trigonometric Functions for Special Angles

QUESTIONING STRATEGIES

How can you determine which quadrant contains the terminal side of an angle in standard position? **Add or subtract a multiple of 2π to obtain a coterminal angle between 0 and 2π. Then use the fact that the quadrantal angles measure $\frac{\pi}{2}$, π, $\frac{3\pi}{2}$, and 2π to locate the terminal side of the angle.**

How can you determine the sign of the trigonometric functions by knowing which quadrant contains the terminal side of the angle? **You can use the signs of the x- and y-coordinates in the quadrant, and the fact that the sign of the cosine is the sign of the x-coordinates, and the sign of the sine is the sign of the y-coordinates. The sign of the tangent is positive in quadrants where the x- and y-values have the same sign and negative where their signs are opposites.**

AVOID COMMON ERRORS

Some students may erroneously determine the reference angle by finding the measure between the terminal side of the angle and the y-axis. Reinforce that reference angles are measured using the x-axis. Students can draw a "bowtie" centered at the origin, as in the Explore, to help them remember this.

DIFFERENTIATE INSTRUCTION

Kinesthetic Experience

A hands-on approach may be helpful for students struggling with the concepts presented in the lesson. Have students draw a unit circle on a piece of graph paper, letting each unit on the graph paper represent 0.1. Have them use a pencil to represent the terminal side of an angle in standard position that measures 0°. Then have them move the pencil through a rotation of, for example, 120°, with the help of a protractor. They can mark the point where the pencil passes through the unit circle and estimate its coordinates. Then have them use a calculator to find the sine and cosine of the angle, and compare the results with their estimates.

Ⓑ $\tan \frac{11\pi}{4}$

Identify the coterminal angle between 0 and 2π. $\frac{11}{4}\pi = 2\pi + \boxed{\frac{3}{4}\pi}$

Find the reference angle for Quadrant $\boxed{\text{II}}$. $\theta' = \boxed{\pi} - \frac{3}{4}\pi$

$\theta' = \boxed{\frac{\pi}{4}}$

Identify the special right triangle angle. $\theta' = \frac{\pi}{4} \times \boxed{\frac{180^\circ}{\pi}} = 45^\circ$

Use the ratios of the sides of a $45^\circ - 45^\circ - 90^\circ$ triangle. $\tan \theta' = \boxed{1}$

Apply the sign of tangent in Quadrant II. $\tan \frac{11\pi}{4} = \boxed{-1}$

Reflect

4. Explain how defining sine, cosine, and tangent in terms of *x*- and *y*-coordinates instead of in terms of the sides of a right triangle also allows these functions to be evaluated at quadrantal angles.

You cannot draw a right triangle for a quadrantal angle, and angles whose measures are multiples of 90° cannot be matched to a reference angle less than 90°. The *x*- and *y*-coordinates of the intersection between the unit circle and the terminal side of an angle are well defined, and easy to determine, for angles whose measures are multiples of 90°.

Your Turn

Evaluate the trigonometric function by using the quadrant and the reference angle to determine the sign and absolute value of the function value.

5. $\sin \frac{5\pi}{6}$

$\theta = \frac{5\pi}{6}$, **Quadrant II**

$\theta' = \pi - \frac{5\pi}{6} = \frac{\pi}{6}$

$\theta' = \frac{\pi}{6} \times \frac{180^\circ}{\pi} = 30^\circ$

$\sin 30^\circ = \frac{1}{2}$

$\sin \frac{5\pi}{6} = \frac{1}{2}$

6. $\cos 7\pi$

$\theta = 7\pi = 6\pi + \pi$, **quadrantal angle**

$\theta' = \pi \times \frac{180^\circ}{\pi} = 180^\circ$

For cosine, use the *x*-coordinate on the left of the unit circle.

$\cos 7\pi = -1$

Explain 2 Evaluating the Basic Trigonometric Functions Using a Calculator

Using coordinates of the unit circle to define trigonometric functions, you can see that any angle measure can be input into the sine and cosine functions. Because tangent has a variable denominator, angles with a unit circle intersection at $x = 0$ give undefined results. This occurs at angles whose measures are $\cdots, -\frac{3\pi}{2}, -\frac{\pi}{2}, \frac{\pi}{2}, \frac{3\pi}{2}, \frac{5\pi}{2}, \cdots$, or $\left(\frac{2n+1}{2}\right)\pi$ for all integers n. These angle measures must be excluded from the domain of the tangent function.

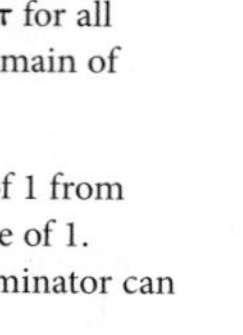

Because both sine and cosine output coordinates at a distance of 1 from the origin, their function values cannot exceed an absolute value of 1. The output of tangent can be arbitrarily large because the denominator can become arbitrarily small (as long as it does not equal 0).

	Sine	Cosine	Tangent
Domain	$\{\theta \mid \theta \in \mathbb{R}\}$	$\{\theta \mid \theta \in \mathbb{R}\}$	$\left\{\theta \mid \theta \neq \frac{(2n+1)\pi}{2}, n \in \mathbb{Z}\right\}$
Range	$\{\theta \mid -1 \leq \theta \leq 1\}$	$\{\theta \mid -1 \leq \theta \leq 1\}$	$\{\theta \mid \theta \in \mathbb{R}\}$

Using trigonometric functions to find coordinates along any circle as a function of an angle is useful for solving real-world applications.

The diagram shows two concentric circles with a single angle inscribed in both. The inner circle is a unit circle, and the outer circle has a radius of r. The two inscribed right triangles are similar —we know this because they have two angles of the same size—, and the coordinates of the outer point can be determined by using the ratios of the sides of similar triangles. The base and height of the inside triangle are $\cos\theta$ and $\sin\theta$ respectively. The ratio of outer and inner widths and outer and inner heights are the same as the ratio of outer and inner hypotenuses, or $\frac{r}{1}$. Thus, the x- and y-coordinates of any point on a circular arc of radius r and angle θ are given by $(r\cos\theta,\ r\sin\theta)$.

The trigonometric ratios can be updated to include the coordinates on any circle with radius r centered at the origin:

$$\sin\theta = \frac{y}{r} \qquad \cos\theta = \frac{x}{r} \qquad \tan\theta = \frac{y}{x}, x \neq 0$$

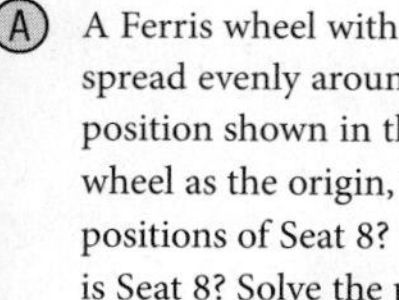

Example 2 **Use trigonometric functions and a calculator to solve the problem.**

(A) A Ferris wheel with a diameter of 45 meters and 24 seats spread evenly around the outside wheel is stopped in the position shown in the diagram. Using the center of the Ferris wheel as the origin, what are the horizontal and vertical positions of Seat 8? How far above the bottom of the wheel is Seat 8? Solve the problem using radians. Give answers to the nearest tenth of a meter.

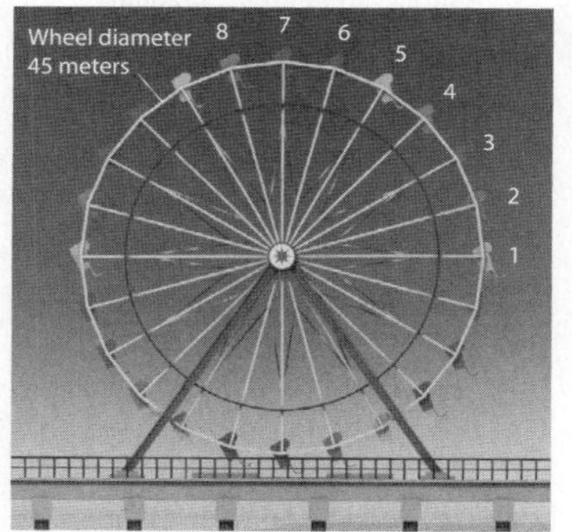

First check that your calculator is in radian mode. On a graphing calculator, the units for angle measure can be changed to radians by pressing MODE and selecting radians.

EXPLAIN 2

Evaluating the Basic Trigonometric Functions Using a Calculator

AVOID COMMON ERRORS

Remind students to check whether their calculators are in degree mode or radian mode prior to using them for trigonometry problems. Finding that a value such as sin(90) is not equal to 1 will be as good an indicator as checking the mode settings.

QUESTIONING STRATEGIES

? Mia used her calculator to find that $\cos\left(\frac{\pi}{8}\right) \approx 0.92$ and $\sin\left(\frac{\pi}{8}\right) \approx 0.38$. What can Mia conclude about the angle that measures $\frac{\pi}{8}$ radians? **Possible answer: The terminal side of the angle in standard position passes through the unit circle at a point that is very close to (0.92, 0.38).**

INTEGRATE MATHEMATICAL PRACTICES

Focus on Technology

MP.5 Ask students to discuss how they could use the sine and cosine functions on the graphing calculator to determine the quadrant in which the terminal side of an angle lies. **Students should recognize that, when used to find the sine and cosine of an angle, the calculator provides the sign of each value. These signs, when used together, can be used to identify the quadrant in which the terminal side of the angle lies.**

Determine the angle between two adjacent seats.

$\theta_{sep} = \frac{2\pi}{24} = \frac{\pi}{12}$

Determine how many seats there are from Seat 8 to Seat 1.

$8 - 1 = 7$

Find the rotation angle of Seat 8.

$\theta = 7\left(\frac{\pi}{12}\right) = \frac{7\pi}{12}$

Find the x- and y-coordinates.

$$(x, y) = (r\cos\theta,\ r\sin\theta)$$
$$= \left(\left(\frac{45}{2}\right)\cos\frac{7\pi}{12}, \left(\frac{45}{2}\right)\sin\frac{7\pi}{12}\right)$$
$$\approx (-5.8, 21.7)$$

Seat 8 is about 5.8 meters to the left and 21.7 meters above the center of the wheel. The center is 22.5 meters above the bottom of the wheel, so Seat 8 is stopped 44.2 meters above the bottom of the wheel.

(B) An airplane begins to descend toward a runway 1 mile away at an angle of $-5°$ to the horizontal. What is its change in elevation after it flies 5000 feet horizontally towards the runway?

First check that your calculator is in degree mode. On a graphing calculator, the units for angle measure can be changed to degrees by pressing MODE and selecting degrees.

Using the beginning of the descent as the origin, the plane's horizontal travel should be treated as the **x**-coordinate. The change in elevation is the **y**-coordinate.

$\tan\theta = \frac{y}{x}$

$\tan(-5°) = \frac{y}{5000}$

$5000\tan(-5°) = y$

$y \approx -437.4$

The elevation drops by about **437.4** feet.

Reflect

7. How could you describe the position of Seat 8 in Example A with a negative angle measure?
Moving clockwise from Seat 1, it is −17 seat intervals to reach Seat 8, so the angle would be (−17)15° = −225°.

LANGUAGE SUPPORT EL

Communicate Math

Provide each student with four drawings of a right triangle drawn within a unit circle whose base is along the positive x-axis, one in each quadrant. Have students label which sides of the triangle represent the sine and cosine of the central angle, and then describe how to determine the tangent.

YourTurn

8. How long a shadow does a 40-foot tall tree cast on the ground if the sun is at an angle of 0.5 radians relative to the horizon? Use a calculator to solve the problem.

Let y represent the height (40 feet) and x the end of the shadow.

$$\tan\theta = \frac{y}{x}$$

$$\tan(0.5) = \frac{40}{x}$$

$$x = \frac{40}{\tan(0.5)}$$

$$\approx 73.2 \text{ feet}$$

The shadow is about 73.2 feet long.

Elaborate

9. Explain the meaning of the message "ERR:DOMAIN" if you try to evaluate $\frac{\pi}{2}$ on a graphing calculator. Why do you get this error message?

This means domain error, or the function was evaluated at a point outside of its domain. Tangent is undefined at $\frac{\pi}{2}$ radians.

10. Explain why it is helpful to find coterminal and reference angles when evaluating trigonometric functions of large positive and negative angles without a calculator.

There are a small number of special angles whose trigonometric function values can be memorized based on the first quadrant. Rather than memorizing the values for the other three quadrants, it is easier to remember how they will be related by sign changes. Similarly, finding a coterminal angle between 0° and 360°, or between 0 and 2π radians, extends the domain of angles whose trigonometric functions can be evaluated without a calculator beyond a single revolution.

11. **Essential Question Check-In** Explain how to define the sine and cosine of an angle in terms of a coordinate on the unit circle.

The sine of an angle is the value of the y-coordinate where the terminal side of the angle intersects the unit circle. The cosine is the value of the x-coordinate where the terminal side of the angle intersects the unit circle.

ELABORATE

QUESTIONING STRATEGIES

How are the sine, cosine, and tangent values of $\frac{2\pi}{3}$, $\frac{4\pi}{3}$, and $\frac{5\pi}{3}$ related to those of $\frac{\pi}{3}$? **Each corresponding function value has the same absolute value. Each may be either the same value or its opposite.**

What is true of the cosine of an angle with its terminal side on the positive or negative y-axis, for any value of r? **It has a value of 0.**

SUMMARIZE THE LESSON

How are the points on the unit circle related to the trigonometric functions? **The x- and y-coordinates of the point on the unit circle through which the terminal side of an angle in standard position passes are the cosine and sine, respectively, of the angle. The tangent is the ratio of the y-coordinate to the x-coordinate.**

EVALUATE

ASSIGNMENT GUIDE

Concepts and Skills	Practice
Explore Using Special Right Triangles in a Unit Circle	Exercise 1
Example 1 Evaluating the Basic Trigonometric Functions for Special Angles	Exercises 2–9, 26
Example 2 Evaluating the Basic Trigonometric Functions Using a Calculator	Exercises 10–25

QUESTIONING STRATEGIES

? How do you find the reference angle for an angle in standard position? **You find the measure of the acute angle formed by the terminal side of the angle and the *x*-axis.**

COGNITIVE STRATEGIES

Students can draw coordinate axes with the letters below in the four quadrants to help them remember which function value is positive in each quadrant.

S	A
T	C

In the diagram, A stands for *all*, S for *sine*, T for *tangent*, and C for *cosine*. The other function values are negative in the given quadrant. A mnemonic for remembering this might be *All Set To Celebrate!* Encourage students to make up their own mnemonics.

Evaluate: Homework and Practice

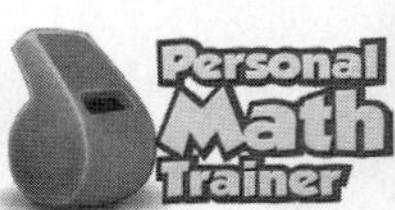

- Online Homework
- Hints and Help
- Extra Practice

1. A right triangle with an angle of approximately 53.1° is inscribed in the first quadrant of the unit circle, with a horizontal length of $\frac{3}{5}$ and a vertical length of $\frac{4}{5}$.

Complete the table for the following trigonometric functions.

Angle of rotation, θ	53.1	126.9	233.1	306.9
$\sin\theta$	$\frac{4}{5}$	$\frac{4}{5}$	$-\frac{4}{5}$	$-\frac{4}{5}$
$\cos\theta$	$\frac{3}{5}$	$-\frac{3}{5}$	$-\frac{3}{5}$	$\frac{3}{5}$
$\tan\theta$	$\frac{4}{3}$	$-\frac{4}{3}$	$\frac{4}{3}$	$-\frac{4}{3}$

Evaluate the trigonometric function without using a calculator. Angles are given in degrees.

2. $\cos 135°$

Quadrant II reference angle:

$\theta' = 180° - 135° = 45°$

$\cos 135° = -\cos 45° = -\frac{\sqrt{2}}{2}$

3. $\tan(-30°)$

$-30° = -360° + 330°$

Quadrant IV reference angle:

$\theta' = 360° - 330° = 30°$

$\tan(-30°) = -\tan 30° = -\frac{\sqrt{3}}{3}$

4. $\sin 480°$

$480° = 360° + 120°$

Quadrant II reference angle:

$\theta' = 180° - 120° = 60°$

$\sin 480° = \sin 60° = \frac{\sqrt{3}}{2}$

5. $\cos 720°$

$720° = 2 \cdot 360° + 0°$

Quadrantal angle; for cosine use the *x*-coordinate on the right of the unit circle:

$\cos 720° = \cos 0° = 1$

Evaluate the trigonometric function without using a calculator. Angles are given in radians.

6. $\cos\frac{7\pi}{4}$

Quadrant IV reference angle:

$\theta' = 2\pi - \frac{7\pi}{4} = \frac{\pi}{4}$

$\cos\frac{7\pi}{4} = \cos\frac{\pi}{4} = \frac{\sqrt{2}}{2}$

7. $\sin\left(-\frac{\pi}{2}\right)$

$-\frac{\pi}{2} = -2\pi + \frac{3\pi}{2}$

Quadrantal angle; for sine, use the *y*-coordinate on the bottom of the unit circle:

$\sin\left(-\frac{\pi}{2}\right) = \sin\frac{3\pi}{2} = -1$

Exercise	Depth of Knowledge (D.O.K.)	COMMON CORE Mathematical Practices
1	**2** Skills/Concepts	**MP.6** Precision
2–9	**2** Skills/Concepts	**MP.7** Using Structure
10–17	**2** Skills/Concepts	**MP.5** Using Tools
18–20	**2** Skills/Concepts	**MP.7** Using Structure
21–25	**2** Skills/Concepts	**MP.4** Modeling
26	**2** Skills/Concepts	**MP.7** Using Structure

8. $\tan\left(-\frac{10\pi}{3}\right)$

$-\frac{10\pi}{3} = (-2)\cdot 2\pi + \frac{2\pi}{3}$

Quadrant II reference angle:

$\theta' = \pi - \frac{2\pi}{3} = \frac{\pi}{3}$

$\tan\left(-\frac{10\pi}{3}\right) = -\tan\frac{\pi}{3} = -\sqrt{3}$

9. $\tan\frac{16\pi}{3}$

$\frac{16\pi}{3} = 2\cdot 2\pi + \frac{4\pi}{3}$

Quadrant III reference angle:

$\theta' = \frac{4\pi}{3} - \pi = \frac{\pi}{3}$

$\tan\frac{16\pi}{3} = \tan\frac{\pi}{3} = \sqrt{3}$

Use a calculator to evaluate the trigonometric function of the angle given in degrees.

10. $\sin 132°$

0.743

11. $\cos(-203°)$

−0.921

12. $\tan 43°$

0.933

13. $\cos 547°$

−0.993

Use a calculator to evaluate the trigonometric function of the angle given in radians.

14. $\sin\left(\frac{5}{8}\pi\right)$

0.924

15. $\cos(1.2\pi)$

−0.809

16. $\tan(10.5)$

1.85

17. $\sin(-3.7)$

0.530

Find a value or an expression for the coordinate on a circle centered at (0, 0) and at an angle θ from the x-axis.

18. radius = 10, $\theta = 135°$, x-coordinate

Quadrant II reference angle

$135° = 180° - 45°$

$x = r\cos\theta$

$x = 10\cos 135°$

$= -10\cos 45°$

$= -10\left(\frac{\sqrt{2}}{2}\right)$

$= -5\sqrt{2}$

19. radius = 5, $\theta = 2.7$ radians, y-coordinate

Use a calculator.

$y = 5\sin 2.7$

$\approx 5(0.4274)$

≈ 2.14

20. radius = r, $\theta = \frac{17\pi}{4}$ radians, x-coordinate

$x = r\cos\frac{17\pi}{4}$

$\frac{17\pi}{4} = 4\pi + \frac{\pi}{4}$

Quadrant I reference angle:

$\cos\frac{17\pi}{4} = \cos\frac{\pi}{4}$

$\cos\frac{17\pi}{4} = \frac{\sqrt{2}}{2}$

$\Rightarrow x = \frac{r\sqrt{2}}{2}$

21. radius = 0.5, $\theta = 2\phi$, y-coordinate

$y = 0.5\sin\theta$

$y = 0.5\sin(2\phi)$

AVOID COMMON ERRORS

Students may correctly find the sine, cosine, and tangent of the reference angle and then forget to adjust the signs of these values. Remind students that drawing the angle in standard position can help them determine the quadrant in which its terminal side is located. This quadrant determines the sign of the values of the trigonometric functions of the angle.

INTEGRATE MATHEMATICAL PRACTICES

Focus on Reasoning

MP.2 Help students to recognize that when they use the ratios of the sides of special triangles to find the values of the trigonometric functions of 30°, 45°, and 60°, they are finding exact values of the functions. Contrast this with the approximations (in most cases) that are obtained by using a calculator.

QUESTIONING STRATEGIES

? Why is the range for sine and cosine between −1 and 1, inclusive? **The sine and cosine are defined using the unit circle. The greatest value either x or y can have is 1 and the least value is −1. Therefore, the range of both functions is between −1 and 1, inclusive.**

Exercise	Depth of Knowledge (D.O.K.)	COMMON CORE Mathematical Practices
27	3 Strategic Thinking H.O.T.	MP.5 Using Tools
28–29	3 Strategic Thinking H.O.T.	MP.8 Patterns

CURRICULUM INTEGRATION

Students may be interested to learn about the many real-world applications of trigonometric functions. Early trigonometric relationships were used around 200 B.C.E. to describe astronomical observations. Today these functions are also used in acoustics, music, optics, electronics, probability, medical imaging, surveying, architecture, electrical engineering, civil engineering, cartography, and computer game development, and other fields. Encourage students to research these applications and share what they learn with the class.

Use trigonometric functions to solve the real-world problems.

22. A swing hangs from a beam 10 feet high, with the seat hanging 2 feet above the ground. In motion, the swing moves back and forth from −130° to −50° to the horizontal. How far forward and back does the swing move along the ground at the extremes?

$r = 10 - 2 = 8$

$x_f = 8\cos(-50°) \approx 5.14$ ft

$x_b = 8\cos(-130°) \approx -5.14$ ft

23. The Americans with Disabilities Act sets the maximum angle for a wheelchair ramp entering a business at 4.76°. Determine the horizontal distance needed to accommodate a ramp that goes up to a door 4 feet off the ground.

$\tan\theta = \frac{y}{x}$

$\tan 4.76° = \frac{4}{x}$

$x(0.0833) = 4$

$x = \frac{4}{0.0833}$

≈ 48 feet

24. Jennifer is riding on a merry-go-round at a carnival that revolves at a speed of 3.3 revolutions per minute. She is sitting 7 feet from the center of the merry-go-round. If Jennifer's starting position is considered to be at 0 radians, what are her *x*- and *y*-coordinates after 57 seconds?

Revolutions $= \left(\frac{57}{60}\right)3.3 = 3.135$

$\theta = 3.135(2\pi) = 6.27\pi$

$(x, y) = \left(7\cos(6.27\pi), 7\sin(6.27\pi)\right)$

$(x, y) \approx (4.63, 5.25)$

25. A car is traveling on a road that goes up a hill. The hill has an angle of 17° relative to horizontal. How high up the hill vertically will the car be after it has traveled 100 yards up the road?

$\sin\theta = \frac{y}{r}$

$\sin 17° = \frac{y}{100}$

$y = 100\sin 17°$

$\approx 100(0.2924)$

≈ 29.24 yards

26. Classify $f(\theta)$ of these trigonometric functions as less than, greater than, or equal to zero.

A. $f(\theta) = \sin\theta$, θ is in quadrant III — A. $f(\theta) < 0$

B. $f(\theta) = \tan\theta$, θ is in quadrant II — B. $f(\theta) < 0$

C. $f(\theta) = \cos\theta$, θ is in quadrant IV — C. $f(\theta) > 0$

D. $f(\theta) = \cos\theta$, $\theta = 180°$ — D. $f(\theta) < 0$

E. $f(\theta) = \tan\theta$, $\theta = 540°$ — E. $f(\theta) = 0$

F. $f(\theta) = \tan\theta$, θ in quadrant I — F. $f(\theta) > 0$

A, B, and D are less than 0. C and F are greater than 0. E is equal to 0.

H.O.T. Focus on Higher Order Thinking

27. **Explain the Error** Sven used his calculator to find $\sin 10°$ and got an answer of approximately -0.5440, which seems wrong given that 10° is in the first quadrant. What did Sven do wrong? What is the correct answer?

Sven used his calculator in radian mode instead of degree mode.

$\sin 10° \approx 0.1736$

28. **Look for a Pattern** Use the reference triangles and your calculator to make an observation about the rate of change of $\tan\theta$ over the interval 0 to 2π. Where does the rate of change increase? Where does it decrease? Are there any intervals where $\tan\theta$ is a decreasing function? Explain.

The rate of change increases as the value of θ goes from 0 to the asymptote at $\frac{\pi}{2}$, and from π to the asymptote at $\frac{3}{2}\pi$. The rate of change decreases as the value of θ goes from the asymptote at $\frac{\pi}{2}$ to π and from the asymptote at $\frac{3}{2}\pi$ to 2π. Tan θ never decreases over any interval. Although the value of $\tan\theta$ jumps from very large to very small as it crosses $\theta = \frac{\pi}{2}$ and $\theta = \frac{3}{2}\pi$, this is not an interval because $\tan\theta$ is not defined at $\frac{\pi}{2}$ and $\frac{3}{2}\pi$.

29. **Analyze Relationships** Use the unit circle and quadrant locations to prove that $\cos(-\theta) = \cos\theta$ for any angle, θ.

Assume θ is in Quadrant I. Then $-\theta$ will be in Quadrant IV. $-\theta$ will have the same reference angle as θ, so their absolute values will be the same. Cosine is positive in both Quadrant I and Quadrant IV, so $\cos\theta$ and $\cos(-\theta)$ will have the same value. If θ is in Quadrant IV, then $-\theta$ is in Quadrant I, and the same reasoning holds. The same pairings work for Quadrants II and III (If θ is in Quadrant II, then $-\theta$ is in Quadrant III, and vice versa. In both cases, the reference angles are the same angle, and the cosine of both θ and $-\theta$ is negative).

INTEGRATE MATHEMATICAL PRACTICES

Focus on Communication

MP.3 It is important that students not lose sight of what the sine, cosine, and tangent of an angle represent. Call upon students to describe what their answers to the exercises represent in terms of the angle and its relationship to the unit circle.

JOURNAL

Have students describe how to use a reference angle to determine the sine and cosine of an angle whose terminal side lies in Quadrant IV.

Lesson Performance Task

In Italy, there is a large circular test track that is used to test race cars and other high-speed automobiles.

a. The track has a radius of 6 kilometers. Find the circumference and area of the track.

$C = 2\pi r$

$= 2\pi(6)$

$= 12\pi$

≈ 37.70 **km**

$A = \pi r^2$

$= \pi(6)^2$

$= 36\pi$

≈ 113.10 **km**^{2}

b. While test-driving a new car, a driver starts at the right-hand side of the circular track, travels in a counter-clockwise direction, and stops $\frac{3}{5}$ of the way around the track. Using the center of the track as the origin and the starting point as the intersection of the x-axis and the circle represented by the track, find the coordinates of the angle where the driver stopped the car.

Find the angle measure of $\frac{3}{5}$ of a circle.

$360° \cdot \frac{3}{5} = 216°$

Find $\cos\theta$ and $\sin\theta$.

$\cos(216°) \approx -0.809$

$\sin(216°) \approx -0.588$

Find $r\cos\theta$ and $r\sin\theta$.

$6\cos(216°) \approx 6(-0.809) = -4.854$

$6\sin(216°) \approx 6(-0.588) = -3.528$

The driver stopped the car approximately at the point $(-4.854, -3.528)$.

c. The driver continues in the same direction, but stops again at the point $(5.3, 2.9)$. What is the car's position on the track relative to its starting point? Did the car make more or less than 1 revolution around the track when it stopped the second time? Explain.

$6 \cos(\theta) = 5.3$

$\cos(\theta) = 0.883$

$\theta = \cos^{-1}(0.883)$

$\theta \approx 27.99°$

$6 \sin(\theta) = 2.9$

$\sin(\theta) = 0.483$

$\theta = \sin^{-1}(0.483)$

$\theta \approx 28.88°$

The approximate angle of the car on the track relative to its starting point is 28°, which represents $\frac{28}{360} = \frac{7}{90} \approx 0.08$, or about $\frac{1}{12}$ of the way around the track. More than one revolution; Because the car's position at its second stopping point is at an angle of 28° relative to its starting point, it had to go around the track more than once to get back to $(5.3, 2.9)$.

d. If the car drove once around the track in 6 minutes and 48 seconds, what is its average velocity? Give your answer in kilometers per hour.

6 minutes 48 seconds is equivalent to 6.8 minutes.

6.8 minutes is equivalent to 0.113 hour.

To find the average velocity, divide the circumference by the number of hours.

$\frac{37.70 \text{ km}}{0.113 \text{ h}} \approx 333.6 \text{ km/h}$

EXTENSION ACTIVITY

Students may be interested in how trigonometry is applied in three dimensions. Have them research the concept of *spherical trigonometry* and how it can be applied to a sphere such as Earth. Note that, for example, a point on Earth can be described in degrees by degrees of latitude from the equator and degrees of longitude from the prime meridian, but also trigonometrically from the center of the earth by what is called a *spherical triangle*. Students may be interested to learn that a spherical triangle can have more than one right angle!

AVOID COMMON ERRORS

Students often think of sine and cosine in that order, and may switch the order when considering coordinates. Remind students that (x, y) is $(r\cos\theta, r\sin\theta)$ and not the reverse. Students should remember that at the starting point, it is y (the sine) that has a value of 0.

INTEGRATE MATHEMATICAL PRACTICES

Focus on Critical Thinking

MP.3 Students should note two things about the velocity of the car. First, the speed of the car is virtually impossible—a speed of 405.27 m/s is about 907 miles per hour. Second, the question posed is a conditional, "If the car…." An answer does not need to be reasonable in the real world if the given premise is impossible and the conditional is proved true.

Scoring Rubric

2 points: Student correctly solves the problem and explains his/her reasoning.

1 point: Student shows good understanding of the problem but does not fully solve or explain his/her reasoning.

0 points: Student does not demonstrate understanding of the problem.

LESSON 17.3

Using a Pythagorean Identity

Common Core Math Standards

The student is expected to:

 F-TF.C.8

Prove the Pythagorean identity $\sin^2(\theta) + \cos^2(\theta) = 1$ and use it to find $\sin(\theta)$, $\cos(\theta)$, or $\tan(\theta)$ given $\sin(\theta)$, $\cos(\theta)$, or $\tan(\theta)$ and the quadrant of the angle.

Mathematical Practices

COMMON CORE MP.1 Problem Solving

Language Objective

Explain to a partner what the Pythagorean Theorem and the Pythagorean identity are and how they are related.

ENGAGE

Essential Question: How can you use a given value of one of the trigonometric functions to calculate the values of the other functions?

The values of the sine, cosine, and tangent functions are connected by the identities $\sin^2(\theta) + \cos^2(\theta) = 1$ and $\tan\theta = \frac{\sin\theta}{\cos\theta}$. Once you know the value of one of the functions, you can use the identities to solve for the others, using the quadrant of the terminal side of θ to assign the correct sign.

PREVIEW: LESSON PERFORMANCE TASK

View the online Engage. Discuss the photo and how light and shadows can help determine where to place a cell tower. Then preview the Lesson Performance Task.

Name ______ Class ______ Date ______

17.3 Using a Pythagorean Identity

Essential Question: How can you use a given value of one of the trigonometric functions to calculate the values of the other functions?

Resource Locker

Explore Proving a Pythagorean Identity

In the previous lesson, you learned that the coordinates of any point (x, y) that lies on the unit circle where the terminal ray of an angle θ intersects the circle are $x = \cos\theta$ and $y = \sin\theta$, and $y = \sin\theta$ that $\tan\theta = \frac{y}{x}$. Combining these facts gives the identity $\tan\theta = \frac{\sin\theta}{\cos\theta}$, which is true for all values of θ where $\cos\theta \neq 0$. In the following Explore, you will derive another identity based on the Pythagorean theorem, which is why the identity is known as a *Pythagorean identity*.

(A) The terminal side of an angle θ intersects the unit circle at the point (a, b) as shown. Write a and b in terms of trigonometric functions involving θ.

$a =$ $\cos\theta$

$b =$ $\sin\theta$

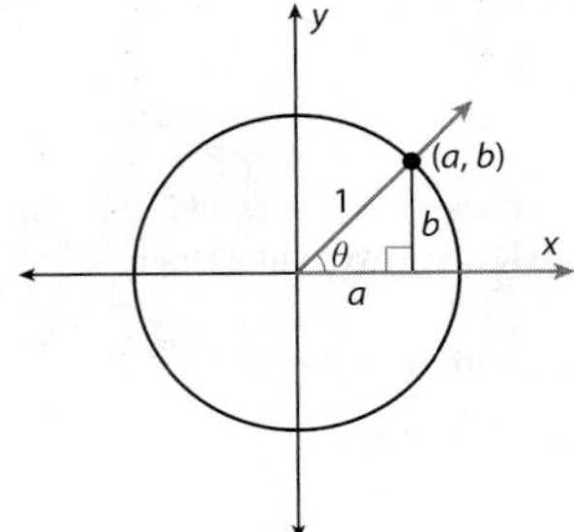

(B) Apply the Pythagorean theorem to the right triangle in the diagram. Note that when a trigonometric function is squared, the exponent is typically written immediately after the name of the function. For instance, $(\sin\theta)^2 = \sin^2\theta$.

Write the Pythagorean Theorem.	$a^2 + b^2 = c^2$
Substitute for a, b, and c.	$(\cos\theta)^2 + (\sin\theta)^2 = 1^2$
Square each expression.	$\cos^2\theta + \sin^2\theta = 1$

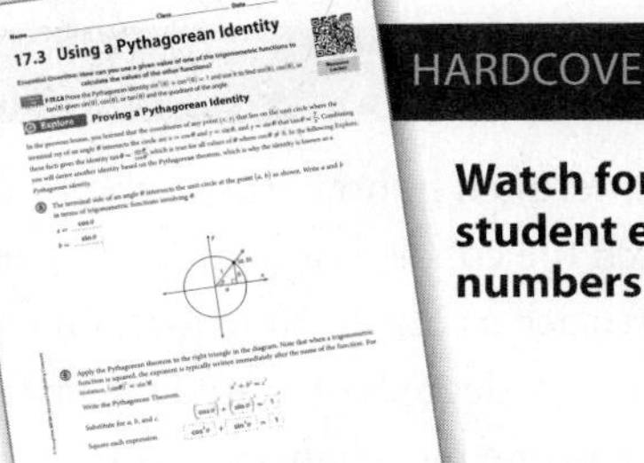

HARDCOVER PAGES 853–864

Watch for the hardcover student edition page numbers for this lesson.

Reflect

1. The identity is typically written with the sine function first. Write the identity this way, and explain why it is equivalent to the one in Step B.
The rewritten identity is $\sin^2\theta + \cos^2\theta = 1$. It is equivalent to the original identity because of the Commutative Property of Addition.

2. Confirm the Pythagorean identity for $\theta = \frac{\pi}{3}$.
$\sin\left(\frac{\pi}{3}\right) = \frac{\sqrt{3}}{2}$ **and** $\cos\left(\frac{\pi}{3}\right) = \frac{1}{2}$**; therefore,**
$\sin^2\theta + \cos^2\theta = \sin^2\left(\frac{\pi}{3}\right) + \cos^2\left(\frac{\pi}{3}\right) = \left(\frac{\sqrt{3}}{2}\right)^2 + \left(\frac{1}{2}\right)^2 = \frac{3}{4} + \frac{1}{4} = 1.$

3. Confirm the Pythagorean identity for $\theta = \frac{3\pi}{4}$.
$\sin\left(\frac{3\pi}{4}\right) = \frac{\sqrt{2}}{2}$ **and** $\cos\left(\frac{3\pi}{4}\right) = -\frac{\sqrt{2}}{2}$**. Therefore,**
$\sin^2\theta + \cos^2\theta = \sin^2\left(\frac{3\pi}{4}\right) + \cos^2\left(\frac{3\pi}{4}\right) = \left(\frac{\sqrt{2}}{2}\right)^2 + \left(-\frac{\sqrt{2}}{2}\right)^2 = \frac{1}{2} + \frac{1}{2} = 1.$

Explain 1 Finding the Value of the Other Trigonometric Functions Given the Value of sin θ or cos θ

You can rewrite the identity $\sin^2\theta + \cos^2\theta = 1$ to express one trigonometric function in terms of the other. As shown, each alternate version of the identity involves both positive and negative square roots. You can determine which sign to use based on knowing the quadrant in which the terminal side of θ lies.

Solve for sin θ	Solve for cos θ
$\sin^2\theta + \cos^2\theta = 1$	$\sin^2\theta + \cos^2\theta = 1$
$\sin^2\theta = 1 - \cos^2\theta$	$\cos^2\theta = 1 - \cos^2\theta$
$\sin\theta = \pm\sqrt{1 - \cos^2\theta}$	$\cos\theta = \pm\sqrt{1 - \sin^2\theta}$

Example 1 **Find the approximate value of each trigonometric function.**

(A) Given that $\sin\theta = 0.766$ where $0 < \theta < \frac{\pi}{2}$, find $\cos\theta$.

Use the identity to solve for $\cos\theta$. $\cos\theta = \pm\sqrt{1 - \sin^2\theta}$

Substitute for $\sin\theta$. $= \pm\sqrt{1 - (0.766)^2}$

Use a calculator, then round. $\approx \pm 0.643$

The terminal side of θ lies in Quadrant I, where $\cos\theta > 0$. So, $\cos\theta \approx 0.643$.

PROFESSIONAL DEVELOPMENT

Integrate Mathematical Practices

This lesson provides an opportunity to address Mathematical Practice **MP.1**, which calls for students to "make sense of problems and persevere in solving them." Students analyze given information and constraints and plan a pathway to the solution. The solution process may involve transforming established identities in order to make use of the given information. In the course of solving the problem, students may revisit the given information to make any additional decisions regarding the solution.

EXPLORE

Proving a Pythagorean Identity

INTEGRATE TECHNOLOGY

Students have the option of completing the Explore activity either in the book or online.

CONNECT VOCABULARY EL

Have the class list expressions that contain the word *identity*, such as *identity theft*, or *student Identity card.* Ask them to discuss the meaning of *identity* in each expression. Remind them that 0 is the *identity element* for addition and 1 is the *identity element* for multiplication. Then have them discuss the use of the word *identity* in the context presented in the lesson.

QUESTIONING STRATEGIES

? How do you know the hypotenuse is equal to 1? **The radius of a unit circle is 1.**

? Is $(\cos\theta)^2$ the same as $\cos^2\theta$? Is $(\sin\theta)^2$ the same as $\sin^2\theta$? **Yes, they are different ways of writing the same thing, because the angle measure is not actually squared.**

? If $\cos^2\theta$ has a value of 0.36, what do you know about $\sin^2\theta$ and $\sin\theta$?
$\sin^2\theta = 1 - 0.36 = 0.64$**, so** $\sin\theta = \sqrt{0.64} = 0.8$**.**

EXPLAIN 1

Finding the Value of the Other Trigonometric Functions Given the Value of sin θ or cos θ

QUESTIONING STRATEGIES

? Is $1 - \sin^2\theta$ ever negative? Why or why not? **No;** $-1 \le \sin\theta \le 1$**, so** $0 \le \sin^2\theta \le 1$**. Therefore,** $1 - \sin^2\theta$ **can never be less than 0.**

QUESTIONING STRATEGIES

Do you need to know the precise value of θ to solve these problems? Why or why not? No; the Pythagorean identity allows you to find the cosine of θ given the sine of θ without knowing the value of θ itself.

Do you need to know the quadrant where θ terminates to solve these problems? Why or why not? Yes; the sign of the answer varies depending on the quadrant in which θ terminates.

AVOID COMMON ERRORS

Students may erroneously reason that since $\sin^2\theta + \cos^2\theta = 1$, $\sin\theta + \cos\theta = \sqrt{1} = 1$. Use a special angle to demonstrate that this is not true, and correct the erroneous reasoning by reminding students that $\sqrt{x^2 + y^2} \neq x + y$.

(B) Given that $\cos\theta = -0.906$ where $\pi < \theta < \frac{3\pi}{2}$, find $\sin\theta$.

Use the identity to solve for $\sin\theta$. $\sin\theta = \pm\sqrt{1 - \cos^2\theta}$

Substitute for $\cos\theta$. $= \pm\sqrt{1 - \left(\boxed{-0.906}\right)^2}$

Use a calculator, then round. $\approx \pm \boxed{0.423}$

The terminal side of θ lies in Quadrant $\boxed{\text{III}}$, where $\sin\theta \boxed{<} 0$. So, $\sin\theta \approx \boxed{-0.423}$.

Reflect

4. Suppose that $\frac{\pi}{2} < \theta < \pi$ instead of $0 < \theta < \frac{\pi}{2}$ in part A of this Example. How does this affect the value of $\sin\theta$?

If $\frac{\pi}{2} < \theta < \pi$, then the terminal side of θ lies in Quadrant II. Since cosine is negative in Quadrant II, the value of $\cos\theta$ would be negative.

5. Suppose that $\frac{3\pi}{2} < \theta < 2\pi$ instead of $\pi < \theta < \frac{3\pi}{2}$ in part B of this Example. How does this affect the value of $\sin\theta$?

If $\frac{3\pi}{2} < \theta < 2\pi$, then the terminal side of θ lies in Quadrant IV. Sine is also negative in Quadrant IV, so the value of $\sin\theta$ would not change.

6. Explain how you would use the results of part A of this Example to determine the approximate value for $\tan\theta$. Then find it.

To determine the approximate value for $\tan\theta$, use the identity $\tan\theta = \frac{\sin\theta}{\cos\theta}$.

$\tan\theta = \frac{0.766}{0.643} \approx 1.191$

Your Turn

7. Given that $\sin\theta = -0.644$ where $\pi < \theta < \frac{3\pi}{2}$, find $\cos\theta$.

$\cos\theta = \pm\sqrt{1 - \sin^2\theta}$

$= \pm\sqrt{1 - (-0.644)^2}$

$\approx \pm 0.765$

Since θ lies in Quadrant III, where $\cos\theta < 0$, $\cos\theta \approx -0.765$.

8. Given that $\cos\theta = -0.994$ where $\frac{\pi}{2} < \theta < \pi$, find $\sin\theta$. Then find $\tan\theta$.

$\sin\theta = \pm\sqrt{1 - \cos^2\theta}$

$= \pm\sqrt{1 - (-0.994)^2}$

$= \pm 0.109$

Since θ lies in Quadrant II, where $\sin\theta > 0$, $\sin\theta \approx 0.109$.

$\tan\theta = \frac{\sin\theta}{\cos\theta} \approx \frac{0.109}{-0.994} \approx -0.110$

COLLABORATIVE LEARNING

Peer-to-Peer Activity

Have students work in pairs. Instruct pairs to write three different identities that show the relationships among the sine, cosine, and tangent functions. Then have them verify each of the three identities for $\theta = 30°$, $\theta = 45°$, and $\theta = 60°$. Have each pair compare their work with that of another pair.

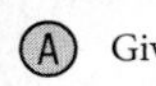 Explain 2

Finding the Value of Other Trigonometric Functions Given the Value of tanθ

If you multiply both sides of the identity $\tan\theta = \frac{\sin\theta}{\cos\theta}$ by $\cos\theta$, you get the identity $\cos\theta\tan\theta = \sin\theta$, or $\sin\theta = \cos\theta\tan\theta$. Also, if you divide both sides of $\sin\theta = \cos\theta\tan\theta$ by $\tan\theta$, you get the identity $\cos\theta = \frac{\sin\theta}{\tan\theta}$. You can use the first of these identities to find the sine and cosine of an angle when you know the tangent.

Example 2 **Find the approximate value of each trigonometric function.**

(A) Given that $\tan\theta \approx -2.327$ where $\frac{\pi}{2} < \theta < \pi$, find the values of $\sin\theta$ and $\cos\theta$.

First, write $\sin\theta$ in terms of $\cos\theta$.

Use the identity $\sin\theta = \cos\theta\tan\theta$. $\quad \sin\theta = \cos\theta\tan\theta$

Substitute the value of $\tan\theta$. $\quad \approx -2.327\cos\theta$

Now use the Pythagorean Identity to find $\cos\theta$. Then find $\sin\theta$.

Use the Pythagorean Identity. $\quad \sin^2\theta = \cos^2\theta = 1$

Substitute for $\sin\theta$. $\quad (-2327\cos\theta)^2 + \cos^2\theta \approx 1$

Square. $\quad 5.415\cos^2\theta + \cos^2\theta \approx 1$

Combine like terms. $\quad 6.415\cos^2\theta \approx 1$

Solve for $\cos^2\theta$. $\quad \cos^2 \approx 0.156$

Solve for $\cos\theta$. $\quad \cos\theta \approx \pm 0.395$

The terminal side of θ lies in Quadrant II, where $\cos\theta < 0$. Therefore, $\cos\theta \approx -0.395$ and $\sin\theta \approx -2.327\cos\theta \approx 0.919$.

(B) Given that $\tan\theta \approx -4.366$ where $\frac{3\pi}{2} < \theta < 2\pi$, find the values of $\sin\theta$ and $\cos\theta$.

First, write $\sin\theta$ in terms of $\cos\theta$.

Use the identity $\sin\theta = \cos\theta\tan\theta$. $\quad \sin\theta = \cos\theta\tan\theta$

Substitute the value of $\tan\theta$. $\quad \approx$ **−4.366** $\cos\theta$

Now use the Pythagorean Identity to find $\cos\theta$. Then find $\sin\theta$.

Use the Pythagorean Identity. $\quad \sin^2\theta + \cos^2\theta = 1$

Substitute for $\sin\theta$. $\quad ($**−4.366** $\cos\theta)^2 + \cos^2\theta \approx 1$

Square. $\quad$ **19.062** $\cos^2\theta + \cos 2\theta \approx 1$

Combine like terms. $\quad$ **20.062** $\cos^2\theta \approx 1$

Solve for $\cos^2\theta$. $\quad \cos^2\theta \approx$ **0.050**

Solve for $\cos\theta$. $\quad \cos\theta \approx$ **0.223**

The terminal side of θ lies in Quadrant **IV**, where $\cos\theta$ **>** 0. Therefore, $\cos\theta \approx$ **0.223** and $\sin\theta \approx$ **−4.366** $\cos\theta \approx$ **−0.974**.

DIFFERENTIATE INSTRUCTION

Multiple Representations

Students may benefit from relating the concepts in this lesson to right triangle trigonometry. For example, if students are given that $\sin\theta = 0.766$ and $0 < \theta < \frac{\pi}{2}$, they can draw a right triangle in the first quadrant, with angle θ at the origin and the adjacent leg on the x-axis. They can then use the definition $\sin\theta = \frac{\text{side opposite}}{\text{hypotenuse}}$ to label the vertical leg 766 units and the hypotenuse 1000 units, and use the Pythagorean Theorem to find the length of the missing leg. Finally, the definitions $\cos\theta = \frac{\text{side adjacent}}{\text{hypotenuse}}$ and $\tan\theta = \frac{\text{side oppositte}}{\text{side adjacent}}$ can be used to find these values. Students can check their results using the methods from the lesson. In doing so, students will likely see the connection between the two methods of solution.

EXPLAIN 2

Finding the Value of the Other Trigonometric Functions Given the Value of tan θ

QUESTIONING STRATEGIES

Is there another way to begin the problem besides writing $\sin\theta$ in terms of $\cos\theta$? **Yes, you can write $\cos\theta$ in terms of $\sin\theta$.**

How can you rewrite the Pythagorean identity with $\cos\theta$ written in terms of $\sin\theta$ and $\tan\theta$? $\sin^2\theta + \left(\frac{\sin\theta}{\tan\theta}\right)^2 = 1$

INTEGRATE TECHNOLOGY

Students can use a graphing calculator to check that the sum of the squares of the values that they find for $\sin\theta$ and $\cos\theta$ is 1. Note that, because the values are approximations, the calculator may return a sum that is not exactly 1.

ELABORATE

QUESTIONING STRATEGIES

? Suppose you know the sine and tangent of an angle. Would you also need to be given information about the quadrant in which the angle terminates in order to find the cosine of the angle? Explain. **No; the signs of the sine and tangent of the angle would be enough information to determine the quadrant in which the angle terminates and, thus, the sign of the cosine.**

INTEGRATE MATHEMATICAL PRACTICES

Focus on Critical Thinking

MP.3 Challenge students to use the identities in the lesson to write a quotient identity that defines in terms of $\cos\theta$. $\tan^2\theta = \frac{1 - \cos^2\theta}{\cos^2\theta}$ or $\tan^2\theta = \frac{1}{\cos^2\theta} - 1$

SUMMARIZE THE LESSON

? If you know the sine of an angle, how can you find the cosine and tangent of the angle? **To find the cosine, you can use the identity $\sin^2\theta + \cos^2\theta = 1$, substitute the given value for $\sin\theta$, and solve for $\cos\theta$. You can then substitute the values of $\sin\theta$ and $\cos\theta$ in the identity $\tan\theta = \frac{\sin\theta}{\cos\theta}$ to find the tangent.**

Reflect

9. In part A of this Example, when you multiplied the given value of $\tan\theta$ by the calculated value of $\cos\theta$ in order to find the value of $\sin\theta$, was the product positive or negative? Explain why this is the result you would expect.

The product was positive. This is expected, since $\sin\theta$ should be positive in Quadrant II.

10. If $\tan\theta = 1$ where $0 < \theta < \frac{\pi}{2}$, show that you can solve for $\sin\theta$ and $\cos\theta$ exactly using the Pythagorean identity. Why is this so?

If $\tan\theta = 1$, then $\sin\theta = \cos\theta$, so $\sin^2\theta + \cos^2\theta = 1$ becomes $2\sin^2\theta = 1$, which gives the result $\sin\theta = \cos\theta = \frac{\sqrt{2}}{2}$. This occurs because θ is the special angle $\frac{\pi}{4}$.

Your Turn

11. Given that $\tan\theta \approx 3.454$ where $\pi < \theta < \frac{3\pi}{2}$, find the values of $\sin\theta$ and $\cos\theta$.

Write $\sin\theta$ in terms of $\cos\theta$.

$\sin\theta = \cos\theta\tan\theta \approx 3.454\cos\theta$

Solve for $\cos\theta$ and $\sin\theta$.

$$\sin^2\theta + \cos^2\theta = 1$$
$$(3.454\cos\theta)^2 + \cos^2\theta \approx 1$$
$$11.930\cos^2\theta + \cos^2\theta \approx 1$$
$$12.930\cos^2\theta \approx 1$$
$$\cos^2\theta \approx 0.0773$$
$$\cos\theta \approx \pm 0.278$$

Since cosine is negative and sine is negative in Quadrant III, $\cos\theta = 0.278$ and $\sin\theta \approx -3.454\cos\theta \approx -0.960$.

Elaborate

12. What conclusions can you draw if you are given only the information that $\tan\theta = -1$?

Possible Answer: Since the tangent is negative, the terminal angle must be either in Quadrant II, where sine is positive and cosine is negative, or in Quadrant IV, where sine is negative and cosine is positive. More specifically, $\sin\theta = \cos\theta$, so $\sin^2\theta + \cos^2\theta = 1$ becomes $2\cos^2 = 1$, so $\cos\theta = \pm\frac{\sqrt{2}}{2}$. Then $\sin\theta = \frac{\sqrt{2}}{2}$ = and $\cos\theta = -\frac{\sqrt{2}}{2}$ or $\sin\theta = -\frac{\sqrt{2}}{2}$ and $\cos\theta = \frac{\sqrt{2}}{2}$.

LANGUAGE SUPPORT EL

Communicate Math

Have students work in pairs. The first student explains what the Pythagorean Theorem is while the second student takes notes. They switch roles and repeat the procedure with the Pythagorean identity. Have them collaborate to describe the relationship between the two, as well as similarities and differences. Encourage students to use pictures and symbols as well as verbal descriptions when explaining to their partners.

13. Discussion Explain in what way the process of finding the sine and cosine of an angle from the tangent ratio is similar to the process of solving a linear equation in two variables by substitution.

When solving a linear equation in two variables, you use one equation to find an expression for one variable in terms of the other, then substitute that expression in the second equation to obtain an equation in one variable that you can solve for that variable and use to find the value of the other variable. When finding the sine and cosine of an angle from the tangent ratio, you use the known tangent value and the identity $\sin\theta = \cos\theta \tan\theta$ to write an expression for $\sin\theta$ in terms of $\cos\theta$, then substitute that expression in the second identity $\sin^2\theta + \cos^2\theta = 1$ to obtain an equation that you can solve for $\cos\theta$, and then use the value of $\cos\theta$ to find the value of $\sin\theta$.

14. Essential Question Check-In If you know only the sine or cosine of an angle and the quadrant in which the angle terminates, how can you find the other trigonometric ratios?

If you know only $\sin\theta$ or $\cos\theta$, you can find the other by substituting the known value in the Pythagorean identity $\sin^2\theta + \cos^2\theta = 1$ and solving for the unknown value. Then you can find the tangent of the angle using the identity $\tan\theta = \frac{\sin\theta}{\cos\theta}$. In all cases, use the quadrant in which the angle terminates to choose the correct sign for the ratio.

Evaluate: Homework and Practice

- Online Homework
- Hints and Help
- Extra Practice

Find the approximate value of each trigonometric function.

1. Given that $\sin\theta = 0.515$ where $0 < \theta < \frac{\pi}{2}$, find $\cos\theta$.

   $\cos\theta = \pm\sqrt{1 - \sin^2\theta} = \pm\sqrt{1 - (0.515)^2} \approx \pm 0.857$

   Since θ lies in Quadrant I, where $\cos\theta > 0$, $\cos\theta \approx 0.857$.

2. Given that $\cos\theta = 0.198$ where $\frac{3\pi}{2} < \theta < 2\pi$, find $\sin\theta$.

   $\sin\theta = \pm\sqrt{1 - \cos^2\theta} = \pm\sqrt{1 - (0.198)^2} \approx \pm 0.980$

   Since θ lies in Quadrant IV, where $\sin\theta < 0$, $\sin\theta \approx -0.980$.

3. Given that $\sin\theta = -0.447$ where $\frac{3\pi}{2} < \theta < 2\pi$, find $\cos\theta$.

   $\cos\theta = \pm\sqrt{1 - \sin^2\theta} = \pm\sqrt{1 - (-0.447)^2} \approx \pm 0.895$

   Since θ lies in Quadrant IV, where $\cos\theta > 0$, $\cos\theta \approx 0.895$.

4. Given that $\cos\theta = -0.544$ where $\frac{\pi}{2} < \theta < 2\pi$, find $\sin\theta$.

   $\sin\theta = \pm\sqrt{1 - \cos^2\theta} = \pm\sqrt{1 - (-0.544)^2} \approx \pm 0.839$

   Since θ lies in Quadrant II, where $\sin\theta > 0$, $\sin\theta \approx 0.839$.

Exercise	Depth of Knowledge (D.O.K.)	COMMON CORE Mathematical Practices
1–16	1 Recall of Information	MP.7 Using Structure
17	1 Recall of Information	MP.6 Precision
18–19	1 Recall of Information	MP.7 Using Structure
20	2 Skills/Concepts	MP.4 Modeling
21	3 Strategic Thinking	MP.4 Modeling
22–23	2 Skills/Concepts H.O.T.	MP.3 Logic
24–25	3 Strategic Thinking H.O.T.	MP.3 Logic

EVALUATE

ASSIGNMENT GUIDE

Concepts and Skills	Practice
Explore Proving a Pythagorean Identity	Exercises 18–19
Example 1 Finding the Value of the Other Trigonometric Functions Given the Value of sin θ or cos θ	Exercises 1–8, 20
Example 2 Finding the Value of the Other Trigonometric Functions Given the Value of tan θ	Exercises 9–17, 21

QUESTIONING STRATEGIES

? If you are given the cosine of an angle, why is it necessary to know in which quadrant the terminal side of the angle lies in order to determine the sine of the angle? **Knowing the quadrant enables you to determine the sign of the sine.**

VISUAL CUES

Suggest that students draw a sketch of the angle described in the problem, placing the terminal side of the angle in the correct quadrant. Students can then write the signs of each of the functions for that quadrant so that they will remember to affix the proper signs to the calculated values.

AVOID COMMON ERRORS

When making a substitution from the transformation of the identity $\tan\theta = \frac{\sin\theta}{\cos\theta}$ into the Pythagorean identity, some students may forget to square the coefficient of the substituted expression. Review that $\sin^2\theta$ means $(\sin\theta)^2$, and the same for cosine, and encourage students to use parentheses when making the substitution.

INTEGRATE TECHNOLOGY

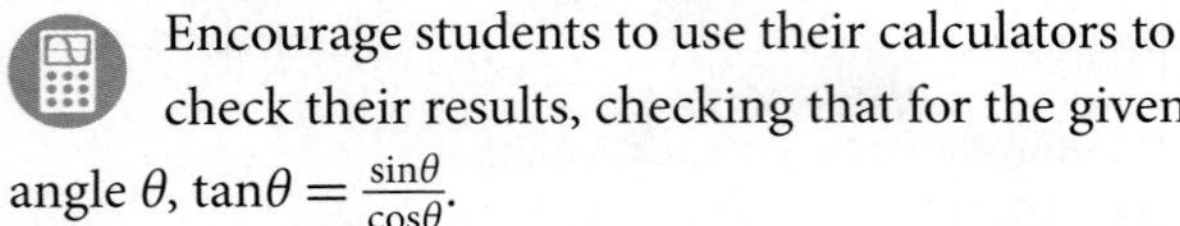

Encourage students to use their calculators to check their results, checking that for the given angle θ, $\tan\theta = \frac{\sin\theta}{\cos\theta}$.

5. Given that $\sin\boldsymbol{\theta} = -0.908$ where $\pi < \boldsymbol{\theta} < \frac{3\pi}{2}$, find $\cos\boldsymbol{\theta}$.

$\cos\theta = \pm\sqrt{1 - \sin^2\theta} = \pm\sqrt{1 - (-0.908)^2} \approx \pm 0.419$

Since θ lies in Quadrant III, where $\cos\theta > 0$, $\cos\theta \approx -0.419$.

6. Given that $\sin\boldsymbol{\theta} = 0.313$ where $\frac{\pi}{2} < \boldsymbol{\theta} < \pi$, find $\cos\boldsymbol{\theta}$.

$\cos\theta = \pm\sqrt{1 - \sin^2\theta} = \pm\sqrt{1 - (-0.313)^2} \approx \pm 0.950$

Since θ lies in Quadrant II, where $\cos\theta < 0$, $\cos\theta \approx -0.950$.

7. Given that $\cos\boldsymbol{\theta} = 0.678$ where $0 < \boldsymbol{\theta} < \frac{\pi}{2}$, find $\sin\boldsymbol{\theta}$.

$\sin\theta = \pm\sqrt{1 - \cos^2\theta} = \pm\sqrt{1 - (-0.678)^2} \approx \pm 0.735$

Since θ lies in Quadrant I, where $\sin\theta > 0$, $\sin\theta \approx 0.735$.

8. Given that $\cos\boldsymbol{\theta} = -0.489$ where $\pi < \boldsymbol{\theta} < \frac{3\pi}{2}$, find $\sin\boldsymbol{\theta}$.

$\sin\theta = \pm\sqrt{1 - \cos^2\theta} = \pm\sqrt{1 - (-0.489)^2} \approx \pm 0.872$

Since θ lies in Quadrant III, where $\sin\theta < 0$, $\sin\theta \approx -0.872$.

Find the approximate value of each trigonometric function.

9. Given that $\tan\boldsymbol{\theta} \approx -3.966$ where $\frac{\pi}{2} < \boldsymbol{\theta} < \pi$, find the values of $\sin\boldsymbol{\theta}$ and $\cos\boldsymbol{\theta}$.

$\sin\theta = \cos\theta\tan\theta \approx -3.966\cos\theta$

$\sin^2\theta + \cos^2\theta = 1$

$(-3.966\cos\theta)^2 + \cos^2\theta \approx 1$

$\cos^2\theta \approx 0.060 \rightarrow \cos\theta \approx \pm 0.245$

In Quad. II, cosine is neg. and sine is pos., so cosine is negative and sine is positive. $\cos\theta \approx -0.245$ and $\sin\theta \approx -3.966\cos\theta \approx 0.972$.

10. Given that $\tan\boldsymbol{\theta} \approx -4.580$ where $\frac{3\pi}{2} < \boldsymbol{\theta} < 2\pi$, find the values of $\sin\boldsymbol{\theta}$ and $\cos\boldsymbol{\theta}$.

$\sin\theta = \cos\theta\tan\theta \approx -4.580\cos\theta$

$\sin^2\theta + \cos^2\theta = 1$

$(-4.580\cos\theta)^2 + \cos^2\theta \approx 1$

$\cos^2\theta \approx 0.046 \rightarrow \cos\theta \approx \pm 0.214$

Since cosine is positive in Quadrant IV, $\cos\theta \approx 0.214$ and $\sin\theta \approx -4.580\cos\theta \approx 0.980$.

11. Given that $\tan\theta \approx 7.549$ where $0 < \theta < \frac{\pi}{2}$, find the values of $\sin\theta$ and $\cos\theta$.

Write $\sin\theta$ in terms of $\cos\theta$.

$\sin\theta = \cos\theta \tan\theta \approx 7.549 \cos\theta$

Solve for $\sin\theta$ and $\cos\theta$.

$$\begin{aligned} \sin^2\theta + \cos^2\theta &= 1 \\ (7.549 \cos\theta)^2 + \cos^2\theta &\approx 1 \\ 56.987 \cos^2\theta + \cos^2\theta &\approx 1 \\ 57.987 \cos^2\theta &\approx 1 \\ \cos^2\theta &\approx 0.017 \\ \cos\theta &\approx \pm 0.130 \end{aligned}$$

Since cosine is positive in Quadrant I, $\cos\theta \approx -0.130$ and $\sin\theta \approx 7.549 \cos\theta \approx 0.981$.

12. Given that $\tan\theta \approx 4.575$ where $\pi < \theta < \frac{3\pi}{2}$, find the values of $\sin\theta$ and $\cos\theta$.

Write $\sin\theta$ in terms of $\cos\theta$.

$\sin\theta = \cos\theta \tan\theta \approx 4.575 \cos\theta$

Solve for $\sin\theta$ and $\cos\theta$.

$$\begin{aligned} \sin^2\theta + \cos^2\theta &= 1 \\ (4.575 \cos\theta)^2 + \cos^2\theta &\approx 1 \\ 20.931 \cos^2\theta + \cos^2\theta &\approx 1 \\ 21.931 \cos^2\theta &\approx 1 \\ \cos^2\theta &\approx 0.046 \\ \cos\theta &\approx \pm 0.214 \end{aligned}$$

Since cosine is negative in Quadrant III, $\cos\theta \approx -0.214$ and $\sin\theta \approx 4.575 \cos\theta \approx -0.979$.

13. Given that $\tan\theta \approx -1.237$ where $\frac{3\pi}{2}, < \theta < 2\pi$ find the values of $\sin\theta$ and $\cos\theta$.

Write $\sin\theta$ in terms of $\cos\theta$.

$\sin\theta = \cos\theta \tan\theta \approx -1.237 \cos\theta$

Solve for $\sin\theta$ and $\cos\theta$.

$$\begin{aligned} \sin^2\theta + \cos^2\theta &= 1 \\ (-1.237 \cos\theta)^2 + \cos^2\theta &\approx 1 \\ 1.530 \cos^2\theta + \cos^2\theta &\approx 1 \\ 2.530 \cos^2\theta &\approx 1 \\ \cos^2\theta &\approx 0.395 \\ \cos\theta &\approx \pm 0.628 \end{aligned}$$

Since cosine is negative in Quadrant IV, $\cos\theta \approx 0.628$ and $\sin\theta \approx -1.237 \cos\theta \approx -0.777$.

14. Given that $\tan\theta \approx 5.632$ where $\pi < \theta < \frac{3\pi}{2}$, find the values of $\sin\theta$ and $\cos\theta$.

Write $\sin\theta$ in terms of $\cos\theta$.

$\sin\theta = \cos\theta \tan\theta \approx 5.632 \cos\theta$

Solve for $\sin\theta$ and $\cos\theta$.

$$\sin^2\theta + \cos^2\theta = 1$$
$$(5.632 \cos\theta)^2 + \cos^2\theta \approx 1$$
$$31.719 \cos^2\theta + \cos^2\theta \approx 1$$
$$32.719 \cos^2\theta \approx 1$$
$$\cos^2\theta \approx 0.031$$
$$\cos\theta \approx \pm 0.176$$

Since cosine is negative in Quadrant III, $\cos\theta \approx -0.176$ and $\sin\theta \approx 5.632 \cos\theta \approx -0.991$.

15. Given that $\tan\theta \approx 6.653$ where $0 < \theta < \frac{\pi}{2}$, find the values of $\sin\theta$ and $\cos\theta$.

Write $\sin\theta$ in terms of $\cos\theta$.

$\sin\theta = \cos\theta \tan\theta \approx 6.653 \cos\theta$

Solve for $\sin\theta$ and $\cos\theta$.

$$\sin^2\theta + \cos^2\theta = 1$$
$$(6.653 \cos\theta)^2 + \cos^2\theta \approx 1$$
$$44.262 \cos^2\theta + \cos^2\theta \approx 1$$
$$45.262 \cos^2\theta \approx 1$$
$$\cos^2\theta \approx 0.022$$
$$\cos\theta \approx \pm 0.148$$

Since cosine is positive in Quadrant I, $\cos\theta \approx -0.148$ and $\sin\theta \approx 6.653 \cos\theta \approx 0.985$.

16. Given that $\tan\theta \approx -9.366$ where $\frac{\pi}{2}, < \theta < \pi$ find the values of $\sin\theta$ and $\cos\theta$.

Write $\sin\theta$ in terms of $\cos\theta$.

$\sin\theta = \cos\theta \tan\theta \approx -9.366 \cos\theta$

Solve for $\sin\theta$ and $\cos\theta$.

$$\sin^2\theta + \cos^2\theta = 1$$
$$(-9.366 \cos\theta)^2 + \cos^2\theta \approx 1$$
$$87.722 \cos^2\theta + \cos^2\theta \approx 1$$
$$88.722 \cos^2\theta \approx 1$$
$$\cos^2\theta \approx 0.011$$
$$\cos\theta \approx \pm 0.105$$

Since cosine is negative in Quadrant II, $\cos\theta \approx -0.105$ and $\sin\theta \approx -9.366 \cos\theta \approx 0.983$.

17. Given the trigonometric function and the location of the terminal angle, state whether the function value will be positive or negative.

A. $\cos\theta$, Quadrant I	**A. Positive**
B. $\sin\theta$, Quadrant IV	**B. Negative**
C. $\tan\theta$, Quadrant II	**C. Negative**
D. $\sin\theta$, Quadrant III	**D. Negative**
E. $\tan\theta$, Quadrant III	**E. Positive**

18. Confirm the Pythagorean identity $\sin^2\theta + \cos^2\theta = 1$ for $\theta = \frac{7\pi}{4}$.

$\sin\left(\frac{7\pi}{4}\right) = -\frac{\sqrt{2}}{2}$ **and** $\cos\left(\frac{7\pi}{4}\right) = \frac{\sqrt{2}}{2}$. **Therefore,**

$$\sin^2\theta + \cos^2\theta = \sin^2\left(\frac{7\pi}{4}\right) + \cos^2\left(\frac{7\pi}{4}\right) = \left(-\frac{\sqrt{2}}{2}\right)^2 + \left(\frac{\sqrt{2}}{2}\right)^2 = \frac{1}{2} + \frac{1}{2} = 1.$$

19. Recall that the equation of a circle with radius r centered at the origin is $x^2 + y^2 = r^2$. Use this fact and the fact that the coordinates of a point on this circle are $(x, y) = (r\cos\theta, r\sin\theta)$ for a central angle θ to show that the Pythagorean identity derived above is true.

$$x^2 + y^2 = r^2 \Rightarrow (r\cos\theta)^2 + (r\sin\theta)^2 = r^2$$

$$r^2\cos^2\theta + r^2\sin^2\theta = r^2 \Rightarrow \cos^2\theta + \sin^2\theta = 1$$

20. Sports A ski supply company is testing the friction of a new ski wax by placing a waxed block on an inclined plane covered with wet snow. The incline plane is slowly raised until the block begins to slide. At the instant the block starts to slide, the component of the weight of the block parallel to the incline, $mg\sin\theta$, and the resistive force of friction, $\mu mg\cos\theta$, are equal, where μ is the coefficient of friction. Find the value of μ to the nearest hundredth if $\sin\theta = 0.139$ at the instant the block begins to slide.

Find $\cos\theta$. Because $\cos\theta$ will be between 0 and 90 degrees, $\cos\theta$ will be positive.

$$\cos\theta = \sqrt{1 - \sin^2\theta} = \sqrt{1 - (0.139)^2} \approx 0.928$$

$$mg\sin\theta = \mu mg\cos\theta \Rightarrow \sin\theta = \mu\cos\theta$$

$$0.139 = \mu\cos\theta$$

$$\mu = \frac{0.139}{\cos\theta} \approx \frac{0.139}{0.928} \approx 0.15$$

21. Driving Tires and roads are designed so that the coefficient of friction between the rubber of the tires and the asphalt of the roads is very high, which gives plenty of traction for starting, stopping, and turning. For a particular road surface and tire, the steepest angle for which a car could rest on the slope without starting to slide has a sine of 0.643. This value satisfies the equation $mg\sin\theta = \mu mg\cos\theta$ where μ is the coefficient of friction. Find the value of μ to the nearest hundredth.

Because $\cos\theta$ will be between 0 and 90 degrees, $\cos\theta$ will be positive.

$$\cos\theta = \sqrt{1 - \sin^2\theta} = \sqrt{1 - (0.643)^2} \approx 0.766$$

$$mg\sin\theta = \mu mg\cos\theta \Rightarrow \sin\theta = \mu\cos\theta$$

$$0.643 = \mu\cos\theta \Rightarrow$$

$$\mu = \frac{0.643}{\cos\theta} \approx \frac{0.643}{0.766} \approx 0.84$$

PEER-TO-PEER DISCUSSION

Ask students to discuss with a partner how they could use what they know about the trigonometry of a right triangle to prove the identity $\tan\theta = \frac{\sin\theta}{\cos\theta}$. Have them discuss their proofs with the class.

Students' work should show that since

$$\sin\theta = \frac{\text{side opposite}}{\text{hypotenuse}} \text{ and}$$

$$\cos\theta = \frac{\text{side adjacent}}{\text{hypotenuse}}, \text{ then}$$

$$\frac{\sin\theta}{\cos\theta} = \frac{\frac{\text{side opposite}}{\text{hypotenuse}}}{\frac{\text{side adjacent}}{\text{hypotenuse}}}$$

$$= \frac{\text{side opposite}}{\text{hypotenuse}} \cdot \frac{\text{hypotenuse}}{\text{side adjacent}}$$

$$= \frac{\text{side opposite}}{\text{side adjacent}}$$

$$= \tan\theta$$

JOURNAL

Have students explain how knowing that the sine of an angle is approximately 0.2588 enables them to find two possible values for the cosine of the angle. Have them find these values, and tell what information would be necessary to decide which of the two possible values is the correct cosine of the angle.

H.O.T. Focus on Higher Order Thinking

22. Explain the Error Julian was given that $\sin\theta = -0.555$ where $\frac{3\pi}{2}, < \theta < 2\pi$ and told to find $\cos\theta$. He produced the following work:

$$\cos\theta = \pm\sqrt{1 - \ \sin^2\theta}$$
$$= \pm\sqrt{1 - \left(-0.555^2\right)}$$
$$\approx \pm 1.144$$

Since $\cos\theta > 0$ when $\frac{3\pi}{2} < \theta < 2\pi$, $\cos\theta \approx 1.144$.

Explain his error and state the correct answer.

Julian added the two quantities inside of the square root together instead of subtracting. He should have noticed, since the cosine of a number is never more than 1. He should have done the following:

$$\cos\theta = \pm\sqrt{1 - \sin^2\theta}$$
$$= \pm\sqrt{1 - (-0.555)^2}$$
$$\approx \pm 0.832$$

Since $\cos\theta > 0$ when $\frac{3\pi}{2} < \theta < 2\pi$, $\cos\theta \approx 0.832$.

Critical Thinking Rewrite each trigonometric expression in terms of cosθ and simplify.

23. $\dfrac{\sin^2\theta}{1 - \cos\theta}$

$$\frac{\sin^2\theta}{1 - \cos\theta}$$
$$= \frac{1 - \cos^2\theta}{1 - \cos\theta}$$
$$= \frac{(1 - \cos\theta)(1 + \cos\theta)}{1 - \cos\theta}$$
$$= 1 + \cos\theta$$

24. $\cos\theta + \sin\theta\cos\theta - \tan\theta + \tan\theta\sin^2\theta$ (Hint: Begin by factoring $\tan\theta$ from the last two terms.)

$$\cos\theta + \sin\theta\cos\theta - \tan\theta + \tan\theta\sin^2\theta$$
$$= \cos\theta + \sin\theta\cos\theta - \tan\theta(1 - \sin^2\theta)$$
$$= \cos\theta + \sin\theta\cos\theta - \tan\theta\cos^2\theta$$
$$= \cos\theta + \sin\theta\cos\theta - \frac{\sin\theta}{\cos\theta}\cos^2\theta$$
$$= \cos\theta + \sin\theta\cos\theta - \sin\theta\cos\theta$$
$$= \cos\theta$$

25. Critical Thinking To what trigonometric function does the expression $\frac{\sqrt{1 - \cos^2\theta}}{\sqrt{1 - \sin^2\theta}}$ simplify? Explain your answer.

The expression $\frac{\sqrt{1 - \cos^2\theta}}{\sqrt{1 - \sin^2\theta}}$ simplifies to $\tan\theta$. If you rewrite $\frac{\sqrt{1 - \cos^2\theta}}{\sqrt{1 - \sin^2\theta}}$ using the Pythagorean Identity, you get the result $\frac{\sqrt{\sin^2\theta}}{\sqrt{\cos^2\theta}}$. Taking the square root results in the expression $\frac{\sin\theta}{\cos\theta}$, which is equivalent to $\tan\theta$.

.esson Performance Task

tower casts a shadow that is 160 feet long at a particular time one orning. With the base of the tower as the origin, east as the positive -axis, and north as the positive y-axis, the shadow at this time is the northwest quadrant formed by the axes. Also at this time, the ngent of the angle of rotation measured so that the shadow lies on e terminal ray is $\tan\theta = -2.545$. What are the coordinates of the p of the shadow to the nearest foot, and what do they indicate?

he coordinates of a point on a circle centered at the rigin with radius r are $r\cos\theta$ and $r\sin\theta$. Use identities elating the sine, cosine, and tangent of an angle to find osθ and sinθ, then use those values to find the coordinates.

irst use the value of the tangent and the identity $\sin\theta = \cos\theta\tan\theta$ to find an expression for sinθ 1 terms of cosθ.

$\text{in}\theta = \cos\theta\tan\theta = -2.545\cos\theta$

ubstitute this expression for sinθ into the Pythagorean identity $\text{in}^2\theta + \cos^2\theta = 1$ to solve for cosθ. Since the shadow is in the northwest, it is in Quadrant II, vhich means that the value of cosθ will be negative.

$$\sin^2\theta + \cos^2\theta = 1$$
$$-2.545\cos\theta)^2 + \cos^2\theta \approx 1$$
$$6.477\cos^2\theta + \cos^2\theta \approx 1$$
$$7.477\cos^2\theta \approx 1$$
$$\cos^2\theta \approx 0.1337$$
$$\cos\theta \approx -0.366$$

ow substitute to find sinθ.

$\text{in}\theta = -2.545\cos\theta \approx -2.545(-0.366) \approx 0.931$

se the fact that $r = 160$ to find the coordinates of the tip of the shadow.

$\cos\theta = 160(-0.366) = -58.56$

$\sin\theta = 160(0.931) = 148.96$

he coordinates are $(-59,149)$. This indicates that the tip of the shadow is about 58 feet west nd 149 feet north of the base of the tower.

EXTENSION ACTIVITY

Your location with respect to two cell towers can be determined by a process called *triangulation*. Have students research how triangulation, a use of angles to find distances, is also employed in other activities, such as mapmaking. Students will encounter and may present the Law of Cosines, which states that $c^2 = a^2 + b^2 - 2ab\cos C$.

INTEGRATE MATHEMATICAL PRACTICES

Focus on Math Connections

MP.1 Students likely have analyzed the relationships between shadow length and other measures, such as object height, in two dimensions. Remind them that they have used indirect measurement and proportion as well as the Pythagorean Theorem to approach these problems. Note that the Lesson Performance Task expands these analyses to allow for positions in all four quadrants using positive and negative coordinate positioning.

CURRICULUM INTEGRATION

Note that a counterclockwise movement of the sun's shadows occurs only in the Southern Hemisphere. Most sundials, which were first introduced in the Northern Hemisphere, assume that shadows move clockwise, and this is also the reason for the development of clockwise-turning clock hands! Point out to students that the sun appears to move in the opposite direction from its shadows—the sun moves counterclockwise in the Northern Hemisphere, so its shadows move in the opposite direction.

Scoring Rubric

2 points: Student correctly solves the problem and explains his/her reasoning.

1 point: Student shows good understanding of the problem but does not fully solve or explain his/her reasoning.

0 points: Student does not demonstrate understanding of the problem.

Study Guide Review

ASSESSMENT AND INTERVENTION

Assign or customize module reviews.

MODULE PERFORMANCE TASK

Mathematical Practices: MP.1, MP.2, MP.4, MP.5, MP.7, MP.8
F-TF.A.1, F-TF.A.3

SUPPORTING STUDENT REASONING

Students should begin this problem by focusing on the information they will need. Here is some of the information they may ask for.

- **Should we use radians or degrees?** Elicit from students why either would produce the same result.
- **Do we have to know the length of the hands on the clock?** Let students know that they only need to find points on the circle's circumference, not points within the circle.

STUDY GUIDE REVIEW

Unit-Circle Definition of Trigonometric Functions

Essential Question: How can the unit-circle definition of trigonometric functions help to solve real-world problems?

Key Vocabulary
angle of rotation (*ángulo de rotación*)
coterminal angles (*ángulos coterminales*)
radian measure (*medida del radián*)
reference angle (*ángulo de referencia*)

KEY EXAMPLE (Lesson 17.1)

A laboratory centrifuge of diameter 12 inches makes approximately 10,000 revolutions in 3 minutes. How long will it take for a test tube in the centrifuge to travel 360,000 degrees? How far will the test tube travel in inches?

$3 \text{ min} \cdot \frac{60 \text{ sec}}{1 \text{ min}} = 180 \text{ sec}$ — Convert minutes per rev. to seconds per rev.

$\frac{360°(10{,}000)}{180 \text{ sec}} = 20{,}000°/\text{sec}$ — Find the angular velocity in terms of degrees/sec.

$\frac{360{,}000°}{\frac{20{,}000°}{1 \text{ sec}}} = 18 \text{ sec}$ — Divide the number of degrees by the velocity.

$S = \theta \cdot \frac{\pi r}{180}$ — Use the formula for arc length to find the distance.

$S = 360{,}000 \cdot \frac{\pi(6)}{180} \approx 37{,}700$

The test tube travels 360,000 degrees in 18 seconds, and travels approximately 37,700 inches.

KEY EXAMPLE (Lesson 17.2)

Evaluate the trigonometric function $\cos \frac{13\pi}{3}$ by using the quadrant and the reference angle to determine the sign and absolute value.

$\frac{13\pi}{3} = 4\pi + \frac{\pi}{3}$ — Identify the coterminal angle between 0 and 2π.

$\theta' = \theta$ — Find the reference angle for quadrant I.

$\vartheta' = \frac{\pi}{3}$

$\theta' = \frac{\pi}{3} \times \frac{180°}{\pi} = 60°$ — Identify the special right triangle angle.

$\cos\theta' = \frac{1}{2}$ — Use the sides of a 30-60-90 triangle.

$\cos \frac{13\pi}{3} = + \cos \frac{\pi}{3}$ — Apply the sign of cosine in quadrant I.

$\cos \frac{13\pi}{3} = \frac{1}{2}$

SCAFFOLDING SUPPORT

- Watch for students using angle measures that are based on the order of the numbers on a clock, rather than according to the unit circle. Remind them that angle measures on the unit circle begin at (1, 0) and proceed counterclockwise, so the "1" on a clock is at 60°, not 30°.

EXERCISES

Use this situation for Exercises 1–6. A merry-go-round of a given radius is traveling at the given rate per minute.

How far, in feet, will a child on the edge of the merry-go-round travel? *(Lesson 17.1)*

1. 4 feet; 270°

Approx. 19 feet

2. 6 feet; 310°

Approx. 32 feet

3. 2 feet; 720°

Approx. 25 feet

4. 3 feet; 90°

Approx. 5 feet

If the radius is 4 feet, how many seconds will it take for the child to travel the given degree distance at the given rate? *(Lesson 17.1)*

5. 3 rev/min; 270°

15 seconds

6. 5 rev/min; 310°

$10.\overline{3}$ seconds

Evaluate the trigonometric function by using the quadrant and the reference angle to determine the sign and absolute value. *(Lesson 17.2)*

7. $\sin \frac{13\pi}{4}$

Approx. –0.707

8. $\tan \frac{4\pi}{3}$

Approx. 1.73

MODULE PERFORMANCE TASK

Telling Time with Trig

An analog clock displays time on a computer screen. It is based on a unit circle, so the programmer can use cosine and sine to specify the positions of the ends of the hands. Draw a clock face and label each of the hour marks with its coordinates. What are the coordinates of each hand at 4:30?

Start by listing in the space below the information you will need to solve the problem. Then use your own paper to complete the task. Be sure to write down all your data and assumptions. Then use graphs, numbers, words, or algebra to explain how you reached your conclusion.

DISCUSSION OPPORTUNITIES

- Lead students in a discussion of how to find the hand positions for other, more difficult times, such as 6:15 or 3:04.
- Discuss with students any patterns they notice in the coordinates on the unit circle.
- Have students discuss possible pros and cons of digital and analog clocks.

SAMPLE SOLUTION

Assumptions

The 12 numbers are evenly spaced on the circumference of a unit circle.

Solution

The angle between two consecutive numbers is $\frac{2\pi}{12}$, or $\frac{\pi}{6}$ radians. Since 1:00 is twice 30° from the x-axis, its coordinates are $\left(\cos 2 \cdot \frac{\pi}{6}, \sin 2 \cdot \frac{\pi}{6}\right) = \left(\frac{1}{2}, \frac{\sqrt{3}}{2}\right)$.

A similar process can be used to find the rest of the coordinates, which are given in the art below.

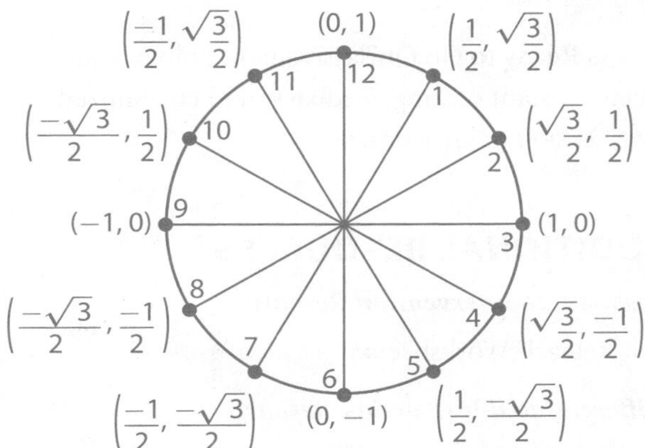

The hour hand rotates $\frac{\pi}{6}$ radians in one hour; the minute hand moves 2π radians in one hour. At 4:30, the minute hand is pointing to the 6 at (0, –1), and the hour hand is halfway between $\frac{11\pi}{6}$ and $\frac{10\pi}{6}$ radians at $\frac{7\pi}{4}$ radians, with coordinates of $\left(\cos \frac{7\pi}{4}, \sin \frac{7\pi}{4}\right)$ or $\left(\frac{1}{2}\sqrt{2}, -\frac{1}{2}\sqrt{2}\right)$.

Assessment Rubric

2 points: Student correctly solves the problem and explains his/her reasoning.

1 point: Student shows good understanding of the problem but does not fully solve or explain his/her reasoning.

0 points: Student does not demonstrate understanding of the problem.

Ready to Go On?

ASSESS MASTERY

Use the assessment on this page to determine if students have mastered the concepts and standards covered in this module.

ASSESSMENT AND INTERVENTION

Access Ready to Go On? assessment online, and receive instant scoring, feedback, and customized intervention or enrichment.

ADDITIONAL RESOURCES

Response to Intervention Resources

- Reteach Worksheets

Differentiated Instruction Resources

- Reading Strategies EL
- Success for English Learners EL
- Challenge Worksheets

Assessment Resources

- Leveled Module Quizzes

17.1–17.3 Unit-Circle Definition of Trigonometric Functions

- Online Homework
- Hints and Help
- Extra Practice

A coin of radius 10 mm is rolled upon the ground at the given rate for the given amount of rotation. State how long it will take the coin to travel the degree measure, and how far in millimeters the coin will go.

1. 180°; 5 rev/sec

0.1 sec; approx. 31.4 mm

2. 360°; 7 rev/sec

approx. 0.14 sec; approx. 62.8 mm

3. 540°; 6 rev/sec

0.25 sec; approx. 94.2 mm

4. 1800°; 4 rev/sec

1.25 sec; approx. 314.2 mm

Evaluate the trigonometric function by using the quadrant and the reference angle to determine the sign and absolute value.

5. $\cos \frac{17\pi}{4}$

approx. 0.707

6. sin 410°

approx. 0.766

Find the approximate value of each trigonometric function.

7. Given $\sin \theta = 0.996$; find $\cos \theta$

approx. ± 0.089

8. Given $\cos \theta = 0.342$; find $\sin \theta$

approx. ± 0.940

ESSENTIAL QUESTION

9. How can the unit-circle definition of trigonometric functions help a racecar driver?

Possible answer: Knowing the diameter of the tires and the distance a driver needs to go in a certain amount of time can help a driver find out how fast he or she needs to be driving in a race to win.

COMMON CORE Common Core Standards

Lesson	Exercise	Math Standards	Mathematical Practices
17.1	1–4	**F-TF.A.1**	**MP.2**
17.2	5	**F-TF.A.2**	**MP.2**
17.2	6	**F-TF.A.2**	**MP.2**
17.3	7	**F-TF.C.8**	**MP.1**
17.3	8	**F-TF.C.8**	**MP.1**

MODULE 17
MIXED REVIEW

Assessment Readiness

1. Consider the radian measure $\frac{16\pi}{5}$. Is the trigonometric equation correct?

   Select Yes or No for A–C.

   A. $\cos \frac{16\pi}{5} \approx -0.809$ ● Yes ○ No

   B. $\tan \frac{16\pi}{5} \approx 0.727$ ● Yes ○ No

   C. $\sin \frac{16\pi}{5} \approx 0.588$ ○ Yes ● No

2. Consider a situation where a colored ring is 10 inches in diameter. Choose True or False for each statement.

   A. If the ring is rolling at a rate of 2 revolutions per second, it will take approximately 0.2 seconds to travel 120°. ● True ○ False

   B. The rate of travel is needed to find the distance the ring will travel in 1080°. ○ True ● False

   C. The radius is needed to find how long it will take the ring to travel 1080°. ○ True ● False

3. Carlos wants to find the value of $\cos \theta$ given $\sin \theta = 0.707$, and he finds that $\cos \theta$ is the same value. Is this possible, or did he make a mistake? Explain.

   His answer is possible. The cosine and sine of an angle can be the same if the angle is 45° or $\frac{\pi}{4}$.

4. Given the equation $y = x(x - 3)(2x + 7)$, find the rational roots. Explain how you determined your answer.

   The rational roots are $x = -3.5, 0, 3$. Possible answer; I found my answers by graphing the equation, then finding where the equation crossed the x-axis.

MIXED REVIEW
Assessment Readiness

ASSESSMENT AND INTERVENTION

Assign ready-made or customized practice tests to prepare students for high-stakes tests.

ADDITIONAL RESOURCES

Assessment Resources

- Leveled Module Quizzes: Modified, B

AVOID COMMON ERRORS

Item 1 When students use a calculator for this problem, they may forget to change from degree mode into radian mode. Remind students that degree mode can only be used for degree measures, and the calculator mode must be changed before it will evaluate radians correctly.

COMMON CORE Common Core Standards

Lesson	Exercise	Math Standards	Mathematical Practices
17.2	1	**F-TF.A.2**	**MP.5**
17.1	2	**F-TF.A.1**	**MP.2**
11.1, 17.3	3*	**N-RN.A.1, F-TF.C.8**	**MP.3**
7.1	4*	**A-APR.B.2**	**MP.6**

* Item integrates mixed review concepts from previous modules or a previous course.

MODULE 18

Graphing Trigonometric Functions

ESSENTIAL QUESTION:

Answer: The sine and cosine functions can be useful for modeling different types of waves, such as sound waves or electromagnetic waves.

PROFESSIONAL DEVELOPMENT VIDEO

Professional Development Video
Author Matt Larson models successful teaching practices in an actual high-school classroom.
Professional Development
my.hrw.com

MODULE 18

Graphing Trigonometric Functions

Essential Question: How can graphing trigonometric functions help to solve real-world problems?

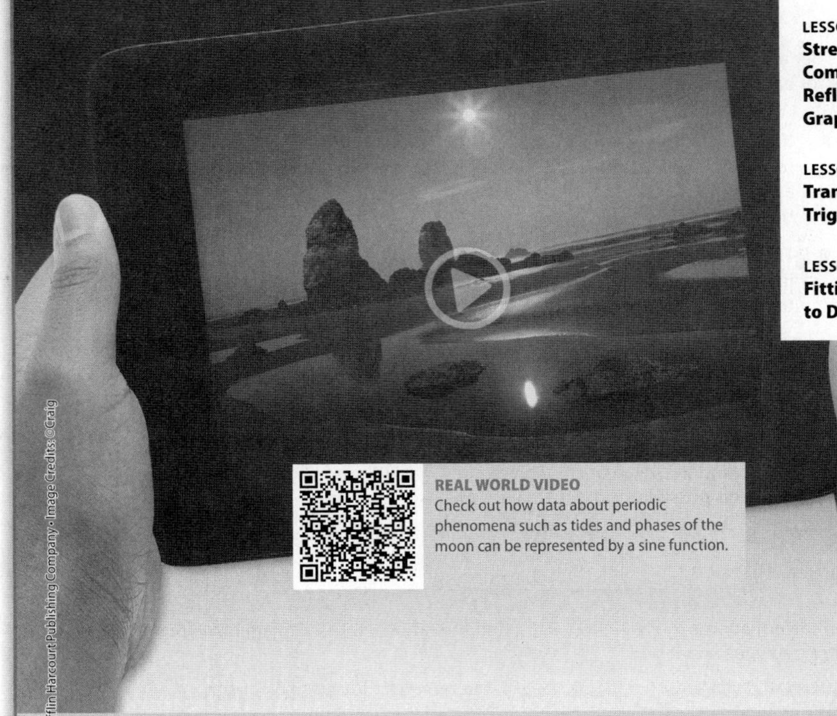

REAL WORLD VIDEO
Check out how data about periodic phenomena such as tides and phases of the moon can be represented by a sine function.

MODULE PERFORMANCE TASK PREVIEW

What's Your Sine?

The moon is visible only because we see the sun's light reflecting from the moon's surface. Depending on where the moon is in its orbit around Earth, we see no moon, a full moon, or any fraction of the moon's surface in between. How can we use a sine function to figure out what fraction of the moon's surface will be lit on any given night? Let's find out!

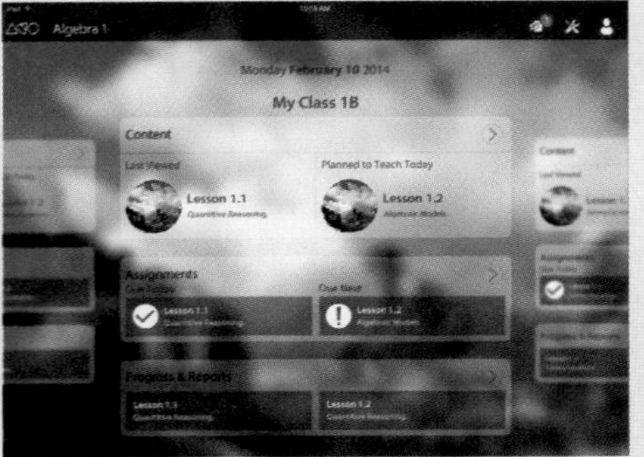

DIGITAL TEACHER EDITION

Access a full suite of teaching resources when and where you need them:

- Access content online or offline
- Customize lessons to share with your class
- Communicate with your students in real-time
- View student grades and data instantly to target your instruction where it is needed most

PERSONAL MATH TRAINER

Assessment and Intervention

Assign automatically graded homework, quizzes, tests, and intervention activities. Prepare your students with updated, Common Core-aligned practice tests.

Complete these exercises to review skills you will need for this chapter.

- Online Homework
- Hints and Help
- Extra Practice

Stretching, Compressing, and Reflecting Quadratic Functions

Example 1 The graph of $g(x) = -2(x+9)^2 - 4$ is vertically compressed by a factor of 0.5 and reflected over the y—axis. Write the new function.

Vertical compression:

$g'(x) = 0.5\left(-2(x+9)^2 - 4\right) = -(x+9)^2 - 2$

Reflection over the y—axis: $g''(x) = -(-x+9)^2 - 2$

The new function is $g''(x) = -(-x+9)^2 - 2$.

Write the new function for $f(x) = (x+1)^2 - 2$ after the given transformation.

1. reflection over x—axis

   $f'(x) = -(x+1)^2 + 2$

2. horizontal compression, factor of 10

   $f'(x) = (10x+1)^2 - 2$

3. vertical stretch, factor of 2

   $f'(x) = 2(x+1)^2 - 4$

Combining Transformations of Quadratic Functions

Example 2 The graph of $f(x) = -2(x+5)^2 + 1$ is transformed 3 units right and 2 units down. Write the new function.

The vertex is $(-5, 1)$. Its location after the transformation is $(-5+3, 1-2)$, or $(-2, -1)$.

The new function is $f'(x) = -2(x+2)^2 - 1$.

Write the new function after the given transformation.

4. $p(x) = 0.1(x-8)^2 + 9$
   5 units left, 6 units down

   $p'(x) = 0.1(x-3)^2 + 3$

5. $q(x) = -0.5(x+2)^2 - 12$
   1 unit right, 9 units up

   $q'(x) = -0.5(x+1)^2 - 3$

6. $h(x) = 0.8(x-8)^2 - 10$
   7 units left, 4 units up

   $h'(x) = 0.8(x-1)^2 - 6$

Response to Intervention			Differentiated Instruction
Tier 1 Lesson Intervention Worksheets	**Tier 2** Strategic Intervention Skills Intervention Worksheets	**Tier 3** Intensive Intervention Worksheets available online	
Reteach 18.1 Reteach 18.2 Reteach 18.3 Reteach 18.4	38 Transforming Linear Functions 39 Transforming Quadratic Functions 42 Combining Transformations … 57 Stretching, Compressing, …	Building Block Skills 40, 43, 45, 102, 103	Challenge worksheets Extend the Math Lesson Activities in TE

Are You Ready?

ASSESS READINESS

Use the assessment on this page to determine if students need strategic or intensive intervention for the module's prerequisite skills.

ASSESSMENT AND INTERVENTION

RtI Response to Intervention TIER 1, TIER 2, TIER 3 SKILLS

Personal Math Trainer will automatically create a standards-based, personalized intervention assignment for your students, targeting each student's individual needs!

ADDITIONAL RESOURCES

See the table below for a full list of intervention resources available for this module.

Response to Intervention Resources also includes:

- Tier 2 Skill Pre-Tests for each Module
- Tier 2 Skill Post-Tests for each skill

LESSON 18.1

Stretching, Compressing, and Reflecting Sine and Cosine Graphs

Common Core Math Standards

The student is expected to:

F-IF.C.7e

Graph exponential and logarithmic functions, showing intercepts and end behavior, and trigonometric functions, showing period, midline, and amplitude. Also F-BF.B.3, F-IF.B.4

Mathematical Practices

MP.7 Using Structure

Language Objective

Complete a table describing the features of sine and cosine graphs.

ENGAGE

Essential Question: What are the key features of the graphs of the sine and cosine functions?

Possible answer: The graph of the sine function has an amplitude of 1, a period of 2π, x-intercepts at, $n\pi$ maximums at $x = \frac{\pi}{2} + 2n\pi$, and minimums at $x = \frac{3\pi}{2} + 2n\pi$, where n is an integer. The graph of the cosine function has an amplitude of 1, a period of 2π, x-intercepts at $\frac{\pi}{2} + n\pi$, maximums at $x = 2n\pi$, and minimums at $x = \pi + 2n\pi$, where n is an integer.

PREVIEW: LESSON PERFORMANCE TASK

View the Engage section online. Discuss the photo and how a trigonometric function can be used to model sounds. Then preview the Lesson Performance Task.

Name ____________ Class ____________ Date ____________

18.1 Stretching, Compressing, and Reflecting Sine and Cosine Graphs

Essential Question: What are the key features of the graphs of the sine and cosine functions?

Explore Graphing the Basic Sine and Cosine Functions

Recall that the points around the unit circle have coordinates $(\cos\theta, \sin\theta)$ as shown.

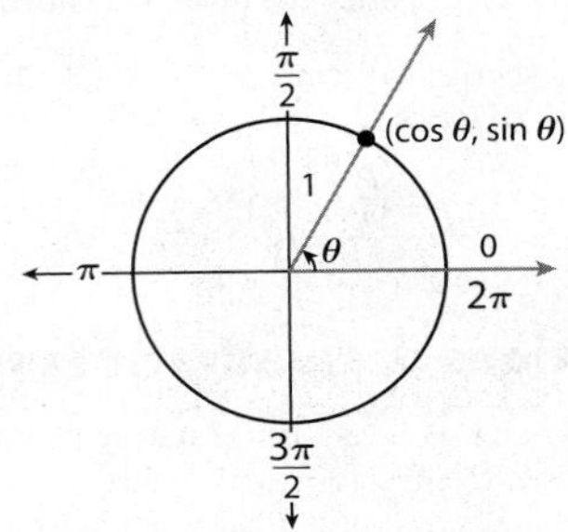

Ⓐ Identify the following points on the graph of the sine function on the interval $[0, 2\pi]$.

A. the three points where x-intercepts occur

B. the point of maximum value

C. the point of minimum value

A. $(0, 0)$, $(\pi, 0)$, and $(2\pi, 0)$

B. $\left(\frac{\pi}{2}, 1\right)$

C. $\left(\frac{3\pi}{2}, -1\right)$

Ⓑ Complete the table of values. Plot the points from the table, and draw a smooth curve through them.

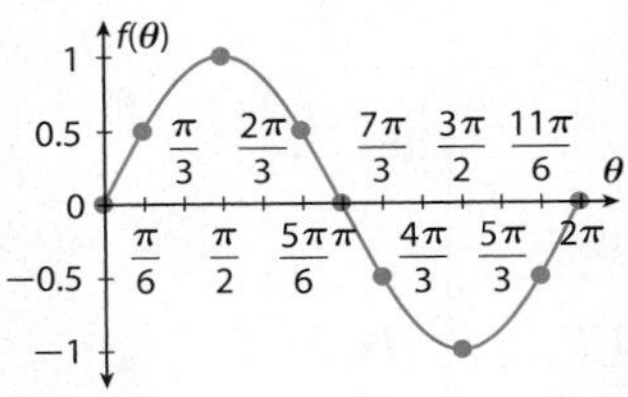

θ	0	$\frac{\pi}{6}$	$\frac{\pi}{2}$	$\frac{5\pi}{6}$	π	$\frac{7\pi}{6}$	$\frac{3\pi}{2}$	$\frac{11\pi}{6}$	2π
$f(\theta) = \sin\theta$	0	0.5	1	0.5	0	−0.5	−1	−0.5	0

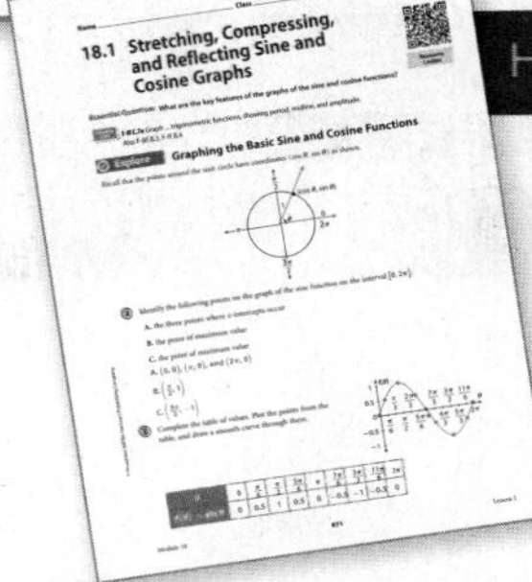

HARDCOVER PAGES 871–888

Watch for the hardcover student edition page numbers for this lesson.

C Identify the following points on the graph of the cosine function on the interval $[0, 2\pi]$.

A. the two points where x-intercepts occur

B. the two points of maximum value

C. the point of minimum value

A. $\left(\frac{\pi}{2}, 0\right)$ **and** $\left(\frac{3\pi}{2}, 0\right)$

B. $(0, 1)$ **and** $(2\pi, 1)$

C. $(\pi, -1)$

D Complete the table of values. Plot the points from the table, and draw a smooth curve through them.

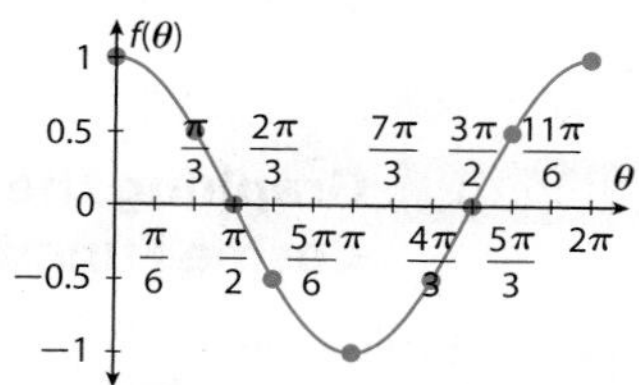

θ	0	$\frac{\pi}{3}$	$\frac{\pi}{2}$	$\frac{2\pi}{3}$	π	$\frac{4\pi}{3}$	$\frac{3\pi}{2}$	$\frac{5\pi}{3}$	2π
$f(\theta) = \cos\theta$	1	0.5	0	−0.5	−1	−0.5	0	0.5	1

Reflect

Give a decimal approximation of $\sin\frac{\pi}{3}$. Check to see whether the curve that you drew passes through the point $\left(\frac{\pi}{3}, \sin\frac{\pi}{3}\right)$. What other points can you check based on the labeling of the θ-axis?

$\sin\frac{\pi}{3} \approx 0.866$; $\left(\frac{2\pi}{3}, 0.866\right)$, $\left(\frac{4\pi}{3}, -0.866\right)$ **and** $\left(\frac{5\pi}{3}, -0.866\right)$

On the interval $0 \le \theta \le 2\pi$, where does the sine function have positive values? Where does it have negative values? Answer the same questions for cosine.

On the interval $0 \le \theta \le 2\pi$, sine has positive values when $0 < \theta < \pi$ and negative values when $\pi < \theta < 2\pi$. Cosine has positive values when $0 < \theta < \frac{\pi}{2}$ and $\frac{3\pi}{2} < \theta < 2\pi$ and negative values when $\frac{\pi}{2} < \theta < \frac{3\pi}{2}$.

What are the minimum and maximum values of $f(\theta) = \sin\theta$ and $f(\theta) = \cos\theta$ on the interval $0 \le \theta \le 2\pi$? Where do the extreme values occur in relation to the θ-intercepts?

The minimum value of $f(\theta) = \sin\theta$ is −1, and the maximum value is 1. These extreme values occur exactly halfway between the θ-intercepts. The minimum value of $f(\theta) = \cos\theta$ is −1, and the maximum value is 1. These extreme values occur exactly halfway between the θ-intercepts.

Describe a rotation that will map the graph of $f(\theta) = \sin\theta$ onto itself on the interval $0 \le \theta \le 2\pi$.

a rotation of 180° clockwise or counterclockwise about the point $(\pi, 0)$

EXPLORE 1

Graphing the Basic Sine and Cosine Functions

INTEGRATE TECHNOLOGY

Students have the option of completing the Explore activity either in the book or online.

CONNECT VOCABULARY EL

Explain the use of the word *periodic* in terms of something that occurs at regular intervals. Ask students to give real-world examples of events or phenomena that occur or repeat at regular intervals. Then extend this idea to the periodic nature of the trigonometric functions.

QUESTIONING STRATEGIES

? Do the graphs represent functions? If so, are they one-to-one? How do you know? **Both graphs pass the vertical line test, so both represent functions. Neither passes the horizontal line test, so the graphs are not one-to-one.**

? What do the five key points of each graph represent? **They represent the x-intercepts and the maximum and minimum points of the graph.**

? What transformation of the graph of $f(x) = \sin x$ produces the graph of $f(x) = \cos x$? **a horizontal translation $\frac{\pi}{2}$ units to the left**

PROFESSIONAL DEVELOPMENT

Math Background

A *periodic function* is a function that repeats its output values at regular intervals called *cycles*. The length of one cycle is the *period* of the function. A function $f(x)$ has period P if $f(x) = f(x + P)$ for all values of x. Consequently, for all integers n, $f(x) = f(x + nP)$. The graph demonstrates for any value x_0, how $f(x_0) = f(x_0 + P) = f(x_0 + 2P) = f(x_0 + 3P)$, and so on. This graph of $f(x)$ coincides with itself after a horizontal translation of P units.

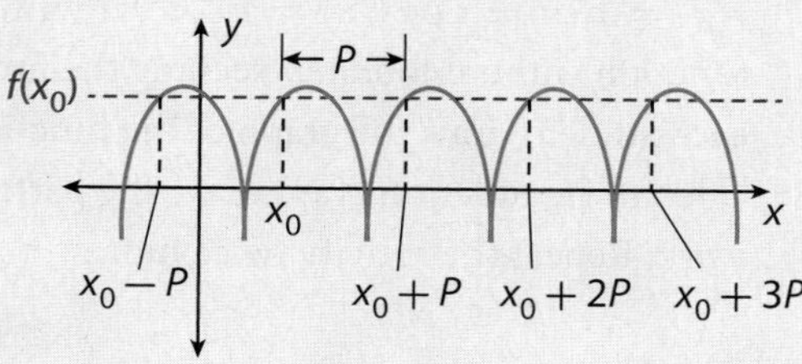

EXPLORE 2

Graphing the Reciprocals of the Basic Sine and Cosine Functions

QUESTIONING STRATEGIES

? What determines the location of an asymptote of the graph of the secant function? **The asymptote occurs where the secant is undefined, which is at values of x for which $\cos x = 0$.**

? For which function is the y-axis an asymptote? How do you explain this? **$f(x) = \csc x$; because $\sin 0 = 0$, and $\csc x = \frac{1}{\sin x}$, the cosecant is undefined at $x = 0$.**

5. Recall that coterminal angles differ by a multiple of 2π and have the same sine value and the same cosine value. This means that the graphs of sine and cosine on the interval $0 \leq \theta \leq 2\pi$ represent one *cycle* of the complete graphs and that the cycles repeat every 2π radians. Use this fact to extend the graphs of $f(\theta) = \sin \theta$ and $f(\theta) = \cos \theta$ to the left and right by 1 cycle.

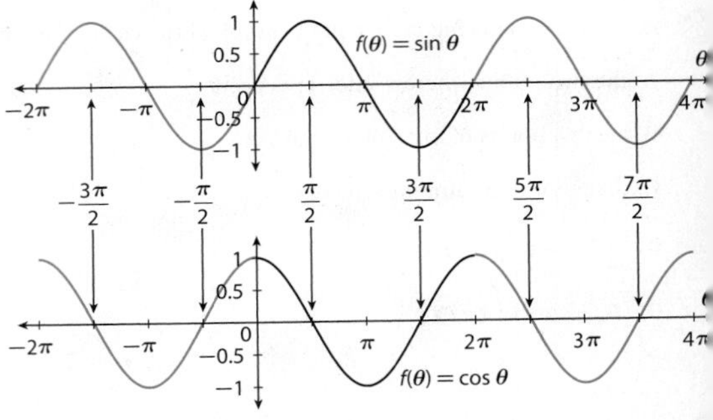

Explore 2 Graphing the Reciprocals of the Basic Sine and Cosine Functions

The **cosecant** and **secant** functions are the reciprocals of the sine and cosine functions, respectively.

$$\csc \theta = \frac{1}{\sin \theta} \qquad \sec \theta = \frac{1}{\cos \theta}$$

(A) Complete the table of values. Note that whenever $\sin \theta = 0$, $\csc \theta$ is undefined.

θ	0	$\frac{\pi}{6}$	$\frac{\pi}{2}$	$\frac{5\pi}{6}$	π	$\frac{7\pi}{6}$	$\frac{3\pi}{2}$	$\frac{11\pi}{6}$	2π
$f(\theta) = \sin \theta$	0	0.5	1	0.5	0	−0.5	−1	−0.5	0
$f(\theta) = \csc \theta$	**undefined**	**2**	**1**	**2**	**undefined**	**−2**	**1**	**−2**	**undefined**

(B) Complete each of the following statements.

A. As $\theta \to 0^+$, $\sin \theta \to$ **0** and $\csc \theta \to$ **∞**.

B. As $\theta \to 0^-$, $\sin \theta \to$ **0** and $\csc \theta \to$ **$-\infty$**.

What does this behavior tell you about the graph of the cosecant function?

The graph has a vertical asymptote at $\theta = 0$.

(C) Sketch the graph of $f(\theta) = \csc \theta$ over the interval $[0, 2\pi]$. Then, extend the graph to the left and right until the entire coordinate plane is filled. Note that the sine function has been plotted for ease of graphing.

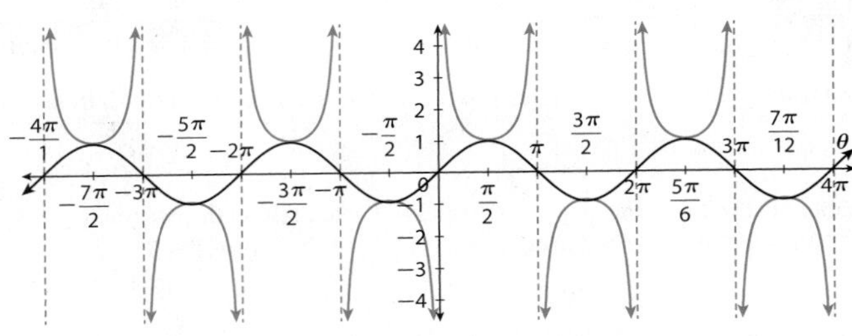

COLLABORATIVE LEARNING

Peer-to-Peer Activity

Have students work in pairs. Provide each pair with an envelope containing 6 strips of paper, each with a different trigonometric function of the form $f(x) = a \sin \frac{1}{b} x$ or $f(x) = a \cos \frac{1}{b} x$ written on it. Instruct students to choose a function without looking, keeping the function hidden from the partner. Have each student draw the graph of the function, then exchange graphs and write the rule for the function graphed by the partner. Have partners check each other's work. Repeat the activity twice more.

Ⓓ Complete the table of values. Note that whenever $\cos\theta = 0$, $\sec\theta$ is undefined.

θ	0	$\frac{\pi}{3}$	$\frac{\pi}{2}$	$\frac{2\pi}{3}$	π	$\frac{4\pi}{3}$	$\frac{3\pi}{2}$	$\frac{5\pi}{3}$	2π
$f(\theta) = \cos\theta$	1	0.5	0	−0.5	−1	−0.5	0	0.5	1
$f(\theta) = \sec\theta$	1	2	undefined	−2	−1	−2	undefined	2	1

Ⓔ Complete each of the following statements.

A. As $\theta \to \frac{\pi}{2}^+$, $\cos\theta \to$ 0 and $\sec\theta \to$ ∞.

B. As $\theta \to \frac{\pi}{2}^-$, $\cos\theta \to$ 0 and $\sec\theta \to$ $-\infty$.

What does this behavior tell you about the graph of the cosecant function?

The graph has a vertical asymptote at $\theta = \frac{\pi}{2}$.

Ⓕ Sketch the graph of $f(\theta) = \sec\theta$ over the interval $[0, 2\pi]$. Then, extend the graph to the left and right until the entire coordinate plane is filled. Note that the cosine function has been plotted for ease of graphing.

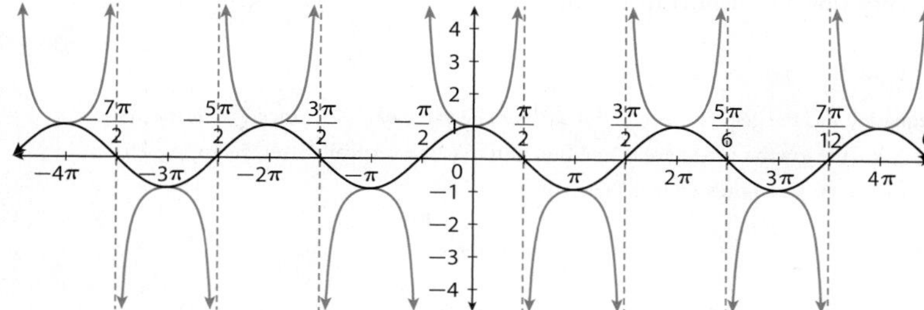

Reflect

6. How do the domain, range, maximum values, and minimum values compare between the sine and cosine functions and their reciprocals?

The domains of the sine and cosine functions are different from that of their reciprocals. The sine and cosine functions have unrestricted domains, but the cosecant and secant functions are not have unrestricted where sin defined $= 0$ and $\cos\theta = 0$, respectively. The ranges of the sine and cosine functions go from −1 to 1, while the ranges of their reciprocals include all y-values other than those between −1 and 1. The sine and cosine functions have a global maximum of 1, while the cosecant and secant functions have a local maximum of −1. Similarly, the sine and cosine functions have a global minimum of −1, while the cosecant and secant functions have a local minimum of 1.

7. Describe the vertical asymptotes of the cosecant and secant functions over the interval $[0, 2\pi]$.

Vertical asymptotes occur at $\theta = 0$, π, and 2π for the cosecant function. Vertical asymptotes occur at $\theta = \frac{\pi}{2}$ and $\frac{3\pi}{2}$ for the secant function.

DIFFERENTIATE INSTRUCTION

Kinesthetic Experience

To make a connection between the unit circle and the graphs of the cosine and sine functions, have students trace the circumference of the unit circle with a finger and note where the x-coordinates are positive, negative, increasing, and decreasing, and also trace along the graph of $f(x) = \cos x$ to see how the changes to the x-coordinate on the unit circle are reflected in the graph of the function. Students can then repeat the activity for $f(x) = \sin x$, observing how it reflects the changes to the y-coordinate.

EXPLAIN 1

Graphing $f(x) = a\sin\left(\frac{1}{b}\right)x$ or $f(x) = a\cos\left(\frac{1}{b}\right)x$

QUESTIONING STRATEGIES

What does one period of $f(x) = \sin x$ or $f(x) = \cos x$ correspond to on the unit circle? **It corresponds to one complete revolution of the terminal side of the angle around the unit circle.**

How can you use the graphs of $f(x) = \sin x$ and $f(x) = \cos x$ to help you draw the graph of $g(x) = a\sin\left(\frac{1}{b}\right)x$ or $g(x) = a\cos\left(\frac{1}{b}\right)x$? **You can start with the graph of the parent function, apply the transformations indicated by *a* and *b* to the key points of the graph, and then use what you know about the shape of the basic graph to sketch the new graph.**

Explain 1 Graphing $f(x) = a\sin\frac{1}{b}x$ or $f(x) = a\cos\frac{1}{b}x$

In the first Explore, you graphed the sine and cosine functions on the interval $0 \le \theta \le 2\pi$, which represents all of the angles of rotation within the first counterclockwise revolution that starts at 0. Your drawings are not the complete graphs, however. They are simply one *cycle* of the graphs.

The graphs of sine and cosine consist of repeated cycles that form a wave-like shape. When a function repeats its values over regular intervals on the horizontal axis as the sine and cosine functions do, the function is called **periodic**, and the length of the interval is called the function's **period**.

The wave-like shape of the sine and cosine functions has a "crest" (where the function's maximum value occurs) and a "trough" (where the function's minimum value occurs). Halfway between the "crest" and the "trough" is the graph's **midline**. The distance that the "crest" rises above the midline or the distance that the "trough" falls below the midline is called the graph's **amplitude**.

Graph the function. Note that for trigonometric functions, the angle θ is the independent variable, and the output $f(\theta)$ is the dependent variable. You can graph these functions on the familiar *xy*-coordinate plane by letting *x* represent the angle and *y* represent the value of the function.

Example 1 **For each trigonometric function, identify the vertical stretch or compression and the horizontal stretch or compression. Then, graph the function and identify its period.**

(A) $y = 3\sin 2x$

The equation has the general form $y = a\sin\frac{1}{b}x$. The value of *a* is 3. Since $\frac{1}{b} = 2$, the value of *b* is $\frac{1}{2}$. So, the graph of the parent sine function must be vertically stretched by a factor of 3 and horizontally compressed by a factor of $\frac{1}{2}$.

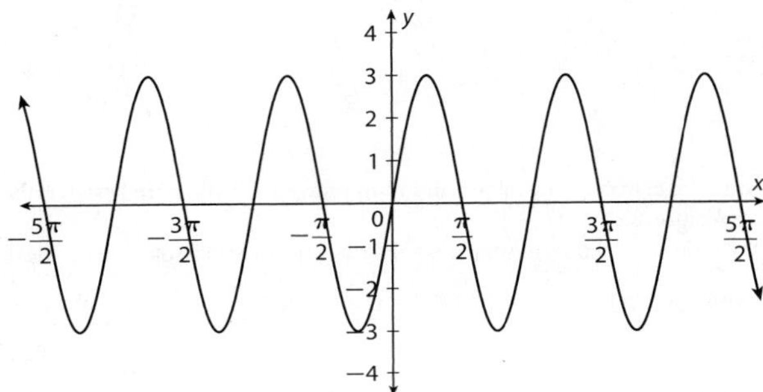

Horizontally stretching or compressing the parent function's graph by a factor of b changes the period of the function. Since the parent function has a period of 2π, multiply 2π by b to obtain the period of the transformed function.

Period: $2\pi \cdot b = 2\pi \cdot \frac{1}{2} = \pi$

LANGUAGE SUPPORT EL

Communicate Math

Have students work in pairs to complete a table like the one below for the general sine and cosine functions $f(x) = a\sin\left(\frac{1}{b}\right)x$ and $f(x) = a\cos\left(\frac{1}{b}\right)x$. They can use this table throughout the lesson.

Graph type	Amplitude	*x*-intercepts	Max.	Min.	Sketch
Sine					
Cosine					

Ⓑ $y = -3\cos\frac{x}{2}$

The equation has the general form $y = a\cos\frac{1}{b}x$. The value of a is $\underline{-3}$. Since $\frac{1}{b} = \boxed{\frac{1}{2}}$, the value of b is $\underline{2}$.

So, the graph of the parent function must be vertically [(stretched)/compressed] by a factor of $\underline{3}$ and horizontally [compressed/(stretched)] by a factor of $\underline{2}$.

Graph the function. Note that since a is negative, the graph will be reflected across the [(x)/y]-axis.

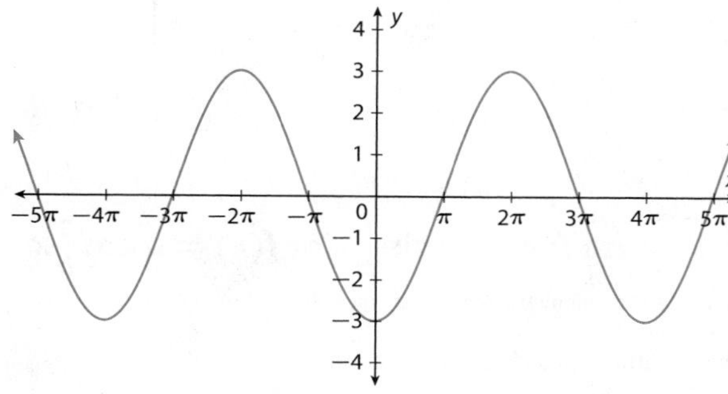

Find the function's period.

$2\pi \cdot b = 2\pi \cdot \boxed{2} = \boxed{4\pi}$

Reflect

8. For the function $y = a\sin\frac{1}{b}x$ or $y = a\cos\frac{1}{b}x$, what is the amplitude, under what circumstances would the function be reflected about the x-axis, and how is the period be determined?

The amplitude is $|a|$, the function would be reflected about the x-axis when the value of a is negative, and the period is determined by multiplying by b.

INTEGRATE TECHNOLOGY

Students can use their graphing calculators to explore the effects of various values of a and b on the parent trigonometric functions. Suggest students graph a parent function and then graph a transformed function to see what effects a and b have on the parent function.

EXPLAIN 2

Writing $f(x) = a\sin\left(\frac{1}{b}\right)x$ or $f(x) = a\cos\left(\frac{1}{b}\right)x$

QUESTIONING STRATEGIES

How can you determine the amplitude of a function by looking at its graph? **Find half the vertical distance between its maximum point (crest) and its minimum point (trough), or find the distance between its midline and either its maximum point or its minimum point.**

How can you determine the period of a function by looking at its graph? **You can determine the horizontal length of one cycle of the graph by finding where the shape of the graph starts to repeat.**

AVOID COMMON ERRORS

Some students may think that if the graph indicates that the period of a sine or cosine function is, for example, $\frac{1}{2}$, the period of the parent function, then the coefficient of x is $\frac{1}{2}$. Help them to see that this horizontal compression is a result of dividing the period of the parent function by 2, so the coefficient of x is 2.

Your Turn

Identify the vertical stretch or compression and the horizontal stretch or compression. Then, graph the function and identify its period.

9. $y = \frac{1}{2}\sin 4x$

$\frac{1}{b} = 4$

$b = \frac{1}{4}$

vertically compressed by a factor of $\frac{1}{2}$ and horizontally compressed by a factor of $\frac{1}{4}$

$2\pi \cdot b = 2\pi \cdot \frac{1}{4} = \frac{\pi}{2}$

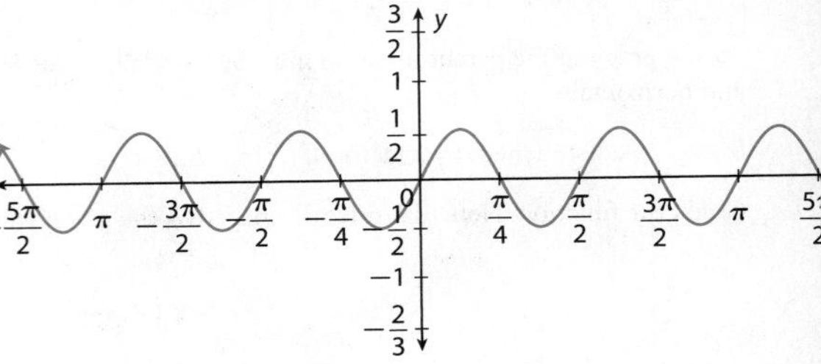

Explain 2 Writing $f(x) = a\sin\frac{1}{b}x$ or $f(x) = a\cos\frac{1}{b}x$

You can write the equation of a trigonometric function if you are given its graph.

Example 2 **Write an equation for each graph.**

Ⓐ Because the graph's y-intercept is 0, the graph is a sine function.

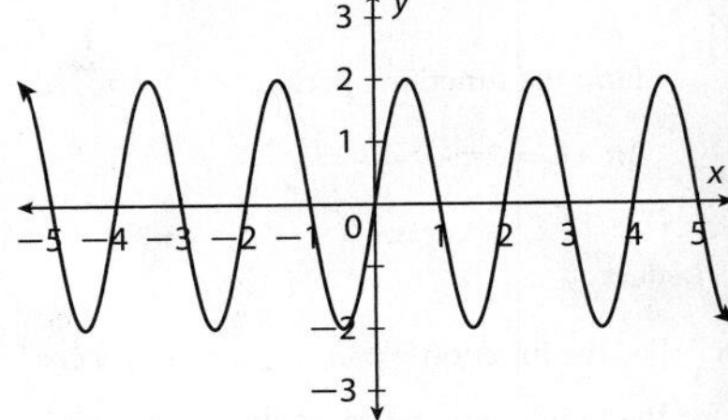

Since the maximum and minimum values are 2 and −2, respectively, the graph is a vertical stretch of the parent sine function by a factor of 2. So, $a = 2$.

The period of the function is 2.

Use the equation $2\pi b = 2$ to find the value of $\frac{1}{b}$.

$2\pi b = 2$

$b = \frac{2}{2\pi}\ \frac{1}{\pi}$

$\frac{1}{b} = \pi$

An equation for the graph is $y = 2\sin \pi x$.

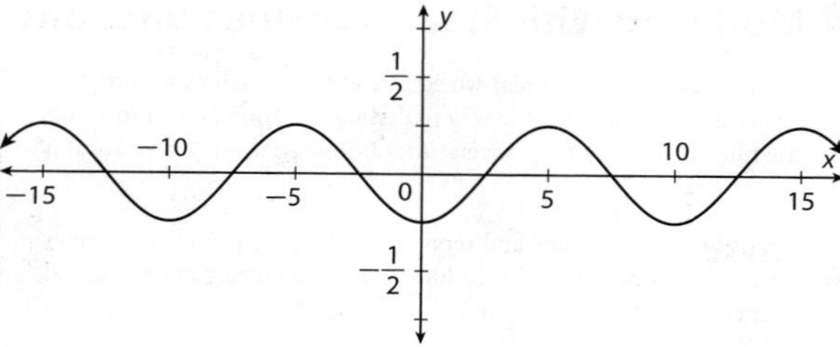

Because the graph's y-intercept is negative, the graph is a [sine/cosine] function reflected across the x-axis.

Since the maximum and minimum in the graph are $\frac{1}{4}$ and $-\frac{1}{4}$, respectively, the graph will be vertical [stretch/compression] of the graph of the parent cosine function by a factor of $\frac{1}{4}$.

The period of the function is 10.

Use the equation $2\pi b =$ 10 to find the value of $\frac{1}{b}$.

$2\pi b = 10$

$b = \frac{10}{2\pi} = \frac{5}{\pi}$

$\frac{1}{b} = \frac{\pi}{5}$

An equation for the graph is $y = -\frac{1}{4} \cos \frac{\pi}{5} x$.

Your Turn

Write an equation for the graph.

10.

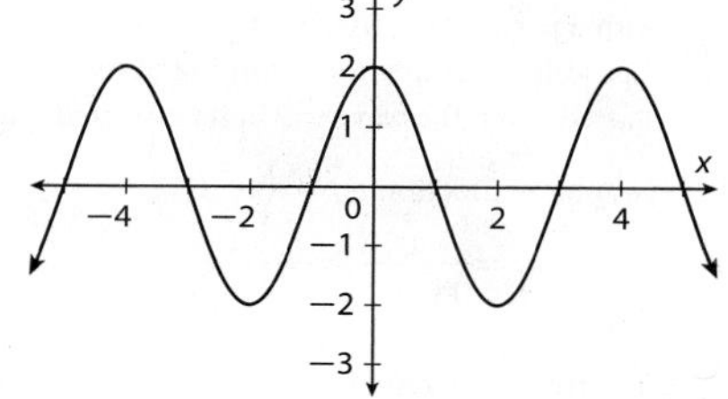

The graph is a cosine function.

$a = 2$

$2\pi b = 4$

$b = \frac{4}{2\pi} = \frac{2}{\pi}$

$\frac{1}{b} = \frac{\pi}{2}$

$y = 2 \cos \frac{\pi}{2} x$

EXPLAIN 3

Modeling with Sine or Cosine Functions

QUESTIONING STRATEGIES

? How does the period help you to graph the function? It tells you the width of each cycle of the curve on the graph.

? How does modeling with a stretched, compressed, or reflected cosine function differ from modeling with the same type of sine function? The y-intercept is 0 for the sine function, but the y-intercept is *not* 0 for the cosine function.

Explain 3 Modeling with Sine or Cosine Functions

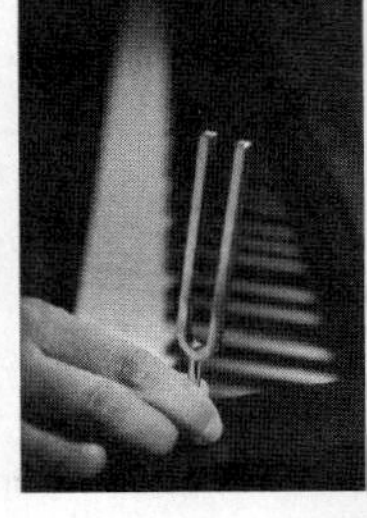

Sine and cosine functions can be used to model real-world phenomena, such as sound waves. Different sounds create different waves. One way to distinguish sounds is to measure *frequency*. **Frequency** is the number of cycles in a given unit of time, so it is the reciprocal of the period of a function.

Hertz (Hz) is the standard measure of frequency and represents one cycle per second. For example, the sound wave made by a tuning fork for middle A has a frequency of 440 Hz. This means that the wave repeats 440 times in 1 second.

As a tuning fork vibrates, it creates fluctuations in air pressure. The maximum change in air pressure, typically measured in pascals, is the sound wave's amplitude.

Example 3 **Graph each function, and then find its frequency. What do the frequency, amplitude, and period represent in the context of the problem?**

Ⓐ **Physics** Use a sine function to graph a sound wave with a period of 0.004 second and an amplitude of 4 pascals.

Graph the function.

$$\text{frequency} = \frac{1}{\text{period}} = \frac{1}{0.004} = 250 \text{ Hz}$$

The frequency represents the number of cycles of the sound wave every second. The amplitude represents the maximum change in air pressure. The period represents the amount of time it takes for the sound wave to repeat.

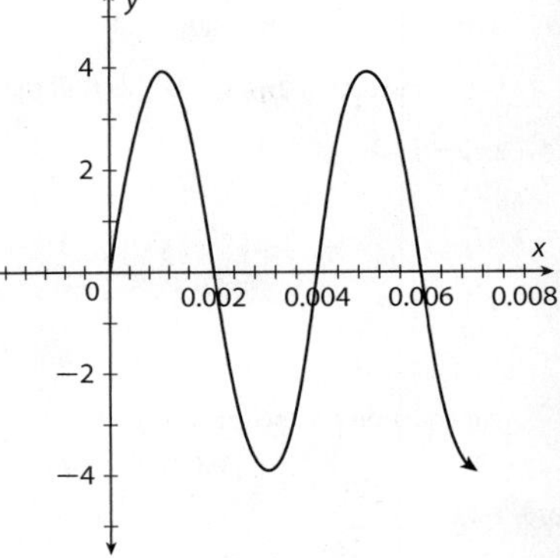

Ⓑ **Physics** Use a cosine function to graph a sound wave with a period of 0.010 second and an amplitude of 3 pascals. Note that the recording of the sound wave started when the wave was at its maximum height.

Graph the function.

$$\text{frequency} = \frac{1}{\text{period}} = \frac{1}{\boxed{0.010}} = \boxed{100} \text{ Hz}$$

The frequency represents the number cycles of the sound wave every **second**. The amplitude represents the maximum change in **air pressure**. The period represents the amount of time it takes for the sound wave to [end/repeat].

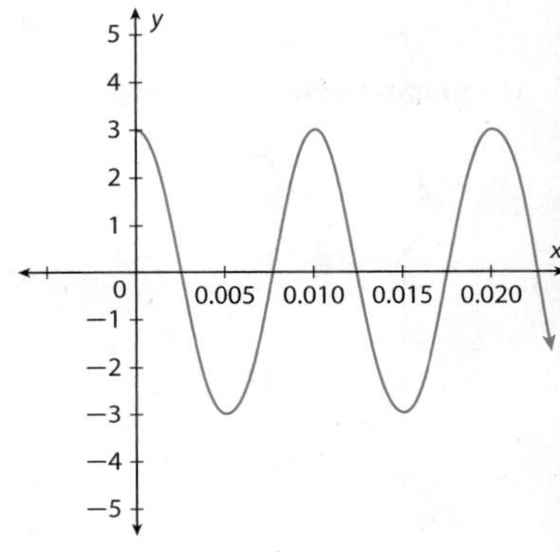

Your Turn

Graph the function, and then find its frequency. What do the frequency, amplitude, and period represent in the context of the problem?

11. A pendulum makes one back-and-forth swing every 1.5 seconds. Its horizontal displacement relative to its position at rest is measured in inches. Starting when the pendulum is 5 inches (its maximum displacement) to the right of its position at rest, use a cosine function to graph the pendulum's horizontal displacement over time.

frequency $= \frac{1}{1.5} \approx 0.67$ Hz

The frequency represents the number of back-and-forth swings per second. The amplitude represents the pendulum's maximum horizontal displacement. The period represents the amount of time it takes the pendulum to complete a back-and-forth swing.

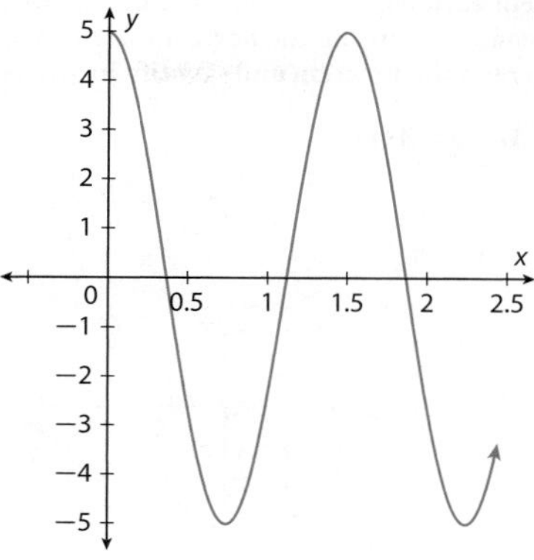

Elaborate

12. The graphs of sine and cosine are periodic functions. Refer to angles of rotation and the unit circle to explain why this is so.

Since one revolution around the unit circle gives all of the possible values of the sine and cosine functions, subsequent revolutions repeat those values.

13. Referring to angles of rotation and the unit circle, explain why $\sin(-\theta) = -\sin\theta$, and why $\cos(-\theta) = \cos\theta$. Use the graphs of $\sin\theta$ and $\cos\theta$ for reference.

Since the angles θ and $-\theta$ intersect the unit circle at points that have the same x-coordinate (cosine value) but opposite y-coordinates (sine value), $\sin(-\theta) = -\sin\theta$, and $\cos(-\theta) = \cos\theta$.

14. How does the unit circle explain why the 2 in $y = \sin 2x$ results in a horizontal compression of the graph of $y = \sin x$?

As the value of x increases from 0 to 2π (one revolution of the circle), the value of $2x$ increases from 0 to 4π (two revolutions of the circle). So, the graph of $y = \sin 2x$ completes two cycles for every one cycle that the graph of $y = \sin x$ completes.

15. Essential Question Check-In What is one key difference between the graphs of the sine and cosine functions?

One key difference is that the sine function always passes through the origin, while the cosine function always passes through the point $(0, a)$, where $|a|$ is the amplitude of the function.

ELABORATE

INTEGRATE MATHEMATICAL PRACTICES

Focus on Communication

MP.3 Have students discuss how the attributes of the graphs of the sine and cosine functions are related to the characteristics of the unit circle.

SUMMARIZE THE LESSON

How do the constants a and b in the functions $f(x) = a\sin\left(\frac{1}{b}\right)x$ or $f(x) = a\cos\left(\frac{1}{b}\right)x$ affect the graphs of the parent trigonometric functions?

The value of a changes the amplitude. The amplitude is $|a|$. If a is negative, the graph is reflected in the x-axis. The value of b changes the period of the function. The period of the transformed function is $\frac{2\pi}{\left|\frac{1}{b}\right|}$.

EVALUATE

ASSIGNMENT GUIDE

Concepts and Skills	Practice
Explore 1 Graphing the Basic Sine and Cosine Functions	Exercise 18
Explore 2 Graphing the Reciprocals of the Basic Sine and Cosine Functions	Exercises 19–22
Example 1 Graphing $f(x) = a\sin\left(\frac{1}{b}\right)x$ or $f(x) = a\cos\left(\frac{1}{b}\right)x$	Exercises 1–6, 17
Example 2 Writing $f(x) = a\sin\left(\frac{1}{b}\right)x$ or $f(x) = a\cos\left(\frac{1}{b}\right)x$	Exercises 7–12
Example 3 Modeling with Sine or Cosine Functions	Exercises 13–16

QUESTIONING STRATEGIES

How do the ranges of $f(x) = \sin x$ and $f(x) = \cos x$ compare? They are the same. The range for both functions is [–1, 1].

How do the zeros of $f(x) = \sin x$ and $f(x) = \cos x$ compare? They are different. The zeros of $f(x) = \sin x$ occur at multiples of π. The zeros of $f(x) = \cos x$ occur at odd multiples of $\frac{\pi}{2}$.

Evaluate: Homework and Practice

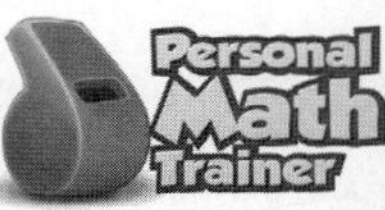

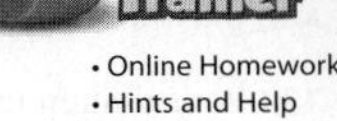

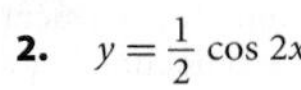

- Online Homework
- Hints and Help
- Extra Practice

For each trigonometric function, identify the vertical stretch or compression and the horizontal stretch or compression. Then, graph the function and identify its period.

1. $y = 4\sin x$

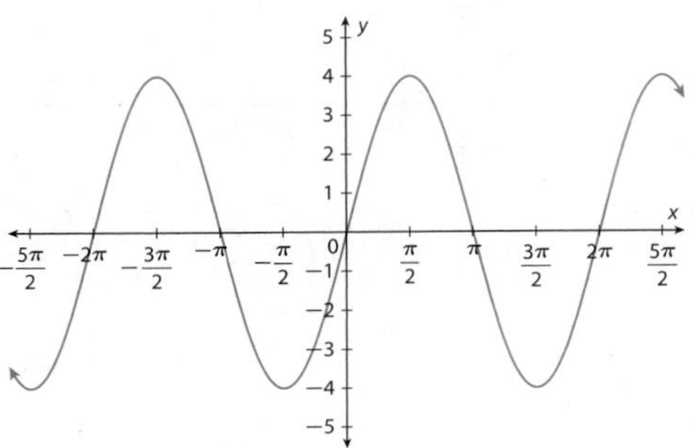

vertically stretched by a factor of 4

period: 2π

2. $y = \frac{1}{2}\cos 2x$

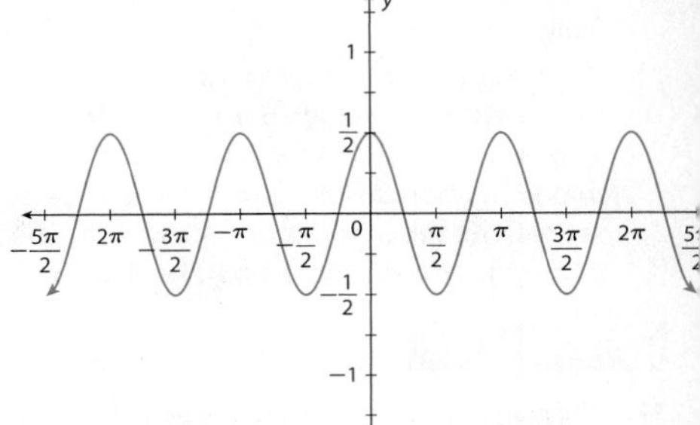

$\frac{1}{b} = 2 \Rightarrow b = \frac{1}{2}$

vertically compressed by a factor of $\frac{1}{2}$;

horizontally compressed by a factor of $\frac{1}{2}$

period: $2\pi \cdot b = 2\pi \cdot \frac{1}{2} = \pi$

3. $y = -3\sin\frac{1}{6}x$

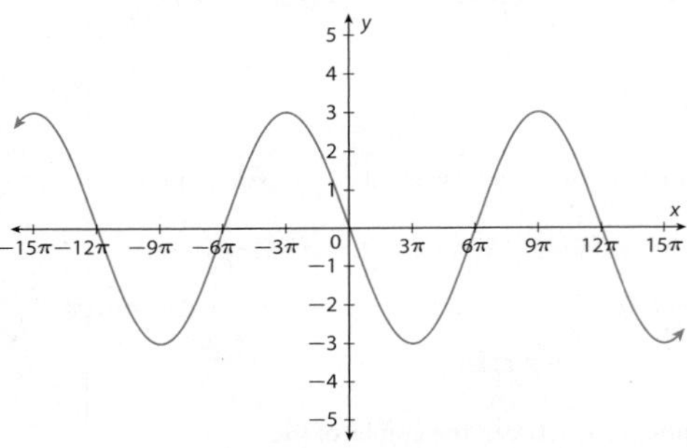

$\frac{1}{b} = \frac{1}{6} \Rightarrow b = 6$

vertically stretched by a factor of 3;

horizontally stretched by a factor of 6;

reflected across the x-axis

period: $2\pi \cdot 6 = 12\pi$

4. $y = -2\cos\frac{1}{3}x$

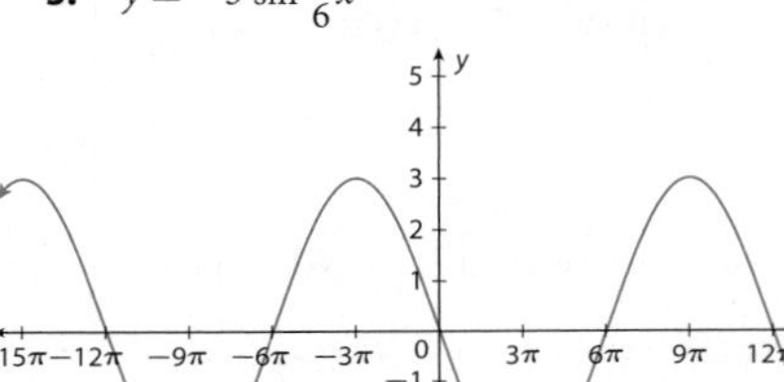

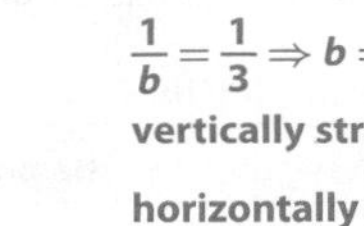

$\frac{1}{b} = \frac{1}{3} \Rightarrow b = 3$

vertically stretched by a factor of 2;

horizontally stretched by a factor of 3;

reflected across the x-axis

period: $2\pi \cdot 3 = 6\pi$

Exercise	Depth of Knowledge (D.O.K.)	COMMON CORE Mathematical Practices
1–6	**1** Recall of Information	**MP.7** Using Structure
7–12	**2** Skills/Concepts	**MP.7** Using Structure
13–16	**1** Recall of Information	**MP.4** Modeling
17	**1** Recall of Information	**MP.7** Using Structure
18–19	**1** Recall of Information	**MP.6** Precision
20	**1** Recall of Information	**MP.7** Using Structure

5. $y = \frac{1}{3} \sin 2x$

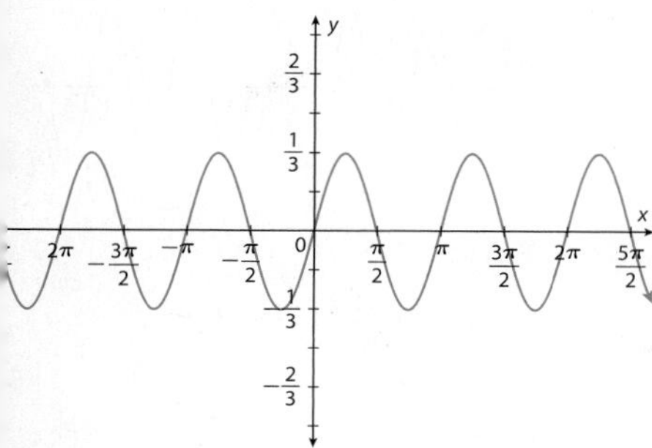

$\frac{1}{b} = 2 \Rightarrow b = \frac{1}{2}$

vertically compressed by a factor of $\frac{1}{3}$;

horizontally compressed by a factor of $\frac{1}{2}$

period: $2\pi \cdot \frac{1}{2} = \pi$

6. $y = -\frac{1}{4} \cos 3x$

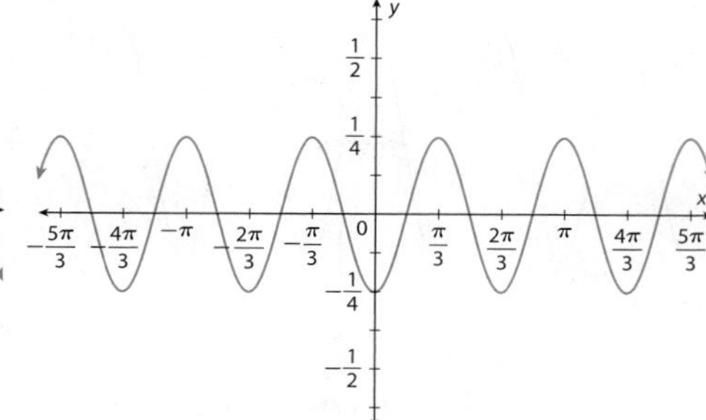

$\frac{1}{b} = 3 \Rightarrow b = \frac{1}{3}$

vertically compressed by a factor of $\frac{1}{4}$;

horizontally compressed by a factor of $\frac{1}{3}$;

reflected across the x-axis

period: $2\pi \cdot \frac{1}{3} = \frac{2\pi}{3}$

Write an equation for each graph.

7.

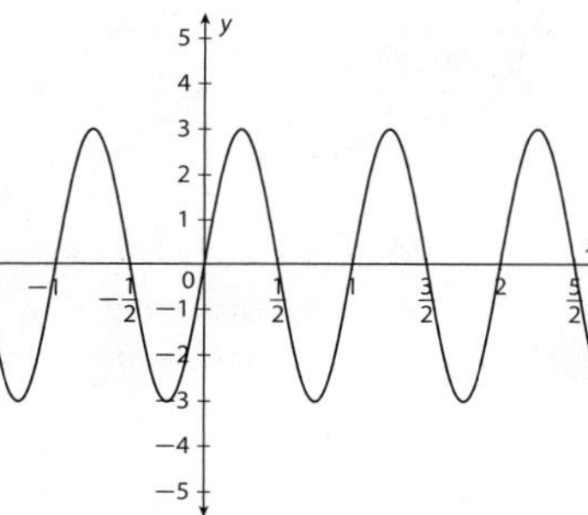

The graph is a sine function.

a = 3

$2\pi b = 1 \Rightarrow b = \frac{1}{2\pi} \Rightarrow \frac{1}{b} = 2\pi$

$y = 3 \sin 2\pi x$

8.

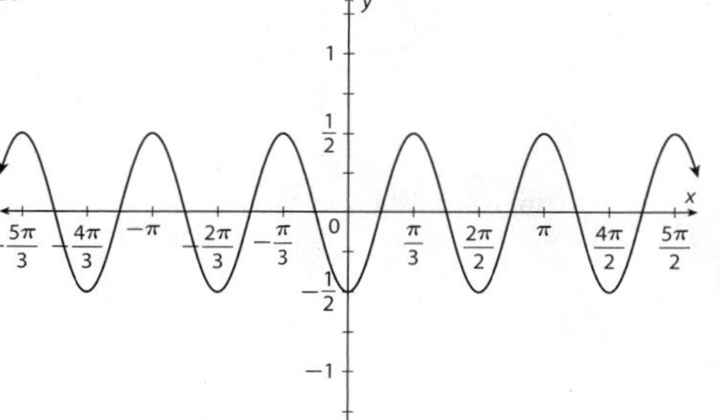

The is a cosine function reflected across the x-axis.

a = $\frac{1}{2}$

$2\pi b = \frac{2\pi}{3} \Rightarrow b \frac{1}{3} \Rightarrow \frac{1}{b} = 3$

$y = -\frac{1}{2} \cos 3x$

INTEGRATE MATHEMATICAL PRACTICES

Focus on Technology

MP.5 Show students how to use a graphing calculator to find the secant or cosecant of a number, and encourage them to use the calculator to check points on their graphs of these functions.

Exercise	Depth of Knowledge (D.O.K.)	COMMON CORE Mathematical Practices
21–22	**1** Recall of Information	**MP.2** Reasoning
23–24	**2** Skills/Concepts H.O.T.	**MP.3** Logic
25	**3** Strategic Thinking H.O.T.	**MP.3** Logic

VISUAL CUES

Suggest that students circle the five key points on the graph of the parent function, so that they can more easily identify and graph the images of these points under the indicated transformation.

AVOID COMMON ERRORS

Students may struggle with the relationship between the period of the function and the coefficient of x in the function rule. Reinforce that the period of the function is the quotient of 2π and the absolute value of the coefficient of x. Help students to see that when this coefficient is a fraction, they must multiply 2π by the absolute value of the *reciprocal* of the fraction in order to obtain the period.

9.

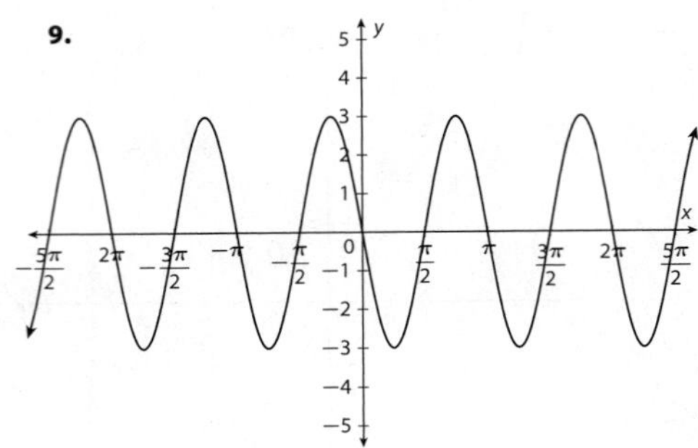

The graph is a sine function reflected across the x-axis.

$a = 3$

$2\pi b = \pi \Rightarrow b = \frac{1}{2} \Rightarrow b = \frac{1}{2} \Rightarrow \frac{1}{b} = 2$

$y = -3 \sin 2x$

10.

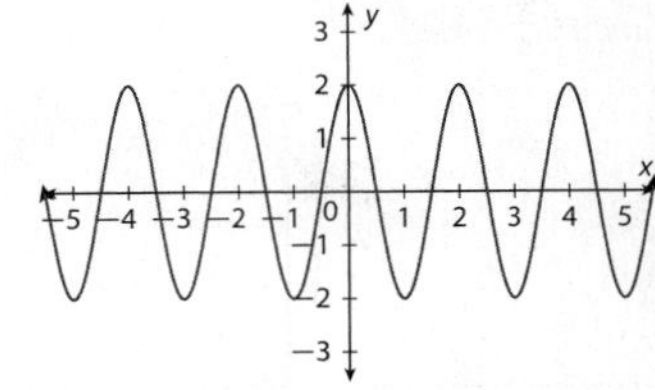

The graph is a cosine function.

$a = 2$

$2\pi b = 2$

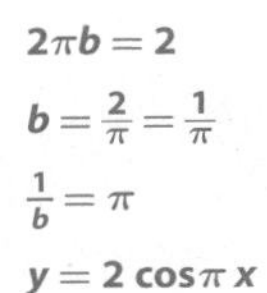

$b = \frac{2}{\pi} = \frac{1}{\pi}$

$\frac{1}{b} = \pi$

$y = 2 \cos \pi x$

11.

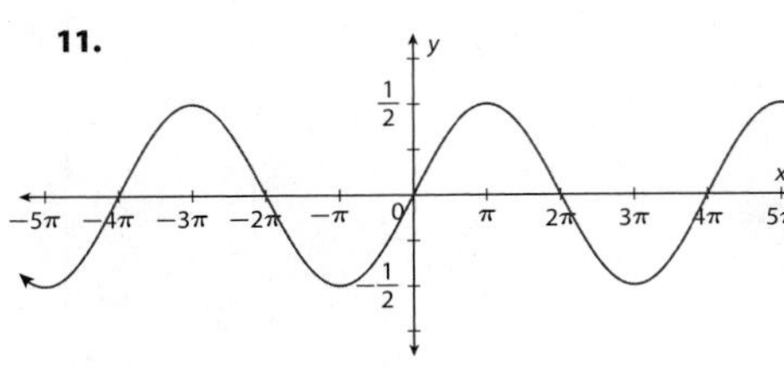

The graph is a sine function.

$a = \frac{1}{2}$

$2\pi b = 4\pi \Rightarrow b = 2 \Rightarrow \frac{1}{b} = \frac{1}{2}$

$y = \frac{1}{2} \sin \frac{1}{2} x$

12.

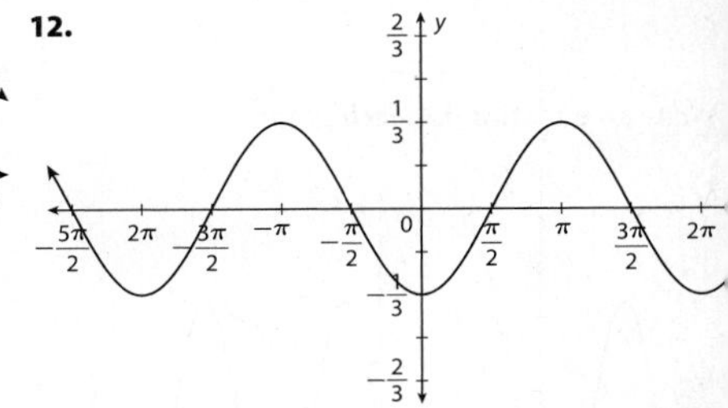

The graph is a cosine function reflected across the x-axis.

$a = \frac{1}{3}$

$2\pi b = 2\pi \Rightarrow b = 1 \Rightarrow \frac{1}{b} \Rightarrow 1$

$y = -\frac{1}{3} \cos x$

ph each function, and then find its frequency. What he frequency, amplitude, and period represent in the text of the problem?

Physics Use a sine function to graph a sound wave with a period of 0.003 second and an amplitude of 2 pascals.

frequency $= \frac{1}{0.003} \approx$ **333 Hz**

The frequency represents the number of cycles of the sound wave every second. The amplitude represents the maximum change in air pressure. The period represents the amount of time it takes for the sound wave to repeat.

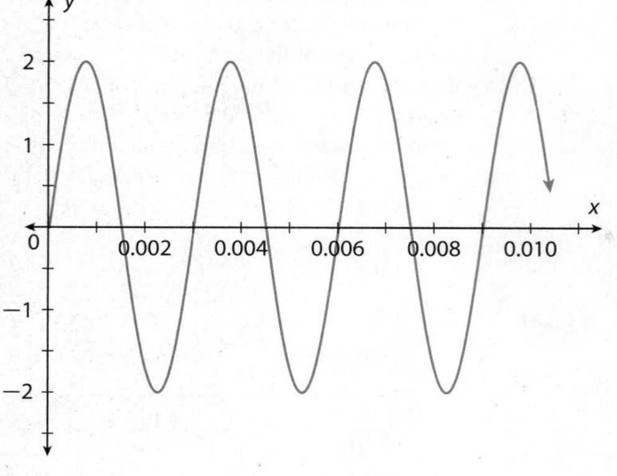

Physics A mass attached to a spring oscillates up and down every 2 seconds. Draw a graph of the vertical displacement of the mass relative to its position at rest if the spring is stretched to a length of 15 cm before the mass is released.

frequency $= \frac{1}{2} =$ **0.15 Hz**

The frequency represents the number of oscillations of the spring every second. The amplitude represents the spring's maximum vertical displacement. The period represents the amount of time that it takes the spring to complete one oscillation.

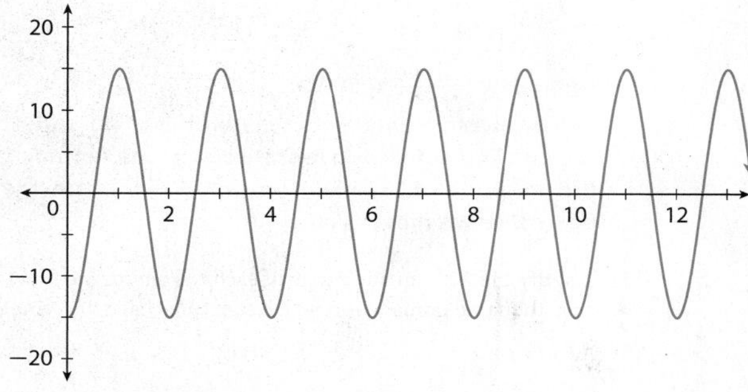

Physics A pendulum is released at a point 5 meters to the right of its position at rest. Graph a cosine function that represents the pendulum's horizontal displacement relative to its position at rest if it completes one back-and-forth swing every π seconds.

frequency $= \frac{1}{\pi} \approx$ **0.32 Hz**

The frequency represents the number of back-and-forth swings every second. The amplitude represents the the pendulum's maximum horizontal displacement. The period represents the amount of time for the pendulum to complete a back-and-forth swing.

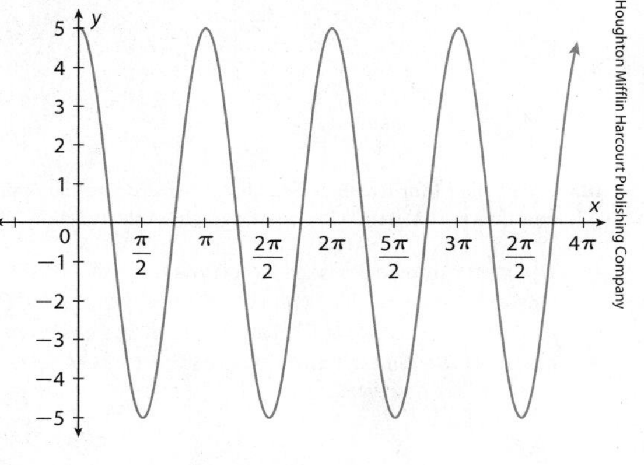

CURRICULUM INTEGRATION

You may wish to have students reinforce their understanding of the terms *amplitude* and *frequency* by investigating their meanings in broadcast media. Radio signals are broadcast on AM (amplitude modulation) and FM (frequency modulation) bands.

INTEGRATE MATHEMATICAL PRACTICES

Focus on Critical Thinking

MP.3 Have students analyze the graphs of $f(x) = \sin x$ and $f(x) = \csc x$ to observe the increasing/decreasing relationship that exists between the reciprocal functions. Ask them to explain *why* the relationship exists. Then have them consider how it is possible for one of the functions to have a bounded range while the other does not.

CONNECT VOCABULARY EL

Ask students to fill out vocabulary cards for the types of functions covered in this lesson (secant, cosecant, periodic) and review these cards frequently.

16. Automobiles Each piston in a car's engine moves up and down in a cylinder and causes a crankshaft to rotate. Suppose a piston starts at the midpoint of a stroke and has a maximum displacement from the midpoint of 50 mm. Also suppose the crankshaft is rotating at a rate of 3000 revolutions per minute (rpm). Use a sine function to graph the piston's displacement relative to the midpoint of its stroke. Note that 60 rpm = 1 revolution per second.

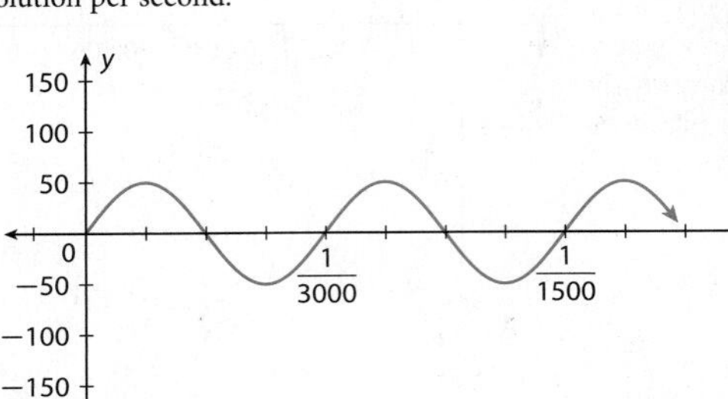

frequency $= \frac{3000}{60} = 50$ Hz

The frequency represents the number of up-and-down movements of the piston every second. The amplitude represents the maximum displacement of the piston relative to the midpoint of a stroke. The period represents the amount of time it takes to make an up-and-down movement.

17. Identify the domain and range of each trigonometric function. State which functions have the same domain and which functions have the same range.

A. $y = \sin x$ — **A. Domain: $\{x \mid x \in R\}$ Range: $\{y \mid -1 \leq y \leq 1\}$**

B. $y = 2\cos x$ — **B. Domain: $\{x \mid -\infty < x < +\infty\}$ Range: $\{y \mid -2 \leq y \leq 2\}$**

C. $y = -3\sin\frac{1}{2}x$ — **C. Domain: $\{x \mid -\infty < x < +\infty\}$ Range: $\{y \mid -3 \leq y \leq 3\}$**

D. $y = -\frac{4}{5}\sin \pi x$ — **D. Domain: $\{x \mid -\infty < x < +\infty\}$ Range: $\{y \mid -\frac{4}{5} \leq y \leq \frac{4}{5}\}$**

E. $y = 2\sin\frac{x}{4}$ — **E. Domain: $\{x \mid -\infty < x < +\infty\}$ Range: $\{y \mid -2 \leq y \leq 2\}$**

A, B, C, D, and E all have the same domain. B and E have the same range.

18. Use Explore 1 for reference. State how the basic sine and cosine functions are similar and how they are different. How are the graphs of the functions geometrically related?

The basic sine and cosine functions have the same period, amplitude, and frequency. However, the graph of the sine function the point $(0, 0)$, while the passes through cosine function the point $(0, 1)$. The graph of the cosine function is a horizontal translation of the graph of the sine function by $\frac{\pi}{2}$ radians to the left.

19. Describe the graphs of the cosecant and secant functions. Note any asymptotes, x-intercepts, and maximum or minimum values.

The graphs of the cosecant and secant functions consist of U-shaped curves that alternate between (a) being above of the x-axis and opening up and (b) being below the x-axis and opening down. The cosecant function has asymptotes at multiples of π, while the secant function has asymptotes at odd multiples of $\frac{\pi}{2}$. Neither function has x-intercepts. Both functions have a local maximum value of -1 and a local minimum value of 1.

20. Compare the two sine functions in terms of their periods.

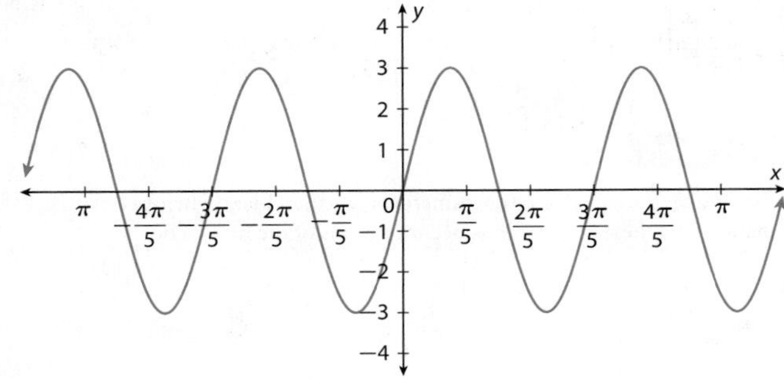

θ	0	$\frac{\pi}{6}$	$\frac{\pi}{2}$	$\frac{5\pi}{6}$	π	$\frac{7\pi}{6}$	$\frac{3\pi}{2}$	$\frac{11\pi}{6}$	2π
$f(\theta) = \sin\theta$	0	1	2	1	0	-1	-2	-1	0

The sine function described by the table has a longer period than the sine function described by the graph. The period is longer by a factor of $\frac{2\pi}{\frac{3\pi}{5}} = \frac{10\pi}{3\pi} = \frac{10}{3}$.

Sketch the graph of a cosecant or secant function, as appropriate, using the provided graph of a sine or cosine function as a reference. Be sure to include asymptotes.

21.

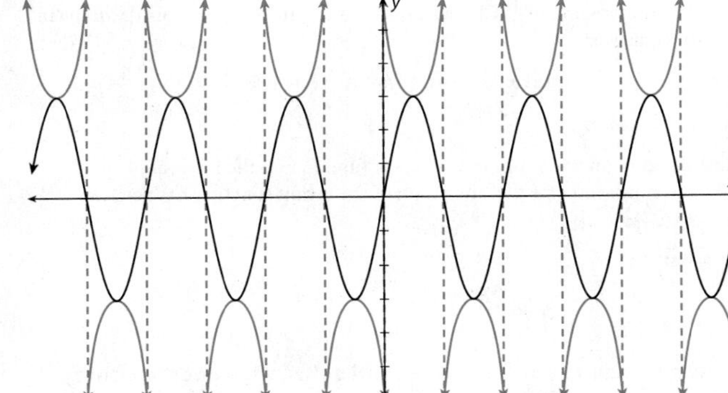

PEER-TO-PEER DISCUSSION

Ask students to work with a partner to explore how they could use the graphs of $f(x) = \sin x$ and $f(x) = \cos x$ to prove the Pythagorean identity $\sin^2 x + \cos^2 x = 1$. **If students graph the two functions on the same coordinate plane, they can then graph the "square" of each function on the same plane by plotting the point (x, y^2) for each point (x, y). Finally, they can plot the points corresponding to the sum of the y-values of the points of the graphs, showing that they all lie on the horizontal line $y = 1$.**

JOURNAL

Have students describe the difference between the graphs of $f(x) = \cos x$ and $g(x) = -2\cos\left(\frac{1}{4}\right)x$.

22.

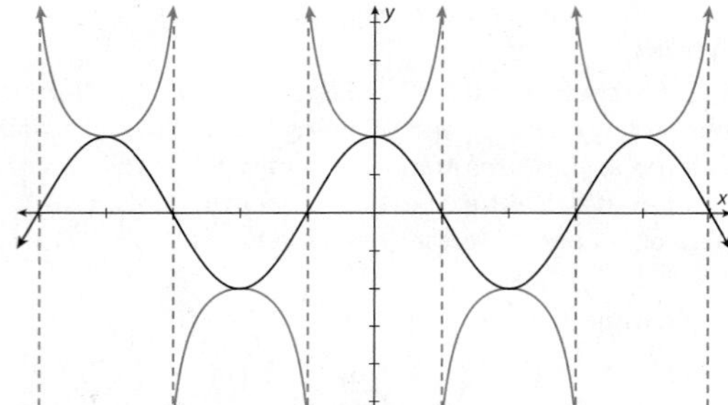

H.O.T. Focus on Higher Order Thinking

23. Critical Thinking Graph the basic sine and cosine functions together. Identify where $\sin \theta = \cos \theta$, and explain where these intersections occur in terms of the unit circle.

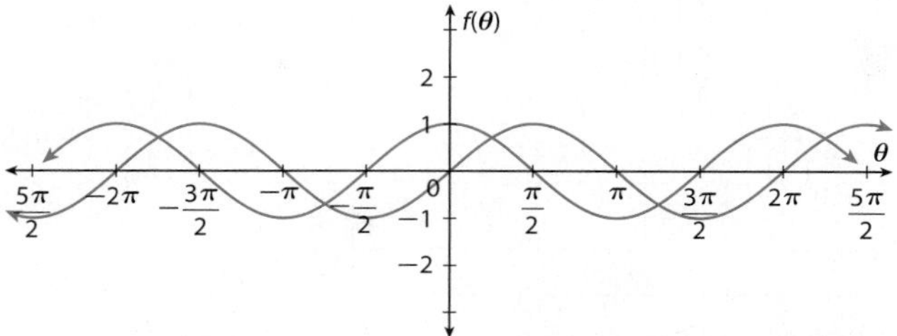

The sine and cosine functions are equal when $\theta = \frac{\pi}{4} + n\pi$, where n is an integer. These angles correspond to the points where the line $y = x$ intersects the unit circle, which means that the x-and y-coordinates of those points are equal.

24. Explain the Error When instructed to write the equation of a sine function with a vertical stretch of 2 and a horizontal compression of $\frac{1}{2}$, Charles produced the answer $y = 2 \sin \frac{1}{2}x$. Explain his error, and state the correct answer.

Charles forgot that a horizontal compression of $\frac{1}{2}$ Means that $b = \frac{1}{2}$ so that $\frac{1}{b} = 2$

The correct answer is $y = 2 \sin 2x$.

25. Critical Thinking State the domain and range of the secant function on the interval $[0, 2\pi]$. Explain how the domain and range indicate that the graph of the secant function has vertical asymptotes.

Domain: $\left\{x \mid 0 < x < \frac{\pi}{2}, \frac{\pi}{2} < x < \frac{3\pi}{2}, \frac{3\pi}{2} < x \le 2\pi\right\}$

Range: $\left\{y \mid -\infty < y \le -1, 1 \le y < +\infty\right\}$

Since the domain does not include $x = \frac{\pi}{2}$ or $x = \frac{3\pi}{2}$, while the range goes to either $+\infty$ or $-\infty$, there has to be vertical asymptotes at $x = \frac{\pi}{2}$ and $x = \frac{3\pi}{2}$.

Lesson Performance Task

A vuvuzela is a plastic horn about 2 feet long and is used during soccer matches in South Africa. If the sound level of the vuvuzela is 120 decibels from 1 meter away, the sound pressure is 20 pascals. A function of the sound pressure P in pascals from the sound wave of a vuvuzela as a function of time t in seconds is approximately $P(t) = 20 \sin(1464.612t)$.

a. Identify the amplitude and period of the sound wave. Explain your findings.

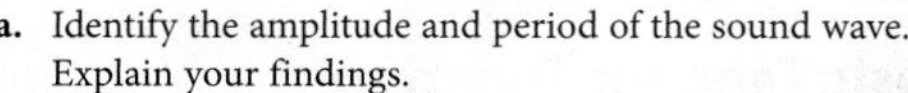

The amplitude is 20 because $a = 20$.

The period is approximately 0.00429 because $2\pi \cdot \frac{1}{|1464.612|} \approx 0.00429$.

b. Use the period of the function to find the frequency of the sound in hertz (Hz). The table shows the notes and frequency of a section of a piano's keyboard. What is the note that the vuvuzela plays? Explain.

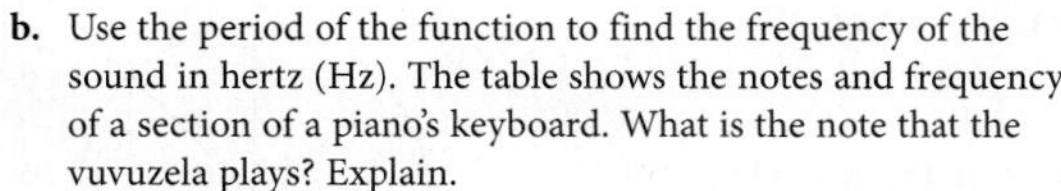

Note	Frequency (Hz)
Middle C	261.626
B	246.942
B-flat	233.082
A	220
A-flat	207.652
G	195.998
G-flat	184.997

Frequency is approximately 233.1 Hz because $\frac{1}{0.00429} \approx 233.1$. The vuvuzela plays a note of B-flat because the frequency of B-flat is approximately the same as the frequency of the sine function.

c. A piano tuner strikes a tuning fork for middle A, which has a frequency 440 Hz, at 80 decibels from 1 meter away, or a sound pressure of 0.2 pascal. What is an equation that represents the sound pressure P in pascals as a function of time t in seconds? Show your work.

The amplitude is equal to the sound pressure, which is 0.2. So, $a = 0.2$.

The period is approximately 0.00227 because $\frac{1}{440} \approx 0.00227$.

So, the coefficient of t is $\approx$ 2767.923 $2\pi \cdot \frac{1}{0.00227}$ and the function is $P(t) = \sin(2767.923t)$.

QUESTIONING STRATEGIES

How does an increase in the sound pressure of the sound wave produced by a vuvuzela, or by striking a key on the piano, affect the wave's amplitude and frequency? **Increasing the sound pressure results in an increase in amplitude; the frequency remains the same.**

AVOID COMMON ERRORS

Students will get incorrect answers if their calculators are in degree mode. Students should make sure that their calculators are set to radian mode. As a quick check, have students try sin 90°. If the result is 1, then the calculator is in degree mode and should be changed.

EXTENSION ACTIVITY

When two sounds with slightly different frequencies are produced at the same time, the sound waves are added together and create a phenomenon known as *beating.* The combined sound will alternate between soft and loud. Have students research beat frequencies, and describe practical applications for this phenomenon (for example, tuning a guitar; police radar; a Doppler pulse probe). Have them consider the sum of two waves with different frequencies, $y_1 + y_2 = a\sin(2\pi f_1 t) + a\sin(2\pi f_2 t)$, and use a trigonometric identity to rewrite this sum as a product. Challenge them to find the beat frequency.

$$y_1 + y_2 = 2a\sin 2\pi\left(\frac{f_1 + f_2}{2}\right)t\cos 2\pi\left(\frac{f_1 - f_2}{2}\right)t;\ f_{beat} = |f_1 - f_2|$$

Scoring Rubric

2 points: Student correctly solves the problem and explains his/her reasoning.

1 point: Student shows good understanding of the problem but does not fully solve or explain his/her reasoning.

0 points: Student does not demonstrate understanding of the problem.

LESSON 18.2

Stretching, Compressing, and Reflecting Tangent Graphs

Common Core Math Standards

The student is expected to:

F-IF.C.7e

Graph exponential and logarithmic functions, showing intercepts and end behavior, and trigonometric functions, showing period, midline, and amplitude. Also F-BF.B.3, F-IF.B.4, F-IF.C.9

Mathematical Practices

MP.7 Using Structure

Language Objective

Work with a partner to complete a table of the features of the sine, cosine, and tangent functions and describe how to graph the functions.

ENGAGE

Essential Question: What are the key features of the graphs of the tangent function?

The graph of the tangent function has a period of π, vertical asymptotes at $x = \frac{\pi}{2} + n\pi$, and x-intercepts at $n\pi$, where n is an integer.

PREVIEW: LESSON PERFORMANCE TASK

View the Engage section online. Discuss the photo and how trigonometry can be used to tell time. Then preview the Lesson Performance Task.

Name ________________ Class ________________ Date ________________

18.2 Stretching, Compressing, and Reflecting Tangent Graphs

Resource Locker

Essential Question: What are the key features of the graph of the tangent function?

Explore Graphing the Basic Tangent Function and Its Reciprocal

Recall that the tangent of an angle can be found from the relationship $\tan\theta = \frac{\sin\theta}{\cos\theta}$. Using the coordinates of the position on the unit circle, $(x, y) = (\cos\theta, \sin\theta)$, the value of the tangent function can also be found from the ratio of y to x.

$\sin\theta > 0$, $\cos\theta < 0$; $\frac{\pi}{2}$; $\sin\theta > 0$, $\cos\theta > 0$; $(\cos\theta, \sin\theta)$; 1; θ; π; 0, 2π; $\sin\theta < 0$, $\cos\theta < 0$; $\frac{3\pi}{2}$; $\sin\theta < 0$, $\cos\theta > 0$

(A) The tangent of an angle is undefined when the denominator of the defining ratio is 0.

As θ increases from 0, the first angle (in radians) at which the tangent becomes undefined is $\frac{\pi}{2}$.

As θ decreases from 0, the first angle (in radians) at which the tangent becomes undefined is $-\frac{\pi}{2}$.

The tangent is defined between these two angles. Use special triangles and the (x, y) coordinates of the unit circle to fill in the table of reference points (the x-intercept and the halfway points):

θ	$-\frac{\pi}{4}$	0	$\frac{\pi}{4}$
$\tan\theta$	−1	0	1

(B) Use your calculator to evaluate tangent as it approaches $\frac{\pi}{2} \approx 1.5708$ and $-\frac{\pi}{2} \approx -1.5708$.

θ	1.492	1.555	1.569	...	$\frac{\pi}{2} \approx 1.5708$
$\tan\theta$	12.66	63.30	556.69	...	Undefined

θ	−1.492	−1.555	−1.569	...	$-\frac{\pi}{2} \approx -1.5708$
$\tan\theta$	−12.66	−63.30	556.69	...	Undefined

The tangent function [increases/decreases] without bound as the angle approaches $\frac{\pi}{2}$ from below, and [increases/decreases] without bound as it approaches $-\frac{\pi}{2}$ from above. There are vertical asymptotes at $\frac{\pi}{2}$ and $-\frac{\pi}{2}$.

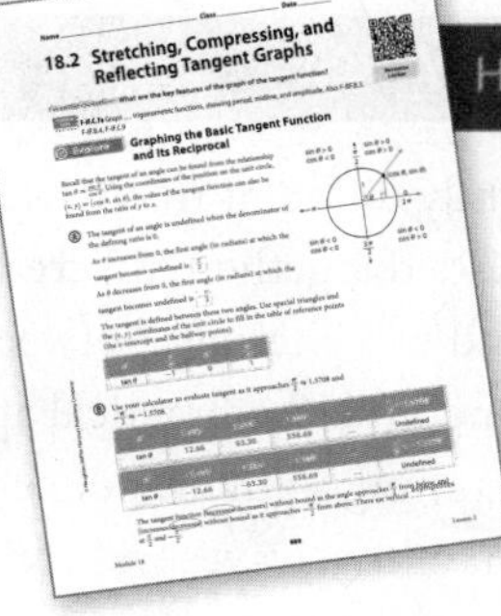

HARDCOVER PAGES 889–904

Watch for the hardcover student edition page numbers for this lesson.

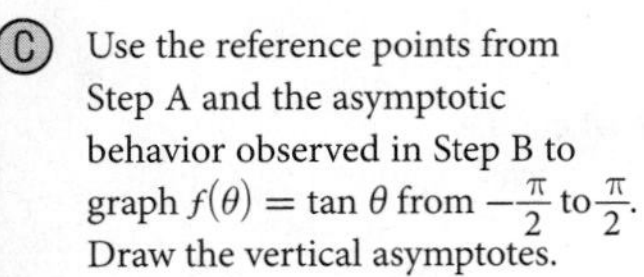

Ⓒ Use the reference points from Step A and the asymptotic behavior observed in Step B to graph $f(\theta) = \tan \theta$ from $-\frac{\pi}{2}$ to $\frac{\pi}{2}$. Draw the vertical asymptotes.

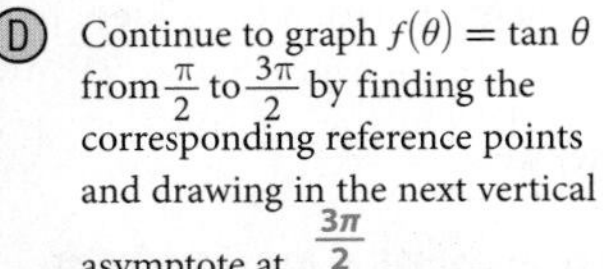

Ⓓ Continue to graph $f(\theta) = \tan \theta$ from $\frac{\pi}{2}$ to $\frac{3\pi}{2}$ by finding the corresponding reference points and drawing in the next vertical asymptote at $\frac{3\pi}{2}$.

θ	$\frac{3\pi}{4}$	π	$\frac{5\pi}{4}$
$\tan\theta$	-1	0	1

Ⓔ Use the same technique to complete the graph from -2π to 4π.

Ⓕ The **cotangent** (or cot) is the reciprocal of the tangent. It can be found by inverting the ratio used to find the tangent of an angle:

$\cot \theta = \frac{1}{\tan \theta} = \frac{\cos \theta}{\sin \theta} = \frac{x}{y}$

Like the tangent function, the graph of cotangent has regular vertical asymptotes, but at angles where $\sin \theta$ is equal to 0. The first interval with positive angle measure and defined values of cotangent is bracketed by vertical asymptotes at $\theta =$ 0 and $\theta =$ π.

Ⓖ Fill in the table of reference points for $\cot \theta$.

θ	$\frac{\pi}{4}$	$\frac{\pi}{2}$	$\frac{3\pi}{4}$
$\cot \theta$	1	0	-1

Cotangent is undefined everywhere tangent is equal to 0, and cotangent is equal to 1 or -1 when tangent is equal to 1 or -1, respectively.

Ⓗ Sketch the asymptotes at 0 and π and use the reference points to sketch the first cycle of $f(\theta) = \cot \theta$. Then continue the graph to the left and right using the same pattern of repeating asymptotes and reference points that you used to plot $f(\theta) = \tan \theta$.

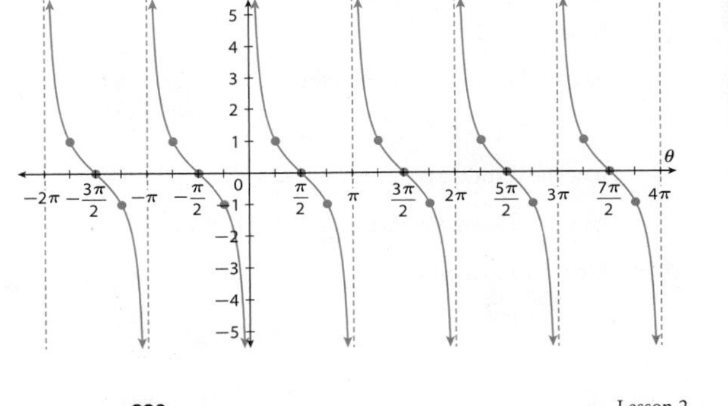

PROFESSIONAL DEVELOPMENT

Math Background

The tangent function has period π. This period is half that of the sine or cosine function. Thus, the graph of the tangent function repeats more frequently on a given interval than does the sine or cosine function. The function $y = \tan x$ is undefined at $x = \frac{\pi}{2} + n\pi$, where n is an integer. Therefore, the graph of $y = \tan x$ has vertical asymptotes at these values of x.

The graph of $y = \tan x$ demonstrates an interesting feature of the function. As x approaches $\frac{\pi}{2}$ from the left, $\tan x$ approaches infinity; as x approaches $\frac{\pi}{2}$ from the right, $\tan x$ approaches negative infinity. The same holds true for each value of x that is an odd multiple of $\frac{\pi}{2}$.

EXPLORE

Graphing the Basic Tangent Function and Its Reciprocal

INTEGRATE TECHNOLOGY

Students have the option of completing the Explore activity either in the book or online.

QUESTIONING STRATEGIES

? How does the domain of the parent tangent function differ from the domains of the parent sine and cosine functions? **The domain of the tangent function is all real numbers except odd multiples of $\frac{\pi}{2}$. The domains of the sine and cosine functions are all real numbers.**

? How does the range of the parent tangent function differ from the ranges of the basic sine and cosine functions? **The range of the tangent function is all real numbers. The ranges of the sine and cosine functions are all real numbers between -1 and 1, inclusive.**

INTEGRATE MATHEMATICAL PRACTICES

Focus on Connections

MP.1 Discuss with students how the tangent and cotangent functions are *discontinuous* functions. Explain that this means, in simple terms, that you cannot draw the graph of the function without lifting your pencil point off the paper. Relate these functions to rational functions with "holes." Lead students to observe that the sine and cosine functions are continuous functions. Tell students that they will learn more about discontinuity in more advanced classes.

AVOID COMMON ERRORS

Some students may mistakenly think that the graph of the cotangent function is the graph of the tangent function reflected across the x-axis. Help them to see that this is not the case, pointing out that the two functions have different asymptotes and x-intercepts.

EXPLAIN 1

Graphing $f(x) = a \tan\left(\frac{1}{b}\right)x$

QUESTIONING STRATEGIES

How do you find the period of the function $f(x) = a \tan\left(\frac{1}{b}\right)x$? **You divide π by the absolute value of the coefficient of x.**

How are the asymptotes of the graph of the parent function affected by the change in the period? **The asymptotes will be at odd multiples of one-half the period.**

How is the point (0, 0) affected by the change in the period? **It is not affected by the change in the period. The point (0, 0) is a point on the transformed graph.**

INTEGRATE TECHNOLOGY

Students can use their graphing calculators to explore the effects of various values of a and b on the parent tangent function. If students graph the parent function and then graph a transformed function, they will see what effects a and b have on the graph.

Reflect

1. Describe the behavior of the graph of the tangent function. Include where the function equals 0, where it has asymptotes, what the period is, and over what regions it is increasing and/or decreasing.
The tangent function is 0 at integer multiples of π, has vertical asymptotes at odd half-integer multiples of π, has a period of π, and is increasing everywhere it is defined.

2. Describe the behavior of the graph of the cotangent function. Include where the function equals 0, where it has asymptotes, what the period is, and over what regions it is increasing and/or decreasing.
The cotangent function is 0 at odd half-integer multiples of π, has vertical asymptotes at integer multiples of π, has a period of π, and is decreasing everywhere it is defined.

3. Use reference angles to explain why the graph of $f(\theta) = \tan\theta$ appears to show $f(-\theta) = -\tan\theta$.
The reference angle for an angle $-\theta$ in quadrant IV is the angle θ in quadrant I, and the sign of the tangent of $-\theta$ is the opposite of the sign of the tangent of θ. The reference angle for an angle $-\theta$ in quadrant III is the same as an angle θ in quadrant II, $\pi - \theta$, with opposite signs for the tangent functions.

Explain 1 Graphing $f(x) = a \tan\left(\frac{1}{b}x\right)$

Tangent functions can be graphed on the x–y–coordinate plane by letting x represent the angle in radians and y represent the value of the function.

The plot of a transformed tangent function can be found from the transformation parameters, as you have done for other families of functions. The parameter a causes the graph to stretch (for $|a| > 1$), compress (for $|a| < 1$), and/or reflect across the x-axis (for $a < 0$). The parameter b controls the horizontal stretches and compressions of the function and the locations of the vertical asymptotes, with the asymptotes $x = \frac{-\pi}{2}$ and $x = \frac{\pi}{2}$ moving in or out to $x = -\frac{b\pi}{2}$ and $x = \frac{b\pi}{2}$. Use the asymptotes to guide your sketch by keeping the curve (or curves if drawing more than one cycle) inside the asymptotes. The other guide to the shape comes from the halfway points at $\left(-\frac{\pi b}{4}, -a\right)$ and $\left(\frac{\pi b}{4}, a\right)$, which correspond to the points $\left(-\frac{\pi}{4}, -1\right)$ and $\left(\frac{\pi}{4}, 1\right)$ in the parent function.

Example 1 **Plot one cycle of the transformed tangent function $g(x)$ on the axes provided with the parent function $f(x) = \tan x$.**

Ⓐ $g(x) = \frac{1}{2}\tan\frac{x}{3}$

Assign values to a and b from the function rule.

$a = \frac{1}{2}, b = 3$

Draw the vertical asymptotes at $x = -\frac{3\pi}{2}$ and $x = \frac{3\pi}{2}$.

Draw the reference points at $\left(-\frac{3\pi}{4}, -\frac{1}{2}\right)$, $(0, 0)$, $\left(\frac{3\pi}{4}, \frac{1}{2}\right)$.

Sketch the function.

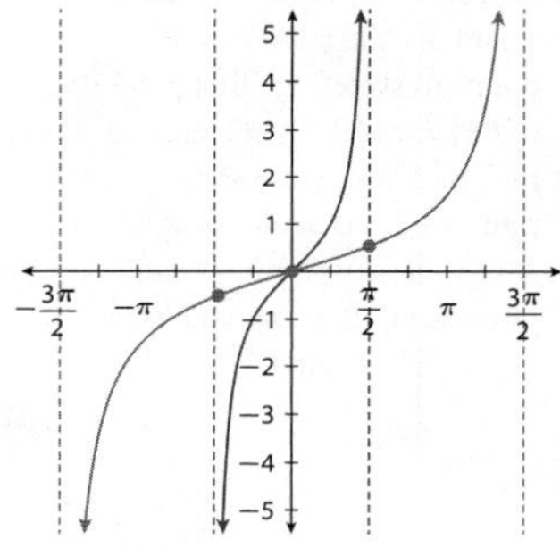

COLLABORATIVE LEARNING

Peer-to-Peer Activity

Have students work in pairs. Instruct each pair to graph three functions of the form $f(x) = a \tan\left(\frac{1}{b}\right)x$, without identifying the function. Have each pair exchange graphs with another pair of students and determine the function rule for each of the graphs they are given. Have students return their work to the pair who drew the graphs and have them check their work. Have students discuss any discrepancies.

Ⓑ $g(x) = -2 \tan 2x$

Assign values to a and b from the function rule.

$a = \boxed{-2}$, $b = \boxed{\frac{1}{2}}$

Draw the vertical asymptotes at $x = \boxed{-\frac{\pi}{4}}$ and

$x = \boxed{\frac{\pi}{4}}$.

Draw the reference points at $\left(\boxed{-\frac{\pi}{8}}, 2\right)$, $\left(\boxed{0}, 0\right)$,

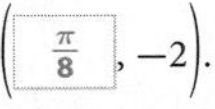

$\left(\boxed{\frac{\pi}{8}}, -2\right)$.

Sketch the function.

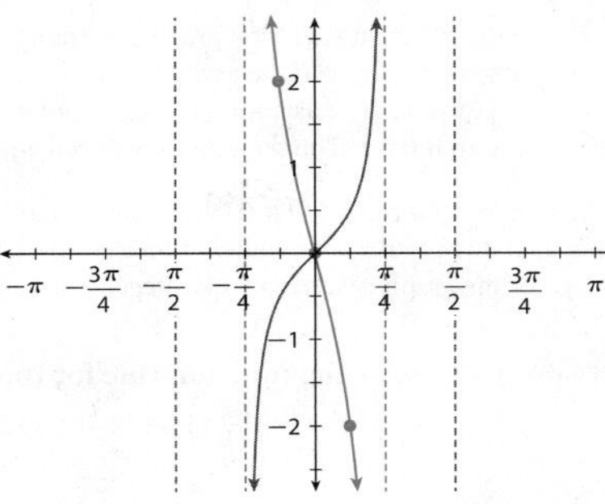

Reflect

4. Why is the vertical stretch parameter, a, referred to as the amplitude when transforming sine and cosine functions, but not tangent functions? If it is not the amplitude, how can it be used to help graph the function?

The amplitude of a periodic function is the distance from the midline to the maximum or minimum. This is a well-defined value for sine and cosine because they have a finite range, but the tangent function is unbounded. For the graph of the tangent function, the points of the graph half-way between the x-intercepts and the asymptotes have a vertical position of a or $-a$.

5. **Make a Conjecture** Do transformed functions of the form $f(x) = a \tan\left(\frac{1}{b}x\right)$ have the same behavior seen in the parent function, that is, $f(-x) = -f(x)$? Explain your answer and how it helps to graph transformed functions.

Yes; $f(-x) = a\tan\left(\frac{-x}{b}\right) = -a\tan\left(\frac{x}{b}\right) = -f(x)$. The graph of the function for $-x$ is the reflection in the x-axis of the corresponding portion of the graph for x.

Your Turn

6. Graph $g(x) = -3 \tan\frac{x}{2}$.

$a = -3$, $b = 2$

Vertical Asymptotes: $x = -\pi$ and $x = \pi$

Reference points: $\left(-\frac{\pi}{2}, 3\right)$, $(0, 0)$, $\left(\frac{\pi}{2}, -3\right)$

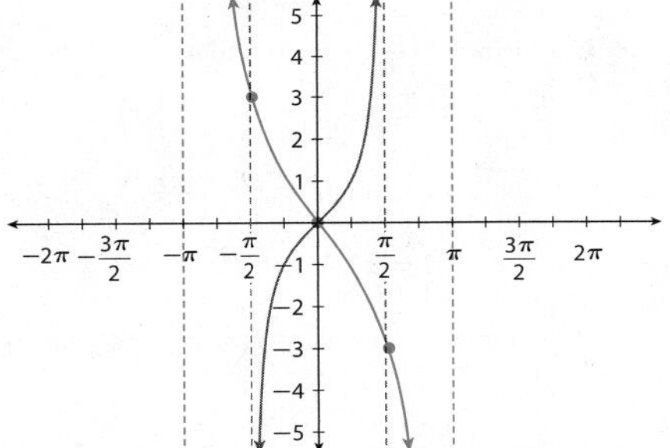

DIFFERENTIATE INSTRUCTION

Kinesthetic Experience

To further make a connection between the unit circle and the graphs of the trigonometric functions described in the previous lesson, have students again trace the circumference of the unit circle with a finger and note the relationship between y-values and x-values, and also trace along the graph of $f(x) = \tan x$ to see how this relationship on the unit circle is reflected in the graph of the function. Have them note, in particular, where the tangent function is undefined.

EXPLAIN 2

Writing $f(x) = a\tan\left(\frac{1}{b}\right)x$

QUESTIONING STRATEGIES

How can you determine the period of the function by looking at its graph? **Determine the distance between two consecutive asymptotes.**

If the graph indicates that the graph of the parent function has been stretched horizontally, is the coefficient of x greater than 1 or less than 1? **less than 1**

Explain 2 Writing $f(x) = a\tan\left(\frac{1}{b}x\right)$

To write the function rule for a graph of a transformed tangent function, identify the value of b from the spacing between the asymptotes. The asymptotes spread apart by a factor of b (or move inward if $|b| < 1$). The asymptotes are the points where the function is undefined, or $\frac{x}{b} = \frac{\pi}{2} + n\pi$, where n is an integer. The separation between any two consecutive asymptotes is $b\pi$.

The parameter a can be found by evaluating $\tan\frac{x}{b}$ at a known point. Finally, unless degrees are specified, the input to the tangent function should be assumed to be in radians, even if the x-axis of the graph is labeled with integers instead of multiples of π.

Example 2 **Write the function rule for the transformed tangent function of the form $f(x) = a\tan\left(\frac{1}{b}x\right)$ from the graph.**

(A) Find b from the distance between the asymptotes.

$\pi b = 1 - (-1)$, so $b = \frac{2}{\pi}$

Substitute the value of b into the function rule.

$f(x) = a\tan\frac{\pi}{2}x$

Use the point $\left(\frac{1}{2}, 2\right)$ to find a.

$2 = a\tan\left(\frac{\pi}{2}\cdot\frac{1}{2}\right)$

$2 = a\tan\frac{\pi}{4}$

$2 = a$

Write the function rule. $f(x) = 2\tan\frac{\pi}{2}x$

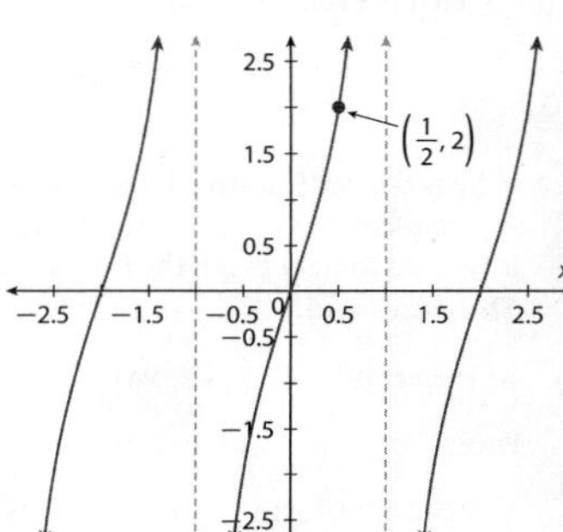

(B) Find b from the distance between the asymptotes.

$\pi b = \boxed{\frac{3\pi}{2}} - \left(\boxed{-\frac{3\pi}{2}}\right)$

$\pi b = \boxed{3\pi}$

$b = \boxed{3}$

Substitute the value of b.

$f(x) = a\tan\boxed{\frac{1}{3}}x$

Use the point $\left(\frac{3\pi}{4}, -2\right)$ to find a.

$\boxed{-2} = a\tan\left(\frac{1}{3}\cdot\boxed{\frac{3\pi}{4}}\right)$

$-2 = a\tan\boxed{\frac{\pi}{4}}$

$-2 = a$

Write the function rule. $f(x) = \boxed{-2}\tan\boxed{\frac{x}{3}}$

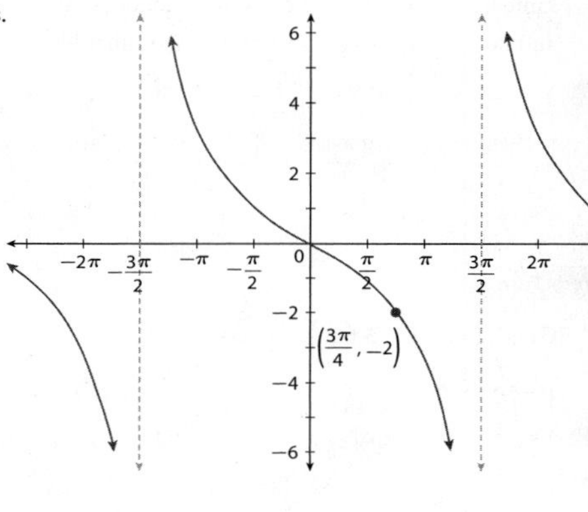

LANGUAGE SUPPORT EL

Communicate Math

Have students work in pairs to complete a table like the one below.

	$f(x) = a\sin\left(\frac{1}{b}\right)x$	$f(x) = a\cos\left(\frac{1}{b}\right)x$	$f(x) = a\tan\left(\frac{1}{b}\right)x$
Graph with key points marked			
Amplitude			
Period			
Asymptotes			
How to graph			

Your Turn

7. Write the function rule for the transformed tangent function from its graph.

$\pi b = \frac{1}{4} - \left(-\frac{1}{4}\right) \Rightarrow b = \frac{1}{2\pi}$

$a \tan 2\pi\left(\frac{1}{8}\right) = \frac{1}{2} \Rightarrow a = \frac{1}{2}$

$f(x) = \frac{1}{2} \tan 2\pi x$

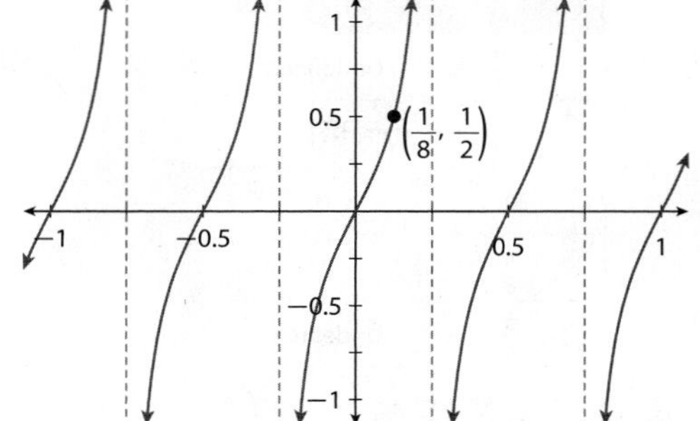

Explain 3 Comparing Tangent Functions

To compare tangent functions expressed in different forms such as graphs, tables, and equations, find the common elements that can be determined from each. Asymptotes are generally easy to recognize, and can be used to determine the period of the function.

Example 3 **Compare the two tangent functions indicated by comparing their periods.**

(A) $f(x)$ is shown in the graph; $g(x) = -\tan \frac{x}{3}$.

The period of $f(x)$ is $\pi - (-\pi) = 2\pi$.

The period of $g(x)$ is $\pi b = 3\pi$.

$g(x)$ has a greater period than $f(x)$.

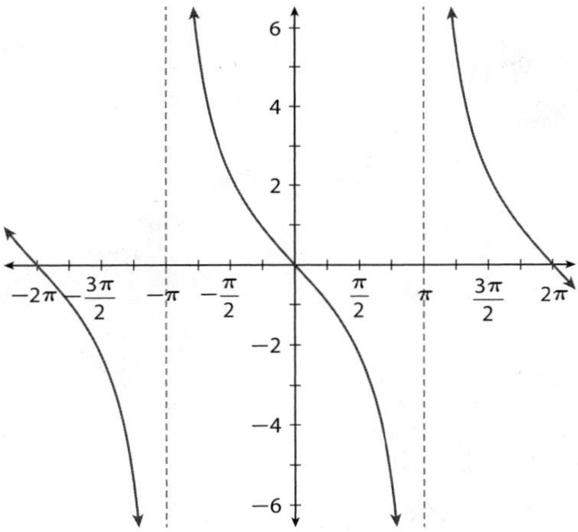

EXPLAIN 3

Comparing Tangent Functions

QUESTIONING STRATEGIES

? If you are given the rule for a tangent function of the form $f(x) = a \tan\left(\frac{1}{b}\right)x$, how can you determine the *y*-values of the halfway points of its graph? The *y*-values will be *a* and −*a*.

INTEGRATE MATHEMATICAL PRACTICES

Focus on Reasoning

MP.2 Ask students to consider and discuss how it is possible that two tangent functions could have different periods, but their graphs have some asymptotes in common. Have them find examples of this, and use their examples to describe what this tells about the relationship between the two functions in terms of the unit circle.

Ⓑ $f(x)$ is shown in the graph; $g(x)$ is shown in the table.

x	$g(x)$
$-\frac{\pi}{4}$	Undefined
$-\frac{\pi}{8}$	-1
0	0
$\frac{\pi}{8}$	1
$\frac{\pi}{4}$	Undefined

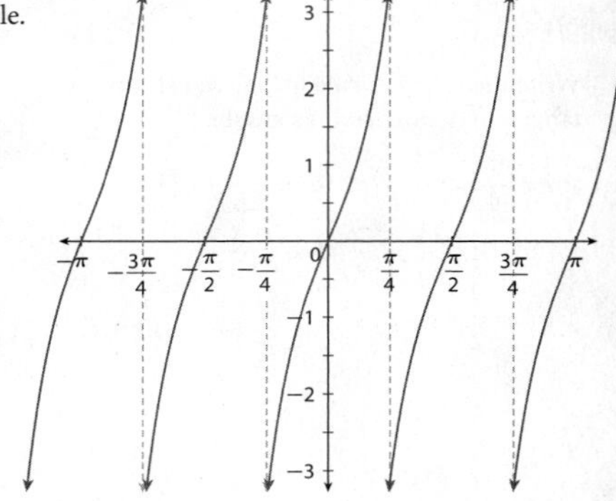

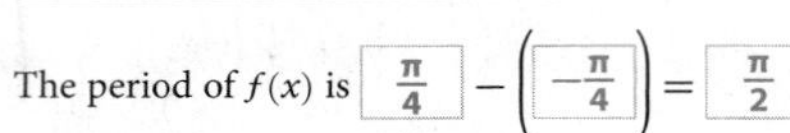

The period of $f(x)$ is $\boxed{\frac{\pi}{4}} - \left(\boxed{-\frac{\pi}{4}}\right) = \boxed{\frac{\pi}{2}}$.

The asymptotes of $g(x)$ can be found where the function is **undefined**.

The period of $g(x)$ is $\boxed{\frac{\pi}{4}} - \left(\boxed{-\frac{\pi}{4}}\right) = \boxed{\frac{\pi}{2}}$.

$g(x)$ has the same period as $f(x)$.

Your Turn

8. $f(x) = 3 \tan \frac{\pi}{3}x$

x	$g(x)$
$-\frac{1}{6}$	Undefined
$-\frac{1}{12}$	-1
0	0
$\frac{1}{12}$	1
$\frac{1}{6}$	Undefined

$f(x)$: $b = \frac{3}{\pi}$

Period $= \pi b = \pi\left(\frac{3}{\pi}\right) = 3$

$g(x)$: Asymptotes at $\frac{-1}{6}$ and $\frac{1}{6}$

Period $= \frac{1}{6} - \left(\frac{-1}{6}\right) = \frac{1}{3}$

The period of $g(x)$ is less than that of $f(x)$.

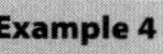 Explain 4 **Modeling with Tangent Functions**

Tangent functions can be used to model real-world situations that relate perpendicular coordinates (x and y or width and height) to an angle.

Example 4 **Read the description and use a tangent function to model the quantities. Use a calculator to make a table of points and graph the model. Describe the significance of the asymptote(s) and determine the domain over which the model works.**

A climber is ascending the face of a 500-foot high vertical cliff at 5 feet per minute. Her climbing partner is observing from 150 feet away. Find the function that describes the amount of time climbing as a function of the angle of elevation of the observer's line-of-sight to the climber. Does the viewing angle ever reach 75 degrees?

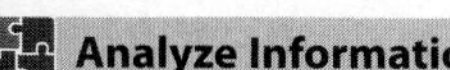 **Analyze Information**

- The distance from the observer to the cliff base is 150 feet.
- The cliff is 500 feet high.
- The climber is climbing at 5 feet per minute.

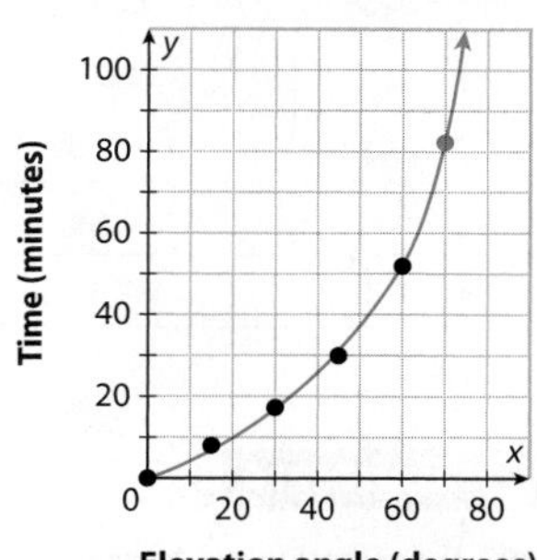

 **Formulate a Plan**

- A vertical line from the cliff base to the climber forms the second leg of a right triangle that can be used to find the appropriate trigonometric ratio.
- Use the right triangle to find a relationship between the height of the climber and the angle of elevation from which the observer is viewing.
- To find the time as a function of the angle, use the speed of the climber to rewrite the tangent expression.

θ	Time (minutes)
0	0.00
15	8.04
30	17.32
45	30.00
60	51.96

 **Solve**

The height as a function of viewing angle is $\tan \theta = \frac{h}{150}$.

The height of the climber is a function of time; $h = 5t$.

Substituting $5t$ for h in the second equation gives:

$$\tan \theta = \frac{5t}{150}$$

$$\tan \theta = \frac{t}{30}$$

$$t = 30 \tan \theta$$

EXPLAIN 4

Modeling with Tangent Functions

INTEGRATE MATHEMATICAL PRACTICES

Focus on Modeling

MP.4 Discuss with students the characteristics of the context that point to the model being that of a tangent function. Have students brainstorm other similar contexts that could also be modeled by a tangent function.

ELABORATE

INTEGRATE MATHEMATICAL PRACTICES

Focus on Patterns

MP.8 Remind students of the connection between the values on the unit circle and the graphs of the trigonometric functions, and ask them to consider *why* the period of the tangent function is π while the periods of the sine and cosine functions are both 2π. Students should focus their attention on the patterns formed by the periodic nature of the unit circle.

SUMMARIZE THE LESSON

? How do the constants a and b in the function $f(x) = a \tan\left(\frac{1}{b}\right)x$ affect the graph of the parent tangent function? The value of a changes the y-value at the halfway points. Those values become a and $-a$. Also, if a is negative, the graph is reflected in the x-axis. The value of b changes the period of the function, and therefore changes the location of the asymptotes. The period of the transformed function is $\frac{\pi}{\left|\frac{1}{b}\right|}$.

Justify and Evaluate

Using the function to calculate time, a viewing angle of 75 degrees should be reached in 111.96 minutes. However, the height at that time would be 559.8 feet, which is higher than the cliff top This means that a viewing angle of 75 degrees is impossible.

Your Turn

9. You observe a model rocket launch from 20 feet away. Find the rule for the rocket's elevation as a function of the elevation angle, and graph it.

$\frac{h}{20} = \tan\theta \Rightarrow h = 20\tan\theta$

Height (feet)	Elevation Angle (degrees)
0	0.00
15	5.36
30	11.55
45	20.00
60	34.64
75	74.64

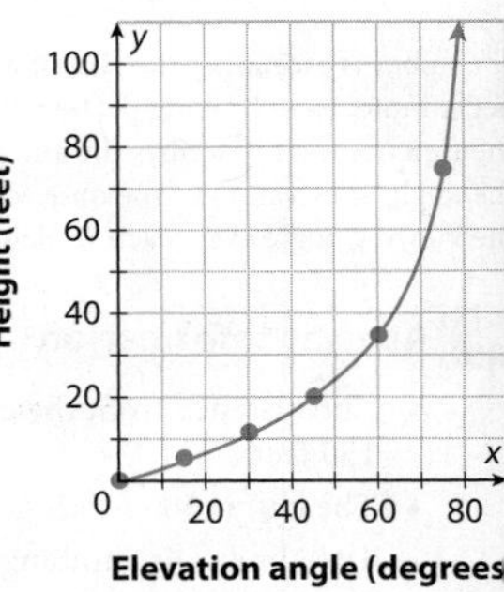

Elaborate

10. If sine, cosine and tangent are all based on coordinates of the unit circle, why do sine and cosine have a domain of all real numbers while the tangent function does not?
Sine and cosine correspond to the coordinates on the unit circles directly, which have values for all angles. Because tangent is a ratio of coordinates, it can become undefined whenever the denominator is 0.

11. Why does the tangent function have a different period than the sine and cosine functions if they are all defined using the unit circle?
The tangent function repeats itself as the angle moves through the entire unit circle, so it has two periods for every one period of the sine and cosine functions.

12. Essential Question Check-in How do the asymptotes and x-intercepts help in graphing the tangent function and its transformations?
There are repeating vertical asymptotes whose spacing comes from the horizontal stretch parameter, b. These guide the sketch of the curve because the curve will approach the asymptote but not cross it. The x-intercepts occur at regular intervals, $n\pi b$, where n is an integer.

Evaluate: Homework and Practice

- Online Homework
- Hints and Help
- Extra Practice

1. Write the rules that describe all asymptotes of the functions $f(x) = \tan x$ and $f(x) = \cot x$.

   For $f(x) = \tan x$, asymptotes are at $x = \frac{\pi}{2} + n\pi$, for all integers n.

   For $f(x) = \cot x$, asymptotes are at $x = n\pi$, for all integers n.

Plot one cycle of the transformed tangent function $g(x)$ on the axes provided with the parent function $f(x) = \tan x$.

2. $g(x) = \tan 3x$

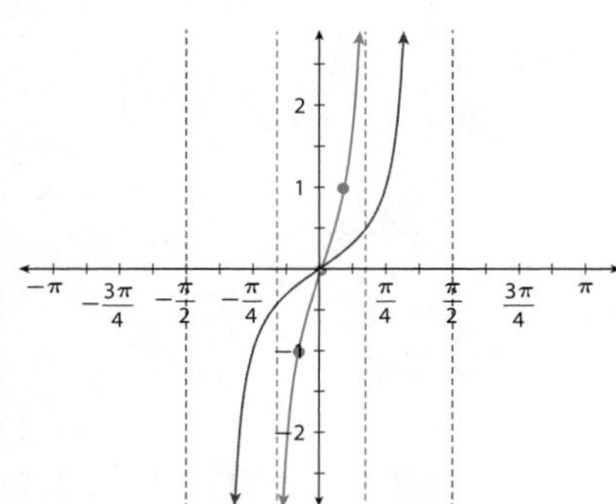

Asymptotes at $x = -\frac{\pi}{6}$ and $x = \frac{\pi}{6}$

Reference points at $\left(-\frac{\pi}{12}, -1\right)$, $(0, 0)$, $\left(\frac{\pi}{12}, 1\right)$

3. $g(x) = 3 \tan \frac{2}{3}x$

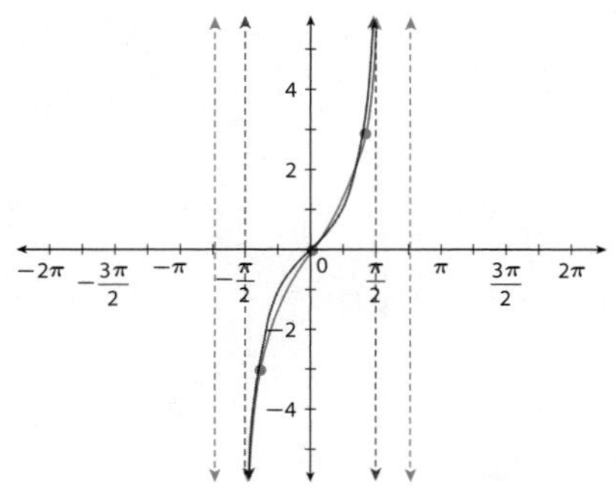

Asymptotes at $x = -\frac{3\pi}{4}$ and $x = \frac{3\pi}{4}$

Reference points at $\left(-\frac{3\pi}{8}, -3\right)$, $(0, 0)$, $\left(\frac{3\pi}{8}, 3\right)$

4. $g(x) = -\tan \frac{x}{3}$

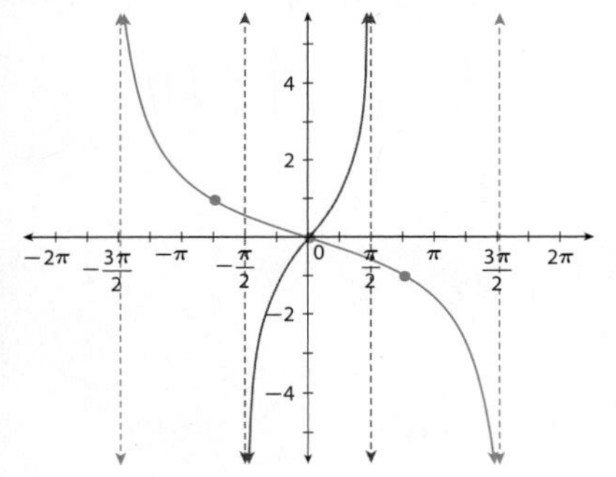

Asymptotes at $x = -\frac{3\pi}{2}$ and $x = \frac{3\pi}{2}$

Reference points at $\left(-\frac{3\pi}{4}, 1\right)$, $(0, 0)$, $\left(\frac{3\pi}{4}, -1\right)$

5. $g(x) = -\frac{1}{4} \tan 4x$

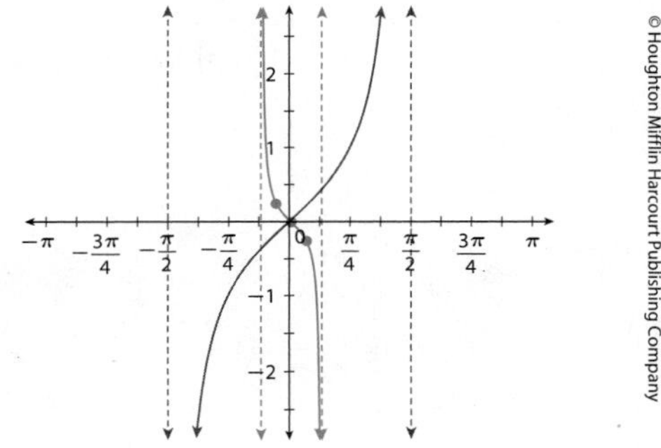

Asymptotes at $x = -\frac{\pi}{8}$ and $x = \frac{\pi}{8}$

Reference points at $\left(-\frac{\pi}{16}, \frac{1}{4}\right)$, $(0, 0)$, $\left(\frac{\pi}{16}, \frac{-1}{4}\right)$

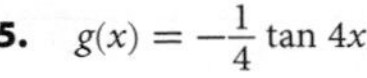

Exercise	Depth of Knowledge (D.O.K.)	COMMON CORE Mathematical Practices
1	**2** Skills/Concepts	**MP.6** Precision
2–9	**2** Skills/Concepts	**MP.7** Using Structure
10–13	**2** Skills/Concepts	**MP.4** Modeling
14–19	**2** Skills/Concepts	**MP.1** Problem Solving
20	**2** Skills/Concepts	**MP.7** Using Structure
21–22	**3** Strategic Thinking H.O.T.	**MP.1** Problem Solving
23	**3** Strategic Thinking H.O.T.	**MP.3** Logic

EVALUATE

ASSIGNMENT GUIDE

Concepts and Skills	Practice
Explore Graphing the Basic Tangent Function and Its Reciprocal	Exercise 1
Example 1 Graphing $f(x) = a \tan\left(\frac{1}{b}\right)x$	Exercises 2–5
Example 2 Writing $f(x) = a \tan\left(\frac{1}{b}\right)x$	Exercises 6–9
Example 3 Comparing Tangent Functions	Exercises 10–13
Example 4 Modeling with Tangent Functions	Exercises 14–19

QUESTIONING STRATEGIES

? How do the x-intercepts and the locations of the asymptotes of the graphs of the tangent and cotangent functions compare? **Where the graph of the tangent function has an x-intercept, the graph of the cotangent function has an asymptote. Where the graph of the cotangent function has an x-intercept, the graph of the tangent function has an asymptote.**

? How does the period of the tangent function compare to the period of the sine function? **The period of the tangent function (π) is half the period of the sine function (2π).**

INTEGRATE MATHEMATICAL PRACTICES

Focus on Critical Thinking

MP.3 Have students discuss why it is incorrect to state that the amplitude of the graph of the function $f(x) = a \tan\left(\frac{1}{b}\right)x$ is $|a|$.

COGNITIVE STRATEGIES

Students are used to making a change in a period by drawing one complete cycle of the sine or cosine curve between the y-axis and the x-value that represents the length of the new period. Help students to see that with the tangent function, it may be easier to consider the y-axis at the center of the cycle, and adjust the graph on either side of the y-axis for the new period, with half the cycle to the left of the axis, and half to the right.

AVOID COMMON ERRORS

Some students may identify the distance from the y-axis to the first asymptote to the right of the y-axis as the period of the transformed function. Remind students that for the tangent function, the y-axis is not an asymptote. Use an example to help them see that the distance they've identified is only half the period.

Write the function rule for the transformed tangent function of the form $g(x) = a\tan\left[\frac{1}{b}x\right]$ from the graph.

6.

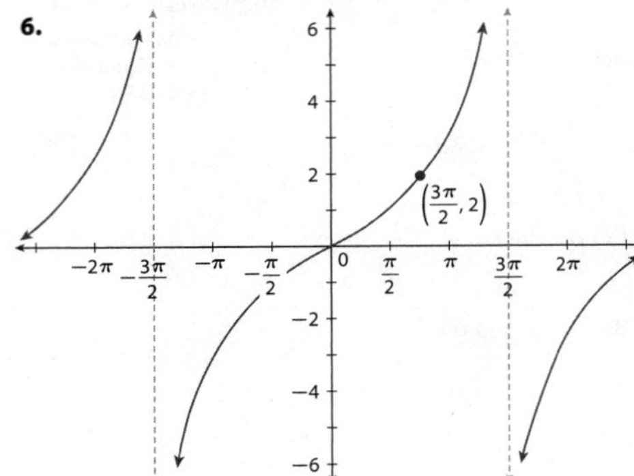

$\pi b = \frac{3\pi}{2} - \left[-\frac{3\pi}{2}\right] \Rightarrow \pi b = 3\pi \Rightarrow b = 3$

$2 = a\tan\frac{1}{3}\left[\frac{3\pi}{4}\right] \Rightarrow 2 = a$

$g(x) = 2\tan\left(\frac{1}{3}\right)x$

7.

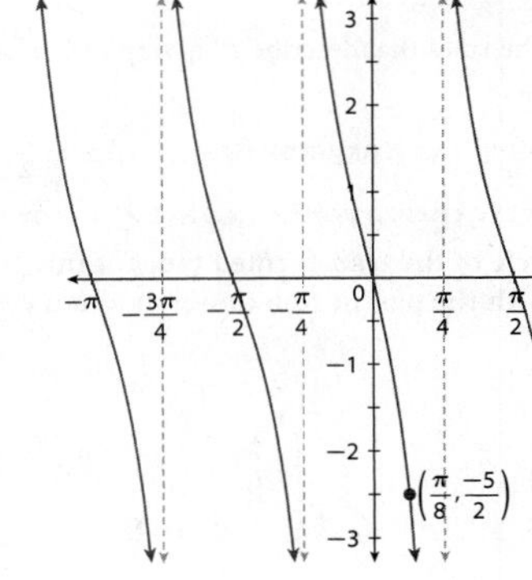

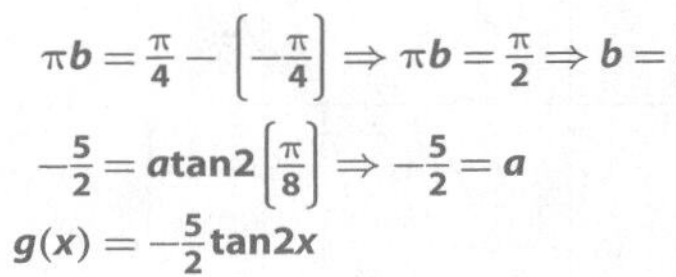

$\pi b = \frac{\pi}{4} - \left[-\frac{\pi}{4}\right] \Rightarrow \pi b = \frac{\pi}{2} \Rightarrow b = \frac{1}{2}$

$-\frac{5}{2} = a\tan 2\left[\frac{\pi}{8}\right] \Rightarrow -\frac{5}{2} = a$

$g(x) = -\frac{5}{2}\tan 2x$

8.

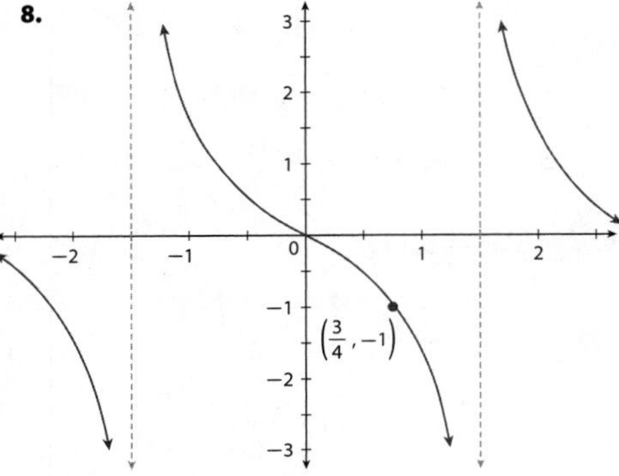

$\pi b = \frac{3}{2} - \left[-\frac{3}{2}\right] \Rightarrow \pi b = 3 \Rightarrow b = \frac{3}{\pi}$

$-1 = a\tan\frac{\pi}{3}\left[\frac{3}{4}\right] \Rightarrow -1 = a$

$g(x) = -\tan\frac{\pi}{3}x$

9.

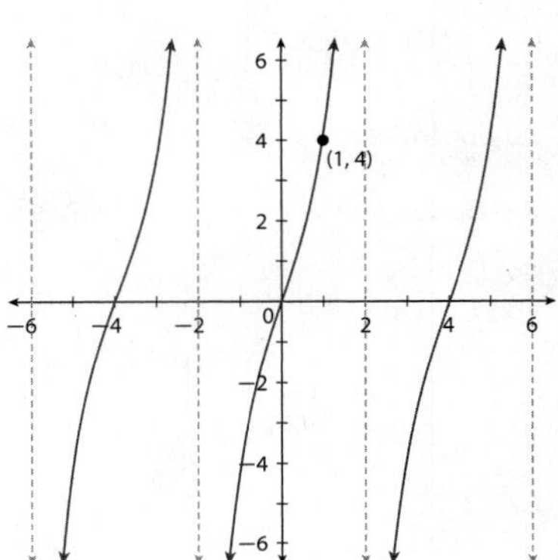

$\pi b = 2 - (-2) \Rightarrow \pi b = 4 \Rightarrow b = \frac{4}{\pi}$

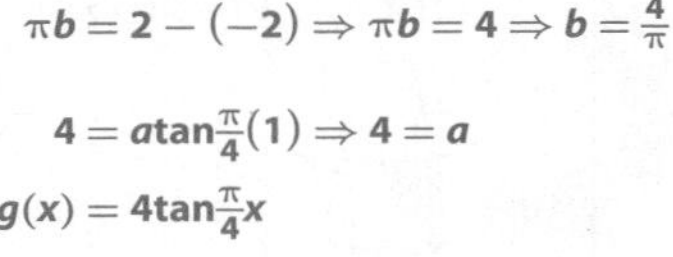

$4 = a\tan\frac{\pi}{4}(1) \Rightarrow 4 = a$

$g(x) = 4\tan\frac{\pi}{4}x$

Compare the two tangent functions indicated by comparing their periods.

10.

x	$f(x)$
−12	undefined
−6	−3
0	0
6	3
12	undefined

$g(x)$ is a tangent function with asymptotes at −10 and 10.

$f(x)$ has asymptotes at −12 and 12, $g(x)$ has asymptotes at −10 and 10. Both are horizontally stretched, but $f(x)$ is stretched more, so $f(x)$ has a greater period than $g(x)$.

11. $f(x) = 3 \tan 4x$; $g(x)$ is a tangent function with midpoints at $-\frac{\pi}{4}$ and $\frac{\pi}{4}$.

$f(x) = 3\tan 4x$

$b = \frac{1}{4}$

$f(x)$ has a period of $\frac{\pi}{4}$.

$g(x)$: halfway points at $-\frac{\pi}{4}$ and $\frac{\pi}{4} \rightarrow$ asymptotes at $-\frac{\pi}{2}$ and $\frac{\pi}{2}$

$g(x)$ has a period of π.

$g(x)$ has a greater period than $f(x)$.

12. $f(x)$ is shown in the graph.

$g(x)$ has a period of 2π.

$f(x)$ has asymptotes at −3 and 3.

$f(x)$ has a period of 6.

$6 < 2\pi \approx 6.28$

$f(x)$ has a lesser period than $g(x)$.

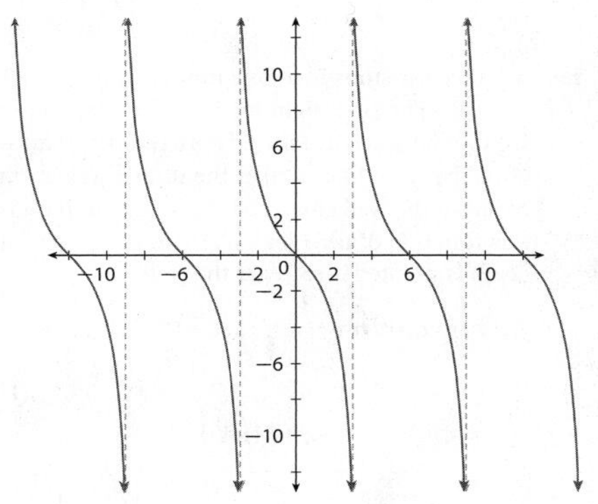

$g(x)$ is a tangent function stretched horizontally by a factor of 2.

13. $f(x) = 3 \tan \pi x$

x	$g(x)$
−1	undefined
$-\frac{1}{2}$	2
0	0
$\frac{1}{2}$	−2
1	undefined

$f(x)$: $b = \frac{1}{\pi}$

Period $= \pi b = \pi\left(\frac{1}{\pi}\right) = 1$

$g(x)$: Asymptotes at −1 and 1

Period $= 1 - (-1) = 2$

$f(x)$ has a lesser period than $g(x)$.

INTEGRATE TECHNOLOGY

Students can use a graphing calculator to check that the functions they write produce the same graph as the given graph.

INTEGRATE MATHEMATICAL PRACTICES

Focus on Communication

MP.3 Ask students to tell which parameter in the function $f(x) = a\tan\left(\frac{1}{b}\right)x$ provides information about the frequency of the function. Have them discuss what the frequency indicates about the graph of the function and, thus, the function values.

14. Sam is watching airplanes fly over his head at an airshow. The airplanes approach from the east at an altitude of 0.1 mile, and cast a shadow directly on the ground below them. Sam watches the airplanes approach and fly past. Counting straight overhead from Sam as an angle of 0°, with angles looking east to the planes measured as positive angles from 0 and angles looking west measured as negative angles from 0, find the distance d of the shadow on the ground from Sam as a function of the angle of Sam's view as the planes approach and fly over.

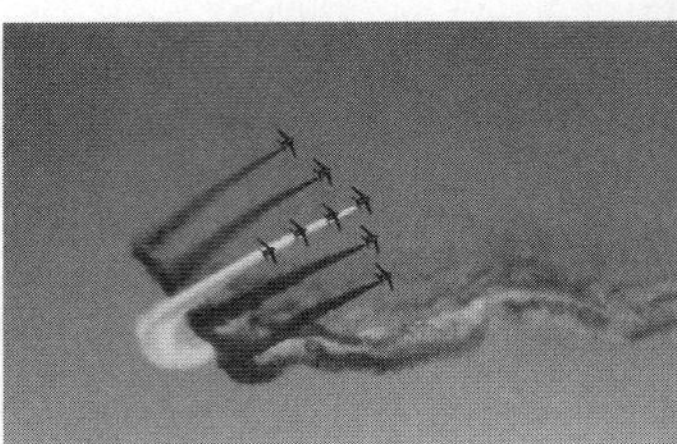

$\frac{d}{0.1} = \tan\theta \Rightarrow d = 0.1\tan\theta$

Angle (degrees)	Distance (miles)
0	0.00
15	0.03
30	0.06
45	0.10
60	0.17
75	0.37

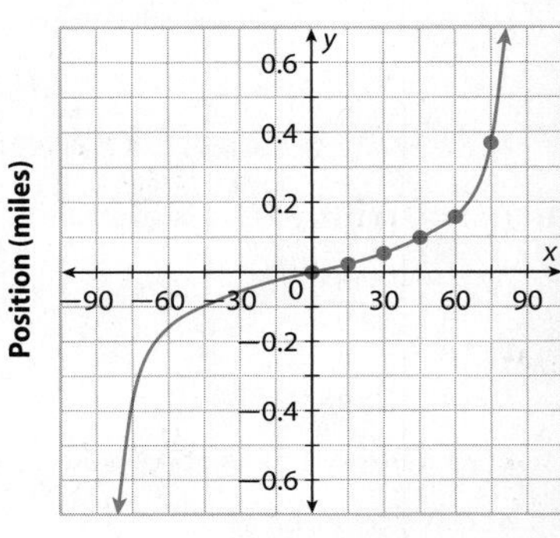

15. A police car stops in a long tunnel and parks 20 feet from the wall. The siren light makes a complete revolution once per second. Find the distance d between the point where the center of the beam of light strikes the tunnel wall at time t and the point on the wall closest to the light's source. Graph the distance as a function of time for $-0.5 < t < 05$ where at time $t = 0$ the beam is pointed directly at the wall.

One revolution = 2π at 1 second, so period = 0.5 sec

$\theta = 2\pi t$

$\frac{d}{20} = \tan\theta \Rightarrow d = 20\tan 2\pi t$

Time (s)	Distance (feet)
0	0.00
0.05	6.50
0.1	14.53
0.15	27.53
0.2	61.55

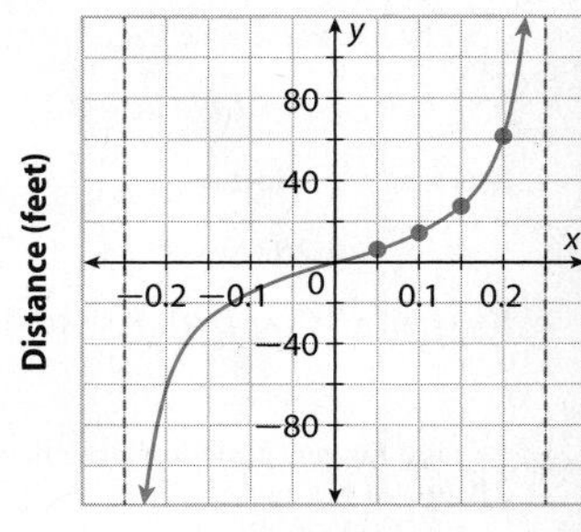

16. A security camera is mounted on the ceiling 10 feet above a long hallway. Find the distance along the hallway of the center of the camera's field of view as a function of the angle the camera makes relative to pointing straight down.

$\frac{d}{10} = \tan\theta \Rightarrow d = 10 \tan\theta$

Angle (degrees)	Distance (feet)
0	0.00
15	2.68
30	5.77
45	10.00
60	17.32
75	37.32

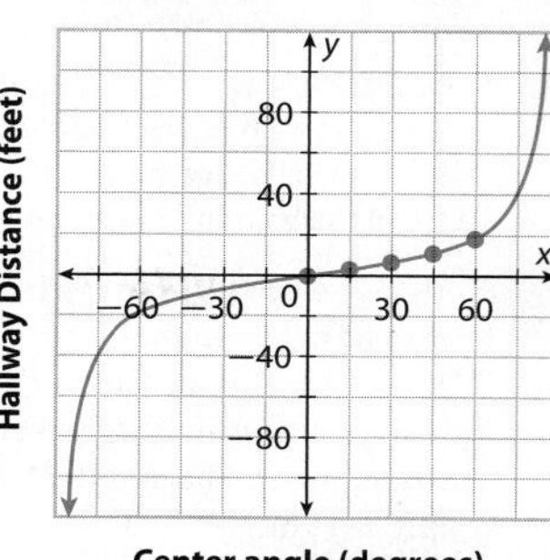

17. At what distances is the shadow when it is at the halfway points of the graph in the airshow example in Exercise 14?

−0.1 mile and 0.1 mile

18. What distances along the hallway are at the center of the view of the security camera when it is at the halfway points of the graph in Exercise 16?

−10 feet and 10 feet

19. At what time is the police siren light shining on the wall at a distance of 20 feet in a negative direction in Exercise 15?

−20 feet corresponds to the halfway point in the negative direction

$\theta = -\frac{\pi}{4} = 2\pi t$

$t = -\frac{1}{8}$ **second**

20. **Multiple Response** The function $g(x) = -3 \tan \pi x$ has which of the following transformations compared to the parent function $f(x) = \tan x$?

(A.) a vertical stretch by a factor of 3

B. a vertical compression by a factor of 3

C. a horizontal stretch by a factor of π

(D.) a horizontal compression by a factor of π

(E.) a reflection over the x-axis

F. a translation up by 3

G. a translation down by 3

COLLABORATIVE LEARNING

Have students work in small groups to make a poster showing the graphs of the three basic trigonometric functions, $f(x) = \sin x$, $f(x) = \cos x$, and $f(x) = \tan x$. Have them mark and label the key points on each graph. Then have them create an example for each function, such as $f(x) = 3 \sin\left(\frac{1}{2}\right)x$, and show how to graph the new function by transforming the graph of the parent function. Have groups share their posters with the class.

PEER-TO-PEER DISCUSSION

Ask students to discuss with a partner how two tangent functions can have different periods yet have the same *y*-values at their halfway points. **Although the *y*-values at the halfway points may be the same, the points will have different *x*-values.**

JOURNAL

Have students describe how to graph the function $f(x) = -3 \tan \left(\frac{1}{2}\right)x$. Then have them compare the graph to that of the parent tangent function.

H.O.T. Focus on Higher Order of Thinking

21. Draw Conclusions In the security camera model of Exercise 16, imagine that the camera has a field of view that is 20° wide (i.e. if the center of the image is looking at 40°, the total image views from 30° to 50°). What center angle views the shortest stretch of the hallway? What center angle views the longest stretch?

For a center position of θ, the camera views from $\theta - 10$ to $\theta + 10$. The length of hallway viewed is given by $10 \tan(\theta + 10) - 10 \tan(\theta - 10)$, or the vertical distance on the graph. The graph is steepest near −90° and 90°, so positioning the camera at −80° or 80° captures the longest stretch of the hallway. The shortest stretch occurs at the least steep portion of the graph, or when $\theta = 0°$.

22. Justify Reasoning In the police siren example of Exercise 15, if the graph were extended to longer times and encompassed more periods of the tangent function, explain whether it would make sense to include all other periods of the tangent function.

For the times when the light is pointing away from the wall it would not make sense to include the plot, even though the tangent function is defined. Only every other period of the tangent function would be included in the graph, since those are the times when the light is hitting the wall (at the other times the light is hitting the opposite wall).

23. Communicate Mathematical Ideas How could you sketch a graph of a tangent function on a coordinate plane with no grid lines (except the *x*- and *y*-axes) that is already showing the sine and cosine functions?

The important reference points and asymptotes of the tangent function all occur at recognizable points in the sine and cosine graphs. The asymptotes will be at the cosine's *x*-intercepts, the tangent's *x*-intercepts will be at the sine's *x*-intercepts, and the halfway points occur where the sine and cosine functions intersect.

Lesson Performance Task

A community on the equator celebrates the equinox by having a festival at the town's sundial. Because the town is located at the equator, the sun rises directly in the east and sets directly in the west, passing directly overhead at solar noon, halfway through the 12 hours of daylight. The sundial rests on the ground, and its gnomon, the pointer that casts the shadow, is 4 feet above the ground. Let x be the angle of the sun from the sundial in degrees and let s be the length of the sundial's shadow in feet, as shown in the figure.

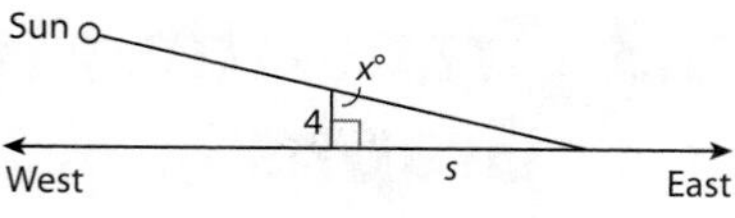

A. Write an equation that expresses the relationship between s and x, and then solve for s. **$\tan x = \frac{s}{4}$, so $4 \tan x = s$**

B. Let the angle off the sundial to the west be negative and the angle off the sundial to the east be positive. Write a function for the length of the sundial's shadow, s, in feet to the east as a function of time t hours after solar noon using the fact that the angle changes by 15° per hour.

Substitute $15t$ for x; $s(x) = 4\tan(x)$, so $s(t) = 4\tan(15t)$

C. Describe the graph of $s(t)$ from part B as a series of transformations from the parent function $f(t) = \tan t$. Also indicate the period of the function.

The graph of $s(t)$ is the graph of $f(t) = \tan t$ stretched vertically by a factor of 4 and compressed horizontally by a factor of $\frac{1}{15}$. The period of the function is $\frac{180}{15} = 12$.

D. Since solar noon occurs at 12:15 p.m. local time, sunrise and sunset occur around 6:15 a.m. and 6:15 p.m., respectively. Complete the table to determine the values of t and $s(t)$, rounding to the nearest hundredth as needed. What is the meaning of the negative values for $s(t)$?

Local Time	t	$s(t)$
6:15 a.m.	−6	undefined
8:15 a.m.	−4	−6.93
10:15 a.m.	−2	−2.31
12:15 p.m.	0	0
2:15 p.m.	2	2.31
4:15 p.m.	4	6.93
6:15 p.m.	6	undefined

The negative values of $s(t)$ mean that the sundial's shadow is pointing to the west.

E. Do the values of $s(t)$ make sense at sunrise and sunset? Explain your reasoning. **The undefined values of $s(t)$ at sunrise and sunset make sense because the sun cannot cast a shadow during those times.**

QUESTIONING STRATEGIES

What is the horizontal stretch or compression of the parent tangent function when a function is written in the form $f(x) = a\tan(px)$? **$\frac{1}{p}$; It is horizontally expanded by a factor of p. If $p < 1$, then it is horizontally compressed.**

AVOID COMMON ERRORS

Students may have trouble recalling the triangle-based definitions of *sine, cosine,* and *tangent.* Encourage students to share any mnemonic devices they have used, such as *Soh-Cah-Toa* or the sentence "**S**addle **o**ur **h**orses, **c**anter **a**way **h**appily **t**o **o**ther **a**dventures." (**S**ine = **o**pposite over **h**ypotenuse, **c**osine = **a**djacent over **h**ypotenuse, and **t**angent = **o**pposite over **a**djacent.)

INTEGRATE TECHNOLOGY

Students can use their graphing calculators to observe how changing the constants a and p in the function $f(x) = a\tan(px)$ affects the graph.

EXTENSION ACTIVITY

Suggest students build their own sundial. Have students research how to construct a horizontal sundial. They should find that the angle the hour line makes with the noon line, θ, can be calculated from the equation $\tan\theta = (\tan t)(\sin L)$, where t is the time measured from noon in angular degrees (with 6 a.m. and 6 p.m. corresponding to 90°), and L is the latitude. Make sure students know how to calculate arctangent.

Scoring Rubric

2 points: Student correctly solves the problem and explains his/her reasoning.

1 point: Student shows good understanding of the problem but does not fully solve or explain his/her reasoning.

0 points: Student does not demonstrate understanding of the problem.

LESSON 18.3

Translating Trigonometric Graphs

Common Core Math Standards

The student is expected to:

COMMON CORE **F-IF.C.7e**

Graph exponential and logarithmic functions, showing intercepts and end behavior, and trigonometric functions, showing period, midline, and amplitude. Also F-BF.B.3, F-IF.B.4, F-IF.C.9

Mathematical Practices

COMMON CORE **MP.7 Using Structure**

Language Objective

Explain to a partner how the constants in the trigonometric functions affect their graphs.

ENGAGE

Essential Question: How do the constants h and k in the functions $f(x) = a\sin\frac{1}{b}(x-h)+k$, $f(x) = a\cos\frac{1}{b}(x-h)+k$, and $f(x) = a\tan\frac{1}{b}(x-h)+k$ affect their graphs?

Changing the value of h translates each graph horizontally, and changing the value of k translates the graph vertically.

PREVIEW: LESSON PERFORMANCE TASK

View the Engage section online. Discuss the photo and how a trigonometric function can be used to model the tides. Then preview the Lesson Performance Task.

Name ______ Class ______ Date ______

18.3 Translating Trigonometric Graphs

Essential Question: How do the constants h and k in the functions $f(x) = a\sin\frac{1}{b}(x-h)+k$, $f(x) = a\cos\frac{1}{b}(x-h)+k$, and $f(x) = a\tan\frac{1}{b}(x-h)+k$ affect their graphs?

Resource Locker

Explore Translating the Graph of a Trigonometric Function

In previous lessons, you saw in what ways the graphs of $f(x) = a\sin\left(\frac{1}{b}\right)x$, $f(x) = a\cos\left(\frac{1}{b}\right)x$, and $f(x) = a\tan\left(\frac{1}{b}\right)x$ were vertical and horizontal shrinks and stretches of the graphs of their parent functions. You saw that the vertical stretches and shrinks changed the amplitude of sine and cosine graphs, but did not change the midline on the x-axis, and the horizontal stretches and compressions changed the period of all of the graphs.

As with other types of functions, you can indicate horizontal and vertical translations in the equations for trigonometric functions. Trigonometric functions in the form $f(x) = a\sin\frac{1}{b}(x-h)+k$, $f(x) = a\cos\frac{1}{b}(x-h)+k$, or $f(x) = a\tan\frac{1}{b}(x-h)+k$ indicate a vertical translation by k and a horizontal translation by h.

(A) Answer the following questions about the graph of $f(x) = 0.5\sin 3x$.

a. What is the period of the graph?

b. What are the first three x-intercepts for $x \geq 0$?

c. What are the maximum and minimum values of the first cycle for $x \geq 0$, and where do they occur?

d. What are the five key points of the graph that represent the values you found?

Use the key points to sketch one cycle of the graph.

a. $b = \frac{1}{3}$, **so period** $= 2\pi \cdot \frac{1}{3} = \frac{2\pi}{3}$

b. The sine function is 0 at the origin, where $x = 0$. It will be 0 at the end of the first cycle from 0, or at $x = \frac{2\pi}{3}$, and also at the halfway point between 0 and $\frac{2\pi}{3}$, or at $x = \frac{\pi}{3}$.

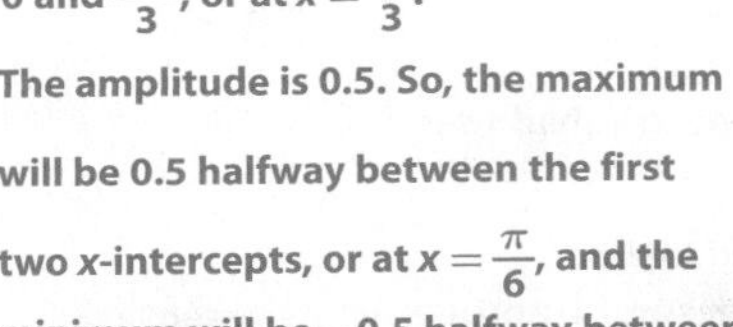

c. The amplitude is 0.5. So, the maximum will be 0.5 halfway between the first two x-intercepts, or at $x = \frac{\pi}{6}$, and the minimum will be −0.5 halfway between the second and third intercepts, or at $x = \frac{\pi}{2}$.

d. $(0,0)$, $\left(\frac{\pi}{6}, 0.5\right)$, $\left(\frac{\pi}{3}, 0\right)$, $\left(\frac{\pi}{2}, -0.5\right)$, $\left(\frac{2\pi}{3}, 0\right)$

HARDCOVER PAGES 905–922

Watch for the hardcover student edition page numbers for this lesson.

(B) Identify h and k for $f(x) = 0.5\sin 3\left(x - \frac{\pi}{3}\right) - 1.5$, and tell what translations they indicate. Find the images of the key points of the graph in Step A. Finally, sketch the graph from Step A again, along with the graph of its image, after the indicated translations.

$h = \frac{\pi}{3}$, $k = -1.5$; the graph will be shifted $\frac{\pi}{3}$ units to the right and 1.5 units down.

Key points:

$\left(0 + \frac{\pi}{3}, 0 - 1.5\right), \left(\frac{\pi}{6} + \frac{\pi}{3}, 0.5 - 1.5\right),$

$\left(\frac{\pi}{3} + \frac{\pi}{3}, 0 - 1.5\right), \left(\frac{\pi}{2} + \frac{\pi}{3}, -0.5 - 1.5\right),$

$\left(\frac{2\pi}{3} + \frac{\pi}{3}, 0 - 1.5\right) \Rightarrow \left(\frac{\pi}{3}, -1.5\right), \left(\frac{\pi}{2}, -1\right), \left(\frac{2\pi}{3}, -1.5\right), \left(\frac{5\pi}{6}, -2\right) (\pi, -1.5)$

(C) Answer the following questions about the graph of $f(x) = 2\tan\frac{1}{2}x$.

a. What is the period of the graph?

b. What is the x-intercept of the graph at or nearest the origin? What are the asymptotes?

c. What are the halfway points on either side of the x-intercept that you found?

d. What are the three key points of the graph that represent the values you found?

Use the key points to sketch one cycle of the graph. Also show the asymptotes.

a. $b = 2$, so period $= \pi \cdot 2 = 2\pi$

b. The tangent function is 0 at the origin, where $x = 0$. The asymptotes are one half of a cycle to the left and right of the intercept, or at $x = \pm\pi$.

c. The halfway points are midway between the x-intercept and the asymptotes, or at $x = \pm\frac{\pi}{2}$. Because $a = 2$, the graph is vertically stretched by a factor of two, so the halfway points are $\left(-\frac{\pi}{2}, -2\right)$ and $\left(\frac{\pi}{2}, 2\right)$.

d. $(0,0), \left(-\frac{\pi}{2}, -2\right), \left(\frac{\pi}{2}, 2\right)$

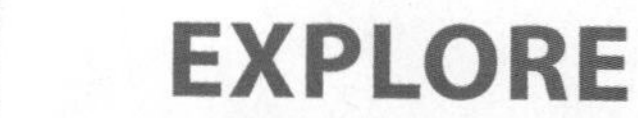

EXPLORE

Translating the Graph of a Trigonometric Function

INTEGRATE TECHNOLOGY

Students have the option of completing the Explore activity either in the book or online.

QUESTIONING STRATEGIES

? If you know the coordinates of the five key points on the graph of $f(x) = a\cos\frac{1}{b}x$, how can you use h and k to find the images of these points in order to graph $f(x) = a\cos\frac{1}{b}(x - h) + k$? **You can add h to each x-coordinate and k to each y-coordinate.**

? How are the asymptotes of the graph of $f(x) = a\tan\frac{1}{b}x$ affected by h and k when the graph is transformed to $f(x) = a\tan\frac{1}{b}(x - h) + k$? **The asymptotes are shifted h units horizontally right if h is positive, left if h is negative. They are not affected by k.**

AVOID COMMON ERRORS

To avoid a common error, it is worth noting that an expression such as $\sin\frac{\pi}{2}(x - 1)$ is equivalent to $\sin\left[\frac{\pi}{2}(x - 1)\right]$ and not equivalent to $\left(\sin\frac{\pi}{2}\right) \cdot (x - 1)$. The use of the extra brackets may be cumbersome, but it serves to eliminate confusion.

PROFESSIONAL DEVELOPMENT

Learning Progressions

Students learned the effects of the values of a and b on the sine, cosine, and tangent functions of the form $f(x) = a\sin\frac{1}{b}x$, etc. Students saw that changing the values of these constants had the same effect on these trigonometric functions as on other types of functions. Students will now study the effects of h and k on trigonometric functions of the form $f(x) = a\sin\frac{1}{b}(x - h) + k$, etc., and they will discover that changing these values translates the graphs of the parent functions horizontally or vertically. The value of h for trigonometric functions indicates the horizontal translation and is called the *phase shift* of the function.

Ⓓ Identify h and k for $f(x) = 2\tan\frac{1}{2}(x + \pi) + 3$, and tell what translations they indicate. Find the images of the key points of the graph in Step A, and the new asymptotes. Finally, sketch the graph from Step A again, along with the graph of its image after the indicated translations. (Note: Show the asymptotes for the translated graph, but not for the original graph.)

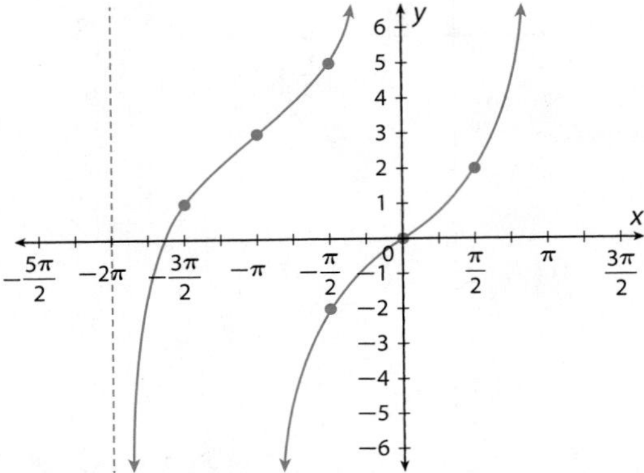

$h = -\pi, k = 3$; the graph will be shifted π units to the left and 3 units up.

Key points:

$$\left(-\frac{\pi}{2} - \pi, -2 + 3\right), \left(0 - \pi, 0 + 3\right), \left(\frac{\pi}{2} - \pi, 2 + 3\right) \Rightarrow \left(-\frac{3\pi}{2}, 1\right), (-\pi, 3), \left(-\frac{\pi}{2}, 5\right)$$

Asymptotes: $x = -\pi - \pi = -2\pi$ and $x = \pi - \pi = 0$

Reflect

1. Suppose that you are told to extend the graph of the translated function you graphed in Step B to the left and to the right. Without actually drawing the graph, explain how you would do this.
First, recognize that the midline of the graph is the horizontal line $y = -1.5$. The graph will intersect the midline every $\frac{\pi}{3}$ units as in the cycle graphed. Indicate these points on the graph. The maximum value of -1 and the minimum value of -2 will repeat every cycle of $\frac{2\pi}{3}$ units along the midline. Indicate these points on the graph, then draw the repeating curve through the key points.

2. What feature of the graphs of the trigonometric functions is represented by the value of the parameter k?
The equation of the midline of the graph is given by $y = k$.

COLLABORATIVE LEARNING

Peer-to-Peer Activity

Have students work in pairs. Provide each pair with a trigonometric function of the form $f(x) = a \sin\frac{1}{b}(x - h) + k$, $f(x) = a \cos\frac{1}{b}(x - h) + k$, or $f(x) = a \tan\frac{1}{b}(x - h) + k$. Have each pair create a table of values for the function, using 8 to12 different values for x. Then have them graph the function using the methods described in the lesson. Have each pair confirm that the points from their table are located on their graph.

Explain 1 Graphing General Trigonometric Functions

Now you can combine all you have learned about the parameters a, b, h, and k in the equations for trigonometric functions to graph functions of the form $f(x) = a\sin\frac{1}{b}(x-h)+k$, $f(x) = a\cos\frac{1}{b}(x-h)+k$, or $f(x) = a\tan\frac{1}{b}(x-h)+k$ directly from their equations without first graphing parent functions.

Example 1 **For the function given, identify the period and the midline of the graph, and where the graph crosses the midline. For a sine or cosine function, identify the amplitude and the maximum and minimum values and where they occur. For a tangent function, identify the asymptotes and the values of the halfway points. Then graph one cycle of the function.**

(A) $f(x) = 3\sin(x-\pi)+1$

Period: $\frac{1}{b} = 1$, so $b = 1$; period $= 2\pi \cdot 1 = 2\pi$

Midline: $y = k$, or $y = 1$

Amplitude: $a = 3$

The point $(0, 0)$ on the graph of the parent function $y = \sin x$ is translated $h = \pi$ units to the right and $k = 1$ unit up to $(\pi, 1)$. The graph also crosses the midline at the endpoint of the cycle , $(\pi + 2\pi, 1) = (3\pi, 1)$ and at the point halfway between $(\pi, 1)$ and $(3\pi, 1)$ or at $(2\pi, 1)$. So, the graph contains $(\pi, 1)$, $(2\pi, 1)$ and $(3\pi, 1)$.

Maximum: $a = 3$ units above the midline, or $k + a = 1 + 3 = 4$; occurs halfway between the first and second midline crossings, or at $x = \frac{\pi + 2\pi}{2} = \frac{3\pi}{2}$. So, the graph contains $\left(\frac{3\pi}{2}, 4\right)$.

Minimum: $a = 3$ units below the midline, or $k - a = 1 - 3 = -2$; occurs halfway between the second and third midline crossings, or at $x = \frac{2\pi + 3\pi}{2} = \frac{5\pi}{2}$. So, the graph contains $\left(\frac{5\pi}{2}, -2\right)$.

Plot the key points found and sketch the graph.

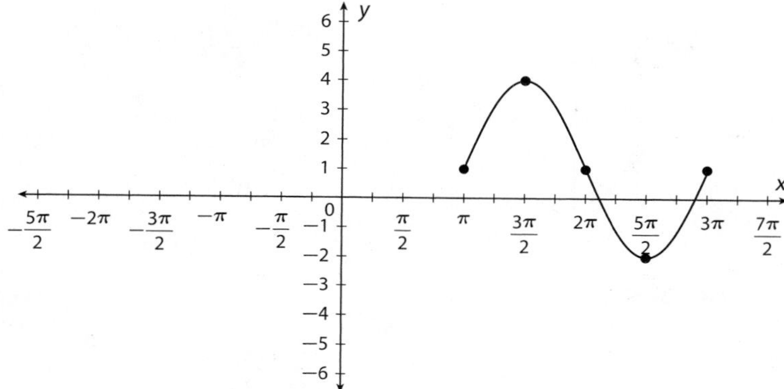

DIFFERENTIATE INSTRUCTION

Kinesthetic Experience

Kinesthetic learners may find it easier to understand the connection between the function rule and its graph by using tracing paper to physically translate the midline of the related sine or cosine graph and apply the phase shift. For example, to graph $f(x) = 3\sin\frac{1}{2}(x-\pi)+4$, students can graph the related function $f(x) = 3\sin\frac{1}{2}x$, trace the graph and the x-axis onto tracing paper, and slide the traced graph so that the axis is located at the new midline, $y = 4$. They can then slide the graph π units to the right horizontally to reflect the phase shift. Have students compare the final location of the graph to the related graph and to the parent graph to see how the parameters affect each graph.

EXPLAIN 1

Graphing General Trigonometric Functions

QUESTIONING STRATEGIES

What is the maximum value of the function $f(x) = a\sin\frac{1}{b}(x-h)+k$? Explain how you know. $|a| + k$; the value of a affects amplitude, so the maximum value before the translation is $|a|$, and k produces a vertical translation of the maximum point.

What are the y-values at the halfway points on the graph of $f(x) = a\tan\frac{1}{b}(x-h)+k$? Explain how you know. $a + k$ and $-a + k$; the values before the translation are a and $-a$, and k produces a vertical translation of each halfway point.

INTEGRATE MATHEMATICAL PRACTICES

Focus on Math Connections

MP.1 Discuss with students the importance of identifying the midline of the graph. Have them describe the role it plays in the graphing of the trigonometric functions. Then explain *inflection point*. Have students practice sketching their graphs with properly-drawn inflection points, paying special attention to the curvature of the pieces of the graph that lie above and below the midline.

CONNECT VOCABULARY EL

Review the different kinds of transformations of graphs with students, making sure they understand what is meant by *stretching* and *compressing*, and *horizontal* and *vertical*.

Ⓑ $f(x) = -2\tan\frac{1}{2}(x - 2\pi) + 2$

Period: $\frac{1}{b} = \boxed{\frac{1}{2}}$, so $b = \boxed{2}$; period $= \boxed{\pi} \cdot 2 = \boxed{2\pi}$

Midline: $y = k$, or $y = \boxed{2}$

The point $(0, 0)$ on the graph of $y = \tan x$ is translated $h = \boxed{2\pi}$ units to the <u>right</u> and $k = \boxed{2}$ units <u>up</u> to $\left(\boxed{2\pi}, \boxed{2}\right)$. There are asymptotes half a cycle to the left and right of this point, or at $x = 2\pi - \boxed{\pi} = \boxed{\pi}$ and $x = 2\pi + \boxed{\pi} = \boxed{3\pi}$.

Halfway points occur halfway between the asymptotes and where the graph crosses its midline, or at

$x = \frac{\boxed{\pi} + 2\pi}{2} = \frac{\boxed{3\pi}}{2}$ and $x = \frac{2\pi + \boxed{3\pi}}{2} = \frac{\boxed{5\pi}}{2}$.

The halfway points of $y = \tan x$ have y-values of -1 and 1. Because $a = \boxed{-2}$ in $f(x) = -2\tan\frac{1}{2}(x - 2\pi) + 2$, the halfway points are reflected across the midline and stretched vertically from it by a factor of $\boxed{2}$. The halfway points are

$\left(\frac{3\pi}{2}, a\left(\boxed{-1}\right) + k\right) = \left(\frac{3\pi}{2}, -2\left(\boxed{-1}\right) + 2\right) = \left(\frac{3\pi}{2}, \boxed{4}\right)$ and

$\left(\frac{5\pi}{2}, a\left(\boxed{1}\right) + k\right) = \left(\frac{5\pi}{2}, -2\left(\boxed{1}\right) + 2\right) = \left(\frac{5\pi}{2}, \boxed{0}\right)$.

Plot the key points found and sketch the graph.

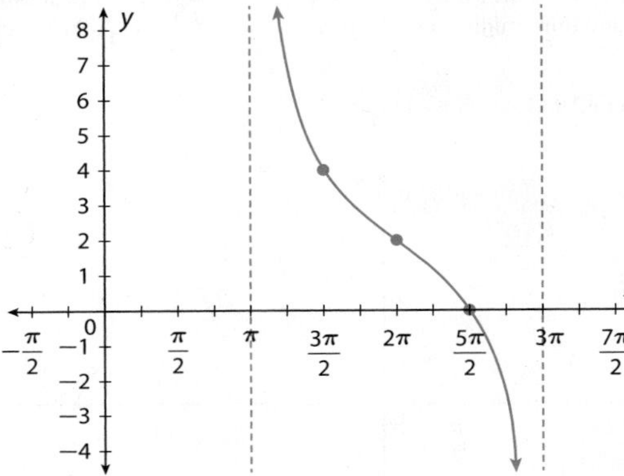

LANGUAGE SUPPORT EL

Communicate Math

Have students work in pairs. The first student explains how, for the graphs of $f(x) = a \sin\frac{1}{b}(x - h) + k$, $f(x) = a \cos\frac{1}{b}(x - h) + k$, and $f(x) = a \cos\frac{1}{b}(x - h) + k$, changing the value of h affects the graph. The second student explains how changing the value of k changes the graphs. Then have them take turns describing the effects of a and b. Listen carefully to the words students use to describe translations, reflections, and stretches.

Your Turn

3. For $f(x) = 2\cos 2\left(x - \frac{\pi}{2}\right) + 1$, identify the period, the midline, where the graph crosses the midline, the amplitude, and the maximum and minimum values and where they occur. Then graph one cycle of the function.

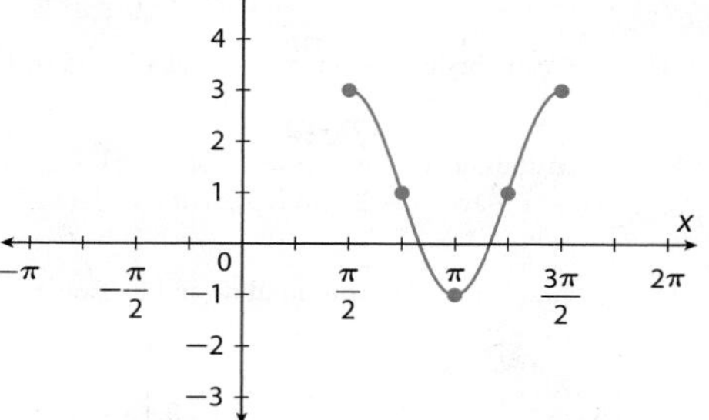

Period: $\frac{1}{b} = 2$, so $b = \frac{1}{2}$; period $= 2\pi \cdot \frac{1}{2} = \pi$

Midline: $y = k$, or $y = 1$

Amplitude: $a = 2$

The point $(0, 1)$ on the graph of $y = \cos x$ is a local maximum, and lies 1 unit above the midline. The corresponding point for $f(x) = 2\cos 2\left(x - \frac{\pi}{2}\right) + 1$ will lie $a(1) = 2(1) = 2$ units above the midline, or at $y = 1 + 2 = 3$. There is also a translation $h = \frac{\pi}{2}$ units to the right. So, $\left(\frac{\pi}{2}, 3\right)$ is on the graph. The next local maximum is one cycle to the right, or at $\left(\frac{\pi}{2} + \pi, 3\right) = \left(\frac{3\pi}{2}, 3\right)$.

Minimum: $a = 2$ units below the midline, or $k - a = 1 - 2 = -1$; occurs one half cycle after the first maximum, or at $x = \frac{\pi}{2} + \frac{\pi}{2} = \pi$. So, $(\pi, -1)$ is on the graph.

The graph crosses its midline halfway between the first maximum and the minimum, and halfway between the minimum and the second maximum, or at $x = \frac{\frac{\pi}{2} + \pi}{2} = \frac{3\pi}{4}$ and $x = \frac{\pi + \frac{3\pi}{2}}{2} = \frac{5\pi}{4}$. So, $\left(\frac{3\pi}{4}, 1\right)$ and $\left(\frac{5\pi}{4}, 1\right)$ are on the graph.

Explain 2 Writing General Trigonometric Functions

Because the equations of $f(x) = a\sin\frac{1}{b}(x - h) + k$, $f(x) = a\cos\frac{1}{b}(x - h) + k$, or $f(x) = a\tan\frac{1}{b}(x - h) + k$ directly reflect the physical features of their graphs, it is straightforward to write an equation given a graph of one of these functions.

Example 2 Write an equation as indicated for the given graph.

(A) a cosine function

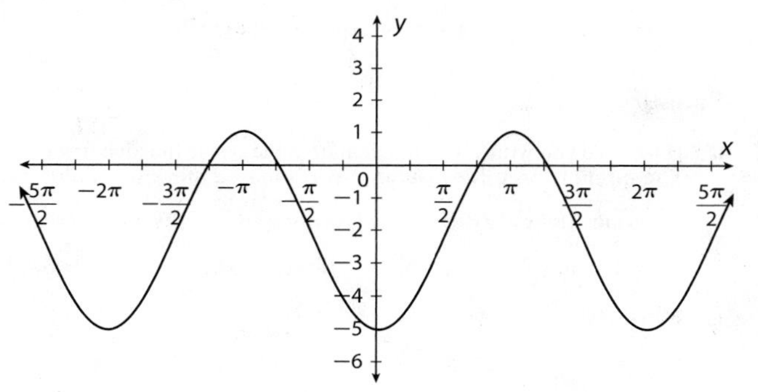

EXPLAIN 2

Writing General Trigonometric Functions

QUESTIONING STRATEGIES

? When writing a function rule for a given graph, why is it important to know whether the graph represents a sine function or a cosine function? **The graphs of the sine and cosine functions are the same shape and one is a horizontal translation of the other, so any given graph of this type can be defined by either function.**

? When writing a function rule for the graph of a tangent function, how can you determine the values of h and k? **Find a point where the graph intersects the translated midline. The x-coordinate of the point is h, and the y-coordinate is k.**

INTEGRATE MATHEMATICAL PRACTICES

Focus on Technology

MP.5 Discuss with students that, due to the periodic nature of the trigonometric functions, infinitely many functions are represented by the same graph. Lead them to see that if a multiple of the period of a function is added to the phase shift, the graph of the new function will be identical to the graph of the original function. For example, since the period of the function

$f(x) = -2\tan\left[\frac{1}{2}\left(x - \frac{\pi}{2}\right)\right] + 1$ is 2π,

adding 2π to the phase shift produces the function $g(x) = -2\tan\left[\frac{1}{2}\left(x - \frac{5\pi}{2}\right)\right] + 1$. Students can use the graphing and table features of a graphing calculator to observe that the graphs of $f(x)$ and $g(x)$ are the same, and to explore other functions that produce identical graphs.

Amplitude: $a = \frac{1-(-5)}{2} = 3$

Midline: $y = -2$, so $k = -2$.

Period: 2π; so, $2\pi \cdot b = 2\pi$, and $b = 1$.

You can obtain a local maximum at $x = -\pi$ by translating the graph of $y = \cos x$ to the left by π units. So, $h = -\pi$.

A cosine equation is $f(x) = 3\cos(x + \pi) - 2$. Notice that the equations $f(x) = 3\cos(x - \pi) - 2$ and $f(x) = -3\cos x - 2$ also represent the graph.

(B) a tangent function with midline and halfway points shown

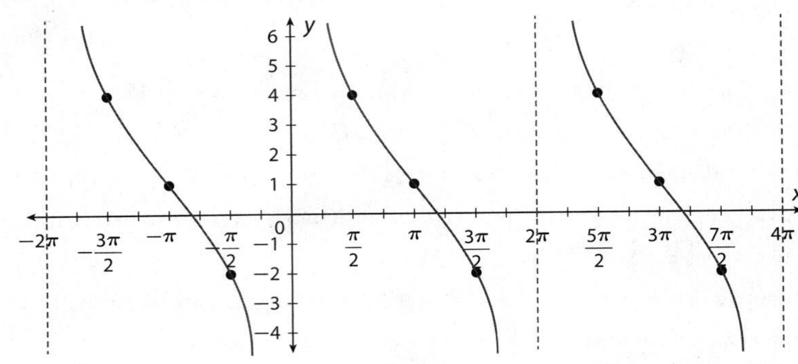

Midline: $y =$ 1, so $k =$ 1.

Period: 2π; so, $\pi \cdot b =$ 2π, and $b =$ 2.

The halfway points lie 3 units above and below the midline, so the graph is vertically (stretched)/shrunk by a factor of 3. Because the graph is falling from left to right for each cycle, the sign of a is (negative)/positive. So, $a =$ −3.

A cycle of the graph crosses the midline at $x = \pi$ instead of at $x = 0$ as for the graph of $y = \tan x$, so you can describe the graph by a translation to the right by π units. So, $h =$ π.

A tangent equation is $f(x) = -3\tan\frac{1}{2}\left(x - \pi\right) + 1$. Notice that the equation $f(x) = -3\tan\frac{1}{2}(x + \pi) + 1$ also represents the graph.

Reflect

4. How could you write a sine function from the cosine function first described by Example 2A?
The midline, amplitude, and maximum and minimum values are the same as with the cosine function. The only difference is a horizontal shift. Because the graph first crosses its midline for $x > 0$ at $x = \frac{\pi}{2}$, it can be described by a sine function where $h = \frac{\pi}{2}$, $k = -2$, $a = 3$, and $b = 1$, or $f(x) = 3\sin\left(x - \frac{\pi}{2}\right) - 2$.

5. What is true in general about the graph of a tangent function of the form $f(x) = a\tan\frac{1}{b}(x - h) + k$ when $a > 0$? when $a < 0$?

When $a > 0$, the graph is always increasing on each cycle. When $a < 0$, the graph is always decreasing on each cycle.

Your Turn

6. Write a sine function for the graph.

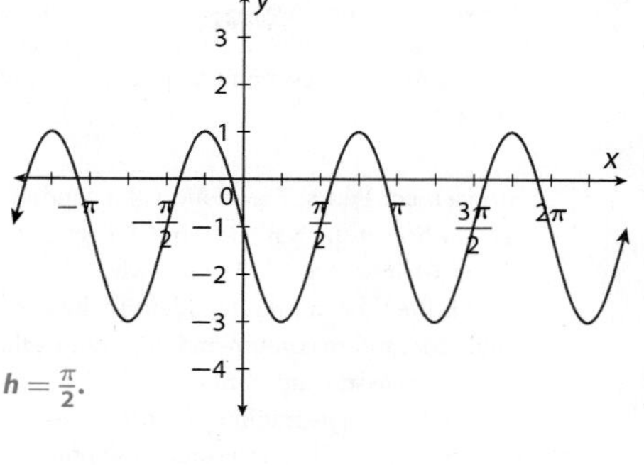

Amplitude: $a = \frac{1 - (-3)}{2} = 2$

Midline: $y = -1$, so $k = -1$.

Period: π; so, $2\pi \cdot b = \pi$, $b = \frac{1}{2}$, and $\frac{1}{b} = 2$.

Because the graph first crosses its midline while rising for $x > 0$ at $x = \frac{\pi}{2}$, it can be represented by a horizontal translation $\frac{\pi}{2}$ units to the right, so $h = \frac{\pi}{2}$.

A sine equation is $f(x) = 2\sin2\left(x - \frac{\pi}{2}\right) - 1$.

(Note that $f(x) = 2\sin2\left(x + \frac{\pi}{2}\right) - 1$ also represents the graph.)

Explain 3 Modeling with General Trigonometric Functions

Many real-world phenomena, such as circular motion and wave motion, involve repeating patterns that are described by trigonometric functions.

Example 3 **Interpret values of trigonometric models.**

(A) **Paddle Wheels** The motion of a point on the outer edge of a riverboat's paddle wheel blade is modeled by $h(t) = 8\sin\frac{\pi}{2}(t - 1) + 6$ where h is the height in feet measured from the water line and t is the time in seconds. Identify the period, midline, amplitude, and maximum and minimum values of the graph. For one cycle starting from $t = 0$, find all points where the graph intersects its midline and the coordinates of any local maxima and minima. Interpret these points in the context of the problem, and graph one cycle.

Period: $\frac{1}{b} = \frac{\pi}{2}$, so $b = \frac{2}{\pi}$, and $2\pi \cdot b = 4$; Midline: $k = 6$, so the midline is $h(t) = 6$.

Amplitude: $a = 8$; Maximum: $k + a = 6 + 8 = 14$; Minimum: $k - a = 6 - 8 = -2$

When $t = 0$, $h(t) = 8\sin\frac{\pi}{2}(0 - 1) + 6 = 8\sin\left(-\frac{\pi}{2}\right) + 6 = 8(-1) + 6 = -2$. So, $(0, -2)$ is on the graph. This is a minimum. There is a second minimum at the end of the cycle at $(0 + 4, -2) = (4, -2)$.

A maximum lies halfway between the x-values of the minima at $x = \frac{0 + 4}{2} = 2$. So, $(2, 14)$ is on the graph.

EXPLAIN 3

Modeling with General Trigonometric Functions

INTEGRATE MATHEMATICAL PRACTICES

Focus on Critical Thinking

MP.3 Ask students to consider the context of the problem, and describe a change to the given situation that would alter one of the parameters in the function. Have them tell what this change would be and how it would affect the graph of the function.

The graph crosses its midline halfway between each local maximum or minimum, or at $x = \frac{0+2}{2} = 1$ and $x = \frac{2+4}{2} = 3$. So, $(1, 6)$ and $(3, 6)$ are on the graph.

The point $(0, -2)$ means that the outer edge of the blade is 2 feet below the water's surface at time $t = 0$. One second later, it is at $(1, 6)$, or 6 feet above the water's surface—the height of the wheel's center. At $(2, 14)$, it reaches its maximum height of 14 feet, is back to the height of the center at $(3, 6)$, and at $(4, -2)$ returns to the lowest point 2 feet below the water at the end of one 4-second cycle.

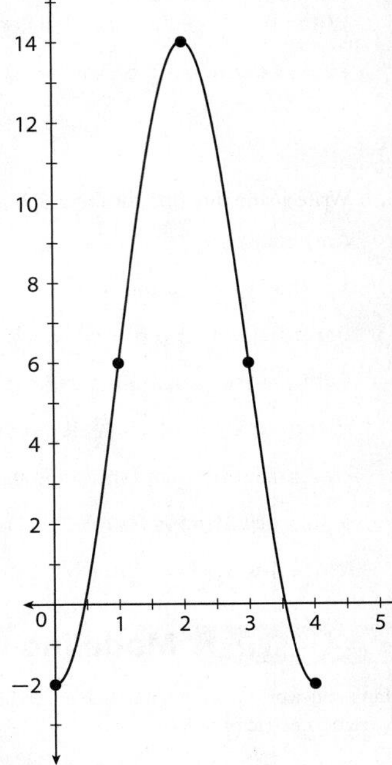

Ⓑ **Amusement Parks** The motion of a gondola car on the Ferris wheel at the Navy Pier in Chicago can be modeled by $h(t) = 70\sin\frac{2\pi}{7}(t - 1.75) + 80$, where h is the height in feet and t is the time in minutes. Identify the period, midline, amplitude, and maximum and minimum values of the graph. For one cycle starting from $t = 0$, find all points where the graph intersects its midline and the coordinates of any local maxima and minima. Interpret these points in the context of the problem, and graph one cycle.

Period: $\frac{1}{b} = \boxed{\frac{2\pi}{7}}$, so $b = \boxed{\frac{7}{2\pi}}$, and $2\pi \cdot b = \boxed{7}$;

Midline: $k = \boxed{80}$, so the midline is $h(t) = \boxed{80}$.

Amplitude: $a = \boxed{70}$; Maximum: $k + a = \boxed{80} + \boxed{70} = \boxed{150}$;

Minimum: $k - a = \boxed{80} - \boxed{70} = \boxed{10}$

When $t = 0$, $h(t) = 70\sin\frac{2\pi}{7}\left(\boxed{0} - 1.75\right) + 80 = 70\sin\left(-\frac{\pi}{\boxed{2}}\right) + 80$

$= 70\left(\boxed{-1}\right) + 80 = \boxed{10}$. So, $\left(0, \boxed{10}\right)$ is on the graph. This is a minimum.

There is a second minimum at the end of the cycle at $\left(0 + \boxed{7}, 10\right)$

$= \left(\boxed{7}, 10.\right)$ A maximum lies halfway between the x-values of the minima

at $x = \frac{0 + \boxed{7}}{2} = \boxed{3.5}$. So, $\left(\boxed{3.5}, \boxed{150}\right)$ is on the graph.

The graph crosses its midline halfway between each local maximum or

minimum, or at $x = \frac{0 + 3.5}{2} = 1.75$ and $x = \frac{3.5 + \boxed{7}}{2} = \boxed{5.25}$.

So, $\left(1.75, \boxed{80}\right)$ and $\left(\boxed{5.25}, \boxed{80}\right)$ are on the graph.

The point $(0, 10)$ means that the gondola is 10 feet above the ground at time $t = 0$. After 1.75 minutes, it is at $(1.75, 80)$, or 80 feet above the ground—the height of the wheel's center. At $(1.75, 150)$ it reaches its maximum height of 150 feet, is back to the height of the center at $(5.25, 80)$, and at $(7, 10)$ returns to the lowest point 10 feet above the ground at the end of one 7-minute cycle.

Your Turn

7. Amusement Parks The height h in feet of a car on a different Ferris wheel can be modeled by $h(t) = -16\cos\frac{\pi}{45}t + 24$, where t is the time in seconds. Identify the period, midline, amplitude, and maximum and minimum values of the graph. For one cycle starting from $t = 0$, find all points where the graph intersects its midline and the coordinates of any local maxima and minima. Interpret these points in the context of the problem, and graph one cycle.

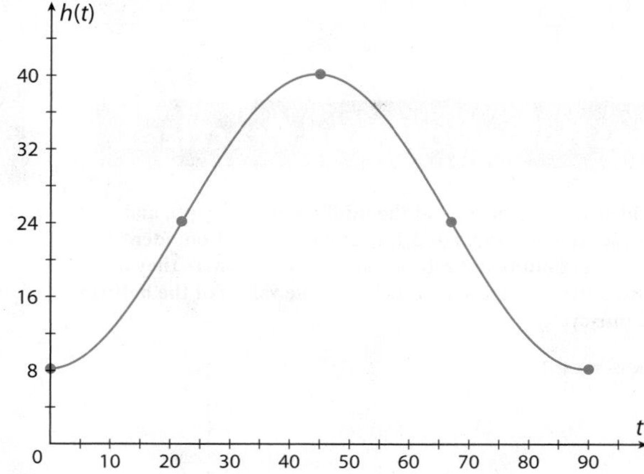

Period: $\frac{1}{b} = \frac{\pi}{45}$, so $b = \frac{45}{\pi}$, and $2\pi \cdot b = 90$; Midline: $k = 24$, so the midline is $h(t) = 24$.

Amplitude: $|a| = 16$; Maximum: $24 + 16 = 40$; Minimum: $24 - 16 = 8$

$h(0) = -16\cos 0 + 24 = 8 \Rightarrow (0, 8)$ is on the graph. This is a minimum.

Second minimum: $(0 + 90, 8) = (90, 8)$

Maximum: $\left(\frac{0+90}{2}, 40\right) = (45, 40)$

Midline crossings: $\left(\frac{0+45}{2}, 24\right) = (22.5, 24)$ and $\left(\frac{45+90}{2}, 24\right) = (67.5, 24)$

$(0, 8)$ means the car is 8 feet above the ground at time $t = 0$; $(22.5, 24)$ means it is at the wheel's center height of 24 feet after 22.5 seconds; at $(45, 40)$ it is at its maximum height of 40 feet; at $(67.5, 24)$ it is back at the wheel's center height; $(90, 8)$ means it is again at the minimum height of 8 feet after a 90-second cycle.

ELABORATE

INTEGRATE MATHEMATICAL PRACTICES

Focus on Critical Thinking

MP.3 Ask students to determine a general rule that can be used to rewrite a cosine function as an equivalent sine function. Have them refer to several graphs to test their rules. You may also want to challenge students to determine a general rule that can be used to rewrite a cotangent function as an equivalent tangent function.

SUMMARIZE THE LESSON

? How are the graphs of $f(x) = a \sin \frac{1}{b}x$ and $g(x) = a \sin \frac{1}{b}(x - h) + k$ alike and how are they different? **They both have the same amplitude and period, but the graph of $g(x)$ is the graph of $f(x)$ translated h units horizontally and k units vertically. The midline of $f(x)$ is the x-axis, whereas the midline of $g(x)$ is the line $y = k$.**

Elaborate

8. How can being given the first local maximum and local minimum of a cosine function $(a > 0)$ help you write its equation?
The horizontal distance from the maximum to the minimum is half of a cycle, so twice the distance is the period. Use the period to find b. The value of a is half the difference between the maximum and minimum values, and k is their average. For a cosine function, a cycle begins at a local maximum. If a maximum is on the y-axis, there is no horizontal shift. If it is translated right or left from there, the distance gives you h.

9. **Essential Question Check-In** How do positive values of h affect the graph of a function in the form $f(x) = a \sin \frac{1}{b}(x - h) + k$? How do negative values of k affect the graph of this function?
Positive values of h will translate the graph to the right h units, while negative values of k will translate the graph down k units.

Evaluate: Homework and Practice

• Online Homework
• Hints and Help
• Extra Practice

For each function, identify the period and the midline of the graph, and where the graph crosses the midline. For a sine or cosine function, identify the amplitude and the maximum and minimum values and where they occur. For a tangent function, identify the asymptotes and the values of the halfway points. Then graph one cycle.

1. $f(x) = -3 \sin(x + \pi) + 1$

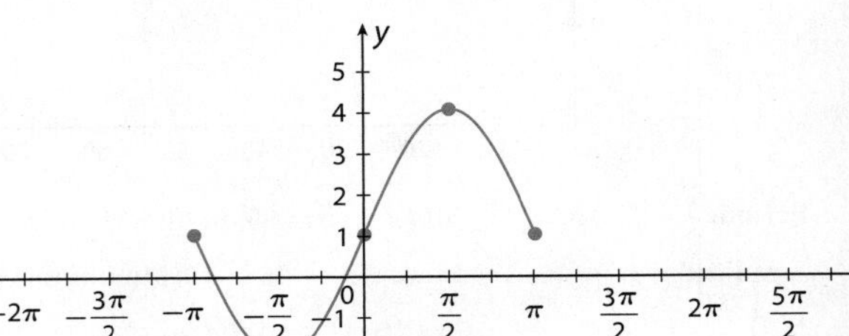

Period: $2\pi \cdot 1 = 2\pi$;
Midline: $y = k$, or $y = 1$;
Amplitude: $|a| = 3$
$h = -\pi, k = 1 \Rightarrow$ image of $(0, 0)$ from $y = \sin x$ is $(-\pi, 1)$; other midline crossings are at cycle halfway point, $(-\pi + \pi, 1) = (0, 1)$ and cycle endpoint, $(-\pi + 2\pi, 1) = (\pi, 1)$. Plot $(-\pi, 1)$, $(0, 1)$, and $(\pi, 1)$. $a < 0$, so the graph is reflected in its midline, and the minimum occurs before the maximum.
Minimum: $k - |a| = 1 - 3 = -2$; occurs at $x = \frac{-\pi + 0}{2} = -\frac{\pi}{2}$. Maximum: $k + |a| = 1 + 3 = 4$; occurs at $x = \frac{0 + \pi}{2} = \frac{\pi}{2}$. Plot $\left(-\frac{\pi}{2}, -2\right)$ and $\left(\frac{\pi}{2}, 4\right)$.

2. $f(x) = 2\cos 3x + 1$

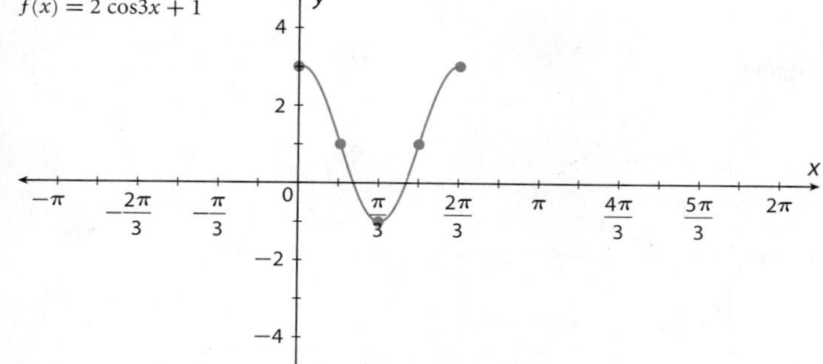

Period: $\frac{1}{b} = 3$, so $b = \frac{1}{3} \Rightarrow 2\pi \cdot b = \frac{2\pi}{3}$; Midline: $y = k$, or $y = 1$; Amplitude: $a = 2$
no horizontal shift
Maximum: $k + a = 1 + 2 = 3$; occurs at beginning and end of cycle at $(0, 3)$ and $\left(\frac{2\pi}{3}, 3\right)$.
Minimum: $k - a = 1 - 2 = -1$; occurs halfway through cycle at $\left(\frac{\pi}{3}, -1\right)$.
Midline crossings: halfway between first maximum and first minimum at $\left(\frac{\pi}{6}, 1\right)$ and halfway between minimum and second maximum at $\left(\frac{\pi}{2}, 1\right)$

3. $f(x) = \tan\frac{1}{2}(x - \pi) + 3$

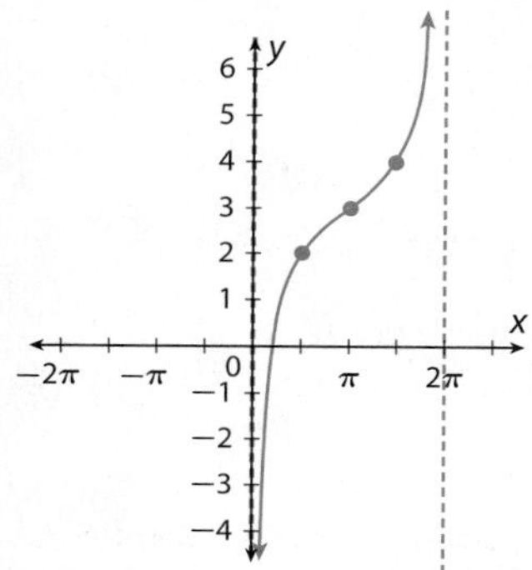

Period: $b = 2 \Rightarrow \pi \cdot b = 2\pi$; Midline: $y = k$, or $y = 3$; $h = \pi \Rightarrow$ midline crossing is translated π units to the right to $(\pi, 3)$; asymptotes are half a cycle to the left and right at $x = \pi - \pi = 0$ and $x = \pi + \pi = 2\pi$.
Halfway points are halfway between the asymptotes and midline crossing, or at $x = \frac{\pi}{2}$ and $x = \frac{3\pi}{2}$. The points are $\left(\frac{\pi}{2}, 3\right)$ and $\left(\frac{3\pi}{2}, 3\right)$.

Exercise	Depth of Knowledge (D.O.K.)	COMMON CORE Mathematical Practices
1–5	**1** Recall of Information	**MP.7** Using Structure
6–7	**2** Skills/Concepts	**MP.7** Using Structure
8–9	**2** Skills/Concepts	**MP.4** Modeling
10	**2** Skills/Concepts	**MP.2** Reasoning
11	**1** Recall of Information	**MP.6** Precision
12–14	**2** Skills/Concepts H.O.T.	**MP.3** Logic

EVALUATE

ASSIGNMENT GUIDE

Concepts and Skills	Practice
Explore Translating the Graph of a Trigonometric Function	Exercise 10
Example 1 Graphing General Trigonometric Functions	Exercises 1–5
Example 2 Writing General Trigonometric Functions	Exercises 6–7
Example 3 Modeling with General Trigonometric Functions	Exercises 8–9

QUESTIONING STRATEGIES

How do you use a, b, h, and k to find the key points of the graph of $f(x) = a \sin\frac{1}{b}(x - h) + k$? **First, use k to find the midline. Plot (h, k). Then use b to determine the period, and plot a point that distance from (h, k) on the midline. Plot the point halfway between the two points. Then use a to determine the amplitude and to plot the crest and the trough.**

AVOID COMMON ERRORS

Some students may apply a phase shift to the graph of a tangent function incorrectly, shifting the asymptotes on either side of the y-axis in opposite directions, as they do when they make a change to the period. Correct this thinking by showing students that this, in turn, changes the period of the function. Reinforce that a phase shift moves the entire graph (asymptotes included) either to the right or to the left.

VISUAL CUES

When they are writing a function rule for a tangent graph, encourage students to circle the point that is the image of the point (0, 0) under the transformation. This may help them remember that the coordinates of this point are h and k, and can help them identify the other key points or features and the parameters needed to write the function rule.

4. $f(x) = 3\sin\frac{\pi}{2}(x - 2) + 3$

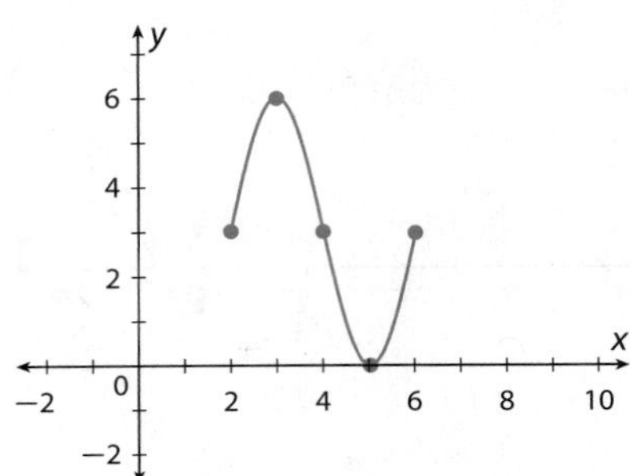

Period: $\frac{1}{b} = \frac{\pi}{2}$, so $b = \frac{2}{\pi} \Rightarrow 2\pi \cdot b = 4$; Midline: $y = k$, or $y = 3$; Amplitude: $a = 3$

$h = 2 \Rightarrow$first midline crossing is translated 2 units to the right to $(2, 3)$; other midline crossings are at cycle halfway point, $(2 + 2, 3) = (4, 3)$, and cycle endpoint, $(2 + 4, 3) = (6, 3$

Maximum: $k + a = 3 + 3 = 6$; occurs when $x = \frac{2+4}{2} = 3$ at $(3, 6)$.

Minimum: $k - a = 2 - 2 = 0$; occurs when $x = \frac{4+6}{2} = 5$ at $(5, 6)$.

Write an equation as indicated for the given graph.

5. a sine function

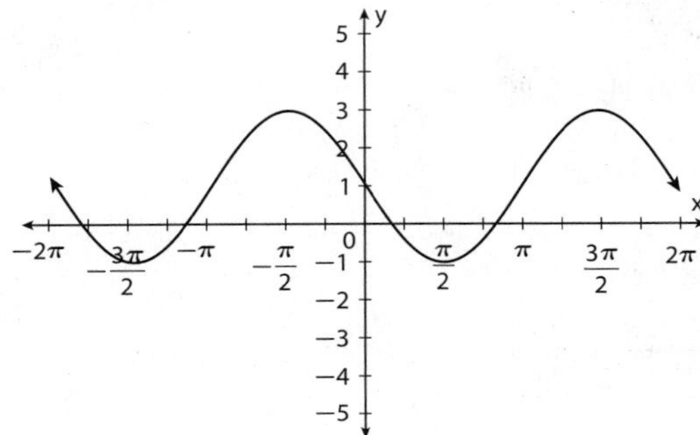

Amplitude: $a = \frac{3-(-1)}{2} = 2$; Midline: $y = 1$, so $k = 1$; Period: 2π; so, $2\pi \cdot b = 2\pi \Rightarrow b = 1$. Graph first crosses midline while rising for $x > 0$ at $x = \pi \Rightarrow$ horizontal translation π units right, so $h = \pi$. An equation is $f(x) = 2\sin(x - \pi) + 1$. (Note that $f(x) = 2\sin(x + \pi) + 1$ also represents the graph.)

6. a cosine function

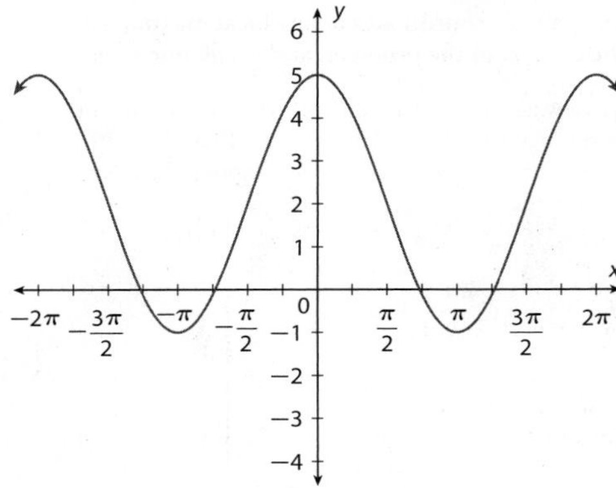

Amplitude: $a = \frac{5-(-1)}{2} = 3$; Midline: $y = 2$, so $k = 2$; Period: 2π, so $b = 1$.

There is no horizontal shift. A cosine equation is $f(x) = 3\cos x + 2$.

7. a tangent function

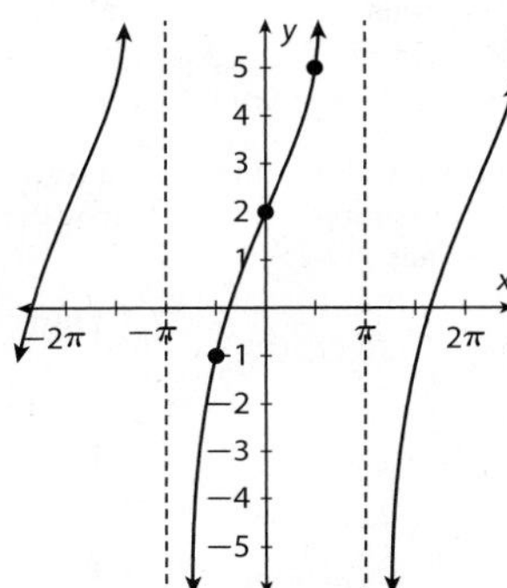

Midline: $y = 2$, so $k = 2$; Period: 2π; so, $\pi \cdot b = 2\pi$, and $b = 2$.

The halfway points lie 3 units above and below the midline, so $a = 3$.

There is no horizontal shift.

An equation is $f(x) = 3\tan\frac{1}{2}x + 2$.

INTEGRATE MATHEMATICAL PRACTICES

Focus on Communication

MP.3 Call upon students to explain how they determined the function rule for a given graph. Their explanations may be helpful for students who are struggling with this skill. Students have different ways of describing and interpreting what they see, and having them verbalize their thought processes may provide other students with an alternate, and perhaps more successful, approach to the solution process.

INTEGRATE TECHNOLOGY

Students can use a graphing calculator to check that the functions they write produce the same graph as the given graph.

For the context described, identify the period, midline, amplitude, and maximum and minimum values of the graph. For one cycle starting from $t = 0$, find all points where the graph intersects its midline and the coordinates of any local maxima and minima. Interpret these points in the context of the problem, and graph one cycle.

8. **Historic Technology** Water turns a water wheel at an old mill. The water comes in at the top of the wheel through a wooden chute. The function $h(t) = 15\cos\frac{\pi}{5}t + 20$ models the height h in feet above the stream into which the water empties of a point on the wheel where t is the time in seconds.

Period: $\frac{1}{b} = \frac{\pi}{5}$, so $b = \frac{5}{\pi}$, and $2\pi \cdot b = 10$;
Midline: $k = 20$, so the midline is $h(t) = 20$.
Amplitude: $a = 15$; **Maximum:** $20 + 15 = 35$;
Minimum: $20 - 15 = 5$

$h(0) = 15\cos 0 + 20 = 35 \Rightarrow (0, 35)$ is on the graph. This is a maximum. The next maximum is one cycle later at $(10, 35)$. A minimum occurs halfway through the cycle at $(5, 5)$.

Midline crossings: halfway between first maximum and minimum at $(2.5, 20)$ and halfway between minimum and second maximum at $(7.5, 20)$.

$(0, 35)$ means the point is at the top of the wheel 35 feet above the stream at time $t = 0$; $(2.5, 20)$ means it is at the wheel's center height of 20 feet after 2.5 seconds; at $(5, 5)$ it is at its minimum height of 5 feet, then back to the center height at $(7.5, 20)$, and finally back to the top of the wheel after 10 seconds.

9. **Games** A toy is suspended 36 inches above the floor on a spring. A child reaches up, pulls the toy, and releases it. The function $h(t) = 10\sin\pi(x - 0.5) + 36$ models the toy's height h in inches above the floor after t seconds.

Period: $\frac{1}{b} = \pi$, so $b = \frac{1}{\pi}$, and $2\pi \cdot b = 2$;
Midline: $k = 36$, so the midline is $h(t) = 36$.
Amplitude: $a = 10$; **Maximum:** $36 + 10 = 46$;
Minimum: $36 - 10 = 26$

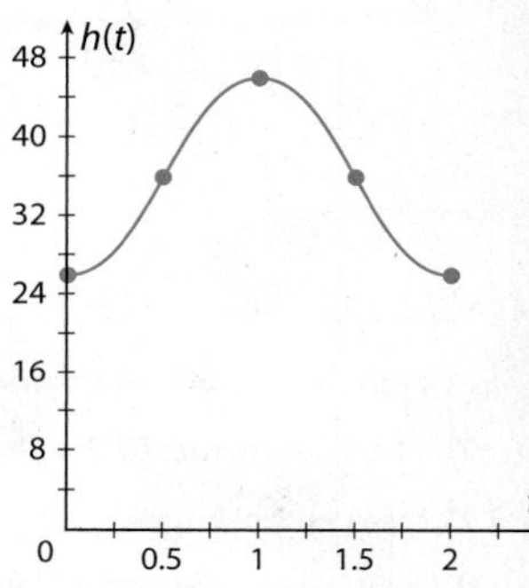

$h(0) = 10\sin\left(-\frac{\pi}{2}\right) + 36 = 26 \Rightarrow (0, 26)$ is on the graph. This is a minimum. The next minimum is one cycle later at $(2, 26)$. A maximum occurs halfway through the cycle at $(1, 46)$. Midline crossings: halfway between first minimum and maximum at $(0.5, 36)$ and halfway between maximum and second minimum at $(1.5, 36)$.

$(0, 26)$ means the toy is at its lowest point 26 inches above the floor $t = 0$; $(0.5, 36)$ means it is at its midline (resting) height of 36 inches after 0.5 second; at $(1, 46)$ it is at its maximum height of 46 inches, then back to the midline height at $(1.5, 36)$, and finally back to the minimum height after 2 seconds.

10. Match each sine function with the cosine function that has the same graph.

A. $y = \sin 2x$	1. $y = \cos\left(x + \frac{\pi}{2}\right) + 1$	A. 3
B. $y = \frac{1}{2}\sin 3x$	2. $y = \frac{1}{2}\cos 4\left(x - \frac{4+\pi}{2}\right)$	B. 5
C. $y = \frac{1}{2}\sin 4(x - 2)$	3. $y = \cos 2\left(x - \frac{\pi}{2}\right)$	C. 2
D. $y = \sin(x - \pi) + 1$	4. $y = \cos(x) + 4$	D. 1
E. $y = \sin\left(x + \frac{\pi}{2}\right) + 4$	5. $y = \frac{1}{2}\cos 3\left(x - \frac{\pi}{2}\right)$	E. 4

11. How do h and k affect the key points of the graphs of sine, cosine, and tangent functions?

The key points are translated h units right for positive h, h units left for negative h, k units up for positive k, and k units down for negative k.

H.O.T. Focus on Higher Order Thinking

12. **Explain the Error** Sage was told to write the equation of a sine function with a period of 2π, an amplitude of 5, a horizontal translation of 3 units right, and a vertical translation of 6 units up. She wrote the equation $f(x) = 5\sin 2\pi(x - 3) + 6$. Explain Sage's error and give the correct equation.

Sage wrote the period, 2π, for $\frac{1}{b}$. The period is $2\pi \cdot b$, so $b = 1$ and $\frac{1}{b} = 1$. The correct equation is $f(x) = 5\sin(x - 3) + 6$.

13. **Critical Thinking** Can any sine or cosine function graph be represented by a sine equation with a positive coefficient a? Explain your answer.

Yes, a sine curve with a negative coefficient a is the same as a curve with a positive coefficient a translated horizontally by half a cycle. For example, the graphs of $y = -\sin x$ and $y = \sin(x + \pi)$ are the same. Also, any cosine curve is the same as a sine curve translated by one fourth of a cycle, so a similar result holds for cosine graphs.

14. **Make a Prediction** What will the graph of the function $f(x) = \cos^2 x + \sin^2 x$ look like? Explain your answer and check it on a graphing calculator.

It will be the horizontal line $y = 1$, because this function represents the Pythagorean identity $\cos^2 x + \sin^2 x = 1$. This makes sense because $\cos^2 x + \sin^2 x$ represents the sum of the squares of the legs of a right triangle in the unit circle with hypotenuse 1, and $1^2 = 1$.

PEER-TO-PEER DISCUSSION

Ask students to work with a partner to write two sine functions, each with a different period, whose graphs have a relative maximum point (crest) at the origin. Have pairs share their functions with the class, and have the class analyze the set of functions to identify their commonalities. **Possible answer: $f(x) = \sin\left(x + \frac{\pi}{2}\right) - 1$ and**

$f(x) = \sin\left[2\left(x + \frac{\pi}{4}\right)\right] - 1$

JOURNAL

Have students describe how to graph the function $f(x) = 3\cos\left[2\left(x - \frac{\pi}{2}\right)\right] - 3$. Then have them compare the graph to that of the parent cosine function.

Lesson Performance Task

At a location off a pier on the Maine coastline, the function $d(t) = 4.36\cos(0.499t) + 8.79$ models the depth d in feet of the water t hours after the first high tide during a first quarter moon.

a. Identify the amplitude and period of the function as well as the equation of the midline. Describe the graph of this function as a series of transformations of the parent function $y = \cos x$.

b. Explain how you can use the cosine function from part A to write a sine function to model the depth of the water. Describe the graph of this function as a series of transformations of the parent function $y = \sin x$.

c. The heights of astronomical tides are affected by the moon phase. A function that models the depth of the water at the same location after the first low tide during a new moon is $d(t) = 6.31\sin[0.503(t - 3.13)] + 8.75$. Identify the amplitude and period of the function as well as the equation of the midline. Describe the graph of this function as a series of transformations of the parent function $y = \sin x$.

(Continued on next page)

a. amplitude: $a = 4.36$ feet; period: $\frac{1}{b} = 0.499$, so $b = \frac{1}{0.499}$, and $2\pi \cdot b = \frac{2\pi}{0.499} \approx 12.59$ hours; equation of midline: $k = 8.79$, so $d(t) = 8.79$; The graph of $d(t)$ is the graph of the parent cosine function stretched horizontally by a factor of 2, stretched vertically by a factor of 4.36, and translated 8.79 feet up.

b. Since a sine function is at the midline when $t = 0$, you can shift the sine function $\frac{1}{4}$ period to the left. One quarter of a period is $\frac{12.59}{4} \approx 3.15$. Therefore, the function $d(t) = 4.36\sin[0.499(t + 3.15)] + 8.79$ can also be used to model the depth of the water. The graph of $d(t)$ is the graph of the parent cosine function stretched horizontally by a factor of 2, translated 3.15 hours to the left, stretched vertically by a factor of 4.36, and translated 8.79 feet up.

c. amplitude: $a = 6.31$ feet; period: $\frac{1}{b} = 0.503$, so $b = \frac{1}{0.503}$, and $2\pi \cdot b = \frac{2\pi}{0.503} \approx 12.49$ hours; equation of midline: $k = 8.75$, so $d(t) = 8.75$; The graph of $d(t)$ is the graph of the parent sine function stretched horizontally by a factor of 1.99, translated 3.13 hours to the right, stretched vertically by a factor of 6.31, and translated 8.75 feet up.

d. Explain how you can use the sine function from part C on the previous page to write a cosine function to model the height of the water. Describe the graph of this function as a series of transformations of the parent function $y = \cos x$.

e. Compare the functions from parts A and B with the functions from parts C and D. How do the tides during a new moon compare to the tides during a first quarter moon?

d. Since a cosine function is at its maximum when $t = 0$, you can shift the cosine function $\frac{1}{4}$ period to the left or right, or approximately 3.125 hours. Therefore, the function $d(t) = 6.31\cos\left[0.503(t - 3.125)\right] + 8.75$ can also be used to model the depth of the water. The graph of $d(t)$ is the graph of the parent cosine function stretched horizontally by a factor of 2, translated horizontally 3.125 hours to the right, stretched vertically by a factor of 6.31, and translated 8.75 feet up.

e. The functions from parts C and D have greater amplitudes and slightly shorter periods than the functions from parts A and B. The equation of the midline is roughly similar for all functions. The tides during a new moon have greater variability than the tides during a first quarter moon. The high tides are higher and the low tides are lower during a new moon than during a first quarter moon, but the mean tides and the periods are about the same.

EXTENSION ACTIVITY

What causes tides, and why are there two high tides every day? Encourage students to research this phenomenon. They should find that the tides are caused by the gravitational attractions among the Earth, moon, and sun. The moon has a greater influence on the tides because of its proximity to Earth. High tides occur on the side of Earth nearest the moon because the moon pulls the water away from the surface. The moon also attracts Earth, so a high tide occurs on the opposite side of the planet as Earth is pulled in the opposite direction from the location of the water.

INTEGRATE MATHEMATICAL PRACTICES

Focus on Technology

MP.5 The graphing calculator may have a trigonometric graphing window available with the **ZOOM** key. Note that graphs in radian and degree mode will appear exactly the same in this window, but the trace functions will show x-values at multiples of 7.5 degrees in degree mode and in multiples of $\frac{\pi}{24}$ in radian mode on some calculators.

INTEGRATE MATHEMATICAL PRACTICES

Focus on Math Connections

MP.1 Note that the phases of the moon are *new moon*, when the angle that the moon appears to make with the Earth and sun is 0°, *first quarter moon* (90°), *full moon* (180°) and *last quarter moon* (90°, or 270° when using the *ecliptic* coordinate system).

Scoring Rubric

2 points: Student correctly solves the problem and explains his/her reasoning.

1 point: Student shows good understanding of the problem but does not fully solve or explain his/her reasoning.

0 points: Student does not demonstrate understanding of the problem.

LESSON 18.4

Fitting Sine Functions to Data

Common Core Math Standards

The student is expected to:

 **F-TF.B.5**

Choose trigonometric functions to model periodic phenomena with specified amplitude, frequency, and midline. Also N-Q.A.2, S-ID.B.6a, A-CED.A.2, F-IF.B.4, A-REI.D.11

Mathematical Practices

 **MP.4 Modeling**

Language Objective

Match sine functions to their graphs and to data sets.

ENGAGE

Essential Question: How can you model data using a sine function?

First, recognize that the data repeat in a wave-shaped pattern. Then, find a model of the form $y = a \sin \frac{1}{b}(x - h) + k$ by estimating the graph's midline to find k, estimating the period to find $\frac{1}{b}$ $\left(\text{because } 2\pi\left(\frac{1}{b}\right) \text{gives the period}\right)$; finding half the vertical distance between peaks and troughs to estimate a; and approximating where the graph intercepts the midline to estimate the horizontal shift h. You can also enter the data on a graphing calculator and use sine regression.

PREVIEW: LESSON PERFORMANCE TASK

View the Engage section online. Discuss the photo and how trigonometry might be related to the cyclical patterns in the incidence of flu. Then preview the Lesson Performance Task.

Name________________ Class__________ Date________

18.4 Fitting Sine Functions to Data

Essential Question: How can you model data using a sine function?

Resource Locker

Explore Roughly Fitting a Sine Function to Data

When the graph of a set of data has a wave-like pattern, you can model the data with a sine function of the form $y = a \sin \frac{1}{b}(x - h) + k$. While it is also possible to use a cosine function as a model, it's not necessary because the basic sine and cosine curves are identical apart from a horizontal translation due to the fact that $\cos x = \sin\left(x + \frac{\pi}{2}\right)$.

Consider Chicago's monthly average temperatures in degrees Fahrenheit.

Month	1	2	3	4	5	6	7	8	9	10	11	12
Average temperature (°F)	23.8	27.7	37.9	48.9	59.1	68.9	74.0	72.4	64.6	52.5	40.3	27.7

(A) Graph the data.

Students only plot points in this step.

They graph the curve in Step F.

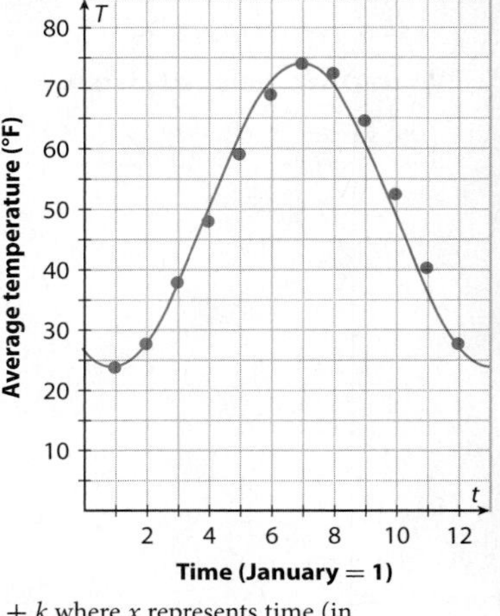

(B) You want to write a model of the form $y = a \sin \frac{1}{b}(x - h) + k$ where x represents time (in months, starting with 1 for January), y represents average monthly temperature (in degrees Fahrenheit), and a, b, h, and k are constants. Begin by finding the value of b.

You know that the parameter b produces a horizontal stretch or compression of the graph of $y = \sin x$ by a factor of b. You also know that the period of $y = \sin x$ is 2π, so the period of $y = a \sin \frac{1}{b}(x-h) + k$ is $2\pi b$. Use this information to find the value of b for the temperature data. Explain your reasoning. Then substitute the value of b into the model.

Because the period of the temperature data is 12 (months), $2\pi b = 12$, so $b = \frac{12}{2\pi} = \frac{6}{\pi}$, and $\frac{1}{b} = \frac{\pi}{6}$. The model becomes $y = a \sin \frac{\pi}{6}(x - h) + k$.

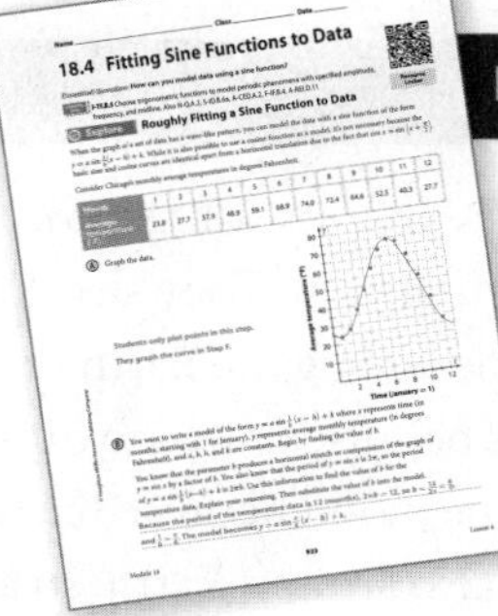

HARDCOVER PAGES 923–936

Watch for the hardcover student edition page numbers for this lesson.

Ⓒ You know that the parameter k produces a vertical translation of the graph of $y = \sin x$. You also know that the graph of $y = \sin x$ has $y = 0$ as its midline, so the graph of $y = a \sin \frac{1}{b}(x - h) + k$ has $y = k$ as its midline. The midline, which is a horizontal line, occurs halfway between the highest and lowest data points. Use this information to find the value of k for the temperature data. Explain your reasoning. Then substitute the value of k into the model.

Because the maximum temperature is 74.0° F and the minimum temperature is 23.8° F, the average of these temperatures is $\frac{74.0 + 23.8}{2} = 48.9$, so $k = 48.9$. The model becomes $y = a \sin \frac{\pi}{6}(x - h) + 48.9$.

Ⓓ You know that the parameter h produces a horizontal translation of the graph of $y = \sin x$. You also know that the graph of $y = \sin x$ crosses its midline at $x = 0$, so the graph of $y = a \sin \frac{1}{b}(x - h) + k$ crosses its midline at $x = h$. Use this information to find the value of h for the temperature data. Explain your reasoning. Then substitute the value of h into the model.

Because the model's midline is $y = 48.9$ and the first occurrence of a temperature close to (actually, equal to) 48.9° F occurs in month 4 (April), $h = 4$. The model becomes $y = a \sin \frac{\pi}{6}(x - 4) + 48.9$.

Ⓔ You know that the parameter a produces a vertical stretch or compression of the graph of $y = \sin x$ as well as a reflection across the midline when a is negative. You also know that the graph of $y = \sin x$ has an amplitude of 1, so the graph of $y = a \sin \frac{1}{b}(x - h) + k$ has an amplitude of $|a|$. The amplitude is half the vertical distance between the highest and lowest data points. Use this information to find the value of a for the temperature data. Explain your reasoning. Then substitute the value of a into the model.

Because the highest data point has a y-coordinate of 74.0 and the lowest data point has a y-coordinate of 23.8, half the difference between these y-coordinates is $\frac{74.0 - 23.8}{2} = 25.1$, so $|a| = 25.1$. Because the temperatures are increasing near $x = 4$, there is no reflection across the midline, so $a = 25.1$. The model becomes $y = 25.1 \sin \frac{\pi}{6}(x - 4) + 48.9$.

Ⓕ Graph the model using the coordinate grid from Step A. **See the graph in Step A.**

Reflect

1. If the temperature data had been given in degrees Celsius rather than degrees Fahrenheit, how would the model change?

The values of the parameters a and k would change to their Celsius equivalents. Everything else in the model would stay the same.

PROFESSIONAL DEVELOPMENT

Learning Progressions

Students have learned how to fit other types of functions to data using both approximation techniques and regression. In this lesson, students expand their knowledge of these techniques to data that can be modeled by the sine function. (Note that data that can be modeled by the sine function can also be modeled by a cosine function.) Students use what they learned in the previous lessons to identify the characteristics of the graph that help them approximate the parameters of the function. They then perform sinusoidal regression on the same set of data, and compare the resulting model to the model they obtained from the visual inspection of the data display.

EXPLORE

Roughly Fitting a Sine Function to Data

INTEGRATE TECHNOLOGY

Students have the option of completing the Explore activity either in the book or online.

QUESTIONING STRATEGIES

? What information helps you to know the period of the function? **the fact that the pattern in the data will repeat every 12 months**

? What information helps you to calculate the amplitude of the function? **The maximum and minimum values—you can find half the difference between them.**

INTEGRATE MATHEMATICAL PRACTICES

Focus on Reasoning

MP.2 Ask students to consider situations in which an *approximation* of the sine function, as opposed to an *exact* model, would be sufficient.

EXPLAIN 1

Fitting a Sine Function to Data Using Technology

INTEGRATE MATHEMATICAL PRACTICES

Focus on Modeling

MP.4 Remind students that, in mathematics, a *regression equation* is *a function that closely models a set of data.* A calculator produces a regression equation by minimizing the overall vertical distances between the data points and the function's graph.

2. If you let t represent time and T represent temperature, what does the model become?
The model becomes $T = 25.1 \sin \frac{\pi}{6}(t-4) + 48.9$.

3. If you define January as month 0 instead of month 1, how does the graph of the data change, and what does the model become?
The graph of the data shifts 1 unit to the left. The model becomes $T = 25.1 \sin \frac{\pi}{6}(t-3) + 48.9$.

Explain 1 Fitting a Sine Function to Data Using Technology

You can obtain a sine model for a set of data by performing sine regression using a graphing calculator in the same way as you would perform linear regression, exponential regression, and so on.

(A) The table gives Chicago's monthly average temperatures as in the Explore. Use a graphing calculator to obtain a sine regression model for the data. Graph the regression model along with the model from the Explore, and compare the models visually.

Month	1	2	3	4	5	6	7	8	9	10	11	12
Average temperature (°F)	23.8	27.7	37.9	48.9	59.1	68.9	74.0	72.4	64.6	52.5	40.3	27.7

Step 1 Enter the data into lists L_1 and L_2. Then press the STAT key and select **C:SinReg** from the **CALC** menu.

So, the regression model is $y = 25.2 \sin(0.5x - 2) + 48.7$.

Step 2 Graph the data, the regression model, and the model $y = 25.1 \sin \frac{\pi}{6}(x-4) + 48.9$ from the Explore. Visually compare the models.

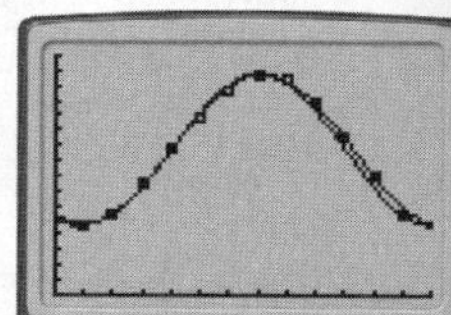

Both models appear to fit the data equally well from $x = 1$ to $x = 8$. For values of x greater than 8, the regression model fits the data better than the rough-fit model from the Explore does.

(B) The table gives the monthly mean minimum temperature, in degrees Celsius, for Canberra, Australia. Roughly fit a sine model of the form $y = a \sin \frac{1}{b}(x-h) + k$ to the data. Then obtain a sine regression model using a graphing calculator. Finally, visually compare the two models in relation to the data.

Month	1	2	3	4	5	6	7	8	9	10	11	12
Minimum temperature (°C)	13.2	13.1	10.7	6.7	3.2	1.0	−0.1	1.0	3.3	6.1	8.8	11.4

COLLABORATIVE LEARNING

Peer-to-Peer Activity

Have students work in pairs. Instruct pairs to research examples of current real-world data that can be modeled using a sine function. Students can use the contexts of the problems in the lesson to help guide them in their searches. Have each pair make a poster using one of the examples they find, showing how the data produces a sinusoidal graph, and explaining *why* the context produces data that approximate a sine function. Have pairs share their posters with the class.

Step 1 Roughly fit a sine model of the form $y = a \sin\frac{1}{b}(x - h) + k$.

- The period $2\pi b$ must equal 12, so $b = \boxed{\frac{6}{\pi}}$ and $\frac{1}{b} = \boxed{\frac{\pi}{6}}$.
- The horizontal midline is halfway between the highest and lowest data points, so $k = \frac{13.2 + (-0.1)}{2} = \boxed{6.55}$.
- The first occurrence of a temperature close to 6.55° C is in month 4, so $h = \boxed{4}$.
- The amplitude is half the vertical distance between the highest and lowest data points, so $|a| = \frac{13.2 - (-0.1)}{2} = \boxed{6.65}$. Because the temperatures are [increasing/decreasing] near $x = 4$, $a = \boxed{-6.65}$.

So, a sine model for the data is $y = \boxed{-6.65} \sin \boxed{\frac{\pi}{6}} \left(x - \boxed{4}\right) + \boxed{6.55}$.

Step 2 Enter the data into a graphing calculator and perform sine regression.

The sine regression model is $y = \boxed{6.65} \sin\left(\boxed{0.51}\,x + \boxed{1.07}\right) + \boxed{6.71}$.

Step 3 Visually compare the two models.

Both models appear to fit the data equally well from $x = 1$ to $x = 10$. For values of x greater than 10, the regression model fits the data [better/worse] than the rough-fit model.

Reflect

4. Rewrite the regression model in Part A so that it has the form $y = a \sin\frac{1}{b}(x - h) + k$. Then compare this form of the regression model with the rough-fit model from the Explore.

$y = 25.2 \sin(0.5x - 2) + 48.6 = 25.2 \sin\frac{1}{2}(x - 4) + 48.6$

The rough-fit model from the Explore is $y = 25.1 \sin\frac{\pi}{6}(x - 4) + 48.9$. Since $\frac{\pi}{6} \approx 0.52$, the two equations are almost identical, with only minor differences between the values of the parameters a, b, and k.

5. **Discussion** Rewrite the regression model in Part B so that it has the form $y = a \sin\frac{1}{b}(x - h) + k$. Then compare this form of the regression model with the rough-fit model in Part B. How can you reconcile any differences you observe?

$y = 6.65 \sin(0.51x + 1.07) + 6.71 \approx 6.65 \sin\frac{1}{1.96}(x + 2.10) + 6.71$

The rough-fit model from Part B is $y = -6.65 \sin\frac{\pi}{6}(x - 4) + 6.55$. The models differ significantly in terms of the sign of the parameter a and the value of the parameter h. However, the two values of h differ by about 6, which is half the period of the two models. When you shift a sine curve by half a period, the shifted curve is a reflection of the original curve across the midline. To compensate for the shift, you can use the opposite of the value of a. So, when you shift the graph of $y = 6.65 \sin\frac{1}{1.96}(x + 2.10) + 6.71$ to the right 6 units, you get the graph of $y = -6.65 \sin\frac{1}{1.96}(x - 3.90) + 6.71$, which is almost identical to the graph of $y = -6.65 \sin\frac{\pi}{6}(x - 4) + 6.55$ since $\frac{1}{1.96} \approx 0.51$ and $\frac{\pi}{6} \approx 0.52$.

QUESTIONING STRATEGIES

How does the regression model produced by the calculator compare to the model obtained in the Explore? **The regression model is more exact, but the two models are fairly close.**

How can you identify the midline of the graph from the regression equation? **The midline is represented in the regression equation by the value of d in $y = a \sin(bx + c) + d$.**

How can you identify the maximum value of the function from the regression equation? **You can add $|a|$ to d.**

AVOID COMMON ERRORS

Students may confuse the value of b displayed by the calculator with $\frac{1}{b}$ in the general form of a sine function, $y = a \sin\frac{1}{b}(x - h) + k$. Explain that the coefficient given by the calculator is actually the reciprocal of the parameter used in the general form of the function. Have students compare the coefficient from the regression equation to the coefficient determined in the Explore.

INTEGRATE TECHNOLOGY

Students can use both the graphing feature and the table feature of a graphing calculator to compare the two models generated for the data.

DIFFERENTIATE INSTRUCTION

Multiple Representations

Students may benefit from a review of why the point of intersection of the two graphs identifies the solution to the problem in Example 2. Remind students that the sine graph represents a function, and the coordinates represent pairs of input and output values. When solving the problem, we are looking for the input value (or values) that produces a particular output value. The horizontal line represents a constant function in which the constant is the particular output value. Therefore, every point at which it intersects the sine wave has, as its y-coordinate, the given output value and, as its x-coordinate, the input value that produces that output value.

EXPLAIN 2

Solving a Real-World Problem Using a Sine Model

QUESTIONING STRATEGIES

For what values of the constant would there be no solution? **values that are not within the range of the function**

What would be true about the graphs of the two functions if this were the case? **The two graphs would not intersect.**

Your Turn

6. The table gives the monthly mean maximum temperature, in degrees Celsius, for Canberra, Australia. Roughly fit a sine model of the form $y = a \sin \frac{1}{b}(x - h) + k$ to the data. Then obtain a sine regression model using a graphing calculator. Finally, visually compare the two models in relation to the data.

Month	1	2	3	4	5	6	7	8	9	10	11	12
Maximum temperature (°C)	28.0	27.1	24.5	20.0	15.6	12.3	11.4	13.0	16.2	19.4	22.7	26.1

Rough-fit model:

$2\pi b = 12$, so $b = \frac{6}{\pi}$ and $\frac{1}{b} = \frac{\pi}{6}$.

$k = \frac{28.0 + 11.4}{2} = 19.7$

The first occurrence of a temperature close to 19.7° C is in month 4, so $h = 4$.

$|a| = \frac{28.0 - 11.4}{2} = 8.3$; since the temperatures are decreasing near $x = 4$, $a = -8.3$.

So, $y = -8.3 \sin \frac{\pi}{6}(x - 4) + 19.7$.

Regression model:

$y = 8.13 \sin(0.52x + 1.05) + 19.79$

Both models fit the data equally well for all values of x.

Explain 2 Solving a Real-World Problem Using a Sine Model

You can use the graph of a sine model to determine when the model takes on a value of interest.

Example 2 **The table gives the amount of daylight, in hours and minutes, in Chicago on the first day of every month. For what period of time during a year does Chicago get a minimum of 12 hours of daylight?**

Day	Jan. 1	Feb. 1	Mar. 1	Apr. 1	May 1	June 1	July 1	Aug. 1	Sept. 1	Oct. 1	Nov. 1	Dec. 1
Amount of daylight (h:min)	9:12	10:03	11:15	12:43	14:02	15:01	15:10	14:24	13:08	11:45	10:22	9:22

Analyze Information

The independent variable in this situation is **time**, given as calendar dates (the first day of every month).

The dependent variable is **amount of daylight**, measured in hours and minutes.

LANGUAGE SUPPORT EL

Communicate Math

Have students work in pairs. Give each pair of students index cards with graphs of sine functions, equations for sine functions, and data sets for those functions. Have them place the cards face down, and take turns turning over three cards at a time, until they find a match for all three.

Formulate a Plan

You want a sine regression model for the data in order to find **the period of time during a year that Chicago gets a minimum of 12 hours of daylight**.

To obtain the model, you need to convert each of the given calendar dates to **the number of days since the start of the year**. You also need to convert each corresponding amount of daylight from hours and minutes to **decimal hours**.

Solve

You can use an online day-of-year calendar to convert the calendar dates to days since the start of the year (assuming it's not a leap year). Converting hours and minutes to decimal hours simply involves dividing the minutes by **60** and adding the result to the hours. Complete the table, giving decimal hours to the nearest hundredth if necessary.

Day	1	32	60	91	121	152	182	213	244	274	305	335
Amount of daylight (hours)	9.2	10.05	11.25	12.72	14.03	15.02	15.17	14.4	13.13	11.75	10.37	9.37

Enter the data into a graphing calculator and perform sine regression. The sine regression model is $y = \boxed{3} \sin\left(\boxed{0.0167}\,x + \boxed{-1.31}\right) + \boxed{12.1}$. Graph the model along with the line $y = \boxed{12}$. Use **5:intersect** from the **CALC** menu to determine the coordinates of each of the points of intersection of the sine curve and the line.

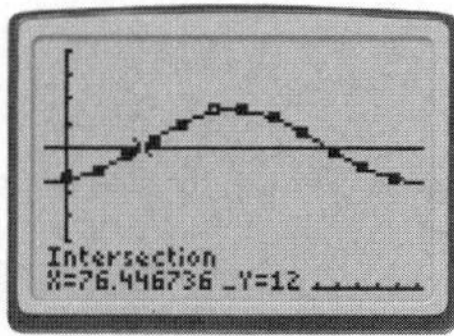

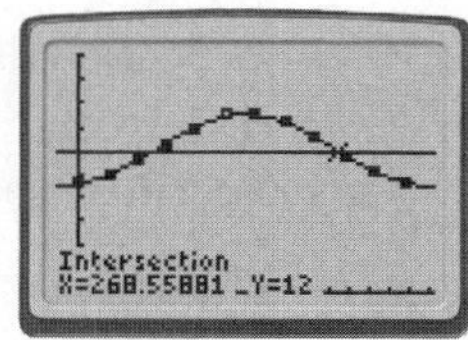

To the nearest whole number, the x-coordinate for the first point of intersection is **76**, and the x-coordinate of the second point of intersection is **269**. Using a day-of-year calendar, you find that 76 corresponds to **March 17** and 269 corresponds to **September 26**. Since the graph of the sine model is above the line between those two dates, Chicago gets a minimum of 12 hours of daylight between **March 17** and **September 26**.

Justify and Evaluate

Looking back at the table of data, you see that the first time the amount of daylight is 12 hours or greater is **April 1** and the last time is **September 1**. These dates fall within the interval you found using the sine regression model, which confirms your answer.

CONNECT VOCABULARY EL

Explain that a *sinusoidal function* is a type of *circular* function. Have students discuss why the term *circular* is an accurate description of the function in the example, and how it provides for the fact that there is more than one solution to the problem.

ELABORATE

INTEGRATE MATHEMATICAL PRACTICES

Focus on Critical Thinking

MP.3 Challenge students to write a cosine function that models any of the data given in the lesson. Have them compare the cosine model to the sine model, and make a generalization about the relationship between sine and cosine functions that model the same set of data.

CONNECT VOCABULARY EL

Have students review the meanings of the terms *"regression"* and *"amplitude"* to help them through this lesson.

SUMMARIZE THE LESSON

? Given a set of data that is sinusoidal in nature, what are some ways to determine a model for the data? **You can plot the data points and approximate the midline and amplitude of the graph. You can also use the graph to identify the period and any phase shift, and then use that information to write the function in the form $y = a \sin \frac{1}{b}(x - h) + k$. Alternatively, you could use a graphing calculator to determine a regression equation.**

Your Turn

7. The table gives the amount of daylight, in hours and minutes, in Sydney, Australia, on the first day of every month. For what period of time during a year does Sydney get a minimum of 12 hours of daylight?

Day	Jan. 1	Feb. 1	Mar. 1	Apr. 1	May 1	June 1	July 1	Aug. 1	Sept. 1	Oct. 1	Nov. 1	Dec. 1
Amount of daylight (h:min)	14:22	13:44	12:49	11:44	10:45	10:03	9:56	10:27	11:23	12:25	13:27	14:13

Data as ordered pairs with days of year and decimal hours: (1, 14.37), (32, 13.73), (60, 12.82), (91, 11.73), (121, 10.75), (152, 10.05), (182, 9.93), (213, 10.45), (244, 11.38), (274, 12.42), (305, 13.45), (335, 14.22)

Sine regression model: $y = 2.25 \sin(0.0165x + 1.87) + 12.2$

Intersection points of the graph of the model and the line $y = 12$: (82, 12) and (262, 12)

So, Sydney gets a minimum of 12 hours of daylight from September 19 to March 23.

Elaborate

8. What pattern must graphed data exhibit in order for a sine function to be an appropriate model for the data?
The graphed data should have a wave-like pattern.

9. When modeling data with the function $y = a \sin \frac{1}{b}(x - h) + k$, how do you use the data to identify a reasonable value for the parameter a?
Identify the maximum and minimum data values and find half their difference. This gives the value of $|a|$. To determine whether the value of a is positive or negative, decide whether the sine curve when $a > 0$ or the sine curve's reflection across the midline (that is, the sine curve when $a < 0$) passes through the data points.

10. When you obtain both a rough-fit sine model and a sine regression model for a set of data, can you compare the constants in the two models directly? Explain.
The rough-fit sine model has the form $y = a \sin \frac{1}{b}(x - h) + k$, while the sine regression model has the form $y = a \sin(bx + c) + d$. The only parameters that you can directly compare are k in the rough-fit model and d in the regression model. To compare the other parameters, you need to rewrite one model in the form of the other.

11. Essential Question Check-In One way to fit a sine model to data is to use the data to identify reasonable values for the parameters a, b, h, and k in $y = a \sin \frac{1}{b}(x - h) + k$. What is another way?
Perform sine regression on a graphing calculator.

Evaluate: Homework and Practice

- Online Homework
- Hints and Help
- Extra Practice

For the situation described:

(a) Graph the data, roughly fit a sine model of the form $y = a \sin \frac{1}{b}(x - h) + k$ to the data, and graph the model on the same grid as the data.

(b) Obtain a sine regression model using a graphing calculator, and then visually compare the two models in relation to the data.

1. The table gives the average monthly temperature in Nashville, Tennessee, in degrees Fahrenheit.

Month	1	2	3	4	5	6	7	8	9	10	11	12
Average temperature (°F)	37.7	41.7	50.0	59.0	67.5	75.7	79.4	78.7	71.5	60.3	49.8	40.4

a. 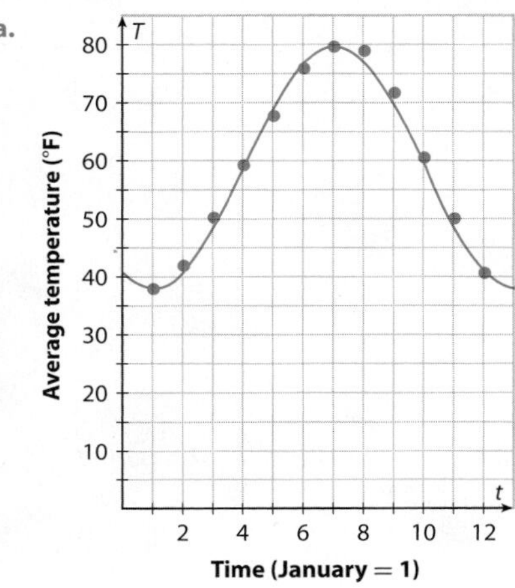

$2\pi b = 12$, so $b = \frac{12}{2\pi} = \frac{6}{\pi}$, and $\frac{1}{b} = \frac{\pi}{6}$.

$k = \frac{79.4 + 37.7}{2} = 58.55$

The first occurrence of a temperature close to 58.55° C is in month 4, so $h = 4$.

$|a| = \frac{79.4 - 37.7}{2} = 20.85$; since the temperatures are increasing near $x = 4$, $a = 20.85$.

So, $y = 20.85 \sin\frac{\pi}{6}(x - 4) + 58.55$.

b. Regression model: $y = 21.02\sin(0.51x - 2.01) + 58.61$

The models are very close together, and both fit the data well for all values of x.

Exercise	Depth of Knowledge (D.O.K.)	COMMON CORE Mathematical Practices
1–4	**2** Skills/Concepts	**MP.5** Using Tools
5	**3** Strategic Thinking H.O.T.	**MP.2** Reasoning
6	**3** Strategic Thinking H.O.T.	**MP.1** Problem Solving
7	**3** Strategic Thinking H.O.T.	**MP.3** Logic

EVALUATE

ASSIGNMENT GUIDE

Concepts and Skills	Practice
Explore Roughly Fitting a Sine Function to Data	
Example 1 Fitting a Sine Function to Data Using Technology	Exercises 1–2
Example 2 Solving a Real-World Problem Using a Sine Model	Exercises 3–4

QUESTIONING STRATEGIES

? How can you use a set of data to approximate the value of a in $y = a \sin \frac{1}{b}(x - h) + k$? **You can subtract the least data value from the greatest data value and take half the difference.**

? How can you use the data to approximate the value of h in $y = a \sin\frac{1}{b}(x - h) + k$? **You can approximate where the graph first intercepts the midline. The x-value of that point is a good approximation of the value of h.**

AVOID COMMON ERRORS

Some students may wrongly interpret the maximum data value as the amplitude of the function. Remind them that the amplitude is the vertical distance between the maximum point and the midline of the graph. Point out that the maximum point is equal to the amplitude only when the midline is the x-axis.

VISUAL CUES

Suggest that students circle the points that appear to be the key points of the graph. They can then use these points to help determine the values of a, b, h, and k in $y = a \sin \frac{1}{b}(x - h) + k$ as they write their models.

TECHNOLOGY

Students can use a calculator to test that the functions they've written produce the ordered pairs in the data. Students should note that since the parameters may have been approximated, the values might not be exact.

2. The table shows the approximate US residential monthly electricity consumption in billions of kilowatt-hours (kWh) for one year where $x = 1$ represents January.

Month	1	2	3	4	5	6	7	8	9	10	11	12
Consumption (billions of kWh)	136	116	106	91	94	114	137	138	115	98	92	124

a.

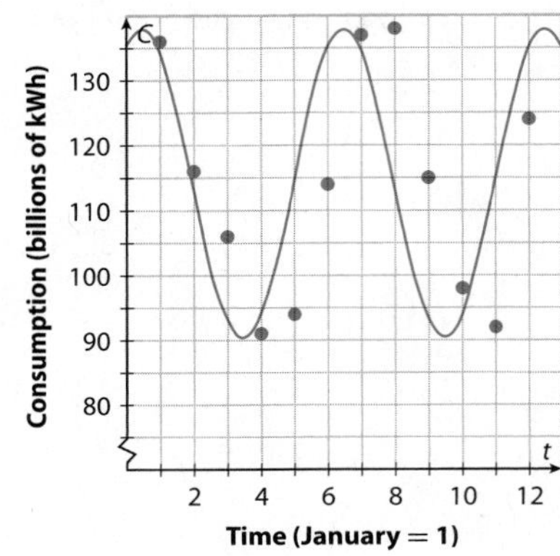

There are two maximums and two minimums during the year, so use a period of 6 months. Then $2\pi b = 6$, so $b = \frac{6}{2\pi} = \frac{3}{\pi}$, and $\frac{1}{b} = \frac{\pi}{3}$.

$k = \frac{138 + 91}{2} = 114.5$

The first occurrence of consumption close to 114.5 billion kWh is in month 2, so $h = 2$.

$|a| = \frac{138 - 91}{2} = 23.5$**; since the consumption is decreasing near $x = 2$, $a = -23.5$.**

So, $y = -23.5\sin\frac{\pi}{3}(x - 2) + 114.5$.

b. Regression model: $y = 22.55\sin(1.00x + 0.53) + 114.16$

Though the rough-fit model has a negative value for *a* and a shift to the right while the regression model has a positive value for *a* and a shift to the left, both curves have similar shapes. Their amplitudes and midlines are almost the same. The period of the rough-fit model is just a little less than that of the regression model. Both curves generally represent the overall behavior of the data, but the regression model clearly fits the data points better. Except for the first two points, the rough-fit curve falls significantly to the left of every data point. The rough-fit curve would be considerably more accurate overall if shifted one month to the right.

For the situation described:

(a) Graph the data, roughly fit a sine model of the form $y = a \sin \frac{1}{b}(x - h) + k$ to the data, and graph the model on the same grid as the data.

(b) Obtain a sine regression model using a graphing calculator, and then visually compare the two models in relation to the data.

(c) Use a graphing calculator and the regression model to answer the question.

3. The table shows the amount of daylight (in minutes) from sunrise to sunset on the 21st day of each month (given as the day of the year) in Green Bay, Wisconsin, where January 1 = day 1.

Day of year	21	52	80	111	141	172	202	233	264	294	325	355
Amount of daylight (minutes)	565	646	732	826	901	933	902	826	733	643	563	530

For about how long each year is the amount of daylight at most 10 hours?

a.

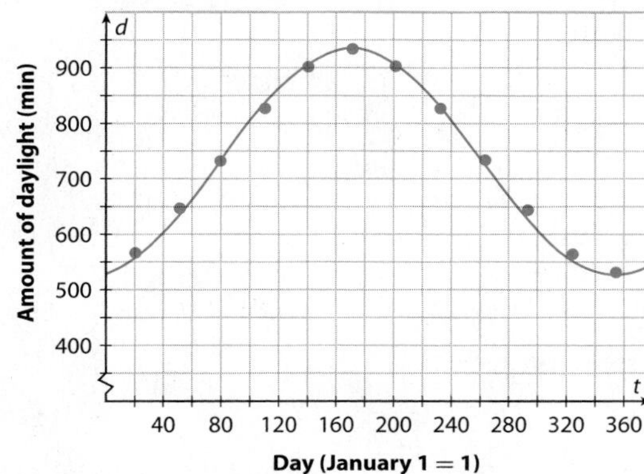

$2\pi b = 365$, so $b = \frac{365}{2\pi}$, and $\frac{1}{b} = \frac{2\pi}{365}$.

$k = \frac{933 + 530}{2} = 731.5$

The first occurrence of an amount of daylight close to 731.5 minutes is day 80 (from the table), so $h = 80$.

$|a| = \frac{933 - 530}{2} = 201.5$; since the amounts of daylight are increasing near $x = 80$, $a = 201.5$.

So, $y = 201.5 \sin \frac{2\pi}{365}(x - 80) + 731.5$.

b. Regression model: $y = 197.8 \sin(0.0168x - 1.32) + 728.7$

Both models fit the data very well for all values of x.

c. Graphing the line $y = 600$ with the regression model graph shows intersection points at about $x = 36$ and about $x = 308$. So, the amount of daylight is at most 10 hours from day 1 through day 36 and from day 308 through day 365, or a total of about $36 + 58 = 94$ days, which is a little over 3 months.

INTEGRATE MATHEMATICAL PRACTICES

Focus on Reasoning

MP.2 Discuss with students the fact that any sinusoid can be modeled by both a sine function and a cosine function. Explain that, typically, the choice is made based upon the type of function that is more convenient for the model. Ask students to consider which type of function they would choose to model a sinusoid whose y-intercept occurs at the minimum value of the function, and to explain their reasoning.

4. The table shows the decimal portion of the moon's surface illuminated from Earth's view at midnight from Washington, D.C., in March, 2014, where x represents the day of the month.

Day	1	3	5	7	9	11	13	15	17	19	21	23	25	27	29	31
Portion of moon illuminated	0.00	0.05	0.19	0.37	0.56	0.74	0.89	0.98	1.00	0.94	0.80	0.60	0.37	0.17	0.03	0.0

A "gibbous moon" refers to the moon phases when more than half of the moon is illuminated, but it is not a full moon. About how long is the period that the moon is either a gibbous moon or a full moon?

a.

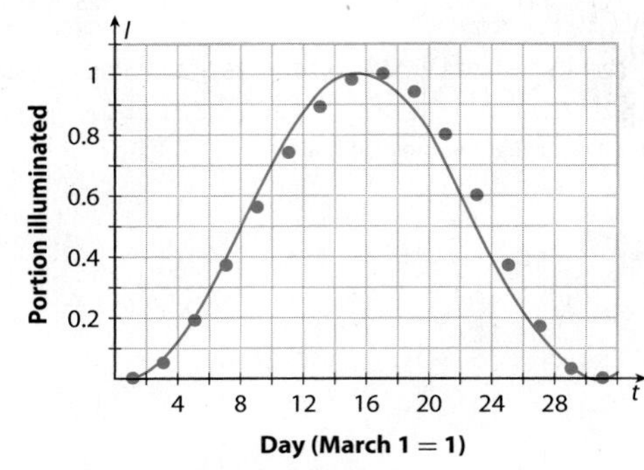

There are minimums at day 1 and day 31, so use a period of 30 days. Then

$2\pi b = 30$, so $b = \frac{30}{2\pi} = \frac{15}{\pi}$, and $\frac{1}{b} = \frac{\pi}{15}$.

$k = \frac{1.00 + 0.00}{2} = 0.50$

Estimating from the graph, it appears the first occurrence of an illumination of about 0.50 should occur on about day 8, so $h = 8$.

$|a| = \frac{1.00 - 0.00}{2} = 0.50$; since the illumination is increasing near $x = 8$, $a = 0.50$.

So, $y = 0.50\sin\frac{\pi}{15}(x - 8) + 0.50$.

b. Regression model: $y = 0.508\sin(0.204x - 1.719) + 0.500$
The models are very similar, and the shapes are very close to identical, but the rough-fit curve tends to lie just a bit left of the points, especially over the second half of the cycle. So, the regression model is a better fit to the data. The estimate of 8 as the first day with an illumination of 0.50 was a little low, and would more accurately have been between day 8 and day 9.

c. Graphing the line $y = 0.50$ with the regression model graph shows intersection points at about $x = 8.4$ and $x = 23.8$. The model predicts the moon will be gibbous or full about 15 days.

H.O.T. Focus on Higher Order Thinking

5. **Make a Conjecture** Why does it make sense that a graphing calculator has a sine regression option but not a cosine regression option?

For cosine and sine functions that have the same amplitude, period, and vertical shift, translating the graph of the cosine function one fourth of a period to the right produces the graph of the sine function, or translating the graph of the sine function one fourth of a period to the left produces the graph of the cosine function. So, if you have a sine regression model, you can rewrite it as a cosine model if desired by a simple horizontal shift.

6. **Critical Thinking** In a science class lab, a mass is suspended from a spring above a tabletop. The mass is pulled down and released. By examining frames from a video as the mass bobs up and down, the class obtains the model $h(t) = 5 \sin 4(t - 0.39) + 10$ for the height h of the mass above the tabletop at time t in seconds. Cassandra notices that after several seconds the mass is not bobbing up and down as far, but it still seems to take about the same time for a cycle. Graph $y = e^{-0.05x}[5 \sin 4(x - 0.39)] + 10$ on a graphing calculator with the original model for $0 \leq x \leq 10$. Explain how this model differs from the original model, and how it might account for Cassandra's observation.

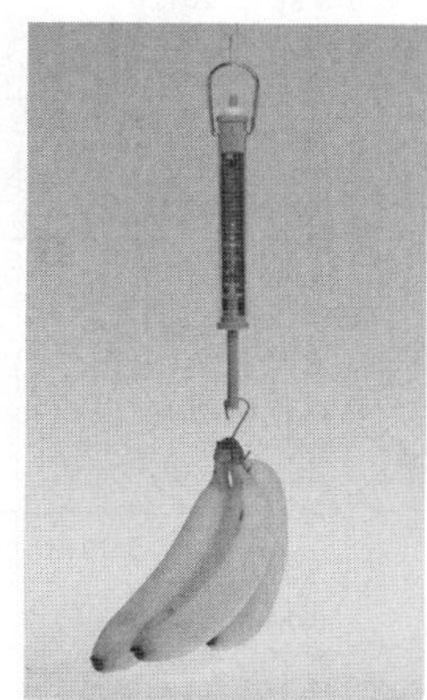

The graph of the new model appears to have the same period, horizontal shift, and midline as that of the original model, but the amplitude is decreasing with time, which matches Cassandra's observation.

7. **Explain the Error** Given a set of data about the Sun's maximum angle θ (in degrees) above the horizon in Boston on any day of the year, Ryan uses his graphing calculator to obtain the regression model $\theta = 23.6 \sin(0.0168t - 1.32) + 47.4$ where t is the number of days since the start of a year. He concludes that the midline of the model's graph is $\theta = 47.4°$ and that the first time during the year that the Sun is reaches this maximum angle in Boston is $t = 1.32$, which corresponds to January 2. What is wrong with Ryan's conclusion? What is the correct conclusion?

The regression model is in the form $y = a\sin(bx + c) + d$ instead of the form $y = a\sin\frac{1}{b}(x - h) + k$. Ryan needs to rewrite the model by factoring out the 0.0168 from the expression $0.0168t - 1.32$:

$$\begin{aligned}\theta &= 23.6 \sin(0.0168t - 1.32) + 47.4 \\ &= 23.6 \sin 0.0168\left(t - \frac{1.32}{0.0168}\right) + 47.4 \\ &\approx 23.6 \sin 0.0168(t - 78.6) + 47.4\end{aligned}$$

So, the first time during the year when the sun reaches a maximum angle of 47.4° above the horizon in Boston is $t = 78.6$, which corresponds to March 20.

PEER-TO-PEER DISCUSSION

Ask students to work with a partner to identify the characteristics of a set of data that indicate that the best model for the data would be a sine function. **The data indicate a periodic function that vacillates between a least value and a greatest value and contain every value in between. The graph of the data is wave-shaped, repeating at regular intervals.**

JOURNAL

Have students describe how to use the attributes of a sinusoidal function to fit a function to a set of appropriately shaped data without the use of technology.

Lesson Performance Task

For two years, a polling agency called a random sample of people every other month and asked them, "Do you think you have or are coming down with a cold or the flu today?" The percentage of those who responded "yes" to the pollsters is shown in the table.

Date	Percentage with cold or flu
January 15, 2012	9.3
March 15, 2012	6.4
May 15, 2012	4.2
July 15, 2012	3.1
September 15, 2012	5.2
November 15, 2012	7.9
January 15, 2013	10.8
March 15, 2013	7.1
May 15, 2013	4.7
July 15, 2013	3.0
September 15, 2013	5.3
November 15, 2013	7.7

a. Are the data periodic? If so, how many cycles do the data represent? Explain your reasoning.

The data are periodic because they repeatedly decrease by 6–8 percentage points over 6 months and then increase by 6–8 percentage points over 6 months. Each cycle lasts 12 months, so the data represent two cycles.

b. When dealing with periodic phenomena, scientists often average corresponding data values from multiple cycles. For instance, for a given location, meteorologists often average the daily high temperatures and the daily low temperatures for corresponding days over a series of years. Why does it make sense to do so?

Averaging "smoothes out" the data. For instance, a high temperature on one day of the year might be much greater than the high temperature on the same day a year later. Averaging replaces many different values for the same point in a cycle with a single "typical" or "normal" value.

c. Complete the table by averaging the corresponding data values from the previous table. Also, replace the calendar dates in the cycle with the number of days since the start of a year (assuming it's not a leap year).

Days since start of year	Percentage with cold or flu
15	10.05
74	6.75
135	4.45
196	3.05
258	5.25
319	7.8

d. Roughly fit a sine model to the data in part c.

Answers may vary. Possible answer:

$2\pi b = 365$, so $b = \frac{365}{2\pi}$ and $\frac{1}{b} = \frac{2\pi}{365}$.

$k = \frac{10.05 + 3.05}{2} = 6.55$

The first occurrence of a percentage close to 6.55 is day 74; since the actual percentage for day 74 is 6.75 and the percentages are decreasing, use a number greater than 74 for h, such as $h = 90$.

$|a| = \frac{10.05 - 3.05}{2} = 3.5$; since the percentages are decreasing near $x = 74$, $a = -3.5$.

So, $y = -3.5 \sin \frac{2\pi}{365}(x - 90) + 6.55$.

e. Use a graphing calculator to obtain a sine regression model for the data in part c. Visually compare this model with your rough-fit model.

Regression model: $y = 4.49 \sin(0.0121x + 2.44) + 7.78$

The regression model fits the data better than the rough-fit model.

f. Use the regression model to determine the period of time during the year when more than 6% of people have a cold or the flu.

Intersection points of the graph of the model and the line $y = 6$: $(92, 6)$ and $(284, 6)$ Day 92 corresponds to April 2, and day 284 corresponds to October 11. The model's graph lies above the line from fall to spring (rather than from spring to fall).

So, more than 6% of people have a cold or flu from mid-October to early April.

EXTENSION ACTIVITY

Climatologists often use sine functions to model weather. Have students pick a city or other location on Earth, then research and model its average monthly rainfall in millimeters. Be sure that locations are chosen from each hemisphere. Have students present and compare models, noting any trends and differences. Students can further research Earth's rainfall patterns and what affects them, such as wind and ocean currents.

QUESTIONING STRATEGIES

? Why is a sine function an appropriate mathematical model for flu data? **The data are relatively cyclical and thus periodic, with low and high points over the course of a year. Other models would have end behavior that rises or falls over long periods of time, or approach an asymptote.**

INTEGRATE MATHEMATICAL PRACTICES

Focus on Critical Thinking

MP.3 Discuss with students how each model might differ if the numbers represented hundreds of residents, rather than percentages, given a population that is relatively constant. Students should note that for each, the model and graph would be the same, and only the real-world interpretation of the units would differ.

Scoring Rubric

2 points: Student correctly solves the problem and explains his/her reasoning.

1 point: Student shows good understanding of the problem but does not fully solve or explain his/her reasoning.

0 points: Student does not demonstrate understanding of the problem.

MODULE 18

Study Guide Review

ASSESSMENT AND INTERVENTION

Assign or customize module reviews.

MODULE PERFORMANCE TASK

Mathematical Practices: MP.1, MP.2, MP.4, MP.6, MP.7, MP.8
F-IF.B.4, F-BF.B.3, F-TF.B.5

SUPPORTING STUDENT REASONING

Students should begin this problem by focusing on the information they will need. Here are some questions students might have.

- **How can I represent the month in my model?** Point out that since the length of a month varies, it would be a better choice to use days instead of months.
- **What should the output of my model be?** The output should be the fraction of the moon that is lit on a particular day.
- **How do I find additional data about the phases of the moon?** They can find data for all of 2014, as well as for other years, at the U.S. Naval Observatory website: http://aa.usno.navy.mil/data/docs/MoonFraction.php

STUDY GUIDE REVIEW

Graphing Trigonometric Functions

MODULE 18

Essential Question: How can graphing trigonometric functions help to solve real-world problems?

Key Vocabulary
amplitude *(amplitude)*
cosecant *(cosecante)*
cotangent *(cotangente)*
frequency *(frecuencia)*
midline *(línea media)*
period *(periodo)*
periodic function *(función periódica)*
secant function *(secante)*

KEY EXAMPLE *(Lesson 18.1)*

Find the amplitude and period of $f(x) = -\frac{1}{2}\cos 2x$.

$a = -\frac{1}{2}, b = 2$ — *Identify a and b by comparing the function with the general equation $f(x) = a\cos b(x-h)+k$ or $f(x) = a\sin b(x-h)+k$.*

amplitude $= |a| = \frac{1}{2}$ period $= \frac{2\pi}{|b|} = \frac{2\pi}{2} = \pi$

KEY EXAMPLE *(Lesson 18.2)*

Find the period, x-intercepts, and asymptotes of $f(x) = \cot \frac{\pi}{2}x$.

$b = \frac{\pi}{2}$ — *Identify b by comparing the function with the general equation $f(x) = \tan bx$ or $f(x) = \cot bx$.*

period $= 2$ — *period $= \frac{\pi}{|b|} = \frac{\pi}{\pi/2} = 2$*

The first x-intercept is at 1. — *Identify the first x-intercept.*

The x-intercepts are at $1 + 2n$. — *Generalize the intercept locations (n = integer).*

The asymptotes are at $x = 2n$. — $x = \frac{\pi n}{|b|} = \frac{\pi n}{\left|\frac{\pi}{2}\right|} = 2n$

KEY EXAMPLE *(Lesson 18.3)*

Find the amplitude, period, horizontal and vertical shifts, maximum, minimum, and midline of $f(x) = 3\cos(x - \pi) - 1$.

$f(x) = 3$	$\cos 1(x$	$-\pi)$	-1
↑	↑	↑	↑
amplitude $= \lvert 3\rvert = 3$	period $\frac{2\pi}{1} = 2\pi$	horizontal shift $= \pi$	vertical shift $= -1$

maximum = amplitude + vertical shift $= 3 + (-1) = 2 \rightarrow (\pi, 2); (3\pi, 2)$

minimum = −amplitude + vertical shift $= -3 + (-1) = -4 \rightarrow (2\pi, -4)$

midline: $y = \frac{\text{maximum} + \text{minimum}}{2} = \frac{2 + (-4)}{2} = -1$

SCAFFOLDING SUPPORT

- If students are having trouble getting started, you might wish to emphasize that the moon's cycles are periodic, so the base function must be periodic, as well.
- Don't let students miss that the first day of the month is the 1st, but functions generally begin with $x = 0$. They need to take this into account.

KEY EXAMPLE (Lesson 18.4)

The table gives information on tides at Canada's Bay of Fundy. Assume that it takes 6.25 hours for the tide to come in and another 6.25 hours for the tide to retreat. Write a cosine function that models the height of the tide over time.

Tides at the Bay of Fundy		
	Time (h)	Height (m)
High Tide	$t = 0$	16.3
Low Tide	$t = 6.25$	0

amplitude: $(0.5)16.3 = 8.15 = a$

period: $12.5 = \frac{2\pi}{|b|} \rightarrow b = \frac{4\pi}{25}$ vertical shift: $(0.5)16.3 = 8.15$

function: $f(x) = 8.15\cos\frac{4\pi}{25}t + 8.15$

EXERCISES

1. Identify the amplitude and period of $f(x) = \frac{\pi}{2}\sin \pi x$ *(Lesson 18.1)*

   amplitude: $\frac{\pi}{2}$; period: 2

2. Identify the period, x-intercepts, and asymptotes of $f(x) = \tan \pi x$. *(Lesson 18.2)*

   period: 1; x-intercepts at n; asymptotes: $x = \frac{1}{2} + n$ where n is an integer.

3. Find the amplitude, period, phase shift, maximum, minimum, and midline of $f(x) = 2\sin\left(x - \frac{\pi}{2}\right) + 3$. *(Lesson 18.3)*

   amplitude: 2; period: 2 π; horizontal shift $\frac{\pi}{2}$ units to the right; vertical shift: 3 units up; maximum: 5; minimum: 1; midline: $y = 3$

MODULE PERFORMANCE TASK

What's Your Sine?

During a new moon, 0% of the moon's surface visible from Earth is illuminated by the Sun. At the full moon, 100% of the moon is lit. Over the course of the year, the moon cycles back and forth between these extremes about every 29.5 days. The table gives the fraction of the moon that was lit on certain days in January 2014.

Day	1	5	10	13	16	20	25	28	31
Fraction Lit	0.00	0.20	0.70	0.92	1.00	0.86	0.40	0.11	0.00

Use this information to find a sine function that models this phenomenon. Then use your model to predict the fraction of the moon's surface that is lit on any given day in 2014.

Start by listing in the space below the information you will need to solve the problem. Then complete the task on your own paper. Use graphs, numbers, words, or algebra to explain how you reached your conclusion.

SAMPLE SOLUTION

The moon's phases vary periodically, so begin with a sine function and transform it to match the data.

The sine function has a range from −1 to 1. To change this range to 0 to 1, compress the function vertically by a factor of 0.5 (range −0.5 to 0.5), then shift it upwards by 0.5 units (range 0 to 1). This gives us $y = 0.5\sin x + 0.5$.

The period of the sine function should change from 2π radians to 29.5 days (as given in the problem). So multiply x by a factor of $\frac{2\pi}{29.5}$.

Now the function is $y = 0.5 + 0.5\sin\left(\frac{2\pi}{29.5}x\right)$.

Finally, shift the function horizontally to match up with the data. The function is close to 0 at $x = -7$ and close to 1 at $x = 8$, so shift it 8 units to the right to agree with the January data.

A completed model for the illumination of the moon is $y = 0.5 + 0.5\sin\left[\frac{2\pi}{29.5}(x - 8)\right]$.

DISCUSSION OPPORTUNITIES

- Have students compare and discuss the differences among their completed models.
- Some students will have chosen a sine function and others may have chosen cosine. Ask them how they would need to change the model if they switched the parent function from one possibility to the other.
- Ask students what other natural occurrences might be modeled by a sine or cosine function.

Assessment Rubric

2 points: Student correctly solves the problem and explains his/her reasoning.

1 point: Student shows good understanding of the problem but does not fully solve or explain his/her reasoning.

0 points: Student does not demonstrate understanding of the problem.

Ready to Go On?

ASSESS MASTERY

Use the assessment on this page to determine if students have mastered the concepts and standards covered in this module.

ASSESSMENT AND INTERVENTION

Access Ready to Go On? assessment online, and receive instant scoring, feedback, and customized intervention or enrichment.

ADDITIONAL RESOURCES

Response to Intervention Resources

- Reteach Worksheets

Differentiated Instruction Resources

- Reading Strategies EL
- Success for English Learners EL
- Challenge Worksheets

Assessment Resources

- Leveled Module Quizzes

Ready to Go On?

18.1–18.4 Graphing Trigonometric Functions

- Online Homework
- Hints and Help
- Extra Practice

1. Find the amplitude, period, phase shift, and x-intercepts of $f(x) = \sin\left(x - \frac{5\pi}{4}\right)$.

amplitude: 1; period: 2 π; phase shift: $\frac{5\pi}{4}$ to the right;

x-intercepts at $\frac{\pi}{4} + n\pi$

2. The displacement in inches of a mass attached to a spring is modeled by $y_1(t) = 3\sin\left(\frac{2\pi}{5}t + \frac{\pi}{2}\right)$, where t is the time in seconds.

a. What is the amplitude of the motion?

3 in.

b. What is the period of the motion?

5 s

c. What is the initial displacement when $t = 0$?

3 in.

3. The paddle wheel of a ship is 11 feet in diameter, revolves 15 times per minute when moving at top speed, and is 2 feet below the water's surface at its lowest point. Using this speed and starting from a point at the very top of the wheel, write a model for the height h (in feet) of the end of the paddle relative to the water's surface as a function of time t (in minutes).

Sample answer: $y = 5.5 \cos(30\pi t) + 3.5$

ESSENTIAL QUESTION

4. What are the key features of the graphs of a trigonometric function and how can you use a trigonometric function to model real-world data?

Sample answer: The keys features of a trigonometric function may include the amplitude, period, x-intercepts, maximum, minimum, asymptotes, horizontal shift, vertical shift, and midline. To model real-world data with a trigonometric function, confirm that the data describe a wave-shaped pattern. If they do, use the data to identify the key features of the wave and then write an equation.

COMMON CORE Common Core Standards

Lesson	exercise	Content Standards	Mathematical Practices
18.3	1	F-IF.C.7e	MP.7
18.1, 18.3	2	F-IF.C.7e	MP.7
18.4	3	F-TF.B.5	MP.4

MODULE 18
MIXED REVIEW

Assessment Readiness

1. Consider the graph of the function $f(x) = \pi\cos\left(x + \frac{\pi}{2}\right) + 2$. Choose True or False for each statement.

   A. The period is π. ○ True ● False
   B. The amplitude is 1. ○ True ● False
   C. The horizontal shift is $-\frac{\pi}{2}$. ● True ○ False

2. Does the given function have an amplitude of 4? Select Yes or No for A–C.

   A. $f(x) = 4\csc x$ ○ Yes ● No
   B. $f(x) = -4\sin \pi x$ ● Yes ○ No
   C. $f(x) = \sin 4x + 4$ ○ Yes ● No

3. A basketball is dropped from a height of 15 feet. Can the height of the basketball be modeled by a trigonometric function? If so, write the function. If not, explain why not.

   No; as the ball bounces it does not return to its original height and therefore is not periodic.

4. In photosynthesis, a plant converts carbon dioxide and water to sugar and oxygen. This process is studied by measuring a plant's carbon assimilation C (in micromoles of CO_2 per square meter per second). For a bean plant, $C(t) = 1.2 \sin \frac{\pi}{12}(t - 6) + 7$, where t is time in hours starting at midnight.

   a. What is the period of the function?
   24 h

   b. What is the maximum and at what time does it occur?
   8.2; noon

MIXED REVIEW
Assessment Readiness

ASSESSMENT AND INTERVENTION

Assign ready-made or customized practice tests to prepare students for high-stakes tests.

ADDITIONAL RESOURCES

Assessment Resources

- Leveled Module Quizzes: Modified, B

AVOID COMMON ERRORS

Item 1 Trigonometric parent functions are different from polynomial functions because they are periodic. This can make their shifts harder to see by eye. Encourage students, if using a calculator to graph a function, to also graph the parent function. This will make the transformations easier to see.

Common Core Standards

Lesson	Items	Math Standards	Mathematical Practices
18.1, 18.3	1	**F-IF.C.7e**	**MP.7**
18.1, 18.3	2	**F-IF.C.7e**	**MP.7**
18.1, 18.2, 18.3, 18.4	3	**F-TF.B.5**	**MP.4**
18.1, 18.3	4	**F-TF.B.5**	**MP.4**

* Item integrates mixed review concepts from previous modules or a previous course.

MIXED REVIEW

Assessment Readiness

ASSESSMENT AND INTERVENTION

Assign ready-made or customized practice tests to prepare students for high-stakes tests.

ADDITIONAL RESOURCES

Assessment Resources

- Leveled Unit Tests: Modified, A, B, C
- Performance Assessment

AVOID COMMON ERRORS

Item 7 Some students have a hard time finding two different ways to approach a problem situation, and instead they pick one way that they like the best. Remind students that knowing multiple methods helps them learn how to approach more kinds of problems.

UNIT 7 MIXED REVIEW

Assessment Readiness

- Online Homework
- Hints and Help
- Extra Practice

1. Consider that $\sin\theta = 0.819$

Select Yes or No for A–C.

A. $\cos\theta = 0.819$ ○ Yes ● No

B. $\cos\theta = -0.574$ ○ Yes ● No

C. $\cos\theta = 0.574$ ● Yes ○ No

2. Consider the graphs of the functions $f(x) = 0.25\cos 4\left(x - \frac{\pi}{2}\right) + 0.5$ and $g(x) = 0.25\cos 4\left(x + \frac{\pi}{2}\right) + 0.5$. Select True or False for each statement.

A. Both graphs look exactly the same. ● True ○ False

B. $g(x)$ is translated up $\frac{\pi}{2}$, and $f(x)$ is translated down $\frac{\pi}{2}$. ○ True ● False

C. $g(x)$ is translated left $\frac{\pi}{2}$, and $f(x)$ is translated right $\frac{\pi}{2}$. ● True ○ False

3. Consider a ball of diameter 10 inches rolling upon the ground at a rate of 20 revolutions per second. Select True or False for each statement.

A. It will take 0.1 second to travel 7200 degrees. ● True ○ False

B. It will take 5 minutes to travel 7200 degrees. ○ True ● False

C. The ball will travel approximately 436 inches if it is rolled for 5000 degrees. ● True ○ False

4. Consider the radian measure $\frac{23\pi}{4}$. Is the trigonometric equation correct?

Select Yes or No for A–C.

A. $\cos\frac{23\pi}{4} \approx -0.707$ ○ Yes ● No

B. $\tan\frac{23\pi}{4} = -1$ ● Yes ○ No

C. $\sin\frac{23\pi}{4} \approx 0.707$ ○ Yes ● No

COMMON CORE

Common Core Standards

Items	Content Standards	Mathematical Practices
1	**F-TF.C.8**	**MP.2**
2*	**F-BF.B.3, F-IF.C.7e**	**MP.6**
3	**F-TF.A.1**	**MP.1**
4	**F-TF-A.2**	**MP.1**
5	**F-IF.C.7e**	**MP.6**
6	**F-TF.B.5**	**MP.3**
7*	**A-REI.B.4b**	**MP.5**

* Item integrates mixed review concepts from previous modules or a previous course.

5. Hannah is graphing the functions $f(x) = 5\sin(x)$ and $g(x) = 5\csc(x)$ on the same coordinate plane. Explain what she should see if she graphs them correctly

Possible answer: $f(x)$ is a wavy line that moves above and below the x axis. $g(x)$ has local maximums and minimums that touch the maximums and minimums of $f(x)$, and then curve in the opposite directions and off the graph.

6. While completing an assignment in class, students were required to recognize the period and amplitude of a trigonometric function without graphing the function. Roland said that the function $f(x) = 4\sin\left(\frac{1}{2}x\right)$ has a period of 4 and an amplitude of $\frac{1}{2}$. Describe and correct his mistake.

He has the period and amplitude reversed. The amplitude should be 4, and the period is $\frac{2\pi}{\frac{1}{2}} = 4\pi$, which stretches the function wider, since a normal period is 2π.

7. Use two different methods to find the roots of the quadratic equation $h(x) = x^2 + 3x - 18$. Explain which methods you used, and why. Did you get the same roots?

$x = -6$ and 3; Possible answer: I used the factoring method to solve the equation, because I noticed that 6 and -3 have a sum of 3, and a product of -18. That gave the factorization of $(x + 6)$ and $(x - 3)$. When setting both sets of parentheses equal to zero, the final answers were $x = -6$ and $x = 3$.; Possible answer: the quadratic equation can also be used: $a = 1$, $b = 3$, and $c = -18$.

$x = \frac{-b \pm \sqrt{b^2 - 4ac}}{2a} = \frac{-3 \pm \sqrt{3^2 - 4(1)(-18)}}{2(1)} = \frac{-3 \pm 9}{2}$ which gives $\frac{6}{2} = 3$ and $\frac{-12}{2} = -6$. The answers are the same.

Performance Tasks

8. When a road has a 6% grade, it rises a vertical distance of 6 ft over a horizontal distance of 100 ft. One of the steepest roads in the U.S. is in San Francisco. Filbert Street between Hyde and Leavenworth has a grade of 31.5%. What is the angle that corresponds to this grade? Show your work.

17.5°; $\tan^{-1}\left(\frac{31.5}{100}\right) = \tan^{-1}(0.315) \approx 17.5°$

PERFORMANCE TASKS

There are three different levels of performance tasks:

*__Novice:__ These are short word problems that require students to apply the math they have learned in straightforward, real-world situations.

**__Apprentice:__ These are more involved problems that guide students step-by-step through more complex tasks. These exercises include more complicated reasoning, writing, and open ended elements.

***__Expert:__ These are open-ended, nonroutine problems that, instead of stepping the students through, ask them to choose their own methods for solving and justify their answers and reasoning.

SCORING GUIDES

Item 8 (2 points) Award the student 1 point for the correct angle and 1 point for showing work.

SCORING GUIDES

Item 9 (6 points)

a. 1 point for correct answer and 1 point for work

b. 2 points for correct distance

c. 2 points for correct distance

Item 10 (6 points)

a. 1 point for the correct function model, and 0.5 point for the correct period, and 0.5 point for the correct amplitude

b. 1 point for a reasonable dew point, and 1 point for the two correct days.

c. 1 point for the correct sine phase shift, and 1 point for the correct cosine phase shift

★★ **9.** A DVD's rotational speed varies from 1530 rpm (revolutions per minute) when the inner edge is being read to 630 rpm when the outer edge is being read.

A. What is the total rotation of the DVD in radians after 10 seconds, if the computer is reading data on the outer edge? Show how you got your answer.

B. In 10 seconds, what linear distance is covered by the part of the DVD that passes under the reader head from part A, which is about 6 cm from the center of the DVD?

C. If the computer is reading data on the inner edge (about 2.5 cm from the center of the DVD), what linear distance is covered by the part of the DVD that passes under the reader head in 10 seconds?

A. $\frac{630 \text{ rev}}{\text{min}} \cdot \frac{\text{min}}{60 \text{ s}} \cdot 10 \text{ s} = 105 \text{ rev} \cdot 2\pi = 210\pi$

B. linear distance = 3958 cm

C. linear distance = 4006 cm

★★★**10.** Belinda recorded the dew point in her hometown in °F each day for a year (not a leap year) and entered the data into her graphing calculator, with $x = 0$ as January 1. She then performed a sinusoidal regression on her graphing calculator as shown.

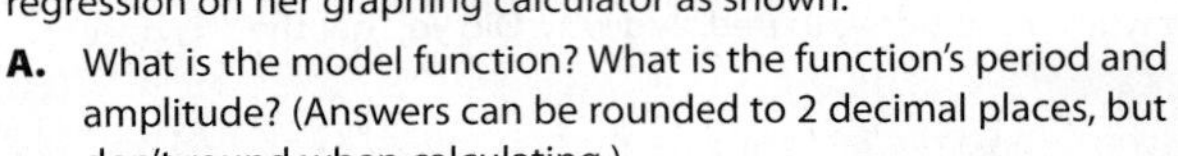

A. What is the model function? What is the function's period and amplitude? (Answers can be rounded to 2 decimal places, but don't round when calculating.)

B. Use the model function to find the approximate dew point on February 20. Also, determine on what day(s) the model says the dew point was 55°F by using your graphing calculator.

C. What is the phase shift of the model function? What would the phase shift have been if the cosine function had been used instead of the sine function in the model? Support your answer.

A. $y \approx 25.00\sin(0.02x - 1.58) + 40.00$; **Period:** $\frac{2\pi}{0.0172134433} \approx 365.02$; **Amplitude: 25.00**

B. Approximate dew point: 23.46 °F; the dew point was 55°F at $x = 129$ and $x = 237$, which was May 10 and August 26.

C. Phase shift: $\frac{-1.583657028}{0.0172134442} = -92.00$, **or 92 units to the right; the phase shift would have been** $92 + \frac{365.02}{4} = 92 + 91.26 = 183.26$ **units to the right if the cosine function had been used, since the cosine function must be translated $\frac{1}{4}$ of its period to the right in order to be equivalent to the sine function.**

MATH IN CAREERS

Boat Builder A side view of a riverboat's paddle wheel is shown. The paddle wheel has a diameter of 16 feet and rotates at a rate of 1 revolution every 4 seconds. Its lowest point

is 2 feet below the water line. The function $h(t) = 8\sin\left[\frac{\pi}{2}(t-1)\right] + 6$ models the motion of

the paddle labeled P. The function gives the "height" (which is negative when the paddle is below the water line) at time t (in seconds).

16 ft

1 revolution every 4 seconds

Water line

2 ft

P

a. Graph the function on the interval $0 \leq t \leq 6$.

b. What is the significance of the graph's t-intercepts in the context of the situation?

c. What is the significance of the maximum and minimum values of h in the context of the situation?

d. If the paddle boat travels a distance of 1 mile in still water, through how many complete rotations will the paddle wheel turn?

a.

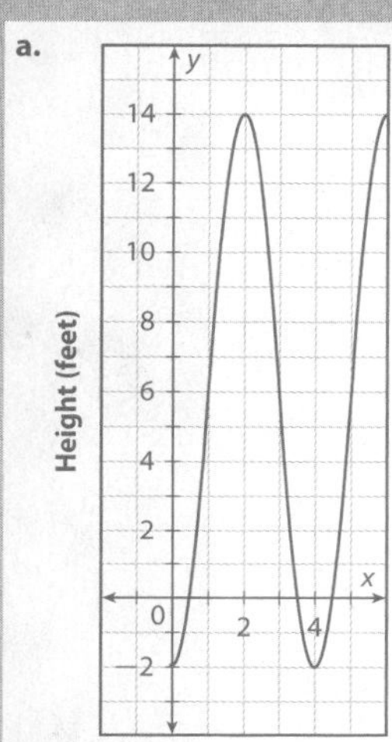

b. They represent each time paddle *P* breaks the surface of the water.

c. The maximum represents the height of paddle *P* when it reaches the top of the wheel, and the minimum represents the "height" of the paddle when it reaches the bottom of the wheel.

d. 105 revolutions

MATH IN CAREERS

Boat Builder In this Unit Performance Task, students can see how a boat builder uses mathematics on the job.

For more information about careers in mathematics as well as various mathematics appreciation topics, visit the American Mathematical Society http://www.ams.org

SCORING GUIDES

Task (6 points)

a. 2 points for a correct graph

b. 1 point for a correct description

c. 2 points for a correct explanation

c. 1 point for a correct answer

UNIT 8

Probability

CONTENTS

Unit Pacing Guide

45-Minute Classes

Module 19

DAY 1	DAY 2	DAY 3	DAY 4	DAY 5
Lesson 19.1	Lesson 19.2	Lesson 19.2	Lesson 19.3	Lesson 19.4
DAY 6				
Module Review and Assessment Readiness				

Module 20

DAY 1	DAY 2	DAY 3	DAY 4	DAY 5
Lesson 20.1	Lesson 20.1	Lesson 20.2	Lesson 20.2	Lesson 20.3
DAY 6				
Module Review and Assessment Readiness				

Module 21

DAY 1	DAY 2	DAY 3	DAY 4	DAY 5
Lesson 21.1	Lesson 21.1	Lesson 21.2	Lesson 21.2	Module Review and Assessment Readiness
DAY 6				
Unit Review and Assessment Readiness				

90-Minute Classes

Module 19

DAY 1	DAY 2	DAY 3
Lesson 19.1	Lesson 19.2 Lesson 19.3	Lesson 19.4 Module Review and Assessment Readiness

Module 20

DAY 1	DAY 2	DAY 3
Lesson 20.1	Lesson 20.2	Lesson 20.3 Module Review and Assessment Readiness

Module 21

DAY 1	DAY 2	DAY 3
Lesson 21.1	Lesson 21.2	Module Review and Assessment Readiness Unit Review and Assessment Readiness

Program Resources

PLAN

HMH Teacher App

Access a full suite of teacher resources online and offline on a variety of devices. Plan present, and manage classes, assignments, and activities.

ePlanner **Easily plan your classes, create and view assignments, and access all program resources with your online, customizable planning tool.**

Professional Development Videos

Authors Juli Dixon and Matt Larson model successful teaching practices and strategies in actual classroom settings.

QR Codes **Scan with your smart phone to jump directly from your print book to online videos and other resources.**

Teacher's Edition

Support students with point-of-use Questioning Strategies, teaching tips, resources for differentiated instruction, additional activities, and more.

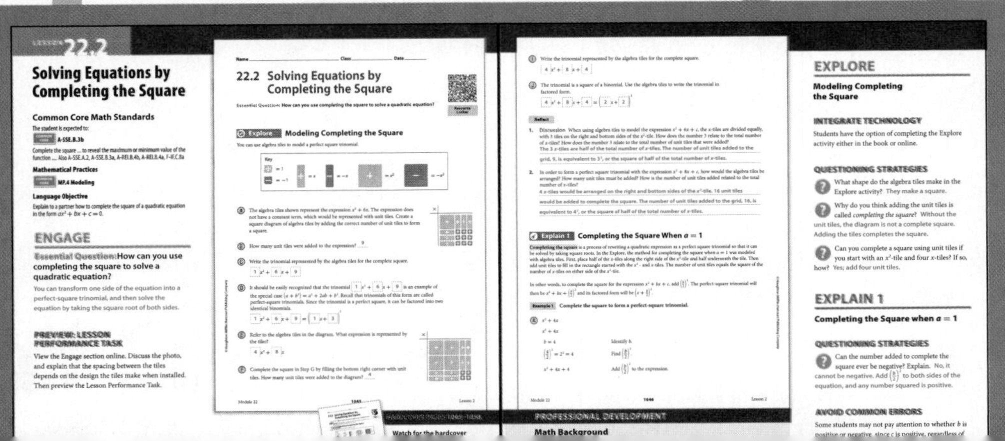

ENGAGE AND EXPLORE

Real-World Videos **Engage students with interesting and relevant applications of the mathematical content of each module.**

Explore Activities

Students interactively explore new concepts using a variety of tools and approaches.

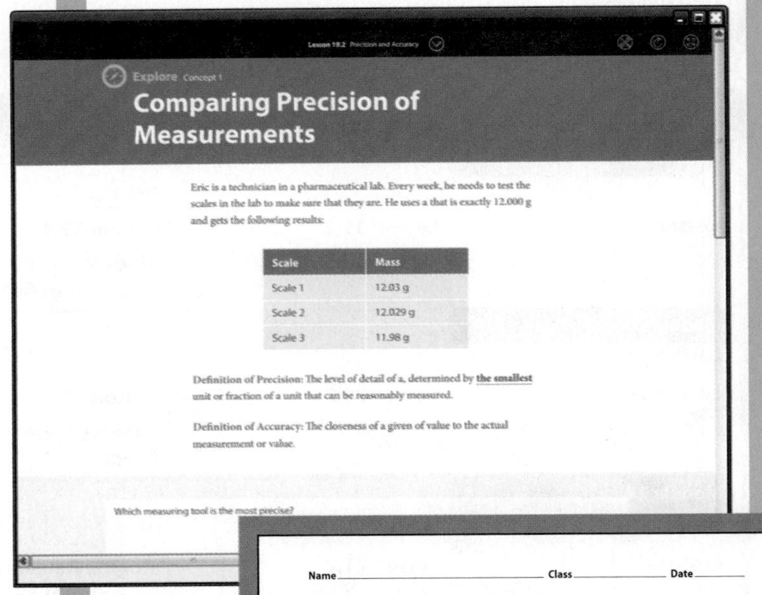

Explore Concept 1
Comparing Precision of Measurements
Eric is a technician in a pharmaceutical lab. Every week, he needs to test the scales in the lab to make sure that they are. He uses a that is exactly 12.000 g and gets the following results:
Scale | Mass
Scale 1 | 12.03 g
Scale 2 | 12.029 g
Scale 3 | 11.98 g
Definition of Precision: The level of detail of a, determined by the smallest unit or fraction of a unit that can be reasonably measured.
Definition of Accuracy: The closeness of a given of value to the actual measurement or value.
Which measuring tool is the most precise?

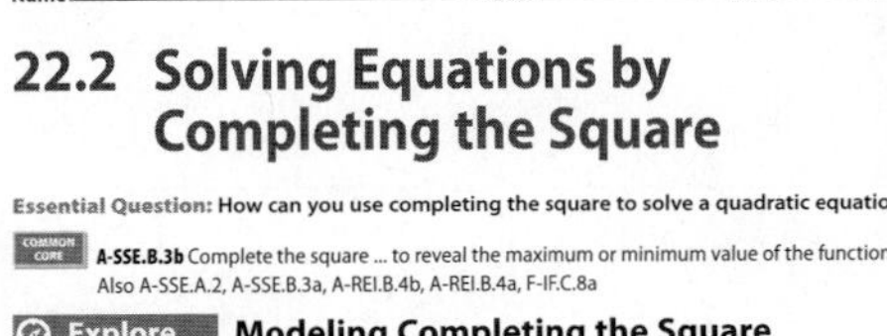

Name ______ Class ______ Date ______

22.2 Solving Equations by Completing the Square

Essential Question: How can you use completing the square to solve a quadratic equation?

A-SSE.B.3b Complete the square ... to reveal the maximum or minimum value of the function ... Also A-SSE.A.2, A-SSE.B.3a, A-REI.B.4b, A-REI.B.4a, F-IF.C.8a

Explore **Modeling Completing the Square**

You can use algebra tiles to model a perfect square trinomial.

Key: $= 1$, $= -1$, $= x$, $= -x$, $= x^2$, $= -x^2$

(A) The algebra tiles shown represent the expression $x^2 + 6x$. The expression does not have a constant term, which would be represented with unit tiles. Create a square diagram of algebra tiles by adding the correct number of unit tiles to form a square.

(B) How many unit tiles were added to the expression? ____

(C) Write the trinomial represented by the algebra tiles for the complete square.

$\square x^2 + \square x + \square$

(D) It should be easily recognized that the trinomial $\square x^2 + \square x + \square$ is an example of

TEACH

Math On the Spot video tutorials, featuring program authors Dr. Edward Burger and Martha Sandoval-Martinez, accompany every example in the textbook and give students step-by-step instructions and explanations of key math concepts.

Interactive Teacher Edition

Customize and present course materials with collaborative activities and integrated formative assessment.

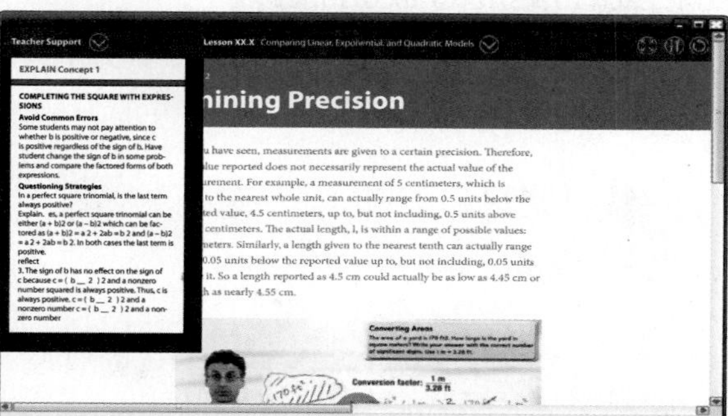

Differentiated Instruction Resources

Support all learners with Differentiated Instruction Resources, including

- **Leveled Practice and Problem Solving**
- **Reading Strategies**
- **Success for English Learners**
- **Challenge**

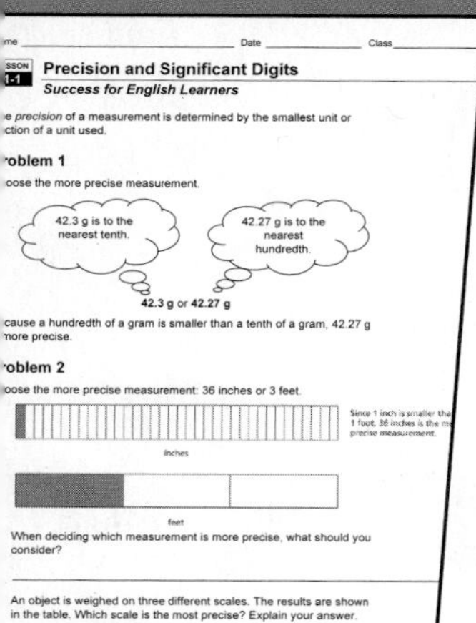

Name ______ Date ______ Class ______

LESSON 1-1 **Precision and Significant Digits**
Success for English Learners

e *precision* of a measurement is determined by the smallest unit or ction of a unit used.

roblem 1

oose the more precise measurement.

42.3 g is to the nearest tenth.

42.27 g is to the nearest hundredth.

42.3 g or **42.27 g**

cause a hundredth of a gram is smaller than a tenth of a gram, 42.27 g more precise.

roblem 2

oose the more precise measurement: 36 inches or 3 feet.

Since 1 inch is smaller tha 1 foot, 36 inches is the m precise measurement.

inches

feet

When deciding which measurement is more precise, what should you consider?

An object is weighed on three different scales. The results are shown in the table. Which scale is the most precise? Explain your answer.

Scale	Measurement

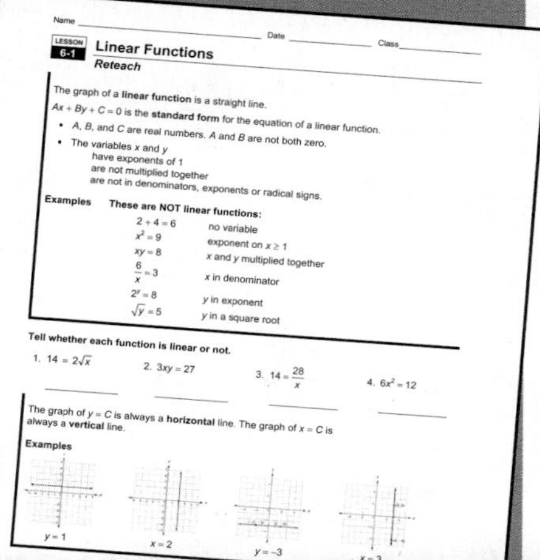

Name ______ Date ______ Class ______

LESSON 6-1 **Linear Functions**
Reteach

The graph of a **linear function** is a straight line.

$Ax + By + C = 0$ is the **standard form** for the equation of a linear function.

- A, B, and C are real numbers. A and B are not both zero.
- The variables x and y
  - have exponents of 1
  - are not multiplied together
  - are not in denominators, exponents or radical signs.

Examples **These are NOT linear functions:**

$2 + 4 = 6$	no variable
$x^2 = 9$	exponent on $x \geq 1$
$xy = 8$	x and y multiplied together
$\frac{6}{x} = 3$	x in denominator
$2^y = 8$	y in exponent
$\sqrt{y} = 5$	y in a square root

Tell whether each function is linear or not.

1. $14 = 2\sqrt{x}$
2. $3xy = 27$
3. $14 = \frac{28}{x}$
4. $6x^2 = 12$

The graph of $y = C$ is always a **horizontal** line. The graph of $x = C$ is always a **vertical** line.

Examples

$y = 1$ $x = 2$ $y = -3$ $x = 3$

ASSESSMENT AND INTERVENTION

The Personal Math Trainer provides online practice, homework, assessments, and intervention. Monitor student progress through reports and alerts. Create and customize assignments aligned to specific lessons or Common Core standards.

- **Practice** – With dynamic items and assignments, students get unlimited practice on key concepts supported by guided examples, step-by-step solutions, and video tutorials.
- **Assessments** – Choose from course assignments or customize your own based on course content, Common Core standards, difficulty levels, and more.
- **Homework** – Students can complete online homework with a wide variety of problem types, including the ability to enter expressions, equations, and graphs. Let the system automatically grade homework, so you can focus where your students need help the most!
- **Intervention** – Let the Personal Math Trainer automatically prescribe a targeted, personalized intervention path for your students.

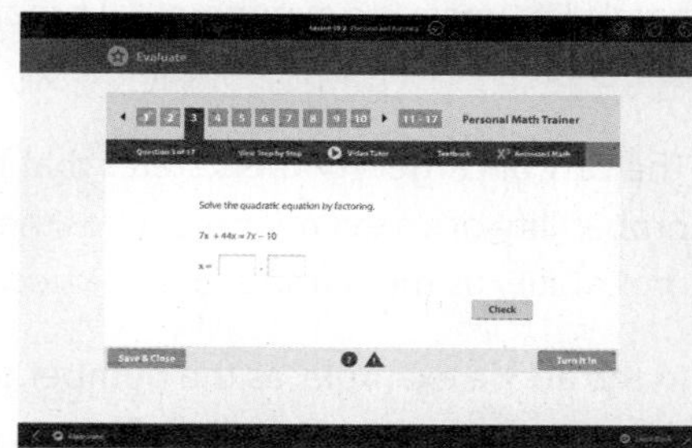

Focus on Higher Order Thinking

Raise the bar with homework and practice that incorporates higher-order thinking and mathematical practices in every lesson.

Assessment Readiness

Prepare students for success on high stakes tests for Algebra 2 with practice at every module and unit

Assessment Resources

Tailor assessments and response to intervention to meet the needs of all your classes and students, including

- Leveled Module Quizzes
- Leveled Unit Tests
- Unit Performance Tasks
- Placement, Diagnostic, and Quarterly Benchmark Tests
- Tier 1, Tier 2, and Tier 3 Resources

Math Background

Probability  S-CP.A.1

LESSON 19.1

A *probability* is *a number between 0 and 1 inclusive that measures the likelihood of an event*. When an event consists of finitely many equally likely outcomes, the *theoretical probability* of the event is *the ratio of the number of outcomes in the event to the total number of possible outcomes.*

The probability of an impossible event is 0; the probability of a certain event is 1. When the set of all possible outcomes is finite, the converses of these statements are also true.

Probabilities may also be found by experimental means. The *experimental probability* of an event is *the ratio of the number of times the event occurs to the total number of trials*. For example, if you toss a coin 100 times and it comes up heads 54 times, the experimental probability of heads is $\frac{54}{100}$, or 0.54.

The Law of Large Numbers states that the experimental probability of an event approaches the theoretical probability as the number of trials becomes arbitrarily large.

In the above example, as the number of coin flips increases, the experimental probability of heads will approach the theoretical probability, 0.5.

Permutations and Combinations  S-CP.B.9

LESSONS 19.2 and 19.3

Combinatorics is the branch of mathematics that deals with arranging and counting finite collections of items.

One of the earliest known uses of combinatorial reasoning is in a medical text from India that dates from the 6th century B.C.E.

The author asserts that six basic tastes—salty, sour, bitter, sweet, hot, and astringent—may be combined to form 63 different taste combinations (6 individual tastes, 15 combinations of two tastes, 20 combinations of three tastes, 15 combinations of four tastes, 6 combinations of five tastes, and 1 combination using all six tastes). This is an example of a combination.

A *combination* is *a grouping of items in which the order does not matter*.

In a permutation, the order of the items does matter.

For a permutation of n items taken r items at a time $\left({}_nP_r\right)$, there are

n choices for the 1st item;

$n - 1$ choices for the 2nd item;

$n - 2$ choices for the 3rd item ; and

$n - (r + 1)$ choices for the last item.

The total number of permutations is the product $n(n-1)(n-2)\ldots\left(n-(r+1)\right)$, or $\frac{n!}{(n-r)!}$.

Consider permutations of 4 numbers taken 3 at a time, shown in the array below. Each row shows six distinct permutations that are equivalent combinations.

123	132	213	231	312	321
124	142	214	241	412	421
134	143	314	341	413	431
234	243	324	342	423	432

In general, for a combination of n items taken r at a time $\left({}_nC_r\right)$, each combination appears $r!$ times in the corresponding list of permutations. In other words, $\left({}_nC_r\right) = \frac{{}_nP_r}{r!} = \frac{n!}{r!(n-r)!}$.

Independent and Dependent Events

S-CP.A.2

LESSONS 20.2 and 20.3

Two events are *independent* if *the occurrence of one does not affect the probability of the other.*

If A and B are independent, then $P(A \text{ and } B)$, also written $P(A \cap B)$, is $P(A) \cdot P(B)$.

More generally, events $A_1, A_2, \ldots, A_n$ are mutually independent if the occurrence of any one does not affect the probability of any other. Then,

$$P(A_1 \cap A_2 \cap \ldots A_n) = P(A_1) \cdot P(A_2) \cdot \ldots \cdot P(A_n).$$

Mutually exclusive events cannot occur in the same trial.

For example, a coin cannot simultaneously show heads and tails.

If A and B are mutually exclusive, then $P(A \text{ or } B)$, also written $P(A \cup B)$, is $P(A) + P(B)$.

This addition rule is generally used when finding probability for a single trial, while the multiplication rule for independent events is usually applied to two or more separate trials, performed either simultaneously or in succession.

If all possible outcomes of an experiment can be expressed as numbers, then the *probability distribution* of the experiment is *a function that pairs each outcome with its probability.*

For example, the probability distribution for rolling a number cube is $P(X) = \frac{1}{6}$, where the input X may be the outcome 1, 2, 3, 4, 5, or 6.

Probability distributions obey all the rules of probability.

That is, for any X, $0 \leq P(X) \leq 1$ and the sum of all the probabilities $P(X)$ over all possible values of X is 1.

If X can take the values $x_1, x_2, \ldots, x_n$ and the corresponding probabilities are $p_1, p_2, \ldots, p_n$, then the expected value for the experiment is $x_1p_1 + x_2p_2 + \ldots + x_np_n$.

The expected value for rolling a number cube is

$$1\left(\frac{1}{6}\right) + 2\left(\frac{1}{6}\right) + 3\left(\frac{1}{6}\right) + 4\left(\frac{1}{6}\right) + 5\left(\frac{1}{6}\right) + 6\left(\frac{1}{6}\right) = \frac{21}{6} = 3.5.$$

The expected value, 3.5, is the average outcome over a large number of trials.

In this sense, it is the "typical" value you expect to roll.

As this example shows, the expected value need not be one of the possible outcomes of the experiment.

Probability

MATH IN CAREERS

Unit Activity Preview

After completing this unit, students will complete a Math in Careers task by tracking the percentages of a population that are afflicted by infections. Critical skills include modeling real-world situations and applying knowledge of overlapping events.

For more information about careers in mathematics as well as various mathematics appreciation topics, visit The American Mathematical Society at http://www.ams.org.

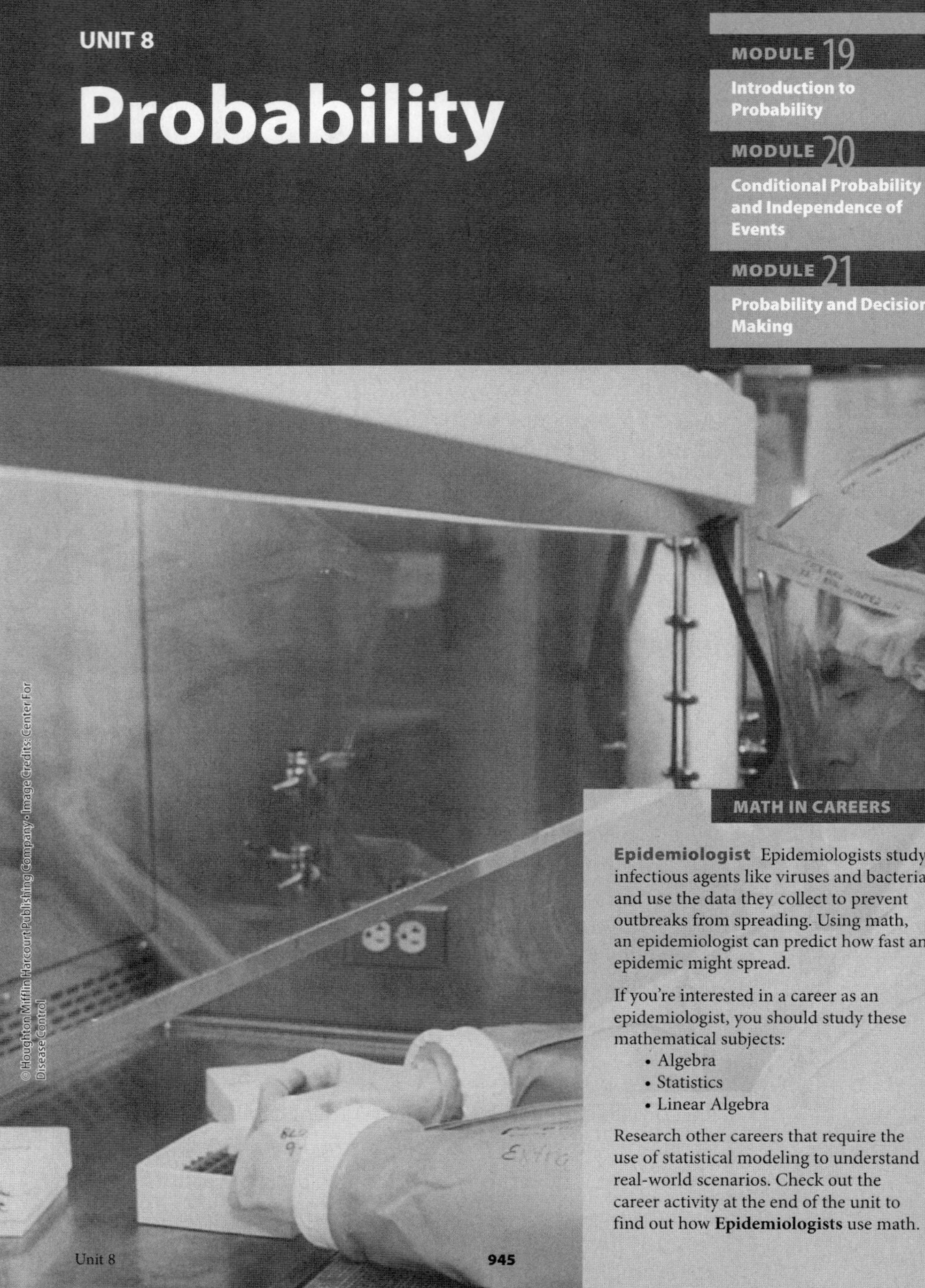

UNIT 8
Probability
MODULE 19
Introduction to Probability
MODULE 20
Conditional Probability and Independence of Events
MODULE 21
Probability and Decision Making
MATH IN CAREERS
Epidemiologist Epidemiologists study infectious agents like viruses and bacteria and use the data they collect to prevent outbreaks from spreading. Using math, an epidemiologist can predict how fast an epidemic might spread.
If you're interested in a career as an epidemiologist, you should study these mathematical subjects:
• Algebra
• Statistics
• Linear Algebra
Research other careers that require the use of statistical modeling to understand real-world scenarios. Check out the career activity at the end of the unit to find out how Epidemiologists use math.
© Houghton Mifflin Harcourt Publishing Company • Image Credits: Center For Disease Control
Unit 8
945

TRACKING YOUR LEARNING PROGRESSION

Before	In this Unit	After
Students understand: • defining trigonometric functions with the unit circle • angles of rotation and radian measure • evaluating trigonometric functions • transformations of the graphs of trigonometric functions	Students will learn about: • probability and set theory • permutations and combinations • independent and dependent events • using probability to make fair decisions	Students will study: • statistics • shape, center, and spread • confidence intervals and margins of error

Reading Start-Up

Visualize Vocabulary

Match the review words to their descriptions to complete the chart.

Word	Description
geometric probability	The use of geometric measures to represent probability
sample space	All possible outcomes of an experiment
event	Any set of outcomes
outcome	A result of an experiment

Vocabulary

Review Words

- ✔ event (*evento*)
- ✔ geometric probability (*probabilidad geométrica*)
- ✔ outcome (*resultado*)
- ✔ sample space (*muestra de espacio*)

Preview Words

combination (*combinación*)
complement (*complementar*)
conditional probability (*probabilidad condicional*)
dependent events (*eventos dependientes*)
element (*elemento*)
empty set (*conjunto vacío*)
factorial (*factorial*)
independent events (*eventos independientes*)
intersection (*intersección*)
permutation (*permutación*)
set (*conjunto*)
subset (*subconjunto*)
union (*unión*)

Understand Vocabulary

Complete the sentences using the preview words.

1. The empty set contains no elements.
2. If the occurrence of one event does not affect the occurrence of another event, then the events are called independent events.
3. A(n) permutation is a group of objects in a particular order.
4. To find the factorial of a positive integer, find the product of the number and all of the positive integers less than the number.

Active Reading

Four-Corner Fold Before beginning the unit, create a four-corner fold for each module. Label each flap with lesson titles from the module. As you study each lesson, write important ideas such as vocabulary, diagrams, and formulas under the appropriate flap. Refer to your layered books as you complete exercises.

Reading Start Up

Have students complete the activities on this page by working alone or with others.

VISUALIZE VOCABULARY

The definition chart helps students review vocabulary associated with probability. If time allows, ask students to provide examples for each term.

UNDERSTAND VOCABULARY

Use the following explanations to help students learn the preview words.

A **set** is a collection of numbers or objects. Each member of the set is an **element**. The **empty set** contains no elements. A **subset** contains elements of a larger set. The **intersection** of two sets contains the elements common to both sets. The **union** of two sets contains all the elements of both sets. The **complement** of an event is all the outcomes in the sample space that are not in the event.

ACTIVE READING

Students can use these reading and note-taking strategies to help them organize and understand the new concepts and vocabulary. Encourage students to include examples to support the vocabulary on the key-term fold. Emphasize the importance to students of continuing to seek as much vocabulary clarification as needed throughout the unit to help them succeed in understanding problem contexts and applications.

ADDITIONAL RESOURCES

Differentiated Instruction

- Reading Strategies EL

Introduction to Probability

ESSENTIAL QUESTION:

Answer: Probability is useful for analyzing the likelihood that a particular event will happen; for example, that a die will show 6 on a throw, or that it will rain.

PROFESSIONAL DEVELOPMENT VIDEO

Professional Development Video

Author Matt Larson models successful teaching practices in an actual high-school classroom.

Professional Development
my.hrw.com

MODULE 19

Introduction to Probability

Essential Question: How can you use probability to solve real-world problems?

REAL WORLD VIDEO
Check out how principles of probability are used to derive and interpret baseball players' statistics.

MODULE PERFORMANCE TASK PREVIEW

Baseball Probability

In this module, you will use concepts of probability to determine the chances of various outcomes for a baseball player at bat. To successfully complete this task, you'll need to calculate a theoretical probability for a real-world situation. Batter up!

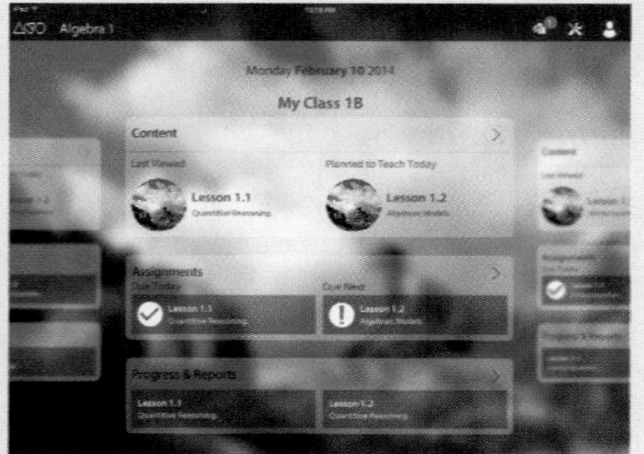

DIGITAL TEACHER EDITION

Access a full suite of teaching resources when and where you need them:

- Access content online or offline
- Customize lessons to share with your class
- Communicate with your students in real-time
- View student grades and data instantly to target your instruction where it is needed most

PERSONAL MATH TRAINER

Assessment and Intervention

Assign automatically graded homework, quizzes, tests, and intervention activities. Prepare your students with updated, Common Core-aligned practice tests.

Complete these exercises to review skills you will need for this module.

Probability of Simple Events

- Online Homework
- Hints and Help
- Extra Practice

Example 1 Find the probability of rolling a 4 when using a normal six-sided die with each side having equal probability.

Each of the six faces has equal probability, so the probability of any face being rolled is $\frac{1}{6}$.

There is only one face with a four on it, so the probability of rolling a four is also $\frac{1}{6}$.

Find each probability.

1. The probability of flipping a coin and getting a heads, given that the probability of getting a tails is the same, and there is no chance that the coin lands on its side. $\frac{1}{2}$
2. The probability of drawing a Jack of Hearts from a 52-card deck given the deck is properly shuffled. $\frac{1}{52}$
3. The probability of any particular day being Sunday. $\frac{1}{7}$

Probability of Compound Events

Example 2 Find the probability of drawing a red card or a black card when the probability of either is $\frac{1}{4}$ and you only draw one card.

Only one card is drawn and either card has a $\frac{1}{4}$ probability, so the probability of drawing one or the other is the sum of their probabilities.

Probability of drawing a red card or black card $\frac{1}{4} + \frac{1}{4} = \frac{1}{2}$.

Find each probability.

4. The probability of rolling a twelve-sided die and getting a 4 or a 6 given the probability of getting a 4 is $\frac{1}{12}$ and is equal to the probability of getting a 6. $\frac{1}{6}$
5. The probability of pulling a red or a blue marble from a jar given the probability of drawing a red marble is $\frac{1}{4}$ and the probability of pulling a blue marble is $\frac{1}{2}$ and you only pull one marble. $\frac{3}{4}$

Response to Intervention			Differentiated Instruction
Tier 1 Lesson Intervention Worksheets	**Tier 2** Strategic Intervention Skills Intervention Worksheets	**Tier 3** Intensive Intervention Worksheets available online	
Reteach 19.1 Reteach 19.2 Reteach 19.3 Reteach 19.4	51 Probability of Compound Events 52 Probability of Simple Events	Building Block Skills 6, 12, 37, 39, 65, 72, 82, 86, 95, 112	Challenge worksheets Extend the Math Lesson Activities in TE

Are You Ready?

ASSESS READINESS

Use the assessment on this page to determine if students need strategic or intensive intervention for the module's prerequisite skills.

ASSESSMENT AND INTERVENTION

Personal Math Trainer

RtI Response to Intervention TIER 1, TIER 2, TIER 3 SKILLS

Personal Math Trainer will automatically create a standards-based, personalized intervention assignment for your students, targeting each student's individual needs!

ADDITIONAL RESOURCES

See the table below for a full list of intervention resources available for this module.

Response to Intervention Resources also includes:

- Tier 2 Skill Pre-Tests for each Module
- Tier 2 Skill Post-Tests for each skill

LESSON 19.1

Probability and Set Theory

Common Core Math Standards

The student is expected to:

 **S-CP.A.1**

Describe events as subsets of a sample space (the set of outcomes) using characteristics ... of the outcomes, or as unions, intersections, or complements of other events ("or," "and," "not").

Mathematical Practices

 **MP.6 Precision**

Language Objective

Explain to a partner how to find the probability of rolling a certain number on a number cube and how to find its complement.

ENGAGE

Essential Question: How are sets and their relationships used to calculate probabilities?

To calculate the probability of an event, you need to know the number of items in the set of outcomes for that event, as well as the number of items in the set of all possible outcomes. The theoretical probability of the event is the ratio of the two numbers.

PREVIEW: LESSON PERFORMANCE TASK

View the Engage section online. Discuss the photograph. Ask students to describe math problems that could be illustrated by the two dogs. Then preview the Lesson Performance Task.

Name ________ Class ________ Date ________

19.1 Probability and Set Theory

Essential Question: How are sets and their relationships used to calculate probabilities?

Resource Locker

Explore Working with Sets

A **set** is a well-defined collection of distinct objects. Each object in a set is called an **element** of the set. A set is often denoted by writing the elements in braces.

The set with no elements is the **empty set**, denoted by $\varnothing$ or $\{\ \}$.

The set of all elements under consideration is the **universal set**, denoted by U.

Identifying the number of elements in a set is important for calculating probabilities.

(A) Use set notation to identify each set described in the table and identify the number of elements in each set.

Set	Set Notation	Number of Elements in the Set
Set A is the set of prime numbers less than 10.	$A = \{2, 3, 5, 7\}$	$n(A) = 4$
Set B is the set of even natural numbers less than 10.	$B = \{2, 4, 6, 8\}$	$n(B) = 4$
Set C is the set of natural numbers less than 10 that are multiple of 4.	$C = \{4, 8\}$	$n(C) = 2$
The universal set is all natural numbers less than 10.	$U = \{1, 2, 3, 4, 5, 6, 7, 8, 9\}$	$n(U) = 9$

HARDCOVER PAGES 949–960

Watch for the hardcover student edition page numbers for this lesson.

The following table identifies terms used to describe relationships among sets. Use sets A, B, C, and U from above. Complete the Example column of the table by drawing the Venn diagrams that include the elements of their associated sets.

Term	Notation	Venn Diagram	Example
Set *C* is a **subset** of set *B* if every element of *C* is also an element of *B*.	$C \subset B$	U; B; C	1,3,5,7,9; 4,8; 2,6
The **intersection** of sets *A* and *B* is the set of all elements that are in both *A and B*.	$A \cap B$	U; A; B	1,9; 4,6,8; 2; 3,5,7
The **union** of sets *A* and *B* is the set of all elements that are in *A or B*.	$A \cup B$	U; A; B	1,9; 3,5,7; 2; 4,6,8
The **complement** of set *A* is the set of all elements in the universal set *U* that are *not* in *A*.	A^C or $\sim A$	U; A	1,4,6,8,9; 2,3,5,7

(B) Since C is a subset of B, then every element of set C, which includes the numbers 4 and 8, is located in oval C. Set B includes the elements of C as well as the additional elements 2 and 6, which are located in oval B outside of oval C. The universal set includes the elements of sets B and C as well as the additional elements 1, 3, 5, 7, and 9, which are located in region U outside of ovals B and C.

(C) In the first row of the table, draw the corresponding Venn diagram that includes the elements of B, C, and U.

See first row of table.

(D) To determine the intersection of A and B, first define the elements of set A and set B separately, then identify all the elements found in both sets A *and* B.

$A = \{2, 3, 5, 7\}$

$B = \{2, 4, 6, 8\}$

$A \cap B = \{2\}$

PROFESSIONAL DEVELOPMENT

Math Background

A German mathematician, Georg Cantor (1845–1918), is considered to be the father of set theory. Cantor discovered that the rational numbers are countable but the real numbers are uncountable.

Two French mathematicians, Blaise Pascal (1623–1662) and Pierre de Fermat (1601–1665), are considered to be the founders of probability theory. The roots of probability theory lie in the letters they exchanged analyzing games of chance.

EXPLORE

Working with Sets

INTEGRATE TECHNOLOGY

Students have the option of doing the Explore activity either in the book or online.

INTEGRATE MATHEMATICAL PRACTICES

Focus on Modeling

MP.4 Discuss how the Venn diagrams provide pictures of set relationships to help students understand the terminology. Encourage students to practice drawing Venn diagrams to use when investigating set theory. For example, discuss how a Venn diagram can make it easier to identify the complement of an intersection.

AVOID COMMON ERRORS

Students may assume that a set that contains only 0 is the same as the empty set. Contrast the empty set, { }, with the set that contains only 0, {0}.

QUESTIONING STRATEGIES

? What word corresponds to the intersection of two sets? Is it *union*? Explain. ***And*** **means the elements are in both sets, which corresponds to the intersection.** ***Or*** **means the elements can be in either set, which corresponds to the union.**

? How is an intersection different from a subset? **The intersection consists of the elements two sets have in common, while all of the elements of a subset lie within the set of which it is a subset.**

? How do you know when sets overlap? **Sets will overlap when they have some elements in common.**

EXPLAIN 1

Calculating Theoretical Probabilities

INTEGRATE MATHEMATICAL PRACTICES

Focus on Math Connections

MP.1 Discuss the set notation used to define theoretical probability. Connect the notation to a word description of the probability ratio, such as, *the ratio of favorable outcomes in sample space to total number of outcomes in sample space.*

AVOID COMMON ERRORS

Students may have difficulty identifying an event based on a union or intersection. Suggest that students draw Venn diagrams to model the experiment. They can begin by defining each set and then create the Venn diagram to show where the sets overlap.

(E) In the second row of the table, draw the Venn Diagram for $A \cap B$ that includes the elements of A, B, and U and the shaded intersection region.

See second row of table.

(F) To determine the union of sets A and B, identify all the elements found in both sets A *or* B by combining all the elements of the two sets into the union set.

$A \cap B = \{2, 3, 4, 5, 6, 7, 8\}$

(G) In the third row of the table, draw the Venn Diagram for $A \cup B$ that includes the elements of A, B, and U and the shaded union region.

See third row of table.

(H) To determine the complement of set A, first identify the elements of set A and universal set U separately, then identify all the elements in the universal set that are *not* in set A.

$A = \{2, 3, 5, 7\}$

$U = \{1, 2, 3, 4, 5, 6, 7, 8, 9\}$

$A^C = \{1, 4, 6, 8, 9\}$

(I) In the fourth row of the table, draw the Venn Diagram for $A \cap B$ that includes the elements of A and U and the shaded region that represents the complement of A.

See fourth row of table.

Reflect

1. **Draw Conclusions** Do sets always have an intersection that is not the empty set? Provide an example to support your conclusion.

   No. Using the example sets above, $A \cap C = \varnothing$ because they do not have any elements in common.

Explain 1 Calculating Theoretical Probabilities

A *probability experiment* is an activity involving chance. Each repetition of the experiment is called a *trial* and each possible result of the experiment is termed an *outcome*. A set of outcomes is known as an *event* and the set of all possible outcomes is called the *sample space*.

The measure of how likely an event is to occur when all the outcomes of an experiment are equally likely is the **theoretical probability**. For an event A in the sample space S, the probability that an event A will occur is given by

$$P(A) = \frac{\text{number of outcomes for the event}}{\text{number of outcomes in the sample space}} = \frac{n(A)}{n(S)}.$$

COLLABORATIVE LEARNING

Small Group Activity

Ask each group to draw a spinner with 6 or 8 equal parts. Then ask them to use letters, colors, or numbers to distinguish each section of the spinner. Have them define two events based on the spinners. For example, if letters are used, the set of vowels and the set of letters in the word *math*. Ask students to find the probability of each event, their complements, their union, and their intersection. Have students share their work. Review which events have a probability of 1, which have a probability of 0, and why.

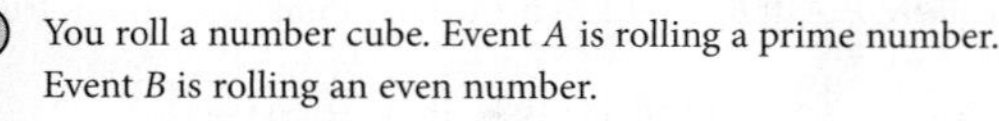

Example 1 **Calculate $P(A)$, $P(A \cup B)$, $P(A \cap B)$, and $P(A^C)$ for each scenario.**

(A) You roll a number cube. Event A is rolling a prime number. Event B is rolling an even number.

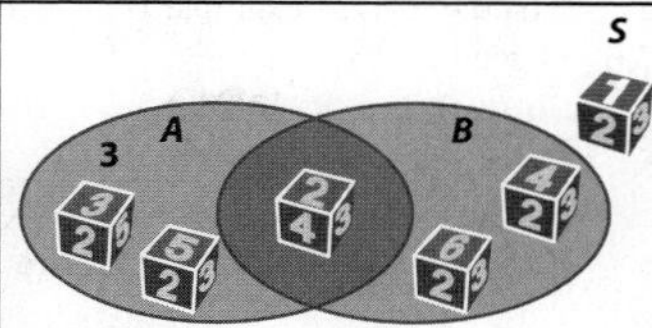

$S = \{1, 2, 3, 4, 5, 6\}$, So $n(S) = 6$. $A = \{2, 3, 5\}$, so $n(A) = 3$.

So, $P(A) = \frac{n(A)}{n(S)} = \frac{3}{6} = \frac{1}{2}$.

$A \cup B = \{2, 3, 4, 5, 6\}$, so $n(A \cup B) = 5$. So, $P(A \cup B) = \frac{n(A \cup B)}{n(S)} = \frac{5}{6}$.

$A \cap B = \{2\}$, so $n(A \cap B) = 1$. So, $P(A \cap B) = \frac{n(A \cap B)}{n(S)} = \frac{1}{6}$

$A^C = \{1, 4, 6\}$, so $n(A^C) = 3$. So, $P(A^C) = \frac{n(A^C)}{n(S)} = \frac{3}{6} = \frac{1}{2}$

(B) Your grocery basket contains one bag of each of the following items: oranges, green apples, green grapes, green broccoli, white cauliflower, orange carrots, and green spinach. You are getting ready to transfer your items from your cart to the conveyer belt for check-out. Event A is picking a bag containing a vegetable first. Event B is picking a bag containing a green food first. All bags have an equal chance of being picked first.

$S = \{$orange, apple, grape, broccoli, cauliflower, carrot, spinach$\}$, so $n(S) = $ **7**

$A = \{$broccoli, cauliflower, **carrot**, **spinach**$\}$, so $n(A) = $ **4**. So $P(A) = \frac{n(\mathbf{A})}{n(\mathbf{S})} = \frac{\mathbf{4}}{\mathbf{7}}$.

$A \cup B = \{$broccoli, **cauliflower**, **carrot**, **spinach**, **apple**, grape$\}$ so $n(A \cup B) = $ **6**

$P(A \cup B) = \frac{\mathbf{n}(\mathbf{A} \cup \mathbf{B})}{\mathbf{n}(\mathbf{S})} = \frac{\mathbf{6}}{\mathbf{7}}$

$A \cap B = \{$**broccoli**, **spinach**$\}$, so $n(A \cap B) = $ **2**

$P(A \cap B) = \frac{\mathbf{n}(\mathbf{A} \cap \mathbf{B})}{\mathbf{n}(\mathbf{S})} = \frac{\mathbf{2}}{\mathbf{7}}$

$P(\mathbf{A^c}) = \frac{\mathbf{n}(\mathbf{A^c})}{\mathbf{n}(\mathbf{S})} = \frac{\mathbf{3}}{\mathbf{7}}$

Order of objects in sets may vary.

QUESTIONING STRATEGIES

When you calculate the theoretical probabilities of events based on the same probability experiment, can the term in the denominator of the probability ratio change? Explain. **No, the term in the denominator corresponds to the sample space, which does not change.**

If a set has no elements, what is the probability of the event represented by the set? Explain. **0, because there are no outcomes in the sample space that correspond to the event**

If the elements of a set are the same as the elements of the sample space, what is the probability of the event represented by the set? Explain. **1, because the number of elements in the set is the same as the number of elements in the sample space**

DIFFERENTIATE INSTRUCTION

Manipulatives

Encourage students to design their own experiments to illustrate what they have learned about probability, such as calculating the complement of rolling a number with a number cube and then attempting to conform the calculation experimentally. Invite students to demonstrate their experiments before the class.

EXPLAIN 2

Using the Complement of an Event

AVOID COMMON ERRORS

Students may have difficulty understanding when to use the complement to find a probability. Point out that students may be able to find the probability directly but that the complement may provide a shortcut. Continue to remind students to create Venn diagrams to help them recognize relationships between sets.

QUESTIONING STRATEGIES

Why are there different equations that relate the probability of an event and its complement? **The three equations state the same relationship in different ways.**

Reflect

2. **Discussion** In Example 1B, which is more likely, $P(A \cup B)$ or $P(A \cap B)$? Do you think this result is true in general? Explain.
Since $P(A \cup B) = \frac{6}{7}$ is larger than $P(A \cap B) = \frac{2}{7}$, the union is more likely than the intersection. Yes, this is generally true since the union set includes all the elements from both events, whereas the intersection set contains only elements present in both sets. However, if $A = B$, then the probability of the union and intersection will be the same.

Your Turn

The numbers 1 through 30 are placed in a hat to determine the order in which students will give an oral report. Event A is being one of the first 10 students to give their report. Event B is picking a multiple of 6. If you pick first, calculate each of the indicated probabilities.

3. $P(A)$
$P(A) = \frac{n(A)}{n(S)} = \frac{10}{30} = \frac{1}{3}$

4. $P(A \cup B)$
$A \cup B = \{1, 2, 3, 4, 5, 6, 7, 8, 9, 10, 12, 18, 24, 30\}$; $P(A \cup B) = \frac{n(A \cup B)}{n(S)} = \frac{14}{30}$

5. $P(A \cap B)$
$A \cup B = \{6\}$; $P(A \cap B) = \frac{n(A \cap B)}{n(S)} = \frac{1}{30}$

6. $P(A^c)$
$A^c = \{11, 12, \ldots, 30\}$; $P(A^c) = \frac{n(A^c)}{n(S)} = \frac{20}{30} = \frac{2}{3}$

Explain 2 Using the Complement of an Event

You may have noticed in the previous examples that the probability of an event occurring and the probability of the event not occurring (i.e., the probability of the complement of the event) have a sum of 1. This relationship can be useful when it is more convenient to calculate the probability of the complement of an event.

Probabilities of an Event and Its Complement	
$P(A) + P(A^c) = 1$	The sum of the probability of an event and the probability of its complement is 1.
$P(A) = 1 - P(A^c)$	The probability of an event is 1 minus the probability of its complement.
$P(A^c) = 1 - P(A)$	The probability of the complement of an event is 1 minus the probability of the event.

LANGUAGE SUPPORT EL

Connect Vocabulary

Have students create a set of cards with diagrams to help them become familiar with the vocabulary introduced in this lesson. Help students connect the vocabulary to the notation used to represent a *set*, an *element*, the *universal set*, a *subset*, *union*, *intersection*, and *complement*. Have students use different colors to highlight and distinguish each relationship.

Example 2 Use the complement to calculate the indicated probabilities.

(A) You roll a blue number cube and a white number cube at the same time. What is the probability that you do not roll doubles?

Step 1 Define the events. Let A be that you do not roll doubles and A^c that you do roll doubles.

Step 2 Make a diagram. A two-way table is one helpful way to identify all the possible outcomes in the sample space.

White Number Cube \ Blue Number Cube	1	2	3	4	5	6
1	1–1	1–2	1–3	1–4	1–5	1–6
2	2–1	2–2	2–3	2–4	2–5	2–6
3	3–1	3–2	3–3	3–4	3–5	3–6
4	4–1	4–2	4–3	4–4	4–5	4–6
5	5–1	5–2	5–3	5–4	5–5	5–6
6	6–1	6–2	6–3	6–4	6–5	6–6

Step 3 Determine $P(A^c)$. Since there are fewer outcomes for rolling doubles, it is more convenient to determine the probability of rolling doubles, which is $P(A^c)$. To determine $n(A^c)$, draw a loop around the outcomes in the table that correspond to (A^c) and then calculate $P(A^c)$.

$$P(A^c) = \frac{n(A^c)}{n(S)} = \frac{6}{36} = \frac{1}{6}$$

Step 4 Determine $P(A)$. Use the relationship between the probability of an event and its complement to determine $P(A)$.

$$P(A) = 1 - P(A^c) = 1 - \frac{1}{6} = \frac{5}{6}$$

So, the probability of not rolling doubles is $\frac{5}{6}$.

(B) One pile of cards contains the numbers 2 through 6 in red hearts. A second pile of cards contains the numbers 4 through 8 in black spades. Each pile of cards has been randomly shuffled. If one card from each pile is chosen at the same time, what is the probability that the sum will be less than 12?

Step 1 Define the events. Let A be the event that the sum is less than 12 and A^c be the event that the sum is not less than 12.

Step 2 Make a diagram. Complete the table to show all the outcomes in the sample space.

Black Spades ♠ \ Red Hearts ♥	2	3	4	5	6
4	4+2	4+3	4+4	4+5	4+6
5	5+2	5+3	5+4	5+5	5+6
6	6+2	6+3	6+4	6+5	6+6
7	7+2	7+3	7+4	7+5	7+6
8	8+2	8+3	8+4	8+5	8+6

Step 3 Determine $P(A^c)$. Circle the outcomes in the table that correspond to A^c, then determine $P(A^c)$.

$$PA^c = \frac{n(A^c)}{n(S)} = \frac{6}{25}$$

Black Spades ♠ \ Red Hearts ♥	2	3	4	5	6
4	4+2	4+3	4+4	4+5	4+6
5	5+2	5+3	5+4	5+5	5+6
6	6+2	6+3	6+4	6+5	(6+6)
7	7+2	7+3	7+4	(7+5)	(7+6)
8	8+2	8+3	(8+4)	(8+5)	(8+6)

ELABORATE

AVOID COMMON ERRORS

Students may have trouble identifying some outcomes associated with an event. Encourage students to carefully identify all outcomes by using tables, lists, or diagrams. They can circle the outcomes of interest (often called the favorable outcomes) in the sample space.

QUESTIONING STRATEGIES

How does listing the elements in a set help you find the probability of an event associated with the set? **The probability is based on the number of elements in the set, so I can just count the elements for the numerator of the probability ratio.**

SUMMARIZE THE LESSON

How can you use set theory to help you calculate theoretical probabilities? **You can use the number of elements in a set to define theoretical probability: the theoretical probability that an event A will occur is given by $P(A) = \frac{n(A)}{n(S)}$, where S is the sample space.**

Step 4 Determine $P(A)$. Use the relationship between the probability of an event and its complement to determine $P(A^c)$.

$$P(A) = \boxed{1} - \boxed{P}\left(\boxed{A^c}\right) = \boxed{1} - \frac{\boxed{6}}{\boxed{25}} = \frac{\boxed{19}}{\boxed{25}}$$

So, the probability that the sum of the two cards is **less than 12** is $\frac{\boxed{19}}{\boxed{25}}$.

Reflect

7. Describe a different way to calculate the probability that the sum of the two cards will be less than 12.
Use the table to count the number of outcomes in event A instead of A^c, which is 19, then divide that by the total number of outcomes to get $\frac{19}{25}$.

Your Turn

One bag of marbles contains two red, one yellow, one green and one blue marble. Another bag contains one marble of each of the same four colors. One marble from each bag is chosen at the same time. Use the complement to calculate the indicated probabilities.

8. Probability of selecting two different colors
$P(A^c) = \frac{5}{20} = \frac{1}{4}$, so $P(A) = 1 - \frac{1}{4} = \frac{3}{4}$.

9. Probability of not selecting a yellow marble
$P(A^c) = \frac{8}{20} = \frac{2}{5}$, so $P(A) = 1 - \frac{2}{5} = \frac{3}{5}$.

Elaborate

10. Can a subset of A contain elements of A^C? Why or why not?
No. The elements of a subset are contained completely within the parent set A, whereas none of the elements of the complement of a set A are in set A by definition, and thus they cannot be in a subset of A.

11. For any set A, what does $A \cap \varnothing$ equal? What does $A \cap \varnothing$ equal? Explain.
The intersection of set A and the empty set is the empty set, $A \cap \varnothing = \varnothing$, since the two sets do not have any elements in common. The union of set A and the empty set is set A, $A \cup \varnothing = A$, since the elements of the union are the elements in set A or the empty set.

12. Essential Question Check-In How do the terms *set*, *element*, and *universal set* correlate to the terms used to calculate theoretical probability?
Possible answer: To calculate probability, you need to know the number of possible outcomes in the sample space, which is like determining the number of elements in the universal set. You also need to know the number of possible outcomes in the defined event, which is like determining the number of elements in the defined set.

Evaluate: Homework and Practice

- Online Homework
- Hints and Help
- Extra Practice

Set A is the set of factors of 12, set B is the set of even natural numbers less than 13, set C is the set of odd natural numbers less than 13, set D is the set of even natural numbers less than 7. The universal set for these questions is the set of natural numbers less than 13.

So $A = \{1, 2, 3, 4, 6, 12\}$, $B = \{2, 4, 6, 8, 10, 12\}$, $C = \{1, 3, 5, 7, 9, 11\}$, $D = \{2, 4, 6\}$, and $U = \{1, 2, 3, 4, 5, 6, 7, 8, 9, 10, 11, 12\}$. Answer each question.

1. Is $D \subset A$? Explain why or why not.
   Yes, because every element of D is also an element of A.

2. Is $B \subset A$? Explain why or why not.
   No, because there is at least one element of B that is not an element of A. For example, 8 is an element of B that is not an element of A.

3. What is $A \cap B$?
   $\{2, 4, 6, 12\}$

4. What is $A \cap C$?
   $\{1, 3\}$

5. What is $A \cup B$?
   $\{1, 2, 3, 4, 6, 8, 10, 12\}$

6. What is $A \cup C$?
   $\{1, 2, 3, 4, 5, 6, 7, 9, 11, 12\}$

7. What is A^C?
   $\{5, 7, 9, 10, 11\}$

8. What is B^C?
   $\{1, 3, 5, 7, 9, 11\}$

You have a set of 10 cards numbered 1 to 10. You choose a card at random. Event A is choosing a number less than 7. Event B is choosing an odd number. Calculate the probability.

9. $P(A)$
   The sample space $S = \{1, 2, 3, 4, 5, 6, 7, 8, 9, 10\}$;
   $A = \{1, 2, 3, 4, 5, 6\}$.
   $P(A) = \frac{n(A)}{n(S)} = \frac{6}{10} = \frac{3}{5}$

10. $P(B)$
    The sample space $S = \{1, 2, 3, 4, 5, 6, 7, 8, 9, 10\}$;
    $B = \{1, 3, 5, 7, 9\}$
    $P(B) = \frac{n(B)}{n(S)} = \frac{5}{10} = \frac{1}{2}$

11. $P(A \cup B)$
    The sample space $S = \{1, 2, 3, 4, 5, 6, 7, 8, 9, 10\}$;
    $A \cup B = \{1, 2, 3, 4, 5, 6, 7, 9\}$
    $P(A \cup B) = \frac{n(A \cup B)}{n(S)} = \frac{8}{10} = \frac{4}{5}$

12. $P(A \cap B)$
    The sample space $S = \{1, 2, 3, 4, 5, 6, 7, 8, 9, 10\}$;
    $A \cap B = \{1, 3, 5\}$
    $P(A \cap B) = \frac{n(A \cap B)}{n(S)} = \frac{3}{10}$

13. $P(A^C)$
    The sample space $S = \{1, 2, 3, 4, 5, 6, 7, 8, 9, 10\}$;
    $A^C = \{7, 8, 9, 10\}$
    $P(A^C) = \frac{n(A^C)}{n(S)} = \frac{4}{10} = \frac{2}{5}$

14. $P(B^C)$
    The sample space $S = \{1, 2, 3, 4, 5, 6, 7, 8, 9, 10\}$;
    $B^C = \{2, 4, 6, 8, 10\}$
    $P(B^C) = \frac{n(B^C)}{n(S)} = \frac{5}{10} = \frac{1}{2}$

Exercise	Depth of Knowledge (D.O.K.)	COMMON CORE Mathematical Practices
1–8	1 Recall of Information	MP.4 Modeling
9–14	1 Recall of Information	MP.2 Reasoning
15–20	2 Skills/Concepts	MP.2 Reasoning
21	3 Strategic Thinking	MP.6 Precision
22	3 Strategic Thinking	MP.4 Modeling
23–26	3 Strategic Thinking	MP.3 Logic
27	3 Strategic Thinking H.O.T.	MP.3 Logic

EVALUATE

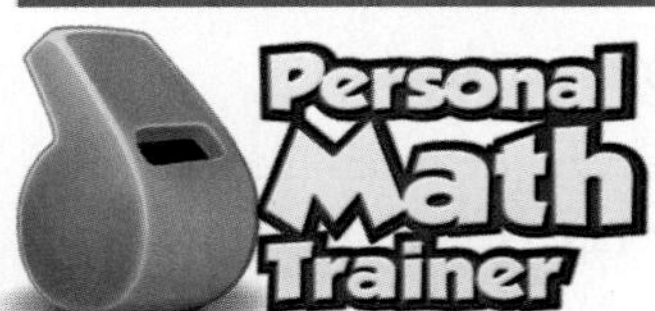

ASSIGNMENT GUIDE

Concepts and Skills	Practice
Explore Working with Sets	Exercises 1–8
Example 1 Calculating Theoretical Probabilities	Exercises 9–14, 22, 26, 29
Example 2 Using the Complement of an Event	Exercises 15–21, 23–25, 27–28

COMMUNICATING MATH

Discuss the importance of understanding the sample space. Encourage students to always list the members of the sample space before they find a probability. Discuss why this can help avoid errors, such as finding the probability of rolling a 2 with a number cube as $\frac{1}{5}$.

INTEGRATE MATHEMATICAL PRACTICES

Focus on Modeling

MP.4 Discuss when a Venn diagram might be useful in solving a probability problem, and when another method might be easier.

INTEGRATE MATHEMATICAL PRACTICES

Focus on Math Connections

MP.1 Review the connection between likelihood and probability with students. Discuss how this can be useful when solving problems. When students calculate the probability of an event, be sure they understand what this means in the context of the original problem. For example, students should recognize that an event with a probability of 0.9 is very likely to occur, while an event with a probability of 0.1 is unlikely to occur.

AVOID COMMON ERRORS

Students may not consider the sample space when finding probabilities. Suggest that they summarize the probability ratio using words before they compute the probability.

Use the complement of the event to find the probability.

15. You roll a 6-sided die. What is the probability that you do not roll a 2?

The probability of rolling a 2, $P(2)$, is $\frac{1}{6}$.

The probability of not rolling a 2 is $1 - P(2) = 1 - \frac{1}{6} = \frac{5}{6}$.

16. You choose a card at random from a standard deck of cards. What is the probability that you do not choose a red king?

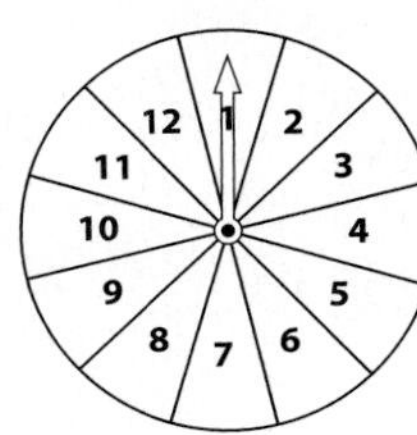

The probability of drawing a red king, $P(\text{red king})$, is $\frac{2}{52} = \frac{1}{26}$.

The probability of not drawing a red king is $1 - P(\text{red king}) = 1 - \frac{1}{26} = \frac{25}{26}$.

17. You spin the spinner shown. The spinner is divided into 12 congruent parts. What is the probability of not spinning a 2?

12, 1, 2, 3, 4, 5, 6, 7, 8, 9, 10, 11

The probability of spinning a 2, $P(2)$, is $\frac{2}{12} = \frac{1}{6}$

The probability of not spinning a 2 is $1 - P(2) = 1 - \frac{1}{6} = \frac{5}{6}$.

18. A bag contains 2 red, 5 blue, and 3 green balls. What is the probability of not choosing a red ball?

The probability of choosing a red ball, $P(\text{red ball})$, is $\frac{2}{10} = \frac{1}{5}$.

The probability of not choosing a red ball is $1 - P(\text{red ball}) = 1 - \frac{1}{5} = \frac{4}{5}$.

19. Cards numbered 1–12 are placed in a bag. What is the probability of not choosing a number less than 5?

The probability of choosing a number less than 5, $P(\text{less than } 5)$, is $\frac{4}{12} = \frac{1}{3}$.

The probability of not choosing a number less than 5 is $1 - P(\text{less than } 5) = 1 - \frac{1}{3} = \frac{2}{3}$.

20. Slips of paper numbered 1–20 are folded and placed into a hat, and then a slip of paper is drawn at random. What is the probability the slip drawn has a number which is not a multiple of 4 or 5?

Multiples of 4 up to 20: 4, 8, 16, 20

Multiples of 5 up to 20: 5, 10, 15, 20

The subset of multiples of 4 or 5 is $\{4, 5, 8, 10, 15, 16, 20\}$.

$P(\text{multiple of 4 or 5}) = \frac{7}{20}$

The probability of not selecting a card that is a multiple of 4 or 5 is $1 - P(\text{multiple of 4 or 5}) = 1 - \frac{7}{20} = \frac{13}{20}$.

$\frac{13}{20}$

Exercise	Depth of Knowledge (D.O.K.)	COMMON CORE Mathematical Practices
28	3 Strategic Thinking H.O.T.	MP.3 Logic
29	3 Strategic Thinking H.O.T.	MP.3 Logic

21. You are going to roll two number cubes, a white number cube and a red number cube, and find the sum of the two numbers that come up.

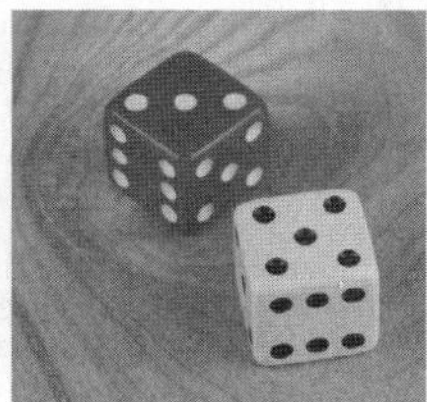

a. What is the probability that the sum will be 6?

There are 36 possible outcomes. There are 5 ways to get a sum of 6: $5 + 1, 4 + 2, 3 + 3, 2 + 4$, and $1 + 5$. So the probability of getting a sum of 6, $P(6)$, is $\frac{5}{36}$.

b. What is the probability that the sum will not be 6?

The probability that the sum will not be 6 is $P(\text{not } 6) = 1 - P(6) = 1 - \frac{5}{36} = \frac{31}{36}$.

22. You have cards with the letters A, B, C, D, E, F, G, H, I, J, K, L, M, N, O, P. Event U is choosing the cards A, B, C or D. Event V is choosing a vowel. Event W is choosing a letter in the word "APPLE". Find $P(U \cap V \cap W)$.

$U \cap V \cap W = \{A\}$; $P(U \cap V \cap W) = \frac{1}{16}$

A standard deck of cards has 13 cards (2, 3, 4, 5, 6, 7, 8, 9, 10, jack, queen, king, ace) in each of 4 suits (hearts, clubs, diamonds, spades). The hearts and diamonds cards are red. The clubs and spades cards are black. Answer each question.

23. You choose a card from a standard deck of cards at random. What is the probability that you do not choose an ace? Explain.

$\frac{12}{13}$; there are 4 aces in the 52-card deck, so $P(\text{ace}) = \frac{4}{52} = \frac{1}{13}$. This means $P(\text{not ace}) = 1 - \frac{1}{13} = \frac{12}{13}$.

24. You choose a card from a standard deck of cards at random. What is the probability that you do not choose a club? Explain.

$\frac{3}{4}$; there are 13 clubs in the 52-card deck, so $P(\text{club}) = \frac{13}{52} = \frac{1}{4}$. This means $P(\text{not club}) = 1 - \frac{1}{4} = \frac{3}{4}$.

25. You choose a card from a standard deck of cards at random. Event A is choosing a red card. Event B is choosing an even number. Event C is choosing a black card. Find $P(A \cap B \cap C)$. Explain.

$A \cap B \cap C = \emptyset$ because you can never draw a card that is both red and black. Therefore, $P(A \cap B \cap C) = 0$.

VISUAL CUES

When students create Venn diagrams to model a sample space and sets, caution them to be sure that an element is not used more than once on the diagram. For example, have students check that a number does not appear both in Set A and in its intersection with Set B.

JOURNAL

Have students write and solve their own probability problems. Remind students to use set notation in their solutions to the problems.

26. You are selecting a card from a standard deck of cards. Match each event with the correct probability. Indicate a match by writing the letter of the event on the line in front of the corresponding probability.

A. Picking a card that is both red and a heart. **B** $\frac{4}{13}$

B. Picking a card that is a heart and an ace. **A** $\frac{1}{4}$

C. Picking a card that is not a heart and not an ace. **C** $\frac{51}{52}$

$P(\text{red} \cap \text{heart}) = \frac{n(\text{red} \cap \text{heart})}{n(\text{deck})} = \frac{13}{52} = \frac{1}{4}$

$P(\text{heart} \cap \text{ace}) = \frac{n(\text{heart} \cap \text{ace})}{n(\text{deck})} = \frac{1}{52}$

$P(\text{not heart} \cap \text{not ace}) = 1 - P(\text{heart} \cap \text{ace}) = 1 - \frac{1}{52} = \frac{51}{52}$; **the only card that is both a heart and an ace is the ace of hearts, so there are 51 cards in the event** $(\text{not heart}) \cap (\text{not ace})$.

H.O.T. Focus on Higher Order Thinking

27. Critique Reasoning A bag contains white tiles, black tiles, and gray tiles. Someone is going to choose a tile at random. $P(W)$, the probability of choosing a white tile, is $\frac{1}{4}$. A student claims that the probability of choosing a black tile, $P(B)$, is $\frac{3}{4}$ since $P(B) = 1 - P(W) = 1 - \frac{1}{4} = \frac{3}{4}$. Do you agree? Explain.

No; choosing a black tile is not the complement of choosing a white tile since the bag also contains gray tiles. It is not possible to calculate $P(B)$ from the given information.

28. Communicate Mathematical Ideas A bag contains 5 red marbles and 10 blue marbles. You are going to choose a marble at random. Event A is choosing a red marble. Event B is choosing a blue marble. What is $P(A \cap B)$? Explain.

0; $A \cap B = \emptyset$ since a marble cannot be both red and blue. So $P(A \cap B) = 0$.

29. Critical Thinking Jeffery states that for a sample space S where all outcomes are equally likely, $0 \leq P(A) \leq 1$ for any subset A of S. Create an argument that will justify his statement or state a counterexample.

Assume A is a subset of S. Then $0 \leq n(A) \leq n(S)$. For example, if S has 10 elements, the number of elements of A is greater than or equal to 0 and less than or equal to 10. No subset of S can have fewer than 0 elements or more than 10 elements. So $0 \leq \frac{n(A)}{n(S)} \leq 1$. When all the outcomes are equally likely, $P(A) = \frac{n(A)}{n(S)}$. Therefore $0 \leq P(A) \leq 1$.

Lesson Performance Task

Is 5 odd or even? Odd, of course. The set of odd numbers is precisely defined, and you can ell at once whether a number is odd or even. In mathematics, a number either belongs or loesn't belong to a set.

1. In the real world, things aren't always so clear. The challenge of classifying dogs is not by whether they're "odd" or "even" but whether they're "big" or "not big." A 250-pound dog is definitely big. Let dogs like that be assigned a "degree of membership" (a measure of how closely they belong to the category) of 1.0. A 5-pound dog is definitely "not big." Let dogs like that be assigned a degree of membership of zero. Other dogs fall somewhere between the two degrees. Copy and complete the graph that's been started here.

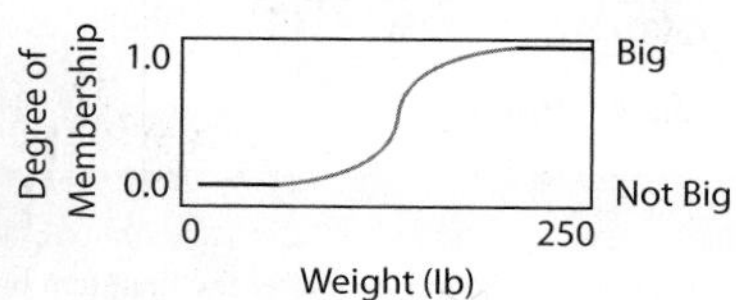

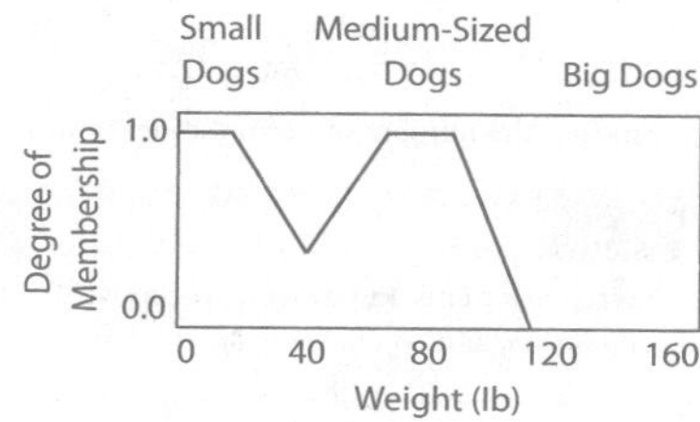

. In 1965, mathematician Lofti Zadeh came up with an idea he called "fuzzy" sets to deal with sets in which membership is not clearly defined. The graph shown here shows three fuzzy sets on the same axes—small dogs, medium-size dogs, and big dogs. Copy the graph and indicate on it each of the following:

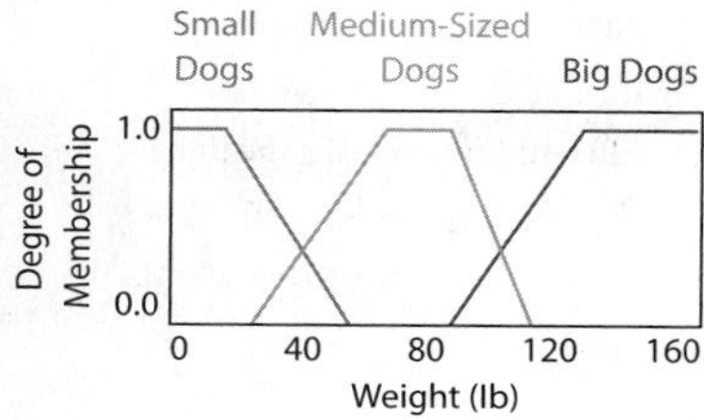

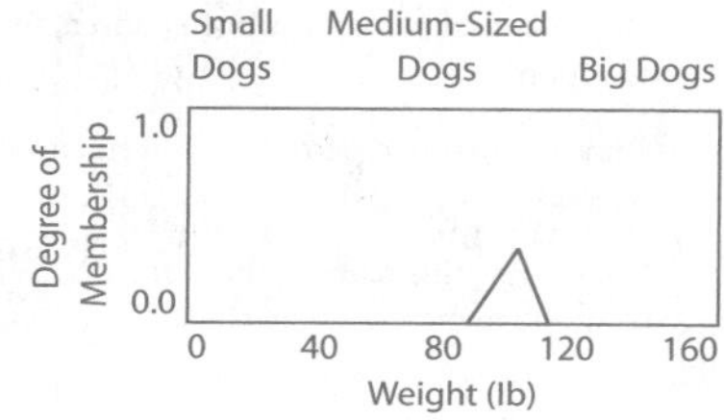

a. the union of "small dogs" and "medium-sized dogs"

b. the intersection of "medium-sized dogs" and "big dogs"

c. the complement of "small dogs"

. Bowzer has a small-dog degree of membership of 0.7 and a medium-size-dog degree of membership of 0.3.

a. What is the degree to which Bowzer belongs to both sets? **0.3**

b. What is the degree to which Bowzer belongs to either the small-dog set or the medium-sized-dog set? **0.7**

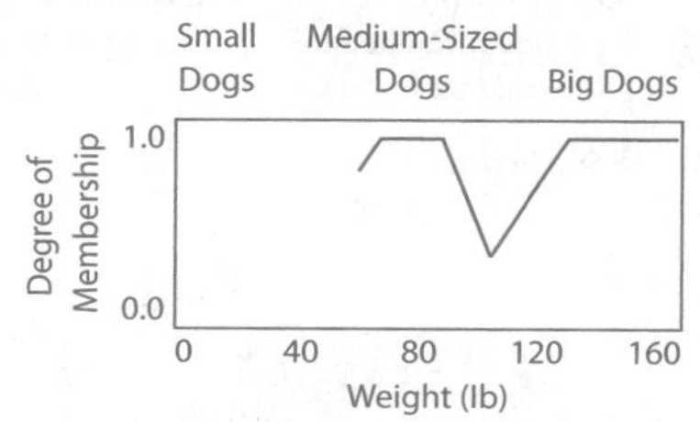

EXTENSION ACTIVITY

Have students draw graphs showing fuzzy sets ranging from cold to hot. (Three sets could show *cold*, *warm*, and *hot*. Four sets could show *cold*, *cool*, *warm*, and *hot*. However, leave the choice of adjectives and the number of sets to students.) The vertical axis should record degrees of membership from 0 to 1. The horizontal axis should show either Fahrenheit or Celsius temperatures. Encourage students to be creative with their graphs, for example, by using colors to distinguish sets from one another. Students should write and answer at least three questions involving unions, intersections, and complements of the sets they have graphed.

INTEGRATE MATHEMATICAL PRACTICES

Focus on Reasoning

MP.2 Call attention to the point in the Lesson Performance Task graph where the green medium-sized dog line and the blue big-dog line intersect. Ask students to give as much information as they can about that point. **Sample answer: The point represents a weight of around 100 pounds and a degree of membership of around 0.3. The point represents the highest degree of membership that a dog of around 100 pounds can obtain simultaneously in both the medium-sized and big-weight categories.**

INTEGRATE MATHEMATICAL PRACTICES

Focus on Critical Thinking

MP.3 Arf has a small-dog degree of membership of x and a medium-sized dog degree of membership of y. Is $x > y$, $x < y$, or does the relationship between x and y depend on Arf's weight? Explain. **The relationship depends on Arf's weight. The red and green graphs intersect at about 40 pounds. If Arf weighs less than 40 pounds, $x > y$. If Arf weighs more than 40 pounds, $x < y$. If Arf weighs 40 pounds, $x = y$.**

Scoring Rubric

2 points: The student's answer is an accurate and complete execution of the task or tasks.

1 point: The student's answer contains attributes of an appropriate response but is flawed.

0 points: The student's answer contains no attributes of an appropriate response.

LESSON 19.2

Permutations and Probability

Common Core Math Standards

The student is expected to:

S-CP.B.9(+)

Use permutations and combinations to compute probabilities of compound events and solve problems.

Mathematical Practices

MP.7 Using Structure

Language Objective

Give an example of a permutation to a partner and explain how you know it is a permutation.

ENGAGE

Essential Question: When are permutations useful in calculating probability?

Permutations are selections of groups of objects in which order is important. So, permutations are used to find the probability of a group of objects being selected in a particular order.

PREVIEW: LESSON PERFORMANCE TASK

View the Engage section online. Discuss the photograph, asking students what it might have to do with probability. Then preview the Lesson Performance Task.

Name ______________ Class ______________ Date ______________

19.2 Permutations and Probability

Essential Question: When listing or choosing a set of objects, when does the order of the objects matter?

Resource Locker

Explore Finding the Number of Permutations

A **permutation** is a selection of a group of objects in which order is important. For example, there are 6 permutations of the letters A, B, and C.

ABC	ACB	BAC	BCA	CAB	CBA

You can find the number of permutations with the **Fundamental Counting Principle**.

Fundamental Counting Principle

If there are n items and a_1 ways to choose the first item, a_2 ways to select the second item after the first item has been chosen, and so on, there are $a_1 \times a_2 \times \ldots \times a_n$ ways to choose n items.

There are 7 members in a club. Each year the club elects a president, a vice president, and a treasurer.

(A) What is the number of permutations of all 7 members of the club?

There are __7__ different ways to make the first selection.

Once the first person has been chosen, there are __6__ different ways to make the second selection.

Once the first two people have been chosen, there are __5__ different ways to make the third selection.

Continuing this pattern, there are __$7 \times 6 \times 5 \times 4 \times 3 \times 2 \times 1 = 5040$__ permutations of all the members of the club.

(B) The club is holding elections for a president, a vice president, and a treasurer. How many different ways can these positions be filled?

There are __7__ different ways the position of president can be filled.

Once the president has been chosen, there are __6__ different ways the position of vice president can be filled. Once the president and vice president have been chosen, there are __5__ different ways the position of treasurer can be filled.

So, there are __$7 \times 6 \times 5 \times = 210$__ different ways that the positions can be filled.

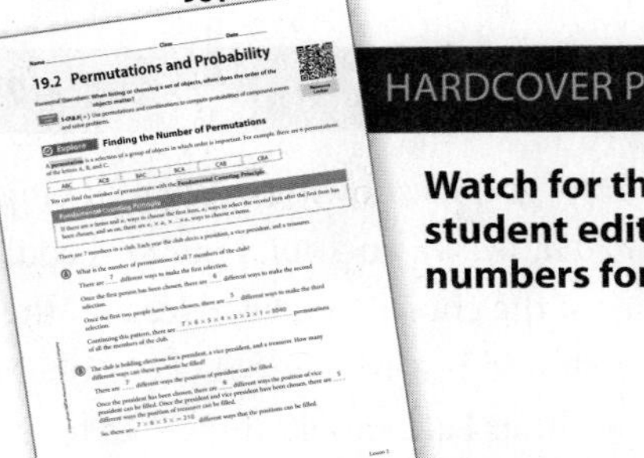

HARDCOVER PAGES 961–972

Watch for the hardcover student edition page numbers for this lesson.

(C) What is the number of permutations of the members of the club who were not elected as officers?

After the officers have been elected, there are 4 members remaining. So there are 4 different ways to make the first selection.

Once the first person has been chosen, there are 3 different ways to make the second selection.

Continuing this pattern, there are $4 \times 3 \times 2 \times 1 = 24$ permutations of the unelected members of the club.

(D) Divide the number of permutations of all the members by the number of permutations of the unelected members.

There are 5040 permutations of all the members of the club.

There are 24 permutations of the non-elected members of the club.

The quotient of these two values is $\frac{5040}{24} = 210$.

Reflect

1. How does the answer to Step D compare to answer to Step B?
Possible answer: The values are the same.

2. **Discussion** Explain the effect of dividing the total number of permutations by the number of permutations of items not selected.
Possible answer: This method can be used to calculate the number of permutations of a group of objects selected from a larger set.

Explain 1 Finding a Probability Using Permutations

The results of the previous section can be generalized to give a formula for permutations. To do so, it is helpful to use *factorials.* For a positive integer n, n **factorial**, written $n!$, is defined as follows.

$$n! = n \times (n-1) \times (n-2) \times \ldots \times 3 \times 2 \times 1$$

That is, $n!$ is the product of n and all the positive integers less than n. Note that 0! is defined to be 1.

In the previous section, the number of permutations of the 7 objects taken 3 at a time is

$$7 \times 6 \times 5 = \frac{7 \times 6 \times 5 \times \cancel{4} \times \cancel{3} \times \cancel{2} \times \cancel{1}}{\cancel{4} \times \cancel{3} \times \cancel{2} \times \cancel{1}} = \frac{7!}{4!} = \frac{7!}{(7-3)!}$$

This can be generalized as follows.

Permutations

The number of permutations of n objects taken r at a time is given by ${}_nP_r = \frac{n!}{(n-r)!}$.

PROFESSIONAL DEVELOPMENT

Learning Progressions

Combinatorics is the branch of mathematics that deals with arranging and counting finite collections of items. This lesson introduces students to permutations, which are groupings of items in which the order of the items matters. In the next lesson, students learn to count combinations, which are groupings of items in which the order does not matter. It is important for students to be able to distinguish between the two counting methods. Both provide useful formulas for counting large collections of items that can be applied to computing the probabilities of events with many equally likely outcomes.

EXPLORE

Finding the Number of Permutations

INTEGRATE TECHNOLOGY

Students have the option of doing the Explore activity either in the book or online.

INTEGRATE MATHEMATICAL PRACTICES

Focus on Reasoning

MP.2 Discuss why developing a counting rule for a group of objects is useful. Check that students recognize how quickly some visualizations become unwieldy, such as making a list or drawing a tree diagram, as the number of objects grows.

QUESTIONING STRATEGIES

? When finding probabilities of groups, what is the effect of specifying that order matters? **Order distinguishes between groups with the same set of elements. For example, AB is not the same as BA if order matters, but it is the same if order does not matter. This affects numbers of outcomes, which affect probabilities of events.**

EXPLAIN 1

Finding a Probability Using Permutations

AVOID COMMON ERRORS

Students may assume that the probability is the ratio of 1 to the permutation. Review the definition of the probability ratio and why a different permutation is needed to count the elements in the numerator and the elements in the denominator.

INTEGRATE TECHNOLOGY

You may want to have students use their calculators to check their work. Graphing calculators have a built-in function that calculates permutations. For example, to find ${}_{10}P_4$, first enter 10. Then press **MATH** and use the arrow keys to choose the **PRB** menu. Select **2:nPr** and press **ENTER**. Now enter 4 and then press **ENTER** to see that ${}_{10}P_4 = 5040$.

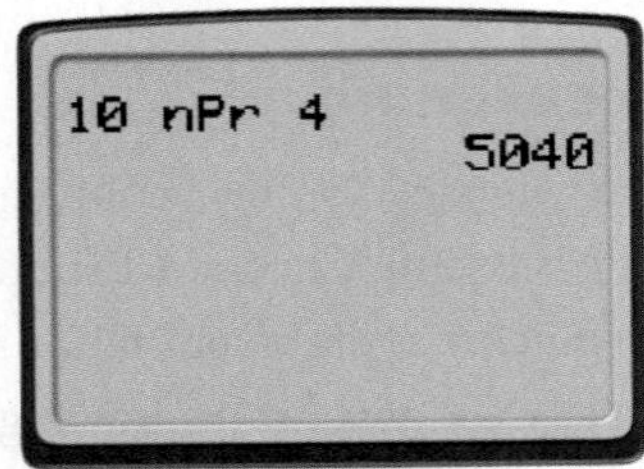

QUESTIONING STRATEGIES

The formula for a permutation is a ratio. Can a permutation ever be a fraction less than 1? Explain. **No, although the formula is a ratio, it always simplifies to a whole number because it is a method for counting arrangements.**

Why is it important to be able to recognize a permutation to count an arrangement of objects? Why can't you just make a list or use a tree diagram? **As the number of objects increases, the number of arrangements in a permutation gets large very quickly, and it becomes impractical and difficult to make a list or use a tree diagram.**

Example 1 **Use permutations to find the probabilities.**

(A) A research laboratory requires a four-digit security code to gain access to the facility. A security code can contain any of the digits 0, 1, 2, 3, 4, 5, 6, 7, 8, and 9, but no digit is repeated. What is the probability that a scientist is randomly assigned a code with the digits 1, 2, 3, and 4 in any order?

The sample space $n(S)$ is the number of permutations of 4 digits selected from 10 digits.

$n(S) = {}_{10}P_4 = \frac{10!}{6!} = 5040$

The event space $n(A)$ is the number of permutations of a security code with the digits 1, 2, 3, and 4.

$n(A) = {}_4P_4 = \frac{4!}{0!} = 24$

The probability of getting a security code with the digits 1, 2, 3, and 4 is

$PA = \frac{n(A)}{n(S)} = \frac{24}{5040} = \frac{1}{210}$

(B) A certain motorcycle license plate consists of 5 digits that are randomly selected. No digit is repeated. What is the probability of getting a license plate consisting of all even digits?

The sample space $n(S)$ is the number of permutations of **5 digits** selected from **10 digits**.

$n(S) = {}_{10}P_{5} = \frac{10!}{5!} = 30,210$

The event space $n(A)$ is the number of permutations of a license plate with **all even digits**.

$n(A) = {}_{5}P_{5} = \frac{5!}{0!} = 120$

The probability of getting a license plate with **all even digits** is

$P(A) = \frac{n(A)}{n(S)} = \frac{120}{30,210} = \frac{4}{1007}$

Your Turn

There are 8 finalists in the 100-meter dash at the Olympic Games. Suppose 3 of the finalists are from the United States.

3. What is the probability that the United States will win all 3 medals in this event?

$n(S) = {}_8P_3 = \frac{8!}{5!} = 336; n(A) = {}_3P_3 = \frac{3!}{0!} = 6$

The probability of the United States winning all 3 medals is $P(A) = \frac{n(A)}{n(S)} = \frac{6}{336} = \frac{1}{56}$.

4. What is the probability that the United States will win no medals in this event?

$n(S) = {}_8P_3 = \frac{8!}{5!} = 336; n(A) = {}_5P_3 = \frac{5!}{2!} = 60$

The probability of the United States winning no medals is $P(A) = \frac{n(A)}{n(S)} = \frac{60}{336} = \frac{5}{28}$.

COLLABORATIVE LEARNING

Peer-to-Peer Activity

Have students work in pairs to confirm that the permutation formulas work. Suggest that they make a list of the number of ways the letters in the word CLUE can be arranged and then find the arrangements using the permutations formula. Next, have them examine what happens to the number of permutations as the number of letters in a word increases by starting a list for the word CLUES. Repeat for the words COOL and TOOT. Have students comment on the usefulness of the permutation formulas when counting items.

Explain 2 Finding the Number of Permutations with Repetition

Up to this point, the problems have focused on finding the permutations of distinct objects. If some of the objects are repeated, this will reduce the number of permutations that are distinguishable.

For example, here are the permutations of the letters A, B, and C.

ABC	ACB	BAC	BCA	CAB	CBA

Next, here are the permutations of the letters M, O, and M. Shading is used to show the different positions of the repeated letter.

MOM	MOM	MMO	MMO	OMM	OMM

Shown without the shading, here are the permutations of the letters M, O, and M.

MOM	MOM	MMO	MMO	OMM	OMM

Notice that since the letter M is repeated, there are only 3 distinguishable permutations of the letters. This can be generalized with a formula for permutations with repetition.

Permutations with Repetition

The number of different permutations of n objects where one object repeats a times, a second object repeats b times, and so on is

$$\frac{n!}{a! \times b! \times \ldots}$$

Example 2 Find the permutations.

(A) How many different permutations are there of the letters in the word ARKANSAS?

There are 8 letters in the word, and there are 3 A's and 2 S's, so the number of permutations of the letters in ARKANSAS is $\frac{8!}{3!2!} = 3360$.

(B) One of the zip codes for Anchorage, Alaska, is 99522. How many permutations are there of the numbers in this zip code?

There are **5** digits in the zip code, and there are **2 nines**, and **2 twos** in the zip code, so the number of permutations of the zip code is

$$\frac{5!}{2!2!} = 30$$

Your Turn

. How many different permutations can be formed using all the letters in MISSISSIPPI?

$\frac{11!}{4!4!2!} = 34,650.$

. One of the standard telephone numbers for directory assistance is 555–1212. How many different permutations of this telephone number are possible?

$\frac{7!}{3!3!2!} = 210.$

DIFFERENTIATE INSTRUCTION

Multiple Representations

Have students calculate the number of permutations in various situations "by hand"; that is, by reasoning about the situation and using multiplication, by making a list, or by drawing tree diagrams. Then ask students what patterns they notice. A common element of every solution should be the product of a string of descending, consecutive integers, letters, or other items. Discuss how students can use this process to help them recall how to find the number of permutations.

EXPLAIN 2

Finding the Number of Permutations with Repetition

INTEGRATE MATHEMATICAL PRACTICES

Focus on Modeling

MP.4 Discuss the importance of identifying the permutation needed to count the sample space separately from the permutation needed to calculate the event when using permutations with probability.

QUESTIONING STRATEGIES

How is the formula for the number of permutations where one object repeats different from the formula for the number of permutations with no repeats? How is it similar? **In both formulas the numerator is n! The denominator of the formula for no repeats is $(n - r)!$, while the denominator for repeats is $a! \cdot b!$ and so on to count the repeating objects.**

EXPLAIN 3

Finding a Probability Using Permutations with Repetition

INTEGRATE MATHEMATICAL PRACTICES

Focus on Communication

MP.3 Discuss how students are able to identify n, r, a, b, and so on to use permutations with repetition to find probabilities.

QUESTIONING STRATEGIES

How can you use what you know about probability to check that the ratio makes sense when finding probability using permutations with or without repetition? **The probability must be between 0 and 1.**

Explain 3 Finding a Probability Using Permutations with Repetition

Permutations with repetition can be used to find probablilities.

Example 3 **The school jazz band has 4 boys and 4 girls, and they are randomly lined up for a yearbook photo.**

Ⓐ Find the probability of getting an alternating boy-girl arrangement.

The sample space $n(S)$ is the number of permutations of 8 objects, with 4 boys and 4 girls.

$n(S)\ \frac{8!}{4!4!} = 70$

The event space $n(A)$ is the number of permutations that alternate boy-girl or girl-boy. The possible permutations are BGBGBGBG or GBGBGBGB.

$n(A) = 2$

The probability of getting an alternating boy-girl arrangement is $P(A) = \frac{n(A)}{n(S)} = \frac{2}{70} = \frac{1}{35}$.

Ⓑ Find the probability of getting all of the boys grouped together.

The sample space $n(S)$ is the number of permutations of **8 students**, with **4 boys and 4 girls**.

$n(S) = \frac{8!}{4!4!} = 70$

The event space $n(A)$ is the number of permutations with **all 4 boys in a row**. The possible permutations are BBBBGGGG, GBBBBGGG, **GGBBBBGG, GGGBBBBG or GGGGBBBB**.

$n(A) = 5$

The probability of getting all the boys grouped together is $P(A) = \frac{n(A)}{n(S)} = \frac{5}{70} = \frac{1}{14}$.

Your Turn

7. There are 2 mystery books, 2 romance books, and 2 poetry books to be randomly placed on a shelf. What is the probability that the mystery books are next to each other, the romance books are next to each other, and the poetry books are next to each other?

$n(S) = \frac{6!}{2!2!2!} = 90$

The event space $n(A)$ is the number of permutations with books from each category next to each other. The possible permutations are MMRRPP, MMPPRR, RRMMPP, RRPPMM, PPMMRR, and PPRRMM.

$n(A) = 6$

The probability of getting all the books from each category next to each other is $P(A) = \frac{n(A)}{n(S)} = \frac{6}{90} = \frac{1}{15}$.

LANGUAGE SUPPORT EL

Connect Vocabulary

Have students look up the meaning of the verb *permute* (it is *to change the order of*). Connect the definition to the mathematical definition of *permutation,* which is *an arrangement of objects in a definite order.*

8. What is the probability that a random arrangement of the letters in the word APPLE will have the two P's next to each other?

The sample space $n(S)$ is the number of permutations of the letters in APPLE, and there are 2 P's, so $n(S) = \frac{5!}{2!} = 60$. Consider the two P's as a single block, so there are 4 positions for the letters to occupy.

$n(A) = 4! = 24$

The probability of getting the two P's next to each other is $P(A) = \frac{n(A)}{n(S)} = \frac{24}{60} = \frac{2}{5}$.

Elaborate

9. If ${}_nP_a = {}_nP_b$, what is the relationship between a and b? Explain your answer.

The equation is true if $\frac{n!}{(n-a)!} = \frac{n!}{(n-b)!}$. This occurs only when $a = b$.

10. It was observed that there are 6 permutations of the letters A, B, and C. They are ABC, ACB, BAC, BCA, CAB, and CBA. If the conditions are changed so that the order of selection does not matter, what happens to these 6 different groups?

Possible answer: They would become a single group of the letters, ABC. The other five groups are duplicates of this result.

11. **Essential Question Check-In** How do you determine whether choosing a group of objects involves permutations?

Possible answer: Permutations are used when the order of selection does matter.

Evaluate: Homework and Practice

- Online Homework
- Hints and Help
- Extra Practice

1. An MP3 player has a playlist with 12 songs. You select the shuffle option for the playlist. In how many different orders can the songs be played?

$12! = 479{,}001{,}600$

The songs can be played in 479,001,600 different orders

2. There are 10 runners in a race. Medals are awarded for 1st, 2nd, and 3rd place. In how many different ways can the medals be awarded?

$10 \times 9 \times 8 = 720$

There are 720 possibilities for awarding medals.

3. There are 9 players on a baseball team. In how many different ways can the coach choose players for first base, second base, third base, and shortstop?

$9 \times 8 \times 7 \times 6 = 3024$

There are 3024 ways to arrange players.

Exercise	Depth of Knowledge (D.O.K.)	COMMON CORE Mathematical Practices
1-11	1 Recall of Information	MP.2 Reasoning
12–15	1 Recall of Information	MP.1 Problem Solving
16–23	2 Skills/Concepts	MP.4 Modeling
24	3 Strategic Thinking H.O.T.	MP.3 Logic
25	3 Strategic Thinking H.O.T.	MP.2 Reasoning
26	3 Strategic Thinking H.O.T.	MP.6 Precision
27	3 Strategic Thinking H.O.T.	MP.3 Logic

ELABORATE

AVOID COMMON ERRORS

Students may be able to identify the permutation needed for one part of the probability ratio but not the other. Remind students to first decide what the sample space is and then use a permutation to count the elements in the sample space. Next, they should use a permutation as needed to count the elements in the event. Review why $n(S)$ is always in the denominator.

SUMMARIZE THE LESSON

What are permutations and how can you use them to calculate probabilities? **A permutation is a group of objects in which order is important. You can use permutations to find the number of outcomes in a sample space or in an event.**

EVALUATE

ASSIGNMENT GUIDE

Concepts and Skills	Practice
Explore Finding the Number of Permutations	Exercises 1–3
Example 1 Finding a Probability Using Permutations	Exercises 4–7, 18–19, 22–23, 26–27
Example 2 Finding the Number of Permutations With Repetition	Exercises 8–24
Example 3 Finding a Probability Using Permutations With Repetition	Exercises 12–17, 20–21, 25

GRAPHIC ORGANIZERS

Have students make a graphic organizer to summarize what they know about permutations. Ask them to include the formulas, with descriptions and examples.

4. A bag contains 9 tiles, each with a different number from 1 to 9. You choose a tile without looking, put it aside, choose a second tile without looking, put it aside, then choose a third tile without looking. What is the probability that you choose tiles with the numbers 1, 2, and 3 in that order?

Let S be the sample space and let A be the event that you choose tiles with the numbers 1, 2, and 3 in that order.

$$n(S) = {}_9P_3 = \frac{9!}{(9-3)!} = \frac{9!}{6!} = 504$$

$$n(A) = 1$$

$$P(A) = \frac{n(A)}{n(S)} = \frac{1}{540}$$

5. There are 11 students on a committee. To decide which 3 of these students will attend a conference, 3 names are chosen at random by pulling names one at a time from a hat. What is the probability that Sarah, Jamal, and Mai are chosen in any order?

Let S be the sample space and let A be the event that Sarah, Jamal, and Mai are chosen in any order.

$$n(S) = {}_{11}P_3 = \frac{11!}{(11-3)!} = \frac{11!}{8!} = 990$$

$$n(A) = {}_3P_3 = \frac{3!}{(3-3)!} = \frac{3!}{0!} = 6$$

$$P(A) = \frac{n(A)}{n(S)} = \frac{6}{990} = \frac{1}{165}$$

6. A clerk has 4 different letters that need to go in 4 different envelopes. The clerk places one letter in each envelope at random. What is the probability that all 4 letters are placed in the correct envelopes?

Let S be the sample space and let A be the event that all 4 letters are placed in the correct envelopes.

$$n(S) = {}_4P_4 = \frac{4!}{(4-4)!} = \frac{4!}{0!} = 24$$

$$n(A) = 1$$

$$P(A) = \frac{n(A)}{n(S)} = \frac{1}{24}$$

7. A swim coach randomly selects 3 swimmers from a team of 8 to swim in a heat. What is the probability that she will choose the three strongest swimmers?

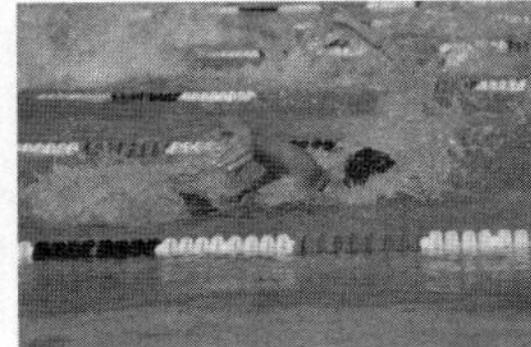

Let S be the sample space and let A be the event that the coach chooses the three strongest swimmers.

$$n(S) = {}_8P_3 = \frac{8!}{(8-3)!} = \frac{8!}{5!} = 336$$

$$n(A) = {}_3P_3 = \frac{3!}{(3-3)!} = \frac{3!}{0!} = 6$$

$$P(A) = \frac{n(A)}{n(S)} = \frac{6}{336} = \frac{1}{56}$$

8. Letter tiles spelling the word ENVELOPE are placed into a bag. How many different sequences of letters can be formed using all the letters in ENVELOPE?

The three letter E's are not distinguishable.

$\frac{_8P_8}{3!} = \frac{8!}{3!} = 6720$

6720 sequences

9. Yolanda has 3 each of red, blue, and green marbles, all the same size. How many possible ways can the 9 marbles be arranged in a row?

$\frac{_9P_9}{3!3!3!} = \frac{9!}{3!3!3!} = 1680$

1680 ways

10. Jane has 16 cards. Ten of the cards look exactly the same and have the number 1 on them. The other 6 cards look exactly the same and have the number 2 on them. Jane is going to make a row containing all 16 cards. How many different ways can she order the row?

$\frac{_{16}P_{16}}{10!6!} = \frac{16!}{10!6!} = 8008$

8008 row arrangements

11. Ramon has 10 cards, each with one number on it. The numbers are 1, 2, 3, 4, 4, 6, 6, 6, 6, 6. Ramon is going to make a row containing all 10 cards. How many different ways can he order the row?

$\frac{_{10}P_{10}}{2!5!} = \frac{10!}{2!5!} = 15{,}120$

15,120 row arrangements

12. A grocer has 5 apples and 5 oranges for a window display. The grocer makes a row of the 10 pieces of fruit by choosing one piece of fruit at random, making it the first piece in the row, choosing a second piece of fruit at random, making it the second piece in the row, and so on. What is the probability that the grocer arranges the fruits in alternating order?

Let *S* be the sample space and let *A* be the event that the grocer arranges the fruits in alternating order. For this problem, it is assumed that the apples are not distinguishable and that the oranges are not distinguishable.

$n(S) = \frac{_{10}P_{10}}{5!5!} = \frac{10!}{5!5!} = 252$

$n(A) = 2$, **AOAOAOAOAO or OAOAOAOAOA**

$P(A) = \frac{n(A)}{n(S)} = \frac{2}{252} = \frac{1}{126}$

13. The letters G, E, O, M, E, T, R, Y are on 8 tiles in a bag, one letter on each tile. If you select tiles randomly from the bag a place them in a row from left to right, what is the probability it will spell out GEOMETRY?

Let *S* be the sample space and let *A* be the event that the tiles spell out GEOMETRY again. The two letter E's are not distinguishable.

$n(S) = \frac{_8P_8}{2!} = \frac{8!}{2!} = 20{,}160$

$n(A) = 1$, **GEOMETRY**

$P(A) = \frac{n(A)}{n(S)} = \frac{1}{20{,}160}$

INTEGRATE MATHEMATICAL PRACTICES

Focus on Math Connections

MP.1 Discuss how to recognize when a probability evaluated using a permutation will be equal to the ratio $\frac{1}{n(S)}$.

AVOID COMMON ERRORS

Students may make errors when simplifying with factorials. Encourage students to write out the product a factorial represents, at least until they are sure which numbers to cancel.

PEER-TO-PEER

Have students work with a partner to write a probability problem about numbers, letters, or both in which a permutation is needed to count the objects. Have students solve their problems. Then ask them to exchange problems with another pair and solve those. Have the pairs review each other's solution methods.

VISUAL CUES

Discuss the locations of and relationship between n and r in the rule for permutations, and how they can be used to help students remember the formula for ${}_nP_r$. Make sure students do not confuse the P in the permutation formula for the P used to denote probability.

14. There are 11 boys and 10 girls in a classroom. A teacher chooses a student at random and puts that student at the head of a line, chooses a second student at random and makes that student second in the line, and so on, until all 21 students are in the line. What is the probability that the teacher puts them in a line alternating boys and girls, where no two of the same gender stand together?

$$n(S) = \frac{{}_{21}P_{21}}{11!10!} = \frac{21!}{11!10!} = 352{,}716$$

Because there are more boys than girls, there is only one way to alternate them: BGBGBGBGBGBGBGBGBGBGB. If a girl started first, the end would have too many boys. So $n(A) = 1$.

$$P(A) = \frac{n(A)}{n(S)} = \frac{1}{352{,}716}$$

15. There are 4 female and 4 male kittens are sleeping together in a row. Assuming that the arrangement is a random arrangement, what is the probability that all the female kittens are together, and all the male kittens are together?

$$n(S) = \frac{{}_8P_8}{4!4!} = \frac{8!}{4!4!} = 70, n(A) = 2, \text{FFFFMMMM or MMMMFFFF}$$

$$P(A) = \frac{n(A)}{n(S)} = \frac{2}{70} = \frac{1}{35}$$

16. If a ski club with 12 members votes to choose 3 group leaders, what is the probability that Marsha, Kevin, and Nicola will be chosen in any order for President, Treasurer, and Secretary?

$$n(S) = {}_{12}P_3 = \frac{12!}{(12-3)!} = \frac{12!}{9!} = 1320, n(A) = {}_3P_3 = \frac{3!}{(3-3)!} = \frac{3!}{0!} = 6$$

$$P(A) = \frac{n(A)}{n(S)} = \frac{6}{1320} = \frac{1}{220}$$

17. There are 7 books numbered 1–7 on the summer reading list. Peter randomly chooses 2 books. What is the probability that Peter chooses books numbered 1 and 2, in either order?

$$n(S) = {}_7P_2 = \frac{7!}{(7-2)!} = \frac{7!}{5!} = 42, n(A) = {}_2P_2 = \frac{2!}{(2-2)!} = \frac{2!}{0!} = 2$$

$$P(A) = \frac{n(A)}{n(S)} = \frac{2}{42} = \frac{1}{21}$$

18. On an exam, you are asked to list 5 historical events in the order in which they occurred. A student randomly orders the events. What is the probability that the student choose the correct order?

$$n(S) = {}_5P_5 = \frac{5!}{(5-5)!} = \frac{5!}{0!} = 120, n(A) = 1$$

$$P(A) = \frac{n(A)}{n(S)} = \frac{1}{120}$$

19. A fan makes 6 posters to hold up at a basketball game. Each poster has a letter of the word TIGERS. Six friends sit next to each other in a row. The posters are distributed at random. What is the probability that TIGERS is spelled correctly when the friends hold up the posters?

Let S be the sample space and let A be the event that that TIGERS is spelled correctly when you hold up the posters.

$n(S) = {}_6P_6 = \frac{6!}{(6-6)!} = \frac{6!}{0!} = 720$

$n(A) = 1$

$P(A) = \frac{n(A)}{n(S)} = \frac{1}{720}$

20. The 10 letter tiles S, A, C, D, E, E, M, I, I, and O are in a bag. What is the probability that the letters S-A-M-E will be drawn from the bag at random, in that order?

Let S be the sample space and let A be the event that the letters S-A-M-E will be drawn from the bag at random, in that order.

$n(S) = \frac{{}_{10}P_4}{2!2!} = \frac{5040}{4} = 1260$

$n(A) = 1$

$P(A) = \frac{n(A)}{n(S)} = \frac{1}{1260}$

21. If three cards are drawn at random from a standard deck of 52 cards, what is the probability that they will all be 7s? (There are four 7s in a standard deck of 52 cards.)

Let S be the sample space and let A be the event that all four cards are 7s.

$n(S) = {}_{52}P_3 = \frac{52!}{(52-3)!} = \frac{52!}{49!} = 132{,}600$

$n(A) = {}_4P_3 = \frac{4!}{(4-3)!} = \frac{4!}{1!} = 24$

$P(A) = \frac{n(A)}{n(S)} = \frac{24}{132{,}600} = \frac{1}{5525}$

22. A shop classroom has ten desks. If there are 6 students in shop class and they choose their desks at random, what is the probability they will sit in the first six desks?

Let S be the sample space and let A be the event that the students sit in the first six desks.

$n(S) = {}_{10}P_6 = \frac{10!}{(10-6)!} = \frac{10!}{4!} = 151{,}200$

$n(S) = {}_6P_6 = \frac{6!}{(6-6)!} = \frac{6!}{0!} = 720$

$P(A) = \frac{n(A)}{n(S)} = \frac{720}{151{,}200} = \frac{1}{210}$

JOURNAL

Have students cite real-world examples of permutations. Have them explain how they know the examples are permutations.

23. Match each event with its probability. All orders are chosen randomly.

A. There are 15 floats that will be in a town parade. Event: The mascot float is chosen to be first and the football team float is chosen to be second.

B. Beth is one of 10 students performing in a school talent show. Event: Beth chosen to be the fifth performer and her best friend is chosen to be fourth.

C. Sylvester is in a music competition with 14 other musicians. Event: Sylvester is chosen to be last, and his two best friends are chosen to be first and second.

C	$\frac{1}{2184}$
A	$\frac{1}{210}$
B	$\frac{1}{90}$

$$P(\text{parade}) = \frac{n(\text{mascot 1st and football 2nd})}{n(\text{all floats in parade})} = \frac{_{13}P_{13}}{_{15}P_{15}} = \frac{1}{210}$$

$$P(\text{talent show}) = \frac{n(\text{Beth 5th and friend 4th})}{n(\text{all contestants})} = \frac{_{8}P_{8}}{_{10}P_{10}} = \frac{1}{90}$$

$$P(\text{music}) = \frac{n(\text{Sylvester 1st, friends 2nd and 3rd})}{n(\text{all musicians})} = \frac{_{11}P_{11}}{_{14}P_{14}} = \frac{1}{2184}$$

H.O.T. Focus on Higher Order Thinking

24. Explain the Error Describe and correct the error in evaluating the expression.

$$_5P_3 = \frac{5!}{3!} = \frac{5 \times 4 \times \cancel{3!}}{\cancel{3!}} = 20$$

The denominator of the first fraction should be $(5 - 3)!$, not 3!; $\frac{5!}{(5-3)!} = \frac{5!}{2!} = 60$.

25. Make a Conjecture If you are going to draw four cards from a deck of cards, does drawing four Aces from the deck have the same probability as drawing four 3s? Explain.

Yes, they have the same probability. The probability of drawing 4 Aces from a deck of cards would be $PA = \frac{nA}{nS} = \frac{_4P_4}{_{52}P_4}$ because the 4 Aces could be drawn in any order, and there are 52 cards in the deck. There are also 4 3s in the deck that could be drawn in any order, so the probability would be the same.

26. Communicate Mathematical Ideas Nolan has Algebra, Biology, and World History homework. Assume that he chooses the order that he does his homework at random. Explain how to find the probability of his doing his Algebra homework first.

If he is doing his Algebra homework first, the only classes that can change are Biology and World History, so $n(A) = {_2P_2}$. The sample space would have all three classes changing, so $n(S) = {_3P_3}$. Since $P(A) = \frac{n(A)}{n(S)} = \frac{_2P_2}{_3P_3} = \frac{2}{6} = \frac{1}{3}$, the probability of Nolan doing his Algebra homework first is $\frac{1}{3}$.

27. Explain the Error A student solved the problem shown. The student's work is also shown. Explain the error and provide the correct answer.

A bag contains 6 tiles with the letters A, B, C, D, E, and F, one letter on each tile. You choose 4 tiles one at a time without looking and line them up from left to right as you choose them. What is the probability that your tiles spell BEAD?

Let S be the sample space and let A be the event that the tiles spell BEAD.

$$n(S) = {}_6P_4 = \frac{6!}{(6-4)!} = \frac{6!}{2!} = 360$$

$$n(A) = {}_4P_4 = \frac{4!}{(4-4)!} = \frac{4!}{0!} = 24$$

$$P(A) = \frac{n(A)}{n(S)} = \frac{24}{360} = \frac{1}{5}$$

$n(A)$ should be 1 since the tiles must appear in the order B-E-A-D. The correct probability is $\frac{1}{360}$.

Lesson Performance Task

How many different ways can a blue card, a red card, and a green card be arranged? The diagram shows that the answer is six.

1. Now solve a similar problem: What is the fewest number of colors needed to color the pattern shown here, so that no two squares sharing a common boundary have the same color? Draw a sketch to show your answer.

   two

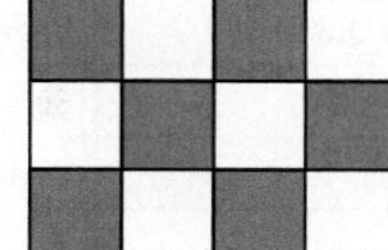

2. Now try this one. Draw a sketch to show your answer.

   three

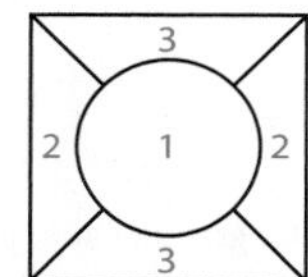

3. In 1974, Kenneth Appel and Wolfgang Haken solved a problem that had confounded mathematicians for more than a century. They proved that no matter how complex a map is, it can be colored in a maximum of four colors, so that no two regions sharing a common boundary have the same color. Sketch the figure shown here. Can you color it in four colors? Can you color it in three colors?

   Four colors are needed.

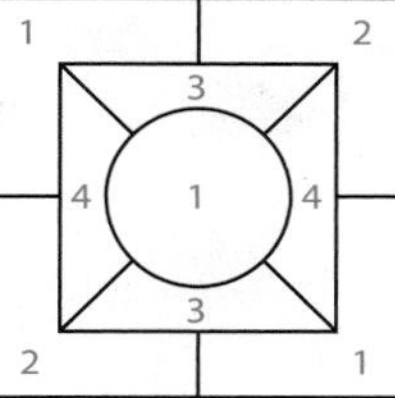

EXTENSION ACTIVITY

Give each student several black-and-white copies of a map of a region containing a complex array of countries, and crayons or colored pencils in four colors. Challenge students to color the map in three colors, following the same restriction stated in the Lesson Performance Task: No two countries sharing a border can have the same color. Regardless of whether the map can be colored in three colors, have students show how it can be colored in four colors.

INTEGRATE MATHEMATICAL PRACTICES

Focus on Modeling

MP.4 Question 3 of the Lesson Performance Task shows a map containing nine regions that cannot be colored with three colors; four colors are required. Challenge students to draw a map containing fewer than nine regions that requires four colors. What is the fewest number of regions a map can contain that requires four colors? **5**

AVOID COMMON ERRORS

Some students may draw a map with two regions that share a vertex point and must be the same color, and think they have disproved the theorem. Remind students that regions only require different colors if they share a boundary, not a corner.

Scoring Rubric

2 points: The student's answer is an accurate and complete execution of the task or tasks.

1 point: The student's answer contains attributes of an appropriate response but is flawed.

0 points: The student's answer contains no attributes of an appropriate response.

LESSON 19.3

Combinations and Probability

Common Core Math Standards

The student is expected to:

COMMON CORE **S-CP.B.9(+)**

Use permutations and combinations to compute probabilities of compound events and solve problems.

Mathematical Practices

COMMON CORE **MP.7 Using Structure**

Language Objective

Give an example of a combination to a partner and explain how you know it is a combination.

ENGAGE

Essential Question: In how many ways can you choose a certain number of objects from a larger group of objects?

You can choose a number of objects in such a way that the order matters, in which case you choose a permutation, or you can choose in such a way that order does not matter, in which case you choose a combination.

PREVIEW: LESSON PERFORMANCE TASK

View the Engage section online. Discuss the photograph. Ask students to guess the location where the photo was taken and describe what is happening there. Then preview the Lesson Performance Task.

Name ____________ Class ________ Date ________

19.3 Combinations and Probability

Essential Question: In how many ways can you choose a certain number of objects from a larger group of objects?

Resource Locker

Explore Finding the Number of Combinations

A **combination** is a selection of a group of objects in which order is unimportant. For example, if 3 letters are chosen from the group of letters A, B, C, and D, there are 4 different combinations.

ABC	ABD	ACD	BCD

A restaurant has 8 different appetizers on the menu, as shown in the table. They also offer an appetizer sampler, which contains any 3 of the appetizers served on a single plate. How many different appetizer samplers can be created? The order in which the appetizers are selected does not matter.

Appetizers	
Nachos	Chicken Wings
Chicken Quesadilla	Vegetarian Egg Rolls
Potato Skins	Soft Pretzels
Beef Chili	Guacamole Dip

(A) Find the number appetizer samplers that are possible if the order of selection does matter. This is the number of permutations of 8 objects taken 3 at a time.

$$_8P_3 = \frac{8!}{(8-3)!} = \frac{8!}{5!} = 336$$

(B) Find the number of different ways to select a particular group of appetizers. This is the number of permutations of 3 objects.

$$_3P_3 = \frac{3!}{(3-3)!} = \frac{3!}{0!} = 6$$

HARDCOVER PAGES 973–984

Watch for the hardcover student edition page numbers for this lesson.

(C) To find the number of possible appetizer samplers, if the order of selection does not matter, divide the answer to part A by the answer to part B.

So the number of appetizer samplers that can be created is $\frac{\boxed{336}}{\boxed{6}} = \boxed{56}$.

Reflect

1. Explain why the answer to Part A was divided by the answer to Part B.
Possible answer: Since the order of selection does not matter, the answer to Part A contained duplications of each possible sampler. Dividing by the answer to Part B removed the duplicates of each sampler.

2. On Mondays and Tuesdays, the restaurant offers an appetizer sampler that contains any 4 of the appetizers listed. How many different appetizer samplers can be created?
The number of appetizer samplers that can be created is $\frac{_8P_4}{_4P_4} = \frac{1680}{24} = 70$.

3. In general, are there more ways or fewer ways to select objects when the order does not matter? Why?
Possible Answer: There are fewer ways to select objects when the order does not matter. This is because multiple selections are counted as the same combination.

Explain 1 Finding a Probability Using Combinations

The results of the previous section can be generalized to give a formula for combinations. In the previous section, the number of combinations of the 8 objects taken 3 at a time is

$$\frac{8 \cdot 7 \cdot 6}{3 \cdot 2 \cdot 1} = \frac{8 \cdot 7 \cdot 6 \cdot \cancel{5} \cdot \cancel{4} \cdot \cancel{3} \cdot \cancel{2} \cdot \cancel{1}}{3 \cdot 2 \cdot 1 \cdot \cancel{5} \cdot \cancel{4} \cdot \cancel{3} \cdot \cancel{2} \cdot \cancel{1}} = \frac{8!}{3!5!} = \frac{8!}{3!(8-3)!}$$

This can be generalized as follows.

Combinations

The number of combinations of n objects taken r at a time is given by

$$_nC_r = \frac{n!}{r!(n-r)!}$$

Example 1 **Find the probabilities.**

(A) There are 4 boys and 8 girls on the debate team. The coach randomly chooses 3 of the students to participate in a competition. What is the probability that the coach chooses all girls?

The sample space $n(S)$ is the number of combinations of 3 students taken from the group of 12 students.

$n(S) = {}_{12}C_3 = \frac{12!}{3!9!} = 220$

The event space $n(A)$ is the number of combinations of 3 girls taken from the set of 8 girls.

$n(A) = {}_8C_3 = \frac{8!}{3!5!} = 56$

The probability that the coach chooses all girls is $P(A) = \frac{n(A)}{n(S)} = \frac{56}{220} = \frac{14}{55}$.

EXPLORE

Finding the Number of Combinations

INTEGRATE TECHNOLOGY

Students have the option of doing the Explore activity either in the book or online.

QUESTIONING STRATEGIES

? Why is it important to distinguish between a permutation and a combination when counting? **They may have a different number of possible arrangements.**

? How can you tell if an arrangement is a combination? **An arrangement is a combination if the order of the items does not matter.**

EXPLAIN 1

Finding a Probability Using Combinations

INTEGRATE TECHNOLOGY

Graphing calculators have a built-in function that calculates combinations. The $_nC_r$ function is available from the **MATH PRB** menu. Have students enter data in the same way they enter n and r when applying the permutation function. For example, to find $_6C_4$, first enter 6. Then press **MATH** and use the arrow keys to choose the **PRB** menu. Select **3:nPr** and press **ENTER**. Now enter 4 and press **ENTER** to see that $_6C_4 = 15$.

PROFESSIONAL DEVELOPMENT

Math Background

In this lesson students are introduced to combinations. A combination of n objects taken r at a time is given by the rule $_nC_r = \frac{n!}{r!(n-r)!}$. Pascal's triangle is a number triangle with rows arranged according to the combination formula, starting with $n = 0$ and continuing indefinitely. Each successive row can be found by adding elements from the row above. It has many fascinating properties, and it can be used as a shortcut in algebra when factoring polynomials.

INTEGRATE MATHEMATICAL PRACTICES

Focus on Reasoning

MP.2 Check that students understand how the formula for the number of combinations of n objects taken r at a time is related to the formula for the number of permutations of n objects taken r at a time. **The number of combinations is equal to the number of permutations divided by $r!$.**

QUESTIONING STRATEGIES

? The formula for the number of combinations is a ratio. Can a combination ever be a fraction less than 1 ? Explain. **No; as with the formula for permutations, although the formula is a ratio, it always simplifies to a whole number because it is a method for counting arrangements.**

? Can the number of combinations ever be equal to the number of permutations? Explain. **only when the combination is taken 1 at a time, when $r = 1$, which is the same as a permutation**

(B) There are 52 cards in a standard deck, 13 in each of 4 suits, clubs, diamonds, hearts, and spades. Five cards are randomly drawn from the deck. What is the probability that all five cards are diamonds?

The sample space $n(S)$ is the number of combinations of **5** cards drawn from 52 cards.

$$n(S) = {}_{52}C_{5} = \frac{52!}{5!47!} = 2{,}598{,}960$$

The event space $n(A)$ is the number of combinations of 5 cards drawn from the **13** diamonds.

$$n(A) = {}_{13}C_{5} = \frac{13!}{5!8!} = 1287$$

The probability of selecting **5** cards that are diamonds is

$$P(A) = \frac{n(A)}{n(S)} = \frac{1287}{2{,}598{,}960} = \frac{33}{66{,}640}$$

Your Turn

4. A coin is tossed 4 times. What is the probability of getting exactly 3 heads?

The sample space $n(S)$ is found by using the Fundamental Counting Principle since each flip can result in heads or tails.

$n(S) = 2 \cdot 2 \cdot 2 \cdot 2 = 2^4 = 16$

The event space $n(A)$ is the number of combinations of 3 heads taken from the set of 4 coin flips, so

$n(A) = {}_4C_3 = \frac{4!}{3!1!} = 4$

The probability of getting exactly 3 heads is

$P(A) = \frac{n(A)}{n(S)} = \frac{4}{16} = \frac{1}{4}$

5. Four cards are randomly drawn from a standard deck. If they are all red (diamonds or hearts), what is the probability they are all the same suit?

The sample space $n(S)$ is the number of combinations of 4 cards drawn from the 26 red card

$n(S) = {}_{26}C_4 = \frac{26!}{4!22!} = 14,950.$

The event space $n(A)$ is the number of combinations of 4 cards drawn from the 13 diamonds

$n(A) = {}_{13}C_4 = \frac{13!}{4!9!} = 715$

The probability of getting all diamonds is

$P(A) = \frac{n(A)}{n(S)} = \frac{715}{14,950} = \frac{11}{230}$

COLLABORATIVE LEARNING

Small Group Activity

Have students create two situations in which 2 out of 16 objects are selected, with order important in one of the situations and not important in the other. Ask students to use the situations to compare and contrast permutations and combinations, explaining why the number of selections is greater in one than in the other, and describing the relationship between the two. Tell students it may be necessary to create several situations in which order is and is not important to be able to describe the relationship between permutations and combinations.

 Explain 2 Finding a Probability Using Combinations and Addition

Sometimes, counting problems involve the phrases "at least" or "at most." For these problems, combinations must be added.

For example, suppose a coin is flipped 3 times. The coin could show heads 0, 1, 2, or 3 times. To find the number of combinations with at least 2 heads, add the number of combinations with 2 heads and the number of combinations with 3 heads $\left({}_3C_2 + {}_3C_3\right)$.

 **Example 2** Find each probability.

Ⓐ A coin is flipped 5 times, and the result of heads or tails is recorded. What is the probability that the result is heads at least 4 times?

The sample space $n(S)$ can be found by using the Fundamental Counting Principle since each flip can result in heads or tails.

$n(S) = 2 \cdot 2 \cdot 2 \cdot 2 \cdot 2 = 2^5 = 32$

Let A be the event that the coin shows heads at least 4 times. This is the sum of 2 events, the coin showing heads 4 times or 5 times. Find the sum of the combinations with 4 heads from 5 coins or with 5 heads from 5 coins.

$n(A) = {}_5C_4 + {}_5C_5 = \frac{5!}{4!1!} + \frac{5!}{5!0!} = 5 + 1 = 6$

The probability that the coin shows at least 4 headsis $P(A) = \frac{n(A)}{n(S)} = \frac{6}{32} = \frac{3}{16}$.

Ⓑ Three standard number cubes are rolled and the result is recorded. What is the probability of at least 2 of the number cubes landing on 6?

The sample space $n(S)$ can be found by using the Fundamental Counting Principle since each roll can result in 1, 2, 3, 4, 5, or 6.

$n(S) = 6^3 = 216$

Let A be the event that at least 2 dice show 6. This is the sum of 2 events, 2 dice showing 6 or 3 dice showing 6. The event of getting 6 on 2 dice occurs 5 times since there are 5 possibilities for the other die.

$n(A) = 5 \cdot {}_3C_2 + {}_3C_3 = 5 \cdot \frac{3!}{2!1!} + \frac{3!}{3!0!} = 15 + 1 = 16$

The probability of getting a 6 at least twice in 3 rolls is $P(A) = \frac{n(A)}{n(S)} = \frac{16}{216} = \frac{2}{27}$.

DIFFERENTIATE INSTRUCTION

Graphic Organizers

Have the class work together to create a graphic organizer that summarizes and demonstrates the rules for counting: the Fundamental Counting Principle, the permutation rule, and the combination rule. For each rule, have students include the formula and an example. Suggest that students highlight words in the examples that indicate why and how the rule is applied.

AVOID COMMON ERRORS

Students may have difficulty using combinations to find probability. Have students break down the probability problem into parts. First find the size of the sample space. Then find the number of outcomes associated with the event. Finally, write the ratio.

EXPLAIN 2

Finding a Probability Using Combinations and Addition

INTEGRATE MATHEMATICAL PRACTICES

Focus on Communication

MP.3 Students may have difficulty recognizing how to use addition with combinations, and understanding why addition is used. Review how to find the probability of simple events that involve addition when rolling a number cube, such as rolling at least a 3 or at most a 4.

QUESTIONING STRATEGIES

When you find a probability using combinations, will both parts of the probability ratio necessarily be combinations? Explain. No, the method used for counting each part of the ratio depends on the problem.

ELABORATE

AVOID COMMON ERRORS

Students sometimes compute a combination for $n(S)$ and then choose the numerator of the probability ratio carelessly. Emphasize the importance of accurately identifying both parts of the probability ratio.

SUMMARIZE THE LESSON

? What are combinations and how can you use them to calculate probabilities? **A combination is a grouping of objects in which order does not matter. You can use combinations to find the number of outcomes in a sample space or in an event.**

Your Turn

6. A math department has a database of 100 true-false questions used to create future exams. A new test is created by randomly selecting 6 questions from the database. What is the probability the new test contains at most 2 questions where the correct answer is "true"?

The sample space $n(S)$ can be found by using the Fundamental Counting Principle since each question is either true or false.

$n(S) = 2 \cdot 2 \cdot 2 \cdot 2 \cdot 2 \cdot 2 = 2^6 = 64$

Let A be the event that at most 2 questions are true. This is the sum of 3 events, 2 true questions, 1 true question, or no true questions.

$n(A) = {}_6C_2 + {}_6C_1 + {}_6C_0 = \frac{6!}{2!4!} + \frac{6!}{1!5!} + \frac{6!}{0!6!} = 15 + 6 + 1 = 22$

The probability that the test contains at most 2 true questions is

$P(A) = \frac{n(A)}{n(S)} = \frac{22}{64} = \frac{11}{32}$

7. There are an equal number of boys and girls in the senior class. If 5 seniors are randomly selected to form the student council, what is the probability the council will contain at least 3 girls?

The sample space $n(S)$ can be found by using the Fundamental Counting Principle since each selection is either a boy or a girl.

$n(S) = 2 \cdot 2 \cdot 2 \cdot 2 \cdot 2 = 2^5 = 32$

Let A be the event that at least 3 girls are selected. This is the sum of 3 events, selecting 3 girls, 4 girls, or 5 girls.

$n(A) = {}_5C_3 + {}_5C_4 + {}_5C_5 = \frac{5!}{3!2!} + \frac{5!}{4!1!} + \frac{5!}{5!0!} = 10 + 5 + 1 = 16$

The probability that the council will contain more girls than boys is

$P(A) = \frac{n(A)}{n(S)} = \frac{16}{32} = \frac{1}{2}$

Elaborate

8. Discussion A coin is flipped 5 times, and the result of heads or tails is recorded. To find the probability of getting tails at least once, the events of 1, 2, 3, 4, or 5 tails can be added together. Is there a faster way to calculate this probability?

Possible Answer: The sum of the probabilities of all possible outcomes is equal to 1. Determine the probability of getting no tails (or 5 heads) and subtract this value from 1.

9. If ${}_nC_a = {}_nC_b$, what is the relationship between a and b? Explain your answer.

The equation is true if $\frac{n!}{a!(n-a)!} = \frac{n!}{b!(n-b)!}$. This will occur when $a = b$ or $a + b = n$.

10. Essential Question Check-In How do you determine whether choosing a group of objects involves combinations?

Possible Answer: Combinations are used when the order of selection does not matter.

LANGUAGE SUPPORT EL

Connect Vocabulary

Have students make a chart to summarize what they know about combinations. **Sample:**

Combination	
Definition	A grouping of objects in which order does not matter
Formula	${}_nC_r = \frac{n!}{r!(n-r)!}$
Example	Combinations of 2 letters from A, B, and C: AB AC BC

Evaluate: Homework and Practice

- Online Homework
- Hints and Help
- Extra Practice

1. A cat has a litter of 6 kittens. You plan to adopt 2 of the kittens. In how many ways can you choose 2 of the kittens from the litter?

$${}_6C_2 = \frac{6!}{2!(6-2!)} = \frac{6!}{2!4!} = \frac{720}{48} = 15 \text{ ways}$$

2. An amusement park has 11 roller coasters. In how many ways can you choose 4 of the roller coasters to ride during your visit to the park?

$${}_{11}C_4 = \frac{11!}{4!(11-4!)} = \frac{11!}{4!7!} = \frac{39{,}916{,}800}{120{,}960} = 330 \text{ ways}$$

3. Four students from 30-member math club will be selected to organize a fundraiser. How many groups of 4 students are possible?

$${}_{30}C_4 = \frac{30!}{4!(30-4!)} = \frac{30!}{4!26!} = 27{,}405 \text{ groups}$$

4. A school has 5 Spanish teachers and 4 French teachers. The school's principal randomly chooses 2 of the teachers to attend a conference. What is the probability that the principal chooses 2 Spanish teachers?

Let S be the sample space and let A be the event that the principal chooses 2 Spanish teachers.

$$n(S) = n(\text{teachers}) = {}_9C_2 = \frac{9!}{2!(9-2!)} = \frac{9!}{2!7!} = \frac{362{,}880}{10{,}080} = 36$$

$$n(A) = n(\text{Spanish}) = {}_5C_2 = \frac{5!}{2!(5-2)!} = \frac{5!}{2!3!} = \frac{120}{12} = 10$$

$$P(A) = \frac{n(A)}{n(S)} = \frac{10}{36} = \frac{5}{18}$$

5. There are 6 fiction books and 8 nonfiction books on a reading list. Your teacher randomly assigns you 4 books to read over the summer. What is the probability that you are assigned all nonfiction books?

Let S be the sample space and let A be the event that you are assigned all nonfiction books.

$$n(S) = n(\text{books}) = {}_{14}C_4 = \frac{14!}{4!(14-4!)} = \frac{14!}{4!10!} = 1001$$

$$n(A) = n(\text{nonfiction}) = {}_8C_4 = \frac{8!}{4!(8-4)!} = \frac{8!}{4!4!} = 70$$

$$P(A) = \frac{n(A)}{n(S)} = \frac{70}{1001} = \frac{10}{143}$$

Exercise	Depth of Knowledge (D.O.K.)	COMMON CORE Mathematical Practices
1–12	**1** Recall of Information	**MP.2** Reasoning
13–14	**2** Skills/Concepts	**MP.4** Modeling
15–20	**2** Skills/Concepts	**MP.1** Problem Solving
21	**2** Skills/Concepts	**MP.4** Modeling
22	**2** Skills/Concepts	**MP.2** Reasoning
23	**3** Strategic Thinking 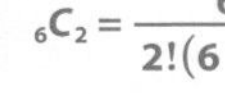 H.O.T.	**MP.3** Logic

EVALUATE

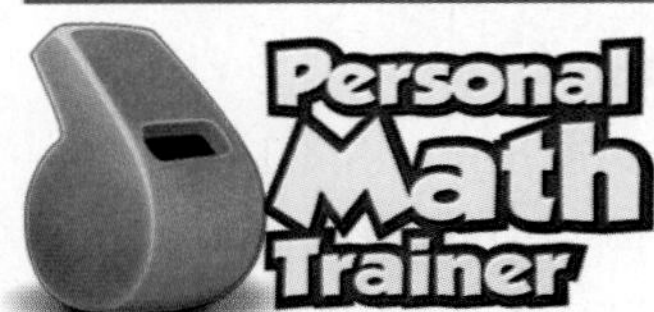

ASSIGNMENT GUIDE

Concepts and Skills	Practice
Explore Finding the Number of Combinations	Exercises 1–3, 22–23, 25–26
Example 1 Finding a Probability Using Combinations	Exercises 4–7, 12–21
Example 2 Finding a Probability Using Combinations and Addition	Exercises 8–11

COMMUNICATING MATH

After students have completed some of the exercises, ask them to discuss how they are able to distinguish combinations and permutations. Then have them explain how they were able to identify n and r in various examples. Ask them to tell whether they find one easier to work with than the other, and why.

INTEGRATE MATHEMATICAL PRACTICES

Focus on Communication

MP.3 Ask students to share their rationales for solving probability problems involving combinations. In particular, have them explain how they computed the values for $n(S)$ and $n(A)$ to find the probability.

AVOID COMMON ERRORS

Students often confuse permutations and combinations. They may not recognize which should be applied or they may apply the wrong formula. Have students begin by deciding whether the order is important or not. Then have them look up the formula. Note that this process may have to be repeated several times to solve a probability problem.

6. A bag contains 26 tiles, each with a different letter of the alphabet written on it. You choose 3 tiles from the bag without looking. What is the probability that you choose the tiles with the letters A, B, and C?

Let S be the sample space and let A be the event that you choose the tiles with the letters A, B, and C.

$$n(S) = {}_{26}C_3 = \frac{26!}{3!(26-3!)} = \frac{26!}{3!23!} = 2600$$

$$n(A) = {}_3C_3 = \frac{3!}{3!(3-3)!} = \frac{3!}{3!0!} = 1 \dashrightarrow P(A) = \frac{n(A)}{n(S)} = \frac{1}{2600}$$

7. You are randomly assigned a password consisting of 6 different characters chosen from the digits 0 to 9 and the letters A to Z. As a percent, what is the probability that you are assigned a password consisting of only letters? Round you answer to the nearest tenth of a percent.

Let S be the sample space and let A be the event that you are assigned a password consisting of only letters.

$$n(S) = n(\text{letters and numbers}) = {}_{36}C_6 = \frac{36!}{6!(36-6!)} = \frac{36!}{6!30!} = 1{,}947{,}792$$

$$n(A) = n(\text{letters}) = {}_{26}C_6 = \frac{26!}{6!(26-6)!} = \frac{26!}{6!20!} = 230{,}230$$

$$P(A) = \frac{n(A)}{n(S)} = \frac{230{,}230}{1{,}947{,}792} \approx 11.8\%$$

8. A bouquet of 6 flowers is made up by randomly choosing between roses and carnations. What is the probability the bouquet will have at most 2 roses?

Let S be the sample space and let A be the event that the bouquet will have at most 2 roses.

$$n(S) = n(\text{two possibilities per flower}) = 2 \cdot 2 \cdot 2 \cdot 2 \cdot 2 \cdot 2 = 2^6 = 64$$

$$n(A) = n(\text{at most 2 roses})$$

$$= {}_6C_2 + {}_6C_1 + {}_6C_0 = 15 + 6 + 1 = 22$$

$$P(A) = \frac{n(A)}{n(S)} = \frac{22}{64} = \frac{11}{32}$$

9. A bag of fruit contains 10 pieces of fruit, chosen randomly from bins of apples and oranges. What is the probability the bag contains at least 6 oranges?

Let S be the sample space and let A be the event that the bag contains at least 6 oranges

$$n(S) = n(\text{two possibilities per fruit}) = 2 \cdot 2 \cdot 2 \cdot 2 \cdot 2 \cdot 2 \cdot 2 \cdot 2 \cdot 2 \cdot 2 = 2^{10} = 1024$$

$$n(A) = n(\text{at least 6 oranges})$$

$$= {}_{10}C_6 + {}_{10}C_7 + {}_{10}C_8 + {}_{10}C_9 + {}_{10}C_{10} = 210 + 120 + 45 + 10 + 1 = 386$$

$$P(A) = \frac{n(A)}{n(S)} = \frac{386}{1024} = \frac{193}{512}$$

Exercise	Depth of Knowledge (D.O.K.)	COMMON CORE Mathematical Practices
24	3 Strategic Thinking H.O.T.	MP.3 Logic
25	3 Strategic Thinking H.O.T.	MP.3 Logic
26	3 Strategic Thinking H.O.T.	MP.3 Logic

10. You flip a coin 10 times. What is the probability that you get at most 3 heads?

Let S be the sample space and let A be the event that you get at most 3 heads.

$n(S) = n(\text{2 possibilities per coin}) = 2 \cdot 2 \cdot 2 \cdot 2 \cdot 2 \cdot 2 \cdot 2 \cdot 2 \cdot 2 \cdot 2 = 2^{10} = 1024$

$n(A) = n(\text{get at most 3 heads})$

$= {}_{10}C_3 + {}_{10}C_2 + {}_{10}C_1 + {}_{10}C_0 = 120 + 45 + 10 + 1 = 176$

$P(A) = \frac{n(A)}{n(S)} = \frac{176}{1024} = \frac{11}{64}$

11. You flip a coin 8 times. What is the probability you will get at least 5 heads?

Let S be the sample space and let A be the event that you get at least 5 heads.

$n(S) = n(\text{2 possibilities per coin}) = 2 \cdot 2 \cdot 2 \cdot 2 \cdot 2 \cdot 2 \cdot 2 \cdot 2 = 2^8 = 256$

$n(A) = n(\text{get at least 5 heads})$

$= {}_8C_5 + {}_8C_6 + {}_8C_7 + {}_8C_8 = 56 + 28 + 8 + 1 = 93$

$P(A) = \frac{n(A)}{n(S)} = \frac{93}{256}$

12. You flip a coin 5 times. What is the probability that every result will be tails?

Let S be the sample space and let A be the event that every result will be tails.

$n(S) = n(\text{two possibilities per flip}) = 2 \cdot 2 \cdot 2 \cdot 2 \cdot 2 = 2^5 = 32$

$n(A) = n(\text{every result is tails}) = {}_5C_5 = 1$

$P(A) = \frac{n(A)}{n(S)} = \frac{1}{32}$

13. There are 12 balloons in a bag: 3 each of blue, green, red, and yellow. Three balloons are chosen at random. Find the probability that all 3 balloons are green.

Let S be the sample space and let A be the event that all 3 balloons are green.

$n(S) = n(\text{choosing 3}) = {}_{12}C_3 = \frac{12!}{3!(12-3)!} = 220$

$n(A) = n(\text{all 3 green}) = {}_3C_3 = 1$

$P(A) = \frac{n(A)}{n(S)} = \frac{1}{220}$

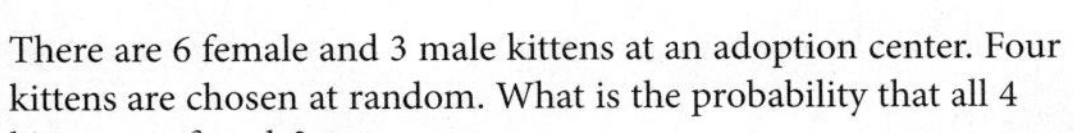

14. There are 6 female and 3 male kittens at an adoption center. Four kittens are chosen at random. What is the probability that all 4 kittens are female?

Let S be the sample space and let A be the event that all 4 kittens are female.

$n(S) = {}_9C_4 = \frac{9!}{4!(9-4!)} = \frac{9!}{4!5!} = 126$

$n(A) = {}_6C_4 = \frac{6!}{4!(6-4)!} = \frac{6!}{4!2!} = 15$

$P(A) = \frac{n(A)}{n(S)} = \frac{15}{126} = \frac{5}{42}$

PEER-TO-PEER

Have students work with a partner to write a probability problem about numbers, letters, or both in which a combination is needed to count the objects. Have students solve their problems. Then ask them to exchange problems with another pair to solve. Have the pairs review each other's solution methods.

AVOID COMMON ERRORS

Students sometimes attempt to simplify permutations or combinations by canceling factors. Remind students of the meaning of factorials, and suggest that they write out the multiplication to determine which factors actually cancel.

There are 21 students in your class. The teacher wants to send 4 students to the library each day. The teacher will choose the students to go to the library at random each day for the first four days from the list of students who have not already gone. Answer each question.

15. What is the probability you will be chosen to go on the first day?

Let S be the sample space and let A be the event that you will be chosen to go on the first day.

$n(S) = n(\text{choosing 4 of 21 students}) = {}_{21}C_4 = \frac{21!}{4!(21-4!)} = \frac{21!}{4!17!} = 5985$

Since you are one group member, the rest of the group members can be made up of any of the 20 remaining students in your class.

$n(A) = n(\text{3 remaining group members}) = {}_{20}C_3 = \frac{20!}{3!(20-3!)} = \frac{20!}{3!17!} = 1140$

$P(A) = \frac{n(A)}{n(S)} = \frac{1140}{5985} = \frac{4}{21}$

16. If you have not yet been chosen to go on days 1–3, what is the probability you will be chosen to go on the fourth day?

12 students have already gone, leaving 9 students to go to the library.

Let S be the sample space and let A be the event that you will be chosen to go on the fourth day.

$n(S) = n(\text{choosing 4 of 9 students}) = {}_9C_4 = \frac{9!}{4!(9-4!)} = \frac{9!}{4!5!} = 126$

Since you are one group member, the rest of the group members can be made up of any of the 8 remaining who have not yet gone.

$n(A) = n(\text{3 remaining group members}) = {}_8C_3 = \frac{8!}{3!(8-3!)} = \frac{8!}{3!5!} = 56$

$P(A) = \frac{n(A)}{n(S)} = \frac{56}{126} = \frac{4}{9}$

17. Your teacher chooses 2 students at random to represent your homeroom. The homeroom has a total of 30 students, including your best friend. What is the probability that you and your best friend are chosen?

Let S be the sample space and let A be the event that you and your best friend are chosen.

$n(S) = n(\text{choosing 2 of 30 students}) = {}_{30}C_2 = 435$

$n(A) = n(\text{you and friend chosen}) = {}_2C_2 = 1$

$P(A) = \frac{n(A)}{n(S)} = \frac{1}{435}$

There are 12 peaches and 8 bananas in a fruit basket. You get a snack for yourself and three of your friends by choosing four of the pieces of fruit at random. Answer each question.

18. What is the probability that all 4 are peaches?

$n(S) = n(\text{fruits}) = {}_{20}C_4 = \frac{20!}{4!(20-4!)} = \frac{20!}{4!16!} = 4845$

$n(A) = n(\text{peaches}) = {}_{12}C_4 = \frac{12!}{4!(12-4!)} = \frac{12!}{4!8!} = 495$

$P(A) = \frac{n(\text{peaches})}{n(\text{fruits})} = \frac{495}{4845} = \frac{33}{323}$

19. What is the probability that all 4 are bananas?

$n(S) = n(\text{fruits}) = {}_{20}C_4 = \frac{20!}{4!(20-4!)} = \frac{20!}{4!16!} = 4845$

$n(A) = n(\text{bananas}) = {}_{8}C_4 = \frac{8!}{4!(8-4)!} = \frac{8!}{4!4!} = 70$

$P(A) = \frac{n(\text{bananas})}{n(\text{fruits})} = \frac{70}{4845} = \frac{14}{969}$

20. There are 30 students in your class. Your science teacher will choose 5 students at random to create a group to do a project. Find the probability that you and your 2 best friends in the science class will be chosen to be in the group.

$n(S) = n(\text{choosing 5 of 30 students})$, $n(A) = n(\text{two additional group members})$

Since 3 of the group members are of you and your friends, the additional 2 group members can come from any combination of the people left in class.

$P(A) = \frac{n(A)}{n(S)} = \frac{{}_{27}C_2}{{}_{30}C_5} = \frac{351}{142{,}506} = \frac{1}{406}$

21. On a television game show, 9 members of the studio audience are randomly selected to be eligible contestants.

a. Six of the 9 eligible contestants are randomly chosen to play a game on the stage. How many combinations of 6 players from the group of eligible contestants are possible?

${}_9C_6 = \frac{9!}{6!(9-6!)} = \frac{9!}{6!3!} = 84$

b. You and your two friends are part of the group of 9 eligible contestants. What is the probability that all three of you are chosen to play the game on stage? Explain how you found your answer.

$n(S) = n(\text{choosing 6}) = {}_9C_6 = 84$

After you and your friends are chosen, 3 other contestants from the pool of 6 can be chosen in any combination, so the number of favorable combinations is ${}_6C_3$.

$n(A) = {}_6C_3 = 20$, $P(A) = \frac{n(A)}{n(S)} = \frac{20}{84} = \frac{5}{21}$

The probability that you and your friends are chosen is $\frac{5}{21}$.

JOURNAL

Have students cite real-world examples of combinations. Have them explain how they know the examples are combinations.

22. Determine whether it would be better to use permutations or combinations to find the number of possibilities in each of the following situations. Select the correct answer for each lettered part.

a. Selecting a group of 5 people from a group of 8 people — ○ permutation ● combination

b. Finding the number of combinations for a combination lock — ● permutation ○ combination

c. Awarding first and second place ribbons in a contest — ● permutation ○ combination

d. Choosing 3 books to read in any order from a list of 7 books — ○ permutation ● combination

a. It doesn't matter what order the people are selected in.

b. Order matters: numbers have to be in a specific order to open the lock.

c. Order matters: awarding Sam first place and Elena second is different from awarding Elena first place and Sam second.

d. It doesn't matter what order the books are listed in.

H.O.T. Focus on Higher Order Thinking

23. **Communicate Mathematical Ideas** Using the letters *A*, *B*, and *C*, explain the difference between a permutation and a combination.

Possible answer: In permutations, order does not matter. In combinations, order does matter. In a permutation of *A*, *B*, and *C*, *ABC* is different from *CBA*, so they would be counted as two different permutations. In a combination, *ABC* is the same as *CBA*, and would not be counted again.

a. **Draw Conclusions** Calculate ${}_{10}C_6$ and ${}_{10}C_4$.

$${}_{10}C_6 = \frac{10!}{6!(10-6)!} = \frac{10!}{6!4!} = \frac{3{,}628{,}800}{17{,}280} = 210$$

$${}_{10}C_4 = \frac{10!}{4!(10-4)!} = \frac{10!}{4!6!} = \frac{3{,}628{,}800}{17{,}280} = 210$$

b. What do you notice about these values? Explain why this makes sense.

${}_{10}C_6 = {}_{10}C_4 = 210$; it makes sense that these values are equal because every combination of 6 objects that are selected has a corresponding combination of 4 objects that are not selected.

c. Use your observations to help you state a generalization about combinations.

In general, ${}_nC_r = {}_nC_{n-r}$.

25. Justify Reasoning Use the formula for combinations to make a generalization about ${}_nC_n$. Explain why this makes sense.

Using the formula for combinations and the fact that $0! = 1$, ${}_nC_n = \frac{n!}{n!(n-n!)} = \frac{n!}{n!0!} = \frac{n!}{n!} = 1$; this makes sense because there is only 1 combination of n objects taken n at a time.

26. Explain the Error Describe and correct the error in evaluating ${}_9C_4$

${}_9C_4 = \frac{9!}{(9-4!)} = \frac{9!}{5!} = 3024$

The answer given was ${}_9P_4$, not ${}_9C_4$; ${}_9C_4 = \frac{9!}{4!(9-4!)} = \frac{9!}{4!5!} = 126$

Lesson Performance Task

1. In the 2012 elections, there were six candidates for the United States Senate in Vermont. In how many different orders, from first through sixth, could the candidates have finished?

2. The winner of the Vermont Senatorial election received 208,253 votes, 71.1% of the total votes cast. The candidate coming in second received 24.8% of the vote. How many votes did the second-place candidate receive? Round to the nearest ten.

3. Following the 2012 election there were 53 Democratic, 45 Republican, and 2 Independent senators in Congress.

   a. How many committees of 5 Democratic senators could be formed?

   b. How many committees of 48 Democratic senators could be formed?

   c. Explain how a clever person who knew nothing about combinations could guess the answer to (b) if the person knew the answer to (a).

4. Following the election, a newspaper printed a circle graph showing the make-up of the Senate. How many degrees were allotted to the sector representing Democrats, how many to Republicans, and how many to Independents?

1. $6! = 6 \cdot 5 \cdot 4 \cdot 3 \cdot 2 \cdot 1 = 720$

2. $\frac{208{,}235}{0.711} = 292{,}901.547117$ **total votes**

$292{,}901.54117 \times 0.248 = 72{,}639.58 \approx 72{,}640$

3. a. ${}_{53}C_5 = \left(\frac{53!}{5! \cdot (53-5)!}\right) = \left(\frac{344{,}362{,}200}{120}\right) = 2{,}869{,}685$

b. ${}_{53}C_{48} = \left(\frac{53!}{48! \cdot (53-48)!}\right) = \left(\frac{344{,}362{,}200}{120}\right) = 2{,}869{,}685$

c. Sample answer: The person could reason that for each committee of 5 Democratic Senators in (a) there were 48 who were not on the committee. So, there is a one-to-one correspondence between the 2,869,685 committees of 5 and the number of groups of 48, making 2,869,685 groups or committees of 48.

4. Democrats $360° \cdot 0.53 = 190.8°$

Republicans $360° \cdot 0.45 = 162°$

Independents $360° \cdot 0.02 = 7.2°$

EXTENSION ACTIVITY

Each day, Senator Smith leaves his office and walks to the Committee Room along a grid of hallways that forms a 5 by 5 square. He moves only right (R) and down (D). The path shown can be written RRRDDDRDDR. The senator has developed a method to use combinations to find the number of different ways he can complete his walk. What is the method? How many ways can he do it? **Find all possible combinations of five R's and five D's; $\frac{10!}{5!5!} = 252$ ways.**

AVOID COMMON ERRORS

In Question 2, students may incorrectly conclude that the winning candidate received 71.1% of the total of 208,253 votes cast. The problem states, however, that 208,253 votes were 71% *of all the votes cast*. The part (208,253) and the percent (71.1) are given and the whole is asked for:

$$\text{whole} = \frac{\text{part}}{\text{percent}} = \frac{208{,}253}{0.711} \approx 292{,}902$$

INTEGRATE MATHEMATICAL PRACTICES

Focus on Patterns

MP.8 Shown below are the first 6 rows of an array called Pascal's Triangle. Each number in the array is found by adding together the two numbers above it.

Row 0	1
Row 1	1 1
Row 2	1 2 1
Row 3	1 3 3 1
Row 4	1 4 6 4 1
Row 5	1 5 10 10 5 1
Row 6	1 6 15 20 15 6 1

Find ${}_3C_2$, ${}_5C_3$, and ${}_6C_4$. Then propose a connection between the terms in the triangle and the quantity ${}_mC_n$. (You'll find the connection easiest to spot by numbering the first term in each row *Term 0*. So, Term 3 in Row 6 is 20.) **${}_mC_n$ equals Term n in Row m.**

What is the 14th term in Row 17 of Pascal's Triangle? **${}_{17}C_{14} = 680$**

Scoring Rubric

2 points: The student's answer is an accurate and complete execution of the task or tasks.

1 point: The student's answer contains attributes of an appropriate response but is flawed.

0 points: The student's answer contains no attributes of an appropriate response.

LESSON 19.4

Mutually Exclusive and Overlapping Events

Common Core Math Standards

The student is expected to:

 **S-CP.A.4**

... Use the two-way table as a sample space to decide if events are independent and to approximate conditional probabilities. Also S-CP.B.7

Mathematical Practices

COMMON CORE **MP.6 Precision**

Language Objective

Give a partner an example of a mutually exclusive event. Explain how you know the events are mutually exclusive. Repeat with an example of overlapping events.

ENGAGE

Essential Question: How are probabilities affected when events are mutually exclusive or overlapping?

The probability of mutually exclusive events is the sum of the individual probabilities, while the probability of overlapping events is the sum of the individual probabilities minus the probability that both events occur.

PREVIEW: LESSON PERFORMANCE TASK

View the Engage section online. Discuss the photograph. Ask students to estimate the probability that two people in the photo have the same birthday. Then preview the Lesson Performance Task.

Name ______ Class ______ Date ______

19.4 Mutually Exclusive and Overlapping Events

Resource Locker

Essential Question: How are probabilities affected when events are mutually exclusive or overlapping?

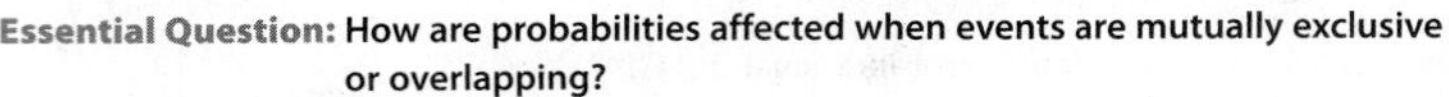

Explore 1 Finding the Probability of Mutually Exclusive Events

Two events are **mutually exclusive events** if they cannot both occur in the same trial of an experiment. For example, if you flip a coin it cannot land heads up and tails up in the same trial. Therefore, the events are mutually exclusive.

A dodecahedral number cube has 12 sides numbered 1 through 12. What is the probability that you roll the cube and the result is an even number or a 7?

(A) Let event A be rolling an even number. Let event B be rolling a 7. Let S be the sample space.

Complete the Venn diagram by writing all outcomes in the sample space in the appropriate region.

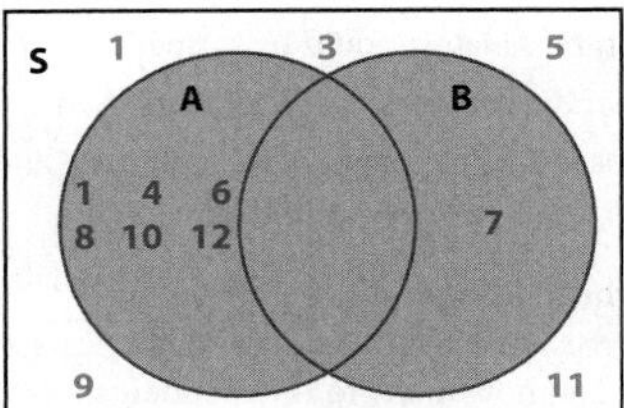

(B) Calculate $P(A)$.

$P(A) = \frac{6}{12} = \frac{1}{2}$

(C) Calculate $P(B)$.

$P(B) = \frac{1}{12}$

(D) Calculate $P(A \text{ or } B)$.

$n(S) = 12$

$n(A \text{ or } B) = n(A) + n(B)$

$= 6 + 1 = 7$

So, $P(A \text{ or } B) = \frac{n(A \text{ or } B)}{n(S)} = \frac{7}{12}$.

(E) Calculate $P(A) + P(B)$. Compare the answer to Step D.

$P(A) + P(B) = \frac{1}{2} + \frac{1}{12} = \frac{7}{12}$

$P(A) + P(B)$ equals $P(A \text{ or } B)$.

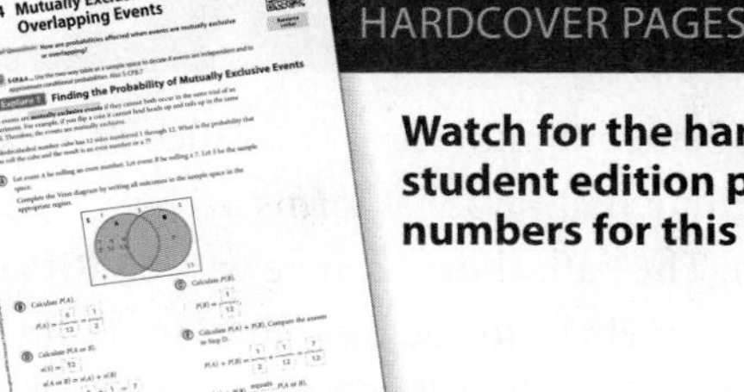

HARDCOVER PAGES 985–996

Watch for the hardcover student edition page numbers for this lesson.

Reflect

1. **Discussion** How would you describe mutually exclusive events to another student in your own words? How could you use a Venn diagram to assist in your explanation?
Possible answer: Mutually exclusive events are events that share no common outcome, meaning that the result of one event cannot be obtained from the result of another event. The Venn diagram could assist in this explanation by visually showing that the events have nothing common because their intersection would be empty.

2. Look back over the steps. What can you conjecture about the probability of the union of events that are mutually exclusive?
The probability of the union of events that are mutually exclusive is equal to the sum of the probabilities of the events.

Explore 2 Finding the Probability of Overlapping Events

The process used in the previous Explore can be generalized to give the formula for the probability of mutually exclusive events.

Mutually Exclusive Events

If A and B are mutually exclusive events, then $P(A \text{ or } B) = P(A) + P(B)$.

Two events are **overlapping events** (or inclusive events) if they have one or more outcomes in common.

What is the probability that you roll a dodecahedral number cube and the result is an even number or a number greater than 7?

(A) Let event A be rolling an even number. Let event B be rolling a number greater than 7. Let S be the sample space.

Complete the Venn diagram by writing all outcomes in the sample space in the appropriate region.

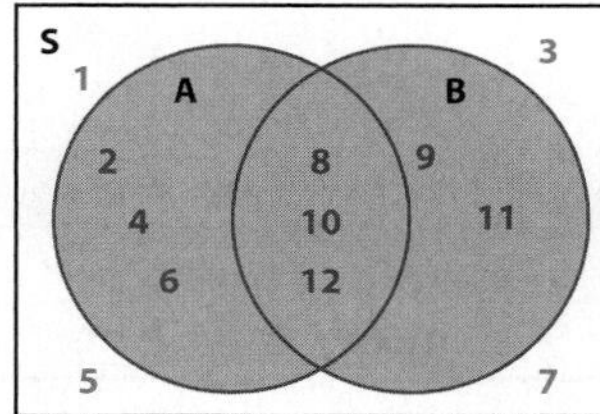

PROFESSIONAL DEVELOPMENT

Integrate Mathematical Practices

This lesson provides an opportunity to address Mathematical Practice **MP.6**, which calls for students to "communicate with precision." In this lesson, students must decide if events are mutually exclusive or overlapping in order to apply the correct version of the Addition Rule. They may examine a variety of representations, including set notation, Venn diagrams, language analysis, and two-way tables, to make and support their decisions.

EXPLORE 1

Finding the Probability of Mutually Exclusive Events

INTEGRATE TECHNOLOGY

Students have the option of doing the Explore activity either in the book or online.

INTEGRATE MATHEMATICAL PRACTICES

Focus on Communication

MP.3 Ask students to give examples of mutually exclusive events using outcomes from different probability experiments, such as a spinner, a number cube, or a deck of cards. Discuss with students how they can be sure the events they describe are mutually exclusive.

QUESTIONING STRATEGIES

? Explain why, in the case of mutually exclusive events, the probability of either event is equal to the sum of the probabilities of each event. **The events have no outcomes in common so the probability will be the total of the individual probabilities.**

? Why is a Venn diagram useful in finding the probability? **The Venn diagram provides a picture of the sets and their outcomes that shows the sets do not overlap.**

EXPLORE 2

Finding the Probability of Overlapping Events

INTEGRATE MATHEMATICAL PRACTICES

Focus on Communication

MP.3 Ask students to give examples of overlapping events using outcomes from different probability experiments, such as a spinner, a number cube, or a deck of cards. Discuss with students how they can be sure the events they describe are overlapping.

INTEGRATE MATHEMATICAL PRACTICES

Focus on Math Connections

MP.1 Review the set notation used for $P(A \text{ or } B)$ and $P(A \text{ and } B)$, as well as how they are represented on Venn diagrams for both mutually exclusive and overlapping events.

INTEGRATE MATHEMATICAL PRACTICES

Focus on Reasoning

MP.2 Discuss why $P(A) + P(B) - P(A \text{ and } B)$ can be used to find any probability $P(A \text{ or } B)$. **For mutually exclusive events, $P(A \text{ and } B) = 0$.**

QUESTIONING STRATEGIES

How is $P(A \text{ or } B)$ different from $P(A \text{ and } B)$? ***Or* refers to the union of the events; *and* refers to the intersection, or overlap, of the events.**

How can a Venn diagram help you remember the Addition Rule for overlapping events? **A Venn diagram shows where the events overlap. This can help me remember to subtract the intersection so it is not counted twice.**

(B) Calculate $P(A)$.

$P(A) = \frac{6}{12} = \frac{1}{2}$

(C) Calculate $P(B)$.

$P(B) = \frac{5}{12}$

(D) Calculate $P(A \text{ and } B)$.

$P(A \text{ and } B) = \frac{3}{12} = \frac{1}{4}$

(E) Use the Venn diagram to find $P(A \text{ or } B)$.

$P(A \text{ or } B) = \frac{8}{12} = \frac{2}{3}$

(F) Now, use $P(A)$, $P(B)$, and $P(A \text{ and } B)$ to calculate $P(A \text{ or } B)$.

$P(A) = \frac{1}{2}$ $\quad P(B) = \frac{5}{12}$ $\quad P(A \text{ and } B) = \frac{1}{4}$

$P(A) + P(B) - P(A \text{ and } B) = \frac{1}{2} + \frac{5}{12} - \frac{1}{4} = \frac{2}{3}$

Reflect

3. Why must you subtract $P(A \text{ and } B)$ from $P(A) + P(B)$ to determine $P(A \text{ or } B)$?
$P(A \text{ and } B)$ must be subtracted from $P(A) + P(B)$ to determine $P(A \text{ or } B)$ because the outcomes they share are counted twice. Therefore, the outcomes in the intersection must be subtracted from the total.

4. Look back over the steps. What can you conjecture about the probability of the union of two events that are overlapping?
The probability of the union of two events that are overlapping is equal to the sum of the probabilities of the two separate events minus the probability of both events.

Explain 1 Finding a Probability From a Two-Way Table of Data

The previous Explore leads to the following rule.

The Addition Rule

$P(A \text{ or } B) = P(A) + P(B) - P(A \text{ and } B)$

Example 1 Use the given two-way tables to determine the probabilities.

(A) $P(\text{senior or girl})$

	Freshman	Sophomore	Junior	Senior	TOTAL
Boy	98	104	100	94	396
Girl	102	106	96	108	412
Total	200	210	196	202	808

To determine $P(\text{senior or girl})$, first calculate $P(\text{senior})$, $P(\text{girl})$, and $P(\text{senior and girl})$.

COLLABORATIVE LEARNING

Peer-to-Peer Activity

Have students work with a partner to describe a situation in which the probability of two events is mutually exclusive. Have them formulate and answer a question about the probability. Repeat with inclusive events. Have students share their problems with the class.

$P(\text{senior}) = \frac{202}{808} = \frac{1}{4}$; $P(\text{girl}) = \frac{412}{808} = \frac{103}{202}$ $P(\text{senior and girl}) = \frac{108}{808} = \frac{27}{202}$

Use the addition rule to determine $P(\text{senior or girl})$.

$$P(\text{senior or girl}) = P(\text{senior}) + P(\text{girl}) - P(\text{senior and girl})$$
$$= \frac{1}{4} + \frac{103}{202} - \frac{27}{202}$$
$$= \frac{253}{404}$$

Therefore, the probability of a student being a senior or a girl is $\frac{253}{404}$.

(B) $P\left((\text{domestic or late})^c\right)$

	Late	On Time	Total
Domestic Flights	12	108	120
International Flights	6	54	60
Total	18	162	180

To determine $P\left((\text{domestic or late})^c\right)$, first calculate $P(\text{domestic or late})$.

$P(\text{domestic}) = \frac{120}{180} = \frac{2}{3}$; $P(\text{late}) = \frac{18}{180} = \frac{1}{10}$; $P(\text{domestic and late}) = \frac{12}{180} = \frac{1}{15}$

Use the addition rule to determine $P(\text{domestic or late})$.

$$P(\text{domestic or late}) = P(\text{domestic}) + P(\text{late}) - P(\text{domestic and late})$$
$$= \frac{2}{3} + \frac{1}{10} - \frac{1}{15} = \frac{7}{10}$$

Therefore, $P\left((\text{domestic or late})^c\right) = 1 - P(\text{domestic or late})$

$$= 1 - \frac{7}{10}$$
$$= \frac{3}{10}$$

EXPLAIN 1

Finding a Probability From a Two-Way Table of Data

AVOID COMMON ERRORS

Students may not use the correct total for the denominator of the probability ratio when they use a two-way table to find a probability. They may use a total from a row or column. As needed, have students extend the table to include a total that shows the sum of the columns is equal to the sum of the rows. This is the total needed for the denominator.

QUESTIONING STRATEGIES

? How do you know the events in the table are inclusive? **Possible answer: The overall total of the rows and columns is the same.**

? How do you identify the value that overlaps to apply the Addition Rule? **The overlap value is in the cell where the column and row intersect.**

DIFFERENTIATE INSTRUCTION

Multiple Representations

Discuss alternate ways to visualize the data in the problems presented. Have students make two-way tables, Venn diagrams, or tree diagrams as alternate ways to view the data and understand the relationships. Discuss the advantages of each representation.

ELABORATE

AVOID COMMON ERRORS

Students may forget to subtract the overlapping probability when finding the probability of overlapping events. Encourage students to draw Venn diagrams to help them remember how to apply the Addition Rule to solve probability problems.

SUMMARIZE THE LESSON

How do you find the probability of mutually exclusive events and overlapping events? **For mutually exclusive events A and B, $P(A \text{ or } B) = P(A) + P(B)$. For overlapping events A and B, $P(A \text{ or } B) = P(A) + P(B) - P(A \text{ and } B)$.**

Your Turn

5. Use the table to determine P(headache or no medicine).

	Took Medicine	No Medicine	TOTAL
Headache	12	15	27
No Headache	48	25	73
TOTAL	60	40	100

$P(\text{headache}) = \frac{27}{100}$; $P(\text{no medicine}) = \frac{40}{100} = \frac{2}{5}$; $P(\text{headache or no medicine}) = \frac{15}{100} = \frac{3}{10}$; $P(\text{headache or no medicine}) = P(\text{headache}) + P(\text{no medicine}) - P(\text{headache and no medicine}) = \frac{27}{100} + \frac{2}{5} - \frac{3}{20} = \frac{13}{25}$ therefore, the probability of a person having a headache or taking no medicine is $\frac{13}{25}$.

Elaborate

6. Give an example of mutually exclusive events and an example of overlapping events.
Possible answer: If you roll a number cube, the event of rolling a 3 and the event of rolling an even number are mutually exclusive because you cannot obtain both outcomes at the same time. If you pull a card from a deck, the event of pulling an ace and the event of pulling a spade are overlapping because you can obtain both outcomes by pulling the ace of spades.

7. Essential Question Check-In How do you determine the probability of mutually exclusive events and overlapping events?
To determine the probability of mutually exclusive events A and B, evaluate $P(A \text{ or } B) = P(A) + P(B)$. To determine the probability of overlapping events A and B, evaluate $P(A \text{ or } B) = P(A) + P(B) - P(A \text{ and } B)$.

Evaluate: Homework and Practice

- Online Homework
- Hints and Help
- Extra Practice

1. A bag contains 3 blue marbles, 5 red marbles, and 4 green marbles. You choose one without looking. What is the probability that it is red or green?
Let S be the sample space, A be the event that you choose a red marble, and B be the event that you choose a green marble. $n(S) = 12$, $n(A \text{ or } B) = n(A) + n(B) = 5 + 4 = 9$; $P(A \text{ or } B) = \frac{n(A \text{ or } B)}{n(S)} = \frac{9}{12} = \frac{3}{4}$; the probability that you choose a red marble or a green marble is $\frac{3}{4}$.

LANGUAGE SUPPORT EL

Connect Vocabulary

For some students, the phrase *overlapping events* may be unclear. Separate the class into groups. Have students work together to create lists of overlapping events other than those in the examples from the lesson.

2. An icosahedral number cube has 20 sides numbered 1 through 20. What is the probability that the result of a roll is a number less than 4 or greater than 11?

Let S be the sample space, A be the event that you roll a number less than 4, and B be the event that you roll a number greater than 11.

$n(S) = 20, n(A \text{ or } B) = n(A) + n(B) = 3 + 9 = 12$

$P(A \text{ or } B) = \frac{n(A \text{ or } B)}{n(S)} = \frac{12}{20} = \frac{3}{5}$

The probability that the result is a number less than 4 or greater than 11 is $\frac{3}{5}$.

3. A bag contains 26 tiles, each with a different letter of the alphabet written on it. You choose a tile without looking. What is the probability that you choose a vowel or a letter in the word GEOMETRY?

Let S be the sample space, A be the event that you choose a vowel, and B be the event that you choose a letter in the word GEOMETRY.

$n(S) = 26, n(A \text{ or } B) = n(A) + n(B) - n(A \text{ and } B) = 5 + 7 - 2 = 10$

$P(A \text{ or } B) = \frac{n(A \text{ or } B)}{n(S)} = \frac{10}{26} = \frac{5}{13}$

The probability that you choose a vowel or a letter in the word GEOMETRY is $\frac{5}{13}$.

4. **Persevere in Problem Solving** You roll two number cubes at the same time. Each cube has sides numbered 1 through 6. What is the probability that the sum of the numbers rolled is even or greater than 9? (*Hint:* Create and fill out a probability chart.)

		Cube 1					
		1	2	3	4	5	6
Cube 2	1	1 + 1	1 + 2	1 + 3	1 + 4	1 + 5	1 + 6
	2	2 + 1	2 + 2	2 + 3	2 + 4	2 + 5	2 + 6
	3	3 + 1	3 + 2	3 + 3	3 + 4	3 + 5	3 + 6
	4	4 + 1	4 + 2	4 + 3	4 + 4	4 + 5	4 + 6
	5	5 + 1	5 + 2	5 + 3	5 + 4	5 + 5	5 + 6
	6	6 + 1	6 + 2	6 + 3	6 + 4	6 + 5	6 + 6

Let S be the sample space, A be the event that the sum of the numbers is even, and B be the event that the sum of the numbers is greater than 9.

$n(S) = 36, n(A \text{ or } B) = n(A) + n(B) - n(A \text{ and } B) = 18 + 6 - 4 = 20$

$P(A \text{ or } B) = \frac{n(A \text{ or } B)}{n(S)} = \frac{20}{36} = \frac{5}{9}$

The probability that the sum of the numbers rolled is even or greater than 9 is $\frac{5}{9}$.

EVALUATE

ASSIGNMENT GUIDE

Concepts and Skills	Practice
Explore 1 Finding the Probability of Mutually Exclusive Events	Exercises 1–2, 22–23
Explore 2 Finding the Probability of Overlapping Events	Exercises 3–4
Example 1 Finding a Probability From a Two-Way Table of Data	Exercises 5–10, 11–21

COMMUNICATING MATH

Discuss the importance of filling in the total values for each row and column when the total values for a two-way table are not given.

Exercise	Depth of Knowledge (D.O.K.)	COMMON CORE Mathematical Practices
1–15	**2** Skills/Concepts	**MP.2** Reasoning
16	**2** Skills/Concepts	**MP.3** Logic
17–21	**2** Skills/Concepts	**MP.1** Problem Solving
22	**3** Strategic Thinking	**MP.3** Logic
23	**3** Strategic Thinking H.O.T.	**MP.3** Logic
24	**3** Strategic Thinking H.O.T.	**MP.4** Modeling
25	**3** Strategic Thinking H.O.T.	**MP.3** Logic

INTEGRATE MATHEMATICAL PRACTICES

Focus on Reasoning

MP.2 Discuss with students why it is easier not to simplify the fractions until after they have used the Addition Rule to calculate probabilities.

AVOID COMMON ERRORS

Students may not recognize overlapping events or may forget to subtract the overlap. Suggest that students first decide if the events can overlap. If so, students should identify the probability of this event first. Discuss how students can use *and* to help them recognize whether events overlap.

The table shows the data for car insurance quotes for 125 drivers made by an insurance company in one week.

	Teen	Adult (20 or over)	Total
0 accidents	15	53	68
1 accident	4	32	36
2+ accidents	9	12	21
Total	28	97	125

You randomly choose one of the drivers. Find each probability.

5. The driver is an adult.

$\frac{\text{Total Adults}}{\text{Total Drivers}} = \frac{97}{125}$

6. The driver is a teen with 0 or 1 accident.

$\frac{\text{Teen with 0 or 1 accident}}{\text{Total Drivers}} = \frac{19}{125}$

7. The driver is a teen.

$\frac{\text{Total Teens}}{\text{Total Drivers}} = \frac{28}{125}$

8. The driver has 2+ accidents.

$\frac{\text{Drivers with 2+ accidents}}{\text{Total Drivers}} = \frac{21}{125}$

9. The driver is a teen and has 2+ accidents.

$\frac{\text{Teens with 2+ accidents}}{\text{Total Drivers}} = \frac{9}{125}$

10. The driver is a teen or a driver with 2+ accidents.

$\frac{\text{Teen or Driver with 2+ accidents}}{\text{Total Drivers}} = \frac{28 + 21 - 9}{125} = \frac{40}{125} = \frac{8}{25}$ or

$\frac{\text{Teen or Driver with 2+ accidents}}{\text{Total Drivers}} = \frac{28}{125} + \frac{21}{125} - \frac{9}{125} = \frac{40}{125} = \frac{8}{25}$

Use the following information for Exercises 11–16. The table shown shows the results of a customer satisfaction survey for a cellular service provider, by location of the customer. In the survey, customers were asked whether they would recommend a plan with the provider to a friend.

	Arlington	Towson	Parkville	Total
Yes	40	35	41	116
No	18	10	6	34
Total	58	45	47	150

One of the customers that was surveyed was chosen at random. Find the probability.

11. The customer was from Towson and said No.

$\frac{\text{Tawson and said no}}{\text{Total}} = \frac{35}{150} = \frac{7}{30}$

12. The customer was from Parkville.

$\frac{\text{Parkville}}{\text{Total}} = \frac{47}{150}$

13. The customer said Yes.

$\frac{\text{Yes}}{\text{Total}} = \frac{116}{150} = \frac{58}{75}$

14. The customer was from Parkville and said Yes.

$\frac{\text{Parkville and said Yes}}{\text{Total}} = \frac{41}{150}$

15. The customer was from Parkville or said Yes.

$\frac{\text{Parkville or said Yes}}{\text{Total}} = \frac{\text{Parkville} + \text{Yes} - \text{Parkville and Yes}}{150} = \frac{47 + 116 - 41}{150} = \frac{122}{150} = \frac{61}{75}$ **or**

$\frac{\text{Parkville or said Yes}}{\text{Total}} = \frac{47}{150} + \frac{116}{150} - \frac{41}{150} = \frac{122}{150} = \frac{61}{75}$

16. Explain the difference between finding the probability that a customer was from Parkville and said Yes, and the probability that the customer was from Parkville or said Yes.

When the conjunction "and" is used, there is a space in the table specifically for that statistic, because they are mutually exclusive events. When the conjunction "or" is used, then they are overlapping events.

Use the following information for Exercises 17–21. Roberto is the owner of a car dealership. He is assessing the success rate of his top three salespeople in order to offer one of them a promotion. Over two months, for each attempted sale, he records whether the salesperson made a successful sale or not. The results are shown in the chart.

	Successful	Unsuccessful	Total
Becky	6	6	12
Raul	4	5	9
Darrell	6	9	15
Total	16	20	36

Roberto chooses one of the attempted sales.

17. Find the probability that the sale was one of Becky's or Darrell's successful sales.

$n(S) = n(\text{total sales}) = 36$

$n(A \cup B) = n(\text{Becky's success or Raul's success})$

$= n(\text{Becky's Success}) + n(\text{Raul's Success}) = 6 + 4 = 10$

$P(A \cup B) = \frac{n(A \cup B)}{n(S)} = \frac{10}{36} = \frac{5}{8}$

The probability that the sale was one of Becky's or Darrell's successful sales is $\frac{5}{8}$.

AVOID COMMON ERRORS

Students might treat inclusive events as mutually exclusive and double count a probability. A total probability greater than 1 could indicate this error. Remind students to consider whether the events can occur simultaneously before they choose the form of the addition rule to use.

18. Find the probability that sale was one of the unsuccessful sales or one of Raul's successful sales.

$n(S) = n(\text{total sales}) = 36$

$n(A \cup B) = n(\text{Unsuccessful or Raul's success})$

$= n(\text{Unsuccessful}) + n(\text{Raul's Success}) = 4 + 20 = 24$

$P(A \cup B) = \frac{n(A \cup B)}{n(S)} = \frac{24}{36} = \frac{2}{3}$

The probability that the sale was one of the unsuccessful sales or one of Raul's successful sales is $\frac{2}{3}$.

19. Find the probability that the sale was one of Darrell's unsuccessful sales or one of Raul's unsuccessful sales.

$n(S) = n(\text{total sales}) = 36$

$n(A \cup B) = n(\text{Darrell's Unsuccessful or Raul's Unsuccessful})$

$= n(\text{Darrell's Unsuccessful}) + n(\text{Raul's Unsuccessful})$

$= 9 + 5 = 14$

$P(A \cup B) = \frac{n(A \cup B)}{n(S)} = \frac{14}{36} = \frac{7}{18}$

The probability that the sale was one of Darrell's unsuccessful sales or one of Raul's unsuccessful sales is $\frac{7}{18}$.

20. Find the probability that the sale was an unsuccessful sale or one of Becky's attempted sales.

$n(S) = n(\text{total sales}) = 36$

$n(A \cup B) = n(\text{Unsuccessful or Becky's})$

$= n(\text{Unsuccessful}) + n(\text{Becky's}) - n(\text{Becky's Unsuccessful})$

$= 20 + 12 - 6 = 26$

$P(A \cup B) = \frac{n(A \cup B)}{n(S)} = \frac{26}{36} = \frac{13}{18}$

The probability that the sale was an unsuccessful sale or one of Becky's attempted sales is $\frac{13}{18}$.

21. Find the probability that the sale was a successful sale or one of Raul's attempted sales.

$n(S) = n(\text{total sales}) = 36$

$n(A \cup B) = n(\text{Successful or Raul's})$

$= n(\text{Successful}) + n(\text{Raul's}) - n(\text{Raul's Successful})$

$= 16 + 9 - 4 = 21$

$P(A \cup B) = \frac{n(A \cup B)}{n(S)} = \frac{21}{36} = \frac{7}{12}$

The probability that the sale was a successful sale or one of Raul's attempted sales is $\frac{7}{12}$.

22. You are going to draw one card from a standard deck of cards. A standard deck of cards has 13 cards (2, 3, 4, 5, 6, 7, 8, 9, 10, jack, queen, king, ace) in each of 4 suits (hearts, clubs, diamonds, spades). The hearts and diamonds cards are red. The clubs and spades cards are black. Which of the following have a probability of less than $\frac{1}{4}$? Choose all that apply.

(a.) Drawing a card that is a spade and an ace

b. Drawing a card that is a club or an ace

c. Drawing a card that is a face card or a club

(d.) Drawing a card that is a black and a heart

e. Drawing a red card and a number card from 2–9

a. $P(\text{spade} \cap \text{ace}) = \dfrac{n(\text{spade} \cap \text{ace})}{n(\text{deck})} = \dfrac{1}{52} < \dfrac{1}{4}$

b. $P(\text{club} \cup \text{ace}) = \dfrac{n(\text{club} \cup \text{ace})}{n(\text{deck})} = \dfrac{n(\text{club}) + n(\text{ace}) - n(\text{club} \cap \text{ace})}{n(\text{deck})} = \dfrac{13 + 4 - 1}{52} = \dfrac{16}{52}$

$= \dfrac{4}{13} > \dfrac{1}{4}$

c. $P(\text{face} \cup \text{club}) = \dfrac{n(\text{face} \cup \text{club})}{n(\text{deck})} = \dfrac{n(\text{face}) + n(\text{club}) - n(\text{face} \cap \text{club})}{n(\text{deck})} = \dfrac{12 + 13 - 3}{52} = \dfrac{22}{52}$

$= \dfrac{11}{26} > \dfrac{1}{4}$

d. $P(\text{black} \cap \text{heart}) = \dfrac{n(\text{black} \cap \text{heart})}{n(\text{deck})} = \dfrac{0}{52} = 0 < \dfrac{1}{4}$

e. $P(\text{red} \cap 2-9) = \dfrac{n(\text{red} \cap 2-9)}{n(\text{deck})} = \dfrac{16}{52} = \dfrac{4}{13} > \dfrac{1}{4}$

H.O.T. Focus on Higher Order Thinking

3. **Draw Conclusions** A survey of 1108 employees at a software company finds that 621 employees take a bus to work and 445 employees take a train to work. Some employees take both a bus and a train, and 321 employees take only a train. To the nearest percent, find the probability that a randomly chosen employee takes a bus or a train to work. Explain.

If 321 employees take only a train, and 445 total employees take a train, then

445 − 321 = 124 people take both a bus and a train to work.

$n(A \cup B) = n(\text{bus}) + n(\text{train}) - n(\text{bus and train}) = 621 + 445 - 124 = 942$

$n(S) = n(\text{total surveyed}) = 1108$

$P(A \cup B) = \dfrac{n(A \cup B)}{n(S)} = \dfrac{942}{1108} = \dfrac{471}{554}$

The probability that a randomly chosen employee takes a bus or a train to work is 85%.

JOURNAL

Have students explain how the probabilities of mutually exclusive and inclusive events are really two versions of the same problem.

24. Communicate Mathematical Ideas Explain how to use a Venn diagram to find the probability of randomly choosing a multiple of 3 or a multiple of 4 from the set of numbers from 1 to 25. Then find the probability.

Let A be the set of multiples of 3 from 1 to 25 and B be the set of multiples of 4 from 1 to 25. Create a Venn diagram representing the sets A and B.

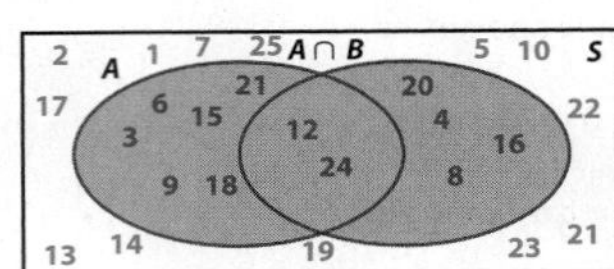

Add the numbers of elements in A and B, and then subtract the number of elements in the overlap to get the numerator of the probability. The denominator is 25.

$n(A \cup B) = 8 + 6 - 2 = 12$

$P(A \cup B) = \frac{12}{25}$

The probability of randomly choosing a multiple of 3 or a multiple of 4 from the set of numbers from 1 to 25 is $\frac{12}{25}$.

25. Explain the Error Sanderson attempted to find the probability of choosing a 10 or a diamond from a standard deck of playing cards. He used the following logic:

Let S be the sample space, A be the event that the card is a 10, and B be the event that the card is a diamond.

There are 52 cards in the deck, so $n(S) = 52$.

There are four 10s in the deck, so $n(A) = 4$.

There are 13 diamonds in the deck, so $n(B) = 13$.

One 10 is a diamond, so $n(A \cap B) = 1$.

$P(A \cup B) = \frac{n(A) \cdot n(B) - n(A \cap B)}{n(S)} = \frac{4 \cdot 13 - 1}{52} = \frac{51}{52}$

Describe and correct Sanderson's mistake.

When finding $n(A \cup B)$, $n(A)$ should be added to $n(B)$, not multiplied.

$P(A \cup B) = \frac{n(A) + n(B) - n(A \cap B)}{n(S)} = \frac{4 + 13 - 1}{52} = \frac{16}{52} = \frac{4}{13}$

Lesson Performance Task

What is the smallest number of randomly chosen people that are needed in order for there to be a better than 50% probability that at least two of them will have the same birthday? The astonishing answer is 23. Follow these steps to find why.

1. Can a person have a birthday on two different days? Use the vocabulary of this lesson to explain your answer.

2. How many pairs of people are there in a group of 23? Explain how you found the answer.

Looking for the probability that two or more people in a group of 23 have matching birthdays is a challenge. Maybe there is one match but maybe there are five matches or seven or fourteen. A much easier way is to look for the probability that there are *no* matches in a group of 23. In other words, all 23 have different birthdays. Then use that number to find the answer.

3. There are 365 possible birthdays in a non-leap year. The probability that a pair of randomly chosen people have the same birthday is $\frac{1}{365}$.

   a. What is the probability that a pair of randomly chosen people have *different* birthdays?

   b. Use your answer to write an expression for the probability that the number of pairs of randomly chosen people in a group of 23 (see your answer to Question 2) have different birthdays.

   c. Evaluate the expression to the nearest ten-thousandth.

   d. How can you use your answer to (c) to find the probability that in a group of 23 randomly chosen people, at least two of them will have the same birthday?

   e. What is the probability that in a group of 23 randomly chosen people, at least two of them will have the same birthday?

1. No; sample answer: The set of days on which you have a birthday and the set when you do not have a birthday are mutually exclusive, not overlapping.

2. 253; $_{23}C_2 = \frac{23!}{2!21!} = \frac{23 \cdot 22}{2}$ 253

3. a. $\frac{364}{365}$

b. $\left(\frac{354}{365}\right)^{253}$

c. 0.4995

d. Subtract the answer from 1 $(= 100\%$ probability$)$.

e. 0.5005, or 50.05%

AVOID COMMON ERRORS

Students hearing the birthday paradox for the first time often misunderstand it as claiming that in a group of 23 randomly chosen people, the chances are better than 50–50 that one of them will have a specific given birthday, say July 23. Students are correct in thinking that that is highly unlikely. Stress that the paradox is that in a random group of 23, the chances are better than 50–50 that *two of them will have the same birthday*. The actual date of the birthday, however, is unstated.

INTEGRATE MATHEMATICAL PRACTICES

Focus on Critical Thinking

MP.3 Tammy's birthday is July 23. How large must a group of randomly chosen people be in order for there to be a better than 50% chance that one of them will have the same birthday she has?
183; $\frac{183}{365} \approx 50.1\%$

EXTENSION ACTIVITY

Present another surprising probability paradox: (1) Mister Jones has two children. The oldest is a girl. What is the probability that the other child is a girl? Explain your reasoning. **$\frac{1}{2}$; 2 possible outcomes for second child: {B, G}; 1 favorable outcome: G** (2) Mister Smith has two children. At least one of them is a girl. What is the probability that the other child is a girl? Explain your reasoning. **$\frac{1}{3}$; 3 possible combinations: {GG, BG, GB}; 1 favorable outcome: GG** It may seem counterintuitive that specifying "at least" changes the probability that the second child will be a girl. To test this, have students flip two coins (H = girl, T = boy). They should ignore TT (boy, boy). If one is a heads, they should count the number of times the other is also a heads.

Scoring Rubric

2 points: The student's answer is an accurate and complete execution of the task or tasks.

1 point: The student's answer contains attributes of an appropriate response but is flawed.

0 points: The student's answer contains no attributes of an appropriate response.

Study Guide Review

ASSESSMENT AND INTERVENTION

Assign or customize module reviews.

MODULE PERFORMANCE TASK

Mathematical Practices: MP.1, MP.2, MP.4, MP.7, MP.8
S-CP.A.1, S-CP.B.9

SUPPORTING STUDENT REASONING

Students should begin this problem by focusing on what information they will need. Here are some issues they might bring up.

- **How to find the probability of getting a hit at bat:** Students can make an organized list that shows the probability of getting a hit in the next turn and then in the next three turns at bat, the least number of turns at bat a player will get in today's game. The probability of getting a hit in three turns will be the sum of the probabilities associated with at least one hit at bat.
- **The probability of getting no hits at bat in one game:** Students can use the organized list to find this value for three turns at bat.
- **How to find the probability of getting exactly one hit at bat:** Students can use the organized list to find this value for three turns at bat. They should add the probabilities for all rows that show exactly one hit in three tries.

Introduction to Probability

Essential Question: How can you use probability to solve real-world problems?

Key Vocabulary
- set *(conjunto, juego)*
- element *(elemento)*
- empty set *(conjunto vacío)*
- universal set *(conjunto universal)*
- subset *(subconjunto)*
- intersection *(intersección)*
- union *(unión)*
- complement *(complementar)*
- theoretical probability *(probabilidad teórica)*
- permutation *(permutación)*
- Fundamental Counting Principle *(principio fundamental de conteo)*
- factorial *(factorial)*
- combination *(combinación)*

KEY EXAMPLE *(Lesson 19.1)*

When rolling two fair number cubes, what is the probability that the sum of the two cubes will not be even or prime?

Event A is the when the sum of the two cubes are either even or prime, so we are looking for the complement of A, or A^C. Also note that $P(A^C) = 1 - P(A)$. When a number cube is rolled there are 6 possible outcomes, so rolling two cubes will have 6^2, or 36, different outcomes. Of those 36, 32 sum to either an even number or a prime number, so $P(A) = \frac{32}{36} = \frac{8}{9}$. Therefore, $P(A^C) = 1 - \frac{8}{9} = \frac{1}{9}$.

KEY EXAMPLE *(Lesson 19.2)*

Ten marbles are placed in a jar. Of the 10 marbles, 3 are blue, 2 are red, 3 are green, 1 is orange, and 1 is yellow. The 10 marbles are randomly placed in a line. What is the probability that all marbles of the same color are next to each other?

Marbles of the same color are indistinguishable objects. The sample space $n(S)$ is the number of permutations of 10 objects, with 3 of one type, 3 of another type, and 2 of a third type.

$$n(S) = \frac{10!}{3!3!2!} = 50{,}400$$

The event space $n(A)$ is the number of permutations that have all marbles of the same color next to each other.

$$n(A) = 5! = 120$$

The probability that all marbles of the same color are next to each other is

$$P(A) = \frac{n(A)}{n(S)} = \frac{120}{50{,}400} = \frac{1}{420}.$$

KEY EXAMPLE *(Lesson 19.3)*

A class of 15 boys and 15 girls is putting together a random group of 3 students to do classroom chores. What is the probability that at least 2 of the students are boys?

The sample space $n(S)$ is the number of combinations of three student groups.

$$n(S) = \frac{30!}{3!27!} = 4060$$

The event space $n(A)$ is the number of combinations of both having 2 boys and having 3 boys in the group. The event of getting 2 boys in the group occurs 15 times, once for each individual girl in the class.

$$n(A) = 15 \cdot {}_{15}C_2 + {}_{15}C_3 = 15 \cdot \frac{15!}{2!13!} + \frac{15!}{3!12!} = 2030$$

The probability that there will be at least 2 boys in the group is $P(A) = \frac{n(A)}{n(S)} = \frac{2030}{4060} = \frac{1}{2}$.

SCAFFOLDING SUPPORT

- Students will first need to calculate the probability of getting a hit in any one turn at bat, using the information given. The probability is the ratio of the number of hits to the number of times at bat. The probability of not getting a hit in any one turn is 1 minus this value.
- To find the probability of any combination of hits and no hits, find the product of the probabilities for each individual event.

EXERCISES

Use the sets below to find the solution set for problems 1–4. *(Lesson 19.1)*

U = {1, 2, 3, 4, 5, 6, 7, 8, 9}

A = {1, 3, 5, 7, 9}

B = {2, 4, 6, 8}

C = {1, 2, 4, 5, 7, 9}

1. $A \cup C$ {1, 2, 3, 4, 5, 7, 8, 9}
2. $B \cap C$ {2, 4}
3. A^C {2, 4, 6, 8}
4. $A \cap B$ {∅}
5. A computer password can use all numbers (0–9) and all letters (*a–z*) that are case sensitive (upper and lower). How many different permutations of 5-figure passwords are there if there is no repeated input? *(Lesson 19.2)* **776520240**
6. Brandon is rolling a 10-sided dice 5 times. What is the probability that he will roll at least two 7s? *(Lesson 19.3)* $\frac{26}{100000}$

Determine if the given event is mutually exclusive. If not, explain why. *(Lesson 19.4)*

7. Rolling a 3 or a 4 on a regular number cube **yes**
8. Drawing a queen or a red card from a standard deck of 52 cards **no; the card can be a red queen**
9. Flipping a coin and it lands on heads or tails **yes**
10. Rolling an even number or a prime number on a number cube **no; 2 is both prime and even**

MODULE PERFORMANCE TASK

Baseball Probability

A baseball player will be batting three times during today's game. So far this season, the player has gotten 109 hits in 325 times at bat. Based on this data, what is the probability that the player will get exactly one hit in today's game? Is that outcome more or less likely than getting no hits?

Start by making notes in the space below about your plan for solving the problem. Then use your own paper to complete the task, using words, numbers, or diagrams to explain how your reached your conclusions.

DISCUSSION OPPORTUNITIES

- There are many baseball games in which a player gets more than three turns at bat. How does this change the probabilities shown in the organized list?
- Why is the probability of getting at least one hit in three turns at bat higher than the probability of getting exactly one hit in three turns at bat?

SAMPLE SOLUTION

Assumption:

The player will continue to bat the same percentage as batted in previous games of the season.

Method:

Find the probability of getting a hit and no hits in any one turn at bat.

Create an organized list to show the possible outcomes for 3 turns at bat by multiplying the probabilities for each outcome.

Use the data from the list to find the probabilities of exactly one hit and no hits.

Find the probability of getting a hit in any one turn.

$\frac{109}{325} \approx 0.335$

The probability of getting no hits is

$1 - 0.335 = 0.665$.

Use these values to calculate the probabilities for all possible outcomes.

At Bat			Calculation	Probability
1	2	3		
H	N	N	$0.335(0.665)^2$	0.148
H	N	H	$0.665(0.335)^2$	0.075
H	H	N	$0.665(0.335)^2$	0.075
H	H	H	$(0.335)^3$	0.037
N	N	N	$(0.665)^3$	0.294
N	H	N	$0.335(0.665)^2$	0.148
N	H	H	$0.665(0.335)^2$	0.075
N	N	H	$0.335(0.665)^2$	0.148
TOTAL				1.000

Since 3 outcomes result in exactly 1 hit in 3 at bats, the probability is 3×0.148 or 0.444. This could also be expressed as 44.4%. This probability is greater than the probability of getting no hits, which is 0.294 or 29.4%.

Assessment Rubric

2 points: Student correctly solves the problem and explains his/her reasoning.

1 point: Student shows good understanding of the problem but does not fully solve or explain.

0 points: Student does not demonstrate understanding of the problem.

Ready to Go On?

ASSESS MASTERY

Use the assessment on this page to determine if students have mastered the concepts and standards covered in this module.

ASSESSMENT AND INTERVENTION

Access Ready to Go On? assessment online, and receive instant scoring, feedback, and customized intervention or enrichment.

ADDITIONAL RESOURCES

Response to Intervention Resources

- Reteach Worksheets

Differentiated Instruction Resources

- Reading Strategies EL
- Success for English Learners EL
- Challenge Worksheets

Assessment Resources

- Leveled Module Quizzes

Ready to Go On?

19.1–19.4 Introduction to Probability

- Online Homework
- Hints and Help
- Extra Practice

Find the probabilities.

1. Twenty-six tiles with the letters A through Z are placed face down on a table and mixed. (For the purpose of this exercise assume that the letter Y is a vowel.) Five tiles are drawn in order. Compute the probability that only consonants are selected.

$n(S) = {}_{26}C_5 = \frac{26!}{5!21!} = 65780, n(A) = {}_{20}C_5 = \frac{20!}{5!15!} = 15504, P(A) = \frac{n(A)}{n(S)} = \frac{15504}{65780} = \frac{3876}{16445}$

2. The two-way table shows the results of a poll in a certain country that asked voters, sorted by political party, whether they supported or opposed a proposed government initiative. Find the given probabilities.

	Party A	Party B	Other Party	No Party	Total
Support	97	68	8	19	192
Oppose	32	81	16	11	140
Undecided	9	23	10	26	68
Total	138	172	34	56	400

a. $P(\text{no party or undecided})$ $\frac{56}{400} + \frac{68}{400} - \frac{26}{400} = \frac{98}{400} = \frac{49}{200}$

b. $P\left((\text{party A or support})^c\right)$ $P\left((\text{party A or support})^c\right) = 1 - P(\text{party A or support}) = 1 - \frac{233}{400} =$

ESSENTIAL QUESTION

3. A teacher is assigning 32 presentation topics to 9 students at random. Each student will get 3 topics, and no topic will be repeated. Somil is very interested in 5 topics. What is the probability that Somil will be assigned at least one of his preferred topics? Explain how you arrived at your answer.

Methods may vary. Somil being assigned at least one of his preferred topics is the complement of Somil being assigned none of his preferred topics. The sample space $n(S)$ is $n(S) = {}_{32}C_3 = \frac{32!}{3!29!} = 4960$. The event space $n(A)$ is the number of combinations of 3 topics in which Somil is not very interested: $n(S) = {}_{27}C_3 = \frac{27!}{3!24!} = 2925$. The probability that Somil is not assigned any of his preferred topics is $P(A) = \frac{n(A)}{n(S)} = \frac{2925}{4960} = \frac{585}{992}$. Thus the probability that Somil is assigned at least one of his preferred topics is $P(A^c) = 1 - P(A) = 1 - P(A) = 1 - \frac{585}{992} = \frac{407}{992}$.

COMMON CORE Common Core Standards

Lesson	Items	Content Standards	Mathematical Practices
19.1, 19.3	1	**S-CP.B.9**	**MP.1**
19.4	2	**S-CP.A.4**	**MP.1**

MODULE 19
MIXED REVIEW

Assessment Readiness

1. Jonah is arranging books on a shelf. The order of the books matters to him. There are 336 ways he can arrange the books. Choose True or False for each statement.
   - **A.** He might arranging 3 books from a selection of 8 different books. ● True ○ False
   - **B.** He might be arranging 4 books from a selection of 8 different books. ○ True ● False
   - **C.** He might be arranging 5 books from a selection of 8 different books. ○ True ● False

2. Decide whether the probability of tossing the given sum with two dice is $\frac{5}{36}$. Select Yes or No for A–C.
   - **A.** A sum of 6. ● True ○ False
   - **A.** A sum of 7. ○ True ● False
   - **A.** A sum of 8. ● True ○ False

3. Let H be the event that a coin flip lands with heads showing, and let T be the event that a flip lands with tails showing. (Note that $P(H) = P(T) = 0.5$.) What is the probability that you will get heads at least once if you flip the coin ten times? Explain your reasoning.

   About 0.999; sample answer: Let A be the probability that heads appears at least once and B be the probability that it doesn't appear.

   $$\begin{aligned} P(A) &= 1 - P(B) \\ &= 1 - P(0.5^{10}) \\ &\approx 1 - .001 \\ &\approx 0.999 \end{aligned}$$

4. There are 8 girls and 6 boys on the student council. How many committees of 3 girls and 2 boys can be formed? Show your work.

   840 committees; $$\begin{aligned} C(8,3) \cdot C(6,2) &= \frac{8 \cdot 7 \cdot \cancel{6} \cdot \cancel{5} \cdot \cancel{4} \cdot \cancel{3} \cdot \cancel{2} \cdot \cancel{1}}{\cancel{5} \cdot \cancel{4} \cdot \cancel{3} \cdot \cancel{2} \cdot \cancel{1} \cdot \cancel{3} \cdot \cancel{2} \cdot 1} \cdot \frac{6 \cdot 5 \cdot \cancel{4} \cdot \cancel{3} \cdot \cancel{2} \cdot \cancel{1}}{\cancel{4} \cdot \cancel{3} \cdot \cancel{2} \cdot \cancel{1} \cdot 2 \cdot 1} \\ &= 56 \cdot 15 \\ &= 840 \end{aligned}$$

Common Core Standards

Lesson	Items	Content Standards	Mathematical Practices
19.2	1	**S-CP.B.9**	**MP.2**
19.1	2	**S-CP.A.1**	**MP.2**
19.1	3	**S-CP.A.1**	**MP.4**
19.3	4	**S-CP.B.9**	**MP.2**

* Item integrates mixed review concepts from previous modules or a previous course.

MIXED REVIEW

Assessment Readiness

ASSESSMENT AND INTERVENTION

Assign ready-made or customized practice tests to prepare students for high-stakes tests.

ADDITIONAL RESOURCES

Assessment Resources

- Leveled Module Quizzes: Modified, B

AVOID COMMON ERRORS

Item 4 Some students have a hard time determining the difference between permutations and combinations. Remind students that with permutations, order matters, and with combinations, order does not matter.

MODULE 20

Conditional Probability and Independence of Events

ESSENTIAL QUESTION:

Answer: Conditional probability and independence of events are useful for analyzing how the occurrence of one event affects the probability of another.

PROFESSIONAL DEVELOPMENT VIDEO

Professional Development Video
Author Matt Larson models successful teaching practices in an actual high-school classroom.
Professional Development
my.hrw.com

MODULE 20

Conditional Probability and Independence of Events

Essential Question: How can you use conditional probability and independence of events to solve real-world problems?

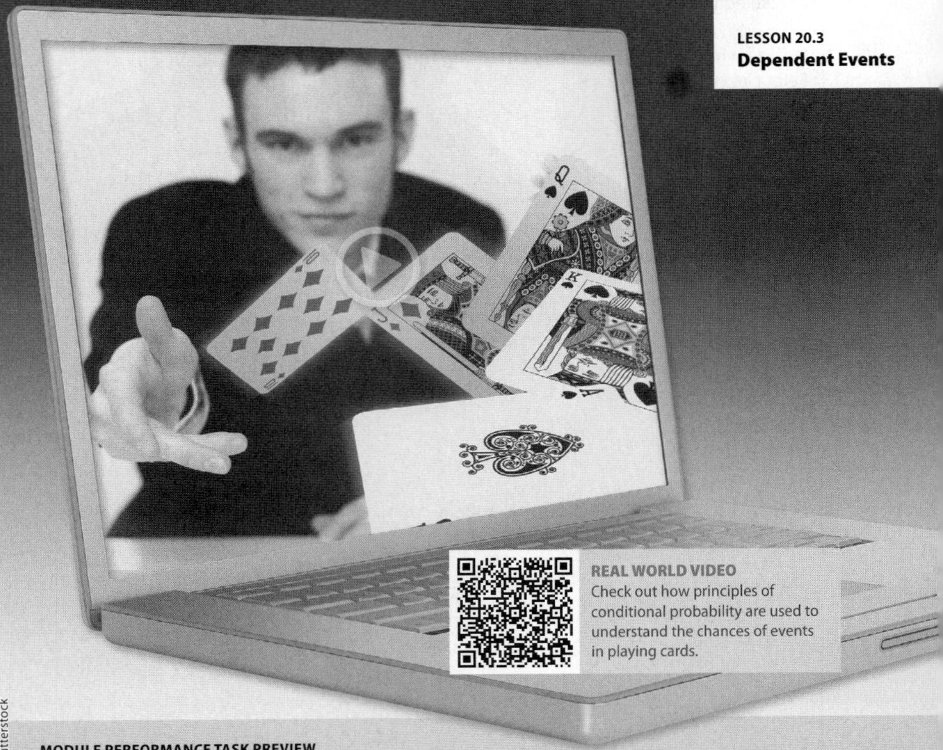

REAL WORLD VIDEO
Check out how principles of conditional probability are used to understand the chances of events in playing cards.

MODULE PERFORMANCE TASK PREVIEW

Playing Cards

In this module, you will use concepts of conditional probability to determine the chance of drawing a hand of cards with a certain property. To successfully complete this task you'll need to master these skills:

- Distinguish between independent and dependent events.
- Apply the conditional probability formula to a real-world situation.
- Use the Multiplication Rule appropriately.

DIGITAL TEACHER EDITION

Access a full suite of teaching resources when and where you need them:

- Access content online or offline
- Customize lessons to share with your class
- Communicate with your students in real-time
- View student grades and data instantly to target your instruction where it is needed most

PERSONAL MATH TRAINER

Assessment and Intervention

Assign automatically graded homework, quizzes, tests, and intervention activities. Prepare your students with updated, Common Core-aligned practice tests.

Complete these exercises to review skills you will need for this module.

- Online Homework
- Hints and Help
- Extra Practice

Probability of Compound Events

Example 1 Find the probability of rolling a pair of six-sided dice and the sum of their faces being even or equal to 3.

3 is not even, so the two probabilities are mutually exclusive. The probability is equal to the sums of the probabilities of rolling an even sum or rolling a sum of 3.

Probability of rolling an even sum $= \frac{9}{36}$ — Count the number of outcomes for the first event.

Probability of rolling a sum of 3 $= \frac{2}{36}$ — Count the number of outcomes for the second event.

Probability of rolling an even sum or a sum of 3 $= \frac{9}{36} + \frac{2}{36} = \frac{11}{36}$

Find each probability.

1. The probability of rolling two dice at the same time and getting a 4 with either die or the sum of the dice is 6. $\frac{7}{18}$
2. The probability of rolling two dice at the same time and getting a 4 with either die and the sum of the dice is 6. $\frac{1}{18}$
3. The probability of pulling a red or a blue marble from a jar given the probability of drawing a red marble is $\frac{1}{2}$ and the probability of pulling a blue marble is $\frac{1}{2}$ and you pull two marbles. 1
4. The probability of pulling a red and a blue marble from a jar given the probability of drawing a red marble is $\frac{1}{2}$ and the probability of pulling a blue marble is $\frac{1}{2}$ and you pull two marbles. $\frac{1}{2}$
5. The probability of flipping a coin three times and getting exactly two heads or at least one tails given the probability of getting a heads is $\frac{1}{2}$ and the probability of getting a tails is $\frac{1}{2}$. $\frac{7}{8}$
6. The probability of flipping a coin three times and getting exactly two heads and at least one tails given the probability of getting a heads is $\frac{1}{2}$ and the probability of getting a tails is $\frac{1}{2}$. $\frac{3}{8}$
7. The probability of flipping a coin three times and getting at least two heads or at least one tails given the probability of getting a heads is $\frac{1}{2}$ and the probability of getting a tails is $\frac{1}{2}$. 1

Response to Intervention			Differentiated Instruction
Tier 1 Lesson Intervention Worksheets	**Tier 2** Strategic Intervention Skills Intervention Worksheets	**Tier 3** Intensive Intervention Worksheets available online	
Reteach 20.1 Reteach 20.2 Reteach 20.3	51 Probability of Compound Events 52 Probability of Simple Events	Building Block Skills 6, 12, 37, 39, 65, 72, 82, 86, 95, 112	Challenge worksheets Extend the Math Lesson Activities in TE

Are You Ready?

ASSESS READINESS

Use the assessment on this page to determine if students need strategic or intensive intervention for the module's prerequisite skills.

ASSESSMENT AND INTERVENTION

RtI Response to Intervention TIER 1, TIER 2, TIER 3 SKILLS

Personal Math Trainer will automatically create a standards-based, personalized intervention assignment for your students, targeting each student's individual needs!

ADDITIONAL RESOURCES

See the table below for a full list of intervention resources available for this module.

Response to Intervention Resources also includes:

- Tier 2 Skill Pre-Tests for each Module
- Tier 2 Skill Post-Tests for each skill

LESSON 20.1

Conditional Probability

Common Core Math Standards

The student is expected to:

 S-CP.A.4

... Use the two-way table ... to approximate conditional probabilities. Also S-CP.A.3, S-CP.A.5, S-CP.B.6

Mathematical Practices

 MP.4 Modeling

Language Objective

Explain to a partner how to find conditional probabilities.

ENGAGE

Essential Question: How do you calculate a conditional probability?

You can calculate the conditional probability $P(A \mid B)$ from a two-way frequency table using the formula $P(A \mid B) = \frac{n(A \cap B)}{n(B)}$. You can also calculate $P(A \mid B)$ using the formula $P(A \mid B) = \frac{P(A \cap B)}{P(B)}$.

PREVIEW: LESSON PERFORMANCE TASK

View the Engage section online. Discuss the photograph. Ask students to identify the celebrity and to describe the reasons for the celebrity's fame. Then preview the Lesson Performance Task.

Name ________ Class ________ Date ________

20.1 Conditional Probability

Essential Question: How do you calculate a conditional probability?

Resource Locker

Explore 1 Finding Conditional Probabilities from a Two-Way Frequency Table

The probability that event A occurs given that event B has already occurred is called the **conditional probability** of A given B and is written $P(A \mid B)$.

One hundred migraine headache sufferers participated in a study of a new medicine. Some were given the new medicine, and others were not. After one week, participants were asked if they had experienced a headache during the week. The two-way frequency table shows the results.

	Took medicine	No medicine	Total
Headache	11	13	24
No headache	54	22	76
Total	65	35	100

Let event A be the event that a participant did not get a headache. Let event B be the event that a participant took the medicine.

(A) To the nearest percent, what is the probability that a participant who took the medicine did not get a headache?

65 participants took the medicine.

Of these, 54 did not get a headache.

So, $P(A \mid B) = \frac{54}{65} \approx 83\%$.

(B) To the nearest percent, what is the probability that a participant who did not get a headache took the medicine?

76 participants did not get a headache.

Of these, 54 took the medicine.

So, $P(B \mid A) = \frac{54}{76} \approx 71\%$.

(C) Let $n(A)$ be the number of participants who did not get a headache, $n(B)$ be the number of participants who took the medicine, and $n(A \cap B)$ be the number of participants who took the medicine and did not get a headache.

$n(A) = 76$ $n(B) = 65$ $n(A \cap B) = 76$

Express $P(A \mid B)$ and $P(B \mid A)$ in terms of $n(A)$, $n(B)$, and $n(A \cap B)$.

$P(B \mid A) = \frac{n(A \cap B)}{n(B)}$ $P(B \mid A) = \frac{n(A \cap B)}{n(A)}$

HARDCOVER PAGES 1003–10

Watch for the hardcover student edition page numbers for this lesson.

Reflect

1. For the question "What is the probability that a participant who did not get a headache took the medicine?", what event is assumed to have already occurred?
   The event that a participant did not get a headache is assumed to have already occurred.

2. In general, does it appear that $P(A \mid B) = P(B \mid A)$? Why or why not?
   No, the calculations of $P(A \mid B)$ and $P(B \mid A)$ in Steps A and B show that these conditional probabilities are not equal, so in general $P(A \mid B) \neq P(B \mid A)$.

Explore 2 Finding Conditional Probabilities from a Two-Way Relative Frequency Table

You can develop a formula for $P(A \mid B)$ that uses relative frequencies (which are probabilities) rather than frequencies (which are counts).

	Took medicine	No medicine	Total
Headache	11	13	24
No headache	54	22	76
Total	65	35	100

(A) To obtain relative frequencies, divide every number in the table by 100, the total number of participants in the study.

	Took medicine	No medicine	Total
Headache	0.11	0.13	0.24
No headache	0.54	0.22	0.76
Total	0.65	0.35	1

(B) Recall that event A is the event that a participant did not get a headache and that event B is the event that a participant took the medicine. Use the relative frequency table from Step A to find $P(A)$, $P(B)$, and $P(A \cap B)$.
$P(A) = 0.76$, $P(B) = 0.65$, and $P(A \cap B) = 0.54$.

(C) In the first Explore, you found the conditional probabilities $P(A \mid B) \approx 83\%$ and $P(B \mid A) \approx 71\%$ by using the frequencies in the two-way frequency table. Use the relative frequencies from the table in Step A to find the equivalent conditional probabilities.

$$P(A \mid B) = \frac{P(A \cap B)}{P(A)} = \frac{0.54}{0.65} \approx 83\ \% \qquad P(B \mid A) = \frac{P(A \cap B)}{P(A)} = \frac{0.54}{0.76} \approx 71\ \%$$

PROFESSIONAL DEVELOPMENT

Learning Progressions

This is the first of three related lessons that cover the concepts of conditional probability, independent events, and dependent events. Many texts begin by defining independent and dependent events. The approach in this module begins with a deeper treatment of conditional probability and then progresses to defining independent and dependent events. This approach gives students many opportunities to work with two-way tables, which they can use to make sense of a wide range of probability and statistics problems as they continue their study of mathematics.

EXPLORE 1

Finding Conditional Probabilities from a Two-Way Frequency Table

INTEGRATE TECHNOLOGY

Students have the option of doing the Explore activity either in the book or online.

QUESTIONING STRATEGIES

? As you read down the column of a two-way table, how do you find the probability that each event happened? **Sample answer: Within the same column, you divide the number of outcomes for each event by the total number of outcomes in that column.**

? What does the notation $P(A \mid B)$ represent? **the conditional probability that event A will happen given that event B has already occurred**

EXPLORE 2

Finding Conditional Probabilities from a Two-Way Relative Frequency Table

INTEGRATE MATHEMATICAL PRACTICES

Focus on Math Connections

MP.1 Two-way frequency tables are efficient ways to express quantitative data that can be categorized by two variables. Point out that there are two formulas for $P(A \mid B)$: $P(A \mid B) = \frac{n(A \cap B)}{n(B)}$ and $P(A \mid B) = \frac{P(A \cap B)}{P(B)}$. It is important for students to be able to identify each of the quantities in the two formulas, and for them to distinguish between $n(B)$, the number of outcomes for B, and $P(B)$, the probability of B.

QUESTIONING STRATEGIES

? What does $A \cap B$ represent in a two-way table? **the number of outcomes that represent both events, *A* and *B***

? What does $n(S)$ represent? **the total number of outcomes in the sample space**

EXPLAIN 1

Using the Conditional Probability Formula

AVOID COMMON ERRORS

Students may be confused about how to find the total number of outcomes in a two-way table. Tell them that the total number of outcomes (the number of outcomes in the sample space) should appear at the lower right corner. It equals the total of the bottom row of the table and the total of the right-most column of the table.

(D) Generalize the results by using $n(S)$ as the number of elements in the sample space (in this case, the number of participants in the study). For instance, you can write $P(A) = \frac{n(A)}{n(S)}$. Write each of the following probabilities in a similar way.

$$P(B) = \frac{n(B)}{n(S)} \qquad P(A \cap B) = \frac{n(A \cap B)}{n(S)} \qquad P(A|B) = \frac{\frac{n(A \cap B)}{n(S)}}{\frac{n(B)}{n(S)}} = \frac{P(A \cap B)}{P(B)}$$

Reflect

3. Why are the two forms of $P(A \cap B)$, $\frac{n(A \cap B)}{n(B)}$ and $\frac{P(A \cap B)}{P(B)}$, equivalent?
   $\frac{n(A \cap B) \div n(S)}{n(B) \div n(S)} = P(A \cap B)$

4. What is a formula for $P(B|A)$ that involves probabilities rather than counts? How do you obtain this formula from the fact that $P(B|A) = \frac{n(A \cap B)}{n(A)}$?
   $P(B|A) = \frac{P(A \cap B)}{P(A)}$**; you divide the numerator and denominator of** $\frac{n(A \cap B)}{n(A)}$ **by** $n(S)$**.**

Explain 1 Using the Conditional Probability Formula

In the previous Explore, you discovered the following formula for the conditional probability.

Conditional Probability

The conditional probability of *A* given *B* (that is, the probability that event *A* occurs given that event *B* occurs) is as follows:

$$P(B|A) = \frac{P(A \cap B)}{P(A)}$$

Example 1 **For a standard deck of playing cards, find the probability that a red card randomly drawn from the deck is a jack.**

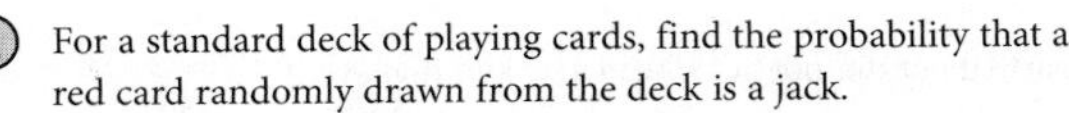

(A) For a standard deck of playing cards, find the probability that a red card randomly drawn from the deck is a jack.

Step 1 Find $P(R)$, the probability that a red card is drawn from the deck.

There are 26 red cards in the deck of 52 cards, so $P(R) = \frac{26}{52}$.

Step 2 Find $P(J \cap R)$, the probability that a red jack is drawn from the deck.

There are 2 red jacks in the deck, so $P(J \cap R) = \frac{2}{52}$.

COLLABORATIVE LEARNING

Small Group Activity

Give groups of students sample two-way tables. Have one student verify all of the totals in the table and give the size of the sample. Ask a second student to explain how to find the conditional probabilities of one column of the table. Then have a third student explain how to find the conditional probabilities of the second column. Have a fourth student verify that the conditional probabilities for the table are consistent with the sample space and are correct. Then have students compare their results, and present them to the class.

Step 3 Substitute the probabilities from Steps 1 and 2 into the formula for conditional probability.

$$P(J|R) = \frac{P(J \cap R)}{P(R)} = \frac{\frac{2}{52}}{\frac{26}{52}}$$

Step 4 Simplify the result.

$$P(J|R) = \frac{\frac{2}{52} \cdot 52}{\frac{26}{52} \cdot 52} = \frac{2}{26} = \frac{1}{13}$$

(B) For a standard deck of playing cards, find the probability that a jack randomly drawn from the deck is a red card.

Step 1 Find $P(J)$, the probability that a jack is drawn from the deck.

There are 4 jacks in the deck of 52 cards, so $P(R) = \frac{4}{52}$.

Step 2 Find $P(J \cap R)$, the probability that a red jack is drawn from the deck.

There are 2 red jacks in the deck, so $P(J \cap R) = \frac{2}{52}$.

Step 3 Substitute the probabilities from Steps 1 and 2 into the formula for conditional probability.

$$P(J|R) = \frac{P(J \cap R)}{P(R)} = \frac{\frac{2}{52}}{\frac{4}{52}}$$

Step 4 Simplify the result.

$$P(J|R) = \frac{\frac{2}{52} \cdot 52}{\frac{4}{52} \cdot 52} = \frac{2}{4} = \frac{1}{2}$$

Your Turn

5. For a standard deck of playing cards, find the probability that a face card randomly drawn from the deck is a king. (The ace is *not* a face card.)

Let F be the event of drawing a face card and K be the event of drawing a king. Then

$$P(F) = \frac{12}{52} \text{ and } P(F \cap K) = \frac{4}{52}, \text{ so } P(K|F) = \frac{P(F \cap K)}{P(F)} = \frac{\frac{4}{52}}{\frac{12}{52}} = \frac{4}{12} = \frac{1}{3}.$$

6. For a standard deck of playing cards, find the probability that a queen randomly drawn from the deck is a diamond.

Let Q be the event of drawing a queen and D be the event of drawing a diamond. Then

$$P(Q) = \frac{4}{52} \text{ and } P(Q \cap D) = \frac{1}{52}, \text{ so } P(D|Q) = \frac{P(Q \cap D)}{PQ} = \frac{\frac{1}{52}}{\frac{4}{52}} = \frac{1}{4}.$$

QUESTIONING STRATEGIES

What is the conditional probability formula, and what does it represent?

$P(A \mid B) = \frac{P(A \cap B)}{P(B)}$; the probability that event A occurs given that event B has already occurred is represented by $P(A \mid B)$, and is equal to the probability that both A and B occur divided by the probability that event B occurs.

INTEGRATE MATHEMATICAL PRACTICES

Focus on Patterns

MP.8 Have students follow a pattern as they find the values to substitute into the conditional probability formula $P(A \mid B) = \frac{P(A \cap B)}{P(B)}$. First, identify which event has already occurred (B, in this case) and find the probability that B occurs (divide the number of B outcomes by the number in the sample space). Then find the number of events that are in the intersection of A and B and calculate the probability that both A and B occur (the sum of A and B divided by the number in the sample space). Finally, substitute the values and divide.

DIFFERENTIATE INSTRUCTION

Modeling

Some students may benefit from a hands-on approach for finding the conditional probabilities for a two-way table. Have groups of students complete a list of questions that they can ask about the table below, such as, "What is the probability that a household owns a dog given that the household owns a cat?" **$15 \div 33 \approx 0.45$**

		Owns a cat	
		Yes	No
Owns a dog	Yes	15	24
	No	18	43

ELABORATE

QUESTIONING STRATEGIES

How can you find conditional probabilities for the data in a two-way table? **Label the events represented by the table as *A* and *B* and use the formula $P(A \mid B) = \frac{n(A \cap B)}{n(B)}$.**

SUMMARIZE THE LESSON

Given a two-way frequency table, how could you quickly verify that it has been filled out correctly? How could you do the same for a two-way relative frequency table? **You could check that the sum of the frequencies in the bottom row and the sum of the frequencies in the right-most column are equal to each other and to the number of outcomes in the sample space; in a two-way relative frequency table, both sums should be equal to 1.**

Elaborate

7. When calculating a conditional probability from a two-way table, explain why it doesn't matter whether the table gives frequencies or relative frequencies.

A conditional probability is a ratio of two frequencies. If you divide those frequencies by the same number to convert them to relative frequencies, their ratio remains unchanged.

8. **Discussion** Is it possible to have $P(B \mid A) = P(A \mid B)$ for some events A and B? What conditions would need to exist?

Yes, it is possible for $P(B \mid A)$ to equal $P(A \mid B)$. This would happen if the probability of event *A* is equal to the probability of event *B*.

9. **Essential Question Check-In** In a two-way frequency table, suppose event A represents a row of the table and event B represents a column of the table. Describe how to find the conditional probability $P(A \mid B)$ using the frequencies in the table.

Divide the frequency that appears in the intersection of the row for *A* and the column for *B* by the total of all frequencies in the row for *B*.

Evaluate: Homework and Practice

• Online Homework
• Hints and Help
• Extra Practice

In order to study the relationship between the amount of sleep a student gets and his or her school performance, a researcher collected data from 120 students. The two-way frequency table shows the number of students who passed and failed an exam and the number of students who got more or less than 6 hours of sleep the night before. Use the table to answer the question.

	Passed exam	Failed exam	Total
Less than 6 hours of sleep	12	10	22
More than 6 hours of sleep	90	8	98
Total	102	18	120

1. To the nearest percent, what is the probability that a student who failed the exam got less than 6 hours of sleep?

Let *L* be the event of getting less than 6 hours of sleep and *F* be the event of failing the exam. Then $P(L \mid F) = \frac{n(L \cap F)}{n(F)} = \frac{10}{18} = \frac{5}{9} \approx 56\%$.

2. To the nearest percent, what is the probability that a student who got less than 6 hours of sleep failed the exam?

Let *L* be the event of getting less than 6 hours of sleep and *F* be the event of failing the exam. Then $P(F \mid L) = \frac{n(L \cap F)}{n(L)} = \frac{10}{22} = \frac{5}{11} \approx 45\%$.

LANGUAGE SUPPORT EL

Connect Vocabulary

To help students describe the events represented in a two-way table and then determine the numbers used to find the conditional probabilities, have them first draw a line around the row or column of a two-way table representing the given information. Then ask them to circle the cell for the probability they are finding in another color. Then ask them to divide the number in that cell by the total in the respective row or column to find the conditional probability.

3. To the nearest percent, what is the probability that a student got less than 6 hours of sleep and failed the exam?

Let L be the event of getting less than 6 hours of sleep, F be the event of failing the exam, and S be the sample space. $P(L \cap F) = \frac{n(L \cap F)}{n(S)} = \frac{10}{120} \approx 8\%$.

4. You have a standard deck of playing cards from which you randomly select a card. Event D is getting a diamond, and event F is getting a face card (a jack, queen, or king).

Show that $P(D|F) = \frac{n(D \cap F)}{n(F)}$ and $P(D|F) = \frac{P(D \cap F)}{P(F)}$ are equal.

$$P(D|F) = \frac{n(D \cap F)}{n(F)} = \frac{3}{12} = \frac{1}{4} \qquad P(D|F) = \frac{P(D \cap F)}{P(F)} = \frac{\frac{3}{52}}{\frac{12}{52}} = \frac{\frac{3}{52} \cdot 52}{\frac{12}{52} \cdot 52} = \frac{3}{12} = \frac{1}{4}$$

The table shows data in the previous table as relative frequencies (rounded to the nearest thousandth when necessary). Use the table for Exercises 5–7.

	Passed exam	Failed exam	Total
Less than 6 hours of sleep	0.100	0.083	0.183
More than 6 hours of sleep	0.750	0.067	0.817
Total	0.850	0.150	1.000

5. To the nearest percent, what is the probability that a student who passed the exam got more than 6 hours of sleep?

Let M be the event of getting more than 6 hours of sleep and Pa be the event of passing the exam. Then $P(M|Pa) = \frac{P(M \cap Pa)}{P(Pa)} = \frac{0.750}{8.850} \approx 0.882 \approx 88\%$.

6. To the nearest percent, what is the probability that a student who got more than 6 hours of sleep passed the exam?

Let M be the event of getting more than 6 hours of sleep and Pa be the event of passing the exam. Then $P(Pa|M) = \frac{n(M \cap Pa)}{n(M)} = \frac{0.750}{0.817} = 0.918 \approx 92\%$.

7. Which is greater, the probability that a student who got less than 6 hours of sleep passed the exam or the probability that a student who got more than 6 hours of sleep failed the exam? Explain.

Let L be the event of getting less than 6 hours of sleep, and let M be the event of getting more than 6 hours of sleep. Let Pa be the event of passing the exam, and let F be the event of failing the exam. Then $P(Pa|L) = \frac{P(L \cap Pa)}{P(L)} = \frac{0.100}{0.183} \approx 0.546 \approx 55\%$, and $P(F|M) = \frac{P(M \cap F)}{P(M)} = \frac{0.067}{0.817} \approx 0.082 \approx 8\%$, so the probability that a student who got less than 6 hours of sleep passed the exam is greater.

Exercise	Depth of Knowledge (D.O.K.)	COMMON CORE Mathematical Practices
1–6	1 Recall of Information	MP.5 Using Tools
7	2 Skills/Concepts	MP.4 Modeling
8–13	1 Recall of Information	MP.5 Using Tools
14	2 Skills/Concepts	MP.4 Modeling
15	2 Skills/Concepts	MP.2 Reasoning
16–20	2 Skills/Concepts	MP.5 Using Tools
21	3 Strategic Thinking H.O.T.	MP.6 Precision
22	3 Strategic Thinking H.O.T.	MP.3 Logic
23	3 Strategic Thinking H.O.T.	MP.2 Reasoning

EVALUATE

ASSIGNMENT GUIDE

Concepts and Skills	Practice
Explore 1 Finding Conditional Probabilities from a Two-Way Frequency Table	Exercises 1–3, 14–15, 20, 22–23
Explore 2 Finding Conditional Probabilities from a Two-Way Relative Frequency Table	Exercises 4–7, 18–19
Example 1 Using the Conditional Probability Formula	Exercises 9–13, 16–17, 21

INTEGRATE MATHEMATICAL PRACTICES

Focus on Math Connections

MP.1 Two-way frequency tables express quantitative data that can be categorized by two variables. *Joint relative frequencies* are the values in each category divided by the total number of values, while *marginal relative frequencies* are found by adding the joint relative frequencies in each row or column. *A conditional relative frequency* is the quotient of a joint relative frequency and the marginal relative frequency. Conditional relative frequencies give an alternate way to find conditional probabilities.

AVOID COMMON ERRORS

Students may assume that B always represents the event assumed to have taken place. Explain that A and B are simply variables and that the conditional probability formula holds true no matter which letters are used. For example, the formula can be used to find the probability of B given A: $P(B \mid A) = \frac{P(A \cap B)}{P(A)}$. Emphasize that the letter *after* the vertical bar represents the event assumed to have taken place, and that its probability will always be in the denominator of the fraction.

You randomly draw a card from a standard deck of playing cards. Let A be the event that the card is an ace, let B be the event that the card is black, and let C be the event that the card is a club. Find the specified probability as a fraction.

8. $P(A \mid B)$ $P(A \mid B) =$

$\frac{P(A \cap B)}{P(B)} = \frac{1}{13}$

9. $P(B \mid A)$ $P(B \mid A) =$

$\frac{P(A \cap B)}{P(A)} = \frac{1}{2}$

10. $P(A \mid C)$ $P(A \mid C) =$

$\frac{P(A \cap C)}{P(C)} = \frac{1}{13}$

11. $P(C \mid A)$ $P(C \mid A) =$

$\frac{P(A \cap C)}{P(A)} = \frac{1}{4}$

12. $P(B \mid C)$ $P(B \mid C) =$

$\frac{P(B \cap C)}{P(C)} = 1$

13. $P(C \mid B)$ $P(C \mid B) =$

$\frac{P(B \cap C)}{P(B)} = \frac{1}{2}$

14. A botanist studied the effect of a new fertilizer by choosing 100 orchids and giving 70% of these plants the fertilizer. Of the plants that got the fertilizer, 40% produced flowers within a month. Of the plants that did not get the fertilizer, 10% produced flowers within a month.

a. Use the given information to complete the two-way frequency table.

	Received fertilizer	Did not receive fertilizer	Total
Did not flower in one month	$70 - 28 = 42$	$30 - 3 = 27$	$42 + 27 = 69$
Flowered in one month	$0.4 \cdot 70 = 28$	$0.1 \cdot 30 = 3$	$28 + 3 = 31$
Total	$0.7 \cdot 100 = 70$	$0.3 \cdot 100 = 30$	100

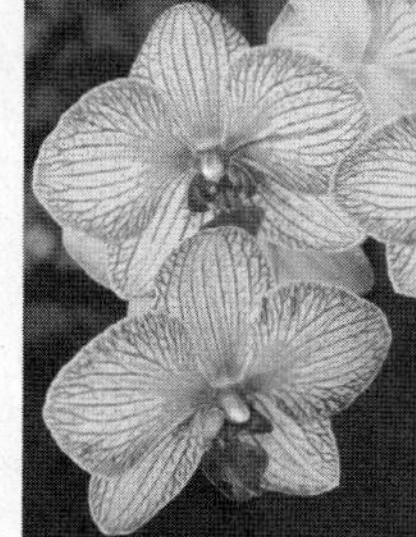

b. To the nearest percent, what is the probability that an orchid that produced flowers got fertilizer?

Let *Fl* be the event that an orchid produced flowers and *Fe* be the event that an orchid got fertilizer. Then $P(Fe \mid Fl) = \frac{n(Fe \cap Fl)}{n(Fl)} = \frac{28}{31} \approx 90\%.$

c. To the nearest percent, what is the probability that an orchid that got fertilizer produced flowers?

Then $P(Fl \mid Fe) = \frac{n(Fe \cap Fl)}{n(Fe)} = \frac{28}{70} = \frac{2}{5} = 40\%.$

15. At a school fair, a box contains 24 yellow balls and 76 red balls. One-fourth of the balls of each color are labeled "Win a prize." Match each description of a probability with its value as a percent.

A. The probability that a randomly selected ball labeled "Win a prize" is yellow — B 76%

B. The probability that a randomly selected ball labeled "Win a prize" is red — D 25%

C. The probability that a randomly selected ball is labeled "Win a prize" and is red — A 24%

D. The probability that a randomly selected yellow ball is labeled "Win a prize" — C 19%

	Winner	Not winner	Total
Red	$\frac{1}{4}(76) = 19$	$\frac{3}{4}(76) = 57$	76
Yellow	$\frac{1}{4}(24) = 6$	$\frac{3}{4}(24) = 18$	24
Total	25	75	100

Let R be the even that a ball is red, Y be the event that a ball is yellow, W be the event that a ball is labeled "Win a prize," and S is the sample space.

A. $P(Y|W) = \frac{n(Y \cap W)}{n(W)} = \frac{6}{25} = 24\%$ C. $P(W \cap R) = \frac{n(W \cap R)}{n(S)} = \frac{19}{100} = 19\%$

B. $P(R|W) = \frac{n(R \cap W)}{n(W)} = \frac{19}{25} = 76\%$ D. $P(W|Y) = \frac{n(Y \cap W)}{n(Y)} = \frac{6}{24} = 25\%$

16. A teacher gave her students two tests. If 45% of the students passed both tests and 60% passed the first test, what is the probability that a student who passed the first test also passed the second?

Let T_1 be the event that a student passed the first test and T_2 be the event that the student passed the second test.

$$P(T_2 | T_1) = \frac{P(T_1 \cap T_2)}{P(T_1)} = \frac{0.45}{0.60} = 0.75 = 75\%$$

17. You randomly select two marbles, one at a time, from a pouch containing blue and green marbles. The probability of selecting a blue marble on the first draw and a green marble on the second draw is 25%, and the probability of selecting a blue marble on the first draw is 56%. To the nearest percent, what is the probability of selecting a green marble on the second draw, given that the first marble was blue?

Let B be the event of selecting a blue marble on the first draw and G be the event of selecting a green marble on the second draw.

$$P(G|B) = \frac{P(B \cap G)}{P(B)} = \frac{0.25}{0.56} \approx 0.45 = 45\%$$

INTEGRATE MATHEMATICAL PRACTICES

Focus on Communication

MP.3 After making a two-way table, have students interpret the tables in terms of percentages. For example, if 10 students in the class own a cat, and 6 of those students also own a dog, have students verbalize that the conditional probability of owning a dog given that they own a cat is $\frac{6}{10} = 60\%$.

You roll two number cubes, one red and one blue. The table shows the probabilities for events based on whether or not a 1 is rolled on each number cube. Use the table to find the specified conditional probability, expressed as a fraction. Then show that the conditional probability is correct by listing the possible outcomes as ordered pairs of the form (number on red cube, number on blue cube) and identifying the successful outcomes.

	Rolling a 1 on the red cube	Not rolling a 1 on the red cube	Total
Rolling a 1 on the blue cube	$\frac{1}{36}$	$\frac{5}{36}$	$\frac{1}{6}$
Not rolling a 1 on the blue cube	$\frac{5}{36}$	$\frac{25}{36}$	$\frac{5}{6}$
Total	$\frac{1}{6}$	$\frac{5}{6}$	1

18. *P*(not rolling a 1 on the blue cube | rolling a 1 on the red cube)

Let $N1B$ be the event that a 1 is not rolled on the blue cube and $1R$ be the event that a 1 is rolled on the red cube.

$$P(N1B \mid 1R) = \frac{n(N1B \cap 1R)}{n(1R)} = \frac{\frac{5}{36}}{\frac{1}{6}} = \frac{\frac{5}{36} \cdot 36}{\frac{1}{6} \cdot 36} = \frac{5}{6}$$

Given that rolling a 1 on the red number cube has occurred, there are 6 possible outcomes (where the ordered pairs give the number on the red cube first): (1, 1), (1, 2), (1, 3), (1, 4), (1, 5), and (1, 6). Of these, the last 5 outcomes are successful because they involve a numbe that is not 1 on the blue cube. So, the probability of not rolling a 1 on the blue cube when a is rolled on the red cube is $\frac{5}{6}$.

19. *P*(not rolling a 1 on the blue cube | not rolling a 1 on the red cube)

Let $N1B$ be the event that a 1 is not rolled on the blue cube and $N1R$ be the event that a 1 is not rolled on the red cube.

$$P(N1B \mid N1R) = \frac{n(N1B \cap N1R)}{n(N1R)} = \frac{\frac{25}{36}}{\frac{5}{6}} = \frac{\frac{25}{36} \cdot 36}{\frac{5}{6} \cdot 36} = \frac{25}{30} = \frac{5}{6}$$

Given that not rolling a 1 on the red number cube has occurred, there are 30 possible outcomes (where the ordered pairs give the number on the red cube first): (2, 1), (2, 2), (2, 3), (2, 4), (2, 5), (2, 6), (3, 1), (3, 2), (3, 4), (3, 5), (3, 6), (4, 1), (4, 2), (4, 3), (4, 4), (4, 5), (4, 6), (5, 1), (5, 2), (5, 3), (5, 4), (5, 5), (5, 6), (6, 1), (6, 2), (6, 3), (6, 4), (6, 5), and (6, 6). Of these, all but 5 outcomes—(2, 1), (3, 1), (4, 1,) (5, 1), and (6, 1)—are successful because the involve a number that is not 1 on the blue cube. So, the probability of not rolling a 1 on the blue cube when a 1 is not rolled on the red cube is $\frac{25}{36} = \frac{5}{6}$.

20. The table shows the results of a quality-control study at a computer factory.

	Shipped	Not shipped	Total
Defective	3	7	10
Not defective	89	1	90
Total	92	8	100

a. To the nearest tenth of a percent, what is the probability that a shipped computer is not defective?

b. To the nearest tenth of a percent, what is the probability that a defective computer is shipped?

Let S be the event that a computer is shipped, D be the event that a computer is defective, and Nd be the even that a computer is not defective.

a. $P(Nd \mid S) = \dfrac{n(Nd \cap S)}{n(S)} = \dfrac{89}{92} \approx 0.967 = 96.7\%$

b. $P(S \mid D) = \dfrac{n(D \cap S)}{n(D)} = \dfrac{3}{10} = 0.3 = 30\%$

H.O.T. Focus on Higher Order Thinking

21. Analyze Relationships In the Venn diagram, the circles representing events A and B divide the sample space S into four regions: the overlap of the circles, the part of A not in the overlap, the part of B not in the overlap, and the part of S not in A or B. Suppose that the area of each region is proportional to the number of outcomes that fall within the region. Which conditional probability is greater: $P(A \mid B)$ or $P(B \mid A)$? Explain.

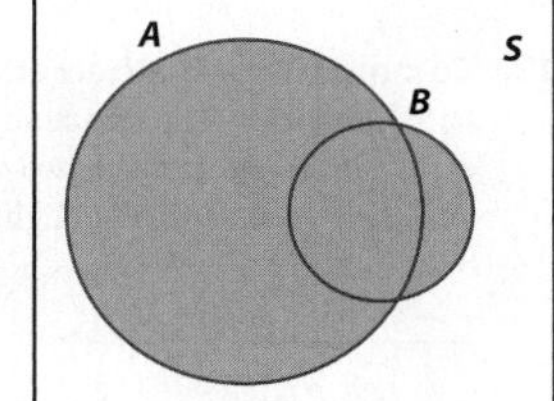

Since $P(A \mid B) = \dfrac{n(A \cap B)}{n(B)}$, you can think of $P(A \mid B)$ as the ratio of the area of the overlap of the circles to the area of the entire circle labeled B. Since more of circle B lies inside the overlap than outside the overlap, $P(A \mid B) > \frac{1}{2}$. On the other hand, since $P(B \mid A) = \dfrac{n(A \cap B)}{n(A)}$, you can think of $P(B \mid A)$ as the ratio of the area of the overlap of the circles to the area of the entire circle labeled A. Since less of circle A lies inside the overlap than outside the overlap, $P(B \mid A) < \frac{1}{2}$. So, $P(A \mid B) > \frac{1}{2} > P(B \mid A)$.

PEER-TO-PEER DISCUSSION

Give students each an example of a two-way table. Ask them to discuss with a partner how to interpret the two variables represented by the table. Then have them describe in their own words the process they would use to find the conditional probabilities for the data given in each cell of the two-way tables.

JOURNAL

Have students explain conditional probability in their own words. Also, ask students to give an example of how to use the formula for conditional probability.

22. Explain the Error A student was asked to use the table shown to find the probability, to nearest percent, that a participant in a study of a new medicine for migraine headaches did not take the medicine, given that the participant reported no headaches.

	Took medicine	No medicine	Total
Headache	11	13	24
No headache	54	22	76
Total	65	35	100

The student made the following calculation.

$P(\text{no medicine} \mid \text{no headache}) = \frac{22}{35} \approx 0.63 = 63\%$

Explain the student's error, and find the correct probability.

The student divided 22, the number of participants who did not take the medicine and did not report headaches, by 35, the number of participants who did not take the medicine. However, the student should have divided 22 by 76, the number of participants who reported no headaches. The correct calculation is $P(\text{no medicine} \mid \text{no headache}) = \frac{22}{76} \approx 0.29 = 29\%$.

23. Communicate Mathematical Ideas Explain how a conditional probability based on a two-way frequency table effectively reduces it to a one-way table. In your explanation, refer to the two-way table shown, which lists frequencies for events A, B, and their complements. Highlight the part of the table that supports your explanation.

	A	Not A	Total
B	$n(A \cap B)$	$n(\text{not } A \cap B)$	$n(B)$
Not B	$n(A \cap \text{not } B)$	$n(\text{not } A \cap \text{not } B)$	$n(\text{not } B)$
Total	$n(A)$	$n(\text{not } A)$	$n(S)$

The conditional probability $P(A \mid B) = \frac{n(A \cap B)}{n(B)}$ restricts the discussion to event B because that event is assumed to have occurred. The numbers used to calculate $P(A \mid B)$ both come from the highlighted row in the table: $n(A \cap B)$ is the number of outcomes in event B that are also in event A, while $n(B)$ is the number of all outcomes in event B. The rest of the table is irrelevant.

Lesson Performance Task

The two-way frequency table gives the results of a survey that asked students this question: Which of these would you most like to meet: a famous singer, a movie star, or a sports star?

	Famous singer	Movie star	Sports star	Total
Boys	20	15	55	90
Girls	40	50	20	110
Total	60	65	75	200

a. Complete the table by finding the row totals, column totals, and grand total.

b. To the nearest percent, what is the probability that a student who chose "movie star" is a girl?

c. To the nearest percent, what is the probability that a student who chose "famous singer" is a boy?

d. To the nearest percent, what is the probability that a boy chose "sports star"?

e. To the nearest percent, what is the probability that a girl chose "famous singer"?

f. To the nearest percent, what is the probability that a student who chose either "famous singer" or "movie star" is a boy?

g. To the nearest percent, what is the probability that a girl did not choose "sports star"?

a. For the following answers, let *B* be the event that a student is a boy, let *G* be the event that a student is a girl, let *FS* be the event that a student chose "famous singer," let *MS* be the event that a student chose "movie star," and let *SS* be the event that a student chose "sports star."

b. $P(G|MS) = \frac{n(G \cap MS)}{n(MS)} = \frac{50}{65} \approx 77\%$

c. $P(B|FS) = \frac{n(B \cap FS)}{n(FS)} = \frac{20}{60} \approx 33\%$

d. $P(SS|B) = \frac{n(B \cap SS)}{n(B)} = \frac{55}{90} \approx 61\%$

e. $P(FS|G) = \frac{n(G \cap FS)}{n(G)} = \frac{40}{110} \approx 36\%$

f. $P(B|(FS \cup MS)) = \frac{n(B \cap (FS \cup MS))}{n(FS \cup MS)} = \frac{35}{125} \approx 28\%$

g. $P(\text{not } SS|G) = \frac{n(G \cap \text{not } SS)}{n(\text{not } SS)} = \frac{90}{125} \approx 72\%$

INTEGRATE MATHEMATICAL PRACTICES

Focus on Patterns

MP.8 When dealing with tables like the ones in the Lesson Performance Task and the Extension Activity, students can check that the cell entries are consistent by (a) adding the row entries (for the Extension Activity, Boys + Girls = 155 + 145 = 300); (b) adding the column entries (Famous Singers + Movie Stars + Sports Star = 80 + 90 + 130 = 300); and (c) checking to see that the sums are equal (300 = 300).

INTEGRATE MATHEMATICAL PRACTICES

Focus on Communication

MP.3 Use the numbers in the "Movie Star" column of the Lesson Performance Task (15 and 50). Write at least four questions beginning with "Find the probability of___" that can be answered by writing a fraction that has either 15 or 50 in the numerator. For each question, give the fraction. **Sample answers: Find the probability that a student who chose "Movie Star" is a boy $\left(\frac{15}{65}\right)$; find the probability that a student who chose "Movie Star" is a girl $\left(\frac{50}{65}\right)$; find the probability that a student who is a boy chose "Movie Star" $\left(\frac{15}{90}\right)$; find the probability that a student who is a girl chose "Movie Star" $\left(\frac{50}{110}\right)$.**

EXTENSION ACTIVITY

Have students fill out a table like the one in the Lesson Performance Task, using these facts: 300 students took part in the survey described in the Task; P(student who chose "Famous Singer" is a girl) $= \frac{7}{10}$; P(student who chose "Sports Star" is a boy) $= \frac{4}{5}$; of those who chose "Movie Star," 30% are boys; 80 students chose "Famous Singer"; 130 students chose "Sports Star."

	Famous Singer	Movie Star	Sports Star
Boys	24	27	104
Girls	56	63	26

Scoring Rubric

2 points: The student's answer is an accurate and complete execution of the task or tasks.

1 point: The student's answer contains attributes of an appropriate response but is flawed.

0 points: The student's answer contains no attributes of an appropriate response.

Independent Events

Common Core Math Standards

The student is expected to:

 S-CP.A.2

Understand that two events *A* and *B* are independent if the probability of *A* and *B* occurring together is the product of their probabilities, ... Also S-CP.A.3, S-CP.A.4, S-CP.A.5

Mathematical Practices

 MP.7 Using Structure

Language Objective

Work with a partner to brainstorm examples of independent events.

ENGAGE

Essential Question: What does it mean for two events to be independent?

Two events are independent provided the occurrence of one event has no effect on the occurrence of the other event. For independent events *A* and *B*, $P(A|B) = P(A)$; that is, the probability of event *A* does not change even when event *B* is assumed to have occurred.

PREVIEW: LESSON PERFORMANCE TASK

View the Engage section online. Discuss the photograph. Ask students to describe differences that they observe in the animals pictured. Then preview the Lesson Performance Task.

Name ______ Class ______ Date ______

20.2 Independent Events

Essential Question: What does it mean for two events to be independent?

Resource Locker

Explore Understanding the Independence of Events

Suppose you flip a coin and roll a number cube. You would expect the probability of getting heads on the coin to be $\frac{1}{2}$ regardless of what number you get from rolling the number cube. Likewise, you would expect the probability of rolling a 3 on the number cube to be $\frac{1}{6}$ regardless of whether of the coin flip results in heads or tails.

When the occurrence of one event has no effect on the occurrence of another event, the two events are called **independent events**.

Ⓐ A jar contains 15 red marbles and 17 yellow marbles. You randomly draw a marble from the jar. Let *R* be the event that you get a red marble, and let *Y* be the event that you get a yellow marble.

Since the jar has a total of 32 marbles, $P(R) = \frac{15}{32}$ and $P(Y) = \frac{17}{32}$.

Ⓑ Suppose the first marble you draw is a red marble, and you put that marble back in the jar before randomly drawing a second marble. Find $P(Y|R)$, the probability that you get a yellow marble on the second draw after getting a red marble on the first draw. Explain your reasoning.

Since the jar still has a total of 32 marbles and 17 of them are yellow, $P(Y|R) = \frac{17}{32}$.

Ⓒ Suppose you *don't* put the red marble back in the jar before randomly drawing a second marble. Find $P(Y|R)$, the probability that you get a yellow marble on the second draw after getting a red marble on the first draw. Explain your reasoning.

Since the jar now has a total of 31 marbles and 17 of them are yellow, $P(Y|R) = \frac{17}{31}$.

Reflect

1. In one case you replaced the first marble before drawing the second, and in the other case you didn't. For which case was $P(Y|R)$ equal to $P(Y)$? Why?
$P(Y|R) = P(Y)$ when the red marble was replaced because the total number of marbles in the jar, and therefore the proportion of marbles that are yellow, stayed the same.

2. In which of the two cases would say the events of getting a red marble on the first draw and getting a yellow marble on the second draw are independent? What is true about $P(Y|R)$ and $P(Y)$ in this case?
The events are independent when the red marble is returned to the jar. In this case, $P(Y|R) = P(Y)$.

HARDCOVER PAGES 1015–103

Watch for the hardcover student edition page numbers for this lesson.

Explain 1 Determining if Events are Independent

To determine the independence of two events A and B, you can check to see whether $P(A|B) = P(A)$ since the occurrence of event A is unaffected by the occurrence of event B if and only if the events are independent.

Example 1 **The two-way frequency table gives data about 180 randomly selected flights that arrive at an airport. Use the table to answer the question.**

	Late Arrival	On Time	Total
Domestic Flights	12	108	120
International Flights	6	54	60
Total	18	162	180

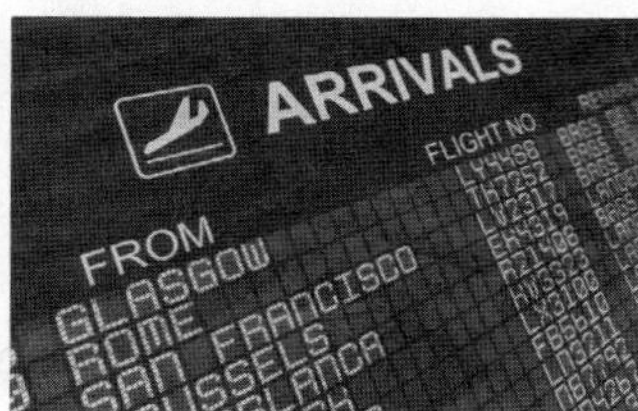

(A) Is the event that a flight is on time independent of the event that a flight is domestic?

Let O be the event that a flight is on time. Let D be the event that a flight is domestic. Find $P(O)$ and $P(O|D)$. To find $P(O)$, note that the total number of flights is 180, and of those flights, there are 162 on-time flights. So, $P(O) = \frac{162}{180} = 90\%$.

To find $P(O|D)$, note that there are 120 domestic flights, and of those flights, there are 108 on-time flights.

So, $P(O|D), = \frac{108}{120} = 90\%$.

Since $P(O|D) = P(O)$, the event that a flight is on time is independent of the event that a flight is domestic.

(B) Is the event that a flight is international independent of the event that a flight arrives late?

Let I be the event that a flight is international. Let L be the event that a flight arrives late. Find $P(I)$ and $P(IL)$. To find $P(I)$, note that the total number of flights is 180, and of those flights, there are 60 international flights. So, $P(I) = \frac{60}{180} = 33\frac{1}{3}\%$.

To find $P(IL)$, note that there are 18 flights that arrive late, and of those flights, there are 6 international flights. So, $P(IL) = \frac{6}{18} = 33\frac{1}{3}\%$.

Since $P(IL) = P(I)$, the event that a flight is international [is/is not] independent of the event that a flight arrives late.

PROFESSIONAL DEVELOPMENT

Math Background

Two events are *independent* if the occurrence of one does not affect the probability of the other. In other words, for independent events A and B, $P(A) = P(A \mid B)$. Note that you can use this criterion to determine if A and B are independent. If A and B are independent, then $P(A \text{ and } B)$, also written $P(A \cap B)$, is $P(A) \cdot P(B)$. More generally, events $A1, A2, \ldots, An$ are *mutually independent* if the occurrence of any one does not affect the probability of any other. Then, $P(A1 \cap A2 \cap \ldots \cap An) = P(A1) \cdot P(A2) \cdot \ldots \cdot P(An)$.

EXPLORE

Understanding the Independence of Events

INTEGRATE TECHNOLOGY

Students have the option of doing the Explore activity either in the book or online.

QUESTIONING STRATEGIES

How can you tell if two events A and B are independent? **If $P(A) = P(A|B)$ or $P(B) = P(B|A)$, then A and B are independent events.**

EXPLAIN 1

Determining if Events are Independent

QUESTIONING STRATEGIES

How can a two-way frequency table help you determine whether two events are independent? **A two-way frequency table makes it easy to find $n(A)$ and $n(A \mid B)$, which you can use to calculate $P(A)$ and $P(A \mid B)$. If the two probabilities are equal, the events are independent.**

AVOID COMMON ERRORS

When given a two-way frequency table, some students may have trouble identifying which values to use to calculate *the probability of A given B*. Encourage them to circle the column that represents event B, and then put another circle around the cell within the column that represents event A. The number in the cell they have circled is $n(A \mid B)$.

EXPLAIN 2

Finding the Probability of Independent Events

INTEGRATE MATHEMATICAL PRACTICES

Focus on Math Connections

MP.1 Point out that independent events are not the same as mutually exclusive events, which are events that cannot occur in the same trial. For example, a coin cannot simultaneously show heads and tails. If A and B are mutually exclusive, then $P(A \text{ or } B)$, also written $P(A \cup B)$, is $P(A) + P(B)$. This addition rule is generally used when finding the probability for a single trial, while the multiplication rule for independent events is usually applied to two or more separate trials, performed either simultaneously or in succession.

QUESTIONING STRATEGIES

? Once you know that two events are independent, how can you find the probability that both events take place? **Multiply the individual probabilities.**

Your Turn

The two-way frequency table gives data about 200 randomly selected apartments in a city. Use the table to answer the question.

	1 Bedroom	2+ Bedrooms	Total
Single Occupant	64	12	76
Multiple Occupants	26	98	124
Total	90	110	200

3. Is the event that an apartment has a single occupant independent of the event that an apartment has 1 bedroom?

Let SO be the event that an apartment has a single occupant, and let $1B$ be the event that an apartment has 1 bedroom. Then $P(SO) = \frac{76}{200} = 38\%$, and $P(SO|1B) = \frac{64}{90} \approx 71\%$. Since $P(SO|1B) \neq P(SO)$, the events are not independent.

4. Is the event that an apartment has 2 or more bedrooms independent of the event that an apartment has multiple occupants?

Let $2B$ represent that an apartment has 2 or more bedrooms, and let MO be the event that an apartment has multiple occupants. Then $P(2B) = \frac{110}{200} = 55\%$, and $P(2B|MO) = \frac{98}{110} \approx 89\%$. Since $P(2B|MO) \neq P(2B)$, the events are not independent.

Explain 2 Finding the Probability of Independent Events

From the definition of conditional probability you know that $P(A|B) = \frac{P(A \cap B)}{P(B)}$ for any events A and B. If those events happen to be independent, you can replace $P(A|B)$ with $P(A)$ and get $P(A) = \frac{P(A \cap B)}{P(B)}$. Solving the last equation for $P(A \cap B)$ gives the following result.

Probability of Independent Events

Events A and B are independent if and only if $P(A \cap B) = P(A) \cdot P(B)$.

Example 2 **Multiply to find the probability of Independent Events.**

Ⓐ Recall the jar with 15 red marbles and 17 yellow marbles from the Explore. Suppose you randomly draw one marble from the jar. After you put that marble back in the jar, you randomly draw a second marble. What is the probability that you draw a yellow marble first and a red marble second?

Let Y be the event of drawing a yellow marble first. Let R be the event of drawing a red marble second. Then $P(Y) = \frac{17}{32}$ and, because the first marble drawn is replaced before the second marble is drawn, $P(R|Y) = P(R)\ \frac{15}{32}$. Since the events are independent, you can multiply their probabilities: $P(Y \cap R) = P(Y) \cdot P(R) = \frac{17}{32} \cdot \frac{15}{32} = \frac{255}{1024} \approx 25\%$.

COLLABORATIVE LEARNING

Small Group Activity

Have students work in groups to do a simple experiment like rolling a number cube twice. Have one student perform the experiment, while another student keeps track of the results both as a table and as a tree diagram. Have a third student determine the sample space for the experiment (for example, HH, HT, TH, TT), and a fourth student explain how to find the probability of the events in the sample space. Ask students to discuss their results, explain why the events are independent, and present their results to the class.

(B) You spin the spinner shown two times. What is the probability that the spinner stops on an even number on the first spin, followed by an odd number on the second spin?

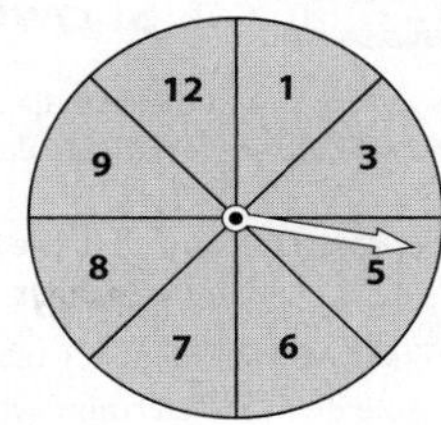

Let E be the event of getting an even number on the first spin. Let O be the event of getting an odd number on the second spin. Then $P(E) = \frac{3}{8}$ and, because the first spin has no effect on the second spin, $P(O|E)\ PO\ \frac{5}{8} =$. Since the events are independent, you can multiply their probabilities:

$P(E \cap O) = P(E) \cdot P(O) = \frac{3}{8} \cdot \frac{5}{8} = \frac{15}{64} \approx$ 23 %.

Reflect

5. In Part B, what is the probability that the spinner stops on an odd number on the first spin, followed by an even number on the second spin? What do you observe? What does this tell you?

The probability of getting an odd number on the first spin followed by an even number on the second spin is $\frac{5}{8} \cdot \frac{3}{8} = \frac{15}{64}$. This value is equal to the probability calculated in Part B. Because the spins are independent of each other, changing the order of the outcomes does not affect the overall probability.

Your Turn

6. You spin a spinner with 4 red sections, 3 blue sections, 2 green sections, and 1 yellow section. If all the sections are of equal size, what is the probability that the spinner stops on green first and blue second?

Let G be the event of getting green with the first spin. Let B be the event of getting blue with the second spin. Then $P(G) = \frac{2}{10} = \frac{1}{5}$ and, because the first spin has no effect on the second spin, $P(B|G) = P(B) = \frac{3}{10}$. Since the events are independent, you can multiply their probabilities: $P(G \cap B) = P(G) \cdot P(B) = \frac{1}{5} \cdot \frac{3}{10} = \frac{3}{50} = 6\%$.

7. A number cube has the numbers 3, 5, 6, 8, 10, and 12 on its faces. You roll the number cube twice. What is the probability that you roll an odd number on both rolls?

Let $O1$ be the event of getting an odd number on the first roll. Let $O2$ be the event of getting an odd number on the second roll. Then $P(O1) = \frac{2}{6} = \frac{1}{3}$ and, because the first roll has no effect on the second roll, $P(O2|O1) = P(O2) = \frac{1}{3}$. Since the events are independent, you can multiply their probabilities: $P(O1 \cap O2) = P(O1) \cdot P(O2) = \frac{1}{3} \cdot \frac{1}{3} = \frac{1}{9} \approx 11\%$.

DIFFERENTIATE INSTRUCTION

Critical Thinking

Distinguish between evaluating $P(A \mid B)$, when it is important to find the conditional probability that event A will occur given that event B has already occurred, and $P(A \text{ and } B)$, when it is important to consider whether events A and B are independent. The division rule $P(A \mid B) = \frac{P(A \cap B)}{P(B)}$ is used to find the conditional probability of A given B, while the multiplication rule $P(A \text{ and } B) = P(A) \cdot P(B)$ is used to find the probability that event A will occur in one trial and event B will occur in another trial, given that one trial does not affect the other.

EXPLAIN 3

Showing that Events are Independent

AVOID COMMON ERRORS

If students are confused about identifying independent events, have them try communicating their results from this lesson orally or in writing. Ask them to check that they are using terms correctly. In particular, be sure students understand that the word *independent* has a specific meaning in probability theory that may be different from its meaning in everyday conversation.

QUESTIONING STRATEGIES

? What are two ways of showing that two events are independent? Show or $P(A) = P(A \mid B)$ or $P(A \text{ and } B) = P(A) \cdot P(B)$.

INTEGRATE MATHEMATICAL PRACTICES

Focus on Patterns

MP.8 Have students follow a pattern to show that events are independent. Have them identify the total number in the sample space. Then ask them to find $P(A)$, $P(B)$, and $P(A \text{ and } B)$ and compare the values. $P(A \text{ and } B) = P(A) \cdot P(B)$ if and only if A and B are independent events.

Explain 3 Showing That Events Are Independent

So far, you have used the formula $P(A \text{ and } B) = P(A) \cdot P(B)$ when you knew that events A and B are independent. You can also use the formula to determine whether two events are independent.

Example 3 **Determine if the events are independent.**

(A) The two-way frequency table shows data for 120 randomly selected patients who have the same doctor. Determine whether a patient who takes vitamins and a patient who exercises regularly are independent events.

	Takes Vitamins	No Vitamins	Total
Regular Exercise	48	28	76
No regular Exercise	12	32	44
Total	60	60	120

Let V be the event that a patient takes vitamins. Let E be the event that a patient exercises regularly.

Step 1 Find $P(V)$, $P(E)$, and $P(V \cap E)$. The total number of patients is 120.

There are 60 patients who take vitamins, so $P(V) = \frac{60}{120} = \frac{1}{2}$.

There are 76 patients who exercise regularly, so $P(B) = \frac{76}{120} = \frac{19}{30}$.

There are 48 patients who take vitamins and exercise regularly, so $P(V \cap E) = \frac{48}{120} = 40\%$.

Step 2 Compare $P(V \cap E)$ and $P(V) \cdot P(E)$.

$P(V) \cdot P(E) = \frac{1}{2} \cdot \frac{19}{30} = \frac{19}{60} \approx 32\%$

Because $P(V \cap E) \neq P(V) \cdot P(E)$, the events are not independent.

(B) The two-way frequency table shows data for 60 randomly selected children at an elementary school. Determine whether a child who knows how to ride a bike and a child who knows how to swim are independent events.

	Knows how to Ride a Bike	Doesn't Know how to Ride a Bike	Total
Knows how to Swim	30	10	40
Doesn't Know how to Swim	15	5	20
Total	45	20	60

Let B be the event a child knows how to ride a bike. Let S be the event that a child knows how to swim.

Step 1 Find $P(B)$, $P(S)$, and $P(B \cap S)$. The total number of children is 60.

There are 45 children who know how to ride a bike, so $P(B) = \frac{45}{60} = \frac{3}{4}$.

There are 40 children who know how to ride a swim, so $P(S) = \frac{40}{60} = \frac{2}{3}$.

There are 30 children who know how to ride a bike and swim, so $P(B \cap S) = \frac{30}{60} = \frac{1}{2}$.

LANGUAGE SUPPORT EL

Connect Vocabulary

Have students create notecards to help them understand the mathematical meaning of *independent*. Ask them to write, on the front of the card, an example of a time in their lives when they acted independently, and then write, on the back, an example of events that are mathematically independent. Connecting the idea to personal experience may help some students remember its meaning and use.

Step 2 Compare $P(B \cap S)$ and $P(B) \cdot P(S)$.

$$P(B) \cdot P(S) = \frac{\boxed{3}}{4} \cdot \frac{\boxed{2}}{3} = \frac{\boxed{1}}{2}$$

Because $P(B \cap S)$ $\boxed{=}$ $P(B) \cdot P(S)$, the, events [(are)/are not] independent.

Your Turn

8. A farmer wants to know if an insecticide is effective in preventing small insects called aphids from damaging tomato plants. The farmer experiments with 80 plants and records the results in the two-way frequency table. Determine whether a plant that was sprayed with insecticide and a plant that has aphids are independent events.

	Has Aphids	No Aphids	Total
Sprayed with Insecticide	12	40	52
Not Sprayed with Insecticide	14	14	28
Total	26	54	80

Let S be the event that a tomato plant was sprayed with insecticide. Let A be the event that a tomato plant has aphids.

$P(S) = \frac{52}{80} = \frac{13}{20}$, $P(A) = \frac{26}{80} = \frac{13}{40}$, **and** $P(S) \cdot P(A) = \frac{13}{40} \cdot \frac{13}{20} = \frac{169}{800} \approx 21\%$.

Because $P(S \cap A) = \frac{12}{80} = \frac{3}{20} = 15\%$ **and** $P(S \cap A) \neq P(S) \cdot P(A)$, **the events are not independent.**

9. A student wants to know if right-handed people are more or less likely to play a musical instrument than left-handed people. The student collects data from 250 people, as shown in the two-way frequency table. Determine whether being right-handed and playing a musical instrument are independent events.

	Right-Handed	Left-Handed	Total
Plays a Musical Instrument	44	6	50
Does not Play a Musical Instrument	176	24	200
Total	220	30	250

Let R be the event that a person is right-handed. Let I be the event that a person plays a musical instrument.

$P(R) = \frac{220}{250} = \frac{22}{25}$, $P(I) = \frac{50}{250} = \frac{1}{5}$, **and** $P(R) \cdot P(I) = \frac{22}{25} \cdot \frac{1}{5} = \frac{22}{125}$.

Because $P(R \cap I) = \frac{44}{450} = \frac{22}{125}$ **and** $P(R \cap I) = P(R) \cdot P(I)$, **the events are independent.**

ELABORATE

QUESTIONING STRATEGIES

How can you find the probability of independent events A and B? Use the multiplication rule $P(A \text{ and } B) = P(A) \cdot P(B)$.

SUMMARIZE THE LESSON

Why is it important that the multiplication rule, $P(A \text{ and } B) = P(A) \cdot P(B)$, is true *if and only if* the events are independent? The fact that it is true if and only if the events are independent means that it can be used to determine whether events are independent, and vice versa.

EVALUATE

ASSIGNMENT GUIDE

Concepts and Skills	Practice
Explore Understanding the Independence of Events	Exercises 1–2
Example 1 Determining if Events are Independent	Exercises 3–4, 20
Example 2 Finding the Probability of Independent Events	Exercises 5–14
Example 3 Showing That Events Are Independent	Exercises 15–19, 21–22

Elaborate

10. What are the ways that you can show that two events A and B are independent?

The ways that you can show that two events A and B are independent are by confirming that $P(A|B) = P(A)$ or that $P(A \text{ and } B) = P(A) \cdot P(B)$.

11. How can you find the probability that two independent events A and B both occur?

Multiply $P(A)$ and $P(B)$

12. Essential Question Check-In Give an example of two independent events and explain why they are independent.

Sample answer: When flipping a coin twice, the events of getting heads on the first flip and on the second flip are independent. The occurrence of getting heads on the first flip does not affect the occurrence of getting heads on the second flip. The probability of getting heads on the second flip is $\frac{1}{2}$ regardless of what happens on the first flip.

Evaluate: Homework and Practice

- Online Homewor
- Hints and Help
- Extra Practice

1. A bag contains 12 red and 8 blue chips. Two chips are separately drawn at random from the bag.

a. Suppose that a single chip is drawn at random from the bag. Find the probability that the chip is red and the probability that the chip is blue.

Let R be the event that the first chip drawn is red. Let B be the even that the second chip drawn is blue.

$P(R) = \frac{12}{20} = \frac{3}{5}$ **and** $P(B) = \frac{8}{20} = \frac{2}{5}$

b. Suppose that two chips are separately drawn at random from the bag and that the first chip is returned to the bag before the second chip is drawn. Find the probability that the second chip drawn is blue given the first chip drawn was red.

$P(B|R) = \frac{8}{20} = \frac{2}{5}$

c. Suppose that two chips are separately drawn at random from the bag and that the first chip is not returned to the bag before the second chip is drawn. Find the probability that the second chip drawn is blue given the first chip drawn was red.

$P(B|R) = \frac{8}{19}$

d. In which situation—the first chip is returned to the bag or not returned to the bag—are the events that the first chip is red and the second chip is blue independent? Explain.

Events R and B are independent when the first chip is returned to the bag because $P(B|R) = P(B)$ in that case

Exercise	Depth of Knowledge (D.O.K.)	COMMON CORE Mathematical Practices
1–2	**1** Recall of Information	**MP.6** Precision
3–14	**2** Skills/Concepts	**MP.5** Using Tools
15–19	**2** Skills/Concepts	**MP.4** Modeling
20	**3** Strategic Thinking H.O.T.	**MP.2** Reasoning
21	**3** Strategic Thinking H.O.T.	**MP.3** Logic
22	**3** Strategic Thinking H.O.T.	**MP.4** Modeling

2. Identify whether the events are independent or not independent.

a. Flip a coin twice and get tails both times. ● Independent ○ Not Independent

b. Roll a number cube and get 1 on the first roll and 6 on the second. ● Independent ○ Not Independent

c. Draw an ace from a shuffled deck, put the card back and reshuffle the deck, and then draw an 8. ● Independent ○ Not Independent

d. Rotate a bingo cage and draw the ball labeled B-4, set it aside, and then rotate the cage again and draw the ball labled N-38. ○ Independent ● Not Independent

Answer the question using the fact that $P(A|B) = P(A)$ only when events A and B are independent.

3. The two-way frequency table shows data for 80 randomly selected people who live in a metropolitan area. Is the event that a person prefers public transportation independent of the event that a person lives in the city?

	Prefers to Drive	Prefers Public Transportation	Total
Lives in the City	12	24	36
Lives in the Suburbs	33	11	44
Total	45	35	80

Let T be the event that a person prefers public transportation. Let C be the event that a person lives in the city. Then $P(T) = \frac{35}{80} \approx 44\%$ and $P(T|C) = \frac{24}{36} \approx 67\%$. Since $P(T|C) \neq P(T)$, the events are not independent.

4. The two-way frequency table shows data for 120 randomly selected people who take vacations. Is the event that a person prefers vacationing out of state independent of the event that a person is a woman?

	Prefers Vacationing Out of State	Prefers Vacationing in State	Total
Men	48	32	80
Women	24	16	40
Total	72	48	120

Let O be the event that a person prefers vacationing out of state. Let W be the event that a person is a woman. Then $P(O) = \frac{72}{120} \approx 60\%$ and $P(O|W) = \frac{24}{40} = 60\%$. Since $P(O|W) = P(O)$, the events are independent.

INTEGRATE MATHEMATICAL PRACTICES

Focus on Modeling

MP.4 To help students describe the independent events represented in a two-way table and then determine the numbers used to find the probabilities, have them also draw a probability tree representing the given information. Then ask them to show the probability for each branch and the calculations for each possible result in the experiment.

AVOID COMMON ERRORS

When students start finding probabilities for successive events, it is easy to confuse the context. Have students read each exercise and highlight the key words and phrases.

INTEGRATE MATHEMATICAL PRACTICES

Focus on Communication

MP.3 Tree diagrams are useful for understanding the formula for the probability of independent events. Ask groups of students to practice constructing tree diagrams from two-way tables, and vice versa.

A jar contains marbles of various colors as listed in the table. Suppose you randomly draw one marble from the jar. After you put that marble back in the jar, you randomly draw a second marble. Use this information to answer the question, giving a probability as a percent and rounding to the nearest tenth of percent when necessary.

Color of Marble	Number of Marbles
Red	20
Yellow	18
Green	12
Blue	10

5. What is the probability that you draw a blue marble first and a red marble second?

Let B be the event of drawing a blue marble first. Let R be the event of drawing a red marble second. Then $P(B) = \frac{10}{60} = \frac{1}{6}$ and, because the first marble drawn is replaced before the second marble is drawn, $P(R|B) = P(R) = \frac{20}{60} = \frac{1}{3}$. Since the events are independent, you can multiply their probabilities: $P(B \cap R) = P(B) \cdot P(R) = \frac{1}{6} \cdot \frac{1}{3} = \frac{1}{18} \approx 5.6\%$.

6. What is the probability that you draw a yellow marble first and a green marble second?

Let Y be the event of drawing a yellow marble first. Let G be the event of drawing a green marble second. Then $P(Y) = \frac{18}{60} = \frac{3}{10}$ and, because the first marble drawn is replaced before the second marble is drawn, $P(G|Y) = P(G) = \frac{12}{60} = \frac{1}{5}$. Since the events are independent, you can multiply their probabilities: $P(Y \cap G) = P(Y) \cdot P(G) = \frac{3}{10} \cdot \frac{1}{5} = \frac{1}{50} = 6\%$.

7. What is the probability that you draw a yellow marble both times?

Let $Y1$ be the event of drawing a blue marble first. Let $Y2$ be the event of drawing a red marble second. Then $P(Y1) = \frac{18}{60} = \frac{3}{10}$ and, because the first marble drawn is replaced before the second marble is drawn, $P(Y2|Y1) = P(Y2) = \frac{18}{60} = \frac{3}{10}$. Since the events are independent, you can multiply their probabilities: $P(Y1 \cap Y2) = P(Y1) \cdot P(Y2) = \frac{3}{10} \cdot \frac{3}{10} = \frac{9}{100} \approx 9\%$.

8. What color marble for the first draw and what color marble for the second draw have the greatest probability of occurring together? What is that probability?

The color marble with the greatest number in the jar has the highest probability of being drawn, so draw a red marble on each draw. Let R1 be the event of drawing a yellow marble first. Let R2 be the event of drawing a yellow marble second. Then $P(R1) = \frac{20}{60} = \frac{1}{3}$ and, because the first marble drawn is replaced before the second marble is drawn, $P(R2|R1) = P(R2) = \frac{20}{60} = \frac{1}{3}$. Since the events are independent, you can multiply their probabilities: $P(R1 \cap R2) = P(R1) \cdot P(R2) = \frac{1}{3} \cdot \frac{1}{3} = \frac{1}{9} = 11.1\%$.

You spin the spinner shown two times. Each section of the spinner is the same size. Use this information to answer the question, giving a probability as a percent and rounding to the nearest tenth of a percent when necessary.

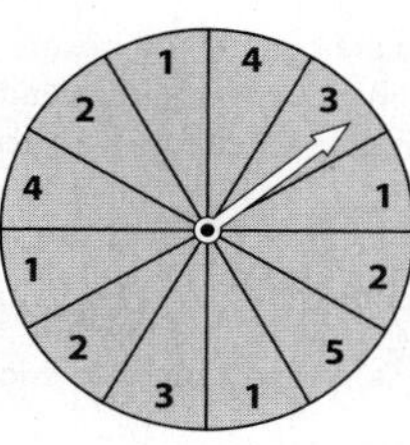

9. What is the probability that the spinner stops on 1 first and 2 second?

$P(1) = \frac{4}{12} = \frac{1}{3}$ and, because the first spin has no effect on the second spin, $P(2|1) = P(2) = \frac{3}{12} = \frac{1}{4}$. Since the events are independent, multiply their probabilities: $P(1 \cap 2) = P(1) \cdot P(2) = \frac{1}{3} \cdot \frac{1}{4} = \frac{1}{12} \approx 8.3\%$.

10. What is the probability that the spinner stops on 4 first and 3 second?

$P(3) = \frac{2}{12} = \frac{1}{6}$ and, because the first spin has no effect on the second spin, $P(4|3) = P(4) = \frac{2}{12} = \frac{1}{6}$. Since the events are independent, multiply their probabilities: $P(4 \cap 3) = P(4) \cdot P(2) = \frac{1}{6} \cdot \frac{1}{6} = \frac{1}{36} \approx 2.8\%$.

11. What is the probability that the spinner stops on an odd number first and an even number second?

Let O be the event of getting an odd number on the first spin. Let E be the event of getting an even number on the second spin. Then $P(O) = \frac{7}{12}$ and, because the first spin has no effect on the second spin, $P(E|O) = P(E) = \frac{5}{12}$. Since the events are independent, multiply their probabilities: $P(O \cap E) = P(O) \cdot P(E) = \frac{7}{12} \cdot \frac{5}{12} = \frac{35}{144} \approx 24.3\%$.

12. What first number and what second number have the least probability of occurring together? What is that probability?

The number that appears least often on the spinner has the lowest probability of occurring, so you want to get 5 on each spin. $P(5) = \frac{1}{12}$ and, because the first spin has no effect on the second spin, $P(5|5) = P(5) = \frac{1}{12}$. Since the events are independent, you can multiply their probabilities: $P(5 \cap 5) = P(5) \cdot P(5) = \frac{1}{12} \cdot \frac{1}{12} = \frac{1}{144} \approx 0.7\%$.

13. Find the probability of getting heads on every toss of a coin when the coin is tossed 3 times.

Let $H1$, $H2$, and $H3$ represent the events of getting heads on the first, second, and third coin tosses, respectively. Because the events are independent, $P(H1 \cap H2 \cap H3) = P(H1) \cdot P(H2) \cdot P(H3) = \frac{1}{2} \cdot \frac{1}{2} \cdot \frac{1}{2} = \frac{1}{8}$.

INTEGRATE MATHEMATICAL PRACTICES

Focus on Math Connections

MP.1 If A and B are independent events, the probability that both A and B occur is given by the multiplication rule $P(A \text{ and } B) = P(A) \cdot P(B)$. More generally, if n independent events occur, then the probability is the product of the n probabilities of the independent events.

14. You are randomly choosing cards, one at a time and with replacement, from a standard deck of cards. Find the probability that you choose an ace, then a red card, and then a face card. (Remember that face cards are jacks, queens, and kings.)

Let A be the event of choosing an ace as the first card. Let R be the event of choosing a red card as the second card. Let F be the event of choosing a face card as the third card. Because you replace each card you choose, the events are independent, and $P(A \cap R \cap F) = P(A) \cdot P(R) \cdot P(F) = \frac{4}{52} \cdot \frac{26}{52} \cdot \frac{12}{52} = \frac{1}{13} \cdot \frac{1}{2} \cdot \frac{3}{13} = \frac{3}{338} \approx 0.9\%$.

Determine whether the given events are independent using the fact that $P(A \text{ and } B) = P(A) \cdot P(B)$ only when events A and B are independent.

15. The manager of a produce stand wants to find out whether there is a connection between people who buy fresh vegetables and people who buy fresh fruit. The manager collects data on 200 randomly chosen shoppers, as shown in the two-way frequency table. Determine whether buying fresh vegetables and buying fresh fruit are independent events.

	Bought Vegetables	No Vegetables	Total
Bought Fruit	56	20	76
No Fruit	49	75	124
Total	105	95	200

Let V be the event that a shopper bought fresh vegetables. Let F be the event that a shopper bought fresh fruit.

$P(V) = \frac{105}{200} = \frac{21}{40}$, $P(F) = \frac{76}{200} = \frac{19}{50}$, and $P(V) \cdot P(F) = \frac{21}{40} \cdot \frac{19}{50} = \frac{399}{2000} \approx 20\%$.

Because $P(V \cap F) = \frac{56}{200} = 28\%$ and $P(V \cap F) \neq P(V) \cdot P(F)$, the events are not independent.

16. The owner of a bookstore collects data about the reading preferences of 60 randomly chosen customers, as shown in the two-way frequency table. Determine whether being a female and preferring fiction are independent events.

	Prefers Fiction	Prefers Nonfiction	Total
Female	15	10	25
Male	21	14	35
Total	36	24	60

Let Fe be the event that a reader is female. Let Fi be the event that a reader prefers fiction.

$P(Fe) = \frac{25}{60} = \frac{5}{12}$, $P(Fi) = \frac{36}{60} = \frac{3}{5}$, and $P(Fe) \cdot P(Fi) = \frac{5}{12} \cdot \frac{3}{5} = \frac{1}{4}$.

Because $P(Fe \cap Fi) = \frac{15}{60} = \frac{1}{4}$ and $P(Fe \cap Fi) = P(Fe) \cdot P(Fi)$, the events are independent.

17. The psychology department at a college collects data about the whether there is relationship between a student's intended career and the student's like or dislike for solving puzzles. The two-way frequency table shows the collected data for 80 randomly chosen students. Determine whether planning for a career in a field involving math or science and a like for solving puzzles are independent events.

	Plans a Career in a Math/Science Field	Plans a Career in a Non-Math/Science Field	Total
Likes Solving Puzzles	35	15	50
Dislikes Solving Puzzles	9	21	30
Total	44	36	80

Let *MS* be the event that a student plans a career in a math/science field. Let *L* be the event that a student likes solving puzzles.

$P(MS) = \frac{44}{80} = \frac{11}{20}$, $P(L) = \frac{50}{80} = \frac{5}{8}$, **and** $P(MS) \cdot P(L) = \frac{11}{20} \cdot \frac{5}{8} = \frac{55}{160} \approx 34\%$.
Because $P(MS \cap L) = \frac{35}{80} \approx 44\%$ **and** $P(MS \cap L) \neq P(MS) \cdot P(L)$, **the events are not independent.**

18. A local television station surveys some of its viewers to determine the primary reason they watch the station. The two-way frequency table gives the survey data. Determine whether a viewer is a man and a viewer primarily watches the station for entertainment are independent events.

	Primarily Watches for Information (News, Weather, Sports)	Primarily Watches for Entertainment (Comedies, Dramas)	Total
Men	28	12	40
Women	35	15	50
Ttotal	63	27	90

Let *M* be the event that a viewer is a man. Let *E* be the event that a viewer primarily watches the station for entertainment.

$P(M) = \frac{40}{90} = \frac{4}{9}$, $P(E) = \frac{27}{90}, \frac{3}{10}$ **and** $P(M) \cdot P(E) = \frac{4}{9} \cdot \frac{3}{10} = \frac{2}{15}$.
Because $P(M \cap E) = \frac{12}{90} = \frac{2}{15}$ **and** $P(MS \cap L) = P(MS) \cdot P(L)$, **the events are independent.**

19. Using what you know about independent events, complete the two-way frequency table in such a way that any event from a column will be independent of any event from a row. Give an example using the table to demonstrate the independence of two events.

	Women	Men	Total
Prefers Writing with a Pen	**40**	**60**	100
Prefers Writing with a Pencil	**20**	**30**	50
Total	60	90	150

The ratio of women to men is 60:90, or 2:3. For independence of events, the 100 people who prefer writing with a pen must also be divided into a ratio of 2:3. Let m represent the common multiplier of 2 and 3, and solve $2m + 3m = 100$ to get $m = 20$. So, there must be $2(20) = 40$ women who prefer writing with a pen and $3(30) = 90$ men who prefer writing with a pen. To find the number of women who prefer writing with a pencil, subtract 40 from 60 to get 20. To find the number of men who prefer writing with a pen, subtract 60 from 90 to get 30.

Examples showing independence of events will vary. Sample answer:

Let W be the event that a person is a woman. Let Pe be the event that a person prefers writing with a pen. $P(W) = \frac{60}{150} = \frac{2}{5}$, $P(Pe) = \frac{100}{150} = \frac{2}{3}$, and $P(W) \cdot P(Pe) = \frac{2}{5} \cdot \frac{2}{3} = \frac{4}{15}$. Since $P(W \cap Pe) = \frac{40}{150} = \frac{4}{15}$ and $P(W \cap Pe) = P(W) \cdot P(Pe)$, the events are independent.

H.O.T. Focus on Higher Order Thinking

20. **Make a Prediction** A box contains 100 balloons. The balloons come in two colors: 80 are yellow and 20 are green. The balloons are also either marked or unmarked: 50 are marked "Happy Birthday!" and 50 are not. A balloon is randomly chosen from the box. How many yellow "Happy Birthday!" balloons must be in the box if the event that a balloon is yellow and the event that a balloon is marked 'Happy Birthday!"' are independent? Explain.

Because half of the balloons are marked "Happy Birthday!", the probability of drawing a "Happy Birthday!" balloon is $\frac{1}{2}$. To be independent of the event that a balloon is yellow, the conditional probability of drawing a balloon marked "Happy Birthday!" given that the balloon is yellow also needs to have a probability of $\frac{1}{2}$. So, $\frac{1}{2}(80) = 40$ yellow "Happy Birthday!" balloons would need to be in the box.

21. Construct Arguments Given that events A and B are independent, prove that the complement of event A, A^c, is also independent of event B.

$P(A^c \mid B) = 1 - P(A \mid B)$	**Definition of complementary events**
$= 1 - P(A)$	**Definition of independent events**
$= P(A^c)$	**Definition of complementary events**

So, events A^c and B are also independent.

22. Multi-Step The two-way frequency table shows two events, A and B, and their complements, A^c and B^c. Let $P(A) = a$ and $P(B) = b$. Using a, b, and the grand total T, form the products listed in the table to find the number of elements in $A \cap B$, $A \cap B^c$, $A^c \cap B$, and $A^c \cap B^c$.

	A	**A^c**	**Total**
B	abT	$(1-a)bT$	
B^c	$a(1-b)T$	$(1-a)(1-b)T$	
Total			T

a. Find the table's missing row and column totals in simplest form.

Row total for event B: $abT + (1-a)bT = [a + (1-a)]bT = bT$

Row total for event B^c: $a(1-b)T + (1-a)(1-b)T = [a + (1-a)](1-b)T = (1-b)T$

Column total for event A: $abT + a(1-b)T = a[b + (1-b)]T = aT$

Column total for event A^c: $(1-a)bT + (1-a)(1-b)T = (1-a)[b + (1-b)]T = (1-a)T$

b. Show that events A and B are independent using the fact that $P(A \mid B) = P(A)$ only when events A and B are independent.

$$P(A|B) = \frac{n(A \cap B)}{n(B)} = \frac{abT}{bT} = a = P(A)$$

c. Show that events A and B^c are independent.

$$P(A|B^c) = \frac{n(A \cap B^c)}{n(B^c)} = \frac{a(1-b)T}{(1-b)T} = a = P(A)$$

d. Show that events A^c and B are independent.

$$P(A^c|B) = \frac{n(A^c \cap B)}{n(B)} = \frac{(1-a)bT}{bT} = 1 - a = P(A^c)$$

e. Show that events A^c and B^c are independent.

$$P(A^c|B^c) = \frac{n(A^c \cap B^c)}{n(B^c)} = \frac{(1-a)(1-b)T}{(1-b)T} = 1 - a = P(A^c)$$

PEER-TO-PEER DISCUSSION

Have students discuss various pairs of independent events that they can create from the spinner below.

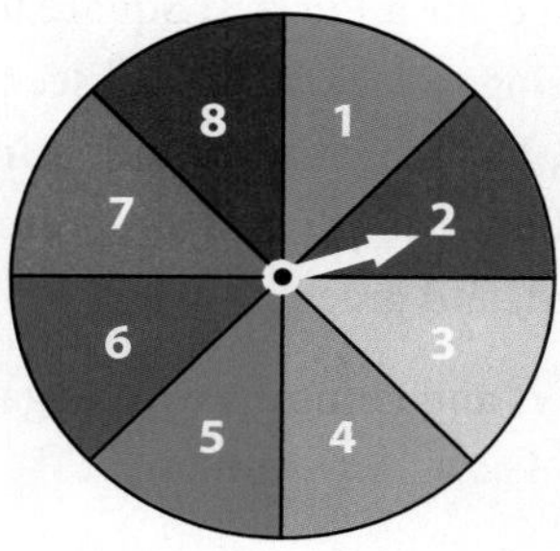

Have them describe in their own words the process they would use to find the probabilities for pairs of independent events.

JOURNAL

Have students explain what is meant by independent events and give an example of how to determine whether two events are independent.

INTEGRATE MATHEMATICAL PRACTICES

Focus on Patterns

MP.8 Megan drew a Punnett Square to find the results of crossing two violet-round seed-yellow seed parents. Let *V*, *R*, and *Y* represent dominant violet, round, and yellow. Let *v*, *r*, and *y* represent recessive white, wrinkled, and green.

How many rows and columns will Megan's Punnett Square have? 8 rows, 8 columns

List the letter groups that will appear atop the columns and beside the rows in the square. *VRY, VRy, VrY, Vry, vRY, vRy, vrY, vry*

What is the probability that a second-generation flower will be white and wrinkled, and have green seeds? $\frac{1}{64}$

Lesson Performance Task

Before the mid-1800s, little was known about the way that plants pass along characteristics such as color and height to their offspring. From painstaking observations of garden peas, the Austrian monk Gregor Mendel discovered the basic laws of heredity. The table shows the results of three of Mendel's experiments. In each experiment, he looked at a particular characteristic of garden peas by planting seeds exclusively of one type.

Characteristic	Type Planted	Results in Second Generation
Flower color	100% violet	705 violet, 224 white
Seed texture	100% round	5474 round, 1850 wrinkled
Seed color	100% yellow	6022 yellow, 2011 green

1. Suppose you plant garden peas with violet flowers and round, yellow seeds. Estimate the probability of obtaining second-generation plants with violet flowers, the probability of obtaining second-generation plants with round seeds, and the probability of obtaining second-generation plants with yellow seeds. Explain how you made your estimates.

Mendel saw that certain traits, such as violet flowers and round seeds, seemed stronger than others, such white flowers and wrinkled seeds. He called the stronger traits "dominant" and the weaker traits "recessive." Both traits can be carried in the genes of a plant, because a gene consists of two *alleles*, one received from the mother and one from the father. (For plants, the "father" is the plant from which the pollen comes, and the "mother" is the plant whose pistil receives the pollen.) When at least one of the alleles has the dominant trait, the plant exhibits the dominant trait. Only when both alleles have the recessive trait does the plant exhibit the recessive trait.

You can use a 2 × 2 Punnett square, like the one shown, to see the results of crossing the genes of two parent plants. In this Punnett square, *V* represents the dominant flower color violet and *v* represents the recessive flower color white. If each parent's genes contain both *V* and *v* alleles, the offspring may receive, independently and with equal probability, either a *V* allele or a *v* allele from each parent.

	V	*v*
V	*VV*	*Vv*
v	*Vv*	*Vv*

2. After planting a first generation of plants exhibiting only dominant traits, Mendel observed that the second generation consisted of plants with a ratio of about 3:1 dominant-to-recessive traits. Does the Punnett square support or refute Mendel's observation? Explain.

3. Draw a 4 × 4 Punnett square for finding the results of crossing two violet-flower-and-round-seed parent plants. Let V and R represent the dominant traits violet flowers and round seeds, respectively. Let v and r represent the recessive traits white flowers and wrinkled seeds, respectively. Each column heading and row heading of your Punnett square should contain a two-letter combination of V or v and R or r. Each cell of your Punnett square will then contain four letters. Use the Punnett square to find the probability that a second-generation plant will have white flowers and round seeds. Explain your reasoning.

1. Estimate the probabilities using Mendel's data: If V represents violet flowers, then $P(V) = \frac{705}{705 + 224} = \frac{705}{929} \approx 76\%$. If R represents round seeds, then $P(R) = \frac{5474}{5474 + 1850} = \frac{5474}{7324} \approx 75\%$. If Y represents yellow seeds, then $P(Y) = \frac{6022}{6022 + 2011} = \frac{6022}{8033} \approx 75\%$.

2. The Punnett square supports Mendel's observation. The combination of alleles in each table cell occurs with a probability of $\frac{1}{2} \cdot \frac{1}{2} = \frac{1}{4}$. Since three of the four table cells contain a dominant V allele, you can expect three-fourths of the offspring to have violet flowers. Since one table cell contains two recessive v alleles, you can expect one-fourth of the offspring to have white flowers. So, the ratio of offspring with violet flowers to offspring with white flowers is $\frac{\frac{3}{4}}{\frac{1}{4}} = \frac{3}{1}$.

3.

	VR	Vr	vR	vr
VR	VVRR	VVRr	VrRR	VvRr
Vr	VVRr	VVrr	VvRr	Vvrr
vR	VvRR	VvRr	vvRR	vvRr
vr	VvRr	Vvrr	vvRr	vvrr

The combination of alleles in each table cell occurs with a probability of $\frac{1}{2} \cdot \frac{1}{2} \cdot \frac{1}{2} \cdot \frac{1}{2} = \frac{1}{16}$. For offspring to have white flowers, which is recessive, a table cell must contain two v alleles. For offspring to have round seeds, which is dominant, a cell must contain two R alleles or a combination of an R allele and an r allele. Three of 16 table cells satisfy those requirements (*vvRR*, *vvRr*, and *vvRr*), giving a probability of $\frac{3}{16}$.

EXTENSION ACTIVITY

Have students work in pairs. Each pair should have two coins and a sheet of paper on which to record their results. Ask students to conduct 50 trials, each time flipping two coins and recording the results (2 heads, a heads and a tails, or 2 tails). Ask them to interpret their results in terms of the laws of heredity discovered by Mendel. Sample answer: We let H represent a dominant trait and T a recessive trait. We interpreted every HH, HT, and TH occurrence as an offspring displaying the dominant trait and every TT occurrence as an offspring displaying the recessive trait. About 75% of our trials resulted in HH, HT, or TH (offspring displaying the dominant trait), closely matching Mendel's results.

INTEGRATE MATHEMATICAL PRACTICES

Focus on Critical Thinking

MP.3 A gardener claimed to have planted 10 violet-round seed-yellow garden pea seeds and to have obtained 10 white-wrinkled seed-green plants. Was the gardener telling the truth? Explain. Sample answer: The gardener's results were possible but highly unlikely. The probability that a single second-generation white-wrinkled seed-green plant will be produced is $\frac{1}{64}$. The probability that 10 will be produced is $\left(\frac{1}{64}\right)^{10}$, which is very small.

Scoring Rubric

2 points: The student's answer is an accurate and complete execution of the task or tasks.

1 point: The student's answer contains attributes of an appropriate response but is flawed.

0 points: The student's answer contains no attributes of an appropriate response.

LESSON 20.3

Dependent Events

Common Core Math Standards

The student is expected to:

COMMON CORE **S-CP.B.8**

Apply the general Multiplication Rule in a uniform probability model, $P(A \text{ and } B) = P(A)P(B|A) = P(B)P(A|B)$, and interpret the answer in terms of the model. Also S-CP.A.3, S-CP.A.4, S-CP.A.5

Mathematical Practices

COMMON CORE **MP.6 Precision**

Language Objective

Work with a partner to brainstorm examples of dependent events.

ENGAGE

Essential Question: How do you find the probability of dependent events?

You can use the Multiplication Rule to find the probability of dependent events.

PREVIEW: LESSON PERFORMANCE TASK

View the Engage section online. Discuss the photograph. Ask students to describe the sport that is pictured. Then preview the Lesson Performance Task.

Name __________ Class __________ Date __________

20.3 Dependent Events

Essential Question: How do you find the probability of dependent events?

Resource Locker

Explore Finding a Way to Calculate the Probability of Dependent Events

You know two tests for the independence of events A and B:

1. If $P(A|B) = P(A)$, then A and B are independent.
2. If $P(A \cap B) = P(A) \cdot P(B)$, then A and B are independent.

Two events that fail either of these tests are **dependent events** because the occurrence of one event affects the occurrence of the other event.

(A) The two-way frequency table shows the results of a survey of 100 people who regularly walk for exercise. Let O be the event that a person prefers walking outdoors. Let M be the event that a person is male. Find $P(O)$, $P(M)$, and $P(O \cap M)$ as fractions. Then determine whether events O and M are independent or dependent.

	Prefers walking outdoors	Prefers walking on a treadmill	Total
Male	40	10	50
Female	20	30	50
Total	60	40	100

$P(O) = \frac{60}{100} = \frac{3}{5}$, $P(M) = \frac{50}{100} = \frac{1}{2}$, and $P(O \cap M) = \frac{40}{100} = \frac{2}{5}$.

Since $P(O) \cdot P(M) = \frac{3}{5} \cdot \frac{1}{2} = \frac{3}{10} \neq P(O \cap M)$, events O and M are dependent.

(B) Calculate the conditional probabilities $P(O|M)$ and $P(M|O)$.

$$P(O|M) = \frac{n(O \cap M)}{n(M)} = \frac{40}{50} = \frac{4}{5}$$

$$P(M|O) = \frac{n(O \cap M)}{n(O)} = \frac{40}{60} = \frac{2}{3}$$

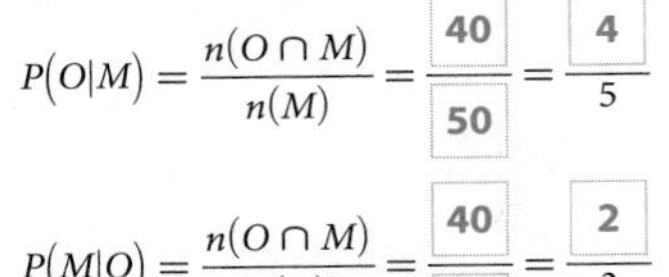

HARDCOVER PAGES **1031–10**

Watch for the hardcover student edition page numbers for this lesson.

Ⓒ Complete the multiplication table using the fractions for $P(O)$ and $P(M)$ from Step A and the fractions for $P(O|M)$ and $P(M|O)$ from Step B.

×	$P(O)$	$P(M)$
$P(O\|M)$	$\frac{3}{5} \cdot \frac{4}{5} = \frac{12}{25}$	$\frac{1}{2} \cdot \frac{4}{5} = \frac{2}{5}$
$P(M\|O)$	$\frac{3}{5} \cdot \frac{2}{3} = \frac{2}{5}$	$\frac{1}{2} \cdot \frac{2}{5} = \frac{1}{5}$

Ⓓ Do any of the four products in Step C equal $P(O \cap M)$, calculated in Step A? If so, which of the four products?

Yes, the products $P(O) \cdot P(M|O)$ and $P(M) \cdot P(O|M)$ both equal $\frac{2}{5}$, the value of $P(O \cap M)$.

Reflect

1. In a previous lesson you learned the conditional probability formula $P(B|A) = \frac{P(A \cap B)}{P(A)}$. How does this formula explain the results you obtained in Step D?

Multiplying both sides of $P(B|A) = \frac{P(A \cap B)}{P(A)}$ by $P(A)$ gives $P(A) \cdot P(B|A) = P(A \cap B)$. Letting $A = O$ and $B = M$ gives $P(O) \cdot P(M|O) = P(O \cap M)$, while letting $A = M$ and $B = O$ gives $P(M) \cdot P(O|M) = P(M \cap O) = P(O \cap M)$.

2. Let F be the event that a person is female. Let T be the event that a person prefers walking on a treadmill. Write two formulas you can use to calculate $P(F \cap T)$. Use either one to find the value of $P(F \cap T)$, and then confirm the result by finding $P(F \cap T)$ directly from the two-way frequency table.

$P(F \cap T) = P(F) \cdot P(T|F)$; $P(F \cap T) = P(T \cap F) = P(T) \cdot P(F|T)$. Using the first of these formulas gives $P(F \cap T) = \frac{50}{100} \cdot \frac{30}{50} = \frac{1}{2} \cdot \frac{3}{5} = \frac{3}{10}$. Calculating $P(T \cap F)$ directly from the table gives $\frac{30}{100} = \frac{3}{10}$.

Explain 1 Finding the Probability of Two Dependent Events

You can use the Multiplication Rule to find the probability of dependent events.

Multiplication Rule

$P(A \cap B) = P(A) \cdot P(B|A)$ where $P(B|A)$ is the conditional probability of event B, given that event A has occurred.

Example 1 **There are 5 tiles with the letters A, B, C, D, and E in a bag. You choose a tile without looking, put it aside, and then choose another tile without looking. Use the Multiplication Rule to find the specified probability, writing it as a fraction.**

PROFESSIONAL DEVELOPMENT

Integrate Mathematical Practices

This lesson provides an opportunity to address Mathematical Practice **MP.6**, which calls for students to "communicate with precision." Students are already familiar with some aspects of probability but, in this lesson, they must analyze whether events are dependent or independent before they find the probabilities of the events. They use multiple representations, including formulas, two-way tables, and tree diagrams, to determine a probability. Students may also make an organized list of all outcomes.

EXPLORE

Finding a Way to Calculate the Probability of Dependent Events

INTEGRATE TECHNOLOGY

Students have the option of doing the Explore activity either in the book or online.

QUESTIONING STRATEGIES

Suppose two events A and B are dependent. How are their probabilities related? **If events A and B are dependent events, $P(A \text{ and } B) = P(A|B) \cdot P(B)$ or $P(A \text{ and } B) = P(B|A) \cdot P(A)$.**

INTEGRATE MATHEMATICAL PRACTICES

Focus on Math Connections

MP.1 Point out that if two events occur with replacement, then the events may not be dependent. For example, if two marbles are drawn from a bag, the events of drawing a marble are dependent. But, if the first marble is replaced before the second one is drawn, then the events become independent, since the first event does not affect the second.

EXPLAIN 1

Finding the Probability of Two Dependent Events

QUESTIONING STRATEGIES

Why is probability of dependent events different from the probability of independent events? **The occurrence of one event affects the probability of the second event.**

AVOID COMMON ERRORS

Help students who are confused about identifying dependent events by having them communicate their results from this lesson orally and in writing. Ask them to check that they are using terms correctly. In particular, be sure students understand that the word *dependent* has a specific meaning in probability theory that may be different from its meaning in everyday conversation.

INTEGRATE MATHEMATICAL PRACTICES

Focus on Math Connections

MP.1 Point out the two different ways to determine the probability of dependent events: (1) by using the formula for the multiplication rule, and (2) by making a tree diagram. You may also wish to tell students that they can determine the probability by thinking about permutations to find the number of outcomes in the sample space and the number of favorable outcomes.

Ⓐ Find the probability that you choose a vowel followed by a consonant.

Let V be the event that the first tile is a vowel. Let C be the event that the second tile is a consonant. Of the 5 tiles, there are 2 vowels, so $P(V) = \frac{2}{5}$.

Of the 4 remaining tiles, there are 3 consonants, so $P(C|V) = \frac{3}{4}$.

By the Multiplication Rule, $P(V \cap C) = P(V) \cdot P(V|C) = \frac{2}{5} \cdot \frac{3}{4} = \frac{6}{20} = \frac{3}{10}$.

Ⓑ Find the probability that you choose a vowel followed by another vowel.

Let $V1$ be the event that the first tile is a vowel. Let $V2$ be the event that the second tile is also a vowel. Of the 5 tiles, there are 2 vowels, so $P(V1) = \frac{2}{5}$.

Of the 4 remaining tiles, there is 1 vowel, so $P(V2|V1) = \frac{1}{4}$.

By the Multiplication Rule, $P(V1 \cap V2) = P(V1) \cdot P(V2|V1) = \frac{2}{5} \cdot \frac{1}{4} = \frac{2}{20} = \frac{1}{10}$.

Your Turn

A bag holds 4 white marbles and 2 blue marbles. You choose a marble without looking, put it aside, and choose another marble without looking. Use the Multiplication Rule to find the specified probability, writing it as a fraction.

3. Find the probability that you remove a white marble followed by a blue marble.

Let *W* be the event that the first marble is white. Let *B* be the event that the second marble is blue.

$P(W) = \frac{4}{6} = \frac{2}{3}$

$P(B|W) = \frac{2}{5}$

$P(W \cap B) = P(W1) \cdot P(B|W) = \frac{2}{3} \cdot \frac{3}{5} = \frac{4}{15}$

4. Find the probability that you choose a white marble followed by another white marble.

Let *W1* be the event that the first marble is a white marble. Let *W2* be the event that the second marble is also a white marble.

$P(W1) = \frac{4}{6} = \frac{2}{3}$

$P(W2|W1) = \frac{3}{5}$

$P(W1 \cap W2) = P(W1) \cdot P(W2|W1) = \frac{2}{3} \cdot \frac{3}{5} = \frac{2}{5}$

COLLABORATIVE LEARNING

Peer-to-Peer Activity

Have students work in pairs. Give each pair a set of 5 to 10 playing cards or numbered index cards. Have students lay out the cards face up, write a list of possible independent and dependent events using the cards, and find the probabilities. Have one student identify the favorable outcomes and the other student identify the sample space for each event.

Explain 2 Finding the Probability of Three or More Dependent Events

You can extend the Multiplication Rule to three or more events. For instance, for three events A, B, and C, the rule becomes $P(A \cap B \cap C) = P(A) \cdot P(B|A) \cdot P(C|A \cap B)$.

Example 2 **You have a key ring with 7 different keys. You're attempting to unlock a door in the dark, so you try keys one at a time and keep track of which ones you try.**

(A) Find the probability that the third key you try is the right one.

Let $W1$ be the event that the first key you try is wrong. Let $W2$ be the event that the second key you try is also wrong. Let R be the event that the third key you try is right.

On the first try, there are 6 wrong keys among the 7 keys, so $P(W1) = \frac{6}{7}$.

On the second try, there are 5 wrong keys among the 6 remaining keys, so $P(W2|W1) = \frac{5}{6}$.

On the third try, there is 1 right key among the 5 remaining keys, so $P(R|W2 \cap W1) = \frac{1}{5}$.

By the Multiplication Rule, $P(W1 \cap W2 \cap R) = P(W1) \cdot P(W2|W1) \cdot P(R|W1 \cap W2) = \frac{6}{7} \cdot \frac{5}{6} \cdot \frac{1}{5} = \frac{1}{7}$.

(B) Find the probability that one of the first three keys you try is right.

There are two ways to approach this problem:

1. You can break the problem into three cases: (1) the first key you try is right; (2) the first key is wrong, but the second key is right; and (3) the first two keys are wrong, but the third key is right.

2. You can use the complement: The complement of the event that one of the first three keys is right is the event that *none* of the first three keys is right.

Use the second approach.

Let $W1$, $W2$, and $W3$ be the events that the first, second, and third keys, respectively, are wrong.

From Part A, you already know that $P(W1) = \frac{6}{7}$ and $P(W2|W1) = \frac{5}{6}$.

On the third try, there are 4 wrong keys among the 5 remaining keys, so $P(W3|W2 \cap W1) = \frac{4}{5}$.

By the Multiplication Rule,

$P(W1 \cap W2 \cap W3) = P(W1) \cdot P(W2|W1) \cdot P(W3|W1 \cap W2) = \frac{6}{7} \cdot \frac{5}{6} \cdot \frac{4}{5} = \frac{4}{7}$

The event $W1 \cap W2 \cap W3$ is the complement of the one you want. So, the probability that one of the first three keys you try is right is $1 - P(W1 \cap W2 \cap W3) = 1 - \frac{4}{7} = \frac{3}{7}$

DIFFERENTIATE INSTRUCTION

Modeling

Help students understand the difference between independent events and dependent events by discussing choosing two colored marbles from a bag: (1) with replacement and (2) without replacement. When you select a marble with replacement, you select the first marble, note its color, put the marble back in the bag, and then choose the second marble. In this case, the two selections are independent events. Without replacement, you select the first marble, put it aside, and then choose the second marble. In this case, the two selections are dependent events because the marble you chose first changed the sample space for your second selection.

EXPLAIN 2

Finding the Probability of Three or More Dependent Events

QUESTIONING STRATEGIES

When does replacement affect independence? **When there is replacement, the events are independent because the outcome of the first event does not affect the probability of the second event.**

Why can you use the multiplication rule $P(A \text{ and } B) = P(A) \cdot P(B|A)$ for both dependent and independent events? **If the events are independent, $P(B|A)$ is equal to $P(B)$.**

INTEGRATE MATHEMATICAL PRACTICES

Focus on Reasoning

MP.2 Ask students if they think that the multiplication rule for dependent events can be extended, as it was for independent events, and why. **Yes; for example, a formula for three events is $P(A \text{ and } B \text{ and } C) = P(A) \cdot P(B \mid A) \cdot P(C \mid A \text{ and } B)$. Since each part of this formula can be found for dependent events, you can extend the rule.**

Reflect

5. In Part B, show that the first approach to solving the problem gives the same result.

Let $W1$ and $W2$ be the events that the first and second keys, respectively, are wrong. Let R be the event that a key is right. Calculate three probabilities: $P(R)$, $P(W1 \cap R)$, and $P(W1 \cap W2 \cap R)$.

There is 1 right key among the 7 keys on the first try, so $P(R) = \frac{1}{7}$.

There are 6 wrong keys among the 7 keys on the first try and then 1 right key among the 6 remaining keys on the second try, so $P(W1 \cap R) = P(W1) \cdot P(R|W1) = \frac{6}{7} \cdot \frac{1}{6} \cdot = \frac{1}{7}$.

From Part A, you know that $P(W1 \cap W2 \cap R) = \frac{1}{7}$.

Because the three events R, $W1 \cap R$, and $W2 \cap W1 \cap R$ are mutually exclusive, the probability that one of the first three keys is right is the sum of the probabilities of those events: $P(R) + P(W1 \cap R) + P(W2 \cap W1 \cap R) = \frac{1}{7} + \frac{1}{7} + \frac{1}{7} = \frac{3}{7}$.

6. In Part A, suppose you don't keep track of the keys as you try them. How does the probability change? Explain.

If you don't keep track of the keys, the probability of trying a wrong key is always $\frac{6}{7}$, and the probability of choosing the right key is always $\frac{1}{7}$. The events $W1$, $W2$, and R are now independent, so you can multiply their probabilities without considering conditional probabilities: $P(W1 \cap W2 \cap R) = P(W1) \cdot P(W2) \cdot P(R) = \frac{6}{7} \cdot \frac{6}{7} \cdot \frac{1}{7} = \frac{36}{343}$

Your Turn

Three people are standing in line at a car rental agency at an airport. Each person is willing to take whatever rental car is offered. The agency has 4 white cars and 2 silver ones available and offers them to customers on a random basis.

7. Find the probability that all three customers get white cars.

Let $W1$, $W2$, and $W3$ be the events that the first, second, and third customers, respectively, get a white car.

$$P(W1 \cap W2 \cap W3) = P(W1) \cdot P(W2|W1) \cdot P(W3|W1 \cap W2)$$
$$= \frac{4}{6} \cdot \frac{3}{5} \cdot \frac{2}{4}$$
$$= \frac{2}{3} \cdot \frac{3}{5} \cdot \frac{1}{2}$$
$$= \frac{1}{5}$$

So, the probability that all three customers get a white car is $\frac{1}{5}$.

LANGUAGE SUPPORT EL

Connect Vocabulary

Help students understand *dependent events* by having them create a poster with examples of dependent events that may be familiar, and that show simple calculations for the probability of the dependent events. You may want to prompt students to highlight the words that correspond to the event that is assumed to have already occurred and have them focus on the fact that this event affects the outcome of the other event.

8. Find the probability that two of the customers get the silver cars and one gets a white car.

Let $W1$ and $S1$ represent the events that the first customer gets a white or silver car, respectively. Let $W2$ and $S2$ represent the events that the second customer gets a white or silver car, respectively. Let $W3$ and $S3$ represent the events that the third customer gets a white or silver car, respectively. Calculate three probabilities: $P(W1 \cap S2 \cap S3)$, $P(S1 \cap W2 \cap S3)$, and $P(S1 \cap S2 \cap W3)$.

$$P(W1 \cap S2 \cap S3) = P(W1) \cdot P(S2|W1) \cdot P(S3|W1 \cap S2) = \frac{4}{6} \cdot \frac{2}{5} \cdot \frac{1}{4} = \frac{1}{15}$$

$$P(S1 \cap W2 \cap S3) = P(S1) \cdot P(W2|S1) \cdot P(S3|S1 \cap W2) = \frac{2}{6} \cdot \frac{4}{5} \cdot \frac{1}{4} = \frac{1}{15}$$

$$P(S1 \cap S2 \cap W3) = P(S1) \cdot P(S2|S1) \cdot P(W3|S1 \cap S2) = \frac{2}{6} \cdot \frac{1}{5} \cdot \frac{4}{4} = \frac{1}{15}.$$

Because the events $W1 \cap S2 \cap S3$, $S1 \cap W2 \cap S3$, and $S1 \cap S2 \cap W3$ are mutually exclusive, you can add their probabilities:

$$P(W1 \cap S2 \cap S3) + P(S1 \cap W2 \cap S3) + P(S1 \cap S2 \cap W3) = \frac{1}{15} + \frac{1}{15} + \frac{1}{15} = \frac{3}{15} = \frac{1}{5}$$

So, the probability that two customers get the silver cars and one gets a white car is $\frac{1}{5}$.

Elaborate

9. When are two events dependent?

Two events are dependent when the occurrence of one event affects the occurrence of the other.

10. Suppose you are given a bag with 3 blue marbles and 2 red marbles, and you are asked to find the probability of drawing 2 blue marbles by drawing one marble at a time and not replacing the first marble drawn. Why does not replacing the first marble make these events dependent? What would make these events independent? Explain.

The first marble you draw changes the sample space for your draw. That is, the occurrence of the event that you get a blue marble on the first draw affects the occurrence of the event that you get a blue marble on the second draw. Replacing the first marble drawn returns the sample space to its original state so that the probability of getting a blue marble doesn't change from one draw to the next, which means that the events are independent.

11. **Essential Question Check-In** According to the Multiplication Rule, when finding $P(A \cap B)$ for dependent events A and B, you multiply $P(A)$ by what?

You multiply $P(A)$ by $P(B|A)$.

ELABORATE

QUESTIONING STRATEGIES

? How is the multiplication rule used to find the probability of dependent or independent events A and B? **Sample answer: If A and B are dependent, then the rule is $P(A \text{ and } B) = P(A) \cdot P(B \mid A)$. If A and B are independent, then $P(B \mid A)$ can be replaced by $P(B)$ and the multiplication rule becomes $P(A \text{ and } B) = P(A) . P(B)$.**

SUMMARIZE THE LESSON

? State the multiplication rule, $P(A \text{ and } B) = P(A) \cdot P(B \mid A)$, in your own words. **The probability that dependent events A and B take place is equal to the product of the probability that A takes place and the probability that B takes place given that A has already occurred.**

EVALUATE

ASSIGNMENT GUIDE

Concepts and Skills	Practice
Explore Finding a Way to Calculate the Probability of Dependent Events	Exercise 1
Example 1 Determining the Probability of Two Dependent Events	Exercises 2–3
Example 2 Finding the Probability of Three or More Dependent Events	Exercises 4–14

INTEGRATE MATHEMATICAL PRACTICES

Focus on Communication

MP.3 Have students work in small groups to explain the difference between dependent and independent events. Then have them explain to each other how to find the probabilities associated with dependent and independent events. Ask them to use examples in their explanations.

Evaluate: Homework and Practice

• Online Homework
• Hints and Help
• Extra Practice

1. Town officials are considering a property tax increase to finance the building of a new school. The two-way frequency table shows the results of a survey of 110 town residents.

	Supports a property tax increase	Does not support a property tax increase	Total
Lives in a household with children	50	20	70
Lives in a household without children	10	30	40
Total	60	50	110

a. Let C be the event that a person lives in a household with children. Let S be the event that a person supports a property tax increase. Are the events C and S independent or dependent? Explain.

$P(C) = \frac{70}{110} = \frac{7}{11}$, $P(S) = \frac{60}{110} = \frac{6}{11}$, and $P(C \cap S) = \frac{50}{110} = \frac{5}{11}$.
Since $P(S) \cdot P(C) = \frac{7}{11} \cdot \frac{6}{11} = \frac{42}{121}$ and $P(C \cap S) = \frac{5}{11} = \frac{55}{121}$,
$P(C) \cdot P(S) \neq P(C \cap S)$, so the events C and S are dependent.

b. Find $P(C|S)$ and $P(S|C)$. Which of these two conditional probabilities can you multiply with $P(C)$ to get $P(C \cap S)$? Which of the two can you multiply with $P(S)$ to get $P(C \cap S)$?

$P(C|S) = \frac{50}{60} = \frac{5}{6}$ and $P(S|C) = \frac{50}{70} = \frac{5}{7}$.

Multiplying $P(C)$ and $P(S|C)$ gives $\frac{7}{11} \cdot \frac{5}{7} = \frac{5}{11} = P(C \cap S)$.

Multiplying $P(S)$ and $P(C|S)$ gives $\frac{6}{11} \cdot \frac{5}{6} = \frac{5}{11} = P(C \cap S)$.

Exercise	Depth of Knowledge (D.O.K.)	COMMON CORE Mathematical Practices
1	2 Skills/Concepts	MP.4 Modeling
2–11	2 Skills/Concepts	MP.1 Problem Solving
12	2 Skills/Concepts H.O.T.	MP.4 Modeling
13	3 Strategic Thinking H.O.T.	MP.3 Logic
14	3 Strategic Thinking H.O.T.	MP.2 Reasoning

2. A mall surveyed 120 shoppers to find out whether they typically wait for a sale to get a better price or make purchases on the spur of the moment regardless of price. The two-way frequency table shows the results of the survey.

	Waits for a Sale	Buys on Impulse	Total
Woman	40	10	50
Man	50	20	70
Total	90	30	120

a. Let W be the event that a shopper is a woman. Let S be the event that a shopper typically waits for a sale. Are the events W and S independent or dependent? Explain.

$P(W) = \frac{50}{120} = \frac{5}{12}$, $PS = \frac{90}{120} = \frac{3}{4}$, **and** $P(W \cap S) = \frac{40}{120} = \frac{1}{3}$.

Since $P(W) \cdot P(S) = \frac{5}{12} \cdot \frac{3}{4} = \frac{5}{16} \neq \frac{1}{3} = P(W \cap S)$, **the events** W **and** S **are dependent.**

b. Find $P(W|S)$ and $P(S|W)$. Which of these two conditional probabilities can you multiply with $P(W)$ to get $P(W \cap S)$? Which of the two can you multiply with $P(S)$ to get $P(W \cap S)$?

$P(W|S) = \frac{40}{90} = \frac{4}{9}$ **and** $P(S|W) = \frac{40}{50} = \frac{4}{5}$. **Multiplying** $P(W)$ **and** $PS|W$ **gives** $\frac{5}{12} \cdot \frac{4}{5} = \frac{1}{3} = P(W \cap S)$. **Multiplying** $P(S)$ **and** $P(W|S)$ **gives** $\frac{3}{4} \cdot \frac{4}{9} = \frac{1}{3} = P(W \cap S)$.

There are 4 green, 10 red, and 6 yellow marbles in a bag. You choose a marble without looking, put it aside, and then choose another marble without looking. Use the Multiplication Rule to find the specified probability, writing it as a fraction.

3. Find the probability that you choose a red marble followed by a yellow marble.

Let R **be the event that the first marble is red. Let** Y **be the event that the second marble is yellow.** $P(R \cap Y) = P(R) \cdot P(Y|R) = \frac{10}{20} \cdot \frac{6}{19} = \frac{3}{19}$

4. Find the probabilty that you choose two yellow marble followed by another yellow marble.

Let $Y1$ **be the event that the first marble is yellow. Let** $Y2$ **be the event that the second marble is yellow.** $P(Y1 \cap Y2) = P(Y1) \cdot P(Y2|Y1) = \frac{6}{20} \cdot \frac{5}{19} = \frac{3}{38}$

5. Find the probability that you choose a red marble, followed by a yellow marble, followed by a green marble.

Let R **be the event that the first marble is red. Let** Y **be the event that the second marble is yellow. Let** G **be the event that the third marble is green.**

$P(R \cap Y \cap G) = P(R) \cdot P(Y|R) \cdot P(G|R \cap Y) = \frac{10}{20} \cdot \frac{6}{19} \cdot \frac{4}{18} = \frac{2}{57}$

6. Find the probability that you choose three red marbles.

Let $R1$, $R2$, **and** $R3$ **be the events that the first, second, and third marbles, respectively, are red.**

$P(R1 \cap R2 \cap R3) = P(R1) \cdot P(R2|R1) \cdot P(R3|R1 \cap R2) = \frac{10}{20} \cdot \frac{9}{19} \cdot \frac{8}{18} = \frac{2}{19}$

AVOID COMMON ERRORS

When students start finding probabilities for events A and B, it is easy to confuse the context. Have students read each exercise and highlight the key words and phrases. Suggest that they first decide whether the given events are dependent or independent. Then have them compute the probability and use it as a guide to determine whether the answer is reasonable.

INTEGRATE MATHEMATICAL PRACTICES

Focus on Modeling

MP.4 Tree diagrams are useful for understanding how to apply the formula for the probability of independent or dependent events. Ask groups of students to practice constructing tree diagrams for various given independent or dependent events A and B, and then use the multiplication rule to find the probabilities. Have them critique each other's work, switch roles, and repeat the exercise several times.

INTEGRATE MATHEMATICAL PRACTICES

Focus on Math Connections

MP.1 Using a smaller sample space may help students see the difference between independent and dependent events. Decrease the size of a sample space for an exercise and have students draw probability trees for two events. One should involve replacement and the other should not. Have students write the probability for each branch of the tree and use them to find the probability for each event.

AVOID COMMON ERRORS

Students should understand that $P(A \mid B)$ is not the same as $P(B \mid A)$, and they should not be confused in the formula $P(A \text{ and } B) = P(A) \cdot P(B \mid A)$. Emphasize that the order of the letters matters, and encourage students to articulate the expressions out loud to reinforce the difference.

The table shows the sums that are possible when you roll two number cubes and add the numbers. Use this information to answer the questions.

+	1	2	3	4	5	6
1	2	3	4	5	6	7
2	3	4	5	6	7	8
3	4	5	6	7	8	9
4	5	6	7	8	9	10
5	6	7	8	9	10	11
6	7	8	9	10	11	12

7. Let A be the event that you roll a 2 on one of the number cubes. Let B be the event that the sum of the numbers on the cubes is 7.

a. Are these events independent or dependent? Explain.

Of the 36 outcomes in the entire table, a sum of 7 appears 6 times, so $P(B) = \frac{6}{36} = \frac{1}{6}$.

Of the 6 outcomes in the row labeled 2 (or the column labeled 2), a sum of 7 appears once, s

$P(B|A) = \frac{1}{6}$. Since $P(B|A)$ $P(A)$, events A and B are independent.

b. What is $P(A \cap B)$?

$P(A \cap B) = P(A) \cdot P(B) = \frac{1}{6} \cdot \frac{1}{6} = \frac{1}{36}$

8. Let A be the event that you roll a 3 on one of the number cubes. Let B be the event that the sum of the numbers on the cubes is 5.

a. Are these events independent or dependent? Explain.

Of the 36 outcomes in the entire table, a sum of 5 appears 4 times, so $P(B) = \frac{4}{36} = \frac{1}{9}$.

Of the 6 outcomes in the row labeled 3 (or the column labeled 3), a sum of 5 appears once, s

$P(B|A) = \frac{1}{6}$. Since $P(B|A) \neq P(A)$, events A and B are dependent.

b. What is $P(A \cap B)$?

$P(A \cap B) = P(A) \cdot P(B|A) = \frac{1}{6} \cdot \frac{1}{6} = \frac{1}{36}$

9. A cooler contains 6 bottles of apple juice and 8 bottles of grape juice. You choose a bottle without looking, put it aside, and then choose another bottle without looking. Match each situation with its probability. More than one situation can have the same probability.

a. Choose apple juice and then grape juice. **D** $\frac{4}{3}$

b. Choose apple juice and then apple juice. **A, C** $\frac{24}{91}$

c. Choose grape juice and then apple juice. **B** $\frac{15}{91}$

d. Choose grape juice and then grape juice.

A1 = apple 1st, A2 = apple 2nd; G1 = grape 1st, G2 = grape 2nd

a. $P(A1) \cdot P(G2|A1) = \frac{6}{14} \cdot \frac{8}{13} = \frac{24}{91}$

c. $P(G1) \cdot P(A2|G1) = \frac{8}{14} \cdot \frac{6}{13} = \frac{24}{91}$

b. $P(A1) \cdot P(A2|A1) = \frac{6}{14} \cdot \frac{5}{13} = \frac{15}{91}$

d. $P(G1) \cdot P(G2|G1) = \frac{8}{14} \cdot \frac{7}{13} = \frac{4}{13}$

10. Jorge plays all tracks on a playlist with no repeats. The playlist he's listening to has 12 songs, 4 of which are his favorites.

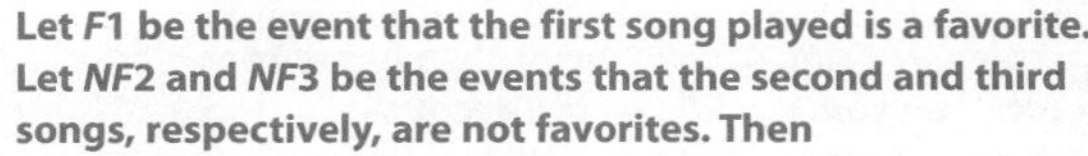

a. What is the probability that the first song played is one of his favorites, but the next two songs are not?

Let $F1$ be the event that the first song played is a favorite. Let $NF2$ and $NF3$ be the events that the second and third songs, respectively, are not favorites. Then

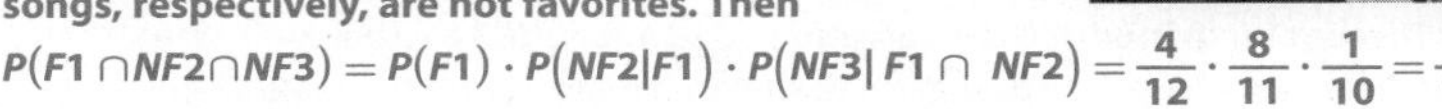

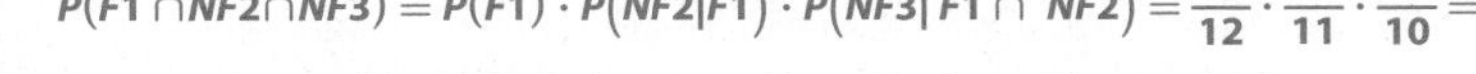

$P(F1 \cap NF2 \cap NF3) = P(F1) \cdot P(NF2|F1) \cdot P(NF3|\, F1 \cap NF2) = \frac{4}{12} \cdot \frac{8}{11} \cdot \frac{1}{10} = \frac{28}{115}.$

b. What is the probability that the first three songs played are all his favorites?

Let $F1$, $F2$, and $F3$ be the events that the first, second, and third songs, respectively, are his favorites. Then $P(F1 \cap F2 \cap F3) = P(F1) \cdot P(F2|F1) \cdot P(F3|\, F1 \cap F2) = \frac{4}{12} \cdot \frac{3}{11} \cdot \frac{2}{10} = \frac{1}{55}.$

c. Jorge can also play the tracks on his playlist in a random order with repeats possible. If he does this, how does your answer to part b change? Explain why.

With repeats allowed, the probability that a favorite song is played is always $\frac{4}{12} = \frac{1}{3}$. The events $F1$, $F2$, and $F3$ are now independent, so you can multiply their probabilities without considering conditional probabilities:
$P(F1 \cap F2 \cap F3) = P(F1) \cdot P(F2) \cdot P(F3) = \frac{1}{3} \cdot \frac{1}{3} \cdot \frac{1}{3} = \frac{1}{27}.$

11. You are playing a game of bingo with friends. In this game, balls are labeled with one of the letters of the word BINGO and a number. Some of these letter-number combinations are written on a bingo card in a 5 × 5 array, and as balls are randomly drawn and announced, players mark their cards if the ball's letter-number combination appears on the cards. The first player to complete a row, column, or diagonal on a card says "Bingo!" and wins the game. In the game you're playing, there are 20 balls left. To complete a row on your card, you need N-32 called. To complete a column, you need G-51 called. To complete a diagonal, you need B-6 called.

a. What is the probability that the next two balls drawn do not have a letter-number combination you need, but the third ball does?

Let $NC1$ and $NC2$ be the events that the letter-number combination on the next ball and the ball after that, respectively, are not what you need. Let $C3$ be the event that the letter-number combination on the third ball is what you need. Then
$P(NC1 \cap NC2 \cap C3) = P(NC1) \cdot P(NC2|NC1) \cdot P(C3|NC1 \cap NC2) = \frac{17}{20} \cdot \frac{16}{19} \cdot \frac{1}{3} = \frac{68}{285}.$

b. What is the probability that none of the letter-number combinations you need is called from the next three balls?

Let $NC1$, $NC2$, and $NC3$ be the events that a letter-number combination you don't need is called from the next ball, the ball after that, or the ball after that, respectively. Then
$P(NC1 \cap NC2 \cap NC3) = P(NC1) \cdot P(NC2|NC1) \cdot P(NC3|NC1 \cap NC2) = \frac{17}{20} \cdot \frac{16}{19} \cdot \frac{15}{18} = \frac{34}{57}.$

JOURNAL

Have students use mathematical notation to define the probability of independent and dependent events. Then have students use their own words to explain what the notation means and how to use it.

H.O.T. Focus on Higher Order Thinking

12. You are talking with 3 friends, and the conversation turns to birthdays.

a. What is the probability that no two people in your group were born in the same month?

Use your birth month as a starting point. Let $NB1$ be the event that friend 1 has a different birth month than you. Let $NB2$ be the event that friend 2 has different birth month than you and friend 1. Let $NB3$ be the event that friend 3 has a different birth month than you, friend 1, and friend 2. Then $P(NB1 \cap NB2 \cap NB3) = P(NB1) \cdot P(NB2|NB1) \cdot P(NB3|NB1 \cap NB2) = \frac{11}{12} \cdot \frac{10}{12} \cdot \frac{9}{12} = \frac{55}{96}$.

b. Is the probability that at least two people in your group were born in the same month greater or less than $\frac{1}{2}$? Explain.

The event that at least two people in your group were born in the same month is the complement of the event in part a. So, the probability that at least two people in your group were born in the same month is $1 - \frac{55}{96} = \frac{41}{96}$, which is less than $\frac{1}{2}$.

c. How many people in a group would it take for the probability that at least two people were born in the same month to be greater than $\frac{1}{2}$? Explain.

Extend the results from part a:
$P((NB1 \cap NB2 \cap NB3) \cap NB4) = P(NB1 \cap NB2 \cap NB3) \cdot P(NB4|NB1 \cap NB2 \cap NB3) = \frac{55}{96} \cdot \frac{8}{12} = \frac{5\ldots}{1\ldots}$
The probability that at least two people in a group of 5 were born in the same month is $1 - \frac{55}{144} = \frac{89}{144}$, which is greater than $\frac{1}{2}$.

13. Construct Arguments Show how to extend the Multiplication Rule to three events *A*, *B*, and *C*.

$P(A \cap B \cap C) = P((A \cap B) \cap C)$	**Group events *A* and *B* as one event.**
$= P(A \cap B) \cdot P(C|A \cap B)$	**Apply the Multiplication Rule to $A \cap B$ and *C*.**
$= P(A) \cdot P(B|A) \cdot P(C|A \cap B)$	**Apply the Multiplication Rule to *A* and *B*.**

14. Make a Prediction A bag contains the same number of red marbles blue marbles. You choose a marble without looking, put it aside, and then choose another marble. Is there a greater-than-50% chance or a less-than-50% chance that you choose two marbles with different colors? Explain.

Let $R1$ and $R2$ be the events that a red marble is drawn on the first and second draws, respectively. Let $B1$ and $B2$ be the events that a blue marble is drawn on the first and second draws, respectively. Let n be the number of marbles of each color. Then $P(R1 \cap B2) = P(R1) \cdot P(B2|R1) = \frac{n}{2n} \cdot \frac{n}{2n-1} = \frac{n^2}{2n(2n-1)}$ and $P(B1 \cap R2) = P(B1) \cdot P(R2|B1) = \frac{n}{2n} \cdot \frac{n}{2n-1} = \frac{n^2}{2n(2n-1)} = \frac{n}{2(2n-1)}$. Since the events $R1 \cap B2$ and $B1 \cap R2$ are mutually exclusive, you can add their probabilities to get the probability of choosing two marbles with different colors:

$\frac{n}{2(2n-1)} + \frac{n}{2(2n-1)} = \frac{n}{2(2n-1)} = \frac{n}{2n-1} = \frac{1}{2-\frac{1}{n}}$. Since the denominator of $\frac{1}{2-\frac{1}{n}}$ is always less than 2 for $n > 0$, the fraction is always greater than $\frac{1}{2}$. So, there is always a greater-than-50% chance that you choose two marbles with different colors.

Lesson Performance Task

To prepare for an accuracy landing competition, a team of skydivers has laid out targets in a large open field. During practice sessions, team members attempt to land inside a target.

Two rectangular targets are shown on each field. Assuming a skydiver lands at random in the field, find the probabilities that the skydiver lands inside the specified target(s).

1. Calculate the probabilities using the targets shown here.

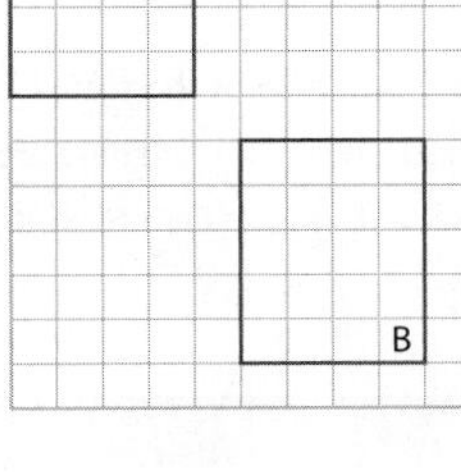

- **a.** $P(A)$ a. 0.12
- **b.** $P(B)$ b. 0.2
- **c.** $P(A \cap B)$ c. 0
- **d.** $P(A \cup B)$ d. 0.32
- **e.** $P(A|B)$ e. 0
- **f.** $P(B|A)$ f. 0

2. Calculate the probabilities using the targets shown here.

- **a.** $P(A)$ a. 0.36
- **b.** $P(B)$ b. 0.14
- **c.** $P(A \cap B)$ c. 0.04
- **d.** $P(A \cup B)$ d. 0.46
- **e.** $P(A|B)$ e. $\frac{2}{7}$
- **f.** $P(B|A)$ f. $\frac{1}{9}$

3. Calculate the probabilities using the targets shown here.

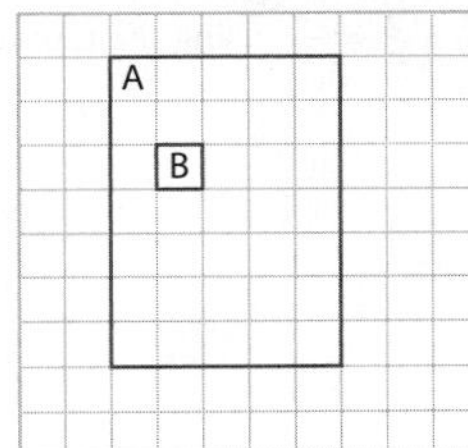

- **a.** $P(A)$ a. 0.35
- **b.** $P(B)$ b. 0.01
- **c.** $P(A \cap B)$ c. 0.01
- **d.** $P(A \cup B)$ d. 0.35
- **e.** $P(A|B)$ e. 1
- **f.** $P(B|A)$ f. $\frac{1}{35}$

INTEGRATE MATHEMATICAL PRACTICES

Focus on Reasoning

MP.2 Two skydiver landing rectangles are outlined on a 10×10 grid. Describe the rectangles if the given probability is true.

- $P(A \text{ and } B) = 0$ The rectangles do not intersect.
- $P(A \text{ or } B) = 1$ the rectangles cover the entire grid.
- $P(A|B) = 1$ Rectangle B is contained in rectangle A.
- $P(B|A) = 0$ The rectangles do not intersect.

INTEGRATE MATHEMATICAL PRACTICES

Focus on Critical Thinking

MP.3 In the 10×10 grid for Question 2 of the Lesson Performance Task, rectangle A measures 6×6 units and rectangle B measures 7×2. Find the dimensions and amount of overlap of two rectangles different from rectangles A and B for which the answers to Questions 2c and 2d are unchanged. Sample answer: rectangle A measures 6×5; rectangle B measures 10×2; amount of overlap: 4 squares.

EXTENSION ACTIVITY

Supply students with grid paper. Ask them to draw a 10×10 grid representing a skydiver landing area. Then have them draw two rectangles, A and B, so that P(A and B) = 0.06 and P(A or B) = 0.58. Ask them to find P(A | B) and P(B | A). Many rectangles A and B are possible. All drawings must show two rectangles with an overlap of 6 squares. Additionally, Area rectangle A, in its entirety, plus Area rectangle B, in its entirety, must equal 64 square units. Sample: rectangle A measuring 6×4 units overlaps by 6 squares rectangle B measuring 8×5 units; $P(A | B) = \frac{3}{20}$ and $P(B | A) = \frac{1}{4}$.

Scoring Rubric

2 points: The student's answer is an accurate and complete execution of the task or tasks.

1 point: The student's answer contains attributes of an appropriate response but is flawed.

0 points: The student's answer contains no attributes of an appropriate response.

Study Guide Review

ASSESSMENT AND INTERVENTION

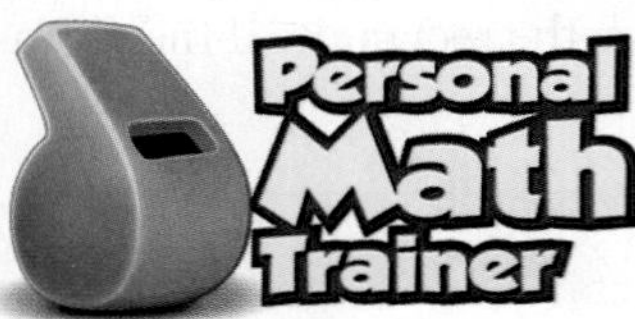

Assign or customize module reviews.

MODULE PERFORMANCE TASK

COMMON CORE

Mathematical Practices: MP.1, MP.2, MP.4, MP.7, MP.8
S-CP.A.1, S-CP.B.6, S-CP.B.8

SUPPORTING STUDENT REASONING

Students should begin this problem by focusing on what information they will need. Here are some issues they might bring up.

- **How to find the probability of choosing one ace from a deck of 52 cards:** There are 4 aces in a deck of 52 cards, so the probability is $\frac{4}{52} = \frac{1}{13}$.
- **If choosing two aces or three aces in a row involves conditional probability:** Yes, because the second event of choosing a second ace in a row depends on a first ace having been chosen. Also, the third event of choosing a third ace in a row depends on the previous two choices being aces.
- **If choosing four cards in a row in which none are aces involves conditional probability:** Yes, because each successive event depends on the previous choice not being an ace.

Conditional Probability and Independence of Events

Essential Question: How can you use statistics and probability to solve real-world problems?

Key Vocabulary
conditional probability (*probabilidad condicional*)
independent events (*eventos independientes*)
dependent events (*eventos dependientes*)

KEY EXAMPLE *(Lesson 20.1)*

Find the probability that a black card drawn from the deck is a queen. (The deck is a standard one of 52 cards.)

The deck has 52 cards and 26 of them are black, so the probability of drawing a black card is $P(B) = \frac{26}{52}$. There are 2 black queens in the deck, so the probability of drawing one of them from the deck is $P(Q \cap B) = \frac{2}{52} = \frac{1}{26}$. Using the formula for conditional probability, $P(Q \mid B) = P\frac{(Q \cap B)}{P(B)} = \frac{\frac{2}{52}}{\frac{26}{52}} = \frac{1}{13}$.

KEY EXAMPLE *(Lesson 20.2)*

Jim rolled a set of two dice. If these are standard 6-sided dice, what is the probability of obtaining 12? (That means the value of the top faces add up to 12.)

The only way to get 12 is for both of the top sides of the dice to be 6. The events of obtaining 6s are independent. Each of these events has the probability of $\frac{1}{6}$ (1 out of 6 options), and the probability of getting 12 is $\frac{1}{6} \cdot \frac{1}{6} = \frac{1}{36}$ by the multiplication rule.

KEY EXAMPLE *(Lesson 20.3)*

What is the probability of selecting 2 blue marbles out of a jar of 20, half of them blue? How did you obtain it?

Let event A be selecting a blue marble on the first pick. Let event B be selecting a blue marble on the second one. The first marble is not replaced, so these are dependent events. Of the 20 marbles, half of them are blue, so $P(A) = \frac{1}{2}$. Of the remaining 19 marbles, 9 of them are blue, so the probability of selecting one is $P(B) = \frac{9}{19}$. Thus, the probability of selecting 2 blue marbles is $P(A \text{ and } B) = \frac{1}{2} \cdot \frac{9}{19} = \frac{9}{38}$, using the multiplication rule.

SCAFFOLDING SUPPORT

- A common error in these types of problems is to forget to subtract one from the sample space after each choice. For example, for the first pick, the sample space is the entire deck of 52 cards. Each time one card is picked, the sample space decreases by 1.
- Students should realize that the probability of not picking an ace can be thought of as the probability of picking a card other than an ace. So for the first pick, there are $\frac{48}{52}$ ways for the first card to not be an ace.

Exercises

Determine the conditional probability. *(Lesson 20.1)*

1. What is the probability that a diamond that is drawn from the deck is a queen?

$P(Q \mid D) = \frac{1}{13}$

2. What is the probability that a queen drawn is a diamond?

$P(D \mid Q) = \frac{1}{4}$

Show that the following situation refers to independent events. *(Lesson 20.2)*

3. Isabelle believes that right- and left-footed soccer players are equally likely to score goals. She collected data from 260 players from a local soccer league. Using the following two-way frequency table, show that being right-footed and scoring goals are independent events.

	Right-Footed	Left-Footed	Total
Has scored a goal	39	13	52
Has not scored a goal	156	52	208
TOTAL	195	65	260

The events are independent because $P(A \text{ and } B) = P(A) \cdot P(B) = \frac{3}{20}$.

Identify whether a situation involves independent or dependent events. *(Lesson 20.3)*

4. Jim has 2 blue, 2 green, and 2 black socks in his drawer. He picks out 2 socks, one after the other. Determine the probability of him getting a matching pair of blue socks.

The events are dependent; $P(A \text{ and } B) = P(A) \cdot P(B \mid A) = \frac{1}{15}$

MODULE PERFORMANCE TASK

Drawing Aces

You have a standard deck of 52 playing cards. You pick three cards in a row without replacement. What is the probability that all three are aces?

Now you replace the three cards, shuffle, and pick four cards in a row without replacement. What is the probability that none are aces?

Begin by making notes in the space below about your plan for approaching this problem. Then complete the task on your own paper, using words, numbers, or diagrams to explain how you reached your conclusions.

DISCUSSION OPPORTUNITIES

- Why is the probability of getting 4 aces in a game of cards so low?
- Why is the probability of getting 3 aces in a row without replacement lower than the probability of getting 3 aces in a row with replacement?

SAMPLE SOLUTION

Let event A be the event that the first card is an ace, so $P(A) = \frac{4}{52} = \frac{1}{13}$ (4 out of 52 options). Let event B be the event that the second card is an ace as well, so $P(B|A) = \frac{3}{51} = \frac{1}{17}$. This is because out of the 51 remaining cards, 3 are aces. Use the multiplication rule.

$P(A \text{ and } B) = P(A) \cdot P(B|A) = \frac{1}{13} \cdot \frac{1}{17} = \frac{1}{221}$

Let event C be picking another ace out of the remaining 50 cards. There are 2 aces left, so $P(C|A \text{ and } B) = \frac{2}{50} = \frac{1}{25}$.

By the multiplication rule:

$$P(A \text{ and } B \text{ and } C) = P(A \text{ and } B) \cdot P(C|A \text{ and } B)$$
$$= \frac{1}{221} \cdot \frac{1}{25} = \frac{1}{5525}$$

The probability of obtaining three aces in three picks is

$P(A \text{ and } B \text{ and } C) = \frac{1}{5525} \approx 0.00018$.

Now, find the probability that four out of four cards picked are not aces. 48 out of 52 cards are not aces in the first draw, then 47 out of 51, and so on.

$P(A) = \frac{48}{52} \cdot \frac{47}{51} \cdot \frac{46}{50} \cdot \frac{45}{49} \approx 0.719$

Assessment Rubric

2 points: Student correctly solves the problem and explains his/her reasoning.

1 point: Student shows good understanding of the problem but does not fully solve or explain.

0 points: Student does not demonstrate understanding of the problem.

Ready to Go On?

ASSESS MASTERY

Use the assessment on this page to determine if students have mastered the concepts and standards covered in this module.

ASSESSMENT AND INTERVENTION

Access Ready to Go On? assessment online, and receive instant scoring, feedback, and customized intervention or enrichment.

ADDITIONAL RESOURCES

Response to Intervention Resources

- Reteach Worksheets

Differentiated Instruction Resources

- Reading Strategies EL
- Success for English Learners EL
- Challenge Worksheets

Assessment Resources

- Leveled Module Quizzes

20.1–20.3 Conditional Probability and Independence of Events

- Online Homework
- Hints and Help
- Extra Practice

Compute the requested probability and explain how you obtained it.

1. A farmer wants to know if a particular fertilizer can cause blackberry shrubs to produce fruit early. Using the following two-way table, compute the probability of a plant producing fruit early without receiving fertilizer.

	Early Fruit	No Fruit	Total
Received Fertilizer	37	3	40
Did not receive fertilizer	19	21	40
TOTAL	56	24	80

In the study, 40 of the shrubs were not given fertilizer. Of these, 19 produced early fruit and the desired probability is $P(A \mid B) = \frac{19}{40} = 47.5\%$.

2. Lisa flipped the same coin twice and recorded the tosses. Determine the probability of her selecting tails on the second try.

The event of selecting tails on the second try does not depend on the first try, and thus i probability is $\frac{1}{2}$. Here she is choosing one option, tails, out of two options, heads or tails

3. Lisa threw the same coin three times. What is the probability she obtained all tails?

The events of selecting tails on different tries are independent, and thus the probability of flipping tails is $\frac{1}{2} \cdot \frac{1}{2} \cdot \frac{1}{2} = \frac{1}{8}$.

ESSENTIAL QUESTION

4. A jar contains 12 pennies, 5 nickels, and 18 quarters. You select 2 coins at random, one after the other. Does selecting a nickel affect the probability of selecting another nickel? Does not selecting a dime affect the probability of selecting a nickel? Describe how you would find the probability of selecting 2 nickels.

Answers may vary. Sample: A dime cannot be selected, so not picking one does not affect the second pick. These are independent events. Selecting two nickels in a row and not replacing the first means that there will be fewer coins to choose from on the second try. These are dependent events. Accordingly, the probability of selecting two nickels in a row is the product of selecting one and then selecting another given that a first one has been picked.

COMMON CORE Common Core Standards

Lesson	Items	Content Standards	Mathematical Practices
20.1	1	S-CP.A.4	MP.6
20.2	2	S-CP.A.2	MP.6
20.2	3	S-CP.A.2	MP.2

MODULE 20
MIXED REVIEW

Assessment Readiness

1. Are the events independent? Choose True or False for each statement.
   A. Picking a penny and a marble out of a jar of pennies and marbles. ● True ○ False
   B. Drawing cards from a deck to form a 4-card hand. ○ True ● False
   C. Choosing a color for a new shirt from a choice of red, yellow, or purple. ● True ○ False

2. Of the boys running for School President, 2 are juniors and 3 are seniors. Of the girls who are running, 4 are juniors and 1 is a senior. Decide whether the situation has a probability of $\frac{2}{5}$. Select Yes or No for A–C.
   A. A girl wins. ○ Yes ● No
   B. A candidate who is a boy is a junior. ● Yes ○ No
   C. A candidate who is a junior is a boy. ○ Yes ● No

3. You shuffle a standard deck of playing cards and deal one card. What is the probability that you deal an ace or a club? Explain your reasoning.

   $\frac{4}{13}$; Sample answer: Four of the 52 cards in the deck are aces, so P(ace) $= \frac{4}{52}$. Thirteen of the cards are clubs, so P(club) $= \frac{13}{52}$. One of the cards, the ace of clubs, is both an ace and a club, so P(ace or clubs) $= \frac{4}{52} + \frac{13}{52} - \frac{1}{52} = \frac{16}{52} = \frac{4}{13}$

4. Claude has 2 jars of marbles. Each jar has 10 blue marbles and 10 green marbles. He selects 2 marbles from each jar. What is the probability they are all blue? Explain your reasoning.

   about 0.056; Sample answer: The probability of choosing 2 blue marbles from 1 jar is $\frac{1}{2} \cdot \frac{9}{19} = \frac{9}{38}$, a pair of dependent events. Picking from different jars is independent, so the probability is $\frac{9}{38} \cdot \frac{9}{38} = \frac{81}{1444} \approx 0.056$.

MIXED REVIEW

Assessment Readiness

ASSESSMENT AND INTERVENTION

Assign ready-made or customized practice tests to prepare students for high-stakes tests.

ADDITIONAL RESOURCES

Assessment Resources

- Leveled Module Quizzes: Modified, B

AVOID COMMON ERRORS

Item 4 Some students will recognize that there are two events but will not see that there are four—two marbles are picked from each of two jars. Remind students to read carefully and consider every event.

COMMON CORE Common Core Standards

Lesson	Items	Content Standards	Mathematical Practices
20.2	1	**S-CP.A.2**	**MP.2**
20.1, 19.1	2*	**S-CP.A.1, S-CP.B.6**	**MP.4**
19.4	3*	**S-CP.B.7**	**MP.3**
20.3	4	**S-CP.A.5**	**MP.3**

* Item integrates mixed review concepts from previous modules or a previous course.

MODULE 21

Probability and Decision Making

ESSENTIAL QUESTION:

Answer: Understanding probability can help you solve real-world problems concerning long-term risk.

PROFESSIONAL DEVELOPMENT VIDEO

Professional Development Video

Author Matt Larson models successful teaching practices in an actual high-school classroom.

Professional Development my.hrw.com

Probability and Decision Making

MODULE 21

Essential Question: How can you use probability to solve real-world problems?

REAL WORLD VIDEO
Physicians today use many sophisticated tests and technologies to help diagnose illnesses, but they must still consider probability in their diagnoses and decisions about treatment

MODULE PERFORMANCE TASK PREVIEW

What's the Diagnosis?

The science of medicine has come a long way since surgeries were performed by the neighborhood barber, and leeches were used to treat just about every ailment. Nevertheless, modern medicine isn't perfect, and widely used tests for diagnosing illnesses aren't always 100 percent accurate. In this module you'll learn how probability can be used to measure the reliability of tests, and then use what you learned to evaluate decisions about a diagnosis.

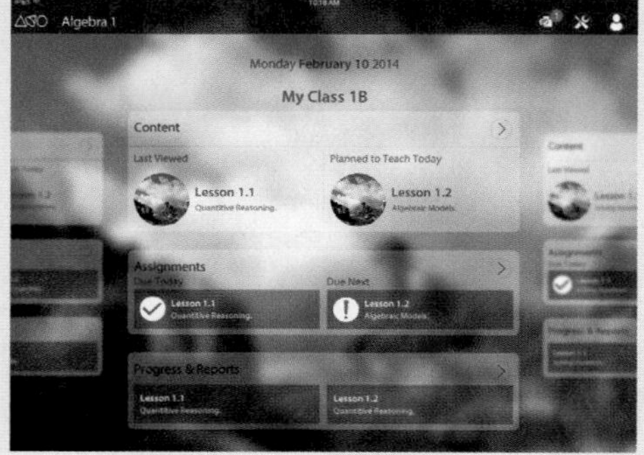

DIGITAL TEACHER EDITION

Access a full suite of teaching resources when and where you need them:

- Access content online or offline
- Customize lessons to share with your class
- Communicate with your students in real-time
- View student grades and data instantly to target your instruction where it is needed most

PERSONAL MATH TRAINER

Assessment and Intervention

Assign automatically graded homework, quizzes, tests, and intervention activities. Prepare your students with updated, Common Core-aligned practice tests.

Complete these exercises to review skills you will need for this chapter.

- Online Homework
- Hints and Help
- Extra Practice

Probability of Simple Events

Example 1 Two 6-sided conventional number cubes are tossed. What is the probability that their sum is greater than 8?

+	1	2	3	4	5	6
1	2	3	4	5	6	7
2	3	4	5	6	7	8
3	4	5	6	7	8	9
4	5	6	7	8	9	10
5	6	7	8	9	10	11
6	7	8	9	10	11	12

There are 10 values greater than 8 and a total number of 36 values.

$$\frac{\text{number of favorable outcomes}}{\text{total number of outcomes}} = \frac{10}{36} = \frac{5}{18}$$

The probability that the sum of the two number cubes is greater than 8 is $\frac{5}{18}$.

Two number cubes are tossed. Find each probability.

1. The sum is prime. $\frac{5}{12}$ **2.** The product is prime. $\frac{1}{6}$ **3.** The product is a perfect square. $\frac{2}{9}$

Making Predictions with Probability

Example 2 A fly lands on the target shown. What is the probability that the fly landed on red?

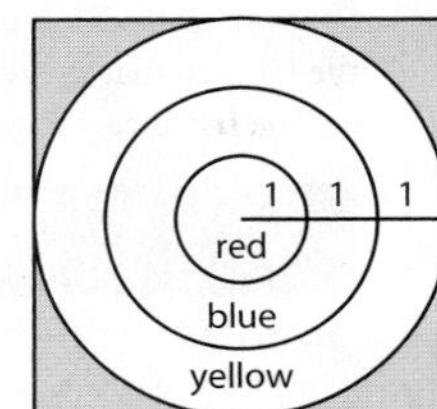

The area of the entire target is 6^2, or 36 units².

Red area is: $A = \pi r^2 = \pi(1)^2 = \pi$.

$$\frac{\text{number of favorable outcomes}}{\text{total number of outcomes}} = \frac{\pi}{36} \approx 8.7\%$$

Use the target to find the percent probability, to the nearest tenth.

4. Blue 26.2% **5.** Yellow or red 52.4% **6.** Not within a circle 21.5%

Are You Ready?

ASSESS READINESS

Use the assessment on this page to determine if students need strategic or intensive intervention for the module's prerequisite skills.

ASSESSMENT AND INTERVENTION

RtI Response to Intervention TIER 1, TIER 2, TIER 3 SKILLS

Personal Math Trainer will automatically create a standards-based, personalized intervention assignment for your students, targeting each student's individual needs!

ADDITIONAL RESOURCES

See the table below for a full list of intervention resources available for this module.

Response to Intervention Resources also includes:

- Tier 2 Skill Pre-Tests for each Module
- Tier 2 Skill Post-Tests for each skill

Response to Intervention			Differentiated Instruction
Tier 1 Lesson Intervention Worksheets	**Tier 2** Strategic Intervention Skills Intervention Worksheets	**Tier 3** Intensive Intervention Worksheets available online	
Reteach 21.1 Reteach 21.2	48 Making Predictions with Probability 52 Probability of Simple Events	Building Block Skills 6, 12, 39, 95	Challenge worksheets Extend the Math Lesson Activities in TE

LESSON 21.1

Using Probability to Make Fair Decisions

Common Core Math Standards

The student is expected to:

COMMON CORE **S-MD.B.6(+)**

Use probabilities to make fair decisions (e.g., drawing by lots, using a random number generator).

Mathematical Practices

MP.4 Modeling

Language Objective

Explain to a partner how to use a random number generator to simulate an experiment.

ENGAGE

Essential Question: How can you use probability to help you make fair decisions?

Probability offers a method for representing a population in an unbiased way so that decisions can be made fairly.

PREVIEW: LESSON PERFORMANCE TASK

View the Engage section online. Discuss the photograph. Ask students to describe the game that is pictured. Then preview the Lesson Performance Task.

Name ________ Class ________ Date ________

21.1 Using Probability to Make Fair Decisions

Resource Locker

Essential Question: How can you use probability to help you make fair decisions?

Explore Using Probabilities When Drawing at Random

You are sharing a veggie supreme pizza with friends. There is one slice left and you and a friend both want it. Both of you have already had two slices. What is a fair way to solve this problem?

(A) Suppose you both decide to have the same amount of pizza. This means that the last slice will be cut into two pieces. Describe a fair way to split this last piece.

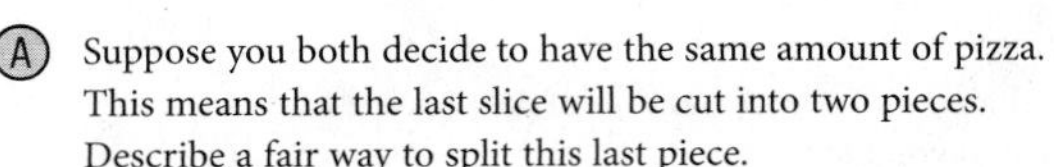

Possible answer: One person gets to cut the pizza into two approximately equal pieces; the other person gets to choose which piece he or she wants.

(B) Suppose instead you decide that one of you will get the whole slice. Complete the table so that the result of each option gives a fair chance for each of you to get the last slice. Why do each of these possibilities give a fair chance?

Option	Result (you get last slice)	Result (friend gets last slice)
Flip a coin	Heads	**Tails**
Roll a standard die	**2, 4, 6**	1, 3, 5
Play Rock, Paper, Scissors	You win.	You **lose**.
Draw lots using two straws of different lengths	**Long straw**	Short straw

For each option, both results have a probability of $\frac{1}{2}$, so both people have the same chance of getting the last slice.

Reflect

1. Suppose, when down to the last piece, you tell your friend, "I will cut the last piece, and I will choose pick which piece you get." Why is this method unfair?
Possible answer: I could cut the slice into two pieces with one much larger than the other and then choose the larger piece for myself.

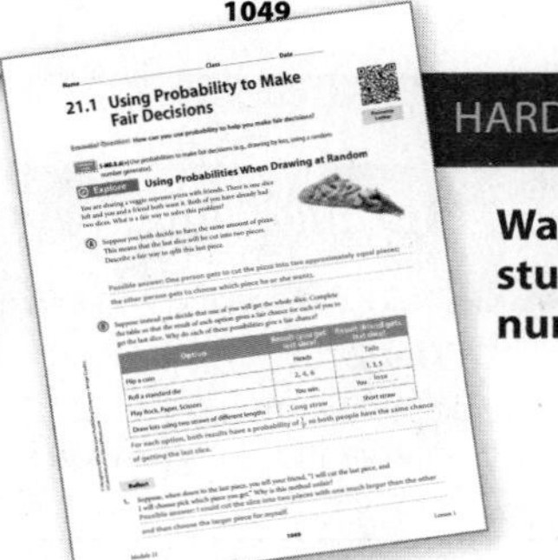

HARDCOVER PAGES 1049–10

Watch for the hardcover student edition page numbers for this lesson.

2. Your friend suggests that you shoot free throws to decide who gets the last piece. Use probability to explain why this might not be a fair way to decide.
Shooting free throws is not a random event. The player with more skill will have a greater probability of winning.

Explain 1 Awarding a Prize to a Random Winner

Suppose you have to decide how to award a prize to a person at an event. You might want every person attending to have the same chance of winning, or you might want people to do something to improve their chance of winning. How can you award the prize fairly?

Example 1 **Explain whether each method of awarding a prize is fair.**

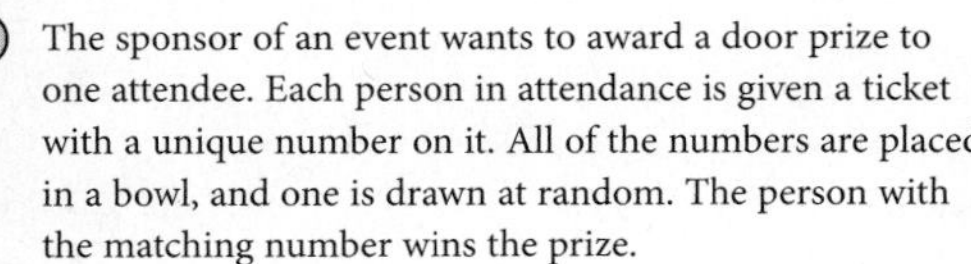

(A) The sponsor of an event wants to award a door prize to one attendee. Each person in attendance is given a ticket with a unique number on it. All of the numbers are placed in a bowl, and one is drawn at random. The person with the matching number wins the prize.

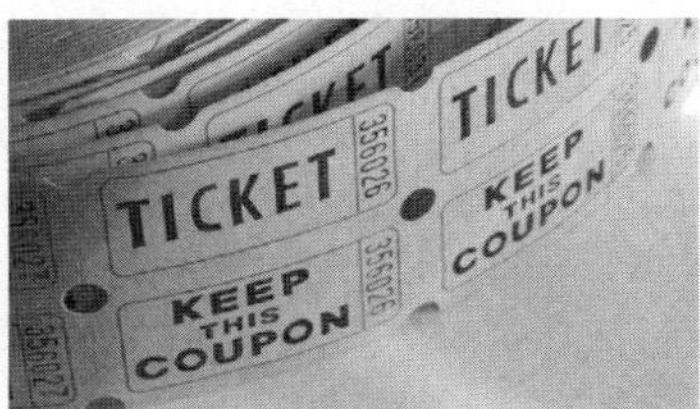

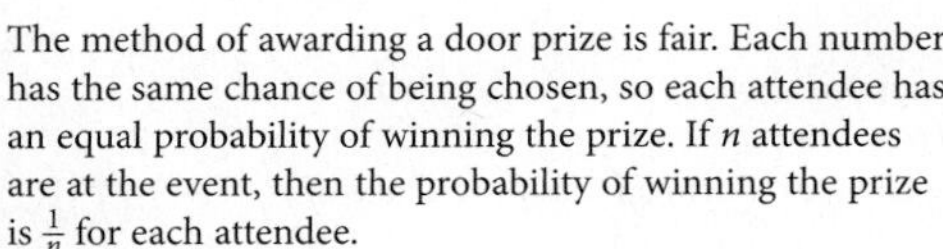

The method of awarding a door prize is fair. Each number has the same chance of being chosen, so each attendee has an equal probability of winning the prize. If n attendees are at the event, then the probability of winning the prize is $\frac{1}{n}$ for each attendee.

(B) A fundraiser includes a raffle in which half of the money collected goes to a charity, and the other half goes to one winner. Tickets are sold for $5 each. Copies of all the tickets are placed in a box, and one ticket is drawn at random. The person with the matching ticket wins the raffle.

The method of choosing a raffle winner is (fair)/not fair because each **ticket** has an equal probability of being drawn.

Reflect

3. In Example 1B, the probability may not be the same for each person to win the raffle. Explain why the method is still fair.
For each ticket, the probability of drawing the matching ticket is the same. A person who buys more tickets should have a better chance of winning.

Your Turn

4. Each month, a company wants to award a special parking space to an employee at random. Describe a fair way to do this. Include a way to ensure that a person doesn't win a second time before each employee has won once.
Possible answer: Choose an employee's name at random from a list of all employees. Each month, remove the previous winners from the list. Once every employee has won once, begin again with the list of all employees.

PROFESSIONAL DEVELOPMENT

Integrate Mathematical Practices

This lesson provides an opportunity to address Mathematical Practice **MP.4**, which calls for students to "represent real-world problems with mathematics." Students are already familiar with some aspects of probability; in this lesson, they will explore random sampling and the probabilities of events. Then they will use probabilities to help them explore the connections among random samples, convenience samples, and fair decision-making.

EXPLORE

Using Probabilities When Drawing at Random

INTEGRATE TECHNOLOGY

Students have the option of doing the Explore activity either in the book or online.

QUESTIONING STRATEGIES

? How can you find the probability that an event does not occur from the probability that an event does occur? **If the events are independent, the probability that an event does not occur is the complement of the probability $P(E)$ that the event does occur, or $1 - P(E)$.**

? How do you know if you have chosen a random sample? **Possible answer: It is random when the probability of your selection has no predictability, and all choices are equally likely.**

EXPLAIN 1

Awarding a Prize to a Random Winner

AVOID COMMON ERRORS

Students may assume that a certain method of awarding a prize is fair without finding the probabilities of the possible outcomes. Remind students that they can be sure a method is fair only if they can show, using probability, that each participant has an equal chance of winning.

QUESTIONING STRATEGIES

? How can you use probability to help make a game fair? **You can use probability to help make sure every player has an equal chance of winning.**

EXPLAIN 2

Solving Real-World Problems Fairly

INTEGRATE TECHNOLOGY

The random number generator of a calculator (**rand**) produces a random decimal number between 0 and 1. This should not be confused with the command to generate random integers, **randInt(1,*n*)**, which produces random integers from 1 to *n*. Point out that spreadsheets can also be used to generate random numbers. Students can use spreadsheets to add the number of trials for an experiment, as well.

QUESTIONING STRATEGIES

How could you use your calculator and the random number generator to generate random integers? **Possible answer: Enter randInt(1,*n*) into the calculator and replace *n* with the highest integer you expect to generate.**

Will every trial using the random number generator produce the same results? Explain. **No; since the integers are generated randomly, each trial should produce a different sequence of random numbers.**

Explain 2 Solving Real-World Problems Fairly

You can use a random number generator to choose a winner of a prize.

Example 2 Use a problem solving plan.

A class of 24 students sold 65 magazine subscriptions to raise money for a trip. As an incentive to participate, you will award a prize to one student in the class. Describe a method of awarding the prize fairly. Use probabilities to explain why your method is fair for the students listed.

Student	Subscriptions Sold
Miri	5
Liam	2
Madison	0

Analyze Information

Identify the important information.

- There are 24 students.
- They sold 65 magazine subscriptions.
- There is one prize, so there will be one winner.

Formulate a Plan

To be fair, students who sold more subscriptions should have a better chance of winning the prize than the students who sold fewer.

Find a method of assigning and choosing chances to win so that the chance of winning is proportional to the number of subscriptions sold.

Solve

The class sold 65 subscriptions, so assign the numbers 1–65 to the students. Each student gets as many numbers as the number of subscriptions he or she sold.

Student	Subscriptions Sold	Numbers Assigned	Probability of Winning
Miri	5	1–5	$\frac{5}{65} \approx 0.077\%$
Liam	2	6, 7	$\frac{2}{65} \approx 0.031\%$
Madison	0	none	$\frac{0}{65} = 0\%$

Then use a calculator to find a random integer from 1 to 65. If the result is 7, then Liam wins the prize.

Justify and Evaluate

This method seems fair/unfair because it gives everyone who sold subscriptions a chance of winning. You could award a prize to the student who sold the most subscriptions, but this might not be possible if multiple students all sold the same number, and it might not seem fair if some students have better access to buyers than others.

COLLABORATIVE LEARNING

Small Group Activity

Have groups of students brainstorm various examples of sampling methods that should produce random, unbiased samples. Have them compare these to methods that would be biased. For example, putting the names of all students into a hat and then drawing ten names should produce a random sample, while selecting student first names that begin with the letter *S* should produce a biased sample, because first names begin with some letters of the alphabet much more often than with other letters, such as *X*.

Reflect

5. A student suggests that it would be better to assign the numbers to students randomly rather than in numerical order. Would doing this affect the probability of winning?
No, each number has the same probability of being chosen, so it does not matter which numbers are assigned to each student.

6. A charity is giving a movie ticket for every 10 coats donated. Jacob collected 8 coats, Ben collected 6, and Ryan and Zak each collected 3. They decide to donate the coats together so that they will get 2 movie tickets. Describe how to use a random number generator to decide which 2 boys get a ticket.
Possible answer: The boys collected a total of 20 coats. Assign Jacob numbers 1–8, Ben 9–14, Ryan 15–17, and Zak 18–20. Use the function randInt (1, 20) to generate 2 random numbers. If the second number is assigned to the boy who won the first ticket, generate another number until someone else wins the second ticket.

Explain 3 Solving the Problem of Points

The decision-making situation that you will apply in this example is based on the "Problem of Points" that was studied by the French mathematicians Blaise Pascal and Pierre de Fermat in the 17th century. Their work on the problem launched the branch of mathematics now known as probability.

Example 3 **Two students, Lee and Rory, find a box containing 100 baseball cards. To determine who should get the cards, they decide to play a game with the rules shown.**

Game Rules

- One of the students repeatedly tosses a coin.
- When the coin lands heads up, Lee gets a point.
- When the coin lands tails up, Rory gets a point.
- The first student to reach 20 points wins the game and gets the baseball cards.

As Lee and Rory are playing the game they are interrupted and are unable to continue. How should the 100 baseball cards be divided between the students given that the game was interrupted at the described moment?

(A) When they are interrupted, Lee has 19 points and Rory has 17 points.

At most, 3 coin tosses would have been needed for someone to win the game.

Make a list of all possible results using H for heads and T for tails. Circle the outcomes in which Lee wins the game.

0T, 3H	1T, 2H	2T, 1H	3T, 0H
HHHH	THH	TTH	TTT
	HTH	THT	
	HHT	HTT	

DIFFERENTIATE INSTRUCTION

Modeling

Some students may benefit from a hands-on approach for learning how to simulate a game with the random integer generator. For example, pairs of students can play a game to see which student gets the highest point total after 10 rolls of a die. Have them discuss the calculator command that is appropriate (**randInt(1,6)**), and how to proceed with the game. Then have students compare their results, declare a winner, play the game again, and compare the results of both games.

AVOID COMMON ERRORS

Some students may not pay attention to the steps used for the problem-solving model. Point out the importance of each step in giving meaning to a problem rather than simply jumping to a solution attempt.

EXPLAIN 3

Solving the Problem of Points

INTEGRATE MATHEMATICAL PROCESSES

Focus on Math Connections

MP.1 Point out that making a list of all possible results for a game helps students see the sample space that is used for the game, which in turn is necessary to calculate the probability of winning the game.

QUESTIONING STRATEGIES

How can you describe the sample space for the results of tossing a coin? **Possible answer: Determine the number of times the coin is tossed and then represent the results of each toss of the coin with "H" for heads and "T" for tails.**

When does tossing a coin simulate the fair outcome of a game? **Possible answer: When there are only two equally likely outcomes possible for a game, then the results of tossing a coin can simulate the two possible outcomes.**

AVOID COMMON ERRORS

Students may not be sure which model to choose to represent the results of a game. Encourage them to determine the model that best simulates the expected results of the game, and then use technology or other means to describe the model mathematically.

There are 8 possible results. Lee wins in 7 of them and Rory wins in 1 of them.

The probability of Lee winning is $\frac{7}{8}$, so he should get $\frac{7}{8}$ of the cards which is 87.5 cards.
The probability of Rory winning is $\frac{1}{8}$, so he should get $\frac{1}{8}$ of the cards which is 12.5 cards.
Rather than split a card into two, they might decide to flip a coin for that card or to let Lee have it because he was more likely to win it.

(B) When they are interrupted, Lee has 18 points and Rory has 17 points.

At most, __four__ more coin tosses would have been needed.

List all possible results. Circle the outcomes in which Lee wins.

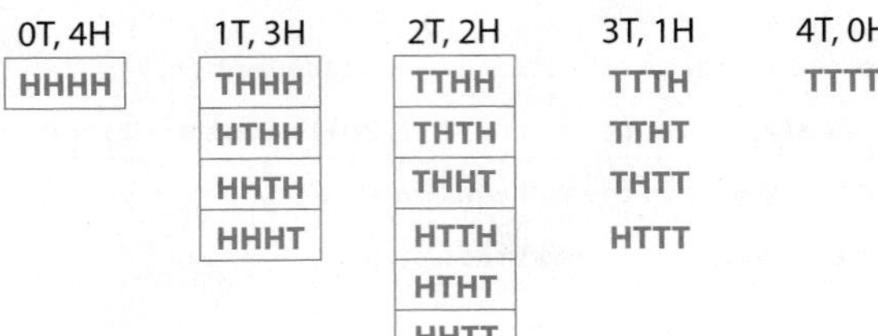

0T, 4H	1T, 3H	2T, 2H	3T, 1H	4T, 0H
HHHH	THHH	TTHH	TTTH	TTTT
	HTHH	THTH	TTHT	
	HHTH	THHT	THTT	
	HHHT	HTTH	HTTT	
		HTHT		
		HHTT		

There are __16__ possible results. Lee wins in __11__ of them and Rory wins in __5__ of them.

The probability of Lee winning is $\frac{11}{16}$, so he should get __69__ cards.

The probability of Rory winning is $\frac{5}{16}$, so he should get __31__ cards.

Reflect

7. **Discussion** A student suggests that a better way to divide the cards in Example 3B would be to split the cards based on the number of points earned so far. Which method do you think is better?

Possible answer: This suggestion would result in dividing the cards about evenly (51 for Lee; 49 for Rory). The solution in the example comes closer to the intended result that one student wins all of the cards.

Your Turn

8. Describe a situation where the game is interrupted, resulting in the cards needing to be divided evenly between the two players.

Possible answer: If the game is interrupted when the players are tied, they each have a probability of winning equal to $\frac{1}{2}$.

LANGUAGE SUPPORT EL

Connect Vocabulary

Students may have difficulty understanding the word *random* as it relates to probability. When discussing randomness with students, you may want to conduct a short experiment with the names of 10 students who play basketball and of 10 students chosen by the last digits of their phone numbers. Ask students how they would design an experiment to find the average height of a high school student. Have them decide which group of students would be a representative sample of the heights of high school students and why.

Elaborate

9. Discussion In the situation described in the Explore, suppose you like the crust and your friend does not. Is there a fair way to cut the slice of pizza that might not result in two equal size pieces?

Possible answer: If you cut the slice so that one piece has all of the crust but less topping, then the crust piece might be larger, but your friend might find it more desirable.

10. How would the solution to Example 2 need to change if there were two prizes to award? Assume that you do not want one student to win both prizes.

You could award the first prize in the same way. Once the first prize is awarded, either all the numbers assigned to that winner have to be ignored when randomly generating a second winning number, or the winner's numbers have to be reassigned to people with the highest numbers. For example, if Liam won the first prize, then his numbers would be reassigned to the person who has the two highest numbers, 64 and 65. Then use randInt (1, 63) to award the second prize.

11. Essential Question Check-In Describe a way to use probability to make a fair choice of a raffle winner.

If people are buying raffle tickets, then each of the *n* tickets should have the same $\left(\frac{1}{n}\right)$ chance of winning. You can select a ticket randomly from a box, or use a random number generator to select the winning number.

Evaluate: Homework and Practice

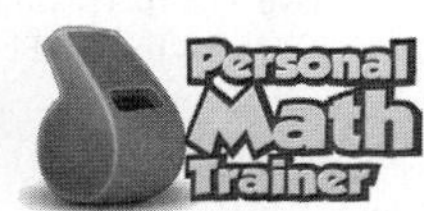

- Online Homework
- Hints and Help
- Extra Practice

1. You and a friend split the cost of a package of five passes to a climbing gym. Describe a way that you could fairly decide who gets to use the fifth pass.

Possible answer: You could split the cost of a sixth pass to the climbing gym so that you each get a third visit for half of the price of an additional pass. Or you could toss a coin and the winner gets the fifth pass. Tossing a coin gives each of you a 50% (or equal) chance of winning the last pass.

2. In addition to prizes for first, second, and third place, the organizers of a race have a prize that they want each participant to have an equal chance of winning. Describe a fair method of choosing a winner for this prize.

If the participants in the race each have a number, the organizers could select a number at random by using a random number generator or by putting slips of paper with each number into a box and randomly choosing one.

Exercise	Depth of Knowledge (D.O.K.)	COMMON CORE Mathematical Practices
1–3	**1** Recall of Information	**MP.2** Reasoning
4	**3** Strategic Thinking	**MP.1** Problem Solving
5–7	**1** Recall of Information	**MP.2** Reasoning
8	**3** Strategic Thinking	**MP.1** Problem Solving
9–11	**1** Recall of Information	**MP.2** Reasoning
12	**3** Strategic Thinking	**MP.1** Problem Solving

ELABORATE

QUESTIONING STRATEGIES

How can you use probability in fair decision-making? Probability gives a quantitative way to choose a random, unbiased sample, which in turn can be used to represent a population so that fair decisions can be made.

SUMMARIZE THE LESSON

How can a random number generator be used to simulate an experiment? Possible answer: Each possible result of an experiment can be assigned a number. When that number is produced by the random number generator, it simulates the corresponding experimental result.

EVALUATE

ASSIGNMENT GUIDE

Concepts and Skills	Practice
Explore Using Probabilities when Drawing at Random	Exercises 1–4
Example 1 Awarding a Prize to a Random Winner	Exercises 9–16
Example 2 Solving Real-World Problems Fairly	Exercises 5–8
Example 3 Solving the Problem of Points	Exercise 17

INTEGRATE MATHEMATICAL PRACTICES

Focus on Math Connections

MP.1 You may want to point out some different samples of a population to help students understand how random samples are different from non-random samples: A systematic sample uses a rule or pattern (like every third student) to select the members; a self-selected sample is one comprised of volunteers; and a convenience sample (like all students in first period lunch) chooses easy to reach members of the population.

Decide whether each method is a fair way to choose a winner if each person should have an equal chance of winning. Explain your answer by evaluating each probability.

3. Roll a standard die. Meri wins if the result is less than 3. Riley wins if the result is greater than 3.
Not fair; $P(\text{Meri wins}) = \frac{2}{6} = \frac{1}{3}$; $P(\text{Riley wins}) = \frac{3}{6} = \frac{1}{2}$

4. Draw a card from a standard deck of cards. Meri wins if the card is red. Riley wins if the card is black.
Fair; $P(\text{Meri wins}) = \frac{26}{52} = \frac{1}{2}$; $P(\text{Riley wins}) = \frac{26}{52} = \frac{1}{2}$

5. Flip a coin. Meri wins if it lands heads. Riley wins if it lands tails.
Fair; $P(\text{Meri wins}) = \frac{1}{2}$; $P(\text{Riley wins}) = \frac{1}{2}$

6. Meri and Riley both jump as high as they can. Whoever jumps higher wins.
Not fair; The person who is the better jumper is most likely to win

7. Roll a standard die. Meri wins if the result is even. Riley wins if the result is odd.
Fair; $P(\text{Meri wins}) = \frac{3}{6} = \frac{1}{2}$; $P(\text{Riley wins}) = \frac{3}{6} = \frac{1}{2}$

8. Draw a stone from a box that contains 5 black stones and 4 white stones. Meri wins if the stone is black. Riley wins if the stone is white.
Not fair; $P(\text{Meri wins}) = \frac{5}{9} \approx 0.56$. $P(\text{Riley wins}) = \frac{4}{9} \approx 0.44$

9. A chess club has received a chess set to give to one of its members. The club decides that everyone should have a chance of winning the set based on how many games they have won this season. Describe a fair method to decide who wins the set. Find the probability that each member will win it.

Member	Games Won	Probability of Winning	Member	Games Won	Probability of Winning
Kayla	30	**0.30**	Hailey	12	**0.12**
Noah	23	**0.23**	Gabe	12	**0.12**
Ava	18	**0.18**	Concour	5	**0.05**

Find the total number of games won: $30 + 23 + 18 + 12 + 12 + 5 = 100$. Assign numbers from 1–100 to the members so each has as many numbers assigned as the number of games won. Then use a random number generator to choose an integer from 1 to 100.

10. Owen, Diego, and Cody often play a game during lunch. When they can't finish, they calculate the probability that each will win given the current state of the game and assign partial wins. Today, when they had to stop, it would have taken at most 56 more moves for one of them to win. Owen would have won 23 of the moves, Diego would have won 18 of them, and Cody would have won 15. To two decimal places, how should they assign partial wins?
Owen: $\frac{23}{56} \approx 0.41$ wins; Diego: $\frac{18}{56} \approx 0.32$ wins; Cody: $\frac{15}{56} \approx 0.27$ wins

Exercise	Depth of Knowledge (D.O.K.)	COMMON CORE Mathematical Practices
13–19	**2** Skills/Concepts	**MP.2** Reasoning
20	**3** Strategic Thinking H.O.T.	**MP.6** Precision
21	**3** Strategic Thinking H.O.T.	**MP.4** Modeling

Represent Real-World Problems Twenty students, including Paige, volunteer to work at the school banquet. Each volunteer worked at least 1 hour. Paige worked 4 hours. The students worked a total of 45 hours. The organizers would like to award a prize to one of the volunteers.

1. Describe a process for awarding the prize so that each volunteer has an equal chance of winning. Find the probability of Paige winning.

   Possible answer: Write the names on slips of paper, place them in a box, and draw a slip at random. The probability of Paige winning is 1 out of 20, or 0.05%.

2. Describe a process for awarding the prize so that each volunteer's chance of winning is proportional to how many hours the volunteer worked. Find the probability of Paige winning.

   Possible answer: Write the names on slips of paper, but for each hour that a student worked, write his or her name on an extra slip. Then draw a slip at random. The probability of Paige winning is 4 out of 45, or about 0.089%.

There are 10,000 seats available in a sports stadium. Each seat has a package beneath it, and 20 of the seats have an, additional prize winning package with a family pass for the entire season.

3. Is this method of choosing a winner for the family passes fair?

   Yes. If the packages were attached randomly, then each seat has an equal chance of having the package containing the family pass.

4. What is the probability of winning a family pass if you attend the game?

   $P(\text{winning}) = \frac{20}{10{,}000} = \frac{1}{500}$

5. What is the probability of not winning a family pass if you attend the game?

   $P(\text{not winning}) = 1 - \left(P(\text{winning})\right) = 1 - \frac{20}{10{,}000} = \frac{9980}{10{,}000} = \frac{499}{500}$

A teacher tells students, "For each puzzle problem you complete, I will assign you a prize entry." In all, 10 students complete 53 puzzle problems. Leon completed 7. To award the prize, the teacher sets a calculator to generate a random integer from 1 to 53. Leon is assigned 18 to 24 as "winners".

6. What is the probability that a specific number is chosen?

   $P(\#) = \frac{\text{one number}}{\text{total numbers}} = \frac{1}{53} \approx 0.0189 \approx 1.89\%$

7. What is the probability that one of Leon's numbers will be chosen?

   $P(\text{leon}) = \frac{\text{Leon's numbers}}{\text{total numbers}} = \frac{7}{53} \approx 0.1321 \approx 13.21\%$

8. What is the probability that one of Leon's numbers will not be chosen?

   $P(\text{not leon's}) = 1 - \frac{\text{Leon's numbers}}{\text{total numbers}} = 1 - \frac{7}{53} \approx 0.8679 \approx 86.79\%$

9. Is this fair to Leon according to the original instructions? Explain.

   Yes. Leon did 7 of the total of 53 completed puzzle problems. He was assigned 7 of the 53 possible winning numbers, and each number has the same chance of being chosen.

AVOID COMMON ERRORS

Students might not understand the importance of an adequate sample size when trying to accurately represent a population for a survey. Point out the need to make the sample size large enough, as well as unbiased, when choosing a sample population.

INTEGRATE MATHEMATICAL PRACTICES

Focus on Math Connections

MP.1 A random sample of a larger population is sometimes called an *unbiased sample* if every other same-sized sample of the same population has an equal chance of being selected. Point out that random sampling is done when it is not convenient or feasible to survey the entire population.

AUDITORY CUES

Arrange students in small groups and have them discuss strategies for some of the exercises. Once they obtain their results, have them explain to one another how probability was used in the solutions.

AVOID COMMON ERRORS

Students may have difficulty understanding either how to generate unique random numbers or what the calculator's output represents. Encourage students to design alternative ways to generate random numbers, including using slips of paper in a bag.

MODELING

Give groups of students a hands-on activity to help them understand how the random-number generator is used to simulate the results of a survey. Have them compare their methods to the methods used in the Explore activity.

JOURNAL

Have students describe how probability can be used to help award a prize fairly.

H.O.T. Focus on Higher Order Thinking

20. Make a Conjecture Two teams are playing a game against one another in class to earn 10 extra points on an assignment. The teacher said that the points will be split fairly between the two teams, depending on the results of the game. If Team A earned 1300 points, and Team B earned 2200 points, describe one way the teacher could split up the 10 extra points. Explain.

Possible answer: Team A should receive $\frac{1300}{3500} = \frac{13}{35} \approx 37\%$ of the 10 extra points, or 3.7 points. Team B should receive $\frac{2200}{3500} = \frac{22}{35} \approx 63\%$, or 6.3 points.

21. Persevere in Problem Solving Alexa and Sofia are at a yard sale, and they find a box of 20 collectible toys that they both want. They can't agree about who saw it first, so they flip a coin until Alexa gets 10 heads or Sofia gets 10 tails. When Alexa has 3 heads and Sofia has 6 tails, they decide to divide the toys proportionally based on the probability each has of winning under the original rules. How should they divide the toys?

It would take at most 10 more flips for one of them to win $\left((10-3)+(10-6)-1\right)$. The number of possible permutations of 10 Hs and Ts is 2^{10} or 1024, so there are 1024 possible results for those 10 flips. In the cases where 7 or more of the flips are heads, Alexa wins. 7H/3T $= \frac{10!}{7! \cdot 3!} = 120$; 8H/2T $= \frac{10!}{8! \cdot 2!} = 45$; 9H/1T $= \frac{10!}{9! \cdot 1!} = 10$; 10H = 1

So Alexa wins in $120 + 45 + 10 + 1 = 176$ of the 1024 possible outcomes. The probability that she will win is $\frac{176}{1024} \approx 0.17$.%. So the probability that Sofia wins is $1 - 0.17 = 0.83$.

To divide the toys, 83% of 20 is 16.6, so Sofia should get 16 or 17 of they toys. Perhaps they could agree that she only gets 16, but gets first choice. Then they take turns choosing until Alexa has 4. Then Sofia gets the rest.

Lesson Performance Task

Three games are described below. For each game, tell whether it is fair (all players are equally likely to win) or unfair (one player has an advantage). Explain how you reached your decision, being sure to discuss how probability entered into your decision.

1. You and your friend each toss a quarter. If two heads turn up, you win. If a head and a tail turn up, your friend wins. If two tails turn up, you play again.
2. You and your friend each roll a die. If the sum of the numbers is odd, you get 1 point. If the sum is even, your friend gets 1 point.
3. You and your friend each roll a die. If the product of the numbers is odd, you get 1 point. If the product is even, your friend gets 1 point.

1. Unfair; table shows that there is a probability of $\frac{1}{4}$ that two heads will turn up, giving you a win, and a probability of $\frac{2}{4} = \frac{1}{2}$ that a head and a tail will turn up, giving your friend a win. Your friend's probability of winning is twice as great as yours, so the game is unfair.

	H	H
H	HH	HT
T	TH	TT

2. Fair; The table shows all of the possible sums when two dice are tossed. Of 36 possible sums, 18 are even, so the probability of rolling even is $\frac{18}{36} = \frac{1}{2}$. Of 36 possible sums, 18 are odd, so the probability of rolling odd is $\frac{18}{36} = \frac{1}{2}$. Both players are equally likely to win, so the game is fair.

+	1	2	3	4	5	6
1	2	3	4	5	6	7
2	3	4	5	6	7	8
3	4	5	6	7	8	9
4	5	6	7	8	9	10
5	6	7	8	9	10	11
6	7	8	9	10	11	12

3. Unfair; The table shows all of the possible products when two dice are tossed. Of 36 possible products, 27 are even, so the probability of rolling even is $\frac{27}{36} = \frac{3}{4}$. Of 36 possible products, 9 are odd, so the probability of rolling odd is $\frac{9}{36} = \frac{1}{4}$. Your friend's probability of winning is three times as great as yours, so the game is unfair.

×	1	2	3	4	5	6
1	1	2	3	4	5	6
2	2	4	6	8	10	12
3	3	6	9	12	15	18
4	4	8	12	16	20	24
5	5	10	15	20	25	30
6	6	12	18	24	30	36

EXTENSION ACTIVITY

Divide students into pairs or teams. Give each pair game-playing materials such as dice, playing cards, blank cards to write on, counters, checkers, spinners, or paper they can use to play games like tic-tac-toe. Have pairs or teams then follow the directions below.

- Make up two games, one fair and one unfair, that utilize their materials.
- Write the rules of the games and the reasons they are fair and unfair.
- Calculate any probabilities associated with the games.
- Play the games and compare the outcomes with the predicted probabilities.

INTEGRATE MATHEMATICAL PRACTICES

Focus on Reasoning

MP.2 Explain how you could change the rules of Game 1 and Game 3 in the Lesson Performance Task to make the games fair. **Possible answers: Game 1: If two heads turn up, you win. If a head and a tail turn up, you play again. If two tails turn up, your friend wins. Game 3: If the product of the numbers is odd, you get 3 points. If the product of the numbers is even, your friend gets 1 point.**

INTEGRATE MATHEMATICAL PRACTICES

Focus on Communication

MP.3 Ask students to describe a simple game that appears to be fair but, due to a small alteration in the construction of the game—a change the player does not know about—is actually unfair. **Possible answer: A spinner with six sections numbered 1 to 6. The player believes that all six sections have the same area, so that all the numbers have a $\frac{1}{6}$ chance of being spun. However, the section numbered 4 is slightly larger than the others, meaning that there is a slightly better chance that 4 will be spun.**

Scoring Rubric

2 points: Student correctly solves the problem and explains his/her reasoning.

1 point: Student shows good understanding of the problem but does not fully solve or explain his/her reasoning.

0 points: Student does not demonstrate understanding of the problem.

LESSON 21.2

Analyzing Decisions

Common Core Math Standards

The student is expected to:

 **S-CP.A.4**

Construct and interpret two-way frequency tables of data when two categories are associated with each object being classified. Use the two-way table as a sample space to decide if events are independent and to approximate conditional probabilities. Also S-CP.A.5, S-MD.B.7(+)

Mathematical Practices

 **MP.2 Reasoning**

Language Objective

State Bayes's Theorem in your own words.

ENGAGE

Essential Question: How can conditional probability help you make real-world decisions?

You can use a two-way table and/or Bayes's Theorem to use given information to calculate a conditional probability. Then you can use the conditional probability to evaluate a decision that may have been made based on the given information.

PREVIEW: LESSON PERFORMANCE TASK

View the Engage section online. Discuss the photograph. Ask students to speculate upon the purpose of the three doors. Then preview the Lesson Performance Task.

Name ______________________ Class ______________ Date ____________

21.2 Analyzing Decisions

Essential Question: How can conditional probability help you make real-world decisions?

Resource Locker

Explore Analyzing a Decision Using Probability

Suppose scientists have developed a test that can be used at birth to determine whether a baby is right-handed or left-handed. The test uses a drop of the baby's saliva and instantly gives the result. The test has been in development, long enough for the scientists to track the babies as they grow into toddlers and to see whether their test is accurate. About 10% of babies turn out to be left-handed.

The scientists have learned that when children are left-handed, the test correctly identifies them as left-handed 92% of the time. Also when children are right-handed, the test correctly identifies them as right-handed 95% of the time.

(A) In the first year on the market, the test is used on 1,000,000 babies. Complete the table starting with the Totals. Then use the given information to determine the expected number in each category.

	Tests Left-handed	Tests Right-handed	Total
Truly Left-handed	**92,000**	**8,000**	**100,000**
Truly Right-handed	**45,000**	**855,000**	**900,000**
Total	**137,000**	**863,000**	**1,000,000**

(B) What is the probability that a baby who tests left-handed actually is left-handed? $\frac{92,000}{137,000} \approx 67.2\%$

(C) What is the probability that a baby who tests right-handed actually is right-handed? $\frac{855,000}{863,000} \approx 99.1\%$

Reflect

1. Is the test a good test of right-handedness?
Yes; 99.1% is a reliable indicator that the baby will be right-handed.

2. A baby is tested, and the test shows the baby will be left-handed. The parents decide to buy a left-handed baseball glove for the baby. Is this a reasonable decision?
No; the test is correct only about $\frac{2}{3}$ of the time when the result is that the baby is left-handed.

HARDCOVER PAGES 1059–10

Watch for the hardcover student edition page numbers for this lesson.

3. Discussion Describe two ways in which the test can become a more reliable indicator of left-handedness.

The obvious way is to improve the test so that it is better than 92% for babies who are really left-handed. But the better way is to improve how the test works on right-handed babies so that there are fewer cases of right-handed babies who test left-handed.

Explore 2 Deriving Bayes' Theorem

You can generalize your results so that they are applicable to other situations in which you want to analyze decisions. Now, you will derive a formula known as Bayes' Theorem.

(A) Complete the steps to derive Bayes' Theorem.

Write the formula for $P(B|A)$. $P(B|A) = \frac{P(A \text{ and } B)}{P(A)}$

Solve for $P(A$ and $B)$. $P(A \text{ and } B) = P(B|A) \cdot P(A)$

Write the formula for $P(A|B)$. $P(A|B) = \frac{P(A \text{ and } B)}{P(B)}$

Substitute the expression for $P(A$ and $B)$. $P(A|B) = \frac{P(B|A) \cdot P(A)}{P(B)}$

(B) Explain how you can use a table giving the number of results for each case to find $P(B)$.

	B	B^c	Total
A	n	p	$n+p$
A^c	m	q	$m+q$
Total	$n+m$	$p+q$	$n+m+p+q$

Divide the total cases resulting in B by the total number of cases. $P(B) = \frac{n+m}{n+m+p+q}$.

(C) Explain how you can use the tree diagram to find $P(B)$.

Add $P(B|A) \cdot P(A)$ and $P(B|A^c) \cdot P(A^c)$.

Test

$P(A)$ $P(A^c)$

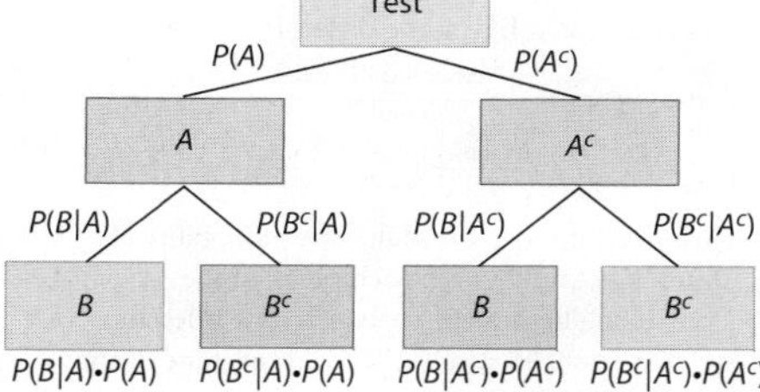

(D) Use your result from Step C to rewrite your final expression from Step A to get another form of Bayes' Theorem.

$$P(A|B) = \frac{P(B|A) \cdot P(A)}{P(B)} = \frac{P(B|A) \cdot P(A)}{P(B|A) \cdot P(A) + P(B|A^c) \cdot P(A^c)}$$

PROFESSIONAL DEVELOPMENT

Math Background

At the heart of this lesson is Bayes's Theorem, a probability formula named after the English mathematician Thomas Bayes (1702–1761). The theorem is useful when you want to "reverse" a conditional probability. For example, you might know the probability that someone who has tuberculosis tests positive for the disease, but you want to know the probability that someone who tests positive actually has tuberculosis. Bayes's Theorem is generally the appropriate tool for calculating this probability. However, since constructing a two-way table seems more intuitive, it is the method used in the lesson.

EXPLORE 1

Analyzing a Decision Using Probability

INTEGRATE TECHNOLOGY

Students have the option of doing the Explore activity either in the book or online.

QUESTIONING STRATEGIES

? Does the size of a population always affect how you solve a problem? **No. Sometimes any size of a population can be used because the size does not affect the relevant percents and probabilities.**

? How can you tell if you have filled in all the relevant cells of a two-way table correctly? **The totals across and down must be correct. The final total must be a sum of the totals in the bottom row.**

EXPLORE 2

Deriving Bayes's Theorem

INTEGRATE MATHEMATICAL PRACTICES

Focus on Critical Thinking

MP.3 Point out that students should focus on interpreting the mathematical results in the context of the situation. When students use Bayes's Theorem to find a conditional probability, the specific value they find for the probability is less important than understanding what this value means. Interpreting the mathematical result is the essential step in determining whether a good decision was made.

QUESTIONING STRATEGIES

When does conditional probability apply to a problem situation? **Possible answer: when the probability of one event is affected by the occurrence of a previous event**

How does a two-way table help you find conditional probabilities? **A two-way table helps you organize information so that the probabilities can be calculated.**

EXPLAIN 1

Using Bayes's Theorem

AVOID COMMON ERRORS

When using Bayes's Theorem, most errors arise from not being able to interpret and represent the conditional probabilities correctly. Suggest that students follow a pattern in identifying and describing each of the probabilities necessary to apply the theorem.

QUESTIONING STRATEGIES

How does Bayes's Theorem help you analyze decisions? **You can use the theorem and the given information to calculate a conditional probability. Then, you can use the conditional probability to evaluate a decision that was based on the given information.**

Reflect

4. Explain in words what each expression means in the context of Explore 1.

$P(A)$ is the probability of actually being left-handed.

$P(B)$ is the probability of testing left-handed.

$P(A|B)$ is **the probability of being left-handed if the baby tests left-handed**.

$P(B|A)$ is **the probability of testing left-handed if the baby is left-handed**.

5. Use Bayes' Theorem to calculate the probability that a baby actually is left-handed, given that the baby tests left-handed. Explain what this probability means.

From the table, $P(B) = \frac{\text{Test left-handed}}{\text{Total tests}} = \frac{137{,}000}{1{,}000{,}000} = 0.137$

$P(A|B) = \frac{0.92 \cdot 0.10}{0.137} \approx 67.2\%$

About 67% of the time, a baby who tests as left-handed will be left-handed.

Explain 1 Using Bayes' Theorem

Bayes' Theorem is a useful tool when you need to analyze decisions.

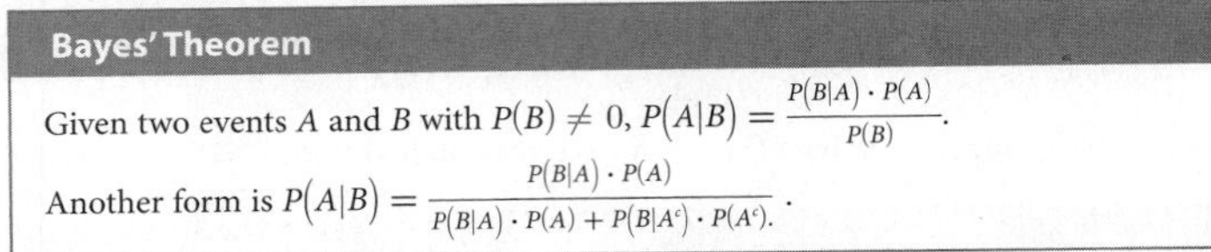

Bayes' Theorem

Given two events A and B with $P(B) \neq 0$, $P(A|B) = \frac{P(B|A) \cdot P(A)}{P(B)}$.

Another form is $P(A|B) = \frac{P(B|A) \cdot P(A)}{P(B|A) \cdot P(A) + P(B|A^c) \cdot P(A^c)}$.

Example 1 **Suppose Walter operates an order-filling machine that has an error rate of 0.5%. He installs a new order-filling machine that has an error rate of only 0.1%. The new machine takes over 80% of the order-filling tasks.**

(A) One day, Walter gets a call from a customer complaining that her order wasn't filled properly. Walter blames the problem on the old machine. Was he correct in doing so? First, find the probability that the order was filled by the old machine given that there was an error in filling the order, $P(\text{old} \mid \text{error})$.

$$P(\text{old}|\text{error}) = \frac{P(\text{error}|\text{old}) \cdot P(\text{old})}{P(\text{error})}$$

$$= \frac{0.005 \cdot (0.20)}{0.001 + 0.0008} = \frac{0.001}{0.0018} = \frac{5}{9} \approx 0.56$$

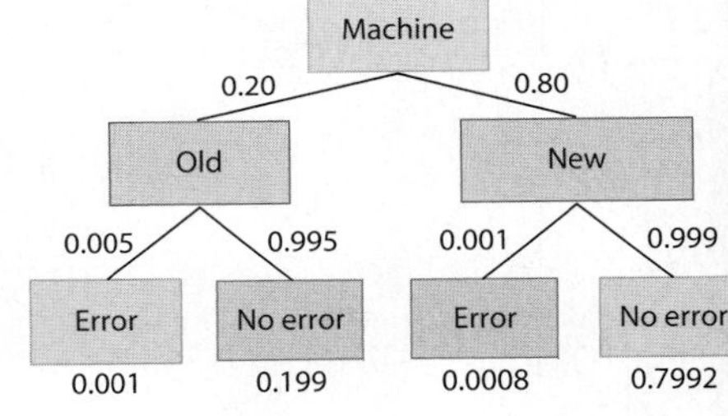

Given that there is a mistake, the probability is about 56% that the old machine filled the order. The probability that the new machine filled the order is $1 - 0.56 = 44\%$. The old machine is only slightly more likely than the new machine to have filled the order. Walter shouldn't blame the old machine.

COLLABORATIVE LEARNING

Small Group Activity

Have groups of students discuss and analyze how the various branches of a tree diagram show the probabilities of the associated events. Have each student tell something about the diagram. For example, "the probabilities of complementary events add to 1." Then have them collate the information and make a conjecture about how to use a tree diagram to find the probability of an event. Invite students to share their information with the class.

Ⓑ Walter needs to increase capacity for filling orders so he increases the number of orders being filled by the old machine to 30% of the total orders. What percent of errors in filled orders are made by the old machine? Is Walter unreasonably increasing the risk of shipping incorrectly filled orders?

Find the probability that **the order was filled by the old machine**

given that **there is an error in filling the package**,

P(**old** | **error**).

Use Bayes' Theorem.

$$P(A|B) = \frac{P(B|A) \cdot P(A)}{P(B)} = \frac{0.005(0.30)}{0.0015 + 0.0007}$$

$$= \frac{0.0015}{0.0022} = \frac{15}{22} \approx 0.68$$

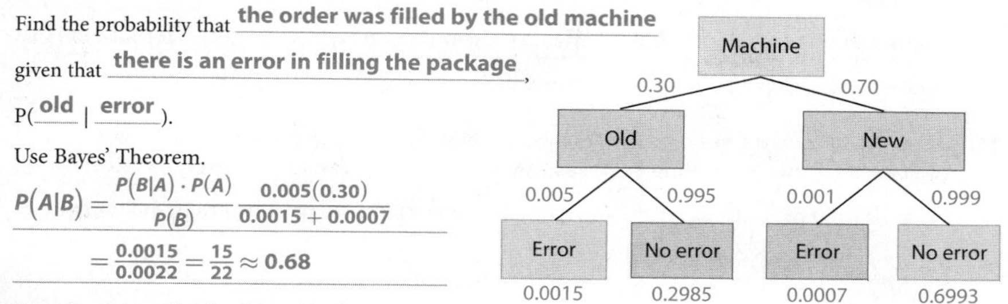

Describe the result of making this change.

Given that there is a mistake, the probability is about 68% that the old machine filled the package. Making this change increases the number of errors by 4 orders for every 10,000 orders. This seems like a worthwhile risk.

Reflect

6. The old machine fills so few orders. How can it be responsible for more than half of the errors?
The error rate of the old machine is five times the error rate of the new machine.

Your Turn

In the situation described in the Explore, suppose the scientists have changed the test so that now it correctly identifies left-handed children 100% of the time, and still correctly identifies right-handed children 95% of the time.

7. Complete the tree diagram.

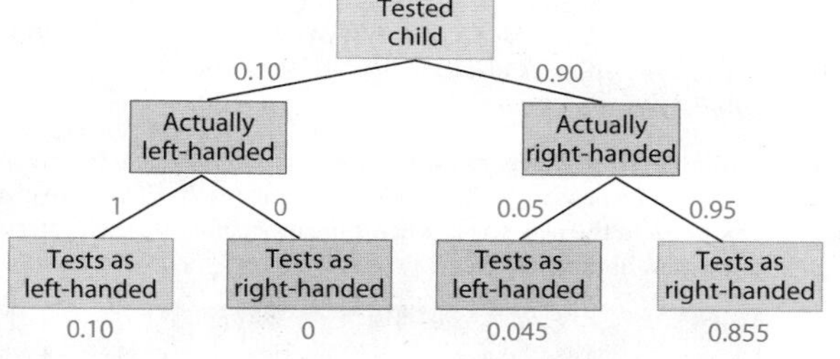

8. With the new test, what is the probability that a child who tests as left-handed will be left-handed? How does this compare to the original test?

$$P(\text{actual}_{\text{left}}|\text{test}_{\text{left}}) = \frac{1 \cdot 0.10}{0.1 + 0.045} = 69\%$$

The probability of the test being correct in this case increases about 2%.

9. With the new test, what is the probability that a child who tests as right-handed will be left-handed? How does this compare to the original test?

$$P(\text{actual}_{\text{right}}|\text{test}_{\text{left}}) = \frac{0.95 \cdot 0.05}{0.10 + 0.045} = 31\%$$

The probability of the test being correct in this case increases about 30%.

INTEGRATE MATHEMATICAL PRACTICES

Focus on Modeling

MP.4 Point out that a tree diagram or a two-way table helps to determine the individual probabilities that are used in Bayes's Theorem. Have students practice making tree diagrams or two-way tables, if necessary, to find each individual probability in the theorem.

DIFFERENTIATE INSTRUCTION

Auditory Cues

Help students understand Bayes's Theorem by having them restate the theorem in their own words and then verbalize how they will apply it. For example, "the probability that event *A* will happen given that event *B* happened is the product of the conditional probability that *B* happens given *A* with the probability of *A*, all divided by the probability of *B*." Stating the theorem in words may help students focus on the values they must find to apply the theorem.

ELABORATE

QUESTIONING STRATEGIES

? How would you say $P(A \mid B)$ in words? How is it different from $P(A)$? The probability of A given B; it is the probability that A occurs if it is given that B has already occurred, instead of simply the probability that A occurs.

SUMMARIZE THE LESSON

? What are some methods of using probability to analyze decisions? You can use two-way tables, tree diagrams, or Bayes's Theorem to calculate conditional probabilities, and then use those results to help you evaluate decisions made on the basis of the probabilities.

Elaborate

10. **Discussion** Compare the probabilities you found in the Explore and Your Turn 8 and 9. Why did the percent of babies who test as right-handed and are actually left-handed increase?
Possible answer: The increased accuracy of the test for left-handed reduced the overall number of tests showing right-handed, so the babies who test right-handed but are left-handed are a larger percent of that group.

11. **Essential Question Check-In** How can you use probability to help you analyze decisions?
You can use a two-way table or Bayes' Theorem to use given information to calculate a conditional probability. Then you can use the conditional probability to evaluate a decision that may have been made based on the given information.

Evaluate: Homework and Practice

- Online Homework
- Hints and Help
- Extra Practice

1. A factory manager is assessing the work of two assembly-line workers. Helen has been on the job longer than Kyle. Their production rates for the last month are in the table. Based on comparing the number of defective products, the manager is considering putting Helen on probation. Is this a good decision? Why or why not?

	Helen	Kyle	Total
Defective	50	20	70
Not defective	965	350	1,315
Total	1,015	370	1,385

No; Of the 1,015 products that Helen completed, 50 were defective, which is about 4.9%. Of the 370 products that Kyle completed, 20 were defective, which is about 5.5%. Neither should be put on probation solely based on these data.

2. **Multiple Step** A reporter asked 150 voters if they plan to vote in favor of a new library and a new arena. The table shows the results. If you are given that a voter plans to vote ***no*** to the new arena, what is the probability that the voter also plans to vote no to the new library?

		Library		
		Yes	No	**Total**
Arena	Yes	21	30	51
	No	57	42	99
	Total	78	72	**150**

$P(\text{no library} \mid \text{no arena}) = \frac{42}{99}$, about 42%

LANGUAGE SUPPORT EL

Connect Vocabulary

If students comprehend some of the concepts in this lesson, provide them the opportunity to listen, share, and interact with other students in groups. Ask each group to make a poster representing a scenario in which one could use Bayes's Theorem to help make a decision, and then present the poster to the class.

3. You want to hand out coupons for a local restaurant to students who live off campus at a rural college with a population of 10,000 students. You know that 10% of the students live off campus and that 98% of those students ride a bike. Also, 62% of the students who live on campus do not have a bike. You decide to give a coupon to any student you see who is riding a bike. Complete the table. Then explain whether this a good decision.

	bike	no bike	Total
on campus	9,000(0.38) = 3,420	9,000(0.62) = 5,580	10,000(0.90) = 9,000
off campus	1,000(0.98) = 980	1,000(0.02) = 20	10,000(0.10) = 1,000
Total	4,400	5,600	10,000

Only 980 of the 4,400 bike-riding students live off campus, so only 22% of the coupons will go to the intended target of students living off campus. Therefore, this is not a good decision.

4. A test for a virus correctly identifies someone who has the virus (by returning a positive result) 99% of the time. The test correctly identifies someone who does not have the virus (by returning a negative result) 99% of the time. It is known that 0.5% of the population has the virus. A doctor decides to treat anyone who tests positive for the virus. Complete the two-way table assuming a total population of 1,000,000 people have been tested. Is this a good decision?

	Tests Positive	Tests Negative	Total
Virus	4,950	50	5,000
No virus	9,950	985,050	995,000
Total	14,900	985,100	1,000,000

Of the 14,900 people who tested positive, only 4,950 actually have the virus. The probability a person who tests positive for the virus actually has it is $\frac{4,950}{14,900}$, or about 33.2%. Most of the patients that the doctor treats for the virus do not need the treatment.

5. It is known that 2% of the population has a certain allergy. A test correctly identifies people who have the allergy 98% of the time. The test correctly identifies people who do not have the allergy 95% of the time. A website recommends that anyone who tests positive for the allergy should begin taking anti-allergy medication. Complete the two-way table. Do you think this is a good recommendation? Why or why not?

	Test Positive	Test Negative	Total
Allergy	196	4	200
No allergy	490	9,310	9,800
Total	686	9,314	10,000

No; Only 196 people out of the 686 who tested positive actually have the allergy. This is about 29% of those who test positive.

Exercise	Depth of Knowledge (D.O.K.)	COMMON CORE Mathematical Practices
1–4	**3** Strategic Thinking	**MP.3** Logic
5	**1** Recall of Information	**MP.5** Using Tools
6–10	**1** Recall of Information	**MP.4** Modeling
11	**1** Recall of Information	**MP.8** Patterns
12	**1** Recall of Information	**MP.5** Using Tools

EVALUATE

ASSIGNMENT GUIDE

Concepts and Skills	Practice
Explore 1 Analyzing a Decisions Using Probability	Exercises 1–4
Explore 2 Deriving Bayes's Theorem	Exercise 5
Example 1 Using Bayes's Theorem	Exercises 6–9

INTEGRATE MATHEMATICAL PRACTICES

Focus on Communication

MP.3 Have students verbalize the solution process in finding conditional probabilities using a two-way table, tree diagram, and Bayes's Theorem. Then have them work in small groups. In each group, have one student pose a conditional probability situation from the real world, or use one of the exercises. The other students should check that conditional probability applies, and then solve the problem.

INTEGRATE MATHEMATICAL PRACTICES

Focus on Reasoning

MP.2 Using probabilities gives a way to quantitatively analyze decisions that need to be made based on the occurrence of past events. Ask students to think of situations that cause decisions to be made independently of the supporting probabilities. For example, a decision to close school for a "snow day" may be made based on factors other than the probability of snow.

6. Use the tree diagram shown.

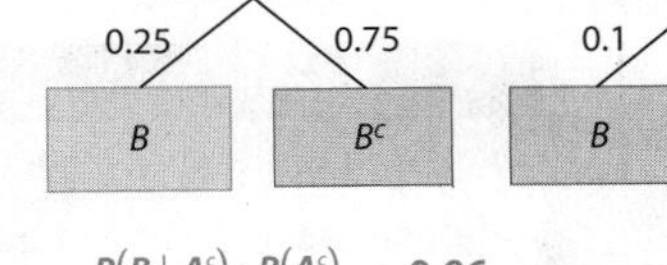
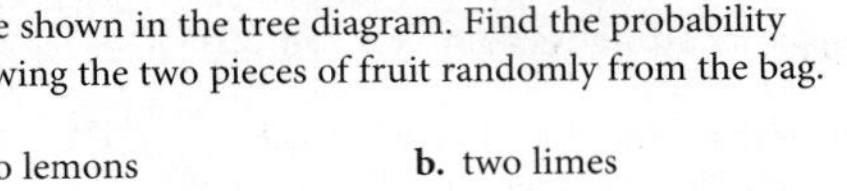
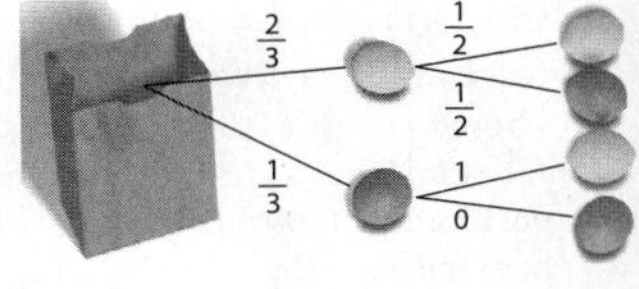

a. Find $P(B|A^c) \cdot P(A^c)$.

$P(B \mid A^c) \cdot P(A^c) = 0.1 \cdot 0.6 = 0.06$

b. Find $P(B)$.

$P(B) = P(B \mid A^c) \cdot P(A^c) + P(B \mid A) \cdot P(A)$

$= 0.06 + 0.25 \cdot 0.4$

$= 0.06 + 0.1 \quad = 0.16$

c. Use Bayes's Theorem to find $P(A^c|B)$. $P(A^c \mid B) = \frac{P(B \mid A^c) \cdot P(A^c)}{P(B)} = \frac{0.06}{0.16} = 0.375$

7. The probabilities of drawing lemons and limes from a bag are shown in the tree diagram. Find the probability of drawing the two pieces of fruit randomly from the bag.

$\frac{2}{3}$, $\frac{1}{3}$, $\frac{1}{2}$, $\frac{1}{2}$, 1, 0

a. two lemons

$\frac{2}{3} \cdot \frac{1}{2} = \frac{1}{3}$

b. two limes

$\frac{1}{3} \cdot 0 = 0$

c. lime, then lemon

$\frac{1}{3} \cdot 1 = \frac{1}{3}.$

d. lemon, then lime

$\frac{2}{3} \cdot \frac{1}{2} + \frac{1}{3} \cdot 1 = \frac{1}{3} + \frac{1}{3} = \frac{2}{3}$

8. **Multiple Step** A school principal plans a school picnic for June 2. A few days before the event, the weather forecast predicts rain for June 2, so the principal decides to cancel the picnic. Consider the following information.

- In the school's town, the probability that it rains on any day in June is 3%.
- When it rains, the forecast correctly predicts rain 90% of the time.
- When it does not rain, the forecast incorrectly predicts rain 5% of the time.

a. Find $P(\text{prediction of rain} \mid \text{rains})$ and $P(\text{rains})$.

$P(\text{prediction of rain} \mid \text{rains}) = 0.9$ (given); $P(\text{rains}) = 0.3$ (given)

b. Complete the tree diagram, and find P (Prediction rains).

P(Prediction of rain) = P(prediction of rain|rains) + P(prediction of rain|does not rain)= 0.027 + 0.0485 = 0.0755

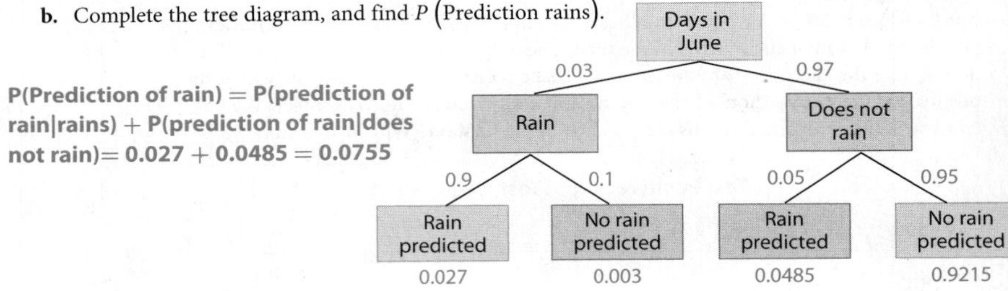

c. Find P(rains| prediction of rain).

$P(\text{rains} \mid \text{prediction of rain}) = \frac{0.9 \cdot 0.03}{0.0755} \approx 0.358 \approx 35.8\%$

d. Is the decision to cancel the picnic reasonable?

No; there is only a 36% chance that it will rain.

Exercise	Depth of Knowledge (D.O.K.)	COMMON CORE Mathematical Practices
13–14	1 Recall of Information	MP.4 Modeling
15–16	3 Strategic Thinking	MP.3 Logic
17	1 Recall of Information	MP.5 Using Tools
18	3 Strategic Thinking H.O.T.	MP.3 Logic
19	3 Strategic Thinking H.O.T.	MP.3 Logic
20	3 Strategic Thinking H.O.T.	MP.3 Logic

9. Pamela has collected data on the number of students in the sophomore class who play a sport or play a musical instrument. She has learned the following.

- 42.5% of all students in her school play a musical instrument.
- 20% of those who play a musical instrument also play a sport.
- 40% of those who play no instrument also play no sport.

Complete the tree diagram. Would it be reasonable to conclude that a student who doesn't play a sport plays a musical instrument?

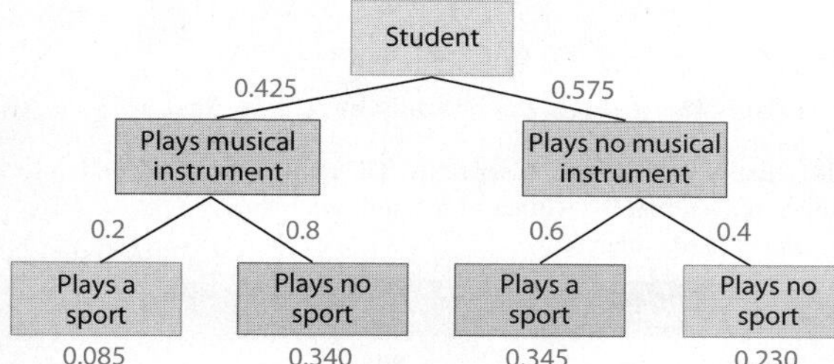

$$\textbf{P(music | no sport)} = \textbf{P(no sport | music)} \cdot \textbf{P(music)} = \frac{\mathbf{0.8 \cdot 0.425}}{\mathbf{0.34 + 0.23}} \approx \mathbf{0.60}$$

The probability that a student plays a musical instrument given that he or she plays no sport is about 60%. So, it is somewhat likely that a student who doesn't play a sport does play an instrument, but it would not be reasonable to assume that this is true.

10. Interpret the Answer Company X supplies 35% of the phones to an electronics store and Company Y supplies the remainder. The manager of the store knows that 25% of the phones in the last shipment from Company X were defective, while only 5% of the phones from Company Y were defective. The manager chooses a phone at random and finds that it is defective. The manager decides that the phone must have come from Company X. Do you think this is a reasonable conclusion? Why or why not?

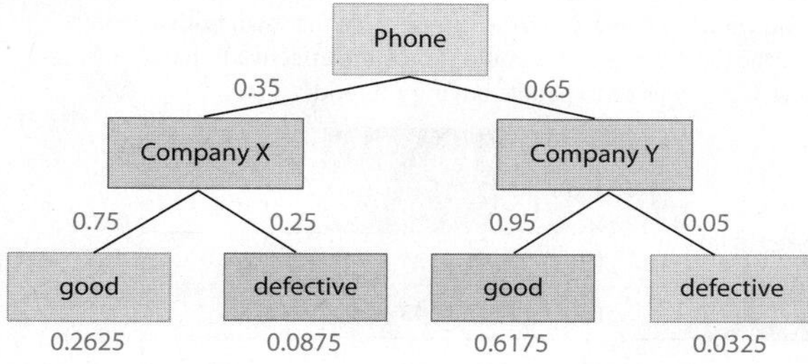

$$\mathbf{P(\text{Company X} \mid \text{defective})} = \frac{\mathbf{P(\text{defective} \mid \text{Company X}) \cdot P(\text{Company X})}}{\mathbf{P(\text{defective})}}$$

$$= \frac{\mathbf{0.0875}}{\mathbf{0.0875 + 0.0325}} \approx \mathbf{0.73}$$

This is a good decision because there is a 73% chance that a defective phone came from Company X.

AVOID COMMON ERRORS

Be sure students understand the difference between probabilities of independent events and of conditional probabilities. Emphasize that conditional probabilities are used for Bayes's Theorem.

11. Suppose that strep throat affects 2% of the population and a test to detect it produces an accurate result 99% of the time. Create a tree diagram and use Bayes Theorem to find the probability that someone who tests positive actually has strep throat.

Person
0.02
0.98
has strep (S)
does not have strep(S^C)
0.99
0.01
0.01
0.99
tests positive (+)
tests negative (−)
tests positive (+)
tests negative (−)
0.0198
0.0002
0.0098
0.9702

$$P(S \mid +) = \frac{P(+ \mid S) \cdot P(S)}{P(+)} = \frac{0.99 \cdot 0.02}{0.99 \cdot 0.02 + 0.01 \cdot 0.98} \approx 0.67$$

About 67% of those tested positively for strep throat actually have strep throat.

12. Fundraising A hand-made quilt is first prize in a fund-raiser raffle. The table shows information about all the ticket buyers. Given that the winner of the quilt is a man, what is the probability that he resides in Sharonville?

	Men	Women	Total
Forestview	35	45	80
Sharonville	15	25	40
Total	50	70	120

$\frac{15}{50} = 0.3 = 30\%$

13. Explain how to derive Bayes' Theorem using the Multiplication Rule.

$P(B) \cdot P(A \mid B) = P(A) \cdot P(B \mid A)$ — $P(B) \cdot P(A \mid B)$ and $P(A) \cdot P(B \mid A)$ are equal

$\frac{P(B) \cdot P(A \mid B)}{P(B)} = \frac{P(A) \cdot P(B \mid A)}{P(B)}$ — Divide each side by P(B).

$P(A \mid B) = \frac{P(A) \cdot P(B \mid A)}{P(B)}$ — Bayes' Theorem

14. Sociology A sociologist collected data on the types of pets in 100 randomly selected households. Suppose you want to offer a service to households that own both a cat and a dog. Based on the data in the table, would it be more effective to hand information to people walking dogs or to people buying cat food?

		Owns a Cat		
		Yes	**No**	**Total**
Owns a Dog	**Yes**	15	24	39
	No	18	43	61
	Total	33	67	100

$P(\text{cat} \mid \text{dog}) = \frac{15}{39} \approx 0.38$ and $P(\text{dog} \mid \text{cat}) = \frac{15}{33} \approx 0.45$, so it would be somewhat more effective to approach people buying cat food.

15. Interpret the Answer It is known that 1% of all mice in a laboratory have a genetic mutation. A test for the mutation correctly identifies mice that have the mutation 98% of the time. The test correctly identifies mice that do not have the mutation 96% of the time. A lab assistant tests a mouse and finds that the mouse tests positive for the mutation. The lab assistant decides that the mouse must have the mutation. Is this a good decision? Complete the tree diagram and explain your answer.

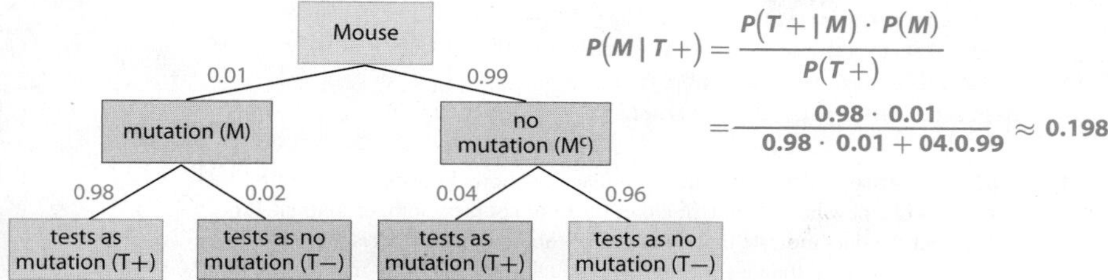

$$P(M \mid T+) = \frac{P(T+ \mid M) \cdot P(M)}{P(T+)}$$

$$= \frac{0.98 \cdot 0.01}{0.98 \cdot 0.01 + 04.0.99} \approx 0.198$$

It is not a good decision, because there is only a 19.8% probability that a mouse that tests positive for the mutation actually has the mutation.

16. Interpret the Answer It is known that 96% of all dogs do not get trained. One professional trainer claims that 54% of trained dogs will sit on one of the first four commands and that no other dogs will sit on command. A condominium community wants to impose a restriction on dogs that are not trained. They want each dog owner to show that his or her dog will sit on one of the first four commands. Assuming that the professional trainer's claim is correct, is this a fair way to identify dogs that have not been trained? Explain.

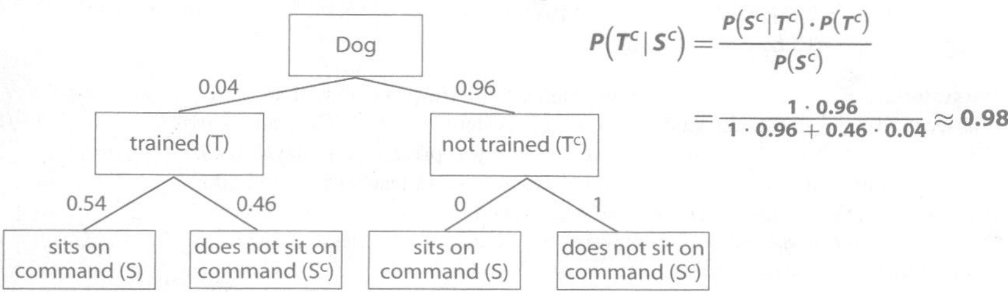

$$P(T^c \mid S^c) = \frac{P(S^c \mid T^c) \cdot P(T^c)}{P(S^c)}$$

$$= \frac{1 \cdot 0.96}{1 \cdot 0.96 + 0.46 \cdot 0.04} \approx 0.98$$

It is fair, because there is a 98% probability that a dog that does not sit on one of the first four commands has not been trained.

17. Multiple Steps Tomas has a choice of three possible routes to work. On each day, he randomly selects a route and keeps track of whether he is late. Based on this 40-day trial, which route makes Tomas least likely to be late for work?

	Late	Not Late
Route A	IIII	𝍸 𝍸
Route B	III	𝍸 II
Route C	IIII	𝍸 𝍸 II

	Late	Not Late	Total
Route *A*	4	10	14
Route *B*	3	7	10
Route *C*	4	12	16

$P(Late \mid A) = \frac{4}{14} \approx 0.29$; $P(Late \mid B) = \frac{3}{10} = 0.3$; $P(Late \mid C) = \frac{4}{16} = 0.25$

Based on the sample, Tomas is least likely to be late if he takes Route *C*.

AUDITORY CUES

Arrange students in small groups and have them discuss the different interpretations that may result from applying Bayes's Theorem. Ask them to brainstorm how the interpretations would change as more information is gathered from a probability experiment.

MODELING

Give groups of students a hands-on activity to help them understand how tree diagrams, two-way tables, and Bayes's Theorem are used to influence decision-making. Have them compare their results to the examples.

JOURNAL

Have students compare two methods of analyzing a decision: making a two-way table, and using Bayes's Theorem. Prompt students to describe the pros and cons of each method.

H.O.T. Focus on Higher Order Thinking

18. Critique Reasoning When Elisabeth saw this tree diagram, she said that the calculations must be incorrect. Do you agree? Justify your answer.

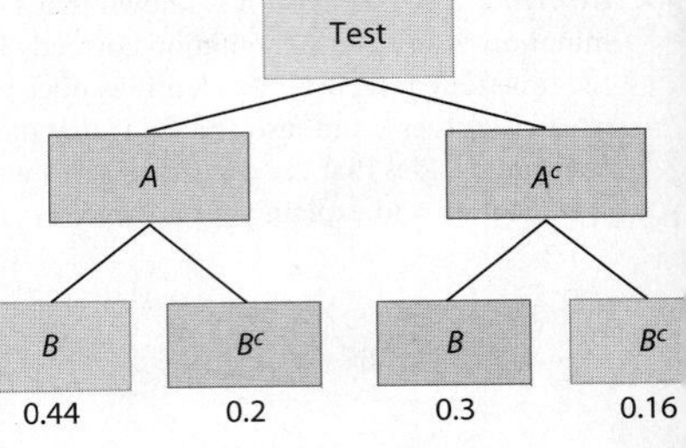

Elisabeth is correct. The sum of the probabilities for the four outcomes is 0.44 + 0.2 + 0.3 + 0.16 = 1.1, but the sum of the probabilities of all possible outcomes must be 1. Therefore, the calculations must be incorrect.

19. Multiple Representations The Venn diagram shows how many of the first 100 customers of a new bakery bought either bread or cookies, both, or neither. Taryn claims that the data indicate that a customer who bought cookies is more likely to have bought bread than a customer who bought bread is likely to have bought cookies. Is she correct?

		Bread		
		Yes	No	Total
Cookies	Yes	18	22	40
	No	54	6	60
	Total	72	28	100

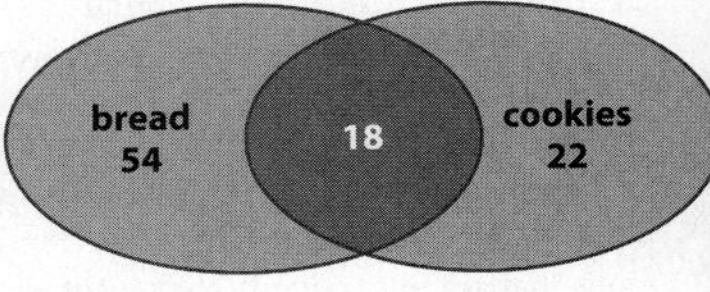

Yes, because $P(B \mid C) = \frac{18}{40} = 0.45$, while $P(C \mid B) = \frac{18}{72} = 0.25$. So, customers who bought cookies also bought bread almost half of the time, while customers who bought bread also bought cookies only a quarter of the time.

20. Persevere in Problem Solving At one high school, the probability that a student is absent today, given that the student was absent yesterday, is 0.12. The probability that a student is absent today, given that the student was present yesterday, is 0.05. The probability that a student was absent yesterday is 0.1. A teacher forgot to take attendance in several classes yesterday, so he assumed that attendance in his class today is the same as yesterday. If there were 40 students in these classes, how many errors would you expect by doing this?

Students present yesterday = 90% of 40 = 36
Students absent yesterday = 10% of 40 = 4

$$P(PY \mid PT) = \frac{P(PT \mid PY) \cdot P(PY)}{P(PT)} = \frac{0.95 \cdot 0.9}{0.95 \cdot 0.9 + 0.88 \cdot 0.1} \approx 0.91;\ 91\% \text{ of } 36 = 33 \text{ students}$$

$$P(AY \mid PT) = \frac{P(PT \mid AY) \cdot P(AY)}{P(PT)} = \frac{0.88 \cdot 0.1}{0.95 \cdot 0.9 + 0.88 \cdot 0.1} \approx 0.09;\ 9\% \text{ of } 36 = 3 \text{ students}$$

$$P(PY \mid AT) = \frac{P(AT \mid PY) \cdot P(PY)}{P(AT)} = \frac{0.05 \cdot 0.9}{0.05 \cdot 0.9 + 0.12 \cdot 0.1} \approx 0.79;\ 79\% \text{ of } 4 = 3 \text{ students.}$$

$$P(AY \mid AT) = \frac{P(AT \mid AY) \cdot P(AY)}{P(AT)} = \frac{0.12 \cdot 0.1}{0.05 \cdot 0.9 + 0.12 \cdot 0.1} \approx 0.\ 21\% \text{ of } 4 = 1 \text{ student}$$

The cases where doing this would cause an error are $P(AY|PT)$ and $P(PY|AT)$. So based on th probabilities, he would have the attendance for yesterday wrong for about 6 students.

Lesson Performance Task

You're a contestant on a TV quiz show. Before you are three doors. Behind two of the doors,, there's a goat. Behind one of the doors, there's a new car. You are asked to pick a door. After you make your choice, the quizmaster opens one of the doors you *didn't* choose, revealing a goat.

Door 1

Door 2

Door 3

Now there are only two doors. You can stick with your original choice or you can switch to the one remaining door. Should you switch?

Intuition tells most people that, with two doors left, there's a 50% probability that they're right and a 50% probability that they're wrong. They conclude that it doesn't matter whether they switch or not.

Does it? Using Bayes' Theorem, it can be shown mathematically that you're much better off switching! You can reach the same conclusion using logical thinking skills. Assume that the car is behind Door #1. (The same reasoning that follows can be applied if the car is behind one of the other doors.) You've decided to switch your choice after the first goat is revealed. There are three possibilities.

1. **If I choose Door #1 first, my switch strategy dictates that I must switch my choice. If the quizmaster opens Door #2 I must switch my choice to Door #3. If the quizmaster opens Door #3 I must switch my choice to Door #2. Either way my strategy is unsuccessful and I lose.**
2. **a. If I choose Door #2 first, the quizmaster must open Door #3 because the car is behind Door #1.**
   b. My switch strategy dictates that I must switch my choice, so I switch to Door #1. My strategy is successful and I win the car.
3. **a. The quizmaster must open Door #2 because the car is behind Door #1.**
   b. My switch strategy dictates that I must switch my choice, so I switch to Door #1. My strategy is successful and I win the car.

$\frac{2}{3}$; I win the car in two of the three case, the two where my first choice is wrong. I lose in only one of the three cases, the one where my first choice is correct.

EXTENSION ACTIVITY

Present the following to pairs of students: *There are three cards in a hat. One card is white on both sides. The second card is white on one side and red on the other. The third card is red on both sides. One card is removed and placed flat on the table. The side showing is red. What is the probability that the other side of the card is red?* Pairs should decide on an answer to the question and be prepared to give their reasoning. The answer seems paradoxical, so students may want to test it experimentally. **$\frac{2}{3}$; the card cannot be white-white, so there are three possible cases. The other side may be (1) white, (2) side 1 of the red-red card, or (3) side 2 of the red-red card. Two of the three possibilities are favorable.**

INTEGRATE MATHEMATICAL PRACTICES

Focus on Modeling

MP.4 Have students work in pairs to create and play games analogous to the game described in the Lesson Performance Task. Students should keep track of the results when they try various strategies for making the correct choice, and compare their results with the claim that switching is the best strategy.

AVOID COMMON ERRORS

Students may have difficulty understanding the logic behind the quizmaster's decision about which door to open after the initial choice has been made, and the reason why switching is a winning strategy in two out of three cases. Have students work in pairs to walk through the steps when the car is behind Door #1, as it is in the Lesson Performance Task; then when it is behind Door #2; and, finally, behind Door #3. Each time, students should begin by making an arbitrary choice of a door, then deciding how the quizmaster will react to the choice, and then seeing the result when they switch the initial choice.

Scoring Rubric

2 points: Student correctly solves the problem and explains his/her reasoning.

1 point: Student shows good understanding of the problem but does not fully solve or explain his/her reasoning.

0 points: Student does not demonstrate understanding of the problem.

Study Guide Review

ASSESSMENT AND INTERVENTION

Assign or customize module reviews.

MODULE PERFORMANCE TASK

Mathematical Practices: MP.1, MP.2, MP.4, MP.5, MP.6, MP.7
S-CP.A.4, S-CP.A.5, S-MD.B.7

SUPPORTING STUDENT REASONING

Here are some questions students might have:

- **What is the "reliability rate" of a diagnostic test?** A test that is 100% reliable always correctly identifies a person who has the illness. A reliability of 85% means that 15% of the time, the test fails to identify a patient who actually has the illness.
- **What is a "false-positive" rate?** A false positive result of a test is one that shows that a patient has the illness, when in fact, he or she does not. A false positive rate of 8% means that of every 100 people who are tested, 8 will test positive for the illness, though they do not have it.

STUDY GUIDE REVIEW

Probability and Decision Making

Essential Question: How can you use probability to solve real-world problems?

KEY EXAMPLE *(Lesson 21.1)*

Determine whether the method of awarding a prize is fair. Explain.

A festival has a baked goods fundraising raffle in which tickets are drawn for winners. The tickets are sold for $2 each, and the purchaser of the ticket places his or her name on the ticket before placing the ticket into a fishbowl on a table. There are 20 cakes for prizes. A ticket is drawn at random from the fishbowl for each cake.

The method of awarding the prize is fair. This is because each ticket has an equal probability of being drawn. For each of n tickets bought, that ticket has a $\frac{1}{n}$ chance of being drawn. The more tickets someone buys, the better chance they have of winning a cake.

KEY EXAMPLE *(Lesson 21.2)*

Suppose Rhonda's Block Warehouse operates a block-making machine that has an error rate of 0.7%. Then Rhonda installs a new block-making machine that has an error rate of only 0.3%. The new machine takes over 75% of the block-making tasks. One day, Rhonda gets a call from a customer complaining that his block is not made properly. Rhonda blames the problem on the old machine. Was she correct in doing so?

Find Event A, Event B, $P(A|B)$, $P(B)$, and $P(A)$.

Event A is the error making the block, Event B is that the old machine made the block, $P(A|B)$ is the error rate of the old machine (0.007), $P(B)$ is the probability the old machine made the block (0.25), and $P(A)$ is $0.75 \cdot 0.003 + 0.25 \cdot 0.007 = 0.004$.

$$P(B|A) = \frac{P(A|B)P(B)}{P(A)} \quad \text{Bayes's Theorem}$$

$$P(\text{old machine}|\text{bad block}) = \frac{0.007 \cdot 0.25}{0.004} \quad \text{Substitute known probabilities}$$

$$P(\text{old machine}|\text{bad block}) = 0.4375 = 43.75\%$$

Given that the probability that a bad block is made by the old machine is less than 50%, Rhonda should not blame the old machine for the bad block.

SCAFFOLDING SUPPORT

- Students will find Bayes' Theorem useful in completing the Performance Task:
$$P(A|B) = \frac{P(B|A) \cdot P(A)}{P(B|A) \cdot P(A) + P(B|\sim A) \cdot P(\sim A)}$$
- If students have trouble using Bayes' Theorem, suggest that they make a two-way table instead, divided into "Test Positive" and "Test Negative" on one side, and "Has Illness" and "Doesn't Have Illness" on the other. Suggest that they use a total of 100,000 patients and fill out the cells using the percentages given in the problem.

EXERCISES

Determine whether the method of awarding a prize is fair. Explain. If it is not fair, describe a way that would be fair. *(Lesson 21.1)*

1. A teacher gives a ticket to each student who earns a 90 or above on any homework assignment. At the end of each week, the teacher draws from the ticket jar and gives the winning student a free homework pass for the next week.

Possible answer: This method of giving out tickets is not fair because it favors the students who make higher grades. A more fair way of distributing tickets would be giving a ticket to any student who turned in homework, regardless of the grade on the assignment.

Suppose that a card dealing machine has a probability of 23% for pulling a face card. An older machine has a 14% chance of pulling a face card. Use Bayes's Theorem to find the probability. *(Lesson 21.2)*

2. If each machine is used 50% of the time, and a face card is the next card drawn, what is the probability the new machine drew the card?

$$P(B|A) = \frac{0.23 \cdot 0.5}{0.185} \approx 0.622 = 62.2\%$$

MODULE PERFORMANCE TASK

What's the Diagnosis?

Lenny works in a factory that makes cleaning products. Lately he has been suffering from headaches. He asks his doctor if the chemicals used in the factory might be responsible for his headaches. The doctor performs a blood test that is routinely used to diagnose the kind of illness Lenny is concerned about.

Use the following facts to gauge the probability that Lenny has the illness if he tests positive:

1. The test has a reliability rate of 85 percent.
2. The test has a false positive rate of 8 percent.
3. The illness affects 2 percent of people who are Lenny's age and who work in conditions similar to those he works in.

Start by listing on your own paper the information you will need to solve the problem. Then complete the task. Use numbers, words, or algebra to explain how you reached your conclusion.

SAMPLE SOLUTION

Apply Bayes' Theorem. Let $P(A)$ represent the probability that Lenny has the illness and let $P(B)$ represent the probability that the text was positive.

$$P(A|B) = \frac{P(B|A) \cdot P(A)}{P(B|A) \cdot P(A) + P(B|\sim A) \cdot P(\sim A)}$$

$$= \frac{0.85 \times 0.03}{0.85 \times 0.03 + 0.08 \times 0.97}$$

$$= \frac{0.0255}{0.0255 + 0.0776}$$

$$= \frac{0.0255}{0.1031}$$

$$\approx 0.247$$

The probability that Lenny has the illness is about 24.7%.

Alternatively, fill out a table, using a total of 100,000 patients who have taken the test:

	Has Illness	Doesn't Have Illness	Total
Test Positive	2,550	7,760	10,310
Test Negative	450	89,240	89,690
Total	3,000	97,000	100,000

In this case, the answer 24.7% is found by dividing 2,550 (the number testing positive who have the illness) by 10,310 (the total number testing positive).

DISCUSSION OPPORTUNITIES

- Ask students to comment on the surprising fact that Lenny's chances of having the illness are only about 25%, even though the test has a seemingly high reliability rate of 85%. **Sample answer: Along with the reliability rate, the false positive rate and the fact that only 2% of people who share Lenny's age and working conditions have the illness both have major effects on the probability that Lenny also has the illness.**

Assessment Rubric

2 points: Student correctly solves the problem and explains his/her reasoning.

1 point: Student shows good understanding of the problem but does not fully solve or explain.

0 points: Student does not demonstrate understanding of the problem.

Ready to Go On?

ASSESS MASTERY

Use the assessment on this page to determine if students have mastered the concepts and standards covered in this module.

ASSESSMENT AND INTERVENTION

Access Ready to Go On? assessment online, and receive instant scoring, feedback, and customized intervention or enrichment.

ADDITIONAL RESOURCES

Response to Intervention Resources

- Reteach Worksheets

Differentiated Instruction Resources

- Reading Strategies EL
- Success for English Learners EL
- Challenge Worksheets

Assessment Resources

- Leveled Module Quizzes

22.1–22.2 Probability and Decision Making

- Online Homework
- Hints and Help
- Extra Practice

Determine whether the method of awarding a prize is fair. Explain briefly.

1. Prize to every 500th customer

Not fair; not everyone can be 500th.

2. Ticket to every customer; drawing

Fair, every customer has a chance.

3. Choose number 1–10; draw number

Fair, each number has equal chance.

4. Ticket to all cars; two to red cars

Not fair; red cars have a higher chance.

Rodney's Repair Service has a lug nut tightening machine that works well 89% of the time. They got a new machine that works well 98% of the time. Each machine is used 50% of the time. Use Bayes's Theorem to find each probability.

5. new machine malfunctioned

$P(B|A) = \frac{0.02 \cdot 0.5}{0.065} \approx 0.154 = 15.4\%$

6. old machine malfunctioned

$P(B|A) = \frac{0.11 \cdot 0.5}{0.065} \approx 0.846 = 84.6\%$

7. old machine worked well

$P(B|A) = \frac{0.89 \cdot 0.5}{0.935} \approx 0.476 = 47.6\%$

8. new machine worked well

$P(B|A) = \frac{0.98 \cdot 0.5}{0.935} \approx 0.524 = 52.4\%$

ESSENTIAL QUESTION

9. How can probability and decision making help the organizer of a raffle?

Possible answer: The organizer of the raffle can make decisions about whether the raffle is fair or not fair. If it is not fair, they can find ways to make the raffle more fair, so more people will be willing to participate.

COMMON CORE Common Core Standards

Lesson	Exercise	Math Standards	Mathematical Practices
21.1	1	**S-MD.B.6**	**MP.6**
21.1	2	**S-MD.B.6**	**MP.6**
21.1	3	**S-MD.B.6**	**MP.6**
21.1	4	**S-MD.B.6**	**MP.6**
21.2	5–8	**S-CP.A.5**	**MP.2**

MODULE 21
MIXED REVIEW

Assessment Readiness

1. Consider the situation. Is the method of awarding the prize fair?

Select Yes or No for **A–C.**

A. Ticket for every \$10 spent — ● Yes ○ No
B. Coupon for every 10 guests — ○ Yes ● No
C. Entry for every mile driven — ○ Yes ● No

2. Consider the situation of having four tiles in a bag spelling M-A-T-H drawn randomly without replacement. Choose True or False for each statement.

A. There is one way to draw all 4 tiles from the bag, if order doesn't matter. — ● True ○ False
B. There are six ways to draw 2 tiles from the bag, if order matters. — ○ True ● False
C. There are twenty four ways to draw 3 tiles from the bag if order matters. — ● True ○ False

3. The band class has two trumpet players. Of the two, the first trumpet player plays a wrong note 4% of the time, and the second trumpet player plays a wrong note 9% of the time. If one song has the first trumpet player playing 75% of the song, and the second trumpet player playing the rest, use Bayes's Theorem to find the probability that a wrong note was played by the second trumpet. Explain whether your answer makes sense.

$P(B|A) = \frac{0.09 \cdot 0.25}{0.0525} \approx 0.429 = 42.9\%$; **Possible answer: It does make sense, because the trumpet player making the most mistakes plays much less of the time, so it would be less likely that the mistake would come from the second trumpet player.**

4. Gerald says that the sequence 4, 16, 64, 256,… can be described by the rule $2 \cdot 2^n = 4^n$. Describe and correct his mistake.

The geometric sequence that would describe the sequence is 4^n, but not $2 \cdot 2^n$. Since the order of operations evaluates exponents first, the 2 and 2 cannot be multiplied to make 4.

Common Core Standards

Lesson	Items	Content Standards	Mathematical Practices
21.1	1	S-MD.B.6	MP.1
19.2, 19.3	2*	S-CP.B.9	MP.2
21.2	3	S-CP.A.5	MP.4
12.2	4*	F-BF.A.2	MP.3

* Item integrates mixed review concepts from previous modules or a previous course.

MIXED REVIEW
Assessment Readiness

ASSESSMENT AND INTERVENTION

Assign ready-made or customized practice tests to prepare students for high-stakes tests.

ADDITIONAL RESOURCES

Assessment Resources

- Leveled Module Quizzes: Modified, B

AVOID COMMON ERRORS

Item 1 Some students have a hard time considering the concept of fairness objectively and will only consider what they personally would consider fair. Remind students that they must use the mathematical definition of fairness to answer correctly.

MIXED REVIEW

Assessment Readiness

ASSESSMENT AND INTERVENTION

Assign ready-made or customized practice tests to prepare students for high-stakes tests.

ADDITIONAL RESOURCES

Assessment Resources

- Leveled Unit Tests: Modified, A, B, C
- Performance Assessment

AVOID COMMON ERRORS

Item 3 Some students will not recognize that drawing the cards are dependent events. Remind students to look for the words "with replacement" for independent events using cards. If the words are not present, it is likely the event is dependent.

UNIT 8 MIXED REVIEW

Assessment Readiness

- Online Homework
- Hints and Help
- Extra Practice

1. Figure *ABCDE* is similar to figure *LMNOP*. Select True or False for each mathematical statement.

A. $\frac{BC}{AE} = \frac{MN}{OP}$ ○ True ● False

B. $\frac{AB}{DE} = \frac{LM}{OP}$ ● True ○ False

C. $\frac{BD}{AE} = \frac{MN}{LP}$ ○ True ● False

2. The transformation $(x, y) \rightarrow (x - 2, y + 1)$ is applied to $\triangle XYZ$. Select True or False for each statement.

A. The area of $\triangle X'Y'Z'$ is the same as the area of $\triangle XYZ$. ● True ○ False

B. The distance from X to X' is equal to the distance from Z to Z'. ● True ○ False

C. The transformation is a rotation. ○ True ● False

3. Does each scenario describe independent events? Select Yes or No for each situation.

A. Drawing two cards from a standard deck of cards that are both aces ○ Yes ● No

B. Rolling a fair number cube twice and getting 6 on both rolls ● Yes ○ No

C. Rolling a 3 on a fair number cube and flipping tails on a fair coin ● Yes ○ No

4. Each student in a class has been assigned at random to draw a parallelogram, a rectangle, a rhombus, or a square. Select True or False for each statement about the likelihood that a student will draw a parallelogram.

A. It is unlikely, but not certain, because the probability is less than 0.5. ○ True ● False

B. It is likely, but not certain, because the probability is more than 0.5. ○ True ● False

C. It is impossible for it not to happen because the probability is 1. ● True ○ False

5. The event A and B are independent. Select True or False for each statement.

A. $P(A \mid B) = P(B \mid A)$ ○ True ● False

B. $P(A \text{ and } B) = P(B) \cdot P(A)$ ● True ○ False

C. $P(A) = P(B)$ ○ True ● False

Common Core Standards

Items	Content Standards	Mathematical Practices
1	G-SRT.A.2	MP.5
2	G-SRT.A.2	MP.6
3*	S-CP.A.2	MP.3, MP.8
4*	S-CP.B.6	MP.3, MP.8
5	S-CP.A.3	MP.2, MP.7
6	S-CP.B.9	MP.2, MP.7

* Item integrates mixed review concepts from previous modules or a previous course.

6. Vera needs to place 15 student volunteers at a local fire station. Five students will wash fire trucks, 7 will be assigned to paint, and 3 will be assigned to wash windows. What is the number of possible job assignments expressed using factorials and as a simplified number?

$\frac{15!}{5! \cdot 7! \cdot 3!}$ or $\frac{15!}{10! \cdot 5!} \cdot \frac{10!}{3! \cdot 7!} \cdot \frac{3!}{0! \cdot 3!}$; 360,360 assignments

7. The table below shows the number of days that a meteorologist predicted it would be sunny and the number of days it was sunny. Based on the data in the table, what is the conditional probability that it will be sunny on a day when the meteorologist predicts it will be sunny? Show your work.

	Sunny	Not Sunny	Total
Predicts Sunny	570	20	590
Does Not Predict Sun	63	347	410
Total	633	367	1000

$\frac{570}{590} \approx 0.966$ or 97%

8. Complete the two-way table below. Then find the fraction of red cards in a standard 52-card deck that have a number on them and find the fraction of numbered cards that are red.

	Red	Black	Total
Number	18	18	36
No Number	8	8	16
Total	26	26	52

Red cards with numbers on them: $\frac{9}{13}$

Numbered cards that are red: $\frac{1}{2}$

Performance Tasks

★ 9. Sixteen cards numbered 1 through 16 are placed face down, and Stephanie chooses one at random. What is the probability that the number on Stephanie's card is less than 5 or greater than 10? Show your work.

The cards that are less than 5: $\{1, 2, 3, 4\}$

The cards that are greater than 10: $\{11, 12, 13, 14, 15, 16\}$

Total number of cards that are either less than 5 or greater than 10: 10

$\frac{10}{16} = \frac{5}{8}$ or about 62.5%

Common Core Standards

Items	Content Standards	Mathematical Practices
7	**S-CP.A.4**	**MP.2, MP.7**
8	**S-CP.A.4**	**MP.1**

* Item integrates mixed review concepts from previous modules or a previous course.

PERFORMANCE TASKS

There are three different levels of performance tasks:

***Novice:** These are short word problems that require students to apply the math they have learned in straightforward, real-world situations.

****Apprentice:** These are more involved problems that guide students step-by-step through more complex tasks. These exercises include more complicated reasoning, writing, and open ended elements.

*****Expert:** These are open-ended, nonroutine problems that, instead of stepping the students through, ask them to choose their own methods for solving and justify their answers and reasoning.

SCORING GUIDES

Item 9 (2 points) Award the student 1 point for the correct answer of $\frac{5}{8}$, and 1 point for showing work.

Item 10 (6 points)

2 points for correct probability for comedies given Class B

2 points for correct probability for Class B given comedies

1 point for explanation

1 point for showing work

Item 11 (6 points)

a. 1 point for correct answers
   1 point for explanation

b. 1 point for correct answer
   1 point for explanation

c. 1 point for correct answer
   1 point for explanation

★★**10.** Students in 4 different classes are surveyed about their favorite movie type. What is the possibility that a randomly selected student in class B prefers comedies? What is the probability that a randomly selected student who prefers comedies is in B class? Explain why the two probabilities are not the same. Show your work.

	A	B	C	D
Action	12	9	8	11
Comedy	13	11	15	4
Drama	6	11	7	18

Total in class B $= 9 + 11 + 11 = 31$

$P(\text{comedies B} \mid \text{class B}) = \frac{11}{31} \approx 35.5\%$

Total that prefer comedies $= 13 + 11 + 15 + 4 = 43$

$P(\text{class B} \mid \text{comedies}) = \frac{11}{43} \approx 25.6\%$

The conditional probabilities are different because the sample spaces are different, with 31 in class B and 43 that prefer comedies.

★★★**11.** A Chinese restaurant has a buffet that includes ice cream for dessert. The table shows the selections made last week.

	Chocolate	Vanilla	Strawberry
Cone	24	18	12
Dish	12	21	15

A. Which flavor is the most popular? Which serving method? Is the combination of the most popular flavor and serving method the most popular dessert choice overall? Explain.

B. Which of the following is more likely? Explain.
- A customer chooses vanilla, given that the customer chose a cone.
- A customer chooses a cone, given that the customer chose vanilla?

C. A class of 24 students gets the buffet for lunch. If they all get ice cream, about how many will get a cone or vanilla? Explain.

A. The most popular are vanilla and cone because they have the largest marginal frequencie

No, the most popular dessert choice is a chocolate cone and not a vanilla cone.

B. $P(\text{vanilla} \mid \text{cone}) = \frac{18}{24 + 18 + 12} \approx 33\%$

$P(\text{cone} \mid \text{vanilla}) = \frac{18}{18 + 21} \approx 46\%$

So a customer chooses a cone, given that the customer chose vanilla is more likely because 46% > 33%.

C. about 18 students because 75 out of 102 is about 73.5%. 73.5% of 24 students is about 18

MATH IN CAREERS

Epidemiologist An epidemiologist is aiding in the treatment of a community plagued by two different infectious agents, X and Z. Each infectious agent must be treated differently with a new treatment if the patient has been infected by both agents. The community has a total population of 15,000 people, where 5% are healthy and 60% are afflicted by the X infection. Unfortunately, the treatment for the X infection fails 35% of the time. The same incident happened to 10 other communities with similar results as the first. What is the probability that people will be healthy? have the X affliction? have the Z affliction? have both afflictions?

Healthy people: 5%, X affliction: 60%, Z affliction: 56%, both: 21%

MATH IN CAREERS

Epidemiologist In this Unit Performance Task, students can see how an epidemiologist uses mathematics on the job.

For more information about careers in mathematics as well as various mathematics appreciation topics, visit the American Mathematical Society http://www.ams.org

SCORING GUIDES

Task (6 points)

2 points for correct probability of X affliction

2 points for correct probability of Z affliction

1 point for correct probability of health

1 point for correct probability of both afflictions

UNIT 9

Statistics

CONTENTS

Unit Pacing Guide

45-Minute Classes

Module 22

DAY 1	DAY 2	DAY 3	DAY 4
Lesson 22.1	**Lesson 22.1**	**Lesson 22.2**	Module Review and Assessment Readiness

Module 23

DAY 1	DAY 2	DAY 3	DAY 4	DAY 5
Lesson 23.1	**Lesson 23.1**	**Lesson 23.2**	**Lesson 23.2**	**Lesson 23.3**

DAY 6
Module Review and Assessment Readiness

Module 24

DAY 1	DAY 2	DAY 3	DAY 4	DAY 5
Lesson 24.1	**Lesson 24.1**	**Lesson 24.2**	**Lesson 24.3**	Module Review and Assessment Readiness

DAY 6
Unit Review and Assessment Readiness

90-Minute Classes

Module 22

DAY 1	DAY 2
Lesson 22.1	**Lesson 22.2** Module Review and Assessment Readiness

Module 23

DAY 1	DAY 2	DAY 3
Lesson 23.1	**Lesson 23.2**	**Lesson 23.3** Module Review and Assessment Readiness

Module 24

DAY 1	DAY 2	DAY 3
Lesson 24.1	**Lesson 24.2** **Lesson 24.3**	Module Review and Assessment Readiness Unit Review and Assessment Readiness

Program Resources

PLAN

HMH Teacher App

Access a full suite of teacher resources online and offline on a variety of devices. Plan present, and manage classes, assignments, and activities.

ePlanner **Easily plan your classes, create and view assignments, and access all program resources with your online, customizable planning tool.**

Professional Development Videos

Authors Juli Dixon and Matt Larson model successful teaching practices and strategies in actual classroom settings.

QR Codes **Scan with your smart phone to jump directly from your print book to online videos and other resources.**

Teacher's Edition

Support students with point-of-use Questioning Strategies, teaching tips, resources for differentiated instruction, additional activities, and more.

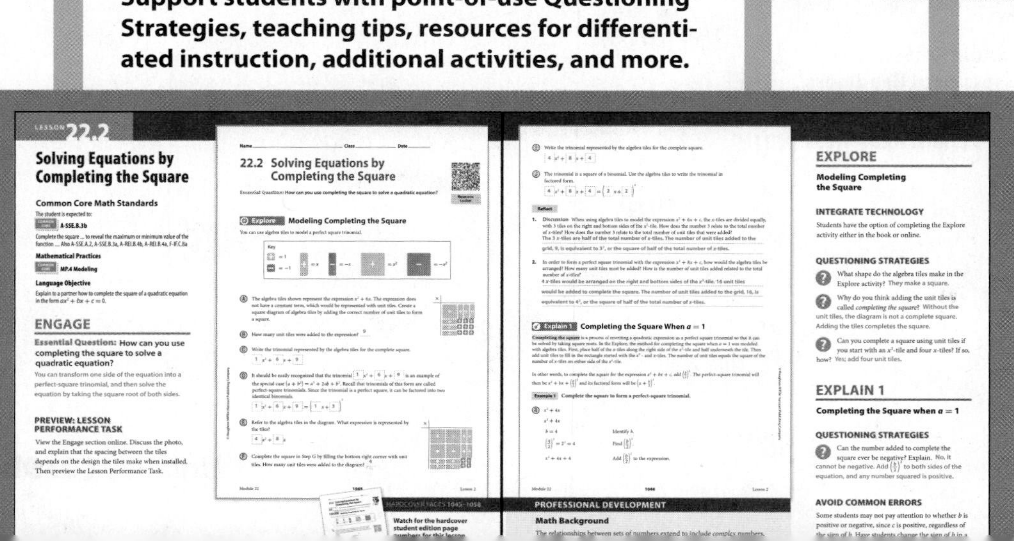

ENGAGE AND EXPLORE

Real-World Videos **Engage students with interesting and relevant applications of the mathematical content of each module.**

Explore Activities

Students interactively explore new concepts using a variety of tools and approaches.

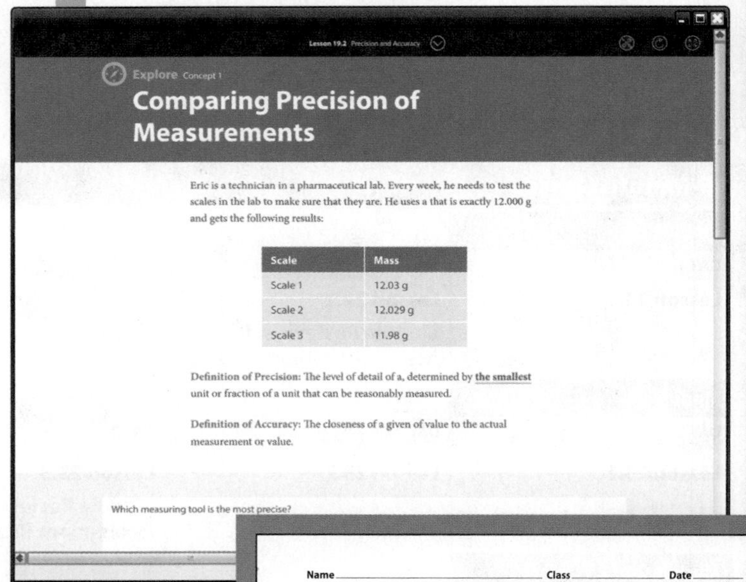
Lesson 19.2 Precision and Accuracy
Explore Concept 1
Comparing Precision of Measurements
Eric is a technician in a pharmaceutical lab. Every week, he needs to test the scales in the lab to make sure that they are. He uses a that is exactly 12.000 g and gets the following results:
Scale | Mass
Scale 1 | 12.03 g
Scale 2 | 12.029 g
Scale 3 | 11.98 g
Definition of Precision: The level of detail of a, determined by the smallest unit or fraction of a unit that can be reasonably measured.
Definition of Accuracy: The closeness of a given of value to the actual measurement or value.
Which measuring tool is the most precise?

Name ____ Class ____ Date ____

22.2 Solving Equations by Completing the Square

Essential Question: How can you use completing the square to solve a quadratic equation?

A-SSE.B.3b Complete the square ... to reveal the maximum or minimum value of the function ... Also A-SSE.A.2, A-SSE.B.3a, A-REI.B.4b, A-REI.B.4a, F-IF.C.8a

Explore **Modeling Completing the Square**

You can use algebra tiles to model a perfect square trinomial.

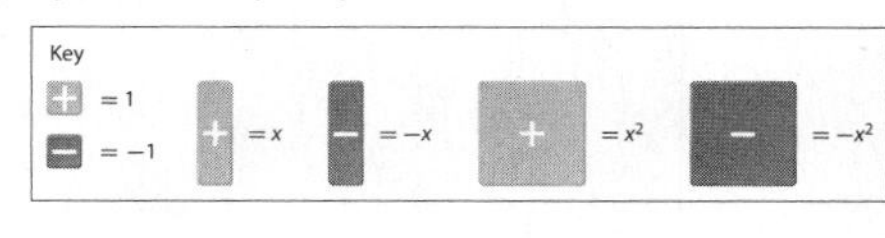
Key
= 1
= −1
= x
= −x
= x²
= −x²

(A) The algebra tiles shown represent the expression $x^2 + 6x$. The expression does not have a constant term, which would be represented with unit tiles. Create a square diagram of algebra tiles by adding the correct number of unit tiles to form a square.

(B) How many unit tiles were added to the expression? ____

(C) Write the trinomial represented by the algebra tiles for the complete square.

$\square x^2 + \square x + \square$

(D) It should be easily recognized that the trinomial $\square x^2 + \square x + \square$ is an example of the special case $(a + b)^2 = a^2 + 2ab + b^2$. Recall that trinomials of this form are called

TEACH

Math On the Spot video tutorials, featuring program authors Dr. Edward Burger and Martha Sandoval-Martinez, accompany every example in the textbook and give students step-by-step instructions and explanations of key math concepts.

Interactive Teacher Edition

Customize and present course materials with collaborative activities and integrated formative assessment.

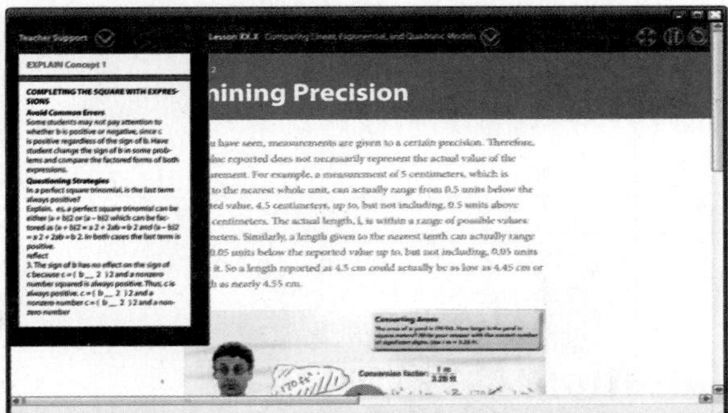

Differentiated Instruction Resources

Support all learners with Differentiated Instruction Resources, including

- **Leveled Practice and Problem Solving**
- **Reading Strategies**
- **Success for English Learners**
- **Challenge**

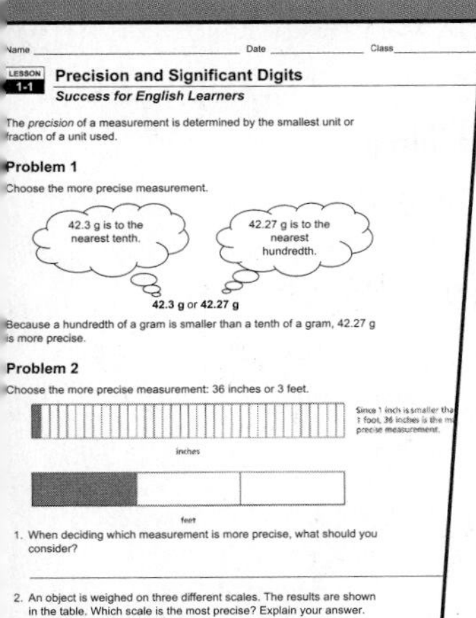

Name ______ Date ______ Class ______

LESSON 1-1 **Precision and Significant Digits**
Success for English Learners

The *precision* of a measurement is determined by the smallest unit or fraction of a unit used.

Problem 1

Choose the more precise measurement.

42.3 g is to the nearest tenth.

42.27 g is to the nearest hundredth.

42.3 g or **42.27 g**

Because a hundredth of a gram is smaller than a tenth of a gram, 42.27 g is more precise.

Problem 2

Choose the more precise measurement: 36 inches or 3 feet.

Since 1 inch is smaller than 1 foot, 36 inches is the more precise measurement.

inches

feet

1. When deciding which measurement is more precise, what should you consider?

2. An object is weighed on three different scales. The results are shown in the table. Which scale is the most precise? Explain your answer.

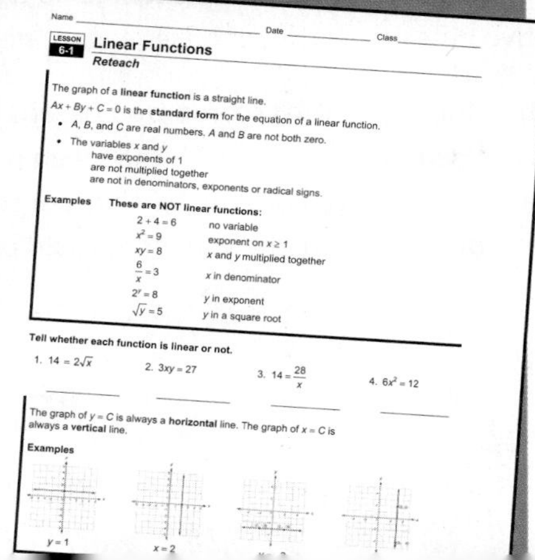

Name ______ Date ______ Class ______

LESSON 6-1 **Linear Functions**
Reteach

The graph of a **linear function** is a straight line.

$Ax + By + C = 0$ is the **standard form** for the equation of a linear function.

- A, B, and C are real numbers. A and B are not both zero.
- The variables x and y
  - have exponents of 1
  - are not multiplied together
  - are not in denominators, exponents or radical signs.

Examples **These are NOT linear functions:**

$2 + 4 = 6$	no variable
$x^2 = 9$	exponent on $x \geq 1$
$xy = 8$	x and y multiplied together
$\frac{6}{x} = 3$	x in denominator
$2^y = 8$	y in exponent
$\sqrt{y} = 5$	y in a square root

Tell whether each function is linear or not.

1. $14 = 2\sqrt{x}$
2. $3xy = 27$
3. $14 = \frac{28}{x}$
4. $6x^2 = 12$

The graph of $y = C$ is always a **horizontal** line. The graph of $x = C$ is always a **vertical** line.

Examples

$y = 1$ $x = 2$

ASSESSMENT AND INTERVENTION

The Personal Math Trainer provides online practice, homework, assessments, and intervention. Monitor student progress through reports and alerts. Create and customize assignments aligned to specific lessons or Common Core standards.

- **Practice** – With dynamic items and assignments, students get unlimited practice on key concepts supported by guided examples, step-by-step solutions, and video tutorials.
- **Assessments** – Choose from course assignments or customize your own based on course content, Common Core standards, difficulty levels, and more.
- **Homework** – Students can complete online homework with a wide variety of problem types, including the ability to enter expressions, equations, and graphs. Let the system automatically grade homework, so you can focus where your students need help the most!
- **Intervention** – Let the Personal Math Trainer automatically prescribe a targeted, personalized intervention path for your students.

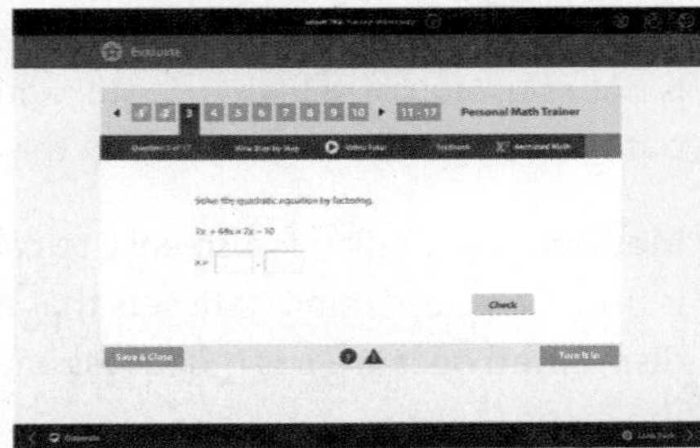

Focus on Higher Order Thinking

Raise the bar with homework and practice that incorporates higher-order thinking and mathematical practices in every lesson.

Assessment Readiness

Prepare students for success on high stakes tests for Algebra 2 with practice at every module and unit

Assessment Resources

Tailor assessments and response to intervention to meet the needs of all your classes and students, including

- Leveled Module Quizzes
- Leveled Unit Tests
- Unit Performance Tasks
- Placement, Diagnostic, and Quarterly Benchmark Tests
- Tier 1, Tier 2, and Tier 3 Resources

Math Background

Mean, Median, and Mode  S-ID.A.2

LESSON 22.2

The *measures of central tendency*—mean, median, and mode—are three ways of summarizing a data set by using a single value. With this goal in mind, students may wonder which measure best represents a particular set of data. Although there is no definitive answer to this question, there are cases in which one measure is clearly more effective at describing a data set than the others. Some general guidelines for choosing a measure to describe a data set can be established.

Mean: The mean (or average) takes every data value into account, is easy to calculate, and works well for describing data sets that are normally distributed. (In a data set that is normally distributed, the graph of the distribution is a bell-shaped curve with the mean at the center.) The mean is not as useful for sets that contain outliers because the outliers can have a large effect on the mean.

Median: The median is also easy to calculate. The median is useful for describing data sets that are not normally distributed because it is much less affected by outliers than the mean.

Mode: The mode is useful when the frequency of data values is important or when the data cluster around multiple values. Among the mean, median, and mode, only the mode can be used to summarize a set of non-numerical data, such as favorite colors.

Each measure provides a slightly different perspective on a data set. The clearest understanding of a dataset is generally obtained when all three measures are considered as a group.

Students should recognize that the mean of a data set need not be one of the data values. The same is true of the median. For example, the data set {10, 20} has a mean and median of 15. On the other hand, the mode, if it exists, must be one of the values in the data set.

Variability 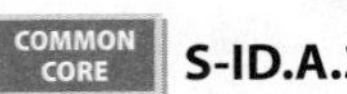 S-ID.A.3

LESSON 22.2

The mean, median, and mode are all ways to describe the "typical" value in a data set. It is also useful to describe the *variability*, or spread, of a data set. The simplest way to quantify variability is with the range.

The *range* of a data set is *the difference between the greatest and least values in the set*. Consider the two data sets shown below. Both have a mean, median, and mode of 5. However, the values in data set B are more spread out, and this is reflected in the fact that the data set has a greater range. The range of data set B is 6, compared with a range of 2 for data set A.

Data Set *A*

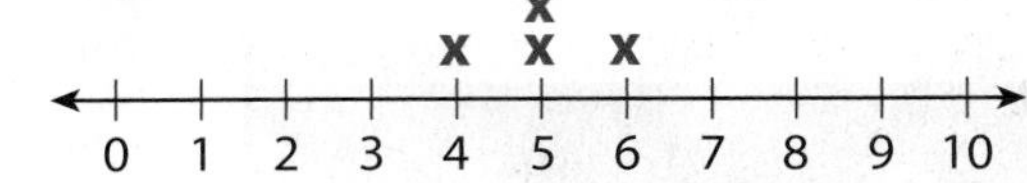

Data Set *B*

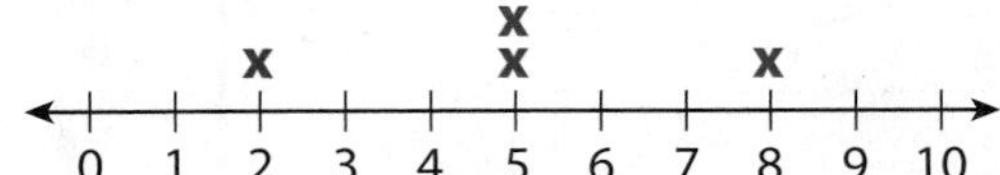

Measures of Variation  S-ID.A.3

LESSON 22.2

A measure of variation describes the spread of a data set. Two of the most useful measures in statistics are the variance and the standard deviation.

Given a set of numerical data, the *variance*, σ_2, is *the average of the squared differences from the mean*.

The differences from the mean are squared so that positive and negative differences do not offset each other.

Suppose the number of runs scored by a baseball team in six games is given by {0, 3, 1, 5, 6, 3}. The mean number of runs is 3 and the variance is about 4.3. Without squaring the differences from the mean, the variance would be 0.

In calculating variance, squaring the differences from the mean may amplify the effect of large differences. To compensate for this and to arrive at a measure of variance more in keeping with the scale of the original data values, statisticians also calculate standard deviation.

The *standard deviation*, σ, is the square root of the variance. Because the standard deviation "undoes" the squaring in the variance, the standard deviation has the same units as the values in the data set.

Probability Distributions  S-MD.A.2

LESSON 23.1

If all possible outcomes of an experiment can be expressed as numbers, then the *probability distribution* of the experiment is *a function that pairs each outcome with its probability.*

For example, the probability distribution for rolling a number cube is $P(X) = \frac{1}{6}$, where the input X may be the outcome 1, 2, 3, 4, 5, or 6.

Probability distributions obey all the rules of probability. That is, for any X, $0 \leq P(X) \leq 1$ and the sum of all the probabilities $P(X)$ over all possible values of X is 1.

If X can take the values $x_1, x_2, \ldots, x_n$ and the corresponding probabilities are $p_1, p_2, \ldots, p_n$, then the expected value for the experiment is $x_1p_1 + x_2p_2 + \ldots + x_np_n$.
The expected value for rolling a number cube is

$$1\left(\frac{1}{6}\right) + 2\left(\frac{1}{6}\right) + 3\left(\frac{1}{6}\right) + 4\left(\frac{1}{6}\right) + 5\left(\frac{1}{6}\right) + 6\left(\frac{1}{6}\right) = \frac{21}{6} = 3.5.$$

The expected value, 3.5, is the average outcome over a large number of trials. In this sense, it is the "typical" value you expect to roll. As this example shows, the expected value need not be one of the possible outcomes of the experiment.

Probability distributions can be based on either discrete or continuous data. Binomial distributions are discrete probability distributions because there are a finite number of possible outcomes. In a continuous probability distribution, the outcome can be any real number—for example, the time it takes to complete a task.

Normal Distributions 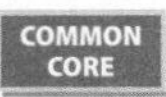 S-ID.A.4

LESSON 23.2

You may be familiar with the bell-shaped curve called *the normal curve.* A *normal distribution* is a *function of the mean and standard deviation of a data set that assigns probabilities to intervals of real numbers associated with continuous random variables.*

The probability assigned to a real-number interval is the area under the normal curve in that interval. Because the area under the curve represents probability, the total area under the curve is 1.

Students should become familiar with the following properties of the normal curve.

- The maximum value of a normal curve occurs at the mean.
- The normal curve is symmetric about a vertical line through the mean.
- The normal curve has a horizontal asymptote at $y = 0$.

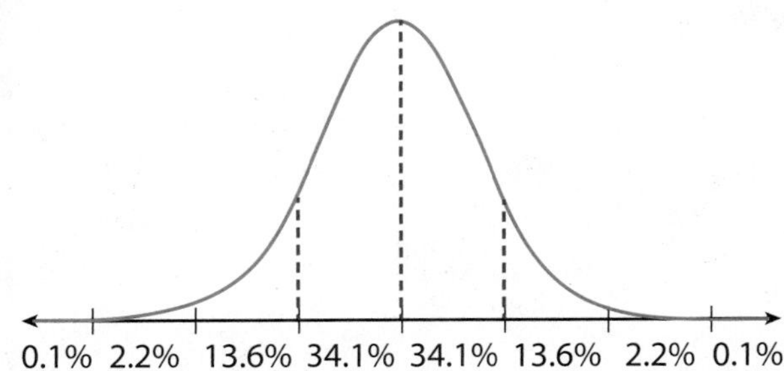

The figure shows the percent of data in a normal distribution that falls within a number of standard deviations from the mean.

The figure shows the following:

- About 68% lie within 1 standard deviation of the mean.
- About 95% lie within 2 standard deviations of the mean.
- More than 99.7% lie within 3 standard deviations of the mean.

UNIT 9

Statistics

MATH IN CAREERS

Unit Activity Preview

After completing this unit, students will complete a Math in Careers task by performing a statistical hypothesis test. Critical skills include writing a null hypothesis, creating visual representations of data, and proving or disproving the null hypothesis.

For more information about careers in mathematics as well as various mathematics appreciation topics, visit The American Mathematical Society at http://www.ams.org.

UNIT 9

Statistics

MODULE 22
Gathering and Displaying Data

MODULE 23
Data Distributions

MODULE 24
Making Inferences from Data

MATH IN CAREERS

Pharmaceutical Scientist
Pharmaceutical scientists work in a variety of capacities, such as inventing and synthesizing new drugs, creating dosage delivery systems, and studying how a particular drug interacts in a living organism. They also design and conduct clinical trials to test the efficacy of novel medications. Pharmaceutical scientists make use of algebra, calculus, and differential equations to model and interpret the effects of a drug and the drug's rate of decay in the body. They also use statistics to help make informed decisions about a medication's usefulness.

If you are interested in a career as a pharmaceutical scientist, you should study these mathematical subjects:

- Algebra
- Statistics
- Calculus
- Differential Equations

Check out the career activity at the end of the unit to find out how **Pharmaceutical Scientists** use math.

TRACKING YOUR LEARNING PROGRESSION

Before	In this Unit	After
Students understand: • probability and set theory • permutations and combinations • independent and dependent events • using probability to make fair decisions	Students will learn about: • statistics • gathering and displaying data • shape, center, and spread • data distributions • confidence intervals and margins of error	Students will study: • simulating distributions • significance tests • hypothesis testing

Reading Start-Up

Visualize Vocabulary

Match the review words to their descriptions to complete the chart.

Word	Description
binomial experiment	A probability experiment with a fixed number of independent trials in which each outcome falls into exactly one of two categories
normal distribution	A bell shaped probability distribution
binomial probability	In a binomial experiment, the probability of r successes $(0 \leq r \leq n)$ is $p(r) = {}_nC_r \cdot p^r q^{n-r}$, with probability of success p and probability of failure q and $p + q = 1$

Vocabulary

Review Words

✔ binomial experiment *(experimento binomial)*
✔ binomial probability *(probabilidad binomial)*
✔ normal distribution *(distribución normal)*

Preview Words

biased sample *(muestra no representativa)*
margin of error *(margen de error)*
null hypothesis *(hipótesis nula)*
observational study *(estudio de observación)*
population *(población)*
probability distribution *(distribución de probabilidad)*
sample *(muestra)*
standard normal value *(valor normal estándar)*
statistic *(estadística)*

Understand Vocabulary

To become familiar with some of the vocabulary terms in the module, consider the following. You may refer to the module, the glossary, or a dictionary.

1. A number that describes a sample is a ___statistic___.
2. A ___biased sample___ does not fairly represent the population.
3. A ___sample___ is a part of the population.
4. The ___null hypothesis___ is an assumption in statistics that there is no difference between the two groups being tested.

Active Reading

Key-Term Fold Before beginning each module in this unit, create a key-term fold to help you learn the definitions in each lesson. Each tab can contain a key term on one side and its definition on the other. When possible, include an example with the definition. Use the key-term fold to quiz yourself on the definitions of the key terms in the unit.

Reading Start Up

Have students complete the activities on this page by working alone or with others.

VISUALIZE VOCABULARY

The information graphic helps students review vocabulary associated with a binomial experiment and binomial probability.

UNDERSTAND VOCABULARY

Use the following explanations to help students learn the preview words.

Binomial experiments are used to model real-world situations in which there are two discrete possible outcomes.

A **sample** is part of a **population**, which is any set of individuals or objects of interest. Samples are used because collecting data on each member in a sample can be time-consuming and expensive. A **biased sample** is not representative of the population. **Statistics** are measures that summarize data, and statistics for a biased sample can be misleading. In science, a hypothesis is an educated guess that guides inquiry. In statistics, a **null hypothesis** is an assumption that can be tested and proved or disproved.

ACTIVE READING

Students can use these reading and note-taking strategies to help them organize and understand the new vocabulary in the unit.

ADDITIONAL RESOURCES

Differentiated Instruction

- Reading Strategies 

Gathering and Displaying Data

ESSENTIAL QUESTION:

Answer: Collecting data in a biased way leads to unreliable results. Displaying data, such as seasonal shifts in customer spending, in charts or graphs gives the retailer a quick understanding of when to prepare for a busy season.

PROFESSIONAL DEVELOPMENT VIDEO

Professional Development Video
Author Matt Larson models successful teaching practices in an actual high-school classroom.
Professional Development
my.hrw.com

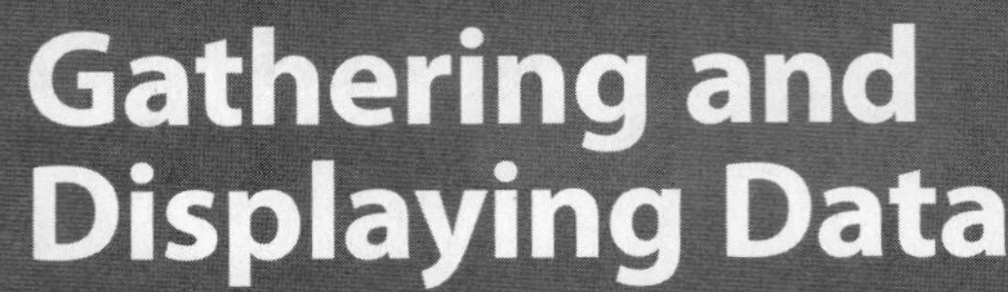
Gathering and
Displaying Data

MODULE 22

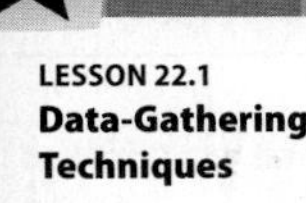

Essential Question: How can gathering and displaying data help to solve real-world problems?

REAL WORLD VIDEO
Unlike packaged foods, fresh fruit and vegetables do not have nutrition labels. Check out some ways we can gather and analyze nutrition data for fresh produce.

MODULE PERFORMANCE TASK PREVIEW

Fruit Nutrition Data

Good nutrition is especially important while you are still growing. You can achieve good nutrition by monitoring the nutrients that you eat. You already know to eat plenty of fruits and vegetables, but how do the nutrients in, say, a pear compare with those of a peach? You've heard that you can't compare apples and oranges, but later on, that's exactly what we'll be doing!

DIGITAL TEACHER EDITION

Access a full suite of teaching resources when and where you need them:

- Access content online or offline
- Customize lessons to share with your class
- Communicate with your students in real-time
- View student grades and data instantly to target your instruction where it is needed most

PERSONAL MATH TRAINER

Assessment and Intervention

Assign automatically graded homework, quizzes, tests, and intervention activities. Prepare your students with updated, Common Core-aligned practice tests.

Are YOU Ready?

Complete these exercises to review skills you will need for this chapter.

- Online Homework
- Hints and Help
- Extra Practice

Two-Way Tables

Example 1 The table shows the number of tickets sold for seats in the four areas of the local playhouse for showings in a three-day period. What percent of the tickets sold for the Saturday showing were for orchestra level seating?

	Friday	Saturday	Sunday
Box	12	4	2
Orchestra	856	891	773
Loge	492	540	411
Balcony	712	695	359

Saturday is the second to last column. The total tickets sold for the Saturday performance were $4 + 891 + 540 + 695$, which is a total of 2130 tickets. The percent of those tickets that were orchestra level is $\frac{891}{2130} \cdot 100$, or about 42%.

Use the table shown to find each percent.

1. What percent of all the loge tickets sold were for the Friday showing? 34%
2. What percent of all tickets sold were for the Sunday showing? 27%
3. What percent of all tickets sold were for seats at either the loge or balcony level? 56%

Box Plots

Example 2 A box plot shows the least and greatest data items, the upper and lower quartiles, and the median of all data. Find the lower quartile of these data:

20, 25, 8, 1, 17, 2, 9, 23, 21, 2, 16, 20

Order the data:

1, 2, 2, 8, 9, 12, 16, 17, 20, 21, 23, 25

The lower quartile is the median of the first half of the data:1, 2, 2, 8, 9, 12. The median is halfway between 2 and 8, which is 5.

Use the data in the example to find each measure.

4. Median 14
5. Upper quartile 20.5
6. Range 24

Response to Intervention			Differentiated Instruction
Tier 1 Lesson Intervention Worksheets	**Tier 2** Strategic Intervention Skills Intervention Worksheets	**Tier 3** Intensive Intervention Worksheets available online	
Reteach 22.1 Reteach 22.2	41 Box Plots 45 Generating Random Samples 46 Histograms 60 Two-Way Tables	Building Block Skills 6, 37, 39, 72, 82, 90, 96, 114, 115, 116, 117, 118	Challenge worksheets Extend the Math Lesson Activities in TE

Are You Ready?

ASSESS READINESS

Use the assessment on this page to determine if students need strategic or intensive intervention for the module's prerequisite skills.

ASSESSMENT AND INTERVENTION

RtI Response to Intervention TIER 1, TIER 2, TIER 3 SKILLS

Personal Math Trainer will automatically create a standards-based, personalized intervention assignment for your students, targeting each student's individual needs!

ADDITIONAL RESOURCES

See the table below for a full list of intervention resources available for this module.

Response to Intervention Resources also includes:

- Tier 2 Skill Pre-Tests for each Module
- Tier 2 Skill Post-Tests for each skill

LESSON 22.1

Data-Gathering Techniques

Common Core Math Standards

The student is expected to:

COMMON CORE **S-IC.A.1**

Understand statistics as a process for making inferences about population parameters based on a random sample from that population.

Mathematical Practices

COMMON CORE **MP.5 Using Tools**

Language Objective

Create a graphic organizer that shows the relationships among population, census, and parameter, as well as sample, sampling, and statistic.

ENGAGE

Essential Question: Under what circumstances should a sample statistic be used as an estimator of a population parameter?

The statistic needs to come from a representative sample, which is most likely to be obtained when the sampling method involves randomness.

PREVIEW: LESSON PERFORMANCE TASK

View the Engage section online. Discuss the photo and how to obtain a representative sample of the student body in order to find out the types of foods most students would choose to eat. Then preview the Lesson Performance Task.

Name ______________________ Class ____________ Date ________

22.1 Data-Gathering Techniques

Resource Locker

Essential Question: Under what circumstances should a sample statistic be used as an estimator of a population parameter?

Explore Finding the Mean of Samples Obtained from Various Sampling Methods

You collect data about a **population** by surveying or studying some or all of the individuals in the population. When *all* the individuals in a population are surveyed or studied, the data-gathering technique is called a **census**. A **parameter** is a number that summarizes a characteristic of the population. When only some of the individuals in a population are surveyed or studied, the data-gathering technique is called **sampling**. A **statistic** is a number that summarizes a characteristic of a sample. Statistics can be used to estimate parameters.

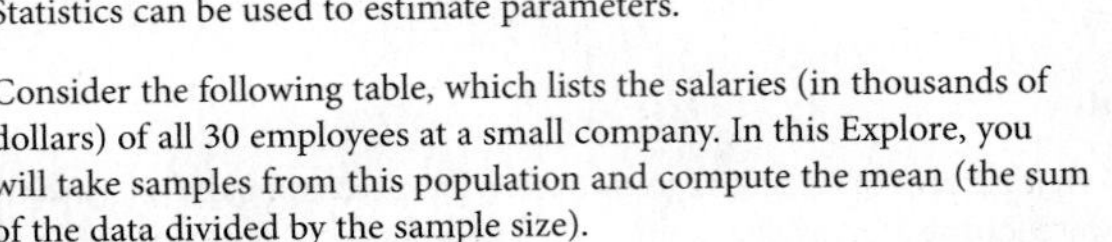

Consider the following table, which lists the salaries (in thousands of dollars) of all 30 employees at a small company. In this Explore, you will take samples from this population and compute the mean (the sum of the data divided by the sample size).

Salaries at a Small Company

21	24	26	28	30	32	33	35	37	41
44	46	47	49	50	51	52	54	55	57
58	62	62	64	64	65	70	71	73	80

(A) Suppose the employees whose salaries are 51, 57, 58, 65, 70, and 73 volunteer to be in the sample. This is called a *self-selected sample*. Compute the sample's mean, rounding to nearest whole number.

$\text{Mean} = \frac{51 + 57 + 58 + 65 + 70 + 73}{6} = \frac{374}{6} \approx 62$

(B) Suppose the six salaries in the first two columns of the table are chosen. This is called a *convenience sample* because the data are easy to obtain. Record the salaries, and then compute the sample's mean, rounding to the nearest whole number.

21, 24, 44, 46, 58, 62; mean $= \frac{21 + 24 + 44 + 46 + 58 + 62}{6} = \frac{255}{6} \approx 43$

(C) Suppose every fifth salary in the list, reading from left to right in each row, is chosen. This is called a *systematic sample*. Record the salaries, and then compute the sample's mean, rounding to the nearest whole number.

30, 41, 50, 57, 64, 80; mean $= \frac{30 + 41 + 50 + 57 + 64 + 80}{6} = \frac{322}{6} \approx 54$

HARDCOVER PAGES 1083–1

Watch for the hardcover student edition page numbers for this lesson.

Ⓓ Label the data in the table with the identifiers 1–10 for the first row, 11–20 for the second row, and 21–30 for the third row. Then use a graphing calculator's random integer generator to generate six identifiers between 1 and 30, as shown. (If any identifiers are repeated, simply generate replacements for them until you have six unique identifiers.) This is called a *simple random sample*. Record the corresponding salaries, and then compute the sample's mean, rounding to the nearest whole number.

Answers will vary. Sample answer based on the random identifiers shown on the calculator screen: 71, 30, 51, 47, 62, 24; mean = $\frac{71 + 30 + 51 + 47 + 62 + 24}{6} = \frac{285}{6} \approx 48$

Reflect

1. Compute the mean of the population. Then list the four samples from best to worst in terms of how well each sample mean estimates the population mean.
Population mean $\approx$ 49; simple random sample, systematic sample, convenience sample, self-selected sample

2. With the way the table is organized, both the convenience sample and the systematic sample have means that are not too far from the population mean. Why?
The data are organized in ascending order. So, choosing every fifth salary for the systematic sample gets some low, some medium, and some high salaries. The same is true when choosing the six salaries in the first two columns of the table for the convenience sample.

Explain 1 Distinguishing Among Sampling Methods

The goal of sampling is to obtain a **representative sample**, because the statistic obtained from the sample is a good estimator of the corresponding population parameter. Some sampling methods can result in **biased samples** that may not be representative of the population and can produce statistics that lead to inaccurate conclusions about the corresponding population parameters.

Sampling Method	Description
Simple random sample	Each individual in the population has an equal chance of being selected.
Self-selected sample	Individuals volunteer to be part of the sample.
Convenience sample	Individuals are selected based on how accessible they are.
Systematic sample	Members of the sample are chosen according to a rule, such as every *n*th individual in the population.
Stratified sample	The population is divided into groups, and individuals from each group are selected (typically through a random sample within each group).
Cluster sample	The population is divided into groups, some of the groups are randomly selected, and either all the individuals in the selected groups are selected or just some of the individuals from the selected groups are selected (typically through a random sample within each selected group).

PROFESSIONAL DEVELOPMENT

Math Background

Sampling involves making observations of or gathering data from a population, either the entire population (a census) or a part of the population (a sample). The goal is to gain knowledge about a population, often to make predictions, or to persuade. Predictions based on statistics have a certain amount of error associated with them. Error can come about from the sampling method used, whether intentional (for example, when using statistics to persuade) or unintentional. A frequent source of error in statistical predictions is bias, which makes it more likely that certain subsets of the population are over-represented in a sample. Sampling methods can affect the statistics gathered and, therefore, the predictions that are based on them.

EXPLORE

Finding the Mean of Samples Obtained from Various Sampling Methods

INTEGRATE TECHNOLOGY

Students have the option of completing the activity either in the book or online.

QUESTIONING STRATEGIES

Are you trying to find a statistic or a parameter? **trying to find a statistic based upon the sample to find the parameter for the population**

EXPLAIN 1

Distinguishing Among Sampling Methods

CONNECT VOCABULARY EL

Relate the word *stratified* to the English prefixes *strati-* and *strato-*, meaning *layer.* Students may be aware that the *stratosphere* is a layer of the atmosphere.

QUESTIONING STRATEGIES

Why might the sample be representative of the population? Why might it not be representative? **It might be representative because it is a random sample. It might not be representative because the sample is small.**

AVOID COMMON ERRORS

Students may prefer to use convenience samples because they are easier. Point out that the results from some convenience samples may be biased, but that other convenience samples may produce good results. For example, if their math class consists of all juniors and they wish to know the percent of students going to the junior prom, using their class as a sample might produce good results.

The Explore showed that simple random samples are likely to be representative of a population (as are other sampling methods that involve randomness) and are therefore preferred over sampling methods that don't involve randomness.

Example 1 **Identify the population, classify the sampling methods, and decide whether the sampling methods could result in a biased sample. Explain your reasoning.**

(A) The officials of the National Football League (NFL) want to know how the players feel about some proposed changes to the NFL rules. They decide to ask a sample of 100 players.

a. The officials choose the first 100 players who volunteer their opinions.

b. The officials randomly choose 3 or 4 players from each of the 32 teams in the NFL.

c. The officials have a computer randomly generate a list of 100 players from a database of all NFL players.

The population consists of the players in the NFL.

a. This is a self-selected sample because the players volunteer their opinions. This could result in a biased sample because the players who feel strongly about the rules would be the first ones to volunteer and get their opinions counted.

b. This is a stratified sample because the players are separated by team and randomly chosen from each team. This is not likely to be biased since the players are chosen randomly and are taken from each team.

c. This is a simple random sample because each player has an equally likely chance of being chosen. This is not likely to be biased since the players are chosen randomly.

(B) Administrators at your school want to know if students think that more vegetarian items should be added to the lunch menu.

a. The administrators survey every 25th student who enters the cafeteria during the lunch period.

b. The administrators survey the first 50 students who get in the lunch line to buy lunch.

c. The administrators use a randomly generated list of 50 students from a master list of all students.

The population consists of **the students at the school**.

a. This is a **systematic** sample because **the rule of every 25th student is used**. This method [is/(isn't)] likely to result in a biased sample because **a wide range of students will be surveyed.**

b. This is a **convenience** sample because **the students are easily accessible**. This method [(is)/isn't] likely to result in a biased sample because **it does not include students who bring their lunch**.

c. This is a **simple random** sample because **each student has an equally likely chance of being chosen**. This method [is/(isn't)] likely to result in a biased sample because **the students are chosen randomly**.

COLLABORATIVE LEARNING

Whole Class Activity

Ask a few students in the class whether they are more interested in music or in art. Use their responses to make a prediction about the whole class. Then ask half the students in the class the same question, and make a second prediction. Finally, direct the question to the entire class and tally the results. Discuss how accurate each prediction is, and whether it is surprising or not that one prediction is more accurate than another.

Your Turn

Identify the population, classify the sampling methods, and decide whether the sampling methods could result in a biased sample. Explain your reasoning.

3. A local newspaper conducts a survey to find out if adult residents of the city think the use of hand-held cell phones while driving in the city should be banned.

a. The newspaper sends a text message to a random selection of 1000 subscribers whose cell phones are listed in the paper's subscription database.

b. Using the 10 neighborhoods into which the city is divided, the newspaper randomly contacts 100 adults living in each of the neighborhoods.

The population consists of adult residents of the city.

a. Simple random sample of subscribers with cell phones; everyone has an equally likely chance of being chosen. Likely to be biased; people who do not use cell phones (or did not give their cell phone numbers to the newspaper) are left out of the survey.

b. Stratified sample; individuals are grouped and a random sample from each group is selected. Not likely to result in a biased sample; a wide range of residents is surveyed.

Explain 2 Making Predictions from a Random Sample

In statistics, you work with data. Data can be **numerical**, such as heights or salaries, or **categorical**, such as eye color or political affiliation. While a statistic like the mean is appropriate for numerical data, an appropriate statistic for categorical data is a **proportion**, which is the relative frequency of a category.

Example 2 **A community health center surveyed a small random sample of adults in the community about their exercise habits. The survey asked whether the person engages in regular cardio exercise (running, walking, swimming, or other) and, if so, what the duration and frequency of exercise are. Of the 25 people surveyed, 10 said that they do engage in regular cardio exercise. The table lists the data for those 10 people. Calculate statistics from the sample, and use the statistics to make predictions about the exercise habits of the approximately 5000 adults living in the community.**

Type of exercise	Duration (minutes spent exercising)	Frequency (times per week)
Running	30	4
Walking	20	5
Running	40	3
Running	60	6
Swimming	40	4
Other	90	2
Running	30	3
Walking	20	5
Running	30	4
Other	120	1

DIFFERENTIATE INSTRUCTION

Kinesthetic Experience

Making flash cards will help students learn the language of statistics. They can add to their cards as the unit progresses. In addition to using the cards for study, students can play games with the flash cards; for example, have one student give clues to a second, who must guess what is on the card.

EXPLAIN 2

Making Predictions from a Random Sample

QUESTIONING STRATEGIES

How could the sampling method be improved to get a more representative sample? **Increase the number of people surveyed, and verify that the people are truthful in their responses.**

What makes a prediction likely to be reliable? **randomness and a sample representative of the population, plus correct calculations**

INTEGRATE TECHNOLOGY

A graphing calculator or spreadsheet can be used to calculate statistics and make projections for the parameters.

CONNECT VOCABULARY EL

Ask students whether *bias* in data reporting and *bias* in society are connected. Note that bias in society is generally intentional, while bias in data may be unintentional.

CONNECT VOCABULARY EL

Ask students to answer the following questions using this vocabulary: *representative, unbiased, population, statistic, parameter.*

What are samples used for and why? **A sample is used to make a prediction about a population when a census is impractical.**

What should be true of a sample in order to make predictions and estimates? **A sample should be both unbiased and representative of every group in the population.**

ELABORATE

INTEGRATE MATHEMATICAL PRACTICES

Focus on Critical Thinking

MP.3 Have students consider a situation in which two different random samples are used, resulting in very different estimates for the population parameters. Students should consider using both samples together to comprise a larger sample.

AVOID COMMON ERRORS

Students may confuse a sample with a census, and assume that they have calculated a statistic when they have actually found the parameter itself for an entire population. Remind students that if every member of a population is sampled, the sample and population are the same.

SUMMARIZE THE LESSON

? What are the different methods for gathering data about a population? **A census, in which information is gathered from every individual in the population, can be used. If a census is impractical, a sampling method can be used. Sampling techniques include random, self-selected, convenience, systematic, stratified, and cluster.**

Ⓐ Calculate the proportion of adults who get regular cardio exercise and the proportion of runners among those who get regular cardio exercise. Use the proportions to predict the number of runners among all adults living in the community.

Proportion of adults who get regular cardio exercise: $\frac{10}{25} = 0.4$ or 40%

Proportion of runners among those who get regular cardio exercise: $\frac{5}{10} = 0.5$ or 50%

To predict the number of runners in the community, multiply the number of adults in the community by the proportion of adults who get regular cardio exercise and then by the proportion of runners among those who get regular cardio exercise.

Predicted number of runners in the community: $5000 \cdot 0.4 \cdot 0.5 = 1000$

Ⓑ Calculate the mean duration of exercise for those who get regular cardio exercise and the mean frequency of exercise for those who get regular cardio exercise. Use the means to predict, for those who get regular cardio exercise, the number of hours spent exercising each week. Show your calculations and include units.

Mean duration of exercise for those who get regular cardio exercise: **48** minutes

Mean frequency of exercise for those who get regular cardio exercise: **3.7** times per week

To predict the number of hours spent exercising, multiply the mean duration of exercise (in minutes) for those who get regular cardio exercise by the mean frequency of exercise (in times per week) for those who get regular cardio exercise. This product will be in minutes per week. To convert to hours per week, also multiply by the conversion factor $\frac{1 \text{ hour}}{60 \text{ minutes}}$.

Predicted time spent exercising: **48** minutes · **3.7** /week · $\frac{1 \text{ hour}}{60 \text{ minutes}} \approx$ **3** hours/week

Reflect

4. Discussion How much confidence do you have in the predictions made from the results of the survey? Explain your reasoning.

Possible answer: The sample was random, which makes the results representative of the population, but the sample size was small, which may not make the results accurate.

Your Turn

5. A ski resort uses the information gained from scanning season ski passes in lift lines to determine how many days out of each season the pass holders ski and how many lift rides they take each day. The table lists the data for a random sample of 16 pass holders. Calculate the mean number of days skied and the mean number of lift rides taken per day. Use the means to predict the number of lift rides taken per season by a pass holder.

Number of days	10	5	2	14	27	3	18	5
Number of lift rides	12	15	6	18	10	6	15	9

Number of days	4	16	7	12	19	14	25	1
Number of lift rides	11	13	14	10	8	6	15	1

Mean number of days skied: 12.125; mean number of lift rides taken per day: 11.625; predicted number of lift rides taken by a pass holder per season:

12.125 days · $\frac{\textbf{11.625 lift rides}}{\textbf{day}} \approx$ **141 lift rides**

LANGUAGE SUPPORT EL

Communicate Math

Have students work in pairs to complete a graphic organizer of relationships like the one below using this list of words: *census, sample, sampling, population, statistic, parameter*. Students should be able to verbalize the relationships.

Population	Sample
↓	↓
Census	Sampling
↓	↓
Parameter	Statistic

Elaborate

6. Name a sampling method that is more likely to produce a representative sample and a sampling method that is more likely to produce a biased sample.
Answers may vary. Possible answer: A simple random sample is more likely to produce a representative sample. A self-selected sample is more likely to produce a biased sample.

7. Why are there different statistics for numerical and categorical data?
Numerical data are numbers that can be ordered (to find the median), summed (to find the mean), and so on. Categorical data are categories, and you cannot perform operations on categories. Instead, you can count the number of individuals in a category (to find the frequency) or find the fraction of all individuals in a category (to obtain the relative frequency).

8. **Essential Question Check-In** Explain the difference between a parameter and a statistic.
A parameter is a number that summarizes a population and is obtained from a census. A statistic is a number that summarizes a sample taken from a population.

Evaluate: Homework and Practice

- Online Homework
- Hints and Help
- Extra Practice

1. A student council wants to know whether students would like the council to sponsor a mid-winter dance or a mid-winter carnival this year. Classify each sampling method.
   a. Survey every tenth student on the school's roster.
   Systematic sample
   b. Survey all students in three randomly selected homerooms.
   Cluster sample
   c. Survey 20 randomly selected freshmen, 20 randomly selected sophomores, 20 randomly selected juniors, and 20 randomly selected seniors.
   Stratified sample
   d. Survey those who ask the council president for a questionnaire.
   Self-selected sample
   e. Survey a random selection of those who happen to be in the cafeteria at noon.
   Convenience sample

2. The officers of a neighborhood association want to know whether residents are interested in beautifying the neighborhood and, if so, how much money they are willing to contribute toward the costs involved. The officers are considering three methods for gathering data:
Method A: Call and survey every tenth resident on the association's roster.
Method B: Randomly select and survey 10 residents from among those who come to the neighborhood block party.
   a. Identify the population.
   The population consists of all residents of the neighborhood.

Exercise	Depth of Knowledge (D.O.K.)	COMMON CORE Mathematical Practices
1–2	1 Recall of Information	MP.3 Logic
3	2 Skills/Concepts	MP.3 Logic
4	1 Recall of Information	MP.3 Logic
5–7	2 Skills/Concepts	MP.3 Logic
8–9	1 Recall of Information	MP.3 Logic
10–11	2 Skills/Concepts	MP.4 Modeling
12–13	2 Skills/Concepts H.O.T.	MP.3 Logic

EVALUATE

ASSIGNMENT GUIDE

Concepts and Skills	Practice
Explore Finding the Mean of Samples Obtained from Various Sampling Methods	Exercise 1
Example 1 Distinguishing Among Sampling Methods	Exercises 2–9
Example 2 Making Predictions from a Random Sample	Exercises 10–11

INTEGRATE MATHEMATICAL PROCESSES

Focus on Reasoning

MP.2 Students should understand the difference between categorical data and numerical data, and that statistics, such as frequency and mode, can be found for categorical data.

AVOID COMMON ERRORS

Students may believe they are calculating parameters when they make predictions, but actual parameters cannot be found through sampling.

COLLABORATIVE LEARNING

Have students design a survey to answer a question about the faculty of the school. Students should come up with one question and two sampling methods that could be used—one that is likely to be representative of the population and one that is not. Tell them to make up results and base a prediction on each method.

b. Which sampling method is most likely to result in a representative sample of the population? Explain.

Method A is most likely to result in a representative sample. If method B is used, those who do not attend the block party would have no chance of being represented.

c. Describe another sampling method that is likely to result in a representative sample of the population.

Possible answer: Randomly select names from the association's roster.

d. Describe the categorical and numerical data that the officers of the neighborhood association want to gather.

Interest in beautifying the neighborhood is categorical. The amounts residents are willing to contribute is numerical.

Decide whether the sampling method could result in a biased sample. Explain your reasoning.

3. On the first day of school, all of the incoming freshmen attend an orientation program. Afterward, the principal wants to learn the opinions of the freshmen regarding the orientation. She decides to ask 25 freshmen as they leave the auditorium to complete a questionnaire.

This sampling method is likely not to be biased since the sample is random and all of the freshmen are available to be chosen.

4. The members of the school drama club want to know how much students are willing to pay for a ticket to one of their productions. They decide that each member of the drama club should ask 5 of his or her friends what they are each willing to pay.

This sampling method could be biased since friends of the club members may be willing to pay more than others.

5. A medical conference has 500 participating doctors. The table lists the doctors' specialties. A researcher wants to survey a sample of 25 of the doctors to get their opinions on proposed new rules for health care providers. Explain why it may be better for the researcher to use a stratified sample rather than a simple random sample.

Doctors from different specialties may have different opinions about the new rules. Using a simple random sample means that dermatologists, as a group, have less of a chance of having their opinions surveyed than any other group, and oncologists have a greater chance than any other group. Using a stratified sample guarantees that the opinions all of five specialties are surveyed.

Specialty	Number of Doctors
Dermatology	40
Geriatrics	120
Oncology	140
Pediatrics	100
Surgery	100

6. A researcher wants to conduct a face-to-face survey of 100 farmers in a large agricultural state to get their opinions about the risks and rewards of farming. The researcher has limited time and budget. Explain why it may be better for the researcher to use a cluster sample based on counties in the state rather than a simple random sample.

By sampling a handful of counties (a cluster sample) and surveying farmers only within those counties, the researcher limits the time and travel costs for the survey.

Exercise	Depth of Knowledge (D.O.K.)	COMMON CORE Mathematical Practices
14	3 Strategic Thinking H.O.T.	MP.3 Logic

Identify the population and the sampling method.

7. A quality control inspector at a computer assembly plant needs to estimate the number of defective computers in a group of 250 computers. He tests 25 randomly chosen computers.

The population consists of all computers at the assembly plant.
This is a simple random sample.

8. The manager of a movie theater wants to know how the movie viewers feel about the new stadium seating at the theater. She asks every 30th person who exits the theater each Saturday night for a month.

The population consists of people who go to the movie theater.
This is a systematic sample.

9. Eric is interested in purchasing a used sports car. He selects the make and model of the car at a website that locates all used cars of that make and model for sale within a certain distance of his home. The website delivers a list of 120 cars that meet his criteria. Eric randomly selects 10 of those cars and records what type of engine and transmission they have, as shown in the table.

Engine (L = liter)	Transmission
3.6 L V6	Manual
3.6 L V6	Automatic
6.2 L V8	Manual
3.6 L V6	Manual
6.2 L Supercharged V8	Manual
3.6 L V6	Automatic
6.2 L V8	Manual
3.6 L V6	Automatic
3.6 L V6	Manual
6.2 L V8	Automatic

a. If Eric can only drive cars with automatic transmissions, predict the number of such cars on the website's list. Show your calculations.

Proportion of cars with an automatic transmission: $\frac{4}{10} = 0.4$ or 40%

Predicted number of cars with an automatic transmission: $120 \cdot 0.4 = 48$

b. Eric knows that the 3.6 L V6 engine takes regular gasoline, but the 6.2 L V8 engine requires premium gasoline. To minimize his fuel costs, he wants a car with the 3.6 L V6 engine. Predict the number of such cars on the website's list. Show your calculations.

Proportion of cars with the 3.6 L V6 engine: $\frac{6}{10} = 0.6$ or 60%

Predicted number of cars with the 3.6 L V6 engine: $120 \cdot 0.6 = 72$

c. Predict the number of cars that have a 3.6 L V6 engine and an automatic transmission. Show your calculations.

Proportion of cars with a 3.6 L V6 engine and an automatic transmission: $\frac{3}{10} = 0.3$ or 30%

Predicted number of cars with a 3.6 L V6 engine and an automatic transmission: $120 \cdot 0.3 = 36$

CONNECT VOCABULARY EL

Help students distinguish among the many terms used for the types of data covered in this lesson. Make connections between the idea of *categorical data* and the descriptions of *categories*, such as gender, age, ethnicity, and so on.

INTEGRATE MATHEMATICAL PRACTICES

Focus on Modeling

MP.4 Explain to students that, although self-selected surveys are not likely to be representative of a general population, they can be useful in determining the opinions of people who already have an interest in an issue. Self-selected surveys also have the benefit of eliminating bias that might stem from direct contact with a surveyor. These two facts can make self-selected surveys especially useful for politicians.

10. A community theater association plans to produce three plays for the upcoming season. The association surveys a random sample of the approximately 7000 households in the community to see if an adult member of the household is interested in attending plays and, if so, what type of plays the person prefers (comedy, drama, or musical), how many members of the household (including the person surveyed) might attend plays, and how many of the three plays those household members might attend. Of the 50 adults surveyed, 12 indicated an interest in attending plays. The table lists the data for those 12 people.

Preferred Type of Play	Number of People Attending	Number of Plays Attending
Comedy	2	1
Musical	3	2
Musical	1	2
Drama	2	3
Comedy	3	2
Comedy	2	3
Musical	4	1
Drama	2	3
Comedy	2	2
Musical	2	3
Comedy	5	1
Drama	1	2

a. Describe the categorical and numerical data gathered in the survey.

Interest in attending plays and preferred type of play are categorical data. Number of household members who might attend plays and number of plays they might attend are numerical data.

b. Calculate the proportion of adults who indicated an interest in attending plays and calculate the proportion of adults who prefer dramas among those who are interested in attending plays. If approximately 15,000 adults live in the community, predict the number of adults who are interested in attending plays that are dramas. Show your calculations.

Proportion of adults interested in attending plays: $\frac{12}{50} = 0.24$ **or 24%**

Proportion of adults who prefer dramas among those who are interested in attending plays: $\frac{3}{12} = 0.25$ **or 25%**

Predicted number of adults who are interested in attending plays that are dramas: $15{,}000 \cdot 0.24 \cdot 0.25 = 900$

c. For an adult with an interest in attending plays, calculate the mean number of household members who might attend plays and the mean number of plays that those household members might attend. Round each mean to the nearest tenth. If the theater association plans to sells tickets to the plays for \$40 each, predict the amount of revenue from ticket sales. Show your calculations and include units.

Mean number of people attending plays: $\frac{29}{12} \approx 2.4$; mean number of plays attended: $\frac{25}{12} \approx 2.1$

Predicted number of households with an adult having an interest in attending plays: $7000 \cdot 0.24 = 1680$

Predicted number of tickets sold: 1680 households $\cdot \frac{2.4 \text{ people}}{\text{household}} \cdot \frac{2.1 \text{ tickets}}{\text{person}} = 8467.2$ tickets

Predicted revenue from ticket sales: 8467.2 tickets $\cdot \frac{\$40}{\text{ticket}} = \$338{,}688$

11. Match each description of a sample on the left with a sampling technique on the right.

A. A television reporter asks people walking by on the street to answer a question about an upcoming election. — C Simple random sample

B. A television reporter randomly selects voting precincts and then contacts voters randomly chosen from a list of registered voters residing in those precincts to ask about an upcoming election. — F Self-selected sample

C. A television reporter contacts voters randomly chosen from a complete list of registered voters to ask about an upcoming election. — A Convenience sample

D. A television reporter contacts every 100th voter from a complete list of registered voters to ask about an upcoming election. — D Systematic sample

E. A television reporter contacts registered voters randomly chosen from every voting precinct to ask about an upcoming election. — E Stratified sample

F. A television reporter asks viewers to call in their response to a question about an upcoming election. — B Cluster sample

H.O.T. Focus on Higher Order Thinking

12. Critical Thinking A reporter for a high school newspaper asked all members of the school's track team how many miles they run each week.

a. What type of data did the reporter gather?
The reporter gathered numerical data.

b. Was the reporter's data-gathering technique a census or a sample? Explain.
It was a census of the track team—unless the reporter's intended population is the entire student body, in which case it was a sample.

c. Are the data representative of the entire student body? Why or why not?
No, the data are not representative of the entire student body; members of the track team most likely run more than members of the entire student body.

INTEGRATE MATHEMATICAL PRACTICES

Focus on Communication

MP.3 Have students research what a Gallup poll is, and write a short report describing the poll and the purpose of the organization that is responsible for Gallup polls.

PEER-TO-PEER DISCUSSION

Give each student six index cards. Tell them to draw a diagram from the *Types of Samples* chart on one side of each card, and then write the corresponding name of the sample on the other side. Have students pair up and take turns quizzing each other with the cards, with one student showing the diagram and the other student giving the name of the sample type. Students can take the cards home and use them as flash cards to study.

JOURNAL

Have students write a journal entry discussing the different types of sampling—random, self-selected, convenience, systematic, stratified, and cluster. The entry should include a description and an example of each type, a reason why you might use each type, and a statement about how representative of the entire population each type is likely to be.

13. Communicate Mathematical Ideas Categorical data can be nominal or ordinal. *Nominal data* refer to categories that do not have any "natural" ordering, while *ordinal data* refer to categories that do have an order. Similarly, numerical data can be discrete or continuous. *Discrete data* are typically counts or scores (which cannot be made more precise), while *continuous data* are typically measurements (which can be made more precise). For each description of a set of data, identify whether the data are nominal, ordinal, discrete, or continuous. Explain your reasoning. Also give another example of the same type of data.

a. A researcher records how many people live in a subject's household.
The data are discrete because how many people live in household is a count. Another example of discrete data: number of televisions in a household.

b. A researcher records the gender of each subject.
The data are nominal because the categories of male and female do not have an order. Another example of nominal data: subject's eye color.

c. A researcher records the amount of time each subject spends using an electronic device during a day.
The data are continuous because time can be measured in hours, minutes, or even seconds. Another example of continuous data: subject's height.

d. A researcher records whether each subject is a young adult, a middle-aged adult, or a senior.
The data are ordinal because the categories have an order from youngest to oldest. Another example of ordinal data: the highest educational degree that a subject has attained (high school diploma, associate's degree, bachelor's degree, and so on).

14. Analyze Relationships The grid represents the entire population of 100 trees in an apple orchard. The values in the grid show the number of kilograms of apples produced by each tree during one year. Given the data, obtain three random samples of size 20 from the population and find the mean of each sample. Discuss how the means of those samples compare with the population mean, which is 68.9.

109	52	62	72	110	61	51	50	100	50
54	104	54	111	74	73	77	68	65	66
108	53	27	75	52	117	76	60	64	67
73	36	103	71	67	60	59	26	80	61
38	63	35	112	75	68	51	72	79	62
58	105	55	53	118	57	101	66	116	31
29	57	74	33	102	69	28	71	30	58
39	55	34	120	64	114	70	113	78	63
107	37	56	25	76	70	69	77	30	115
56	40	106	32	119	65	80	78	79	59

Answers will vary. The mean for any given sample is likely to fall between 57.5 and 80.3.

Lesson Performance Task

Think about your school's cafeteria and the food it serves. Suppose you are given the opportunity to conduct a survey about the cafeteria.

a. Identify the population to be surveyed.

b. Write one or more survey questions. For each question, state whether it will generate numerical data or categorical data.

c. Assuming that you aren't able to conduct a census of the population, describe how you could obtain a representative sample of the population.

d. Suppose you asked a random sample of 25 students in your school whether they were satisfied with cafeteria lunches and how often in a typical week they brought their own lunches. The tables give the results of the survey. If the school has 600 students, use the results to predict the number of students who are satisfied with cafeteria lunches and the number of lunches brought to school in a typical week.

Satisfied with cafeteria lunches?	
Response	**Number**
Yes	18
No	7

Bring own lunches how often in a week?	
Response	**Number**
5 times	2
4 times	1
3 times	4
2 times	2
1 time	4
0 times	12

a. Answers may vary. Possible answer: All students who attend the school. (Alternatively, the population might be only students who sometimes or always eat the cafeteria's lunches.)

b. Answers may vary. Possible answers: The question "Are you satisfied with cafeteria lunches?" would generate categorical data, while the question "In a typical week, how often do you bring your own lunch?" would generate numerical data.

c. Answers may vary. Possible answer: If a complete roster of students is available, assign numerical IDs to the students and use a random number generator to obtain a list of IDs. Otherwise, use a systematic sample of students in the cafeteria during each of the school's lunch periods.

d. From the first table, the proportion of students who are satisfied with cafeteria lunches is $\frac{18}{25} = 0.72$, so the predicted number of students in the school who are satisfied is $600 \cdot 0.72 = 432$. From the second table, the mean number of lunches brought to school by a student in a typical week is $\frac{2 \cdot 5 + 1 \cdot 4 + 4 \cdot 3 + 2 \cdot 2 + 4 \cdot 1 + 12 \cdot 0}{25} = 1.36$, so the predicted number of lunches brought to school by all students is $600 \cdot 1.36 = 816$.

EXTENSION ACTIVITY

Have students research the meaning of the expression *margin of error* and a formula for finding it when sampling *n* people. Then have them find the percent margin of error for a poll of 2400 people. Have them consider standard error margins for political surveys, for example. Note that margin of error will be discussed further in Lesson 24.3, in the study of data distributions. **A margin of error is the amount of miscalculation allowed in computing data; margin of error $= \pm \frac{1}{\sqrt{n}}$, where n represents the number of data values in the set; margin of error $= \pm \frac{1}{\sqrt{2400}} \approx \pm 0.02$ or, about 2%.**

CONNECT VOCABULARY EL

Discuss the fact that, in an ice cream parlor, paint store, or fabric store, a customer can ask for a *sample* before deciding to make a purchase. Ask students how this type of sample is similar to polling a sample of a population. Students should make the connection that, in both situations, a small portion of the whole is evaluated in order to make a decision about the whole.

QUESTIONING STRATEGIES

? Under what circumstances would you take a census rather than a sample of the school population? **Possible answer: If the food supplier needed to prepare specific lunches for those students who have food allergies, the chef would need to know how many such lunches to prepare.**

INTEGRATE MATHEMATICAL PRACTICES

Focus on Reasoning

MP.2 Discuss why you would not want to poll the first 30 students entering the cafeteria at a specific time of day. Look for student responses such as the following: The first 30 students might be closest to the cafeteria, or the hungriest, or have different needs. They would be more likely to be the same age or to arrive in groups of the same gender or from the same location. Using data from such a poll would create a bias in favor of that group's preferences.

Scoring Rubric

2 points: Student correctly solves the problem and explains his/her reasoning.

1 point: Student shows good understanding of the problem but does not fully solve or explain his/her reasoning.

0 points: Student does not demonstrate understanding of the problem.

LESSON 22.2

Shape, Center, and Spread

Common Core Math Standards

The student is expected to:

COMMON CORE **S-ID.A.4**

Use the mean and standard deviation of a data set to fit it to a normal distribution and to estimate population percentages. Recognize that there are data sets for which such a procedure is not appropriate. Use calculators, spreadsheets, and tables to estimate areas under the normal curve.

Mathematical Practices

COMMON CORE **MP.2 Reasoning**

Language Objective

Have students work in pairs to fill in a table showing the shape of distributions of data.

ENGAGE

Essential Question: Which measures of center and spread are appropriate for a normal distribution, and which are appropriate for a skewed distribution?

For a normal distribution, it's appropriate to use either a combination of mean and standard deviation or a combination of median and IQR. For a skewed distribution, only a combination of median and IQR should be used because mean and standard deviation are sensitive to the data values in the tail of the distribution

PREVIEW: LESSON PERFORMANCE TASK

View the online Engage. Discuss what kinds of data might be collected and compared with the normally-distributed data when a pet visits the veterinarian. Then preview the Lesson Performance Task.

Name __________ Class __________ Date __________

22.2 Shape, Center, and Spread

Essential Question: Which measures of center and spread are appropriate for a normal distribution, and which are appropriate for a skewed distribution?

Resource Locker

Explore 1 Seeing the Shape of a Distribution

"Raw" data values are simply presented in an unorganized list. Organizing the data values by using the frequency with which they occur results in a **distribution** of the data. A distribution may be presented as a frequency table or as a data display. Data displays for numerical data, such as line plots, histograms, and box plots, involve a number line, while data displays for categorical data, such as bar graphs and circle graphs, do not. Data displays reveal the shape of a distribution.

The table gives data about a random sample of 20 babies born at a hospital.

Baby	Birth Month	Birth Weight (kg)	Mother's Age
1	5	3.3	28
2	7	3.6	31
3	11	3.5	33
4	2	3.4	35
5	10	3.7	39
6	3	3.4	30
7	1	3.5	29
8	4	3.2	30
9	7	3.6	31
10	6	3.4	32

Baby	Birth Month	Birth Weight (kg)	Mother's Age
11	9	3.6	33
12	10	3.5	29
13	11	3.4	31
14	1	3.7	29
15	6	3.5	34
16	5	3.8	30
17	8	3.5	32
18	9	3.6	30
19	12	3.3	29
20	2	3.5	28

(A) Make a line plot for the distribution of birth months.

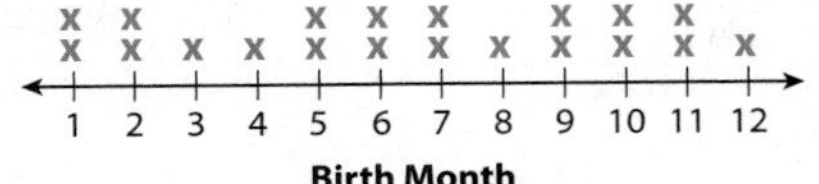

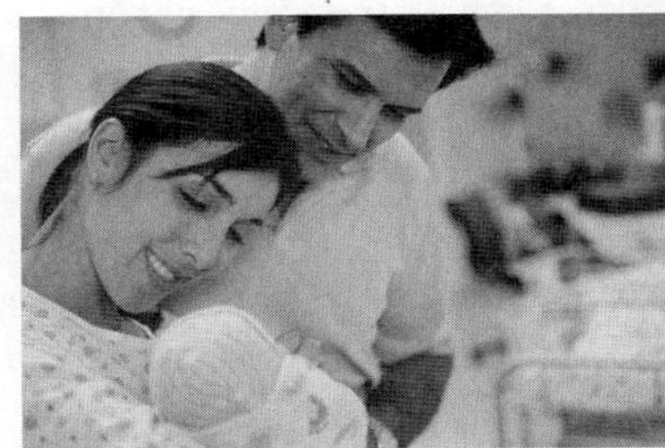

HARDCOVER PAGES 1095–11

Watch for the hardcover student edition page numbers for this lesson.

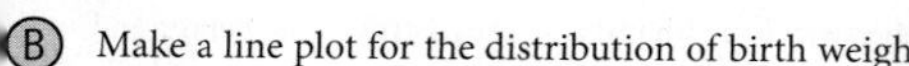
(B) Make a line plot for the distribution of birth weights.

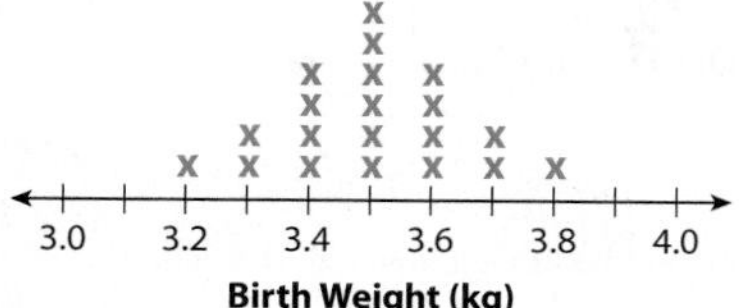

(C) Make a line plot for the distribution of mothers' ages.

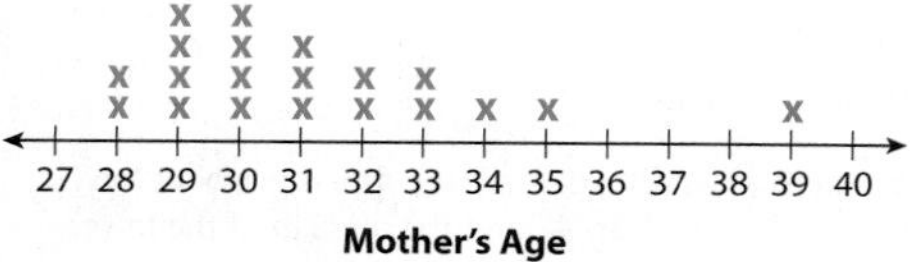

Reflect

1. Describe the shape of the distribution of birth months.
The distribution is fairly level; that is, the data are more or less evenly distributed.

2. Describe the shape of the distribution of birth weights.
The distribution is mounded and symmetric.

3. Describe the shape of the distribution of mothers' ages.
The distribution is mounded and asymmetric; that is, it trails off more to the right than to the left.

Explore 2 Relating Measures of Center and Spread to the Shape of a Distribution

As you saw in the previous Explore, data distributions can have various shapes. Some of these shapes are given names in statistics.

A distribution whose shape is basically level (that is, it looks like a rectangle) is called a **uniform distribution**.

A distribution that is mounded in the middle with symmetric "tails" at each end (that is, it looks bell-shaped) is called a **normal distribution**.

A distribution that is mounded but not symmetric because one "tail" is much longer than the other is called a **skewed distribution**. When the longer "tail" is on the left, the distribution is said to be *skewed left*. When the longer "tail" is on the right, the distribution is said to be *skewed right*.

The figures show the general shapes of normal and skewed distributions.

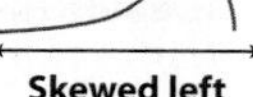
Skewed left

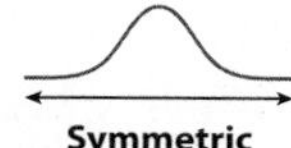
Symmetric

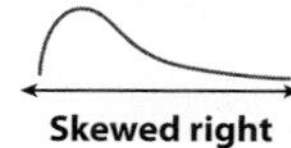
Skewed right

PROFESSIONAL DEVELOPMENT

Integrate Mathematical Practices

The Explore activities in this lesson provide opportunities to address Mathematical Practice **MP.2**, which asks students to "reason abstractly and quantitatively." Students review various ways to display data, and they learn to recognize various shapes of data distributions. They also calculate measures of center and spread and relate them to the shapes of the distributions. Finally, they learn that certain measures of center and spread are better statistics for non-normal distributions.

EXPLORE 1

Seeing the Shape of a Distribution

INTEGRATE TECHNOLOGY

Students have the option of completing the activity either in the book or online.

QUESTIONING STRATEGIES

? What values are on the number lines for line plots, histograms, and box plots? **the data values**

? What does the height of each vertical stack of X's in the line plots represent? **the number of times each value occurs, or frequencies**

EXPLORE 2

Relating Measures of Center and Spread to the Shape of a Distribution

AVOID COMMON ERRORS

When using multiple lists in a calculator, students can confuse them or end up with mismatched data. Students should write down what set of data is in each list to help them avoid confusion.

QUESTIONING STRATEGIES

? What information does a data display give you? **the shape of the data distribution** What information do the mean and median give you? **the center of the distribution** What information do the standard deviation and interquartile range give you? **the spread of the distribution**

? Which types of distributions are relatively balanced about the measure of central tendency and which are not? **Uniform and normal distributions are balanced, skewed distributions are not.**

Shape is one way of characterizing a data distribution. Another way is by identifying the distribution's center and spread. You should already be familiar with the following measures of center and spread:

- The *mean* of n data values is the sum of the data values divided by n. If $x_1, x_2, \ldots, x_n$ are data values from a sample, then the mean $\overline{x}$ is given by:

$$\overline{x} = \frac{x_1 + x_2 + \cdots + x_n}{n}$$

- The *median* of n data values written in ascending order is the middle value if n is odd, and is the mean of the two middle values if n is even.
- The *standard deviation* of n data values is the square root of the mean of the squared deviations from the distribution's mean. If $x_1, x_2, \ldots, x_n$ are data values from a sample, then the standard deviation s is given by:

$$s = \sqrt{\frac{(x_1 - \overline{x})^2 + (x_2 - \overline{x})^2 + \cdots + (x_n - \overline{x})^2}{n}}$$

- The *interquartile range*, or IQR, of data values written in ascending order is the difference between the median of the upper half of the data, called the *third quartile* or Q_3, and the median of the lower half of the data, called the *first quartile* or Q_1. So, IQR $= Q_3 - Q_1$.

To distinguish a population mean from a sample mean, statisticians use the Greek letter mu, written μ, instead of $\overline{x}$. Similarly, they use the Greek letter sigma, written σ, instead of s to distinguish a population standard deviation from a sample standard deviation.

Ⓐ Use a graphing calculator to compute the measures of center and the measures of spread for the distribution of baby weights and the distribution of mothers' ages from the previous Explore. Begin by entering the two sets of data into two lists on a graphing calculator as shown.

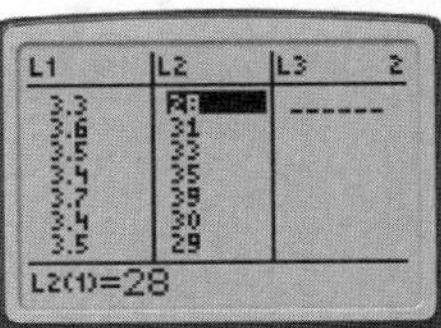

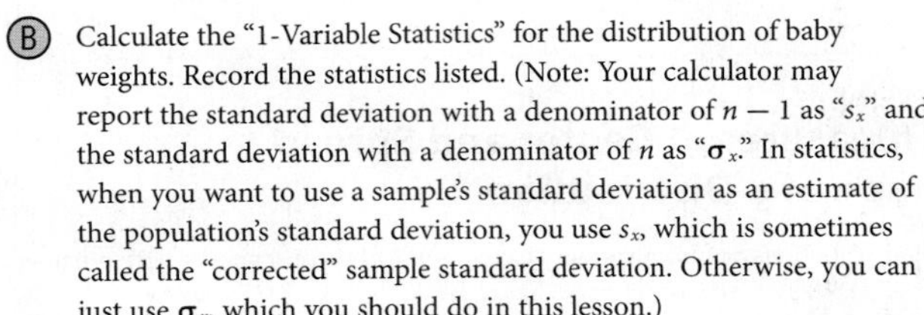

Ⓑ Calculate the "1-Variable Statistics" for the distribution of baby weights. Record the statistics listed. (Note: Your calculator may report the standard deviation with a denominator of $n - 1$ as "s_x," and the standard deviation with a denominator of n as "σ_x." In statistics, when you want to use a sample's standard deviation as an estimate of the population's standard deviation, you use s_x, which is sometimes called the "corrected" sample standard deviation. Otherwise, you can just use σ_x, which you should do in this lesson.)

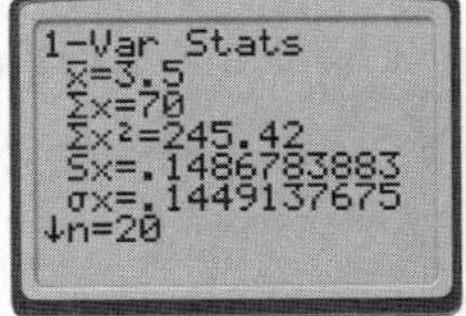

$\overline{x} =$ **3.5** Median $=$ **3.5**

$s \approx$ **0.14** IQR $= Q_3 - Q_1 =$ **0.2**

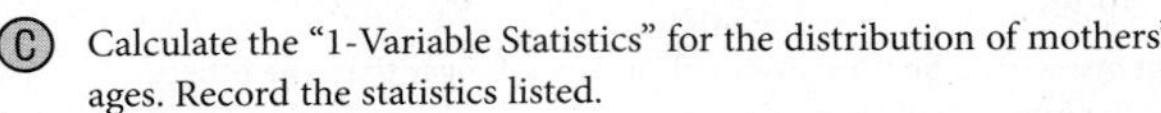

Ⓒ Calculate the "1-Variable Statistics" for the distribution of mothers' ages. Record the statistics listed.

$\overline{x} =$ **31.15** Median $=$ **30.5**

$s \approx$ **2.6** IQR $= Q_3 - Q_1 =$ **3.5**

COLLABORATIVE LEARNING

Whole Class Activity

Have students work in pairs. Assign pairs to find either the number of United States Representatives or the number of electoral votes for each state, or provide this information. Have each pair work together to make a poster with a histogram and an analysis of the data.

Gather together as a class to compare the two types of posters to see how the two posters are related. Have students describe the similarities and differences.

Reflect

4. What do you notice about the mean and median for the symmetric distribution (baby weights) as compared with the mean and median for the skewed distribution (mothers' ages)? Explain why this happens.
The mean and median for a symmetric distribution are equal, but the mean and median for a skewed distribution are not. This happens because the mean is pulled toward the data values in the longer tail, but the median is not.

5. The standard deviation and IQR for the skewed distribution are significantly greater than the corresponding statistics for the symmetric distribution. Explain why this makes sense.
The data are more spread out in the skewed distribution, so the measures of spread should be greater.

6. Which measures of center and spread would you report for the symmetric distribution? For the skewed distribution? Explain your reasoning.
Report either the mean and standard deviation or the median and IQR for the symmetric distribution, but use only the median and IQR for the skewed distribution because the mean and standard deviation are too sensitive to the data values in the long tail.

Explain 1 Making and Analyzing a Histogram

You can use a graphing calculator to create a histogram of numerical data using the viewing window settings Xmin (the least x-value), Xmax (the greatest x-value), and Xscl (the width of an interval on the x-axis, which becomes the width of the histogram).

Example 1 **Use a graphing calculator to make a histogram of the given data and then analyze the graph.**

(A) a. Make a histogram of the baby weights from Explore 1. Based on the shape of the distribution, identify what type of distribution it is.

Begin by turning on a statistics plot, selecting the histogram option, and entering the list where the data are stored.

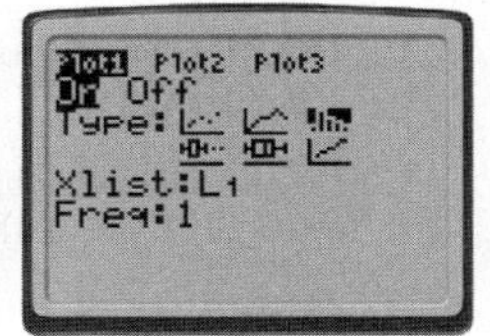

Set the viewing window. To obtain a histogram that looks very much like the line plot that you drew for this data set, use the values shown. Xscl determines the width of each bar, so when Xscl = 0.1 and Xmin = 3.15, the first bar covers the interval $3.15 \leq x < 3.25$, which captures the weight 3.2 kg.

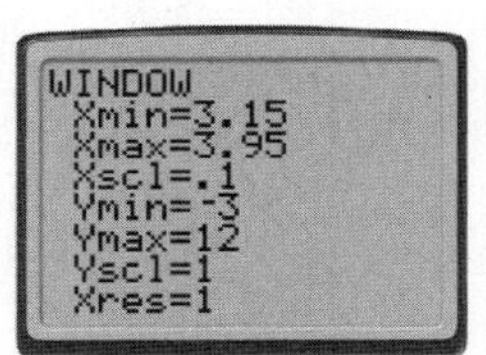

DIFFERENTIATE INSTRUCTION

Kinesthetic Experience

Have students make flash cards for the vocabulary, and add them to their flash cards from the previous lesson. Group students in pairs. Have students shuffle their own cards. One student in each pair puts the cards down with the terms showing; the other student puts them down with definitions showing. Students take turns placing a card with a definition on top of a card with the matching term. Students get a point for each correct match. Have each turn begin with the student who is about to match cards either accepting or challenging the previous match. If the student correctly challenges a match, he or she earns a point and the opponent loses a point. If the challenging student is incorrect, he or she loses a point and a turn.

EXPLAIN 1

Making and Analyzing a Histogram

QUESTIONING STRATEGIES

How do you set **Xmin** and **Xscl** when using a graphing calculator to make a histogram? **One method is to set XMin at or below the least value and choose Xscl so that each data value in L1 is a separate bar.**

How are the shapes of the line plot and the histogram for birth weight related? **The shapes are the same; both represent a normal distribution.**

INTEGRATE MATHEMATICAL PRACTICES

Focus on Math Connections

MP.1 Remind students that they might think of the standard deviation as the expected, or usual, variation of the data from the mean.

INTEGRATE MATHEMATICAL PRACTICES

Focus on Technology

MP.5 Encourage students to examine the features of their graphing calculators. Some have **Zoom** options such as **ZoomStat** that give a good initial window for a histogram.

CONNECT VOCABULARY EL

Write the names of the types of distributions and the measures of center on the board, and leave them there throughout the lesson. This will keep students who might have trouble memorizing the terms from having to flip back to the first page of the lesson while they are working.

Draw the histogram by pressing GRAPH. You can obtain the heights of the bars by pressing TRACE and using the arrow keys.

The distribution has a central mound and symmetric tails, so it is a normal distribution.

b. By examining the histogram, determine the percent of the data that are within 1 standard deviation ($s \approx 0.14$) of the mean ($\bar{x} = 3.5$). That is, determine the percent of the data in the interval $3.5 - 0.14 < x < 3.5 + 0.14$, or $3.36 < x < 3.64$. Explain your reasoning.

The bars for x-values that satisfy $3.36 < x < 3.64$ have heights of 4, 6, and 4, so 14 data values out of 20, or 70% of the data, are in the interval.

c. Suppose one of the baby weights is chosen at random. By examining the histogram, determine the probability that the weight is more than 1 standard deviation above the mean. That is, determine the probability that the weight is in the interval $x > 3.5 + 0.14$, or $x > 3.64$. Explain your reasoning.

The bars for x-values that satisfy $x > 3.64$ have heights of 2 and 1, so the probability that the weight is in the interval is $\frac{3}{20} = 0.15$ or 15%.

(B) The table gives the lengths (in inches) of the random sample of 20 babies from Explore 1.

Baby	Baby Length (in.)
1	17
2	21
3	20
4	19
5	22
6	19
7	20

Baby	Baby Length (in.)
8	18
9	21
10	19
11	21
12	20
13	19
14	22

Baby	Baby Length (in.)
15	20
16	23
17	20
18	21
19	18
20	20

a. Make a histogram of the baby lengths. Based on the shape of the distribution, identify what type of distribution it is.

The distribution has a central mound and symmetric tails, so it is a **normal** distribution.

b. By examining the histogram, determine the percent of the data that are within 2 standard deviations ($s \approx 1.4$) of the mean ($\bar{x} = 20$). Explain your reasoning.

The interval for data that are within 2 standard deviations of the mean is

17.2 $< x <$ **22.8**. The bars for x-values that satisfy **17.2** $< x <$ **22.8** have heights of **2, 4, 6, 4, and 2**, so **18** data values out of 20, or **90** % of the data, are in the interval.

LANGUAGE SUPPORT EL

Communicate Math

Have students work with a partner to fill in a table like the one below using both words and labeled drawings or pictures. Students should be able to label and describe the meaning of each part of a normal distribution graph with respect to the data.

Type of Distribution	Graph	Description
Normal distribution		
Skewed right		
Skewed left		
Uniform distribution		

c. Suppose one of the baby lengths is chosen at random. By examining the histogram,determine the probability that the length is less than 2 standard deviations below the mean. Explain your reasoning.

The interval for data that are less than 2 standard deviations below the mean is $x <$ **17.2**. The only bar for x-values that satisfy $x <$ **17.2** has a height of **1**, so the probability that the length is in the interval is $\frac{1}{20}$ = **0.05** or **5** %.

Your Turn

7. The table lists the test scores of a random sample of 22 students who are taking the same math class.

Student	Math test scores
1	86
2	78
3	95
4	83
5	83
6	81
7	87
8	81

Student	Math test scores
9	90
10	85
11	83
12	99
13	81
14	75
15	85

Student	Math test scores
16	83
17	83
18	70
19	73
20	79
21	85
22	83

a. Use a graphing calculator to make a histogram of the math test scores. Based on the shape of the distribution, identify what type of distribution it is.

The distribution has a central mound and symmetric tails, so it is a normal distribution.

b. By examining the histogram, determine the percent of the data that are within 2 standard deviations ($s \approx 6.3$) of the mean ($\bar{x} \approx 83$). Explain your reasoning.

The interval for data that are within 2 standard deviations of the mean is $70.4 < x < 95.6$. The bars for x-values that satisfy $70.4 < x < 95.6$ have heights of 1, 1, 1, 1, 3, 6, 3, 1, 1, 1, and 1, so 20 data values out of 22, or about 91% of the data, are in the interval.

c. Suppose one of the math test scores is chosen at random. By examining the histogram, determine the probability that the test score is less than 2 standard deviations below the mean. Explain your reasoning.

The interval for data that are less than 2 standard deviations below the mean is $x < 70.4$. The only bar for x-values that satisfy $x < 70.4$ has a height of 1, so the probability that the test score is in the interval is $\frac{1}{22} \approx 0.05$.

Explain 2 Making and Analyzing a Box Plot

A box plot, also known as a box-and-whisker plot, is based on five key numbers: the minimum data value, the first quartile of the data values, the median (second quartile) of the data values, the third quartile of the data values, and the maximum data value. A graphing calculator will automatically compute these values when drawing a box plot. A graphing calculator also gives you two options for drawing box plots: one that shows outliers and one that does not. For this lesson, choose the second option.

EXPLAIN 2

Making and Analyzing a Box Plot

AVOID COMMON ERRORS

Students may use the mean as the measure of central tendency in a box plot. Emphasize that box plots involve dividing the data into four groups, with the median dividing the data into two groups of equal number and the quartiles further dividing each of those groups into two groups.

QUESTIONING STRATEGIES

? How do you find the interquartile range (IQR)? **Calculate Q3 – Q1, which is the median of the upper half of the data minus the median of the lower half of the data.**

? Describe what the IQR corresponds to on the box plot. **the width of the box**

INTEGRATE MATHEMATICAL PRACTICES

Focus on Math Connections

MP.1 Emphasize that extreme values usually do not affect the interquartile range, but may greatly affect the range.

CONNECT VOCABULARY EL

The concept of *spread* arises frequently in data analysis. Make sure students understand that when you use the word *spread,* you are referring to how the data are spread as well as how they are displayed.

Example 2 **Use a graphing calculator to make a box plot of the given data and then analyze the graph.**

(A) **a.** Make a box plot of the mothers' ages from Explore 1. How does the box plot show that this skewed distribution is skewed right?

Begin by turning on a statistics plot, selecting the second box plot option, and entering the list where the data are stored.

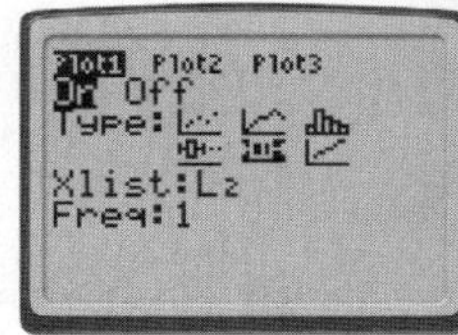

Set the viewing window. Use the values shown.

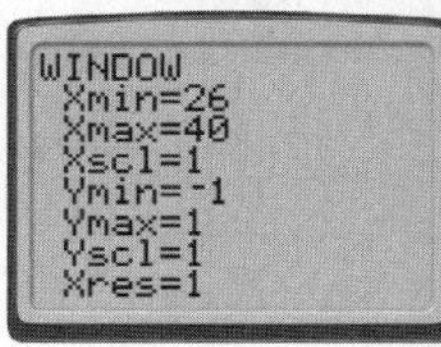

Draw the box plot by pressing GRAPH. You can obtain the box plot's five key values by pressing TRACE and using the arrow keys.

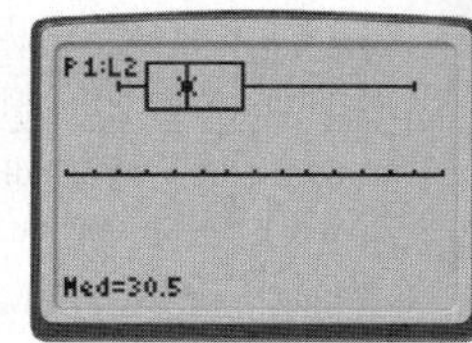

The part of the box to the right of the median is slightly wider than the part to the left, and the "whisker" on the right is much longer than the one on the left, so the distribution is skewed right.

b. Suppose one of the mothers' ages is chosen at random. Based on the box plot and not the original set of data, what can you say is the approximate probability that the age falls between the median, 30.5, and the third quartile, 32.5? Explain your reasoning.

The probability is about 25%, or 0.25, because Q_1, the median, and Q_3 divide the data into four almost-equal parts.

(B) The list gives the ages of a random sample of 16 people who visited a doctor's office one day.

80, 52, 78, 64, 70, 80, 78, 35, 78, 74, 82, 73, 80, 75, 62, 80

a. Make a box plot of the ages. How does the box plot show that this skewed distribution is skewed left?

The part of the box to the left of the median is slightly wider than the part to the right and the "whisker" on the left is much longer than the one on the right, so the distribution is skewed left.

b. Suppose one of the ages is chosen at random. Based on the box plot and not the original set of data, what can you say is the approximate probability that the age falls between the first quartile, 67, and the third quartile, 80? Explain your reasoning.

The probability is about **50**%, or **0.5**, because Q_1, the median, and Q_3 divide the data into **four** almost-equal parts and there are two parts that each represent about **25**% of the data between the first and third quartiles.

Your Turn

8. The list gives the starting salaries (in thousands of dollars) of a random sample of 18 positions at a large company. Use a graphing calculator to make a box plot and then analyze the graph.

40, 32, 27, 40, 34, 25, 37, 39, 40, 37, 28, 39, 35, 39, 40, 43, 30, 35

a. Make a box plot of the starting salaries. How does the box plot show that this skewed distribution is skewed left?

The part of the box to the right of the median is slightly wider than the part to the left, and the "whisker" on the right is longer than the one on the left, so the distribution is skewed right.

b. Suppose one of the starting salaries is chosen at random. Based on the box plot and not the original set of data, what can you say is the approximate probability that the age is greater than the third quartile, 40? Explain your reasoning.

The probability is about 75%, or 0.75, because Q_1, the median, and Q_3 divide the data into four almost-equal parts and there are three parts that each represent about 25% of the data from the first quartile to the maximum value.

Elaborate

9. Explain the difference between a normal distribution and a skewed distribution.

A normal distribution is mound-shaped with two symmetric tails. The mean and median of a normal distribution are equal or almost equal. A skewed distribution is also mound-shaped but one tail is noticeably longer than the other. The mean is usually greater than the median in a right-skewed distribution and less than the median in a left-skewed distribution.

10. **Discussion** Describe how you can use a line plot, a histogram, and a box plot of a set of data to answer questions about the percent of the data that fall within a specified interval.

All three types of data displays organize numerical data using a number line. A line plot preserves the data values, and you can simply count the number of data values that fall within a specified interval. A histogram uses the heights of bars to indicate the number of data values in intervals of equal width, and you can sum the heights of the bars whose intervals are part of the specified interval. A box plot shows the points that divide the data into four equal parts, so the specified interval must be expressed in terms of the dividing points (quartiles), which means that the corresponding percent of the data will be a multiple of 25%.

ELABORATE

INTEGRATE MATHEMATICAL PRACTICES

Focus on Critical Thinking

MP.3 Challenge students to find a way to "flip" a skewed box plot so that it keeps the same minimum and maximum values. Subtracting each value from the sum of these two values will produce this result.

AVOID COMMON ERRORS

Students who depend on technology to calculate standard deviation need to know whether the result is σ, the population standard deviation or s, the sample standard deviation. The sample standard deviation will be slightly larger, as the quotient in the calculation is $n - 1$ rather than n. For large values of n there will be little difference between the values.

SUMMARIZE THE LESSON

? How can you use shape, center, and spread to characterize a data distribution? **The shape of the distribution of a data set can be shown by displaying the data as a line plot, as a histogram, or as a box plot. The measures of center and spread can be used to summarize the distribution. Normal distributions can be summarized using either the mean and standard deviation or the median and IQR, while skewed distributions should be summarized using only the median and IQR.**

EVALUATE

ASSIGNMENT GUIDE

Concepts and Skills	Practice
Explore 1 Seeing the Shape of a Distribution	Exercise 1
Explore 2 Relating Measures of Center and Spread to the Shape of a Distribution	Exercises 4, 7
Example 1 Making and Analyzing a Histogram	Exercises 2–3
Example 2 Making and Analyzing a Box Plot	Exercises 5–6

CONNECT VOCABULARY EL

Remind students that the word *normal*, as used in mathematics, does not mean the same thing as *good* or *healthy,* as it might, for example, in the sentence "the patient's temperature is normal." A *normal curve* simply represents one kind of distribution with certain characteristics.

INTEGRATE MATHEMATICAL PRACTICES

Focus on Critical Thinking

MP.3 Have students analyze a set of data that has a small interquartile range but a large range, and have them describe how the data are distributed. The data are clustered around the median and have some extreme values.

11. Essential Question Check-In Why are the mean and standard deviation not appropriate statistics to use with a skewed distribution?

Because the mean and standard deviation are calculated using every data value, data values that are much larger or smaller than the other data values can have a significant impact on those statistics. So, the mean and standard deviation may be too sensitive to the data values in the longer tail of a skewed distribution.

Evaluate: Homework and Practice

- Online Homework
- Hints and Help
- Extra Practice

1. Make a line plot of the data. Based on the shape of the distribution, identify what type of distribution it is.

a. Ages of children: 4, 9, 12, 8, 7, 8, 7, 10, 8, 9, 6, 8

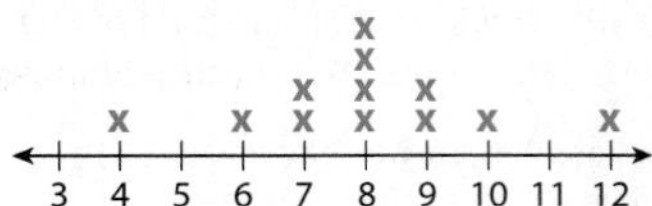

The distribution has a central mound and symmetric tails, so it is a normal distribution.

b. Scores on a test: 80, 78, 70, 77, 75, 77, 76, 66, 77, 76, 75, 77

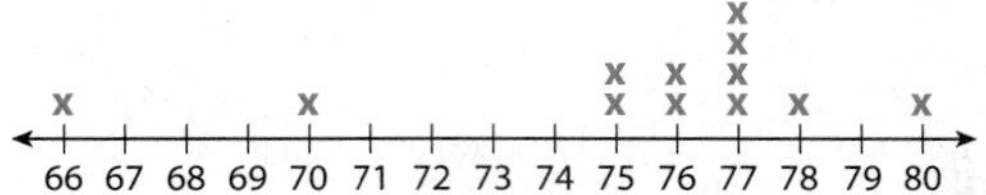

The distribution has a central mound and asymmetric tails with the longer tail on the left, so it is a left-skewed distribution.

c. Salaries (in thousands of dollars) of employees: 35, 35, 36, 40, 37, 36, 37, 35, 35, 38, 36, 34

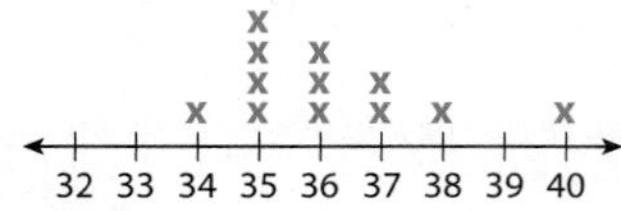

The distribution has a central mound and asymmetric tails with the longer tail on the right, so it is a right-skewed distribution.

Exercise	Depth of Knowledge (D.O.K.)	COMMON CORE Mathematical Practices
1	**1** Recall of Information	**MP.3** Logic
2	**1** Recall of Information	**MP.5** Using Tools
3	**2** Skills/Concepts	**MP.4** Modeling
4–5	**2** Skills/Concepts	**MP.3** Logic
6–7	**1** Recall of Information	**MP.5** Using Tools
8–10	**3** Strategic Thinking H.O.T.	**MP.3** Logic

In Exercises 2–3, use the data in the table. The table gives the heights and weights of a random sample of 14 college baseball players.

Height (in.)	Weight (lb)
70	160
69	165
72	170
70	170
68	150
71	175
70	160
69	165
71	165
70	170
67	155
69	165
71	165
73	185

2. a. Find the mean, median, standard deviation, and IQR of the height data.

$\bar{x} = 70$ **Median $= 70$**

$s \approx 1.5$ **IQR $= Q_3 - Q_1 = 2$**

b. Use a graphing calculator to make a histogram of the height data. Based on the shape of the distribution, identify what type of distribution it is.

The distribution has a central mound and fairly symmetric tails, so it is a normal distribution.

c. By examining the histogram of the height distribution, determine the percent of the data that fall within 1 standard deviation of the mean. Explain your reasoning.

The interval for data that are within 1 standard deviation of the mean is $68.5 < x < 71.5$. The bars for x-values that satisfy $68.5 < x < 71.5$ have heights of 3, 4, and 3, so 10 data values out of 14, or about 71% of the data, are in the interval.

AUDITORY CUES

The word *quartile* sounds like *quarter*, which suggests fourths.

AVOID COMMON ERRORS

Students may assume that if one side of a box plot is longer than the other, the longer side represents more data. Remind students that a longer side indicates the same amount of data, but a wider spread, showing that the values are farther apart from each other.

INTEGRATE MATHEMATICAL PRACTICES

Focus on Math Connections

MP.1 Emphasize that the advantage of using a box plot instead of a line plot is that it is easier to see the range, median, and other features of the data. The disadvantage of a box plot is that the values of the individual data cannot be seen.

d. Suppose one of the heights is chosen at random. By examining the histogram, determine the probability that the height is more than 1 standard deviation above the mean. Explain your reasoning.

The interval for data that are more than 1 standard deviation above the mean is $x > 71.5$.

The bars for x-values that satisfy $x > 71.5$ have heights of 1 and 1, so the probability that a height is in the interval is $\frac{2}{14} \approx 0.14$.

3. **a.** Find the mean, median, standard deviation, and IQR of the weight data.

$\bar{x} \approx 166$ Median $= 165$

$s \approx 8.2$ IQR $= Q_3 - Q_1 = 10$

b. Use a graphing calculator to make a histogram of the weight data. Based on the shape of the distribution, identify what type of distribution it is.

The distribution has a central mound and fairly symmetric tails, so it is a normal distribution.

c. By examining the histogram, determine the percent of the weight data that are within 2 standard deviations of the mean. Explain your reasoning.

The interval for data that are within 2 standard deviations of the mean is $149.6 < x < 182.$ The bars for x-values that satisfy $149.6 < x < 182.4$ have heights of 1, 1, 2, 5, 3, and 1, so 13 data values out of 14, or about 93% of the data, are in the interval.

d. Suppose one of the weights is chosen at random. By examining the histogram, determine the probability that the weight is less than 1 standard deviation above the mean. Explain your reasoning.

The interval for data that are less than 1 standard deviation above the mean is $x < 174.2$. The bars for x-values that satisfy $x < 174.2$ have heights of 1, 1, 2, 5, and 3, so the probability that a weight is in the interval is $\frac{12}{14} \approx 0.86$ or 86%.

4. The line plot shows a random sample of resting heart rates (in beats per minute) for 24 adults.

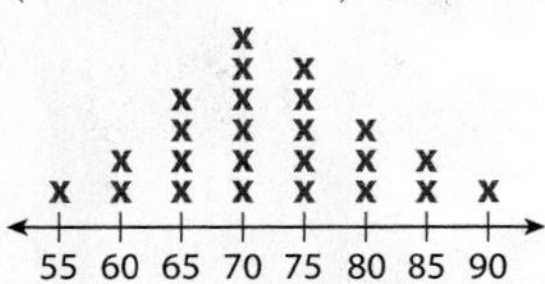

Resting Heart Rate

a. Find the mean, median, standard deviation, and IQR of the heart rates.

$\bar{x} \approx 72$ **Median $= 70$**

$s \approx 8.4$ **IQR $= Q_3 - Q_1 = 12.5$**

b. By examining the line plot, determine the percent of the data that are within 1 standard deviation of the mean. Explain your reasoning.

The interval for data that are within 1 standard deviation of the mean is $63.6 < x < 80.4$. This interval includes heart rates of 65, 70, 75, and 80, which have frequencies of 4, 6, 5, and 3, respectively. So, 18 data values out of 24, or 75% of the data, are in the interval.

c. Suppose one of the heart rates is chosen at random. By examining the line plot, determine the probability that the heart rate is more than 1 standard deviation below the mean. Explain your reasoning.

The interval for data that are more than 1 standard deviation below the mean is $x > 63.6$. This interval includes heart rates of 65, 70, 75, 80, 85, and 90, which have frequencies of 4, 6, 5, 3, 2, and 1, respectively. So, the probability that a heart rate is in the interval is $\frac{21}{24} = 0.875$ or 87.5%.

5. The list gives the prices (in thousands of dollars) of a random sample of houses for sale in a large town.

175, 400, 325, 350, 500, 375, 350, 375, 400, 375, 250, 400, 200, 375, 400, 400, 375, 325, 400, 350

a. Find the mean, median, standard deviation, and IQR of the house prices. How do these statistics tell you that the distribution is not symmetric?

$\bar{x} = 355$ **Median $= 375$**

$s \approx 72.28$ **IQR $= Q_3 - Q_1 = 62.5$**

The mean and median are significantly different, which indicates that the distribution is not symmetric.

b. Use a graphing calculator to make a box plot of the house prices. How does the box plot show that this skewed distribution is skewed left?

The part of the box to the left of the median is slightly wider than the part to the right, and the "whisker" on the left is longer than the one on the right, so the distribution is skewed left.

c. Suppose one of the house prices is chosen at random. Based on the box plot and not the original set of data, what can you say is the approximate probability that the price falls between the first and the third quartiles? Explain your reasoning.

The probability is about 50%, or 0.50, because Q_1, the median, and Q_3 divide the data into four almost-equal parts and there are two parts that each represent about 25% of the data between the first and third quartiles.

INTEGRATE MATHEMATICAL PRACTICES

Focus on Technology

MP.5 Remind students that the **TRACE** feature of a graphing calculator can be used to find the quartiles for a data set graphed as a box plot.

6. The line plot shows a random sample of the amounts of time (in minutes) that an employee at a call center spent on the phone with customers.

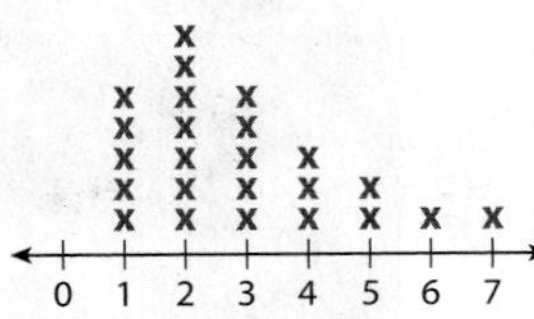

Time Spent With Customer

a. Do you expect the mean to be equal to, less than, or greater than the median? Explain.

The mean should be greater than the median because the distribution is right-skewed and the mean will be pulled toward the right tail.

b. Find the mean, median, standard deviation, and IQR of the time data. Do these statistics agree with your answer for part a?

$\bar{x} = 2.875$ Median $= 2.5$

$s \approx 1.6$ IQR $= Q_3 - Q_1 = 2$

Yes, the mean is greater than the median.

c. Use a graphing calculator to make a box plot of the time data. How does the box plot show that the distribution is skewed right?

The part of the box to the right of the median is wider than the part to the left, and the "whisker" on the left is longer than the one on the right.

d. Suppose one of the times spent with a customer is chosen at random. Based on the box plot and not the original set of data, what can you say is the approximate probability that the time is greater than the third quartile? Explain your reasoning.

The probability is about 25%, or 0.25, because Q_1, the median, and Q_3 divide the data into four almost-equal parts.

7. Classify each description as applying to a normal distribution or a skewed distribution.

A. Histogram is mound-shaped with two symmetric tails.	● Normal	○ Skewed
B. Mean and median are equal or almost equal.	● Normal	○ Skewed
C. Box plot has one "whisker" longer than the other.	○ Normal	● Skewed
D. Histogram is mounded with one tail longer than the other.	○ Normal	● Skewed
E. Box plot is symmetric with respect to the median.	● Normal	○ Skewed
F. Mean and median are significantly different.	○ Normal	● Skewed

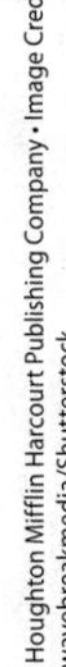

H.O.T. Focus on Higher Order Thinking

8. **Explain the Error** A student was given the following data and asked to determine the percent of the data that fall within 1 standard deviation of the mean.

20, 21, 21, 22, 22, 22, 22, 23, 23, 23, 23, 24, 24, 24, 24, 24, 25, 25, 25, 26, 26, 26, 27, 27, 28

The student gave this answer: "The interval for data that are within 1 standard deviation of the mean is $24 - 3.5 < x < 24 + 3.5$, or $21.5 < x < 27.5$. The bars for x-values that satisfy $21.5 < x < 27.5$ have heights of 4, 4, 5, 3, 3, and 2, so 21 data values out of 25, or about 84% of the data, are in the interval." Find and correct the student's error.

The median of the data is 24, and the IQR is 3.5, so the student used the median and IQR, rather than the mean and standard deviation, to define the interval for data that are within 1 standard deviation of the mean. Since the mean of the data is 23.88 and the standard deviation is about 2.03, the student should have used the interval $23.88 - 2.03 < x < 23.88 + 2.03$, or $21.85 < x < 25.91$. The bars for x-values that satisfy $21.85 < x < 25.91$ have heights of 4, 4, 5, and 3, so 16 data values out of 25, or about 64% of the data, are in the interval.

9. **Analyze Relationships** The list gives the number of siblings that a child has from a random sample of 10 children at a daycare center.

5, 2, 3, 1, 0, 2, 3, 1, 2, 1

a. Use a graphing calculator to create a box plot of the data. Does the box plot indicate that the distribution is normal or skewed? Explain.
Although the two parts of the box in the box plot have the same width, the box plot shows that the distribution is skewed right because the right "whisker" is longer than the left one.

b. Find the mean, median, standard deviation, and IQR of the sibling data. What is the relationship between the mean and median?
$\bar{x} = 2$ Median $= 2$
$s \approx 1.3$ IQR $= Q_3 - Q_1 = 2$
The mean and median are equal.

c. Suppose that an 11th child at the daycare is included in the random sample, and that child has 1 sibling. How does the box plot change? How does the relationship between the mean and median change?
The box plot does not change.
$\bar{x} = 1.9$ Median $= 2$
$s \approx 1.3$ IQR $= Q_3 - Q_1 = 2$
The mean is less than the median.

d. Suppose that a 12th child at the daycare is included in the random sample, and that child also has 1 sibling. How does the box plot change? How does the relationship between the mean and median change?
The part of the box to the right of the median is now wider than the part to the left, and the right "whisker" is now even longer than the left one.
$\bar{x} \approx 1.8$ Median $= 1.5$
$s \approx 1.3$ IQR $= Q_3 - Q_1 = 1.5$
The mean is greater than the median.

AVOID COMMON ERRORS

Students may decide to divide the number of data by 4 to get the lower quartile and upper quartile. Reinforce that these quartiles are defined as the medians of the upper and lower halves of the data as determined by the median.

PEER-TO-PEER DISCUSSION

Group students in pairs. Ask one student in each pair to give values for the quartiles, range, and interquartile range. Then have the other student determine a set of data that fits these values and graph the data as a box plot. As an extension, have the students write a problem that fits the data.

JOURNAL

Have students write a journal entry in which they draw a normal distribution and a skewed distribution. Next to the drawings, have students list the measures of center and spread that are used for each type of distribution and explain why.

e. What is the general rule about the relationship between the mean and median when a distribution is skewed right? What has your investigation of the sibling data demonstrated about this rule?

The general rule is that when a distribution is skewed right, the mean is greater than the median because the mean is increased by the data in the tail on the right. The investigation of the sibling data shows that this rule doesn't always apply.

10. Draw Conclusions Recall that a graphing calculator may give two versions of the standard deviation. The population standard deviation, which you can also use for the "uncorrected" sample standard deviation, is $\sigma_x = \sqrt{\frac{(x_1-\bar{x})^2 + (x_2-\bar{x})^2 + \cdots + (x_n-\bar{x})^2}{n}}$.

The "corrected" sample standard deviation is $s_x = \sqrt{\frac{(x_1-\bar{x})^2 + (x_2-\bar{x})^2 + \cdots + (x_n-\bar{x})^2}{n-1}}$.

Write and simplify the ratio $\frac{\sigma_x}{s_x}$. Then determine what this ratio approaches as n increases without bound. What does this result mean in terms of finding standard deviations of samples?

$$\frac{\sigma_x}{s_x} = \frac{\sqrt{\frac{(x_1-\bar{x})^2 + (x_2-\bar{x})^2 + \cdots + (x_n-\bar{x})^2}{n}}}{\sqrt{\frac{(x_1-\bar{x})^2 + (x_2-\bar{x})^2 + \cdots + (x_n-\bar{x})^2}{n-1}}} = \sqrt{\frac{\frac{(x_1-\bar{x})^2 + (x_2-\bar{x})^2 + \cdots + (x_n-\bar{x})^2}{n}}{\frac{(x_1-\bar{x})^2 + (x_2-\bar{x})^2 + \cdots + (x_n-\bar{x})^2}{n-1}}} = \sqrt{\frac{n-1}{n}}$$

. As n increases without bound, $\frac{n-1}{n}$ approaches 1, so $\frac{\sigma_x}{s_x}$ approaches $\sqrt{1}$, or 1. This means that as the sample size increases, the two forms of the standard deviation get closer to being equal.

Lesson Performance Task

The table gives data about a random sample of 16 cats brought to a veterinarian's office during one week.

Sex	Weight (pounds)	Age (years)
Male	12	11
Female	9	2
Female	8	12
Male	10	15
Female	10	10
Male	11	10
Male	10	11
Male	11	7

Sex	Weight (pounds)	Age (years)
Female	9	5
Male	12	8
Female	7	13
Male	11	11
Female	10	13
Male	13	9
Female	8	12
Female	9	16

a. Find the mean, median, standard deviation, and IQR of the weight data. Do the same for the age data.

b. Use a graphing calculator to make a histogram of the weight data and a separate histogram of the age data. Based on the shape of each distribution, identify what type of distribution it is. Explain your reasoning.

c. By examining the histogram of the weight distribution, determine the percent of the data that fall within 1 standard deviation of the mean. Explain your reasoning.

d. For the age data, $Q_1 = 8.5$ and $Q_3 = 12.5$. By examining the histogram of the age distribution, find the probability that the age of a randomly chosen cat falls between Q_1 and Q_3. Why does this make sense?

e. Investigate whether being male or female has an impact on a cat's weight and age. Do so by calculating the mean weight and age of female cats and the mean weight and age of male cats. For which variable, weight or age, does being male or female have a greater impact? How much of an impact is there?

a. Weight data: $\bar{x} = 10$ Median = 10; $s \approx 1.6$ $IQR = Q_3 - Q_1 = 2$

Age data: $\bar{x} \approx 10.3$ Median = 11; $s \approx 3.5$ $IQR = Q_3 - Q_1 = 4$

b. The weight distribution has a central mound and symmetric tails, so it is a normal distribution. The age distribution has a central mound and a left tail that is longer than the right tail, so it is a skewed-left distribution.

c. The interval for weight data that are within 1 standard deviation of the mean is $8.4 < x < 11.6$. The bars for x-values that satisfy $8.4 < x < 11.6$ have heights of 3, 4, and 3, so 10 data values out of 16, or 62.5% of the weight data, are in the interval.

d. The bars for x-values that satisfy $8.5 < x < 12.5$ have heights of 1, 2, 3, and 2, so the probability that a randomly chosen cat is between 8.5 and 12.5 years old is $\frac{8}{16} = 0.5$ or 50%. This makes sense because Q_1, the median, and Q_3 divide the data into four almost-equal parts and there are two parts that each represent about 25% of the data between the first and third quartiles.

e. For female cats, the mean weight is 8.75 pounds, and the mean age is about 10.4 years. For male cats, the mean weight is 11.25 pounds, and the mean age is about 10.3 years. Being male or female appears to have an impact on weight but not on age. On average, male cats weigh 2.5 pounds more than female cats.

EXTENSION ACTIVITY

Have students compare the formulas for sample standard deviation, S, and population standard deviation, σ. They should calculate for both very small samples and very large samples. Then have students research to find reasons for dividing the summation by n and the other by $n - 1$.

Note that S is considered an *unbiased estimate* of the standard deviation of the population and is based on the concept of *degrees of freedom*. One degree of freedom is lost due to the fact that the sample and the complement of the sample must total the entire population. Dividing by $n - 1$ compensates for the information in the population that is not within the sample.

QUESTIONING STRATEGIES

Why might you be interested only in the sample standard deviation and not in the population standard deviation? **Possible answer: You might be interested only in the subset of the population because the rest of the population will not be affected by any decisions made from the data.**

Why do we square the differences between data values and the mean? Why not just add the differences from the mean? **The sum of the differences is 0, so the mean difference will always be 0. This provides no insight with respect to the data.**

INTEGRATE MATHEMATICAL PRACTICES

Focus on Technology

MP.5 In calculating the distribution of data, what does each of the six symbols on the calculator screen represent? **$\bar{x}$ represents the mean. $\sum x$ represents the sum of the data. $\sum x^2$ represents the sum of squares of the data. S_x represents the sample standard deviation. σ_x represents the population standard deviation. n represents the total number of items entered in the list of data.**

Scoring Rubric

2 points: Student correctly solves the problem and explains his/her reasoning.

1 point: Student shows good understanding of the problem but does not fully solve or explain his/her reasoning.

0 points: Student does not demonstrate understanding of the problem.

Study Guide Review

ASSESSMENT AND INTERVENTION

Assign or customize module reviews.

MODULE PERFORMANCE TASK

COMMON CORE

Mathematical Practices: : MP.1, MP.2, MP.4, MP.5, S-ID.A.1, S-ID.A.2

SUPPORTING STUDENT REASONING

Students should begin this problem by considering different ways to display the data. Here is some of the information they may ask for.

- **Are there any ways of displaying data that we should not be considering?** Ask students to consider the pros and cons of various displays and to choose the one that best compares the nutrients of the ten fruits.
- **Does all the data need to fit in one display?** Students should create as many displays as needed to easily compare the nutrients of one fruit to those of the other nine.

STUDY GUIDE REVIEW

Gathering and Displaying Data

MODULE 22

Essential Question: How can gathering and displaying data help solve real-world problems?

Key Vocabulary
population *(población)*
census *(censo)*
parameter *(parámetro)*
sample *(muestra)*
sampling statistic *(estadística)*
representative sample *(muestra representantiva)*
biased sample *(muestra no representantiva)*
numerical data *(datos numéricos)*
categorical data *(datos categóricos)*
proportion *(proporción)*
distribution *(distribución)*
uniform distribution *(distribución uniforme)*
normal distribution *(distribución normal)*
skewed distribution *(distribución asimétrica)*

KEY EXAMPLE *(Lesson 22.1)*

A local community center surveyed a small random sample of people in the community about their time spent volunteering. The survey asked whether the person engaged in regular volunteer work (food kitchen, hospital, community center, or other) and, if so, the duration and frequency of the volunteer work.

Of the 20 people surveyed, 8 said they do engage in regular volunteer work. The table lists the data for those 8 people.

Type of Work	Duration (hours)	Days per Week
Food Kitchen	2	5
Hospital	3	3
Hospital	2	4
Food Kitchen	5	3
Comm. Center	4	5
Hospital	2	4
Other	3	5
Comm. Center	2	4

Calculate statistics from the sample, and use the statistics to make predictions about the volunteering habits of the approximately 10,000 people living in the community.

Proportion of adults who volunteer $= \frac{8}{20} = 0.4 = 40\%$

Proportion of hospital volunteers $= \frac{3}{8} = 0.375 = 37.5\%$

Use proportion and a verbal model to predict the number of hospital volunteers among all people living in the community.

Total hospital volunteers = Community × Prop. of Volunteers × Prop. of Hospital Volunteers
$= 10{,}000 \times 0.4 \times 0.375 = 1500$

KEY EXAMPLE *(Lesson 22.2)*

Using the volunteer table, make a line plot for the distribution of hours, and a line plot for the distribution of frequency (days per week).

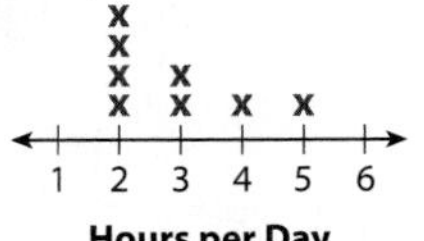

This line plot is skewed left.

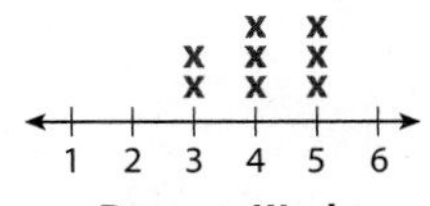

This line plot has a nearly uniform distribution.

SCAFFOLDING SUPPORT

- Some students may need extra time to experiment with different displays to choose the best display.
- You may wish to intervene if most students are creating a different display for each type of fruit. Elicit from students various other options and have them compare pros and cons of a couple of different display types for these data.

EXERCISES

A local high school surveys a random sample of students out of a total of approximately 2500 students to see if a student is interested in attending sporting events and, if so, what type of sporting events the person prefers (football, baseball, volleyball, or track), how many friends they would bring along, and how many events they would be willing to attend a year.

Of the 25 students surveyed, 10 indicated an interest in attending sporting events. The table lists the data for those 10 people.

Sporting Event	Number of Friends	Number of Events
Football	3	5
Football	0	6
Baseball	2	4
Volleyball	2	8
Football	5	7
Track	1	3
Football	3	4
Volleyball	2	5
Baseball	4	2
Track	3	3

1. Using the statistics from the sample, create a verbal model to predict the number of students likely to attend a track meet, then predict the total attendance when they bring their friends. *(Lesson 22.1)*

Total student attendees = Total students × prop. of students willing to attend sporting events × prop. of students willing to attend track meets = $2500 \times \frac{10}{25} \times \frac{2}{10} = 2500 \times 0.4 \times 0.2 = 200$.

Total attendance with friends = $2500 \times \frac{10}{25} \times \left(\frac{1}{10}(2) + \frac{1}{10}(4)\right) = 600$

MODULE PERFORMANCE TASK

Fruit Nutrition Data

The table compares the nutritional values of ten fruits. Specifically, the table shows how much of the recommended daily allowance of three different nutrients is met by a serving of each fruit.

You want to display the data so you can pick up a piece of fruit and know how it compares nutritionally to the other nine fruits. Make appropriate data representations and use them to describe the distributions for each of these data sets. Then, pick one fruit and use your data representations to compare it with the other fruits.

Start on your own paper by listing information you will need to solve the problem. Then use graphs, numbers, tables, words, or algebra to explain how you reached your conclusion.

	Percentage of Daily Value		
Fruit	Potassium	Fiber	Vitamin C
Apple	7	20	8
Banana	13	12	15
Cantaloupe	7	4	80
Cherries	10	4	15
Orange	7	12	130
Peach	7	8	15
Pear	5	24	10
Pineapple	3	4	50
Strawberries	5	8	160
Watermelon	8	4	25

SAMPLE SOLUTION

Start with potassium. Order the potassium percent levels from least to greatest:
3, 5, 5, 7, 7, 7, 7, 8, 10, 13

- The minimum is 3, the first quartile is 5, the median is 7, the third quartile is 8, and the maximum is 13.

We have all we need to create a box plot for potassium:

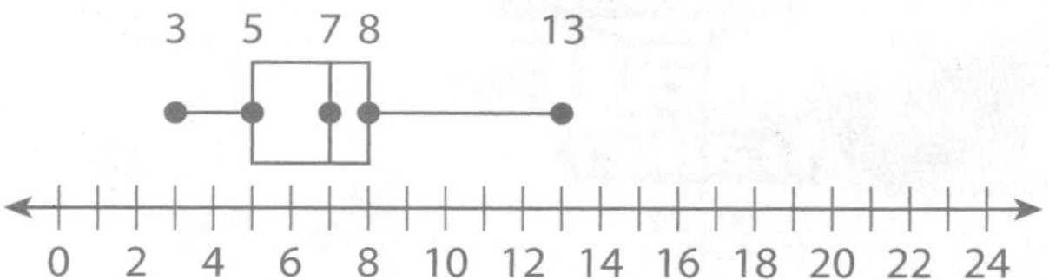

Use a similar process to create box plots for fiber and vitamin C:

Fiber:

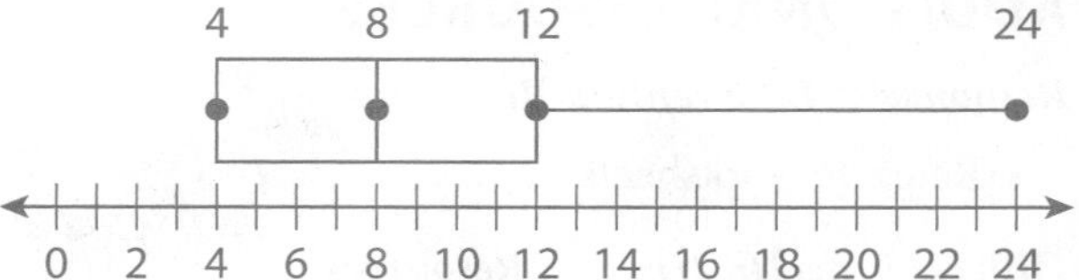

Vitamin C:

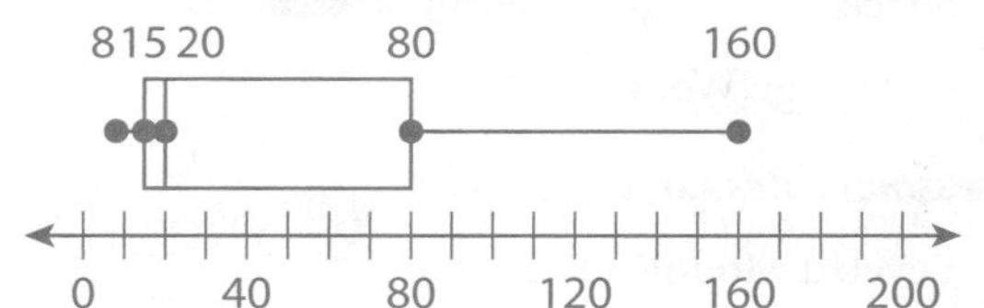

From the box plots, we can see that the distribution for potassium is relatively symmetrical, the distribution for fiber is skewed to the right, and the distribution for Vitamin C is heavily skewed to the right.

By comparing the data values for a banana to the box plots, you can see that, relative to other fruits, a banana is very rich in potassium, above average in fiber, but poor in vitamin C.

DISCUSSION OPPORTUNITIES

- Discuss with students what made them choose the display choice they did. Also ask them what characteristics of the other display choices caused them to be rejected.
- Discuss with students the benefits of potassium, fiber, and vitamin C. Ask them what other nutrients are important to a healthy diet.

Assessment Rubric

2 points: Student correctly solves the problem and explains his/her reasoning.

1 point: Student shows good understanding of the problem but does not fully solve or explain his/her reasoning.

0 points: Student does not demonstrate understanding of the problem.

Ready to Go On?

ASSESS MASTERY

Use the assessment on this page to determine if students have mastered the concepts and standards covered in this module.

ASSESSMENT AND INTERVENTION

Access Ready to Go On? assessment online, and receive instant scoring, feedback, and customized intervention or enrichment.

ADDITIONAL RESOURCES

Response to Intervention Resources

- Reteach Worksheets

Differentiated Instruction Resources

- Reading Strategies EL
- Success for English Learners EL
- Challenge Worksheets

Assessment Resources

- Leveled Module Quizzes

Ready to Go On?

23.1–23.2 Gathering and Displaying Data

- Online Homework
- Hints and Help
- Extra Practice

Use the table for exercises 1–4.

A local business surveys a random sample of about 500 employees to see if they are working overtime and, if so, how many hours per week and how many weeks per month. The company has four types of employees: sales, engineer, manager, and clerical.

The 40 employees surveyed were evenly split between the four employment categories. Ten worked overtime last month. The table lists the data for those 10 people.

Employee	Avg. Overtime/Week	Weeks/ Month
Manager	8	3
Manager	10	2
Sales	3	1
Engineer	2	1
Manager	8	2
Clerical	8	2
Sales	4	3
Engineer	3	1
Manager	7	3
Sales	2	2

1. Predict the number of managers working overtime out of the employees of the company.

   50 managers

2. Predict the number of sales people working overtime out of the employees of the company.

   Approximately 38 sales people

3. Create the line plot for the number of weeks per month the sample of employees works overtime.

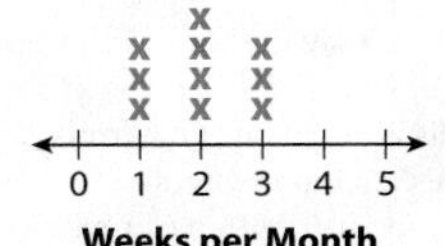

ESSENTIAL QUESTION

4. How can gathering and displaying data help a business owner?

   Possible answer: A business owner can use data to keep track of sales, or of how many hours employees are working.

COMMON CORE Common Core Standards

Lesson	*Exercise*	Math Standards	Mathematical Practices
22.1	1	**S-ID.A.4**	**MP.1**
22.1	2	**S-ID.A.4**	**MP.1**
22.2	3	**S-IC.A.1**	**MP.7**

MODULE 22
MIXED REVIEW

Assessment Readiness

1. Consider the equation $y = \frac{3x-2}{x+2}$. Is the function defined for the value of x? Select Yes or No for A–C.

   A. $x = 2$ ● Yes ○ No
   B. $x = -2$ ○ Yes ● No
   C. $x = 0$ ● Yes ○ No

2. Consider the distribution of data on line plots. Choose True or False for each statement.

   A. A distribution that is "skewed" has most of the data in the middle with two tails on each side. ○ True ● False
   B. A "uniform" distribution has a data distribution that is basically level, though it doesn't have to be exactly level. ● True ○ False
   C. A distribution that is "normal" looks bell-shaped. ● True ○ False

3. The junior class at a local school would like to survey students to pick a theme for the junior-senior prom. They are considering the following survey methods:
   - Survey every tenth student in the junior and senior classes on the school roster.
   - Survey every fifteenth student on the school roster for freshman through seniors.
   - Survey those who happen to be standing around outside in the morning before the first bell rings.

   Which sampling method would most likely result in a theme that would please those attending the prom? Explain.

   Possible answer: It is a junior-senior prom, so the second and third survey would include people who would not be able to attend the prom. The first survey method is the only method that includes only those able to attend.

4. Solve the equation $2x^2 + 6x + 10 = 0$ for all values of x. Explain the method you used, and why.

   $x = \frac{-3 \pm i\sqrt{11}}{2}$; **Possible answer: The discriminant was negative, so I continued through with the quadratic formula, because I knew the answer would be imaginary.**

Common Core Standards

Lesson	Exercise	Math Standards	Mathematical Practices
8.2, 8.3	1*	F-IF.C.7, A-APR.D.7	MP.1
22.2	2	S-ID.A.4	MP.6
22.1	3	S-IC.B.3	MP.4
3.3	4*	N-CN.C.7	MP.5

* Item integrates mixed review concepts from previous modules or a previous course.

MIXED REVIEW

Assessment Readiness

ASSESSMENT AND INTERVENTION

Assign ready-made or customized practice tests to prepare students for high-stakes tests.

ADDITIONAL RESOURCES

Assessment Resources

- Leveled Module Quizzes: Modified, B

AVOID COMMON ERRORS

Item 1 Many students will forget that a denominator of zero means that a value is undefined, and they will instead consider it equal to zero. Remind students that they can also graph rational functions on the calculator and check the table, which will show an error when asked to evaluate an undefined value.

Data Distributions

ESSENTIAL QUESTION:

Answer: Understanding normal relationships between data sets, such as height and age from 0 to 20 years, helps doctors identify possible illnesses or disorders.

PROFESSIONAL DEVELOPMENT VIDEO

Professional Development Video
Author Matt Larson models successful teaching practices in an actual high-school classroom.
Professional Development
my.hrw.com

MODULE 23

Data Distributions

Essential Question: How can you use data distributions to solve real-world problems?

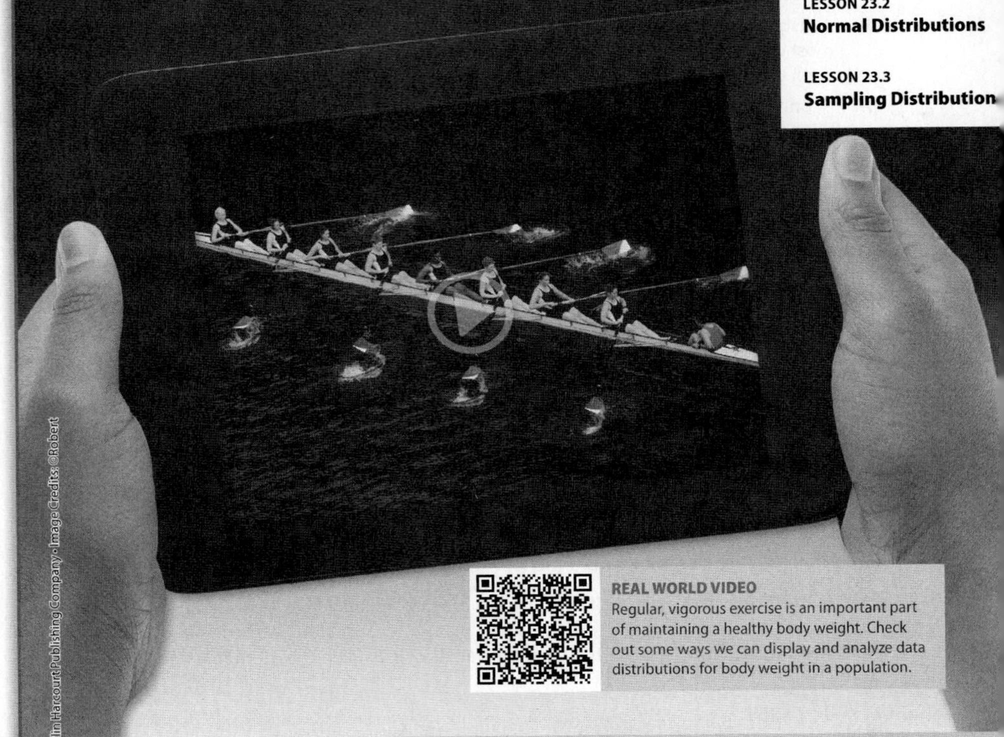

REAL WORLD VIDEO
Regular, vigorous exercise is an important part of maintaining a healthy body weight. Check out some ways we can display and analyze data distributions for body weight in a population.

MODULE PERFORMANCE TASK PREVIEW

BMI and Obesity

Health experts use a variety of statistics to measure the overall health of a population. One of these is body mass index (BMI), which uses a person's weight and height to produce a number that describes whether he or she is overweight, underweight, or normal. How many people are within the normal range? How many are obese? These are weighty questions! An ounce of curiosity is all we will need to figure them out at the end of the module.

Module 1 1115

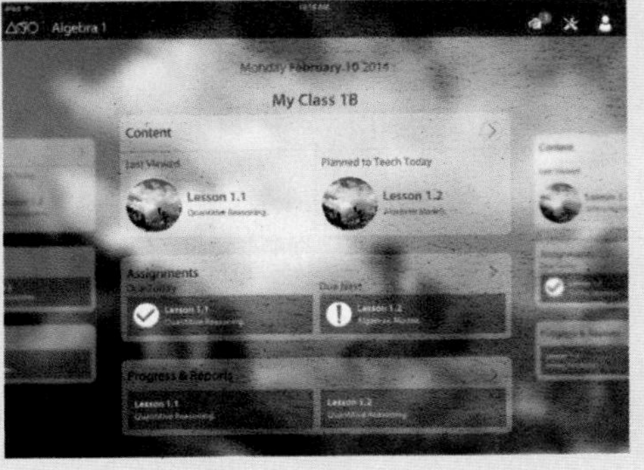

DIGITAL TEACHER EDITION

Access a full suite of teaching resources when and where you need them:

- Access content online or offline
- Customize lessons to share with your class
- Communicate with your students in real-time
- View student grades and data instantly to target your instruction where it is needed most

PERSONAL MATH TRAINER

Assessment and Intervention

Assign automatically graded homework, quizzes, tests, and intervention activities. Prepare your students with updated, Common Core-aligned practice tests.

Are YOU Ready?

Complete these exercises to review skills you will need for this chapter.

Measures of Center and Spread

- Online Homework
- Hints and Help
- Extra Practice

Example 1 Find the median, mean, and range of these ordered data.

8, 15, 15, 26, 33, 49, 50, 54

Median: $\frac{26 + 33}{2} = 29.5$

Mean: $\frac{8 + 15 + 15 + 26 + 33 + 49 + 50 + 54}{8} = 31.25$

Range: $54 - 8 = 46$

Find the median, mean, and range.

1. 16, 38, 12, 19, 40

med: 19; mean: 25; range: 28

2. 14, 4, 10, 6, 16, 9, 1, 2, 5, 3

med: 5.5; mean: 7; range: 15

3. 15, 8, 12, 1, 10, 2

med: 9; mean: 8; range: 14

Normal Distributions

Example 2 The graph shows a normal distribution of Intelligence Quotient (IQ) scores. What percent of the population has an IQ score greater than the mean?

The curve is symmetrical about an IQ score of 100, which is the mean. So 50% of the population has an IQ score greater than the mean.

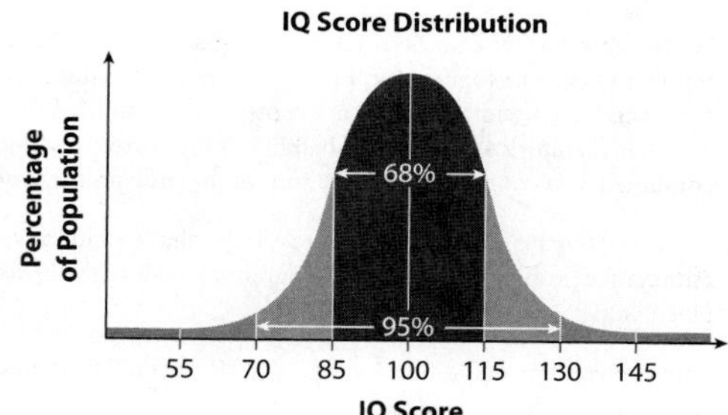

Use the graph to answer the questions.

4. What percent of the population has an IQ score above 130?

2.5%

5. What percent of the population has an IQ score above 115?

16%

6. What percent of the population has an IQ score between 70 and 85?

13.5%

Response to Intervention			Differentiated Instruction
Tier 1 Lesson Intervention Worksheets	**Tier 2** Strategic Intervention Skills Intervention Worksheets	**Tier 3** Intensive Intervention Worksheets available online	
Reteach 23.1 Reteach 23.2 Reteach 23.3	43 Data Distributions and Outliers 49 Measures of Center and Spread 50 Normal Distributions	Building Block Skills 72, 115, 116, 117	Challenge worksheets Extend the Math Lesson Activities in TE

Are You Ready?

ASSESS READINESS

Use the assessment on this page to determine if students need strategic or intensive intervention for the module's prerequisite skills.

ASSESSMENT AND INTERVENTION

Personal Math Trainer

RtI Response to Intervention TIER 1, TIER 2, TIER 3 SKILLS

Personal Math Trainer will automatically create a standards-based, personalized intervention assignment for your students, targeting each student's individual needs!

ADDITIONAL RESOURCES

See the table below for a full list of intervention resources available for this module.

Response to Intervention Resources also includes:

- Tier 2 Skill Pre-Tests for each Module
- Tier 2 Skill Post-Tests for each skill

LESSON 23.1

Probability Distributions

Common Core Math Standards

The student is expected to:

 **S-IC.A.2**

Decide if a specified model is consistent with results from a given data-generating process, e.g., using simulation. Also A-APR.C.5(+), S-CP.B.7

Mathematical Practices

 **MP.7 Using Structure**

Language Objective

Work with a partner to fill in a chart describing empirical, theoretical, and cumulative probability.

ENGAGE

Essential Question: What is a probability distribution for a discrete random variable, and how can it be displayed?

A probability distribution shows the probability (either empirical or theoretical) associated with each possible value of the random variable. The distribution can be displayed using a histogram with bars that are centered on the possible values and having a height equal to the probability for that value.

PREVIEW: LESSON PERFORMANCE TASK

View the Engage section online. Discuss the photo and how a census can provide information that can be used to calculate a probability. Then preview the Lesson Performance Task.

Name ______ Class ______ Date ______

23.1 Probability Distributions

Essential Question: What is a probability distribution for a discrete random variable, and how can it be displayed?

Resource Locker

Explore Using Simulation to Obtain an Empirical Probability Distribution

A **random variable** is a variable whose value is determined by the outcome of a probability experiment. For example when you roll a number cube, you can use the random variable X to represent the number you roll. The possible values of X are 1, 2, 3, 4, 5, and 6.

A **probability distribution** is a data distribution that gives the probabilities of the values of a random variable. A probability distribution can be represented by a histogram in which the values of the random variable—that is, the possible outcomes—are on the horizontal axis, and probabilities are on the vertical axis. The probability distribution for rolling a number cube is shown. Notice that it is a uniform distribution.

Probability: $\frac{3}{6}$, $\frac{2}{6}$, $\frac{1}{6}$

1 2 3 4 5 6

Result of rolling a number cube

When the values of a random variable are discrete, as is the case for rolling a number cube, a histogram for the probability distribution typically shows bars that each have a width of 1 and are centered on a value of the variable. The area of each bar therefore equals the probability of the corresponding outcome, and the combined areas of the bars are the sum of the probabilities, which is 1.

A **cumulative probability** is the probability that a random variable is less than or equal to a given value. You can find cumulative probabilities from a histogram by adding the areas of the bars for all outcomes less than or equal to the given value.

Suppose you flip a coin 5 times in a row. Use a simulation to determine the probability distribution for the number of times the coin lands heads up.

(A) When you flip a coin, the possible outcomes are heads and tails. Use a graphing calculator to generate the integers 0 and 1 randomly, associating each 0 with tails and each 1 with heads.

randInt(0,1)
0
1
0
1
0

To do the simulation, press MATH and then select the probability (**PRB**) menu. Choose **5:randInt** and enter a 0, a comma, a 1, and a closing parenthesis. Now press ENTER 5 times to generate a group of 0s and 1s. This simulates one trial (that is, one set of 5 coin flips).

Carry out 4 trials and record your results in the table. **Answers will vary. Possible answer:**

Trial	1	2	3	4
Number of heads	2	1	2	3

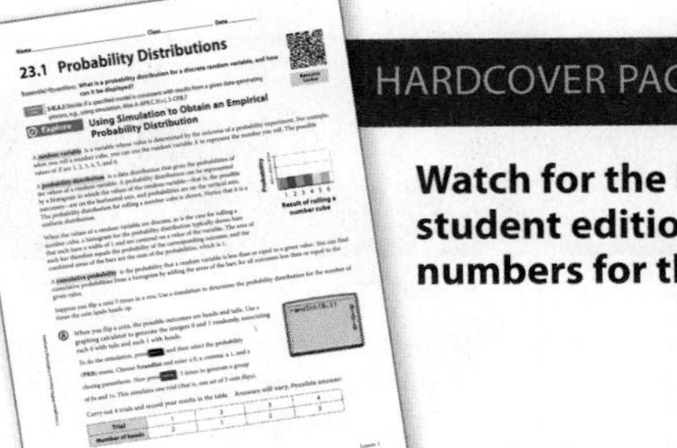

HARDCOVER PAGES 1117–1

Watch for the hardcover student edition page numbers for this lesson.

Ⓑ Report your results to your teacher in order to combine everyone's results. Use the combined class data to complete the table. To find the relative frequency for an outcome, divide the frequency of the outcome by the total number of trials in the class and round to the nearest hundredth.

Answers will vary. Possible answer (based on 60 trials):

Number of heads	0	1	2	3	4	5
Frequency	5	9	18	16	7	5
Relative frequency	0.08	0.15	0.30	0.27	0.12	0.08

Ⓒ Enter the outcomes (0 through 5) into your calculator as list L_1. Enter the relative frequencies as list L_2. Make a histogram by turning on a statistics plot, selecting the histogram option, and using L_1 for Xlist and L_2 for Freq as shown. Then set the viewing window as shown. Finally, press GRAPH to obtain a histogram like the one shown. Describe the shape of the probability distribution.

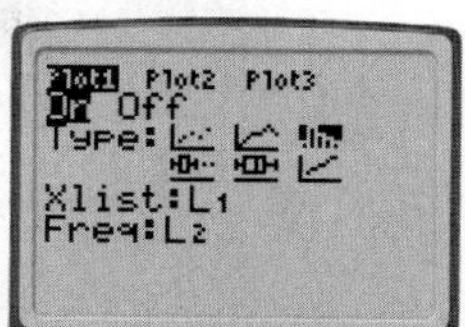

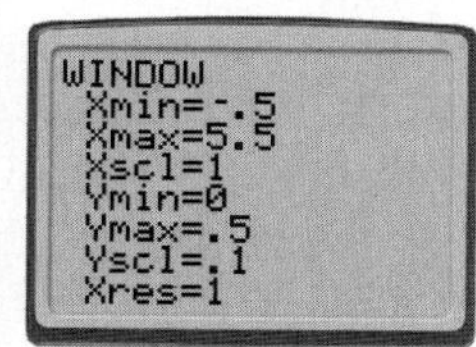

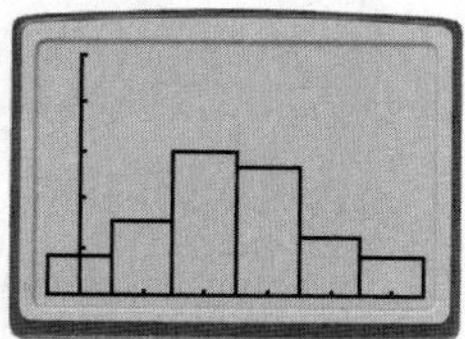

The distribution is mounded and has tails that are roughly symmetric, so the distribution is approximately normal.

Reflect

1. **Discussion** If you flipped a coin 5 times and got 5 heads, would this cause you to question whether the coin is fair? Why or why not?
Answers may vary. Possible answer: The probability of getting 5 heads in 5 flips with a fair coin is very low, so I might question whether the coin is fair.

PROFESSIONAL DEVELOPMENT

Integrate Mathematical Practices

This lesson provides an opportunity to address Mathematical Practice **MP.7**, which asks students to "look for and make use of structure." Students will use histograms to display and analyze probability distributions. They will recognize the difference between a theoretically generated probability distribution and an experimentally generated probability distribution. They will be able to explain why theoretical and experimental probability distributions are not necessarily the same, and when they should expect them to be more alike (which happens as the number of trials in the experiment increases).

EXPLORE

Using Simulation to Obtain an Empirical Probability Distribution

INTEGRATE TECHNOLOGY

Students have the option of completing the Explore activity either in the book or online.

QUESTIONING STRATEGIES

? How do the values on the x-axis of a probability distribution compare to those on the x-axis for a data distribution histogram? **For a data distribution histogram, the x-axis shows data values (or groups of data values). For a probability distribution, the x-axis shows possible outcomes (that is, the values of the random variable).**

? How do the values on the y-axis of a probability distribution compare to those on the x-axis for a data distribution histogram? **For a data distribution histogram, the y-axis shows the frequency of each data value (or group of data values). For a probability distribution, the y-axis shows the probability of each outcome.**

INTEGRATE MATHEMATICAL PRACTICES

Focus on Modeling

MP.4 Ask students to discuss how generating random numbers models flipping a coin. Students should observe that the random numbers are divided into two groups of equal size, and since the numbers are generated randomly, you are as likely to get a number in the first group as you are to get a number in the second group. This is the same situation as flipping a coin—you are as likely to get heads as you are to get tails on each flip.

INTEGRATE TECHNOLOGY

Discuss with students the use of the calculator's random number generator to simulate the trials in the experiment. Lead students to observe that generating the data in this way guarantees that the results reflect those that would be produced by a fair coin. Point out that this may be preferable to using an actual coin, on the chance that the coin or tossing process is not fair.

AVOID COMMON ERRORS

Students may, in error, use the frequencies of each outcome to draw their histograms. Reinforce that since the histogram represents a *probability* distribution, the histogram must be drawn using the *relative* frequencies, which are the probabilities of occurrence for each possible value of the random variable.

CONNECT VOCABULARY EL

Ask students if they know what *accumulate* means. to increase in amount gradually Then explain that *cumulative* is an adjective that means increasing in amount by *successive* (one after another) additions.

EXPLAIN 1

Displaying and Analyzing a Theoretical Probability Distribution

INTEGRATE MATHEMATICAL PRACTICES

Focus on Math Connections

MP.1 You may want to review Pascal's Triangle and its relationship to binomial probability. Students can use the appropriate values from the triangle to help calculate the probabilities.

Explain 1 Displaying and Analyzing a Theoretical Probability Distribution

Recall that a binomial experiment involves repeated trials where each trial has only two outcomes: success or failure. The probability of success on each trial is p, and the probability of failure on each trial is $q = 1 - p$. The binomial probability of r successes in n trials is given by $P(X = r) = {}_nC_r\, p^r q^{n-r}$.

Example 1 **Calculate all the theoretical probabilities for the given binomial experiment. Then draw a histogram of the probability distribution, observe its shape, and use it to find the specified probabilities.**

A binomial experiment consists of flipping a fair coin for 5 trials where getting heads is considered a success. Find the probability of getting 3 or more heads and the probability of getting at least 1 head.

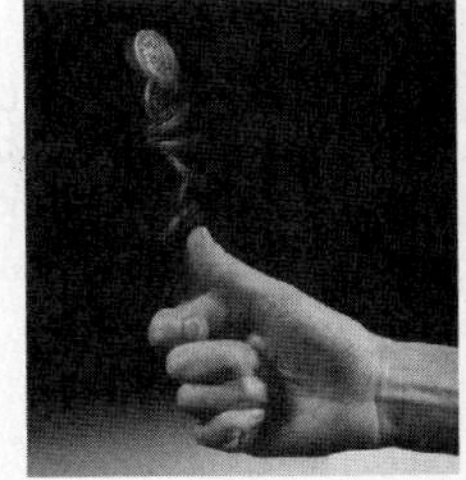

To calculate the probabilities, set n equal to 5 and let r range from 0 to 5 in ${}_nC_r\, p^r q^{n-r}$. Since the coin is fair, $p = \frac{1}{2}$ and $q = \frac{1}{2}$.

Number of heads	0	1	2	3	4	5
Theoretical probability	$\frac{1}{32}$	$\frac{5}{32}$	$\frac{10}{32}$	$\frac{10}{32}$	$\frac{5}{32}$	$\frac{1}{32}$

Create a histogram.

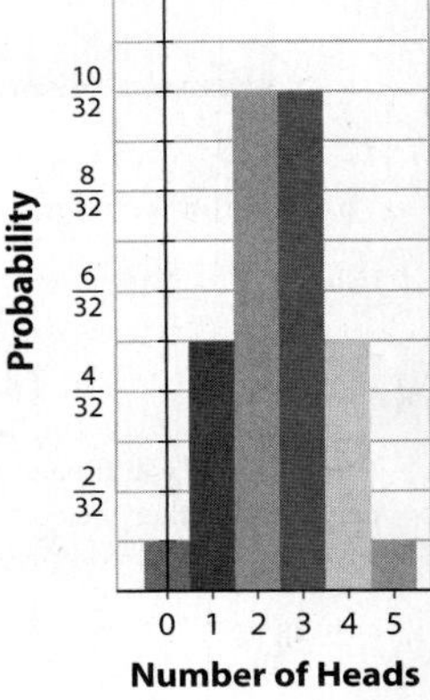

The distribution is mounded and has symmetric tails, so it is a normal distribution.

The probability of getting 3 or more heads:

$$P(X \geq 3) = P(X = 3) + P(X = 4) + P(X = 5)$$
$$= \frac{10}{32} + \frac{5}{32} + \frac{1}{32}$$
$$= \frac{16}{32} = 0.5$$

The probability of getting at least 1 head:

$$P(X \geq 1) = 1 - P(X = 0)$$
$$= 1 - \frac{1}{32}$$
$$= \frac{31}{32} \approx 0.969$$

COLLABORATIVE LEARNING

Whole Class Activity

Have students work as a class to design and perform an experiment that simulates the tossing of a coin that is *not* fair. Have them decide the degree of bias of the coin, and use this measure to design the simulation. Have each student perform a certain number of trials of the experiment. Then combine the results to form one set of data for the class. Have students determine the probability distribution and construct the related histogram. Have them analyze the results, and use them to critique the design of their simulation.

Ⓑ A binomial experiment consists of flipping a biased coin for 5 trials where getting heads is considered a success. The coin lands heads up 75% of the time. Find the probability of getting 3 or more heads and the probability of getting at least 1 head.

To calculate the probabilities, set n equal to 5 and let r range from 0 to 5 in ${}_nC_r\, p^r q^{n-r}$.
Since the coin is biased such that it lands head up 75% of the time, $p = \frac{3}{4}$ and $q = \boxed{\frac{1}{4}}$.

Number of heads	0	1	2	3	4	5
Theoretical probability	$\frac{1}{1024}$	$\frac{15}{1024}$	$\frac{90}{1024}$	$\frac{270}{1024}$	$\frac{405}{1024}$	$\frac{243}{1024}$

Create a histogram.

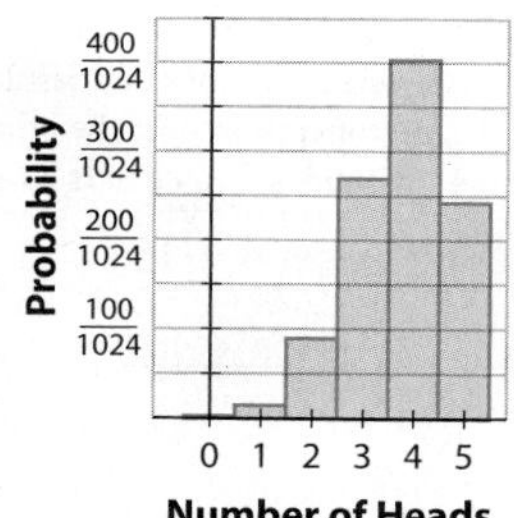

The distribution is mounded and has a tail to the left, so the distribution is skewed left.

The probability of getting 3 or more heads:

$P(X \geq 3) = P(X = 3) + P(X = 4) + P(X = 5)$

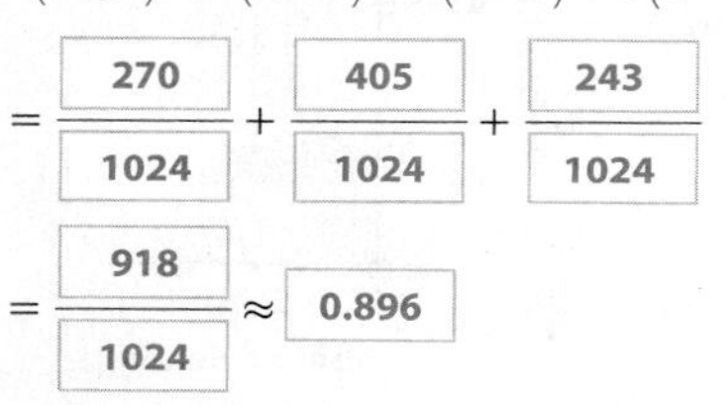

$= \frac{270}{1024} + \frac{405}{1024} + \frac{243}{1024}$

$= \frac{918}{1024} \approx 0.896$

The probability of getting at least 1 head:

$P(X \geq 1) = 1 - P(X = 0)$

$= 1 - \frac{1}{1024}$

$= \frac{1023}{1024} \approx 0.999$

QUESTIONING STRATEGIES

How would you describe the shape of the histogram? **It is mound-shaped and symmetric, with high probabilities in the middle tapering to low probabilities at the ends.**

What does the shape of the histogram indicate? **You are least likely to get the outcomes represented by the bars on the far ends, slightly more likely to get the outcomes represented by the bars as you move towards the middle, and most likely to get the outcomes represented by the bars in the middle.**

How does the shape of the histogram in Part A of the Example compare to that from the Explore? How do you explain this difference? **The histogram in the Example is perfectly symmetrical, while the one from the Explore is not. This is because the histogram in the Explore was based on experimental results, which only approximate the theoretical results.**

DIFFERENTIATE INSTRUCTION

Kinesthetic Experience

Some students may better understand the process and the meaning of the results of a coin-flipping experiment if they perform the experiment using an actual coin rather than the random number generator on a calculator. Have students work in pairs, flipping the coin and recording the results. Have each pair complete the given number of trials, and then combine their results with those of other pairs to create a table of the data and the related probabilities. Have each student draw a histogram for the probability distribution. Students might also compare their results with those obtained from the random number generator.

Reflect

2. Why are the probabilities in the histogram you made in the Explore different from the probabilities given in the histogram from Part A?
The histogram in the Explore was based on experimental probabilities, so there is randomness in the results.

3. For which coin, the fair coin in Part A or the biased coin in Part B, is flipping a coin 5 times and getting 5 heads more likely to occur? Explain.
The biased coin in Part B is more likely to produce 5 heads in 5 flips because $P(X = 5) = \frac{1}{32} \approx 0.031$ for the fair coin, and $P(X = 5) = \frac{243}{1024} \approx 0.237$ (about 7.6 times more likely) for the biased coin.

4. **Discussion** Can you definitively conclude whether a coin that results in repeated heads when flipped is fair or biased? What might make you favor one conclusion over the other?
Answers may vary. Possible answer: Assume the coin is fair so long as a result is not very unlikely. Determining when a result crosses over into being very unlikely is debatable, however.

Your Turn

Calculate all the theoretical probabilities for the given binomial experiment. Then draw a histogram of the probability distribution, observe its shape, and use it to find the specified probabilities.

5. A binomial experiment consists of flipping a biased coin for 4 trials where getting heads is considered a success. The coin lands heads up 40% of the time. Find the probability of getting 2 or more heads and the probability of getting fewer than 4 heads.

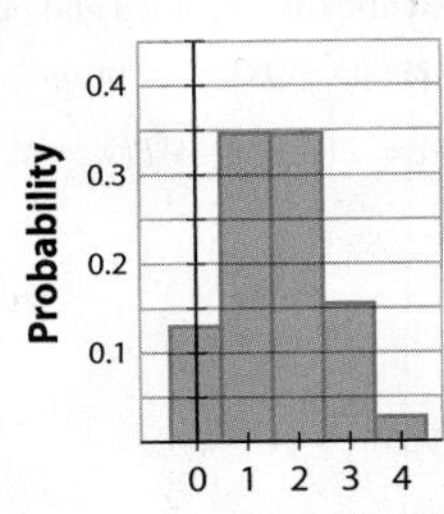

Number of heads	0	1	2	3	4
Theoretical probability	0.1296	0.3456	0.3456	0.1536	0.0256

The distribution is slightly skewed right.

$$\begin{aligned} P(X \geq 2) &= P(X = 2) + P(X = 3) + P(X = 4) \\ &= 0.3456 + 0.1536 + 0.0256 \\ &= 0.5248 \end{aligned}$$

$$\begin{aligned} P(X < 4) &= 1 - P(X = 4) \\ &= 1 - 0.0256 \\ &= 0.9744 \end{aligned}$$

LANGUAGE SUPPORT EL

Communicate Math

Have students work in pairs to complete a table like the one below. Be sure that students understand the differences among the types and how the distributions would differ.

Type of Probability	Description	Example
Empirical probability		
Theoretical probability		
Cumulative probability		

Your Turn

6. A binomial experiment consists of flipping a biased coin for 4 trials where getting tails is considered a success. The coin lands heads up 40% of the time. Find the probability of getting 2 or more tails and the probability of getting fewer than 4 tails.

Number of heads	0	1	2	3	4
Theoretical probability	0.0256	0.1536	0.3456	0.3456	0.1296

The distribution is slightly skewed left.

$P(X \geq 2) = P(X = 2) + P(X = 3) + P(X = 4)$

$= 0.3456 + 0.1536 + 0.0256$

$= 0.5248$

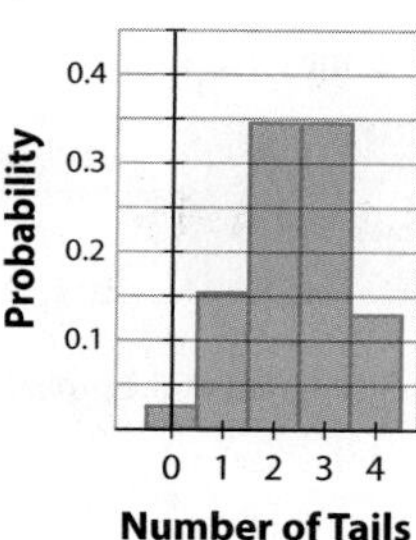

$P(X < 4) = 1 - P(X = 4)$

$= 1 - 0.1296$

$= 0.8704$

Elaborate

7. What is a random variable, and what makes a random variable discrete?
A random variable is a variable whose value is determined by the outcome of a probability experiment. If the outcomes are distinct, such as whole numbers, the random variable is discrete.

8. How can a histogram for a probability distribution be used to calculate a cumulative probability?
The probability is the sum of the areas of the bars in the histogram. The bars correspond to the values of the random variable that are less than or equal to a given value.

9. **Essential Question Check-In** What is a probability distribution for a discrete random variable?
A probability distribution shows the probability (either empirical or theoretical) associated with each possible value of the random variable.

ELABORATE

INTEGRATE MATHEMATICAL PRACTICES

Focus on Critical Thinking

MP.3 Ask students to describe the types of problems that require the calculation of a cumulative probability. Have them brainstorm different real-world scenarios in which the determination of cumulative probabilities would play an important role in decision-making.

INTEGRATE TECHNOLOGY

The graphing calculator command **Int(100*rand)+1** can be used to generate random numbers from 1 to 100. Alternatively, a spreadsheet can generate these random numbers when the command **=INT(RAND()*100+1)** is entered into a cell.

SUMMARIZE THE LESSON

How do you construct a histogram for a probability distribution based on the data from a binomial experiment? **Determine the different numbers of possible successes, and use them to label the *x*-axis. Label the *y*-axis from 0 to 1 to show the probabilities. Then, divide the number of successes for each possible value of the random variable by the total number of outcomes to find the probability for each value, and draw a bar to the height that would indicate that probability.**

EVALUATE

ASSIGNMENT GUIDE

Concepts and Skills	Practice
Explore Using Simulation to Obtain an Empirical Probability Distribution	
Example 1 Displaying and Analyzing a Theoretical Probability Distribution	Exercises 1–7

QUESTIONING STRATEGIES

What can you conclude about a binomial experiment if the histogram for the probability distribution is skewed? **The probabilities of the two outcomes were not equally likely.**

If a binomial experiment consists of two equally likely outcomes, what will the histogram of the theoretical probability distribution look like? **It will be mound-shaped and symmetric, with high probabilities in the middle, tapering to low probabilities at the ends.**

AVOID COMMON ERRORS

Some students may have trouble making the connection between the outcome of a trial of an experiment and the value of the random variable associated with that outcome. Help to clarify this by encouraging students to determine the possible values of the random variable and describe what each value represents, before performing the experiment.

Evaluate: Homework and Practice

- Online Homework
- Hints and Help
- Extra Practice

1. A spinner has three equal sections, labeled 1, 2, and 3. You spin the spinner twice and find the sum of the two numbers the spinner lands on.

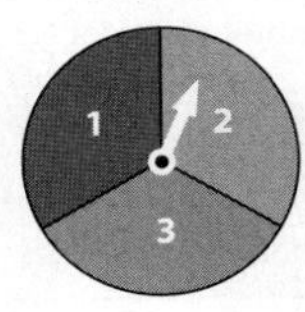

a. Let X be a random variable that represents the sum of the two numbers. What are the possible values of X?
2, 3, 4, 5, and 6

b. Complete the table.

Sum	2	3	4	5	6
Probability	$\frac{1}{9}$	$\frac{2}{9}$	$\frac{3}{9}$	$\frac{2}{9}$	$\frac{1}{9}$

c. Make a histogram of the probability distribution.

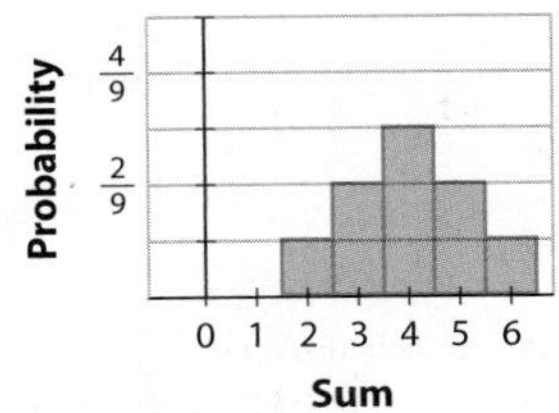

d. What is the probability that the sum is not 2? How is this probability represented in the histogram?
The probability is $\frac{8}{9}$. This is the sum of the areas of the bars for the outcomes 3, 4, 5, and 6.

Exercise	Depth of Knowledge (D.O.K.)	COMMON CORE Mathematical Practices
1	**2** Skills/Concepts	**MP.2** Reasoning
2	**2** Skills/Concepts	**MP.6** Precision
3	**2** Skills/Concepts	**MP.5** Using Tools
4	**2** Skills/Concepts	**MP.7** Using Structure
5	**2** Skills/Concepts	**MP.2** Reasoning
6	**2** Skills/Concepts	**MP.6** Precision
7	**2** Skills/Concepts	**MP.3** Logic

2. You roll two number cubes at the same time. Let X be a random variable that represents the absolute value of the difference of the numbers rolled.

a. What are the possible values of X?
0, 1, 2, 3, 4, and 5

b. Complete the table.

Absolute difference	0	1	2	3	4	5
Probability	$\frac{6}{36}$	$\frac{10}{36}$	$\frac{8}{36}$	$\frac{6}{36}$	$\frac{4}{36}$	$\frac{2}{36}$

c. Is this probability distribution symmetric? Why or why not?
No; the probability distribution is skewed right because in a histogram of the distribution, the tallest bar would occur at 1, with bars to the right decreasing in height.

d. Find the probability of getting a difference greater than 3.
$P(X > 3) = P(X = 4) + P(X = 5) = \frac{4}{36} + \frac{2}{36} = \frac{6}{36} = \frac{1}{6}$

3. A trick coin is designed to land heads up with a probability of 80%. You flip the coin 7 times.

a. Complete the table?

Number of heads	0	1	2	3	4	5	6	7
Theoretical probability	$\frac{1}{78,125}$	$\frac{28}{78,125}$	$\frac{336}{78,125}$	$\frac{2240}{78,125}$	$\frac{8960}{78,125}$	$\frac{21,504}{78,125}$	$\frac{28,672}{78,125}$	$\frac{16,384}{78,125}$

b. Make a histogram of the probability distribution.

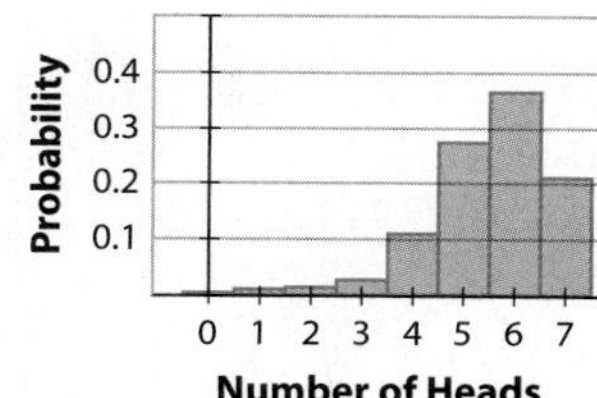

c. What is the probability of getting 6 or 7 heads?
$P(X = 6) + P(X = 7) = \frac{28,672}{78,125} + \frac{16,384}{78,125} = \frac{45,056}{78,125} \approx 0.577$

d. What is the probability of getting 4 or more heads?
$P(X \geq 4) = P(X = 4) + P(X = 5) + P(X = 6) + P(X = 7)$

$= \frac{8960}{78,125} + \frac{21,504}{78,125} + \frac{28,672}{78,125} + \frac{16,384}{78,125}$

$= \frac{75,520}{78,125} \approx 0.967$

INTEGRATE MATHEMATICAL PRACTICES

Focus on Reasoning

MP.2 Ask students to consider what must be true about the sum of the probabilities in a probability distribution. **The sum must be 1.** Ask them explain why this is so. Then encourage them to use this fact to check their work.

Exercise	Depth of Knowledge (D.O.K.)	COMMON CORE Mathematical Practices
8–10	3 Strategic Thinking H.O.T.	MP.3 Logic

PEER-TO-PEER DISCUSSION

Ask students to discuss with a partner how the histograms for the probability distributions of two binomial experiments would differ if the probability of success in Experiment A was 20% and the probability of success in Experiment B was 60%. **The histogram for Experiment A would be greatly skewed to the right, while the histogram for Experiment B would be slightly skewed to the left.**

e. Which is greater, the probability of getting an even number of heads or the probability of getting an odd number of heads?

The probability of getting an even number of heads is $P(X = 0) + P(X = 2) + P(X = 4) + P(X = 6) = \frac{1}{78,125} + \frac{336}{78,125} + \frac{8960}{78,125} + \frac{28,672}{78,125} = \frac{37,969}{78,125}$, while the probability of getting an odd number of heads is $P(X = 1) + P(X = 3) + P(X = 5) + P(X = 7) = \frac{28}{78,125} + \frac{2240}{78,125} + \frac{21,504}{78,125} + \frac{16,384}{78,125} = \frac{40,156}{78,125}$. So, the probability of getting an odd number of heads is greater.

f. Suppose you flip a coin 7 times and get 7 heads. Based on what you know now, would you question whether the coin is fair? Why or why not?

Answers may vary. Possible answer: The probability of getting 7 heads in 7 flips of a fair coin is $\frac{1}{2}^7 = \frac{1}{128} \approx 0.008$. The probability of getting 7 heads in 7 flips of the trick coin is $\frac{16,384}{78,125} \approx 0.210$. Since getting 7 heads on the trick coin is more than 26 times as likely to occur as getting 7 heads on the fair coin, I would question whether the coin is fair.

4. You flip a coin 4 times in a row. The histogram shows the theoretical probability distribution for this situation.

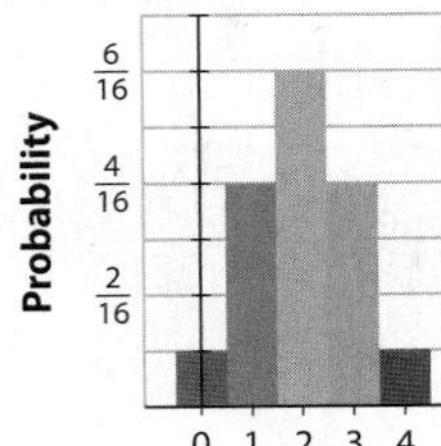

a. What is the probability of getting 3 or more heads?

$P(X \geq 3) = P(X = 3) + P(X = 4)$

$= \frac{4}{16} + \frac{1}{16}$

$= \frac{5}{16} = 0.3125$

b. What is the probability of getting at most 2 heads?

$P(X \leq 2) = 1 - P(X \geq 3)$

$= 1 - 0.3125$

$= 0.6875$

c. How do you know that the coin is fair?

The coin is fair because the distribution shown in the histogram is perfectly symmetric. If the probability of getting heads were not $\frac{1}{2}$, then the distribution would be skewed.

5. A spinner has 4 equal sections that are labeled 1, 2, 3, and 4. You spin the spinner twice and find the sum of the 2 numbers it lands on. Let X be a random variable that represents the sum of the 2 numbers.

a. Complete the table.

Sum	2	3	4	5	6	7	8
Frequency	1	2	3	4	3	2	1
Probability	$\frac{1}{16}$	$\frac{2}{16}$	$\frac{3}{16}$	$\frac{4}{16}$	$\frac{3}{16}$	$\frac{2}{16}$	$\frac{1}{16}$

b. Make a histogram of the probability distribution.

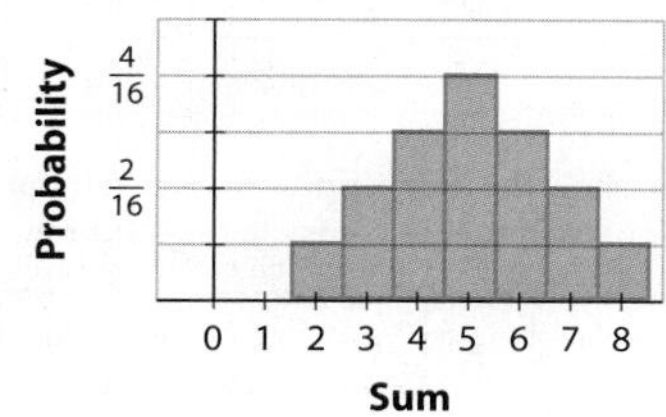

c. What is the probability of getting a sum of 6 or more?

$$P(X \geq 6) = P(X=6) + P(X=7) + P(X=8)$$
$$= \frac{3}{16} + \frac{2}{16} + \frac{1}{16}$$
$$= \frac{6}{16} = 0.375$$

d. Without actually calculating any probabilities, determine the relationship between $P(X > 5)$ and $P(X < 5)$. Explain your reasoning.

$P(X > 5) = P(X < 5)$ because the histogram of the probability distribution is symmetric with respect to $x = 5$.

COMMUNICATING MATH

Test for understanding by having students describe what their histograms indicate about the results of a given experiment, and what overall conclusions they can draw.

COLLABORATIVE LEARNING

Have students work in small groups to make a poster showing the difference between a frequency histogram and a histogram for a probability distribution. Have them generate or gather a set of data that they can use to construct both displays. Have them compare the two types of histograms, pointing out how they differ and how they are related.

6. You roll 2 number cubes at the same time. Let X be a random variable that represents the sum of the numbers rolled.

a. Complete the table to show the sums that are possible. In the table, the row heads are the numbers that are possible on one number cube, and the column heads are the numbers that are possible on the other number cube.

	1	2	3	4	5	6
1	2	3	4	5	6	7
2	3	4	5	6	7	8
3	4	5	6	7	8	9
4	5	6	7	8	9	10
5	6	7	8	9	10	11
6	7	8	9	10	11	12

b. Complete the second row of the table to show the number of ways that you can get each sum. Then find the probability of each sum to complete the third row.

Sum	2	3	4	5	6	7	8	9	10	11	12
Frequency	1	2	3	4	5	6	5	4	3	2	1
Probability	$\frac{1}{36}$	$\frac{2}{36}$	$\frac{3}{36}$	$\frac{4}{36}$	$\frac{5}{36}$	$\frac{6}{36}$	$\frac{5}{36}$	$\frac{4}{36}$	$\frac{3}{36}$	$\frac{2}{36}$	$\frac{1}{36}$

c. Make a histogram of the probability distribution.

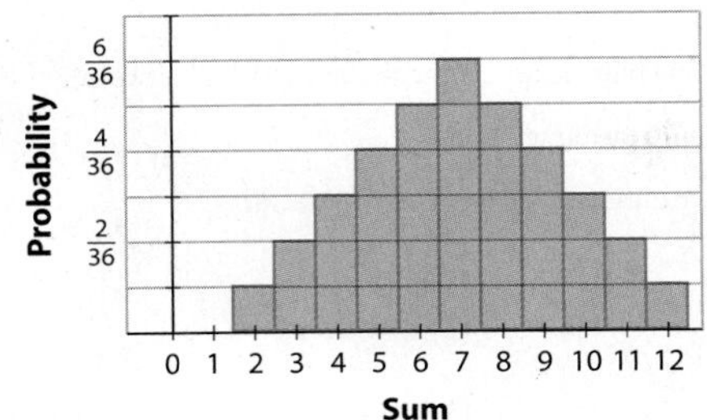

d. What is the probability that you roll a sum of 5 or less?

$P(X \le 5) = P(X = 2) + P(X = 3) + P(X = 4) + P(X = 5)$

$= \frac{1}{36} + \frac{2}{36} + \frac{3}{36} + \frac{4}{36} = \frac{10}{36} \approx 0.278$

e. What is the probability that you roll a sum of 12 four times in a row? If this happened, would you question whether the number cubes are fair?

The probability of rolling a sum of 12 four times in a row is $\left(\frac{1}{36}\right)^4 = \frac{1}{1{,}679{,}616} \approx 0.0000006$. This probability is so low that it calls into question the fairness of the number cubes.

7. A fair coin is flipped 6 times. Match each specified probability on the left with its value on the right. (A value on the right may apply to more than one specified probability on the left.)

A. The probability of getting at least 4 heads — B $\frac{7}{64}$

B. The probability of getting no more than 1 head — C $\frac{21}{64}$

C. The probability of getting 1 or 2 heads — A, D $\frac{11}{32}$

D. The probability of getting no more than 2 heads — E, F $\frac{1}{2}$

E. The probability of getting an even number of heads

F. The probability of getting an odd number of heads

A. $P(X \geq 4) = P(X = 4) + P(X = 5) + P(X = 6) = \frac{15}{64} + \frac{6}{64} + \frac{1}{64} = \frac{22}{64} = \frac{11}{32}$

B. $P(X \leq 1) = P(X = 0) + P(X = 1) = \frac{1}{64} + \frac{6}{64} = \frac{7}{64}$

C. $P(X = 1) + P(X = 2) = \frac{6}{64} + \frac{15}{64} = \frac{21}{64}$

D. $P(X \leq 2) = P(X = 0) + P(X = 1) + P(X = 2) = \frac{1}{64} + \frac{6}{64} + \frac{15}{64} = \frac{22}{64} = \frac{11}{32}$

E. $P(X = 0) + P(X = 2) + P(X = 4) + P(X = 6) = \frac{1}{64} + \frac{15}{64} + \frac{15}{64} + \frac{1}{64} = \frac{32}{64} = \frac{1}{2}$

F. $P(X = 1) + P(X = 3) + P(X = 5) = \frac{6}{64} + \frac{20}{64} + \frac{6}{64} = \frac{32}{64} = \frac{1}{2}$

H.O.T. Focus on Higher Order Thinking

. **Represent Real-World Situations** About 19.4% of the U.S. population that is 25 years old and over have a bachelor's degree only, and 10.5% have an advanced degree.

a. Find the probability that of 6 randomly selected people who are 25 years old or over, 4 have at least a bachelor's degree.

The probability that a person who is 25 years old or over has at least a bachelor's degree is $0.194 + 0.105 \approx 0.3$. So, the probability that 4 of 6 randomly selected people who are 25 years old or over have at least a bachelor's degree is about ${}_6C_4\,(0.3)^4\,(0.7)^2 \approx 0.0595$.

b. Find the probability that of 6 randomly selected people who are 25 years old or over, 4 do not have even a bachelor's degree.

The probability that a person who is 25 years old or over doesn't have at least a bachelor's degree is about $1 - 0.3 = 0.7$. So, the probability that 4 of 6 randomly selected people who are 25 years old or over don't have even a bachelor's degree is about ${}_6C_4\,(0.7)^4\,(0.3)^2 \approx 0.324$.

JOURNAL

Have students describe why the histogram for the empirical probability distribution of an experiment could be different from the histogram for the theoretical probability distribution of the same experiment.

c. Suppose all 6 of 6 randomly selected people have advanced degrees. Would you question the probability model? Explain.

The probability that all 6 have an advanced degree is $(0.105)^6 \approx 0.00000134$. This seems very unlikely. I might question whether the selection process was truly random, thinking instead that the sampling method was biased (for instance, it was a self-selected sample of people who read a professional journal, or it was random sample of a subset of the population, such as people living in a city where scientific research or high tech is a large part of the local economy).

9. Justify Reasoning Describe a way to get fair results from a coin that you suspect is biased. Explain how you know that the process is fair.

Rather than flip the coin just once, flip the coin twice. If you flip the coin twice and the results match, then completely disregard the results. If you flip the coin twice and the results are different, then use the first result and disregard the second result. To see why the process is fair, let p be the probability of getting heads and $1 - p$ be the probability of getting tails. For a biased coin, $p \neq 1 - p$. Assume that both probabilities are nonzero. Then the probability of getting two heads is p^2, the probability of getting two tails is $(1 - p)^2$, and these probabilities are not equal if p and $1 - p$ are not equal. However, the probability of getting heads followed by tails is $p(1 - p)$, the probability of getting tails followed by heads is $(1 - p)p$, and these probabilities are equal. So, by going with heads when heads appear first and going with tails when tails appear first, the two outcomes have equal probability, and the results are fair.

10. Construct Arguments Use the formula $P(X = r) = {}_nC_r\, p^r q^{n-r}$ for a binomial experiment to explain why the probability distribution for the number of heads obtained when a fair coin is flipped n times is symmetric.

Because the coin is fair, $p = \frac{1}{2}$ and $q = \frac{1}{2}$, so the formula becomes $P(X = r) = {}_nC_r\, p^r q^{n-r} = {}_nC_r \left(\frac{1}{2}\right)^r \left(\frac{1}{2}\right)^{n-r} = {}_nC_r \left(\frac{1}{2}\right)^n$. Because $\left(\frac{1}{2}\right)^n$ is a constant for a given value of n, the only variable factor is ${}_nC_n$ which gives the number of ways that r (where r ranges from 0 to n) of n flips of the coin can result in heads. But for every way there is to obtain r heads, there is a corresponding way to obtain $n - r$ heads by simply switching heads and tails. (For instance, one way to obtain 2 heads in 7 flips of a coin is HTTTHTT, and the corresponding way to obtain 5 heads in 7 flips is THHHTHH.) This means that ${}_nC_r \left(\frac{1}{2}\right)^n = {}_nC_{n-r} \left(\frac{1}{2}\right)^n$, so $P(X = r) = P(X = n - r)$, which shows that the probability distribution is symmetric.

Lesson Performance Task

According to the U.S. Census, in 2010 the number of people 18 years old or over in the U.S. was 229.1 million, and of those people, 129.5 million were married.

a. Find the probability that of 10 randomly selected people 18 years old or over, 6 are married.

b. Consider a survey where all 10 of the people surveyed are married. What conclusion might you draw about that survey?

a. The probability that a randomly selected person 18 years old or over is married is $\frac{129.5}{229.1} \approx 0.565$. The probability that of 10 randomly selected people 18 years old and over, 6 are married is ${}_{10}C_6\,(0.565)^6(0.435)^4 = 210(0.565)^6(0.435)^4 \approx 0.245$.

b. The probability that of 10 randomly selected people 18 years old and over, all 10 are married is ${}_{10}C_{10}\,(0.565)^{10}(0.435)^0 = (0.565)^{10} \approx 0.003$. This probability is low and might call into question whether the survey was actually random or representative of the general U.S. population.

EXTENSION ACTIVITY

Have students find United States Census information about the voter turnout (the percent of voting-age population that voted) in the 2012 Presidential election and in the most recent midyear election, a non-Presidential election in which voting is for Congressional representatives. Then have them consider a "sample" small town with a number of people of voting age, find the number expected to vote in each election, and perform a simulation to estimate these numbers. Ask students to present and compare their findings.

AVOID COMMON ERRORS

Urge students solving without a calculator to check their substitutions in the expression ${}_nC_x p^x q^{n-x}$ before computing. The sum of the exponents must be n and $p + q = n$. The exponents in the expression should also match the factorials in the denominator of ${}_nC_x$.

INTEGRATE MATHEMATICAL PRACTICES

Focus on Technology

MP.5 To calculate combinations, ${}_nC_r$, using a graphing calculator, press the value for ***n***, and then the **MATH** key. Then press the right arrow key three times to scroll right to **PRB**. Press 3 to select the combination formula. Type the value for ***r*** and press **ENTER**.

Scoring Rubric

2 points: Student correctly solves the problem and explains his/her reasoning.

1 point: Student shows good understanding of the problem but does not fully solve or explain his/her reasoning.

0 points: Student does not demonstrate understanding of the problem.

LESSON 23.2

Normal Distributions

Common Core Math Standards

The student is expected to:

COMMON CORE **S-ID.A.4**

Use the mean and standard deviation of a data set to fit it to a normal distribution and to estimate population percentages. Recognize that there are data sets for which such a procedure is not appropriate. Use calculators, spreadsheets, and tables to estimate areas under the normal curve.

Mathematical Practices

COMMON CORE **MP.1 Problem Solving**

Language Objective

Work with a partner to sketch and label the standard deviations above and below the mean in two different normal distributions.

ENGAGE

Essential Question: How do you find percents of data and probabilities of events associated with normal distributions?

If a given data value is 1, 2, or 3 standard deviations from the mean, use the fact that 68% of the data are within 1 standard deviation of the mean, 95% of the data are within 2 standard deviations of the mean, and 99.7% of the data are within 3 standard deviations of the mean. If the data value is not 1, 2, or 3 standard deviations from the mean, calculate *z*-scores and use the standard normal table.

PREVIEW: LESSON PERFORMANCE TASK

View the Engage section online. Discuss the photo and how a census can provide information that can be used to calculate a probability. For example, if you know how many people older than 18 are married, you can select 10 people over 18 at random and find the probability that all 10 of them would be married. Then preview the Lesson Performance Task.

Name ______ Class ______ Date ______

23.2 Normal Distributions

Resource Locker

Essential Question: How do you find percents of data and probabilities of events associated with normal distributions?

Explore 1 Substituting a Normal Curve for a Symmetric Histogram

The table below gives the mass (in kilograms) of 20 babies at birth. You know that there are 20 babies, because that is the sum of the frequencies. You also know that the masses are normally distributed because the mass with the greatest frequency occurs at the center of the distribution and the other frequencies taper off symmetrically from that center. The mean of the data is 3.5 kg, and the standard deviation is 1.4 kg.

You can use a graphing calculator to draw a smooth bell-shaped curve, called a *normal curve*, that captures the shape of the histogram. A normal curve has the property that the area under the curve (and above the *x*-axis) is 1. This means that you must adjust the heights of the bars in the histogram so that the sum of the areas of the bars is 1.

(A) Find the relative frequency of each mass.

Mass (kg)	3.2	3.3	3.4	3.5	3.6	3.7	3.8
Frequency	1	2	4	6	4	2	1
Relative frequency	$\frac{1}{20} = 0.05$	0.1	0.2	0.3	0.2	0.1	0.05
Adjusted bar height	$\frac{0.05}{0.1} = 0.5$	1	2	3	2	1	0.5

(B) What is the sum of the relative frequencies? 1

(C) For a given mass, the relative frequency is the area that you want the bar to have. Since you used a bar width of 0.1 when you created the histogram, the area of the bar is $0.1h$ where h is the height of the bar. You want $0.1h$ to equal the relative frequency f, so solve $0.1h = f$ for h to find the adjusted bar height. Complete this row in the table.

(D) Enter each mass from the table into L_1 on your graphing calculator. Then enter each adjusted bar height into L_2.

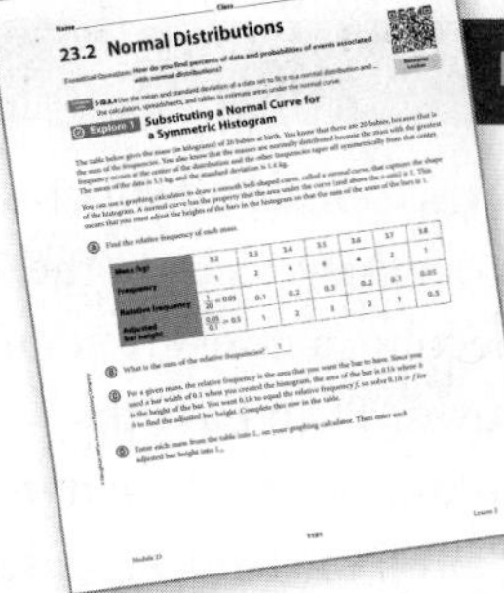

HARDCOVER PAGES 1131–114

Watch for the hardcover student edition page numbers for this lesson.

Ⓔ Turn on a statistics plot and select the histogram option. For Xlist, enter L_1. For Freq, enter L_2. Set the graphing window as shown. Then press GRAPH.

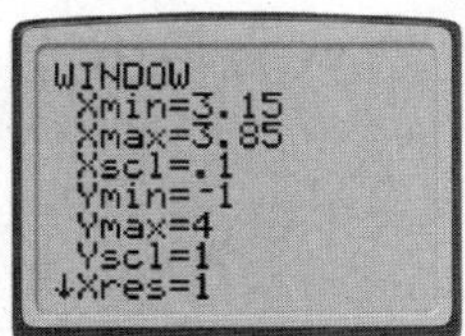

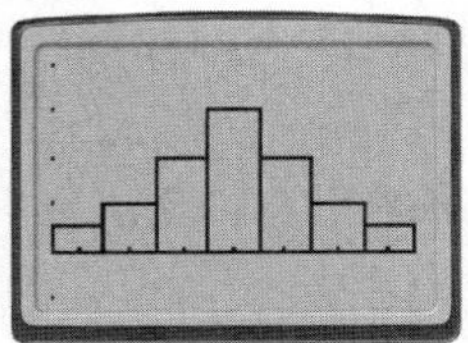

Ⓕ Your calculator has a built-in function called a *normal probability density function*, which you can access by pressing 2nd VARS and selecting the first choice from the DISTR (distribution) menu. When entering this function to be graphed, you must include the mean and standard deviation of the distribution by entering **normalpdf(X, 3.5, 0.14)**. When you press GRAPH, the calculator will draw a normal curve that fits the histogram.

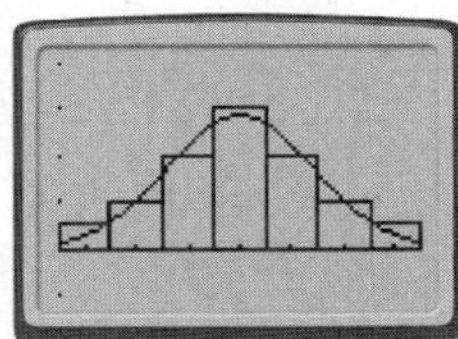

Reflect

1. Describe the end behavior of the normal probability density function.

$f(x)$ approaches 0 as x increases or decreases without bound.

2. **Discussion** If the area under the normal curve is 1, then what is the area under the curve to the left of the mean, 3.5? Describe how to obtain this area using the bars in the histogram. Show that your method gives the correct result.

0.5; add the areas of the first three bars plus half the area of the fourth bar:

$0.05 + 0.1 + \frac{1}{2}(0.3) = 0.5$ (since bar area = relative frequency)

3. Explain how you can use the bars in the histogram to estimate the area under the curve within 1 standard deviation of the mean, which is the interval from $3.5 - 0.14 = 3.36$ to $3.5 + 0.14 = 3.64$ on the x-axis. Then find the estimate.

The interval "captures" the middle three bars, so the sum of the areas of those bars should give an estimate of the area under the curve: $0.2 + 0.3 + 0.2 = 0.7$

4. Explain how you can use the bars in the histogram to estimate the area under the curve within 2 standard deviations of the mean, which is the interval from $3.5 - 2(0.14) = 3.22$ to $3.5 + 2(0.14) = 3.78$ on the x-axis. Then find the estimate.

The interval "captures" the middle five bars, so the sum of the areas of those bars gives an estimate of the area under the curve: $0.1 + 0.2 + 0.3 + 0.1 = 0.9$

EXPLORE

Substituting a Normal Curve for a Symmetric Histogram

INTEGRATE TECHNOLOGY

Students have the option of completing the Explore activity either in the book or online.

QUESTIONING STRATEGIES

Why is the sum of the relative frequencies 1? **The sum is 1 because the sum represents the whole sample or, in terms of percent, 100% of the sample.**

Why were adjustments made to the heights of the bars? **They were adjusted in order to make the sum of all the areas of the bars in the histogram 1.**

What value does the area under the normal curve between two specific x-values represent? **It represents the probability that the outcome will be between those two x-values.**

INTEGRATE MATHEMATICAL PRACTICES

Focus on Math Connections

MP.1 Help students see that a normal curve is a graphic representation of the concepts of mean and standard deviation. Have students identify those elements for the curves pictured in the lesson.

PROFESSIONAL DEVELOPMENT

Math Background

The general shape of a normal probability distribution, also called a Gaussian distribution, is that of a bell. The exact shape of the bell is determined by the distribution's mean and standard deviation. The graph of a normal probability distribution is called a normal curve and is given by the equation

$$y = \frac{1}{\sqrt{2\pi\sigma^2}} e^{-\frac{(x-\mu)^2}{2\sigma^2}}$$

where μ is the mean and σ is the standard deviation. The mean and standard deviation can be found from the data. Students should be able to draw a histogram from data and sketch a smooth, "best-fit" normal curve by hand.

EXPLAIN 1

Finding Areas Under a Normal Curve

QUESTIONING STRATEGIES

? What does the 68-95-99.7 rule tell you about a set of data that is normally distributed with mean μ? **It says that 68% of the data falls within one standard deviation of μ, 95% falls within 2 standard deviations of μ, and 99.7% falls within 3 standard deviations of μ.**

? How can you use the 68-95-99.7 rule to determine the percent of the data that falls more than 3 standard deviations above the mean? **Since 99.7% of the data falls within 3 standard deviations of the mean, subtract 99.7 from 100, and divide the difference by 2 (since half of this percentage represents the data that fall below 3 standard deviations below the mean).**

INTEGRATE MATHEMATICAL PRACTICES

Focus on Communication

MP.3 Ask students to use their own words to describe what the normal curve and the 68-95-99.7 rule indicate about a set of data in which the mean is 30 and the standard deviation is 5.

INTEGRATE MATHEMATICAL PRACTICES

Focus on Reasoning

MP.2 Discuss with students how the 68-95-99.7 rule helps to describe how "typical" a data value is for a normally distributed data set. Help them to understand the relationship between the percents and the probability distribution of the data.

Explain 1 Finding Areas Under a Normal Curve

All normal curves have the following properties, sometimes collectively called the 68–95–99.7 rule:

- 68% of the data fall within 1 standard deviation of the mean.
- 95% of the data fall within 2 standard deviations of the mean.
- 99.7% of the data fall within 3 standard deviations of the mean.

A normal curve's symmetry allows you to separate the area under the curve into eight parts and know the percent of the data in each part.

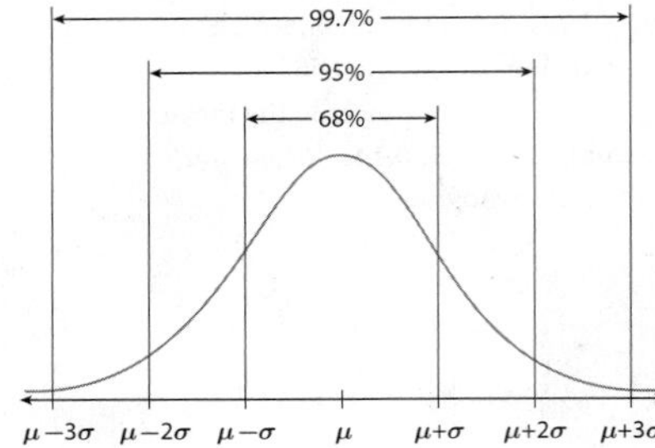

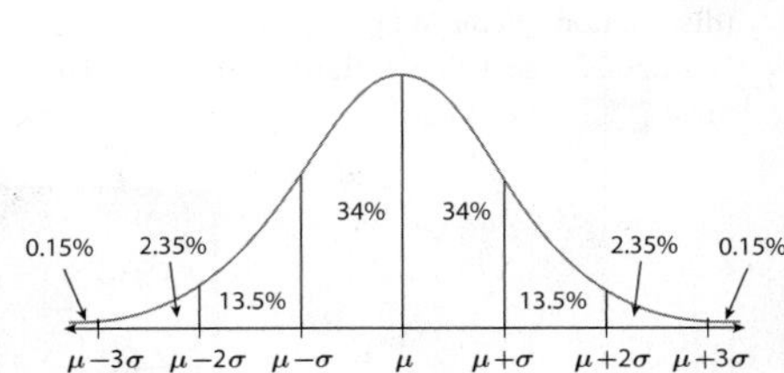

Example 1 **Suppose the heights (in inches) of men (ages 20–29) years old in the United States are normally distributed with a mean of 69.3 inches and a standard deviation of 2.92 inches. Find each of the following.**

(A) The percent of men who are between 63.46 inches and 75.14 inches tall.

63.46 inches is 5.84 inches, or 2 standard deviations, below the mean.

75.14 inches is 5.84 inches, or 2 standard deviations, above the mean.

95% of the data in a normal distribution fall within 2 standard deviations of the mean.

So, 95% of males are between 63.46 inches and 75.14 inches tall.

(B) The percent of men who are taller than 72.22 inches.

72.22 inches is **2.92** inches, or **1** standard deviation(s), above the mean.

When the area under a normal curve is separated into eight parts, the parts that satisfy the condition that the height will be greater than 72.22 inches have percents of **13.5%, 2.35%, and 0.15%**.

The sum of these percents is **16** %.

So, **16** % of males are taller than 72.22 inches.

COLLABORATIVE LEARNING

Peer-to-Peer Activity

Have students work in pairs. Instruct each pair to use the data in Example 2 to create a quiz containing 4 problems similar to those in the Example, and an answer key for their quiz. Have pairs exchange and take each other's quizzes. Then have the students return their quizzes to the original pair for grading, and reconcile any discrepancies.

Your Turn

Suppose the heights (in inches) of men (ages 20–29) in the United States are normally distributed with a mean of 69.3 inches and a standard deviation of 2.92 inches. Find each of the following.

5. The percent of men who are between 60.54 inches and 78.06 inches tall.
60.54 and 78.06 are both 3 standard deviations from the mean; 99.7%

6. The percent of men who are shorter than 60.54 inches.
60.54 is 3 standard deviations below the mean; 0.15%.

Explain 2 Using the Standard Normal Distribution

The **standard normal distribution** has a mean of 0 and a standard deviation of 1. A data value x from a normal distribution with mean μ and standard deviation σ can be standardized by finding its **z-score** using the formula $z = \frac{x - \mu}{\sigma}$.

Areas under the standard normal curve to the left of a given z-score have been computed and appear in the standard normal table below. This table allows you to find a greater range of percents and probabilities than you can using μ and multiples of σ. For example, the area under the curve to the left of the z-score 1.3 is 0.9032. (In the table, "0.0000+" means slightly more than 0, and "1.0000−" means slightly less than 1.)

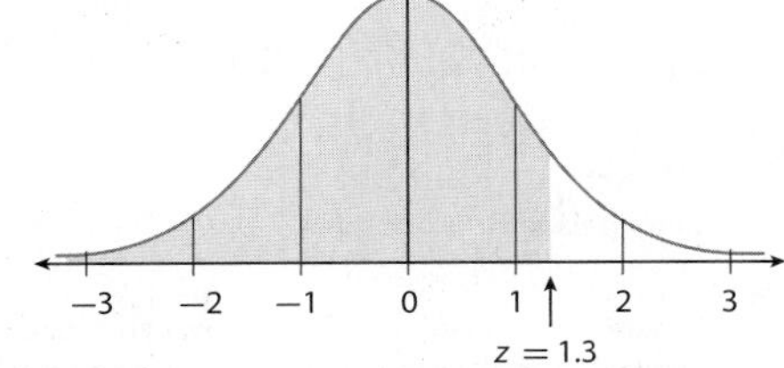

Standard Normal Table

z	.0	.1	.2	.3	.4	.5	.6	.7	.8	.9
−3	0.0013	0.0010	0.0007	0.0005	0.0003	0.0002	0.0002	0.0001	0.0001	0.0000+
−2	0.0228	0.0179	0.0139	0.0107	0.0082	0.0062	0.0047	0.0035	0.0026	0.0019
−1	0.1587	0.1357	0.1151	0.0968	0.0808	0.0668	0.0548	0.0446	0.0359	0.0287
−0	0.5000	0.4602	0.4207	0.3821	0.3446	0.3085	0.2743	0.2420	0.2119	0.1841
0	0.5000	0.5398	0.5793	0.6179	0.6554	0.6915	0.7257	0.7580	0.7881	0.8159
1	0.8413	0.8643	0.8849	0.9032	0.9192	0.9332	0.9452	0.9554	0.9641	0.9713
2	0.9772	0.9821	0.9861	0.9893	0.9918	0.9938	0.9953	0.9965	0.9974	0.9981
3	0.9987	0.9990	0.9993	0.9995	0.9997	0.9998	0.9998	0.9999	0.9999	1.000−

Example 2 **Suppose the heights (in inches) of women (ages 20–29) in the United States are normally distributed with a mean of 64.1 inches and a standard deviation of 2.75 inches. Find the percent of women who are no more than 65 inches tall and the probability that a randomly chosen woman is between 60 inches and 63 inches tall.**

Analyze Information

The mean of the heights is 64.1 inches.

The standard deviation of the heights is 2.75 inches.

DIFFERENTIATE INSTRUCTION

Multiple Representations

To help students who may be having difficulty understanding how the normal curve relates to a set of data, have them take a specific set of normally distributed data with a given mean and standard deviation, draw a sketch of the normal curve, and beneath μ, $\mu + \sigma$, $\mu + 2\sigma$, etc., write the values that correspond to these quantities. Have them label the sections of the graph with the percentages defined by the 64-95-99.7 rule. Then have them plot the actual data values from the data set along the horizontal axis to see how the graph relates to the spread of the data.

EXPLAIN 2

Using the Standard Normal Distribution

INTEGRATE MATHEMATICAL PRACTICES

Focus on Modeling

MP.4 Discuss with students that no distribution fits a normal distribution perfectly but many are close to normal, such as heights of males or females, and standardized test scores. Discuss the importance of standardizing. By standardizing, you can compare values from groups with different means and standard deviations.

AVOID COMMON ERRORS

When finding a z-score, students may subtract the x-value from the mean instead of the mean from the x-value. Explain that any value greater than the mean must have a positive z-score, and any value less than the mean must have a negative z-score. Keeping this in mind will help students notice when they have made this error.

QUESTIONING STRATEGIES

? What is the meaning of the number read from the standard normal table for a given z-score? The number is the probability that a randomly selected data value will have a z-score less than or equal to the given z-score.

? How do you find the probability that a data value exceeds a given z-score? Subtract the probability obtained from the standard normal table for the given z-score from 1.

ELABORATE

INTEGRATE MATHEMATICAL PRACTICES

Focus on Critical Thinking

MP.3 Have students consider a normal distribution with mean μ and standard deviation σ, and ask them to find the z-score that corresponds to μ. Have them justify their results and explain the related percent from the standard normal table. Then have them make a conjecture about the z-score for $\mu + \sigma$, test their conjectures, and generalize their findings.

SUMMARIZE THE LESSON

? What is the normal curve, and how does it, in conjunction with the 68-95-99.7 rule, describe a set of normally distributed data? **It is the bell-shaped curve approximated by the histogram for the probability distribution for a set of normally distributed data. It shows how the data clusters about the mean, with 68% of the data falling within 1 standard deviation of the mean, 95% of the data falling within 2 standard deviations of the mean, and 99.7% of the data falling within 3 standard deviations of the mean.**

Formulate a Plan

Convert the heights to **z-scores** and use the **standard normal table** to find the probabilities needed.

Solve

First, find the percent of women who are no more than 65 inches tall.

Convert 65 to a z-score (to the nearest tenth): $z_{65} = \frac{65 - \mu}{\sigma} = \frac{65 - \boxed{64.1}}{\boxed{2.75}} \approx \boxed{0.3}$

Recognize that the phrase "no more than 65 inches" means that $z \le z_{65}$. Read the decimal from the appropriate row and column of the standard normal table: **0.6179**

Write the decimal as a percent: **61.79%**

Next, find the probability that a randomly chosen woman is between 60 inches and 63 inches tall.

Convert 60 to a z-score: $z_{60} = \frac{60 - \mu}{\sigma} = \frac{60 - \boxed{64.1}}{\boxed{2.75}} \approx \boxed{-1.5}$

Convert 63 to a z-score: $z_{63} = \frac{63 - \mu}{\sigma} = \frac{63 - \boxed{64.1}}{\boxed{2.75}} = \boxed{-0.4}$

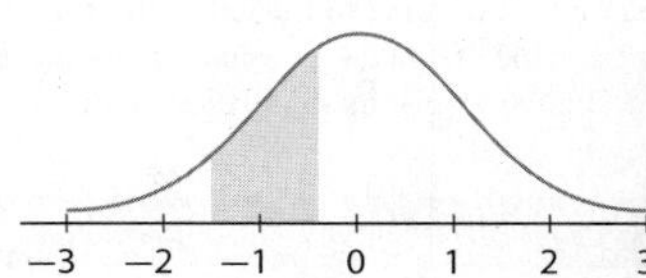

Because the standard normal table gives areas under the standard normal curve to the left of a given z-score, you find $P(z_{60} \le z \le z_{63})$ by subtracting $P(z \le z_{60})$ from $P(z \le z_{63})$. Complete the following calculation using the appropriate values from the table:

$P(z_{60} \le z \le z_{63}) = P(z \le z_{63}) - P(z \le z_{60}) =$ **0.3446 − 0.0668 = 0.2778**

Write the decimal as a percent: **27.78%**

Justify and Evaluate

65 inches is slightly **greater** than the mean height. Since all the heights up to the mean represent **50** % of the data, it makes sense that all the heights up to 65 inches are slightly **more** than 50%. Heights from 60–63 inches are within the area for heights less than 65 inches but there are fewer, so it makes sense that the probability is **less** than 50%.

Your Turn

Suppose the heights (in inches) of adult females (ages 20–29) in the United States are normally distributed with a mean of 64.1 inches and a standard deviation of 2.75 inches.

7. Find the percent of women who are at least 66 inches tall.

   $z_{66} = \frac{66 - 64.1}{2.75} \approx 0.7; P(z \ge z_{66}) = 1 - P(z \le z_{66}) = 1 - 0.7580 = 0.242$, or about 24.2%

8. Find the percent of women who are less than or equal to 61.6 inches tall.

   $z_{61.6} = \frac{61.6 - 64.1}{2.75} \approx -0.9; P(z \le z_{61.6}) = 0.1841$, or about 18.41%

LANGUAGE SUPPORT EL

Communicate Math

Have students work in pairs to discuss what two different normal distributions might look like, and have one student sketch a narrow one and the other sketch a wide one. The pairs should talk about how to show what 1 standard deviation, 2 standard deviations, and 3 standard deviations from the mean are in each sketch, and the percentages attached to each.

Elaborate

9. Explain how you know that the area under a normal curve between $\mu + \sigma$ and $\mu + 2\sigma$ represents 13.5% of the data if you know that the percent of the data within 1 standard deviation of the mean is 68% and the percent of the data within 2 standard deviations of the mean is 95%.

The difference between 95% and 68% is 27%; the symmetry of the curve tells you that this difference is split evenly between the interval from $\mu - 2\sigma$ to $\mu - \sigma$ and the interval from $\mu + \sigma$ to $\mu + 2\sigma$, so each interval represents 13.5% of the data.

10. How can you use the 68-95-99.7 rule and the symmetry of a normal curve to find the percent of normally distributed data that are less than 1 standard deviation above the mean?

The symmetry of a normal curve tells you that 50% of the data are below the mean. Knowing that 68% of the data are within that 1 standard deviation of the mean tells you that 34% of the data fall between the mean and 1 standard deviation above the mean. Then 50% + 34% = 84% of the data are less than 1 standard deviation above the mean.

11. Essential Question Check-In Explain what a *z*-score is and how it's used.

A *z*-score represents the number of standard deviations that a data value is above or below the mean. *z*-scores are used to find probabilities based on the areas under the standard normal curve given in the standard normal table.

Evaluate: Homework and Practice

- Online Homework
- Hints and Help
- Extra Practice

1. The first calculator screen shows the probability distribution when 6 coins are flipped and the number of heads is counted. The second screen shows the probability distribution of the number of correct answers given by a group of people on a 6-question quiz. For which distribution is it reasonable to use a normal curve as an approximation? Why?

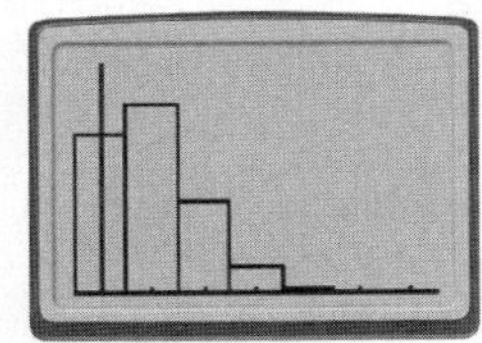

It is reasonable to use a normal curve for the distribution of heads when 6 coins are flipped because the distribution is symmetric and follows a bell-shaped curve.

Exercise	Depth of Knowledge (D.O.K.)	COMMON CORE Mathematical Practices
1	**1** Recall of Information	**MP.3** Logic
2–9	**2** Skills/Concepts	**MP.4** Modeling
10–15	**2** Skills/Concepts	**MP.6** Precision
16–22	**2** Skills/Concepts	**MP.5** Using Tools
23–24	**3** Strategic Thinking H.O.T.	**MP.3** Logic
25	**3** Strategic Thinking H.O.T.	**MP.2** Reasoning

EVALUATE

ASSIGNMENT GUIDE

Concepts and Skills	Practice
Explore Substituting a Normal Curve for a Symmetric Histogram	Exercise 1
Example 1 Finding Areas Under a Normal Curve	Exercises 2–9
Example 2 Using the Standard Normal Distribution	Exercises 10–22

QUESTIONING STRATEGIES

Why is the area to the left of a negative *z*-score always less than 0.5? **A negative *z*-score corresponds to a data value that lies below the mean. Since the area to the left of the mean is 0.5, the area to the left of any number less than the mean will be less than 0.5.**

Why do you have to subtract to find the area between two *z*-scores? **The table gives the percentages *below* each of the *z*-scores, so you have to subtract the lesser percent from the greater percent to find the difference between them.**

VISUAL CUES

Suggest that students draw and shade normal curves to model each exercise. They can then use their models to check their answers for reasonableness.

AVOID COMMON ERRORS

Students may make calculation errors based on the faulty thinking that the percent of the data that lies between the mean and 3 standard deviations above (or below) the mean is 50%. Correct this thinking by pointing out the tails of the curve that extend beyond the points $\mu + 3\sigma$ and $\mu - 3\sigma$, and emphasizing that these unbounded regions each make up a small percentage of the area that lies above or below the mean.

INTEGRATE MATHEMATICAL PRACTICES

Focus on Reasoning

MP.2 Discuss with students how standardization and *z*-scores make it possible to compare two sets of related data that may have different means and standard deviations. Use an example, such as the heights of male basketball players and the heights of female basketball players, to illustrate this concept.

A college-entrance exam is designed so that scores are normally distributed with a mean of 500 and a standard deviation of 100.

2. What percent of exam scores are between 400 and 600?

Both 400 and 600 are 1 standard deviation from the mean, so 68%.

3. What is the probability that a randomly chosen exam score is above 600?

600 is 1 standard deviation above the mean. When the area under a normal curve is separated into eight parts, the parts that satisfy the condition that the score will be greater than 600 have percents of 13.5%, 2.35%, and 0.15%. The sum of these percents is 16%, or 0.16.

4. What is the probability that a randomly chosen exam score is less than 300 or greater than 700?

300 is 2 standard deviations below the mean and 700 is 2 standard deviations above the mean. 95% of the data fall within 2 standard deviations of the mean, so the probability that an exam score is less than 300 or greater than 700 is 100% − 95% = 5%, or 0.05.

5. What is the probability that a randomly chosen exam score is above 300?

$1 - (0.0015 + 0.0235) = 0.975$

Flight 202's arrival time is normally distributed with a mean arrival time of 4:30 p.m. and a standard deviation of 15 minutes. Find the probability that a randomly chosen arrival time is within the given time period.

6. After 4:45 p.m.

$0.135 + 0.0235 + 0.0015 = 0.16$

7. Between 4:15 p.m. and 5:00 p.m.

$0.68 + 0.135 = 0.815$

8. Between 3:45 p.m. and 4:30 p.m.

$0.5000 - 0.0015 = 0.4985$

9. By 4:45 p.m.

$0.50 + 0.34 = 0.84$

Suppose the scores on a test given to all juniors in a school district are normally distributed with a mean of 74 and a standard deviation of 8. Find each of the following using the standard normal table.

10. Find the percent of juniors whose score is no more than 90.

$z_{90} = \frac{90 - \mu}{\sigma} = \frac{90 - 74}{8} = 2$; 0.9772, or about 98%

11. Find the percent of juniors whose score is between 58 and 74.

$z_{58} = \frac{58 - \mu}{\sigma} = \frac{58 - 74}{8} = -2$; $z_{74} = \frac{74 - \mu}{\sigma} = \frac{74 - 74}{8} = 0$; $0.5000 - 0.0228 = 0.4772$, or about 48%

12. Find the percent of juniors whose score is at least 74.

74 is the mean, so the percent is 50%.

13. Find the probability that a randomly chosen junior has a score above 82.

$z_{82} = \frac{82 - \mu}{\sigma} = \frac{82 - 74}{8} = 1$; $1 - 0.8413 = 0.1587$

14. Find the probability that a randomly chosen junior has a score between 66 and 90.

$z_{66} = \frac{66 - \mu}{\sigma} = \frac{66 - 74}{8} = -1$; $z_{90} = \frac{90 - \mu}{\sigma} = \frac{90 - 74}{8} = 2$; $0.9772 - 0.1587 = 0.8185$

15. Find the probability that a randomly chosen junior has a score below 74.

74 is the mean, so the probability is 0.5.

Graphing Calculator **On a graphing calculator, you can use the function normalcdf(lower bound, upper bound, μ, σ) to find the area under a normal curve for values of x between a specified lower bound and a specified upper bound. You can use $-1\text{E}99$ as the lower bound to represent negative infinity and $1\text{E}99$ as the upper bound to represent positive infinity. Suppose that cans of lemonade mix have amounts of lemonade mix that are normally distributed with a mean of 350 grams and a standard deviation of 4 grams. Use this information and a graphing calculator to answer each question.**

16. What percent of cans have less than 338 grams of lemonade mix?

normalcdf$(-1\text{E}99, 338, 350, 4) \approx 0.001$

17. What is the probability that a randomly chosen can has between 342 grams and 350 grams of lemonade mix?

normalcdf$(342, 350, 350, 4) \approx 0.477$

18. What is the probability that a randomly chosen can has less than 342 grams or more than 346 grams of lemonade mix?

normalcdf$(-1\text{E}99, 342, 350, 4) \approx 0.023$; normalcdf$(346, 1\text{E}99, 350, 4) \approx 0.841$; $0.841 + 0.023 = 0.864$

Spreadsheet **In a spreadsheet, you can use the function NORM.DIST(upper bound, μ, σ, TRUE) to find the area under a normal curve for values of x less than or equal to a specified upper bound. Suppose the heights of all the children in a state are normally distributed with a mean of 45 inches and a standard deviation of 6 inches. Use this information and a spreadsheet to answer each question.**

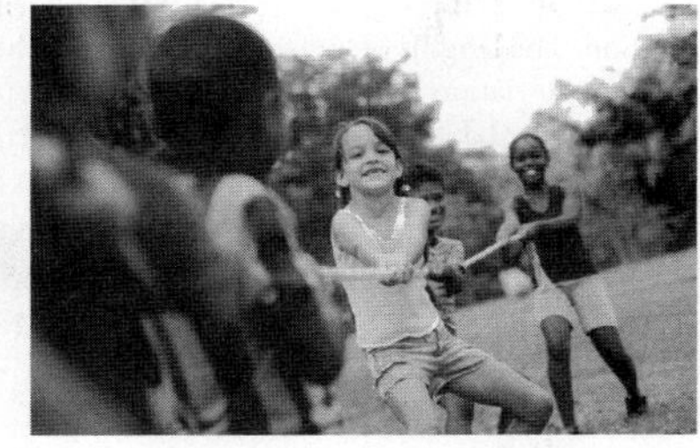

19. What is the probability that a randomly chosen child is less than 40 inches tall?

NORM.DIST$(40, 45, 6, \text{TRUE}) \approx 0.2023$

20. What is the probability that a randomly chosen child is greater than 47 inches tall?

NORM.DIST$(47, 45, 6, \text{TRUE}) \approx 0.6306$; $1 - 0.6306 = 0.3694$

21. What percent of children are between 50 and 53 inches tall?

NORM.DIST$(50, 45, 6, \text{TRUE}) \approx 0.7977$; NORM.DIST$(53, 45, 6, \text{TRUE}) \approx 0.9088$; $0.9088 - 0.7977 = 0.1111$; About 11.11% of children are between 50 and 53 inches tall.

22. What is the probability that a randomly chosen child is less than 38 inches tall or more than 51 inches tall?

NORM.DIST$(38, 45, 6, \text{TRUE}) \approx 0.1217$; NORM.DIST$(51, 45, 6, \text{TRUE}) \approx 0.8413$; $1 - 0.8413 = 0.1587$; $0.1587 + 0.1217 = 0.2804$

INTEGRATE MATHEMATICAL PRACTICES

Focus on Math Connections

MP.1 The Central Limit Theorem states that the distribution of the means of random samples, rather than the actual data, are normally distributed for large sample sizes. So normal distributions can be used to describe the averages of data that do not necessarily have a normal distribution themselves.

PEER-TO-PEER DISCUSSION

Ask students to discuss with a partner how, if you know the mean and standard deviation of a set of normally distributed data, you can find the data value that has a given z-score. Have students write a formula that can be used to find this value. The formula for finding a z-score can be transformed to $x = z\sigma + \mu$, showing how the data value x can be calculated from the three given measures.

JOURNAL

Have students explain how to use the standard normal table to find the probability of an event, given the mean and standard deviation of a normal distribution. Have them create an example to illustrate their explanations.

H.O.T. Focus on Higher Order Thinking

23. Explain the Error A student was asked to describe the relationship between the area under a normal curve for all x-values less than a and the area under the normal curve for all x-values greater than a. The student's response was "Both areas are 0.5 because the curve is symmetric." Explain the student's error.

The student's answer is only correct if a is the mean. If a is not the mean, the area for the x-values less than a is p, and the area for x-values greater than a is $1 - p$.

24. Make a Conjecture A local orchard packages apples in bags. When full, the bags weigh 5 pounds each and contain a whole number of apples. The weights are normally distributed with a mean of 5 pounds and a standard deviation of 0.25 pound. An inspector weighs each bag and rejects all bags that weigh less than 5 pounds. Describe the shape of the distribution of the weights of the bags that are not rejected.

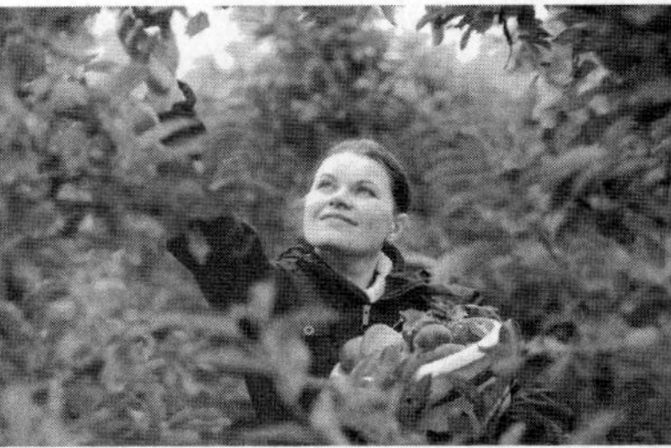

The shape of the distribution will be the right half of a normal curve because all values below the mean are rejected.

25. Analyze Relationships A biologist is measuring the lengths of frogs in a certain location. The lengths of 20 frogs are shown. If the mean is 7.4 centimeters and the standard deviation is 0.8 centimeter, do the data appear to be normally distributed? Complete the table and explain.

Length (cm)				
7.5	5.8	7.9	7.6	8.1
7.9	7.1	5.9	8.4	7.3
7.1	6.4	8.3	8.4	6.7
8.1	7.8	5.9	6.8	8.1

			Values $\leq x$	
z	Area $\leq z$	x	Projected	Actual
−2	0.02	5.8	$0.02 \cdot 20 = 0.4 \approx 0$	1
−1	0.16	6.6	$0.16 \cdot 20 = 3.2 \approx 3$	4
0	0.5	7.4	$0.5 \cdot 20 = 10$	9
1	0.84	8.2	$0.84 \cdot 20 = 16.8 \approx 17$	17
2	0.98	9	$0.98 \cdot 20 = 19.6 \approx 20$	20

The projected number of values that corresponds to each value of z is close to the actual number of data values. The data appear to be normally distributed.

Lesson Performance Task

Suppose a nurse records the temperatures of healthy men and women. The table represents the means and standard deviations of the data.

	Women	Men
°F	98.4 ± 0.7 °F	98.1 ± 0.7 °F
°C	36.9 ± 0.4 °C	36.7 ± 0.4 °C

A. What is the range of temperatures for 1, 2, and 3 standard deviations for both women and men? (Give temperatures in both degrees Fahrenheit and degrees Celsius.)

Women

1 standard deviation: 97.7 °F to 99.1 °F; 36.5 °C to 37.3 °C

2 standard deviations: 97 °F to 99.8 °F; 36.1 °C to 37.7 °C

3 standard deviations: 96.3 °F to 100.5 °F; 35.7 °C to 38.1 °C

Men

1 standard deviation: 97.4 °F to 98.8 °F; 36.3 °C to 37.1 °C

2 standard deviations: 96.7 °F to 99.5 °F; 35.9 °C to 37.5 °C

3 standard deviations: 96 °F to 100.2 °F; 35.5 °C to 37.9 °C

B. Assuming a normal distribution, find the probability that a randomly selected man's temperature is between 96.7 °F and 97.4 °F.

97.4 is 1 standard deviation below the mean.

68% of the data fall between 97.4 °F and 98.8 °F.

96.7 is 2 standard deviations below the mean.

95% of the data fall between 96.7 °F and 99.5 °F.

The difference is 27%.

$\frac{0.27}{2} = 0.135$

The probability that a randomly selected man's temperature is between 96.7 °F and 97.4 °F is 0.135.

C. A fever is considered medically significant if body temperature reaches 100.4 °F (38 °C). What can you observe about this temperature?

It is about 3 standard deviations above the mean for both men and women, which is higher than almost all (about 99.85% of) normal body temperatures.

EXTENSION ACTIVITY

Have students come up with an idea for a survey of students in the school that would collect data that should be normally distributed. Ask them to use the standard normal curve to predict the number of students who should fall within one standard deviation of the mean, two standard deviations of the mean, and so on. Then, if it is feasible, have students conduct the survey and find out whether their actual data is normally distributed.

CONNECT VOCABULARY EL

Describe how a person might *deviate* partly or completely from guidelines or from a plan. Connect this to the concept that data may deviate from the mean.

INTEGRATE MATHEMATICAL PRACTICES

Focus on Modeling

MP.1 Students may benefit by representing the mean temperatures and temperatures representing 1, 2, and 3 standard deviations from the mean on a number line, with the standard deviation ranges marked below the line and the relevant temperatures above the line. By using two number lines, one above the other, students can compare these temperatures for the genders.

Scoring Rubric

2 points: Student correctly solves the problem and explains his/her reasoning.

1 point: Student shows good understanding of the problem but does not fully solve or explain his/her reasoning.

0 points: Student does not demonstrate understanding of the problem.

Sampling Distributions

Common Core Math Standards

The student is expected to:

 **S-IC.B.4**

Use data from a sample survey to estimate a population mean or proportion; develop a margin of error through the use of simulation models for random sampling.

Mathematical Practices

 **MP.6 Precision**

Language Objective

Work with a partner to compare and contrast the standard error of the mean and the standard error of the proportion.

ENGAGE

Essential Question: How is the mean of a sampling distribution related to the population mean or proportion?

The mean of the sampling distribution of the sample mean is equal to the population mean. Similarly, the mean of the sampling distribution of the sample proportion is equal to the population proportion.

PREVIEW: LESSON PERFORMANCE TASK

View the Engage section online. Discuss the photo and note that the U.S. Census Bureau gathers data on the number of people in each household and the number of households that have each number of people, and that sampling could be used to find relevant probabilities. Then preview the Lesson Performance Task.

Name ______________ Class ______________ Date ______________

23.3 Sampling Distributions

Essential Question: How is the mean of a sampling distribution related to the corresponding population mean or population proportion?

Resource Locker

Explore 1 Developing a Distribution of Sample Means

The tables provide the following data about the first 50 people to join a new gym: member ID number, age, and sex.

ID	Age	Sex	ID	Age	Sex	ID	Age	Sex	ID	Age	Sex	ID	Age	Sex
1	30	M	11	38	F	21	74	F	31	32	M	41	46	M
2	48	M	12	24	M	22	21	M	32	28	F	42	34	F
3	52	M	13	48	F	23	29	F	33	35	M	43	44	F
4	25	F	14	45	M	24	48	M	34	49	M	44	68	M
5	63	F	15	28	F	25	37	M	35	18	M	45	24	F
6	50	F	16	39	M	26	52	F	36	56	F	46	34	F
7	18	F	17	37	F	27	25	F	37	48	F	47	55	F
8	28	F	18	63	F	28	44	M	38	38	F	48	39	M
9	72	M	19	20	M	29	29	F	39	52	F	49	40	F
10	25	F	20	81	F	30	66	M	40	33	F	50	30	F

(A) Enter the age data into a graphing calculator and find the mean age μ and standard deviation σ for the population of the gym's first 50 members. Round each statistic to the nearest tenth.

$\mu \approx 41.2$; $\sigma \approx 15.3$

(B) Use a graphing calculator's random number generator to choose a sample of 5 gym members. Find the mean age $\bar{x}$ for your sample. Round to the nearest tenth.

Answers will vary. Possible answer: $\bar{x} = 39.5$

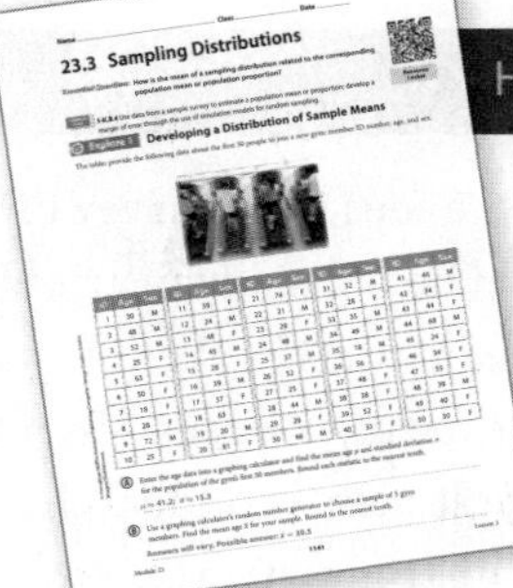

HARDCOVER PAGES 1141–11

Watch for the hardcover student edition page numbers for this lesson.

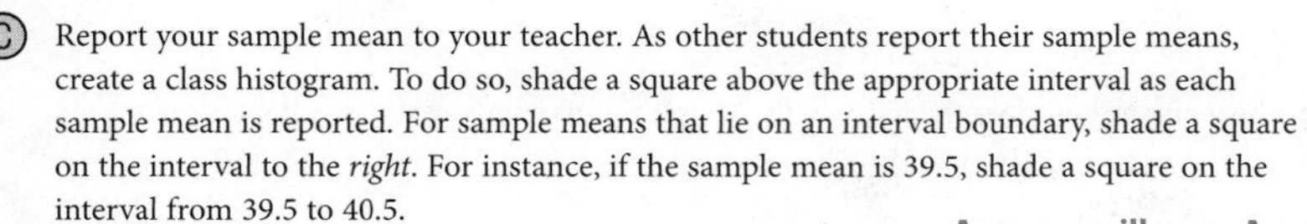

Ⓒ Report your sample mean to your teacher. As other students report their sample means, create a class histogram. To do so, shade a square above the appropriate interval as each sample mean is reported. For sample means that lie on an interval boundary, shade a square on the interval to the *right*. For instance, if the sample mean is 39.5, shade a square on the interval from 39.5 to 40.5.

Make your own copy of the class histogram using the grid shown. **Answers will vary. A possible histogram is shown.**

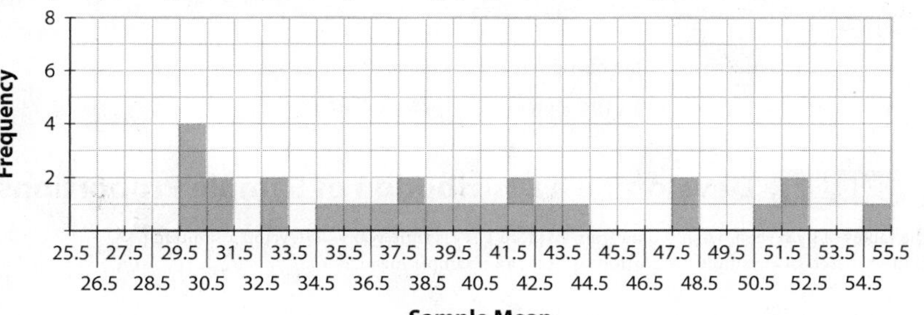

Ⓓ Calculate the mean of the sample means, $\mu_{\bar{x}}$, and the standard deviation of the sample means, $\sigma_{\bar{x}}$.

Answers will vary. Possible answer: $\mu_{\bar{x}} = 39.8$; $\sigma_{\bar{x}} = 7.9$

Ⓔ Now use a graphing calculator's random number generator to choose a sample of 15 gym members. Find the mean for your sample. Round to the nearest tenth.

Answers will vary. Possible answer: $\bar{x} = 40.5$

Ⓕ Report your sample mean to your teacher. As other students report their sample means, create a class histogram and make your own copy of it. **Answers will vary. A possible histogram is shown.**

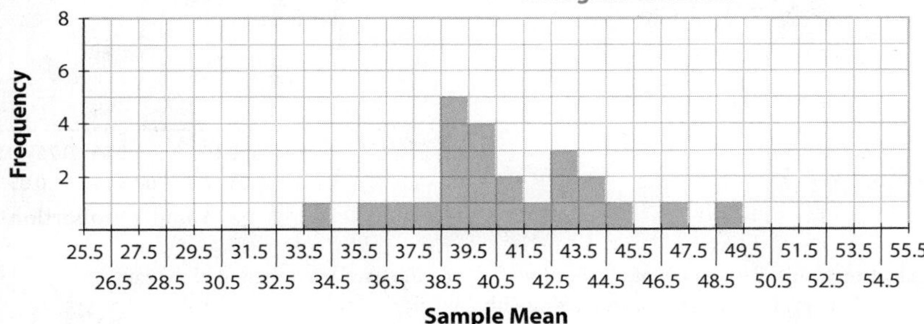

Ⓖ Calculate the mean of the sample means, $\mu_{\bar{x}}$, and the standard deviation of the sample means, $\sigma_{\bar{x}}$.

Answers will vary. Possible answer: $\mu_{\bar{x}} = 40.8$; $\sigma_{\bar{x}} = 3.4$

PROFESSIONAL DEVELOPMENT

Learning Progressions

In previous lessons, students constructed probability distributions, and they explored normal distributions in detail. In this lesson, students will construct distributions of data obtained from different samples of the same population. Students should understand that the mean and standard deviation for a sample usually will not match the statistics for the entire population or for a different sample of the same population. Students will learn how to use population statistics to determine the likelihood that a sample will have certain characteristics. In the next lesson they will build on this knowledge to make predictions about population parameters from sample statistics.

EXPLORE 1

Developing a Distribution of Sample Means

INTEGRATE TECHNOLOGY

Students will use graphing calculators to first calculate the mean and standard deviation of a population, then randomly select samples from that population, and finally calculate statistics for the distribution of sample means. This simulation will enable them to see the effect of sample size on how closely the sample means approximate the population mean.

QUESTIONING STRATEGIES

How can you change the way a sample is selected to make the sample mean better match the population mean? **Increase the sample size. As the sample size increases, the sample mean approaches the population mean.**

EXPLORE 2

Developing a Distribution of Sample Proportions

QUESTIONING STRATEGIES

What is the difference between this sampling distribution and the one in the first Explore activity? **The first one was a distribution of sample means, while this is a distribution of sample proportions.**

INTEGRATE MATHEMATICAL PRACTICES

Focus on Reasoning

MP.2 When creating a histogram of sample proportions for a sample size of 5, ask students why there are only a few different values for the sample proportion, even when many samples are selected. Students should recognize that the only possible values for the proportion are 0, 0.2, 0.4, 0.6, 0.8 and 1.

Reflect

1. In the class histograms, how does the mean of the sample means compare with the population mean?
   The mean of the sample means is close to the population mean.

2. What happens to the standard deviation of the sample means as the sample size increases?
   The standard deviation of the sample means decreases.

3. What happens to the shape of the histogram as the sample size increases?
   The histogram gets closer to the shape of a normal distribution.

Explore 2 Developing a Distribution of Sample Proportions

Use the tables of gym membership data from Explore 1. This time you will develop a sampling distribution based on a sample proportion rather than a sample mean.

(A) Find the proportion p of female gym members in the population.

$p = 0.6$

(B) Use a graphing calculator's random number generator to choose a sample of 5 gym members. Find the proportion $\hat{p}$ of female gym members for your sample.

Answers will vary. All sample proportions will be 0, 0.2, 0.4, 0.6, 0.8, or 1.

(C) Report your sample proportion to your teacher. As other students report their sample proportions, create a class histogram and make your own copy of it.

Answers will vary. A possible histogram is shown.

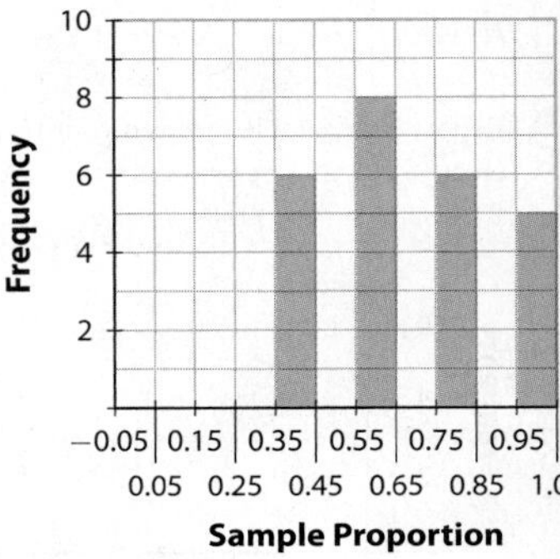

(D) Calculate the mean of the sample proportions, $\mu_{\hat{p}}$, and the standard deviation of the sample proportions, $\sigma_{\hat{p}}$. Round to the nearest hundredth.

Answers will vary. Possible answer: $\mu_{\hat{p}} = 0.68$; $\sigma_{\hat{p}} = 0.21$

(E) Now use your calculator's random number generator to choose a sample of 10 gym members. Find the proportion of female members $\hat{p}$ for your sample.

Answers will vary. All sample proportions will be 0, 0.1, 0.2, ..., 0.9, or 1.

COLLABORATIVE LEARNING

Peer-to-Peer Activity

Have students work in pairs. Give each pair the mean and standard deviation for a population. Have each student choose a sample size, determine the standard error of the mean for that sample size, and identify an interval that contains either 68%, 95%, or 99.7% of the sample means. Next, have students tell their partners the sample size they used and the upper and lower bounds of the interval they found. Have each student calculate the percent of sample means that fall within the partner's interval. Have partners check each other's results.

(F) Report your sample proportion to your teacher. As other students report their sample proportions, create a class histogram and make your own copy of it.

Answers will vary. A possible histogram is shown.

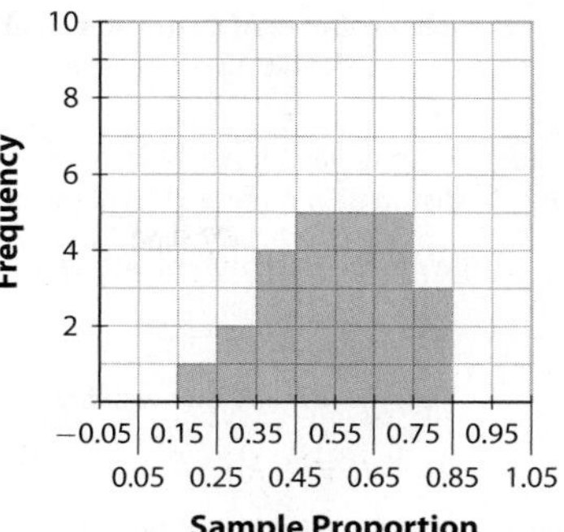

(G) Calculate the mean of the sample proportions, $\mu_{\hat{p}}$, and the standard deviation of the sample proportions, $\sigma_{\hat{p}}$. Round to the nearest hundredth.

Answers will vary. Possible answer: $\mu_{\hat{p}} = 0.55$; $\sigma_{\hat{p}} = 0.16$

Reflect

4. In the class histograms, how does the mean of the sample proportions compare with the population proportion?

The mean of the sample proportions is close to the population proportion.

5. What happens to the standard deviation of the sample proportions as the sample size increases?

The standard deviation of the sample proportions decreases.

Explain 1 Using the Sampling Distribution of the Sample Mean

The histograms that you made in the two Explores are *sampling distributions*. A **sampling distribution** shows how a particular statistic varies across all samples of n individuals from the same population. In Explore 1, you approximated sampling distributions of the sample mean, $\bar{x}$, for samples of size 5 and 15. (The reason your sampling distributions are approximations is that you did not find *all* samples of a given size.)

The mean of the sampling distribution of the sample mean is denoted $\mu_{\bar{x}}$. The standard deviation of the sampling distribution of the sample mean is denoted $\sigma_{\bar{x}}$ and is also called the **standard error of the mean**.

In Explore 1, you may have discovered that $\mu_{\bar{x}}$ is close to $\bar{x}$ regardless of the sample size and that $\sigma_{\bar{x}}$ decreases as the sample size n increases. You based these observations on simulations. When you consider all possible samples of n individuals, you arrive at one of the major theorems of statistics.

Properties of the Sampling Distribution of the Sample Mean

If a random sample of size n is selected from a population with mean μ and standard deviation σ, then

1. $\mu_{\bar{x}} = \mu$,
2. $\sigma_{\bar{x}} = \frac{\sigma}{\sqrt{n}}$, and
3. the sampling distribution of the sample mean is normal if the population is normal; for all other populations, the sampling distribution of the mean approaches a normal distribution as n increases.

The third property stated above is known as the Central Limit Theorem.

EXPLAIN 1

Using the Sampling Distribution of the Sample Mean

QUESTIONING STRATEGIES

If you create two sampling distributions by randomly selecting samples from the same population, with one distribution having samples of size 25 and the other having samples of size 100, how will the standard errors of the means of the two distributions compare? Explain. The standard error of the mean for samples of 100 will be half as large as the standard error for samples of 25. Standard error is inversely proportional to the square root of the sample size, so quadrupling the sample size reduces the standard error by a factor of 2.

INTEGRATE TECHNOLOGY

Review how to use a graphing calculator to find the probability that a value in a normal distribution is between two specified values. Find the cumulative distribution function by going to the **DISTR** menu and selecting **2:normalcdf(**, and entering the given information in the correct order (smaller value, larger value, mean, standard deviation) to find the probability. To find the probability that a quantity is less than a given value, enter **−1 EE 99** for the lower value. To find the probability that a quantity is greater than a given value, enter **1 EE 99** for the upper value.

AVOID COMMON ERRORS

Remind students that when using a calculator to find the probability that the mean of a sample is between two given values (or above or below a given value), they must first calculate $\sigma_{\bar{x}}$, the standard error of the mean, then use that value as the standard deviation that they enter on the calculator. If, instead, they use the standard deviation of the population, they will obtain an incorrect result.

Example 2 **Boxes of Cruncho cereal have a mean mass of 323 grams with a standard deviation of 20 grams.**

(A) For random samples of 36 boxes, what interval centered on the mean of the sampling distribution captures 95% of the sample means?

Write the given information about the population and a sample.

$\mu = 323 \qquad \sigma = 20 \qquad n = 36$

Find the mean of the sampling distribution of the sample mean and the standard error of the mean.

$\mu_{\bar{x}} = \mu = 323 \qquad \sigma_{\bar{x}} = \frac{\sigma}{\sqrt{n}} = \frac{20}{\sqrt{36}} = \frac{20}{6} \approx 3.3$

The sampling distribution of the sample mean is approximately normal. In a normal distribution, 95% of the data fall within 2 standard deviations of the mean.

$\mu_{\bar{x}} - 2\sigma_{\bar{x}} = 323 - 2(3.3) = 316.4 \qquad \mu_{\bar{x}} + 2\sigma_{\bar{x}} = 323 + 2(3.3) = 329.6$

So, for random samples of 36 boxes, 95% of the sample means fall between 316.4 grams and 329.6 grams.

(B) What is the probability that a random sample of 25 boxes has a mean mass of at most 325 grams?

Write the given information about the population and the sample.

$\mu = 323 \qquad \sigma = 20 \qquad n = 25$

Find the mean of the sampling distribution of the sample mean and the standard error of the mean.

$\mu_{\bar{x}} = \mu = 323 \qquad \sigma_{\bar{x}} = \frac{\sigma}{\sqrt{n}} = \frac{20}{\sqrt{25}} = \frac{20}{5} = 4$

The sampling distribution of the sample mean is approximately normal. Use a graphing calculator to find $P(\bar{x} \leq 325)$.

$P(\bar{x} \leq 325) = \text{normalcdf}(-1\text{E}99, 325, 323, 4) \approx 0.69$

So, the probability that the random sample has a mean mass of at most 325 grams is about 0.69.

Your Turn

Boxes of Cruncho cereal have a mean mass of 323 grams with a standard deviation of 20 grams.

6. For random samples of 50 boxes, what interval centered on the mean of the sampling distribution captures 99.7% of the sample means?

$\mu_{\bar{x}} = \mu = 323 \qquad \sigma_{\bar{x}} = \frac{\sigma}{\sqrt{n}} = \frac{20}{\sqrt{50}} \approx 2.8$

The sampling distribution of the sample mean is approximately normal. In a normal distribution, 99.7% of the data fall within 3 standard deviations of the mean.

$\mu_{\bar{x}} - 3\sigma_{\bar{x}} = 323 - 3(2.8) = 314.6 \qquad \mu_{\bar{x}} - 3\sigma_{\bar{x}} = 323 - 3(2.8) = 331.4$

So, for random samples of 50 boxes, 99.7% of the sample means fall between 314.6 grams and 331.4 grams.

7. What is the probability that a random sample of 100 boxes has a mean mass of at least 320 grams?

$\mu_{\bar{x}} = \mu = 323$ $\sigma_{\bar{x}} = \frac{\sigma}{\sqrt{n}} = \frac{20}{\sqrt{100}} = \frac{20}{10} = 2$

The sampling distribution of the sample mean is approximately normal.
$P(\bar{x} \geq 320) = \text{normalcdf}(320, 1E99, 323, 2) \approx 0.93$

So, the probability that the random sample has a mean mass of at least 320 grams is about 0.93.

Explain 2 Using the Sampling Distribution of the Sample Proportion

When you work with the sampling distribution of a sample proportion, p represents the proportion of individuals in the population that have a particular characteristic (that is, the proportion of "successes") and $\hat{p}$ is the proportion of successes in a sample. The mean of the sampling distribution of the sample proportion is denoted $\mu_{\hat{p}}$. The standard deviation of the sampling distribution of the sample proportion is denoted $\sigma_{\hat{p}}$ and is also called the **standard error of the proportion**.

Properties of the Sampling Distribution of the Sample Proportion

If a random sample of size n is selected from a population with proportion p of successes, then

1. $\mu_{\hat{p}} = p$,
2. $\sigma_{\hat{p}} = \sqrt{\frac{p(1-p)}{n}}$, and
3. if both np and $n(1-p)$ are at least 10, then the sampling distribution of the sample proportion is approximate normal.

Example 2 **40% of the students at a university live off campus. When sampling from this population, consider "successes" to be students who live off campus.**

(A) For random samples of 50 students, what interval centered on the mean of the sampling distribution captures 95% of the sample proportions?

Write the given information about the population and a sample.

$p = 0.4$ $n = 50$

Find the mean of the sampling distribution of the sample proportion and the standard error of the proportion.

$\mu_{\hat{p}} = p = 0.4$ $\sigma_{\hat{p}} = \sqrt{\frac{p(1-p)}{n}} = \sqrt{\frac{0.4(1-0.4)}{50}} \approx 0.069$

Check that np and $n(1-p)$ are both at least 10.

$np = 50 \cdot 0.4 = 20$ $n(1-p) = 50 \cdot 0.6 = 30$

Since np and $n(1-p)$ are both greater than 10, the sampling distribution of the sample proportion is approximately normal. In a normal distribution, 95% of the data fall within 2 standard deviations of the mean.

$\mu_{\hat{p}} - 2\sigma_{\hat{p}} = 0.4 - 2(0.069) = 0.262$ $\mu_{\hat{p}} + 2\sigma_{\hat{p}} = 0.4 + 2(0.069) = 0.538$

So, for random samples of 50 students, 95% of the sample proportions fall between 26.2% and 53.8%.

LANGUAGE SUPPORT ELL

Communicate Math

Have students work with a partner to compare and contrast the standard error of the mean and the standard error of the proportion. Monitor students' use of terminology to learn what words and concepts are difficult for them to understand or to communicate.

EXPLAIN 2

Using the Sampling Distribution of the Sample Proportion

QUESTIONING STRATEGIES

How are the mean and standard deviation of the sampling distribution of a sample proportion similar to and different from the mean and standard deviation of the sampling distribution of a sample mean? **In both cases, the mean of the sampling distribution is equal to the corresponding value (mean or proportion) for the population. However, the standard deviation is calculated somewhat differently for sample means and sample proportions.**

INTEGRATE MATHEMATICAL PRACTICES

Focus on Critical Thinking

MP.3 Discuss with students the criteria for determining whether a sampling distribution is approximately normal. If the population is normally distributed, the sampling distribution of the sample mean will also be normal. Also, the sampling distribution of a sample mean approaches a normal distribution as the sample size n increases. The distribution is approximately normal when n is very large, but we do not have precise definitions of "approximately normal" or "very large."

For the sampling distribution of a sample proportion, how close the distribution is to normal depends on both n and the proportion p. If p is very large or very small, n must be especially large for the distribution to be approximately normal. We can use the rule of thumb that says that if both np and $n(1-p)$ are at least 10, we can consider the distribution approximately normal.

(B) What is the probability that a random sample of 25 students has a proportion of at most 37%?

Write the given information about the population and the sample, where a success is a student who lives off campus.

$p = \boxed{0.4}$ $n = \boxed{25}$

Find the mean of the sampling distribution of the sample proportion and the standard error of the proportion.

$\mu_{\hat{p}} = p = \boxed{0.4}$ $\sigma_{\hat{p}} = \sqrt{\frac{p(1-p)}{n}} = \sqrt{\frac{\boxed{0.4}\left(1 - \boxed{0.4}\right)}{\boxed{25}}} = \boxed{0.098}$

Check that np and $n(1-p)$ are both at least 10.

$np = \boxed{25} \cdot \boxed{0.4} = \boxed{10}$ $n(1-p) = \boxed{25} \cdot \boxed{0.6} = \boxed{15}$

Since np and $n(1-p)$ are greater than or equal to 10, the sampling distribution of the sample proportion is approximately normal. Use a graphing calculator to find $P(\hat{p} \le 0.37)$.

$P(\hat{p} \le 0.37) = \text{normalcdf}\left(-1\text{E}99, \boxed{0.37}, \boxed{0.4}, \boxed{0.098}\right) \approx \boxed{0.38}$

So, the probability that the random sample has a proportion of at most 37% is about 0.38.

YourTurn

40% of the students at a university live off campus. When sampling from this population, consider "successes" to be students who live off campus.

8. For random samples of 80 students, what interval centered on the mean of the sampling distribution captures 68% of the sample proportions?

$\mu_{\hat{p}} = p = 0.4$ $\sigma_{\hat{p}} = \sqrt{\frac{p(1-p)}{n}} = \sqrt{\frac{0.4(1-0.4)}{80}} \approx 0.055$

Since $np = 32$, $n(1-p) = 48$, and both are greater than 10, the sampling distribution is approximately normal. In a normal distribution, 68% of the data fall within 1 standard deviation of the mean.

$\mu_{\hat{p}} - \sigma_{\hat{p}} = 0.4 - 0.055 = 0.345$ $\mu_{\hat{p}} + \sigma_{\hat{p}} = 0.4 + 0.055 = 0.445$

So, for random samples of 80 students, 68% of the sample proportions fall between 34.5% and 45.5%.

9. What is the probability that a random sample of 60 students includes more than 18 students who live off campus?

$\mu_{\hat{p}} = p = 0.4$ $\sigma_{\hat{p}} = \sqrt{\frac{p(1-p)}{n}} = \sqrt{\frac{0.41(-0.4)}{60}} \approx 0.063$

Since $np = 24$, $n(1-p) = 36$, and both are greater than 10, the sampling distribution is approximately normal.

$\hat{p}_{min} = \frac{18}{60} = 0.3$

$P(\hat{p} > 0.3) = \text{normalcdf}(0.3, 1E99, 0.4, 0.063) \approx 0.94$

So, the probability that the random sample includes more than 18 students who live off campus is about 0.94.

Elaborate

10. What is a sampling distribution?
A sampling distribution is a distribution that shows how a particular statistic varies across all samples of *n* individuals from the same population.

11. What allows you to conclude that 95% of the sample means in a sampling distribution are within 2 standard deviations of the population mean?
The Central Limit Theorem says that the sampling distribution of the sample mean is normal or approximately normal, so 95% of the sample means will fall within 2 standard deviations of the mean of the sampling distribution, but the mean of the sampling distribution is equal to the population mean, so 95% of the sample means will fall within 2 standard deviations of the population mean.

12. When finding a sample mean or a sample proportion, why is using the greatest sample size possible (given constraints on the cost and time of sampling) a desirable thing to do?
Increasing the sample size decreases the variation in the sampling distribution, which in turn means that the sample mean or sample proportion will be more accurate because it is more likely to fall closer to the population mean or the population proportion.

13. **Essential Question Check-In** When you repeatedly take random samples of the same size from a population, what does the mean of the samples approximate?
The mean of the samples approximates the population mean (if the data are numerical) or the population proportion (if the data are categorical).

ELABORATE

INTEGRATE MATHEMATICAL PRACTICES

Focus on Communication

MP.3 Ask students to describe different methods for determining the probability that a sample mean or proportion falls between two given values. They should understand that if the given values are multiples of a standard deviation away from the mean of the sampling distribution, they can use the known percentages of data that fall within 0, 1, 2, or 3 standard deviations of the mean. If not, they can calculate *z*-scores for the given values and look up the corresponding probabilities on a standard normal table. Alternatively, they can use the cumulative distribution function on a graphing calculator.

SUMMARIZE THE LESSON

? Given the mean and standard deviation of a population, how can you determine the mean and standard deviation of a sampling distribution of sample means? **The mean of the sampling distribution of the sample mean is equal to the mean of the population. To find the standard deviation, divide the population standard deviation by the square root of the sample size.**

EVALUATE

ASSIGNMENT GUIDE

Concepts and Skills	Practice
Explore 1 Developing a Distribution of Sample Means	Exercise 1
Explore 2 Developing a Distribution of Sample Proportions	Exercise 18
Example 1 Using the Sampling Distribution of the Sample Mean	Exercises 2–9
Example 2 Using the Sampling Distribution of the Sample Proportion	Exercises 10–17

AVOID COMMON ERRORS

When finding the probability that a sample has a value within a given range, remind students to pay attention to whether they are working with sample means or sample proportions, so that they use the correct formula for the standard deviation of the sample distribution.

Evaluate: Homework and Practice

- Online Homework
- Hints and Help
- Extra Practice

1. The general manager of a multiplex theater took random samples of size 10 from the audiences attending the opening weekend of a new movie. From each sample, the manager obtained the mean age and the proportion of those who said they liked the movie. The sample means and sample proportions are listed in the tables.

Sample number	Sample mean (age)	Sample proportion (liked the movie)
1	22.1	0.6
2	25.7	0.9
3	24.8	0.7
4	24.3	0.7
5	23.9	0.8
6	23.3	0.6
7	22.8	0.5
8	24.0	0.8
9	25.1	0.7
10	23.6	0.7

Sample number	Sample mean (age)	Sample proportion (liked the movie)
11	24.2	0.5
12	26.4	0.6
13	25.9	0.7
14	23.8	0.8
15	21.1	0.7
16	24.4	0.7
17	23.9	0.6
18	25.1	0.7
19	24.7	0.9
20	22.9	0.6

a. Based on the 20 samples, what is the best estimate for the mean age of all the people who saw the movie? Explain.

The best estimate of the population mean is the mean of the sample means: $\mu_{\bar{x}} = 24.1$.

b. Based on this sample, what is the best estimate for the proportion of all the people who saw the movie and liked it? Explain.

The best estimate of the population proportion is the mean of the sample proportions: $\mu_{\hat{p}} = 0.69$.

c. What could the manager have done to improve the accuracy of both estimates?

The manager could have improved the accuracy of the estimates by using a sample size greater than 10.

Exercise	Depth of Knowledge (D.O.K.)	COMMON CORE Mathematical Practices
1	**1** Recall of Information	**MP.5** Using Tools
2–5	**2** Skills/Concepts	**MP.5** Using Tools
6–9	**2** Skills/Concepts	**MP.6** Precision
10–13	**2** Skills/Concepts	**MP.5** Using Tools

On a standardized science test, the seniors at Fillmore High School have a mean score of 425 with a standard deviation of 80.

2. For random samples of 30 seniors, what interval centered on the mean of the sampling distribution captures 95% of the mean scores?

$\mu_{\bar{x}} = \mu = 425; \sigma_{\bar{x}} = \frac{\sigma}{\sqrt{n}} = \frac{80}{\sqrt{30}} \approx 14.6$

$\mu_{\bar{x}} - 2\sigma_{\bar{x}} = 425 - 2(14.6) = 395.8$

$\mu_{\bar{x}} + 2\sigma_{\bar{x}} = 425 + 2(14.6) = 454.2$

So, for random samples of 30 seniors, 95% of the sample means fall between 395.8 and 454.2.

3. For random samples of 100 seniors, what interval centered on the mean of the sampling distribution captures 68% of the mean scores?

$\mu_{\bar{x}} = \mu = 425; \sigma_{\bar{x}} = \frac{\sigma}{\sqrt{n}} = \frac{80}{\sqrt{100}} = 8$

$\mu_{\bar{x}} - \sigma_{\bar{x}} = 425 - 8 = 417$

$\mu_{\bar{x}} + \sigma_{\bar{x}} = 425 + 8 = 433$

So, for random samples of 100 seniors, 68% of the sample means fall between 417 and 433.

4. What is the probability that a random sample of 50 seniors has a mean score of at most 415?

$\mu_{\bar{x}} = \mu = 425; \sigma_{\bar{x}} = \frac{\sigma}{\sqrt{n}} = \frac{80}{\sqrt{50}} \approx 11.3$

$P(\bar{x} \leq 415) =$ normalcdf $(-1\text{E}99, 415, 425, 11.3) \approx 0.19$

So, the probability that a random sample of 50 seniors has a mean score of at most 415 is about 0.19.

5. What is the probability that a random sample of 25 seniors has a mean score of at least 430?

$\mu_{\bar{x}} = \mu = 425; \sigma_{\bar{x}} = \frac{\sigma}{\sqrt{n}} = \frac{80}{\sqrt{25}} = 16$

$P(\bar{x} \geq 430) =$ normalcdf $(430, 1\text{E}99, 425, 16) \approx 0.38$

So, the probability that a random sample of 25 seniors has a mean score of at least 430 is about 0.38.

For Exercises 6–9, use the following information: The safety placard on an elevator states that up to 8 people (1200 kilograms) can ride the elevator at one time. Suppose the people who work in the office building where the elevator is located have a mean mass of 80 kilograms with a standard deviation of 25 kilograms.

6. For random samples of 8 people who work in the office building, what interval centered on the mean of the sampling distribution captures 95% of the mean masses?

$\mu_{\bar{x}} = \mu = 80; \frac{\sigma}{\sqrt{n}} = \frac{25}{\sqrt{8}} \approx 8.8$

$\mu_{\bar{x}} - 2\sigma_{\bar{x}} = 80 - 2(8.8) = 62.4$ $\quad \mu_{\bar{x}} + 2\sigma_{\bar{x}} = 80 + 2(8.8) = 97.6$

So, for random samples of 8 people who work in the office building, 95% of the sample means fall between 62.4 kilograms and 97.6 kilograms.

VISUAL CUES

When finding an interval that captures a given percentage of the sample means or proportions, encourage students to look back at the figure in the previous lesson that divides the normal curve into parts and indicates what percent of the data in a normal distribution are contained in each part. This visual representation may make it easier for visual learners to identify the required interval.

Exercise	Depth of Knowledge (D.O.K.)	COMMON CORE Mathematical Practices
14–17	**2** Skills/Concepts	**MP.6** Precision
18	**2** Skills/Concepts	**MP.3** Logic
19	**2** Skills/Concepts H.O.T.	**MP.3** Logic
20	**3** Strategic Thinking H.O.T.	**MP.6** Precision
21	**3** Strategic Thinking H.O.T.	**MP.3** Logic

AVOID COMMON ERRORS

When using a graphing calculator to determine the probability that a sample mean or proportion is above or below a given value, students will obtain incorrect results if they enter the given information in the wrong order. Remind them to read each problem carefully. If the problem asks about means or proportions that are "more than" a certain value, that value should be the first number entered in the calculator's cumulative distribution function. For questions about means or proportions that are "at most" a certain value, that value should be the second number entered.

7. For random samples of 8 people who work in the office building, what interval centered on the mean of the sampling distribution captures 99.7% of the mean masses?

$\mu_{\bar{x}} = \mu = 80$; $\sigma_{\bar{x}} = \frac{\sigma}{\sqrt{n}} = \frac{25}{\sqrt{8}} \approx 8.8$

$\mu_{\bar{x}} - 3\sigma_{\bar{x}} = 80 - 3(8.8) = 53.6$

$\mu_{\bar{x}} + 3\sigma_{\bar{x}} = 80 + 3(8.8) = 106.4$

So, for random samples of 8 people who work in the office building, 99.7% of the sample means fall between 53.6 kilograms and 106.4 kilograms.

8. What is the probability that a random sample of 8 people who work in the office building has a mean mass of at most 90 kilograms?

$\mu_{\bar{x}} = \mu = 80$; $\sigma_{\bar{x}} = \frac{\sigma}{\sqrt{n}} = \frac{25}{\sqrt{8}} \approx 8.8$

$P(\bar{x} \le 90) = \text{normalcdf}(-1\text{E}99, 90, 80, 8.8) \approx 0.87$

So, the probability that a random sample of 8 people who work in the office building has a mean mass of at most 90 kilograms is about 0.87.

9. Based on the elevator's safety placard, what is the maximum mean mass of 8 people who can ride the elevator at one time? What is the probability that a random sample of 8 people who work in the office building exceeds this maximum mean mass?

The maximum mean mass of 8 people who can ride the elevator at one time is $\frac{1200}{8} = 150$ **kilograms.**

$\mu_{\bar{x}} = \mu = 80$; $\sigma_{\bar{x}} = \frac{\sigma}{\sqrt{n}} = \frac{25}{\sqrt{8}} \approx 8.8$

$P(\bar{x} > 150) = \text{normalcdf}(150, 1\text{E}99, 80, 8.8) \approx 0.00000000000000091$

So, the probability that a random sample of 8 people who work in the office building has a mean mass that exceeds 150 kilograms is less than one quadrillionth

A popcorn manufacturer puts a prize in 25% of its bags of popcorn. When sampling from this population, consider "successes" to be bags of popcorn containing a prize.

10. For random samples of 100 bags of popcorn, what interval centered on the mean of the sampling distribution captures 95% of the sample proportions?

$\mu_{\hat{p}} = p = 0.25$; $\sigma_{\hat{p}} = \sqrt{\frac{p(1-p)}{n}} = \sqrt{\frac{0.25(1-0.25)}{100}} \approx 0.043$

Since $np = 25$, $n(1-p) = 75$, **and both are greater than 10, the sampling distribution is approximately normal.**

$\mu_{\hat{p}} - 2\sigma_{\hat{p}} = 0.25 - 2(0.043) = 0.164$

$\mu_{\hat{p}} + 2\sigma_{\hat{p}} = 0.25 + 2(0.043) = 0.336$

So, for random samples of 100 bags of popcorn, 95% of the sample proportions fall between 16.4% and 33.6%.

11. For random samples of 80 bags of popcorn, what interval centered on the mean of the sampling distribution captures 68% of the sample proportions?

$\mu_{\hat{p}} = p = 0.25; \sigma_{\hat{p}} = \sqrt{\frac{p(1-p)}{n}} = \sqrt{\frac{0.25(1-0.25)}{80}} \approx 0.048$

Since $np = 20$, $n(1-p) = 60$, and both are greater than 10, the sampling distribution is approximately normal.

$\mu_{\hat{p}} - \sigma_{\hat{p}} = 0.25 - 2(0.048) = 0.202$

$\mu_{\hat{p}} + \sigma_{\hat{p}} = 0.25 + 2(0.048) = 0.298$

So, for random samples of 80 bags of popcorn, 68% of the sample proportions fall between 20.2% and 29.8%.

12. What is the probability that a random sample of 120 bags of popcorn has prizes in at most 30% of the bags?

$\mu_{\hat{p}} = p = 0.25; \sigma_{\hat{p}} = \sqrt{\frac{p(1-p)}{n}} = \sqrt{\frac{0.25(1-0.25)}{120}} \approx 0.040$

Since $np = 30$, $n(1-p) = 90$, and both are greater than 10, the sampling distribution is approximately normal.

$P(\hat{p} \leq 0.3) = \text{normalcdf}(-1\text{E}99, 0.3, 0.25, 0.04) \approx 0.89$

So, the probability that a random sample of 120 bags of popcorn has prizes in at most 30% of the bags is about 0.89.

13. What is the probability that a random sample of 60 bags has prizes in more than 12 bags?

$\mu_{\hat{p}} = p = 0.25; \sigma_{\hat{p}} = \sqrt{\frac{p(1-p)}{n}} = \sqrt{\frac{0.25(1-0.25)}{60}} \approx 0.056$

Since $np = 15$, $n(1-p) = 45$, and both are greater than 10, the sampling distribution is approximately normal.

$\hat{p}_{\text{min}} = \frac{12}{60} = 0.2$

$P(\hat{p} > 0.2) = \text{normalcdf}(-0.2, 1\text{E}99, 0.25, 0.056) \approx 0.81$

So, the probability that a random sample of 60 bags of popcorn has prizes in more than 12 bags is about 0.81.

About 28% of students at a large school play varsity sports. When sampling from this population, consider "successes" to be students who play varsity sports.

14. For random samples of 75 students, what interval centered on the mean of the sampling distribution captures 95% of the sample proportions?

$\mu_{\hat{p}} = p = 0.28$

$$\sigma_{\hat{p}} = \sqrt{\frac{p(1-p)}{n}} = \sqrt{\frac{0.28(1-0.28)}{75}} \approx 0.052$$

Since $np = 21$, $n(1-p) = 54$, and both are greater than 10, the sampling distribution is approximately normal.

$\mu_{\hat{p}} - 2\sigma_{\hat{p}} = 0.28 - 2(0.052) = 0.176$

$\mu_{\hat{p}} + 2\sigma_{\hat{p}} = 0.28 + 2(0.052) = 0.384$

So, for random samples of 75 students, 95% of the sample proportions fall between 17.6% and 38.4%.

15. For random samples of 100 students, what interval centered on the mean of the sampling distribution captures 99.7% of the sample proportions?

$$\mu_{\hat{p}} = p = 0.28; \sigma_{\hat{p}} = \sqrt{\frac{p(1-p)}{n}} = \sqrt{\frac{0.28(1-0.28)}{100}} \approx 0.045$$

Since $np = 28$, $n(1-p) = 72$, and both are greater than 10, the sampling distribution is approximately normal.

$\mu_{\hat{p}} - 3\sigma_{\hat{p}} = 0.28 - 3(0.045) = 0.145$

$\mu_{\hat{p}} + 3\sigma_{\hat{p}} = 0.28 + 3(0.045) = 0.415$

So, for random samples of 100 students, 99.7% of the sample proportions fall between 14.5% and 41.5%.

16. What is the probability that a random sample of 45 students includes more than 18 students who play varsity sports?

$$\mu_{\hat{p}} = p = 0.28; \sigma_{\hat{p}} = \sqrt{\frac{p(1-p)}{n}} = \sqrt{\frac{0.28(1-0.28)}{45}} \approx 0.067$$

Since $np = 12.6$, $n(1-p) = 32.4$, and both are greater than 10, the sampling distribution is approximately normal.

$$\hat{p}_{\min} = \frac{18}{45} = 0.4$$

$P(\hat{p} > 0.4) =$ **normalcdf (0.4, 1E99, 0.28, 0.067)** ≈ 0.037

So, the probability that a random sample of 45 students includes more than 18 students who play varsity sports is about 0.037.

17. What is the probability that a random sample of 60 students includes from 12 to 24 students who play varsity sports?

$\mu_{\hat{p}} = p = 0.28$; $\sigma_{\hat{p}} = \sqrt{\frac{p(1-p)}{n}} = \sqrt{\frac{0.28(1-0.28)}{60}} \approx 0.058$

Since $np = 16.8$, $n(1-p) = 43.2$, and both are greater than 10, the sampling distribution is approximately normal.

$\hat{p}_{min} = \frac{12}{60} = 0.2$; $\hat{p}_{max} = \frac{24}{60} = 0.4$

$P(0.2 \le \hat{p} \le 0.4) = \text{normalcdf}(0.2, 0.4, 0.28, 0.058) \approx 0.90$

So, the probability that a random sample of 60 students includes from 12 to 24 students who play varsity sports is about 0.90.

18. Among the 450 seniors in a large high school, 306 plan to be in college in the fall following high school graduation. Suppose random samples of 100 seniors are taken from this population in order to obtain sample proportions of seniors who plan to be college in the fall. Which of the following are true statements? Select all that apply.

a. Every sample proportion is 0.68.

b. The mean of the sampling distribution of the sample proportion is 0.68.

c. The standard error of the proportion is about 0.047.

d. The standard error of the proportion is about 0.0047.

e. The sampling distribution of the sample proportion is skewed.

f. The sampling distribution of the sample proportion is approximately normal.

The population proportion is $p = \frac{306}{450} = 0.68$. This is also the mean of the sampling distribution of the sample proportion. However, sample proportions obtained from individual samples will vary. So, A is false, and B is true.

For random samples of size 100, the standard error of the proportion is $\sigma_{\hat{p}} = \sqrt{\frac{0.68(1-0.68)}{100}} \approx 0.047$. So, C is true, and D is false.

Because $np = 100(0.68) = 68$, $n(1-p) = 100(0.32) = 32$, and both are greater than 10, the sampling distribution of the sample proportion is approximately normal. So, E is false, and F is true.

Answers: B, C, F

INTEGRATE MATHEMATICAL PRACTICES

Focus on Reasoning

MP.2 To help students see that the formula for $\sigma_{\hat{p}}$ (the standard error of the proportion) is actually a special case of the formula for $\sigma_{\bar{x}}$ (the standard error of the mean), you can show them the derivation of a formula for the standard deviation of a population consisting of categorical data that either meet or do not meet a criterion:

Let each data value that meets the criterion be 1, and let each data value that doesn't meet the criterion be 0. This effectively converts the categorical data into numerical data. Assume that a proportion p of the population has a value of 1, while a proportion $1 - p$ has a value of 0. Then the mean value of the population is $p(1) + (1 - p)(0) = p$. The deviation of each 1 from the mean is $1 - p$, while the deviation of each 0 from the mean is $0 - p$, or $-p$. The standard deviation can be calculated by multiplying each fraction of the population by its squared deviation from the mean, then taking the square root:

$$\sigma = \sqrt{p(1-p)^2 + (1-p)(-p)^2},$$

which can be simplified to $\sigma = \sqrt{p(1-p)}$.
The standard deviation of the sampling distribution of the mean is, therefore,
$\sigma_{\bar{x}} = \frac{\sigma}{\sqrt{n}} = \frac{\sqrt{p(1-p)}}{\sqrt{n}} = \sqrt{\frac{p(1-p)}{n}}$, which exactly matches the formula for $\sigma_{\hat{p}}$.

JOURNAL

Have students create a flow chart showing how to determine the interval that contains 95% of the means of random samples of size n taken from a population whose mean and standard deviation are known.

H.O.T. Focus on Higher Order Thinking

19. Explain the Error A student was told that a population has a mean of 400 and a standard deviation of 25. The student was asked to find the probability that a random sample of size 45 taken from the population has a mean of at most 401. The student entered normalcdf $(-1E99, 401, 400, 25)$ on a graphing calculator and got a probability of about 0.516. What did the student do wrong? Show how to find the correct answer.

The student used the standard deviation of the population rather than the standard deviation of the sampling distribution.

$$\sigma_{\bar{x}} = \frac{\sigma}{\sqrt{n}} = \frac{25}{45} \approx 3.73$$

$$P(\bar{x} \leq 401) = \text{normalcdf}\,(-1E99, 401, 400, 3.73) \approx 0.606$$

20. Draw Conclusions Amanda plans to use random sampling to estimate the percent of people who are truly ambidextrous (that is, they do not have a dominant right or left hand). She suspects that the percent is quite low, perhaps as low as 1%. If she wants the sampling distribution of the sample proportion to be approximately normal, what minimum sample size should she use? Explain.

The sampling distribution of the sample proportion is approximately normal provided $np = 10$. Substituting 0.01 for p and solving for n gives $n = 1000$. So, the minimum sample size should be 1000.

21. Check for Reasonableness Given that about 90% of people are right-handed, you are interested in knowing what percent of people put their right thumb on top when they clasp their hands. Having no other information to go on, you assume that people who put their right thumb on top when they clasp their hands are those who are also right-handed. You then take a random sample of 100 people and find that 60 put their right thumb on top when they clasp their hands. Does this result lead you to question your assumption? Explain why or why not.

The assumption that people who put their right thumb on top when they clasp their hands are those who are also right-handed means that the population proportion p for right thumb on top should equal 0.9. For random samples of size 100, $np = 100(0.9) = 90$ and $n(1 - p) = 100(0.1) = 10$, so the sampling distribution of the sample proportion should be approximately normal with mean $\mu_{\hat{p}} = 0.9$ and standard deviation $\sigma_{\hat{p}} = \sqrt{\frac{0.9(1 - 0.9)}{100}} = 0.03$. Since $\frac{0.6 - 0.9}{0.03} = -10$, your random sample has produced a sample proportion that is 10 standard deviations below the mean. This result is so unlikely that you should reject your assumption.

Lesson Performance Task

Among the data that the U.S. Census Bureau collects are the sizes of households, as shown in the table.

Number of people in household	Number of households	Number of people
1	31,886,794	**31,886,794**
2	38,635,170	**77,270,340**
3	18,044,529	**54,133,587**
4	15,030,350	**60,121,400**
5	6,940,508	**34,702,540**
6	2,704,873	**16,229,238**
7 or more	1,749,501	**12,246,507**

a. In the table above, assume that you can simply use 7 as the number of people in households with 7 or more people. Complete the third column of the table. Then use that column to approximate the population mean μ (that is, the mean number of people in a household). Explain your reasoning.

Divide the total number of households by the total number of people living in those households.

$$\frac{31{,}886{,}794 + 77{,}270{,}340 + 54{,}133{,}587 + 60{,}121{,}400 + 34{,}702{,}540 + 16{,}229{,}238 + 12{,}246{,}507}{31{,}886{,}794 + 38{,}635{,}170 + 18{,}044{,}529 + 15{,}030{,}350 + 6{,}940{,}508 + 2{,}704{,}873 + 1{,}749{,}501} = \frac{286{,}590{,}406}{114{,}991{,}725} \approx 2.49$$

So, the approximate population mean is about 2.49.

b. Is the actual population mean greater than or less than the mean that you calculated? Explain.

The actual population mean is greater because the "7 or more" category includes households with 7 people, 8 people, 9 people, and so on. So, the actual number of people living in those households is greater than 12,246,507, which makes the numerator of $\frac{286{,}590{,}406}{114{,}991{,}725}$ greater, which in turn makes the mean greater.

c. Given that $\mu \approx 2.49$ and $\sigma \approx 1.42$, find the probability that a random sample of 100 households in the United States has a mean size of 2.3 people or less.

$\mu_{\bar{x}} = \mu \approx 2.49$; $\sigma_{\bar{x}} = \frac{\sigma}{\sqrt{n}} \approx \frac{1.42}{\sqrt{100}} = 0.142$

$P(\bar{x} \leq 2.3) = \text{normalcdf}\,(-1\text{E}99, 2.3, 2.49, 0.142) \approx 0.09$

d. Given that $\mu \approx 2.49$ and $\sigma \approx 1.42$, find the probability that a random sample of 100 households in the United States has a mean size of 2.6 people or more.

$\mu_{\bar{x}} = \mu \approx 2.49$; $\sigma_{\bar{x}} = \frac{\sigma}{\sqrt{n}} = \frac{1.42}{\sqrt{100}} = 0.142$

$P(\bar{x} \geq 2.6) = \text{normalcdf}\,(2.6, 1\text{E}99, 2.49, 0.142) \approx 0.22$

EXTENSION ACTIVITY

Have different students choose a sample of either 200, 400, or 600 households; different ranges for the number of people in the household (for example 1 to 3); and then find the probability that, out of a random sample of that many households in the United States, the mean household size will be within that range. Have students compare their results and how the different sample sizes affected their results.

AVOID COMMON ERRORS

Recommend that students organize the information they need for the Lesson Performance Task in a table.

Lower bound	Upper bound	Population mean	Standard deviation

This will help students enter and track numbers in their correct order.

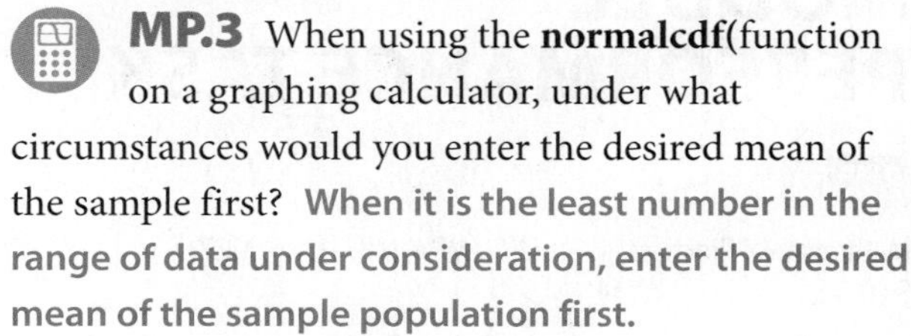

INTEGRATE MATHEMATICAL PRACTICES

Focus on Critical Thinking

MP.3 When using the **normalcdf(**function on a graphing calculator, under what circumstances would you enter the desired mean of the sample first? **When it is the least number in the range of data under consideration, enter the desired mean of the sample population first.**

Scoring Rubric

2 points: Student correctly solves the problem and explains his/her reasoning.

1 point: Student shows good understanding of the problem but does not fully solve or explain his/her reasoning.

0 points: Student does not demonstrate understanding of the problem.

MODULE 23

Study Guide Review

ASSESSMENT AND INTERVENTION

Assign or customize module reviews.

MODULE PERFORMANCE TASK

Mathematical Practices: MP.1, MP.2, MP.4, MP.5, MP.6, MP.7
S-ID.A.4

SUPPORTING STUDENT REASONING

Students should begin this problem by considering different ways to display the data. Here is some of the information they may ask for.

- **What about the left side of the curve?** The left side of the curve is on underweight people in the population. Explain that the focus of this problem is on subjects carrying excess weight.
- **Can we round normal curve percentages to whole percents?** Ask students to be as precise as possible on this problem.
- **What technique should we use to find the percentage?** Explain that any technique is acceptable, as long as it yields a reasonably accurate percentage.

STUDY GUIDE REVIEW

Data Distributions

MODULE 23

Essential Question: How can data distributions help solve real-world problems?

Key Vocabulary
random variable (*variable aleatoria*)
probability distribution (*distribución de probabilidad*)
cumulative probability (*probabilidad acumulativa*)
sampling distribution (*distribución muestral*)
standard error of the mean (*error típico de la media*)

KEY EXAMPLE *(Lesson 23.1)*

A spinner has four equal sections that are labeled 1, 2, 3, and 4. A die has six sides labeled 1, 2, 3, 4, 5, and 6. You spin the spinner and roll the die, then find the sum of the two numbers. Let x be a random variable that represents the sum of the two numbers. Make a histogram of the probability distribution of x.

First, complete the table. Then, make a histogram of the probability distribution.

Sum	2	3	4	5	6	7	8	9	10
Frequency	1	2	3	4	4	4	3	2	1
Probability	$\frac{1}{24}$	$\frac{2}{24}$	$\frac{3}{24}$	$\frac{4}{24}$	$\frac{4}{24}$	$\frac{4}{24}$	$\frac{3}{24}$	$\frac{2}{24}$	$\frac{1}{24}$

Probability: $\frac{4}{24}$, $\frac{3}{24}$, $\frac{2}{24}$, $\frac{1}{24}$
Sum: 2 3 4 5 6 7 8 9

KEY EXAMPLE *(Lesson 23.3)*

Suppose the heights (in feet) of oak trees in the United States are normally distributed with a mean of 68.5 feet and a standard deviation of 12 feet. Find the percent of trees that are no more than 72 feet tall.

$z_{72} = \frac{72 - \mu}{\sigma} = \frac{72 - 68.5}{12} \approx 0.3$ — Convert 72 to a z – score

$z \le z_{72}$, so 0.6179 — Read from standard normal table.

62% — Write decimal as percent.

KEY EXAMPLE *(Lesson 23.3)*

Suppose the average birth weight of a full-term newborn is approximately 7.5 pounds with a standard deviation of 2 pounds. You choose a random sample at the hospital of 20 newborn weights. What is the probability that your sample has a mean weight of up to 7.75 pounds?

$\mu = 7.5, \sigma = 2, n = 20$ — Write the given information.

$\mu_x = \mu = 7.5, \sigma_{\bar{x}} = \frac{\sigma}{\sqrt{20}} = \frac{2}{\sqrt{20}} \approx 0.447$ — Find the mean of the sampling distribution and the standard error.

$z_{7.25} = \frac{7.75 - 7.5}{0.447} \approx 0.6$ — Convert 7.75 to a z – score.

$P(z \le z_{7.25}) = 0.7257 = 73\%$ — Use the standard normal table.

SCAFFOLDING SUPPORT

- For students who need more support, you may want to show a normal curve with the percentages for each standard deviation.
- Students may confuse the BMI ranges for being categorized as overweight or obese with the values given for mean and standard deviation of BMI. Note that these are two independent measures, and being overweight does not correspond to (for example) being one standard deviation above the mean.

EXERCISES

Complete the frequency table, then create the histogram of the probability distribution.

1. **A spinner has five equal sections labeled 1, 2, 3, 4, and 5. You spin the spinner twice, then find the sum of the two numbers.** *(Lesson 23.1)*

Sum	2	3	4	5	6	7	8	9	10
Frequency	1	2	3	4	5	4	3	2	1
Probability	$\frac{1}{25}$	$\frac{2}{25}$	$\frac{3}{25}$	$\frac{4}{25}$	$\frac{5}{25}$	$\frac{4}{25}$	$\frac{3}{25}$	$\frac{2}{25}$	$\frac{1}{25}$

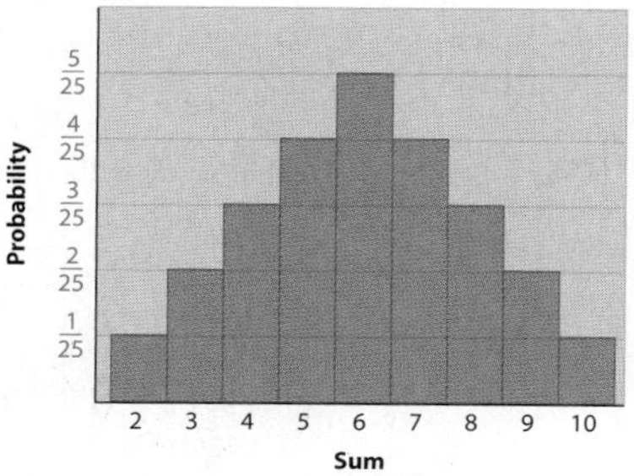

Suppose the mean weight (in pounds) of a newborn elephant is 200 pounds with a standard deviation of 23 pounds. *(Lesson 23.2, 24.3)*

2. Find the percent of elephants that are no more than 212 pounds.

Approx. 70%

3. Find the percent of elephants that are no more than 205 pounds.

Approx. 58%

4. If you take a sampling of 15 elephants, what is the probability that your sample has a mean weight of up to 198?

Approx. 38%

MODULE PERFORMANCE TASK

BMI and Obesity

You can calculate your BMI (body mass index) by dividing your weight in kilograms by the square of your height in meters. A person with a BMI from 18.5 to 24.9 is considered to have a healthy weight. An overweight adult has a BMI from 25.0 to 29.9. An obese person has a BMI greater than 29.9.

The BMI of 18-year-old males is approximately normally distributed with a mean of 24.2 and a standard deviation of 5.1. What percent of 18-year-old males are overweight? What percentage are obese?

Start on your own paper by listing information you will need to solve the problem. Then use graphs, numbers, tables, words, or algebra to explain how you reached your conclusion.

SAMPLE SOLUTION

First, calculate the z-scores for BMIs of 25.0 and 29.9:

$$z = \frac{x - \text{mean}}{\text{st. dev.}}$$

$$z = \frac{25.0 - 24.2}{5.1} \approx 0.157$$

$$z = \frac{29.9 - 24.2}{5.1} \approx 1.118$$

Rounding to the nearest tenth and using the standard normal table, we find that $P(z \leq 0.2) = 0.5793$, and $P(z \leq 1.1) = 0.8643$.

Overweight males have BMIs less than 29.9 but not less than 25.0, so find $P(0.2 \leq z \leq 1.1)$:

$0.8643 - 0.5793 = 0.285$

About 28.5% of 18-year-old males are overweight.

Obese males have BMIs over 29.9, so find $P(z > 1.1)$:

$1 - 0.8643 = 0.1357$

About 13.57% of 18-year-old males are obese.

(Using a more precise method, such as a graphing calculator, will give values of about 30.58% for overweight males and about 13.19% for obese males.)

DISCUSSION OPPORTUNITIES

- Have students discuss the solution methods they used and their advantages and drawbacks. Potential methods could include using the standard normal table, a graphing calculator, a spreadsheet program, or estimating using the 68-95-99.7 rule.

Assessment Rubric

2 points: Student correctly solves the problem and explains his/her reasoning.

1 point: Student shows good understanding of the problem but does not fully solve or explain his/her reasoning.

0 points: Student does not demonstrate understanding of the problem.

Ready to Go On?

ASSESS MASTERY

Use the assessment on this page to determine if students have mastered the concepts and standards covered in this module.

ASSESSMENT AND INTERVENTION

Access Ready to Go On? assessment online, and receive instant scoring, feedback, and customized intervention or enrichment.

ADDITIONAL RESOURCES

Response to Intervention Resources

- Reteach Worksheets

Differentiated Instruction Resources

- Reading Strategies EL
- Success for English Learners EL
- Challenge Worksheets

Assessment Resources

- Leveled Module Quizzes

Ready to Go On?

23.1–23.3 Data Distributions

- Online Homework
- Hints and Help
- Extra Practice

At a local company, the ages of all new employees hired during the last 10 years are normally distributed. The mean age is 35 years old, with a standard deviation of 10 years.

1. Find the percent of new employees that are no more than 27 years old.

Approx. 21%

2. Find the percent of new employees that are no more than 39 years old.

Approx. 66%

3. Find the percent of new employees that are at least 27 years old.

Approx. 79%

4. If you were to take a sampling of 10 employees, what is the probability your mean age will be at least 32?

Approx. 18%

5. If you were to take a sampling of 10 employees, what is the probability your mean age will be at least 38?

Approx. 82%

ESSENTIAL QUESTION

6. How could data distributions help a doctor do his or her job? Give an example.

Possible answer: If the results of a medicine are normally distributed by effectiveness at different ages, then a doctor would know what age the medicine would be more effective for before prescribing it.

COMMON CORE Common Core Standards

Lesson	Items	Content Standards	Mathematical Practices
23.2	1	S-ID.A.4	MP.1
23.2	2	S-ID.A.4	MP.1
23.2	3	S-ID.A.4	MP.1
23.3	4	S-IC.B.4	MP.2
23.3	5	S-IC.B.4	MP.2

MODULE 23
MIXED REVIEW

Assessment Readiness

1. Consider the histogram. Does the statement correctly describe the histogram? Select Yes or No for **A–C.**

   A. There are 16 data values. ● Yes ○ No

   B. Data is spread between 5 sums. ○ Yes ● No

   C. Each sum is equally likely. ○ Yes ● No

2. Consider the shape of a histogram with a normal distribution. Choose True or False for each statement.

   A. A histogram with normal distribution increases, but never decreases. ○ True ● False

   B. A histogram with normal distribution makes a bell curve. The bell could be wide or tall. ● True ○ False

   C. A histogram with normal distribution has the same shape as a line plot with normal distribution. ● True ○ False

3. A local zoo plans to add a new animal display according to the desires of the community members who spend the most time at the zoo. They are considering the following survey methods:

   - Put a survey up on their website and solicit responses from those visiting the site.
   - Survey every 12th customer buying a ticket for the zoo.
   - Survey every annual zoo pass purchaser.

   Which sampling method would most likely result in a theme that would please those who spend the most time at the zoo? Explain.

   Possible answer: Annual zoo pass purchasers would be the most likely to spend the most time at the zoo. Those would be the people whom the zoo wants to target.

4. Suppose the average time a student spends on homework at a certain school is 3.75 hours a night, with a standard deviation of 1.5 hours. You choose a random sample of 20 students. What is the probability that your sample has a mean time of up to 4.25 hours? Explain.

   Approx. 93%; Possible answer: First, I divided the standard deviation (1.5) by the square root of the sample set (20). Then, I found the difference between the means and divided by the first quotient. Then, I compared it to the standard normal table.

Common Core Standards

Lesson	Items	Content Standards	Mathematical Practices
23.1	1	**S-IC.A.2**	**MP.7**
22.2, 23.2	2*	**S-ID.A.4**	**MP.6**
21.1, 21.2	3*	**S-MD.B.6**	**MP.5**
23.3	4	**S-IC.B.4**	**MP.2**

* Item integrates mixed review concepts from previous modules or a previous course.

MIXED REVIEW

Assessment Readiness

ASSESSMENT AND INTERVENTION

Assign ready-made or customized practice tests to prepare students for high-stakes tests.

ADDITIONAL RESOURCES

Assessment Resources

- Leveled Module Quizzes: Modified, B

AVOID COMMON ERRORS

Item 2 Some students may mistake normal distributions for regular distributions, in which everything has an equally likely chance and the data form a rectangle. Remind students that a normal distribution is shaped like a bell.

Making Inferences from Data

ESSENTIAL QUESTION:

Answer: New medicines are tested to see how they affect the human body. If the drug has negative effects or only minimal positive effects, the company may decide to abandon its production or to try to make it more effective.

PROFESSIONAL DEVELOPMENT VIDEO

Professional Development Video

Author Matt Larson models successful teaching practices in an actual high-school classroom.

Professional Development my.hrw.com

MODULE 24

Making Inferences from Data

Essential Question: How can making inferences from data help to solve real-world problems?

REAL WORLD VIDEO
Competitive athletes train hard and are always looking for training techniques that might give them an advantage over their competitors. How can we use data to make judgments about the effectiveness of various training strategies?

MODULE PERFORMANCE TASK PREVIEW

Sports Nutrition

The greatest sports players have to be in their best health in order to play at a high level. They exercise regularly and avoid unhealthy habits. Coaches tell them what to eat and what not to eat to play a good game. But really, how necessary is good nutrition for great athletic performance? By the end of this module, you'll have the means to answer this question.

DIGITAL TEACHER EDITION

Access a full suite of teaching resources when and where you need them:

- Access content online or offline
- Customize lessons to share with your class
- Communicate with your students in real-time
- View student grades and data instantly to target your instruction where it is needed most

PERSONAL MATH TRAINER

Assessment and Intervention

Assign automatically graded homework, quizzes, tests, and intervention activities. Prepare your students with updated, Common Core-aligned practice tests.

Complete these exercises to review skills you will need for this chapter.

- Online Homework
- Hints and Help
- Extra Practice

Trend Lines and Predictions

Example 1 A pet store asked loyal customers the weight of their dog and monthly budgeted expenses for owning it. The scatter plot shows the results of this survey with a line of best fit. Approximate the monthly cost of a dog weighing 40 pounds.

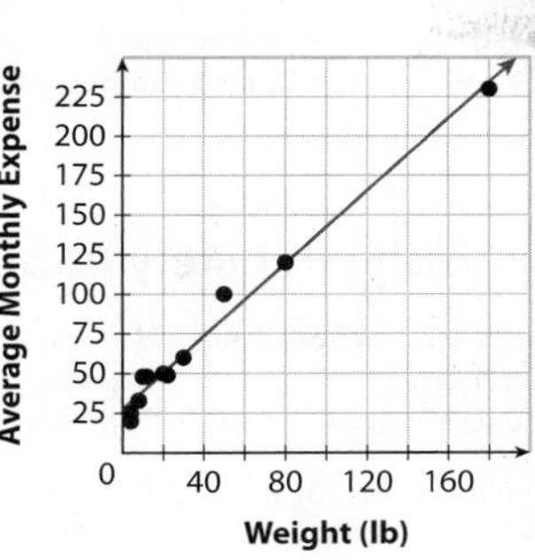

According to the graph, when $x = 40$ lbs, the expected monthly cost is about $75.

Find the expected monthly cost of owning a dog at the given weight.

1. 60 lb

About $100

2. 100 lb

About $140

3. 150 lb

About $200

Making Inferences From a Random Sample

Example 2 A product quality engineer takes a random sample of 200 widgets and finds that 15 of them are defective. At this factory, the rule is if the defect rate is greater than 8.5%, the assembly line needs to be shut down for retooling. Should the engineer shut down the assembly line?

No. In the sample, only $\frac{15}{200} = 7.5\%$ of the widgets were defective.

For each sample size and number of defective widgets, should the engineer close down the assembly line or not? Explain.

4. Sample size = 5; defective widgets = 1

No. The defect rate is 20%, but the sample size is too small to make an accurate inference.

5. Sample size = 150; defective widgets = 27

Yes. The defect rate is 18% and the sample size is large, so there is enough evidence to shut down the assembly line.

Are You Ready?

ASSESS READINESS

Use the assessment on this page to determine if students need strategic or intensive intervention for the module's prerequisite skills.

ASSESSMENT AND INTERVENTION

Personal Math Trainer

RtI Response to Intervention TIER 1, TIER 2, TIER 3 SKILLS

Personal Math Trainer will automatically create a standards-based, personalized intervention assignment for your students, targeting each student's individual needs!

ADDITIONAL RESOURCES

See the table below for a full list of intervention resources available for this module.

Response to Intervention Resources also includes:

- Tier 2 Skill Pre-Tests for each Module
- Tier 2 Skill Post-Tests for each skill

Response to Intervention			Differentiated Instruction
Tier 1 Lesson Intervention Worksheets	**Tier 2** Strategic Intervention Skills Intervention Worksheets	**Tier 3** Intensive Intervention Worksheets available online	
Reteach 24.1 Reteach 24.2 Reteach 24.3	47 Making Inferences from a Random Sample 54 Scatter Plots and Association 59 Trend Lines and Predictions	Building Block Skills 6, 20, 39, 43, 45, 47, 54, 70, 89, 90, 91, 114	Challenge worksheets Extend the Math Lesson Activities in TE

LESSON 24.1

Confidence Intervals and Margins of Error

Common Core Math Standards

The student is expected to:

COMMON CORE **S-IC.B.4**

Use data from a sample survey to estimate a population mean or proportion; develop a margin of error through the use of simulation models for random sampling.

Mathematical Practices

COMMON CORE **MP.4 Modeling**

Language Objective

Work with a partner to label the formula for the confidence interval for a population proportion.

ENGAGE

Essential Question: How do you calculate a confidence interval and a margin of error for a population proportion or population mean?

To calculate a confidence interval, use the formula $\hat{p} - z_c\sqrt{\frac{\hat{p}(1-\hat{p})}{n}} \le p \le \hat{p} + z_c\sqrt{\frac{\hat{p}(1-\hat{p})}{n}} \le$, where p is the proportion of successes in a population, $\hat{p}$ is the sample proportion, n is the sample size, and z_c depends on the desired degree of confidence. To calculate a confidence interval for a population mean, use the formula $\bar{x} - z_c\frac{\sigma}{\sqrt{n}} \le \mu \le \bar{x} + z_c\frac{\sigma}{\sqrt{n}}$, where μ is the mean of a normally distributed population, $\bar{x}$ is the sample mean, σ is the population standard deviation, and z_c depends on the desired degree of confidence. For both the population proportion and the population mean, the margin of error is half the length of the confidence interval.

PREVIEW: LESSON PERFORMANCE TASK

View the Engage section online. Discuss the photo and how different proportions from samples might represent populations where the proportions are equal. Then preview the Lesson Performance Task.

Name________ Class________ Date________

24.1 Confidence Intervals and Margins of Error

Resource Locker

Essential Question: How do you calculate a confidence interval and a margin of error for a population proportion or population mean?

Explore Identifying Likely Population Proportions

In a previous lesson, you took samples from a population whose parameter of interest is known in order to see how well a sample statistic estimated that parameter. In this lesson, you will estimate a population parameter using a statistic obtained from a random sample, and you will quantify the accuracy of that estimate.

Suppose you survey a random sample of 50 students at your high school and find that 40% of those surveyed attended the football game last Saturday. Although you cannot survey the entire population of students, you would still like to know what population proportions are reasonably likely in this situation.

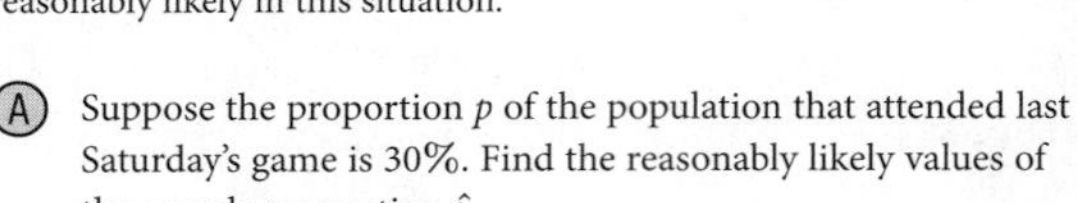

(A) Suppose the proportion p of the population that attended last Saturday's game is 30%. Find the reasonably likely values of the sample proportion $\hat{p}$.

In this case, $p =$ **0.3** and $n =$ **50**.

$\mu_{\hat{p}} = p =$ **0.3** and $\sigma_{\hat{p}} = \sqrt{\frac{p(1-p)}{n}} = \sqrt{\frac{0.3(1-0.3)}{50}} \approx$ **0.065**

(B) The reasonably likely values of $\hat{p}$ fall within 2 standard deviations of $\mu_{\hat{p}}$.

$\mu_{\hat{p}} - 2\sigma_{\hat{p}} =$ **0.3** $- 2($**0.065**$) =$ **0.17**

$\mu_{\hat{p}} + 2\sigma_{\hat{p}} =$ **0.3** $+ 2($**0.065**$) =$ **0.43**

(C) On the graph, draw a horizontal line segment at the level of 0.3 on the vertical axis to represent the interval of likely values of $\hat{p}$ you found in Step B.

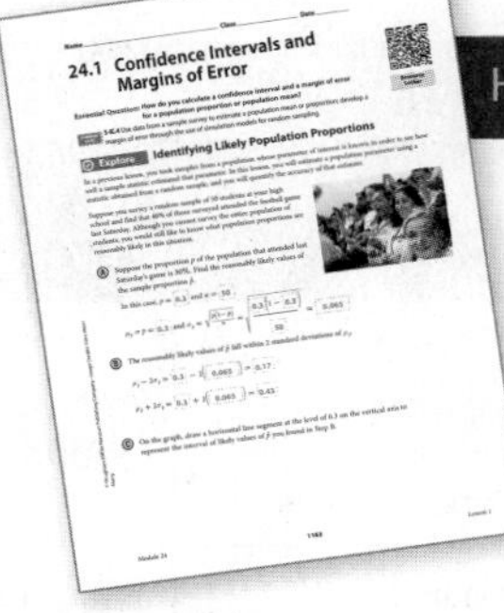

HARDCOVER PAGES 1163–11

Watch for the hardcover student edition page numbers for this lesson.

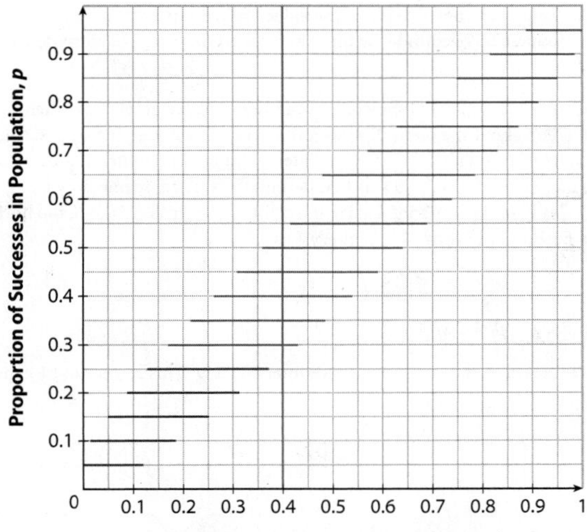

(D) Now repeat the process for $p = 0.35$, 0.4, 0.45, and so on to complete the graph in Step C. You may wish to divide up the work with other students and pool your findings.

(E) Draw a vertical line at 0.4 on the horizontal axis. This represents $\hat{p} = 0.4$. The line segments that this vertical line intersects are the population proportions for which a sample proportion of 0.4 is reasonably likely.

Reflect

1. **Discussion** Is it possible that 30% of all students at your school attended last Saturday's football game? Is it likely? Explain.
It is both possible and likely. Since $p = 0.3$, the interval of likely sample proportions for a sample of 50 students is 0.17 to 0.43, which includes $\hat{p} = 0.4$.

2. **Discussion** Is it possible that 60% of all students at your school attended last Saturday's football game? Is it likely? Explain.
It is possible but unlikely. Since $p = 0.6$, the interval of likely sample proportions for a sample of 50 students is 0.46 to 0.74, which does not include $\hat{p} = 0.4$.

3. **Discussion** Based on your graph, which population proportions do you think are reasonably likely? Why?
The proportions from 30% to 50% are reasonably likely because these population proportions have intervals of likely sample proportions that include $\hat{p} = 0.4$.

Explain 1 Finding a Confidence Interval for a Population Proportion

A **confidence interval** is an approximate range of values that is likely to include an unknown population parameter. The *level* of a confidence interval, such as 95%, gives the probability that the interval includes the true value of the parameter.

PROFESSIONAL DEVELOPMENT

Learning Progressions

In the previous lesson, students learned that the individual sample means or sample proportions within a sampling distribution vary, forming an approximately normal distribution having a standard deviation that they learned how to calculate. In the previous lesson, the population parameters (population mean and standard deviation for numerical data and population proportion for categorical data) were known. This lesson extends their knowledge to populations whose mean or proportion is not known. Students will learn how to determine, with a certain degree of confidence, that the population mean or proportion is within a particular range of values.

EXPLORE

Identifying Likely Population Proportions

INTEGRATE TECHNOLOGY

Students have the option of completing the confidence interval activity either in the book or online.

QUESTIONING STRATEGIES

? How does the sample size affect the reasonably likely values of the sample proportion $\hat{p}$? **As the sample size increases, the range of the reasonably likely values of the sample proportion $\hat{p}$ decreases.**

? If you drew a conclusion that would be reasonably likely for the sample size of 50 students, could you draw this same conclusion if all numbers in the given situation stayed the same except that the sample size was 100 instead of 50? Explain your reasoning. **No; a population proportion would no longer be reasonably likely. If you drew the graph for a sample size of 100 students, the vertical line segment might not intersect the horizontal line segment on the graph.**

AUDITORY CUES

The probability notation $\hat{p}$, a letter p with a caret or circumflex above it, is sometimes referred to as "*p*-hat." Help students to understand that this notation connects the probability to confidence intervals.

EXPLAIN 1

Finding a Confidence Interval for a Population Proportion

QUESTIONING STRATEGIES

? Based on the given random sample, two different researchers made different, reasonable statements about the data. What could be the reason for the discrepancy? **Possible answer: The researchers made their statements with different confidence intervals.**

AVOID COMMON ERRORS

Some students may be confused about why they substitute p for $\mu_{\hat{p}}$ when finding a confidence interval. Point out that this is done so that the horizontal line segment is used to find the interval on the vertical line segment that captures all the likely population proportions.

Recall that when data are normally distributed, 95% of the values fall within 2 standard deviations of the mean. Using this idea in the Explore, you found a 95% confidence interval for the proportion of all students who attended the football game last Saturday.

The graph that you completed in the Explore is shown. You can see from the graph that when the horizontal line segment at $p = 0.4$ is rotated 90° about the point (0.4, 0.4), it becomes a vertical line segment that captures all of the likely population proportions. Since you already know the interval on the horizontal axis that defines the horizontal segment, you can find the interval on the vertical axis that defines the vertical segment by using the fact that $\mu_{\hat{p}} = p$ and interchanging the variables $\hat{p}$ on the horizontal axis) and p (on the vertical axis). So, the horizontal axis interval $\mu_{\hat{p}} - 2\sigma_{\hat{p}} \le \hat{p} \le \mu_{\hat{p}} + 2\sigma_{\hat{p}}$ becomes the vertical axis interval as follows:

Replace $\mu_{\hat{p}}$ with p. $\quad p - 2\sigma_{\hat{p}} \le \hat{p} \le p + 2\sigma_{\hat{p}}$

Interchange $\hat{p}$ and p. $\quad \hat{p} - 2\sigma_{\hat{p}} \le p \le \hat{p} + 2\sigma_{\hat{p}}$

In this case, the vertical axis interval is the 95% confidence interval for p. This result can be generalized to a c% confidence interval for p.

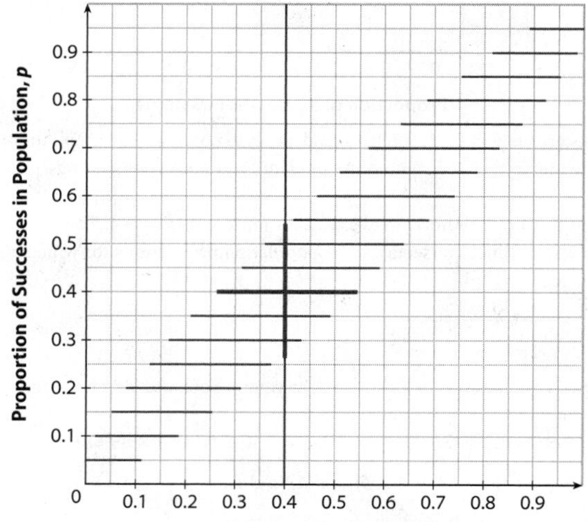

A Confidence Interval for a Population Proportion

A c% confidence interval for the proportion p of successes in a population is given by $\hat{p} - z_c\sqrt{\frac{\hat{p}(1-\hat{p})}{n}} \le p \le \hat{p} + z_c\sqrt{\frac{\hat{p}(1-\hat{p})}{n}}$, where $\hat{p}$ is the sample proportion, n is the sample size, and z_c depends upon the desired degree of confidence.

In order for this interval to describe the value of p reasonably accurately, three conditions must be met:

1. There are only two possible outcomes associated with the parameter of interest. The population proportion for one outcome is p, and the proportion for the other outcome is $1 - p$.
2. $n\hat{p}$ and $n(1 - \hat{p})$ must both be at least 10.
3. The size of the population must be at least 10 times the size of the sample, and the sample must be random.

COLLABORATIVE LEARNING

Small Group Activity

Have students discuss the formula used to find a confidence interval for a population mean, and how it applies only when the scores are normally distributed. Then have them share and discuss examples of scores that are distributed so that the given formula for a confidence interval should *not* be used and explain why. **Possible answer: Examples include distributions of the scores that are uniform, skewed left, or skewed right. When a distribution is skewed, conclusions based on the use of the given formula for a confidence interval are invalid.**

Use the values in the table for z_c. Note that you should use 1.96 rather than 2 for $z_{95\%}$ for greater accuracy.

Desired degree of confidence	90%	95%	99%
Value of z_c	1.645	1.96	2.576

Example 1 **In a random sample of 100 four-year-old children in the United States, 76 were able to write their name. Find the specified confidence interval for the proportion p of four-year-olds in the United States who can write their name.**

(A) Find a 95% confidence interval.

Identify the sample size n, the proportion $\hat{p}$ of four-year-olds in the sample who can write their name, and the value of z_c for a 95% confidence interval.

$n = 100$ $\quad \hat{p} = 0.76$ $\quad z_c = 1.96$

Substitute the values of n, $\hat{p}$, and z_c into the formulas for the endpoints of the confidence interval. Simplify and round to two decimal places.

$$\hat{p} - z_c\sqrt{\frac{\hat{p}(1-\hat{p})}{n}} = 0.76 - 1.96\sqrt{\frac{0.76(1-0.76)}{100}} \approx 0.68$$

$$\hat{p} + z_c\sqrt{\frac{\hat{p}(1-\hat{p})}{n}} = 0.76 + 1.96\sqrt{\frac{0.76(1-0.76)}{100}} \approx 0.84$$

So, you can state with 95% confidence that the proportion of all four-year-olds in the United States who can write their name lies between 68% and 84%.

(B) Find a 99% confidence interval.

Identify the sample size n, the proportion $\hat{p}$ of four-year-olds in the sample who can write their name, and the value of z_c for a 99% confidence interval.

$n =$ 100 $\quad \hat{p} =$ 0.76 $\quad z_c =$ 2.576

Substitute the values of n, $\hat{p}$, and z_c into the formulas for the endpoints of the confidence interval. Simplify and round to two decimal places.

$$\hat{p} - z_c\sqrt{\frac{\hat{p}(1-\hat{p})}{n}} = 0.76 - 2.576\sqrt{\frac{0.76(1-0.76)}{100}} \approx 0.65$$

$$\hat{p} + z_c\sqrt{\frac{\hat{p}(1-\hat{p})}{n}} = 0.76 + 2.576\sqrt{\frac{0.76(1-0.76)}{100}} \approx 0.87$$

So, you can state with 99% confidence that the proportion of all four-year-olds in the United States who can write their name lies between 65% and 87%.

DIFFERENTIATE INSTRUCTION

Communicating Math

Students may benefit from seeing some real-world situations in which statistics are reported with a specified level of confidence. Academic journals in fields ranging from science and medicine to psychology and business often display detailed information resulting from surveys in a table format, often with a confidence level indicated at the bottom. Although the statistics used may go beyond what is covered in this lesson, students can see that level of confidence is a component of many statistical analyses.

EXPLAIN 2

Finding a Confidence Interval for a Population Mean

QUESTIONING STRATEGIES

Suppose the confidence level in a given situation is reduced. Would the confidence interval for the mean test score among all students be wider or narrower than the confidence interval for the mean test score among all students when the confidence level is higher? Explain your reasoning. The confidence interval for a lower confidence level will be narrower than the confidence interval for a higher confidence level. As the confidence interval becomes wider, it is more likely that the mean test score among all students will fall within that confidence interval; therefore, the confidence level increases.

Reflect

4. **Discussion** Do the data from the sample of four-year-old children satisfy the three conditions for using the confidence interval formula? Explain.
   Yes, because a child either can or cannot write his or her name, $n\hat{p} = 100(0.76) = 76$ and $n(1 - \hat{p}) = 100(0.24) = 24$, which are both greater than 10, and the population of four-year-olds in the United States is far greater than $10n = 10(100) = 1000$.

5. **Discussion** Does increasing the value of c increase or decrease the range of values for a confidence interval of a population proportion? Explain why it happens mathematically and why it makes sense.
   Increasing the value of c increases the range of values because the amount that is being added or subtracted from $\hat{p}$ increases. This makes sense because in order to have a higher level of confidence that you've "caught" the population proportion, you need to cast a wider "net."

Your Turn

6. Isabelle surveys a random sample of 80 voters in her large town and finds that 46 support raising property taxes in order to build a new library. Find a 95% confidence interval for the proportion p of all voters in Isabelle's town who support raising property taxes in order to build a new library.

$n = 80 \qquad \hat{p} = \frac{46}{80} = 0.575 \qquad z_c = 1.96$

$\hat{p} - z_c\sqrt{\frac{\hat{p}(1-\hat{p})}{n}} = 0.575 - 1.96\sqrt{\frac{0.575(1-0.575)}{80}} \approx 0.47$

$\hat{p} + z_c\sqrt{\frac{\hat{p}(1-\hat{p})}{n}} = 0.575 + 1.96\sqrt{\frac{0.575(1-0.575)}{80}} \approx 0.68$

So with 95% confidence, the proportion of all voters in Isabelle's town who support raising property taxes in order to build a new library lies between 47% and 68%.

Explain 2 Finding a Confidence Interval for a Population Mean

You can use reasoning similar to the argument in the Explore to develop a formula for a confidence interval for a population mean.

A Confidence Interval for a Population Mean

A c% confidence interval for the mean μ in a normally distributed population is given by $\bar{x} - z_c\frac{\sigma}{\sqrt{n}} \leq \mu \leq \bar{x} + z_c\frac{\sigma}{\sqrt{n}}$, where $\bar{x}$ is the sample mean, n is the sample size, σ is the population standard deviation, and z_c depends upon the desired degree of confidence.

Note that it is assumed that the population is normally distributed and that you know the population standard deviation σ. In a more advanced statistics course, you can develop a confidence interval that does not depend upon a normally distributed population or knowing the population standard deviation.

Example 2 **For the given situation, find the specified confidence interval for the population mean.**

(A) In a random sample of 20 students at a large high school, the mean score on a standardized test is 610. Given that the standard deviation of all scores at the school is 120, find a 99% confidence interval for the mean score among all students at the school.

LANGUAGE SUPPORT EL

Communicate Math

Have students work in pairs to identify the parts of this formula for a population proportion, asking them to identify and label what the p values, as well as n and z, represent:

$$\hat{p} - z_c\sqrt{\frac{\hat{p}(1-\hat{p})}{n}} \leq p \leq \hat{p} + z_c\sqrt{\frac{\hat{p}(1-\hat{p})}{n}}$$

Identify the sample size n, the sample mean $\bar{x}$, the population standard deviation σ, and the value of z_c for a 99% confidence interval.

$n = 20$ $\bar{x} = 610$ $\sigma = 120$ $z_c = 2.576$

Substitute the values of n, $\bar{x}$, σ, and z_c into the formulas for the endpoints of the confidence interval. Simplify and round to the nearest whole number.

$\bar{x} - z_c\frac{\sigma}{\sqrt{n}} = 610 - 2.576 \cdot \frac{120}{\sqrt{20}} \approx 541$ $\bar{x} + z_c\frac{\sigma}{\sqrt{n}} = 610 + 2.576 \cdot \frac{120}{\sqrt{20}} \approx 679$

So, you can state with 99% confidence that the mean score among all students lies between 541 and 679.

(B) In a random sample of 30 students at a large high school, the mean score on a standardized test is 1514. Given that the standard deviation of all scores at the school is 141, find a 95% confidence interval for the mean score among all students at the school.

Identify the sample size n, the sample mean $\bar{x}$, the population standard deviation σ, and the value of z_c for a 95% confidence interval.

$n =$ **30** $\bar{x} =$ **1514** $\sigma =$ **141** $z_c =$ **1.96**

Substitute the values of n, $\bar{x}$, σ, and z_c into the formulas for the endpoints of the confidence interval. Simplify and round to the nearest whole number.

$$\bar{x} - z_c\frac{\sigma}{\sqrt{n}} = 1514 - 1.96 \cdot \frac{141}{\sqrt{30}} \approx 1464$$

$$\bar{x} + z_c\frac{\sigma}{\sqrt{n}} = 1514 + 1.96 \cdot \frac{141}{\sqrt{30}} \approx 1564$$

So, you can state with 95% confidence that the mean score among all students at the school lies between **1464** and **1564**.

Reflect

7. What must you assume about the test scores of all students to use the formula for the confidence interval?
You must assume that the scores are normally distributed.

Your Turn

8. In a random sample of 42 employees in a large company, the mean weekly number of minutes spent exercising is 86. Given that the standard deviation of all employees is 22.4, find a 99% confidence interval for the mean weekly number of minutes spent exercising among all employees in the company.

$n = 42$ $\bar{x} = 86$ $\sigma = 22.4$ $z_c = 2.576$

$\bar{x} - z_c\frac{\sigma}{\sqrt{n}} = 86 - 2.576 \cdot \frac{22.4}{\sqrt{42}} \approx 77$ $\bar{x} + z_c\frac{\sigma}{\sqrt{n}} = 86 + 2.576 \cdot \frac{22.4}{\sqrt{42}} \approx 95$

So with 99% confidence, the mean weekly number of minutes spent exercising among all employees in the company lies between 77 minutes and 95 minutes.

AVOID COMMON ERRORS

Remind students that the formula used will produce valid results only when the population is normally distributed.

EXPLAIN 3

Choosing a Sample Size

QUESTIONING STRATEGIES

A researcher wants to decrease the margin of error in a study surveying a random sample of students that represents a much larger population of students. Due to cost considerations, the sample size cannot be increased. How could the researcher accomplish the goal of decreasing the margin of error? **The researcher could decrease the confidence level for the results of the survey, which will decrease the margin of error.**

INTEGRATE MATHEMATICAL PRACTICES

Focus on Reasoning

MP.2 Explain to students that when designing a survey, researchers can use a formula that allows them to calculate the sample size they need to obtain a desired margin of error and confidence level. Have students discuss why they would want to use a smaller rather than a larger sample size, such as the cost of the survey, convenience in conducting the survey, and time considerations. Have students consider how the advantages of choosing a larger sample size may outweigh the disadvantages, despite the fact that choosing a smaller sample size saves money, effort, and time.

Explain 3 Choosing a Sample Size

In Part B of Example 2, you found the 95% confidence interval $1464 \le \bar{x} \le 1564$, which is a range of values centered at $\bar{x} = 1514$. You can write the confidence interval as 1514 ± 50, where 50 is called the *margin of error*. The **margin of error** is half the length of a confidence interval.

Margin of Error for a Population Proportion

The margin of error E for the proportion of successes in a population with sample proportion $\hat{p}$ and sample size n is given by $E = z_c\sqrt{\frac{\hat{p}(1-\hat{p})}{n}}$, where z_c depends on the degree of the confidence interval.

Margin of Error for a Population Mean

The margin of error E for the mean in a normally distributed population with standard deviation σ, sample mean $\bar{x}$, and sample size n is given by $E = z_c\frac{\sigma}{\sqrt{n}}$, where z_c depends on the degree of the confidence interval.

From the formulas you can see that the margin of error decreases as the sample size n increases. This suggests using a sample that is as large as possible. However, it is often more practical to determine a margin of error that is acceptable and then calculate the required sample size.

Example 3 **Find the appropriate sample size for the given situation.**

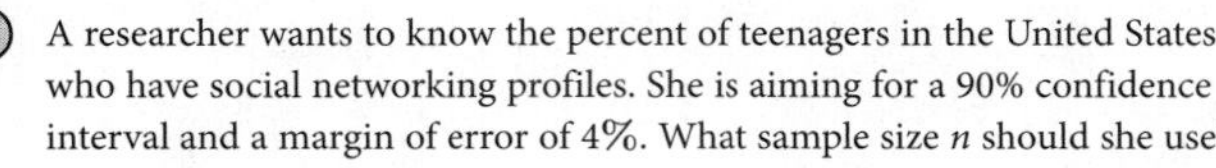

(A) A researcher wants to know the percent of teenagers in the United States who have social networking profiles. She is aiming for a 90% confidence interval and a margin of error of 4%. What sample size n should she use?

Step 1 Rewrite the margin-of-error formula for a population proportion by solving for n.

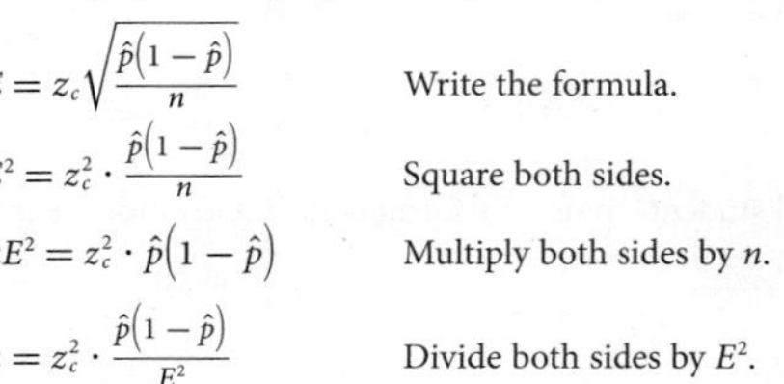

$E = z_c\sqrt{\frac{\hat{p}(1-\hat{p})}{n}}$ Write the formula.

$E^2 = z_c^2 \cdot \frac{\hat{p}(1-\hat{p})}{n}$ Square both sides.

$nE^2 = z_c^2 \cdot \hat{p}(1-\hat{p})$ Multiply both sides by n.

$n = z_c^2 \cdot \frac{\hat{p}(1-\hat{p})}{E^2}$ Divide both sides by E^2.

Step 2 Estimate the value of $\hat{p}$.

The researcher has not conducted the survey and is trying to find $\hat{p}$. So, she must estimate $\hat{p}$ as 0.5, which is the value of $\hat{p}$ that makes the expression $\hat{p}(1-\hat{p})$ as large as possible.

Step 3 Identify the values of E and z_c.

E is the margin of error written as a decimal and z_c is the z-score that corresponds to a 90% confidence interval. So, $E = 0.04$ and $z_c = 1.645$.

Step 4 Substitute the values of $\hat{p}$, E, and z_c in the rewritten margin-of-error formula from Step 1.

$$n = z_c^2 \cdot \frac{\hat{p}(1-\hat{p})}{E^2} = \frac{(1.645)^2 \cdot 0.5\,(1-0.5)}{(0.04)^2} \approx 423$$

So, the researcher should survey a random sample of 423 teenagers.

(B) Caleb is a restaurant manager and wants to know the mean number of seconds it takes to complete a customer's order. He is aiming for a 95% confidence interval and a margin of error of 6 seconds. Based on past experience, Caleb estimates the population standard deviation to be 21 seconds. What sample size n should he use?

Step 1 Rewrite the margin-of-error formula for a population mean by solving for n.

$E = z_c \frac{\sigma}{\sqrt{n}}$ Write the formula.

$E^2 = z_c^2 \cdot \frac{\sigma^2}{n}$ Square both sides.

$nE^2 = z_c^2 \cdot \sigma^2$ Multiply both sides by n.

$n = \frac{z_c^2 \cdot \sigma^2}{E^2}$ Divide both sides by E^2.

Step 2 Identify the values of E, σ, and z_c.

E is the margin of error, σ is the population standard deviation, and z_c is the z-score that corresponds to a 95% confidence interval. So, $E =$ 6, $\sigma =$ 21 and $z_c =$ 1.96.

Substitute the values of E, σ, and z_c in the margin of error for a population mean formula that was solved for n.

$$n = \frac{(1.96)^2 (21)^2}{(6)^2} \approx 47$$

So, Caleb should survey a random sample of 47 orders.

Reflect

9. **Discussion** In Part A, do you expect the sample size to increase or decrease if the researcher decides she wants a smaller margin of error? Explain using the margin-of-error formula for a population proportion.
The sample size must increase. A smaller margin of error means that the value of E is smaller, which means that the value of E^2 is also smaller. Dividing $z_c^2 \cdot \hat{p}(1-\hat{p})$ by a smaller value of E^2 results in a larger value of n.

10. **Discussion** In Part B, do you expect the sample size to increase or decrease if Caleb decides he wants a 99% confidence interval instead of a 95% confidence interval? Explain using the margin-of-error formula for a population mean.
The sample size must increase. A higher level of confidence means that the value of z_c is greater, which means that the value of z_c^2 is also greater. Multiplying $\frac{\sigma^2}{E^2}$ by a greater value of z_c^2 results in a greater value of n.

ELABORATE

INTEGRATE MATHEMATICAL PRACTICES

Focus on Critical Thinking

MP.3 Make sure that students are comfortable with analyzing the problem statement for the data set and determining which of the formulas in this unit may apply to the problem. Have them highlight the key words in the problem statement that lead them to choose a formula, and then ask them to give the restrictions or parameters that allow them to use the formula.

CONNECT VOCABULARY EL

Have students use note cards to create a list of words that are associated with finding confidence intervals and margin of error for a population proportion or population mean. This list can be used to choose or eliminate formulas that do not apply for a given sample population or for a problem statement about the population.

SUMMARIZE THE LESSON

Have students make a graphic organizer outlining the processes for calculating a confidence interval for a population proportion and a population mean. Include information about calculating the margin of error, as well as steps for choosing a sample size.

Your Turn

11. Zoe is an editor of a newspaper in a state capital and wants to know the percent of residents in her state who are in favor of banning the use of handheld cell phones while driving, a bill that is being considered in the state legislature. After researching similar polls conducted in other states, she estimates that $\hat{p} = 0.35$. She is aiming for a 95% confidence interval and a margin of error of 5%. What sample size n should Zoe use?

$E = 0.05$ and $z_c = 1.96$

$$n = \frac{(1.96)^2 \cdot 0.35(1 - 0.35)}{(0.05)^2} \approx 350$$

So, Zoe should survey a random sample of 350 state residents.

Elaborate

12. How can an interval that captures 95% of the sample proportions in a sampling distribution be used to find a 95% confidence interval for a population proportion?

Since the interval $\mu_{\hat{p}} - 2\sigma_{\hat{p}} \le \hat{p} \le \mu_{\hat{p}} + 2\sigma_{\hat{p}}$ captures 95% of the sample proportions in a sampling distribution, the 95% confidence interval for a population proportion is found by substituting p for $\mu_{\hat{p}}$ and interchanging $\hat{p}$ and p. This yields $\hat{p} - 2\sigma_{\hat{p}} \le p \le \hat{p} + 2\sigma_{\hat{p}}$, which can also be written as $\hat{p} - 2\sqrt{\frac{\hat{p}(1-\hat{p})}{n}} \le p \le \hat{p} + 2\sqrt{\frac{\hat{p}(1-\hat{p})}{n}}$.

13. Describe how increasing the sample size affects the confidence interval of a population mean.

Increasing the sample size decreases the value of $z_c\frac{\sigma}{\sqrt{n}}$, which means that the endpoints of the confidence interval become closer to each other.

14. Essential Question Check-in What is the relationship between a confidence interval and a margin of error for a population proportion or population mean?

The margin of error is half the length of the confidence interval.

Evaluate: Homework and Practice

- Online Homework
- Hints and Help
- Extra Practice

Identify the values of the sample proportion $\hat{p}$ that fall within 2 standard deviations of the given population proportion p for each situation.

1. Suppose that 44% of all employees at a large company attended a recent company function. Alannah plans to survey a random sample of 32 employees to estimate the population proportion. What are the values of $\hat{p}$ that she is likely to obtain?

$\mu_{\hat{p}} = p = 0.44, n = 32$

$\sigma_{\hat{p}} = \sqrt{\frac{0.44(1-0.44)}{32}} \approx 0.088$

$\mu_{\hat{p}} - 2\sigma_{\hat{p}} = 0.44 - 2(0.088) \approx 0.26$ $\quad \mu_{\hat{p}} + 2\sigma_{\hat{p}} = 0.44 + 2(0.088) \approx 0.62$

So, the reasonably likely values of the sample proportion are between 26% and 62%.

2. Suppose the proportion p of a school's students who oppose a change to the school's dress code is 73%. Nicole surveys a random sample of 56 students to find the percent of students who oppose the change. What are the values of $\hat{p}$ that she is likely to obtain?

$\mu_{\hat{p}} = p = 0.73, n = 56$

$\sigma_{\hat{p}} = \sqrt{\frac{0.73(1-0.73)}{56}} \approx 0.059$

$\mu_{\hat{p}} - 2\sigma_{\hat{p}} = 0.73 - 2(0.059) \approx 0.61$ $\quad \mu_{\hat{p}} + 2\sigma_{\hat{p}} = 0.73 + 2(0.059) \approx 0.85$

So, the reasonably likely values of the sample proportion are between 61% and 85%.

For the given situation, find the specified confidence interval for the population proportion.

3. Hunter surveys a random sample of 64 students at his community college and finds that 37.5% of the students saw a film at the local movie theater in the last 30 days. Find a 90% confidence interval for the proportion p of all students at the community college who saw a film at the movie theater in the last 30 days.

$n = 56 \quad \hat{p} = 0.375 \quad z_c = 1.645$

$\hat{p} - z_c\sqrt{\frac{\hat{p}(1-\hat{p})}{n}} = 0.375 - 1.645\sqrt{\frac{0.375(1-0.375)}{64}} \approx 0.275$

$\hat{p} + z_c\sqrt{\frac{\hat{p}(1-\hat{p})}{n}} = 0.375 + 1.645\sqrt{\frac{0.375(1-0.375)}{64}} \approx 0.475$

With 90% confidence, the proportion of all students who saw a film at the movie theater in the last 30 days lies between 27.5% and 47.5%.

Exercise	Depth of Knowledge (D.O.K.)	COMMON CORE Mathematical Practices
1–13	**2** Skills/Concepts	**MP.4** Modeling
14	**3** Strategic Thinking	**MP.1** Problem Solving
15	**2** Skills/Concepts	**MP.6** Precision
16–17	**3** Strategic Thinking H.O.T.	**MP.2** Reasoning
18	**3** Strategic Thinking H.O.T.	**MP.2** Logic

EVALUATE

ASSIGNMENT GUIDE

Concepts and Skills	Practice
Explore Identifying Likely Population Proportions	Exercises 1–2
Example 1 Finding a Confidence Interval for a Population Proportion	Exercises 3–6
Example 2 Finding a Confidence Interval for a Population Mean	Exercises 7–10
Example 3 Choosing a Sample Size	Exercises 11–15

INTEGRATE MATHEMATICAL PRACTICES

Focus on Modeling

MP.4 Remind students to check on the restrictions needed to apply each formula, including the size of the sample, before choosing a formula for a given exercise.

INTEGRATE MATHEMATICAL PRACTICES

Focus on Communication

MP.3 Students may miss the nuances of explanations in English regarding statistics and probability not being hard and fast rules, but providing information about what is likely to happen. Ask students to explain to each other what a *margin of error* is and why we even calculate it to begin with; this will provide information about what they understand.

4. In a random sample of 300 U.S. households, 111 households have a pet dog. Find a 99% confidence interval for the proportion p of all U.S. households that have a pet dog.

$n = 300 \quad \hat{p} = \frac{111}{300} = 0.37 \quad z_c = 2.576$

$$\hat{p} - z_c\sqrt{\frac{\hat{p}(1-\hat{p})}{n}} = 0.37 - 2.576\sqrt{\frac{0.37(1-0.37)}{300}} \approx 0.298$$

$$\hat{p} + z_c\sqrt{\frac{\hat{p}(1-\hat{p})}{n}} = 0.37 + 2.576\sqrt{\frac{0.37(1-0.37)}{300}} \approx 0.442$$

With 99% confidence, the proportion of U.S. households that have a pet dog lies between 29.8% and 44.2%.

5. A quality control team at a company that manufactures digital utility meters randomly selects 320 meters and finds 12 to be defective. Find a 95% confidence interval for the proportion p of all digital utility meters that the company manufactures and are defective.

$n = 320 \quad \hat{p} = \frac{12}{320} = 0.0375 \quad z_c = 1.96$

$$\hat{p} - z_c\sqrt{\frac{\hat{p}(1-\hat{p})}{n}} = 0.0375 - 1.96\sqrt{\frac{0.0375(1-0.0375)}{320}} \approx 0.017$$

$$\hat{p} + z_c\sqrt{\frac{\hat{p}(1-\hat{p})}{n}} = 0.0375 + 1.96\sqrt{\frac{0.0375(1-0.0375)}{320}} \approx 0.058$$

With 95% confidence, the proportion of digital utility meters that are defective lies between 1.7% and 5.8%.

6. In a random sample of 495 four-year-olds in a state, 54.7% can provide the first and last name of at least one parent or guardian. Find a 99% confidence interval for the proportion p of all four-year-olds in the state who can provide the first and last name of at least one parent or guardian.

$n = 495 \quad \hat{p} = 0.547 \quad z_c = 2.576$

$$\hat{p} - z_c\sqrt{\frac{\hat{p}(1-\hat{p})}{n}} = 0.547 - 2.576\sqrt{\frac{0.547(1-0.547)}{495}} \approx 0.489$$

$$\hat{p} + z_c\sqrt{\frac{\hat{p}(1-\hat{p})}{n}} = 0.547 + 2.576\sqrt{\frac{0.547(1-0.547)}{495}} \approx 0.605$$

With 99% confidence, the proportion of four-year-olds in the state who can provide the first and last name of at least one parent or guardian lies between 48.9% and 60.5%.

For the given situation, find the specified confidence interval for the population mean.

7. An online website that tracks gas prices surveys a random sample of 73 gas stations in a state and finds that the mean price of 1 gallon of regular gasoline is $3.576. If the website estimates from past surveys that the population standard deviation is $0.117, find a 95% confidence interval for the mean price of regular gasoline in the state.

$n = 73 \quad \bar{x} = 3.576 \quad \sigma = 0.117 \quad z_c = 1.96$

$\bar{x} - z_c\frac{\sigma}{\sqrt{n}} = 3.576 - 1.96 \cdot \frac{0.117}{\sqrt{73}} \approx 3.549 \qquad \bar{x} + z_c\frac{\sigma}{\sqrt{n}} = 3.576 + 1.96 \cdot \frac{0.117}{\sqrt{73}} \approx 3.603$

With 95% confidence, the mean price of 1 gallon of regular gasoline in the state lies between $3.549 and $3.603.

8. Caiden manages the security team at a large airport and surveys a random sample of 149 travelers. He finds that the mean amount of time that it takes passengers to clear security is 28.3 minutes. From past experience, Caiden estimates that the population standard deviation is 6.4 minutes. Find a 90% confidence interval for the mean amount of time that it takes passengers to clear security.

$n = 149 \quad \bar{x} = 28.3 \quad \sigma = 6.4 \quad z_c = 1.645$

$\bar{x} - z_c\frac{\sigma}{\sqrt{n}} = 28.3 - 1.645 \cdot \frac{6.4}{\sqrt{149}} \approx 27.4 \qquad \bar{x} + z_c\frac{\sigma}{\sqrt{n}} = 28.3 + 1.645 \cdot \frac{6.4}{\sqrt{149}} \approx 29.2$

With 90% confidence, the mean amount of time that it takes passengers to clear security at the airport lies between 27.4 minutes and 29.2 minutes.

9. A quality control team at a company that manufactures smartphones measures the battery life of 24 randomly selected smartphones and finds that the mean amount of continuous video playback from a full charge is 12.70 hours. Given that the population standard deviation is 0.83 hour, find a 99% confidence interval for the mean amount of continuous video playback from a full charge.

$n = 24 \quad \bar{x} = 12.70 \quad \sigma = 0.83 \quad z_c = 2.576$

$\bar{x} - z_c\frac{\sigma}{\sqrt{n}} = 12.70 - 2.576 \cdot \frac{0.83}{\sqrt{24}} \approx 12.26 \qquad \bar{x} + z_c\frac{\sigma}{\sqrt{n}} = 12.70 + 2.576 \cdot \frac{0.83}{\sqrt{24}} \approx 13.14$

With 99% confidence, the mean amount of continuous video playback from a full charge lies between 12.26 hours and 13.14 hours.

COLLABORATIVE LEARNING

Have students work in small groups to make a poster showing how to choose a formula to find a confidence interval for a population proportion or for a population mean. Give each group a different data set to use and have them identify each of the parameters for the formula. Then have each group present its poster to the rest of the class, and ask for a volunteer from the group to explain the poster.

AVOID COMMON ERRORS

Watch for students who do not use the correct formulas for the given problem situation. Remind students that the formula used for a population mean will produce valid results only when the population is normally distributed.

10. Stephen surveys 53 randomly selected students at his large high school and finds that the mean amount of time spent on homework per night is 107.9 minutes. Given that the population standard deviation is 22.7 minutes, find a 90% confidence interval for the mean amount of time students at the school spend on homework per night.

$n = 53 \quad \bar{x} = 107.9 \quad \sigma = 22.7 \quad z_c = 1.645$

$\bar{x} - z_c\frac{\sigma}{\sqrt{n}} = 107.9 - 1.645 \cdot \frac{22.7}{\sqrt{53}} \approx 102.8 \quad \bar{x} + z_c\frac{\sigma}{\sqrt{n}} = 107.9 + 1.645 \cdot \frac{22.7}{\sqrt{53}} \approx 113.0$

With 90% confidence, the mean amount of time students spend on homework per night lies between 102.8 minutes and 113.0 minutes.

Find the appropriate sample size for the given situation.

11. Executives at a health insurance company want to know the percent of residents in a state who have health insurance. Based on data from other states, they estimate that $\hat{p} = 0.8$. They are aiming for a 99% confidence interval and a margin of error of 1.5%. What sample size n should they use?

$E = 0.015$ and $z_c = 2.576 \qquad n = \frac{(2.576)^2 \cdot 0.8(1-0.8)}{(0.015)^2} \approx 4719$

So, the executives should survey a random sample of 4719 state residents.

12. Tyler is a manager at a utility company and wants to know the mean amount of electricity that residential customers consume per month. He is aiming for a 90% confidence interval and a margin of error of 10 kilowatt-hours (kWh). From past experience, Tyler estimates that the population standard deviation is 91.1 kWh. What sample size n should he use?

$E = 10, \sigma = 91.1$, and $z_c = 1.645 \qquad n = \frac{(1.645)^2(91.1)^2}{10^2} \approx 225$

So, Tyler should survey a random sample of 225 residential customers.

13. Teneka is a restaurant owner and wants to know the mean amount of revenue per day. She is aiming for a 95% confidence interval and a margin of error of \$200. Given that the population standard deviation is \$870, what sample size should Teneka use?

$E = 200, \sigma = 870$, and $z_c = 1.96 \qquad n = \frac{(1.96)^2(870)^2}{200^2} \approx 73$

So, Teneka should survey a random sample of revenues from 73 days.

14. Biology Miranda is a biologist who is measuring the lengths of randomly selected frogs of the same species from two locations.

a. Miranda measures the lengths of 25 frogs from location A and finds that the mean length is 7.35 cm. Given that the population standard deviation is 0.71 cm, find a 95% confidence interval for the mean length of frogs from location A.

$n = 25 \quad \bar{x} = 7.35 \quad \sigma = 0.71 \quad z_c = 1.96$

$\bar{x} - z_c\frac{\sigma}{\sqrt{n}} = 7.35 - 1.96 \cdot \frac{0.71}{\sqrt{25}} \approx 7.07 \qquad \bar{x} + z_c\frac{\sigma}{\sqrt{n}} = 7.35 + 1.96 \cdot \frac{0.71}{\sqrt{25}} \approx 7.63$

With 95% confidence, the mean length of frogs from location A lies between 7.07 cm and 7.63 cm.

b. Miranda measures the lengths of 20 frogs from location B and finds that the mean length is 7.17 cm. Given that the population standard deviation is 0.69 cm, find a 95% confidence interval for the mean length of frogs from location B.

$n = 20 \quad \bar{x} = 7.17 \quad \sigma = 0.69 \quad z_c = 1.96$

$\bar{x} - z_c\frac{\sigma}{\sqrt{n}} = 7.17 - 1.96 \cdot \frac{0.69}{\sqrt{20}} \approx 6.87 \qquad \bar{x} + z_c\frac{\sigma}{\sqrt{n}} = 7.17 + 1.96 \cdot \frac{0.69}{\sqrt{20}} \approx 7.47$

With 95% confidence, the mean length of frogs from location B lies between 6.87 cm and 7.47 cm.

c. Is it clear that the mean length of frogs from one location is greater than the mean length of frogs from the other location? Explain your reasoning.

No, because the confidence intervals of the two locations overlap between 7.07 and 7.47 cm, which is a significant portion of each confidence interval.

15. Which of the following sets of desired margin of error E, desired confidence level c, and given sample proportion $\hat{p}$ or population standard deviation σ require a sample size of at least 100? Select all that apply.

A. $E = 0.1$, $c = 95\%$, $\hat{p} = 0.5$

B. $E = 1000$, $c = 99\%$, $\sigma = 4000$

C. $E = 0.04$, $c = 90\%$, $\hat{p} = 0.9$

D. $E = 4$, $c = 95\%$, $\sigma = 18.6$

E. $E = 0.06$, $c = 99\%$, $\hat{p} = 0.3$

F. $E = 50$, $c = 90\%$, $\sigma = 309$

A. $n = \frac{(1.96)^2 \cdot 0.5(1 - 0.5)}{(0.1)^2} \approx 96$

B. $n = \frac{(2.576)^2 (4000)^2}{(1000)^2} \approx 106$

C. $n = \frac{(1.645)^2 \cdot 0.9(1 - 0.9)}{(0.04)^2} \approx 152$

D. $n = \frac{(1.96)^2 (18.6)^2}{(4)^2} \approx 83$

E. $n = \frac{(2.576)^2 \cdot 0.3(1 - 0.3)}{(0.06)^2} \approx 387$

F. $n = \frac{(1.645)^2 (309)^2}{(50)^2} \approx 103$

Answers: B, C, E, F

INTEGRATE MATHEMATICAL PRACTICES

Focus on Reasoning

MP.2 When students are making a statement about a confidence interval, ask them to make sure the statement makes sense with respect to the original data set. Have them justify their work in terms of different confidence intervals, including 90%, 95%, or 99% intervals, and describe the differences created by choosing a different percentage.

WHOLE CLASS DISCUSSION

Lead a class discussion about how to explain the relationship between a margin of error and a confidence interval. Ask students to include the restrictions that apply for finding a margin of error or a confidence interval.

JOURNAL

Have students use words, formulas, graphs, calculators, and/or tables to explain how to find the confidence interval for a population proportion and for a population mean.

H.O.T. Focus on Higher Order Thinking

16. **Multiple Representations** The margin of error E for the proportion of successes in a population may be estimated by $\frac{1}{\sqrt{n}}$, where n is the sample size. Explain where this estimate comes from. Assume a 95% confidence interval.

Since $z_c = 1.96 \approx 2$ and $\hat{p}$ is assumed to be 0.5,

$$E = z_c\sqrt{\frac{\hat{p}(1-\hat{p})}{n}} = 2\sqrt{\frac{0.5(0.5)}{n}} = 2\sqrt{\frac{1}{4n}} = \frac{2}{2}\sqrt{\frac{1}{n}} = \frac{1}{\sqrt{n}}.$$

17. **Draw Conclusions** In the Explore, you wrote an interval of the form $\mu_{\hat{p}} - 2\sigma_{\hat{p}} < \hat{p} < \mu_{\hat{p}} + 2\sigma_{\hat{p}}$ that captures 95% of the sample proportions. You know that $\mu_{\hat{p}} = p$, so you can rewrite the interval as $p - 2\sigma_{\hat{p}} < \hat{p} < p + 2\sigma_{\hat{p}}$. Solve this compound inequality for p. What does this result tell you?

$$p - 2\sigma_{\hat{p}} < \hat{p} < p + 2\sigma_{\hat{p}}$$

$$-2\sigma_{\hat{p}} < \hat{p} - p < 2\sigma_{\hat{p}}$$

$$-\hat{p} - 2\sigma_{\hat{p}} < -p < -\hat{p} + 2\sigma_{\hat{p}}$$

$$\hat{p} + 2\sigma_{\hat{p}} > p > \hat{p} - 2\sigma_{\hat{p}}$$

$$\hat{p} - 2\sigma_{\hat{p}} < p < \hat{p} + 2\sigma_{\hat{p}}$$

The last inequality gives the confidence interval for the population proportion p.

18. **Explain the Error** A quality assurance team for an LED bulb manufacturer tested 400 randomly selected LED bulbs and found that 6 are defective. A member of the team performed the following calculations to obtain a 95% confidence interval for the proportion p of LED bulbs that are defective. Explain the error.

$n = 400 \qquad \hat{p} = \frac{6}{400} = 0.015 \qquad z_c = 1.96$

$$\hat{p} - z_c\sqrt{\frac{\hat{p}(1-\hat{p})}{n}} = 0.015 - 1.96\sqrt{\frac{0.015(1-0.015)}{400}} \approx 0.003$$

$$\hat{p} + z_c\sqrt{\frac{\hat{p}(1-\hat{p})}{n}} = 0.015 + 1.96\sqrt{\frac{0.015(1-0.015)}{400}} \approx 0.027$$

With 95% confidence, the proportion of LED bulbs that are defective lies between 0.3% and 2.7%.

In order for a confidence interval to describe the value of p reasonably accurately, both $n\hat{p}$ and $n(1-\hat{p})$ must be at least 10. Since only 6 LED bulbs are defective, $n\hat{p} = 6$, which is less than 10. So, the confidence interval may not be reasonably accurate.

Lesson Performance Task

Between 2010 and 2011, a research group conducted a survey of young working women and men, ages 18 to 34. Of the 610 women surveyed, 66% indicated that being successful in a high-paying career is either "one of the most important things" or "very important" in their lives. Of the 703 men surveyed, only 59% replied that they attach such importance to career.

a. Find a 95% confidence interval for each sample proportion.

$z_{95\%} = 1.96$

Women:

$$\hat{p}_w - z_c\sqrt{\frac{\hat{p}_w(1-\hat{p}_w)}{n_w}} \le p_w \le \hat{p}_w + z_c\sqrt{\frac{\hat{p}_w(1-\hat{p}_w)}{n_w}}$$

$$0.66 - 1.96\sqrt{\frac{0.66(1-0.66)}{610}} \le p_w \le 0.66 + 1.96\sqrt{\frac{0.66(1-0.66)}{610}}$$

$$0.622 \le p_w \le 0.698$$

Men:

$$\hat{p}_m - z_c\sqrt{\frac{\hat{p}_m(1-\hat{p}_m)}{n_m}} \le p_m \le \hat{p}_m + z_c\sqrt{\frac{\hat{p}_m(1-\hat{p}_m)}{n_m}}$$

$$0.59 - 1.96\sqrt{\frac{0.59(1-0.59)}{703}} \le p_m \le 0.59 + 1.96\sqrt{\frac{0.59(1-0.59)}{703}}$$

$$0.554 \le p_m \le 0.626$$

b. Find the margin of error for each result at the 95% confidence level.

Women:

$$E_w = z_c\sqrt{\frac{\hat{p}_w(1-\hat{p}_w)}{n}}$$

$$= 1.96\sqrt{\frac{0.66(1-0.66)}{610}}$$

$$\approx 0.038$$

Men:

$$E_m = z_c\sqrt{\frac{\hat{p}_m(1-\hat{p}_m)}{n}}$$

$$= 1.96\sqrt{\frac{0.59(1-0.59)}{703}}$$

$$\approx 0.036$$

c. Is it possible that the population proportions could actually be equal? Explain.

It is possible for the population proportions to be equal because the confidence intervals overlap between 0.622 and 0.626. However, it is unlikely that the population proportions are equal as the confidence intervals barely overlap each other.

EXTENSION ACTIVITY

Have students research Slovin's formula and find how it is used. Students should be able to demonstrate a calculation using the formula. **Slovin's formula is used to determine a sample size when nothing about the behavior of a population is known. Slovin's formula states, for n samples and a population of N, where e represents the error tolerance, $n = \frac{N}{1 + Ne^2}$. So, for 95% confidence, e is 5% or 0.05. For a population size of 5000, $n = \frac{5000}{1 + 5000(0.05)^2} \approx 370.37$, so the sample size would be 371. Note that when e is 0.05, the maximum sample size needed is 400, but when e is 0.01, the maximum is 10,000.**

INTEGRATE TECHNOLOGY

This Lesson Performance Task and others like it can be solved using a graphing calculator if the total population n is known. First, multiply the total population by the percent to find the x-value. Then press the **STAT** key. Scroll right to **TESTS**. Scroll down to **A:1-PropZInterval** and press **ENTER**.

Scroll down to enter the values for x and n. Enter 0.95 for the **C-Level**, which is the confidence level. Scroll down to click on **Calculate**. The window then shows the confidence interval, the $\hat{p}$ -value, and the value for n.

LANGUAGE SUPPORT EL

Margin of error and confidence levels are closely related in statistics as well as in human relationships. As the number of errors a person makes increases, our confidence in that person decreases. Likewise, in statistics, we find the interval in which we can be confident of extremely few errors. That is why we choose a high confidence level at or near 95% and a low error level at or near 5%.

Scoring Rubric

2 points: Student correctly solves the problem and explains his/her reasoning.

1 point: Student shows good understanding of the problem but does not fully solve or explain his/her reasoning.

0 points: Student does not demonstrate understanding of the problem.

LESSON 24.2

Surveys, Experiments, and Observational Studies

Common Core Math Standards

The student is expected to:

 S-IC.B.3

Recognize the purposes of and differences among sample surveys, experiments, and observational studies; explain how randomization relates to each. Also S-IC.B.6

Mathematical Practices

 MP.3 Logic

Language Objective

Work with a partner to discuss a Venn diagram describing when to use surveys, experiments, or observational studies.

ENGAGE

Essential Question: What kinds of statistical research are there, and which ones can establish cause-and-effect relationships between variables?

Statistical research can include surveys, observational studies, and experiments. While surveys measure variables and observational studies may show associations between variables, only experiments can establish cause-and-effect relationships between variables.

PREVIEW: LESSON PERFORMANCE TASK

View the Engage section online. Discuss the photo and the need to analyze the validity of a study based on a report of the findings. Then preview the Lesson Performance Task.

Name __________ Class __________ Date __________

24.2 Surveys, Experiments, and Observational Studies

Resource Locker

Essential Question: What kinds of statistical research are there, and which ones can establish cause-and-effect relationships between variables?

Explore Recognizing Different Forms of Statistical Research

Statistical research takes various forms depending on whether the purpose of the research is to measure a variable in a population, to see if there is evidence of an association between two variables, or to determine whether one variable actually influences another variable.

Suppose a graduate school researcher is considering three studies related to math and music. One study involves asking a random sample of high school students in a large school district whether they listen to music while doing math homework. A second study involves asking a random sample of students at a large university whether they are majoring in math and whether they also play a musical instrument or sing. A third study involves a group of adult participants where half will be randomly assigned either to listen to classical music for 15 minutes before taking a logical reasoning test or to listen to white noise for 15 minutes before taking the same test.

(A) Which study appears to look for an association between two variables without actively manipulating either one? What are those variables?

The study that looks for an association between two variables is the one that asks a random sample of students at a large university whether they are majoring in math and whether they play a musical instrument or sing. The variables are whether the student has mathematical ability and whether the student has musical ability.

(B) Which study appears to be looking for evidence that one variable actually influences another variable? What are those variables, and which one is manipulated to see if it influences the other?

The study that looks for evidence that one variable influences another is the one that randomly assigns adult participants to listen to classical music or white noise before taking a logical reasoning test. The variables are the type of sound being played and the listeners' performance on the logical reasoning test. The type of sound being played is manipulated to see if it influences listeners' performance on the test.

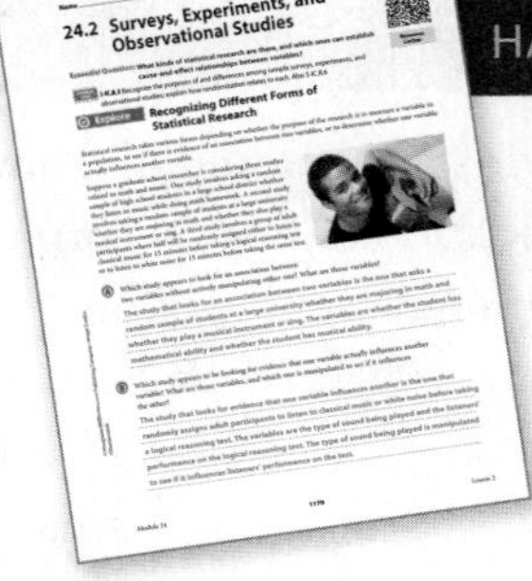

HARDCOVER PAGES 1179–11

Watch for the hardcover student edition page numbers for this lesson.

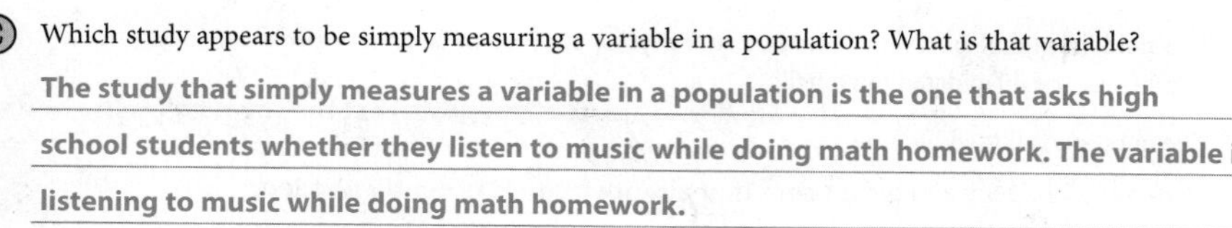

(C) Which study appears to be simply measuring a variable in a population? What is that variable?

The study that simply measures a variable in a population is the one that asks high school students whether they listen to music while doing math homework. The variable is listening to music while doing math homework.

Reflect

1. **Discussion** Describe the type of result or conclusion the researcher might obtain from each study.

For the first study, the researcher can determine the proportion of high school students who listen to music while doing math homework but cannot determine whether listening to music has any influence on learning math. For the second study, the researcher might be able to identify an association between mathematical ability and musical ability but not the reason why the two are linked. For the third study, the researcher might find that listening to music has a positive impact, a negative impact, or no impact (compared with listening to white noise) on performance on a test of logical reasoning.

Explain 1 Detecting Errors in Surveys

A **survey** measures characteristics of interest about a population using a sample selected from the population. As you saw in a previous lesson, a sample needs to be representative of the population in order for the measurements obtained from the sample to be accurate. Random sampling is generally the best way to ensure representation.

Even when random sampling is used, a survey's results can have errors. Some of the sources of errors are:

- *Biased questions:* The wording of questions in a survey can influence the way people respond to questions. Survey questions need to be worded in a neutral, unbiased way.
- *Interviewer effect:* If an interviewer asks the questions in a survey, the person being interviewed may give inaccurate responses to avoid being embarrassed.
- *Nonresponse:* Some people may be difficult to contact, or they may simply refuse to participate once contacted. If nonresponse rates are higher for certain subgroups of a population, then those subgroups will be underrepresented in the survey results.

Example 1 **Explain why the results of each survey are likely to be inaccurate, and then suggest a way to improve the accuracy of the survey.**

(A) The owner of a business, conducts interviews with a random sample of employees to have them rate how satisfied they are with their jobs.

Since the interviewer is the owner of the business, the employees may not be completely open about any job dissatisfaction they may have. The employees may feel that their job security is at stake. A better survey would involve a neutral interviewer or allow the employees to respond anonymously.

PROFESSIONAL DEVELOPMENT

Integrate Mathematical Practices

This lesson provides an opportunity to address Mathematical Practice **MP.3**, which calls for students to "construct viable arguments and critique the reasoning of others." By looking at media reports about research studies and identifying the type of statistical research based on given information, students can determine whether or not the conclusions in the media report are valid. For example, if the research is an observational study rather than an experiment, students will be able to critique any conclusions that try to establish a cause-and-effect relationship between variables.

EXPLORE

Recognizing Different Forms of Statistical Research

INTEGRATE TECHNOLOGY

Students have the option of completing the Explore activity either in the book or online.

QUESTIONING STRATEGIES

? Consider each of the studies described. Of what use might the results of each study be to the researcher? Answers may vary.

EXPLAIN 1

Detecting Errors in Surveys

QUESTIONING STRATEGIES

? Are biased questions in a survey always intentional on the part of the person designing the survey? No, often the bias is unintentional, which is why it is a good idea to have someone uninvolved with the survey look at the questions before the survey is administered.

? Many surveys are conducted over the telephone. How could using only landline phones to conduct a survey affect the outcome? People with only cell phones will not be included. Those people may be younger or more urban than people with only landline phones and therefore be underrepresented in the survey.

CONNECT VOCABULARY EL

Have students explain to each other what the difference is between a *treatment group* and a *control group*. Explain that sometimes control groups are called *comparison groups*, because they are being compared to the group receiving the treatment or intervention.

INTEGRATE MATHEMATICAL PRACTICES

Focus on Reasoning

MP.2 Have students discuss in greater depth the concept of biased questioning in surveys. Have them give examples of biased questions, explain why they are biased, and offer ways to rework the questions to make them unbiased.

EXPLAIN 2

Distinguishing Between Observational Studies and Experiments

QUESTIONING STRATEGIES

? What is an example of a situation for which an observational study would be better than an experiment? Possible answer: If the treatment being imposed in an experiment could be harmful, then an observational study would be better. For example, if researchers want to study whether eating fried food every day increases cholesterol, it would be better to conduct an observational study of people who already report that they eat fried food every day rather than ask people to engage in the potentially harmful behavior as a treatment in an experiment.

AVOID COMMON ERRORS

Results of observational studies are often incorrectly interpreted as establishing a cause-and-effect relationship. Remind students that observational studies can establish only an association between a factor and a characteristic of interest.

Ⓑ In a random sample of town residents, a survey asks, "Are you in favor of a special tax levy to renovate the dilapidated town hall?"

The question is biased because **the word "dilapidated" suggests that the town hall is in a state of disrepair, which makes it seem that a renovation is urgently needed.**

A better survey would **begin with a factual list of repairs that need to be made and then ask, "Are you in favor of a special tax levy to make these repairs?"**

Reflect

2. Even if the survey question in Part B is revised to avoid being biased, do the people surveyed have enough information to give an informed and accurate response? Explain.
"No, because most people responding to the survey will want to know the amount of the tax levy. Residents may be likely to respond negatively out of fear that their taxes will increase too much without that knowledge.

Your Turn

Explain why the results of the survey are likely to be inaccurate, and then suggest a way to improve the accuracy of the survey.

3. A teacher conducts one-on-one interviews with a random sample of her students to get feedback on her teaching methods.
Since the interviewer is the teacher, students may not be open about any dissatisfaction they may have with her teaching methods. The students may feel that how the teacher grades them will be influenced by their responses. A better survey would allow the students to respond anonymously.

Explain 2 Distinguishing Between Observational Studies and Experiments

In an **observational study**, researchers determine whether an existing condition, called a *factor*, in a population is related to a characteristic of interest. For instance, an observational study might be used to find the incidence of heart disease among those who smoke. In the study, being a smoker is the factor, and having heart disease is the characteristic of interest.

In an **experiment**, researchers create a condition by imposing a treatment on some of the subjects of the experiment. For instance, an experiment might be conducted by having some people with eczema take a vitamin E pill daily, and then observing whether their symptoms improve. In the experiment, taking the vitamin E pill is the treatment, and improvement of symptoms is the characteristic of interest.

Generally, an experiment is preferred over an observational study because an experiment allows researchers to manipulate one variable to see its effect on another. However, there may be practical or unethical reasons against performing an experiment. For example, it would be unethical to ask people to smoke in order to study the effects of smoking on their health. Instead, an observational study should be performed using people who already smoke.

COLLABORATIVE LEARNING

Peer-to-Peer Activity

Have students work in pairs. Ask each pair to brainstorm to identify a question for a research study that could be addressed through either an experiment or an observational study. Have them describe how they would design each study. Finally, have them determine which method is better and why. Have pairs share their work with the class.

Example 2 **Determine whether each research study is an observational study or an experiment. Identify the factor if it is an observational study or the treatment if is an experiment. Also identify the characteristic of interest.**

(A) Researchers measure the cholesterol of 50 subjects who report that they eat fish regularly and 50 subjects who report that they do not eat fish regularly.

This research study is an observational study. The factor is whether people eat fish regularly, and the characteristic of interest is cholesterol level.

(B) Researchers have 100 subjects with high cholesterol take fish oil pills daily for two months. They monitor the cholesterol of the subjects during that time.

This research study is an **experiment**. The factor/(treatment) is **taking fish oil pills daily**. The characteristic of interest is **cholesterol level**.

Reflect

4. **Discussion** Suppose the researchers in Part A find that considerably more people who eat fish regularly have normal cholesterol levels than those who do not eat fish regularly. Is it reasonable to conclude that eating fish regularly has an effect on cholesterol? Explain.

It is not reasonable to make that conclusion because there may be other factors that the people who eat fish regularly have in common, such as a better diet or regular exercise, and it may be those factors that have an effect on cholesterol.

Your Turn

Determine whether the research study is an observational study or an experiment. Identify the factor if it is an observational study or the treatment if is an experiment. Also identify the characteristic of interest.

5. Researchers monitor the driving habits of 80 subjects in their twenties and 80 subjects in their fifties for one month by using a GPS device that tracks location and speed.

This research study is an observational study. The factor is a person's age and the characteristic of interest is the person's driving habits.

Explain 3 Identifying Control Groups and Treatment Groups in Experiments

Whether a study is observational or experimental, it should be comparative in order to establish a connection between the factor or treatment and the characteristic of interest. For instance, determining the rate of car accidents among people who talk on cell phones while driving is not instructive unless you compare it with the rate of car accidents among people who don't talk on cell phones while driving and find that it is significantly different.

EXPLAIN 3

Identifying Control Groups and Treatment Groups in Experiments

QUESTIONING STRATEGIES

An experiment involves testing the effectiveness of a new drug. Why does giving the subjects in the control group a pill that does not contain the drug make the results more valid than if the subjects in the control group did not take any pill at all? **Possible answer: If subjects in the control group did not take a pill, then the placebo effect (in the treatment group) could make it difficult to interpret the results of the experiment. If the treatment group had different outcomes from the control group, researchers could not tell whether the result was due to the drug in the pill or merely to the effect of taking a pill.**

DIFFERENTIATE INSTRUCTION

Kinesthetic Experience

Students may benefit from acting out interview and telephone surveys. Have students design survey questions, including questions that may be biased. Challenge the class to identify potential sources of error for each survey and suggest ways that the accuracy of the survey can be improved.

INTEGRATE MATHEMATICAL PRACTICES

Focus on Communication

MP.3 Discuss with students the importance of randomization in a controlled experiment. Help them recognize that randomization produces reliable results that would be valid for another randomized group. Lead them to conclude that randomization allows generalization of the results.

While a comparative observational study can suggest a relationship between two variables, such as cell phone use while driving and car accidents, it cannot establish a cause-and-effect relationship because there can be *confounding variables* (also called *lurking variables*) that influence the results. For instance, perhaps people who talk on cell phones while driving are more likely to drive aggressively, so it is the aggressive driving (not the cell phone use) that leads to a higher rate of car accidents.

In an experiment, randomization can remove the problem of a confounding variable by distributing the variable among the groups being compared so that its influence on the groups is more or less equal. Therefore, the best way to establish a cause-and-effect relationship between two variables is through a **randomized comparative experiment** where subjects are randomly divided into two groups: the *treatment group*, which is given the treatment, and the *control group*, which is not.

Example 3 **Identify the treatment, characteristic of interest, control group, and treatment group for the given experiment. Assume all subjects of the research are selected randomly.**

Ⓐ To see whether zinc has an effect on the duration of a cold, researchers have half of the subjects take tablets containing zinc at the onset of cold symptoms and the other half take tablets without any zinc. The durations of the colds are then recorded.

The treatment is having subjects take tablets that contain zinc at the onset of cold symptoms.
The characteristic of interest is the duration of the cold.
The control group consists of subjects who took tablets without zinc.
The treatment group consists of subjects who took tablets containing zinc.

Ⓑ To see whether regular moderate exercise has an effect on blood pressure, researchers have half of the subjects set aside 30 minutes daily for walking and the other half not do any walking beyond their normal daily routines. The subjects also take and record their blood pressure at the same time each day.

The treatment is having subjects **walk for 30 minutes daily**.

The characteristic of interest is **blood pressure**.

The control group consists of subjects who **do not do any walking beyond their normal daily routines**.

The treatment group consists of subjects who **walked for 30 minutes daily.**.

Your Turn

6. Identify the treatment, characteristic of interest, control group, and treatment group for the following experiment. Assume all subjects of the research are selected randomly.

To see whether reviewing for a test with a classmate improves scores, researchers ask half of the subjects to study with a classmate and the other half to study alone. The test scores are then recorded.

The treatment is studying for the test with a classmate.
The characteristic of interest is the student's test score.
The control group consists of subjects who study for the test alone.
The treatment group consists of subjects who study for the test with a classmate.

LANGUAGE SUPPORT EL

Communicate Math

Have students work with a partner to create a Venn diagram like the one shown for the types of sampling methods. Have them try to describe situations that could apply for each of the 7 regions, if possible. Students should begin to realize that there are situations where only one or possibly two of the sampling methods are useful, and one is generally preferred.

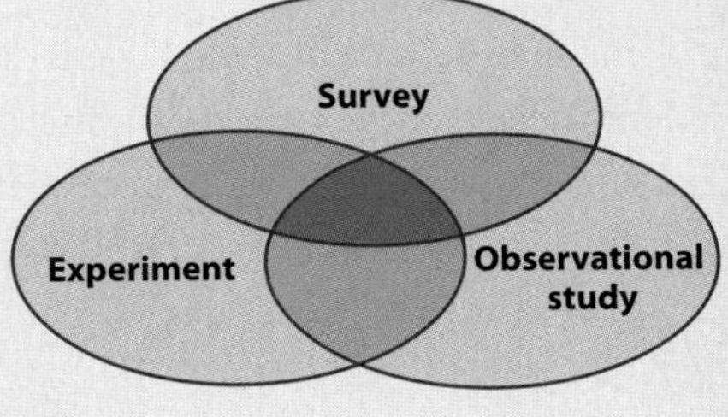

Explain 4 Evaluating a Media Report of Statistical Research

When you encounter media reports of statistical research in your daily life, you should judge any reported conclusions on the basis of how the research was conducted. Among the questions you should consider are the following:

- Is the research a survey, an observational study, or an experiment? In broad terms, a survey simply measures variables, an observational study attempts to find an association between variables, and an experiment attempts to establish a cause-and-effect relationship between variables.
- Was randomization used in conducting the research? As you know, random sampling is considered the best way to obtain a representative sample from a population and therefore get accurate results. Randomization also helps to dilute the effects of confounding variables.
- Does the report include the details of the research, such as sample size, statistics, and margins of error? The details help you judge how much confidence to have in the results of the research or how much importance to place on the results.

Example 4 **Evaluate the article by answering the following questions.**

- Is this a survey, an observational study, or an experiment? How do you know?
- Was randomization used in the research? If so, how?
- What details of the research does the article include? Is any important information missing?

(A)

Caring Doctors Shorten and Ease the Common Cold

Researchers have found that among patients with colds, those who gave their doctors perfect scores on a questionnaire measuring empathy have colds that did not last as long and were less severe. Empathy on the part of doctors included making patients feel at ease, listening to their concerns, and showing compassion.

A total of 350 subjects who were experiencing the onset of a cold were randomly assigned to one of three groups: no doctor-patient interaction, standard interaction, and enhanced interaction. Only subjects in the third group saw doctors who had been coached on being empathetic.

- Is this a survey, an observational study, or an experiment? How do you know?
  This study is an experiment because treatments were imposed on two groups of patients: those who had a standard interaction with a doctor and those who had an enhanced interaction with a doctor.
- Was randomization used in the research? If so, how?
  Randomization was used by randomly assigning subjects to a control group or one of two treatment groups.
- What details of the research does the article include? Is any important information missing?
  The report includes the number of subjects but no statistics, such as measures of cold duration or severity.

EXPLAIN 4

Evaluating a Media Report of Statistical Research

INTEGRATE MATHEMATICAL PRACTICES

Focus on Critical Thinking

MP.3 Students may be surprised to learn that many media reports of research that implies a cause-and-effect relationship are based on observational studies or surveys. Such conclusions may not be valid. Encourage students to find examples of this type of misuse of statistics in current media reports.

Fitness in Teen Years May Guard Against Heart Trouble Later

A study of almost 750,000 Swedish men suggests people who are aerobically fit as teenagers are less likely to have a heart attack later in life. Each 15 percent increase in the level of aerobic fitness as a teenager is associated with an 18 percent reduced risk of a heart attack 30 years later. Overall, teens and young adults who participate in regular cardiovascular training have a 35 percent reduced risk of a heart attack later in life.

The researchers analyzed medical data from men drafted into the nation's army, which requires a test of aerobic fitness at the time of induction. National health registers provided information on heart attacks the men had later in life.

- Is this a survey, an observational study, or an experiment? How do you know?
  This study is an observational study because the factor of aerobic fitness as a teenager is being related to the characteristic of interest, which is the risk of having a heart attack later in life.
- Was randomization used in the research? If so, how?
  Randomization was not used in the research because all of the subjects were male draftees in the Swedish army. The subjects may not be representative of all adults because women were obviously excluded, and they may not be representative all adult males because only Swedish males were studied.
- What details of the research does the article include? Is any important information missing?
  The report includes the sample size and the following statistics: each 15 percent increase in the level of aerobic fitness as a teenager is associated with an 18 percent reduced risk of a heart attack 30 years later, and teens and young adults who participate in regular cardiovascular training have an overall 35 percent reduced risk of a heart attack later in life (presumably compared with teens and young adults who don't participate in regular cardiovascular training). What is missing is how the researchers defined "level of aerobic fitness" and "regular cardiovascular training" as well as how they calculated their reported statistics.

Reflect

7. **Discussion** What conclusion do you draw from the report in Part A? How much confidence do you have in that conclusion? Why?
   Answers may vary. Possible answer: A doctor should be empathetic because empathy causes a patient's cold to be shorter and milder. My confidence about the conclusion of the research is relatively high because it seems that the research was a comparative randomized experiment and involved a substantial number of subjects.

Your Turn

8. Evaluate the article by answering the following questions.

- Is this a survey, an observational study, or an experiment? How do you know?
- Was randomization used in the research? If so, how?
- What details of the research does the article include? Is any important information missing?

> **Study Finds One in Seven Would Fail Kitchen Inspection**
>
> Research suggests that at least one in seven home kitchens would flunk a health inspection that is given to restaurants. Only 61 percent of home kitchens would get an A or B if put through a restaurant inspection, compared with 98 percent of Los Angeles County restaurants. At least 14 percent of home kitchens would fail. The results are based on a questionnaire about food safety administered on the Internet and taken by about 13,000.

This study is a survey because a characteristic of interest (knowledge of food safety) was measured. Randomization was not used in the research because people volunteered to take the Internet questionnaire, which means that those who are interested in food safety are more likely to take the questionnaire. The report includes the sample size of 13,000 and the statistics that 61 percent of home kitchens would earn an A or B on a restaurant inspection and 14 percent would fail, but it is missing the margins of error for these statistics.

Elaborate

9. What are some sources of errors in a survey? Why should these errors be avoided?

Some sources of errors in surveys are biased questions, the interviewer effect, and nonresponse. These errors should be avoided so that the data from the survey are accurate.

10. Describe the difference between a factor in an observational study and a treatment in an experiment.

A factor in an observational study is an existing condition in a population that researchers want to relate to a characteristic of interest. A treatment in an experiment is a condition that researchers impose on subjects to see if it influences the characteristic of interest.

11. Explain what confounding variables are and describe how they are handled in a randomized experiment.

Confounding variables are variables that may influence the results of an observational study or experiment but that are not taken into account. A randomized comparative experiment distributes the confounding variables among the groups being compared so that their influence on each group is about equal.

12. Essential Question Check-in How do the three kinds of statistical research discussed in this lesson study a characteristic of interest in a population?

A survey measures a characteristic of interest, an observational study looks for an association between a factor and a characteristic of interest, and an experiment imposes a treatment to see if it influences a characteristic of interest.

ELABORATE

QUESTIONING STRATEGIES

? Why is it important that subjects in a randomized comparative experiment be randomly assigned to the treatment group and the control group? **Randomization minimizes bias and ensures that the groups are, theoretically, similar in all ways before the treatment is applied.**

SUMMARIZE THE LESSON

? What is the main difference between an observational study and an experiment? **An observational study is a study that is used to determine whether a condition that already exists in a population is related to a characteristic of interest. An experiment is a study that involves imposing a treatment on a group, and seeing whether the treatment has an effect on the characteristic of interest.**

EVALUATE

ASSIGNMENT GUIDE

Concepts and Skills	Practice
Explore Recognizing Different Forms of Statistical Research	Exercise 1
Example 1 Detecting Errors in Surveys	Exercises 2–3
Example 2 Distinguishing Between Observational Studies and Experiments	Exercises 4–8
Example 3 Identifying Control Groups and Treatment Groups in Experiments	Exercises 9–12
Example 4 Evaluating a Media Report of Statistical Research	Exercises 13–15

QUESTIONING STRATEGIES

What is the purpose of the control group in a randomized comparative experiment? **Since subjects in the control group are not given the treatment, researchers can conclude that any changes that are exhibited by subjects in the treatment group and not by the subjects in the control group are due to the treatment.**

Evaluate: Homework and Practice

- Online Homework
- Hints and Help
- Extra Practice

1. Members of a research team are considering three studies related to sleep and learning. The first study involves comparing the scores on a post-study test of learning from two groups of randomly chosen adults, with one group getting at least 7 hours of sleep per night for a week and the other group getting at most 6 hours of sleep per night for a week. A second study involves asking a random sample of students at a large university to report the average number of hours of sleep they get each night and their college grade point average. A third study involves asking a random sample of high school students in a large school district whether they feel they get enough sleep to stay alert throughout the school day.

   a. Which study appears to look for an association between two variables without actively manipulating either one? What are those variables?

   The study that looks for an association between two variables is the one that asks a random sample of students at a large university how much sleep they get and what their college grade point average is. The variables are average daily amount of sleep and academic performance (as indicated by college grade point average).

   b. Which study appears to be looking for evidence that one variable actually influences another variable? What are those variables, and which one is manipulated to see if it influences the other?

   The study that looks for evidence that one variable influences another is the one that randomly assigns adults to a group that gets at least 7 hours of sleep per night for a week or to a group that gets at most 6 hours per night of sleep for a week, with a test of learning given afterward. The variables are the daily amount of sleep and the ability to learn (as indicated by a score on a test). The amount of sleep is manipulated to see if it influences ability to learn.

   c. Which study appears to be simply measuring a variable in a population? What is that variable?

   The study that simply measures a variable in a population is the one that involves asking high school students whether they feel they get enough sleep to stay alert throughout the school day. The variable is getting enough sleep to feel alert throughout the school day.

Explain why the results of each survey are likely to be inaccurate and then suggest a way to improve the accuracy of the survey.

2. A store offers its customers a chance to win a cash prize if they call a toll-free number on a receipt and participate in a customer satisfaction survey.

   Survey respondents are only those who bought something and are self-selected. These customers may be inclined to rate their satisfaction high in the belief that doing so will increase their chances of winning the cash prize. A better way is to randomly ask customers to complete a quick survey as they are leaving the store, regardless of whether they made a purchase.

Exercise	Depth of Knowledge (D.O.K.)	COMMON CORE Mathematical Practices
1	**1** Recall of Information	**MP.3** Logic
2–3	**2** Skills/Concepts	**MP.3** Logic
4–12	**1** Recall of Information	**MP.6** Precision
13–14	**2** Skills/Concepts	**MP.3** Logic
15	**1** Recall of Information	**MP.6** Precision
16	**2** Skills/Concepts H.O.T.	**MP.3** Logic
17–18	**3** Strategic Thinking H.O.T.	**MP.1** Problem Solving

3. A reporter for a local newspaper asks a random sample of people attending a holiday parade, "Since this holiday parade is so popular, do you support having the city provide the support for a larger parade next year?"

The reporter asks only people who are attending the parade and are more likely to support having a larger parade in the future, so there is nonresponse from people who do not attend the parade. Also, the phrase "since this holiday parade is so popular" biases the question. A better method is to ask a random sample of all residents a question that does not mention the popularity of this year's parade.

Determine whether each research study is an observational study or an experiment. Identify the factor if it is an observational study or the treatment if is an experiment. Also identify the characteristic of interest.

4. Researchers found that of patients who had been taking a bone-loss drug for more than five years, a high percentage of patients also had an uncommon type of fracture in the thigh bone.

This is an observational study. The factor is taking a bone-loss drug for more than five years. The characteristic of interest is an uncommon type of fracture in the thigh bone.

5. Researchers found that when patients with chronic illnesses were randomly divided into two groups, the group that got regular coaching by phone from health professionals to help them manage their illnesses had lower monthly medical costs than the group that did not get the coaching.

This study is an experiment. The treatment is the regular coaching by phone from health professionals that one group got. The characteristic of interest is the monthly medical costs.

6. A caretaker at a zoo is studying the effect of a new diet on the health of the zoo's elephants. She continues to feed half of the elephants their existing food, switches the other half to a new diet, and then monitors the health of the elephants.

This study is an experiment. The treatment is the new diet that is given to half of the elephants. The characteristic of interest is the health of the elephants.

7. A school district wants to know whether there is a relationship between students' standardized test scores and the amount of time they spend on extracurricular activities. The school board surveys students from each school in the system to gather data about the average number of hours per week spent on extracurricular activities and each student's most recent test scores.

This is an observational study. The factor is the average number of hours per week a student spent on extracurricular activities. The characteristic of interest is the student's most recent standardized test score.

AVOID COMMON ERRORS

Students may forget to consider the placebo effect when determining the validity of the conclusions drawn from a study. Remind students that they need to analyze the design of the study and consider whether a treatment may be having an effect simply because the subjects in the treatment group are receiving it.

CURRICULUM INTEGRATION

Many scientific experiments involve applying a treatment or action that will affect a variable in the experiment. Ask students if they have conducted these types of experiments in their science classes. Have them explain how they measured the effect of the treatment.

8. Researchers want to know the effect of vitamin C as a dietary supplement on blood pressure. Half of the randomly assigned subjects take one 1000-milligram tablet of vitamin C daily for six months while the other half of the subjects take one placebo tablet daily for six months. The blood pressure of all subjects is taken weekly.

This study is an experiment. The treatment is taking a tablet of vitamin C daily for a month. The characteristic of interest is the subjects' blood pressure.

Identify the treatment, characteristic of interest, control group, and treatment group for the given experiment. Assume all subjects of the research are selected randomly.

9. A restaurant manager wants to know whether to keep using orange slices as a garnish or to change to tangerine slices. All of the subjects are blindfolded. Half of the subjects are asked to eat orange slices, and the other half are asked to eat tangerine slices. All subjects are asked whether they like the taste of the fruit.

The treatment is giving subjects the tangerine slices. The characteristic of interest is whether the subjects like the taste of the fruit. The control group consists of the subjects who are given the orange slices (the current garnish), and the treatment group consists of the subjects who are given the tangerine slices.

10. A pharmaceutical company wants to know about the side effects of a new cholesterol medication. Out of 400 randomly selected volunteers who currently take the existing cholesterol medication, the researchers switch the old drug with the new drug for 200 of them, and continue to give the other 200 the old drug. They then monitor the two groups for side effects.

The treatment is the new cholesterol drug. The characteristic of interest is the side effects of the new drug. The control group consists of subjects who continue to use the old drug. The treatment group consists of subjects who are given the new drug.

11. A park service wants to determine whether reintroducing a particular species of underwater plant to the lakes in the park system would be beneficial to a particular species of fish living in the lakes. The researchers reintroduce the plant in one lake. One year later, they study the health of the fish population in the lake where the plant was reintroduced, as well as in an ecologically similar lake without the plant.

The treatment is reintroducing the underwater plant in one lake. The characteristic of interest is the health of the fish population. The control group consists of the fish in the lake without the plant. The treatment group consists of the fish in the lake with the plant.

12. A research team wants to know whether a new formula for a laundry detergent is more effective than the existing formula. The team members first wash a variety of fabrics with a variety of stains using the detergent with the new formula, and then they wash the same pairings of fabrics and stains using the detergent with the existing formula. They then compare the extent to which the stains have been eliminated.

The treatment is washing the fabrics using the detergent with the new formula. The characteristic of interest is the extent to which stains are eliminated. The control group consists of the fabrics with stains that are washed using the detergent with the existing formula. The treatment group consists of the fabrics with stains that are washed using the detergent with the new formula.

Evaluate each article by answering the following questions.

- Is this a survey, an observational study, or an experiment? How do you know?
- Was randomization used in the research? If so, how?
- What details of the research does the article include? Is any important information missing?

13.

Doctors Work When Sick

Doctors know that they can get sick from their patients, but when they are sick themselves, do they stay away from their patients? Researchers asked 537 doctors-in-training to anonymously report whether they had worked while sick during the past year. The researchers found that 58% said they had worked once while sick and 31% said they had worked more than once while sick.

This study is a survey because the only variable is doctors who work while sick. The report does not say whether random sampling was used but only doctors-in-training were surveyed. The report includes the sample size and sample proportions but does not include the margins of error.

14.

Antibiotic Use Tied to Asthma and Allergies

Antibiotic use in infants is linked to asthma and allergies, according to a study involving 1401 children. Researchers asked mothers how many doses of antibiotics their children received before 6 months of age as well as whether their children had developed asthma or allergies by age 6. Children who received just one dose of antibiotics were 40% more likely to develop asthma or allergies. The risk jumped to 70% for children who received two doses.

This is an observational study because two variables, antibiotic use and occurrence of asthma and allergies, are compared but no treatment is imposed. The report does not say whether subjects were chosen at random. The report gives the sample size and the increased risks of developing asthma or allergies.

INTEGRATE MATHEMATICAL PRACTICES

Focus on Communication

MP.3 Have students consider an online advertisement that asks you to participate in a survey. The survey asks how much time you spend online each week. Ask students to consider the bias in this method and suggest a method more likely to produce a random sample.

JOURNAL

Have students compare and contrast surveys, observational studies, and experiments. For each type of research, have them describe how the data are gathered, and what conclusions can be determined from the results.

15. Which of the following research topics are best addressed through an observational study? Select all that apply.

    A. Does listening to loud music with headphones affect a person's hearing?

    B. Does second-hand smoke affect the health of pets?

    C. Does a particular medication make seasonal allergy symptoms less severe?

    D. Does increasing the number of stoplights per mile on a road decrease the number of car accidents on the road?

    E. Does drinking sports drinks before and while playing a game of baseball increase the number of runs scored?

    F. Does a certain toothpaste prevent cavities in children better than another toothpaste?

    A, B, D

H.O.T. Focus on Higher Order Thinking

16. **Draw Conclusions** Randomly assigning subjects to the control group or the treatment group for an experiment means that if a difference between the two groups is observed at the conclusion of the experiment, then the difference must be due either to chance or to the treatment. How do you think a researcher can conclude that the difference is due to the treatment?

    The researcher must show that the difference is so unusual that it is highly unlikely to have occurred by chance.

17. **Critique Reasoning** Consider the following experiment: Mr. Jones wants to know what the condition of his deck would be if he did not continue to reapply wood sealant to it every spring to protect it. This spring, he uses the sealant on the entire deck except for several adjacent boards. He then observes how exposure to the weather affects those boards in relation to the rest of the deck.

    Lindsay claims that the part of the deck to which the sealant is applied constitutes the treatment group because that is the part that is actually "treated." Is she correct? Explain.

    Lindsay is incorrect because Mr. Jones is determining the effect of the board's exposure to the weather, which is the treatment. The part of the deck with the sealant is the control group because it is not exposed to the weather, and Mr. Jones has applied the sealant every spring.

18. **Persevere in Problem Solving** Give an example of a question that could be better answered by gathering data in an observational study than it could by gathering data in an experiment. Explain why an observational study would be more appropriate. Then describe an observational study that would answer the question.

    Answers will vary. Possible answer: "Does the length of people's commutes affect their health?" is a question that could be better answered by doing an observational study because it is impractical to manipulate people's commutes for an experiment. The study could involve asking a random sample of people how much time they spend each workday commuting to and from work as well as questions about their physical, emotional, and mental health.

Lesson Performance Task

Using an online search engine, look for a research-based article that interests you about teen health, teen fitness, or teen nutrition using the search terms "teen health articles," "teen fitness articles," or "teen nutrition articles." Print the article to give to your teacher, and include your analysis of the research on which the article is based. Your analysis should address the following points:

- On what type of research study is the article based? How do you know?
- Was randomization used in conducting the research? If so, how?
- What details about the research does the article include? Are there any details that appear to be missing?
- What is your overall evaluation of the research? How much importance do you place on the conclusions drawn from the research? Explain.

Answers will vary. You may wish to evaluate students' work by using a rubric based on the four points that the task asks students to address.

EXTENSION ACTIVITY

Have students write a proposal to prove or disprove a theory they have about teen nutrition. Have them explain why they would base their conclusions on an observational study or an experimental study. They should provide as much information as is needed to set up and proceed with the study. If the proposal seems reasonable and student interest is high, encourage the student to proceed with the study. Invite other classmates to assist the student, if needed.

QUESTIONING STRATEGIES

How can you tell whether research is based on an observational study or on an experiment? **An experiment imposes a change and then observes the response. An observational study observes how the population responds to existing changes.**

What are some of the indications that a report is not valid? **Possible answer: Pertinent information might be missing; randomization was not used; there was no control group; or, the control group and test group are not enough alike.**

INTEGRATE MATHEMATICAL PRACTICES

Focus on Technology

MP.5 Have students use the Internet to find related studies that support or disprove the conclusions made in the article they found. Have them compare the studies to see which has the stronger argument.

Scoring Rubric

2 points: Student correctly solves the problem and explains his/her reasoning.

1 point: Student shows good understanding of the problem but does not fully solve or explain his/her reasoning.

0 points: Student does not demonstrate understanding of the problem.

LESSON 24.3

Determining the Significance of Experimental Results

Common Core Math Standards

The student is expected to:

 **S-IC.B.5**

Use data from a randomized experiment to compare two treatments; use simulations to decide if differences between parameters are significant.

Mathematical Practices

 **MP.3 Logic**

Language Objective

Explain how to determine when an observed difference between the control and treatment groups is likely to be caused by the treatment.

ENGAGE

Essential Question: In an experiment, when is an observed difference between the control group and treatment group likely to be caused by the treatment?

In an experiment, the null hypothesis states that any observed difference between the control and the treatment groups is due to chance. However, if the probability of randomly getting such a difference (or a more extreme difference) is very low, then the null hypothesis can be rejected, and the standard practice is to attribute the cause of the difference to the treatment. You can use a permutation test to determine whether a difference between means for the control and the treatment groups is statistically significant.

PREVIEW: LESSON PERFORMANCE TASK

View the Engage section online. Discuss the photo and how a test might be conducted to see if using a cell phone while driving decreases reaction time more than listening to music. Then preview the Lesson Performance Task.

Name ________________ Class ________________ Date ________________

24.3 Determining the Significance of Experimental Results

Essential Question: In an experiment, when is an observed difference between the control group and treatment group likely to be caused by the treatment?

Resource Locker

Explore 1 Formulating the Null Hypothesis

You can think of every randomized comparative experiment as a test of a *null hypothesis*. The **null hypothesis** states that any difference between the control group and the treatment group is due to chance. In other words, the null hypothesis is the assumption that the treatment has no effect.

An unusual experimental result may be *statistically significant*. The determination of **statistical significance** is based on the probability of randomly getting a result that is the same as, or more extreme than, the result obtained from the experiment under the assumption that the null hypothesis is true. A low probability of getting the result, or a more extreme result, by chance is evidence in favor of rejecting the null hypothesis.

A statistically significant result does not prove that the treatment has an effect; the null hypothesis may still be true, and a rare event may simply have occurred. Nevertheless, standard practice in statistics is to reject the null hypothesis in favor of the *alternative hypothesis* that the result is, in fact, due to the treatment.

(A) Suppose 10 people with colds are treated with a new formula for an existing brand of cold medicine, and 10 other people with colds are treated with the original formula. The mean recovery times for the two groups are compared.

The null hypothesis is that the mean recovery times for the two groups will be [very different/about the same].

(B) Suppose that the mean recovery time for both groups is 5 days. Does the result of the experiment appear to be statistically significant? Explain your reasoning.

No, the result does not appear to be statistically significant because there is no difference between the control group and the treatment group.

(C) Suppose a potential growth agent is sprayed on the leaves of 12 emerging ferns twice a week for a month. Another 12 emerging ferns are not sprayed with the growth agent. The mean stalk lengths of the two groups of ferns are compared after a month.

State the null hypothesis.

The null hypothesis is that the mean stalk lengths of the two groups of ferns will be about the same.

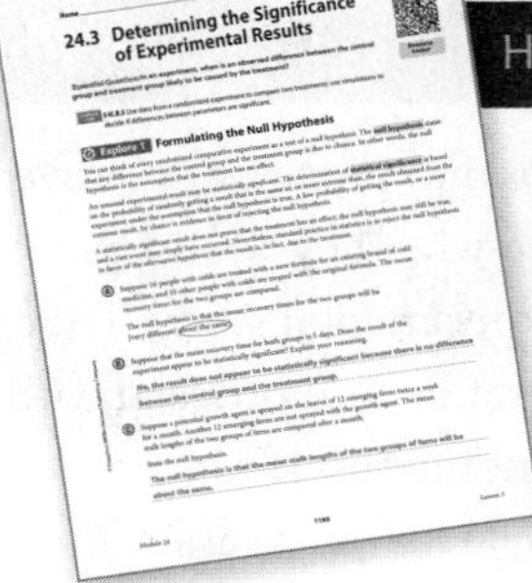

HARDCOVER PAGES 1193–12

Watch for the hardcover student edition page numbers for this lesson.

(D) Suppose that the treated ferns had a mean stalk length that is twice the mean stalk length of the untreated ferns. Does the result of the experiment appear to be statistically significant? Explain your reasoning.

Yes, the result appears to be statistically significant because the difference between the control group and the treatment group is so dramatic.

Reflect

1. **Discussion** In the U.S. legal system, a defendant is assumed innocent until guilt is proved beyond a reasonable doubt. How is what happens with a null hypothesis like what happens with a defendant?
A null hypothesis (like innocence) is assumed to be true unless the experimental evidence (like evidence of guilt) is so substantial that it allows you to reject the null hypothesis (innocence).

2. Does the experimental result in Step B prove that the new formula is no more effective than the original formula? Explain.
No, the result does not prove that the new formula is no more effective than the old; it just does not provide evidence that the new formula is more effective than the old.

3. Does the experimental result in Step D prove that the growth agent works? Explain.
No, the result does not prove that the growth agent works; it only provides evidence that rejecting the assumption that the growth agent has no effect is reasonable.

Explore 2 Simulating a Resampling Distribution

Suppose a company that offers a college entrance exam prep course wants to demonstrate that its course raises test scores. The company recruits 20 students and randomly assigns half of them to a treatment group, where subjects take the course before taking the college entrance exam, and half to a control group, where subjects do not take the course before taking the exam. The table shows the exam scores of the 10 students in each group. How can you tell whether the course actually improved the scores of the students in the treatment group?

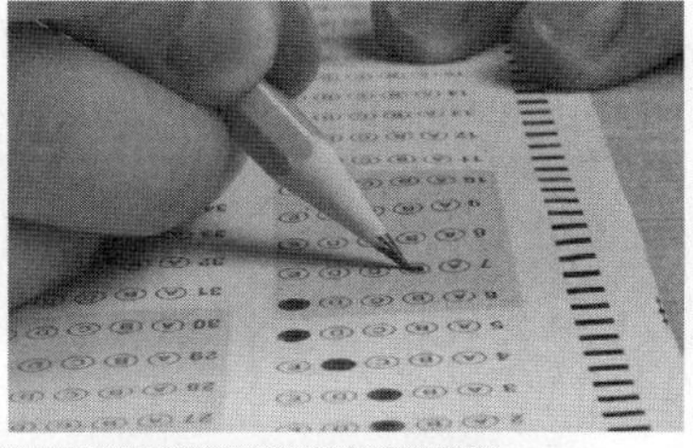

	College Entrance Exam Scores				
Treatment group	1440	1610	1430	1700	1690
	1570	1480	1620	1780	2010
Control group	1150	1500	1050	1600	1460
	1860	1350	1750	1680	1330

One thing you could do is compute the mean exam score for each group to see if the means are different. Obviously, the company expects the treatment group's mean to be greater than the control group's mean. But even if that is the case, how do you know that the difference in the means can be attributed to the treatment and not to chance? In other words, how do you know if the difference is statistically significant?

EXPLORE 1

Formulating the Null Hypothesis

INTEGRATE TECHNOLOGY

Students have the option of completing the null hypothesis activity either in the book or online.

QUESTIONING STRATEGIES

? Why does a result have to be rare (that is, have a very low probability of occurrence) for the null hypothesis to be rejected? Why couldn't any result that shows a difference between the treatment and control groups be evidence that the treatment has an effect? **There is always going to be some variation within a group and therefore some difference between two groups regardless of whether a treatment has an effect. This is why the null hypothesis says that any difference between the groups is simply due to chance. Only when a difference between the treatment and control groups is rare should the null hypothesis be called into question and the treatment deemed to have an effect.**

AVOID COMMON ERRORS

Some students may be confused about why, when a null hypothesis is rejected, it is reasonable to accept the alternative hypothesis that the result is due to the *treatment*. Point out that the reason that other factors can be ruled out is that the experiment was randomized. That is, subjects were randomly assigned to the treatment and control groups, thereby distributing the effects of other factors between them. The only factor that makes the two groups different is the treatment.

PROFESSIONAL DEVELOPMENT

Math Background

In this lesson, students either accept or reject a null hypothesis for a randomized comparative experiment. Working under the assumption that the null hypothesis is true, students use the data from an experiment to generate a resampling distribution, which is approximately normal. If the experimental result falls somewhere in the middle 90% (or 95% or even 99%) of the resampling distribution, there is no reason to reject the null hypothesis, so the result is not statistically significant. But if the result falls outside the middle, the null hypothesis is rejected and the result is called statistically significant.

EXPLORE 2

Simulating a Resampling Distribution

QUESTIONING STRATEGIES

Is it possible to have a simulation in which the mean score difference between two groups is greater than the mean score difference between the control and treatment groups? Explain. **Yes; for example, if the calculator's random integer generator happens to assign the ten highest scores to one group and the ten lowest scores to the other group, then the difference between the mean scores for the two groups will be greater than the difference between the mean scores for the control and treatment groups.**

Are three simulations enough to tell you anything about the significance of the difference in mean scores between the control group and the treatment group? **Answers will vary depending on the outcomes of the simulations. Students will generally find that the absolute value of the difference between the mean scores for the two groups is much less than the difference between the control and the treatment groups. However, three simulations are not enough to get an accurate sense of the resampling distribution.**

LANGUAGE SUPPORT EL

This is a heavily nuanced lesson, and sometimes these nuances in English are difficult for English learners to grasp. Make sure students understand why *P*-values are calculated, and why causation and correlation are not automatically assumed when there is a change for the treatment group.

The null hypothesis for this experiment is that the college entrance exam prep course has no effect on a student's score. Under this assumption, it doesn't matter whether a student is in the treatment group or the control group. Since each group is a sample of the students, the means of the two samples should be about equal. In fact, any random division of the 20 students into two groups of 10 should result in two means whose difference is relatively small and a matter of chance. This technique of scrambling the data, called *resampling*, allows you to create a *resampling distribution* of the differences of means for every possible pairing of groups with 10 students in each. You can test the null hypothesis by using the resampling distribution to find the likelihood, given that the null hypothesis is true, of getting a difference of means at least as great as the actual experimental difference. The test is called a **permutation test**, also known as a *randomization test.*

Use the table of exam scores to construct a resampling distribution for the difference of means, assuming that the null hypothesis is true. Then determine the significance of the actual experimental result.

(A) State the null hypothesis in terms of the difference of the two group means.

The difference of the two group means is about 0.

(B) Calculate the mean score for the treatment group, $\overline{x}_T$, and the mean score for the control group, $\overline{x}_C$. Then find the difference of the means.

$\overline{x}_T = 1633$; $\overline{x}_C = 1473$; $\overline{x}_T - \overline{x}_C = 160$

(C) Label the data in the table with the identifiers 1 through 20. Then follow these steps to complete each of the following tables.

- Use a graphing calculator's random integer generator to generate a list of 10 identifiers between 1 and 20 with no identifiers repeated.
- Record the scores that correspond to those identifiers as the scores for Group A. Record the remaining 10 scores as the scores for Group B.
- Find $\overline{x}_A$, $\overline{x}_B$, and $\overline{x}_A - \overline{x}_B$, and record them in the table.

Answers will vary. Possible answers appear in each table.

	Resampling 1					Means	Difference of means
Group A	1750	1460	1330	1480	1570	$\overline{x}_A = 1536$	$\overline{x}_A - \overline{x}_B = -34$
	1610	1700	1350	1430	1680		
Group B	1440	1690	1620	1780	2010	$\overline{x}_B = 1570$	
	1150	1500	1050	1600	1860		

COLLABORATIVE LEARNING

Small Group Activity

Have students discuss how to use graphing calculators to generate random numbers that can be used for simulating a sampling distribution as well as calculating the sample mean. Then have each student run another experiment using a different sample mean and discuss with the group the results in terms of how that mean affects whether the null hypothesis will be accepted or rejected.

	Resampling 2					Means	Difference of means
Group A	1570	1680	1150	1350	1610	$\bar{x}_A = 1559$	$\bar{x}_A - \bar{x}_B = 12$
	1750	1440	2010	1330	1700		
Group B	1430	1690	1480	1620	1780	$\bar{x}_B = 1547$	
	1500	1050	1600	1460	1860		

	Resampling 3					Means	Difference of means
Group A	1600	1860	1460	1330	1350	$\bar{x}_A = 1551$	$\bar{x}_A - \bar{x}_B = -4$
	1610	1780	1750	1150	1620		
Group B	1440	1430	1700	1690	1570	$\bar{x}_B = 1555$	
	1480	2010	1500	1050	1680		

Ⓓ Report the differences of means that you found for simulations 1–3 to your teacher so that your teacher can create a frequency table and histogram of the class results. You should make your own copy of the frequency table and histogram using the table and grid shown.

Answers will vary. Possible answers:

Interval	Frequency
$-320 \le x < -240$	1
$-240 \le x < -160$	7
$-160 \le x < -80$	19
$-80 \le x < 0$	26
$0 \le x < 80$	23
$80 \le x < 160$	11
$160 \le x < 240$	2
$240 \le x < 320$	1

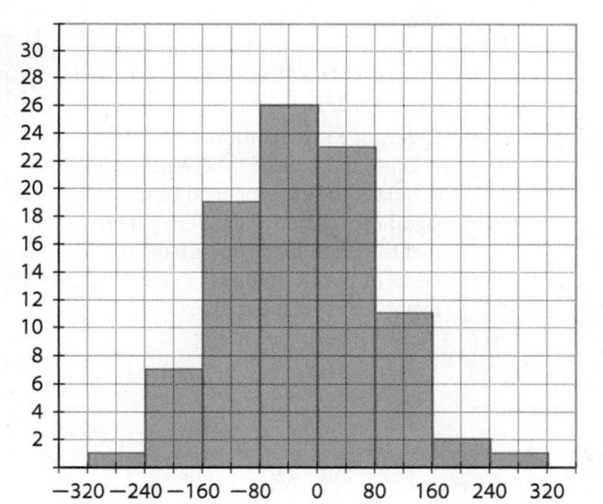

DIFFERENTIATE INSTRUCTION

Auditory Cues

Help students understand the permutation test by having them restate how to find the number of permutations of n distinct objects, or $n! = n(n-1)(n-2)...1$. Then explain that, since the labels used for the treatment group and the control group are not distinct, the formula for the number of resamples becomes $\frac{n}{n_1! \cdot n_2! \ldots n_L!}$, where L is the total number of labels used. Ask students to tell in their own words whether they have generated all possible resamples, and then verbalize when the permutation test gives statistically significant results. Stating how to use the permutation test in their own words may help students focus on the values they must find to apply the test.

EXPLAIN 1

Performing a Permutation Test

QUESTIONING STRATEGIES

A critic might claim that there could be other reasons for the observed difference in the mean scores of the treatment and control groups in any given experiment and the conclusion drawn from a permutation test. Do you agree or disagree? Explain. **Disagree: An external factor in the experiment should have been randomly distributed between the two groups, so its influence on the results should be inconsequential. What distinguishes the treatment group from the control group is the treatment itself.**

AVOID COMMON ERRORS

When students use a frequency table or histogram in a permutation test to find the probability that a difference of means is at least as great as the difference they recorded for the control and treatment groups in the experiment, they may include only the frequencies for the interval in which the difference occurs. Remind students that they must find the sum of frequencies for all the intervals including and above the difference.

Reflect

4. **Discussion** Would you say that the resampling distribution provides sufficient evidence to reject the null hypothesis? Explain your reasoning.
Answers may vary. Possible answer: There are very few results in the resampling distribution that are greater than or equal to 160, so the probability of getting such results is low, and I would reject the null hypothesis.

Explain 1 Performing a Permutation Test

Once you use the resampling distribution to calculate the probability, called the *P–value*, of randomly getting a result that is the same as, or more extreme than, the result obtained from the experiment under the assumption that the null hypothesis is true, you can determine the significance of the result. Statisticians commonly use the following levels of significance:

- When $P > 0.10$, the result is *not significant*. The null hypothesis is not rejected.
- When $0.10 \leq P < 0.05$, the result is *marginally significant*. You can reject the null hypothesis at the 10% significance level.
- When $0.05 \leq P < 0.01$, the result is *significant*. You can reject the null hypothesis at the 5% significance level.
- When $P \leq 0.01$, the result is *highly significant*. You can reject the null hypothesis at the 1% significance level.

Example 1 **Determine the experimental result's significance and state a conclusion.**

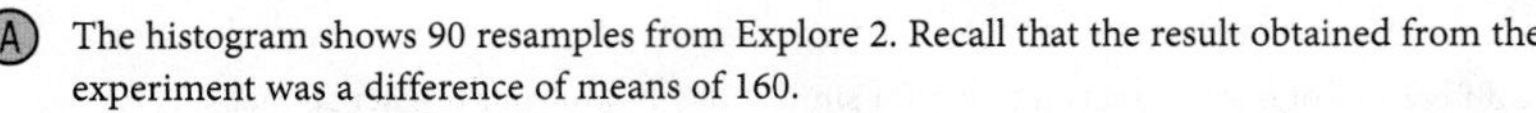

(A) The histogram shows 90 resamples from Explore 2. Recall that the result obtained from the experiment was a difference of means of 160.

Step 1 Calculate the *P*-value.
Divide the sum of the frequencies for the intervals $160 \leq x < 240$ and $240 \leq x < 320$ by the sum of all frequencies (the total number of resamples). So, $P(x \geq 160) = \frac{2+1}{90} \approx 0.03$.

Step 2 Determine the significance.
Because the *P*-value is between 0.05 and 0.01, the experimental result is significant. Reject the null hypothesis that the exam prep course has no effect in favor of the alternative hypothesis that the course has a positive effect.

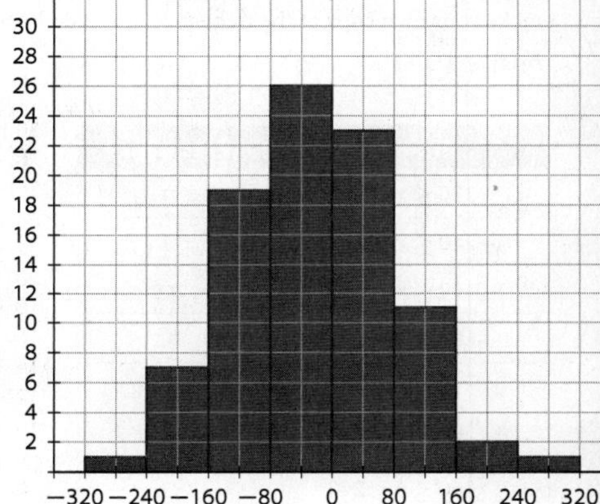

LANGUAGE SUPPORT EL

Communicate Math

Have students work in pairs. Have each student explain to the other how to determine when an observed difference between the control group and treatment group is likely to be caused by the treatment. They should use terms such as *null hypothesis* and *alternative hypothesis*. Have the students collaborate to write out their steps in a flow chart or graphic organizer.

Ⓑ A textbook company has created an electronic version of one of its books and wants to know what effect, if any, using the e-book has on student learning. A teacher who has two classes that already use the textbook agrees, with the permission of the school district, to participate in a research study. One of the classes uses the e-book for the next unit of instruction while the other class continues to use the print version of the book. After teaching the unit, the teacher gives the same test to both classes. The mean score for the class using the e-book is 82.3, while the mean score for the class using the print book is 78.2.

The resampling distribution for the difference of mean test scores, given that the null hypothesis is true, is normal with a mean of 0 and a standard error of 2. The distribution is shown.

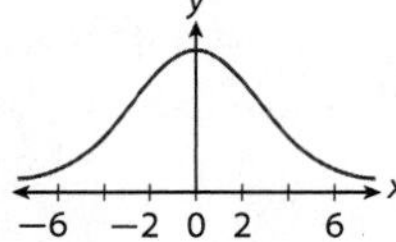

Step 1 State the null hypothesis in terms of the difference of the mean test scores.

The difference of the mean test scores using the e-book and the print book is about 0.

Step 2 Identify the treatment group and its mean test score, $\bar{x}_T$, as well as the control group and its mean test score, $\bar{x}_C$. Then find $\bar{x}_T - \bar{x}_C$.

Treatment group: **class using e-book**

$\bar{x}_C =$ **82.3**

Control group: **class using print book**

$\bar{x}_C =$ **78.2**

$\bar{x}_T - \bar{x}_C =$ **4.1**

Step 3 Use the resampling distribution to determine the significance of the experimental result.

The interval $-2(\,\mathbf{2}\,) \le x \le 2(\,\mathbf{2}\,)$, or $\mathbf{-4} \le x \le \mathbf{4}$, captures the middle 95% of the differences of the means in the resampling distribution.

The experimental result is [significant/not significant] because it falls [inside/outside] the interval. [Reject/Don't reject] the null hypothesis that the e-book had no effect on student learning. [Accept/Don't accept] the alternative hypothesis that the e-book had an effect on student learning.

(Circled: significant, outside, Reject, Accept)

Reflect

5. Which part of this example, Part A or Part B, involves a *one-tailed* test and which part involves a *two-tailed* test? Explain your reasoning.

Part A involves a one-tailed test because the alternative hypothesis is that the treatment improved exam scores. The *P*-value is calculated using only one tail of the resampling distribution. Part B involves a two-tailed test because the alternative hypothesis is that the treatment has an effect (without specifying the direction of the effect). A result that falls in either tail (outside the middle 95%) is significant.

ELABORATE

INTEGRATE MATHEMATICAL PRACTICES

Focus on Math Connections

MP.1 Make sure that students are comfortable with identifying the null hypothesis. Have them highlight the key words in the problem statement that lead them to formulate a null hypothesis, and then ask them to state the conditions that will cause them to reject or accept the null hypothesis.

CONNECT VOCABULARY EL

Help students to understand how the expression *statistically significant* is used to interpret the P-*value,* the probability that a difference of means is *at least as great* as the difference recorded in a frequency table or histogram. Point out the algebraic interpretation of the *P*-value and how the algebraic categories are used to tell whether experimental results are statistically significant.

SUMMARIZE THE LESSON

Have students make a graphic organizer outlining the steps for formulating a null hypothesis and using a permutation test to determine whether experimental results are statistically significant.

Your Turn

Determine the experimental result's significance and state a conclusion.

6. In another experiment for the same company that offers the college entrance exam prep course, $\bar{x}_T = 1632$, $\bar{x}_C = 1370$, and the resampling distribution is normal with a mean of 0 and a standard error of 83.

$\bar{x}_T - \bar{x}_C = 262$

Since 3 standard errors above the mean is $3(83) = 249$, the experimental result falls in the part of the tail of the resampling distribution that is more than 3 standard errors above the mean. This means that the *P*-value for the experimental result is less than 0.15%, or 0.0015, according to the 68-95-99.7 rule for normal distributions, so the result is highly significant. Reject the null hypothesis that the exam prep course has no effect in favor of the alternative hypothesis that the course has a positive effect.

7. Suppose a teacher at a different school agrees to participate in the same research study using the e-book. For this school, the mean score for the class using the e-book is 81.7, while the mean score for the class using the print book is 77.9. The resampling distribution for this school is the same as the resampling distribution for the first school.

$\bar{x}_T - \bar{x}_C = 3.8$

The experimental result is not significant because it falls inside the interval that captures the middle 95% of the differences of the means in the resampling distribution. The null hypothesis cannot be rejected. In this case, the conclusion is that the e-book had no effect on student learning.

Elaborate

8. Describe how to obtain a resampling distribution given the data from an experiment.

A resampling distribution is based on the assumption that the null hypothesis is true. The data from an experiment are randomly reassigned to the treatment and control groups, the mean for each group is calculated, and then the difference of the two means is calculated and included in the resampling distribution.

9. Describe how to perform a permutation test using a resampling distribution.

Use the resampling distribution to determine the probability of getting a result the same as, or more extreme than, the result obtained from the experiment. If the probability is 10% or less, reject the null hypothesis in favor of the alternative hypothesis.

10. Essential Question Check-In To what does the null hypothesis attribute any difference between the control group and the treatment group? To what does the alternative hypothesis attribute a difference?

The null hypothesis says that any difference between the control group and the treatment group is due to chance. The alternative hypothesis attributes any difference to the treatment.

Evaluate: Homework and Practice

- Online Homework
- Hints and Help
- Extra Practice

1. A research dietitian is investigating whether the consumption of fish improves the strength of bones in older adults. Two hundred older adults are recruited for an experiment in which half are asked to eat fish at least three times per week while the other half maintains their regular diet. The dietitian measures the bone density of the subjects at the beginning and end of the experiment and calculates the mean change in bone density for the two groups.

   a. State the null hypothesis for this experiment.

   The null hypothesis is that the mean change in bone density for the two groups will be about the same.

   b. If the dietitian finds that the difference of the mean changes in bone density for the two groups is not statistically significant, how does the dietitian interpret the results of the experiment?

   The null hypothesis cannot be rejected, so the dietitian must conclude that the consumption of fish does not improve the strength of bones in older adults.

2. An agricultural researcher investigates a new fertilizer by planting a field of corn using the new fertilizer and another field using standard fertilizer. At the end of the growing season, the researcher measures the corn yield from each plant in each field and then calculates the mean corn yields for both fields.

   a. State the null hypothesis for this experiment.

   The null hypothesis is that the mean corn yields for the two fields are about the same.

   b. If the researcher finds that the mean corn yield for the field with the new fertilizer is greater than the mean corn yield for the field with standard fertilizer and that the difference of the mean yields is statistically significant, how does the researcher interpret the results of the experiment?

   The null hypothesis can be rejected, so the researcher can conclude that the new fertilizer improves corn yield.

In Exercises 3 and 4, follow these steps for creating a resampling distribution using a combination of a spreadsheet and a graphing calculator. (The steps assume 10 data values for the control group and 10 for the treatment group. You will need to make adjustments for different numbers of data values.)

Step 1 Enter the original data from the experiment in column A of a spreadsheet. List all the treatment group's data first, followed by all the control group's data. Then calculate the difference of the means by entering = **AVERAGE(A1:A10)** − **AVERAGE(A11:A20)**in cell A21.

Step 2 In cell B1, enter = **RAND()** and fill down to cell B20.

Exercise	Depth of Knowledge (D.O.K.)	COMMON CORE Mathematical Practices
1–4	**1** Recall of Information	**MP.3** Logic
5	**2** Skills/Concepts	**MP.6** Precision
6	**2** Skills/Concepts	**MP.5** Using Tools
7	**2** Skills/Concepts	**MP.6** Precision
8	**2** Skills/Concepts H.O.T.	**MP.3** Logic
9–10	**3** Strategic Thinking H.O.T.	**MP.3** Logic

EVALUATE

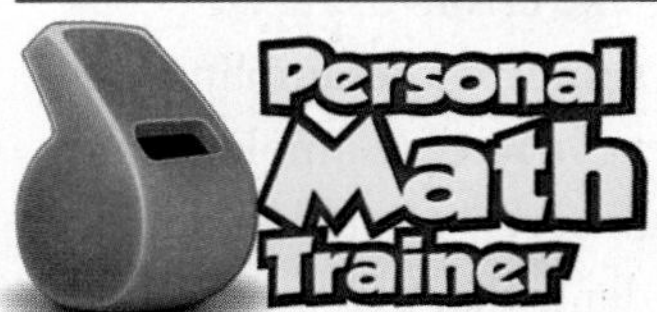

ASSIGNMENT GUIDE

Concepts and Skills	Practice
Explore 1 Formulating the Null Hypothesis	Exercises 1–4
Explore 2 Simulating a Resampling Distribution	Exercises 5–6
Example 1 Performing a Permutation Test	Exercise 7

INTEGRATE MATHEMATICAL PRACTICES

Focus on Modeling

MP.4 Remind students to use a histogram to show a resampling distribution along with the actual difference of means from the experiment to calculate the *P*-value and determine the result's significance level.

AVOID COMMON ERRORS

Watch for students who make errors using a spreadsheet to help them simulate a resampling distribution. As with other forms of technology, the spreadsheet will yield results even when the inputs are incorrect. Remind students that they need to understand well the processes of performing a simulation and doing a permutation test before using the technology. This will help them spot results that are not compatible with the data.

Step 3 Select the rows containing the data and choose **Sort...** from the **Data** drop-down menu. In the dialog box, indicate that you want the data sorted on **Column B.**

Step 4 Clicking OK in the dialog box puts the random numbers in numerical order and rearranges the data from the experiment at the same time. The first 10 data values become the new treatment group, and the last 10 become the new control group. Notice that the difference of the means in cell A21 is also recalculated.

Step 5 Enter the difference of the means in List 1 of a graphing calculator. Then return to the spreadsheet, highlight cell B1, and fill down to the last data value. Doing so creates a new list of random numbers in column B.

Step 6 Repeat Steps 3–5 as many times as desired. Then use the graphing calculator to obtain a histogram of the simulated resampling distribution and use trace to obtain the frequencies of the bars in the histogram in order to perform a permutation test.

3. A psychology researcher is testing whether it's possible to reduce test anxiety and improve test performance by having people write about their thoughts and feelings before taking a test. The researcher recruits 20 people, randomly assigning half to the control group, who sit quietly for 15 minutes before taking a test of general knowledge, and the other half to the treatment group, who write about their thoughts and feelings for 15 minutes before taking the same test. The table lists the scores on the test.

Control group	88	72	75	63	81	77	68	78	82	66
Treatment group	89	82	74	83	78	76	71	80	88	69

a. State the null hypothesis for the experiment.

The null hypothesis is that the mean score on the test is the about the same for the two groups.

b. Calculate the mean score for the treatment group, $\bar{x}_T$, and the mean score for the control group, $\bar{x}_C$. Then find the difference of the means.

$\bar{x}_T = 79; \bar{x}_C = 75; \bar{x}_T - \bar{x}_C = 4$

c. Use a spreadsheet and a calculator to obtain at least 50 resamples of the data.

Interval	Frequency
$-8 \leq x < -4$	5
$-4 \leq x < 0$	18
$0 \leq x < 4$	21
$4 \leq x < 8$	5

Answers will vary. Possible answers (based on 50 resamples) are given in the table.

d. Calculate the *P*-value.

Answers will vary. Possible answer: $P(x \geq 4) = \frac{5}{50} = 0.10$

e. Determine the experimental result's significance and state a conclusion.

Answers may vary. Possible answer: Because the *P*-value equals 0.10, the result is marginally significant. The null hypothesis can be rejected. So, writing about thoughts and feelings for 15 minutes before taking a test improves test performance.

4. A medical researcher is testing a new gel coating for a pill and wants to know if it improves absorption into the bloodstream. The 12 subjects in the control group are asked to take the pill with the original coating, and the 12 subjects in the treatment group are asked to take the pill with the new coating. Blood samples are drawn from each subject 1 hour after ingesting a pill. The measured drug levels, in micrograms per milliliter, are listed in the table.

Control group	34	26	33	27	36	29	39	33	25	34	37	31
Treatment group	35	36	37	35	29	31	33	40	37	36	20	39

a. State the null hypothesis for the experiment.

The null hypothesis is that the mean level of the drug in the blood is about the same for the two groups.

b. Calculate the mean drug level for the treatment group, $\overline{x}_T$, and the mean drug level for the control group, $\overline{x}_C$. Then find the difference of the means.

$\overline{x}_T = 34; \overline{x}_C = 32; \overline{x}_T - \overline{x}_C = 2$

c. Use a spreadsheet and a calculator to obtain at least 50 resamples of the data.

Answers will vary. Possible answers (based on 50 resamples):

Interval	Frequency
$-6 \leq x < -4$	0
$-4 \leq x < -2$	7
$-2 \leq x < 0$	15
$0 \leq x < 2$	19
$2 \leq x < 4$	7
$4 \leq x < 6$	2

d. Calculate the *P*-value.

Answers will vary. Possible answer: $P(x \geq 2) = \frac{7+2}{50} = 0.18$

e. Determine the experimental result's significance and state a conclusion.

Answers may vary. Possible answer: Because the *P*-value is greater than 0.10, the result is not significant. The null hypothesis cannot be rejected. So, the new pill had no effect on absorption.

COOPERATIVE LEARNING

Have students work in small groups to make a poster showing how to identify the null hypothesis for an experiment and then perform a simulation of the experiment using a test group and a control group. Give each group a different data experiment to simulate and have them perform the simulation to find and interpret the *P*-value of the results. Then have each group present its poster to the rest of the class, and ask for a volunteer from the group to explain the poster.

5. A research gerontologist is interested in finding ways to help seniors who suffer from insomnia. She conducts an experiment in which 50 elderly volunteers are randomly assigned to two groups, one that receives informational brochures about insomnia and one that receives two in-person therapy sessions and two follow-up phone calls on how to overcome insomnia. Both groups are monitored for the amount of sleep they get each night. After 1 month, the mean change in the amount of sleep that each group gets is calculated and found to be 0.2 hour for the group that gets brochures and 1.4 hours for the group that gets therapy sessions and phone calls.

a. State the null hypothesis for the experiment.

The null hypothesis is that the mean change in the amount of sleep that each group gets is about the same.

b. Identify the treatment group and its mean test score, $\overline{x}_T$, as well as the control group and its mean test score, $\overline{x}_C$. Then find $\overline{x}_T - \overline{x}_C$.

Treatment group: those who receive therapy sessions and follow-up phone calls; $\overline{x}_T = 1.4$

Control group: those who receive informational brochures; $\overline{x}_C = 0.2$

$\overline{x}_T - \overline{x}_C = 1.2$

c. The resampling distribution for the difference of the mean change in the amount of sleep, given that the null hypothesis is true, is normal with a mean of 0 and a standard error of 0.5. What interval captures 95% of the differences of the means in the resampling distribution?

$2(-0.5) \leq x \leq 2(0.5)$, or $-1 \leq x \leq 1$

d. Determine the experimental result's significance and state a conclusion.

The experimental result is significant because it falls outside the interval $-1 \leq x \leq 1$. Reject the null hypothesis that the therapy sessions and phone calls had no effect on the amount of sleep in favor of the alternative hypothesis that the therapy sessions and phone calls improved sleep.

6. A public health researcher is interested in knowing whether the calories that teenagers consume at fast food restaurants is affected by listing calorie counts on restaurant menu boards. He recruits 50 teenagers each from two localities, one where fast food restaurants are not required to post calorie counts and one where they are. The teenagers are asked to keep the receipt each time they eat at a fast food restaurant so that the researcher can determine the calorie count for the meal. The researcher finds that the mean calorie count for the teenagers living where restaurants do not post calorie counts is 554, while the mean calorie count for the teenagers living where restaurants do post calorie counts is 486.

a. State the null hypothesis for the experiment.

The null hypothesis is that the mean calorie count for each group is about the same.

b. Identify the treatment group and its mean test score, $\bar{x}_T$, as well as the control group and its mean test score, $\bar{x}_C$. Then find $\bar{x}_T - \bar{x}_C$.

Treatment group: those who eat at fast food restaurants where calorie counts are posted; $\bar{x}_T = 486$

Control group: those who eat at fast food restaurants where calorie counts are not posted; $\bar{x}_C = 554$

$\bar{x}_T - \bar{x}_C = -68$

c. The resampling distribution for the difference of the mean calorie counts, given that the null hypothesis is true, is normal with a mean of 0 and a standard error of 40. What interval captures 95% of the differences of means in the resampling distribution?

$-2(40) \leq x \leq 2(40)$, or $-80 \leq x \leq 80$

d. Determine the experimental result's significance and state a conclusion.

The experimental result is not significant because it falls inside the interval. The null hypothesis cannot be rejected. So, the posting of calorie counts on restaurant menu boards has no effect on the calories that teenagers consume at fast food restaurants.

WHOLE CLASS DISCUSSION

Lead a class discussion about the relationship between a *P*-value and a result that is or is not statistically significant. Ask students to use the *P*-value to characterize the significance of experimental results they have found.

7. A research botanist is investigating the health of plants that have been genetically engineered to be more disease resistant. The botanist measures the nitrogen levels in two groups of plants, ones that have been genetically engineered and ones that have not. Using the data from the experiment, the botanist creates the resampling distribution shown. The random variable X represents the difference of the mean nitrogen level for the genetically engineered plants and the mean nitrogen level for the standard plants. Use the resampling distribution to classify the significance of each value of X.

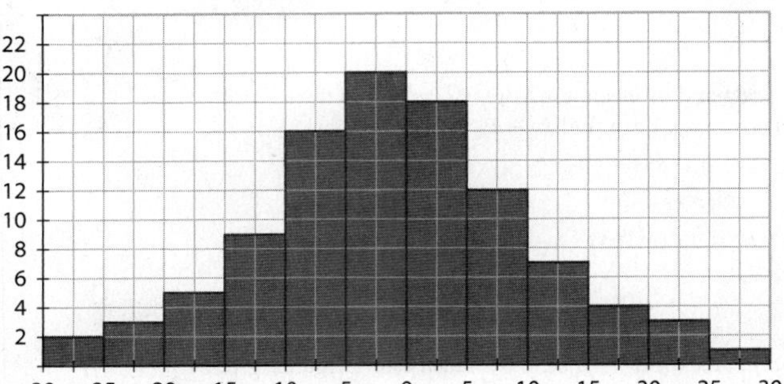

A. $X = 25$
- ● Highly significant
- ○ Significant
- ○ Marginally significant
- ○ Not significant

B. $X = 15$
- ○ Highly Significant
- ○ Significant
- ● Marginally significant
- ○ Not significant

C. $X = -20$
- ○ Highly Significant
- ● Significant
- ○ Marginally significant
- ○ Not significant

D. $X = -10$
- ○ Highly Significant
- ○ Significant
- ○ Marginally significant
- ● Not significant

A. $P(X \geq 25) = \frac{1}{100} = 0.01$**. Since** $P \leq 0.01$**, the difference is highly significant.**

B. $P(X \geq 15) = \frac{4+3+1}{100} = 0.08$**. Since** $0.10 \leq P < 0.05$**, the difference is marginally significant.**

C. $P(X \leq -20) = \frac{3+2}{100} = 0.05$**. Since** $0.05 \leq P < 0.01$**, the difference is significant.**

D. $P(X \leq -10) = \frac{9+5+3+2}{100} = 0.19$**. Since** $P \geq 0.10$**, the difference is not significant.**

H.O.T. Focus on Higher Order Thinking

Draw Conclusions The reason that the statistical test you used in this lesson is called a *permutation* test is that the process of resampling assigns different permutations of the labels "treatment" and "control" to the data from an experiment. Although the number of permutations of n distinct objects is $n!$, the objects in this case are some number of "treatment" labels and some number of "control" labels, so the objects are not distinct. When a set of n objects contains n_1 copies of the first object, n_2 copies of the second object, …, and n_L copies of the last object, then the formula for the number of permutations of the n objects becomes $\frac{n!}{n_1! \cdot n_2! \cdot \ldots \cdot n_L!}$.

a. Recall that in Explore 2, you had a control group with 10 students and a treatment group of 10 students. How many permutations of the "treatment" and "control" labels are possible? Did your class generate all possible resamples?

$\frac{20!}{10! \cdot 10!} = 184{,}756$**; no**

b. Suppose your class had generated all possible resamples. Explain why the resampling distribution would be perfectly symmetric and centered on 0.

For every treatment group and control group for which a difference of means equals *x*, you can switch the labels on the two groups and obtain a difference of means that equals $-x$. The sum of all possible differences of means is 0, so the mean of the differences is 0.

Communicate Mathematical Ideas The table shows measurements obtained from an experiment involving 3 subjects in the control group and 3 subjects in the treatment group.

Control group	2	4	3
Treatment group	9	10	5

a. How many distinct resamples of the data are possible? Explain your reasoning.

Use the permutations formula from the previous exercise to get $\frac{6!}{3! \cdot 3!} = 20$. Alternatively, think in terms of taking 6 data values and assigning 3 of them, without regard to order, to the control group (with the rest assigned to the treatment group). Then, ${}_6C_3 = 20$.

b. Calculate the difference of the means for the given treatment and control groups. Is this difference significant at the 5% level using a one-tailed test? Explain why or why not.

$\bar{x}_T - \bar{x}_C = 8 - 3 = 5$. Because the greatest data values are in the treatment group, this difference of means is greater than any other difference possible using resamples of the given data.

So, $P(x \geq 5) = \frac{1}{20} = 0.05$, and the difference is significant at the 5% level using a one-tailed test.

JOURNAL

Have students use frequency tables and histograms to explain how to use simulations to compare two treatments and decide whether differences between parameters are significant.

10. Explain the Error A student was given the resampling distribution shown and asked to determine the *P*–value when the actual difference of means for the treatment and control groups from an experiment is 30. The student gave the answer $\frac{4}{77} \approx 0.052$. Is the student correct? Explain.

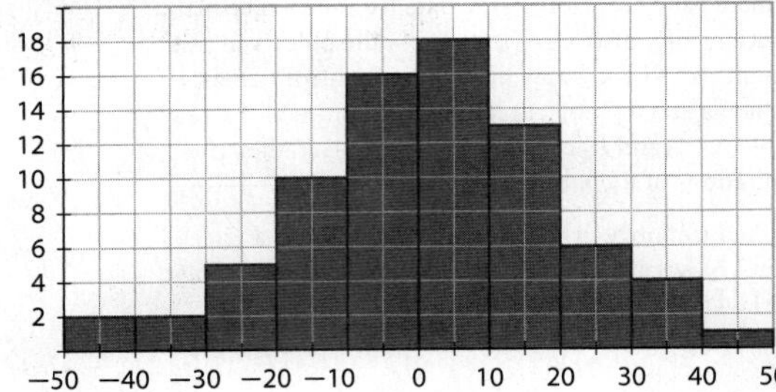

The student is not correct. He or she included the frequency only for the interval in which the difference occurs. The *P*-value is the probability of getting the result *or a more extreme result*. So, the student must find the sum of the frequencies for all the intervals to the right of 30 on the *x*-axis. The correct *P*-value is $\frac{5}{77} \approx 0.065$.

Lesson Performance Task

Researchers conducted an experiment where 12 teenage subjects were asked to use a driving simulator. At random intervals, a signal changed from green to red. Subjects were told to press a "brake" button as soon as they noticed that the signal changed to red. Each subject used the simulator under two conditions: while talking on a cell phone with a friend (the treatment) and while music was playing from a radio (the control). The table gives the data from the experiment.

Subject	Reaction Time (milliseconds)	
	Cell Phone (Treatment)	Radio (Control)
A	565	471
B	585	544
C	564	529
D	581	613
E	604	531
F	567	597
G	523	535
H	549	556
I	561	474
J	551	508
K	610	551
L	579	462

a. Calculate the mean reaction for the treatment, $\bar{x}_C$, and the mean reaction time for the control, $\bar{x}_C$. Then find the difference of the means.

$$\bar{x}_T = \frac{565 + 585 + 564 + 581 + 604 + 567 + 523 + 549 + 561 + 551 + 610 + 579}{12} \approx 569.92$$

$$\bar{x}_C = \frac{471 + 544 + 529 + 613 + 531 + 597 + 535 + 556 + 474 + 508 + 551 + 462}{12} \approx 530.92$$

$\bar{x}_T - \bar{x}_C = 39$

EXTENSION ACTIVITY

Have students research the difference between z-values and t-values in hypothesis testing. Students can verify the results of this Lesson Performance Task by using a 2-tailed t-test. They can use an Excel spreadsheet to help them. **The difference in means is 39, $n = 12$ for both groups, the standard deviation for the cellphone group is 24.017, the standard deviation for the control group is 47.129. $t = 2.6676$, and the 2-tailed t-test table shows the critical value at 2.0739, which is greater than t. Therefore, reject the null hypothesis. The two methods give the same result.**

INTEGRATE TECHNOLOGY

Suggest that students use a spreadsheet to calculate the two means and difference in means.

QUESTIONING STRATEGIES

? What is a good P-value to use if you want to be very sure not to reject the null hypothesis if the two population means are not actually different? Why? **Possible answer: 0.01, because results of less than 0.01 are highly significant**

? How does the number 0 relate to the null hypothesis? **Possible answer: If the observed difference between the control group and the treatment group is due to chance, then the mean difference in reaction times from 0 should be statistically insignificant.**

? What is a good P-value to use if you want to be very sure not to reject a null hypothesis that the two means are not significantly different? **Possible answer: 0.01**

INTEGRATE MATHEMATICAL PRACTICES

Focus on Math Connections

MP.1 In statistical analysis, a Type I error is rejecting a null hypothesis that is actually true. A Type II error is accepting a null hypothesis that is actually false. Ask students what each type of error would mean in terms of this situation, and what the ramifications would be of making either type of error.

Scoring Rubric

2 points: Student correctly solves the problem and explains his/her reasoning.

1 point: Student shows good understanding of the problem but does not fully solve or explain his/her reasoning.

0 points: Student does not demonstrate understanding of the problem.

b. Because this experiment involved obtaining both the control data and the treatment data from the same subjects, resampling the data involves maintaining the pairing of the data but randomizing the order of the data within pairs. The table shows one resample where a coin was flipped for each of the 12 subjects. If the coin landed heads up, then the subject's reaction times were kept as they are. However, if the coin landed tails up, then the subject's reaction times were swapped. Using the data for the resample, find $\bar{x}_T$, $\bar{x}_C$, and $\bar{x}_T - \bar{x}_C$. How does the difference of the means for the resample compare with the difference of the means you obtained in part a?

Subject	Treatment Reaction Time (milliseconds)	Control Reaction Time (milliseconds)	Treatment Reaction Time for Resample	Control Reaction Time for Resample
A	565	471	565	471
B	585	544	544	585
C	564	529	564	529
D	581	613	581	613
E	604	531	531	604
F	567	597	567	597
G	523	535	535	523
H	549	556	549	556
I	561	474	474	561
J	551	508	551	508
K	610	551	551	610
L	579	462	462	579

$$\bar{x}_T = \frac{565 + 544 + 564 + 581 + 531 + 567 + 535 + 549 + 474 + 551 + 551 + 462}{12} = 539.5$$

$$\bar{x}_C = \frac{471 + 585 + 529 + 613 + 604 + 597 + 523 + 556 + 561 + 508 + 610 + 579}{12} \approx 561.33$$

$$\bar{x}_T - \bar{x}_C = -21.83$$

The difference of the means for the resample is 60.83 milliseconds less than the difference of the means from part a. The fact that the difference of the means for the resample is negative means that the mean control reaction time was greater than the mean treatment reaction time for the resample, which was not the case for the original data.

c. State the null hypothesis for the experiment.

The null hypothesis is that mean reaction times for driving while talking on a cell phone and driving while listening to music are about the same.

d. Under the assumption that the null hypothesis is true, researchers resampled the data 1000 times and obtained the resampling distribution shown in the table. Use the table to find the probability that a difference of the means from the resampling distribution is at least as great as the difference of the means that you found in part a.

Interval	Frequency
$-61 \le x < -41$	5
$-41 \le x < -21$	89
$-21 \le x < -1$	390
$-1 \le x < 19$	408
$19 \le x < 39$	102
$39 \le x < 59$	6

$P(x \ge 39) = \frac{6}{1000} = 0.006$

e. Using the *P*-value you obtained in part d, state the significance of the experimental result and the conclusion you can draw from the permutation test.

Since the *P*-value is less than 0.01, the experimental result is highly significant. So, reject the null hypothesis that the mean reaction times for driving while talking on a cell phone and driving while listening to music are about the same in favor of the alternative hypothesis that the mean reaction time for driving while talking on a cell phone is substantially greater than the mean reaction time for driving while listening to music.

MODULE 24

Study Guide Review

ASSESSMENT AND INTERVENTION

Assign or customize module reviews.

MODULE PERFORMANCE TASK

COMMON CORE

Mathematical Practices: MP.1, MP.2, MP.4, MP.5, MP.6, MP.7, MP.8
S-IC.B.5

SUPPORTING STUDENT REASONING

Students should begin this problem by focusing on what information they will need. Here are some issues they might bring up.

- **How should we figure out whether the difference is statistically significant?** Remind students about resampling and permutation tests. If students are interested in calculating significance more directly, you may wish to tell them that the name of appropriate test is the *two-sample T-test* and have them research further. Be prepared to provide additional support.
- **How many times should we perform the simulation?** If time allows, tell students that at least 25 simulations would be best. Alternatively, have each student perform a simulation a few times, then collect and pool the data for the class.

STUDY GUIDE REVIEW

Making Inferences from Data

MODULE 24

Essential Question: How can making inferences from data help to solve real-world problems?

Key Vocabulary
confidence interval *(intervalo de confianza)*
margin of error *(margen de error)*
survey *(estudio)*
observational study *(estudio de observación)*
experiment *(experimento)*
randomized comparative experiment *(experimento comparative aleatorizado)*
null hypothesis *(hipótesis nula)*
statistically significant *(estadísticamente significativa)*
resampling *(remuestro)*
permutation test *(prueba de permutación)*

KEY EXAMPLE *(Lesson 24.1)*

In a random sample of 100 clothing buyers at a particular clothing store, 64 bought a pair of jeans. Find a 90% confidence interval for the proportion p of clothing buyers at that particular store who will buy jeans.

$n = 100$
$\hat{p} = 0.64$
$z_c = 1.645$

Determine the sample size n, the proportion $\hat{p}$, and the value of z_c for a 90% confidence interval.

Substitute into the formulas for the endpoints of the confidence interval.

$$\hat{p} - z_c\sqrt{\frac{\hat{p}(1-\hat{p})}{n}} = 0.64 - 1.645\sqrt{\frac{0.64(1-0.64)}{100}} \approx 0.56$$

$$\hat{p} + z_c\sqrt{\frac{\hat{p}(1-\hat{p})}{n}} = 0.64 + 1.645\sqrt{\frac{0.64(1-0.64)}{100}} \approx 0.72$$

So, you can state with 90% confidence that the proportion of people that will buy jeans at that particular store lies between 0.56 and 0.72.

KEY EXAMPLE *(Lesson 24.2)*

Explain why the results of the survey are likely to be inaccurate, and then suggest a way to improve the accuracy of the survey.

Mr. Culberson, the owner of a sporting goods company, conducts one-on-one interviews with a random sample of employees to have them rate how satisfied they are with the quality of the goods they sell.

Because the person conducting the survey is the owner of the company, the employees may not be completely open about their feelings of the products. Some employees may not even buy the products. A better survey would involve a neutral interviewer, allow employees to respond anonymously, or to interview customers instead of employees.

In a random sample of town residents, a survey asks, "Are you in favor of a special tax levy to renovate the sad state of the city park?"

The question is biased because the words "sad state" suggest that the park is in such a state that it needs to be fixed, which makes it seem that the tax levy is necessary. The question should begin with a factual list of improvements, and then a question like, "Are you in favor of a tax levy to make improvements to the park?"

SCAFFOLDING SUPPORT

- For a one-tailed T-test, the actual P-value is about 0.0177. If students perform 50 simulations and find that the actual difference between means is exceeded more than a couple of times, it's a strong indication that something has gone wrong with their simulation setup.
- Students who are interested in finding the precise P-value can be pointed toward the **2-SampTTest** option on their graphing calculators.

EXERCISES

In a random sample of 50 parfait buyers at Yo-Gurt Shop, 37 used vanilla frozen yogurt for their parfait. Find the proportion. *(Lesson 24.1)*

1. Find a 99% confidence interval for the proportion p of parfait purchasers who will use vanilla frozen yogurt.

   Between 0.58 and 0.90

2. If the survey were expanded to 100 buyers, and 89 used vanilla frozen yogurt, find a 90% confidence interval for the proportion p of parfait purchasers who will use vanilla frozen yogurt.

   Between 0.84 and 0.94

Explain why the results of the survey are likely to be inaccurate. *(Lesson 24.2)*

3. A survey of favorite sports for the school is taken after football practice.

   The survey is biased toward football by asking mostly football players.

   The survey should include more than just football players.

MODULE PERFORMANCE TASK

Sports Nutrition

Twenty-four athletes training for the Olympics were randomly assigned to one of two groups for a sports nutrition study. The treatment group received a daily dosage of a particular nutritional supplement for 6 weeks. The control group received a placebo. Each athlete's power output was tested before and after the 6-week training period. Researchers reported the following gains for each athlete in watts per kilogram of body mass.

	Increase in Power (watts/kg of body mass)			
Treatment Group	0.52	0.21	0.38	0.36
	0.39	0.30	0.46	0.33
	0.41	0.53	0.27	0.40
Control Group	0.32	0.39	0.25	0.29
	0.28	0.41	0.18	0.28
	0.19	0.42	0.33	0.26

What is the difference in means between the treatment and control groups? Is this difference statistically significant? Start on your own paper by listing information you will need to solve the problem. Be sure to write down all your data and assumptions. Then use graphs, numbers, tables, words, or algebra to explain how you reached your conclusion.

SAMPLE SOLUTION

The mean of the treatment group is 0.38, and the mean of the control group is 0.30. The difference in means is 0.08.

The null hypothesis is that the supplement has no effect on an athlete's power output. To test, set up a simulation using Excel. For each simulation, randomly assign all data values to the treatment and control groups. Keep track of how many times the difference in means is 0.08 or more.

After 50 simulations, the difference in means was 0.08 or more only once. The *P*-value is therefore $\frac{1}{50} = 0.02$. This is less than 0.05, so the simulations suggest that the result is statistically significant, and the supplement does have a positive effect on power output in athletes.

DISCUSSION OPPORTUNITIES

- What other concerns might there be for an athlete deciding whether or not to use a particular supplement?
- Discuss with students the fairness of using a performance-enhancing supplement in athletic competitions if the opposing team has no access to it.

Assessment Rubric

2 points: Student correctly solves the problem and explains his/her reasoning.

1 point: Student shows good understanding of the problem but does not fully solve or explain.

0 points: Student does not demonstrate understanding of the problem.

Ready to Go On?

ASSESS MASTERY

Use the assessment on this page to determine if students have mastered the concepts and standards covered in this module.

ASSESSMENT AND INTERVENTION

Access Ready to Go On? assessment online, and receive instant scoring, feedback, and customized intervention or enrichment.

ADDITIONAL RESOURCES

Response to Intervention Resources

- Reteach Worksheets

Differentiated Instruction Resources

- Reading Strategies EL
- Success for English Learners EL
- Challenge Worksheets

Assessment Resources

- Leveled Module Quizzes

Ready to Go On?

25.1–25.3 Making Inferences from Data

- Online Homework
- Hints and Help
- Extra Practice

State the null hypothesis.

1. Ten plants are given a new plant food once a week, in addition to regular watering. Ten other plants are only watered regularly. After one month, the mean heights of the two groups of plants are compared.

The null hypothesis is that both groups will have the same growth.

2. A sample group of patients suffering from frequent headaches are given a new medicine designed to significantly reduce the number of headaches per month. Another group of patients also suffering from frequent headaches are given a sugar pill. After 6 months, the mean numbers of headaches are compared for the two groups.

The null hypothesis is that both groups would have the same mean number of headaches.

Find the proportion.

3. A local school took a random sample of 500 students, in which 378 carried backpacks. Find the proportion of students who carry backpacks with a 95% confidence interval.

Between 0.72 and 0.79

ESSENTIAL QUESTION

4. How can making inferences from data help a test-prep writer?

Possible answer: After writing the preparation materials, the writer can test the effectiveness of the test preparation curriculum by comparing control groups to groups who use the materials.

COMMON CORE Common Core Standards

Lesson	Exercise	Math Standards	Mathematical Practices
24.3	1	S-IC.B.5	MP.6
24.3	2	S-IC.B.5	MP.6
24.1	3	S-IC.B.4	MP.7

MODULE 24
MIXED REVIEW

Assessment Readiness

1. A local band took a survey of 100 local music listeners about their favorite type of music. The results are as follows: 36 stated they preferred rock, 32 stated they preferred country, 25 stated they preferred hip-hop, and 7 stated they had no preference. Any probability uses a 95% confidence interval.

   Select Yes or No for A–C.

   A. The data have a normal distribution. ○ Yes ● No
   B. probability of country: between 0.23 and 0.41 ● Yes ○ No
   C. probability of rock: between 0.27 and 0.45 ● Yes ○ No

2. Consider the situation where a company is testing a new pair of shoes. They give 20 runners a pair of their redesigned shoes and 20 runners a pair of the previous model of shoes. After one month, they will be testing the amount of wear on the shoes. Choose True or False for each statement.

   A. The null hypothesis would be that both shoes wear the same amount. ● True ○ False
   B. A potential problem with the test is not knowing how much each runner runs in a week. This cannot be avoided. ○ True ● False
   C. The desired hypothesis for the shoe company would be that the older shoes worked better than the redesigned ones. ○ True ● False

3. A local political group is taking surveys of potential voters in the next election. They are calling voters registered in the Democratic Party to see which candidate is most likely to win the election for mayor. Explain why the results of the survey are likely to be inaccurate, and then suggest a way to improve the accuracy of the survey.

   The survey is biased, because they are only calling those registered with the Democratic Party. The results of the survey would be better if they called representatives from the overall registered voters in the city, regardless of party affiliation.

4. What type of function is illustrated by the points $(-1, 16)$, $(0, 4)(1, 1)$, $\left(2, \frac{1}{4}\right)$ and $\left(3, \frac{1}{16}\right)$? Explain your answer.

   Exponential decay function; Whenever x increases by 1, $f(x)$ is multiplied by the common ratio of $\frac{1}{4}$. Since the ratio is less than 1, the points represent exponential decay.

Common Core Standards

Lesson	Exercise	Math Standards	Mathematical Practices
23.2, 24.1	1*	S-ID.A.4, S-IC.B.4	MP.2
24.2, 24.3	2	S-IC.B.3, S-IC.B.5	MP.6
24.2	3	S-IC.B.3	MP.6
13.1	4*	F-LE.A.2	MP.2

* Item integrates mixed review concepts from previous modules or a previous course.

MIXED REVIEW

Assessment Readiness

ASSESSMENT AND INTERVENTION

Assign ready-made or customized practice tests to prepare students for high-stakes tests.

ADDITIONAL RESOURCES

Assessment Resources

- Leveled Module Quizzes: Modified, B

AVOID COMMON ERRORS

Item 4 Some students may have a hard time recognizing the type of function because the coordinates include fractions. Remind students that they can convert the fractions to decimals if that will make the function easier to recognize.

MIXED REVIEW

Assessment Readiness

ASSESSMENT AND INTERVENTION

Assign ready-made or customized practice tests to prepare students for high-stakes tests.

ADDITIONAL RESOURCES

Assessment Resources

- Leveled Unit Tests: Modified, A, B, C
- Performance Assessment

AVOID COMMON ERRORS

Item 7 Some students have a hard time recognizing mistakes in a stepped-out solution. Encourage students to solve the problem their own way, and then compare it to the given way to find the mistakes.

UNIT 9 MIXED REVIEW

Assessment Readiness

- Online Homework
- Hints and Help
- Extra Practice

1. Consider a survey to pick a new sport to add to the school. Is the suggested sampling method likely to result in an accurate result?

   Select Yes or No for A–C.

   A. survey every 10 attendees at a football game ○ Yes ● No
   B. survey every teacher ○ Yes ● No
   C. survey every 20 students on the school roster ● Yes ○ No

2. Consider a situation where a pizza company wants to improve its sauce. They give each of 15 testers two unlabeled samples of pizza; one with the new sauce and one with the old sauce.

   Select True or False for each statement.

   A. The null result would be both sauces tasting the same. ● True ○ False
   B. The desired result would be the customers preferring the new sauce. ● True ○ False
   C. The undesired result would be that the customers cannot tell between the two sauces. ○ True ● False

3. Consider the survey where a company owner, Ms. Baker, takes a random sample of her customers' names and their opinion about the quality of her product in return for a free donut.

   Select True or False for each statement.

   A. The survey is biased because the customers may not be honest to the owner of the company since they have to give their names. ● True ○ False
   B. The survey would be more accurate if Ms. Baker would allow customers to survey anonymously. ● True ○ False
   C. All customers will be honest if they get a free donut for completing the survey. ○ True ● False

4. Consider each equation. Does the equation have at least 2 real roots?

   Select Yes or No for A–C.

   A. $f(x) = x^2 - 6$ ● Yes ○ No
   B. $f(x) = x^2 + 2$ ○ Yes ● No
   C. $f(x) = (x^2 - 2)(x + 2)(x - 4)$ ● Yes ○ No

COMMON CORE

Common Core Standards

Items	Content Standards	Mathematical Practices
1	S-IC.B.3	MP.2
2	S-IC.B.5	MP.5
3	S-IC.B.3	MP.5
4*	A-SSE.B.3a, F-IF.C.7c	MP.2
5	S-ID.A.4	MP.6
6	S-IC.B.4	MP.4
7*	A-REI.B.3	MP.3

* Item integrates mixed review concepts from previous modules or a previous course.

5. Describe the difference between a normal distribution and a uniform distribution.

Possible answer: A normal distribution looks like it has a bell curve. A uniform distribution looks more like a rectangle, where everything has an equal likelihood of happening.

6. Suppose the average time a student spends traveling to school via walking, car, or bus is 22 minutes, with a standard deviation of 12 minutes. You choose a random sample of 100 students. What is the probability that your sample has a mean time up to 24 minutes? Explain.

96%; Possible answer: 96% of the data would lie under the curve up to the standard normal of 1.7.

7. Karissa solved the absolute value equation $5 = 2|x - 3| + 2$ as shown. Describe and correct Karissa's mistake(s).

$5 = 2\|x - 3\| + 2$	Subtract 2 from both sides.
$3 = 2\|x - 3\|$	Divide both sides by 2.
$1.5 = \|x - 3\|$	Separate equation into two equations.
$1.5 = x - 3$ and $-1.5 = x - 3$	Solve for x.
$x = -1.5$ and $x = -4.5$	

Karissa did not solve the final equations correctly. Instead of doing the opposite operation to isolate the variable, she did the same operation. The correct answers are $x = 1.5$ and $x = 4.5$.

Performance Tasks

8. Samples of the ages of members of two different athletic clubs in Smithville are shown.

Membership Information	
Power-Pump Gym	24, 28, 44, 50, 31, 20, 25, 54, 27, 19, 23, 37, 42, 25, 29, 40
Smithville Racket Club	14, 49, 30, 17, 28, 71, 64, 29, 12, 28, 60, 51, 23, 59, 66, 23

A. Determine the mean and standard deviation for each data set. Round to the nearest age.

B. What do the samples say about the age of a typical member at each club? Explain.

A. Power-Pump Gym: mean 32, standard deviation 11; Smithville Racket Club: mean 39, standard deviation 20

B. Possible answer: the ages at the racket club are more spread out; the gym has younger members on average.

PERFORMANCE TASKS

There are three different levels of performance tasks:

***Novice:** These are short word problems that require students to apply the math they have learned in straightforward, real-world situations.

****Apprentice:** These are more involved problems that guide students step-by-step through more complex tasks. These exercises include more complicated reasoning, writing, and open ended elements.

*****Expert:** These are open-ended, nonroutine problems that, instead of stepping the students through, ask them to choose their own methods for solving and justify their answers and reasoning.

SCORING GUIDES

Item 8 (2 points) Award 1 point for correct mean and standard deviation, and 1 point for analysis.

SCORING GUIDES

Item 9 (6 points)

a. 1 point per aspect named (3 points total)

b. 1 point per statement about reasoning (3 points total)

Item 10 (6 points)

a. 1 point for the correct answer, and 1 point for the correct explanation

b. 2 points for the correct answer

c. 2 points for the correct explanation

★★ **9.** A cable company wants to know if customers that pay for DVR service (to record shows) would cancel it if the ads in the shows could not be skipped when shows are viewed. A report from a survey shows that only 12% of customers that pay for DVR would cancel it.

A. Name at least three aspects of the survey that you would want to know more about to help determine if the report is valid.

B. The cable company ultimately wants more of its customers to pay for DVR service, since only 29% of customers currently subscribe to this service. How might this information affect the company's decision to disable fast-forwarding of ads? Write 3 statements about your reasoning.

A. **Possible answer: the number of people surveyed, whether the survey was random, and how the survey was conducted, such as exactly what group was surveyed (a particular region for example), or how the 12% was determined (for example, does it include respondents that were not sure if they would cancel DVR service).**

B. **Possible answer: This affects the decision because the 29% of customers that buy DVR service may still decrease by about 12%. Also, customers interested in buying the DVR service may not, if they know that they cannot fast-forward through ads. Lastly, customers in general may be dissatisfied with a negative change in the service and look for alternative services.**

★★★**10.** The United States Association of Table Tennis (USATT) uses a rating system for members. The ratings are normally distributed with a mean of 1400 and a standard deviation of 490.

A. Ernesto says that about a third of all members have a rating between 900 and 1400. Is this correct? Explain.

B. An "expert" player is considered to have a rating of at least 1900. About what percent of members are *not* "experts"?

C. A USATT club in New York has 73 members. The club has an average member rating of 1870. Explain why the members of the club do not reflect the distribution of all USATT members.

A. **Yes; about 34.1% of members have a rating between the mean and one standard deviation below the mean. Because $1400 - 490 = 910$ is a little more than 900, and 34.1% is a little more than one third, the given statement is correct.**

B. **about 84%**

C. **All of the members of a particular club do not constitute a random sample. A random sample would mean that each member of the USATT had an equal chance of being selected for the sample.**

Pharmaceutical Scientist A pharmaceutical scientist is testing whether a certain medication for raising glucose levels is more effective at higher doses. In a random trial, the fasting glucose levels of 5 patients being treated at a normal dose (Group A) and 5 patients being tested at a high dose (Group B) were recorded. The glucose levels in mmol/L are shown in the table.

A	5.4	5.7	4.8	4.3	4.6
B	5.5	5.1	4.2	5.9	4.9

a. State the null hypothesis for the experiment.

b. Compare the results for the control group and the treatment group using box plots.

c. Do you think that the researcher has enough evidence to reject the null hypothesis?

a. The population average of glucose levels of the drug will be the same for the control group (A) and the treatment group (B).

b.

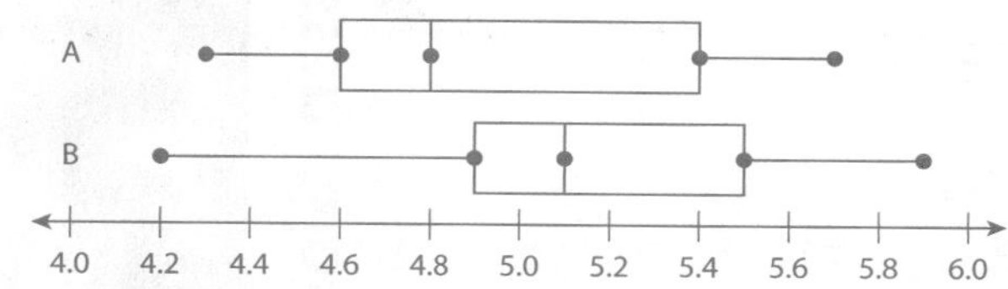

c. Sample answer: If anything, the treatment group actually shows a tendency toward higher glucose levels. The researcher cannot reject the null hypotheses, which means that the medication is probably just as effective at the normal dose as it is at the high dose.

MATH IN CAREERS

Pharmaceutical Scientist In this Unit Performance Task, students can see how a pharmaceutical scientist uses mathematics on the job.

For more information about careers in mathematics as well as various mathematics appreciation topics, visit the American Mathematical Society http://www.ams.org

SCORING GUIDES

Task (6 points)

a. 1 point for the correct null hypothesis

b. 3 points for correct box plots

c. 2 points for a correct explanation

Glossary/Glosario

A

ENGLISH	SPANISH	EXAMPLES
absolute value of a complex number The absolute value of $a + bi$ is the distance from the origin to the point (a, b) in the complex plane and is denoted $\lvert a + bi \rvert = \sqrt{a^2 + b^2}$.	**valor absoluto de un número complejo** El valor absoluto de $a + bi$ es la distancia desde el origen hasta el punto (a, b) en el plano complejo y se expresa $\lvert a + bi \rvert = \sqrt{a^2 + b^2}$.	$\lvert 2 + 3i \rvert = \sqrt{2^2 + 3^2} = \sqrt{13}$
absolute value of a real number The absolute value of x is the distance from zero to x on a number line, denoted $\lvert x \rvert$. $\lvert x \rvert = \begin{cases} x & \text{if } x \geq 0 \\ -x & \text{if } x < 0 \end{cases}$	**valor absoluto de un número real** El valor absoluto de x es la distancia desde cero hasta x en una recta numérica y se expresa $\lvert x \rvert$. $\lvert x \rvert = \begin{cases} x & \text{si } x \geq 0 \\ -x & \text{si } x < 0 \end{cases}$	$\lvert 3 \rvert = 3$ $\lvert -3 \rvert = 3$
absolute-value function A function whose rule contains absolute-value expressions.	**función de valor absoluto** Función cuya regla contiene expresiones de valor absoluto.	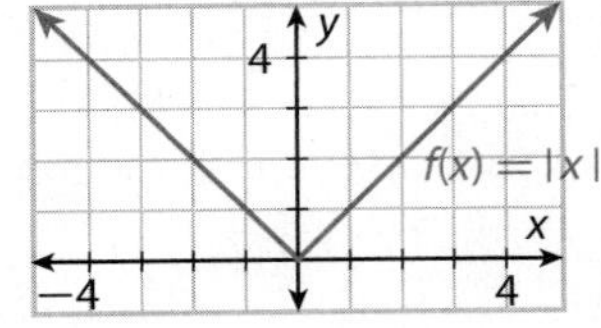
amplitude The amplitude of a periodic function is half the difference of the maximum and minimum values (always positive).	**amplitud** La amplitud de una función periódica es la mitad de la diferencia entre los valores máximo y mínimo (siempre positivos).	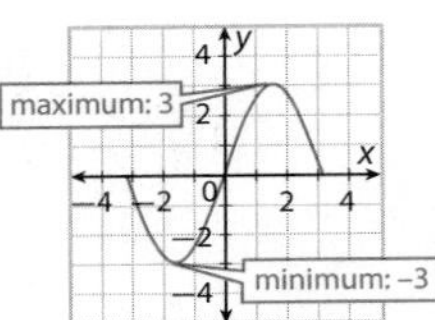 amplitude $= \frac{1}{2}\left[3 - (-3)\right] = 3$
angle of depression The angle formed by a horizontal line and a line of sight to a point below.	**ángulo de depresión** Ángulo formado por una recta horizontal y una línea visual a un punto inferior.	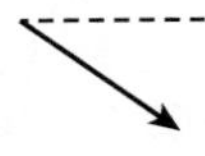
angle of elevation The angle formed by a horizontal line and a line of sight to a point above.	**ángulo de elevación** Ángulo formado por una recta horizontal y una línea visual a un punto superior.	
angle of rotation An angle formed by a rotating ray, called the terminal side, and a stationary reference ray, called the initial side.	**ángulo de rotación** Ángulo formado por un rayo en rotación, denominado lado terminal, y un rayo de referencia estático, denominado lado inicial.	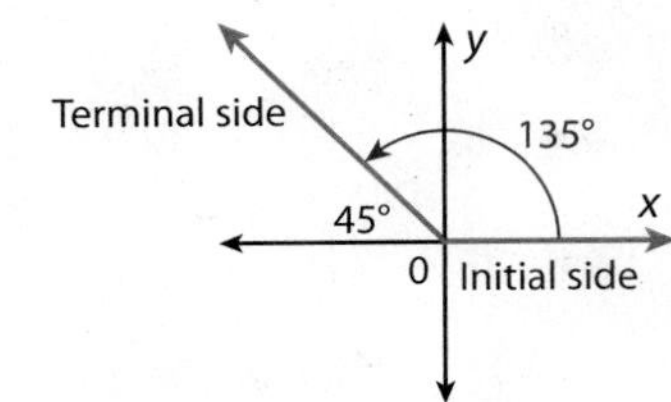

Glossary/Glosario

ENGLISH	SPANISH	EXAMPLES
arithmetic sequence A sequence whose successive terms differ by the same nonzero number d, called the *common difference*.	**sucesión aritmética** Sucesión cuyos términos sucesivos difieren en el mismo número distinto de cero d, denominado *diferencia común*.	4, 7, 10, 13, 16, ... $+3 + 3 + 3 + 3$ $d = 3$
arithmetic series The indicated sum of the terms of an arithmetic sequence.	**serie aritmética** Suma indicada de los términos de una sucesión aritmética.	$4 + 7 + 10 + 13 + 16 + \ldots$
asymptote A line that a graph approaches as the value of a variable becomes extremely large or small.	**asíntota** Línea recta a la cual se aproxima una gráfica a medida que el valor de una variable se hace sumamente grande o pequeño.	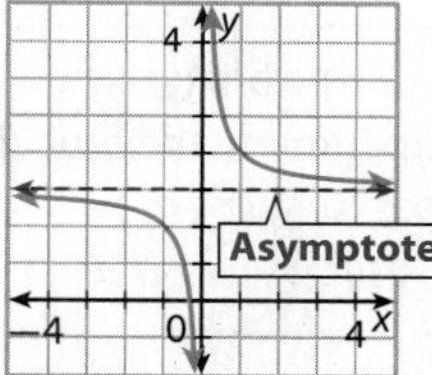
augmented matrix A matrix that consists of the coefficients and the constant terms in a system of linear equations.	**matriz aumentada** Matriz formada por los coeficientes y los términos constantes de un sistema de ecuaciones lineales.	System of equations: $3x + 2y = 5$, $2x - 3y = 1$ Augmented matrix: $\left[\begin{array}{cc\|c} 3 & 2 & 5 \\ 2 & -3 & 1 \end{array}\right]$
average rate of change The ratio of the change in the function values, $f(x_2) - f(x_1)$ to the change in the x-values, $x_2 - x_1$.	**tasa de cambio promedio** Razón entre el cambio en los valores de la función, $f(x_2) - f(x_1)$ y el cambio en los valores de x, $x_2 - x_1$.	
axis of symmetry A line that divides a plane figure or a graph into two congruent reflected halves.	**eje de simetría** Línea que divide una figura plana o una gráfica en dos mitades reflejadas congruentes.	Axis of symmetry; $y = \|x\|$

B

ENGLISH	SPANISH	EXAMPLES
base of an exponential function The value of b in a function of the form $f(x) = ab^x$, where a and b are real numbers with $a \neq 0$, $b > 0$, and $b \neq 1$.	**base de una función exponencial** Valor de b en una función del tipo $f(x) = ab^x$, donde a y b son números reales con $a \neq 0$, $b > 0$, y $b \neq 1$.	$f(x) = 5(2)^x$ — base (2)
biased sample A sample that does not fairly represent the population.	**muestra no representativa** Muestra que no representa adecuadamente una población.	
binomial A polynomial with two terms.	**binomio** Polinomio con dos términos.	$x + y$ $2a^2 + 3$ $4m^3n^2 + 6mn^4$

ENGLISH	SPANISH	EXAMPLES
binomial experiment A probability experiment consists of n identical and independent trials whose outcomes are either successes or failures, with a constant probability of success p and a constant probability of failure q, where $q = 1 - p$ or $p + q = 1$.	**experimento binomial** Experimento de probabilidades que comprende n pruebas idénticas e independientes cuyos resultados son éxitos o fracasos, con una probabilidad constante de éxito p y una probabilidad constante de fracaso q, donde $q = 1 - p$ o $p + q = 1$.	A multiple-choice quiz has 10 questions with 4 answer choices. The number of trials is 10. If each question is answered randomly, the probability of success for each trial is $\frac{1}{4} = 0.25$ and the probability of failure is $\frac{3}{4} = 0.75$.
binomial probability In a binomial experiment, the probability of r successes $(0 \leq r \leq n)$ is $P(r) = {}_nC_r \cdot p^r q^{n-r}$.	**probabilidad binomial** En un experimento binomial, la probabilidad de r éxitos $(0 \leq r \leq n)$ es $P(r) = {}_nC_r \cdot p^r q^{n-r}$.	In the binomial experiment above, the probability of randomly guessing 6 problems correctly is $P = {}_{10}C_6\,(0.25)^6\,(0.75)^4 \approx 0.016$.
Binomial Theorem For any positive integer n, $(x+y)^n = {}_nC_0\,x^n y^0 + {}_nC_1\,x^{n-1} y^1 + {}_nC_2\,x^{n-2} y^2 + \ldots + {}_nC_{n-1}\,x^1 y^{n-1} + {}_nC_n\,x^0 y^n$.	**Teorema de los binomios** Dado un entero positivo n, $(x+y)^n = {}_nC_0\,x^n y^0 + {}_nC_1\,x^{n-1} y^1 + {}_nC_2\,x^{n-2} y^2 + \ldots + {}_nC_{n-1}\,x^1 y^{n-1} + {}_nC_n\,x^0 y^n$.	$(x+2)^4 = {}_4C_0\,x^4 2^0 + {}_4C_1\,x^3 2^1 + {}_4C_2\,x^2 2^2 + {}_4C_1\,x^1 2^3 + {}_4C_4 x^0 2^4 = x^4 + 8x^3 + 24x^2 + 32x + 16$
branch of a hyperbola One of the two symmetrical parts of the hyperbola.	**rama de una hipérbola** Una de las dos partes simétricas de la hipérbola.	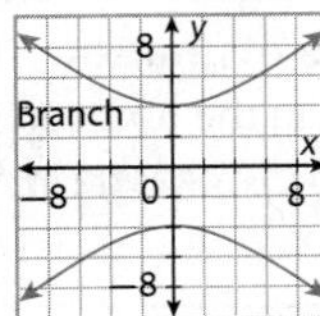

C

ENGLISH	SPANISH	EXAMPLES
categorical data Data that represent observations or attributes that can be sorted into groups or categories.	**datos categóricos** Datos que representan observaciones o atributos que pueden ser clasificados en grupos o categorías.	
census A survey of an entire population.	**censo** Estudio de una población entera.	
closure A set of numbers is said to be closed, or to have closure, under a given operation if the result of the operation on any two numbers in the set is also in the set.	**cerradura** Se dice que un conjunto de números es cerrado, o tiene cerradura, respecto de una operación determinada, si el resultado de la operación entre dos numerous cualesquiera del conjunto también está en el conjunto.	The natural numbers are closed under addition because the sum of two natural numbers is always a natural number.
coefficient matrix The matrix of the coefficients of the variables in a linear system of equations.	**matriz de coeficientes** Matriz de los coeficientes de las variables en un sistema lineal de ecuaciones.	System of equations: $2x + 3y = 11$, $5x - 4y = 16$; Coefficient matrix: $\begin{bmatrix} 2 & 3 \\ 5 & -4 \end{bmatrix}$

Glossary/Glosario

ENGLISH	SPANISH	EXAMPLES
combination A selection of a group of objects in which order is *not* important. The number of combinations of *r* objects chosen from a group of *n* objects is denoted ${}_nC_r$.	**combinación** Selección de un grupo de objetos en la cual el orden *no* es importante. El número de combinaciones de *r* objetos elegidos de un grupo de *n* objetos se expresa así: ${}_nC_r$.	For 4 objects *A*, *B*, *C*, and *D*, there are ${}_4C_2 = 6$ different combinations of 2 objects: *AB, AC, AD, BC, BD, CD*.
common difference In an arithmetic sequence, the nonzero constant difference of any term and the previous term.	**diferencia común** En una sucesión aritmética, diferencia constante distinta de cero entre cualquier término y el término anterior.	In the arithmetic sequence 3, 5, 7, 9, 11, ..., the common difference is 2.
common logarithm A logarithm whose base is 10, denoted $\log_{10}$ or just log.	**logaritmo común** Logaritmo de base 10, que se expresa $\log_{10}$ o simplemente log.	$\log 100 = \log_{10} 100 = 2$, since $10^2 = 100$.
common ratio In a geometric sequence, the constant ratio of any term and the previous term.	**razón común** En una sucesión geométrica, la razón constante *r* entre cualquier término y el término anterior.	In the geometric sequence 32, 16,18, 4, 2 ..., the common ratio is $\frac{1}{2}$.
complement of an event All outcomes in the sample space that are not in an event *E*, denoted $\bar{E}$.	**complemento de un suceso** Todos los resultados en el espacio muestral que no están en el suceso *E* y se expresan $\bar{E}$.	In the experiment of rolling a number cube, the complement of rolling a 3 is rolling a 1, 2, 4, 5, or 6.
completing the square A process used to form a perfect-square trinomial. To complete the square of $x^2 + bx$, add $\left(\frac{b}{2}\right)^2$.	**completar el cuadrado** Proceso utilizado para formar un trinomio cuadrado perfecto. Para completar el cuadrado de $x^2 + bx$, hay que sumar $\left(\frac{b}{2}\right)^2$.	$x^2 + 6x + \blacksquare$ Add $\left(\frac{6}{2}\right)^2 = 9$. $x^2 + 6x + 9$ $(x + 3)^2$ *is a perfect square.*
complex conjugate The complex conjugate of any complex number $a + bi$, denoted $\overline{a + bi}$, is $a - bi$.	**conjugado complejo** El conjugado complejo de cualquier número complejo $a + bi$, expresado como $\overline{a + bi}$, es $a - bi$.	$\overline{4 + 3i} = 4 - 3i$ $\overline{4 - 3i} = 4 + 3i$
complex fraction A fraction that contains one or more fractions in the numerator, the denominator, or both.	**fracción compleja** Fracción que contiene una o más fracciones en el numerador, en el denominador, o en ambos.	$\dfrac{\frac{1}{2}}{1 + \frac{2}{3}}$
complex number Any number that can be written as $a + bi$, where *a* and *b* are real numbers and $i = \sqrt{-1}$.	**número complejo** Todo número que se puede expresar como $a + bi$, donde *a* y *b* son números reales e $i = \sqrt{-1}$.	$4 + 2i$ $5 + 0i = 5$ $0 - 7i = -7i$
complex plane A set of coordinate axes in which the horizontal axis is the real axis and the vertical axis is the imaginary axis; used to graph complex numbers.	**plano complejo** Conjunto de ejes cartesianos en el cual el eje horizontal es el eje real y el eje vertical es el eje imaginario; se utiliza para representar gráficamente números complejos.	Imaginary axis 2i 0 + 0i Real axis −2 2 −2i

ENGLISH	SPANISH	EXAMPLES
composition of functions The composition of functions f and g, written as $(f \circ g)(x)$ and defined as $f(g(x))$ uses the output of $g(x)$ as the input for $f(x)$.	**composición de funciones** La composición de las funciones f y g, expresada como $(f \circ g)(x)$ y definida como $f(g(x))$ utiliza la salida de $g(x)$ como la entrada para $f(x)$.	If $f(x) = x^2$ and $g(x) = x + 1$, the composite function $(f \circ g)(x) = (x + 1)^2$.
compound event An event made up of two or more simple events.	**suceso compuesto** Suceso formado por dos o más sucesos simples.	In the experiment of tossing a coin and rolling a number cube, the event of the coin landing heads and the number cube landing on 3.
compound interest Interest earned or paid on both the principal and previously earned interest, found using the formula $A(t) = P\left(1 + \frac{r}{n}\right)^{nt}$ where A is the final amount, P is the principal, r is the interest rate given as a decimal, n is the number of times interest is compounded, and t is the time.	**interés compuesto** Interés ganado o pagado tanto sobre el capital inicial como sobre el interés previamente ganado. Se halla usando la fórmula $A(t) = P\left(1 + \frac{r}{n}\right)^{nt}$, donde A es la cantidad final, P es el capital inicial, r es la tasa de interés indicada en forma de número decimal, n es el número de veces que se reinvierte el interés y t es el tiempo.	
compression A transformation that pushes the points of a graph horizontally toward the y-axis or vertically toward the x-axis.	**compresión** Transformación que desplaza los puntos de una gráfica horizontalmente hacia el eje y o verticalmente hacia el eje x.	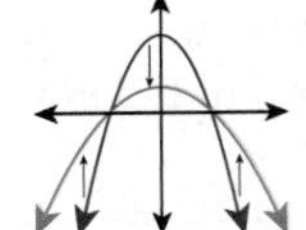
conditional probability The probability of event B, given that event A has already occurred or is certain to occur, denoted $P(B \mid A)$; used to find probability of dependent events.	**probabilidad condicional** Probabilidad del suceso B, dado que el suceso A ya ha ocurrido o es seguro que ocurrirá, expresada como $P(B \mid A)$; se utiliza para calcular la probabilidad de sucesos dependientes.	
confidence interval An approximate range of values that is likely to include an unknown population parameter.	**intervalo de confianza** Un rango aproximado de valores que probablemente incluirá un parámetro de población desconocido.	
conic section A plane figure formed by the intersection of a double right cone and a plane. Examples include circles, ellipses, hyperbolas, and parabolas.	**sección cónica** Figura plana formada por la intersección de un cono regular doble y un plano. Algunos ejemplos son círculos, elipses, hipérbolas y parábolas.	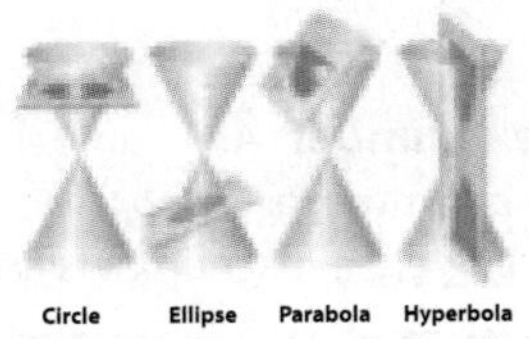
conjugate axis The axis of symmetry of a hyperbola that separates the two branches of the hyperbola.	**eje conjugado** Eje de simetría de una hipérbola que separa las dos ramas de la hipérbola.	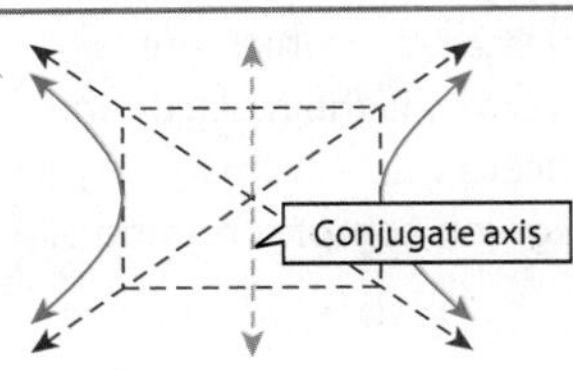

ENGLISH	SPANISH	EXAMPLES

constraint One of the inequalities that define the feasible region in a linear-programming problem.

restricción Una de las desigualdades que definen la región factible en un problema de programación lineal.

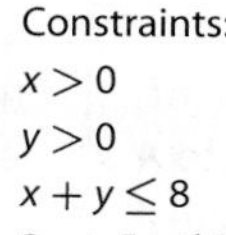

Constraints:
$x > 0$
$y > 0$
$x + y \leq 8$
$3x + 5y \leq 30$

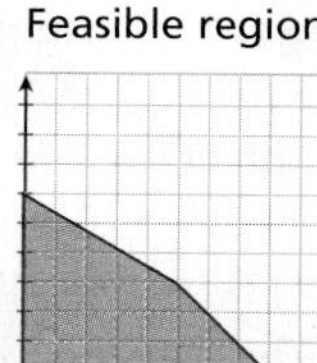

continuous function A function whose graph is an unbroken line or curve with no gaps or breaks.

función continua Función cuya gráfica es una línea recta o curva continua, sin espacios ni interrupciones.

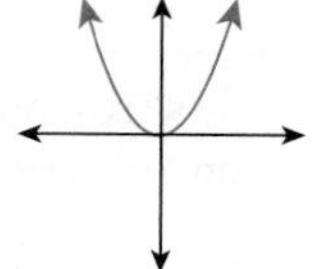

contradiction An equation that has no solutions.

contradicción Ecuación que no tiene soluciones.

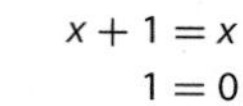

$x + 1 = x$
$1 = 0x$

correlation A measure of the strength and direction of the relationship between two variables or data sets.

correlación Medida de la fuerza y dirección de la relación entre dos variables o conjuntos de datos.

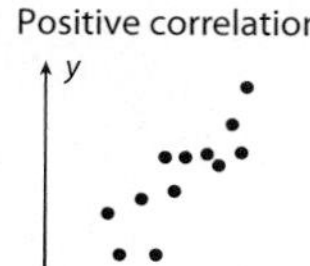

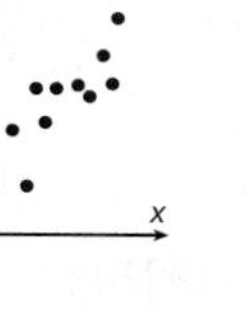

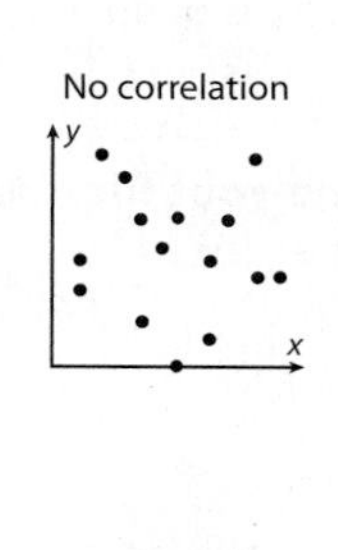

correlation coefficient A number r, where $-1 \leq r \leq 1$, that describes how closely the points in a scatter plot cluster around the least–squares line.

coeficiente de correlación Número r, donde $-1 \leq r \leq 1$, que describe a qué distancia de la recta de mínimos cuadrados se agrupan los puntos de un diagrama de dispersión.

An r–value close to 1 describes a strong positive correlation.
An r–value close to 0 describes a weak correlation or no correlation.
An r–value close to -1 describes a strong negative correlation.

cosecant In a right triangle, the cosecant of angle A is the ratio of the length of the hypotenuse to the length of the side opposite A. It is the reciprocal of the sine function.

cosecante En un triángulo rectángulo, la cosecante del ángulo A es la razón entre la longitud de la hipotenusa y la longitud del cateto opuesto a A. Es la inversa de la función seno.

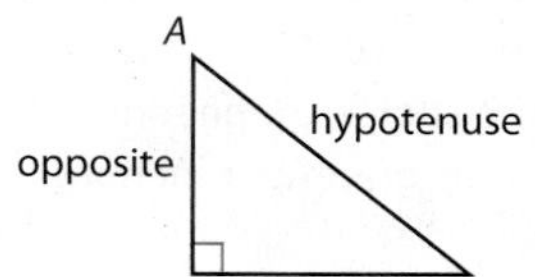

$$\csc A = \frac{\text{hypotenuse}}{\text{opposite}} = \frac{1}{\sin A}$$

cosine In a right triangle, the cosine of angle A is the ratio of the length of the side adjacent to angle A to the length of the hypotenuse. It is the reciprocal of the secant function.

coseno En un triángulo rectángulo, el coseno del ángulo A es la razón entre la longitud del cateto adyacente al ángulo A y la longitud de la hipotenusa. Es la inversa de la función secante.

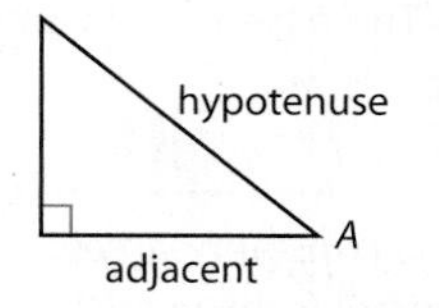

$$\cos A = \frac{\text{adjacent}}{\text{hypotenuse}} = \frac{1}{\sec A}$$

ENGLISH	SPANISH	EXAMPLES
cotangent In a right triangle, the cotangent of angle A is the ratio of the length of the side adjacent to A to the length of the side opposite A. It is the reciprocal of the tangent function.	**cotangente** En un triángulo rectángulo, la cotangente del ángulo A es la razón entre la longitud del cateto adyacente a A y la longitud del cateto opuesto a A. Es la inversa de la función tangente.	opposite, A, adjacent $\cot A = \frac{\text{adjacent}}{\text{opposite}} = \frac{1}{\tan A}$
coterminal angles Two angles in standard position with the same terminal side.	**ángulos coterminales** Dos ángulos en posición estándar con el mismo lado terminal.	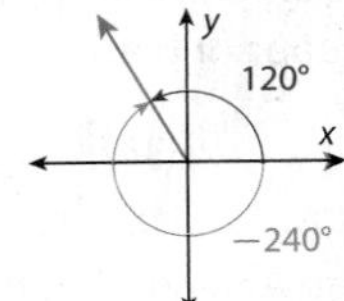
critical values Values that separate the number line into intervals that either contain solutions or do not contain solutions.	**valores críticos** Valores que separan la recta numérica en intervalos que contienen o no contienen soluciones.	
cube-root function The function $f(x) = \sqrt[3]{x}$.	**función de raíz cúbica** La función $f(x) = \sqrt[3]{x}$.	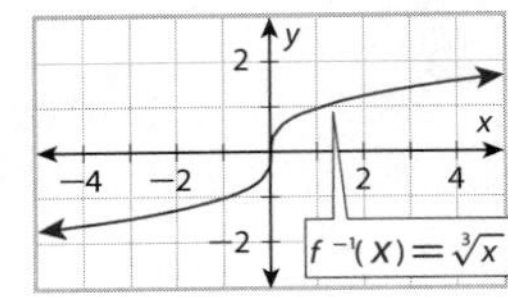
cubic function A polynomial function of degree 3.	**función cúbica** Función polinomial de grado 3.	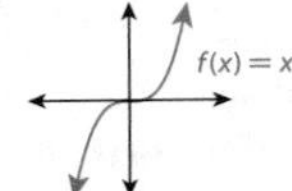
cumulative probability The probability that a random variable is less than or equal to a given value.	**probabilidad acumulada** La probabilidad de que una variable aleatoria sea menor o igual que un valor determinado.	
cycle of a periodic function The shortest repeating part of a periodic graph or function.	**ciclo de una función periódica** La parte repetida más corta de una gráfica o función periódica.	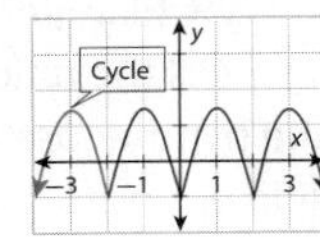

D

ENGLISH	SPANISH	EXAMPLES
decay factor The base $1 - r$ in an exponential expression.	**factor decremental** Base $1 - r$ en una expresión exponencial.	$2(0.93)^t$ decay factor (representing $1 - 0.07$)
decay rate The constant percent decrease, in decimal form, in an exponential decay function.	**tasa de disminución** Disminución porcentual constante, en forma decimal, en una función de disminución exponencial.	In the function $f(t) = a(1 - 0.2)^t$, 0.2 is the decay rate.

Glossary/Glosario

ENGLISH	SPANISH	EXAMPLES
decreasing A function is decreasing on an interval if $f(x_1) > f(x_2)$ when $x_1 > x_2$ for any x-values x_1 and x_2 from the interval.	**decreciente** Una función es decreciente en un intervalo si $f(x_1) > f(x_2)$ cuando $x_1 > x_2$ dados los valores de x, x_1 y x_2, pertenecientes al intervalo.	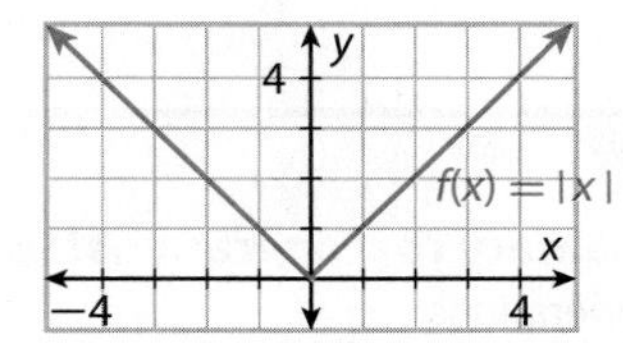 $f(x)$ is decreasing on the interval $x < 0$.
degree of a monomial The sum of the exponents of the variables in the monomial.	**grado de un monomio** Suma de los exponentes de las variables del monomio.	$4x^2y^5z^3$ Degree: $2 + 5 + 3 = 10$ 5 Degree: 0 $(5 = 5x^0)$
degree of a polynomial The degree of the term of the polynomial with the greatest degree.	**grado de un polinomio** Grado del término del polinomio con el grado máximo.	$3x^2y^2 + 4xy^5 - 12x^3y^2$ Degree 6 Degree 4 Degree 6 Degree 5
dependent events Events for which the occurrence or nonoccurrence of one event affects the probability of the other event.	**sucesos dependientes** Dos sucesos son dependientes si el hecho de que uno de ellos se cumpla o no afecta la probabilidad del otro.	From a bag containing 3 red marbles and 2 blue marbles, drawing a red marble, and then drawing a blue marble without replacing the first marble.
dependent system A system of equations that has infinitely many solutions.	**sistema dependiente** Sistema de ecuaciones que tiene infinitamente muchas soluciones.	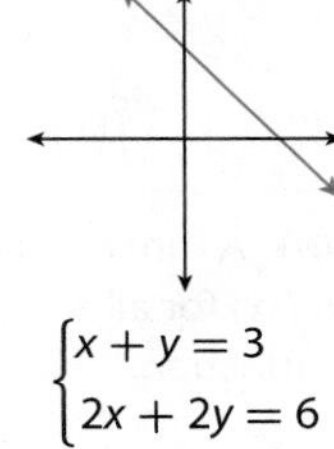 $\begin{cases} x + y = 3 \\ 2x + 2y = 6 \end{cases}$
difference of two squares A polynomial of the form $a^2 - b^2$, which may be written as the product $(a + b)(a - b)$.	**diferencia de dos cuadrados** Polinomio del tipo $a^2 - b^2$, que se puede expresar como el producto $(a + b)(a - b)$.	$x^2 - 4 = (x + 2)(x - 2)$
directrix A fixed line used to define a *parabola*. Every point on the parabola is equidistant from the directrix and a fixed point called the *focus*.	**directriz** Línea fija utilizada para definir una *parábola*. Cada punto de la parábola es equidistante de la directriz y de un punto fijo denominado *foco*.	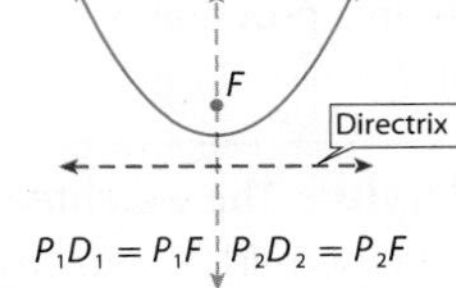
discontinuous function A function whose graph has one or more jumps, breaks, or holes.	**función discontinua** Función cuya gráfica tiene uno o más saltos, interrupciones u hoyos.	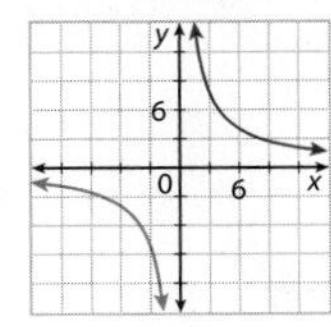
discriminant The discriminant of the quadratic equation $ax^2 + bx + c = 0$ is $b^2 - 4ac$.	**discriminante** El discriminante de la ecuación cuadrática $ax^2 + bx + c = 0$ es $b^2 - 4ac$.	The discriminant of $2x^2 - 5x - 3 = 0$ is $(-5)^2 - 4(2)(-3) = 25 + 24 = 49$.
distribution A set of numerical data that you can graph using a data display that involves a number line, such as a line plot, histogram, or box plot.	**distribución** Un conjunto de datos numéricos que se pueden representar gráficamente mediante una representación de datos que incluye una recta numérica, como un diagrama de puntos, un histograma o un diagrama de cajas.	

ENGLISH	SPANISH	EXAMPLES

E

elementary row operations *See* row operations.	**operaciones elementales de fila** *Véase* operaciones de fila.	
elimination A method used to solve systems of equations in which one variable is eliminated by adding or subtracting two equations of the system.	**eliminación** Método utilizado para resolver sistemas de ecuaciones por el cual se elimina una variable sumando o restando dos ecuaciones del sistema.	
empty set A set with no elements.	**conjunto vacío** Conjunto sin elementos.	The solution set of $\lvert x \rvert < 0$ is the empty set, $\{\ \}$, or $\emptyset$.
end behavior The trends in the y-values of a function as the x-values approach positive and negative infinity.	**comportamiento extremo** Tendencia de los valores de y de una función a medida que los valores de x se aproximan al infinito positivo y negativo.	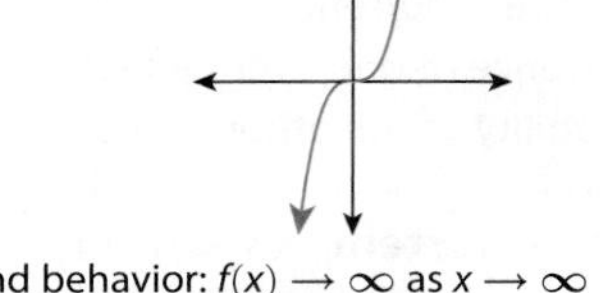 End behavior: $f(x) \to \infty$ as $x \to \infty$ $f(x) \to -\infty$ as $x \to -\infty$
even function A function in which $f(-x) = f(x)$ for all x in the domain of the function.	**función par** Función en la que para todos los valores de x dentro del dominio de la función.	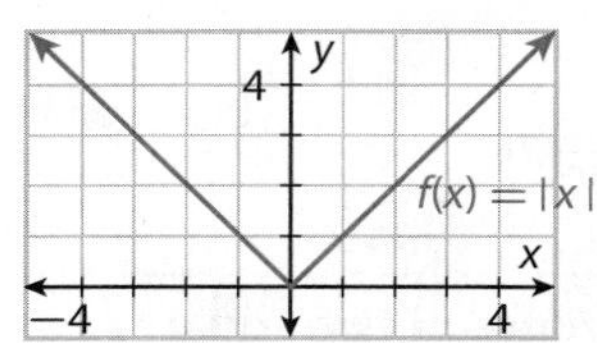 $f(x) = \lvert x \rvert$ is an even function.
event An outcome or set of outcomes in a probability experiment.	**suceso** Resultado o conjunto de resultados en un experimento de probabilidad.	In the experiment of rolling a number cube, the event "an odd number" consists of the outcomes 1, 3, and 5.
expected value The weighted average of the numerical outcomes of a probability experiment.	**valor esperado** Promedio ponderado de los resultados numéricos de un experimento de probabilidad.	The table shows the probability of getting a given score by guessing on a three-question quiz. **Score**: 0, 1, 2, 3 **Probability**: 0.42, 0.42, 0.14, 0.02 The expected value is a score of $0(0.42) + 1(0.42) + 2(0.14) + 3(0.02) = 0.76$.
experiment An operation, process, or activity in which outcomes can be used to estimate probability.	**experimento** Una operación, proceso o actividad cuyo resultado se puede usar para estimar la probabilidad.	Tossing a coin 10 times and noting the number of heads.
experimental probability The ratio of the number of times an event occurs to the number of trials, or times, that an activity is performed.	**probabilidad experimental** Razón entre la cantidad de veces que ocurre un suceso y la cantidad de pruebas, o veces, que se realiza una actividad.	Kendra made 6 of 10 free throws. The experimental probability that she will make her next free throw is $P(\text{free throw}) = \frac{\text{number made}}{\text{number attempted}} = \frac{6}{10}$.

ENGLISH	SPANISH	EXAMPLES
explicit formula A formula that defines the *n*th term a_n, or general term, of a sequence as a function of *n*.	**fórmula explícita** Fórmula que define el enésimo término a_n, o término general, de una sucesión como una función de *n*.	Sequence: 4, 7, 10, 13, 16, 19, … Explicit formula: $a_n = 1 + 3n$
exponential decay An exponential function of the form $f(x) = ab^x$ in which $0 < b < 1$. If *r* is the rate of decay, then the function can be written $y = a(1 - r)^t$, where *a* is the initial amount and *t* is the time.	**decremento exponencial** Función exponencial del tipo $f(x) = ab^x$ en la cual $0 < b < 1$. Si *r* es la tasa decremental, entonces la función se puede expresar como $y = a(1 - r)^t$, donde a es la cantidad inicial y *t* es el tiempo.	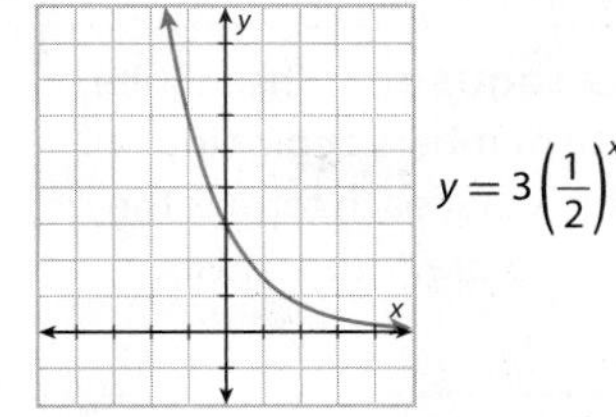
exponential equation An equation that contains one or more exponential expressions.	**ecuación exponencial** Ecuación que contiene una o más expresiones exponenciales.	$2^{x+1} = 8$
exponential function A function of the form $f(x) = ab^x$, where *a* and *b* are real numbers with $a \neq 0$, $b > 0$, and $b \neq 1$.	**función exponencial** Función del tipo $f(x) = ab^x$, donde *a* y *b* son números reales con $a \neq 0$, $b > 0$ y $b \neq 1$.	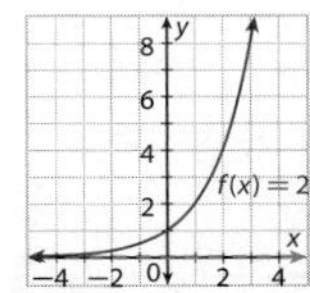
exponential growth An exponential function of the form $f(x) = ab^x$ in which $b > 1$. If *r* is the rate of growth, then the function can be written $y = a(1 + r)^t$, where *a* is the initial amount and *t* is the time.	**crecimiento exponencial** Función exponencial del tipo $f(x) = ab^x$ en la que $b > 1$. Si *r* es la tasa de crecimiento, entonces la función se puede expresar como $y = a(1 + r)^t$, donde *a* es la cantidad inicial y *t* es el tiempo.	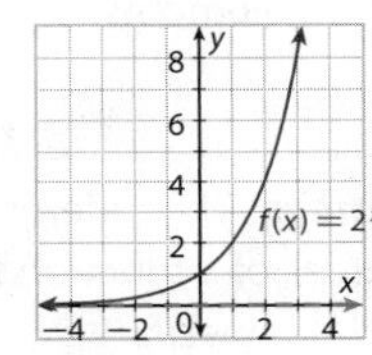
exponential regression A statistical method used to fit an exponential model to a given data set.	**regresión exponencial** Método estadístico utilizado para ajustar un modelo exponencial a un conjunto de datos determinado.	ExpReg y=a*b^x a=814.9602955 b=1.379191229 r²=.9962061645 r=.9981012797
extraneous solution A solution of a derived equation that is not a solution of the original equation.	**solución extraña** Solución de una ecuación derivada que no es una solución de la ecuación original.	To solve $\sqrt{x} = -2$, square both sides; $x = 4$. ***Check*** $\sqrt{4} = -2$ is false; so 4 is an extraneous solution.

F

Factor Theorem For any polynomial $P(x)$, $(x - a)$ is a factor of $P(x)$ if and only if $P(a) = 0$.	**Teorema del factor** Dado el polinomio $P(x)$, $(x - a)$ es un factor de $P(x)$ si y sólo si $P(a) = 0$.	$(x - 1)$ is a factor of $P(x) = x^2 - 1$ because $P(1) = 1^2 - 1 = 0$.

ENGLISH	SPANISH	EXAMPLES
factorial If n is a positive integer, then n factorial, written $n!$, is $n \cdot (n-1) \cdot (n-2) \cdot \ldots \cdot 2 \cdot 1$. The factorial of 0 is defined to be 1.	**factorial** Si n es un entero positivo, entonces el factorial de n, expresado como $n!$, es $n \cdot (n-1) \cdot (n-2) \cdot \ldots \cdot 2 \cdot 1$ Por definición, el factorial de 0 será 1.	$7! = 7 \cdot 6 \cdot 5 \cdot 4 \cdot 3 \cdot 2 \cdot 1 = 5040$ $0! = 1$
Fibonacci sequence The infinite sequence of numbers beginning with 1, 1 such that each term is the sum of the two previous terms.	**sucesión de Fibonacci** Sucesión infinita de números que comienza con 1, 1 de forma tal que cada término es la suma de los dos términos anteriores.	1, 1, 2, 3, 5, 8, 13, 21, …
finite geometric series A geometric series in which the sum of a finite number of terms of a geometric sequence is found.	**serie geométrica finita** Una serie geométrica en la que se halla la suma de un número finito de términos de una secuencia geométrica.	
finite sequence A sequence with a finite number of terms.	**sucesión finita** Sucesión con un número finito de términos.	1, 2, 3, 4, 5
finite set A set with a definite, or finite, number of elements.	**conjunto finito** Conjunto con un número de elementos definido o finito.	$\{2, 4, 6, 8, 10\}$
first differences The differences between y-values of a function for evenly spaced x-values.	**primeras diferencias** Diferencias entre los valores de y de una función para valores de x espaciados uniformemente.	*x*: 0, 1, 2, 3 *y*: 3, 7, 11, 15 first differences +4 +4 +4
focus (pl. foci) of a parabola A fixed point F used with a *directrix* to define a *parabola*.	**foco de una parábola** Punto fijo F utilizado con una *directriz* para definir una *parábola*.	Focus F
frequency of a data value The number of times the value appears in the data set.	**frecuencia de un valor de datos** Cantidad de veces que aparece el valor en un conjunto de datos.	In the data set 5, 6, 6, 6, 8, 9, the data value 6 has a frequency of 3.
frequency of a periodic function The number of cycles per unit of time. Also the reciprocal of the period.	**frecuencia de una función periódica** Cantidad de ciclos por unidad de tiempo. También es la inversa del periodo.	The function $y = \sin(2x)$ has a period of π and a frequency of $\frac{1}{\pi}$.
function rule An algebraic expression that defines a function.	**regla de función** Expresión algebraica que define una función.	$f(x) = 2x^2 + 3x - 7$ function rule

ENGLISH	SPANISH	EXAMPLES
Fundamental Counting Principle For n items, if there are m_1 ways to choose a first item, m_2 ways to choose a second item after the first item has been chosen, and so on, then there are $m_1 \cdot m_2 \cdot \ldots \cdot m_n$ ways to choose n items. 	**Principio fundamental de conteo** Dados n elementos, si existen m_1 formas de elegir un primer elemento, m_2 formas de elegir un segundo elemento después de haber elegido el primero, y así sucesivamente, entonces existen $m_1 \cdot m_2 \cdot \ldots \cdot m_n$ formas de elegir n elementos.	If there are 4 colors of shirts, 3 colors of pants, and 2 colors of shoes, then there are $4 \cdot 3 \cdot 2 = 24$ possible outfits.

G

ENGLISH	SPANISH	EXAMPLES
Gaussian Elimination An algorithm for solving systems of equations using matrices and row operations to eliminate variables in each equation in the system.	**Eliminación Gaussiana** Algoritmo para resolver sistemas de ecuaciones mediante matrices y operaciones de fila con el fin de eliminar variables en cada ecuación del sistema.	
general form of a conic section $Ax^2 + Bxy + Cy^2 + Dx + Ey + F = 0$, where A and B are not both 0.	**forma general de una sección cónica** $Ax^2 + Bxy + Cy^2 + Dx + Ey + F = 0$, donde A y B no son los dos 0.	A circle with a vertex at $(1, 2)$ and radius 3 has the general form $x^2 + y^2 - 2x - 4y - 4 = 0$.
geometric mean In a geometric sequence, a term that comes between two given nonconsecutive terms of the sequence. For positive numbers a and b, the geometric mean is $\sqrt{ab}$.	**media geométrica** En una sucesión geométrica, un término que se encuentra entre dos términos no consecutivos dados de la sucesión. Dados los números positivos a y b, la media geométrica es $\sqrt{ab}$.	The geometric mean of 4 and 9 is $\sqrt{4(9)} = \sqrt{36} = 6$.
geometric probability A form of theoretical probability determined by a ratio of geometric measures such as lengths, areas, or volumes.	**probabilidad geométrica** Una forma de la probabilidad teórica determinada por una razón de medidas geométricas, como longitud, área o volumen.	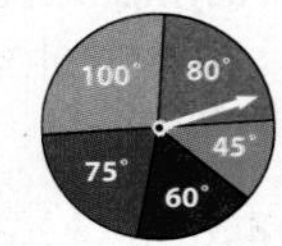 The probability of the pointer landing the 80° angle is $\frac{2}{9}$.
geometric sequence A sequence in which the ratio of successive terms is a constant r, called the common ratio, where $r \neq 0$ and $r \neq 1$.	**sucesión geométrica** Sucesión en la que la razón de los términos sucesivos es una constante r, denominada razón común, donde $r \neq 0$ y $r \neq 1$.	1, 2, 4, 8, 16, ... $\cdot 2$ $\cdot 2$ $\cdot 2$ $\cdot 2$ $r = 2$
geometric series The indicated sum of the terms of a geometric sequence.	**serie geométrica** Suma indicada de los términos de una sucesión geométrica.	$1 + 2 + 4 + 8 + 16 + \ldots$

ENGLISH	SPANISH	EXAMPLES
greatest-integer function A function denoted by $f(x) = [x]$ or $f(x) = \lfloor x \rfloor$ in which the number x is rounded down to the greatest integer that is less than or equal to x.	**función de entero mayor** Función expresada como $f(x) = [x]$ o $f(x) = \lfloor x \rfloor$ en la cual el número x se redondea hacia abajo hasta el entero mayor que sea menor que o igual a x.	$\lfloor 4.98 \rfloor = 4$ $\lfloor -2.1 \rfloor = -3$
growth factor The base $1 + r$ in an exponential expression.	**factor de crecimiento** La base $1 + r$ en una expresión exponencial.	$12{,}000(1 + 0.14)^t$ ↑ growth factor
growth rate The constant percent increase, in decimal form, in an exponential growth function.	**tasa de crecimiento** Aumento porcentual constante, en forma decimal, en una función de crecimiento exponencial.	In the function $f(t) = a(1 + 0.3)^t$, 0.3 is the growth rate.

H

Heron's Formula A triangle with side lengths a, b, and c has area $A = \sqrt{s(s-a)(s-b)(s-c)}$, where s is one-half the perimeter, or $s = \frac{1}{2}(a + b + c)$.	**fórmula de Herón** Un triángulo con longitudes de lado a, b y c tiene un área $A = \sqrt{s(s-a)(s-b)(s-c)}$, donde s es la mitad del perímetro ó $s = \frac{1}{2}(a + b + c)$.	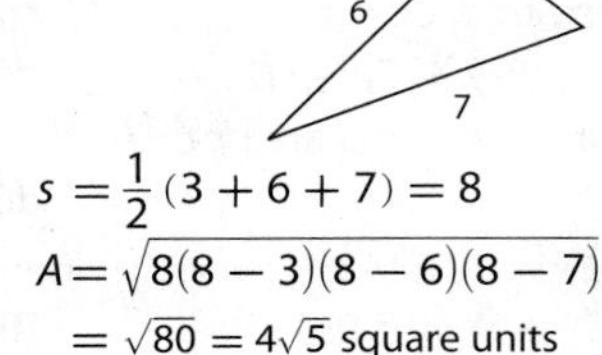 $s = \frac{1}{2}(3 + 6 + 7) = 8$ $A = \sqrt{8(8-3)(8-6)(8-7)}$ $= \sqrt{80} = 4\sqrt{5}$ square units
hole (in a graph) An omitted point on a graph. If a rational function has the same factor $x - b$ in both the numerator and the denominator, and the line $x = b$ is not a vertical asymptote, then there is a hole in the graph at the point where $x = b$.	**hoyo (en una gráfica)** Punto omitido en una gráfica. Si una función racional tiene el mismo factor $x - b$ tanto en el numerador como en el denominador, y la línea $x = b$ no es una asíntota vertical, entonces hay un hoyo en la gráfica en el punto donde $x = b$.	$f(x) = \frac{(x-2)(x+2)}{(x+2)}$ has a hole at $x = -2$. 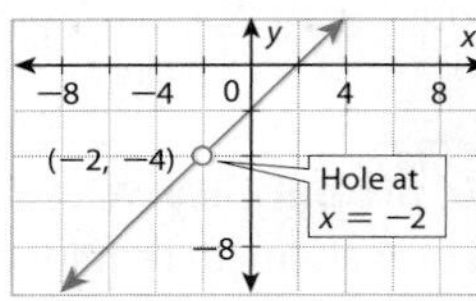
hypothesis testing A type of testing used to determine whether the difference in two groups is likely to be caused by chance.	**comprobación de hipótesis** Tipo de comprobación que sirve para determinar si el azar es la causa probable de la diferencia entre dos grupos.	

I

imaginary axis The vertical axis in the complex plane, it graphically represents the purely imaginary part of complex numbers.	**eje imaginario** Eje vertical de un plano complejo. Representa gráficamente la parte puramente imaginaria de los números complejos.	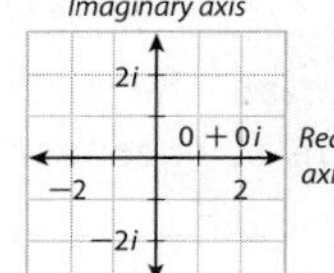

Glossary/Glosario

ENGLISH	SPANISH	EXAMPLES

imaginary number The square root of a negative number, written in the form *bi*, where *b* is a real number and *i* is the imaginary unit, $\sqrt{-1}$. Also called a *pure imaginary number*.

número imaginario Raíz cuadrada de un número negativo, expresado como *bi*, donde *b* es un número real e *i* es la unidad imaginaria, $\sqrt{-1}$. También se denomina *número imaginario puro*.

$$\sqrt{-16} = \sqrt{16} \cdot \sqrt{-1} = 4i$$

---

imaginary unit The unit in the imaginary number system, $\sqrt{-1}$.

unidad imaginaria Unidad del sistema de números imaginarios, $\sqrt{-1}$.

$$\sqrt{-1} = i$$

---

inconsistent system A system of equations or inequalities that has no solution.

sistema inconsistente Sistema de ecuaciones o desigualdades que no tiene solución.

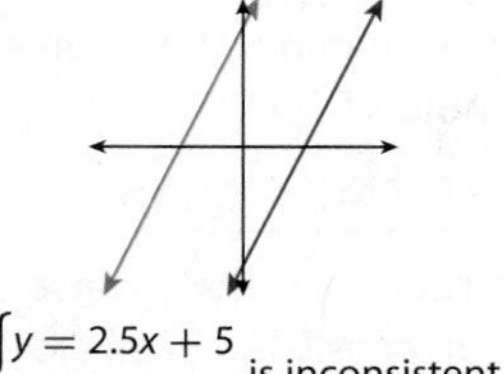

$\begin{cases} y = 2.5x + 5 \\ y = 2.5x - 5 \end{cases}$ is inconsistent.

Increasing A function is increasing on an interval if $f(x_1) < f(x_2)$ when $x_1 < x_2$ for any *x*-values x_1 and x_2 from the interval.

creciente Una función es creciente en un intervalo si $f(x_1) < f(x_2)$ cuando $x_1 < x_2$ dados los valores de x, x_1 y x_2, pertenecienlos al intervalo.

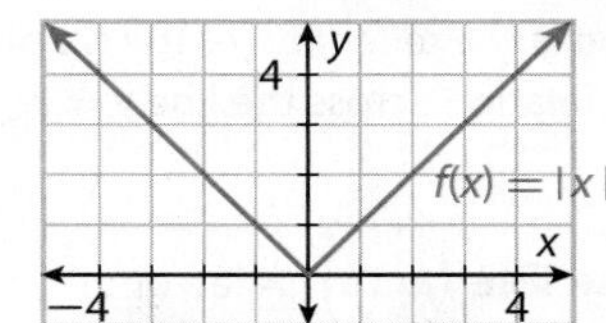

$f(x)$ is increasing on the interval $x > 0$.

---

independent events Events for which the occurrence or non-occurrence of one event does not affect the probability of the other event.

sucesos independientes Dos sucesos son independientes si el hecho de que se produzca o no uno de ellos no afecta la probabilidad del otro suceso.

From a bag containing 3 red marbles and 2 blue marbles, drawing a red marble, replacing it, and then drawing a blue marble.

---

independent system A system of equations that has exactly one solution.

sistema independiente Sistema de ecuaciones que tiene exactamente una solución.

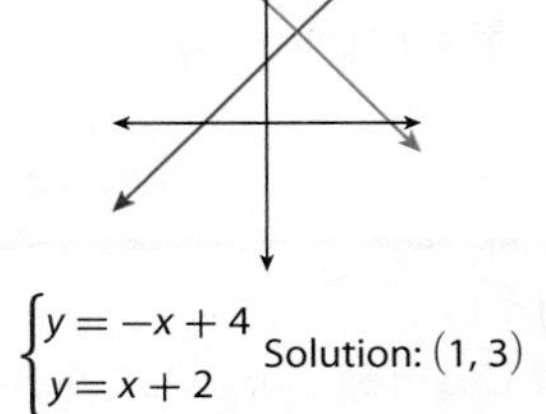

$\begin{cases} y = -x + 4 \\ y = x + 2 \end{cases}$ Solution: $(1, 3)$

---

independent variable The input of a function; a variable whose value determines the value of the output, or dependent variable.

variable independiente Entrada de una función; variable cuyo valor determina el valor de la salida, o variable dependiente.

$y = 2x + 1$

↑ independent variable

---

initial side The ray that lies on the positive *x*-axis when an angle is drawn in standard position.

lado inicial El rayo que se encuentra en el eje positivo *x* cuando se traza un ángulo en la posición estándar.

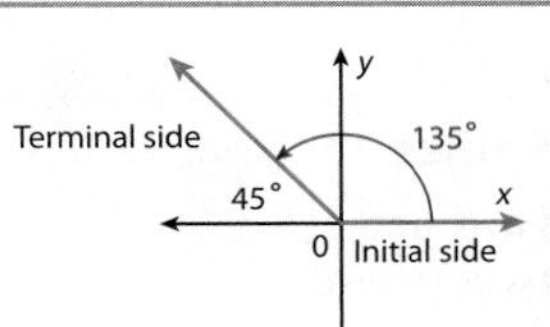

ENGLISH	SPANISH	EXAMPLES

interval notation A way of writing the set of all real numbers between two endpoints. The symbols [and] are used to include an endpoint in an interval, and the symbols (and) are used to exclude an endpoint from an interval.

notación de intervalo Forma de expresar el conjunto de todos los números reales entre dos extremos. Los símbolos [y] se utilizan para incluir un extremo en un intervalo y los símbolos (y) se utilizan para excluir un extremo de un intervalo.

Interval notation	Set-builder notation
(a, b)	$\{x \mid a < x < b\}$
$(a, b]$	$\{x \mid a < x \leq b\}$
$[a, b)$	$\{x \mid a \leq x < b\}$
$[a, b]$	$\{x \mid a \leq x \leq b\}$

inverse function The function that results from exchanging the input and output values of a one-to-one function. The inverse of $f(x)$ is denoted $f^{-1}(x)$.

función inversa Función que resulta de intercambiar los valores de entrada y salida de una función uno a uno. La función inversa de $f(x)$ se expresa $f^{-1}(x)$

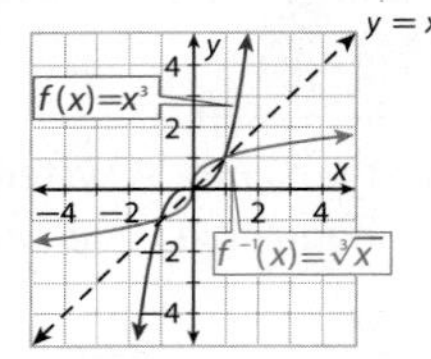

inverse relation The inverse of the relation consisting of all ordered pairs (x, y) is the set of all ordered pairs (y, x). The graph of an inverse relation is the reflection of the graph of the relation across the line $y = x$.

relación inversa La inversa de la relación que consta de todos los pares ordenados (x, y) es el conjunto de todos los pares ordenados (y, x). La gráfica de una relación inversa es el reflejo de la gráfica de la relación sobre la línea $y = x$.

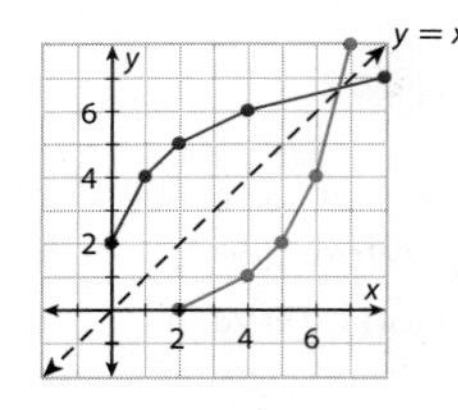

irreducible factor A factor of degree 2 or greater that cannot be factored further.

factor irreductible Factor de grado 2 o mayor que no se puede seguir factorizando.

$x^2 + 7x + 1$

joint relative frequency The ratio of the frequency in a particular category divided by the total number of data values.

frecuencia relativa conjunta La razón de la frecuencia en una determinada categoría dividida entre el número total de valores.

Law of Cosines For $\triangle ABC$ with side lengths a, b, and c,
$a^2 = b^2 + c^2 - 2bc \cos A$
$b^2 = a^2 + c^2 - 2ac \cos B$
$c^2 = a^2 + b^2 - 2ab \cos C$.

Ley de cosenos Dado $\triangle ABC$ con longitudes de lado a, b y c,
$a^2 = b^2 + c^2 - 2bc \cos A$
$b^2 = a^2 + c^2 - 2ac \cos B$
$c^2 = a^2 + b^2 - 2ab \cos C$

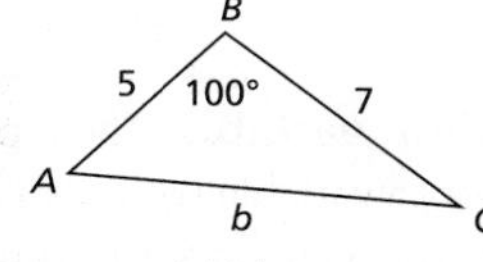

$b^2 = 7^2 + 5^2 - 2(7)(5)\cos 100°$
$b^2 \approx 86.2$
$b \approx 9.3$

Law of Sines For $\triangle ABC$ with side lengths a, b, and c,
$\frac{\sin A}{a} = \frac{\sin B}{b} = \frac{\sin C}{c}$.

Ley de senos Dado $\triangle ABC$ con longitudes de lado a, b y c,
$\frac{\text{sen} A}{a} = \frac{\text{sen} B}{b} = \frac{\text{sen} C}{c}$.

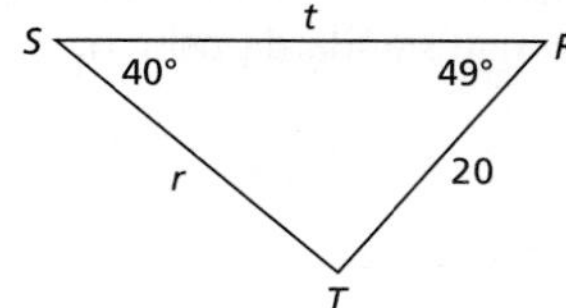

$\frac{\sin 49°}{r} = \frac{\sin 40°}{20}$
$r = \frac{20 \sin 49°}{\sin 40°} \approx 23.5$

ENGLISH	SPANISH	EXAMPLES
leading coefficient The coefficient of the first term of a polynomial in standard form.	**coeficiente principal** Coeficiente del primer termino de un polinomio en forma estandar	$3x^2 + 7x - 2$ ↑ Leading coefficient
limit For an infinite arithmetic series that converges, the number that the partial sums approach.	**límite** Para un serie que coverge, el número que se aproximan las sumas.	The series $\frac{1}{2} + \frac{1}{4} + \frac{1}{8} + \frac{1}{16} + \ldots$ has a limit of 1.
line of best fit The line that comes closest to all of the points in a data set.	**línea de mejor ajuste** Línea que más se acerca a todos los puntos de un conjunto de datos.	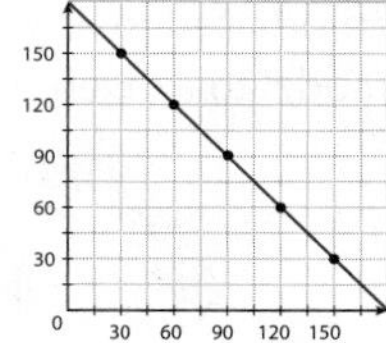
linear equation in three variables An equation with three distinct variables, each of which is either first degree or has a coefficient of zero.	**ecuación lineal en tres variables** Ecuación con tres variables diferentes, sean de primer grado o tengan un coeficiente de cero.	$5 = 3x + 2y + 6z$
linear regression A statistical method used to fit a linear model to a given data set.	**regresión lineal** Método estadístico utilizado para ajustar un modelo lineal a un conjunto de datos determinado.	
linear system A system of equations containing only linear equations.	**sistema lineal** Sistema de ecuaciones que contiene sólo ecuaciones lineales.	$\begin{cases} y = 2x + 1 \\ x + y = 8 \end{cases}$
local maximum For a function f, $f(a)$ is a local maximum if there is an interval around a such that $f(x) < f(a)$ for every x-value in the interval except a.	**máximo local** Dada una función f, $f(a)$ es el máximo local si hay un intervalo en a tal que $f(x) < f(a)$ para cada valor de x en el intervalo excepto a.	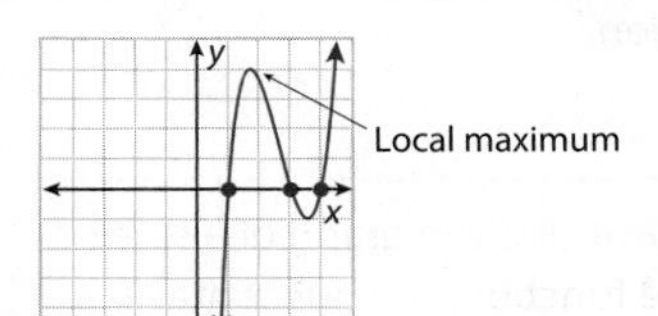
local minimum For a function f, $f(a)$ is a local minimum if there is an interval around a such that $f(x) > f(a)$ for every x-value in the interval except a.	**mínimo local** Dada una función f, $f(a)$ es el mínimo local si hay un intervalo en a tal que $f(x) > f(a)$ para cada valor de x en el intervalo excepto a.	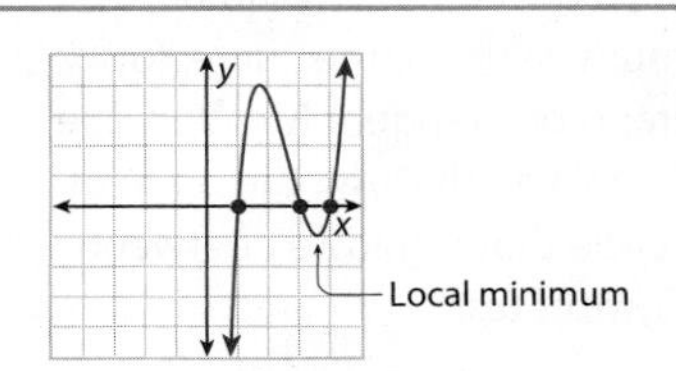
logarithm The exponent that a specified base must be raised to in order to get a certain value.	**logaritmo** Exponente al cual debe elevarse una base determinada a fin de obtener cierto valor.	$\log_2 8 = 3$, because 3 is the power that 2 is raised to in order to get 8; or $2^3 = 8$.
logarithmic equation An equation that contains a logarithm of a variable.	**ecuación logarítmica** Ecuación que contiene un logaritmo de una variable.	$\log x + 3 = 7$

ENGLISH	SPANISH	EXAMPLES
logarithmic function A function of the form $f(x) = \log_b x$, where $b \neq 1$ and $b > 0$, which is the inverse of the exponential function $f(x) = b^x$.	**función logarítmica** Función del tipo $f(x) = \log_b x$, donde $b \neq 1$ y $b > 0$, que es la inversa de la función exponencial $f(x) = b^x$.	$f(x) = \log_4 x$
logarithmic regression A statistical method used to fit a logarithmic model to a given data set.	**regresión logarítmica** Método estadístico utilizado para ajustar un modelo logarítmico a un conjunto de datos determinado.	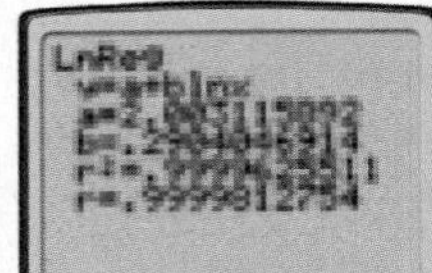

M

ENGLISH	SPANISH	EXAMPLES
margin of error In a random sample, it defines an interval, centered on the sample percent, in which the population percent is most likely to lie.	**margen de error** En una muestra aleatoria, define un intervalo, centrado en el porcentaje de muestra, en el que es más probable que se encuentre el porcentaje de población.	
matrix A rectangular array of numbers.	**matriz** Arreglo rectangular de números.	$\begin{bmatrix} 1 & 0 & 3 \\ -2 & 2 & -5 \\ 7 & -6 & 3 \end{bmatrix}$
maximum value of a function The *y*-value of the highest point on the graph of the function.	**máximo de una función** Valor de *y* del punto más alto en la gráfica de la función.	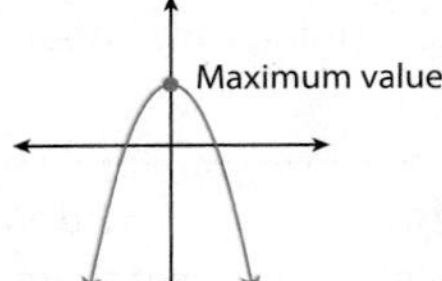
midline For the graph of a sine or cosine function, the horizontal line halfway between the maximum and minimum values of the curve; for the graph of a tangent function, the horizontal line through the point of each cycle that is midway between the asymptotes.	**línea media** En la gráfica de una función seno o coseno, la línea horizontal a medio camino entre los valores máximo y mínimo de la curva; en la gráfica de una función tangente, la línea horizontal que atraviesa el punto de cada ciclo que está a medio camino entre las asíntotas.	
minimum value of a function The *y*-value of the lowest point on the graph of the function.	**mínimo de una función** Valor de *y* del punto más bajo en la gráfica de la función.	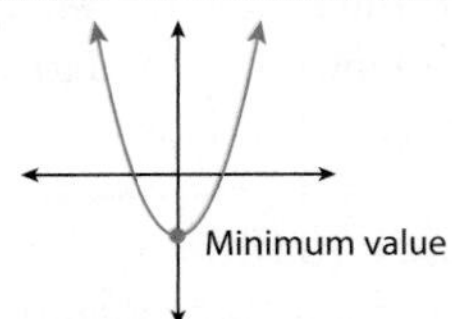
monomial A number or a product of numbers and variables with whole-number exponents, or a polynomial with one term.	**monomio** Número o producto de números y variables con exponentes de números cabales, o polinomio con un término.	$8x$, 9, $3x^2y^4$

ENGLISH	SPANISH	EXAMPLES
multiple root A root r is a multiple root when the factor $(x - r)$ appears in the equation more than once.	**raíz múltiple** Una raíz r es una raíz múltiple cuando el factor $(x - r)$ aparece en la ecuación más de una vez.	3 is a multiple root of $P(x) = (x - 3)^2$.
multiplicity If a polynomial $P(x)$ has a multiple root at r, the multiplicity of r is the number of times $(x - r)$ appears as a factor in $P(x)$.	**multiplicidad** Si un polinomio $P(x)$ tiene una raíz múltiple en r, la multiplicidad de r es la cantidad de veces que $(x - r)$ aparece como factor en $P(x)$.	For $P(x) = (x - 3)^2$, the root 3 has a multiplicity of 2.
mutually exclusive events Two events are mutually exclusive if they cannot both occur in the same trial of an experiment.	**sucesos mutuamente excluyentes** Dos sucesos son mutuamente excluyentes si ambos no pueden ocurrir en la misma prueba de un experimento.	In the experiment of rolling a number cube, rolling a 3 and rolling an even number are mutually exclusive events.

N

ENGLISH	SPANISH	EXAMPLES
natural logarithm A logarithm with base e, written as ln.	**logaritmo natural** Logaritmo con base e, que se escribe ln.	$\ln 5 = \log_e 5 \approx 1.6$
natural logarithmic function The function $f(x) = \ln x$, which is the inverse of the natural exponential function $f(x) = e^x$. Domain is $\{x \mid x > 0\}$; range is all real numbers	**función logarítmica natural** Función $f(x) = \ln x$, que es la inversa de la función exponencial natural $f(x) = e^x$. El dominio es $\{x \mid x > 0\}$; el rango es todos los números reales.	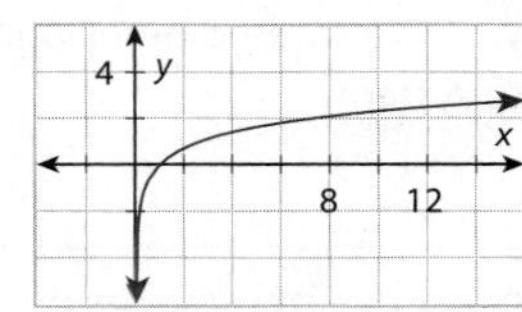
nonlinear system of equations A system in which at least one of the equations is not linear.	**sistema no lineal de ecuaciones** Sistema en el cual por lo menos una de las ecuaciones no es lineal.	$\begin{cases} y = 2x^2 \\ y = -3^2 + 5 \end{cases}$
normal distribution A distribution that is mounded in the middle with symmetric "tails" at each end, forming a bell shape.	**distribución normal** Una distribución que está elevada en el centro con "colas" simétricas en los extremos, lo que forma la figura de una campana.	
***n*th root** The nth root of a number a, written as $\sqrt[n]{a}$ or $a^{\frac{1}{n}}$, is a number that is equal to a when it is raised to the nth power.	**enésima raíz** La enésima raíz de un número a, que se escribe como $\sqrt[n]{a}$ or $a^{\frac{1}{n}}$, es un número igual a a cuando se eleva a la enésima potencia.	$\sqrt[5]{32} = 2$, because $2^5 = 32$.
null hypothesis The assumption made that any difference between the control group and the treatment group in an experiment is due to chance, and not to the treatment.	**hipótesis nula** La suposición de que cualquier diferencia entre el grupo de control y el grupo de tratamiento en un experimento se debe al azar, no al tratamiento.	

ENGLISH	SPANISH	EXAMPLES
numerical data Data that represent quantities or observations that can be measured.	**datos numéricos** Datos que representan cantidades u observaciones que pueden medirse.	

O

ENGLISH	SPANISH	EXAMPLES
observational study A study that observes individuals and measures variables without controlling the individuals or their environment in any way.	**estudio de observación** Estudio que permite obsérvar a individuos y medir variables sin controlar a los individuos ni su ambiente.	
odd function A function in which $f(-x) = -f(x)$ for all x in the domain of the function.	**función impar** Función en la que $f(-x) = -f(x)$ para todos los valores de x dentro del dominio de la función	$f(x) = x^3$ $f(x) = x^3$ is an odd function.
one-to-one function A function in which each y-value corresponds to only one x-value. The inverse of a one-to-one function is also a function.	**función uno a uno** Función en la que cada valor de y corresponde a sólo un valor de x. La inversa de una función uno a uno es también una función.	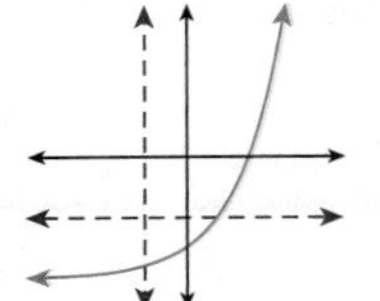
ordered triple A set of three numbers that can be used to locate a point (x, y, z) in a three-dimensional coordinate system.	**tripleta ordenada** Conjunto de tres números que se pueden utilizar para ubicar un punto (x, y, z) en un sistema de coordenadas tridimensional.	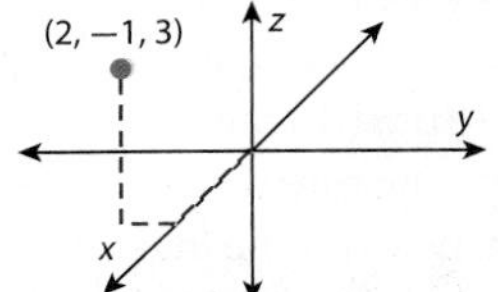
overlapping events Events in the sample space of a probability experiment that have one or more outcomes in common.	**eventos solapados** Eventos en el espacio muestral de un experimento de probabilidad que tienen uno o más resultados en común.	

P

ENGLISH	SPANISH	EXAMPLES
parabola The shape of the graph of a quadratic function. Also, the set of points equidistant from a point F, called the focus, and a line d, called the *directrix*.	**parábola** Forma de la gráfica de una función cuadrática. También, conjunto de puntos equidistantes de un punto F, denominado *foco*, y una línea d, denominada *directriz*.	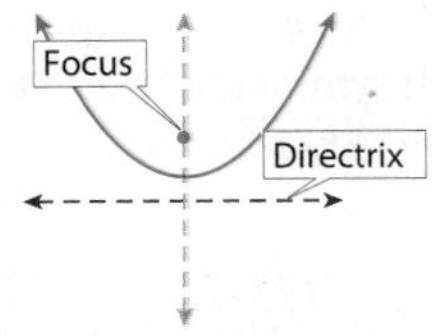
parameter One of the constants in a function or equation that may be changed. Also the third variable in a set of parametric equations.	**parámetro** Una de las constantes en una función o ecuación que se puede cambiar. También es la tercera variable en un conjunto de ecuaciones paramétricas.	$y = (x - h)^2 + k$ parameters
parent cube root function The function $f(x) = \sqrt[3]{x}$.	**función madre de la raíz cúbica** Función del tipo $f(x) = \sqrt[3]{x}$.	$f(x) = \sqrt[3]{x}$

Glossary/Glosario

ENGLISH	SPANISH	EXAMPLES
parent function The simplest function with the defining characteristics of the family. Functions in the same family are transformations of their parent function.	**función madre** La función más básica con las características de la familia. Las funciones de la misma familia son transformaciones de su función madre.	$f(x) = x^2$ is the parent function for $g(x) = x^2 + 4$ and $h(x) = 5(x + 2)^2 - 3$.
parent square root function The function $f(x) = \sqrt{x}$, where $x \geq 0$.	**función madre de la raíz cuadrada** Función del tipo $f(x) = \sqrt{x}$, donde $x \geq 0$.	$f(x) = \sqrt{x}$
partial sum Indicated by $S_n = \sum_{i=1}^{n} a_i$, the sum of a specified number of terms n of a sequence whose total number of terms is greater than n.	**suma parcial** Expresada por $S_n = \sum_{i=l}^{n} a_i$, la suma de un número específico n de términos de una sucesión cuyo número total de términos es mayor que n.	For the sequence $a_n = n^2$, the fourth partial sum of the infinite series $\sum_{k=1}^{\infty} k^2$ is $\sum_{k=1}^{4} k^2 = 1^2 + 2^2 + 3^2 + 4^2 = 30$.
Pascal's triangle A triangular arrangement of numbers in which every row starts and ends with 1 and each other number is the sum of the two numbers above it.	**triángulo de Pascal** Arreglo triangular de números en el cual cada fila comienza y termina con 1 y cada uno de los demás números es la suma de los dos números que están encima de él.	1 1 1 1 2 1 1 3 3 1 1 4 6 4 1
perfect-square trinomial A trinomial whose factored form is the square of a binomial. A perfect-square trinomial has the form $a^2 - 2ab + b^2 = (a - b)^2$ or $a^2 + 2ab + b^2 = (a + b)^2$.	**trinomio cuadrado perfecto** Trinomio cuya forma factorizada es el cuadrado de un binomio. Un trinomio cuadrado perfecto tiene la forma $a^2 - 2ab + b^2 = (a - b)^2$ o $a^2 + 2ab + b^2 = (a + b)^2$.	$x^2 + 6x + 9$ is a perfect square trinomial, because $x^2 + 6x + 9 = (x + 3)^2$.
period of a periodic function The length of a cycle measured in units of the independent variable (usually time in seconds). Also the reciprocal of the frequency.	**periodo de una función periódica** Longitud de un ciclo medido en unidades de la variable independiente (generalmente el tiempo en segundos). También es la inversa de la frecuencia.	Period; y; x; −3; −1; 1; 3
periodic function A function that repeats exactly in regular intervals, called *periods*.	**función periódica** Función que se repite exactamente a intervalos regulares denominados *periodos*.	Period; y; x; −3; −1; 1; 3
permutation An arrangement of a group of objects in which order is important. The number of permutations of r objects from a group of n objects is denoted ${}_nP_r$.	**permutación** Arreglo de un grupo de objetos en el cual el orden es importante. El número de permutaciones de r objetos de un grupo de n objetos se expresa ${}_nP_r$.	For 4 objects *A*, *B*, *C*, and *D*, there are ${}_4P_2 = 12$ different permutations of 2 objects: *AB*, *AC*, *AD*, *BC*, *BD*, *CD*, *BA*, *CA*, *DA*, *CB*, *DB*, and *DC*.

ENGLISH	SPANISH	EXAMPLES
permutation test A significance test performed on the results of an experiment by forming every possible regrouping of all the data values taken from the control and treatment groups into two new groups, finding the distribution of the differences of the means for all of the new group pairings, and then finding the likelihood, given that the null hypothesis is true, of getting a difference of means at least as great as the original experimental difference.	**prueba de permutación** Una prueba de significancia realizada sobre los resultados de un experimento al formar todos los reagrupamientos posibles de todos los valores de datos tomados de los grupos de control y de tratamiento en dos nuevos grupos, hallar la distribución de las diferencias de las medias para todos los emparejamientos nuevos, y luego hallar la probabilidad, suponiendo que la hipótesis nula es verdadera, de obtener una diferencia de medias al menos tan grande como la diferencia experimental original.	
phase shift A horizontal translation of a periodic function.	**cambio de fase** Traslación horizontal de una función periódica.	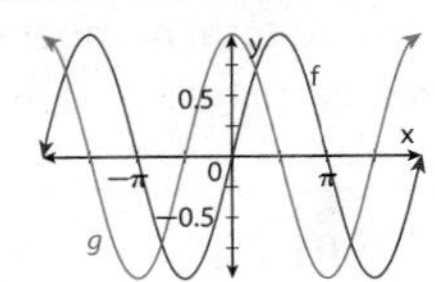 g is a phase shift of f $\frac{\pi}{2}$ units left.
piecewise function A function that is a combination of one or more functions.	**función a trozos** Función que es una combinación de una o más funciones.	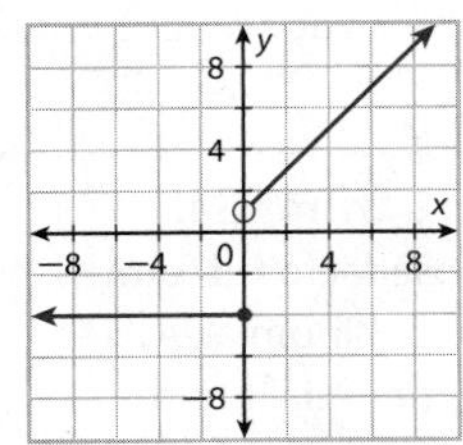 $f(x) = \begin{cases} -4 & \text{if } x \leq 0 \\ x+1 & \text{if } x > 0 \end{cases}$
polynomial A monomial or a sum or difference of monomials.	**polinomio** Monomio o suma o diferencia de monomios.	$2x^2 + 3x - 7$
polynomial function A function whose rule is a polynomial.	**función polinomial** Función cuya regla es un polinomio.	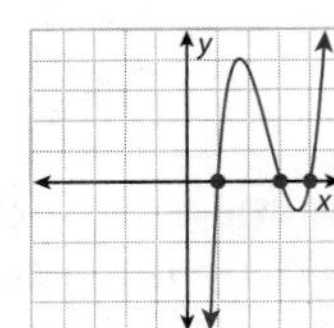 $f(x) = x^3 - 8x^2 + 19x - 12$
polynomial identity A mathematical relationship equating one polynomial quantity to another.	**identidad de polinomios** Relación matemática que iguala una cantidad polinomial con otra.	$(x^4 - y^4) = (x^2 + y^2)(x^2 - y^2)$
population The entire group of objects or individuals considered for a survey.	**población** Grupo completo de objetos o individuos que se desea estudiar.	In a survey about the study habits of high school students, the population is all high school students.
probability A number from 0 to 1 (or 0% to 100%) that is the measure of how likely an event is to occur.	**probabilidad** Número entre 0 y 1 (o entre 0% y 100%) que describe cuán probable es que ocurra un suceso.	A bag contains 3 red marbles and 4 blue marbles. The probability of choosing a red marble is $\frac{3}{7}$.

ENGLISH	SPANISH	EXAMPLES
probability distribution for an experiment The function that pairs each outcome with its probability.	**distribución de probabilidad para un experimento** Función que asigna a cada resultado su probabilidad.	A number cube is rolled 10 times. The results are shown in the table. (see table below)
probability sample A sample in which every member of the population being sampled has a nonzero probability of being selected.	**muestra de probabilidad** Muestra en la que cada miembro de la población que se estudia tiene una probabilidad distinta de cero de ser elegido.	
pure imaginary number *See* imaginary number.	**número imaginario puro** Ver número imaginario.	$3i$

Outcome	1	2	3	4	5	6
Probability	$\frac{1}{10}$	$\frac{1}{5}$	$\frac{1}{5}$	0	$\frac{3}{10}$	$\frac{1}{5}$

ENGLISH	SPANISH	EXAMPLES
quadratic equation An equation that can be written in the form $ax^2 + bx + c = 0$, where a, b, and c are real numbers and $a \neq 0$.	**ecuación cuadrática** Ecuación que se puede expresar como $ax^2 + bx + c = 0$, donde a, b y c son números reales y $a \neq 0$.	$x^2 + 3x - 4 = 0$ $x^2 - 9 = 0$
Quadratic Formula The formula $x = \frac{-b \pm \sqrt{b^2 - 4ac}}{2a}$, which gives solutions, or roots, of equations in the form $ax^2 + bx + c = 0$, where $a \neq 0$.	**fórmula cuadrática** La fórmula $x = \frac{-b \pm \sqrt{b^2 - 4ac}}{2a}$, que da soluciones, o raíces, para las ecuaciones del tipo $ax^2 + bx + c = 0$, donde $a \neq 0$.	The solutions of $2x^2 - 5x - 3 = 0$ are given by $x = \frac{-(-5) \pm \sqrt{(-5)^2 - 4(2)(-3)}}{2(2)}$ $= \frac{5 \pm \sqrt{25 + 24}}{4} = \frac{5 \pm 7}{4}$; $x = 3$ or $x = -\frac{1}{2}$.
quadratic function A function that can be written in the form $f(x) = ax^2 + bx + c$, where a, b, and c are real numbers and $a \neq 0$, or in the form $f(x) = a(x - h)^2 + k$, where a, h, and k are real numbers and $a \neq 0$.	**función cuadrática** Función que se puede expresar como $f(x) = ax^2 + bx + c$, donde a, b y c son números reales y $a \neq 0$, o como $f(x) = a(x - h)^2 + k$, donde a, h y k son números reales y $a \neq 0$.	$f(x) = x^2 - 6x + 8$
quadratic model A quadratic function used to represent a set of data.	**modelo cuadrático** Función cuadrática que se utiliza para representar un conjunto de datos.	(see table below) A quadratic model for the data is $f(x) = x^2 + 3.3x - 2.6$.
quadratic regression A statistical method used to fit a quadratic model to a given data set.	**regresión cuadrática** Método estadístico utilizado para ajustar un modelo cuadrático a un conjunto de datos determinado.	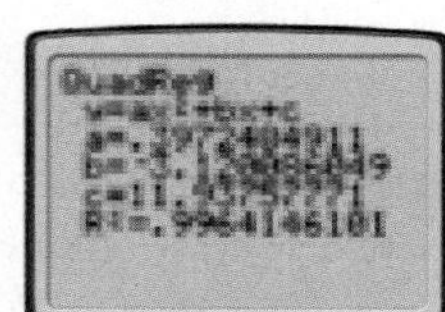

x	4	6	8	10
$f(x)$	27	52	89	130

ENGLISH	SPANISH	EXAMPLES
R		
radian A unit of angle measure based on arc length. In a circle of radius r, if a central angle has a measure of 1 radian, then the length of the intercepted arc is r units. 2π radians $= 360°$ 1 radian $\approx 57°$	**radián** Unidad de medida de un ángulo basada en la longitud del arco. En un círculo de radio r, si un ángulo central mide 1 radián, entonces la longitud del arco abarcado es r unidades. 2π radianes $= 360°$ 1 radián $\approx 57°$	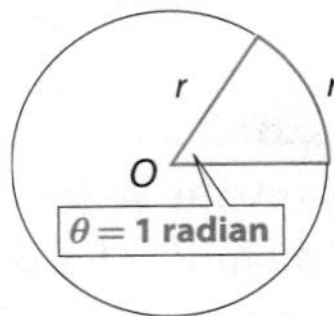
radical An indicated root of a quantity.	**radical** Raíz indicada de una cantidad.	$\sqrt{36} = 6,\ \sqrt[3]{27} = 3$
radical equation An equation that contains a variable within a radical.	**ecuación radical** Ecuación que contiene una variable dentro de un radical.	$\sqrt{x+3} + 4 = 7$
radical function A function whose rule contains a variable within a radical.	**función radical** Función cuya regla contiene una variable dentro de un radical.	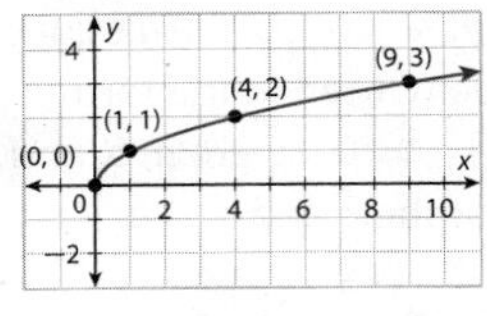 $f(x) = \sqrt{x}$
radicand The expression under a radical sign.	**radicando** Número o expresión debajo del signo de radical.	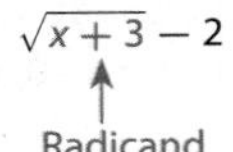
random variable A variable whose value is determined by the outcome of a probability experiment.	**variable aleatoria** Una variable cuyo valor viene determinado por el resultado de un experimento de probabilidad.	
randomized comparative experiment An experiment in which the individuals are assigned to the control group or the treatment group at random, in order to minimize bias.	**experimento comparativo aleatorizado** Experimento en el que se elige al azar a los individuos para el grupo de control o para el grupo experimental, a fin de minimizar el sesgo.	
range of a function or relation The set of output values of a function or relation.	**rango de una función o relación** Conjunto de los valores desalida de una función o relación.	The range of $y = x^2$ is $\left\{y \mid y \geq 0\right\}$.
rational equation An equation that contains one or more rational expressions.	**ecuación racional** Ecuación que contiene una o más expresiones racionales.	$\frac{x+2}{x^2+3x-1} = 6$
rational exponent An exponent that can be expressed as $\frac{m}{n}$ such that if m and n are integers, then $b^{\frac{m}{n}} = \sqrt[n]{b^m} = \left(\sqrt[n]{b}\right)^m$.	**exponente racional** Exponente quese puede expresar como $\frac{m}{n}$ tal que, si m y n son números enteros, entonces $b^{\frac{m}{n}} = \sqrt[n]{b^m} = \left(\sqrt[n]{b}\right)^m$	$4^{\frac{3}{2}} = \sqrt{4^3} = \sqrt{64} = 8$ $4^{\frac{3}{2}} = \left(\sqrt{4}\right)^3 = 2^3 = 8$

Glossary/Glosario

ENGLISH	SPANISH	EXAMPLES
rational expression An algebraic expression whose numerator and denominator are polynomials and whose denominator has a degree ≥ 1.	**expresión racional** Expresión algebraica cuyo numerador y denominador son polinomios y cuyo denominador tiene un grado ≥ 1.	$\frac{x+2}{x^2+3x-1}$
rational function A function whose rule can be written as a rational expression.	**función racional** Función cuya regla se puede expresar como una expresión racional.	$f(x) = \frac{x+2}{x^2+3x-1}$
real axis The horizontal axis in the complex plane; it graphically represents the real part of complex numbers.	**eje real** Eje horizontal de un plano complejo. Representa gráficamente la parte real de los números complejos.	Imaginary axis; $2i$; $0+0i$; Real axis; -2; 2; $-2i$
recursive rule A rule for a sequence in which one or more previous terms are used to generate the next term.	**Regla recurrente** Regla para una sucesión en la cual uno o más términos anteriores se utilizan para generar el término siguiente.	For the sequence 5, 7, 9, 11, ..., a recursive rule is $a_1 = 5$ and $a_n = a_{n-1} + 2$.
reduced row-echelon form A form of an augmented matrix in which the coefficient columns form an identity matrix.	**forma escalonada reducida por filas** Forma de matriz aumentada en la que las columnas de coeficientes forman una matriz de identidad.	$\left[\begin{array}{cc\|c} 1 & 0 & -1 \\ 0 & 1 & 3 \end{array}\right]$
reference angle For an angle in standard position, the reference angle is the positive acute angle formed by the terminal side of the angle and the x-axis.	**ángulo de referencia** Dado un ángulo en posición estándar, el ángulo de referencia es el ángulo agudo positivo formado por el lado terminal del ángulo y el eje x.	y; $135°$; $45°$; x; 0
reflection A transformation that reflects, or "flips," a graph or figure across a line, called the line of reflection, such that each reflected point is the same distance from the line of reflection but is on the opposite side of the line.	**reflexión** Transformación que refleja, o invierte, una gráfica o figura sobre una línea, llamada la línea de reflexión, de manera tal que cada punto reflejado esté a la misma distancia de la línea de reflexión pero que se encuentre en el lado opuesto de la línea.	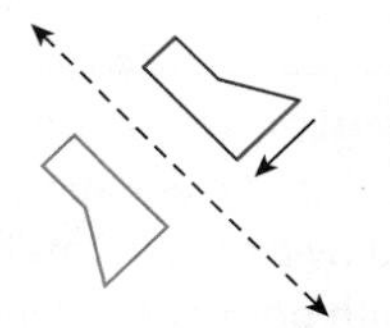
regression The statistical study of the relationship between variables.	**regresión** Estudio estadístico de la relación entre variables.	
Remainder Theorem If the polynomial function $P(x)$ is divided by $x - a$, then the remainder r is $P(a)$.	**Teorema del resto** Si la función polinomial $P(x)$ se divide entre $x - a$, entonces, el residuo r será $P(a)$.	
representative sample A sample that is a good estimator for its corresponding population parameter.	**muestra representativa** Una muestra que es un buen estimador para su parámetro de población correspondiente.	

ENGLISH	SPANISH	EXAMPLES
rotation A transformation that rotates or turns a figure about a point called the center of rotation.	**rotación** Transformación que hace rotar o girar una figura sobre un punto llamado centro de rotación.	
row operation An operation performed on a row of an augmented matrix that creates an equivalent matrix.	**operación por filas** Operación realizada en una fila de una matriz aumentada que crea una matriz equivalente.	$\left[\begin{array}{cc\|c} 2 & 0 & -2 \\ 0 & 1 & 3 \end{array}\right] = \left[\begin{array}{cc\|c} \frac{1}{2}(2) & \frac{1}{2}(0) & \frac{1}{2}(-1) \\ 0 & 1 & 3 \end{array}\right] = \left[\begin{array}{cc\|c} 1 & 0 & -1 \\ 0 & 1 & 3 \end{array}\right]$
row-reduction method The process of performing elementary row operations on an augmented matrix to transform the matrix to reduced row echelon form.	**método de reducción por filas** Proceso por el cual se realizan operaciones elementales de filas en una matriz aumentada para transformar la matriz en una forma reducida de filas escalonadas.	$\left[\begin{array}{cc\|c} 2 & 0 & -2 \\ 0 & 1 & 3 \end{array}\right] = \left[\begin{array}{cc\|c} \frac{1}{2}(2) & \frac{1}{2}(0) & \frac{1}{2}(-1) \\ 0 & 1 & 3 \end{array}\right] = \left[\begin{array}{cc\|c} 1 & 0 & -1 \\ 0 & 1 & 3 \end{array}\right]$

S

sample A part of the population.	**muestra** Una parte de la población.	In a survey about the study habits of high school students, a sample is a survey of 100 students.
sample space The set of all possible outcomes of a probability experiment.	**espacio muestral** Conjunto de todos los resultados posibles en un experimento de probabilidades.	In the experiment of rolling a number cube, the sample space is 1, 2, 3, 4, 5, 6.
sampling distribution A distribution that shows how a particular statistic varies across all samples of *n* individuals from the same population.	**distribución de muestreo** Una distribución que muestra de qué manera una determinada estadística varía a lo largo de todas las muestras de *n* individuos de la misma población.	
second-degree equation in two variables An equation constructed by adding terms in two variables with powers no higher than 2.	**ecuación de segundo grado en dos variables** Ecuación compuesta por la suma de términos en dos variables con potencias no mayores a 2.	$ax^2 + by^2 + cx + dy + e = 0$
second differences Differences between first differences of a function.	**segundas diferencias** Diferencias entre las primerasdiferencias de una función.	x: 0, 1, 2, 3; y: 1, 4, 9, 16 first differences +3 +5 +7 second differences +2 +2
self-selected sample A sample in which members volunteer to participate.	**muestra de voluntarios** Muestra en la que los miembros se ofrecen voluntariamente para participar.	
sequence A list of numbers that often form a pattern.	**sucesión** Lista de números que generalmente forman un patrón.	1, 2, 4, 8, 16, ...

Glossary/Glosario

ENGLISH	SPANISH	EXAMPLES
series The indicated sum of the terms of a sequence.	**serie** Suma indicada de los términos de una sucesión.	$1 + 2 + 4 + 8 + 16 + \ldots$
set A collection of items called elements.	**conjunto** Grupo de componentes denominados elementos.	$\{1, 2, 3\}$
set-builder notation A notation for a set that uses a rule to describe the properties of the elements of the set.	**notación de conjuntos** Notación para un conjunto que se vale de una regla para describir las propiedades de los elementos del conjunto.	$\{x \mid x > 3\}$ read, "The set of all x such that x is greater than 3."
simple event An event consisting of only one outcome.	**suceso simple** Suceso que contiene sólo un resultado.	In the experiment of rolling a number cube, the event consisting of the outcome 3 is a simple event.
simulation A model of an experiment, often one that would be too difficult or time-consuming to actually perform.	**simulación** Modelo de un experimento; generalmente se recurre a la simulación cuando realizar dicho experimento sería demasiado difícil o llevaría mucho tiempo.	A random number generator is used to simulate the roll of a number cube.
sine In a right triangle, the ratio of the length of the side opposite $\angle A$ to the length of the hypotenuse.	**seno** En un triángulo rectángulo, razón entre la longitud del cateto opuesto a $\angle A$ y la longitud de la hipotenusa.	opposite hypotenuse A $\sin A = \frac{\text{opposite}}{\text{hypotenuse}}$.
skewed distribution A distribution that is mounded but not symmetric because one "tail" is much longer than the other.	**distribución sesgada** Una distribución que está elevada pero no es simétrica porque una de las "colas" es mucho más larga que la otra.	
square-root function A function whose rule contains a variable under a square-root sign.	**función de raíz cuadrada** Función cuya regla contiene una variable bajo un signo de raíz cuadrada.	(0, 0), (1, 1), (4, 2), (9, 3) $f(x) = \sqrt{x}$
standard deviation A measure of dispersion of a data set. The standard deviation σ is the square root of the variance.	**desviación estándar** Medida de dispersión de un conjunto de datos. La desviación estándar σ es la raíz cuadrada de la varianza.	Data set: $\{6, 7, 7, 9, 11\}$ Mean: $\frac{6+7+7+9+11}{5} = 8$ Variance: $\frac{1}{5}(4 + 1 + 1 + 1 + 9) = 3.2$ Standard deviation: $\sigma = \sqrt{3.2} \approx 1.8$
standard error of the mean The standard deviation of the sampling distribution of the sample mean, denoted $\sigma_{\bar{x}}$.	**error estándar de la media** La desviación estándar de la distribución de muestreo de la media de la muestra, que se indica así: $\sigma_{\bar{x}}$.	

ENGLISH	SPANISH	EXAMPLES
standard error of the proportion The standard deviation of the sampling distribution of the sample proportion, denoted $\sigma_{\hat{p}}$.	**error estándar de la proporción** La desviación estándar de la distribución de muestreo de la proporción de la muestra, que se indica así: $\sigma_{\hat{p}}$.	
standard form of a polynomial A polynomial in one variable is written in standard form when the terms are in order from greatest degree to least degree.	**forma estándar de un polinomio** Un polinomio de una variable se expresa en forma estándar cuando los términos se ordenan de mayor a menor grado.	$3x^3 - 5x^2 + 6x - 7$
standard form of a quadratic equation $ax^2 + bx + c = 0$, where a, b, and c are real numbers and $a \neq 0$.	**forma estándar de una ecuación** cuadrática $ax^2 + bx + c = 0$, donde a, b y c son números reales y $a \neq 0$.	$2x^2 + 3x - 1 = 0$
standard normal distribution A normal distribution that has a mean of 0 and a standard deviation of 1.	**distribución normal estándar** Una distribución normal que tiene una media de 0 y una desviación estándar de 1.	
standard normal value A value that indicates how many standard deviations above or below the mean a particular value falls, given by the formula $z = \frac{x - \mu}{\sigma}$, where z is the standard normal value, x is the given value, μ is the mean, and σ is the standard deviation of a standard normal distribution.	**valor normal estándar** Valor que indica a cuántas desviaciones estándar por encima o por debajo de la media se encuentra un determinado valor, dado por la fórmula $z = \frac{x - \mu}{\sigma}$, donde z es el valor normal estándar, x es el valor dado, μ es la media y σ es la desviación estándar de una distribución normal estándar.	
standard position An angle in standard position has its vertex at the origin and its initial side on the positive x–axis.	**osición estándar** Ángulo cuyo vértice se encuentra en el origen y cuyo lado inicial se encuentra sobre el eje x.	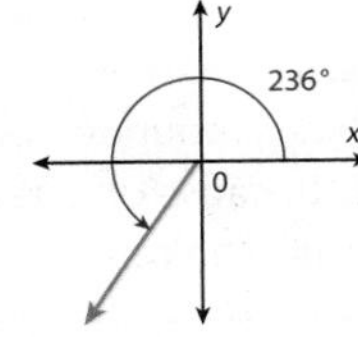
statistic A number that describes a sample.	**estadística** Número que describe una muestra.	
statistical significance A determination that the likelihood that an experimental result occurred by chance is so low that a conclusion in favor of rejecting the null hypothesis is justified.	**significación estadística** Una determinación de que la probabilidad de que un resultado experimental ocurriera por azar es tan reducida que está justificada una conclusión a favor de rechazar la hipótesis nula.	
step function A piecewise function that is constant over each interval in its domain.	**función escalón** Función a trozos que es constante en cada intervalo en su dominio.	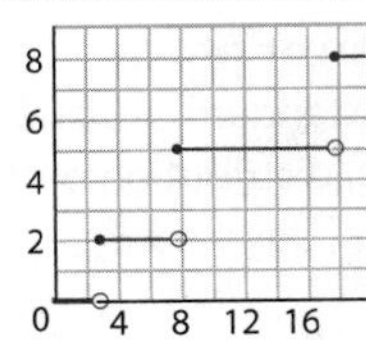

ENGLISH	SPANISH	EXAMPLES
stretch A transformation that pulls the points of a graph horizontally away from the *y*-axis or vertically away from the *x*-axis.	**estiramiento** Transformación que desplaza los puntos de una gráfica en forma horizontal alejándolos del eje y o en forma vertical alejándolos del eje *x*.	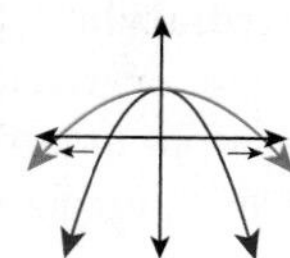
summation notation A method of notating the sum of a series using the Greek letter $\sum$ (capital *sigma*).	**notación de sumatoria** Método de notación de la suma de una serie que utiliza la letra griega $\sum$ (SIGMA mayúscula).	$\sum_{n=1}^{5} 3k = 3 + 6 + 9 + 12 + 15 = 45$
survey A data collection tool that uses questions to measure characteristics of interest about a population using a sample selected from the population.	**encuesta** Una herramienta para recopilar datos que usa preguntas para medir las características de interés sobre una población mediante una muestra seleccionada de entre la población.	
synthetic division A shorthand method of dividing by a linear binomial of the form $(x - a)$ by writing only the coefficients of the polynomials.	**división sintética** Método abreviado de división que consiste en dividir por un binomio lineal del tipo $(x - a)$ escribiendo sólo los coeficientes de los polinomios.	$(x^3 - 7x + 6) \div (x - 2)$ $\begin{array}{r\|rrrr} 2 & 1 & 0 & -7 & 6 \\ & & 2 & 4 & 6 \\ \hline & 1 & 2 & -3 & 0 \end{array}$ $(x^3 - 7x + 6) \div (x - 2) = x^2 + 2x - 3$
synthetic substitution The process of using synthetic division to evaluate a polynomial $p(x)$ when $x = c$.	**sustitución sintética** Proceso que consiste en usar la división sintética para evaluar un polinomio $p(x)$ cuando $x = c$.	
system of equations A set of two or more equations that have two or more variables.	**sistema de ecuaciones** Conjunto de dos o más ecuaciones que contienen dos o más variables.	$\begin{cases} 2x + 3y = -1 \\ x^2 = 4 \end{cases}$
system of linear inequalities A system of inequalities in two or more variables in which all of the inequalities are linear.	**sistema de desigualdades lineales** Sistema de desigualdades en dos o más variables en el que todas las desigualdades son lineales.	$\begin{cases} 2x + 3y \geq -1 \\ x - 3y < 4 \end{cases}$

T

ENGLISH	SPANISH	EXAMPLES
term of a sequence An element or number in the sequence.	**término de una sucesión** Elemento o número de una sucesión.	5 is the third term in the sequence 1, 3, 5, 7, . . .
terminal side For an angle in standard position, the ray that is rotated relative to the positive *x*-axis.	**lado terminal** Dado un ángulo en una posición estándar, el rayo que rota en relación con el eje positivo *x*.	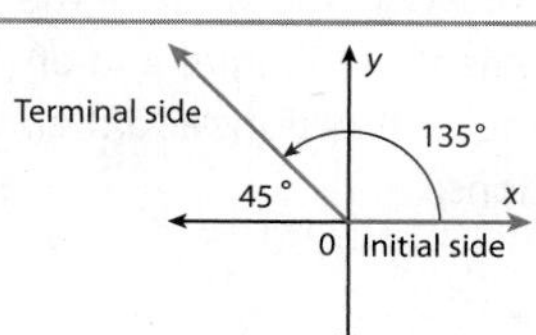

ENGLISH	SPANISH	EXAMPLES
theoretical probability The ratio of the number of equally likely outcomes in an event to the total number of possible outcomes.	**probabilidad teórica** Razón entre el número de resultados igualmente probables de un suceso y el número total de resultados posibles.	The theoretical probability of rolling an odd number on a number cube is $\frac{3}{6} = \frac{1}{2}$.
three-dimensional coordinate system A space that is divided into eight regions by an *x*-axis, a *y*-axis, and a *z*-axis. The locations, or coordinates, of points are given by ordered triples.	**sistema de coordenadas tridimensional** Espacio dividido en ocho regiones por un eje *x*, un eje *y* y un eje *z*. Las ubicaciones, o coordenadas, de los puntos son dadas por tripletas ordenadas.	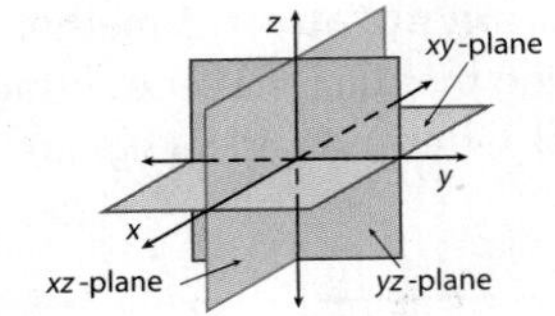
transformation A change in the position, size, or shape of a figure or graph.	**transformación** Cambio en la posición, tamaño o forma de una figura o gráfica.	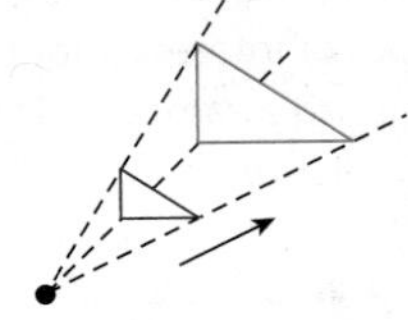
translation A transformation that shifts or slides every point of a figure or graph the same distance in the same direction.	**traslación** Transformación en la que todos los puntos de una figura se mueven la misma distancia en la misma dirección.	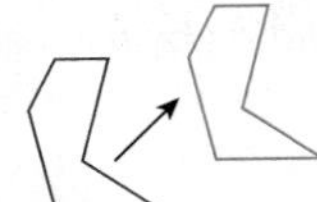
trial In probability, a single repetition or observation of an experiment.	**prueba** En probabilidad, una sola repetición u observación de un experimento.	In the experiment of rolling a number cube, each roll is one trial.
trigonometric function A function whose rule is given by a trigonometric ratio.	**función trigonométrica** Función cuya regla es dada por una razón trigonométrica.	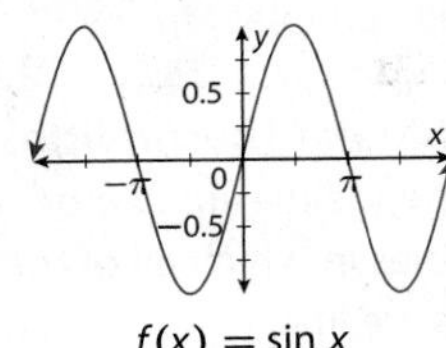 $f(x) = \sin x$
trigonometric ratio Ratio of the lengths of two sides of a right triangle.	**razón trigonométrica** Razón entre dos lados de un triángulo rectángulo.	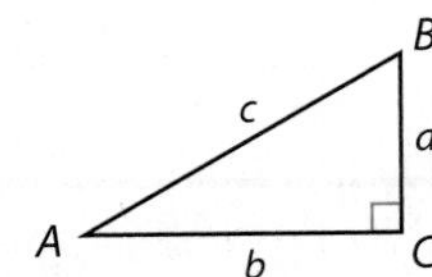 $\sin A = \frac{a}{c}$, $\cos A = \frac{b}{c}$, $\tan A = \frac{a}{b}$
trigonometry The study of the measurement of triangles and of trigonometric functions and their applications.	**trigonometría** Estudio de la medición de los triángulos y de las funciones trigonométricas y sus aplicaciones.	
trinomial A polynomial with three terms.	**trinomio** Polinomio con tres términos.	$4x^2 + 3xy - 5y^2$

ENGLISH	SPANISH	EXAMPLES
turning point A point on the graph of a function that corresponds to a local maximum (or minimum) where the graph changes from increasing to decreasing (or vice versa).	**punto de inflexión** Punto de la gráfica de una función que corresponde a un máximo (o mínimo) local donde la gráfica pasa de ser creciente a decreciente (o viceversa).	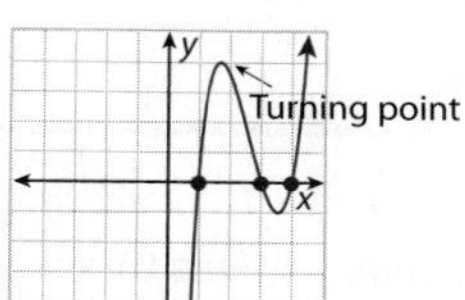

U

uniform distribution A distribution that is basically level, forming a shape that looks like a rectangle.	**distribución uniforme** Una distribución que es básicamente llana, formando una figura similar a un rectángulo.	
unit circle A circle with a radius of 1, centered at the origin.	**círculo unitario** Círculo con un radio de 1, centrado en el origen.	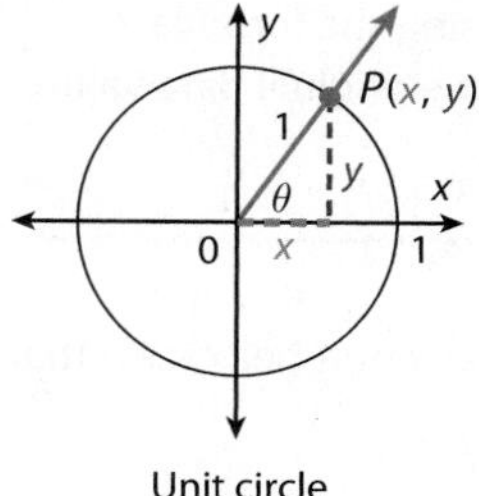 Unit circle

V

variance The average of squared differences from the mean. The square root of the variance is called the *standard deviation*.	**varianza** Promedio de las diferencias cuadráticas en relación con la media. La raíz cuadrada de la varianza se denomina *desviación estándar*.	Data set: is $\{6, 7, 7, 9, 11\}$ Mean: $\frac{6+7+7+9+11}{5} = 8$ Variance: $\frac{1}{5}(4+1+1+1+9) = 3.2$
vertex form of a quadratic function A quadratic function written in the form $f(x) = a(x-h)^2 + k$, where a, h, and k are constants and (h, k) is the vertex.	**forma en vértice de una función cuadrática** Una función cuadrática expresada en la forma $f(x) = a(x-h)^2 + k$, donde a, h y k son constantes y (h, k) es el vértice.	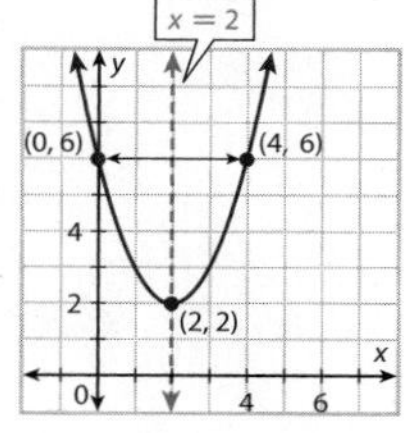 $f(x) = (x-2)^2 + 2$
vertex of an absolute-value graph The point where the axis of symmetry intersects the graph.	**vértice de una gráfica de valor absoluto** Punto donde en el eje de simetría interseca la gráfica.	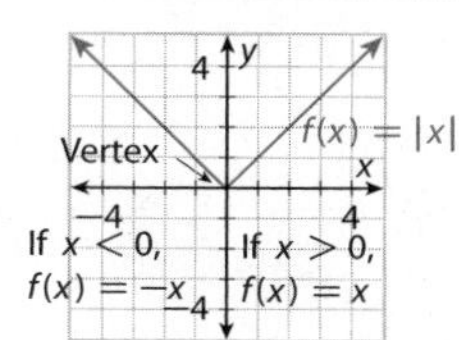
vertex of a parabola The highest or lowest point on the parabola.	**vértice de una parábola** Punto más alto o más bajo de una parábola.	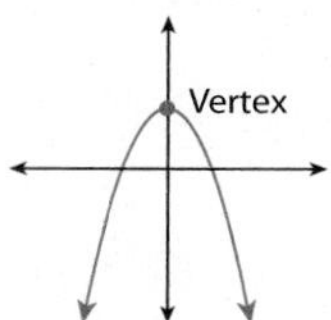

ENGLISH	SPANISH	EXAMPLES

Z

z-axis The third axis in a three-dimensional coordinate system.

eje z Tercer eje en un sistema de coordenadas tridimensional.

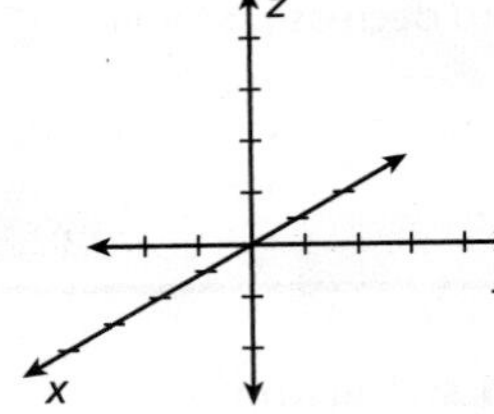

z-score A standardized data value from a normal distribution with mean μ and standard deviation σ found by using the formula $z = \frac{x-\mu}{\sigma}$ where x is the original data value.

puntaje z Un valor de datos estandarizado de una distribución normal con una media μ y una desviación estándar σ que se halla usando la fórmula $z = \frac{x-\mu}{\sigma}$, donde x es el valor de datos original.

zero of a function For the function f, any number x such that $f(x) = 0$.

cero de una función Dada la función f, todo número x tal que $f(x) = 0$.

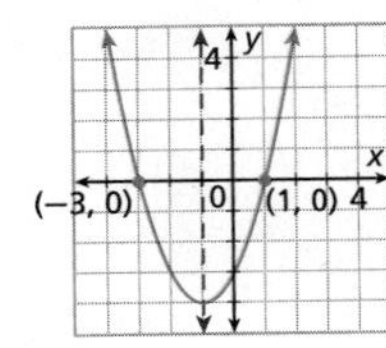

The zeros of $f(x) = x^2 + 2x - 3$ are −3 and 1.

Index

Index locator numbers are in Module. Lesson form. For example, 2.1 indicates Module 2, Lesson 1 as listed in the Table of Contents.

A

B

C

D

E

F

G

H

I

L

M

N

O

P

Q

R

Table of Measures

LENGTH

1 inch = 2.54 centimeters

1 meter = 39.37 inches

1 mile = 5,280 feet

1 mile = 1760 yards

1 mile = 1.609 kilometers

1 kilometer = 0.62 mile

MASS/WEIGHT

1 pound = 16 ounces

1 pound = 0.454 kilograms

1 kilogram = 2.2 pounds

1 ton = 2000 pounds

CAPACITY

1 cup = 8 fluid ounces

1 pint = 2 cups

1 quart = 2 pints

1 gallon = 4 quarts

1 gallon = 3.785 liters

1 liter = 0.264 gallons

1 liter = 1000 cubic centimeters

Symbols

Symbol	Meaning
$\neq$	is not equal to
$\approx$	is approximately equal to
10^2	ten squared; ten to the second power
$2.\overline{6}$	repeating decimal 2.66666...
$\lvert -4 \rvert$	the absolute value of negative 4
$\sqrt{}$	square root
π	pi: (about 3.14)
$\perp$	is perpendicular to
$\parallel$	is parallel to
$\overleftrightarrow{AB}$	line *AB*
$\overrightarrow{AB}$	ray *AB*
$\overline{AB}$	line segment *AB*
$m\angle A$	measure of $\angle A$

Formulas

Triangle	$A = \frac{1}{2}bh$	Pythagorean Theorem	$a^2 + b^2 = c^2$
Parallelogram	$A = bh$	Quadratic Formula	$x = \frac{-b \pm \sqrt{b^2 - 4ac}}{2a}$
Circle	$A = \pi r^2$	Arithmetic Sequence	$a_n = a_1 + (n - 1)d$
Circle	$C = \pi d$ or $C = 2\pi r$	Geometric Sequence	$a_n = a_1 r^{n-1}$
General Prisms	$V = Bh$	Geometric Series	$S_n = \frac{a_1 - a_1 r^n}{1 - r}$ *where* $r \neq 1$
Cylinder	$V = \pi r^2 h$	Radians	1 *radian* $= \frac{180}{\pi}$ *degrees*
Sphere	$V = \frac{4}{3}\pi r^3$	Degrees	1 *degree* $= \frac{\pi}{180}$ *radians*
Cone	$V = \frac{1}{3}\pi r^2 h$	Exponential Growth/Decay	$A = A_0 e^{k(t - t_0)} + B_0$
Pyramid	$V = \frac{1}{3}Bh$